DAD,
Christmas 1999
with Love - Sam, Patte, Annie & Sammy

DA COACH

DA COACH

Rich Wolfe

TRIUMPH
BOOKS
CHICAGO

This book is available in quantity at special discounts for your group or organization. For more information, contact:

Triumph Books
601 South LaSalle Street
Chicago, Illinois 60605
(312) 939-3330 FAX (312) 663-3557

Book design by Patricia Frey
Cover design by Mike Mulligan

Rights/Permissions: Rich Wolfe

Every effort to secure permission to reproduce copyrighted material has been made. Apologies are made for any errors or omissions.

Front cover photo: Heinz Kluetmeier/Sports Illustrated
Back cover photo: Greg Heisler/ESPN the Magazine

Printed in the United States of America

ISBN 1-57243-383-3

Table of Contents

Acknowledgements

A project like this would not have been possible without the help of good friends like Jon Spoelstra, Dale Ratermann, John Counsell, Jim Murray, Gene Cervelli, Cappy Gagnon, and Jim Wisniewski; real professionals like Russ Russell at *The Dallas Cowboys Weekly*, Paul Jensen of the Arizona Cardinals, Ken Valdiserri of the Chicago Bears, Ed Rose of the *Beaver County Times*, Ben Manges of the University of Pittsburgh Athletic Department, Jim Prokell, and Beano Cook; and especially the wonderful people like Kathy and Steve Moffit at Petty Motorsports in Greensboro, NC, and Ann Verhulst at Old World Industries in Northbrook, IL. Thanks should also go to Peter Bannon at Sports Publishing Inc., and Ernie Roth and John Nolan at Contemporary Books; previous Ditka book authors Don Pierson and Armen Keyteyian for their kind offers of help; and outstanding writers like Gregg Lewis, Bob Verdi, Pat Smith, John Tullius, and Bob Greene.

But the biggest thanks go to prolific author Peter Golenbock, for his research notes; Richard Whittingham, the author of many books, including the four best-written books about the Chicago Bears; and Ellen Brewer, the smartest, most beautiful woman in the whole state of Oklahoma and the Sooner State's best typist since a senior at Henryetta (OK) High School named Troy Aikman won the Oklahoma State Boys' Typing Championship in 1984.

*To Gene Cervelli and Jon Spoelstra,
good friends and great guys.*

To Special K, who is great in every way.

Introduction

Why a book on Ditka? Because Ditka is a character at a time when the world is running out of characters. Orthodox behavior has totally stifled creativity. Posturing and positioning one's image in order to maximize income has replaced honesty and bluntness. Political correctness has made phonies out of too many. But not Ditka—when he said New Orleans was filthy, he was right. In 1997, when he said Doug Flutie could play in the NFL and that he wanted to sign him for the Saints, he was right, even though the critics laughed at him.

Recently I did a book on Harry Caray—a character if ever there was one. One of the people I interviewed for Harry's book was Mike Ditka, a guy I've always liked. He was a great interview, very generous with his time, and really interesting. We talked about Harry Caray for five minutes, about football for five minutes, and about life in general for almost an hour. Most impressive was his conversation about his personal spiritual evolution and the effect it's had on his life.

So doing a book on Ditka seemed a natural progression. He was a character. I liked him, it would be fun, and you just knew there would be a lot of good stories. And what an experience it's been. The gentleness in the voices of fierce competitors like Jerry West and Gale Sayers was surprising. Beano Cook was a riot. The sincerity and drive of Coach Dave McGinnis made me realize the Bears made a bad mistake in not hiring him. The Varmint brothers deserve an entire book of their own. The Kyle Petty people were the most professional, and in a really nice way. Ditka was blunt, which was fine, and wary, which is understandable. Hall of Famer Jack Ham was nicely businesslike, humble, and quick-witted, but the athletic department at his alma mater, Penn State, was exactly the opposite.

The world was different when I was young. For one thing, it was flat, according to my sons. Notre Dame University is 307 miles from my hometown of Lost Nation, Iowa, and Lost Nation, Iowa, is about a million miles from Notre Dame. So it was with more than a little trepidation that I left the farm in the early sixties and headed to South Bend on a baseball scholarship. But I thought, "How tough could it be?" In Iowa, there were four colleges bigger than Notre Dame. I quickly found out that Notre Dame was another planet athletically. Fifty-one of my schoolmates would be drafted by the NFL or the AFL. My roommate would later play for the New York Mets. Four pitchers on the baseball team would also make the major leagues and one of them would play several years in the NBA. A Heisman trophy winner lived in the dormitory adjacent to mine. Because of alphabetical seating, I sat next to Carl Yastrzemski in a couple of fall classes. The sons of Stan Musial, Eddie Arcaro, and Don Dunphy were also students at that time. Don Criqui was a student-station sports announcer. A freshman basketball teammate of mine was Jon Spoelstra, who later became president and/or general manager of three NBA teams. And Don Ohlmeyer, who started Monday Night Football and also inaugurated the Skins Game in golf, was a classmate.

For a sports fan like me it was an exhilarating experience. But the one athlete who really stood out to this wide-eyed freshman was an end from Pitt named Mike Ditka. Better on defense than offense, the meanest, strongest, and toughest athlete I had ever seen, before or since—guys like Ditka simply didn't exist where I came from.

I know what you're thinking: Didn't this gifted writer just end a sentence with a preposition? Yep. 'Cause that's just how most people talk, including me. This is a book written by a sports fan for other sports fans—not for publishers, not for editors, not for critics.

It's not to say we don't take criticism well. If you have any, just jot them down on the back of a twenty-dollar bill and send them to my attention in care of the publisher.

This book is mainly about Mike Ditka, but there will be a fair amount of meandering into areas that seemed too interesting not to include. We'll eavesdrop and find out some fascinating tidbits about Ann-Margret, the Chicago Cubs, Leon Spinks, and the Dallas Cowboys, among others.

The best thing about athletes, particularly the older ones, is that they tell great stories. The best thing about writing a book is meeting these people, getting to know them, and sharing the laughter. As you will see, some remember the same events differently, but all of them rejoice in the memories.

Enjoy your reading, 'cause this book could turn you into "park bench" material.

> Rich Wolfe
> October, 1999
> Pittsburgh, Pennsylvania

Chapter I

Ken Clapper

Joseph Haller

Jerry West

Foge Fazio

Don Hennon

Paul Martha

Beano Cook

George Kiseda

Maury Youmans

photo courtesy of *Dallas Cowboys Weekly*

College Days

STEALING DITKA
KEN CLAPPER

As an undergraduate at Pitt, Ken Clapper never went to a single Pitt football game. Yet he was the key to recruiting Pitt's legendary Mike Ditka. Clapper has had a very successful career in the insurance business in Altoona, which is about two hours east of Pittsburgh.

A few years ago, I was chairman of the cancer drive in Blair County, Pennsylvania. Seated beside me at the kickoff luncheon was Joe Paterno. I told Joe the story about how I stole Ditka from Penn State, and he could hardly eat his lunch.

It was the summer of 1957 and I got a call from Pitt's coach. We were good friends. John said, "Are you having some baseball thing over there next week?" I said, "Yeah, we're having the national amateur baseball federation." He said, "There was a left fielder on the Pittsburgh team. He's a good football player. He's going to Penn State. But at least touch base with him. His name's Mike Ditka."

So the Pittsburgh team came in and they stayed at a real cruddy hotel—it was just the luck of the draw. I tracked him down. I said, "Mike, would you like to go to dinner?" I took him to dinner, we had a nice chat, but I didn't really make any progress. So I followed the Pittsburgh team the next day and that night I again asked, "Mike, want to go to dinner?" I don't know what made me say it. At dinner I asked Mike, "What do you think you want to do in life?" "Oh," he said, "I think I want to be a dentist, maybe even an oral surgeon." I said, "Well, we just had a new oral surgery clinic open up here recently. Would you like to see it?" He said, "Yeah, I'd like to see it." He was nice. He wasn't a smarty like he is now.

Joe Paterno

So I talked to the manager of the Pittsburgh team. I said, "Could we take Ditka through the oral surgery clinic?" He said, "Yeah, on the way out of town." They were eliminated on Thursday, and they stopped by on the way out of town.

I got the oral surgeon, Joe Haller, off the golf course. He didn't even change his shoes—he was still wearing his golf shoes. The team parked outside the clinic. We took Ditka in and talked to him about dentistry, oral surgery, and things of this type.

Meanwhile, the team was waiting outside for Ditka. We were ready to close the thing down, and Ditka looked at me and said, "Mr. Clapper, do you think Mr. Engle would be mad if I changed my mind and decided to go to Pitt?" I said, "Oh no, Mike. Mr. Engle is interested in your education as well as your football." He said, "Well, I think that's what I'll do." He went outside, got in the car, and started back home. I called John and said, "John, get your ass down to Aliquippa with your feet under the kitchen table. We've got Ditka." He said, "You've got to be kidding; he's committed to Penn State." I said, "Just do what I tell you." John drove to Aliquippa and Ditka said, "Yeah, I want to go to Pitt."

They took Ditka, a high school fullback by the name of J. M. Cunningham, and another player to Pitt, and they registered them

> Q: Red Grange was nicknamed "Old Seventy-Seven," "The Wheaton Iceman," and "The Galloping Ghost." What was his fourth nickname?
> A: Red. His first name was Harold.

for classes. Then they took them to Lake Erie and hid them for three days. After school had started, they brought them down and put them in classes.

In the meantime, Paterno, who was an assistant at Penn at the time, was over at the Pitt campus, saying, "I know you've got Ditka here somewhere." He never found Ditka until after Ditka was in class. That is how Ditka got to Pitt. He came to Altoona intending to go to Penn State, and left here going to Pitt.

"I think I want to be a dentist, maybe even an oral surgeon."

I don't know how he did in that baseball tournament. But he was a good baseball player. And he's liable to hit you for writing this book.

DR. MIKE DITKA
JOSEPH HALLER

Joseph Haller is a retired oral surgeon from Altoona, Pennsylvania, now living in Vero Beach, Florida. It was in his clinic that Ditka decided to become a dentist and enroll in the University of Pittsburgh, thus forsaking Joe Paterno and the Nittany Lions.

We had a guy who really promoted Pitt like crazy—Kenny Clapper. I had never heard of Mike Ditka before Kenny Clapper got a hold of me and wanted me to meet him. Ditka was in Altoona playing in a baseball tournament. Kenny wanted Ditka to meet me because he wanted Ditka to go to dental school at Pitt. One of the reasons Ditka went to Pitt was because he had a chance to get into one of the professional schools—either medicine or dentistry. Those other schools like Penn State didn't have a dental school.

They took me off the golf course to meet him. I walked into my clinic with my golf shoes on. I'm a neural and oral facial surgeon. I do all the facial stuff—give people new chins, new jaws, etc. They wanted him to see that. I worked him over a little bit and finally he decided to go. I'll tell you one thing—he wanted to be a doctor.

We told Ditka that if he was a good enough student to get into Pitt, he probably could get into dental school, because the coach at Pitt used to get a lot of guys into dental school.

The other players were sitting out front in their cars, waiting for him. He was still in his baseball uniform. I was in my golfing outfit. My office and golf course were only ten minutes from where they were playing baseball. He was at the clinic for about an hour or an hour and a half. The only other person with him was Kenny Clapper from Altoona. Kenny was a big supporter of Pitt for many years, and he wanted Ditka to go to Pitt. He was actually more responsible for Ditka going to Pitt than I was. He wanted me to add some muscle to it. I knew everybody over at Pitt, and Kenny knew I could get Ditka into the dental school since the dean was a good friend of mine. I was a trustee and I was also on the state dental board.

My first impression of Ditka was that he was a big, strong kid. They told me that he was a good football player and a good baseball player. I was impressed with the guy, and he seemed pretty sincere. He expressed himself very well. I said, "Are you sure you want to go to dental school?" He said, "Yes, that's what I want to be." Of course, he never got that far. He made out better; he ended up a coach.

I've seen Ditka quite a few times since then. Three years ago, I played in a tournament in California for Frank Sinatra before he died. Ditka always played in those tournaments, and I had a chance to talk to him a little bit. He didn't remember me.

> **He wanted to be a doctor . . . He made out better; he ended up a coach.**

Mike Ditka is the only man to score a Super Bowl touchdown and coach a Super Bowl winner.

DEATH WISH
JERRY WEST

Jerry West, such an NBA legend that he was the model for the NBA logo, was arguably the best defensive guard ever. He is the only MVP of an NBA Finals who played for the losing team. His long and successful career as a Hall of Fame player, coach, and general manager began in his hometown of Cabin Creek, West Virginia, and continued on to the courts of West Virginia University.

The University of Pittsburgh was our biggest and most bitter rival because the two schools were only about ninety minutes apart. We would win the games at our court in Morgantown fairly easily. We would never be threatened as much as when we played at Pitt. The games at Pitt were really hard-fought, close games, very competitive and very physical.

In 1958, during my junior year, we played a game at Pitt. It was a field house-like place, and around their court they had a running track. At one end of the court, there was no seating, just a curtain and, behind that, the running track.

> Q: What was the previous name of the Big Ten Conference?
> A: It was called the Big Nine after the University of Chicago dropped out following the 1939 season. It became the Big Ten again when Michigan State joined in the early 1950s.

Of course, I had no idea who Mike Ditka was, but I met him that night. Early in the game, I faked out my defender and was driving for an easy layup. Ditka absolutely creamed me and deposited me over this curtain that kept dust off the floor. While I was scraping cinders off my arms and legs, one of my teammates said something to him. Ditka called him a "snake," but to use the language, called him a particular kind of snake, and said he would break his neck. All throughout the game, you knew Mike was around. He was just an aggressive player.

Was Ditka a good player?

"Oh, Mike was a great football player."

No, I mean, was Ditka a good basketball player?

"Like I told you, Mike was an excellent football player."

photo courtesy of the University of Pittsburgh

MEMORIES OF "THE HAMMER"
FOGE FAZIO

Foge Fazio is the assistant coach for the Minnesota Vikings and a former Pitt head coach. The Coriapolis, Pennsylvania, native has played with and against Ditka since childhood.

Mike went to a larger high school than I did, but I knew him then and watched him play. He was a year behind me at the University, and we were on teams together. We also played American Legion baseball against each other.

During his sophomore year he went out for the basketball team at Pitt and made the team. We were playing at West Virginia, and they put him in the game. Jerry West and all those guys just got the hell out of the way. His nickname was "the Hammer." Naturally, Mike was the hammer and the enforcer, but he also liked to shoot the ball. He would take a couple of shots now and then, and we would be sitting in the stands going crazy cheering for him.

Mike is such a competitor. He was playing shortstop in one of our games, and someone hit a ball out to center field, where his brother Ashton was playing. Ashton came in and got the ball, but he didn't throw it to the cut-off guy. Mike was so pissed he threw his hat down and went after Ashton. Ashton saw him coming, took off running, and went over a chain-link fence to get out of his way. The game was delayed until Mike got back, and then they had to put in a new center fielder. I don't think Mike caught up with Ashton, but I'm sure he got him later at home. Mike was a good shortstop. He had great range and was a good hitter and leader, just like he was in football.

We were playing Boston College at Boston College my senior year. In those days, when we scored a touchdown we had to line up and kick off. So basically we were on the kickoff cover team, too. If you started on defense and offense, you had to cover the kickoffs.

I'm sure he was bruised as hell, but you never would have known it.

It was a pretty tough game and we had just pulled ahead of them. Mike was all fired up, running up and down the line, smacking guys on their helmets. He smacked one guard, Norton, and almost knocked him down. I saw him coming and ducked. Then he went up to Jimbo Cunningham, who was a big, tough fullback. He smacked Jimbo on the head and they almost got into a fistfight. People had to separate them right there before the kickoff.

One week we were getting ready to play Syracuse, the national champions. On the Thursday before the game, we were at our place doing a practice session without pads. They threw a long pass to Mike and he went down the field and caught it. Just as he caught it, he ran smack into the blocking sled, which was a two-man steel sled without the pads. A hush fell over the whole place. He just jumped right up. He had a big gash on his hand, and I'm sure he was bruised as hell, but you never would have known it. He still came out and played that Saturday. Most people would have been lying in the hospital. He is just a tough, tough individual.

Mike would somehow go off his block and just knock the hell out of the ball carrier. He was a crusher.

We played a 5–3 defense. I played outside linebacker either beside Mike or just behind him. I'd go to make a tackle, and all at once I would hear a "boom"—Mike would somehow go off his block and just knock the hell out of the ball carrier, before I could get there. I was shocked when he went to the NFL and played tight end. I thought for sure he would be a linebacker or a defensive end. He was a crusher. He was an outstanding defensive man.

I went to the Patriots in 1960. I was cut and went back to see Pitt play Michigan State at Pitt Stadium.

Pitt had to play at 10:00 in the morning so they could get their game out of the way. A big fight broke out between Herb Adderley and Mike Ditka on the field. They probably would still be fighting today, like two gladiators on the field, but some people broke it up. It was one of those rambunctious deals that was momentous at the time.

When I got the head coaching job at Pitt, Mike called and said, "The Italian kid from Coriapolis who went to Pitt and the Slovac kid from Aliquippa who went to Pitt now become head coaches on the same day." He even put that in his book.

We played Illinois one year when the NFL was on strike. Mike came down to the game and gave my players a pep talk and really fired them up. They all knew who Mike was.

He is such a loyal guy. Every year he holds a golf tournament for his high school in Aliquippa. At one time, with the factory, they were probably graduating four or five hundred kids; now, they are graduating about one hundred. He holds the golf tournament to raise money not only for the football program, but for scholarships for needy kids. One year he had just had one of his hips replaced. Another year he played after a knee operation. He is very loyal to his hometown, and he always has been.

We played in an alumni game in the spring of 1977. I was the linebacker coach for Jackie Sherrill at the time and we all played in the game. Mike was coaching the Dallas Cowboys at the time and he came back and played defense. We were thirty-seven years old. But that's the kind of guy he is. He gives back to the people in his hometown.

Q: Who is the only college football player to be MVP of four bowl games?

A: Bo knows it's Bo Jackson, Auburn '82, '83, '84, '85. Marvin Graves of Syracuse came close, winning every year but his senior year. Bo is the only NFL back to have earned two touchdown runs of over ninety yards from a scrimmage.

EXTRA-LARGE PANTIES FOR TWO ALL-AMERICANS
DON HENNON

Although he is only 5'9", Don Hennon became the first All-American basketball player in University of Pittsburgh history. He was Mike Ditka's friend and fraternity brother, and is now a successful surgeon in the Pittsburgh area.

M ike was a good basketball player; he was a very coordinated and talented athlete. He not only played basketball, he also played football and baseball and was a wrestling champ for the interfraternity council. He was an all-around athlete and a real good guy.

He was a junior, one year behind me. When they were initiating us into the fraternity, they had us run around in the basement of the fraternity house in women's panties. We were running around in the basement, and one of the brothers took some ice cubes, pulled Mike's pants back, and dumped the ice down his panties. Mike didn't say anything, but I saw him walk over to a table where there were about a half dozen eggs in a container. He picked the eggs up, went over to the guy—who was wearing a brand new suit—and smashed them over his head. Eggs were running all over him. I thought, "Oh, my goodness, we're going to get thrown out of here for sure." But they didn't throw us out; they went ahead and let us join. What a sight: this guy was all dressed up and thought he was doing something, and BOOM! Eggs all over him.

TAKING CARE OF BUSINESS

PAUL MARTHA

Paul Martha attended Pitt with Mike Ditka, and later went on to enjoy a professional career with the Pittsburgh Steelers and the Denver Broncos.

photo courtesy of the University of Pittsburgh

When I was recruited by Pitt, Mike and I worked a construction job together. He kind of took care of me. We were building a Kaufmann's department store in Monroeville. No one ever fooled around with Michael; therefore, no one ever fooled around with me. Construction is construction and it can get a little physical, but no one ever got physical with Michael.

Michael was a very physical guy, but I never saw him get in a fight. No one really wanted to fight him because he was bigger than most people. He was just Mike Ditka, and people didn't fool around with Mike Ditka.

I think he was a junior then, and I was about to become a freshman. I never really played with Mike, but I played against him when he was with the Bears and I was with the Steelers. In college, we scrimmaged, but we never played on the same team because freshmen weren't eligible in those days.

He was just Mike Dikta, and people didn't fool around with Mike Dikta.

I did play some basketball games with him. I played for Pitt for two years, and we would scrimmage the varsity. Michael wasn't a player with a lot of finesse; he was a big guy and very physical. West Virginia had a good team—Jerry West, Clint Kishbaugh—but we were a little more physical than they were.

He was a pretty good baseball player. He played center field. We both played for the Lawrenceville Tigers, a sandlot team, in Pittsburgh. It was good baseball. A lot of minor league players came back and played.

One season Pitt played USC, and the McKeevers twins, who starred for Southern Cal, gave Ditka a tough time. They picked on him, and the crowd (this part of Pittsburgh was a tough crowd) got on Michael about the McKeevers. The crowd was more Pittsburgh fans than Pitt fans, so they got on Michael. He wasn't doing too well—he had struck out once and had dropped a fly ball—so they got on him. He was out in center field, and I played shortstop. Right in the middle of the inning, he started in from center field, and I said, "Michael, where are you going?" He said, "I've got to take care of business." He just cleaned out the stands; they saw him coming and they just left. Bingo, everybody was immediately gone. Then he came back to center field.

He could have played professional baseball. But in those days, it wasn't worth the effort because they sent you down to the Mexican League. It was a lot easier to play college football.

> The rings for the Super Bowl winners cost twice as much as the rings for the losers.

ACHILLES
BEANO COOK

photo courtesy of ESPN/Rick LaBrache

Beano Cook is ESPN's resident college football expert. He still resides in his native Pittsburgh and has known Ditka for a long time.

I first heard about Ditka when he was still a junior in high school. He was a pretty good player; they won a league championship. I heard about him then, but I really started to hear about him in the fall of 1956. The two football players I heard about a lot were Myron Pottios, who ended up captain at Notre Dame, and Mike Ditka, who ended up captain at Pitt.

Everybody wanted Ditka. He was supposed to go to Penn State, but for some reason he changed his mind around August 5 and went to Pitt. Joe Paterno was recruiting for Penn State's head coach Rip Engle, and he had Ditka all set for Penn State. Paterno still says it was his toughest recruiting loss.

Ditka came to Pitt to study dentistry. Can't you see Ditka doing somebody's teeth? Picture Mike putting the novocaine in: "What do you mean, novocaine? Why do you want novocaine? You've got to be a man. Here's the drill." I can just see him opening somebody's mouth and sticking those goddamn things in.

Freshmen couldn't play in those days but the varsity players talked about him. Every so often they scrimmaged and someone would say, "Ditka's some player; he's a rock." When you saw him for the first time, you just had the feeling that this guy was special. I've been wrong before, I guess, but I was right about him; I knew he was special right away, and he was.

Bob Anderson, who played for Army in 1958, Ditka's sophomore year, was a great All-American. He tells a story about the Pitt-Army game in 1958 that cost Army the national title. It was 14–14. Pitt brought the third team ends in, and this guy just about killed Anderson. He found out later that the guy was Mike Ditka.

This was 1958. Nobody knew who the players were. You knew the players in your conference, the Notre Dame quarterback, and that's it. Now they know all their names because of publicity. Later, Anderson said, "You know, I just never got hit like that." He wasn't expecting that from a substitute end.

On the last play of the game against Army, Pitt threw a long pass that was intercepted. Ditka came back to help make the tackle, and he was injured. As he was being carried off the field, an Army player came up to him and said, "You, Mike Ditka, are the greatest football player I've ever seen." He had his arms around the trainer and another player. The trainer told me that story. Mike would not have told me that; he was modest. He wanted to win, but he didn't care about personal glory. He just wanted to win.

The first game Ditka ever started was against Notre Dame at Pittsburgh in 1958. The day before the game, Terry Brennan, Notre Dame's coach, said, "All I know is if I had Mike Ditka, I would start him." The score was 29–26 Pitt. Ditka caught a fourth down pass

In the 1970s, a St. Louis football Cardinals fan bought an ad in the *St. Louis Post-Dispatch* offering to sell the "Official Cardinals' Playbook" with "all five plays illustrated, including the squib punt."

that kept the drive alive in the last two minutes, and Pitt scored with eleven seconds to go. That's the game that cost Terry Brennan his job, or so they say.

In those days, Ditka might have been a hell-raiser, but he didn't get into trouble. If you told him to be there at 4:00, he was there at 4:00.

His dad was a steelworker. There were people in that area who said, "Don't take Mike! He's nothing but a trouble-maker. His dad's a union organizer." But the doctors, dentists, and coaches who recruited for Pitt in the Beaver Valley said, "That's crazy; the kid's a great football player."

He wanted to win, but he didn't care about personal glory.

I think he was captain of all the postseason games. Ditka was something. In his senior year, seven of the ten opponents voted for all-opponent teams, and he made all seven! Of the other three, he definitely would have made two; I don't know about the third one. So, if all the teams had voted, he definitely would have made nine out of ten.

In 1959, Syracuse won the national title. The game was over when Art Baker danced into the end zone for one touchdown—he just high-stepped it in. The next year, on the first or second play, Ditka looked Baker over and said, "We're going to see if you do any high-stepping this year," and Pitt beat them 10–0. That was a great Syracuse team—they hadn't lost a game since 1958 and this was late October or November. Pitt upset them 10–0 and Baker didn't do any high-stepping!

When Mike played basketball, the opponents' screens completely disappeared. Pitt played Kentucky one year and gave them a pretty good game. They were setting up the screens, so Ditka went in. The screens parted like the Red Sea; they had probably been belted by him a couple of times before. Adolph Rupp, the legendary Kentucky coach, was screaming, "You're pretty rough out there." And Ditka said, "Well, you've got a bunch of guys who are, too."

During the one year Mike played basketball, I got on the officials at Duke and they kicked me out of the pressroom. Young Mike, on the way back to Pitt, came over and said, "Beano, I'll even that over when we play them in October."

In an earlier life, Dikta was probably Achilles.

I saw Bill Murray (Duke's coach) after the 1959 game and he said, "Our plane looked like a hospital." Ditka had laid out half the team! He wasn't a dirty player. He was just as tough as they come.

He also played baseball at Pitt. You should have seen him—temper, strike out. Ditka had a temper—he's always had a temper—but he would hit the ball a mile sometimes.

In 1963, Ditka made the greatest run in NFL history. It was November 24 at Pitt Stadium. The Bears were losing 17–10, Ditka caught the pass, and four or five guys bounced off him. It was unbelievable, but nobody saw it because the games weren't televised then, because of the Kennedy assassination. But now the play is famous and everybody's seen it, because word got around. The game ended in a tie, but the Bears were fighting to win the division. They won the division and beat the Giants 14–10 in Wrigley Field to win the championship.

In an earlier life, Ditka was probably Achilles—a great, great fighter—and he came back as Mike Ditka. He was unbelievable—he gave one hundred percent in every play.

A SPECIAL CASE
GEORGE KISEDA

George Kiseda wrote for the Pittsburgh Sun Telegraph *during Ditka's college days. He went on to successful stints with the* New York Times *and the* Los Angeles Times.

I only covered Ditka in college; I never had any contact with him after that. I have to admit that I, along with a lot of other writers, didn't realize at the time what a good source Ditka would have been for anecdotes and quotes.

You could tell he was good in college; you didn't have to be that sharp to know that. He played two ways. Instead of a tight end, Army's Red Blaik introduced the "lonely end." The lonely end would split way out wide. Pitt did that with Ditka; he was the lonely end and he was also the punter.

He made the greatest run in NFL history. You can see it every once in a while on NFL highlight films—it was in a game against the Steelers at Forbes Field. If I'm not mistaken, they played the game the weekend that Kennedy was assassinated, and there was a lot of criticism of them for that. He made that unbelievable run after he caught a pass, and he just steamrollered the guys, just ran right over them. It was at least three sure tackles.

I realized he was really different, a special case, after reading about him once he became a pro. When I read about him, I said, "Jeez, this guy's a treasure, and we just weren't on top of it then."

We didn't interview the individual players in those days, in the '50s. One guy was assigned to write the game story and somebody else did the dressing room story. If you were doing the game story, you really didn't even go to the dressing rooms after the game. Now, that would be unheard of; you couldn't hold your job now if you did that.

Bronco Terrell Davis demands that the nameplate above his locker always must read "Joe Abdullah," and Bronco center Tom Maler won't wash his practice gear during the year because he feels that he's giving the equipment "natural seasoning" to shield him from "evil spirits."

A GENEROUS SPEAKER
MAURY YOUMANS

Maury Youmans was a member of Syracuse University's 1959 National Championship team and later enjoyed a fine career with the Chicago Bears and the Dallas Cowboys.

My son was in high school the year the Bears won the Super Bowl, in 1986. He went to a small Catholic school, Saint Petersburg Catholic, and before the Bears won, the school asked me if I could get Mike Ditka to be a speaker. I was pretty sure I couldn't, but I was willing to call and ask him. I congratulated him on winning the playoff game and on going to the Super Bowl, and told him about the banquet the school had planned and asked if he could speak at it. He said no, that he was busy on that date, but that he had two other dates open and if I was willing to switch, he would do it. The school checked and they were able to switch, and then they asked me how much he charged. So I called him up. I said, "Mike, we've arranged the date, and by the way, I don't know what you charge. I'll be glad to send an airline ticket."

He laughed and said, "Maury, you can't afford me. But for you and for the kids, I'll do it for whatever honorarium you can arrange to give me." So I think we gave him $1,000, when he was used to getting $10,000 to $15,000. By then, they had won the Super Bowl, and it couldn't have been better for our group.

I played against him in college but had no idea who he was. We played Pittsburgh my senior year and we trounced them pretty good, but I don't remember him in particular in that game. We were always friends, but we weren't real close. I didn't buddy around with him. He buddied around with Stan Mikita.

I never thought Ditka would coach. But I guess if you spend any time with Landry, and you're willing to assist him, then you've got the basis to be a great NFL coach.

The 1943 Heisman winner, Angelo Bertelli, started the first six games for Notre Dame, went to boot camp because of World War II, and was replaced by Johnny Lujack. Notre Dame is the only team ever to have two Heisman Trophy winners on the same roster.

Chapter 2

Dick Butkus

Doug Buffone

Gale Sayers

Mike Pyle

Gary Ballman

Frank Clarke

Walt Garrison

Donnie Tolbert

Hollywood Henderson

Jim McMahon

Mike Singletary

photo courtesy of *Dallas Cowboys Weekly*

Players

photo courtesy of the Chicago Bears

A BEAR OF A PARTY
DICK BUTKUS

Dick Butkus was a fullback at a Chicago vocational high school who wanted to attend Notre Dame. When he was told they would not accept married students, Butkus went to the University of Illinois instead and became the greatest player in their history. Butkus joined the Bears in 1965, but his wonderful career with the team was cut short by knee injuries.

One day, I got my first hint that just maybe I was beginning to be accepted by some of the older players. O'Bradovich came over to me on the practice field and said that if I was a good boy I might be invited to Bob Wetoska's birthday party—an annual, semisecret affair held at a local saloon in Rensselaer. The party was not so much to mark another year in Wetoska's life as to celebrate the end of our two-a-day practice hell. Bob was a veteran offensive tackle and a co-captain. I respected him a great deal.

When I joined the veterans at the party later on, I found out that everybody was invited. So much for O'Bradovich's private invitation—and my thinking I was becoming accepted. Strong safety Richie Petitbon was there, along with reserve quarterback Frank Budka, Mike Ditka, defensive end Doug Atkins, and all the other rookies, including running back Brian Piccolo, who never had to go through the ragging I did.

The beer began to flow immediately, and pretty soon someone suggested a drinking contest among the rookies. O'B nominated me to represent the defense because he remembered my high guzzling aptitude from that first semester at Illinois. Somebody picked Piccolo to swig for the offense. This pleased me. It meant payback time for all the snide comments and insults I received from the veterans while Brian usually got off unscathed.

Ditka wrapped his head with a bandanna and declared himself the referee. A table was cleared and two large glasses of beer were set down. Brian and I faced off on either side of the table. Ditka slapped his big mitts, signaling the start, and I drained my glass before Brian barely had his to his lips. Applause and hoots and hollers from the defense rocked the saloon, and the gambling began. Petitbon and O'B bankrolled the effort, and pretty soon I was beating everyone the offense threw at me.

> The Chicago Bears have the most members in the Hall of Fame, with twenty-eight. They have the most wins, with more than six hundred. They have the most numbers retired, with thirteen.

After about an hour of this, I was getting pretty shitfaced. But I was still functioning. Then someone yelled, "Hey! We have to get to our meeting! It's almost seven!" Chairs scraped back as everyone got up to leave. Everyone except Doug Atkins, that is. He was standing at the door with a bottle of Wild Turkey, informing us that nobody was going anywhere. As big as some of us were, Doug Atkins was in a league by himself. I never saw anybody like Atkins. Nobody ever saw anybody like Atkins. Six-foot-eight, 275 pounds, and not enough fat on him to cook an egg. On top of that, he was not your typical gentle giant. Dougie's exploits were legendary in pro football camps from Baltimore to Oakland.

Dikta wrapped his head with a bandanna and declared himself the referee.

Finally someone promised him that we would come right back after the meeting, so Doug said, "Well, okay then. But first everyone has to take a swig of this Wild Turkey."

So we all lined up and took our medicine, which did not sit all that well on top of a couple of gallons of beer. I jumped in my Buick Riviera and flew to the local hall where we held our team meetings. As I arrived at the building, I neglected to hit the brakes in a timely manner, and the car stopped halfway up the stairs leading to the front door. I'm lucky I didn't kill anyone. Inside, Frank Budka produced one of those plastic horns the fans use to make noise at games, and he started blowing into it, which got everybody's attention. Happy as hell with himself, he belted out a song:

> Hooray for Halas, hooray at last!
> Hooray for Halas, he's a horse's ass!

Just as Budka was finishing his solo, in walked the old man—with rockets going off in his eyes. He ripped the horn out of Rudy's hand and rapped him over the head with it a couple of times. Then he said in that grating voice, "You son of a bitch! You're drunk! Now quiet down, all of you—you crazy bastards! Break into your groups, NOW!"

Everybody got real quiet and I noticed that Atkins was sitting there in the back, shaking his head in dismay at such juvenile behavior, while up front Papa Bear, with his big hands on his hips, started in again, cursing everybody's mother. Over to one side, George Allen was waiting for the thunder to subside, and I was thinking, "Wow, so this is the NFL!"

When Halas finally calmed down, our defensive unit gathered around Allen. Seeing—and no doubt smelling—our advanced state of intoxication, Allen quickly reduced his syllabus to a few simple points and let us out of school early. We promptly returned to the saloon, but Atkins got there first and took his position at the doorway. Our ticket inside was another swallow of that Wild Turkey.

That was my first of many team parties.

> The Oakland Raiders do not retire numbers.
> Neither do the Dallas Cowboys—but they do put
> the number in a Circle of Honor.

A CERTAIN EDGE
DOUG BUFFONE

Doug Buffone, a native of Yatesboro, Pennsylvania, joined the Chicago Bears in 1966 as a fourth-round draft pick from the University of Louisville. After an outstanding fourteen-year career with the Bears, Buffone quickly became a force in the Chicago sports radio market.

Both Ditka and I are from western Pennsylvania, where football is king and everything rotates around it. The first time I played against Ditka was prior to the College All-Stars game in 1966. We were playing the Packers that year; the Packers were the champs. We wanted to get tuned up for the Packers, so the All-Stars went down to the Chicago Bears' training camp in Renssalaer, Indiana, to scrimmage the Bears. Of course, I was going to be a Bear after the All-Stars game was over.

We went down and scrimmaged the Bears. I lined up in my outside linebacker position, and of course that position was right on top of the tight end. That tight end was Mike Ditka. It was a hell of a day. It got so damn bad that he started telling me which way the plays were going so we could make a play. The guy was beating me to death; they were running over me and everything else. After the scrimmage was over, I asked myself, "Do I belong in the National Football League?" It was a tough day.

After the scrimmage, we went back to our camp in Evanston. We practiced, we played the Packers, and we got beat. Afterward, I joined the Chicago Bears. I think I was able to become an NFL linebacker, who eventually would play fourteen years, because my first year was pure hell. Can you imagine looking into Ditka's face every day? I was probably the only guy who was happy when he was traded to Philadelphia at the end of that year. We were always fighting—it was World War III every day. Once, in the middle of the season, someone was talking about the opponents, and I heard Ditka say, "Yeah, that fucking Buffone, he gives me more trouble than anybody." That made me feel pretty good because in practice I was going after him. That's the way you have to play if you want to survive. That's why he was Iron Mike.

In '67 and '68, after Mike was traded to Philadelphia, I played against him. By that time I knew him inside and out, and I knew it was going to be a long day. Mike liked to hit people—that was part of being a linebacker. Everyone thought he could catch the ball; I thought he was one of the best blockers around. When he did come out and block you, he was deadly. He would literally come out and drill you. I've played with some of the best, and you have to have this certain edge, this certain attitude, to play the game. You need it to be successful, at least for longevity in the game.

When I heard Ditka was hired in Dallas, I thought, "Look out. He'll put Landry in a booth." In fact, I had Dan Reeves on my radio show and he and I were talking about it. Mike and Dan were two different guys. Mike was wild and tough. Dan Reeves was

> The Chicago Bears wear blue and orange
> because those are the colors that team
> founder George Halas wore when he played
> for the University of Illinois.

also very intense, but he was more of a quiet type—a gentleman. I told Dan Reeves I didn't know how they meshed. Tom Landry was so stoic, standing on the sidelines with his little hat on. Even when it rained, he never got wet. You never got a chance to look at him. Ditka was wild and churlish, but that was something the Dallas Cowboys needed, and I think Tom Landry

Halas knew that Dikta would sell in Chicago. They needed someone with attitude.

realized that. They became great friends. And Ditka and Dan Reeves always had the highest praise for Tom Landry, although everybody thought Tom Landry was a cold fish.

Before I knew Ditka was hired as head coach of the Bears, I got a call from George Allen, who had drafted me in 1966. He had left the Bears after a falling out with George Halas. Allen called and talked to me about how he wanted to be the Bears' new head coach.

At this time, I didn't know anything about Mike Ditka becoming coach of the Bears. So I called George Halas and talked to him about Allen. That's when Halas told me, "I've got to bring back the tradition of the Chicago Bears, bring back the two-fisted, Grabowski-type deal, so I really want Mike Ditka as my head coach." I knew that deep down Halas had an affection for Ditka because they came from the same mold. I honestly believe they are the same person. They have the same attitude, the same toughness. Halas knew that Ditka would sell in Chicago, and he also knew that he had to turn his team around somehow. They needed someone with an attitude. The city needed an emotional lift; I think that's why he went with Mike Ditka.

I started doing radio shows when I retired after the 1979–80 season. Now I have a show on The Score (WSCR) in Chicago with Norm VanLier called "The Bull and the Bear."

Ditka does radio work for us at The Score. Before he left Chicago, he did an hour show on our station every week, so I saw him quite a bit. He also has a restaurant in town, so he goes back and forth a lot.

Chicago loves him because he's a Hall of Famer who played football here on a championship team in 1963, and because he took the team to the Super Bowl in 1985. He represents what the people in this town like about football. It's got to be tough. They want to know that you're going to go out there and knock somebody on their ass, and they want you to win while you're doing it. They want you to be physical and they want you to be tough. That sounds just like Mike Ditka, doesn't it? They fell in love with Ditka, and to this day I get phone calls all the time: "Bring back the Coach. Bring back the Coach."

> Quarterback Brad Johnson, who started more games at Florida State in basketball than he did in football, is the only NFL quarterback in history to complete a touchdown pass to himself.

THE TOUGHEST MAN ON THE FIELD
GALE SAYERS

photo courtesy of the Chicago Bears

Gale Sayers was born in Wichita, Kansas, but grew up in Omaha, Nebraska. He is the youngest player ever to be inducted into the Hall of Fame, and also had the shortest career of any inductee, just seven years. Many consider him the greatest running back in NFL history. He now owns Gale Sayers Computer Supplies in Mount Prospect, Illinois.

When I came out of Kansas I didn't know anything about the Bears. I played offense and Mike played offense, but I didn't know anything else about him. I had heard of George Halas, but I didn't know a whole lot about the players. I just wanted to make the ball club. When I got to the Bears, I saw how intense Mike was, and I thought it was great because you have to be that way in pro football.

When I was with the Bears, I never really hung around with Mike that much. Most of the white players lived on the North Side of Chicago, and most of the black players lived on the South Side of Chicago. The only time we saw each other was when we practiced or played a game; we really never saw each other socially unless we attended team parties and things like that. But it wasn't anything like, "We don't want to be around you." It was just the way it happened.

I remember Mike as a very, very tough football player. If you didn't hustle, he would get on your tail. When the game was on

the line, Mike was there. Even when he was hurt, he would take shots in his knees and ankles to play, because Mike Ditka on one leg is better than a second-string tight end on three legs. He always gave 110 percent on every play—he was a tremendous football player.

Dick Butkus was also a tough player; he played every down like it was the last down. It was the same with Mike—he played every down like it was the last, and he would block, catch passes, and do anything he could to win a football game. This is what I admired about him.

Sometime in their pasts, somebody—whether a parent, a high school coach, or a college coach—told them, "If you want to be a great player, you have to go out all the way on every play." Somebody said to them, "Hey, if you're going to be great, you can't do it half the time, or three plays out of four, or two plays out of four; you have to do it every play." Somebody told them that, just like somebody told me that. My grade school coach said, "Gale, you've got a lot of talent, but you have to use it. You have to prepare yourself, because if you don't, you'll waste your talent." I really believe that somebody told them, "Hey, you have to be the toughest man on the field," and they believed that. I know Dick believed that, and I'm pretty sure Mike believed that, too.

I was very surprised to find out that Tom Landry had hired Mike as an assistant. When Landry hired Mike, it was the beginning of the end of hard-nosed coaches grabbing your helmet and cussing you out. Mike was the end of that era; he could still do that to some of his players. Today you can't do that.

When the game was on the line, Mike was there.

Will he be successful at New Orleans? I don't know. He sold the house when he got Ricky Williams, so I hope he is successful, because he's going to be gone if he's not. If Williams does get hurt, Mike's in real trouble. You can say what you want about Mike. He's probably a good coach and a good motivator, but you still have to have talented players; it's as simple as that. I don't care how good of a motivator you are, if the people on the field don't have the talent, you're not going to be a good coach.

The Los Angeles Rams were the first NFL team to wear helmets with a logo. The logo was designed by a player, Fred Gehrke. The Cleveland Browns are the only team with no logo.

photo courtesy of the Chicago Bears

DITKA THE GRABOWSKI
MIKE PYLE

Mike Pyle and Mike Ditka both joined the Bears as rookies in 1961 and were roommates the night before every Bears away game, until Ditka was traded to the Eagles for Jack Concannon in 1967. Pyle was a well-established radio personality in Chicago by the time Ditka returned fifteen years later to guide the Bears. That commenced a ten-year-long relationship as Pyle hosted Ditka's "Coaches' Show" during Ditka's entire reign.

ROOMIES

Ditka and I were roommates on the road from the time we both joined the Bears in 1961 until he was traded to the Philadelphia Eagles in 1967. There were three of us coming from the All-Star camp, so at least two of us were going to room together, and somehow the draw paired Mike and I. I got along well with Mike and I think he got along well with me, and it stayed that way for the six years that Mike played for the Bears. What an interesting combination—a guy from Winnetka who went to Yale and a guy from Aliquippa who went to Pittsburgh. But we were friends right from the start.

I never heard of Ditka when I was in college. I first heard of him when the Bears drafted him in the first round and drafted me in the seventh round. We played college football for four years at the same time, but the Pittsburgh teams weren't great teams and I was an Ivy Leaguer.

I only remember one time that Ditka came out on the wrong side of a scuffle. It was in Sonoma, California, where we would practice, between the San Francisco and LA games. There were no big jets in those days to fly us home in between games. One day in practice, Mike ran a pattern against the backups who ran the plays of the team we were going to play. He thought the safety, Don Mullins, had held him or something, and he charged him. But Mullins was a safety and pretty quick, and all he did was sidestep Ditka and get his fist inside that stupid single-bar helmet Ditka always wore. Ditka caused the impact; he ran into the fist. Forty guys fell dead silent as Ditka went down to his knees, but didn't collapse. He got up and went back to the huddle. He said, "I got whupped!" Can you imagine what the media in Chicago would do with a story like that nowadays?

BYE-BYE BIRDIE

I went to high school with Ann-Margret Olsen. In high school, she was a beautiful young girl. I knew her well, but she wasn't a part of my group. Several guys in my class dated girls in her class—her best friends. But she wasn't as popular as she could have been; her parents were from Sweden, and they were really tough.

When Ditka and I were rookies with the Bears in '61, we went to LA for our first game. I don't think I'd ever been to LA before. Ann-Margret was in LA because she didn't finish at Northwestern; George Burns discovered her and took her out there. When I arrived, I called one of my New Trier classmates, Tom, who was in the Marine Corps at Camp Pendleton. He came over and picked me up where we were staying in LA. I couldn't get Ann-Margret's phone number, but I had her apartment number. We drove over to see her, and her mother was there. Ann was making "Bye-Bye Birdie" in Dallas at the time. Tom and I had to sit and talk with Mrs. Olsen for three hours. It was not what we had planned.

The next year, I called her. Halas had us staying in Long Beach—forty miles from where she lived. I was really lucky this time. I got her on the phone, but I didn't get to see her because we had meetings. So I offered her a couple of game tickets and she said, "Sure."

She came to the game with a starlet friend. After the game, I came out of the locker room at the Coliseum, and she was there. She threw her arms around me, gave me a kiss, and introduced me to her friend. I had to get on a bus to leave, so we walked up the ramp at

> Q: Which Heisman Trophy winner made the most money?
> A: 1959 winner Billy Cannon of LSU. A successful dentist, he nevertheless spent several years in jail for counterfeiting.

Walter Payton, Mike Ditka, and Mike Pyle

photo courtesy of Mike Pyle

the Coliseum. This is when Mike Pyle became a veteran. I was still a rookie until after this game, when the rest of the team saw me kissing Ann-Margret goodbye at the bus door. Then Ann-Margret and her friend walked around the bus and it almost tipped over. From then on, I was a veteran.

I talked to Ann-Margret about a year ago. She's extremely nice. She never forgot where she came from, which is good.

THE REAL STORY

In his autobiography, Ditka tells a story I know very well, about staying out after curfew at training camp. In the book, Mike said I was the guy who ran into a wire fence, but it was Ditka. I'll tell the story the correct way.

We'd been forced to come back early from a preseason game just so Halas could get us back in camp, because he wanted to know where everybody was. The whole team was madder than hell. A handful of us went to Brook Country Club, where you could get a beer on Sunday; you couldn't do that anywhere else in Indiana. Rick Casares, Ditka, Roger Davis, Richie Petitbon, myself, and a few other players were there. We were mad, and we started bitching about how Halas treated us and what he made us do. We were getting madder and madder, and drinking more and more. Several guys said, "We've got to go back to training camp." But Ditka, Petitbon, Casares, and I decided not to go back. It got to be 12:00, and the club closed up. We drove back to camp in Rich Casares's Lincoln. Ditka said—and this is the truth—"We're going to get caught by the Silver Bullet (a retired cop who spied on the team for Halas)."

> **I don't think Ditka has ever felt pain; I don't think he even has a pain threshold.**

It was me or Richie Petitbon who said, "Let's sneak into the cafeteria." We were hungry since we hadn't had dinner, so we decided to break into the cafeteria. Ditka said, "I'm not going to break into the cafeteria." He jumped out of the car, ran across the field to our dorm, and ran into the wire. If I had run into that wire, I would have woken up everyone in the place, because I don't like pain. I don't think Ditka has ever felt pain; I don't think he even has a pain threshold.

When I saw Ditka the next day, it looked like he had cut his legs off running full speed into the wire. He was the guy who ran into the wire, not me. The three of us sneaked into the cafeteria, ate a bunch of food, and went back to the dorm.

That night, when we came back and parked after Ditka ran out of the car, the Bullet saw three people in Casares's car. The next day,

Halas called everybody up after practice and said, "You know, some of your teammates don't have much respect for the rest of the team. There were three guys who stayed out after curfew last night. They really don't have much respect for the rest of you. There were three people, but I only know whose car it was, and your buddy Rick Casares doesn't have much respect for you guys. The other two guys don't either; I'm going to fine Rick Casaras $1,500 and see if he has any friends."

When we broke and started heading for the locker room, I ran up to Richie Petitbon. I said to Rich, "Let's go have some fun with Rick." So Richie and I ran up to Casares. We said, "Rick, that's really too bad. Who were the other two guys?" He just laughed. Later, I asked Rick if he ever got fined that $1,500, because sometimes, if we had a good season, Halas would forgive those fines. But Rick said, "Yeah." And I said, "Rick, I owe you money." He said, "Don't worry about it. I wouldn't take it if you gave it to me." That's the kind of guy he was.

THE CAST

Mike rarely played in training camp. The rest of us would play a lot and be tired going into the season; we'd really have to work hard to get some spring back in our legs because training camp was so tough. But since Mike did everything at full speed, he was generally hurt during training camp.

If Ditka stayed out at night, he worked harder the next day. He worked hard to pay the fiddler, and as a result, he probably had more strains and pulled muscles than most guys. The rest of us

> Joe Theismann holds the NFL record for the shortest punt that wasn't blocked—one yard.

might try to ease up a little bit if we had a hangover or felt bad, but Mike would have a lot of injuries because he worked as hard as he could work.

One year—I think it was his first year—he hurt his foot. The doctors put a cast on it and told him he couldn't practice for three to four weeks. After about two weeks, Mike cut the cast off himself, went out, and started practicing. He ended up breaking his arch, and he missed three or four games. That was the most amazing thing I ever saw—Mike cutting his own cast off to go out and practice. Pain did not get in his way.

I think Mike would agree that cutting off that cast and breaking his arch probably caused his first hip replacement. I've talked to Mike about it over the years. He started running in Dallas, and then went into an absolute fitness craze right at the end of his career. He was getting older like everyone does—he wasn't as quick and he was losing some of his skills. So he went on a fitness tear, and the weight loss from the running probably kept him in the game a year or two longer. He continued to run when he was coaching, and it got to the point where he would run five or six miles, seven days a week. He and Diana once joined my wife and I and a couple of other couples in Aspen, and he would get up, run four miles, and then ski all day. We all thought he was absolutely nuts. Well, it turned out that running on that bad foot for all those years led to him destroying his hip and needing a hip replacement. I was able to track the damage back to when he cut his cast off as a rookie.

> In the early part of the twentieth century, a college football game was seventy minutes long and five yards got you a first down.

CO-CAPTAINS

When Ditka and I were rookies together in 1961, the NFL was just beginning to gain fame. The NFL's growth really became accepted by the public during the fifties. The 1958 championship game in New York that the Colts won in overtime was the beginning of a period of recognition for the National Football League. National publicity, like the TV show "The Violent World of Sam Huff," began after that '58 game.

So Ditka and I came in right at the beginning of the real growth of the National Football League. It was an interesting time, because the game was growing in popularity, but we still played exhibition games in those little towns. We didn't have full stadiums. We had full crowds at Wrigley Field, but even in the early '60s the league

As wild as Ditka is on the outside, he's got the strongest motivational, inspirational, and competitive core of any man I've ever known.

was changing. Around the time I started, a rule was passed that a stadium had to have a minimum of 55,000 or 60,000 seats. We never could put more than 45,000 in Wrigley Field, but the NFL let Halas play there until 1970 because he was the founder of the league.

In 1971, Halas and the Bears were forced to go to Soldier Field, which is the worst stadium in the league. It was built for a World's Fair, not for anything competitive. It was built with 112,000 seats along the sidelines, for which you would have to have a three-hundred-yard football field. It was just an odd stadium that wasn't built around a football field. It is better now; they've rebuilt it many times, but even with all the rebuilding it's still the worst stadium in pro football. When people ask why I say that, it's because it's a shallow stadium. If you sit low on the fifty-yard line, you can't see over the crown on the field. If you sit high, even though they're probably the best seats, you are a mile from the field. It's not bad from the players' point of view; there is a nice field, but it's not a durable field. Any bad weather will really mess it up.

I was the captain of the team for seven of my nine years. During the 1963 training camp, George Halas asked both Ditka and I if we'd be the co-captains of the offensive team. That was the year we won the championship, and it was Mike's and my first year as co-captains for the offense. Mike was a captain until he left in 1967, and I was a captain until I left after 1969. The two previous captains—linebacker Bill George and Stan Jones on offense—had been captains for many years. Halas went to four captains. We never had elections; we were just appointed.

As wild as Ditka is on the outside, he's got the strongest motivational, inspirational, and competitive core of any man I've ever known. I've known guys who've played with the same intensity, but I think Mike is the best.

Mike got into a contract argument with George Halas. Mike always represented himself; none of us had agents in those days. Halas wouldn't talk to an agent. Ditka told a newspaper writer that Halas threw nickels around like manhole covers, and the writer printed it. It's a wonderful line, but right after it was printed, Halas traded him. But Ditka still had plenty of playing left. And it sure wasn't a good trade.

> The first Super Bowl, in 1967 at the Los Angeles Coliseum, had 32,000 empty seats even though the most expensive ticket was $12.00, not $275.00 like it is today.

THE RADIO SHOW

I hosted a radio show with Mike the whole time he was in Chicago. A lot of people thought that would be the end of my radio career, because when you're the moderator and you've got one of the best-known sports celebrities in America, you can't have a personality on the show. The general manager of the station said I was doing the wrong thing by hosting the Ditka show, but I loved doing it because Ditka and I had been friends for a long time, and I made more money working with Ditka. The station manager said, "You know the game of football, but you'll never be able to express an opinion when you've got Ditka as the master." But I made more money with Ditka than if I had my own show and could say, "Ditka's right" or "Ditka's wrong."

In 1987, there was a bitter players' strike. I was the president of the NFL Players' Association when we registered with the National Labor Relations Board in the winter of 1968. During the strike I would ask my questions, and obviously I was a strong supporter of the players' side. Mike, like always, was not diplomatic, and he'd get mad at me and we'd argue on the air. It was good radio, but if that had not have happened, the players might not have been as mad at him. Mike would publicly give his opinion on the air, and I loved generating it because I knew quite a bit about the other side. Ditka's position wasn't popular with the players, but how in the hell could they fight his position—how can a group of employees fight an employer who pays people that much money to do what they love to do?

He just said, "Don't tell me about all these other issues—free agency, equitable treatment, and all the other things that the union would argue and fight for. Why would you ever want to interrupt or disturb people who pay you that much to do what you love to do most?"

I felt his philosophy was oversimplified, and we sure had some interesting shows because of that. But today I believe that Mike's more right than I am. I'm turning the corner, because the game of football is nowhere near as good as it was a few years ago. It's not as enjoyable. The games are not as much fun with so many players changing teams every year.

Ditka is still extremely popular in Chicago because he's one of those unique celebrity personalities who's hard to get to know. It's the Grabowski thing—he really hit a chord with his behavior and actions. That is what the Midwest is about, and he wouldn't be as popular in New York City or Los Angeles. He's a Midwestern, provincial Chicago Grabowski. Once you like a Midwesterner, you like him forever.

Ditka's position wasn't popular with the players, but how in the hell could they fight his position?

Normally, our show was on Monday nights, but one time the Bears played the Monday night before Election Day and we did the show on Tuesday night. For some reason, we had to pretape it; we weren't doing it live, and we couldn't take phone calls. So I had to change the format if I wasn't going to take phone calls. I could have talked to Mike for an hour, but I thought I would try to make it better. So I got George Connors and Doug Buffone to come into the studio. I was trying to get players from different eras, so I got Roland Harper, a younger guy who started in 1975 with Payton, on the phone. As I recall, Roland Harper said about two things because Doug Buffone, who played with Ditka, and George Connors ("Mr. Chicago") took over. Doug said "Mike, in the game yesterday, you had a player who didn't call an audible and instead ran a play that couldn't be run against the particular defense that had been called. You couldn't run that play against that defense. Why didn't the quarterback change that play?"

Now, this was insider stuff. Doug's the only guy who would have recognized that defense. Mike used to yell at callers—that's why he was so good on the radio. When callers would ask stupid questions, Ditka would say, "That's a stupid question and I'm not going to answer it." That was great

Ditka would say, "That's a stupid question and I'm not going to answer it."

radio. But in this case, he said, "You know, Doug, you're right." I never heard Ditka tell a person asking a question that he was right. He said "You're right, he should have called an audible." Doug was so happy that he said, "Maybe part of your game plan was wrong." Then everyone was talking offense and defense and getting the coach to tell them how the offenses and plays are designed, and why they were in the game plan. I was personally fascinated.

Both Harry Caray and Mike Ditka had the ability not to be diplomatic and the courage to say what they thought. I think that's the reason for Mike's popularity. The other guys, the Brickhouses of the world, were always being careful.

The last year we did the show, the season was going badly. We were on the Score radio (WSCR), and we had to have the Score guys on every week. They were doing it to get rid of me, and they did, when Mike was fired. They typed me as a WGN man, a company man, an easy man who never got tough. When we did the show on WMAQ, they hired Chet Coppock and asked if I minded if he was on the show.

So I had to use Chet on the air with Ditka. Chet felt this was a platform for him to get tough with the coach, and he'd ask these tough questions. Mike would say, "I don't want to answer that," or he would direct an answer to Chet, and not to the audience. I would defend my style with the media, the fans, and everyone else.

They called me a company man and said I asked easy questions. I asked questions that Mike Ditka answered. I thought my job was to get as much information about the Chicago Bears and his coaching techniques as I could. To me, that's the mission of a radio interviewer. No, I didn't get credited with asking a tough question, but I didn't need that. I was trying to get information on the Bears and on what Mike Ditka was doing. When we had the show on WGN, the managers would tell me that I shouldn't do the show because I didn't get to talk about what I knew about the Bears and the game. I said, "Well, that's a concession I make. If I wanted to sit here and argue with Ditka, I don't think Ditka would want me as the moderator. Mike isn't trying to be a radio star. He gets paid a bunch of money and he knows it's in his best interest to communicate with the fans. That's the reason he's doing it. Does he want to argue with me on the radio?" That's what the Chet Coppocks, the Mike Norths, and the other guys do.

I moved the show to the Score. The Score wanted it and it was the best show they had on the air in 1992, the last season Ditka coached the Bears. As part of the deal, the Score wanted their guys on the air. The Score guys would sit behind me while I tried to control the show. I would try to steer Mike on to something that went on in the game the day before. The guys sitting behind me would interrupt my question line because they wanted to get all the air time. I'd give them the standard radio hand signals, and they would not take my signals. I hated the experience because I didn't like any of the guys on the Score. If that's talk radio, then I'm going to plant flowers or get in another business.

> The Packers have sold out every game since 1960 and at $30 have the lowest average ticket price in the NFL.

My favorite radio story about Ditka took place while we were doing the Ditka show with Chet Coppock on WMAQ. I would do two or three shows every summer at training camp. The radio station would send an engineer and equipment up, and I would do a show with Ditka in his office after practice. It was always a fun show and a relaxed atmosphere. One year, we had a little trouble taking phone calls since I was the only one doing the show in Platteville. We had to have someone in the studio in Chicago answer the phones and hang them up. Chet said he would take care of the phones. I got on the phone with Chet before the show and said, "Chet, I want you to know that I'm the guy who interviews Mike on this program. You're going to have control of the microphones in Chicago. I don't want you to do all the talking. Yes, I need you to answer the phones. You can ask your questions as you normally do, but it's my show. I want to control it."

The show started and Chet was just carrying on. About two minutes into his carrying on, my wife pulled a deck of cards out of her purse, looked at Mike and looked at me, and we both nodded "yes." I took the deck of cards. I was the moderator of the show. Ditka was the star of the show. I dealt a hand of gin. Mike and I, during the first half hour of the show, played three hands of gin while Chet talked. Occasionally Mike would have to answer a question. I'd have to do a commercial cue or ask a question, but we played three hands of gin in Mike's office in Platteville while Coppock carried on and wouldn't give us the microphone.

In 1992, Ditka was angry most of the time because he was being criticized by the press and his team wasn't winning. He was coaching a team that had been totally dismantled by McCaskey. He had had a great team that had won the championship in '85, and had only had a couple of bad playoff games because of injured quarterbacks in '86 and '87. He could have easily won three championships. It wasn't that he was a bad coach. With Jim McMahon hurt going into the playoffs in '86 and '87, they weren't going to win a championship. With McMahon they might have. But everybody said his coaching wasn't any good.

Getting fired was the best thing that could have happened to Mike at the time.

Ditka would never admit that he didn't have the talent to win. He kept wanting to win and it really hurt him that he couldn't. It created a stress and an inability to coach as well, because he was still trying to be good with less talent. It wasn't Mike's fault. It was the guy who owned and dismantled the team. When Wilber Marshall went to the Redskins for $6 million, there were fourteen unsigned players, of which seven or eight were starters. Anybody who could spell football could have made that deal and gotten Marshall away from the Bears. They knew the Bears wouldn't match it. You don't pay a guy like Wilber Marshall $6 million in 1986 and 1987 and have fourteen other guys unsigned. But McCaskey hadn't taken care of business, and that's why Wilber Marshall left. Then he lost Willie Gault because he argued with him about a little money, and he lost Otis Wilson. He lost one guy after another because of mismanagement, and Ditka was trying to win with a terrible team. So he was mad.

Getting fired was the best thing that could have happened to Mike at the time. The Bears were a bad football team and Mike was one of the most popular sports celebrities in the country. He still does a radio show in Chicago and he's in his third year as coach of the New Orleans Saints. Now that's blind loyalty.

DITKA THE MAN

Ditka is good at golf; he can hit the ball far, but he really works on the short game. And he's got a great touch. That's why he could play to a five handicap. I don't know what his handicap is now with his leg problems. I've watched him work at it—he chips and putts and works on the fine game all the time. He's totally committed. He'd spend ten hours a day in the winter at Bob O'Link at their indoor range hitting golf balls. That's how you get good.

My wife and I hosted a birthday party for Mike every year. It was a fun party with lots of funny gifts. Once, at around the fifth year, Diana showed up and Ditka wasn't there. Diana got mad and called Bob O'Link. The man at Bob O'Link said, "He doesn't want to be interrupted, Mrs. Ditka." So Diana made me call. I called and got the same thing. I said, "Give him a message, please." He was three hours late for his own birthday party.

The next year, Candy and I decided that everybody would wear the same thing—a shirt that said something like "Another Year, Same Shit." We'd even gotten one for Diana. Ditka, after arriving late, got a shirt, too, but his said "The Big Shit."

Because of his competitiveness, Mike doesn't take practical joking well. So he's the best guy to play a practical joke on. He doesn't laugh it off easily.

Neill Armstrong ended his four-year head coaching stint with the Bears at the end of the 1981 season. He was not an inspirational coach, but he was a very smart and a neat guy, and I loved him. I did the radio show with him every year he coached. He was a good coach, but he didn't have that motivational, inspirational energy. If you're a sports coach, one of the most important things you have to do is make sure that your players are giving everything they have, and that they're not taking anything home with them. Well, he had

Mike Ditka's life expectancy in war or combat would be about a second and a half, because that's the only speed he knows.

a team that didn't care and didn't leave everything on the field, so I knew they had to do something, and Ditka was the kind of guy they needed. He'd never even been a coordinator, but he had respect for George Halas and a love of Chicago and the Chicago Bears' tradition. That's why he was absolutely the best choice they could have made. The team had a bunch of guys who might have had the potential to be good players, but they weren't mentally tough. Ditka knew how to make them that.

The first years were fun. I could tell what had happened in a game by listening to his press conference after the game. If he was mad or he yelled, I could tell he was the guy who had made the mistakes. The more he yelled about the things that happened, the more he was covering up for his inability to admit that he might have made a mistake or done something wrong.

He can admit he screwed up and mean it. He does it regularly. He's very capable of humility. When he admits he made a mistake, he means it and will stand by it, but it may not be for forty-eight hours or so. The first time the Bears played the Dallas Cowboys after he joined the team as head coach in '82, something happened in the first half and I thought Mike had screwed up. I wasn't sure, but after listening to the postgame interview and hearing him bitch about the

> The Arizona Cardinals are the only NFL team to play in a college stadium—Arizona State's Sun Devil Stadium.

things they did, I said, "It was Mike's fault." I could tell by the way he bellowed and screamed at everybody. He got mad at the media, got mad at the press, got mad at the team. He got mad at everybody. It was because Landry beat him, because Landry outcoached him.

I realized the level of Ditka's intensity as a competitor—not just as an athlete, but in everything he does—the first time I saw him compete. I saw that at the All-Star camp in '61. The next closest in intensity would probably be Dick Butkus. You could make an argument that Butkus was as intense or even more intense than Mike. The only way I've ever been able to describe it is that Mike Ditka's life expectancy in war or combat would be about a second and a half, because that's the only speed he knows.

There are lot of guys with that kind of competitiveness who aren't big enough or strong enough or fast enough to play on the big-time teams. Probably the biggest mistake the NFL makes in scouting players today is not giving enough importance to character. They've got all those rating methods, but I still think they make a big mistake in not judging character. To Ditka, character is very important and has brought guys in that most thought couldn't be players. It's not how big and strong and fast you are, it's how big your heart is. "Are you a football player?"—that's the question. Football is not an easy game to play because you've got to have skills and you've got to have brains. You've got to be smart to play football.

> Q: How did the San Diego Chargers get their name?
> A: The Chargers were originally the Los Angeles Chargers in 1960, the first year of the AFL. They were owned by Barron Hilton of the Hilton Hotel chain. Hilton owned the Carte Blanche credit card company and named the team to promote the card.

photo courtesy of *Dallas Cowboys Weekly*

IN THE WRONG PLACE AT THE WRONG TIME
GARY BALLMAN

Gary Ballman played with Ditka in Philadelphia in 1967 and 1968.

I first met Mike when NY Giant Andy Robestelli put twelve guys together—me, Ron Kramer, Mike Ditka, and nine others—to do marketing stuff for Allied Chemical Corporation. They had about six different divisions and we would sign autographs and go to banquets as guest speakers.

I was an end and an outside receiver for the Eagles. I was happy to see Ditka come to Philly. He had just had an operation on his foot and he wasn't the same guy, though he had a very high tolerance for pain.

Once, our trainer used some kind of weird detergent and we all had jock rash. We were up in Reading, Pennsylvania. There were hooks in the locker room that came down from the ceiling for drying out uniforms and stuff. They gave us some of this stuff to put on the rash. It burned like you wouldn't believe. Mike was standing beneath the hooks, and he put that stuff on and jumped up and hit a hook. He needed about six stitches in his head. It was the most injury he had that season. He just happened to be in the wrong place at the wrong time.

One time I played golf with Mike at Bala Country Club in Philadelphia. I was getting my woods refinished so I was just hitting irons. We were playing a $5 Nassau and he got so pissed off he threw his clubs in the lake. I never saw a guy as competitive as Mike—he hates to lose.

I didn't think Mike had the temperament to be a head coach. But he's a very bright guy. After he was traded to the Cowboys, I was traveling through Dallas and I gave him a call. We went out to lunch and he told me that he had learned more at Dallas than he ever would have thought. At that time, Dallas was *the* team. Ditka said he learned more from Landry and from their system than from everywhere else combined.

> The Bengals, owned by Paul Brown, were named after the Massillon (Ohio) High School Tigers, whom Brown coached before he became head coach of Ohio State and the Cleveland Browns.

Mike Ditka photo courtesy of *Dallas Cowboys Weekly*

ON THE LOOKOUT
FRANK CLARKE

Clarke, a Beloit, Wisconsin, native, spent eleven years in the NFL as an outstanding receiver, primarily with the Dallas Cowboys.

I n '62 I was on the verge of breaking a seventeen-games-in-a-row touchdown record. I had fourteen games in a row with three games to go, and in a game against Washington I got hurt. I was coming down to block the linebacker, and the guy viciously kneed me in the thigh with all his force, giving me severe internal bleeding.

I was still on the sidelines when the Giants beat us, and I also had to miss the next game when we lost to the Bears by a point. I watched from the sidelines as Dandy Don Meredith played a great game, throwing four touchdown passes. The other thing I remember from that game was seeing the Bears' Mike Ditka catch passes and look for people to run over. He was amazing. I never saw any receiver catch the ball and look for people to run over. Of course, you pay the price when you want that kind of contact. At the end of his career, he could hardly walk.

When offered the coaching job at Marshall University, Bobby Bowden changed his mind at the last minute and turned it down. Less than two years later, the entire Marshall staff and team were killed in a plane crash. A few years later, he had a similar change of heart with LSU. LSU's next choice was Bo Rein.

A few months after taking the job, Rein used a private jet on a recruiting trip to Shreveport, Louisiana. On the return leg of the flight, the pilot and Rein were overcome by fumes and the plane flew pilotless across the southeastern United States before running out of gas and crashing into the Atlantic Ocean near Bermuda, killing Rein and the pilot.

THE MONK
WALT GARRISON

The pride of Lewisville, Texas, and Oklahoma State University, Walt Garrison began his nine-year pro career with the Cowboys in 1968, one year before Ditka joined the team. He became successful on the rodeo circuit after his football career ended.

Getting Ditka, a future Hall of Famer with a reputation for bloodlust, to play for the Cowboys was Tom Landry's idea. A few days after the '69 season, Tom Landry called Ditka, who had been feuding with Philadelphia coach Joe Kuharich while spending much of his season with the Eagles drinking heavily. Ditka was thinking about retiring, even though he still had a year left on his contract.

Landry told him, "We don't even know if you can play anymore, but we're going to bring you down and take a look at you and see if you can play a few more years." Ditka had always hated the Cowboys because of their arrogance and their goody-two-shoes image, but he despised Kuharich more, and agreed to come if Landry could swing a trade for him. Just prior to the '69 season, the Cowboys shipped Dave McDaniels, a second-round draft choice who turned out to be one of Gil Brandt's mistakes, to Philadelphia in exchange for the eight-year veteran.

Ditka created headlines a week before the '69 season began when he was involved in an early-morning accident after a night on the town. He weighed 235 pounds, and because of his fat jowls halfback Walt Garrison started calling him "Monk," short for "Chipmunk." Garrison, who enjoyed watching a good train wreck, was fascinated by the unpredictable Ditka.

TAUNTING DITKA

When Ditka joined the Cowboys, defensive backs Charlie Waters and Cliff Harris used to taunt him: "Yeah, Mike, you've got some great moves." And they'd swivel their heads back and forth indicating the extent of Ditka's "moves."

In practice, Charlie and Cliff would cover Monk like paint. They'd be all over him because he couldn't beat them deep and they knew it. So they didn't have to be honest. Ditka was slower than the last day of school. He would try his damnedest when he was running his routes to get those two little bastards up close enough so he could give them a forearm to the chops. Right before he made his cut, he'd try to cream our cornerbacks.

That was Ditka.

LIKE PULLING TEETH

Ditka got his teeth knocked out in an auto accident the year he joined us. He flipped his car over a parked car, went through the windshield, and broke his jaw.

The dentist told Ditka, "We can wire your teeth shut, but you can't play tomorrow. Or we can pull them."

Ditka said, "Pull the sonuvabitches."

As it turned out, they had to wire his jaw shut anyway because it was broken. But he played all the same. You could hear him out on the field breathing through his teeth. "Hiss-haw, hiss-haw, hiss-haw"—he sounded like a rabid hound. You could hear that mad dog Ditka cussing even with his mouth wired shut: "God da otherrucker."

Man, that Ditka was mean. He walked into a restaurant one night, walked over to a table with some chairs stacked on it, raked them all off with his big old forearm, and motioned for us to come on over and sit down.

Nobody said a word. I know why, too. Ditka had the foulest temper of any man I've ever met. It was so bad people used to get him mad just to see what he'd do. He could lose control in a slim second and anything could happen. That was the fun of it—the element of surprise.

PANDEMONIUM, DITKA-STYLE

Ditka was a madman. It was always a circus when Mike would play cards. He had a terrible temper when he played cards; he'd even throw chairs across the room. He was a bad card player who hated to lose, and he had a terrible temper. Put them all together, and you've got pandemonium, Ditka-style.

They let him play because before he got mad, he'd lose all his money. He was so competitive he'd stick with lousy cards, and everyone knew it. It was like having your own personal ATM machine.

> During Super Bowl III, when the Jets upset the Baltimore Colts, Joe Namath did not attempt a pass in the 4th quarter.

We usually played a card game called boo-ray before a game, and of course Monk would lose his ass and get so mad he'd start throwing chairs across the room. Hell, Ditka was throwing chairs when Bobby Knight over at

It was always a circus when Mike would play cards.

Indiana University was still using his to sit in. Ditka's big ol' chipmunk cheeks would turn red. Then he'd take the deck of cards and tear them in half and throw the sonuvabitches in the air like confetti.

Lee Roy Jordan would say, "Well, it looks like the game's over."

"Game ain't over till I get a chance to win this money back," Ditka would scream.

Ditka would stay in a hand and try to beat you when he had nothing, and everybody knew it. He was so competitive he wanted to win even if he had an eight-high nothing. As soon as he got pissed off, he'd bet and bet no matter what he had. And we all knew it.

All you could hear through the halls at night was Ditka screaming. You knew Monk was losing again.

They played mostly for markers in camp. Then at the end of camp they'd settle up. By the end of camp, Ditka didn't have any money, of course, and he owed thousands. There was no way he could pay it all. He owed one guy $1,200, another guy $1,500, another guy $2,000. And so he'd go up to each guy and say, "How much on the dollar would you like? Twenty cents on the dollar? I mean, how much actual cash will you take for what I owe you? No way I can pay twelve hundred."

The funny thing is that nobody was really pissed off. The money came so easy from Monk, if they got twenty cents on the dollar it was better than winning straight from somebody else.

Lee Roy Jordan was the only guy who was really upset about the transactions. Lee Roy was smart. He wouldn't drink, he'd just sit there and play his cards while everybody else was drunk as hell, screaming and yelling, laughing and swearing. And, of course, Lee Roy was eating them up.

> **He was so competitive he'd stick with lousy cards, and everyone knew it. It was like having your own personal ATM machine.**

Once, Buddy Dial was out a grand to Lee Roy, Chuck Howley owed him a bunch, and Monk, of course, had signed over his mortgage and his first-born child.

The gambling got so bad that when it came time for the first exhibition game, players were more concerned about who was going to get cut and leave without paying than they were about the team. Guys would be trying to make another player look good just so Landry wouldn't cut his ass and take their winnings with him.

Landry got pissed off one time about the gambling, so he got up in a meeting and said, "No more cards. No more gambling. It's disrupting the team."

So we all went back to our rooms after the meeting and decided that since nobody would get a chance to win any money back, all bets were off. We were going to just tear up all the "owsies."

Lee Roy tore up $5,000 or $6,000 worth of IOU's. And five days later the sonuvabitches were playing again. Why not? They suddenly had all this money saved up that they hadn't lost yet.

YOU CAN GET HURT PLAYING THIS GAME

(Dan) Reeves and (Dave) Manders played Landry and Ditka in tennis one evening at training camp at the apartments at Cal Lutheran, where a lot of young couples go with their kids. Everything was real nice and sociable until Ditka got behind. Then he started up. "S--t! How did I miss that shot! I hate this game!" He was yelling at the top of his lungs, and mothers were scattering around, trying to get their kids out of earshot. They might as well have moved them to Arizona as loud as Ditka was cussing.

The whole time Landry never said a word. Finally, Ditka missed a shot, slammed his racket down, smashed it all to hell, and threw what was left of it at the net. Well, the damn thing went under the net, skipped along the court, and hit Landry in the ankles. Tom was hopping around, hurting like hell, and he looked over at Reeves and said, "Boy, you can get hurt playing this game."

I used to go golfing with Ditka and Reeves and Dave Edwards. Mike threw his club after about every shot. He used to throw stuff all over. I'd just started playing golf, and I thought it was part of the game: get mad, throw a club, cuss, beat your club on the ground, break the damn thing, throw it in the lake—I thought that was how you played golf.

Monk would throw a club over in the woods and I'd go on over there and get it and put it in my bag. That's how I got my first set of clubs.

Troy Aikman wrote a book which had nothing to do with football. It was a kids' book called *Things Change*, and it sold an astonishing 200,000 copies.

LUCIFER ON WHEELS

A group of the Cowboys started riding motorcycles. On Mondays after the game, we'd usually go to Grapevine Lake and ride out in the dirt all day. Ditka bought a 125cc. Yeah, Ditka was a madman.

Ditka was a madman. He bought a yellow Yamaha, but that didn't fit Mike's image of himself so he painted it black.

He bought a yellow Yamaha, but that didn't fit Mike's image of himself so he painted it black. He bought a black leather jacket and black leather pants and a black helmet. Man, he looked like Lucifer on wheels. The only problem was that he couldn't ride worth beans. The place where we used to go riding a lot had a hill with a creek at the bottom. Monk would always try to jump the creek, and every time he'd miss and hit the other bank. BAM! "Goddamnit!" He'd start that thing up again, go back, and try to jump it again. BAM! "Goddamnit!" He'd get up and go again. BAM! "Goddamnit!"

But what really pissed Ditka off was that Cliff and Charlie could hop that creek like it was a puddle, and they'd yell back at Mike, "Come on, you fat chipmunk!" and ride off. Ditka hated those two little bastards, so he'd go back and BAM! "Goddamnit!"

A few years later, we were playing St. Louis at Texas Stadium and he was the special teams coach that year. The officials were flagging Mike's guys all day long, and Ditka was stomping and cussing and fuming along the sidelines. Finally, the officials told him he had better take it easy or he was gone.

Well, it got to be the fourth quarter and they flagged his team one more time, this time for offsides. Ditka went out onto the field and was real calm, and he said to the official, "Excuse me, sir. Are you a member of the Fellowship of Christian Athletes?"

The official kind of looked at him like, huh? "No," he said. "Then f--k you!" Ditka yelled. Landry just melted on the sidelines. They took Ditka away after that.

CONQUERING THE MOUNTAIN

After the Super Bowl one year a bunch of Cowboys went skiing in Vail, Colorado. There were about eight couples—Ditka, Manders, Reeves, Lee Roy, myself, and our wives among them.

Well, Ditka couldn't ski for shit, but of course that didn't mean anything to him. With him, it was always full-speed ahead, even if you didn't know what you were doing. The rest of us were all pretty good skiers, so we took the chair lift to the top of the mountain and Ditka came right along with us. His wife at the time, Marge, went along, too. She was wearing a purple outfit that must have cost her a couple of grand, at least. She had on purple pants, purple boots, a purple jacket, a purple hat, and a blond wig. She looked sensational!

Well, she came off that chair lift at the top and it was all iced over. She flew right off that mountain and rolled over and over a few times and her blond wig and purple hat flew right off and rolled a couple hundred feet down the mountain.

While the rest of us picked her up, Mike took off. She was really pissed. We were all asking how she was and her husband was off skiing in the other direction. He couldn't have cared less. Hey, he had a job to do. He had to conquer that mountain.

> The first black Chicago Bears quarterback was aptly named Willie Thrower.

photo courtesy of *Dallas Cowboys Weekly*

It took Mike about an hour to ski down that hill. He'd ski across and fall. Then he'd get up and cuss awhile, and then he'd ski across and fall and cuss some more. By the time he got down to the bottom, he had fallen so many times his sweater was soaked and it had stretched all the way down to his knees. It looked like a trench coat and he looked like a walrus. He had snot and ice frozen in his mustache and he was sweating like a bull on mating day. This mother was hot!

I figured Mike had to be so miserable when we finally got him down that all he'd want to do would be to go in the lodge and drink. Wrong. Not Ditka. He got down to the bottom of the slope, took one final head-over-ashcan fall, stood up, and said, "Let's go again!"

BAD FOR BUSINESS

Ditka opened a dinner-dance club in Dallas called The Sportspage, and it did unbelievable business. People were lined up on the side-walk every night begging to get a table. And on Sundays after the game, you couldn't buy your way in. That's where all the players went after the game so it attracted a crowd. People would get to drink and dance and see all their football heroes up close.

That went on for two and a half years. Then all of a sudden Ditka thought he was a restaurant tycoon instead of just a damn good tight end. So he took his profits and opened up a joint in Richardson, Texas, called The Hungry Hunter. They served wild boar, bear meat, quail—stuff like that. Hell, they even had ostrich eggs.

When Mike opened that place he figured he'd retire in two years. But the damn place didn't do any business. How many times do you say to your wife, "Geez, honey, you know what I really feel like tonight? An ostrich egg!"

After that fiasco, Ditka bought some land in Wolf Creek Pass and opened up a ski area. I don't know what Mike thought he knew about skiing, but it wasn't enough. They didn't get any snow the first year and the place bombed.

So, in the end, he blew most of the money he'd made on The Sportspage trying to hit another big one. Before he knew it, he was back at tight end with nothing in the bank and a few good years left in him. Good thing he knew how to coach.

Ditka also owned a bar with Dave Edwards in Houston. I walked in one night and there was Mike.

"How's it going, Mike?" I asked him.

"Well, it's great," Ditka says. "But those Varmint brothers came in last week. I told them to drink what they wanted and they just got drunker than hell. They were slobbering and pinching the girls and pulling their dresses over their heads. I'd have asked them to leave but I didn't know how. Finally, they got ready to go. Then Don got up on the stage with the band and there's slobber coming out of his mouth, and he yells, 'Hey, turn that off. I got something to say.' "

"So they turned the music off and Tolbert screams, 'I'll see all you sonuvabitches later.' "

> At halftime of a New Orleans Saints game in 1968, Charleston Heston drove a chariot and rode an ostrich while filming the movie Number One.

"They finally stumbled out of the place," Ditka said. "Now that's hard on business."

Ditka didn't have much luck with his friends in football. They were the main attraction of the place but they were also big pains. I was there the night E. J. Holub, the behemoth linebacker for the Kansas City Chiefs, came in. Only problem was he came in on a horse. And it wasn't no Shetland pony either. Damn thing looked like a Clydesdale.

We were all in there after the game and we looked up and saw E. J. on his trusty steed. He came right through the front doors of Ditka's place, went down the stairs, backed that baby right up in the corner, and yelled, "Y'all get my horse some beer."

He sat on that horse for an hour just sipping beer and bullshitting. Then he rode on out of there the same way he came in. And there was poor old Ditka in the back of the bar with this sorry look on his face, watching his investment go to hell.

"Ah, geez," he said. "Now that's hard on business."

photo courtesy of *Dallas Cowboys Weekly*

"TEX" DITKA, AMARILLO SLIM, AND THE VARMINT BROTHERS
DONNIE TOLBERT

The Varmint brothers are legendary in NFL circles and to anyone who was connected with the league in the 1960s and early 1970s. Donnie, Diron, Paul, and Charlie Tolbert are from the University of Texas in Richmond. Diron spent most of his career with the LA Rams and the Washington Redskins, while Donnie spent the majority of his career with the Dallas Cowboys. They spent many a memorable occasion with Mike Ditka. Although they have calmed down in recent years and are now respectable businessmen, they still cut a wide swathe in the NFL.

Doff Briscoe (now the ex-governor of Texas) was running for governor, and Dan Reeves and Walt Garrison were riding the wagon of a guy named Ben Barnes, who at that time was the lieutenant governor of Texas. So a guy named Lee Roy Caffey, who played for the Cowboys, said, "Hey, let's get some guys and back Briscoe." Briscoe flew into Dallas, and we went up and met him to have dinner and a few drinks. Then we all went out to Texas Instruments and shook hands with everybody coming onto the line in the morning. We made a few stops and he was really appreciative. He was running about third in the ranking.

About two weeks later, they caught Ben Barnes in a bank scandal. Our man Briscoe went straight to the top. He won the nomination and won as governor of Texas. He said to us, "I want to take you guys on a big hunt."

So we got all our guys together and drove from Austin out to San Antonio airport. We were picking up Dave Edwards, Craig Morton, and Mike Ditka. They had all worked for Briscoe. We got to the airport and said, "Where the hell is Ditka? That son of a bitch didn't even show up." Then Ditka stepped out from behind a column where he had been hiding and said, "I knew I was in trouble when I saw all them damn Boone's Farm bottles come flying out of the car."

We got down to the ranch, rode around, hunted, and had a big time, and that night they got into a poker game. A bunch of judges were there, and Doff had also invited all his bankers and everyone on his board of directors. We all had dinner, had a few drinks, and carried on. Then they decided to play poker. A bunch of them wanted to play, and they weren't playing penny ante—they were playing pot limit. Ditka sat down next to a judge and got on him because the judge had all the damn chips. Ditka said, "You little son of a bitch, call or get out of the game."

He had a case of twelve-year-old St. James scotch. They were all raising hell. They were playing high-low split and had a two-pot game. The judge still had all the chips. Ditka said, "Deal the damn

> In 1961, Alabama assistant football coach
> Howard Schnellenberger personally picked up
> Joe Namath in Beaver Falls, Pennsylvania, and
> drove him to the Alabama campus in Tuscaloosa.

cards. You run a kangaroo court down there in Commerce, I know you do."

They were raising hell, so one of Doff's guys came over and said, "Any of you all want to go out and shoot a mountain lion?" So four or five of us went with him. On the way out there we caught a small jackrabbit. We brought it back to the house with us.

It was way more cursing than God likes to hear from a football person during peacetime.

When we got back, they were still playing cards, and Ditka was still on the judge. He was saying the same things: "You little sawed-off son of a bitch, running a kangaroo court, deal the cards." The judge had all these cards, and he said, "What was the name of that little game we were playing? How do you play this game, little fellers?" And Ditka said, "You got all the chips and you're asking what kind of a game we're playing?"

I said, "Look at Ditka. He's in there raising hell, just tearing every-body every way. Let's get the rabbit and put it in Ditka's bed." So I went outside and got the rabbit.

Ditka, Dave Edwards, my brother Diron Tolbert, and my old room-mate Eddie Padgett were in the Sam Rayburn suite. This wasn't a camp house—this was plush. The Sam Rayburn suite was beautiful and immaculate—the beds were made and it had a big sleeping porch. There were about twelve to fifteen of us, and we all loudly crept into the suite. Dave Edwards said, "What are you all doing?"

We asked him which bed was Ditka's. Then we took the rabbit and put it between Ditka's pillows.

Ditka came in at about 2:00 in the morning. He pulled the covers back and laid his head down, right on the rabbit. You could have heard him holler all the way to Mexico City; it was hilarious. He was after us all the next day. He said, "You all have had it." It was way more cursing than God likes to hear from a football person during peacetime.

When he got up the next day, he and the judge were the best of friends. They were inseparable; they rode all over the ranch, hugging each other and telling each other what buddies they were. And just the night before they were killing each other.

> Q: What comic strip characters are named after sports figures?
> A: The B. C. character in "Doonesbury" is named after former Yale and Cleveland Browns quarterback Brian Dowling. The title character in the current sports comic strip "Gil Thorp" is named for Gil Hodges and Jim Thorpe.

photo courtesy of *Dallas Cowboys Weekly*

NO AD-LIBBING
THOMAS "HOLLYWOOD" HENDERSON

Hollywood Henderson was a controversial linebacker for the Cowboys in the 1970s. Drafted in a low round out of Langston University in Oklahoma, a virtually unknown school for football, Henderson soon made a mark on the Cowboys scene with his running talents.

T he Cowboys' opponent in Super Bowl X in 1976 was the Pittsburgh Steelers, a powerful defensive team that was back for its second year in a row. Pittsburgh had defeated Minnesota by a score of 16–6 in Super Bowl IX, in which the Steelers held Fran Tarkenton to six points, a testament to their defense's quickness. "Mean" Joe Greene, Ernie Holmes, Dwight

White, and L. C. Greenwood were a formidable front line, and middle linebacker Jack Lambert was a wild man in the mold of Dick Butkus.

On the urging of special teams coach Mike Ditka, the Cowboys' game plan began with a surprise. Though Thomas Henderson was a linebacker, he could run the 40 in 4.5. Against the Cardinals on a reverse he had run a kickoff back ninety-seven yards for a touchdown, and before the game Ditka explained to the rookie that he was to do it again. For one of the few times in his life, Thomas Henderson had butterflies.

The coach I had the best relationship with that first year was Mike Dikta.

Let me tell you how I was feeling before that game. Here's a guy who had witnessed his mother shoot his stepfather with a gun nine years before, whose best friend had been shot at close range and killed six years before, and who had graduated from Langston University just one year before. I had played one season in the NFL and had run for a touchdown. But to be in the Super Bowl—that was a different story.

Before the game, I had already wrapped myself up. I had on the elbow pads, the hand pads, and all this extra padding, because I was going to kick butt on those special teams. Then, after we warmed up, Ditka came over to me and said, "If we win the toss, we're going with the reverse." So I had to take all that padding off. I had to put stickum on. It scared me to death! I was like, "You're going to let me handle the ball the first play of the Super Bowl?"

There have been times in my life when I've been afraid, but this was the first stage fright I have ever had. It was all that pressure. Coach Landry was very concerned that a linebacker was handling the ball. He liked the results, but he was always nervous about a linebacker handling the ball, which is a legitimate concern. I agreed with Landry at that moment: "I'm a linebacker. Give the ball to somebody else." But on the other hand, I was like, "Give me the ball. Let's go." I was a running back in high school, in my early days; I knew how to run.

Ditka was a very intense man. All he wanted you to do was do your job and do it right.

They kicked it off, I faked my little deal, Preston Pearson took it deep, and I had to go around. I was standing on the thirty-yard line, and I had to go back to him at about the ten. He started my way and I went his way. He gave the ball to me, and I took it the other way, and a wall set up. When I turned the corner, everything looked pretty good, except the Steelers weren't quite as fooled as the Cardinals had been a few weeks earlier. At some point, I thought I could have cut back.

But instead I ran the play the way it was designed. I didn't freelance and try to make something happen. Ditka liked that. He didn't like you to go out there and start doing your own tap dance. "No ad-libbing, goddamn it," he'd say.

The coach I had the best relationship with that first year was Mike Ditka. He was an offensive coach and a special teams coach. He liked the way I got things done. To this day, Ditka will say, "Thomas Henderson was a good football player. He's crazy as hell, but he's a good football player." He'll say that because all the coaches who ever coached me never saw me back down. You'll watch films on a player and he'll get hurt and wince and run or dodge. They never saw me back down. I don't have that in me.

Ditka was a very intense man. All he wanted you to do was do your job and do it right. He would tell me to go down the field and do this or that, and I did it. And he never saw me back down.

I remember playing one of my finest games in Super Bowl XII in 1978. Ditka, the consummate competitor, said to me, "Thomas," —and he knew I loved doing shit like this—"on the first punt, if you get a shot at Rick Upchurch, take the penalty. Just take him out. Don't hurt him, but get his attention. Make sure he's going to be looking for you the rest of the day." We were all afraid of Rick Upchurch. We felt that he could beat us returning kickoffs and punts.

I flew down the field with my mission orders, and I took a fifteen-yard penalty. I just creamed Upchurch. I came over to the sideline, and Ditka had moved away, so I had to see Landry. I said to him, "Well, Ditka told me to do that." Landry turned to look for Ditka and he couldn't even find him!

> The oldest NFL record belongs to George Halas.
> He made the longest fumble return for a
> touchdown (ninety-seven yards) in 1923.

THE MONSTER OF THE MIDWAY
JIM McMAHON

Jim McMahon, a graduate of Brigham Young, was a first-round draft pick for the Chicago Bears in 1982. He played with the Bears for seven years, and led the team to their 1985 Super Bowl win. McMahon retired in 1996.

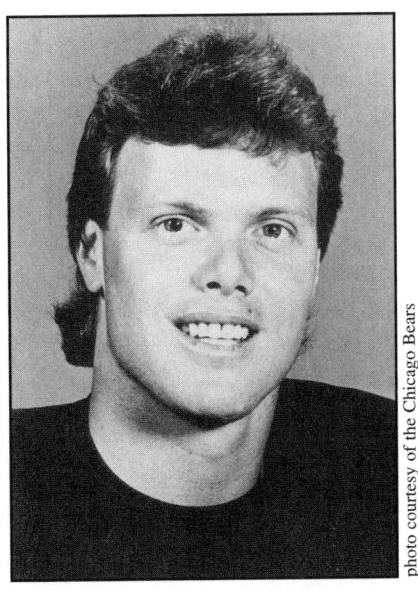

photo courtesy of the Chicago Bears

For many years, American Airlines hosted an annual golf outing featuring their best corporate customers playing with famous athletes. The tournament rotated among the top golf resorts in North America. In February 1986, the tournament paid its third visit to Scottsdale, Arizona. It was less than a month after the Bears won the Super Bowl. Of all the famous athletes playing, Jim McMahon was easily the most in demand.

The final day of the tournament was one of the worst ever weather-wise. It was cold, windy, and rainy. If ever an athlete could beg off signing autographs without an explanation, that was the day. When McMahon came off the eighteenth green, every fan still braving the elements was waiting for him. He stood there for almost an hour signing autographs and posing for pictures. Someone asked him what Scottsdale bar he was going to that evening. He looked up from his signing and replied, "I'm going to the best bar in the world tonight—my mother-in-law's house in San Francisco."

Before I went up to my first Bears camp in Platteville, Wisconsin, I didn't know anything at all about Mike Ditka. All I knew of the Bears was Brian Piccolo, Gale Sayers, and Dick Butkus. I grew up in the Bay area, so I was a Raiders/49ers fan; those were my teams.

I liked Ditka's attitude. I liked the fact that his number one priority was to win. That's why you play sports and that's why you compete—to win. Every player wants to do his best, but hell, it's no fun unless you win.

Ditka and I would have a run-in every week. Our goals were the same; he just had a different opinion on how to achieve those goals. When I was on the field, I felt that was my job. I felt like, I know what the hell I'm doing—just leave me alone. He wanted to call all the plays and do this and that. But I was taught in college that if you see something to exploit, exploit it. Since we didn't throw the ball a lot, if I got a chance to change the play to a pass, I would do it. We'd scream and yell at each other, because his natural tendency was to blow up if something didn't work. Then we'd watch the film and he'd say, "Well, now I see why you did what you did." I think he eventually just figured out that I knew what the hell I was doing. That's why the guys playing now are struggling. If the headsets go out, they can't call a play. They're so reliant on their coaches to spoon-feed them everything. Hell, I don't know what they learn in college anymore.

I told Mike many times I wished I had played with him. He played the game the way it's supposed to be played. He didn't think I studied enough. I told him if he'd ever been in the huddle with me, he'd have a different opinion. I said to him, "You know, you don't have to be a rocket scientist to run this offense. You could be brain-dead almost." The offense didn't change in the seven years I was there.

O. J. Simpson's cousin is Ernie Banks. Their grandfathers were twin brothers.

I didn't socialize with Mike, but I played a lot of golf with his wife, Diana. She would always say, "Mike likes you a lot." I'd say, "Then why is he cussing me out every Sunday?" I used to play with her and her friends all the time; she was great. His regular game was cards. I heard a lot of stories about him throwing chairs and card tables through the wall, just because he wanted to win. He hates losing. I hate losing as much as him. Any game Ditka plays—air hockey, pool, golf—he wants to win. That's where you separate the men from the boys. If you're going to do something, be the best at it. You have to have it inside you to win. You've got to have that something inside you that says you're not going to lose that game.

> **I liked Dikta's attitude. I liked the fact that his number one priority was to win.**

In '85, I watched from the sidelines as the Minnesota game slipped away. You could see it in the guys' faces when they came off the field. I was yelling at Mike to let me in. I had been in traction on the Monday and Tuesday before the game. I got out of the hospital Wednesday morning, went to practice that afternoon, and then flew up to Minnesota Thursday morning for the Thursday night game. Not only were my back and neck screwed up, I also had an infected turf burn on my leg. My damn calf was twice as big as my thigh.

On my very first play he called a screen pass, and I didn't throw the screen. I stumbled away from the center, I was so wobbly. I knew it was a blitz, which is man-to-man coverage, and a screen is not very good against that unless you use a technique we called "the spy." I happened to look downfield and saw Willie Gault running his guy off like he was supposed to on a screen. He was ten yards past his man, so I just threw it to him. Mike was yelling at me as I came off the field, "Damn it, what play did you call?" I told him I had called the screen pass he gave me. He said, "Why'd you throw it to Willie?" I said, "Because he was open. We scored, what are you mad about?" I think he thought I did everything just to piss him off, but I did it to amuse myself. Sitting in those meetings a couple of hours a day bored me. I'm a player; I just want to play. I didn't practice a whole lot in my career, and it didn't seem to hurt me.

PERSONALITY CONFLICTS

Ditka and I have had our moments, and we probably always will. He said I did certain things for the sole purpose of aggravating him, but I really didn't. I didn't wake up every morning wondering, "How can I annoy Ditka today?" It's hard enough just to wake up in the morning, let alone think and plot.

> **I told Mike many times I wished I had played with him.**

I was hurt one season, and we didn't talk for a few weeks. We never exchanged a civil word. Jerry Vainisi even called me up to his office one day after practice, sat me down, and told me I had to resolve my personality conflict with Mike. Personality conflict? What personality conflict? I was injured. I wasn't playing. There was no reason for him to talk to me, or for me to talk to him.

Besides, Ditka did talk to me, as he pointed out when someone asked him about the situation. He came over to me on the sidelines in Dallas and screamed, "Shut the f--k up, McMahon!" That's talking, isn't it? And I know it was Mike, because his veins were sticking out of his neck and his face was red as a beet, like it was ready to explode. That had to be my good friend Sybil, the one who wears a necktie on the sidelines, the one we all figured would strangle himself someday with that same necktie. He'll get mad and he'll reach to make that knot tighter, and by the time the paramedics get to him with the oxygen it'll be too late.

I remember clearly why he screamed at me in Dallas. That was the game in which we humiliated the Cowboys 44–0. Steve Fuller started for us at quarterback, and he did a great job. Our defense was awesome, as usual. I was yelling from the bench for our guys to really give it to the Dallas quarterback, Danny White, which they eventually did.

"Shut the f--k up, McMahon!" Ditka roared. "What's the problem, Mike?" I asked. "They get Danny White hurt, and they'll put in (Gary) Hogeboom, and he's better than White," Ditka said. "So shut up."

I just walked away from him. That was the same day he got mad at me because of the way I was dressed. I had on a normal shirt and faded blue jeans. He got mad because he thought I didn't look presentable. Hell, I had on a pair of ostrich boots that were worth more than his entire wardrobe. Mike doesn't worry about the unimportant things. Most of the time, anyway.

We had another episode later in the season at Giants Stadium when we played the New York Jets. I called an audible and Walter Payton just got smashed on the play, sort of like when I screwed up early in the Super Bowl. When I got back to the sidelines, I could see that Mike wasn't in the best of moods. I don't know how I was able to make that deduction. Maybe it was the fact that, with sixty thousand people screaming in the arena, Mike's voice was the only one anybody heard.

> In 1999, Monday Night Football became the longest-running prime-time entertainment series ever, breaking a tie with Walt Disney at twenty-nine years.

photo courtesy of the Chicago Bears

"You motherf--ker," he yelled at me. "F--k you," I said.

The national TV cameras recorded our little conversation. That was a Saturday in December. The next day, when a lot of pro football games were being played, the people from CBS asked me to stay over in New York to appear on the NFL Today show.

Naturally, they had those film clips ready, and naturally, they asked me about the incident.

"Well," I said, "that about sums up our relationship." I never lie, particularly on Sundays.

But Mike has mellowed since we both came to the Bears in 1982. He was really uptight when he started as coach. One of the worst things he did was get all over guys for making mistakes. He'd take them out of games, scream at them in public, and go crazy on the sidelines. It got so bad that the players couldn't relax, because they were afraid of what Ditka might do if they dropped a pass or missed an assignment. He could really get out of control, and so badly that he'd lose his grasp on the game itself. He was the Monster of the Midway.

Ditka was just as hard on himself. We heard stories about some of the wild things he did as an assistant with the Cowboys before he left Dallas for Chicago. He could throw a pretty mean clipboard, we were told. He could throw a pretty good fit, too. Mike Ditka had a major-league temper.

We found that out after our fourth game of the 1983 season, which we lost in overtime to Baltimore, 22–19. Ditka came into the locker room and started pounding on an equipment locker. All of a sudden, he looked up at the trainer and said, "I think I broke my hand." He had. We didn't know whether to laugh or cry.

SPECIAL WINE

During the last couple of years we were together, Ditka wasn't quite as high-strung, and that helped the players play better. The fact that we were 18–1 probably helped us get away with things we never would have gotten away with otherwise, but the point is that Ditka was most concerned with how we played on Sunday. He didn't bug us about some of the nutty things we said or did.

Of course, he said and did some pretty strange things himself. There was that sixth game of 1985, when we whipped the 49ers in San Francisco 26–10. That win not only kept us unbeaten at 6–0, it repaid the 49ers for knocking us out of the playoffs the year before. Mike really wanted to win that game. He told us that if we won, he'd share some of his special wine on the long flight back to Chicago that night.

Well, we never got to taste any of that wine. Later, we found out why. Mike had tasted all of the wine himself. He was smashed, hammered, bobbing, and weaving. There's no way he should have been allowed to drive home that night. Vainisi felt the same way and offered him a lift. Apparently, the police felt the same way, too.

Five minutes after we left O'Hare Airport, Ditka was pulled over for drunk driving. He had said something on TV after the game about how he might celebrate a little on the plane, to the point where he might not be able to see when he got back home. Evidently, the Illinois State Police were watching.

A few of us took the same highway home, and he damn near ran over a couple of guys. He was all over the road. He would have killed himself if he hadn't have been stopped by the cops. When we caught up to where he'd been nailed, we saw his car and the police car on the side of the road. Nobody pulled over. We just honked our horns and drove on by. I guess his wife, Diana, had to come and get him.

The next morning, I heard about it on the radio on the way to Halas Hall. So had most of the other guys. Naturally, it was a hot topic in the locker room, and when Mike held his meeting, he didn't look too good. He looked like a coach who hadn't lost a game, but had lost his license for a few months.

"Fellas . . . I did something very stupid last night," he said. There were a few of us in the room coughing loudly to keep from cracking up. That must have been real special wine indeed.

Ironically, this guy who could pound the streets at night with the best of them later told my roommate, Kurt Becker, and me to watch ourselves. I had a bad first half in Tampa one year, and he came over

> The NFL since 1968 has given every player the Wonderlic test (a human resources test measuring the ability to acquire and use job knowledge). In a recent year, 118,549 non-NFL people took the test and only 4 had a perfect score of 50. In thirty years, the only NFL player with a perfect score was Pat McInally of Harvard in 1968. McInally starred with the Cincinnati Bengals as tight end and punter.

to me and said, "That's what you get for staying out all night." I hadn't been out all night, or even half the night, but that was Mike.

Ditka also warned Becker that alcohol and football don't mix. He told Becker that he would fine us one week's paycheck if we were caught breaking curfew, and that management might have to put a cage around our room on the road just to keep us in at night. This from a coach who got picked up by the police for driving under the influence! That never happened to me. Besides, I don't mix my alcohol with football. I don't mix my alcohol with anything. I prefer beer. It's much better for you than wine.

I'm not saying Mike is a hypocrite, he just does some weird things. He's a born-again Christian who says he's very religious, which is fine. But I guess for three hours every Sunday that doesn't hold, because I wouldn't even use some of the words that come out of his mouth when he's coaching. I've never even heard some of those words!

FINDING OURSELVES

Mike Ditka just wants to win. He wants to win more than anything.

Every so often, he'd give us that same line: "If you forty-five guys don't want to play, we'll go out and get forty-five guys who do." That was part of his "prima donna" speech. When you hear that twice a week, it tends to get old. Mike has to get some new material.

Still, he was great at keeping his players levelheaded. He had to have known that the 1985 Bears didn't have a whole lot of attitude problems. Just like he had to have known that we weren't a bunch of prima donnas. We worked our butts off, and he knew it. But whether he wanted us to know he knew is another matter. He was forever reviewing films of Sunday victories on Monday and knocking us down to size.

For instance, we finished one regular season in Detroit. We beat the Lions 37–17 to finish 15–1. It wasn't a great performance, and we realized that, but it got the job done. After the game, Ditka told us we were full of horsefeathers and that we had no chance in the playoffs if we continued to play that way. We had just won a game on the road by twenty points to go 15–1, and he was giving us grief.

"You've got a couple days off for Christmas, fellas," he said. "I hope you go home and find yourselves."

> **I never looked at Ditka, but I don't imagine he found anything funny in my sick and sarcastic humor.**

On the flight home that night—it was a short one, so we didn't have any special wine on board—I slipped up front and grabbed hold of the public-address system. I told the guys we were about to land and that they should have a happy holiday, but that above all, they should try to find themselves. When I walked to the back of the plane, the guys were roaring. I never looked at Ditka, but I don't imagine he found anything funny in my sick and sarcastic humor.

I do think, though, that deep down Ditka respects a guy who will stand up for what he believes in. He might even like me for that, in some strange way, because that's the way he is. Mike doesn't watch every word he says. He's not afraid to say something that's going to motivate the next week's opponent, because he knows next week's game is going to be won on the field, not in the newspapers. It's you against us, baby. Let's see who's better. Let's see who's stronger. That's the way Mike operates. That's the way I think.

Considering his background as a bona fide free spirit, I don't think

Mike expected us all to be the same, on the field or off. He knows that you can't lock forty-five guys in their rooms at 8:00 the night before a game. Some guys will stay in, which is fine. I couldn't. For one thing, I couldn't sleep that well or that long before a game. I liked to go out and have a few beverages and relax. Sometimes I forgot to check the clock, but it's ridiculous to be knocking on the doors of grown men to make sure they haven't broken curfew. Fortunately, Mike wasn't into that. Every once in a while he'd give you a little message, to let you know that he was watching. But when you win like we won, a good coach is going to let a lot slide.

Is Mike Ditka a good coach? Well, he knows the game, but he gets a little wrapped up in his innovations sometimes. That's surprising, I know, because he is a basic guy, no frills. But Mike did spend a lot of time in Dallas under Tom Landry, the head coach of the Cowboys, and he got caught up with movement and all those different formations. That's great stuff, if you know what you're doing. The thing is, the more complex you make the game, the more chances you have to make mistakes. If it were up to me, football would be as simple as possible. Mike is that way, deep down, but every once in a while, when he puts his thinking cap on, you never know quite what to expect.

He can be very stubborn, too. I've talked to his assistant coaches, and they say he's a good guy to work for. He listens, he can have some fun, and he doesn't demand that you spend twenty-four hours a day on the job, looking at films and all that, even though he is in his office at 5:00 A.M. during the season. I don't know when he sees his family. His assistants also say that Mike's pretty good at taking a game plan that's been carefully drawn up by the staff, then changing it all around to do it his way.

Maybe he is a genius in a way. Not with the X's and O's, but in getting players to be committed to win. When I first got to the Bears, the attitude wasn't very good. He said there were too many guys around whose highlight of the week wasn't game day, but payday. You don't want to pay the price, he said, you're just putting in time and going through the motions.

I'll give Ditka full credit for getting rid of those players. He let them know that he wanted no part of them, and he gave them a chance to do it his way. When they didn't, they were gone. That's what got that ball rolling—the selection of the right forty-five guys. Mike was right when he said that some of our so-called second- or third-stringers might not have had the ability that other players on teams that didn't win the Super Bowl had. But our guys were perfect for us; they fit in just right.

Mike, as committed as he is to God, doesn't believe it's God's will when you lose a game. We had a few players who would pray in the shower room, all by themselves. These were the same guys who would drop a pass and say, "Well, He meant it that way." Well, I believe in God, and I believe that God's will is that everybody tries his hardest, everybody tries to succeed, and everybody tries to win. You can use God as an inspiration, but not as a crutch.

That was just one of the factions, or cliques, that used to hurt the Bears. When you have a few guys going off by themselves to pray before a game, it sort of sets them apart. A lot of people would have trouble believing this, but I said a little prayer to God before every game, too. I asked him to help me do my best and to help me stay healthy for my family's sake. But I didn't run off and pray away from my teammates. And if I played a lousy game, I didn't say it

> In football pileups, Walter Payton used to lay at the bottom and untie his opponents' shoelaces. That's why a lot of defenders put tape over their laces today.

was the Lord's will.

I'm partial, of course. I think if you have forty-five beer-drinking fools who love each other, you have a good chance of having a good football team. Judging by some of the things Mike's done as a coach, I have to think he partly agrees. After Ditka came, we didn't have the divisions in the team we used to have. We didn't have the offense on one side of the room and the

> **They say that there's a lot of Mike Dikta in me, and a lot of me in Mike Dikta.**

defense on another side, blaming each other. We were all together, and Ditka was a big reason for that. He kept stressing that you can't be pointing fingers, that it's not the offensive team or the defensive team that matters. It's the team, period. The Bears.

Ditka could get under your skin at times, that's for sure. He'd get you furious enough at him that you'd go out and knock a guy's block off, just to get him off your back, just to prove him wrong. Ditka was pretty smart that way. He kept pushing and pushing until you were right at the edge. But he also knew when to lift you up. He's a man's man, when you get right down to it.

As serious as he is, Mike can make you laugh. He could make some really strong pregame speeches, but he could also go the other way. The Saturday night before the Super Bowl, he showed up for our meeting and it was obvious he wasn't going to give us the "Win one for the Gipper" business. Instead, he started imitating some of the bizarre things that had taken place that week, especially those things involving me.

He wore sunglasses, he brought up the headbands and the acupuncture, and then he turned around and dropped his pants right in our faces. That was his way of toasting my sore behind, I suppose. That was also his way of mimicking what I'd done earlier that week, when a helicopter flew over our secret practice session. I flipped them a moon, just to show everybody where I hurt. Mike was just trying to act as demented as me. It worked. It was pretty funny.

They say there's a lot of Mike Ditka in me, and a lot of me in Mike Ditka. That might be true. Some of the things he did made me mad and some of the things I did made him mad. But we both wanted to do the same thing: win and let the rest take care of itself. I'd still call him if I was in trouble or if I needed help. I'd want him on my side in a fight. And, if we were teammates, I'm sure we'd go out for a few beers—unless, of course, he wanted to drink wine. In that case, I'd make sure to drive him home.

One of the things about Ditka, who was a mean and rough tight end for the Bears when they won the NFL title in 1963, is that he was a hell-raiser as a player. There's this story about George Halas showing films one day when he was still the coach. He was pointing out some things about the next opponent—strengths, weaknesses, that sort of thing. All of a sudden, Mike stood up in the back of the room and yelled at the top of his lungs, "F--k 'em!" I don't know if the story is true, but it sure sounds like Ditka.

So does that anecdote about how Ditka was fighting with Halas, trying to get a raise. Ditka got angry and frustrated and said, "The old man throws quarters around like manhole covers." Way to go, Mike! That's what I mean when I say Ditka probably would have been a great guy to have as a teammate, a lot more fun that he was to have as a coach. We would have probably been out drinking every night. I know he would have been out every night. I know I would have been out every night. It only stands to reason that we would have gone out together every night.

SEPARATING THE MEN FROM THE BOYS
MIKE SINGLETARY

Mike Singletary exploded onto the Chicago sports scene in 1981 as the Bears' first-round draft pick from Baylor University. He quickly established himself among the very top Bears players of all time with his savage play and wide-eyed intensity.

photo courtesy of the Chicago Bears

I'll never forget the first day I saw Ditka. Intensity oozed from his pores. That first day, you knew change was ahead. But for good or for bad, no one was quite sure. He instructed Ted Plumb, our receivers coach, to call roll. *Roll.* "Well, fellas," Ditka said, calling us together for the first time, "we have only forty-nine players, and we're going to get out here, and we're going to see who's best. We're going to separate the men from the boys around here, and see who wants to work and who doesn't. If you don't want to win, if you don't want to sacrifice, then you don't want to be here."

Even if you did want to "be here," there were times when you didn't. He had two mini-camps, and one was in Scottsdale, Arizona. It was ninety degrees in the shade, and the training regimen was more Green Beret than Bear. Forty-yard dashes until we dropped. Run here. Sprint there. Miles and miles before we slept. The mumbling and grumbling would have been louder if anyone had had enough strength to speak. "I want football players," he said time and time

photo courtesy of the Chicago Bears

again. "Too many guys around here have too many things going on outside of football."

It boiled down to one word: pride. Pride in yourself. Pride in your teammates. Pride in your commitment to improve. "I'm proudest of being a Bear," he would say. Ditka! It even sounded tough. From that first day, I never doubted his ability to unify and push his team in a positive direction.

His golden rule was that you played by his. He never begged us to do anything. If he said the meeting was at 9:00 A.M., he didn't mean 8:59 or 9:01. You did things a certain way—his way—or you were cut. Yet, at the same time that he was filling the waiver wires, you sensed that he would accept deviation, a free spirit or two. And even though the papers were already calling Halas's hiring of him "madness" and knocking Ditka's intelligence, Ditka was going about his business, building a bond between offense and defense that never before existed.

"You don't win games with defense," he said. "It takes offense, special teams. We're not going to win until everyone does his job, because winning and losing depends on all three." He didn't care whom we played. "They're playing the Bears! The Bears!" There was nothing phony about him. You'd see him in his office at 5:30 A.M., jogging the halls, then again at midnight, turning off the lights. He wanted to be the best. That's all I knew about him. We rarely talked—only once or twice a season in depth—but I knew all I needed to know, or wanted to know. He wanted to be the best. That was good enough for me.

But the transition wasn't easy. He cleaned house for one year. In a way, he reminded me of a tailor, because whenever someone wasn't putting out or was getting too big for his britches, Ditka would always be there to cut him down to size. If he sensed a certain swagger seeping into your step, or a head beginning to swell, he always reached for the scissors. Chop, chop. "Hey, just look at it this way," he'd say. "You could be working for a living. And really, what can you do? I don't think half of you are smart enough to get a job. We don't need you. If you want to leave and get a better deal, fine. Leave."

> **I'll never forget the first day I saw Dikta. Intensity oozed from his pores.**

In the strike-shortened season of 1982, we went 3–6, and the press was screaming for Ditka's scalp. McMahon was hot and cold, still learning the offense, and we were still a year away from a block-buster draft.

Halas had died in October 1982, at the age of eighty-eight, and was replaced by Bears president Mike McCaskey, a Yale graduate, ex-Peace Corps volunteer, Harvard professor, and author of a book on management. Despite the eighteen months remaining on his three-year contract, Ditka wasn't sure where he stood with McCaskey, a man with a corporate outlook on life who was in the process of restructuring our front office, paying particular attention to improving our scouting department. We had only two scouts for fifty states, the smallest such department in the league. McCaskey was fully aware that only one pick past the fourth round had ever made our club between 1978 and 1982.

The changes paid off in 1983. Big-time talent arrived in the form of Jimbo Covert, Willie Gault, Mike Richardson, Dave Duerson, Pat Dunsmore, Richard Dent, and Mark Bortz. I had made All-Pro my second season, and had signed a six-year, $1.6-million deal with the Bears, much of the money deferred. The contract had been negotiated by Tom Williams, my friend in Houston. "Treat me fair," I said. "I want to die a Bear." My only stipulation: if at any time this contract becomes unfair, we'll work together to bring it up to date.

Except for my rookie year in 1981, Mike was the only head coach I ever had in the pros.

Q: Pat Summerall's real first name is George. Why is he called Pat?

A: Because when he was a kicker with the New York Giants football team, the newspapers would always print: "P.A.T. Summerall." P.A.T. stood for "Point After Touchdown."

MIKE DITKA ON DUANE THOMAS

photo courtesy of *Dallas Cowboys Weekly*

Duane Thomas was a big factor in us winning. He was a good football player. He was a good all-around receiver, runner, and blocker. He was a fluid runner who never took a real hard hit. He was like Jim Brown. He knew how to give and go, slip and slide—all that stuff. He was an excellent blocker, which people didn't know. Dan Reeves worked with him and said, "That guy is really smart." He knew the fullback and halfback spots. He had to know both because Walt Garrison got hurt and Duane had to go to fullback with Calvin Hill at halfback.

But it was just uncomfortable and no fun to be around him. Once we were playing the Giants in Yankee Stadium. I always made a habit of going up and wishing everybody good luck before a game. I went up to Duane and just patted him on the back and said, "Good luck." He didn't acknowledge it. I went on my way. We played the game. The following Tuesday, I was sitting beside my locker reading the paper in Dallas before practice and he came up to me and said, "Hey, man, don't ever hit me on the back before a game. It breaks my concentration."

I said, "Hey, Duane, go f--k yourself."

That was our conversation.

Chapter 3

photo courtesy of *Dallas Cowboys Weekly*

Dave McGinnis

Rick Jago

Tom Hurvis

Mac Chuchill

Kyle Petty

Jim Rittenberg

Bob Costas

Buddy Diliberto

Mike North

Skip Bayless

Greg Aiello

Vince Tobin

Colleagues

A CLASS ACT
DAVE McGINNIS

photo courtesy of the Arizona Cardinals

Dave McGinnis grew up in the west Texas town of Snyder and starred at TCU. He is one of the few people ever to turn down a head coaching job in the NFL, despite never having held one previously. The Chicago Bears' Mike McCaskey brought the offer to replace Dave Wannstedt to McGinnis in early 1999. McGinnis said thanks but no thanks. He is now a defensive coordinator with the Arizona Cardinals.

Turning down the head coaching job with the Bears in early 1999 was an easy decision to make. I wanted that job so badly, but it was an easy decision to make because everything that is supposed to be there for something to be right was absent. Ditka was one of the first guys to call me, because I had talked to him extensively when I had been up there to interview. He said, "Kid, you're one in a thousand who would have turned it down. If I could right now, I'd come through this phone and kiss you right on the mouth."

It was just incredible, and not only for the people in Chicago. I've still got stacks of mail from executives and assistant coaches in the league who knew what was going wrong. It just points out that there is no right way to do the wrong thing. Something was wrong at the very beginning.

It was extremely, extremely hard to turn it down, believe me. But I knew taking it wasn't right. As I said in my exit interview at O'Hare, I wasn't angry; I was very sad. I was extremely sad that it was handled the way it was. You grow up with

> **"If I could right now, I'd come through this phone and kiss you right on the mouth."**

principles and things that you know are right, and you can't compromise those for power, and that's what I told Michael. If I compromise my vows for the power, the position, and the money, when I get up in front of this team I'm nobody. When I get up in front of this city, I'm nobody. Because I'm here for a reason: because you respect what I stand for. This is not what I stand for—all of the bluster and everything that goes on. It's like Ditka; people don't know that Mike is very, very religious and spiritual. He'll deal with you—look you straight in the eye and deal with you—from the heart.

I said to the Bears, "Regardless of how much money you put on this table now, bypass me, because you've lost what is important." That's exactly the way I felt. It's very important to get those positions, but it's more important to take them and be able to be an example when you've got them. If you're in that kind of position, you need to have some influence, and the influence has to be positive. If you can't be positive, you take the position in an underhanded manner—just because of the money.

Ever since the Chicago thing, I've been doing some head-hunting. It's incredible, the response I've received from what happened in Chicago. It helps me to know that some people, especially some owners in this league, do realize how important it is, especially in this climate, to have someone the players can look up to and know is honest.

If you've lived the right way and continue to do the right thing, it will come out and show itself, because there is no right way to do the wrong thing. That other stuff is very temporal and it can't last forever.

It was really a shock when we all got canned in Chicago in '93. I really didn't believe it was going to happen, just because of all that Ditka had done. And like anything else, you run through cycles in this league, so I don't know about all the maneuverings behind the scenes. But we didn't expect it, and when it came, it came as a shock and was very sad.

Just to see the way he handled that—with dignity and confidence and very real emotion. He cried. Because Mike Ditka's a very real guy.

He loved the Bears, and he's a tough guy who's not afraid to cry and show you his emotions. That's another thing that endeared him to the team. Some of the greatest times with him were on those Saturday nights before the ballgames. He would get up with impassioned speeches the guys knew weren't contrived, especially when we were getting ready to play the Packers. During those years, you could feel and see Halas and Lombardi coming out of him. As a coach getting ready to play a ballgame, you were sitting on edge. But even as a fan of the game, you could feel the history coming out of every pore of Ditka's body when he was talking about the game and what it meant. I think that's what

> Q: Name three players who quit baseball to star in the NFL and to whom George Steinbrenner gave $100,000 in Yankee bonuses.
> A: John Elway, Deion Sanders, and Billy Cannon Jr.

He loved the Bears, and he's a tough guy who's not afraid to cry and show you his emotions.

made him so successful, when he can get a group of men to be as passionate as he is. And that's what he tries to do wherever he is.

We were all at the office when the other shoe fell. We went to the press conference and it was a very emotional, very traumatic time, as it was again in the days afterward, when he gathered us all together. Then he brought us each in individually to talk to us. He told me, "I'll do anything I can to help you. You've been loyal to me, and believe me, from now on, I'll always help you and you can always count on me. And don't worry about me. I'll be fine." It was such a class act.

PEAK PERFORMERS
RICK JAGO

Rick Jago is the marketing direc-
tor for Old World Industries,
which makes Peak Performance
Antifreeze.

photo courtesy of Rick Jago

T he whole theme was being a "Peak Performer." These guys (Ditka, Petty, and Gretzky) were peak performers. The campaign was really quite well done and I give a lot of credit to the guys who did it. It lasted for about four years. We were all under contract for three years; I think Kyle did it a little longer because he carried the Peak Banner for quite a long time on his car. We then went into sponsoring actual races in Dover, Delaware, under the Peak name, and then we launched the Spitfire brand of spark plugs.

I came in and took over sports marketing as a marketing manager, so I worked with Kyle, Gretzky, and Ditka. Ditka was quite an individual. One time we had to do a deal with him in Chicago, and he was going to speak to the automotive industry on our behalf. Their meeting was at McCormick Place. The entire automotive industry was there for their after-market show. I met him there. He was kind of hacked off because he never does anything in season. This was a Monday in season and he agreed to do it—he was a good guy in that way. He wasn't happy about it; I remember him grumbling at me the whole way—with the cigar in his mouth-"I don't do anything in season."

He transcended football and was famous even in racing.

We sat down in a room full of about a thousand people, and he got up there and was the most sparkling, pleasant speaker. He just turned it on in front of all those people. He lived up to his commitment; he didn't really have to because he never did things in season. But he did it and he really wowed the whole crowd. He knew how important it was—all of our competitors, customers, and retailers were there. He was a very interesting guy.

The biggest coup of the whole campaign was when Kyle Petty was going to run in the Daytona 500 and Mike Ditka was brought down to be an honorary member of Petty's crew. He was wearing the Peak jacket, the uniform—all that stuff. He was so big at the time that CBS, who was broadcasting the race, made a big deal about Mike Ditka being at the Daytona 500; they even brought him up to the booth and interviewed him. He transcended football and was famous even in racing.

> Announcer Tim Green, an eight-year NFL veteran, was a valedictorian at Syracuse and has written four football-related books. He is the only valedictorian in NFL history.

photo courtesy of Old World Industries

THE DOMINANT PLAYER
TOM HURVIS

Tom Hurvis is the founder and chairman of Old World Industries, which makes Peak Performance Antifreeze.

I had a very good relationship with Ditka and I like the guy a lot. You either like him or you don't like him. Ditka was on Kyle Petty's pit crew at Daytona and we got incredible press. He was on the ten o'clock news everywhere in the country, and it didn't cost us a penny except for what we paid Ditka. He loved it; NASCAR loved it. It was an incredible promotion.

When we were talking to Ditka about going down to Daytona, he said, "Earnhardt makes two and a half million dollars. I gotta meet that guy."

So we took him down to Daytona, and he was like a magnet there. It was right before the race and all the drivers came out of their pits and huddled around him. Then Earnhardt came up behind him and gave him a shot in the shoulder with his elbow. Ditka turned around, and they hugged each other. They had never met. It just shows you the tremendous respect people have for Ditka.

He had a lot of guts and did exactly what he wanted to do.

I was in the helicopter that brought Gretzky down from San Francisco to Ditka in LA, where Ditka gave this great speech about how he met Gretzky and how Gretzky slaughtered him up in Canada. Ditka was coaching junior hockey and Gretzky scored twenty goals in the first quarter.

Once, we were shooting a commercial in Chicago with Ditka, Gretzky, and Petty. Gretzky and Petty were there for about fifteen minutes, and everybody was looking at them and talking. Then Ditka came in and it was like Gretzky and Petty had disappeared. All of a sudden, he took over. He was the animal; he was the dominant player.

What was unusual about those guys was that every one of them was a terrific interview. Actually, the smoothest was Petty, but Gretzky was damn good. Ditka was so impatient about everything. You'd take one shot and that would be it; he'd say, "Well, hell, you took it once."

One day I got this phone call from Ditka, and he said, "Tom, this relationship's gotta change. I didn't get my check." I said, "Well, Mike, I sent the check to you." He was really pissed and he said, "You're probably going to ruin this whole relationship that we have." So I said, "Look, I sent it to you. I don't know what happened, but I sent it to you." I hung up the phone and called his secretary. She hadn't given it to him yet. So he would have just ripped my head off for nothing.

I was on the board of his charity. I never socialized with him but we had extremely good rapport. He said, "Look, Tom, I'll push Peak as much as I can, just send me a set of golf clubs and shirts." We had a very good relationship; I liked Ditka because I'm pretty direct, too. I loved the fact that the guy was pretty candid and said exactly what was on his mind. I know a lot of people really don't like Ditka. He was a wild man and he drank a lot—I know all about his failures—but the guy's honest. He's straightforward and says it like it is, and I like that. I love the guy; I think he had a lot of guts and did exactly what he wanted to do. He did a good job—he won the Super Bowl.

> The revenue from one home football game at schools like Michigan and Tennessee pay for all the athletic scholarships in all their sports for the entire school year.

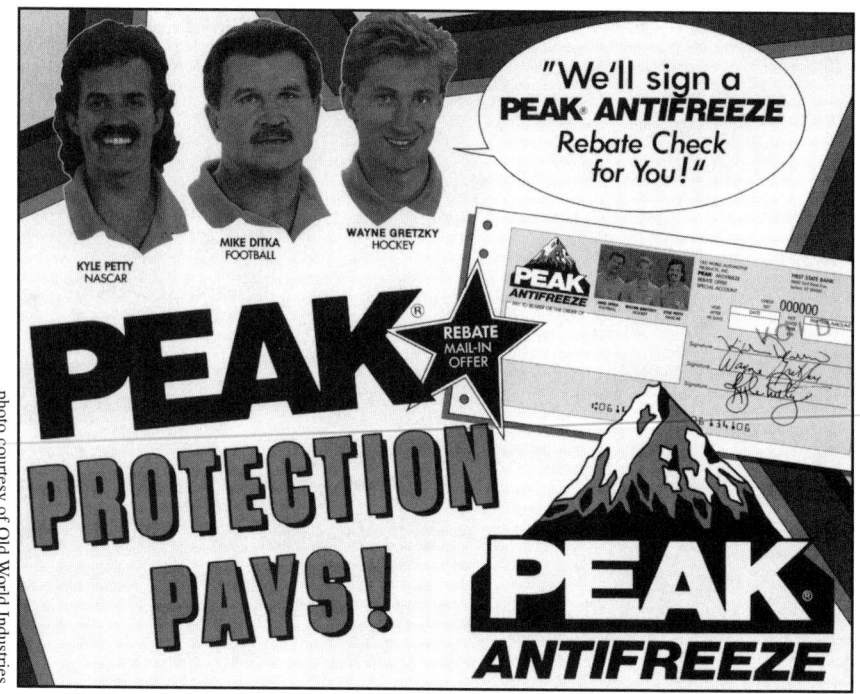

DITKA AND THE PRETTY BOY
MAC CHURCHILL

Mac Churchill, retired now in Naples, Florida, was the ad genius at J. Walter Thompson who decided to put Wayne Gretzky, Mike Ditka, and Kyle Petty together for Peak Performance Antifreeze in the mid-'80s.

Kyle had long hair; he was a hippie type at the time. Every woman alive walks into a room and falls in love with Kyle. He's a very handsome guy—he could have been a movie star.

Ditka walked in, and there's this guy who's almost pretty, and I thought, "Geez, this may not work well." But by the end of the first day of shooting, they became truly good friends. At first, I wasn't sure how it would work. I could imagine Ditka saying, "Aw, this is one of those pretty boys."

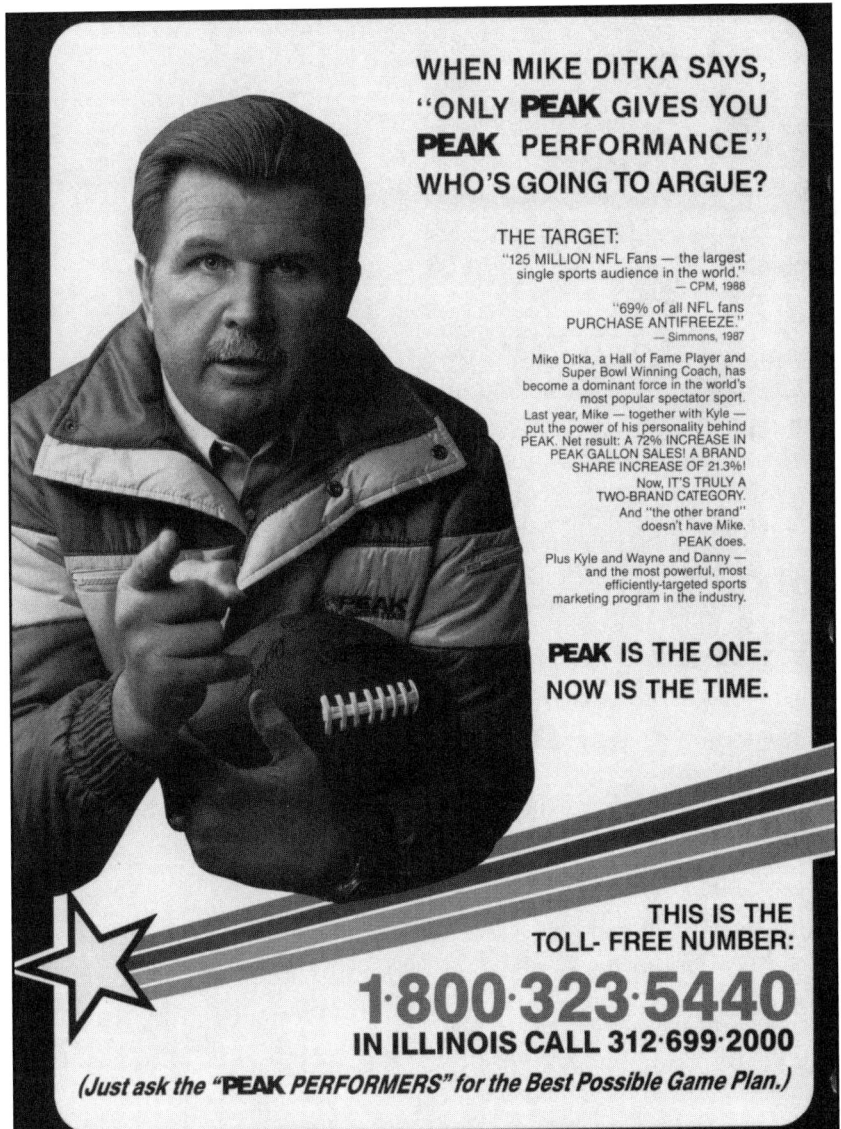

WHEN MIKE DITKA SAYS, "ONLY **PEAK** GIVES YOU **PEAK** PERFORMANCE" WHO'S GOING TO ARGUE?

THE TARGET:

"125 MILLION NFL Fans — the largest single sports audience in the world."
— CPM, 1988

"69% of all NFL fans PURCHASE ANTIFREEZE."
— Simmons, 1987

Mike Ditka, a Hall of Fame Player and Super Bowl Winning Coach, has become a dominant force in the world's most popular spectator sport.

Last year, Mike — together with Kyle — put the power of his personality behind PEAK. Net result: A 72% INCREASE IN PEAK GALLON SALES! A BRAND SHARE INCREASE OF 21.3%!

Now, IT'S TRULY A TWO-BRAND CATEGORY.

And "the other brand" doesn't have Mike.

PEAK does.

Plus Kyle and Wayne and Danny — and the most powerful, most efficiently-targeted sports marketing program in the industry.

PEAK IS THE ONE.
NOW IS THE TIME.

THIS IS THE TOLL- FREE NUMBER:

1·800·323·5440
IN ILLINOIS CALL 312·699·2000

(Just ask the "PEAK PERFORMERS" for the Best Possible Game Plan.)

photo courtesy of Old World Industries

DOING IT RIGHT THE FIRST TIME
KYLE PETTY

Kyle Petty has carved out his own superlative career on the NASCAR circuit, following in the footsteps of his father, Richard Petty.

Ditka ended up on my pit crew because we were both spokespersons for Peak Antifreeze, out of Des Plaines, Illinois. I drove a racecar for them and had for a couple of years. When Chicago went on their tear with the Bears, I became the East Coast and Southeast spokesperson for Peak. Ditka did the Midwest and Wayne Gretzky did California and Canada. Peak brought Ditka down one year for the race and he gave the team a pep talk. We were running like junk, we were terrible, but he gave us a pep talk before we ran the race and we thought we could beat the world. It was pretty cool to be around somebody who motivated like that.

We did a couple of commercials together, and I thought he was a great guy. When we were doing the commercials, he was very intense and focused on what he was doing. I get a little out in left field sometimes and just have a good time, so I'm not as intense as he is. We would go in and they would give us our lines. He's so intense that he wants to do it right the first time. He wants to please and he wants to do it right. But I could never tell if he was doing it right, or if the director was just afraid to tell him to do it again.

I saw him again after he had his heart attack, and he was a different person. He wasn't as intense; he was enjoying life and having a better time. The first time we worked together, he was a bit upset if we were supposed to start at 1:00 and we didn't start until 1:15. The second time, if we started at 1:15, he was okay.

I could never tell if he was doing it right, or if the director was just afraid to tell him to do it again.

He was in our pit at the Daytona race in '89 or '90, and he came down and saw the guys do a pit stop. It's pretty incredible to watch a group of guys go over a wall and change four tires and put twenty-one gallons of gas in a car in about sixteen or seventeen seconds. I think he had a new respect not only for what the racecar drivers did, but for what the pit guys did, too. Racing is a team sport, just like football was at the time.

All football fans have heard of Ditka, so I knew who he was. I'm a huge football fan, and I follow the conference that he coached in because I've always been a Packers fan.

I have not seen Ditka in person—only on TV in those dreadlocks—since those days. I have to admit: he looked good in the dreadlocks. And even if he didn't look good, you're not going to hear Kyle Petty say he didn't look good, because he's a pretty big guy.

Pete Rozelle never let an NFL game start later than 4:00 P.M. local time, other than the Monday night game, so that little kids could see the entire game before bedtime.

WILLING THE TEAM
DAVE McGINNIS

Mike Ditka was at his best when things were really tight. During a lot of ballgames in Chicago, he would basically will the team through the game. I can remember the first ballgame after the strike in 1987. The strike year was very, very hard in Chicago. We had started off the season 4–0. We were completely ahead of everyone. Then came the strike. The union held all their strike meetings in Chicago. When we came back, it was a very tense situation. Then we went down to play Tampa Bay. Of course, Tampa was having a hard time ever even scoring on the Bears, and we found ourselves down in the ballgame.

I can remember Mike standing up at halftime and saying, "Regardless of what has gone on in the past, you and we are still the Chicago Bears. You are the Chicago Bears, and you will be victorious." Once we went out there on the field, he went up and down the sideline, and it was like he was willing us. Neal Anderson would make a first down just by about the length of the football, and Ditka was right there on the sideline. If Neal Anderson needed four yards, Ditka was standing at four and a half to bring him across to that part. And we ended up winning that ballgame.

I can also remember a Monday night ballgame when we played Houston in the Astrodome. P. T. Willis got sacked right before halftime and Ditka was just livid. He came in the locker room, picked up a laundry cart full of towels—there's no telling how much it weighed—and just threw the laundry cart. The strength coach came over afterward and asked him, "Coach, can I get you something to drink?" He said, "Yeah, I need something to drink. I need some poison." Then the strength coach, who is very strong, tried to move the laundry cart back over to where it was supposed to be, and he couldn't pick it up.

When Vince Tobin got the defensive coordinator's job in 1986, Mike told Vince he wanted to hire a young linebacker coach. He brought several guys in to interview. Vince brought me in because I had been associated with Vince at Missouri.

I came in and started talking to him. Ditka said, "I have talked to some people about you." This was right after they had won the Super Bowl, and he said, "Now, tell me, if we're out there on the field, and you're coaching Mike Singletary, Otis Wilson, and Wilber Marshall—does that make any difference to you, or does making them better players than they are today make a difference to you?" I said, "Coach, I want to make them better players than they are today." He said, "Never, ever forget that. Never forget that. You're the guy I want for the job."

Tex Schramm's first name is "Texas" even though he was born in California.

DITKA'S CITY LIGHTS
JIM RITTENBERG

Jim Rittenberg is one of the most successful restaurant and night-club owners in the history of the city of Chicago. He has started several dozen successful nightspots, including Juke Box Saturday Night and Faces, as well as starting Ditka's City Lights in the mid-'80s. Jim Rittenberg is the man who made Harry Caray the "Mayor of Rush Street." Jim now runs Mother Hubbard's restaurant in downtown Chicago.

I knew Ditka's City Lights was going to be busy; I had projections at five million. I had a great location—sixty thousand cars went by it every day. We opened in late '86 and I left in '91, and it closed about thirteen to fourteen months later. It wasn't going to be a celebrity joint until Jerry Vainisi approached us.

The nightclub was going to be called Faces, and the restaurant was going to be called Coach's Club. The restaurant was only 2,700 square feet of the 16,000 total square feet. Ditka's City Lights was a name I coined. I was trying to come up with a nightlife name for the nightclub. So we called it Ditka's Restaurant, and we called the back part City Lights Nightclub. That's where the big money was. I projected five million in the offering. I think we did $9.7 million one year.

I think Ditka added a good twenty-five to thirty percent to the gross, mostly for the restaurant business. The restaurant business is not as profitable as the nightclub business. Ditka was a pretty good sport about doing commercials for the restaurant. They were all pretty humorous. He did his Grabowski shuffle at the restaurant—that was kind of funny.

I would watch what he did, like the chewing gum incident in San Francisco. Then we went out and picked up all kinds of Wrigley chewing gum and handed it out to people after they ate dinner. When he had the heart attack, we came out with "Holy Mike's Mackerel." We tied in with the Heart Association and donated fifty cents from every order because mackerel is

When he had the heart attack, we came out with "Holy Mike's Mackerel."

very high in the acids that help prevent heart disease. When Buddy Ryan choked on a pork chop, I sent an order of pork chops to his hotel room when he was in town to play the Bears. I sent pork chops to Letterman to get him to talk about the restaurant on TV.

We were famous for our pork chops. The location I wanted was next to Carson's Rib Joint and surrounded by steak houses and pasta houses, so I needed a signature item that nobody else had. I couldn't do steaks because we had Morton's and Gene & Georgetti's. I couldn't do pasta because I was across from Leno's. I didn't want to do ribs because I was next door to Carson's Ribs. So I came up with pork chops. Everybody liked pork chops; it fit with the Ditka image. I said two is not enough, so I threw a third pork chop on the menu. They all yelled at me. They said, "Why are you putting a third pork chop on there?" I said, "Listen, this is what you're going to build a restaurant around." That was the beginning of the huge baked potatoes, too. It was more than anybody could eat: a baked potato the size of a football—a huge potato— and three pork chops rather than two, so you actually got a pound and a half of pork chops.

At Ditka's it was always jammed. We had a thing called The Coach's Club, and it was $40 for all you could eat and all you could drink when you watched the games on Sundays. I think that's what sparked those cornballs from "Saturday Night Live"—where they did "all you can eat when you watch the games." Those guys would sit around, dressed in Bears' colors. I've got to believe that somebody who came up with that idea had to have been in the restaurant.

Everybody liked pork chops; it fit with the Ditka image.

Every Sunday starting before kickoff at 11:30, we'd open the bar and a big buffet. The buffet had the pork chops and everything. It lasted until 3:30, until after the game was over. These guys had the same table every week and they dressed in the Bears' colors, and each week they'd get a prize—a hat or a T-shirt or something. They were diehards.

The NFL talked to me and said, "You can't show those games out of market; it's illegal." We were one of only two places in Chicago that had satellites. Gamekeepers on Armitage and Ditka's were the only two places. We had big screens and big satellite dishes. This was '85, '86, and '87; it hadn't been done yet.

The NFL said, "Not all our games are legal. We'd hate to have to bust a place with Ditka's name on it." I said, "Listen, if you make everybody else stop, I'll stop, but it isn't fair to stop me and not anybody else."

We just kept on showing them and the problem went away. They never enforced it. But later they came out with a plan where you had to pay for it. And that was fine with us.

They didn't have sports bloopers on tape then; we made our own sports bloopers. When people were waiting two hours for a table, we would run the sports bloopers to try to shorten their perception of time. We called the bloopers the "Ditka Dogs," since they all started with the dogs that run and jump over things and fall. We had a whole crew that did nothing but make bloopers. We had a TV and radio station—we did all our own editing and all our own production. The dancing waiters and waitresses in the nightclub were called "City Lights Skyliners." I actually had a choreographer work with them each week. So three or four times during the night we would stop, they would come out on the dance floor, and they would do a theme. Sometimes it would be a Chicago theme, sometimes an athletic theme, sometimes a Bears theme.

Ditka was nice to the people and came up to them. We used to have to cordon him off sometimes if there were too many people, but he was always nice to the little guys when they came up for autographs. He was always friendly. If he was impatient, he was impatient more or less with the staff. He wasn't like a Harry Caray, who would walk around from table to table, saying, "Hey, how are you?" "What's going on?" or "Hey, sweetheart. Give me a kiss." He wasn't a Harry Caray, but at the same time he was very positive, a real asset.

Ditka handled the football market. I hired Doug Buffone to represent us. That was interesting. When we did the parties, people would ask, "Will Coach Ditka be there?" If Coach Ditka wasn't going to be there, he'd make sure one of the players or one of his ex-teammates was there. It was always Doug Buffone. If Coach couldn't make it, he'd call his pal, Doug Buffone, and Doug would come down.

We had a tape made up of Doug Buffone, "Old No. 55," we called it, because a lot of people didn't know who Doug Buffone was. Doug was a great player, and we'd show him smashing heads, etc.

> Dean Cain, who played Superman on TV,
> holds the NCAA record for most
> interceptions in one season.

If Coach Ditka wasn't going to be there, he'd make sure one of the players or one of his ex-teammates was there.

We'd say, "And here he is, ladies and gentlemen, to say hello to you—Coach Ditka's best buddy, Doug Buffone." Doug would come in and say, "Coach called me yesterday to come down. He couldn't make it today, but you guys are important," and we'd pay Doug a fee. Doug was happy because at the time it was a nice little gig for him. He and I were friends for years.

We also had Leon Spinks working for us at Ditka's City Lights. Johnathan Brandemeir was a real hot disk jockey in town, and Johnathan needed someone to get Leon a job here in Chicago. He said, "If you can get him a job, I'll give you so much press and so much PR. It doesn't make any difference what you pay him, I'll give you ten times that."

So I had a meeting with Brandemeir and Leon Spinks, and we decided to hire Leon. We paid Leon—no secret—$700 a week. We put him in a tuxedo and we had a tape made up of when he beat Muhammad Ali for the championship. We'd show the last round, when he beat Ali. Then we'd say, "And now, ladies and gentlemen, I'd like you to welcome our host here at Ditka's Restaurant, Leon Spinks." Then Leon would come out. Now, people loved Leon, he was so friendly. Leon would walk around, shake hands, smile, pose for pictures. But Leon didn't do the parties. I still had Doug Buffone for the parties, and I had Leon going out and doing appearances for the restaurant.

That was his job, he was a PR figure. It really helped because we had a lot of Europeans come into the place from the hotels. They don't know what a Ditka was. When you think about it—he's a football coach. That's good. But he's one of twenty-eight football coaches, and Leon Spinks was one of four living heavyweight champions of the world, so we would introduce him. So these people from Europe would come from the hotels to see Leon Spinks.

Leon was just a hoot. A part of his deal was that he could eat for free. So I caught him walking out with lobsters and pork chops; he would go back in the kitchen and the guys were afraid to say no to him.

- George Halas and Marv Levy are the only men in their 70s to have coached NFL teams.
- Levy is the only head coach in any major sport to be Phi Beta Kappa.

photo courtesy of NBC/Paul Drinkwater

A STRAIGHTFOR-WARD GUY
BOB COSTAS

This Long Island native and St. Louis resident has handled a wide array of assignments since joining NBC in 1980. Just prior to that he called play-by-play for the Chicago Bulls' telecasts.

Ditka was seemingly straightforward. He was more likely than most people on television to say what he really felt about something. There was less of a filter between his first honest thought and what he might say, which is one of the reasons for his popularity. It may be the reason why he sometimes got himself into controversy. People found a genuineness in him, because he gave an honest reaction rather than a carefully thought-through presentation.

I have played golf with Ditka in the past. He was always amused by my ineptitude and how poorly I played. I'm a little better now. He was a great joker and storyteller; there was a different joke or story for each of the eighteen holes. He has difficulty with his knee or hip, and was limping around quite a bit. He's not as competitive on the golf course. He wanted to play well, but he was not competitive. He has always been great and friendly to me.

THE BIG LEBOWSKI
BUDDY DILIBERTO

photo courtesy of Buddy Diliberto/WWL 870AM

Buddy Diliberto has been a fixture in the New Orleans sports scene for many years and did radio shows with Mike Ditka before Ditka became head coach of the Saints.

On Wednesday nights during the football season, Ditka would fly down. He was actually working through Casino Magic then. They'd play golf with some of the high rollers, and I'd do that hour show on WWL with Mike from Casino Magic in Bay St. Louis, Mississippi, in '94 and '95, before he had anything to do with the Saints.

Actually, it was through that show in '95 that I realized how much he wanted to get back in the game. He was bitching about it and I said, "Are you really serious?" He said, "Yeah." So I went to see the governor. I had been so critical of the Saints operation I was sort of persona non grata, so I couldn't go to the Saints owner because he wouldn't give me the time of day. So I inquired who had the owner's ear. It was Governor Edwards, the guy who got DeBartolo kicked out of the league. I made a phone call and went up to visit with him for about an hour, telling him why I thought Ditka would be a good fit here.

He endorsed the idea and said he would talk to Benson about it. That was during the '95 season. At the end of the '95 season,

Benson didn't make a move. Everyone expected he was going to fire Jim Mora and make a move at that time. But he kept everybody for another year—well, it turned out not to be a full year because Mora quit in the middle of the '96 season. The governor told me he then talked to Benson.

I was convinced Ditka would be a good coach because of his background and because of all that he had accomplished in Chicago with the Super Bowl team. One thing I was convinced about—and this was proven right—I knew he'd be very marketable. I'm still keeping an open mind as to what kind of coach I think he is. I know this town because I'm a native and I knew that the sale of the Saints' season tickets was going into a freefall. I knew if you brought in Mike Ditka, all of a sudden this town would jump on the bandwagon again. Now, like everything else, within two or three years he's got to do something on the field, otherwise that confidence starts dwindling. So consequently, in my opinion, 1999 is sort of a watershed year. I don't think the owner will fire him, but as far as the confidence of the community is concerned, this is a watershed year.

I call him The Big Lebowski. You saw that movie; to me, that's exactly what he is. Here's an example: The week of the draft, they had this press conference and everyone was asking, "Would Mike do this, draft that guy?" They have it every year, so Ditka was sitting up there with the Director of Scouting. Anyway, I asked the question, and they went on about how they were doing everything they could to move up so they could get Ricky Williams. I asked the question, "Suppose that doesn't work; you can't make that deal,

> Q: What is in the NFL penalty flags that make them go straight down instead of fluttering?
> A: Uncooked popcorn. When an official throws his flag and then sees another infraction, he throws his cap.

nobody'll go for it, and you don't get a shot at Ricky Williams? Somebody else drafts him. But the other running back, Edgerrin James, if he is there when you all pick, would you go for him?" Ditka's answer was, "Well, he's a good back, but you know we've got Troy Davis. I don't see any difference in those two." Well, only a Big Lebowski would say something like that. I mean, you have Troy Davis come in and he absolutely embarrasses us and runs nowhere.

He chewed the guy out just like he would chew a quarterback out after he had thrown an interception.

He talked about how everybody was going to gang up on Ricky Williams. So consequently, he's trying to field the type of passing game they're going to have this year. He wants his quarterbacks to complete sixty-five percent of their passes. If anybody's watching the quarterbacks the Saints have, they couldn't complete sixty-five percent on the sidelines playing pitch and catch. The fact of the matter is, very few quarterbacks in the league, no matter who they are, ever complete sixty-five percent of their passes. I don't think he ever thinks before he talks.

It was great when we had our radio show. He wasn't in coaching then, so he would give very candid and humorous opinions. Now, with the shoe on the other foot, he was telling me recently how negative I am. I'm negative. And I burst out laughing. He didn't think I was negative in '94 and '95.

We were doing a show on WWL, the biggest station in the area, so the casino wanted to get a sports show on WWL. They went with the idea that they could deliver Mike Ditka if WWL would put it on. WWL's point at the time was "Why do we want Mike

I don't think he ever thinks before he talks.

Ditka? We've got Buddy, he's our sports talk guy. Everything's going fine as far as ratings and everything like that." From that, they said, "Why don't we put the two of them together?" So consequently, Casino Magic was the one who delivered Ditka. Naturally, my attitude was "Absolutely, I'd love to do that." I had never really met him—I had done interviews with him, like in the Super Bowl when they were playing New Orleans. I grew up with Richie Petitbon; we're real good friends. We vacation together almost every year. He had played with him and I knew a lot about him. But other than doing interviews with him, I had never really met him until those shows in the casino.

Usually after the show we would go over to the dice table and play some dice. He's a big player on the dice table. One particular night the dice table was pretty filled, but Ditka got his bets all over the place. One person got the dice, and he was obviously not interested in the game—he was talking to the girl next to him. Well, it was his turn to roll the dice and he just kind of flings them out—sort of a limp fling—and he's not paying attention to the game. All of a sudden, Ditka yells at him from the other end of the table, "Goddamn it, if you want to play dice, roll the dice like you mean something, like you want to play, instead of that little flicking kind of thing." The guy's mouth opened like the end of the Mississippi. He chewed the guy out just like he would chew a quarterback out after he had thrown an interception—after he had done something the coach had told him not to do. The freaking guy almost died just listening to the cussing. The rest of us at the table just kind of smiled.

After one of the games last year, Ditka was so upset at the blocking of his wide receivers that on Monday when he had his press conference, he said that the Country Day wide receivers blocked better than our wide receivers. Country Day is a little private school that's about a mile away from the Saints camp. I do a show with him every Tuesday night at the restaurant, and who shows up but the whole corps of Country Day wide receivers to offer him their services. Man, he got a big kick out of that. We put them on live: "We heard you needed us, and we want to help. We're ready to suit up."

Red Grange was not the most famous person coached by the legendary Bob Zuppke. When Zuppke coached high school football in suburban Chicago, one of his players was Ernest Hemingway.

photo courtesy of SCORE radio 1160AM

AN AVERAGE GUY
MIKE NORTH

Mike North has been a fixture on Score radio and in sports talk radio in Chicago for the last ten years.

About three years ago, I was hosting a golf tournament for the Italian-American Sports Hall of Fame on the South Side of Chicago. Ditka called me the night before the tournament and asked me if I wanted to go to Bay St. Louis, Mississippi. I was hosting the golf outing on a Wednesday; on Tuesday night he called and said, "Hey, kid, how'd you like to go to Bay St. Louis, Mississippi, with me tomorrow? I got a radio show to shoot with Buddy Diliberto. It's from Casino Magic."

Well, I'm just a regular guy—I'm not used to this. I asked, "What are we going to do, take United?" He said, "No, no, no. Meet me at Palwaukee airport." So I left the golf outing at about 2:00 to be at Palwaukee airport at 3:30. We jumped on this Lear jet and flew to Mississippi. There was a buffet on the plane, and his wife, my wife, and another couple were with us. We flew out there and took a limo from the airport in Mississippi.

He didn't have to do the show until 6:30, so we did a little gambling. Then we did this hour-long radio show—me, him, and Diliberto. Afterward, we ate, and I was back home in Chicago by 10:30 and watching the Letterman show. That's the way the guy is. He just jumps on flights, spends maybe four hours somewhere, and then leaves. I'm not used to this kind of thing—I can't believe it.

If you look at the Bear logo and a picture of him, there's not much difference. He's a human being in a bear's hat.

I golfed with him in the Score golf outing, and one of my shots almost hit him on the head. He was on the foursome in front of me. He turned around, and I almost had a heart attack. He said, "Who did that?" Nobody would answer.

The first year I worked for him, each host for the Score did a week with him from his restaurant in Chicago. I did the show with him and we got into this philosophical football argument. He said to me during a commercial break, "How come you're not afraid of me?" I had never met the guy, but I always respected him and loved him as a coach. I said, "Because my dad was tougher than you. Why would I be afraid of you when I wasn't afraid of my dad?" Ever since then we got along great. He intimidated a lot of the hosts. He scares players when they walk in to see him in his office. Most guys are intimidated by him. But I think that's what makes it fun. He's a big guy, and he looks like a bear—he looks like the Bears logo. If you look at the Bear logo and a picture of him, there's not much difference. He's a human being in a bear's hat.

I loved him when I was growing up in Chicago; he left in 1966. We loved him as kids. We saw him catch touchdown passes in Dallas. But when he got the job with the Bears, we were all thrilled. All the writers in Chicago thought he'd only last a year, because of his feistiness, because they didn't think he could do it, because he was a special teams coach. They thought Halas picked the wrong guy—they didn't think he had the mental makeup to be a coach. But he was exactly the guy the Bears needed. He still is the biggest name in Chicago next to Michael Jordan.

He's an average guy. He'll still go out, hang around, have drinks. He's been in Chicago for the last month. He's the New Orleans coach, but he's in Chicago all the time. He's got a restaurant here; you see him on Rush Street. He's a big kid, that's what he is. He's a cool guy to hang out with. He comes across as a blue-collar guy, even though he's got all the money in the world. He reminds me of a guy who would live in a bungalow on the southwest side. He's that kind of guy.

He's a great speaker when he does commercials. He never makes a mistake; he does everything in one take whether it's radio or TV. He's very intelligent.

He and Harry were at Ditka's O'Hare, doing a Budweiser spot, and Ditka did his line perfectly. Now, Ditka's one of those guys who, once he does it, he wants to go. But he had to stay in the commer-

The Rams, who began as the Cleveland Rams, were named for the Fordham University team.

cial spot because Harry kept flubbing his lines. Harry'd say, "I'm sorry, Mike." And Ditka would say, "Come on, Harry, take your time, you'll get it done." Twenty minutes later, Harry was still screwing up his lines. But they finally got it done. You could see that Mike was becoming impatient even though he loved Harry, because Mike Ditka doesn't waste any time. He wanted in and he wanted out. It was hilarious to listen to those two do the outtakes.

He should have never been let go as Bears coach.

He should have never been let go as Bears coach. I think we would be a playoff team right now if he hadn't been let go. Every coach who has been at a place for any amount of time has had bad times—like Shula. Things happen, it's cyclical, but Ditka would have had them back on their feet already. Since he's been gone, nothing's gone right.

There are still guys who, like him, have the killer instinct. The Bill Parcells, the Bobby Knights, and people like that prove that the days of the Ditkas aren't gone. But I think there are less than more. If Ditka was still head coach of this team, there'd still be rabid interest in him. None of the common guys wanted him fired. The common people, the blue-collar guys, never wanted him fired. He had two losing seasons, and McCaskey couldn't wait for him to lose; McCaskey was afraid of him. So McCaskey got rid of him instead of trying to work things out. I think the only fault Ditka had was that he thought he was never going to get fired. That's why he never tried to play politics, though he's not that kind of guy anyway. He's not going to BS anybody. He's a straight-shooting guy, and that's what I love about him.

LEARNING UNDER GOD'S COACH
SKIP BAYLESS

Skip is an Oklahoma City native, a Vanderbilt graduate, a long-time Dallas sports writer, and now a columnist for the Chicago Tribune. *He is the author of several best-selling sports books, including* God's Coach *and* The Boys.

A friend of mine and I went out to play golf in Dallas in March 1981, in early spring. We got to the club and some big cold front blew through, what we used to call a norther in Dallas. The temperature dropped, the wind kicked up, and the wind chill was probably in the 20s or 30s. We were having lunch, watching this happen, and we said, "That's enough, we're not going to play today." It would have been our first time to play that spring. We continued having lunch, talking and laughing about how people were driving off the course in their carts because they just couldn't take it anymore.

As we sat there, we could see up the ninth fairway. There was one guy left, playing his way toward the clubhouse up number nine. We both remarked that the guy must be an idiot to still be out there playing by himself. The wind was blowing into his face. He was just hitting shot after shot up the fairway into the teeth of the wind. It was blowing so hard he was having trouble advancing the ball. Anyone would in that kind of wind—it was forty miles per hour.

The guy finally got up on the green, which was near the window where we were sitting, and I looked down and said, "I think that's Mike Ditka," who at that point was not a big deal in Dallas because he was a special teams coach. I was amazed that it was Mike Ditka who was still out there playing in that wind.

Not only did he putt out, but he got in his cart, drove past our window, and went to the tenth tee. He was still going, and he kept playing through the afternoon in that wind chill. Maybe people in Chicago would have thought it was like springtime, but to us in Dallas, it was too cold to be playing golf. Probably too cold to be playing football.

When Mike Ditka was Landry's receivers' coach, a story circulated in the locker room about what a "crazy mother" Ditka was. After one practice, as the receivers ran halfhearted sprints, Ditka challenged them to a fistfight. Right there, all at once—Drew Pearson, Butch Johnson, Tony Hill, Billy Joe DuPree, Doug Cosbie. "Come on, you pussies!" Ditka yelled as Landry looked on. There were no takers.

Now, of course, it seems that every other Saints practice ends with Coach Ditka challenging half the squad to a rumble. But in the Cowboys structure, Ditka seemed to have enough loose screws to build an entire robot. He was Landry's token maniac.

But Ditka also was as shrewd as Tex Schramm. He knew he could get away with an occasional explosion as long as he paid the proper homage to Mount Landry. Ditka kissed Landry's, well, hat. All Landry's top assistants did—Ditka, Dan Reeves, John Mackovic,

Academic All-American teams have been picked every year since 1952. Nebraska leads all colleges by a wide margin in number of players selected.

Gene Stallings. Today they tell interviewers that coaching under Landry was among their "greatest" experiences, but it wasn't then. One thing they learned in Dallas was that it isn't always wise to be honest, especially about legends.

> **Ditka seemed to have enough loose screws to build an entire robot. He was Landry's token maniac.**

When they were under Landry, they always filled newspaper stories with awe over him. They publicly accepted their ridiculously limited amount of input and responsibility. They arrived early for coaches' meetings and mostly deferred to Landry's one-way thinking. "Assistants," Drew Pearson said, "could act like little kids, peeking around the corner to see if Landry was coming. They were even more afraid of him than the players were. Once when I was coaching, my daughter didn't have a ride home from school, and I absolutely had to go get her and miss some of practice. The other assistants said, 'You can't miss practice.' They thought I was crazy. But I just said, well, I'll have to suffer the consequences. Coach Landry didn't really say anything."

But Pearson, who lasted just one year as an assistant, had no life-or-death ambition to become a head coach. The others knew that if they could live with their head coach, they'd have a better chance of becoming one. Serving under God's Coach made for a blinding resume. If an assistant was good enough for Tom Landry, he was good enough for an owner in search of a Landry.

One morning at camp I wandered into the TV room of the coaches' dorm and found Ditka intently watching a soap opera.

"You always watch this?" I asked.

"Don't tell anybody," Ditka said, grinning. He eyed me a second and said, "You don't swallow the party line around here, do you? I like that." And Ditka winked at me.

Associating with God's Coach certainly didn't hurt "crazy" Ditka. When the Bears called Ditka in 1982, several Chicago writers called me to ask if the guy was sane. I told them I wasn't sure he had enough of a handle on his temper to last as a head coach, but I stressed that Ditka knew how to play the game, both on the field and behind the microphone.

As Bears coach, Ditka actually became a phone pal of Landry's. They talked once or so a week. Landry volunteered to serve as a character witness when Ditka was arrested for DWI in 1985. You got the feeling Landry wished he could be a little more like Ditka, not to intoxication, but a little more spontaneous and outwardly emotional. But did Ditka and Reeves keep in touch with Landry the way you do with a tough professor or a commanding officer? It's difficult to imagine Ditka or Reeves calling Landry to shoot the breeze or, for that matter, Landry chatting at length with anyone but Alicia. But in a profession without much security or mercy, continuing a relationship with Landry can't hurt your image.

Landry delighted in talking to the media about the success of his "sons," Ditka and Reeves, especially as the Cowboys were less and less successful. But he never was able to replace what Ditka and Reeves did for his Cowboys teams. They could keep a Butch Johnson from flying off the handle and the lid from flying off Landry's locker room.

> Rich Kotite, former head coach of the Eagles and the Jets, was once Muhammad Ali's sparring partner in Miami.

Doug Todd and Greg Aiello   photo courtesy of *Dallas Cowboys Weekly*

AMERICA'S TEAM
GREG AIELLO

Greg Aiello is a fine Notre Dame man who used to be the Public Relations Director for the Dallas Cowboys. Now he's the head of Public Relations for the National Football League.

The term "America's Team" for the Dallas Cowboys came into play when Ditka was coaching in Dallas. My colleague, Doug Todd, who died a couple of years ago, actually came up with the phrase and put it on a NFL Films highlight show. It was 1979, the year I got there. Doug came up with the term, but we always just passed it off on NFL Films so it wouldn't sound too arrogant.

The Cowboys had been to five Super Bowls; in their fifth Super Bowl of the '70s, they lost in a 35–31 game to Pittsburgh. It was January, in the 1978–79 season, and they were trying to come up with some concept for the film because they had lost the Super Bowl. They had won it the year before. Bob Ryan actually came up with the theme—that the Cowboys had transcended Dallas and were a national team. They had all this footage of the Cowboys and their fans

Mike Ditka was sort of the anti-Landry in a lot of ways.

on the road, and they were batting around ideas for what to call the team. Doug Todd came up with "America's Team." They decided that was the one.

It was during that 1979 season that it started to catch on. When we went on the road, writers just started picking up on the idea, and we helped sell it. The Cowboys were the most popular team at that time. We promoted it and the media responded to it because it was legitimate. It was a phenomenon.

What I remember about Mike Ditka in those Dallas days were the characteristics that everyone later came to enjoy and appreciate after he went to Chicago and became a national celebrity. I remember his intensity, his emotions, and the way he could express himself.

He and Dan Reeves were big buddies. They were partners; they'd played together. And now they were young coaches under Tom Landry, so they ran around together. Ditka was considered sort of half-crazy. If you were with the Cowboys, a head coach was supposed to be like Tom Landry, and Mike Ditka was sort of the anti-Landry in a lot of ways. He was so emotional and intense and seemingly out of control at times, to the point where no one in Dallas really envisioned Mike Ditka as a future head coach, because Tom Landry was the model.

And yet the interesting thing was that Tom loved Ditka. Maybe because Tom appreciated that Ditka had things that Tom didn't have, in terms of his way of expressing himself and his intensity—his emotions. Tom also appreciated his commitment to the game and his passion for football.

They seem like opposites, but yet Tom really loved Ditka. So it was somewhat surprising when all of a sudden he was named the head coach of the Bears. And he was a special teams coach with Dallas. That's somewhat of an unusual jump, going from special teams coach to head coach. It was somewhat surprising in that sense, but he went on to enjoy great success and is an outstanding football leader.

In my first year with Dallas, we played up at Pittsburgh. This was a big rivalry at the time; they were the defending Super Bowl champs. We played two Super Bowls against them. There was a little scuffle along our sideline involving Ron Johnson—I think he was a rookie cornerback with the Steelers—and Dikta came running up the sideline with a football in his hand and sort of leaned over and fired this football at Ron Johnson's head. The official threw a flag for a fifteen-yard penalty. That's something Tom Landry would never do. And something you wouldn't expect a head coach to do. But it was part of Dikta's intensity.

> Bronko Nagurski played nine years for the Chicago Bears and had exactly one one hundred-yard rushing game.

A FRIEND FOR LIFE
DAVE McGINNIS

photo courtesy of *Dallas Cowboys Weekly*

Mike Ditka and his wife were extremely good to my wife and I the whole time we were in Chicago. Mike Ditka has done so much for me during my career— even today I could pick up the phone and call him and ask for anything, and he would do it.

When he got out, you knew— because of the way the situation was when it ended and because of his resolve and how strong a personality he is—you knew that he would be back in the ballgame.

People don't even know the extent of what Mike Ditka has done in his charitable works. To see him around those kids in Misericordia, how involved he was and how gentle he was—it's incredible. The strength coach on the Bears' staff during the time Ditka was there had a child who was born diagnosed with Down's syndrome. I remember Mike Ditka going to that coach's house, talking to them and sitting and holding that child. Just to see Mike holding that little girl and being as loving as he was—these are things that people don't know, that he's really a wonderful, wonderful man who is very well grounded.

I can remember when we were coaching at the Senior Bowl one year, and he would take us out, as a staff, every night to eat. It was out of the question for anybody but Mike to pay. And the way he is treated—it was like moving around the city of Mobile every night with a rock star, because of the way the people reacted when they saw him.

When Dikta enters a place, everybody recognizes and knows and identifies with him immediately.

We went overseas to play; we went to Berlin, to Sweden, to London. When Ditka enters a place, everybody recognizes and knows and identifies with him immediately. I can remember one time in Goteberg, Sweden, when we all came back from dinner and sat down in the lobby of a Swedish hotel. Before we knew it, it was midnight and there had to be four hundred people in that lobby, just sitting, and Mike was not holding court, but involving everybody in what was going on. He has that type of personality that draws everything to him. It was like being with a rock star.

I can remember the first year Mike put on a golf tournament in Aliquippa, and we all went back there. Some of the best times we had were at the Old Mill Inn. There were guys sitting there who knew Ditka when he was little and were talking to him about the time he chased his brother around the Little League field. And Mike would sit right there with them.

That is the plus of the man: he has gotten so large, yet he has retained who he really is and that is what endears him to so many people. That's why I count him as a very good friend and why we are so close, because he has got deep, deep roots and deep values, he is a spiritual guy, and he is so loyal. If you are loyal to Mike Ditka, you have got a friend for life. He is so solid and so grounded, and he has got so much—as we say in west Texas—bottom to him and so much inside of him. Immediately, if you are that kind of person, people are going to attach themselves to you. To this day, I know I can believe what Mike Ditka tells me, and that he would do anything for me. All this about his temper, it's only because he wants everybody involved with him to be as passionate about what they're doing as he is.

I can remember when my wife and I got married in Chicago. I'm from west Texas; my wife is from Colby, in western Kansas. I invited Mike and Diana to the wedding and to the reception, just because it's what you do.

We got married on May 6, and it snowed that day, believe it or not. I remember Mike rented a limo and brought several office employees down to the wedding, stayed at the wedding, and then came to the reception. And it

If you are loyal to Mike Ditka, you have got a friend for life.

was not just a cursory appearance; he sat at that reception for three hours. He signed autographs for every little aunt from west Texas and western Kansas, took every picture—everything they wanted.

We had a nice reception at a hotel on the North Shore. A waiter said to me, "David, coach Ditka would like to buy some champagne for the reception." I said, "No, no, we've already got champagne for the reception." He said, "NO, COACH DITKA WANTS . . ." Obviously, he bought the best—Dom Perignon—and sat there, and it was the most gracious thing I have ever seen.

There was no telling how much money he was making for appearances at that time in his career. Yet he stayed there all day and signed autographs, posed for pictures, kissed little aunts and grandmas, and shook everybody's hand, and really just sat and mixed. It was a wonderful, wonderful thing. And I told him days afterward, "Mike, I sincerely appreciate it." He said, "David, I wouldn't have expected to do anything else. What did you expect?"

Mike is a guy who is very perceptive, and that's what makes you feel good. Once Mike Ditka counts you as a friend, he's very perceptive and he understands. It's just like you or I.

You can tell when someone is genuine or not. And that, I think, is his greatest attribute. He really is able to see. He knows which button to push on which players because he understands personalities. He knows. He's wonderful to watch, and I learned a lot as a young coach about the way he would push the buttons of individual players and then how he would push the button of the team as a whole—different ways, different times. He's a master at it, and you can see why he's a tremendous competitor, why he was so successful as a player, and now why he is so successful as a coach.

> The Rose Bowl parade originally had nothing to
> do with the Rose Bowl football game.
> It was a celebration in Pasadena for
> the ripening of the oranges.

DOING THINGS THE RIGHT WAY
VINCE TOBIN

photo courtesy of the Chicago Bears

Vince Tobin has been the head football coach of the Arizona Cardinals since the ouster of Buddy Ryan. Ironically, it was Tobin who had the unenviable task of replacing Buddy Ryan after the Bears' Super Bowl championship in 1986.

I grew up on a farm near Burlington Junction, Missouri, and played football at the University of Missouri. I worked for the Columbia Neighborhood Youth Corps in Columbia, which was part of the poverty program for the Great Society under Lyndon Johnson. The more money they poured into it, the more I became the guy who filled out paperwork and sent it to Washington. I didn't want to do it anymore, so I went and talked to the coaches to see if they could get me a high school coaching job. They were expanding their staff and they hired me as an assistant coach. I went right in and coached there for nine years. I left in 1977 and went to Canada to coach the BC Lions of the Canadian Football League for three years. When I left, I went to the USFL and worked with Jim Mora and the Philadelphia Stars for three years. We were 15–3 our first year and 16–2 our next year, and we won the championship two out of three years. We played in the championship game all three years. When that league folded, I went to Chicago and stayed there.

He tries to do things the right way and expects other people to do things the right way.

Before Buddy Ryan took the Philadelphia Eagles job in 1986, Jim Mora had an opportunity to take three jobs: he could have taken the Eagles job, the St. Louis job, or the New Orleans job. Jim Finks went to New Orleans. He had been the Bears' general manager and had hired my brother Bill, who worked for the Bears as their personnel director. When Finks went to New Orleans, he in turn called Jim Mora about taking the New Orleans job. Jim went down and accepted it. When Jim dropped out of the Philadelphia Eagles job, Buddy Ryan got it. I was on my way to New Orleans to be with Jim Mora. I hadn't signed a contract or accepted the job or anything.

Mike Ditka called me the night before I left to go to New Orleans and asked me if I'd be interested in coming to the Bears as an offensive coordinator. So I went down to New Orleans, met with Jim, and told him that Mike had called and I was interested in talking to him about a job. Ditka was coming down there for the scouting combine, so I met with him about two days after I had gotten to New Orleans and interviewed with him. He offered me the job and I accepted. It was a bang-bang thing—it's not like he interviewed a lot of people. He interviewed me and offered me the job.

With all that had happened, Mike never once second guessed me on any call. When I first started he said, "The defense is yours to do with as you see fit." I certainly respected him for that, because if I hadn't have had his support, it would have been a hard act to follow. We had some problems, but in '86 the team ended up better in almost every defensive statistic than they had in '85. We set the record in 1986 for the fewest points allowed, and that record still stands today.

Mike is a Christian. He believes very strongly that God has a plan for everybody's life and that He's got a plan for his life. Mike is very committed to that. As Mike will tell you, he tries to control his temper, but it sometimes gets the best of him. He tries to do things the right way and expects other people to do things the right way.

When the ax came down in Chicago in January 1993, we were all shocked. It was done very, very clumsily, after the season was over. The owner was gone and we were sitting there twisting in the wind for about eight or ten days until he came back. They released Mike, and it was a very emotional time.

We had had a down year that year, and it gave ownership an opening and they took advantage of it. Every team has down years, but they've had a down cycle ever since Ditka left, I know that.

Barry Sanders was tackled for losses fourteen percent of the time. On approximately four hundred carries, he lost more than one thousand yards.

DITKA ON FAME AND RELIGION

I do influence a lot of people, sometimes in a good way and sometimes in a bad way. I think the only way you can influence people is through your life, not by something they read about you. Some people are going to like it and some aren't. I get it all the time; I get people who are great fans, and I get people who don't like me at all. And that's fine. There's nobody who is totally liked, no matter who it is. There's somebody that will find something wrong with Ernie Banks—let's face it. People are like that.

My involvement with Misericordia started when someone invited me to a golf tournament and I met Sister Rosemary. She said, "Why don't you come visit the place?" I did, and I realized it's not so much what you give, but what you get. You get a lot more than you give. It's become the love of my life. I deal with an institution down here (in New Orleans) called St. Michael's School for Special Children. There's Sister Rosemary in Chicago, and there's Sister Lillian here. These are people who devote their lives to taking care of special children. Whether it be the Special Olympics or something else, people like that love unconditionally. As healthy human beings, we have a tendency to put special conditions on anything—especially our love: how much we're going to give, who we're going to give it to, why we're going to give it to them. We find problems with everything. We think, "Oh, he's good for this reason," or "He's bad for that reason." But the love of these children is unconditional. The Bible says: "Unless you become as little children you can't enter the kingdom of heaven." What the Bible is talking about is: simply the ability to love and to treat people with love. Kids don't find too many problems with anybody else—that's a fact. That's what He was saying.

I've got a long way to go in life. I've got a lot of problems. I work on them. I don't think people really care—and I'm being honest with you—what my religious preferences are. I am what I am. I've learned one thing: I can't worry too much about what people think about me in life. I really can't. I have enough trouble worrying about what I'm doing myself. What they think is not going to bother me a whole lot.

I don't believe the good things that are said about me and I don't believe the bad things that are said about me. What I do know is who I am and what I'm trying to do in life. Everybody knows everything there is to know about me. When the last chapter is written, it's going to be written in New Orleans.

Chapter 4

Tom Landry

Jim Stamborski

Grant DePorter

Butch McGuire

Dan Reeves

Chet Coppock

Don Pierson

Keith Buchert

Tom Dreesen

Robert Smigel

photo courtesy of *Dallas Cowboys Weekly*

Fans and Friends

A COMPETITIVE NATURE

TOM LANDRY

photo courtesy of *Dallas Cowboys Weekly*

The Dallas Cowboys were not the first NFL team to play in Texas. Before the Cowboys started in 1960, there was an NFL team that played in Dallas for one year in 1952. The franchise, formerly the New York Yanks franchise, moved to Dallas and became the Dallas Texans. In their very first game, their first touchdown was the result of a fumbled punt by a New York Giants player, Tom Landry, the same Tom Landry who would coach the Cowboys for the first twenty-nine years of their existence.

We got Ditka in '69 in an offseason trade with Philadelphia. He had been sent from the Bears to the Eagles a few years after he angered George Halas by considering a jump to the rival AFL. To be perfectly honest, when Mike came to the Cowboys, he wasn't worth shooting. His knees were bad, his legs were gone. But he worked diligently with our weight coach to build his legs back up to the point where he made a valuable contribution to the Cowboys' offense for the next several years. Mike immediately proved he was not only a smart player, but also a tough competitor who wouldn't let anything keep him from playing.

A little more than a week before the season opener, an automobile accident left Ditka shaken and badly bruised, and four of his front teeth loose. A dentist told Mike he should sit out for a few weeks to allow the teeth time to tighten back up.

Mike just looked at the man and said, "Pull them." The dentist decided to fit him with a special rubber mouthpiece instead. Mike played his first game as a Cowboy the next week.

To be perfectly honest, when Mike came to the Cowboys, he wasn't worth shooting.

After I was fired in 1989, my wife and I were at our home in Palm Springs, at the time when the NFL held its annual spring meetings in Palm Springs. We didn't go to any of the meetings, of course, but Mike and Diana Ditka, Dan and Pam Reeves, and Gene and Ruth Ann Stallings called and invited Alicia and I to join them for dinner at a local restaurant.

It felt like old times. Gene Stallings, an old Bear Bryant protégé out of the University of Alabama, worked with me for fourteen years before he left to become head coach of the Cardinals in 1986. He is a fine football man and a dear friend, and there's no one I respect more as a family man and a father than Gene.

Mike played and coached under me for thirteen years before he took over as coach of the Chicago Bears. Danny played and coached with me for sixteen years. The two of them were as much like sons as assistants. In fact, I sometimes had to give them a little stern fatherly advice.

I remember one day when they got so worked up at the officials that I sat them down after the game and said, "I think I'd rather lose a football game than ever have my assistants act that way on the sidelines again."

I don't know of anyone more fiercely competitive than Mike and Dan. And not just about football. I used to play a little tennis with them during training camps. For them, tennis was a contact sport. They'd rather knock their partner down trying to get to a drop shot than lose an uncontested point.

Even across the net from Mike you weren't safe. You never knew what he'd do if he missed a particularly frustrating shot. I've seen him smash his racket on the court until it looked like an aluminum pretzel, then bend it back into its approximate original shape and go on with the match. One day he blew a shot and angrily slung his racket at the net and missed, hitting me on the ankle and sending me hopping around the court on one foot.

They were just as competitive in whatever they did. Danny brought a dartboard to Thousand Oaks one year and hung it on the wall of his dorm room. He and Mike went at it with such a vengeance they had to pay for a new wall when we broke training camp.

So we had a lot of memories to talk about and a lot of laughter to share in that Palm Springs restaurant. In fact, our evening together was such a poignant reminder of all that we'd enjoyed, all the associations that would never be again, that Alicia broke down and cried for the first time since my firing. For my sake, she'd been so strong for so long. It was like everything finally hit her. A wonderful part of our life was really over. Sensing that completely, she finally let down and cried. But it was okay; we were among loving friends.

> Q: What two college football teams play at Rice Stadium?
> A: Rice University in Houston and the University of Utah in Salt Lake. Both stadiums are named Rice.

ONE OF US
JIM STAMBORSKI

Jim Stamborski defied all the odds and lived the dream of many sports fans. He wrote a book about his biggest sports hero—Mike Ditka.

I grew up in southern California. My father was transferred to Chicago in 1960, and that's when I became a Bears fan. The '60s were a time of great Bears teams, culminating in 1963 with the Bears' 14–10 championship victory over the Giants at Wrigley Field. From that point on, the Bears were my favorite team. I really liked Ditka and Bill Wade a lot. The Bears were a great team at that time—when they truly were "Monsters of the Midway."

It was fun following Ditka's career. Anyone who saw him play that season saw a very crucial game. Every time you see a Ditka highlight film, you see him plowing through the whole Steelers team and scoring a touchdown. That was a tremendous run; it was unbelievable.

You ask people in Aliquippa, Pennsylvania, about Mike, or people he has visited in the hospital when they were sick, or his friends and acquaintances, and they all have something really nice to say about him. This thing about his ex-players not liking him is a big fallacy, a big myth. Jim Harbaugh has nothing but the highest praise for Mike Ditka, and it's the same with Jim McMahon and Mike

Tomczak. You saw him grabbing their helmets or reaming them out on the sidelines, but they have a tremendous amount of respect for Mike, as do almost all the players who have played for him. It really is surprising when you consider his reputation of being a hard-nosed guy.

A lot of people forget that Mike Ditka played the game. He played the game as a Hall of Famer, and now he's a coach, so he knows what the game is about. He constantly talks to players about the love of the game, and tells them not to be in it just for the money. He was very upset when the players went on strike in '87, and he basically said that free agency was going to kill football. And if you look at it right now, free agency is a big problem. Ditka was right.

He is so popular because he is one of us— honest, hardworking.

He was right about Doug Flutie, too, and a lot of people don't give him credit for that. Everybody laughed when Mike drafted Doug Flutie, and look what he did. He went to the Canadian Football League, set all the records, came back to the NFL, and had an outstanding season for Buffalo. Nobody remembers that about Mike Ditka. Ditka tried to sign Flutie and Cunningham for New Orleans, too. Everybody laughed and said, "There's no way." But Ditka is a tremendous evaluator of talent, and he's a gambler, too. Look at this riverboat gamble with Ricky Williams. You've got to love it.

I think he is so popular because he is one of us—honest, hardworking, a guy who busted his ass to get where he wanted to go and is honest, straightforward, loyal, and a straight-shooter. He's had his ups and downs, just like all of us. He can walk into any bar, in any steel mill town, in Chicago, in New Orleans, or any other place, and sit down, have a shot and a beer with somebody, and talk about life.

He was a bust-out player, by his own admission, when he left the Bears. But he worked hard; he's a hard worker. He knows what it's like to have a boss who gives him a hard time. He knows what it's like to be a player. He knows what it's like to be a human being— to be out there, busting your ass to make a few dollars. That's what I like about Mike Ditka. He doesn't forget his roots. He's a steel mill kid. He'll tell you that he got to where he is by working harder than everybody else. That's what we're all about. That's what we have to do in life.

But he's done it with class, dignity, and honesty, and he's done it with great humor. Mike Ditka is atypical of a celebrity, and of course when you're different, people seem to gravitate to you because you're unusual. Any coach has his guarded moments—he will or won't say certain things. Ditka is unusual because he's an honest, straightforward, no-nonsense kind of guy. You never know what he is going to say, because he is totally and completely honest with his feelings. He will say things that, before they even come out of his mouth, he knows will upset people and get him in trouble.

But he'd say, "Hey, that's the way I am. Take it or leave it." When Ditka complained in the paper about Refrigerator Perry's wife cooking too much for him, he got reamed. But he came out and said, "I apologize. I've learned my lesson. I probably shouldn't have said it." That's the way he is; he just laid it all out there.

How many people do you know who are totally honest in the public eye and in private, too? That really intrigued me about Ditka. He doesn't care what he says as long as he feels it's honest. He doesn't care if it's not the politically correct thing to say. When he said recently that downtown New Orleans was full of trash and they should clean it up,

> Quarterback Chris Chandler is married to
> John Brodie's daughter.

it was true, but he got roasted for it. He got roasted for his honesty. That's what we admire—hard work, honesty, and loyalty. That's Mike Ditka.

Just before the playoff game with the Rams, somebody said, "How would you describe this game?" Ditka said, "Well, this is the Smiths versus the Grabowskis." Everybody laughed, and

"The Grabowskis know who they are. My team is full of Grabowskis."

the guy said, "What do you mean by 'the Grabowskis'?" And Ditka said, "The Grabowskis know who they are. My team is full of Grabowskis." So of course, sociologists came on the scene and examined it, and one guy was pretty close when he said, "A Grabowski is a person who understands the sustained pushing of the rock up the hill." I thought that was a really good description, because, hey, that's Chicago.

That's what Chicago is about. Ethnic people keep pushing that rock up that hill every single day, trying to get a better job, trying to get a better house, trying to get a better education for their kids, trying to pay their bills—simple things like that. That's what that is: the sustained pushing of the rock up the hill. That's Chicago and Pittsburgh. That's the connection, and I think Mike Ditka feels that right down to his very soul.

Ditka's father was a steel mill guy, a very tough guy—the kind of guy who had a little union off to the side that dealt with the train transport. Those steel mill towns in Pennsylvania are like castles—there is one big, long bridge that goes into the steel mill, and the whole town is built around it. Mike Ditka Sr., and about thirty guys held off about six thousand people when they went on strike. They blocked the bridge with axe handles and wouldn't let anyone through until they made their point.

When I was in Pittsburgh I talked to a couple of guys, like the guy who was driving the shuttle, and asked them, "What do you think of Mike Ditka?" "Mike Ditka's the greatest; his family's the greatest," they would say. The guy driving the shuttle started telling me stories about his father or grandfather having the locker next to Mike Ditka's dad. He just kept saying what wonderful people they are, and how they retired in Aliquippa when they could have gone anywhere. They retired to the hill on top of Aliquippa where all the steel workers retired.

Ditka goes back to Aliquippa every year, holds a golf tournament, and supports the football team. The whole community has basically changed now, but he supports the team and the city. If you ask people in Aliquippa what they think of Mike Ditka, they will tell you he is the greatest.

I had become a big fan of Mike Ditka, and like all of Chicago, I was thrilled when the Bears won the 1985 Super Bowl championship. A few years later, I began to follow Mike Ditka's career. I thought to myself, "This guy is a very interesting person." I decided I wanted to go back through old newspapers to find out if Mike Ditka was consistent from day one—from January 20, 1982, when he became the Bears' coach—and throughout his career with the Bears.

Not only did I find that Ditka was consistent, I also found a whole universe of wonderful things about him. I discovered that he was intelligent, witty, and the most intense competitor—all these great things came out of my research. When I came home from work, I would go through the papers or go to the library and look up quotes about Mike Ditka. I realized that he was a totally unique person. The man was just incredible. I began to find a lot of little threads in Mike Ditka's personality.

One of those was his loyalty to the Bears organization. That basically occurred because George Halas took a chance and named an assistant coach at Dallas to be the head coach of the Bears. Mike Ditka came out of nowhere. When he was hired, everybody in the Chicago media said, "Mike Ditka? You've got to be kidding me. Who is he?" Mike Ditka said, "In three years, we're going to be at the Super Bowl." And everybody laughed at him. They said, "He's off his rocker; there's no way this collection of Bears is ever going to do anything." Of course, they won the Super Bowl in 1985, and the rest is history.

There are some myths about why George Halas picked Ditka, because when Halas introduced him to the press, he said, "I've been working on this plan for several years. This plan is now complete with the hiring of Mike Ditka." Well, that's not exactly the way it happened.

The Thanksgiving before Halas hired Ditka in January, he saw Ditka on television with the Cowboys, and he saw him throw his clipboard into the stands. According to one of the members of the team who was with him at the time, Halas said, "That's him, that's my coach." So there was no long-range plan.

I also found out that Mike Ditka came cheap, which for George Halas was really important. Halas didn't pay him much, and Ditka said, "Well, I don't really care what he's paying me, because if I win it's not going to matter, and if I lose it's not going to matter." So Ditka knew exactly what he was getting into.

Q: What consumer product is named after a school's mascot?
A: Gatorade. It was developed by a professor at the University of Florida under a grant from

I ended up collecting about four thousand quotes covering 1982 to 1987, and I thought that I had enough material for a book. I thought that other Bears fans might enjoy reading it, and if they didn't, I'd have something I could keep and refer to. It turned out to be highly entertaining, and there was a lot of insight into the Bears personalities at the time—people like Jim McMahon and the Fridge. There was a lot of really good stuff in the book.

I looked at publishers in Chicago and mailed a draft out to six of them. Three actually called me back, which really surprised me. Chicago Review Press liked it, and they picked it up. They wanted to know if Mike Ditka had approved of the book or knew anything about it. When I said "no," they asked me to send a draft of the book to him and get something in writing from him saying that he liked the book or the concept. I didn't think there was any way he was going to do that. But I called his secretary, Mary Albright, explained who I was, and told her that I wanted to send Coach Ditka a copy of the book to see if he liked it. She said, "Okay, no problem."

I later found out that she is Mike Ditka's agent, and has been for many years, which says a lot about the man. A man whose secretary is also his agent—in this day and age, that's really fantastic. I sent the manuscript to him and called her a couple of times and couldn't get through. Finally I got through to her, and I asked if Ditka liked the book. She said, "Let me put it to you this way. He comes in at about 5:00 in the morning and I heard him back in his office laughing hysterically." I asked her if he would mind sending a little letter saying he liked the book. I thought it was really an imposition at the time, but, true to form, Mike Ditka actually sent me a letter congratulating me on the book and wishing me well on the project. He doesn't know who I am. I'm not a professional author. For Mike Ditka to do that for somebody as insignificant as me in the whole scheme of things—that just really floored me. But Mike Ditka does that for people.

It was exciting to walk into a bookstore and see my name on books. I did a couple of radio shows, and I did one with Wally Phillips, who was like an icon in Chicago. I was totally impressed with Wally Phillips because he actually read the book before he interviewed me. He loved the book and as a result of that a lot of people read it. I've never heard anything negative said about it.

That's because they get the total picture of Mike Ditka; they get the funny Mike Ditka, the young Mike Ditka, the competitive Mike Ditka, the creative Mike Ditka—they get the full picture. It really made me feel good to know that people weren't getting just one side of him, like "da Coach," some kind of media creation; they got to see the whole man.

> **They said, "He's off his rocker; there's no way this collection of Bears is ever going to do anything."**

This is a man who makes mistakes and admits he makes mistakes. He was arrested for drunk driving and was very apologetic about it. He gets mad at people in the media, at fans—it's all right there in the book. Like Mike Ditka says, "Why should I be anything else than who I am? This is me. Take it or leave it."

He is just a total up-front, honest personality, and this is what I love about the guy. But because he is that way, people are always trying to take cheap shots at him. He got some cheap shots from columnists in Chicago toward the end of his career, and he definitely got some cheap shots from Armen Keteyian, who wrote *Monster of the Midway*. That stuff really bothers him and it bothers me too, because it's not accurate.

People don't realize that Ditka was operating with one hand tied behind his back a lot of the time he was in Chicago. He had a big problem with Mike McCaskey. When you go through the book, you can see the threads of the problem. You can see when things started happening. First, Jim McMahon had a problem in his rear, so he went to an acupuncturist. Mike McCaskey, behind the scenes—and even out front to the media—made a big deal about it, saying, "Why is the coach stepping into this?" It was almost like he was saying, "If they lose, it's because Ditka allowed an acupuncturist to treat McMahon's butt." Of course, Jim McMahon really reamed out McCaskey, and I don't think it sat very well with him. Right after they won the Super Bowl, Wilber Marshall got away to the Redskins.

Then the real crusher came in '86, when McCaskey fired Jerry Vainisi, Ditka's closest friend in football. And then after that there was the problem with the strike. That kind of stuff created real problems. Then there was the Jim Harbaugh quarterback pick, which Mike Ditka knew nothing about. They made some bad drafts that I don't think Ditka was involved in, but it was still on Ditka's record. He had all that stuff against him.

But Mike Ditka will always be loyal to the Bears organization. The Halas/McCaskey family had to take McCaskey out of his job as CEO for the Bears because he screwed up the team, but Mike didn't criticize or say anything about him. Then they let Mike Ditka get away, and I think a lot of Chicagoans wanted to lynch them for that.

I lived in Chicago until 1988, when I got a job in North Miami. In 1995, one of my friends told me that Ditka was going to be doing a heart unit dedication at Baptist Hospital in Miami, and thought I should go down to see him. So I grabbed a couple of my books and went down there. They had a big tent set up. Mike limped up to the stage, because his hip is so bad, and gave a very stirring talk. Mike Ditka is a big guy on quotes, and he was quoting Abraham Lincoln in his speech. He gave a tremendous talk about modern-day athletes, Abraham Lincoln, and what's important in life—really inspirational words.

Afterward, he took a couple of questions. I raised my hand and he picked me right away. I said, "Coach Ditka, I'm your greatest fan." Then I asked him a two-part question that I thought would allow him to expound on his football philosophy. The second part was "Would you ever consider coaching the Dolphins?" Everybody laughed when I said that. The first part was: "When you first took over the Bears on January 20, 1982, you talked about having ACEs, which is an acronym for attitude, character, and enthusiasm. Would you describe what you meant by that?" He went off on that for a while. He was smiling when he answered the second part. He was very diplomatic. He said, "Well, Coach Shula (the Dolphins coach at the time) can coach as long as he wants, but if he ever leaves, I might be interested and someone can talk to me." It was kind of a noncommittal answer, but that's when I knew he was coming back to football. There was no question about it.

Then he had a little autograph signing. I brought my books up to him and said, "Coach Ditka, I don't know if you remember me—" And he said, "Of course I remember you." I don't know if he did or not, but it was a great thing to say.

> Yvonne Davis is married to 1946 Heisman winner Glenn Davis. Before that she was married to the 1954 Heisman winner, the late Alan Ameche.

photo courtesy of Harry Caray's Restaurant

GO TO DITKA'S
GRANT DePORTER

Grant DePorter is the managing partner of Harry Caray's Restaurant in Chicago. When Harry Caray's opened in late 1987, Ditka's City Lights was the most popular nightspot in the Windy City. The menu at Caray's under "Pork Chops" said, "Go to Ditka's."

I think part of the reason Harry Caray's existed is because Ditka was around, and Harry liked to see what Mike was doing. So when Harry was approached about doing his own restaurant, he already knew about Ditka's. They were friends; they liked each other. Harry would eat at Ditka's. We were an Italian steakhouse, and that first year we had a plain pork chop on the menu, which was what Ditka's was known for. We didn't do it after that first year.

Mike has eaten here many times and has always been great. Mike always liked Harry because he was a big St. Louis Cardinals baseball fan when he was growing up in Pennsylvania. Stan Musial, the great Cardinal, was from Donora, Pennsylvania, near where Ditka was raised, and Ditka used to listen to the Cardinals' night games on KMOX in St. Louis, where Harry broadcast from 1945 to 1969.

Part of the reason Harry Caray's existed is because Dikta was around, and Harry liked to see what Mike was doing.

Two of the greatest quarterbacks of all time, Johnny Unitas and Dan Marino, have the same middle name—Constantine.

THE AVERAGE CHICAGOAN
BUTCH McGUIRE

Butch McGuire has owned Butch McGuire Saloon, a Chicago institution, for more than forty years.

I knew Mike when he was a Bears football player. The Bears used to frequent us on Monday afternoons at about 2:00 or 3:00 P.M. We were usually very happy to see them leave at about 5:00 or 5:30. From our place, they would go to Pat Herrons'.

You can't even get near Ditka. The downside of having professional athletes as customers is the jock sniffers that come around when they're there. That is the problem—it's not the athletes themselves. I don't know about the new, modern athletes. I think they really have a lot of problems. But Ditka and his fellow players were all good guys.

Mike represents the average Chicagoan.

The Green Bay guys used to hang around our saloon whenever they were in town. A lot of them came here when they weren't playing. The group that was with Paul Hornung was different. Paul still comes in when he is in town. Today's professional athlete, in my estimation, is nothing but a rich bum, with rare exceptions. The great ones, like Singletary, who is a wonderful, intelligent gentleman—you never saw his face. Chasing broads and hanging around saloons—that just wasn't his game.

Mike represents the average Chicagoan. He was a hardworking son of an immigrant who was successful in high school and college athletics and went on to become a very well-known professional athlete. His teammates loved him. Halas loved him. He was their leader. The guys would get out of line, and he would whip them back in line. He was good for the Bears, and the Bears were obviously good for him. I think everybody still wishes he coached the Bears. The McCaskey kid was the fly in the ointment. Ditka had a fine organization and McCaskey just decided to break it up. He wouldn't let Ditka draft whom he wanted. It was a horror show for Ditka; it was just tragic.

The average NFL salary is more than $800,000.

Mike Ditka

HE HATES TO LOSE
DAN REEVES

Dan Reeves played with the Cowboys for eight years and has been Ditka's buddy since they were teammates in 1968. After serving as Tom Landry's assistant in Dallas, Reeves went on to coach the Denver Broncos, the New York Giants, and the Atlanta Falcons, where he is today.

We were playing gin rummy one night in 1968, and after Ditka lost a couple of hands he picked up a chair and threw it across the room. All four legs stuck in the wall. All I could say was, "God, this guy hates to lose."

THE KILLER INSTINCT
CHET COPPOCK

Chet Coppock is arguably the best sports talk radio host in America.

photo courtesy of WMAQ 670AM

There is no one I've ever had greater admiration for than George Halas. I recall telling him that I thought Ditka was a logical choice for the Bears' coach because the ball club for so long had lacked anything resembling a killer instinct. There were Fencik and Plank and a handful of other guys, but as a collective unit there was no energy in the ball club. It was a very indifferent football team.

Then Ditka arrived. I called the old man the night before he arrived, and George was like a kid under the Christmas tree. He kept talking about how wonderful it was to have Mike Ditka come back to Chicago. I remember the press conference that took place in Halas's office. There were so many reporters and cameramen, they were actually standing on top of Halas's desk. Rudy Custer, who was George's business manager, was telling the cameramen to "get the hell off of the desk." By contrast, when Abe Gibron took over the ball club in 1972, there couldn't have been more than a dozen people at his press conference. It really wasn't a press conference so much as a shouting match between Mugs Halas and Bill Gleason about how the Bears were being covered.

I had the good fortune to be with Ditka and Mike Pyle up in Ditka's suite the night before the Bears played New England in Super Bowl

XX. That was not their big game that year; the big game was when they knocked off the Giants in the first round of the playoffs. When they shut out Parcells, put Joe Morris under wraps, took Phil Simms completely out of his element, and blanked the Giants, that, for all practical purposes, was when the Chicago Bears were crowned the National Football League champions.

The point at which the club really began to emerge was in 1984, when they beat the Raiders. During that game, you knew you were looking at something very, very special. Now, I have seen the team play some physical football games. In 1968, when Sayers ran for 205 yards in Green Bay, there was absolutely nothing short of manslaughter going on between the two ball clubs. But after that 1984 game against the Raiders, I remember Merlin Olsen, who worked that ballgame for NBC with Dickie Enberg, saying that he had never seen a more violent football game.

When I was with Mike the night before the Super Bowl in 1986, and we were doing his radio show on WMAQ radio, I remember this remarkable aura of tranquility permeating Ditka's suite. There was no feeling of impending confrontation. There was no feeling that the next day was a mission from God, or that Armstrong was going to land on the moon. He appeared to have a very cut-and-dried attitude about the whole thing.

I always got a kick out of the way Ditka operated on his show. Here's this guy from Aliquippa, Pennsylvania, who has a lot of savvy. It used to kill me to watch him do his radio show. He would put one half of the headset up to his ear, and he would sit there and watch television. But he was still so adept at answering questions and maintaining the flow of the show.

> Joe Klecko is only player to be All-NFL
> at three positions.

Ditka's just a very gifted guy. There isn't a doubt in my mind that if Ditka had wanted to be a broadcaster, he could have been one in the conventional sense, and not just a studio host. He could have been a sportscaster in the classic sense of the word. When I finally began to take him on, in 1992 when the ball club was playing badly, I felt like Mike had run his course. It was very difficult for me to suggest that it was time for Ditka to step down.

For a long time after that, Mike and I really didn't speak to each other. Finally, sometime in 1995, one of my local friends said, "You know, Ditka and you had a pretty good friendship. Why don't you contact him and at least try to reopen the friendship?" So I wrote Mike a letter. It was not a syrupy apology letter; it was just a letter in which I said, "I hope you know I respect you and think you're a hell of a guy. The Hall of Fame waited much too long to put you in." He wrote me back this very simple letter, but I've never forgotten how beautiful it was in its simplicity: "I don't hold grudges. You remain one of my friends. God bless you. Mike Ditka."

I'm not sure if Mike Ditka has ever found complete happiness.

That meant a lot to me, because I think we tend to look at him and see this larger-than-life, complex figure who's just a series of contradictions.

Another great story about Mike takes place during his first year back in Chicago. He hadn't yet coached a ballgame. There was a charity golf tournament for NFL alumni in the summer of 1982, and I was emceeing it out at Beverly Golf Club. Former Bears great Eddie Sprinkle was in charge of the tournament; he was one of the sweetest guys in the world. I thought that with Ditka being back in town as the new head coach with a new regime, it would be great to have Mike speak to the crowd. I asked him, "Mike, do you mind doing ten minutes?" "Oh sure," he said. "No problem."

So the banquet started rolling—but no Ditka. Dinner was served—still no Ditka. I walked up to one of his assistant coaches and said, "Where's Mike?" "I have no idea," he said. So I walked downstairs to the locker room. And there was Mike, playing cards with Reggie Fleming. I said, "Coach, we need you in about twenty minutes. Can you walk up?"

After twenty minutes, there was still no Ditka. I called up Earl Morrall, the former Lion, to speak. I called up Jimmie Taylor. Then I sneaked down to the locker room to get Ditka. He was lying against the locker, completely asleep. Well, not asleep—he was drunk.

A GREAT COACH

Ditka's unpredictability factor is so unreal. Who in the world trades the entire store for a running back? Only Ditka would have the rocks to do something like that.

The young Mike Ditka used to hang out at Chicago Stadium and was nuts about the Blackhawks. He used to sit in the front row at the turn behind the glass. He was a huge hockey fan. He was nuts about Bobby Hull and Stan Mikita. He was everything a man's man was supposed to be.

There is a part of Mike Ditka that Mike Ditka will never sell. And there's a part of Mike Ditka that leaves him something less than

> In order to host the Pro Bowl from 1994 to 1998, the state of Hawaii had to donate the use of the stadium and guarantee the NFL $1 million income each year.

fully complete. Mike will have friendships that are absolutely locked in stone, and something will go wrong and he just won't be able to leverage them back into a rightful position. In Mike's case, it's almost like he thinks that his masculinity would be threatened if he were to do that. It's very unfortunate.

I'm not sure if Mike Ditka has ever found complete happiness. I'll give you a great story about Mike. The

> **I think in his own mind, Mike feels that there is a group of people who refuse to recognize him as a so-called "great coach."**

Bears danced on Ray Berry's face at the Super Bowl. The ballgame was over twenty seconds after the coin toss. The next day, I was hosting the Ditka show on WMAQ out of the studios at the Merchandise Mart. My first question was something about winning the ballgame. It was obvious that Mike was very relaxed. The first thing he said to me was "They're lucky we didn't score sixty points on them." He said it with a very sardonic and sarcastic feel to his voice, but you got the sense that maybe he felt that people hadn't paid enough homage to the Bears, or to him.

I don't think Mike would admit that he battles to this day for the respect of former 49ers coach Bill Walsh. That is why Mike has very derisively called him a genius. I think in his own mind, Mike feels that there is a group of people who refuse to recognize him as a so-called "great coach." I absolutely do. But I think there is a part of Mike that has always sought a certain kind of parental approval, especially since he and his father were not particularly close. I don't think Mike has to prove a damn thing to anybody.

ONE TAKE EACH

I was waxed at Channel 5 in November of 1983. It came out of nowhere. I was making a lot of money—I had more than a million dollars of contract money. So I was fighting for a settlement. My wife was pregnant; my life was up in the air—the whole nine yards.

Lo and behold, as a part of the settlement, I wound up at WMAQ radio as the sports director. I was going to launch a brand new vehicle—not a sports talk show, but a sports magazine format in which I would have four or five live guests per night. I asked Mike if he would come down to the studio and cut a couple of promos for me.

As it happened, about a week later, Mike and I were both appearing at a banquet. He was the principal speaker and I was the emcee. I said, "Why don't you stop by afterward?" I told him not to park at the Merchandise Mart because it was inside. But he got confused and had to park outside the Mart.

Now, he had just had significant surgery, and he was on crutches. The windchill factor was about twenty-five below, and he was only wearing a sports coat. The poor guy walked over on crutches.

By the time he got there, he was absolutely crimson. I thought, "My God, do I call a paramedic and have him treated for frostbite?" It was 8:00. I had a tape recorder and I turned it on. I told Mike, "You have about twenty-eight and one-half seconds, so let's talk about you." I knew he was frozen to death, he hurt like hell, and he didn't want to be there, but he did two spots—one take each. One take each! No one does that, not even experienced old pros. But Ditka did.

DON'T SAY NO TO HIM

Everyone knows about Mike's inability to separate the various components of his relationships. I think there's a part of Mike that has that old-fashioned, western Pennsylvania mentality. Part of it is defiance, and part of it is trying to please a father figure that he felt was never quite pleased by him.

The great thing about Jerry Vainisi, who was the Bears' general manager when Ditka was coach, was that on the days Mike was pissed off, Jerry would go back and pour him a scotch on the rocks. He

Don't you ever say no to this guy.

was a shoulder for Mike to lean on. There were times, in my opinion, when Vainisi may have saved Ditka from self-destruction. Of course, now they aren't nearly as close as they once were.

Another example is Steve Kasor, who was Ditka's special teams coach in Chicago for the entire run. He told me that he couldn't even get a call in to Ditka about getting a job with the New Orleans Saints. Kasor feels terribly left out by Ditka. He's not the only one.

Ditka reminds me a lot of Bobby Knight. I played golf one day with Bobby and Doc, the Indiana team doctor and a local fixture in Bloomington, and Sam Carmichael, who owned a beautiful course between Bloomington and Indianapolis. We played golf, wrapped up the round, hung around for a while, and then our wives joined us.

My wife Nancy, Doc's wife, and Sam Carmichael's wife all drove up to meet us. We were all going to have dinner together that night. Then Knight said, "All right, you guys all go home, Coppock's going to ride with me."

So I rode with Bobby. We got back to the university, and boom! What happens? We sat there talking for an hour, then two hours, and then we finally got showered. Three hours had gone by, and we didn't get to the restaurant until 9:30. Everybody else was there by 6:00.

We walked in, and Nancy didn't say a word. Nobody said a word. They were all too afraid. I was even tempted to say, "Bobby, for

God's sake, we've got to get the hell out of here." But you just don't do that with a guy like Bobby.

There are those people in life who people strive to be close to, and as a result will put up with any number of idiosyncrasies that are either particular, or spoiled, or just screwed up. Ditka and Bobby Knight both fall into that category. I think Lombardi probably fell into that category, and Auerbach, too. The list goes on and on.

One thing you have to remember about Ditka: Don't you ever say no to this guy. Don't you ever suggest that he can't do something, because he'll ram it right down your throat.

AN IMPOSING FIGURE

Ditka got in a fight in the first game he ever played, on September 13, 1961. It was the Vikings' first game in Minneapolis, and the Bears got creamed by Tarkenton, who was a rookie for the Vikings. Norm Van Brocklin, the Dutchman, was the Vikings' head coach.

Ditka hauled off and slugged one of his own teammates, Ted Karras, Alex Karras's brother. Ditka apparently was upset about the way Karras was playing. He was furious that the Bears got trampled in their opener, so he hauled off and took a swing at his teammate.

With the sponsors, Ditka was tremendous—when he wanted to be. That was part of Ditka's unpredictability factor, and you either had to learn to accept it or you had to walk away from it. A lot of the players could not deal with it. The bulk of the press, whether they would admit it or not, were absolutely scared to death of Ditka.

After all, he was such an imposing figure and an enormous physical specimen. The guy was a combination of Hulk Hogan and Sonny Liston.

> Jim Thorpe was the first president of the NFL.

DITKA, THE WRITE WAY
DON PIERSON

photo courtesy of *Chicago Tribune*

Don Pierson writes for the Chicago Tribune *and is the author of* Ditka: An Autobiography, *which was published in 1986.*

I was covering the Bears for the *Tribune* and a publisher called up and asked if we would be interested in writing a book about Ditka. We weren't, but he talked us into it, and I'm glad we did it.

During the writing of the book, Ditka was terrific—very accessible. We worked out a deal: I would come to his home at a certain time and if it wasn't convenient, we would do it when it was. We weren't going to make this a pain in the ass; we were going to have fun doing it. He was always very professional about it and I don't think he ever changed the schedule. We must have talked for thirty or thirty-five hours.

That '85 season was great, and every win would have helped us sell the book, but the publisher didn't care whether the Bears won or not after they sold enough books to pay us off. It should have gone coast to coast, but they didn't care about distribution at all. You couldn't get that book. McMahon's book sold 300,000 copies. Ditka was always mad about that—that McMahon sold more books than he did.

LOOK WHO'S COMING TO DINNER
KEITH BUCHERT

Keith Buchert owns the Timbers Supper Club in Platteville, Wisconsin, where the Chicago Bears have trained every summer since 1984.

Mike Ditka dined here frequently. Prior to the breakup of camp, he would bring all his coaches in for dinner. He always left every server a hundred-dollar tip—he was just a great guy and a good customer.

Once, Refrigerator Perry and Steve McMichael came in. They were sitting in the bar having cocktails. At the time, Ditka was putting the heat on Perry to lose weight. Perry and McMichael ordered an appetizer tray, and Perry made a stick man out of the carrots and celery and bribed one of the waiters to take it over to Ditka's table.

Another time, after they won the Super Bowl, he was sitting in the lounge, which was full of people. Somebody said, "Mike, what does that Super Bowl ring look like?" So he took it off and passed it around the bar so everybody could look at it. I thought that was nice.

He was always very gracious and never forgot who his fans were. He was never offended by anyone asking for an autograph. One time a woman saw him here, and she pointed and said, "Oh my gosh, it's Mike Ditka." He happened to see that, and he walked over to her table and gave her a little kiss. She thought that was just great.

He always left every server a hundred-dollar tip.

After Ditka left, attendance kind of went down.

I ran into him at the restaurant show in Chicago and we talked. I said, "We really miss you at the Timbers." We were at the ESPN booth, and they were taking pictures. He signed one "Good luck to all of you at the Timbers." He said he'd had some great times at the Timbers and remembered us well.

Kansas City's Arrowhead Stadium was the first stadium designed exclusively for football. It opened in 1972 next door to Royals Stadium.

A NEIGHBORHOOD KIND OF GUY
TOM DREESEN

A native of the Chicago sub-urbs, comedian Tom Dreesen was Frank Sinatra's opening act for thirteen years. He's a member of a celebrity golf tour and often plays with Mike Ditka.

Ditka was so popular in Chicago for the same reasons Harry Caray was popular in Chicago. Chicagoans are different from the residents of most other cities because they live in such a blue-collar town. Harry reminded you of a bartender in the corner tavern. Mike reminds you of a guy who would have a bar called "Iron Mike's"—he's a neighborhood kind of guy.

Ditka, no matter what he does, no matter what he accomplishes, no matter where he goes, will always be the kind of guy neighborhood guys feel they can approach. And they do, by the way. They walk up to him all the time in bars.

But when they look Ditka in the eye, they also know they can't give him a ration of shit. If they give Ditka shit he'll look at them with the coldest eyes you've ever seen in your life. He can freeze you right in your spot.

I've seen him do that to football teams. I've seen him go in at halftime and blow the roof off the locker room. And I've heard him tell his players, "When you get your check, back up to get it, because you sure as hell didn't earn it today."

I thought Ditka would be a good coach for the Bears because he was what they needed at the time, and he had a bundle of talent. Now those Bears days are gone, and I wonder how he'll do in New Orleans. There are prima donnas in football today; they play for the money and not for the game. It's all special teams now—this guy coaches the defense, that guy coaches the quarterbacks, this guy coaches the downtrodden and the meek.

Mike is an intense coach; it's his way or the highway. But as tough and as strong as Mike Ditka is, he is very gentle when he sees a child, and certainly if he sees a disabled child. He just

He can freeze you right in your spot.

melts. As strong as he is, he's also very compassionate and very sensitive to other people.

Mike's about a five-handicap golfer—extremely intense. One time he missed a lob shot on the side of the green, and he promptly left the green, took a sand wedge, and beat it against the side of a tree until it shattered. Either the tree or the sand wedge was going to go, and it turned out it was the sand wedge.

Mike calls me to do shows since I am a master of ceremonies. I have done so many of those things, and Mike was on the dais with me at the Harry Caray roast, so when the time came, Mike wanted me to be the master of ceremonies for his charity.

I've stayed in his home on the North Side of Chicago. His wife Diana is perfect for him. She's a southern gal who adores him. That's her man. She allows him the freedom to be himself. You can't throw a harness around a guy like Ditka. If you do, he'll just drag you along like a mule plowing the fields.

When Mike Ditka was playing and he got the football, he wasn't the fastest guy in the world, but it took two trucks to bring him down.

If Mike Ditka ran for office, he could have done just what Jesse Ventura did.

When he got the ball, he simply did not want to be tackled. Sometimes it would take half the team to bring him down. His legs would still be pumping. That's the kind of football player he was, and that's the kind of person he is. He's a straight ahead, dig in, put your head in, and go for it kind of guy.

Mike is up in years now, but I have seen people come up to him in Iron Mike's and want his autograph. Some people are really nice, and then there are those guys with the big beer bellies and crew cuts who you know are just looking for some shit. They're just looking to argue with him so they can go home and tell everybody they got into it with Ditka. But the way Mike looks at them, and the way he answers them, they know immediately they've got the wrong guy.

In a neighborhood, it's almost like a fort. In the old days, the pioneers in the wilderness carved out a fort to protect themselves from the elements. The neighborhood tavern is like that; it's where everybody goes.

Chicago was a city of boundaries for many, many years. The Irish took over here. The Polish took over there. The Italians took over there. The blacks took over there. There were neighborhoods. When you got inside your neighborhood, there was a comfort there, a safety.

The people who stood out the most in those neighborhoods were those who told the truth. If they said they would be there at 9:00, they were there at 9:00. If they said they were going to help you move at 9:00 on Saturday morning, and even if they were out drinking until 5:00 in the morning, they still had to be there at 9:00 because you're only as good as your word. All my life I've told my children: you're judged by two things—your work and your word. If this is your work, whatever it is, do it the best that you can. If this is your word, never, ever go back on it.

Mike Ditka exemplifies all that. His work ethic cannot be denied, nor can his word. Mike is the kind of guy who, right or wrong, tells it like it is. That's why he was such a big hit on NBC. I was with him just before he took the coaching job in New Orleans, and I thought he was crazy for taking it, because we loved to hear what he would say on the air. For instance, a young football quarterback would be doing this or that and would be holding out. One of the coaches would say, "Well, you've got to talk to him and get hold of his agent." Mike would say, "What he needs is a good slap in the face." And everybody would say, "Yeah, that's exactly what he needs." Mike said that about that quarterback, Jeff George, who gave everybody so many problems everywhere he went. Mike said it on national television. Everybody in every bar in every city said, "Yeah." Because he speaks like us. That's the way you talk in the neighborhoods. Mike doesn't pull any punches. He doesn't speak out of both sides of his mouth.

Today, in a time when voter apathy is up, young people have no respect whatsoever for anyone who runs for office. Why did Jesse Ventura, a wrestler, become a governor? If Mike Ditka ran for office, he could have done just what Jesse Ventura did. Common people would have voted for him because he told it like it was.

> Pat Riley never played college football but was drafted by the Dallas Cowboys. His brother, Lee, played seven years in the NFL.

photo courtesy of *Dallas Cowboys Weekly*

DRESSED TO IMPRESS
PALMER PYLE

Brother of Mike Pyle, Palmer had a stellar high school career in suburban Chicago and starred at Michigan State. After a successful pro career with the Eagles and the Raiders, Palmer became a radio executive in Phoenix, Las Vegas, Jacksonville, and Michigan.

O n Tuesdays, we'd all go out and hit the town after practice. Every Wednesday, Mike would come to practice in a suit so he could go right back to the same places to apologize. I remember that vividly.

DA BEARS
ROBERT SMIGEL

In the early 1990s, the "Saturday Night Live" cast started performing a skit entitled "Sports Fans." Robert Smigel was the key player in that scenario, which allowed such phrases as "da Coach," "da Bears," and "da Bulls," to become part of America's lingo.

I grew up in New York, but I lived in Chicago in the early '80s. I was there taking improv classes. I'm a huge sports fan. I always thought New York was the be-all and end-all, but when I went to Chicago I could see it was a better sports town than any town I'd ever seen. The fans were so devoted and so hilarious, because with devotion often comes insanity. There was a crazy element to the fans—how they took stuff seriously but often with good humor.

That's when I really started noticing the look that a lot of Chicago fans have. It was the beefiness that naturally accumulates from years of sausage eating and beer drinking, the proud, oversized aviator shades that had gone out of style about five years earlier, and the thick mustache, which was very Ditka-like. So I started making fun of the fans and their cocky attitudes.

That's what led to the sketch that Bob Odenkirk and I came up with for "Saturday Night Live." I actually performed the sketch in Chicago before we were both writers for SNL five years later.

Suddenly, "da Bears" and "da Bulls" became catchphrases in Chicago. In the script I didn't even spell it "da," I just wrote " the" and we pronounced it "da." I didn't know it was going be a catchphrase. Then we did the sketch again when George Wendt came on

The holy trinity was basically God, Ditka, and Halas.

the show, and I started seeing these banners at Bulls games on ESPN that said "da Bulls." Then the Bulls started inviting us to their championship celebrations. I realized that this had turned into something.

Ditka was just a natural extension of the sketch. The fans would elevate the Bears to this godlike status, and the holy trinity was basically God, Ditka, and Halas. We did one bit speculating on the seating arrangements up in heaven—there's God, then there's Halas and Jesus and Brian Piccolo.

Ditka has such a quintessential Chicago look that he became the role model for our characters—he embodied everything that was masculine and proper and good on the planet. The characters would rhapsodize about his hair and how sharp it was, and his brain—they'd say that when the coach passes, at least science will have the benefit of examining his brain. The mother lode of information that would come forth would be blinding. It's a complex network of nerve endings covered with a very sharp haircut.

We did the sketch eight times on "Saturday Night" over a period of about five years. It was like a brush fire. It started as "da Bears," then it became "da Bulls," and then it became a national thing. Then it sort of got embraced by rap music. It first began with us making fun of these white guys with Chicago accents.

It took on a life of its own in ways that I didn't ever envision. Jim Downey, the producer at the time, says it's the most repeated catchphrase of any catchphrase that was manufactured on SNL. There are catchphrases that people have said in real life that then become famous on SNL. This was something that just came out of nothing, and he thought it was the most ubiquitous manufactured catch-phrase in the show's history.

I named the characters Super Fans because I remembered a guy in Chicago who went to Cubs games and wore a super hero costume. He called himself "Super Fan." This was in the early '80s. I thought, "That's what these guys would call themselves on their radio show."

Joe Mantegna was Bill Swerski, and when George Wendt hosted the next time we did it we made him Bob Swerski, Bill's brother. From then on Bob always did it because Bill was out recovering from another heart attack; he was always recovering from heart attacks. We named them after Chuck Swersky, a sportscaster in Chicago. Bob Odenkirk picked the name Swerski. We spelled it with an "i" instead of with a "y." Chris Farley was Todd O'Connor. Mike Meyers was in the sketch, too. His character's name was Pat Arnold. My character's name was Carl Wollarski.

I don't usually perform on SNL, but Jim Downey placed me in the sketch because he was from Joliet, near Chicago, and he didn't feel like anybody else was doing the accent as well. So he wanted me in there. He used to call me the metronome for the sketch because if I did a few lines with a perfect accent the whole sketch would sound a little better in his mind.

He actually felt like I did the accent better than George Wendt, who grew up on the South Side of Chicago. Farley grew up in Madison, Wisconsin. Mike Meyers grew up in Canada, so he was at a disadvantage, too. But for some reason, I had a natural affinity for "dat particular accent as per Jim Downey's ear."

> Greasy Neale is the only person to play in a World Series, coach a Rose Bowl team, and coach an NFL champion.

I always thought that no one would get the joke outside of Chicago. After that first season, we only did it twice. It was a phenomenon in Chicago because it coincided with the Bulls winning their first championship, so everything magnified intensely because of all the excitement. Then we were invited to do a comic relief tribute to Michael Jordan the summer after they won the championship. Michael Jordan participated in a sketch on the stage of the Chicago Theater and we had a blast. Then we were invited to do a Bears thing at the Super Bowl. We did all these crazy things over the years.

We actually stepped onto the field before a Bears playoff game in December 1991, when they played the Cowboys. The three of us— George Wendt, Chris Farley, and I— went out to the middle of the field and they introduced us. Then at halftime we participated in the field goal competition for the kids. Farley went first; he took a huge fall and rolled around in the mud and got a huge laugh. I was next and I thought, "There's no way I can top Farley comedically, so I'm actually going to try to kick the ball through." But I had to do it in a funny way, so I held my beer as I did it. I kicked a field goal with a crappy little sneaker. I just managed to kick a twenty yarder and I got a huge cheer. Then I cockily held up my beer and took the applause. It was surreal. George Wendt went last, and he had a great way to finish it off. He called an audible and had me hike the ball to him, and Farley lined up on defense. I threw a block on Farley and George ran in for a touchdown. It was the dumbest thing ever, and it got the biggest cheer. It was completely moronic.

After Ditka was fired, we brought the characters back and they wrote a letter of protest to Michael McCaskey. The whole sketch

> In the 1931 Rose Bowl, "Five Yards" Fogarty
> carried the ball twenty-five times and gained
> exactly five yards each time.

was just us sitting at a table listening while George Wendt wrote this letter of protest. We were giving back all our Bears paraphernalia—ridiculous Bears hats, underwear, a sandwich Mike Singletary had taken a bite out of that we had saved since 1986—just ridiculous souvenirs. Ditka agreed to do it, which was weird because it was the week he was fired. We had somebody go to his house in Chicago to shoot him reading the letter in his basement. On the raw footage it was pretty crappy. It was really funny because the camera guy kept wanting him to do one more take. Ditka said, "What are you talking about, how many times can I do this thing?" It was not the week to ask for extra takes.

> **He embodied everything that was masculine and proper and good on the planet.**

We did this whole sketch where he was reading the letter, and then we dissolved to him chewing gum and reading the letter. The letter suggested that Ditka should be an astronaut, since now the only thing left for him to do was to go to the moon. He called NASA and they didn't think it was such a good idea.

He did something for us as coach of the Saints, too. We went to New Orleans and taped him in his office. He had a phone conversation with Chris Farley. In the sketch, the Super Fans were all in withdrawal because Ditka had moved to New Orleans, and we were all confused. One guy had willingly deprogrammed himself to become a Saints fan. Another guy had lost his mind and moved to the exact middle point between New Orleans and Chicago, which was a gas station in the middle of Tennessee. He had cut his uniform in half—with the Bears on one side and the Saints on the other—and he had attached the sides with nacho cheese. Farley's character was in a mental hospital because he was in denial and kept insisting it was

1986 and the Bears were 9–0. So Ditka had to talk him down and tell him to move on with his life.

Ditka was a great sport about it. I think he loved it. We used his restaurant, Ditka's City Lights, and he was thrilled because we always showed it at the beginning of the sketch. We pretended that that was where the sketch was taking place. In the opening of the sketch, we would play "Sweet Home Chicago," and there was a fake banner outside of the photo of Ditka's that said, "Every Sunday, Bob Swerski's Super Fans on WCBN Radio," or something like that. Whenever I was in Chicago I would go to Ditka's restaurant and they would treat me like a king. I would get a free meal and royal treatment.

> In 1941, Buff Donelli was the head football coach for the Pittsburgh Steelers and Duquesne University.

DIKTA ON HIS BEAR DAYS

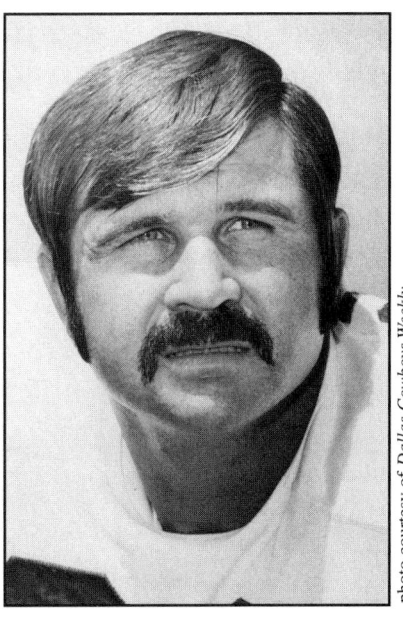

I was tremendously proud to put on a Bears uniform. I knew very little about the Bears until I was drafted by them in 1961 because I was from Pennsylvania and mostly followed the Pittsburgh Steelers and Philadelphia Eagles. But the more I found out about the Bears, the more I liked the team; they played the kind of football that I believed in, and Coach Halas taught the kind of football I believed in. The Bears were the Monsters of the Midway, or the bullies, or whatever you want to call them, and that's the way I thought the game was supposed to be played.

I was with the College All-Stars in 1961, and we scrimmaged the Bears. I did not make any friends on the team. I ran over a couple of guys, which did not sit well with them. We played the Philadelphia Eagles, who had won the NFL title the year before. We had some very good ballplayers.

I think the first friend I made on the team was Bill George. Bill was a Pennsylvania kid from the coal mine area of western Pennsylvania. He kind of took me under his wing and helped me a little bit. And I remember Larry Morris and some of the other guys. Harlon Hill was a lot of help to me. Harlon was a great guy. It was toward the end of his career, and he spent a good amount of time working with me. He was also playing, and I think they were planning on converting him to tight end. I think they even tried him on defense because his days as a wide receiver were over, but in my day he was one of the great wide receivers.

I didn't have an agent when I came to Chicago. I don't have an agent now. I don't believe in agents. I know what I'm worth and I wouldn't fool anybody about that. My agents were myself and my dad. I was very flattered at the time to be drafted into the NFL when I was coming out of college. I didn't know if I would play in the National Football League. It was actually George Allen who signed me—he was the Bears' assistant defensive coach at the time. He said, "You know, I'm paying you more money than the Bears have paid any rookie since Red Grange," or something like that, and I knew he was lying, but still I had to laugh.

My first impression of George Halas was that he was the leader. What he said went; he was the boss, period. I saw him as being in control and very authoritative. He was the guy who got his way almost all the time, either when dealing with the Bears or the NFL.

I came to our first training camp pretty well prepared. At Pitt we worked as hard as anybody. Our coach was a stickler for hard work and tough training. Since I was used to working hard, training camp was not that difficult for me.

There was, of course, a difference from college football. At Pitt I'd played defense and blocked a lot. Catching passes was rarely on the agenda. With the Bears my job was to catch balls and block, and that was a big change for me. So when I was drafted by the Bears in '61, I went to Chicago early and worked out. That was the year

In the 1983 Holiday Bowl, Brigham Young University quarterback Steve Young caught the winning touchdown pass in a 21–17 victory over Missouri.

the Bears traded for Bill Wade. Sid Luckman was there as an assistant coach, and he really helped me tremendously in becoming a receiver. He took the time to work with me and teach me how to catch a ball. Not that I couldn't catch the ball—I led the team at Pitt in receiving my senior year with fourteen catches or so, which tells you what our passing game was like. Sid guided me, and Bill Wade worked with me, throwing the ball to me; we just did it over and

> **It was a different game then. We were all part of football as a sport, and it's not like that anymore; it's big business.**

over. We worked out down at Soldier Field in those days even though we played at Wrigley Field. We worked for about three or four weeks in the summer, and it really helped me for training camp.

It was a different game then, too. We were all part of football as a sport, and it's not like that anymore; it's big business. We were part of pro football when it was played more for the love of the game. We played hard together on the field and off the field, and we had fun.

We were much more together as a group in those days. It was nothing for all of us to meet at a place and have a beer together or a sandwich. I think we did much more of that than the players do today.

There was also a strong camaraderie. Maybe there wasn't a great love, but there was always a great respect between our offense and defense. I always felt that. We knew that we were a team that won because of our defense, yet offensively we tried to do the things we had to do.

One of the things I did that first summer when I came to Chicago early, besides catching passes and working out, was watch a lot of *game film. One day I was watching a film of the Bears playing the Lions, and I remember Joe Fortunato rushing a passer. Jim Gibbons was Detroit's tight end, and he was on the right end's side. Joe got outside of Gibbons and gave him the clothesline, took him all the way to the quarterback with him, and just dropped them both. Coach Halas happened to be in the room at the time, and he said, "Did you see that?"*

I said, "Yeah, do they always do that to the tight ends?" And he said, "Not if you don't let them." I said, "Well, I'll try not to let them then." Fortunato was just a big, impressive guy and a hell of a football player.

Our finest season, of course, was 1963. The first thing I remember about that season was when we played the Giants in the preseason. We beat them, and after the game Coach Halas called me in and asked me about where I thought we could go that year. I said I thought we could win it all.

I also remember the '63 games against Green Bay, which were tremendous games. We won both (at Green Bay, 10–3, and at Wrigley Field, 26–7)—not an easy chore when they had Vince Lombardi on the sideline and players like Starr, Nitschke, Taylor, Kramer, and Davis on the field.

The game in Pittsburgh was memorable, as was the tie at the end of the year against the Vikings (which we had to get), and the game against Detroit (which we had to win), when Davey Whitsell intercepted a pass and saved the game. After all those games and the things that happened in them, the championship game against the Giants was almost anticlimactic, but it was a great game—the

> Clemson University started the Booster Club concept with IPTAY (I Pay Ten a Year). Rivals claim it stands for "It's Probation Time Again, Y'all."

league's top offense (Giants) against the best defense (Bears).

The play that everybody seems to remember was in the Steelers game that year. (Ditka took a short pass and rambled sixty-three yards, shedding at least five tacklers to set up the game-tying field goal.) I don't really know that it was the best play I ever made, because if it had been the best, I would have scored a touchdown and I would have outrun that last guy. I was very tired at that point. That play was near the end of the game, and I'd played the whole game. I remember that because Wade wanted me to run a deep pattern, and I said, "No, I can't," and I told him what play to run. I said, "I'll hook up about twelve yards down, you throw me the ball, and maybe I can get across midfield." I felt that if we hit another pass or two, maybe we could score a touchdown or at least kick another field goal. Then, during my run, all those guys missed me, but I started running out of gas, and when the last guy hit me, I went down. So I wasn't going too fast. On the play after that—I had come out of the game—Wade threw a perfect pass to Bo Farrington, hit him right between the numbers in the end zone, and he dropped it. So we had to kick a field goal to tie it. When you think about the little things that made that season, it's kind of crazy. At any rate, we ended up half a game ahead of Green Bay and went out and whipped the Giants for the title.

We had some great players then. Bill George was definitely one of the all-time greatest players. There's no question in my mind about Doug Atkins, either. I don't think Dick Butkus had a peer at middle linebacker; he played the position ferociously. Bill George played it a little differently. So did Joe Schmidt of Detroit. But Butkus, Ray Nitschke of Green Bay, and Jack Lambert of Pittsburgh, they played it like: "I'm just going to kick the shit out of these guys; I've got no friends on the other side. Don't take any prisoners." I respected them for that.

There were other damn good players too: linebackers Joe Fortunato and Larry Morris, defensive end Ed O'Bradovich, tackles Fred Williams and Stan Jones. In the secondary we had Rosey Taylor, Richie Petitbon, Bennie McRae, and Davey Whitsell. So it was a very solid football team. We had J. C. Caroline backing up in the offense, and one of the game's greatest running backs and a very underrated player, Willie Galimore. I saw him after he had about five knee surgeries, but he could still fly. I never saw anybody cut and run like he could. He was very similar to Gale Sayers, but actually I thought he was faster than Gale. I don't know that he could cut as well as Gale, but they were very similar. Then, of course, we had Joe Marconi and Rick Casares at fullback, and Rudy Bukich and Bill Wade at quarterback. On the line were Bob Wetoska, Ted Karras, and Herm Lee. There was Mike Pyle at center. Bo Farrington and Johnny Morris were the wide receivers. It was a solid football team. In passing we couldn't match Baltimore's personnel, which included Johnny Unitas and Raymond Berry, but we got the job done.

Galimore and Farrington were killed at the next training camp in 1964. It was a terrible shock. You're with the guys one night, you leave a meeting with them, you have a bite to eat with them, and then it's over, forever. They went over to the country club to watch the Olympics and eat pizza. Because somebody had misplaced a road sign, they ran off the road when they were coming back, hooked a wheel, and the car flipped over. They both were killed. I

The youngest coaches in NFL history were Harlan Svare, thirty-one, 1962, Rams; David Shula, thirty-two, Bengals, 1992; John Madden, thirty-three, Raiders 1969; Don Shula, thirty-three, Colts, 1963.

can remember the shock of everyone at training camp, and it was terrible.

I played against some tough guys. Ray Nitschke of the Packers—he was as tough as they come. Willie Wood, up in Green Bay, was a really rugged defensive back; I had great respect for him. And, of course, I had to play against Herb Adderley. Another tough one was a kid out of the 49ers, Jimmy Johnson, a great defensive back. During my career, most of the trouble seemed to come from the Packers guys, like Willie Davis. Another tough guy I played against was Bill Pellington, at Baltimore—he'd knock people down with his fist.

It was really something to go against the Packers in those days. There's always been a great rivalry between the Bears and Green Bay.

Gino Marchetti—I respected him so much. He was just a great football player. If you can block Marchetti and you can block Willie Davis, you can block anybody. Another tough one was Alex Karras from Detroit. He was pretty damn tough. There was a linebacker out of San Francisco who played in the '70s, Dave Wilcox. He played against us at the end of my Bears career, and then when I was playing at Dallas. He was a very underrated football player.

I had a couple of good run-ins with Sam Huff of the Giants, but I had great respect for Sam because he played the game the way I did. He played hard like I did, and we both felt that you can't worry about who is going to get mad at you out there as a result. If they get mad at you, they get mad at you. Sam didn't have to be big, he played so well. He wasn't small, though—I think he played linebacker at about 230 or 235 pounds.

The two best teams of my time were the Packers and the Colts. Baltimore, talent-wise, might even have been better than the Packers. They finally won the NFL championship in 1964.

It was really something to go against the Packers in those days. There's always been a great rivalry between the Bears and Green Bay. But we had a good rivalry with Baltimore, too, in those days. In fact, we had a lot of intense rivalries, including Detroit and Minnesota.

I came back to the Bears in 1982. George Halas called me. I had written him a letter some years before and had told him that if the opportunity ever arose, I would really appreciate at least talking about the possibility of coaching the Bears. And so he called me and asked if I would come in and have a talk. Actually, he didn't call me first; he called the Cowboys for permission to talk to me, and Tex Schramm, the president of the Cowboys, told me that I could. Then Halas called me at home one night and said, "Fly in and come to my apartment. Don't tell anyone about it." So that's what I did.

We sat down and talked. It was very informal, at the kitchen table. At the time, all the fair-haired guys were coming in, the new geniuses of football. I think Mr. Halas was trying to check me out to see if I was one of them, and so he asked me what my philosophy of football was. I kind of laughed and said, "You know I don't think that's important. First of all, my philosophy is the same as yours, and that's strictly to win. How we do it? We have our methods and we have our ideas. But if you're asking me if I am going to go out and throw the ball all over the ballpark like it's a wounded duck, no, I'm going to play football and teach good, basic fundamentals."

He offered me a two-year contract, but I said I wouldn't take a two-year contract; it would have to be a three-year contract, period. I said two years wasn't enough. And it wouldn't have been. He said, "Fine," and gave me the other year. It was not a very lucrative con-

tract, but it didn't matter. That was never important; the opportunity was what was important.

He gave me that opportunity, and I'm forever grateful. It's just a shame that he couldn't have stayed around to see all the good things that happened to the Bears in the 1980s. But I think he knows they happened. I think he had an inkling that they were going to happen, I really do. It's also a shame he didn't get a chance to see the '85 team, because it may have been as good a Bears team as there ever was.

In the beginning, when I first got out of playing the game, I wanted to stay with the game by coaching. I managed to do that. But I knew it would be a while before I was ready to take on a head coaching job. In fact, I never wanted to be head coach, per se. I had a good job as an assistant coach with the Dallas Cowboys, and that's a pretty secure job if you do your job. It was good because the Cowboys had won and were a very stable organization. I was working for Tom Landry and Tex Schramm, two people I loved and respected.

Everybody started talking about head coaching jobs when Dan Reeves, another of our assistants at Dallas at the time, got the Denver Broncos job.

The only job I ever wanted was the Bears job. Nobody was going to call me from New York or Atlanta or any of those kinds of teams. I was committed to the Bears' type of football—the kind George Halas had fostered. Anybody can think what they want to think or write what they want to write—it was just meant to be. That's all

> The Jacksonville Jaguars were the first major team in any sport to be completely anti-smoking in every way.

there was to it. You can call it fate, but that's how it was meant to be. I don't think anybody could have written a script with the sense of destiny I felt, beginning with my coming to Chicago in '61 and my travels and my return in '82, twenty years later.

The year 1985 was truly special. I thought we would be a pretty good football team. I thought we would be a team that would never knuckle under to anybody. I knew we were going to be tough. And then everything just came together.

We won most of the early games with offense; our defense was not sure yet. They were still getting their feet wet, and everybody had kind of picked on them. Other teams knew when we were blitzing and this and that, but once the defense cranked it up it didn't matter if they knew or not, because nobody could stop them. As the season went along, our cornerbacks got more confidence. By the end of the year, you could see from the other teams playing us that they didn't want any part of those guys, nor did they want any part of our defensive line or linebackers—Hampton, Dent, Perry, McMichael, Singletary, Marshall, and Otis Wilson. Those guys were just awfully good. And they were brutal.

We just surged to the Super Bowl, and that is the best feeling there is. Of all the feelings I've ever had, to be the head coach of a Super Bowl-winning football team is the finest, because it's a total team effort. It's nothing I did, and it's nothing any one individual on the team did; it was a collective effort by everybody in the organization from top to bottom. There were so many people to thank, even people who were gone, like Jim Finks, who had helped put the pieces in place with his excellent draft picks, and Jerry Vainisi and Bill McGrane from the front office. It was a terrific organization. It seemed like everybody worked for a common goal that year, and that's what we tried to get back. That's such a hard thing to reestablish once you have done it, because people get caught up in the whole idea of why you win or how important they were in the scheme of things instead of realizing that they were just part of the reason, and not the whole reason.

We would have made history if we would have beaten Miami in 1985, but they outcoached us. Don Shula outcoached us. They didn't outplay us—our guys were really playing hard—they just outcoached us, and I'm willing to admit that.

If we had not have lost that game, I'm not sure we would have gone all the way. I thought that the loss regenerated everything, that it just pissed everybody off: staff, players, everybody. So we went out and rededicated ourselves. When we hit the playoffs, we shut out two teams, we just rolled over them. We did everything right. We peaked at the right time.

Of course, we had Walter Payton that year. As a football player he was simply the best I've ever seen. I'm talking about the whole package—what you give to the game, what you take from the game, your attitude on and off the field, how you handle the media and the press, and how you play the game. He played the game with great enthusiasm and fervor, and he was exceptional. Walter was a great runner, and he was also a great blocker. He did everything—he could have played defense if we'd have put him over there, and he'd have played it pretty darn good.

I think today we have to be careful not to lose sight of football as a great sport. The game has become very big and reaches tens of millions of people each week of the season, and everybody is entitled to his piece of the game. Yet I still say that our game, the game played in the National Football League, is a very good product, and I don't think there are a lot of reasons to change everything every year. It's a good product, and we have to be careful that we don't take what is good about the product and get rid of it. This game has been played for a long time—more than eighty years—and will be played eighty more. We should not spend our time worrying about making the game shorter or speeding it up. If it's a good game, it's a good game. Think of all the great individual games we've been fortunate to watch; think of the great performances, the great plays, the great team efforts—that's NFL football.

We have to be careful not to lose sight of the game itself and the glory connected with it.

The first stadium to have a corporate sponsor was Rich Stadium (1973) in Buffalo.

Chapter 5

Chip Caray

Gary Pressy

John McDonough

Mary Therese Kraft

photo courtesy of the Chicago Cubs

Take Me Out to the Ballgame

photo courtesy of the Chicago Cubs

A WRIGLEY FIELD MOMENT
CHIP CARAY

Chip Caray, grandson of the legendary Harry Caray and son of the longtime Atlanta Braves announcer Skip Caray, has been an announcer with the Chicago Cubs since 1998.

He was late getting here. Usually the guys sit and enjoy the game in one of the luxury boxes with our marketing staff. He was out playing golf and got stuck in the infamous Chicago traffic. The game's going on and we're not sure if and when he's going to get here. The seventh inning comes along, and there's no Ditka, so Steve (Stone) grabs the microphone and says, "Well, fans, it's the seventh-inning stretch and we've got good news and bad news. The good news is Mike Ditka was scheduled to do it.

The bad news is he's not here. So Chip and I are going to have to fill in and 'pinch-sing' for him." The crowd, of course, turns around and starts to boo us unmercifully.

Then all of a sudden Steve gets a cue from one of the marketing guys, who says, "Wait a minute, Ditka's in the house." Well, Ditka, as you know, has bad knees, bad hips, and a bad back from all those NFL days, and he's trudging up the ramps of the ballpark with that cigar sticking out of his mouth. He dashes into the booth. Just as Steve says he's here, he walks in, there is thunderous applause, he comes down, he knows he's late. He's out of breath, takes one giant gasp of air, and then of course lets out that famous rendition of "Take Me Out to the Ballgame."

He did it in his own inimitable way.

Like everybody else, I thought the way he was singing was hilarious. He knew he was late, he was rushing, he didn't want to let anybody down. I think the anticipation is always the hardest part for people who don't sing or speak in public, and Mike obviously has never been a guy who's afraid to say what's on his mind. I think he just wanted to get it over with and get it out as quickly as he could. He certainly did it in his own inimitable way. That's the way he coached the Bears. He just rode his bicycle straight through, as it were. It was great; it was wonderful.

As soon as it was over, it was almost like he had run fifty sets of forty-yard wind sprints. But he did a great job. It was certainly the most memorable rendition that we had ever heard. It was a true story: he was just stuck in traffic. We're glad he made it because it made all the highlight shows and will forever live on as one of those Wrigley Field "moments" that no one will ever forget.

photo courtesy of the Chicago Cubs

Ditka is a big baseball fan and very knowledgeable about the sport. One time he was invited to throw out the first pitch at a Cubs game. The catcher for the ceremonial first pitch was Joe Girardi. Girardi was holding a football in his right hand, but he kept it hidden behind his back. He caught Ditka's first pitch one-handed, stood up, and fired the football right at Ditka as the crowd went wild. That scene was replayed on practically every sports show in the country that evening.

Then there's the Kevin Hickey story. He pitched for the White Sox in 1983 but was released after going 1–2 with five saves. On a postgame show, after he was let go, Hickey mentioned that he needed a job. The host of the show called Mike Ditka. Hickey became a doorman at Ditka's City Lights and was in the training program when the Baltimore Orioles' general manager Roland Hemond went to eat at Ditka's, saw Hickey, and signed him for the Orioles.

photo courtesy of Gary Pressy

SINGING TOO FAST
GARY PRESSY

Gary Pressy is the organist who accompanied Ditka at Wrigley Field.

He was going to sing in the bottom of the seventh, but he ran a little late because he was playing golf and traffic was backed up. So we go into the bottom of the seventh, and Steve Stone takes the microphone and says, "The coach hasn't arrived. I guess I have to do it." Then all of a sudden here he comes. He bolts like a bat out of hell; he grabs the microphone, and in his Knute Rockne style of "Take Me Out to the Ballgame," he starts. I'm five booths down from where he is, and I'm just holding on to the key like I do with everybody. Then he starts—it looks like a polka tempo so I'm going to have to pick it up. About a quarter of the way or halfway through, I caught up with him. He went on and I just kept up with him.

The amazing part is that we scored seven runs in the bottom of the inning. We scored a touchdown—he was rallying the troops! Usually the performers come into the booth before they sing and we go over it: How are you going to sing—like a one, a two, a three? Let me hear you.

> **It was like a 33 rpm record going at 78 rpm.**

He came late so he just came right to the booth, and I picked up his tempo. He was ahead of me, but I said, "No, no, I'm going to catch up with him." I started speeding up and I caught up to him. People didn't know what was going on. I say it was like a 33 rpm record going at 78 rpm.

Actually, I never met him that day. I did talk to him on the phone the next day. He said, "Well, I knew the organist was good. He'd keep up with anybody." Then I met him personally on Opening Day 1999, and he said, "Now listen, I'm not going to do it too fast." He did it the regular way.

Harry's the one who put Wrigley on the map with "Take Me Out to the Ballgame." I don't know who's been the best. Vince Scully was excellent; he did it like an Irish tenor. He appreciates the song and what it means to baseball. We had Kenny Rogers, the singer, not the pitcher. He did an excellent job. He came into the booth afterward and said, "I want to thank you. It's an honor." I said, "No, I want to thank you." We've had Walter Payton, Ernie Banks, Muhammad Ali. He couldn't sing, but he was there. You get to play it with all these people in different fields—Hall of Famers, singers, actors, announcers—it's great.

Ditka wasn't even the worst singer to do it. Harry was no Frank Sinatra, so if someone sang it off key, so be it. I think it turned out great when Ditka did it the first time, because it put "Take Me Out

It put "Take Me Out to the Ballgame" on the map.

to the Ballgame" on the map. After that, everybody was saying, "Now who's going to sing?"

Mike Ditka epitomizes Chicago. He was a hardworking, put-it-on-the-line type of player, and they loved that. I still see tapes of him in that game against Pittsburgh, the day after Kennedy got shot, when he ran through the whole team. He went eighty-five yards. Chicago loves that personality. And if you win, that's the icing on the cake. Since he left, the Bears have never been the same. In that one season, 1985, I can't remember a more dominant football team, and the fans loved it. He would tell the media off in no uncertain terms. He didn't care. He told the Vikings he had roller skates on in Minnesota. They loved that. That's what Chicago is.

> The Tampa Bay Buccaneers have never returned a kickoff for a touchdown. In a 1998 game between the Ravens and the Vikings, three kickoffs were returned for touchdowns within seven minutes.

photo courtesy of the Chicago Cubs

SINGING AT WRIGLEY
JOHN McDONOUGH

John is the Chicago Cubs' Vice President of Marketing and Broadcasting.

I had known Mike for a while. I noticed that he was at Harry's funeral; they were close. They are kind of built out of the same cloth—two guys who have won decisive victories over life. They both play offense.

When we asked Ditka to sing, we didn't know if he could sing or not, but we're finding out that not many of them can. I think Mike's rendition has garnered more attention than anyone we've had.

We've had the biggest of the biggest of the biggest of the big, and Ditka has superceded them all.

I don't think anyone's ever heard a rendition as aggressive, as loud, as bombastic or enthusiastic as that one, before or since.

Mary Therese Kraft, the young woman in our office, actually made the original contact, but when he was aware of our marketing strategy, he was flattered. He made time to do it and was very gracious about it.

There was one out in the seventh inning and he wasn't here yet. I called up to the booth and told Steve Stone and Chip Caray, our announcers, "It doesn't look like he's going to make it. You go ahead without him." Right away, there were two outs. We heard that Ditka was in the parking lot and were hoping the hitter would foul a few off—which he did. The guy stepped out of the box at the same time Ditka was running up the ramp. Well, sure enough, the guy made the third out. It was show time. "All right, ladies and gentlemen, unfortunately the coach is not with us," they said. And it was just a crescendo—a loud crescendo—of boos.

Had those fans not responded so negatively, Chip and Steve would have gone ahead. All of a sudden, almost like it was scripted out of central casting in Hollywood, Ditka appeared. He took on this persona of the coach and just let it rip. I don't think anyone's ever heard a rendition as aggressive, as loud, as bombastic or enthusiastic as that one, before or since.

The funny part about it is that with all those other obstacles—bad hips, etc.—he still made it. If you've ever been to our press box, it's the stairway to heaven. It's a long way. So it adds to the lore. We were behind in the game and after Ditka got here, he fired up the troops. It's one of the funniest pieces of video I've ever seen. It actually has won some video awards from Major League Baseball.

I didn't know whether to laugh or cry because we're trying to make this tribute to Harry somewhat dignified and honorable and respectful, yet lighthearted. Ditka's rendition took this to a brand new dimension. When you turned on the news that night, it led off every sportscast, including ESPN, FOX, and all the local news and sports shows. They played it for days and days. Then I had dinner with Mike in February of '99. We wanted to do Opening Day 1999 under the theme: "This time he's on time."

> Pullman, Washington, home of Washington State University, has a population of twenty-five thousand. Martin Stadium, the home stadium for the Washington State Cougars, holds thirty-eight thousand.

photo courtesy of the Chicago Cubs

HARRY MUST BE LAUGHING IN HEAVEN
MARY THERESE KRAFT

Mary Therese Kraft is a fine young Notre Dame graduate who has the envious task of inviting singers to sing "Take Me Out the Ballgame" at Wrigley Field during the seventh-inning stretch. Singing the song is a tribute to Harry Caray and has become a popular tradition at Wrigley Field.

We invited Mike Ditka to sing "Take Me Out to the Ballgame." When he accepted we were ecstatic. The plan was for him to arrive at the ballpark directly after his golf game. The game started, and we were all running around in a panic trying to find out where he was. We called the restaurant and they said he was at the golf course. The golf course called and said, "Oh, he just left." This all happened in about the fifth inning.

We had a security person posted in the parking lot and one with me up in the booth. We just waited for him to come. As it turned out, we had to decide whether we were going to go with him or not. He arrived with two outs in the top of the seventh inning. My intern at the time, Doug Thompson, was with the security guard and they ran him up there. They radioed up to us and said Ditka had arrived. So we told our PA announcer and our message board operator, "He's here, he's in the building—we're going to go with Ditka." Then all of a sudden the third out was made. Poor Steve Stone, who's a riot, did such a great job of holding the crowd. He said, "We have an announcement: Ditka's in the building but he's not here yet, so I may have to sing by myself." The crowd started booing, not because they didn't want to hear Steve but because everyone was anticipating Mike Ditka.

In the meantime, our security guard was running this poor guy— who has had two hip surgeries and a heart attack—up our back stairway, which has about three flights of stairs and four ramps. We got him up to the top of the stairway, and Steve Stone said, "The coach has arrived." Everybody in the crowd just went crazy. We told him we were going to prep him on the way up and that we'd been waiting for him. We meant that we were not going to sing without him. But I think he thought we meant that we weren't going to start the

> Only two teams in the last quarter century have won college football's national title with a freshman quarterback: Miami in 1983 with Bernie Kosar and Oklahoma in 1985 with Jamelle Holieway.

game until he sang. So he just belted it out like no other. Oh, it was so funny, and his expression after was just the most comical thing we saw all year.

Everyone's faces were in a state of confusion. They started to sing with him, but just couldn't keep up. Everyone started with "Take me out to the ballgame," but they just lost him after that. This had never happened; the seventh inning stretch was not sung. Everyone was just in awe. Our organist Gary Pressy kept right up with him. He followed him to a T, which is amazing. It was unreal. As soon as he finished, everyone was like, "What just happened?" The bleacher section did a chorus of their own and sang the whole song over again because it was just too fast.

> **We got him up to the top of the stairway, and Steve Stone said, "The coach has arrived." Everybody in the crowd just went crazy.**

My heart has never beaten so fast. It went from a total state of panic—"I have no idea where he is"—to "Okay, he's here, let's run him up." Then we just took a huge breath, and it didn't hit anybody until that night when it was aired across the country on ESPN and CNN. Diana, his wife, called and asked for a copy of it, because she hadn't seen it. People were just calling like crazy. They were laughing and saying it was the best rendition. When you look at it, you know Harry has to be laughing hysterically in heaven because it was so Harry-esque and so Ditka-esque. The way he said, "One, two, three strikes you're out"—it was a riot.

He could not have been nicer. He stayed on the air with Chip and Steve; they couldn't even cut to a commercial because it was so late. He was wonderful. He interviewed with the press and was so apologetic. He said, "I'm so sorry; I didn't realize it would take so long to get here from the golf course. I got stuck on Addison." We ask everybody who sings to autograph the score and some baseballs to auction off at the end of the season. He said, "Oh, I'll sign anything you want. I feel terrible." I asked if he would mind going on WGN radio, and he said, "Oh, I'll do anything, I feel so bad." He was funny.

I had never met him before in person, and he was great. He took pictures with everybody, signed anything anybody wanted him to sign, and did a great interview with the media. He was wonderful, and I think he really loved it. He won an award for us, which really put this entire "seventh-inning stretch" song on the map. From that point on, we had people calling us up to offer to sing because of the exposure he was able to get for us.

Ditka sang on Opening Day 1999, and I have to say that he still can't carry a tune. Our theme this year was: "This time he's on time." This time he sang much slower. I think it was important to him to come back and do it again and do it right. He's not a strong singer, but he's a phenomenal guy all around. When we approached him this year, we told him about the award that MLB had presented to us because of his performance; I think he was kind of in awe. Major League Baseball gave us the award for "Blooper of the Year." It probably isn't something to be too proud of, but it was pretty funny.

Ditka is such an amazing icon; it's really impressive. You see that stern face, that rugged blue-collar persona on TV, the Ditka that

When Mack Brown became the head coach at the University of Texas, he became the second-highest-paid college football coach ever, yet he had never even won a conference title.

When you look at it, you know Harry has to be laughing hysterically in heaven because it was so Harry-esque and so Ditka-esque.

broke his arm in the locker room when he was so mad—this rough, tough guy. The first time I met him, I was almost taken aback. His face is such a caricature. Here is a man who is no longer affiliated with Chicago—he coaches an opposing team now and just has a restaurant in Chicago—but is loved more than any other Chicagoan right now, and that is really impressive. The fans still love the coach and think of him as Chicago's.

We had a hard time, because usually we play music, make an announcement, and lead up to who's going to sing. Of course, we didn't want to play anything Saints-related, and we almost didn't want to play anything Bears-related, since he's not head coach anymore. So we just played "Chicago," because that's what he is. He is Chicago. My generation, especially, admires him. He's got that Midwest mentality that everybody appreciates and associates with. It's that rugged image of someone who worked hard all his life, has definite morals and ethics, or at least is someone you can respect. Who doesn't really appreciate and support that?

> More NFL games have been played at Wrigley Field than at any other stadium in the country. Mile High Stadium in Denver is in second place.

MIKE DITKA ON HARRY CARAY

photo courtesy of Dallas Cowboys Weekly

It's hard to describe Harry without getting into a long description. He really enjoyed life. He was fun to be around. And he was real. He was genuine. There was no phoniness to Harry Caray. I loved him for that. He didn't make it a secret that when he wanted a beer, he had a beer. There was no put-on, no front. He was just real people.

He took time with people. That's the thing I noticed. Every time I was with him, he always took time with people. He always signed the autographs. He talked to the people. A lot of it could have been very aggravating, but he did it. A lot of celebrities won't do that, and I thought that was one of the greatest things about him.

Ditka's famed restaurant on Chicago's West Ontario Street pre-dated Harry Caray's eatery as a trendy place. But Caray's had the staying power. Ditka now is associated with another restaurant a few blocks further east, in the Streeterville area. Caray did patronize the original Ditka's.

Harry was at Ditka's City Lights a few times. Actually, the guy who put Harry in business with his restaurant, Ben Stein, was a partner in our business for a while.

Harry and I shot a commercial up at the bar at Ditka's (Restaurant) by the (O'Hare) airport. It was funnier than heck, because it was not very hard to do, but Harry had had a few pops and he was continuing to drink his Budweiser as we were trying to do the shoot. Oh my gosh. It took him about twenty-five to thirty shoots to get it. After a while, I was the problem because I was laughing so hard at him. But he was beautiful.

He loved the Cubs. He had a strong relationship with the Cardinals and he worked for the White Sox. But I don't think any relationship was as strong as his with the Cubs. I think he probably agonized more over that relationship than over any of the others. He really just wanted them to win.

Even I'm pulling for the Cubs now. Believe me.

Alabama has the most college football bowl wins with twenty-eight and the most losses with twenty. Southern Cal is second with twenty-five and thirteen.

BIBLIOGRAPHY

Anderson, Terry. *The Movement and the Sixties.* New York: Oxford University Press, 1995.

Bahas, Dr. Gabriel. *Keep off the Grass.* Pleasantville, N.Y.: Readers Digest Press, 1976.

Bayless, Skip. *The Boys: Jones vs. Johnson and the Feud that Rocked America's Team.* New York: Pocket Books, 1994.

Bayless, Skip. *God's Coach.* New York: Simon & Schuster, 1990.

Blair, Sam. *Dallas Cowboys: Pro or Con?* New York: Doubleday, 1970.

Dent, Jim. *King of the Cowboys: The Life and Times of Jerry Jones.* Holbrook, Mass.: Adams Publishing, 1995.

Dorsett, Tony, with Harvey Frommer. *Running Tough.* New York: Doubleday, 1989.

Garrison, Walt, and John Tullius. *Once a Cowboy.* New York: Random House, 1988.

Gent, Pete. *North Dallas Forty.* New York: William Morrow, 1973.

Goodman, Michael E. *Chicago Bears* (NFL Today). Mankato, Minn.: Creative Education, 1996.

Harris, David. *The League: The Rise and Decline of the NFL.* New York: Bantam Books, 1986.

Henderson, Thomas "Hollywood," and Peter Knobler. *Out of Control: Confessions of an NFL Casualty.* New York: G. P. Putnam & Sons, 1987.

Johnson, Jimmy, as told to Ed Hinton. *Turning the Thing Around.* New York: Hyperion, 1993.

Keteyian, Armen. *Ditka: Monster of the Midway.* New York: Pocket Books, 1992.

Kowat, Don. *The Rich Who Own Sports.* New York: Random House, 1977.

Lamb, Kevin. *Portrait of Victory: Chicago Bears 1985.* Provo, Utah: Final Four Publications, 1986.

Landry, Tom, with Gregg Lewis. *Tom Landry: An Autobiography.* New York: Zondervan Publishing, 1990.

Leslie, Warren. *Dallas City Limit.* New York: Grossman Publishers, 1964.

Mausser, Wayne. *Chicago Bears Facts and Trivia* (Sports Facts and Trivia). South Bend, Ind.: E. B. Houchin Company, 1997.

Nolen, Claude H. *The Negro's Image in the South: The Anatomy of White Supremacy.* Louisville: University of Kentucky Press, 1967.

O'Connor, Richard. *The Oil Barons: Men of Greed and Grandeur.* Boston: Little, Brown, 1971.

Payne, Darwin. *Big D: Triumphs and Troubles of an American Supercity in The 20th Century*. Dallas: Three Forks Press, 1994.

Priestly, James. *A Saga of Wealth*. New York: G. P. Putnam & Sons, 1978.

Rentzel, Lance. *When All the Laughter Died in Sorrow*. New York: Saturday Review Press, 1972.

Rothaus, James R. *The Chicago Bears*. Mankato, Minn.: Creative Education, 1981.

St. John, Bob. *The Landry Legend*. Dallas: Word Books, 1989.

St. John, Bob. *Landry: The Man Inside*. Dallas: Word Books, 1979.

St. John, Bob. *Tex!: The Man Who Built the Cowboys*. New York: Prentice Hall, 1988.

Schapp, Dick. *Quarterbacks Have All the Fun*. Chicago: Playboy Press, 1974.

Singletary, Mike, and Armen Keteyian. *Calling the Shots: Inside the Chicago Bears*. Chicago: Contemporary Books, 1986.

Smith, Emmitt, with Steve Delsohn. *The Emmitt Zone*. New York: Crown, 1994.

Stamborski. Jim. *Don't Get Me Wrong: Mike Ditka's Insights, Outbursts, Kudos, and Comebacks*. Chicago: Chicago Review Press, 1988.

Staubach, Roger, with Frank Luksa. *Time Enough to Win*. Waco, Tex.: Word Incorporated, 1980.

Stowers, Carlton. *Journey to Triumph*. Dallas: Taylor Publishing, 1982.

Switzer, Barry, with Bud Shrake. *Bootlegger's Boy*. New York: William Morrow, 1990.

Thomas, Duane, and Paul Zimmerman. *Duane Thomas and the Fall of America's Team*. New York: Warner Books, 1988.

Toomay, Pat. *The Crunch*. New York: W. W. Norton, 1975.

Vass, George. *George Halas and the Chicago Bears*. Chicago: Regnery, 1971.

Whittingham, Richard. *Bears: In Their Own Words: Chicago Bear Greats Talk About the Team, the Game, the Coaches, and the Times of Their Lives*. Chicago: Contemporary Books, 1992.

Whittingham, Richard. *The Chicago Bears: An Illustrated History*. Chicago: Rand McNally, 1979.

Whittingham, Richard. *The Chicago Bears: From George Halas to Super Bowl XX, an Illustrated History*. New York: Simon and Schuster, 1986.

Wiley, Ralph. *Why Black People Tend to Shout*. New York: Birch Lane Press, 1991.

Wismer, Harry. *The Public Calls It Sport*. New York: Prentice Hall, 1965.

Wolfe, Jane. *The Murchisons: The Rise and Fall of a Texas Dynasty*. New York: St. Martin's Press, 1989.

About Rich...

Rich Wolfe was raised near Lost Nation, Iowa, played basketball and baseball at Notre Dame, and has lived in Scottsdale, Arizona, since 1975. He is a sports marketing consultant, has owned a minor league basketball team, and currently owns a Central Hockey League franchise. His previous books are *Sports Fans Who Made Headlines* and *I Remember Harry Caray.*

Publisher's Note

An editor's nightmare . . . One day out of nowhere, a jumbled pile of fifty incomplete transcriptions with no corresponding photographs gets dumped on your desk along with marching orders to turn them into a coherent, complete book in less than three weeks. You have a crazed author and a demanding, knows-enough-to-be-dangerous publisher to contend with, as well as a few other projects on your plate.

What do you do? What would Mike Ditka do?

You grit your teeth, clench your fists—and make it happen. And that's just what the editorial department at Triumph Books did.

And then there's Rich Wolfe, a one-man wrecking crew, who came up with the concept and burned up the phone lines to get the raw material for this book. Rich exploded onto the scene at our offices eight weeks prior to his demanded project completion date with guns blazing, holding an oversized plastic garbage bag filled with soggy papers, transcription tapes, and his signature case of Diet Coke™. Go get 'em, Rich!

Also, to the publisher of Mike Ditka's autobiography, Aaron Cohodes: it was a heck of a ride—a blessing and a curse rolled into one (though still trying to get a handle on the blessing part).

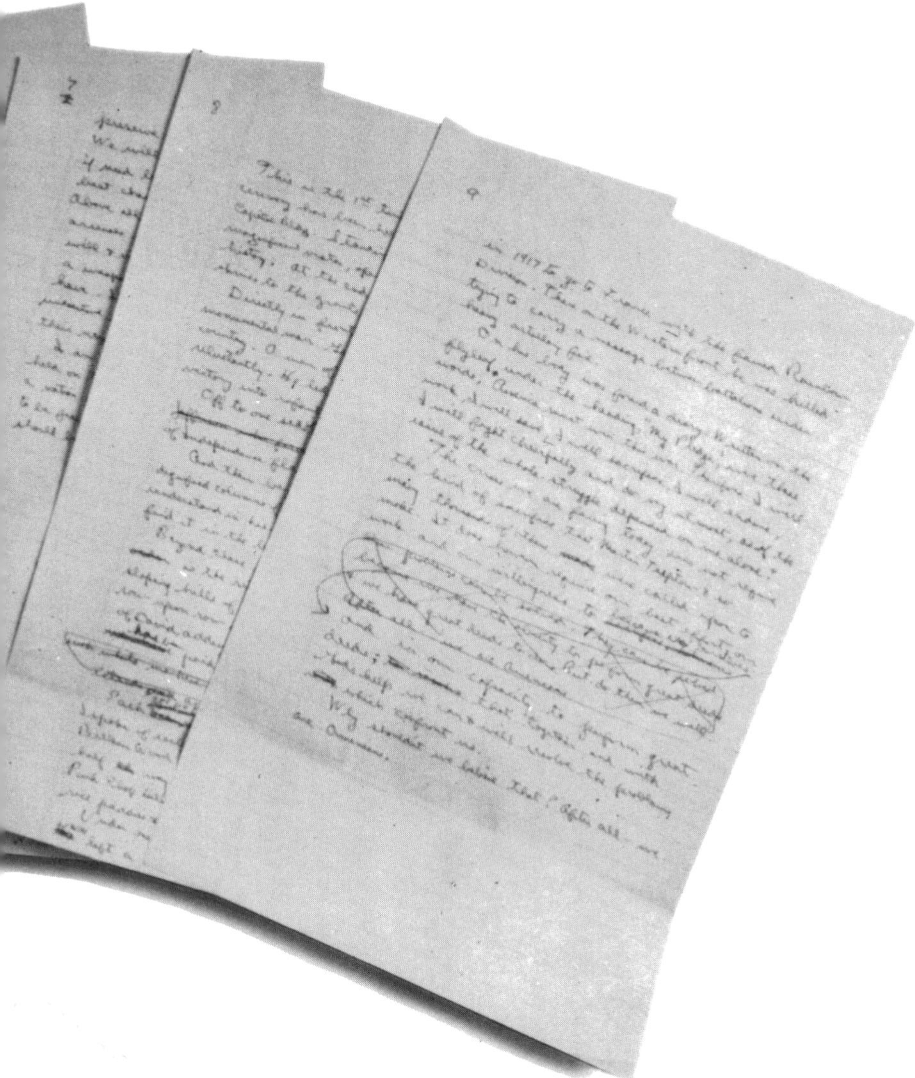

SPEAKING MY MIND

— BY —

Ronald Reagan

SELECTED SPEECHES

SIMON AND SCHUSTER
NEW YORK · LONDON · TORONTO · SYDNEY · TOKYO

SIMON AND SCHUSTER
SIMON & SCHUSTER BUILDING
ROCKEFELLER CENTER
1230 AVENUE OF THE AMERICAS
NEW YORK, NEW YORK 10020

SIMON AND SCHUSTER AND COLOPHON ARE REGISTERED TRADEMARKS OF
SIMON & SCHUSTER, INC.
DESIGNED BY EVE METZ
MANUFACTURED IN THE UNITED STATES OF AMERICA

1   3   5   7   9   10   8   6   4   2

LIBRARY OF CONGRESS CATALOGING IN PUBLICATION DATA
REAGAN, RONALD.
SPEAKING MY MIND: SELECTED SPEECHES/RONALD REAGAN.
P.   CM.
INCLUDES INDEX.
1. UNITED STATES—POLITICS AND GOVERNMENT—1981–1989.
2. CALIFORNIA—POLITICS AND GOVERNMENT—1951–   I. TITLE.
E838.5.R435   1989   89-35533
973.927′092—DC20   CIP
ISBN 0-671-68857-X

ISBN 0-671-69146-5   II

ISBN 0-671-69187-2   I

To the American people

ACKNOWLEDGMENTS

There are so many people who have helped to make this book possible. First and foremost, there is Landon Parvin, whose contribution has been immeasurable. I shall be indebted to him forever.

And I'd also like to thank Kathy Osborne, who is as kind and competent an assistant as anyone could wish, and Misty Church, one of my loyal researchers at the White House, who looked over the manuscript to be sure everything was in order. The people at Simon and Schuster have been a terrific group—Michael Korda, Lydia Buechler, Eve Metz. You would be surprised by all the people it takes to put out a book. And, of course, the highly respected literary agent Mort Janklow brought it all together.

I'd also like to thank all those who had anything to do with my speeches over the years—from the individuals who sent me the moving letters that I loved to put in my speeches to my staff who assisted me in getting the ideas together in the first place. One of the people I was most impressed with at the White House was Nancy Roberts, who worked under great pressure typing my speeches, sometimes still typing last-minute changes as I was heading for the helicopter to take off for the event.

And, most of all, I'd like to express my gratitude to the American people, who listened to what I had to say and responded with support and even affection.

I thank you all.

Contents

CONTENTS

1984

1985

1986

CONTENTS

1987

1988

CONTENTS

1989

Foreword

I can't help but imagine someone a couple hundred years from now stumbling upon this very book in a forgotten trunk somewhere. By then, these pages will be dry and crumbly—not to mention me, who will be long gone and buried. But I'd like to think that if a future reader sits down to browse through this selection of speeches, he would come to know me both as a president and as a person. I hope that the reader would also come to learn something about the America that I knew and loved.

This is not a book about policies. I've not felt compelled to include a speech on education, another on agriculture, another on social security, and so forth. I've not included a single one of my State of the Union addresses. My purpose has not been to give a definitive history of the Reagan years.

No, what I've done is this. I've selected a group of speeches that will give anyone who's interested some insights into who I am, where I came from, what I believe, and what I tried to do as a result. I hope this collection also tells a certain story; it does in my mind. I'll leave it up to the reader to interpret that story for himself or herself.

The speeches selected from my White House years are verbatim transcripts with no deletions for misstatements I may have made or for hopes I voiced that never came true. I didn't want to edit the texts because I didn't want to edit history. I'll just take my chances.

Speechmaking has played a major role in my life. Some of my critics over the years have said that I became president because I was an actor who knew how to give a good speech. I suppose that's not too far wrong. Because an actor knows two important things—to be honest in what he's doing and to be in touch with the audience. That's not bad advice for a politician either. My actor's instinct simply told me to speak the truth as I saw it and felt it.

I don't believe my speeches took me as far as they did merely because of my rhetoric or delivery, but because there were certain basic truths in them that the average American citizen recognized. When I first began speaking of political things, I could feel that people were as frustrated about the government as I was. What I said simply made sense to the guy on the street, and it's the guy on the street who elects presidents of the United States.

And that's exactly what happened to me.

The
California
Years

Remarks at the
Kiwanis International Convention

ST. LOUIS, MISSOURI
JUNE 21, 1951

Let me begin by telling you how an actor like myself started giving speeches in the first place. If you didn't sing or dance in the Hollywood of my day, you wound up as an after-dinner speaker. Personal appearances were part of a performer's life. People wanted to see and hear the actors and actresses of the screen in the flesh.

As a board member and later president of the Screen Actors Guild, I found myself out on the "mashed potato" circuit fairly regularly. I made Hollywood the subject of my speeches, trying to correct some of the misimpressions about the gaudy, bawdy Hollywood lifestyle created by gossip columnists and fan magazines among others.

Looking back, I realize that even then I was discussing political issues. I remember speaking about a plan that was introduced in the United States Senate to license actors. Congress would do the licensing and only performers who met certain moral standards would be allowed to act in movies. The outrage of this kind of government intrusion became part of my speeches. I pointed out there were two United States senators in prison at the time and no actors. That always got a laugh.

I would also point out ways in which my colleagues in Hollywood were discriminated against by government in terms of taxes and so forth. This was how I learned government had an adversarial relationship with its own business community. Increasingly after my speeches, I would find individuals waiting to tell me what they were putting up with in their own professions or industries. Gradually the Hollywood part of my speech grew shorter and shorter until eventually it was barely an introduction to a speech in which I exposed government's growing unfairness to the citizenry and called for action to make government once again the servant of "we the people."

Ten years after the bare-boned little speech you're about to read, I was speaking fifty solid minutes on the abuses of government. People often found it odd that an actor would be concerned with such things. I guess they forgot I was also a citizen.

But, I'm getting ahead of myself. Let me first give you my basic Hollywood speech. The one you're about to read was to the Kiwanis International Convention in St. Louis in 1951. Of course, I would ad-lib the latest anecdote I'd heard and personalize the remarks for the audience, but it's from this plain little acorn of a speech that my political speechmaking grew.

I WOULD LIKE TO TALK to you as a travel narrator would talk about a very strange and foreign land. But it is a foreign land which has more actual press coverage than any other locality in the world except the capital in Washington, D.C. Some 450 correspondents cover the daily activities of the motion picture industry in Hollywood, California. Yet this remains the least-discovered place on earth.

Probably more misconceptions and misinformation exist about the people I work with, the people in my industry and my town, than any other spot on earth. Part of this is due to the fact that among these 450 newspaper people that are there doing an honest job of gathering and reporting news we have attracted many camp followers. These are people who do not have the journalistic integrity to go through the task of gathering and reporting news honestly. With only a few hundred newsworthy names to deal with every day and a column to fill, they have chosen the easy path of gossip. They have the mistaken idea that the American people want to hear the worst instead of the best. And when they are hardpressed to fill their columns, they invent what does not happen.

The result is that among you and your communities and out through America there exists an idea that the people of motion pictures are crazy, extravagant, immoral, fickle, and are flitting from one husband or wife to the other, with no regard for each other. There exists also the idea that if we are interested in politics at all, it is because we are Communists.

The statements I have just made are not out of my own mind but are the result of a survey to find out what you people do think about those of us in Hollywood. Consequently, you will be a little surprised to learn that the people of motion pictures are not the troubadours, the strolling players who used to come into your town and live out of a trunk for a week and then pass on. Being a part of the community now, and because the mechanical nature of motion pictures is so difficult, they have to go to work in the morning like everyone else, and they come home in the evening like everyone else. They have lawns to mow and they own their own homes. Seventy percent of them are high-school graduates or better, as against the national average of 28 percent. Seventy-nine percent of the people in my industry are married; 70 percent to their first husband or wife; 70 percent of them have children; 61 percent of them are regular members and attendants at the churches of Hollywood.

They constitute 1 percent of the population of Los Angeles. They contribute annually 12 percent of all the money in Los Angeles that is contributed to charity. Twenty-five percent of the personnel in the motion picture business were in the armed forces in the last war.

We are pretty proud of the fact that our government says that in the ideological struggle that is going on on the screens of the world, it is the American motion picture, not with its message picture, just showing our store windows in the street scenes with the things that Americans can buy, our parking lots, our streets with the automobiles, our shots of American working men driving those automobiles, that is holding back the flood of propaganda from the other side of the Iron Curtain. Last, but not least, we are most proud of the great tribute that was paid to us by the Kremlin in Moscow, when recently it said, "The worst enemy of the people, the worst tool of degenerate capitalism that must be destroyed is the motion picture screen of Hollywood, California." We are very proud of that tribute.

Well, these are just a few of the things about our community that make us rather proud. Some of the things we feel a little badly about. We feel badly that the divorce rate in Hollywood is 29.9 percent. We feel worse that the national average is 40 percent. We wish that the rest of the country could catch up with us.

Because the public has a misconception about us and because there is so much apathy about us, certain enemies of ours—enemies of democracy and our way of life—think they have found a leak in the dike. They have found a way to attack some of our American institutions and our American principles by way of the motion picture industry. What we must all learn is that you can't lose a freedom anyplace without losing freedom everyplace.

If you are going to let one segment of society or one area of the country become maligned without insisting that the truth be known, all other segments and areas are subject to similar fates.

You know that the Communists have tried to invade our industry and that we have fought them to the point where we now have them licked. But there are other more insidious and less obvious inroads being made at our democratic institutions by way of the motion picture industry. For example, no industry has been picked for such discriminatory taxes as have the individuals in the industry of motion pictures, and you don't realize that because the average citizen is too prone to say, "They are all overpaid in Hollywood, so let it go at that," but if they can get away with it there, it is aimed at your pocketbook and you are next.

Another one of the insidious infiltrations and the worst on our American freedom is by way of censorship. There isn't an American who wouldn't stand up and strike back at the imposition of controls on our freedom of press and freedom of speech, and yet here, for the last fifteen years, we have been permitting it in spite of a self-imposed production code by the motion picture industry. We have political censorship in eight states and over two hundred cities in the United States.

Do you realize that we are raising an entire generation of Americans in this way to assume that it is all right for someone to tell them what they can see and hear from a motion picture screen? Isn't it a rather short step from there when they have grown up to tell those same people, "Well, we might go just a little further. It is all right for us to tell you what you can read." And from there you don't have very far to go to telling them what they can say and then what they can think.

I wanted to correct the misconceptions about Hollywood so you could take a word or two of it back to your communities because this is your struggle, not alone ours. The reason I want to say all of this to you and ask you to take it back to your communities is because we feel that we are operating in the best manner of free enterprise, because never once has our industry asked for government aid nor any subsidy of any kind. We still stand today as one of the greatest fields of opportunity. We are in the American way. You can come into our field and the heights are unlimited, based only upon your ability and your talent.

We feel that you people should join us now in the struggle to preserve some of these freedoms, some of these American principles that are being nibbled away through our industry. In short, we would like to invite you to be on our side because we feel that we have been on your side for a very long time.

Televised Nationwide Address
on Behalf of
Senator Barry Goldwater

OCTOBER 27, 1964

What happened after a while was that my speeches were no
longer personal-appearance gimmicks. I genuinely had a cause
—exposing big government and its intrusive, domineering
ways. During this period, I was host for a television show called
GE Theater. As part of my arrangement, the company would

make me available to local Rotary Clubs, Chambers of Commerce, and other organizations in those towns where GE had plants and offices.

My speeches began getting nationwide attention as these organizations would reprint and distribute my remarks. During this time I was told that I was the most popular speaker in the country after President Kennedy. And after a while I noticed something very interesting. I would go into a city and find out at the other end of town, there'd be a member of the Kennedy cabinet. After a while I realized it was deliberate. I guess I was getting too much attention to suit them.

You should know that I had been a lifelong Democrat until the 1960s. My first vote was cast for Franklin Delano Roosevelt. He campaigned on a platform of reducing federal spending, eliminating useless federal boards and commissions, and returning authority to the states, the communities, and the people, which, he said, had been unjustly seized by the federal government.

The theme of my speeches had been along these lines. But one day I came home from a speaking trip and said to Nancy that it had just dawned on me that I'd been making these speeches on what I thought was wrong with government and then every four years I'd campaign for the people who were doing these things.

So finally I changed parties, and in 1964 I became cochairman of Californians for Barry Goldwater. I went up and down the state with a campaign speech I'd written that wasn't too different in tone and message from my GE presentations. The speech seemed to go over very well.

One night a few weeks before the election I addressed a fundraiser at the Coconut Grove in Los Angeles. When the evening was over, a delegation of high-powered Republicans waited for me. They asked whether I would deliver that same speech on nationwide TV if they raised the money to buy the time. I said yes and suggested that, instead of just having me in a studio alone, they bring in an audience to get a little better feel. They readily agreed.

A few days before the speech, Senator Goldwater himself called me and mentioned canceling the address. His people told him that I talked about social security, and he'd been getting kicked all over the place on the issue. I explained to him that I'd been making the speech all over the state and nobody had ever said anything.

His people apparently wanted to repeat some show of former president Eisenhower and him strolling around fields at Ike's farm outside Gettysburg. I said, "Barry, I can't just turn the time over to you, because it's not mine to give. A private group bought this time."

Well, he said, "I haven't seen the speech or heard it, let me call you back." So he got a copy of the sound track and listened to it. I'm told that when he heard it, he said, "Well, what the hell's wrong with that?"

I was getting a little scared, though, thinking that this was pretty big-league stuff for me to be going nationwide for a candidate for president. I started having second thoughts and thinking, "Holy Toledo, here's a man running for president and his people think something else could be better. Maybe they're right."

The night that the tape of the speech was to air on NBC, Nancy and I went over to another couple's home to watch it. Everyone thought I'd done well, but still you don't always know about these things. The phone rang about midnight. It was a call from Washington, D.C., where it was three A.M. One of Barry's staff called to tell me that the switchboard was still lit up from the calls pledging money to his campaign. I then slept peacefully. The speech raised $8 million and soon changed my entire life.

Here's that speech. Although I didn't put a title on it, it later became known as "A Time for Choosing."

Announcer. The following prerecorded political program is sponsored by TV for Goldwater-Miller on behalf of Barry

Goldwater, Republican candidate for president of the United States. Ladies and gentlemen, we take pride in presenting a thoughtful address by Ronald Reagan. Mr. Reagan . . .

Ronald Reagan. Thank you very much. Thank you, and good evening. The sponsor has been identified, but unlike most television programs, the performer hasn't been provided with a script. As a matter of fact, I have been permitted to choose my own words and discuss my own ideas regarding the choice that we face in the next few weeks.

I have spent most of my life as a Democrat. I recently have seen fit to follow another course. I believe that the issues confronting us cross party lines. Now, one side in this campaign has been telling us that the issues of this election are the maintenance of peace and prosperity. The line has been used "We've never had it so good!"

But I have an uncomfortable feeling that this prosperity isn't something upon which we can base our hopes for the future. No nation in history has ever survived a tax burden that reached a third of its national income. Today thirty-seven cents out of every dollar earned in this country is the tax collector's share, and yet our government continues to spend 17 million dollars a day more than the government takes in. We haven't balanced our budget twenty-eight out of the last thirty-four years. We have raised our debt limit three times in the last twelve months, and now our national debt is one and a half times bigger than all the combined debts of all the nations of the world. We have 15 billion dollars in gold in our treasury— we don't own an ounce. Foreign dollar claims are 27.3 billion dollars, and we have just had announced that the dollar of 1939 will now purchase forty-five cents in its total value.

As for the peace that we would preserve, I wonder who among us would like to approach the wife or mother whose husband or son has died in Vietnam and ask them if they think this is a peace that should be maintained indefinitely. Do they mean peace, or do they mean we just want to be left in peace? There can be no real peace while one American is dying someplace in the world for the rest of us. We are at war with the most dangerous enemy that has ever faced mankind in his long climb from the swamp to the stars, and it has been said if we lose that war, and in so doing lose this way of freedom of ours, history will record with the greatest astonishment that those who had the most to lose did the least to prevent its happening. Well, I think it's time we ask ourselves if we still know the freedoms that were intended for us by the Founding Fathers.

Not too long ago two friends of mine were talking to a Cuban refugee, a businessman who had escaped from Castro, and in the midst of his story one of my friends turned to the other and said, "We don't know how lucky we are." And the Cuban stopped and said, "How lucky you are! I had someplace to escape to." In that sentence he told us the entire story. If we lose freedom here, there is no place to escape to. This is the last stand on earth.

And this idea that government is beholden to the people, that it has no other source of power except the sovereign people, is still the newest and most unique idea in all the long history of man's relation to man. This is the issue of this election. Whether we believe in our capacity for self-government or whether we abandon the American Revolution and confess that a little intellectual elite in a far-distant capital can plan our lives for us better than we can plan them ourselves.

You and I are told increasingly that we have to choose between a left or right, but I would like to suggest that there is no such thing as a left or right. There is only an up or down—up to man's age-old dream—the ultimate in individual freedom consistent with law and order—or down to the ant heap of totalitarianism, and regardless of their sincerity, their humanitarian motives, those who would trade our freedom for security have embarked on this downward course.

In this vote-harvesting time they use terms like the "Great Society," or as we were told a few days ago by the President, we must accept a "greater government activity in the affairs of the people." But they have been a little more explicit in the past and among themselves—and all of the things that I now will

26

quote have appeared in print. These are not Republican accusations. For example, they have voices that say "the cold war will end through our acceptance of a not undemocratic socialism." Another voice says that the profit motive has become outmoded, it must be replaced by the incentives of the welfare state; or our traditional system of individual freedom is incapable of solving the complex problems of the twentieth century.

Senator Fulbright has said at Stanford University that the Constitution is outmoded. He referred to the president as our moral teacher and our leader, and he said he is hobbled in his task by the restrictions in power imposed on him by this antiquated document. He must be freed so that he can do for us what he knows is best.

And Senator Clark of Pennsylvania, another articulate spokesman, defines liberalism as "meeting the material needs of the masses through the full power of centralized government." Well, I for one resent it when a representative of the people refers to you and me—the free men and women of this country—as "the masses." This is a term we haven't applied to ourselves in America. But beyond that, "the full power of centralized government"—this was the very thing the Founding Fathers sought to minimize. They knew that governments don't control *things*. A government can't control the economy without controlling people. And they knew when a government sets out to do that, it must use force and coercion to achieve its purpose. They also knew, those Founding Fathers, that outside of its legitimate functions, government does nothing as well or as economically as the private sector of the economy.

Now, we have no better example of this than the government's involvement in the farm economy over the last thirty years. Since 1955 the cost of this program has nearly doubled. One-fourth of farming in America is responsible for 85 percent of the farm surplus. Three-fourths of farming is out on the free market and has known a 21 percent increase in the per capita consumption of all its produce. You see, that one-fourth of farming is regulated and controlled by the federal government. In the last three years we have spent forty-three dollars in the feed grain program for every dollar bushel of corn we don't grow.

Senator Humphrey last week charged that Barry Goldwater as president would seek to eliminate farmers. He should do his homework a little better, because he will find out that we have had a decline of 5 million in the farm population under these government programs. He will also find that the Democratic administration has sought to get from Congress an extension of the farm program to include that three-fourths that is now free. He will find that they have also asked for the right to imprison farmers who wouldn't keep books as prescribed by the federal government. The secretary of agriculture asked for the right to seize farms through condemnation and resell them to other individuals. And contained in that same program was a provision that would have allowed the federal government to remove 2 million farmers from the soil.

At the same time there has been an increase in the Department of Agriculture employees. There is now one for every thirty farms in the United States, and still they can't tell us how sixty-six shiploads of grain headed for Austria disappeared without a trace, and Billie Sol Estes never left shore!

Every responsible farmer and farm organization has repeatedly asked the government to free the farm economy, but who are farmers to know what is best for them? The wheat farmers voted against a wheat program. The government passed it anyway. Now the price of bread goes up; the price of wheat to the farmers goes down.

Meanwhile, back in the city, under urban renewal the assault on freedom carries on. Private property rights are so diluted that public interest is almost anything that a few government planners decide it should be. In a program that takes from the needy and gives to the greedy, we see such spectacles as in Cleveland, Ohio, a million-and-a-half-dollar building completed only three years ago must be destroyed to make way for what government officials call a "more compatible use of the land." The President tells us he is now going to start building public housing units in the thousands where heretofore we have only built them in the hundreds. But FHA and the Veterans Administration tell us that they have 120,000 housing units they've taken back through mortgage foreclosures.

For three decades we have sought to solve the problems of unemployment through government planning, and the more the plans fail, the more the planners plan. The latest is the Area Redevelopment Agency. They have just declared Rice County, Kansas, a depressed area. Rice County, Kansas, has two hundred oil wells, and the 14,000 people there have over thirty million dollars on deposit in personal savings in their banks. When the government tells you you are depressed, lie down and be depressed!

We have so many people who can't see a fat man standing beside a thin one without coming to the conclusion that the fat man got that way by taking advantage of the thin one! So they are going to solve all the problems of human misery through government and government planning. Well, now if government planning and welfare had the answer, and they've had almost thirty years of it, shouldn't we expect government to read the score to us once in a while? Shouldn't they be telling us about the decline each year in the number of people needing help? . . . the reduction in the need for public housing?

But the reverse is true. Each year the need grows greater, the program grows greater. We were told four years ago that seventeen million people went to bed hungry each night. Well, that was probably true. They were all on a diet! But now we are told that 9.3 million families in this country are poverty-stricken on the basis of earning less than $3,000 a year. Welfare spending is ten times greater than in the dark depths of the Depression. We are spending 45 billion dollars on welfare. Now do a little arithmetic, and you will find that if we divided the 45 billion dollars up equally among those 9 million poor families, we would be able to give each family $4,600 a year, and this added to their present income should eliminate poverty! Direct aid to the poor, however, is running only about $600 per family. It seems that someplace there must be some overhead.

So now we declare "war on poverty," or "you, too, can be a Bobby Baker!" How do they honestly expect us to believe that if we add 1 billion dollars to the 45 billion we are spending . . . one more program to the thirty-odd we have—and remember, this new program doesn't replace any, it just duplicates existing programs . . . do they believe that poverty is suddenly going to disappear by magic? Well, in all fairness I should explain that there is one part of the new program that isn't duplicated. This is the youth feature. We are now going to solve the dropout problem, juvenile delinquency, by reinstituting something like the old CCC camps, and we are going to put our young people in camps, but again we do some arithmetic, and we find that we are going to spend each year just on room and board for each young person that we help $4,700 a year! We can send them to Harvard for $2,700! Don't get me wrong. I'm not suggesting that Harvard is the answer to juvenile delinquency!

But seriously, what are we doing to those we seek to help? Not too long ago, a judge called me here in Los Angeles. He told me of a young woman who had come before him for a divorce. She had six children, was pregnant with her seventh. Under his questioning, she revealed her husband was a laborer earning $250 a month. She wanted a divorce so that she could get an $80 raise. She is eligible for $330 a month in the Aid to Dependent Children Program. She got the idea from two women in her neighborhood who had already done that very thing.

Yet anytime you and I question the schemes of the do-gooders, we are denounced as being against their humanitarian goals. They say we are always "against" things, never "for" anything. Well, the trouble with our liberal friends is not that they are ignorant, but that they know so much that isn't so! We are for a provision that destitution should not follow unemployment by reason of old age, and to that end we have accepted social security as a step toward meeting the problem.

But we are against those entrusted with this program when they practice deception regarding its fiscal shortcomings, when they charge that any criticism of the program means that we want to end payments to those people who depend on them for a livelihood. They have called it insurance to us in a hundred million pieces of literature. But then they appeared before the Supreme Court and they testified that it was a welfare program. They only use the term "insurance" to sell it to the people. And they said social security dues are a tax for the general use of the government, and the government has used that tax. There is no fund, because Robert Byers, the actuarial head, appeared before a congressional committee and admitted that social security as of this moment is $298 billion in the hole! But he said there should be no cause for worry because as long as they have the power to tax, they could always take away from the people whatever they needed to bail them out of trouble! And they are doing just that.

A young man, twenty-one years of age, working at an average salary . . . his social security contribution would, in the open market, buy him an insurance policy that would guarantee $220 a month at age sixty-five. The government promises 127! He could live it up until he is thirty-one and then take out a policy that would pay more than social security. Now, are we so lacking in business sense that we can't put this program on a sound basis so that people who do require those payments will find that they can get them when they are due . . . that the cupboard isn't bare? Barry Goldwater thinks we can.

At the same time, can't we introduce voluntary features that would permit a citizen to do better on his own, to be excused upon presentation of evidence that he had made provisions for the nonearning years? Should we not allow a widow with children to work, and not lose the benefits supposedly paid for by her deceased husband? Shouldn't you and I be allowed to declare who our beneficiaries will be under these programs, which we cannot do? I think we are for telling our senior citizens that no one in this country should be denied medical care because of a lack of funds. But I think we are against forcing all citizens, regardless of need, into a compulsory government program, especially when we have such examples, as announced last week, when France admitted that their medicare program was now bankrupt. They've come to the end of the road.

In addition, was Barry Goldwater so irresponsible when he suggested that our government give up its program of deliberate planned inflation so that when you do get your social security pension, a dollar will buy a dollar's worth, and not forty-five cents' worth?

I think we are for the international organization, where the nations of the world can seek peace. But I think we are against subordinating American interests to an organization that has become so structurally unsound that today you can muster a two-thirds vote on the floor of the General Assembly among nations that represent less than 10 percent of the world's population. I think we are against the hypocrisy of assailing our allies because here and there they cling to a colony, while we engage in a conspiracy of silence and never open our mouths about the millions of people enslaved in Soviet colonies in the satellite nations.

I think we are for aiding our allies by sharing of our material blessings with those nations which share in our fundamental beliefs, but we are against doling out money government to government, creating bureaucracy, if not socialism, all over the world. We set out to help 19 countries. We are helping 107. We spent $146 billion. With that money, we bought a 2-million-dollar yacht for Haile Selassie. We bought dress suits for Greek undertakers, extra wives for Kenya government officials. We bought a thousand TV sets for a place where they have no electricity. In the last six years, fifty-two nations have bought $7 billion of our gold, and all fifty-two are receiving foreign aid from us. No government ever voluntarily reduces itself in size. Government programs, once launched, never disappear. Actually, a government bureau is the nearest thing to eternal life we'll ever see on this earth!

Federal employees number 2.5 million, and federal, state, and local, one out of six of the nation's work force is employed by government. These proliferating bureaus with their thousands of regulations have cost us many of our constitutional safeguards. How many of us realize that today federal agents can invade a man's property without a warrant? They can impose a fine without a formal hearing, let alone a trial by jury, and they can seize and sell his property in auction to enforce the payment of that fine. In Chicot County, Arkansas, James Wier overplanted his rice allotment. The government obtained a $17,000 judgment, and a U.S. marshal sold his 950-acre farm at auction. The government said it was necessary as a warning to others to make the system work! Last February 19th, at the University of Minnesota, Norman Thomas, six times candidate for president on the Socialist Party ticket, said, "If Barry Goldwater became president, he would stop the advance of socialism in the United States." I think that's exactly what he will do!

As a former Democrat, I can tell you Norman Thomas isn't the only man who has drawn this parallel to socialism with the present administration. Back in 1936, Mr. Democrat himself, Al Smith, the great American, came before the American people and charged that the leadership of his party was taking the party of Jefferson, Jackson, and Cleveland down the road under the banners of Marx, Lenin, and Stalin. And he walked away from his party, and he never returned to the day he died, because to this day, the leadership of that party has been taking that party, that honorable party, down the road in the image of the labor socialist party of England. Now it doesn't require expropriation or confiscation of private property or business to impose socialism upon a people. What does it mean whether you hold the deed or the title to your business or property if the government holds the power of life and death over that business or property? Such machinery already exists. The government can find some charge to bring against any concern it chooses to prosecute. Every businessman has his own tale of harassment. Somewhere a perversion has taken place. Our natural, inalienable rights are now considered to be a dispensation from government, and freedom has never been so fragile, so close to slipping from our grasp as it is at this moment. Our Democratic opponents seem unwilling to debate these issues. They want to make you and I think that this is a contest between two men

. . . that we are to choose just between two personalities. Well, what of this man they would destroy . . . and in destroying, they would destroy that which he represents, the ideas that you and I hold dear.

Is he the brash and shallow and trigger-happy man they say he is? Well, I have been privileged to know him "when." I knew him long before he ever dreamed of trying for high office, and I can tell you personally I have never known a man in my life I believe so incapable of doing a dishonest or dishonorable thing.

This is a man who in his own business, before he entered politics, instituted a profit-sharing plan, before unions had ever thought of it. He put in health and medical insurance for all his employees. He took 50 percent of the profits before taxes and set up a retirement plan, and a pension plan for all his employees. He sent monthly checks for life to an employee who was ill and couldn't work. He provided nursing care for the children of mothers who work in the stores. When Mexico was ravaged by the floods from the Rio Grande, he climbed in his airplane and flew medicine and supplies down there.

An ex-GI told me how he met him. It was the week before Christmas during the Korean War, and he was at the Los Angeles airport trying to get a ride home to Arizona, and he said that there were a lot of servicemen there and no seats available on the planes. Then a voice came over the loudspeaker and said, "Any men in uniform wanting a ride to Arizona, go to runway such-and-such," and they went down there, and there was a fellow named Barry Goldwater sitting in his plane. Every day in the weeks before Christmas, all day long, he would load up the plane, fly to Arizona, fly them to their homes, then fly back over to get another load.

During the hectic split-second timing of a campaign, this is a man who took time out to sit beside an old friend who was dying of cancer. His campaign managers were understandably impatient, but he said, "There aren't many left who care what happens to her. I'd like her to know that I care." This is a man who said to his nineteen-year-old son, "There is no foundation like the rock of honesty and fairness, and when you begin to

34

build your life upon that rock, with the cement of the faith in God that you have, then you have a real start!" This is not a man who could carelessly send other people's sons to war. And that is the issue of this campaign that makes all of the other problems I have discussed academic, unless we realize that we are in a war that must be won.

Those who would trade our freedom for the soup kitchen of the welfare state have told us that they have a utopian solution of peace without victory. They call their policy "accommodation." And they say if we only avoid any direct confrontation with the enemy, he will forget his evil ways and learn to love us. All who oppose them are indicted as warmongers. They say we offer simple answers to complex problems. Well, perhaps there is a simple answer . . . not an easy one . . . but a simple one, if you and I have the courage to tell our elected officials that we want our *national* policy based upon what we know in our hearts is morally right.

We cannot buy our security, our freedom from the threat of the bomb by committing an immorality so great as saying to a billion human beings now in slavery behind the Iron Curtain, "Give up your dreams of freedom because to save our own skin, we are willing to make a deal with your slave-masters." Alexander Hamilton said, "A nation which can prefer disgrace to danger is prepared for a master, and deserves one!" Let's set the record straight. There is no argument over the choice between peace and war, but there is only one guaranteed way you can have peace . . . and you can have it in the next second . . . surrender!

Admittedly there is a risk in any course we follow other than this, but every lesson in history tells us that the greater risk lies in appeasement, and this is the specter our well-meaning liberal friends refuse to face . . . that their policy of accommodation is appeasement, and it gives no choice between peace and war, only between fight or surrender. If we continue to accommodate, continue to back and retreat, eventually we have to face the final demand—the ultimatum. And what then? When Nikita Khrushchev has told his people he knows what our answer will be? He has told them that we are retreating under the pressure of the cold war, and someday when the time comes to deliver the ultimatum, our surrender will be voluntary because by that time we will have been weakened from within spiritually, morally, and economically. He believes this because from our side he has heard voices pleading for "peace at any price" or "better Red than dead," or as one commentator put it, he would rather "live on his knees than die on his feet." And therein lies the road to war, because those voices don't speak for the rest of us. You and I know and do not believe that life is so dear and peace so sweet as to be purchased at the price of chains and slavery. If nothing in life is worth dying for, when did this begin—just in the face of this enemy?—or should Moses have told the children of Israel to live in slavery under the pharaohs? Should Christ have refused the cross? Should the patriots at Concord Bridge have thrown down their guns and refused to fire the shot heard round the world? The martyrs of history were not fools, and our honored dead who gave their lives to stop the advance of the Nazis didn't die in vain! Where, then, is the road to peace? Well, it's a simple answer after all.

You and I have the courage to say to our enemies, "There is a price we will not pay." There is a point beyond which they must not advance! This is the meaning in the phrase of Barry Goldwater's "peace through strength!" Winston Churchill said that "the destiny of man is not measured by material computation. When great forces are on the move in the world, we learn we are spirits—not animals." And he said, "There is something going on in time and space, and beyond time and space, which, whether we like it or not, spells duty." You and I have a rendezvous with destiny. We will preserve for our children this, the last best hope of man on earth, or we will sentence them to take the last step into a thousand years of darkness.

We will keep in mind and remember that Barry Goldwater has faith in us. He has faith that you and I have the ability and the dignity and the right to make our own decisions and determine our own destiny.

Thank you.

Eisenhower College Fund-Raiser

WASHINGTON, D.C.
OCTOBER 14, 1969

Little did I know then how my life was going to change. Now, although I had always believed in people participating in elections—after all, I'd been elected president of my union—never for a minute did I want to change my line of work. I hadn't the slightest interest in public office. Indeed, in my mind, it was completely unexciting and unattractive compared to show business.

There was no evidence of any change for the next year after the Goldwater speech, but then one evening as the 1966 gubernatorial race in California began to appear on the horizon, I had callers.

Some of them were the same ones who had financed my speech for Goldwater. They waded right in. They told me the California Republican party was split right down the middle by the previous campaign, and I was the only one who could unite the party and defeat the incumbent governor. They never told me I'd make a good governor; they just told me I could win.

I said that I had no intention of seeking public office. I told them to pick a candidate and I'd work for him as I did for Goldwater, and that was final.

Well, they didn't take it as final. They kept coming back and with reinforcements. Finally, I told them if they would make it possible for me to go up and down the state accepting speaking engagements for six months, I'd come back and tell them if they were right or wrong about me being a candidate. I felt sure that the people would accept me as a campaigner for someone else, but not as a candidate myself. After all, I was "just an actor."

But again the people seemed to respond to the message that I was bringing them. They, too, had the idea I should be a candidate. Pretty soon Nancy and I were having trouble sleeping —what if those people were right?

So I gave in and said I'd be a candidate, although in my heart I really believed I'd be back in show business come election day. The people had a different idea. They elected me governor of California. I began applying the conservative principles I'd simply been talking about to running a state government. This isn't the place to run down how we did this. But one issue does stand out during my years in the statehouse in Sacramento— the turmoil on the campuses.

You know, the odd thing is that when I was campaigning for governor, I went on campuses quite a lot and was well received. I think it was because I was running against the establishment, which was represented by the then governor, Pat Brown. When I became governor, I then became the establishment, and there was a time I would've caused a riot by just stepping onto the campus at Berkeley for example.

Thinking back, I'm amazed how intimidated the educational system was by the student rebellion. Free speech was accorded only to the rowdies who had the bullhorn. I regret to say this attitude still is prevalent on many of our campuses. But to show you how tense the campuses were back in the sixties, while I was governor the chancellor at UCLA once canceled the playing of the national anthem at commencement exercises because it might be provocative. I know, I was there.

The following speech focused on the turmoil on our campuses. I'm quite proud I never lost faith in our young people even though I was burned in effigy so regularly I must have helped gasoline sales. In retrospect, it's clear that my faith in them was not misplaced. They became my strongest supporters as president. And my affection and respect for them grows daily.

Y OU HAVE DONE ME an honor for which I will ever be grateful in allowing me to be here and to share this occasion with you.

In this day when image-making occupies the time and energy of so many, I am quite cognizant of the effort to portray me as an anti-intellectual holding little regard for higher education. It is frustrating, to say the least.

We have been brought together here tonight remembering a man we held in high esteem and for whom we felt a great personal warmth and affection. At the ground-breaking for Eisenhower College, my good friend Bob Hope commented that the school is a monument, "a living monument to a monumental man." Bob said, "The general believed that education was something more than one of freedom's blessings, education was freedom—freedom of the mind to search for and find a better way of life for all mankind."

The general's great and good friend Winston Churchill said, "The destiny of man is not measured by material computation. When great forces are on the move in the world, we learn we are spirits—not animals. There is something going on in time and space, and beyond time and space, which, whether we like it or not, spells duty."

How appropriate to this man we could refer to as President, or as General, but who is enshrined in so many hearts as "Ike."

His was a lifetime devoted to duty. He said, in expressing his pride in the college which he wanted to be "of benefit to the young people of the nation" that "we must, all of us, have a sharper understanding of how we are to exercise the rights of citizenship—and to discharge its duties." He spent his life preserving the American tradition. He was trained in the science of war, but he called it "man's greatest stupidity," and his dream for all of us was a world at peace.

Still, he knew that his craft—his profession—was an absolute necessity in this world, for there is a price on peace and sometimes the price is more than free men can pay.

There is one with us here tonight who knows the weight of duty and knows, too, that the price of immediate peace could be a thousand years of darkness for generations yet unborn.

Parades are held in the name of peace, but some of those who march carry the flag of a nation that has killed almost 40,000 of our young men. We have a right to suspect that at least some of those who arrange the parades are less concerned with peace than with lending comfort and aid to the enemy.

Many of our universities, which should be committed to learning and free inquiry, will close down their classes in what is called a Vietnam Moratorium Day—which, probably, is correctly named, for there will be a moratorium on free discussion. A decision has been reached by the national Vietnam Day committee—but those responsible for the safety and security of this nation and its people, those with access to all the facts and information on the situation, will simply be told by the self-anointed.

And some young Americans living today will die tomorrow as the enemy frames his strategy to add fuel to the demonstrations in our streets.

I know it is something of a cliché to draw a parallel between the rise and fall of Rome and our own republic. Certainly, in academic circles, this is so, and yet the parallel is there in such detail as to be almost eerie.

Dr. Robert Strausz-Hupé recently published a series of articles based on the observations of historians such as Spengler, De Reincourt, Ferrero, and Gibbon. The history of the Roman Empire has been better recorded and documented than almost all of the great civilizations of the past.

We know it started with a kind of pioneer heritage not unlike our own. Then it entered into its two centuries of greatness, reaching its height in the second of those two centuries, going into its decline and collapse in the third. However, the signs of decay were becoming apparent in the latter years of that second century.

We are approaching the end of our second century. It has been pointed out that the days of democracy are numbered once the belly takes command of the head. When the less affluent feel the urge to break a commandment and begin to covet that which their more affluent neighbors possess, they are tempted to use their votes to obtain instant satisfaction. Then equal opportunity at the starting line becomes an extended guarantee of at least a tie at the finish of the race. Under the euphemism "the greatest good for the greatest number," we destroy a system which has accomplished just that and move toward the managed economy which strangles freedom and mortgages generations yet to come.

We've known rioting in our streets. The abuse of drugs and narcotics soars, particularly among our young people. We have campus demonstrations to force the college to divorce itself from participating in the defense of the nation. We no longer walk in the countryside or on our city streets after dark without fear. The jungle seems to be closing in on this little plot we've been trying to civilize for 6,000 years. Half of those who commit crime have not yet reached the age of eighteen, and half of all the crimes are committed in a desperate frenzy to finance addiction to narcotics.

All of us are disturbed at the virus that has infected the campus, and no doubt we could top each other with frightening and unbelievable stories. Hardly a day passes without the mail bringing new evidence of the campus revolt—a leaflet entitled "The Need to Fight the Cops," a pamphlet explaining how to make and throw firebombs.

One day I listened to a tape recording of a so-called student meeting where plans for campus disruption were being discussed. Explicit directions were given on how to start fires, and subsequently there were fifty fires started in the buildings of the campus in one day. Continuing to listen to the tape, we hear a voice say, "If in the process it becomes necessary to kill, you will kill."

One is gripped by an overwhelming sense of unreality—unreality that it's happening at all, but even more frightening at

41

how close we've come to accepting this as normal. Dr. Spock's babies have grown up—which is probably more than we can say for him. Certainly he served us better when his concern was pabulum and potty training.

Last year, on our California campuses, one million dollars' worth of damage was done by arson and vandalism and there were three murders. Two young people live with mangled hands and sightless eyes. One, a twenty-year-old girl, was picking up the mail delivery in a college administration office when the bomb went off. The other, a nineteen-year-old boy, in the dark hours of the morning was planting a bomb—a symbol of his rage and hatred.

How and when did all this begin? It began the first time someone old enough to know better declared it was no crime to break the law in the name of social protest. It started with those who proclaimed, in the name of academic freedom, that the campus was a sanctuary immune to the laws and rules that govern the rest of us. It began with those who, in the name of change and progress, decided they could scrap all the time-tested wisdom man has accumulated in his climb from the swamp to the stars. Simply call its constricting tradition and morality the dead hand of the past and wipe it out as a discipline no longer binding on us.

St. Thomas Aquinas warned teachers they must never dig a ditch in front of a student that they failed to fill in. To clearly raise doubts and to ever seek and never find is to be in opposition to education and progress. To discuss freely all sides of all questions without values is to ensure the creation of a generation of uninformed and talkative minds. Our obligation is to help our young people find truth and purpose, to find identity and goal.

I've talked of those already in rebellion—club and torch in hand. Admittedly only a few. But there is a ferment involving the great majority of our young men and women. They have complaints and their complaints are legitimate. They want to invest their energy and their idealism in causes they believe in. They refuse to become numbers in a computer in some kind of diploma factory where they lose their identity and are spewed from the assembly line in four years stamped "educated" . . . but no one really knows who they are or where they were during all those four years. These young people want a reordering of the priorities—let "publish or perish" and research come along behind teaching in the order of importance.

Is it possible that all of the ferment and rebellion is in reality a cry for help? All the more poignant because it has gone unheeded?

I stood one day in the giant field house of one of our Midwestern universities. There were about 4,000 townspeople and 10,000 students in the tiers of seats extending around the oval and all the way to the ceiling. The program called for a question-and-answer period, and one question from an adult had to do with the rebellion of youth against all the principles and standards we had known and tried to pass on to them.

I almost answered the question with a question because frankly I wasn't sure I had the answer. But then I suggested that perhaps young people aren't rebelling against our standards— they are rebelling because they don't think we *ourselves* are living by the standards we've tried to teach them. There was a second of silence and then the 10,000 young people came to their feet with a roar I'll never forget.

Have they lost faith in our standards or have they lost faith in us? Do they doubt our willingness to practice what we preach? Where were we when God was expelled from the classroom?

Last year the banks and financial institutions of this country lost $117 million—not to masked bandits, but to petty pilfering by employees. Retail establishments lose $4 billion a year to a kind of self-declared fringe benefit on the part of employees who take home samples.

What about us when that youngster comes home from the practice field telling how he learned to get away with holding illegally on a block? How many times have they seen us look over our shoulder and fudge on the stop sign if no policeman was in sight? As the country pastor said, "The fellow who left the gate open is only slightly more guilty than the one who saw it open and didn't close it."

Is is possible that much of what frightens and disturbs us actually started with us? With a gradual and silent erosion of our own moral code? Are *we* the lost generation?

No government at any level and for any price can afford the police necessary to assure our safety and our freedom unless the overwhelming majority of us are guided by an inner personal code of morality.

On the deck of the tiny *Arabella* off the coast of Massachusetts in 1630, John Winthrop gathered the little band of pilgrims together and spoke of the life they would have in that land they had never seen.

"We shall be as a city upon a hill. The eyes of all the people are upon us, so that if we shall deal falsely with our God in this work we have undertaken and so cause Him to withdraw His present help from us, we shall be made a story and a byword through all the world."

To you who are considering what you can do to support Eisenhower College, I tell you that without such schools, this shining dream of John Winthrop's may well become the taste of ashes in our mouths.

They are an educational whetstone, serving to hone the educational process, helping to improve the public, tax-supported system, keeping it competitive in the drive for excellence. By that very competition they help preserve the public institutions from political interference, guaranteeing a measure of academic freedom they could never attain by themselves.

General Eisenhower commended those who give of their time and their sustenance to bring this college into being and to keep it alive. He knew that institutions such as Eisenhower College are essential to America. They provide leadership out of all proportion to their size. America will be needing them more and more in the days ahead.

You—ladies and gentlemen of the world of commerce and the professions—you can make no greater investment in freedom than your contributions to independent schools and colleges in this country.

Having a captive audience of the makeup of this one, I go even farther. I dare to hope that one day the federal government will grant tax credits—not deductions but tax credits—for at least a portion of the tuition fees paid by parents sending their sons and daughters to such colleges. I even dare to hope that we will explore the possibility of extending federal aid, not through more bureaucracy, but by creating tax credits for contributions to schools and colleges—within a prescribed limit, of course, as to the overall amount.

If we are to win the battle where it is being fought today, in the minds and hearts of our young people, I pray that you will keep alive this dream of a man named Ike—this viable force that will help ensure the preservation of our American culture and our heritage.

Robert Taylor Eulogy

LOS ANGELES, CALIFORNIA
JUNE 11, 1969

Now, you might wonder why I put this eulogy to Robert Taylor in here. It obviously has nothing to do with my being governor or the development of my political thought.

I placed this among the collection because I honestly believe eulogies have significance, and I included many eulogies in this book because I believe they are some of the most important speeches I've ever given. I don't mean because they changed the face of the nation in any way, but because it's a very great responsibility to capture the spirit of an individual and what he or she meant to the world.

You can give comfort. You can give perspective. To be asked to give a eulogy is a great honor because you have the power to sum up a human life. I've always taken this power quite seriously.

I liked Bob Taylor a lot. We were good friends; and since I still think about him now and then, I guess you could say I miss him.

How to say farewell to a friend named Bob. He'd probably say, "Don't make any fuss. I wouldn't want to cause any trouble."

How to speak of Robert Taylor—one of the truly great and most enduring stars in the golden era of Hollywood. What can we say about a boy named—well, a boy from Nebraska with an un-Nebraska-like name of Spangler Arlington Brugh.

Perhaps that's as good a starting point as any. A young man, son of a Nebraska doctor, coming to California—to Pomona —for his last years in college, and from there the story reads like a script from one of those early musicals. And it happens to the last person in the world who would have thought that great fame was in store for him.

There was the college play, the talent scout, and most improbable of all, the coincidence of timing that found him in an MGM casting office on the day that had been picked for the testing of a prospective actress. Who can we get to do the scene with her? What about that kid in the outer office? When the test was over, they didn't hire her, they hired him. And I suppose that would be first-act curtain.

And the second act followed the same pattern—was almost a repeat. A newly signed contract player getting a minor role in a picture. No one remembers who had the principal roles— most have forgotten even the title of the picture. But when it was previewed, everyone wanted to know who was Robert Taylor—a young man with the name that sounded like one the studio would think up and become instead Robert Taylor, a name with a kind of honest Midwest sound.

MGM was a giant and the home of giants. It had the greatest stars in an era when Hollywood was a Mount Olympus peopled with godlike stars—Gable, Tracy, Grant, Montgomery, Colman, Cooper, the Barrymores. And there were goddesses to match—Garbo, Shearer, Crawford, Irene Dunne. Bob Taylor became one of the all-time greats of motion picture stardom. Twenty-four years at that one studio, MGM, alone. Thirty-five years before the public. His face, instantly recognizable in every corner of the world. His name a new one—a household word.

And all of this came to be in one sudden, dazzling burst. To simply appear in public caused a traffic jam. There has never been anything like it before or since—possibly the only thing that can compare to it—Rudolph Valentino, and why not? Because on all of Mount Olympus, he was the most handsome.

Now there were those in our midst who worked very hard to bring him down with the label "pretty boy." And of course, there's that standard Hollywood rule that true talent must never be admitted as playing a part in success if the individual is too handsome or too beautiful.

It's only in the recent years of our friendship that I've been able to understand how painful all of this must have been to him—to a truly modest man—because he was modest to the point of being painfully shy. In all of the years of stardom, he never got quite over being genuinely embarrassed at the furor that his appearance created. He went a long way to avoid putting himself in a position where he could become the center of attention.

And in these later years I have learned . . . and not by any complaints from him—complaining wasn't a part of him . . . but I have learned of something else that must have been hard for him to bear: that idea that just a handsome face was responsible for his success—that he wasn't truly an actor. Because Bob had one intolerance—he had no patience with those who came into the business with the idea that they could shortcut hard work and substitute gimmicks for craftsmanship.

He respected his profession and he was a superb master of it. He took a quiet pride in his work. He was a pro, and the "pretty boy" tag couldn't begin to survive roles like *Magnificent Obsession, Camille, Waterloo Bridge, Johnny Eager, Quo Vadis.*

It takes a rare and unique actor to be believable, as he was believable, in costume epics like *Ivanhoe, Knights of the Round Table,* and also, at the same time, as a fighter in *The Crowd Roars* and the almost psychopathic *Billy the Kid.* Some of his pictures live on as true classics, and generally, the standard is so high that in retrospect it would appear his modesty caused this industry to underrate the caliber of this man who was truly a star among stars.

And yet, none of this is what brought us together here today.

Perhaps each one of us has his own different memory, but I'll bet that somehow they all add up to "nice man." Mervyn Le Roy, who directed so many of his great pictures, speaks of his always showing consideration for everyone who worked with him. Artie Deutsch said he never worked in a company where he wasn't well-loved, well-liked, even beloved, by cast and crew.

His quiet and disciplined manner had a steadying effect on every company he was ever in, and at the same time, throughout this country, there are hundreds of men who remember him because he taught them to fly. He sought combat duty in World War II as a Navy flier, and he wound up teaching others—and I'll bet he taught 'em good. There was no caste system in his love of humanity.

Today I am sure there is sorrow among the rugged men in the Northwest who run the swift water of the Rogue River and who knew him as one of them. There are cowpokes up in a valley in Wyoming who remember him and mourn—mourn a man who rode and hunted with them. And millions and millions of people who only knew him by way of the silver screen, and they remember with gratitude that in the darkened theater he never embarrassed them in front of their children.

I know that some night on the late, late show I'm going to see him resplendent in white tie and tails dining at Delmonico's, and I am sure I'll smile—smile at Robert Spangler Arlington Brugh Taylor, because I'll remember how a fellow named Bob really preferred blue jeans and boots. And I'll see him squinting through the smoke of a barbecue as I have seen him a hundred times.

He loved his home and everything that it meant. Above all, he loved his family and his beautiful Ursula—lovely Manuela, all grown up; little Tessa; Terry, his son, a young man in whom he had such great pride.

(To the family) In a little while the hurt will be gone. Time will do that for you. Then you will find you can bring out your memories. You can look at them—take comfort from their warmth. As the years go by you will be very proud. Not so much of the things that we have talked about here—you are going to be proud of simple things. Things not so stylish in certain circles today, but that just makes them a little more rare and of greater value. Simple things he had, like honor and honesty, responsibility to those he worked for and who worked for him, standing up for what he believed, and yes, even a simple old-fashioned love for his country, and above all, an inner humility.

(To the children) I think, too, that he'd want me to tell you how very much he loved your mother. What happiness she brought him and how wonderful she is. The papers say he was in the hospital seven times; actually he was out of the hospital seven times. He needed the strength that he could only get from being in that home so filled with her presence.

He spoke to me of this just a few days ago. It was uppermost in his mind, and I am sure he meant for me to tell you something that he wanted above all else. Ursula, there is just one last thing that only you can do for him—be happy. This was his last thought to me.

I don't pretend to know God's plan for each one of us, but I have faith in His infinite mercy. Bob had great success in the work he loved, and he returned each day from that work with the knowledge there were those who waited affectionately for the sound of his footsteps.

Syndicated Radio Shows

I've always loved radio. My first job out of college was as a radio sportscaster, and it was one of the happiest times of my life. I had a fun job, a new car, a certain amount of fame and recognition there in the Midwest. I was having a good time. Eventually I got a crack at working in motion pictures, and I left radio, but it always had a certain hold on my heart.

After I left the governorship, I got into radio again—this time doing syndicated commentaries. Writing these pieces was a lot harder than sportscasting. In fact, it was something of a grind turning these things out. But I'll tell you what these commentaries did. They kept my name before the public while I was out of office, and they did something else that was probably more important. The commentaries forced me to have a broader, more national outlook on issues than perhaps I had when I was governor. They forced me to articulate my opinions on a whole range of matters, which I think in turn helped prepare me for my run for the presidency.

The following two commentaries embody beliefs that became central to my political philosophy.

A N UNBORN CHILD's property rights are protected by law—its right to life is not. I'll be right back.

Eight years ago when I became governor, I found myself involved almost immediately in a controversy over abortion. It was a subject I'd never given much thought to and one for which I didn't really have an opinion. But now I was governor, and abortion turned out to be something I couldn't walk away from.

A bill had been introduced in the California legislature to make abortion available upon demand. The pro and anti forces were already marshaling their troops, and emotions were running high. Then the author of the bill sent word down that he'd amend his bill to anything I felt I could sign. The ball—to coin a cliché—was in my court. Suddenly I had to have a position on abortion.

I did more studying and soul-searching than on anything that was to face me as governor. I discovered that neither medicine, law, or theology had really found a common ground on the subject. Some believed an unborn child was no more than a growth on the body female and she should be able to remove it as she would her appendix. Others felt a human life existed from the moment the fertilized egg was implanted in the womb. Strangely enough, the same legislature that couldn't agree on abortion had unanimously passed a law making it murder to abuse a pregnant woman so as to cause the death of her unborn child.

Another inconsistency—the unborn have property rights protected by law. A man can will his estate to his wife and children and any children yet to be born of his marriage. Yet the proposed abortion law would deny the unborn the protection of the law in preserving its life.

I went to the lawyers on my staff and posed a hypothetical question. What if a pregnant woman became a widow during her pregnancy and found her husband had left his fortune to her and the unborn child. Under the proposed abortion law, she could take the life of her child and inherit all of her husband's estate. Wouldn't that be murder for financial gain? The only answer I got was that they were glad I wasn't asking the questions on the bar exam.

There is a quite common acceptance in medical circles that the cell—let's call it the egg—once it has been fertilized is on its way as a human being with individual physical traits and personality characteristics already determined.

My answer as to what kind of abortion bill I could sign was one that recognized an abortion is the taking of a human life. In our Judeo-Christian religion we recognize the right to take life in defense of our own. Therefore an abortion is justified when done in self-defense. My belief is that a woman has the right to protect her own life and health against even her own unborn child. I believe also that just as she has the right to defend herself against rape, she should not be made to bear a child resulting from the violation of her person and therefore abortion is an act of self-defense.

I know there will be disagreements with this view, but I can find no evidence whatsoever that a fetus is not a living human being with human rights. This is Ronald Reagan. Thanks for listening.

ANYONE WHO HAS BEEN plagued by bureaucratic nonsense, forms to fill out, regulations to comply with even though they make little sense, has to be a fan of a mayor in Texas. I'll be right back.

The mayor of Midland, Texas, Ernest Angelo, will see that Midland never suffers the problems of New York City. As a matter of fact, New York City would never have suffered the problems of New York City if it had had a few Ernie Angelos in City Hall these past twenty years.

As a former governor, I can testify as to the ridiculous demands inflicted on state and local government by the paper pushers of the Potomac. And I know any of you listening who are in business or farming can reel off personal horror stories of the hours spent filling out government-required paperwork and bowing to the demands of senseless regulations. Well, give a listen. You'll enjoy the mayor of Midland's revenge.

Mayor Angelo struggled through a bureaucratic jungle of red tape in the U.S. Department of Housing and Urban Development to obtain for his city some federal funds that were due. It took him eight long, frustrating months of paperwork, questionnaires in duplicate, triplicate, and quadruplicate before he broke through into daylight.

Then one day the regional office of HUD (that's bureaucratese for the Housing and Urban Development agency) requested a reserved parking space at the Midland Municipal Airport. Mayor Angelo was delighted to comply with the request—if HUD would do a little complying.

He sent a letter to the Dallas regional office of HUD with copies to the President, Secretary Carla Hills, and a few others in Washington. His letter requested three executed and fourteen confirmed copies of their application. It further said, "Submit the make and model of the proposed vehicle to be parked in the space together with certified assurance that everyone connected with the manufacture, servicing, and operating of same was paid according to wage scale in compliance with requirements of the Davis-Bacon Act.

"Submit a genealogical table for everyone who will operate said vehicle so that we can ascertain that there will be a precisely exact equal percentage of whites, blacks, and other minorities, as well as women and elderly.

"Submit certified assurances that all operators of said vehicle and any filling station personnel that service same will be equipped with steel-toed boots, safety goggles, and crash helmets, and that the vehicle will be equipped with at least safety belts and an air bag in compliance with the Occupational Safety and Health Act.

"Submit environmental impact statements"—well, you get the idea. His letter went on for quite a few additional paragraphs citing all the red-tape requirements (so dear to the hearts of those who toil on the banks of the Potomac) that would have to be complied with before favorable consideration could be given to their request for a parking space.

Then Mayor Angelo added a postscript. He told them they could have their parking space without complying with all the aforementioned red tape.

I hope he made his point because the General Accounting Office in Washington estimates the yearly cost of regulations at $60 billion. The Federal Trade Commission puts it at $80 billion—all waste due to regulatory overkill. Probably the correct figure is nearer the $130 billion the Council of Economic Advisers estimate is prorated out at $2,000 per family.

Maybe we'll talk some more about this tomorrow. This is Ronald Reagan. Thanks for listening.

1981

Inaugural Address

I know, the last thing you read I was an ex-governor doing radio commentaries, and now I'm about to be sworn in as president of the United States. Well, yes, a lot happened in between, but it really didn't have much to do with any particular speech. The speeches I gave in 1976 when I ran against President Ford for the Republican nomination and the speeches I gave in the 1980 race against President Carter were simply refinements of the basic ideas I'd been talking about sixteen years earlier in the Goldwater speech.

In fact, that's one of my theories about political speechmaking. You have to keep pounding away with your message, year after year, because that's the only way it will sink into the collective consciousness. I'm a big believer in stump speeches— speeches you can give over and over again with slight variations. Because if you have something you believe in deeply, it's worth repeating time and again until you achieve it. You also get better at delivering it.

I do think, however, that my faith in the American people and in what they could do had a special resonance in 1980. The Democratic party's leaders would never admit this, but the simple fact is that they had lost faith in the citizens and the future of our country. They couldn't see this, but the American people

59

did, and they elected me the fortieth president of the United States.

The year 1981 was one of applying the conservative princi-ples that I had so long espoused to national government. The great exercise was almost cut short by Mr. Hinckley's bullet, which got within an inch of my heart. That slowed me down for a couple of months, but in a way it allowed the pressure for change to build, so that when I was back in the fray I had momentum on my side. I had an agenda. I had things that I wanted to accomplish. I began outlining all that with my inau-gural address.

SENATOR HATFIELD, Mr. Chief Justice, Mr. President, Vice President Bush, Vice President Mondale, Senator Baker, Speaker O'Neill, Reverend Moomaw, and my fellow citizens.

To a few of us here today this is a solemn and most momen-tous occasion, and yet in the history of our nation it is a com-monplace occurrence. The orderly transfer of authority as called for in the Constitution routinely takes place, as it has for almost two centuries, and few of us stop to think how unique we really are. In the eyes of many in the world, this every-four-year ceremony we accept as normal is nothing less than a mir-acle.

Mr. President, I want our fellow citizens to know how much you did to carry on this tradition. By your gracious cooperation in the transition process, you have shown a watching world that we are a united people pledged to maintaining a political system which guarantees individual liberty to a greater degree than any other, and I thank you and your people for all your help in maintaining the continuity which is the bulwark of our republic.

The business of our nation goes forward. These United States are confronted with an economic affliction of great propor-tions. We suffer from the longest and one of the worst sustained inflations in our national history. It distorts our economic decisions, penalizes thrift, and crushes the struggling young and the fixed-income elderly alike. It threatens to shatter the lives of millions of our people.

Idle industries have cast workers into unemployment, human misery, and personal indignity. Those who do work are denied a fair return for their labor by a tax system which penalizes successful achievement and keeps us from maintaining full productivity.

But great as our tax burden is, it has not kept pace with public spending. For decades we have piled deficit upon deficit, mortgaging our future and our children's future for the temporary convenience of the present. To continue this long trend is to guarantee tremendous social, cultural, political, and economic upheavals.

You and I, as individuals, can, by borrowing, live beyond our means, but for only a limited period of time. Why, then, should we think that collectively, as a nation, we're not bound by that same limitation? We must act today in order to preserve tomorrow. And let there be no misunderstanding: We are going to begin to act, beginning today.

The economic ills we suffer have come upon us over several decades. They will not go away in days, weeks, or months, but they will go away. They will go away because we as Americans have the capacity now, as we've had in the past, to do whatever needs to be done to preserve this last and greatest bastion of freedom.

In this present crisis, government is not the solution to our problem; government is the problem. From time to time we've been tempted to believe that society has become too complex to be managed by self-rule, that government by an elite group is superior to government for, by, and of the people. Well, if no one among us is capable of governing himself, then who among us has the capacity to govern someone else? All of us together, in and out of government, must bear the burden. The solutions we seek must be equitable, with no one group singled out to pay a higher price.

We hear much of special interest groups. Well, our concern

must be for a special interest group that has been too long neglected. It knows no sectional boundaries or ethnic and racial divisions, and it crosses political party lines. It is made up of men and women who raise our food, patrol our streets, man our mines and factories, teach our children, keep our homes, and heal us when we're sick—professionals, industrialists, shopkeepers, clerks, cabbies, and truck drivers. They are, in short, "we the people," this breed called Americans.

Well, this administration's objective will be a healthy, vigorous, growing economy that provides equal opportunities for all Americans, with no barriers born of bigotry or discrimination. Putting America back to work means putting all Americans back to work. Ending inflation means freeing all Americans from the terror of runaway living costs. All must share in the productive work of this "new beginning," and all must share in the bounty of a revived economy. With the idealism and fair play which are the core of our system and our strength, we can have a strong and prosperous America, at peace with itself and the world.

So, as we begin, let us take inventory. We are a nation that has a government—not the other way around. And this makes us special among the nations of the earth. Our government has no power except that granted it by the people. It is time to check and reverse the growth of government, which shows signs of having grown beyond the consent of the governed.

It is my intention to curb the size and influence of the federal establishment and to demand recognition of the distinction between the powers granted to the federal government and those reserved to the states or to the people. All of us need to be reminded that the federal government did not create the states; the states created the federal government.

Now, so there will be no misunderstanding, it's not my intention to do away with government. It is rather to make it work —work with us, not over us; to stand by our side, not ride on our back. Government can and must provide opportunity, not smother it; foster productivity, not stifle it.

If we look to the answer as to why for so many years we

achieved so much, prospered as no other people on earth, it was because here in this land we unleashed the energy and individual genius of man to a greater extent than has ever been done before. Freedom and the dignity of the individual have been more available and assured here than in any other place on earth. The price for this freedom at times has been high, but we have never been unwilling to pay that price.

It is no coincidence that our present troubles parallel and are proportionate to the intervention and intrusion in our lives that result from unnecessary and excessive growth of government. It is time for us to realize that we're too great a nation to limit ourselves to small dreams. We're not, as some would have us believe, doomed to an inevitable decline. I do not believe in a fate that will fall on us no matter what we do. I do believe in a fate that will fall on us if we do nothing. So, with all the creative energy at our command, let us begin an era of national renewal. Let us renew our determination, our courage, and our strength. And let us renew our faith and our hope.

We have every right to dream heroic dreams. Those who say that we're in a time when there are no heroes, they just don't know where to look. You can see heroes every day going in and out of factory gates. Others, a handful in number, produce enough food to feed all of us and then the world beyond. You meet heroes across a counter, and they're on both sides of that counter. There are entrepreneurs with faith in themselves and faith in an idea who create new jobs, new wealth and opportunity. They're individuals and families whose taxes support the government and whose voluntary gifts support church, charity, culture, art, and education. Their patriotism is quiet, but deep. Their values sustain our national life.

Now, I have used the words "they" and "their" in speaking of these heroes. I could say "you" and "your," because I'm addressing the heroes of whom I speak—you, the citizens of this blessed land. Your dreams, your hopes, your goals are going to be the dreams, the hopes, and the goals of this administration, so help me God.

We shall reflect the compassion that is so much a part of

your makeup. How can we love our country and not love our countrymen; and loving them, reach out a hand when they fall, heal them when they're sick, and provide opportunity to make them self-sufficient so they will be equal in fact and not just in theory?

Can we solve the problems confronting us? Well, the answer is an unequivocal and emphatic "yes." To paraphrase Winston Churchill, I did not take the oath I've just taken with the intention of presiding over the dissolution of the world's strongest economy.

In the days ahead I will propose removing the roadblocks that have slowed our economy and reduced productivity. Steps will be taken aimed at restoring the balance between the various levels of government. Progress may be slow, measured in inches and feet, not miles, but we will progress. It is time to reawaken this industrial giant, to get government back within its means, and to lighten our punitive tax burden. And these will be our first priorities, and on these principles there will be no compromise.

On the eve of our struggle for independence a man who might have been one of the greatest among the Founding Fathers, Dr. Joseph Warren, president of the Massachusetts Congress, said to his fellow Americans, "Our country is in danger, but not to be despaired of. . . . On you depend the fortunes of America. You are to decide the important questions upon which rests the happiness and the liberty of millions yet unborn. Act worthy of yourselves."

Well, I believe we, the Americans of today, are ready to act worthy of ourselves, ready to do what must be done to ensure happiness and liberty for ourselves, our children, and our children's children. And as we renew ourselves here in our own land, we will be seen as having greater strength throughout the world. We will again be the exemplar of freedom and a beacon of hope for those who do not now have freedom.

To those neighbors and allies who share our freedom, we will strengthen our historic ties and assure them of our support and firm commitment. We will match loyalty with loyalty. We will strive for mutually beneficial relations. We will not use our friendship to impose on their sovereignty, for our own sovereignty is not for sale.

As for the enemies of freedom, those who are potential adversaries, they will be reminded that peace is the highest aspiration of the American people. We will negotiate for it, sacrifice for it; we will not surrender for it, now or ever.

Our forbearance should never be misunderstood. Our reluctance for conflict should not be misjudged as a failure of will. When action is required to preserve our national security, we will act. We will maintain sufficient strength to prevail if need be, knowing that if we do so we have the best chance of never having to use that strength.

Above all, we must realize that no arsenal or no weapon in the arsenals of the world is so formidable as the will and moral courage of free men and women. It is a weapon our adversaries in today's world do not have. It is a weapon that we as Americans do have. Let that be understood by those who practice terrorism and prey upon their neighbors.

I'm told that tens of thousands of prayer meetings are being held on this day, and for that I'm deeply grateful. We are a nation under God, and I believe God intended for us to be free. It would be fitting and good, I think, if on each Inaugural Day in future years it should be declared a day of prayer.

This is the first time in our history that this ceremony has been held, as you've been told, on this West Front of the Capitol. Standing here, one faces a magnificent vista, opening up on this city's special beauty and history. At the end of this open mall are those shrines to the giants on whose shoulders we stand.

Directly in front of me, the monument to a monumental man, George Washington, father of our country. A man of humility who came to greatness reluctantly. He led America out of revolutionary victory into infant nationhood. Off to one side, the stately memorial to Thomas Jefferson. The Declaration of Independence flames with his eloquence. And then, beyond the Reflecting Pool, the dignified columns of the Lincoln Memorial.

Whoever would understand in his heart the meaning of America will find it in the life of Abraham Lincoln.

Beyond those monuments to heroism is the Potomac River, and on the far shore the sloping hills of Arlington National Cemetery, with its row upon row of simple white markers bearing crosses or Stars of David. They add up to only a tiny fraction of the price that has been paid for our freedom.

Each one of those markers is a monument to the kind of hero I spoke of earlier. Their lives ended in places called Belleau Wood, the Argonne, Omaha Beach, Salerno, and halfway around the world on Guadalcanal, Tarawa, Pork Chop Hill, the Chosin Reservoir, and in a hundred rice paddies and jungles of a place called Vietnam.

Under one such marker lies a young man, Martin Treptow, who left his job in a small town barbershop in 1917 to go to France with the famed Rainbow Division. There, on the western front, he was killed trying to carry a message between battalions under heavy artillery fire.

We're told that on his body was found a diary. On the flyleaf under the heading "My Pledge," he had written these words: "America must win this war. Therefore I will work, I will save, I will sacrifice, I will endure, I will fight cheerfully and do my utmost, as if the issue of the whole struggle depended on me alone."

The crisis we are facing today does not require of us the kind of sacrifice that Martin Treptow and so many thousands of others were called upon to make. It does require, however, our best effort and our willingness to believe in ourselves and to believe in our capacity to perform great deeds, to believe that together with God's help we can and will resolve the problems which now confront us.

And after all, why shouldn't we believe that? We are Americans.

God bless you, and thank you.

Remarks at a Luncheon for Members of the Baseball Hall of Fame

STATE DINING ROOM

MARCH 27, 1981

One of the great things about being president is that you can invite anyone you want to lunch or dinner, and chances are they'll come. I don't remember exactly how this event got on the schedule, but it's representative of the kind of fun you can have even living in a museum called the White House.

As you may know, I love to tell stories, and boy, did I get to tell my share to these guys. There's something very therapeutic about hearing laughter and about laughing yourself. I believe there is some basis to this business about laughter being able to heal. So can friendship, which is what I considered this gathering to be all about.

The President. Gentlemen, go ahead with your coffee and all, but I know that time is getting by and we have a few remarks.

I'm delighted—well, I can't tell you how thrilled to have you all here. And over there at the other table is a ballplayer who is delighted to be here, Vice President George Bush, and he did play. But I want to tell you, you span the years for me, and all these young gentlemen here that are growing up as ballplayers. It's a delight to have all of you here.

The nostalgia is bubbling within me, and I may have to be dragged out of here because of all the stories that are coming up in my mind. Baseball—I had to finally confess over here, no, I didn't play when I was young. I went down the football path. But I did play in a way, as Bob Lemon well knows, I was old Grover Cleveland Alexander, and I've been very proud of that. It was a wonderful experience.

There were quite a few ballplayers, including Bob Lemon, who were on the set for that picture. And I remember one day when they wanted some shots of me pitching, but kind of close up—so, they wanted me to throw past the camera, and they had a fellow back there—well, Al Lyons, one of the ballplayers that was there, was going to catch the ball back there and then toss it back over the camera to me. And the cam was getting these close shots for use wherever they could use them. And he was on one side of the camera, and my control wasn't all that it should be at one point, and I threw it on the other side of the camera. And he speared it with his left hand with no glove on. He was a left-hander, and after he brought the ball to me, and he said, "Alex, I'm sorry I had to catch your blazer bare-handed." [*Laughter*] He didn't suffer any pain, I am sure of it.

But I remember we had a fellow that I'm sure some of you know and remember, Metkovitch. And Metkovitch, during the day's shooting, would memorize everyone's lines. And then if we were on location and got in the bus to go back in from location, he would now play all the scenes for us on the bus. [*Laughter*] So, thinking about this, one day, on the process screen, an umpire behind him, he was at the plate, and they wanted a shot of a ballplayer at the plate. And the director said, "There are no lines, but you'll know what to say." He said, "The umpire's going to call it a strike," and he said, "You don't think it's a strike. So, do what you do in a ball game when you think it's a bad call." And extroverted Metkovitch, who was so happy to play all the scenes, was standing up at the plate, and if you looked closely, you could see that the bat was beginning to shake a little bit—[*Laughter*]—and the ball came by on an after play and the umpire bellowed out, "Strike one!" and Metkovitch lowered the bat and he says, "Gee, that was no strike." [*Laughter*] The picture wasn't a comedy, so we couldn't leave it in.

But you know, I've always been sorry about one thing. Alex is in the Hall of Fame and deservedly so. Everyone knows that great 1926 World Series, when he had won two games, received the greatest ovation anyone's ever received, and then was called on in the seventh inning with the bases loaded, no one out, and one of the most dangerous hitters in baseball at the plate. And he came in and saved the game. The tragedy that I've always regretted is that the studio was unwilling to reveal in the picture, was afraid to reveal what I think was the best-kept secret in sports.

A bad habit of Alex's was widely heralded and took something away from his luster. But they wouldn't let us use the actual word of what was behind, maybe, his bad habit. Alex was an epileptic. And when he was arrested and picked up for being drunk in a gutter, as he once was, he wasn't at all. But he would rather take that than admit to the disease that plagued him all his life.

But he also, early in his baseball career, was hit in the head going from first base down to second on a throw from second; they caught him right in the head. And he was out of baseball for a while, and they didn't know whether forever, because he had double vision. And he kept experimenting, trying to find out if there wasn't some way that he could pitch. And he went to a minor league club and asked for a tryout, and the manager got up at the plate and said, "Well, go on out on the mound and throw me a few." Alex broke three of his ribs on the first pitch. [*Laughter*] His experiment had been that he thought that if he closed one eye and threw, he'd only—[*Laughter*]—and the friend that was with him when they were thrown out of the ball park said, "What happened?" And he said, "I closed the wrong eye." [*Laughter*]

But there are men in this room that were playing when I was

69

broadcasting, and I promised to say something here to a great Cub fan that we have at the table that would make him feel good. I was broadcasting the Cubs when the only mathematical possibility—and Billy Herman will remember this very well—that the Cubs had of winning the pennant was to win the last twenty-one games of the season. And they did. And I was so imbued with baseball by that time that I know you're not supposed to talk about a no-hitter while it's going on because you'll jinx them. So, there I was, a broadcaster, and never mentioned once in the twenty-one games—and I was getting as uptight as they were—and never mentioned the fact that they were at sixteen, they were at seventeen, and that they hadn't lost a game, because I was afraid I'd jinx them. But anyway, they did it and it's still in the record books.

What isn't in the record books is Billy Jurges staying at the plate, I think, the longest of any ballplayer in the history of the game. I was doing the games by telegraphic report, and the fellow on the other side of a window with a little slit underneath, the headphones on, getting the dot-and-dash Morse code from the ball park, would type out the play. And the paper would come through to me—it would say, "S1C." Well you're not going to sell any Wheaties yelling "S1C!" [*Laughter*] So, I'd say, "And so-and-so comes out of the windup, here's the pitch, and it's a called strike, breaking over the outside corner to so-and-so, who'd rather have a ball someplace else and so forth and backed out there."

Well, I saw him start to type, and I started—Dizzy Dean was on the mound—and I started the ball on the way to the plate —or him in the windup and he, Curly, the fellow on the other side, was shaking his head, and I thought he just—maybe it was a miraculous play or something. But when the slip came through it said, "The wire's gone dead." Well, I had the ball on the way to the plate. [*Laughter*] And I figured real quick, I could say we'll tell them what had happened and then play transcribed music. But in those days there were at least seven or eight other fellows that were doing the same ball game. I didn't want to lose the audience.

So, I thought real quick, "There's one thing that doesn't get in the score book," so I had Billy foul one off. And I looked at Curly, and Curly just went like this; so I had him foul another one. And I had him foul one back at third base and described the fight between the two kids that were trying to get the ball. [*Laughter*] Then I had him foul one that just missed being a home run, about a foot and a half. And I did set a world record for successive fouls or for someone standing there, except that no one keeps records of that kind. And I was beginning to sweat, when Curly sat up straight and started typing, and he was nodding his head, "Yes." And the slip came through the window, and I could hardly talk for laughing, because it said, "Jurges popped out on the first ball pitch." [*Laughter*]

But those were wonderful days, not only playing the part, but some of you here, I think, will—I'm going to tell another story here that has been confirmed for me by Waite Hoyt. Those of you who played when the Dodgers were in Brooklyn know that Brooklynese have a tendency to refer to someone by the name of Earl as "oil." But if they want a quart of oil in the car, they say, "Give me a quart of earl." And Waite was sliding into second. And he twisted his ankle. And instead of getting up, he was lying there, and there was a deep hush over the whole ball park. And then a Brooklyn voice was heard above all that silence and said, "Gee, Hurt is hoyt." [*Laughter*]

But, I can't take any more time doing this or we'd be here all day. They tell me that I'm supposed to go out there in front of the door to the Blue Room, and because I haven't been able to say hello to all of you in here and, as I say, there are many of you that were playing when I broadcast in those telegraphic report games, and not only re-created but—as I just told you— now and then created some of the ball game. But I understand that we're going to have a chance outside here—kind of a line where I can say hello and good-bye at the same time to each one of you.

And now I'm going to present—the commissioner has something here that I think should be said. Commissioner, come on up here.

*Mr. Kuhn.** Okay, fine. I just wanted to take a moment on behalf of all of us gathered here together to thank the President for his great kindness in having us all here today.

I'm going to borrow a line from the man I talked to yesterday who's sitting here in the room, Mr. President, Bob Howsam. When Bob and I were talking, I said, "I'll see you there tomorrow, won't I?" And Bob's a member of our executive council from the Cincinnati Reds sitting over here, and he said, "Commissioner, I will never be so proud or so old that I won't be thrilled to set foot in the White House and say hello to the President of the United States." And I think on behalf of us all, I can say we're very thrilled to be here, to be with you, to share with you some anecdotes about the game of baseball.

I want to just do one little thing that I found. I want to say to the President on behalf of baseball that I think we have contributed mightily to the President's situation here in Washington, because he was a Cubs fan, as you can tell. And I've got an article I found in the *Chicago Tribune* which plainly indicates that baseball has prepared him for his career here. It says, "For four years, Ronald Reagan broadcast games of the Cubs and in the process became that rarest of nature's noblemen," Dave Broder, "a Cub fan. Nothing before or since those four years has prepared him more fully to face with fortitude the travails of the Oval Office. As a Cub fan, he learned that virtue will not necessarily prevail over chicanery, that swift failure follows closely on the heels of even the most modest success, that the world mocks those who are pure in heart, but slow of foot. But"—and here's the good news, Mr. President—"but that the bitterest disappointment will soon yield to the hope and promise of a new season."

We thank you from the bottoms of our heart for your kindness and generosity here today.

Mr. Stack. I'm Ed Stack, the president of the Baseball Hall of Fame, and I have a couple presentations I'd like to make.

* Bowie Kuhn, Commissioner of the American Baseball Association.

Before the luncheon, the President greeted the commissioner and myself in the Oval Office and was very gracious to sign our historic presidential baseball, which we have on display at the Baseball Hall of Fame in Cooperstown. He added his signature to the baseballs that have been signed by all the presidents since William Howard Taft. And tomorrow morning, it'll be on display in Cooperstown for the millions of visitors to see when they come through the shrine.

Also, we presented the President with a lifetime gold pass to the Baseball Hall of Fame, and we hope that he will use it many times in the future.

I'd like to ask the President to accept from us a couple of gifts. The first gift that we have to present is something that Billy Martin sent from Oakland. Bill heard about the luncheon and asked that I present this to the President. And if he could open it and show the audience, I think he'll enjoy it.

[*The President was presented with an Oakland A's team jacket.*]

The President. Hey, look, Ma, I made the team! [*Laughter*] I hope he hasn't got this too big. [*Laughter*] A little big.

Well, I thank him very much. I thank all of you.

Address to the Nation on the Economy

OVAL OFFICE

FEBRUARY 5, 1981

A major reason I was elected president was because the American economy had become a basket case. Here we were, a country bursting with economic promise, and yet our political leadership had gone out of its way to frustrate America's natu-

ral economic strength. It made no sense. My attitude had always been—let the people flourish.

With the help of some Democratic "boll weevils" in Congress, we enacted the largest tax and budget cuts in history. Later we would enact the most extensive reform ever of the tax code. In the process, we cut inflation, interest rates, and unemployment. The consequence is that we have enjoyed the longest peacetime economic expansion in our nation's history.

The following speech was my first appeal to the American people about the economic crisis we were facing. There would be many more appeals over the years. Some I would win, some I would lose, such as my continual fights with Congress to get control of the budget deficit. The Congress of the United States today is a captive of the special interest groups and totally unable to balance the budget. I am convinced we'll never have a balanced budget unless we have a constitutional amendment requiring one.

To make clear the erosion of our nation's economy, I used some coins in this speech to show how inflation had eaten into the value of a dollar. The commentators all noted how effective this was. I guess my acting background did pay off now and then.

G OOD EVENING.

I'm speaking to you tonight to give you a report on the state of our nation's economy. I regret to say that we're in the worst economic mess since the Great Depression.

A few days ago I was presented with a report I'd asked for, a comprehensive audit, if you will, of our economic condition. You won't like it. I didn't like it. But we have to face the truth and then go to work to turn things around. And make no mistake about it, we can turn them around.

I'm not going to subject you to the jumble of charts, figures, and economic jargon of that audit, but rather will try to explain where we are, how we got there, and how we can get back. First, however, let me just give a few "attention getters" from the audit.

The federal budget is out of control, and we face runaway deficits of almost $80 billion for this budget year that ends September 30th. That deficit is larger than the entire federal budget in 1957, and so is the almost $80 billion we will pay in interest this year on the national debt.

Twenty years ago, in 1960, our federal government payroll was less than $13 billion. Today it is 75 billion. During these twenty years our population has only increased by 23.3 percent. The federal budget has gone up 528 percent.

Now, we've just had two years of back-to-back double-digit inflation—13.3 percent in 1979. 12.4 percent last year. The last time this happened was in World War I.

In 1960 mortgage interest rates averaged about 6 percent. They're two and a half times as high now, 15.4 percent.

The percentage of your earnings the federal government took in taxes in 1960 has almost doubled.

And finally there are 7 million Americans caught up in the personal indignity and human tragedy of unemployment. If they stood in a line, allowing three feet for each person, the line would reach from the coast of Maine to California.

Well, so much for the audit itself. Let me try to put this in personal terms. Here is a dollar such as you earned, spent, or saved in 1960. And here is a quarter, a dime, and a penny—thirty-six cents. That's what this 1960 dollar is worth today. And if the present world inflation rate should continue three more years, that dollar of 1960 will be worth a quarter. What initiative is there to save? And if we don't save we're short of the investment capital needed for business and industry expansion. Workers in Japan and West Germany save several times the percentage of their income that Americans do.

What's happened to that American dream of owning a home? Only ten years ago a family could buy a home, and the monthly payment averaged little more than a quarter—twenty-seven cents out of each dollar earned. Today, it takes forty-two cents out of every dollar of income. So, fewer than one out of eleven families can afford to buy their first new home.

Regulations adopted by government with the best of intentions have added $666 to the cost of an automobile. It is estimated that altogether regulations of every kind, on shopkeepers, farmers, and major industries, add $100 billion or more to the cost of the goods and services we buy. And then another 20 billion is spent by government handling the paperwork created by those regulations.

I'm sure you're getting the idea that the audit presented to me found government policies of the last few decades responsible for our economic troubles. We forgot or just overlooked the fact that government—any government—has a built-in tendency to grow. Now, we all had a hand in looking to government for benefits as if government had some source of revenue other than our earnings. Many if not most of the things we thought of or that government offered to us seemed attractive.

In the years following the Second World War it was easy, for a while at least, to overlook the price tag. Our income more than doubled in the twenty-five years after the war. We increased our take-home pay in those twenty-five years by more than we had amassed in all the preceding one hundred and fifty years put together. Yes, there was some inflation, 1 or 1½ percent a year. That didn't bother us. But if we look back at those golden years, we recall that even then voices had been raised, warning that inflation, like radioactivity, was cumulative and that once started it could get out of control.

Some government programs seemed so worthwhile that borrowing to fund them didn't bother us. By 1960 our national debt stood at $284 billion. Congress in 1971 decided to put a ceiling of 400 billion on our ability to borrow. Today the debt is 934 billion. So-called temporary increases or extensions in the debt ceiling have been allowed twenty-one times in these ten years, and now I've been forced to ask for another increase in the debt ceiling or the government will be unable to function past the middle of February—and I've only been here sixteen days. Before we reach the day when we can reduce the debt ceiling, we may in spite of our best efforts see a national debt in excess of a trillion dollars. Now, this is a figure that's literally beyond our comprehension.

We know now that inflation results from all that deficit spending. Government has only two ways of getting money other than raising taxes. It can go into the money market and borrow, competing with its own citizens and driving up interest rates, which it has done, or it can print money, and it's done that. Both methods are inflationary.

We're victims of language. The very word "inflation" leads us to think of it as just high prices. Then, of course, we resent the person who puts on the price tags, forgetting that he or she is also a victim of inflation. Inflation is not just high prices; it's a reduction in the value of our money. When the money supply is increased but the goods and services available for buying are not, we have too much money chasing too few goods. Wars are usually accompanied by inflation. Everyone is working or fighting, but production is of weapons and munitions, not things we can buy and use.

Now, one way out would be to raise taxes so that government need not borrow or print money. But in all these years of government growth, we've reached, indeed surpassed, the limit of our people's tolerance or ability to bear an increase in the tax burden. Prior to World War II, taxes were such that on the average we only had to work just a little over one month each year to pay our total federal, state, and local tax bill. Today we have to work four months to pay that bill.

Some say shift the tax burden to business and industry, but business doesn't pay taxes. Oh, don't get the wrong idea. Business is being taxed, so much so that we're being priced out of the world market. But business must pass its costs of operations —and that includes taxes—on to the customer in the price of the product. Only people pay taxes, all the taxes. Government just uses business in a kind of sneaky way to help collect the taxes. They're hidden in the price; we aren't aware of how much tax we actually pay.

Today this once great industrial giant of ours has the lowest rate of gain in productivity of virtually all the industrial nations with whom we must compete in the world market. We can't even hold our own market here in America against foreign automobiles, steel, and a number of other products. Japanese production of automobiles is almost twice as great per worker as it is in America. Japanese steelworkers outproduce their American counterparts by about 25 percent.

Now, this isn't because they're better workers. I'll match the American working man or woman against anyone in the world. But we have to give them the tools and equipment that workers in the other industrial nations have.

We invented the assembly line and mass production, but punitive tax policies and excessive and unnecessary regulations plus government borrowing have stifled our ability to update plant and equipment. When capital investment is made, it's too often for some unproductive alterations demanded by government to meet various of its regulations. Excessive taxation of individuals has robbed us of incentive and made overtime unprofitable.

We once produced about 40 percent of the world's steel. We now produce 19 percent. We were once the greatest producer of automobiles, producing more than all the rest of the world combined. That is no longer true, and in addition, the "Big Three," the major auto companies in our land, have sustained tremendous losses in the past year and have been forced to lay off thousands of workers.

All of you who are working know that even with cost-of-living pay raises, you can't keep up with inflation. In our progressive tax system, as you increase the number of dollars you earn, you find yourself moved up into higher tax brackets, paying a higher tax rate just for trying to hold your own. The result? Your standard of living is going down.

Over the past decades we've talked of curtailing government spending so that we can then lower the tax burden. Sometimes we've even taken a run at doing that. But there were always those who told us that taxes couldn't be cut until spending was reduced. Well, you know, we can lecture our children about extravagance until we run out of voice and breath. Or we can cure their extravagance by simply reducing their allowance.

It's time to recognize that we've come to a turning point. We're threatened with an economic calamity of tremendous proportions, and the old business-as-usual treatment can't save us. Together, we must chart a different course.

We must increase productivity. That means making it possible for industry to modernize and make use of the technology which we ourselves invented. That means putting Americans back to work. And that means above all bringing government spending back within government revenues, which is the only way, together with increased productivity, that we can reduce and, yes, eliminate inflation.

In the past we've tried to fight inflation one year and then, with unemployment increased, turn the next year to fighting unemployment with more deficit spending as a pump primer. So, again, up goes inflation. It hasn't worked. We don't have to choose between inflation and unemployment—they go hand in hand. It's time to try something different, and that's what we're going to do.

I've already placed a freeze on hiring replacements for those who retire or leave government service. I've ordered a cut in government travel, the number of consultants to the government, and the buying of office equipment and other items. I've put a freeze on pending regulations and set up a task force under Vice President Bush to review regulations with an eye toward getting rid of as many as possible. I have decontrolled oil, which should result in more domestic production and less dependence on foreign oil. And I'm eliminating that ineffective Council on Wage and Price Stability.

But it will take more, much more. And we must realize there is no quick fix. At the same time, however, we cannot delay in implementing an economic program aimed at both reducing tax rates to stimulate productivity and reducing the growth in government spending to reduce unemployment and inflation.

On February 18th, I will present in detail an economic program to Congress embodying the features I've just stated. It will propose budget cuts in virtually every department of government. It is my belief that these actual budget cuts will only be part of the savings. As our cabinet secretaries take charge of their departments, they will search out areas of waste, extravagance, and costly overhead which could yield additional and substantial reductions.

Now, at the same time we're doing this, we must go forward with a tax relief package. I shall ask for a 10-percent reduction across the board in personal income tax rates for each of the next three years. Proposals will also be submitted for accelerated depreciation allowances for business to provide necessary capital so as to create jobs.

Now, here again, in saying this, I know that language, as I said earlier, can get in the way of a clear understanding of what our program is intended to do. Budget cuts can sound as if we're going to reduce total government spending to a lower level than was spent the year before. Well, this is not the case. The budgets will increase as our population increases, and each year we'll see spending increases to match that growth. Government revenues will increase as the economy grows, but the burden will be lighter for each individual, because the economic base will have been expanded by reason of the reduced rates.

Now, let me show you a chart that I've had drawn to illustrate how this can be.

Here you see two trend lines. The bottom line shows the increase in tax revenues. The red line on top is the increase in government spending. Both lines turn upward, reflecting the giant tax increase already built into the system for this year 1981, and the increases in spending built into the '81 and '82 budgets and on into the future. As you can see, the spending line rises at a steeper slant than the revenue line. And that gap between those lines illustrates the increasing deficits we've been running, including this year's $80-billion deficit.

Now, in the second chart, the lines represent the positive effects when Congress accepts our economic program. Both lines continue to rise, allowing for necessary growth, but the gap narrows as spending cuts continue over the next few years until finally the two lines come together, meaning a balanced budget.

I am confident that my administration can achieve that. At that point tax revenues, in spite of rate reductions, will be increasing faster than spending, which means we can look forward to further reductions in the tax rates.

Now, in all of this we will, of course, work closely with the Federal Reserve System toward the objective of a stable monetary policy.

Our spending cuts will not be at the expense of the truly needy. We will, however, seek to eliminate benefits to those who are not really qualified by reason of need.

As I've said before, on February 18th I will present this economic package of budget reductions and tax reform to a joint session of Congress and to you in full detail.

Our basic system is sound. We can, with compassion, continue to meet our responsibility to those who, through no fault of their own, need our help. We can meet fully the other legitimate responsibilities of government. We cannot continue any longer our wasteful ways at the expense of the workers of this land or of our children.

Since 1960 our government has spent $5.1 trillion. Our debt has grown by 648 billion. Prices have exploded by 178 percent. How much better off are we for all that? Well, we all know we're very much worse off. When we measure how harshly these years of inflation, lower productivity, and uncontrolled government growth have affected our lives, we know we must act and act now. We must not be timid. We will restore the freedom of all men and women to excel and to create. We will unleash the energy and genius of the American people, traits which have never failed us.

To the Congress of the United States, I extend my hand in cooperation, and I believe we can go forward in a bipartisan manner. I've found a real willingness to cooperate on the part of Democrats and members of my own party.

To my colleagues in the executive branch of government and

to all federal employees, I ask that we work in the spirit of service.

I urge those great institutions in America, business and labor, to be guided by the national interest, and I'm confident they will. The only special interest that we will serve is the interest of all the people.

We can create the incentives which take advantage of the genius of our economic system—a system, as Walter Lippmann observed more than forty years ago, which for the first time in history gave men "a way of producing wealth in which the good fortune of others multiplied their own."

Our aim is to increase our national wealth so all will have more, not just redistribute what we already have, which is just a sharing of scarcity. We can begin to reward hard work and risk-taking, by forcing this government to live within its means.

Over the years we've let negative economic forces run out of control. We stalled the judgment day, but we no longer have that luxury. We're out of time.

And to you, my fellow citizens, let us join in a new determination to rebuild the foundation of our society, to work together, to act responsibly. Let us do so with the most profound respect for that which must be preserved as well as with sensitive understanding and compassion for those who must be protected.

We can leave our children with an unrepayable massive debt and a shattered economy, or we can leave them liberty in a land where every individual has the opportunity to be whatever God intended us to be. All it takes is a little common sense and recognition of our own ability. Together we can forge a new beginning for America.

Thank you, and good night.

Statement on the Air Traffic Controllers' Strike

WHITE HOUSE ROSE GARDEN
AUGUST 3, 1981

I'm not very good at firing people; maybe it goes back to the fact that as a child I can remember my father being out of work. I know the hardship and dislocation it can cause a family. But I also believe that people should keep their word when they make a promise. This is why I fired the air controllers.

As a former union president myself, I couldn't go along with the controllers violating not only the law, but their own pledges, not to strike. I also don't believe government employees have the right to strike, because the strike is against their fellow citizens, not some moneyed employer.

This episode was an early test of my administration's resolve. We had the choice of caving in to unreasonable demands while keeping our air traffic system operating without incident, or of taking a stand for what we thought was right with the risk of throwing the system into possible chaos. I felt we had to do what was right. This decision forced us to train almost an entirely new crop of air traffic controllers. It took years for our air traffic system to return to normal. I think the principle was worth the price.

Most often it's not how handsomely or eloquently you say something, but the fact that your words mean something. That's the case here.

T HIS MORNING AT SEVEN A.M. the union representing those who man America's air traffic control facilities called a strike. This was the culmination of seven months of negotiations between the Federal Aviation Administration and the union. At one point in these negotiations agreement was reached and signed by both sides, granting a $40 million increase in salaries and benefits. This is twice what other government employees can expect. It was granted in recognition of the difficulties inherent in the work these people perform. Now, however, the union demands are seventeen times what had been agreed to—$681 million. This would impose a tax burden on their fellow citizens which is unacceptable.

I would like to thank the supervisors and controllers who are on the job today, helping to get the nation's air system operating safely. In the New York area, for example, four supervisors were scheduled to report for work, and seventeen additionally volunteered. At National Airport a traffic controller told a newsperson he had resigned from the union and reported to work because, "How can I ask my kids to obey the law if I don't?" This is a great tribute to America.

Let me make one thing plain. I respect the right of workers in the private sector to strike. Indeed, as president of my own union, I led the first strike ever called by that union. I guess I'm maybe the first one to ever hold this office who is a lifetime member of an AFL-CIO union. But we cannot compare labor-management relations in the private sector with government. Government cannot close down the assembly line. It has to provide without interruption the protective services which are government's reason for being.

It was in recognition of this that the Congress passed a law forbidding strikes by government employees against the public safety. Let me read the solemn oath taken by each of these employees, a sworn affidavit, when they accepted their jobs: "I am not participating in any strike against the Government of the United States or any agency thereof, and I will not so participate while an employee of the Government of the United States or any agency thereof."

It is for this reason that I must tell those who fail to report for duty this morning they are in violation of the law, and if they do not report for work within forty-eight hours, they have forfeited their jobs and will be terminated.

Remarks at the Eighty-fourth Annual Dinner of the Irish American Historical Society

NEW YORK CITY
NOVEMBER 6, 1981

On more than one occasion I got into scraps in the schoolyard because of some Protestant kid saying that the Catholic church basement was filled with rifles in preparation for the Pope's takeover of the United States. My father went to that church. I knew the story wasn't true; he had told me so. But there was a prejudice against Catholics in those days. At one time there was also a prejudice against the Irish in this country.

My father was both—Irish and Catholic. My mother was of English and Scottish descent and took my brother and me to the Protestant church. But I think anyone who's the least bit Irish, however, likes to consider himself so and wear a bit of the green. In any event, I've always considered myself an Irishman, and I love Irish events, such as this dinner I attended in New York.

D R. CAHILL,* I thank you and all those who are responsible for this great honor. And I want to say that I happen to know that there is one among us here who has known, also, today,

* Dr. Kevin Cahill, president of the Society.

the same joy and even greater, if possible, than I could feel. And that is Dr. Cahill himself, who this morning was presented by Cardinal Cooke, on behalf of the Pope, the Grand Cross Pro Merito Melitensi. He is the first American to ever receive this award.

Your Eminence, the other clergy here at the head table, the other distinguished guests, and one in particular that I might pick out and mention, Teddy Gleason of the International Longshoremen's Association. And I mention him because on Sunday he is going to celebrate the forty-second anniversary of his thirty-ninth birthday. Teddy, I've found that for some time, that makes it much easier to greet each one of these annual occasions.

But I do thank you very much. You know, there is the legend in Ireland of the happy colleen of Ballisodare who lived gaily among the wee people, the tiny people, for seven years, and then when she came home discovered that she had no toes. She had danced them off. I feel happy enough—when I get home tonight I'm going to count mine. [*Laughter*]

Nancy is sorry that she couldn't be here, and so am I. She sent her warm regards and her regrets. Unfortunately, on the last trip into town she picked up the bug.

Now, I'm happy to say that's not a situation for me, like the two sons of Ireland who were in the pub one evening and one asked the other about his wife. And he said, "Oh, she's terribly sick." He said, "She's terribly ill." And the other one says, "Oh, I'm sorry to hear that." But he said, "Is there any danger?" "Oh," he said, "no. She's too weak to be dangerous anymore." [*Laughter*]

A writer for the Irish press who was based in Washington, a correspondent for the press there, stated to me the other day— or stated the other day about me—that I have only recently developed a pride in my Irish heritage or background, and that up till now I have had an apathy about it. Well, let me correct the record. That is not so. I have been troubled until fairly recently about a lack of knowledge about my father's history.

My father was orphaned at age six. He knew very little about his family history. And so I grew up knowing nothing more beyond him than an old photograph, a single photo that he had of his mother and father, and no knowledge of that family history. But somehow, a funny thing happened to me on the way to Washington. [*Laughter*] When I changed my line of work about a year ago, it seemed that I became of a certain interest to people in Ireland, who very kindly began to fill me in. And so I have learned that my great-grandfather took off from the village of Ballyporeen in County Tipperary to come to America. And that isn't the limit to all that I have learned about that.

Some years ago, when I was just beginning in Hollywood in the motion picture business, I had been sentenced for the few years I'd been there to movies that the studio didn't want good, it wanted them Thursday. [*Laughter*]

And then came that opportunity that every actor asks for or hopes for, and that was a picture that was going to be made and the biography of the late Knute Rockne, the great immortal coach of Notre Dame. Pat O'Brien was to play Rockne. And there was a part in there that from my own experience as a sports announcer I had long dreamed of, the part of George Gipp. And generously, Pat O'Brien, who was then a star at the studio, held out his hand to a young aspiring actor, and I played Gipp. Pat playing Rockne, he himself will say, was the high point of his theatrical career. My playing "The Gipp" opened the door to stardom and a better kind of picture.

I've been asked at times, "What's it like to see yourself in the old movies, the reruns on TV?" It's like looking at a son you never knew you had. [*Laughter*] But I found out—in learning about my own heritage, going back to Ballyporeen—that, believe it or not, what a small world it is, Pat O'Brien's family came from Ballyporeen.

But I've been filled-in much more since. An historian has informed me that our family was one of the four tribes of Tara, and that from the year 200 until about 900 A.D., they defended the only pass through the Slieve Bloom Mountains. They held it for all those centuries and adopted the motto, "The Hills

Forever." And that, too, is strange, because for the better part of nine months now, I've been saying much the same thing, only in the singular: "The Hill Forever." Capitol Hill, that is. [*Laughter*]

I do remember my father telling me once when I was a boy, and with great pride he said to me, "The Irish are the only people in the country, in America, that built the jails and then filled them." [*Laughter*] I was a little perturbed even then, at that tender age, because at the sound of pride in his voice and from the way I'd been raised, I couldn't quite understand why that was something to be proud of, until I then later learned, which he had never explained to me, that he was referring to the fact that the overwhelming majority of men wearing the blue of the police department in America were of Irish descent.

You know, those weren't the only jobs that were open to the Irish. Back in the high day of vaudeville, long before sound pictures drove it out, there were, very popular in this country, comedians who would reach great stardom in vaudeville with a broad German accent. German comedians coming on *"Ach und Himmel Sie der."* What is little known in show business is that almost without exception, they were Irish. Their wit and humor that made them comedians, they came by naturally and honestly.

I was on a mission to England for our government some ten years ago. I should say to Europe, to several countries, and finally wound up and the last country was Ireland.

On the last day in Ireland, I was taken to Cashel Rock. I didn't know at that time that it's only twenty-five miles from Ballyporeen. But I do know that the young Irish guide who was showing us around the ruins of the ancient cathedral, there on the rock, finally took us to the little cemetery. We walked with great interest and looked at those ancient tombstones and the inscriptions.

And then we came to one and the inscription said: "Remember me as you pass by, for as you are, so once was I. But as I am, you too will be, so be content to follow me." And that was too much for the Irish wit and humor of someone who came after, because underneath was scratched: "To follow you I am content, I wish I knew which way you went." [*Laughter*]

But the Irish, like many, a great many of the people and like my grandfather, great-grandfather, were driven to the New World by famine and by tragedies of other kinds. The Irish—they built the railroads, they opened the West wearing the blue and gold of the United States Cavalry. There was John L. Sullivan, the heavyweight champion of the world, writers like Eugene O'Neill, clergy like Cardinal Cooke, and even physicians to the Pope like Dr. Cahill.

And it goes all the way back in our history. George Washington said, "When our friendless standard was first unfurled, who were the strangers who first mustered around our staff? And when it reeled in the fight, who more brilliantly sustained it than Erin's generous sons?" And a century and a half later, who else than George M. Cohan would write of the Grand Old Flag, the Stars and Stripes, and Yankee Doodle Dandy with the line, "I'm a real live nephew of my Uncle Sam."

There must have been a divine plan that brought to this blessed land people from every corner of the earth. And here, those people kept their love for the land of their origin at the same time that they pledged their love and loyalty to this new land, this great melting pot. They worked for it, they fought for it, and yes, they died for it—and none more bravely than Erin's generous sons.

Tragedy, as I've said, very often was the impetus that sent many to America. Today, as has been said here already tonight, there is tragedy again in the Emerald Isle. The cardinal prayed and His Holiness, the Pope, pleaded for peace when he visited Ireland. I think we all should pray that responsible leaders on both sides and the governments of the United Kingdom and the Republic of Ireland can bring peace to that beautiful isle once again. And once again, we can join John Locke in saying, "O Ireland, isn't it grand you look—like a bride in her rich adornment? And with all the pent-up love in [of] my heart, I bid you top o' the mornin'!"

No, I have no apathy, no feeling at all, I am just so grateful that among the other things that happened when I was allowed to move into public housing—[*Laughter*]—I had a chance, finally, to learn of the very rich heritage that my father had left me.

And I can only say once again, with heartfelt thanks, I wear this * and take it home with a feeling of great honor, and say something that I know to all of you is as familiar as "top o' the mornin' " or anything else. That is: "May the road rise beneath your feet, the sun shine warm upon your face, and the wind be always at your back, and may God, until we meet again, hold you in the hollow of His hand."

Thank you.

* The President was presented with a medal representing the Society's highest award.

Remarks at the
Conservative Political Action Conference

WASHINGTON, D.C.
MARCH 20, 1981

I went to these Conservative Political Action Conference events almost every year I was president. I attended before I was president, too. These were my people, the people who had labored for the conservative cause when it seemed like a hopeless endeavor. These were the people who fought the cause for individual liberty and freedom when the government seemed to be getting more powerful by the day. They were the people who persevered, and I can't tell you how much I admire them for their tenacity and their hope.

I also can't tell you how embattled we felt over the years. The pundits and the intelligentsia often treated us as if we were some kind of Neanderthals, our brains developed barely enough to come into our caves out of the rain. We were often ridiculed and usually dismissed. Such treatment only strengthened our ideals and our resolve.

The speech you're about to read is special because it marked a coming home. The evening was a celebration of what we'd worked so long for—a conservative president in the White House.

93

Mr. chairman* and Congressman Mickey Edwards, thank you very much. My goodness, I can't realize how much time has gone by, because I remember when I first knew Mickey, he was just a clean-shaven boy. [*Laughter*] But thank you for inviting me here once again. And as Mickey told you, with the exception of those two years, it is true about how often I've been here. So, let me say now that I hope we'll be able to keep this tradition going forward and that you'll invite me again next year.

And in the rough days ahead, and I know there will be such days, I hope that you'll be like the mother of the young lad in camp when the camp director told her that he was going to have to discipline her son. And she said, "Well, don't be too hard on him. He's very sensitive. Slap the boy next to him, and that will scare Irving." [*Laughter*] But let us also, tonight, salute those with vision who labored to found this group—the American Conservative Union, the Young Americans for Freedom, *National Review* and *Human Events*.

It's been said that anyone who seeks success or greatness should first forget about both and seek only the truth, and the rest will follow. Well, fellow truth seekers, none of us here tonight—contemplating the seal on this podium and a balanced budget in 1984—can argue with that kind of logic. For whatever history does finally say about our cause, it must say: The conservative movement in twentieth-century America held fast through hard and difficult years to its vision of the truth. And history must also say that our victory, when it was achieved, was not so much a victory of politics as it was a victory of ideas, not so much a victory for any one man or party as it was a victory for a set of principles—principles that were protected and nourished by a few unselfish Americans through many grim and heartbreaking defeats.

Now, you are those Americans that I'm talking about. I

* James Lacey, national chairman of the Young Americans for Freedom.

wanted to be here not just to acknowledge your efforts on my behalf, not just to remark that last November's victory was singularly your victory, not just to mention that the new administration in Washington is a testimony to your perseverance and devotion to principle, but to say simply, "Thank you," and to say those words not as a president, or even as a conservative; thank you as an American. I say this knowing that there are many in this room whose talents might have entitled them to a life of affluence but who chose another career out of a higher sense of duty to country. And I know, too, that the story of their selflessness will never be written up in *Time* or *Newsweek* or go down in the history books.

You know, on an occasion like this it's a little hard not to reminisce, not to think back and just realize how far we've come. The Portuguese have a word for such recollection—*saudade*—a poetic term rich with the dreams of yesterday. And surely in our past there was many a dream that went aglimmering and many a field littered with broken lances.

Who can forget that July night in San Francisco when Barry Goldwater told us that we must set the tides running again in the cause of freedom, and he said, "until our cause has won the day, inspired the world, and shown the way to a tomorrow worthy of all our yesteryears"? And had there not been a Barry Goldwater willing to take that lonely walk, we wouldn't be here talking of a celebration tonight.

But our memories are not just political ones. I like to think back about a small artfully written magazine named *National Review*, founded in 1955 and ridiculed by the intellectual establishment because it published an editorial that said it would stand athwart the course of history yelling, "Stop!" And then there was a sprightly written newsweekly coming out of Washington named *Human Events* that many said would never be taken seriously, but it would become later "must reading" not only for Capitol Hill insiders but for all of those in public life.

How many of us were there who used to go home from meetings like this with no thought of giving up, but still find

95

ourselves wondering in the dark of night whether this much-loved land might go the way of other great nations that lost a sense of mission and a passion for freedom?

There are so many people and institutions who come to mind for their role in the success we celebrate tonight. Intellectual leaders like Russell Kirk, Friedrich Hayek, Henry Hazlitt, Milton Friedman, James Burnham, Ludwig von Mises—they shaped so much of our thoughts.

It's especially hard to believe that it was only a decade ago, on a cold April day on a small hill in upstate New York, that another of these great thinkers, Frank Meyer, was buried. He'd made the awful journey that so many others had: He pulled himself from the clutches of "The God That Failed," and then in his writing fashioned a vigorous new synthesis of traditional and libertarian thought—a synthesis that is today recognized by many as modern conservatism.

It was Frank Meyer who reminded us that the robust individualism of the American experience was part of the deeper current of Western learning and culture. He pointed out that a respect for law, an appreciation for tradition, and regard for the social consensus that gives stability to our public and private institutions, these civilized ideas must still motivate us even as we seek a new economic prosperity based on reducing government interference in the marketplace.

Our goals complement each other. We're not cutting the budget simply for the sake of sounder financial management. This is only a first step toward returning power to the states and communities, only a first step toward reordering the relationship between citizen and government. We can make government again responsive to people not only by cutting its size and scope and thereby ensuring that its legitimate functions are performed efficiently and justly.

Because ours is a consistent philosophy of government, we can be very clear: We do not have a social agenda, separate, separate economic agenda, and a separate foreign agenda. We have one agenda. Just as surely as we seek to put our financial house in order and rebuild our nation's defenses, so too we seek to protect the unborn, to end the manipulation of schoolchildren by utopian planners, and permit the acknowledgment of a Supreme Being in our classrooms just as we allow such acknowledgments in other public institutions.

Now, obviously we're not going to be able to accomplish all this at once. The American people are patient. I think they realize that the wrongs done over several decades cannot be corrected instantly. You know, I had the pleasure in appearing before a Senate committee once while I was still governor, and I was challenged because there was a Republican president in the White House who'd been there for several months—why we hadn't then corrected everything that had been done. And the only way I could think to answer him is I told him about a ranch many years ago that Nancy and I acquired. It had a barn with eight stalls in it in which they had kept cattle, and we wanted to keep horses. And I was in there day after day with a pick and a shovel, lowering the level of those stalls, which had accumulated over the years. [*Laughter*] And I told this senator who'd asked that question that I discovered that you did not undo in weeks or months what it had taken some fifteen years to accumulate.

I also believe that we conservatives, if we mean to continue governing, must realize that it will not always be so easy to place the blame on the past for our national difficulties. You know, one day the great baseball manager Frankie Frisch sent a rookie out to play center field. The rookie promptly dropped the first fly ball that was hit to him. On the next play he let a grounder go between his feet and then threw the ball to the wrong base. Frankie stormed out of the dugout, took his glove away from him, and said, "I'll show you how to play this position." And the next batter slammed a line drive right over second base. Frankie came in on it, missed it completely, fell down when he tried to chase it, threw down his glove, and yelled at the rookie, "You've got center field so screwed up nobody can play it." [*Laughter*]

The point is we must lead a nation, and that means more than criticizing the past. Indeed, as T. S. Eliot once said, "Only by acceptance of the past will you alter its meaning."

Now, during our political efforts, we were the subject of much indifference and oftentimes intolerance, and that's why I hope our political victory will be remembered as a generous one and our time in power will be recalled for the tolerance we showed for those with whom we disagree.

But beyond this, beyond this we have to offer America and the world a larger vision. We must remove government's smothering hand from where it does harm; we must seek to revitalize the proper functions of government. But we do these things to set loose again the energy and the ingenuity of the American people. We do these things to reinvigorate those social and economic institutions which serve as a buffer and a bridge between the individual and the state—and which remain the real source of our progress as a people.

And we must hold out this exciting prospect of an orderly, compassionate, pluralistic society—an archipelago of prospering communities and divergent institutions—a place where a free and energetic people can work out their own destiny under God.

I know that some will think about the perilous world we live in and the dangerous decade before us and ask what practical effect this conservative vision can have today. When Prime Minister Thatcher was here recently we both remarked on the sudden, overwhelming changes that had come recently to politics in both our countries.

At our last official function, I told the Prime Minister that everywhere we look in the world the cult of the state is dying. And I held out hope that it wouldn't be long before those of our adversaries who preach the supremacy of the state were remembered only for their role in a sad, rather bizarre chapter in human history. The largest planned economy in the world has to buy food elsewhere or its people would starve.

We've heard in our century far too much of the sounds of anguish from those who live under totalitarian rule. We've seen too many monuments made not out of marble or stone but out of barbed wire and terror. But from these terrible places have come survivors, witnesses to the triumph of the human spirit over the mystique of state power, prisoners whose spiritual values made them the rulers of their guards. With their survival, they brought us "the secret of the camps," a lesson for our time and for any age: Evil is powerless if the good are unafraid.

That's why the Marxist vision of man without God must eventually be seen as an empty and a false faith—the second-oldest in the world—first proclaimed in the Garden of Eden with whispered words of temptation: "Ye shall be as gods." The crisis of the Western World, Whittaker Chambers reminded us, exists to the degree in which it is indifferent to God. "The Western World does not know it," he said about our struggle, "but it already possesses the answer to this problem —but only provided that its faith in God and the freedom He enjoins is as great as communism's faith in man."

This is the real task before us: to reassert our commitment as a nation to a law higher than our own, to renew our spiritual strength. Only by building a wall of such spiritual resolve can we, as a free people, hope to protect our own heritage and make it someday the birthright of all men.

There is, in America, a greatness and a tremendous heritage of idealism which is a reservoir of strength and goodness. It is ours if we will but tap it. And, because of this—because that greatness is there—there is need in America today for a reaffirmation of that goodness and a reformation of our greatness.

The dialog and the deeds of the past few decades are not sufficient to the day in which we live. They cannot keep the promise of tomorrow. The encrusted bureaucracies and the ingrained procedures which have developed of late respond neither to the minority nor the majority. We've come to a turning point. We have a decision to make. Will we continue with yesterday's agenda and yesterday's failures, or will we reassert our ideals and our standards, will we reaffirm our faith, and renew our purpose? This is a time for choosing.

I made a speech by that title in 1964. I said, "We've been

told increasingly that we must choose between left or right." But we're still using those terms—left or right. And I'll repeat what I said then in '64. "There is no left or right. There's only an up or down": up to the ultimate in individual freedom, man's age-old dream, the ultimate in individual freedom consistent with an orderly society—or down to the totalitarianism of the ant heap. And those today who, however good their intentions, tell us that we should trade freedom for security are on that downward path.

Those of us who call ourselves conservative have pointed out what's wrong with government policy for more than a quarter of a century. Now we have an opportunity to make policy and to change our national direction. All of us in government—in the House, in the Senate, in the executive branch—and in private life can now stand together. We can stop the drain on the economy by the public sector. We can restore our national prosperity. We can replace the overregulated society with the creative society. We can appoint to the bench distinguished judges who understand the first responsibility of any legal system is to punish the guilty and protect the innocent. We can restore to their rightful place in our national consciousness the values of family, work, neighborhood, and religion. And finally, we can see to it that the nations of the world clearly understand America's intentions and respect our resolve.

Now we have the opportunity—yes, and the necessity—to prove that the American promise is equal to the task of redressing our grievances and equal to the challenge of inventing a great tomorrow.

This reformation, this renaissance, will not be achieved or will it be served by those who engage in political claptrap or false promises. It will not be achieved by those who set people against people, class against class, or institution against institution. So, while we celebrate our recent political victory we must understand there's much work before us: to gain control again of government, to reward personal initiative and risk-taking in the marketplace, to revitalize our system of federalism, to strengthen the private institutions that make up the independent sector of our society, and to make our own spiritual affirmation in the face of those who would deny man has a place before God. Not easy tasks perhaps. But I would remind you as I did on January 20th, they're not impossible, because, after all, we're Americans.

This year we will celebrate a victory won two centuries ago at Yorktown, the victory of a small, fledgling nation over a mighty world power. How many people are aware—I've been told that a British band played the music at that surrender ceremony because we didn't have a band. [*Laughter*] And they played a tune that was very popular in England at the time. Its title was "The World Turned Upside Down." I'm sure it was far more appropriate than they realized at that moment. The heritage from that long, difficult struggle is before our eyes today in this city, in the great halls of our government and in the monuments to the memory of our great men.

It is this heritage that evokes the images of a much-loved land, a land of struggling settlers and lonely immigrants, of giant cities and great frontiers, images of all that our country is and all that we want her to be. That's the America entrusted to us, to stand by, to protect, and yes, to lead her wisely.

Fellow citizens, fellow conservatives, our time is now. Our moment has arrived. We stand together shoulder to shoulder in the thickest of the fight. If we carry the day and turn the tide, we can hope that as long as men speak of freedom and those who have protected it, they will remember us, and they will say, "Here were the brave and here their place of honor."

Thank you.

Remarks on the Departure of the U.S. Delegation to Funeral Services for President Anwar Sadat

WHITE HOUSE SOUTH LAWN
OCTOBER 8, 1981

When news of President Sadat's assassination came, both Nancy and I had the same feeling—this is personal with us. He had crossed the line from that of simply another head of state with whom we did business to something more. Our sense of loss was personal with him, and we still keep in contact with Mrs. Sadat, whom we also greatly admire.

Just two months before, he had made an official state visit to the U.S. There were welcoming ceremonies with twenty-one–gun salutes, substantive meetings, and a state dinner with toasts to each other's health and friendship. And then it seemed he no sooner returned home than he was gone.

Anwar was a warm human being who didn't hold back from personalizing things. He had a wonderful laugh and a remarkable courage. He was one of a kind, and it's a damn shame we lost him.

Former presidents Nixon, Ford, and Carter led our official delegation to his funeral. I delivered the following remarks on the South Lawn of the White House on a cold, rainy evening before they departed.

ON BEHALF OF THE COUNTRY, I want to express a heartfelt thanks to Presidents Nixon, Ford, and Carter, and Mrs. Carter, for undertaking this sad mission. Their presence in Cairo will express to the Egyptian people the depth of America's grief and sorrow at the loss of a great leader and a beloved friend.

Today the American people stand beside the Egyptian people —the people of a new nation with the people of an ancient land; people of the West with the people of the East. We stand together in mourning the loss of Anwar Sadat and rededicating ourselves to the cause for which he so willingly gave his life.

There are times, there are moments in history, when the martyrdom of a single life can symbolize all that's wrong with an age and all that is right about humanity. The noble remnants of such lives—the spoken words of an Illinois lawyer who lived in this house, the diary of a young Dutch schoolgirl, the final moments of a soldier-statesman from Mit Abu el-Qum—can gain the force and power that endures and inspires and wins the ultimate triumph over the forces of violence, madness, and hatred.

Anwar Sadat, a man of peace in a time of violence, understood his age. In his final moments, as he had during all his days, he stood in defiance of the enemies of peace, the enemies of humanity. Today, those of us who follow him can do no less. And so to those who rejoice in the death of Anwar Sadat, to those who seek to set class against class, nation against nation, people against people, those who would choose violence over brotherhood and who prefer war over peace, let us stand in defiance and let our words of warning to them be clear: In life you feared Anwar Sadat, but in death you must fear him more. For the memory of this good and brave man will vanquish you. The meaning of his life and the cause for which he stood will endure and triumph. Not too long ago, he was asked in an interview if he didn't fear the possibility of the kind of violence that has now just taken his life. And he said, "I will not die one hour before God decides it is time for me to go."

Again, a heartfelt thank you to these men here, these three who are making this mission on behalf of our country. I thank you, and if I may, in the language of my own ancestry, say: Until we meet again, may God hold you in the hollow of His hand.

1982

Address to Members of the British Parliament

PALACE OF WESTMINSTER
JUNE 8, 1982

We had a rough year economically and politically in 1982. The recession, which began under my predecessor, hit full force in 1982. My Democratic opponents in the Congress began blaming our economic program, which they called Reaganomics, for the recession even before our tax and budget cuts had gone into effect. That really burned me up. Of course, after our program took effect and began turning the economy around, they didn't call it Reaganomics anymore. Unfortunately, that was too late for the congressional elections, in which the Republicans lost a number of seats.

But I think the real story of 1982 is that we began applying conservatism to foreign affairs. When I came into office, I believed there had been mistakes in our policy toward the Soviets in particular. I wanted to do some things differently, like speaking the truth about them for a change, rather than hiding reality behind the niceties of diplomacy. In the section for next year, for example, you'll see that I even called them an evil empire. That woke everybody up.

This speech before the British Parliament examined the West's concepts of democracy and its attitude toward communism and is probably one of the most important speeches I gave as president. What eventually flowed from it became known as the Reagan Doctrine, which was our often controversial policy of supporting those fighting for freedom and against communism wherever we found them. And we found them in such places as Afghanistan, Nicaragua, and Angola.

This address also fit into my plan of speaking my mind about communism. In retrospect, I am amazed that our national leaders had not philosophically and intellectually taken on the principles of Marxist-Leninism. We were always too worried we would offend the Soviets if we struck at anything so basic. Well, so what? Marxist-Leninist thought is an empty cupboard. Everyone knew it by the 1980s, but no one was saying it. I decided to articulate a few of these things.

I think our honesty helped the Soviets face up to their own weaknesses and uncertain future. General Secretary Gorbachev has had the foresight to see things previous Soviet leaders had been unwilling to see. We'll talk about my friend Gorbachev later. This speech is before his time.

M Y LORD CHANCELLOR, Mr. Speaker:

The journey of which this visit forms a part is a long one. Already it has taken me to two great cities of the West, Rome and Paris, and to the economic summit at Versailles. And there, once again, our sister democracies have proved that even in a time of severe economic strain, free peoples can work together freely and voluntarily to address problems as serious as inflation, unemployment, trade, and economic development in a spirit of cooperation and solidarity.

Other milestones lie ahead. Later this week, in Germany, we and our NATO allies will discuss measures for our joint defense and America's latest initiatives for a more peaceful, secure world through arms reductions.

Each stop of this trip is important, but among them all, this moment occupies a special place in my heart and in the hearts of my countrymen—a moment of kinship and homecoming in these hallowed halls.

Speaking for all Americans, I want to say how very much at home we feel in your house. Every American would, because this is, as we have been so eloquently told, one of democracy's shrines. Here the rights of free people and the processes of representation have been debated and refined.

It has been said that an institution is the lengthening shadow of a man. This institution is the lengthening shadow of all the men and women who have sat here and all those who have voted to send representatives here.

This is my second visit to Great Britain as president of the United States. My first opportunity to stand on British soil occurred almost a year and a half ago when your prime minister graciously hosted a diplomatic dinner at the British Embassy in Washington. Mrs. Thatcher said then that she hoped I was not distressed to find staring down at me from the grand staircase a portrait of His Royal Majesty King George III. She suggested it was best to let bygones be bygones, and in view of our two countries' remarkable friendship in succeeding years, she added that most Englishmen today would agree with Thomas Jefferson that "a little rebellion now and then is a very good thing." [*Laughter*]

Well, from here I will go to Bonn and then Berlin, where there stands a grim symbol of power untamed. The Berlin Wall, that dreadful gray gash across the city, is in its third decade. It is the fitting signature of the regime that built it.

And a few hundred kilometers behind the Berlin Wall, there is another symbol. In the center of Warsaw, there is a sign that notes the distances to two capitals. In one direction it points toward Moscow. In the other it points toward Brussels, headquarters of Western Europe's tangible unity. The marker says that the distances from Warsaw to Moscow and Warsaw to Brussels are equal. The sign makes this point: Poland is not East or West. Poland is at the center of European civilization. It has contributed mightily to that civilization. It is doing so today by being magnificently unreconciled to oppression.

Poland's struggle to be Poland and to secure the basic rights we often take for granted demonstrates why we dare not take those rights for granted. Gladstone, defending the Reform Bill of 1866, declared, "You cannot fight against the future. Time is on our side." It was easier to believe in the march of democracy in Gladstone's day—in that high noon of Victorian optimism.

We're approaching the end of a bloody century plagued by a terrible political invention—totalitarianism. Optimism comes less easily today, not because democracy is less vigorous, but because democracy's enemies have refined their instruments of repression. Yet optimism is in order, because day by day democracy is proving itself to be a not-at-all-fragile flower. From Stettin on the Baltic to Varna on the Black Sea, the regimes planted by totalitarianism have had more than thirty years to establish their legitimacy. But none—not one regime—has yet been able to risk free elections. Regimes planted by bayonets do not take root.

The strength of the Solidarity movement in Poland demonstrates the truth told in an underground joke in the Soviet Union. It is that the Soviet Union would remain a one-party nation even if an opposition party were permitted, because everyone would join the opposition party. [*Laughter*]

America's time as a player on the stage of world history has been brief. I think understanding this fact has always made you patient with your younger cousins—well, not always patient. I do recall that on one occasion, Sir Winston Churchill said in exasperation about one of our most distinguished diplomats: "He is the only case I know of a bull who carries his china shop with him." [*Laughter*]

But witty as Sir Winston was, he also had that special attribute of great statesmen—the gift of vision, the willingness to see the future based on the experience of the past. It is this sense of history, this understanding of the past that I want to talk with you about today, for it is in remembering what we share of the past that our two nations can make common cause for the future.

We have not inherited an easy world. If developments like the Industrial Revolution, which began here in England, and the gifts of science and technology have made life much easier for us, they have also made it more dangerous. There are threats now to our freedom, indeed to our very existence, that other generations could never even have imagined.

There is first the threat of global war. No president, no congress, no prime minister, no parliament can spend a day entirely free of this threat. And I don't have to tell you that in today's world the existence of nuclear weapons could mean, if not the extinction of mankind, then surely the end of civilization as we know it. That's why negotiations on intermediate-range nuclear forces now under way in Europe and the START talks—Strategic Arms Reduction Talks—which will begin later this month, are not just critical to American or Western policy; they are critical to mankind. Our commitment to early success in these negotiations is firm and unshakable, and our purpose is clear: reducing the risk of war by reducing the means of waging war on both sides.

At the same time there is a threat posed to human freedom by the enormous power of the modern state. History teaches the dangers of government that overreaches—political control taking precedence over free economic growth, secret police, mindless bureaucracy, all combining to stifle individual excellence and personal freedom.

Now, I'm aware that among us here and throughout Europe there is legitimate disagreement over the extent to which the public sector should play a role in a nation's economy and life. But on one point all of us are united—our abhorrence of dictatorship in all its forms, but most particularly totalitarianism and the terrible inhumanities it has caused in our time—the great purge, Auschwitz and Dachau, the gulag, and Cambodia.

Historians looking back at our time will note the consistent restraint and peaceful intentions of the West. They will note that it was the democracies who refused to use the threat of their nuclear monopoly in the forties and early fifties for territorial or imperial gain. Had that nuclear monopoly been in the hands of the Communist world, the map of Europe—indeed, the world—would look very different today. And certainly they will note it was not the democracies that invaded Afghanistan or suppressed Polish Solidarity or used chemical and toxic warfare in Afghanistan and Southeast Asia.

If history teaches anything, it teaches self-delusion in the face of unpleasant facts is folly. We see around us today the marks of our terrible dilemma—predictions of doomsday, antinuclear demonstrations, an arms race in which the West must, for its own protection, be an unwilling participant. At the same time we see totalitarian forces in the world who seek subversion and conflict around the globe to further their barbarous assault on the human spirit. What, then, is our course? Must civilization perish in a hail of fiery atoms? Must freedom wither in a quiet, deadening accommodation with totalitarian evil?

Sir Winston Churchill refused to accept the inevitability of war or even that it was imminent. He said, "I do not believe that Soviet Russia desires war. What they desire is the fruits of war and the indefinite expansion of their power and doctrines. But what we have to consider here today while time remains is the permanent prevention of war and the establishment of conditions of freedom and democracy as rapidly as possible in all countries."

Well, this is precisely our mission today: to preserve freedom as well as peace. It may not be easy to see; but I believe we live now at a turning point.

In an ironic sense Karl Marx was right. We are witnessing today a great revolutionary crisis, a crisis where the demands of the economic order are conflicting directly with those of the political order. But the crisis is happening not in the free, non-Marxist West, but in the home of Marxist-Leninism, the Soviet Union. It is the Soviet Union that runs against the tide of history by denying human freedom and human dignity to its citizens. It also is in deep economic difficulty. The rate of growth in the national product has been steadily declining since the fifties and is less than half of what it was then.

The dimensions of this failure are astounding: A country

which employs one-fifth of its population in agriculture is unable to feed its own people. Were it not for the private sector, the tiny private sector tolerated in Soviet agriculture, the country might be on the brink of famine. These private plots occupy a bare 3 percent of the arable land but account for nearly one-quarter of Soviet farm output and nearly one-third of meat products and vegetables. Overcentralized, with little or no incentives, year after year the Soviet system pours its best resources into the making of instruments of destruction. The constant shrinkage of economic growth combined with the growth of military production is putting a heavy strain on the Soviet people. What we see here is a political structure that no longer corresponds to its economic base, a society where productive forces are hampered by political ones.

The decay of the Soviet experiment should come as no surprise to us. Wherever the comparisons have been made between free and closed societies—West Germany and East Germany, Austria and Czechoslovakia, Malaysia and Vietnam—it is the democratic countries that are prosperous and responsive to the needs of their people. And one of the simple but overwhelming facts of our time is this: Of all the millions of refugees we've seen in the modern world, their flight is always away from, not toward the Communist world. Today on the NATO line, our military forces face east to prevent a possible invasion. On the other side of the line, the Soviet forces also face east to prevent their people from leaving.

The hard evidence of totalitarian rule has caused in mankind an uprising of the intellect and will. Whether it is the growth of the new schools of economics in America or England or the appearance of the so-called new philosophers in France, there is one unifying thread running through the intellectual work of these groups—rejection of the arbitrary power of the state, the refusal to subordinate the rights of the individual to the superstate, the realization that collectivism stifles all the best human impulses.

Since the exodus from Egypt, historians have written of those who sacrificed and struggled for freedom—the stand at Thermopylae, the revolt of Spartacus, the storming of the Bastille, the Warsaw uprising in World War II. More recently we've seen evidence of this same human impulse in one of the developing nations in Central America. For months and months the world news media covered the fighting in El Salvador. Day after day we were treated to stories and film slanted toward the brave freedom fighters battling oppressive government forces in behalf of the silent, suffering people of that tortured country.

And then one day those silent, suffering people were offered a chance to vote, to choose the kind of government they wanted. Suddenly the freedom fighters in the hills were exposed for what they really are—Cuban-backed guerrillas who want power for themselves, and their backers, not democracy for the people. They threatened death to any who voted, and destroyed hundreds of buses and trucks to keep the people from getting to the polling places. But on election day, the people of El Salvador, an unprecedented 1.4 million of them, braved ambush and gunfire, and trudged for miles to vote for freedom.

They stood for hours in the hot sun waiting for their turn to vote. Members of our Congress who went there as observers told me of a woman who was wounded by rifle fire on the way to the polls, who refused to leave the line to have her wound treated until after she had voted. A grandmother, who had been told by the guerrillas she would be killed when she returned from the polls, and she told the guerrillas, "You can kill me, you can kill my family, kill my neighbors, but you can't kill us all." The real freedom fighters of El Salvador turned out to be the people of that country—the young, the old, the in-between.

Strange, but in my own country there's been little if any news coverage of that war since the election. Now, perhaps they'll say it's—well, because there are newer struggles now.

On distant islands in the South Atlantic young men are fighting for Britain. And yes, voices have been raised protesting their sacrifice for lumps of rock and earth so far away. But those young men aren't fighting for mere real estate. They fight for a cause—for the belief that armed aggression must not be allowed to succeed, and the people must participate in the decisions of government—[*Applause*]—the decisions of government under the rule of law. If there had been firmer support for that principle some forty-five years ago, perhaps our generation wouldn't have suffered the bloodletting of World War II.

In the Middle East now the guns sound once more, this time in Lebanon, a country that for too long has had to endure the tragedy of civil war, terrorism, and foreign intervention and occupation. The fighting in Lebanon on the part of all parties must stop, and Israel should bring its forces home. But this is not enough. We must all work to stamp out the scourge of terrorism that in the Middle East makes war an ever-present threat.

But beyond the trouble spots lies a deeper, more positive pattern. Around the world today, the democratic revolution is gathering new strength. In India a critical test has been passed with the peaceful change of governing political parties. In Africa, Nigeria is moving in remarkable and unmistakable ways to build and strengthen its democratic institutions. In the Caribbean and Central America, sixteen of twenty-four countries have freely elected governments. And in the United Nations, eight of the ten developing nations which have joined that body in the past five years are democracies.

In the Communist world as well, man's instinctive desire for freedom and self-determination surfaces again and again. To be sure, there are grim reminders of how brutally the police state attempts to snuff out this quest for self-rule—1953 in East Germany, 1956 in Hungary, 1968 in Czechoslovakia, 1981 in Poland. But the struggle continues in Poland. And we know that there are even those who strive and suffer for freedom within the confines of the Soviet Union itself. How we conduct ourselves here in the Western democracies will determine whether this trend continues.

No, democracy is not a fragile flower. Still it needs cultivating. If the rest of this century is to witness the gradual growth of freedom and democratic ideals, we must take actions to assist the campaign for democracy.

Some argue that we should encourage democratic change in

right-wing dictatorships, but not in Communist regimes. Well, to accept this preposterous notion—as some well-meaning people have—is to invite the argument that once countries achieve a nuclear capability, they should be allowed an undisturbed reign of terror over their own citizens. We reject this course.

As for the Soviet view, Chairman Brezhnev repeatedly has stressed that the competition of ideas and systems must continue and that this is entirely consistent with relaxation of tensions and peace.

Well, we ask only that these systems begin by living up to their own constitutions, abiding by their own laws, and complying with the international obligations they have undertaken. We ask only for a process, a direction, a basic code of decency, not for an instant transformation.

We cannot ignore the fact that even without our encouragement there has been and will continue to be repeated explosions against repression and dictatorships. The Soviet Union itself is not immune to this reality. Any system is inherently unstable that has no peaceful means to legitimize its leaders. In such cases, the very repressiveness of the state ultimately drives people to resist it, if necessary, by force.

While we must be cautious about forcing the pace of change, we must not hesitate to declare our ultimate objectives and to take concrete actions to move toward them. We must be staunch in our conviction that freedom is not the sole prerogative of a lucky few, but the inalienable and universal right of all human beings. So states the United Nations Universal Declaration of Human Rights, which, among other things, guarantees free elections.

The objective I propose is quite simple to state: to foster the infrastructure of democracy, the system of a free press, unions, political parties, universities, which allows a people to choose their own way to develop their own culture, to reconcile their own differences through peaceful means.

This is not cultural imperialism, it is providing the means for genuine self-determination and protection for diversity. Democracy already flourishes in countries with very different cultures and historical experiences. It would be cultural condescension, or worse, to say that any people prefer dictatorship to democracy. Who would voluntarily choose not to have the right to vote, decide to purchase government propaganda handouts instead of independent newspapers, prefer government- to worker-controlled unions, opt for land to be owned by the state instead of those who till it, want government repression of religious liberty, a single political party instead of a free choice, a rigid cultural orthodoxy instead of democratic tolerance and diversity?

Since 1917 the Soviet Union has given covert political training and assistance to Marxist-Leninists in many countries. Of course, it also has promoted the use of violence and subversion by these same forces. Over the past several decades, West European and other Social Democrats, Christian Democrats, and leaders have offered open assistance to fraternal, political, and social institutions to bring about peaceful and democratic progress. Appropriately, for a vigorous new democracy, the Federal Republic of Germany's political foundations have become a major force in this effort.

We in America now intend to take additional steps, as many of our allies have already done, toward realizing this same goal. The chairmen and other leaders of the national Republican and Democratic party organizations are initiating a study with the bipartisan American Political Foundation to determine how the United States can best contribute as a nation to the global campaign for democracy now gathering force. They will have the cooperation of congressional leaders of both parties, along with representatives of business, labor, and other major institutions in our society. I look forward to receiving their recommendations and to working with these institutions and the Congress in the common task of strengthening democracy throughout the world.

It is time that we committed ourselves as a nation—in both the public and private sectors—to assisting democratic development.

We plan to consult with leaders of other nations as well.

There is a proposal before the Council of Europe to invite parliamentarians from democratic countries to a meeting next year in Strasbourg. That prestigious gathering could consider ways to help democratic political movements.

This November in Washington there will take place an international meeting on free elections. And next spring there will be a conference of world authorities on constitutionalism and self-government hosted by the Chief Justice of the United States. Authorities from a number of developing and developed countries—judges, philosophers, and politicians with practical experience—have agreed to explore how to turn principle into practice and further the rule of law.

At the same time, we invite the Soviet Union to consider with us how the competition of ideas and values—which it is committed to support—can be conducted on a peaceful and reciprocal basis. For example, I am prepared to offer President Brezhnev an opportunity to speak to the American people on our television if he will allow me the same opportunity with the Soviet people. We also suggest that panels of our newsmen periodically appear on each other's television to discuss major events.

Now, I don't wish to sound overly optimistic, yet the Soviet Union is not immune from the reality of what is going on in the world. It has happened in the past—a small ruling elite either mistakenly attempts to ease domestic unrest through greater repression and foreign adventure, or it chooses a wiser course. It begins to allow its people a voice in their own destiny. Even if this latter process is not realized soon, I believe the renewed strength of the democratic movement, complemented by a global campaign for freedom, will strengthen the prospects for arms control and a world at peace.

I have discussed on other occasions, including my address on May 9th, the elements of Western policies toward the Soviet Union to safeguard our interests and protect the peace. What I am describing now is a plan and a hope for the long term—the march of freedom and democracy which will leave Marxism-Leninism on the ash heap of history as it has left other tyrannies which stifle the freedom and muzzle the self-expression of the people. And that's why we must continue our efforts to strengthen NATO even as we move forward with our Zero-Option initiative in the negotiations on intermediate-range forces and our proposal for a one-third reduction in strategic ballistic missile warheads.

Our military strength is a prerequisite to peace, but let it be clear we maintain this strength in the hope it will never be used, for the ultimate determinant in the struggle that's now going on in the world will not be bombs and rockets, but a test of wills and ideas, a trial of spiritual resolve, the values we hold, the beliefs we cherish, the ideals to which we are dedicated.

The British people know that, given strong leadership, time, and a little bit of hope, the forces of good ultimately rally and triumph over evil. Here among you is the cradle of self-government, the mother of parliaments. Here is the enduring greatness of the British contribution to mankind, the great civilized ideas: individual liberty, representative government, and the rule of law under God.

I've often wondered about the shyness of some of us in the West about standing for these ideals that have done so much to ease the plight of man and the hardships of our imperfect world. This reluctance to use those vast resources at our command reminds me of the elderly lady whose home was bombed in the Blitz. As the rescuers moved about, they found a bottle of brandy she'd stored behind the staircase, which was all that was left standing. And since she was barely conscious, one of the workers pulled the cork to give her a taste of it. She came around immediately and said, "Here now—there now, put it back. That's for emergencies." [*Laughter*]

Well, the emergency is upon us. Let us be shy no longer. Let us go to our strength. Let us offer hope. Let us tell the world that a new age is not only possible but probable.

During the dark days of the Second World War, when this island was incandescent with courage, Winston Churchill exclaimed about Britain's adversaries, "What kind of a people do they think we are?" Well, Britain's adversaries found out what extraordinary people the British are. But all the democracies paid a terrible price for allowing the dictators to underestimate us. We dare not make that mistake again. So, let us ask ourselves, "What kind of people do we think we are?" And let us answer, "Free people, worthy of freedom and determined not only to remain so but to help others gain their freedom as well."

Sir Winston led his people to great victory in war and then lost an election just as the fruits of victory were about to be enjoyed. But he left office honorably, and as it turned out, temporarily, knowing that the liberty of his people was more important than the fate of any single leader. History recalls his greatness in ways no dictator will ever know. And he left us a message of hope for the future, as timely now as when he first uttered it, as opposition leader in the Commons nearly twenty-seven years ago, when he said, "When we look back on all the perils through which we have passed and at the mighty foes that we have laid low and all the dark and deadly designs that we have frustrated, why should we fear for our future? We have," he said, "come safely through the worst."

Well, the task I've set forth will long outlive our own generation. But together, we too have come through the worst. Let us now begin a major effort to secure the best—a crusade for freedom that will engage the faith and fortitude of the next generation. For the sake of peace and justice, let us move toward a world in which all people are at last free to determine their own destiny.

Thank you.

-- Thank you. Boy, I cleaned up -- a Golden E pin, a bust in
my honor, and induction into the Eureka Athletic Hall of
Fame. I've been lucky enough to receive a couple other
~~I thought I'd reached the pinnacle when~~
commendations from our alma mater. listen to what the 1931
said that as
Prism had to say, "Dutch Reagan, president of the Booster
Club, received commendation for his part in managing the
committees in charge of the homecoming festivities." . . .
remember first what I said. There are a few
I Wish I could manage the committees in the Congress with as
congressional committees I'd like to manage.
much success.

I've stopped telling anyone about receiving Eureka Centennial
-- I was telling some people the other day that in 1955 I
Citation in 1955. People thought it referred to my centennial.
received Eureka's Centennial Citation. They thought that
was wonderful because I didn't look that old. And you know
there's a Reagan Memorabilia Collection on campus. Ed Meese
is scared to death that after we leave office, he's going to
be in it.

I've spent the day in a warm flood of
- But, honestly, today genuinely has caused a flood of
nostalgia.
memories for me. you must be feeling the same way. And I know you're feeling the very same
emotions. Eureka is something that's in all our hearts.

Eureka College Alumni Dinner

PEORIA, ILLINOIS
MAY 9, 1982

*While I was back in Illinois giving a commencement address at
my alma mater, I also attended an alumni dinner. This was
pure heaven for me. I love Eureka College. It's a very small
school without a national Ivy League reputation, but if I had it
to do all over again, I'd go right back there for my education.*

*The advantage of a smaller school is that you can't be anon-
ymous. On these megacampuses with tens of thousands of students, you can get lost. You can escape being part of campus*

life. In small schools, everybody is part of college life. You're asked to do things because they always need people on this committee or that one.

Also in small schools, the faculty has personal knowledge of you. In my day, the professors would know who your steady girl was or whom you were dating. Sometimes a professor would ask you to watch his house for him while he and his wife went out for the evening. Now, there's no reason in Eureka, Illinois, for someone to watch your house. But the professor knew full well this would give you a chance to sit in front of the fire with a girl.

I genuinely enjoy reminiscing and I did my share of it that evening.

W ELL, I THANK JUST EVERYBODY. I've cleaned up—a Golden E pin, a plaque, a bust in my honor, being in the Eureka Athletic Hall of Fame. I thought I had reached the pinnacle when the 1931 *Prism* said that as president of the Booster Club I received commendation for my part in managing the committees in charge of the homecoming festivities. [*Laughter*] You don't know how much I wish I could remember what I did. [*Laughter*] There are a few committees on Capitol Hill that need some managing right now. [*Laughter*]

But, Mac,* this—if we could have gotten this many people to a football game on a Saturday afternoon, we wouldn't have had to wear the same pants two or three years. [*Laughter*] We could have had you new uniforms. But I'm not quite sure whether I got this for three years as guard or for making some touchdowns for Notre Dame at Warner Brothers. [*Laughter*]

I was interviewed just the other day before I came out here by a reporter from the *Bloomington Pantagraph*, who came up and wanted to talk all about memories, Illinois here and Eureka

---

* William McNett, president of the Eureka College Alumni Association.

College and all. And then he said, "Well now, there's a story going around about you scoring a touchdown against Normal in the last minutes of play." And that just goes to show you how stories can get stretched. [*Laughter*] I can tell you about that touchdown.

We were one point ahead, as I remember. And there was just seconds to go. I'd been in the entire game, and Normal was passing, throwing bombs all over. And I finally decided because —you remember that no one in our backfield was over about five nine or ten in those days, so our pass defense wasn't all it should be if anyone on the other side was taller than they were. So, I used to charge against my man and then when I felt it was going to be a pass, duck back into the secondary and see if I could help cover for passes.

And I saw everyone sucked over to one side of the field, and this Normal fellow—never forget that bright red jersey—going down the field all by himself. And I took out after him. And pretty soon, as he was looking back, I knew the ball must be coming. And I turned around and here it came, and I went up in the air, I got it, but by this time, as I say, having been in the entire game, I knew that there wasn't anything left in me. There was a lineman's dream, a guard way over on the sideline, about seventy-five yards from the goal line but a clear field down that sideline. But coming down with the ball, I thought if I just juggle it for a second or two, he'll tackle me. We still win the ball game, and I won't have to run. [*Laughter*]

Well, I juggled it and I bent over, and I juggled it some more and nothing happened. [*Laughter*] And just as I started to raise my head, he put his arms around me and said, "Tag, you're it." [*Laughter*]

At the same moment, I saw a substitute coming in for me, I knew. And I started for the sideline, and one Ralph McKenzie, very serious of face—indeed, angry of face—said, "What happened to you?" And all I could say was, "I'm tired." [*Laughter*] But that—I told the reporter—that was my touchdown that was never made, my lineman's dream.

You know, one thing I've stopped talking about is that—

receiving Eureka's centennial citation in 1955. Too many people began to think it was *my* centennial. [*Laughter*]

But I've spent the day in a warm flood of nostalgia, as I'm sure a great many of you have. You must be feeling the same way. Eureka is in all our hearts. And it gave me the greatest happiness today to be on the campus and to see today's students and to see that that same spirit and that same love is there among them every bit as great as it has been among us. They'll carry the memory of days at Eureka as abundantly and warm as we have carried them.

I got a letter a few months ago from Mrs. Lee Putnam, class of '50. Lee, are you here someplace? There. Hey, you don't mind if I let them in on your letter. Lee is the daughter of Professor Tom Wiggins, our English professor that so many of us remember so well. And she wrote me this letter about some of the memories that she had of her recollections of the 1930s at Eureka. Well, if she was the class of '50, she had to be pretty young in the 1930s. But she said they're vivid—"faculty teas before the fireplace; Daddy reading; Mother playing the piano; bluebooks being graded; having Carl Sandburg as an overnight guest; and eating canned salmon, spinach, and baked beans night after night. [*Laughter*] The college had an arrangement with the Happy Hour Canning Factory in Bloomington which allowed us to order canned goods, since no salaries were paid during that time." And that's right.

"We also received dairy products from the college farm run by Frank Felter. I was too young to be aware then, but the entire community must have pitched in to save Eureka College." And that is what happened.

Day after day in those classrooms, those professors just as if they were getting paid on time—I've thought about that sometimes when I see some teachers' strikes lately. But I believe that that spirit is still at Eureka—in the town, the faculty, and the students.

And Lee, I have to tell you a memory that I have of your father—God bless him. It seems that the late Bud Cole—God rest his soul—and I were declared ineligible if we did not take a makeup exam, and it was the day before the homecoming game. So, we went over to the gym that afternoon, and we got into our football uniforms. And then we went up in the Burgess Hall to the classroom where your father was there. And he gave us each two questions and said, "Take your choice of one." And he said, "I'll be in the Administration Building if you need me." And we finished the exam in quick time and went out to the field, convinced that we had passed the exam—and we had —and were able to play the next day in the game. That spirit of Eureka lasts not only four years but a lifetime, and that's why there are so many of you gathered here this evening.

And by the way, I want to thank Lee for writing. I don't know quite what to make of this, but later in the letter she writes, "My sister Barbara Cooper is a sergeant in Burbank, California, Police Department and has met you." [Laughter] Wait till the press gets hold of that. [Laughter]

But I can't tell you how wonderful it has been. The only fly in the ointment—the thing that's really wrong is that today is over, and now we turn back into pumpkins again because we can't even stay for dinner. This is the first time I've been a before-dinner speaker—been an after-dinner speaker many times. But we have to go out and get in that airplane and be on our way. So, we have to leave. But to be here among you again —everyone in Washington that's in government should have to, at regular intervals, have this kind of an experience, because there is a real difference between the real world and what's on the other side of the Potomac.

So, from one Red Devil to all the others—[Laughter]—hail to maroon and gold, and hail to our alma mater, and I think all of us should pledge in our hearts that it will be there long after we're gone doing for young people what it did for all of us.

God bless you, and I wish we could stay and say hello to every one of you. It's been a very thrilling and exciting time for us. And I leave greatly rewarded.

I have one little story I just want to tell before I go. [Laughter] I'm having a hard time getting away from here. For my graduation speech, we had decided in Washington that I should make a speech on the world situation and our plans for attempting disarmament, reduction of nuclear weapons, and so forth. And they were talking about what would be a proper forum in which to make this speech before I go to Europe at the end of this month to meet with our allies and all. And I said, "I have the perfect forum: I am making a speech in Illinois." And I reminded them of Winnie Churchill making a speech at a little college in Missouri some years ago in which he coined the term "Iron Curtain."

So, I said, we'll make the speech there. But to those who were there today, I told them of a little story that illustrates the humor of the Russian people and their cynicism about their way of life and their government. And I had to choose between two. So, I won't repeat the one that I told there today—[*Laughter*]—but the one I wanted to tell and didn't—and this is truly —the jokes—I've come to be a collector of these that the Russian people tell among themselves that reveals their feeling about their government.

And it has to do with when Brezhnev first became president. And he invited his elderly mother to come up and see his suite of offices in the Kremlin and then put her in his limousine and drove her to his fabulous apartment there in Moscow. And in both places, not a word. She looked; she said nothing. Then he put her in his helicopter and took her out to the country home outside Moscow in a forest. And again, not a word. Finally, he put her in his private jet and down to the shores of the Black Sea to see that marble palace which is known as his beach

home. And finally she spoke. She said, "Leonid, what if the Communists find out?" [*Laughter*]

We love you. We envy you for being able to stay, and God bless all of you.

Thank you.

Remarks at the Recommissioning
of the USS *New Jersey*

LONG BEACH, CALIFORNIA
DECEMBER 28, 1982

I believe another reason the American people voted me in was to rebuild our nation's military, which was in a state of disrepair and neglect. For too long, our leaders had thought we could have a strong military on the cheap, and so it was the military budget that was always cut. Eventually the American people no longer felt secure, and I hope they elected me to do something about it. We had our work cut out for us. As I often said during the campaign of 1980, we had planes that couldn't fly and ships that couldn't leave port. Really, that was no exaggeration.

Military hardware and readiness were only part of the problem. We had a serious morale problem in the military as well. The self-esteem of our people in uniform had been going down since Vietnam. Maybe I had seen too many war movies, the heroics of which I sometimes confused with real life, but common sense told me something very essential—you can't have a fighting force without an esprit de corps.

So one of my first priorities was to rebuild our military and, just as important, our military's morale. The recommissioning of the New Jersey *is representative of what we had to do.*

Secretary Lehman,* I thank you. Captain Fogarty, the officers and members of the crew, the other distinguished guests:

Secretary of Defense Weinberger would be here, but with all of us here he felt that someone had to stay in Washington and mind the store.

Surrounded by all this Navy blue and gold, I've had the strange feeling that I'm back on the set filming *Hellcats of the Navy*. [*Laughter*] That was a picture that was based on a great, victorious operation of the Navy in World War II in the Sea of Japan called Operation Hellcat. I remember at the time I was in love with my leading lady. She is Nancy, my wife, and I'm still in love with her, but I have to confess that today I find myself developing a great respect for the leading lady in these ceremonies. She's gray, she's had her face lifted, but she's still in the prime of life, a gallant lady: the *New Jersey*.

I'm honored to be here for the recommissioning of this mighty force for peace and freedom. Putting this great ship back to work protecting our country represents a major step toward fulfilling our pledge to rebuild America's military capabilities. It marks the resurgence of our nation's strength. It's a strength we can afford. We cannot afford to lose it.

Since the founding of our armed forces during the Revolutionary War, our country has always done without large standing armies and navies. Our great success story—unique in history—has been based on peaceful achievements in every sphere of human experience. In our two centuries of continuous democracy, we've been the envy of the world in technology, commerce, agriculture, and economic potential.

Our status as a free society and world power is not based on brute strength. When we've taken up arms, it has been for the defense of freedom for ourselves and for other peaceful nations

* Secretary of the Navy John Lehman.

who needed our help. But now, faced with the development of weapons with immense destructive power, we've no choice but to maintain ready defense forces that are second to none. Yes, the cost is high, but the price of neglect would be infinitely higher.

Another great power in the world sees its military forces in a different light. The Soviet Union has achieved sheer power status only by—or I should say superpower status—only by virtue of its military might. It has done so by sacrificing and ignoring achievement in virtually any and every other field.

In contrast, America's strength is the bedrock of the free world's security, for the freedom we guard is not just our own. But over the past years we began to drift dangerously away from what was so clearly our responsibility. From 1970 to 1979, our defense spending, in constant dollars, decreased by 22 percent. The Navy, so vital to protecting our interests in faraway trouble spots, shrank—as you've been told by the secretary—from more than 1,000 ships to 453.

Potential adversaries saw this unilateral disarmament, which was matched in all the other services, as a sign of weakness and a lack of will necessary to protect our way of life. While we talked of détente, the lessening of tensions in the world, the Soviet Union embarked on a massive program of militarization. Since around 1965, they have increased their military spending, nearly doubling it over the past fifteen years.

In a free society such as ours, where differing viewpoints are permitted, there will be people who oppose defense spending of any kind at any level. There are others who believe in defense, but who mistakenly feel that the Department of Defense is inherently wasteful and unconcerned about cost-cutting. Well, they're dead wrong.

Waste in government spending of any kind is an ever-present threat. But I can assure our fellow citizens there is no room for waste in our national defense. A dollar wasted is a dollar lost in the crucial effort to build a safer future for our people. Secretary Weinberger and the members of this administration are committed to spending what is necessary for defense to secure the peace and not a penny more. As the recommissioning of this ship demonstrates, we are rearming with prudence, using existing assets to the fullest.

To those who've been led to believe that we've gone overboard on national security needs and are spending a disproportionate share on the military, let me state: This is not true.

In spite of all the sound and fury that we hear and read, defense spending as a percentage of gross national product is well below what it was in the Eisenhower and Kennedy years. The simple fact is that, by reforming defense procurement, by stressing efficiencies and economies in weapons system production, we have been able to structure and fund a defense program our nation can afford. It meets the threat, and it provides wages and benefits that are more akin to what our men and women in uniform deserve.

Already, we're realizing tremendous dividends from our defense program. The readiness of our forces is dramatically improved. As you've just been told, we're more than meeting our recruitment goals. And we've had congressional support for such key initiatives as the purchase of two aircraft carriers, the B-1 bomber, and the C-5 transport plane.

As a nation, we're committed to take every step to reduce substantially the possibility of nuclear war, while providing an unshakable deterrent to such a war for ourselves and our allies. To this end, we're closing the window of vulnerability by instituting a comprehensive strategic force modernization program.

But while we do this, we're advancing vigorous arms control proposals aimed at deep and verifiable reductions in strategic nuclear missiles. We have proposed that intermediate-range nuclear missiles in Europe be reduced to zero on both sides at the same time we cut conventional forces in Europe to balanced levels. And I may say, the news is encouraging. The Soviet Union has met us halfway on the zero option. They've agreed to zero on our part. [*Laughter*]

We can't shut our eyes to the fact that, as the Soviet military power increased, so did their willingness to embark on military adventures. The scars are plainly evident in a number of Third

World countries. We're also aware that, though the Soviet Union is historically a land power—virtually self-sufficient in mineral and energy resources and land-linked to Europe and the vast stretches of Asia—it has created a powerful, blue-ocean navy that cannot be justified by any legitimate defense need. It is a navy built for offensive action, to cut the free world's supply lines and render impossible the support, by sea, of free world allies.

By contrast, the United States is a naval power by necessity, critically dependent on the transoceanic import of vital strategic materials. Over 90 percent of our commerce between the continents moves in ships. Freedom to use the seas is our nation's lifeblood. For that reason, our Navy is designed to keep the sea-lanes open worldwide, a far greater task than closing those sea-lanes at strategic choke points.

Maritime superiority for us is a necessity. We must be able in time of emergency to venture in harm's way, controlling air, surface, and subsurface areas to assure access to all the oceans of the world. Failure to do so will leave the credibility of our conventional defense forces in doubt.

We are, as I said, building a 600-ship fleet, including 15 carrier battle groups. But numbers are not the final test. Those ships must be highly capable.

The *New Jersey* and her sister ships can outgun and outclass any rival platform. This 58,000-ton ship, whose armor alone weighs more than our largest cruiser, is being recommissioned at no more than the cost of a new 4,000-ton frigate. The "Big J" is being reactivated with the latest in missile electronic warfare and communications technology. She's more than the best means of quickly adding real firepower to our Navy; she's a shining example of how this administration will rebuild America's armed forces on budget and on schedule and with the maximum cost-effective application of high technology to existing assets.

The *New Jersey*'s mission is to conduct prompt and sustained operations worldwide, in support of our national interests. In some cases, deployment of the *New Jersey* will free up our overstressed aircraft carriers for other uses. While the aircraft carrier remains the foundation of American naval power, the battleship will today be the sovereign of the seas. In support of amphibious operations, the *New Jersey*'s 16-inch guns can deliver shells as heavy as an automobile with pinpoint accuracy. And with a speed of thirty-five knots, the *New Jersey* will be among the fastest ships afloat.

History tells us that a delegate to the Continental Congress called the creation of our Navy "the maddest idea in the world." Well, we've been questioned for bringing back this battleship. Yet, I would challenge anyone who's been aboard or even seen the *New Jersey* to argue its value. It seems odd and a little ironic to me that some of the same critics who accuse us of chasing technology and gold-plating our weapons systems have led the charge against the superbly cost-effective and maintainable *New Jersey*. I doubt if there's a better example of the cost-consciousness of this administration than the magnificent ship that we're recommissioning today.

However, even with maximum efficiency and an eye toward making every dollar count, we must not fool ourselves. Providing an adequate defense is not cheap. The price of peace is always high, but considering the alternative, it's worth it.

Teddy Roosevelt said it well. "We Americans have many grave problems to solve, many threatening evils to fight, and many deeds to do if, as we hope and believe, we have the wisdom, the strength, the courage, and the virtue to do them. But we must face facts as they are. Our nation is that one among all nations of the earth which holds in its hands the fate of the coming years."

Today, I'd like to take this opportunity to thank all of those who worked on the *New Jersey*. You're a great team, and you did an outstanding job in putting her back into fighting trim. You represent a new spirit, a new sense of responsibility that we must have in all our shipyards and defense-related industries if public support for our vital task is to be maintained.

This ship, as the secretary told us, was brought in on time and on budget. And from all reports, the craftsmanship and professionalism of those involved in the project were superior, and I'm pleased to have the opportunity to extend the thanks of a grateful nation.

The *New Jersey,* like any ship in our fleet, will depend on the ability, dedication, and yes, patriotism of you here who are her crew. You're the elite. Six thousand applied for 1,500 crew spaces on the *New Jersey.* I have no doubt, too, that from among your ranks will come the Spruances and the Halseys and the Thompsons of tomorrow.

A few moments ago I quoted Teddy Roosevelt. Most people remember him as a man of strength and vitality, and yes, some have an image of a warlike man always spoiling for a fight. Well, let us remember, he won the Nobel Peace Prize, an honor bestowed upon him for his courageous and energetic efforts to end the Russo-Japanese war. He knew the relationship between peace and strength. And he knew the importance of a strong navy.

"The Navy of the United States," he said, "is the right arm of the United States and is emphatically the peacemaker. Woe to our country if we permit that right arm to become palsied or even to become flabby and inefficient."

Well, the *New Jersey* today becomes our 514th ship and represents our determination to rebuild the strength of America's right arm so that we can preserve the peace.

After valiant service in Vietnam and after saving the lives of countless marines, the *New Jersey* was decommissioned in 1969. During that solemn ceremony, her last commanding officer, Captain Robert Penniston, spoke prophetically when he suggested that this mighty ship "rest well, yet sleep lightly, and hear the call, if again sounded, to provide firepower for freedom."

Well, the call has been sounded. America needs the battleship once again to provide firepower for the defense of freedom and above all, to maintain the peace. She will truly fulfill her mission if her firepower never has to be used.

Captain Fogarty, I hereby place the United States Ship *New Jersey* in commission.

God bless, and Godspeed.

Thank you, John. Nancy and I are delighted to be with you
this morning and honored to be in such distinguished company.

General Dozier, I
you only consider doin
going to pull rank on

We want to give t
want to salute the Ita
rescue, and, Jim, we
your gallantry; and sai
said that a hero is no
brave five minutes lon
longer.

Now we know why t
celebration. Last yea
something else -- my
don't worry because I
commissioned him for
Abraham was 100 and h
truly amazing. He li
put $2,000 a year into
Many of you chose
that has particular r
who dreamt he walked
walked, above him in

Page 2

experience of his life. Reaching the end of the beach, and as
he looked back and saw two sets of footprints
places only one.

We turned
would walk with
hand. Why did Y
of greatest need
leave you. Wher
them that I car
And now we've s
God carried him
We need only th
" . . . weeping
morning." [Ps

Speaking
for all your p
are put here t
did not and I
whatever

I also b
a country cre
voluntary com
law, with fa

there's
needs y

Ou
involve

Page 3

Sometimes, we seem to have strayed from that noble
beginning -- strayed from our conviction that standards of right
and wrong do exist and must be lived up to. God, the source of
our knowledge   public schools. He
gives us His
condone the t

We canno
but
turn away fr

I wonde
waiting for
Him and eac
meaning to

There
and a will
People hav
they do i
does.

Well
Good Sam
wounds o

Page 4

From
churches and synagogues to take the lead
restoring our spirit of neighbor caring for neighbor.

We know what you are already doing, and, believe me, we
grateful. If all of you worked for the Federal Government, y
would be classified "essential." We need you, now more than
ever.

the private sec   pick up -- do
for dollar -- every Federal program being reduced.
We're not asking you to replace what hasn't worked. No

We want you to raise our spirits and reach into our pocket
spark the conviction in us all that we should be doing God's wo
on Earth.

We will never find every answer, solve every problem, heal
every wound, or live all our dreams. But we _can_ do a lot, if we
walk together down that one path we know provides real hope. We
have His promise that what we give in love will be given back
many times over. Love will never fail.

So, let us rekindle the fire of our faith.

Let our wisdom be vindicated by our deeds.

when our work is done, we can say -- we have fought the
good fight, we have finished the race, we have kept the faith.

Thank you. God bless you.

Annual National Prayer Breakfast

WASHINGTON, D.C.
FEBRUARY 4, 1982

I went to the national prayer breakfasts almost every year. It's a gathering of people who come together because of their belief in prayer. I never came away from one of these sessions without feeling stronger for it. It's a remarkable feeling to know that people are praying for you and for your strength. I know first-hand. I felt those prayers when I was recovering from that bullet.

I find this sort of interesting. When I played football in college, I always said a prayer while waiting for the kickoff. I never asked to win. I prayed to do my best. I prayed that no one got hurt. And I prayed I would have no regrets when the game was over because I had done my utmost. Years later, I realized that this was almost the identical prayer I was saying as president. I find that prayer does sustain and guide.

By the way, the General Dozier I mention in the following remarks is the U.S. general who was kidnapped by terrorists and then dramatically rescued by Italian police.

T HANK YOU VERY MUCH, John*, all our friends and distinguished guests here at the head table, and all of you very distinguished people. Nancy and I are delighted to be with you this morning, and are honored to be here.

---

* Senator John Stennis of Mississippi.

General Dozier, I know you don't like being praised for what you only consider was doing your duty. Forgive me, I'm going to pull rank on you. [*Laughter*] We want to give thanks to God for answering our prayers. We want to salute the Italian authorities for their brilliant rescue, and Jim, we just want to thank both you and Judith for your gallantry. Welcome home, soldier.

Someone once said that a hero is no braver than any other man. He's just brave five minutes longer. Well, General, you were brave forty-two days longer. And now we know why prayer breakfasts are a time for praise and celebration.

Last year, you all helped me begin celebrating the thirty-first anniversary of my thirty-ninth birthday. [*Laughter*] And I must say that all of those pile up, an increase of numbers, don't bother me at all, because I recall that Moses was 80 when God commissioned him for public service, and he lived to be 120. [*Laughter*] And Abraham was 100 and his wife Sarah 90 when they did something truly amazing—[*Laughter*]—and he lived to be 175. Just imagine if he had put $2,000 a year into his IRA account. [*Laughter*]

Those of you who were here last year might remember that I shared a story by an unknown author, a story of a dream he had had. He had dreamt, as you recall, that he walked down the beach beside the Lord. And as they walked, above him in the sky was reflected each experience of his life. And then reaching the end of the beach, he looked back and saw the two sets of footprints extending down the way, but suddenly noticed that every once in a while there was only one set of footprints. And each time, they were opposite a reflection in the sky of a time of great trial and suffering in his life. And he turned to the Lord in surprise and said, "You promised that if I walked with You, You would always be by my side. Why did You desert me in my times of need?" And the Lord said, "My beloved child, I wouldn't desert you when you needed Me. When you see only one set of footprints, it was then that I carried you."

Well, when I told that story last year, I said I knew, having only been here in this position for a few weeks, that there would be many times for me in the days ahead when there would be only one set of footprints and I would need to be carried, and if I didn't believe that I would be, I wouldn't have the courage to do what I was doing.

Shortly thereafter, there came a moment when, without doubt, I was carried. And now, we've seen in General Dozier's life such a moment. Well, God is with us. We need only to believe. The psalmist says, "Weeping may endure for a night, but joy cometh in the morning."

Speaking for Nancy and myself, we thank you for your faith and for all your prayers on our behalf. And it is true that you can sense and feel that power.

I've always believed that we were, each of us, put here for a reason, that there is a plan, somehow a divine plan for all of us. I know now that whatever days are left to me belong to Him.

I also believe this blessed land was set apart in a very special way, a country created by men and women who came here not in search of gold, but in search of God. They would be free people, living under the law with faith in their Maker and their future.

Sometimes, it seems we've strayed from that noble beginning, from our conviction that standards of right and wrong do exist and must be lived up to. God, the source of our knowledge, has been expelled from the classroom. He gives us His greatest blessing, life, and yet many would condone the taking of innocent life. We expect Him to protect us in a crisis, but turn away from Him too often in our day-to-day living. I wonder if He isn't waiting for us to wake up.

There is, as Pete* so eloquently said, in the American heart a spirit of love, of caring, and a willingness to work together. If we remember the parable of the Good Samaritan, he crossed the road, knelt down, and bound up the wounds of the beaten traveler, the Pilgrim, and then carried him into the nearest town. He didn't just hurry on by into town and then look up a

* Senator Pete V. Domenici of New Mexico.

caseworker and tell him there was a fellow back out on the road that looked like he might need help.

Isn't it time for us to get personally involved, for our churches and synagogues to restore our spirit of neighbor caring for neighbor? But talking to this particular gathering, I realize I'm preaching to the choir. If all of you worked for the federal government, you would be classified as essential. We need you now more than ever to remind us that we should be doing God's work on earth. We'll never find every answer, solve every problem, or heal every wound, but we can do a lot if we walk together down that one path that we know provides real hope.

You know, in one of the conflicts that was going on throughout the past year when views were held deeply on both sides of the debate, I recall talking to one senator who came into my office. We both deeply believed what it was we were espousing, but we were on opposite sides. And when we finished talking, as he rose, he said, "I'm going out of here and do some praying." And I said, "Well, if you get a busy signal, it's me there ahead of you." [*Laughter*]

We have God's promise that what we give will be given back many times over, so let us go forth from here and rekindle the fire of our faith. Let our wisdom be vindicated by our deeds.

We are told in II Timothy that when our work is done, we can say, "We have fought the good fight. We have finished the race. We have kept the faith." This is an evidence of it.

I hope that on down through the centuries not only is this great land preserved but this great tradition is preserved and that all over the land there will always be this one day in the year when we remind ourselves of what our real task is.

God bless you. Thank you.

Christmas Day Radio Address to the Nation

DECEMBER 25, 1982

When I became president, I got back in the radio business again. I gave a five-minute radio address every Saturday at noon eastern standard time. The first one was in April of 1982, and by the time I finished at the end of my two terms, I'd done 331 of these weekly broadcasts, almost a year of Saturdays.

The shows gave me a chance to talk about what was current in the news that week and to get things off my chest. It also gave me a chance to share items that came across my desk, like letters and newspaper clippings and such, with the American people. The following radio piece fits in the latter category.

MERRY CHRISTMAS from the White House. Nancy and I wish we could personally thank the thousands of you who've sent us holiday cards, greetings, and messages. Each one is moving and tells a story of its own—a story of love, hope, prayer, and patriotism. And each one has helped to brighten our Christmas.

Some of the most moving have come from fellow citizens who, unlike most of us, are not spending Christmas day at the family hearth, surrounded by friends and loved ones. I'm thinking of the twelve U.S. marines who sent us a card from Beirut, Lebanon, where they'll spend their Christmas helping to rebuild the shattered hopes for peace in a suffering land. And I'm thinking of the petty officer serving aboard the USS *Enterprise* who asked that we remember him and his shipmates this holiday season. "Christmas in the Indian Ocean is *no* fun," he writes, "but it's for a very good cause."

Well, that's right, sailor. You're serving a very good cause, indeed. On this, the birthday of the Prince of Peace, you and your comrades serve to protect the peace He taught us. You may be thousands of miles away, but to us here at home, you've never been closer.

One of my favorite pieces of Christmas mail came early this year, a sort of modern American Christmas story that took place not in our country's heartland, but on the troubled waters of the South China Sea last October. To me, it sums up so much of what is best about the Christmas spirit, the American character, and what this beloved land of ours stands for—not only to ourselves but to millions of less fortunate people around the globe.

I want to thank Mr. Gary Kemp of Neenah, Wisconsin, for bringing it to my attention. It's a letter from Ordnance Man, First Class, John Mooney, written to his parents from aboard the aircraft carrier *Midway* on October 15th. But it's a true Christmas story in the best sense.

"Dear Mom and Dad," he wrote, "today we spotted a boat in the water, and we rendered assistance. We picked up sixty-five Vietnamese refugees. It was about a two-hour job getting everyone aboard, and then they had to get screened by intelligence and checked out by medical and fed and clothed and all that.

"But now they're resting on the hangar deck, and the kids— most of them seem to be kids . . . are sitting in front of probably the first television set they've ever seen, watching *Star Wars*. Their boat was sinking as we came alongside. They'd been at sea five days and had run out of water. All in all, a couple of more days and the kids would have been in pretty bad shape.

"I guess once in a while," he writes, "we need a jolt like that for us to realize why we do what we do and how important, really, it can be. I mean, it took a lot of guts for those parents to make a choice like that to go to sea in a leaky boat in hope of finding someone to take them from the sea. So much risk! But apparently they felt it was worth it rather than live in a Communist country.

"For all of our problems, with the price of gas, and not being able to afford a new car or other creature comforts this year ... I really don't see a lot of leaky boats heading out of San Diego looking for the Russian ships out there. ...

"After the refugees were brought aboard, I took some pictures, but as usual I didn't have my camera with me for the REAL picture—the one blazed in my mind. ...

"As they approached the ship, they were all waving and trying as best they could to say, 'Hello, America sailor! Hello, freedom man!' It's hard to see a boat full of people like that and not get a lump somewhere between chin and belly button. And it really makes one proud and glad to be an American. People were waving and shouting and choking down lumps and trying not to let other brave men see their wet eyes. A lieutenant next to me said, 'Yeah, I guess it's payday in more ways than one.' (We got paid today.) And I guess no one could say it better than that.

"It reminds us all of what America has always been—a place a man or woman can come to for freedom. I know we're crowded and we have unemployment and we have a real burden with refugees, but I honestly hope and pray we can always find room. We have a unique society, made up of castoffs of all the world's wars and oppressions, and yet we're strong and free. We have one thing in common—no matter where our forefathers came from, we believe in that freedom.

"I hope we always have room for one more person, maybe an Afghan or a Pole or someone else looking for a place ... where he doesn't have to worry about his family's starving or a knock on the door in the night ... and where all men who truly seek freedom and honor and respect and dignity for themselves and their posterity can find a place where they can . . . finally see their dreams come true and their kids educated and become the next generation of doctors and lawyers and builders and soldiers and sailors.

"Love, John."

Well, I think that letter just about says it all. In spite of everything, we Americans are still uniquely blessed, not only with the rich bounty of our land but by a bounty of the spirit —a kind of year-round Christmas spirit that still makes our country a beacon of hope in a troubled world and that makes this Christmas and every Christmas even more special for all of us who number among our gifts the birthright of being an American.

Until next week, thanks for listening. Merry Christmas, and God bless you.

1983

Address on Central America
Before a Joint Session of the Congress

APRIL 27, 1983

In my mind, 1983 is the year of regional conflicts—the horrible bombing of our Marine barracks in Beirut, the rescue of Grenada, and the solidifying of the Marxist-Leninist regime in Nicaragua. The situation in Lebanon would return to haunt me in the form of an increasing number of American hostages over there. The situation in Nicaragua would continue to defy resolution because of the weakness of Congress in supporting peoples willing to fight for their freedom.

This address before the Congress deals with the struggle for democracy in Central America and was the first major speech I gave on the subject. I was to give many, many more in my attempts to bring pressure on Nicaragua's Sandinista government. Our best hope for democracy in Nicaragua was and remains the contras, the freedom fighters whom the Democratic Congress kept pulling the rug out from under. History will judge the Congress's grudging and constantly changing policy toward the contras as a disgrace.

I could never seem to convince the Congress what was going on down there. The Nicaraguans had a very sophisticated disinformation campaign that completely bamboozled many on Capitol Hill. Congressional delegations would go to Nicaragua and simply be shown what the Sandinistas wanted them to see. I also honestly believe the Sandinistas hoodwinked many in the American press.

One day I saw an article in the paper about a Catholic bishop from Iowa who had led some Nicaraguan refugees out of Nicaragua and across the border into Honduras. The story said they had been attacked by the contras and rescued by the Sandinistas. Well, I found this disturbing if true, so I tracked him down and called him. He said, yes, he did lead some of his people out, but that the story was exactly backward—they were attacked by the Sandinistas and rescued by the contras.

On two different occasions I met with Nicaraguan clergymen who'd had their ears cut off with bayonets by the Sandinistas for preaching. I remember one man's story in particular. The Sandinistas had tied this one young Nicaraguan preacher to a tree and cut off his ears. They then cut his throat and ruthlessly said, "Now call upon your God. Maybe He can help you." The clergyman's congregation got to him before he bled to death. He himself told me that story in the Oval Office of the White House. Both ministers were available to the press, and yet their stories never appeared in the major papers or on the evening news.

M R. SPEAKER, MR. PRESIDENT, distinguished members of the Congress, honored guests, and my fellow Americans:

A number of times in past years, members of Congress and a president have come together in meetings like this to resolve a crisis. I have asked for this meeting in the hope that we can prevent one.

It would be hard to find many Americans who aren't aware of our stake in the Middle East, the Persian Gulf, or the NATO line dividing the free world from the Communist bloc. And the same could be said for Asia.

But in spite of, or maybe because of, a flurry of stories about places like Nicaragua and El Salvador and yes, some concerted propaganda, many of us find it hard to believe we have a stake in problems involving those countries. Too many have thought of Central America as just that place way down below Mexico that can't possibly constitute a threat to our well-being. And that's why I've asked for this session. Central America's problems do directly affect the security and the well-being of our own people. And Central America is much closer to the United States than many of the world trouble spots that concern us. So, we work to restore our own economy; we cannot afford to lose sight of our neighbors to the south.

El Salvador is nearer to Texas than Texas is to Massachusetts. Nicaragua is just as close to Miami, San Antonio, San Diego, and Tucson as those cities are to Washington, where we're gathered tonight.

But nearness on the map doesn't even begin to tell the strategic importance of Central America, bordering as it does on the Caribbean—our lifeline to the outside world. Two-thirds of all our foreign trade and petroleum pass through the Panama Canal and the Caribbean. In a European crisis at least half of our supplies for NATO would go through these areas by sea. It's well to remember that in early 1942, a handful of Hitler's submarines sank more tonnage there than in all of the Atlantic Ocean. And they did this without a single naval base anywhere in the area. And today, the situation is different. Cuba is host to a Soviet combat brigade, a submarine base capable of servicing Soviet submarines, and military air bases visited regularly by Soviet military aircraft.

Because of its importance, the Caribbean Basin is a magnet for adventurism. We're all aware of the Libyan cargo planes refueling in Brazil a few days ago on their way to deliver "medical supplies" to Nicaragua. Brazilian authorities discovered the so-called medical supplies were actually munitions and prevented their delivery.

You may remember that last month, speaking on national television, I showed an aerial photo of an airfield being built on the island of Grenada. Well, if that airfield had been completed, those planes could have refueled there and completed their journey.

If the Nazis during World War II and the Soviets today could recognize the Caribbean and Central America as vital to our interests, shouldn't we, also? For several years now, under two administrations, the United States has been increasing its defense of freedom in the Caribbean Basin. And I can tell you tonight, democracy is beginning to take root in El Salvador, which, until a short time ago, knew only dictatorship.

The new government is now delivering on its promises of democracy, reforms, and free elections. It wasn't easy, and there was resistance to many of the attempted reforms, with assassinations of some of the reformers. Guerrilla bands and urban terrorists were portrayed in a worldwide propaganda campaign as freedom fighters, representative of the people. Ten days before I came into office, the guerrillas launched what they called "a final offensive" to overthrow the government. And their radio boasted that our new administration would be too late to prevent their victory.

Well, they learned that democracy cannot be so easily defeated. President Carter did not hesitate. He authorized arms and munitions to El Salvador. The guerrilla offensive failed, but not America's will. Every president since this country assumed global responsibilities has known that those responsibilities could only be met if we pursued a bipartisan foreign policy.

As I said a moment ago, the government of El Salvador has been keeping its promises, like the land reform program which is making thousands of farm tenants, farm owners. In a little over three years, 20 percent of the arable land in El Salvador has been redistributed to more than 450,000 people. That's one in ten Salvadorans who have benefited directly from this program.

El Salvador has continued to strive toward an orderly and democratic society. The government promised free elections. On March 28th, a little more than a year ago, after months of campaigning by a variety of candidates, the suffering people of El Salvador were offered a chance to vote, to choose the kind of government they wanted. And suddenly, the so-called freedom fighters in the hills were exposed for what they really are —a small minority who want power for themselves and their backers, not democracy for the people. The guerrillas threatened death to anyone who voted. They destroyed hundreds of buses and trucks to keep the people from getting to the polling places. Their slogan was brutal: "Vote today, die tonight." But on election day, an unprecedented 80 percent of the electorate braved ambush and gunfire and trudged for miles, many of them, to vote for freedom. Now, that's truly fighting for freedom. We can never turn our backs on that.

Members of this Congress who went there as observers told me of a woman who was wounded by rifle fire on the way to the polls, who refused to leave the line to have her wound treated until after she had voted. Another woman had been told by the guerrillas that she would be killed when she returned from the polls, and she told the guerrillas, "You can kill me, you can kill my family, you can kill my neighbors. You can't kill us all." The real freedom fighters of El Salvador turned out to be the people of that country—the young, the old, the in-between—more than a million of them out of a population of less than 5 million. The world should respect this courage and not allow it to be belittled or forgotten. And again I say, in good conscience, we can never turn our backs on that.

The democratic political parties and factions in El Salvador are coming together around the common goal of seeking a political solution to their country's problems. New national elections will be held this year, and they will be open to all political parties. The government has invited the guerrillas to participate in the election and is preparing an amnesty law. The people of El Salvador are earning their freedom, and they deserve our moral and material support to protect it.

Yes, there are still major problems regarding human rights, the criminal justice system, and violence against noncombatants. And like the rest of Central America, El Salvador also faces severe economic problems. But in addition to recession-depressed prices for major agricultural exports, El Salvador's economy is being deliberately sabotaged.

Tonight in El Salvador—because of ruthless guerrilla attacks —much of the fertile land cannot be cultivated; less than half the rolling stock of the railways remains operational; bridges, water facilities, telephone and electric systems have been destroyed and damaged. In one twenty-two-month period, there were five thousand interruptions of electrical power. One region was without electricity for a third of the year.

I think Secretary of State Shultz put it very well the other day: "Unable to win the free loyalty of El Salvador's people, the guerrillas," he said, "are deliberately and systematically depriving them of food, water, transportation, light, sanitation, and jobs. And these are the people who claim they want to help the common people." They don't want elections because they know they'd be defeated. But as the previous election showed, the Salvadoran people's desire for democracy will not be defeated.

The guerrillas are not embattled peasants, armed with muskets. They're professionals, sometimes with better training and weaponry than the government's soldiers. The Salvadoran battalions that have received U.S. training have been conducting themselves well on the battlefield and with the civilian population. But so far, we've only provided enough money to train one Salvadoran soldier out of ten, fewer than the number of guerrillas that are trained by Nicaragua and Cuba.

And let me set the record straight on Nicaragua, a country next to El Salvador. In 1979 when the new government took over in Nicaragua, after a revolution which overthrew the authoritarian rule of Somoza, everyone hoped for the growth of democracy. We in the United States did, too. By January of 1981, our emergency relief and recovery aid to Nicaragua totaled $118 million—more than provided by any other developed country. In fact, in the first two years of Sandinista rule, the United States directly or indirectly sent five times more aid to Nicaragua than it had in the two years prior to the revolution. Can anyone doubt the generosity and the good faith of the American people?

These were hardly the actions of a nation implacably hostile to Nicaragua. Yet, the government of Nicaragua has treated us as an enemy. It has rejected our repeated peace efforts. It has broken its promises to us, to the Organization of American States, and most important of all, to the people of Nicaragua.

No sooner was victory achieved than a small clique ousted others who had been part of the revolution from having any voice in the government. Humberto Ortega, the minister of defense, declared Marxism-Leninism would be their guide, and so it is.

The government of Nicaragua has imposed a new dictatorship. It has refused to hold the elections it promised. It has seized control of most media and subjects all media to heavy prior censorship. It denied the bishops and priests of the Roman Catholic Church the right to say Mass on radio during Holy Week. It insulted and mocked the Pope. It has driven the Miskito Indians from their homelands, burning their villages, destroying their crops, and forcing them into involuntary internment camps far from home. It has moved against the private sector and free labor unions. It condoned mob action against Nicaragua's independent human rights commission and drove the director of that commission into exile.

In short, after all these acts of repression by the government, is it any wonder that opposition has formed? Contrary to propaganda, the opponents of the Sandinistas are not diehard supporters of the previous Somoza regime. In fact, many are anti-Somoza heroes and fought beside the Sandinistas to bring down the Somoza government. Now they've been denied any part in the new government because they truly wanted democracy for Nicaragua and they still do. Others are Miskito Indians fighting for their homes, their lands, and their lives.

The Sandinista revolution in Nicaragua turned out to be just an exchange of one set of autocratic rulers for another, and the people still have no freedom, no democratic rights, and more poverty. Even worse than its predecessor, it is helping Cuba and the Soviets to destabilize our hemisphere.

Meanwhile, the government of El Salvador, making every effort to guarantee democracy, free labor unions, freedom of religion, and a free press, is under attack by guerrillas dedicated to the same philosophy that prevails in Nicaragua, Cuba, and yes, the Soviet Union. Violence has been Nicaragua's most important export to the world. It is the ultimate in hypocrisy for the unelected Nicaraguan government to charge that we seek their overthrow, when they're doing everything they can to bring down the elected government of El Salvador. [*Applause*] Thank you. The guerrilla attacks are directed from a headquarters in Managua, the capital of Nicaragua.

But let us be clear as to the American attitude toward the government of Nicaragua. We do not seek its overthrow. Our interest is to ensure that it does not infect its neighbors through the export of subversion and violence. Our purpose, in conformity with American and international law, is to prevent the flow of arms to El Salvador, Honduras, Guatemala, and Costa Rica. We have attempted to have a dialog with the government of Nicaragua, but it persists in its efforts to spread violence.

We should not, and we will not, protect the Nicaraguan government from the anger of its own people. But we should, through diplomacy, offer an alternative. And as Nicaragua ponders its options, we can and will—with all the resources of diplomacy—protect each country of Central America from the danger of war.

Even Costa Rica, Central America's oldest and strongest democracy—a government so peaceful it doesn't even have an army—is the object of bullying and threats from Nicaragua's dictators.

Nicaragua's neighbors know that Sandinista promises of peace, nonalliance, and nonintervention have not been kept. Some thirty-six new military bases have been built. There were only thirteen during the Somoza years. Nicaragua's new army numbers 25,000 men, supported by a militia of 50,000. It is the largest army in Central America, supplemented by 2,000 Cuban military and security advisers. It is equipped with the most modern weapons—dozens of Soviet-made tanks, 800 Soviet-bloc trucks, Soviet 152-millimeter howitzers, 100 antiaircraft guns, plus planes and helicopters. There are additional thousands of civilian advisers from Cuba, the Soviet Union, East Germany, Libya, and the PLO. And we're attacked because we have 55 military trainers in El Salvador.

The goal of the professional guerrilla movements in Central

America is as simple as it is sinister: to destabilize the entire region from the Panama Canal to Mexico. And if you doubt beyond this point, just consider what Cayetano Cárpio, the now-deceased Salvadoran guerrilla leader, said earlier this month. Cárpio said that after El Salvador falls, El Salvador and Nicaragua would be "arm-in-arm and struggling for the total liberation of Central America."

Nicaragua's dictatorial junta, who themselves made war and won power operating from bases in Honduras and Costa Rica, like to pretend that they are today being attacked by forces based in Honduras. The fact is, it is Nicaragua's government that threatens Honduras, not the reverse. It is Nicaragua who has moved heavy tanks close to the border, and Nicaragua who speaks of war. It was Nicaraguan radio that announced on April 8th the creation of a new, unified, revolutionary coordinating board to push forward the Marxist struggle in Honduras.

Nicaragua, supported by weapons and military resources provided by the Communist bloc, represses its own people, refuses to make peace, and sponsors a guerrilla war against El Salvador.

President Truman's words are as apt today as they were in 1947 when he, too, spoke before a joint session of the Congress:

"At the present moment in world history, nearly every nation must choose between alternate ways of life. The choice is not too often a free one. One way of life is based upon the will of the majority and is distinguished by free institutions, representative government, free elections, guarantees of individual liberty, freedom of speech and religion, and freedom from political oppression. The second way of life is based upon the will of a minority forcibly imposed upon the majority. It relies upon terror and oppression, a controlled press and radio, fixed elections, and the suppression of personal freedoms.

"I believe that it must be the policy of the United States to support free peoples who are resisting attempted subjugation by armed minorities or by outside pressures. I believe that we must assist free peoples to work out their own destinies in their own way. I believe that our help should be primarily through economic and financial aid which is essential to economic stability and orderly political processes.

"Collapse of free institutions and loss of independence would be disastrous not only for them but for the world. Discouragement and possibly failure would quickly be the lot of neighboring peoples striving to maintain their freedom and independence."

The countries of Central America are smaller than the nations that prompted President Truman's message. But the political and strategic stakes are the same. Will our response—economic, social, military—be as appropriate and successful as Mr. Truman's bold solutions to the problems of postwar Europe?

Some people have forgotten the successes of those years and the decades of peace, prosperity, and freedom they secured. Some people talk as though the United States were incapable of acting effectively in international affairs without risking war or damaging those we seek to help.

Are democracies required to remain passive while threats to their security and prosperity accumulate? Must we just accept the destabilization of an entire region from the Panama Canal to Mexico on our southern border? Must we sit by while independent nations of this hemisphere are integrated into the most aggressive empire the modern world has seen? Must we wait while Central Americans are driven from their homes like the more than a million who've sought refuge out of Afghanistan, or the one and a half million who have fled Indochina, or the more than a million Cubans who have fled Castro's Caribbean utopia? Must we, by default, leave the people of El Salvador no choice but to flee their homes, creating another tragic human exodus?

I don't believe there's a majority in the Congress or the country that counsels passivity, resignation, defeatism, in the face of this challenge to freedom and security in our own hemisphere. [*Applause*] Thank you. Thank you.

I do not believe that a majority of the Congress or the country is prepared to stand by passively while the people of Central America are delivered to totalitarianism and we ourselves are left vulnerable to new dangers.

Only last week, an official of the Soviet Union reiterated Brezhnev's threat to station nuclear missiles in this hemisphere, five minutes from the United States. Like an echo, Nicaragua's Comandante Daniel Ortega confirmed that, if asked, his country would consider accepting those missiles. I understand that today they may be having second thoughts.

Now, before I go any further, let me say to those who invoke the memory of Vietnam, there is no thought of sending American combat troops to Central America. They are not needed— [*Applause*]

Thank you. And, as I say, they are not needed, and indeed, they have not been requested there. All our neighbors ask of us is assistance in training and arms to protect themselves while they build a better, freer life.

We must continue to encourage peace among the nations of Central America. We must support the regional efforts now under way to promote solutions to regional problems.

We cannot be certain that the Marxist-Leninist bands who believe war is an instrument of politics will be readily discouraged. It's crucial that we not become discouraged before they do. Otherwise, the region's freedom will be lost and our security damaged in ways that can hardly be calculated.

If Central America were to fall, what would the consequences be for our position in Asia, Europe, and for alliances such as NATO? If the United States cannot respond to a threat near our own borders, why should Europeans or Asians believe that we're seriously concerned about threats to them? If the Soviets can assume that nothing short of an actual attack on the United States will provoke an American response, which ally, which friend will trust us then?

The Congress shares both the power and the responsibility for our foreign policy. Tonight, I ask you, the Congress, to join me in a bold, generous approach to the problems of peace and poverty, democracy and dictatorship in the region. Join me in a program that prevents Communist victory in the short run, but goes beyond, to produce for the deprived people of the area the reality of present progress and the promise of more to come.

Let us lay the foundation for a bipartisan approach to sustain the independence and freedom of the countries of Central America. We in the administration reach out to you in this spirit.

We will pursue four basic goals in Central America:

First, in response to decades of inequity and indifference, we will support democracy, reform, and human freedom. This means using our assistance, our powers of persuasion, and our legitimate leverage to bolster humane democratic systems where they already exist and to help countries on their way to that goal complete the process as quickly as human institutions can be changed. Elections in El Salvador and also in Nicaragua must be open to all, fair and safe. The international community must help. We will work at human rights problems, not walk away from them.

Second, in response to the challenge of world recession and, in the case of El Salvador, to the unrelenting campaign of economic sabotage by the guerrillas, we will support economic development. And by a margin of two to one our aid is economic now, not military. Seventy-seven cents out of every dollar we will spend in the area this year goes for food, fertilizers, and other essentials for economic growth and development. And our economic program goes beyond traditional aid. The Caribbean Initiative introduced in the House earlier today will provide powerful trade and investment incentives to help these countries achieve self-sustaining economic growth without exporting U.S. jobs. Our goal must be to focus our immense and growing technology to enhance health care, agriculture, industry, and to ensure that we who inhabit this interdependent region come to know and understand each other better, retaining our diverse identities, respecting our diverse traditions and institutions.

And *third,* in response to the military challenge from Cuba and Nicaragua—to their deliberate use of force to spread tyranny—we will support the security of the region's threatened nations. We do not view security assistance as an end in itself, but as a shield for democratization, economic development, and diplomacy. No amount of reform will bring peace so long as guerrillas believe they will win by force. No amount of economic help will suffice if guerrilla units can destroy roads and bridges and power stations and crops, again and again, with impunity. But with better training and material help, our neighbors can hold off the guerrillas and give democratic reform time to take root.

And *fourth,* we will support dialog and negotiations both among the countries of the region and within each country. The terms and conditions of participation in elections are negotiable. Costa Rica is a shining example of democracy. Honduras has made the move from military rule to democratic government. Guatemala is pledged to the same course. The United States will work toward a political solution in Central America which will serve the interests of the democratic process.

To support these diplomatic goals, I offer these assurances: The United States will support any agreement among Central American countries for the withdrawal, under fully verifiable and reciprocal conditions, of all foreign military and security advisers and troops. We want to help opposition groups join the political process in all countries and compete by ballots instead of bullets. We will support any verifiable, reciprocal agreement among Central American countries on the renunciation of support for insurgencies on neighbors' territory. And finally, we desire to help Central America end its costly arms race and will support any verifiable, reciprocal agreements on the nonimportation of offensive weapons.

To move us toward these goals more rapidly, I am tonight announcing my intention to name an ambassador at large as my special envoy to Central America. He or she will report to me through the secretary of state. The ambassador's responsibilities will be to lend U.S. support to the efforts of regional governments to bring peace to this troubled area and to work

Mr. Speaker, Mr. President, distinguished members of Congress, honored guests & my fellow Americans.

A number of times in past years members of Congress & a Pres. have come together in meetings like this to resolve a crisis. I have asked for this meeting in the hope that we can prevent one.

It would be hard to find many Americans who aren't aware of our stake in the Middle East, the Persian gulf or the Nato line dividing the free world from the Communist bloc. The same ... be said for Asia.

But in spite of or maybe ... of stories about places like ... and yes some concerted propa... find it hard to believe we ... problems involving three countri... a place "way down below Me... constitutes a threat to our well...

That is why I have aske... Central America problems do ... security & well being of our ... America is much closer to th... the nearest trouble spots that ...

El Salvador is closer to Tx... Mass., Nicaragua is closer to Mia... San Antonio, Los Angeles & Denver... are to Wash. where we are ga...

But just nearness on the map ... strategic importance of Central Amer... on the Caribbean — our lifeline to t... almost half of our foreign tra... oil pass through the Panama Ca... In a European crisis ⅔ of ours me... would go through these areas by... to Europe. It is well to reme... 1942 a handful of Hitlers subma... tonnage there than in all of the... And they did this without a se... anywhere in the area.

Page 2

Central America is much closer to the U...
trouble spots that concern us. El Salv...
than Texas is to Massachusetts. Nicara...
New Orleans, Houston, Los Angeles, and ...
are to Washington where we are gathered...

But nearness on the map doesn't tel...
importance of Central America, bordering...
Caribbean — our lifeline to the outside...
all our foreign trade tonnage and crude ...
Panama Canal and the Caribbean. In a Eur...
of our mobilization requirements would go...
sea. It is well to remember that in earl...
Hitler's submarines sank more tonnage ther...
Atlantic Ocean. And they did this without...
anywhere in the area.

Today, the Soviets are diligently ply...
host to a Soviet combat brigade, a submari...
servicing Soviet nuclear submarines, and m...
visited regularly by Soviet aircraft.

Because of its importance, the Caribbe...
of adventurism. We're all aware of the Lib...
refueling in Brazil on their way to deliver ...
Nicaragu... Brazilian authorities discovered ...
... documented their delivery...

Page 3

If the Nazis during World War II and ...
consider the Caribbean and Central America...
interests, shouldn't we also?

For several years now, under two adm...
States has been increasing its defense of ...
Caribbean Basin. And I can tell you toni...
beginning to blossom in El Salvador. The...
delivering on its promises of democracy, ...
elections. It wasn't easy and there was...
the attempted reforms with assassination ...
Guerrilla bands and urban terrorists we...
worldwide propaganda campaign as freedo...
of the people. Ten days before I came ...
guerrillas launched what they called a ...
overthrow the government. Their radio ...
Administration would be too late to pr...
learned democracy cannot be so easily ...

President Carter had not hesitat...
ammunition, and military trainers to ...
offensive failed, but not America's ...

As I said a moment ago, the gov...
promises, like the land reform progr...
of farm tenants, farm owners. In a ...
20 percent of the arable land in El ...
... to more than 450,000 ...
... directly benefitted ...

Page 4

... El Salvad...
democratic soc...
March 28th, 1...
campaigning b...
El Salvador w...
of government ...
fighters in ...
small minori...
not democrac...
anyone who ...
to keep the ...
slogan was ...
day, an un...
and gunfir...
truly figh...

Member ...
of a woma...
who refus...
after she ...
guerrill...
and she ...
family, ...
freedom...
that co...
1 milli...
The wo...
belitt...

Page 8

... we seek their overthrow when they are doing everything they ca...
to bring down the elected government of El Salvador. The gov...
... in Nicaragua ... the American attitude toward ...

But let us be clear as to what is overthrow. Our ...
government of Nicaragua. We do not seek it does not infect its neighbor...
interest is to insure that it does not infect its neighbors ...
through the export of subversion and violence. Our purpos...
conformity with American and international law, is to pre...
flow of arms to El Salvador, Guatemala, and Costa Rica...
... to ... dialogue, ... the government of ...
... our ... persisted in its efforts to spread violence.

It is Nicaragua's government that has moved heavy ...
not the reverse. It is Nicaragua that speaks of war ...
close to the border; Nicaragua that has push forward ...
stockpiles weapons inside Honduras. And it is Radio ...
announced a new revolutionary board to push forward ...
Marxist-Leninist struggle in Honduras.

Even Costa Rica, Central America's oldest and ...
democracy, a government so peaceful it does not e...
army, is the object of bullying and threats from ...
military dictators.

Nicaragua's neighbors know that Sandinista ...
peace, non-alliance, and non-intervention have ...
Some 37 new military bases have been built — ...
during the Somoza years.

Nicaragua's new army numbers 25,000 men ...
militia of 50,000. It is the largest army ...
supplemented by 2,000 quote, unquote Cuban ...

Page 9

equipped with the most modern weapons, Soviet tank... so more
Soviet 152mm Howitzers, 100 Anti aircraft guns other defenses
... artillery, and helicopter...
... hundreds of advisors from the Soviet Union, East ...
and the P.L.O. ... we have 55 militar...
El Salvador.

The goal of the professional guerrilla movem...
America is as simple as it is sinister — to des...
entire region from the Panama Canal to Mexico. ...
on this point, let me read you what a leader of ...
guerrillas told the Mexican magazine Proceso: ...
process of Central America is a single process. ...
one are the triumphs of the other · · · Guatem...
hour. Honduras its. Costa Rica, too, will hav...
glory. The first note was heard in Nicaragua, ...

... hemisp...
... that on fa...
... consequ...
... allian...
... with a...
... or Asi...

From the desk of President Ronald Reagan

Nicaraguas mil. junta who
themselves made war & won p...
from operating from bases in...
& Costa Rica likes to pretend ...
are today being attacked from ...
forces based in Honduras. T...
fact is it is Nicaragua's g...
that threatens Honduras ...
the reverse.

It is Nicaragua who h...
moved heavy tanks close to ...
border; Nicaragua who speaks...
and encamped on radio. Ap...
the creation of a new revol...
Revolutionary board commi...
board to push forward t...
marxist struggle in H...

Nicaragua supported by
weapons & mil. resources provided by the
Communist bloc represses it's own people,
refuses to make peace, & sponsors a
guerrilla war against El Salvador.

- 13 -
(NEW PAGE 13)

I believe that our help sho...
through economic and financia...
to economic stability and ord...
processes."

"... Collapse of free insti...
of independence would be disa...
them but for the world. Disc...
failure would quickly be the ...
peoples striving to maintain ...
independence."

The size and the power of the ...
America are smaller than ~~Greece and Tu~~ the nations of...
and strategic stakes are similar. Will...
social, military — be as appropriate a...
Truman's bold solutions to the problems ...

Some people have forgotten the ...
years — and the decades of peace, pro...
secured.

Some people talk as though the ...
incapable of acting effectively in inte...
without risking war or damaging those w...

Some people think we cannot en...
without producing "another Vietnam." ...
how often and how successfully Americ...
help others defend themselves.

The political parties and factions in El Salvador are coming together -- they now share the common goal of seeking a political solution to their country's problems. New national elections will be held this year and they will be open to all political parties. The people of El Salvador are earning their freedom they deserve our moral and material support to protect it.

Yes, there are still major problems regarding human ri the criminal justice system, and violence against non-comb And like the rest of Central America, El Salvador also f severe economic problems. But, in addition to recession-depressed prices for major agricultural expo El Salvador's economy is being deliberately sabotaged

Tonight in El Salvador -- because of guerrilla much of the fertile land cannot be cultivated; les rolling stock of the railways remains operational facilities, telephone and electrical systems hav and damaged.

I think Secretary of State Shultz put it day: "Unable to win the free loyalty of El S the guerrillas are deliberately and systemat of food, water, transportation, light, san these are the people who claim they want people."

They don't want elections because defeated. But as the previous electio people's desire for democracy will no

---

The government of Nicaragua has imposed a new dictatorship; it has refused to hold the elections it promised; it has seized control of all media except a lone newspaper that it subjects to heavy prior censorship; it denied the bishops and priests of the Roman Catholic Church the right to say Mass on television during Holy Week; it insulted and mocked the Pope; it has driven the Miskito Indians from their homelands -- burning their villages, destroying their crops, and forcing them into involuntary internment in camps far from home; it has moved against the private sector and free labor unions; it condoned mob action against Nicaragua's independent human rights commission and drove the director of that Commission into exile.

In short, after all these acts of repression by the government, is it any wonder opposition has formed? Contrary to propaganda, the opponents of the Sandinistas are not die-hard

In fact, many are anti-Somoza been denied any part in democracy for Nicaragua and still do. Others are Miskito Indians fighting for their homes, lands, and lives.

Meanwhile, the government of El Salvador, making every effort to guarantee democracy, free labor unions, freedom of religion, and a free press, is under attack by guerrillas dedicated to the same philosophy that prevails in guerrillas Cuba, and, yes, the Soviet Union. Violence has been Nicaragua, most important export to the world. Violence has been Nicaragua, hypocrisy for the unelected Nicaraguan government to charge that

---

required to remain passive and prosperity accumulate?

destabilization of an enti to Mexico?

nations of this hemisphere aggressive empire the mod

aided by a massive, world terrorists, the U.S. is nd women willing to ris eserve their countrie hools, fishing rights

en from their home t refuge outside east Asians who h s who have escape enjoyed the high believe United States m, in the fac

---

freedom and security in our hemisphe I believe that a majori is prepared to stand by passively government to stand by while the p America are delivered to vulnerable to ne dangers.

Only last week an official Office reiterated Brezhnev's th missiles in this hemisphere -- United States. Daniel Ortega confirmed that, consider accepting those miss

---

Present course is We must continue to encourage peace among the nations of Central America. We must support the regional efforts to promote solutions to regional problems.

The Congress shares the responsibility for our foreign policy.

Tonight, I join me in a new, bolder, more generous approach to the problems of peace and poverty, democracy and dictatorship in the region.

Join me in a program that includes preventing Communist victory in the short run, but goes beyond it to produce for the chronically deprived people of the area the reality of present progress and the promise of more to come.

Tonight, I America and the Caribbean a new plan for Central the Truman Doctrine and Marshall Plans were to those of.

The problems are not identical. Neither are the great importance. The stakes are both of can be the same. The spirit of determination and generosity at once the complexity of the problems -- at once economic, social and military -- is similar -- and so is the

closely with the Congress to assure the fullest possible, bipartisan coordination of our policies toward the region.

What I'm asking for is prompt congressional approval for the full reprogramming of funds for key current economic and security programs so that the people of Central America can hold the line against externally supported aggression. In addition, I am asking for prompt action on the supplemental request in these same areas to carry us through the current fiscal year and for early and favorable congressional action on my requests for fiscal year 1984.

And finally, I am asking that the bipartisan consensus, which last year acted on the trade and tax provisions of the Caribbean Basin Initiative in the House, again take the lead to move this vital proposal to the floor of both chambers. And as I said before, the greatest share of these requests is targeted toward economic and humanitarian aid, not military.

What the administration is asking for on behalf of freedom in Central America is so small, so minimal, considering what is at stake. The total amount requested for aid to all of Central America in 1984 is about $600 million. That's less than one-tenth of what Americans will spend this year on coin-operated video games.

In summation, I say to you that tonight there can be no question: The national security of all the Americas is at stake in Central America. If we cannot defend ourselves there, we cannot expect to prevail elsewhere. Our credibility would collapse, our alliances would crumble, and the safety of our homeland would be put in jeopardy.

We have a vital interest, a moral duty, and a solemn responsibility. This is not a partisan issue. It is a question of our meeting our moral responsibility to ourselves, our friends, and our posterity. It is a duty that falls on all of us—the President, the Congress, and the people. We must perform it together. Who among us would wish to bear responsibility for failing to meet our shared obligation?

Thank you, God bless you, and good night.

Remarks on Greeting the Finalists
of the National Spelling Bee

WHITE HOUSE ROSE GARDEN
JUNE 6, 1983

I put this little thing in because I wanted to give you a feel for the small things that presidents do. You meet with spelling bee finalists; you meet with championship sports teams; you receive a live turkey every year before Thanksgiving, although I don't think we ever ended up eating one of those birds. It would be like eating an acquaintance. Anyway, if you add all these things up, they say something about our culture and our people and the American identity.

H ELLO THERE. Well, first let me welcome all of you spellers to the White House and let me compliment you—and that's compliment with an "i," not complement with an "e." I want to compliment you with an "i" on your accomplishments. You're the 137 finalists out of 8 to 9 million students who participated in this National Spelling Bee. That's quite an honor, and you should be very proud.

You know, because of this event, I learned that the study of spelling is called orthography. Orthography—that's o-r-t-h-o-g-r-a- . . .uh . . . p . . . ummm . . . [*Laughter*] . . . ummm . . .

h-y. [*Laughter*] No, I'm sure you already knew that, and you were just proving it, but I thought I'd give you that just in case they asked for it on Wednesday.

But all of us are proud not only of your spelling ability but of your determination to increase your knowledge. I wish all American students were as interested in their studies as you evidently are and have been. And I wish all teachers and parents took an interest in their children's educational development as your parents and teachers have taken in yours.

Now, on Wednesday, you're going to be feeling the pressure of the competition. But I want you to know that you're already —all of you—winners in my book and in the hearts of your hometowns. So, enjoy the competition and enjoy your trip to Washington. I hope you've been having some fun and seeing some of the sights here.

I'm told you're on your way to a barbecue. That sounds like fun, so I don't want to hold you up. But again, let me wish you all the best of luck on Wednesday. And remember, "i" before "e" except after "c." [*Laughter*] That ought to help a little.

You know, I have to tell you one story. People can get so sure of themselves. I know you must have heard, or read in your studies, about the author of many years ago, Mark Twain. Mark Twain was on a ship going across to Europe. And in the dining salon that night at dinner, someone wanting to impress him at the table asked him to pass the sugar and then said, "Mr. Twain, don't you think it's unusual that sugar is the only word in our language in which 's-u' has the 'shu' sound?" And Mark Twain said: "Are you sure?" [*Laughter*]

Well, good luck to all of you, and as I say, you're all winners, and you all have every reason to be proud. So win, lose, or tie, we're proud of all of you. And I maybe have time to just come down and say hello to a few of you here, and I'm going to do that.

Remarks on the Anniversary
of Martin Luther King, Jr.'s, Birth

EAST ROOM OF THE WHITE HOUSE
JANUARY 15, 1983

For all of my so-called powers of communication, I was never able to convince many black citizens of my commitment to their needs. They often mistook my belief in keeping the government out of the average American's life as a cover for doing nothing about racial injustice.

I think of all things that were said about me during my presidency, this charge bothers me the most personally. I abhor racism. These skinheads and white supremacist groups have no place in this country. They are not what we are about, and I wish they would just vaporize.

Now, there's no denying that during my presidency I had a cool relationship with most national black leaders. They fault me for many things, and I fault them for making the plight of poor black people even worse. I know that statement will raise a ruckus, but it's what I think. Many of these leaders over the past twenty years have been so wed to the big-government, status-quo thinking that they have done a terrible disservice to the independence and aspirations of many black Americans. Fortunately, some wonderfully gifted conservative black thinkers have emerged during the 1980s. I hope their influence grows in proportion to their independent brilliance.

I don't know whether Martin Luther King, Jr., would have

fallen into the trap of the status quo or not, but he certainly was a great leader at a time when this country needed him. I didn't appreciate what a remarkable man he was while he was living. But I suppose that's the way it is with prophets. You sometimes don't know their impact and importance until they're gone.

T HANK YOU ALL FOR BEING HERE. And let me especially thank the Harlem Boys' Choir. From what we've just heard, I think that you fellows could show the famous Vienna Boys' Choir a thing or two.

But welcome, all of you, to the White House on this special day. Earlier today on my radio broadcast I spoke of Dr. King's character and contributions. Now let me speak a little more personally about the man who tumbled the wall of racism in our country. Though Dr. King and I may not have exactly had identical political philosophies, we did share a deep belief in freedom and justice under God.

Freedom is not something to be secured in any one moment of time. We must struggle to preserve it every day. And freedom is never more than one generation away from extinction.

History shows that Dr. King's approach achieved great results in a comparatively short time, which was exactly what America needed. Let me read you part of what he wrote from a jail cell:

"When you suddenly find your tongue twisted as you seek to explain to your six-year-old daughter why she can't go to a public amusement park that's just been advertised on television; when you take a cross-country drive and find it necessary to sleep night after night in the uncomfortable corners of your automobile because no motel will accept you; when you're humiliated day in and day out by nagging signs reading 'white' and 'colored,' then you can understand why we find it difficult to wait."

PRESIDENTIAL REMARKS: MARTIN LUTHER KING BIRTHDAY RECEPTION
                        SATURDAY, JANUARY

Thank you all for being here, and
the Harlem Boys Choir. From what we ju
fellows could show the Vienna Boys Cho
Welcome, all of you, to the White Hous

Earlier today in my radio speech
character and contributions. Now, I
more personally about this man who t
our country.

Though Dr. King and I may not
philosophies, we ~~shared~~ DID SHARE a deep bel
under God. Freedom is not someth
~~It is~~ never more ~~than I~~
moment in time. We must struggle
History shows that Dr. King's ap
a comparatively short time -- w
needed. Let me read you part o
~~Birmingham Jail~~. ~~He wrote~~, ".
tongue twisted as you seek to
daughter why she can't go to
just been advertised on television
cross-
night
motel
by nag
will u

THNK U ALL ... BEING HR. & LET ME U
ESPCLY THNK ... HARLEM BOYS. CHOIR.
FRM. WHT. ... JUST HRD. ... THINK U
FELLOWS CLD. SHO ... FAMOUS VIENNA
BOYS. CHOIR. ... TH
... U ... W.H. ... T
EARLIER TODAY ...
... SPOKE ... DRK
NOW ... LK. ...
PERSNLY ABT ...
"RACISM ...
& I MAY N
POL. PHLGS
BLF. "FR
FRDM. ... A
"ANY I
STRUGG
... NEVR ...
EXTIR ...
COLOR
"FND
JR. F
W

APPROACH. ACHVD. GRT. RESULTS IN
"COMPARITIVY SHORT TM. - WCH
WS. EXACTLY WHT. AM. NDD. J LET
ME. RD. U. PRT. ... WHT. AM. WROTE ... JAIL
CELL - " ... WHN. U SUDDNLY FND. YR.
TONGUE TWISTD ... GO ... PUB. AMU
YR. G.YR. ... ADVRTSD ... TV
GO ... PUB. AMU ... SEEK. "XPLAIN
ADVRTSD ... TV ... NT.

HE LIFTD. HVY. BURDN FRM. TH
CO. J AS SURELY ... BLCK. AM's ...
SCARRD ... YOKE ... SLAVRY - AM's. "SCARRD
INDIGNTE ... & ... "BE HONEST ... SO. THS
BFR. - J MNY. AM's. DID NOT FULLY
REALIZE ... HVY. AM's. BURDN WS.
GN. LIFTD. & ... DR. KING
US. - ALL. US. ARE.
MN. J IN MNY

& ESPCLY ... POL. LF. ... SPOKN ... (4
GRT. DEAL. ABT. ... "NATURE & SPIRIT ...
AM's.) BLV ... VAST MAJORITY ... AM's.
SHR. ... SPIRIT WTH. DR. K. J HE SD.
" ... GOAL. AM. "FRDM. ") ... SD. ... AM
P. ... INFECTD ... DEN. IDEALS ... & THI
"FOUND HOPE J ... SD. ... BLVD. ...
GRT VAULTS "OPP. ... THS. NAT."
" GENUINELY BLVD. ... POTENTIAL ... A
SM. ONE REMRKD ... "COMFORT" HV
"FRND MAY ... TKN. AWY - BUT NOT
" HVNG HD ONE J WL. AM. MAT
LOST ... COMFORT & COURAGE ... DR. K
PERSNL PRSENC BUT ... NOT REALLY
EVRY TM ... BLCK W. CASTS ... BA
DR. K. ... THR. J EVRY TM ... BLCK
"HIRED "GOOD JOB - DR. K.
EVRY TM ... BLCK. CHLD. RCVS ...
DR. K. ... THR. J EVRY TM ... BLCK

" ... ELECTD ... PUB. OFFICE - DR. K. THR. (S
& EVRY TM. B. & W. AM's. WRK. SO. ... SO.
... BETTR FUTURE DR. K. ... THR. J ... WTH
US & ... VRY MUCH TODAY. J M. L. K.
USED ... SPK ... HS. ABIDNG FAITH ...
AM. & ... FUT. ... MNKIND. J ... DR. K.
WHT. IS ... WHT. OUGHT. BE J & ...
DEDICATED ... LF ... THT. DRM. J ... REJECTD
HS. DRM ... BCM ... REALITY J MUCH ...
STILL ... BE ACHVD. J DR. K's. FAITH
"CONTINU ... BEACN ... HOPE ... US ALGAS
"CONTINU ... STRV TOGETHR ... MK. AM.
" NAT. ... KNEW ... CLD. BCM. J SO THNK
U ... SHARING ... VRY SPCL. DAY ... US AS
" GATHR. HR. ... REMEMBR "GRT. AM -
MN. ... VISION & ... MN. ... PC. J THNK
U. & GOD BLSS !!

Martin Luther King, Jr., burned with the gospel of freedom, and that flame in his heart lit the way for millions. What he accomplished—not just for black Americans, but for all Americans—he lifted a heavy burden from this country. As surely as black Americans were scarred by the yoke of slavery, America was scarred by injustice. Many Americans didn't fully realize how heavy America's burden was until it was lifted. Dr. King did that for us, all of us.

Abraham Lincoln freed the black man. In many ways, Dr. King freed the white man. How did he accomplish this tremendous feat? Where others—white and black—preached hatred, he taught the principles of love and nonviolence. We can be so thankful that Dr. King raised his mighty eloquence for love and hope rather than for hostility and bitterness. He took the tension he found in our nation, a tension of injustice, and channeled it for the good of America and all her people.

Throughout my life, and especially my political life, I've spoken a great deal about the nature and spirit of America. I believe the vast majority of Americans share that spirit with Dr. King. He said, "The goal of America is freedom." He said, "The American people are infected with democratic ideals." And there he found hope. He said he believed there were great vaults of opportunity in this nation. He genuinely believed in the potential of America.

Someone has remarked, the comfort of having a friend may be taken away but not that of having had a friend. Well, America may have lost the comfort and courage of Dr. King's presence, but we've not really lost him. Every time a black woman casts a ballot, Martin King is there. Every time a black man is hired for a good job, Dr. King is there. Every time a black child receives a sound education, Dr. King is there. Every time a black person is elected to public office, Dr. King is there. Every time black and white Americans work side by side for a better future, Dr. King is there. He's with us, and with us very much today.

Martin Luther King used to speak of his abiding faith in America and the future of mankind. He rejected what is for what ought to be, and he dedicated his life to that dream. Much of his dream has become reality, but much is still to be achieved. Dr. King's faith will continue to be a beacon of hope for us all as we continue to serve together to make America the nation that we knew it could become.

So, thank you for this very special day, for being with us as we gather here to remember a great American—a man of vision, a man of peace. Thank you, and God bless you.

Remarks at the
Annual Convention of the
National Association of Evangelicals

ORLANDO, FLORIDA
MARCH 8, 1983

This is the "evil empire" speech that was so often quoted as defining my attitude toward the Soviets. At the time it was portrayed as some kind of know-nothing, archconservative statement that could only drive the Soviets to further heights of paranoia and insecurity.

For too long our leaders were unable to describe the Soviet Union as it actually was. The keepers of our foreign-policy knowledge—in other words, most liberal foreign-affairs scholars, the State Department, and various columnists—found it illiberal and provocative to be so honest. I've always believed, however, that it's important to define differences, because there are choices and decisions to be made in life and history.

The Soviet system over the years has purposely starved, murdered, and brutalized its own people. Millions were killed; it's all right there in the history books. It put other citizens it dis-

agreed with into psychiatric hospitals, sometimes drugging them into oblivion. Is the system that allowed this not evil? Then why shouldn't we say so? Even the Soviets themselves are now admitting to annihilating their own people during Stalin's era.

I could not in good conscience today call the Soviet Union an evil empire. As I write this, the Soviets have just conducted the most democratic elections since their revolution. Remarkable things are happening under Mikhail Gorbachev.

In addition to taking a hard line on the morality of the Soviet Union, this speech also outlines my opinions on a number of other moral issues.

REVEREND CLERGY ALL, Senator Hawkins, distinguished members of the Florida congressional delegation, and all of you:

I can't tell you how you have warmed my heart with your welcome. I'm delighted to be here today.

Those of you in the National Association of Evangelicals are known for your spiritual and humanitarian work. And I would be especially remiss if I didn't discharge right now one personal debt of gratitude. Thank you for your prayers. Nancy and I have felt their presence many times in many ways. And believe me, for us they've made all the difference.

The other day in the East Room of the White House at a meeting there, someone asked me whether I was aware of all the people out there who were praying for the President. And I had to say, "Yes, I am. I've felt it. I believe in intercessionary prayer." But I couldn't help but say to that questioner after he'd asked the question that—or at least say to them that if sometimes when he was praying he got a busy signal, it was just me in there ahead of him. [*Laughter*] I think I understand how Abraham Lincoln felt when he said, "I have been driven many times to my knees by the overwhelming conviction that I had nowhere else to go."

From the joy and the good feeling of this conference, I go to a political reception. [*Laughter*] Now, I don't know why, but that bit of scheduling reminds me of a story—[*Laughter*]—which I'll share with you.

An evangelical minister and a politician arrived at Heaven's gate one day together. And St. Peter, after doing all the necessary formalities, took them in hand to show them where their quarters would be. And he took them to a small, single room with a bed, a chair, and a table and said this was for the clergyman. And the politician was a little worried about what might be in store for him. And he couldn't believe it then when St. Peter stopped in front of a beautiful mansion with lovely grounds, many servants, and told him that these would be his quarters.

And he couldn't help but ask, he said, "But wait, how—there's something wrong—how do I get this mansion while that good and holy man only gets a single room?" And St. Peter said, "You have to understand how things are up here. We've got thousands and thousands of clergy. You're the first politician who ever made it." [*Laughter*]

But I don't want to contribute to a stereotype. [*Laughter*] So I tell you there are a great many God-fearing, dedicated, noble men and women in public life, present company included. And yes, we need your help to keep us ever mindful of the ideas and the principles that brought us into the public arena in the first place. The basis of those ideals and principles is a commitment to freedom and personal liberty that, itself, is grounded in the much deeper realization that freedom prospers only where the blessings of God are avidly sought and humbly accepted.

The American experiment in democracy rests on this insight. Its discovery was the great triumph of our Founding Fathers, voiced by William Penn when he said: "If we will not be governed by God, we must be governed by tyrants." Explaining the inalienable rights of men, Jefferson said, "The God who gave us life, gave us liberty at the same time." And it was George Washington who said that "of all the dispositions and habits which lead to political prosperity, religion and morality are indispensable supports."

And finally, that shrewdest of all observers of American democracy, Alexis de Tocqueville, put it eloquently after he had gone on a search for the secret of America's greatness and genius—and he said: "Not until I went into the churches of America and heard her pulpits aflame with righteousness did I understand the greatness and the genius of America. . . . America is good. And if America ever ceases to be good, America will cease to be great."

Well, I'm pleased to be here today with you who are keeping America great by keeping her good. Only through your work and prayers and those of millions of others can we hope to survive this perilous century and keep alive this experiment in liberty, this last, best hope of man.

I want you to know that this administration is motivated by a political philosophy that sees the greatness of America in you, her people, and in your families, churches, neighborhoods, communities—the institutions that foster and nourish values like concern for others and respect for the rule of law under God.

Now, I don't have to tell you that this puts us in opposition to, or at least out of step with, a prevailing attitude of many who have turned to a modern-day secularism, discarding the tried and time-tested values upon which our very civilization is based. No matter how well intentioned, their value system is radically different from that of most Americans. And while they proclaim that they're freeing us from superstitions of the past, they've taken upon themselves the job of superintending us by government rule and regulation. Sometimes their voices are louder than ours, but they are not yet a majority.

An example of that vocal superiority is evident in a controversy now going on in Washington. And since I'm involved, I've been waiting to hear from the parents of young America. How far are they willing to go in giving to government their prerogatives as parents?

Let me state the case as briefly and simply as I can. An organization of citizens, sincerely motivated and deeply concerned about the increase in illegitimate births and abortions involving girls well below the age of consent, some time ago established a nationwide network of clinics to offer help to these girls and, hopefully, alleviate this situation. Now, again, let me say, I do not fault their intent. However, in their well-intentioned effort, these clinics have decided to provide advice and birth control drugs and devices to underage girls without the knowledge of their parents.

For some years now, the federal government has helped with funds to subsidize these clinics. In providing for this, the Congress decreed that every effort would be made to maximize parental participation. Nevertheless, the drugs and devices are prescribed without getting parental consent or giving notification after they've done so. Girls termed "sexually active"—and that has replaced the word "promiscuous"—are given this help in order to prevent illegitimate birth or abortion.

Well, we have ordered clinics receiving federal funds to notify the parents such help has been given. One of the nation's leading newspapers has created the term "squeal rule" in editorializing against us for doing this, and we're being criticized for violating the privacy of young people. A judge has recently granted an injunction against an enforcement of our rule. I've watched TV panel shows discuss this issue, seen columnists pontificating on our error, but no one seems to mention morality as playing a part in the subject of sex.

Is all of Judeo-Christian tradition wrong? Are we to believe that something so sacred can be looked upon as a purely physical thing with no potential for emotional and psychological harm? And isn't it the parents' right to give counsel and advice to keep their children from making mistakes that may affect their entire lives?

Many of us in government would like to know what parents think about this intrusion in their family by government. We're going to fight in the courts. The right of parents and the rights of family take precedence over those of Washington-based bureaucrats and social engineers.

But the fight against parental notification is really only one example of many attempts to water down traditional values and even abrogate the original terms of American democracy. Freedom prospers when religion is vibrant and the rule of law under God is acknowledged. When our Founding Fathers passed the First Amendment, they sought to protect churches from government interference. They never intended to construct a wall of hostility between government and the concept of religious belief itself.

The evidence of this permeates our history and our government. The Declaration of Independence mentions the Supreme Being no less than four times. "In God We Trust" is engraved on our coinage. The Supreme Court opens its proceedings with a religious invocation. And the members of Congress open their sessions with a prayer. I just happen to believe the schoolchildren of the United States are entitled to the same privileges as Supreme Court justices and congressmen.

Last year, I sent the Congress a constitutional amendment to restore prayer to public schools. Already this session, there's growing bipartisan support for the amendment, and I am calling on the Congress to act speedily to pass it and to let our children pray.

Perhaps some of you read recently about the Lubbock school case, where a judge actually ruled that it was unconstitutional for a school district to give equal treatment to religious and nonreligious student groups, even when the group meetings were being held during the students' own time. The First Amendment never intended to require government to discriminate against religious speech.

Senators Denton and Hatfield have proposed legislation in the Congress on the whole question of prohibiting discrimination against religious forms of student speech. Such legislation could go far to restore freedom of religious speech for public school students. And I hope the Congress considers these bills quickly. And with your help, I think it's possible we could also get the constitutional amendment through the Congress this year.

More than a decade ago, a Supreme Court decision literally wiped off the books of fifty states statutes protecting the rights of unborn children. Abortion on demand now takes the lives of up to one and a half million unborn children a year. Human life legislation ending this tragedy will someday pass the Congress, and you and I must never rest until it does. Unless and until it can be proven that the unborn child is not a living entity, then its right to life, liberty, and the pursuit of happiness must be protected.

You may remember that when abortion on demand began, many, and indeed, I'm sure many of you, warned that the practice would lead to a decline in respect for human life, that the philosophical premises used to justify abortion on demand would ultimately be used to justify other attacks on the sacredness of human life—infanticide or mercy killing. Tragically enough, those warnings proved all too true. Only last year a court permitted the death by starvation of a handicapped infant.

I have directed the Health and Human Services Department to make clear to every health care facility in the United States that the Rehabilitation Act of 1973 protects all handicapped persons against discrimination based on handicaps, including infants. And we have taken the further step of requiring that each and every recipient of federal funds who provides health care services to infants must post and keep posted in a conspicuous place a notice stating that "discriminatory failure to feed and care for handicapped infants in this facility is prohibited by federal law." It also lists a twenty-four-hour, toll-free number so that nurses and others may report violations in time to save the infant's life.

In addition, recent legislation introduced in the Congress by Representative Henry Hyde of Illinois not only increases restrictions on publicly financed abortions, it also addresses this whole problem of infanticide. I urge the Congress to begin hearings and to adopt legislation that will protect the right of life to all children, including the disabled or handicapped.

Now, I'm sure that you must get discouraged at times, but you've done better than you know, perhaps. There's a great spiritual awakening in America, a renewal of the traditional values that have been the bedrock of America's goodness and greatness.

One recent survey by a Washington-based research council concluded that Americans were far more religious than the people of other nations; 95 percent of those surveyed expressed a belief in God and a huge majority believed the Ten Commandments had real meaning in their lives. And another study has found that an overwhelming majority of Americans disapprove of adultery, teenage sex, pornography, abortion, and hard drugs. And this same study showed a deep reverence for the importance of family ties and religious belief.

I think the items that we've discussed here today must be a key part of the nation's political agenda. For the first time the Congress is openly and seriously debating and dealing with the prayer and abortion issues—and that's enormous progress right there. I repeat: America is in the midst of a spiritual awakening and a moral renewal. And with your biblical keynote, I say today, "Yes, let justice roll on like a river, righteousness like a never-failing stream."

Now, obviously, much of this new political and social consensus I've talked about is based on a positive view of American history, one that takes pride in our country's accomplishments and record. But we must never forget that no government schemes are going to perfect man. We know that living in this world means dealing with what philosophers would call the phenomenology of evil or, as theologians would put it, the doctrine of sin.

There is sin and evil in the world, and we're enjoined by Scripture and the Lord Jesus to oppose it with all our might. Our nation, too, has a legacy of evil with which it must deal. The glory of this land has been its capacity for transcending the moral evils of our past. For example, the long struggle of minority citizens for equal rights, once a source of disunity and civil war, is now a point of pride for all Americans. We must never go back. There is no room for racism, anti-Semitism, or other forms of ethnic and racial hatred in this country.

I know that you've been horrified, as have I, by the resurgence of some hate groups preaching bigotry and prejudice. Use the mighty voice of your pulpits and the powerful standing of your churches to denounce and isolate these hate groups in our midst. The commandment given us is clear and simple: "Thou shalt love thy neighbor as thyself."

But whatever sad episodes exist in our past, any objective observer must hold a positive view of American history, a history that has been the story of hopes fulfilled and dreams made into reality. Especially in this century, America has kept alight the torch of freedom, but not just for ourselves but for millions of others around the world.

And this brings me to my final point today. During my first press conference as president, in answer to a direct question, I pointed out that, as good Marxist-Leninists, the Soviet leaders have openly and publicly declared that the only morality they recognize is that which will further their cause, which is world revolution. I think I should point out I was only quoting Lenin, their guiding spirit, who said in 1920 that they repudiate all morality that proceeds from supernatural ideas—that's their name for religion—or ideas that are outside class conceptions. Morality is entirely subordinate to the interests of class war. And everything is moral that is necessary for the annihilation of the old, exploiting social order and for uniting the proletariat.

Well, I think the refusal of many influential people to accept this elementary fact of Soviet doctrine illustrates a historical reluctance to see totalitarian powers for what they are. We saw this phenomenon in the 1930s. We see it too often today.

This doesn't mean we should isolate ourselves and refuse to seek an understanding with them. I intend to do everything I can to persuade them of our peaceful intent, to remind them that it was the West that refused to use its nuclear monopoly in

the forties and fifties for territorial gain and which now pro-
poses a 50-percent cut in strategic ballistic missiles and the
elimination of an entire class of land-based, intermediate-range
nuclear missiles.

At the same time, however, they must be made to understand
we will never compromise our principles and standards. We
will never give away our freedom. We will never abandon our
belief in God. And we will never stop searching for a genuine
peace. But we can assure none of these things America stands
for through the so-called nuclear freeze solutions proposed by
some.

The truth is that a freeze now would be a very dangerous
fraud, for that is merely the illusion of peace. The reality is that
we must find peace through strength.

I would agree to a freeze if only we could freeze the Soviets'
global desires. A freeze at current levels of weapons would
remove any incentive for the Soviets to negotiate seriously in
Geneva and virtually end our chances to achieve the major arms
reductions which we have proposed. Instead, they would
achieve their objectives through the freeze.

A freeze would reward the Soviet Union for its enormous and
unparalleled military buildup. It would prevent the essential
and long overdue modernization of United States and allied
defenses and would leave our aging forces increasingly vulnerable. And an honest freeze would require extensive prior negotiations on the systems and numbers to be limited and on the
measures to ensure effective verification and compliance. And
the kind of a freeze that has been suggested would be virtually
impossible to verify. Such a major effort would divert us completely from our current negotiations on achieving substantial
reductions.

A number of years ago, I heard a young father, a very prominent young man in the entertainment world, addressing a tremendous gathering in California. It was during the time of the
cold war, and communism and our own way of life were very
much on people's minds. And he was speaking to that subject.
And suddenly, though, I heard him saying, "I love my little girls

more than anything—" And I said to myself, "Oh, no, don't. You can't—don't say that." But I had underestimated him. He went on: "I would rather see my little girls die now, still believing in God, than have them grow up under communism and one day die no longer believing in God."

There were thousands of young people in that audience. They came to their feet with shouts of joy. They had instantly recognized the profound truth in what he had said, with regard to the physical and the soul and what was truly important.

Yes, let us pray for the salvation of all of those who live in that totalitarian darkness—pray they will discover the joy of knowing God. But until they do, let us be aware that while they preach the supremacy of the state, declare its omnipotence over individual man, and predict its eventual domination of all peoples on the earth, they are the focus of evil in the modern world.

It was C. S. Lewis who, in his unforgettable *Screwtape Letters,* wrote: "The greatest evil is not done now in those sordid 'dens of crime' that Dickens loved to paint. It is not even done in concentration camps and labor camps. In those we see its final result. But it is conceived and ordered (moved, seconded, carried and minuted) in clean, carpeted, warmed, and well-lighted offices, by quiet men with white collars and cut fingernails and smooth-shaven cheeks who do not need to raise their voice."

Well, because these "quiet men" do not "raise their voices," because they sometimes speak in soothing tones of brotherhood and peace, because, like other dictators before them, they're always making "their final territorial demand," some would have us accept them at their word and accommodate ourselves to their aggressive impulses. But if history teaches anything, it teaches that simpleminded appeasement or wishful thinking about our adversaries is folly. It means the betrayal of our past, the squandering of our freedom.

So, I urge you to speak out against those who would place the United States in a position of military and moral inferiority. You know, I've always believed that old Screwtape reserved his best efforts for those of you in the church. So, in your discus-

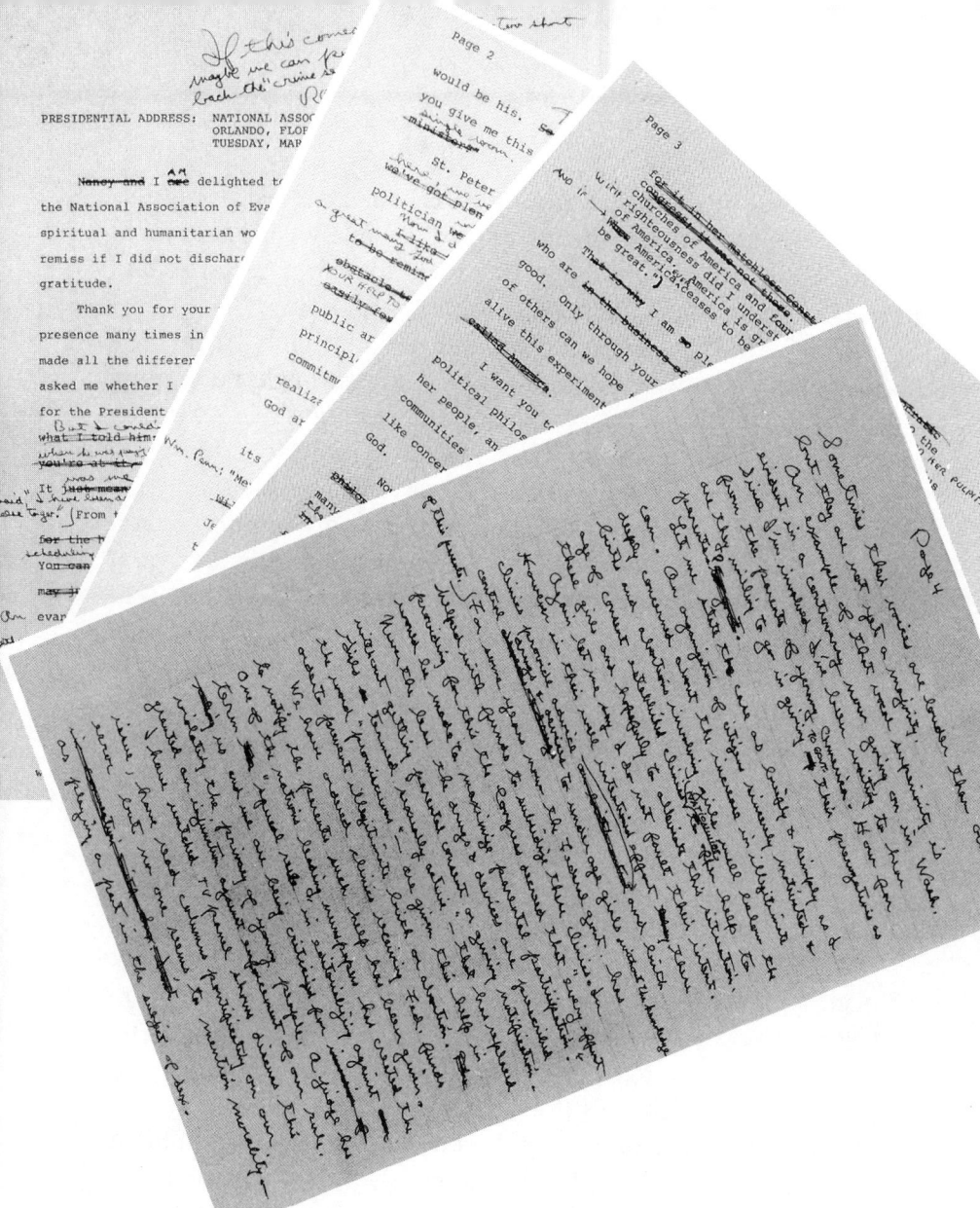

sions of the nuclear freeze proposals, I urge you to beware the temptation of pride—the temptation of blithely declaring yourselves above it all and label both sides equally at fault, to ignore the facts of history and the aggressive impulses of an evil empire, to simply call the arms race a giant misunderstanding and thereby remove yourself from the struggle between right and wrong and good and evil.

I ask you to resist the attempts of those who would have you withhold your support for our efforts, this administration's efforts, to keep America strong and free, while we negotiate real and verifiable reductions in the world's nuclear arsenals and one day, with God's help, their total elimination.

While America's military strength is important, let me add here that I've always maintained that the struggle now going on for the world will never be decided by bombs or rockets, by armies or military might. The real crisis we face today is a spiritual one; at root, it is a test of moral will and faith.

Whittaker Chambers, the man whose own religious conversion made him a witness to one of the terrible traumas of our time, the Hiss-Chambers case, wrote that the crisis of the Western world exists to the degree in which the West is indifferent to God, the degree to which it collaborates in communism's attempt to make man stand alone without God. And then he said, for Marxism-Leninism is actually the second-oldest faith, first proclaimed in the Garden of Eden with the words of temptation, "Ye shall be as gods."

The Western world can answer this challenge, he wrote, "but only provided that its faith in God and the freedom He enjoins is as great as communism's faith in Man."

I believe we shall rise to the challenge. I believe that communism is another sad, bizarre chapter in human history whose last pages even now are being written. I believe this because the source of our strength in the quest for human freedom is not material, but spiritual. And because it knows no limitation, it must terrify and ultimately triumph over those who would enslave their fellow man. For in the words of Isaiah: "He giveth power to the faint; and to them that have no might He increased strength. . . . But they that wait upon the Lord shall renew their strength; they shall mount up with wings as eagles; they shall run, and not be weary. . . ."

Yes, change your world. One of our Founding Fathers, Thomas Paine, said, "We have it within our power to begin the world over again." We can do it, doing together what no one church could do by itself.

God bless you, and thank you very much.

Remarks on Awarding the
U.S. Coast Guard Medal
Posthumously to Arland D. Williams, Jr.

OVAL OFFICE

JUNE 6, 1983

I've always felt that heroes were very important to our nation. They bind us together; they give us strength that we can do great things. I felt that part of my job as president was to let our people know how many heroes we had in this country. Arland Williams, Jr., was one of the best. I wish I had known him.

The President. We're here to honor Arland Williams, Jr. Virtually everyone in the United States knows of his heroism and knows of his deed, but very few, if any, knew his name. Those of us who do know of his bravery have remembered him only as the "unknown hero." And that was in the terrible tragedy that took place down here on January 13th, 1982, when the plane crashed into the bridge and into the ice-covered Potomac. And for a long, long time we have known of the one man who repeatedly handed the line from the helicopter to others that he thought were in a worse situation than he was, saving five people in all. And then when the helicopter went back for him, he was no longer there.

And now an investigation by the Coast Guard and a thorough study has made it known that Arland Williams, Jr., was the hero who gave his life that others might live. And we have here his family—Arland and Virginia Williams; his son and daughter, Arland and Leslie—and the Vice Commander of the Coast Guard. And we are awarding to him this medal—some 607, I think it is, have been given in the one hundred years' history of the medal. There is a gold and silver medal. Two gold were given to other heroes in this same tragedy, two silver, and now this one.

And *Time* magazine said, "If the man in the water gave a lifeline to the people gasping for survival, he was likewise giving a lifeline to those who observed him." And I think that is true, because all of us had to stand a little taller witnessing this heroic deed and knowing now the man who gets the credit.

And now would you read the citation?

Vice Admiral Stabile. Mr. President, I'd be happy to.

"The secretary of transportation takes pleasure in presenting the Gold Lifesaving Medal posthumously to Arland D. Williams, Jr., for acts as set forth in the following citation:

"For extreme and heroic daring on the afternoon of 13 January 1982, following the crash of an airplane in the Potomac River in Washington, D.C. Mr. Williams was a passenger on an Air Florida 737 that crashed in a blinding snowstorm into the Fourteenth Street Bridge that crosses the Potomac River and connects Washington, D.C., and Northern Virginia. After hitting the bridge, the plane plunged into the frozen waters of the Potomac River. Mr. Williams was seated in the rear section of the plane, which was partially above the water. When a U.S. Park Police helicopter arrived to commence rescue efforts, Mr. Williams, although injured, quickly realized that he was trapped in his seat by a jammed seat belt. As the helicopter lowered a line to the survivors for towing them to shore, Mr. Williams, acknowledging the fact that he was trapped, refused to grab the line and passed it on to the other injured persons. The helicopter crew rescued five other survivors and then returned to Mr. Williams. He could not be found as he had sunk beneath the icy waters. By not grabbing the rescue line and occupying valuable time in what would probably have been a futile attempt to pull himself free, other survivors, who might have perished if they had been in the frigid waters much longer, were saved. Mr. Williams sacrificed his own life so that others may live. Mr. Williams's unselfish actions and valiant service reflect the highest credit upon himself and were in keeping with the highest traditions of humanitarian service."

Signed, Elizabeth Hanford Dole, Secretary of Transportation.

The President. Mrs. Williams, I hope that you'll receive this medal for your son. And to his son and daughter, let me just say you can live with tremendous pride in your father.

Address to the Nation
on Events in Lebanon and Grenada

OVAL OFFICE
OCTOBER 27, 1983

George Shultz invited us down to Augusta one October week-end to golf. It was a weekend that I will never forget. Nancy and I were put up in the cottage Ike used when he frequented the links there. The weekend would have been eventful enough by the fact that a gunman took over the pro shop and held two of my staff hostage. Fortunately, the matter ended peacefully.

I can't say the same for the other events of that weekend. I guess it was three or four in the morning when the telephone rang. We had received a request for help from half a dozen countries in the Caribbean telling us they knew they were next in line to fall because of what was happening on their sister island of Grenada, where armed thugs backed by Cubans had taken over. The other islands said they didn't have the power to do any-thing by themselves and that they needed our help in addition.

I immediately called a meeting in the cottage. I knew if we turned them down, we might as well forget any relationship with other countries in the Americas. I gave the go-ahead. Grenada was so close to Cuba that I said this deal has to be the best-kept secret in town until it's under way. Only a very few outside the Pentagon knew what we were planning. Even though I'd given the go-ahead on the operation, we decided to stay in Augusta so as not to tip anyone off about what we were up to.

Then something happened that caused us to leave immediately for Washington. We received word on the bombing of our Marine barracks in Lebanon. Our boys got hit with two thousand pounds of TNT loaded onto a truck piloted by a suicide driver.

That was our hope—to bring some relief to the people of that suffering, violent place. Those boys gave their lives because of our ideal that life should have some peace to it. We can't abandon our hopes, but my how it still hurts to have lost those young men. Sending our boys to that place is the most anguishing regret of my years as president.

The following is the speech I gave to the American people on the events of that week.

M Y FELLOW AMERICANS:

Some two months ago we were shocked by the brutal massacre of 269 men, women, and children, more than 60 of them Americans, in the shooting down of a Korean airliner. Now, in these past several days, violence has erupted again, in Lebanon and Grenada.

In Lebanon, we have some 1,600 marines, part of a multinational force that's trying to help the people of Lebanon restore order and stability to that troubled land. Our marines are assigned to the south of the city of Beirut, near the only airport operating in Lebanon. Just a mile or so to the north is the Italian contingent and not far from them, the French and a company of British soldiers.

This past Sunday, at twenty-two minutes after six Beirut time, with dawn just breaking, a truck, looking like a lot of other vehicles in the city, approached the airport on a busy main road. There was nothing in its appearance to suggest it was any different than the trucks or cars that were normally seen on and around the airport. But this one was different. At the wheel was a young man on a suicide mission.

The truck carried some 2,000 pounds of explosives, but there was no way our marine guards could know this. Their first warning that something was wrong came when the truck crashed through a series of barriers, including a chain-link fence and barbed wire entanglements. The guards opened fire, but it was too late. The truck smashed through the doors of the headquarters building in which our marines were sleeping and instantly exploded. The four-story concrete building collapsed in a pile of rubble.

More than two hundred of the sleeping men were killed in that one hideous, insane attack. Many others suffered injury and are hospitalized here or in Europe.

This was not the end of the horror. At almost the same instant, another vehicle on a suicide and murder mission crashed into the headquarters of the French peacekeeping force, an eight-story building, destroying it and killing more than fifty French soldiers.

Prior to this day of horror, there had been several tragedies for our men in the multinational force. Attacks by snipers and mortar fire had taken their toll.

I called bereaved parents and/or widows of the victims to express on behalf of all of us our sorrow and sympathy. Sometimes there were questions. And now many of you are asking: Why should our young men be dying in Lebanon? Why is Lebanon important to us?

Well, it's true, Lebanon is a small country, more than five and a half thousand miles from our shores on the edge of what we call the Middle East. But every president who has occupied this office in recent years has recognized that peace in the Middle East is of vital concern to our nation and, indeed, to our allies in Western Europe and Japan. We've been concerned because the Middle East is a powder keg; four times in the last thirty years, the Arabs and Israelis have gone to war. And each time, the world has teetered near the edge of catastrophe.

The area is key to the economic and political life of the West. Its strategic importance, its energy resources, the Suez Canal, and the well-being of the nearly 200 million people living there —all are vital to us and to world peace. If that key should fall into the hands of a power or powers hostile to the free world, there would be a direct threat to the United States and to our allies.

We have another reason to be involved. Since 1948 our nation has recognized and accepted a moral obligation to assure the continued existence of Israel as a nation. Israel shares our democratic values and is a formidable force an invader of the Middle East would have to reckon with.

For several years, Lebanon has been torn by internal strife. Once a prosperous, peaceful nation, its government had become ineffective in controlling the militias that warred on each other. Sixteen months ago, we were watching on our TV screens the shelling and bombing of Beirut, which was being used as a fortress by PLO bands. Hundreds and hundreds of civilians were being killed and wounded in the daily battles.

Syria, which makes no secret of its claim that Lebanon should be a part of a Greater Syria, was occupying a large part of Lebanon. Today, Syria has become a home for 7,000 Soviet advisers and technicians who man a massive amount of Soviet weaponry, including SS-21 ground-to-ground missiles capable of reaching vital areas of Israel.

A little over a year ago, hoping to build on the Camp David accords, which had led to peace between Israel and Egypt, I proposed a peace plan for the Middle East to end the wars between the Arab states and Israel. It was based on U.N. resolutions 242 and 338 and called for a fair and just solution to the Palestinian problem, as well as a fair and just settlement of issues between the Arab states and Israel.

Before the necessary negotiations could begin, it was essential to get all foreign forces out of Lebanon and to end the fighting there. So, why are we there? Well, the answer is straightforward: to help bring peace to Lebanon and stability to the vital Middle East. To that end, the multinational force was created to help stabilize the situation in Lebanon until a government could be established and a Lebanese army mobilized to restore Lebanese sovereignty over its own soil as the foreign forces withdrew. Israel agreed to withdraw as did Syria, but Syria then reneged on its promise. Over 10,000 Palestinians who had been bringing ruin down on Beirut, however, did leave the country.

Lebanon has formed a government under the leadership of President Gemayel, and that government, with our assistance and training, has set up its own army. In only a year's time, that army has been rebuilt. It's a good army, composed of Lebanese of all factions.

A few weeks ago, the Israeli army pulled back to the Awali River in southern Lebanon. Despite fierce resistance by Syrian-backed forces, the Lebanese army was able to hold the line and maintain the defensive perimeter around Beirut.

In the year that our marines have been there, Lebanon has made important steps toward stability and order. The physical presence of the marines lends support to both the Lebanese government and its army. It allows the hard work of diplomacy to go forward. Indeed, without the peacekeepers from the U.S., France, Italy, and Britain, the efforts to find a peaceful solution in Lebanon would collapse.

As to that narrower question—what exactly is the operational mission of the marines—the answer is, to secure a piece of Beirut, to keep order in their sector, and to prevent the area from becoming a battlefield. Our marines are not just sitting in an airport. Part of their task is to guard that airport. Because of their presence, the airport has remained operational. In addition, they patrol the surrounding area. This is their part—a limited, but essential part—in the larger effort that I've described.

If our marines must be there, I'm asked, why can't we make them safer? Who committed this latest atrocity against them and why?

Well, we'll do everything we can to ensure that our men are as safe as possible. We ordered the battleship *New Jersey* to join our naval forces offshore. Without even firing them, the threat of its 16-inch guns silenced those who once fired down on our marines from the hills, and they're a good part of the reason we suddenly had a cease-fire. We're doing our best to make our forces less vulnerable to those who want to snipe at them or send in future suicide missions.

Secretary Shultz called me today from Europe, where he was meeting with the foreign ministers of our allies in the multinational force. They remain committed to our task. And plans were made to share information as to how we can improve security for all our men.

We have strong circumstantial evidence that the attack on the marines was directed by terrorists who used the same method to destroy our embassy in Beirut. Those who directed this atrocity must be dealt justice, and they will be. The obvious purpose behind the sniping and, now, this attack was to weaken American will and force the withdrawal of U.S. and French forces from Lebanon. The clear intent of the terrorists was to eliminate our support of the Lebanese government and to destroy the ability of the Lebanese people to determine their own destiny.

To answer those who ask if we're serving any purpose in being there, let me answer a question with a question. Would the terrorists have launched their suicide attacks against the multinational force if it were not doing its job? The multinational force was attacked precisely because it is doing the job it was sent to do in Beirut. It is accomplishing its mission.

Now then, where do we go from here? What can we do now to help Lebanon gain greater stability so that our marines can come home? Well, I believe we can take three steps now that will make a difference.

First, we will accelerate the search for peace and stability in that region. Little attention has been paid to the fact that we've had special envoys there working, literally, around the clock to bring the warring factions together. This coming Monday in

Geneva, President Gemayel of Lebanon will sit down with other factions from his country to see if national reconciliation can be achieved. He has our firm support. I will soon be announcing a replacement for Bud McFarlane, who was preceded by Phil Habib. Both worked tirelessly and must be credited for much if not most of the progress we've made.

Second, we'll work even more closely with our allies in providing support for the government of Lebanon and for the rebuilding of a national consensus.

Third, we will ensure that the multinational peacekeeping forces, our marines, are given the greatest possible protection. Our commandant of the Marine Corps, General Kelley, returned from Lebanon today and will be advising us on steps we can take to improve security. Vice President Bush returned just last night from Beirut and gave me a full report of his brief visit.

Beyond our progress in Lebanon, let us remember that our main goal and purpose is to achieve a broader peace in all of the Middle East. The factions and bitterness that we see in Lebanon are just a microcosm of the difficulties that are spread across much of that region. A peace initiative for the entire Middle East, consistent with the Camp David accords and U.N. resolutions 242 and 338, still offers the best hope for bringing peace to the region.

Let me ask those who say we should get out of Lebanon: If we were to leave Lebanon now, what message would that send to those who foment instability and terrorism? If America were to walk away from Lebanon, what chance would there be for a negotiated settlement, producing a unified democratic Lebanon?

If we turned our backs on Lebanon now, what would be the future of Israel? At stake is the fate of only the second Arab country to negotiate a major agreement with Israel. That's another accomplishment of this past year, the May 17th accord signed by Lebanon and Israel.

If terrorism and intimidation succeed, it'll be a devastating blow to the peace process and to Israel's search for genuine security. It won't just be Lebanon sentenced to a future of chaos. Can the United States, or the free world, for that matter, stand by and see the Middle East incorporated into the Soviet bloc? What of Western Europe's and Japan's dependence on Middle East oil for the energy to fuel their industries? The Middle East is, as I've said, vital to our national security and economic well-being.

Brave young men have been taken from us. Many others have been grievously wounded. Are we to tell them their sacrifice was wasted? They gave their lives in defense of our national security every bit as much as any man who ever died fighting in a war. We must not strip every ounce of meaning and purpose from their courageous sacrifice.

We're a nation with global responsibilities. We're not somewhere else in the world protecting someone else's interests; we're there protecting our own.

I received a message from the father of a marine in Lebanon. He told me, "In a world where we speak of human rights, there is a sad lack of acceptance of responsibility. My son has chosen the acceptance of responsibility for the privilege of living in this country. Certainly in this country one does not inherently have rights unless the responsibility for these rights is accepted." Dr. Kenneth Morrison said that while he was waiting to learn if his son was one of the dead. I was thrilled for him to learn today that his son Ross is alive and well and carrying on his duties in Lebanon.

Let us meet our responsibilities. For longer than any of us can remember, the people of the Middle East have lived from war to war with no prospect for any other future. That dreadful cycle must be broken. Why are we there? Well, a Lebanese mother told one of our ambassadors that her little girl had only attended school two of the last eight years. Now, because of our presence there, she said her daughter could live a normal life.

With patience and firmness, we can help bring peace to that strife-torn region—and make our own lives more secure. Our role is to help the Lebanese put their country together, not to do it for them.

Now, I know another part of the world is very much on our minds, a place much closer to our shores: Grenada. The island is only twice the size of the District of Columbia, with a total population of about 110,000 people.

Grenada and a half dozen other Caribbean islands here were, until recently, British colonies. They're now independent states and members of the British Commonwealth. While they respect each other's independence, they also feel a kinship with each other and think of themselves as one people.

In 1979 trouble came to Grenada. Maurice Bishop, a protégé of Fidel Castro, staged a military coup and overthrew the government which had been elected under the constitution left to the people by the British. He sought the help of Cuba in building an airport, which he claimed was for tourist trade, but which looked suspiciously suitable for military aircraft, including Soviet-built long-range bombers.

The six sovereign countries and one remaining colony are joined together in what they call the Organization of Eastern Caribbean States. The six became increasingly alarmed as Bishop built an army greater than all of theirs combined. Obviously, it was not purely for defense.

In this last year or so, Prime Minister Bishop gave indications that he might like better relations with the United States. He even made a trip to our country and met with senior officials of the White House and the State Department. Whether he was serious or not, we'll never know. On October 12th, a small group in his militia seized him and put him under arrest. They were, if anything, more radical and more devoted to Castro's Cuba than he had been.

Several days later, a crowd of citizens appeared before Bishop's home, freed him, and escorted him toward the headquarters of the military council. They were fired upon. A number, including some children, were killed, and Bishop was seized. He and several members of his cabinet were subsequently executed, and a twenty-four-hour shoot-to-kill curfew was put in effect. Grenada was without a government, its only authority exercised by a self-proclaimed band of military men.

There were then about one thousand of our citizens on Grenada, eight hundred of them students in St. George's University Medical School. Concerned that they'd be harmed or held as hostages, I ordered a flotilla of ships, then on its way to Lebanon with marines, part of our regular rotation program, to circle south on a course that would put them somewhere in the vicinity of Grenada in case there should be a need to evacuate our people.

Last weekend, I was awakened in the early morning hours and told that six members of the Organization of Eastern Caribbean States, joined by Jamaica and Barbados, had sent an urgent request that we join them in a military operation to restore order and democracy to Grenada. They were proposing this action under the terms of a treaty, a mutual assistance pact that existed among them.

These small, peaceful nations needed our help. Three of them don't have armies at all, and the others have very limited forces. The legitimacy of their request, plus my own concern for our citizens, dictated my decision. I believe our government has a responsibility to go to the aid of its citizens, if their right to life and liberty is threatened. The nightmare of our hostages in Iran must never be repeated.

We knew we had little time and that complete secrecy was vital to ensure both the safety of the young men who would undertake this mission and the Americans they were about to rescue. The Joint Chiefs worked around the clock to come up with a plan. They had little intelligence information about conditions on the island.

We had to assume that several hundred Cubans working on the airport could be military reserves. Well, as it turned out, the number was much larger, and they were a military force. Six hundred of them have been taken prisoner, and we have discovered a complete base with weapons and communications equipment, which makes it clear a Cuban occupation of the island had been planned.

Two hours ago we released the first photos from Grenada. They included pictures of a warehouse of military equipment—

one of three we've uncovered so far. This warehouse contained weapons and ammunition stacked almost to the ceiling, enough to supply thousands of terrorists. Grenada, we were told, was a friendly island paradise for tourism. Well, it wasn't. It was a Soviet-Cuban colony, being readied as a major military bastion to export terror and undermine democracy. We got there just in time.

I can't say enough in praise of our military—Army rangers and paratroopers, Navy, Marine, and Air Force personnel—those who planned a brilliant campaign and those who carried it out. Almost instantly, our military seized the two airports, secured the campus where most of our students were, and are now in the mopping-up phase.

It should be noted that in all the planning, a top priority was to minimize risk, to avoid casualties to our own men and also the Grenadian forces as much as humanly possible. But there were casualties, and we all owe a debt to those who lost their lives or were wounded. They were few in number, but even one is a tragic price to pay.

It's our intention to get our men out as soon as possible. Prime Minister Eugenia Charles of Dominica—I called that wrong; she pronounces it Dominica—she is chairman of OECS. She's calling for help from Commonwealth nations in giving the people their right to establish a constitutional government on Grenada. We anticipate that the governor general, a Grenadian, will participate in setting up a provisional government in the interim.

The events in Lebanon and Grenada, though oceans apart, are closely related. Not only has Moscow assisted and encouraged the violence in both countries, but it provides direct support through a network of surrogates and terrorists. It is no coincidence that when the thugs tried to wrest control over Grenada, there were thirty Soviet advisers and hundreds of Cuban military and paramilitary forces on the island. At the moment of our landing, we communicated with the governments of Cuba and the Soviet Union and told them we would offer shelter and security to their people on Grenada. Regrettably, Castro ordered his men to fight to the death, and some did. The others will be sent to their homelands.

You know, there was a time when our national security was based on a standing army here within our own borders and shore batteries of artillery along our coasts, and of course, a navy to keep the sea-lanes open for the shipping of things necessary to our well-being. The world has changed. Today, our national security can be threatened in faraway places. It's up to all of us to be aware of the strategic importance of such places and to be able to identify them.

Sam Rayburn once said that freedom is not something a nation can work for once and win forever. He said it's like an insurance policy; its premiums must be kept up to date. In order to keep it, we have to keep working for it and sacrificing for it just as long as we live. If we do not, our children may not know the pleasure of working to keep it, for it may not be theirs to keep.

In these last few days, I've been more sure than I've ever been that we Americans of today will keep freedom and maintain peace. I've been made to feel that by the magnificent spirit of our young men and women in uniform and by something here in our nation's capital. In this city, where political strife is so much a part of our lives, I've seen Democratic leaders in the Congress join their Republican colleagues, send a message to the world that we're all Americans before we're anything else, and when our country is threatened, we stand shoulder to shoulder in support of our men and women in the armed forces.

May I share something with you I think you'd like to know? It's something that happened to the commandant of our Marine Corps, General Paul Kelley, while he was visiting our critically injured marines in an Air Force hospital. It says more than any of us could ever hope to say about the gallantry and heroism of these young men, young men who serve so willingly so that others might have a chance at peace and freedom in their own lives and in the life of their country.

I'll let General Kelley's words describe the incident. He spoke of a "young marine with more tubes going in and out of his body than I have ever seen in one body.

"He couldn't see very well. He reached up and grabbed my four stars, just to make sure I was who I said I was. He held my hand with a firm grip. He was making signals, and we realized he wanted to tell me something. We put a pad of paper in his hand—and he wrote 'Semper Fi.' "

Well, if you've been a marine or if, like myself, you're an admirer of the marines, you know those words are a battle cry, a greeting, and a legend in the Marine Corps. They're marine shorthand for the motto of the Corps—"Semper Fidelis"—"always faithful."

General Kelley has a reputation for being a very sophisticated general and a very tough marine. But he cried when he saw those words, and who can blame him?

That marine and all those others like him, living and dead, have been faithful to their ideals. They've given willingly of themselves so that a nearly defenseless people in a region of great strategic importance to the free world will have a chance someday to live lives free of murder and mayhem and terrorism. I think that young marine and all of his comrades have given every one of us something to live up to.

They were not afraid to stand up for their country or, no matter how difficult and slow the journey might be, to give to others that last, best hope of a better future. We cannot and will not dishonor them now and the sacrifices they've made by failing to remain as faithful to the cause of freedom and the pursuit of peace as they have been.

I will not ask you to pray for the dead, because they're safe in God's loving arms and beyond need of our prayers. I would like to ask you all—wherever you may be in this blessed land —to pray for these wounded young men and to pray for the bereaved families of those who gave their lives for our freedom.

God bless you, and God bless America.

1984

Remarks on Accepting the GOP
Presidential Nomination

DALLAS, TEXAS
AUGUST 23, 1984

The story of 1984 is the election. The economy was humming, the world was fairly quiet, the wheels of government were turning, so the nation and the media focused on politics.

Even though campaigning can become a grind with so many stops you don't know where you are, it can also be invigorating. It really does get your adrenaline pumping when people respond so warmly and enthusiastically toward you.

The 1984 campaign was nothing if not enthusiastic. A member of my staff who's been reviewing some of the videotapes of the campaign asked me the other day if you can feel an audience's adulation. I said that, yes, you could. (In fact, I bet I have a better idea of what it feels like to be a rock star than most twenty-year-olds.) So then he said, "Well, how do you handle it?" I said, "I pray that I will be deserving." I always tried to remember that; otherwise the power goes to your head, and the history books are littered with such unsavory people.

Now the other thing that I always tried to remember was to campaign as if I was one vote behind. Because if you think you're going to win, you won't do what you need to do. In the '84 convention speech, I think it shows I was running pretty hard and taking nothing for granted. I went after my opponent and his fellow Democrats. You have to draw the line so people will know who you are and what you value.

The President. Mr. Chairman, Mr. Vice President, delegates to this convention, and fellow citizens:

In seventy-five days, I hope we enjoy a victory that is the size of the heart of Texas. Nancy and I extend our deep thanks to the Lone Star State and the "Big D"—the city of Dallas—for all their warmth and hospitality.

Four years ago I didn't know precisely every duty of this office, and not too long ago, I learned about some new ones from the first graders of Corpus Christi School in Chambersburg, Pennsylvania. Little Leah Kline was asked by her teacher to describe my duties. She said: "The President goes to meetings. He helps the animals. The President gets frustrated. He talks to other Presidents." How does wisdom begin at such an early age?

Tonight, with a full heart and deep gratitude for your trust, I accept your nomination for the presidency of the United States. I will campaign on behalf of the principles of our party which lift America confidently into the future.

America is presented with the clearest political choice of half a century. The distinction between our two parties and the different philosophy of our political opponents are at the heart of this campaign and America's future.

I've been campaigning long enough to know that a political party and its leadership can't change their colors in four days. We won't, and no matter how hard they tried, our opponents didn't in San Francisco. We didn't discover our values in a poll taken a week before the convention. And we didn't set a weathervane on top of the Golden Gate Bridge before we started talking about the American family.

The choices this year are not just between two different personalities or between two political parties. They're between two different visions of the future, two fundamentally different ways of governing—their government of pessimism, fear, and limits, or ours of hope, confidence, and growth.

Their government sees people only as members of groups; ours serves all the people of America as individuals. Theirs lives in the past, seeking to apply the old and failed policies to an era that has passed them by. Ours learns from the past and strives to change by boldly charting a new course for the future. Theirs lives by promises, the bigger, the better. We offer proven, workable answers.

Our opponents began this campaign hoping that America has a poor memory. Well, let's take them on a little stroll down memory lane. Let's remind them of how a 4.8-percent inflation rate in 1976 became back-to-back years of double-digit inflation—the worst since World War I—punishing the poor and the elderly, young couples striving to start their new lives, and working people struggling to make ends meet.

Inflation was not some plague borne on the wind; it was a deliberate part of their official economic policy, needed, they said, to maintain prosperity. They didn't tell us that with it would come the highest interest rates since the Civil War. As average monthly mortgage payments more than doubled, home building nearly ground to a halt; tens of thousands of carpenters and others were thrown out of work. And who controlled both houses of the Congress and the executive branch at that time? Not us, not us.

Campaigning across America in 1980, we saw evidence everywhere of industrial decline. And in rural America, farmers' costs were driven up by inflation. They were devastated by a wrongheaded grain embargo and were forced to borrow money at exorbitant interest rates just to get by. And many of them didn't get by. Farmers have to fight insects, weather, and the marketplace; they shouldn't have to fight their own government.

The high interest rates of 1980 were not talked about in San Francisco. But how about taxes? They were talked about in San Francisco. Will Rogers once said he never met a man he didn't like. Well, if I could paraphrase Will, our friends in the other party have never met a tax they didn't like or hike.

Under their policies, tax rates have gone up three times as

much for families with children as they have for everyone else over these past three decades. In just the five years before we came into office, taxes roughly doubled.

Some who spoke so loudly in San Francisco of fairness were among those who brought about the biggest single, individual tax increase in our history in 1977, calling for a series of increases in the social security payroll tax and in the amount of pay subject to that tax. The bill they passed called for two additional increases between now and 1990, increases that bear down hardest on those at the lower income levels.

The Census Bureau confirms that, because of the tax laws we inherited, the number of households at or below the poverty level paying federal income tax more than doubled between 1980 and 1982. Well, they received some relief in 1983, when our across-the-board tax cut was fully in place. And they'll get more help when indexing goes into effect this January.

Our opponents have repeatedly advocated eliminating indexing. Would that really hurt the rich? No, because the rich are already in the top brackets. But those working men and women who depend on a cost-of-living adjustment just to keep abreast of inflation would find themselves pushed into higher tax brackets and wouldn't even be able to keep even with inflation because they'd be paying a higher income tax. That's bracket creep; and our opponents are for it, and we're against it.

It's up to us to see that all our fellow citizens understand that confiscatory taxes, costly social experiments, and economic tinkering were not just the policies of a single administration. For the twenty-six years prior to January of 1981, the opposition party controlled both houses of Congress. Every spending bill and every tax for more than a quarter of a century has been of their doing.

About a decade ago, they said federal spending was out of control, so they passed a budget control act and, in the next five years, ran up deficits of $260 billion. Some control.

In 1981 we gained control of the Senate and the executive branch. With the help of some concerned Democrats in the

House we started a policy of tightening the federal budget instead of the family budget.

A task force chaired by Vice President George Bush—the finest vice president this country has ever had—it eliminated unnecessary regulations that had been strangling business and industry.

And while we have our friends down memory lane, maybe they'd like to recall a gimmick they designed for their 1976 campaign. As President Ford told us the night before last, adding the unemployment and inflation rates, they got what they called a misery index. In '76 it came to 12½ percent. They declared the incumbent had no right to seek reelection with that kind of a misery index. Well, four years ago, in the 1980 election, they didn't mention the misery index, possibly because it was then over 20 percent. And do you know something? They won't mention it in this election either. It's down to 11.6 and dropping.

By nearly every measure, the position of poor Americans worsened under the leadership of our opponents. Teenage drug use, out-of-wedlock births, and crime increased dramatically. Urban neighborhoods and schools deteriorated. Those whom government intended to help discovered a cycle of dependency that could not be broken. Government became a drug, providing temporary relief, but addiction as well.

And let's get some facts on the table that our opponents don't want to hear. The biggest annual increase in poverty took place between 1978 and 1981—over 9 percent each year, in the first two years of our administration. Well, I should—pardon me— I didn't put a period in there. In the first two years of our administration, that annual increase fell to 5.3 percent. And 1983 was the first year since 1978 that there was no appreciable increase in poverty at all.

Pouring hundreds of billions of dollars into programs in order to make people worse off was irrational and unfair. It was time we ended this reliance on the government process and renewed our faith in the human process.

In 1980 the people decided with us that the economic crisis was not caused by the fact that they lived too well. Government lived too well. It was time for tax increases to be an act of last resort, not of first resort.

The people told the liberal leadership in Washington, "Try shrinking the size of government before you shrink the size of our paychecks."

Our government was also in serious trouble abroad. We had aircraft that couldn't fly and ships that couldn't leave port. Many of our military were on food stamps because of meager earnings, and reenlistments were down. Ammunition was low, and spare parts were in short supply.

Many of our allies mistrusted us. In the four years before we took office, country after country fell under the Soviet yoke. Since January 20th, 1981, not one inch of soil has fallen to the Communists.

The Audience. Four more years! Four more years! Four more years!

The President. All right.

The Audience. Four more years! Four more years! Four more years!

The President. But worst of all, Americans were losing the confidence and optimism about the future that has made us unique in the world. Parents were beginning to doubt that their children would have the better life that has been the dream of every American generation.

We can all be proud that pessimism is ended. America is coming back and is more confident than ever about the future. Tonight, we thank the citizens of the United States whose faith and unwillingness to give up on themselves or this country saved us all.

Together, we began the task of controlling the size and activities of the government by reducing the growth of its spending while passing a tax program to provide incentives to increase productivity for both workers and industry. Today, a working family earning $25,000 has about $2,900 more in purchasing power than if tax and inflation rates were still at the 1980 level.

Today, of all the major industrial nations of the world, America has the strongest economic growth; one of the lowest inflation rates; the fastest rate of job creation—6½ million jobs in the last year and a half—a record 600,000 business incorporations in 1983; and the largest increase in real, aftertax personal income since World War II. We're enjoying the highest level of business investment in history, and America has renewed its leadership in developing the vast new opportunities in science and high technology. America is on the move again and expanding toward new eras of opportunity for everyone.

Now, we're accused of having a secret. Well, if we have, it is that we're going to keep the mighty engine of this nation revved up. And that means a future of sustained economic growth without inflation that's going to create for our children and grandchildren a prosperity that finally will last.

Today our troops have newer and better equipment; their morale is higher. The better armed they are, the less likely it is they will have to use that equipment. But if, heaven forbid, they're ever called upon to defend this nation, nothing would be more immoral than asking them to do so with weapons inferior to those of any possible opponent.

We have also begun to repair our valuable alliances, especially our historic NATO alliance. Extensive discussions in Asia have enabled us to start a new round of diplomatic progress there.

In the Middle East, it remains difficult to bring an end to historic conflicts, but we're not discouraged. And we shall always maintain our pledge never to sell out one of our closest friends, the State of Israel.

Closer to home, there remains a struggle for survival for free Latin American states, allies of ours. They valiantly struggle to prevent Communist takeovers fueled massively by the Soviet Union and Cuba. Our policy is simple: We are not going to betray our friends, reward the enemies of freedom, or permit fear and retreat to become American policies—especially in this hemisphere.

None of the four wars in my lifetime came about because we were too strong. It's weakness that invites adventurous adversaries to make mistaken judgments. America is the most peaceful, least warlike nation in modern history. We are not the cause of all the ills of the world. We're a patient and generous people. But for the sake of our freedom and that of others, we cannot permit our reserve to be confused with a lack of resolve.

Ten months ago, we displayed this resolve in a mission to rescue American students on the imprisoned island of Grenada. Democratic candidates have suggested that this could be likened to the Soviet invasion of Afghanistan—

The Audience. Boo-o-o!

The President. —the crushing of human rights in Poland or the genocide in Cambodia.

The Audience. Boo-o-o!

The President. Could you imagine Harry Truman, John Kennedy, Hubert Humphrey, or Scoop Jackson making such a shocking comparison?

The Audience. No!

The President. Nineteen of our fine young men lost their lives on Grenada, and to even remotely compare their sacrifice to the murderous actions taking place in Afghanistan is unconscionable.

There are some obvious and important differences. First, we were invited in by six East Caribbean states. Does anyone seriously believe the people of Eastern Europe or Afghanistan invited the Russians?

The Audience. No!

The President. Second, there are hundreds of thousands of Soviets occupying captive nations across the world. Today, our combat troops have come home. Our students are safe, and freedom is what we left behind in Grenada.

There are some who've forgotten why we have a military. It's not to promote war; it's to be prepared for peace. There's a sign over the entrance to Fairchild Air Force Base in Washington State, and that sign says it all: "Peace is our profession."

Our next administration—

The Audience. Four more years! Four more years! Four more years!

The President. All right.

The Audience. Four more years! Four more years! Four more years!

The President. I heard you. And that administration will be committed to completing the unfinished agenda that we've placed before the Congress and the nation. It is an agenda which calls upon the national Democratic leadership to cease its obstructionist ways.

We've heard a lot about deficits this year from those on the other side of the aisle. Well, they should be experts on budget deficits. They've spent most of their political careers creating deficits. For forty-two of the last fifty years, they have controlled both houses of the Congress.

The Audience. Boo-o-o!

The President. And for almost all of those fifty years, deficit spending has been their deliberate policy. Now, however, they call for an end to deficits. They call them ours. Yet, at the same time, the leadership of their party resists our every effort to bring federal spending under control. For three years straight, they have prevented us from adopting a balanced budget amendment to the Constitution. We will continue to fight for that amendment, mandating that government spend no more than government takes in.

And we will fight, as the vice president told you, for the right of a president to veto items in appropriations bills without having to veto the entire bill. There is no better way than the line-item veto, now used by governors in forty-three states to cut out waste in government. I know. As governor of California, I successfully made such vetos over nine hundred times.

Now, their candidate, it would appear, has only recently found deficits alarming. Nearly ten years ago he insisted that a $52-billion deficit should be allowed to get much bigger in order to lower unemployment, and he said that sometimes "we need a deficit in order to stimulate the economy."

The Audience. Boo-o-o!

The President. As a senator, he voted to override President Ford's veto of billions of dollars in spending bills and then voted no on a proposal to cut the 1976 deficit in half.

The Audience. Boo-o-o!

The President. Was anyone surprised by his pledge to raise your taxes next year if given the chance?

The Audience. No!

The President. In the Senate, he voted time and again for new taxes, including a 10-percent income tax surcharge, higher taxes on certain consumer items. He also voted against cutting the excise tax on automobiles. And he was part and parcel of that biggest single, individual tax increase in history—the social security payroll tax of 1977. It tripled the maximum tax and still didn't make the system solvent.

The Audience. Boo-o-o!

The President. If our opponents were as vigorous in supporting our voluntary prayer amendment as they are in raising taxes, maybe we could get the Lord back in the schoolrooms and drugs and violence out.

Something else illustrates the nature of the choice Americans must make. While we've been hearing a lot of tough talk on crime from our opponents, the House Democratic leadership continues to block a critical anticrime bill that passed the Republican Senate by a 91-to-1 vote. Their burial of this bill means that you and your families will have to wait for even safer homes and streets.

There's no longer any good reason to hold back passage of tuition tax credit legislation. Millions of average parents pay their full share of taxes to support public schools while choosing to send their children to parochial or other independent schools. Doesn't fairness dictate that they should have some help in carrying a double burden?

When we talk of the plight of our cities, what would help more than our enterprise zones bill, which provides tax incentives for private industry to help rebuild and restore decayed areas in seventy-five sites all across America? If they really wanted a future of boundless new opportunities for our citizens, why have they buried enterprise zones over the years in committee?

Our opponents are openly committed to increasing our tax burden.

The Audience. Boo-o-o!

The President. We are committed to stopping them, and we will.

They call their policy the new realism, but their new realism is just the old liberalism. They will place higher and higher taxes on small businesses, on family farms, and on other working families so that government may once again grow at the people's expense. You know, we could say they spend money like drunken sailors, but that would be unfair to drunken sailors [*Laughter*]—

The Audience. Four more years! Four more years! Four more years!

The President. All right. I agree.

The Audience. Four more years! Four more years! Four more years!

The President. I was going to say, it would be unfair, because the sailors are spending their own money. [*Laughter*]

Our tax policies are and will remain prowork, progrowth, and profamily. We intend to simplify the entire tax system—to make taxes more fair, easier to understand, and most important, to bring the tax rates of every American further down, not up. Now, if we bring them down far enough, growth will continue strong; the underground economy will shrink; the world will beat a path to our door; and no one will be able to hold America back; and the future will be ours.

The Audience. U.S.A.! U.S.A.! U.S.A.!

The President. All right. Another part of our future, the greatest challenge of all, is to reduce the risk of nuclear war by reducing the levels of nuclear arms. I have addressed parliaments, have spoken to parliaments in Europe and Asia during these last three and a half years, declaring that a nuclear war cannot be won and must never be fought. And those words, in those assemblies, were greeted with spontaneous applause.

There are only two nations who by their agreement can rid the world of those doomsday weapons—the United States of America and the Soviet Union. For the sake of our children and the safety of this earth, we ask the Soviets—who have walked out of our negotiations—to join us in reducing and yes, ridding the earth of this awful threat.

When we leave this hall tonight, we begin to place those clear choices before our fellow citizens. We must not let them be confused by those who still think that GNP stands for gross national promises. [*Laughter*] But after the debates, the position papers, the speeches, the conventions, the television commercials, primaries, caucuses, and slogans—after all this, is there really any doubt at all about what will happen if we let them win this November?

The Audience. No!

The President. Is there any doubt that they will raise our taxes?

The Audience. No!

The President. That they will send inflation into orbit again?

The Audience. No!

The President. That they will make government bigger than ever?

The Audience. No!

The President. And deficits even worse?

The Audience. No!

The President. Raise unemployment?

The Audience. No!

The President. Cut back our defense preparedness?

The Audience. No!

The President. Raise interest rates?

The Audience. No!

The President. Make unilateral and unwise concessions to the Soviet Union?

The Audience. No!

The President. And they'll do all that in the name of compassion.

The Audience. Boo-o-o!

The President. It's what they've done to America in the past. But if we do our job right, they won't be able to do it again.

The Audience. Reagan! Reagan! Reagan!

The President. It's getting late.

The Audience. Reagan! Reagan! Reagan!

The President. All right. In 1980 we asked the people of America, "Are you better off than you were four years ago?" Well, the people answered then by choosing us to bring about a change. We have every reason now, four years later, to ask that same question again, for we have made a change.

The American people joined us and helped us. Let us ask for their help again to renew the mandate of 1980, to move us further forward on the road we presently travel, the road of common sense, of people in control of their own destiny; the road leading to prosperity and economic expansion in a world at peace.

As we ask for their help, we should also answer the central question of public service: Why are we here? What do we believe in? Well for one thing, we're here to see that government continues to serve the people and not the other way around. Yes, government should do all that is necessary, but only that which is necessary.

We don't lump people by groups or special interests. And let me add, in the party of Lincoln, there is no room for intolerance and not even a small corner for anti-Semitism or bigotry of any kind. Many people are welcome in our house, but not the bigots.

We believe in the uniqueness of each individual. We believe in the sacredness of human life. For some time now we've all fallen into a pattern of describing our choice as left or right. It's become standard rhetoric in discussions of political philosophy. But is that really an accurate description of the choice before us?

Go back a few years to the origin of the terms and see where left or right would take us if we continued far enough in either direction. Stalin. Hitler. One would take us to Communist totalitarianism; the other to the totalitarianism of Hitler.

Isn't our choice really not one of left or right, but of up or down? Down through the welfare state to statism, to more and more government largesse accompanied always by more government authority, less individual liberty, and ultimately, totalitarianism, always advanced as for our own good. The alternative is the dream conceived by our Founding Fathers, up to the ultimate in individual freedom consistent with an orderly society.

We don't celebrate dependence day on the Fourth of July. We celebrate Independence Day.

The Audience. U.S.A.! U.S.A.! U.S.A.!

The President. We celebrate the right of each individual to be recognized as unique, possessed of dignity and the sacred right to life, liberty, and the pursuit of happiness. At the same time, with our independence goes a generosity of spirit more evident here than in almost any other part of the world. Recognizing the equality of all men and women, we're willing and able to lift the weak, cradle those who hurt, and nurture the bonds that tie us together as one nation under God.

Finally, we're here to shield our liberties, not just for now or for a few years but forever.

Could I share a personal thought with you tonight, because tonight's kind of special to me. It's the last time, of course, that I will address you under these same circumstances. I hope you'll invite me back to future conventions. Nancy and I will be forever grateful for the honor you've done us, for the opportunity to serve, and for your friendship and trust.

I began political life as a Democrat, casting my first vote in 1932 for Franklin Delano Roosevelt. That year, the Democrats called for a 25-percent reduction in the cost of government by abolishing useless commissions and offices and consolidating departments and bureaus, and giving more authority to state governments. As the years went by and those promises were forgotten, did I leave the Democratic Party, or did the leadership of that party leave not just me but millions of patriotic Democrats who believed in the principles and philosophy of that platform?

One of the first to declare this was a former Democratic nominee for president—Al Smith, the Happy Warrior, who went before the nation in 1936 to say, on television—or on radio—that he could no longer follow his party's leadership and that he was "taking a walk." As Democratic leaders have taken their party further and further away from its first principles, it's no surprise that so many responsible Democrats feel that our platform is closer to their views, and we welcome them to our side.

Four years ago we raised a banner of bold colors—no pale pastels. We proclaimed a dream of an America that would be "a shining city on a hill."

We promised that we'd reduce the growth of the federal government, and we have. We said we intended to reduce interest rates and inflation, and we have. We said we would reduce taxes to provide incentives for individuals and business to get our economy moving again, and we have. We said there must be jobs with a future for our people, not government make-work programs, and, in the last nineteen months, as I've said, six and a half million new jobs in the private sector have been created. We said we would once again be respected throughout the world, and we are. We said we would restore our ability to protect our freedom on land, sea, and in the air, and we have.

We bring to the American citizens in this election year a record of accomplishment and the promise of continuation.

We came together in a national crusade to make America great again, and to make a new beginning. Well, now it's all coming together. With our beloved nation at peace, we're in the midst of a springtime of hope for America. Greatness lies ahead of us.

Holding the Olympic games here in the United States began defining the promise of this season.

The Audience. U.S.A.! U.S.A.! U.S.A.!

The President. All through the spring and summer, we marveled at the journey of the Olympic torch as it made its passage east to west. Over nine thousand miles, by some four thousand runners, that flame crossed a portrait of our nation.

From our Gotham City, New York, to the Cradle of Liberty, Boston, across the Appalachian springtime, to the City of the

Big Shoulders, Chicago. Moving south toward Atlanta, over to St. Louis, past its Gateway Arch, across wheatfields into the stark beauty of the Southwest and then up into the still, snow-capped Rockies. And after circling the greening Northwest, it came down to California, across the Golden Gate and finally into Los Angeles. And all along the way, that torch became a celebration of America. And we all became participants in the celebration.

Each new story was typical of this land of ours. There was Ansel Stubbs, a youngster of ninety-nine, who passed the torch in Kansas to four-year-old Katie Johnson. In Pineville, Kentucky, it came at one A.M., so hundreds of people lined the streets with candles. At Tupelo, Mississippi, at seven A.M. on a Sunday morning, a robed church choir sang "God Bless America" as the torch went by.

That torch went through the Cumberland Gap, past the Martin Luther King, Jr., Memorial, down the Santa Fe Trail, and alongside Billy the Kid's grave.

In Richardson, Texas, it was carried by a fourteen-year-old boy in a special wheelchair. In West Virginia the runner came across a line of deaf children and let each one pass the torch for a few feet, and at the end these youngsters' hands talked excitedly in their sign language. Crowds spontaneously began singing "America the Beautiful" or "The Battle Hymn of the Republic."

And then, in San Francisco a Vietnamese immigrant, his little son held on his shoulders, dodged photographers and policemen to cheer a nineteen-year-old black man pushing an eighty-eight-year-old white woman in a wheelchair as she carried the torch.

My friends, that's America.

The Audience. U.S.A.! U.S.A.! U.S.A.!

The President. We cheered in Los Angeles as the flame was carried in and the giant Olympic torch burst into a billowing fire in front of the teams, the youth of 140 nations assembled on the floor of the Coliseum. And in that moment, maybe you were struck as I was with the uniqueness of what was taking place before a hundred thousand people in the stadium, most of them citizens of our country, and over a billion worldwide watching on television. There were athletes representing 140 countries here to compete in the one country in all the world whose people carry the bloodlines of all those 140 countries and more. Only in the United States is there such a rich mixture of races, creeds, and nationalities—only in our melting pot.

And that brings to mind another torch, the one that greeted so many of our parents and grandparents. Just this past Fourth of July, the torch atop the Statue of Liberty was hoisted down for replacement. We can be forgiven for thinking that maybe it was just worn out from lighting the way to freedom for 17 million new Americans. So, now we'll put up a new one.

The poet called Miss Liberty's torch the "lamp beside the golden door." Well, that was the entrance to America, and it still is. And now you really know why we're here tonight.

The glistening hope of that lamp is still ours. Every promise, every opportunity is still golden in this land. And through that golden door our children can walk into tomorrow with the knowledge that no one can be denied the promise that is America.

Her heart is full; her door is still golden, her future bright. She has arms big enough to comfort and strong enough to support, for the strength in her arms is the strength of her people. She will carry on in the eighties unafraid, unashamed, and unsurpassed.

In this springtime of hope, some lights seem eternal; America's is.

Thank you, God bless you, and God bless America.

Remarks at the U.S. Ranger Monument

POINTE DU HOC, FRANCE
JUNE 6, 1984

This was an emotional day. The ceremonies honoring the fortieth anniversary of D day became more than commemorations. They became celebrations of heroism and sacrifice. This place, Pointe du Hoc, in itself was moving and majestic. I stood there on that windswept point with the ocean behind me. Before me were the boys who forty years before had fought their way up from the ocean. Some rested under the white crosses and Stars of David that stretched out across the landscape. Others sat right in front of me. They looked like elderly businessmen, yet these were the kids who climbed the cliffs.

W<small>E'RE HERE TO MARK</small> that day in history when the Allied armies joined in battle to reclaim this continent to liberty. For four long years, much of Europe had been under a terrible shadow. Free nations had fallen, Jews cried out in the camps, millions cried out for liberation. Europe was enslaved, and the world prayed for its rescue. Here in Normandy the rescue began. Here the Allies stood and fought against tyranny in a giant undertaking unparalleled in human history.

We stand on a lonely, windswept point on the northern shore of France. The air is soft, but forty years ago at this moment, the air was dense with smoke and the cries of men, and the air was filled with the crack of rifle fire and the roar of cannon. At dawn, on the morning of the 6th of June, 1944, 225 Rangers jumped off the British landing craft and ran to the bottom of these cliffs. Their mission was one of the most difficult and daring of the invasion: to climb these sheer and desolate cliffs and take out the enemy guns. The Allies had been told that some of the mightiest of these guns were here and they would be trained on the beaches to stop the Allied advance.

The Rangers looked up and saw the enemy soldiers—at the edge of the cliffs shooting down at them with machine guns and throwing grenades. And the American Rangers began to climb. They shot rope ladders over the face of these cliffs and began to pull themselves up. When one Ranger fell, another would take his place. When one rope was cut, a Ranger would grab another and begin his climb again. They climbed, shot back, and held their footing. Soon, one by one, the Rangers pulled themselves over the top, and in seizing the firm land at the top of these cliffs, they began to seize back the continent of

Europe. Two hundred and twenty-five came here. After two days of fighting, only ninety could still bear arms.

Behind me is a memorial that symbolizes the Ranger daggers that were thrust into the top of these cliffs. And before me are the men who put them there.

These are the boys of Pointe du Hoc. These are the men who took the cliffs. These are the champions who helped free a continent. These are the heroes who helped end a war.

Gentlemen, I look at you and I think of the words of Stephen Spender's poem. You are men who in your "lives fought for life . . . and left the vivid air signed with your honor."

I think I know what you may be thinking right now—thinking "we were just part of a bigger effort; everyone was brave that day." Well, everyone was. Do you remember the story of Bill Millin of the 51st Highlanders? Forty years ago today, British troops were pinned down near a bridge, waiting desperately for help. Suddenly, they heard the sound of bagpipes, and some thought they were dreaming. Well, they weren't. They looked up and saw Bill Millin with his bagpipes, leading the reinforcements and ignoring the smack of bullets into the ground around him.

Lord Lovat was with him—Lord Lovat of Scotland, who calmly announced when he got to the bridge, "Sorry I'm a few minutes late," as if he'd been delayed by a traffic jam, when in truth he'd just come from the bloody fighting on Sword Beach, which he and his men had just taken.

There was the impossible valor of the Poles who threw themselves between the enemy and the rest of Europe as the invasion took hold, and the unsurpassed courage of the Canadians who had already seen the horrors of war on this coast. They knew what awaited them there, but they would not be deterred. And once they hit Juno Beach, they never looked back.

All of these men were part of a roll call of honor with names that spoke of a pride as bright as the colors they bore: The Royal Winnipeg Rifles, Poland's 24th Lancers, the Royal Scots Fusiliers, the Screaming Eagles, the Yeomen of England's armored divisions, the forces of Free France, the Coast Guard's "Matchbox Fleet," and you, the American Rangers.

Forty summers have passed since the battle that you fought here. You were young the day you took these cliffs; some of you were hardly more than boys, with the deepest joys of life before you. Yet, you risked everything here. Why? Why did you do it? What impelled you to put aside the instinct for self-preservation and risk your lives to take these cliffs? What inspired all the men of the armies that met here? We look at you, and somehow we know the answer. It was faith and belief; it was loyalty and love.

The men of Normandy had faith that what they were doing was right, faith that they fought for all humanity, faith that a just God would grant them mercy on this beachhead or on the next. It was the deep knowledge—and pray God we have not lost it—that there is a profound moral difference between the use of force for liberation and the use of force for conquest. You were here to liberate, not to conquer, and so you and those others did not doubt your cause. And you were right not to doubt.

You all knew that some things are worth dying for. One's country is worth dying for, and democracy is worth dying for, because it's the most deeply honorable form of government ever devised by man. All of you loved liberty. All of you were willing to fight tyranny, and you knew the people of your countries were behind you.

The Americans who fought here that morning knew word of the invasion was spreading through the darkness back home. They fought—or felt in their hearts, though they couldn't know in fact, that in Georgia they were filling the churches at four A.M., in Kansas they were kneeling on their porches and praying, and in Philadelphia they were ringing the Liberty Bell.

Something else helped the men of D day: their rock-hard belief that Providence would have a great hand in the events that would unfold here; that God was an ally in this great cause. And so, the night before the invasion, when Colonel Wolverton asked his parachute troops to kneel with him in prayer, he told them: Do not bow your heads, but look up so you can see God and ask His blessing in what we're about to do. Also that night, General Matthew Ridgway on his cot, listening in the darkness for the promise God made to Joshua: "I will not fail thee nor forsake thee."

These are the things that impelled them; these are the things that shaped the unity of the Allies.

When the war was over, there were lives to be rebuilt and governments to be returned to the people. There were nations to be reborn. Above all, there was a new peace to be assured. These were huge and daunting tasks. But the Allies summoned strength from the faith, belief, loyalty, and love of those who fell here. They rebuilt a new Europe together.

There was first a great reconciliation among those who had been enemies, all of whom had suffered so greatly. The United States did its part, creating the Marshall Plan to help rebuild our allies and our former enemies. The Marshall Plan led to the Atlantic alliance—a great alliance that serves to this day as our shield for freedom, for prosperity, and for peace.

In spite of our great efforts and successes, not all that followed the end of the war was happy or planned. Some liberated countries were lost. The great sadness of this loss echoes down to our own time in the streets of Warsaw, Prague, and East Berlin. Soviet troops that came to the center of this continent did not leave when peace came. They're still there, uninvited, unwanted, unyielding, almost forty years after the war. Because of this, allied forces still stand on this continent. Today, as forty years ago, our armies are here for only one purpose—to protect and defend democracy. The only territories we hold are memorials like this one and graveyards where our heroes rest.

We in America have learned bitter lessons from two world wars: It is better to be here ready to protect the peace, than to take blind shelter across the sea, rushing to respond only after freedom is lost. We've learned that isolationism never was and never will be an acceptable response to tyrannical governments with an expansionist intent.

But we try always to be prepared for peace; prepared to deter aggression; prepared to negotiate the reduction of arms; and yes, prepared to reach out again in the spirit of reconciliation. In truth, there is no reconciliation we would welcome more than a reconciliation with the Soviet Union, so, together, we can lessen the risks of war, now and forever.

It's fitting to remember here the great losses also suffered by the Russian people during World War II: 20 million perished, a terrible price that testifies to all the world the necessity of ending war. I tell you from my heart that we in the United States do not want war. We want to wipe from the face of the earth the terrible weapons that man now has in his hands. And I tell you, we are ready to seize that beachhead. We look for some sign from the Soviet Union that they are willing to move forward, that they share our desire and love for peace, and that they will give up the ways of conquest. There must be a changing there that will allow us to turn our hope into action.

We will pray forever that someday that changing will come. But for now, particularly today, it is good and fitting to renew our commitment to each other, to our freedom, and to the alliance that protects it.

We are bound today by what bound us forty years ago, the same loyalties, traditions, and beliefs. We're bound by reality. The strength of America's allies is vital to the United States, and the American security guarantee is essential to the continued freedom of Europe's democracies. We were with you then; we are with you now. Your hopes are our hopes, and your destiny is our destiny.

Here, in this place where the West held together, let us make a vow to our dead. Let us show them by our actions that we understand what they died for. Let our actions say to them the words for which Matthew Ridgway listened: "I will not fail thee nor forsake thee."

Strengthened by their courage, heartened by their valor and borne by their memory, let us continue to stand for the ideals for which they lived and died.

Thank you very much, and God bless you all.

Remarks at the Normandy Invasion Ceremony

OMAHA BEACH, FRANCE
JUNE 6, 1984

Later that same afternoon, I attended a joint U.S.–French ceremony commemorating D day at the Omaha Beach Memorial. A young woman had sent me a beautiful letter about her father, who had participated in the invasion. I had decided to read the letter aloud to the audience because it was so deeply moving and meaningful, but I hadn't expected to fight back the tears. Her words affected me more than I had anticipated as I started reading them. The young woman was right in the front row and I could see her crying. I know she must have been the apple of her father's eye. I know he must have been very proud of this wonderful, loving young woman.

Mr. President,* distinguished guests, we stand today at a place of battle, one that forty years ago saw and felt the worst of war. Men bled and died here for a few feet of—or inches of sand, as bullets and shellfire cut through their ranks. About them, General Omar Bradley later said, "Every man who set foot on Omaha Beach that day was a hero."

No speech can adequately portray their suffering, their sacrifice, their heroism. President Lincoln once reminded us that through their deeds, the dead of battle have spoken more eloquently for themselves than any of the living ever could. But we can only honor them by rededicating ourselves to the cause for which they gave a last full measure of devotion.

Today we do rededicate ourselves to that cause. And at this place of honor, we're humbled by the realization of how much so many gave to the cause of freedom and to their fellow man.

Some who survived the battle of June 6, 1944, are here today. Others who hoped to return never did.

"Someday, Lis, I'll go back," said Private First Class Peter Robert Zanatta, of the 37th Engineer Combat Battalion, and first assault wave to hit Omaha Beach. "I'll go back, and I'll see it all again. I'll see the beach, the barricades, and the graves."

Those words of Private Zanatta come to us from his daughter, Lisa Zanatta Henn, in a heartrending story about the event her father spoke of so often. "In his words, the Normandy invasion would change his life forever," she said. She tells some of his stories of World War II but says of her father, "The story to end all stories was D day.

"He made me feel the fear of being on that boat waiting to land. I can smell the ocean and feel the seasickness. I can see the looks on his fellow soldiers' faces—the fear, the anguish, the uncertainty of what lay ahead. And when they landed, I can feel the strength and courage of the men who took those first

* President François Mitterrand of France.

steps through the tide to what must have surely looked like instant death."

Private Zanatta's daughter wrote to me: "I don't know how or why I can feel this emptiness, this fear, or this determination, but I do. Maybe it's the bond I had with my father. All I know is that it brings tears to my eyes to think about my father as a twenty-year-old boy having to face that beach."

The anniversary of D day was always special for her family. And like all the families of those who went to war, she describes how she came to realize her own father's survival was a miracle: "So many men died. I know that my father watched many of his friends be killed. I know that he must have died inside a little each time. But his explanation to me was, 'You did what you had to do, and you kept on going.' "

When men like Private Zanatta and all our allied forces stormed the beaches of Normandy forty years ago they came not as conquerors, but as liberators. When these troops swept across the French countryside and into the forests of Belgium and Luxembourg they came not to take, but to return what had been wrongly seized. When our forces marched into Germany, they came not to prey on a brave and defeated people, but to nurture the seeds of democracy among those who yearned to be free again.

We salute them today. But Mr. President, we also salute those who, like yourself, were already engaging the enemy inside your beloved country—the French Resistance. Your valiant struggle for France did so much to cripple the enemy and spur the advance of the armies of liberation. The French Forces of the Interior will forever personify courage and national spirit. They will be a timeless inspiration to all who are free and to all who would be free.

Today, in their memory, and for all who fought here, we celebrate the triumph of democracy. We reaffirm the unity of democratic peoples who fought a war and then joined with the vanquished in a firm resolve to keep the peace.

From a terrible war we learned that unity made us invincible; now, in peace, that same unity makes us secure. We sought to bring all freedom-loving nations together in a community dedicated to the defense and preservation of our sacred values. Our alliance, forged in the crucible of war, tempered and shaped by the realities of the postwar world, has succeeded. In Europe, the threat has been contained, the peace has been kept.

Today the living here assembled—officials, veterans, citizens—are a tribute to what was achieved here forty years ago. This land is secure. We are free. These things are worth fighting and dying for.

Lisa Zanatta Henn began her story by quoting her father, who promised that he would return to Normandy. She ended with a promise to her father, who died eight years ago of cancer: "I'm going there, Dad, and I'll see the beaches and the barricades and the monuments. I'll see the graves, and I'll put flowers there just like you wanted to do. I'll feel all the things you made me feel through your stories and your eyes. I'll never forget what you went through, Dad, nor will I let anyone else forget. And Dad, I'll always be proud."

Through the words of his loving daughter, who is here with us today, a D day veteran has shown us the meaning of this day far better than any president can. It is enough for us to say about Private Zanatta and all the men of honor and courage who fought beside him four decades ago: We will always remember. We will always be proud. We will always be prepared, so we may always be free.

Thank you.

Remarks to the Citizens of Ballyporeen

BALLYPOREEN, IRELAND
JUNE 3, 1984

So this was home. This was where my people came from in ages past. That's the great thing about America, we all come from someplace else. We all have roots that reach somewhere far away. Even the Native American Indian apparently came across from Asia when there was a land bridge leading to North America tens of thousands of years ago. We all have another home.

I N THE BUSINESS that I formerly was in, I would have to say this is a very difficult spot—to be introduced to you who have waited so patiently—following this wonderful talent that we've seen here. And I should have gone on first, and then you should have followed—[*Laughter*]—to close the show. But thank you very much.

Nancy and I are most grateful to be with you here today, and I'll take a chance and say, *muintir na hEireann* [people of Ireland]. Did I get it right? [*Applause*] All right. Well, it's difficult to express my appreciation to all of you. I feel like I'm about to drown everyone in a bath of nostalgia. Of all the honors and gifts that have been afforded me as president, this visit is the one that I will cherish dearly. You see, I didn't know much about my family background—not because of a lack of interest, but because my father was orphaned before he was six years old. And now thanks to you and the efforts of good people who have dug into the history of a poor immigrant family, I know at last whence I came. And this has given my soul a new contentment. And it is a joyous feeling. It is like coming home after a long journey.

You see, my father, having been orphaned so young, he knew nothing of his roots also. And, God rest his soul, I told the father, I think he's here, too, today, and very pleased and happy to know that this is whence he came.

Robert Frost, a renowned American poet, once said, "Home is the place where, when you have to go there, they have to take you in." [*Laughter*] Well, it's been so long since my great-grandfather set out that you don't have to take me in. So, I'm certainly thankful for this wonderful homecoming today. I can't think of a place on the planet I would rather claim as my roots more than Ballyporeen, County Tipperary.

My great-grandfather left here in a time of stress, seeking to better himself and his family. From what I'm told, we were a poor family. But my ancestors took with them a treasure, an indomitable spirit that was cultivated in the rich soil of this county.

And today I come back to you as a descendant of people who are buried here in paupers' graves. Perhaps this is God's way of reminding us that we must always treat every individual, no matter what his or her station in life, with dignity and respect. And who knows? Someday that person's child or grandchild might grow up to become the prime minister of Ireland or president of the United States.

Looking around town today, I was struck by the similarity between Ballyporeen and the small town in Illinois where I was born, Tampico. Of course, there's one thing you have that we didn't have in Tampico. We didn't have a Ronald Reagan Lounge in town. [*Laughter*] Well, the spirit is the same, this spirit of warmth, friendliness, and openness in Tampico and Ballyporeen, and you make me feel very much at home.

What unites us is our shared heritage and the common values of our two peoples. So many Irish men and women from every walk of life played a role in creating the dream of America. One was Charles Thompson, Secretary of the Continental Congress, and who designed the first Great Seal of the United States. I'm certainly proud to be part of that great Irish American tradition. From the time of our revolution when Irishmen filled the ranks of the Continental Army, to the building of the railroads, to the cultural contributions of individuals like the magnificent tenor John McCormack and the athletic achievements of the great heavyweight boxing champion John L. Sullivan—all of them are part of a great legacy.

Speaking of sports, I'd like to take this opportunity to congratulate an organization of which all Irish men and women can be proud, an organization that this year is celebrating its one-hundredth anniversary: the Gaelic Athletic Association. I understand it was formed a hundred years ago in Tipperary to foster the culture and games of traditional Ireland. Some of you may be aware that I began my career as a sports announcer—a sports broadcaster—so I had an early appreciation for sporting competition. Well, congratulations to all of you during this GAA centennial celebration.

I also understand that not too far from here is the home of the great Irish novelist Charles Joseph Kickham. The Irish identity flourished in the United States. Irish men and women proud of their heritage can be found in every walk of life. I even have some of them in my cabinet. One of them traces his maternal roots to Mitchellstown, just down the road from Ballyporeen. And he and I have almost the same name. I'm talking about Secretary of the Treasury Don Regan.

He spells it R-e-g-a-n. We're all of the same clan, we're all cousins. I tried to tell the secretary one day that his branch of the family spelled it that way because they just couldn't handle as many letters as ours could. [*Laughter*] And then I received a paper from Ireland that told me that the clan to which we belong, that in it those who said "Regan" and spelled it that way were the professional people and the educators, and only the common laborers called it "Reagan." [*Laughter*] So, meet a common laborer.

The first job I ever got—I was fourteen years old, and they put a pick and a shovel in my hand and my father told me that that was fitting and becoming to one of our name.

The bond between our two countries runs deep and strong, and I'm proud to be here in recognition and celebration of our ties that bind. My roots in Ballyporeen, County Tipperary, are little different from millions of other Americans who find their roots in towns and counties all over the Isle of Erin. I just feel exceptionally lucky to have this chance to visit you.

Last year a member of my staff came through town and recorded some messages from you. It was quite a tape, and I was moved deeply by the sentiments that you expressed. One of your townsmen sang me a bit of a tune about Sean Tracy, and a few lines stuck in my mind. They went like this—not that I'll sing—"And I'll never more roam, from my own native home, in Tipperary so far away."

Well, the Reagans roamed to America, but now we're back. And Nancy and I thank you from the bottom of our hearts for coming out to welcome us, for the warmth of your welcome. God bless you all.

Remarks at the Al Smith Dinner

NEW YORK CITY
OCTOBER 18, 1984

These Al Smith dinners in New York are charity fund-raising dinners that politicians like to attend, especially in election years. I guess you could be cynical and say it's because of the Catholic vote, but it's more than that. The evenings often have a special feeling of warmth. Sometimes you're expected to be funny, sometimes sentimental. This evening in 1984, I decided to talk about my friend Cardinal Cooke, who ministered to me after the assassination attempt on my life. He had recently died and I just wanted to say a few words about him.

T HANK YOU VERY MUCH. I have to catch the shuttle. [*Laughter*]

May it please Your Excellency, Archbishop O'Connor, and members of the reverend clergy, Governor Cuomo, Senators Moynihan and D'Amato, Mayor Koch, and Mr. Toastmaster, Sonny Werblin, and distinguished friends:

I thank you for that welcome.

I must say, I have traveled the banquet circuit for many years. I've never quite understood the logistics of dinners like this, and how the absence of one individual could cause three of us to not have seats. [*Laughter*] But that's enough of that. [*Laughter*]

I'm grateful for your invitation and honored to be here. And I can't help but feel that four great Americans are with us here in spirit tonight: Al Smith, of course, the Happy Warrior, whom time and respect and affectionate memory have elevated beyond partisanship; the beloved Francis Cardinal Spellman, whose remarkable works of charity so notably include his establishment of this Al Smith Dinner thirty-eight years ago; the great Jewish philanthropist Charles Silver. He was enlisted by Cardinal Spellman as chairman of these dinners and raised millions for hospitals serving all faiths; and finally, Terence Cardinal Cooke, that gentle soul whom I, for one, shall never forget.

All of them are gone now, gone to God—Cardinal Cooke and Charlie Silver within a year's passing, as you've been told. And all of them personify the great commandment—to love our fellow man.

Here we are, then, at the height of a season marked by differences of opinion, and yet, all this striving and all these contesting issues fade to insignificance in the clear light of example that these four men set for us, each one in his own unique way: Al Smith, in his lifelong struggles for the working man and woman; Cardinal Spellman, as a prince and builder of the church; Charles Silver, as a friend and colleague in ecumenical service to humanity; and Cardinal Cooke, whom I knew best in circumstances of dire spiritual need.

Nothing could have meant more to me and to Nancy than Cardinal Cooke's visit with us at the White House while I was recovering from young Mr. Hinckley's unwelcome attentions. His Eminence offered prayers and encouragement that maintained us in a time of genuine personal need—a need far more serious, I know now, than we or almost anyone at the time realized.

And so it was only natural that Nancy and I should have been so profoundly grief-stricken upon learning in August of last year that the cardinal was dying. Together, we telephoned our dear friend in New York to tell him of our heartfelt prayers for him and to thank him once again for all he had done to comfort and reassure us in our hour of need. Our prayerful concern for the cardinal, I assured him, was shared by millions of other Americans grateful for all that he had done on behalf of his country.

His letter of September 15th, which followed our call, said our prayers, good wishes, and loving concern "are a source of great comfort to me." But then he wrote, "I want you to know that I'm offering my prayers and my suffering for the gift of God's peace among all the members of His human family."

Nancy and I will always be grateful that we were able to visit him in New York and, as it turned out, only days before his death. We were told that when we arrived that he had been in great pain for the previous forty-eight hours, so much so that they'd feared he wouldn't be able to receive us. But when we arrived, he was so much like his old self, it was hard to believe that he was desperately ill.

Being Terence Cooke, he couldn't resist doing a little lobbying in behalf of a cause that concerned him: "As a nation known for its compassion," he said, "the United States has accomplished so much through the years in advancing the cause of international justice and peace through its programs of economic assistance to the less fortunate peoples of the world." And then he acknowledged the appropriation that I had approved for help to sub-Saharan African nations.

He also talked of my problems, and he said, "When I join the Lord, I'll continue to pray for you." He paused, and then, with something of an abashed or self-deprecatory smile, very simply he added, "Maybe I'm being a little presumptuous in assuming I'll be with the Lord." Well, eleven days later he left us, and none of us have any doubt that he joined the Lord.

I have presumed to share this personal experience with you tonight because it says so much about our gentle friend, Terence Cooke. It says much also about Al Smith and Cardinal Spellman and Charlie Silver, for, linked in charity, linked in service, linked in humanity, they are linked by this occasion.

I think it should make us proud to have known these great Americans and their works of love for their fellow man. I think it should make us just a little bit prouder than ever to be Americans.

Archbishop O'Connor, I know that you're profoundly aware of the great tradition in which you now pursue God's work. And in this you have my every good wish and, I know, those also of a grateful nation. And if you wouldn't think that I was invading your field, could I just say, in addition to a heartfelt thank you to all of you, God bless you.

Remarks at a Rally
in Fairfield, Connecticut

OCTOBER 26, 1984

This speech was typical of the stump speech I delivered out on the hustings. I'd give it or an alternate almost everywhere I went with small variations for the audience and for the local Republican candidates running for office. I don't know why, but during the '84 campaign the audiences seemed to get caught up in the spirit of things and they'd start chanting or yelling things out to me. It was really quite a party, a Republican party as things turned out. The year came to a close with a landslide under our belt and another four-year lease on the White House.

The President. Well, it's great to be here in Fairfield and back in Connecticut again. And I'm proud to be here today with your Congressman Stu McKinney. We need him back in Washington. And that goes for Congresswoman Nancy Johnson, too. She's had a first, great term, and we need her back in Washington.

Today I want to ask everyone in Connecticut to help out this administration by sending Larry Denardis back to the Congress from the third district, electing Herschel Klein in the first district, and Roberta Koontz in the second, and John Rowland in the fifth.

I am always glad to visit again with the good people who

have given America some of its greatest Republicans—John Davis Lodge, Clare Boothe Luce, and yes, a fellow named George Bush. He's a great friend, a strong right arm, and I think the finest vice president this country's ever had.

I would also like to say hello to Donna and Bruce Keith, whose son, Jeff, is undertaking a courageous task to raise money for the American Cancer Society. Jeff, as you probably all know, is running from Boston to Los Angeles, and Nancy and I met him on Monday in Kansas City—where I'd gone for a little fracas of my own. Jeff's run is not only an inspiration, it's a challenge to all of us to go as far as our abilities will take us—and a little bit farther. And I think that all of you probably are well aware of what he's doing and are proud of him, as we all are.

Now, you know that Nathan Hale was from Connecticut. Now, I'm not going to claim he was a Republican; that would be almost as bad as my opponent invoking the name of Harry Truman to defend his defense policies. I hope you've all noticed that my opponent, who back in the primaries sounded like he thought the world was *Mr. Rogers' Neighborhood*—[*Laughter*]—has suddenly discovered that America has some dangerous adversaries out there. The man who, all his years in the Senate, voted against every weapons system except slingshots—[*Laughter*]—is now talking tough about our adversaries and the need for national security.

Audience member. He doesn't know what he's talking about!

The President. You're right. [*Laughter*] He doesn't. For those of you who are too far away to hear, a lady up here said, "He doesn't know what he's talking about." [*Laughter*] She's absolutely right.

And last-minute conversions aren't going to hide the fact that these liberal Democrats don't represent traditional Democrats anymore. You know, national Democrats used to fight for the working families of America, and now all they seem to fight for are the special interests and their own left-wing ideology. We have a tremendous opportunity this year to join with a lot of disaffected Democrats and independents to send a message back to Washington, a message that says the American people want a Congress that won't stalemate or obstruct our agenda for hope and new opportunity for the future.

Abe Lincoln said we must disenthrall ourselves with the past, and then we will save our country. Well, four years ago that's just what we did. We made a great turn. We got out from under the thrall of a government which we had hoped would make our lives better, but which wound up trying to live our lives for us. The power of the federal government, that it had over the decades, created great chaos—economic, social, and international. And our leaders were adrift, rudderless, without compass.

Four years ago we began to navigate by some certain, fixed principles. Our North Star was freedom, and common sense our constellations. We knew that economic freedom meant paying less of the American family's earnings to the government, and so we cut personal tax rates by 25 percent.

We knew that inflation, the quiet thief, was stealing our savings, and the highest interest rates since the Civil War were making it impossible for people to own a home or start an enterprise. And let me interject a news note, in case you've been busy this morning and haven't heard it: Led by Morgan, the bank, two other major banks joined them, and the prime rate came down to 12 percent as of this morning. And I'm sure that the other banks will soon follow.

The Audience. Four more years! Four more years! Four more years!

The President. All right. You'd better let me talk; it looks like it's going to rain.

We knew that our national military defense had been weakened, so we decided to rebuild and be strong again. And this we knew would enhance the chances for peace throughout the world.

It was a second American revolution, and it's only just begun. But America is back, a giant, powerful in its renewed spirit, its growing economy, powerful in its ability to defend itself and secure the peace, and powerful in its ability to build a new future. And you know something? That's not debatable.

Yet four years after our efforts began small voices in the night are sounding the call to go back—back to the days of drift, the days of torpor, timidity, and taxes. My opponent this year is known to you, but perhaps we can gain greater insight into the world he would take us back to if we take a look at his record.

His understanding of economics is well demonstrated by his predictions. Just before we took office, he said our economic program is obviously, murderously, inflationary. That was just before we lowered inflation from 12.4 down to around 4 percent. And just after our tax cuts, he said the most he could see was an anemic recovery. And that was right before the United States economy created more than 6 million new jobs in twenty-one months.

My opponent said our policies would deliver a misery index the likes of which we haven't seen for a long time. Now, there he was partially right. You know you get the misery index by adding the rate of unemployment to the rate of inflation. They invented that in 1976, during the campaign that year. They said that Jerry Ford had no right to ask for reelection because his misery index was 12.6. Now, they didn't mention the misery index in the 1980 election, probably because it had gone up to more than 20. And they aren't talking too much about it in this campaign, because it's down around 11.

He said that decontrol of oil, the oil prices, would cost American consumers more than $36 billion a year. Well, we decontrolled oil prices. It was one of the first things we did. And the price of gas went down eight cents a gallon.

Now, I have something figured out here—that maybe all we have to do to get the economy in absolutely perfect shape is to persuade my opponent to predict absolute disaster. [Laughter]

He says he cares about the middle class, but he boasts, "I have consistently supported legislation, time after time, which increases taxes on my own constituents." Doesn't that make you just want to be one of his constituents?

The Audience. No!

The President. He's no doubt proud of the fact that as senator he voted sixteen times to increase taxes on the American people.

The Audience. Boo-o-o!

The President. But this year he's outdone himself. He's already promised, of course, to raise your taxes. But if he's to keep all the promises that he's made in this campaign—we figured it out by computer—he will have to raise your taxes $1,890 for every household in this country.

The Audience. Boo-o-o!

The President. That's better than $150 a month, that's the Mondale mortgage. But his economic plan has two basic parts: raise your taxes, and then raise them again. But I've got news for him: The American people don't want his tax increases, and he isn't going to get them.

If he got them, if he got those tax increases, it would stop the recovery. But I tell you, he did give me an idea: If I can figure out how to dress like his tax program, I'll go out on Halloween and scare the devil out of all the neighbors. [*Laughter*]

If his campaign were a television show, it would be *Let's Make a Deal.* You give up your prosperity to see what surprise he has for you behind the curtain. [*Laughter*] If his plan were a Broadway show, it would be *Promises, Promises.* [*Laughter*] And if the administration that he served in as vice president were a book, you'd have to read it from the back end to the front to get a happy ending.

He sees an America in which every day is tax day, April 15th. But we see an America in which every day is Independence Day, July 4th. We want to lower your tax rates so that your families will be stronger, our economy will be stronger, and America will be stronger.

I'm proud to say that during these last four years, not one square inch of territory in the world has been lost to Communist aggression. And the United States is more secure than it was four years ago.

But my opponent sees a different world. Some time back he said the old days of a Soviet strategy of suppression by force are over. That was just before the Soviets invaded Czechoslovakia. After they invaded Afghanistan, he said, "It just baffles me why the Soviets these last few years have behaved as they have." But then, there's so much that baffles him. [*Laughter*]

One year ago we liberated Grenada from Communist thugs who had taken over that country, and my opponent called what we did a violation of international law that erodes our moral authority to criticize the Soviets.

The Audience. Boo-o-o!

The President. Well, there's nothing immoral about rescuing American students whose lives are in danger. But by the time my opponent decided that action was justified, the students were long since home.

After the Sandinista revolution in Nicaragua, he praised it. He said, "Winds of democratic progress are stirring where they have long been stifled." But we all know that the Sandinistas immediately began to persecute the genuine believers in democracy and export terror. They went on to slaughter the Miskito Indians, abuse and deport church leaders, practice anti-Semitism, slander the Pope, and move to kill free speech. Don't you think it's time my opponent stood up, spoke out, and condemned the Sandinista crimes? [*Applause*]

More recently, he refused, or failed to repudiate the Reverend Jesse Jackson, when he went to Havana and then stood with Fidel Castro and cried: "Long live President Fidel Castro! Long live Che Guevara!"

The Audience. Boo-o-o!

The President. But let me try to put this in perspective. The 1984 election is not truly a partisan contest. I was a Democrat once myself, and for a long time, a large part of my life. But in those days, its leaders didn't belong to the "blame America first" crowd. Its leaders were men like Harry Truman, who understood the challenges of our times. They didn't reserve all their indignation for America. They knew the difference between freedom and tyranny and they stood up for one and damned the other.

To all the good Democrats who respect that tradition, I say —and I hope there are many present—you're not alone. We're asking you to come walk with us down the new path of hope and opportunity, and we'll make it a bipartisan salvation of our country.

This month an American woman walked in space—Kathryn Sullivan—and she made history. And she returned to a space shuttle in which some of the great scientific and medical advances of the future will be made. Cures for diabetes and heart disease may be possible up there; advances in technology and communications. But my opponent led the fight in the United States Senate against the entire shuttle program and called it a horrible waste.

Well, we support the space shuttle, and we've committed America to meet a great challenge—to build a permanently manned space station before this decade is out.

And now, I've probably been going on for too long up here—

The Audience. No!

The President. —but I just want to say the point is we were right when we made a great turn in 1980. Incidentally, I was mistaken when I said there "before this decade is out." I should say within ten years—a decade—we're hoping for that space station.

We were right to take command of the ship, stop its aimless drift, and get moving again. And we were right when we stopped sending out SOS and starting saying U.S.A.!

The Audience. U.S.A.! U.S.A.! U.S.A.!

The President. You are right. The United States was never meant to be a second-best nation. And like our Olympic athletes, this nation should set its sights on the stars and go for the gold.

If America could bring down inflation from, as I said, 12.4 percent to 4, then we can bring inflation from 4 percent down to zero. If lowering your tax rates led to the best expansion in thirty years, then we can lower them again and keep America growing into the twenty-first century.

If we could create 6 million new jobs in twenty-one months, and some 9 million new businesses be incorporated in eighteen months, then we can make it possible for every American— young, old, black, or white—who wants, to find a job.

If our states and municipalities can establish enterprise zones to create economic growth, then we can elect people to Congress who will free our enterprise-zones bill from Tip O'Neill —it's been there for more than two years—so that we can provide hope and opportunity for the most distressed areas of America.

If we can lead a revolution in technology, push back the frontiers of space, then we can provide our workers—in industries old and new—all that they need. I say that American workers provided with the right tools can outproduce, outcompete, and outsell anyone in the world.

Audience member. Give 'em hell!

The President. Someone said, "Give 'em hell." Harry Truman —when they said that to Harry Truman, he said tell them the truth, and they'll think it's hell. Well, if our grassroots drive to restore excellence in education could reverse a twenty-year decline in scholastic aptitude test scores—which it has—then we can keep raising those scores and restoring American academic excellence second to none.

If our crackdown on crime could produce the sharpest drop ever in the crime index, then we can keep cracking down until our families and friends can walk our streets again without being afraid.

And if we could reverse the decline in our military defenses and restore respect for America, then we can make sure this nation remains strong enough to protect freedom and peace for us, for our children, and for our children's children.

And if we make sure that America is strong and prepared for peace, then we can begin to reduce nuclear weapons and one day banish them entirely from the earth. And that is our goal.

If we can strengthen our economy, strengthen our security, and strengthen the values that bind us, then America will become a nation ever greater in art and learning, greater in the love and worship of the God who made us and Who has blessed us as no other people on earth have ever been blessed.

To the young people of our country—and I'm so happy to see so many of them here—let me, if I could, say to you young people: You are what this election is all about—you and your future.

Your generation is something special. Your love of country and idealism are unsurpassed. And it's our highest duty to make certain that you have an America every bit as full of opportunity, hope, confidence, and dreams as we had when we were your age.

You know, last Sunday night I didn't get to finish what I started to say, was going to finish with in that debate, so I can finish it now. I was talking about you young people. And I've seen you all across this country, and you are special. And what I was going to say was that my generation—and a few generations between mine and yours—that we grew up in an America where we took it for granted that you could fly as high and as far as your own strength and ability would take you. And it is our sacred responsibility—those several generations I've just mentioned—to make sure that we hand you an America that is free in a world that is at peace. And we're going to do it.

The Audience. Four more years! Four more years! Four more years!

The President. All right. Thank you. I really hadn't thought about it, but you've talked me into it. You know, if we can, all of us together—we're part of a great revolution, and it's only just begun. America is never going to give up its special mission on this earth—never. There are new worlds on the horizon, and we're not going to stop until we all get there together.

America's best days are yet to come. And I know it may drive my opponents up the wall, but I'm going to say it anyway: You ain't seen nothin' yet.

The Audience. Reagan! Reagan! Reagan!

The President. Thank you very much. Thank you, and God bless you all.

1985

Address to the Nation
on the Upcoming
U.S.–Soviet Summit in Geneva

OVAL OFFICE
NOVEMBER 14, 1985

The U.S.–Soviet summit is the lead for 1985. Who would have guessed it? Here I was, the great anti-Communist, heading off for a meeting with the leader of the evil empire.

Actually, it did not surprise me at all. The only reason I'd never met with General Secretary Gorbachev's predecessors was because they kept dying on me—Brezhnev, Chernenko, Andropov. Then along came Gorbachev. He was different in style, in substance, and, I believe, in intellect from previous Soviet leaders. He is a man who takes chances and that's what you need for progress. He is a remarkable force for change in that country.

We first met in Geneva. My team had set up a guesthouse away from the main meeting area where Gorbachev and I could talk one-on-one. He jumped at the chance when I suggested we sneak away. And there we sat and talked for hours in front of a roaring fire. I opened by telling him that ours was a unique situation—two men who together had the power to bring on World War III. By the same token we had the capability to bring about world peace. I said, "We don't mistrust each other because we're armed. We're armed because we mistrust each other." I asked him how, in addition to eliminating the arms, how could we eliminate the mistrust?

I did not know when I left for that meeting in Geneva, I would eventually call Mikhail Gorbachev a friend. I did not know what to expect. This is the speech I gave to the American people as I prepared to depart for Geneva.

M<small>Y FELLOW</small> A<small>MERICANS</small>:

Good evening. In thirty-six hours I will be leaving for Geneva for the first meeting between an American president and a Soviet leader in six years. I know that you and the people of the world are looking forward to that meeting with great interest, so tonight I want to share with you my hopes and tell you why I am going to Geneva.

My mission, stated simply, is a mission for peace. It is to engage the new Soviet leader in what I hope will be a dialog for peace that endures beyond my presidency. It is to sit down across from Mr. Gorbachev and try to map out, together, a basis for peaceful discourse even though our disagreements on fundamentals will not change. It is my fervent hope that the two of us can begin a process which our successors and our peoples can continue—facing our differences frankly and openly and beginning to narrow and resolve them; communicating effectively so that our actions and intentions are not misunderstood; and eliminating the barriers between us and cooperating wherever possible for the greater good of all.

This meeting can be an historic opportunity to set a steady, more constructive course to the twenty-first century. The history of American-Soviet relations, however, does not augur well for euphoria. Eight of my predecessors—each in his own way in his own time—sought to achieve a more stable and peaceful relationship with the Soviet Union. None fully succeeded; so, I don't underestimate the difficulty of the task ahead. But these sad chapters do not relieve me of the obligation to try to make this a safer, better world. For our children, our grandchildren, for all mankind—I intend to make the effort. And with your prayers and God's help, I hope to succeed. Success at the summit, however, should not be measured by any short-term agreements that may be signed. Only the passage of time will tell us whether we constructed a durable bridge to a safer world. This, then, is why I go to Geneva—to build a foundation for lasting peace.

When we speak of peace, we should not mean just the absence of war. True peace rests on the pillars of individual freedom, human rights, national self-determination, and respect for the rule of law. Building a safer future requires that we address candidly all the issues which divide us and not just focus on one or two issues, important as they may be. When we meet in Geneva, our agenda will seek not just to avoid war, but to strengthen peace, prevent confrontation, and remove the sources of tension. We should seek to reduce the suspicions and mistrust that have led us to acquire mountains of strategic weapons. Since the dawn of the nuclear age, every American president has sought to limit and end the dangerous competition in nuclear arms. I have no higher priority than to finally realize that dream. I've said before, I will say again: A nuclear war cannot be won and must never be fought. We've gone the extra mile in arms control, but our offers have not always been welcome.

In 1977 and again in 1982, the United States proposed to the Soviet Union deep reciprocal cuts in strategic forces. These offers were rejected out-of-hand. In 1981 we proposed the complete elimination of a whole category of intermediate-range nuclear forces. Three years later, we proposed a treaty for a global ban on chemical weapons. In 1983 the Soviet Union got up and walked out of the Geneva nuclear arms control negotiations altogether. They did this in protest because we and our European allies had begun to deploy nuclear weapons as a counter to Soviet SS-20s aimed at our European and other allies. I'm pleased now, however, with the interest expressed in reducing offensive weapons by the new Soviet leadership. Let me repeat tonight what I announced last week. The United States is prepared to reduce comparable nuclear systems by 50 percent. We seek reductions that will result in a stable balance between us with no first-strike capability and verified full compliance. If we both reduce the weapons of war there would be no losers, only winners. And the whole world would benefit if we could both abandon these weapons altogether and move to nonnuclear defensive systems that threaten no one.

But nuclear arms control is not of itself a final answer. I told four Soviet political commentators two weeks ago that nations do not distrust each other because they're armed; they arm themselves because they distrust each other. The use of force, subversion, and terror has made the world a more dangerous place. And thus, today there's no peace in Afghanistan; no peace in Cambodia; no peace in Angola, Ethiopia, or Nicaragua. These wars have claimed hundreds of lives and threaten to spill over national frontiers. That's why in my address to the United Nations, I proposed a way to end these conflicts: a regional peace plan that calls for negotiations among the warring parties—withdrawal of all foreign troops, democratic reconciliation, and economic assistance.

Four times in my lifetime, our soldiers have been sent overseas to fight in foreign lands. Their remains can be found from Flanders Field to the islands of the Pacific. Not once were those young men sent abroad in the cause of conquest. Not once did they come home claiming a single square inch of some other country as a trophy of war. A great danger in the past, however, has been the failure by our enemies to remember that while we Americans detest war, we love freedom and stand ready to sacrifice for it. We love freedom not only because it's practical and beneficial but because it is morally right and just.

In advancing freedom, we Americans carry a special burden —a belief in the dignity of man in the sight of the God who gave birth to this country. This is central to our being. A century and a half ago, Thomas Jefferson told the world, "The mass of mankind has not been born with saddles on their backs. . . ." Freedom is America's core. We must never deny it nor forsake it. Should the day come when we Americans remain silent in the face of armed aggression, then the cause of America, the cause of freedom, will have been lost and the great heart of this country will have been broken. This affirmation of freedom is not only our duty as Americans, it's essential for success at Geneva.

Freedom and democracy are the best guarantors of peace. History has shown that democratic nations do not start wars. The rights of the individual and the rule of law are as fundamental to peace as arms control. A government which does not respect its citizens' rights and its international commitments to protect those rights is not likely to respect its other international undertakings. And that's why we must and will speak in Geneva on behalf of those who cannot speak for themselves. We are not trying to impose our beliefs on others. We have a right to expect, however, that great states will live up to their international obligations.

Despite our deep and abiding differences, we can and must prevent our international competition from spilling over into violence. We can find, as yet undiscovered, avenues where American and Soviet citizens can cooperate fruitfully for the benefit of mankind. And this, too, is why I'm going to Geneva. Enduring peace requires openness, honest communications, and opportunities for our peoples to get to know one another directly. The United States has always stood for openness. Thirty years ago in Geneva, President Eisenhower, preparing for his first meeting with the then Soviet leader, made his Open Skies proposal and an offer of new educational and cultural exchanges with the Soviet Union. He recognized that removing the barriers between people is at the heart of our relationship. He said: "Restrictions on communications of all kinds, including radio and travel, existing in extreme form in some places, have operated as causes of mutual distrust. In America, the fervent belief in freedom of thought, of expression, and of movement is a vital part of our heritage."

Well, I have hopes that we can lessen the distrust between us, reduce the levels of secrecy, and bring forth a more open world. Imagine how much good we could accomplish, how the cause of peace would be served, if more individuals and families from our respective countries could come to know each other in a personal way. For example, if Soviet youth could attend American schools and universities, they could learn firsthand what spirit of freedom rules our land and that we do not wish the Soviet people any harm. If American youth could do likewise, they could talk about their interests and values and hopes for the future with their Soviet friends. They would get firsthand knowledge of life in the U.S.S.R., but most important, they would learn that we're all God's children with much in common. Imagine if people in our nation could see the Bolshoi Ballet again, while Soviet citizens could see American plays and hear groups like the Beach Boys. And how about Soviet children watching *Sesame Street.*

We've had educational and cultural exchanges for twenty-five years and are now close to completing a new agreement. But I feel the time is ripe for us to take bold new steps to open the way for our peoples to participate in an unprecedented way in the building of peace. Why shouldn't I propose to Mr. Gorbachev at Geneva that we exchange many more of our citizens from fraternal, religious, educational, and cultural groups? Why not suggest the exchange of thousands of undergraduates each year, and even younger students who would live with a host family and attend schools or summer camps? We could look to increased scholarship programs, improve language studies, conduct courses in history, culture, and other subjects, develop new sister cities, establish libraries and cultural centers, and yes, increase athletic competition. People of both our nations love sports. If we must compete, let it be on the playing fields and not the battlefields. In science and technology, we could launch new joint space ventures and establish joint medical research projects. In communications, we'd like to see more appearances in the other's mass media by representatives of both our countries. If Soviet spokesmen are free to appear on American television, to be published and read in the American press, shouldn't the Soviet people have the same right to see, hear, and read what we Americans have to say? Such proposals will not bridge our differences, but people-to-people contacts can build genuine constituencies for peace in both countries. After all, people don't start wars, governments do.

Let me summarize, then, the vision and hopes that we carry with us to Geneva. We go with an appreciation, born of experience, of the deep differences between us—between our values, our systems, our beliefs. But we also carry with us the determination not to permit those differences to erupt into confrontation or conflict. We do not threaten the Soviet people and never will. We go without illusion, but with hope, hope that progress can be made on our entire agenda. We believe that progress can be made in resolving the regional conflicts now burning on three continents, including our own hemisphere. The regional plan we proposed at the United Nations will be raised again at Geneva. We're proposing the broadest people-to-people exchanges in the history of American-Soviet relations, exchanges in sports and culture, in the media, education, and the arts. Such exchanges can build in our societies thousands of coalitions for cooperation and peace. Governments can only do so much. Once they get the ball rolling, they should step out of the way and let people get together to share, enjoy, help, listen, and learn from each other, especially young people.

Finally, we go to Geneva with the sober realization that nuclear weapons pose the greatest threat in human history to the survival of the human race, that the arms race must be stopped. We go determined to search out and discover common ground —where we can agree to begin the reduction, looking to the eventual elimination, of nuclear weapons from the face of the earth. It is not an impossible dream that we can begin to reduce nuclear arsenals, reduce the risk of war, and build a solid foundation for peace. It is not an impossible dream that our children and grandchildren can someday travel freely back and forth between America and the Soviet Union; visit each other's homes; work and study together; enjoy and discuss plays, music, television, and root for teams when they compete.

These, then, are the indispensable elements of a true peace: the steady expansion of human rights for all the world's peoples; support for resolving conflicts in Asia, Africa, and Latin

America that carry the seeds of a wider war; a broadening of people-to-people exchanges that can diminish the distrust and suspicion that separate our two peoples; and the steady reduction of these awesome nuclear arsenals until they no longer threaten the world we both must inhabit. This is our agenda for Geneva; this is our policy; this is our plan for peace.

We have cooperated in the past. In both world wars, Americans and Russians fought on separate fronts against a common enemy. Near the city of Murmansk, sons of our own nation are buried, heroes who died of wounds sustained on the treacherous North Atlantic and North Sea convoys that carried to Russia the indispensable tools of survival and victory. While it would be naive to think a single summit can establish a permanent peace, this conference can begin a dialog for peace. So, we look to the future with optimism, and we go to Geneva with confidence.

Both Nancy and I are grateful for the chance you've given us to serve this nation and the trust you've placed in us. I know how deep the hope of peace is in her heart, as it is in the heart of every American and Russian mother. I received a letter and picture from one such mother in Louisiana recently. She wrote, "Mr. President, how could anyone be more blessed than I? These children you see are mine, granted to me by the Lord for a short time. When you go to Geneva, please remember these faces, remember the faces of my children—of Jonathan, my son, and of my twins, Lara and Jessica. Their future depends on your actions. I will pray for guidance for you and the Soviet leaders." Her words "my children" read like a cry of love. And I could only think how that cry has echoed down through the centuries, a cry for all the children of the world, for peace, for love of fellow man. Here is the central truth of our time, of any time, a truth to which I've tried to bear witness in this office.

When I first accepted the nomination of my party, I asked you, the American people, to join with me in prayer for our nation and the world. Six days ago in the Cabinet Room, religious leaders—Ukrainian and Greek Orthodox bishops, Catholic church representatives, including a Lithuanian bishop,

Protestant pastors, a Mormon elder, and Jewish rabbis—made me a similar request. Well, tonight I'm honoring that request. I'm asking you, my fellow Americans, to pray for God's grace and His guidance for all of us at Geneva, so that the cause of true peace among men will be advanced and all of humanity thereby served.

Good night, and God bless you.

Remarks at Bergen-Belsen Concentration Camp

AND

Bitburg Air Base

FEDERAL REPUBLIC OF GERMANY

MAY 5, 1985

I really created quite a controversy when I decided to go to a cemetery in Bitburg, West Germany, where two thousand German war dead were buried. What we didn't know when we said yes was that forty-eight members of the Nazi SS were also buried there. When our advance people had gone over, snow covered the SS graves so our people didn't see them.

The problem was that we couldn't back out without offending our German hosts, who would've taken this as quite a slap.

By the same token, many people in our own country were deeply hurt that I would go where storm troopers were buried because of what those monsters had done. Holocaust survivor Elie Wiesel emotionally pleaded to me at the White House, "Mr. President, that is not your place." Even Nancy thought I should stay away.

I made the decision, however, that we must go. I didn't feel that we could ask new generations of Germans to live with this guilt forever without any hope of redemption. They were not alive during World War II. These young people should not be made to bear the burden. Many of their grandfathers died in that war. These men weren't Nazis; they didn't work in the concentration camps; they were just soldiers doing their job of fighting a war.

Later, I also learned that several of the Nazi storm troopers buried there were buried in prisoner uniforms. They were killed by their fellow SS members for helping concentration camp prisoners. I received letters to this effect from Jewish survivors. I remember one man wrote me that he was in the camp at the age of sixteen. One of the SS kept him from being executed by hiding him.

The following two sets of remarks I've put together because

they are related. A little after noon, I laid a wreath at Bergen-Belsen concentration camp for those who had been murdered there. What an emotional place that is. And the remarkable thing is that every year schoolchildren from all over Germany go there so that they will learn what happened and so that they will not forget. From that ceremony, I went to the cemetery at Bitburg and laid a wreath for the soldiers who are interred there. I actually made my remarks about Bitburg not at the cemetery, but at the air base nearby.

CHANCELLOR KOHL and honored guests, this painful walk into the past has done much more than remind us of the war that consumed the European continent. What we have seen makes unforgettably clear that no one of the rest of us can fully understand the enormity of the feelings carried by the victims of these camps. The survivors carry a memory beyond anything that we can comprehend. The awful evil started by one man, an evil that victimized all the world with its destruction, was uniquely destructive of the millions forced into the grim abyss of these camps.

Here lie people—Jews—whose death was inflicted for no reason other than their very existence. Their pain was borne only because of who they were and because of the God in their prayers. Alongside them lay many Christians—Catholics and Protestants.

For year after year, until that man and his evil were destroyed, hell yawned forth its awful contents. People were brought here for no other purpose but to suffer and die—to go unfed when hungry, uncared for when sick, tortured when the whim struck, and left to have misery consume them when all there was around them was misery.

I'm sure we all share similar first thoughts, and that is: What of the youngsters who died at this dark stalag? All was gone for them forever—not to feel again the warmth of life's sunshine and promise, not the laughter and the splendid ache of growing up, nor the consoling embrace of a family. Try to think of being young and never having a day without searing emotional and physical pain—desolate, unrelieved pain.

Today, we've been grimly reminded why the commandant of this camp was named "the Beast of Belsen." Above all, we're struck by the horror of it all—the monstrous, incomprehensible horror. And that's what we've seen but is what we can never understand as the victims did. Nor with all our compassion can we feel what the survivors feel to this day and what they will feel as long as they live. What we've felt and are expressing with words cannot convey the suffering that they endured. That is why history will forever brand what happened as the Holocaust.

Here, death ruled, but we've learned something as well. Because of what happened, we found that death cannot rule forever, and that's why we're here today. We're here because humanity refuses to accept that freedom of the spirit of man can ever be extinguished. We're here to commemorate that life triumphed over the tragedy and the death of the Holocaust—overcame the suffering, the sickness, the testing, and yes, the gassings. We're here today to confirm that the horror cannot outlast hope, and that even from the worst of all things, the best may come forth. Therefore, even out of this overwhelming sadness, there must be some purpose, and there is. It comes to us through the transforming love of God.

We learn from the Talmud that "it was only through suffering that the children of Israel obtained three priceless and coveted gifts: The Torah, the Land of Israel, and the World to Come." Yes, out of this sickness—as crushing and cruel as it was—there was hope for the world as well as for the world to come. Out of the ashes—hope, and from all the pain—promise.

So much of this is symbolized today by the fact that most of the leadership of free Germany is represented here today. Chancellor Kohl, you and your countrymen have made real the renewal that had to happen. Your nation and the German people have been strong and resolute in your willingness to confront and condemn the acts of a hated regime of the past. This reflects the courage of your people and their devotion to freedom and justice since the war. Think how far we've come from that time when despair made these tragic victims wonder if anything could survive.

As we flew here from Hanover, low over the greening farms and the emerging springtime of the lovely German countryside, I reflected, and there must have been a time when the prisoners at Bergen-Belsen and those of every other camp must have felt the springtime was gone forever from their lives. Surely we can understand that when we see what is around us—all these children of God under bleak and lifeless mounds, the plainness of which does not even hint at the unspeakable acts that created them. Here they lie, never to hope, never to pray, never to love, never to heal, never to laugh, never to cry.

And too many of them knew that this was their fate, but that was not the end. Through it all was their faith and a spirit that moved their faith.

Nothing illustrates this better than the story of a young girl who died here at Bergen-Belsen. For more than two years Anne Frank and her family had hidden from the Nazis in a confined annex in Holland where she kept a remarkably profound diary. Betrayed by an informant, Anne and her family were sent by freight car to Auschwitz and finally here to Bergen-Belsen.

Just three weeks before her capture, young Anne wrote these words: "It's really a wonder that I haven't dropped all my ideals because they seem so absurd and impossible to carry out. Yet I keep them because in spite of everything I still believe that people are good at heart. I simply can't build up my hopes on a foundation consisting of confusion, misery, and death. I see the world gradually being turned into a wilderness. I hear the ever approaching thunder which will destroy us too; I can feel the suffering of millions and yet, if I looked up into the heavens I think that it will all come right, that this cruelty too will end and that peace and tranquility will return again." Eight months later, this sparkling young life ended here at Bergen-Belsen. Somewhere here lies Anne Frank.

Everywhere here are memories—pulling us, touching us, making us understand that they can never be erased. Such memories take us where God intended His children to go—toward learning, toward healing, and above all, toward redemption. They beckon us through the endless stretches of our heart to the knowing commitment that the life of each individual can change the world and make it better.

We're all witnesses; we share the glistening hope that rests in every human soul. Hope leads us, if we're prepared to trust it, toward what our President Lincoln called the better angels of our nature. And then, rising above all this cruelty, out of this tragic and nightmarish time, beyond the anguish, the pain, and the suffering for all time, we can and must pledge: Never again.

T HANK YOU VERY MUCH. I have just come from the cemetery where German war dead lay at rest. No one could visit there without deep and conflicting emotions. I felt great sadness that history could be filled with such waste, destruction, and evil, but my heart was also lifted by the knowledge that from the ashes has come hope and that from the terrors of the past we have built forty years of peace, freedom, and reconciliation among our nations.

This visit has stirred many emotions in the American and German people, too. I've received many letters since first deciding to come to Bitburg cemetery; some supportive, others deeply concerned and questioning, and others opposed. Some old wounds have been reopened, and this I regret very much because this should be a time of healing.

To the veterans and families of American servicemen who still carry the scars and feel the painful losses of that war, our gesture of reconciliation with the German people today in no way minimizes our love and honor for those who fought and died for our country. They gave their lives to rescue freedom in its darkest hour. The alliance of democratic nations that guards the freedom of millions in Europe and America today stands as living testimony that their noble sacrifice was not in vain.

No, their sacrifice was not in vain. I have to tell you that nothing will ever fill me with greater hope than the sight of two former war heroes who met today at the Bitburg ceremony; each among the bravest of the brave; each an enemy of the other forty years ago; each a witness to the horrors of war. But today they came together, American and German, General Matthew B. Ridgway and General Johanner Steinhoff, reconciled and united for freedom. They reached over the graves to one another like brothers and grasped their hands in peace.

To the survivors of the Holocaust: Your terrible suffering has made you ever vigilant against evil. Many of you are worried that reconciliation means forgetting. Well, I promise you, we will never forget. I have just come this morning from Bergen-Belsen, where the horror of that terrible crime, the Holocaust, was forever burned upon my memory. No, we will never forget, and we say with the victims of that Holocaust: Never again.

The war against one man's totalitarian dictatorship was not like other wars. The evil war of Nazism turned all values upside down. Nevertheless, we can mourn the German war dead today as human beings crushed by a vicious ideology.

There are over two thousand buried in Bitburg cemetery. Among them are forty-eight members of the SS—the crimes of the SS must rank among the most heinous in human history—but others buried there were simply soldiers in the German Army. How many were fanatical followers of a dictator and willfully carried out his cruel orders? And how many were conscripts, forced into service during the death throes of the Nazi war machine? We do not know. Many, however, we know from the dates on their tombstones, were only teenagers at the time. There is one boy buried there who died a week before his sixteenth birthday.

There were thousands of such soldiers to whom Nazism meant no more than a brutal end to a short life. We do not believe in collective guilt. Only God can look into the human heart, and all these men have now met their supreme judge, and they have been judged by Him as we shall all be judged.

Our duty today is to mourn the human wreckage of totalitarianism, and today in Bitburg cemetery we commemorated the potential good in humanity that was consumed back then, forty years ago. Perhaps if that fifteen-year-old soldier had lived, he would have joined his fellow countrymen in building this new democratic Federal Republic of Germany, devoted to human dignity and the defense of freedom that we celebrate today. Or perhaps his children or his grandchildren might be among you here today at the Bitburg Air Base, where new generations of Germans and Americans join together in friendship and common cause, dedicating their lives to preserving peace and guarding the security of the free world.

Too often in the past each war only planted the seeds of the next. We celebrate today the reconciliation between our two nations that has liberated us from that cycle of destruction. Look at what together we've accomplished. We who were enemies are now friends; we who were bitter adversaries are now the strongest of allies.

In the place of fear we've sown trust, and out of the ruins of war has blossomed an enduring peace. Tens of thousands of Americans have served in this town over the years. As the mayor of Bitburg has said, in that time there have been some six thousand marriages between Germans and Americans, and many thousands of children have come from these unions. This is the real symbol of our future together, a future to be filled with hope, friendship, and freedom.

The hope that we see now could sometimes even be glimpsed in the darkest days of the war. I'm thinking of one special story —that of a mother and her young son living alone in a modest cottage in the middle of the woods. And one night as the Battle of the Bulge exploded not far away, and around them, three young American soldiers arrived at their door—they were standing there in the snow, lost behind enemy lines. All were frostbitten; one was badly wounded. Even though sheltering the enemy was punishable by death, she took them in and made them a supper with some of her last food. Then, they heard another knock at the door. And this time four German soldiers stood there. The woman was afraid, but she quickly said with a firm voice, "There will be no shooting here." She made all the soldiers lay down their weapons, and they all joined in the makeshift meal. Heinz and Willi, it turned out, were only sixteen; the corporal was the oldest at twenty-three. Their natural suspicion dissolved in the warmth and the comfort of the cottage. One of the Germans, a former medical student, tended the wounded American.

But now, listen to the rest of the story through the eyes of one who was there, now a grown man, but that young lad that had been her son. He said: "Then Mother said grace. I noticed that there were tears in her eyes as she said the old, familiar words, 'Komm, Herr Jesus. Be our guest.' And as I looked around the table, I saw tears, too, in the eyes of the battle-weary soldiers, boys again, some from America, some from Germany, all far from home."

That night—as the storm of war tossed the world—they had their own private armistice. And the next morning, the German corporal showed the Americans how to get back behind their own lines. And they all shook hands and went their separate ways. That happened to be Christmas day, forty years ago.

Those boys reconciled briefly in the midst of war. Surely we allies in peacetime should honor the reconciliation of the last forty years.

To the people of Bitburg, our hosts and the hosts of our servicemen, like that generous woman forty years ago, you make us feel very welcome. Vielen dank. [Many thanks.]

And to the men and women of Bitburg Air Base, I just want to say that we know that even with such wonderful hosts, your job is not an easy one. You serve around the clock far from home, always ready to defend freedom. We're grateful, and we're very proud of you.

Four decades ago we waged a great war to lift the darkness of evil from the world, to let men and women in this country and in every country live in the sunshine of liberty. Our victory was great, and the Federal Republic, Italy, and Japan are now in the community of free nations. But the struggle for freedom is not complete, for today much of the world is still cast in totalitarian darkness.

Twenty-two years ago President John F. Kennedy went to the Berlin Wall and proclaimed that he, too, was a Berliner. Well, today freedom-loving people around the world must say: I am a Berliner. I am a Jew in a world still threatened by anti-Semitism. I am an Afghan, and I am a prisoner of the gulag. I am a refugee in a crowded boat foundering off the coast of Vietnam. I am a Laotian, a Cambodian, a Cuban, and a Miskito Indian in Nicaragua. I, too, am a potential victim of totalitarianism.

The one lesson of World War II, the one lesson of Nazism, is that freedom must always be stronger than totalitarianism and that good must always be stronger than evil. The moral measure of our two nations will be found in the resolve we show to preserve liberty, to protect life, and to honor and cherish all God's children.

That is why the free, democratic Federal Republic of Germany is such a profound and hopeful testament to the human spirit. We cannot undo the crimes and wars of yesterday nor call the millions back to life, but we can give meaning to the past by learning its lessons and making a better future. We can let our pain drive us to greater efforts to heal humanity's suffering.

Today I've traveled 220 miles from Bergen-Belsen and, I feel, forty years in time. With the lessons of the past firmly in our minds, we've turned a new, brighter page in history.

One of the many who wrote me about this visit was a young woman who had recently been bas mitzvahed. She urged me to lay the wreath at Bitburg cemetery in honor of the future of Germany. And that is what we've done.

On this fortieth anniversary of World War II, we mark the day when the hate, the evil, and the obscenities ended, and we commemorate the rekindling of the democratic spirit in Germany.

There's much to make us hopeful on this historic anniversary. One of the symbols of that hate—that could have been that hope, a little while ago, when we heard a German band playing the American national anthem and an American band playing the German national anthem. While much of the world still huddles in the darkness of oppression, we can see a new dawn of freedom sweeping the globe. And we can see in the new democracies of Latin America, in the new economic freedoms and prosperity in Asia, in the slow movement toward peace in the Middle East, and in the strengthening alliance of democratic nations in Europe and America that the light from that dawn is growing stronger.

Together, let us gather in that light and walk out of the shadow. Let us live in peace.

Thank you, and God bless you all.

Remarks on Presenting
the Presidential Medal
of Freedom to Mother Teresa

WHITE HOUSE ROSE GARDEN
JUNE 20, 1985

Mother Teresa is a fascinating slip of a woman, so filled with love for every human being. And she is something of a pamphleteer as well. A member of my staff one time reached out to shake her hand and Mother Teresa said, "Love God," and stuck out a pamphlet extolling Jesus instead. That person now has the pamphlet framed. Mother Teresa would sometimes write me when she needed something in particular for her work, and we'd usually find a way to get it to her through a corporation or the government. I believe she is a living saint.

The President. This great house receives many great visitors, but none more special or more revered than our beloved guest today. A month ago, we awarded the Medal of Freedom to thirteen heroes who have done their country proud. Only one of the recipients could not attend because she had work to do —not special work, not unusual work for her, but everyday work which is both special and urgent in its own right. Mother Teresa was busy, as usual, saving the world. And I mean that quite literally. And so we rather appreciated her priorities, and we're very happy, indeed, that she could come to America this week.

Now, a moment ago, I said we'd awarded the Medal of Freedom to heroes who've done our country proud. And I believe Mother Teresa might point out here that she is most certainly not an American but a daughter of Yugoslavia, and she has not spent her adult life in this country but in India. However, it simply occurred to us when we wanted to honor her that the goodness in some hearts transcends all borders and all narrow nationalistic considerations.

Some people, some very few people are, in the truest sense, citizens of the world; Mother Teresa is. And we love her so much we asked her to accept our tribute, and she graciously accepted. And I will now read the citation.

"Most of us talk about kindness and compassion, but Mother Teresa, the saint of the gutters, lives it. As a teenager, she went to India to teach young girls. In time, Mother Teresa began to work among the poor and the dying of Calcutta. Her order of the Missionaries of Charity has spread throughout the world, serving the poorest of the poor.

"Mother Teresa is a heroine of our times. And to the many honors she has received, including the Nobel Peace Prize, we add, with deep affection and endless respect, the Presidential Medal of Freedom."

[*At this point, the President presented the award to Mother Teresa.*]

May I say that this is the first time I've given the Medal of Freedom with the intuition that the recipient might take it home, melt it down, and turn it into something that can be sold to help the poor. [*Laughter*]

And I want to thank you for something, Mother Teresa. Your great work and your life have inspired so many Americans to become personally involved, themselves, in helping the poor. So many men and women in every area of life, in government and the private sector, have been led by the light of your love, and they have given greatly of themselves. And we thank you for your radiant example.

Mother Teresa. I am most unworthy of this generous gift of our president, Mr. Reagan, and his wife and you people of United States. But I accept it for the greater glory of God and in the name of the millions of poor people that this gift, in spirit and in love, will penetrate the hearts of the people. For in giving it to me, you are giving it to them, to my hands, with your great love and concern.

I've never realized that you loved the people so tenderly. I had the experience, I was last time here, a sister from Ethiopia found me and said, "Our people are dying. Our children are dying. Mother, do something." And the only person that came in my mind while she was talking, it was the President. And immediately I wrote to him, and I said, "I don't know, but this is what happened to me." And next day it was that immediately he arranged to bring food to our people. And I can tell you the gift that has come from your people, from your country, has brought life—new life—to our suffering people in Ethiopia.

I also want to thank the families here in United States for their continual and delicate love that they have given, and they have shown, by leaving their children to become sisters and to serve the poor throughout the world. We are now over the world and trying to bring the tenderness and the love of Jesus.

And you, you cannot go where we go. You cannot do what we do. But together, we are doing something beautiful for God. And my gratitude to you, President, and your family and to your people. It's my prayer for you that you may grow in holiness to this tender love for the poorest of the poor. But this love begins at home, in your own family, and it begins by praying together. Prayer gives a clean heart, and a clean heart can see God. And if you see God in each other, you will have love, peace, joy together. And works of love are works of peace. And love begins at home.

So, my sisters, brothers, and fathers, you are going—and all our poor people, thousands and thousands and thousands of people that we deal with, I bring their gratitude to you. And keep the joy of loving. Love them, and begin in your own family first. And that love will penetrate right through the furthest place where no one has ever been—there is that tenderness and love of Christ.

And remember that whatever you do to the least, you do it to Him, Jesus said. You did it to me. What a wonderful opportunity for each one of us to be twenty-four hours with Jesus. And in doing what we are doing, as He said, if you receive a little child in my name, you receive me. If you give a glass of water in my name, you give it to me. What a wonderful and beautiful tenderness and love of Christ for each one of us.

So, once more, I want to thank you for this beautiful gift, which I am sure it will bring great joy to our people by sharing it with them.

God bless you and keep you in His heart.

Remarks at the
Conservative Political Action Conference

WASHINGTON, D.C.
MARCH 1, 1985

You may wonder why I've selected another speech from one of these CPAC gatherings. Well, this is a good representation of what I was trying to accomplish at the start of my second term. These friends were the base of everything that I was trying to do. What I'm saying in this speech to my fellow conservatives could actually serve as the inaugural address for my second term.

T HANK YOU, Vice Chairman Linen,* for those very kind words. I'm grateful to the American Conservative Union, Young Americans for Freedom, *National Review, Human Events,* for organizing this wonderful evening. When you work in the White House, you don't get to see your old friends as much as you'd like. And I always see the CPAC speech as my opportunity to "dance with the one that brung ya."

There's so much I want to talk about tonight. I've been think-

---

* James A. Linen, vice chairman of the American Conservative Union.

ing, in the weeks since the inauguration, that we are at an especially dramatic turning point in American history. And just putting it all together in my mind, I've been reviewing the elements that have led to this moment.

Ever since FDR and the New Deal, the opposition party, and particularly those of a liberal persuasion, have dominated the political debate. Their ideas were new; they had momentum; they captured the imagination of the American people. The left held sway for a good long time. There was a right, but it was, by the forties and fifties, diffuse and scattered, without a unifying voice.

But in 1964 came a voice in the wilderness—Barry Goldwater; the great Barry Goldwater, the first major party candidate of our time who was a true-blue, undiluted conservative. He spoke from principle, and he offered vision. Freedom—he spoke of freedom: freedom from the government's increasing demands on the family purse, freedom from the government's increasing usurpation of individual rights and responsibilities, freedom from the leaders who told us the price of world peace is continued acquiescence to totalitarianism. He was ahead of his time. When he ran for president, he won six states and lost forty-four. But his candidacy worked as a precursor of things to come.

A new movement was stirring. And in the 1960s Young Americans for Freedom is born; *National Review* gains readership and prestige in the intellectual community; *Human Events* becomes a major voice on the cutting edge. In the seventies the antitax movement begins. Actually, it was much more than an antitax movement, just as the Boston Tea Party was much more than antitax initiative. [*Laughter*] In the late seventies Proposition 13 and the Sagebrush Rebellion; in 1980, for the first time in twenty-eight years, a Republican Senate is elected; so, may I say, is a conservative president. In 1984 that conservative administration is reelected in a forty-nine-state sweep. And the day the votes came in, I thought of Walt Whitman: "I hear America singing." [*Laughter*]

This great turn from left to right was not just a case of the pendulum swinging—first, the left holds sway and then the right, and here comes the left again. The truth is, conservative thought is no longer over here on the right; it's the mainstream now.

And the tide of history is moving irresistibly in our direction. Why? Because the other side is virtually bankrupt of ideas. It has nothing more to say, nothing to add to the debate. It has spent its intellectual capital, such as it was—[Laughter]—and it has done its deeds.

Now, we're not in power now because they failed to gain electoral support over the past fifty years. They did win support. And the result was chaos, weakness, and drift. Ultimately, though, their failures yielded one great thing—us guys. [Laughter] We in this room are not simply profiting from their bankruptcy; we are where we are because we're winning the contest of ideas. In fact, in the past decade, all of a sudden, quietly, mysteriously, the Republican Party has become the party of ideas.

We became the party of the most brilliant and dynamic young minds. I remember them, just a few years ago, running around scrawling Laffer curves on table napkins—[Laughter] —going to symposia and talking about how social programs did not eradicate poverty, but entrenched it; writing studies on why the latest weird and unnatural idea from the social engineers is weird and unnatural. [Laughter] You were there. They were your ideas, your symposia, your books, and usually somebody else's table napkins. [Laughter]

All of a sudden, Republicans were not defenders of the status quo but creators of the future. They were looking at tomorrow with all the single-mindedness of an inventor. In fact, they reminded me of the American inventors of the nineteenth and twentieth centuries who filled the world with light and recorded sound.

The new conservatives made anew the connection between economic justice and economic growth. Growth in the economy would not only create jobs and paychecks, they said; it would enhance familial stability and encourage a healthy optimism about the future. Lower those tax rates, they said, and let the economy become the engine of our dreams. Pull back regulations, and encourage free and open competition. Let the men and women of the marketplace decide what they want.

But along with that, perhaps the greatest triumph of modern conservatism has been to stop allowing the left to put the average American on the moral defensive. By average American I mean the good, decent, rambunctious, and creative people who raise the families, go to church, and help out when the local library holds a fund-raiser; people who have a stake in the community because they are the community.

These people had held true to certain beliefs and principles that for twenty years the intelligentsia were telling us were hopelessly out of date, utterly trite, and reactionary. You want prayer in the schools? How primitive, they said. You oppose abortion? How oppressive, how antimodern. The normal was portrayed as eccentric, and only the abnormal was worthy of emulation. The irreverent was celebrated, but only irreverence about certain things: irreverence toward, say, organized religion, yes; irreverence toward establishment liberalism, not too much of that. They celebrated their courage in taking on safe targets and patted each other on the back for slinging stones at a confused Goliath, who was too demoralized and really too good to fight back.

But now one simply senses it. The American people are no longer on the defensive. I believe the conservative movement deserves some credit for this. You spoke for the permanent against the merely prevalent, and ultimately you prevailed.

I believe we conservatives have captured the moment, captured the imagination of the American people. And what now? What are we to do with our success? Well, right now, with conservative thought accepted as mainstream thought and with the people of our country leading the fight to freedom, now we must move.

You remember your Shakespeare: "There is a tide in the affairs of men which, taken at the flood, leads on to fortune.

Omitted, all the voyage of their life is bound in shallows and in miseries. On such a full sea are we now afloat. And we must take the current when it serves, or lose our ventures." I spoke in the—[*Applause*]. It's typical, isn't it? I just quoted a great writer, but as an actor, I get the bow. [*Laughter*]

I spoke in the State of the Union of a second American revolution, and now is the time to launch that revolution and see that it takes hold. If we move decisively, these years will not be just a passing era of good feeling, not just a few good years, but a true golden age of freedom.

The moment is ours, and we must seize it. There's work to do. We must prolong and protect our growing prosperity so that it doesn't become just a passing phase, a natural adjustment between periods of recession. We must move further to provide incentive and make America the investment capital of the world.

We must institute a fair tax system and turn the current one on its ear. I believe there is natural support in our country for a simplified tax system, with still-lower tax rates but a broader base, with everyone paying their fair share and no more. We must eliminate unproductive tax shelters. Again, there is natural support among Americans, because Americans are a fair-minded people.

We must institute enterprise zones and a lower youth minimum wage so we can revitalize distressed areas and teenagers can get jobs. We're going to take our revolution to the people, all of the people. We're going to go to black Americans and members of all minority groups, and we're going to make our case.

Part of being a revolutionary is knowing that you don't have to acquiesce to the tired, old ideas of the past. One such idea is that the opposition party has black America and minority America locked up, that they own black America. Well, let me tell you, they own nothing but the past. The old alignments are no longer legitimate, if they ever were.

We're going to reach out, and we need your help. Conservatives were brought up to hate deficits, and justifiably so. We've long thought there are two things in Washington that are unbalanced—the budget and the liberals. [*Laughter*]

But we cannot reduce the deficit by raising taxes. And just so that every "i" is dotted and every "t" is crossed, let me repeat tonight for the benefit of those who never seem to get the message: We will not reduce the deficit by raising taxes. We need more taxes like John McLaughlin* needs assertiveness training. [*Laughter*]

Now, whether government borrows or increases taxes, it will be taking the same amount of money from the private economy, and either way, that's too much. We must bring down government spending. We need a constitutional amendment requiring a balanced budget. It's something that forty-nine states already require—no reason the federal government should be any different.

We need the line-item veto, which forty-three governors have —no reason that the president shouldn't. And we have to cut waste. The Grace commission has identified billions of dollars that are wasted and that we can save.

But the domestic side isn't the only area where we need your help. All of us in this room grew up, or came to adulthood, in a time when the doctrine of Marx and Lenin was coming to divide the world. Ultimately, it came to dominate remorselessly whole parts of it. The Soviet attempt to give legitimacy to its tyranny is expressed in the infamous Brezhnev doctrine, which contends that once a country has fallen into Communist darkness, it can never again be allowed to see the light of freedom.

Well, it occurs to me that history has already begun to repeal that doctrine. It started one day in Grenada. We only did our duty, as a responsible neighbor and a lover of peace, the day we went in and returned the government to the people and rescued our own students. We restored that island to liberty. Yes, it's only a small island, but that's what the world is made of—small islands yearning for freedom.

* Washington executive editor, *National Review* magazine.

There's much more to do. Throughout the world the Soviet Union and its agents, client states, and satellites are on the defensive—on the moral defensive, the intellectual defensive, and the political and economic defensive. Freedom movements arise and assert themselves. They're doing so on almost every continent populated by man—in the hills of Afghanistan, in Angola, in Kampuchea, in Central America. In making mention of freedom fighters, all of us are privileged to have in our midst tonight one of the brave commanders who lead the Afghan freedom fighters—Abdul Haq. Abdul Haq, we are with you.

They are our brothers, these freedom fighters, and we owe them our help. I've spoken recently of the freedom fighters of Nicaragua. You know the truth about them. You know who they're fighting and why. They are the moral equal of our Founding Fathers and the brave men and women of the French Resistance. We cannot turn away from them, for the struggle here is not right versus left; it is right versus wrong.

Now, I am against sending troops to Central America. They are simply not needed. Given a chance and the resources, the people of the area can fight their own fight. They have the men and women. They're capable of doing it. They have the people of their country behind them. All they need is our support. All they need is proof that we care as much about the fight for freedom seven hundred miles from our shores as the Soviets care about the fight against freedom five thousand miles from theirs. And they need to know that the U.S. supports them with more than just pretty words and good wishes. We need your help on this, and I mean each of you—involved, active, strong, and vocal. And we need more.

All of you know that we're researching nonnuclear technologies that may enable us to prevent nuclear ballistic missiles from reaching U.S. soil or that of our allies. I happen to believe —logic forces me to believe—that this new defense system, the Strategic Defense Initiative, is the most hopeful possibility of our time. Its primary virtue is clear. If anyone ever attacked us, Strategic Defense would be there to protect us. It could conceivably save millions of lives.

SDI has been criticized on the grounds that it might upset any chance of an arms control agreement with the Soviets. But SDI is arms control. If SDI is, say, 80 percent effective, then it will make any Soviet attack folly. Even partial success in SDI would strengthen deterrence and keep the peace. And if our SDI research is successful, the prospects for real reduction in U.S. and Soviet offensive nuclear forces will be greatly enhanced.

It is said that SDI would deal a blow to the so-called East-West balance of power. Well, let's think about that. The Soviets already are investing roughly as much on strategic defenses as they are on their offensive nuclear forces. This could quickly tip the East-West balance if we had no defense of our own. Would a situation of comparable defenses threaten us? No, for we're not planning on being the first to use force.

As we strive for our goal of eventual elimination of nuclear weapons, each side would retain a certain amount of defensive —or of, I should say, destructive power—a certain number of missiles. But it would not be in our interest, or theirs, to build more and more of them.

Now, one would think our critics on the left would quickly embrace, or at least be open-minded about a system that promises to reduce the size of nuclear missile forces on both sides and to greatly enhance the prospects for real arms reductions. And yet we hear SDI belittled by some with nicknames, or demagogued with charges that it will bring war to the heavens.

They complain that it won't work, which is odd from people who profess to believe in the perfectability of man—machines after all. [Laughter] And man—machines are so much easier to manipulate. They say it won't be 100 percent effective, which is odd, since they don't ask for 100 percent effectiveness in their social experiments. [Laughter] They say SDI is only in the research stage and won't be realized in time to change things. To which, as I said last month, the only reply is: Then let's get started.

Now, my point here is not to question the motives of others. But it's difficult to understand how critics can object to exploring the possibility of moving away from exclusive reliance upon nuclear weapons. The truth is, I believe that they find it difficult to embrace any idea that breaks with the past, that breaks with consensus thinking and the common establishment wisdom. In short, they find it difficult and frightening to alter the status quo.

And what are we to do when these so-called opinion leaders of an outworn philosophy are out there on television and in the newspapers with their steady drumbeat of doubt and distaste? Well, when all you have to do to win is rely on the good judgment of the American people, then you're in good shape, because the American people have good judgment. I know it isn't becoming of me, but I like to think that maybe forty-nine of our fifty states displayed that judgment just a few months ago. [*Laughter*]

What we have to do, all of us in this room, is get out there and talk about SDI. Explain it, debate it, tell the American people the facts. It may well be the most important work we do in the next few years. And if we try, we'll succeed. So, we have great work ahead of us, big work. But if we do it together and with complete commitment, we can change our country and history forever.

Once during the campaign, I said, "This is a wonderful time to be alive." And I meant that. I meant that we're lucky not to live in pale and timid times. We've been blessed with the opportunity to stand for something—for liberty and freedom and fairness. And these are things worth fighting for, worth devoting our lives to. And we have good reason to be hopeful and optimistic.

We've made much progress already. So, let us go forth with good cheer and stout hearts—happy warriors out to seize back a country and a world to freedom.

Thank you, and God bless you.

Remarks at the Memorial Service for Members of the 101st Airborne Division

FORT CAMPBELL, KENTUCKY

DECEMBER 16, 1985

Why is it so many tragedies seem to occur before Christmas? As you may recall, a plane full of our soldiers was heading home to the U.S. for the holidays. At six forty-five P.M. on December 12, the plane crashed after refueling in Gander, Newfoundland. A few days later I attended a memorial service with family members and friends.

Many people have commented to me about the comfort Nancy and I tried to give the families. My remarks were always designed to give those grieving something to cling to so that they knew their loved ones didn't die in vain. Words do help, but so can simply going from one family to the next and offering personal condolences. So many would just come into your arms sobbing.

I can't remember which memorial service it was—either this one or the ceremony for the crew of the Stark *or the one for the astronauts. But Nancy and I were going from person to person trying to help with the grief and I came to a little boy. As I took his small hand, he said to me, "Please bring my daddy home."*

I cannot describe to you the anguish.

WE ARE HERE in the name of the American people. The passing of American soldiers killed as they returned from difficult duty abroad is marked by our presence here. At this point the dimensions of the tragedy are known to almost every person in the country. Most of the young men and women we mourn were returning to spend the holidays with their families. They were full of happiness and laughter as they pushed off from Cairo, and those who saw them at their last stop spoke of how they were singing Christmas carols. They were happy; they were returning to kith and kin.

And then the terrible crash, the flags lowered to half-staff, and the muffled sobs, and we wonder: How this could be? How could it have happened, and why? We wonder at the stark tragedy of it all, the enormity of the loss. For lost were not only the 248 but all of the talent, the wisdom, and the idealism that they had accumulated; lost, too, were their experience and their enormous idealism. Who else but an idealist would choose to become a member of the armed forces and put himself or herself in harm's way for the rest of us? Who but the idealist would go to hard duty in one of the most troubled places of the world and go not as a matter of conquest, but as a force that existed to keep the peace?

Some people think of members of the military as only warriors, fierce in their martial expertise. But the men and women we mourn today were peacemakers. They were there to protect life and preserve a peace, to act as a force for stability and hope and trust. Their commitment was as strong as their purpose was pure. And they were proud. They had a rendezvous with destiny and a potential they never failed to meet. Their work was a perfect expression of the best of the Judeo-Christian tradition. They were the ones of whom Christ spoke when He said, "Blessed *are* the peacemakers: for they shall be called the children of God."

Tragedy is nothing new to mankind, but somehow it's always a surprise, never loses its power to astonish. Those of us who did not lose a brother or a son or daughter or friend or father are shaken nonetheless. And we all mourn with you. We cannot fully share the depth of your sadness, but we pray that the special power of this season will make its way into your sad hearts and remind you of some old joys; remind you of the joy it was to know these fine young men and women, the joy it was to witness the things they said and the jokes they played, the kindnesses they did, and how they laughed. You were part of that, and you who mourn were a part of them. And just as you think today of the joy they gave you, think for a moment of the joy you gave them and be glad. For love is never wasted; love is never lost. Love lives on and sees us through sorrow. From the moment love is born, it is always with us, keeping us aloft in the time of flooding and strong in the time of trial.

You do not grieve alone. We grieve as a nation, together, as together we say good-bye to those who died in the service of their country. In life they were our heroes, in death our loved ones, our darlings. They were happy and singing, and they were right: They were going home. And so, we pray: Receive, O Lord, into your heavenly kingdom the men and women of the 101st Airborne, the men and women of the great and fabled Screaming Eagles. They must be singing now, in their joy, flying higher than mere man can fly and as flights of angels take them to their rest.

I know that there are no words that can make your pain less or make your sorrow less painful. How I wish there were. But of one thing we can be sure—as a poet said of other young soldiers in another war: They will never grow old; they will always be young. And we know one thing with every bit of our thinking: They are now in the arms of God.

God bless you.

1986

Address to the Nation
on the U.S. Air Strike Against Libya

OVAL OFFICE

APRIL 14, 1986

I suppose if I had to choose the worst year of my presidency it would be 1986. The Challenger *exploded, throwing the nation into shock, grief, and doubt. The Republicans lost control of the Senate, making progress on tough issues even more unlikely with the Democrats now controlling both houses of Congress. My meeting with Gorbachev in Iceland fell apart and ended in disappointment. And what's more, the Iran/contra controversy began to break. On the up side, we passed some historic tax reform legislation and rededicated Lady Liberty in one of the most breathtaking ceremonies I've ever seen.*

One of the most newsworthy events of the year was our air raid on Libya. We had irrefutable proof that Colonel Qadhafi was responsible for bombing a disco in West Germany that had killed some U.S. military people. We also had proof Qadhafi's terrorists were responsible for shooting up an airport. The terrorists had used Tunisian passports, passports that Qadhafi had confiscated when he ejected the Tunisian workers from Libya.

We had to show him he couldn't get away with such things. We had absolutely no intention of hitting civilian buildings, including his—although to be honest I wouldn't have shed any tears if that stray bomb that got his tent had gotten him, too. I

*have to say that he quieted down after the attack. I guess he's
sane enough to understand that we would retaliate anytime we
had proof linking him to terrorist acts.*

MY FELLOW AMERICANS:

At seven o'clock this evening eastern time, air and naval
forces of the United States launched a series of strikes against
the headquarters, terrorist facilities, and military assets that
support Mu'ammar Qadhafi's subversive activities. The attacks
were concentrated and carefully targeted to minimize casualties
among the Libyan people, with whom we have no quarrel.

From initial reports, our forces have succeeded in their mission. Several weeks ago in New Orleans I warned Colonel
Qadhafi we would hold his regime accountable for any new
terrorist attacks launched against American citizens. More
recently I made it clear we would respond as soon as we
determined conclusively who was responsible for such attacks.

On April 5th in West Berlin a terrorist bomb exploded in a
nightclub frequented by American servicemen. Sergeant Kenneth Ford and a young Turkish woman were killed and 230
others were wounded, among them some 50 American military
personnel. This monstrous brutality is but the latest act in Colonel Qadhafi's reign of terror. The evidence is now conclusive
that the terrorist bombing of La Belle discotheque was planned
and executed under the direct orders of the Libyan regime. On
March 25th, more than a week before the attack, orders were
sent from Tripoli to the Libyan People's Bureau in East Berlin
to conduct a terrorist attack against Americans to cause maximum and indiscriminate casualties. Libya's agents then planted
the bomb. On April 4th the People's Bureau alerted Tripoli that
the attack would be carried out the following morning. The
next day they reported back to Tripoli on the great success of
their mission.

Our evidence is direct; it is precise; it is irrefutable. We have solid evidence about other attacks Qadhafi has planned against the United States installations and diplomats and even American tourists.

Thanks to close cooperation with our friends, some of these have been prevented. With the help of French authorities, we recently aborted one such attack: a planned massacre, using grenades and small arms, of civilians waiting in line for visas at an American embassy.

Colonel Qadhafi is not only an enemy of the United States. His record of subversion and aggression against the neighboring states in Africa is well documented and well known. He has ordered the murder of fellow Libyans in countless countries. He has sanctioned acts of terror in Africa, Europe, and the Middle East, as well as the Western Hemisphere.

Today we have done what we had to do. If necessary, we shall do it again. It gives me no pleasure to say that, and I wish it were otherwise.

Before Qadhafi seized power in 1969, the people of Libya had been friends of the United States. And I'm sure that today most Libyans are ashamed and disgusted that this man has made their country a synonym for barbarism around the world. The Libyan people are a decent people caught in the grip of a tyrant.

To our friends and allies in Europe who cooperated in today's mission, I would only say you have the permanent gratitude of the American people. Europeans who remember history understand better than most that there is no security, no safety, in the appeasement of evil. It must be the core of Western policy that there be no sanctuary for terror. And to sustain such a policy, free men and free nations must unite and work together.

Sometimes it is said that by imposing sanctions against Colonel Qadhafi or by striking at his terrorist installations we only magnify the man's importance, that the proper way to deal with him is to ignore him. I do not agree. Long before I came into this office, Colonel Qadhafi had engaged in acts of international terror, acts that put him outside the company of civilized men. For years, however, he suffered no economic or political or military sanction; and the atrocities mounted in number, as did the innocent dead and wounded. And for us to ignore by inaction the slaughter of American civilians and American soldiers, whether in nightclubs or airline terminals, is simply not in the American tradition. When our citizens are abused or attacked anywhere in the world on the direct orders of a hostile regime, we will respond so long as I'm in this Oval Office. Self-defense is not only our right, it is our duty. It is the purpose behind the mission undertaken tonight, a mission fully consistent with Article 51 of the United Nations Charter.

We believe that this preemptive action against his terrorist installations will not only diminish Colonel Qadhafi's capacity to export terror, it will provide him with incentives and reasons to alter his criminal behavior. I have no illusion that tonight's action will ring down the curtain on Qadhafi's reign of terror. But this mission, violent though it was, can bring closer a safer and more secure world for decent men and women. We will persevere.

This afternoon we consulted with the leaders of Congress regarding what we were about to do and why. Tonight I salute the skill and professionalism of the men and women of our armed forces who carried out this mission. It's an honor to be your commander in chief.

We Americans are slow to anger. We always seek peaceful avenues before resorting to the use of force—and we did. We tried quiet diplomacy, public condemnation, economic sanctions, and demonstrations of military force. None succeeded. Despite our repeated warnings, Qadhafi continued his reckless policy of intimidation, his relentless pursuit of terror. He counted on America to be passive. He counted wrong.

I warned that there should be no place on earth where terrorists can rest and train and practice their deadly skills. I meant it. I said that we would act with others, if possible, and alone if necessary to ensure that terrorists have no sanctuary anywhere. Tonight, we have.

Thank you, and God bless you.

Address to the Nation
on the *Challenger* Disaster

OVAL OFFICE
JANUARY 28, 1986

The sight of the Challenger *exploding is seared into each of our minds. A few days after the explosion, I attended a memorial service in Houston for the crew. I stood next to Jane Smith, the wife of Michael Smith, one of the crewmen on the* Challenger.

She gave me a most remarkable gift, a three-by-five card that her husband had written before the flight and left on the bedroom dresser. He wrote about the importance of their mission. It was such a personal, generous gift that I didn't feel right keeping it. I made a copy, which is shown here, and gave her back the original. I'll never forget her generosity in offering me that part of her husband's final days.

I delivered the following message to the American people on nationwide radio and television a few hours after the disaster.

LADIES AND GENTLEMEN, I'd planned to speak to you tonight to report on the state of the Union, but the events of earlier today have led me to change those plans. Today is a day for mourning and remembering.

Nancy and I are pained to the core by the tragedy of the shuttle *Challenger*. We know we share this pain with all of the people of our country. This is truly a national loss.

Nineteen years ago, almost to the day, we lost three astronauts in a terrible accident on the ground. But we've never lost an astronaut in flight; we've never had a tragedy like this. And perhaps we've forgotten the courage it took for the crew of the shuttle; but they, the *Challenger* Seven, were aware of the dangers, but overcame them and did their jobs brilliantly. We mourn seven heroes: Michael Smith, Dick Scobee, Judith Resnik, Ronald McNair, Ellison Onizuka, Gregory Jarvis, and Christa McAuliffe. We mourn their loss as a nation together.

For the families of the seven, we cannot bear, as you do, the full impact of this tragedy. But we feel the loss, and we're thinking about you so very much. Your loved ones were daring and brave, and they had that special grace, that special spirit that says, "Give me a challenge and I'll meet it with joy." They had a hunger to explore the universe and discover its truths. They wished to serve, and they did. They served all of us.

We've grown used to wonders in this century. It's hard to dazzle us. But for twenty-five years the United States space

"FOR MAN, THERE IS NO REST AND NO ENDING
HE MUST GO ON -- CONQUEST BEYOND CONQUEST;
THIS LITTLE PLANET, AND ITS WINDS AND
WAYS, AND ALL THE LAWS OF MIND AND
MATTER THAT RESTRAIN HIM. THEN
THE PLANETS ABOUT HIM, AND, AT LAST
OUT ACROSS THE IMMENSITY TO THE
STARS. AND WHEN HE HAS CONQUERED ALL
THE DEEPS OF SPACE AND ALL THE MYSTERIES
OF TIME .. STILL HE WILL BE BUT BEGINNING"

ASTRONAUT MICHAEL SMITH, QUOTING H. G. WELLS.

program has been doing just that. We've grown used to the idea of space, and perhaps we forget that we've only just begun. We're still pioneers. They, the members of the *Challenger* crew, were pioneers.

And I want to say something to the schoolchildren of America who were watching the live coverage of the shuttle's takeoff. I know it is hard to understand, but sometimes painful things like this happen. It's all part of the process of exploration and discovery. It's all part of taking a chance and expanding man's horizons. The future doesn't belong to the fainthearted; it belongs to the brave. The *Challenger* crew was pulling us into the future, and we'll continue to follow them.

I've always had great faith in and respect for our space program, and what happened today does nothing to diminish it. We don't hide our space program. We don't keep secrets and cover things up. We do it all up front and in public. That's the way freedom is, and we wouldn't change it for a minute.

We'll continue our quest in space. There will be more shuttle flights and more shuttle crews and yes, more volunteers, more civilians, more teachers in space. Nothing ends here; our hopes and our journeys continue.

I want to add that I wish I could talk to every man and woman who works for NASA or who worked on this mission and tell them: "Your dedication and professionalism have moved and impressed us for decades. And we know of your anguish. We share it."

There's a coincidence today. On this day 390 years ago, the great explorer Sir Francis Drake died aboard ship off the coast of Panama. In his lifetime the great frontiers were the oceans, and a historian later said, "He lived by the sea, died on it, and was buried in it." Well, today we can say of the *Challenger* crew: Their dedication was, like Drake's, complete.

The crew of the space shuttle *Challenger* honored us by the manner in which they lived their lives. We will never forget them, nor the last time we saw them, this morning, as they prepared for their journey and waved good-bye and "slipped the surly bonds of earth" to "touch the face of God."

Remarks at a Dinner
Honoring Tip O'Neill

WASHINGTON, D.C.
MARCH 17, 1986

Tip O'Neill, the former Speaker of the House of Representatives, is a Democratic politician of the old school. They really don't make them like him anymore, and I'm not saying they should, but he is quite a character.

After I got into office I went to see Tip up on Capitol Hill. And then Nancy and I had Tip and his wife, Millie, down to dinner at the White House. And so I was surprised to see one day in the paper that he was beating my brains out on some issue or another, so I called him up. I said, "Tip, I thought we had something going here?" And Tip said, "Well, old buddy, that's politics. We're friends after six P.M."

Sometimes when he came to see me, I'd set my watch up so that it would be six.

REVEREND CLERGY, Mr. Prime Minister,* Mr. Speaker, ladies and gentlemen, I want to begin tonight by saying how touched I am to know that Tip wanted me here this evening. [*Laughter*] Why, he even called me himself last week and said, "Mr. President, make sure you don't miss the dinner Tuesday night." [*Laughter*]

But to be honest, I've always known that Tip was behind me —[*Laughter*]—even if it was only at the State of the Union Address. As I made each proposal, I could hear Tip whispering to George Bush, "Forget it. No way. Fat chance." [*Laughter*]

I think it was inevitable, though, that there'd be a standoff between us. Imagine one Irishman trying to corner another Irishman in the Oval Office. [*Laughter*] But despite all this, Tip wanted me here. He said that since it was March 17th, it was only fitting that someone drop by who actually had known St. Patrick. [*Laughter*] And that's true, Tip, I did know St. Patrick. In fact, we both changed to the same political party at about the same time. [*Laughter*]

Now, it's true that Tip and I have our political disagreements. Sure, I said some things about Tip, and Tip said some things about me. But that's all history. And anyway, you know how it is, I forget. [*Laughter*] I just follow that old motto "Forgive and forget." Or is it "Forget and forgive." [*Laughter*]

Ladies and gentlemen, I think you know Tip and I've been kidding each other for some time now. And I hope you also know how much I hope this continues for many years to come. A little kidding is, after all, a sign of affection, the sort of things that friends do to each other. And Mr. Speaker, I'm grateful you have permitted me in the past, and I hope in the future, that singular honor, the honor of calling you my friend. I think the fact of our friendship is testimony to the political system

---

* Prime Minister Garret FitzGerald of Ireland.

that we're part of and the country we live in, a country which permits two not-so-shy and not-so-retiring Irishmen to have it out on the issues, rather than on each other or their countrymen.

But in addition to celebrating a country and a personal friendship, I wanted to come here tonight to join you in saluting Tip O'Neill, to salute him for the years of dedication and devotion to country. Tip's recollections of politics go back, of course, far beyond my own. [*Laughter*] He's seen some who play the game well and others who do not. He's seen some who love politics and some who came to it only out of a sense of duty. But through it all, Tip has been a vital and forceful part of America's political tradition, a tradition that he has truly enriched.

Yet Tip O'Neill represents far more than just this political tradition. Deep within, too, is the memory of places like Back Bay and south Boston, the docks, the piers, those who came off the ships in Boston Harbor seeking a better land, a better way for their children. And they found that something better. They rose above the prejudice and the hardship.

Tip would see one of his contemporaries become president— John F. Kennedy would be sixty-eight today, had he lived. And Tip can remember those golden hours better than most in this room. And then, not too many years later, there was another of immigrant stock who would become Speaker of the House. In so short a time, so much leadership from one city, one place, one people. How fitting that Boston College, a place that became to so many of those new arrivals a symbol of moving upward and onward; how fitting that Boston College, whose towers on the heights have reached to heaven's own blue for so many, should sponsor this salute to Tip O'Neill. Tip, you are a true son of Boston College and our friend. And we salute you.

You are also a leader of the nation, and for that we honor you. But you also embody so much of what this nation is all about, the hope that is America. So, you make us proud as well, my friend, you make us proud.

Thank you. God bless you all.

Remarks at the Statue of Liberty Centennial Ceremonies

GOVERNORS ISLAND

JULY 3, 1986

This was one of the grandest occasions I attended while I was president. What an uplifting experience unveiling the spruced-up lady and relighting her torch. And the thousands and thousands of people who came to celebrate were wonderful. The police told us that even with these great crowds there was never any jostling. Everyone was trying to help make things go smoothly.

We had several events in the area over the course of a couple

*of days, and every time we would come and go, our helicopter
would circle around the top of the statue. I was carried away.
She was so feminine, which I never realized before. I told
Nancy, "This is the other woman in my life."*

T HANK YOU. And Lee Iacocca,* thank you on behalf of all
America.

President and Madame Mitterrand, my fellow Americans:

The ironworkers from New York and New Jersey who came
here to begin restoration work were at first puzzled and a bit
put off to see foreign workers, craftsmen from France, arrive.
Jean Wiart, the leader of the French workers, said his countrymen understood. After all, he asked, how would Frenchmen
feel if Americans showed up to help restore the Eiffel Tower?

But as they came to know each other—these Frenchmen and
Americans—affections grew; and so, too, did perspectives. The
Americans were reminded that Miss Liberty, like the many millions she's welcomed to these shores, is of foreign birth, the gift
of workers, farmers, and shopkeepers and children who donated hundreds of thousands of francs to send her here. They
were the ordinary people of France. This statue came from their
pockets and from their hearts.

The French workers, too, made discoveries. Monsieur Wiart,
for example, normally lives in a 150-year-old cottage in a small
French town, but for the last year he's been riding the subway
through Brooklyn. "A study in contrasts," he said—contrasts
indeed. But he has also told the newspapers that he and his
countrymen learned something else at Liberty Island. For the
first time, they worked in proximity with Americans of Jewish,
black, Italian, Irish, Russian, Polish, and Indian backgrounds.

* Lee Iacocca was chairman of the Statue of Liberty and Ellis Island Foundation,
which was responsible for raising funds for the restoration of the statue.

"Fascinating," he said, "to see different ethnic and national types work and live so well together."

Well, it's how we like to think of America. And it's good to know that Miss Liberty is still giving life to the dream of a new world where old antagonisms could be cast aside and people of every nation could live together as one.

It's especially fitting that this lesson should be relived and relearned here by Americans and Frenchmen. President Mitterrand, the French and American people have forged a special friendship over the course of two centuries. Yes, in the 1700s, France was the midwife of our liberty. In two world wars, America stood with France as she fought for her life and for civilization. And today, Mr. President, with infinite gentleness, your countrymen tend the final resting places, marked now by rows of white crosses and stars, of more than 60,000 Americans who remain on French soil, a reminder since the days of Lafayette of our mutual struggles and sacrifices for freedom. So, tonight, as we celebrate the friendship of our two nations, we also pray: May it ever be so. God bless America, and *vive la France.*

And yet, my fellow Americans, it is not only the friendship of two peoples but the friendship of all peoples that brings us here tonight. We celebrate something more than the restoration of this statue's physical grandeur. Another worker here, Scott Aronsen, a marble restorer, has put it well: "I grew up in Brooklyn and never went to the Statue of Liberty. But when I first walked in there to work, I thought about my grandfathers coming through here." And which of us does not think of other grandfathers and grandmothers, from so many places around the globe, for whom this statue was the first glimpse of America.

"She was silhouetted very clear," one of them wrote about standing on deck as their ship entered New York Harbor. "We passed her very slowly. Of course we had to look up. She was beautiful." Another talked of how all the passengers rushed to one side of the boat for a fast look at their new home and at her. "Everybody was crying. The whole boat bent toward her. She was beautiful with the early morning light."

To millions returning home, especially from foreign wars, she was also special. A young World War I captain of artillery described how, on a troopship returning from France, even the most hard-bitten veteran had trouble blinking back the tears. "I've never seen anything that looked so good," that doughboy, Harry Truman, wrote to his fiancée, Bess, back in Independence, Missouri, "as the Liberty Lady in New York Harbor."

And that is why tonight we celebrate this mother of exiles who lifts her light beside the golden door. Many of us have seen the picture of another worker here, a tool belt around his waist, balanced on a narrow metal rod of scaffolding, leaning over to place a kiss on the forehead of Miss Liberty. Tony Soraci, the grandson of immigrant Italians, said it was something he was proud to do, "something to tell my grandchildren."

Robert Kearney feels the same way. At work on the statue after a serious illness, he gave $10,000 worth of commemorative pins to those who visited here. Part of the reason, he says, was an earlier construction job over in Hoboken and his friend named Blackie. They could see the harbor from the building they were working on, and every morning Blackie would look over the water, give a salute, and say, "That's my gal."

Well, the truth is, she's everybody's gal. We sometimes forget that even those who came here first to settle the new land were also strangers. I've spoken before of the tiny *Arabella,* a ship at anchor just off the Massachusetts coast. A little group of Puritans huddled on the deck. And then John Winthrop, who would later become the first governor of Massachusetts, reminded his fellow Puritans there on that tiny deck that they must keep faith with their God, that the eyes of all the world were upon them, and that they must not forsake the mission that God had sent them on, and they must be a light unto the nations of all the world—a shining city upon a hill.

Call it mysticism if you will, I have always believed there was some divine providence that placed this great land here between the two great oceans, to be found by a special kind of people from every corner of the world, who had a special love for freedom and a special courage that enabled them to leave their own land, leave their friends and their countrymen, and come to this new and strange land to build a new world of peace and freedom and hope.

Lincoln spoke about hope as he left the hometown he would never see again to take up the duties of the presidency and bring America through a terrible civil war. At each stop on his long train ride to Washington, the news grew worse: The nation was dividing; his own life was in peril. On he pushed, undaunted. In Philadelphia he spoke in Independence Hall, where eighty-five years earlier the Declaration of Independence had been signed. He noted that much more had been achieved there than just independence from Great Britain. It was, he said, "hope to the world, future for all time."

Well, that is the common thread that binds us to those Quakers on the tiny deck of the *Arabella*, to the beleaguered farmers and landowners signing the Declaration in Philadelphia in that hot Philadelphia hall, to Lincoln on a train ready to guide his people through the conflagration, to all the millions crowded in the steerage who passed this lady and wept at the sight of her, and those who've worked here in the scaffolding with their hands and with their love—Jean Wiart, Scott Aronsen, Tony Soraci, Robert Kearney, and so many others.

We're bound together because, like them, we, too, dare to hope—hope that our children will always find here the land of liberty in a land that is free. We dare to hope, too, that we'll understand our work can never be truly done until every man, woman, and child shares in our gift, in our hope, and stands with us in the light of liberty—the light that, tonight, will shortly cast its glow upon her, as it has upon us for two centuries, keeping faith with a dream of long ago and guiding millions still to a future of peace and freedom.

And now we will unveil that gallant lady. Thank you, and God bless you all.

Remarks on Signing
the Tax Reform Act into Law

WHITE HOUSE SOUTH LAWN

OCTOBER 22, 1986

This legislation really gets to the heart of my conservative economic principles. A nation will prosper if the government will just get out of the way and give the people an incentive to work and produce. This act wouldn't have passed without the active support of the Democratic Congress. This was truly a bipartisan measure.

The act gave the United States the lowest federal income tax rates of any major industrialized nation in the world and one of the fairest systems as well. More than four million lower-

income households were relieved of their federal tax burden entirely.

The top personal tax rate dropped from 70 percent in 1981 to between 28 and 33 percent in 1988, the lowest since 1931. Eighty percent of all Americans now pay a flat 15 percent or owe no income tax at all.

I know that reading about taxes is pretty dull stuff, but I hope you won't skip the following remarks because I think we really accomplished something for the American people.

WELL, THANK YOU, and welcome to the White House. In a moment I'll be sitting at that desk, taking up a pen, and signing the most sweeping overhaul of the Tax Code in our nation's history. To all of you here today who've worked so long and hard to see this day come, my thanks and the thanks of a nation go out to you.

The journey's been long, and many said we'd never make it to the end. But as usual the pessimists left one thing out of their calculations: the American people. They haven't made this the freest country and the mightiest economic force on this planet by shrinking from challenges. They never gave up. And after almost three years of commitment and hard work, one headline in the *Washington Post* told the whole story: "The Impossible Became the Inevitable," and the dream of America's fair-share tax plan became a reality.

When I sign this bill into law, America will have the lowest marginal tax rates and the most modern tax code among major industrialized nations, one that encourages risk-taking, innovation, and that old American spirit of enterprise. We'll be refueling the American growth economy with the kind of incentives that helped create record new businesses and nearly 11.7 million jobs in just forty-six months. Fair and simpler for most Americans, this is a tax code designed to take us into a future of technological invention and economic achievement, one that will keep America competitive and growing into the twenty-first century.

But for all tax reform's economic benefits, I believe that history will record this moment as something more: as the return to the first principles. This country was founded on faith in the individual, not groups or classes, but faith in the resources and bounty of each and every separate human soul. Our Founding Fathers designed a democratic form of government to enlist the individual's energies and fashioned a Bill of Rights to protect its freedoms. And in so doing, they tapped a wellspring of hope and creativity that was to completely transform history.

The history of these United States of America is indeed a history of individual achievement. It was their hard work that built our cities and farmed our prairies; their genius that continually pushed us beyond the boundaries of existing knowledge, reshaping our world with the steam engine, polio vaccine, and the silicon chip. It was their faith in freedom and love of country that sustained us through trials and hardships and through wars, and it was their courage and selflessness that enabled us to always prevail.

But when our Founding Fathers designed this government—of, by, and for the people—they never imagined what we've come to know as the progressive income tax. When the income tax was first levied in 1913, the top rate was only 7 percent on people with incomes over $500,000. Now, that's the equivalent of multimillionaires today. But in our lifetime we've seen marginal tax rates skyrocket as high as 90 percent, and not even the poor have been spared.

As tax rates escalated, the Tax Code grew ever more tangled and complex, a haven for special interests and tax manipulators, but an impossible frustration for everybody else. Blatantly unfair, our Tax Code became a source of bitterness and discouragement for the average taxpayer. It wasn't too much to call it un-American.

Meanwhile, the steeply progressive nature of the tax struck at the heart of the economic life of the individual, punishing that special effort and extra hard work that has always been the driving force of our economy. As government's hunger for ever more revenues expanded, families saw tax cuts—or taxes, I should say—cut deeper and deeper into their paychecks; and taxation fell most cruelly on the poor, making a difficult climb up from poverty even harder.

Throughout history, the oppressive hand of government has fallen most heavily on the economic life of the individuals. And more often than not, it is inflation and taxes that have undermined livelihoods and constrained their freedoms. We should not forget that this nation of ours began in a revolt against oppressive taxation. Our Founding Fathers fought not only for our political rights but also to secure the economic freedoms without which these political freedoms are no more than a shadow.

In the last twenty years we've witnessed an expansion and strengthening of many of our civil liberties, but our economic liberties have too often been neglected and even abused. We protect the freedom of expression of the author, as we should, but what of the freedom of expression of the entrepreneur, whose pen and paper are capital and profits, whose book may be a new invention or small business? What of the creators of our economic life, whose contributions may not only delight the mind but improve the condition of man by feeding the poor with new grains, bringing hope to the sick with new cures, banishing ignorance with wondrous new information technologies?

And what about fairness for families? It's in our families that America's most important work gets done: raising our next generation. But over the last forty years, as inflation has shrunk the personal exemption, families with children have had to shoulder more and more of the tax burden. With inflation and bracket-creep also eroding incomes, many spouses who would rather stay home with their children have been forced to go looking for jobs.

And what of America's promise of hope and opportunity, that with hard work even the poorest among us can gain the security and happiness that is the due of all Americans? You can't put a price tag on the American dream. That dream is the heart and soul of America; it's the promise that keeps our nation forever good and generous, a model and hope to the world.

For all these reasons, this tax bill is less a freedom—or a reform, I should say—than a revolution. Millions of working poor will be dropped from the tax rolls altogether, and families will get a long-overdue break with lower rates and an almost doubled personal exemption. We're going to make it economical to raise children again.

Flatter rates will mean more reward for that extra effort, and banishing loopholes and a minimum tax will mean that everybody and every corporation pay their fair share. And that's why I'm certain that the bill I'm signing today is not only an historic overhaul of our Tax Code and a sweeping victory for fairness, it's also the best antipoverty bill, the best profamily measure, and the best job-creation program ever to come out of the Congress of the United States.

And now that we've come this far, we cannot, and we will not, allow tax reform to be undone with tax rate hikes. We must restore certainty to our Tax Code and our economy. And I'll oppose with all my might any attempt to raise tax rates on the American people, and I hope that all here will join with me to make permanent the historic progress of tax reform.

I think all of us here today know what a Herculean effort it took to get this landmark bill to my desk. That effort didn't start here in Washington, but began with the many thinkers who have struggled to return economics to its classical roots—to an understanding that ultimately the economy is not made up of aggregates like government spending and consumer demand, but of individual men and women, each striving to provide for his family and better his or her lot in life.

But we must also salute those courageous leaders in the Congress who've made this day possible. To Bob Packwood, Dan Rostenkowski, Russell Long, John Duncan, and Majority Leader Bob Dole; to Jack Kemp, Bob Kasten, Bill Bradley, and Dick Gephardt, who pioneered with their own versions of tax reform—I salute all of you and all the other members of the

Senate and House whose efforts paid off and whose votes finally won the day.

And last but not least, the many members of the administration who must often have felt that they were fighting a lonely battle against overwhelming odds—particularly my two incomparable secretaries of the treasury, Don Regan and Jim Baker —and I thank them from the bottom of my heart.

I feel like we just played the World Series of tax reform— [*Laughter*]—and the American people won.

Address to the Nation
on Return from Meeting
with General Secretary Gorbachev

OVAL OFFICE
OCTOBER 13, 1986

I think the television cameras captured very accurately the look of disappointment on my face when I finally left the meeting in Reykjavik, Iceland, with General Secretary Gorbachev.

Mikhail and I had gotten into a discussion of the total elimination of nuclear weapons. Yes, it was breathtaking. The U.S. delegation was supposed to be on our way home, but naturally we stayed through Sunday because we seemed to be making real progress.

Finally after making all this progress, Mikhail said it all hinged on us stopping our Strategic Defense Initiative program, what others call our Star Wars plan to protect ourselves from incoming nuclear missiles. Gorbachev hadn't mentioned this condition before.

Well, I gave him several arguments. I didn't want him to think we were developing this technology only to be better prepared for a fight, so I offered to give it away. He said, "I don't believe you." I said, "Well, maybe you're judging by your own people."

He repeated that none of the progress we discussed was possible unless we dropped SDI. I eventually blew my top and said, "There's no way." And we left.

On returning home, I made the following speech explaining to the American people what had happened to our hopes.

G OOD EVENING.

As most of you know, I've just returned from meetings in Iceland with the leader of the Soviet Union, General Secretary Gorbachev. As I did last year when I returned from the summit conference in Geneva, I want to take a few moments tonight to share with you what took place in these discussions.

The implications of these talks are enormous and only just beginning to be understood. We proposed the most sweeping and generous arms control proposal in history. We offered the complete elimination of all ballistic missiles—Soviet and American—from the face of the earth by 1996. While we parted company with this American offer still on the table, we are closer than ever to agreements that could lead to a safer world without nuclear weapons.

But first, let me tell you that from the start of my meetings with Mr. Gorbachev, I have always regarded you, the American people, as full participants. Believe me, without your support none of these talks could have been held, nor could the ultimate aims of American foreign policy—world peace and freedom—be pursued. And it's for these aims I went the extra mile to Iceland.

Before I report on our talks, though, allow me to set the stage by explaining two things that were very much a part of our talks: one a treaty and the other a defense against nuclear missiles, which we're trying to develop. Now, you've heard their titles a thousand times—the ABM treaty and SDI. Well, those letters stand for: ABM, antiballistic missile; SDI, Strategic Defense Initiative.

Some years ago, the United States and the Soviet Union agreed to limit any defense against nuclear missile attacks to the emplacement in one location in each country of a small number of missiles capable of intercepting and shooting down incoming nuclear missiles, thus leaving our real defense—a policy called mutual assured destruction, meaning if one side launched a nuclear attack, the other side could retaliate. And this mutual threat of destruction was believed to be a deterrent against either side striking first.

So here we sit, with thousands of nuclear warheads targeted on each other and capable of wiping out both our countries. The Soviets deployed the few antiballistic missiles around Moscow as the treaty permitted. Our country didn't bother deploying because the threat of nationwide annihilation made such a limited defense seem useless.

For some years now we've been aware that the Soviets may be developing a nationwide defense. They have installed a large, modern radar at Krasnoyarsk, which we believe is a critical part of a radar system designed to provide radar guidance for antiballistic missiles protecting the entire nation. Now, this is a violation of the ABM treaty.

Believing that a policy of mutual destruction and slaughter of their citizens and ours was uncivilized, I asked our military, a few years ago, to study and see if there was a practical way to destroy nuclear missiles after their launch but before they can reach their targets, rather than to just destroy people. Well, this is the goal for what we call SDI, and our scientists researching such a system are convinced it is practical and that several years down the road we can have such a system ready to deploy. Now incidentally, we are not violating the ABM treaty, which permits such research. If and when we deploy, the treaty also allows withdrawal from the treaty upon six months' notice. SDI, let me make it clear, is a nonnuclear defense.

So, here we are at Iceland for our second such meeting. In the first, and in the months in between, we have discussed ways to reduce and in fact eliminate nuclear weapons entirely. We and the Soviets have had teams of negotiators in Geneva trying to work out a mutual agreement on how we could reduce or eliminate nuclear weapons. And so far, no success.

On Saturday and Sunday, General Secretary Gorbachev and his foreign minister, Shevardnadze, and Secretary of State George Shultz and I met for nearly ten hours. We didn't limit ourselves to just arms reductions. We discussed what we call violation of human rights on the part of the Soviets—refusal to let people emigrate from Russia so they can practice their religion without being persecuted, letting people go to rejoin their families, husbands, and wives—separated by national borders —being allowed to reunite.

In much of this, the Soviet Union is violating another agreement—the Helsinki accords they had signed in 1975. Yuriy Orlov, whose freedom we just obtained, was imprisoned for pointing out to his government its violations of that pact, its refusal to let citizens leave their country or return. We also discussed regional matters such as Afghanistan, Angola, Nicaragua, and Cambodia. But by their choice, the main subject was arms control.

We discussed the emplacement of intermediate-range missiles in Europe and Asia and seemed to be in agreement they could be drastically reduced. Both sides seemed willing to find a way to reduce, even to zero, the strategic ballistic missiles we have aimed at each other. This then brought up the subject of SDI.

I offered a proposal that we continue our present research. And if and when we reached the stage of testing, we would sign, now, a treaty that would permit Soviet observation of such tests. And if the program was practical, we would both eliminate our offensive missiles, and then we would share the benefits of advanced defenses. I explained that even though we would have done away with our offensive ballistic missiles, having the defense would protect against cheating or the possibility of a madman, sometime, deciding to create nuclear missiles. After all, the world now knows how to make them. I likened it to our keeping our gas masks, even though the nations of the world had outlawed poison gas after World War I.

We seemed to be making progress on reducing weaponry, although the General Secretary was registering opposition to SDI and proposing a pledge to observe ABM for a number of years as the day was ending.

Secretary Shultz suggested we turn over the notes our notetakers had been making of everything we'd said to our respective teams and let them work through the night to put them together and find just where we were in agreement and what differences separated us. With respect and gratitude, I can inform you those teams worked through the night till six-thirty A.M.

Yesterday, Sunday morning, Mr. Gorbachev and I, with our foreign ministers, came together again and took up the report of our two teams. It was most promising. The Soviets had asked for a ten-year delay in the deployment of SDI programs.

In an effort to see how we could satisfy their concerns— while protecting our principles and security—we proposed a ten-year period in which we began with the reduction of all strategic nuclear arms, bombers, air-launched cruise missiles, intercontinental ballistic missiles, submarine-launched ballistic missiles, and the weapons they carry. They would be reduced 50 percent in the first five years. During the next five years, we would continue by eliminating all remaining offensive ballistic missiles, of all ranges. And during that time, we would proceed with research, development, and testing of SDI—all done in conformity with ABM provisions. At the ten-year point, with all ballistic missiles eliminated, we could proceed to deploy advanced defenses, at the same time permitting the Soviets to do likewise.

And here the debate began. The General Secretary wanted wording that, in effect, would have kept us from developing the SDI for the entire ten years. In effect, he was killing SDI.

And unless I agreed, all that work toward eliminating nuclear weapons would go down the drain—canceled.

I told him I had pledged to the American people that I would not trade away SDI, there was no way I could tell our people their government would not protect them against nuclear destruction. I went to Reykjavik determined that everything was negotiable except two things: our freedom and our future. I'm still optimistic that a way will be found. The door is open, and the opportunity to begin eliminating the nuclear threat is within reach.

So you can see, we made progress in Iceland. And we will continue to make progress if we pursue a prudent, deliberate, and above all, realistic approach with the Soviets. From the earliest days of our administration this has been our policy. We made it clear we had no illusions about the Soviets or their ultimate intentions. We were publicly candid about the critical moral distinctions between totalitarianism and democracy. We declared the principal objective of American foreign policy to be not just the prevention of war, but the extension of freedom. And we stressed our commitment to the growth of democratic government and democratic institutions around the world.

And that's why we assisted freedom fighters who are resisting the imposition of totalitarian rule in Afghanistan, Nicaragua, Angola, Cambodia, and elsewhere. And finally, we began work on what I believe most spurred the Soviets to negotiate seriously: rebuilding our military strength, reconstructing our strategic deterrence, and above all, beginning to work on the Strategic Defense Initiative.

And yet, at the same time, we set out these foreign policy goals and began working toward them. We pursued another of our major objectives: that of seeking means to lessen tensions with the Soviets and ways to prevent war and keep the peace.

Now, this policy is now paying dividends—one sign of this in Iceland was the progress on the issue of arms control. For the first time in a long while, Soviet-American negotiations in the area of arms reductions are moving, and moving in the right direction—not just toward arms control, but toward arms reduction.

But for all the progress we made on arms reductions, we must remember there were other issues on the table in Iceland, issues that are fundamental. As I mentioned, one such issue is human rights. As President Kennedy once said, "And is not peace, in the last analysis, basically a matter of human rights?"

I made it plain that the United States would not seek to exploit improvement in these matters for purposes of propaganda. But I also made it plain, once again, that an improvement of the human condition within the Soviet Union is indispensable for an improvement in bilateral relations with the United States. For a government that will break faith with its own people cannot be trusted to keep faith with foreign powers. So, I told Mr. Gorbachev—again in Reykjavik, as I had in Geneva—we Americans place far less weight upon the words that are spoken at meetings such as these than upon the deeds that follow. When it comes to human rights and judging Soviet intentions, we're all from Missouri—you got to show us.

Another subject area we took up in Iceland also lies at the heart of the differences between the Soviet Union and America. This is the issue of regional conflicts. Summit meetings cannot make the American people forget what Soviet actions have meant for the peoples of Afghanistan, Central America, Africa, and Southeast Asia. Until Soviet policies change, we will make sure that our friends in these areas—those who fight for freedom and independence—will have the support they need.

Finally, there was a fourth item. And this area was that of bilateral relations, people-to-people contacts. In Geneva last year, we welcomed several cultural exchange accords; in Iceland, we saw indications of more movement in these areas. But let me say now: The United States remains committed to people-to-people programs that could lead to exchanges between not just a few elite, but thousands of everyday citizens from both our countries.

So, I think, then, that you can see that we did make progress in Iceland on a broad range of topics. We reaffirmed our four-point agenda. We discovered major new grounds of agreement. We probed again some old areas of disagreement.

And let me return again to the SDI issue. I realize some Americans may be asking tonight: Why not accept Mr. Gorbachev's demand? Why not give up SDI for this agreement?

Well, the answer, my friends, is simple. SDI is America's insurance policy that the Soviet Union would keep the commitments made at Reykjavik. SDI is America's security guarantee if the Soviets should—as they have done too often in the past —fail to comply with their solemn commitments. SDI is what brought the Soviets back to arms control talks at Geneva and Iceland. SDI is the key to a world without nuclear weapons.

The Soviets understand this. They have devoted far more resources, for a lot longer time than we, to their own SDI. The world's only operational missile defense today surrounds Moscow, the capital of the Sovet Union.

What Mr. Gorbachev was demanding at Reykjavik was that the United States agree to a new version of a fourteen-year-old ABM treaty that the Soviet Union has already violated. I told him we don't make those kinds of deals in the United States.

And the American people should reflect on these critical questions: How does a defense of the United States threaten the Soviet Union or anyone else? Why are the Soviets so adamant that America remain forever vulnerable to Soviet rocket attack? As of today, all free nations are utterly defenseless against Soviet missiles—fired either by accident or design. Why does the Soviet Union insist that we remain so—forever?

So, my fellow Americans, I cannot promise, nor can any president promise, that the talks in Iceland or any future discussions with Mr. Gorbachev will lead inevitably to great breakthroughs or momentous treaty signings. We will not abandon the guiding principle we took to Reykjavik. We prefer no agreement than to bring home a bad agreement to the United States.

And on this point, I know you're also interested in the question of whether there will be another summit. There was no indication by Mr. Gorbachev as to when or whether he plans to travel to the United States, as we agreed he would last year in Geneva. I repeat tonight that our invitation stands, and that we continue to believe additional meetings would be useful. But that's a decision the Soviets must make.

But whatever the immediate prospects, I can tell you that I'm ultimately hopeful about the prospects for progress at the summit and for world peace and freedom. You see, the current summit process is very different from that of previous decades. It's different because the world is different; and the world is different because of the hard work and sacrifice of the American people during the past five and a half years. Your energy has restored and expanded our economic might. Your support has restored our military strength. Your courage and sense of national unity in times of crisis have given pause to our adversaries, heartened our friends, and inspired the world. The Western democracies and the NATO alliance are revitalized; and all across the world, nations are turning to democratic ideas and the principles of the free market. So, because the American people stood guard at the critical hour, freedom has gathered its forces, regained its strength, and is on the march.

So, if there's one impression I carry away with me from these October talks, it is that, unlike the past, we're dealing now from a position of strength. And for that reason, we have it within our grasp to move speedily with the Soviets toward even more breakthroughs. Our ideas are out there on the table. They won't go away. We're ready to pick up where we left off. Our negotiators are heading back to Geneva, and we're prepared to go forward whenever and wherever the Soviets are ready. So, there's reason, good reason, for hope.

I saw evidence of this in the progress we made in the talks with Mr. Gorbachev. And I saw evidence of it when we left Iceland yesterday, and I spoke to our young men and women at our naval installation at Keflavik—a critically important base far closer to Soviet naval bases than to our own coastline.

As always, I was proud to spend a few moments with them and thank them for their sacrifices and devotion to country.

They represent America at her finest: committed to defend not only our own freedom but the freedom of others who would be living in a far more frightening world were it not for the strength and resolve of the United States.

"Whenever the standard of freedom and independence has been . . . unfurled, there will be America's heart, her benedictions, and her prayers," John Quincy Adams once said. He spoke well of our destiny as a nation. My fellow Americans, we're honored by history, entrusted by destiny with the oldest dream of humanity—the dream of lasting peace and human freedom.

Another president, Harry Truman, noted that our century had seen two of the most frightful wars in history and that "the supreme need of our time is for man to learn to live together in peace and harmony." It's in pursuit of that ideal I went to Geneva a year ago and to Iceland last week. And it's in pursuit of that ideal that I thank you now for all the support you've given me, and I again ask for your help and your prayers as we continue our journey toward a world where peace reigns and freedom is enshrined.

Thank you, and God bless you.

Meeting with Hostage David Jacobsen and Reporters

WHITE HOUSE ROSE GARDEN
NOVEMBER 7, 1986

I found this little episode interesting because it deals more with what presidents can't say than what they can. It also previews one of the biggest controversies of my presidency.

David Jacobsen was the second hostage we had gotten out as a result of our secret negotiations with a group of Iranians who we thought were more moderate. To this day, I don't know what happened to those Iranians after the Iran/contra thing burst into the headlines. I don't know if they're dead or gone underground or just lying low. Anyway, back then they told us that two more hostages would be released in forty-eight hours.

About this same time, a rag of a newspaper in Beirut reported that we had sold arms to Iranians in return for hostages. Well, of course, the press had all sorts of questions at a very delicate time in terms of getting those other two hostages out. I found Mr. Jacobsen's plea to the press so compelling I decided I'd just put it in here. He made his points much more eloquently than I could ever have. We never did get those other two people out.

The President. Ladies and gentlemen, you know who our guest is today, and I know that he has a few words for you. And I think a great many prayers have been answered by his presence here in our country.

Mr. Jacobsen. I certainly have some words, and I would like to read them. I usually like to speak extemporaneously. But we have our people being held prisoners, and I'd like to just preface my remarks by one simple statement.

And what I say today, what you report, what you speculate upon is heard throughout the entire world within twenty-four hours. A simple speculation on your part could cause the death of my dear friend Tom Sutherland, or Terry Anderson, or Joe Cicippio, or any other of the other hostages. And I would ask that you would be responsible and please do not engage in unreasonable and unrealistic speculations. Be intellectually honest. I ask of you, I plead for you: I am worried about what you might say, or someone else, might result in a death of somebody that I love. I don't want that on my conscience, and I don't think you want it on yours.

So, I have a brief statement that I've written, and I'm happy to read it. And it's a thrill to be here.

Mr. President, you can't really imagine—and Mrs. President —can't imagine my joy of being here with you on this very special day. For seventeen long months, I never lost hope of being a free man again. I prayed long and hard. And my dear family—my six wonderful children are here, are with me here today—and my friends—they kept the faith, and they never lost hope despite many, many frustrations. And that knowledge kept me going.

And freedom is a very precious gift, and I really learned it in a very personal manner. Freedom is a very precious gift, and one that we Americans sometimes take for granted. When freedom is taken away, the loss is immense. But that same hope and that faith and that optimism that sustained the founders of our country, of this great land, during the periods of our adversity as a nation also kept my spirits high during my long captivity.

And Mr. President, I know that you and many others in and out of the administration of this government have worked long and hard on my behalf and on the behalf of the other captives and you continue to do so for the others that are still being held hostage. And in particular, there are a number of independent people, religious leaders and others, that deserve special praise for their independent efforts.

Terry Waite, who is one of those great humanitarians, who has given so much of himself so that I may be free—Terry Waite did it as a free man, free of all governments and any type of deals. Terry did it as a humanitarian. The families of Terry Anderson, Tom Sutherland, Joe Cicippio, and the other innocent people still being held hostage should not give up hope.

Contact by you, Mr. President, and others in the administration and especially those very special people in the State Department, who have maintained frequent contact with our families, help our dear ones sustain their hope. And I know, Mr. President, that you have sought our freedom from the day that the first American was taken hostage, and I know that you have not rested, nor will you rest, until every American is home free.

And Mr. President, you really have my eternal gratitude. You're the leader of a truly great country, and I'm proud to be an American. And I really want to thank you very, very much. You're quite a man.

The President. Thank you.

Mr. Jacobsen. Thank you. And please, please, in your comments and evaluations, be responsible. Thank you.

Q. Mr. President, the Iranians are saying that if you'll release some of those weapons, they'll intercede to free the rest of the hostages. Will you?

The President. Bill [Bill Plante, CBS News], I think in view of this statement, this is just exactly what I tried to say last night. There's no way that we can answer questions having anything to do with this without endangering the people we're trying to rescue.

Q. Could you just tell us whether Secretary of State Shultz agrees with your policy or disagrees and has protested as has been reported?

The President. We have all been working together.

Q. And Secretary Shultz supports the policy, and so does Cap Weinberger?

The President. Yes.

Q. Why not dispel the speculation by telling us exactly what happened, sir?

The President. Because it has to happen again and again and again until we have them all back. And anything that we tell about all the things that have been going on in trying to effect his rescue endangers the possibility of further rescue.

Q. Your own party's majority leader says you're rewarding terrorists.

Mr. Jacobsen. Please, you didn't hear what I said at the beginning. Unreasonable speculation on your part can endanger their lives. I would like to take some time now and talk. But this is a day of joy for me. I have my children inside. I want to share it with them. And I want Terry Anderson to share the same joy with his family. And I want Tom Sutherland to share the joy with his family. And in the name of God, would you please just be responsible and back off. Thank you.

Q. Mr. Jacobsen, how are we to know what is responsible and what is not?

1987

Remarks on Signing
the INF Treaty

WHITE HOUSE EAST ROOM
DECEMBER 8, 1987

The country had a good year in 1987. The economic recovery continued and we signed an historic agreement with the Soviet Union eliminating an entire class of nuclear weapons—the intermediate range ones that had been stationed in Europe. Privately, we—and especially Nancy—had a rough year. In October, Nancy had a mastectomy, and before she even had time to recover from the surgery, her mother died. And during the first part of the year, my credibility with the American people according to the polls dropped to an all-time low because of the continuing Iran/contra matter. Although my relationship with the people would soon recover, this was a source of great personal pain to me at the time.

The big news of the year, however, was the INF agreement. We signed it in the East Room of the White House. I believe this proves what progress can be made when we bargain from a position of strength and determination. I don't think the agreement would have been possible without our defense buildup. I also don't think it would have been possible before Gorbachev. He's quite a fellow.

He has a different attitude from previous Soviet leaders regarding not only arms reductions but the need to restructure the Soviet system itself. I've been a little concerned about his safety as a result. Why don't I let you read something I wrote in my diary earlier in 1987 to explain what I mean:

> *... then a fine meeting with XXX. Very interesting—suggested maybe I should go to Moscow instead of Gorbachev coming here. Then XXX dropped the bomb. A top Soviet official [said] Gorbachev might well be killed if he came here. There is so much opposition to what he's trying to do in Russia—they could murder him here and then pin the whole thing on us. I don't find the warning at all outlandish. The KGB is capable of doing just that.*

Although I knew that our security people had done everything possible to protect him, when he did come over in December I don't mind telling you I thought about his safety. He's a smart man, so he could have done some handpicking of the Soviet agents he brought with him to the U.S. I don't know. But you can understand why his security and our security people were so jumpy when he got out of his limo on the streets of downtown Washington to shake a few hands.

But his trip here to sign the INF agreement was a big success. He's not above trying to bamboozle you as he tried to do to us in Reykjavik by raising the SDI thing at the last moment, but I believe he is a reasonable man. He is, as Margaret Thatcher once said, a man we can do business with.

And that is exactly what we did that day in December.

The President. Thank you all very much. Welcome to the White House.

This ceremony and the treaty we're signing today are both excellent examples of the rewards of patience. It was over six years ago, November 18, 1981, that I first proposed what would come to be called the zero option. It was a simple proposal—one might say, disarmingly simple. [*Laughter*] Unlike treaties in the past, it didn't simply codify the status quo or a new arms buildup; it didn't simply talk of controlling an arms race. For the first time in history, the language of "arms control" was replaced by "arms reduction"—in this case, the complete elimination of an entire class of U.S. and Soviet nuclear missiles.

Of course, this required a dramatic shift in thinking, and it took conventional wisdom some time to catch up. Reaction, to say the least, was mixed. To some the zero option was impossibly visionary and unrealistic; to others merely a propaganda ploy. Well, with patience, determination, and commitment, we've made this impossible vision a reality.

General Secretary Gorbachev, I'm sure you're familiar with Ivan Krylov's famous tale about the swan, the crawfish, and the pike. It seems that once upon a time these three were trying to move a wagonload together. They hitched and harnessed themselves to the wagon. It wasn't very heavy, but no matter how hard they worked, the wagon just wouldn't move. You see, the swan was flying upward; the crawfish kept crawling backward; the pike kept making for the water. The end result was that they got nowhere, and the wagon is still there to this day. Well, strong and fundamental moral differences continue to exist between our nations. But today, on this vital issue, at least, we've seen what can be accomplished when we pull together.

The numbers alone demonstrate the value of this agreement. On the Soviet side, over 1,500 deployed warheads will be removed, and all ground-launched intermediate-range missiles, including the SS-20s, will be destroyed. On our side, our entire complement of Pershing II and ground-launched cruise missiles, with some 400 deployed warheads, will all be destroyed. Additional backup missiles on both sides will also be destroyed.

But the importance of this treaty transcends numbers. We have listened to the wisdom in an old Russian maxim. And I'm sure you're familiar with it, Mr. General Secretary, though my pronunciation may give you difficulty. The maxim is: *Dovorey no provorey*—trust, but verify.

The General Secretary. You repeat that at every meeting. [*Laughter*]

The President. I like it. [*Laughter*]

This agreement contains the most stringent verification regime in history, including provisions for inspection teams actually residing in each other's territory and several other forms of on-site inspection, as well. This treaty protects the interests of America's friends and allies. It also embodies another important principle: the need for *glasnost,* a greater openness in military programs and forces.

We can only hope that this history-making agreement will not be an end in itself but the beginning of a working relationship that will enable us to tackle the other urgent issues before us: strategic offensive nuclear weapons, the balance of conventional forces in Europe, the destructive and tragic regional conflicts that beset so many parts of our globe, and respect for the human and natural rights God has granted to all men.

To all here who have worked so hard to make this vision a reality: Thank you, and congratulations—above all to Ambassadors Glitman and Obukhov.* To quote another Russian proverb—as you can see, I'm becoming quite an expert—[*Laughter*] —in Russian proverbs: "The harvest comes more from sweat than from the dew."

So, I'm going to propose to General Secretary Gorbachev that we issue one last instruction to you: Get some well-deserved rest. [*Laughter*]

The General Secretary. We're not going to do that. [*Laughter*]

The President. Well, now, Mr. General Secretary, would you like to say a few words before we sign the treaty?

The General Secretary. Mr. President, ladies and gentlemen, comrades:

* Ambassador Maynard W. Glitman, U.S. Negotiator on Intermediate-Range Nuclear Forces, and Ambassador Aleksey Obukhov, Deputy Head of the Soviet Nuclear and Space Arms Delegation.

Succeeding generations will hand down their verdict on the importance of the event which we are about to witness. But I will venture to say that what we are going to do, the signing of the first-ever agreement eliminating nuclear weapons, has a universal significance for mankind, both from the standpoint of world politics and from the standpoint of humanism.

For everyone, and above all, for our two great powers, the treaty whose text is on this table offers a big chance at last to get onto the road leading away from the threat of catastrophe. It is our duty to take full advantage of that chance and move together toward a nuclear-free world, which holds out for our children and grandchildren and for their children and grandchildren the promise of a fulfilling and happy life without fear and without a senseless waste of resources on weapons of destruction.

We can be proud of planting this sapling, which may one day grow into a mighty tree of peace. But it is probably still too early to bestow laurels upon each other. As the great American poet and philosopher Ralph Waldo Emerson said: "The reward of a thing well done is to have done it."

So, let us reward ourselves by getting down to business. We have covered a seven-year-long road, replete with intense work and debate. One last step toward this table, and the treaty will be signed.

May December 8, 1987, become a date that will be inscribed in the history books, a date that will mark the watershed separating the era of a mounting risk of nuclear war from the era of a demilitarization of human life.

Remarks at the Memorial Service
for Malcolm Baldrige

THE NATIONAL CATHEDRAL
WASHINGTON, D.C.
JULY 29, 1987

Mac Baldrige, my secretary of commerce, was a great guy. He told me this story one day when we were horseback riding down at the Marine base in Quantico, Virginia, south of Washington.

His first job was as a cowpuncher when he was fourteen years old. He loved rodeos and riding and roping, but at the age of twenty-eight he was told he could never ride or do anything athletic again because of arthritis of the spine. At one point, he was taking up to fifteen or thirty pills a day—in any event a great many. One day he said to hell with it. He said, "I love to ride and I don't care what the doctors say." So he just started riding again and rodeoing again. Well, it was great therapy. He told me that jumping off a horse and wrestling a calf to the ground was his miracle cure.

In the end, he died when his horse fell on him in a rodeo event, but something tells me that's the way Mac would have wanted to go.

Midge, Megan, Molly,* distinguished ladies and gentlemen:

The day I called Mac Baldrige to ask him to join the cabinet, I was told by Midge I would have to call back later. He was out on his horse roping and couldn't come to the phone. Right then I knew he was the kind of man I wanted.

It's a gift to be simple, we're told. If that means to hold simple, strong, and decent values, Mac had that gift. You could see it in the way he moved around the White House. He seemed to know everyone, not just those in the public eye but the secretaries and assistants, as well. And he treated everyone with the same measure of courtesy and respect, from his driver to the President. He never judged a man or woman by rank or trappings. Despite his many remarkable successes, worldly success was not the way he measured people. No, money was not, position was not, qualities of character were. Honesty, courage, industry, and humility—these were his yardsticks. And if you had these simple qualities, you'd made it in his eyes, whether you were rich or poor, famous or unknown.

Language was one way he decided if you were his kind of person. It's well-known now that he insisted on simple language in memos at the Commerce Department. He banned phrases that were vague or redundant. He once said that the thing he liked about cowboys was that they didn't talk unless they had something to say, and when they said something, they meant it. To him, simple language did not mark a simple mind, but a strong and fearless one. It was a sign of those who didn't hide their meaning behind a cloud of ambiguous words.

Mac, of course, never hid his opinions. Even if the tide was against him, he was forceful and clear and unflinching. I always knew where he stood, and so did the country. I could always count on him for the truth as he saw it, no matter how unpleasant or unpopular. There were times the Cabinet came down on an issue twelve to one, and he was on the short end. But I knew

---

* Malcolm Baldrige's wife and two daughters.

that if he believed something that others didn't, he wouldn't rein himself in and follow the herd. He would step forward and be clear.

What I'm saying about Mac Baldrige adds up to a simple but extraordinary quality that I would call, more than anything else, American. In his directness, in his honesty, in his independence, in his disregard for rank, in his courage, he embodied the best of the American spirit. I suppose we think of that spirit as living most of all in cowboys. And that's why I've always suspected that it was more than just roping and his place here in Washington that got Mac voted into the Cowboy Hall of Fame. He belonged there. It was in his blood. It was in his heart and soul.

Let me say a word about his many contributions to his country. These were not simple, although they were built on simple principles, principles like his reverence for the independence of the American character, for the freedom that lets independence flourish, and for the opportunities of a free society.

Mac was an architect of American international economic policy during years in which that policy moved to center stage. He also helped shape our policy toward East-West trade in a period in which that was a source of new questions and concerns. And perhaps the least recognized of his major achievements was the securing of trade ties with China. In just four years since his 1983 visit to China, trade has become a pillar of the Sino-American relationship.

To contribute so much required skill and persistence—qualities Mac had in abundance. It also required vision, vision not only for dealing with immediate issues but for the future of the entire world and its economy, as well.

I always prized the quality of Mac's vision. He had the capacity to look up from the dust of the plains to the distant mountains. He never forgot that all the skirmishes and battles over trade policy that we have here in Washington and around the world have one final goal: We're building a world in which our children and grandchildren will live. And we who love freedom and revere the dignity of humanity have a sacred duty to make that an open world of real hope and abundant opportunity, a world in which the spirit of freedom—yes, what you might call that part of the American spirit that lives in all of mankind—in which that spirit can ride across an open range toward the peaks beyond.

I'm told that Mac's staff had orders to interrupt him at whatever time of the day with calls from only two people. I was one, and any cowboy who rang up was the other. Well, I'm honored to have been in that company. Mac, as we know, left us while he was doing what he loved most. And now, whenever any of us wants to ring him up, we'll have to remind ourselves that he's out on a horse somewhere, and we'll just have to wait. Yet in his simplicity, he has entered the company of the men and women who have shaped our nation and its destiny, and he will live in that company forever.

Yes, there is sorrow, but the sorrow is with us and for us. We must believe that door is opened that God promised and he has just gone through that door into another life, where there is no more pain, no more sorrow. And we must believe that we, too, will one day go through that door and join him again.

Thank you. God bless you.

Remarks at a Ceremony
Honoring Residents of Chase, Maryland

OLD EXECUTIVE OFFICE BUILDING
FEBRUARY 3, 1987

I'm quite taken with heroes. And the wonderful thing is that they're all around us in our daily lives. During my presidency, I consistently tried to focus attention on those average Americans who are quietly heroic. And there are so many of them that I think this must just be part of the American character.

In the following ceremony, we honored an entire small community for their response to a terrible train wreck.

I<small>T'S AN HONOR</small> to have you all here at the White House. Now, I know that must sound strange. Most people think of it as an honor to be invited here, and that includes myself. I remember how humble I felt on that day in 1980 when the American people first asked me to come here. But today the tables are turned. For by your deeds, you and the members of your community have honored all America. You've shown us all, once again, the love and courage, the self-sacrifice and eagerness to help and serve those in need—in short, the qualities that for generations have been the heart of American life.

It was an ordinary winter's day at the end of the New Year's weekend. Some of you were hanging out laundry. Some of you were about to watch the football game. And then something happened—investigators are still piecing together just what it was—and your community was face-to-face with the worst accident in Amtrak history. And that's when, on that ordinary day, the people of Chase, Maryland, showed that what we take as ordinary in America is really very wonderful and special, very extraordinary.

Robert Booker and his cousin, Michael Cooper, were among the first on the scene. Robert climbed into a burning car. He couldn't save everyone. And I know that he and all of you've thought a great deal since that day about those whom God took into His arms, but also remember that there are many who are alive today because of your strength and courage. You gave to scores of people the gift of life.

As Michael and Robert worked together helping to pull people out of the train, Eve Booker and Juanita Mattes helped to care for the injured, cleaning their wounds, wrapping them, covering them with blankets from their homes to keep them warm. As one reporter wrote of Eve and Juanita: "They acted quickly, calmly, heroically. But when the night ended, the fifteen-year-olds wept."

Well, those stories of sacrifice and love were repeated hundreds of times that day. All of you and your neighbors helped people escape the wreck, helped care for them, feed them, and gave them shelter. Nancy Tharpe said there were forty-five passengers in her house on that Sunday. As Bob Cooper said later, "Everybody just chipped in and did what they had to do." And as a result, most of the passengers were out of the train even before the emergency crews arrived. In the hours and days that followed, you took into your homes not only the victims of the crash but rescue workers and reporters, too. I don't want to forget the magnificent work of those workers or the people who, within hours, lined up to give blood for the victims. They made us all proud, too.

Some have talked since about how amazing you were, and I know that Cathi Fischer spoke for all of you when she told a reporter, "I don't think it was anything remarkable. I think if it had been another community, they would have done the same thing." But that's just the point; you all did what Americans have done for more than two centuries: When others were in need, you didn't point to the other guys. You just rolled up your sleeves and went to work.

Not long ago a commentator on the network news show said that we Americans had become selfish, only out for ourselves, had lost our dedication to community and country. I know he's paid well to give his wisdom to the country each and every week. But for my money, the true wisdom is in Cathi Fischer's words, and the best answer to him is your example.

Yes, on an ordinary day in January, Americans in an ordinary American community showed extraordinary courage, self-sacrifice, and love for their fellow man. And when it was all over, you didn't brag and shout. You just went back to your daily work. But you left behind a gift not just for crash victims but for all of us. Your strength strengthened all Americans. Your spirit will long inspire and guide us all. And as president, I just asked you here today so I could say thanks.

Thank you all, and God bless you all.

And now I'd like to award the Private Sector Initiatives Commendation to the community of Chase, Maryland. And Robert Booker, will you please step forward and receive this? This is in recognition of the exemplary community service in the finest American tradition.

Thank you all very much. And just for my curiosity, where are the two young ladies sitting that that night cried? I know they're out there with you someplace. There you are. Well, God bless you.

Well, again, I hate to walk away and leave, but they tell me I've still got things to do over there. I haven't told this for a long time, but I got some letters from some young people when I first arrived in Washington. And one of them that always appealed to me was from a little girl and she wrote—and very informed about the things that were facing me and the problems I had to solve and everything. And when she finished she said, "Now, get back to the Oval Office, and get to work." [*Laughter*] So, that's what I'll do. Thank you all.

Address to the Nation
on the Tower Commission Report

OVAL OFFICE
MARCH 4, 1987

The Iran/contra mess got even worse in 1987. I had appointed a commission headed by former senator John Tower to get to the bottom of what had actually happened. The commission's report did not give us a clean bill of health. Something clearly went wrong with our initial plan.

I'm going to cover this more completely in my memoirs, but I get beside myself when I think that people believe I would actually trade arms for hostages. I fully realize that few people buy my argument, but for history's sake I simply feel compelled to make it.

The way I saw it was like this. If your child was kidnapped and someone who wasn't the kidnapper came to you and offered to help you find your child, I think most parents would take that help even if it cost you some money. By the same reasoning, I did not see it as trading arms for hostages because we were dealing with Iranian intermediaries, not the kidnap-

pers themselves. I know it may be a fine line to most people, but it's what I believed then and what I still believe.

I have to say that in looking back I wonder if this whole thing wasn't a setup, a sting operation, by the Iranians. Maybe we were conned into believing these were moderate Iranians seeking to reach out to the West, while in reality they were working directly for the Ayatollah just to get some arms. Who knows? Whatever the real story, the whole thing ended in a mess, but it certainly wasn't the end of the world as some up on Capitol Hill were wailing.

This address is the one I made to the people following the release of the Tower Commission's report.

My fellow Americans:

I've spoken to you from this historic office on many occasions and about many things. The power of the presidency is often thought to reside within this Oval Office. Yet it doesn't rest here; it rests in you, the American people, and in your trust. Your trust is what gives a president his powers of leadership and his personal strength, and it's what I want to talk to you about this evening.

For the past three months, I've been silent on the revelations about Iran. And you must have been thinking: "Well, why doesn't he tell us what is happening? Why doesn't he just speak to us as he has in the past when we've faced troubles or trage-dies?" Others of you, I guess, were thinking: "What's he doing hiding out in the White House?" Well, the reason I haven't spoken to you before now is this: You deserve the truth. And as frustrating as the waiting has been, I felt it was improper to come to you with sketchy reports, or possibly even erroneous statements, which would then have to be corrected, creating even more doubt and confusion. There's been enough of that.

I've paid a price for my silence in terms of your trust and confidence. But I've had to wait, as you have, for the complete story. That's why I appointed Ambassador David Abshire as my special counselor to help get out the thousands of documents to the various investigations. And I appointed a special review board, the Tower Board, which took on the chore of pulling the truth together for me and getting to the bottom of things. It has now issued its findings.

I'm often accused of being an optimist, and it's true I had to hunt pretty hard to find any good news in the Board's report. As you know, it's well stocked with criticisms, which I'll discuss in a moment; but I was very relieved to read this sentence: ". . . the Board is convinced that the President does indeed want the full story to be told." And that will continue to be my pledge to you as the other investigations go forward.

I want to thank the members of the panel: former senator John Tower, former secretary of state Edmund Muskie, and former national security adviser Brent Scowcroft. They have done the nation, as well as me personally, a great service by submitting a report of such integrity and depth. They have my genuine and enduring gratitude.

I've studied the Board's report. Its findings are honest, convincing, and highly critical; and I accept them. And tonight I want to share with you my thoughts on these findings and report to you on the actions I'm taking to implement the Board's recommendations.

First, let me say I take full responsibility for my own actions and for those of my administration. As angry as I may be about activities undertaken without my knowledge, I am still accountable for those activities. As disappointed as I may be in some who served me, I'm still the one who must answer to the American people for this behavior. And as personally distasteful as I find secret bank accounts and diverted funds—well, as the Navy would say, this happened on my watch.

Let's start with the part that is the most controversial. A few months ago I told the American people I did not trade arms for hostages. My heart and my best intentions still tell me that's true, but the facts and the evidence tell me it is not. As the Tower Board reported, what began as a strategic opening to

337

Iran deteriorated, in its implementation, into trading arms for hostages. This runs counter to my own beliefs, to administration policy, and to the original strategy we had in mind. There are reasons why it happened, but no excuses. It was a mistake.

I undertook the original Iran initiative in order to develop relations with those who might assume leadership in a post-Khomeini government. It's clear from the Board's report, however, that I let my personal concern for the hostages spill over into the geopolitical strategy of reaching out to Iran. I asked so many questions about the hostages' welfare that I didn't ask enough about the specifics of the total Iran plan.

Let me say to the hostage families: We have not given up. We never will. And I promise you we'll use every legitimate means to free your loved ones from captivity. But I must also caution that those Americans who freely remain in such dangerous areas must know that they're responsible for their own safety.

Now, another major aspect of the Board's findings regards the transfer of funds to the Nicaraguan contras. The Tower Board wasn't able to find out what happened to this money, so the facts here will be left to the continuing investigations of the court-appointed Independent Counsel and the two congressional investigating committees. I'm confident the truth will come out about this matter, as well. As I told the Tower Board, I didn't know about any diversion of funds to the contras. But as president, I cannot escape responsibility.

Much has been said about my management style, a style that's worked successfully for me during eight years as governor of California and for most of my presidency. The way I work is to identify the problem, find the right individuals to do the job, and then let them go to it. I've found this invariably brings out the best in people. They seem to rise to their full capability, and in the long run you get more done.

When it came to managing the NSC staff, let's face it, my style didn't match its previous track record. I've already begun correcting this. As a start, yesterday I met with the entire professional staff of the National Security Council. I defined for them the values I want to guide the national security policies of this country. I told them that I wanted a policy that was as justifiable and understandable in public as it was in secret. I wanted a policy that reflected the will of the Congress as well as of the White House. And I told them that there'll be no more free-lancing by individuals when it comes to our national security.

You've heard a lot about the staff of the National Security Council in recent months. Well, I can tell you, they are good and dedicated government employees, who put in long hours for the nation's benefit. They are eager and anxious to serve their country.

One thing still upsetting me, however, is that no one kept proper records of meetings or decisions. This led to my failure to recollect whether I approved an arms shipment before or after the fact. I did approve it; I just can't say specifically when. Well, rest assured, there's plenty of record keeping now going on at 1600 Pennsylvania Avenue.

For nearly a week now, I've been studying the Board's report. I want the American people to know that this wrenching ordeal of recent months has not been in vain. I endorse every one of the Tower Board's recommendations. In fact, I'm going beyond its recommendations so as to put the house in even better order.

I'm taking action in three basic areas: personnel, national security policy, and the process for making sure that the system works. *First,* personnel—I've brought in an accomplished and highly respected new team here at the White House. They bring new blood, new energy, and new credibility and experience.

Former senator Howard Baker, my new chief of staff, possesses a breadth of legislative and foreign affairs skills that's impossible to match. I'm hopeful that his experience as minority and majority leader of the Senate can help us forge a new partnership with the Congress, especially on foreign and national security policies. I'm genuinely honored that he's given up his own presidential aspirations to serve the country as my chief of staff.

Frank Carlucci, my new national security adviser, is respected for his experience in government and trusted for his judgment and counsel. Under him, the NSC staff is being rebuilt with proper management discipline. Already, almost half the NSC professional staff is comprised of new people.

Yesterday I nominated William Webster, a man of sterling reputation, to be director of the Central Intelligence Agency. Mr. Webster has served as director of the FBI and as a U.S. District Court judge. He understands the meaning of "rule of law."

So that his knowledge of national security matters can be available to me on a continuing basis, I will also appoint John Tower to serve as a member of my Foreign Intelligence Advisory Board. I am considering other changes in personnel, and I'll move more furniture, as I see fit, in the weeks and months ahead.

Second, in the area of national security policy, I have ordered the NSC to begin a comprehensive review of all covert operations. I have also directed that any covert activity be in support of clear policy objectives and in compliance with American values. I expect a covert policy that if Americans saw it on the front page of their newspaper, they'd say, "That makes sense." I have had issued a directive prohibiting the NSC staff itself from undertaking covert operations—no ifs, ands, or buts. I have asked Vice President Bush to reconvene his task force on terrorism to review our terrorist policy in light of the events that have occurred.

Third, in terms of the process of reaching national security decisions, I am adopting in total the Tower report's model of how the NSC process and staff should work. I am directing Mr. Carlucci to take the necessary steps to make that happen. He will report back to me on further reforms that might be needed. I've created the post of NSC legal adviser to assure a greater sensitivity to matters of law.

I am also determined to make the congressional oversight process work. Proper procedures for consultation with the Congress will be followed, not only in letter but in spirit. Before the end of March, I will report to the Congress on all the steps I've taken in line with the Tower Board's conclusions.

Now, what should happen when you make a mistake is this: You take your knocks, you learn your lessons, and then you move on. That's the healthiest way to deal with a problem. This in no way diminishes the importance of the other continuing investigations, but the business of our country and our people must proceed. I've gotten this message from Republicans and Democrats in Congress, from allies around the world, and—if we're reading the signals right—even from the Soviets. And of course, I've heard the message from you, the American people.

You know, by the time you reach my age, you've made plenty of mistakes. And if you've lived your life properly—so, you learn. You put things in perspective. You pull your energies together. You change. You go forward.

My fellow Americans, I have a great deal that I want to accomplish with you and for you over the next two years. And the Lord willing, that's exactly what I intend to do.

Good night, and God bless you.

Remarks at the Memorial Service
for Crew Members of the USS *Stark*

MAYPORT NAVAL STATION
JACKSONVILLE, FLORIDA
MAY 22, 1987

Another heartbreaking memorial. It was always agony delivering them, but I felt that as commander in chief it was my duty. I felt it was important to be there with the families.

One of the hardest things for a president to do is to send our boys into harm's way. The USS Stark was mistakenly attacked by an Iraqi fighter jet while patrolling the Persian Gulf. There was a lot of debate at the time about whether we should keep the sea-lanes open. I think it is clear now that this decision helped to bring the war between Iran and Iraq to an end. Some of our seamen paid a price for this with their lives.

Not too long after the loss, I saw something that caught my eye in the paper. The widow of one of the crewmen had found her husband's Bible, scorched on the outside but otherwise intact, amid the warped metal and ashes of his bunk. It was the only thing that survived the attack.

OUR TASK TODAY is simple and sad: to remember, to pay tribute to those we loved.

For some of us here today, our love is the unquenchable, unforgetting love of a wife or child for a fallen father, of a mother or father for a fallen son. For others of us, this love, while more distant, is still anguished and grieving; ours is a love for a fallen countryman who died so that we, a free people, might live and this great nation endure.

Even as we hear these words, we understand again their inadequacy. We appreciate anew Lincoln's humble wisdom at Gettysburg. When brave men die, it is their deeds, not our words, that are remembered. It is their sacrifice, not our brief recollection, that offers everlasting testimony to their love for others, and their love for us.

But we're human, and today we know such great heartache. So, we come to this place to seek the simple assurance of each other and the hope of finding a higher meaning, a greater purpose. And so we ask: Why did this happen? Why to them? Could anything be worth such a sacrifice? And these fallen, whom we knew and loved but rarely thought of as great men or legends, can we now truly say they are heroes? And even if we can, would we not rather have them back, ordinary men again perhaps, but still ours to hold and keep?

The answers are hard. Hard because memory forces some of us to remember other faraway places which Americans have never heard of until their sons and brothers and fathers and friends fell there. Each Memorial Day, and especially with the news of the past week, my own mind has turned many times to the great war of forty-six years ago. Few of us who lived through it can ever forget those opening months of conflict, when our nation and our fighting men were so sorely tested.

In later years, in the South Pacific campaign, American sailors would speak often of the bravery of the marines they put on the beaches to fight and die; but one night, especially, off a place called Guadalcanal, as the shellfire lit the darkness in one of the most violent surface actions ever seen, it was the marines who stood in awe and in silent tribute to the men of the United States Navy. Hopelessly outnumbered and outgunned, a small group of U.S. ships had taken on a powerful enemy fleet. And though five Medals of Honor were won and the enemy was turned back and Guadalcanal was saved, the price was so high and the burden so heavy—nine ships and hundreds of young lives. And none of us who were alive then can forget the special burden of grief borne by Mr. and Mrs. Thomas Sullivan of Waterloo, Iowa. They would remember forever the autumn afternoon they learned that their sons—George, Francis, Joseph, Madison, and Albert—The Five Sullivans as we knew them then, would not be coming home.

But while our sorrow was great in those days, I cannot help but tell you this morning that in some ways it was easier to bear then, because it was easier to understand why we were there and why we were fighting. The burden of our own time is so different. And when young Americans like those of the USS *Stark* die in far-off seas, we learn again how right President Kennedy was when he spoke of the sacrifices asked by a "hard and bitter peace" and our own "long twilight struggle."

Even at moments like these, then, we must address directly the reason the USS *Stark* and her men were there in the Persian Gulf. You're entitled to know the importance of the role that their valor played in keeping our world safe for peace and freedom. There's a reason why since 1949 American ships have patrolled the gulf. Every American president since World War II has understood the strategic importance of this region: It is a region that is a crossroads for three continents and the starting place for the oil that is the lifeblood of much of the world economy, especially those of our allies in Europe. Even more important, this is a region critical to avoiding larger conflict in the tinderbox that is the Middle East, and our role there is essential to building the conditions for peace in that troubled, dangerous part of the world. And it is this objective that has guided us as we've sought to end the brutal war between Iran and Iraq, a war that has gone on for over six and a half terrible years and taken such an awful toll on human life.

Peace is at stake here, and so too is our own nation's security and our freedom. Were a hostile power ever to dominate this strategic region and its resources, it would become a choke-point for freedom—that of our allies and our own. And that's why we maintain a naval presence there. Our aim is to prevent, not to provoke, wider conflict, to save the many lives that further conflict would cost us.

The fallen sailors of the USS *Stark* understood their obligations; they knew the importance of their job. So, too, I believe that most Americans today know the price of freedom in this uneasy world. They know that to retreat or withdraw would only repeat the improvident mistakes of the past and hand final victory to those who seek war, who make war, who know it would only invite further aggression and tragedy. So, it's a simple truth we reaffirm here today: Young Americans of the USS *Stark* gave up their lives so that the terrible moments of the past would not be repeated, so that wider war and greater conflict could be avoided, so that thousands, and perhaps millions, of others might be spared the final sacrifice these men so willingly made.

So, we ask again: Were they heroes? "Heroes are not supermen," Herman Wouk once reminded us, "they're good men, and embodied by the cast of destiny, the virtue of a whole people in a great hour." And writing of the thousands of such heroes in our nation, men and women who wear our country's uniform in this troubled peace of ours, he asked us to never forget "to reassure them that their hard, long training is needed, that love of country is noble, that self-sacrifice is rewarding, that to be ready to fight for freedom fills a man with a sense of worth like nothing else." And he said, "If America is still the great beacon in dense gloom, the promise to hundreds of millions of the oppressed that liberty exists, that it is the shining future, that they can throw off their tyrants, and learn freedom and cease learning war, then we still" need heroes "to stand guard in the night."

The men of the USS *Stark* stood guard in the night. One of our ambassadors paid them this tribute: "They were tough, they were brave, they were great." Well, they were great, and those that died did embody the best of us. Yes, they were ordinary men who did extraordinary things. Yes, they were heroes. And because they were heroes, let us not forget this: That for all the lovely spring and summer days we will never share with them again, for every Thanksgiving and Christmas that will seem empty without them, there will be other moments, too, moments when we see the light of discovery in young eyes, eyes that see for the first time the world around them and know the sweep of history and wonder, "Why is there such a place as America, and how is it that such a precious gift is mine?"

And we can answer them. We can answer them by telling of this day and those that we come to honor here. And it's then we'll see understanding in those young eyes; it is then they will know the same gratitude and pride that we share today, the gratitude and pride Americans feel always for those who suffer and die so that the precious gift of America might always be ours.

The men of the USS *Stark* have protected us; they have done their duty. Now let us do ours. Senior Chief Gary Clinefelter showed us how yesterday. He had volunteered to work at the coordinating center here for the families when he received word that his own son, Seaman Brian Clinefelter, previously listed as missing in action, was among the confirmed dead. "I need to keep working," he said. He stayed at his post; he carried on.

Well, so, too, we must carry on. We must stay at our post. We must keep faith with their sacrifice. In our great hour, we must answer, as did they, the call of history. It's a summons that, as a nation or a people, we did not seek, but it is a call we cannot shirk or refuse—a call to wage war against war, to stand for freedom until freedom can stand alone, to live for liberty until liberty is the blessing and birthright of every man, woman, and child on this earth.

And let us remember a final duty: to understand that these men made themselves immortal by dying for something immortal, that theirs is the best to be asked of any life—a sharing of

the human heart, a sharing in the infinite. In giving themselves for others, they made themselves special, not just to us but to their God. "Greater love than this has no man than to lay down his life for his friends." And because God is love, we know He was there with them when they died and that He is with them still. We know they live again, not just in our hearts but in His arms. And we know they've gone before to prepare a way for us.

So, today we remember them in sorrow and in love. We say good-bye. And as we submit to the will of Him who made us, we pray together the words of scripture: "Lord, now let thy servants go in peace, Thy word has been fulfilled."

May I point out again, so many of you have known long months of separation from your loved ones, from these young men. You were separated by distance, by miles of land and ocean. Now you are separated again, not just by territorial limits but because they have stepped through that door that God has promised all of us. They do live now in a world where there is no sorrow, no pain. And they await us, and we shall all be together again.

God bless you.

Remarks at the Brandenburg Gate

WEST BERLIN

JUNE 12, 1987

The Brandenburg Gate and the Berlin Wall separate Berlin into East and West. In spite of the changes that are going on in Communist countries, especially the Soviet Union, that wall is a reminder of the difference between freedom and totalitarianism. The people of East Berlin are walled in with barbed wire and booby-trapped explosives.

Our advance people had put up speakers aimed at East Berlin, hoping that my speech might be heard on the other side. I could see the East German police keeping people away so that they couldn't hear. They simply don't realize it's going to take more than that to keep out the stirrings of freedom.

There's a couple sentences in this speech about tearing down the wall and opening the gate that I like quite a bit, and it actually makes the speech. I'm told that the State Department and the National Security Council thought the lines were too provocative.

Just because our relationship with the Soviet Union is improving doesn't mean we have to begin denying the truth. That is what got us into such a weak position with the Soviet Union in the first place. The line stayed and got quite a reaction from the crowd.

T HANK YOU VERY MUCH.

Chancellor Kohl, Governing Mayor Diepgen, ladies and gentlemen:

Twenty-four years ago, President John F. Kennedy visited Berlin, speaking to the people of this city and the world at the City Hall. Well, since then two other presidents have come, each in his turn, to Berlin. And today I, myself, make my second visit to your city.

We come to Berlin, we American presidents, because it's our duty to speak, in this place, of freedom. But I must confess, we're drawn here by other things as well: by the feeling of history in this city, more than five hundred years older than our own nation; by the beauty of the Grünewald and the Tiergarten; most of all, by your courage and determination.

Perhaps the composer Paul Lincke understood something about American presidents. You see, like so many presidents before me, I come here today because wherever I go, whatever I do: *Ich hab noch einen Koffer in Berlin.* [I still have a suitcase in Berlin.]

Our gathering today is being broadcast throughout Western Europe and North America. I understand that it is being seen and heard as well in the East. To those listening throughout Eastern Europe, I extend my warmest greetings and the goodwill of the American people. To those listening in East Berlin, a special word: Although I cannot be with you, I address my remarks to you just as surely as to those standing here before me. For I join you, as I join your fellow countrymen in the West, in this firm, this unalterable belief: *Es gibt nur ein Berlin.* [There is only one Berlin.]

Behind me stands a wall that encircles the free sectors of this city, part of a vast system of barriers that divides the entire continent of Europe. From the Baltic, south, those barriers cut across Germany in a gash of barbed wire, concrete, dog runs, and guard towers. Farther south, there may be no visible, no obvious wall. But there remain armed guards and checkpoints all the same—still a restriction on the right to travel, still an instrument to impose upon ordinary men and women the will of a totalitarian state. Yet it is here in Berlin where the wall emerges most clearly; here, cutting across your city, where the news photo and the television screen have imprinted this brutal division of a continent upon the mind of the world. Standing before the Brandenburg Gate, every man is a German, separated from his fellow men. Every man is a Berliner, forced to look upon a scar.

President von Weizsäcker has said, "The German question is open as long as the Brandenburg Gate is closed." Today I say: As long as this gate is closed, as long as this scar of a wall is permitted to stand, it is not the German question alone that remains open, but the question of freedom for all mankind. Yet I do not come here to lament. For I find in Berlin a message of hope, even in the shadow of this wall, a message of triumph.

In this season of spring in 1945, the people of Berlin emerged from their air-raid shelters to find devastation. Thousands of miles away, the people of the United States reached out to help. And in 1947 Secretary of State—as you've been told—George Marshall announced the creation of what would become known as the Marshall Plan. Speaking precisely forty years ago this month, he said: "Our policy is directed not against any country or doctrine, but against hunger, poverty, desperation, and chaos."

In the Reichstag a few moments ago, I saw a display commemorating this fortieth anniversary of the Marshall Plan. I was struck by the sign on a burnt-out, gutted structure that was being rebuilt. I understand that Berliners of my own generation can remember seeing signs like it dotted throughout the western sectors of the city. The sign read simply: "The Marshall Plan is helping here to strengthen the free world." A strong, free world in the West, that dream became real. Japan rose from ruin to become an economic giant. Italy, France, Belgium—virtually every nation in Western Europe saw political and economic rebirth; the European Community was founded.

In West Germany and here in Berlin, there took place an economic miracle, the *Wirtschaftswunder*. Adenauer, Erhard,

Reuter, and other leaders understood the practical importance of liberty—that just as truth can flourish only when the journalist is given freedom of speech, so prosperity can come about only when the farmer and businessman enjoy economic freedom. The German leaders reduced tariffs, expanded free trade, lowered taxes. From 1950 to 1960 alone, the standard of living in West Germany and Berlin doubled.

Where four decades ago there was rubble, today in West Berlin there is the greatest industrial output of any city in Germany—busy office blocks, fine homes and apartments, proud avenues, and the spreading lawns of parkland. Where a city's culture seemed to have been destroyed, today there are two great universities, orchestras and an opera, countless theaters, and museums. Where there was want, today there's abundance —food, clothing, automobiles—the wonderful goods of the Ku'damm. From devastation, from utter ruin, you Berliners have, in freedom, rebuilt a city that once again ranks as one of the greatest on earth. The Soviets may have had other plans. But my friends, there were a few things the Soviets didn't count on—*Berliner Herz, Berliner Humor, ja, und Berliner Schnauze.* [Berliner heart, Berliner humor, yes, and a Berliner *Schnauze.*] [*Laughter*]

In the 1950s, Khrushchev predicted: "We will bury you." But in the West today, we see a free world that has achieved a level of prosperity and well-being unprecedented in all human history. In the Communist world, we see failure, technological backwardness, declining standards of health, even want of the most basic kind—too little food. Even today, the Soviet Union still cannot feed itself. After these four decades, then, there stands before the entire world one great and inescapable conclusion: Freedom leads to prosperity. Freedom replaces the ancient hatreds among the nations with comity and peace. Freedom is the victor.

And now the Soviets themselves may, in a limited way, be coming to understand the importance of freedom. We hear much from Moscow about a new policy of reform and openness. Some political prisoners have been released. Certain foreign news broadcasts are no longer being jammed. Some economic enterprises have been permitted to operate with greater freedom from state control.

Are these the beginnings of profound changes in the Soviet state? Or are they token gestures, intended to raise false hopes in the West, or to strengthen the Soviet system without changing it? We welcome change and openness; for we believe that freedom and security go together, that the advance of human liberty can only strengthen the cause of world peace. There is one sign the Soviets can make that would be unmistakable, that would advance dramatically the cause of freedom and peace.

General Secretary Gorbachev, if you seek peace, if you seek prosperity for the Soviet Union and Eastern Europe, if you seek liberalization: Come here to this gate! Mr. Gorbachev, open this gate! Mr. Gorbachev, tear down this wall!

I understand the fear of war and the pain of division that afflict this continent—and I pledge to you my country's efforts to help overcome these burdens. To be sure, we in the West must resist Soviet expansion. So we must maintain defenses of unassailable strength. Yet we seek peace; so we must strive to reduce arms on both sides.

Beginning ten years ago, the Soviets challenged the Western alliance with a grave new threat, hundreds of new and more deadly SS-20 nuclear missiles, capable of striking every capital in Europe. The Western alliance responded by committing itself to a counterdeployment unless the Soviets agreed to negotiate a better solution; namely, the elimination of such weapons on both sides. For many months, the Soviets refused to bargain in earnestness. As the alliance, in turn, prepared to go forward with its counterdeployment, there were difficult days—days of protests like those during my 1982 visit to this city—and the Soviets later walked away from the table.

But through it all, the alliance held firm. And I invite those who protested then—I invite those who protest today—to mark this fact: Because we remained strong, the Soviets came back to the table. And because we remained strong, today we have within reach the possibility, not merely of limiting the growth of arms, but of eliminating, for the first time, an entire class of nuclear weapons from the face of the earth.

As I speak, NATO ministers are meeting in Iceland to review the progress of our proposals for eliminating these weapons. At the talks in Geneva, we have also proposed deep cuts in strategic offensive weapons. And the Western allies have likewise made far-reaching proposals to reduce the danger of conventional war and to place a total ban on chemical weapons.

While we pursue these arms reductions, I pledge to you that we will maintain the capacity to deter Soviet aggression at any level at which it might occur. And in cooperation with many of our allies, the United States is pursuing the Strategic Defense Initiative—research to base deterrence not on the threat of offensive retaliation, but on defenses that truly defend; on systems, in short, that will not target populations, but shield them. By these means we seek to increase the safety of Europe and all the world. But we must remember a crucial fact: East and West do not mistrust each other because we are armed; we are armed because we mistrust each other. And our differences are not about weapons but about liberty. When President Kennedy spoke at the City Hall those twenty-four years ago, freedom was encircled, Berlin was under siege. And today, despite all the pressures upon this city, Berlin stands secure in its liberty. And freedom itself is transforming the globe.

In the Philippines, in South and Central America, democracy has been given a rebirth. Throughout the Pacific, free markets are working miracle after miracle of economic growth. In the industrialized nations, a technological revolution is taking place —a revolution marked by rapid, dramatic advances in computers and telecommunications.

In Europe, only one nation and those it controls refuse to join the community of freedom. Yet in this age of redoubled economic growth, of information and innovation, the Soviet Union faces a choice: It must make fundamental changes, or it will become obsolete.

Today thus represents a moment of hope. We in the West stand ready to cooperate with the East to promote true openness, to break down barriers that separate people, to create a safer, freer world. And surely there is no better place than Berlin, the meeting place of East and West, to make a start. Free people of Berlin: Today, as in the past, the United States stands for the strict observance and full implementation of all parts of the Four Power Agreement of 1971. Let us use this occasion, the 750th anniversary of this city, to usher in a new era, to seek a still fuller, richer life for the Berlin of the future. Together, let us maintain and develop the ties between the Federal Republic and the Western sectors of Berlin, which is permitted by the 1971 agreement.

And I invite Mr. Gorbachev: Let us work to bring the Eastern and Western parts of the city closer together, so that all the inhabitants of all Berlin can enjoy the benefits that come with life in one of the great cities of the world.

To open Berlin still further to all Europe, East and West, let us expand the vital air access to this city, finding ways of making commercial air service to Berlin more convenient, more comfortable, and more economical. We look to the day when West Berlin can become one of the chief aviation hubs in all central Europe.

With our French and British partners, the United States is prepared to help bring international meetings to Berlin. It would be only fitting for Berlin to serve as the site of United Nations meetings, or world conferences on human rights and arms control or other issues that call for international cooperation.

There is no better way to establish hope for the future than to enlighten young minds, and we would be honored to sponsor summer youth exchanges, cultural events, and other programs for young Berliners from the East. Our French and British friends, I'm certain, will do the same. And it's my hope that an authority can be found in East Berlin to sponsor visits from young people of the Western sectors.

One final proposal, one close to my heart: Sport represents a source of enjoyment and ennoblement, and you may have noted that the Republic of Korea—South Korea—has offered to permit certain events of the 1988 Olympics to take place in the North. International sports competitions of all kinds could take place in both parts of this city. And what better way to demonstrate to the world the openness of this city than to offer in some future year to hold the Olympic games here in Berlin, East and West?

In these four decades, as I have said, you Berliners have built a great city. You've done so in spite of threats—the Soviet attempts to impose the East-mark, the blockade. Today the city thrives in spite of the challenges implicit in the very presence of this wall. What keeps you here? Certainly there's a great deal to be said for your fortitude, for your defiant courage. But I believe there's something deeper, something that involves Berlin's whole look and feel and way of life—not mere sentiment. No one could live long in Berlin without being completely disabused of illusions. Something instead, that has seen the difficulties of life in Berlin but chose to accept them, that continues to build this good and proud city in contrast to a surrounding totalitarian presence that refuses to release human energies or aspirations. Something that speaks with a powerful voice of affirmation, that says yes to this city, yes to the future, yes to freedom. In a word, I would submit that what keeps you in Berlin is love—love both profound and abiding.

Perhaps this gets to the root of the matter, to the most fundamental distinction of all between East and West. The totalitarian world produces backwardness because it does such violence to the spirit, thwarting the human impulse to create, to enjoy, to worship. The totalitarian world finds even symbols of love and of worship an affront. Years ago, before the East Germans began rebuilding their churches, they erected a secular structure: the television tower at Alexander Platz. Virtually ever since, the authorities have been working to correct what they view as the tower's one major flaw, treating the glass sphere at the top with paints and chemicals of every kind. Yet even today when the sun strikes that sphere—that sphere that towers over all Berlin—the light makes the sign of the cross. There in Berlin, like the city itself, symbols of love, symbols of worship, cannot be suppressed.

As I looked out a moment ago from the Reichstag, that embodiment of German unity, I noticed words crudely spray-painted upon the wall, perhaps by a young Berliner: "This wall will fall. Beliefs become reality." Yes, across Europe, this wall will fall. For it cannot withstand faith; it cannot withstand truth. The wall cannot withstand freedom.

And I would like, before I close, to say one word. I have read, and I have been questioned since I've been here about certain demonstrations against my coming. And I would like to say just one thing, and to those who demonstrate so. I wonder if they have ever asked themselves that if they should have the kind of government they apparently seek, no one would ever be able to do what they're doing again.

Thank you and God bless you all.

Remarks at the Memorial Service for Edith Luckett Davis

ST. THOMAS THE APOSTLE ROMAN CATHOLIC CHURCH PHOENIX, ARIZONA OCTOBER 31, 1987

Nancy and her mother were as close to each other as anything I've ever seen. They would talk every night. Even a couple of years after Edie's death, Nancy is still recovering.

I was crazy about my mother-in-law. In fact, after I met her I was never able to tell another mother-in-law joke again, which is something considering how much I like to tell stories. When I became president, Edie would call me whenever she heard a good joke, and she especially enjoyed those that were a little risqué. She was a remarkable woman and I miss her, too.

Father John Doran. We want to welcome all of you to St. Thomas the Apostle Parish. In a sense, it's a home parish for Edie, for though she was not a Catholic, she began coming to this parish in 1951, when we were a little barracks built on the back of the property.

And she, as a matter of fact, became one of the first benefactors of this parish, where she came one Sunday in the old, cold barracks—and we were sitting on folding chairs—and she said, "We've got to do something about this parish." So, she went back up to the Biltmore, and she said, "There's a bunch of you rich Catholics around here, and you've got to do something for that young, little"—years ago—"young, little priest that is trying to build a parish. Now, I'm going to give a bingo game Sunday night, and you're going to come, and you're going to dish out." And thus it happened. When she said something, it happened. And she came down the next day very gleefully with a pocket—or with a bagful of money that she had made for the parish that night.

So, that was her beginning here, and it carried on. As the parish grew, she continued to be a part of it. And one day about eighteen years ago, when Edie wasn't feeling particularly well at that time, Loyal got me aside, and he said, "Father, you've got to make a promise to me." I said, "What?" He said, "When Edie dies, you've got to bury her, and you've got to bury her down in that church, where she's been going all these years."

So, we are fulfilling a promise. And Nancy and I looked at each other the other night, and we said, "We're fulfilling a promise to Edie. We're also fulfilling a promise to Loyal."

So, it is very appropriate that you join with us today, as we say a very happy word of memory to a very happy person. So, we continue now.

The President. How do we say good-bye to someone we've loved for so long, someone of innate tenderness who loved us? Indeed, she loved all humankind. We all have our memories, precious memories. I became acquainted with Deedie by telephone. When Nancy and I were courting, if she were calling

358

her mother or her mother calling her and I was there, she—well, she introduced me to Deedie on the phone. And then she would put me on the phone to visit for a while. And it was quite a time before we met face-to-face, but when we did, we were already close friends.

To paraphrase Winston Churchill, meeting her was "like opening a bottle of champagne." Nancy and I spent our honeymoon with Deedie and Loyal here in Arizona. And after getting to know her and after a period of that kind together, I have to tell you I have never been able to tell a mother-in-law story or joke since.

Somerset Maugham wrote a line that could have been for her: "When you have loved as she has loved, you grow old beautifully."

Many people who only knew about Deedie will remember her as the lady who headed up the great fund-raising charity in Chicago for twenty-five years. Many more will remember her for all that she did here in Phoenix, raising millions of dollars, particularly for children who were disabled or handicapped. But there are countless more individuals who will remember her for what she did for them, personally, when they had a problem or a trouble or something that made them need help.

She didn't just recognize the cop on the corner; they were personal friends. She knew countless other people who just crossed her path—delivery boys, the cleaning woman, Dr. Loyal's patients, and yes, his students in the medical school at Northwestern University.

My first inkling of how well she was known and loved came some years ago when, at that time, my television sponsor had brought me to Chicago to appear at a kind of forum. It ran late, and I came out; it was dark. And I was supposed to meet Deedie and Loyal. They had told me the name of the cafe, and I was to meet them for dinner. And I told the doorman about this and that I needed some instructions as to where was that cafe. And was it far enough away that I needed transportation?

And in doing so, I, without realizing it, I told him who I was meeting. And he just raised his hand when I said that name.

And he left me and went out to the curb, and he started looking, I suppose, for a cab. But the traffic was stopped for the stoplight on the corner, and there was a police car. And he waved the police car over to the curb, and he told them about me and who I was meeting and that I needed to get there. And the next thing I knew, I was a passenger in a police car with two officers who knew Deedie Davis and who drove me right to the door as quickly as they could.

On another occasion, Nancy and I were coming into Chicago on the overnight train from New York, getting in early in the morning in the midst of a blizzard. And there wasn't a redcap in sight. The porters on the cars took the luggage off and sat it down there on the ramp. We were quite a ways from the station.

In that blizzard, and all up and down the train, were all the passengers trying to sort out the luggage and trying to find their own bags. And Nancy and I looked up, and coming down the ramp was Deedie, arm in arm with two redcaps. [*Laughter*] They were having quite a conversation. And as they got closer, I heard she was talking to one about his daughter, and by name. She knew his daughter, also, and how was she getting along in school? And by that time they were close to us. And Deedie said, "Oh, this is my son and daughter. Could you help them with their luggage?" And so the five of us went back up the ramp. And now Edie was arm in arm with both of us, and the two redcaps were carrying our baggage past hundreds of passengers who had no such help.

I remembered one thing that I've never forgotten. She said to her two friends when they caught up with us that I was her son and Nancy her daughter. She didn't say son-in-law.

She gave wit and charm and kindliness throughout all of her life. She also raised a son who was a respected surgeon, an honorable man, caring father and husband. And she gave the world a loving daughter, a woman who has made my life complete.

In the midst of our grief, Dick and Nancy, I hope you'll take

How do we say good-bye to someone we've loved for so long, someone of such innate tenderness who loved us. Dedie loved all humankind.

We all have our memories - precious memories. I became acquainted with Dedie by telephone. When Nancy & I were _____ courting, if I were there when Nancy was phoning her mother, Dedie could hear she _____ _____ _____

...

for what she did for them personally when they had need for help of whatever kind.

She didn't just recognize the cop on the corner & know him as a personal guard. Just as she knew countless other people who crossed her path - delivery boys, the cleaning woman, Bi Lo; _____ his medical

My first inkling of _____ come some years ago _____ looked me to _____ in Chi. Coming out _____ behind schedule. I _____ due at a dinner and _____ other directions - no _____

...

snow. There wasn't a red-cap in sight. Passengers the whole length of the train were trying to get their bags together in the freezing cold, ourselves included. Suddenly we looked up and saw Dedie coming down the ramp arm in arm with 2 redcaps. As they got closer it was apparent they were old friends. Dedie was inquiring about the daughter of one of them & how she was doing in school. As they reached us she said, "Oh, this is my son & daughter - could you give them a hand with their luggage?" Back of the ramp we went - the 5 of us, this time Dedie was arm in arm with us and she red caps had our bags. We passed the hundreds of passengers still trying to sort out their luggage. Ours were the only 2 red caps in the entire station. She had said "My son & daughter" not

She gave the world love & charm & kindness. She who reared a son who is a respected surgeon, a honorable man & a caring father & husband. And she gave the world a loving daughter — a woman who has made my life complete. And in the midst of our _____ _____ comfort in this _____

...

Where she is - the smiling, loving Dedie we all remember. She is there once again - hand in hand with Sagal - surrounded by other loved ones who preceded her. And yes she is here in this place today looking at us with love - but she wants all of us to be happy - knowing that one day we'll all be together again. And if I know Dedie that other life will be even better because she's been promised there's no pain.

comfort from this: that you were loving children, and you made Deedie happy and very proud.

Yes, all of us who are gathered here feel great sorrow. But let's be sure we know the sorrow is for ourselves, for the loss that we now feel. But let us realize that Deedie has just gone through a door from this life to that other life that God promised us, that life that is eternal, where no one is old, where there's no pain or sorrow, and where she is a smiling and loving Deedie we all remember, now once again hand in hand with Loyal, surrounded by others of her loved ones who have preceded her there.

And she's looking back on us with that loving kindness. Yes, she's here. She's seeing us and hearing us now. She's wanting us to be happy in knowing that one day, we will all be together again. And if I know Deedie, that other life that we've been promised will even be better, because she's been there for a while before we arrived.

1988

Veterans Day Ceremony

I feel very good about the last year of my presidency. Things really came together. I worked hard to elect George Bush as president. The trip to Moscow was a big success. The economy continued to expand with more people at work than ever in our history. And as journalist Lou Cannon has said of my last year in the White House—I was president until the moment I left the place. I like that.

If I had to pick out one speech in 1988 that most represented what I had accomplished over my two terms in office, the following speech might be the one. I feel very good when people say that one of my accomplishments was restoring the spirit and faith of America, because I tried very hard to do that. I think one area where there may be evidence of this is the attitude toward our Vietnam veterans.

A good friend of mine, Dennis LeBlanc, fought in Vietnam. Only three were left alive out of his squadron. When he came back to college, the kids found out he'd been in Vietnam; they called him murderer and shunned him. What kind of welcome home was that for a young man who had risked his life for his country? It hurt when I first heard that story.

One of the best letters I ever received as president was from a Vietnam veteran in Texas who said that I'd helped him hold his head up. If I did have anything to do with that, my entire two terms in office would be worth it.

WELL, THANK YOU, JACK WHEELER,* thank you very much. I shall treasure that gift. And to all of you, thanks, and good morning.

Before I begin, let me take a moment to congratulate the Vietnam Veterans Memorial Fund and the other distinguished guests without whom the construction and operation of this memorial would not have been possible. Let me also say that America is grateful to the hundreds of Vietnam veterans who, when I asked them to join my administration, did so, and have and are serving our nation so proudly. For your devotion to America, I salute you.

We're gathered today, just as we have gathered before, to remember those who served, those who fought, those still missing, and those who gave their last full measure of devotion for our country. We're gathered at a monument on which the names of our fallen friends and loved ones are engraved, and with crosses instead of diamonds beside them, the names of those whose fate we do not yet know. One of those who fell wrote, shortly before his death, these words: "Take what they have left and what they have taught you with their dying and keep it with your own. And take one moment to embrace those gentle heroes you left behind."

Well, today, Veterans Day, as we do every year, we take that moment to embrace the gentle heroes of Vietnam and of all our wars. We remember those who were called upon to give all a person can give, and we remember those who were prepared to make that sacrifice if it were demanded of them in the line of duty, though it never was. Most of all, we remember the devotion and gallantry with which all of them ennobled their nation as they became champions of a noble cause.

I'm not speaking provocatively here. Unlike the other wars

---

* John Wheeler, chairman of the Vietnam Veterans Memorial Fund. He gave the President a bronze replica of the "Three Fighting Men" statue, which is a part of the memorial.

of this century, of course, there were deep divisions about the wisdom and rightness of the Vietnam War. Both sides spoke with honesty and fervor. And what more can we ask in our democracy? And yet after more than a decade of desperate boat people, after the killing fields of Cambodia, after all that has happened in that unhappy part of the world, who can doubt that the cause for which our men fought was just? It was, after all, however imperfectly pursued, the cause of freedom; and they showed uncommon courage in its service. Perhaps at this late date we can all agree that we've learned one lesson: that young Americans must never again be sent to fight and die unless we are prepared to let them win.

But beyond that, we remember today that all our gentle heroes of Vietnam have given us a lesson in something more: a lesson in living love. Yes, for all of them, those who came back and those who did not, their love for their families lives. Their love for their buddies on the battlefields and friends back home lives. Their love of their country lives.

This memorial has become a monument to that living love. The thousands who come to see the names testify to a love that endures. The messages and mementos they leave speak with a whispering voice that passes gently through the surrounding trees and out across the breast of our peaceful nation. A childhood teddy bear, a photograph of the son or daughter born too late to know his or her father, a battle ribbon, a note—there are so many of these, and all are testimony to our living love for them. And our nation itself is testimony to the love our veterans have had for it and for us. Our liberties, our values, all for which America stands is safe today because brave men and women have been ready to face the fire at freedom's front. And we thank God for them.

Yes, gentle heroes and living love and our memories of a time when we faced great divisions here at home. And yet if this place recalls all this, both sweet and sad, it also reminds us of a great and profound truth about our nation: that from all our divisions we have always eventually emerged strengthened. Perhaps we are finding that new strength today, and if so, much of it comes from the forgiveness and healing love that our Vietnam veterans have shown.

For too long a time, they stood in a chill wind, as if on a winter night's watch. And in that night, their deeds spoke to us, but we knew them not. And their voices called to us, but we heard them not. Yet in this land that God has blessed, the dawn always at last follows the dark, and now morning has come. The night is over. We see these men and know them once again —and know how much we owe them, how much they have given us, and how much we can never fully repay. And not just as individuals but as a nation, we say we love you.

These days, we show our love in many ways—some of it through the government. We now fly the POW–MIA flag at this memorial on Memorial Day, Veterans Day, and POW–MIA Recognition Day. This is a small gesture, but a significant one. America also keeps a vigil for those who have not yet returned. We have negotiated with the Vietnamese to bring our nation's sons home, and for the first time, too, have joint teams investigating remote areas of Vietnam that might shed light on the fate of those we list as missing. In Laos, we have also begun a new round of surveys and excavations of crash sites. And we have told Hanoi that it must prove to the American people through its cooperation whether men are still being held against their will in Indochina. Otherwise we will assume some are, and we will do everything we can to find them.

Here, at home, a new Department of Veterans Affairs and extended veterans benefits are merely outward and visible signs of an inward and invisible grace that has come to our land. Vietnam service is once more universally recognized as a badge of pride. Four years ago, I noted that this healing had begun and that I hoped that before my days as commander in chief were over it would be completed. Well, now as I approach the end of my service and I see Vietnam veterans take their rightful place among America's heroes, it appears to me that we have healed. And what can I say to our Vietnam veterans but, Welcome home.

Now before I go, as have so many others, Nancy and I

wanted to leave a note at the wall. And if I may read it to you before doing so, we will put this note here before we leave:

"Our young friends—yes, young friends, for in our hearts you will always be young, full of the love that is youth, love of life, love of joy, love of country—you fought for your country and for its safety and for the freedom of others with strength and courage. We love you for it. We honor you. And we have faith that, as He does all His sacred children, the Lord will bless you and keep you, the Lord will make His face to shine upon you and give you peace, now and forever more."

Thank you all, and God bless you.

Remarks at the White House Correspondents Dinner

WASHINGTON, D.C.
APRIL 21, 1988

One thing I kept wanting to put in this book was a speech from one of the humorous dinners and roasts I frequently attended —the Alfalfa Dinner, the Radio and TV Correspondents Dinner, the Gridiron Dinner, and so forth. I would go every year to these things, and the format calls for you to be funny. The problem is that political humor just doesn't read very funny a few years after the fact.

I thought I would put this one in, however, just to give you a feel for these events.

T HANK YOU ALL, and I'm delighted to be here. My, what a crowd. Looks like the index of Larry Speakes's book. [*Laughter*] It's good to see Norm Sandler,* and your incoming president, Jerry O'Leary.

In his book, Larry said that Jerry used to fill his coat pockets with pastry. Jerry denies it. Earlier tonight, just to be safe, I told him, keep his hands off my dinner roll. [*Laughter*] Larry also said that preparing me for a press conference was like reinventing the wheel. It's not true. I was around when the wheel was invented, and it was easier. [*Laughter*] But even Howard Baker's writing a book about me. It's called *Three by Five, the Measure of a Presidency.* [*Laughter*] Mike Deaver, in his book, said that I had a short attention span. Well, I was going to reply to that, but—oh, what the hell, let's move on to something else. [*Laughter*]

Now, I forgot to acknowledge Yakov Smirnov. I've heard him before, and he's a very funny man. And I just have an idea here. Why don't you and I have a little fun? How would you like to go to the summit as my interpreter? [*Laughter*]

But the media has certainly had a lot to report on lately. I thought it was extraordinary that Richard Nixon went on *Meet the Press* and spent an entire hour with Chris Wallace, Tom Brokaw, and John Chancellor. That should put an end to that talk that he's been punished enough. [*Laughter*] And of course, you've been reporting on the New York primary. I'm afraid that Dukakis's foreign policy views are a little too far left for me. He wants no U.S. military presence in Korea anymore, no U.S. military presence in Central America, and no U.S. military presence at the Pentagon. [*Laughter*] Dukakis got great news today, though, about the Jimmy Carter endorsement—he isn't getting it. [*Laughter*]

George Bush is doing well. George has been a wonderful vice president, but nobody's perfect. [*Laughter*] I put him in charge

* The outgoing president of the Association.

of antiterrorism, and the McLaughlin Group is still on the air. [*Laughter*] But with so much focus on the presidential election, I've been feeling a little lonely these days. I'm so desperate for attention I almost considered holding a news conference. [*Laughter*] I've even had time to watch the Oscars. I was a little disappointed in that movie *The Last Emperor.* I thought it was going to be about Don Regan. [*Laughter*]

Of course, I still have lots of work here. There is that Panamanian business going on. One thing I can't figure: If the Congress wants to bring the Panamanian economy to its knees, why doesn't it just go down there and run it? [*Laughter*]

Ladies and gentlemen, this is the last White House Correspondents Dinner that I'll be attending. We've had our disagreements over the years, but the time I've spent with you has been very educational. [*Laughter*] I used to think the fourth estate was one of Walter Annenberg's homes. [*Laughter*]

As my good-bye, I'm not going to stand up here and deliver one of those worn-out sentimental homilies about the press and the presidency. Neither of us would believe it. [*Laughter*] A president may like members of the press personally, and I do—Jerry and Norm and Johanna and Lou and so many others of you—but a president institutionally seeks to wield power to accomplish his goals for the people. The press complicates the wielding of that power by using its own great power, and that makes for friction. Every president will try to use the press to his best advantage and to avoid those situations that aren't to his advantage. To do otherwise results in a diminution of his leadership powers. The press is not a weak sister that needs bracing. It has more freedom, more influence, than ever in our history. The press can take care of itself quite nicely. And a president should be able to take care of himself as well. So, what I hope my epitaph will be with the White House correspondents, what every president's epitaph should be with the press is this: He gave as good as he got. [*Laughter*] And that I think will make for a healthy press and a healthy presidency. And I think all that's left to say is to thank you for inviting me, and thank you for your hospitality.

Remarks and
Question-and-Answer Session
with Students at
Moscow State University

MAY 31, 1988

The trip to Moscow was one of the most intriguing experiences of my years in office. You can understand more about a place by just seeing it. One thing I noticed was that there is such a visible break in the history of the Russian people. It's right there in the architecture.

You see the splendor and glory of the czars, such as I saw at the Kremlin Palace, and Nancy also saw at some of the marvelous palaces in Leningrad. It's no wonder there was a revolution. The wealth of that country was obviously bled from the people for the personal benefit of the czars. And then you see the drab, gray, cold structures of communism. And again you see that the people don't have a lot because the wealth of the country is used to support the state, only this time it is the Communist government and its military that eats up whatever wealth there is.

The architecture of Moscow State University is quite ominous. The university is housed in this threatening, yes, evil-looking, building erected by Stalin. But speaking to these

students, I felt I could have been speaking to students any-
where. The coldness disappeared.

What a step forward it was just being there in that audito-
rium with the big bust of Lenin right behind me. I couldn't
speak to the entire student body because the hall wasn't large
enough, so the Soviets only let in students who were members
of the Young Communist League. I didn't know that at the
time, but it didn't seem to make any difference because I could
feel that I was still getting a good reaction. I could see the
students turn to each other and nod every once in a while,
occasionally smile. I came away from there with a very good
feeling.

I had complete freedom to explain America to these young
Communists. This is how I made our case.

The President. Thank you, Rector Logunov, and I want to
thank all of you very much for a warm welcome. It's a great
pleasure to be here at Moscow State University, and I want to
thank you all for turning out. I know you must be very busy
this week, studying and taking your final examinations. So, let
me just say *zhelayu vam uspekha* [I wish you success]. Nancy
couldn't make it today because she's visiting Leningrad, which
she tells me is a very beautiful city, but she, too, says hello and
wishes you all good luck.

Let me say it's also a great pleasure to once again have this
opportunity to speak directly to the people of the Soviet Union.
Before I left Washington, I received many heartfelt letters and
telegrams asking me to carry here a simple message, perhaps,
but also some of the most important business of this summit: It
is a message of peace and goodwill and hope for a growing
friendship and closeness between our two peoples.

As you know, I've come to Moscow to meet with one of your
most distinguished graduates. In this, our fourth summit, General Secretary Gorbachev and I have spent many hours together, and I feel that we're getting to know each other well.
Our discussions, of course, have been focused primarily on

many of the important issues of the day, issues I want to touch on with you in a few moments. But first I want to take a little time to talk to you much as I would to any group of university students in the United States. I want to talk not just of the realities of today but of the possibilities of tomorrow.

Standing here before a mural of your revolution, I want to talk about a very different revolution that is taking place right now, quietly sweeping the globe without bloodshed or conflict. Its effects are peaceful, but they will fundamentally alter our world, shatter old assumptions, and reshape our lives. It's easy to underestimate because it's not accompanied by banners or fanfare. It's been called the technological or information revolution, and as its emblem, one might take the tiny silicon chip, no bigger than a fingerprint. One of these chips has more computing power than a roomful of old-style computers.

As part of an exchange program, we now have an exhibition touring your country that shows how information technology is transforming our lives—replacing manual labor with robots, forecasting weather for farmers, or mapping the genetic code of DNA for medical researchers. These microcomputers today aid the design of everything from houses to cars to spacecraft; they even design better and faster computers. They can translate English into Russian or enable the blind to read or help Michael Jackson produce on one synthesizer the sounds of a whole orchestra. Linked by a network of satellites and fiber-optic cables, one individual with a desktop computer and a telephone commands resources unavailable to the largest governments just a few years ago.

Like a chrysalis, we're emerging from the economy of the Industrial Revolution—an economy confined to and limited by the earth's physical resources—into, as one economist titled his book, "the economy in mind," in which there are no bounds on human imagination and the freedom to create is the most precious natural resource. Think of that little computer chip. Its value isn't in the sand from which it is made but in the microscopic architecture designed into it by ingenious human minds. Or take the example of the satellite relaying this broadcast around the world, which replaces thousands of tons of copper mined from the earth and molded into wire. In the new economy, human invention increasingly makes physical resources obsolete. We're breaking through the material conditions of existence to a world where man creates his own destiny. Even as we explore the most advanced reaches of science, we're returning to the age-old wisdom of our culture, a wisdom contained in the book of Genesis in the Bible: In the beginning was the spirit, and it was from this spirit that the material abundance of creation issued forth.

But progress is not foreordained. The key is freedom—freedom of thought, freedom of information, freedom of communication. The renowned scientist, scholar, and founding father of this university, Mikhail Lomonosov, knew that. "It is common knowledge," he said, "that the achievements of science are considerable and rapid, particularly once the yoke of slavery is cast off and replaced by the freedom of philosophy." You know, one of the first contacts between your country and mine took place between Russian and American explorers. The Americans were members of Cook's last voyage on an expedition searching for an Arctic passage; on the island of Unalaska, they came upon the Russians, who took them in, and together, with the native inhabitants, held a prayer service on the ice.

The explorers of the modern era are the entrepreneurs, men with vision, with the courage to take risks and faith enough to brave the unknown. These entrepreneurs and their small enterprises are responsible for almost all the economic growth in the United States. They are the prime movers of the technological revolution. In fact, one of the largest personal computer firms in the United States was started by two college students, no older than you, in the garage behind their home. Some people, even in my own country, look at the riot of experiment that is the free market and see only waste. What of all the entrepreneurs that fail? Well, many do, particularly the successful ones; often several times. And if you ask them the secret of their success, they'll tell you it's all that they learned in their struggles along the way; yes, it's what they learned from failing. Like an athlete in competition or a scholar in pursuit of the truth, experience is the greatest teacher.

And that's why it's so hard for government planners, no matter how sophisticated, to ever substitute for millions of individuals working night and day to make their dreams come true. The fact is, bureaucracies are a problem around the world. There's an old story about a town—it could be anywhere—with a bureaucrat who is known to be a good-for-nothing, but he somehow had always hung on to power. So one day, in a town meeting, an old woman got up and said to him: "There is a folk legend here where I come from that when a baby is born, an angel comes down from heaven and kisses it on one part of its body. If the angel kisses him on his hand, he becomes a handyman. If he kisses him on his forehead, he becomes bright and clever. And I've been trying to figure out where the angel kissed you so that you should sit there for so long and do nothing." [*Laughter*]

We are seeing the power of economic freedom spreading around the world. Places such as the Republic of Korea, Singapore, Taiwan, have vaulted into the technological era, barely pausing in the industrial age along the way. Low-tax agricultural policies in the subcontinent mean that in some years India is now a net exporter of food. Perhaps most exciting are the winds of change that are blowing over the People's Republic of China, where one-quarter of the world's population is now getting its first taste of economic freedom. At the same time, the growth of democracy has become one of the most powerful political movements of our age. In Latin America in the 1970s, only a third of the population lived under democratic government; today over 90 percent does. In the Philippines, in the Republic of Korea, free, contested, democratic elections are the order of the day. Throughout the world, free markets are the model for growth. Democracy is the standard by which governments are measured.

We Americans make no secret of our belief in freedom. In fact, it's something of a national pastime. Every four years the American people choose a new president, and 1988 is one of those years. At one point there were thirteen major candidates running in the two major parties, not to mention all the others, including the Socialist and Libertarian candidates—all trying to get my job. About 1,000 local television stations, 8,500 radio stations, and 1,700 daily newspapers—each one an independent, private enterprise, fiercely independent of the government —report on the candidates, grill them in interviews, and bring them together for debates. In the end, the people vote; they decide who will be the next president.

But freedom doesn't begin or end with elections. Go to any American town, to take just an example, and you'll see dozens of churches, representing many different beliefs—in many places, synagogues and mosques—and you'll see families of every conceivable nationality worshiping together. Go into any schoolroom, and there you will see children being taught the Declaration of Independence, that they are endowed by their Creator with certain unalienable rights—among them life, liberty, and the pursuit of happiness—that no government can justly deny; the guarantees in their Constitution for freedom of speech, freedom of assembly, and freedom of religion.

Go into any courtroom, and there will preside an independent judge, beholden to no government power. There every defendant has the right to a trial by a jury of his peers, usually twelve men and women—common citizens; they are the ones, the only ones, who weigh the evidence and decide on guilt or innocence. In that court, the accused is innocent until proven guilty, and the word of a policeman or any official has no greater legal standing than the word of the accused.

Go to any university campus, and there you'll find an open, sometimes heated discussion of the problems in American society and what can be done to correct them. Turn on the television, and you'll see the legislature conducting the business of government right there before the camera, debating and voting on the legislation that will become the law of the land. March in any demonstration, and there are many of them; the people's right of assembly is guaranteed in the Constitution and protected by the police. Go into any union hall, where the members know their right to strike is protected by law. As a matter of fact, one of the many jobs I had before this one was being president of a union, the Screen Actors Guild. I led my union out on strike, and I'm proud to say we won.

But freedom is more even than this. Freedom is the right to question and change the established way of doing things. It is the continuing revolution of the marketplace. It is the understanding that allows us to recognize shortcomings and seek solutions. It is the right to put forth an idea, scoffed at by the experts, and watch it catch fire among the people. It is the right to dream—to follow your dream or stick to your conscience, even if you're the only one in a sea of doubters. Freedom is the recognition that no single person, no single authority or government has a monopoly on the truth, but that every individual life is infinitely precious, that every one of us put on this world has been put there for a reason and has something to offer.

America is a nation made up of hundreds of nationalities. Our ties to you are more than ones of good feeling; they're ties of kinship. In America, you'll find Russians, Armenians, Ukrainians, peoples from Eastern Europe and Central Asia. They come from every part of this vast continent, from every continent, to live in harmony, seeking a place where each cultural heritage is respected, each is valued for its diverse strengths and beauties and the richness it brings to our lives. Recently, a few individuals and families have been allowed to visit relatives in the West. We can only hope that it won't be long before all are allowed to do so and Ukrainian Americans, Baltic Americans, Armenian Americans, can freely visit their homelands, just as the Irish American visits his.

Freedom, it has been said, makes people selfish and materialistic, but Americans are one of the most religious peoples on earth. Because they know that liberty, just as life itself, is not earned but a gift from God, they seek to share that gift with the world. "Reason and experience," said George Washington in his farewell address, "both forbid us to expect that national morality can prevail in exclusion of religious principle. And it is substantially true, that virtue or morality is a necessary spring of popular government." Democracy is less a system of government than it is a system to keep government limited, unintrusive; a system of constraints on power to keep politics and government secondary to the important things in life, the true sources of value found only in family and faith.

But I hope you know I go on about these things not simply to extol the virtues of my own country but to speak to the true greatness of the heart and soul of your land. Who, after all, needs to tell the land of Dostoevski about the quest for truth, the home of Kandinski and Scriabin about imagination, the rich and noble culture of the Uzbek man of letters Alisher Navoi about beauty and heart? The great culture of your diverse land speaks with a glowing passion to all humanity. Let me cite one of the most eloquent passages on human freedom. It comes, not from the literature of America, but from this country, from one of the greatest writers of the twentieth century, Boris Pasternak, in the novel *Dr. Zhivago.* He writes: "I think that if the beast who sleeps in man could be held down by threats—any kind of threat, whether of jail or of retribution after death—then the highest emblem of humanity would be the lion tamer in the circus with his whip, not the prophet who sacrificed himself. But this is just the point—what has for centuries raised man above the beast is not the cudgel, but an inward music—the irresistible power of unarmed truth."

The irresistible power of unarmed truth. Today the world looks expectantly to signs of change, steps toward greater freedom in the Soviet Union. We watch and we hope as we see positive changes taking place. There are some, I know, in your society who fear that change will bring only disruption and discontinuity, who fear to embrace the hope of the future. Sometimes it takes faith. It's like that scene in the cowboy movie *Butch Cassidy and the Sundance Kid,* which some here in Moscow recently had a chance to see. The posse is closing in on the two outlaws, Butch and Sundance, who find themselves trapped on the edge of a cliff, with a sheer drop of hundreds of feet to the raging rapids below. Butch turns to Sundance and says their only hope is to jump into the river below, but Sundance refuses. He says he'd rather fight it out with the posse, even though they're hopelessly outnumbered. Butch says that's suicide and urges him to jump, but Sundance still refuses and finally admits, "I can't swim." Butch breaks up laughing and says, "You crazy fool, the fall will probably kill you." And, by the way, both Butch and Sundance made it, in case you didn't see the movie. I think what I've just been talking about is *perestroika* and what its goals are.

But change would not mean rejection of the past. Like a tree growing strong through the seasons, rooted in the earth and drawing life from the sun, so, too, positive change must be rooted in traditional values—in the land, in culture, in family and community—and it must take its life from the eternal things, from the source of all life, which is faith. Such change will lead to new understandings, new opportunities, to a broader future in which the tradition is not supplanted but finds its full flowering. That is the future beckoning to your generation.

At the same time, we should remember that reform that is not institutionalized will always be insecure. Such freedom will always be looking over its shoulder. A bird on a tether, no matter how long the rope, can always be pulled back. And that is why, in my conversation with General Secretary Gorbachev, I have spoken of how important it is to institutionalize change —to put guarantees on reform. And we've been talking together about one sad reminder of a divided world: the Berlin Wall. It's time to remove the barriers that keep people apart.

I'm proposing an increased exchange program of high school students between our countries. General Secretary Gorbachev mentioned on Sunday a wonderful phrase you have in Russian for this: "Better to see something once than to hear about it a hundred times." Mr. Gorbachev and I first began working on this in 1985. In our discussion today, we agreed on working up to several thousand exchanges a year from each country in the near future. But not everyone can travel across the continents and oceans. Words travel lighter, and that's why we'd like to make available to this country more of our 11,000 magazines and periodicals and our television and radio shows that can be beamed off a satellite in seconds. Nothing would please us more than for the Soviet people to get to know us better and to understand our way of life.

Just a few years ago, few would have imagined the progress our two nations have made together. The INF treaty, which General Secretary Gorbachev and I signed last December in Washington and whose instruments of ratification we will exchange tomorrow—the first true nuclear arms reduction treaty in history, calling for the elimination of an entire class of U.S. and Soviet nuclear missiles. And just sixteen days ago, we saw the beginning of your withdrawal from Afghanistan, which gives us hope that soon the fighting may end and the healing may begin and that that suffering country may find self-determination, unity, and peace at long last.

It's my fervent hope that our constructive cooperation on these issues will be carried on to address the continuing destruction of conflicts in many regions of the globe and that the serious discussions that led to the Geneva accords on Afghanistan will help lead to solutions in southern Africa, Ethiopia, Cambodia, the Persian Gulf, and Central America.

I have often said: Nations do not distrust each other because they are armed; they are armed because they distrust each other. If this globe is to live in peace and prosper, if it is to embrace all the possibilities of the technological revolution, then nations must renounce, once and for all, the right to an expansionist foreign policy. Peace between nations must be an enduring goal, not a tactical stage in a continuing conflict.

I've been told that there's a popular song in your country— perhaps you know it—whose evocative refrain asks the question, "Do the Russians want a war?" In answer it says: "Go ask that silence lingering in the air, above the birch and poplar there; beneath those trees the soldiers lie. Go ask my mother, ask my wife; then you will have to ask no more, 'Do the Russians want a war?' " But what of your onetime allies? What of those who embraced you on the Elbe? What if we were to ask the watery graves of the Pacific or the European battlefields where America's fallen were buried far from home? What if we were to ask their mothers, sisters, and sons, do Americans want war? Ask us, too, and you'll find the same answer, the same longing in every heart. People do not make wars; governments do. And no mother would ever willingly sacrifice her sons for territorial gain, for economic advantage, for ideology. A people free to choose will always choose peace.

Americans seek always to make friends of old antagonists. After a colonial revolution with Britain, we have cemented for all ages the ties of kinship between our nations. After a terrible civil war between North and South, we healed our wounds and found true unity as a nation. We fought two world wars in my lifetime against Germany and one with Japan, but now the Federal Republic of Germany and Japan are two of our closest allies and friends.

Some people point to the trade disputes between us as a sign of strain, but they're the frictions of all families, and the family of free nations is a big and vital and sometimes boisterous one. I can tell you that nothing would please my heart more than in my lifetime to see American and Soviet diplomats grappling with the problem of trade disputes between America and a growing, exuberant, exporting Soviet Union that had opened up to economic freedom and growth. And as important as these official people-to-people exchanges are, nothing would please me more than for them to become unnecessary, to see travel between East and West become so routine that university students in the Soviet Union could take a month off in the summer and just like students in the West do now, put packs on their backs and travel from country to country in Europe with barely a passport check in between. Nothing would please me more than to see the day that a concert promoter in, say, England could call up a Soviet rock group, without going through any government agency, and have them playing in Liverpool the next night. Is this just a dream? Perhaps. But it is a dream that is our responsibility to have come true.

Your generation is living in one of the most exciting, hopeful times in Soviet history. It is a time when the first breath of freedom stirs the air and the heart beats to the accelerated rhythm of hope, when the accumulated spiritual energies of a long silence yearns to break free. I am reminded of the famous passage near the end of Gogol's *Dead Souls*. Comparing his nation to a speeding troika, Gogol asks what will be its destination. But he writes, "There was no answer save the bell pouring forth marvelous sound."

We do not know what the conclusion will be of this journey, but we're hopeful that the promise of reform will be fulfilled. In this Moscow spring, this May 1988, we may be allowed that hope: that freedom, like the fresh green sapling planted over Tolstoi's grave, will blossom forth at last in the rich fertile soil of your people and culture. We may be allowed to hope that the marvelous sound of a new openness will keep rising through, ringing through, leading to a new world of reconciliation, friendship, and peace.

Thank you all very much, and *da blagoslovit vas gospod*— God bless you.

Mr. Logunov. Dear friends, Mr. President has kindly agreed to answer your questions. But since he doesn't have too much time, only fifteen minutes—so, those who have questions, please ask them.

Q. And this is a student from the history faculty, and he says that he's happy to welcome you on behalf of the students of the university. And the first question is that the improvement in the relations between the two countries has come about during your tenure as president, and in this regard he would like to ask the following question. It is very important to get a handle on the question of arms control and specifically, the limitation of strategic arms. Do you think that it will be possible for you and the General Secretary to get a treaty on the limitation of strategic arms during the time that you are still president?

The President. Well, the arms treaty that is being negotiated now is the so-called START treaty, and it is based on taking the intercontinental ballistic missiles and reducing them by half, down to parity between our two countries. Now, this is a much more complicated treaty than the INF treaty, the intermediate-range treaty, which we have signed and which our two govern-ments have ratified and is now in effect. So, there are many things still to be settled. You and we have had negotiators in Geneva for months working on various points of this treaty. Once we had hoped that maybe, like the INF treaty, we would have been able to sign it here at this summit meeting. It is not completed; there are still some points that are being debated. We are both hopeful that it can be finished before I leave office, which is in the coming January, but I assure you that if it isn't —I assure you that I will have impressed on my successor that we must carry on until it is signed. My dream has always been that once we've started down this road, we can look forward to a day, you can look forward to a day, when there will be no more nuclear weapons in the world at all.

Q. The question is: The universities influence public opinion, and the student wonders how the youths have changed since the days when you were a student up until now?

The President. Well, wait a minute. How you have changed since the era of my own youth?

Q. How just students have changed, the youth have changed. You were a student. [Laughter] At your time there were one type. How they have changed?

The President. Well, I know there was a period in our country when there was a very great change for the worst. When I was governor of California, I could start a riot just by going to a campus. But that has all changed, and I could be looking out at an American student body as well as I'm looking out here and would not be able to tell the difference between you.

I think that back in our day—I did happen to go to school, get my college education in a unique time; it was the time of the Great Depression, when, in a country like our own, there was 25 percent unemployment and the bottom seemed to have fallen out of everything. But we had—I think what maybe I should be telling you from my point here, because I graduated in 1932, that I should tell you that when you get to be my age, you're going to be surprised how much you recall the feelings you had in these days here and that how easy it is to understand the young people because of your own having been young once. You know an awful lot more about being young than you do about being old. [*Laughter*]

And I think there is a seriousness, I think there is a sense of responsibility that young people have, and I think that there is an awareness on the part of most of you about what you want your adulthood to be and what the country you live in—you want it to be. And I have a great deal of faith. I said the other day to seventy-six students—they were half American and half Russian. They had held a conference here and in Finland and then in the United States, and I faced them just the other day, and I had to say—I couldn't tell the difference looking at them, which were which, but I said one line to them. I said I believe that if all the young people of the world today could get to know each other, there would never be another war. And I think that of you. I think that of the other students that I've addressed in other places.

And of course, I know also that you're young and therefore there are certain things that at times take precedence. I'll illustrate one myself. Twenty-five years after I graduated, my alma mater brought me back to the school and gave me an honorary degree. And I had to tell them they compounded a sense of guilt I had nursed for twenty-five years because I always felt the first degree they gave me was honorary. [*Laughter*] You're great. Carry on.

Q. Mr. President, you have just mentioned that you welcome the efforts—settlement of the Afghanistan question and the difference of other regional conflicts. What conflicts do you mean? Central America conflicts, Southeast Asian, or South African?

The President. Well, for example, in South Africa, where Namibia has been promised its independence as a nation—another new African nation. But it is impossible because of a civil war going on in another country there, and that civil war is being fought on one side by some 30,000 to 40,000 Cuban troops who have gone from the Americas over there and are fighting on one side with one kind of authoritative government. When that country was freed from being a colony and given its independence, one faction seized power and made itself the government of that nation. And leaders of another—seemingly the majority of the people had wanted simply the people to have the right to choose the government that they wanted, and that is the civil war that is going on. But what we believe is that those foreign soldiers should get out and let them settle it, let the citizens of that nation settle their problems.

And the same is true in Nicaragua. Nicaragua has been— Nicaragua made a promise. They had a dictator. There was a revolution, there was an organization that—and was aided by others in the revolution, and they appealed to the Organization of American States for help in getting the dictator to step down and stop the killing. And he did. But the Organization of American States had asked, what are the goals of the revolution? And they were given in writing, and they were the goals of pluralistic society, of the right of unions and freedom of speech and press and so forth and free elections—a pluralistic society. And then the one group that was the best organized among the revolutionaries seized power, exiled many of the other leaders, and has its own government, which violated every one of the promises that had been made. And here again, we want—we're trying to encourage the getting back those—or making those promises come true and letting the people of that particular country decide their fate.

Q. Esteemed Mr. President, I'm very much anxious and concerned about the destiny of 310 Soviet soldiers being missing in Afghanistan. Are you willing to help in their search and their return to the motherland?

The President. Very much so. We would like nothing better than that.

Q. The reservation of the inalienable rights of citizens guaranteed by the Constitution faces certain problems; for example, the right of people to have arms, or for example, the problem appears, an evil appears whether spread of pornography or narcotics is compatible with these rights. Do you believe that these problems are just unavoidable problems connected with democracy, or they could be avoided?

The President. Well, if I understand you correctly, this is a question about the inalienable rights of the people—does that include the right to do criminal acts—for example, in the use of drugs, and so forth? No. [*Applause*] No, we have a set of laws. I think what is significant and different about our system is that every country has a constitution, and most constitutions or practically all of the constitutions in the world are documents in which the government tells the people what the people can do. Our Constitution is different, and the difference is in three words; it almost escapes everyone. The three words are "We the people." Our Constitution is a document in which we the people tell the government what its powers are. And it can have no powers other than those listed in that document. But very carefully, at the same time, the people give the government the power with regard to those things which they think would be destructive to society, to the family, to the individual and so forth—infringements on their rights. And thus, the government can enforce the laws. But that has all been dictated by the people.

Q. Mr. President, from history I know that people who have been connected with great power, with big posts, say good-bye, leave these posts with great difficulty. Since your term of office is coming to an end, what sentiments do you experience and whether you feel like, if, hypothetically, you can just stay for another term? [*Laughter*]

The President. Well, I'll tell you something. I think it was a kind of revenge against Franklin Delano Roosevelt, who was elected four times—the only president. There had kind of grown a tradition in our country about two terms. That tradition was started by Washington, our first president, only because there was great talk at the formation of our country that we might become a monarchy, and we had just freed ourselves from a monarchy. So, when the second term was over, George Washington stepped down and said he would do it—stepping down—so that there would not get to be the kind of idea of an inherited aristocracy. Well, succeeding presidents—many of them didn't get a chance at a second term; they did one term and were gone. But that tradition kind of remained. But it was just a tradition. And then Roosevelt ran the four times—died very early in his fourth term. And suddenly, in the atmosphere at that time, they added an amendment to the Constitution that presidents could only serve two terms.

When I get out of office—I can't do this while I'm in office, because it will look as if I'm selfishly doing it for myself—when I get out of office, I'm going to travel around, what I call the mashed-potato circuit—that is the after-dinner speaking to luncheon groups and so forth—I'm going to travel around and try to convince the people of our country that they should wipe out that amendment to the Constitution because it was an interference with the democratic rights of the people. The people should be allowed to vote for who they wanted to vote for, for as many times as they want to vote for him; and that it is they who are being denied a right. But you see, I will no longer be president then, so I can do that and talk for that.

There are a few other things I'm going to try to convince the people to impress upon our Congress, the things that should be done. I've always described it that if—in Hollywood, when I was there, if you didn't sing or dance, you wound up as an after-dinner speaker. And I didn't sing or dance. [*Laughter*] So, I have a hunch that I will be out on the speaking circuit, telling about a few things that I didn't get done in government, but urging the people to tell the Congress they wanted them done.

Q. Mr. President, I've heard that a group of American Indians have come here because they couldn't meet you in the United

States of America. If you fail to meet them here, will you be able to correct it and to meet them back in the United States?

The President. I didn't know that they had asked to see me. If they've come here or whether to see them there—[*Laughter*]—I'd be very happy to see them.

Let me tell you just a little something about the American Indian in our land. We have provided millions of acres of land for what are called preservations—or reservations, I should say. They, from the beginning, announced that they wanted to maintain their way of life, as they had always lived there in the desert and the plains and so forth. And we set up these reservations so they could, and have a Bureau of Indian Affairs to help take care of them. At the same time, we provide education for them—schools on the reservations. And they're free also to leave the reservations and be American citizens among the rest of us, and many do. Some still prefer, however, that way—that early way of life. And we've done everything we can to meet their demands as to how they want to live. Maybe we made a mistake. Maybe we should not have humored them in that wanting to stay in that kind of primitive lifestyle. Maybe we should have said, no, come join us; be citizens along with the rest of us. As I say, many have; many have been very successful.

And I'm very pleased to meet with them, talk with them at any time and see what their grievances are or what they feel they might be. And you'd be surprised: Some of them became very wealthy because some of those reservations were overlaying great pools of oil, and you can get very rich pumping oil. And so, I don't know what their complaint might be.

Q. Mr. President, I'm very much tantalized since yesterday evening by the question, why did you receive yesterday—did you receive and when you invite yesterday—refuseniks or dissidents? And for the second part of the question is, just what are your impressions from Soviet people? And among these dissidents, you have invited a former collaborator with a fascist, who was a policeman serving for fascists.

The President. Well, that's one I don't know about, or maybe the information hasn't been all given out on that. But you have to understand that Americans come from every corner of the world. I received a letter from a man that called something to my attention recently. He said, you can go to live in France, but you cannot become a Frenchman; you can go to live in Germany, you cannot become a German—or a Turk or a Greek or whatever. But he said anyone, from any corner of the world, can come to live in America and become an American.

You have to realize that we are a people that are made up of every strain, nationality, and race of the world. And the result is that when people in our country think someone is being mistreated or treated unjustly in another country, these are people who still feel that kinship to that country because that is their heritage. In America, whenever you meet someone new and become friends, one of the first things you tell each other is what your bloodline is. For example, when I'm asked, I have to say Irish, English, and Scotch—English and Scotch on my mother's side, Irish on my father's side. But all of them have that.

Well, when you take on to yourself a wife, you do not stop loving your mother. So, Americans all feel a kind of a kinship to that country that their parents or their grandparents or even some great-grandparents came from; you don't lose that contact. So, what I have come and what I have brought to the General Secretary—and I must say he has been very cooperative about it—I have brought lists of names that have been brought to me from people that are relatives or friends that know that or that believe that this individual is being mistreated here in this country, and they want him to be allowed to emigrate to our country. Some are separated families.

One that I met in this, the other day, was born the same time I was. He was born to Russian parents who had moved to America, oh, way back in the early 1900s, and he was born in 1911. And then sometime later, the family moved back to Russia. Now he's grown, has a son. He's an American citizen. But they wanted to go back to America and being denied on the grounds that, well, they can go back to America, but his son married a Russian young lady, and they want to keep her from going back. Well, the whole family said, no, we're not going to leave her alone here. She's a member of the family now. Well, that kind of a case is brought to me personally, so I bring it to the General Secretary. And as I say, I must say, he has been most helpful and most agreeable about correcting these things.

Now, I'm not blaming you; I'm blaming bureaucracy. We have the same type of thing happen in our own country. And every once in a while, somebody has to get the bureaucracy by the neck and shake it loose and say, Stop doing what you're doing. And this is the type of thing and the names that we have brought. And it is a list of names, all of which have been brought to me personally by either relatives or close friends and associates. [*Applause*] Thank you very much. You're all very kind. I thank you very much. And I hope I answered the questions correctly. Nobody asked me what it was going to feel like to not be president anymore. I have some understanding, because after I'd been governor for eight years and then stepped down, I want to tell you what it's like. We'd only been home a few days, and someone invited us out to dinner. Nancy and I both went out, got in the backseat of the car, and waited for somebody to get in front and drive us. [*Laughter*]

[*At this point, Rector Logunov presented the President with a gift.*]

That is beautiful. Thank you very much.

Remarks at a Campaign Rally for Vice President George Bush

SAN DIEGO, CALIFORNIA
NOVEMBER 7, 1988

I traditionally ended my campaigns in San Diego. I ended my campaign for the election of George Bush as president at the same place. I think it was starting to dawn on me that my days as president were disappearing rapidly. This was the last stop of the last campaign that I would ever be a vital part of again. I felt a little like a boxer hanging up his gloves. I think maybe it shows a little.

The President. Thank you very much and good Duke, thank you very much for that kind introduction. I think some thanks should go also to the Coronado High School Band and the Torrey Pines High School Band. And also I understand that some people that played a helping hand in bringing this all together happened to be my fraternity brothers from San Diego State, my fellow TEKEs. Thank you. I was told back there at Eureka College when I became a member of Tau Kappa Epsilon that it was a fraternity for life. But now let me say hello to Earl Cantos; * to Congressmen Duncan Hunter and Bill Lowery; and to a great future congressman we'll all be proud of, Rob Butterfield; and to one of America's greatest governors, George

* Chairman of the San Diego Republican Party.

393

Deukmejian; and to one of the finest senators I know, Pete Wilson.

Now, before I start, I have a message from my roommate to every young person here. She told me to say: Please, for your parents, for your friends, for your country, but most of all for yourselves, just say no to drugs and alcohol.

The Audience. Just say no! Just say no! Just say no!

The President. All right. You know, some time ago I told Britain's prime minister, Margaret Thatcher, that if her people had come over this ocean out here instead of the Atlantic the capital of the United States would be in California. But more and more over the last eight years, I've come to realize what a good thing it was for the settling of our continent that the pioneers had to go east to west rather than the other way around. After all, if they'd started out here in our beautiful state with all we have, they'd never have wanted to leave. Instead of "Westward Ho!" their motto would have been what mine has become: "There's no place like home."

Now, please forgive me if from time to time over the next few minutes, there seems to be a lump in my throat and a catch in my voice. This is a special moment for me in a special place and yes, with special people. I closed both of my campaigns for the presidency right here in San Diego. And you see, there was a reason for that. You see, when the parades have ended, the shouting is over, the speeches are done, and the final bell has sounded, a fighter wants to return to his corner and be with family and friends while he waits for the verdict of the judges. And whenever I finish in San Diego, I feel I'm with family, and I know I'm with friends. I love San Diego.

A lot of people have been mighty surprised how far you and I have gone together in our crusade over the years. I remember a story that made the rounds the time I first ran for office. Someone told my old boss Jack Warner that I'd announced for governor. And Jack thought about it for just a second, and then he said, "No, Jimmy Stewart for governor; Ronald Reagan for best friend."

But this year my name is not on the ballot. And it won't appear on a ballot ever again, unless, of course, you—

The Audience. Boo!

The President. No, no—unless you count the one that someone up there casts when your time is done and the moment has arrived for His verdict, which, when all is said and done, is the only election that really counts. But if my name isn't on your ballot tomorrow, something more important is: a principle, a legacy. No, this is not the end of an era; it's a time to refresh and strengthen the new beginning we started eight years ago. At stake are the very things you and I have been working for and fighting for ever since we first joined together almost a quarter of a century ago and set out to restore our state and then our nation. They add up to the difference between candidates who promise that come January "the Reagan era is over" and those who say, "Read my lips: No new taxes." Yes, it's the difference between the liberals and the men and women on the Republican ticket, candidates like this district's next congressman, Rob Butterfield; Senator Pete Wilson; and the next president of the United States of America, George Bush.

And that's why I'm here today: to ask you to turn out to vote tomorrow for our entire federal, state, and local Republican ticket so that our principles survive, our legacy endures, and our truth goes marching on. I've dedicated myself this autumn to making sure that all we've begun these past eight years continues. In the House of Representatives, in the Senate, in the White House, and in the state legislatures—which will redraw congressional district lines after the 1990 census, and through that act profoundly shape the course of the entire nation in the next decade—yes, on every level, the election this year is about what the Vice President called the other day the big issues: freedom; peace; opportunity; respect of government for family and community; the safety of law-abiding citizens; and whether we remain true to our national mission of standing with those who, like our Founding Fathers, would battle against tyranny and for liberty. It's about the values that have made America the greatest, freest nation on earth, as Lincoln said, "the last best hope" of humanity. And we're determined to keep it that way.

I've seen some press reports these last few weeks noting how I've been campaigning so hard for Republican candidates. And they say few other presidents have done what I've done. Well, of course, few other presidents have had the opportunity to be succeeded by a man as good as George Bush or to stump for candidates as good as Pete Wilson and Rob Butterfield. But I'll let you in on a little secret: I'm not doing this just for George Bush or Pete Wilson or our Republican candidates on all levels around the nation. I'm doing it for the country, of course, but for someone else as well—actually for two other people.

He was the best storyteller I've ever heard and the strongest man of principle I've ever known. He believed in honesty and hard work. He was filled with a love of justice and a hatred of bigotry. Once he was out on the road—he was a shoe salesman, traveling around northern Illinois in the winter. And this was in the depths of the Depression. And in a midst of a blizzard, he went into a small-town hotel in the town he was going through. And as he signed his name and the clerk saw the name, which was a very Irish name—"Oh," he said, "you're going to love it here." And then he told him why: Because that hotel would not allow people of a certain faith to stay there. And this man picked up his suitcase and said, "Then I don't stay here." And he spent the night in his car in the snow, caught near-pneumonia, and a short time later had the first heart attack of the several that led to his death.

We called him Jack. And just as he was strong, his wife, Nelle, was filled with goodness and love. In the darkest days of the Depression, when they themselves could barely scrape by, no one ever came to their door in need of a meal who Nelle sent away empty-handed. I'm proud of many things I've done in my life, including more than a few in the last eight years; but nothing has ever given me as much satisfaction as when, after several years in California, I could bring my mother and father out here and give them a home, the first they had ever owned.

So, you see, I'm campaigning this year also for them. A son of Jack and Nelle Reagan never walked away from a battle on principle. This year's election is that kind of fight. And by darn, we're going to win it.

Think of all those who depend on us and the principles we Republicans stand for. Young people just getting out of school, looking for their first job, and able to find it because our recovery has created an average of a quarter of a million new jobs each month for the last seventy-one months. Young couples looking for their first home, who can afford it because we've brought mortgage rates down by a third since we took office. Mothers and fathers trying to keep within the family budget—cutting inflation by two-thirds and bringing the top personal income tax rate that most families pay down to 15 percent has made their lives a lot better.

But these aren't the only people who depend on our success. Tomorrow on the plains of Afghanistan and in jungles around the world, freedom fighters will huddle close to their radios, hoping to catch word that the administration in America will remain their friend. In cells across the globe, political prisoners will await anxiously for assurance that America has chosen strength over weakness, because for many of them, our strength is all that keeps their hope alive.

Just on the plane coming out here I read a letter I had just received. It was a couple thanking me for the fact that they are now in the United States after having spent more than seven years in the prisons and psychiatric wards of the Soviet Union. But all these people—they depend on us, and so help me God, we won't let them down.

And there's some other very special people we won't let down, either. There's no change during our administration of which I'm prouder than that our young men and women once more take pride in wearing the uniform of the United States of America. Thanks to their valor, in the last eight years not one square inch of land anywhere in the world has been lost to communism. And in fact, we've rescued one tiny nation, Grenada, from communism.

This year, we're facing a liberal campaign of unusual deception. First our opponents wanted to conceal their ideology. It took us three months to drag the "L" word out of them. [*Laughter*] And now they're trying to hide what side they're on. They say that they're on your side, but you tell me, yes or no, and shout it loud and clear: When their candidates for president, U.S. senator, and Congress refuse to rule out raising your taxes and have already made their marks as world-class big spenders in state or federal government, are they on your side?

The Audience. No!

The President. When their candidates for president and U.S. senator, as well as for Congress and other posts, have a history of nominating and supporting judges who oppose the death penalty and, all in all, are strictly for the birds—if you know what I mean—[*Laughter*]—are they on your side?

The Audience. No!

The President. I like this audience.

The Audience. Reagan! Reagan! Reagan!

The President. Thank you. Wait a minute, I've got one more. I like this audience, I said, but one last question.

Audience member. We love you!

The President. When their candidates consistently support cutting back on the very weapons—including our Strategic Defense Initiative, SDI—that have forced the Soviets to seek to negotiate serious arms reductions with us, and when they seem to believe that a strong defense is what gets talked about in Right Guard commercials—[*Laughter*]—and that a strong Navy is the color of a suit—[*Laughter*]—when they do all this, are they on your side?

The Audience. No!

The President. Our liberal friends just never seem to learn: You can't be for big government, big taxes, and big bureaucracy and still be for the little guy. In the race for the White House only one guy is for the little guy, and that guy is George Bush. And in the Senate race, that guy is Pete Wilson. In this district, in the House of Representatives, it's Rob Butterfield. And in the state legislature, it's Byron Wear, Steve Baldwin, Carol Bentley, and our other great Republican candidates.

Yes, from top to bottom, the election this year is a referendum on liberalism. Do we want to risk going back to the old, failed liberal policies of the past?

The Audience. No!

The President. Or do we build on the successes of the present—

The Audience. Yes!

The President. —to expand the chances of peace and prosperity in the future?

Consider for a moment the people you'll be sending to Washington tomorrow. Congress and the president are equal branches of government. When you vote for the Senate or for your local congressional seat, you're voting for the direction of the country and the world as much as when you vote for president. And since we have to ride two horses, Congress and the president, across every stream, shouldn't they both be going in the same direction? [*Applause*] Everyone on our ticket—led by George Bush, Pete Wilson and Rob Butterfield—is going the same way. And come to think of it, that's my way, too.

Take our great senator and, I hope, our next great senator as well, Pete Wilson. Pete Wilson, George Bush, and I have been a team: The Three Musketeers—one for all and all for the taxpayers and against the special interests. Now, you know, in Washington, Pete's been named "Watchdog of the Treasury" —five times he's been named that. He's guarding it against liberals like his opponent. He'll work with the new president and not try to cut him off at the knees every chance he gets. Nancy and I cast our absentee ballots last week. And I know I shouldn't tell you this, but we voted, and I hope you will, too, for a great team: Pete Wilson and the entire Republican team.

Last week a major national newspaper ran a story about one of our own liberal California congressmen. In it, he spelled out to the reporter how he tells constituents he's for a strong defense, while voting for less defense, and how he opposed the death penalty amendment to the drug bill, but says he's for the death penalty when he's back home. And then he got down to business. Quoting now, "He wants it understood that a President Bush would get no quarter from him. Any budget proposal will have to include higher taxes, he says, whether a president likes it or not. 'Otherwise, we're going to go after him.' " Well, if you ask me, it's time we went after them, and some of the people to do it are Bill Lowery, Ron Packard, Duncan Hunter, and Rob Butterfield.

We must not forget what we're up against, but we all must never forget what we're for. A poet once wrote: "I have fallen in love with American names," and Americans love no name better than the name of "freedom." Well, in this campaign, and so many others, I've heard America singing, and its song is "freedom." You can hear it in the shipyards near here, as men and women go to work. You can hear it in offices, factories, schools, and stores all over our land. You can hear it when a young man or woman dreams of striking out alone and becoming part of the great boom in entrepreneurship that has created virtually all of the new jobs in America in recent years: 84—or 80.4 million new jobs in these several years. You can hear it in the prayers from every church, synagogue, temple, and mosque in our land. Yes, "one nation, under God, indivisible"—all in the name of glorious freedom.

You know, some years ago two friends of mine were talking with a Cuban refugee who had escaped from Castro. In the midst of the tale of horrible experiences, one friend turned to the other and said, "We don't know how lucky we are." And the Cuban stopped and said, "How lucky you are? I had someplace to escape to." Well, let's keep it that way.

How sacred is our trust—we to whom God has given the

custody of the name and the song of "freedom." America represents something universal in the human spirit. I received a letter not long ago from a man who said, "You can go to Japan to live, but you cannot become Japanese. You can go to France, and you'd live and not become a Frenchman. You can go to live in Germany or Turkey, and you won't become a German or a Turk." But then he added, "Anybody from any corner of the world can come to America to live and become an American."

John Adams once said that "the way to secure liberty is to place it in the people's hands. . . ." And that's what America is: we, the people, holding liberty in our hands. This year I did something I thought that no American president would ever have an opportunity to do. There in the Lenin Hills, at Moscow State University—no TEKE chapter there—[*Laughter*]—I addressed Soviet students, spoke to them, and my speech was about the wonder and glory of human and individual freedom. Now, think of those students. Only if they're very lucky and rise high in the Communist Party will any one of them ever have the influence that each American has just by walking into the voting booth.

So, let me ask you one or two more questions. And I'm asking for a commitment, so if you shout yes, be sure you mean it.

Tomorrow, will you show up at the polls and vote?

The Audience. Yes!

The President. Will you get your friends and neighbors also to vote?

The Audience. Yes!

The President. For the state legislature, will you vote for Byron Wear, Steve Baldwin, Carol Bentley, and the entire Republican team?

The Audience. Yes!

The President. Will you vote to reelect Congressmen Bill Lowery, Ron Packard, and Duncan Hunter and to elect Rob Butterfield?

The Audience. Yes!

The President. And will you vote for Pete Wilson in the United States Senate?

The Audience. Yes!

The President. And will you make George Bush the next president of the United States of America?

The Audience. Yes! Bush! Bush! Bush!

The President. The same thing I'm asking you I've asked our country this year. Eight years ago, America said it's time for a change. Well, we've heard some talk like that in this campaign. Well, we are the change. Won't you stand by the change? We started it eight years ago. Stand by the Republican ticket, and I don't mind if you stand by me.

So, now we come to the end of this last campaign, and I just hope that Nelle and Jack are looking down on us right now and nodding their heads and saying their kid did them proud. And I hope that someday your children and grandchildren will tell of the time that a certain president came to town at the end of a long journey and asked their parents and grandparents to join him in setting America on the course to the new millennium, and that a century of peace, prosperity, opportunity, and hope had followed. So, if I could ask you just one last time. Tomorrow, when mountains greet the dawn, would you go out there and win one for the Gipper?

Thank you, and God bless you all.

Tribute to Mrs. Reagan

At the Republican Convention in 1988, my daughter Maureen organized a lunch in honor of Nancy in order to raise money for Nancy's campaign against drug abuse.

We have a drug crisis in this country that has been building for years. It started with the permissive attitudes toward drugs in the sixties and seventies. I think more than anyone else in this country Nancy helped change the United States's attitude toward drugs. She helped educate an entire nation. She warned of the destructiveness of drugs way back in the early eighties when comedians were still joking about the pleasures of getting high. She foretold the consequences of drugs when many Americans considered drug use a matter of personal choice.

I think history will prove her to be one of the most farsighted first ladies this nation has ever had.

It's a wonderful feeling to be so proud of the person you love. I tried to put a few of these sentiments into words at this tribute.

Mrs. Reagan. Well, wait till I tell my husband about this. [*Laughter*] Maureen, you really did surprise me—everything. I was told that this was going to be a surprise luncheon. I was not to ask any questions, which I didn't, so that I never knew what exactly was going to happen. But really, I do thank you. Thank you. And I want to thank Rich Little, my good friend, and Barbara Cook, who was so wonderful and sang my favorite song, and everybody who spoke up here so nicely about me. I appreciate it so much. And all these wonderful kids—I mean, you were the topping on the cake. And the contribution, of course, was—I never, never expected—the whole thing has been a big, big surprise.

Well, now, if I can come down to earth for a minute here. You know, obviously, this convention is a very warm and nostalgic one for my husband and me. We can't help but think of previous conventions and all the remarkable people that we've met over the years. So many memories come flooding back: Kansas City, Detroit, Dallas. The Republican Party has given Ronnie and me eight of the most wonderful years we ever had. Of course, sometimes they were a little bit frustrating and a little bit frightening, but they were wonderful. So, I'd like to express our thanks to you for giving us those years.

But you know, there are cycles and rhythms to life. There are times to enter, times to stay, and times to leave. And today the curtain begins to close on the Reagan era of the Republican Party. We've had a wonderful run. But the time has come for the Bushes to step into the political leading roles, and for the Reagans to step into the wings. And that's as it should be.

During our two terms together, George and Bar have been totally supportive and helpful and gracious. And they have our gratitude and affection. My husband couldn't have selected a better vice president than George Bush. He's a man of integrity and conscience and loyalty—qualities that aren't always in great abundance in Washington. And I know I couldn't have found a warmer, more considerate, more caring counterpart than Barbara Bush. And I think she'll make a remarkable First Lady.

So, I want to thank George and Bar for that letter that they sent also. And I want to thank all of you here and so many others who aren't here, who have stood by us over these past eight years. I can't tell you how important it is to know that you have friends. So, to my friends, I say a very heartfelt thank you. Thank you very much.

Maureen Reagan. We have one more surprise for you. It wouldn't be complete to pay a tribute to the First Lady of the United States without the real leader of the Republican Party, President Ronald Reagan.

The President. I came over on such short notice that I haven't had a chance to read my remarks yet. [*Laughter*] But the speechwriters usually do a pretty good job, so I'll just begin.

I've known the guest of honor for many years. [*Laughter*] Well, yes, that's true. [*Laughter*] She was once one of the original members of the Reagan inner circle—[*Laughter*]—well, I can't dispute that—[*Laughter*]—who's been involved in some of the most delicate White House matters, such as high-level staff—maybe I better do this by myself. [*Laughter*]

In fact, I've been thinking for several days about what exactly I wanted to say today and how to put Nancy's role in my life in perspective for you. But what do you say about someone who gives your life meaning? What do you say about someone who's always there with support and understanding, someone who makes sacrifices so that your life will be easier and more successful? Well, what you say is that you love that person and treasure her. I simply can't imagine the last eight years without Nancy. The presidency wouldn't have been the joy it's been for me without her there beside me. And that second-floor living quarters in the White House would have seemed a big and lonely spot without her waiting for me every day at the end of the day. You know, she once said that a president has all kinds of advisers and experts who look after his interests when it comes to foreign policy or the economy or whatever, but no one who looks after his needs as a human being. Well, Nancy has done that for me through recuperations and crises. Every president should be so lucky.

I think it's all too common in marriages that, no matter how much partners love each other, they don't thank each other enough. And I suppose I don't thank Nancy enough for all that she does for me. So, Nancy, in front of all your friends here today, let me say, thank you for all you do. Thank you for your love. And thank you for just being you.

Mrs. Reagan. Oh, dear!

The President. You going to puddle up?

Mrs. Reagan. Yes.

1989

Farewell Address to the Nation

OVAL OFFICE
JANUARY 11, 1989

Before I say my formal good-bye, maybe I should tell you what I'm up to now that I'm out of office. Well, I'm still giving speeches, still sounding off about those things I didn't get accomplished while I was president.

High on my agenda are three things. First, I'm out there stumping to help future presidents—Republican or Democrat —get the tools they need to bring the budget under control. And those tools are a line-item veto and a constitutional amendment to balance the budget. Second, I'm out there talking up the need to do something about political gerrymandering. This is the practice of rigging the boundaries of congressional districts. It is the greatest single blot on the integrity of our nation's electoral system, and it's high time we did something about it. And third, I'm talking up the idea of repealing the Twenty-second Amendment to the Constitution, the amendment that prevents a president from serving more than two terms. I believe it's a preemption of the people's right to vote for whomever they want as many times as they want.

So I'm back where I came in—out there on the mashed potato circuit. I have a feeling I'll be giving speeches until I'm called to the great beyond and maybe even after. All it will take is for St. Peter to say, "Ronald Wilson Reagan, what do you have to say for yourself? Speak up."

"Well, sir, unaccustomed as I am . . ."

Mᵧ ғᴇʟʟᴏw Aᴍᴇʀɪᴄᴀɴs:

This is the thirty-fourth time I'll speak to you from the Oval Office and the last. We've been together eight years now, and soon it'll be time for me to go. But before I do, I wanted to share some thoughts, some of which I've been saving for a long time.

It's been the honor of my life to be your president. So many of you have written the past few weeks to say thanks, but I could say as much to you. Nancy and I are grateful for the opportunity you gave us to serve.

One of the things about the presidency is that you're always somewhat apart. You spend a lot of time going by too fast in a car someone else is driving, and seeing the people through tinted glass—the parents holding up a child, and the wave you saw too late and couldn't return. And so many times I wanted to stop and reach out from behind the glass, and connect. Well, maybe I can do a little of that tonight.

People ask how I feel about leaving. And the fact is, "parting is such sweet sorrow." The sweet part is California, and the ranch and freedom. The sorrow—the good-byes, of course, and leaving this beautiful place.

You know, down the hall and up the stairs from this office is the part of the White House where the president and his family live. There are a few favorite windows I have up there that I like to stand and look out of early in the morning. The view is over the grounds here to the Washington Monument, and then the Mall and the Jefferson Memorial. But on mornings when the humidity is low, you can see past the Jefferson to the river, the Potomac, and the Virginia shore. Someone said that's the view Lincoln had when he saw the smoke rising from the Battle of Bull Run. I see more prosaic things: the grass on the banks, the morning traffic as people make their way to work, now and then a sailboat on the river.

I've been thinking a bit at that window. I've been reflecting on what the past eight years have meant and mean. And the image that comes to mind like a refrain is a nautical one—a small story about a big ship, and a refugee and a sailor. It was back in the early eighties, at the height of the boat people. And the sailor was hard at work on the carrier *Midway,* which was patrolling the South China Sea. The sailor, like most American servicemen, was young, smart, and fiercely observant. The crew spied on the horizon a leaky little boat. And crammed inside were refugees from Indochina hoping to get to America. The *Midway* sent a small launch to bring them to the ship and safety. As the refugees made their way through the choppy seas, one spied the sailor on deck and stood up and called out to him. He yelled, "Hello, American sailor. Hello, freedom man."

A small moment with a big meaning, a moment the sailor, who wrote it in a letter, couldn't get out of his mind. And when I saw it, neither could I. Because that's what it was to be an American in the 1980s. We stood, again, for freedom. I know we always have, but in the past few years the world again, and in a way, we ourselves—rediscovered it.

It's been quite a journey this decade, and we held together through some stormy seas. And at the end, together, we are reaching our destination.

The fact is, from Grenada to the Washington and Moscow summits, from the recession of '81 to '82, to the expansion that began in late '82 and continues to this day, we've made a difference. The way I see it, there were two great triumphs, two things that I'm proudest of. One is the economic recovery, in which the people of America created—and filled—19 million new jobs. The other is the recovery of our morale. America is respected again in the world and looked to for leadership.

Something that happened to me a few years ago reflects some of this. It was back in 1981, and I was attending my first big economic summit, which was held that year in Canada. The meeting place rotates among the member countries. The opening meeting was a formal dinner for the heads of government of the seven industrialized nations. Now, I sat there like the new kid in school and listened, and it was all François this and

Helmut that. They dropped titles and spoke to one another on a first-name basis. Well, at one point I sort of leaned in and said, "My name's Ron." Well, in that same year, we began the actions we felt would ignite an economic comeback—cut taxes and regulation, started to cut spending. And soon the recovery began.

Two years later another economic summit, with pretty much the same cast. At the big opening meeting we all got together, and all of a sudden, just for a moment, I saw that everyone was just sitting there looking at me. And then one of them broke the silence. "Tell us about the American miracle," he said.

Well, back in 1980, when I was running for president, it was all so different. Some pundits said our programs would result in catastrophe. Our views on foreign affairs would cause war. Our plans for the economy would cause inflation to soar and bring about economic collapse. I even remember one highly respected economist saying, back in 1982, that "the engines of economic growth have shut down here, and they're likely to stay that way for years to come." Well, he and the other opinion leaders were wrong. The fact is, what they called "radical" was really "right." What they called "dangerous" was just "desperately needed."

And in all of that time I won a nickname, "The Great Communicator." But I never thought it was my style or the words I used that made a difference: It was the content. I wasn't a great communicator, but I communicated great things, and they didn't spring full bloom from my brow, they came from the heart of a great nation—from our experience, our wisdom, and our belief in the principles that have guided us for two centuries. They called it the Reagan revolution. Well, I'll accept that, but for me it always seemed more like the great rediscovery, a rediscovery of our values and our common sense.

Common sense told us that when you put a big tax on something, the people will produce less of it. So, we cut the people's tax rates, and the people produced more than ever before. The economy bloomed like a plant that had been cut back and could now grow quicker and stronger. Our economic program brought about the longest peacetime expansion in our history: real family income up, the poverty rate down, entrepreneurship booming, and an explosion in research and new technology. We're exporting more than ever because American industry became more competitive and at the same time, we summoned the national will to knock down protectionist walls abroad instead of erecting them at home. Common sense also told us that to preserve the peace, we'd have to become strong again after years of weakness and confusion. So, we rebuilt our defenses, and this New Year we toasted the new peacefulness around the globe. Not only have the superpowers actually begun to reduce their stockpiles of nuclear weapons—and hope for even more progress is bright—but the regional conflicts that rack the globe are also beginning to cease. The Persian Gulf is no longer a war zone. The Soviets are leaving Afghanistan. The Vietnamese are preparing to pull out of Cambodia, and an American-mediated accord will soon send 50,000 Cuban troops home from Angola.

The lesson of all this was, of course, that because we're a great nation, our challenges seem complex. It will always be this way. But as long as we remember our first principles and believe in ourselves, the future will always be ours. And something else we learned: Once you begin a great movement, there's no telling where it will end. We meant to change a nation, and instead, we changed a world.

Countries across the globe are turning to free markets and free speech and turning away from the ideologies of the past. For them, the great rediscovery of the 1980s has been that, lo and behold, the moral way of government is the practical way of government: Democracy, the profoundly good, is also the profoundly productive.

When you've got to the point when you can celebrate the anniversaries of your thirty-ninth birthday, you can sit back sometimes, review your life, and see it flowing before you. For me there was a fork in the river, and it was right in the middle of my life. I never meant to go into politics. It wasn't my intention when I was young. But I was raised to believe you had to pay your way for the blessings bestowed on you. I was happy with my career in the entertainment world, but I ultimately went into politics because I wanted to protect something precious.

Ours was the first revolution in the history of mankind that truly reversed the course of government, and with three little words: "We the people." "We the people" tell the government what to do, it doesn't tell us. "We the people" are the driver, the government is the car. And we decide where it should go, and by what route, and how fast. Almost all the world's constitutions are documents in which governments tell the people what their privileges are. Our Constitution is a document in which "We the people" tell the government what it is allowed to do. "We the people" are free. This belief has been the underlying basis for everything I've tried to do these past eight years.

But back in the 1960s, when I began, it seemed to me that we'd begun reversing the order of things—that through more and more rules and regulations and confiscatory taxes, the government was taking more of our money, more of our options, and more of our freedom. I went into politics in part to put up my hand and say, "Stop." I was a citizen politician, and it seemed the right thing for a citizen to do.

I think we have stopped a lot of what needed stopping. And I hope we have once again reminded people that man is not free unless government is limited. There's a clear cause and effect here that is as neat and predictable as a law of physics: As government expands, liberty contracts.

Nothing is less free than pure communism, and yet we have, the past few years, forged a satisfying new closeness with the Soviet Union. I've been asked if this isn't a gamble, and my answer is no because we're basing our actions not on words but deeds. The détente of the 1970s was based not on actions but promises. They'd promise to treat their own people and the people of the world better. But the gulag was still the gulag, and the state was still expansionist, and they still waged proxy wars in Africa, Asia, and Latin America.

Well, this time, so far, it's different. President Gorbachev has brought about some internal democratic reforms and begun the withdrawal from Afghanistan. He has also freed prisoners whose names I've given him every time we've met.

But life has a way of reminding you of big things through small incidents. Once, during the heady days of the Moscow summit, Nancy and I decided to break off from the entourage one afternoon to visit the shops on Arbat Street—that's a little street just off Moscow's main shopping area. Even though our visit was a surprise, every Russian there immediately recognized us and called out our names and reached for our hands. We were just about swept away by the warmth. You could almost feel the possibilities in all that joy. But within seconds, a KGB detail pushed their way toward us and began pushing and shoving the people in the crowd. It was an interesting moment. It reminded me that while the man on the street in the Soviet Union yearns for peace, the government is Communist. And those who run it are Communists, and that means we and they view such issues as freedom and human rights very differently.

We must keep up our guard, but we must also continue to work together to lessen and eliminate tension and mistrust. My view is that President Gorbachev is different from previous Soviet leaders. I think he knows some of the things wrong with his society and is trying to fix them. We wish him well. And we'll continue to work to make sure that the Soviet Union that eventually emerges from this process is a less threatening one. What it all boils down to is this. I want the new closeness to continue. And it will, as long as we make it clear that we will continue to act in a certain way as long as they continue to act in a helpful manner. If and when they don't, at first pull your punches. If they persist, pull the plug. It's still trust but verify. It's still play, but cut the cards. It's still watch closely. And don't be afraid to see what you see.

I've been asked if I have any regrets. Well, I do. The deficit is one. I've been talking a great deal about that lately, but tonight isn't for arguments. And I'm going to hold my tongue. But an observation: I've had my share of victories in the Congress, but what few people noticed is that I never won anything you didn't win for me. They never saw my troops, they never saw Reagan's regiments, the American people. You won every battle with every call you made and letter you wrote demanding action. Well, action is still needed. If we're to finish the job, Reagan's regiments will have to become the Bush brigades. Soon he'll be the chief, and he'll need you every bit as much as I did.

Finally, there is a great tradition of warnings in presidential farewells, and I've got one that's been on my mind for some time. But oddly enough it starts with one of the things I'm proudest of in the past eight years: the resurgence of national pride that I called the new patriotism. This national feeling is good, but it won't count for much, and it won't last unless it's grounded in thoughtfulness and knowledge.

An informed patriotism is what we want. And are we doing a good enough job teaching our children what America is and what she represents in the long history of the world? Those of us who are over thirty-five or so years of age grew up in a different America. We were taught, very directly, what it means to be an American. And we absorbed, almost in the air, a love of country and an appreciation of its institutions. If you didn't get these things from your family, you got them from the neighborhood, from the father down the street who fought in Korea or the family who lost someone at Anzio. Or you could get a sense of patriotism from school. And if all else failed, you could get a sense of patriotism from the popular culture. The movies celebrated democratic values and implicitly reinforced the idea that America was special. TV was like that, too, through the midsixties.

But now, we're about to enter the nineties, and some things have changed. Younger parents aren't sure that an unambivalent appreciation of America is the right thing to teach modern children. And as for those who create the popular culture, well-grounded patriotism is no longer the style. Our spirit is back, but we haven't reinstitutionalized it. We've got to do a better job of getting across that America is freedom—freedom of speech, freedom of religion, freedom of enterprise. And freedom is special and rare. It's fragile; it needs production [*protection*].

So, we've got to teach history based not on what's in fashion but what's important: Why the Pilgrims came here, who Jimmy Doolittle was, and what those thirty seconds over Tokyo meant. You know, four years ago on the fortieth anniversary of D day, I read a letter from a young woman writing of her late father, who'd fought on Omaha Beach. Her name was Lisa Zanatta Henn, and she said, "we will always remember, we will never forget what the boys of Normandy did." Well, let's help her keep her word. If we forget what we did, we won't know who we are. I'm warning of an eradication of the American memory that could result, ultimately, in an erosion of the American spirit. Let's start with some basics: more attention to American history and a greater emphasis on civic ritual. And let me offer lesson number one about America: All great change in America begins at the dinner table. So, tomorrow night in the kitchen I hope the talking begins. And children, if your parents haven't been teaching you what it means to be an American, let 'em know and nail 'em on it. That would be a very American thing to do.

And that's about all I have to say tonight. Except for one thing. The past few days when I've been at that window upstairs, I've thought a bit of the "shining city upon a hill." The phrase comes from John Winthrop, who wrote it to describe the America he imagined. What he imagined was important because he was an early Pilgrim, an early freedom man. He journeyed here on what today we'd call a little wooden boat; and like the other Pilgrims, he was looking for a home that would be free.

I've spoken of the shining city all my political life, but I don't know if I ever quite communicated what I saw when I said it. But in my mind it was a tall proud city built on rocks stronger than oceans, wind-swept, God-blessed, and teeming with people of all kinds living in harmony and peace, a city with free ports that hummed with commerce and creativity, and if there had to be city walls, the walls had doors and the doors were open to anyone with the will and the heart to get here. That's how I saw it, and see it still.

And how stands the city on this winter night? More prosperous, more secure, and happier than it was eight years ago. But more than that; after two hundred years, two centuries, she still stands strong and true on the granite ridge, and her glow has held steady no matter what storm. And she's still a beacon, still a magnet for all who must have freedom, for all the pilgrims from all the lost places who are hurtling through the darkness, toward home.

We've done our part. And as I walk off into the city streets, a final word to the men and women of the Reagan revolution, the men and women across America who for eight years did the work that brought America back. My friends: We did it. We weren't just marking time. We made a difference. We made the city stronger. We made the city freer, and we left her in good hands. All in all, not bad, not bad at all.

And so, good-bye, God bless you, and God bless the United States of America.

The Wit and Wisdom of Ronald Reagan

SELECTED BY THE EDITORS

"You know, Senator Kennedy was at a dinner just recently, the ninetieth birthday party for former governor and ambassador Averell Harriman. Teddy Kennedy said that Averell's age was only half as old as Ronald Reagan's ideas. And you know, he's absolutely right. The Constitution is almost two hundred years old, and that's where I get my ideas."

—*November 13, 1981*

"Since I came to the White House, I've gotten two hearing aids, had a colon operation, a prostate operation, skin cancer, and I've been shot . . . damn thing is, I never felt better."

—*March 28, 1987*

"Government does not solve problems; it subsidizes them."

—*December 11, 1972*

"Many governments oppress their people and abuse human rights . . . I have one question for those rulers: If communism is the wave of the future, why do you still need walls to keep people in and armies of secret police to keep them quiet?"

—*July 19, 1983*

"Well, I know this. I've laid down the law, though, to everyone from now on about anything that happens: no matter what time it is, wake me . . . even if it's in the middle of a cabinet meeting."

—*April 13, 1984*

"And that, in my view, is what the whole controversy comes down to. Are you entitled to the fruits of your own labor or does government have some presumptive right to spend and spend and spend?"

—*July 27, 1981*

"It's true hard work never killed anybody, but I figure, why take the chance?"

—*March 28, 1987*

"And to every person trapped in tyranny . . . our message must be: Your struggle is our struggle, your dream is our dream, and someday, you, too, will be free."

—*July 19, 1983*

"History's no easy subject. Even in my day it wasn't, and we had so much less of it to learn then."

—*September 10, 1987*

"All of these men were different, but they shared this in common: They loved America very much. There was nothing they wouldn't do for her. And they loved with the sureness of the young."

—*Arlington Cemetery, May 25, 1986*

"These last weeks have really been hectic what with Libya, Nicaragua, and the budget and taxes. I don't know about you, but I've been working long hours. I've really been burning the midday oil."

—*April 17, 1986*

"In this two-hundredth anniversary year of our Constitution, you and I stand on the shoulders of giants—men whose words and deeds put wind in the sails of freedom . . . We will be guided tonight by their acts, and we will be guided forever by their words."

—*January 27, 1987*

"I couldn't play baseball because I couldn't see good enough. That's why I turned to football. The ball was bigger, and so were the fellows."

—*June 22, 1981*

"The future belongs to the free."

—*May 6, 1985*

"I heard one presidential candidate say that what this country needed was a president for the nineties. I was set to run again. I thought he said a president *in* his nineties."

—*April 28, 1987*

"Are you better off today than you were four years ago?"

—*1980 campaign*

"Sometimes when I'm faced with an unbeliever, an atheist, I am tempted to invite him to the greatest gourmet dinner that one could ever serve, and when we finished eating that magnificent dinner, to ask him if he believes there's a cook."

—*May 30, 1988*

"If I'm ever in need of any transplants, I've got parts they don't make anymore."

—*February 10, 1986*

"To those who are fainthearted and unsure, I have this message: If you're afraid of the future, then get out of the way, stand aside. The people of this country are ready to move again."

—*September 29, 1982*

"Recession is when your neighbor loses his job. Depression is when you lose yours. And recovery is when Jimmy Carter loses his."

—*1980 campaign*

"We've polished up the American dream."

—*July 8, 1987*

"Sometimes, I can't help but feel the First Amendment is being turned on its head. Because ask yourselves: Can it really be true that the First Amendment can permit Nazis and Ku Klux Klansmen to march on public property, advocate the extermination of people of the Jewish faith and the subjugation of blacks, while the same amendment forbids our children from saying a prayer in school?"

—*February 25, 1984*

"The other day the *Washington Post* ran a story heralding the return of spring, and I thought it was just another one of the reports on the political campaign. The headline said, 'The Sap is Running Again.' "

—*April 13, 1984*

"Nations crumble from within when the citizenry asks of government those things which the citizenry might better provide for itself."

—*April 7, 1975*

"We should end those negotiations on giving away the Panama Canal and tell General Torrijos—we bought it, we paid for it, we built it, and we're going to keep it."

—*1976 Republican primary campaign*

"History will ask and our answer will determine the fate of freedom for a thousand years. Did a nation born of hope lose hope? Did a people forged by courage find courage wanting? Did a generation steeled by hard war and a harsh peace forsake honor at the moment of great climactic struggle for the human spirit?"

—*May 17, 1981*

"With the Iran thing occupying everyone's attention, I was thinking: Do you remember the flap when I said, 'We begin bombing in five minutes'? Remember when I fell asleep during my audience with the Pope? Remember Bitburg? . . . Boy, those were the good old days."

—*March 28, 1987*

"At my age I didn't go to Washington to play politics as usual."

—*October 29, 1982*

"We are with you, Germany; you are not alone."

—*June 9, 1982*

"If the Soviet Union let another political party come into existence, they would still be a one-party state, because everybody would join the other party."

—*June 23, 1983*

"My young friends, history is a river that may take us as it will. But we have the power to navigate, to choose direction, and make our passage together."

—*April 30, 1984*

"Somebody asked me one day why we didn't put a stop to Sam's [correspondent Sam Donaldson] shouting questions at us when we're out on the South Lawn. We can't. If we did, the starlings would come back."

—*May 18, 1983*

"I will not exploit my opponent's youth and inexperience."

—*when asked in the 1984 presidential debate with Walter Mondale about the age issue*

"The federal government has taken too much tax money from the people, too much authority from the states, and too much liberty with the Constitution."

—*February 9, 1982*

"A friend of mine was asked to a costume ball a short time ago. He slapped some egg on his face and went as a liberal economist."

—*February 11, 1988*

"We have to keep in mind we are a nation under God, and if we ever forget that, we'll be just a nation under."

—*May 23, 1983*

"How can the leadership of the other side, as they did last week, open each session of their great convention with an injunction to the Lord, and end each session with a prayer to God, and still insist on denying that right to a child in a public school?"

—*July 26, 1984*

"Seventy-five years ago I was born in Tampico, Illinois, in a little flat above the bank building. We didn't have any other contact with the bank than that."

—*February 6, 1986*

"We were poor when I was young, but the difference then was that the government didn't come around telling you you were poor."

—*July 6, 1986*

"My whole family were Democrats. As a matter of fact, I had an uncle who won a medal once for never having missed voting in an election for fifteen years . . . and he'd been dead for fourteen."

—*August 9, 1973*

"Please tell me you're Republicans."

—*to doctors preparing to operate following the assassination attempt, March 30, 1981*

"I let football and other extracurricular activities eat into my study time with the result that my grade average was closer to the C level required for eligibility than it was to straight A's. And even now I wonder what I might have accomplished if I'd studied harder."

—*May 9, 1982*

"The West won't contain communism, it will transcend communism."

—*May 17, 1981*

"Freedom should be the right to be stupid if you want to be."

—*February 13, 1973*

"The American people weren't put on this earth to become managers of decline."

—*November 16, 1982*

"Heroes may not be braver than anyone else. They're just braver five minutes longer."

—*December 22, 1982*

"And I also remember something that Thomas Jefferson once said: 'We should never judge a president by his age, only by his works.' And ever since he told me that . . .'"

—*February 6, 1984*

"We cannot play innocents abroad in a world that is not innocent."

—*February 6, 1985*

"What our critics really believe is that those in Washington know better how to spend your money than you, the people, do. But we're not going to let them do it, period."

—*June 30, 1982*

"If the federal government had been around when the Creator was putting His hand to this state, Indiana wouldn't be here. It'd still be waiting for an environmental impact statement."

—*February 9, 1982*

"The best view of big government is in the rearview mirror as you're driving away from it."

—*March 24, 1982*

"You know, I keep remembering there would always be a picture of a president standing in the Oval Office looking out the window—usually the picture was from behind. And he's standing there, and then his words are quoted as a tag for the picture about this is the loneliest place and so forth. I don't know about them. I haven't been lonely one minute."

—*farewell to the White House staff, January 18, 1989*

Index

SAUNDERS

Comprehensive Review *for the*

NCLEX-RN®
EXAMINATION

SAUNDERS

EDITION 4

Comprehensive Review *for the*
NCLEX-RN®
EXAMINATION

LINDA ANNE SILVESTRI, MSN, RN
Instructor of Nursing
Salve Regina University
Newport, Rhode Island
President
Nursing Reviews, Inc.
and
Professional Nursing Seminars, Inc.
Charlestown, Rhode Island
Instructor: NCLEX-RN® and NCLEX-PN® Review Courses

SAUNDERS

ELSEVIER

SAUNDERS
ELSEVIER

11830 Westline Industrial Drive
St. Louis, Missouri 63146

SAUNDERS COMPREHENSIVE REVIEW FOR THE NCLEX-RN®
EXAMINATION

ISBN: 978-1-4160-3708-8

Copyright © 2008 by Saunders, an imprint of Elsevier Inc.

Notice

NCLEX® and NCLEX-RN® are registered trademarks and service marks of the National Council of State Boards of Nursing, Inc.

Previous editions copyrighted 1999, 2002, 2005

ISBN: 978-1-4160-3708-8

Managing Editor: Nancy O'Brien
Developmental Editor: Charlene R.M. Ketchum
Publishing Services Manager: John Rogers
Senior Project Manager: Doug Turner
Multimedia Producer: David Rushing
Designer: Margaret Reid

Printed in Canada

Last digit is the print number: 9 8 7 6 5 4 3 2 1

To my parents,
To my mother, **Frances Mary,**
and in loving memory of my father, **Arnold Lawrence,**
who taught me to always love, care,
and be the best that I could be.

About the Author

Linda Anne Silvestri

As a child, I always dreamed of becoming either a nurse or a teacher. Initially I chose to become a nurse because I really wanted to help others, especially those who were ill. Then I realized that both of my dreams could come true and I could be both a nurse and a teacher. So I pursued my dreams.

I received my diploma in nursing at Cooley Dickinson Hospital School of Nursing in Northampton, Massachusetts. Afterwards, I worked at Baystate Medical Center in Springfield, Massachusetts. At Baystate Medical Center, I cared for clients in acute medical-surgical units, the intensive care unit, the emergency department, pediatric units, and other acute care units. Later I received an associate degree from Holyoke Community College in Holyoke, Massachusetts, my Bachelor of Science in Nursing from American International College in Springfield, Massachusetts, and my Master of Science in Nursing from Anna Maria College in Paxton, Massachusetts, with a dual major in Nursing Management and Patient Education. Currently I am working on my doctorate in Nursing at the University of Nevada, Las Vegas, and I am planning to do research related to success on the NCLEX examination. I am also a member of the Honor Society of Nursing, Sigma Theta Tau International, and the Eastern Nursing Research Society.

As a native of Springfield, Massachusetts, I began my teaching career in 1981 as an instructor of medical-surgical nursing and leadership-management nursing at Baystate Medical Center School of Nursing. In 1989, I relocated to Rhode Island and began teaching advanced medical-surgical nursing and psychiatric nursing to RN and LPN students at the Community College of Rhode Island. While I was teaching there, a group of students approached me for help in preparing for the NCLEX-RN examination. I have always had a very special interest in test success for nursing students because of my own personal experiences with testing. Success with testing was never easy for me, and as a student I needed to find methods and strategies that would bring success. My own difficult experiences and my desire and dedication to help nursing students overcome the obstacles associated with testing inspired me to write the many products that would foster success with testing. I used my experiences as a student, nursing educator, and item writer for the NCLEX examinations as I developed a comprehensive review course to prepare nursing graduates for the NCLEX-RN examination.

Later in 1994, I began teaching medical-surgical nursing at Salve Regina University in Newport, Rhode Island, and remain there as an adjunct faculty member. I also prepare nursing students at Salve Regina University for the NCLEX-RN examination.

In 1991, I established Professional Nursing Seminars, Inc., and in 2000, I established Nursing Reviews, Inc. Both companies are dedicated to conducting review courses for the NCLEX-RN and the NCLEX-PN examinations and assisting nursing graduates to achieve their goals of becoming Registered Nurses or Licensed Practical/Vocational Nurses.

Today, I conduct review courses for the NCLEX examinations throughout New England and am the successful author of numerous review products. I am so pleased that you have decided to join me in your journey to success in testing for nursing examinations and for the NCLEX-RN examination!

Contributors

JoAnn Acierno, BSN, RN
Assistant Professor
Bachelor of Science in Nursing Program
Clarkson College
Omaha, Nebraska
Chapter 55: Gastrointestinal System
Chapter 56: Gastrointestinal Medications

Katherine H. Dimmock, JD, EdD, MSN, RN
Dean and CEO
Columbia College of Nursing, Inc.
Milwaukee, Wisconsin
Chapter 7: Ethical and Legal Issues
*Chapter 8: Leadership, Delegating, and Prioritizing Client
Care*

Mary L. Dowell, PhD, RN, BC
Professor
University of Mary Hardin Baylor
Belton, Texas
Chapter 26: Labor and Delivery
Chapter 27: Problems With Labor and Delivery
Chapter 28: The Postpartum Period
Chapter 29: Postpartum Complications
Chapter 30: Care of the Newborn
Chapter 31: Maternity and Newborn Medications
*Chapter 35: Neurological, Cognitive, and Psychosocial
Disorders*
Chapter 36 Eye, Ear, and Throat Disorders
Chapter 40: Metabolic and Endocrine Disorders
Chapter 41: Renal and Urinary Disorders

Julie Eggert, PhD, GNP-C, AOCN
Associate Professor
School of Nursing
Clemson University
Clemson, South Carolina
Chapter 32: Theories of Growth and Development
Chapter 33: Developmental Stages
Chapter 34: Care of the Older Client

Cynthia A. Gaudet, MSN, RN
Nursing Instructor
American International College
Springfield, Massachusetts
Chapter 49: Integumentary System
Chapter 50: Integumentary Medications

Karen Clark Griffith, PhD, RN
Assistant Professor
College of Nursing
The University of Iowa
Iowa City, Iowa
Chapter 42: Integumentary Disorders
Chapter 43: Musculoskeletal Disorders
Chapter 44: Hematological Disorders

Sheila C. Grossman, PhD, APRN-BC
Professor and Director
FNP Track
Fairfield University School of Nursing
Fairfield, Connecticut
Chapter 69: Immune Disorders
Chapter 70: Immunologic Medications

Amy Zlomek Hedden, RN, MS, NP
Associate Professor
Pediatric Content Expert
Department of Nursing
California State University, Bakersfield;
Registered Nurse
Bakersfield Memorial Hospital
Bakersfield, California
Chapter 47: Infectious and Communicable Diseases

Beverly K. Hogan, APRN, BC
School of Nursing
University of Alabama at Birmingham
Birmingham, Alabama
*Chapter 71: Foundations of Psychiatric Mental Health
    Nursing:*
Chapter 72: Models of Care
Chapter 73: Mental Health Disorders
Chapter 74: Addictions
Chapter 75: Crisis Theory and Intervention
Chapter 76: Psychiatric Medications

Katje A. Koning, RN
Graduate, Nursing
University of Connecticut
Storrs, Connecticut
*Chapter 4: The NCLEX-RN® Examination: From a
    Student's Perspective*

Lois S. Marshall, PhD, RN
Nurse Researcher Scholar in Residence
Honor Society of Nursing, Sigma Theta Tau
    International;
Nurse Education Consultant
LSM Educational Consulting
Miami, Florida
Chapter 37: Respiratory Disorders
Chapter 38: Cardiovascular Disorders
Chapter 39: Gastrointestinal Disorders
Chapter 45: Oncological Disorders
Chapter 46: Acquired Immunodeficiency Syndrome
*Chapter 48: Pediatric Medication Administration and
    Calculations*

Dorothy Mae Mathers, MSN, RN
Associate Professor
Pennsylvania College of Technology
Williamsport, Pennsylvania
Chapter 53: Endocrine System
Chapter 54: Endocrine Medications

Ellyn E. Matthews, PhD, RN, AOCN, CRNI
Assistant Professor
University of Colorado at Denver and Health Sciences
    Center
Denver, Colorado
Chapter 51: Oncological Disorders
Chapter 52: Antineoplastic Medications

Ellen C. McElroy, BSN, RN
Assistant Professor
School of Nursing
University of Alabama at Birmingham
Birmingham, Alabama
*Chapter 71: Foundations of Psychiatric Mental Health
    Nursing*
Chapter 72: Models of Care
Chapter 73: Mental Health Disorders
Chapter 74: Addictions
Chapter 75: Crisis Theory and Intervention
Chapter 76: Psychiatric Medications

Lolita T. O'Donnell, RN, MSN, PhD
Assistant Professor
George Mason University
Fairfax, Virginia
Chapter 63: The Eye and the Ear
Chapter 64: Ophthalmic and Otic Medications

Kathleen A. Ohman, EdD, MS, RN, CCRN
Professor of Nursing
College of St. Benedict/St. John's University
St. Joseph, Minnesota;
Registered Nurse
St. Cloud Hospital
St. Cloud, Minnesota
Chapter 61: Renal System
Chapter 62: Renal Medications

Emily Porterfield, RN, LDN
Consulting Dietitian
Freelance Copyeditor and Proofreader
Greenville, North Carolina
Chapter 6: Cultural Diversity and Health Practices
Chapter 12: Nutrition
Chapter 13: Parenteral Nutrition

Donna Russo, RN, MSN, CCRN
Nursing Instructor
Frankford Hospital School of Nursing
Philadelphia, Pennsylvania
Chapter 59: Cardiovascular Disorders
Chapter 60: Cardiovascular Medications

Shirley Sherrick-Escamilla, PhD(c), MSN, RNC
Assistant Professor
University of Detroit Mercy
Detroit, Michigan
Chapter 22: Female Reproductive System
Chapter 23: Obstetrical Assessment
Chapter 24: Prenatal Period
Chapter 25: Risk Conditions Related to Pregnancy

Fran Soukup, RN, MSN, EdS
Faculty
Excelsior College
Albany, New York
Chapter 65: Neurological System
Chapter 66: Neurological Medications

Bethany Hawes Sykes, EdD, RN, CEN, CCRN
Adjunct Faculty
Department of Nursing
Salve Regina University
Newport, Rhode Island
Chapter 16: Provision of a Safe Environment
Chapter 17: Administration of Medication and Intravenous Solutions
Chapter 18: Basic Life Support
Chapter 19: Perioperative Nursing Care
Chapter 20: Positioning Clients
Chapter 21: Care of a Client With a Tube

Linda D. Taylor, PhD(c), RN, OCN
Assistant Professor
St. Anthony College of Nursing
Rockford, Illinois
Chapter 57: Respiratory System
Chapter 58: Respiratory Medications

Laurent W. Valliere, BS
Vice President
Professional Nursing Seminars, Inc.
Charlestown, Rhode Island
Chapter 3: Pathways to Success

Vicki L. Vann, MS, ARNP
Nursing Education Specialist
Department of Nursing Research and Education
H. Lee Moffitt Cancer Center & Research Institute
Tampa, Florida
Chapter 9: Fluids and Electrolytes
Chapter 10: Acid-Base Balance
Chapter 11: Laboratory Values
Chapter 14: Intravenous Therapy
Chapter 15: Administration of Blood Products

Danette Wood, EdD, MSN, RN, CCRN
Associate Professor
Bachelor of Science in Nursing Program Director
School of Nursing
Georgia Southern University
Statesboro, Georgia
Chapter 67: Musculoskeletal System
Chapter 68: Musculoskeletal Medications

ITEM WRITERS

Barbara Cornett, PhD, CNS, RN, CHES
Professor
Otterbein College
Westerville, Ohio

Katherine A. Fletcher, RN, PhD, CS
Clinical Associate Professor
University of Kansas School of Nursing
Kansas City, Kansas

Marilyn Johnessee Greer, MS, RN
Associate Professor of Nursing
Rockford College
Rockford, Illinois

Juanita F. Johnson, PhD, RN
Adjunct Professor of Nursing
School of Nursing
Oklahoma Baptist University
Shawnee, Oklahoma

Susan A. Moore RN, PhD
Assistant Professor
Loewenberg School of Nursing
University of Memphis
Memphis, Tennessee

Bruce Austin Scott, MSN, APRN, BC
Nursing Instructor
San Joaquin Delta College
Stockton, California

Mary M. Smith, MSN, RN
Lecturer
School of Nursing
College of Health and Human Services
University of North Carolina at Charlotte
Charlotte, North Carolina

Sharon Souter, RN, PhD
Director of the Bachelor of Nursing Program
Patty Hanks Shelton School of Nursing
Abilene, Texas

Linda Turchin, RN, BSN, MSN
Assistant Professor of Nursing
Department of Nursing
Fairmont State University
Fairmont, West Virginia

Cheryle I. Whitney, RN, MSN
ciwhitney & associates, L.L.C.
President
The Woodlands, Texas

Chris Winkelman, RN, PhD, CNP, CCRN
Assistant Professor
Frances Payne Bolton School of Nursing
Case Western Reserve University
Cleveland, Ohio

The author and publisher would also like to acknowledge the following individuals for contributions to the previous editions of this book:

Marion G. Anema, PhD, RN
Nashville, Tennessee

Marianne P. Barba, MS, RN, CPC
Coventry, Rhode Island

Carol A. Baxter, EdD, RN
Philadelphia, Pennsylvania

Eloise M. Brotzman, MSEd, MSN, RNC
Bethlehem, Pennsylvania

Reitha Cabaniss, MSN, RN
Sumiton, Alabama

Janice Almon Call, MSN, RN, C
Gainesville, Texas

Darlene Nebel Cantu, MSN, RNC
San Antonio, Texas

Heather Carlson, RN
Newport, Rhode Island

Elizabeth M. Carson, EdD, RN
Rockford, Illinois

Shannon Chase, RN
Newport, Rhode Island

Jane Anne Claffy, MSN, RNC
Germantown, New York

Alice D. Coomes, MSN, RN
Owensboro, Kentucky

Gloria Coschigano, MSN, RN, CS
Valhalla, New York

Nancy Wilson Darland, MSN, RNC, CNS
Ruston, Louisiana

Jean W. Davis, EdD, RN, CS
Miami Shores, Florida

Jean DeCoffe, MSN, RN
Milton, Massachusetts

Carole A. Devine, MSN, RN
Kingston, Rhode Island

Kerry H. Fater, PhD, RN, CS
Newport, Rhode Island

Ginette G. Ferszt, PhD, RN, CS
Kingston, Rhode Island

Cathy Fortenbaugh, MSN, RN, AOCN, CNS, C
Philadelphia, Pennsylvania

Jane H. Freeman, EdD, RN
Jacksonville, Alabama

Rita S. Glazebrook, PhD, RN, CNP
Northfield, Minnesota

Kimberly Green, RN
Newport, Rhode Island

Joyce Hammer, MSN, RN
Detroit, Michigan

Jacqueline Lynne Harris, MNSc, RN, ONC
Searcy, Arkansas

Mary Ann Hogan, MSN, RN, CS
Amherst, Massachusetts

Mary Kathleen Jackson, BSN, RN, CPN
Whiteville, North Carolina

Gail M. Johnson, EdD, MSN, RN, CNAA, BC
Trenton, New Jersey

Katherine Theresa Jorgensen, MSN, RN, MA
Vermillion, South Dakota

Elisa Mangosing Lemmon, MSN, RN, C
Newport News, Virginia

Teresa Leonard, MSN, RN, CCRN
Florence, Alabama

Carol O. Long, PhD, RN
Tempe, Arizona

Marilyn Lusk, MSN, MS, RN
Kingman, Arizona

Linda Ann Martin, MSN, RN, APN-C
Trenton, New Jersey

Jo Ann Barnes Mullaney, PhD, RN, CS
Newport, Rhode Island

Betsy J. Nield, MS, RNC
Warwick, Rhode Island

Tina Nink, MSN, RN, FNP
Oglesby, Illinois

Patricia A. Parsons, MSN, MS, RN
Austin, Minnesota

Elizabeth Phillip, MSN, RN
Bethlehem, Pennsylvania

Tommie Wright Pniewski, MSN, RN, CNAA
Hopkinsville, Kentucky

Ethel Pruden, MSN, RN
Savannah, Georgia

Marion Sawyier, MSN, RN
Albuquerque, New Mexico

Nancy Schlapman, PhD, RN
Kokomo, Indiana

Jane Schlickau, MN, RN, ARNP, CTN
Winfield, Kansas

Joan Schmitke, DSN, APRN, FNP, BC
Richmond, Kentucky

Geneva Scott, MSN, RN, BSS
Weatherford, Texas

Shellie Simons, MS, RN
Boston, Massachusetts

Marian I. Stewart, MSN, RN
Lynchburg, Tennessee

Lynn Tesh, MSN, RN
Asheboro, North Carolina

Cheryl J. Vitacco-Grab, MSN, RNC
Lancaster, Pennsylvania

Loretta A. Wack, MSN, PNP, FNP
Weyers Cave, Virginia

Mary Hauser Whitaker, MSN, RN
Richmond, Kentucky

Terry Yoesting, MS, RN
Denison, Texas

ANCILLARY CO-AUTHOR

Lois S. Marshall, PhD, RN
Nurse Researcher Scholar in Residence
Honor Society of Nursing, Sigma Theta Tau
    International;
Nurse Education Consultant
LSM Educational Consulting
Miami, Florida

*The author would like to acknowledge the book contributors
for their assistance with the ancillary materials.*

Reviewers

Jacqueline B. Arnett, BSN, CPN
Registered Nurse, Educator, Author
Oro Valley, Arizona

Joanna E. Cain, BSN, BA, RN
President
Auctorial Pursuits Incorporated
Wilmington, North Carolina

Judy M. Cole, MSN, RNC
Clinical Educator
Obstetrics Department
Saint Francis Hospital;
Adjunct Faculty
Lowenberg School of Nursing
University of Memphis;
Adjunct Faculty
School of Nursing
Southwest Tennessee Community College
Memphis, Tennessee

Faith Darilek, MSN, RN
Nursing Professor
The Victoria College
Victoria, Texas

Jill M. Espelin, MSN, RN
Clinical Faculty
School of Nursing
University of Connecticut
Storrs, Connecticut

Mary Fabick, MSN, MEd, RN, CEN
Associate Professor of Nursing
Milligan College
Milligan College, Tennessee

Vivian A. Gaits RN, APRN-BC, AOCN, CHPN, CRNI
Clinical Assistant Professor of Nursing
Joint Practice Clinician
UMDNJ/RCNJ/EHMC Joint BSN at Englewood
    Hospital
Englewood, New Jersey

Margaret M. Gingrich, MSN, RN
Professor
Harrisburg Area Community College
Harrisburg, Pennsylvania

Mary Ann Glendon, PhD, MSN, RN
Associate Professor
Southern Connecticut State University
New Haven, Connecticut

Frances Harden-Fanning, MSN, RN
Lecturer
College of Nursing
University of Kentucky
Lexington, Kentucky

Jill Hasley, MNSc, APRN-BC
Program Director
Arkansas Rural Nursing Education Consortium
    (ARNEC)
Nashville, Arkansas

Mary A. Kindred Ludvigsen, APRN-BC, FNP
Assistant Professor of Nursing
MacMurray College
Jacksonville, Illinois

Kathryn Magorian, RN, MSN
Assistant Professor of Nursing
Mount Marty College
Yankton, South Dakota

Diana King Mixon, BSN, MSN
Associate Professor
Boise State University
Boise, Idaho

Deborah Poling, MSN, APRN, BC, ANP, FNP
Assistant Professor
Department of Nursing
Regis University
Denver, Colorado

Sharon R. Redding, MN, RN, CNE
Associate Professor of Nursing
Division of Health Care Professions
College of Saint Mary
Omaha, Nebraska

Katherine Roberts, MS, RN
Assistant Professor of Nursing
Lamar University
Beaumont, Texas

Linda Rodebaugh, EdD, MSN, RN
Associate Professor
School of Nursing
University of Indianapolis
Indianapolis, Indiana

Bonnie Schmidt, RN, MSN
Nursing Instructor
University of Wisconsin Oshkosh
Oshkosh, Wisconsin

Chris Seckman, MSN, RN
Associate Professor
College of Nursing
University of Missouri-St. Louis
St. Louis, Missouri

Louis Stackler, BA, MA, ADN, BSN, MS
Instructor, CNS
Tulsa Technology Center
Tulsa, Oklahoma

Catherine Thillen, RN, BSN, MEd, MSN, APRN, BC
Advanced Practice Nurse
Medical-Surgical Clinical Nurse Specialist
St. Francis Hospital
Memphis, Tennessee

Donna Wilsker, MSN, RN
Assistant Professor
Lamar University
Beaumont, Texas

Connie S. Wilson, EdD, RN
Professor of Nursing
University of Indianapolis
Indianapolis, Indiana

Vivian K. Wong, RN, CNS, PhD
Associate Professor
San Jose State University
San Jose, California

Preface

"*To know that even one life has breathed easier because you have lived, this is to have succeeded.*"

Ralph Waldo Emerson

Welcome to *Saunders Pyramid to Success!*

AN ESSENTIAL RESOURCE FOR TEST SUCCESS

Saunders Comprehensive Review for the NCLEX-RN® Examination is one of a series of products designed to assist you in achieving your goal of becoming a registered nurse. This text will provide you with a comprehensive review of all of the nursing content areas specifically related to the new 2007 test plan for the NCLEX-RN examination as implemented by the National Council of State Boards of Nursing. This resource will help you achieve success on your nursing examinations during nursing school and on the NCLEX-RN examination.

ORGANIZATION

This text contains 20 units and 76 chapters. The chapters are designed to identify specific components of nursing content. The chapters contain practice questions, both multiple choice and alternate item formats, which reflect the chapter content and the 2007 test plan for the NCLEX-RN exam. The final unit contains a 75-question Comprehensive Test.

The new test plan identifies a framework based on *Client Needs*. These Client Needs categories include Safe and Effective Care Environment; Health Promotion and Maintenance; Psychosocial Integrity; and Physiological Integrity. *Integrated Processes* are also identified as a component of the test plan. These include Caring; Communication and Documentation; Nursing Process; and Teaching and Learning. All of the chapters address the components of the test plan framework.

SPECIAL FEATURES OF THE BOOK

Pyramid Terms

Each content area, presented as either a chapter or a unit, begins with *Pyramid Terms* and their definitions. These terms are important to the content contained in the chapter. In addition, the Pyramid Terms are in bold type throughout the content section.

Pyramid to Success

The *Pyramid to Success*, a unit or chapter introduction, provides you with an overview of the chapter or the unit, guidance and direction regarding the focus of review in the particular content area, and its relative importance to the 2007 test plan for the NCLEX-RN exam. Specific nursing content areas, as specified in the test plan, are identified. The Pyramid to Success reviews the Client Needs and the Integrated Processes as they pertain to the content in that unit or chapter. These points are the specific components to keep in mind as you review the chapter outline.

Pyramid Points

Pyramid Points ▲ are the icons that are placed next to specific content areas throughout the chapters. The Pyramid Points provide you with immediate identification of content that is important in your preparation for the NCLEX-RN examination. These icons identify content areas that typically appear on the NCLEX-RN examination.

Practice Questions

While preparing for the NCLEX-RN examination, it is crucial for students to practice questions. This book contains 1000 practice multiple choice and alternate item format questions in NCLEX-style format. The accompaning CD includes all of the questions from the book, plus additional questions for a total of 4214 questions.

Multiple Choice and Alternate Item Format Questions

Each content chapter is followed by a practice test. Each practice test contains several *Multiple Choice* questions and an *Alternate Item Format* question. The alternate item format question may be presented as a fill-in-the-blank question, a multiple response question, a prioritizing (ordered response) question, a figure/illustration (hot spot) question, or a chart/exhibit question. These questions provide you with practice in prioritizing, decision-making, and critical thinking skills.

Heart and Lung Sound Questions

The accompanying CD also contains *Sound Questions* representative of content addressed in the 2007 test plan for the NCLEX-RN exam. These questions are in NCLEX-style format, and each question presents an audio sound as a component of the question.

Answer Section

The answer sections for each practice question include the correct answer, rationale, test-taking strategy, question categories, and reference source. The structure for the answer section is unique and provides the following information:

The Rationale: The rationale gives you critical insights and information about correct and incorrect options.

Test-Taking Strategy: The test-taking strategy maps out a logical path for selecting the correct option and assists you in selecting an answer to a question on which you might have to guess. Specific suggestions for review are identified in the test-taking strategy.

Question Categories: Each question is identified based on the categories used by the test plan for the NCLEX-RN exam. Additional content categories are provided with each question to help you identify areas in need of review. The categories identified with each practice question include Level of Cognitive Ability, Client Needs, Integrated Process, and the specific nursing Content Area. All categories are identified by their full names so that you do not need to memorize codes or abbreviations.

Reference: A reference, including a page number, is provided so you can easily find the information that you need to review in your undergraduate nursing textbooks.

PHARMACOLOGY AND MEDICATION CALCULATIONS REVIEW

Students consistently state that pharmacology is an area with which they need help. The 2007 test plan for the NCLEX-RN exam incorporates pharmacology in the examination to a greater extent than in the past. Therefore, pharmacology chapters have been included for your review and practice. This book includes 13 pharmacology chapters, a medication and intravenous calculation chapter, and a pediatric medication calculation chapter. Each of these chapters is followed by a practice test that uses the same question format as described earlier. This book contains more than 200 pharmacology questions. Additional pharmacology questions can be found on the accompanying CD.

NCLEX-RN® REVIEW CD

Packaged in this book is a CD containing more than 4200 practice questions. This CD also includes a 75-question Assessment Pretest that provides you with feedback on your strengths and weaknesses. The results of your Assessment Pretest will generate an individualized study calendar to guide you in your preparation for the NCLEX-RN examination. This CD also includes the alternate item format questions and the sound questions. This Windows- and Macintosh-compatible program offers three testing modes for review, including quiz, study, and exam.

HOW TO USE THIS BOOK

Saunders Comprehensive Review for the NCLEX-RN® Examination is especially designed to help you with your successful journey to the peak of the *Saunders Pyramid to Success*, becoming a registered nurse. As you begin your journey through this book, you will be introduced to all of the important points regarding the 2007 NCLEX-RN examination, the process of testing, and the unique and special tips regarding how to prepare yourself for this very important examination.

You should begin your process through the *Saunders Pyramid to Success* by reading Unit I and becoming familiar with the important points regarding the NCLEX-RN examination. Read the chapter from the nursing graduate who recently passed the examination and note what she has to say about the examination. The test-taking strategy chapter will provide you with those important strategies that will guide you in selecting the correct option or assist you in selecting an answer to a question on which you must guess. Read this chapter and practice these strategies as you proceed through your journey with this book. Continue your journey by reading each of the chapters and content areas. Review the Pyramid Terms and the Pyramid to Success and identify the Client Needs and Integrated Processes specific to the test plan in that area. Read each of the content areas, focusing on the Pyramid Points that identify those areas most likely to be tested on the NCLEX-RN examination.

As you read each chapter, identify your strengths and those areas in need of further review. Highlight these areas and test your strengths and abilities by taking all of the practice tests provided at the end of the chapters. Be sure to read all of the rationales and the test-taking strategies. The rationale provides you with the significant information regarding both the correct and incorrect options. The test-taking strategy offers you a logical path for selecting the correct option and identifies the content area that you need to review if you had difficulty with the question. Use the reference source listed so you can easily find the information that you need to review.

After reviewing all of the chapters in the book, turn to Unit XX, the Comprehensive Test. Take this examination and then review each question, answer, and rationale. Identify any areas requiring further review; then take the time to review those areas again. Finally, use the CD and begin by taking the Assessment Pretest. Then review your individualized study calendar to guide you in preparing for the NCLEX-RN examination.

After using this book to review specific content areas, continue on your journey through the *Saunders Pyramid to Success* with the companion book, *Saunders Q&A Review for the NCLEX-RN® Examination*, for additional practice questions. The companion book and its accompanying CD offer you more than 5000 practice questions on specific areas outlined by the 2007 test plan for the NCLEX-RN exam. With practice questions uniquely focused on the Client Needs and the Integrated Processes, you can assess your level of competence.

Saunders Online Review Course for the NCLEX-RN® Examination is another valuable resource to use in preparing for the examination. This course consists of 10 modules and 47 lessons. Every lesson contains content for review, illustrations, animations, practice questions, and a case study followed by questions related to the case study. After each module is a 100-question exam that is made up of questions representative of the content in the module lessons. There is also a Pretest

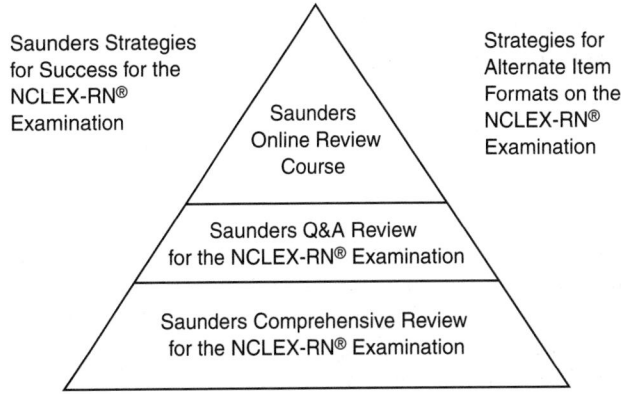

Exam that generates an individualized study calendar, a Comprehensive (Cumulative) Exam, and a CAT (computerized adaptive testing) Exam. The course provides you with a systematic and individualized method for preparing to take the NCLEX-RN examination.

Two other extremely valuable resources that will ensure your success in testing are *Saunders Strategies for Success for the NCLEX-RN® Examination* and *Saunders Alternate Item Formats on the NCLEX-RN® Examination*. *Saunders Strategies for Success for the NCLEX-RN® Examination* book and accompanying CD provide all of the test-taking strategies that will help you pass your nursing examinations and the NCLEX-RN examination. The chapters describe all of the test-taking strategies, include several sample questions that illustrate how to use the strategy, and provide an additional 500 practice questions, including multiple choice and alternate item format questions.

Saunders Alternate Item Formats on the NCLEX-RN® Examination focuses specifically on the alternate item format questions that will appear on your nursing examinations and on the NCLEX-RN examination. This resource is organized by the Client Needs component of the test plan, provides an accompanying CD, and includes more than 275 alternate item format questions, including fill-in-the blank, multiple response, prioritizing (ordered response), figure/illustration (hot spot), and chart/exhibit questions. A total of 15 sound questions are also included on the accompanying CD.

Good luck with your journey through the *Saunders Pyramid to Success*. I wish you continued success throughout your new career as a Registered Nurse!

Linda Anne Silvestri, MSN, RN

Acknowledgments

Sincere appreciation and warmest thanks are extended to the many individuals who in their own ways have contributed to the publication of this book.

First, I want to thank all of my nursing students at the Community College of Rhode Island in Warwick who approached me in 1991 and persuaded me to help them prepare to take the NCLEX-RN examination. Their enthusiasm and inspiration led to the commencement of my professional endeavors in conducting review courses for the NCLEX-RN exam for nursing students. I also thank the numerous nursing students who have attended my review courses for their willingness to share their needs and ideas. Their input has certainly added a special uniqueness to this publication.

I wish to acknowledge all of the nursing faculty who taught in my review courses for the NCLEX-RN exam. Their commitment, dedication, and expertise has certainly assisted nursing students in achieving success with the NCLEX-RN exam. Additionally, I want to acknowledge Laurent W. Valliere for his contribution to this publication, for teaching in my review courses for the NCLEX-RN exam, and for his commitment and dedication in helping my nursing students prepare for the NCLEX-RN exam from a non-academic point of view. A special thank you also goes to Katje A. Koning, RN, for writing a chapter for this book about her experiences with preparing for and taking the NCLEX-RN examination. I also want to acknowledge Lois Marshall for her enormous contributions to the Instructor's Electronic Resource accompanying this text. Thank you for making this an invaluable resource, Lois!

I sincerely acknowledge and thank two very important individuals from Elsevier Health Sciences. I thank Nancy O'Brien, Managing Editor, for all of her assistance throughout the preparation of this edition and for her continuous enthusiasm, support, and expert professional guidance. And a very special thank you extends to Charlene Ketchum, Developmental Editor. Charlene has provided me with a tremendous amount of support throughout this publication. Her planning and expert organizational and prioritizing skills kept me organized. She was an expert at keeping in order the enormous amount of work that I submitted for manuscript production. Thank you, Charlene!

A special thank you and acknowledgment goes to two important individuals, Dianne E. Ventrice and Lawrence Fiorentino. They provided continuous support and dedication to my work in both the NCLEX exam review courses and in reference support and other secretarial responsibilities for the fourth edition of this book.

I want to acknowledge all of the staff at Elsevier Health Sciences for their tremendous assistance throughout the preparation and production of this publication. A special thank you to all of them. I thank all of the special people in the production department, Doug Turner, Project Manager; John Rogers, Publishing Services Manager; David Rushing, Multimedia Producer; and Margaret Reid, Designer, who all played such significant roles in finalizing this publication. I sincerely thank those in the marketing department who helped with the promotion of this book including Bob Boehringer, Segment Marketing Director; Kathy Mantz, Group Segment Manager; Dan Hughes, Marketing Manager; and Susan Adkisson, Marketing Coordinator.

I would also like to acknowledge Patricia Mieg, former Educational Sales Representative, who encouraged me to submit my ideas and initial work for the first edition of this book to the W.B. Saunders Company.

I want to acknowledge my parents, who opened my door of opportunity in education. I thank my mother, Frances Mary, for all of her love, support, and assistance as I continuously worked to achieve my professional goals. I thank my father, Arnold Lawrence, who always provided insightful words of encouragement. My memories of his love and support will always remain in my heart. I am certain that he would be very proud of my professional accomplishments.

I also thank my sister, Dianne Elodia, my brother, Lawrence Peter, and my niece, Gina Marie, who were continuously supportive, giving, and helpful during my research and preparation of this publication.

I want to acknowledge all of the contributors who reviewed and updated the content and practice questions and the item writers who updated and provided many of the practice questions. I also thank the many faculty and student reviewers for their thoughts and ideas. A very special thank you to all of you!

I also need to thank Salve Regina University for the opportunity to educate nursing students in the baccalaureate nursing program and for its support during my research and writing of this publication. I would like to especially acknowledge my colleagues, Dr. Peggy Mat-

teson, Dr. Ellen McCarty, Dr. JoAnn Mullaney, Dr. Jane McCool, and Dr. Bethany Sykes for all of their support and encouragement.

I wish to acknowledge the Community College of Rhode Island, which provided me the opportunity to educate nursing students in the Associate Degree of Nursing Program, and a special thank you to Patricia Miller, MSN, RN, and Michelina McClellan, MS, RN, from Baystate Medical Center, School of Nursing, in Springfield, Massachusetts, who were my first mentors in nursing education.

Lastly, a very special thank you to all my nursing students, past, present and future. All of you light up my life! Your love and dedication to the profession of nursing and your commitment to provide health care will bring never-ending rewards!

Linda Anne Silvestri, MSN, RN

Contents

NCLEX-RN® Exam Preparation

The NCLEX-RN® Examination

▲ THE PYRAMID TO SUCCESS

Welcome to the Pyramid to Success.

Saunders Comprehensive Review for the NCLEX-RN® Examination is specially designed to help you begin your successful journey to the peak of the pyramid, becoming a registered nurse. As you begin your journey, you will be introduced to all the important points regarding the NCLEX-RN examination and the process of testing and to the unique and special tips regarding how to prepare yourself for this important examination. You will read what a nursing graduate who recently passed the NCLEX-RN examination has to say about the test. All the important test-taking strategies are detailed. These details will guide you in selecting the correct option or assist you in selecting an answer to a question at which you must guess.

Each of the content areas in this book begins with the Pyramid to Success. The Pyramid to Success addresses specific points related to the NCLEX-RN examination, including the Pyramid Terms, and the Client Needs and Integrated Processes as identified in the test plan framework for the examination. Pyramid Terms are key words that are defined and are set in boldface throughout each chapter to direct your attention to those significant points for the examination. The Client Needs and the Integrated Processes specific to the content of the chapter are identified.

Throughout each chapter, you will find Pyramid Point bullets that identify areas most likely to be tested on the NCLEX-RN examination. Read each chapter, and identify your strengths and areas that are in need of further review. Test your strengths and abilities by taking all the practice tests provided in this book. Be sure to read all the rationales and test-taking strategies. The rationale provides you with significant information regarding the correct and incorrect options. The test-taking strategy provides you with the logical path to selecting the correct option. The test-taking strategy also identifies the content area to review, if required. The reference source and page number are provided so that you can find the information easily that you need to review. Each question is coded based on the level of cognitive ability, the Client Needs category, the Integrated Process, and the nursing content area.

Following the completion of your comprehensive review in this book, continue on your journey through the Pyramid to Success with the companion book, *Saunders Q&A Review for the NCLEX-RN® Examination,* which provides you with more than 5000 practice questions based on the NCLEX-RN examination test plan framework, with a specific focus on Client Needs and Integrated Processes. Then, you will be ready for the *Saunders Online Review Course for the NCLEX-RN® Examination.* Additional products in Saunders Pyramid to Success include *Saunders Strategies for Success for the NCLEX-RN® Examination* and *Saunders Strategies for Alternate Item Formats on the NCLEX-RN® Examination.* These products are described below.

The *Saunders Online Review Course for the NCLEX-RN® Examination* addresses all areas of the test plan identified by the National Council of State Boards of Nursing (NCSBN). The course contains a pretest that provides feedback regarding your strengths and weaknesses and that generates an individualized study schedule in a calendar format. Content review includes practice questions and case studies, figures and illustrations, a glossary, and animations and videos. A cumulative examination and a computer adaptive test (CAT) are also key components of the online review course. The types of practice questions in this course include multiple choice, fill in the blank, multiple response, those that require you to prioritize (ordered response), and questions containing figures (hot spots) that may require you to use the computer mouse to answer.

The *Saunders Strategies for Success for the NCLEX-RN® Examination* focuses on the test-taking strategies that will help you pass your nursing examinations while in nursing school and will prepare you for the NCLEX-RN examination. The chapters describe all the test-taking strategies and include several sample questions that illustrate how to use the test-taking strategy. There are a total of 500 practice questions that accompany this book. All the practice questions are reflective of the framework and the content identified in the current NCLEX-RN test plan and include multiple-choice and alternate item format questions.

The *Saunders Strategies for Alternate Item Formats on the NCLEX-RN® Examination* differs from all the other products in the Saunders Pyramid to Success in that it contains only alternate item format questions. It provides you with all the information needed about all types of alternate item format questions that may appear on your nursing examinations and on the NCLEX-RN examination. It contains 265 practice alternate item format questions and 15 heart and lung sounds questions to prepare you for your nursing examinations and for that most important examination, the NCLEX-RN. All the products in Saunders Pyramid to Success can be obtained online by visiting http://www.elsevierhealth.com or by calling 800-426-4545.

Let's begin our journey through the Pyramid to Success.

THE EXAMINATION PROCESS

An important step in the Pyramid to Success is to become as familiar as possible with the examination process. A significant amount of anxiety can occur in candidates facing the challenge of this examination. Knowing what the examination is all about and knowing what you will encounter during the process of testing will assist in alleviating fear and anxiety. The information contained in this chapter addresses the procedures related to the development of the NCLEX-RN examination test plan, the components of the test plan, and the answers to the questions most commonly asked by nursing students and graduates preparing to take the NCLEX-RN examination. The information contained in this chapter related to the test plan was obtained from the NCSBN Web site (http://www.ncsbn.org) and from the National Council of State Boards of Nursing Test Plan for the NCLEX-RN Examination (effective date, April 2007). You can obtain additional information regarding the test and its development by accessing the NCSBN Web site or by writing to the National Council of State Boards of Nursing, 111 East Wacker Drive, Suite 2900, Chicago, IL 60601.

COMPUTER ADAPTIVE TESTING

The acronym *CAT* stands for computer adaptive test, which means that the examination is created as the test taker answers each question. All the test questions are categorized based on the test plan structure and the level of difficulty of the question. As you answer a question, the computer determines your competency based on the answer you selected. If you selected a correct answer to a question, the computer scans the question bank and selects a more difficult question. If you selected an incorrect answer, the computer scans the question bank and selects an easier question. This process continues until the test plan requirements are met and a reliable pass or fail decision is made.

When a test question is presented on the computer screen, you must answer it or the test will not move on. This means that you will not be able to skip questions, go back and review questions, or go back and change answers. Remember, in a CAT examination, once an answer is recorded, all subsequent questions administered depend, to an extent, on the answer selected for that question. Skipping and returning to earlier questions are not compatible with the logical methodology of a computer adaptive test. The inability to skip questions or go back to change previous answers will not be a disadvantage to you. Actually, you will not fall into that "trap" of changing a correct answer to an incorrect one with the CAT system.

If you are faced with a question that contains unfamiliar content, you may need to guess at the answer. There is no penalty for guessing on this examination. Remember, with most of the questions, the answer will be right there in front of you. If you need to guess, use your nursing knowledge to its fullest extent, as well as all the test-taking strategies that you have practiced in this review program.

You do not need any computer experience to take this examination. A keyboard tutorial is provided and administered to all test takers at the start of the examination. The tutorial will instruct you on the use of the on-screen optional calculator, the use of the mouse, and how to record an answer. In addition to the traditional four-option multiple-choice question, the tutorial also provides instructions on how to respond to alternate item format questions. A proctor is present to assist in explaining the use of the computer to ensure your full understanding of how to proceed.

DEVELOPMENT OF THE TEST PLAN AND ITEM WRITERS

The test plan for the NCLEX-RN examination is developed by the NCSBN. As an initial step in the test development process, the NCSBN considers the legal scope of nursing practice as governed by state laws and regulations, including the nurse practice act, and uses these laws to define the areas on the examination that will assess the competence of a candidate (test taker) for licensure.

The NCSBN also conducts a practice analysis study to determine the framework for the test plan for the examination. The participants in this study include newly licensed registered nurses from all types of basic education programs. The NCSBN provides participants with a list of nursing activities and asks them about the frequency of performing these specific activities, their impact on maintaining client safety, and the setting where the activities were performed. A panel of experts at the NCSBN analyzes the results of the study and makes decisions regarding the test plan framework. Because nursing practice continues to change, the NCSBN conducts this study every 3 years. The results of this study, most recently conducted in 2005, provided the structure for the test plan implemented in April 2007.

The NCSBN selects question (item) writers after an extensive application process. The writers are registered nurses who hold a master's degree or a higher degree. Many of the writers are nursing educators; however, a nurse currently employed in clinical nursing practice and working directly with nurses who have entered practice within the last 12 months may be selected to participate in this process. Question writers voluntarily submit an application to become a writer and must meet specific criteria established by the council to be accepted as participants in the process.

THE TEST PLAN

The content of the NCLEX-RN examination reflects the activities that a newly licensed, entry-level registered nurse must be able to perform to provide clients with safe and effective nursing care. The questions are written to address the levels of cognitive ability, Client Needs, and Integrated Processes as identified in the test plan developed by the NCSBN (Box 1-1).

Levels of Cognitive Ability

The examination for licensure as a registered nurse may include questions at the cognitive levels of knowledge, comprehension, application, and analysis. However, most questions are written at the application or higher levels of cognitive ability, such as the analysis level, because the practice of nursing requires critical thinking in

decision making. This means that the test taker will be required to analyze and apply the information provided in the test question. Box 1-2 presents an example of a question that requires you to analyze data to determine the nursing intervention.

Client Needs

In the test plan implemented in April 2007, the NCSBN has identified a test plan framework based on Client Needs. The NCSBN identifies four major categories of Client Needs. Some of these categories are further divided into subcategories. The Client Needs categories include Safe and Effective Care Environment, Health Promotion and Maintenance, Psychosocial Integrity, and Physiological Integrity (Table 1-1).

Safe and Effective Care Environment

The Safe and Effective Care Environment category includes two subcategories, Management of Care and Safety and Infection Control. According to the NCSBN, Management of Care (13% to 19% of questions) addresses content that tests the nurse's knowledge, skills, and ability required to ensure a safe care delivery setting to protect clients, families, significant others, visitors, and health care personnel. The NCSBN indicates that Safety and Infection Control (8% to 14% of questions) addresses content that tests the nurse's knowledge, skills, and ability required to protect clients, families, significant others, visitors, and health care personnel from health and environmental hazards. Box 1-3 presents examples of questions that address these two subcategories.

Health Promotion and Maintenance

The Health Promotion and Maintenance category (6% to 12% of questions) addresses the principles related to growth and development. According to the NCSBN, this Client Needs category also addresses content that tests the nurse's knowledge, skills, and ability required to assist the client, family members, and significant others to prevent health problems, to recognize alterations in health, and to develop health practices that promote and support wellness. See Box 1-4 for an example of a question in this Client Needs category.

Psychosocial Integrity

The Psychosocial Integrity category (6% to 12% of questions) addresses content that tests the nurse's knowledge, skills, and ability required to promote and support the client, client's family, and significant other's ability to cope, adapt, and problem solve during stressful events. The NCSBN also indicates that this Client Needs category addresses the emotional, mental, and social well-being of the client, family, or significant other, and the knowledge, skills, and ability required to

---

BOX 1-1

Examination Questions

Each examination question addresses the following:
  A level of cognitive ability
  A Client Needs category
  An Integrated Process

BOX 1-2

Level of Cognitive Ability

LEVEL OF COGNITIVE ABILITY: APPLICATION*

A child has just returned from surgery and has a hip spica cast. The nurse should take which priority action at this time?

1. Elevate the head of the bed.
2. Assess the circulatory status.
3. Abduct the hips using pillows.
4. Turn the child on the right side.

Answer: 2

This question requires the test taker to determine the priority nursing action for a child following application of a hip spica cast. During the first few hours after a cast is applied, the priority concern is swelling, which may cause the cast to act as a tourniquet and obstruct circulation. Therefore, circulatory assessment is the priority. Elevating the head of the bed of a child in a hip spica cast would cause discomfort. Using pillows to abduct the hips is not necessary because a hip spica cast immobilizes the hip and knee. Turning the child from side to side at least every 2 hours is important because it allows the body cast to dry evenly and prevents complications related to immobility; however, it is not a higher priority than checking circulation.

*Reference: Hockenberry, M., & Wilson, D. (2007). *Wong's nursing care of infants and children* (8th ed., pp. 1756-1757). St. Louis: Mosby.

LEVEL OF COGNITIVE ABILITY: ANALYSIS†

A client is receiving tobramycin (Nebcin). The nurse determines that the client is responding well to the medication therapy if which of the following laboratory results is noted?

1. Sodium level, 145 mEq/L; chloride level, 106 mEq/L
2. Sodium level, 140 mEq/L; potassium level, 3.9 mEq/L
3. White blood cell count, 8,000/mm^3; creatinine level, 0.9 mg/dL
4. White blood cell count, 15,000/mm^3; blood urea nitrogen level, 38 mg/dL

Answer: 3

This question requires the test taker to determine the action of the medication and its effectiveness based on laboratory values. Tobramycin is an antibiotic (aminoglycoside) that causes nephrotoxicity and ototoxicity. The medication is working if the white blood cell (WBC) count drops back into the normal range and kidney function remains normal. Option 4 indicates an abnormal WBC count and options 1 and 2 are unrelated to the use of this medication.

†Reference: Hodgson, B., & Kizior, R. (2007). *Saunders nursing drug handbook 2007* (p. 1144). Philadelphia: W.B. Saunders.

TABLE 1-1

Client Needs Categories and Percentage of Questions on the NCLEX-RN® Examination

Client Needs Category	Percentage of Questions
SAFE AND EFFECTIVE CARE ENVIRONMENT	
Management of Care	13-19
Safety and Infection Control	8-14
HEALTH PROMOTION AND MAINTENANCE	6-12
PSYCHOSOCIAL INTEGRITY	6-12
PHYSIOLOGICAL INTEGRITY	
Basic Care and Comfort	6-12
Pharmacological and Parenteral Therapies	13-19
Reduction of Risk Potential	13-19
Physiological Adaptation	11-17

care for the client with an acute or chronic mental illness. See Box 1-5 for an example of a question in this Client Needs category.

Physiological Integrity

The Physiological Integrity category includes four subcategories, Basic Care and Comfort, Pharmacological and Parenteral Therapies, Reduction of Risk Potential,

and Physiological Adaptation. The NCSBN describes these subcategories as follows. Basic Care and Comfort (6% to 12% of questions) addresses content that tests the nurse's knowledge, skills, and ability required to provide comfort and assistance to the client in the performance of activities of daily living. Pharmacological and Parenteral Therapies (13% to 19% of questions) addresses content that tests the nurse's knowledge, skills, and ability required to administer medications and parenteral therapies. Reduction of Risk Potential (13% to 19% of questions) addresses content that tests the nurse's knowledge, skills, and ability required to prevent complications or health problems related to the client's condition or any prescribed treatments or procedures. Physiological Adaptation (11% to 17% of questions) addresses content that tests the nurse's knowledge, skills, and ability required to provide care to clients with acute, chronic, or life-threatening conditions. See Box 1-6 for examples of questions in this Client Needs category.

Integrated Processes

The NCSBN identifies four processes that are fundamental to the practice of nursing. These processes are a component of the test plan and are incorporated throughout the major categories of Client Needs. The Integrated Processes include caring, communication and documentation, nursing process (assessment, analysis, planning,

---

BOX 1-3
Safe and Effective Care Environment

MANAGEMENT OF CARE*

A client arrives at the emergency department complaining of acute right lower quadrant abdominal pain. Laboratory tests are performed and the nurse notes that the client's white blood cell (WBC) count is elevated. The nurse reviews the physician's orders and contacts the physician to question which order, if noted, in the client's record?

1. Maintain an NPO status.
2. Apply a cold pack to the abdomen.
3. Administer 30 mL of Milk of Magnesia (MOM).
4. Initiate an intravenous (IV) line for the administration of IV fluids.

Answer: 3

This question is an example of a question that represents the subcategory Management of Care in the Client Needs category of Safe and Effective Care Environment. It requires you to analyze the data provided in the question to determine which physician's order should be questioned to protect the client from harm. Appendicitis should be suspected in a client with an elevated WBC count complaining of acute right lower quadrant abdominal pain. The client would be NPO and given IV fluids in preparation for possible surgery. Cold packs may be ordered for comfort. Laxatives are not ordered because, if appendicitis is present, the effect of the laxative may cause a rupture, with resultant peritonitis.

*Reference: Ignatavicius, D., & Workman, M. (2006). Medical-surgical nursing: Critical thinking for collaborative care (5th ed., p. 1340). Philadelphia: W.B. Saunders.

SAFETY AND INFECTION CONTROL†

A hospitalized client is diagnosed with urethritis caused by a chlamydial infection. The nurse instructs the nursing assistant about which measure to use to prevent contracting the infection during care?

1. Contact isolation
2. Enteric precautions
3. Standard precautions
4. Use of gloves and a mask

Answer: 3

This question addresses the subcategory Safety and Infection Control in the Client Needs category Safe and Effective Care Environment and addresses content related to protection from infection. Chlamydia is a sexually transmitted disease and requires no special precautions other than standard precautions. Caregivers cannot acquire the disease during administration of care, and using standard precautions is the only measure that needs to be used.

†Reference: Ignatavicius, D., & Workman, M. (2006). *Medical-surgical nursing: Critical thinking for collaborative care* (5th ed., p. 1895). Philadelphia: W.B. Saunders.

BOX 1-4
Health Promotion and Maintenance

A 7-year-old child is hospitalized with a fracture of the femur and is placed in traction. In meeting the developmental needs of the child, the nurse selects which of the following play activities for the child?

1. A board game
2. A large puzzle
3. A finger-painting set
4. A coloring book with crayons

Answer: 1

This question addresses the Client Needs category Health Promotion and Maintenance and specifically relates to the principles of growth and development of a school-age child. The school-age child becomes organized with more direction with play activities. Such activities include collections, drawing, construction, dolls, pets, guessing games, board games, riddles, hobbies, competitive games, and listening to the radio or television. Option 2 is appropriate for a toddler. Options 3 and 4 are appropriate for a preschooler.

Reference: Hockenberry, M., & Wilson, D. (2007). *Wong's nursing care of infants and children* (8th ed., pp. 724-725). St. Louis: Mosby.

BOX 1-5
Psychosocial Integrity

A client with ovarian cancer says to the nurse, "If I can just live long enough to attend my daughter's graduation, I'll be ready to die." The nurse determines that the client is experiencing which phase of coping?

1. Isolation
2. Bargaining
3. Depression
4. Acceptance

Answer: 2

This question addresses the Client Needs category Psychosocial Integrity, and the content addresses coping mechanisms. Bargaining is the phase of coping in which the dying person tries to negotiate, as in this case, making deals with their God or fate. Options 1, 3, and 4 also identify phases of coping but these phases are not indicative of the client's statement.

Reference: Potter, P., & Perry, A. (2005). *Fundamentals of nursing* (6th ed., p. 570). St. Louis: Mosby.

BOX 1-6

Physiological Integrity

BASIC CARE AND COMFORT

A nurse provides instructions to a client about the use of a cane and watches as the client uses it. Which observation by the nurse indicates the need to provide additional instructions to the client?

1. The client holds the cane on the strong side.
2. The client holds the cane about 6 inches to the side of the foot.
3. The client flexes the elbow at a 15- to 30-degree angle when holding the cane in place.
4. The client moves the cane and the stronger leg forward first and then moves the weaker leg forward.

Answer: 4

This question addresses the subcategory Basic Care and Comfort in the Client Needs category Physiological Integrity and addresses client mobility and promoting assistance in an activity of daily living. Note the subject of the question, the need for the nurse to provide additional instructions. Visualize each option in terms of its safety in performing ambulation regarding the use of a cane to direct you to the option that is unsafe. The weaker leg is moved forward to the cane so that body weight is divided between the cane and stronger leg. The stronger leg is then advanced past the cane so that the weaker leg and body weight are supported by the cane.

Reference: Potter, P., & Perry, A. (2005). *Fundamentals of nursing* (6th ed., p. 948). St. Louis: Mosby.

PHARMACOLOGICAL AND PARENTERAL THERAPIES

A nurse is caring for a client with hypertension receiving torsemide (Demadex) 5 mg orally daily. Which laboratory finding indicates to the nurse that the client might be experiencing an adverse reaction related to the medication?

1. A chloride level of 98 mEq/L
2. A sodium level of 135 mEq/L
3. A potassium level of 3.1 mEq/L
4. A blood urea nitrogen level (BUN) of 15 mg/dL

Answer: 3

This question addresses the subcategory of Pharmacological and Parenteral Therapies in the Client Needs category Physiological Integrity. Torsemide is a loop diuretic. The medication can produce acute, profound water loss, volume and electrolyte depletion, dehydration, decreased blood volume, and circulatory collapse. Option 3 is the only option that indicates electrolyte depletion, because the normal potassium level is 3.5 to 5.1 mEq/L. The normal chloride level is 98 to 107 mEq/L. The normal sodium level is 135 to 145 mEq/L. The normal BUN level is 5 to 20 mg/dL.

Reference: Hodgson, B., & Kizior, R. (2007). *Saunders nursing drug handbook 2007* (p. 1156). Philadelphia: W.B. Saunders.

REDUCTION OF RISK POTENTIAL

A magnetic resonance imaging (MRI) procedure is prescribed for a client with a suspected brain tumor. The nurse implements which action to prepare the client for this test?

1. Keeps the client NPO for 6 hours prior to the test
2. Shaves the groin for insertion of a femoral catheter
3. Removes all metal-containing objects from the client
4. Instructs the client in inhalation techniques for the administration of the radioiostope

Answer: 3

This question addresses the subcategory of Reduction of Risk Potential in the Client Needs category Physiological Integrity and the nurse's responsibilities in preparing the client for the diagnostic test. During an MRI, radiofrequency pulses in a magnetic field are converted into pictures. All metal objects, such as rings, bracelets, hairpins, earrings, and watches, should be removed. In addition, a history should be taken to ascertain whether the client has any internal metallic devices, such as orthopedic hardware, pacemakers, or shrapnel. For an abdominal MRI scan, the client is usually NPO. NPO status is not necessary for a MRI scan of the head. The groin may be shaved for an angiogram and inhalation of the radioisotope may be prescribed with positron emission tomography (PET).

Reference: Chernecky, C., & Berger, B. (2004). *Laboratory tests and diagnostic procedures* (4th ed., pp. 754, 886). Philadelphia: W.B. Saunders.

PHYSIOLOGICAL ADAPTATION

A nurse reviews the blood gas results of a client with pneumonia and determines that the client is experiencing respiratory acidosis. Which of the following validates the nurse's findings?

1. pH 7.45, Pco_2 52 mm Hg
2. pH 7.35, Pco_2 40 mm Hg
3. pH 7.25, Pco_2 50 mm Hg
4. pH 7.50, Pco_2 30 mm Hg

Answer: 3

This question addresses the subcategory of Physiological Adaptation in the Client Needs category Physiological Integrity. The normal pH is 7.35 to 7.45. The normal Pco_2 is 35 to 45 mm Hg. In respiratory acidosis, the pH is down and the Pco_2 is up. Options 1 and 4 reflect an elevated pH that indicates an alkalotic condition. Option 2 reflects a normal blood gas result. The content addressed in this question relates to an acid-base imbalance, an alteration in body systems.

Reference: Ignatavicius, D., & Workman, M. (2006). *Medical-surgical nursing: Critical thinking for collaborative care* (5th ed., pp. 286-287). Philadelphia: W.B. Saunders.

A client is scheduled for angioplasty. The client says to the nurse, "I'm so afraid that it will hurt, and will make me worse off than I am." The nurse makes which best statement to the client?
1. "Can you tell me what you understand about the procedure?"
2. "Your fears are a sign that you really should have this procedure."
3. "Try not to worry. This is a well-known and easy procedure for the doctor."
4. "Those are very normal fears, but please be assured that everything will be okay."

Answer: 1

This question addresses the Integrated Process of Caring. Option 1 is a therapeutic communication technique that explores the client's feelings, determines the level of client understanding about the procedure, and displays caring. Option 2 demeans the client and does not encourage further sharing by the client. Option 3 diminishes the client's feelings by directing attention away from the client and to the physician's importance. Option 4 does not address the client's fears and puts the client's feelings on hold.

Reference: Potter, P., & Perry, A. (2005) *Fundamentals of nursing* (6th ed., pp. 437-442). St. Louis: Mosby.

implementation, and evaluation), and teaching and learning. See Box 1-7 for an example of a question that incorporates the Integrated Process of caring.

TYPES OF QUESTIONS ON THE EXAMINATION

The types of questions that may be administered on the examination include multiple choice, fill in the blank, multiple response, prioritizing (ordered response), chart or exhibit, and questions that contain a figure or illustration (hot spot). Some questions may require you to use the mouse and cursor on the computer. For example, you may be presented with a visual that displays the arterial vessels of an adult client. In this illustration, you may be asked to "point and click" (using the mouse) on the area where the dorsalis pedis pulse could be felt. The NCSBN provides specific directions for you to follow with these questions to guide you in your process of testing. Be sure to read these directions as they appear on the computer screen.

Multiple-Choice Questions

Most of the questions that you will be asked to answer will be in the multiple-choice format. These questions provide you with data about a particular client situation and four answers or options.

A physician orders an intravenous dose of 200,000 units of penicillin G benzathine (Bicillin) for an adult client. The label on the 10-mL ampule sent from the pharmacy reads penicillin G benzathine (Bicillin), 300,000 units/mL. The nurse prepares how much medication to administer the correct dose? (Round to the nearest tenth.)

Answer: 0.7

In this question, you need to use the formula for calculating a medication dose. Once you determine the dose, you will need to type in your answer. In this particular question, you are asked to round to the nearest tenth. Always follow the specific directions noted on the computer screen when answering the question. Also, remember that there will be an onscreen calculator on the computer for your use, if needed.

Reference: Potter, P., & Perry, A. (2005) *Fundamentals of nursing* (6th ed., pp. 835-836). St. Louis: Mosby.

Fill-in-the-Blank Questions

Fill-in-the-blank questions may ask you to perform a medication calculation, determine an intravenous flow rate, or calculate an intake or output record on a client. You will need to type in your answer. See Box 1-8 for an example.

Multiple Response Questions

For a multiple response question, you will be asked to select or check all the options, such as nursing interventions, that relate to the information in the question. No partial credit is given for correct selections. You need to do exactly as the question asks, which will be to select all the options that apply. See Box 1-9 for an example.

Prioritizing (Ordered Response) Questions

In this type of question, you will be asked to use the computer mouse to drag and drop your nursing actions in order of priority. Information will be presented in a question and, based on the data, you need to determine what you will do first, second, third, and so forth. See Box 1-10 for an example.

Figure or Illustration (Hot Spot) Questions

A question with a figure or illustration will ask you to answer the question based on the figure or illustration. The question could contain a chart, table, or a figure or illustration. You also may be asked to use the computer mouse to point and click on a specific area in the visual. A figure or illustration may appear in any type of ques-

BOX 1-9

Multiple Response Question

An emergency room nurse is caring for a child suspected of acute epiglottitis. Select all nursing interventions that apply in the care of the child.
- ❑ 1. Obtain a throat culture
- ☑ 2. Ensure a patent airway
- ☑ 3. Prepare the child for a chest x-ray
- ❑ 4. Maintain the child in a supine position
- ☑ 5. Obtain a pediatric-size tracheostomy tray
- ☑ 6. Place the child on an oxygen saturation monitor

In a multiple response question, you will be asked to select or check all the options, such as nursing interventions, that relate to the information in the question. To answer this question, recall that acute epiglottitis is a serious obstructive inflammatory process that requires immediate intervention. To reduce respiratory distress, the child should sit upright. Examination of the throat with a tongue depressor or attempting to obtain a throat culture is contraindicated because the examination can precipitate further obstruction. The child is placed on an oxygen saturation monitor to monitor oxygenation status. A lateral neck and chest x-ray is obtained to determine the degree of obstruction, if present. Intubation may be necessary if respiratory distress is severe. Remember, follow the specific directions given on the computer screen.

Reference: Hockenberry, M., & Wilson, D. (2007). Wong's nursing care of infants and children (8th ed., pp. 1330-1332). St. Louis: Mosby.

tion, including a multiple-choice question. See Box 1-11 for an example.

Chart or Exhibit Questions

In this type of question, you will be presented with a problem and a chart or exhibit. You will need to refer to the information in the chart or exhibit to answer the question. See Box 1-12 for an example.

REGISTERING TO TAKE THE EXAMINATION

The initial step in the registration process is to submit an application to the state board of nursing in the state in which you intend to obtain licensure. You need to obtain information from the board of nursing regarding the specific registration process because the process may vary from state to state. In most states, you may register for the examination through the Internet, by mail, or by telephone. The NCLEX candidate Web site is http://www.vue.com/nclex. Following the registration instructions and completing the registration forms precisely and accurately are important. Registration forms not properly completed or not accompanied by the proper fees in the required method of payment will be returned to you and will delay testing. You must pay a fee for taking the examination, and you also may have to pay additional fees to the board of nursing in the state in

BOX 1-10

Prioritizing (Ordered Response) Question

A nurse is preparing to suction a client who has a tracheostomy tube and gathers the supplies needed for the procedure. In order of priority, list the actions that the nurse takes to perform this procedure. (Number 1 is the first priority action and number 6 is the last action)
- 4. Hyperoxygenate the client.
- 1. Place the client in a semi-Fowler's position.
- 2. Turn on the suction device and set the regulator at 80 mm Hg.
- 3. Apply gloves and attach the suction tubing to the suction catheter.
- 5. Insert the catheter into the tracheostomy until resistance is met and then pull back 1 cm.
- 6. Apply intermittent suction and slowly withdraw the catheter while rotating it back and forth.

This question requires you to list in order of priority the nursing actions that should be taken to suction a client who has a tracheostomy tube. The nurse would position the client first and then turn the suction device on and set the regulator. The nurse then dons gloves and attaches the suction tubing to the suction catheter. The nurse would hyperoxygenate the client both before and after suctioning. The nurse then inserts the catheter into the tracheostomy until resistance is met and pulls back 1 cm, applies intermittent suction, and slowly withdraws the catheter while rotating it back and forth. Remember that the client and equipment are prepared before performing the procedure. Also, remember that on the NCLEX examination, you will use the drag and drop feature with the computer mouse to place the actions in order of priority.

Reference: Elkin, M., Perry, A., & Potter, P. (2004). Nursing interventions and clinical skills (3rd ed., pp. 763-765). St. Louis: Mosby.

which you are applying. You will be sent a confirmation indicating that your registration was received. If you do not receive a confirmation within 4 weeks of submitting your registration, you should contact the candidate services (at the NCLEX candidate Web site, http://www.vue.com/nclex).

AUTHORIZATION TO TEST FORM

Once your eligibility to test has been determined by the board of nursing in the state in which licensure is requested, your registration form is processed and an Authorization to Test form will be sent to you. You cannot make an appointment until the board of nursing declares eligibility and you receive an Authorization to Test form. The examination will take place at a Pearson Professional Center, and you can make an appointment through the Internet (http://www.vue.com/nclex) or by telephone. You can schedule an appointment at any Pearson Professional Center. You do not have to take the examination in the same state in which you are seeking licensure. A confirmation of your appointment will be sent to you.

BOX 1-11
Figure or Illustration Question

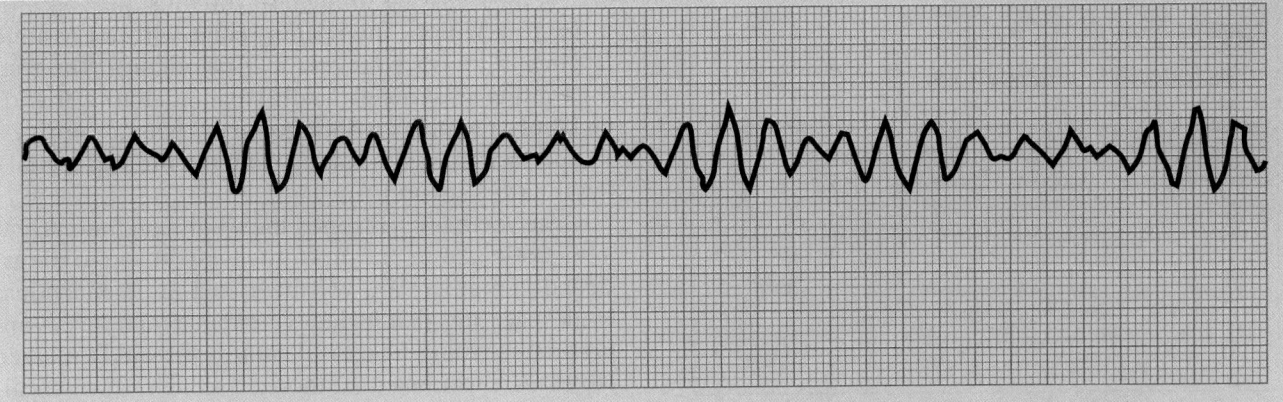

FIG. 1-1   Rhythm strip. (From Ignatavicius, D., & Workman, M. [2006]. *Medical-surgical nursing: Critical thinking for collaborative care* [5th ed., p. 731]. Philadelphia: W.B. Saunders.)

The nurse notes this cardiac rhythm on a client's cardiac monitor and prepares to administer which priority measure?
1. Defibrillation
2. Insertion of a tracheotomy tube
3. Measurement of the blood pressure
4. Application of oxygen via tight face mask

Answer: 1

This question requires you to identify the cardiac rhythm and then determine the priority nursing action. The goal of treatment for ventricular fibrillation (VF) is to terminate the VF immediately. Therefore, if the client experiences ventricular fibrillation, the priority is to defibrillate the client immediately. If the VF does not terminate after three rapid successive shocks of increasing energy, the nurse and resuscitation team must resume cardiopulmonary resuscitation and provide airway management via oxygen and antidysrhythmic therapy. If VF is successfully converted to an organized rhythm, the nurse continues supportive therapy and assists the physician in treating potential causes of VF and preventing its recurrence. Measurement of the blood pressure is not the priority intervention, although vital signs measurement is part of monitoring during supportive therapy. Option 2 is an unnecessary action.

Reference: Ignatavicius, D. & Workman, M. (2006). *Medical-surgical nursing: Critical thinking for collaborative care* (5th ed., pp. 731-732). Philadelphia: Saunders.

The Authorization to Test form contains important information, including your test authorization number, candidate identification number, and an expiration date. Note the expiration date on the form because you must take the test by this date. You also need to take your Authorization to Test form to the test center on the day of your examination. You will not be admitted to the examination if you do not have it.

If for any reason you need to cancel or reschedule your appointment to test, you can make the change on the candidate Web site (http://www.vue.com/nclex) or by calling candidate services. The change needs to be made 1 full business day (24 hours) before your scheduled appointment. If you fail to arrive for the examination or fail to cancel your appointment to test without providing appropriate notice, you will forfeit your examination fee and your Authorization to Test will be invalidated. This information will be reported to the board of nursing in the state in which you have applied for licensure, and you will be required to register and pay the testing fees again.

It is important that you arrive at the testing center at least 30 minutes before the test is scheduled. If you arrive late for the scheduled testing appointment, you may be required to forfeit your examination appointment. If it is necessary to forfeit your appointment, you will need to reregister for the examination and pay an additional fee. The board of nursing will be notified that you did not take the test. A few days before your scheduled date of testing, take the time to drive to the testing center to determine its exact location, the length of time required to arrive to that destination, and any potential obstacles that might delay you, such as road construction, traffic, or parking sites.

SPECIAL TESTING CIRCUMSTANCES

If you require special testing accommodations, you should contact the board of nursing before submitting a registration form. The board of nursing will provide the procedures for the request. The board of nursing must authorize special testing accommodations. Following board of nursing approval, the NCSBN reviews the requested accommodations and also must approve the request. If the request is approved, the testing appointment must be made by the NCLEX Program Coor-

BOX 1-12
Chart or Exhibit Question

CLIENT'S CHART:

HISTORY	MEDICATIONS	DIAGNOSTIC TESTS
Diabetes mellitus Atrial fibrillation Hypertension Gout	NPH insulin 16 units subcutaneous daily Allopurinol (Zyloprim) 100 mg po daily Atorvastatin (Lipitor) 10 mg po daily Furosemide (Lasix) 40 mg po daily Lanoxin (Digoxin) 0.125 mg po daily	Electrocardiogram: normal Chest x-ray: normal

Prednisone (Deltasone) is prescribed for a hospitalized client. Which laboratory result should the nurse monitor most closely?
1. Lipase level
2. Chloride level
3. Uric acid level
4. Blood glucose level
   Answer: 4

This chart or exhibit question provides you with data from a client's medical chart, identifies a medication, and asks about the laboratory result that needs to be monitored most closely. Read all the data in the question and the client's chart. Use nursing knowledge about the interactions and effects of prednisone (Deltasone) and recall that this medication may increase the blood glucose level.

Reference: Mosby. (2006). *Mosby's 2006 drug consult for nurses* (2006) (p. 1140). St. Louis: Mosby.

dinator, whom you can contact by calling NCLEX candidate services. If it is necessary, you must cancel or reschedule an appointment through the NCLEX Program Coordinator.

THE TESTING CENTER

The test center is designed to ensure complete security of the testing process. Strict candidate identification requirements have been established. To be admitted to the testing center, you must bring the Authorization to Test form, along with two forms of identification. Both forms of identification must be signed and current or nonexpired, and one must contain a recent photograph of you. The name on the photograph identification must be the same as the name on the Authorization to Test form. A digital fingerprint, signature, and photograph will be taken at the test center and will accompany the NCLEX exam results to confirm your identity. Also, if you leave the testing room for any reason, you may be required to be fingerprinted again to be readmitted to the room.

Personal belongings are not allowed in the testing room. Secure storage will be provided for you; however, storage space is limited, so you must plan accordingly. In addition, the testing center will not assume responsibility for your personal belongings. The testing waiting areas are generally small; therefore, friends or family members who accompany you are not permitted to wait in the testing center while you are taking the examination.

Once you have completed the admission process and a brief orientation, the proctor will escort you to the assigned computer. You will be seated at an individual work space area that includes computer equipment, appropriate lighting, an erasable note board, and a marker. No items, including unauthorized scratch paper, are allowed into the testing room. Electronic devices such as watches, beepers, or cell phones, are not allowed in the testing room. Eating, drinking, or the use of tobacco is not allowed in the testing room. You will be observed at all times by the test proctor while taking the examination. Additionally, video and audio recordings of all test sessions are made. Pearson Professional Centers has no control over the sounds made by typing on the computer by others. If these sounds are distracting, raise your hand to summon the proctor. Earplugs are available on request.

You must follow the directions given by the test center staff and must remain seated during the test, except when authorized to leave. If you think that you have a problem with the computer, need an additional note board, need to take a break, or need the test proctor for any reason, you must raise your hand.

TESTING TIME

The maximum testing time is 6 hours; this period includes the tutorial, the sample items, all breaks, and the examination. All breaks are optional. If you take a break, you must leave the testing room and, when you return, you may be required to provide a fingerprint to be readmitted to the testing room.

LENGTH OF THE EXAMINATION

The minimum number of questions that you will need to answer is 75. Of these 75 questions, 60 will be operational (scored) questions and 15 will be pretest (unscored) questions. The maximum number of questions in the test is 265. Fifteen of the total number of questions that you need to answer will be pretest (unscored) questions.

The pretest questions are questions that may be presented as scored questions on future examinations. These pretest questions are not identified as such. In other words, you do not know which questions are the pretest (unscored) questions.

PASS-OR-FAIL DECISIONS

All the examination questions are categorized by test plan area and level of difficulty. This is an important point to keep in mind when you consider how the computer makes a pass-or-fail decision because a pass-or-fail decision is not based on a percentage of correctly answered questions.

After the minimum number of questions have been answered (75 questions), the computer compares the test-taker's ability level to the standard required for passing. The standard required for passing is set based on the expert judgment of several individuals appointed by the NCSBN. If the test-taker is clearly above the passing standard, then the test-taker passes the examination. If the test-taker is clearly below the passing standard, then the test-taker fails the examination. If the computer is not able to determine clearly whether the test-taker has passed or failed because the test-taker's ability is close to the passing standard, then the computer continues asking questions. After each question, the computer determines the test-taker's ability and, when it becomes clear on which side of the passing standard the test-taker falls (above the standard or below the standard), the examination ends. If the test-taker is administered the maximum number of questions (265 questions), the computer will make a pass-or-fail decision by recomputing the test-taker's final ability level, based on every question answered, and comparing it with the passing standard. If the ability level is above the passing standard, the test-taker passes. If the ability level is not above the passing standard, the test-taker fails.

If the examination ends because you have run out of time, the computer may not have enough information to make a clear pass-or-fail decision. If this is the case, the computer will review the test-taker's performance during testing. If the test-taker's ability was consistently above the passing standard specifically on the last 60 questions, the test-taker passes. If the test-taker's ability falls to or below the passing standard, even once, the test-taker fails.

COMPLETING THE EXAMINATION

Once the examination has ended, you will complete a brief computer-delivered questionnaire about your testing experience. After you complete this questionnaire, you need to raise your hand to summon the test proctor. The test proctor will collect and inventory all note boards and then permit you to leave.

PROCESSING RESULTS

Every computerized examination is scored twice, once by the computer at the testing center and then again after the examination is transmitted to Pearson Professional Centers. No results are released at the test center. The board of nursing will mail your results to you about 1 month after you take the examination. You should not call Pearson Professional Centers, NCSBN, candidate services, or the state board of nursing for results. In some states, results can be obtained via the state Web site or via an NCSBN telephone results service. Information about obtaining NCLEX results by this method can be obtained on the NCSBN Web site under candidate services.

CANDIDATE PERFORMANCE REPORT

A candidate performance report is provided to a test-taker who failed the examination. This report provides the test-taker with information about her or his strengths and weaknesses in relation to the test plan and provides a guide for studying and retaking the examination. The test-taker should refer to the state board of nursing in the state in which licensure is sought for procedures regarding when the examination can be taken again.

INTERSTATE ENDORSEMENT

Because the NCLEX-RN examination is a national examination, you can apply to take the examination in any state. Once licensure is received, you can apply for interstate endorsement, which is obtaining another license in another state to practice nursing in that state. The procedures and requirements for interstate endorsement may vary from state to state, and these procedures can be obtained from the state board of nursing in the state in which endorsement is sought. You may also be allowed to practice nursing in another state if the state has enacted a nurse licensure compact. The state boards of nursing can be accessed via the NCSBN Web site at http://www.ncsbn.org.

NURSE LICENSURE COMPACT

It may be possible to hold one license from the state of residency and practice nursing in another state under the mutual recognition model of nursing licensure if the state has enacted a nurse licensure compact. To obtain information about the nurse licensure compact and the states that are part of this interstate compact, access the National Council of State Boards of Nursing Web site at http://www.ncsbn.org.

ADDITIONAL INFORMATION ABOUT THE EXAMINATION

Additional information regarding the NCLEX-RN examination can be obtained from the National Council of State Boards of Nursing, 111 East Wacker Drive, Suite 2900, Chicago, IL 60601. The telephone number for the testing service is (866) 293-9600. The Web site is http://www.ncsbn.org.

REFERENCES

Chernecky, C., & Berger, B. (2004). *Laboratory tests and diagnostic procedures* (4th ed.). Philadelphia: W.B. Saunders.

Elkin, M., Perry, A., & Potter, P. (2004) *Nursing interventions and clinical skills* (3rd ed.). St. Louis: Mosby.

Hockenberry, M., & Wilson, D. (2007). *Wong's nursing care of infants and children* (8th ed.). St. Louis: Mosby.

Hodgson, B., & Kizior, R. (2007). *Saunders nursing drug handbook* 2007. Philadelphia: W.B. Saunders.

Ignatavicius, D., & Workman, M. (2006). *Medical-surgical nursing: Critical thinking for collaborative care* (5th ed.). Philadelphia: W.B. Saunders.

Mosby. (2006). *Mosby's 2006 drug consult for nurses.* St. Louis: Mosby, p. 1140.

National Council of State Boards (Eds.). (2007). *2007 NCLEX-RN® detailed test plan.* Chicago: Author.

National Council of State Boards of Nursing. http://www.ncsbn.org.

Potter, P., & Perry, A. (2005) *Fundamentals of nursing* (6th ed.). St. Louis: Mosby.

Preparation for the NCLEX-RN®
Exam: Transitional Issues
for the Foreign-Educated Nurse

This chapter provides information regarding the certification processes that you will have to pursue to become a registered nurse in the United States. An important factor to consider as you pursue this process is that some requirements may vary from state to state. Therefore, as a first step in the process, you need to contact the board of nursing in the state in which you are planning to obtain licensure. You can obtain contact information for each state board of nursing through the National Council of State Boards of Nursing (NCSBN) Web site at http://www.ncsbn.org. Once you have accessed the NCSBN Web site, select the link titled "Boards of Nursing." Additionally, you can write to the NCSBN regarding the NCLEX exam. The address is 111 East Wacker Drive, Suite 2900, Chicago, IL 60601. The telephone number for the NCSBN is (312) 525-3600; the fax number is (312) 279-1032.

An additional step in the process of obtaining information about becoming a registered nurse in the U.S. is to access the NCSBN Web site at http://www.ncsbn.org and obtain information provided for international nurses in the NCLEX Web site link. The NCSBN provides information about some of the data that you will need to obtain as an international nurse seeking licensure as a registered nurse in the United States and about credentialing agencies.

This chapter provides information about the Commission on Graduates of Foreign Nursing Schools (CGFNS) credentialing program. The NCSBN Web site (http://www.ncsbn.org) can provide information about additional credentialing agencies. The credentialing agency needs to follow the standards identified by the professional credentialing association, such as the National Association of Credential Evaluation Services (NACES; http://www.naces.org). Therefore, it is important to obtain contact information about credentialing agencies from the NCSBN. Also, because

criteria can change, it is recommended that you access the NCSBN Web site to obtain the most up to date information about the credentialing process and obtaining a license to practice as a registered nurse in the United States.

VISASCREEN

United States immigration law requires certain health care professionals to successfully complete a screening program before receiving an occupational visa (Section 343 of the Illegal Immigration Reform and Immigration Responsibility Act of 1996). Therefore, you are required to obtain a VisaScreen certificate.

The CGFNS is an organization that offers this federal screening program. The International Commission on Health Care Professions, a division of the CGFNS, administers the VisaScreen. The VisaScreen components include an educational analysis, license verification, assessment of proficiency in the English language, and an examination that tests nursing knowledge. This chapter describes each of these components. Once the applicant successfully achieves each component, the applicant is presented with a VisaScreen certificate. You can obtain information related to the VisaScreen through the CGFNS Web site at http://www.cgfns.org.

Educational Analysis

The educational analysis component requires the following:

1. Applicant must present proof of completion of senior secondary school education, separate from any professional certification.
2. Applicant must present proof of completion from a government-approved professional health care program of at least 2 years in length.

3. Applicant must provide documentation that he or she has completed a minimum number of clock and/or credit hours in specific theoretical and clinical areas while in nursing school.

Licensure Verification

The applicant must present all current and past licensure for review.

Proficiency in the English Language

The applicant must submit proof of a passing score on an approved U.S. Department of Education and Health and Human Services English language proficiency examination. Box 2-1 lists English proficiency examinations and testing organizations. The credentialing agency will also provide you with information about English language proficiency examinations.

Testing Nursing Knowledge

An examination to test nursing knowledge includes the following:
1. The 1-day qualifying examination that is administered as part of the process for obtaining a CGFNS certificate tests nursing knowledge; therefore, a CGFNS certificate provides proof of adequate nursing knowledge. This qualifying examination is described in "Components of the CGFNS Certification Program."

BOX 2-1

English Language Proficiency Exam and Testing Organizations

Tests Administered by the Educational Testing Service (ETS) Worldwide
Test of English as a Foreign Language (TOEFL)
Test of English for International Communication (TOEIC)
Contact information:
Educational Testing Service (ETS)
P.O. Box 6151
Princeton, NJ 08541-6151
Telephone: (609) 771-7100
E mail: toefl@ets.org

International English Language Testing System (IELTS)*
Contact information:
International English Language Testing System
IELTS Administrator
Cambridge Examinations and IELTS International
100 East Corson Street, Suite 200
Pasadena, CA 91103
Telephone: (626) 564-2954
E mail: ielts@ceii.org
Web site: http://www.ielts.org

*Jointly managed by British Council and IELTS Australia.

---

2. A foreign-educated nurse who is licensed and practicing nursing in the United States also is required to obtain a VisaScreen and provide proof of adequate nursing knowledge; if the nurse does not have a CGFNS certificate, the nurse may be granted eligibility to take the NCLEX exam to provide this proof.

STATE REQUIREMENTS

Most states in the United States require that you receive certification from the CGFNS or another credentialing agency before you can be eligible to take the NCLEX exam. If the state in which you intend to obtain licensure does not require certification, it may require submission of some of the same documents that the CGFNS or other credentialing agency requires. Therefore, in addition to what the CGFNS or other credentialing agency requires, a state may require the following:
1. Proof of citizenship or lawful alien status
2. Official transcripts of educational credentials sent directly to the agency and board of nursing from the school of nursing
3. Validation of theoretical instruction and clinical practice in a variety of nursing areas, including but not limited to medical nursing, surgical nursing, pediatric nursing, maternity and newborn nursing, community and public health nursing, and mental health nursing. Validation of professional nursing course work may also be required.
4. Copy of nursing license and/or diploma
5. Proof of proficiency in the English language
6. Photographs of the applicant
7. Application fees

THE COMMISSION ON GRADUATES OF FOREIGN NURSING SCHOOLS

The CGFNS provides a certification program for nurses educated and licensed outside the United States.

The certificate program offered by the CGFNS is a requirement of most state boards of nursing, and the certificate may be required before you can take the NCLEX exam. The certificate program ensures that you are eligible and qualified to meet licensure and other practice requirements in the United States, and it also predicts your success on the NCLEX exam. This program also assists you in obtaining your VisaScreen certificate. You can obtain additional information relating to the CGFNS and its certification program through the CGFNS Web site at http://www.cgfns.org.

Eligibility for the CGFNS Certification Program

The CGFNS Certification Program is designed for nurses educated outside the United States who hold an initial and current registration or licensure as a first-level general registered nurse. According to the CGFNS, a first-level nurse is called a registered nurse or professional nurse in most countries. As a general nurse, the foreign-educated nurse must have obtained theoretical instruction and clinical practice in a variety of nursing areas. These nursing areas include but are not limited to medical nursing, surgical nursing, pediatric nursing, maternity and newborn nursing, community public health nursing, and mental health nursing. If the nurse educated outside the United States does not meet these requirements, the nurse is not eligible for the certification program.

Components of the CGFNS Certification Program

The CGFNS Certification Program contains three parts, and you must complete all parts successfully to be awarded a CGFNS Certificate. The three parts include a credentials review, a 1-day qualifying examination that tests nursing knowledge, and an English language proficiency examination. You can take the qualifying and English language proficiency examinations at various locations throughout the world. This provides the applicant the opportunity to obtain the CGFNS Certificate before coming to the United States or traveling to other countries to take the NCLEX exam. These three parts of the certificate program are described next.

Credentials Review

The CGFNS requires validation of education and a licensing history of the applicant to ensure that the applicant has the appropriate credentials to seek certification. The CGFNS must receive transcripts and validation documents from the nursing program and licensing agency. The CGFNS does not accept transcripts and validation documents from the applicant. The specific credentialing requirements are similar to those needed for the VisaScreen certificate and include the following:

1. Completion of a senior secondary school education
2. Graduation from a government-approved nursing program of at least 2 years in length
3. Acquisition of theoretical instruction and clinical practice in the areas of medical nursing, surgical nursing, pediatric nursing, maternity and newborn nursing, community public health nursing, and mental health nursing
4. Possession of a full and unrestricted license or registration to practice as a first-level general nurse in the country where he or she completed her or his general nursing education
5. Possession of a current license or registration as a first-level general nurse

Qualifying Examination

The qualifying examination tests the applicant's knowledge in nursing in the areas of adult health, pediatrics, maternity and newborn, mental health, and community public health. The examination is designed to ensure that the applicant has the knowledge to provide nursing care to various client groups at the same level as recent U.S. nursing graduates.

English Language Proficiency Examination

The applicant must take and pass an English language proficiency examination. You can take the examination before or after the qualifying examination. The English language proficiency examination needs to be taken from a testing organization approved by the CGFNS, and the applicant must apply directly to the testing organization to take the examination. The scores must be sent directly to the CGFNS from the testing organization. The CGFNS will not accept test scores from the applicant. Box 2-1 lists the types of English proficiency examinations, approved testing organizations, and their contact information. The CGFNS or other credentialing agency will provide you with current information about these approved testing organizations.

The CGFNS or other credentialing agency may identify certain applicants as exempt from the English language proficiency requirement. For an applicant to be exempt, the applicant must meet all the following criteria: native language is English; country of nursing education was Australia, Canada (except Quebec), New Zealand, the United Kingdom, or Trinidad and Tobago; and the language of instruction and language of textbooks was English. Because these criteria may change, it is recommended that you obtain current information from the credentialing agency.

Once you successfully have met each of the three required components of the CGFNS Certification Program, the CGFNS will issue a certificate of completion. Unless the state in which you intend to obtain licensure indicates additional requirements, and if you have received your VisaScreen certificate, you will be eligible to take the NCLEX exam.

REGISTERING TO TAKE THE NCLEX® EXAM

If you are planning to take the examination in the United States, the initial step in the registration process is to submit an application to the state board of nursing in the state in which you intend to obtain licensure. You need to obtain information from the board of nursing regarding the specific registration process because the process may vary from state to state. In most states, you may register for the examination through the Internet, by mail, or by telephone. The NCLEX candidate Web site is http://www.vue.com/nclex. You must follow the registration instructions and complete the registration forms precisely and accurately. Registration forms not properly completed, or not accompanied by the proper fees in the required method of payment, will be returned to you and will delay testing. You must pay a fee for taking the examination, and you also may have to pay additional fees to the board of nursing in the state in which you are applying. You will be sent a confirmation indicating that your registration was received. If you do not receive a confirmation within 4 weeks of submitting your registration, you should contact the candidate services. You can obtain information regarding candidate services at the candidate Web site at http://www.vue.com/nclex.

Once the board of nursing in the state in which you request licensure has verified your eligibility to take the examination, the board will process your registration form and send you an Authorization to Test form. You cannot make an appointment until the board of nursing declares eligibility and you receive an Authorization to Test form. The examination will take place at a Pearson Professional Center, and you can make an appointment through the Internet or by telephone. You can schedule an appointment at any Pearson Professional Center. You do not have to take the examination in the same state in which you are seeking licensure. A confirmation of your appointment will be sent to you. For additional information regarding the NCLEX exam and testing procedures, refer to Chapter 1. You can also obtain information about the registration process and testing procedures from the NCSBN Web site at http://www.ncsbn.org.

NCLEX examination testing abroad is also available in some countries. Current international testing sites are Australia, Canada, England, Germany, Hong Kong, India, Japan, Mexico, Puerto Rico, South Korea, and Taiwan. These testing sites provide the nurse who is interested in becoming a licensed nurse in the United States an opportunity to pass the NCLEX examination before traveling to the United States. It is recommended that you visit the NCLEX Web site for current information about international testing sites.

PREPARING TO TAKE THE NCLEX® EXAM

The challenge that is presented to you is one that requires patience and endurance. The positive result of your endeavor certainly will reward you professionally and give you the personal satisfaction of knowing that you have become part of a family of highly skilled professionals, registered nurses. You have successfully completed the requirements to become eligible to take the NCLEX exam and now you have one more important goal to achieve: to pass the exam.

I highly recommend adequate preparation for the NCLEX examination, because the examination is difficult. An important step that you have taken in preparing is that you are using this book, *Saunders Comprehensive Review for the NCLEX-RN® Examination*. Once you have reviewed the content and answered the practice questions, the next step in your journey to success is to use the companion book, *Saunders Q&A Review for the NCLEX-RN® Examination*; this provides you with more than 5000 practice questions based on the NCLEX-RN examination test plan framework, with a specific focus on Client Needs and Integrated Processes. Additional resources to prepare you for this examination are the *Saunders Strategies for Success for the NCLEX-RN® Examination*, *Saunders Strategies for Alternate Item Formats on the NCLEX-RN® Examination*, and the *Saunders Online Review Course for the NCLEX-RN® Examination*. These products are described below. All these products can be obtained online by visiting http://www.elsevierhealth.com or by calling 800-426-4545.

The *Saunders Strategies for Success for the NCLEX-RN® Examination* focuses on the test-taking strategies that will help prepare you for the NCLEX-RN examination. The chapters describe all the test-taking strategies and include several sample questions that illustrate how to use the test-taking strategy. There are a total of 500 practice questions that accompany this book. All the practice questions are reflective of the framework and content identified in the current NCLEX-RN test plan and include multiple-choice and alternate item format questions.

The *Saunders Strategies for Alternate Item Formats on the NCLEX-RN® Examination* differs from all of the other products in that it contains *only* alternate item format questions. It provides you with all the information that you will need about all types of alternate item format questions that may appear on the NCLEX-RN examination. It contains 265 practice alternate item format questions and 15 heart and lung sounds questions.

The *Saunders Online Review Course for the NCLEX-RN® Examination* addresses all areas of the test plan identified by the National Council of State Boards of Nursing. The course contains a pretest that provides feedback regarding your strengths and weaknesses and generates an individualized study schedule in a calendar format. Content review includes practice questions and case studies, figures and illustrations, a glossary, and animations and videos. A cumulative examination and a computer adaptive test (CAT) are also key components of the online review course. The types of practice questions in this course include multiple choice, fill in the blank, multiple response, those that require you to prioritize (ordered response), and questions containing figures (hot spots) that may require you to use the computer mouse to answer.

Finally, never lose sight of your goal. Patience and dedication will contribute significantly to your achieving the status of registered nurse. Remember, success is climbing a mountain, facing the challenge of obstacles, and reaching the top of the mountain. I wish you the best success in your journey and beginning your career as a registered nurse in the United States of America.

REFERENCES

Commission on Graduates of Foreign Nursing Schools. http://www.cgfns.org.
Educational Testing Service, Princeton, NJ. http://www.ets.org/toefl.
International English Language Testing System. http://www.ielts.org.
National Council of State Boards of Nursing. http://www.ncsbn.org.

Pathways to Success

▲ THE PYRAMID TO SUCCESS

Preparing to take the NCLEX-RN examination can produce a great deal of anxiety. You may be thinking that the NCLEX-RN is the most important examination you will ever have to take, and that it reflects the culmination of everything that you have worked so hard for. NCLEX-RN is an important examination because receiving that nursing license means that you can begin your career as a registered nurse. Your success on the NCLEX-RN involves getting rid of all your thoughts that allow this examination to appear overwhelming and intimidating. Such thoughts will take complete control over your destiny. A positive attitude, a structured plan for preparation, and maintaining control in your pathway to success will ensure achievement in reaching the peak of the Pyramid to Success (Fig. 3-1).

PATHWAYS TO SUCCESS (Box 3-1)

The Foundation

The foundation of pathways to success begins with a positive attitude, the belief that you will achieve success, and developing control. It also includes developing a list of your personal short- and long-term goals and a plan for preparation. A positive attitude, belief in yourself, control, and a list of personal goals will lead you to becoming a registered nurse. Without these components, your pathway to success leads to nowhere and has no endpoint. You will expend energy and valuable time in your journey, lack control over where you are heading, and experience exhaustion without any accomplishment. Therefore, it is imperative that you take the time to develop that positive attitude and establish your short- and long-term goals.

Where do you start? To begin this process, find a location that offers solitude. Sit or lie in a comfortable position, close your eyes, relax, inhale deeply, hold your

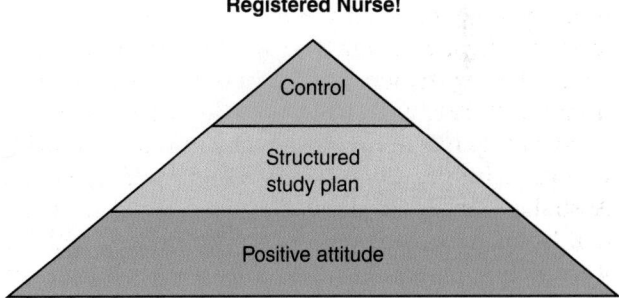

FIG. 3-1 The Pyramid to Success.

breath to a count of four, exhale slowly and, again, relax. Repeat this breathing exercise several times until you begin to feel relaxed, free from anxiety, and in control of your destiny. Allow your mind to become void of all the mind chatter; now you are in control and your mind can see for miles. Your highway of life has a multitude of destinations to which you may travel. Next, reflect on all that you have accomplished and the path that brought you to where you are today. Keep a journal of your reflections as you plan the order of your journey to the Pyramid to Success.

The List

It is time to create "The List." "The List" is your set of short- and long-term goals. At this time, you may or may not have a scheduled date for taking the NCLEX-RN examination. Therefore, begin by developing the goals that you wish to accomplish today, tomorrow, over the next month, and in the future. Allow yourself the opportunity to list all that is flowing from your mind. Write your goals in your personal journal. When "The List" is complete, it is time to put it away for 2 or 3 days. After 2 or 3 days, retrieve and review "The List"

BOX 3-1
Pathways to Success

THE FOUNDATION
Maintaining a positive attitude
Thinking about short- and long-term realistic goals
Preparing a plan for preparation
Maintaining control

THE LIST
Journaling short- and long-term realistic goals

THE PLAN FOR PREPARATION
Developing a study plan and schedule
Deciding on the place to study
Balancing personal and work obligations with the study schedule
Sharing the study schedule and personal needs with others
Implementing the study plan

POSITIVE PAMPERING
Planning time for exercise and fun activities
Establishing healthy eating habits
Including activities in the schedule that provide positive mental stimulation

FINAL PREPARATION
Reviewing goals
Identifying goals achieved
Remaining focused to complete the plan of study
Writing down the date and time of the examination and posting it next to your name with the letters R.N. following, and the word "yes!"
Planning a test drive to the testing center
Relaxing activities on the day before the examination

THE DAY OF THE EXAMINATION
Grooming yourself for success
Eating a healthy and nutritious breakfast
Maintaining a confident and positive attitude
Maintaining control
Meeting the challenges of the day
Reaching the peak of the Pyramid to Success

BOX 3-2
Developing a Plan for Study

Do I work better alone or in a group study environment?
If I work best in a group, does the group consist of one, two, or more study partners?
Who are these study partners?
How long should my study sessions last?
Does the time of day that I study make a difference for me?
Do I retain more if I study in the morning?
How does my work schedule affect my study pattern?
How do I balance my family obligations with my need to study?
Do I have a comfortable study area at home or do I need to find another environment that is conducive to my study needs?

adhere to it. This consistency will provide advantages to you and to those supporting you. A daily schedule allows you to plan your content areas for study more carefully. Stick to your plan of study. Adherence to the plan helps you develop a rhythm that can only enhance your retention and positive momentum. Those who are supporting you will share this rhythm and will be able to schedule their activities and lives better when you are consistent with your study schedule. You are moving forward, and you are in control.

The length of the study session will depend on you and your ability to focus and concentrate. What you need to think about is quality rather than quantity when you are deciding on a realistic amount of time for each session. Plan to schedule, at the very least, 2 hours of quality time daily. If you can spend more than 2 hours, then by all means do so.

You may be asking yourself, "What do you mean by quality time?" Quality time means spending uninterrupted quiet time at your study session. This may mean that you will have to isolate yourself for these study sessions. Think again about what has worked for you during nursing school when you studied for examinations; select a study place now that has worked for you in the past. If you have a special study room at home that you have always used, then plan your study sessions in that special room. If you have always studied at a library, then plan your study sessions at the library. If you plan to study at home, make the time spent studying uninterrupted and quiet. Sometimes, it is difficult to balance your study time with your family obligations and possibly a work schedule but, if you can, plan your study time when you know that you will be at home alone. Try to eliminate anything that may be distracting during your study time. For example, unplug your telephone or shut off your cell phone so that you will not be disturbed. If you have small children, plan your study time during their nap time or during their school hours.

and begin the process of planning to prepare for the NCLEX-RN examination.

The Plan for Preparation

Now that you have "The List" in order, look at the goals that relate to studying for the licensing exam. The first task is to decide what study pattern works best for you. Think about what has worked most successfully for you in the past. There are questions that must be addressed to develop your plan for study, identified in Box 3-2.

The plan must include a schedule. Use a calendar to plan and document the times and nursing content areas for your study sessions. Establish a realistic schedule that includes your daily, weekly, and future goals, and

"The Plan" must include how you will manage your study needs and the demands of your work, family, and friends. Take time to think about how you will balance your everyday commitments with your plan for study. Your family and friends are key players in your life and are going to become part of your Pyramid to Success. After you have established your study needs, communicate your needs and the importance of your study plan in achieving your goal of becoming a registered nurse to your family and friends.

A difficult part of the plan may be how to deal with those family members and friends who choose not to participate in your plan for success. What if an individual chooses not to be part of your plan? For example, what do you do if a friend asks you to go to a movie and it is your scheduled study time? Your friend may say, "Come on. Take some time off. You have plenty of time to study. Study later when we get back!" Then you are faced with a decision. You must weigh all the factors carefully. You must keep your goals in mind and remember that your need for positive momentum is critical. Your decision may not be an easy one, but it must be one that will help ensure that your goal of becoming a registered nurse is achieved. Remember, a positive momentum and meeting your goals is most important.

POSITIVE PAMPERING

What is positive pampering? This means that you must continue to care for yourself holistically. Positive momentum can be maintained only if you are properly balanced. Proper exercise, diet, and positive mental stimulation are critical to achieving your goal of becoming a registered nurse. Just as you have developed a schedule for study, you should have a schedule that includes some fun and some form of physical activity. It is your choice—aerobics, running, walking, weight lifting, bowling, or whatever makes you feel good about yourself. Time spent away from the hard study schedule and devoted to some form of fun and physical exercise pays you back 100-fold. You will feel alive and more energetic with a schedule that includes these activities.

Establish healthy eating habits. Stay away from fatty foods because they will slow you down. Eat lighter meals and eat more frequently. Include complex carbohydrates in your diet for energy, and be careful not to include too much caffeine in your daily diet. Continue to feel good about yourself, because you are in control.

Take the time to pamper yourself with activities that make you feel even better about who you are. Make dinner reservations at your favorite restaurant with someone who is special and is supporting your goal to become a registered nurse. Take walks in a place that has a particular tranquility that enables you to reflect on the positive momentum that you have achieved and maintained. Whatever it is, wherever it takes you, allow yourself the time to do some positive pampering.

FINAL PREPARATION

You have established the foundation of your Pyramid to Success. You have developed your list of goals and your study plan and have maintained your positive momentum. You are moving forward, and you are in control. When you receive your date and time for the NCLEX-RN examination, you may immediately think, "I am not ready!" Stop! Reflect on all that you have achieved. Think about your goal achievement and the organization of the positive life momentum with which you have surrounded yourself. Think about all those who love and support your effort to become a registered nurse. Believe that the challenge that awaits you is one that you have successfully prepared for and will lead you to your goal, becoming a registered nurse.

Take a deep breath and organize the remaining days so that they support your educational and personal needs. Support your positive momentum with a visual technique. Write your name in large letters, and write the letters *R.N.* after it. Post one or more of these visual reinforcements in areas that you frequent. This form of visual motivational technique works for many preparing for this examination.

Through all that you have accomplished so far, it is imperative that you not fall into the trap of expecting too much of yourself. The idea of perfection must not drive you to a point that causes your positive momentum to hesitate. You must believe in who you are, as you are, and stay focused on your goal. Allow yourself the opportunity to continue to carry out your plan in a manner that is most conducive to who you are, not someone else. The date and time are at hand. Write down the date and time, and underneath write the word "yes." Post this next to your name, plus R.N.

You must ensure that you have command over how to get to the testing center. A test run is a must. Time the drive, and allow for road construction or whatever might occur to slow traffic down. On the test run, when you arrive at the test facility, you may want to walk into it. Go on in and become familiar with the lobby and the surroundings. This may help alleviate some of the peripheral nervousness associated with entering an unknown building. Remember, you must do whatever it takes to keep yourself in control. If familiarizing yourself with the facility will help you maintain positive momentum, by all means be sure to do so. Who is in control? You are!

It is time to check your study plan and make the necessary adjustments now that a firm date and time are set. Adjust your review so that it flows to your needs and that your study plan ends 2 days before the examination. Remember, the mind is like a muscle. If it is overworked, it has no strength or stamina. Your strategy is to rest the body and mind on the day before the examination. Your strategy is to stay in control and allow yourself the opportunity to be absolutely fresh and attentive on the day of the examination. This will help you control the nervousness that is natural, achieve the clear thought processes required, and feel confident that you have done all that is necessary to prepare and conquer this challenge. The day before the examination is to be one of pleasure. Treat yourself to what you enjoy the most.

Relax! You have prepared yourself well for the challenge of tomorrow. Allow yourself a good night's sleep, and wake up on the day of the examination knowing that you are absolutely ready to succeed. Look at your name with R.N. after it and the word "yes!"

THE DAY OF THE EXAMINATION (Box 3-3)

Wake up believing in yourself and that all you have accomplished is about to propel you to the professional level of registered nurse. Allow yourself plenty of time, eat a nutritious breakfast, and groom yourself for success. You are ready to meet the challenges of the day and overcome any obstacle that may face you. Today will soon be history, and tomorrow will bring you the enve-

---

BOX 3-3

Day of the Examination

Breathe: Inhale deeply, hold your breath to a count of four, exhale slowly.
Believe: Have positive thoughts today and always about your achievements.
Control: You are in command.
Believe: This is your day.
Visualize: Registered Nurse with your name.

---

lope on which you read your name with the words "Registered Nurse" after it.

Be proud and confident of your achievements. You have worked hard to achieve your goal of becoming a registered nurse. If you believe in yourself and your goals, no one person or obstacle can move you off the pathway that leads to success, to the peak of the Pyramid!

Congratulations and I wish you the very best in your career as a registered nurse.

The NCLEX-RN® Examination: From a Student's Perspective

We nursing students are already test experts! We have taken so many exams in so many formats that one more is just further evidence that we have been well prepared. This was the cornerstone of my studying technique for the NCLEX-RN. I have studied for the SAT, GRE, and countless course exams and have done well thus far, so I decided that I would just stick with what worked for me.

Preparations for past exams usually started with reading over notes and textbooks to review and assess what information was comfortable and what needed work. Then, I went over questions and took notes on the items I could not answer correctly. Finally, I made note cards of the difficult stuff and carried them with me to the gym, or the coffee shop, or the line at the bank (seriously).

This was just how I prepared for the NCLEX-RN exam as well. I took a course though my school that reviewed content and test-taking techniques, and then I used an NCLEX-RN study book to work countless test questions. Finally, I kept premade NCLEX study cards with me so I could review even more questions if I had a few minutes. After each example test, I would look to the answer key for the questions I got wrong and go through the rationale to find out how I could answer that type of question correctly when it really counted.

Timing was one concern of mine for which I received differing advice. Some people recommended a month or more for studying before the exam, and others claimed that if I waited too long I would forget what I had learned. How did I resolve this issue? I decided to go back to my original plan—rely on my past successes. I usually gave myself 2 weeks for studying before an exam, so I scheduled the NCLEX-RN for 2 weeks after the review class.

My original schedule was complicated by the winter holidays, which threw a wrench in the works! I had set a three test-a-day plan, but could not possibly get that done with all my family events and obligations. I freaked out for a moment; I was definitely going to fail now! But a few calming friends and cups of tea later, I realized that life always happens regardless of our well-intentioned plans. There were always end-of-semester parties and I was packing to move during final exams. Sticking to the plan was less important than getting in quality studying when I could.

In the end, I completed about 75% of the studying that I had intended to do, and spent the day before the exam relaxing and eating well. As with my studying, I followed my regular routine for eating and sleeping before the NCLEX-RN. Some people recommended carb loading or superhydrating, but I do not usually do that, so I figured it could mess me up for the big day. I went to bed at my usual time of midnight, ate my usual breakfast of cereal and coffee, and wore my usual clothes (that I set out the night before, just to be safe).

At the exam facility, I actually met a few of my classmates! We shared how our nerves were feeling and encouraged each other. After all, we had come through a full nursing curriculum and study course in preparation for that day. If there is anything I could recommend to my fellow test-takers for the NCLEX-RN, it is to take your time reading the questions and answer options, as well as question type. It is not a race, and you only get to see each item once. There is no going back to reread or change your answer, so work on each question carefully, and then forget about it! That is the beauty of a computer-based test. You really get to give everything to each item, ensuring that you do your best.

Some people used the earplugs and some did not. It was so quiet in the testing room that you could hear a pin drop, so I did not feel them necessary. The temperature was comfortable, but I was glad I had worn a couple of layers to adjust if necessary. One mistake I did make was forgetting to use the bathroom before sitting down to take the test. I definitely suggest making sure you are comfortable before entering the testing area.

However, as I have emphasized throughout my journey, rely on your past success and follow what makes you feel comfortable. You are the expert on what works best for you. Be confident, be patient, be yourself, and it will all come together to become the RN you were meant to be!

Test-Taking Strategies

A. Pyramid Points
   1. Avoid asking yourself, "Well, what if.....?" because this will lead you right into the "forbidden" area, reading into the question.
   2. Focus only on the information in the question, read every word, and make a decision about what the question is asking.
   3. Look for the strategic words in the question, such as *immediate, initial, first, priority, side effect,* or *toxic effect;* strategic words make a difference with regard to what the question is asking about.
   4. In multiple-choice questions, multiple response questions, or questions that require you to number in order of priority, read every choice or option presented before selecting answers.
   5. Always use the process of elimination when choices or options are presented; once you have eliminated options, reread the question before selecting your final choice(s).
   6. With questions that require you to fill in the blank, focus on the information in the question and determine what the question is asking; if the question requires you to calculate a medication dose, an intravenous flow rate, or intake and output amounts, recheck your work in calculating and always use the on-screen calculator to verify the answer.
   7. Remember, avoid asking yourself the "forbidden" words, "Well, what if.....?", when deciding on an answer to a question.

BOX 5-1
Pyramid to Success

Avoid asking yourself, "Well, what if.....?" because this will lead you right into reading into the question.

Focus only on the information in the question, read every word, and make a decision regarding what the question is asking.

Look for the strategic words in the question; strategic words make a difference with regard to what the question is asking about.

Always use the process of elimination when choices or options are presented; once you have eliminated options, reread the question before selecting your final choice or choices.

Determine if the question is a positive or negative event query.

Use all your nursing knowledge, your clinical experiences, and your test-taking skills and strategies to answer the question.

B. The parts of a question (Box 5-3)
   1. The parts of a question include the event, which is a client or clinical situation, the event query, and the options or answers. A fill-in-the-blank question will not contain options and some figure or illustration (hot spot) questions may or may not contain options.
   2. The event provides you with the content about the client or clinical situation that you need to think about when answering the question.
   3. The event query asks something specific about the content of the event.
   4. The options are all the answers provided with the question.

Practice Question: Avoiding the "What if...."
Syndrome and Reading into the Question

A nurse is caring for a hospitalized client with a diagnosis of congestive heart failure who suddenly complains of shortness of breath and dyspnea. The nurse takes which *immediate* action?
1. Calls the physician
2. Administers oxygen to the client
3. Elevates the head of the client's bed
4. Prepares to administer furosemide (Lasix)
Answer: 3
Test-Taking Strategy: Now, you may immediately think, the client has developed pulmonary edema, a complication of congestive heart failure, and needs a diuretic. Although pulmonary edema is a complication of congestive heart failure, there is no information in the question that indicates the presence of pulmonary edema. The question simply states that the client suddenly complains of shortness of breath and dyspnea. Read the question carefully. Note the strategic word *immediate* and focus on the subject, the client's complaints. Although the physician may need to be notified, this is not the immediate action. A physician's order is needed to administer oxygen. Furosemide is a diuretic and may or may not be prescribed for the client. Because there is no information in the question that indicates the presence of pulmonary edema, option 3 is correct. The question is asking you for a nursing action, so that's what you need to look for as you eliminate the incorrect options. Use nursing knowledge and test-taking strategies to assist in answering the question.

Reference: Ignatavicius, D., & Workman, M. (2006). *Medical-surgical nursing: Critical thinking for collaborative care* (5th ed., p. 755). Philadelphia: W.B. Saunders.

Multiple-Choice Question: Event, Event Query, and Options

Event: A nurse caring for a client with myocardial infarction is helping the client fill out the diet menu request form.
Event Query: The nurse recommends that the client select which of the following beverages from the menu?
Options:
1. Tea
2. Cola
3. Coffee
4. Fruit juice
Answer: 4
Test-Taking Strategy: Focus on the client's diagnosis and recall that caffeine needs to be eliminated from the diet because of its stimulating effects. Also note that options 1, 2, and 3 are comparative or alike in that they are all products that contain caffeine. This will direct you to the correct option.

Reference: Black, J., & Hawks, J. (2005). *Medical-surgical nursing: Clinical management for positive outcomes* (7th ed., p. 1706). Philadelphia: W.B. Saunders.

Common Strategic Words

Best
Early or late
First
Immediately
Initial
Most appropriate or least appropriate
Most likely or least likely

5. In a multiple-choice question, there will be four options and you must select one; read every option carefully and think about the event and the event query as you use the process of elimination.
6. In a multiple-response question, there will be several options and you must select all options that apply to the event in the question; visualize the event, and use your nursing knowledge and your clinical experiences to answer the question.
7. In a prioritizing (ordered response) question, you will be required to list in order of priority certain nursing interventions or other data; visualize the event, and use your nursing knowledge and clinical experiences to answer the question.
8. A chart or exhibit question will most likely contain options; read the question carefully and all of the information in the chart or exhibit before selecting an answer.

III. **THE STRATEGIC WORDS** (Boxes 5-4 and 5-5)
A. Strategic words focus your attention on a critical point to consider when answering the question and will assist you in eliminating the incorrect options.
B. Some strategic words may indicate that all the options are correct, and that it will be necessary to prioritize to select the correct option (Box 5-6).
C. As you read the question, look for the strategic words; strategic words make a difference with regard to the focus of the question.

IV. **THE SUBJECT OF THE QUESTION** (Box 5-7)
A. The subject of the question is the specific topic that the question is asking about.
B. Identifying the subject of the question will assist in eliminating the incorrect options and direct you to selecting the correct option.

V. **POSITIVE AND NEGATIVE EVENT QUERIES** (Boxes 5-8 and 5-9)
A. A positive event query uses strategic words that ask you to select an option that is correct; for example, the event query may read, "Which statement by a

Practice Question: Strategic Words

A nurse is caring for a client who just returned from the recovery room after undergoing abdominal surgery. The nurse monitors the client for which *early* sign of hypovolemic shock?
1. Lethargy
2. Increased pulse rate
3. Increased depth of respiration
4. Decreased deep tendon reflexes
   Answer: 2

Test-Taking Strategy: Note the strategic word *early*. Focusing on this strategic word and recalling that the earliest clinical signs of hypovolemic shock are cardiovascular changes will direct you to the correct option. Although lethargy, increased depth of respirations, and decreased or absent deep tendon reflexes occur in hypovolemic shock, these are not early signs. Rather, they occur as the shock progresses. Remember to look for strategic words.

Reference: Ignatavicius, D., & Workman, M. (2006). *Medical-surgical nursing: Critical thinking for collaborative care* (5th ed., p. 825). Philadelphia: W.B. Saunders.

BOX 5-6
Common Strategic Words That Indicate the Need to Prioritize

Best
Essential
First
Highest priority
Immediate
Initial
Most appropriate or least appropriate
Most important
Most likely or least likely
Next
Primary
Vital

client *indicates an understanding* of the side effects of the prescribed medication?"
B. A negative event query uses strategic words that ask you to select an option that is an incorrect item or statement; for example, the event query may read, "Which statement by a client *indicates a need for further teaching* about the side effects of the prescribed medication?"

VI. QUESTIONS THAT REQUIRE PRIORITIZING
A. Questions in the examination may require you to use the skill of prioritizing nursing actions.
B. Look for the strategic words in the question that indicate the need to prioritize (see Box 5-6).
C. Remember, when a question requires prioritization, all options may be correct and you need to determine the correct order of action.

BOX 5-7
The Subject of the Question

A client with glaucoma is receiving acetazolamide (Diamox). The nurse understands that the purpose of this medication for this client is which of the following?
1. To prevent hypertension
2. To prevent hyperthermia
3. To decrease intraocular pressure
4. To maintain an adequate blood pressure for cerebral perfusion
   Answer: 3

Test-Taking Strategy: Focus on the subject, the purpose of the medication for a client with glaucoma. Use your nursing knowledge, clinical experiences, and test-taking skills and strategies to answer the question. Recalling that acetazolamide is a carbonic anhydrase inhibitor, and is used in the client with glaucoma to decrease the formation of aqueous humor, will direct you to the correct option. The other options are not actions of this medication. Also, note the relationship between the client's diagnosis and the correct option.

Reference: Hodgson, B., & Kizior, R. (2007). *Saunders nursing drug handbook 2007* (p. 14). Philadelphia: W.B. Saunders.

BOX 5-8
Practice Question: Positive Event Query

A client with suspected meningitis is being scheduled for diagnostic tests. The nurse anticipates that which diagnostic test will *most likely* be prescribed to *confirm* the diagnosis?
1. Lumbar puncture
2. Electromyography
3. Serum electrolytes
4. White blood cell count
   Answer: 1

Test-Taking Strategy: This question identifies an example of a positive event query. Note the strategic words *most likely* and *confirm*. Focus on the diagnosis presented in the question and the associated pathophysiology to assist in directing you to option 1. Remember, meningitis is an acute or chronic inflammation of the meninges and the cerebrospinal fluid. The confirming diagnostic test used in meningitis is the lumbar puncture. A white blood cell count and serum electrolyte test may also be performed. Electromyography is not a confirming diagnostic test. Remember that positive event queries ask you to select an option that is a correct item or statement.

Reference: Ignatavicius, D., & Workman, M. (2006). *Medical-surgical nursing: Critical thinking for collaborative care* (5th ed., p. 956). Philadelphia: W.B. Saunders.

D. Strategies to use to prioritize include the ABCs (airway, breathing, and circulation), Maslow's Hierarchy of Needs theory, and the steps of the nursing process.
E. The ABCs (Box 5-10)
   1. Use the ABCs—airway, breathing, and circulation—when selecting an answer or determining the order of priority.

BOX 5-9

Practice Question: Negative Event Query

A nurse has reinforced discharge instructions to a client who has undergone a right mastectomy with axillary lymph node dissection. Which statement by the client indicates a *need for further instruction* regarding home care measures?
1. "It is all right to use a straight razor to shave under my arms."
2. "I need to be sure that I do not have blood pressures or blood drawn from my right arm."
3. "I should inform all of my other health care providers that I have had this surgical procedure."
4. "I need to be sure to wear thick mitt hand covers or use thick pot holders when I am cooking and touching hot pans."

Answer: 1

Test-Taking Strategy: This question identifies an example of a negative event query question. Note the strategic words *need for further instruction*. These strategic words indicate that you need to select an option that identifies an incorrect client statement. Recalling that edema and infection are the concerns with this client and that the client needs to be instructed in the measures that will avoid trauma to the affected arm will direct you to the correct option.

Reference: Lewis, S., Heitkemper, M., Dirksen, S., Graber-O'Brien, P. & Bucher, L. (2007). *Medical-surgical nursing: Assessment and management of clinical problems* (7th ed., pp. 1359-1360). St. Louis: Mosby.

BOX 5-10

Practice Question: Use of the ABCs

The client with a diagnosis of cancer is receiving morphine sulfate for pain. When preparing the plan of care for the client, the nurse includes which priority action?
1. Monitor stools.
2. Encourage fluid intake.
3. Monitor the urine output.
4. Encourage the client to cough and deep-breathe.

Answer: 4

Test-Taking Strategy: Use the ABCs—airway, breathing, and circulation—as a guide to direct you to the correct option. Recall that morphine sulfate suppresses the cough reflex and the respiratory reflex. Although options 1, 2, and 3 are components of the plan of care, the correct option addresses airway. Remember, use the ABCs, airway, breathing, and circulation, to prioritize.

Reference: Hodgson, B., & Kizior, R. (2007). *Saunders nursing drug handbook 2007* (p. 797). Philadelphia: W.B. Saunders.

2. Remember the order of priority—airway, breathing, and circulation.
3. Airway is always the first priority!
F. Maslow's Hierarchy of Needs theory (Box 5-11; Fig. 5-1)
1. According to Maslow's Hierarchy of Needs theory, physiological needs are the priority, followed by safety and security needs, love and be-

BOX 5-11

Practice Question: Maslow's Hierarchy of Needs Theory

A nurse caring for a client experiencing dystocia reviews the client's plan of care and determines that which intervention is the *highest priority*?
1. Providing emotional support to the client
2. Explaining to family members about what is happening to the client
3. Monitoring for changes in the physical condition of the mother and fetus
4. Reinforcing breathing techniques learned in childbirth preparatory classes

Answer: 3

Test-Taking Strategy: All the options are correct and would be implemented during the care of this client. However, note the strategic words *highest priority* and use Maslow's Hierarchy of Needs theory to prioritize, remembering that physiological needs come first. Using this guideline will direct you to option 3. Also, note that option 3 is the only option that addresses both the mother and fetus.

Reference: Lowdermilk, D., & Perry, S. (2006). *Maternity nursing* (7th ed., pp. 782, 790). St. Louis: Mosby.

longing needs, self-esteem needs and, finally, self-actualization needs; therefore, select the option or determine the order of priority by addressing physiological needs first.
2. When a physiological need is not addressed in the question or noted in one of the options, continue to use Maslow's Hierarchy of Needs theory as a guide and look for the option that addresses safety.
G. Steps of the nursing process
1. Use the steps of the nursing process to prioritize.
2. The steps include assessment, analysis, planning, implementation, and evaluation and are followed in this order.
3. Assessment
   a. Assessment questions address the process of gathering subjective and objective data relative to the client, confirming that data, and communicating and documenting the data.
   b. Remember that assessment is the first step in the nursing process.
   c. When you are asked to select your first, immediate, or initial nursing action, follow the steps of the nursing process to prioritize when selecting the correct option.
   d. Look for strategic words in the options that reflect assessment (Box 5-12).
   e. If an option contains the concept of assessment or the collection of client data, the best choice is to select that option (Box 5-13).
   f. If an assessment action is not one of the options, follow the steps of the nursing process

Nursing Priorities from Maslow's Hierarchy

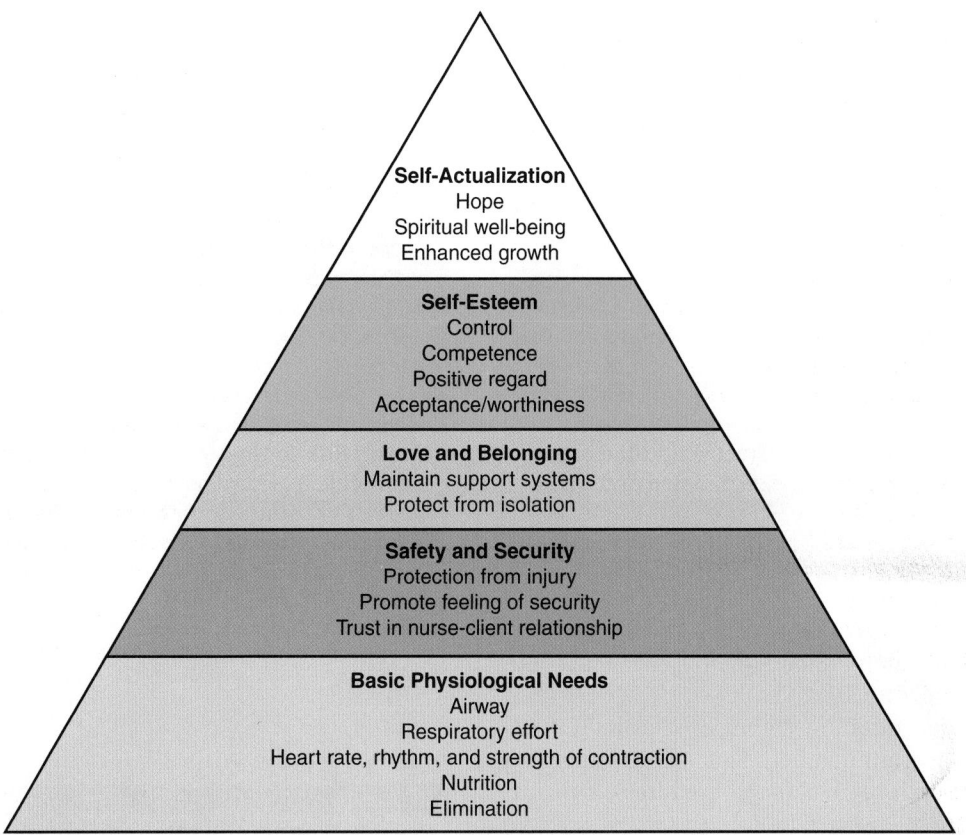

Self-Actualization
Hope
Spiritual well-being
Enhanced growth

Self-Esteem
Control
Competence
Positive regard
Acceptance/worthiness

Love and Belonging
Maintain support systems
Protect from isolation

Safety and Security
Protection from injury
Promote feeling of security
Trust in nurse-client relationship

Basic Physiological Needs
Airway
Respiratory effort
Heart rate, rhythm, and strength of contraction
Nutrition
Elimination

FIG. 5-1 Using Maslow's hierarchy to establish priorities. (From Harkreader, H., & Hogan, M.A. [2004]. *Fundamentals of nursing: Caring and clinical judgment* [2nd ed.]. Philadelphia: W.B. Saunders.)

BOX 5-12
Assessment: Strategic Words

Ascertain
Assess
Check
Collect
Determine
Find out
Gather
Identify
Monitor
Observe
Obtain information
Recognize

BOX 5-13
Practice Question: The Nursing Process—Assessment

A client who has had an application of a right long arm cast complains of pain at the wrist when the arm is passively moved. The nurse should *first:*
1. Elevate the arm.
2. Document the findings.
3. Medicate with an additional dose of an opioid.
4. Check for paresthesias and paralysis of the right arm.
Answer: 4

Test-Taking Strategy: Note the strategic word *first*. Use the steps of the nursing process to answer the question, remembering that assessment is the first step. The only option that addresses assessment is option 4. Options 1, 2, and 3 address the implementation step of the nursing process. Also, these options are inaccurate first actions and the casted arm should have already been elevated (option 1). The client may be experiencing compartment syndrome, a complication following trauma to the extremities and application of a cast. Additional data need to be collected to determine if this complication is present. Remember, assessment is the first step in the nursing process.

Reference: Ignatavicius, D., & Workman, M. (2006). *Medical-surgical nursing: Critical thinking for collaborative care* (5th ed., p. 1197). Philadelphia: W.B. Saunders.

as your guide to select your first, immediate, or initial action.

    g. Possible exception to the guideline—if the question presents an emergency situation, read carefully; in an emergency situation, an intervention may be the priority.

4. Analysis (Box 5-14)

    a. Analysis questions are the most difficult questions because they require understanding of the principles of physiological responses and

BOX 5-14
Practice Question: The Nursing Process—Analysis

A nurse is reviewing the laboratory results of an infant suspected of having hypertrophic pyloric stenosis. Which of the following laboratory findings would the nurse most likely expect to note in this infant?
1. A blood pH of 7.30
2. A blood pH of 7.50
3. A blood bicarbonate level of 19 mEq/L
4. A blood bicarbonate level of 22 mEq/L
   Answer: 1

Test-Taking Strategy: An understanding of the physiology associated with hypertrophic pyloric stenosis and recalling that metabolic alkalosis is likely to occur as a result of vomiting is necessary. Next, the nurse must know which laboratory findings would be noted in this acid-base condition. Analysis of this data will direct you to the correct option. Remember, analysis is the second step of the nursing process.

Reference: Hockenberry, M., & Wilson, D. (2007). *Wong's nursing care of infants and children* (8th ed., p. 1419). St. Louis: Mosby.

require interpretation of the data based on assessment.
   b. Analysis questions require critical thinking and determining the rationale for therapeutic interventions that may be addressed in the question.
   c. Analysis questions may address the formulation of a nursing diagnosis and the communication and documentation of the results of the process of analysis.
5. Planning (Box 5-15)
   a. Planning questions require prioritizing nursing diagnoses, determining goals and outcome criteria for goals of care, developing the plan of care, and communicating and documenting the plan of care.
   b. Regarding nursing diagnoses, remember that actual client problems rather than potential or at-risk client problems will most likely be the priority.
6. Implementation (Box 5-16)
   a. Implementation questions address the process of organizing and managing care, counseling and teaching, providing care to achieve established goals, supervising and coordinating care, and communicating and documenting nursing interventions.
   b. Focus on a nursing action rather than on a medical action when you are answering a question, unless the question is asking you what prescribed medical action is anticipated.
   c. On NCLEX-RN, the only client that you need to be concerned about is the client in the question that you are answering; avoid the "What if......?" syndrome and remember that

BOX 5-15
Practice Question: The Nursing Process—Planning

A nurse develops a plan of care for a client with a cataract. Which nursing diagnosis is the priority?
1. Fear related to loss of eyesight
2. Risk for Injury related to decreased vision
3. Disturbed Sensory Perception (visual) related to ocular lens opacity
4. Social Isolation related to decreased ability to mobilize in the community
   Answer: 3

Test-Taking Strategy: This question relates to planning nursing care and asks you to identify the priority nursing diagnosis. Use Maslow's Hierarchy of Needs theory to answer the question. Remembering that physiological needs are the priority will direct you to option 3. Although Risk for Injury is a potential rather than an actual problem, according to Maslow's Hierarchy of Needs theory, safety is the second priority. Fear and Social Isolation are psychosocial needs and would be the last priorities in this situation. Remember, planning is the third step of the nursing process.

Reference: Ignatavicius, D., & Workman, M. (2006). *Medical-surgical nursing: Critical thinking for collaborative care* (5th ed., p. 1094). Philadelphia: W.B. Saunders.

BOX 5-16
Practice Question: The Nursing Process—Implementation

A nurse is caring for a hospitalized client with angina pectoris who begins to experience chest pain. The nurse administers a sublingual nitroglycerin (Nitrostat) tablet sublingually as prescribed, but the pain is unrelieved. The nurse should take which action next?
1. Reposition the client.
2. Contact the physician.
3. Call the client's family.
4. Administer another nitroglycerin tablet.
   Answer: 4

Test-Taking Strategy: Implementation questions address the process of organizing and managing care. This question also requires that you prioritize the nursing actions. Note the strategic word *next* and that the client is hospitalized. Recalling that the nurse would administer three nitroglycerin tablets 5 minutes apart from each other to relieve chest pain will assist in directing you to option 4. Remember, implementation is the fourth step of the nursing process.

Reference: Hodgson, B., & Kizior, R. (2007). *Saunders nursing drug handbook 2007*. Philadelphia: W.B. Saunders, p. 845.

the client in the question on the computer screen is your only assigned client.
   d. Answer the question from a textbook and ideal perspective and remember that the nurse has all the time and resources needed and readily available at the client's bedside.

Practice Question: The Nursing Process—Evaluation

A nurse provides instructions to a pregnant woman about food items to consume that contain folic acid. Which statement, made by the client, *indicates adequate understanding* of these food items?
1. "I will eat yogurt every day."
2. "I will eat a banana every day."
3. "A glass of milk a day will be sufficient."
4. "Green leafy vegetables, whole grains, and fruits are important to eat."
   Answer: 4

   Test-Taking Strategy: Note the strategic words *indicates adequate understanding*. These words indicate that this is an evaluation-type question. Options 1 and 3 can be eliminated first because they are comparative or alike options in that both yogurt and milk are dairy products and are high in calcium. To select from the remaining options, remember that bananas are high in potassium. Remember, evaluation is the fifth step of the nursing process.

Reference: Lowdermilk, D., & Perry, S. (2006). *Maternity nursing* (7th ed., p. 289). St. Louis: Mosby.

   e. Avoid the "What if......?" syndrome and remember that you do not need to run to the treatment room to obtain supplies, for example, sterile gloves, because the sterile gloves will be at the client's bedside.
7. Evaluation (Box 5-17)
   a. Evaluation questions focus on comparing the actual outcomes of care with the expected outcomes, and communicating and documenting findings.
   b. These questions focus on assisting in determining the client's response to care, and identifying factors that may interfere with achieving expected outcomes.
   c. In an evaluation question, watch for negative event queries, because they are frequently used in evaluation-type questions.

VII. CLIENT NEEDS
A. Safe and Effective Care Environment
   1. These questions test the concepts that the nurse provides nursing care, collaborates with other health care team members to facilitate effective client care, and protects clients, significant others, and health care personnel from environmental hazards.
   2. Focus on safety in these types of questions, and remember the importance of hand washing, call bells, bed positioning, the appropriate use of side rails, and the use of standard and other precautions.
B. Physiological Integrity
   1. These questions test the concepts that the nurse provides comfort and assistance in the perfor-

mance of activities of daily living and provides care related to the administration of medications and parenteral therapies.
   2. These questions also address the nurse's ability to reduce the client's potential for developing complications or health problems related to treatments, procedures, or existing conditions, and providing care to clients with acute, chronic, or life-threatening physical health conditions.
   3. Focus on Maslow's Hierarchy of Needs theory in these types of questions and remember that physiological needs are a priority and are addressed first.
   4. Use the ABCs, airway, breathing, and circulation, and the steps of the nursing process when selecting an option addressing physiological integrity.
C. Psychosocial Integrity
   1. These questions test the concepts that the nurse provides nursing care that promotes and supports the emotional, mental, and social well-being of the client and significant other(s).
   2. Content addressed in these questions relates to supporting and promoting the client's or significant other(s)' ability to cope, adapt, or problem-solve in situations such as illnesses, disabilities, or stressful events such as abuse, neglect, or violence.
   3. In this Client Needs category you may be asked communication-type questions that relate to how you would respond to a client, a client's family member or significant other, or other health care team members.
   4. Use therapeutic communication techniques to answer communication questions because of their effectiveness in the communication process.
   5. Remember to select the option that focuses on the client's, client's family member, or significant other's thoughts, feelings, concerns, anxieties, or fears (Box 5-18).
D. Health Promotion and Maintenance
   1. These questions test the concepts that the nurse provides and assists in directing nursing care to promote and maintain health.
   2. Content addressed in these questions relates to assisting the client and significant other(s) during the normal expected stages of growth and development, from conception through advanced old age, and providing client care related to the prevention and early detection of health problems.
   3. Use the Teaching and Learning theory if the question addresses client teaching, remembering that the client's willingness, desire, and readiness to learn is the first priority.
   4. Watch for negative event queries because they are frequently used in questions that address

BOX 5-18

Practice Question: Communication

A client scheduled for bowel surgery states to the nurse, "I'm not sure if I should have this surgery." Which response by the nurse is appropriate?
1. "It's your decision."
2. "Don't worry. Everything will be fine."
3. "Why don't you want to have this surgery?"
4. "Tell me what concerns you have about the surgery."
   Answer: 4

   Test-Taking Strategy: Use therapeutic communication techniques to answer communication questions and remember to focus on the client's thoughts, feelings, concerns, anxieties, and fears. Option 4 is the only option that addresses the client's concern. Option 1 is a blunt response and does not address the client's concern. Option 2 provides false reassurance. Option 3 can make the client feel defensive. Remember, use therapeutic communication techniques and focus on the client.

Reference: Potter, P., & Perry, A. (2005). *Fundamentals of nursing* (6th ed., pp. 437-442). St. Louis: Mosby.

Health Promotion and Maintenance and client education.

VIII. ELIMINATING COMPARATIVE OR ALIKE OPTIONS (Box 5-19)
A. When reading the options, look for options that are comparative or alike; these options will include a similar concept or nursing action.
B. Comparative or alike options can be eliminated as possible answers.

IX. ELIMINATE OPTIONS CONTAINING CLOSE-ENDED WORDS (Box 5-20)
A. Close-ended words include *all, always, every, must, none, never,* and *only.*
B. Eliminate options that contain close-ended words because these words infer a fixed or extreme meaning; these types of options are usually incorrect.
C. Options that contain open-ended words such as *may, usually, normally, commonly,* or *generally* should be considered as possible correct options.

X. LOOK FOR THE UMBRELLA OPTION (Box 5-21)
A. When answering a question, look for the umbrella option.
B. The umbrella option is one that is a broad or universal statement and that usually contains the concepts of the other options within it.
C. The umbrella option will be the correct answer

XI. USE THE GUIDELINES FOR DELEGATING AND MAKING ASSIGNMENTS (Box 5-22)
A. You may be asked a question that will require you to decide how you will delegate a task or assign clients to other health care providers.

BOX 5-19

Practice Question: Eliminate Comparative or Alike Options

A nurse is caring for a group of clients. On review of the clients' medical records, the nurse determines that which client is at risk for excess fluid volume?
1. The client on diuretics
2. The client with renal failure
3. The client with an ileostomy
4. The client on gastrointestinal suctioning
   Answer: 2

   Test-Taking Strategy: Focus on the subject of the question, the client at risk for excess fluid volume. Think about the pathophysiology associated with each condition identified in the options. The only client who retains fluid is the client with renal failure. The client on diuretics, the client with an ileostomy, and the client on gastrointestinal suctioning all lose fluid. Remember, eliminate comparative or alike options.

Reference: Ignatavicius, D., & Workman, M. (2006). *Medical-surgical nursing: Critical thinking for collaborative care* (5th ed., p. 223). Philadelphia: W.B. Saunders.

BOX 5-20

Practice Question: Eliminate Options That Contain Close-Ended Words

A client will undergo a barium swallow and the nurse provides preprocedure instructions to the client. The nurse instructs the client to:
1. Avoid eating or drinking after midnight before the test.
2. Limit self to only two cigarettes on the morning of the test.
3. Have a clear liquid breakfast only on the morning of the test.
4. Take all routine medications with a glass of water on the morning of the test.
   Answer: 1

   Test-Taking Strategy: Note the close-ended word *only* in options 2 and 3, and *all* in option 4. Remember, eliminate options that contain close-ended words because these options are usually incorrect. Also, note that options 2, 3, and 4 are comparative or alike options in that they all involve taking in something on the morning of the examination.

Reference: Ignatavicius, D., & Workman, M. (2006). *Medical-surgical nursing: Critical thinking for collaborative care* (5th ed., p. 1243). Philadelphia: W.B. Saunders.

B. Focus on the information in the question and what task or assignment is to be delegated.
C. Once you have determined what task or assignment is to be delegated, consider the client's needs and match the client's needs with the scope of practice of the health care providers identified in the question.
D. The nurse practice act and any practice limitations define which aspects of care can be dele-

BOX 5-21
Practice Question: Look for the Umbrella Option

A nurse is developing a plan of care for a client with Menière's disease. The priority nursing interventions should focus on which of the following?
1. Safety measures
2. Dietary restrictions
3. Activity limitations
4. Knowledge about medication therapy

Answer: 1

Test-Taking Strategy: Focus on the client's disorder, Menière's disease, and recall the pathophysiology associated with this disease. All the options identify a component of the plan of care for this client, but remember that safety is a priority. Also, note that option 1 is the umbrella option in that it is a broad statement or intervention.

Reference: Ignatavicius, D., & Workman, M. (2006). *Medical-surgical nursing: Critical thinking for collaborative care* (5th ed., pp. 1132-1133). Philadelphia: W.B. Saunders.

BOX 5-22
Practice Question: Use the Guidelines for Delegating and Assignment-Making

A nurse is planning the client assignments for the day and has a licensed practical nurse (LPN) and a nursing assistant on the nursing team. Which client would the nurse *most appropriately* assign to the LPN?
1. A client who is scheduled for an electrocardiogram and a chest x-ray
2. A client with stable congestive heart failure who has early-stage Alzheimer's disease
3. A client who was treated for dehydration and is weak and needs assistance with bathing
4. A client with emphysema who is receiving oxygen at 2 L by nasal cannula and becomes dyspneic on exertion

Answer: 4

Test-Taking Strategy: The nurse would most appropriately assign the client with emphysema to the LPN. This client has an airway problem and has the highest priority needs of the clients presented in the options. The clients described in options 1, 2, and 3 can be cared for appropriately by the nursing assistant. Remember, match the client's needs with the scope of practice of the health care provider.

Reference: Huber, D. (2006). *Leadership and nursing care management* (3rd ed., pp. 546-550). Philadelphia: W.B. Saunders.

BOX 5-23
Practice Question: Answering Pharmacology Questions

Quinapril hydrochloride (Accupril) is prescribed as adjunctive therapy in the treatment of heart failure. After administering the first dose, the nurse monitors which of the following *most closely*?
1. Respirations
2. Urine output
3. Lung sounds
4. Blood pressure

Answer: 4

Test-Taking Strategy: Focus on the name of the medication and note the strategic words *most closely*. This tells you that all the options may be correct and that you must prioritize. Recall that the medication names of most angiotensin-converting enzyme (ACE) inhibitors end with "*-pril*" and that these medications are used to treat hypertension. Excessive hypotension ("first-dose syncope") can occur in clients with heart failure or in clients who are severely salt- or volume-depleted. Although respirations, urine output, and lung sounds would be monitored, the nurse would *most closely* monitor the client's blood pressure.

Reference: Hodgson, B., & Kizior, R. (2007). *Saunders nursing drug handbook 2007* (p. 996). Philadelphia: W.B. Saunders.

usually perform certain invasive tasks such as dressings, suctioning, urinary catheterization, and administering medications orally or by subcutaneous or intramuscular injection.

G. The registered nurse can perform the tasks that a licensed practical nurse can perform and is responsible for assessment and planning care, analyzing client data, implementing and evaluating client care, supervising care, initiating teaching, and administering medications intravenously.

XII. ANSWERING PHARMACOLOGY QUESTIONS (Box 5-23)

A. If you are familiar with the medication, use nursing knowledge to answer the question.

B. Remember that the question will identify both the generic name and trade name of the medication.

C. If the question identifies a medical diagnosis, then try to form a relationship between the medication and the diagnosis; for example, you can determine that cyclophosphamide (Cytoxan) is an antineoplastic medication if the question refers to a client with breast cancer who is taking this medication.

D. Try to determine the classification of the medication being addressed to assist in answering the question. Identifying the classification will assist in determining a medication's action and/or side effects; for example, diltiazem (*Cardi*zem) is a cardiac medication.

gated and which must be performed by the registered nurse.

E. Generally, noninvasive interventions such as skin care, range-of-motion exercises, ambulation, grooming, and hygiene measures can be assigned to a nursing assistant.

F. A licensed practical nurse can perform the tasks that a nursing assistant can perform and also can

E. Recognize the common side effects associated with each medication classification and then relate the appropriate nursing interventions to each side effect; for example, if a side effect is hypertension, then the associated nursing intervention would be to monitor the blood pressure.

F. Learn medications that belong to a classification by commonalities in their medication names; for example, medications that are xanthine bronchodilators end with "*-line*" (e.g., theophyl*line*).

G. Look at the medication name and use medical terminology to assist in determining the medication action; for example, *Lopressor* lowers (*lo*) the blood pressure (*pressor*).

H. If the question requires a medication calculation, remember that a calculator is available on the computer; talk yourself through each step to be sure the answer makes sense, and recheck the calculation before answering the question, particularly if the answer seems like an unusual dosage.

I. Pharmacology: Pyramid Points to remember
   1. Generally, the client should not take an antacid with medication because the antacid will affect the absorption of the medication.
   2. Enteric-coated and sustained-release tablets should not be crushed; also, capsules should not be opened.
   3. The client should never adjust or change a medication dose or abruptly stop taking a medication.
   4. The nurse never adjusts or changes the client's medication dosage and never discontinues a medication.
   5. The client needs to avoid taking any over-the-counter medications or any other medications, such as herbal preparations, unless they are approved for use by the health care provider.
   6. The client needs to avoid consuming alcohol.
   7. Medications are never administered if the order is difficult to read, is unclear, or identifies a medication dose that is not a normal one.

REFERENCES

Black, J., & Hawks, J. (2005). *Medical-surgical nursing: Clinical management for positive outcomes* (7th ed.). Philadelphia: W.B. Saunders.

Hockenberry, M., & Wilson, D. (2007). *Wong's nursing care of infants and children* (8th ed.). St. Louis: Mosby.

Hodgson, B., & Kizior, R. (2007). *Saunders nursing drug handbook 2007*. Philadelphia: W.B. Saunders.

Huber, D. (2006). *Leadership and nursing care management* (3rd ed.). Philadelphia: W.B. Saunders.

Ignatavicius, D., & Workman, M. (2006). *Medical-surgical nursing: Critical thinking for collaborative care* (5th ed.). Philadelphia: W.B. Saunders.

Lewis, S., Heitkemper, M., & Dirksen, S., Graber-O'Brien, P. & Bucher, L. (2007). *Medical-surgical nursing: Assessment and management of clinical problems* (7th ed.). St. Louis: Mosby.

Lowdermilk, D., & Perry, S. (2006). *Maternity nursing* (7th ed.) St. Louis: Mosby.

National Council of State Boards (Eds.). (2007). *2007 NCLEX-RN® detailed test plan*. Chicago: Author.

National Council of State Boards of Nursing. http://www.ncsbn.org.

Potter, P., & Perry, A. (2005) *Fundamentals of nursing* (6th ed.). St. Louis: Mosby.

Issues in Nursing

Cultural Diversity and Health Practices

PYRAMID TERMS

acculturation Process of learning norms, beliefs, and behavioral expectations of a group other than one's own group.

belief Something accepted as true by a culture.

cultural assimilation Process in which individuals from a minority group are absorbed by the dominant culture and take on the characteristics of the dominant culture.

cultural competence The acquisition of knowledge, understanding, and appreciation of a culture that facilitates the provision of culturally appropriate health care.

cultural diversity The differences among groups of people that result from ethnic, racial, and cultural variables.

cultural imposition The tendency to impose one's own beliefs, values, and patterns of behavior on individuals from another culture.

culture The dynamic network of knowledge, beliefs, patterns of behavior, ideas, attitudes, values, and norms that are unique to a particular group of people.

dominant culture The group whose values prevail within a society.

ethnic group A group of people within a culture who share an identity based on race, religion, color, national origin, or language.

ethnicity An individual's identification of self as part of an ethnic group.

ethnocentrism An assumption of cultural superiority and an inability to accept the ways of another culture.

minority group An ethnic, cultural, racial, or religious group that constitutes less than a numerical majority of the population.

race A grouping of people based on biological similarities. Members of a racial group have similar physical characteristics, such as blood group, facial features, and color of skin, hair, and eyes.

racism Discrimination directed toward individuals or groups who are perceived to be inferior because of biological differences; often accompanied by oppression.

stereotyping An expectation that all people within the same racial, ethnic, or cultural group act alike and share the same beliefs and attitudes.

subculture A group of people with characteristic patterns of behavior that distinguish the group from the larger culture or society.

values Principles and standards that have meaning and worth to an individual, family, group, community, or culture.

THE PYRAMID TO SUCCESS

Often, nurses care for clients who come from ethnic, cultural, or religious backgrounds that are different from their own. Awareness of and sensitivity to the unique health and illness beliefs and practices are essential for the delivery of safe and effective care. Acknowledgment and acceptance of cultural differences with a nonjudgmental attitude are essential to providing culturally sensitive care. The belief underlying the NCLEX-RN examination test plan is that persons are unique individuals and define their own systems of daily living, which reflect their values, motives, and lifestyles. The Integrated Processes addressed in this chapter are Caring, Communication and Documentation, Nursing Process, and Teaching/Learning.

CLIENT NEEDS

Safe and Effective Care Environment

Acting as a client advocate

Ensuring ethical practices

Ensuring legal rights and responsibilities

Establishing priorities

Maintaining confidentiality

Providing continuity of care

Respecting the client's control of personal environment and property

Upholding client rights

Health Promotion and Maintenance

Considering cultural issues related to family systems and family planning

Identifying changes related to the aging process

Preventing disease

Promoting health and wellness

Providing health screening

Respecting lifestyle choices

Psychosocial Integrity

Assisting the client to use coping mechanisms effectively

Identifying the client's support systems

Identifying cultural diversity issues

Identifying end-of-life care issues

Identifying family dynamics as they relate to the client's culture

Providing a therapeutic environment

Respecting religious and spiritual influences on health

Using therapeutic communication techniques

Physiological Integrity

Identifying the cultural considerations related to alternative and complementary therapies

Identifying the cultural issues related to receiving blood and blood products

Implementing therapeutic procedures

Providing nonpharmacological comfort interventions

Providing nutrition and oral hydration (Boxes 6-1 and 6-2)

Providing palliative care

Using cultural concepts in illness management

BOX 6-1
Dietary Preferences

AFRICAN AMERICANS
Fried foods
Pork, greens, rice
Some pregnant African-American women engage in pica.

ASIAN AMERICANS
Soy sauce
Raw fish
Rice

EUROPEAN (WHITE) ORIGIN AMERICANS
Carbohydrates (potatoes)
Red meat

HISPANIC AMERICANS
Beans
Fried foods
Spicy foods
Tortillas
Carbonated beverages

AMERICAN INDIANS, ALEUTS, ESKIMOS
Blue cornmeal
Fish
Game
Fruits and berries
Navajos prefer meat and blue cornmeal and tend to avoid consumption of milk.

I. AFRICAN AMERICANS

A. Communication
   1. Members are competent in standard English and in black English, a variation based on pronunciation, grammar, and vocabulary.
   2. Head nodding does not necessarily mean agreement.
   3. Prolonged eye contact may be interpreted as rudeness or aggressive behavior.
   4. Nonverbal communication is important.
   5. Personal questions asked on initial contact with a person may be viewed as intrusive.

B. Time orientation and personal space preferences
   1. Time orientation varies according to age, socioeconomics, and subgroups and may include past, present, or future orientation.
   2. Members may be late for an appointment because relationships and events may be deemed more important than being on time.
   3. Members are comfortable with close personal space when interacting with family and friends.

C. Social roles
   1. Large extended family networks are important; older adults are respected.
   2. Many households are headed by a single-parent woman.
   3. Religious **beliefs** and church affiliation are sources of strength.

D. Health and illness
   1. Religious **beliefs** profoundly affect ideas about health and illness.
   2. Members believe that illness can be prevented by nutritious meals, exercise in fresh air, and cleanliness.

E. Health risks
   1. Sickle cell anemia
   2. Hypertension
   3. Heart disease
   4. Cancer
   5. Lactose intolerance
   6. Diabetes mellitus
   7. Obesity
   8. Human immunodeficiency virus (HIV) and acquired immunodeficiency syndrome (AIDS)

F. Interventions
   1. Recognize the presence of many individual and subgroup variations.

BOX 6-2
Religions and Dietary Practices

SEVENTH DAY ADVENTIST (CHURCH OF GOD)
Alcohol and caffeinated beverages are prohibited.
Many are lacto-ovo vegetarians; those who eat meat avoid pork.
Overeating is prohibited; 5 to 6 hours between meals without snacking is practiced.

BUDDHISM
Alcohol is prohibited.
Many are lacto-ovo vegetarians.
Some eat fish and some avoid only beef.

ROMAN CATHOLICISM
They avoid meat on Ash Wednesday and Fridays of Lent.
They practice optional fasting during Lent season.
Children and the ill are exempt from fasting.

CHURCH OF JESUS CHRIST OF LATTER-DAY SAINTS (MORMON)
Alcohol, coffee, and tea are prohibited.
Consumption of meat is limited.
The first Sunday of the month is optional for fasting.

HINDUISM
Many are vegetarians. Those who eat meat do not eat beef or pork.
Fasting rituals vary.
Children are not allowed to participate in fasting.

ISLAM
Pork, birds of prey, alcohol, and any meat product not ritually slaughtered are prohibited.
During the month of Ramadan, fasting occurs during the daytime.

JEHOVAH'S WITNESS
Any foods to which blood has been added are prohibited.
They can eat animal flesh that has been drained.

JUDAISM
Orthodox believers must adhere to dietary kosher laws:
  Meats allowed include animals that are vegetable eaters, cloven-hoofed animals, and animals that are ritually slaughtered.
  Fish that have scales and fins are allowed.
  Any combination of meat and milk is prohibited.
During Yom Kippur, 24-hour fasting is observed.
Pregnant women and those who are seriously ill are exempt from fasting.
During Passover, only unleavened bread is eaten.

PENTECOSTAL (ASSEMBLY OF GOD)
Alcohol is prohibited.
Members avoid consumption of anything to which blood has been added.
Some individuals avoid pork.

EASTERN ORTHODOX
During Lent, all animal products, including dairy products, are forbidden.
Fasting occurs during Advent.
Exceptions from fasting include illness and pregnancy.

---

2. Build a relationship based on trust.
3. Clarify the meaning of the client's verbal and nonverbal behavior.
4. Be flexible and avoid rigidity in scheduling care.
5. Encourage family involvement.
6. Alternative modes of healing may include herbs, prayer, and laying on of hands.

II. ASIAN AMERICANS
A. Communication
   1. Languages include Chinese, Japanese, Korean, Vietnamese, and English.
   2. Silence is valued.
   3. Eye contact may be considered inappropriate or disrespectful.
   4. Criticism or disagreement is not expressed verbally.
   5. Head nodding does not necessarily mean agreement.
   6. The word "no" may be interpreted as disrespect for others.

B. Time orientation and personal space preferences
   1. Time orientation reflects respect for the past but includes emphasis on the present and future.
   2. Preference is for a formal personal space, except with family and close friends.
   3. Usually, members do not touch others during conversation.
   4. Touching is unacceptable with members of the opposite gender.
   5. The head is considered to be sacred; therefore, touching someone on the head is disrespectful.
C. Social roles
   1. Members are devoted to tradition.
   2. Large extended-family networks are common.
   3. Loyalty to immediate and extended family and honor are valued.
   4. Family unit is structured and hierarchical.
   5. Men have the power and authority, and women are expected to be obedient.
   6. Education is viewed as important.

7. Religions include Taoism, Buddhism, Confucianism, Shintoism, Hinduism, Islam, and Christianity.
8. Social organizations are strong within the community.

D. Health and illness
1. Health is a state of physical and spiritual harmony with nature and a balance between positive and negative energy forces (yin and yang).
2. A healthy body is viewed as a gift from the ancestors.
3. Illness is viewed as an imbalance between yin and yang.
4. Yin foods are cold and yang foods are hot; one eats cold foods when one has a hot illness and one eats hot foods when one has a cold illness.
5. Illness is also attributed to prolonged sitting or lying or to overexertion.

E. Health risks
1. Hypertension
2. Heart disease
3. Cancer
4. Lactose intolerance
5. Thalassemia

F. Interventions
1. Avoid physical closeness and excessive touching; only touch a client's head when necessary, informing the client before doing so.
2. Limit eye contact.
3. Avoid gesturing with hands.
4. If possible, a female client prefers a female health care provider.
5. Clarify responses to questions and expectations of the health care provider.
6. Be flexible and avoid rigidity in scheduling care.
7. Encourage family involvement.
8. Alternative modes of healing may include herbs, acupuncture, restoration of balance with foods, massage, and offering of prayers and incense.

III. EUROPEAN (WHITE) ORIGIN AMERICANS

A. Communication
1. Languages include national languages and English.
2. Silence can be used to show respect or disrespect for another, depending on the situation.
3. Eye contact is viewed as indicating trustworthiness.

B. Time orientation and personal space preferences
1. Members are future oriented.
2. Time is valued; members tend to be on time and to be impatient with people who are not on time.
3. Members may be aloof and tend to avoid close physical contact.
4. Handshakes may be used for formal greetings.

C. Social roles
1. The nuclear family is the basic unit; the extended family is also important.
2. The man is the dominant figure, but a variation of gender roles exists within families and relationships.
3. Religion includes Judeo-Christian **beliefs**.
4. Community social organizations are important.

D. Health and illness
1. Health is usually viewed as an absence of disease or illness.
2. Members have a tendency to be stoical when expressing physical concerns.
3. Members primarily rely on the modern Western health care delivery system.

E. Health risks
1. Cancer
2. Heart disease
3. Diabetes mellitus
4. Obesity
5. Hypertension

F. Interventions
1. Monitor and assess the client's body language.
2. Respect the client's personal space and time.

IV. HISPANIC AMERICANS

A. Communication
1. Languages include Spanish and Portuguese.
2. Members tend to be verbally expressive, yet confidentiality is important.
3. Avoiding eye contact with a person in authority indicates respect and attentiveness.
4. Direct confrontation is disrespectful and the expression of negative feelings is impolite.
5. Dramatic body language, such as gestures or facial expressions, is used to express emotion or pain.

B. Time orientation and personal space preferences
1. Members are oriented more to the present.
2. Members may be late for an appointment because relationships and events are valued more than being on time.
3. Members are comfortable in close proximity with family, friends, and acquaintances.
4. Members are very tactile and use embraces and handshakes.
5. Members value the physical presence of others.
6. Politeness and modesty are essential.

C. Social roles
1. The nuclear family is the basic unit; also, large, extended-family networks are common.
2. The extended family is highly regarded.
3. Needs of the family take precedence over an individual family member's needs.
4. Depending on age and **acculturation** factors, men are the decision makers and breadwinners and women are the caretakers and homemakers.

5. Religions include Catholicism and evangelicalism.
6. Members have strong church affiliations.
7. Social organizations are strong within the community.
   D. Health and illness
   1. Health may be viewed as a reward from God or a result of good luck.
   2. Health results from a state of balance between "hot and cold" forces and "wet and dry" forces.
   3. Illness may be viewed as a result of God's punishment for sins.
   4. Members may adhere to folk medicine traditions.

▲ E. Health risks
   1. Lactose intolerance
   2. Diabetes mellitus
   3. Parasites
   4. Hypertension
   5. Heart disease
   6. Obesity

▲ F. Interventions
   1. Allow time for the client to discuss treatment options with family members.
   2. Protect privacy.
   3. Offer to call clergy because of the significance of religious practices related to illnesses.
   4. Ask if it would be all right to touch a child before examining him or her.
   5. Be flexible regarding time of arrival for appointments and avoid rigidity in scheduling care.
   6. Alternative modes of healing include herbs, consultation with lay healers, restoration of balance with hot or cold foods, prayer, and religious medals.

V. NATIVE AMERICANS

▲ A. Communication
   1. Languages include English, Navajo, and other tribal languages.
   2. Silence indicates respect for the speaker.
   3. Members speak in a low tone of voice and expect others to be attentive.
   4. Eye contact is viewed as a sign of disrespect.
   5. Body language is important.
   B. Time orientation and personal space preferences
   1. Oriented more to the present.
   2. Personal space is important.
   3. Members will lightly touch another person's hand during greetings.

▲ 4. Massage is used for the newborn infant to promote bonding between the infant and mother.
▲ 5. Some tribes may prohibit touching of a dead body.
   C. Social roles
   1. Members are family oriented.
   2. Basic family unit is the extended family, which often includes persons from several households.

3. In some tribes, grandparents are viewed as family leaders.
4. Elders are honored.
5. Children are taught to respect traditions.
6. The father does all the work outside the home and the mother assumes responsibility for domestic duties.
7. Sacred myths and legends provide spiritual guidance.
8. Religion and healing practices are integrated.
9. Community social organizations are important.
   D. Health and illness
   1. Health is a state of harmony between the person, family, and environment.
   2. Illness is caused by supernatural forces and disequilibrium between the person and environment.
   3. Traditional health and illness **beliefs** may continue to be observed, including natural and religious folk medicine tradition.
   E. Health risks
   1. Alcohol abuse
   2. Obesity
   3. Heart disease
   4. Diabetes mellitus
   5. Tuberculosis
   6. Arthritis
   7. Lactose intolerance
   8. Gallbladder disease
   9. American Eskimos susceptible to glaucoma
   F. Interventions
   1. Clarify communication.
   2. Understand that the client may be attentive, even when eye contact is absent.
   3. Be attentive to your own use of body language.
   4. Obtain input from members of the extended family.
   5. Encourage the client to personalize space in which health care is delivered; for example, encourage the client to bring personal items or objects to the hospital.
   6. In the home, assess for the availability of running water and modify infection control and hygiene practices as necessary.
   7. Alternative modes of healing include herbs, restoration of balance between the person and the universe, and consultation with traditional healers.

VI. AMISH AMERICANS (Fig. 6-1)
A. Cultural **beliefs** and practices (Box 6-3)
B. Interventions
   1. Speak to both the husband and wife regarding health care decisions, because they consider themselves partners in family life.
   2. Health instructions must be given in a simple, clear language.

3. Most Amish need to have church (bishop and community) permission to be hospitalized, because it is the community that will come together to help pay the costs.

4. Usually, they do not have health insurance, because it is a "worldly product" and may show a lack of faith in God.

FIG. 6-1 Amish woman quilting. From Giger, J., & Davidhizar, R. (2004). *Transcultural nursing: Assessment and intervention* (4th ed.). St. Louis: Mosby.

5. Barriers to modern health care include distance, lack of transportation, cost, and language (most do not understand scientific jargon).

VII. END-OF-LIFE ISSUES (Box 6-4)

A. Christian Science religion is unlikely to use medical means to prolong life.

B. Those in the Jewish faith generally oppose prolonging life after irreversible brain damage.

C. Eastern Orthodox religions, Muslims, and Orthodox Jews may prohibit, oppose, or discourage autopsy.

D. Muslims prohibit organ donation.

E. The Amish permit organ donation with the exception of heart transplants (the heart is the soul of the body).

F. Buddhists in America encourage organ donation and consider it an act of mercy.

G. The Mormon, Eastern Orthodox, Islamic, and Jewish (Conservative and Orthodox) faiths discourage, oppose, or prohibit cremation.

H. Hindus prefer cremation and cast the ashes in a holy river.

I. Hispanic and Latino groups
   1. The family generally makes decisions and may request to withhold the diagnosis or prognosis from the client.
   2. Extended-family members often are involved in end-of-life care (pregnant women may be pro-

---

BOX 6-3

Amish Americans: Cultural Beliefs and Practices

Amish maintain a culture distinct and separate from the non-Amish.

They usually speak a German dialect called Pennsylvania Dutch.

German language is used during worship; English is learned in school.

Men follow the laws of the Hebrew Scriptures with regard to beards (mustaches are not grown because of the long-perceived association of mustaches with the military).

Men usually dress in a plain, dark-colored suit; women usually wear a plain dress with long sleeves, bonnet, and apron.

Women are not allowed to hold positions of power in the congregational organization.

Marriage outside the faith is not allowed.

Family life has a patriarchal structure.

Although the roles of the women are considered equally important to those of men, they are very unequal in terms of authority.

Unmarried women remain under the authority of their father.

Wives are submissive to their husbands.

Amish generally remain separate from the rest of the world, physically and socially.

They reject materialism and worldliness.

Some Amish would prefer not to be photographed.

They value living simply and may choose to avoid technology, such as electricity and cars.

Amish highly value responsibility, generosity, and helping others.

They often work as farmers, builders, quilters, and homemakers.

Amish use traditional health care and alternative health care measures and practices, such as healers, herbs, and massage.

They believe that health is a gift from God, but that clean living and a balanced diet help maintain it.

Amish have lower risk factors for disease than the general population because of their work in manual labor, consumption of fresh foods, and rare consumption of tobacco and alcohol.

Many choose not to have health insurance and maintain mutual aid funds for Amish members to help with medical costs.

Funerals are conducted in the home without a eulogy, flower decorations, or any other display; caskets are plain and simple, without adornment.

At death, a woman is usually buried in her bridal dress.

One is believed to live on after death, either with eternal reward in heaven or punished in hell.

hibited from caring for the dying or attending funerals).

3. Several family members may be at the dying client's bedside.
4. Vocal expression of grief and mourning are acceptable and expected.
5. Members refuse procedures that alter the body, such as organ donation or autopsy.
6. Dying at home may be considered bad luck.

J. African Americans
1. Members discuss issues with the spouse or older family member (elders are held in high respect).
2. Family is highly valued and is central to the care of the terminally ill.
3. Open displays of emotion are common and accepted.
4. Organ and blood donation usually are not allowed.
5. Members prefer to die at home.

K. Chinese Americans
1. Family members may make decisions about care and often do not tell the client the diagnosis or prognosis.
2. Dying at home may be considered bad luck.
3. Organ donation is usually not allowed.

L. Native Americans
1. Family meetings may be held to make decisions about end-of-life and the type of treatments that should be pursued.
2. Some tribes avoid contact with the dying (may prefer to die in the hospital).

VIII. COMPLEMENTARY AND ALTERNATIVE MEDICINE (CAM)
A. Description
1. Therapies are used in addition to conventional treatment to provide healing resources and focus on the mind-body connection.

BOX 6-4

Religion and End-of-Life Care

CHRISTIANITY
Catholic and Orthodox religions
A priest anoints the sick.
Other sacraments before death include reconciliation and holy communion.

PROTESTANT
No last rites (anointing of the sick is accepted by some groups).
Prayers are given to offer comfort and support.

CHURCH OF JESUS CHRIST OF LATTER-DAY SAINTS (MORMONS)
May administer a sacrament if the client requests.

JEHOVAH'S WITNESS
Do not believe in sacraments.
Will be excommunicated if they receive a blood transfusion.

ISLAM
Second-degree male relatives such as cousins or uncles should be the contact person and determine whether the client and/or family should be given information about the client.
Client may choose to face Mecca (west or southwest in the United States).
The head should be elevated above the body.
Discussions about death usually are not welcomed.
Stopping medical treatment is against the will of Allah (Arabic word for God).
Grief may be expressed through slapping or hitting the body.
If possible, only a same-gender Muslim should handle the body after death; if not possible, non-Muslims should wear gloves so as not to touch the body.

JUDAISM
Prolongation of life is important (a client on life support must remain so until death).
A dying person should not be left alone (a rabbi's presence is desired).
Autopsy and cremation are forbidden.

HINDUISM
Rituals include tying a thread around the neck or wrist of the dying person, sprinkling the person with special water, and placing a leaf of basil on their tongue.
After death, the sacred threads are not removed and the body is not washed.

BUDDHISM
A shrine to Buddha may be placed in the client's room.
Time for meditation at the shrine is important and should be respected.
Clients may refuse medications that may alter their awareness (such as opioids).
After death, a monk may recite prayers for 1 hour (need not be done in the presence of the body).

AMISH AMERICANS
Funerals are conducted in the home without a eulogy, flower decorations, or any other display; caskets are plain and simple, without adornment.
At death, a woman is usually buried in her bridal dress.
One is believed to live on after death, either with eternal reward in heaven or punished in hell.

BOX 6-5

Categories of Complementary and Alternative Medicine (CAM)

Whole medical systems
Mind-body medicine
Biologically based practices
Manipulative and body-based practices
Energy medicine

2. Included are high-risk therapies (some that are invasive) and low-risk therapies (those that are noninvasive).
3. The National Center for Complementary and Alternative Medicine has proposed a classification system that includes five categories of complementary and alternative types of therapy (Box 6-5).
B. Whole medical systems
   1. Traditional Chinese medicine (TCM): Focuses on restoring and maintaining a balanced flow of vital energy; interventions include acupressure, acupuncture, herbal therapies, diet, meditation, tai chi, and qi gong (exercise that focuses on breathing, visualization, and movement).
   2. Ayurveda: Focuses on the balance of mind, body, and spirit; interventions include diet, medicinal herbs, detoxification, massage, breathing exercises, meditation, and yoga.
   3. Homeopathy: Focuses on healing and interventions consisting of small doses of specially prepared plant and mineral extracts that assist in the innate healing process of the body.
   4. Naturopathy: Focuses on enhancing the natural healing responses of the body; interventions include nutrition, herbology, hydrotherapy, acupuncture, physical therapies, and counseling.
C. Mind-body medicine
   1. Mind-body medicine focuses on the interactions among the brain, mind, body, and behavior and on the powerful ways in which emotional, mental, social, spiritual, and behavioral factors can directly affect health.
   2. Interventions include biofeedback, hypnosis, relaxation therapy, meditation, visual imagery, yoga, tai chi, qi gong, cognitive-behavioral therapies, group support, autogenic training, and spirituality.
D. Biologically based practices (Box 6-6)
   1. Biologically based therapies in CAM use substances found in nature, such as herbs, foods, and vitamins.
   2. Therapies include botanicals, prebiotics and probiotics, whole-food diets, functional foods, animal-derived extracts, vitamins, minerals, fatty acids, amino acids, and proteins.

BOX 6-6

Biologically Based Practices

AROMATHERAPY
The use of topical or inhaled oils (plant extracts) that will promote and maintain health

HERBAL THERAPIES
The use of herbs derived from mostly plant sources that will maintain and restore balance and health

MACROBIOTIC DIET
Diet high in whole-grain cereals, vegetables, beans, sea vegetables, and vegetarian soups
Elimination of meat, animal fat, eggs, poultry, dairy products, sugars, and artificially produced food from the diet

ORTHOMOLECULAR THERAPY
Focus on nutritional balance, including the use of vitamins, essential amino acids, essential fats, and minerals

E. Manipulative and body-based practices
   1. Interventions involve manipulation and movement of the body by a therapist.
   2. Interventions include practices such as chiropractic and osteopathic manipulation, massage therapy, and reflexology.
F. Energy medicine
   1. Energy therapies focus on energy originating within the body or on energy from other sources.
   2. Interventions include sound energy therapy, light therapy, acupuncture, qi gong, reiki and johre, therapeutic touch, intercessory prayer, whole medical systems, and magnetic therapy.

IX. HERBAL THERAPIES (Box 6-7)
A. Herbal therapy is the use of herbs (plant or a plant part) for its therapeutic value on health.
B. Some herbs have been determined to be safe, yet some herbs, even in small amounts, can be toxic.
C. If the client is taking prescription medications, the client should consult with the health care provider regarding the use of herbs because serious herb-medication interactions can occur.
D. Client teaching points
   1. Discuss herbal therapies with the health care provider before use.
   2. Contact the physician if any side effects of the herbal substance occur.
   3. Contact the health care provider before stopping the use of a prescription medication.
   4. Avoid using herbs to treat a serious medical condition such as heart disease.
   5. Avoid taking herbs if pregnant or attempting to get pregnant or if nursing.

Aloe: Antiinflammatory and antimicrobial effect; accelerates wound healing

Angelica: Antispasmodic and vasodilator; balances the effects of estrogen

Bilberry: Improves microcirculation in the eyes

Black cohosh: Produces estrogen-like effects

Cat's claw: Antioxidant; stimulates the immune system, lowers the blood pressure

Chamomile: Antispasmodic and antiinflammatory; produces a mild sedative effect

Dehydroepiandrosterone (DHEA): Converts to androgens and estrogen; slows the effects of aging; used for erectile dysfunction

Echinacea: Stimulates the immune system

Evening primrose: Assists with the metabolism of fatty acid

Feverfew: Antiinflammatory; used for migraine headaches, arthritis, and fever

Garlic: Antioxidant; used to lower cholesterol levels

Ginger: Antiemetic; used for nausea and vomiting

Ginkgo biloba: Antioxidant; used to improve memory

Ginseng: Increases physical endurance and stamina; used for stress and fatigue

Glucosamine: An amino acid that assists in the synthesis of cartilage

Goldenseal: Antiinflammatory and antimicrobial used to stimulate the immune system; has an anticoagulant effect and may increase blood pressure

Kava: Antianxiety and skeletal muscle relaxant; produces a sedative effect

Melatonin: A hormone that regulates sleep; used for insomnia

Milk thistle: Antioxidant; stimulates the production of new liver cells, reduces liver inflammation; used for liver and gallbladder disease

Peppermint oil: Antispasmodic; used for irritable bowel syndrome

St. John's wort: Antibacterial, antiviral, antidepressant

Saw palmetto: Antiestrogen activity; used for urinary tract infections and benign prostatic hypertrophy

Valerian: Used to treat nervous disorders such as anxiety, restlessness, and insomnia

Zinc: Antiviral; stimulates the immune system

6. Do not give herbs to infants or young children.
7. Purchase herbal supplements only from a reputable manufacturer; the label should contain the scientific name of the herb, name and address of the manufacturer, batch or lot number, date of manufacture, and expiration date.
8. Adhere to the recommended dose; if herbal preparations are taken in high doses, they can be toxic.
9. Moisture, sunlight, and heat may alter the components of herbal preparations.

10. If surgery is planned, the herbal therapy may need to be discontinued 2 to 3 weeks before surgery.

X. **LOW-RISK THERAPIES**
A. Low-risk therapies are those that have no adverse effects and, when implementing care, can be used by the nurse who has training and experience in their use.
B. Common low-risk therapies
  1. Meditation
  2. Relaxation techniques
  3. Imagery
  4. Music therapy
  5. Massage
  6. Touch
  7. Laughter and humor
  8. Spiritual measures, such as prayer

XI. **NURSING CONSIDERATIONS**
A. Principle: If health care recommendations, interventions, or treatments do not fit within the client's cultural **values**, they will not be followed.
B. Assessment skills: Be alert to cues regarding eye contact, personal space, time concepts, and understanding of the recommended plan of care.
C. Knowledge: Learn about the **cultures** of clients with whom you will be working; also, learn from your clients about their health care practices.
D. Flexibility: Allow for variation in accomplishing goals of health care; negotiate with the client until a mutually agreeable plan has been established.
E. Communication principles
  1. Treat each client and those accompanying the client with respect.
  2. Appreciate the differences and diversity of **beliefs** about health, illness, and treatment modalities.
  3. Ask who has been consulted about the illness or condition and what treatments were recommended by the consultant.
  4. Clarify perceptions of what the client has said or done and about the client's expectations of the health care provider.
  5. If language barriers pose a problem, seek an interpreter; avoid using family members as interpreters, except as a last resort.

PRACTICE QUESTIONS

1. A nurse in an ambulatory care clinic is performing an admission assessment for an African-American client scheduled for a cataract removal with an intraocular lens implant. Which question would be inappropriate for the nurse to ask on an initial assessment?
   1. "Do you ever experience chest pain?"
   2. "Do you have any difficulty breathing?"
   3. "Do you have a close family relationship?"
   4. "Do you frequently have episodes of headache?"

2. A nurse is providing discharge instructions to a Chinese client regarding prescribed dietary modifications. During the teaching session, the client continuously turns away from the nurse. Which nursing action is appropriate?
    1. Continue with the instructions, verifying client understanding.
    2. Walk around the client so that the nurse constantly faces the client.
    3. Give the client a dietary booklet and return later to continue with the instructions.
    4. Tell the client about the importance of the instructions for the maintenance of health care.

3. A nurse is preparing a plan of care for a client who is a Jehovah's Witness. The client has been told that surgery is necessary. The nurse considers the client's religious preferences in developing the plan of care and documents that:
    1. Faith healing is practiced primarily.
    2. Medication administration is not allowed.
    3. Surgery is prohibited in this religious group.
    4. The administration of blood and blood products is forbidden.

4. Which of the following meal trays would be appropriate for the nurse to deliver to a client of Jewish faith who follows a kosher diet?
    1. Pork roast, rice, vegetables, mixed fruit, milk
    2. Crab salad on a croissant, vegetables with dip, potato salad, milk
    3. Sweet and sour chicken with rice and vegetables, mixed fruit, juice
    4. Fettuccini Alfredo with shrimp and vegetables, salad, mixed fruit, iced tea

5. An ambulatory care nurse is discussing preoperative procedures with a Chinese-American client who is scheduled for surgery the following week. During the discussion, the client continually smiles and nods the head. The nurse interprets this nonverbal behavior as:
    1. Reflecting a cultural value.
    2. An acceptance of the treatment.
    3. The client is agreeable to the required procedures.
    4. The client understands the preoperative procedures.

6. A Chinese-American client experiencing anemia, which is believed to be a yin disorder, is likely to treat it with:
    1. Magnetic therapy.
    2. Intercessory prayer.
    3. Foods considered to be yin.
    4. Foods considered to be yang.

7. The role of the nurse regarding complementary and alternative medicine (CAM) should include:
    1. Recommending herbal remedies that the client should use.
    2. Educating the client about "good" versus "bad" therapies.
    3. Discouraging the client from using any alternative therapies.
    4. Educating the client about therapies that he or she is using or is interested in using.

8. A nursing student is discussing cultural diversity issues in a clinical conference when a nursing instructor asks the student to describe ethnocentrism. Which statement by the student indicates a lack of understanding of the issue of ethnocentrism?
    1. "It is a tendency to view one's own ways as best."
    2. "It is acting in a manner that is superior to other cultures."
    3. "It is imposing one's beliefs on individuals from another culture."
    4. "It is believing that one's own way is the only acceptable way."

9. When communicating with a culturally diverse client who speaks a different language, the best practice for the nurse is to:
    1. Speak loudly and slowly.
    2. Stand close to the client and speak loudly.
    3. Arrange for an interpreter when communicating with the client.
    4. Speak to the client and family together to increase the chances that the topic will be understood.

10. A nurse educator asks a student to list the five categories of complementary and alternative medicine (CAM), developed by the National Center for Complementary and Alternative Medicine (NCCAM), to a group of nursing students. Which of the following, if stated by the nursing student, would indicate an understanding of the five categories of CAM?
    1. Herbology, hydrotherapy, acupuncture, nutrition, and chiropractic care
    2. Mind-body medicine, traditional Chinese medicine, homeopathy, naturopathy, and healing touch
    3. Biologically based practices, body-based practices, magnetic therapy, massage therapy, and Trager body work
    4. Whole medical systems, mind-body medicine, biologically based practices, manipulative and body-based practices, and energy medicine

11. Which of the following clients has the lowest risk of obesity and diabetes mellitus?
    1. A 45-year-old Native-American male
    2. A 23-year-old Asian-American female
    3. A 35-year-old Hispanic-American male
    4. A 40-year-old African-American female

12. A nurse is bathing a hospitalized Native American client of the Navajo culture and notes that the client avoids eye contact during the procedure. The

nurse makes which interpretation about the client's behavior?
1. The client is depressed.
2. The client is displaying disrespectful mannerisms.
3. The client is displaying behavior that is a common cultural action.
4. The client is humiliated because of the need to be cared for by someone else.

13. An antihypertensive medication has been prescribed for a client with hypertension. The client tells the clinic nurse that she would like to take an herbal substance to help lower her blood pressure. The nurse should take which appropriate action?
1. Tell the client that herbal substances are not safe and should never be used.
2. Advise the client to discuss the use of an herbal substance with the physician.
3. Teach the client how to take her blood pressure so that it can be monitored closely.
4. Tell the client that if she takes the herbal substance she will need to have her blood pressure checked frequently.

14. A nurse educator is providing in-service education to the nursing staff regarding transcultural nursing care when a staff member asks the nurse educator to describe the concept of acculturation. The appropriate response is which of the following?

1. "It is a subjective perspective of the person's heritage and a sense of belonging to a group."
2. "It is a group of individuals in a society who are culturally distinct and have a unique identity."
3. "It is a process of learning a different culture to adapt to a new or changing environment."
4. "It is a group that shares some of the characteristics of the larger population group of which it is a part."

15. The nurse understands that which of the following statements regarding herbal therapies is true?
1. Zinc is used for insomnia.
2. Ginger is used to improve memory.
3. Echinacea is used for erectile dysfunction.
4. Black cohosh produces estrogen-like effects.

ALTERNATE ITEM FORMAT: MULTIPLE RESPONSE

16. Which of the following are low-risk therapies? Select all that apply.
❏ 1. Herbs
❏ 2. Prayer
❏ 3. Touch
❏ 4. Massage
❏ 5. Relaxation
❏ 6. Acupuncture
Answer: _____

ANSWERS

1. **3**
Rationale: In the African-American culture, asking personal questions on the initial contact or meeting is considered intrusive. African Americans are highly verbal and express feelings openly to family or friends, but what transpires within the family is viewed as private. Cardiovascular, respiratory, and neurological assessments include physiological assessments, which are the priority assessments.
Test-Taking Strategy: Use Maslow's Hierarchy of Needs theory to answer the question. Note the strategic words *inappropriate* and *initial*. Options 1, 2, and 4 address physiological needs. Option 3 addresses the psychosocial need. Review characteristics of the African-American culture if you had difficulty with this question.
Level of Cognitive Ability: Application
Client Needs: Psychosocial Integrity
Integrated Process: Nursing Process—assessment
Content Area: Fundamental skills
Reference: Potter, P. & Perry, A. (2005) *Fundamentals of nursing* (6th ed., p. 124). St. Louis: Mosby.

2. **1**
Rationale: Most Chinese maintain a formal distance with others, which is a form of respect. Many Chinese are uncomfortable with face-to-face communications, especially when eye

contact is direct. If the client turns away from the nurse during a conversation, the most appropriate action is to continue with the conversation. Walking around to the client so that the nurse faces the client is in direct conflict with the cultural practice. The client may consider returning later to continue with the explanation as a rude gesture. Telling the client about the importance of the instructions for the maintenance of health care may be viewed as degrading.
Test-Taking Strategy: Use the process of elimination. Eliminate options 3 and 4 first because these actions are nontherapeutic. From the remaining options, option 1 is the therapeutic action. If you had difficulty with this question, review the communication practices of this cultural group.
Level of Cognitive Ability: Application
Client Needs: Psychosocial Integrity
Integrated Process: Nursing Process—implementation
Content Area: Fundamental skills
Reference: Jarvis, C. (2004). *Physical examination and health assessment* (4th ed., pp. 68, 70). Philadelphia: W.B. Saunders.

3. **4**
Rationale: Among Jehovah's Witnesses, surgery is not prohibited, but the administration of blood and blood products is forbidden. Faith healing is forbidden in this religious group. Administration of medication is an acceptable practice, except if the medication is derived from blood products.

Test-Taking Strategy: Use the process of elimination, recalling that the administration of blood and any associated blood products is forbidden in this religious group. Review the characteristics of this religious group if you had difficulty with this question.
Level of Cognitive Ability: Application
Client Needs: Psychosocial Integrity
Integrated Process: Communication and Documentation
Content Area: Fundamental skills
Reference: Potter, P., & Perry, A. (2005). *Fundamentals of nursing* (6th ed., p. 133). St. Louis: Mosby.

4. **3**
Rationale: In the Jewish religion, those who are kosher believe that the dairy-meat combination is not acceptable. Pork and pork products are not allowed in the traditional Jewish religion. Only fish that have scales and fins are allowed; meats that are allowed include animals that are vegetable eaters, cloven-hoofed, and ritually slaughtered.
Test-Taking Strategy: Use the process of elimination, recalling that the dairy-meat combination is not acceptable in those in this religious group who follow the kosher tradition. Option 2 contains crab and milk, and option 1 contains pork roast and milk. Option 4 can be eliminated because it includes shrimp. Review the dietary rules of this religious group if you had difficulty with this question.
Level of Cognitive Ability: Application
Client Needs: Psychosocial Integrity
Integrated Process: Nursing Process—implementation
Content Area: Fundamental skills
Reference: Mahan, L.K., & Escott-Stump, S. (2004). *Krause's food, nutrition, & diet therapy* (11th ed., p. 385). Philadelphia: W.B. Saunders.

5. **1**
Rationale: Nodding or smiling by a Chinese-American client may reflect only the cultural value of interpersonal harmony. This nonverbal behavior may not be an indication of agreement with the speaker, an acceptance of the treatment, or an understanding of the procedure.
Test-Taking Strategy: Use the process of elimination. Eliminate options 2 and 3 first because they are comparative or alike. From the remaining options, select option 1 because it is characteristic of Chinese-American culture. In addition, option 4 is an incorrect interpretation of the client's nonverbal behavior. Review the cultural characteristics of the Chinese-American population if you had difficulty with this question.
Level of Cognitive Ability: Comprehension
Client Needs: Psychosocial Integrity
Integrated Process: Nursing Process—assessment
Content Area: Fundamental skills
Reference: Jarvis, C. (2004). *Physical examination and health assessment* (4th ed., p. 65). Philadelphia: W.B. Saunders.

6. **4**
Rationale: In the yin and yang theory, health is believed to exist when all aspects of the person are in perfect balance. Yin foods are cold and yang foods are hot. Cold foods are eaten when one has a hot illness and hot foods are eaten when one

has a cold illness. Options 1 and 2 are not associated with the yin and yang theory.
Test-Taking Strategy: Use the process of elimination and knowledge regarding the theory of yin and yang. Remember that cold foods are eaten when one has a hot illness and hot foods are eaten when one has a cold illness. If you are unfamiliar with this theory, review its elements.
Level of Cognitive Ability: Comprehension
Client Needs: Psychosocial Integrity
Integrated Process: Nursing Process—planning
Content Area: Fundamental skills
Reference: Potter, P., & Perry, A. (2005). *Fundamentals of nursing* (6th ed., p. 1286). St. Louis: Mosby.

7. **4**
Rationale: Complementary (alternative) therapies include a wide variety of treatment modalities that are used in addition to conventional therapy to treat a disease or illness. Educating the client about therapies that he or she uses or is interested in using is the nurse's role. Options 1, 2, and 3 are all inappropriate actions for the nurse to take.
Test-Taking Strategy: Use therapeutic communication techniques. Eliminate options 1, 2, and 3 because they are nontherapeutic. Option 4 is the only option that is appropriate. Review therapeutic communication techniques if you had difficulty with this question.
Level of Cognitive Ability: Application
Client Needs: Physiological Integrity
Integrated Process: Nursing Process—implementation
Content Area: Fundamental skills
Reference: Mahan, L.K., & Escott-Stump, S. (2004). *Krause's food, nutrition, & diet therapy* (11th ed., pp. 491-492, 1227). Philadelphia: W.B. Saunders.

8. **3**
Rationale: Ethnocentrism is a tendency to view one's own way of life as the most desirable, acceptable, or best and to act in a superior manner toward another culture. Cultural imposition is the tendency to impose one's own beliefs, values, and patterns of behavior on individuals from another culture.
Test-Taking Strategy: Use the process of elimination and note the strategic words *indicates a lack of understanding* in the question. Also, note that options 1, 2, and 4 are comparative or alike. If you had difficulty with this question, review culturally related concepts.
Level of Cognitive Ability: Comprehension
Client Needs: Psychosocial Integrity
Integrated Process: Teaching and Learning
Content Area: Fundamental skills
Reference: Jarvis, C. (2004). *Physical examination and health assessment* (4th ed., p. 40). Philadelphia: W.B. Saunders.

9. **3**
Rationale: Arranging for an interpreter would be the best practice when communicating with a client who speaks a different language. Options 1 and 2 are inappropriate and are ineffective ways in which to communicate. Option 4 is inappropriate because it violates privacy and does not ensure correct translation.

Test-Taking Strategy: Note the strategic words *best practice* in the question. To begin answering this question, eliminate options 1 and 2 because they are nontherapeutic actions. From the remaining options, focus on the strategic word *best* to direct you to option 3. Review these communication techniques if you had difficulty with this question.
Level of Cognitive Ability: Application
Client Needs: Psychosocial Integrity
Integrated Process: Communication and Documentation
Content Area: Fundamental skills
References: Jarvis, C. (2004). *Physical examination and health assessment* (4th ed., p. 68). Philadelphia: W.B. Saunders.
Lewis, S., Heitkemper, M., & Dirksen, S. (2004). *Medical-surgical nursing: Assessment and management of clinical problems* (6th ed., p. 27). St. Louis: Mosby.

10. **4**
Rationale: The five categories of complementary and alternative medicine (CAM) include whole medical systems, mind-body medicine, biologically based practices, manipulative and body-based practices, and energy medicine. The other options contain therapies within each category of CAM.
Test-Taking Strategy: Use knowledge of the five categories of CAM to assist in answering this question. Noting that the question asks about categories, not therapies, will assist in answering correctly. Review CAM if you had difficulty with this question.
Level of Cognitive Ability: Comprehension
Client Needs: Psychosocial Integrity
Integrated Process: Teaching and Learning
Content Area: Fundamental skills
References: Lewis, S., Heitkemper, M., & Dirksen, S. (2004). *Medical-surgical nursing: Assessment and management of clinical problems* (6th ed., pp. 95-97). St. Louis: Mosby.
Potter, P., & Perry, A. (2005). *Fundamentals of nursing* (6th ed., pp. 913-915). St. Louis: Mosby.

11. **2**
Rationale: Asian Americans have the lowest risk of obesity and diabetes mellitus from the options provided. Native Americans, African Americans, and Hispanic Americans have a high risk of obesity and diabetes mellitus.
Test-Taking Strategy: Note the strategic words *lowest risk, obesity,* and *diabetes mellitus.* Think about the health practices of each cultural group to direct you to option 2. If you had difficulty with this question, review the characteristics of this culture.
Level of Cognitive Ability: Comprehension
Client Needs: Health Promotion and Maintenance
Integrated Process: Nursing Process—assessment
Content Area: Fundamental skills
Reference: Giger, J.N., & Davidhizar, R.E. (2004). *Transcultural nursing: Assessment and intervention* (4th ed., pp. 201-202, 241-242, 267-268). St. Louis: Mosby.

12. **3**
Rationale: Native American clients often avoid eye contact when being cared for by health care personnel. In this culture, eye contact is considered a sign of disrespect. Therefore,

this client's action is culturally appropriate behavior. Options 1, 2, and 4 are inappropriate interpretations of the client's behavior.
Test-Taking Strategy: Use the process of elimination and knowledge regarding the culturally appropriate behaviors of Navajo clients. Remember that, in this culture, eye contact is considered a sign of disrespect. If you had difficulty with this question, review the characteristics of this culture.
Level of Cognitive Ability: Comprehension
Client Needs: Psychosocial Integrity
Integrated Process: Nursing Process—analysis
Content Area: Fundamental Skills
Reference: Jarvis, C. (2004). *Physical examination and health assessment* (4th ed., pp. 68, 70). Philadelphia: W.B. Saunders.

13. **2**
Rationale: Although herbal substances may have some beneficial effects, not all herbs are safe to use. Clients who are being treated with conventional medication therapy should be advised to avoid herbal substances with similar pharmacological effects because the combination may lead to an excessive reaction or to unknown interaction effects. Therefore, the nurse would advise the client to discuss the use of the herbal substance with the physician. Options 1, 3, and 4 are inappropriate nursing actions.
Test-Taking Strategy: Use the process of elimination. Eliminate option 1 first because of the close-ended word *never.* Next, eliminate options 3 and 4 because they are comparative or alike. Review the limitations associated with the use of herbal substances if you had difficulty with this question.
Level of Cognitive Ability: Application
Client Needs: Physiological Integrity
Integrated Process: Nursing Process—implementation
Content Area: Fundamental skills
Reference: Potter, P. ,& Perry, A. (2005). *Fundamentals of nursing* (6th ed., pp. 922-923). St. Louis: Mosby.

14. **3**
Rationale: Acculturation is a process of learning a different culture to adapt to a new or changing environment. Option 1 describes ethnic identity. Option 2 describes an ethnic group. Option 4 describes a subculture.
Test-Taking Strategy: Knowledge regarding the descriptions and definitions of the foundational concepts related to culture is required to answer this question. Focusing on the word *acculturation* and thinking about its definition will direct you to option 3. Review these concepts if you are unfamiliar with them.
Level of Cognitive Ability: Comprehension
Client Needs: Psychosocial Integrity
Integrated Process: Teaching and Learning
Content Area: Fundamental Skills
Reference: Potter, P., & Perry, A. (2005). *Fundamentals of nursing* (6th ed., p. 120). St. Louis: Mosby.

15. **4**
Rationale: Black cohosh produces estrogen-like effects. Zinc stimulates the immune system and is used for its antiviral properties. Echinacea stimulates the immune system and ginger is used for nausea and vomiting.

Test-Taking Strategy: Note the strategic word *true* and use the process of elimination and knowledge regarding herbal therapies. Options 1, 2 and 3 can be eliminated because the herb identified does not correlate with the correct therapeutic property. If you had difficulty with this question, review commonly used herbs and their therapeutic properties.
Level of Cognitive Ability: Comprehension
Client Needs: Physiological Integrity
Integrated Process: Teaching and Learning
Content Area: Fundamental skills
References: Hodgson, B., & Kizior, R. (2007). *Saunders nursing drug handbook 2007* (pp. 145, 1261). Philadelphia: W.B. Saunders.
Mahan, L.K., & Escott-Stump, S. (2004). *Krause's food, nutrition, & diet therapy* (11th ed., pp. 482-487). Philadelphia: W.B. Saunders.

ALTERNATE ITEM FORMAT: MULTIPLE RESPONSE

16. **2, 3, 4, 5**
Rationale: Low-risk therapies include meditation, relaxation techniques, imagery, music therapy, massage, touch, laughter and humor, and spiritual measures, such as prayer. The other options are not considered low-risk therapies.
Test-Taking Strategy: Use knowledge of low-risk complementary and alternative therapies. Focusing on the strategic words *low-risk* will direct you to the correct options. Review complementary and alternative medicine (CAM) and low-risk therapies if you had difficulty with this question.
Level of Cognitive Ability: Comprehension
Client Needs: Psychosocial Integrity
Integrated Process: Teaching and Learning
Content Area: Fundamental skills
Reference: Lewis, S., Heitkemper, M., & Dirksen, S. (2004). *Medical-surgical nursing: Assessment and management of clinical problems* (6th ed., pp. 97-108). St. Louis: Mosby.

REFERENCES

Giger, J.N., & Davidhizar, R.E. (2004). *Transcultural nursing: Assessment and intervention* (4th ed.). St. Louis: Mosby.

Hodgson, B., & Kizior, R. (2007). *Saunders nursing drug handbook 2007*. Philadelphia: W.B. Saunders.

Jarvis, C. (2004). *Physical examination and health assessment* (4th ed.). Philadelphia: W.B. Saunders.

Lewis, S., Heitkemper, M., & Dirksen, S. (2004). *Medical-surgical nursing: Assessment and management of clinical problems* (6th ed.). St. Louis: Mosby.

Mahan, L.K., & Escott-Stump, S. (2004). *Krause's food, nutrition, & diet therapy* (11th ed.). Philadelphia: W.B. Saunders.

National Council of State Boards (Eds.). (2007). *2007 NCLEX-RN® detailed test plan*. Chicago: Author.

Potter, P., & Perry, A. (2005). *Fundamentals of nursing* (6th ed.). St. Louis: Mosby.

Ethical and Legal Issues

PYRAMID TERMS

advance directive A written document (sometimes called a living will) recognized by state law that provides directions concerning the provision of care when a client is unable to make his or her own treatment choices.

advocacy Acting on the behalf of the client and protecting the client's rights to make his or her own decisions.

consent Voluntary act whereby a person agrees to allow someone else to do something.

ethics The distinction between right and wrong based on a body of knowledge, not just based on opinions.

HIPAA (Health Insurance Portability and Accountability Act) A federal law that establishes standards for the privacy and security of health information as well as a standard for electronic data interchange of health information.

informed consent A client's understanding of the reason for the proposed intervention, with its benefits and risks, and agreement with the treatment by signing a consent form.

law A system composed of general rules governing conduct and the procedures for resolving disputes when rules are not followed.

malpractice Failure to meet the standards of acceptable care, which results in harm to another person.

negligence Failure to provide care that a reasonable person ordinarily would use in a similar circumstance.

Patient's Bill of Rights The rights and responsibilities of clients receiving care.

values Beliefs and attitudes that may influence behavior and the process of decision making.

▲ THE PYRAMID TO SUCCESS

Across all settings in the practice of nursing, nurses frequently are confronted with ethical and legal issues related to client care. The professional nurse has the responsibility to be aware of the ethical principles, laws, and guidelines related to providing safe and quality care to clients. In the Pyramid to Success, focus on ethical practices; the nurse practice act and client's rights, particularly confidentiality and informed consent; advocacy, documentation, advance directives, and cultural, religious, and spiritual issues. The Integrated Processes addressed in this chapter are Caring, Communication and Documentation, Nursing Process, and Teaching/Learning.

CLIENT NEEDS
Safe and Effective Care Environment

Acting as an advocate
Advance directives documents
Confidentiality and information security issues related to the client's health care
Continuous quality improvement procedures
Ensuring client rights
Establishing priorities
Ethical practice in health care
Issues surrounding informed consent
Legal responsibilities and information technology related to client care
Resource management
Use of incident reports

Health Promotion and Maintenance

Developmental stages and transitions
Family systems
Lifestyle choices of the client

Psychosocial Integrity

Abuse and neglect issues
Available support systems
Chemical dependency
Coping mechanisms
Cultural, spiritual, and religious issues
End of life and grief and loss

Physiological Integrity

Alterations in body systems
Palliative and comfort care for the client
Unexpected responses to therapies

I. ETHICS

A. Description: The branch of philosophy concerned with the distinction between right and wrong based on a body of knowledge, not just based on opinions

B. Morality: Behavior in accordance with customs or tradition, usually reflecting personal or religious beliefs

C. Ethical principles: Codes that direct or govern nursing actions (Box 7-1)

D. **Values:** Beliefs and attitudes that may influence behavior and the process of decision making

E. **Values** clarification: Process of analyzing one's own **values** to understand more completely what is truly important

F. Ethical codes
   1. Ethical codes provide broad principles for determining and evaluating client care.
   2. These codes are not legally binding but, in most states, the board of nursing has authority to reprimand nurses for unprofessional conduct that results from violation of the ethical codes.
   3. Specific ethical codes are as follows:
      a. The Code for Nurses developed by the International Council of Nurses
      b. American Nurses Association Code of Ethics (Box 7-2)

G. Ethical dilemma
   1. An ethical dilemma occurs when there is a conflict between two or more ethical principles.
   2. No correct decision exists.
   3. The nurse must make a choice between two alternatives that are equally unsatisfactory.
   4. Such dilemmas may occur as a result of differences in cultural or religious beliefs.
   5. Ethical reasoning is the process of thinking through what one should do in an orderly and systematic manner to provide justification for actions based on principles.

H. Advocate
   1. A person who speaks up for or acts on the behalf of the client, protects the client's right to make his or her own decisions, and upholds the principle of fidelity.
   2. An advocate represents the client's viewpoint to others.
   3. An advocate avoids letting personal **values** influence **advocacy** for the client and supports the

---

BOX 7-1
Ethical Principles

Autonomy	Respect for an individual's right to self-determination
Nonmaleficence	The obligation to do or cause no harm to another
Beneficence	The duty to do good to others and to maintain a balance between benefits and harms; paternalism is an undesirable outcome of beneficence, in which the health care provider decides what is best for the client and encourages the client to act against his or her own choices
Justice	The equitable distribution of potential benefits and tasks determining the order in which client's should be cared for
Veracity	The obligation to tell the truth
Fidelity	The duty to do what one has promised

BOX 7-2
American Nurses Association Code of Ethics

The nurse, in all professional relationships, practices with compassion and respect for the inherent dignity, worth and uniqueness of every individual, unrestricted by considerations of social or economic status, personal attributes, or the nature of health problems.

The nurse's primary commitment is to the patient, whether an individual, family, group, or community.

The nurse promotes, advocates for, and strives to protect the health, safety, and rights of the client.

The nurse is responsible and accountable for individual nursing practice and determines the appropriate delegation of tasks consistent with the nurse's obligation to provide optimum patient care.

The nurse owes the same duties to self as to others, including the responsibility to preserve integrity and safety, to maintain competence, and to continue personal and professional growth.

The nurse participates in establishing, maintaining, and improving health care environments and conditions of employment conducive to the provision of quality health care and consistent with the values of the profession through individual and collective action.

The nurse participates in the advancement of the profession through contributions to practice, education, administration, and knowledge development.

The nurse collbatorates with other health professionals and the public in promoting community, national, and international efforts to meet health needs.

The profession of nursing, as represented by associations and their members, is responsible for articulating nursing values, for maintaining the integrity of the profession and its practice, and for shaping social policy.

From American Nurses Association. (2001). *Code of ethics for nurses with interpretive statements.* Washington, DC: American Nurses Publishing.

client's decision, even when it conflicts with his or her own preferences or choices.

I. **Ethics** committees
1. **Ethics** committees take a multidisciplinary approach to facilitate dialogue regarding ethical dilemmas.
2. These committees develop and establish policies and procedures to facilitate the prevention and resolution of dilemmas.

II. REGULATION OF NURSING PRACTICE
A. Nurse practice act
1. A series of statutes that have been enacted by each state legislature to regulate the practice of nursing in that state.
2. Nurse practice acts set educational requirements for the nurse, distinguish between nursing practice and medical practice, and define the scope of nursing practice.
3. Additional issues covered by nurse practice acts include licensure requirements for protection of the public, grounds for disciplinary action, rights of the nurse licensee if a disciplinary action is taken, and related topics.
4. All nurses are responsible for knowing the provisions of the act of the state or province in which they work.
B. Standards of care
1. Standards of care are guidelines that identify what the client can expect to receive in terms of nursing care.
2. The guidelines determine whether nurses have performed duties in an appropriate manner.
3. If a nurse does not perform duties within accepted standards of care, the nurse places himself or herself in jeopardy of legal action.
4. If a nurse is named as a defendant in a **malpractice** lawsuit and proceedings show that the nurse followed neither the accepted standards of care outlined by the state or province nursing practice act nor the policies of the employing institution, the nurse's legal liability is clear.
C. Employee guidelines
1. Respondent superior: Employer will be held liable for any negligent acts of an employee if the alleged negligent act occurred during the employment relationship and was within the scope of the employee's responsibilities.
2. Contracts
   a. Nurses are responsible for carrying out the terms of a contractual agreement with the employing agency and the client.
   b. The nurse employee relationship is governed by established employee handbooks and client care policies and procedures that create obligations, rights, and duties between those parties.
3. Institutional policies
   a. Written policies and procedures of the employing institution detail how nurses are to perform their duties.
   b. Policies and procedures are usually specific and describe the expected behavior on the part of the nurse.
   c. Although policies are not **laws**, courts generally rule against nurses who violate policies.
   d. If the nurse practices nursing according to client care policies and procedures established by the employer, functions within the job responsibility, and provides care consistently in a non-negligent manner, the nurse minimizes the potential for liability.
D. Hospital staffing
1. Charges of abandonment may be made against nurses who "walk out" when staffing is inadequate.
2. Nurses in short staffing situations are obligated to make a report to the nursing administration.
E. Floating
1. Floating is an acceptable, legal practice used by health care facilities to alleviate under- and over-staffing.
2. Legally, a nurse cannot refuse to float unless a union contract guarantees that nurses can work only in a specified area or the nurse can prove lack of knowledge for the performance of assigned tasks.
3. Nurses in a floating situation must not assume responsibility beyond their level of experience or qualification.
4. Nurses who float should inform the supervisor of any lack of experience in caring for the type of clients on the new nursing unit.
5. The nurse should request and be given orientation to the new unit.
F. Disciplinary action
1. Boards of nursing may deny, revoke, or suspend any license to practice as a registered nurse, according to their statutory authority.
2. Causes for disciplinary action are as follows:
   a. Unprofessional conduct
   b. Conduct that could affect the health and welfare of the public adversely
   c. Breach of client confidentiality
   d. Failure to use sufficient knowledge, skills, or nursing judgment
   e. Physically or verbally abusing a client
   f. Assuming duties without sufficient preparation
   g. Knowingly delegating to unlicensed personnel nursing care that places the client at risk for injury

BOX 7-3
Types of Law

CONTRACT LAW
Contract law is concerned with enforcement of agreements among private individuals.

CIVIL LAW
Civil law is concerned with relationships among persons and the protection of a person's rights.
Violation may cause harm to an individual or property, but no grave threat to society exists.

CRIMINAL LAW
Criminal law is concerned with relationships between individuals and governments and with acts that threaten society and its order; a crime is an offense against society that violates a law and is defined as a misdemeanor (less serious nature) or felony (serious nature).

TORT LAW
A tort is a civil wrong, other than a breach in contract, in which the law allows an injured person to seek damages from a person who caused the injury.

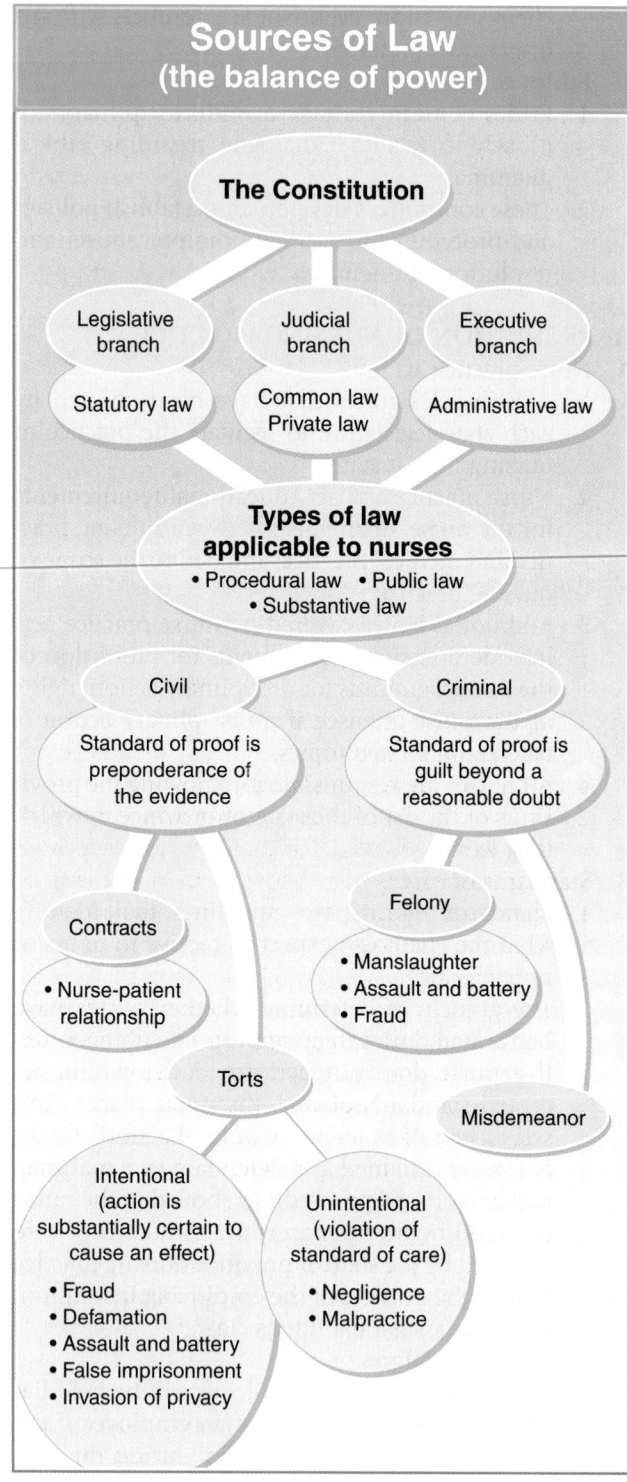

Sources of Law
(the balance of power)

The Constitution

Legislative branch — Judicial branch — Executive branch

Statutory law — Common law Private law — Administrative law

Types of law applicable to nurses
• Procedural law • Public law
• Substantive law

Civil — Criminal

Standard of proof is preponderance of the evidence

Standard of proof is guilt beyond a reasonable doubt

Contracts

Felony

• Nurse-patient relationship

• Manslaughter
• Assault and battery
• Fraud

Torts

Misdemeanor

Intentional (action is substantially certain to cause an effect)
• Fraud
• Defamation
• Assault and battery
• False imprisonment
• Invasion of privacy

Unintentional (violation of standard of care)
• Negligence
• Malpractice

FIG. 7-1 Sources of law for nursing practice. (From Harkreader, H., & Hogan, M.A. (2004). *Fundamentals of nursing: Caring and clinical judgment.* [2nd ed.]. Philadelphia: W.B. Saunders.)

---

    h. Failure to maintain an accurate record for each client
    i. Falsifying a client's record
    j. Leaving a nursing assignment without properly notifying appropriate personnel

III. LEGAL LIABILITY

A. **Laws**
1. Nurses are governed by civil and criminal **law** in roles as providers of services, employees of institutions, and private citizens.
2. A nurse has a personal and legal obligation to provide a standard of client care expected of a reasonably competent professional nurse.
3. Professional nurses are held responsible (liable) for harm resulting from their negligent acts or their failure to act.

B. Types of laws (Box 7-3; Fig. 7-1)

C. **Negligence** and **malpractice** (Box 7-4)
1. **Negligence** is conduct that falls below the standard of care.
2. **Negligence** can include acts of commission and acts of omission.
3. A nurse who does not meet appropriate standards of care may be held liable.
4. **Malpractice** is **negligence** on the part of a nurse.
5. **Malpractice** is determined if the nurse owed a duty to the client and did not carry out the duty, and the client was injured because the nurse failed to perform the duty.
6. Proof of liability
    a. Duty: At the time of injury, a duty existed between the plaintiff and the defendant.

    b. Breach of duty: The defendant breached duty of care to the plaintiff.
    c. Proximate cause: The breach of the duty was the legal cause of injury to the client.
    d. Damage or injury: The plaintiff experienced

BOX 7-4
Negligent Acts

Medication errors that result in injury to the client

Intravenous administration errors such as incorrect flow rates or failure to monitor a flow rate that results in injury to the client

Falls that occur as a result of failure to provide safety to the client

Failure to use sterile technique when indicated

Failure to check equipment for proper functioning

Burns sustained by the client as a result of failure to monitor bath temperature or equipment

Failure to monitor a client's condition

Failure to report changes in the client's condition to the physician

Failure to provide a complete report to the oncoming nursing staff

Modified from Potter, P., & Perry, A. (2005). *Fundamentals of nursing* (6th ed.). St. Louis: Mosby.

injury or damages or both and can be compensated by **law.**

D. Professional liability insurance
   1. Nurses need their own liability insurance for protection against **malpractice** lawsuits.
   2. Having their own insurance provides nurses protection as individuals and allows nurses to have an attorney present who has only the nurses' interests in mind.
E. Good Samaritan **laws**
   1. State legislatures pass Good Samaritan **laws,** which may vary from state to state.
   2. These **laws** encourage health care professionals to assist in emergency situations without fear of being sued for the care provided.
   3. These **laws** limit liability and offer legal immunity for persons helping in an emergency, provided that they give reasonable care.
   4. Immunity from suit applies only when all conditions of the state **law** are met, such as the health care provider receives no compensation for the care provided and the care given is not intentionally negligent.
F. Controlled substances
   1. The nurse should adhere to facility policies and procedures concerning administration of controlled substances, which are governed by federal and state **laws.**
   2. Controlled substances must be kept locked securely, and only authorized personnel should have access to them.

IV. **COLLECTIVE BARGAINING**
A. Collective bargaining is a formalized decision-making process between representatives of management and representatives of labor to negotiate wages and conditions of employment.

B. When collective bargaining breaks down because the parties cannot reach an agreement, the employees usually call a strike.
C. Striking presents a moral dilemma to many nurses because nursing practice is a service to people.
D. The United American Nurses (UAN), American Federation of Labor and Congress of Industrial Organizations (AFL-CIO), is an affiliate of both the American Nurses Association and the AFL-CIO. UAN staff nurses set the standard for RNs in organizing, collective bargaining, and contracts. Additional information can be obtained at http://www.uannurse.org.

V. **LEGAL RISK AREAS**
A. Assault
   1. Assault occurs when a person puts another person in fear of a harmful or offensive contact.
   2. The victim fears and believes that harm will result as a result of the threat.
B. Battery is an intentional touching of another's body without the other's **consent.**
C. Invasion of privacy includes violating confidentiality, intruding on private client or family matters, and sharing client information with unauthorized persons.
D. False imprisonment
   1. False imprisonment occurs when a client is not allowed to leave a health care facility when there is no legal justification to detain the client.
   2. False imprisonment occurs when restraining devices are used without an appropriate clinical need.
   3. A client can sign an Against Medical Advice form when the client refuses care and is competent to make decisions.
   4. The nurse should document circumstances in the medical record to avoid allegations by the client that cannot be defended.
E. Defamation is a false communication or a careless disregard for the truth that causes damage to someone's reputation, either in writing (libel) or verbally (slander).
F. Fraud results from a deliberate deception intended to produce unlawful gains.

VI. **CLIENT'S RIGHTS**
A. Description
   1. The client's rights document, also called the **Patient's Bill of Rights**, reflects acknowledgment of a client's right to participate in her or his health care with an emphasis on client autonomy.
   2. The document provides a list of the rights of the client and responsibilities that the hospital cannot violate (Box 7-5).
   3. The client's rights affect the relationship between the client and health care provider and between

BOX 7-5
Patient's Rights When Hospitalized

Right to considerate and respectful care
Right to be informed about illness, possible treatments, likely outcome, and to discuss this information with the physician
Right to know the names and roles of the persons who are involved in care
Right to consent or refuse a treatment
Right to have an advance directive
Right to privacy
Right to expect that medical records are confidential
Right to review the medical record and to have information explained
Right to expect that the hospital will provide necessary health services
Right to know if the hospital has relationships with outside parties that may influence treatment or care
Right to consent or refuse to take part in research
Right to be told of realistic care alternatives when hospital care is no longer appropriate
Right to know about hospital rules that affect treatment and about charges and payment methods

From Christensen, B., & Kockrow, E. (2003). *Foundations of nursing* (4th ed.). St. Louis: Mosby; and modified from American Hospital Association: *A patient's bill of rights*. (1992). http://www.patienttalk.info/AHA-Patient_Bill_of_Rights.htm.

BOX 7-6
Laws and Standards

AMERICAN HOSPITAL ASSOCIATION
Issued a patients' bill of rights

AMERICAN NURSES ASSOCIATION
Developed the Code for Nurses, which defines the nurse's responsibility for upholding the client's rights

MENTAL HEALTH SYSTEMS ACT
Developed rights for the mentally ill client

JOINT COMMISSION ON ACCREDITATION OF HEALTHCARE ORGANIZATIONS
Developed policy statements on the rights of the mentally ill.

BOX 7-7
Rights for the Mentally Ill

Right to be treated with dignity and respect
Right to communicate with persons outside the hospital
Right to keep clothing and personal effects with them
Right to religious freedom
Right to be employed
Right to manage property
Right to execute wills
Right to enter into contractual agreements
Right to make purchases
Right to education
Right to habeas corpus (written request for release from the hospital)
Right to an independent psychiatric examination
Right to civil service status, including the right to vote
Right to retain licenses, privileges, or permits
Right to sue or be sued
Right to marry or divorce
Right to treatment in the least restrictive setting
Right not to be subject to unnecessary restraints
Right to privacy and confidentiality
Right to informed consent
Right to treatment and to refuse treatment
Right to refuse participation in experimental treatments or research

Modified from Stuart, G., & Laraia, M. (2005). *Principles and practice of psychiatric nursing* (8th ed.). St. Louis: Mosby.

the client and health care delivery system and protect the client's ability to determine the level and type of care received.

4. Several laws and standards pertain to client's rights (Box 7-6).

B. Rights for the mentally ill (Box 7-7)
   1. The Mental Health Systems Act created rights for the mentally ill.
   2. The Joint Commission has developed policy statements on the rights of the mentally ill.
   3. Psychiatric facilities are required to have a client's bill of rights posted in a visible area.

▲ C. Organ donation and transplantation
   1. Client has the right to decide to become an organ donor and a right to refuse organ transplantation as a treatment option.
   2. An individual who is at least 18 years of age may indicate a wish to become a donor on his or her driver's license (state-specific) or in an **advance directive**.
   3. The Uniform Anatomical Gift Act provides a list of individuals who can provide **informed consent** for the donation of a deceased individual's organs.
   4. The United Network for Organ Sharing sets the criteria for organ donations.
   5. Some organs, such as the heart, lungs, and liver, can be obtained only from a person who is on mechanical ventilation and has suffered brain death, whereas other organs or tissues can be removed several hours after death.
   6. Donor must be free of infectious disease and cancer.
   7. Requests to a family for organ donation from the deceased family member usually are done by the physician or nurse specially trained for making such requests.

8. Donation of organs does not delay funeral arrangements, no obvious evidence that the organs were removed from the body shows when the body is dressed, and the family incurs no cost for removal of the organs donated.

D. Religious beliefs: Organ donation and transplantation
   1. Catholic Church: Organ donation and transplants are acceptable.
   2. Orthodox Church: Church discourages organ donation.
   3. Islam (Muslim) beliefs: Body parts may not be removed or donated for transplantation.
   4. Jehovah's Witness: An organ transplant may be accepted, but the organ must be cleansed with a nonblood solution before transplantation.
   5. Orthodox Judaism
      a. All body parts removed during autopsy must be buried with the body because it is believed that the entire body must be returned to the earth; hence, organ donation may not be considered by family members.
      b. Organ transplantation may be allowed with the rabbi's approval.

▲ VII. INFORMED CONSENT
   A. Description
      1. **Informed consent** is the client's approval (or that of the client's legal representative) to have his or her body touched by a specific individual.
      2. **Consents**, or releases, are legal documents that indicate the client's permission to perform surgery, perform a treatment, or give information to a third party.
      3. Types of **consents** (Box 7-8)
      4. **Informed consent** indicates the client's participation in the decision regarding health care.
      5. The client must be informed, in understandable terms, of the risks and benefits of the surgery or treatment, what the consequences are for not having the surgery or procedure performed, treatment options, and the name of the health care provider performing the surgery or procedure.
      6. A client's questions about the surgery or procedure must be answered before signing the **consent**.
      7. A **consent** must be signed freely by the client without threat or pressure and must be witnessed (witness must be an adult).
      8. A client who has been medicated with sedating medications or any other medications that can affect the client's cognitive abilities should not be asked to sign a **consent**.
      9. Legally, the client must be mentally and emotionally competent to give **consent**.

BOX 7-8
Types of Consents

ADMISSION AGREEMENT
Admission agreements are obtained at the time of admission and identify the health care agency's responsibility to the client.

BLOOD TRANSFUSION CONSENT
A blood transfusion consent indicates that the client was informed of the benefits and risks of the transfusion.
   Some clients hold religious beliefs that would prohibit them from receiving a blood transfusion, even in a life-threatening situation.

SURGICAL CONSENT
Surgical consent is obtained for all surgical or invasive procedures or diagnostic tests that are invasive.
   The physician, surgeon, or anesthesiologist who performs the operative or other procedure is responsible for explaining the procedure, its risks and benefits, and possible alternative options.

RESEARCH CONSENT
The research consent obtains permission from the client regarding participation in a research study.
   The consent informs the client about the possible risks, consequences, and benefits of the research.

SPECIAL CONSENTS
Special consents are required for the use of restraints, photographing the client, disposal of body parts during surgery, donating organs after death, or performing an autopsy.

BOX 7-9
Mentally or Emotionally Incompetent Clients

Declared incompetent
Unconscious
Under the influence of alcohol or drugs
Chronic dementia or other mental deficiency

---

10. If a client is declared mentally or emotionally incompetent, the next of kin, appointed guardian (appointed by the court), or the durable power of attorney has legal authority to give **consent** (Box 7-9).
11. A competent client over 18 years of age must sign the **consent**.
12. In most states, when a nurse is involved in the **informed consent** process, the nurse is witnessing only the signature of the client on the **informed consent** form.
13. An **informed consent** can be waived for urgent medical or surgical intervention as long as institutional policy so indicates.

14. A client has the right to refuse information and waive the **informed consent** and undergo treatment, but this decision must be documented in the medical record.
15. A client may withdraw **consent** at any time.

B. Minors
1. A minor is a client under legal age as defined by state statute (usually younger than 18 years).
2. A minor may not give legal consent, and consent must be obtained from a parent or the legal guardian.
3. Parental or guardian consent should be obtained before treatment is initiated for a minor, except in the following cases: in an emergency; in situations in which the consent of the minor is sufficient, such as treatment related to substance abuse, treatment of a sexually transmitted disease, human immunodeficiency virus testing and acquired immunodeficiency syndrome treatment, birth control services, pregnancy, or psychiatric services; emancipated minor; or if a court order or other legal authorization has been obtained.

C. Emancipated minor
1. An emancipated minor has established independence from the parents through marriage, pregnancy, service in the armed forces, or by a court order.
2. An emancipated minor is considered legally capable of signing an **informed consent**.

▲ VIII. **HEALTH INSURANCE PORTABILITY AND ACCOUNTABILITY ACT**

A. Description
1. The **Health Insurance Portability and Accountability Act (HIPAA)** describes how personal health information (PHI) may be used and how the client can obtain access to the information.
2. Personal health information includes individually identifiable information that relates to the client's past, present, or future health; treatment; and payment for health care services.
3. The act requires health care agencies to keep PHI private, provides information to the client about the legal responsibilities regarding privacy, and explains the client's rights with respect to PHI.
4. The client has various rights as a consumer of health care under **HIPAA**, and any client requests may need to be placed in writing; a fee may be attached to certain client requests.
5. The client may file a complaint if the client believes that privacy rights have been violated.

B. Client's rights
1. To inspect a copy of PHI
2. To ask the health care agency to amend the PHI that is contained in a record if the PHI is inaccurate

3. To request a list of disclosures made regarding the PHI as specified by **HIPAA**
4. To request to restrict how the health care agency uses or discloses PHI regarding treatment, payment, or health care services unless information is needed to provide emergency treatment
5. To request that the health care agency communicates with the client in a certain way or at a certain location; the request must specify how or where the client wishes to be contacted.
6. To request a paper copy of the **HIPAA** notice

C. Health care agency use and disclosure of PHI
1. The health care agency obtains PHI in the course of providing or administering health insurance benefits.
2. Use or disclosure of PHI may be done for the following:
    a. Health care payment purposes
    b. Health care operations purposes
    c. Treatment purposes
    d. Providing information about health care services
    e. Data aggregation purposes to make health care benefit decisions
    f. Administering health care benefits
3. Additional uses or disclosures of PHI (Box 7-10)

BOX 7-10

Uses or Disclosures of Personal Health Information

Compliance with legal proceedings or for limited law enforcement purposes

To a family member or significant other in a medical emergency

To a personal representative appointed by the client or designated by law

For research purposes in limited circumstances

To a coroner, medical examiner, or funeral director about a deceased person

To an organ procurement organization in limited circumstances

To avert a serious threat to the client's health or safety or the health or safety of others

To a governmental agency authorized to oversee the health care system or government programs

To the Department of Health and Human Services for the investigation of compliance with the Health Insurance Portability and Accountability Act or to fulfill another lawful request

To federal officials for lawful intelligence or national security purposes

To protect health authorities for public health purposes

To appropriate military authorities if a client is a member of the armed forces

In accordance with a valid authorization signed by the client

Modified from U.S. Department of Health and Human Services Office for Civil Rights. (2006). *HIPAA Administration Simplification Regulation Text.* http://www.hhs.gov/ocr/ AdminSimpRegText.pdf.

IX. CLIENT PRIVACY
A. Client's right to protection against unreasonable and unwarranted interference into private affairs
B. Violations (Box 7-11)

X. CONFIDENTIALITY
A. Description
 1. Clients have a right to privacy in the health care system.
 2. A special relationship exists between the client and nurse, in which information discussed will not be shared with a third party who is not directly involved in the client's care.
B. Nurse's responsibility
 1. Nurses are bound to protect client confidentiality by most nurse practice acts, by ethical principles and standards, and by institutional and agency policies and procedures.
 2. Disclosure of confidential information exposes the nurse to liability for invasion of the client's privacy.
 3. The nurse needs to protect the client from indiscriminate disclosure of health care information that may cause harm (Box 7-12).
C. Medical records
 1. Medical records are confidential.
 2. The client has the right to read the medical record and have copies of the record.
 3. Only staff members directly involved in care have legitimate access to a client's record; these may include physicians and nurses caring for the client, technicians, therapists, social workers, unit secretaries, client advocates, administrators (for statistical analysis, staffing, quality care re-

view). Others must ask permission from the client to review a record.
 4. The medical record is sent to the records or the health information department after discharge of the client from the health care facility.
D. Computerized medical records
 1. Health care employees should have access only to the client's records in the nursing unit or work area.
 2. Confidentiality can be protected by the use of special computer access codes to limit what employees can find in computer systems.
 3. The use of a password or identification code is needed to enter and sign off a computer system.
 4. A password or identification code should never be shared with another person.
 5. Personal passwords should be changed periodically to prevent unauthorized computer access.
E. In research, any information provided by the client is not to be reported in any manner that identifies the client and is not to be made accessible to anyone outside the research team.

XI. LEGAL SAFEGUARDS
A. Risk management
 1. Risk management is a planned method to identify, analyze, and evaluate risks followed by a plan for reducing the frequency of accidents and injuries.
 2. Programs are based on a systematic reporting system for incidents or unusual occurrences.
B. Incident reports (Box 7-13)
 1. The report is used as a means of identifying risk situations and improving client care.
 2. Follow specific documentation guidelines.
 3. Fill out the report completely, accurately, and factually.
 4. The report form should not be copied or placed in the client's record.
 5. Make no reference to the incident report form in the client's record.

BOX 7-11
Violations and Invasion of the Client's Privacy

Taking photographs of the client
Release of medical information to an unauthorized person, such as a member of the press, family, friend, or neighbor of the client, without the client's permission
Use of the client's name or picture for the health care agency's sole advantage
Intrusion by the health care agency regarding the client's affairs
Publication of information about the client
Publication of embarrassing facts
Public disclosure of private information
Leaving the curtains or room door open while a treatment or procedure is being performed
Allowing individuals to observe a treatment or procedure without the client's consent
Leaving a confused or agitated client sitting in the nursing unit hallway
Interviewing a client in a room with only a curtain between clients or where conversation can be overheard
Accessing medical records when unauthorized to do so

BOX 7-12
Maintenance of Confidentiality

Not discussing client issues with other clients or uninvolved staff in the client's care
Not sharing health care information with others without the client's consent (includes family members or friends of the client)
Keeping all information about a client private and not revealing it to someone not directly involved in care
Sharing client information only in private and secluded areas
Protecting the medical record from all unauthorized readers

BOX 7-13

Incidents That Need to be Reported

Accidental omission of ordered therapies
Circumstances that led to injury or a risk for client injury
Client falls
Medication administration errors
Needle stick injuries
Procedure-related or equipment-related accidents
A visitor having symptoms of an illness

BOX 7-14

Telephone Orders

Date and time the entry.
Repeat the order to the physician and record the order.
Sign the order; begin with "t.o." (telephone order),
    write the physician's name, and then sign the order.
If another nurse witnessed the order, that nurse's signature follows.
The physician needs to countersign the order within a
    time frame according to agency policy.

BOX 7-15

Components of a Medication Order

Date and time the order was written
Medication name
Medication dosage
Route of administration
Frequency of administration
Physician's or health care provider's signature

BOX 7-16

Documentation Guidelines

Use a black-colored ink pen for narrative documentation.
Date and time entries.
Provide objective, factual, and complete documentation.
Document care, medications, treatments, and procedures
    as soon as possible after completion.
Document client responses to interventions.
Document consent for or refusal of treatments.
Document calls made to other health care providers.
Do not document for others or change documentation
    for other individuals.
Sign and title each entry.
Use quotes as appropriate for subjective data.
Use correct spelling, grammar, and punctuation.
Avoid unacceptable abbreviations.
Avoid judgmental or evaluative statements, such as "un-
    cooperative client."
Do not leave blank spaces on documentation forms.
Follow agency policies when an error is made (draw one
    line through the error, initial, and date).
Follow agency guidelines regarding late entries.
Use only the user identification code, name, or password
    for computerized documentation.
Never lend access identification computer codes to an-
    other person.
Maintain privacy and confidentiality of documented in-
    formation printed from the computer.

6. The report is not a substitute for a complete entry in the client's record regarding the incident.
C. Safeguarding valuables
1. Client's valuables should be given to a family member or secured for safekeeping in a stored and locked designated location, such as the agency's safe, and the location of the client's valuables is documented per agency policy.
2. Many health care agencies require a client to sign a release to free the agency of the responsibility for lost valuables.
3. A client's wedding band can be taped in place unless a risk exists for swelling of the hands or fingers.
4. Religious items, such as medals or scapulars, may be pinned to the client's gown if allowed by agency policy.
▲ D. Physicians' orders
1. A nurse is obligated to carry out a physician's order except when the nurse believes an order to be inappropriate or inaccurate.
2. A nurse carrying out an inaccurate order may be legally responsible for any harm suffered by the client.
3. The nurse should clarify with the physician an unclear or inappropriate order.
4. If no resolution occurs regarding the order in question, the nurse should contact the nurse manager or supervisor.
5. The nurse should follow specific guidelines for telephone orders (Box 7-14).

6. The nurse should ensure that all components of a medication order are documented (Box 7-15).
E. Documentation
1. Documentation is legally required by accrediting agencies, state licensing laws, and state nurse and medical practice acts.
2. The nurse should follow agency guidelines and procedures (Box 7-16).
F. Client and family teaching
1. Provide complete instructions in a language that the client or family can understand.
2. Document client and family teaching, what was taught, evaluation of understanding, and who was present during the teaching.
3. Inform the client of what could happen if information shared during teaching is not followed.

XII. LEGAL DOCUMENTS

A. Patient Self-Determination Act
1. The Patient Self-Determination Act became a **law** in the United States in 1990 and was implemented in all health care institutions.
2. Clients must be provided with information about their rights to identify written directions about the care that they wish to receive in the event that they become incapacitated and are unable to make health care decisions.
3. On admission to a health care facility, the client is asked about the existence of an **advance directive**; if one exists, it must be documented and included as part of the medical record.
4. If the client signs an **advance directive** at the time of admission, it must be documented in the client's medical record.

B. **Advance directives**
1. An **advance directive** is a written document (sometimes called a living will) recognized by state **law** that provides directions concerning the provision of care when a client is unable to make his or her own treatment choices.
2. The **advance directive** also may include naming a relative or friend (health care proxy) who will make health care decisions in the event of the client's incapacitation.

C. Living will
1. An **advance directive** lists the medical treatment that a client chooses to omit or refuse if the client becomes unable to make decisions and is terminally ill.
2. States have their own requirements for executing living wills, but, in general, two witnesses, neither of whom can be a relative or physician, are needed when the client signs the living will.

D. Durable powers of attorney is a legal document that appoints a person (health care proxy) chosen by the client to carry out the client's wishes as expressed in the **advance directive** or to make decisions on the client's behalf when the client can no longer make decisions.

E. Do not resuscitate (DNR) orders
1. The DNR is an order written by a physician when a client has indicated a desire to be allowed to die if the client suffers cardiac and/or respiratory arrest.
2. The client or his or her legal representative must provide **informed consent** for the DNR status.
3. The DNR order must be defined clearly so that other treatment, not refused by the client, will be continued.
4. The DNR order must be reviewed regularly according to agency policy.
5. All health care personnel must know whether a client has a DNR order.
6. A nurse who attempts to resuscitate a client who has an order for DNR would be acting without the client's consent and committing battery.
7. The nurse must follow specific agency guidelines regarding when and under what circumstances a verbal DNR order is acceptable.

F. The nurse's role
1. Discussing **advance directives** with the client opens the communication channel to establish what is important to the client and what the client may view as promoting life versus prolonging dying.
2. The nurse needs to ensure that the client has been provided with information about the right to identify written directions about the care that the client wishes to receive.
3. On admission to a health care facility, the nurse determines whether an **advance directive** exists and ensures that it is part of the medical record.
4. The nurse ensures that the physician has been notified of the presence of an **advance directive**.
5. All health care workers need to follow the directions of an advance directive to be immune from liability.
6. Some agencies have specific policies that prohibit a nurse from signing as a witness to a legal document such as a living will.
7. If a nurse witnesses a legal document, the nurse must document the event and the factual circumstances surrounding the signing in the medical record.
8. Documentation as a witness should include who was present, any significant comments by the client, and the nurse's observations of the client's conduct during this process.

XIII. REPORTING RESPONSIBILITIES

A. Nurses are required to report certain communicable diseases or criminal activities such as abuse, gunshot or stab wounds, assaults, homicides, and suicides to the appropriate authorities.

B. The impaired nurse
1. If a nurse suspects that a co-worker is abusing chemicals, and thus potentially jeopardizing a client's safety, the nurse must report the individual to the nursing administration in a confidential manner. (Client safety is always the first priority.)
2. Nursing administration then notifies the board of nursing regarding the nurse's behavior.

C. Occupational Safety and Health Act
1. The Occupational Safety and Health Act (OSHA) requires that an employer provide a safe workplace for employees according to regulations.
2. Employees confidentially can report working conditions that violate regulations.

3. An employee who reports unsafe working conditions cannot be retaliated against by the employer.

D. Sexual harassment

1. Sexual harassment is prohibited by state and federal **laws**.
2. Sexual harassment includes unwelcome conduct of a sexual nature.
3. Follow agency policies and procedures to handle reporting a concern or complaint.

PRACTICE QUESTIONS

1. The nurse has just assisted a client back to bed after a fall. The nurse and physician have assessed the client, and have determined that the client is not injured. After completing the incident report, the nurse should take which action next?
   1. Reassess the client.
   2. Conduct a staff meeting to describe the fall.
   3. Document in the nurse's notes that an incident report was completed.
   4. Contact the nursing supervisor to update information regarding the fall.

2. A client arrives in the emergency room and is assessed by the nurse. The client is staggering, confused, and verbally abusive, complains of a headache from drinking alcohol, and is asking for medication. The nurse explains to the client that the physician will need to perform an assessment before the administration of medication. When the client becomes verbally abusive, the nurse obtains leather restraints and threatens to place the client in the restraints. With which of the following can the client legally charge the nurse as a result of the nursing action?
   1. Assault
   2. Battery
   3. Negligence
   4. Invasion of privacy

3. The nurse calls the physician regarding a new medication order because the dosage prescribed is higher than the recommended dosage. The nurse is unable to locate the physician and the medication is due to be administered. Which action should the nurse take?
   1. Contact the nursing supervisor.
   2. Administer the dose prescribed.
   3. Hold the medication until the physician can be contacted.
   4. Administer the recommended dose until the physician can be located.

4. A nursing graduate is employed as a staff nurse in a local hospital. During orientation, the new graduate asks the nurse educator about the need to obtain professional liability insurance. The appropriate response by the nurse educator is:
   1. "It is very expensive and not necessary."
   2. "The hospital's liability insurance will cover your actions."
   3. "The majority of suits are filed against physicians and the hospital."
   4. "Nurses are encouraged to have their own professional liability insurance."

5. The registered nurse arrives at work and is told to report (float) to the intensive care unit (ICU) for the day because the ICU is understaffed and needs additional nurses to care for the clients. The nurse has never worked in the ICU. The nurse should take which action first?
   1. Call the hospital lawyer.
   2. Refuse to float to the ICU.
   3. Call the nursing supervisor.
   4. Report to the ICU and identify tasks that can be performed safely.

6. The nurse gives an inaccurate dose of a medication to a client. Following assessment of the client, the nurse completes an incident report. The nurse notifies the nursing supervisor of the medication error and calls the physician to report the occurrence. The nurse who administered the inaccurate medication dose understands that:
   1. The error will result in suspension.
   2. The incident will be reported to the board of nursing.
   3. The incident will be documented in the personnel file.
   4. An incident report needs to be completed and is a method of promoting quality care and risk management.

7. A nurse who works on the night shift enters the medication room and finds a co-worker with a tourniquet wrapped around the upper arm. The co-worker is about to insert a needle, attached to a syringe containing a clear liquid, into the antecubital area. The appropriate initial action by the nurse is which of the following?
   1. Call security.
   2. Call the police.
   3. Call the nursing supervisor.
   4. Lock the co-worker in the medication room until help is obtained.

8. A hospitalized client tells the nurse that a living will is being prepared and that the lawyer will be bringing the will to the hospital today for witness signatures. The client asks the nurse for assistance in obtaining a witness to the will. The appropriate response to the client is which of the following?
   1. "I will sign as a witness to your signature."
   2. "You will need to find a witness on your own."
   3. "Whoever is available at the time will sign as a witness for you."

4. "I will call the nursing supervisor to seek assistance regarding your request."

9. The nurse has made an error in documenting an assessment finding on a client and obtains the client's record to correct the error. The nurse corrects the error by:
   1. Documenting a late entry into the client's record.
   2. Trying to erase the error for space to write in the correct data.
   3. Using whiteout to delete the error to write in the correct data.
   4. Drawing one line through the error, initialing and dating the line, and then documenting the correct information.

10. The nurse employed in a hospital is waiting to receive a report from the laboratory via the facsimile (fax) machine. The fax machine activates and the nurse expects the report but instead receives a sexually oriented photograph. The appropriate initial nursing action is to:
    1. Call the police.
    2. Cut up the photograph and throw it away.
    3. Call the nursing supervisor and report the incident.
    4. Call the laboratory and ask for the individual's name who sent the photograph.

11. The nursing instructor provides a lecture to nursing students regarding the issue of client's rights and asks a nursing student to identify a situation that represents an example of invasion of client privacy. Which of the following, if identified by the student, indicates an understanding of a violation of this client right?
    1. Performing a procedure without consent
    2. Threatening to give a client a medication
    3. Telling the client that he or she cannot leave the hospital
    4. Observing care provided to the client without the client's permission

12. The nursing staff is sitting in the lounge taking their morning break. A nursing assistant tells the group that she thinks that the unit secretary has acquired immunodeficiency syndrome (AIDS) and proceeds to tell the nursing staff that the secretary probably contracted the disease from her husband, who is supposedly a drug addict. Which legal tort has the nursing assistant violated?
    1. Libel
    2. Slander
    3. Assault
    4. Negligence

13. The nurse hears a client calling out for help, hurries down the hallway to the client's room, and finds a client lying on the floor. The nurse performs a thorough assessment, assists the client back to bed, notifies the physician of the incident, and completes an incident report. Which of the following should the nurse document on the incident report?
    1. The client fell out of bed.
    2. The client climbed over the side rails.
    3. The client was found lying on the floor.
    4. The client became restless and tried to get out of bed.

14. A client is brought to the emergency room by emergency medical services (EMS) after being hit by a car. The name of the client is not known and the client has sustained a severe head injury and multiple fractures, and is unconscious. An emergency craniotomy is required. Regarding informed consent for the surgical procedure, which of the following is the best action?
    1. Obtain a court order for the surgical procedure.
    2. Transport the victim to the operating room for surgery.
    3. Call the police to identify the client and locate the family.
    4. Ask the EMS team to sign the informed consent.

15. An 87-year-old woman is brought to the emergency room for treatment of a fractured arm. On physical assessment, the nurse notes old and new ecchymotic areas on the client's chest and legs and asks the client how the bruises were sustained. The client, although reluctant, tells the nurse in confidence that her son frequently hits her if supper is not prepared on time when he arrives home from work. Which of the following is the appropriate nursing response?
    1. "Oh, really. I will discuss this situation with your son."
    2. "This is a legal issue, and I must tell you that I will need to report it."
    3. "Let's talk about the ways you can manage your time to prevent this from happening."
    4. "Do you have any friends that can help you out until you resolve these important issues with your son."

ALTERNATE FORMAT ITEM: PRIORITIZING (ORDERED RESPONSE)

A client involved in a head-on automobile crash has awakened from a coma and asks for her husband, who was killed in the same accident. The family does not want the client to know at this time that her husband has died. The family wants all nursing staff to tell the client that the husband was taken by helicopter to another hospital, has a head injury, and is in the intensive care unit. Because the American Nurses Association Code of Ethics requires the nurse to preserve integrity, but the nurse wants to follow the family's instruction, the nurse faces an ethical dilemma. Number in order the steps for systematic processing of the ethical dilemma. Number 1 is the first step and number 6 is the last step.

___ Evaluate the action.
___ Verbalize the problem.

___ Negotiate the outcome.
___ Consider possible courses of action.
___ Gather all of the information relevant to the case.
___ Examine and determine one's own values on the issues.

ANSWERS

1. **1**
Rationale: The client's fall should be treated as private information and shared on a "need to know" basis. Communication regarding the event should involve only those participating in the client's care. An incident report is a problem-solving document; however, its completion is not documented in the nurse's notes. If the nursing supervisor has been made aware of the incident, the supervisor will contact the nurse if status update is desired. After a client's fall, the nurse must frequently reassess the client, because potential complications do not always appear immediately after the fall.
Test-Taking Strategy: Focus on the data in the question and the subject, the next nursing action. Using the steps of the nursing process will direct you to option 1. Review guidelines related to incident reports and care to the client after sustaining a fall if you had difficulty with this question.
Level of Cognitive Ability: Application
Client Needs: Physiological Integrity
Integrated Process: Nursing Process—implementation
Content Area: Fundamental skills
Reference: Potter, P., & Perry, A. (2005). *Fundamentals of nursing* (6th ed., pp. 411, 419). St. Louis: Mosby.

2. **1**
Rationale: An assault occurs when a person puts another person in fear of a harmful or offensive contact. For this intentional tort to be actionable, the victim must be aware of the threat of harmful or offensive contact. Battery is the actual contact with one's body. Negligence involves actions below the standards of care. Invasion of privacy occurs with unreasonable intrusion into the individual's private affairs.
Test-Taking Strategy: Use the process of elimination. Note the strategic word *threatens* in the question. This word should direct you to option 1. If you had difficulty with this question, review the descriptions associated with the terms in each option.
Level of Cognitive Ability: Comprehension
Client Needs: Safe and Effective Care Environment
Integrated Process: Nursing Process—implementation
Content Area: Fundamental skills
Reference: Potter, P., & Perry, A. (2005). *Fundamentals of nursing* (6th ed., p. 413). St. Louis: Mosby.

3. **1**
Rationale: If the physician writes an order that requires clarification, the nurse's responsibility is to contact the physician for clarification. If there is no resolution regarding the order because the physician cannot be located or because the order remains as it was written after talking with the physician, the

nurse then should contact the nurse manager or nursing supervisor for further clarification as to what the next step should be. Under no circumstances should the nurse proceed to carry out the order until obtaining clarification.
Test-Taking Strategy: Use the process of elimination and eliminate options 2 and 4 first because they are comparative or alike and are unsafe actions. Holding the medication can result in client injury. The nurse needs to take action. Option 1 clearly identifies the required action in this situation. Review nursing responsibilities related to the physician's orders if you had difficulty with this question.
Level of Cognitive Ability: Application
Client Needs: Safe and Effective Care Environment
Integrated Process: Nursing Process—implementation
Content Area: Fundamental skills
Reference: Potter, P., & Perry, A. (2005). *Fundamentals of nursing* (6th ed., p. 419). St. Louis: Mosby.

4. **4**
Rationale: Nurses need their own professional liability insurance for protection against malpractice law suits. Nurses erroneously assume that they are protected by an agency's professional liability policies. Usually, when a nurse is sued, the employer also is sued for the nurse's actions or inactions. Even though this is the norm, nurses are encouraged to have their own professional liability insurance.
Test-Taking Strategy: Note that the subject of the question relates to "obtaining professional liability insurance." This subject should direct you to option 4. Review liability related to malpractice insurance if you had difficulty with this question.
Level of Cognitive Ability: Comprehension
Client Needs: Safe and Effective Care Environment
Integrated Process: Teaching and Learning
Content Area: Fundamental skills
Reference: Potter, P., & Perry, A. (2005). *Fundamentals of nursing* (6th ed., p. 418). St. Louis: Mosby.

5. **4**
Rationale: Floating is an acceptable legal practice used by hospitals to solve their understaffing problems. Legally, a nurse cannot refuse to float unless a union contract guarantees that nurses can work only in a specified area or the nurse can prove the lack of knowledge for the performance of assigned tasks. When encountering this situation, the nurse should set priorities and identify potential areas of harm to the client. The nursing supervisor is called if the nurse is expected to perform tasks that he or she cannot safely perform. Calling the hospital lawyer is a premature action.

Test-Taking Strategy: Use the process of elimination, noting the strategic word *first*. Eliminate option 2 first because of the word *refuse*. Next, eliminate options 1 and 3 because they are premature actions. Review nursing responsibilities related to floating if you had difficulty with this question.
Level of Cognitive Ability: Application
Client Needs: Safe and Effective Care Environment
Integrated Process: Nursing Process—implementation
Content Area: Fundamental skills
Reference: Potter, P., & Perry, A. (2005). *Fundamentals of nursing* (6th ed., pp. 418-419). St. Louis: Mosby.

6. **4**
Rationale: Documentation of unusual occurrences, incidents, and accidents and of the nursing actions taken as a result of the occurrence is internal to the institution or agency and allows the nurse and administration to review the quality of care and determine any potential risks present. Based on the information provided in the question, the nurse's error will not result in suspension, nor will it be documented in the personnel file. The error and the situation presented in the question are not a reason for notifying the board of nursing.
Test-Taking Strategy: Focus on the information provided in the question. Use the process of elimination and knowledge regarding the purpose of incident reports to assist in eliminating options 1, 2, and 3. Note that the correct option is also the umbrella option. If you had difficulty with this question, review the purpose of incident reports.
Level of Cognitive Ability: Comprehension
Client Needs: Safe and Effective Care Environment
Integrated Process: Nursing Process—implementation
Content Area: Fundamental skills
Reference: Potter, P., & Perry, A. (2005). *Fundamentals of nursing* (6th ed., pp. 419, 497). St. Louis: Mosby.

7. **3**
Rationale: Nurse practice acts require reporting impaired nurses. The board of nursing has jurisdiction over the practice of nursing and may develop plans for treatment and supervision of the impaired nurse. This incident needs to be reported to the nursing supervisor, who will then report to the board of nursing and other authorities, such as the police, as required. The nurse may call security if a disturbance occurs, but no information in the question supports this need, and therefore this is not the initial action. Option 4 is an inappropriate and unsafe action.
Test-Taking Strategy: Note the strategic words *initial action*. Eliminate option 4 first because this is an inappropriate and unsafe action. Recall the lines of organizational structure to assist in directing you to option 3. If you had difficulty with this question, review the nurse's responsibilities when substance abuse is suspected or occurs in the workplace.
Level of Cognitive Ability: Application
Client Needs: Safe and Effective Care Environment
Integrated Process: Nursing Process—implementation
Content Area: Fundamental skills
Reference: Ignatavicius, D., & Workman, M. (2006). *Medical-surgical nursing: Critical thinking for collaborative care* (5th ed., p. 93). Philadelphia: W.B. Saunders.

8. **4**
Rationale: Living wills are required to be in writing and signed by the client. The client's signature must be witnessed by specified individuals or notarized. Many states prohibit any employee, including a nurse of a facility where the client is receiving care, from being a witness. Option 2 is nontherapeutic and not a helpful response. The nurse should seek the assistance of the nursing supervisor.
Test-Taking Strategy: Note the strategic word *appropriate*. Options 1 and 3 are comparative or alike and should be eliminated first. Option 2 is eliminated because it is a nontherapeutic response. Review legal implications associated with wills if you had difficulty with this question.
Level of Cognitive Ability: Application
Client Needs: Safe and Effective Care Environment
Integrated Process: Nursing Process—implementation
Content Area: Fundamental skills
References: Ignatavicius, D., & Workman, M. (2006). *Medical-surgical nursing: Critical thinking for collaborative care* (5th ed., p. 106). Philadelphia: W.B. Saunders.
Potter, P., & Perry, A. (2005). *Fundamentals of nursing* (6th ed., pp. 409-410). St. Louis: Mosby.

9. **4**
Rationale: If the nurse makes an error in documenting in the client's record, the nurse should follow agency policies to correct the error. This includes drawing one line through the error, initialing and dating the line, and then documenting the correct information. A late entry is used to document additional information not remembered at the initial time of documentation. Erasing data from the client's record and the use of whiteout are prohibited.
Test-Taking Strategy: Use the process of elimination and principles related to documentation. Recalling that alterations to a client's record are to be avoided will assist in eliminating options 2 and 3. From the remaining options, focusing on the subject of the question and using knowledge regarding the principles related to documentation easily will direct you to option 4. Review these principles if you had difficulty with this question.
Level of Cognitive Ability: Application
Client Needs: Safe and Effective Care Environment
Integrated Process: Communication and Documentation
Content Area: Fundamental skills
Reference: Potter, P., & Perry, A. (2005). *Fundamentals of nursing* (6th ed., pp. 836, 841). St. Louis: Mosby.

10. **3**
Rationale: Sexual harassment in the workplace is prohibited by state and federal laws. Sexually suggestive jokes, touching, pressuring a co-worker for a date, and open displays of or transmitting sexually oriented photographs or posters are examples of conduct that could be considered sexual harassment by another worker. If the nurse believes that he or she is being subjected to unwelcome sexual conduct, these concerns should be reported to the nursing supervisor immediately. Option 1 is unnecessary at this time. Options 2 and 4 are not appropriate initial actions.
Test-Taking Strategy: Note the strategic word *initial*. This may indicate that one or more than one of the options is partially

or totally correct. Use the skills of prioritizing to select the correct option. Remember that using the organizational channels of communication is best. This will assist in directing you to option 3. Review nursing responsibilities when sexual harassment occurs in the workplace if you had difficulty with this question.
Level of Cognitive Ability: Application
Client Needs: Safe and Effective Care Environment
Integrated Process: Nursing Process—implementation
Content Area: Fundamental skills
Reference: Huber, D. (2006). *Leadership and nursing care management* (3rd ed., pp. 679, 681, 683, 685). Philadelphia: W.B. Saunders.

11. **4**
Rationale: Invasion of privacy takes place with unreasonable intrusion into an individual's private affairs. Performing a procedure without consent is an example of battery. Threatening to give a client a medication constitutes assault. Telling the client that the client cannot leave the hospital constitutes false imprisonment.
Test-Taking Strategy: The strategic words in the question are *invasion of client privacy.* Focus on these strategic words to direct you to option 4. If you had difficulty with this question, review those situations that include invasion of privacy.
Level of Cognitive Ability: Comprehension
Client Needs: Safe and Effective Care Environment
Integrated Process: Caring
Content Area: Fundamental skills
Reference: Potter, P., & Perry, A. (2005). *Fundamentals of nursing* (6th ed., pp. 413-414). St. Louis: Mosby.

12. **2**
Rationale: Defamation is a false communication or a careless disregard for the truth that causes damage to someone's reputation, either in writing (libel) or verbally (slander). An assault occurs when a person puts another person in fear of a harmful or an offensive contact. Negligence involves the actions of professionals that fall below the standard of care for a specific professional group.
Test-Taking Strategy: Use the process of elimination and eliminate options 3 and 4 first. Recalling that slander constitutes verbal defamation will direct you to option 2. If you had difficulty with this question, review the torts identified in each option.
Level of Cognitive Ability: Comprehension
Client Needs: Safe and Effective Care Environment
Integrated Process: Nursing Process—implementation
Content Area: Fundamental skills
Reference: Potter, P., & Perry, A. (2005). *Fundamentals of nursing* (6th ed., p. 414). St. Louis: Mosby.

13. **3**
Rationale: The incident report should contain the client's name, age, and diagnosis. The report should contain a factual description of the incident, any injuries experienced by those involved, and the outcome of the situation. Option 3 is the only option that describes the facts as observed by the nurse. Options 1, 2, and 4 are interpretations of the situation and are not factual information as observed by the nurse.

Test-Taking Strategy: Use the process of elimination and read the information contained in the question to select the correct option. Remember to focus on factual information when documenting, and avoid including interpretations. This will direct you to option 3. Review documentation principles related to incident reports if you had difficulty with this question.
Level of Cognitive Ability: Application
Client Needs: Safe and Effective Care Environment
Integrated Process: Communication and Documentation
Content Area: Fundamental skills
Reference: Potter, P., & Perry, A. (2005). *Fundamentals of nursing* (6th ed., pp. 481-482). St. Louis: Mosby.

14. **2**
Rationale: Generally, there are two situations in which informed consent of an adult client is not needed. One is when an emergency is present and delaying treatment for the purpose of obtaining informed consent would result in injury or death to the client. The second is when the client waives the right to give informed consent. Option 1 will delay emergency treatment and option 4 is inappropriate. Although option 3 may be pursued, it is not the best action.
Test-Taking Strategy: Use the process of elimination. Recalling that when an emergency is present and a delay in treatment for the purpose of obtaining informed consent could result in injury or death will direct you to option 2. Review the issues surrounding informed consent if you had difficulty with this question.
Level of Cognitive Ability: Application
Client Needs: Safe and Effective Care Environment
Integrated Process: Nursing Process—implementation
Content Area: Fundamental skills
References: Ignatavicius, D., & Workman, M. (2006). *Medical-surgical nursing: Critical thinking for collaborative care* (5th ed., p. 857). Philadelphia: W.B. Saunders.
Potter, P., & Perry, A. (2005). *Fundamentals of nursing* (6th ed., pp. 416-417). St. Louis: Mosby.

15. **2**
Rationale: Confidential issues are not to be discussed with nonmedical personnel or the client's family or friends without the client's permission. Clients should be assured that information is kept confidential, unless it places the nurse under a legal obligation. The nurse must report situations related to child or elder abuse, gunshot wounds, and certain infectious diseases. Options 1, 3, and 4 do not address the legal implications of the situation and do not ensure a safe environment for the client.
Test-Taking Strategy: Use the process of elimination and knowledge regarding the nursing responsibilities related to reporting obligations. Options 1, 3, and 4 should be eliminated because they are comparative or alike in that they do not protect the client from injury. Review the nursing responsibilities related to reporting obligations if you had difficulty with this question.
Level of Cognitive Ability: Application
Client Needs: Safe and Effective Care Environment
Integrated Process: Nursing Process—implementation
Content Area: Fundamental skills
Reference: Potter, P., & Perry, A. (2005). *Fundamentals of nursing* (6th ed., pp. 391-392, 433). St. Louis: Mosby.

ALTERNATE FORMAT ITEM: PRIORITIZING (ORDERED RESPONSE)

Answer: 6, 3, 5, 4, 1, 2

Rationale: Ethical reasoning is the process of thinking through what one ought to do in an orderly and systematic manner to provide justification for actions based on principles. First, the nurse determines whether or not the issue involves an ethical dilemma and gathers information that is relevant to the case. Next, the nurse undertakes personal value clarification and identifies his or her own values regarding the issue. Third, the nurse verbalizes the problem in a simple sentence. Fourth, the nurse considers possible courses of action. In this case, the nurse may choose to seek the counsel of the agency's ethicist regarding the issue. Fifth, the nurse negotiates the outcome by developing a confidence in her or his own point of view with deep respect for the opinions of others. In this case, the nurse may negotiate with the family to determine a course of action that will allow the nurse to preserve integrity and yet allow the family to determine when the client should be informed of the tragic loss. Finally, the nurse evaluates the action.

Level of Cognitive Ability: Application
Client Needs: Psychosocial Integrity
Integrated Process: Nursing Process—implementation
Content Area: Fundamental Skills
Reference: Potter, P., & Perry, A. (2005). *Fundamentals of nursing* (6th ed., p. 398). St. Louis: Mosby.

REFERENCES

American Hospital Association: *A patient's bill of rights.* (1992). http://www.patienttalk.info/AHA-Patient_Bill_of_Rights.htm.

Harkreader, H., & Hogan, M.A. (2004). *Fundamentals of nursing: Caring and clinical judgment* (2nd ed.). Philadelphia: W.B. Saunders.

Huber, D. (2006). *Leadership and nursing care management* (3rd ed.). Philadelphia: W.B. Saunders.

Ignatavicius, D., & Workman, M. (2006). *Medical-surgical nursing: Critical thinking for collaborative care* (5th ed.). Philadelphia: W.B. Saunders.

National Council of State Boards (Eds.). (2007). *2007 NCLEX-RN® detailed test plan.* Chicago: Author.

Potter, P., & Perry, A. (2005). *Fundamentals of nursing* (6th ed.). St. Louis: Mosby.

Stuart, G., & Laraia, M. (2005). *Principles and practice of psychiatric nursing* (8th ed.). St. Louis: Mosby.

United American Nurses. (2000). *UAN Resolutions.* http://www.uan-nurse.org/who/resolution/2000/17.html.

U.S. Department of Health and Human Services Office for Civil Rights. (2006). *HIPAA Administration Simplification Regulation Text.* http://www.hhs.gov/ocr/ AdminSimpRegText.pdf.

Leadership, Delegating, and Prioritizing Client Care

PYRAMID TERMS

accountability   A moral concept that involves acceptance by the professional nurse of the consequences of a decision or action.

authority   Legitimate power or official right to act.

case management   An interdisciplinary health care delivery system designed to promote appropriate use of hospital personnel and material resources to maximize the health care agency's revenues while providing for optimal outcome of care.

change   A dynamic process that leads to an alteration in behavior.

critical path   An effective clinical management system for monitoring care and for reducing or controlling the length of hospital stay.

delegation   The process of transferring a selected nursing task in a situation to an individual who is competent to perform that specific task.

empowerment   An interpersonal process of enabling others to do for themselves.

leadership   An interpersonal process that involves motivating and guiding others to achieve goals.

management   The accomplishment of tasks by one self or by directing others.

power   The ability to do or act that results in the achievement of desired results.

prioritizing   Deciding which needs or problems require immediate action and which ones could tolerate a delay in response until a later time because they are not urgent.

responsibility   The duty to act.

variances   Actual deviations or detours from the critical paths.

▲ THE PYRAMID TO SUCCESS

The professional nurse is a leader and a manager. As described in the NCLEX-RN examination test plan, the professional nurse needs to provide integrated,

cost-effective care to clients by coordinating, supervising, and collaborating with members of the multidisciplinary health care team. A primary Pyramid Point focuses on the skills required to prioritize client care activities. Pyramid Points also focus on concepts of leadership and management, case management, resource management, the change process, and the process of delegation. The Integrated Processes addressed in this chapter include Caring, Communication and Documentation, Nursing Process, and Teaching/Learning.

CLIENT NEEDS   ▲

Safe and Effective Care Environment

Case management concepts
Consulting with members of the health care team
Continuous (total) quality improvement and effective client care outcomes
Delegating client care activities
Establishing priorities related to client care activities
Identifying professional practice limitations
Implementing cost-effective measures when providing nursing care
Leadership and management skills
Performance improvement (quality assurance)
Supervising the delivery of client care
Using appropriate health care resources
Variance analysis

Health Promotion and Maintenance

Client's ability to perform self-care
Disease prevention measures and health and wellness
Health promotion programs
Health screening

Psychosocial Integrity

Available support systems
Cultural, spiritual, and religious issues
Therapeutic interactions with others

Physiological Integrity

Ensuring that palliative and comfort care is provided to the client
Potential for alterations in body systems
Unexpected responses to therapy

I. HEALTH CARE DELIVERY

A. Managed care
1. Managed care is designed to control the cost of health services and promote a continuum of care through the development and use of integrated services.
2. Managed care uses a select group of providers who agree to a predetermined payment before delivering care.
3. Client care is outcome driven and is managed by a case management process.
4. Managed care emphasizes the promotion of health, client education and responsible self-care, early identification of disease, and the use of health care resources.

B. **Case management**
1. **Case management** is an organized system for delivering health care to an individual client or a group of clients throughout their illnesses.
2. **Case management** includes assessment and development of a plan of care, coordination of all services, referral, and follow-up.

C. Case manager
1. A professional nurse is a nurse who assumes **responsibility** for coordinating the client's care from admission and following discharge.
2. The case manager establishes a plan of care with the client, coordinates any consultations and referrals, and facilitates discharge.

D. **Critical path**
1. This is a multidisciplinary treatment plan that identifies the clinical interventions over a projected length of hospital stay or a projected time frame for specific case types.
2. All members of the health care team work with one plan to achieve the same client outcomes.
3. The goal of a **critical path** is to anticipate and recognize negative **variance** (i.e., problematic differences) early so that appropriate action can be taken and positive client outcomes can result.
4. **Variance** (difference)
   a. Actual deviations or detours from a **critical path** are **variances**.

b. Positive **variance** occurs when a client achieves maximum benefit and is discharged earlier than anticipated on the **critical path**.
c. Negative **variance** occurs when untoward events prevent a timely discharge and the length of hospital stay is longer than planned for a client on a specific **critical path**.
d. **Variance** analysis is a continuous process that the case manager and other caregivers conduct by comparing the specific client outcomes with the expected outcomes described on the **critical path**.
e. Accurate monitoring of the **critical path** with **variance** analysis can estimate the financial impact of actual client outcomes on the health care facility, especially when the client is not achieving expected outcomes.
f. If the **variance** is predictable, negotiation with health care insurers for an additional length of health care facility stay cost coverage can maximize client care revenues.
g. If the **variance** is not predicted and additional cost coverage is not negotiated with health care insurers, the hospital will not be reimbursed for a longer period of client care.

E. CareMaps
1. A CareMap is a model for a **critical path**.
2. The CareMap incorporates day-to-day expected client outcomes and those outcomes anticipated at discharge or at the end of a treatment phase.
3. The CareMap outlines clinical assessments, treatments and procedures, dietary interventions, activity and exercise therapies, client education, and discharge planning.

F. Nursing care plan
1. A nursing care plan is a written guideline and communication tool that identifies the client's pertinent assessment data, problems and nursing diagnoses, goals, interventions, and expected outcomes.
2. The plan enhances continuity of care by identifying specific nursing actions necessary to achieve the goals of care.
3. The client and family are involved in developing the plan of care, and the plan identifies short-term and long-term goals.
4. Client problems, goals, interventions, and expected outcomes are documented in the care plan, which provides a framework for evaluation of the client's response to nursing actions.

II. FORMAL ORGANIZATIONS

A. An organization's mission statement communicates in broad terms its reason for existence, the geographic area that the organization serves, and attitudes, beliefs, and values from which the organization functions.

B. Goals and objectives are measurable activities specific to the development of designated services and programs of an organization.

C. The organizational chart depicts and communicates how activities are arranged, how **authority** relationships are defined, and how communication channels are established.

D. Policies, procedures, and protocols
1. Policies are guidelines that define the organization's standpoint on courses of action.
2. Procedures are based on policy and define methods for tasks.
3. Protocols prescribe a specific course of action for a specific type of client or problem.

E. Centralization is the making of decisions by a limited number of individuals at the top of the organization or by managers of a department or unit, and decisions are communicated thereafter to the employees.

F. Decentralization is the distribution of **authority** throughout the organization to allow for increased **responsibility** and delegation in **decision making**.

▲ III. **CONTINUOUS (TOTAL) QUALITY IMPROVEMENT**

A. The total quality improvement program focuses on processes or systems that significantly contribute to effective client care outcomes.

B. When total quality improvement is part of the philosophy of a health care agency, every staff member becomes involved in ways to improve client care and outcomes.

C. The quality of a health care organization is defined in its mission statement and in the philosophy of the nursing department. These statements also identify how nurses are to perform, identify the services that are made available to the client, and provide directions for professional standards and care guidelines that should support positive client outcomes completely.

D. The Joint Commission describes quality improvement as an approach to the continuous assessment and improvement of the methods of providing health care to meet the needs of others.

E. The total quality improvement process is similar to the nursing process and involves a multidisciplinary approach

F. An outcome describes the most positive response to care.

G. Comparison of client responses to the expected outcomes indicates whether the interventions are effective, whether the client has progressed, how well standards are met, and whether changes are necessary.

H. The evaluation of health care is a process used to determine the quality of care and service provided to clients.

I. The nurse has the responsibility to recognize trends in nursing practice, identify recurrent problems, and initiate opportunities to improve the quality of care.

IV. **NURSING DELIVERY SYSTEMS** ▲

A. Functional nursing
1. Functional nursing involves a task approach to client care, with major tasks being delegated by the charge nurse to individual members of the team.
2. The goals are concerned with work productivity at the lowest possible cost.
3. Tasks generally are assigned to the lowest skilled paid workers who are available to do the work.

B. Team nursing
1. The team generally is led by a registered nurse who is responsible for assessing, developing nursing diagnoses, planning, and evaluating each client's plan of care.
2. Each staff member works fully within the realm of his or her educational and clinical expertise and job description.
3. Each staff member is accountable for client care and outcomes of care delivered in accordance with the licensing and practice scope as determined by health care agency policy and state law.
4. Team nursing is characterized by a high degree of respect for and maturity of team members and a high degree of communication and collaboration among members.

C. Primary nursing
1. Focuses on client outcomes as opposed to nursing tasks
2. Is concerned with keeping the nurse at the bedside, actively involved in client care, while planning goal-directed, individualized care

V. **PROFESSIONAL RESPONSIBILITIES**

A. **Accountability** ▲
1. The process that mandates that individuals have an obligation (or duty) to act and are answerable for their actions
2. Involves assuming only the responsibilities that are within one's scope of practice and not assuming **responsibility** for activities in which competence has not been achieved
3. Involves admitting mistakes rather than blaming others and evaluating the outcomes of one's own actions
4. Includes a **responsibility** to the client to be competent, render nursing services in accordance with standards of nursing practice, and adhere to the professional ethics code

B. **Leadership** (Box 8-1) ▲
1. **Leadership** is the interpersonal process that involves motivating and guiding others (followers) to achieve goals.

BOX 8-1

Leadership Behaviors

Treats followers as unique individuals
Inspires followers and stimulates critical thinking
Shows followers how to think about old problems in
    new ways
Is visible to followers, is flexible, and provides guidance,
    assistance, and feedback
Communicates a vision, establishes trust, and empowers
    followers
Motivates followers to achieve goals

Modified from Huber, D. (2006). *Leadership and nursing care management* (3rd ed.). Philadelphia: W.B. Saunders.

---

2. **Leadership** is a method of modeling accountable behavior to others (followers).
3. Followership is an interpersonal process of participation.

C. **Leadership** styles
1. Autocratic **leadership**
   a. An autocratic leader is focused and maintains strong control, makes decisions, and addresses all problems.
   b. An autocratic leader dominates the group and commands rather than seeks suggestions or input.
2. Democratic **leadership**
   a. This is also called participative **leadership**.
   b. It is based on the belief that every group member should have input into the development of goals and problem solving.
   c. A democratic leader acts primarily as a facilitator and resource person and is concerned for each member of the group.
   d. Democratic leadership is a more "talk with the members" **leadership** style and much less authoritarian than the autocratic **leadership** style.
3. Laissez-faire **leadership**
   a. A laissez-faire leader assumes a passive, nondirective, and inactive approach and relinquishes part or all of the **leadership** responsibilities to the members of the group.
   b. Decision making is left to the group, with the laissez-faire leader providing little if any guidance, support, or feedback.
4. Situational **leadership**
   a. Situational **leadership** uses a combination of styles based on the current circumstances and events.
   b. Situational **leadership** styles are assumed according to the needs of the group and the tasks to be achieved.

D. **Leadership** qualities (Box 8-2)
1. Communication
   a. Leaders listen actively to others.

BOX 8-2

Leadership Qualities

Effective communicator
Credibility
Critical thinker
Initiator of action
Risk taker
Is persuasive and influences followers

---

   b. Leaders communicate in an assertive manner and speak directly and honestly to others.
   c. Leaders differentiate among aggressive, passive, and assertive behaviors to communicate appropriately in a given situation.
2. Credibility
   a. Demonstration of **leadership** skills enhances a nurse's **accountability**.
   b. Individuals who perform well are those who can influence others.
   c. Both leaders and managers need to demonstrate attributes that support credibility.
3. Critical thinking
   a. A critical thinker is an individual with an open-minded, questioning attitude.
   b. To be effective, a leader must be a critical thinker.
4. Initiation of action
   a. A leader initiates processes and measures to solve problems and puts ideas into action.
   b. If an approach is ineffective, a leader demonstrates flexibility and is not hesitant to try another approach.
5. Risk taking
   a. Taking risks involves acting to solve problems.
   b. Risk-taking activities are goal-directed.
   c. A leader considers risks when making decisions.
   d. An effective leader institutes measures to minimize risk, along with problem solving.
6. Persuasiveness and influence
   a. Leaders motivate and inspire others to achieve goals.
   b. Leaders understand how to use **power** effectively and do not dominate but rather motivate others.
   c. Persuasiveness can create enthusiasm, encourage collaboration, and increase cohesiveness among team members.

E. **Management** is the accomplishment of tasks by oneself or by directing others.
F. Steps of the **management** process (Box 8-3; Fig. 8-1)
G. Problem-solving process and decision making
1. Problem solving involves obtaining information and using it to reach an acceptable solution to a problem.

BOX 8-3

Functions of Management

Planning: Determining objectives and identifying methods that lead to the achievement of those objectives
Organizing: Using resources (human and material) to achieve predetermined outcomes
Directing: Guiding and motivating others to meet the expected outcomes
Controlling: Using performance standards as criteria for measuring success and taking corrective action

TABLE 8-1

Similarities of the Problem-Solving Process and Nursing Process

Problem-Solving Process	Nursing Process
Identifying a problem and collecting data about the problem	Assessment
Determining the exact nature of the problem	Analysis
Deciding on a plan of action	Planning
Carrying out the plan	Implementation
Evaluating the plan	Evaluation

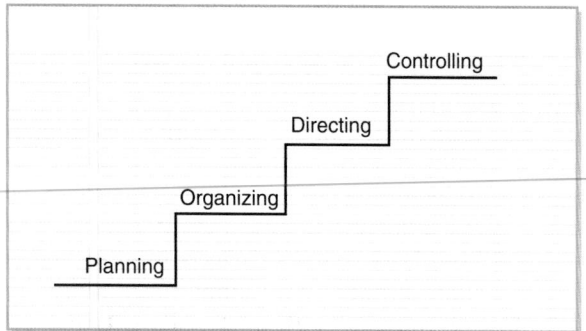

FIG. 8-1   Four steps of the managament process. (From Huber, D. [2000]. *Leadership and nursing care management* [2nd ed.]. Philadelphia: W.B. Saunders.)

BOX 8-4

Types of Power

Reward: Ability to provide incentives
Coercive: Ability to punish
Referent: Based on attraction
Expert: Based on having an expert knowledge base and skill level
Legitimate: Based on a position in society
Personal: Derived from a high degree of self-confidence
Informational: When one person provides explanations why another should behave in a certain way

2. Decision making involves identifying a problem and deciding which alternative(s) can best achieve objectives.
3. Steps of the problem-solving process are similar to the steps of the nursing process (Table 8-1).

H. Types of managers
1. Frontline manager
   a. Frontline managers function in supervisory roles closely identified with the actual delivery of client care.
   b. Frontline roles include those of charge nurse, team leader, and client care coordinator.
   c. Frontline managers coordinate the activity of all staff who provide client care and supervise team members during the manager's period of accountability.
2. Middle manager
   a. Middle manager roles include unit manager and supervisor.
   b. A middle manager's responsibilities include supervising staff, preparing budgets, preparing work schedules, writing and implementing policies that guide client care and unit operations, and maintaining the quality of client services.
3. Nurse executive
   a. A nurse executive is a top level nurse manager and may be the director of nursing services or the vice president for client care services.

   b. The nurse executive supervises a number of departments and works closely with the administrative team of the organization.
   c. The nurse executive ensures that all client care provided by nurses is consistent with the objectives of the health care organization.

VI. **POWER**
A. **Power** is the ability to do or act to achieve desired results.
B. Powerful persons are able to modify behavior and influence others to **change**, even when others are resistant to **change**.
C. Effective nurse leaders use **power** to improve the delivery of care and to enhance the profession.
D. **Power** that is effective is power that is shared.
E. Types of **power** (Box 8-4)

VII. **EMPOWERMENT**
A. **Empowerment** is an interpersonal process of enabling others to do for themselves.
B. **Empowerment** occurs when individuals are able to influence what happens to them more effectively.
C. **Empowerment** involves open communication, mutual goal setting, and decision making.
D. Nurses can empower clients through teaching and advocacy.

VIII. **THE CHANGE PROCESS**
A. **Change** is a dynamic process that leads to an alteration in behavior.

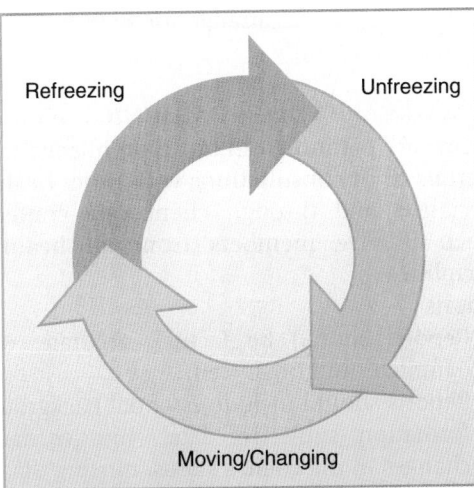

FIG. 8-2 Elements of a successful change. (From Huber, D. [2000]. *Leadership and nursing care management* [2nd ed.]. Philadelphia: W.B. Saunders.)

BOX 8-5
Reasons For Resisting Change

CONFORMITY
One goes along with others to avoid conflict.

DISSIMILAR BELIEFS AND VALUES
Differences can impede positive change.

HABIT
Routine, set behaviors are often hard to change.

SECONDARY GAINS
Benefits or payoff are present and so desirable that there is no incentive to change.

THREATS TO SATISFY BASIC NEEDS
Change may be perceived as a threat to self-esteem, security, or survival.

FEAR
One fears failure or has fear of the unknown.

---

1. Kurt Lewin's basic concepts of the **change** process includes three elements for successful **change**: unfreezing, moving and changing, and refreezing (Fig. 8-2).
   a. Unfreezing is the first phase of the process during which the problem is identified and individuals involved gather facts and evidence supporting a basis for **change**.
   b. During the moving and changing phase, **change** is planned and implemented.
   c. Refreezing is the last phase of the process during which the **change** becomes stabilized.
2. The leadership style influences the approach to initiating the **change** process.
B. Types of **change**
   1. Planned **change**: A deliberate effort to improve a situation
   2. Unplanned **change**: **Change** that is unpredictable but is beneficial and may go unnoticed
C. Resistance to **change** (Box 8-5)
   1. Resistance to **change** occurs when an individual rejects proposed new ideas without critically thinking about the proposal.
   2. **Change** requires energy.
   3. The **change** process does not guarantee positive outcomes.
D. Overcoming barriers
   1. Create a flexible and adaptable environment.
   2. Encourage those involved to plan and set goals for **change**.
   3. Include all involved in the plan for **change**.
   4. Focus on the benefits of the **change** in relation to improvement of client care.
   5. Delineate the drawbacks from failing to make the **change** in relation to client care.
   6. Evaluate the **change** process on an ongoing basis, and keep everyone informed of the progress.
   7. Provide positive feedback to all involved.
   8. Commit to the time it takes to **change**.

IX. CONFLICT
A. Conflict arises from a perception of incompatibility or difference in beliefs, attitudes, values, goals, priorities, or decisions.
B. Types of conflict
   1. Intrapersonal: Occurs within a person
   2. Interpersonal: Occurs between and among clients, nurses, or other staff members
   3. Organizational: Occurs when an employee confronts policies and procedures of the organization
C. Modes of conflict resolution
   1. Avoidance
      a. Avoiders are unassertive and uncooperative.
      b. Avoiders do not pursue their own needs, goals, or concerns, and they do not assist others to pursue theirs.
      c. Avoiders postpone dealing with the issue.
   2. Accommodation
      a. Accommodators neglect their own needs, goals, or concerns (unassertive) while trying to satisfy those of others.
      b. Accommodators obey and serve others and often feel resentment and disappointment because he or she "gets nothing in return."
   3. Competition
      a. Competitors pursue their own needs and goals at the expense of others.
      b. Competitors also may stand up for rights and defend important principles.
   4. Compromise
      a. Compromisers are assertive and cooperative.

b. Compromisers work creatively and openly to find the solution that most fully satisfies all important goals and concerns to be achieved.

▲ **X. ROLES OF HEALTH CARE TEAM MEMBERS**
A. Nurse roles are as follows:
1. Promote health and prevent disease
2. Provide comfort and care to clients
3. Make decisions
4. Act as client advocate
5. Lead and manage the nursing team
6. Serve as case manager
7. Function as a rehabilitator
8. Communicate effectively
9. Educate clients, families, and communities as well as health team members
10. Act as a resource person
11. Allocate resources in a cost-effective manner
B. Physician: The physician diagnoses and treats disease.
C. Physician assistant
1. The physician assistant acts to a limited extent in the role of the physician during the physician's absence
2. The physician assistant conducts physical examinations, performs diagnostic procedures, assists in the operating room and emergency room, and performs treatments.
3. Certified and licensed physician assistants in some states have prescriptive powers.
D. Physical therapist: A physical therapist assists in examining, testing, and treating the physically disabled.
E. Occupational therapist: An occupational therapist develops adaptive devices that help chronically ill or handicapped clients perform activities of daily living.
F. Respiratory therapist: A respiratory therapist delivers treatments designed to improve the client's ventilation and oxygenation status.
G. Nutritionist: The nutritionist or dietitian assists in planning dietary measures to improve or maintain a client's nutritional status.
H. Continuing care nurse: This nurse coordinates discharge plans for the client.
I. Assistive personnel, including the nursing assistant, unlicensed personnel, and client care technicians, help the registered nurse with specified tasks and functions.
J. Pharmacist: The pharmacist formulates and dispenses medications.
K. Social worker: The social worker counsels clients and families.
L. Pastoral care: The cleric offers spiritual support and guidance to clients and families.
M. Administrative staff: Administrative or support staff members organize and schedule diagnostic tests

and procedures and arrange for services needed by the client and family.

XI. HEALTH CARE TEAM COMMUNICATION ▲
A. Client care planning can be accomplished through referrals to or consultations with other health care specialists and through client care conferences, which involve members from all health care disciplines.
B. Reports
1. Reports should be factual, accurate, current, complete, and organized.
2. Reports should include essential background information, subjective data, objective data, any changes in the client's status, nursing diagnoses, treatments and procedures, medication administration, client teaching, discharge planning, family information, the client's response to treatments and procedures, and the client's priority needs.
3. Change of shift report
a. The report facilitates continuity of care among nurses who are responsible for a client.
b. The report may be written, oral, audiotaped, or provided during walking rounds at the client's bedside.
c. The report describes the client's health status and informs the nurse on the next shift about the client's needs and priorities for care.
4. Telephone reports
a. Purposes include informing a physician of a client's change in status; communicating information about a client's transfer to or from another unit or facility; and obtaining results of laboratory or diagnostic tests.
b. The telephone report should be documented and should include when the call was made, who made the call, who was called, to whom information was given, what information was given, and what information was received.
5. Transfer reports
a. Transferring nurse reports provide continuity of care and may be given by telephone or in person (Box 8-6).
b. Receiving nurse should repeat transfer information to ensure client safety and ask questions to clarify information about the client's status.

XII. CONSULTATION WITH THE HEALTH CARE TEAM ▲
A. Consultation is a process in which a specialist is sought to identify methods of care or treatment plans to meet the needs of a client.
B. Consultation is needed when the nurse encounters a problem that cannot be solved using nursing knowledge, skills, and available resources.

BOX 8-6
Transfer Reports

Client's name, age, physician, and diagnoses
Current health status and plan of care
Client's needs and priorities for care
Any assessments or interventions that need to be performed after transfer, such as laboratory tests, medication administration, or dressing changes
Need for any special equipment
Additional considerations such as allergies, resuscitation status, precautionary considerations, or family issues

BOX 8-7
Discharge Teaching

How to administer prescribed medications
Side effects of medications that need to be reported to the physician
Prescribed dietary and activity measures
Complications of the medical condition that need to be reported to the physician
How to perform prescribed treatments
How to use any special equipment prescribed for the client
Schedule for any home care services that are planned
How to access available community resources
When to obtain follow-up care

C. Consultation also is needed when the exact problem remains unclear; a consultant can objectively and more clearly assess and identify the exact nature of the problem.
D. Rapid response teams are being developed within hospitals to provide nursing staff with internal consultative services provided by expert clinicians.
E. Rapid response teams are used to assist nursing staff with early detection and resolution of client problems.

▲ **XIII. DISCHARGE PLANNING**
A. Discharge planning begins when the client is admitted to the hospital or health care facility.
B. Discharge planning is a multidisciplinary process that ensures that the client has a plan for continuing care after leaving the health care facility and assists in the client's transition from one environment to another.
C. All caregivers need to be involved in discharge planning, and referrals to other health care professionals or agencies may be needed. A physician's order may be needed for the referral, and the referral needs to be approved by the client's health care insurer.
D. The nurse should anticipate the client's discharge needs and make the referral as soon as possible (involve the client and family in the referral process).
E. The nurse needs to educate the client and family regarding care at home (Box 8-7).

▲ **XIV. PERFORMANCE IMPROVEMENT (QUALITY ASSURANCE)**
A. Description
1. Performance improvement is a process of evaluating the outcome of care measured against predetermined standards.
2. Aspects of care that represent the predetermined standards are selected, criteria for achievement of the standards are identified, and the methods of monitoring are defined.
3. Compliance in achieving the predetermined standards is measured and ways to improve compliance are sought, if needed.

B. A retrospective ("looking back") audit is an evaluation method used to inspect the medical record after the client's discharge for documentation of compliance with the standards.
C. A concurrent ("at the same time") audit is an evaluation method used to inspect the nursing staff's compliance with predetermined standards and criteria while the nurses are providing care during the client's stay.
D. The quality assurance staff, charge nurse, or nurse educator may perform the review; a peer review approach may be implemented, in which each member of the nursing staff reviews other staff members' compliance with predetermined standards and criteria.

XV. DELEGATION AND ASSIGNMENTS ▲
A. **Delegation**
1. **Delegation** is a process of transferring performance of a selected nursing task in a situation to an individual who is competent to perform that specific task.
2. **Delegation** involves achieving outcomes and sharing activities with other individuals who have the **authority** to accomplish the task.
3. The nurse practice act and any practice limitations define which aspects of care can be delegated and which must be performed by the registered nurse.
4. Even though a task may be delegated to someone, the nurse who delegates maintains **accountability** for the overall nursing care of the client.
5. Only the task, not the ultimate **accountability**, may be delegated to another.
B. Principles and guidelines of delegating (Box 8-8)
C. Assignments
1. Assignment is transferring performance of client care activities to specific staff members.
2. Guidelines for client care assignments
   a. Always ensure client safety.
   b. Be aware of individual variations in work abilities.

BOX 8-8

Principles and Guidelines of Delegating

Delegate the right task to the right delegatee. Be familiar with the experience of the delegatees, their scopes of practice, their job descriptions, agency policy and procedures, and the state nurse practice act.

Provide clear directions about the task and ensure that the delegatee understands the expectations.

Determine the degree of supervision that may be required.

Provide the delegatee with the authority to complete the task; provide a deadline for completion of the task.

Evaluate the outcome of care that has been delegated.

Provide feedback to the delegatee regarding his or her performance.

Generally noninvasive interventions such as skin care, range-of-motion exercises, ambulation, grooming, and hygiene measures can be assigned to a nursing assistant.

A licensed practical nurse (LPN) or licensed vocational nurse (LVN) can perform not only the tasks that a nursing assistant can perform but also can perform certain invasive tasks, such as dressings changes, suctioning, urinary catheterization, and medication administration (oral, subcutaneous, and intramuscular) according to the education and job description of the LPN or LVN.

The registered nurse can perform the tasks that a LPN or LVN can perform and is responsible for assessment and planning care, initiating teaching, and administering medications intravenously.

c. Determine which tasks can be delegated and to whom.

d. Match the task to the delegatee based on the nurse practice act and appropriate position descriptions.

e. Provide directions that are clear, concise, accurate, and complete.

f. Validate the person's understanding of the directions.

g. Communicate a feeling of confidence to the delegate, and provide feedback promptly after the task is performed.

h. Maintain continuity of care as much as possible when assigning client care.

▲ XVI. TIME MANAGEMENT

A. Description

1. Time **management** is a technique designed to assist in completing tasks within a definite time period.

2. Learning how, when, and where to use one's time and establishing personal goals and time frames are part of time **management.**

3. Time **management** requires an ability to anticipate the day's activities, to combine activities when possible, and not to be interrupted by nonessential activities.

4. Time **management** involves efficiency in completing tasks as quickly as possible and effectiveness in deciding on the most important task to do (i.e., prioritizing) and doing it correctly.

B. Principles and guidelines

1. Identify tasks, obligations, and activities, and write them down.

2. Organize the work day; identify which tasks must be completed in specified time frames.

3. Prioritize client needs according to importance.

4. Anticipate the needs of the day and provide time for unexpected and unplanned tasks that may arise.

5. Focus on beginning the daily tasks, working on the most important first while keeping goals in mind; look at the final goal for the day, which helps in the breakdown of tasks into manageable parts.

6. Begin client rounds at the beginning of the shift, collecting data on each assigned client.

7. Delegate tasks when appropriate.

8. Keep a daily hour-by-hour log to assist in providing structure to the tasks that must be accomplished, and cross tasks off the list as they are accomplished.

9. Use health care agency resources wisely, anticipating resource needs, and gather the necessary supplies before beginning the task.

10. Organize paperwork and continuously document task completion and necessary client data throughout the day (i.e., documentation should be concurrent with completion of a task or observation of pertinent client data).

11. At the end of the day, evaluate the effectiveness of time management.

XVII. PRIORITIZING CARE

A. **Prioritizing** is deciding which needs or problems require immediate action and which ones could tolerate a delay in response until a later time because they are not urgent.

B. Guidelines for **prioritizing** (Box 8-9)

C. Setting priorities for client teaching

1. Determine client's immediate learning needs.

2. Review the learning objectives established for the client.

3. Determine what the client perceives as important.

4. Assess the client's anxiety level and the time available to teach.

D. Prioritizing when caring for a group of clients

1. Identify the problems of each client.

2. Review nursing diagnoses.

3. Determine which client problems are most urgent based on basic needs, the client's changing or unstable status, and complexity of the client's problems.

BOX 8-9
Guidelines for Prioritizing

The nurse and the client mutually rank the client's needs in order of importance based on the client's preferences and expectations, safety, and physical and psychological needs; what the client sees as his or her priority needs may be different from what the nurse sees as the priority needs.

Priorities are classified as high, intermediate, or low.

Client needs that are life-threatening or that could result in harm to the client if they are left untreated are high priorities.

Nonemergency and non–life-threatening client needs are intermediate priorities.

Client needs that are not related directly to the client's illness or prognosis are low priorities.

When providing care, the nurse needs to decide which needs or problems require immediate action and which ones could be delayed until a later time because they are not urgent.

The nurse considers client problems that involve actual or life-threatening concerns before potential health-threatening concerns.

When prioritizing care, the nurse must consider time constraints and available resources.

Problems identified as important by the client must be given high priority.

The nurse can use the ABCs—airway, breathing, and circulation—as a guide when determining priorities; client needs related to maintaining a patent airway are always the priority.

The nurse can use Maslow's Hierarchy of Needs theory as a guide to determine priorities and identify the levels of physiological needs, safety, love and belonging, self-esteem, and self-actualization (basic needs are met before moving to other needs in the hierarchy).

The nurse can use the steps of the nursing process as a guide to determine priorities, remembering that assessment is the first step of the nursing process.

BOX 8-10
Types of Disasters

HUMAN-MADE DISASTERS
Dam failures resulting in flooding
Hazardous substance accidents such as pollution, chemical spills, or toxic gas leaks
Accidents involving release of radioactive material
Resource shortages such as food, water, and electricity
Structural collapse, fire, or explosions
Terrorist attacks such as bombing, riots, and bioterrorism
Mass transportation accidents

NATURAL DISASTERS
Blizzards
Communicable disease epidemics
Cyclones
Droughts
Earthquakes
Floods
Forest fires
Hailstorms
Hurricanes
Landslides
Mudslides
Tidal waves
Tornadoes
Volcanic eruptions

---

4. Anticipate the time that it may take to care for the priority needs of the clients.
5. Combine activities, if possible, to resolve more than one problem at a time.
6. Involve the client in his or her care as much as possible.

▲ XVIII. DISASTERS AND DISASTER PLANNING
  A. Description
    1. A disaster is any human-made or natural event that causes destruction and devastation that cannot be alleviated without assistance (Box 8-10).
    2. Internal disasters are those that occur within a health care agency (e.g., health care agency fire, structural collapse), whereas external disasters include those that occur outside the health care agency (e.g., mass transit accident that could send hundreds of clients to emergency departments).
    3. A disaster preparedness plan is a formal plan of action for coordinating the response of the health care agency staff in the event of a disaster in the health care agency or surrounding community.
  B. American Red Cross (ARC)
    1. Has been given **authority** by the federal government to provide disaster relief.
    2. All ARC disaster relief assistance is free, and local offices are located across the United States.
    3. Participates with the government in developing and testing community disaster plans.
    4. Identifies and trains personnel for disaster response.
    5. Works with businesses and labor organizations to identify resources and individuals for disaster work.
    6. Educates the public about ways to prepare for a disaster.
    7. Operates shelters, provides assistance to meet immediate emergency needs, and provides disaster health services, including crisis counseling.
    8. Handles inquiries from family members.
    9. Coordinates relief activities with other agencies.
    10. Nurses are involved directly with the ARC and assume functions such as managers, supervisors, and educators of first aid; they also participate in disaster preparedness and disaster relief

BOX 8-11
Federal Emergency Management Agency: Four Disaster Management Phases

Mitigation
Preparedness
Response
Recovery

BOX 8-12
Federal Emergency Management Agency Levels of Disaster

LEVEL III DISASTER
A minor disaster that involves a minimal level of damage but could result in a presidential declaration of an emergency

LEVEL II DISASTER
A moderate disaster that likely will result in a presidential declaration of an emergency, with moderate federal assistance

LEVEL I DISASTER
A massive disaster that involves significant damage and results in a presidential disaster declaration, with major federal involvement and full engagement of federal, regional, and national resources

programs and provide services, such as blood collection drives and immunization programs.

C. Phases of disaster **management**
1. The Federal Emergency Management Agency (FEMA) identifies four disaster **management** phases: mitigation, preparedness, response, and recovery (Box 8-11).
2. Mitigation encompasses the following:
   a. Actions or measures that can prevent the occurrence of a disaster or reduce the damaging effects of a disaster
   b. Determination of the community hazards and community risks (actual and potential threats) before a disaster occurs
   c. Awareness of available community resources and community health personnel to facilitate mobilization of activities and minimize chaos and confusion if a disaster occurs
   d. Determination of the resources available for care to infants, older clients, the disabled, and those with chronic health problems
3. Preparedness encompasses the following:
   a. Plans for rescue, evacuation, and caring for disaster victims
   b. Plans for training disaster personnel and gathering resources, equipment, and other materials needed for dealing with the disaster
   c. Identification of specific responsibilities for various disaster response personnel
   d. Establishment of a community disaster plan and an effective public communication system
   e. Development of an emergency medical system and a plan for activation
   f. Verification of proper functioning of emergency equipment
   g. Collection of anticipatory provisions and creation of a location for providing food, water, clothing, shelter, other supplies, and needed medicine
   h. Inventory of supplies on a regular basis and replenishment of outdated supplies
   i. Practice of community disaster plans (mock disaster drills)
4. Response
   a. Response includes putting disaster planning services into action and the actions taken to save lives and prevent further damage.

   b. Primary concerns include safety, physical health, and mental health of the victims and members of the disaster response team.
5. Recovery
   a. Recovery includes actions taken to return to a normal situation following the disaster.
   b. Recovery includes preventing debilitating effects and restoring personal, economic, and environmental health and stability to the community.

D. Levels of disaster:
1. FEMA identifies three levels of disaster with FEMA response (Box 8-12).
2. Once a federal emergency has been declared, the federal response plan may take effect and activate emergency support functions.
3. The emergency support functions of the ARC include performing emergency first aid, sheltering, feeding, providing a disaster welfare information system, and coordinating bulk distribution of emergency relief supplies.
4. Disaster medical assistant teams (teams of specially trained personnel) can be activated and sent to a disaster site to provide triage and medical care to victims until they can be evacuated to a hospital.

E. Nurse's role in disaster planning
1. Personal and professional preparedness
   a. Make personal and family preparations (Box 8-13).
   b. Be aware of the disaster plan at the place of employment and in the community.
   c. Maintain certification in disaster training and in cardiopulmonary resuscitation.
   d. Participate in mock disaster drills.
   e. Prepare professional emergency response items, such as a copy of the nursing license, personal health care equipment such as a

---

BOX 8-13

Emergency Plans and Supplies

Plan a meeting place for family members.
Identify where to go if an evacuation is necessary.
Determine when and how to turn off water, gas, and electricity at main switches.
Locate the safe spots in the home for each type of disaster.
Replace water supply every 3 months and food supply every 6 months.
Include the following supplies:
  A 3-day supply of water (1 gallon per person per day)
  A 3-day supply of nonperishable food
  Clothing and blankets
  A first-aid kit
  Adequate supply of prescription medication
  Battery-operated radio
  Flashlight and batteries
  Credit card, cash, or traveler's checks
  An extra set of car keys and a full tank of gas in the car
  Sanitation supplies for washing, toileting, and for disposing of trash
  An extra pair of eyeglasses
  Special items for infants, the older client, or the disabled
  Items needed for a pet such as food, water, and leash
  Important documents in a waterproof case

---

stethoscope, cash, warm clothing, record-keeping materials, and other nursing care supplies.

2. Disaster response
   a. In the heath care agency setting, if a disaster occurs, the agency disaster preparedness plan (emergency response plan) is activated immediately, and the nurse responds by following the directions identified in the plan.
   b. In the community setting, if the nurse is the first responder to a disaster, the nurse would care for the victims by attending to those with life-threatening problems first; once rescue workers arrive at the scene, immediate plans for triage should begin.
▲ F. Triage
   1. In a disaster or war, triage consists of brief assessment of victims that allows the nurse to classify victims according to the severity of the injury, urgency of treatment, and place for treatment.
   2. In an emergency department, triage consists of brief assessment of clients that allows the nurse to classify clients according to their need for care and establishing priorities of care; the type of illness or injury, the severity of the problem, and the resources available govern the process.
G. Triage rating systems: Various rating systems are used in clinical settings, and the nurse must be familiar with the rating system in the health care agency in which he or she is employed (Box 8-14).

BOX 8-14

Triage Rating Systems

FIVE-TIER SYSTEM (MOST OFTEN USED IN MILITARY TRIAGE)
1. Victim is dead or will die.
2. Life-threatening (emergent): Victim has life-threatening injuries, but they are readily correctable.
3. Urgent: Victim must be treated within 1 to 2 hours.
4. Delayed (nonurgent): Victim is noncritical or ambulatory; victim has minimal injury and no immediate treatment is necessary.
5. No injury: No treatment is necessary.

FOUR-TIER SYSTEM
1. Immediate (emergent): Victim is seriously injured but has a reasonable chance for survival.
2. Delayed (nonurgent): Victim can wait for care after simple first aid.
3. Expectant: Victim is extremely critical and dying.
4. Minimal (nonurgent): Victim has no impairment of function and can treat self or be treated by a nonprofessional.

THREE-TIER SYSTEM (COMMONLY USED IN HEALTH CARE AGENCIES)
1. Life threatening (emergent): Victim has life-threatening injuries, but they are readily correctable.
2. Urgent: Victim must be treated within 1 to 2 hours.
3. Delayed (nonurgent): Victim has no injury, is noncritical, or is ambulatory.

TWO-TIER SYSTEM
1. Immediate: Category includes victims who have life-threatening injuries that are readily correctable on the scene (emergent) and victims who must be treated within 1 to 2 hours (urgent).
2. Delayed (nonurgent): Category includes victims who have no injuries or noncritical injuries, are ambulatory, are dying, or are dead.

Modified from Mosby. (2002). *Mosby's medical, nursing, and allied health dictionary* (6th ed.). (2002). St. Louis: Mosby.

H. Emergency department triage system
   1. A commonly used rating system in an emergency department is a three-tier system that uses the categories of emergent, urgent, and nonurgent and also may identify these categories by color coding or numbers (Box 8-15).
   2. The nurse needs to be familiar with the triage system of the health care agency.
   3. When caring for the client who has died, the nurse needs to recognize the importance of family and religious rituals and provide support to loved ones.
   4. Organ donation procedures of the health care agency need to be addressed if appropriate.
I. Client assessment in the emergency department
   1. Primary assessment
      a. The purpose of primary assessment is to identify any client problem that poses an immediate or potential threat to life.

BOX 8-15
Emergency Department Triage

EMERGENT (RED): PRIORITY 1 (HIGHEST)
This classification is given to clients who have life-threatening injuries and need immediate attention and continuous evaluation, but have a high probability for survival once stabilized.

Such clients include those with trauma, chest pain, severe respiratory distress or cardiac arrest, limb amputation, acute neurological deficits, and those who have sustained chemical splashes to the eyes.

URGENT (YELLOW): PRIORITY 2
This classification is given to clients who require treatment and whose injuries have complications that are not life-threatening, provided that they are treated within 1 to 2 hours; these clients require continuous evaluation every 30 to 60 minutes thereafter.

Such clients include those with a simple fracture, asthma without respiratory distress, fever, hypertension, abdominal pain, or a renal stone.

NONURGENT (GREEN): PRIORITY 3
This classification is given to clients with local injuries who do not have immediate complications and who can wait several hours for medical treatment; these clients require evaluation every 1 to 2 hours thereafter.

Such clients include those with conditions such as a minor laceration, sprain, or cold symptoms.

b. The nurse gathers information primarily through objective data and, on finding any abnormalities, immediately initiates interventions.
c. The nurse uses the ABCs—airway, breathing, and circulation—as a guide in assessing the client's needs and also assesses the client who has sustained a traumatic injury for signs of a head injury or cervical spine injury.
2. Secondary assessment
a. The nurse performs secondary assessment following the primary assessment and after treatment for any primary problems identified.
b. Secondary assessment identifies any other life-threatening problems that the client might be experiencing.
c. The nurse obtains subjective and objective data, including a history, general overview, vital sign measurements, neurological assessment, pain assessment, and a complete or focused physical assessment.

PRACTICE QUESTIONS

1. A new unit nurse manager is holding her first staff meeting. The manager greets the staff and comments that she has been employed to bring about performance improvement. The manager provides a plan that she developed, as well as a list of tasks and activities for which each staff member must volunteer to perform. In addition, she instructs staff members to report any problems directly to her. What type of leadership style do the new manager's characteristics suggest?
   1. Autocratic
   2. Situational
   3. Democratic
   4. Laissez-faire

2. A nurse employed in an emergency department is assigned to triage clients arriving to the emergency room for treatment on the evening shift. The nurse should assign highest priority to which of the following clients?
   1. A client complaining of muscle aches, a headache, and malaise
   2. A client who twisted her ankle when she fell while rollerblading
   3. A client with a minor laceration on the index finger sustained while cutting an eggplant
   4. A client with chest pain who states that he just ate pizza that was made with a very spicy sauce

3. A new nursing graduate is attending an agency orientation regarding the nursing model of practice implemented in the health care facility. The nurse is told that the nursing model is a team nursing approach. The nurse understands that planning care delivery will be based on which characteristic of this type of nursing model of practice?
   1. A task approach method is used to provide care to clients.
   2. Managed care concepts and tools are used in providing client care.
   3. An RN (registered nurse) leads nursing personnel in providing care to a group of clients.
   4. A single RN is responsible for providing nursing care to a group of clients.

4. The nurse manager has implemented a change in the method of the nursing delivery system from functional to team nursing. A nursing assistant is resistant to the change and is not taking an active part in facilitating the process of change. Which of the following is the best approach in dealing with the nursing assistant?
   1. Ignore the resistance.
   2. Exert coercion with the nursing assistant.
   3. Provide a positive reward system for the nursing assistant.
   4. Confront the nursing assistant to encourage verbalization of feelings regarding the change.

5. The RN is planning the client assignments for the day. Which of the following is the most appropriate assignment for the nursing assistant?
   1. A client requiring a colostomy irrigation
   2. A client receiving continuous tube feedings

3. A client who requires urine specimen collections
4. A client with difficulty swallowing food and fluids

6. The RN employed in a long-term care facility is planning assignments for the clients on a nursing unit. The RN needs to assign four clients and has a licensed practical (vocational) nurse and three nursing assistants on a nursing team. Which of the following clients would the nurse most appropriately assign to the licensed practical (vocational) nurse?
   1. The client who requires a bed bath
   2. An older client requiring frequent ambulation
   3. A client who requires a 24-hour urine collection
   4. A client with an abdominal wound requiring wound irrigations and dressing changes every 3 hours

7. The RN has received the assignment for the day shift. After making initial rounds and checking all of the assigned clients, which client will the RN plan to care for first?
   1. A client who is ambulatory
   2. A client scheduled for physical therapy at 1 PM
   3. A client with a fever who is diaphoretic and restless
   4. A postoperative client who has just received pain medication

8. The nurse is assigned to care for four clients. In planning client rounds, which client should the nurse assess first?
   1. A client scheduled for a chest x-ray
   2. A client requiring daily dressing changes
   3. A postoperative client preparing for discharge
   4. A client receiving oxygen via nasal cannula who had difficulty breathing during the previous shift

9. The nurse is giving a bed bath to an assigned client when a nursing assistant enters the client's room and tells the nurse that another assigned client is in pain and needs pain medication. The appropriate nursing action is which of the following?
   1. Finish the bed bath and then administer the pain medication to the other client.
   2. Ask the nursing assistant to find out when the last pain medication was given to the client.
   3. Ask the nursing assistant to tell the client in pain that medication will be administered as soon as the bed bath is complete.
   4. Cover the client, raise the side rails, tell the client that you will return shortly, and administer the pain medication to the other client.

10. The nurse manager of a critical care unit must speak to a staff nurse about an employment issue, tardiness. Nearly every day during the past week, the staff nurse has been from 5 to 20 minutes late, missing portions of the daily client status conferences. The manager had verbally counseled the staff nurse 3 months prior to the latest incidence of tardiness about the same issue. When they meet, the nurse manager's best approach to the staff nurse is to:
    1. Send the staff nurse to the Human Resources Department for counseling.
    2. Ask the staff nurse to tell the manager about the facts surrounding the tardiness.
    3. Inform the staff nurse that, based on unreliability caused by tardiness issues, the nurse is terminated.
    4. Provide the staff nurse with a detailed notice of intent to terminate if any further incident of tardiness occurs.

ALTERNATE ITEM FORMAT: CHART OR EXHIBIT WITH PRIORITIZING (ORDERED RESPONSE)

The home health care nurse is planning client visits and nursing activities for the day. The nurse begins the visits at 9 AM. All clients live within a 5-mile radius. List in order of priority how the nurse should plan the order of the assignments for the day? (Number 1 is the first client and/or nursing activity for the day and number 6 is the last.)

CHART/EXHIBIT
CLIENT ASSIGNMENT AND NURSING ACTIVITIES
____ The client requiring admission
____ The client being visited by the home health aide
____ The client regarding supervision of the dressing change
____ First dressing change for the client requiring twice-daily dressing changes
____ Second dressing change for the client requiring twice-daily dressing changes
____ The client with diabetes mellitus who needs a fasting blood glucose level drawn

ANSWERS

1. **1**

Rationale: The autocratic leader is focused, maintains strong control, makes decisions, and, addresses all problems. Furthermore, the autocrat dominates the group and commands rather than seeks suggestions or input. In this situation, the manager addresses a problem (performance improvement) with the staff, designs a plan without input, and wants all problems reported directly back to her. A situational leader will use a combination of styles, depending on the needs of the group and the tasks to be achieved. The situational leader would work with the group to validate that the information that the leader gained as a new employee was accurate and that a problem existed, and would then take the time to get to know the group and determine which approach to change (if needed) would work best according to the needs of the group and the nature and substance of the change that was required. A democratic leader is participative and would likely meet with each staff person individually to determine the staff member's perception of the problem. The democratic leader would also speak with the staff about any issues and ask the staff for input with developing a plan. A laissez-faire leader is passive and nondirective. The laissez-faire leader would state what the problem was and inform the staff that the staff needed to come up with a plan to "fix it."

Test-Taking Strategy: Focus on the data in the question and note the strategic words *provides a plan that she developed, each staff member must volunteer to perform* and *instructs staff members to report any problems directly to her.* Remember, autocratic managers take control and dominate. Review the various types of leadership styles if you had difficulty with this question.

Level of Cognitive Ability: Comprehension
Client Needs: Safe and Effective Care Environment
Integrated Process: Nursing Process/Planning
Content Area: Leadership/Management
Reference: Marriner-Tomey, A. (2004). *Guide to nursing management and leadership* (7th ed., pp. 167-176). St. Louis: Mosby.

2. **4**

Rationale: In an emergency department, triage involves brief client assessment to classify clients according to their need for care and includes establishing priorities of care. The type of illness or injury, the severity of the problem, and the resources available govern the process. Clients with trauma, chest pain, severe respiratory distress or cardiac arrest, limb amputation, acute neurological deficits, and those who have sustained chemical splashes to the eyes are classified as emergent and are the number 1 priority. Clients with conditions such as a simple fracture, asthma without respiratory distress, fever, hypertension, abdominal pain, or a renal stone have urgent needs and are classified as number 2 priority. Clients with conditions such as a minor laceration, sprain, or cold symptoms are classified as nonurgent and are the number 3 priority.

Test-Taking Strategy: Note the strategic words highest priority. Use the ABCs—airway, breathing, and circulation—to direct you to option 4. A client experiencing chest pain is always classified as priority number 1 until a myocardial infarction has been ruled out. Review the triage classification system commonly used in a hospital emergency department if you had difficulty with this question.

Level of Cognitive Ability: Application
Client Needs: Safe and Effective Care Environment
Integrated Process: Nursing Process—implementation
Content Area: Delegating/Prioritizing
References: Ignatavicius, D., & Workman, M. (2006). *Medical-surgical nursing: Critical thinking for collaborative care* (5th ed., pp. 161-162). Philadelphia: W.B. Saunders.
Lewis, S., Heitkemper, M., & Dirksen, S. (2004). *Medical-surgical nursing: Assessment and management of clinical problems* (6th ed., p. 1846). St. Louis: Mosby.

3. **3**

Rationale: In team nursing, nursing personnel are led by a registered nurse leader in providing care to a group of clients. Option 1 identifies functional nursing. Option 2 identifies a component of case management. Option 4 identifies primary nursing.

Test-Taking Strategy: Note that the subject of the question relates to team nursing. Keep this subject in mind and use the process of elimination. Option 3 is the only option that identifies the concept of a team approach. Review the various types of nursing delivery systems if you had difficulty with this question.

Level of Cognitive Ability: Comprehension
Client Needs: Safe and Effective Care Environment
Integrated Process: Nursing Process—planning
Content Area: Leadership/Management
References: Huber, D. (2006). *Leadership and nursing care management* (3rd ed., pp. 317, 322). Philadelphia: W.B. Saunders.
Potter, P., & Perry, A. (2005). *Fundamentals of nursing* (6th ed., p. 373). St. Louis: Mosby.

4. **4**

Rationale: Confrontation is an important strategy to meet resistance head on. Face-to-face meetings to confront the issue at hand will allow verbalization of feelings, identification of problems and issues, and development of strategies to solve the problem. Option 1 will not address the problem. Option 2 may produce additional resistance. Option 3 may provide a temporary solution to the resistance but will not address the concern specifically.

Test-Taking Strategy: Use the process of elimination. Options 1 and 2 easily can be eliminated first. From the remaining options, select option 4 over option 3 because this option specifically addresses the subject and would provide problem-solving measures. If you had difficulty with this question, review the strategies associated with dealing with resistance to change.

Level of Cognitive Ability: Application
Client Needs: Safe and Effective Care Environment
Integrated Process: Nursing Process—implementation
Content Area: Leadership/Management
References: Huber, D. (2006). *Leadership and nursing care management* (3rd ed., p. 527). Philadelphia: W.B. Saunders.
Potter, P., & Perry, A. (2005). *Fundamentals of nursing* (6th ed., p. 440). St. Louis: Mosby.

5. **3**

Rationale: The nurse must determine the most appropriate assignment based on the skills of the staff member and the needs of the client. In this case, the most appropriate assignment for a nursing assistant would be to care for the client who requires urine specimen collections. The nursing assistant is skilled in this procedure. Colostomy irrigations and tube feedings are not performed by unlicensed personnel. The client with difficulty swallowing food and fluids is at risk for aspiration.

Test-Taking Strategy: Note the strategic words, *most appropriate*, and note the subject, an assignment to a nursing assistant. Eliminate option 4 first because of the words *difficulty swallowing*. Next, eliminate options 1 and 2 because they are comparative or alike and are both invasive procedures. Review the principles of delegation if you had difficulty with this question.

Level of Cognitive Ability: Application
Client Needs: Safe and Effective Care Environment
Integrated Process: Nursing Process—planning
Content Area: Delegating/Prioritizing
References: Huber, D. (2006). *Leadership and nursing care management* (3rd ed., p. 546). Philadelphia: W.B. Saunders.
Potter, P., & Perry, A. (2005). *Fundamentals of nursing* (6th ed., pp. 42, 350, 378). St. Louis: Mosby.

6. 4
Rationale: When delegating nursing assignments, the nurse needs to consider the skills and educational level of the nursing staff. Collecting a 24-hour urine sample, giving a bed bath, and assisting with frequent ambulation can be provided most appropriately by the nursing assistant. The licensed practical (vocational) nurse is skilled in wound irrigations and dressing changes and most appropriately would be assigned to the client who needs this care.

Test-Taking Strategy: Use the process of elimination and knowledge regarding the principles of delegation and assignment making. Focus on the subject, assignment to a licensed practical/vocational nurse. Recall that education and job position as described by the nurse practice act and employee guidelines need to be considered when delegating activities and making assignments. Options 1, 2, and 3 easily can be eliminated because a nursing assistant can perform these tasks. If you had difficulty with this question, review the principles of delegation and assignment making.

Level of Cognitive Ability: Application
Client Needs: Safe and Effective Care Environment
Integrated Process: Nursing Process—planning
Content Area: Delegating/Prioritizing
References: Huber, D. (2006). *Leadership and nursing care management* (3rd ed., pp. 545-546). Philadelphia: W.B. Saunders.
Potter, P., & Perry, A. (2005). *Fundamentals of nursing* (6th ed., pp. 41-42, 378). St. Louis: Mosby.

7. 3
Rationale: The RN would plan to care for the client who has a fever and is diaphoretic and restless first because this client's needs are the priority. Waiting for pain medication to take effect before providing care to the postoperative client is best. The client who is ambulatory and the client scheduled for physical therapy later in the day do not have priority needs related to care.

Test-Taking Strategy: Note the strategic words *care for first* and use principles related to prioritizing. Noting the words *diaphoretic* and *restless* will assist in directing you to this option. Re-

view the principles related to prioritizing if you had difficulty with this question.

Level of Cognitive Ability: Application
Client Needs: Safe and Effective Care Environment
Integrated Process: Nursing Process—planning
Content Area: Delegating/Prioritizing
References: Huber, D. (2006). *Leadership and nursing care management* (3rd ed., p. 167). Philadelphia: W.B. Saunders.
Potter, P., & Perry, A. (2005). *Fundamentals of nursing* (6th ed., pp. 267-268). St. Louis: Mosby.

8. 4
Rationale: Airway is always a highest priority, and the nurse would attend to the client who has been experiencing an airway problem first. The clients described in options 1, 2, and 3 have needs that would be identified as intermediate priorities.

Test-Taking Strategy: Use Maslow's Hierarchy of Needs theory and the ABCs—airway, breathing, and circulation—to answer the question. Remember that airway is always the highest priority. This will direct you to option 4. Review principles related to prioritizing if you had difficulty with this question.

Level of Cognitive Ability: Application
Client Needs: Safe and Effective Care Environment
Integrated Process: Nursing Process—planning
Content Area: Delegating/Prioritizing
Reference: Potter, P., & Perry, A. (2005). *Fundamentals of nursing* (6th ed., pp. 267-268, 1247). St. Louis: Mosby.

9. 4
Rationale: The nurse is responsible for the care provided to assigned clients. The appropriate action in this situation is to provide safety to the client who is receiving the bed bath and prepare to administer the pain medication. Options 1 and 3 delay the administration of medication to the client in pain. Option 2 is not a responsibility of the nursing assistant.

Test-Taking Strategy: Use the process of elimination and principles related to priorities of care. Options 1 and 3 delay the administration of pain medication, and option 2 is not a responsibility of the nursing assistant. The appropriate action is to plan to administer the medication. Review principles related to priorities of care if you had difficulty with this question.

Level of Cognitive Ability: Application
Client Needs: Safe and Effective Care Environment
Integrated Process: Nursing Process—implementation
Content Area: Delegating/Prioritizing
References: Jarvis, C. (2004). *Physical examination and health assessment* (4th ed., p. 4). Philadelphia: W.B. Saunders.
Potter, P., & Perry, A. (2005). *Fundamentals of nursing* (6th ed., pp. 267-268, 1030). St. Louis: Mosby.

10. 4
Rationale: In general, the process for corrective action begins with an oral reprimand and then a written reprimand. In addition to the written reprimand, the manager should be prepared to work with the staff nurse to develop a plan of action. The manager must notify the staff nurse, in writing, of the potential for termination based on tardiness. If this were the first instance, the manager would ask the staff nurse to describe the facts surrounding the tardiness in order for the manager to assist the staff nurse with problem-solving strate-

gies or to examine the need for moving the staff nurse to a different shift, if indicated. Managers are expected to deal with personnel issues, and tardiness is a frequent problem that managers face. Human resources serves as a support to the actions of the manager, but does not assume the role of dealing with the employee. Managers must give notice prior to termination as a risk management strategy.
Test-Taking Strategy: Note that the series of tardinesses are the second offense. Remember that the process for corrective action begins with an oral reprimand and then a written reprimand. Review the principles and processes of disciplinary action if you had difficulty with this question.
Level of Cognitive Ability: Application
Client Needs: Safe and Effective Care Environment
Integrated Process: Nursing Process/Implementation
Content Area: Leadership/Management
Reference: Marriner-Tomey, A. (2004). *Guide to nursing management and leadership* (7th ed., pp. 418-425) St. Louis: Mosby.

ALTERNATE ITEM FORMAT: CHART OR EXHIBIT WITH PRIORITIZING (ORDERED RESPONSE)

Answer: 5, 3, 4, 2, 6, 1
Rationale: The nurse would plan to visit the client with diabetes mellitus first and draw the fasting blood glucose level because this client needs to remain NPO until the blood is drawn. This client would also not be able to take any medication, such as insulin, until the blood is drawn. The nurse would plan to see the client requiring twice-daily dressing changes next because the dressing changes should be spaced as far apart as possible. The nurse then would plan to see the

client being visited by the home health aide and provide instructions and directions to the home health aide regarding care to the client. The nurse then would visit the client regarding supervision of the dressing change and would perform the admission last because that may take more time than the other clients. The nurse then would return to the client requiring the second twice-daily dressing change.
Test-Taking Strategy: Note the needs of the client and the role of the nurse in caring for each of the clients. Noting that the client with diabetes mellitus needs to remain NPO until the blood is drawn will assist in determining that this client needs to be visited first. Noting that the client requiring twice-daily dressing changes will need to be seen twice will assist in determining the next and last client visit of the day, because dressing changes should be spaced as far apart as possible. Next, note that the home health aide will be with the client at 10 AM; this client will be seen next. From the remaining clients, select the client requiring a supervised dressing change to be seen next because the client admission may take time. If you had difficulty with this question, review the process of planning care and time management.
Level of Cognitive Ability: Application
Client Needs: Safe and Effective Care Environment
Integrated Process: Nursing Process—planning
Content Area: Delegating/Prioritizing
References: Huber, D. (2006). *Leadership and nursing care management* (3rd ed., p. 83). Philadelphia: W.B. Saunders.
Potter, P., & Perry, A. (2005). *Fundamentals of nursing* (6th ed., pp. 377-378). St. Louis: Mosby.

REFERENCES

Cohen, E., & Cesta, T. (2005). *Nursing case management: From essentials to advanced practice applications* (4th ed.). St. Louis: Mosby.
Huber, D. (2006). *Leadership and nursing care management* (3rd ed.). Philadelphia: W.B. Saunders.
Ignatavicius, D., & Workman, M. (2006). *Medical-surgical nursing: Critical thinking for collaborative care* (5th ed.). Philadelphia: W.B. Saunders.
Jarvis, C. (2004). *Physical examination and health assessment* (4th ed.). Philadelphia: W.B. Saunders.
Lewis, S., Heitkemper, M., & Dirksen, S. (2004). *Medical-surgical nursing: Assessment and management of clinical problems* (6th ed.). St. Louis: Mosby.

Marriner-Tomey, A. (2004). *Guide to nursing management and leadership,* (7th ed.). St. Louis: Mosby.
Mosby. (2002). *Mosby's medical, nursing, and allied health dictionary* (6th ed.). St. Louis: Mosby.
National Council of State Boards (Eds.). (2007). *2007 NCLEX-RN® detailed test plan.* Chicago: Author.
Potter, P., & Perry, A. (2005). *Fundamentals of nursing* (6th ed.). St. Louis: Mosby.

Nursing Sciences

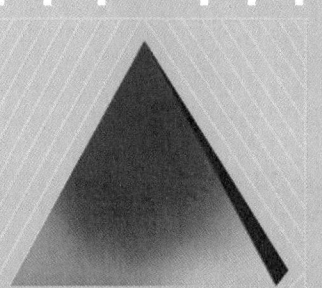

Fluids and Electrolytes

PYRAMID TERMS

calcium A mineral element needed for the process of bone formation, coagulation of blood, excitation of cardiac and skeletal muscle, maintenance of muscle tone, conduction of neuromuscular impulses, and the synthesis and regulation of the endocrine and exocrine glands. The normal adult level is 8.6 to 10.0 mg/dL.

fluid volume deficit Dehydration in which the fluid intake of the body is not sufficient to meet the fluid needs of the body.

fluid volume excess Fluid intake or fluid retention that exceeds the fluid needs of the body. Also called overhydration or fluid overload.

homeostasis The tendency of biological systems to maintain relatively constant conditions in the internal environment while continuously interacting with and adjusting to changes originating within or outside the system.

hypercalcemia A serum calcium level that exceeds 10.0 mg/dL.

hyperkalemia A serum potassium level that exceeds 5.1 mEq/L.

hypermagnesemia A serum magnesium level that exceeds 2.6 mg/dL.

hypernatremia A serum sodium level that exceeds 145 mEq/L.

hyperphosphatemia A serum phosphorus level that exceeds 4.5 mg/dL.

hypocalcemia A serum calcium level less than 8.6 mg/dL.

hypokalemia A serum potassium level less than 3.5 mEq/L.

hypomagnesemia A serum magnesium level less than 1.6 mg/dL.

hyponatremia A serum sodium level less than 135 mEq/L.

hypophosphatemia A serum phosphorus level less than 2.7 mg/dL.

magnesium Concentrated in the bone, cartilage, and within the cell itself; required for the use of adenosine triphosphate (ATP) as a source of energy. It is necessary for the action of numerous enzyme systems such as carbohydrate metabolism, protein synthesis, nucleic acid synthesis, and contraction of muscular tissue. It also regulates neuromuscular activity and the clotting mechanism. The normal adult level is 1.6 to 2.6 mg/dL.

potassium A principle electrolyte of intracellular fluid and the primary buffer within the cell itself. It is needed for nerve conduction, muscle function, acid-base balance, and osmotic pressure. Along with calcium and magnesium, it controls the rate and force of contraction of the heart and thus cardiac output. The normal adult level is 3.5 to 5.1 mEq/L.

phosphorus Needed for generation of bony tissue. It functions in the metabolism of glucose and lipids, in the maintenance of acid-base balance, and in the storage and transfer of energy from one site in the body to another. Phosphorus levels are evaluated in relation to calcium levels because of their inverse relationships; when calcium levels are decreased, phosphorus levels are increased, and when phosphorus levels are decreased, calcium levels are increased. The normal adult level is 2.7 to 4.5 mg/dL.

sodium An abundant electrolyte that maintains osmotic pressure and acid-base balance and transmits nerve impulses. The normal adult level is 135 to 145 mEq/L.

THE PYRAMID TO SUCCESS

Pyramid Points focus primarily on the assessment of a fluid and electrolyte imbalance, interventions, and evaluating the expected outcomes. Fluids and electrolytes constitute a content area that is sometimes complex and difficult to understand. The nurse must understand cell functions and properties and the concepts related to body fluids as outlined in this chapter. Pyramid Points focus on the common fluid and electrolyte disturbances. As you review this content, focus on the Pyramid Points related to the causes, assessment findings, and related treatments. In any fluid or electrolyte imbalance, nursing interventions include monitoring significant laboratory results and monitoring the client's cardiovascular, respiratory, gastrointestinal, neuromuscular, renal, and central nervous system status. Integrated Processes addressed in this chapter are Caring, Communication and Documentation, Nursing Process, and Teaching/Learning.

▲ CLIENT NEEDS

Safe and Effective Care Environment

Consulting with members of the health care team

Establishing priorities for care

Handling hazardous and infectious materials to prevent injury to health care personnel and others

Maintaining medical and surgical asepsis and preventing infection in the client when samples for laboratory studies are obtained or when intravenous solutions are administered

Maintaining standard, transmission-based, and other precautions to prevent transmission of infection to self and others

Preventing accidents and ensuring safety of the client when an imbalance exists, particularly when changes in cardiovascular, respiratory, gastrointestinal, neuromuscular, renal, or central nervous systems occur, or when the client is at risk for complications such as seizures, respiratory depression, or dysrhythmias

Health Promotion and Maintenance

Implementing health screening and monitoring for the potential risk for a fluid and electrolyte imbalance

Providing education related to medication and diet management

Providing education related to the potential risk for a fluid and electrolyte imbalance, measures to prevent an imbalance, signs and symptoms of an imbalance, and actions to take if signs and symptoms develop

Psychosocial Integrity

Providing reassurance to the client who is experiencing a fluid or electrolyte imbalance

Providing support and continuously informing the client of the purposes for prescribed interventions

Physiological Integrity

Assessing for expected and unexpected responses to therapeutic interventions and documenting findings

Assisting in managing emergencies

Identifying clients who are at risk for a fluid or electrolyte imbalance

Monitoring for complications related to the imbalance

Monitoring of laboratory values

BOX 9-1

Properties of Electrolytes and Their Components

ATOM

An atom is the smallest part of an element that still has the properties of the element.

The atom is composed of particles known as the proton (positive charge), neutron (neutral), and electron (negative charge).

Protons and neutrons are in the nucleus of the atom; therefore, the nucleus is positively charged.

Electrons carry a negative charge and revolve around the nucleus.

As long as the number of electrons is the same as the number of protons, the atom has no net charge; that is, it is neither positive nor negative.

Atoms may gain, lose, or share electrons and then are no longer neutral.

MOLECULE

A molecule is two or more atoms that combine to form a substance.

ION

An ion is an atom that carries an electrical charge because it has gained or lost electrons.

Some ions carry a negative electrical charge and some carry a positive charge.

CATION

A cation is an ion that carries a positive charge and has given away or lost electrons.

The result is fewer electrons than protons, and the result is a positive charge.

ANION

An anion is an ion that has gained electrons and therefore carries a negative charge.

When an ion has gained or taken on electrons, it assumes a negative charge and the result is a negatively charged ion.

▲ I. CONCEPTS OF FLUID AND ELECTROLYTE BALANCE

A. Electrolytes

1. Description: A substance that is dissolved in solution and some of its molecules split or dissociate into electrically charged atoms or ions (Box 9-1)

2. Measurement
   a. The metric system is used to measure volumes of fluids—liters (L) or milliliters (mL).
   b. The unit of measure that expresses the combining activity of an electrolyte is the milliequivalent (mEq).
   c. One milliequivalent (1 mEq) of any cation will always react chemically with 1 mEq of an anion.
   d. Milliequivalents provide information about the number of anions or cations available to combine with other anions or cations.

B. Body fluid compartments
   1. Description
      a. Fluid in each of the body compartments contains electrolytes.

b. Each compartment has a particular composition of electrolytes, which differs from that of other compartments.

c. To function normally, body cells must have fluids and electrolytes in the right compartments and in the right amounts.

d. Whenever an electrolyte moves out of a cell, another electrolyte moves in to take its place.

e. The numbers of cations and anions must be the same for **homeostasis** to exist.

f. Compartments are separated by semipermeable membranes.

2. Intravascular compartment: Refers to fluid inside a blood vessel

3. Intracellular compartment
   a. The intracellular compartment refers to all fluid inside the cell.
   b. Most bodily fluids are inside the cell.

4. The extracellular compartment is the fluid outside the cell.
   a. The extracellular compartment includes the interstitial fluid, which is fluid between cells (sometimes called the third space), blood, lymph, bone, connective tissue, water, and transcellular fluid.
   b. Transcellular fluid is the fluid in various parts of the body, such as peritoneal fluid, pleural fluid, cerebrospinal fluid, and synovial fluid.

▲ C. Third-spacing
1. Third-spacing is the accumulation and sequestration of trapped extracellular fluid in an actual or potential body space as a result of disease or injury.
2. The trapped fluid represents a volume loss and is unavailable for normal physiological processes.
3. Fluid may be trapped in body spaces such as the pericardial, pleural, peritoneal, or joint cavities, the bowel, or the abdomen, or within soft tissues after trauma or burns.
4. Assessing the intravascular fluid loss caused by third-spacing is difficult. The loss may not be reflected in weight changes or intake and output records and may not become apparent until after organ malfunction occurs.

▲ D. Edema
1. Edema is an excess accumulation of fluid in the interstitial space.
2. Localized edema occurs as a result of traumatic injury from accidents or surgery, local inflammatory processes, or burns.
3. Generalized edema, also called anasarca, is an excessive accumulation of fluid in the interstitial space throughout the body and occurs as a result of conditions such as cardiac, renal, or liver failure.

E. Body fluid
1. Description
   a. Body fluids transport nutrients to the cells and carry waste products from the cells.
   b. Total body fluid (intracellular and extracellular) amounts to about 60% of body weight in the adult, 55% in the older adult, and 80% in the infant.
   c. Thus, infants and the older adult are at a higher risk for fluid-related problems than younger adults; children have a greater proportion of body water than adults and the older adult has the least proportion of body water.

2. Constituents of body fluids
   a. Body fluids consist of water and dissolved substances.
   b. The largest single fluid constituent of the body is water.
   c. Some substances, such as glucose, urea, and creatinine, do not dissociate in solution; that is, they do not separate from their complex forms into simpler substances when they are in solution.
   d. Other substances do dissociate; for example, when **sodium** chloride is in a solution, it dissociates or separates into two parts or elements.

F. Body fluid transport
1. Diffusion
   a. Diffusion is the process whereby a solute (substance that is dissolved) may spread through a solution or solvent (solution in which the solute is dissolved).
   b. Diffusion of a solute will spread the molecules from an area of higher concentration to an area of lower concentration.
   c. A permeable membrane will allow substances to pass through it without restriction.
   d. A selectively permeable membrane will allow some solutes to pass through without restriction but will prevent other solutes from passing freely.
   e. Diffusion occurs within fluid compartments and from one compartment to another if the barrier between the compartments is permeable to the diffusing substances.

2. Osmosis
   a. Osmotic pressure is the force that draws the solvent from a less concentrated solute through a selectively permeable membrane into a more concentrated solute, thus tending to equalize the concentration of the solvent.
   b. If a membrane is permeable to water but not to all the solutes present, the membrane is a selective or semipermeable membrane.

c. Osmosis is the movement of solvent molecules across a membrane in response to a concentration gradient, usually from a solution of lower to one of higher solute concentration.

d. When a more concentrated solution is on one side of a selectively permeable membrane and a less concentrated solution is on the other side, a pull called osmotic pressure draws the water through the membrane to the more concentrated side or the side with more solute.

3. Filtration
   a. Filtration is the movement of solutes and solvents by hydrostatic pressure.
   b. The movement is from an area of higher pressure to an area of lower pressure.

4. Hydrostatic pressure
   a. Hydrostatic pressure is the force exerted by the weight of a solution.
   b. When a difference exists in the hydrostatic pressure on two sides of a membrane, water and diffusible solutes move out of the solution that has the higher hydrostatic pressure by the process of filtration.
   c. At the arterial end of the capillary, the hydrostatic pressure is higher than the osmotic pressure; therefore, fluids and diffusible solutes move out of the capillary.
   d. At the venous end, the osmotic pressure or pull is higher than the hydrostatic pressure, and fluids and some solutes move into the capillary.
   e. The excess fluid and solutes remaining in the interstitial spaces are returned to the intravascular compartment by the lymph channels.

5. Osmolality
   a. Osmolality refers to the number of osmotically active particles/kilogram of water; it is the concentration of a solution.
   b. In the body, osmotic pressure is measured in milliosmoles (mOsm).
   c. The normal osmolality of plasma is 270 to 300 milliosmoles/kilogram (mOsm/kg) water.

G. Movement of body fluid
   1. Description
      a. Cell membranes separate the interstitial fluid from the intravascular fluid.
      b. Cell membranes are selectively permeable; that is, the cell membrane and the capillary wall will allow water and some solutes free passage through them.
      c. Several forces affect the movement of water and solutes through the walls of cells and capillaries.
      d. The greater the number of particles within the cell, the more pressure exists to force the water through the cell membrane.

   e. If the body loses more electrolytes than fluids, as can happen in diarrhea, then the extracellular fluid will contain fewer electrolytes or less solute than the intracellular fluid.
   f. Fluids and electrolytes must be kept in balance for health; when they remain out of balance, death can occur.

   2. Isotonic solutions
      a. When the solutions on both sides of a selectively permeable membrane have established equilibrium or are equal in concentration, they are isotonic.
      b. An example of an isotonic solution is 0.9% sodium chloride, which is referred to as isotonic saline solution or normal saline solution.
      c. Isotonic solutions are isotonic to human cells, and thus very little osmosis occurs; isotonic solutions have the same osmolality as body fluids.
      d. Other solutions that are isotonic are 5% dextrose in water, 5% dextrose in 0.225% saline, and Ringer's lactate solution.

   3. Hypotonic solutions
      a. When a solution contains a lower concentration of salt or solute than another more concentrated solution, it is considered hypotonic.
      b. A hypotonic solution has less salt or more water than an isotonic solution; these solutions have lower osmolality than body fluids.
      c. 0.45% sodium chloride, 0.225% sodium chloride, and 0.33% sodium chloride are examples of hypotonic solutions.
      d. Hypotonic solutions are hypotonic to the cells; therefore, osmosis would continue in an attempt to bring about balance or equality.

   4. Hypertonic solutions
      a. A solution that has a higher concentration of solutes than another less concentrated solution is hypertonic; these solutions have a higher osmolality than body fluids.
      b. Hypertonic solutions include 3% sodium chloride, 5% sodium chloride, 10% dextrose in water, 5% dextrose in 0.9% sodium chloride, 5% dextrose in 0.45% sodium chloride, and 5% dextrose in Ringer's lactate solution.
      c. Refer to Table 14-1 (Chap. 14) for a list of isotonic, hypotonic, and hypertonic solutions.

   5. Osmotic pressure
      a. The amount of osmotic pressure is determined by the concentration of solutes in solution.
      b. When the solutions on each side of a selectively permeable membrane are equal in concentration, they are isotonic.

c. A hypotonic solution has less solute than an isotonic solution, whereas a hypertonic solution contains more solute.

d. A solvent will move from the less concentrated solute side to the more concentrated solute side to equalize concentration.

6. Active transport

a. If an ion is to move through a membrane from an area of lower concentration to an area of higher concentration, an active transport system is necessary.

b. An active transport system moves molecules or ions against concentration and osmotic pressure.

c. Metabolic processes in the cell supply the energy for active transport.

d. Substances that are transported actively through the cell membrane include ions of **sodium, potassium, calcium,** iron, and hydrogen, some of the sugars, and the amino acids.

▲ H. Body fluid excretion (Box 9-2)

1. Description

a. Fluids leave the body by several routes, including the skin, lungs, gastrointestinal tract, and kidneys.

b. The kidneys excrete the largest quantity of fluid.

c. As long as all organs are functioning normally, the body is able to maintain balance in its fluid content.

2. Skin

a. Water is lost through the skin in the amount of about 400 mL/day.

b. The amount of water lost by perspiration varies according to the temperature of the environment and of the body, but the average amount of loss by perspiration alone is 100 mL/day.

c. Water lost through the skin is called insensible loss (the individual is unaware of losing that water).

3. Lungs

a. Water is lost from the lungs through expired air that is saturated with water vapor.

b. The amount of water lost from the lungs varies with the rate and the depth of respiration.

c. The average amount of water lost from the lungs is about 350 mL/day.

d. Water lost from the lungs is called insensible loss.

4. Gastrointestinal tract

a. Large quantities of water are secreted into the gastrointestinal tract, but almost all this fluid is reabsorbed.

b. A large volume of electrolyte-containing liquids moves into the gastrointestinal tract and then returns again into the extracellular fluid.

c. The average amount of water lost in the feces is 150 mL/day, equal to the amount of water gained through the oxidation of foods.

d. Severe diarrhea results in the loss of large quantities of fluids and electrolytes.

5. Kidneys

a. The kidneys play a major role in regulating fluid and electrolyte balance.

b. Normal kidneys can adjust the amount of water and electrolytes leaving the body.

c. The quantity of fluid excreted by the kidneys is determined by the amount of water ingested and the amount of waste and solutes excreted.

d. The usual urine output is about 1500 mL/day; however, this varies greatly depending on fluid intake, amount of perspiration, and other factors.

I. Body fluid replacement

1. Description: Water enters the body through three sources—orally ingested liquids, water in foods, and water formed by oxidation of foods.

2. Amounts

a. The average total amount of water taken into the body by all three sources is 2500 mL/day.

b. About 10 mL of water is released by the metabolism of each 100 calories of fat, carbohydrates, or proteins.

3. Electrolytes

a. Electrolytes are present in foods and liquids.

b. With a normal diet, an excess of essential electrolytes is taken in and the unused electrolytes are excreted.

J. Maintaining fluid and electrolyte balance

1. Description

a. **Homeostasis** is a term that indicates the relative stability of the internal environment.

b. Concentration and composition of body fluids must be nearly constant.

c. In a client, when one of the substances is deficient, either fluids or electrolytes, the substance must be replaced normally by the intake of food and water or by therapy such as intravenous solutions and medications.

d. When the client has an excess of fluid or electrolytes, therapy is directed toward assisting the body to eliminate the excess.

BOX 9-2

Daily Body Fluid Excretion

Skin by diffusion: 400 mL
Skin by perspiration: 100 mL
Lungs: 350 mL
Feces: 150 mL
Kidneys: 1500 mL

2. The kidneys play a major role in controlling all types of balance in fluid and electrolytes.
3. The adrenal glands, through the secretion of aldosterone, also aid in controlling extracellular fluid volume by regulating the amount of sodium reabsorbed by the kidneys.
4. Antidiuretic hormone from the pituitary gland regulates the osmotic pressure of extracellular fluid by regulating the amount of water reabsorbed by the kidney.

II. FLUID VOLUME DEFICIT

A. Description
  1. Dehydration occurs when the fluid intake of the body is not sufficient to meet the fluid needs of the body.
  2. The goal of treatment is to restore fluid volume, replace electrolytes as needed, and eliminate the cause of the **fluid volume deficit**.
B. Types of **fluid volume deficits**
  1. Isotonic dehydration
    a. Water and dissolved electrolytes are lost in equal proportions.
    b. Known as hypovolemia, isotonic dehydration is the most common type of dehydration.
    c. Isotonic dehydration results in decreased circulating blood volume and inadequate tissue perfusion.
  2. Hypertonic dehydration
    a. Water loss exceeds electrolyte loss.
    b. The clinical problems that occur result from alterations in the concentrations of specific plasma electrolytes.
    c. Fluid moves from the intracellular compartment into the plasma and interstitial fluid spaces, causing cellular dehydration and shrinkage.
  3. Hypotonic dehydration
    a. Electrolyte loss exceeds water loss.
    b. The clinical problems that occur result from fluid shifts between compartments, causing a decrease in plasma volume.
    c. Fluid moves from the plasma and interstitial fluid spaces into the cells, causing a plasma volume deficit and causing the cells to swell.
C. Causes of **fluid volume** deficits
  1. Isotonic dehydration
    a. Inadequate intake of fluids and solutes
    b. Fluid shifts between compartments
    c. Excessive losses of isotonic body fluids
  2. Hypertonic dehydration—conditions that increase fluid loss, such as excessive perspiration, hyperventilation, ketoacidosis, prolonged fevers, diarrhea, early-stage renal failure, and diabetes insipidus

  3. Hypotonic dehydration
    a. Chronic illness
    b. Excessive fluid replacement (hypotonic)
    c. Renal failure
    d. Chronic malnutrition
D. Assessment
  1. Cardiovascular
    a. Thready, increased pulse rate
    b. Decreased blood pressure and orthostatic (postural) hypotension
    c. Flat neck and hand veins in dependent positions
    d. Diminished peripheral pulses
  2. Respiratory: Increased rate and depth of respirations
  3. Neuromuscular
    a. Decreased central nervous system activity, from lethargy to coma
    b. Fever
  4. Renal
    a. Decreased urinary output
    b. Increased urinary specific gravity
  5. Integumentary
    a. Dry skin
    b. Poor turgor, tenting present
    c. Dry mouth
  6. Gastrointestinal
    a. Decreased motility and diminished bowel sounds
    b. Constipation
    c. Thirst
    d. Decreased body weight
  7. Hypotonic dehydration: skeletal muscle weakness
  8. Hypertonic dehydration
    a. Hyperactive deep tendon reflexes
    b. Pitting edema
  9. Laboratory findings
    a. Increased serum osmolality
    b. Increased hematocrit
    c. Increased blood urea nitrogen (BUN) level
    d. Increased serum **sodium** level
E. Interventions
  1. Monitor cardiovascular, respiratory, neuromuscular, renal, integumentary, and gastrointestinal status.
  2. Prevent further fluid losses and increase fluid compartment volumes to normal ranges.
  3. Provide oral rehydration therapy if possible and intravenous (IV) fluid replacement if the dehydration is severe; monitor intake and output.
  4. Generally, isotonic dehydration is treated with isotonic fluid solutions, hypertonic dehydration with hypotonic fluid solutions, and hypotonic dehydration with hypertonic fluid solutions.

5. Administer medications as prescribed such as antidiarrheal, antimicrobial, antiemetic, and antipyretic medications, to correct the cause and treat any symptoms.
6. Administer oxygen as prescribed.
7. Monitor electrolyte values and prepare to administer medication to treat an imbalance, if present.

III. FLUID VOLUME EXCESS

A. Description
   1. Fluid intake or fluid retention exceeds the fluid needs of the body.
   2. **Fluid volume excess** also is called overhydration or fluid overload.
   3. The goal of treatment is to restore fluid balance, correct electrolyte imbalances if present, and eliminate or control the underlying cause of the overload.
B. Types
   1. Isotonic overhydration
      a. Known as hypervolemia, isotonic overhydration results from excessive fluid in the extracellular fluid compartment.
      b. Only the extracellular fluid compartment is expanded, and fluid does not shift between the extracellular and intracellular compartments.
      c. Isotonic overhydration causes circulatory overload and interstitial edema; when severe or when it occurs in a client with poor cardiac function, congestive heart failure and pulmonary edema can result.
   2. Hypertonic overhydration
      a. Occurrence of hypertonic overhydration is rare and is caused by an excessive **sodium** intake.
      b. Fluid is drawn from the intracellular fluid compartment; the extracellular fluid volume expands, and the intracellular fluid volume contracts.
   3. Hypotonic overhydration
      a. Hypotonic overhydration is known as water intoxication.
      b. The excessive fluid moves into the intracellular space, and all body fluid compartments expand.
      c. Electrolyte imbalances occur as a result of dilution.
C. Causes
   1. Isotonic overhydration
      a. Inadequately controlled IV therapy
      b. Renal failure
      c. Long-term corticosteroid therapy
   2. Hypertonic overhydration
      a. Excessive **sodium** ingestion

b. Rapid infusion of hypertonic saline
      c. Excessive **sodium** bicarbonate therapy
   3. Hypotonic overhydration
      a. Early renal failure
      b. Congestive heart failure
      c. Syndrome of inappropriate antidiuretic hormone secretion
      d. Inadequately controlled IV therapy
      e. Replacement of isotonic fluid loss with hypotonic fluids
      f. Irrigation of wounds and body cavities with hypotonic fluids
D. Assessment
   1. Cardiovascular
      a. Bounding, increased pulse rate
      b. Elevated blood pressure
      c. Distended neck and hand veins
      d. Elevated central venous pressure
   2. Respiratory
      a. Increased respiratory rate (shallow respirations)
      b. Dyspnea
      c. Moist crackles on auscultation
   3. Neuromuscular
      a. Altered level of consciousness
      b. Headache
      c. Visual disturbances
      d. Skeletal muscle weakness
      e. Paresthesias
   4. Integumentary
      a. Pitting edema in dependent areas
      b. Skin pale and cool to touch
   5. Increased motility in the gastrointestinal tract
   6. Isotonic overhydration results in liver enlargement and ascites.
   7. Hypotonic overhydration results in the following:
      a. Polyuria
      b. Diarrhea
      c. Nonpitting edema
      d. Dysrhythmias
      e. Projectile vomiting
   8. Laboratory findings
      a. Decreased serum osmolality
      b. Decreased hematocrit
      c. Decreased BUN level
      d. Decreased serum **sodium** level
      e. Decreased urine specific gravity
E. Interventions
   1. Monitor cardiovascular, respiratory, neuromuscular, renal, integumentary, and gastrointestinal status.
   2. Prevent further fluid overload, and restore normal fluid balance.
   3. Administer diuretics; osmotic diuretics typically are prescribed first to prevent severe electrolyte imbalances.

4. Restrict fluid and **sodium** intake.
5. Monitor intake and output and weight.
6. Monitor electrolyte values, and prepare to administer medication to treat an imbalance if present.

IV. HYPONATREMIA
A. Description
   1. **Hyponatremia** is a serum **sodium** level lower than 135 mEq/L (Box 9-3).
   2. **Sodium** imbalances usually are associated with fluid volume imbalances.
▲ B. Causes
   1. Increased **sodium** excretion
      a. Excessive diaphoresis
      b. Diuretics
      c. Vomiting
      d. Diarrhea
      e. Wound drainage, especially gastrointestinal
      f. Renal disease
      g. Decreased secretion of aldosterone
   2. Inadequate **sodium** intake
      a. Nothing by mouth
      b. Low-salt diet
   3. Dilution of serum **sodium**
      a. Excessive ingestion of hypotonic fluids or irrigation with hypotonic fluids
      b. Renal failure
      c. Freshwater drowning
      d. Syndrome of inappropriate antidiuretic hormone secretion
      e. Hyperglycemia
      f. Congestive heart failure
▲ C. Assessment
   1. Cardiovascular
      a. Symptoms vary with changes in vascular volume
      b. Normovolemic: Rapid pulse rate; normal blood pressure
      c. Hypovolemic: Thready, weak, rapid pulse rate; hypotension; flat neck veins; normal or low central venous pressure
      d. Hypervolemic: Rapid, bounding pulse; blood pressure normal or elevated; normal or elevated central venous pressure
   2. Respiratory: shallow, ineffective respiratory movements as a late manifestation related to skeletal muscle weakness
   3. Neuromuscular
      a. Generalized skeletal muscle weakness that is worse in the extremities
      b. Diminished deep tendon reflexes
▲ 4. Cerebral function
      a. Headache
      b. Personality changes
      c. Confusion
      d. Seizures
      e. Coma

BOX 9-3
Sodium

NORMAL VALUE
135 to 145 mEq/L

COMMON FOOD SOURCES
Bacon
Butter
Canned food
Cheese, such as American or cottage cheese
Frankfurters
Ketchup
Lunch meat
Milk
Mustard
Processed food
Snack food
Soy sauce
Table salt
White and whole-wheat bread

---

   5. Gastrointestinal
      a. Increased motility and hyperactive bowel sounds
      b. Nausea
      c. Abdominal cramping and diarrhea
   6. Renal
      a. Decreased urinary specific gravity
      b. Increased urinary output
D. Interventions
   1. Monitor cardiovascular, respiratory, neuromuscular, cerebral, renal, and gastrointestinal status. ▲
   2. If **hyponatremia** is accompanied by a fluid deficit (hypovolemia), IV sodium chloride infusions are administered to restore **sodium** content and fluid volume.
   3. If **hyponatremia** is accompanied by fluid excess (hypervolemia), osmotic diuretics are administered to promote the excretion of water rather than **sodium**.
   4. If the cause is inappropriate or excessive secretion of antidiuretic hormone, medications that antagonize antidiuretic hormone, such as lithium and demeclocycline (Declomycin), may be administered.
   5. Instruct client to increase oral **sodium** intake ▲ and inform the client about the foods to include in the diet (see Box 9-3).
   6. If the client is taking lithium, monitor the lith- ▲ ium level, because **hyponatremia** can cause diminished lithium excretion, resulting in toxicity.

V. HYPERNATREMIA ▲
A. Description: **Hypernatremia** is a serum sodium level that exceeds 145 mEq/L (see Box 9-3).

B. Causes
   1. Decreased **sodium** excretion
      a. Corticosteroids
      b. Cushing's syndrome
      c. Renal failure
      d. Hyperaldosteronism
   2. Increased **sodium** intake: Excessive oral **sodium** ingestion or excessive administration of **sodium**-containing IV fluids
   3. Decreased water intake: Nothing by mouth
   4. Increased water loss: Increased rate of metabolism, fever, hyperventilation, infection, excessive diaphoresis, watery diarrhea, diabetes insipidus

C. Assessment
   1. Cardiovascular: Heart rate and blood pressure that respond to vascular volume status
   2. Respiratory: Pulmonary edema if hypervolemia is present
   3. Neuromuscular
      a. Early: Spontaneous muscle twitches; irregular muscle contractions
      b. Late: Skeletal muscle weakness; deep tendon reflexes diminished or absent
   4. Central nervous system
      a. Altered cerebral function is the most common manifestation of **hypernatremia**.
      b. Normovolemia or hypovolemia: Agitation, confusion, seizures
      c. Hypervolemia: Lethargy, stupor, coma
   5. Renal
      a. Increased urinary specific gravity
      b. Decreased urinary output
   6. Integumentary
      a. Dry skin
      b. Presence or absence of edema, depending on fluid volume changes

D. Interventions
   1. Monitor cardiovascular, respiratory, neuromuscular, cerebral, renal, and integumentary status.
   2. If the cause is fluid loss, prepare to administer IV infusions.
   3. If the cause is inadequate renal excretion of **sodium**, prepare to administer diuretics that promote **sodium** loss.
   4. Restrict **sodium** and fluid intake as prescribed (see Box 9-3).

VI. HYPOKALEMIA
A. Description
   1. **Hypokalemia** is a serum **potassium** level lower than 3.5 mEq/L (Box 9-4).
   2. **Potassium** deficit is potentially life-threatening because every body system is affected.

B. Causes
   1. Actual total body **potassium** loss
      a. Excessive use of medications such as diuretics or corticosteroids

---

BOX 9-4
Potassium

NORMAL VALUE
3.5 to 5.1 mEq/L

COMMON FOOD SOURCES
Avocado
Bananas
Cantaloupe
Carrots
Fish
Mushrooms
Oranges
Potatoes
Pork, beef, veal
Raisins
Spinach
Strawberries
Tomatoes

---

      b. Increased secretion of aldosterone, such as in Cushing's syndrome
      c. Vomiting, diarrhea
      d. Wound drainage, particularly gastrointestinal
      e. Prolonged nasogastric suction
      f. Excessive diaphoresis
      g. Renal disease impairing reabsorption of **potassium**
   2. Inadequate **potassium** intake: nothing by mouth
   3. Movement of **potassium** from the extracellular fluid to the intracellular fluid
      a. Alkalosis
      b. Hyperinsulinism
   4. Dilution of serum **potassium**
      a. Water intoxication
      b. Intravenous therapy with **potassium**-poor solutions

C. Assessment
   1. Cardiovascular
      a. Thready, weak, irregular pulse
      b. Peripheral pulses weak
      c. Orthostatic hypotension
      d. Electrocardiogram changes: ST depression, shallow, flat or inverted T wave, and prominent U wave (Table 9-1)
   2. Respiratory
      a. Shallow, ineffective respirations that result from profound weakness of the skeletal muscles of respiration
      b. Diminished breath sounds
   3. Neuromuscular
      a. Anxiety, lethargy, confusion, coma
      b. Skeletal muscle weakness, eventual flaccid paralysis
      c. Loss of tactile discrimination
      d. Deep tendon hyporeflexia

TABLE 9-1

Electrocardiographic Changes in Electrolyte Imbalances

Electrolyte Imbalance	Electrocardiographic Changes
Hypocalcemia	Prolonged ST interval
	Prolonged QT interval
Hypercalcemia	Shortened ST segment
	Widened T wave
Hypokalemia	ST depression
	Shallow, flat, or inverted T wave
	Prominent U wave
Hyperkalemia	Tall peaked T waves
	Flat P waves
	Widened QRS complex
	Prolonged PR interval
Hypomagnesemia	Tall T waves
	Depressed ST segment
Hypermagnesemia	Prolonged PR interval
	Widened QRS complexes

4. Gastrointestinal
   a. Decreased motility, hypoactive to absent bowel sounds
   b. Nausea, vomiting, constipation, abdominal distention
   c. Paralytic ileus
5. Renal
   a. Decreased urinary specific gravity
   b. Increased urinary output

D. Interventions
   1. Monitor cardiovascular, respiratory, neuromuscular, gastrointestinal, and renal status, and place on a cardiac monitor.
   2. Monitor electrolyte values.
   3. Administer **potassium** supplements orally or intravenously, as prescribed.
   4. Oral **potassium** supplements
      a. Oral **potassium** supplements may cause nausea and vomiting and they should not be taken on an empty stomach; if the client complains of abdominal pain, distention, nausea, vomiting, diarrhea, or gastrointestinal bleeding, the supplement may need to be discontinued.
      b. Liquid **potassium** chloride has an unpleasant taste and should be taken with juice or another liquid.
   5. Take the following precautions with intravenously administered **potassium**:
      a. **Potassium** is never given by IV push or by the intramuscular or subcutaneous route.
      b. A dilution of no more than 1 mEq/10 mL of solution is recommended.
      c. After adding **potassium** to an IV solution, rotate and invert the bag to ensure that the **potassium** is distributed evenly throughout the IV solution.

      d. Ensure that the IV bag containing **potassium** is properly labeled.
      e. The maximum recommended infusion rate is 5 to 10 mEq/hr, never to exceed 20 mEq/hr under any circumstances.
      f. A client receiving more than 10 mEq/hr should be placed on a cardiac monitor and monitored for cardiac changes, and the infusion should be controlled by an infusion device.
      g. **Potassium** infusion can cause phlebitis; therefore, the nurse should assess the IV site frequently for signs of phlebitis or infiltration. If either of these occurs, the infusion is stopped immediately.
      h. The nurse should assess renal function before administering **potassium** and monitor intake and output during administration.
   6. Institute safety measures for the client experiencing muscle weakness.
   7. If the client is taking a **potassium**-losing diuretic, it may be discontinued; a **potassium**-sparing diuretic may be prescribed.
   8. Instruct the client about foods that are high in **potassium** content (see Box 9-4).

VII. HYPERKALEMIA
A. Description: **Hyperkalemia** is a serum **potassium** level that exceeds 5.1 mEq/L (see Box 9-4).
B. Causes
   1. Excessive **potassium** intake
      a. Overingestion of **potassium**-containing foods or medications, such as **potassium** chloride or salt substitutes
      b. Rapid infusion of **potassium**-containing IV solutions
   2. Decreased **potassium** excretion
      a. **Potassium**-sparing diuretics
      b. Renal failure
      c. Adrenal insufficiency, such as in Addison's disease
   3. Movement of **potassium** from the intracellular fluid to the extracellular fluid
      a. Tissue damage
      b. Acidosis
      c. Hyperuricemia
      d. Hypercatabolism
C. Assessment
   1. Cardiovascular
      a. Slow, weak, irregular heart rate
      b. Decreased blood pressure
      c. Electrocardiographic changes: Tall peaked T waves, flat P waves, widened QRS complexes, and prolonged PR intervals (Table 9-1)
   2. Respiratory: Profound weakness of the skeletal muscles leading to respiratory failure
   3. Neuromuscular

a. Early: Muscle twitches, cramps, paresthesias (tingling and burning followed by numbness in the hands and feet and around the mouth)

b. Late: Profound weakness, ascending flaccid paralysis in the arms and legs (trunk, head, and respiratory muscles become affected when the serum potassium level reaches a lethal level)

4. Gastrointestinal

a. Increased motility, hyperactive bowel sounds

b. Diarrhea

▲ D. Interventions

1. Monitor cardiovascular, respiratory, neuromuscular, renal, and gastrointestinal status; place the client on a cardiac monitor.

2. Discontinue IV potassium (keep the IV catheter patent), and hold oral **potassium** supplements.

3. Initiate a **potassium**-restricted diet.

4. Prepare to administer **potassium**-excreting diuretics if renal function is not impaired.

5. If renal function is impaired, prepare to administer **sodium** polystyrene sulfonate (Kayexalate), a cation exchange resin that promotes gastrointestinal **sodium** absorption and **potassium** excretion.

6. Prepare the client for dialysis if **potassium** levels are critically high.

7. Prepare for the IV administration of hypertonic glucose with regular insulin to move excess **potassium** into the cells.

8. Monitor renal function.

9. When blood transfusions are prescribed for a client with a **potassium** imbalance, the client should receive fresh blood, if possible; transfusions of stored blood may elevate the **potassium** level because the breakdown of older blood cells releases **potassium**.

10. Teach the client to avoid foods high in **potassium** (see Box 9-4).

11. Instruct the client to avoid the use of salt substitutes or other **potassium**-containing substances.

▲ VIII. HYPOCALCEMIA

A. Description: **Hypocalcemia** is a serum **calcium** level lower than 8.6 mg/dL (Box 9-5).

B. Causes

1. Inhibition of **calcium** absorption from the gastrointestinal tract

▲ a. Inadequate oral intake of **calcium**

▲ b. Lactose intolerance

c. Malabsorption syndromes such as celiac sprue or Crohn's disease

▲ d. Inadequate intake of vitamin D

e. End-stage renal disease

2. Increased **calcium** excretion

a. Renal failure, polyuric phase

b. Diarrhea

BOX 9-5
Calcium

NORMAL VALUE
8.6 to 10.0 mg/dL

COMMON FOOD SOURCES
Cheese
Collard greens
Milk and soy milk
Rhubarb
Sardines
Spinach
Tofu
Yogurt

---

c. Steatorrhea

d. Wound drainage, especially gastrointestinal ▲

3. Conditions that decrease the ionized fraction of **calcium**

a. Hyperproteinemia

b. Alkalosis

c. Medications such as **calcium** chelators or binders

d. Acute pancreatitis

e. **Hyperphosphatemia** ▲

f. Immobility ▲

g. Removal or destruction of the parathyroid ▲ glands

C. Assessment ▲

1. Cardiovascular

a. Decreased heart rate

b. Hypotension

c. Diminished peripheral pulses

d. Electrocardiographic changes: Prolonged ▲ ST interval, prolonged QT interval (see Table 9-1)

2. Respiratory: Not directly affected; however, respiratory failure or arrest can result from decreased respiratory movement because of muscle tetany or seizures.

3. Neuromuscular

a. Irritable skeletal muscles: Twitches, cramps, ▲ tetany, seizures

b. Painful muscle spasms in the calf or foot during periods of inactivity

c. Paresthesias followed by numbness that may ▲ affect the lips, nose, and ears in addition to the limbs

d. Positive Trousseau's and Chvostek's signs ▲ (Fig. 9-1)

e. Hyperactive deep tendon reflexes ▲

f. Anxiety, irritability

4. Gastrointestinal

a. Increased gastric motility; hyperactive bowel ▲ sounds

b. Abdominal cramping, diarrhea

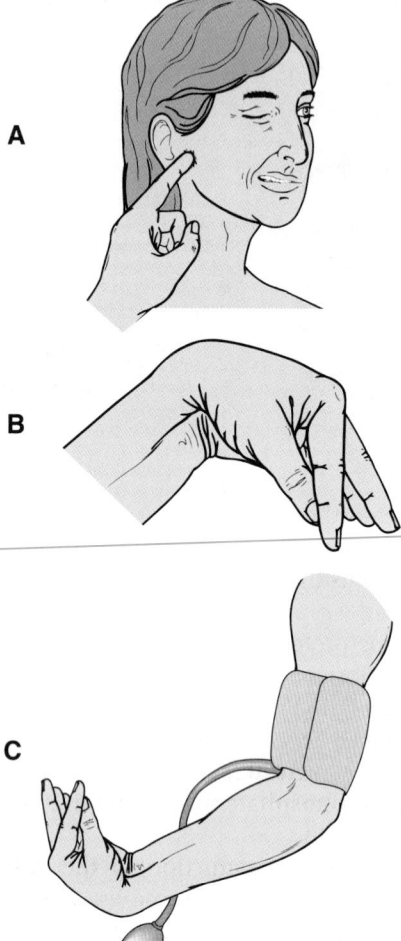

FIG. 9-1 Tests for hypocalcemia. **A,** Chvostek's sign is contraction of facial muscles in response to a light tap over the facial nerve in front of the ear. **B,** Trousseau's sign is a carpal spasm induced by inflating a blood pressure cuff **(C)** above the systolic pressure for a few minutes. (From Lewis, S., Heitkemper, M., & Dirksen, S. [2004]. *Medical-surgical nursing* [6th ed.]. St. Louis: Mosby.)

D. Interventions
1. Monitor cardiovascular, respiratory, neuromuscular, and gastrointestinal status; place the client on a cardiac monitor.
2. Administer **calcium** supplements orally or **calcium** intravenously.
3. When administering **calcium** intravenously, warm the injection solution to body temperature before administration and administer slowly; monitor for electrocardiographic changes, observe for infiltration, and monitor for **hypercalcemia**.
4. Administer medications that increase **calcium** absorption.
   a. Aluminum hydroxide reduces serum **phosphorus** levels, causing the countereffect of increasing **calcium** levels.

   b. Vitamin D aids in the absorption of **calcium** from the intestinal tract.
5. Provide a quiet environment to reduce environmental stimuli.
6. Initiate seizure precautions.
7. Move the client carefully, and monitor for signs of a fracture.
8. Keep 10% **calcium** gluconate available for treatment of acute **calcium** deficit.
9. Instruct the client to consume foods high in **calcium** (see Box 9-5).

IX. HYPERCALCEMIA
A. Description: **Hypercalcemia** is a serum **calcium** level that exceeds 10.0 mg/dL (see Box 9-5).
B. Causes
1. Increased **calcium** absorption
   a. Excessive oral intake of **calcium**
   b. Excessive oral intake of vitamin D
2. Decreased **calcium** excretion
   a. Renal failure
   b. Use of thiazide diuretics
3. Increased bone resorption of **calcium**
   a. Hyperparathyroidism
   b. Hyperthyroidism
   c. Malignancy (bone destruction from metastatic tumors)
   d. Immobility
   e. Use of glucocorticoids
4. Hemoconcentration
   a. Dehydration
   b. Use of lithium
   c. Adrenal insufficiency
C. Assessment
1. Cardiovascular
   a. Increased heart rate in the early phase, bradycardia that can lead to cardiac arrest in late phases
   b. Increased blood pressure
   c. Bounding, full peripheral pulses
   d. Electrocardiographic changes: Shortened ST segment, widened T wave (see Table 9-1)
2. Respiratory: ineffective respiratory movement as a result of profound skeletal muscle weakness
3. Neuromuscular
   a. Profound muscle weakness
   b. Diminished or absent deep tendon reflexes
   c. Disorientation, lethargy, coma
4. Renal
   a. Increased urinary output leading to dehydration
   b. Formation of renal calculi
5. Gastrointestinal
   a. Decreased motility and hypoactive bowel sounds
   b. Anorexia, nausea, abdominal distention, constipation

D. Interventions
1. Monitor cardiovascular, respiratory, neuromuscular, renal, and gastrointestinal status; place the client on a cardiac monitor.
2. Discontinue IV infusions of solutions containing calcium and oral medications containing **calcium** or vitamin D.
3. Discontinue thiazide diuretics and replace with diuretics that enhance the excretion of **calcium**.
4. Administer medications as prescribed that inhibit **calcium** resorption from the bone, such as **phosphorus**, calcitonin (Calcimar), bisphosphonates, and prostaglandin synthesis inhibitors (aspirin, nonsteroidal antiinflammatory drugs).
5. Prepare the client with severe **hypercalcemia** for dialysis if medications fail to reduce the serum **calcium** level.
6. Move the client carefully and monitor for signs of a fracture.
7. Monitor for flank or abdominal pain, and strain the urine to check for the presence of urinary stones.
8. Instruct the client to avoid foods high in **calcium** (see Box 9-5).

X. HYPOMAGNESEMIA
A. Description: **Hypomagnesemia** is a serum **magnesium** level lower than 1.6 mg/dL (Box 9-6).
B. Causes
1. Insufficient **magnesium** intake
   a. Malnutrition and starvation
   b. Vomiting or diarrhea
   c. Malabsorption syndrome
   d. Celiac disease
   e. Crohn's disease
2. Increased **magnesium** secretion
   a. Medications such as diuretics
   b. Chronic alcoholism

BOX 9-6

Magnesium

NORMAL VALUE
1.6 to 2.6 mg/dL

COMMON FOOD SOURCES
Avocado
Canned white tuna
Cauliflower
Green leafy vegetables such as spinach and broccoli
Milk
Oatmeal
Peanut butter
Peas
Pork, beef, chicken
Potatoes
Raisins
Yogurt

---

3. Intracellular movement of **magnesium**
   a. Hyperglycemia
   b. Insulin administration
   c. Sepsis
C. Assessment
1. Cardiovascular
   a. Electrocardiographic changes: Tall T waves, depressed ST segments (see Table 9-1)
   b. Tachycardia
   c. Hypertension
2. Gastrointestinal
   a. Decreased motility; decreased bowel sounds
   b. Anorexia, nausea, abdominal distention
3. Respiratory: Shallow respirations
4. Neuromuscular
   a. Twitches; paresthesias
   b. Positive Trousseau's and Chvostek's signs
   c. Hyperreflexia
   d. Tetany, seizures
5. Central nervous system
   a. Irritability
   b. Confusion
D. Interventions
1. Monitor cardiovascular, gastrointestinal, respiratory, neuromuscular, and central nervous system status; place the client on a cardiac monitor.
2. Because **hypocalcemia** frequently accompanies **hypomagnesemia**, interventions also aim to restore normal serum **calcium** levels.
3. Administer **magnesium** sulfate by the IV route in severe cases (intramuscular injections cause pain and tissue damage); monitor serum **magnesium** levels frequently.
4. Initiate seizure precautions.
5. Monitor for reduced deep tendon reflexes, suggesting **hypermagnesemia**, during the administration of **magnesium**.
6. Oral preparations of **magnesium** may cause diarrhea and increase **magnesium** loss.
7. Instruct the client to increase the intake of foods that contain **magnesium** (see Box 9-6).

XI. HYPERMAGNESEMIA
A. Description: **Hypermagnesemia** is a serum **magnesium** level that exceeds 2.6 mg/dL (see Box 9-6).
B. Causes
1. Increased **magnesium** intake
   a. **Magnesium**-containing antacids and laxatives
   b. Excessive administration of **magnesium** intravenously
2. Decreased renal excretion of **magnesium** as a result of renal insufficiency
C. Assessment
1. Cardiovascular
   a. Bradycardia, dysrhythmias
   b. Hypotension

c. Electrocardiographic changes: Prolonged PR interval, widened QRS complexes (see Table 9-1)

2. Respiratory: Respiratory insufficiency when the skeletal muscles of respiration are involved

3. Neuromuscular
   a. Diminished or absent deep tendon reflexes
   b. Skeletal muscle weakness

4. Central nervous system: Drowsiness and lethargy that progresses to coma

D. Interventions

1. Monitor cardiovascular, respiratory, neuromuscular, and central nervous system status; place the client on a cardiac monitor.

2. Diuretics are prescribed to increase renal excretion of **magnesium**.

3. Intravenously administered **calcium** chloride or **calcium** gluconate may be prescribed to reverse the effects of **magnesium** on cardiac muscle.

4. Instruct the client to restrict dietary intake of **magnesium**-containing foods (see Box 9-6).

5. Instruct the client to avoid the use of laxatives and antacids containing **magnesium**.

XII. HYPOPHOSPHATEMIA

A. Description

1. **Hypophosphatemia** is a serum **phosphorus** level lower than 2.7 mg/dL (Box 9-7).

2. A decrease in the serum **phosphorus** level is accompanied by an increase in the serum **calcium** level.

B. Causes

1. Insufficient **phosphorus** intake: Malnutrition and starvation

2. Increased **phosphorus** excretion
   a. Hyperparathyroidism
   b. Malignancy
   c. Use of aluminum hydroxide–based or **magnesium**-based antacids

3. Intracellular shift
   a. Hyperglycemia
   b. Respiratory alkalosis

C. Assessment

1. Cardiovascular

BOX 9-7
Phosphorus

NORMAL VALUE
2.7 to 4.5 mg/dL

COMMON FOOD SOURCES
Fish
Organ meats
Nuts
Pork, beef, chicken
Whole-grain breads and cereals

---

a. Decreased contractility and cardiac output
   b. Slowed peripheral pulses

2. Respiratory: shallow respirations

3. Neuromuscular
   a. Weakness
   b. Decreased deep tendon reflexes
   c. Decreased bone density that can cause fractures and alterations in bone shape
   d. Rhabdomyolysis

4. Central nervous system
   a. Irritability
   b. Confusion
   c. Seizures

5. Hematological
   a. Decreased platelet aggregation and increased bleeding
   b. Immunosuppression

D. Interventions

1. Monitor cardiovascular, respiratory, neuromuscular, central nervous system, and hematological status.

2. Discontinue medications that contribute to **hypophosphatemia**.

3. Administer **phosphorus** orally along with a vitamin D supplement.

4. Prepare to administer **phosphorus** intravenously when serum **phosphorus** levels fall below 1 mg/dL and when the client experiences critical clinical manifestations.

5. Administer intravenous **phosphorus** slowly because of the risks associated with **hyperphosphatemia**.

6. Assess the renal system before administering **phosphorus**.

7. Move the client carefully, and monitor for signs of a fracture.

8. Instruct the client to increase intake of **phosphorus**-containing foods while decreasing the intake of **calcium**-containing foods (Box 9-7; see Box 9-5).

XIII. HYPERPHOSPHATEMIA

A. Description

1. **Hyperphosphatemia** is a serum **phosphorus** level that exceeds 4.5 mg/dL (see Box 9-7).

2. Most body systems tolerate elevated serum **phosphorus** levels well.

3. An increase in the serum **phosphorus** level is accompanied by a decrease in the serum **calcium** level.

4. The problems that occur in **hyperphosphatemia** center on the **hypocalcemia** that results when serum **phosphorus** levels increase.

B. Causes

1. Decreased renal excretion resulting from renal insufficiency

2. Tumor lysis syndrome

3. Increased intake of **phosphorus**, including dietary intake or overuse of phosphate-containing laxatives or enemas
4. Hypoparathyroidism

C. Assessment: Refer to assessment of hypocalcemia.

D. Interventions
1. Interventions entail the management of **hypocalcemia**.
2. Administer phosphate-binding medications that increase fecal excretion of **phosphorus** by binding **phosphorus** from food in the gastrointestinal tract.
3. Instruct the client to avoid phosphate-containing medications, including laxatives and enemas.
4. Instruct the client to decrease the intake of food that is high in **phosphorus** (see Box 9-7).
5. Instruct the client in medication administration: take phosphate-binding medications, emphasizing that they should be taken with meals or immediately after meals.

PRACTICE QUESTIONS

1. A nurse is reading a physician's progress notes in the client's record and reads that the physician has documented "insensible fluid loss of approximately 800 mL daily." The nurse understands that this type of fluid loss can occur through:
   1. The skin
   2. Urinary output
   3. Wound drainage
   4. The gastrointestinal tract

2. A nurse is assigned to care for a group of clients. On review of the clients' medical records, the nurse determines that which client is at risk for deficient fluid volume?
   1. A client with a colostomy
   2. A client with congestive heart failure
   3. A client with decreased kidney function
   4. A client receiving frequent wound irrigations

3. A nurse caring for a client who has been receiving intravenous diuretics suspects that the client is experiencing a deficient fluid volume. Which assessment finding would the nurse note in a client with this condition?
   1. Lung congestion
   2. Decreased hematocrit
   3. Increased blood pressure
   4. Decreased central venous pressure (CVP)

4. A nurse is assigned to care for a group of clients. On review of the clients' medical records, the nurse determines that which client is at risk for excess fluid volume?
   1. The client taking diuretics
   2. The client with renal failure
   3. The client with an ileostomy
   4. The client who requires gastrointestinal suctioning

5. The nurse is caring for a client with congestive heart failure. On assessment, the nurse notes that the client is dyspneic and that crackles are audible on auscultation. The nurse suspects excess fluid volume. What additional signs would the nurse expect to note in this client if excess fluid volume is present?
   1. Weight loss
   2. Flat neck and hand veins
   3. An increase in blood pressure
   4. A decreased central venous pressure (CVP)

6. A nurse is preparing to care for a client with a potassium deficit. The nurse reviews the client's record and determines that the client was at risk for developing the potassium deficit because the client:
   1. Has renal failure.
   2. Requires nasogastric suction.
   3. Has a history of Addison's disease.
   4. Is taking a potassium-sparing diuretic.

7. A nurse reviews a client's electrolyte laboratory report and notes that the potassium level is 3.2 mEq/L. Which of the following would the nurse note on the electrocardiogram as a result of the laboratory value?
   1. U waves
   2. Absent P waves
   3. Elevated T waves
   4. Elevated ST segment

8. A nursing student needs to administer potassium chloride intravenously as prescribed to a client with hypokalemia. The nursing instructor determines that the student is unprepared for this procedure if the student states that which of the following is part of the plan for preparation and administration of the potassium?
   1. Obtaining a controlled IV infusion pump
   2. Monitoring urine output during administration
   3. Diluting in appropriate amount of normal saline
   4. Preparing the medication for bolus administration

9. A nurse instructs a client at risk for hypokalemia about the foods high in potassium that should be included in the daily diet. The nurse determines that the client understands the food sources of potassium if the client states that the food item lowest in potassium is:
   1. Apples
   2. Carrots
   3. Spinach
   4. Avocado

10. A nurse caring for a group of clients reviews the electrolyte laboratory results and notes a potassium level of 5.5 mEq/L on one client's laboratory report. The nurse understands that which client is

at highest risk for the development of a potassium value at this level?
1. The client with colitis
2. The client with Cushing's syndrome
3. The client who has been overusing laxatives
4. The client who has sustained a traumatic burn

11. A nurse reviews the electrolyte results of an assigned client and notes that the potassium level is 5.4 mEq/L. Which of the following would the nurse expect to note on the electrocardiogram as a result of the laboratory value?
1. ST depression
2. Inverted T wave
3. Prominent U wave
4. Tall peaked T waves

12. A nurse caring for a group of clients reviews the electrolyte laboratory results and notes a sodium level of 130 mEq/L on one client's laboratory report. The nurse understands that which client is at highest risk for the development of a sodium value at this level?
1. The client with renal failure
2. The client who is taking diuretics
3. The client with hyperaldosteronism
4. The client who is taking corticosteroids

13. A nurse is caring for a client with acute congestive heart failure who is receiving high doses of a diuretic. On assessment, the nurse notes that the client has flat neck veins, generalized muscle weakness, and diminished deep tendon reflexes. The nurse suspects hyponatremia. What additional signs would the nurse expect to note in this client if hyponatremia were present?
1. Dry skin
2. Decreased urinary output
3. Hyperactive bowel sounds
4. Increased specific gravity of the urine

14. A nurse is caring for a client with a nasogastric tube. Nasogastric tube irrigations are prescribed to be performed once every shift. The client's serum electrolyte results indicate a potassium level of 4.5 mEq/L and a sodium level of 132 mEq/L. Based on these laboratory findings, the nurse selects which solution to use for the nasogastric tube irrigation?
1. Tap water
2. Sterile water
3. Sodium chloride
4. Distilled water

15. A nurse is reviewing laboratory results and notes that a client's serum sodium level is 150 mEq/L. The nurse reports the serum sodium level to the physician and the physician prescribes dietary instructions based on the sodium level. Which food item does the nurse instruct the client to avoid?
1. Peas
2. Cauliflower

3. Low-fat yogurt
4. Processed oat cereals

16. A nurse is reviewing a client's laboratory report and notes that the serum calcium level is 4.0 mg/dL. The nurse understands that which condition most likely caused this serum calcium level?
1. Prolonged bed rest
2. Renal insufficiency
3. Hyperparathyroidism
4. Excessive ingestion of vitamin D

17. A nurse is assessing a client with a suspected diagnosis of hypocalcemia. Which of the following clinical manifestations would the nurse expect to note in the client?
1. Twitching
2. Negative Trousseau's sign
3. Hypoactive bowel sounds
4. Hypoactive deep tendon reflexes

18. A nurse caring for a client with hypocalcemia would expect to note which of the following changes on the electrocardiogram?
1. Widened T wave
2. Prominent U wave
3. Prolonged QT interval
4. Shortened ST segment

19. A nurse caring for a client with severe malnutrition reviews the laboratory results and notes a magnesium level of 1.0 mg/dL. Which electrocardiographic change would the nurse expect to note based on the magnesium level?
1. Prominent U waves
2. Prolonged PR interval
3. Depressed ST segment
4. Widened QRS complexes

20. A nurse reviews a client's laboratory report and notes that the client's serum phosphorus level is 2.0 mg/dL. Which condition most likely caused this serum phosphorus level?
1. Alcoholism
2. Renal insufficiency
3. Hypoparathyroidism
4. Tumor lysis syndrome

ALTERNATE ITEM FORMAT: MULTIPLE RESPONSE

The nurse provides instructions to a client with a low magnesium level about the foods that are high in magnesium and tells the client to consume which foods? Select all that apply.
❏ 1. Peas
❏ 2. Bacon
❏ 3. Oranges
❏ 4. Cauliflower
❏ 5. Peanut butter
❏ 6. Canned white tuna

ANSWERS

1. **1**
Rationale: Sensible losses are those of which the person is aware, such as through wound drainage, gastrointestinal tract losses, and urination. Insensible losses may occur without the person's awareness. Insensible losses occur daily through the skin and the lungs.
Test-Taking Strategy: Note that the subject of the question is insensible fluid loss. Use the process of elimination, noting that options 2, 3, and 4 are comparative or alike. In options 2, 3 and 4, these types of losses can be measured for accurate output. Fluid loss through the skin cannot be measured accurately, only approximated. If you had difficulty with this question, review the difference between sensible and insensible fluid loss.
Level of Cognitive Ability: Comprehension
Client Needs: Physiological Integrity
Integrated Process: Communication and Documentation
Content Area: Fundamental skills
Reference: Ignatavicius, D., & Workman, M. (2006). *Medical-surgical nursing: Critical thinking for collaborative care* (5th ed., p. 203). Philadelphia: W.B. Saunders.

2. **1**
Rationale: Causes of deficient fluid volume include vomiting, diarrhea, conditions that cause increased respirations or increased urinary output, insufficient IV fluid replacement, draining fistulas, and the presence of an ileostomy or colostomy. A client with congestive heart failure or decreased kidney function, or a client receiving frequent wound irrigations, is at risk for excess fluid volume.
Test-Taking Strategy: Read the question carefully, noting that it asks for the client at risk for a deficit. Read each option and think about the fluid imbalance that can occur in each. The clients presented in options 2, 3, and 4 retain fluid. The only condition that can cause a deficit is the condition noted in option 1. If you had difficulty with this question, review the causes of deficient fluid volume.
Level of Cognitive Ability: Analysis
Client Needs: Physiological Integrity
Integrated Process: Nursing Process—assessment
Content Area: Fundamental skills
References: Black, J., & Hawks, J. (2005). *Medical-surgical nursing: Clinical management for positive outcomes* (7th ed., pp. 223, 2494). Philadelphia: W.B. Saunders.
Ignatavicius, D., & Workman, M. (2006). *Medical-surgical nursing: Critical thinking for collaborative care* (5th ed., p. 1324). Philadelphia: W.B. Saunders.

3. **4**
Rationale: Assessment findings in a client with a deficient fluid volume include increased respirations and heart rate, decreased central venous pressure (CVP), weight loss, poor skin turgor, dry mucous membranes, decreased urine volume, increased specific gravity of the urine, increased hematocrit, and altered level of consciousness. The normal CVP is between 4 and 11 cm H_2O. A client with dehydration has a low CVP. The assessment findings in options 1, 2, and 3 are seen in a client with excess fluid volume.
Test-Taking Strategy: Use the process of elimination and focus on the subject, deficient fluid volume. Eliminate options

1 and 3 first. Lung congestion is noted in excess fluid volume, as is increased blood pressure. From the remaining options, recall that central venous pressure reflects the pressure under which blood is returned to the superior vena cava and right atrium. Therefore, pressure (volume) would be decreased in a deficient fluid volume. If you had difficulty with this question, review the assessment findings noted in deficient fluid volume.
Level of Cognitive Ability: Analysis
Client Needs: Physiological Integrity
Integrated Process: Nursing Process—assessment
Content Area: Fundamental skills
References: Lewis, S., Heitkemper, M., & Dirksen, S. (2004). *Medical-surgical nursing: Assessment and management of clinical problems* (6th ed., p. 339). St. Louis: Mosby.
Potter, P., & Perry, A. (2005). *Fundamentals of nursing* (6th ed., p. 1144). St. Louis: Mosby.

4. **2**
Rationale: The causes of excess fluid volume include decreased kidney function, congestive heart failure, the use of hypotonic fluids to replace isotonic fluid losses, excessive irrigation of wounds and body cavities, and excessive ingestion of sodium. The client taking diuretics, the client with an ileostomy, and the client who requires gastrointestinal suctioning are at risk for deficient fluid volume.
Test-Taking Strategy: Use the process of elimination and focus on the subject, excess fluid volume. Read each option and think about the fluid imbalance that can occur in each. The clients presented in options 1, 3, and 4 lose fluid. The only condition that can cause an excess is the condition noted in option 2. If you had difficulty with this question, review the causes of excess fluid volume.
Level of Cognitive Ability: Analysis
Client Needs: Physiological Integrity
Integrated Process: Nursing Process—assessment
Content Area: Fundamental skills
Reference: Potter, P., & Perry, A. (2005). *Fundamentals of nursing* (6th ed., p. 1144). St. Louis: Mosby.

5. **3**
Rationale: Assessment findings associated with excess fluid volume include cough, dyspnea, crackles, tachypnea, tachycardia, an elevated blood pressure and a bounding pulse, an elevated CVP, weight gain, edema, neck and hand vein distention, altered level of consciousness, and a decreased hematocrit. Options 1, 2, and 4 identify signs noted in deficient fluid volume.
Test-Taking Strategy: Use the process of elimination and knowledge regarding the assessment findings in excess fluid volume. Note that options 1, 2, and 4 are similar or alike in that each of these signs reflects a decrease. Option 3 reflects an increase. If you had difficulty with this question, review the assessment findings noted in excess fluid volume.
Level of Cognitive Ability: Analysis
Client Needs: Physiological Integrity
Integrated Process: Nursing Process—assessment
Content Area: Fundamental skills
Reference: Lewis, S., Heitkemper, M., & Dirksen, S. (2004). *Medical-surgical nursing: Assessment and management of clinical problems* (6th ed., p. 339). St. Louis: Mosby.

6. 2

Rationale: Potassium-rich gastrointestinal fluids are lost through gastrointestinal suction, placing the client at risk for hypokalemia. The client with renal failure or Addison's disease and the client taking a potassium-sparing diuretic are at risk for hyperkalemia.

Test-Taking Strategy: Use the process of elimination. Note that the subject of the question is a potassium deficit. Option 2 is the only option that identifies a loss of body fluid. If you had difficulty with this question, review the causes of hypokalemia.

Level of Cognitive Ability: Analysis
Client Needs: Physiological Integrity
Integrated Process: Nursing Process—assessment
Content Area: Fundamental skills
References: Ignatavicius, D., & Workman, M. (2006). *Medical-surgical nursing: Critical thinking for collaborative care* (5th ed., pp. 226-227). Philadelphia: W.B. Saunders.
Potter, P., & Perry, A. (2005). *Fundamentals of nursing* (6th ed., pp. 1141-1142). St. Louis: Mosby.

7. 1

Rationale: A serum potassium level lower than 3.5 mEq/L indicates hypokalemia. Potassium deficit is a common electrolyte imbalance and is potentially life-threatening. Electrocardiographic changes include inverted T waves, ST segment depression, and prominent U waves. Absent P waves are not a characteristic of hypokalemia.

Test-Taking Strategy: From the information in the question, you need to determine that the client is experiencing hypokalemia. From this point, you must know the electrocardiographic changes that are expected when hypokalemia exists. If you had difficulty with this question, review the electrocardiographic changes that occur in hypokalemia.

Level of Cognitive Ability: Analysis
Client Needs: Physiological Integrity
Integrated Process: Nursing Process—analysis
Content Area: Fundamental skills
Reference: Lewis, S., Heitkemper, M., & Dirksen, S. (2004). *Medical-surgical nursing: Assessment and management of clinical problems* (6th ed., pp. 342-344). St. Louis: Mosby.

8. 4

Rationale: Potassium chloride administered intravenously must always be diluted in IV fluid and infused via a pump or controller. The usual concentration of IV potassium chloride is 20 to 40 mEq/L. Potassium chloride is never given by bolus (IV push). Giving potassium chloride by IV push can result in cardiac arrest. Dilution in normal saline is recommended, but dextrose solution is avoided because this type of solution increases intracellular potassium shifting. The IV bag containing the potassium chloride is always gently agitated before hanging. The IV site is monitored closely because potassium chloride is irritating to the veins and the risk of phlebitis exists. The nurse monitors urinary output during administration and contacts the physician if the urinary output is less than 30 mL/hr.

Test-Taking Strategy: Use the process of elimination and knowledge regarding the administration of potassium chloride intravenously. Noting the strategic word *unprepared* in the question and *bolus* in option 4 will direct you to the correct option. Review the administration of potassium chloride if you had difficulty with this question.

Level of Cognitive Ability: Analysis
Client Needs: Physiological Integrity
Integrated Process: Teaching and Learning
Content Area: Pharmacology
Reference: Gahart, B., & Nazareno, A. (2006). *2006 intravenous medications* (22nd ed., p. 1022). St. Louis: Mosby.

9. 1

Rationale: A medium apple provides about 159 mg of potassium. A large carrot provides 341 mg, spinach ($3\frac{1}{2}$ oz) provides 470 mg, and a medium avocado provides 1097 mg of potassium.

Test-Taking Strategy: Note the strategic words *lowest in potassium*. Recalling the potassium content of the foods identified in the options will direct you to option 1. Review the foods that are high and low in potassium content if you had difficulty with this question.

Level of Cognitive Ability: Comprehension
Client Needs: Health Promotion and Maintenance
Integrated Process: Nursing Process—evaluation
Content Area: Fundamental skills
Reference: Grodner, M., Long, S., & DeYoung, S. (2004). *Foundations and clinical applications of nutrition: A nursing approach.* (3rd ed., p. 611). St. Louis: Mosby.

10. 4

Rationale: A serum potassium level higher than 5.1 mEq/L indicates hyperkalemia. Clients who experience cellular shifting of potassium in the early stages of massive cell destruction, such as with trauma, burns, sepsis, or metabolic or respiratory acidosis, are at risk for hyperkalemia. The client with Cushing's syndrome or colitis and the client who has been overusing laxatives are at risk for hypokalemia.

Test-Taking Strategy: Use the process of elimination. Eliminate option 1 and 3 first because they are similar or alike, with both reflecting a gastrointestinal loss. From the remaining options, recalling that cell destruction causes potassium shifts will assist in directing you to the correct option. Remember that Cushing's syndrome presents a risk for hypokalemia and that Addison's disease presents a risk for hyperkalemia. If you had difficulty with this question, review the risk factors associated with hyperkalemia.

Level of Cognitive Ability: Analysis
Client Needs: Physiological Integrity
Integrated Process: Nursing Process—assessment
Content Area: Fundamental skills
Reference: Potter, P., & Perry, A. (2005). *Fundamentals of nursing* (6th ed., pp. 1141-1142). St. Louis: Mosby.

11. 4

Rationale: A serum potassium level higher than 5.1 mEq/L indicates hyperkalemia. Electrocardiographic changes include flat P waves, prolonged PR intervals, widened QRS complexes, and tall peaked T waves.

Test-Taking Strategy: From the information in the question, you need to determine that this condition is a hyperkalemic one. From this point, you must know the electrocardiographic changes that are expected when hyperkalemia exists. If you had difficulty with this question, review the normal serum

potassium level and the electrocardiographic changes that occur in hyperkalemia.
Level of Cognitive Ability: Analysis
Client Needs: Physiological Integrity
Integrated Process: Nursing Process—analysis
Content Area: Fundamental skills
Reference: Lewis, S., Heitkemper, M., & Dirksen, S. (2004). *Medical-surgical nursing: Assessment and management of clinical problems* (6th ed., p. 343). St. Louis: Mosby.

12. **2**
Rationale: Hyponatremia is evidenced by a serum sodium level lower than 135 mEq/L. Hyponatremia can occur in the client taking diuretics. The client taking corticosteroids and the client with renal failure or hyperaldosteronism are at risk for hypernatremia.
Test-Taking Strategy: Use the process of elimination. First, determine that the client is experiencing hyponatremia. Next, you must know the causes of hyponatremia to direct you to option 2. Review the normal serum sodium level and the causes of hyponatremia if you had difficulty with this question.
Level of Cognitive Ability: Analysis
Client Needs: Physiological Integrity
Integrated Process: Nursing Process—assessment
Content Area: Fundamental skills
Reference: Potter, P., & Perry, A. (2005) *Fundamentals of nursing* (6th ed., p. 1141). St. Louis: Mosby.

13. **3**
Rationale: Hyperactive bowel sounds indicate hyponatremia. Options 1, 2, and 4 are signs of hypernatremia. In hyponatremia, increased urinary output and decreased specific gravity of the urine would be noted. Dry skin occurs in deficient fluid volume.
Test-Taking Strategy: Focus on the data in the question and the subject of the question. Recalling the signs of hyponatremia will direct you to option 3. If you had difficulty with this question, review the assessment signs associated with hyponatremia and hypernatremia.
Level of Cognitive Ability: Analysis
Client Needs: Physiological Integrity
Integrated Process: Nursing Process—assessment
Content Area: Fundamental skills
References: Ignatavicius, D., & Workman, M. (2006). *Medical-surgical nursing: Critical thinking for collaborative care* (5th ed., p. 234). Philadelphia: W.B. Saunders.
Potter, P., & Perry, A. (2005). *Fundamentals of nursing* (6th ed., p. 1141). St. Louis: Mosby.

14. **3**
Rationale: A potassium level of 4.5 mEq/L is within normal range. A sodium level of 132 mEq/L is low, indicating hyponatremia. In clients with hyponatremia, sodium chloride (isotonic) should be used rather than water for gastrointestinal irrigations.
Test-Taking Strategy: Use the process of elimination. Eliminate options 1, 2, and 4 because they are comparative or alike (sterile water, tap water, and distilled water). Also, recalling that the serum sodium level identified in the question indicates hyponatremia will direct you to option 3. If you had difficulty with this question, review the care of the client experiencing hyponatremia.

Level of Cognitive Ability: Application
Client Needs: Physiological Integrity
Integrated Process: Nursing Process—implementation
Content Area: Fundamental skills
Reference: Ignatavicius, D., & Workman, M. (2006). *Medical-surgical nursing: Critical thinking for collaborative care* (5th ed., p. 235). Philadelphia: W.B. Saunders.

15. **4**
Rationale: The normal serum sodium level is 135 to 145 mEq/L. A serum sodium level of 150 mEq/L indicates hypernatremia. Based on this finding, the nurse would instruct the client to avoid foods high in sodium. Low-fat yogurt, cauliflower, and peas are good food sources of phosphorus. Processed foods are high in sodium content.
Test-Taking Strategy: First, you must determine that the client has hypernatremia. Next, note the strategic word *avoid* in the question. Eliminate options 1 and 2 first because these are vegetables. From the remaining options, note the word *processed* in option 4. Processed foods tend to be higher in sodium content. Review foods high in sodium content if you had difficulty with this question.
Level of Cognitive Ability: Application
Client Needs: Health Promotion and Maintenance
Integrated Process: Teaching and Learning
Content Area: Fundamental skills
Reference: Grodner, M., Long, S., & DeYoung, S. (2004). *Foundations and clinical applications of nutrition: A nursing approach* (3rd ed., p. 609). St. Louis: Mosby.

16. **1**
Rationale: The normal serum calcium level is 8.6 to 10.0 mg/dL. A client with a serum calcium level of 4.0 mg/dL is experiencing hypocalcemia. The excessive ingestion of vitamin D and hyperparathyroidism are causative factors associated with hypercalcemia. End-stage renal disease, rather than renal insufficiency, is a cause of hypocalcemia. Prolonged bed rest is a cause of hypocalcemia. Although immobilization initially can cause hypercalcemia, the long-term effect of prolonged bed rest is hypocalcemia.
Test-Taking Strategy: Note the strategic words *most likely*. First, you must determine that the client is experiencing hypocalcemia. This should assist in eliminating option 4. Next, you must recall the causative factors associated with hypocalcemia to direct you to option 1. If you had difficulty with the question, review the causative factors associated with hypocalcemia.
Level of Cognitive Ability: Analysis
Client Needs: Physiological Integrity
Integrated Process: Nursing Process—assessment
Content Area: Fundamental skills
Reference: Potter, P., & Perry, A. (2005). *Fundamentals of nursing* (6th ed., p. 1142). St. Louis: Mosby.

17. **1**
Rationale: Signs of hypocalcemia include paresthesias followed by numbness, hyperactive deep tendon reflexes, and a positive Trousseau's or Chvostek's sign. Additional signs of hypocalcemia include increased neuromuscular excitability, muscle cramps, twitching, tetany, seizures, irritability, and anxiety. Gastrointestinal symptoms include increased gastric motility, hyperactive bowel sounds, abdominal cramping, and diarrhea.

Test-Taking Strategy: Use the process of elimination, noting that options 2, 3, and 4 are comparative or alike in that they reflect a hypoactivity. The option that is different is option 1. Review the assessment signs and symptoms noted in hypocalcemia if you had difficulty with this question.
Level of Cognitive Ability: Analysis
Client Needs: Physiological Integrity
Integrated Process: Nursing Process—assessment
Content Area: Fundamental skills
Reference: Ignatavicius, D., & Workman, M. (2006). *Medical-surgical nursing: Critical thinking for collaborative care* (5th ed., p. 238). Philadelphia: W.B. Saunders.

18. **3**
Rationale: Electrocardiographic changes that occur in a client with hypocalcemia include a prolonged ST or QT interval. A shortened ST segment and a widened T wave occur with hypercalcemia. Prominent U waves occur with hypokalemia.
Test-Taking Strategy: Use knowledge regarding the electrocardiographic changes that occur in a calcium imbalance to answer the question. Remember that hypocalcemia causes a prolonged ST or QT interval. If you had difficulty with this question, review the electrocardiographic changes that occur in these conditions.
Level of Cognitive Ability: Analysis
Client Needs: Physiological Integrity
Integrated Process: Nursing Process—assessment
Content Area: Fundamental skills
Reference: Ignatavicius, D., & Workman, M. (2006). *Medical-surgical nursing: Critical thinking for collaborative care* (5th ed., p. 696). Philadelphia: W.B. Saunders.

19. **3**
Rationale: The normal magnesium level is 1.6 to 2.6 mg/dL. A magnesium level of 1.0 mg/dL indicates hypomagnesemia. In hypomagnesemia, the nurse would note tall T waves and a depressed ST segment. Options 2 and 4 would be noted in a client experiencing hypermagnesemia. Prominent U waves occur with hypokalemia.
Test-Taking Strategy: First, you must determine that the client is experiencing hypomagnesemia. Next, identify the electrocardiographic changes that occur in this condition. If you had difficulty with this question, review the normal magnesium level and the electrocardiographic changes that occur in hypomagnesemia and hypermagnesemia.
Level of Cognitive Ability: Analysis
Client Needs: Physiological Integrity

Integrated Process: Nursing Process—assessment
Content Area: Fundamental skills
Reference: Ignatavicius, D., & Workman, M. (2006). *Medical-surgical nursing: Critical thinking for collaborative care* (5th ed., p. 243). Philadelphia: W.B. Saunders.

20. **1**
Rationale: The normal serum phosphorus level is 2.7 to 4.5 mg/dL. The client is experiencing hypophosphatemia. Causative factors relate to malnutrition or starvation and the use of aluminum hydroxide–based or magnesium-based antacids. Malnutrition is associated with alcoholism. Hypoparathyroidism, tumor lysis syndrome, and renal insufficiency are causative factors of hyperphosphatemia.
Test-Taking Strategy: First you must determine that the client is experiencing hypophosphatemia. From this point, you must know the causes of hypophosphatemia. If you had difficulty with this question, review the causative factors associated with hypophosphatemia.
Level of Cognitive Ability: Analysis
Client Needs: Physiological Integrity
Integrated Process: Nursing Process—assessment
Content Area: Fundamental skills
Reference: Huether, S., & McCance, K. (2004). *Understanding pathophysiology* (3rd ed., p. 119). St. Louis: Mosby.

ALTERNATE ITEM FORMAT: MULTIPLE RESPONSE

Answer: 1, 4, 5, 6
Rationale: The normal magnesium level is 1.6 to 2.6 mg/dL. Common food sources of magnesium include avocado, canned white tuna, cauliflower, green leafy vegetables such as spinach and broccoli, milk, oatmeal, peanut butter, peas, pork, beef, chicken, potatoes, raisins, and yogurt. Bacon is high in sodium. Oranges are high in potassium.
Test-Taking Strategy: Focus on the subject, foods high in magnesium. Read each food item and recall that bacon is high in sodium and oranges are high in potassium. Review the food items high in magnesium if you had difficulty with this question.
Level of Cognitive Ability: Application
Client Needs: Physiological Integrity
Integrated Process: Teaching and Learning
Content Area: Fundamental Skills
Reference: Ignatavicius, D., & Workman, M. (2006). *Medical-surgical nursing: Critical thinking for collaborative care* (5th ed., pp. 205, 207). Philadelphia: W.B. Saunders.

REFERENCES

Black, J., & Hawks, J., (2005). *Medical-surgical nursing: Clinical management for positive outcomes* (7th ed.). Philadelphia: W.B. Saunders.

Chernecky, C., & Berger, B. (2001). *Laboratory tests and diagnostic procedures* (3rd ed.). Philadelphia: W.B. Saunders.

Gahart, B., & Nazareno, A. (2006). *2006 intravenous medications* (22nd ed.). St. Louis: Mosby.

Grodner, M., Long, S., & DeYoung, S. (2004). *Foundations and clinical applications of nutrition: A nursing approach* (3rd ed.). St. Louis: Mosby.

Hodgson, B., & Kizior, R. (2007). *W.B. Saunders nursing drug handbook 2007.* Philadelphia: W.B. Saunders.

Huether, S., & McCance, K. (2004). *Understanding pathophysiology* (3rd ed.). St. Louis: Mosby.

Ignatavicius, D., & Workman, M. (2006). *Medical-surgical nursing: Critical thinking for collaborative care* (5th ed.). Philadelphia: W.B. Saunders.

Lewis, S., Heitkemper, M., & Dirksen, S. (2004). *Medical-surgical nursing: Assessment and management of clinical problems* (6th ed.). St. Louis: Mosby.

National Council of State Boards (Eds.). (2007). *2007 NCLEX-RN® detailed test plan.* Chicago: Author.

Potter, P., & Perry, A. (2005). *Fundamentals of nursing* (6th ed.). St. Louis: Mosby.

Acid-Base Balance

PYRAMID TERMS

Allen's test A test to assess for collateral circulation to the hand by evaluating the patency of the radial and ulnar arteries.

metabolic acidosis A total concentration of buffer base that is lower than normal, with a relative increase in the hydrogen ion concentration. This results from loss of buffer bases or retention of too many acids without sufficient bases, and occurs in conditions such as renal failure and diabetic ketoacidosis, from the production of lactic acid, and from the ingestion of toxins, such as acetylsalicylic acid (aspirin).

metabolic alkalosis A deficit or loss of hydrogen ions or acids or an excess of base (bicarbonate) that results from the accumulation of base or from a loss of acid without a comparable loss of base in the body fluids. This occurs in conditions resulting in hypovolemia, the loss of gastric fluid, excessive bicarbonate intake, the massive transfusion of whole blood, and hyperaldosteronism.

respiratory acidosis A total concentration of buffer base that is lower than normal, with a relative increase in hydrogen ion concentration; thus, a greater number of hydrogen ions is circulating in the blood than the buffer system can absorb. This is caused by primary defects in the function of the lungs or by changes in normal respiratory patterns as a result of secondary problems. Any condition that causes an obstruction of the airway or depresses respiratory status can cause respiratory acidosis.

respiratory alkalosis A deficit of carbonic acid or a decrease in hydrogen ion concentration that results from the accumulation of base or from a loss of acid without a comparable loss of base in the body fluids. This occurs in conditions that cause overstimulation of the respiratory system.

▲ THE PYRAMID TO SUCCESS

Acid-base imbalance is a content area that sometimes is viewed as complex and difficult to understand. You must understand the description of each imbalance and then review the causes of each disorder, correlating the pathophysiology with each cause. From this point, note the assessment signs related to each disorder and the treatment associated with the clinical manifestations. Maintenance of a patent airway is a priority. The nurse also needs to monitor vital signs, cardiovascular status, neurological status, intake and output, laboratory values, and arterial blood gas values. Remember, safety and seizure precautions may need to be initiated. Integrated Processes addressed in this chapter are Caring, Communication and Documentation, Nursing Process, and Teaching/Learning.

CLIENT NEEDS
Safe and Effective Care Environment

Establishing priorities
Maintaining medical and surgical asepsis
Maintaining standard, transmission-based, and other precautions
Obtaining informed consent for invasive procedures
Preventing accidents
Providing safety for the client during implementation of various treatments for the acid-base imbalance

Health Promotion and Maintenance

Identifying clients at risk for an acid-base imbalance
Performing physical assessment techniques
Preventing disease
Promoting health and wellness
Teaching the client and family about prevention, early detection, and treatment measures for health disorders

Psychosocial Integrity

Identifying support systems
Monitoring for sensory and perceptual alterations
Providing emotional support to the client and family

Physiological Integrity

Administering and monitoring medications, intravenous fluids, and other therapeutic interventions

Assisting with diagnostic tests

Monitoring for alterations in body systems

Monitoring for changes in status and for complications

Monitoring for expected effects of pharmacological and parenteral therapies

Monitoring laboratory values

Obtaining an arterial blood gas specimen and analyzing the results

Providing basic care and comfort

Providing wound care when blood is obtained for an arterial blood gas study

Reducing the likelihood that an acid-base imbalance will occur

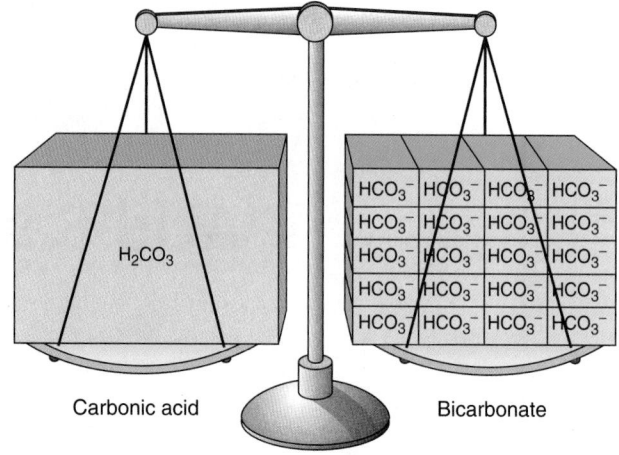

FIG. 10-1 Normal ratio of carbonic acid to bicarbonate is 1:20. (From Ignatavicius, D., & Workman, M. [2006]. *Medical-surgical nursing: Critical thinking for collaborative care* [5th ed.]. Philadelphia: W.B. Saunders.)

I. HYDROGEN IONS, ACIDS, AND BASES

A. Hydrogen ions
   1. Vital to life
   2. Expressed as pH
   3. Circulate in the body in two forms:
      a. Volatile hydrogen of carbonic acid
      b. Nonvolatile form of hydrogen and organic acids
B. Acids
   1. Acids are produced as end products of metabolism.
   2. Acids contain hydrogen ions and are hydrogen ion donors, which means that acids give up hydrogen ions to neutralize or decrease the strength of an acid or to form a weaker base.
   3. The strength of an acid is determined by the number of hydrogen ions it contains.
   4. The number of hydrogen ions in body fluid determines its acidity, alkalinity, or neutrality.
   5. The lungs excrete 13,000 to 30,000 mEq/day of volatile hydrogen in the form of carbonic acid as carbon dioxide (CO_2).
   6. The kidneys excrete 50 mEq/day of nonvolatile acids.
C. Bases
   1. Contain no hydrogen ions.
   2. Are hydrogen ion acceptors; they accept hydrogen ions from acids to neutralize or decrease the strength of a base or to form a weaker acid.

II. REGULATORY SYSTEMS FOR HYDROGEN ION CONCENTRATION IN THE BLOOD

A. Buffers
   1. Buffers are the fastest acting regulatory system.
   2. Provide immediate protection against changes in hydrogen ion concentration in the extracellular fluid.
   3. Buffers are reactors that function only to keep the pH within the narrow limits of stability when too much acid or base is released into the system, and buffers absorb or release hydrogen ions as needed.
   4. Buffers serve as a transport mechanism that carries excess hydrogen ions to the lungs.
   5. Once the primary buffer systems react, they are consumed; this leaves the body less able to withstand further stress until they are replaced.
B. Primary buffer systems in extracellular fluid
   1. Hemoglobin system
      a. Red blood cells contain hemoglobin.
      b. System maintains acid-base balance by a process called chloride shift.
      c. Chloride shifts in and out of the cells in response to the level of O_2 in the blood.
      d. For each chloride ion that leaves a red blood cell, a bicarbonate ion enters.
      e. For each chloride ion that enters a red blood cell, a bicarbonate ion leaves.
   2. Plasma protein system
      a. The system functions along with the liver to vary the amount of hydrogen ions in the chemical structure of plasma proteins.
      b. Plasma proteins have the ability to attract or release hydrogen ions.
   3. Carbonic acid–bicarbonate system
      a. Primary buffer system in the body.
      b. The system maintains a pH of 7.4 with a ratio of 20 parts bicarbonate (HCO_3^-) to 1 part carbonic acid (H_2CO_3) (Fig. 10-1).
      c. This ratio (20:1) determines the hydrogen ion concentration of body fluid.
      d. Carbonic acid concentration is controlled by the excretion of CO_2 by the lungs; the rate and depth of respiration change in response to changes in the CO_2.
      e. The kidneys control the bicarbonate concentration and selectively retain or excrete bicarbonates in response to bodily needs.

4. Phosphate buffer system
   a. System is present in the cells and body fluids and is especially active in the kidneys.
   b. System acts like bicarbonate and neutralizes excess hydrogen ions.
C. Lungs
   1. The lungs are the second defense of the body and interact with the buffer system to maintain acid-base balance.
   2. In acidosis, the pH decreases and the respiratory rate and depth increase in an attempt to exhale acids. The carbonic acid created by the neutralizing action of bicarbonate can be carried to the lungs, where it is reduced to CO_2 and water and exhaled; thus hydrogen ions are inactivated and exhaled.
   3. In alkalosis, the pH increases and the respiratory rate and depth decrease; CO_2 is retained and carbonic acid increases to neutralize and decrease the strength of excess bicarbonate.
   4. The action of the lungs is reversible in controlling an excess or deficit.
   5. The lungs can hold hydrogen ions until the deficit is corrected or can inactivate hydrogen ions, changing the ions to water molecules to be exhaled along with CO_2, thus correcting the excess.
   6. The process of correcting a deficit or excess takes 10 to 30 seconds to complete.
   7. The lungs are capable of inactivating only hydrogen ions carried by carbonic acid; excess hydrogen ions created by other mechanisms must be excreted by the kidneys.
D. Kidneys
   1. The ultimate correction of acid-base disturbances depends on the kidneys, even though the renal excretion of acids and alkalis occurs more slowly.
   2. Compensation requires a few hours to several days; however, the compensation is more thorough and selective than that of other regulators, such as the buffer systems and lungs.
   3. In acidosis, the pH decreases and excess hydrogen ions are secreted into the tubules and combine with buffers for excretion in the urine.
   4. In alkalosis, the pH increases and excess bicarbonate ions move into the tubules, combine with sodium, and are excreted in the urine.
   5. Selective regulation of bicarbonate occurs in the kidneys.
      a. The kidneys restore bicarbonate by excreting hydrogen ions and retaining bicarbonate ions.
      b. Excess hydrogen ions are excreted in the urine in the form of phosphoric acid.
      c. The alteration of certain amino acids in the renal tubules results in a diffusion of ammonia into the kidneys; the ammonia combines with excess hydrogen ions and is excreted in the urine.

E. Potassium (K^+)
   1. Potassium plays an exchange role in maintaining acid-base balance.
   2. The body changes the potassium level by drawing hydrogen ions into the cell or by pushing them out of the cell.
   3. The potassium level changes to compensate for hydrogen ion level changes (Fig. 10-2).
      a. In acidosis, the body protects itself from the acidic state by moving hydrogen ions into the cell. Therefore, potassium moves out to make room for hydrogen ions and the serum potassium level increases.
      b. In alkalosis, the cells release hydrogen ions into the blood in an attempt to increase the acidity of the blood; this forces the serum potassium into the cell and potassium levels decrease.

III. RESPIRATORY ACIDOSIS

A. Description: The total concentration of buffer base is lower than normal, with a relative increase in hydrogen ion concentration; thus, a greater number of hydrogen ions is circulating in the blood than can be absorbed by the buffer system.
B. Causes (Box 10-1)
   1. **Respiratory acidosis** is caused by primary defects in the function of the lungs or changes in normal respiratory patterns.
   2. Any condition that causes an obstruction of the airway or depresses the respiratory system can cause **respiratory acidosis**.
   3. Asthma: Spasms resulting from allergens, irritants, or emotions cause the smooth muscles of the bronchioles to constrict, resulting in ineffective gas exchange.
   4. Atelectasis: Excessive mucus collection, with the collapse of alveolar sacs caused by mucous plugs, infectious drainage, or anesthetic medications, results in ineffective gas exchange.
   5. Brain trauma: Excessive pressure on the respiratory center or medulla oblongata depresses respirations.
   6. Bronchiectasis: Bronchi become dilated as a result of inflammation, and destructive changes and weakness in the walls of the bronchi occur.
   7. Bronchitis: Inflammation causes airway obstruction, resulting in inadequate gas exchange.
   8. Central nervous system (CNS) depressants such as sedatives, opioids, and anesthetics depress the respiratory center, leading to hypoventilation; carbon dioxide is retained and the hydrogen ion concentration increases.
   9. Emphysema: Loss of elasticity of alveolar sacs restricts air flow in and out, primarily out, leading to an increased CO_2 level.
   10. Hypoventilation: Carbon dioxide is retained and the hydrogen ion concentration increases,

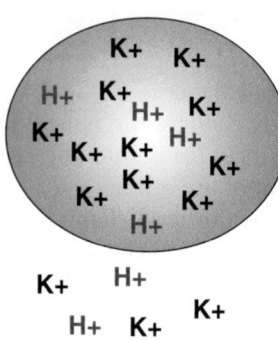

Under normal conditions, the intracellular potassium content is much greater than that of the extracellular fluid. The concentration of hydrogen ions is low in both compartments.

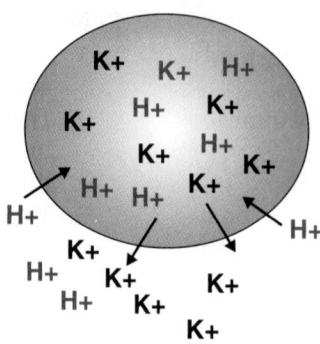

In acidosis, the extracellular hydrogen ion content increases, and the hydrogen ions move into the intracellular fluid. To keep the intracellular fluid electrically neutral, an equal number of potassium ions leave the cell, creating a relative hyperkalemia.

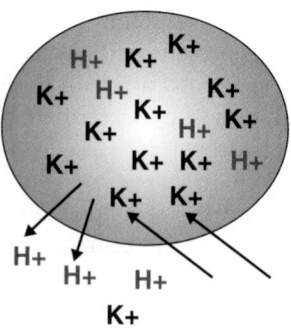

In alkalosis, more hydrogen ions are present in the intracellular fluid than in the extracellular fluid. Hydrogen ions move from the intracellular fluid into the extracellular fluid. To keep the intracellular fluid electrically neutral, potassium ions move from the extracellular fluid into the intracellular fluid, creating a relative hypokalemia.

FIG. 10-2 Movement of potassium in response to changes in the extracellular fluid hydrogen ion concentration. (From Ignatavicius, D. & Workman, M. [2006]. *Medical-surgical nursing: Critical thinking for collaborative care* [5th ed.]. Philadelphia: W.B. Saunders. Courtesy of M. Linda Workman.)

BOX 10-1

Some Causes Of Respiratory Acidosis

Asthma
Atelectasis
Brain trauma
Bronchiectasis
Bronchitis
Central nervous system depressants
Emphysema
Hypoventilation
Pulmonary edema
Pneumonia
Pulmonary emboli

---

leading to the acidic state; carbonic acid is retained and the pH decreases.

11. Pulmonary edema: Extracellular accumulation of fluid in pulmonary tissue causes disturbances in alveolar diffusion and perfusion.

12. Pneumonia: Excess mucus production and lung congestion cause airway obstruction, resulting in inadequate gas exchange.

13. Pulmonary emboli: Emboli cause a pulmonary and airway obstruction, resulting in inadequate gas exchange.

C. Assessment: In an attempt to compensate, the kidneys will retain bicarbonate and excrete excess hydrogen ions into the urine (Table 10-1).

D. Interventions

1. Monitor for signs of respiratory distress.
2. Administer oxygen as prescribed.
3. Place the client in a semi-Fowler's position, unless contraindicated.
4. Encourage and assist the client to turn, cough, and deep-breathe.
5. Prepare to administer respiratory treatments as prescribed.
6. Encourage hydration to thin secretions, unless excess fluid intake is contraindicated.
7. Suction the client's airway, if necessary.
8. Reduce restlessness by improving ventilation rather than by administering tranquilizers, sedatives, or opioids because these medications further depress respirations.
9. Monitor electrolyte values, particularly the potassium level.
10. Administer antibiotics for respiratory infection or other medications as prescribed.
11. Prepare for endotracheal intubation and mechanical ventilation if CO_2 levels rise above 50 mm Hg and if signs of respiratory distress are present.

IV. **RESPIRATORY ALKALOSIS** (Table 10-2)
A. Description: A deficit of carbonic acid and a decrease in hydrogen ion concentration that results from the accumulation of base or from a loss of acid without a comparable loss of base in the body fluids.
B. Causes (Box 10-2)

TABLE 10-1

Clinical Manifestations of Acidosis

Respiratory ($\uparrow Pco_2$)	Metabolic ($\downarrow HCO_3^-$)
NEUROLOGICAL	
Drowsiness	Drowsiness
Disorientation	Confusion
Dizziness	Headache
Headache	Coma
Coma	
CARDIOVASCULAR	
$\downarrow$Blood pressure	$\downarrow$Blood pressure
Ventricular fibrillation (related to hyperkalemia from compensation)	Dysrhythmias (related to hyperkalemia from compensation)
Warm, flushed skin (related to peripheral vasodilation)	Warm, flushed skin (related to peripheral vasodilation)
GASTROINTESTINAL	
No significant findings	Nausea, vomiting, diarrhea, abdominal pain
NEUROMUSCULAR	
Seizures	No significant findings
RESPIRATORY	
Hypoventilation with hypoxia (lungs are unable to compensate when there is a respiratory problem)	Deep, rapid respirations (compensatory action by the lungs)

Modified from Lewis, S., Heitkemper, M., & Dirksen, S. (2004). *Medical-surgical nursing: Assessment and management of clinical problems* (6th ed.). St. Louis: Mosby.

TABLE 10-2

Clinical Manifestations of Alkalosis

Respiratory ($\downarrow Pco_2$)	Metabolic ($\uparrow HCO_3^-$)
NEUROLOGICAL	
Lethargy	Drowsiness
Light-headedness	Dizziness
Confusion	Nervousness
	Confusion
CARDIOVASCULAR	
Tachycardia	Tachycardia
Dysrhythmias (related to hypokalemia from compensation)	Dysrhythmias (related to hypokalemia from compensation)
GASTROINTESTINAL	
Nausea	Anorexia
Vomiting	Nausea
Epigastric pain	Vomiting
NEUROMUSCULAR	
Tetany	Tremors
Numbness	Hypertonic muscles
Tingling of extremities	Muscle cramps
Hyperreflexia	Tetany
Seizures	Tingling of fingers and toes
	Seizures
RESPIRATORY	
Hyperventilation (lungs are unable to compensate when there is a respiratory problem)	Hypoventilation (compensatory action by the lungs)

Modified from Lewis, S., Heitkemper, M., & Dirksen, S. (2004). *Medical-surgical nursing: Assessment and management of clinical problems* (6th ed.). St. Louis: Mosby.

BOX 10-2

Some Causes of Respiratory Alkalosis

Fever
Hyperventilation
Hypoxia
Hysteria
Overventilation by mechanical ventilators
Pain

1. **Respiratory alkalosis** results from conditions that cause overstimulation of the respiratory system.
2. Fever: Causes increased metabolism, resulting in overstimulation of the respiratory system.
3. Hyperventilation: Rapid respirations cause the blowing off of CO_2, leading to a decrease in carbonic acid.
4. Hypoxia: Stimulates the respiratory center in the brainstem, which causes an increase in the respiratory rate in order to increase oxygen; this causes hyperventilation, which results in a decrease in the CO_2 level.
5. Hysteria: Hysteria often is neurogenic and related to a psychoneurosis; however, this condition leads to vigorous breathing and excessive exhaling of CO_2.
6. Overventilation by mechanical ventilators: The administration of O_2 and the depletion of CO_2 can occur from mechanical ventilation, causing the client to be hyperventilated.
7. Pain: Overstimulation of the respiratory center in the brainstem results in a carbonic acid deficit.

C. Assessment: Initially the hyperventilation and respiratory stimulation will cause abnormal rapid respirations (tachypnea); in an attempt to compensate, the kidneys will excrete excess circulating bicarbonate into the urine (see Table 10-2)
D. Interventions
   1. Monitor for signs of respiratory distress.
   2. Provide emotional support and reassurance to the client.
   3. Encourage appropriate breathing patterns.

4. Assist with breathing techniques and breathing aids as prescribed.
   a. Voluntary holding of the breath
   b. Use of a rebreathing mask as prescribed
   c. Carbon dioxide breaths as prescribed (rebreathing into a paper bag)
5. Provide cautious care with ventilator clients so that they are not forced to take breaths too deeply or rapidly.
6. Monitor electrolyte values, particularly potassium and calcium levels.
7. Administer medications as prescribed.
8. Prepare to administer calcium gluconate for tetany as prescribed.

V. METABOLIC ACIDOSIS

A. Description: A total concentration of buffer base that is lower than normal, with a relative increase in the hydrogen ion concentration, resulting from loss of too much base and/or retention of too much acid.
B. Causes (Box 10-3)
   1. Diabetes mellitus or diabetic ketoacidosis: An insufficient supply of insulin causes increased fat metabolism, leading to an excess accumulation of ketones or other acids; the bicarbonate then ends up being depleted.
   2. Excessive ingestion of acetylsalicylic acid (aspirin) causes an increase in the hydrogen ion concentration.
   3. High-fat diet: A high intake of fat causes a much too rapid accumulation of the waste products of fat metabolism, leading to a buildup of ketones and acids.
   4. Insufficient metabolism of carbohydrates: When the O_2 supply is not sufficient for the metabolism of carbohydrates, lactic acid is produced and lactic acidosis results.
   5. Malnutrition: Improper metabolism of nutrients causes fat catabolism, leading to an excess buildup of ketones and acids.
   6. Renal insufficiency or renal failure results in the following:
      a. Increased waste products of protein metabolism are retained.
      b. Acids increase, and bicarbonate is unable to maintain acid-base balance.

7. Severe diarrhea: Intestinal and pancreatic secretions are normally alkaline; therefore excessive loss of base leads to acidosis.
C. Assessment: In an attempt to compensate for the acidosis, hyperpnea with Kussmaul's respiration occurs as the lungs attempt to exhale the excess CO_2 (see Table 10-1).
D. Interventions
   1. Monitor for signs of respiratory distress.
   2. Assess level of consciousness for central nervous system depression.
   3. Monitor intake and output and assist with fluid and electrolyte replacement as prescribed.
   4. Prepare to administer solutions intravenously as prescribed to increase the buffer base.
   5. Initiate safety and seizure precautions.
   6. Monitor the serum potassium level closely; as metabolic acidosis resolves, potassium will move back into the cell and the serum potassium level will decrease.
E. Interventions in diabetes mellitus and diabetic ketoacidosis
   1. Give insulin as prescribed to hasten the movement of serum glucose into the cell, thereby decreasing the concurrent ketosis.
   2. When glucose is being properly metabolized, the body will stop converting fats to glucose.
   3. Monitor for circulatory collapse caused by polyuria, which may result from the hyperglycemic state; osmotic diuresis may lead to extracellular volume deficit.
F. Interventions in renal failure
   1. In renal failure, dialysis may be used to remove protein and waste products, thereby lessening the acidotic state.
   2. A diet low in protein and high in calories will decrease the amount of protein waste products; this in turn will lessen the acidosis.

VI. METABOLIC ALKALOSIS

A. Description: A deficit of carbonic acid and a decease in hydrogen ion concentration that results from the accumulation of base or from a loss of acid without a comparable loss of base in the body fluids.
B. Causes (Box 10-4)
   1. **Metabolic alkalosis** results from a dysfunction of metabolism that causes an increased amount of available base solution in the blood or a decrease in available acids in the blood.

BOX 10-3
Some Causes of Metabolic Acidosis

Diabetes mellitus or diabetic ketoacidosis
Excessive ingestion of acetylsalicylic acid (aspirin)
High-fat diet
Insufficient metabolism of carbohydrates
Malnutrition
Renal insufficiency or renal failure
Severe diarrhea

BOX 10-4
Some Causes of Metabolic Alkalosis

Diuretics
Excessive vomiting or gastrointestinal suctioning
Hyperaldosteronism
Ingestion of and/or infusion of excess sodium bicarbonate
Massive transfusion of whole blood

2. Diuretics: The loss of hydrogen ions and chloride from diuresis causes a compensatory increase in the amount of bicarbonate in the blood.
3. Excessive vomiting or gastrointestinal suctioning leads to an excessive loss of hydrochloric acid.
4. Hyperaldosteronism: Increased renal tubular re-absorption of sodium occurs, with the resultant loss of hydrogen ions.
5. Ingestion of and/or infusion of excess sodium bicarbonate causes an increase in the amount of base in the blood.
6. Massive transfusion of whole blood: The citrate anticoagulant used for the storage of blood is metabolized to bicarbonate.

C. Assessment: In an attempt to compensate, respiratory rate and depth decrease to conserve CO_2 (see Table 10-2).

D. Interventions
1. Monitor for signs of respiratory distress.
2. Monitor potassium and calcium serum levels.
3. Institute safety precautions.
4. Prepare to administer medications as prescribed to promote the kidney excretion of bicarbonate.
5. Prepare to replace potassium chloride as prescribed.
6. Treat the underlying cause of the alkalosis.

VII. ARTERIAL BLOOD GASES (Box 10-5)
A. Collection of an arterial blood gas specimen
1. Obtain vital signs.
2. Determine whether the client has an arterial line in place.
3. Perform the **Allen's test** to determine the presence of collateral circulation (Box 10-6).
4. Assess factors that may affect the accuracy of the results, such as changes in the O_2 settings, suctioning within the last 20 minutes, and client's activities.
5. Provide emotional support to the client.
6. Assist with the specimen draw by preparing a heparinized syringe.
7. Apply pressure immediately to the puncture site following the blood draw; maintain pressure for 5 minutes, or for 10 minutes if the client is taking anticoagulants.
8. Appropriately label the specimen and transport it on ice to the laboratory.
9. On the laboratory form, record the client's temperature and the type of supplemental oxygen that the client is receiving.

B. Respiratory acid-base imbalances (Table 10-3)
1. Remember, the respiratory function indicator is the P_{CO_2}.
2. In a respiratory imbalance, you will find an opposite relationship between the pH and the P_{CO_2}; in other words, the pH will be elevated with a decreased P_{CO_2} (alkalosis) or the pH will be decreased with an elevated P_{CO_2} (acidosis).
3. Look at the pH and the P_{CO_2} to determine whether the condition is a respiratory problem.
4. **Respiratory acidosis**: The pH is decreased; the P_{CO_2} is elevated.
5. **Respiratory alkalosis**: The pH is elevated; the P_{CO_2} is decreased.

C. Metabolic acid-base imbalances (see Table 10-3)
1. Remember, the metabolic function indicator is the bicarbonate ion (HCO_3^-).
2. In a metabolic imbalance, you will find a corresponding relationship between the pH and the HCO_3^-; in other words, the pH will be elevated and the HCO_3^- will be elevated (alkalosis), or the pH will be decreased and the HCO_3^- will be decreased (acidosis).
3. Look at the pH and the HCO_3^- to determine

BOX 10-6

Performing the Allen's Test

Apply direct pressure over the client's ulnar and radial arteries simultaneously.

While applying pressure, ask the client to open and close the hand repeatedly; the hand should blanch.

Release pressure from the ulnar artery while compressing the radial artery and assess the color of the extremity distal to the pressure point.

If pinkness fails to return within 6 seconds, the ulnar artery is insufficient, indicating that the radial artery should not be used for obtaining a blood specimen.

BOX 10-5

Normal Arterial Blood Gas Values

pH	7.35-7.45
P_{CO_2}	35-45 mm Hg
HCO_3^-	22-27 mEq/L
P_{O_2}	80-100 mm Hg

TABLE 10-3

Acid-Base Imbalances: Usual Laboratory Value Changes

Imbalance	pH	HCO_3^-	Pa_{O_2}	Pa_{CO_2}	K^+
Respiratory acidosis	Decreased	Increased	Decreased	Increased	Increased
Respiratory alkalosis	Increased	Decreased	Normal	Deceased	Decreased
Metabolic acidosis	Decreased	Decreased	Normal	Normal or decreased	Increased
Metabolic alkalosis	Increased	Increased	Normal	Normal or increased	Decreased

BOX 10-7

Analyzing Arterial Blood Gas Results

If you can remember the following Pyramid Points and Pyramid Steps, you will be able to analyze any blood gas report.

PYRAMID POINTS

In acidosis, the pH is decreased.
In alkalosis, the pH is elevated.
The respiratory function indicator is the P_{CO_2}.
The metabolic function indicator is the bicarbonate ion (HCO_3^-).

PYRAMID STEPS

Pyramid Step 1

Look at the blood gas report. Look at the pH. Is the pH elevated or decreased? If the pH is elevated, it reflects alkalosis. If the pH is decreased, it reflects acidosis.

Pyramid Step 2

Look at the P_{CO_2}. Is the P_{CO_2} elevated or decreased? If the P_{CO_2} reflects an opposite relationship to the pH, then you know that the condition is a respiratory imbalance. If the P_{CO_2} does not reflect an opposite relationship to the pH, then move on to Pyramid Step 3.

Pyramid Step 3

Look at the HCO_3^-. Does the HCO_3^- reflect a corresponding relationship with the pH? If it does, then the condition is a metabolic imbalance.

Pyramid Step 4

Remember, compensation has occurred if the pH is in a normal range of 7.35 to 7.45. If the pH is not within normal range, look at the respiratory or metabolic function indicators.

Respiratory Imbalances

If the condition is a respiratory imbalance, look at the HCO_3^- to determine the state of compensation.

If the HCO_3^- is normal, then the condition is uncompensated. If the HCO_3^- is abnormal, then the condition is partial compensation.

Metabolic Imbalances

If the condition is a metabolic imbalance, look at the P_{CO_2} to determine the state of compensation.

If the P_{CO_2} is normal, then the condition is uncompensated. If the P_{CO_2} is abnormal, then the condition is partial compensation.

whether the condition is a metabolic problem.
4. **Metabolic acidosis**: The pH is decreased; the HCO_3^- is decreased.
5. **Metabolic alkalosis**: The pH is elevated; the HCO_3^- is elevated.

D. Compensation
1. **Respiratory acidosis** and **respiratory alkalosis**
   a. When compensation has occurred, the pH will be within normal limits.
   b. The blood gas result reflects partial compensation if the HCO_3^- is abnormal.
   c. The blood gas result reflects an uncompen-

sated condition if the HCO_3^- is normal.
2. **Metabolic acidosis** and **metabolic alkalosis**
   a. When compensation has occurred, the pH will be within normal limits.
   b. The blood gas result reflects partial compensation if the P_{CO_2} is abnormal.
   c. The blood gas result reflects an uncompensated condition if the P_{CO_2} is normal.
E. Steps for analyzing arterial blood gas results (Box 10-7)

PRACTICE QUESTIONS

1. A client with a 3-day history of nausea and vomiting presents to the emergency department. The client is hypoventilating and has a respiratory rate of 6 breaths/ min. The electrocardiogram (ECG) monitor displays tachycardia, with a heart rate of 120 beats/min. Arterial blood gases are drawn and the nurse reviews the results, expecting to note which of the following?
   1. A decreased pH and an increased CO_2
   2. An increased pH and a decreased CO_2
   3. A decreased pH and a decreased HCO_3^-
   4. An increased pH with an increased HCO_3^-

2. A client who is found unresponsive has arterial blood gases drawn and the results indicate the following: pH is 7.12, P_{CO_2} is 90 mm Hg, and HCO_3^- is 22 mEq/L. The nurse interprets the results as indicating which condition?
   1. Metabolic acidosis with compensation
   2. Respiratory acidosis with compensation
   3. Metabolic acidosis without compensation
   4. Respiratory acidosis without compensation

3. A nurse plans care for a client with chronic obstructive pulmonary disease, knowing that the client is most likely to experience what type of acid-base imbalance?
   1. Metabolic acidosis
   2. Metabolic alkalosis
   3. Respiratory acidosis
   4. Respiratory alkalosis

4. A nurse reviews the blood gas results of a client with Guillain-Barré syndrome. The nurse analyzes the results and determines that the client is experiencing respiratory acidosis. Which of the following validates the nurse's findings?
   1. pH 7.25, P_{CO_2} 50 mm Hg
   2. pH 7.35, P_{CO_2} 40 mm Hg
   3. pH 7.50, P_{CO_2} 52 mm Hg
   4. pH 7.52, P_{CO_2} 28 mm Hg

5. A nurse is caring for a client who is on a mechanical ventilator. Blood gas results indicate a pH of 7.50 and a P_{CO_2} of 30 mm Hg. The nurse has determined that the client is experiencing respiratory alkalosis. Which laboratory value would most likely be noted in this condition?

1. Sodium level of 145 mEq/L
2. Potassium level of 3.0 mEq/L
3. Magnesium level of 2.0 mg/dL
4. Phosphorus level of 4.0 mg/dL

6. A nurse reviews the arterial blood gas results of a client and notes the following: pH 7.45, PCO_2 of 30 mm Hg, and HCO_3^- of 22 mEq/L. The nurse analyzes these results as indicating which condition?
   1. Metabolic acidosis, compensated
   2. Respiratory alkalosis, compensated
   3. Metabolic alkalosis, uncompensated
   4. Respiratory acidosis, uncompensated

7. A client is scheduled for blood to be drawn from the radial artery for an arterial blood gas determination. Before the blood is drawn, an Allen's test is performed to determine the adequacy of the:
   1. Ulnar circulation
   2. Carotid circulation
   3. Femoral circulation
   4. Popliteal circulation

8. A nurse is caring for a client with a nasogastric tube that is attached to low suction. The nurse monitors the client, knowing that the client is at risk for which acid-base disorder?
   1. Metabolic acidosis
   2. Metabolic alkalosis
   3. Respiratory acidosis
   4. Respiratory alkalosis

9. A nurse caring for a client with an ileostomy understands that the client is most at risk for developing which acid-base disorder?

1. Metabolic acidosis
2. Metabolic alkalosis
3. Respiratory acidosis
4. Respiratory alkalosis

10. A nurse is caring for a client with diabetic ketoacidosis and documents that the client is experiencing Kussmaul's respirations. Based on this documentation, which of the following did the nurse observe?
    1. Respirations that cease for several seconds
    2. Respirations that are regular but abnormally slow
    3. Respirations that are labored and increased in depth and rate
    4. Respirations that are abnormally deep, regular, and increased in rate

ALTERNATE ITEM FORMAT: PRIORITIZING (ORDERED RESPONSE)

A nurse is preparing to obtain an arterial blood gas specimen from a client and plans to perform the Allen's test on the client. Number in order of priority the steps for performing the Allen's test. (Number 1 is the first step and number 6 is the last step.)

_____ Document the findings
_____ Explain the procedure to the client.
_____ Release pressure from the ulnar artery.
_____ Apply pressure over the ulnar and radial arteries.
_____ Ask the client to open and close the hand repeatedly.
_____ Assess the color of the extremity distal to the pressure point.

ANSWERS

1. **4**

Rationale: Clients experiencing nausea and vomiting would most likely present with metabolic alkalosis resulting from loss of gastric acid, thus causing the pH and HCO_3^- to increase. Symptoms experienced by the client would include hypoventilation and tachycardia. Option 1 reflects a respiratory acidotic condition. Option 2 reflects a respiratory alkalotic condition. Option 3 reflects a metabolic acidotic condition.

Test-Taking Strategy: Focus on the data in the question and note that the client is vomiting. Recalling that vomiting would most likely cause metabolic alkalosis will assist in directing you to option 4. Review the causes of metabolic alkalosis if you had difficulty with this question.
Level of Cognitive Ability: Analysis
Client Needs: Physiological Integrity
Integrated Process: Nursing Process—analysis
Content Area: Fundamental Skills
Reference: Lewis, S., Heitkemper, M., & Dirksen, S. (2004). *Medical-surgical nursing: Assessment and management of clinical problems* (6th ed., pp. 351-352). St. Louis: Mosby.

2. **4**

Rationale: The acid-base disturbance is respiratory acidosis without compensation. The normal pH is 7.35 to 7.45. The normal PCO_2 is 35 to 45 mm Hg. In respiratory acidosis the pH

is decreased and the PCO_2 is elevated. The normal bicarbonate (HCO_3^-) level is 22 to 27 mEq/L. Because the bicarbonate is still within normal limits, the kidneys have not had time to adjust for this acid-base disturbance. Therefore, the condition is without compensation. Options 1, 2, and 3 are incorrect.

Test-Taking Strategy: Use the process of elimination. Remember that in a respiratory imbalance you will find an opposite response between the pH and the PCO_2. Also, remember that the pH is decreased in an acidotic condition and that compensation is reflected by a normal pH. Review the interpretation of arterial blood gas values if you had difficulty with this question.
Level of Cognitive Ability: Analysis
Client Needs: Physiological Integrity
Integrated Process: Nursing Process—analysis
Content Area: Fundamental skills
Reference: Lewis, S., Heitkemper, M., & Dirksen, S. (2004). *Medical-surgical nursing: Assessment and management of clinical problems* (6th ed., pp. 351-352). St. Louis: Mosby.

3. **3**

Rationale: Respiratory acidosis is most often caused by hypoventilation. Chronic respiratory acidosis is most commonly caused by chronic obstructive pulmonary disease. In end-stage disease, pathological changes lead to airway collapse, air trapping, and disturbance of ventilation-perfusion relationships. Options 1, 2, and 4 are incorrect options.

Test-Taking Strategy: Use the process of elimination. Note the strategic words *most likely*. Remembering that hypoventilation results in respiratory acidosis will direct you to option 3. Review the causes of respiratory acidosis if you had difficulty with this question.
Level of Cognitive Ability: Comprehension
Client Needs: Physiological Integrity
Integrated Process: Nursing Process—planning
Content Area: Fundamental skills
Reference: Ignatavicius, D., & Workman, M. (2006). *Medical-surgical nursing: Critical thinking for collaborative care* (5th ed., pp. 283, 598-599). Philadelphia: W.B. Saunders.

4. **1**
Rationale: The normal pH is 7.35 to 7.45. The normal P_{CO_2} is 35 to 45 mm Hg. In respiratory acidosis, the pH is decreased and the P_{CO_2} is elevated. Option 2 identifies normal values. Option 3 identifies an alkalotic condition. Option 4 identifies respiratory alkalosis.
Test-Taking Strategy: Use the process of elimination. Remember that in a respiratory imbalance you will find an opposite response between the pH and the P_{CO_2}. Also, remember that the pH is decreased in an acidotic condition. Option 2 reflects a normal blood gas result. Options 3 and 4 reflect an elevated pH, which indicates an alkalotic condition. Option 1 is the only option that reflects an acidotic condition. Review blood gas analysis if you had difficulty with this question.
Level of Cognitive Ability: Analysis
Client Needs: Physiological Integrity
Integrated Process: Nursing Process—analysis
Content Area: Fundamental skills
References: Chernecky, C., & Berger, B. (2004). *Laboratory tests and diagnostic procedures* (4th ed., p. 245). Philadelphia: W.B. Saunders.
Ignatavicius, D. & Workman, M. (2006). *Medical-surgical nursing: Critical thinking for collaborative care* (5th ed., p. 1009). Philadelphia: W.B. Saunders.

5. **2**
Rationale: Clinical manifestations of respiratory alkalosis include headache, tachypnea, paresthesias, tetany, vertigo, convulsions, hypokalemia, and hypocalcemia. Options 1, 3, and 4 identify normal laboratory values. Option 2 identifies the presence of hypokalemia.
Test-Taking Strategy: Use the process of elimination and knowledge regarding the clinical manifestations of respiratory alkalosis and normal laboratory values to answer the question. The only abnormal laboratory value is the potassium level, option 2. Review the clinical manifestations of respiratory alkalosis and normal laboratory values if you had difficulty with this question.
Level of Cognitive Ability: Comprehension
Client Needs: Physiological Integrity
Integrated Process: Nursing Process—analysis
Content Area: Fundamental skills
Reference: Potter, P., & Perry, A. (2005). *Fundamentals of nursing* (6th ed., pp.1144-1145). St. Louis: Mosby.

6. **2**
Rationale: The normal pH is 7.35 to 7.45. In a respiratory condition, an opposite effect will be seen between the pH and the P_{CO_2}. In this situation, the pH is at the high end of the normal value and the P_{CO_2} is low. In an alkalotic condition, the pH is elevated. Therefore, the values identified in the question indicate a respiratory alkalosis. Compensation occurs when the pH returns to a normal value. Because the pH is in the normal range at the high end, compensation has occurred.
Test-Taking Strategy: Remember that in a respiratory imbalance you will find an opposite response between the pH and the P_{CO_2} as indicated in the question. Therefore, you can eliminate options 1 and 3. Also, remember that the pH increases in an alkalotic condition and compensation occurs, as evidenced by a normal pH. Option 2 reflects a respiratory alkalotic condition and compensation and describes the blood gas values as indicated in the question. Review the steps related to reading blood gas values if you had difficulty with this question.
Level of Cognitive Ability: Analysis
Client Needs: Physiological Integrity
Integrated Process: Nursing Process—analysis
Content Area: Fundamental skills
References: McLean, B. (2005). Acid-base imbalances. In Baird MS, Keen JH, Swearingen PL (Eds.): *Manual of critical care nursing* (5th ed., pp. 566-581). St. Louis: Mosby.
Potter, P., & Perry, A. (2005). *Fundamentals of nursing* (6th ed., p. 1145). St. Louis: Mosby.

7. **1**
Rationale: Before radial puncture for obtaining an arterial specimen for arterial blood gases, you should perform an Allen's test to determine adequate ulnar circulation. Failure to determine the presence of adequate collateral circulation could result in severe ischemic injury to the hand if damage to the radial artery occurs with arterial puncture. Options 2, 3, and 4 are incorrect options.
Test-Taking Strategy: Use the process of elimination and knowledge regarding the purpose and procedure for the Allen's test. Remember that the purpose of this test is to assess the adequacy of the ulnar circulation. Review the purpose and procedure of the Allen's test if you had difficulty with this question.
Level of Cognitive Ability: Comprehension
Client Needs: Physiological Integrity
Integrated Process: Nursing Process—assessment
Content Area: Fundamental skills
References: Chernecky, C., & Berger, B. (2004). *Laboratory tests and diagnostic procedures* (4th ed.), p. 248. Philadelphia: W.B. Saunders.
Potter, P., & Perry, A. (2005). *Fundamentals of nursing* (6th ed., pp. 731-732). St. Louis: Mosby.

8. **2**
Rationale: Loss of gastric fluid via nasogastric suction or vomiting causes metabolic alkalosis as a result of the loss of hydrochloric acid. Options 1, 3, and 4 are incorrect.
Test-Taking Strategy: Remembering that a client receiving nasogastric suction loses hydrochloric acid will direct you to the option identifying an alkalotic condition. Because the question addresses a situation other than a respiratory one, the acid-base disorder would be a metabolic condition. If you had difficulty with this question, review the causes of metabolic alkalosis.

Level of Cognitive Ability: Comprehension
Client Needs: Physiological Integrity
Integrated Process: Nursing Process—analysis
Content Area: Fundamental skills
References: Ignatavicius, D., & Workman, M. (2006). *Medical-surgical nursing: Critical thinking for collaborative care* (5th ed., pp. 288-289). Philadelphia: W.B. Saunders.
Potter, P., & Perry, A. (2005). *Fundamentals of nursing* (6th ed., p. 1145). St. Louis: Mosby.

9. **1**
Rationale: Intestinal secretions are high in bicarbonate and may be lost through enteric drainage tubes or an ileostomy, or with diarrhea. These conditions result in metabolic acidosis. Options 2, 3, and 4 are incorrect because they do not occur in the client with an ileostomy.
Test-Taking Strategy: Use the process of elimination. Note that the client's condition described in the question is a gastrointestinal disorder. This will direct you toward a metabolic disorder. Remembering that intestinal fluids are primarily alkaline will assist you in selecting the correct option. When excess bicarbonate is lost, acidosis will result. If you had difficulty with this question, review the causes of metabolic acidosis.
Level of Cognitive Ability: Comprehension
Client Needs: Physiological Integrity
Integrated Process: Nursing Process—analysis
Content Area: Fundamental skills
Reference: Ignatavicius, D., & Workman, M. (2006). *Medical-surgical nursing: Critical thinking for collaborative care* (5th ed., p. 1327). Philadelphia: W.B. Saunders.

10. **4**
Rationale: Kussmaul's respirations are abnormally deep, regular, and increased in rate. Apnea is described as respirations that cease for several seconds. In bradypnea, respirations are regular but abnormally slow. In hyperpnea, respirations are labored and increased in depth and rate.
Test-Taking Strategy: Use the process of elimination and knowledge of the description of Kussmaul's respirations. Recalling that this type of respiration occurs in diabetic ketoacidosis will direct you to option 4. Review the characteristics of this type of respiration if you had difficulty with this question.
Level of Cognitive Ability: Comprehension

Client Needs: Physiological Integrity
Integrated Process: Nursing Process—assessment
Content Area: Fundamental skills
References: Ignatavicius, D., & Workman, M. (2006). *Medical-surgical nursing: Critical thinking for collaborative care* (5th ed., p. 1327). Philadelphia: W.B. Saunders.
Potter, P., & Perry, A. (2005). *Fundamentals of nursing* (6th ed., pp. 650, 1088). St. Louis: Mosby.

ALTERNATE ITEM FORMAT: PRIORITIZING (ORDERED RESPONSE)

Answer: 6, 1, 4, 2, 3, 5
Rationale: The Allen's test is performed before obtaining an arterial blood specimen from the radial artery to determine the presence of collateral circulation and the adequacy of the ulnar artery. Failure to determine the presence of adequate collateral circulation could result in severe ischemic injury to the hand if damage to the radial artery occurs with arterial puncture. The nurse first would explain the procedure to the client. To perform the test, the nurse applies direct pressure over the client's ulnar and radial arteries simultaneously. While applying pressure, the nurse asks the client to open and close the hand repeatedly; the hand should blanch. The nurse then releases pressure from the ulnar artery while compressing the radial artery and assesses the color of the extremity distal to the pressure point. If pinkness fails to return within 6 seconds, the ulnar artery is insufficient, indicating that the radial artery should not be used for obtaining a blood specimen. Finally, the nurse documents the findings.
Test-Taking Strategy: Recalling that the procedure needs to be explained to the client will assist in determining the first action. Next, think about the purpose and reason for performing this test and visualize the procedure. This will assist in determining the steps for performing the Allen's test. Remember, the nurse would document the findings last. Review this test if you had difficulty with this question.
Level of Cognitive Ability: Application
Client Needs: Physiological Integrity
Integrated Process: Nursing Process—assessment
Content Area: Delegating/Prioritizing
Reference: Potter, P., & Perry, A. (2005). *Fundamentals of nursing* (6th ed., pp. 731-732). St. Louis: Mosby.

REFERENCES

Black, J., & Hawks, J. (2005). *Medical-surgical nursing: Clinical management for positive outcomes* (7th ed.). Philadelphia: W.B. Saunders.

Chernecky, C., & Berger, B. (2004). *Laboratory tests and diagnostic procedures* (4th ed.). Philadelphia: W.B. Saunders.

Ignatavicius, D., & Workman, M. (2006). *Medical-surgical nursing: Critical thinking for collaborative care* (5th ed.). Philadelphia: W.B. Saunders.

Lewis, S., Heitkemper, M., & Dirksen, S. (2004). *Medical-surgical nursing: Assessment and management of clinical problems* (6th ed.). St. Louis: Mosby.

McLean, B. (2005). Acid-base imbalances. *In* Baird MS, Keen JH, Swearingen PL (Eds.): *Manual of critical care nursing* (5th ed.). St. Louis: Mosby.

National Council of State Boards of Nursing (Eds.). (2007). *2007 NCLEX-RN® detailed test plan.* Chicago: Author.

Potter, P., & Perry, A. (2005). *Fundamentals of nursing* (6th ed.). St. Louis: Mosby.

Laboratory Values

PYRAMID TERMS

blood   The liquid pumped by the heart through the arteries, veins, and capillaries. It is composed of a clear yellow fluid, called plasma, formed elements, and cell types with different functions (Fig. 11-1).

blood cell   Any of the formed elements of the blood, including red cells (erythrocytes), white cells (leukocytes), and platelets (thrombocytes).

plasma   The watery, straw-colored, fluid part of lymph and the blood in which the formed elements (blood cells) are suspended. It is made up of water, electrolytes, protein, glucose, fats, bilirubin, and gases, and is essential for carrying the cellular elements of the blood through the circulation.

serum   The clear and thin fluid part of blood that remains after coagulation. Serum contains no blood cells, platelets, or fibrinogen.

venipuncture   Puncture into a vein to obtain a blood specimen for testing; the antecubital veins are the veins of choice because of ease of access.

▲ THE PYRAMID TO SUCCESS

This chapter identifies the normal adult values for the most common laboratory tests. It is important to remember that normal laboratory values may vary slightly, depending on the laboratory setting and equipment used in testing. If you are familiar with the normal values, you will be able to determine whether an abnormality exists when a laboratory value is presented in a question. The questions on the NCLEX-RN examination related to laboratory values require you to identify whether the laboratory value is normal or abnormal, and then you are required to think critically about the effects of the laboratory value in terms of the client. Pyramid Points focus on knowledge of the normal values for the most common laboratory tests, therapeutic serum medication levels of commonly prescribed medications, and determination of the need to implement

specific actions based on the findings. Remember that most blood samples should not be drawn during hemodialysis. When a question is presented on the NCLEX-RN examination regarding a specific laboratory value, note the disorder presented in the question and the associated body organ affected as a result of the disorder. This process will assist you in determining the correct answer. For example, if the question asks about the immune status of a client receiving chemotherapy, assessment of laboratory values will focus on the white blood cell count and the neutrophils. You will need to analyze these results as possibly being low and determine the specific client need, which in this case would be the risk for infection. In the client receiving chemotherapy who has a low white blood cell count, your plan centers on the immune system and protecting that client from infection. Implementation focuses on preventive interventions related to infection, perhaps protective isolation measures. Evaluation may focus on maintenance of a normal temperature in the client. Integrated Processes addressed in this chapter are Caring, Communication and Documentation, Nursing Process, and Teaching/Learning. Box 11-1 lists the abbreviations found in laboratory values.

CLIENT NEEDS   ▲
Safe and Effective Care Environment

Applying principles of infection control

Ensuring medical and surgical asepsis when obtaining a specimen

Implementing procedures for handling hazardous and infectious materials

Maintaining standard, transmission-based, and other precautions

Obtaining informed consent for specific procedures

Verifying the identity of the client

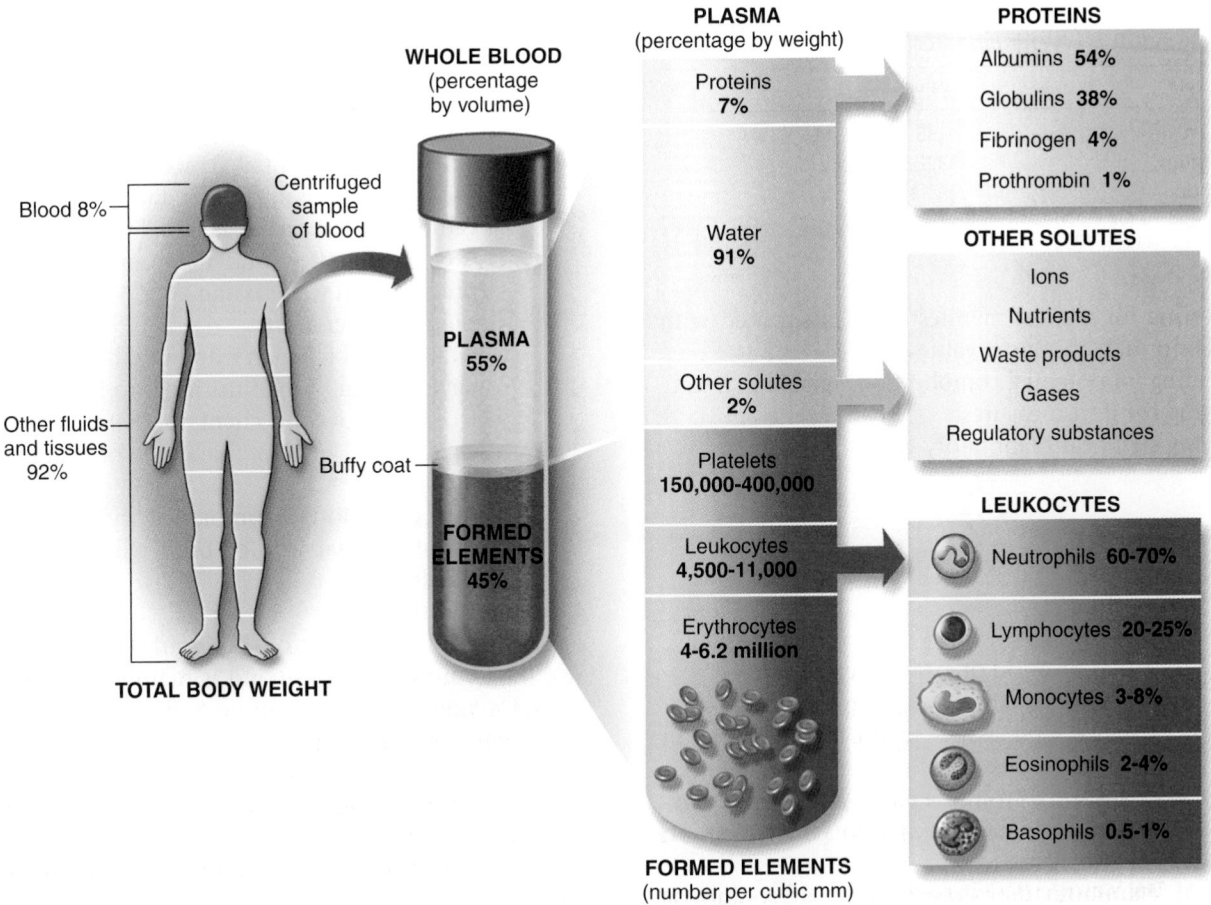

FIG. 11-1 Approximate values for the components of blood in a normal adult. (Modified from Thibodeau, G.A., & Patton, K.T. [2005]. *The human body in health and disease* [4th ed.]. St. Louis: Mosby.)

BOX 11-1
Pyramid Abbreviations

ABBREVIATION	DEFINITION
g/dL	grams per deciliter
mcg/dL	micrograms per deciliter
mg/dL	milligrams per deciliter
mEq/L	milliequivalents per liter
units/L	units per liter
mm/hr	millimeters per hour
IU/L	International units per liter
mcg/mL	micrograms per milliliter
ng/mL	nanograms per milliliter
microunits/mL	microunits per milliliter
mL/kg	milliliters per kilogram
mm³	millimeters cubed
μL	microliters

Health Promotion and Maintenance

Discussing the importance of follow-up laboratory studies

Identifying community resources available for the follow-up

Implementing post-test procedures

Monitoring for signs and symptoms that indicate the need to notify the health care provider

Preparing the client for the laboratory test

Psychosocial Integrity

Communicating the purpose of the laboratory test to the client

Communicating with the client regarding the laboratory results

Describing specific interventions or home care measures required based on the results

Providing emotional support during testing

Physiological Integrity

Determining the need to implement specific actions based on the laboratory results

Identifying normal values for the most common laboratory tests

Identifying therapeutic serum medication levels of commonly prescribed medications

TABLE 11-1

Normal Adult Electrolyte Values

Electrolyte	Value
Sodium	135-145 mEq/L
Potassium	3.5-5.1 mEq/L
Chloride	98-107 mEq/L
Bicarbonate (venous)	22-29 mEq/L

Monitoring for clinical manifestations associated with an abnormal laboratory value
Monitoring for potential complications related to a test
Providing comfort measures
Reporting significant laboratory values

I. ELECTROLYTES (Table 11-1)

A. **Serum** sodium
   1. Description
      a. A major cation of extracellular fluid
      b. Maintains osmotic pressure and acid-base balance, and assists in the transmission of nerve impulses
      c. Is absorbed from the small intestine and excreted in the urine in amounts dependent on dietary intake
      d. Minimum daily requirement of sodium is approximately 15 mEq
   2. Nursing consideration: Drawing **blood** samples soon after an intravenous (IV) infusion of sodium chloride will increase the level, producing an inaccurate result.
B. **Serum** potassium
   1. Description
      a. A major intracellular cation; it regulates cellular water balance, electrical conduction in muscle cells, and acid-base balance.
      b. The body obtains potassium through dietary ingestion and the kidneys preserve or excrete potassium, depending on cellular need.
      c. Potassium levels are used to evaluate cardiac function, renal function, gastrointestinal function, and the need for IV replacement therapy.
   2. Nursing considerations
      a. Prolonged use of a tourniquet and clenching and unclenching the hand before venous sampling can increase the level, producing an inaccurate result.
      b. Do not draw **blood** from a site where an IV infusion exists.
      c. If the client is receiving potassium supplementation, note this on the laboratory form.
      d. Clients with elevated white **blood cell** counts and platelet counts may have falsely elevated potassium levels.

C. **Serum** chloride
   1. Description
      a. A hydrochloric acid salt that is the most abundant body anion in the extracellular fluid
      b. Functions to counterbalance cations, such as sodium, and acts as a buffer during oxygen and carbon dioxide exchange in red **blood cells**
      c. Aids in digestion and maintaining osmotic pressure and water balance
   2. Nursing considerations
      a. Draw **blood** from an extremity that does not have normal saline infusing into it.
      b. Do not allow the client to clench and unclench his or her hand before drawing **blood**.
      c. Any condition accompanied by prolonged vomiting, diarrhea, or both will alter chloride levels.
D. **Serum** bicarbonate
   1. Description: Is part of the bicarbonate-carbonic acid buffering system and is mainly responsible for regulating the pH of body fluids
   2. Nursing considerations
      a. Ingestion of acidic or alkaline solutions may cause increased or decreased results, respectively.
      b. Prolonged tourniquet application before the **blood** draw increases the **serum** bicarbonate level.

II. COAGULATION STUDIES

A. Activated partial thromboplastin time (aPTT)
   1. Description
      a. The aPTT evaluates how well the coagulation sequence is functioning by measuring the amount of time it takes in seconds for recalcified citrated **plasma** to clot after partial thromboplastin is added to it.
      b. The test screens for deficiencies and inhibitors of all factors, except VII and XIII.
      c. Usually, the aPTT is used to monitor heparin therapy and screen for coagulation disorders.
   2. Value: 20 to 36 seconds, depending on the type of activator used
   3. Nursing considerations
      a. If the client is receiving intermittent heparin therapy, draw the **blood** sample 1 hour before the next scheduled dose.
      b. Do not draw samples from an arm into which heparin is infusing.
      c. Transport specimen to the laboratory immediately.
      d. The aPTT should be between 1.5 and 2.5 times normal when the client is receiving heparin therapy; if the value is prolonged, initiate bleeding precautions.

B. Prothrombin time (PT) and international normalized ratio (INR)
1. Description
   a. Prothrombin is a vitamin K–dependent glycoprotein produced by the liver that is necessary for fibrin clot formation.
   b. Each laboratory establishes a normal or control value based on the method used to perform the PT test.
   c. The PT measures the amount of time it takes in seconds for clot formation and is used to monitor response to warfarin sodium (Coumadin) therapy or to screen for dysfunction of the extrinsic clotting system resulting from liver disease, vitamin K deficiency, or disseminated intravascular coagulation.
   d. A PT value within 2 seconds (plus or minus) of the control is considered normal.
   e. The INR standardized the PT ratio and is calculated in the laboratory setting by raising the observed PT ratio to the power of the international sensitivity index specific to the thromboplastin reagent used.
   f. The INR measures the effects of oral anticoagulants.
2. Values
   a. PT: 9.6 to 11.8 seconds (male adult); 9.5 to 11.3 seconds (female adult)
   b. INR: 2.0 to 3.0 for standard warfarin therapy
   c. INR: 3.0 to 4.5 for high-dose warfarin therapy
3. Nursing considerations
   a. A baseline PT should be drawn before anticoagulation therapy is started; note the time of collection on the laboratory form.
   b. Provide direct pressure to the **venipuncture** site for 3 to 5 minutes if a coagulation defect is present.
   c. Concurrent warfarin therapy with heparin therapy can lengthen the PT for up to 5 hours after dosing.
   d. Diets high in green leafy vegetables can increase the absorption of vitamin K, which shortens the PT.
   e. Orally administered anticoagulation therapy usually maintains the PT at 1.5 to 2 times the laboratory control value.
   f. A PT longer than 30 seconds places the client at risk for bleeding.
C. Clotting time
1. Description: The time required for the interaction of all factors involved in the clotting process
2. Value: 8 to 15 minutes
3. Nursing considerations
   a. The client should not receive heparin therapy for 3 hours before specimen collection because the heparin therapy will affect the results.

   b. The test result is falsely prolonged by any anticoagulant therapy, test tube agitation, or exposure of the specimen to high temperature changes.
D. Platelet count
1. Description
   a. Platelets function in hemostatic plug formation, clot retraction, and coagulation factor activation.
   b. Platelets are produced by the bone marrow to function in hemostasis.
2. Value: 150,000 to 400,000 cells/mm^3
3. Nursing considerations
   a. Monitor the **venipuncture** site for bleeding in clients with known thrombocytopenia.
   b. High altitudes, chronic cold weather, and exercise increase platelet counts.
   c. Bleeding precautions should be instituted in clients with a low platelet count.

III. ERYTHROCYTE STUDIES
A. Erythrocyte sedimentation rate
1. Description
   a. Rate at which erythrocytes settle out of anticoagulated **blood** in 1 hour
   b. A nonspecific test used to detect illnesses associated with acute and chronic infection, inflammation, advanced neoplasm, and tissue necrosis or infarction
2. Value: 0 to 30 mm/hr, depending on age of client
3. Nursing consideration: Fasting is not necessary, but a fatty meal may cause **plasma** alterations.
B. Hemoglobin and hematocrit
1. Description
   a. Hemoglobin is the main component of erythrocytes and serves as the vehicle for transporting oxygen and carbon dioxide.
   b. Hemoglobin determinations are important in identifying anemia.
   c. Hematocrit represents red **blood cell** mass and is an important measurement in the identification of anemia or polycythemia (Table 11-2).
2. Nursing consideration: Fasting is not required.
C. **Serum** iron
1. Description
   a. Iron is found predominantly in hemoglobin.
   b. Iron acts as a carrier of oxygen from the lungs to the tissues and indirectly aids in the return of carbon dioxide to the lungs.
   c. Iron aids in diagnosing anemias and hemolytic disorders.
2. Normal values
   a. Male adult: 65 to 175 mcg/dL
   b. Female adult: 50 to 170 mcg/dL

TABLE 11-2	
Normal Adult Blood Components	
Blood Component	**Normal Value**
HEMOGLOBIN	
Male adult	14-16.5 g/dL
Female adult	12-15 g/dL
HEMATOCRIT	
Male adult	42%-52%
Female adult	35%-47%
IRON	
Male adult	65-175 mcg/dL
Female adult	50-170 mcg/dL
RED BLOOD CELLS	
Male adult	4.5-6.2 million/μL
Female adult	4.0-5.5 million/μL

TABLE 11-3	
Normal Adult Serum Enzymes/Cardiac Markers	
Serum Enzyme	**Normal Value**
Creatine kinase (CK)	26-174 units/L
Creatine kinase isoenzymes	
CK-MB	0%-5% of total
CK-MM	95%-100% of total
CK-BB	0%
Lactate dehydrogenase	140-280 units/L
Lactate dehydrogenase iso-enzymes	
LDH1	14%-26%
LDH2	29%-39%
LDH3	20%-26%
LDH4	8%-16%
LDH5	6%-16%
Troponin I	<0.6 ng/mL; >1.5 ng/mL indicates myocardial infarction
Troponin T	>0.1-0.2 ng/mL indicates myocardial infarction
Myoglobin	<90 mcg/L; elevation could indicate myocardial infarction

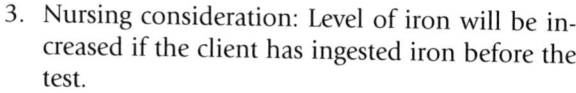

3. Nursing consideration: Level of iron will be increased if the client has ingested iron before the test.

D. Red **blood cell** (RBC) count (erythrocytes)
   1. Description
      a. Red **blood cells** function in hemoglobin transport, which results in delivery of oxygen to the body tissues.
      b. Red **blood cells** are formed by red bone marrow, have a life span of 120 days, and are removed from the **blood** via the liver, spleen, and bone marrow.
      c. The red **blood cell** count aids in diagnosing anemias and **blood** dyscrasias.
      d. The red **blood cell** count evaluates the ability of the body to produce red **blood cells** in sufficient numbers.
   2. Values
      a. Female adult: 4 to 5.5 million cells/μL
      b. Male adult: 4.5 to 6.2 million cells/μL
   3. Nursing consideration: Fasting is not required.

IV. **SERUM ENZYMES AND CARDIAC MARKERS** (Table 11-3)
A. Creatine kinase (CK)
   1. Description
      a. Creatine kinase is an enzyme found in muscle and brain tissue that reflects tissue catabolism resulting from cell trauma.
      b. The CK level begins to rise within 6 hours of muscle damage, peaks at 18 hours, and returns to normal in 2 to 3 days.
      c. The test for CK is performed to detect myocardial or skeletal muscle damage or central nervous system damage; a normal CK value is 26 to 174 units/L.

   d. Isoenzymes include CK-MB (cardiac), CK-BB (brain), and CK-MM (muscles).
   e. Isoenzyme CK-MB is found mainly in cardiac muscle, CK-BB is found mainly in brain tissue, and CK-MM is found mainly is skeletal muscle.
   2. Values
      a. CK-MB: 0% to 5% of total
      b. CK-MM: 95% to 100% of total
      c. CK-BB: 0%
   3. Nursing considerations
      a. If the test is to evaluate skeletal muscle, instruct the client to avoid strenuous physical activity for 24 hours before the test.
      b. Also instruct the client to avoid ingestion of alcohol for 24 hours before the test.
      c. Invasive procedures and intramuscular injections may falsely elevate CK levels.
B. Lactate dehydrogenase (LDH)
   1. Description
      a. The LDH isoenzymes affected by acute myocardial infarction are LDH1 and LDH2.
      b. The LDH level begins to rise about 24 hours after myocardial infarction and peaks in 48 to 72 hours; thereafter, it returns to normal, usually within 7 to 14 days.
      c. The presence of an LDH flip (when LDH1 is higher than LDH2) is helpful in diagnosing a myocardial infarction.

2. Nursing considerations
   a. The LDH isoenzyme levels should be interpreted in view of the clinical findings.
   b. Testing should be repeated on 3 consecutive days.

C. Troponins
   1. Description
      a. Troponin is a regulatory protein found in striated muscle (skeletal and myocardial).
      b. Increased amounts of troponins are released into the bloodstream when an infarction causes damage to the myocardium.
      c. Levels elevate as early as 3 hours after myocardial injury. Troponin I levels may remain elevated for 7 to 10 days and troponin T levels may remain elevated for up to 10 to 14 days.
      d. Serial measurements are important to compare with a baseline test.
   2. Values
      a. Troponin I: Value usually is lower than 0.6 ng/mL; higher than 1.5 ng/mL is consistent with a myocardial infarction.
      b. Troponin T: Higher than 0.1 to 0.2 ng/mL is consistent with a myocardial infarction.
   3. Nursing considerations
      a. Testing is repeated in 12 hours, followed by daily testing for 3 to 5 days.
      b. Rotate **venipuncture** sites.

D. Myoglobin
   1. Description
      a. It is an oxygen-binding protein found in striated (cardiac and skeletal) muscle that releases oxygen at very low tensions.
      b. Any injury to skeletal muscle will cause a release of myoglobin into the **blood**.
   2. Values: Normal value is lower than 90 mcg/L; an elevation could indicate myocardial infarction.
   3. Nursing considerations
      a. The level can rise as early as 2 hours after a myocardial infarction, with a rapid decline in the level after 7 hours.
      b. Because the myoglobin level is not cardiac-specific and rises and falls so rapidly, its use in diagnosing myocardial infarction may be limited.

V. SERUM GASTROINTESTINAL STUDIES

A. Albumin
   1. Description
      a. A main **plasma** protein of **blood**
      b. Maintains oncotic pressure and transports bilirubin, fatty acids, medications, hormones, and other substances that are insoluble in water
      c. Is increased in conditions such as dehydration, diarrhea, and metastatic carcinoma; is decreased in conditions such as acute infection, ascites, and alcoholism
      d. Presence of detectable albumin, or protein, in the urine is indicative of abnormal renal function
   2. Value: 3.4 to 5 g/dL
   3. Nursing consideration: Perform **venipuncture** from an extremity that does not have an IV infusion.

B. Alkaline phosphatase
   1. Description
      a. Alkaline phosphatase is an enzyme normally found in bone, liver, intestine, and placenta.
      b. The level rises during periods of bone growth, liver disease, and bile duct obstruction.
   2. Value: 4.5 to 13 King-Armstrong units/dL
   3. Nursing considerations
      a. The client may need to fast 12 hours before the test.
      b. Hepatotoxic medications administered within 12 hours before specimen collection can cause a falsely elevated value.
      c. Transport the specimen to the laboratory immediately.

C. Ammonia
   1. Description
      a. Ammonia is a byproduct of protein catabolism; most of it is created by bacteria acting on proteins present in the gut.
      b. Ammonia is metabolized by the liver and excreted by the kidneys as urea.
      c. Elevated levels resulting from hepatic dysfunction may lead to encephalopathy.
      d. Venous ammonia levels are not a reliable indicator of hepatic coma.
   2. Value: 35 to 65 mg/dL
   3. Nursing considerations
      a. Instruct the client to fast, except for water, and to refrain from smoking for 8 to 10 hours before the test; smoking increases ammonia levels.
      b. Place the specimen in ice and transport to the laboratory immediately.

D. Amylase
   1. Description
      a. This enzyme, produced by the pancreas and salivary glands, aids in the digestion of complex carbohydrates and is excreted by the kidneys.
      b. In acute pancreatitis, the amylase level is greatly increased; the level starts rising 3 to 6 hours after the onset of pain, peaks at about 24 hours, and returns to normal in 2 to 3 days after the onset of pain.
   2. Value: 25 to 151 units/L
   3. Nursing considerations
      a. On the laboratory form, list the medications that the client has taken during the previous 24 hours before the test.

b. Note that many medications may cause false-positive or false-negative results.

c. Results are invalidated if the specimen was obtained less than 72 hours after cholecystography with radiopaque dyes.

E. Lipase

1. Description

   a. This pancreatic enzyme converts fats and triglycerides into fatty acids and glycerol.

   b. Elevated lipase levels occur in pancreatic disorders; elevations may not occur until 24 to 36 hours after the onset of illness and may remain elevated for up to 14 days.

2. Value: 10 to 140 units/L

3. Nursing considerations: Endoscopic retrograde cholangiopancreatography (ERCP) may increase lipase activity.

▲ F. Bilirubin

1. Description

   a. Bilirubin is produced by the liver, spleen, and bone marrow and is also a byproduct of hemoglobin breakdown.

   b. Total bilirubin levels can be broken down into direct bilirubin, which is excreted primarily via the intestinal tract, and indirect bilirubin, which circulates primarily in the bloodstream.

   c. Total bilirubin levels increase with any type of jaundice; direct and indirect bilirubin levels help differentiate the cause of the jaundice.

2. Values

   a. Bilirubin, direct (conjugated): 0 to 0.3 mg/dL

   b. Bilirubin, indirect (unconjugated): 0.1 to 1.0 mg/dL

   c. Bilirubin, total: Lower than 1.5 mg/dL

3. Nursing considerations

   a. Instruct the client to eat a diet low in yellow foods, such as carrots, yams, yellow beans, and pumpkins, for 3 to 4 days before the **blood** is drawn.

   b. Instruct the client to fast for 4 hours before the **blood** is drawn.

   c. Note that results will be elevated with the ingestion of alcohol or the administration of morphine sulfate, theophylline, ascorbic acid (vitamin C), or acetylsalicylic acid (aspirin).

   d. Note that results are invalidated if the client has received a radioactive scan within 24 hours before the test.

▲ G. Lipids

1. Description

   a. **Blood** lipids consist primarily of cholesterol, triglycerides, and phospholipids.

   b. Lipid assessment includes total cholesterol, high-density lipoprotein (HDL), low-density lipoprotein (LDL), and triglycerides.

c. Cholesterol is present in all body tissues and is a major component of low-density lipoproteins, brain and nerve cells, cell membranes, and some gallbladder stones.

d. Triglycerides constitute a major part of very low-density lipoproteins and a small part of low-density lipoproteins.

e. Triglycerides are synthesized in the liver from fatty acids, protein, and glucose, and are obtained from the diet.

f. Increased cholesterol levels, LDL levels, and triglyceride levels place the client at risk for coronary artery disease

g. HDL helps protect against the risk of coronary artery disease

2. Values:

   a. Cholesterol: 140 to 199 mg/dL

   b. Low-density lipoproteins: Lower than 130 mg/dL

   c. High-density lipoproteins: 30 to 70 mg/dL

   d. Triglycerides: Lower than 200 mg/dL

3. Nursing considerations

   a. Oral contraceptives may increase the lipid level.

   b. Instruct the client to abstain from foods and fluid, except for water, for 12 to 14 hours and from alcohol for 24 hours before the test.

   c. Instruct the client to completely avoid high-cholesterol foods the evening meal before the test.

H. Protein

1. Description

   a. Protein reflects the total amount of albumin and globulins in the **plasma**.

   b. Protein regulates osmotic pressure and comprises coagulation factors for hemostasis, enzymes, hormones, tissue growth and repair, and pH buffers.

   c. Increased in conditions such as Addison's disease, autoimmune collagen disorders, chronic infection, and Crohn's disease.

   d. Decreased in conditions such as burns, cirrhosis, edema, and severe hepatic disease.

2. Value: 6.0 to 8.0 g/dL

3. Nursing considerations

   a. Do not draw **blood** from an extremity with an IV infusion.

   b. Instruct the client to avoid a high-fat diet for 8 hours before the test.

I. Uric acid

1. Description

   a. Uric acid is formed as the purines adenine and guanine and are metabolized continuously during the formation and degradation of DNA and RNA. It is also formed from the metabolism of dietary purines.

b. Elevated amounts of uric acid deposit in joints and soft tissue and cause gout.

c. Conditions of increased cellular turnover, as well as slowed renal excretion of uric acid, may cause hyperuricemia.

d. Elevated levels of urinary uric acid precipitate into urate stones in the kidneys.

2. Values
   a. Male adult: 4.5 to 8 mg/dL
   b. Female adult: 2.5 to 6.2 mg/dL

3. Nursing considerations
   a. Instruct the client to fast for 8 hours before the test.
   b. Aminophylline, caffeine, and vitamin C may cause falsely elevated results.

VI. GLUCOSE STUDIES

A. Fasting **blood** glucose

1. Description
   a. Glucose is a monosaccharide found in fruits and is formed from the digestion of carbohydrates and the conversion of glycogen by the liver.
   b. Glucose is the main source of cellular energy for the body and is essential for brain and erythrocyte function.
   c. Fasting **blood** glucose levels are used to help diagnose diabetes mellitus and hypoglycemia (Table 11-4).

2. Nursing considerations
   a. Instruct the client to fast for 8 to 12 hours before the test.
   b. Instruct a client with diabetes mellitus to withhold morning insulin or oral hypoglycemic medication until after the **blood** is drawn.

B. Glucose tolerance test (see Table 11-4)

1. Description
   a. The glucose tolerance test aids in the diagnosis of diabetes mellitus.
   b. If the glucose levels peak at higher than normal at 1 and 2 hours after injection or inges-

tion of glucose and are slower than normal to return to fasting levels, then diabetes mellitus is confirmed.

2. Nursing considerations
   a. Instruct the client to eat a high-carbohydrate (200- to 300-g) diet for 3 days before the test.
   b. Instruct the client to avoid alcohol, coffee, and smoking for 36 hours before the test.
   c. Instruct the client to fast for 10 to 16 hours before the test.
   d. Instruct the client to avoid strenuous exercise for 8 hours before and after the test.
   e. Instruct the client with diabetes mellitus to withhold morning insulin or oral hypoglycemic medication.
   f. Instruct the client that the test will take 3 to 5 hours, requires intravenous or oral administration of glucose, and multiple **blood** samples.

C. Glycosylated hemoglobin

1. Description
   a. Glycosylated hemoglobin is **blood** glucose bound to hemoglobin.
   b. Hemoglobin A_{1c} (glycosylated hemoglobin A; HbA_{1c}) is a reflection of how well **blood** glucose levels have been controlled for the past 3 to 4 months.
   c. Hyperglycemia in diabetics is usually a cause of an increase in the hemoglobin A_{1c}.

2. Values
   a. Values are expressed as a percentage of the total hemoglobin.
   b. Diabetics with good control: 7% or lower
   c. Diabetics with fair control: 7% to 8%
   d. Diabetics with poor control: Higher than 8%

3. Nursing consideration: Fasting is not required before the test.

D. Glycosylated **serum** albumin (fructosamine)

1. Description
   a. Reflects average **serum** glucose levels over a period of 2 to 3 weeks
   b. More sensitive to recent changes than the HbA_{1c}

2. Values: Normal ranges vary according to method of testing used; nondiabetic client, 1.5 to 2.7 mmol/L; diabetic client, 2.0 to 5.0 mmol/L.

3. Nursing consideration: The client needs to fast for 12 hours before the test.

VII. RENAL FUNCTION STUDIES

A. **Serum** creatinine

1. Description
   a. Creatinine is a specific indicator of renal function.
   b. Increased levels of creatinine indicate a slowing of the glomerular filtration rate.

TABLE 11-4

Normal Adult Glucose Values

Measurement Setting	Normal Value
Glucose, fasting	70-110 mg/dL
Glucose monitoring (capillary blood)	60-110 mg/dL
Glucose tolerance test, oral	
Baseline fasting	70-110 mg/dL
30-min fasting	110-170 mg/dL
60-min fasting	120-170 mg/dL
90-min fasting	100-140 mg/dL
120-min fasting	70-120 mg/dL
Glucose, 2-hr postprandial	<140 mg/dL

2. Value: 0.6 to 1.3 mg/dL
3. Nursing consideration: Instruct the client to avoid excessive exercise for 8 hours and excessive red meat intake for 24 hours before the test.

B. **Blood** urea nitrogen
  1. Description
      a. Urea nitrogen is the nitrogen portion of urea, a substance formed in the liver through an enzymatic protein breakdown process.
      b. Urea is normally freely filtered through the renal glomeruli, with a small amount reabsorbed in the tubules and the remainder excreted in the urine.
      c. Elevated levels indicate a slowing of the glomerular filtration rate.
  2. Value: 8 to 25 mg/dL
  3. Nursing consideration: Creatinine and urea nitrogen levels should be analyzed when renal function is evaluated.

VIII. **ELEMENTS**
  A. Calcium
    1. Description
        a. Calcium is a cation absorbed into the bloodstream from dietary sources and functions in bone formation, nerve impulse transmission, and contraction of myocardial and skeletal muscles.
        b. Calcium aids in **blood** clotting by converting prothrombin to thrombin.
    2. Value: 8.6 to 10.0 mg/dL
    3. Nursing considerations
        a. Instruct the client to eat a diet with a normal calcium level (800 mg/day) for 3 days before the test.
        b. Instruct the client that fasting may be required for 8 hours before the test.
  B. Magnesium
    1. Description
        a. Magnesium is used as an index to determine metabolic activity and renal function.
        b. Magnesium is needed in the **blood**-clotting mechanism, regulates neuromuscular activity, acts as a cofactor that modifies the activity of many enzymes, and has an effect on the metabolism of calcium.
    2. Value: 1.6 to 2.6 mg/dL
    3. Nursing considerations
        a. Prolonged use of magnesium products will cause increased **serum** levels.
        b. Long-term parenteral nutrition therapy or excessive loss of body fluids may decrease **serum** levels.
  C. Phosphorus
    1. Description
        a. Phosphorus is important in bone formation, energy storage and release, urinary acid-base buffering, and carbohydrate metabolism.
        b. Phosphorus is absorbed from food and is excreted by the kidneys.
        c. High concentrations of phosphorus are stored in bone and skeletal muscle.
    2. Value: 2.7 to 4.5 mg/dL
    3. Nursing considerations: Instruct the client to fast before the test.

IX. **THYROID STUDIES**
  A. Description
    1. Thyroid studies are performed if a thyroid disorder is suspected.
    2. Thyroid studies are helpful to differentiate primary thyroid disease from secondary causes and from abnormalities in thyroxine-binding globulin levels.
  B. Values
    1. Thyroid-stimulating hormone (also called thyrotropin): 0.2 to 5.4 microunits/mL
    2. Thyroxine (T_4): 5.0 to 12.0 mcg/dL
    3. Thyroxine, free (FT_4): 0.8 to 2.4 ng/dL
    4. Triiodothyronine (T_3): 80 to 230 ng/dL
  C. Nursing consideration: Test results may be invalid if the client has undergone a radionuclide scan within 7 days before the test.

X. **WHITE BLOOD CELL COUNT**
  A. Description
    1. White **blood cells** function in the immune defense system of the body
    2. The white **blood cell** count assesses leukocyte distribution.
  B. Value: 4,500 to 11,000 cells/mm^3 (Table 11-5)
  C. Nursing considerations
    1. A "shift to the left" means that an increased number of immature neutrophils is present in the **blood**.
    2. A low total white **blood cell** count with a left shift indicates a recovery from bone marrow depression or an infection of such intensity that the demand for neutrophils in the tissue is higher than the capacity of the bone marrow to release them into the circulation.

TABLE 11-5

Normal Adult White Blood Cell Differential Count

Cell Type	Percentage and Count
Neutrophils	56% or 1800-7800 cells/mm^3
Bands	3% or 0-700 cells/mm^3
Eosinophils	2.7% or 0-450 cells/mm^3
Basophils	0.3% or 0-200 cells/mm^3
Lymphocytes	34% or 1000-4800 cells/mm^3
Monocytes	4% or 0-800 cells/mm^3

3. A high total white **blood cell** count with a left shift indicates an increased release of neutrophils by the bone marrow in response to an overwhelming infection or inflammation.

4. A "shift to the right" means that cells have more than the usual number of nuclear segments; found in liver disease, Down syndrome, or megaloblastic and pernicious anemia.

XI. HEPATITIS TESTING

A. Description
   1. Tests include radioimmunoassay, enzyme-linked immunosorbent assay (ELISA), and microparticle enzyme immunoassay.
   2. Serological tests for specific hepatitis virus markers assist in defining the specific type of hepatitis.

B. Values
   1. The presence of immunoglobulin M (IgM) antibody to hepatitis A virus and the presence of the total antibody to hepatitis A virus identify the disease.
   2. Detection of hepatitis B core antigen (HBcAg), envelope antigen (HBeAg), and surface antigen (HBsAg), or their corresponding antibodies, constitutes hepatitis B assessment.
   3. Hepatitis C is confirmed by the presence of antibodies to hepatitis C virus.
   4. Serological hepatitis D virus determination is made by detection of the hepatitis D antigen (HDAg) early in the course of the infection and by detection of anti–hepatitis D virus antibody in the later disease stages.
   5. Specific serological tests for hepatitis E virus include detection of IgM and IgG antibodies to hepatitis E.
   6. Hepatitis G virus has been found in some **blood** donors (donated **blood**), IV drug users, hemodialysis clients, and clients with hemophilia; however, hepatitis G virus does not appear to cause significant liver disease.

C. Nursing consideration: If the radioimmunoassay technique is being used, the injection of radionuclides within 1 week before the **blood** test is performed may cause falsely elevated results.

XII. HUMAN IMMUNODEFICIENCY VIRUS (HIV) AND ACQUIRED IMMUNODEFICIENCY SYNDROME (AIDS) TESTING

A. Description
   1. Testing detects HIV, which is the cause of AIDS.
   2. Tests used to determine the presence of antibodies to HIV include ELISA, Western blot, and immunofluorescence assay (IFA).
   3. A single reactive ELISA test by itself cannot be used to diagnose HIV and should be repeated in duplicate with the same **blood** sample; if the result is repeatedly reactive, follow-up tests using Western blot or IFA should be performed.
   4. A positive Western blot or IFA result is considered confirmatory for HIV.
   5. A positive ELISA result that fails to be confirmed by Western blot or IFA should not be considered negative, and repeat testing should take place in 3 to 6 months.

B. CD4$^+$ T cell counts
   1. This cell count monitors the progression of HIV.
   2. As the disease progresses, usually the number of CD4$^+$ T-cells decreases, with a resultant decrease in immunity.
   3. Normal CD4$^+$ T-cell count is between 500 and 1600 cells/L.
   4. Generally, the immune system remains healthy with CD4$^+$ T-cell counts higher than 500 cells/L.
   5. Immune system problems occur when the CD4$^+$ T-cell count is between 200 and 499 cells/L.
   6. Severe immune system problems occur when the CD4$^+$ T-cell count is lower than 200 cells/L.

C. CD4-to-CD8 ratio
   1. This ratio monitors the progression of disease.
   2. The normal ratio is approximately 2:1.

D. Viral culture involves placing the infected client's **blood cells** in a culture medium and measuring the amount of reverse transcriptase activity over a specified period of time.

E. Viral load testing measures the presence of HIV viral genetic material (RNA) or another viral protein in the client's **blood**.

F. The p24 antigen assay quantifies the amount of HIV viral core protein in the client's **serum**.

G. Oral testing for HIV
   1. This uses a device that is placed against the gum and cheek for 2 minutes
   2. Fluid (not saliva) is drawn into an absorbable pad, which, in an HIV-positive individual, contains antibodies.
   3. The pad is placed in a solution and a specified observable change is noted if the test result is positive.
   4. If the result is positive, a **blood** test is needed to confirm the results.

H. Home test kits for HIV
   1. A drop of **blood** is placed on a test card with a special code number; the card is mailed to the laboratory for testing for the HIV antibodies.
   2. The individual receives the results by calling a special telephone number and entering the special code number; test results are then given.

I. Nursing considerations
   1. Maintain issues of confidentiality surrounding HIV and AIDS testing.
   2. Follow prescribed state regulations and protocols related to reporting positive test results.

XIII. URINE TESTS (Table 11-6)

XIV. THERAPEUTIC SERUM MEDICATION LEVELS
(Table 11-7)

TABLE 11-6

Normal Adult Values: Urine Tests

Name of Test	Value
Color	Pale yellow
Odor	Specific aromatic odor, similar to ammonia
Turbidity	Clear
pH	4.5-7.8
Specific gravity	1.016 to 1.022
Glucose	<0.5 g/day
Ketones	None
Protein	None
Bilirubin	None
Casts	None to few
Crystals	None
Bacteria	None or <1000/mL
Red blood cells	<3 cells/HPF
White blood cells	≤4 cells/HPF
Chloride	110-250 mEq/24 hr
Magnesium	7.3-12.2 HPF, High-powered field.
Potassium	25-125 mEq/24 hr
Sodium	40-220 mEq/24 hr
Uric acid	250-750 mg/24 hr

HPF, High-powered field.

TABLE 11-7

Therapeutic Serum Medication Levels

Medication	Therapeutic Range
Acetaminophen (Tylenol)	10-20 mcg/mL
Amikacin (Amikin)	25-30 mcg/mL
Amitriptyline	120-150 ng/mL
Carbamazepine (Tegretol)	5-12 mcg/mL
Chloramphenicol (Chloromycetin)	10-20 mcg/mL
Desipramine (Norpramin)	150-300 ng/mL
Digoxin (Lanoxin)	0.5-2 ng/mL
Disopyramide (Norpace)	2-5 mcg/mL
Ethosuximide (Zarontin)	40-100 mcg/mL
Gentamicin	5-10 mcg/mL
Imipramine (Tofranil)	150-300 ng/mL
Lidocaine (Xylocaine)	1.5-5 mcg/mL
Lithium (Lithobid)	0.5-1.3 mEq/L
Magnesium sulfate	4-7 mg/dL
Phenobarbital (Luminal)	10-30 mcg/mL
Phenytoin (Dilantin)	10-20 mcg/mL
Propranolol (Inderal)	50-100 ng/mL
Salicylate	100-250 mcg/mL
Theophylline (aminophylline; Theo-Dur)	10-20 mcg/mL
Tobramycin (Nebcin)	5-10 mcg/mL
Valproic acid (Depakene)	50-100 mcg/mL

PRACTICE QUESTIONS

1. A client is brought to the emergency room stating that he has accidentally been taking two times his prescribed dose of warfarin (Coumadin) for the past week. After noting that the client has no evidence of obvious bleeding, the nurse plans to do which of the following next?
   1. Prepares to administer an antidote
   2. Draws a sample for type and crossmatch and transfuse the client
   3. Draws a sample for an activated partial thromboplastin time (aPTT) level
   4. Draws a sample for prothrombin (PT) and international normalized ratio (INR) level

2. The nurse is assigned to a 40-year-old client who has a diagnosis of chronic pancreatitis. The nurse reviews the laboratory result, anticipating a laboratory report that indicates a serum amylase level of:
   1. 45 units/L
   2. 100 units/L
   3. 300 units/L
   4. 500 units/L

3. A 22-year-old adult has a cholesterol blood test done at a screening clinic sponsored by a local health club. The nurse volunteering at the screening teaches the client that diet and exercise should be used as health measures to keep the total cholesterol level below:
   1. 80 mg/dL
   2. 200 mg/dL
   3. 250 mg/dL
   4. 300 mg/dL

4. A client has been admitted to the hospital for urinary tract infection and dehydration. The nurse determines that the client has received adequate volume replacement if the blood urea nitrogen level drops to:
   1. 3 mg/dL
   2. 15 mg/dL
   3. 29 mg/dL
   4. 35 mg/dL

5. A client arrives in the emergency room complaining of chest pain that began 4 hours ago. A troponin T blood specimen is obtained, and the results indicate a level of 0.6 ng/mL. The nurse interprets that this result indicates:
   1. A normal level
   2. A low value that indicates possible gastritis
   3. A level that indicates a myocardial infarction
   4. A level that indicates the presence of possible angina

6. A client is suspected of having a myocardial infarction. The nurse assesses for elevations in which of the following isoenzyme values reported with the creatine kinase level?
   1. MM
   2. MB

3. BB
4. MK

7. An adult client has had laboratory work done as part of a routine physical examination. The nurse interprets that the client may have a mild degree of renal insufficiency if which of the following serum creatinine levels is noted?
   1. 0.2 mg/dL
   2. 0.5 mg/dL
   3. 1.9 mg/dL
   4. 3.5 mg/dL

8. A client with a history of a seizure disorder who has been compliant with medication therapy is admitted to the hospital with seizure activity. Phenytoin (Dilantin) is administered to the client intravenously, and subsequently a sample for the serum phenytoin level is drawn. The nurse determines that the medication therapy has been most effective if the laboratory result is:
   1. 3 mcg/mL
   2. 8 mcg/mL
   3. 16 mcg/mL
   4. 24 mcg/mL

9. A client with atrial fibrillation who is receiving maintenance therapy of warfarin sodium (Coumadin) has a prothrombin time of 35 seconds. Based on the prothrombin time, the nurse anticipates which of the following orders?
   1. Adding a dose of heparin sodium
   2. Holding the next dose of warfarin
   3. Increasing the next dose of warfarin
   4. Administering the next dose of warfarin

10. A client who takes theophylline for chronic obstructive pulmonary disease is seen in the urgent care center for respiratory distress. Once the client is stabilized, the nurse begins discharge teaching. The nurse would be especially vigilant to include information about complying with medication therapy if the client's baseline theophylline level was:
    1. 10 mcg/mL
    2. 12 mcg/mL
    3. 15 mcg/mL
    4. 18 mcg/mL

11. The nurse checks the laboratory result for a serum digoxin level that was determined for a client earlier in the day and notes that the result is 2.4 ng/mL. Which of the following is the most important action on the part of the nurse?
    1. Notify the physician.
    2. Check the client's last pulse rate.
    3. Record the normal value on the client's flow sheet.
    4. Administer the next dose of the medication as scheduled.

12. A client is receiving a continuous intravenous infusion of heparin sodium to treat deep vein thrombosis. The client's activated partial thromboplastin (aPTT) time is 65 seconds. The client's baseline before the initiation of therapy was 30 seconds. The nurse anticipates that which action is needed?
    1. Discontinuing the heparin infusion
    2. Increasing the rate of the heparin infusion
    3. Decreasing the rate of the heparin infusion
    4. Leaving the rate of the heparin infusion as is

13. An adult client who had preadmission testing before surgery had blood drawn for serum electrolyte testing. The nurse should report which of the following abnormal values to the surgeon's office preoperatively?
    1. Sodium, 148 mEq/L
    2. Chloride, 101 mEq/L
    3. Potassium, 3.8 mEq/L
    4. Bicarbonate, 26 mEq/L

14. A client with a history of cardiac disease is due for a morning dose of furosemide (Lasix). Which serum potassium level should be reported to the surgeon before administering the dose of furosemide?
    1. 3.2 mEq/L
    2. 3.8 mEq/L
    3. 4.2 mEq/L
    4. 4.8 mEq/L

15. An adult client with a history of gastrointestinal bleeding has a platelet count of 300,000 cells/mm³. Which action by the nurse is most appropriate after seeing the laboratory results?
    1. Report the abnormally low count.
    2. Report the abnormally high count.
    3. Place the client on bleeding precautions.
    4. Place the normal report in the client's medical record.

16. An adult client with cirrhosis has been following a diet with optimal amounts of protein because neither an excess nor a deficiency of protein has been helpful. The nurse evaluates the client's status as being most satisfactory if the total protein level is which of the following values?
    1. 0.4 g/dL
    2. 3.7 g/dL
    3. 6.4 g/dL
    4. 9.8 g/dL

17. An adult client was diagnosed with acute pancreatitis 9 days ago. The nurse interprets that the client is recovering from this episode if the serum lipase level decreases to which of the following values, which is just below the upper limit of normal?
    1. 20 units/L
    2. 80 units/L
    3. 135 units/L
    4. 350 units/L

18. An adult female client has a hemoglobin level of 10.8 g/dL. The nurse interprets that this result is most likely caused by which of the following conditions noted in the client's history?
    1. Dehydration
    2. Heart failure
    3. Iron deficiency anemia
    4. Chronic obstructive pulmonary disease

19. A client with diabetes mellitus has a glycosylated hemoglobin A_{1c} level of 9%. Based on this test result, the nurse plans to teach the client about the need to:
    1. Avoid infection
    2. Take in adequate fluids
    3. Prevent and recognize hypoglycemia
    4. Prevent and recognize hyperglycemia

20. The nurse is caring for a client with a diagnosis of cancer who is immunosuppressed. The nurse would consider implementing neutropenic precautions if the client's white blood cell count was which of the following?

1. 2,000 cells/mm³
2. 5,800 cells/mm³
3. 8,400 cells/mm³
4. 11,500 cells/mm³

ALTERNATE ITEM FORMAT: MULTIPLE RESPONSE

Several laboratory tests are prescribed for a client, and the nurse reviews the results of the tests. Select the laboratory test results that are abnormal.

❏ 1. Calcium, 7.0 mg/dL
❏ 2. Magnesium, 1.0 mg/dL
❏ 3. Phosphorus, 3.6 mg/dL
❏ 4. Neutrophils, 1000/mm³
❏ 5. Serum creatinine, 1.0 mg/dL
❏ 6. White blood cells, 3000/mm³

ANSWERS

1. **4**

Rationale: The next action is to draw a sample for PT and INR level to determine the client's anticoagulation status and risk for bleeding. These results will provide information as to how to best treat this client if an antidote (vitamin K) or blood transfusion is needed. The aPTT monitors the effects of heparin therapy.

Test-Taking Strategy: Use a process of elimination. Eliminate option 3 because it is unrelated to warfarin therapy and relates to heparin therapy. Next, eliminate options 1 and 2 because these therapies would not be implemented unless the PT and INR levels are known. Review care to the client receiving warfarin therapy and the purpose of the PT and INR if you had difficulty with this question.

Level of Cognitive Ability: Analysis
Client Needs: Physiological Integrity
Integrated Process: Nursing Process—analysis
Content Area: Fundamental Skills
Reference: Lehne, R.A. (2004). *Pharmacology for nursing care* (5th ed., p. 552). St. Louis: W.B. Saunders.

2. **3**

Rationale: The normal serum amylase level is 25 to 151 units/L. With chronic cases of pancreatitis, the rise in serum amylase levels usually does not exceed three times the normal value. In acute pancreatitis, the value may exceed five times the normal value. Options 1 and 2 are within normal limits. Option 4 is an extremely elevated level seen in acute pancreatitis.

Test-Taking Strategy: Use the process of elimination and note the strategic word *chronic* in the question. Recalling the normal amylase level and focusing on the strategic word will direct you to option 3. Review this level and the findings in chronic pancreatitis if you had difficulty with this question.

Level of Cognitive Ability: Analysis
Client Needs: Physiological Integrity
Integrated Process: Nursing Process—analysis
Content Area: Adult health—gastrointestinal
References: Chernecky, C., & Berger, B. (2004). *Laboratory tests*

and diagnostic procedures (4th ed., p. 172). Philadelphia: W.B. Saunders.
Ignatavicius, D., & Workman, M. (2006). *Medical-surgical nursing: Critical thinking for collaborative care* (5th ed., p. 1406). Philadelphia: W.B. Saunders.

3. **2**

Rationale: The nurse should counsel the client to keep the total cholesterol level under 200 mg/dL. This will aid in the prevention of atherosclerosis, which can lead to a number of cardiovascular disorders later in life. Options 3 and 4 are elevated values and place the client at risk for cardiovascular disease. Although option 1 is a low cholesterol level, option 2 identifies the realistic value to assist in preventing cardiovascular disease.

Test-Taking Strategy: Recalling that the normal cholesterol level ranges from 140 to 199 mg/dL and noting the subject of the question will direct you to option 2. Because of the importance of the health problems caused by atherosclerosis and cardiovascular disease, review this laboratory test.

Level of Cognitive Ability: Application
Client Needs: Health Promotion and Maintenance
Integrated Process: Teaching and Learning
Content Area: Adult health—cardiovascular
Reference: Chernecky, C., & Berger, B. (2004). *Laboratory tests and diagnostic procedures* (4th ed., p. 369). Philadelphia: W.B. Saunders.

4. **2**

Rationale: The normal blood urea nitrogen level is 8 to 25 mg/dL. Values such as those in options 3 and 4 reflect continued dehydration. Option 1 reflects a lower than normal value, which may occur with fluid volume overload, among other conditions.

Test-Taking Strategy: Use the process of elimination and knowledge of the normal blood urea nitrogen level to answer the question. Option 2 is the only option that identifies a normal value. Review this laboratory test if you had difficulty with this question.

Level of Cognitive Ability: Analysis
Client Needs: Physiological Integrity
Integrated Process: Nursing Process—evaluation
Content Area: Adult health—renal
Reference: Chernecky, C., & Berger, B. (2004). *Laboratory tests and diagnostic procedures* (4th ed., p. 1111). Philadelphia: W.B. Saunders.

5. **3**
Rationale: Troponin is a regulatory protein found in striated muscle. The troponins function together in the contractile apparatus for striated muscle in skeletal muscle and in the myocardium. Increased amounts of troponins are released into the bloodstream when an infarction causes damage to the myocardium. A troponin T value that is higher than 0.1 to 0.2 ng/mL is consistent with a myocardial infarction. A normal troponin I level is lower than 0.6 ng/mL.
Test-Taking Strategy: Note that the subject of the question relates to the troponin T. Knowing that a level higher than 0.1 to 0.2 ng/mL is consistent with a myocardial infarction will direct you to option 3. Review this diagnostic test if you are unfamiliar with it.
Level of Cognitive Ability: Analysis
Client Needs: Physiological Integrity
Integrated Process: Nursing Process—analysis
Content Area: Adult health—cardiovascular
References: Chernecky, C., & Berger, B. (2004). *Laboratory tests and diagnostic procedures* (4th ed., p. 1094). Philadelphia: W.B. Saunders.
Ignatavicius, D., & Workman, M. (2006). *Medical-surgical nursing: Critical thinking for collaborative care* (5th ed., p. 694). Philadelphia: W.B. Saunders.

6. **2**
Rationale: Creatine kinase (CK) is a cellular enzyme that can be fractionated into three isoenzymes. The MB band reflects CK from cardiac muscle. This is the level that elevates with myocardial infarction. The MM band reflects CK from skeletal muscle. The BB band reflects CK from the brain. There is no MK band.
Test-Taking Strategy: To answer this question correctly, you must have specific knowledge of the isoenzymes produced with elevations in the CK level. Eliminate option 4 because there is no MK band. From the remaining options, recall that the MB band reflects CK from cardiac muscle. Review this important laboratory value for detecting myocardial infarction if you had difficulty with this question.
Level of Cognitive Ability: Comprehension
Client Needs: Physiological Integrity
Integrated Process: Nursing Process—assessment
Content Area: Adult health—cardiovascular
References: Ignatavicius, D., & Workman, M. (2006). *Medical-surgical nursing: Critical thinking for collaborative care* (5th ed., p. 845). Philadelphia: W.B. Saunders.
Pagana, K., & Pagana, T. (2006). *Mosby's manual of diagnostic and laboratory tests* (3rd ed., p. 202). St. Louis: Mosby.

7. **3**
Rationale: The normal serum creatinine level for adults is 0.6 to 1.3 mg/dL. The client with a mild degree of renal insufficiency would have a slightly elevated level. A creatinine level of 0.2 mg/dL is low, and a level of 0.5 mg/dL is just below

normal. A creatinine level of 3.5 mg/dL may be associated with acute or chronic renal failure.
Test-Taking Strategy: Note the strategic word *mild*. This tells you that the correct option will be an abnormal value but perhaps not the most abnormal of all the options. Recall the normal value for this common laboratory test to direct you to option 3. Review the normal value for this laboratory test if you had difficulty with this question.
Level of Cognitive Ability: Analysis
Client Needs: Physiological Integrity
Integrated Process: Nursing Process—analysis
Content Area: Adult health—renal
References: Chernecky, C., & Berger, B. (2004). *Laboratory tests and diagnostic procedures* (4th ed., p. 428). Philadelphia: W.B. Saunders.
Ignatavicius, D., & Workman, M. (2006). *Medical-surgical nursing: Critical thinking for collaborative care* (5th ed., p. 1740). Philadelphia: W.B. Saunders.

8. **3**
Rationale: The therapeutic range for serum phenytoin (Dilantin) level is 10 to 20 mcg/mL. If the level is below the therapeutic range, the client may continue to experience seizure activity. If the level is too high, the client could experience phenytoin toxicity.
Test-Taking Strategy: Use the process of elimination. Recalling that the therapeutic range is 10 to 20 mcg/mL will direct you to option 3. Learn this therapeutic range if you had difficulty with this question.
Level of Cognitive Ability: Comprehension
Client Needs: Physiological Integrity
Integrated Process: Nursing Process—evaluation
Content Area: Adult health—neurological
Reference: Chernecky, C., & Berger, B. (2004). *Laboratory tests and diagnostic procedures* (4th ed., p. 869). Philadelphia: W.B. Saunders.

9. **2**
Rationale: The normal prothrombin time (PT) is 9.6 to 11.8 seconds (male adult) or 9.5 to 11.3 seconds (female adult). A therapeutic PT level is 1.5 to 2.0 times higher than the normal level. Because the value of 35 seconds is high (and perhaps near the critical range), the nurse should anticipate that the client would not receive further doses at this time.
Test-Taking Strategy: Use the process of elimination, recalling that the normal PT is 9.6 to 11.8 seconds (male adult) or 9.5 to 11.3 seconds (female adult) and that a therapeutic PT level is 1.5 to 2.0 times higher than the normal level. If this question was difficult, review this laboratory test and the expected level if the client is receiving warfarin sodium.
Level of Cognitive Ability: Analysis
Client Needs: Physiological Integrity
Integrated Process: Nursing Process—analysis
Content Area: Adult health—cardiovascular
Reference: Chernecky, C., & Berger, B. (2004). *Laboratory tests and diagnostic procedures* (4th ed., p. 920). Philadelphia: W.B. Saunders.

10. **1**
Rationale: The therapeutic range for the serum theophylline level is 10 to 20 mcg/mL. If the level is below the therapeutic range, the client may experience frequent exacerbations of the

disorder. Although all the options identify values within the therapeutic range, option 1 is the option that reflects a need for compliance with medication.

Test-Taking Strategy: Use the process of elimination. Note the strategic words *especially vigilant.* Recalling the therapeutic level of theophylline will direct you to option 1. Review this therapeutic range if you had difficulty with this question.

Level of Cognitive Ability: Comprehension
Client Needs: Physiological Integrity
Integrated Process: Teaching and Learning
Content Area: Adult health—respiratory
Reference: Chernecky, C., & Berger, B. (2004). *Laboratory tests and diagnostic procedures* (4th ed., p. 1040). Philadelphia: W.B. Saunders.

11. 1

Rationale: The normal therapeutic range for digoxin is 0.5 to 2.0 ng/mL. A level of 2.4 ng/mL exceeds the therapeutic range and indicates toxicity. The most important action is to notify the physician, who may give further orders about holding further doses of digoxin. Option 3 is incorrect because the level is not normal. The next dose should not be administered because the serum digoxin level exceeds the therapeutic range. Checking the client's last pulse rate is not incorrect but may have limited value in this situation. Depending on the time that has elapsed since the last assessment, a current assessment of the client's status may be more useful.

Test-Taking Strategy: Use the process of elimination and note the strategic words *most important action.* To choose correctly, you must be familiar with the therapeutic range for this medication and note that the level of 2.4 ng/mL is a toxic one. If this question was difficult, review the information on this commonly used medication and measurement of its therapeutic serum level.

Level of Cognitive Ability: Application
Client Needs: Physiological Integrity
Integrated Process: Nursing Process—implementation
Content Area: Adult health—cardiovascular
Reference: Chernecky, C., & Berger, B. (2004). *Laboratory tests and diagnostic procedures* (4th ed., p. 477). Philadelphia: W.B. Saunders.

12. 4

Rationale: The normal activated partial thromboplastin time (aPTT) varies between 20 and 36 seconds, depending on the type of activator used in testing. The therapeutic dose of heparin for treatment of deep vein thrombosis is to keep the aPTT between 1.5 and 2.5 times normal. Thus, the client's aPTT is within the therapeutic range, and the dose should remain unchanged.

Test-Taking Strategy: To answer this question accurately, you must be familiar with the normal aPTT level and the therapeutic level needed following institution of heparin therapy. Remember that the normal range is 20 to 36 seconds and that the aPTT should be between 1.5 and 2.5 times normal when the client is receiving heparin therapy. If this question was difficult, review this laboratory test and the expected level if the client is receiving heparin.

Level of Cognitive Ability: Analysis
Client Needs: Physiological Integrity
Integrated Process: Nursing Process—analysis

Content Area: Adult health—cardiovascular
References: Chernecky, C., & Berger, B. (2004). *Laboratory tests and diagnostic procedures* (4th ed., pp. 138-140). Philadelphia: W.B. Saunders.
Gahart, B., & Nazareno, A. (2006). *2006 intravenous medications* (22nd ed., p. 633). St. Louis: Mosby.

13. 1

Rationale: The normal serum electrolyte ranges for adults are as follows: sodium, 135 to 145 mEq/L; potassium, 3.5 to 5.1 mEq/L; chloride, 98 to 107 mEq/L; and bicarbonate (venous), 22 to 29 mEq/L. The only abnormal value identified in the options is the serum sodium level. The nurse reports any abnormal preoperative laboratory value to the surgeon's office.

Test-Taking Strategy: Use the process of elimination and knowledge of the normal serum electrolyte values to direct you to option 1. If this question was difficult, memorize these common laboratory values.

Level of Cognitive Ability: Application
Client Needs: Physiological Integrity
Integrated Process: Nursing Process—implementation
Content Area: Fundamental skills
Reference: Chernecky, C., & Berger, B. (2004). *Laboratory tests and diagnostic procedures* (4th ed., p. 492). Philadelphia: W.B. Saunders.

14. 1

Rationale: The normal serum potassium level in the adult is 3.5 to 5.1 mEq/L. Option 1 is the only value that falls below the therapeutic range. Administering furosemide to a client with a low potassium level and a history of cardiac problems could precipitate ventricular dysrhythmias. Options 2, 3, and 4 are within the normal range.

Test-Taking Strategy: Use the process of elimination and knowledge of the normal serum potassium level to answer this question. This will assist you in identifying the value that is not within normal range. Remember, the normal serum potassium level in the adult is 3.5 to 5.1 mEq/L. If this question was difficult, memorize this common laboratory value.

Level of Cognitive Ability: Comprehension
Client Needs: Physiological Integrity
Integrated Process: Nursing Process—planning
Content Area: Adult health—cardiovascular
Reference: Chernecky, C., & Berger, B. (2004). *Laboratory tests and diagnostic procedures* (4th ed., p. 887). Philadelphia: W.B. Saunders.

15. 4

Rationale: A normal platelet count ranges from 150,000 to 400,000 cells/mm³. The nurse should place the report containing the normal laboratory value in the client's medical record. A platelet count of 300,000 cells/mm³ is not an elevated count. The count also is not low; therefore, bleeding precautions are not needed.

Test-Taking Strategy: Use the process of elimination. Remember that options that are comparative or alike are not likely to be correct. With this in mind, eliminate options 1 and 3 first. From the remaining options, you must be familiar with the normal range for this laboratory test. Review this normal laboratory value if you had difficulty with this question.

Level of Cognitive Ability: Application

Client Needs: Physiological Integrity
Integrated Process: Nursing Process—implementation
Content Area: Adult health—gastrointestinal
Reference: Pagana, K., & Pagana, T. (2006). *Mosby's manual of diagnostic and laboratory tests* (3rd ed., p. 409). St. Louis: Mosby.

16. **3**
Rationale: The normal range for total serum protein level in the adult client is 6.0 to 8.0 g/dL. The client with cirrhosis often has low total protein levels as a result of inadequate nutrition. Excess protein is not helpful, though, because a function of the liver is to metabolize protein. A diseased liver may not metabolize protein well. Options 1 and 2 identify low values, and option 4 identifies a high protein value.
Test-Taking Strategy: Use the process of elimination. Note the strategic words *most satisfactory*. Recalling the normal total protein level will direct you to option 3. Review this laboratory range if you had difficulty with this question.
Level of Cognitive Ability: Comprehension
Client Needs: Physiological Integrity
Integrated Process: Nursing Process—evaluation
Content Area: Adult health—gastrointestinal
Reference: Pagana, K., & Pagana, T. (2005). *Mosby's diagnostic and laboratory test reference* (7th ed., p. 758). St. Louis: Mosby.

17. **3**
Rationale: The normal serum lipase level is 10 to 140 units/L. The client who is recovering from acute pancreatitis usually has elevated lipase levels for about 10 days after the onset of symptoms. This makes lipase a valuable test in monitoring the client's pancreatic function because serum amylase levels usually return to normal 3 days after the onset of symptoms. Option 3 is the only option that contains a value just below the upper limit of normal.
Test-Taking Strategy: Use the process of elimination and knowledge of the serum lipase level to answer this question. Noting the strategic words *just below the upper limit of normal* will assist in directing you to option 3. Review the range for this laboratory value if you had difficulty with this question.
Level of Cognitive Ability: Analysis
Client Needs: Physiological Integrity
Integrated Process: Nursing Process—evaluation
Content Area: Adult health—gastrointestinal
Reference: Chernecky, C., & Berger, B. (2004). *Laboratory tests and diagnostic procedures* (4th ed., p. 724). Philadelphia: W.B. Saunders.

18. **3**
Rationale: The normal hemoglobin level for an adult female client is 12 to 15 g/dL. Iron deficiency anemia can result in lower hemoglobin levels. Dehydration may increase the hemoglobin level by hemoconcentration. Heart failure and chronic obstructive pulmonary disease may increase the hemoglobin level as a result of the body's need for more oxygen-carrying capacity.
Test-Taking Strategy: Use the process of elimination. Evaluate each of the options in terms of whether each is likely to raise or lower the hemoglobin level. Also, note the relationship between *hemoglobin level* in the question and option 3. Review

the normal hemoglobin level if you had difficulty with this question.
Level of Cognitive Ability: Analysis
Client Needs: Physiological Integrity
Integrated Process: Nursing Process—analysis
Content Area: Fundamental skills
References: Chernecky, C., & Berger, B. (2004). *Laboratory tests and diagnostic procedures* (4th ed., p. 639). Philadelphia: W.B. Saunders.
Ignatavicius, D., & Workman, M. (2006). *Medical-surgical nursing: Critical thinking for collaborative care* (5th ed., p. 894). Philadelphia: W.B. Saunders.

19. **4**
Rationale: In the test result for glycosylated hemoglobin A_{1c}, 7% or less indicates good control, 7% to 8% indicates fair control, and 8% or higher indicates poor control. This test measures the amount of glucose that has become permanently bound to the red blood cells from circulating glucose. Elevations in the blood glucose level will cause elevations in the amount of glycosylation. Thus, the test is useful in identifying clients who have periods of hyperglycemia that are undetected in other ways. Elevations indicate continued need for teaching related to the prevention of hyperglycemic episodes.
Test-Taking Strategy: Use the process of elimination and knowledge regarding the values for this test and their significance to answer the question. Focusing on the level identified in the question will assist in directing you to option 4. If you had difficulty with this question or are unfamiliar with this test, review this content.
Level of Cognitive Ability: Application
Client Needs: Health Promotion and Maintenance
Integrated Process: Nursing Process—planning
Content Area: Adult health—endocrine
References: Chernecky, C., & Berger, B. (2004). *Laboratory tests and diagnostic procedures* (4th ed., p. 615). Philadelphia: W.B. Saunders.
Ignatavicius, D., & Workman, M. (2006). *Medical-surgical nursing: Critical thinking for collaborative care* (5th ed., pp. 882, 1507). Philadelphia: W.B. Saunders.

20. **1**
Rationale: The normal white blood cell count ranges from 4,500 to 11,000/mm³. The client who is immunosuppressed has a decrease in the number of circulating white blood cells. The nurse implements neutropenic precautions when the client's values fall sufficiently below the normal level. The specific value for implementing neutropenic precautions usually is determined by agency policy. Options 2, 3, and 4 are normal values.
Test-Taking Strategy: Use the process of elimination. Recalling that the normal white blood cell count is 4,500 to 11,000/mm³ will direct you to option 1. Review this hematological test if you had difficulty with this question.
Level of Cognitive Ability: Analysis
Client Needs: Physiological Integrity
Integrated Process: Nursing Process—planning
Content Area: Adult health—oncology
References: Pagana, K., & Pagana, T. (2006). *Mosby's manual of diagnostic and laboratory tests* (3rd ed., p. 537). St. Louis: Mosby.

ALTERNATE ITEM FORMAT: MULTIPLE RESPONSE

Answer: 1, 2, 4, 6

Rationale: The normal values include the following: white blood cells, 4,500 to 11,000/mm³; neutrophils, 56%, or 1,800 to 7,800/mm³; phosphorus, 2.7 to 4.5 mg/dL; magnesium, 1.6 to 2.6 mg/dL; calcium, 8.6 to 10.0 mg/dL; and serum creatinine, 0.6 to 1.3 mg/dL.

Test-Taking Strategy: Note the word *abnormal* in the question. Knowledge of the normal laboratory values for these studies will assist in answering this question. Review these normal values if you had difficulty with this question.

Level of Cognitive Ability: Comprehension
Client Needs: Physiological Integrity
Integrated Process: Nursing Process—assessment
Content Area: Fundamental skills
References: Lewis, S., Heitkemper, M., & Dirksen, S. (2004). *Medical-surgical nursing: Assessment and management of clinical problems* (6th ed., pp. 700, 1034, 1163, 1263-1264). St. Louis: Mosby.
Pagana, K., & Pagana, T. (2006). *Mosby's manual of diagnostic and laboratory tests* (3rd ed., p. 537). St. Louis: Mosby.

REFERENCES

Black, J., & Hawks, J., (2005). *Medical-surgical nursing: Clinical management for positive outcomes* (7th ed.). Philadelphia: W.B. Saunders.

Chernecky, C., & Berger, B. (2004). *Laboratory tests and diagnostic procedures* (4th ed.). Philadelphia: W.B. Saunders.

Gahart, B., & Nazareno, A. (2006). *2006 Intravenous medications* (22nd ed.). St. Louis: Mosby.

Ignatavicius, D., & Workman, M. (2006). *Medical-surgical nursing: Critical thinking for collaborative care* (5th ed.). Philadelphia: W.B. Saunders.

Lehne, R.A. (2004). *Pharmacology for nursing care* (5th ed.). St. Louis: W.B. Saunders.

Lewis, S., Heitkemper, M., & Dirksen, S. (2004). *Medical-surgical nursing: Assessment and management of clinical problems* (6th ed.). St. Louis: Mosby.

National Council of State Boards of Nursing (Eds.). (2007). *2007 NCLEX-RN® detailed test plan*. Chicago: Author.

Pagana, K., & Pagana, T. (2006). *Mosby's manual of diagnostic and laboratory tests* (3rd ed.). St. Louis: Mosby.

Potter, P., & Perry, A. (2005). *Fundamentals of nursing* (6th ed.). St. Louis: Mosby.

12

Nutrition

PYRAMID TERMS

absorption Passage of digested nutrients through the wall of the stomach or small intestine into the blood or lymph system.

digestion The breakdown of carbohydrates, fats, and proteins into monosaccharides, fatty acids, and amino acids.

enteral nutrition Administration of nutrition with liquefied foods into the gastrointestinal tract via a tube.

malnutrition Deficiency of the nutrients required for development and maintenance of the human body.

metabolism Ongoing chemical process within the body that converts digested nutrients into energy for the functioning of body cells.

nutrients Carbohydrates, fats or lipids, proteins, vitamins, minerals, electrolytes, and water that must be supplied in adequate amounts to provide energy, growth, development, and maintenance of the human body.

▲ THE PYRAMID TO SUCCESS

Nutrition is a basic need that must be met for all clients. Nurses must have the knowledge required to educate and care for healthy clients and for clients with nutritional needs or disorders requiring alterations in dietary measures. The NCLEX-RN examination addresses the dietary measures required for basic needs and for particular body system alterations. When presented with a question related to nutrition, consider the client's diagnosis and the particular requirement or restriction necessary for treatment of the disorder. Pyramid Points focus on the common types of therapeutic diets, nutrients contained in food items, and supplemental or enteral feedings. Integrated Processes addressed in this chapter include Caring, Communication and Documentation, Nursing Process, and Teaching/Learning.

CLIENT NEEDS   ▲

Safe and Effective Care Environment

Consulting with members of the health care team regarding dietary needs
Obtaining informed consent for invasive procedures
Maintaining medical and surgical asepsis
Maintaining standard, transmission-based, and other precautions

Health Promotion and Maintenance

Initiating health promotion programs
Performing physical assessment
Preventing disease
Promoting health and wellness
Providing dietary teaching

Psychosocial Integrity

Considering cultural preferences related to nutritional patterns and lifestyle choices
Identifying coping mechanisms
Identifying religious and spiritual influences on health

Physiological Integrity

Assessing elimination patterns
Monitoring for alteration in body systems
Monitoring of enteral feedings and the client's ability to tolerate feedings
Monitoring of fluid and electrolyte balance
Monitoring of laboratory values
Monitoring of nutritional intake and oral hydration

I. NUTRIENTS
  A. Carbohydrates (Box 12-1)
    1. The preferred source of energy
    2. Include sugars, starches, and cellulose and provide 4 cal/g
    3. Promote normal fat **metabolism**, spare protein, and enhance lower gastrointestinal function.
    4. Major food sources of carbohydrates include milk, grains, fruits, and vegetables.
    5. Inadequate carbohydrate intake affects **metabolism**.
  B. Fats (Box 12-2)
    1. Provide a concentrated source and a stored form of energy
    2. Protect internal organs and maintain body temperature
    3. Enhance **absorption** of the fat-soluble vitamins
    4. Provide 9 cal/g
    5. Inadequate fat intake leads to clinical manifestations of sensitivity to cold, skin lesions, increased risk of infection, and amenorrhea in women.
    6. Diets high in fat can lead to obesity and increase the risk of cardiovascular disease and some cancers.
  C. Proteins (Box 12-3)
    1. Made from amino acids, are critical to all aspects of growth and development of body tissues, and provide 4 cal/g
    2. Build and repair body tissues, regulate fluid balance, maintain acid-base balance, produce antibodies, provide energy, and produce enzymes and hormones
    3. Essential amino acids are required in the diet because the body cannot manufacture them.
    4. High-quality proteins or complete proteins such as eggs, dairy products, meat, fish, and poultry contain adequate amounts of essential amino acids.
    5. Foods that do not contain the essential amino acids in sufficient amounts are lower-quality or incomplete proteins.
    6. Inadequate protein can cause protein energy **malnutrition** and severe wasting of fat and muscle tissue.
  D. Vitamins (Box 12-4)
    1. Facilitate **metabolism** of proteins, fats, and carbohydrates and act as catalysts for metabolic functions
    2. Promote life and growth processes and maintain and regulate body functions
    3. Fat-soluble vitamins A, D, E, and K can be stored in the body, so an excess can cause toxicity.
    4. The B vitamins and vitamin C are water-soluble vitamins, are not stored in the body, and can be excreted in the urine.
    5. Vitamin K acts as a catalyst for facilitating blood-clotting factors, especially prothrombin.
    6. Vitamin C functions in the production of collagen, a vital component in wound healing.
    7. Vitamin A maintains eyesight and epithelial linings.
  E. Minerals (Box 12-5)
    1. Components of hormones, cells, tissues, and bones
    2. Act as catalysts for chemical reactions and enhancers of cell function

---

BOX 12-1
Food Sources of Carbohydrates

CELLULOSE	STARCH
Apples	Barley
Beans	Beets, carrots, and peas
Bran	Corn
Cabbage	Oats
	Potatoes and pasta
FRUCTOSE	Rye
Fruits	Wheat
Honey	
	SUCROSE
GLUCOSE	Apricots
Carrots	Granulated table sugar
Corn	Honeydew and cantaloupe
Dates	Molasses
Grapes	Peaches
Oranges	Peas and corn
	Plums
LACTOSE	
Milk	

BOX 12-2
Food Sources of Fats

CHOLESTEROL	POLYUNSATURATED FATS
Animal products	Corn oil
Egg yolks	Safflower oil
Liver and organ meats	Sunflower oil
Shellfish	
	SATURATED FATS
MONOUNSATURATED FATS	Beef
Duck and goose	Butter
Eggs	Hard yellow cheeses
Olive and peanut oils	Luncheon meats

BOX 12-3
Food Sources of Protein

Bread and cereal products
Dairy products
Dried beans
Eggs
Meats, fish, and poultry

BOX 12-4
Food Sources of Vitamins

WATER-SOLUBLE VITAMINS
Folic acid: Green, leafy vegetables; liver, beef, and fish; legumes; grapefruit and oranges
Niacin: Meats, poultry, fish, beans, peanuts, grains
Vitamin B_1 (thiamine): Pork and nuts, whole-grain cereals, and legumes
Vitamin B_2 (riboflavin): Milk, lean meats, fish, grains
Vitamin B_6 (pyridoxine): Yeast, corn, meat, poultry, fish
Vitamin B_{12} (cobalamin): Meat, liver
Vitamin C (ascorbic acid): Citrus fruits, tomatoes, broccoli, cabbage

FAT-SOLUBLE VITAMINS
Vitamin A: Liver, egg yolk, whole milk, green or orange vegetables, fruits
Vitamin D: Fortified milk, fish oils, cereals
Vitamin E: Vegetable oils; green, leafy vegetables; cereals; apricots, apples, and peaches
Vitamin K: Green leafy vegetables; cauliflower and cabbage

BOX 12-5
Food Sources of Minerals

CALCIUM
Broccoli
Carrots
Cheese
Collard greens
Green beans
Milk
Rhubarb
Spinach
Tofu
Yogurt, low-fat

CHLORIDE
Salt

MAGNESIUM
Avocado
Canned white tuna
Cauliflower
Cooked rolled oats
Green leafy vegetables
Low-fat yogurt
Milk
Peanut butter
Peas
Pork, beef, chicken
Potatoes
Raisins

PHOSPHORUS
Fish
Nuts
Organ meats
Pork, beef, chicken
Whole-grain breads and cereals

POTASSIUM
Avocado
Bananas
Cantaloupe
Carrots
Fish

POTASSIUM—cont'd
Mushrooms
Oranges
Pork, beef, veal
Potatoes
Raisins
Spinach
Strawberries
Tomatoes

SODIUM
American cheese
Bacon
Butter
Canned food
Cottage cheese
Cured pork
Hot dogs
Ketchup
Lunch meat
Milk
Mustard
Processed food
Snack food
Soy sauce
Table salt
White and whole-wheat bread

IRON
Breads and cereals
Dark green vegetables
Egg yolk
Liver
Meats

ZINC
Eggs
Leafy vegetables
Meats
Protein-rich foods

3. Almost all foods contain some form of minerals.
4. A deficiency of minerals can occur in chronically ill or hospitalized clients.
5. Electrolytes play a major role in osmolality and body water regulation, acid-base balance, enzyme reactions, and neuromuscular activity (see Chap. 9 for additional information regarding electrolytes).

II. FOOD GUIDE PYRAMID (Fig. 12-1)
A. The food guide pyramid (MyPyramid)
 1. Provides individualized guidance to healthy eating and physical activity.
 2. Activity: Illustrated by the person climbing the steps in Figure 12-1; symbolizes the importance of finding a balance between food and physical activity
 3. Food groups, illustrated by the bands on the pyramid in Figure 12-1, include grains, vegetables, fruits, milk, and meat and beans.
 4. MyPyramid provides recommendations regarding physical activity and the amounts and types of foods for each food group.
B. Shape of the pyramid
 1. The wide base of each food group band on the pyramid indicates foods with little or no solid fats or added sugars; these are foods that should be eaten most often.
 2. The narrower part of the food group band indicates foods containing more added sugars and solid fats; these foods should be eaten less often

(increased activity is needed when these foods are eaten).

III. THERAPEUTIC DIETS
A. Clear liquid diet
 1. Indications
  a. Provides fluids and some electrolytes to prevent dehydration
  b. Used as an initial feeding after complete bowel rest

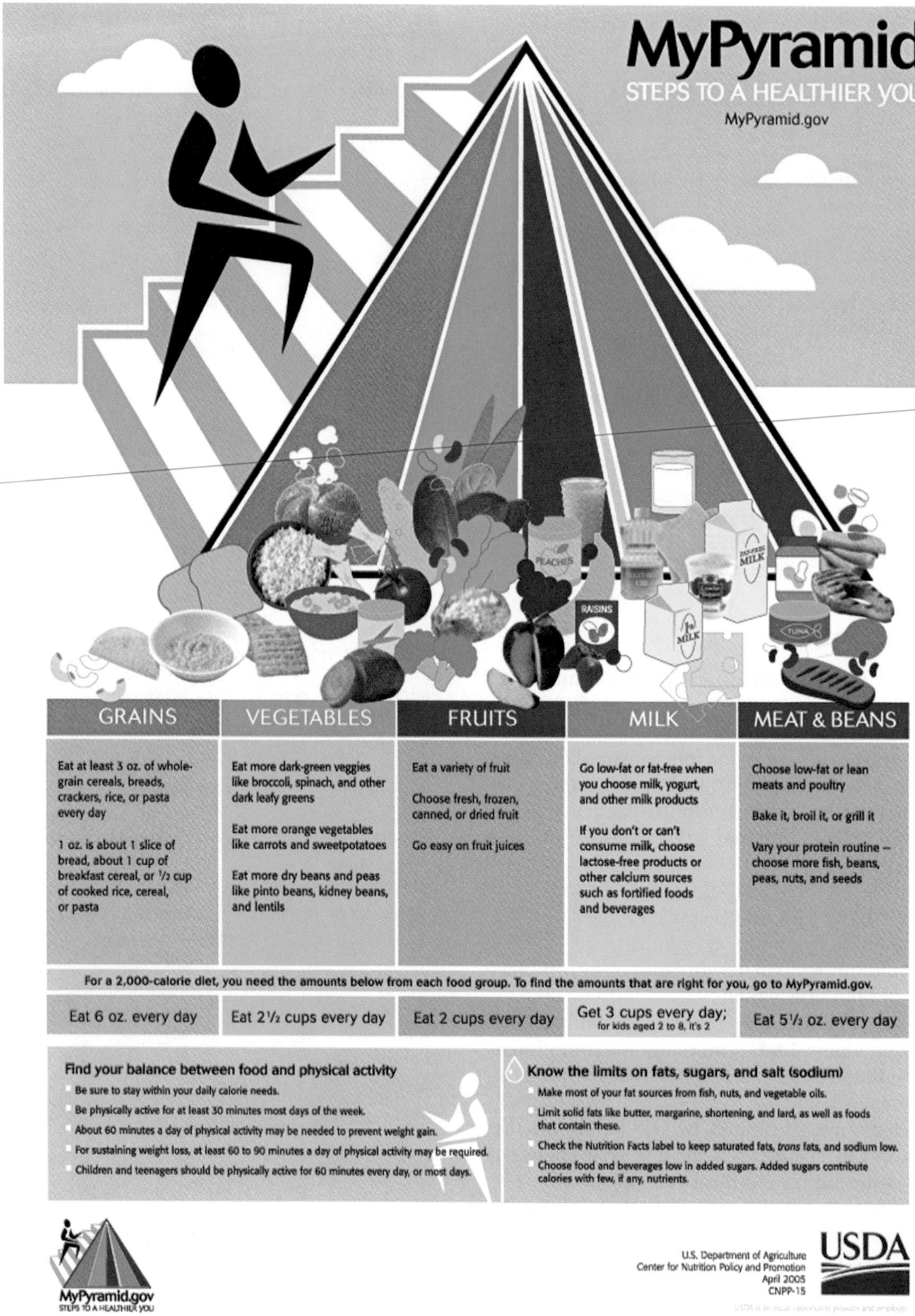

MyPyramid
STEPS TO A HEALTHIER YOU
MyPyramid.gov

GRAINS	VEGETABLES	FRUITS	MILK	MEAT & BEANS
Eat at least 3 oz. of whole-grain cereals, breads, crackers, rice, or pasta every day 1 oz. is about 1 slice of bread, about 1 cup of breakfast cereal, or ½ cup of cooked rice, cereal, or pasta	Eat more dark-green veggies like broccoli, spinach, and other dark leafy greens Eat more orange vegetables like carrots and sweetpotatoes Eat more dry beans and peas like pinto beans, kidney beans, and lentils	Eat a variety of fruit Choose fresh, frozen, canned, or dried fruit Go easy on fruit juices	Go low-fat or fat-free when you choose milk, yogurt, and other milk products If you don't or can't consume milk, choose lactose-free products or other calcium sources such as fortified foods and beverages	Choose low-fat or lean meats and poultry Bake it, broil it, or grill it Vary your protein routine — choose more fish, beans, peas, nuts, and seeds

For a 2,000-calorie diet, you need the amounts below from each food group. To find the amounts that are right for you, go to MyPyramid.gov.

Eat 6 oz. every day	Eat 2½ cups every day	Eat 2 cups every day	Get 3 cups every day; for kids aged 2 to 8, it's 2	Eat 5½ oz. every day

Find your balance between food and physical activity
- Be sure to stay within your daily calorie needs.
- Be physically active for at least 30 minutes most days of the week.
- About 60 minutes a day of physical activity may be needed to prevent weight gain.
- For sustaining weight loss, at least 60 to 90 minutes a day of physical activity may be required.
- Children and teenagers should be physically active for 60 minutes every day, or most days.

Know the limits on fats, sugars, and salt (sodium)
- Make most of your fat sources from fish, nuts, and vegetable oils.
- Limit solid fats like butter, margarine, shortening, and lard, as well as foods that contain these.
- Check the Nutrition Facts label to keep saturated fats, trans fats, and sodium low.
- Choose food and beverages low in added sugars. Added sugars contribute calories with few, if any, nutrients.

MyPyramid.gov
STEPS TO A HEALTHIER YOU

U.S. Department of Agriculture
Center for Nutrition Policy and Promotion
April 2005
CNPP-15

USDA

USDA is an equal opportunity provider and employer.

FIG. 12-1 MyPyramid. (From U.S. Department of Agriculture. http://www.mypyramid.gov.)

c. Used initially to feed a malnourished person or a person who has not had any oral intake for some time

d. Used for bowel preparation for surgery or tests and also postoperatively in clients with fever, vomiting, or diarrhea

e. Used for gastroenteritis or pancreatitis

2. Nursing considerations

a. Clear liquid diet is deficient in energy (calories) and many **nutrients**

b. Easily digested and absorbed

c. Contributes minimal residue in the gastrointestinal tract

d. Can be unappetizing and boring

e. Intended for short-term use or as a transition diet

f. Consists of clear liquids or foods that are relatively transparent to light and are liquid at body temperature

g. Foods include items such as water, clear fat-free broth or bouillon, clear carbonated beverages, gelatin, hard candy, lemonade, Popsicles, diluted fruit juices such as apple juice, and regular or decaffeinated coffee or tea.

h. The nurse should limit the amount of caffeine consumed by the client because caffeine can cause an upset stomach and sleeplessness.

i. The client may have salt or sugar.

j. Dairy products and fruit juices with pulp are not allowed.

B. Full liquid diet

1. Indication: May be used as a transition diet after clear liquids following surgery or for clients who have difficulty chewing, swallowing, or tolerating solid foods.

2. Nursing considerations

a. A full liquid diet is nutritionally deficient in energy (calories) and many **nutrients**.

b. The diet includes clear and opaque liquid foods and those that are liquid at body temperature.

c. Foods include all clear liquids and items such as plain ice cream, sherbet, breakfast drinks, milk, pudding and custard, soups that are strained, cream-based soups, refined cooked cereals, fruit juices, and strained vegetable juices.

d. Use of a complete nutritional liquid supplement is often necessary to meet nutrient needs for clients on a full liquid diet for more than 3 days.

C. Mechanically altered diet

1. Indications

a. Provides foods that have been mechanically altered in texture to require minimal chewing

b. Used for clients who have difficulty chewing but tolerate more variety in texture than a liquid diet offers

c. Used for clients who have dental problems, surgery of the head or neck, or dysphagia (requires swallowing evaluation and may require thickened liquids)

2. Nursing considerations

a. Degree of texture modification depends on individual need, including pureed, mashed, ground, or chopped.

b. Foods to be avoided in mechanically altered diets include nuts, dried fruits, raw fruits and vegetables, fried foods, tough, smoked, or salted meats, and foods with coarse textures.

D. Soft diet

1. Indications

a. Used for clients who have difficulty chewing or swallowing

b. Used for clients who have ulcerations of the mouth or gums, oral surgery, broken jaw, plastic surgery of the head or neck, or dysphagia or for the client who has had a stroke

2. Nursing considerations

a. Clients with mouth sores should be served foods at cooler temperatures.

b. Clients who have difficulty chewing and swallowing because of dry mouth can increase salivary flow by sucking on sour candy.

c. Encourage the client to eat a variety of foods.

d. Provide plenty of fluids with meals to ease chewing and swallowing of foods.

e. Drinking fluids through a straw may be easier than drinking from a cup or glass.

f. These are foods that normally have a soft texture and are not mechanically altered.

g. Foods that contain nuts or seeds, which easily can become trapped in the mouth and cause discomfort, need to be avoided.

h. Raw fruits and vegetables, fried foods, and whole grains need to be avoided.

E. Low-residue, low-fiber diet

1. Indications

a. Supplies foods that are least likely to form an obstruction when the intestinal tract is narrowed by inflammation or scarring or when gastrointestinal motility is slowed

b. Used during acute phases of gastrointestinal disorders such as diverticulitis, Crohn's disease, and ulcerative colitis

2. Nursing considerations

a. Foods that are low in residue include white bread, refined cooked cereals, cooked potatoes without skins, white rice, and refined pasta.

b. Foods to limit or avoid are raw fruits (except bananas), vegetables, nuts and seeds, plant fiber, and whole grains.

c. Dairy products should be limited to two servings a day.

F. High-fiber diet

1. Indication: Used for constipation, diverticulosis, diabetes mellitus, obesity, and hyperlipidemia

2. Nursing considerations

a. Provides 20 to 35 g of dietary fiber daily

b. Adds volume and weight to the stool and speeds the movement of undigested materials through the intestine

c. Consists of fruits and vegetables and whole grain products.

d. Increase fiber gradually and provide adequate fluids to reduce possible undesirable side effects such as abdominal cramps, bloating, diarrhea, and dehydration.

e. Gas-forming foods should be limited (Box 12-6)

G. Cardiac diet (Box 12-7; see Box 12-2)

1. Indications

a. Indicated for atherosclerosis, diabetes mellitus, hyperlipidemia, hypertension, myocardial infarction

b. Reduces the risk of heart disease

BOX 12-6

Gas-Forming Foods

Apples	Figs
Artichokes	Honey
Barley	Melons
Beans	Milk
Bran	Molasses
Broccoli	Nuts
Brussels sprouts	Onions
Cabbage	Radishes
Celery	Soybeans
Cherries	Wheat
Coconuts	Yeast
Eggplant	

BOX 12-7

Sodium-Free Spices and Flavorings

Allspice	Ginger
Almond extract	Lemon extract
Bay leaves	Maple extract
Caraway seeds	Marjoram
Cinnamon	Mustard powder
Curry powder	Nutmeg
Garlic powder or garlic	

---

2. Nursing consideration: Restricts saturated fat, *trans*-fat, cholesterol, and sodium

H. Fat-restricted diet

1. Indications

a. Used to reduce symptoms of abdominal pain, steatorrhea, flatulence, and diarrhea associated with high intakes of dietary fat, and to decrease nutrient losses caused by ingestion of dietary fat in individuals with malabsorptive disorders

b. Used for clients with malabsorption disorders, pancreatitis, gallbladder disease, and gastroesophageal reflux

2. Nursing considerations

a. Restricts amount of total fat, including saturated, *trans*-, polyunsaturated, and monounsaturated.

b. Clients with malabsorption may also have difficulty tolerating fiber and lactose.

c. Vitamin and mineral deficiencies may occur in clients with diarrhea or steatorrhea.

d. A fecal fat test indicates fat malabsorption with excretion of more than 6 to 8 g fat (or more than 10% of fat consumed) per day during the 3 days of specimen collection.

I. High-calorie, high-protein diet

1. Indication: Used for severe stress, burns, wounds, cancer, human immunodeficiency virus, acquired immunodeficiency syndrome, chronic obstructive pulmonary disease (COPD), respiratory failure, or any other type of debilitating disease

2. Nursing considerations

a. Encourage nutrient-dense, high-calorie, high-protein foods such as whole milk and milk products, peanut butter, nuts and seeds, beef, chicken, fish, pork, and eggs.

b. Some high-calorie foods include sugar, cream, gravy, oil, butter, mayonnaise, dried fruit, avocado, and honey.

c. Encourage snacks between meals, such as milkshakes, instant breakfasts, and nutritional supplements.

J. Carbohydrate-consistent diet

1. Indication: Used for clients with diabetes mellitus, hypoglycemia, hyperglycemia, and obesity

2. Nursing considerations

a. The Exchange System for Meal Planning, developed by the American Dietetic Association and the American Diabetes Association, is a food guide that may be recommended.

b. The Exchange System groups foods according to the amounts of the carbohydrates, fats, and proteins they contain.

c. Major food groups include the carbohydrate, meat and meat substitute, and fat groups.

K. Sodium-restricted diet (see Box 12-7)
1. Indication: Used for hypertension, congestive heart failure, renal disease, cardiac disease, and liver disease
2. Nursing considerations
   a. Individualized; can include 4 g of sodium daily (no added salt diet), 2 to 3 g of sodium daily (moderate restriction), 1 g of sodium daily (strict restriction), or 500 mg of sodium daily (severe and seldom prescribed)
   b. Encourage intake of fresh foods, rather than processed foods, which contain higher amounts of sodium.
   c. Canned, frozen, instant, smoked, pickled, and boxed foods usually contain higher amounts of sodium. Lunch meats, soy sauce, salad dressings, fast foods, soups, and snacks such as potato chips and pretzels also contain large amounts of sodium.
   d. Certain medications contain significant amounts of sodium.
   e. Salt substitutes may be used to improve palatability; most salt substitutes contain large amounts of potassium and should not be used by clients with renal disease.
L. Protein-restricted diet
1. Indication: Used for renal disease and liver disease.
2. Nursing considerations
   a. Provide enough protein to maintain nutritional status but not an amount that will allow the buildup of waste products from protein **metabolism** (40 to 60 g of protein daily).
   b. The less protein allowed, the more important it becomes that all protein in the diet be of high biological value (contain all essential amino acids in recommended proportions).
   c. An adequate total energy intake from foods is critical for clients on protein-restricted diets (protein will be used for energy, rather than for protein synthesis).
   d. Special low-protein products, such as pastas, bread, cookies, wafers, and gelatin made with wheat starch, can improve energy intake and add variety to the diet.
   e. Carbohydrates in powdered or liquid forms can provide additional energy.
   f. Vegetables and fruits contain some protein and, for very low-protein diets, these foods must be calculated into the diet.
   g. Foods are limited from the milk, meat, bread, and starch exchange.
M. Renal diet (see Boxes 12-3 and 12-5)
1. Indication: Used for the client with acute or chronic renal failure and those requiring hemodialysis or peritoneal dialysis

2. Nursing considerations
   a. Controlled amounts of protein, sodium, phosphorus, calcium, potassium, and fluids may be prescribed; may also need modification in fiber, cholesterol, and fat based on individual requirements.
   b. Most clients receiving dialysis need to restrict fluids (Box 12-8).
N. Potassium-modified diet (see Box 12-5)
1. Indications
   a. Low-potassium diet is indicated for hyperkalemia, which may be caused by impaired renal function, hypoaldosteronism, Addison's disease, angiotensin-converting enzyme inhibitor medications, immunosuppressive medications, potassium-sparing diuretics, and chronic hyperkalemia.
   b. High-potassium diet is indicated for hypokalemia, which may be caused by renal tubular acidosis, gastrointestinal losses (diarrhea, vomiting), intracellular shifts, potassium-wasting diuretics, antibiotics, mineralocorticoid or glucocorticoid excess resulting from primary or secondary aldosteronism, Cushing's syndrome, or exogenous steroid use.
2. Nursing considerations
   a. Foods that are low in potassium include applesauce, green beans, cabbage, lettuce, peppers, grapes, blueberries, cooked summer squash, cooked turnip greens, fresh pineapple and raspberries.
   b. Box 12-5 lists foods that are high in potassium.
O. High-calcium diet
1. Indication: Calcium is needed during bone growth and in adulthood to prevent osteoporosis and to facilitate vascular contraction, vasodilation, muscle contraction, and nerve transmission.
2. Nursing considerations
   a. Primary dietary sources of calcium are dairy products (see Chap. 9, Box 9-5, for food items high in calcium).
   b. Lactose-intolerant clients should incorporate nondairy sources of calcium into their diet regularly.
P. Low-purine diet
1. Indication: Used for gout, kidney stones, and elevated uric acid levels

---

BOX 12-8

Measures to Relieve Thirst

Chew gum or suck hard candy.
Freeze fluids so they take longer to consume.
Add lemon juice to water to make it more refreshing.
Gargle with refrigerated mouthwash.

2. Nursing considerations
   a. Purine is a precursor for uric acid, which forms stones and crystals.
   b. Foods to restrict include anchovies, herring, mackerel, sardines, scallops, glandular meats, gravies, meat extracts, wild game, goose, and sweetbreads.

Q. High-iron diet
   1. Indication: Used for clients with anemia
   2. Nursing considerations
      a. The high-iron diet replaces iron deficit from inadequate intake or loss.
      b. The diet includes organ meats, meat, egg yolks, whole-wheat products, dark green leafy vegetables, dried fruit, and legumes.

R. Miscellaneous diets: See Chapter 9, Boxes 9-3, 9-4, 9-6, and 9-7, for foods high in sodium, potassium, magnesium, and phosphorus, respectively.

IV. VEGETARIAN DIETS

A. Types (Box 12-9)
B. Nursing considerations
   1. Ensure that the client eats a sufficient amount of varied foods to meet nutrient and energy needs.
   2. Clients should be educated about consuming complementary proteins over the course of each day to ensure that all essential amino acids are provided.
   3. Potential deficiencies in vegetarian diets include energy, protein, vitamin B_{12}, zinc, iron, calcium, omega-3 fatty acids, and vitamin D (if limited exposure to sunlight).
   4. To enhance **absorption** of iron, vegetarians should include a good source of iron and vitamin C with each meal.
   5. Foods commonly eaten include tofu, tempeh, soy milk and soy products, meat analogues, legumes, nuts and seeds, sprouts, and a variety of fruits and vegetables.

BOX 12-9

Types of Vegetarian Diets

LACTO-OVO VEGETARIAN
Includes eggs and dairy products, but excludes meat, poultry, and seafood

LACTO VEGETARIAN
Includes dairy products, but excludes eggs, meat, poultry, and seafood

VEGAN
Excludes animal products

PESCO VEGETARIAN
Includes seafood, but excludes meat, poultry, eggs, and dairy products

---

6. Soy protein is considered equivalent in quality to animal protein.

V. ENTERAL NUTRITION

A. Description: Provides liquefied foods into the gastrointestinal tract via a tube
B. Indications
   1. When the gastrointestinal tract is functional but oral intake is not meeting estimated nutrient needs
   2. Used for clients with swallowing problems, burns, major trauma, liver or other organ failure, or severe **malnutrition**
C. Nursing considerations
   1. Clients with lactose intolerance need to be placed on lactose-free formulas.
   2. See Chapter 21 for information regarding the administration of gastrointestinal tube feedings.

PRACTICE QUESTIONS

1. The nurse instructs a client with renal failure who is receiving hemodialysis about dietary modifications. The nurse determines that the client understands these dietary modifications if the client selects which items from the dietary menu?
   1. Cream of wheat, blueberries, coffee
   2. Sausage and eggs, banana, orange juice
   3. Bacon, cantaloupe melon, tomato juice
   4. Cured pork, grits, strawberries, orange juice

2. The nurse is conducting a dietary assessment on a client who is on a vegan diet. The nurse plans to provide dietary teaching focusing on foods high in which vitamin that may be lacking in a vegan diet?
   1. Vitamin A
   2. Vitamin B_{12}
   3. Vitamin C
   4. Vitamin E

3. A client with hypertension has been told to maintain a diet low in sodium. A nurse who is teaching this client about foods that are allowed would plan to include which food item in a list provided to the client?
   1. Tomato soup
   2. Boiled shrimp
   3. Instant oatmeal
   4. Summer squash

4. A client who is recovering from surgery has been advanced from a clear liquid diet to a full liquid diet. The client is looking forward to the diet change because he has been "bored" with the clear liquid diet. The nurse would offer which full liquid item to the client?
   1. Tea
   2. Gelatin

3. Custard
4. Popsicle
5. The nurse is teaching a client who has iron deficiency anemia about foods she should include in her diet. The nurse determines that the client understands the dietary modifications if she selects which of the following from her menu?
   1. Nuts and milk
   2. Coffee and tea
   3. Cooked rolled oats and fish
   4. Oranges and dark green leafy vegetables
6. A nurse is planning to teach a client with malabsorption syndrome about the necessity of following a low-fat diet. The nurse develops a list of high-fat foods to avoid and includes which food item on the list?
   1. Oranges
   2. Broccoli
   3. Cream cheese
   4. Broiled haddock
7. A client who recently has been started on enteral feedings begins to complain of abdominal cramping, followed by the passage of two liquid stools. A nurse notes that the client has abdominal distention as well. The nurse reviews the nutritional content on the label of the can of feeding to see if it has which of the following ingredients?
   1. Lactose
   2. Sucrose
   3. Fructose
   4. Maltose
8. A client is recovering from abdominal surgery and has a large abdominal wound. A nurse encourages the client to eat which food item that is naturally high in vitamin C to promote wound healing?
   1. Milk
   2. Oranges

3. Bananas
4. Chicken
9. A nurse is caring for a client with cirrhosis of the liver. To minimize the effects of the disorder, the nurse teaches the client about foods that are high in thiamine. The nurse determines that the client has the best understanding of the dietary measures to follow if the client states an intention to increase the intake of:
   1. Pork
   2. Milk
   3. Chicken
   4. Broccoli
10. The nurse is instructing a client with hypertension on the importance of choosing foods low in sodium. The nurse should teach the client to limit which of the following foods?
    1. Apples
    2. Bananas
    3. Smoked sausage
    4. Steamed vegetables

ALTERNATE ITEM FORMAT: MULTIPLE RESPONSE

A postoperative client has been placed on a clear liquid diet. Select the items that the client is allowed to consume on this diet. Select all that apply.
❏ 1. Broth
❏ 2. Coffee
❏ 3. Gelatin
❏ 4. Pudding
❏ 5. Vegetable juice
❏ 6. Pureed vegetables

ANSWERS

1. **1**
Rationale: The diet for a client with renal failure who is receiving hemodialysis should include controlled amounts of sodium, phosphorus, calcium, potassium, and fluids. Options 2, 3, and 4 are high in sodium, phosphorus and potassium.
Test-Taking Strategy: Use the process of elimination and focus on the client's diagnosis. Noting the items sausage (option 2), bacon (option 3), and cured pork (option 4) will assist in eliminating these options. Review dietary guidelines for the client with renal failure if you had difficulty with this question.
Level of Cognitive Ability: Analysis
Client Needs: Physiological Integrity
Integrated Process: Nursing Process/Evaluation
Content Area: Adult health—renal

Reference: Lewis, S., Heitkemper, M., & Dirksen, S. (2004). *Medical-surgical nursing: Assessment and management of clinical problems* (6th ed., p. 1215). St. Louis: Mosby.

2. **2**
Rationale: Vegans do not consume any animal products. Vitamin B_{12} is found in animal products and therefore would most likely be lacking in a vegan diet. Vitamins A, C, and E are found in fresh fruits and vegetables, which are consumed in a vegan diet.
Test-Taking Strategy: Focus on the subject, a vegan diet. Recalling the food items eaten and restricted in this diet will direct you to the correct option. Review vegan diets and sources of vitamins if you had difficulty with this question.
Level of Cognitive Ability: Application
Client Needs: Health Promotion and Maintenance
Integrated Process: Teaching and Learning

Content Area: Fundamental Skills
Reference: Lewis, S., Heitkemper, M., & Dirksen, S. (2004). *Medical-surgical nursing: Assessment and management of clinical problems* (6th ed., p. 972). St. Louis: Mosby.

3. **4**
Rationale: Foods that are lower in sodium include fruits and vegetables (option 4), because they do not contain physiological saline. Highly processed or refined foods (options 1 and 3) are higher in sodium unless their food labels specifically state "low sodium." Saltwater fish and shellfish are high in sodium.
Test-Taking Strategy: Use the process of elimination. Begin to answer this question by eliminating option 2, recalling that saltwater fish and shellfish are high in sodium. Next, eliminate options 1 and 3 because they are processed foods. Review the foods that are high in sodium if you had difficulty with this question.
Level of Cognitive Ability: Application
Client Needs: Physiological Integrity
Integrated Process: Teaching and Learning
Content Area: Adult health—cardiovascular
References: Grodner, M., Long, S., & DeYoung, S. (2004). *Foundations and clinical applications of nutrition: A nursing approach* (3rd ed., p. 609). St. Louis: Mosby.
Nix, S. (2005). *Williams basic nutrition and diet therapy* (12th ed., p. 359). St. Louis: Mosby.

4. **3**
Rationale: Full liquid food items include items such as plain ice cream, sherbet, breakfast drinks, milk, pudding and custard, soups that are strained, and strained vegetable juices. A clear liquid diet consists of foods that are relatively transparent. The food items in options 1, 2, and 4 are clear liquids.
Test-Taking Strategy: Focus on the subject, a full liquid item. Remember that a clear liquid diet consists of foods that are relatively transparent. This will assist you in eliminating options 1, 2, and 4. Review food items allowed on a clear liquid diet and a full liquid diet if you had difficulty with this question.
Level of Cognitive Ability: Application
Client Needs: Physiological Integrity
Integrated Process: Nursing Process/Implementation
Content Area: Adult health—gastrointestinal
Reference: Grodner, M., Long, S., & DeYoung, S. (2004). *Foundations and clinical applications of nutrition: A nursing approach* (3rd ed., p. 417). St. Louis: Mosby.

5. **4**
Rationale: Dark green leafy vegetables are a good source of iron and oranges are a good source of vitamin C, which enhances iron absorption. All other options are not food sources that are high in iron and vitamin C.
Test-Taking Strategy: Use knowledge of foods high in iron and vitamin C and recall that vitamin C enhances iron absorption. Use the process of elimination to eliminate options 1, 2, and 3 because they do not contain sources of iron and vitamin C. Review food sources of vitamins and minerals if you had difficulty with this question.
Level of Cognitive Ability: Analysis
Client Needs: Physiological Integrity
Integrated Process: Nursing Process/Evaluation

Content Area: Fundamental skills
Reference: Mahan, L. K., & Escott-Stump, S. (2004). *Krause's food, nutrition, & diet therapy* (11th ed., p. 544). Philadelphia: W.B. Saunders.

6. **3**
Rationale: Fruits and vegetables tend to be lower in fat because they do not come from animal sources. Fish is also naturally lower in fat. Cream cheese is a high-fat food.
Test-Taking Strategy: Use the process of elimination and focus on the subject of the question, the high-fat food. Options 1 and 2 (fruit and vegetable) can be eliminated first. From the remaining options, remember that cheese is high in fat content. Review foods that are high in fat content if you had difficulty with this question.
Level of Cognitive Ability: Application
Client Needs: Health Promotion and Maintenance
Integrated Process: Teaching and Learning
Content Area: Adult health—cardiovascular
Reference: Grodner, M., Long, S., & DeYoung, S. (2004). *Foundations and clinical applications of nutrition: A nursing approach* (3rd ed., p. 123). St. Louis: Mosby.

7. **1**
Rationale: Several tube feeding formulas contain lactose. A client with an unreported history of lactose intolerance would develop symptoms such as abdominal cramping, distention, and the passage of liquid stool in response to nutritional therapy with these formulas. If the client is diagnosed as lactose intolerant, a lactose-free formula should be prescribed by the physician. This will resolve the client's symptoms and promote adequate nutrition for the client.
Test-Taking Strategy: Focus on the data in the question. Recalling the association of the symptoms experienced by the client with the symptoms of lactose intolerance will direct you to the correct option. If you had difficulty with this question, review the symptoms of lactose intolerance and the nursing considerations related to enteral feedings.
Level of Cognitive Ability: Analysis
Client Needs: Physiological Integrity
Integrated Process: Nursing Process/Assessment
Content Area: Fundamental skills
Reference: Nix, S. (2005). *Williams basic nutrition and diet therapy* (12th ed., p. 26). St. Louis: Mosby.

8. **2**
Rationale: Citrus fruits and juices are especially high in vitamin C. Bananas are high in potassium. Meats and dairy products are two food groups that are high in the B vitamins.
Test-Taking Strategy: Note the strategic words *naturally high* in the question. Use the process of elimination, recalling that citrus fruits and juices are high in vitamin C. Review the foods high in vitamin C if you are unfamiliar with them.
Level of Cognitive Ability: Application
Client Needs: Health Promotion and Maintenance
Integrated Process: Teaching and Learning
Content Area: Fundamental skills
Reference: Grodner, M., Long, S., & DeYoung, S. (2004). *Foundations and clinical applications of nutrition: A nursing approach* (3rd ed., pp. 180-181). St. Louis: Mosby.

9. 1
Rationale: The client with cirrhosis needs to consume foods high in thiamine. Thiamine is present in a variety of foods of plant and animal origin. Pork products are especially rich in this vitamin. Other good food sources include nuts, whole grain cereals, and legumes. Milk contains vitamins A, D, and B$_2$. Poultry contains niacin. Broccoli contains vitamins C, E, and K and folic acid.
Test-Taking Strategy: Note the strategic words *best understanding* in the stem of the question. This may indicate that more than one option may be a food that contains thiamine. Remembering that pork products are especially rich in thiamine will direct you to option 1. Review food items high in thiamine if you had difficulty with this question.
Level of Cognitive Ability: Analysis
Client Needs: Physiological Integrity
Integrated Process: Nursing Process—evaluation
Content Area: Adult health—gastrointestinal
Reference: Grodner, M., Long, S., & DeYoung, S. (2004). *Foundations and clinical applications of nutrition: A nursing approach* (3rd ed., p. 170). St. Louis: Mosby.

10. 3
Rationale: Smoked foods are high in sodium. Options 1, 2, and 4 are fruits and vegetables that are low in sodium.
Test-Taking Strategy: Note the strategic word *limit* and use the process of elimination, recalling the food items that are high in sodium. If you had difficulty with this question, review foods high in sodium.
Level of Cognitive Ability: Application
Client Needs: Physiological Integrity

Integrated Process: Teaching and Learning
Content Area: Adult health—cardiovascular
Reference: Barker, H., & Aldrich, C. (2004). *Nutrition and dietetics for health care* (10th ed., p. 247). Edinburgh: Churchill Livingstone.

ALTERNATE ITEM FORMAT: MULTIPLE RESPONSE

Answer: 1, 2, 3
Rationale: A clear liquid diet consists of foods that are relatively transparent to light and are clear and liquid at room and body temperature. These foods include items such as water, bouillon, clear broth, carbonated beverages, gelatin, hard candy, lemonade, Popsicles, and regular or decaffeinated coffee or tea. The incorrect food items are items that are allowed on a full liquid diet.
Test-Taking Strategy: Focus on the subject, a clear liquid diet. Recalling that a clear liquid diet consists of foods that are relatively transparent to light and are clear will assist in answering the question. Review foods allowed on a clear and full liquid diet if you had difficulty with this question.
Level of Cognitive Ability: Application
Client Needs: Physiological Integrity
Integrated Process: Nursing Process—implementation
Content Area: Fundamental skills
References: Grodner, M., Long, S., & DeYoung, S. (2004). *Foundations and clinical applications of nutrition: A nursing approach* (3rd ed., pp. 415-417). St. Louis: Mosby.
Potter, P., & Perry, A. (2005). *Fundamentals of nursing* (6th ed., p. 1298). St. Louis: Mosby.

REFERENCES

Barker, H., & Aldrich, C. (2004). *Nutrition and dietetics for health care* (10th ed.). Edinburgh: Churchill Livingstone.
Grodner, M., Long, S., & DeYoung, S. (2004). *Foundations and clinical applications of nutrition: A nursing approach* (3rd ed.). St. Louis: Mosby.
Hodgson, B., & Kizior, R. (2007). *Saunders nursing drug handbook 2007*. Philadelphia: W.B. Saunders.
Ignatavicius, D. & Workman, M. (2006). *Medical-surgical nursing: Critical thinking for collaborative care* (5th ed.). Philadelphia: W.B. Saunders.
Mahan, L. K., & Escott-Stump, S. (2004). *Krause's food, nutrition, & diet therapy* (11th ed.). Philadelphia: W.B. Saunders.
National Council of State Boards of Nursing (Eds.). (2007). *2007 NCLEX-RN® detailed test plan*. Chicago: Author.
Nix, S. (2005). *Williams basic nutrition and diet therapy* (12th ed.). St. Louis: Mosby.
Potter, P., & Perry, A. (2005). *Fundamentals of nursing* (6th ed.). St. Louis: Mosby.

13

Parenteral Nutrition

PYRAMID TERMS

fat emulsion (lipids) Preparation administered during parenteral nutrition therapy to prevent fatty acid deficiency.

parenteral nutrition (PN) The administration of nutrition through a central or peripheral intravenous catheter; also known as hyperalimentation.

peripheral parenteral nutrition (PPN) Parenteral nutrition administered through a peripheral vein in an extremity; also known as partial parenteral nutrition.

total parenteral nutrition (TPN) Parenteral nutrition administered through a central vein, such as the subclavian vein; also known as central parenteral nutrition.

▲ THE PYRAMID TO SUCCESS

The NCLEX-RN examination test plan addresses parenteral nutrition (PN) as related content in the Client Needs area of Physiological Integrity, Pharmacological and Parenteral Therapies. Pyramid Points focus on the administration of PN and fat emulsions, nursing interventions, and the interventions required in monitoring for complications. Pyramid Points also focus on home care instructions for the client receiving PN at home. Integrated Processes addressed in this chapter are Communication and Documentation, Caring, Nursing Process, and Teaching/Learning.

▲ CLIENT NEEDS

Safe and Effective Care Environment

Consulting with members of the health care team, including the dietitian

Handling hazardous and infectious materials

Initiating home health care referral

Maintaining medical and surgical asepsis to prevent infection

Maintaining standard, transmission-based, and other precautions

Obtaining informed consent for venous access and placement of the catheter

Health Promotion and Maintenance

Promoting health and wellness related to nutrition

Providing client and family education regarding monitoring for complications

Providing client and family education regarding the administration of PN at home

Psychosocial Integrity

Discussing role changes related to the client's need to receive PN

Identifying support systems in the home to assist with the administration of PN

Physiological Integrity

Assessing the central venous access device for administering TPN

Monitoring for expected effects

Monitoring laboratory values

Monitoring nutritional needs

Monitoring for potential complications

Providing comfort and assistance in the performance of activities of daily living

Promoting rest and sleep

▲

I. PARENTERAL NUTRITION (PN)

A. Description

  1. Supplies nutrients via the veins

  2. Supplies carbohydrates in the form of dextrose, fats in an emulsified form, proteins in the form

of amino acids, vitamins, minerals, electrolytes, and water

3. Prevents subcutaneous fat and muscle protein from being catabolized by the body for energy

B. Indications

1. Clients with severely dysfunctional or nonfunctional gastrointestinal tracts who are unable to process nutrients may benefit from **PN**.

2. Clients who can take some oral nutrition, but not enough to meet their nutrient requirements, may benefit from **PN**.

3. Clients with multiple gastrointestinal surgeries, gastrointestinal trauma, severe intolerance to enteral feedings, or intestinal obstructions, or who need to rest the bowel for healing, may benefit from **PN**.

4. Clients with acquired immunodeficiency syndrome, cancer, burn injuries, malnutrition, or clients receiving chemotherapy may benefit from **PN**.

5. **PN** is the least desirable form of nutrition and is used when there is no other nutritional alternative.

C. **Types of PN** (Fig. 13-1)

1. Total parenteral nutrition (TPN)

   a. **TPN** is administered through central access when the client requires a larger concentration of carbohydrates (higher than 10% glucose concentration).

   b. The subclavian or internal jugular veins are used when **TPN** is a short-term intervention (shorter than 4 weeks).

   c. When **TPN** is anticipated for an extended period (longer than 4 weeks), a more permanent catheter, such as a peripherally inserted central catheter (PICC) line, a tunneled catheter, or an implanted vascular access device, is used.

2. **Peripheral parenteral nutrition (PPN)**

   a. **Peripheral parenteral nutrition** is administered through a peripheral vein, typically in the arm.

   b. **Peripheral parenteral nutrition** is used for short periods (5 to 7 days) and when the client needs only small concentrations of carbohydrates, fats, and proteins.

   c. **Peripheral parenteral nutrition** is used to deliver isotonic or mildly hypertonic solutions; the delivery of highly hypertonic solutions into peripheral veins can cause sclerosis, phlebitis, or swelling.

II. COMPONENTS OF PARENTERAL NUTRITION

A. Carbohydrates

1. Mainly in the form of dextrose (glucose), with concentrations ranging from 5% to 70%.

2. The strength of the dextrose solution prescribed depends on the client's nutritional needs and on agency protocols.

3. Typically provide 60% to 70% of calorie (energy) needs.

4. Dextrose provides 3.4 kcal/g.

B. Amino acids

1. Concentrations range from 3.5% to 20%; lower concentrations are most commonly used for **PPN** and higher concentrations are most often administered through a central vein.

2. Amino acid solutions provide approximately 4 kcal/g of protein.

3. About 15% to 20% of total energy needs should come from protein.

C. **Fat emulsion (lipids)**

1. Provides up to 30% of calorie (energy) needs

2. Provides nonprotein calories and prevents or corrects fatty acid deficiency

3. Available in concentrations of 10%, 20%, and 30%, providing 1.1, 2.0, and 3.0 kcal/mL, respectively

4. Lipid solutions are isotonic and therefore can be administered through a peripheral or central vein.

5. Most **fat emulsions** are prepared from soybean or safflower oil with egg yolk to provide emulsification; the primary components are linoleic, oleic, palmitic, linolenic, and stearic acids.

6. **Lipids** contain egg yolk phospholipids, and should not be given to clients with egg allergies.

7. Glucose-intolerant clients or clients with diabetes mellitus may benefit from receiving a larger percentage of their **PN** from **lipids**; this can help control blood glucose levels and lower insulin requirements caused by infused dextrose.

8. Examine the bottle for separation of emulsion into layers or fat globules or for the accumula-

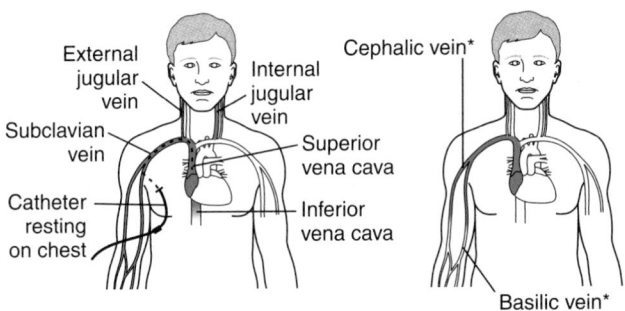

Central line access

External jugular vein
Subclavian vein
Catheter resting on chest
Internal jugular vein
Superior vena cava
Inferior vena cava

Peripheral line access

Cephalic vein*
Basilic vein*

* Access points for catheter (long line) peripheral feeding. Peripheral feeding using a cannula device may be administered through any vein.

FIG. 13-1 Parenteral nutrition access routes. (From Byrom, S.E. [2002]. *Pocket guide to nutrition and dietetics.* Edinburgh: Churchill Livingstone.)

BOX 13-1

Signs of an Adverse Reaction to Lipids

Chest and back pain
Chills
Cyanosis
Diaphoresis
Dyspnea
Fever
Flushing
Headache
Nausea and vomiting
Pressure over the eyes
Thrombophlebitis
Vertigo

---

tion of froth; if observed, do not use and return the solution to the pharmacy.

9. Additives should not be put into the **fat emulsion** solution.

10. Infuse solution initially at 1 mL/min, monitor vital signs every 10 minutes, and observe for adverse reactions for the first 30 minutes of the infusion; if signs of an adverse reaction occur, stop the infusion and notify the physician (Box 13-1).

11. If no adverse reaction occurs, adjust the flow rate to the prescribed rate.

12. Monitor serum **lipids** 4 hours after discontinuing the infusion.

D. Vitamins
  1. **PN** solutions usually contain a standard multivitamin preparation to meet most vitamin needs and prevent deficiencies.
  2. Individual vitamin preparations can be added, as needed.

E. Minerals and trace elements: Commercial mineral and trace element preparations are available in different concentrations to promote normal metabolism.

F. Water: The amount of water needed in a **PN** solution is determined by electrolyte balance and fluid requirements.

G. Electrolytes: Electrolyte requirements for individuals receiving **PN** therapy vary, depending on body weight, presence of malnutrition or catabolism, degree of electrolyte depletion, changes in organ function, ongoing electrolyte losses, and the disease process.

H. Insulin: May be added to control the blood glucose level because of the high concentration of glucose in the **PN** solution.

I. Heparin: may be added to reduce the buildup of a fibrinous clot at the catheter tip.

III. ADMINISTRATION

A. Types of infusion
  1. Continuous **PN**
    a. Infused continuously over 24 hours
    b. Most commonly used in a hospital setting
    c. Less risk of complications
  2. Cyclic **PN**
    a. Generally are 8- to 16-hour infusions that are usually given at night
    b. Allows client requiring **PN** on long-term basis to participate in activities of daily living without inconvenience of IV bag and pump set
    c. Monitor glucose levels closely
    d. Preferable for use in home settings

B. Types of **PN** solutions
  1. 2-in-1 solution
    a. Combines dextrose and amino acids in one solution.
    b. An in-line filter (0.22 μm) is placed in the dextrose–amino acid line to ensure sterility.
    c. **Lipids** are administered peripherally or by "piggybacking" them into the central line via a Y connector.
    d. **Lipids** are administered through separate tubing attached below the filter of the main IV administration because particles in the **fat emulsion** are too large to pass through filters.
  2. Total nutrient admixture (TNA), or 3-in-1 solutions
    a. Combines dextrose, amino acids, and **lipids** in one solution.
    b. A 1.2-μm filter or larger should be used because the lipid particles are too large to pass through a 0.22-μm filter.

C. Discontinuing **PN** therapy
  1. Gradually decrease the flow rate for 1 to 2 hours while increasing oral intake (this assists in preventing hypoglycemia).
  2. After removing the catheter, change the dressing daily until the wound heals.
  3. Encourage oral nourishment.
  4. Record oral intake, body weight, and laboratory results of serum electrolyte and glucose levels.

IV. COMPLICATIONS

A. Description
  1. Pneumothorax and air embolism are associated with central line placement; air embolism is also associated with tubing changes (Table 13-1).
  2. Other complications include infection (catheter-related), hypervolemia, and metabolic alterations such as hyperglycemia and hypoglycemia; these complications are usually caused by the **parenteral nutrition** solution itself.

B. Air embolism
  1. Instruct the client in the Valsalva maneuver for IV tubing and cap changes.
  2. For tubing and cap changes, place the client in the Trendelenburg position (if not contraindicated) with the head turned in the opposite di-

TABLE 13-1

Complications of Parenteral Nutrition (PN)

Complication	Possible Cause	Signs or Symptoms	Intervention	Prevention
Air embolism	Catheter system opened or IV tubing disconnected Air entry on IV tubing changes	Apprehension Chest pain Dyspnea Hypotension Loud churning sound heard over pericardium on auscultation Rapid and weak pulse Respiratory distress	Clamp the catheter. Place the client in a left-side lying position with the head lower than the feet. Notify the physician. Administer oxygen.	Make sure all catheter connections are secure. Clamp the catheter when not in use. Instruct the client in the Valsalva maneuver for tubing and cap changes. For tubing and cap changes, place the client in the Trendelenburg position (if not contraindicated), with the head turned in the opposite direction of the insertion site.
Hyperglycemia	Client receiving solution too quickly Not enough insulin Infection	Coma (when severe) Confusion Diaphoresis Elevated blood glucose level (>200 mg/dL) Excessive thirst Fatigue Kussmaul's respirations Restlessness Weakness	Notify the physician. The infusion rate may need to be slowed. Administer Regular insulin as prescribed. Monitor blood glucose levels.	Assess the client for a history of glucose intolerance. Assess the client's medication history. Begin infusion at a slow rate as prescribed. Monitor blood glucose levels. Use strict aseptic technique.
Hypervolemia	Excessive fluid administration or administration of fluid too rapidly Renal dysfunction Heart failure Hepatic failure	Bounding pulse Crackles on lung auscultation Headache Increased blood pressure Jugular vein distention Weight gain greater than desired	Slow or stop IV infusion. Restrict fluids. Administer diuretics. Use dialysis (in extreme cases).	Assess client's history for risk for hypervolemia. Administer solution via an electronic infusion device. Monitor intake and output. Monitor weight daily.
Hypoglycemia	PN abruptly discontinued Too much insulin being administered	Anxiety Diaphoresis Hunger Low blood glucose level (<70 mg/dL) Shakiness Weakness	Intravenous dextrose is administered. Monitor blood glucose level.	Gradually decrease PN solution when discontinued. Infuse 10% dextrose at same rate as the PN to prevent hypoglycemia when the PN solution is discontinued. Monitor glucose levels when insulin is being given.

Continued

rection of the insertion site (increases intrathoracic venous pressure).

3. Check all catheter connections and secure (use tape per agency protocol) tubing connections.

4. If an air embolism is suspected, do the following:

a. Clamp the intravenous catheter.

b. Place the client in a left side-lying position with the head lower than the feet (to trap air in right side of the heart).

c. Notify the physician.

d. Administer oxygen as prescribed.

TABLE 13-1

Complications of Parenteral Nutrition (PN)—cont'd

Complication	Possible Cause	Signs or Symptoms	Intervention	Prevention
Infection	Poor aseptic technique Catheter contamination Contamination of solution	Chills Fever Elevated white blood cell count Erythema or drainage at insertion site	Remove catheter. Send the catheter tip to the laboratory for culture. Prepare to obtain blood cultures. Prepare for antibiotic administration.	Use strict aseptic techniques. Monitor temperature. Assess IV site for signs of infection. Change site dressing, solution, and tubing as specified by agency policy. Do not disconnect tubing unnecessarily.
Pneumothorax	Incorrect catheter placement	Absence of breath sounds on affected side Chest or shoulder pain Sudden shortness of breath Tachycardia Cyanosis	Small pneumothorax may resolve. Larger pneumothorax may require chest tube.	Monitor for signs of pneumothorax. Obtain a chest x-ray after insertion of the catheter to ensure proper catheter placement. PN is not initiated until correct catheter placement is verified and the absence of pneumothorax is confirmed.

C. Hyperglycemia
1. Assess the client for a history of glucose intolerance.
2. Assess the client's medication history (corticosteroids may increase the blood glucose level).
3. Begin infusion at a slow rate (usually 40 to 60 mL/hr) as prescribed.
4. Monitor blood glucose levels every 4 to 6 hours or according to agency protocol.
5. Administer Regular insulin as prescribed.

D. Hypervolemia
1. Hypervolemia occurs if the client receives the IV solution too rapidly.
2. **Parenteral nutrition** is always delivered via an electronic infusion device.
3. Never increase the infusion rate to "catch up" if the IV infusion gets behind.
4. Monitor intake and output.
5. Weigh the client daily (ideal weight gain is 1 to 2 lb/week).

E. Hypoglycemia
1. Monitor the blood glucose level.
2. Gradually decrease the infusion when discontinuing **PN**.
3. When an infusion of hypertonic glucose is stopped, an infusion of 10% dextrose should be instituted and maintained for 1 to 2 hours to prevent hypoglycemia.
4. Assess blood glucose level 1 hour after discontinuing **PN**.
5. Prepare for the administration of glucose or intravenous dextrose if hypoglycemia occurs.

F. Infection
1. Use strict aseptic technique; because the **PN** solution has a high concentration of glucose, it is a medium for bacterial growth.
2. Monitor temperature; in the event of fever, suspect sepsis.
3. Assess the IV site for redness, swelling, tenderness, or drainage.
4. Change **PN** solution every 12 to 24 hours or according to agency protocol.
5. Change IV tubing every 24 hours or according to agency protocol.
6. Change dressing at the IV site every 48 hours or according to agency protocol.
7. If signs of infection occur at the site, do the following:
   a. The IV line must be removed and restarted at a different site.
   b. Remove the tip of the IV catheter and send it to the laboratory for culture.
   c. Prepare the client for blood cultures.

G. Pneumothorax
1. Monitor for signs of pneumothorax.
2. After insertion of the catheter, obtain a portable chest x-ray film to confirm correct catheter placement and to detect the presence of a pneumothorax; **parenteral nutrition** is not initiated until verification of correct catheter placement and the absence of pneumothorax.
3. After confirmation of catheter placement and the absence of pneumothorax, **parenteral nutrition** is initiated.

V. ADDITIONAL NURSING CONSIDERATIONS

A. Always check the **PN** solution with the physician's order to ensure that the prescribed components are contained in the solution.

B. To prevent infection and solution incompatibility, IV medications and blood are not given through the **PN** line.

C. Monitor partial thromboplastin time and prothrombin time for clients receiving anticoagulants.

D. Monitor electrolyte and albumin levels and liver and renal function studies.

E. In severely dehydrated clients, the albumin level may drop initially, because the treatment restores hydration.

F. With severely malnourished clients, monitor for "refeeding syndrome" (a rapid drop in potassium, magnesium, and phosphate serum levels).

G. Abnormal liver function values may indicate intolerance to or an excess of **fat emulsion** or problems with metabolism with glucose and protein.

H. Abnormal renal function tests may indicate an excess of amino acids.

I. **Parenteral nutrition** solutions should be stored under refrigeration and administered within 24 hours from the time that they were prepared (remove from refrigerator 0.5 to 1 hour before use).

J. **Parenteral nutrition** solutions that are cloudy or darkened should not be used and should be returned to the pharmacy.

K. Additions to **PN** solutions should be made in the pharmacy and not on the nursing unit.

VI. HOME CARE INSTRUCTIONS (Box 13-2)

BOX 13-2
Home Care Instructions

Teach caregiver how to administer and maintain parenteral nutrition fluids.

Teach caregiver how to change a sterile dressing.

Obtain a daily weight at the same time of day in the same clothes.

Stress that a weight gain of more than 3 lb/week may indicate excessive fluid intake and should be reported.

Monitor the blood glucose level and report abnormalities immediately.

Check for signs and symptoms of infection, thrombosis, air embolism, and catheter displacement.

Instruct in the importance of reporting signs and symptoms of complications.

Symptoms of an air embolus should be taught to another person in the client's home.

For symptoms of thrombosis, the client should report edema of the arm or at the catheter insertion site, neck pain, and jugular vein distention.

Leaking of fluid from the insertion site or pain or discomfort as the fluids are infused may indicate displacement of the catheter; this must be reported immediately.

PRACTICE QUESTIONS

1. The nurse plans care for a client receiving total parenteral nutrition (TPN), understanding that which of the following statements regarding TPN and peripheral parenteral nutrition (PPN) is true?
   1. TPN is usually indicated for clients needing long-term nutritional support, whereas PPN is for short-term support.
   2. TPN is used to deliver isotonic or mildly hypertonic solutions, whereas PPN is used to deliver highly hypertonic solutions.
   3. PPN is indicated for clients needing more than 2000 cal, whereas TPN is indicated for clients needing less than 2000 cal.
   4. PPN is indicated for clients who are NPO (nothing by mouth), whereas TPN is indicated for clients who need to supplement oral intake.

2. A nurse is preparing to care for a client who will receive parenteral nutrition (PN) support. The client is receiving dextrose, amino acids, and lipids all in one solution (total nutrient admixture). The nurse plans to do which of the following?
   1. Use a 1.2-μm filter.
   2. Use a 0.22-μm filter to ensure sterility.
   3. Use a 0.10-μm filter to ensure sterility.
   4. Administer the solution without a filter.

3. A client is receiving nutrition by means of parenteral nutrition (PN). A nurse monitors the client for complications of the therapy and assesses the client for which of the following signs of hyperglycemia?
   1. Fever, weak pulse, and thirst
   2. Nausea, vomiting, and oliguria
   3. Sweating, chills, and abdominal pain
   4. Weakness, thirst, and increased urine output

4. At 8 AM, a nurse checks the amount of solution left in a parenteral nutrition (PN) infusion bag for an assigned client. It is a 3000-mL bag with 1000 mL remaining. The solution is running at a rate of 100 mL/hr. The bag was hung the previous day at noon. The nurse plans to change the infusion bag and tubing today at:
   1. Noon
   2. 2 PM
   3. 4 PM
   4. 8 PM

5. A nurse is changing the central line dressing of a client receiving parenteral nutrition (PN) and notes that the catheter insertion site appears reddened. The nurse next assesses which of the following items?
   1. Client's temperature
   2. Expiration date on the bag
   3. Time of last dressing change
   4. Tightness of tubing connections

6. A nurse is preparing to hang fat emulsion (lipids) and notes that fat globules are visible at the top of the solution. The nurse takes which of the following actions?
   1. Rolls the bottle of solution gently.
   2. Obtains a different bottle of solution.
   3. Shakes the bottle of solution vigorously.
   4. Runs the bottle of solution under warm water.

7. A client is being weaned from parenteral nutrition (PN) and is expected to begin taking solid food today. The ongoing solution rate has been 100 mL/hr. A nurse anticipates that which of the following orders regarding the PN solution will accompany the diet order?
   1. Discontinue the PN.
   2. Decrease PN rate to 50 mL/hr.
   3. Hang 1000 mL 0.9% normal saline.
   4. Continue current infusion rate orders for PN.

8. A nurse is preparing to change the total parenteral nutrition (TPN) solution bag and tubing. The client's central venous line is located in the right subclavian vein. The nurse asks the client to take which most essential action during the tubing change?
   1. Breathe normally.
   2. Turn the head to the right.
   3. Exhale slowly and evenly.
   4. Take a deep breath, hold it, and bear down.

9. A client with total parenteral nutrition (TPN) infusing has disconnected the tubing from the central line catheter. A nurse assesses the client and suspects an air embolism. The nurse should immediately place the client in which position?
   1. On the left side, with the head lower than the feet
   2. On the left side, with the head higher than the feet
   3. On the right side, with the head lower than the feet
   4. On the right side, with the head higher than the feet

10. A client receiving parenteral nutrition (PN) complains of a headache. A nurse notes that the client has an increased blood pressure, bounding pulse, jugular vein distention, and crackles bilaterally. The nurse interprets that the client is experiencing which complication of PN therapy?
    1. Sepsis
    2. Air embolism
    3. Hypervolemia
    4. Hyperglycemia

11. A client receiving parenteral nutrition (PN) suddenly spikes a fever. A nurse notifies the physician, and the physician initially orders that the solution and tubing be changed. The nurse should do which of the following with the discontinued materials?
    1. Discard them in the unit trash.
    2. Return them to the hospital pharmacy.
    3. Send them to the laboratory for culture.
    4. Save them for return to the manufacturer.

12. A nurse enters the room of a client receiving parenteral nutrition (PN) and discovers that the electronic infusion pump has been shut off. After checking the line for patency and restarting the infusion, the nurse assesses the client for which of the following signs and symptoms?
    1. Fever and chills
    2. Dyspnea and hypotension
    3. Weakness, thirst, and excessive urination
    4. Weakness, shakiness, diaphoresis, and complaints of hunger

13. A nurse is making initial rounds at the beginning of the shift and notes that the parenteral nutrition (PN) bag of an assigned client is empty. Which of the following solutions readily available on the nursing unit should the nurse hang until another PN solution is mixed and delivered to the nursing unit?
    1. 5% dextrose in water
    2. 10% dextrose in water
    3. 5% dextrose in Ringer's lactate
    4. 5% dextrose in 0.9% sodium chloride

14. At the beginning of a shift, a nurse assesses a client receiving parenteral nutrition (PN) with fat emulsion (lipids) piggybacked to the line. The nurse notes that the fat emulsion tubing has a 0.22-μm filter. Which of the following actions by the nurse is appropriate?
    1. Leave the system alone.
    2. Check the line for patency.
    3. Inspect the filter for clogging.
    4. Replace with a tubing without a filter.

15. A nurse is monitoring the status of a client's fat emulsion (lipid) infusion and notes that the infusion is 1 hour behind. Which of the following actions by the nurse is appropriate?
    1. Adjust the infusion rate to catch up over the next hour.
    2. Increase the infusion rate to catch up over the next 2 hours.
    3. Ensure that the fat emulsion infusion rate is infusing at the prescribed rate.
    4. Adjust the infusion rate to run wide open until the solution is back on time.

16. A client receiving parenteral nutrition (PN) in the home setting has a weight gain of 5 lb in 1 week. The nurse next assesses the client to detect the presence of which of the following?
    1. Thirst
    2. Polyuria
    3. Decreased blood pressure
    4. Crackles on auscultation of the lungs

17. A nurse is caring for a restless client who is beginning nutritional therapy with parenteral nutrition (PN). The nurse should plan to ensure that which of the following is done to prevent the client from injury?

1. Calculate daily intake and output.
2. Monitor the temperature once daily.
3. Secure all connections in the PN system.
4. Monitor blood glucose levels every 12 hours.

18. A client has been discharged to home on parenteral nutrition (PN). With each visit, a home care nurse assesses which of the following parameters most closely in monitoring this therapy?
   1. Pulse and weight
   2. Temperature and weight
   3. Pulse and blood pressure
   4. Temperature and blood pressure

19. A nurse is caring for a group of adult clients on an acute care medical-surgical nursing unit. The nurse understands that which of the following clients would be the least likely candidate for parenteral nutrition (PN)?
   1. A 66-year-old client with extensive burns
   2. A 42-year-old client who has had an open cholecystectomy
   3. A 27-year-old client with severe exacerbation of Crohn's disease
   4. A 35-year-old client with persistent nausea and vomiting from chemotherapy

20. A nurse is preparing to hang the first bag of total parenteral nutrition (TPN) solution via the central line of an assigned client. The nurse obtains which most essential piece of equipment before hanging the solution?
   1. Urine test strips
   2. Blood glucose meter
   3. Electronic infusion pump
   4. Noninvasive blood pressure monitor

ALTERNATE ITEM FORMAT: PRIORITIZING (ORDERED RESPONSE)

A nurse is monitoring a client receiving parenteral nutrition. The client suddenly develops respiratory distress, dyspnea, and chest pain, and the nurse suspects air embolism. Number the actions that the nurse would take in order of priority. (Number 1 is the first action and number 6 is the last action.)

_____ Administer oxygen.
_____ Contact the physician.
_____ Document the occurrence
_____ Take the client's vital signs.
_____ Clamp the intravenous catheter.
_____ Position the client in left Trendelenburg position.

ANSWERS

1. **1**
Rationale: TPN is usually indicated for clients receiving long-term nutritional support and PPN is usually used for short-term support. PPN can supplement oral intake, whereas TPN is usually administered to clients who are NPO. TPN can provide a greater number of calories than PPN. PPN is used to deliver isotonic or mildly hypertonic solutions and TPN can be used to deliver highly hypertonic solutions.
Test-Taking Strategy: Note the strategic words *TPN, PPN,* and *true* and remember that for an option to be correct, all parts of that option must be correct. Remembering that the "T" in "TPN" means "total" will assist in directing you to option 1. Review the types of parenteral nutrition (PN) if you had difficulty with this question.
Level of Cognitive Ability: Comprehension
Client Needs: Physiological Integrity
Integrated Process: Nursing Process—planning
Content Area: Fundamental skills
Reference: Mahan, L. K., & Escott-Stump, S. (2004). *Krause's food, nutrition, & diet therapy* (11th ed., p. 544). Philadelphia: W.B. Saunders.

2. **1**
Rationale: A total nutrient admixture (TNA) is a solution that combines dextrose, amino acids, and lipids in one solution. A 1.2-µm filter or larger filter should be used because the lipid particles are too large to pass through a smaller (0.22- or 0.10-µm) filter. A 0.22-µm filter is used for 2-in-1 solutions containing only dextrose and amino acids. A 0.10-µm filter is smaller than a 1.2-µm filter. Administering the solution without using a filter is not an appropriate action.

Test-Taking Strategy: Use the process of elimination and note that dextrose, amino acids, and lipids are all in one solution. Recall that total nutrient admixture (TNA) or 3-in-1 solutions contain lipids, which are too large to pass through 0.22-µm filters. Begin to answer this question by eliminating options 2 and 3 because the filters are too small for lipid particles to pass through. Choose option 1 over option 4 because a 1.2-µm filter would be the correct size to allow lipid particles to pass through. Review the types of PN solutions and the appropriate filter sizes if you had difficulty with this question.
Level of Cognitive Ability: Application
Client Needs: Physiological Integrity
Integrated Process: Nursing Process—planning
Content Area: Fundamental skills
References: Lewis, S., Heitkemper, M., & Dirksen, S. (2004). *Medical-surgical nursing: Assessment and management of clinical problems* (6th ed., p. 989). St. Louis: Mosby.
Perry, A., & Potter, P. (2006). *Clinical nursing skills & techniques* (6th ed., p. 1062). St. Louis: Mosby.

3. **4**
Rationale: The high glucose concentration in PN places the client at risk for hyperglycemia. Signs of hyperglycemia include excessive thirst, fatigue, restlessness, confusion, weakness, Kussmaul's respirations, diuresis, and coma, when hyperglycemia is severe. If the client has these symptoms, the blood glucose level should be checked immediately. Options 1, 2, and 3 do not identify signs specific to hyperglycemia.
Test-Taking Strategy: Use the process of elimination. Remember that for an option to be correct, all of the parts of that option must be correct. Begin to answer this question by eliminating options 1 and 3 because chills and fever are in-

dicative of infection. Choose option 4 over option 2 because the client with hyperglycemia has increased urine output rather than decreased urine output. Review the signs of hyperglycemia if you had difficulty with this question.
Level of Cognitive Ability: Comprehension
Client Needs: Physiological Integrity
Integrated Process: Nursing Process—assessment
Content Area: Fundamental skills
Reference: Perry, A., & Potter, P. (2006). *Clinical nursing skills & techniques* (6th ed., p. 1050). St. Louis: Mosby.

4. **1**
Rationale: Parenteral nutrition solution should be changed every 24 hours because the PN solution is a high-concentrate glucose solution and is a medium for bacterial growth. Infection control is also aided by use of aseptic technique with bag and tubing changes. Most agencies recommend that tubing be changed every 24 hours along with the bag, although some agencies recommend changing tubing every 48 to 72 hours. The nurse always should adhere to specific agency policies. Options 2, 3, and 4 identify insufficient time frames and present the risk for infection.
Test-Taking Strategy: Use the process of elimination. Recalling that the infusion bag should be changed every 24 hours will direct you to the correct option. Review the principles related to the prevention of infection in the client receiving PN if you had difficulty with this question.
Level of Cognitive Ability: Application
Client Needs: Physiological Integrity
Integrated Process: Nursing Process—planning
Content Area: Fundamental skills
Reference: Gahart, B., & Nazareno, A. (2006). *2006 intravenous medications* (22nd ed., p. 1055). St. Louis: Mosby.

5. **1**
Rationale: Redness at the catheter insertion site is a possible indication of infection. The nurse would next assess for other signs of infection. Of the options given, the temperature is the next item to assess. The tightness of tubing connections should be assessed each time the PN is checked; loose connections would result in leakage, not skin redness. The expiration date on the bag is a viable option, but this also should be checked at the time the solution is hung and with each shift change. The time of the last dressing change should be checked with each shift change.
Test-Taking Strategy: Note the strategic word *next*. This question requires that you prioritize based on the information provided in the question. Also note the relationship between *site appears reddened* in the question and the word *temperature* in the correct option. Focusing on the subject of infection will direct you to option 1. Review the signs of infection in the client receiving PN if you had difficulty with this question.
Level of Cognitive Ability: Application
Client Needs: Physiological Integrity
Integrated Process: Nursing Process—assessment
Content Area: Fundamental skills
References: Black, J., & Hawks, J. (2005). *Medical-surgical nursing: Clinical management for positive outcomes* (7th ed., pp. 708-709). Philadelphia: W.B. Saunders.
Perry, A., & Potter, P. (2006). *Clinical nursing skills & techniques* (6th ed., pp. 1055, 1060). St. Louis: Mosby.

6. **2**
Rationale: The nurse should examine the bottle of fat emulsion for separation of emulsion into layers or fat globules or for the accumulation of froth. The nurse should not hang a fat emulsion if any of these are observed and should return the solution to the pharmacy. Options 1, 3, and 4 are inappropriate actions.
Test-Taking Strategy: Use the process of elimination. Remember that options that are comparative or alike are not likely to be correct. With this in mind, eliminate options 1 and 3 first. Select between the remaining options by recalling the significance of fat globules in the solution. Also, think about the potential adverse effect of fat globules entering the client's bloodstream. Review the procedure for administering fat emulsion if you had difficulty with this question.
Level of Cognitive Ability: Application
Client Needs: Physiological Integrity
Integrated Process: Nursing Process—implementation
Content Area: Fundamental skills
References: Gahart, B., & Nazareno, A. (2006). *2006 intravenous medications* (22nd ed., p. 540). St. Louis: Mosby.
Lehne, R. (2004). *Pharmacology for nursing care* (5th ed., p. 863). Philadelphia: W.B. Saunders.
Lewis, S., Heitkemper, M., & Dirksen, S. (2004). *Medical-surgical nursing: Assessment and management of clinical problems* (6th ed., p. 989). St. Louis: Mosby.

7. **2**
Rationale: When a client begins eating a regular diet after a period of receiving parenteral nutrition, the PN is decreased gradually. Parenteral nutrition that is discontinued abruptly can cause hypoglycemia. Clients often have anorexia after being without food for some time, and the digestive tract also is not used to producing the digestive enzymes that will be needed. Gradually decreasing the infusion rate allows the client to remain adequately nourished during the transition to a normal diet and prevents the occurrence of hypoglycemia. Even before clients are started on a solid diet, they are given clear liquids followed by full liquids to further ease the transition. A solution of normal saline will not provide the glucose needed during the transition of discontinuing the PN and also could cause the client to experience hypoglycemia.
Test-Taking Strategy: Use the process of elimination and note the strategic word *weaned* in the question. Recalling the effects of PN and the complications that occur will direct you to option 2. If you had difficulty with this question, review the concepts related to discontinuing PN solution.
Level of Cognitive Ability: Analysis
Client Needs: Physiological Integrity
Integrated Process: Nursing Process—analysis
Content Area: Fundamental skills
Reference: Lewis, S., Heitkemper, M., & Dirksen, S. (2004). *Medical-surgical nursing: Assessment and management of clinical problems* (6th ed., p. 990). St. Louis: Mosby.

8. **4**
Rationale: The client should be asked to perform the Valsalva maneuver during tubing changes. This helps avoid air embolism during tubing changes. The nurse asks the client to take a deep breath, hold it, and bear down. If the IV line is on the

right, the client turns his or her head to the left. This position will increase intrathoracic pressure. Options 1 and 3 are inappropriate and could cause the potential for an air embolism during the tubing change.
Test-Taking Strategy: Note the strategic words *most essential.* Use the process of elimination, recalling that air embolism is a complication that can occur during tubing changes. This will direct you to option 4. Review the procedure for PN bag and tubing change if you had difficulty with this question.
Level of Cognitive Ability: Application
Client Needs: Physiological Integrity
Integrated Process: Nursing Process—implementation
Content Area: Fundamental skills
References: Ignatavicius, D., & Workman, M. (2006). *Medical-surgical nursing: Critical thinking for collaborative care* (5th ed., p. 257). Philadelphia: W.B. Saunders.
Perry, A., & Potter, P. (2006). *Clinical nursing skills & techniques* (6th ed., p. 1053). St. Louis: Mosby.

9. **1**
Rationale: When air embolism is suspected, the client should be placed in a left side-lying position. The head should be lower than the feet. This position is used to try to minimize the effect of the air traveling as a bolus to the lungs by trapping it in the right side of the heart. Options 2, 3, and 4 are incorrect positions if an air embolism is suspected.
Test-Taking Strategy: Use the process of elimination and recall that the goal is to trap air in the right side of the heart. This will direct you to option 1. If you had difficulty with this question, review the immediate interventions when air embolism is suspected.
Level of Cognitive Ability: Application
Client Needs: Physiological Integrity
Integrated Process: Nursing Process—implementation
Content Area: Fundamental skills
Reference: Perry, A., & Potter, P. (2006). *Clinical nursing skills & techniques* (6th ed., p. 1050). St. Louis: Mosby.

10. **3**
Rationale: The client's signs and symptoms are consistent with hypervolemia. The increased intravascular volume increases the blood pressure, whereas the pulse rate increases as the heart tries to pump the extra fluid volume. The volume also causes neck vein distention and shifting of fluid into the alveoli, resulting in lung crackles. The signs and symptoms presented in the question do not indicate hyperglycemia, air embolism, or sepsis.
Test-Taking Strategy: Use the process of elimination, focusing on the signs and symptoms presented in the question. Recalling the signs of hypervolemia will direct you to option 3. If you had difficulty with this question, review the signs of hypervolemia.
Level of Cognitive Ability: Analysis
Client Needs: Physiological Integrity
Integrated Process: Nursing Process—analysis
Content Area: Fundamental skills
Reference: Lewis, S., Heitkemper, M., & Dirksen, S. (2004). *Medical-surgical nursing: Assessment and management of clinical problems* (6th ed., p. 990). St. Louis: Mosby.

11. **3**
Rationale: When the client who is receiving PN spikes a temperature, a catheter-related infection should be suspected. The solution and tubing should be changed, and the discontinued materials should be cultured for infectious organisms. The other options are incorrect.
Test-Taking Strategy: Use the process of elimination. Identifying the subject of the question, infection, and correlating the elevated temperature with infection associated with the IV should direct you to option 3. Review the procedure when infection is suspected in the client receiving PN if you had difficulty with this question.
Level of Cognitive Ability: Application
Client Needs: Physiological Integrity
Integrated Process: Nursing Process—implementation
Content Area: Fundamental skills
Reference: Lewis, S., Heitkemper, M., & Dirksen, S. (2004). *Medical-surgical nursing: Assessment and management of clinical problems* (6th ed., p. 989). St. Louis: Mosby.

12. **4**
Rationale: If the pump that is infusing PN shuts off for a period of time, the nurse assesses the client for signs and symptoms of hypoglycemia. These signs include weakness, shakiness, headache, anxiety, diaphoresis, and complaints of hunger. The blood glucose level will be lower than 70 mg/dL. The other signs and symptoms described are those of infection (option 1), air embolism (option 2), and hyperglycemia (option 3).
Test-Taking Strategy: Use the process of elimination and focus on the subject of the question, that the infusion pump has been shut off. Recall that the client is at risk for hypoglycemia when the PN is stopped or discontinued. Next, recalling the signs of hypoglycemia will direct you to option 4. Review the complications associated with PN and the signs of complications if you had difficulty with this question.
Level of Cognitive Ability: Analysis
Client Needs: Physiological Integrity
Integrated Process: Nursing Process—assessment
Content Area: Fundamental skills
References: Lewis, S., Heitkemper, M., & Dirksen, S. (2004). *Medical-surgical nursing: Assessment and management of clinical problems* (6th ed., p. 990). St. Louis: Mosby.
Perry, A., & Potter, P. (2006). *Clinical nursing skills & techniques* (6th ed., p. 1056). St. Louis: Mosby.

13. **2**
Rationale: The solution containing the highest amount of glucose should be hung until the new PN solution becomes available. Because PN solutions contain high glucose concentrations, the 10% dextrose in water solution is the best of the choices presented. The solution selected should be one that minimizes the risk of hypoglycemia. Options 1, 3, and 4 will not be as effective in minimizing the risk of hypoglycemia.
Test-Taking Strategy: Use the process of elimination, recalling that this particular client is at risk for hypoglycemia. With this in mind, you would then select the solution that minimizes this risk to the client. Also, remember that options that are comparative or alike are not likely to be correct. Each of the incorrect options represents a solution that contains 5% dextrose. Review the nursing actions to prevent hypoglycemia in

the client receiving PN if you had difficulty with this question.
Level of Cognitive Ability: Application
Client Needs: Physiological Integrity
Integrated Process: Nursing Process—implementation
Content Area: Fundamental skills
Reference: Gahart, B., & Nazareno, A. (2006). *2006 intravenous medications* (22nd ed., p. 1056). St. Louis: Mosby.

14. 4
Rationale: The appropriate action by the nurse is to replace the tubing. A 0.22-μm filter is appropriate for the administration of PN, but fat emulsion should be administered without a filter. If fat emulsion is mixed into the PN solution, then a 1.2-μm or larger filter should be used to allow the fat emulsion to pass through. Therefore, options 1, 2, and 3 are incorrect.
Test-Taking Strategy: Use the process of elimination, recalling that fat emulsion should be administered without a filter. This will direct you to option 4. If you had difficulty with this question, review the procedure for the administration of fat emulsion.
Level of Cognitive Ability: Application
Client Needs: Physiological Integrity
Integrated Process: Nursing Process—implementation
Content Area: Fundamental skills
References: Lewis, S., Heitkemper, M., & Dirksen, S. (2004). *Medical-surgical nursing: Assessment and management of clinical problems* (6th ed., p. 989). St. Louis: Mosby.
Perry, A., & Potter, P. (2006). *Clinical nursing skills & techniques* (6th ed., p. 1062). St. Louis: Mosby.

15. 3
Rationale: The nurse should not increase the rate of a fat emulsion to make up the difference if the infusion timing falls behind. Doing so could place the client at risk for fat overload. The same principle applies to PN; increasing the rate suddenly in this case could cause hyperglycemia and fluid overload. Therefore, options 1, 2, and 4 are incorrect.
Test-Taking Strategy: Note the strategic word *appropriate*. Remember also that options that are comparative or alike are not likely to be correct. This guides you to eliminate options 1 and 2 first. Choose option 3 over option 4, recalling that the nurse never increases the infusion rate or adjusts an infusion rate to run wide open if an infusion is behind. Review these safety principles if you had difficulty with this question.
Level of Cognitive Ability: Application
Client Needs: Physiological Integrity
Integrated Process: Nursing Process—implementation
Content Area: Fundamental skills
References: Lewis, S., Heitkemper, M., & Dirksen, S. (2004). *Medical-surgical nursing: Assessment and management of clinical problems* (6th ed., p. 989). St. Louis: Mosby.
Perry, A., & Potter, P. (2006). *Clinical nursing skills & techniques* (6th ed., pp. 1062-1063). St. Louis: Mosby.

16. 4
Rationale: Optimal weight gain on PN is 1 to 2 lb/week. The client who has a weight gain of 5 lb/week while receiving PN is likely to have fluid retention that can result in hypervolemia. Signs of hypervolemia include increased blood pressure, crackles on lung auscultation, a bounding pulse, jugular

vein distention, headache, and weight gain more than desired. Options 1 and 2 are associated with hyperglycemia. Option 3 is likely to be noted in deficient fluid volume.
Test-Taking Strategy: Focus on the subject of the question, a weight gain of 5 lb in 1 week. This should direct your thinking to the potential for hypervolemia. With this in mind, use the process of elimination, selecting the option that identifies the signs of hypervolemia. If you had difficulty with this question, review the signs and symptoms of complications associated with the administration of PN.
Level of Cognitive Ability: Analysis
Client Needs: Physiological Integrity
Integrated Process: Nursing Process—assessment
Content Area: Fundamental skills
Reference: Perry, A., & Potter, P. (2006). *Clinical nursing skills & techniques* (6th ed., p. 1060). St. Louis: Mosby.

17. 3
Rationale: The nurse should plan to secure all connections in the tubing (tape is used per agency protocol). This will help prevent the restless client from pulling the connections apart accidentally. The nurse should also monitor intake and output, but this does not relate specifically to a risk for injury as presented in the question. Also, options 2 and 4 do not relate to a risk for injury as presented in the question. In addition, the client's temperature and blood glucose levels are monitored more frequently than the time frames identified in the options to detect signs of infection and hyperglycemia, respectively.
Test-Taking Strategy: Note the strategic words *restless, ensure, prevent,* and *injury*. Focus on the subject of the question, and use the process of elimination to direct you to option 3. Review the precautions related to PN if you had difficulty with this question.
Level of Cognitive Ability: Application
Client Needs: Safe and Effective Care Environment
Integrated Process: Nursing Process—planning
Content Area: Fundamental skills
Reference: Perry, A., & Potter, P. (2006). *Clinical nursing skills & techniques* (6th ed., p. 1057). St. Louis: Mosby.

18. 2
Rationale: The client receiving parenteral nutrition (PN) at home should have her or his temperature monitored as a means of detecting infection, which is a potential complication of this therapy. An infection also could result in sepsis because the catheter is in a blood vessel. The client's weight is monitored as a measure of the effectiveness of this nutritional therapy and to detect hypervolemia. The pulse and blood pressure are important parameters to assess, but they do not relate specifically to the effects of PN.
Test-Taking Strategy: Note the strategic words *most closely,* which tell you that more than one or all the options may be partially or totally correct. Remember also that when there are multiple parts to an option, all the parts must be correct for that option to be correct. Recalling that infection and hypervolemia are complications of PN and that weight is monitored as a measure of the effectiveness of this nutritional therapy will direct you to option 2. Review these important assessments if you had difficulty with this question.
Level of Cognitive Ability: Application
Client Needs: Physiological Integrity

Integrated Process: Nursing Process—assessment
Content Area: Fundamental skills
References: Black, J., & Hawks, J. (2005). *Medical-surgical nursing: Clinical management for positive outcomes* (7th ed., pp. 707-708). Philadelphia: W.B. Saunders.
Ignatavicius, D., & Workman, M. (2006). *Medical-surgical nursing: Critical thinking for collaborative care* (5th ed., p. 1433). Philadelphia: W.B. Saunders.
Perry, A., & Potter, P. (2006). *Clinical nursing skills & techniques* (6th ed., p. 1055). St. Louis: Mosby.

19. **2**
Rationale: Parenteral nutrition is indicated in clients whose gastrointestinal tracts are not functional or who cannot take in a diet enterally for extended periods. Examples of these conditions include those of the clients identified in options 1, 3, and 4. Other clients would be those who have had extensive surgery, have multiple fractures, are septic, or have advanced cancer or acquired immunodeficiency syndrome. The client with the open cholecystectomy is not a candidate because this client would resume a regular diet within a few days following surgery.
Test-Taking Strategy: Note the strategic words *least likely*, which tell you that the correct option is the client who does not require this type of nutritional support. Use nursing knowledge of these various conditions and baseline knowledge of the purposes of PN to make your selection. Review the indications for PN if you had difficulty with this question.
Level of Cognitive Ability: Analysis
Client Needs: Physiological Integrity
Integrated Process: Nursing Process—assessment
Content Area: Fundamental skills
References: Black, J., & Hawks, J. (2005). *Medical-surgical nursing: Clinical management for positive outcomes* (7th ed., p. 820). Philadelphia: W.B. Saunders.
Ignatavicius, D., & Workman, M. (2006). *Medical-surgical nursing: Critical thinking for collaborative care* (5th ed., p. 1400). Philadelphia: W.B. Saunders.

20. **3**
Rationale: The nurse obtains an electronic infusion pump before hanging a TPN solution. Because of the high glucose content, use of an infusion pump is necessary to ensure that the solution does not infuse too rapidly or fall behind. Because the client's blood glucose level is monitored every 4 to 6 hours during administration of TPN, a blood glucose meter also will be needed, but this is not the most essential item needed before hanging the solution. Urine test strips (to mea-

sure glucose) rarely are used because of the advent of blood glucose monitoring. A noninvasive blood pressure monitor is unnecessary for this procedure.
Test-Taking Strategy: Note the strategic words *most essential*. They tell you that the correct option identifies the item needed to start the infusion. Use the process of elimination and knowledge of the procedure for initiating TPN to direct you to option 3. Review these procedures if you had difficulty with this question.
Level of Cognitive Ability: Application
Client Needs: Physiological Integrity
Integrated Process: Nursing Process—planning
Content Area: Fundamental skills
References: Lewis, S., Heitkemper, M., & Dirksen, S. (2004). *Medical-surgical nursing: Assessment and management of clinical problems* (6th ed., p. 989). St. Louis: Mosby.
Potter, P., & Perry, A. (2005). *Fundamentals of nursing* (6th ed., pp. 1160-1161). St. Louis: Mosby.

ALTERNATE ITEM FORMAT: PRIORITIZING (ORDERED RESPONSE)

Answer: 4, 3, 6, 5, 1, 2
Rationale: If air embolism is suspected, the nurse would first clamp the intravenous catheter to prevent the embolism from traveling through the heart to the pulmonary system. The nurse would next place the client in a left side-lying position with the head lower than the feet (to trap air in right side of the heart). The nurse would notify the physician and administer oxygen as prescribed. The nurse would monitor the client closely and take the client's vital signs. Finally, the nurse documents the occurrence.
Test-Taking Strategy: Think about the pathophysiology and effects of an air embolism. Recalling that a primary concern is that the embolism will travel to the pulmonary system will assist in determining that the catheter needs to be clamped first and that the client needs to be positioned to trap the air in the right side of the heart. Because this event is an emergency, the nurse notifies the physician next and the physician will provide an order for oxygen, if necessary. The nurse monitors the client and takes the client's vital signs frequently.
Level of Cognitive Ability: Application
Client Needs: Physiological Integrity
Integrated Process: Nursing Process—implementation
Content Area: Delegating/Prioritizing
References: Perry, A., & Potter, P. (2006). *Clinical nursing skills & techniques* (6th ed., p. 1050). St. Louis: Mosby.
Potter, P., & Perry, A. (2005). *Fundamentals of nursing* (6th ed., pp. 1315-1316). St. Louis: Mosby.

REFERENCES

Black, J., & Hawks, J., (2005). *Medical-surgical nursing: Clinica management for positive outcomes* (7th ed.). Philadelphia: W.B. Saunders.
Gahart, B., & Nazareno, A. (2006). *2006 intravenous medications* (22nd ed.). St. Louis: Mosby.
Ignatavicius, D., & Workman, M. (2006). *Medical-surgical nursing: Critical thinking for collaborative care* (5th ed.). Philadelphia: W.B. Saunders.
Lehne, R. (2004). *Pharmacology for nursing care* (5th ed.). Philadelphia: W.B. Saunders.
Lewis, S., Heitkemper, M., & Dirksen, S. (2004). *Medical-surgical nursing: Assessment and management of clinical problems* (6th ed.). St. Louis: Mosby.

Mahan, L. K., & Escott-Stump, S. (2004). *Krause's food, nutrition, & .diet therapy* (11th ed.). Philadelphia: W.B. Saunders.
National Council of State Boards of Nursing (Eds.). (2007). *2007 NCLEX-RN® detailed test plan.* Chicago: Author.
Perry, A., & Potter, P. (2006). *Clinical nursing skills & techniques* (6th ed.). St. Louis: Mosby.
Potter, P., & Perry, A. (2005). *Fundamentals of nursing* (6th ed.). St. Louis: Mosby.

Intravenous Therapy

PYRAMID TERMS

air embolism An obstruction caused by a bolus of air that enters the vein through an inadequately primed intravenous line, from a loose connection, during a tubing change, or during removal of an intravenous line.

catheter embolism An obstruction caused by breakage of the catheter tip during intravenous line insertion or removal.

hypertonic Solutions that are more concentrated or have a higher osmolality than body fluids.

hypotonic Solutions that are more dilute or have a lower osmolality than body fluids.

infiltration Seepage of intravenous fluid out of the vein and into the surrounding interstitial spaces.

isotonic Solutions that have the same osmolality as body fluids.

phlebitis An inflammation of the vein that can occur from mechanical or chemical (medication) trauma or from a local infection.

▲ THE PYRAMID TO SUCCESS

Professional nurses are responsible for managing and providing care to clients receiving intravenous (IV) therapy. Pyramid Points focus on the safety measures required to initiate and maintain an IV line. Assessment of the client for allergies, including latex sensitivity, before initiation of an IV line is a critical nursing responsibility. Additional nursing responsibilities include monitoring for complications related to the IV line and initiating the measures required when an IV complication occurs. Pyramid Points focus on the signs and symptoms of infection, infiltration, phlebitis, circulatory overload, and air embolism and the treatment measures associated with each. Integrated Processes addressed in this chapter include Caring, Communication and Documentation, Nursing Process, and Teaching/Learning.

CLIENT NEEDS

Safe and Effective Care Environment

Applying principles of infection control
Consulting with members of the health care team
Establishing priorities
Handling hazardous or infectious materials safely
Maintaining medical and surgical asepsis during handling of equipment and supplies
Maintaining standard, transmission-based, and other precautions
Obtaining informed consent for invasive procedures
Preventing errors in administering IV fluids

Health Promotion and Maintenance

Assessing the client's ability to perform self-care
Considering lifestyle choices related to home care of the IV line
Evaluating the client's home environment for self-care modifications
Promoting health and wellness
Teaching the client and family about care of the IV line

Psychosocial Integrity

Assessing coping mechanisms
Assessing the client's emotional response to treatment
Identifying support systems in the home for caring for the IV line

Physiological Integrity

Assessing central venous access devices
Initiating immediate interventions if a complication occurs
Maintaining intravenous therapy

Monitoring for complications of IV therapy

Monitoring for expected effects of IV therapy

Monitoring laboratory values for fluid and electrolyte imbalances

I. INTRAVENOUS THERAPY

A. Purpose and uses
1. Used to sustain clients who are unable to take substances orally
2. Replaces water, electrolytes, and nutrients more rapidly than oral administration
3. Provides immediate access to the vascular system for the rapid delivery of specific solutions without the time required for gastrointestinal tract absorption
4. Provides a vascular route for the administration of medication or blood components

B. Types of solutions (Table 14-1)
1. **Isotonic** solutions
   a. Have the same osmolality as body fluids
   b. Increase extracellular fluid volume
   c. Do not enter the cells because no osmotic force exists to shift the fluids
2. **Hypotonic** solutions
   a. Are more dilute solutions and have a lower osmolality than body fluids
   b. Cause the movement of water into cells by osmosis
   c. Should be administered slowly to prevent cellular edema
3. **Hypertonic** solutions
   a. Are more concentrated solutions and have a higher osmolality than body fluids
   b. Concentrate extracellular fluid and cause movement of water from cells into the extracellular fluid by osmosis
4. Colloids
   a. Also called plasma expanders
   b. Pull fluid from the interstitial compartment into the vascular compartment
   c. Used to increase the vascular volume rapidly, such as in hemorrhage or severe hypovolemia

II. INTRAVENOUS DEVICES

A. Intravenous cannulas
1. Steel needles or butterfly sets
   a. The set is a wing-tip needle with a metal cannula, plastic or rubber wings, and a plastic catheter or hub.
   b. The needle is 0.5 to 1.5 inches in length, with needle gauge sizes from 16 to 26.
   c. Intravenous cannulas are used when the infusion time will be short.
   d. **Infiltration** is more common with these devices.
   e. The butterfly infusion set commonly is used in children and older clients, whose veins are likely to be small or fragile.
2. Plastic cannulas
   a. Plastic cannulas may be an over-the-needle device or an in-needle catheter and are used primarily for short-term therapy.
   b. The over-the-needle device is preferred for rapid infusion and is more comfortable for the client.
   c. The in-needle catheter can cause **catheter embolism** if the tip of the cannula breaks.

B. Intravenous gauges
1. The gauge refers to the diameter of the lumen of the needle or cannula.
2. The smaller the gauge number, the larger the diameter of the lumen; the larger the gauge number, the smaller the diameter of the lumen.
3. The size of the gauge used depends on the solution to be administered and the diameter of the available vein.
4. Large-diameter lumens (smaller gauge numbers) allow a higher fluid rate than smaller diameter lumens and allow the administration of higher concentrations of solutions.
5. For rapid emergency fluid administration, blood products, or anesthetics, large-diameter lumen needles or cannulas are used, such as a 14-, 16-, 18-, or 19-gauge.
6. For peripheral fat infusions (lipids), a 20- or 21-gauge lumen or cannula is used.

TABLE 14-1

Types of Intravenous Solutions

Solution	Tonicity
0.9% saline (NS)	Isotonic
5% dextrose in water (D$_5$W)	Isotonic
5% dextrose in 0.225% saline D$_5$W/$^1/_4$ NS	Isotonic
Lactated Ringer's solution	Isotonic
0.45% saline ($^1/_2$ NS)	Hypotonic
0.225% saline ($^1/_4$ NS)	Hypotonic
0.33% saline ($^1/_3$ NS)	Hypotonic
3% saline (3% NS)	Hypertonic
5% saline (5% NS)	Hypertonic
10% dextrose in water (D$_{10}$W)	Hypertonic
5% dextrose in 0.9% saline D$_5$W/NS	Hypertonic
5% dextrose in 0.45% saline D$_5$W/$^1/_2$ NS)	Hypertonic
5% dextrose in lactated Ringer's solution	Hypertonic
Dextran	Colloid
Albumin	Colloid

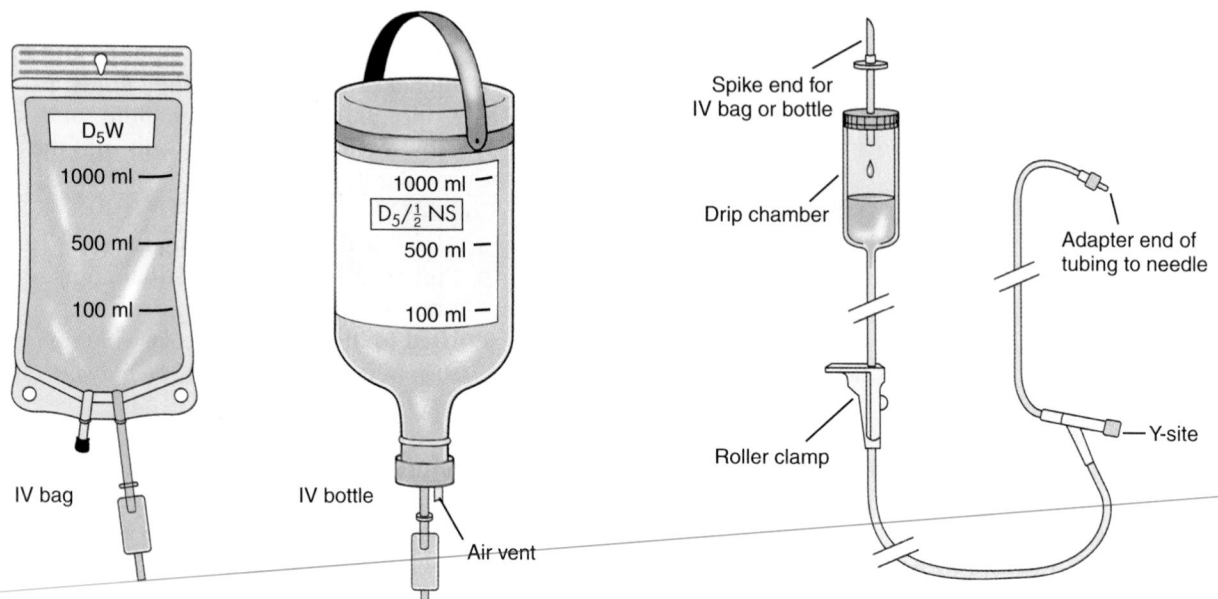

FIG. 14-1   Intravenous containers. (From Kee, J. L., & Marshall, S. M. [2004]. *Clinical calculations: With applications to general and specialty areas* [5th ed]. Philadelphia: W.B. Saunders.)

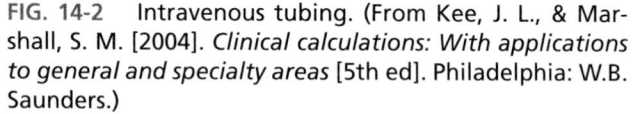

FIG. 14-2   Intravenous tubing. (From Kee, J. L., & Marshall, S. M. [2004]. *Clinical calculations: With applications to general and specialty areas* [5th ed]. Philadelphia: W.B. Saunders.)

7. For standard IV fluid and clear liquid IV medications, a 22- or 24-gauge lumen or cannula is used.
8. If the client has very small veins, a 24- to 25-gauge lumen or cannula is used.

C. IV containers (Fig. 14-1)
   1. Container may be glass or plastic.
   2. Squeeze the plastic bag to ensure intactness and assess the glass bottle for any cracks before hanging.
   3. Do not write on the plastic IV bag with a marking pen because the ink may be absorbed through the plastic into the solution.
   4. Use a label and a ballpoint pen for marking the bag, placing the label onto the bag.

D. Intravenous tubing (Fig. 14-2)
   1. Intravenous tubing contains a spike end for the bag or bottle, drip chamber, roller clamp, Y site, and adapter end for attachment to the needle.
   2. Extension tubing is available for children, clients who are restless, or clients who have special mobility needs.
   3. Shorter secondary tubing is used for piggyback solutions, connecting them to the injection sites nearest to the drip chamber (Fig. 14-3).
   4. Special tubing is used for medication that absorbs into plastic.
   5. Vented and nonvented tubing are available.
      a. A vent allows air to enter the IV container as the fluid leaves.
      b. A vented adapter can be used to add a vent to a nonvented IV tubing system.

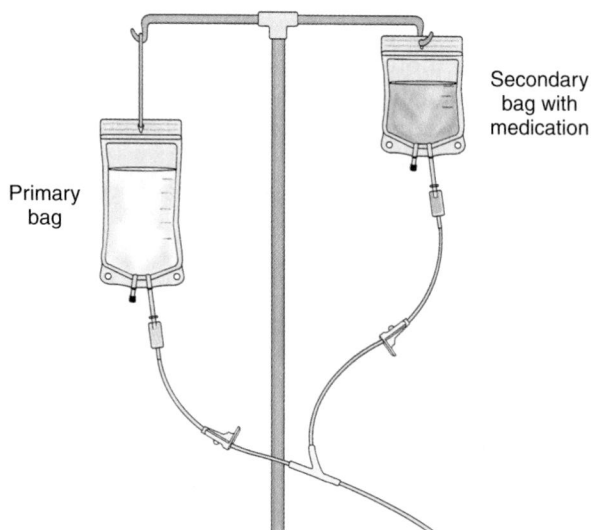

FIG. 14-3   Secondary bag with medication. (Modified from Kee, J. L., & Marshall, S. M. [2004]. *Clinical calculations: With applications to general and specialty areas* [5th ed]. Philadelphia: W.B. Saunders.)

      c. Use nonvented tubing for flexible containers.
      d. Use vented tubing for glass or rigid plastic containers to allow air to enter and displace the fluid as it leaves; fluid will not flow from a rigid IV container unless it is vented.

E. Drip chambers (Fig. 14-4)
   1. Macrodrip chamber
      a. The chamber is used if the solution is thick or is to be infused rapidly.

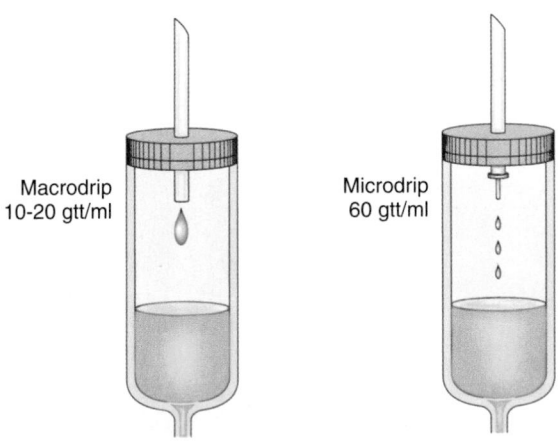

Macrodrip
10-20 gtt/ml

Microdrip
60 gtt/ml

FIG. 14-4 Macrodrip and microdrip sizes. (From Kee, J. L., & Marshall, S. M. [2004]. *Clinical calculations: With applications to general and specialty areas* [5th ed]. Philadelphia: W.B. Saunders.)

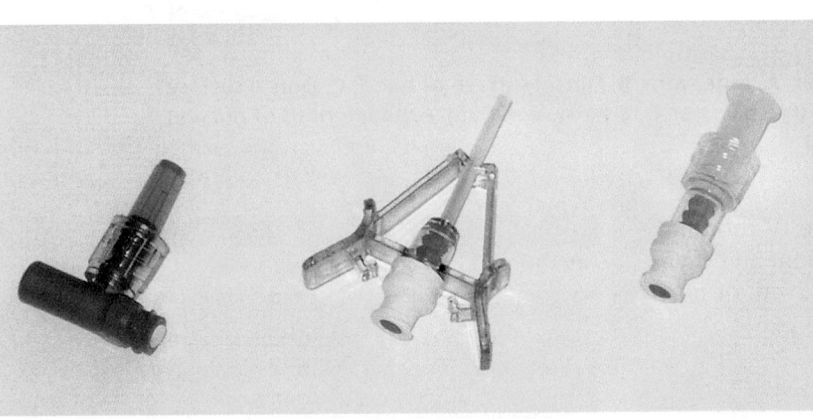
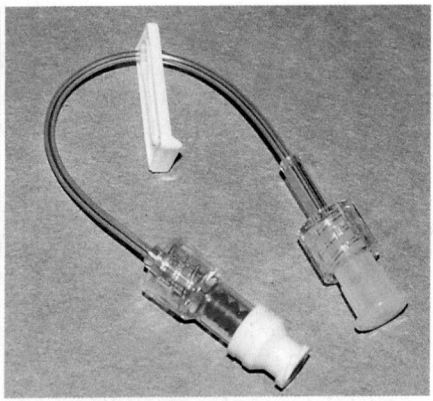

FIG. 14-5 Needleless infusion devices. (From Kee, J. L., & Marshall, S. M. [2004]. *Clinical calculations: With applications to general and specialty areas* [5th ed]. Philadelphia: W.B. Saunders.)

  b. The drop factor varies from 10 to 20 drops/mL.
  c. Read the tubing package to determine how many drops per milliliter are delivered (drop factor).
 2. Microdrip chamber
  a. Normally, the chamber has a short vertical metal piece where the drop forms.
  b. The chamber delivers about 60 drops/mL.
  c. Read the tubing package to determine how many drops per milliliter are delivered (drop factor).
  d. Microdrip chambers are used if fluid will be infused at a slow rate (less than 50 mL/hr).
  e. Microdrip chambers are used if the solution contains potent medication that needs to be titrated, such as in a critical care setting or in pediatrics.
 F. Filters
 1. Filters provide protection by preventing particles from entering the client's veins.
 2. They are used in IV lines to trap small particles such as undissolved antibiotics or salt or medications that have precipitated in solution.

 3. Assess the agency policy regarding the use of filters.
 4. A 0.22-µm filter is used for most solutions, a 1.2-µm for solutions containing lipids or albumin, and a special filter for blood components.
 5. Change filters every 24 to 72 hours (depending on agency policy) to prevent bacterial growth.
 G. Needleless infusion devices (Fig. 14-5)
 1. Needleless infusion devices include recessed needles, plastic cannulas, and one-way valves; these systems decrease the exposure to contaminated needles.
 2. Do not administer parenteral nutrition or blood products through a one-way valve.
 H. Intermittent infusion devices
 1. Intermittent infusion devices are used when intravascular accessibility is desired for intermittent administration of medications by IV push or IV piggyback.
 2. Patency is maintained by periodic flushing with normal saline solution (sodium chloride and normal saline are interchangeable names).
 3. Depending on agency policy, when administering medication, flush with 1 to 2 mL of normal

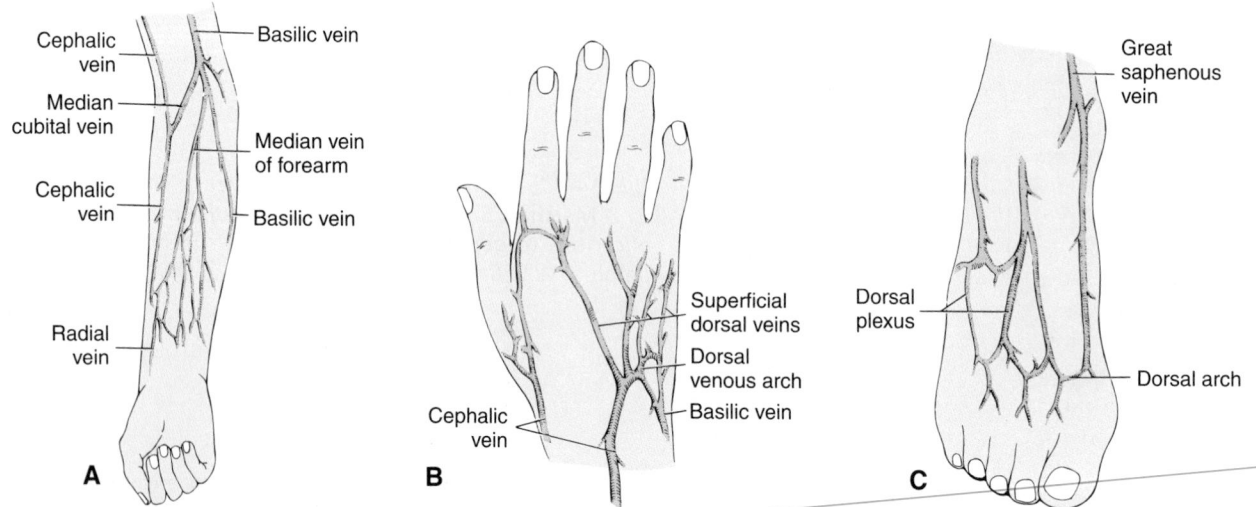

FIG. 14-6 Common IV sites. **A,** Inner arm. **B,** Dorsal surface of hand. **C,** Dorsal surface of the foot (children only). (From Potter, P., & Perry, A. [2005]. *Fundamentals of nursing* [6th ed.]. St. Louis: Mosby.)

saline to confirm placement of the IV cannula; administer the prescribed medication, and then flush the cannula again with 1 to 2 mL of normal saline to maintain patency.

III. LATEX ALLERGY
A. Assess the client for an allergy to latex.
B. Intravenous supplies, including IV catheters, IV tubing, IV ports (particularly IV rubber injection ports), rubber stoppers on multidose vials, and adhesive tape, may contain latex.
C. Latex-safe IV supplies need to be used for clients with a latex allergy.
D. A three-way stopcock, rather than a rubber injection port, needs to be used on plastic tubing.
E. See Chapter 69 for additional information regarding latex allergy.

IV. SELECTION OF A PERIPHERAL IV SITE
A. Veins in the hand, forearm, and antecubital fossa are suitable sites (Fig. 14-6).
B. Veins in the lower extremities (legs and feet) are not suitable for an adult client because of the risk of thrombus formation and possible pooling of medication in areas of decreased venous return (Box 14-1).
C. Veins in the scalp and feet may be suitable sites for infants (see Fig. 14-6).
D. The most frequently used sites are the veins of the forearm because the bones of the forearm act as a natural support and splint.
E. Assess the veins of both arms closely before selecting a site.
F. Start the IV infusion distally to provide the option of proceeding up the extremity if the vein is ruptured or **infiltration** occurs; if **infiltration** occurs

> **BOX 14-1**
> **Peripheral Intravenous Sites to Avoid**
>
> Edematous extremity
> An arm that is weak, traumatized, or paralyzed
> The arm on the same side as a mastectomy
> An arm that has an arteriovenous fistula or shunt for dialysis
> Infected skin tissue

from the antecubital vein, the lower veins in the same arm usually cannot be used for further puncture sites.
G. Determine the client's dominant side, and select the opposite side for a venipuncture site.
H. Bending the elbow on the arm with an IV may easily obstruct the flow of solution, causing **infiltration** that could lead to thrombophlebitis.
I. Avoid checking the blood pressure on the arm receiving the IV infusion if possible.
J. Do not place restraints over the venipuncture site.
K. Use an armboard as needed when the venipuncture site is located in an area of flexion.

V. ADDITION OF MEDICATION TO AN IV SOLUTION
A. Assess for compatibility of the medication and solution.
B. When adding medication to the IV bag, mix the bag end to end several times before hanging it to disperse the medication.
C. Ensure that the medication can be mixed in soft plastic because some medications absorb into the soft plastic and should be mixed only in glass.

VI. ADMINISTRATION OF IV SOLUTIONS

A. Check the IV solution against the physician's orders for the type, amount, percentage of solution, and rate of flow.

B. Assess the health status and medical disorders of the client.

C. Identify client conditions that contraindicate use of a particular IV solution.

D. Wash hands thoroughly before inserting an IV line and before working with an IV line.

E. Use sterile technique when inserting an IV line and when changing the dressing over the IV site.

F. When inserting an IV line, clean the skin with an antimicrobial solution, using an inner to outer circular motion, or as specified by the agency policy.

G. Prime the IV tubing to remove air from the system.

H. Change the venipuncture site every 48 to 72 hours, depending on agency policy.

I. Change the IV dressing every 72 hours, when the dressing is wet or contaminated, or as specified by the agency policy.

J. Change the IV tubing every 24 to 72 hours, depending on agency policy.

K. Label the tubing, dressing, and solution bags clearly, indicating the date and time when changed.

L. Do not let an IV bag or bottle of solution hang for more than 24 hours because of the potential for bacterial contamination and possibly sepsis.

M. Do not allow the IV tubing to touch the floor because of the potential for bacterial contamination.

N. Before adding medications to solutions, swab access ports with 70% alcohol, another equally effective solution, or as specified by the agency policy.

VII. PRECAUTIONS FOR IV LINES

A. On insertion, an IV line can cause initial pain and discomfort for the client.

B. An IV puncture provides a route of entry for microorganisms into the body.

C. Medications administered by the IV route enter the blood immediately, and any adverse reactions or allergic responses can occur immediately.

D. Fluid (circulatory) overload or electrolyte imbalances can occur from excessive or too rapid infusion of IV fluids.

E. Incompatibilities between certain solutions and medications can occur.

F. Clients with respiratory, cardiac, renal, or liver diseases, older clients, and very young persons cannot tolerate an excessive fluid volume, and the risk of fluid overload exists with these clients.

G. A client with congestive heart failure usually is not given a solution containing saline because this type of fluid encourages the retention of water and would therefore exacerbate heart failure by increasing the fluid overload.

H. A client with diabetes mellitus usually does not receive dextrose (glucose) solutions.

I. Lactated Ringer's solution contains potassium and should not be administered to clients with renal failure.

VIII. COMPLICATIONS (Table 14-2)

A. Air embolism
   1. Description: A bolus of air enters the vein through an inadequately primed IV line, from a loose connection, during tubing change, or during removal of the IV.
   2. Prevention and interventions
      a. Prime tubing with fluid before use, and monitor for any air bubbles in the tubing.
      b. Secure all connections

TABLE 14-2

Signs of Complications of Intravenous Therapy

Complication	Signs
Air embolism	Tachycardia
	Dyspnea
	Hypotension
	Cyanosis
	Decreased level of consciousness
Catheter embolism	Decrease in blood pressure
	Pain along the vein
	Weak, rapid pulse
	Cyanosis of the nail beds
	Loss of consciousness
Circulatory overload	Increased blood pressure
	Distended jugular veins
	Rapid breathing
	Dyspnea
	Moist cough and crackles
Electrolyte overload	Signs depend on the specific electrolyte overload imbalance
Hematoma	Ecchymosis, immediate swelling and leakage of blood at the site, and hard and painful lumps at the site
Infection	Local—redness, swelling, and drainage at the site
	Systemic—chills, fever, malaise, headache, nausea, vomiting, backache, tachycardia
Infiltration	Edema, pain, and coolness at the site; may or may not have a blood return
Phlebitis	Heat, redness, tenderness at the site
	Not swollen or hard
	Intravenous infusion sluggish
Thrombophlebitis	Hard and cordlike vein
	Heat, redness, tenderness at site
	Intravenous infusion sluggish
Tissue damage	Skin color changes, sloughing of the skin, discomfort at the site

c. Replace the IV fluid before the bag or bottle is empty.

d. Monitor for signs of **air embolism**, including tachycardia, dyspnea, hypotension, cyanosis, and decreased level of consciousness; a loud churning sound heard over the pericardium that results from air in the right ventricle may be audible.

e. If **air embolism** is suspected, clamp the tubing, turn the client on the left side with the head of the bed lowered (Trendelenburg position) to trap the air in the right atrium, and notify the physician.

B. **Catheter embolism**

1. Description: An obstruction that results from breakage of the catheter tip during intravenous line insertion or removal.

2. Prevention and interventions

a. Monitor for signs of **catheter embolism**, including a decrease in blood pressure, pain along the vein, weak and rapid pulse, cyanosis of the nail beds, and loss of consciousness.

b. Remove the catheter carefully.

c. Inspect the catheter when removed.

d. If the catheter tip has broken off, place a tourniquet as proximally as possible to the IV site on the affected limb, notify the physician immediately, prepare to obtain an x-ray, and prepare the client for surgery to remove the catheter piece(s), if necessary.

C. Circulatory overload

1. Description

a. Circulatory overload also is known as fluid overload.

b. Circulatory overload results from the administration of fluids too rapidly or in a client at risk for fluid overload.

2. Prevention and interventions

a. Identify clients at risk for circulatory overload.

b. Calculate and monitor the drip (flow) rate frequently.

c. Use an infusion controller device and frequently check the drip rate or pump setting, particularly in clients at risk for overload.

d. Add a time strip to the IV bag or bottle.

e. Monitor for signs of circulatory overload, including increased blood pressure, distended jugular veins, rapid breathing, dyspnea, moist cough, and crackles.

f. If circulatory overload occurs, decrease the flow rate to a minimum at a keep vein open rate, elevate the head of the bed, keep the client warm, assess lung sounds, assess for edema, and notify the physician.

g. Document the assessment and actions taken.

D. Electrolyte overload

1. Description: An electrolyte imbalance caused by too rapid or excessive infusion or by use of an inappropriate intravenous solution

2. Prevention and interventions

a. Assess laboratory value reports.

b. Verify the correct solution.

c. Calculate and monitor the flow rate.

d. Use an infusion controller device, and frequently check the flow rate or pump setting.

e. Add a time strip (label) to the IV bag or bottle.

f. Place a medication sticker on the bag or bottle if a medication, such as potassium chloride, has been added to the IV solution.

g. Monitor for signs of an electrolyte imbalance, and notify the physician if they occur.

E. Hematoma

1. Description: The collection of blood in the tissues after an unsuccessful venipuncture or after the venipuncture site is discontinued and blood continues to ooze into the tissue

2. Prevention and interventions

a. When starting an IV, avoid piercing the posterior wall of the vein.

b. Do not apply a tourniquet to the extremity immediately after an unsuccessful venipuncture.

c. When discontinuing an IV, apply pressure to the site for at least 1 minute and elevate the extremity; apply pressure longer for clients with a bleeding disorder or who are taking anticoagulants.

d. Monitor for ecchymosis, immediate swelling and leakage of blood at the site, and hard and painful lumps at the site.

e. If a hematoma develops, elevate the extremity and apply pressure and ice as prescribed.

F. Infection

1. Description

a. Infection occurs from the entry of microorganisms into the body through the venipuncture site.

b. Venipuncture interrupts the integrity of the skin, the first line of defense against infection.

c. The longer the therapy continues, the greater the risk of infection.

d. Infection can occur locally at the IV insertion site or systemically from the entry of microorganisms into the body.

2. At-risk clients

a. Immunocompromised clients with diseases such as cancer or acquired immunodeficiency syndrome are at risk for infection.

b. Clients receiving treatments such as chemotherapy who have an altered or lowered white blood cell count are at risk for infection.

c. Older clients, because aging alters the effectiveness of the immune system, are at risk for infection.

3. Prevention and interventions

a. Assess the client for predisposition to or risk for infection.

b. Maintain strict asepsis when caring for the IV site.

c. Monitor for signs of local infection, such as redness, swelling, and drainage at the IV site.

d. Monitor for signs of systemic infection, such as chills, fever, malaise, headache, nausea, vomiting, backache, and tachycardia.

e. Monitor white blood cell counts.

f. Check fluid containers for cracks, leaks, cloudiness, or other evidence of contamination.

g. Change tubing and site dressing every 24 to 72 hours according to agency policy.

h. Use antimicrobial ointment at the IV site.

i. Label the IV site, bag or bottle, and tubing with the date and time to ensure that these are changed on time according to agency policy.

j. Ensure that the IV solution is not hanging for more than 24 hours.

k. If infection occurs, discontinue the IV, place the venipuncture device in a sterile container for possible culture, and notify the physician.

l. Prepare to obtain blood cultures as prescribed if infection occurs.

m. Restart an IV in the opposite arm to differentiate sepsis (systemic infection) from local infection at the IV site.

n. Document assessment of the finding related to infection.

G. **Infiltration**

1. Description

a. **Infiltration** is a form of tissue damage; it is also called extravasation.

b. **Infiltration** is seepage of the intravenous fluid out of the vein and into the surrounding interstitial spaces.

c. **Infiltration** occurs when an access device has become dislodged or perforates the wall of the vein or when venous backpressure occurs because of a clot or venospasm.

2. Prevention and interventions

a. Avoid venipuncture over an area of flexion.

b. Anchor the cannula and a loop of tubing securely with tape.

c. Use an armboard or splint as needed if the client is restless or active.

d. Assess the IV site for pain, edema, or coolness, comparing it with the opposite extremity.

e. Monitor the IV rate for a decrease or a cessation of flow.

f. Evaluate the IV site for **infiltration** by occluding the vein proximal to the IV site. If the IV

fluid continues to flow, the cannula is probably outside the vein (infiltrated); if the IV flow stops after occlusion of the vein, the IV device is still in the vein.

g. Lower the IV fluid container below the IV site, and monitor for the appearance of blood in the IV tubing; if blood appears, the IV device is most likely in the vein.

h. If **infiltration** has occurred, remove the IV device immediately.

i. Do not rub an infiltrated area, which can cause the development of a hematoma.

j. If **infiltration** has occurred, elevate the extremity and apply compresses (warm or cool, depending on the IV solution that was infusing and the physician's order) over the affected area.

k. Document the assessment of the infiltration, its effects, and the action taken.

H. **Phlebitis** and thrombophlebitis

1. Description

a. **Phlebitis** is an inflammation of the vein that can occur from mechanical or chemical (medication) trauma or from a local infection.

b. **Phlebitis** can cause the development of a clot (thrombophlebitis).

2. Prevention and interventions

a. Use an IV cannula smaller than the vein, and avoid using very small veins when administering irritating solutions.

b. Avoid using the lower extremities (legs and feet) as an access area for the IV.

c. Avoid venipuncture over an area of flexion.

d. Anchor the cannula and a loop of tubing securely with tape.

e. Use an armboard or splint as needed if the client is restless or active.

f. Change the venipuncture site every 48 to 72 hours, depending on agency policy.

g. If **phlebitis** occurs, remove the IV device immediately and restart it in the opposite extremity.

h. Notify the physician if **phlebitis** is suspected, and apply warm, moist compresses, as prescribed.

i. If thrombophlebitis occurs, never irrigate the IV catheter; remove the IV, notify the physician, and restart the IV in the opposite extremity.

j. Document assessment of the **phlebitis** or thrombophlebitis and its effects.

I. Tissue damage

1. Description

a. Tissues most commonly damaged include the skin, veins, and subcutaneous tissue.

b. Tissue damage can be uncomfortable and can cause permanent negative effects.

2. Prevention and interventions
   a. Use a careful and gentle approach when applying a tourniquet.
   b. Avoid tapping the skin over the vein when starting an IV.
   c. Monitor for ecchymosis when penetrating the skin with the cannula.
   d. Assess for any allergies to tape or dressing adhesives.
   e. Monitor for skin color changes, sloughing of the skin, or discomfort at the IV site.
   f. Notify the physician if tissue damage is suspected.
   g. Document assessment of the tissue damage and its effects.

IX. CENTRAL VENOUS CATHETERS

A. Description
   1. Central venous catheters (Fig. 14-7) are used to deliver hyperosmolar solutions, measure central venous pressure, infuse parenteral nutrition, or infuse multiple IV solutions or medications.
   2. Catheter position is determined by radiography after insertion.
   3. The catheter may have a single, double, or triple lumen.
   4. The catheter may be inserted peripherally and threaded through the basilic or cephalic vein into the superior vena cava, inserted centrally through the internal jugular or subclavian veins,

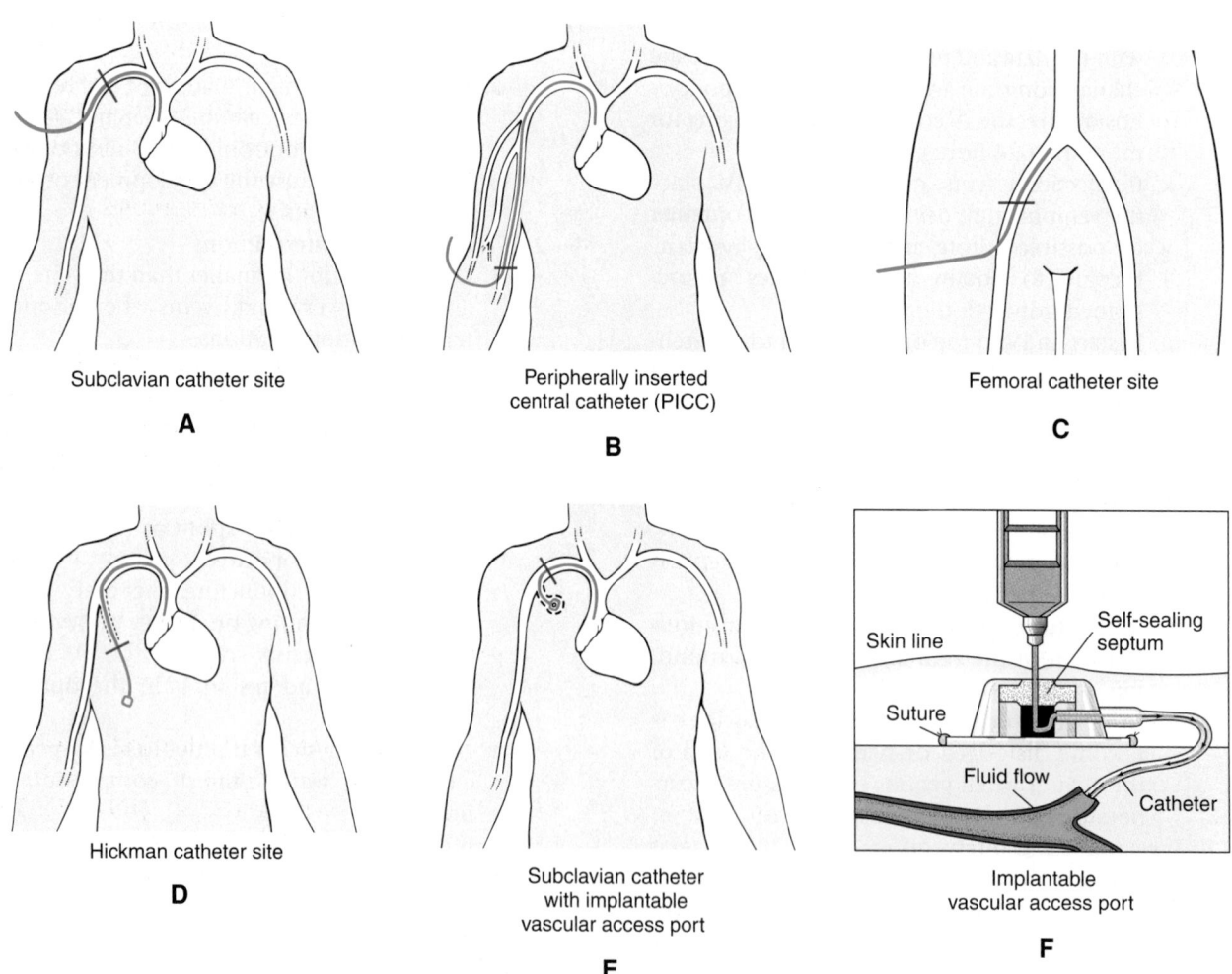

Subclavian catheter site
A

Peripherally inserted central catheter (PICC)
B

Femoral catheter site
C

Hickman catheter site
D

Subclavian catheter with implantable vascular access port
E

Skin line
Self-sealing septum
Suture
Fluid flow
Catheter

Implantable vascular access port
F

FIG. 14-7 Central venous access site(s). **A,** Subclavian catheter. **B,** Peripherally inserted central catheter. **C,** Femoral catheter. **D,** Hickman catheter. **E,** Subclavian catheter with implantable vascular access port. **F,** Implantable vascular access port. (From Kee, J. L., & Marshall, S. M. [2004]. *Clinical calculations: With applications to general and specialty areas* [5th ed]. Philadelphia: W.B. Saunders; F redrawn from Winters, B. [1984]. Implantable vascular access devices. *Oncology Nursing Forum*, 11, 25-30.)

or surgically tunneled through subcutaneous tissue into the cephalic vein.

5. With multilumen catheters, more than one medication can be administered at the same time without incompatibility problems, and only one insertion site is present.

▲ 6. For central line insertion, tubing change, and line removal, place the client in Trendelenburg position if not contraindicated, or supine position, and instruct the client to perform Valsalva's maneuver to increase pressure in the central veins when the IV system is open.

B. Tunneled central venous catheters
1. A more permanent type of catheter, such as the Hickman, Broviac, or Groshong catheter, is used for long-term IV therapy.
2. The catheter may be single lumen or multilumen.
3. The catheter is inserted in the operating room, and the catheter is threaded into the lower part of the vena cava at the entrance of the right atrium.
4. The catheter will be fitted with an intermittent infusion device to allow access as needed and to keep the system closed and intact.
▲ 5. Patency is maintained by flushing with a diluted heparin solution or normal saline solution, depending on the type of catheter and as per agency policy.

C. Vascular access ports (implantable port)
▲ 1. Surgically implanted under the skin, ports such as a Port-a-Cath, Mediport, or Infusaport are used for long-term administration of repeated IV therapy.
▲ 2. For access, the port requires palpation and injection through the skin into the self-sealing port with a noncoring needle, such as a Huber-point needle.
3. Patency is maintained by periodic flushing with a diluted heparin solution as prescribed and as per agency policy.

D. Peripherally inserted central catheter (PICC) line
1. The catheter is used for long-term IV therapy, frequently in the home.
2. The basilic vein usually is used, but the median cubital and cephalic veins in the antecubital area also can be used.
3. The catheter is threaded so that the catheter tip may terminate in the subclavian vein or superior vena cava.
4. A small amount of bleeding may occur at the time of insertion and may continue for 24 hours, but bleeding thereafter is not expected.
5. **Phlebitis** is a common complication.
6. Insertion is below the heart level; therefore, **air embolism** is not common.

PRACTICE QUESTIONS

1. A client recently diagnosed with a myocardial infarction and impaired renal function is recuperating on the step-down cardiac unit. The client's blood pressure has been borderline low and intravenous (IV) fluids have been infusing at 100 mL/hr via a central line catheter in the right internal jugular for approximately 24 hours to increase renal output and maintain the blood pressure. On entering the client's room, the nurse notes that the client is breathing rapidly and is coughing. The nurse determines that the client is most likely experiencing which complication of intravenous therapy?
   1. Hematoma
   2. Systemic infection
   3. Electrolyte overload
   4. Circulatory overload

2. A client involved in a motor vehicle crash presents to the emergency department with severe internal bleeding. The client is severely hypotensive and unresponsive. The nurse anticipates that which intravenous solution will most likely be prescribed to increase intravascular volume, replace immediate blood loss, and increase blood pressure?
   1. 0.45% sodium chloride
   2. 0.33% sodium chloride
   3. 0.225% sodium chloride
   4. Lactated Ringer's solution

3. The nurse is planning to provide a list of instructions to a client being discharged to home with a peripherally inserted central catheter (PICC). The nurse would avoid writing which of the following incorrect items on the instruction sheet?
   1. Wear a Medic-Alert tag or bracelet.
   2. Have a repair kit available in the home for use if needed.
   3. Keep the insertion site protected when in the shower or bath.
   4. Keep activity level to a minimum while this catheter is in place.

4. The nurse is assessing the IV dressing of a client with a peripheral intravenous infusion running. The date on the dressing is 7/25 (July 25). The nurse documents on the client's record that the dressing should be changed on which of the following dates?
   1. 7/26
   2. 7/28
   3. 7/30
   4. 8/1

5. The nurse is making initial rounds on the nursing unit to assess the condition of assigned clients. The nurse notes that a client's intravenous (IV) site is cool, pale, and swollen, and the solution is not infus-

ing. The nurse concludes that which of the following complications has been experienced by the client?
1. Infection
2. Phlebitis
3. Infiltration
4. Thrombosis

6. A client rings the call bell and complains of pain at the site of an intravenous (IV) infusion. The nurse assesses the site and determines that the client has developed phlebitis. The nurse avoids which action in the care of this client?
   1. Notifies the physician.
   2. Applies warm moist packs to the site.
   3. Discontinues the IV catheter at that site.
   4. Starts a new IV line in a proximal portion of the same vein.

7. A client had a 1000-mL bag of 5% dextrose in 0.9% sodium chloride hung at 3 PM. The nurse making rounds at 3:45 PM finds that the client is complaining of a pounding headache and is dyspneic, experiencing chills, and apprehensive, with an increased pulse rate. The intravenous (IV) bag has 400 mL remaining. The nurse should take which of the following actions first?
   1. Call the physician.
   2. Slow the IV infusion.
   3. Sit the client up in bed.
   4. Remove the IV catheter.

8. The nurse has an order to hang an IV bag of 1000 mL 5% dextrose in water with 20 mEq potassium chloride. The nurse should plan to do which of the following immediately after injecting the potassium chloride into the port of the intravenous (IV) bag?
   1. Rotate the bag gently.
   2. Attach the tubing to the client.
   3. Prime the tubing with the IV solution.
   4. Check the solution for yellowish discoloration.

9. The nurse is inserting an intravenous line into a client's vein. After the initial stick, the nurse continues to advance the catheter if the nurse notes that
   1. The catheter advances easily.
   2. The vein is distended under the needle.
   3. The client does not complain of discomfort.
   4. Blood return shows in the backflash chamber of the catheter.

10. The nurse notes that the site of a client's peripheral intravenous (IV) catheter is reddened, warm, painful, and slightly edematous proximal to the insertion point of the IV catheter. After taking appropriate steps to care for the client, the nurse documents in the medical record that the client experienced:
    1. Phlebitis of the vein.
    2. Infiltration of the IV line.
    3. Hypersensitivity to the IV solution.
    4. Allergic reaction to the IV catheter material.

11. The nurse is preparing a continuous intravenous (IV) infusion at the medication cart. As the nurse goes to attach the distal end of the IV tubing to a needleless device, the exposed tubing drops and hits the top of the medication cart. Which of the following is the appropriate action by the nurse?
    1. Obtain new IV tubing.
    2. Attach a new needleless device.
    3. Wipe the distal end of the tubing with Betadine.
    4. Scrub the needleless device with an alcohol swab.

12. A client is hypovolemic and plasma expanders are not available. The nurse anticipates that which of the following solutions available on the nursing unit will be prescribed by the physician?
    1. 5% dextrose in water
    2. 0.9% sodium chloride
    3. 0.45% sodium chloride
    4. 5% dextrose in 0.45% sodium chloride

13. The nurse hears an attending physician asking an intern to prescribe a hypotonic intravenous (IV) solution for a client. Which of the following IV solutions would the nurse expect the intern to prescribe?
    1. 5% dextrose in water
    2. 10% dextrose in water
    3. 0.45% sodium chloride
    4. 5% dextrose in 0.9% sodium chloride

14. A physician has written an order to discontinue an intravenous line. The nurse obtains which of the following supplies from the unit supply area for applying pressure to the site after removing the intravenous (IV) catheter?
    1. Alcohol swab
    2. Betadine swab
    3. Adhesive bandage
    4. Sterile 2 × 2 gauze

15. A client has just undergone insertion of a central venous catheter at the bedside. The nurse would be sure to check the results of which of the following before initiating the flow rate of the client's IV solution at 100 mL/hr?
    1. Serum osmolality
    2. Serum electrolyte levels
    3. Portable chest x-ray film
    4. Intake and output record

ALTERNATE ITEM FORMAT: FILL IN THE BLANK

The nurse is completing a time tape for a 1000-mL IV bag that is scheduled to infuse over 8 hours. The nurse has just placed the 11:00 AM marking at the 500-mL level. The nurse would place the mark for noon at which numerical level (mL) on the time tape?

_____ mL

ANSWERS

1. **4**

Rationale: Circulatory (fluid overload) is a complication of intravenous therapy. Signs include rapid breathing, dyspnea, a moist cough, and crackles. When circulatory overload is present, the client's blood pressure would also increase. Hematoma is characterized by ecchymosis, swelling, and leakage at the IV insertion site, and hard and painful lumps at the site. Systemic infection is characterized by chills, fever, malaise, headache, nausea, vomiting, backache, and tachycardia. Signs of electrolyte imbalance depends on the specific electrolyte.

Test-Taking Strategy: Focus on the data in the question. Noting that the client is experiencing rapid breathing and is coughing will assist in directing you to the correct option. Review the signs of complications of IV therapy if you had difficulty with this question.

Level of Cognitive Ability: Analysis
Client Needs: Physiological Integrity
Integrated Process: Nursing Process—analysis
Content Area: Fundamental skills
Reference: Lewis, S., Heitkemper, M., & Dirksen, S. (2004). *Medical-surgical nursing: Assessment and management of clinical problems* (6th ed., p.749). St. Louis: Mosby.

2. **4**

Rationale: The goal of therapy with this client is to expand intravascular volume as quickly as possible. Lactated Ringer's (hypertonic solution) would increase intravascular volume and immediately replace lost fluid volume until a transfusion could be administered, resulting in an increase in the client's blood pressure. The solutions in options 1, 2, and 3 would not be given to this client because they are hypotonic solutions and, instead of increasing intravascular space, the solutions would move into the cells via osmosis.

Test-Taking Strategy: Focus on the data in the question, noting that the client requires increased intravascular volume. Recalling IV fluid types and how hypotonic and hypertonic solutions function within the intravascular space will direct you to the correct option. Review these types of IV fluids if you had difficulty with this question.

Level of Cognitive Ability: Analysis
Client Needs: Physiological Integrity
Integrated Process: Nursing Process—analysis
Content Area: Fundamental skills
Reference: Lewis, S., Heitkemper, M., & Dirksen, S. (2004). *Medical-surgical nursing: Assessment and management of clinical problems* (6th ed., p. 715). St. Louis: Mosby.

3. **4**

Rationale: The client should be taught that only minor activity restrictions apply with this type of catheter. The client should protect the site during bathing and should carry or wear a Medic-Alert identification. The client should have a repair kit in the home for use as needed because the catheter is for long-term use.

Test-Taking Strategy: Use the process of elimination and note the strategic words *avoid* and *incorrect*. Recalling that the PICC is for long-term use will assist in directing you to option 4. To keep activity to a minimum with such a catheter is unreason-able. Review home care instructions for a client with a PICC if you had difficulty with this question.

Level of Cognitive Ability: Application
Client Needs: Physiological Integrity
Integrated Process: Teaching and Learning
Content Area: Fundamental skills
Reference: Perry, A., & Potter, P. (2006). *Clinical nursing skills & techniques* (6th ed., pp. 926, 929). St. Louis: Mosby.

4. **2**

Rationale: The IV site dressing should be changed every 48 to 72 hours, which is every 2 to 3 days. With an insertion date of 7/25, the due date for change, depending on agency policy, would be 7/27 or 7/28. It would be unnecessary, uncomfortable, and not cost-effective to change the site dressing daily (option 1). Changing the site dressing every 5 or 7 days (options 3 and 4) would place the client at higher risk for infection or other catheter complications.

Test-Taking Strategy: Use the process of elimination. Recalling that the IV site dressing should be changed every 48 to 72 hours will direct you to option 2. Review the standard accepted guidelines for intravenous site maintenance if you had difficulty with this question.

Level of Cognitive Ability: Application
Client Needs: Safe and Effective Care Environment
Integrated Process: Communication and Documentation
Content Area: Fundamental skills
References: Ignatavicius, D., & Workman, M. (2006). *Medical-surgical nursing: Critical thinking for collaborative care* (5th ed., p. 256). Philadelphia: W.B. Saunders.
Perry, A., & Potter, P. (2006). *Clinical nursing skills & techniques* (6th ed., p. 925). St. Louis: Mosby.
Potter, P., & Perry, A. (2005). *Fundamentals of nursing* (6th ed., p. 1187). St. Louis: Mosby.

5. **3**

Rationale: An infiltrated IV is one that has dislodged from the vein and is lying in subcutaneous tissue. Pallor, coolness, and swelling are the results of IV fluid being deposited in the subcutaneous tissue. When the pressure in the tissues exceeds the pressure in the tubing, the flow of the IV solution will stop. The corrective action is to remove the catheter and start a new IV line at another site. The other three options are likely to be accompanied by warmth at the site, not coolness.

Test-Taking Strategy: Use the process of elimination, focusing on the clinical manifestations identified in the question. Noting the strategic word *cool* in the question will direct you to option 3. Review the signs of infiltration if you had difficulty with this question.

Level of Cognitive Ability: Analysis
Client Needs: Physiological Integrity
Integrated Process: Nursing Process—assessment
Content Area: Fundamental skills
References: Ignatavicius, D., & Workman, M. (2006). *Medical-surgical nursing: Critical thinking for collaborative care* (5th ed., p. 259). Philadelphia: W.B. Saunders.
Perry, A., & Potter, P. (2006). *Clinical nursing skills & techniques* (6th ed., pp. 918-919). St. Louis: Mosby.
Potter, P., & Perry, A. (2005). *Fundamentals of nursing* (6th ed., p. 1173). St. Louis: Mosby.

6. 4

Rationale: The nurse should discontinue the IV at the phlebitic site and apply warm moist compresses to the area to speed resolution of the inflammation. Because phlebitis has occurred, the nurse also notifies the physician about the IV complication. The nurse should restart the IV in a vein other than the one that has developed phlebitis.

Test-Taking Strategy: Use the process of elimination and note the strategic word *avoids*. This tells you that the correct option is an incorrect nursing action. Recalling that the nurse should restart the IV in a vein other than the one that has developed phlebitis will direct you to option 4. Review nursing interventions related to phlebitis if you had difficulty with this question.

Level of Cognitive Ability: Application
Client Needs: Physiological Integrity
Integrated Process: Nursing Process—implementation
Content Area: Fundamental skills
References: Ignatavicius, D., & Workman, M. (2006). *Medical-surgical nursing: Critical thinking for collaborative care* (5th ed., p. 260). Philadelphia: W.B. Saunders.
Potter, P., & Perry, A. (2005). *Fundamentals of nursing* (6th ed., p. 1173). St. Louis: Mosby.

7. 2

Rationale: The client's symptoms are compatible with circulatory overload. This may be verified by noting that 600 mL has infused in the course of 45 minutes. The first action of the nurse is to slow the infusion. Other actions may follow in rapid sequence. The nurse may elevate the head of the bed to aid the client's breathing, if necessary. The nurse also notifies the physician immediately. The IV catheter is not removed; it may be needed once the complication has been resolved.

Test-Taking Strategy: Use the process of elimination and note the strategic word *first*. This tells you that more than one or all of the options are likely to be correct actions, and the nurse needs to prioritize them according to a time sequence. You must be able to recognize the signs of circulatory overload. From this point, select the option that provides the intervention specific to circulatory overload. Review nursing actions related to this complication if you had difficulty with this question.

Level of Cognitive Ability: Application
Client Needs: Physiological Integrity
Integrated Process: Nursing Process—implementation
Content Area: Delegating/prioritizing
References: Ignatavicius, D., & Workman, M. (2006). *Medical-surgical nursing: Critical thinking for collaborative care* (5th ed., p. 262). Philadelphia: W.B. Saunders.
Potter, P., & Perry, A. (2005). *Fundamentals of nursing* (6th ed., p. 1173). St. Louis: Mosby.

8. 1

Rationale: After adding a medication to a bag of intravenous (IV) solution, the nurse should agitate or rotate the bag gently to mix the medication evenly in the solution. The nurse should then attach a completed medication label. The nurse can then prime the tubing. The IV solution should have been checked for discoloration before the medication was added to the solution. The tubing is attached to the client last.

Test-Taking Strategy: Use the process of elimination and note the strategic words *immediately after injecting*. They imply a

correct time sequence, and you need to prioritize. Visualize and think through the steps of adding medication to an IV bag, and make your choice accordingly. Review the procedure for adding potassium chloride to an IV bag if you had difficulty with this question.

Level of Cognitive Ability: Application
Client Needs: Physiological Integrity
Integrated Process: Nursing Process—implementation
Content Area: Pharmacology
Reference: Potter, P., & Perry, A. (2005). *Fundamentals of nursing* (6th ed., pp. 894-896). St. Louis: Mosby.

9. 4

Rationale: The IV catheter has entered the lumen of the vein successfully when blood backflash shows in the IV catheter. The vein should have been distended by the tourniquet before the vein was cannulated. Client discomfort varies with the client, the site, and the nurse's insertion technique and is not a reliable measure of catheter placement. The nurse should not advance the catheter until placement in the vein is verified by blood return.

Test-Taking Strategy: Use the process of elimination, focusing on the subject of the question: correct placement of an IV catheter. Noting the strategic words *blood return* in option 4 will direct you to this option. Review the steps for inserting an IV catheter if you had difficulty with this question.

Level of Cognitive Ability: Application
Client Needs: Physiological Integrity
Integrated Process: Nursing Process—implementation
Content Area: Fundamental skills
References: Perry, A., & Potter, P. (2006). *Clinical nursing skills & techniques* (6th ed., p. 912). St. Louis: Mosby.
Potter, P., & Perry, A. (2005). *Fundamentals of nursing* (6th ed., pp. 1167-1168). St. Louis: Mosby.

10. 1

Rationale: Phlebitis at an IV site can be distinguished by client discomfort at the site and by redness, warmth, and swelling proximal to the catheter. If phlebitis occurs, the nurse should discontinue the IV line and insert a new IV line at a different site. Coolness at the site would be noted if the IV catheter was infiltrated. An allergic reaction produces a rash, redness, and itching. A major reaction, such as hypersensitivity, can cause dyspnea, a swollen tongue, and cyanosis.

Test-Taking Strategy: Use the process of elimination. Remember that options that are comparative or alike are not likely to be correct. In this situation, options 3 and 4 are comparative or alike and therefore are eliminated. Choose option 1 over option 2 after recalling the signs of common IV complications. Review the signs and symptoms of phlebitis if you had difficulty with this question.

Level of Cognitive Ability: Analysis
Client Needs: Physiological Integrity
Integrated Process: Communication and Documentation
Content Area: Fundamental skills
References: Ignatavicius, D., & Workman, M. (2006). *Medical-surgical nursing: Critical thinking for collaborative care* (5th ed., p. 260). Philadelphia: W.B. Saunders.
Potter, P., & Perry, A. (2005). *Fundamentals of nursing* (6th ed., p. 1173). St. Louis: Mosby.

11. 1
Rationale: The nurse should obtain a new IV tubing because contamination has occurred and could cause systemic infection to the client. Wiping with Betadine is insufficient and would be contraindicated anyhow because the tubing will be attached directly to an angiocatheter in the client's vein. The needleless device has not been contaminated and does not need replacement or cleaning.
Test-Taking Strategy: Use the process of elimination and knowledge of basic infection control measures and intravenous therapy concepts to answer this question. Clearly, only one option is correct. Remember that if an item is contaminated, discard it and obtain a new sterile item. Review aseptic technique if you had difficulty with this question.
Level of Cognitive Ability: Application
Client Needs: Safe and Effective Care Environment
Integrated Process: Nursing Process—implementation
Content Area: Fundamental skills
Reference: Ignatavicius, D., & Workman, M. (2006). *Medical-surgical nursing: Critical thinking for collaborative care* (5th ed., p. 250). Philadelphia: W.B. Saunders.

12. 4
Rationale: A solution of 5% dextrose in 0.45% sodium chloride is hypertonic. An advantage of hypertonic solutions is that they may be used to treat hypovolemia when plasma expanders are not readily available. Options 1 and 2 are isotonic solutions. Option 3 is a hypotonic solution.
Test-Taking Strategy: Use the process of elimination. Noting the strategic word *hypovolemic* will assist in directing you to option 4 if you are familiar with the IV solutions that are hypertonic. If this question was difficult, review the nature and purposes of hypertonic, isotonic, and hypotonic IV solutions.
Level of Cognitive Ability: Analysis
Client Needs: Physiological Integrity
Integrated Process: Nursing Process—analysis
Content Area: Fundamental skills
References: Ignatavicius, D., & Workman, M. (2006). *Medical-surgical nursing: Critical thinking for collaborative care* (5th ed., pp. 213, 247). Philadelphia: W.B. Saunders.
Potter, P., & Perry, A. (2005). *Fundamentals of nursing* (6th ed., pp. 1136, 1396). St. Louis: Mosby.

13. 3
Rationale: Hypotonic solutions contain a lower concentration of salt or more water than an isotonic solution. A solution of 0.45% sodium chloride is hypotonic. A solution of 5% dextrose in water (D_5W) is isotonic. Solutions of 10% dextrose in water ($D_{10}W$) and 5% dextrose in 0.9% sodium chloride are hypertonic solutions.
Test-Taking Strategy: Use the process of elimination. Note that options 1, 2, and 4 are comparative or alike. All these solutions contain dextrose. Option 3 is different from the other options. If you had difficulty with this question, review the tonicity of the various IV solutions.
Level of Cognitive Ability: Analysis
Client Needs: Physiological Integrity

Integrated Process: Nursing Process—planning
Content Area: Fundamental skills
References: Ignatavicius, D., & Workman, M. (2006). *Medical-surgical nursing: Critical thinking for collaborative care* (5th ed., pp. 213, 247). Philadelphia: W.B. Saunders.
Potter, P., & Perry, A. (2005). *Fundamentals of nursing* (6th ed., pp. 1136, 1196). St. Louis: Mosby.

14. 4
Rationale: A dry sterile dressing such as a sterile 2 × 2 is used to apply pressure to the discontinued IV site. This material is absorbent, sterile, and nonirritating. A Betadine swab or an alcohol swab would irritate the opened puncture site and would not stop the blood flow. An adhesive bandage may be used to cover the site once hemostasis has occurred.
Test-Taking Strategy: Use the process of elimination and note the strategic words *applying pressure*. Visualize this procedure, thinking about each of the items identified in the options to direct you to option 4. Review this basic procedure if you had difficulty with this question.
Level of Cognitive Ability: Application
Client Needs: Physiological Integrity
Integrated Process: Nursing Process—implementation
Content Area: Fundamental skills
References: Ignatavicius, D., & Workman, M. (2006). *Medical-surgical nursing: Critical thinking for collaborative care* (5th ed., p. 258). Philadelphia: W.B. Saunders.
Perry, A., & Potter, P. (2006). *Clinical nursing skills & techniques* (6th ed., pp. 937-938). St. Louis: Mosby.
Potter, P., & Perry, A. (2005). *Fundamentals of nursing* (6th ed., p. 1190). St. Louis: Mosby.

15. 3
Rationale: Before beginning administration of IV solution, the nurse should assess whether the chest radiograph reveals that the central catheter is in the proper place. This is necessary to prevent infusion of IV fluid into pulmonary or subcutaneous tissues. The other options represent items that are useful for the nurse to be aware of in the general care of this client, but they do not relate to this procedure.
Test-Taking Strategy: Use the process of elimination and note the words *central venous catheter at the bedside*. Recalling the potential complications associated with the insertion of central venous catheters will direct you to option 3. Review the principles of care for a central venous catheter after insertion if you had difficulty with this question.
Level of Cognitive Ability: Application
Client Needs: Physiological Integrity
Integrated Process: Nursing Process—assessment
Content Area: Fundamental skills
References: Ignatavicius, D., & Workman, M. (2006). *Medical-surgical nursing: Critical thinking for collaborative care* (5th ed., p. 250). Philadelphia.
Lewis, S., Heitkemper, M., & Dirksen, S. (2004). *Medical-surgical nursing: Assessment and management of clinical problems* (6th ed., p. 313). St. Louis: Mosby.

ALTERNATE ITEM FORMAT: FILL IN THE BLANK

Answer: 375.

Rationale: If the IV is scheduled to run over 8 hours, then the hourly rate is 125 mL/hr. Using 500 mL as the reference point, the next hourly marking would be at 375 mL, which is 125 mL less than 500.

Test-Taking Strategy: Use basic principles related to pharmacology math and IV administration to answer this question. If this question was difficult, review the concepts related to marking an IV solution by using a time tape.

Level of Cognitive Ability: Application
Client Needs: Physiological Integrity
Integrated Process: Nursing Process—implementation
Content Area: Fundamental skills
Reference: Potter, P., & Perry, A. (2005). *Fundamentals of nursing* (6th ed., p. 831). St. Louis: Mosby.

REFERENCES

Ignatavicius, D., & Workman, M. (2006). *Medical-surgical nursing: Critical thinking for collaborative care* (5th ed.). Philadelphia: W.B. Saunders.

Lewis, S., Heitkemper, M., & Dirksen, S. (2004). *Medical-surgical nursing: Assessment and management of clinical problems* (6th ed.). St. Louis: Mosby.

National Council of State Boards of Nursing (Eds.). (2007). *2007 NCLEX-RN® detailed test plan*. Chicago: Author.

Potter, P., & Perry, A. (2005). *Fundamentals of nursing* (6th ed.). St. Louis: Mosby.

Perry, A., & Potter, P. (2006). *Clinical nursing skills & techniques* (6th ed.). St. Louis: Mosby.

Administration of Blood Products

PYRAMID TERMS

ABO A type of antigen system. The ABO type of the donor should be compatible with the recipient's. Type A can match with type A or O; type B can match with type B or O; type O can match only with type O; type AB can match with type A, B, or O.

autologous donation A donation of the client's own blood before a scheduled procedure.

blood salvage An autologous donation that involves suctioning blood from body cavities, joint spaces, or other closed body sites during a procedure.

circulatory overload A complication resulting from the infusion of blood at a rate too rapid for the size, cardiac status, or clinical condition of the recipient.

compatibility Matching of blood from two persons by two different types of antigen systems, ABO and Rh, present on the membrane surface of the red blood cells, to prevent a transfusion reaction.

crossmatching The testing of the donor's blood and the recipient's blood for compatibility.

designated donor A compatible donor who has been selected by the recipient.

fresh frozen plasma A blood product administered to increase the level of clotting factors in clients with such a deficiency.

iron overload A delayed transfusion complication that occurs in clients who are chronically dependent on blood transfusions, such as clients with anemia or thrombocytopenia.

platelets A blood product administered to clients with low platelet counts and to thrombocytopenic clients who are bleeding actively or are scheduled for an invasive procedure.

red blood cells A blood product used to replace erythrocytes lost as a result of trauma or surgical interventions or in clients with bone marrow suppression.

Rh factor Rh stands for Rhesus factor. A person having the factor is Rh positive; a person lacking the factor is Rh negative. The presence or absence of Rh antigens on the surface of red blood cells (RBCs) determines the classification as Rh positive or Rh negative.

septicemia The presence of infective agents or their toxins in the bloodstream. Septicemia is a serious infection and must be treated promptly; otherwise, the infection leads to circulatory collapse, profound shock, and death.

transfusion reaction A hemolytic reaction caused by blood type or Rh incompatibility. An allergic transfusion reaction most often occurs in clients with a history of allergy. A febrile transfusion reaction most commonly occurs in clients with antibodies directed against the transfused white blood cells. A bacterial transfusion reaction occurs after transfusion of contaminated blood products.

whole blood Whole blood is composed of red blood cells, plasma, and plasma proteins and is administered primarily to treat hypovolemic shock resulting from hemorrhage.

THE PYRAMID TO SUCCESS

Pyramid Points focus on the safe administration of blood components, managing and providing care related to the procedure for administering blood components, and monitoring for complications. Focus is on the safe procedure for administering blood products and on the signs and symptoms of transfusion reaction. Pyramid Points also focus on the immediate interventions if a transfusion reaction occurs, and evaluation and documentation of expected and unexpected effects of the therapy. Integrated Processes addressed in this chapter are Caring, Communication and Documentation, Nursing Process, and Teaching/Learning.

CLIENT NEEDS

Safe and Effective Care Environment

Establishing priorities of care
Ensuring ethical practice and legal responsibilities
Handling of hazardous and infectious materials
Implementing standard, transmission-based, and other precautions

Maintaining continuity of care and providing close supervision during a blood transfusion

Maintaining medical and surgical asepsis

Obtaining informed consent for the administration of blood products

Upholding client rights

Health Promotion and Maintenance

Identifying lifestyle choices related to receiving a blood transfusion

Providing client education about the signs of a transfusion reaction

Psychosocial Integrity

Ensuring therapeutic interactions with the client regarding the procedure for blood administration

Identifying religious, spiritual, and cultural considerations related to blood administration

Physiological Integrity

Administering blood products safely

Assessing venous access devices for blood administration

Documenting the client's response to receiving the blood product

Managing medical emergencies if a transfusion reaction or other complication occurs

Monitoring for complications related to blood administration

Monitoring for expected effects

Monitoring laboratory values

I. TYPES OF BLOOD COMPONENTS

A. Packed **red blood cells**
1. **Red blood cells** are a blood product used to replace erythrocytes.
2. Each unit increases the hemoglobin level by 1 g/dL and hematocrit by 2% to 3%; the change in laboratory values takes 4 to 6 hours after completion of the blood transfusion.
3. Evaluation of an effective response is based on the resolution of the symptoms of anemia and an increase in the erythrocyte count.

B. **Platelets**
1. Platelets are used to treat thrombocytopenia and platelet dysfunctions.
2. **Crossmatching** is not required but usually is done (platelet concentrates contain few **red blood cells**).
3. The volume in a unit of **platelets** may vary; always check the bag for the volume of the blood component (in milliliters).

4. **Platelets** are administered immediately on receipt from the blood bank and are given rapidly, usually over 15 to 30 minutes.
5. Evaluation of an effective response is based on improvement in the platelet count, and platelet counts normally are evaluated 1 hour and 18 to 24 hours after the transfusion.

C. **Fresh frozen plasma**
1. **Fresh frozen plasma** may be used to provide clotting factors or volume expansion; it contains no platelets.
2. **Fresh frozen plasma** is infused within 2 hours of thawing, while clotting factors are still viable, and is infused as rapidly as possible.
3. **Rh compatibility** and **ABO compatibility** are required for the transfusion of plasma products.
4. Evaluation of an effective response is assessed by monitoring coagulation studies, particularly the prothrombin time and the partial thromboplastin time, and resolution of hypovolemia.

D. Albumin
1. Albumin is prepared from plasma and can be stored for 5 years.
2. It is used to treat hypovolemic shock or hypoalbuminemia.
3. Albumin, 25g/100 mL, is equal to 500 mL of plasma.

E. Cryoprecipitates
1. Prepared from **fresh frozen plasma** and can be stored for 1 year; once thawed, the product must be used.
2. Used to replace clotting factors, especially factor VIII and fibrinogen.

II. TYPES OF BLOOD DONATIONS

A. Autologous
1. A donation of the client's own blood before a scheduled procedure is autologous; it reduces the risk of disease transmission and potential transfusion complications.
2. **Autologous donation** is not an option for a client with leukemia or bacteremia.
3. A donation can be made every 3 days as long as the hemoglobin remains within a safe range.
4. Donations should begin within 5 weeks of the transfusion date and end at least 3 days before the date of transfusion.

B. Blood salvage
1. **Blood salvage** is an **autologous donation** that involves suctioning blood from body cavities, joint spaces, or other closed body sites.
2. Blood may need to be "washed," a special process that removes tissue debris before reinfusion.

C. **Designated donor**

TABLE 15-1

Compatibility Chart for Red Blood Cell Transfusions

Donor	Recipient			
	A	B	AB	O
A	X		X	
B		X	X	
AB			X	
O	X	X	X	X

From Ignatavicius, D., & Workman, M. (2006). Medical-surgical nursing: Critical thinking for collaborative care (5th ed.). Philadelphia: W.B. Saunders.

1. Designated donation occurs when recipients select their own compatible donors.
2. Donation does not reduce the risk of contracting infections transmitted by the blood; however, recipients feel more comfortable identifying their donors.

III. COMPATIBILITY (Table 15-1)

A. Client (the recipient) blood samples are drawn and labeled at the client's bedside at the time the blood sample is drawn; the client is asked to state his or her name, which is compared with the name on the client's identification band or bracelet.

B. The recipient's **ABO** type and **Rh** type are identified.

C. An antibody screen is done to determine the presence of antibodies other than anti-A and anti-B.

D. Crossmatching is done, in which donor red blood cells are combined with the recipient's serum and Coombs' serum; the crossmatch is compatible if no red blood cell agglutination occurs.

E. The universal red blood cell donor is O negative; the universal recipient is AB positive.

IV. INFUSION CONTROLLERS AND PUMPS

A. Infusion controllers and pumps may be used to administer blood products if they are designed to function with opaque solutions; however, the negative pressure exerted by the cassette of the machine can cause hemolysis of **red blood cells**.

B. Always consult manufacturer guidelines for the controller or pump.

C. Special manual pressure cuffs may be used to increase the flow rate but it should not exceed 300 mm Hg.

D. Standard sphygmomanometer cuffs are not to be used to increase the flow rate because they do not exert uniform pressure against all parts of the bag.

V. BLOOD WARMERS

A. Blood warmers may be used to prevent hypothermia and adverse reactions when several units of blood are being administered.

B. Special warmers have been designed for this purpose, and only devices specifically tested and approved for this use can be used.

C. Do not warm blood products in a microwave or in hot water.

VI. PRECAUTIONS AND NURSING RESPONSIBILITIES (Box 15-1)

VII. COMPLICATIONS (Box 15-2)

A. **Transfusion reactions**

1. Description
   a. A **transfusion reaction** is an adverse reaction that occurs as a result of receiving a blood transfusion
   b. Types of **transfusion reactions** include hemolytic, allergic, febrile or bacterial reactions, **circulatory overload,** or transfusion-associated graft-versus-host disease (GVHD).

2. Signs of an immediate **transfusion reaction**
   a. Chills and diaphoresis
   b. Muscle aches, back pain, or chest pain
   c. Rashes, hives, itching, and swelling
   d. Rapid, thready pulse
   e. Dyspnea, cough, or wheezing
   f. Pallor and cyanosis
   g. Apprehension
   h. Tingling and numbness
   i. Headache
   j. Nausea, vomiting, abdominal cramping, and diarrhea

3. Signs of a **transfusion reaction** in an unconscious client
   a. Weak pulse
   b. Fever
   c. Tachycardia or bradycardia
   d. Hypotension
   e. Visible hemoglobinuria
   f. Oliguria or anuria

4. Delayed **transfusion reactions**
   a. Reactions can occur days to years after a transfusion.
   b. Signs include fever, mild jaundice, and a decreased hematocrit level.

5. Interventions
   a. Stop the transfusion.
   b. Keep the intravenous line open with 0.9% normal saline.
   c. Notify the physician and blood bank.
   d. Remain with the client, observing signs and symptoms and monitoring vital signs as often as every 5 minutes.
   e. Prepare to administer emergency medications such as antihistamines, vasopressors, fluids, and corticosteroids, as prescribed.
   f. Obtain a urine specimen for laboratory studies.

BOX 15-1
Precautions and Nursing Responsibilities

GENERAL PRECAUTIONS

A large volume of refrigerated blood infused rapidly through a central catheter into the ventricle of the heart can cause cardiac dysrhythmias.

No solution other than normal saline should be added to blood components.

Medications are never added to blood components or piggybacked into a blood transfusion.

To avoid the risk of septicemia, infusions (1 unit) should not exceed 4 hours.

The blood administration set should be changed every 4 to 6 hours, with each unit of blood, or according to institution policy, to reduce the risk of septicemia.

Always check the blood bag for the date of expiration; components expire at midnight on the day marked on the bag unless otherwise specified.

Inspect the blood bag for leaks, abnormal color, clots, and bubbles.

Blood must be administered as soon as possible (within 20 to 30 minutes) from its being received from the blood bank, because this is the maximal allowable time out of monitored storage.

Never refrigerate blood in refrigerators other than those used in blood banks; if the blood is not administered within 20 to 30 minutes, return it to the blood bank.

The recommended rate of infusion varies with the blood component being transfused and depends on the client's condition; generally, blood is infused as quickly as the client's condition allows.

Components containing few red blood cells and platelets may be infused rapidly, but caution should be taken to avoid circulatory overload.

The nurse should measure vital signs and assess lung sounds before the transfusion and again after the first 15 minutes and every hour until 1 hour after the transfusion is completed.

BLOOD BANK PRECAUTIONS

Blood will be released from the blood bank only to personnel specified by agency policy.

The name and identification number of the intended recipient must be provided to the blood bank, and a documented permanent record of this information must be maintained.

Blood should be transported from the blood bank to only one client at a time to prevent blood delivery to the wrong client.

CLIENT IDENTITY AND COMPATIBILITY

The most critical phase of the transfusion is confirming product compatibility and verifying client identity.

Two licensed nurses need to check the physician's order, the client's identity, and the client's identification band or bracelet and number, verifying that the name and number are identical to those on the blood component tag.

At the bedside, the nurse asks the client to state his or her name, and the nurse compares the name with the name on the identification band or bracelet.

The nurse checks the blood bag tag, label, and blood requisition form to ensure that ABO and Rh types are compatible.

If the nurse notes any inconsistencies when verifying client identity and compatibility, the nurse notifies the blood bank immediately.

CLIENT ASSESSMENT

Assess for any cultural or religious beliefs regarding blood transfusions.

A Jehovah's Witness cannot receive blood or blood products; this group believes that blood transfusions have eternal consequences.

Ensure that an informed consent has been obtained.

Determine whether the client has ever experienced any previous reactions to blood transfusions.

Check the client's vital signs; assess renal, circulatory, and respiratory status and the client's ability to tolerate intravenously administered fluids.

If the client's temperature is elevated, notify the physician before beginning the transfusion; a fever may be a cause for delaying the transfusion in addition to masking a possible symptom of an acute transfusion reaction.

ADMINISTRATION OF THE TRANSFUSION

Maintain standard, transmission-based, and other precautions as necessary.

Insert an intravenous (IV) line and infuse normal saline; maintain the infusion at a keep vein open rate.

An 18- or 19-gauge IV needle will be needed to achieve a maximum flow rate of blood products and prevent damage to red blood cells; if a smaller gauge needle must be used, red blood cells may be diluted with normal saline.

A central catheter is an acceptable venous access option for blood transfusions.

Always check the bag for the volume of the blood component.

Blood products should be infused through administration sets designed specifically for blood; use a Y-tubing or straight tubing blood administration set that contains a filter designed to trap fibrin clots and other debris that accumulate during blood storage (Fig. 15-1).

Premedicate the client with acetaminophen (Tylenol) or diphenhydramine (Benadryl), as prescribed, if the client has a history of adverse reactions; if prescribed, oral medications should be administered 30 minutes before the transfusion is started, and intravenously administered medications may be given immediately before the transfusion is started.

Instruct the client to report anything unusual immediately.

Determine the rate of infusion by the physician's order or, if not specified, by agency policy.

Begin the transfusion slowly under close supervision; if no reaction is noted within the first 15 minutes, the flow can be increased to the prescribed rate.

Continued

BOX 15-1
Precautions and Nursing Responsibilities—cont'd

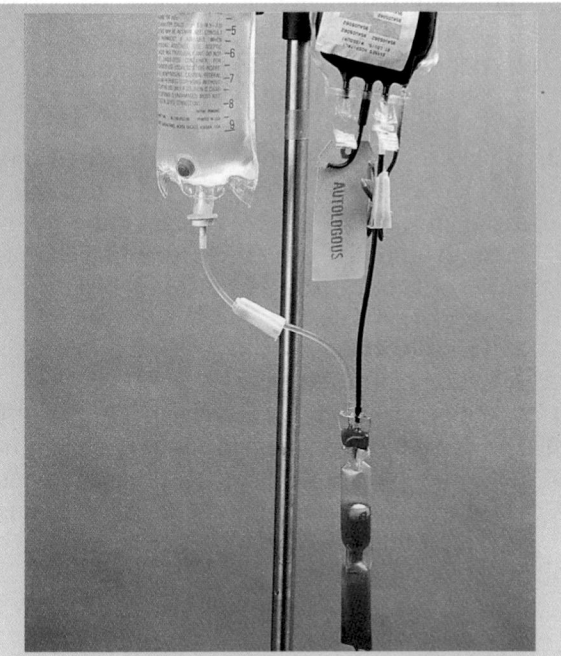

FIG. 15-1   Tubing for blood administration has an in-line filter. (From Potter, P., & Perry, A. [2005]. Fundamentals of nursing [6th ed.]. St. Louis: Mosby.

During the transfusion, monitor the client for signs and symptoms of a transfusion reaction; the first 15 minutes of the transfusion are the most critical, and the nurse must stay with the client.

If a major ABO incompatibility exists or a severe allergic reaction occurs, the reaction is usually evident within the first 50 mL of the transfusion.

Document the client's tolerance to the administration of the blood product.

Monitor appropriate laboratory values and document effectiveness of treatment related to the specific type of blood product.

REACTIONS TO THE TRANSFUSION

If a transfusion reaction occurs, stop the transfusion, change the IV tubing down to the IV site, keep the IV line open with normal saline, notify the physician and blood bank, and return the blood bag and tubing to the blood bank.

Do not leave the client alone, and monitor the client for any life-threatening symptoms.

Obtain appropriate laboratory samples according to agency policies, such as blood and urine samples (free hemoglobin indicates that red blood cells were hemolyzed).

g. Return blood bag, tubing, attached labels, and transfusion record to the blood bank.

B. **Circulatory overload**
1. Description: Caused by the infusion of blood at a rate too rapid for the client to tolerate
2. Assessment
   a. Cough, dyspnea, chest pain, and wheezing on auscultation of the lungs
   b. Headache
   c. Hypertension
   d. Tachycardia and a bounding pulse
   e. Distended neck veins
3. Interventions
   a. Slow the rate of infusion.
   b. Place the client in an upright position, with the feet in a dependent position.
   c. Notify the physician.
   d. Administer oxygen, diuretics, and morphine sulfate, as prescribed.
   e. Monitor for dysrhythmias.
   f. Phlebotomy also may be a method of pre-scribed treatment in a severe case.

C. **Septicemia**
1. Description: Occurs with the transfusion of blood that is contaminated with microorganisms
2. Assessment
   a. Rapid onset of chills and a high fever
   b. Vomiting
   c. Diarrhea

BOX 15-2
Complications of a Blood Transfusion

Transfusion reactions
Circulatory overload
Septicemia
Iron overload
Disease transmission
Hypocalcemia
Hyperkalemia

   d. Hypotension
   e. Shock
3. Interventions
   a. Notify the physician.
   b. Obtain blood cultures and cultures of the blood bag.
   c. Administer oxygen, intravenous fluids, anti-biotics, vasopressors, and corticosteroids as ordered.

D. **Iron overload**
1. Description: A delayed transfusion complication that occurs in clients who are chronically depen-dent on blood transfusions, such as clients with anemia or thrombocytopenia
2. Assessment
   a. Vomiting
   b. Diarrhea

c. Hypotension

      d. Altered hematological values

  3. Interventions

      a. Deferoxamine (Desferal), administered intravenously or subcutaneously, removes accumulated iron via the kidneys.

      b. Urine turns red as iron is excreted after the administration of deferoxamine; treatment is discontinued when serum iron levels return to normal.

E. Disease transmission

  1. A disease commonly transmitted is hepatitis C, which is manifested by anorexia, nausea, vomiting, dark urine, and jaundice; the symptoms usually occur within 4 to 6 weeks after the transfusion.

  2. Other infectious agents and diseases transmitted by blood transfusion include hepatitis B virus, human immunodeficiency virus, human herpesvirus type 6, Epstein-Barr virus, human T-cell leukemia, cytomegalovirus, and malaria.

  3. Donor screening has greatly reduced the risk of transmission of infectious agents; additionally, antibody testing of donors for human immunodeficiency virus has greatly reduced the risk of transmission.

F. Hypocalcemia

  1. Citrate in transfused blood binds with calcium and is excreted.

  2. Assess serum calcium level before and after transfusion.

  3. Monitor for signs of hypocalcemia (hyperactive reflexes, paresthesias, tetany, muscle cramps, positive Trousseau's sign, positive Chvostek's sign).

  4. Slow the transfusion and notify the physician if signs of hypocalcemia occur.

G. Hyperkalemia

  1. Stored blood liberates potassium through hemolysis.

  2. The older the blood, the greater the risk of hyperkalemia; therefore, clients at risk for hyperkalemia, such as those with renal insufficiency or renal failure, should receive fresh blood.

  3. Assess the date on the blood and the serum potassium level before and after the transfusion.

  4. Monitor the potassium level and for signs of hyperkalemia (paresthesias, weakness, abdominal cramps, diarrhea, and dysrhythmias).

  5. Slow the transfusion and notify the physician if signs of hyperkalemia occur.

PRACTICE QUESTIONS

1. A client receiving a transfusion of packed red blood cells (PRBCs) begins to vomit. The nurse takes the client's blood pressure and it is 90/50 mm Hg, from a baseline of 125/78 mm Hg. The client's temperature is 100.8° F orally, from a baseline of 99.2° F orally. The nurse determines that the client may be experiencing which complication of a blood transfusion?
   1. Septicemia
   2. Hyperkalemia
   3. Circulatory overload
   4. Delayed transfusion reaction

2. The nurse who is about to begin a blood transfusion knows that blood cells start to deteriorate after a certain period of time. Which of the following items is important to check regarding the age of blood cells before the transfusion is begun?
   1. Expiration date
   2. Presence of clots
   3. Blood group and type
   4. Blood identification number

3. The nurse is told by a physician that a client in hypovolemic shock will require plasma expansion. The nurse anticipates receiving an order to transfuse which product?
   1. Albumin
   2. Platelets
   3. Cryoprecipitate
   4. Packed red blood cells

4. A physician tells a client that the client needs a blood transfusion and that a blood sample must be drawn first for blood typing and crossmatching. After the physician leaves, the client asks the nurse, "What exactly is a blood type, anyway?" The nurse responds with which of the following statements?
   1. "The blood type represents an antigen found on the surface of the red blood cell."
   2. "The blood type represents an antibody found on the surface of the red blood cell."
   3. "The blood type represents an antibody that normally circulates in the blood plasma."
   4. "The blood type represents an antigen that normally circulates in the blood plasma."

5. A client requiring surgery is anxious about the possible need for a blood transfusion during or after the procedure. The nurse advises the client to do which of the following to reduce the risk of possible transfusion complications?
   1. Give an autologous blood donation before the surgery.
   2. Ask a friend or family member to donate blood ahead of time.
   3. Take iron supplements before surgery to boost hemoglobin levels.
   4. Request that any donated blood be screened twice by the blood bank.

6. A client with severe blood loss resulting from multiple trauma requires rapid transfusion of several units of blood. The nurse asks another health team member to obtain which device for use during the

transfusion procedure to help reduce the risk of cardiac dysrhythmias?
1. Pulse oximetry
2. Cardiac monitor
3. Infusion controller
4. Blood-warming device

7. The nurse enters a client's room to assess the client, who began receiving a blood transfusion 45 minutes earlier, and notes that the client is flushed and dyspneic. On assessment, the nurse auscultates the presence of crackles in the lung bases. The nurse determines that this client most likely is experiencing which complication of blood transfusion therapy?
1. Bacteremia
2. Hypovolemia
3. Fluid overload
4. Transfusion reaction

8. The nurse determines that a client is having a transfusion reaction. After the nurse stops the transfusion, which action should immediately be taken next?
1. Remove the IV line.
2. Run normal saline at a keep vein open rate.
3. Run a solution of 5% dextrose in water.
4. Obtain a culture of the tip of the catheter device removed from the client.

9. The nurse has discontinued a unit of blood that was infusing into a client because the client experienced a transfusion reaction. After documenting the incident appropriately, the nurse sends the blood bag and tubing to which of the following departments?
1. Blood Bank
2. Risk Management
3. Environmental Services
4. Infection Control Department

10. The nurse has just received a unit of packed red blood cells from the blood bank for transfusion to an assigned client. The nurse is careful to select tubing especially made for blood products, knowing that this tubing is manufactured with:
1. An air vent.
2. An in-line filter.
3. A microdrip chamber.
4. Tinted tubing to protect the blood from light.

11. Packed red blood cells have been prescribed for a client with low hemoglobin and hematocrit levels. The nurse takes the client's temperature before hanging the blood transfusion and records 100.6° F orally. Which of the following is the appropriate nursing action?
1. Begin the transfusion as prescribed.
2. Delay hanging the blood and notify the physician.
3. Administer an antihistamine and begin the transfusion.
4. Administer two tablets of acetaminophen (Tylenol) and begin the transfusion.

12. The nurse has received an order to transfuse a client with a unit of packed red blood cells. Before explaining the procedure to the client, the nurse asks which initial question?
1. "Have you ever had a transfusion before?"
2. "Why do you think that you need the transfusion?"
3. "Have you ever gone into shock for any reason in the past?"
4. "Do you know the complications and risks of a transfusion?"

13. The nurse is picking up a unit of packed red blood cells at the hospital blood bank. After putting the pen down, the nurse glances at the clock, which reads 1:00. The nurse calculates that the transfusion must be started by:
1. 1:30
2. 2:00
3. 2:30
4. 3:00

14. A client has received a transfusion of platelets. The nurse evaluates that the client is benefiting most from this therapy if the client exhibits which of the following?
1. Increased hematocrit level
2. Increased hemoglobin level
3. Decline of elevated temperature to normal
4. Decreased oozing of blood from puncture sites and gums

15. The nurse has just obtained a unit of blood from the blood bank to transfuse into a client as ordered. Before preparing the blood for transfusion, the nurse next looks for which of the following members of the health care team to assist in checking the unit of blood?
1. Phlebotomist
2. Medical student
3. Registered nurse
4. Blood bank technician

16. The nurse has obtained a unit of blood from the blood bank and has checked the blood bag properly with another nurse. Just before beginning the transfusion, the nurse assesses which of the following items?
1. Vital signs
2. Skin color
3. Urine output
4. Latest hematocrit level

17. The nurse has just received an order to transfuse a unit of packed red blood cells for an assigned client. Approximately how long will the nurse need to stay with the client to ensure that a transfusion reaction is not occurring?
1. 5 minutes
2. 15 minutes
3. 30 minutes
4. 45 minutes

18. A client has an order to receive a unit of packed red blood cells. The nurse should obtain which of the following intravenous (IV) solutions from the IV storage area to hang with the blood product at the client's bedside?
    1. Lactated Ringer's
    2. 0.9% sodium chloride
    3. 5% dextrose in 0.9% sodium chloride
    4. 5% dextrose in 0.45% sodium chloride

19. The nurse listening to morning report learns that an assigned client received a unit of granulocytes the previous evening. The nurse makes a note to assess the results of which of the following daily serum laboratory studies to assess the effectiveness of the transfusion?
    1. Hematocrit level
    2. Erythrocyte count
    3. Hemoglobin level
    4. White blood cell count

20. A client is brought to the emergency room having experienced blood loss related to an arterial laceration. Fresh frozen plasma (FFP) is ordered and transfused to replace fluid and blood loss. The nurse understands that the rationale for transfusing FFP in this client is:
    1. To treat the loss of platelets
    2. To promote rapid volume expansion

3. That the transfusion must be done slowly
4. That it will increase the hemoglobin and hematocrit levels

ALTERNATE ITEM FORMAT: PRIORITIZING (ORDERED RESPONSE)

A unit of packed red blood cells has been prescribed for a client with low hemoglobin and hematocrit levels. The nurse notifies the blood bank of the order, and a blood specimen is drawn from the client for typing and crossmatching. The nurse receives a telephone call from the blood bank and is informed that the unit of blood is ready for administration. Number the actions in order of priority that the nurse should take to administer the blood. (Number 1 is the first action and number 6 is the last action.)

_____ Hang the bag of blood
_____ Obtain the unit of blood from the blood bank.
_____ Ensure that an informed consent has been signed.
_____ Verify the physician's order for the blood transfusion.
_____ Insert an 18- or 19- gauge IV catheter into the client.
_____ Ask a licensed nurse to assist in confirming blood compatibility and verifying client identity.

ANSWERS

1. **1**

Rationale: Septicemia occurs with the transfusion of blood contaminated with microorganisms. Signs include chills, fever, vomiting, diarrhea, hypotension, and the development of shock. Hyperkalemia causes weakness, paresthesias, abdominal cramps, diarrhea, and dysrhythmias. Circulatory overload causes cough, dyspnea, chest pain, wheezing, tachycardia, and hypertension. A delayed transfusion reaction can occur days to years after a transfusion. Signs include fever, mild jaundice, and a decreased hematocrit level.
Test-Taking Strategy: Focus on the data in the question. Noting that the client's temperature is elevated will direct you to option 1. Review the signs of complications of a blood transfusion if you had difficulty with this question.
Level of Cognitive Ability: Analysis
Client Needs: Physiological Integrity
Integrated Process: Nursing Process—analysis
Content Area: Fundamental skills
Reference: Potter, P., & Perry, A. (2005). *Fundamentals of nursing* (6th ed., p. 1192). St. Louis: Mosby.

2. **1**

Rationale: The nurse notes the expiration date on the unit of blood to ensure that the blood is fresh. Blood cells begin to deteriorate over time, so safe storage usually is limited to 35 days. Careful notation of the expiration date by the nurse is an essential part of the verification process before hanging a unit of blood. The nurse also notes the blood identification (unit) number, blood group and type, and client's name. The nurse

also inspects the unit of blood for clots and returns the unit to the blood bank if clots are noted.
Test-Taking Strategy: Use the process of elimination and note that the strategic word in this question is *deteriorate*. To answer this question correctly, you must know which part of the pretransfusion verification procedure relates to the *freshness* of the unit of blood. Keeping this in mind should allow you to eliminate each of the incorrect options systematically. Review the procedure for checking blood if you had difficulty with this question.
Level of Cognitive Ability: Application
Client Needs: Physiological Integrity
Integrated Process: Nursing Process—implementation
Content Area: Fundamental skills
Reference: Ignatavicius, D., & Workman, M. (2006). *Medical-surgical nursing: Critical thinking for collaborative care* (5th ed., p. 913). Philadelphia: W.B. Saunders.

3. **1**

Rationale: Albumin may be used as a plasma expander. Platelets are used when the client's platelet count is low. Cryoprecipitate is useful in treating bleeding from hemophilia or disseminated intravascular coagulopathy because it is rich in clotting factors. Packed red blood cells replace erythrocytes and are not a plasma expander.
Test-Taking Strategy: Use the process of elimination, noting the strategic words *require plasma expansion*. Recalling the composition of each of the blood components identified in the options will direct you to option 1. If you had difficulty with this question, review the various blood component therapies.
Level of Cognitive Ability: Analysis

Client Needs: Physiological Integrity
Integrated Process: Nursing Process—analysis
Content Area: Fundamental skills
Reference: Ignatavicius, D., & Workman, M. (2006). *Medical-surgical nursing: Critical thinking for collaborative care* (5th ed., p. 870). Philadelphia: W.B. Saunders.

4. 1
Rationale: The major blood types are A, B, AB, and O. The blood type indicates an antigen found on the surface of the red blood cell. Acute hemolytic transfusion reaction (ABO incompatibility) can occur if a client receives blood that is not compatible with his or her blood type. Acute hemolytic reaction is the most serious adverse reaction to a blood transfusion.
Test-Taking Strategy: Use the process of elimination and specific knowledge related to the meaning of blood groups. Remember that the blood type indicates an antigen found on the surface of the red blood cell. If you had difficulty with this question, review these concepts.
Level of Cognitive Ability: Analysis
Client Needs: Physiological Integrity
Integrated Process: Nursing Process—analysis
Content Area: Fundamental skills
References: Ignatavicius, D., & Workman, M. (2006). *Medical-surgical nursing: Critical thinking for collaborative care* (5th ed., p. 913). Philadelphia: W.B. Saunders.
Potter, P., & Perry, A. (2005). *Fundamentals of nursing* (6th ed., pp. 1190-1192). St. Louis: Mosby.

5. 1
Rationale: Donating autologous blood to be reinfused as needed during or after surgery reduces the risk of possible transfusion complications. The next most effective way is to ask a family member to donate blood before surgery. Blood banks do not provide extra screening on request. Preoperative iron supplements are helpful for iron deficiency anemia but are not helpful in replacing blood lost during the surgery.
Test-Taking Strategy: Use the process of elimination and focus on the subject to reduce the risk of possible transfusion complications. Recalling that an autologous transfusion is the collection of the client's own blood will direct you to option 1. Review the concepts related to disease transmission and blood donation procedures if you had difficulty with this question.
Level of Cognitive Ability: Application
Client Needs: Physiological Integrity
Integrated Process: Nursing Process—implementation
Content Area: Fundamental skills
References: Ignatavicius, D., & Workman, M. (2006). *Medical-surgical nursing: Critical thinking for collaborative care* (5th ed., p. 334). Philadelphia: W.B. Saunders.
Potter, P., & Perry, A. (2005). *Fundamentals of nursing* (6th ed., p. 1190). St. Louis: Mosby.

6. 4
Rationale: If several units of blood are to be administered, a blood warmer should be used. Rapid transfusion of cool blood places the client at risk for cardiac dysrhythmias. To prevent this, the nurse warms the blood as needed, using a blood-warming device. Pulse oximetry and cardiac monitoring equipment are useful for the early assessment of complications but do not reduce the occurrence of cardiac dysrhythmias. Elec-

tronic infusion devices are not helpful in this case because the infusion must be rapid, and infusion devices generally are used to control the flow rate. In addition, not all infusion devices are made to handle blood or blood products.
Test-Taking Strategy: Use the process of elimination and note the strategic words *rapid* and *reduce the risk*. These words tell you that the infusions will infuse quickly and that the correct option is the one that will minimize the risk of cardiac dysrhythmias. Eliminate option 1 and 2 first because these items are used to assess for rather than reduce the risk of complications. From the remaining options, use knowledge related to the complications of transfusion therapy and note the relationship between the words *several units of blood* in the question and *blood warming device* in the correct option. Review the concepts related to the use of a blood warmer if you had difficulty with this question.
Level of Cognitive Ability: Application
Client Needs: Physiological Integrity
Integrated Process: Nursing Process—planning
Content Area: Fundamental skills
References: Perry, A., & Potter, P. (2006) *Clinical nursing skills & techniques* (6th ed., p. 970). St. Louis: Mosby.
Potter, P., & Perry, A. (2005). *Fundamentals of nursing* (6th ed., p. 1191). St. Louis: Mosby.

7. 3
Rationale: With fluid overload, the client has the presence of crackles in addition to dyspnea. An allergic reaction, which is one type of blood transfusion reaction, would produce symptoms such as flushing, dyspnea, itching, and a generalized rash. Hypovolemia is not a complication of a blood transfusion. With bacteremia, the client would have a fever, which is not part of the clinical picture presented.
Test-Taking Strategy: Use the process of elimination, noting the strategic words *most likely*. Read the question carefully and focus on the symptoms identified in the question. Eliminate option 2 first because it is not a complication of a blood transfusion. Next, eliminate option 1 because no information in the question indicates that the client has an elevated temperature. From the remaining options, focusing on the strategic words *crackles in the lung bases* will direct you to option 3. Review the complications of blood transfusion therapy if you had difficulty with this question.
Level of Cognitive Ability: Analysis
Client Needs: Physiological Integrity
Integrated Process: Nursing Process—analysis
Content Area: Fundamental skills
Reference: Perry, A., & Potter, P. (2006). *Clinical nursing skills & techniques* (6th ed., p. 977). St. Louis: Mosby.

8. 2
Rationale: If the nurse suspects a transfusion reaction, the nurse stops the transfusion and infuses normal saline at a keep vein open rate pending further physician orders. This maintains a patent IV access line and aids in maintaining the client's intravascular volume. The nurse would not discontinue the IV line because then there would be no IV access route. Obtaining a culture of the tip of the catheter device removed from the client is incorrect. First, the catheter should not be removed. Second, cultures are performed when infection, not transfusion reaction, is suspected. Normal saline is the solution of choice over

solutions containing dextrose because saline does not cause red blood cells to clump.

Test-Taking Strategy: Use the process of elimination, noting the strategic word *next*. Knowing that the IV should not be removed or discontinued assists in eliminating options 1 and 4. Recalling that normal saline, not dextrose, is used when administering a unit of blood will direct you to option 2. Review care for the client with a transfusion reaction if you had difficulty with this question.

Level of Cognitive Ability: Application
Client Needs: Physiological Integrity
Integrated Process: Nursing Process—implementation
Content Area: Delegating/Prioritizing
References: Perry, A., & Potter, P. (2006). *Clinical nursing skills & techniques* (6th ed., p. 977). St. Louis: Mosby.
Potter, P., & Perry, A. (2005). *Fundamentals of nursing* (6th ed., pp. 1191-1193). St. Louis: Mosby.

9. **1**

Rationale: The nurse returns the blood transfusion bag containing any remaining blood to the blood bank. This allows the blood bank to complete any follow-up testing procedures needed once a transfusion reaction has been documented. The other options are incorrect.

Test-Taking Strategy: Use the process of elimination and specific knowledge related to routine transfusion-related procedures to answer the question. Recalling that blood is issued from the blood bank will help you to eliminate each of the incorrect options. Review nursing responsibilities for when a transfusion reaction occurs if you had difficulty with this question.

Level of Cognitive Ability: Application
Client Needs: Physiological Integrity
Integrated Process: Nursing Process—implementation
Content Area: Fundamental skills
References: Perry, A. & Potter, P. (2006). *Clinical nursing skills & techniques* (6th ed., p. 968). St. Louis: Mosby.
Potter, P., & Perry, A. (2005). *Fundamentals of nursing* (6th ed., p. 1193). St. Louis: Mosby.

10. **2**

Rationale: The tubing used for blood administration has an in-line filter. The filter helps ensure that any particles larger than the size of the filter are caught in the filter and are not infused into the client. The tubing should be macrodrip, not microdrip, to allow blood to flow freely through the drip chamber. An air vent is unnecessary because the blood bag is not made of glass. Option 4 is incorrect and, in addition, blood does not need to be protected from light.

Test-Taking Strategy: Use the process of elimination. Read each option carefully and visualize the process of blood administration. Remember that tubing used for blood administration has an in-line filter. Review concepts related to tubing used for blood administration if you had difficulty with this question.

Level of Cognitive Ability: Application
Client Needs: Physiological Integrity
Integrated Process: Nursing Process—implementation
Content Area: Fundamental skills
References: Ignatavicius, D., & Workman, M. (2006). *Medical-surgical nursing: Critical thinking for collaborative care* (5th ed., pp. 913-914). Philadelphia: W.B. Saunders.

Potter, P., & Perry, A. (2005). *Fundamentals of nursing* (6th ed., p. 1191). St. Louis: Mosby.

11. **2**

Rationale: If the client has a temperature higher than 100° F, the unit of blood should not be hung until the physician is notified and has the opportunity to give further orders. The physician likely will prescribe that the blood be administered regardless of the temperature, but the decision is not within the nurse's scope of practice to make. The other options are incorrect.

Test-Taking Strategy: Use the process of elimination. Eliminate options 1, 3, and 4 because they all indicate beginning the transfusion. Review the nursing responsibilities before administering a blood transfusion if you had difficulty with this question.

Level of Cognitive Ability: Application
Client Needs: Physiological Integrity
Integrated Process: Nursing Process—implementation
Content Area: Fundamental skills
Reference: Ignatavicius, D., & Workman, M. (2006). *Medical-surgical nursing: Critical thinking for collaborative care* (5th ed., p. 914). Philadelphia: W.B. Saunders.

12. **1**

Rationale: Asking the client about personal experience with transfusion therapy provides a good starting point for client teaching about this procedure. Options 3 and 4 are not helpful because they may elicit a fearful response from the client. Although determining whether the client knows the reason for the transfusion is important, option 2 is not an appropriate statement in terms of eliciting information from the client regarding an understanding of the need for the transfusion.

Test-Taking Strategy: Use the process of elimination and note that the strategic words in the question are *initial question*. This tells you that the correct option is the best starting point for discussion about the transfusion therapy. Options 3 and 4 have emotionally laden trigger words, including *gone into shock* and *risks*, respectively, which make them incorrect. From the remaining options, focus on the strategic words and use therapeutic communication techniques to direct you to option 1. Review pretransfusion assessment procedures if you had difficulty with this question.

Level of Cognitive Ability: Application
Client Needs: Physiological Integrity
Integrated Process: Nursing Process—assessment
Content Area: Fundamental skills
References: Ignatavicius, D., & Workman, M. (2006). *Medical-surgical nursing: Critical thinking for collaborative care* (5th ed., p. 913). Philadelphia: W.B. Saunders.
Perry, A., & Potter, P. (2006). *Clinical nursing skills & techniques* (6th ed., pp. 972, 977). St. Louis: Mosby.
Potter, P., & Perry, A. (2005). *Fundamentals of nursing* (6th ed., p. 1190). St. Louis: Mosby.

13. **1**

Rationale: Blood must be hung as soon as possible (within 30 minutes) after obtaining it from the blood bank. After that time, the blood temperature will be higher than 50° F and could be unsafe for use. For this reason options 2, 3, and 4 are incorrect.

Test-Taking Strategy: Use the process of elimination. You should know that blood must be hung within 30 minutes

after obtaining it from the blood bank to answer this question correctly. Review the standard procedures related to safe blood administration if you had difficulty with this question.
Level of Cognitive Ability: Application
Client Needs: Physiological Integrity
Integrated Process: Nursing Process—planning
Content Area: Fundamental skills
References: Ignatavicius, D., & Workman, M. (2006). *Medical-surgical nursing: Critical thinking for collaborative care* (5th ed., p. 914). Philadelphia: W.B. Saunders.
Lewis, S., Heitkemper, M., & Dirksen, S. (2004). *Medical-surgical nursing: Assessment and management of clinical problems* (6th ed., p. 747). St. Louis: Mosby.

14. **4**
Rationale: Platelets are necessary for proper blood clotting. The client with insufficient platelets may exhibit frank bleeding or oozing of blood from puncture sites, wounds, and mucous membranes. Increased hemoglobin and hematocrit levels would occur when the client has received a transfusion of red blood cells. An elevated temperature would decline to normal after infusion of granulocytes if those cells were instrumental in fighting infection in the body.
Test-Taking Strategy: Use the process of elimination and knowledge regarding the potential uses and benefits of the various types of blood product transfusions. Eliminate options 1 and 2 first because they are comparative or alike. From the remaining options, recalling that platelets are necessary for proper blood clotting will direct you to option 4. If this question was difficult, review the types of blood products available for transfusion.
Level of Cognitive Ability: Analysis
Client Needs: Physiological Integrity
Integrated Process: Nursing Process—evaluation
Content Area: Fundamental skills
References: Ignatavicius, D., & Workman, M. (2006). *Medical-surgical nursing: Critical thinking for collaborative care* (5th ed., p. 915). Philadelphia: W.B. Saunders.
Perry, A., & Potter, P. (2006). *Clinical nursing skills & techniques* (6th ed., p. 971). St. Louis: Mosby.

15. **3**
Rationale: Two registered nurses (RNs) or one RN and a licensed practical nurse (LPN) (depending on agency policy) must check the label on the blood product together against the client's identification number, blood group, and complete name. This minimizes the risk of error in checking information on the blood bag and thereby minimizes the risk of harm or injury to the client. A blood bank technician will verify data with the nurse when the blood is obtained from the blood bank, but will not verify information on the nursing unit or at the client's bedside. The other options are also incorrect.
Test-Taking Strategy: Use the process of elimination and specific knowledge of blood administration methods and techniques. Remember that two RNs or one RN and a licensed practical nurse (depending on agency policy) must check the blood product together. Review the procedures related to checking blood before administration if you had difficulty with this question.
Level of Cognitive Ability: Application
Client Needs: Physiological Integrity
Integrated Process: Nursing Process—planning

Content Area: Fundamental skills
References: Ignatavicius, D., & Workman, M. (2006). *Medical-surgical nursing: Critical thinking for collaborative care* (5th ed., p. 914). Philadelphia: W.B. Saunders.
Potter, P., & Perry, A. (2005). *Fundamentals of nursing* (6th ed., p. 1191). St. Louis: Mosby.

16. **1**
Rationale: A change in vital signs during the transfusion from baseline may indicate that a transfusion reaction is occurring. This is why the nurse assesses vital signs before the procedure and again after the first 15 minutes. The other options do not identify assessments that are required just before beginning a transfusion.
Test-Taking Strategy: Use the process of elimination and note the strategic words *just before beginning the transfusion*. This tells you that more than one of the options may be partially or totally correct and that the correct option needs to be assessed for possible comparison during the transfusion. Use the ABCs—airway, breathing, and circulation—to direct you to option 1. Review the nursing interventions for preparing to administer a blood transfusion if you had difficulty with this question.
Level of Cognitive Ability: Application
Client Needs: Physiological Integrity
Integrated Process: Nursing Process—assessment
Content Area: Fundamental skills
References: Ignatavicius, D., & Workman, M. (2006). *Medical-surgical nursing: Critical thinking for collaborative care* (5th ed., p. 913). Philadelphia: W.B. Saunders.
Potter, P., & Perry, A. (2005). *Fundamentals of nursing* (6th ed., p. 1191) St. Louis: Mosby.

17. **2**
Rationale: The nurse must remain with the client for the first 15 minutes of a transfusion, which is usually when a transfusion reaction may occur. This enables the nurse to detect a reaction and intervene quickly. The nurse engages in safe nursing practice by obtaining coverage for the other assigned clients during this time. Options 1, 3, and 4 are incorrect.
Test-Taking Strategy: Use the process of elimination and knowledge regarding blood transfusion procedures to answer this question. Remember, the client must be monitored directly for the first 15 minutes of the transfusion. Review the nursing responsibilities involved in beginning a blood transfusion if you had difficulty with this question.
Level of Cognitive Ability: Application
Client Needs: Physiological Integrity
Integrated Process: Nursing Process—planning
Content Area: Fundamental skills
Reference: Ignatavicius, D., & Workman, M. (2006). *Medical-surgical nursing: Critical thinking for collaborative care* (5th ed., p. 914). Philadelphia: W.B. Saunders.
Potter, P., & Perry, A. (2005). *Fundamentals of nursing* (6th ed., p.1191). St. Louis: Mosby.

18. **2**
Rationale: Sodium chloride 0.9% (normal saline) is a standard isotonic solution used to precede and follow infusion of blood products. Dextrose is not used because it could result in clumping and subsequent hemolysis of red blood cells. Lactated Ringer's is not the solution of choice with this procedure.

Test-Taking Strategy: Use the process of elimination and eliminate options 3 and 4 first because they are comparative or alike in that both solutions contain dextrose. From the remaining options, remember that normal saline is the solution compatible with red blood cells. If this question was difficult, review the procedures related to the administration of blood.
Level of Cognitive Ability: Application
Client Needs: Physiological Integrity
Integrated Process: Nursing Process—implementation
Content Area: Fundamental skills
Reference: Ignatavicius, D., & Workman, M. (2006). *Medical-surgical nursing: Critical thinking for collaborative care* (5th ed., p. 913). Philadelphia: W.B. Saunders.

19. **4**
Rationale: The client who has neutropenia may receive a transfusion of granulocytes, or white blood cells. These clients often have severe infections and are unresponsive to antibiotic therapy. The nurse notes the results of follow-up white blood cell counts to evaluate the effectiveness of the therapy. The nurse also continues to monitor the client for signs and symptoms of infection. Erythrocyte count and hemoglobin and hematocrit levels are determined after transfusion of packed red blood cells.
Test-Taking Strategy: Use the process of elimination. Recalling that granulocytes are a component of white blood cells will assist in directing you to option 4. In addition, note that options 1, 2, and 3 are comparative or alike in that these options all refer to erythrocytes. Review the key points related to types of blood products if you had difficulty with this question.
Level of Cognitive Ability: Analysis
Client Needs: Physiological Integrity
Integrated Process: Nursing Process—evaluation
Content Area: Fundamental skills
Reference: Ignatavicius, D., & Workman, M. (2006). *Medical-surgical nursing: Critical thinking for collaborative care* (5th ed., pp. 915-916). Philadelphia: W.B. Saunders.

20. **2**
Rationale: Fresh frozen plasma is often used for volume expansion as a result of fluid and blood loss. It does not contain platelets, so it is not used to treat any type of low platelet count disorder. It is rich in clotting factors and can be thawed quickly and transfused quickly. It will not specifically increase the hemoglobin and hematocrit level.
Test-Taking Strategy: Focus on the data in the question. Note the relationship between the words *experienced blood loss* and option 2. Review the purpose and use for FFP if you had difficulty with this question.
Level of Cognitive Ability: Analysis
Client Needs: Physiological Integrity

Integrated Process: Nursing Process—analysis
Content Area: Fundamental skills
Reference: Lewis, S., Heitkemper, M., & Dirksen, S. (2004). *Medical-surgical nursing: Assessment and management of clinical problems* (6th ed., p. 748). St. Louis: Mosby.

ALTERNATE ITEM FORMAT: PRIORITIZING (ORDERED RESPONSE)

Answer: 6, 4, 2, 1, 3, 5
Rationale: The nurse would first verify the physician's order for the blood transfusion and ensure that the client has been informed about the procedure and has signed an informed consent. Once this has been done, the nurse would ensure that at least an 18- or 19-gauge intravenous needle is inserted into the client. Blood has a thicker and stickier consistency than intravenous solutions, and using an 18- or 19-gauge catheter ensures that the bore of the catheter is large enough to prevent damage to the blood cells. Next, the blood is obtained from the blood bank, once the nurse is sure that the client has been informed and has an adequate access for administering the blood. Once the blood has been obtained, two registered nurses, or one registered and a licensed practical nurse (depending on agency policy), must together check the label on the blood product against the client's identification number, blood group, and complete name. This minimizes the risk of error in checking information on the blood bag and thereby minimizes the risk of harm or injury to the client. The nurse should measure vital signs and assess lung sounds and then hang the transfusion.
Test-Taking Strategy: Remember that a physician's order is needed for treatments and procedures. This will direct you to the first nursing action. Recalling that the client needs to be informed about a procedure will assist in determining that the next action would be to ensure that the client has signed a consent form. Next, remember that client preparation for the procedure is important. You would not obtain the blood from the blood bank unless the client was prepared; therefore, the nurse would ensure that the client had an adequate intravenous access. Once blood is obtained, remember that verifying compatibility and client identity is critical before hanging the blood. Review the procedure for administering blood if you had difficulty with this question.
Level of Cognitive Ability: Application
Client Needs: Physiological Integrity
Integrated Process: Nursing Process—implementation
Content Area: Delegating/Prioritizing
References: Ignatavicius, D., & Workman, M. (2006). *Medical-surgical nursing: Critical thinking for collaborative care* (5th ed., p. 914). Philadelphia: W.B. Saunders.
Potter, P., & Perry, A. (2005). *Fundamentals of nursing* (6th ed., pp. 1190-1191). St. Louis: Mosby.

REFERENCES

Ignatavicius, D., & Workman, M. (2006). *Medical-surgical nursing: Critical thinking for collaborative care* (5th ed.). Philadelphia: W.B. Saunders.

Lewis, S., Heitkemper, M., & Dirksen, S. (2004). *Medical-surgical nursing: Assessment and management of clinical problems* (6th ed.). St. Louis: Mosby.

National Council of State Boards of Nursing (Eds.). (2007). *2007 NCLEX-RN® detailed test plan.* Chicago: Author.

Pagana, K., & Pagana, T. (2006). *Mosby's manual of diagnostic and laboratory tests* (3rd ed.) St.. Louis: Mosby.

Perry, A., & Potter, P. (2006). *Clinical nursing skills & techniques* (6th ed.). St. Louis: Mosby.

Potter, P., & Perry, A. (2005). *Fundamentals of nursing* (6th ed.). St. Louis: Mosby.

Fundamental Skills

Provision of a Safe Environment

PYRAMID TERMS

chemical restraints Medications given to inhibit a specific behavior or movement.

environmental safety Removing items from the environment and avoiding situations or events that place the client at risk for accidental injury.

health care–associated (nosocomial) infections Infections acquired in the hospital or other health care facility that were not present or incubating at the time of the client's admission; also referred to as hospital-acquired infections.

physical hazards Any situation or event that places the client at risk for accidental injury or death.

physical restraints Devices applied to restrict a client's movement.

poison Any substance that impairs health or destroys life when ingested, inhaled, or otherwise absorbed by the body.

standard precautions Guidelines used by all health care providers for all clients to reduce the risk of infection for clients and caregivers.

transmission-based precautions Guidelines used in addition to standard precautions for specific syndromes that are highly suggestive of infections until a diagnosis is confirmed.

warfare agent Biological or chemical substances that can cause mass destruction or fatality.

▲ THE PYRAMID TO SUCCESS

Safety and Infection Control is a subcategory of the Client Needs component, Safe and Effective Care Environment, of the NCLEX-RN examination test plan. Pyramid Points focus on maintaining environmental safety, preventing accidents, using restraints, priority nursing actions in the event of a disaster, and biological and chemical warfare agents. Pyramid Points also focus on standard and transmission-based precautions and the measures required to handle hazardous or infectious materials. The Integrated Processes addressed in this chapter include Caring, Communication and Documentation, Nursing Process, and Teaching/Learning.

CLIENT NEEDS

Safe and Effective Care Environment

Disaster planning and biological and chemical warfare agents

Ensuring that client's rights are upheld, including informed consent

Establishing priorities

Following guidelines regarding the use of restraints

Handling hazardous and infectious materials safely

Maintaining precautions to prevent accidents

Using standard, transmission-based, and other infection-control precautions

Health Promotion and Maintenance

Assisting clients and families to identify environmental hazards in the home

Performing home safety assessments

Teaching clients and families about accident prevention

Teaching clients and families about measures to be implemented in an emergency or disaster

Teaching clients and families about preventing the spread of infection

Psychosocial Integrity

Assessing the client for sensory/perceptual alterations

Identifying cultural and religious lifestyles

Identifying support systems

187

Physiological Integrity

Assisting the client with activities of daily living

Implementing priority nursing actions in an emergency or disaster

Managing and providing care to clients with infectious diseases

Providing comfort and assistance to the client

Using assistive devices to prevent injury

I. ENVIRONMENTAL SAFETY

A. Fire safety (Box 16-1)
   1. Keep open spaces free of clutter.
   2. Clearly mark fire exits.
   3. Know the locations of all fire alarms, exits, and extinguishers (Box 16-2; Table 16-1).
   4. Know the telephone number for reporting fires.
   5. Know the fire drill and evacuation plan of the agency.
   6. Never use the elevator in the event of a fire.
   7. Turn off oxygen and appliances in the vicinity of the fire.

BOX 16-1

Priority Actions in the Event of a Fire

Remember the mnemonic RACE to set priorities in the event of a fire:

R, Rescue: Remove all clients from the vicinity of a fire.

A, Alarm: Activate the fire alarm; report a fire before attempting to extinguish it.

C, Confine: Close doors and windows when a fire is detected.

E, Extinguish: Extinguish the fire, using the appropriate fire extinguisher.

BOX 16-2

Using a Fire Extinguisher

Remember the mnemonic PASS to use a fire extinguisher:

P: Pull the pin.

A: Aim at the base of the fire.

S: Squeeze the handles.

S: Sweep the fire from side to side.

TABLE 16-1

Types of Fire Extinguishers

Type	Class of Fire
A	Wood, cloth, upholstery, paper, rubbish, plastic
B	Flammable liquids or gases, grease, tar, oil-based paint
C	Electrical equipment

8. In the event of a fire, if a client is on life support, maintain respiratory status manually with an Ambu bag (resuscitation bag) until the client is moved away from the threat of the fire and can be placed back on life support.
9. In the event of a fire, ambulatory clients can be directed to walk by themselves to a safe area and, in some cases, may be able to assist in moving clients in wheelchairs.
10. Bedridden clients generally are moved from the scene of a fire by stretcher, their bed, or wheelchair.
11. If a client must be carried from the area of a fire, appropriate transfer techniques need to be used.
12. If fire department personnel are at the scene of the fire, they can help evacuate clients.

B. Electrical safety
   1. Electrical equipment must be maintained in good working order and should be grounded.
   2. Use a three-pronged electrical cord.
   3. In a three-pronged electrical cord, the third longer prong of the cord is the ground; the other two prongs carry the power to the piece of electrical equipment.
   4. Any electrical equipment that the client brings into the health care facility must be inspected for safety before use.
   5. Check electrical cords and outlets for exposed, frayed, or damaged wires.
   6. Avoid overloading any circuit.
   7. Read warning labels on all equipment; never operate unfamiliar equipment.
   8. Use safety extension cords only when absolutely necessary, and tape them to the floor with electrical tape.
   9. Never run electrical wiring under carpets.
   10. Never pull a plug by using the cord; always grasp the plug itself.
   11. Never use electrical appliances near sinks, bathtubs, or other water sources.
   12. Always disconnect a plug from the outlet before cleaning equipment or appliances.
   13. If a client receives an electrical shock, turn off the electricity before touching the client.

C. Radiation safety
   1. Know the protocols and guidelines of the health care agency.
   2. Label potentially radioactive material.
   3. To reduce exposure to radiation, do the following:
      a. Limit the time spent near the source.
      b. Make the distance from the source as great as possible.
      c. Use a shielding device such as a lead apron.
   4. Monitor radiation exposure with a film badge.
   5. Place the client who has a radiation implant in a private room.
   6. Never touch dislodged radiation implants.

D. Disposal of infectious wastes
  1. Handle all infectious materials as a hazard.
  2. Dispose of waste in designated areas only, using proper containers for disposal.
  3. Ensure that infectious material is labeled properly.
  4. Needles should not be recapped, bent, or broken.
  5. Dispose of all sharps immediately after use in closed, puncture-resistant disposal containers that are leakproof and labeled or color-coded.
E. Physiological changes in the older client that increase the risk of accidents (Box 16-3)
F. Measures to prevent falls (Box 16-4)
G. Restraints
  1. Restraints are protective devices used to limit the physical activity of a client or to immobilize a client or an extremity.
  2. **Physical restraints** restrict client movement through the application of a device.
  3. **Chemical restraints** are medications given to inhibit a specific behavior or movement.
  4. Interventions (Fig. 16-1)
    a. When restraints are necessary, the physician's orders should state the type of restraint, identify specific client behaviors for which restraints are to be used, and identify a limited time frame for use.
    b. Physicians' orders for restraints should be renewed within a specific time frame according to the policy of the agency.
    c. Restraints are not to be ordered PRN—that is, as needed.
    d. The reason for the restraints should be given to the client and the family, and their permission should be sought.
    e. Restraints should not interfere with any treatments or affect the client's health problem.
    f. Use a half-bow or safety knot (quick release tie) to secure the device to the bed frame or chair, not to the side rails.
    g. Ensure that enough slack is on the straps to allow some movement of the body part.
    h. Assess skin integrity and neurovascular and circulatory status every 30 minutes and remove the restraint at least every 2 hours to permit muscle exercise and to promote circulation.
    i. Continually assess and document the need for restraints (Box 16-5).
  5. Alternatives to restraints
    a. Orient the client and family to the surroundings.
    b. Explain all procedures and treatments to the client and family.

BOX 16-3
Physiological Changes in the Older Client That Increase the Risk of Accidents

MUSCULOSKELETAL CHANGES
Strength and function of muscles decrease.
Joints become less mobile and bones become brittle.
Postural changes and limited range of motion occur.

NERVOUS SYSTEM CHANGES
Voluntary and autonomic reflexes become slower.
Decreased ability to respond to multiple stimuli occurs.
Decreased sensitivity to touch occurs.

SENSORY CHANGES
Decreased vision and lens accommodation and cataracts develop.
Delayed transmission of hot and cold impulses occurs.
Impaired hearing develops, with high-frequency tones less perceptible.

GENITOURINARY CHANGES
Increased nocturia and occurrences of incontinence may occur.

Modified from Potter A., and Perry, P. (2005). *Fundamentals of nursing* (6th ed.). St. Louis: Mosby.

BOX 16-4
Measures to Prevent Falls

Assess the client's risk for falling.
Assign the client at risk for falling to a room near the nurses' station.
Alert all personnel to the client's risk for falling.
Orient the client to physical surroundings.
Instruct the client to seek assistance when getting up.
Explain the use of the call bell system.
Keep the bed in the low position with side rails up, if required.
Lock all beds, wheelchairs, and stretchers.
Keep personal items within reach.
Eliminate clutter and obstacles in the client's room.
Provide adequate lighting.
Reduce bathroom hazards.
Maintain the client's toileting schedule throughout the day.

BOX 16-5
Documentation Points With the Use of a Restraint

Reason for restraint
Method of restraint
Date and time of application of restraint
Duration of use of restraint and client's response
Release from restraint with periodic exercise and circulatory, neurovascular, and skin assessment
Assessment of continued need for restraint
Evaluation of client's response

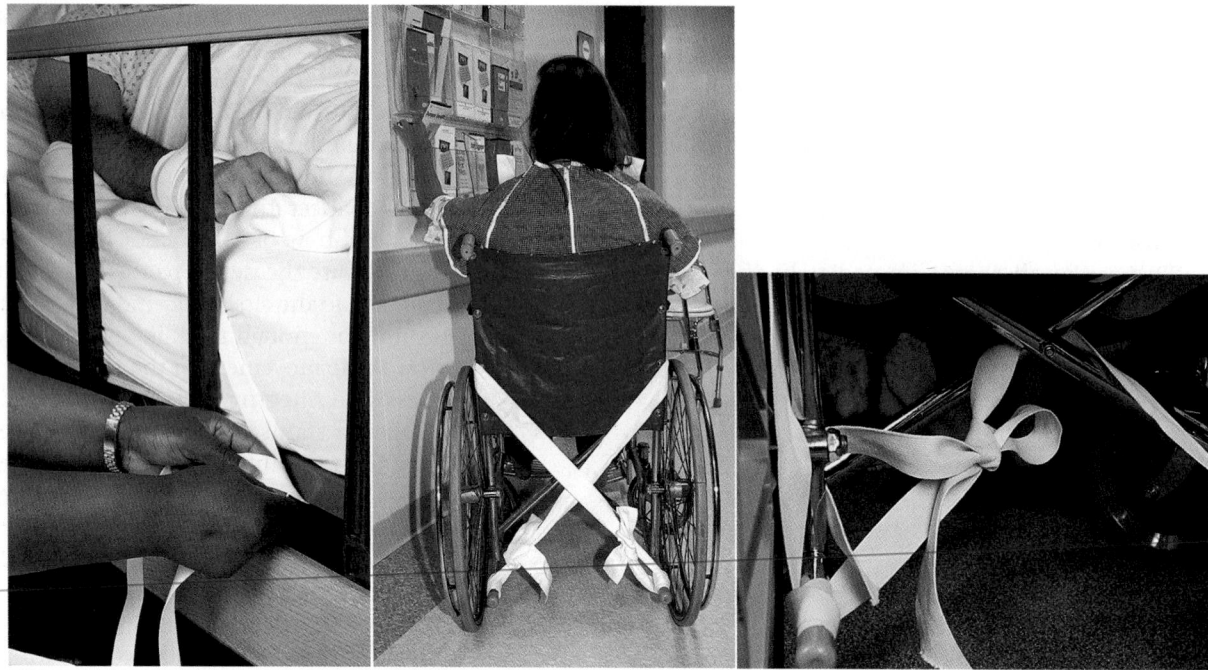

FIG. 16-1 Applying physical restraints. (From Elkin, M., Perry, A., and Potter, P. [2004]. *Nursing interventions and clinical skills* [3rd ed.]. St. Louis: Mosby.)

c. Encourage family and friends to stay with the client, and use sitters for clients who need supervision.

d. Assign confused and disoriented clients to rooms near the nurses' station.

e. Provide appropriate visual and auditory stimuli to the client, such as clocks, calendars, television, and a radio.

f. Place familiar items, such as family pictures, near the client's bedside.

g. Maintain toileting routines.

h. Eliminate bothersome treatments, such as tube feedings, as soon as possible.

i. Evaluate all medications that the client is receiving.

j. Use relaxation techniques with the client.

k. Institute exercise and ambulation schedules as the client's condition allows.

H. Poisons

1. A **poison** is any substance that impairs health or destroys life when ingested, inhaled, or otherwise absorbed by the body.

2. Specific antidotes or treatments are available only for some types of **poisons**.

3. The capacity of body tissue to recover from a **poison** determines the reversibility of the effect.

4. **Poison** can impair the respiratory, circulatory, central nervous, hepatic, gastrointestinal, and renal systems of the body.

5. The toddler, the preschooler, and the young school-age child must be protected from accidental poisoning. ▲

6. In older adults, diminished eyesight and impaired memory may result in accidental ingestion of poisonous substances or an overdose of prescribed medications. ▲

7. A Poison Control Center phone number should be visible on the telephone in homes with small children; in all cases of suspected poisoning, the number should be called immediately. ▲

8. Interventions ▲

a. Remove any obvious materials from the mouth, eyes, or body area immediately.

b. Identify the type and amount of substance ingested.

c. Call the Poison Control Center before attempting an intervention.

d. If the victim vomits or vomiting is induced, save the vomitus if requested to do so, and deliver it to the Poison Control Center.

e. If instructed by the Poison Control Center to take the person to the emergency department, call an ambulance.

f. Never induce vomiting following ingestion of lye, household cleaners, grease, or petroleum products. ▲

g. Never induce vomiting in an unconscious victim.

BOX 16-6
Common Drug-Resistant Nosocomial Infections

Vancomycin-resistant enterococci
Methicillin-resistant *Staphylococcus aureus*
Multidrug-resistant tuberculosis

II. HEALTH CARE–ASSOCIATED (NOSOCOMIAL) INFECTIONS (Box 16-6)

A. **Health care–associated (nosocomial) infections** also are referred to as hospital-acquired infections.

B. Such infections are infections acquired in a hospital or other health care facility that were not present or incubating at the time of a client's admission.

C. Illness impairs the normal defense mechanisms of the body.

▲ D. The hospital environment provides exposure to a variety of virulent organisms that the client has not been exposed to in the past; therefore, the client has not developed resistance to these organisms.

▲ E. Infections can be transmitted by health care personnel who fail to practice proper hand washing procedures or fail to change gloves between client contacts.

F. Many health care agencies have dispensers containing an alcohol-based solution for hand rubs mounted at the entrance to each client's room.

▲ III. STANDARD PRECAUTIONS

A. Description

▲ 1. Nurses must practice **standard precautions** with all clients in any setting, regardless of the diagnosis or presumed infectiousness.

2. **Standard precautions** promote hand washing and the use of gloves, masks, eye protection, and gowns, when appropriate, for client contact.

▲ 3. These precautions apply to blood, all body fluids (whether or not they contain blood), secretions and excretions, nonintact skin, and mucous membranes.

▲ B. Interventions

▲ 1. Handle all blood and body fluids from all clients as if they were contaminated.

2. Wash hands between client contacts; after contact with blood, body fluids, secretions or excretions, nonintact skin, or mucous membranes; after contact with equipment or contaminated articles; and immediately after removing gloves.

3. Wear gloves when touching blood, body fluids, secretions, excretions, nonintact skin, mucous membranes, or contaminated items; remove gloves and wash hands between client care contacts.

4. Wear masks, eye protection, or face shields if client care activities may generate splashes or sprays of blood or body fluid.

5. Wear gowns if soiling of clothing is likely from blood or body fluid; wash hands after removing a gown.

6. Clean and reprocess client care equipment properly and discard single-use items.

7. Place contaminated linen in leakproof bags and handle to prevent skin and mucous membrane exposure.

8. Use needleless devices or special needle safety ▲ devices whenever possible to reduce the risk of needlesticks and sharps injuries to health care workers.

9. Discard all sharp instruments and needles in a ▲ puncture-resistant container; dispose of needles uncapped or use a mechanical device for recapping the needle, if necessary and available.

10. Clean spills of blood or body fluids with a ▲ solution of bleach and water (diluted 1:10) or agency-approved disinfectant.

IV. TRANSMISSION-BASED PRECAUTIONS

A. **Transmission-based precautions** include airborne, ▲ droplet, and contact precautions

B. Airborne precautions

1. Diseases
   a. Measles
   b. Chickenpox (varicella)
   c. Disseminated varicella zoster
   d. Tuberculosis

2. Barrier protection ▲
   a. Single room maintained under negative pressure; door is kept closed except when someone is entering or exiting the room
   b. Negative airflow pressure used in the room, with a minimum of 6 to 12 air exchanges per hour depending on the health care agency
   c. Ultraviolet germicide irradiation or high-efficiency particulate air filter used in the room
   d. Mask or personal respiratory protection device used
   e. Mask placed on client when client needs to leave the room; client leaves the room only if necessary

C. Droplet precautions

1. Diseases
   a. Adenovirus
   b. Diphtheria (pharyngeal)
   c. Epiglottitis
   d. Influenza
   e. Meningitis
   f. Mumps
   g. Mycoplasmal pneumonia or meningococcal pneumonia
   h. Parvovirus B19
   i. Pertussis

      j. Pneumonia

      k. Rubella

      l. Scarlet fever

      m. Sepsis

      n. Streptococcal pharyngitis

  2. Barrier protection

      a. Private room or cohort client

      b. Use of a mask

      c. Mask placed on client when client is out of the room; client leaves the room only if necessary

D. Contact precautions

  1. Diseases

      a. Colonization or infection with a multidrug-resistant organism

      b. Enteric infections, such as *Clostridium difficile*

      c. Respiratory infections, such as respiratory syncytial virus

      d. Wound infections

      e. Skin infections, such as cutaneous diphtheria, herpes simplex, impetigo, pediculosis, scabies, staphylococcus, and varicella zoster

      f. Eye infection such as conjunctivitis

  2. Barrier protection

      a. Private room or cohort client

      b. Use of gloves and a gown when in contact with the client

V. DISASTERS

A. Know the disaster plan of the agency.

B. Internal disasters are those in which the agency is in danger.

C. External disasters occur in the community, and victims will be brought to the health care facility for care.

D. When the health care agency is notified of a disaster, the nurse would follow the guidelines specified in the disaster plan of the agency.

E. See Chapter 8 for additional information on disaster planning.

VI. BIOLOGICAL WARFARE AGENTS

A. A **warfare agent** is a biological or chemical substance that can cause mass destruction or fatality.

B. Anthrax (Fig. 16-2)

  1. The disease is caused by *Bacillus anthracis* and can be contracted through the digestive system, abrasions in the skin, or inhalation through the lungs.

  2. Anthrax is transmitted by direct contact with bacteria and spores; spores are dormant encapsulated bacteria that become active when they enter a living host (no person-to-person spread) (Box 16-7).

  3. The infection is carried to the lymph node and then spreads to the rest of the body by way of the

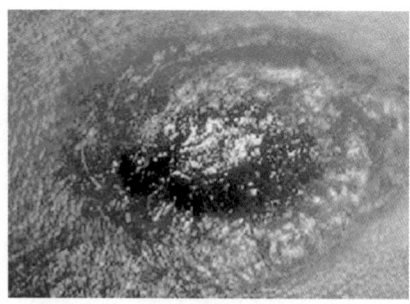

FIG. 16-2   Anthrax. (From *Mosby's dictionary of medicine, nursing, and health professions* [7th ed.]. St. Louis: Mosby.)

BOX 16-7

Anthrax: Transmission and Symptoms

SKIN

Spores enter the skin through cuts and abrasions and are contacted by handling contaminated animal skin products.

Infection starts with an itchy bump like a mosquito bite that progresses to a small liquid-filled sac.

The sac becomes a painless ulcer with an area of black, dead tissue in the middle.

Toxins destroy surrounding tissue.

GASTROINTESTINAL

Infection occurs following the ingestion of contaminated undercooked meat.

Symptoms begin with nausea, loss of appetite, and vomiting.

The disease progresses to severe abdominal pain, vomiting of blood, and severe diarrhea.

INHALATION

Infection is caused by the inhalation of bacterial spores, which multiply in the alveoli.

The disease begins with the same symptoms as the flu, including fever, muscle aches, and fatigue.

Symptoms suddenly become more severe with the development of breathing problems and shock.

Toxins cause hemorrhage and destruction of lung tissue.

---

blood and lymph; high levels of toxins lead to shock and death.

  4. In the lungs, anthrax can cause buildup of fluid, tissue decay, and death (fatal if untreated).

  5. A blood test is available to detect anthrax (magnifies DNA from the blood sample and matches it to anthrax DNA).

  6. Anthrax is treated with ciprofloxacin (Cipro), doxycycline, or penicillin.

  7. The vaccine has limited availability.

C. Smallpox (Fig. 16-3)

  1. Smallpox is transmitted in air droplets and by handling contaminated materials and is highly contagious.

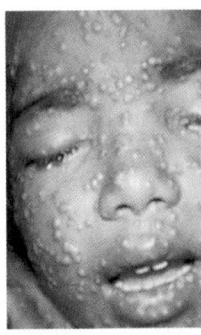 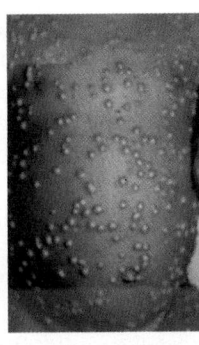 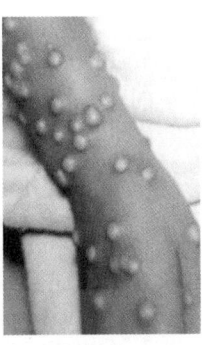

FIG. 16-3 Smallpox. (From McKinney, E., James, S., Murray, S., & Ashwill, J. [2005]. *Maternal-child nursing* [2nd ed.]. Philadelphia: W.B. Saunders. Courtesy of Centers for Disease Control and Prevention. [2002]. *Evaluating patients for smallpox.* Atlanta: Author.)

2. Symptoms begin 7 to 17 days after exposure and include fever, back pain, vomiting, malaise, and headache.
3. Papules develop 2 days after symptoms develop and progress to pustular vesicles that are abundant on the face and extremities initially.
4. A vaccine is available to those at risk for exposure to smallpox.

D. Botulism
1. Botulism is a serious paralytic illness caused by a nerve toxin produced by the bacterium *Clostridium botulinum* (death can occur within 24 hours).
2. Its spores are found in the soil and can spread through the air or food (improperly canned food) or via a contaminated wound.
3. It cannot be spread from person to person.
4. Symptoms include abdominal cramps, diarrhea, nausea and vomiting, double vision, blurred vision, drooping eyelids, difficulty swallowing or speaking, dry mouth, and muscle weakness.
5. Neurological symptoms begin 12 to 36 hours after ingestion of foodborne botulism and 24 to 72 hours after inhalation and can progress to paralysis of the arms, legs, trunk, or respiratory muscles (mechanical ventilation is necessary).
6. If diagnosed early, foodborne and wound botulism can be treated with an antitoxin that blocks the action of toxin circulating in the blood.
7. Other treatments include induction of vomiting, enemas, and penicillin.
8. No vaccine is available.

E. Plague
1. Plague is caused by *Yersinia pestis*, a bacteria found in rodents and fleas.
2. Plague is contracted by being bitten by a rodent or flea that is carrying the plague bacterium, by the ingestion of contaminated meat, or by handling an animal infected with the bacteria.
3. Transmission is by direct person-to-person spread.

4. Forms include bubonic (most common), pneumonic, and septicemic (most deadly).
5. Symptoms usually begin within 1 to 3 days and include fever, chest pain, lymph node swelling, and a productive cough (hemoptysis).
6. The disease rapidly progresses to dyspnea, stridor, and cyanosis; death occurs from respiratory failure, shock, and bleeding.
7. Antibiotics are only effective if administered immediately; medications of choice include streptomycin or gentamicin.
8. A vaccine is available.

F. Tularemia
1. Tularemia (also called deer fly fever or rabbit fever) is an infectious disease of animals caused by the bacillus *Francisella tularensis.*
2. The disease is transmitted by ticks, deer flies, or contact with an infected animal.
3. Symptoms include fever, headache, an ulcerated skin lesion with localized lymph node enlargement, eye infections, gastrointestinal ulcerations, or pneumonia.
4. Treatment is with antibiotics.
5. Recovery produces lifelong immunity (a vaccine is available).

G. Hemorrhagic fever
1. Hemorrhagic fever is caused by several viruses, including Marburg, Lassa, Junin, and Ebola.
2. The virus is carried by rodents and mosquitoes.
3. The disease can be transmitted by direct person-to-person spread via body fluids.
4. Symptoms include fever, headache, malaise, conjunctivitis, nausea, vomiting, hypotension, hemorrhage of tissues and organs, and organ failure.
5. No known specific treatment is available; treatment is symptomatic.

VII. CHEMICAL WARFARE AGENTS
A. Sarin
1. Sarin is a highly toxic nerve gas that can cause death within minutes of exposure.
2. It enters the body through the eyes and skin and acts by paralyzing the respiratory muscles.
B. Phosgene is a colorless gas normally used in chemical manufacturing that if inhaled at high concentrations for a long enough period will lead to severe respiratory distress, pulmonary edema, and death.
C. Mustard gas is yellow to brown and has a garlic-like odor that irritates the eyes and causes skin burns and blisters.
D. Ionizing radiation
1. Acute radiation exposure develops after a substantial exposure to radiation.
2. Exposure can occur from external radiation or internal absorption.
3. Symptoms depend on the amount of exposure to the radiation and range from nausea and

vomiting, diarrhea, fever, electrolyte imbalances, and neurological and cardiovascular impairment to leukopenia, purpura, hemorrhage, and death.

▲ VIII. NURSE'S ROLE FOR EXPOSURE TO WARFARE AGENTS

A. Be aware that initially, a bioterrorism attack may resemble a naturally occurring outbreak of an infectious disease.

B. Nurses and other health care workers must be prepared to assess and determine what type of event occurred, the number of clients who may be affected, and how and when clients will be expected to arrive.

C. It is essential to determine any changes in the microorganism that may increase its virulence or make it resistant to conventional antibiotics or vaccines.

D. See Chapter 8 for additional information on disasters and disaster planning.

PRACTICE QUESTIONS

1. The nurse is caring for a client diagnosed with meningitis and implements which transmission-based precautions for this client?
   1. Private room or cohort client
   2. Personal respiratory protection device
   3. Private room with negative airflow pressure
   4. Mask worn by staff when the client needs to leave the room

2. A nurse is giving a report to a nursing assistant who will be caring for a client who has hand restraints. The nurse instructs the nursing assistant to assess the skin integrity of the restrained hands:
   1. Every 2 hours
   2. Every 3 hours
   3. Every 4 hours
   4. Every 30 minutes

3. A nurse is planning care for a client with an internal radiation implant. Which of the following is an inappropriate component for the nurse to include in the plan of care?
   1. Wearing gloves when emptying the client's bedpan
   2. Keeping all linens in the room until the implant is removed
   3. Wearing a lead apron when providing direct care to the client
   4. Placing the client in a semiprivate room at the end of the hallway

4. A mother calls a neighbor who is a nurse and tells the nurse that her 3-year-old child has just ingested liquid furniture polish. The nurse would direct the mother immediately to:
   1. Induce vomiting.
   2. Call an ambulance.

3. Call the Poison Control Center.
4. Bring the child to the emergency department.

5. An emergency department nurse receives a telephone call and is informed that a tornado has hit a local residential area and that numerous casualties have occurred. The victims will be brought to the emergency room. The initial nursing action is which of the following?
   1. Prepare the triage rooms.
   2. Activate the agency disaster plan.
   3. Obtain additional supplies from the central supply department.
   4. Obtain additional nursing staff to assist in treating the casualties.

6. A client is diagnosed with a nosocomial infection caused by methicillin-resistant *Staphylococcus aureus* and contact precautions are initiated. The nurse prepares to provide colostomy care to the client and obtains which of the following protective items needed to perform this procedure?
   1. Gloves and a gown
   2. Gloves and goggles
   3. Gloves, gown, and shoe protectors
   4. Gloves, gown, goggles, and a face shield

7. A nurse enters a client's room and finds that the wastebasket is on fire. The nurse immediately assists the client out of the room. The next nursing action would be to:
   1. Call for help.
   2. Extinguish the fire.
   3. Activate the fire alarm.
   4. Confine the fire by closing the room door.

8. A nurse enters the nursing lounge and discovers that a chair is on fire. She activates the alarm, closes the lounge door, and obtains the fire extinguisher to extinguish the fire. The nurse pulls the pin on the fire extinguisher. The next appropriate action for the use of the fire extinguisher is to:
   1. Aim at the base of the fire.
   2. Squeeze the handle on the extinguisher.
   3. Sweep the fire from side to side with the extinguisher.
   4. Sweep the fire from top to bottom with the extinguisher.

9. A nurse is preparing to initiate an intravenous line containing a high dose of potassium chloride and plans to use an intravenous infusion pump. The nurse brings the pump to the bedside, prepares to plug the pump cord into the wall, and notes that no receptacle is available in the wall socket. Which of the following is the appropriate nursing action?
   1. Initiate the intravenous line without the use of a pump.
   2. Contact the electrical maintenance department for assistance.

3. Plug in the pump cord in the available plug above the room sink.
4. Use an extension cord from the nurses' lounge for the pump plug.

10. A nurse obtains an order from a physician to restrain a client by using a jacket restraint and instructs a nursing assistant to apply the restraint to the client. Which observation by the nurse indicates inappropriate application of the restraint by the nursing assistant?
   1. A safety knot in the restraint straps
   2. Restraint straps that are safely secured to the side rails
   3. Jacket restraint straps that do not tighten when force is applied against them
   4. Jacket restraint secured so that two fingers can slide easily between the restraint and the client's skin

ALTERNATE ITEM FORMAT: MULTIPLE RESPONSE

A community health nurse is providing a teaching session about terrorism to members of the community and is discussing information regarding anthrax. The nurse tells those attending that anthrax can be transmitted by which route(s)?
❏ 1. Bites from ticks or deer flies
❏ 2. Inhalation of bacterial spores
❏ 3. Through a cut or abrasion in the skin
❏ 4. Direct contact with an infected individual
❏ 5. Sexual contact with an infected individual
❏ 6. Ingestion of contaminated undercooked meat

ANSWERS

1. **1**
Rationale: Meningitis is transmitted by droplet infection. Precautions for this disease include a private room or cohort client and use of a standard precaution mask. Private negative airflow pressure rooms and personal respiratory protection devices are required for clients with airborne disease such as tuberculosis (TB). When appropriate, a mask must be worn by the client and not the staff when the client leaves the room.
Test-Taking Strategy: Use the process of elimination to determine the correct precaution needs for this client. Focusing on the client's diagnosis and recalling that meningitis is transmitted by droplets will direct you to option 1. If you had difficulty with this question, review transmission-based categories, including precaution criteria.
Level of Cognitive Ability: Application
Client Needs: Safe and Effective Care Environment
Integrated Process: Nursing Process—implementation
Content Area: Fundamental skills
Reference: Potter, A., and Perry, P. (2005). *Fundamentals of nursing* (6th ed., p. 965). St. Louis: Mosby.

2. **4**
Rationale: The nurse should instruct the nursing assistant to assess restraints and skin integrity every 30 minutes. Agency guidelines regarding the use of restraints should always be followed.
Test-Taking Strategy: Use the process of elimination. In this situation, selecting the option that identifies the most frequent time frame is best. Review the guidelines related to the use of restraints if you had difficulty with this question.
Level of Cognitive Ability: Application
Client Needs: Safe and Effective Care Environment
Integrated Process: Teaching and Learning
Content Area: Leadership/Management
Reference: Ignatavicius, D., & Workman, M. (2006). *Medical-surgical nursing: Critical thinking for collaborative care* (5th ed., p. 45). Philadelphia: W.B. Saunders.

3. **4**
Rationale: A private room with a private bath is essential if a client has an internal radiation implant. This is necessary to prevent accidental exposure of other clients to radiation. Options 1, 2, and 3 are accurate interventions for a client with a radiation implant.
Test-Taking Strategy: Use the process of elimination and note the strategic words *inappropriate component*. Option 1 can be eliminated first because this is a component of standard precautions for all clients. Options 2 and 3 can be eliminated next because they directly relate to radiation safety. Review radiation safety principles if you had difficulty with this question.
Level of Cognitive Ability: Application
Client Needs: Safe and Effective Care Environment
Integrated Process: Nursing Process—planning
Content Area: Fundamental skills
Reference: Ignatavicius, D., & Workman, M. (2006). *Medical-surgical nursing: Critical thinking for collaborative care* (5th ed., p. 490). Philadelphia: W.B. Saunders.

4. **3**
Rationale: If a poisoning occurs, the Poison Control Center should be contacted immediately. Vomiting should not be induced if the victim is unconscious or if the substance ingested is a strong corrosive or petroleum product. Bringing the child to the emergency department or calling an ambulance would not be the initial action because this would delay treatment. The Poison Control Center may advise the mother to bring the child to the emergency department and, if this is the case, the mother should call an ambulance.
Test-Taking Strategy: Use the process of elimination and note the strategic word *immediately*. Eliminate options 2 and 4 because these options will delay treatment. Recalling that vomiting should not be induced if a corrosive substance was ingested will assist in eliminating option 1. Review poison control measures if you had difficulty with this question.
Level of Cognitive Ability: Application
Client Needs: Safe and Effective Care Environment

Integrated Process: Nursing Process—implementation
Content Area: Fundamental skills
Reference: Potter, P., & Perry, A. (2005). *Fundamentals of nursing* (6th ed., p. 992). St. Louis: Mosby.

5. **2**

Rationale: In an external disaster, many victims may be brought to the emergency department for treatment. Although options 1, 3, and 4 may be components of preparing for the casualties, the initial nursing action must be to activate the disaster plan.
Test-Taking Strategy: Use the process of elimination to determine the priority action. Note the strategic word *initial* in the event query. Note that option 2 is the umbrella option. Review procedures related to management of a disaster if you had difficulty with this question.
Level of Cognitive Ability: Application
Client Needs: Safe and Effective Care Environment
Integrated Process: Nursing Process—implementation
Content Area: Fundamental skills
Reference: Ignatavicius, D., & Workman, M. (2006). *Medical-surgical nursing: Critical thinking for collaborative care* (5th ed., pp. 167-168). Philadelphia: W.B. Saunders.

6. **4**

Rationale: Goggles and a face shield are worn to protect the mucous membranes of the eyes during interventions that may produce splashes of blood, body fluids, secretions, or excretions. In addition, contact precautions require the use of gloves, and a gown should be worn if direct client contact is anticipated. Shoe protectors are not necessary.
Test-Taking Strategy: Note the strategic words *contact precautions* and *colostomy.* Use the process of elimination and visualize care for this client to determine the necessary items required in caring for this client. If you had difficulty with this question, review transmission-based precautions.
Level of Cognitive Ability: Application
Client Needs: Safe and Effective Care Environment
Integrated Process: Nursing Process—implementation
Content Area: Fundamental skills
Reference: Ignatavicius, D., & Workman, M. (2006). *Medical-surgical nursing: Critical thinking for collaborative care* (5th ed., pp. 513-514). Philadelphia: W.B. Saunders.

7. **3**

Rationale: The order of priority in the event of a fire is to rescue the clients who are in immediate danger. The next step is to activate the fire alarm. The fire then is confined by closing all doors and, finally, the fire is extinguished.
Test-Taking Strategy: Remember the mnemonic *RACE* to prioritize in the event of a fire. *R* is rescue clients in immediate danger, *A* is alarm (sound the alarm), *C* is confine the fire by closing all doors, and *E* is extinguish or evacuate. If you had difficulty with this question, review the principles related to fire safety.
Level of Cognitive Ability: Application
Client Needs: Safe and Effective Care Environment
Integrated Process: Nursing Process—implementation
Content Area: Fundamental skills
Reference: Potter, P., & Perry, A. (2005). *Fundamentals of nursing* (6th ed., p. 991). St. Louis: Mosby.

8. **1**

Rationale: A fire can be extinguished or by using a fire extinguisher. To use the extinguisher, pull the pin first. The nurse then aims at the base of the fire. The extinguisher is squeezed and the fire is extinguished by sweeping from side to side to coat the area evenly.
Test-Taking Strategy: Remember the mnemonic *PASS* to prioritize in the use of a fire extinguisher. *P* is pull the pin, *A* is aim at the base of the fire, *S* is squeeze the handle, and *S* is sweep from side to side to coat the area evenly. If you had difficulty with this question, review the steps in the appropriate use of a fire extinguisher.
Level of Cognitive Ability: Application
Client Needs: Safe and Effective Care Environment
Integrated Process: Nursing Process—implementation
Content Area: Fundamental skills
Reference: Potter, P., & Perry, A. (2005). *Fundamentals of nursing* (6th ed., p. 992). St. Louis: Mosby.

9. **2**

Rationale: The nurse needs to use hospital resources for assistance. A regular extension cord should not be used because it poses the risk of fire. The use of electrical appliances near a sink also presents a hazard. An intravenous line that contains a high dose of potassium chloride should be administered by the use of a pump.
Test-Taking Strategy: Use the process of elimination. Noting the strategic words *high dose* in the question will assist in eliminating option 1. Recalling safety issues related to electrical hazards will assist in eliminating options 3 and 4. If you had difficulty with this question, review the interventions related to electrical safety.
Level of Cognitive Ability: Application
Client Needs: Safe and Effective Care Environment
Integrated Process: Nursing Process—implementation
Content Area: Fundamental skills
Reference: Potter, P., & Perry, A. (2005). *Fundamentals of nursing* (6th ed., pp. 992-993). St. Louis: Mosby.

10. **2**

Rationale: The restraint straps are secured to the bed frame and never to the side rail to avoid accidental injury in the event that the side rail is released. A half-bow or safety knot should be used for applying a restraint because it does not tighten when force is applied against it and it allows quick and easy removal of the restraint in case of an emergency. The jacket restraint should be secure, and one to two fingers should slide easily between the restraint and the client's skin.
Test-Taking Strategy: Use the process of elimination and note the strategic words *indicates inappropriate application.* These words indicate a negative event query and ask you to select an option that is an incorrect observation. This indicates that you are looking for an option that identifies an inaccurate measure related to the application of restraints. Read each option carefully. The words *secured to the side rails* in option 2 should direct your attention to this as an inappropriate action. Review guidelines related to the application of restraints if you had difficulty with this question.
Level of Cognitive Ability: Analysis
Client Needs: Safe and Effective Care Environment

Integrated Process: Teaching and Learning
Content Area: Fundamental skills
Reference: Ignatavicius, D., & Workman, M. (2006). *Medical-surgical nursing: Critical thinking for collaborative care* (5th ed., pp. 44-45). Philadelphia: W.B. Saunders.

ALTERNATE ITEM FORMAT: MULTIPLE RESPONSE

Answer: 2, 3, 6
Rationale: Anthrax is caused by *Bacillus anthracis* and can be contracted through the digestive system, abrasions in the skin, or inhaled through the lungs. It cannot be spread from person to person or animal to person and it is not contracted via bites from ticks or deer flies.

Test-Taking Strategy: Knowledge regarding the methods of contracting anthrax is needed to answer this question. Remember that it is not spread by person-to-person contact or contracted via tick or deer fly bites. Review information related to this infection if you had difficulty with this question.
Level of Cognitive Ability: Application
Client Needs: Safe and Effective Care Environment
Integrated Process: Teaching and Learning
Content Area: Fundamental skills
Reference: Ignatavicius, D., & Workman, M. (2006). *Medical-surgical nursing: Critical thinking for collaborative care* (5th ed., p. 519). Philadelphia: W.B. Saunders.

REFERENCES

Ignatavicius, D., & Workman, M. (2006). *Medical-surgical nursing: Critical thinking for collaborative care* (5th ed.). Philadelphia: W.B. Saunders.

Lewis, S., Heitkemper, M., & Dirksen, S. (2004). *Medical-surgical nursing: Assessment and management of clinical problems* (6th ed.). St. Louis: Mosby.

National Council of State Boards of Nursing (Eds.). (2007). *2007 NCLEX-RN® detailed test plan.* Chicago: Author.

Perry, A., & Potter, P. (2006). *Clinical nursing skills & techniques* (6th ed.). St. Louis: Mosby.

Potter, P., & Perry, A. (2005). *Fundamentals of nursing* (6th ed.). St. Louis: Mosby.

Administration of Medication and Intravenous Solutions

PYRAMID TERMS

conversion The first step in the calculation of a medication problem.

generic name Also known as the nonproprietary name of a medication, or the U.S. adopted name; each medication has only one generic name.

medication reconciliation An organized process to avoid medication errors by comparing the client's medication orders to all the medications that the client has been previously taking.

milliequivalent An expression of the number of grams of a medication contained in 1 mL of a solution; abbreviated mEq.

parenteral Given by injection, such as by the intravenous, intramuscular, subcutaneous, or intradermal route.

percentage solution The number of grams of a medication per 100 mL of solution.

ratio solution The number of grams of a medication per total milliliters of solution.

reconstitution Dissolving a powder in a sterile diluent before use, usually in sterile water or normal saline.

trade name Also known as the proprietary or brand name of a medication. The trade name is the name under which a medication is marketed. A medication can have many trade names; therefore, trade names must be approved by the U.S. Food and Drug Administration (FDA) to ensure that no two trade names are alike.

unit A measurement of a medication in terms of its action, not its physical weight.

▲ THE PYRAMID TO SUCCESS

When a medication or intravenous calculation question is presented, a nurse should always use the appropriate formula to solve the problem. The nurse should not use shortcuts to make these calculations. The problem and answer should be expressed in the correct units of measure. Be careful with decimal points. Correct placement of the decimal point is important or the answer will be incorrect. When solving a medication calculation problem, the nurse determines whether the answer is within reason and makes sense. In the clinical setting, the nurse should always seek assistance if unsure of the accuracy of a calculation.

On the NCLEX-RN examination, the fill-in-the-blank questions may require that you calculate a medication dose or an intravenous flow rate. You will be provided with a computer on-screen calculator for these medication and intravenous problems. Even if you use the calculator to calculate dosages and flow rates, you must check the calculation before selecting an option or typing the answer. Follow the formula, place the decimal point in the correct place, and check the accuracy of the calculation. Remember, practice makes perfect. The Integrated Processes addressed in this chapter are Caring, Communication and Documentation, Nursing Process, and Teaching/Learning.

CLIENT NEEDS ▲

Safe and Effective Care Environment

Calculating medication doses and intravenous flow rates
Handling hazardous and infectious materials
Maintaining client's rights
Maintaining medical and surgical asepsis
Maintaining standard and other precautions
Preventing errors
Using equipment safely

Health Promotion and Maintenance

Performing a physical assessment of a client
Preventing diseases
Respecting lifestyle choices
Teaching the client about prescribed medication(s) or intravenous (IV) therapy

Psychosocial Integrity

Identifying support systems
Identifying the cultural, religious, and spiritual factors influencing health
Interacting therapeutically with the client and family
Identifying the use of coping mechanisms

Physiological Integrity

Administering medications and IV therapy
Assessing for expected and unexpected effects of pharmacological therapy
Identifying the adverse effects of and contraindications to medication or IV therapy
Monitoring for alterations in body systems
Monitoring laboratory values

I. MEDICATION ADMINISTRATION (Box 17-1)

II. DRUG MEASUREMENT SYSTEMS

A. Metric system (Box 17-2)
   1. The basic **units** of metric measures are meter, liter, and gram.
   2. Meter measures length, liter measures volume, gram measures mass.
B. Apothecary and household systems (Box 17-3)
   1. The apothecary and household systems are the oldest of the medication measurement systems.
   2. Apothecary measures such as grain, dram, minim, and ounce are not commonly used in the clinical setting.

3. Commonly used household measures include drop, teaspoon, tablespoon, ounce, pint, and cup.
C. Additional common drug measures
   1. **Milliequivalent**
      a. **Milliequivalent** is abbreviated mEq.
      b. The **milliequivalent** is an expression of the number of grams of a medication contained in 1 mL of a solution.
      c. For example, the measure of serum potassium is given in **milliequivalents**.
   2. **Unit**
      a. **Unit** measures a medication in terms of its action, not its physical weight.
      b. For example, penicillin, heparin sodium, and insulin are measured in **units**.

III. CONVERSIONS

A. Conversion between metric **units** (Box 17-4)
   1. The metric system is a decimal system; therefore, **conversions** between the **units** in this system can be done by dividing or multiplying by 1000 or by moving the decimal point three places to the right or three places to the left.
   2. In the metric system, to convert larger to smaller, multiply by 1000 or move the decimal point three places to the right.

BOX 17-1
Medication Administration

Assess the medication order.
Ask the client about a history of allergies.
Assess the client's current condition and the purpose for the medication or intravenous solution.
Determine the client's understanding regarding the purpose of the prescribed medication or need for intravenous solution.
Teach the client about the medication and about self-administration at home.
Identify and address concerns (social, cultural, religious) that the client may have about taking the medication.
Assess the need for conversion when preparing a dose of medication for administration to the client.
Assess the six rights of medication administration: right medication, right dose, right client, right route, right time, and right documentation.
Assess the vital signs before administering medication, when appropriate.
Document the administration of the prescribed therapy and client's response to the therapy.

BOX 17-2
Metric System

ABBREVIATIONS	EQUIVALENTS
meter: m	1 mcg = 0.000001 g
liter: L	1 mg = 1000 mcg or 0.001 g
milliliter: mL	1 g = 1000 mg
kilogram: kg	1 kg = 1000 g
gram: g	1 kg = 2.2 lb
milligram: mg	1 mL = 0.001 L
microgram: mcg	

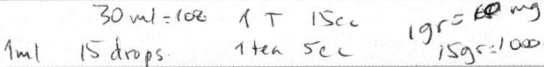

BOX 17-3
Apothecary and Household Systems

ABBREVIATIONS	EQUIVALENTS
Apothecary (Weight)	1 gr = 60-65 mg
grain: gr	5 gr = 300-325 mg
ounce: oz	15 gr = 1000 mg or 1 g
Household (Volume)	$\frac{1}{150}$ gr = 0.4 mg
drops: gtt	1 fl oz = 30 mL
teaspoon: t or tsp	1 T = 15 mL or 3 tsp
tablespoon: T or tbs	1 t or tsp = 5 mL
fluid ounce: fl oz	1 C = 8 fl oz
cup: C	1 qt = 946 mL or 0.946 L
pint: pt	1 qt = 2 pt or 32 fl oz
quart: qt	1 pt = 16 fl oz
Household (Weight)	16 oz = 1 lb
pound: lb	2.2 lb = 1 kg

BOX 17-4
Conversion Between Metric Units

PROBLEM 1
Convert 2 g to milligrams.
Solution
Change a larger unit to a smaller unit.
2 g = 2000 mg (moving decimal three places to right)

PROBLEM 2
Convert 250 mL to liters.
Solution
Change a smaller unit to a larger unit.
250 mL = 0.25 L (moving decimal three places to left)

BOX 17-5
Ratio and Proportion

Ratio: The relationship between two numbers, separated by a colon—for example, 1:2 (1 to 2).
Proportion: The relationship between two ratios, separated by a double colon (::) or an equal sign (=).
Formula:
H (on hand):V (vehicle) :: (=) (desired dose):X (unknown)
To solve a ratio and proportion problem: The middle numbers (means) are multiplied and the end numbers (extremes) are multiplied.

SAMPLE PROBLEM
H = 1
V = 2
Desired dose = 3
X = unknown
Set up the formula:
1:2::3:X
Solve: Multiply means and extremes.
1X = 6
X = 6

BOX 17-6
Calculating Equivalents Between Two Systems

Calculating equivalents between two systems may be done by using the method of ratio and proportion.

PROBLEM
The physician orders nitroglycerin, grain (gr) $\frac{1}{150}$. The medication label reads 0.4 milligram (mg) per tablet. The nurse prepares to administer how many tablets to the client?
Ratio and Proportion Formula
H (on hand):V (vehicle) :: (=) (desired dose):X
1 gr:60 mg :: $\frac{1}{150}$ gr:mg
$60 \times \frac{1}{150} = X$
X = 0.4 mg (1 tablet)

BOX 17-7
Celsius and Fahrenheit Temperature

FAHRENHEIT TO CELSIUS
To convert Fahrenheit to Celsius, subtract 32 and divide the result by 1.8.
Formula:
$$C = \frac{(F - 32)}{1.8}$$

CELSIUS TO FAHRENHEIT
To convert Celsius to Fahrenheit, multiply by 1.8 and add 32.
Formula:
$$F = (1.8 \times C) + 32$$

5. Calculating equivalents between two systems may be done by using the method of ratio and proportion (Boxes 17-5 and 17-6).

IV. CELSIUS AND FAHRENHEIT TEMPERATURE (Box 17-7)
A. To convert Fahrenheit to Celsius, subtract 32 and divide the result by 1.8.
B. To convert Celsius to Fahrenheit, multiply by 1.8 and add 32.

V. MEDICATION LABELS
A. A medication label contains the **generic name** and the **trade name** of the medication.
B. Always check expiration dates on medication labels.

VI. MEDICATION ORDERS (Box 17-8)
A. In a medication order, the name of the medication is written first, followed by the dosage, route, and frequency (depending on the frequency of the order, times of administration are usually established by the health care agency and written in an agency policy).
B. Medication orders need to be written using accepted abbreviations, acronyms, and symbols

3. In the metric system, to convert smaller to larger, divide by 1000 or move the decimal point three places to the left.
B. **Conversion** between household and metric systems
   1. Household and metric measures are equivalent and not equal measures.
   2. **Conversion** to equivalent measures between systems is necessary when a medication order is written in one system but the medication label is stated in another.
   3. Medications are not always ordered and prepared in the same system of measurement; therefore, **conversion** of **units** from one system to another is necessary.
   4. **Conversion** is the first step in the calculation of dosages.

Name of client
Date and time when order is written
Name of medication to be given
Dosage of medication
Medication route
Time and frequency of administration
Signature of person writing the order

approved by The Joint Commission; also follow agency guidelines.

C. If the nurse has any questions about or sees inconsistencies in the written order, the nurse must contact the person who wrote the order immediately and must verify the order.

VII. ORAL MEDICATIONS

A. Scored tablets contain an indented mark to be used for possible breakage into partial doses; when necessary, scored tablets (those marked for division) can be divided into halves or quarters.

B. Enteric-coated tablets and sustained-released capsules delay absorption until the medication reaches the small intestine; these medications should not be crushed.

C. Capsules contain a powdered or oily medication in a gelatin cover.

D. Orally administered liquids are supplied in solution form and contain a specific amount of medication in a given amount of solution, as stated on the label.

E. The medicine cup
1. The medicine cup has a capacity of 30 mL or 1 oz.
2. The medicine cup is used for orally administered liquids.
3. The medicine cup is calibrated to measure teaspoons, tablespoons, and ounces.
4. To pour accurately, place the medication cup on a level surface at eye level and then pour the liquid while reading the measuring markings.

F. Volumes of less than 5 mL are measured by using a syringe with the needle removed.

G. A calibrated dropper is used for giving medicine to children or for adding small amounts of liquid to water or juice; calibrations are in milliliters or drops.

VIII. PARENTERAL MEDICATIONS

A. **Parenteral** always means an injection route and **parenteral** medications are administered by intravenous, intramuscular, subcutaneous, or intradermal injection.

B. **Parenteral** medications are packaged in single-use ampules, in single- and multiple-use rubber-stoppered vials, and in premeasured syringes and cartridges.

C. The nurse should not administer more than 3 mL per intramuscular or 1 mL per subcutaneous injection site; larger volumes are difficult for an injection site to absorb and, if prescribed, need to be verified.

D. Always question and verify excessively large or small volumes of medication.

E. The standard 3-mL syringe is used to measure most injectable medications and is calibrated in tenths (0.1) of a milliliter (Fig. 17-1).

F. The calibrations on a syringe are read from the top black ring on the syringe, not the middle section and not the bottom ring.

G. Prefilled medication cartridge (Fig. 17-2)
1. The medication cartridge slips into the cartridge holder, which provides a plunger for injection of the medication.
2. The cartridge is designed to provide sufficient capacity to allow for the addition of a second medication when combined dosages are prescribed.
3. The prefilled medication cartridge is to be used once and discarded; if a nurse is to give less than the full single dose provided, the nurse needs to discard the extra amount before giving the client the injection, following agency policies and procedures.

H. Standard medication doses for adults are to be rounded to the nearest tenth (0.1 mL) of a milliliter and measured on the milliliter scale; for example, 1.25 mL is rounded to 1.3 mL.

I. When volumes larger than 3 mL are required, the nurse may use a 5-mL syringe; these syringes are calibrated in fifths (0.2 mL) (Fig. 17-3).

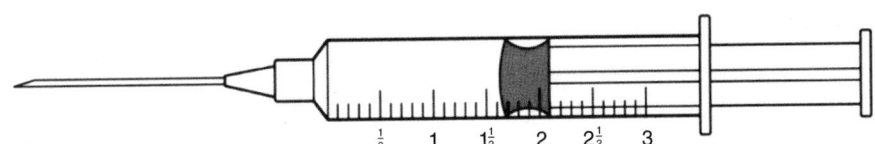

FIG. 17-1 Three-milliliter syringe. (From Kee, J., & Marshall, S. [2004]. *Clinical calculations: With applications to general and specialty areas* [5th ed.]. Philadelphia: W.B. Saunders.)

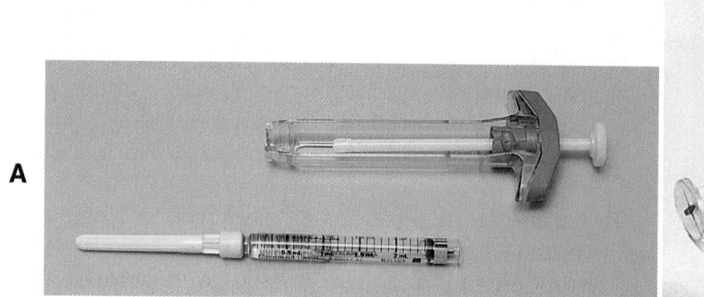
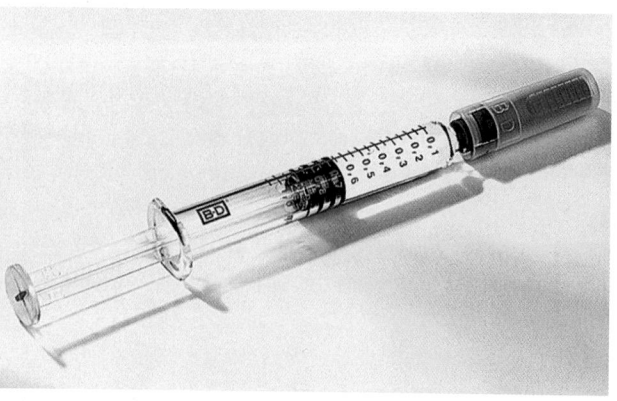

FIG. 17-2 **A,** Tubex syringe with cartridge. **B,** BD Hypak prefilled syringe. (From Kee, J., & Marshall, S. [2000]. *Clinical calculations: With applications to general and specialty areas* [4th ed.]. Philadelphia: W.B. Saunders. **A,** Courtesy of Wyeth-Ayerst Laboratories, Philadelphia; **B,** courtesy of Becton, Dickinson, Franklin Lakes, NJ.)

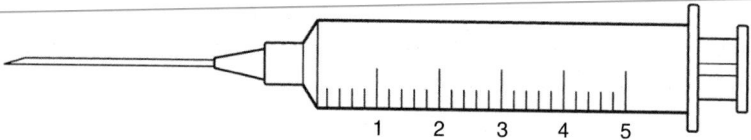

FIG. 17-3 Five-milliliter syringe. (From Kee, J., & Marshall, S. [2004]. *Clinical calculations: With applications to general and specialty areas* [5th ed.]. Philadelphia: W.B. Saunders.)

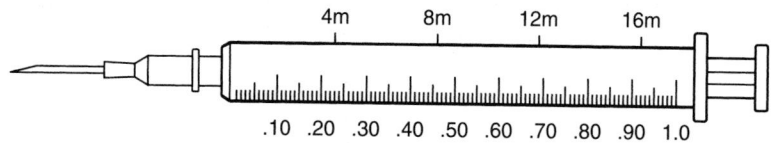

FIG. 17-4 Tuberculin syringe. (From Kee, J., & Marshall, S. [2004]. *Clinical calculations: With applications to general and specialty areas* [5th ed.]. Philadelphia: W.B. Saunders.)

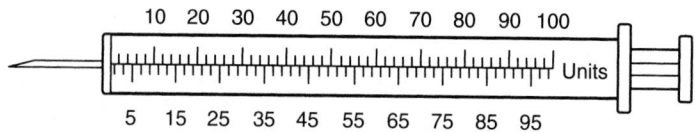

FIG. 17-5 Insulin syringe. (From Kee, J., & Marshall, S. [2004]. *Clinical calculations: With applications to general and specialty areas* [5th ed.]. Philadelphia: W.B. Saunders.)

J. Syringes sized 10, 20, and 50 mL are available and may be used for medication administration requiring dilution.

K. Tuberculin syringe (Fig. 17-4)
   1. The tuberculin syringe holds 1 mL and is used to measure small or critical amounts of medication, such as allergen extract, vaccine, or a child's medication.
   2. The syringe is calibrated in hundredths (0.01) of a milliliter, with each one tenth (0.1) marked on the metric scale.

L. Insulin syringe (Fig. 17-5)
   1. The standard 100-unit insulin syringe is calibrated for 100 **units** of insulin (100 **units** = 1 mL); low-dose insulin syringes ($\frac{1}{2}$- and 1-mL sizes) may also be used when administering smaller insulin doses.
   2. Insulin should not be measured in any other type of syringe.
   3. When the insulin order states to combine regular and NPH insulin, remember "RN": draw Regular insulin first, and then draw the NPH insulin.

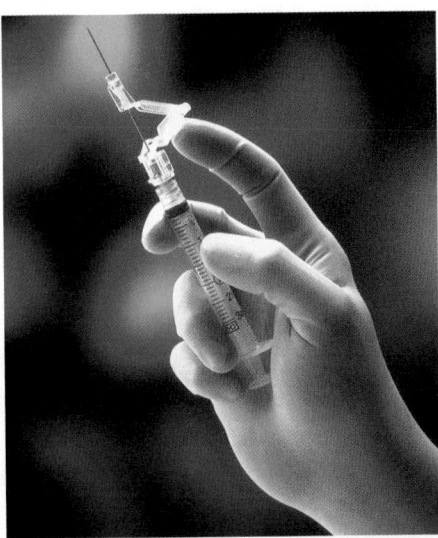

FIG. 17-6 SafetyGlyde needle, one type of safety needle. (From Kee, J., & Marshall, S. [2004]. *Clinical calculations: With applications to general and specialty areas* [5th ed.]. Philadelphia: W.B. Saunders. Courtesy of Becton, Dickinson, Franklin Lakes, NJ.).

M. Safety needles
   1. Contain shielding devices are available to reduce the incidence of needlestick injuries (Fig. 17-6).
   2. See Chapter 14 (Fig. 14-5) for examples of needleless medication administration infusion devices.

IX. INJECTABLE MEDICATIONS IN POWDER FORM
A. Some medications become unstable when stored in solution form and are therefore packaged in powder form.
B. Powders must be dissolved with a sterile diluent before use; usually, sterile water or normal saline is used. The dissolving procedure is called **reconstitution** (Box 17-9).

X. CALCULATING THE CORRECT DOSAGE
   (Boxes 17-10 and 17-11)
A. When calculating dosages of oral medications, check the calculation and question an order if the calculation calls for more than three tablets.
B. When calculating dosages of **parenteral** medications, check the calculation and question an order if the amount to be given is too large a dose.
C. Regardless of the source of an error, if a nurse gives an incorrect dose, the nurse is legally responsible for the action.
D. Be sure that all measures are in the same system, and that all **units** are in the same size, converting when necessary; carefully consider what is the reasonable amount of the medication that should be administered.
E. Round standard injection doses to tenths and measure in a 3-mL syringe.

BOX 17-9
Reconstitution

In reconstituting the medication, locate the instructions on the label or in the vial package insert, and read and follow the directions carefully.
   Instructions will state the volume of diluent to be used and the resulting volume of the reconstituted medication.
   Often, the powdered medication adds volume to the solution in addition to the amount of diluent added.
   When reconstituting a multiple-dose vial, label the medication vial with the date and time of preparation, your initials, and the date of expiration.
   Indicating the strength per volume on the medication label also is important.
   The total volume of the prepared solution will exceed the volume of the diluent added.

BOX 17-10
Standard Formula for Calculating a Medication Dosage

$$\frac{D}{A} \times Q = X$$

D (desired) is the dosage that the physician ordered.
A (available) is the dosage strength as stated on the medication label.
Q (quantity) is the volume or form in which the dosage strength is available, such as tablets, capsules, or milliliters.

BOX 17-11
Formulas for Intravenous Calculations

FLOW RATES
$$\frac{\text{Total volume} \times \text{drop factor}}{\text{Time in minutes}} = \text{drops per minute}$$

INFUSION TIME
$$\frac{\text{Total volume to infuse}}{\text{Milliliters per hour being infused}} = \text{infusion time}$$

NUMBER OF MILLILITERS PER HOUR
$$\frac{\text{Total volume in milliliters}}{\text{Number of hours}} = \text{number of milliliters per hour}$$

F. Round small, critical amounts or children's doses to hundredths and measure in the 1-mL tuberculin syringe.

XI. PERCENTAGE AND RATIO SOLUTIONS
A. **Percentage solutions**
   1. Express the number of grams of the medication per 100 mL of solution.

2. For example, calcium gluconate 10% is 10 g of pure medication per 100 mL of solution.

B. **Ratio solutions**
   1. Express the number of grams of the medication per total milliliters of solution.
   2. For example, epinephrine 1:1000 is 1 g of pure medication per 1000 mL solution.

XII. INTRAVENOUS FLOW RATES (see Box 17-11)

A. Monitor IV flow rate every 30 minutes for adults and every 15 minutes for children.
B. If an IV is running behind schedule, collaborate with the physician to determine the client's ability to tolerate an increased flow rate, particularly for clients with cardiac, pulmonary, renal, or neurological conditions.
C. The nurse should never increase the rate (speed up) of an IV infusion to catch up if the infusion is running behind schedule.
D. Whenever a prescribed IV rate is increased, the nurse should assess the client for increased heart rate, increased respirations, or increased lung congestion, which could indicate fluid overload.
E. Intravenously administered fluids are ordered most frequently based on milliliters per hour to be administered.
F. The volume per hour ordered is administered by setting the flow rate, which is counted in drops per minute.
G. Most flow rate calculations involve changing milliliters per hour into drops per minute.
H. Intravenous tubing
   1. Intravenous tubing is calibrated in drops per milliliter, and this calibration is needed for calculating flow rates.
   2. A standard or macrodrip set is used for routine adult IV administrations; depending on the manufacturer and type of tubing, the set will require 10, 15, or 20 gtt to equal 1 mL.
   3. A minidrip or microdrip set is used when more exact measurements are needed, such as in intensive care units and pediatric units.
   4. In a minidrip or microdrip set, 60 gtt is usually equal to 1 mL.
   5. The calibration, in drops per milliliter, is written on the IV tubing package.

XIII. ELECTRONIC IV FLOW RATE REGULATORS

A. Controller
   1. The controller works on the same principle of gravity as a regular IV drip, with the rate of flow being maintained by rapid compression and decompression of the IV tubing by the machine.
   2. The desired flow rate is set on the controller in milliliters per hour.

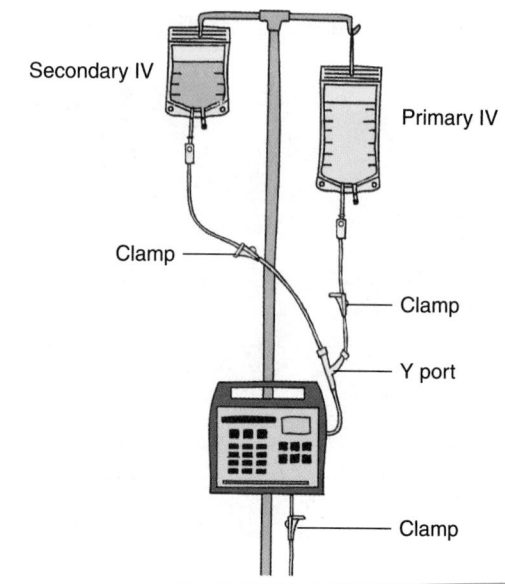

FIG. 17-7 Infusion pump. (From Kee, J., & Marshall, S. [2004]. *Clinical calculations: With applications to general and specialty areas* [5th ed.]. Philadelphia: W.B. Saunders.)

   3. Because controllers work by gravity, the height of the solution bag is critical; the bag must be maintained a minimum of 36 inches above the controller.
   4. The nurse should continue to assess the amount of IV solution in the IV container and monitor the controller to ensure proper functioning of the machine.

B. Pump (Fig. 17-7)
   1. A pump is different from a controller in that it physically pumps fluids against resistance.
   2. Gravity is not a factor in the use of a pump, and the height of the IV solution container is not a critical factor.
   3. The flow rate on a pump is set in milliliters per hour.
   4. The nurse should continue to assess the amount of IV solution in the IV container and monitor the pump to ensure proper functioning of the machine.

XIV. CALCULATION OF INFUSIONS ORDERED BY UNIT DOSAGE PER HOUR

A. The most common medications that will be ordered by **unit** dosage per hour and run by continuous infusion are heparin sodium and regular insulin.
B. Calculation of these infusions can be done by a two-step process (Box 17-12).
   1. Determine the amount of medication per 1 mL.
   2. Determine the infusion rate or milliliters per hour.

BOX 17-12

Infusions Ordered by Unit Dosage per Hour

Calculation of these problems can be done by a two-step process:
1. Determine the amount of medication per 1 mL.
2. Determine the infusion rate or milliliters per hour.

PROBLEM 1
Order: Continuous heparin sodium by IV at 1000 units per hour
Available: IV bag of 500 mL D$_5$W with 20,000 units of heparin sodium
How many milliliters per hour are required to administer the correct dose?
Solution
Step 1: Calculate the units per milliliter.

$$\frac{\text{Known amount of medication in solution}}{\text{Total volume of diluent}} = \text{amount of medication per milliliter}$$

$$\frac{20,000 \text{ units}}{500 \text{ mL}} = 40 \text{ units/1 mL}$$

Step 2: Calculate milliliters per hour.

$$\frac{\text{Dose per hour desired}}{\text{Concentration per milliliter}} = \text{infusion rate, or milliliter per hour}$$

$$\frac{1000 \text{ units}}{40 \text{ units}} = 25 \text{ mL/hr}$$

PROBLEM 2
Order: Continuous regular insulin by IV at 10 units per hour
Available: IV bag of 100 mL NS with 50 units regular insulin
How many milliliters per hour are required to administer the correct dose?
Solution
Step 1: Calculate the units per milliliter.

$$\frac{\text{Known amount of medication in solution}}{\text{Total volume of diluent}} = \text{amount of medication per milliliter}$$

$$\frac{50 \text{ units}}{100 \text{ mL}} = 0.5 \text{ units per milliliter}$$

Step 2: Calculate milliliters per hour.

$$\frac{\text{Dose per hour desired}}{\text{Concentration per milliliter}} = \text{infusion rate, or milliliters per hour}$$

$$\frac{10 \text{ units}}{0.5 \text{ units/mL}} = 20 \text{ mL/hr}$$

PRACTICE QUESTIONS: ALTERNATE ITEM FORMAT (FILL IN THE BLANK)

1. The physician's order reads vancomycin (Vancocin) 500 mg in 250 mL of 5% dextrose in water and administer over 2 hours. The drop factor is 10 drops/mL. A nurse sets the flow rate at how many drops per minute? (Round answer to the nearest whole number.)

   Answer: _____ drops per minute

2. A physician orders 1000 mL of normal saline (NS) to infuse over 12 hours. The drop factor is 15 drops/1 mL. A nurse prepares to set the flow rate at how many drops per minute? (Round answer to the nearest whole number.)

   Answer: _____ drops per minute

3. A physician orders an intravenous (IV) dose of 400,000 units of penicillin G benzathine (Bicillin). The label on the 10-mL ampule sent from the pharmacy reads penicillin G benzathine (Bicillin), 300,000 units/mL. A nurse prepares how much medication to administer the correct dose? (Round answer to the nearest tenth.)

   Answer: _____ mL

4. A physician's order reads potassium chloride 30 mEq to be added to 1000 mL normal saline (NS) and to be administered over a 10-hour period. The label on the medication bottle reads 40 mEq/20 mL. A nurse prepares how many milliliters of potassium chloride to administer the correct dose of medication?

   Answer: _____ mL

5. A physician orders 3000 mL of 5% dextrose in water (D$_5$W) to infuse over a 24-hour period. The drop factor is 10 drops/1 mL. A nurse sets the flow rate at how many drops per minute? (Round answer to the nearest whole number.)

   Answer: _____ drops per minute

6. A physician's order reads clindamycin phosphate (Cleocin Phosphate) 0.3 g in 50 mL normal saline (NS) to be administered intravenously over 30 minutes. The medication label reads clindamycin phosphate (Cleocin Phosphate) 900 mg in 6 mL. A nurse prepares how many milliliters of the medication to administer the correct dose?

   Answer: _____ mL

7. A physician's order reads phenytoin (Dilantin) 0.2 g orally twice daily. The medication label states 100-mg capsules. A nurse prepares how many capsule(s) to administer one dose?

   Answer: _____ capsule(s)

8. A physician orders 1000 mL of ½ normal saline (NS) to infuse over 8 hours. The drop factor is 15 drops/1 mL. The nurse sets the flow rate at how many drops per minute? (Round answer to the nearest whole number.)

   Answer: _____ drops per minute

9. A physician orders 2000 mL of 5% dextrose and ½ normal saline (NS) to infuse over 24 hours. The drop factor is 15 drops/1 mL. A nurse sets the flow rate at how many drops per minute? (Round answer to the nearest whole number.)

   Answer: _____ drops per minute

10. A physician orders heparin sodium, 1300 units/hr by continuous intravenous (IV) infusion. The pharmacy prepares the medication and delivers an IV bag labeled heparin sodium 20,000 units/250 mL D_5W. An infusion pump must be used to administer the medication. The nurse sets the infusion pump at how many milliliters per hour to deliver 1300 units/hr? (Round answer to the nearest whole number.)

    Answer: _____ mL per hour

11. A physician's order reads cyanocobalamin (vitamin B_{12}) 1000 mcg by the intramuscular route. The medication label reads cyanocobalamin (vitamin B_{12}) 0.5 mg/mL. A nurse prepares the medication and administers how many milliliters to the client?

    Answer: _____ mL

12. A physician orders 3000 mL of D_5W to be administered over a 24-hour period. A nurse determines that how many milliliters per hour will be administered to the client?

    Answer: _____ mL per hour

13. Gentamicin sulfate, 80 mg in 100 mL normal saline (NS), is to be administered over 30 minutes. The drop factor is 10 drops/mL. A nurse sets the flow rate at how many drops per minute? (Round answer to the nearest whole number.)

    Answer: _____ drops per minute

14. A physician's order reads levothyroxine (Synthroid), 150 mcg orally daily. The medication label reads Synthroid, 0.1 mg/tablet. A nurse administers how many tablet(s) to the client?

    Answer: _____ tablet(s)

15. Cefuroxime sodium, 1 g in 50 mL normal saline (NS), is to be administered over 30 minutes. The drop factor is 15 drops/mL. A nurse sets the flow rate at how many drops per minute?

    Answer: _____ drops per minute

16. A physician orders 1000 mL D_5W to infuse at a rate of 125 mL/hr. A nurse determines that it will take how many hours for 1 L to infuse?

    Answer: _____ hour(s)

17. A physician orders 500 mL of normal saline (NS) to infuse over 5 hours. The drop factor is 10 drops/1 mL. A nurse sets the flow rate at how many drops per minute? (Round answer to the nearest whole number.)

    Answer: _____ drops per minute

18. A physician orders 1 unit of packed red blood cells to infuse over 4 hours. The unit of blood contains 250 mL. The drop factor is 10 drops/1 mL. A nurse prepares to set the flow rate at how many drops per minute? (Round answer to the nearest whole number.)

    Answer: _____ drops per minute

19. A physician's order reads morphine sulfate, 8 mg stat. The medication ampule reads morphine sulfate, 10 mg/mL. A nurse prepares how many milliliters to administer the correct dose?

    Answer: _____ mL

20. A physician orders regular insulin, 8 units/hr by continuous intravenous (IV) infusion. The pharmacy prepares the medication and then delivers an IV bag labeled 100 units of regular insulin in 100 mL normal saline (NS). An infusion pump must be used to administer the medication. The nurse sets the infusion pump at how many milliliters per hour to deliver 8 units/hr?

    Answer: _____ mL

21. The physician orders ketorolac 15 mg intravenous push (IVP). The medication vial states 30 mg/ 1 mL. How many milliliters will the nurse administer?

    Answer: _____ mL

ANSWERS: ALTERNATE ITEM FORMAT (FILL IN THE BLANK)

1. **21**

Rationale: Use the intravenous (IV) flow rate formula.

Formula:

$$\frac{\text{Total volume} \times \text{drop factor}}{\text{Time in minutes}} = \text{drops per minute}$$

$$\frac{250 \text{ mL} \times 10 \text{ gtt}}{120 \text{ minutes}} = \frac{2500}{120} = 20.8 \text{ or } 21 \text{ drops per minute}$$

Test-Taking Strategy: Use the formula for calculating IV flow rates when answering the question. Once you have performed the calculation, verify your answer using a calculator and make sure that the answer makes sense. Remember to round the answer to the nearest whole number. Review IV infusion rates if you had difficulty with this question.

Level of Cognitive Ability: Application
Client Needs: Physiological Integrity
Integrated Process: Nursing Process—implementation
Content Area: Fundamental skills
Reference: Potter, P., & Perry, A. (2005). *Fundamentals of nursing* (6th ed., pp.1175-1176). St. Louis: Mosby.

2. **21**

Rationale: Use the intravenous (IV) flow rate formula.

Formula:

$$\frac{\text{Total volume} \times \text{drop factor}}{\text{Time in minutes}} = \text{drops per minute}$$

$$\frac{1000 \text{ mL} \times 15 \text{ gtt}}{720 \text{ minutes}} = \frac{15,000}{720} = 20.8, \text{ or } 21 \text{ drops per minute}$$

Test-Taking Strategy: Use the formula for calculating IV flow rates when answering the question. Once you have performed the calculation, verify your answer using a calculator and make sure that the answer makes sense. Remember to round the answer to the nearest whole number. Review IV infusion rates if you had difficulty with this question.

Level of Cognitive Ability: Application
Client Needs: Physiological Integrity
Integrated Process: Nursing Process—planning
Content Area: Fundamental skills
Reference: Potter, P., & Perry, A. (2005). *Fundamentals of nursing* (6th ed., p. 835). St. Louis: Mosby.

3. **1.3**

Rationale: Use the medication dose formula.

Formula:

$$\frac{\text{Desired} \times \text{mL}}{\text{Available}} = \text{milliliters per dose}$$

$$\frac{400,000 \text{ units} \times 1 \text{ mL}}{300,000 \text{ units}} = \text{milliliters per dose}$$

$$\frac{400,000}{300,000} = 1.33 = 1.3 \text{ mL}$$

Test-Taking Strategy: Follow the formula for the calculation of the correct medication dose. Once you have performed the calculation, verify your answer using a calculator and make sure that the answer makes sense. Remember to round the answer to the nearest tenth. If you had difficulty with this question, review medication calculation problems.

Level of Cognitive Ability: Application
Client Needs: Physiological Integrity

Integrated Process: Nursing Process—implementation
Content Area: Fundamental skills
Reference: Kee, J. & Marshall, S. (2004). *Clinical calculations: With applications to general and specialty areas* (5th ed., p. 156). Philadelphia: W.B. Saunders.

4. **15**

Rationale: Use the medication calculation formula.

Formula:

$$\frac{\text{Desired} \times \text{mL}}{\text{Available}} = \text{milliliters per dose}$$

$$\frac{30 \text{ mEq} \times 20 \text{ mL}}{40 \text{ mEq}} = 15 \text{ mL}$$

Test-Taking Strategy: Follow the formula for the calculation of the correct medication dose. Once you have performed the calculation, verify your answer using a calculator and make sure that the answer makes sense. If you had difficulty with this question, review medication calculation problems.

Level of Cognitive Ability: Application
Client Needs: Physiological Integrity
Integrated Process: Nursing Process—implementation
Content Area: Fundamental skills
Reference: Harkreader, H., & Hogan, M.A. (2004). *Fundamentals of nursing: Caring and clinical judgment* (2nd ed., p. 408). Philadelphia: W.B. Saunders.

5. **21**

Rationale: Use the IV flow rate formula.

Formula:

$$\frac{\text{Total volume} \times \text{drop factor}}{\text{Time in minutes}} = \text{drops per minute}$$

$$\frac{3000 \text{ mL} \times 10 \text{ gtt}}{1440 \text{ minutes}} = \frac{30,000}{1440} = 20.8, \text{ or } 21 \text{ drops per minute}$$

Test-Taking Strategy: Use the formula for calculating IV flow rates when answering the question. Once you have performed the calculation, verify your answer using a calculator and make sure that the answer makes sense. Remember to round the answer to the nearest whole number. Review IV infusion rates if you had difficulty with this question.

Level of Cognitive Ability: Application
Client Needs: Physiological Integrity
Integrated Process: Nursing Process—implementation
Content Area: Fundamental skills
Reference: Harkreader, H., & Hogan, M.A. (2004). *Fundamentals of nursing: Caring and clinical judgment* (2nd ed., p. 598). Philadelphia: W.B. Saunders.

6. **2**

Rationale: You must convert 0.3 g to milligrams. In the metric system, to convert larger to smaller, multiply by 1000 or move the decimal three places to the right. Therefore, 0.3 g = 300 mg. Following conversion from grams to milligrams, use the formula to calculate the correct dose.

Formula:

$$\frac{\text{Desired} \times \text{mL}}{\text{Available}} = \text{milliliters per dose}$$

$$\frac{300 \text{ mg} \times 6 \text{ mL}}{900 \text{ mg}} = \frac{1800}{900} = 2 \text{ mL}$$

Test-Taking Strategy: In this medication calculation problem, first you must convert grams to milligrams. Once you have

performed the calculation, verify your answer using a calculator and make sure that the answer makes sense. If you had difficulty with this question, review medication calculation problems.
Level of Cognitive Ability: Application
Client Needs: Physiological Integrity
Integrated Process: Nursing Process—implementation
Content Area: Fundamental skills
Reference: Potter, P., & Perry, A. (2005). *Fundamentals of nursing* (6th ed., p. 835). St. Louis: Mosby.

7. 2
Rationale: You must convert 0.2 g to milligrams. In the metric system, to convert larger to smaller, multiply by 1000 or move the decimal three places to the right. Therefore, 0.2 g equals 200 mg. After conversion from grams to milligrams, use the formula to calculate the correct dose.
Formula:

$$\frac{\text{Desired} \times \text{capsule(s)}}{\text{Available}} = \text{capsule(s) per dose}$$

$$\frac{200 \text{ mg} \times 1 \text{ capsule}}{100 \text{ mg}} = 2 \text{ capsules}$$

Test-Taking Strategy: In this medication calculation problem, first you must convert grams to milligrams. Once you have done the conversion and reread the medication calculation problem, you will know that two capsules is the correct answer. Recheck your work using a calculator and make sure that the answer makes sense. If you had difficulty with this question, review medication calculation problems.
Level of Cognitive Ability: Application
Client Needs: Physiological Integrity
Integrated Process: Nursing Process—implementation
Content Area: Fundamental skills
Reference: Potter, P., & Perry, A. (2005). *Fundamentals of nursing* (6th ed., p. 835). St. Louis: Mosby.

8. 31
Rationale: Use the intravenous (IV) flow rate formula.
Formula:

$$\frac{\text{Total volume} \times \text{drop factor}}{\text{Time in minutes}} = \text{drops per minute}$$

$$\frac{1000 \text{ mL} \times 15 \text{ gtt}}{480 \text{ minutes}} = \frac{15,000}{480} = 31.2, \text{ or } 31 \text{ drops per minute}$$

Test-Taking Strategy: Use the formula for calculating IV flow rates when answering the question. Once you have performed the calculation, verify your answer using a calculator and make sure that the answer makes sense. Remember to round the answer to the nearest whole number. Review IV infusion rates if you had difficulty with this question.
Level of Cognitive Ability: Application
Client Needs: Physiological Integrity
Integrated Process: Nursing Process—implementation
Content Area: Fundamental skills
Reference: Kee, J., & Marshall, S. (2004). *Clinical calculations: With applications to general and specialty areas* (5th ed., p. 202). Philadelphia: W.B. Saunders.

9. 21
Rationale: Use the intravenous (IV) flow rate formula.
Formula:

$$\frac{\text{Total volume} \times \text{drop factor}}{\text{Time in minutes}} = \text{drops per minute}$$

$$\frac{2000 \text{ mL} \times 15 \text{ gtt}}{1440 \text{ minutes}} = \frac{30,000}{1440} = 20.8, \text{ or } 21 \text{ drops per minute}$$

Test-Taking Strategy: Use the formula for calculating IV flow rates when answering the question. Once you have performed the calculation, verify your answer using a calculator and make sure that the answer makes sense. Remember to round the answer to the nearest whole number. Review IV infusion rates if you had difficulty with this question.
Level of Cognitive Ability: Application
Client Needs: Physiological Integrity
Integrated Process: Nursing Process—implementation
Content Area: Fundamental skills
Reference: Harkreader, H., & Hogan, M.A. (2004). *Fundamentals of nursing: Caring and clinical judgment* (2nd ed., p. 598). Philadelphia: W.B. Saunders.

10. 16
Rationale: Calculation of this problem requires a two-step process. First, you need to determine the amount of heparin sodium in 1 mL. The next step is to determine the infusion rate, or milliliters per hour.
Step 1:

$$\frac{\text{Known amount of medication in solution}}{\text{Total volume of diluent}} =$$

amount of medication per milliliter

$$\frac{20,000 \text{ units}}{250 \text{ mL}} = 80 \text{ units/mL}$$

Step 2:

$$\frac{\text{Dose per hour desired}}{\text{Concentration per milliliter}} =$$

infusion rate, or milliliters per hour

$$\frac{1300 \text{ units}}{80 \text{ units/mL}} = 16.25, \text{ or } 16 \text{ mL/hr}$$

Test-Taking Strategy: Read the question carefully, noting that two steps are required to solve this medication problem. Follow the formula, verify your answer using a calculator, and make sure that the answer makes sense. Remember to round the answer to the nearest whole number. If you had difficulty with this question, learn these steps now. These steps can be used for similar medication problems related to the administration of heparin sodium or regular insulin by IV infusion.
Level of Cognitive Ability: Application
Client Needs: Physiological Integrity
Integrated Process: Nursing Process—implementation
Content Area: Fundamental skills
Reference: Kee, J., & Marshall, S. (2004). *Clinical calculations: With applications to general and specialty areas* (4th ed., p. 204). Philadelphia: W.B. Saunders.

11. **2**

Rationale: You must convert 1000 mcg to milligrams (mg). In the metric system, to convert smaller to larger, divide by 1000 or move the decimal three places to the left. Therefore, 1000 mcg equals 1 mg. Next, use the formula to calculate the correct dose.

Formula:

$$\frac{Desired \times mL}{Available} = milliliters\ per\ dose$$

$$\frac{1\ mg \times 1\ mL}{0.5\ mg} = \frac{1}{0.5} = 2\ mL$$

Test-Taking Strategy: In this medication calculation problem, first you must convert micrograms to milligrams. Once you have performed the calculation, verify your answer using a calculator and make sure that the answer makes sense. If you had difficulty with this question, review medication calculation problems.
Level of Cognitive Ability: Application
Client Needs: Physiological Integrity
Integrated Process: Nursing Process—implementation
Content Area: Fundamental skills
Reference: Potter, P., & Perry, A. (2005). *Fundamentals of nursing* (6th ed., p. 835). St. Louis: Mosby.

12. **125**

Rationale: Use the intravenous (IV) formula to determine milliliters per hour.

Formula:

$$\frac{Total\ volume\ in\ milliliters}{Number\ of\ hours} = milliliters\ per\ hour$$

$$\frac{3000\ mL}{24\ hours} = 125\ mL/hr$$

Test-Taking Strategy: Read the question carefully, noting that the question is asking about milliliters per hour to be administered to the client. Use the formula for calculating milliliters per hour. Once you have performed the calculation, verify your answer using a calculator and make sure that the answer makes sense. Review the IV formula for calculating milliliters per hour if you had difficulty with this question.
Level of Cognitive Ability: Comprehension
Client Needs: Physiological Integrity
Integrated Process: Nursing Process—planning
Content Area: Fundamental skills
Reference: Harkreader, H., & Hogan, M.A. (2004). *Fundamentals of nursing: Caring and clinical judgment* (2nd ed., p. 598). Philadelphia: W.B. Saunders.

13. **33**

Rationale: Use the intravenous (IV) flow rate formula.

Formula:

$$\frac{Total\ volume \times drop\ factor}{Time\ in\ minutes} = drops\ per\ minute$$

$$\frac{100\ mL \times 10\ gtt}{30\ minutes} = \frac{1000}{30} = 33.3,\ or\ 33\ drops\ per\ minute$$

Test-Taking Strategy: Use the formula for calculating IV flow rates when answering the question. Once you have performed the calculation, verify your answer using a calculator and make sure that the answer makes sense. Remember to round the answer to the nearest whole number. Review IV infusion rates if you had difficulty with this question.

Level of Cognitive Ability: Application
Client Needs: Physiological Integrity
Integrated Process: Nursing Process—implementation
Content Area: Fundamental skills
Reference: Kee, J., & Marshall, S. (2004). *Clinical calculations: With applications to general and specialty areas* (5th ed., p. 202). Philadelphia: W.B. Saunders.

14. **1.5**

Rationale: You must convert 150 mcg to milligrams. In the metric system, to convert smaller to larger, divide by 1000 or move the decimal three places to the left. Therefore, 150 mcg equals 0.15 mg. Next, use the formula to calculate the correct dose.

Formula:

$$\frac{Desired}{Available} \times tablet = tablets\ per\ dose$$

$$\frac{0.15\ mg}{0.1\ mg} \times 1\ tablet = 1.5\ tablets$$

Test-Taking Strategy: In this medication calculation problem, first you must convert micrograms to milligrams. Next, follow the formula for the calculation of the correct dose, verify your answer using a calculator, and make sure that the answer makes sense. If you had difficulty with this question, review medication calculation problems.
Level of Cognitive Ability: Application
Client Needs: Physiological Integrity
Integrated Process: Nursing Process—implementation
Content Area: Fundamental skills
Reference: Potter, P., & Perry, A. (2005). *Fundamentals of nursing* (6th ed., p. 835). St. Louis: Mosby.

15. **25**

Rationale: Use the intravenous (IV) flow rate formula.

Formula:

$$\frac{Total\ volume \times drop\ factor}{Time\ in\ minutes} = drops\ per\ minute$$

$$\frac{50\ mL \times 15\ gtt}{30\ minutes} = \frac{750}{30} = 25\ drops\ per\ minute$$

Test-Taking Strategy: Use the formula for calculating IV flow rates when answering the question. Once you have performed the calculation, verify your answer using a calculator and make sure that the answer makes sense. Review IV infusion rates if you had difficulty with this question.
Level of Cognitive Ability: Application
Client Needs: Physiological Integrity
Integrated Process: Nursing Process—implementation
Content Area: Fundamental skills
Reference: Harkreader, H., & Hogan, M.A. (2004). *Fundamentals of nursing: Caring and clinical judgment* (2nd ed., p. 598). Philadelphia: W.B. Saunders.

16. **8**

Rationale: You must determine that 1 L equals 1000 mL. Next, use the formula for determining infusion time in hours.

Formula:

$$\frac{Total\ volume\ to\ infuse}{Milliliters\ per\ hour\ being\ infused} = infusion\ time$$

$$\frac{1000\ mL}{125\ mL} = 8\ hours$$

Test-Taking Strategy: Read the question carefully, noting that the question is asking about infusion time in hours. First, convert 1 L to milliliters. Next, use the formula for determining infusion time in hours. Verify your answer using a calculator and make sure that the answer makes sense. Review the IV formula for calculating infusion time if you had difficulty with this question.
Level of Cognitive Ability: Comprehension
Client Needs: Physiological Integrity
Integrated Process: Nursing Process—planning
Content Area: Fundamental skills
Reference: Kee, J., & Marshall, S. (2004). *Clinical calculations: With applications to general and specialty areas* (5th ed., p. 202). Philadelphia: W.B. Saunders.

17. 17
Rationale: Use the intravenous (IV) flow rate formula.
Formula:

$$\frac{Total\ volume \times drop\ factor}{Time\ in\ minutes} = drops\ per\ minute$$

$$\frac{500\ mL \times 10\ gtt}{300\ minutes} = \frac{5000}{300} = 16.6,\ or\ 17\ drops\ per\ minute$$

Test-Taking Strategy: Use the formula for calculating IV flow rates when answering the question. Once you have performed the calculation, verify your answer using a calculator and make sure that the answer makes sense. Remember to round the answer to the nearest whole number. Review IV infusion rates if you had difficulty with this question.
Level of Cognitive Ability: Application
Client Needs: Physiological Integrity
Integrated Process: Nursing Process—implementation
Content Area: Fundamental skills
References: Harkreader, H., & Hogan, M.A. (2004). *Fundamentals of nursing: Caring and clinical judgment* (2nd ed., p. 598). Philadelphia: W.B. Saunders.

18. 10
Rationale: Use the IV flow rate formula.
Formula:

$$\frac{Total\ volume \times drop\ factor}{Time\ in\ minutes} = drops\ per\ minute$$

$$\frac{250\ mL \times 10\ gtt}{240\ minutes} = \frac{2500}{240} = 10.4,\ or\ 10\ drops\ per\ minute$$

Test-Taking Strategy: Use the formula for calculating IV flow rates when answering the question. Once you have performed the calculation, verify your answer using a calculator and make sure that the answer makes sense. Remember to round the answer to the nearest whole number. Review IV infusion rates if you had difficulty with this question.
Level of Cognitive Ability: Application
Client Needs: Physiological Integrity
Integrated Process: Nursing Process—planning
Content Area: Fundamental skills
Reference: Kee, J., & Marshall, S. (2004). *Clinical calculations: With applications to general and specialty areas* (5th ed., p. 202). Philadelphia: W.B. Saunders.

19. 0.8
Rationale: Use the formula to calculate the correct dose.
Formula:

$$\frac{Desired \times mL}{Available} = milliliters\ per\ dose$$

$$\frac{8\ mg \times 1\ mL}{10\ mg} = 0.8\ mL$$

Test-Taking Strategy: Follow the formula for the calculation of the correct dose. Once you have performed the calculation, verify your answer using a calculator and make sure that the answer makes sense. If you had difficulty with this question, review medication calculation problems.
Level of Cognitive Ability: Application
Client Needs: Physiological Integrity
Integrated Process: Nursing Process—planning
Content Area: Fundamental skills
Reference: Potter, P., & Perry, A. (2005). *Fundamentals of nursing* (6th ed., p. 835). St. Louis: Mosby.

20. 8
Rationale: Calculation of this problem requires a two-step process. First, you need to determine the amount of regular insulin in 1 mL. The next step is to determine the infusion rate, or milliliters per hour.
Formula:
Step 1:

$$\frac{Known\ amount\ of\ medication\ in\ solution}{Total\ volume\ of\ diluent} = amount\ of\ medication\ per\ milliliter$$

$$\frac{100\ units}{100\ mL} = 1\ unit/mL$$

Step 2:

$$\frac{Dose\ per\ hour\ desired}{Concentration\ per\ milliliter} = infusion\ rate,\ or\ milliliters\ per\ hour$$

$$\frac{8\ units}{1\ unit/mL} = 8\ mL/hr$$

Test-Taking Strategy: Read the question carefully, noting that two steps are required to solve this medication problem. Once you have performed the calculation, verify your answer using a calculator and make sure that the answer makes sense. These steps can be used for similar medication problems related to the administration of heparin sodium or regular insulin by IV infusion. Learn these steps if you had difficulty with this question.
Level of Cognitive Ability: Application
Client Need: Physiological Integrity
Integrated Process: Nursing Process—implementation
Content Area: Fundamental skills
Reference: Kee, J., & Marshall, S. (2004). *Clinical calculations: With applications to general and specialty areas* (4th ed., p. 204). Philadelphia: W.B. Saunders.

21. **0.5**
Rationale: Use the medication calculation formula.
Formula:

$$\frac{\text{Desired} \times \text{mL}}{\text{Available}} = \text{milliliters per dose}$$

$$\frac{15 \text{ mg} \times 1 \text{ mL}}{30 \text{ mg}} = 0.5 \text{ mL}$$

Test-Taking Strategy: Follow the formula for the calculation of the correct dose. Once you have performed the calculation, verify your answer using a calculator and make sure that the answer makes sense. If you had difficulty with this question, review medication calculation problems.
Level of Cognitive Ability: Application
Client Needs: Physiological Integrity
Integrated Process: Nursing Process—implementation
Content Area: Fundamental skills
Reference: Potter, P., & Perry, A. (2005). *Fundamentals of nursing* (6th ed., pp. 835-836). St. Louis: Mosby.

REFERENCES

Elkin, M., Perry, A., & Potter, P. (2004). *Nursing interventions and clinical skills* (3rd ed). St. Louis: Mosby.

Harkreader, H., & Hogan, M.A. (2004). *Fundamentals of nursing: Caring and clinical judgment* (2nd ed.). Philadelphia: W.B. Saunders.

Kee, J., & Marshall, S. (2004). *Clinical calculations: With applications to general and specialty areas* (5th ed.). Philadelphia: W.B. Saunders.

Lehne, R. (2007). *Pharmacology for nursing care* (6th ed.). Philadelphia: W.B. Saunders.

National Council of State Boards of Nursing (Eds.). (2007). *2007 NCLEX-RN® detailed test plan.* Chicago: Author.

Potter, P., & Perry, A. (2005). *Fundamentals of nursing* (6th ed.). St. Louis: Mosby.

Basic Life Support

PYRAMID TERMS

automated external defibrillator (AED) Machine that converts ventricular fibrillation into a perfusing rhythm and allows for early defibrillation by first responders.

basic life support (BLS) Provision of oxygen to the brain, heart, and other vital organs until help arrives.

cardiopulmonary resuscitation (CPR) An interchangeable term for basic life support.

head tilt–chin lift Preferred method to open a victim's airway.

Heimlich maneuver Method to relieve a foreign body airway obstruction.

jaw thrust maneuver Method used to open a victim's airway if a neck injury is suspected.

▲ THE PYRAMID TO SUCCESS

The Pyramid to Success focuses on the emergency measures related to performing basic life support measures. Focus on the points related to the breaths and compression ratio with one-person and two-person adult cardiopulmonary resuscitation (CPR) and CPR in the infant and the child. Pyramid Points focus on airway management in CPR and on performing the Heimlich maneuver to relieve a foreign body airway obstruction. Focus on the correct hand placements for cardiac compressions and on the differences between the adult, the child, and the infant. For the health care provider, before initiating CPR, the initial action is to determine unresponsiveness. Remember the ABCDs—airway, breathing, circulation, and defibrillation or definitive treatment—when performing CPR. The Integrated Processes addressed in this chapter include Caring, Communication and Documentation, Nursing Process, and Teaching/Learning.

CLIENT NEEDS ▲

Safe and Effective Care Environment

Acting as an advocate regarding the client's wishes
Considering ethical and legal responsibilities
Establishing priorities
Following advance directives regarding the client's documented requests
Implementing standard, transmission-based, and other precautions
Upholding client's rights

Health Promotion and Maintenance

Performing the techniques of physical assessment
Providing health promotion programs
Teaching significant others to perform CPR and the Heimlich maneuver

Psychosocial Integrity

Considering the client's cultural, religious, and spiritual preferences
Discussing end-of-life and grief and loss issues
Providing emotional support to significant others

Physiological Integrity

Administering emergency medications and intravenous solutions
Documenting the client's response to basic life support measures
Handling medical emergencies
Identifying alterations in the cardiopulmonary system
Performing CPR or the Heimlich maneuver
Using special equipment

I. BASIC LIFE SUPPORT (BLS) (Box 18-1)
  A. **Basic life support** is providing oxygen to the brain, heart, and other vital organs until help arrives.
  B. **Basic life support** also is known as **cardiopulmonary resuscitation (CPR).**

II. ADULT CPR GUIDELINES FOR THE HEALTH CARE PROVIDER (HCP) (Box 18-2) (Table 18-1)
  A. Description: An adult is defined as a person who is an adolescent or older (for lay rescuers, adults are defined as those 8 years of age or older).
  B. Airway
    1. Remember, for the health care provider (HCP), assessment is the first step of the nursing process; assessing a victim of sudden illness or accident for unconsciousness is the initial action (assess for 5 to 10 seconds)
    2. Gently shake the victim's shoulders and ask "Are you OK?"; be alert to the potential for a head or neck injury.
    3. Call the emergency response number when the victim is found unconscious; if asphyxial arrest is likely, call after five cycles (2 minutes) of **CPR.**
    4. Place the victim in a supine position on a firm, flat surface (logroll the victim, using spine precautions).
      a. One-person rescue: The rescuer is positioned on his or her knees, perpendicular to the victim's sternum and facing the victim.
      b. Two-person rescue: One rescuer faces the victim, kneeling perpendicular to the victim's head, maintains an open airway, monitors the carotid pulse, and performs the rescue breathing; the second rescuer moves to the opposite side and faces the victim, kneeling perpendicular to the victim's sternum, and performs the chest compressions.
      c. When two rescuers are present during **CPR,** the rescuers should rotate the compressor role every 2 minutes.
      d. The rescuers apply gloves and face shields, if available.
    5. Open the airway.
    6. The **head tilt–chin lift** is the preferred method for opening the airway; if the victim has a neck injury, the **jaw thrust maneuver** is used to open the airway (Figs. 18-1 and 18-2).
    7. Look for any foreign material, liquids, or solids in the victim's mouth; wipe out any foreign material with a hooked index or middle finger.
  C. Breathing
    1. Assess breathing and maintain an open airway.
    2. The rescuer places his or her ear over the victim's nose and mouth and looks for the chest to rise and fall, listens for air moving in and out of the lungs, and feels for the flow of air (Fig. 18-3).
    3. For the breathing victim, do the following:
      a. Place the victim on his or her side if no cervical trauma is suspected; logroll the victim onto the side as a unit (without twisting) to help maintain an open airway and decrease the risk of aspiration.
      b. If trauma or injury is suspected, do not move the victim.
    4. For the nonbreathing victim, do the following:
      a. Maintain the **head tilt–chin lift;** pinch the nostrils closed, and give two, effective breaths at 1 second per breath (Fig. 18-4).
      b. Allow the chest to recoil (return to normal position) completely after each compression, and use approximately equal compression and relaxation times.
      c. Avoid delivering breaths that are too large or too forceful.
      d. Attempt to use a resuscitation bag or face shield, if available, ensuring an adequate air seal; allow the victim to exhale fully between breaths.
      e. If unsuccessful at giving the breath, reposition the victim's head and try again (improper chin and head position is the most common cause of difficulty in ventilating the victim).
      f. If still unsuccessful, check the victim's mouth for a foreign body or for loose dentures (re-

---

BOX 18-1

The ABCDs of Basic Life Support for the Health Care Provider

A: Airway
B: Breathing
C: Circulation
D: Defibrillation or definitive treatment
Each step of the ABCDs of basic life support begins with assessment.

BOX 18-2

Pyramid Points: When to Stop CPR

Avoid interruptions in cardiopulmonary resuscitation (CPR).

STOP CPR ONLY IF THE FOLLOWING OCCUR(S):
Pulse and respiration return.
Emergency medical help arrives.
Administration of the automated external defibrillator.
A physician declares the victim deceased.
Additional Pyramid Point: In a non–health care setting, another indication to stop CPR would be that the rescuer was exhausted and physically unable to continue performing CPR.

TABLE 18-1

Summary of Basic Life Support ABCD Maneuvers for Infants, Children, and Adults

Maneuver*	Adult†	Child‡	Infant§
Activate (call) emergency response number (one rescuer).	Call when victim is found unresponsive. HCP: If asphyxial arrest is likely, call after five cycles (2 min) of cardiopulmonary resuscitation (CPR).	Call after performing five cycles of CPR. For sudden unwitnessed collapse, call after verifying that victim is unresponsive.	Call after performing five cycles of CPR. For sudden unwitnessed collapse, call after verifying that victim is unresponsive.
AIRWAY BREATHS	Head tilt–chin lift (HCP: If trauma is suspected, use jaw thrust.) Two effective breaths at 1 sec per breath	Head tilt–chin lift (HCP: If trauma is suspected, use jaw thrust.) Two effective breaths at 1 sec per breath	Head tilt–chin lift (HCP: If trauma is suspected, use jaw thrust.) Two effective breaths at 1 sec per breath
HCP: Rescue breathing without chest compressions	10-12 breaths/min (one breath every 5-6 sec)	12-20 breaths/min (one breath every 3-5 sec)	12-20 breaths/min (one breath every 3-5 sec)
HCP: Rescue breathing for CPR with advanced airway	8-10 breaths/min (one breath every 6-8 sec)	8-10 breaths/min (one breath every 6-8 sec)	8-10 breaths/min (one breath every 6-8 sec)
Foreign body airway obstruction	Abdominal thrusts	Back slaps and chest thrusts	Back slaps and chest thrusts
CIRCULATION			
HCP: Pulse check (10 sec or less)	Carotid artery	HCP can use femoral artery in child	Brachial or femoral artery
Compression landmarks	Center of chest, between nipples	Center of chest, between nipples	Just below nipple line
Compression method: Push hard and fast. Allow complete recoil.	Two hands: Heel of one hand, other hand on top	Two hands: Heel of one hand with second on top *or* One hand: Heel of one hand only	One rescuer: two fingers HCP, two rescuers: Two-thumb–encircling hands technique
Compression depth	1½-2 inches	Approximately ⅓ to ½ the depth of the chest	Approximately ⅓ to ½ the depth of the chest
Compression rate	Approximately 100 per minute	Approximately 100 per minute	Approximately 100 per minute
Compression-to-ventilation ratio	30:2 (one or two rescuers)	30:2 (single rescuer) HCP: 15:2 (two rescuers)	30:2 (single rescuer) HCP: 15:2 (two rescuers)
DEFIBRILLATION			
Automatic external defibrillator (AED)	Use adult pads. Do not use child pads or a child system. HCP: For out-of-hospital response, you may provide five cycles (2 min) of CPR before shock if response time is longer than 4-5 min and arrest was not witnessed.	HCP: Use AED as soon as possible for sudden and in-hospital collapse. All: After five cycles of CPR (out of hospital). Use child pads and system for child 1-8 yr old if available. If child pads and system are not available, use adult AED and pads.	No recommendation for infants younger than 1 yr old

*Maneuver performed only by health care provider indicated by HCP.
†For lay rescuers, adults are defined as those 8 years of age or older; for HCPs, adolescent or older.
‡For lay rescuers, children are those 1-8 years of age; for HCPs, 1 year to adolescent.
§For all rescuers, infants are defined as those younger than 1 year of age.
With permission from American Heart Association. (2005-2006). Highlights of the 2005 American Heart Association guidelines for cardiopulmonary resuscitation and emergency cardiovascular care. *Currents in Emergency Cardiovascular Care,* 16(4), 15.

move dentures only if they interfere with the mouth seal), clear the airway, and try to ventilate again.

g. Be alert to gastric distention when giving ventilations.

5. Mouth to nose: This method is recommended when ventilating through the victim's mouth is impossible, the mouth cannot be opened, the mouth is seriously injured, or a tight mouth-to-mouth seal is difficult to achieve.

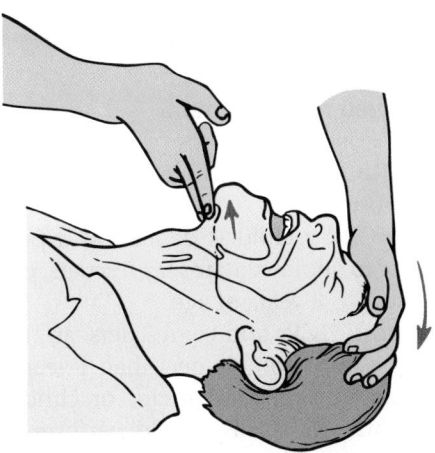

FIG. 18-1   Opening the airway using the head tilt–chin lift maneuver. (From Lewis, S.M., Heitkemper, M.M., & Dirksen, S.R. [2004]. *Medical-surgical nursing: Assessment and management of clinical problems* [6th ed.]. St. Louis: Mosby.)

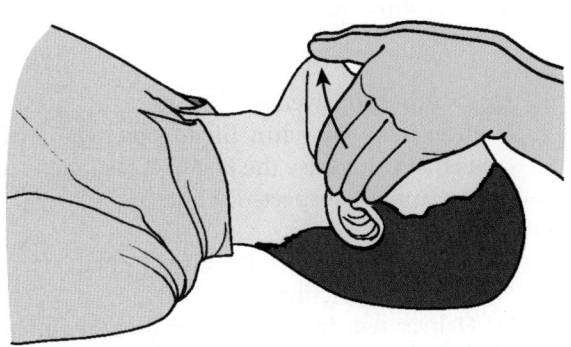

FIG. 18-2   Opening the airway using the jaw thrust maneuver. (From Harkreader, H., & Hogan, M.A. [2004]. *Fundamentals of nursing: Caring and clinical judgment* [2nd ed.]. Philadelphia: W.B. Saunders. Used with permission of the American Heart Association. [1992]. Guidelines for cardiopulmonary resuscitation and emergency cardiac care: An international consensus on science and circulation, *Circulation*, 102(Suppl), 217-222.]

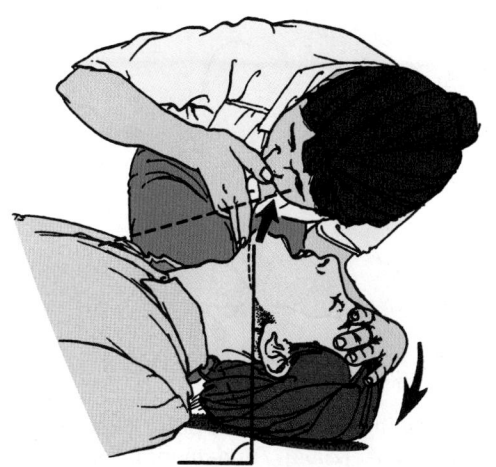

FIG. 18-3   Listening and feeling for exhalation. (From Harkreader, H., & Hogan, M.A. [2004]. *Fundamentals of nursing: Caring and clinical judgment.* (2nd ed.). Philadelphia: W.B. Saunders. From Emergency Cardiac Care Committee and Subcommittees, American Heart Association. [1992]. Guidelines for cardiopulmonary resuscitation and emergency cardiac care. Part VIII: Ethical consideration in resuscitation. *Journal of the American Medical Association,* 268[16], 2282-2288.)

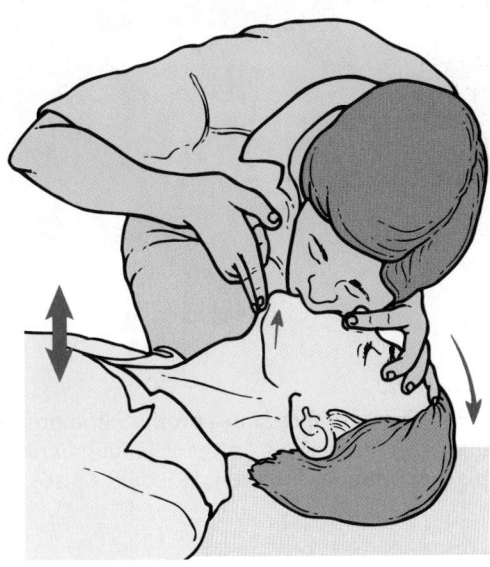

FIG. 18-4   The chin is lifted and brought forward; the nostrils are then closed and two effective breaths are given at 1 second per breath. (From Lewis, S.M., Heitkemper, M.M., & Dirksen, S.R. [2004]. *Medical-surgical nursing: Assessment and management of clinical problems* [6th ed.]. St. Louis: Mosby.)

6. Mouth to stoma (advanced airway)
   a. This method is used for the victim who has had a laryngectomy or has an advanced airway such as tracheostomy; to be effective, an adequate seal over the victim's mouth and nose is necessary.
   b. With an advanced airway (endotracheal tube, laryngeal airway, tracheostomy, esophagotracheal Combitube), 8 to 10 breaths per minute (one breath every 6 to 8 seconds) is delivered

D. Circulation
   1. Palpate the carotid artery to assess circulation; always check for the absence of a pulse before beginning chest compressions on the victim (Fig. 18-5).
   2. Maintain an open airway and palpate for a carotid pulse for 10 seconds or less.
   3. If there is a pulse, continue to give 10 to 12 breaths per minute.
   4. If there is no pulse, chest compressions should begin.

E. Chest compression landmarks: center of the chest, between the nipples

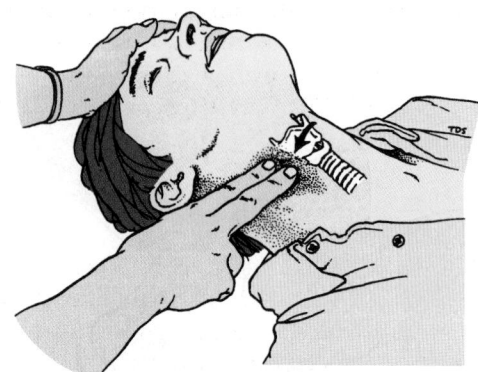

FIG. 18-5 Feeling for the carotid pulse. (From Harkreader, H., & Hogan, M.A. [2004]. *Fundamentals of nursing: Caring and clinical judgment* (2nd ed.). Philadelphia: W.B. Saunders. From Emergency Cardiac Care Committee and Subcommittees, American Heart Association. [1992]. Guidelines for cardiopulmonary resuscitation and emergency cardiac care. Part VIII: Ethical consideration in resuscitation. *Journal of the American Medical Association,* 268[16], 2282-2288.)

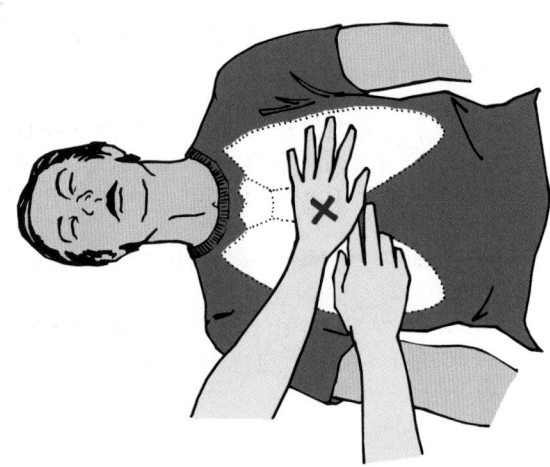

FIG. 18-6 Chest compression—proper hand position for an adult. (From Perry A., & Potter, P. [2006]. *Clinical nursing skills & techniques* [6th ed.]. St. Louis: Mosby.)

F. Chest compression method (Fig. 18-6)
   1. The rescuer uses two hands; the heel of one hand is placed on the landmark and the other hand is placed on top.
   2. The rescuer should push hard and fast and avoid interrupted compressions (every time chest compressions are stopped, blood flow stops as well).
   3. The rescuer should allow for complete recoil between compressions.
   4. Compression depth should be $1\frac{1}{2}$ to 2 inches.
   5. Compression rate is approximately 100 times per minute.
   6. The compression to ventilation ratio is 30:2 (for both one or two rescuers).

G. Complications of chest compressions
   1. Laceration of internal organs
   2. Punctured lungs
   3. Fractured ribs or sternum

III. **PEDIATRIC CPR GUIDELINES FOR THE HCP**
A. Description
   1. For HCPs, a child is defined as a person from 1 year to adolescent; for lay rescuers, children are those 1 to 8 years of age.
   2. For both HCPs and lay rescuers, an infant is defined as a person younger than 1 year of age.
   3. For an unresponsive infant or child, the lone (one rescuer) HCP should perform five cycles (about 2 minutes of **CPR**) and then call the emergency response number; the HCP must assess the most likely cause of the arrest.
   4. If the infant or child has a sudden witnessed collapse, the collapse is likely to be cardiac in origin (hypoxic cardiac arrest); in this situation, the HCP should call the emergency response number after verifying that the victim is unresponsive.
B. Airway
   1. Assess unresponsiveness.
   2. Use the **head tilt–chin lift** to open the airway (the HCP would use the **jaw thrust maneuver** if neck trauma is suspected).
C. Breathing
   1. Breathing victim: Keep the airway open.
   2. Nonbreathing victim
      a. Deliver two initial effective breaths (breaths that cause a visible chest rise) to the infant or child at 1 second per breath; 12 to 20 breaths per minute are then delivered (one breath every 3 to 5 seconds)
      b. With the infant, provide ventilations by mouth to mouth and nose.
      c. With the larger child, provide ventilations by mouth to mouth.
      d. For the child or infant with an advanced airway, 8 to 10 breaths per minute (one breath every 6 to 8 seconds) are delivered.
D. Circulation
   1. Assess circulation for no more than 10 seconds.
   2. If the victim is older than 1 year, assess circulation via the carotid or femoral pulse.
   3. If the victim is younger than 1 year, assess circulation via the brachial or femoral pulse.
   4. If there is a pulse, continue to give 12 to 20 breaths per minute (one breath every 3 to 5 seconds).
   5. If there is no pulse, chest compressions should begin.
   6. Chest compression landmarks
      a. Child: Center of the chest between the nipples
      b. Infant: Just below the nipple line

7. Chest compression method
   a. Child: Use of two hands with the heel of one hand on the chest and the second hand on top; or, use one hand with the heel of one hand only on the chest.
   b. Infant: One rescuer uses two fingers; two rescuers use two-thumb–encircling hands technique.
   c. Compression depth: $\frac{1}{3}$ to $\frac{1}{2}$ the depth of the chest
   d. Compression rate: Approximately 100 per minute
   e. Compression to ventilation ratio: 30:2 for a single rescuer; 15:2 for two rescuers

IV. AUTOMATED EXTERNAL DEFIBRILLATOR (AED) BY THE HCP
   A. Description
      1. The **automated external defibrillator** is used to convert ventricular fibrillation into a perfusing rhythm.
      2. The **AED** differentiates nonventricular from ventricular fibrillation rhythms and allows for early defibrillation by first responders.
      3. The use of **AEDs** is recommended for children in cardiac arrest 1 year of age and older (not recommended for infants younger than 1 year).
      4. For sudden witnessed arrest in the child or adult in the out-of-hospital setting, the health care provider should phone the emergency response number, retrieve the **AED**, and return to the victim to perform **CPR** and use the **AED**.
   B. Adult
      1. Adult pads need to be used (child pads or a child system cannot be used on an adult).
      2. Out-of-hospital response: Provide five cycles (2 minutes) of **CPR** before defibrillating if response time was longer than 4 to 5 minutes and the arrest was not witnessed.
   C. Child
      1. Child pads and child system are used for the child 1 to 8 years of age, if available (if child pads and system are not available, adult **AED** and pads are used).
      2. Out-of-hospital response: Provide five cycles of **CPR** before defibrillating.
   D. Interventions
      1. Attach **AED** pads to the victim.
      2. Turn on the **AED** and push the button to activate the analyzer.
      3. Follow instructions given for the **AED**, usually "assess," "stand back," "shock," and "reassess."
      4. **CPR** guidelines to treat cardiac arrest associated with ventricular fibrillation (VF) or pulseless ventricular tachycardia (VT) recommend the delivery of single shocks followed immediately by a period of **CPR**; interruptions of chest compressions to check circulation should not be done until about five cycles or approximately 2 minutes of **CPR** have been provided after the shock.

V. FOREIGN BODY AIRWAY OBSTRUCTION (FBAO)
   A. General guidelines
      1. The HCP needs to distinguish choking victims who require treatment (abdominal thrusts or back slaps and chest thrusts) from those who do not (*mild* versus *severe* airway obstruction).
      2. Signs of severe airway obstruction include poor air exchange and increased breathing difficulty, a silent cough, cyanosis, or inability to speak or breathe.
      3. Every time the airway is opened (with a **head tilt–chin lift**) to deliver rescue breaths, the rescuer should look in the mouth and remove an object only if one is seen.
      4. Blind finger sweeps in the mouth should not be performed.
      5. Abdominal thrusts are used for the adult; back slaps and chest thrusts are used for the child and infant.
   B. Conscious adult
      1. Ask the victim, "Are you choking?" (the victim will not be able to speak or cough if he or she is choking); if the victim nods yes, help is needed.
      2. Relieve the obstruction by the **Heimlich maneuver** (Box 18-3 and Fig. 18-7).
      3. Continue abdominal thrusts until the object is dislodged or the victim becomes unconscious.
   C. Unconscious adult
      1. Assess unconsciousness.
      2. Call for help
      3. Perform the **head tilt–chin lift** technique.
      4. Open the airway and look in the mouth; remove an object only if one is seen.
      5. Attempt ventilation.
      6. Reposition the head if unsuccessful; reattempt ventilation.
      7. Relieve the obstruction by the **Heimlich maneuver** with five abdominal thrusts.
      8. To perform the **Heimlich maneuver**, straddle the victim's thighs, place the heel of one hand on top of the other, between the umbilicus and xiphoid process, and give five abdominal thrusts in and up with the heel of the bottom hand.
      9. Reattempt ventilation.
      10. Repeat the sequence of **head tilt–chin lift**, breaths, and **Heimlich maneuver** until successful.
      11. Be sure to assess for the victim's carotid pulse and for the presence of spontaneous respirations.
      12. Perform rescue breathing or **CPR,** if required.

BOX 18-3
Heimlich Maneuver

Stand behind the victim.
Place arms around the victim's waist.
Make a fist.
Place the thumb side of the fist just above the umbilicus (belly button) and well below the xiphoid process.
Perform five quick in and up abdominal thrusts (between the umbilicus and the xiphoid process).
Use chest thrusts for the obese or the advanced pregnancy victim.

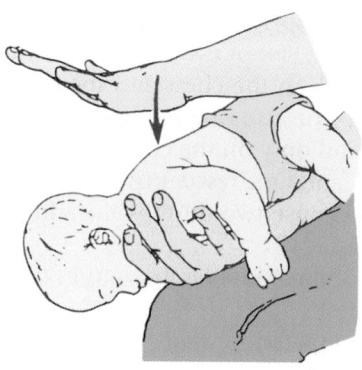

FIG. 18-8 Clearing airway obstruction in an infant. (From Christensen, B., & Kockrow, E. [2006]. *Foundations of nursing* [5th ed.]. St. Louis: Mosby.)

FIG. 18-7 Heimlich maneuver. (From Christensen, B., & Kockrow, E. [2006]. *Foundations of nursing* [5th ed.]. St. Louis: Mosby.)

D. Choking child or infant
   1. Foreign body airway obstruction requiring intervention is when signs of severe airway obstruction exist.
   2. For the conscious child:
      a. Assess for obstruction by asking the child, "Are you choking?" If the victim nods yes, help is needed.
      b. Relieve the obstruction by the **Heimlich maneuver** until the obstruction is dislodged or the child becomes unconscious.
   3. For the unconscious child, do the following:
      a. Assess unconsciousness.
      b. Open the airway by the **head tilt–chin lift** technique.
      c. Check for breathing and look for a foreign object (remove only if seen).
      d. Attempt ventilation.
      e. If unsuccessful, reposition the head; reattempt ventilation.
      f. Relieve the obstruction by using the **Heimlich maneuver**.
      g. Look in the mouth and remove a foreign object only if one is seen.
      h. Reattempt ventilation.
      i. Repeat the sequence.

   4. For the conscious infant, do the following:
      a. Assess for obstruction and note if mild or severe airway obstruction exists.
      b. Relieve the obstruction by five back slaps and five chest thrusts (Fig. 18-8).
      c. Straddle the infant over the arm, place the infant's head lower than the trunk, and support the head firmly, holding the jaw.
      d. Give five back slaps with the heel of the hand between the shoulder blades.
      e. Turn the infant; place the head lower than the trunk.
      f. Give five chest thrusts at the same location as for chest compressions.
      g. Check for the object and remove, if visible.
      h. Continue until the object is removed or the infant becomes unconscious.
   5. For the unconscious infant, do the following:
      a. Assess unconsciousness by gentle taps.
      b. Open the airway by the **head tilt–chin lift** technique and check for breathing.
      c. Look in the mouth and remove any visualized foreign object every time the airway is opened.
      d. Attempt ventilation.
      e. Reposition the head if unsuccessful; reattempt ventilation.
      f. Relieve the obstruction by five back slaps and five chest thrusts.
      g. Reattempt ventilation and repeat the sequence.

VI. **PREGNANT OR OBESE VICTIM**
A. **Heimlich maneuver** and relieving a foreign body airway obstruction
   1. Place the arms under the woman's axilla and across the chest.
   2. Place the thumb side of a clenched fist against the middle of the sternum, and place the other hand over the fist.

3. Perform backward chest thrusts until the foreign body is expelled or until the woman becomes unconscious.
4. If she becomes unconscious, place her on her back; a wedge, such as a pillow or rolled blanket, should be placed under the right abdominal flank and hip to displace the uterus to the left side of the abdomen.
5. If unable to ventilate, position the hands as for chest compressions and deliver chest thrusts firmly to remove the obstruction.

B. Defibrillation in the pregnant client: If defibrillation is needed, place the paddles one rib interspace higher than usual because the heart is displaced slightly by the enlarged uterus.

PRACTICE QUESTIONS

1. A nurse understands that which of the following is a correct guideline for adult cardiopulmonary resuscitation (CPR) for a health care provider?
   1. One breath should be given for every five compressions.
   2. Two breaths should be given for every 15 compressions.
   3. Initially, two quick breaths should be given as rapidly as possible.
   4. Each rescue breath should be given over 1 second and should produce visible chest rise.
2. A nurse attempts to relieve an airway obstruction on a 3-year-old conscious child. The nurse performs this maneuver by placing his or her hands between the:
   1. Groin and the abdomen.
   2. Umbilicus and the groin.
   3. Lower abdomen and the chest.
   4. Umbilicus and the xiphoid process.
3. A nurse is performing cardiopulmonary resuscitation (CPR) on a 7-year-old child. The nurse delivers how many breaths per minute to the child?
   1. 6
   2. 8
   3. 10
   4. 20
4. A nurse is performing cardiopulmonary resuscitation (CPR) on an infant. When performing chest compressions, the nurse understands that the compression rate is at least:
   1. 60 times per minute
   2. 80 times per minute
   3. 100 times per minute
   4. 160 times per minute
5. A nursing instructor teaches a group of students about basic life support (BLS). The instructor asks a student to identify the most appropriate location to assess the pulse of an infant younger than 1 year of age. Which of the following, if stated by the student,

would indicate that the student understands the appropriate assessment procedure?
   1. Radial
   2. Carotid
   3. Brachial
   4. Popliteal
6. A nurse is teaching cardiopulmonary resuscitation (CPR) to a group of nursing students. The nurse asks a student to describe the reason why blind finger sweeps are avoided in infants. The nurse determines that the student understands this reason if the student makes which statement?
   1. "The object may have been swallowed."
   2. "The infant may bite down on the finger."
   3. "The mouth is too small to see the object."
   4. "The object may be forced back farther into the throat."
7. A nurse is performing cardiopulmonary resuscitation (CPR) on an adult client. The nurse understands that when performing chest compressions, one should depress the sternum:
   1. $^3/_4$ to 1 inch
   2. $^1/_2$ to $^3/_4$ inch
   3. $1^1/_2$ to 2 inches
   4. $2^1/_2$ to 3 inches
8. A nursing instructor asks a nursing student to describe the procedure for performing the Heimlich maneuver on an unconscious pregnant woman at 8 months' gestation. The student describes the procedure correctly if the student states that she or he will:
   1. Place the hands in the pelvis to perform the thrusts.
   2. Perform abdominal thrusts until the object is dislodged.
   3. Perform left lateral abdominal thrusts until the object is dislodged.
   4. Place a rolled blanket under the right abdominal flank and hip area.
9. The nurse is teaching cardiopulmonary resuscitation to a group of community members. The nurse tells the group that when performing chest compressions on children and infants, the sternum should be depressed:
   1. $1^1/_2$ to 2 inches
   2. $2^1/_2$ to 3 inches
   3. $^1/_3$ to $^1/_2$ the depth of the chest
   4. Deep enough to make a finger impression
10. A nurse is teaching adult cardiopulmonary resuscitation (CPR) guidelines to a group of laypeople. The nurse tells the group that how many chest compressions are delivered with every two rescue breaths?
    1. 10
    2. 15
    3. 20
    4. 30
11. A nurse on the day shift walks into a client's room and finds the client unresponsive. The client is not

breathing and does not have a pulse, and the nurse immediately calls out for help. The next nursing action is which of the following?
1. Open the airway.
2. Give the client oxygen.
3. Start chest compressions.
4. Ventilate with a mouth-to-mask device.

12. A nurse witnesses a neighbor's husband sustain a fall from the roof of his house. The nurse rushes to the victim and determines the need to open the airway. The nurse opens the airway in this victim by using which method?
1. Flexed position
2. Head tilt–chin lift
3. Jaw thrust maneuver
4. Modified head tilt–chin lift

ALTERNATE ITEM FORMAT: PRIORITIZING (ORDERED RESPONSE)

A nursing student is asked to describe the correct steps for performing adult cardiopulmonary resuscitation (CPR). Number in order of priority the steps of adult CPR. (Number 1 is the first step and number 6 is the last step.)

_____ Initiate breathing
_____ Open the client's airway
_____ Determine breathlessness
_____ Perform chest compressions
_____ Check for a pulse at the carotid artery
_____ Determine unconsciousness by shaking the client and asking "Are you OK?"

ANSWERS

1. **4**

Rationale: In adult CPR, each rescue breath should be given over 1 second and should produce a visible chest rise. Excessive ventilation (too many breaths per minute or breaths that are too large or forceful) may be harmful and should not be performed. Health care providers should employ a 30:2 compression-to-ventilation ratio for the adult victim. Options 1, 2, and 3 are incorrect.
Test-Taking Strategy: Read each option carefully. Noting the words *visible chest rise* in option 4 will direct you to this option. Review CPR guidelines for the adult if you had difficulty with this question.
Level of Cognitive Ability: Comprehension
Client Needs: Physiological Integrity
Integrated Process: Nursing Process—implementation
Content Area: Fundamental skills
Reference: American Heart Association. (2005-2006). Highlights of the 2005 American Heart Association guidelines for cardiopulmonary resuscitation and emergency cardiovascular care. *Currents in Emergency Cardiovascular Care, 16*(4), 13.

2. **4**

Rationale: To perform the Heimlich maneuver on a child, the rescuer stands behind the victim and places the arms directly under the victim's axillae and around the victim. The rescuer places the thumb side of one fist against the victim's abdomen in the midline, slightly above the umbilicus and well below the tip of the xiphoid process. The rescuer grasps the fist with the other hand and delivers up to five thrusts. One must take care not to touch the xiphoid process or the lower margins of the rib cage because force applied to these structures may damage internal organs. Options 1, 2, and 3 are incorrect hand placements.
Test-Taking Strategy: Use the process of elimination, noting the age of the child. Eliminate options 1 and 2 first because they are comparative or alike. From the remaining options, considering the anatomical location and the effect of the maneuver in dislodging an obstruction will direct you to option 4. If you had difficulty with this question, review the correct hand placement for the Heimlich maneuver.

Level of Cognitive Ability: Application
Client Needs: Physiological Integrity
Integrated Process: Nursing Process—implementation
Content Area: Child health
References: Hockenberry, M., Wilson, D., & Winkelstein, M. (2005). *Wong's essentials of pediatric nursing* (7th ed., p. 836). St. Louis: Mosby.
Ignatavicius, D., & Workman, M. (2006). *Medical-surgical nursing: Critical thinking for collaborative care* (5th ed., p. 570). Philadelphia: W.B. Saunders.

3. **4**

Rationale: In a child between the ages of 1 and 8 years, 12 to 20 breaths per minute are delivered. Options 1, 2, and 3 are incorrect.
Test-Taking Strategy: Use the process of elimination and note the age of the child. Recalling the normal respiratory rate in a child at this age will assist in directing you to option 4. If you had difficulty with this question, review CPR guidelines for a child.
Level of Cognitive Ability: Application
Client Needs: Physiological Integrity
Integrated Process: Nursing Process—implementation
Content Area: Child health
References: McKinney, E., James, S., Murray, S., & Ashwill, J. (2005). *Maternal-child nursing* (2nd ed., pp. 861, 863). St. Louis: W.B. Saunders.
Perry, A., & Potter, P. (2006). *Clinical nursing skills & techniques* (6th ed., p. 888). St. Louis: Mosby.

4. **3**

Rationale: In an infant, the rate of chest compressions is at least 100 times per minute. Options 1 and 2 identify rates that are too low, and option 4 identifies a rate that is too high.
Test-Taking Strategy: Use the process of elimination, considering the normal heart rate of an infant. Eliminate options 1 and 2 because of the low rates identified in the options. Eliminate option 4 because this rate would be much too rapid for an infant. If you had difficulty with this question, review CPR for an infant.

Level of Cognitive Ability: Application
Client Needs: Physiological Integrity
Integrated Process: Nursing Process—implementation
Content Area: Child health
References: McKinney, E., James, S., Murray, S., & Ashwill, J. (2005). *Maternal-child nursing* (2nd ed., p. 863). St. Louis: W.B. Saunders.
Perry, A., & Potter, P. (2006). *Clinical nursing skills & techniques* (6th ed., p. 888). St. Louis: Mosby.

5. 3
Rationale: To assess a pulse in an infant (younger than 1 year of age), the pulse is checked at the brachial or femoral artery. The infant's relatively short fat neck makes palpation of the carotid artery difficult. The popliteal and radial pulses are also difficult to palpate in an infant.
Test-Taking Strategy: Use the process of elimination and knowledge regarding circulatory assessment in an infant. Considering the body structure of an infant will assist in directing you to option 3. Review cardiac assessment and BLS for an infant if you had difficulty with this question.
Level of Cognitive Ability: Comprehension
Client Needs: Physiological Integrity
Integrated Process: Nursing Process—evaluation
Content Area: Child health
Reference: McKinney, E., James, S., Murray, S., & Ashwill, J. (2005). *Maternal-child nursing* (2nd ed., p. 862). St. Louis: W.B. Saunders.

6. 4
Rationale: Blind finger sweeps are not recommended for infants and children because of the risk of forcing the object farther down into the airway. Options 1, 2, and 3 are not related directly to the subject of the question.
Test-Taking Strategy: Use the ABCDs—airway, breathing, circulation, and defibrillation or definitive treatment—to answer this question. Option 4 addresses the concern of airway patency. If you had difficulty with this question, review obstructed airway management for an infant or a child.
Level of Cognitive Ability: Comprehension
Client Needs: Physiological Integrity
Integrated Process: Nursing Process—evaluation
Content Area: Child health
References: McKinney, E., James, S., Murray, S., & Ashwill, J. (2005). *Maternal-child Nursing* (2nd ed., p. 862). St. Louis: W.B. Saunders.
Perry, A., & Potter, P. (2006). *Clinical nursing skills & techniques* (6th ed., p. 888). St. Louis: Mosby.

7. 3
Rationale: When performing cardiopulmonary resuscitation (CPR) on an adult client, the sternum is depressed $1\frac{1}{2}$ to 2 inches. Options 1 and 2 identify compression depths that would be ineffective in an adult. Option 4 identifies a depth that could cause injury to the client.
Test-Taking Strategy: Note the strategic word *adult* in the question. Consider the normal body structure of an adult to assist in directing you to option 3. If you had difficulty with this question, review the procedure for performing adult CPR.
Level of Cognitive Ability: Application
Client Needs: Physiological Integrity

Integrated Process: Nursing Process—implementation
Content Area: Adult health—cardiovascular
Reference: Perry, A., & Potter, P. (2006). *Clinical nursing skills & techniques* (6th ed., p. 888). St. Louis: Mosby.

8. 4
Rationale: To perform the Heimlich maneuver on an unconscious woman in an advanced stage of pregnancy, place the woman on her back. Place a wedge, such as a pillow or rolled blanket, under the right abdominal flank and hip to displace the uterus to the left side of the abdomen. Options 1, 2, and 3 are incorrect and can harm the woman and the fetus.
Test-Taking Strategy: Use the process of elimination and note that the client is an unconscious pregnant woman at 8 months' gestation. Recall the concepts associated with hypotension and vena cava syndrome to assist in directing you to option 4. Review the principles associated with performing the Heimlich maneuver on a pregnant woman if you had difficulty with this question.
Level of Cognitive Ability: Analysis
Client Needs: Physiological Integrity
Integrated Process: Nursing Process—evaluation
Content Area: Maternity—antepartum
Reference: Lowdermilk, D., & Perry, A. (2004). *Maternity and women's health care* (8th ed., pp. 917-918). St. Louis: Mosby.

9. 3
Rationale: When performing cardiopulmonary resuscitation (CPR) on infants and children, the sternum is depressed one third to one half the depth of the sternum. Options 1, 2, and 4 could be ineffective and harmful to both children and infants.
Test-Taking Strategy: Focus on the data in the question and note that the question addresses infants and children. Think about the body size of the infant and child to direct you to option 3. If you had difficulty with this question, review the procedure for performing layperson CPR compressions.
Level of Cognitive Ability: Application
Client Needs: Physiological Integrity
Integrated Process: Teaching and Learning
Content Area: Child health
Reference: American Heart Association. (2005-2006). Highlights of the 2005 American Heart Association guidelines for cardiopulmonary resuscitation and emergency cardiovascular care. *Currents in Emergency Cardiovascular Care, 16*(4), 6.

10. 4
Rationale: When performing cardiopulmonary resuscitation (CPR) on adults, the ratio of chest compressions to breaths is 30:2. Therefore, options 1, 2, and 3 are incorrect.
Test-Taking Strategy: Focus on the data in the question, the ratio of chest compressions to breaths for an adult. Remember, for an adult, the ratio is 30:2. If you had difficulty with this question, review the procedure for performing CPR.
Level of Cognitive Ability: Application
Client Needs: Physiological Integrity
Integrated Process: Teaching and Learning
Content Area: Adult health—cardiovascular
Reference: American Heart Association. (2005-2006). Highlights of the 2005 American Heart Association guidelines for cardiopulmonary resuscitation and emergency cardiovascular care. *Currents in Emergency Cardiovascular Care, 16*(4), 7.

11. **1**

Rationale: The next nursing action would be to open the airway. Ventilation cannot be initiated unless the airway is opened. Chest compressions are started after opening the airway and initiating ventilation. Oxygen may be helpful at some point, but the airway is opened first.

Test-Taking Strategy: Visualize the steps of basic life support (BLS) to answer the question. Recalling the ABCDs—airway, breathing, circulation, defibrillation or definitive treatment—will assist in directing you to option 1. Review the steps of BLS if you had difficulty with this question.

Level of Cognitive Ability: Application
Client Needs: Physiological Integrity
Integrated Process: Nursing Process—implementation
Content Area: Delegating/Prioritizing
Reference: Ignatavicius, D., & Workman, M. (2006). *Medical-surgical nursing: Critical thinking for collaborative care* (5th ed., p. 161). Philadelphia: W.B. Saunders.

12. **3**

Rationale: If a neck injury is suspected, the jaw thrust maneuver is used to open the airway. The head tilt–chin lift maneuver produces hyperextension of the neck and could cause complications if a neck injury is present. A flexed position is an inappropriate position for opening the airway.

Test-Taking Strategy: Use the process of elimination. Eliminate options 2 and 4 first because they are comparative or alike. Next, eliminate option 1 because this position would not open the airway. If you had difficulty with this question, review the appropriate methods to open an airway.

Level of Cognitive Ability: Application

Client Needs: Physiological Integrity
Integrated Process: Nursing Process—implementation
Content Area: Adult health—neurological
Reference: Perry, A., & Potter, P. (2006). *Clinical nursing skills & techniques* (6th ed., p. 890). St. Louis: Mosby.

ALTERNATE ITEM FORMAT: PRIORITIZING (ORDERED RESPONSE)

Answer: 4, 2, 3, 6, 5, 1
Rationale: The sequence for basic CPR for health care providers is as follows. After determining unconsciousness, the airway is opened and breathlessness is determined. Next, the health care provider delivers effective breaths that produce a visible rise in the chest, followed by assessing the carotid artery for presence of a pulse. In the absence of any pulse, chest compressions are provided at an adequate rate and depth that will allow adequate chest recoil, with minimal interruptions in chest compressions.

Test-Taking Strategy: Remember that determining unresponsiveness is the first action. Next, use the ABCs, airway, breathing, and circulation, to determine the correct order of action. Review the procedure for performing CPR if you had difficulty with this question.

Level of Cognitive Ability: Application
Client Needs: Physiological Integrity
Integrated Process: Nursing Process/Implementation
Content Area: Delegating/Prioritizing
Reference: American Heart Association. (2005-2006). Highlights of the 2005 American Heart Association guidelines for cardiopulmonary resuscitation and emergency cardiovascular care. *Currents in Emergency Cardiovascular Care*, 16(4), 11.

REFERENCES

American Heart Association. (1992). Guidelines for cardiopulmonary resuscitation and emergency cardiac care. Part VIII: Ethical considerations in resuscitation. *Journal of the American Medical Association*, 268(16), 2282–2288.

American Heart Association. (2005-2006). Highlights of the 2005 American Heart Association guidelines for cardiopulmonary resuscitation and emergency cardiovascular care. *Currents in Emergency Cardiovascular Care*, 16(4).

Christensen, B., & Kockrow (2006). *Foundations of nursing* (5th ed.). St. Louis: Mosby.

Elkin, M., Perry, A., & Potter, P. (2004). *Nursing interventions and clinical skills* (3rd ed.). St. Louis: Mosby.

Harkreader, H., & Hogan, M.A. (2004). *Fundamentals of nursing: Caring and clinical judgment* (2nd ed.). Philadelphia: W.B. Saunders.

Hockenberry, M., Wilson, D., & Winkelstein, M. (2005). *Wong's essentials of pediatric nursing* (7th ed.). St. Louis: Mosby.

Ignatavicius, D., & Workman, M. (2006). *Medical-surgical nursing: Critical thinking for collaborative care* (5th ed.). Philadelphia: W.B. Saunders.

Lewis, S.M., Heitkemper, M.M., & Dirksen, S.R. (2004). *Medical-surgical nursing: Assessment and management of clinical problems* (6th ed.). St. Louis: Mosby.

Lowdermilk, D. & Perry, A. (2004). *Maternity and women's health care* (8th ed.). St. Louis: Mosby.

McKinney, E., James, S., Murray, S., & Ashwill, J. (2005). *Maternal-child nursing* (2nd ed.). St. Louis: W.B. Saunders.

National Council of State Boards of Nursing (Eds.). (2007). *2007 NCLEX-RN® detailed test plan*. Chicago: Author.

Perry, A., & Potter, P. (2006). *Clinical nursing skills & techniques* (6th ed.). St. Louis: Mosby.

Perioperative Nursing Care

PYRAMID TERMS

atelectasis   A collapsed or airless state of the lung that may be the result of airway obstruction caused by accumulated secretions or failure of the client to deep breathe; a common postoperative complication that usually occurs 1 to 2 days after surgery.

extended postoperative stage   The period of at least 1 to 4 days after surgery.

immediate postoperative stage   The period of 1 to 4 hours after surgery.

intermediate postoperative stage   The period of 4 to 24 hours after surgery.

perioperative nursing   Nursing care given before (preoperative), during (intraoperative), and after surgery (postoperative).

wound dehiscence   Separation of the wound edges.

wound evisceration   Protrusion of internal organs through an incision.

THE PYRAMID TO SUCCESS

Pyramid Points focus on teaching the client and family or significant other in the preoperative stage, preparing the client for the operative procedure, ensuring that prescribed preoperative tests and procedures such as x-ray films or laboratory studies have been performed, and ensuring that the results of the tests and procedures are within expected ranges and are documented. In the postoperative stage, Pyramid Points focus on monitoring for surgical complications and on the implementation of initial nursing measures if a complication arises. Pyramid Points also focus on preparing the client for discharge, teaching related to the prescribed treatments, and the mobilization of home care support services, as needed. The Integrated Processes addressed in this chapter include Caring, Communication and Documentation, Nursing Process, and Teaching/Learning.

CLIENT NEEDS

Safe and Effective Care Environment

Ensuring that advance directives documents are in the client's medical record
Establishing priorities
Informing the client of the surgical process
Initiating referrals to home care and other support services
Maintaining confidentiality
Maintaining standard precautions
Maintaining surgical asepsis
Obtaining informed consent for the surgical procedure
Preventing a surgical infection
Providing safety to the medicated client
Upholding client's rights

Health Promotion and Maintenance

Discussing expected body image changes
Identifying lifestyle choices
Performing techniques of physical assessment
Providing client and family teaching related to the prescribed discharge plan
Providing health and wellness teaching to prevent complications

Psychosocial Integrity

Assessing psychosocial concerns
Assisting the client to develop coping methods
Communicating therapeutically
Identifying support systems
Identifying unexpected body image changes
Promoting an environment that will allow the client to express concerns

Physiological Integrity

Administering intravenous (IV) fluids and blood products safely

Administering preoperative and postoperative medications safely

Initiating nursing interventions when surgical complications arise

Monitoring for unexpected responses to treatments and procedures

Monitoring for surgical complications

Monitoring for wound infection

Providing basic care and comfort

Providing respiratory therapy

I. PREOPERATIVE CARE

A. Obtaining informed consent
1. The surgeon is responsible for obtaining the consent for surgery.
2. No sedation should be administered to the client before the client signs the consent.
3. Minors (clients under 18 years old) may need a parent or legal guardian to sign the consent form.
4. Older clients may need a legal guardian to sign the consent form.
5. The nurse may witness the client's signing of the consent form, but the nurse must be sure that the client has understood the surgeon's explanation of the surgery.
6. The nurse needs to document the witnessing of the signing of the consent form after the client acknowledges understanding the procedure.

B. Nutrition
1. Review the physician's orders regarding the NPO status before surgery.
2. Withhold solid foods and liquids for 6 to 8 hours before general anesthesia and for approximately 3 hours before surgery with local anesthesia to avoid aspiration.
3. Insert an IV line and administer IV fluids, if ordered.
4. Administer parenteral nutrition, as ordered, to clients who are malnourished, have protein or metabolic deficiencies, or cannot ingest foods.

C. Elimination
1. If the client is to have intestinal or abdominal surgery, an enema, laxative, or both may be prescribed the day or night before surgery.
2. The client should void immediately before surgery.

3. Insert a Foley catheter, if ordered.
4. If a Foley catheter is in place, it should be emptied immediately before surgery, and the nurse should document the amount and characteristics of the urine.

D. Surgical site
1. Clean the surgical site with a mild antiseptic soap the night before surgery, as prescribed.
2. Shave the operative site, as prescribed.
3. Hair should be shaved only if it will interfere with the surgical procedure and only if prescribed.

E. Preoperative client teaching
1. Inform the client about what to expect postoperatively.
2. Inform the client to notify the nurse if the client experiences any pain postoperatively and that pain medication will be prescribed and given as the client requests.
3. Inform the client that requesting an opioid (narcotic) after surgery will not make the client a drug addict.
4. Demonstrate the use of a client-controlled analgesia pump if its use is prescribed.
5. Instruct the client to use noninvasive pain relief techniques such as relaxation, distraction techniques, and guided imagery before the pain occurs and as soon as the pain is noticed.
6. The nurse should instruct the client not to smoke for at least 24 hours before surgery.
7. Instruct the client in deep-breathing and coughing techniques, use of incentive spirometry, and the importance of performing the techniques postoperatively to prevent the development of pneumonia and **atelectasis** (Box 19-1; Fig. 19-1).
8. Instruct the client in leg and foot exercises to prevent venous stasis of blood and to facilitate venous blood return (Fig. 19-2; see Box 19-1).
9. Instruct the client in how to splint an incision, turn, and reposition (Fig. 19-3; see Box 19-1).
10. Inform the client of any invasive devices that may be needed after surgery, such as a nasogastric tube, drain, Foley catheter, epidural catheter, or intravenous or subclavian lines.
11. Instruct the client not to pull on any of the invasive devices, because they will be removed as soon as possible.

F. Psychosocial preparation
1. Be alert to the client's level of anxiety.
2. Answer any questions or concerns that the client may have regarding surgery.
3. Allow time for privacy for the client to prepare for surgery psychologically.
4. Provide support and assistance as needed.
5. Take cultural aspects into consideration when providing care (Box 19-2)

G. Preoperative checklist
1. Ensure that the client is wearing an identification bracelet.
2. Assess for allergies (see Chap. 69 for information on latex allergy).

BOX 19-1
Client Teaching

DEEP-BREATHING AND COUGHING EXERCISES
Instruct the client that a sitting position gives the best lung expansion for coughing and deep-breathing exercises.
Instruct the client to breathe deeply three times, inhaling through the nostrils and exhaling slowly through pursed lips.
Instruct the client that the third breath should be held for 3 seconds; then, the client should cough deeply three times.
The client should perform this exercise every 1 to 2 hours.

INCENTIVE SPIROMETRY
Instruct the client to assume a sitting or upright position.
Instruct the client to place the mouth tightly around the mouthpiece.
Instruct the client to inhale slowly to raise and maintain the flow rate indicator between the 600 and 900 marks.
Instruct the client to hold the breath for 5 seconds, and then to exhale through pursed lips.
Instruct the client to repeat this process 10 times every hour.

LEG AND FOOT EXERCISES
Gastrocnemius (calf) pumping: Instruct the client to move both ankles by pointing the toes up and then down.
Quadriceps (thigh) setting: Instruct the client to press the back of the knees against the bed, and then to relax the knees; this contracts and relaxes the thigh and calf muscles to prevent thrombus formation.
Foot circles: Instruct the client to rotate each foot in a circle.
Hip and knee movements: Instruct the client to flex the knee and thigh and to straighten the leg and hold the position for 5 seconds before lowering (not performed if the client is having abdominal surgery or if the client has a back problem).

SPLINTING OF THE INCISION
If the surgical incision is abdominal or thoracic, instruct the client to place a pillow, or one hand with the other hand on top, over the incisional area.
During deep breathing and coughing, the client presses gently against the incisional area to splint or support it.

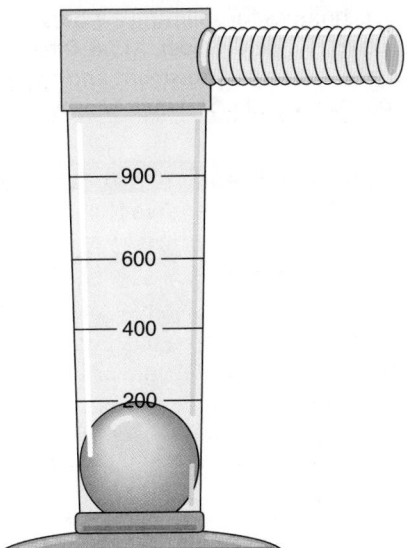

FIG. 19-1 Incentive spirometer. (From Phipps, W., Monahan, F., Sands, J. et al. [2003]. *Medical-surgical nursing: Health and illness perspectives* [7th ed.]. St. Louis: Mosby.)

3. Review the preoperative checklist to be sure that each item is addressed before the client is transported to surgery.
4. Ensure that informed consent forms have been signed for the operative procedure, any blood transfusions, disposal of a limb, or surgical sterilization procedures.
5. Ensure that a history and physical examination have been completed and documented in the client's record. (Box 19-3)
6. Ensure that consultation requests have been completed and documented in the client's record.
7. Ensure that prescribed laboratory results are documented in the client's record.
8. Ensure that the electrocardiogram and chest radiography reports are documented in the client's record.
9. Ensure that a blood type, screen, type, and cross-match are performed and documented in the client's record.
10. Remove jewelry, makeup, dentures, hairpins, nail polish (depending on agency procedures), glasses, and prostheses.
11. Document that valuables have been given to the client's family members or locked in the hospital safe.
12. Document the last time that the client ate or drank.
13. Document that the client voided before surgery.
14. Document that the prescribed preoperative medication was given (Box 19-4).
15. Monitor and document the client's vital signs.
H. Preoperative medications
1. Prepare to administer preoperative medications as prescribed or on call to the operating room immediately before surgery.

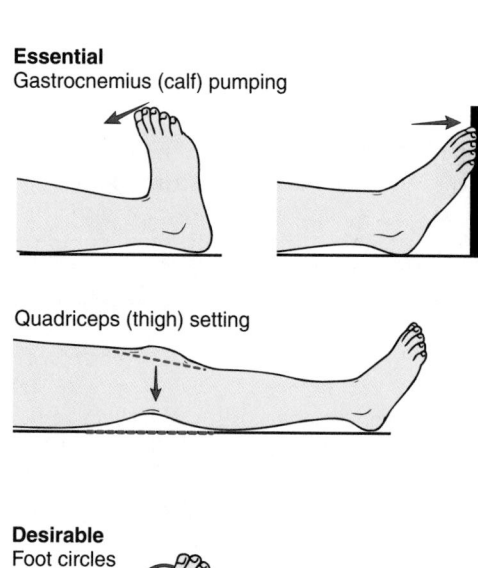

Essential
Gastrocnemius (calf) pumping

Quadriceps (thigh) setting

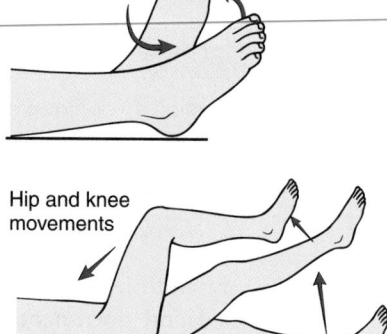

Desirable
Foot circles

Hip and knee
movements

FIG. 19-2 Postoperative leg exercises. (From Lewis, S., Heitkemper, M., & Dirksen, S. [2004]. *Medical-surgical nursing: Assessment and management of clinical problems* [6th ed.]. St. Louis: Mosby.)

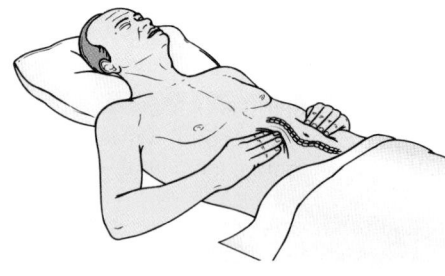

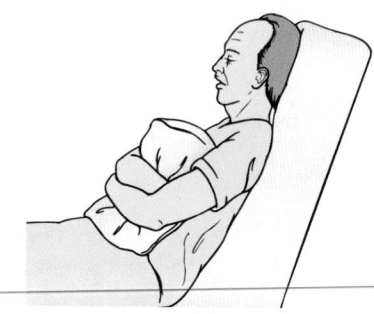

FIG. 19-3 Techniques for splinting a wound when coughing. (From Lewis, S., Heitkemper, M., & Dirksen, S. [2004]. *Medical-surgical nursing: Assessment and management of clinical problems* [6th ed.]. St. Louis: Mosby.)

2. Instruct the client about the desired effects of the preoperative medication.

3. After administering the preoperative medications, keep the client in bed with the side rails up.

4. Place the call bell next to the client; instruct the client not to get out of bed and to call for assistance if needed.

I. Arrival in the operating room

1. Guidelines to eliminate wrong site and wrong procedure surgery

   a. The nurse and surgeon ensure that the operative site has been appropriately marked (the surgeon uses indelible ink to mark the operative site).

   b. Just before starting the surgical procedure, a time out is conducted with all members of the operative team present to identify the appropriate surgical site again.

2. When the client arrives in the operating room, the operating room nurse will verify the identification bracelet with the client's verbal response and will review the client's chart.

BOX 19-2

Cultural Aspects of Perioperative Nursing Care

Cultural assessment includes questions related to:
  Primary language spoken
  Feelings related to surgery and pain
  Pain management
  Expectations
  Support systems
  Feelings toward self
Allow a family member to be present when and if appropriate.
Secure the help of a professional interpreter to communicate with non-English speaking clients.
Use pictures or phrase cards to communicate and assess the non-English speaking client's perception of pain or other feelings
Provide preoperative and postoperative educational materials in the appropriate language.

Modified from Potter, P., & Perry, A. (2005). *Fundamentals of nursing* (6th ed.). St. Louis: Mosby.

3. The client's chart will be checked for completeness and reviewed for informed consent forms, history and physical examination, and allergic reaction information.

4. Physicians' orders will be verified and implemented.

BOX 19-3

Medical Conditions That Increase the Risk of Surgery

Bleeding disorders such as thrombocytopenia, hemophilia
Diabetes mellitus
Chronic pain
Heart disease, such as a recent myocardial infarction, dysrhythmia, congestive heart failure, or peripheral vascular disease
Obstructive sleep apnea
Upper respiratory infection

Liver disease
Fever
Chronic respiratory disease, such as emphysema, bronchitis, or asthma
Immunological disorders, such as leukemia, AIDS, bone marrow depression, or the use of chemotherapy or immunosuppressive agents
Abuse of street drugs

AIDS, Acquired immunity deficiency syndrome.
Modified from Potter, P., & Perry, A. (2005). *Fundamentals of nursing* (6th ed.). St. Louis: Mosby.

BOX 19-4

Substances That Can Affect the Client in Surgery

ANTIBIOTICS
Antibiotics potentiate the action of anesthetic agents.

ANTICHOLINERGICS
Medications with anticholinergic effects increase the potential for confusion.

ANTICOAGULANTS
Anticoagulants alter normal clotting factors and increase the risk of hemorrhaging.
 Aspirin (acetylsalicylic acid) and nonsteroidal anti-inflammatory drugs are commonly used medications that can alter clotting mechanisms.
 These medications should be discontinued at least 48 hours before surgery or as specified by the surgeon.

ANTICONVULSANTS
Long-term use of certain anticonvulsants can alter the metabolism of anesthetic agents.

ANTIDEPRESSANTS
Antidepressants may lower the blood pressure during anesthesia.

ANTIDYSRHYTHMICS
Antidysrhythmic medications reduce cardiac contractility and impair cardiac conduction during anesthesia.

ANTIHYPERTENSIVES
Antihypertensive medications can interact with anesthetic agents and cause bradycardia, hypotension, and impaired circulation.

CORTICOSTEROIDS
Corticosteroids cause adrenal atrophy and reduce the ability of the body to withstand stress.
 Before and during surgery, dosages may be increased temporarily.

DIURETICS
Diuretics potentiate electrolyte imbalances after surgery.

HERBAL SUBSTANCES
Herbal substances can interact with anesthesia and cause a variety of adverse effects. These substances may need to be stopped at a specific time before surgery. During the preoperative period, the client needs to be asked if he or she is taking an herbal substance.

INSULIN
The need for insulin after surgery in a diabetic may be reduced because the client's nutritional intake is decreased, or the need for insulin may be increased because of the stress response and intravenous administration of glucose solutions.

---

 5. The IV line may be initiated at this time, if prescribed.
 6. The anesthesia team will administer the prescribed anesthesia.

II. POSTOPERATIVE CARE
A. **Immediate postoperative stage**
 1. Description: The period of 1 to 4 hours after surgery
 2. Respiratory system
  a. Monitor vital signs.
  b. Monitor airway patency and adequate ventilation because prolonged mechanical ventilation during anesthesia may affect postoperative lung function.
  c. Remember that extubated clients who are lethargic may not be able to maintain an airway.
  d. Monitor for secretions; if the client is unable to clear the airway by coughing, suction the secretions from the client's airway.
  e. Observe chest movement for symmetry and the use of accessory muscles.
  f. Monitor oxygen administration if prescribed.
  g. Monitor pulse oximetry.
  h. Encourage deep breathing and coughing exercises as soon as possible.

▲ i. Note the rate, depth, and quality of respirations; the respiratory rate should be higher than 10 and lower than 30 breaths/min.

j. Assess breath sounds—stridor, wheezing, or a crowing sound can indicate partial obstruction, bronchospasm, or laryngospasm; crackles or rhonchi may indicate pulmonary edema.

▲ k. Monitor for signs of respiratory distress, **atelectasis**, or other respiratory complications.

3. Cardiovascular system
   a. Assess the skin and check capillary refill.
   b. Assess peripheral pulses.
   c. Assess for peripheral edema.

▲ d. Monitor for bleeding.
   e. Assess the pulse for rate and rhythm; a bounding pulse may indicate hypertension, fluid overload, or excitement.
   f. Monitor for signs of hypertension and hypotension.
   g. Monitor for cardiac dysrhythmias.
   h. Assess for Homans' sign, particularly in clients who were in the lithotomy position during surgery.

4. Musculoskeletal system
   a. Assess the client for movement of the extremities.
   b. Review physician's orders regarding client positioning or restrictions.

▲ c. Unless contraindicated, place the client in a low Fowler's position after surgery to increase the size of the thorax for lung expansion.

▲ d. Avoid positioning the client in a supine position until pharyngeal reflexes have returned.

▲ e. If the client is comatose or semicomatose, position on the side and keep an oral airway in place.

5. Neurological system
   a. Assess level of consciousness.
   b. Frequent periodic attempts to awaken the client should continue until the client awakens.

▲ c. Orient the client to the environment.
   d. Speak in a soft tone; filter out extraneous noises in the environment.
   e. Maintain body temperature and prevent heat loss by providing the client with warm blankets and raising the room temperature as necessary.

6. Temperature control
   a. Monitor temperature.
   b. Monitor for signs of hypothermia that may result from anesthesia, a cool operating room, or exposure of the skin and internal organs during surgery.

▲ c. Apply warm blankets and continue oxygen as prescribed if the client is shivering.

7. Integumentary system
   a. Assess surgical site, drains, and wound ▲ dressings.
   b. Monitor for and document any drainage or bleeding from the surgical site.
   c. Assess the skin for redness, abrasions, or breakdown that may have resulted from surgical positioning.

8. Fluid and electrolyte balance
   a. Monitor IV fluid administration as prescribed.
   b. Record intake and output.
   c. Monitor for signs of hypocalcemia, hyperglycemia, and metabolic or respiratory acidosis ▲ or alkalosis.

9. Gastrointestinal system
   a. Monitor for nausea and vomiting.
   b. Maintain patency of the nasogastric tube if present.
   c. Monitor for abdominal distention.
   d. Monitor for return of bowel sounds. ▲

10. Renal system
    a. Assess the bladder for distention.
    b. Monitor color, quantity, and quality of urine output if a Foley catheter is present.
    c. Expect the client to void 6 to 8 hours after the ▲ surgical procedure, depending on the type of anesthesia administered.

11. Pain management
    a. Assess for pain.
    b. Assess the type of anesthetic used and pre- ▲ operative medication that the client received, and note whether the client received any pain medications in the postanesthesia period.
    c. Inquire about the type and location of pain.
    d. Ask the client to rate the degree of pain on a scale of 1 to 10, with 10 being the most severe.
    e. If the client is unable to rate the pain with a numerical pain scale, then use a descriptor scale that lists words that describe different levels of pain intensity, such as *no pain*, *mild pain*, *moderate pain*, and *severe pain*.
    f. For children older than 4 or 5 years of age, the Wong-Baker FACES Pain Rating Scale can be used to rate the pain level; the scale provides the child the opportunity to choose a face that shows "how much hurt he or she has now."
    g. Monitor for objective data related to pain, ▲ such as facial expressions, body gestures, increased pulse rate, increased blood pressure, and increased respirations.
    h. Inquire about the effectiveness of the last pain medication.
    i. Administer pain medication as prescribed.
    j. Ensure that the client with a client-controlled analgesia pump understands how to use it.

k. If an opioid (narcotic) has been prescribed, during the initial administration, assess the client every 30 minutes for respiratory rate and pain relief.

l. Use noninvasive measures to relieve postoperative pain, including distraction, comfort measures, positioning, backrubs, and providing a quiet and restful environment.

m. Document effectiveness of the pain medication and noninvasive pain relief measures.

B. **Intermediate postoperative stage**

1. Description: The period of 4 to 24 hours after surgery

2. Respiratory system
   a. Monitor vital signs.
   b. Continue the same assessments as during the immediate stage.
   c. Monitor patency of airway, verifying that the lungs are clear on auscultation or describe sounds heard.
   d. Encourage deep breathing and coughing.

3. Cardiovascular system
   a. Monitor circulatory status, such as peripheral pulses, capillary refill, and the absence of edema, numbness, and tingling.
   b. Encourage the use of antiembolism stockings, if prescribed, to promote venous return, strengthen muscle tone, and prevent pooling of blood in the extremities.

4. Musculoskeletal system
   a. Assess for range of motion in all extremities.
   b. Encourage ambulation; before ambulation, instruct the client to sit at the edge of the bed with his or her feet supported to assume balance.
   c. If the client is unable to get out of bed, turn the client every 1 to 2 hours.

5. Neurological system
   a. Assess level of consciousness.
   b. Maintain orientation to the environment.

6. Integumentary system
   a. Assess surgical site and drains.
   b. Monitor body temperature and wound for signs of infection.
   c. Maintain a dry, intact dressing.
   d. Reinforce the wound with a sterile dressing if necessary, and notify the physician if bleeding occurs from the site.
   e. Change dressings as prescribed, noting the amount of bleeding or drainage, odor, and intactness of sutures or staples.
   f. Use an abdominal binder for obese and debilitated individuals to prevent dehiscence of the incision (Fig. 19-4).
   g. Drains should be patent, with minimal bleeding or drainage.

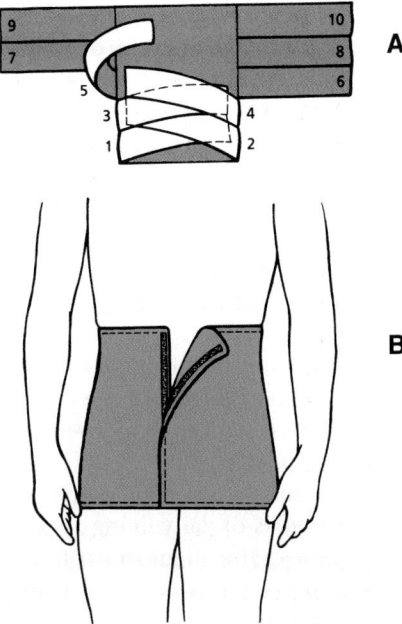

FIG. 19-4 Abdominal binders. **A,** Scultetus. **B,** Straight. (From Elkin, M., Perry, A., & Potter, P. [2004]. *Nursing interventions and clinical skills* (3rd ed.) St. Louis: Mosby.)

h. Prepare to assist with the removal of drains (as prescribed by the physician) when the drainage amount becomes insignificant.

7. Gastrointestinal system
   a. Monitor intake and output.
   b. Monitor for nausea and vomiting.
   c. Turn the client to a side-lying position if vomiting occurs and have suctioning equipment available and ready to use.
   d. Administer frequent oral care, at least every 2 hours.
   e. Maintain the NPO status until the gag reflex and peristalsis return.
   f. Continue IV fluids as prescribed until the client can tolerate fluids.
   g. When oral fluids are permitted, start with ice chips and water.
   h. Ensure that the client advances to clear liquids and then to a regular diet, as prescribed.
   i. Assess for bowel sounds in all four quadrants.
   j. Monitor the client for passing flatus and encourage ambulation.

8. Renal system
   a. Monitor urinary output (should be more than 30 mL/hr).
   b. If the client does not have a Foley catheter, the client is expected to void within 6 to 8 hours postoperatively; ensure that the amount is at least 200 mL.

9. Pain management: Continue with assessments and interventions as during the immediate stage.

C. **Extended postoperative stage**
1. Description: The period of at least 1 to 4 days postoperatively
2. Interventions
   a. Continue to assess and observe the client's body systems during this stage.
   b. Monitor for signs of infection, such as redness, swelling, and tenderness at the surgical site, fever, and leukocytosis.
   c. Encourage active range-of-motion exercises every 2 hours.
   d. Continue to encourage ambulation to promote peristalsis and the passage of flatus.
   e. Increase ambulation every day to increase muscle strength.
   f. Encourage the client to perform as many of activities of daily living as possible.
   g. Instruct the client to eat foods that are high in protein and vitamin C content to promote wound healing.

III. **PNEUMONIA AND ATELECTASIS**
A. Description (Box 19-5; Fig. 19-5)
1. Pneumonia: An inflammation of the alveoli caused by an infectious process that may develop 3 to 5 days postoperatively as a result of infection, aspiration, or immobility
2. **Atelectasis**: A collapse of the alveoli with retained mucous secretions; the most common postoperative complication, usually occurring 1 to 2 days postoperatively
B. Assessment
1. Assess for factors that may increase the risk of pneumonia and **atelectasis**.
2. Dyspnea and increased respiratory rate.
3. Crackles over involved lung area.
4. Elevated temperature.
5. Productive cough and chest pain.
C. Interventions
1. Assess lung and breath sounds.
2. Reposition the client every 1 to 2 hours.
3. Encourage the client to deep-breathe, cough, and use the incentive spirometer.
4. Provide chest physiotherapy and postural drainage, as prescribed.
5. Use suction to clear secretions if the client is unable to cough.
6. Encourage fluid intake and early ambulation.

IV. HYPOXIA
A. Description: An inadequate concentration of oxygen in arterial blood (see Box 19-5).
B. Assessment
1. Restlessness
2. Dyspnea
3. Hypertension
4. Tachycardia

BOX 19-5
Postoperative Complications

Constipation	Shock
Hemorrhage	Thrombophlebitis
Hypoxia	Urinary retention
Paralytic ileus	Wound dehiscence
Pneumonia and atelectasis	Wound evisceration
Pulmonary embolism	Wound infection

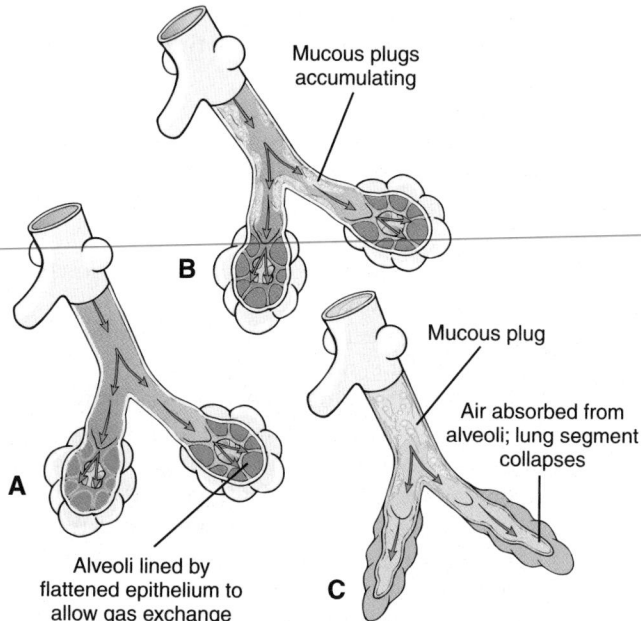

FIG. 19-5   Postoperative atelectasis. **A,** Normal bronchiole and alveoli. **B,** Mucous plug in bronchiole. **C,** Collapse of alveoli caused by atelectasis following absorption of air. (From Lewis, S., Heitkemper, M., & Dirksen, S. [2004]. *Medical-surgical nursing: Assessment and management of clinical problems* [6th ed.]. St. Louis: Mosby.)

5. Diaphoresis
6. Cyanosis
C. Interventions
1. Monitor for signs of hypoxia.
2. Notify the physician and eliminate the cause of hypoxia.
3. Monitor lung sounds and pulse oximetry.
4. Administer oxygen as prescribed.
5. Encourage deep breathing and coughing and use of the incentive spirometer.
6. Turn and reposition the client.

V. PULMONARY EMBOLISM
A. Description: An embolus blocking the pulmonary artery and disrupting blood flow to one or more lobes of the lung; presence of a pulmonary embolism may be life-threatening and requires emergency action (see Box 19-5).
B. Assessment
1. Dyspnea
2. Sudden sharp chest or upper abdominal pain

3. Cyanosis
4. Tachycardia
5. A drop in blood pressure
C. Interventions
1. Notify the physician immediately.
2. Monitor vital signs.
3. Administer oxygen and medications as prescribed.

VI. HEMORRHAGE
A. Description: The loss of a large amount of blood externally or internally in a short time period (see Box 19-5)
B. Assessment
1. Restlessness
2. Weak and rapid pulse
3. Hypotension
4. Tachypnea
5. Cool, clammy skin
6. Reduced urine output
C. Interventions
1. Provide pressure to the site of bleeding.
2. Notify the physician immediately.
3. Administer oxygen, as prescribed.
4. Administer IV fluids and blood, as prescribed.
5. Prepare the client for a surgical procedure, if necessary.

VII. SHOCK
A. Description: Loss of circulatory fluid volume, which usually is caused by hemorrhage (see Box 19-5)
B. Assessment: Similar to assessment findings in hemorrhage
C. Interventions
1. If shock develops, elevate the legs.
2. If the client had spinal anesthesia, do not elevate the legs any higher than placing them on the pillow; otherwise, the diaphragm muscles could be impaired.
3. Notify the physician.
4. Determine and treat the cause of shock.
5. Administer oxygen, as prescribed.
6. Monitor level of consciousness.
7. Monitor vital signs for increased pulse or decreased blood pressure.
8. Monitor intake and output.
9. Assess color, temperature, turgor, and moisture of the skin and mucous membranes.
10. Administer IV fluids, blood, and colloid solutions, as prescribed.

VIII. THROMBOPHLEBITIS
A. Description (see Box 19-5)
1. Thrombophlebitis is an inflammation of a vein, often accompanied by clot formation.
2. Veins in the legs are affected most commonly.
B. Assessment
1. Vein inflammation

2. Aching or cramping pain
3. Vein feels hard and cordlike and is tender to touch
4. Elevated temperature
5. Positive Homans' sign
C. Interventions
1. Monitor legs for swelling, inflammation, pain, tenderness, venous distention, and cyanosis and notify the physician if any of these signs are present.
2. Elevate the extremity 30 degrees without allowing any pressure on the popliteal area.
3. Encourage the use of antiembolism stockings as prescribed; remove stockings twice a day to wash and inspect the legs.
4. Use an intermittent pulsatile compression device as prescribed (Fig. 19-6).
5. Perform passive range-of-motion exercises every 2 hours if the client is confined to bed rest.
6. Encourage early ambulation, as prescribed.
7. Do not allow the client to dangle the legs.
8. Instruct the client not to sit in one position for an extended period of time.
9. Administer anticoagulants such as heparin sodium or warfarin (Coumadin), as prescribed.

IX. URINARY RETENTION
A. Description
1. Urinary retention (see Box 19-5) is an involuntary accumulation of urine in the bladder as a result of loss of muscle tone.
2. It is caused by the effects of anesthetics or opioid analgesics and appears 6 to 8 hours after surgery.
B. Assessment
1. Inability to void
2. Restlessness and diaphoresis
3. Lower abdominal pain
4. Distended bladder
5. Hypertension
6. On percussion, bladder sounds like a drum

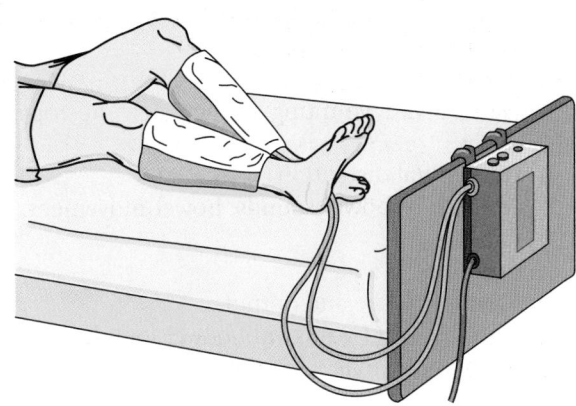

FIG. 19-6 Intermittent pulsatile compression device. (From Phipps, W., Monahan, F., Sands, J. et al. [2003]. *Medical-surgical nursing: Health and illness perspectives* [7th ed.]. St. Louis: Mosby.)

C. Interventions
1. Monitor for voiding.
2. Assess for a distended bladder.
3. Encourage ambulation when prescribed.
4. Encourage fluid intake unless contraindicated.
5. Assist the client to void by helping to stand.
6. Provide privacy.
7. Pour warm water over the perineum or allow the client to hear running water to promote voiding.
8. Contact the physician and catheterize the client as prescribed after all noninvasive techniques have been attempted.

X. CONSTIPATION

A. Description
1. Constipation (see Box 19-5) is an abnormal infrequent passage of stool.
2. When the client resumes a solid diet postoperatively, failure to pass stool within 48 hours is a cause for concern.

B. Assessment
1. Abdominal distention
2. Absence of bowel movements
3. Anorexia, headache, and nausea

C. Interventions
1. Assess bowel sounds.
2. Encourage fluid intake up to 3000 mL/day unless contraindicated.
3. Encourage early ambulation.
4. Encourage consumption of fiber foods unless contraindicated.
5. Administer stool softeners and laxatives, as prescribed.
6. Provide privacy and adequate time for bowel elimination.

XI. PARALYTIC ILEUS

A. Description
1. Paralytic ileus (see Box 19-5) is failure of appropriate forward movement of bowel contents.
2. The condition may occur as a result of anesthetic medications or of manipulation of the bowel during the surgical procedure.

B. Assessment
1. Nausea and vomiting immediately postoperatively
2. Abdominal distention
3. Absence of bowel sounds, bowel movement, or flatus

C. Interventions
1. Monitor intake and output.
2. Maintain NPO status until bowel sounds return.
3. Maintain patency of a nasogastric tube if in place.
4. Encourage ambulation.
5. Administer IV fluids or parenteral nutrition, as prescribed.

6. Administer medications as prescribed to increase gastrointestinal motility and secretions.
7. If ileus occurs, it is treated first nonsurgically with bowel decompression by insertion of an nasogastric tube attached to intermittent or constant suction.

XII. WOUND INFECTION

A. Description
1. Wound infection (see Box 19-5) is caused by poor aseptic technique or a contaminated wound before surgical exploration.
2. Infection usually occurs 3 to 6 days after surgery.
3. Purulent material may exit from the drains or separated wound edges.

B. Assessment
1. Fever and chills
2. Warm, tender, painful, and inflamed incision site
3. Edematous skin at the incision and tight skin sutures
4. Elevated white blood cell count

C. Interventions
1. Monitor temperature.
2. Monitor incision site for approximation of suture line, edema, or bleeding, and signs of infection (*REEDA*: *r*edness, *e*rythema, *e*cchymosis, *d*rainage, *a*pproximation of the wound edges); notify the physician if signs of wound infection are present.
3. Maintain patency of drains, and assess drainage amount, color, and consistency.
4. Keep drain and tubes away from the incision line, and maintain asepsis.
5. Change the dressing, as prescribed.
6. Administer antibiotics, as prescribed.

XIII. WOUND DEHISCENCE

A. Description
1. **Wound dehiscence** (Fig. 19-7; see Box 19-5) is separation of the wound edges at the suture line.
2. Dehiscence usually occurs 6 to 8 days after surgery.

B. Assessment
1. Increased drainage
2. Opened wound edges
3. Appearance of underlying tissues through the wound

C. Interventions
1. Place the client in a low Fowler's position with the knees bent to prevent abdominal tension on an abdominal suture line.
2. Cover the wound with a sterile normal saline dressing.
3. Notify the physician.
4. Prevent wound infection through strict asepsis.

5. Administer antiemetics as prescribed to prevent vomiting and further strain on the abdominal incision.
6. Instruct the client to splint the abdominal incision when coughing.

XIV. WOUND EVISCERATION
A. Description
1. **Wound evisceration** (see Box 19-5 and Fig. 19-7) is protrusion of the internal organs through an incision.
2. Evisceration is most common among obese clients, clients who have had abdominal surgery, or those who have poor wound-healing ability.
3. Evisceration usually occurs 6 to 8 days after surgery.
4. **Wound evisceration** is an emergency.
B. Assessment
1. Discharge of serosanguineous fluid from a previously dry wound
2. The appearance of loops of bowel or other abdominal contents through the wound
3. Client reports feeling a popping sensation after coughing or turning
C. Interventions
1. Place the client in a low Fowler's position with the knees bent to prevent abdominal tension.
2. Cover the wound with a sterile normal saline dressing.
3. Notify the physician.
4. Prevent wound infection through strict asepsis.

5. Administer antiemetics as prescribed to prevent vomiting and further strain on the incision.
6. Instruct the client to splint the incision when coughing.
7. Monitor for signs of shock.

XV. AMBULATORY SURGERY
A. General criteria for client discharge
1. Client is alert and oriented.
2. Client has voided.
3. Client has no respiratory distress.
4. Client is able to ambulate, swallow, and cough.
5. Client has minimal pain.
6. Client is not vomiting.
7. Client has minimal, if any, bleeding from the incision site.
8. Client has a responsible adult available to drive the client home.
9. The surgeon has signed a release form.
B. Discharge teaching (Box 19-6)
1. Discharge teaching should be performed before the date of the scheduled procedure.

BOX 19-6
Postoperative Discharge Teaching

Assess the client's readiness to learn, educational level, and desire to change or modify lifestyle.
Assess the need for resources needed for home care.
Demonstrate care of the incision and how to change the dressing.
Instruct the client to cover the incision with plastic if showering is allowed.
Be sure the client is provided with a 48-hour supply of dressings for home use.
Instruct the client on the importance of returning to the physician's office for follow-up.
Instruct the client that sutures usually are removed in the physician's office 7 to 10 days after surgery.
Inform the client that staples are removed 7 to 14 days after surgery and that the skin may become slightly reddened when they are ready to be removed.
Steri-Strips may be applied to provide extra support after the sutures are removed.
Instruct the client on the use of medications, their purpose, dosages, administration, and side effects.
Instruct the client on diet and to drink six to eight glasses of liquid a day.
Instruct the client about activity levels and to resume normal activities gradually.
Instruct the client to avoid lifting for 6 weeks if a major surgical procedure was performed.
Instruct the client with an abdominal incision not to lift anything weighing 10 lb or more and not to engage in any activities that involve pushing or pulling.
The client usually can return to work in 6 to 8 weeks as prescribed by the physician.
Instruct the client about the signs and symptoms of complications and when to call a physician.

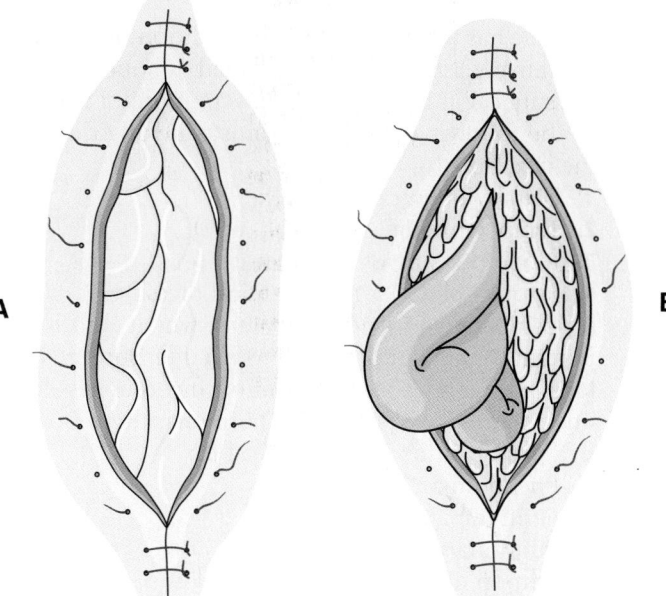

A   **B**

FIG. 19-7   **A,** Wound dehiscence. **B,** Wound evisceration. (From Phipps, W., Monahan, F., Sands, J. Marek, et al. [2003]. *Medical-surgical nursing: Health and illness perspectives* [7th ed.]. St. Louis: Mosby.)

2. Provide written instructions to the client and family regarding the specifics of care.
3. Instruct the client and family about postoperative complications that can occur.
4. Provide appropriate resources for home care support.
5. Instruct the client not to drive for 24 hours after general anesthesia.
6. Instruct the client to call the surgeon, ambulatory center, or emergency department if postoperative problems occur.
7. Instruct the client to keep follow-up appointments with the surgeon.

PRACTICE QUESTIONS

1. A nurse assesses a client's surgical incision for signs of infection. Which finding by the nurse would be interpreted as a normal finding at the surgical site?
   1. Red, hard skin
   2. Serous drainage
   3. Purulent drainage
   4. Warm, tender skin

2. When performing a surgical dressing change of a client's abdominal dressing, a nurse notes an increase in the amount of drainage and separation of the incision line. The underlying tissue is visible to the nurse. The nurse should do which of the following in the initial care of this wound?
   1. Leave the incision open to the air to dry the area.
   2. Irrigate the wound and apply a sterile dry dressing.
   3. Apply a sterile dressing soaked with normal saline.
   4. Apply a sterile dressing soaked in povidone-iodine (Betadine).

3. A nurse is monitoring the status of a postoperative client. The nurse would become most concerned with which of the following signs that could indicate an evolving complication?
   1. Increasing restlessness
   2. A negative Homans' sign
   3. Hypoactive bowel sounds in all four quadrants
   4. Blood pressure of 110/70 mm Hg and a pulse of 86 beats/min

4. A nurse is reviewing a physician's order sheet for a preoperative client that states that the client must be NPO after midnight. The nurse would telephone the physician to clarify whether which of the following medications should be given to the client and not withheld?
   1. Ferrous sulfate
   2. Prednisone (Deltasone)
   3. Cyclobenzaprine (Flexeril)
   4. Conjugated estrogen (Premarin)

5. A client who has undergone preadmission testing has had blood drawn for serum laboratory studies, including a complete blood count, coagulation studies, and electrolytes and creatinine levels. Which of the following laboratory results should be reported to the surgeon's office by the nurse, knowing that it could cause surgery to be postponed?
   1. Sodium, 141 mEq/L
   2. Hemoglobin, 8.0 g/dL
   3. Platelets, 210,000/mm³
   4. Serum creatinine, 0.8 mg/dL

6. A nurse in a surgical unit receives a postoperative client from the postanesthesia care unit. After the initial assessment of the client, the nurse plans to continue with postoperative assessment activities:
   1. Every hour for 2 hours, and then every 4 hours as needed.
   2. Every 30 minutes for the first hour, every hour for 2 hours, and then every 4 hours as needed.
   3. Every 15 minutes for the first hour, every 30 minutes for 2 hours, every hour for 4 hours, and then every 4 hours as needed.
   4. Every 5 minutes for the first half-hour, every 15 minutes for 2 hours, every 30 minutes for 4 hours, and then every hour as needed.

7. A nurse receives a telephone call from the postanesthesia care unit stating that a client is being transferred to the surgical unit. The nurse plans to do which of the following first on arrival of the client?
   1. Assess the patency of the airway.
   2. Check tubes or drains for patency.
   3. Check the dressing to assess for bleeding.
   4. Assess the vital signs to compare with preoperative measurements.

8. A nurse has just reassessed the condition of a postoperative client who was admitted 1 hour ago to the surgical unit. The nurse plans to monitor which of the following parameters most carefully during the next hour?
   1. Urinary output of 20 mL/hr
   2. Temperature of 37.6° C (99.6° F)
   3. Blood pressure of 100/70 mm Hg
   4. Serous drainage on the surgical dressing

9. A postoperative client asks a nurse why it is so important to deep-breathe and cough after surgery. In formulating a response, the nurse incorporates the understanding that retained pulmonary secretions in a postoperative client can lead to:
   1. Pneumonia
   2. Fluid imbalance
   3. Pulmonary edema
   4. Carbon dioxide retention

10. A client is admitted to a surgical unit postoperatively with a wound drain in place. Which action should the nurse avoid in the care of the drain?
    1. Check the drain for patency.
    2. Observe for bright red bloody drainage.

3. Curl the drain tightly and tape it firmly to the body.

4. Maintain aseptic technique when emptying the drain.

11. A nurse is developing a plan of care for a preoperative client who has a latex allergy. Which intervention should be included in the plan?
    1. Avoid using medications from glass ampules.
    2. Avoid using IV tubing that is made of polyvinyl chloride.
    3. Use medications that are from ampules with rubber stoppers.
    4. Apply a cloth barrier to the client's arm under a blood pressure cuff when taking the blood pressure.

12. A nurse is developing a plan of care for a client scheduled for surgery. The nurse should include which activity in the nursing care plan for the client on the day of surgery?
    1. Have the client void immediately before surgery.
    2. Avoid oral hygiene and rinsing with mouthwash.
    3. Verify that the client has not eaten for the last 24 hours.
    4. Report immediately any slight increase in blood pressure or pulse.

13. A nurse is developing a list of home care instructions for a client being discharged after a laparoscopic cholecystectomy. Which of the following instructions would be least appropriate to include in the postoperative discharge plan of care?
    1. Wound care
    2. Follow-up care
    3. Activity restrictions
    4. Deep-breathing exercises

14. A nurse is monitoring a postoperative client after abdominal surgery for signs of complications. The nurse assesses the client for the presence of Homans' sign and determines that this sign is positive if which of the following is noted?
    1. Incisional pain
    2. Absent bowel sounds
    3. Pain with dorsiflexion of the foot
    4. Crackles on auscultation of the lungs

15. An operating room nurse is positioning a client on the operating room table to prevent the client's extremities from dangling over the sides of the table. A nursing student who is observing for the day asks the nurse why this is so important. The nurse responds that this is done primarily to prevent:
    1. An increase in pulse rate.
    2. A drop in blood pressure.
    3. Nerve and muscle damage.
    4. Muscle fatigue in the extremities.

16. A client with a perforated gastric ulcer is scheduled for surgery. The client cannot sign the operative consent form because of sedation from opioid analgesics that have been administered. The nurse should take which appropriate action in the care of this client?
    1. Obtain a court order for the surgery.
    2. Send the client to surgery without the consent form being signed.
    3. Have the hospital chaplain sign the informed consent immediately.
    4. Obtain a telephone consent from a family member, following agency policy.

17. A preoperative client expresses anxiety to a nurse about upcoming surgery. Which response by the nurse is most likely to stimulate further discussion between the client and the nurse?
    1. "If it's any help, everyone is nervous before surgery."
    2. "I will be happy to explain the entire surgical procedure to you."
    3. "Can you share with me what you've been told about your surgery?"
    4. "Let me tell you about the care you'll receive after surgery and the amount of pain you can anticipate."

18. A nurse is conducting preoperative teaching with a client about the use of an incentive spirometer. The nurse should include which piece of information in discussions with the client?
    1. Inhale as rapidly as possible.
    2. Keep a loose seal between the lips and the mouthpiece.
    3. After maximum inspiration, hold the breath for 15 seconds and exhale.
    4. The best results are achieved when sitting up or with the head of the bed is elevated 45 to 90 degrees.

19. A nurse has conducted preoperative teaching for a client scheduled for surgery in 1 week. The client has a history of arthritis and has been taking acetylsalicylic acid (aspirin). The nurse determines that the client needs additional teaching if the client states:
    1. "Aspirin can cause bleeding after surgery."
    2. "Aspirin can cause my ability to clot blood to be abnormal."
    3. "I need to discontinue the aspirin 48 hours before the scheduled surgery."
    4. "I need to continue to take the aspirin until the day of surgery."

20. A nurse is preparing a preoperative client for transfer to the operating room. The nurse should take which action in the care of this client at this time?
    1. Ensure that the client has voided.
    2. Administer all the daily medications.
    3. Practice postoperative breathing exercises.
    4. Verify that the client has not eaten for the last 24 hours.

ALTERNATE ITEM FORMAT: MULTIPLE RESPONSE

A client who has had abdominal surgery complains of feeling as though "something gave way" in the incisional site. The nurse removes the dressing and notes the presence of a loop of bowel protruding through the incision. Which nursing interventions should the nurse take? Select all that apply.

☑ 1. Contact the surgeon.
☐ 2. Instruct the client to remain quiet.
☐ 3. Prepare the client for wound closure.
☑ 4. Document the findings and actions taken
☐ 5. Place a sterile saline dressing and ice packs over the wound.
☐ 6. Place the client in a supine position without a pillow under the head.

ANSWERS

1. **2**

Rationale: Serous drainage is an expected finding at a surgical site. The other options indicate signs of wound infection. Signs and symptoms of infection include warm, red, and tender skin around the incision. Purulent material may exit from drains or from separated wound edges. Infection may be caused by poor aseptic technique and a contaminated wound before surgical exploration. Wound infection usually appears 3 to 6 days after surgery. The client also may have a fever and chills.

Test-Taking Strategy: Use the process of elimination, noting the strategy words *normal finding*. Recalling the signs of a wound infection and noting these strategy words will direct you to option 2. Review the signs of a wound infection if you had difficulty with this question.

Level of Cognitive Ability: Analysis
Client Needs: Physiological Integrity
Integrated Process: Nursing Process—assessment
Content Area: Fundamental skills
Reference: Ignatavicius, D., & Workman, M. (2006). *Medical-surgical nursing: Critical thinking for collaborative care* (5th ed., p. 345). Philadelphia: W.B. Saunders.

2. **3**

Rationale: Wound dehiscence is the separation of wound edges at the suture line. Signs and symptoms include increased drainage and the appearance of underlying tissues. Dehiscence usually occurs 6 to 8 days after surgery. The client should be instructed to remain quiet and to avoid coughing or straining. The client should be positioned to prevent further stress on the wound (semi-Fowler's). Sterile dressings soaked with sterile normal saline should be used to cover the wound. The nurse must notify the physician after applying this initial dressing to the wound. Options 1, 2, and 4 are incorrect.

Test-Taking Strategy: Use the process of elimination. Eliminate option 1 first because this action would dry the wound and also present a risk of infection to the underlying tissues. Eliminate options 2 and 4 next because a dry dressing and a dressing soaked with povidone-iodine will irritate the exposed body tissues. Review initial nursing care when dehiscence or evisceration occurs if you had difficulty with this question.

Level of Cognitive Ability: Application
Client Needs: Physiological Integrity
Integrated Process: Nursing Process—implementation
Content Area: Fundamental skills
Reference: Ignatavicius, D., & Workman, M. (2006). *Medical-surgical nursing: Critical thinking for collaborative care* (5th ed., pp. 346, 350-351). Philadelphia: W.B. Saunders.

3. **1**

Rationale: Increasing restlessness is a sign that requires continuous and close monitoring because it could indicate a potential complication, such as hemorrhage, shock, or pulmonary embolism. Hypoactive bowel sounds heard in all four quadrants are a normal occurrence, as is a negative Homans' sign. (A positive Homans' sign may indicate thrombophlebitis.) A blood pressure of 110/70 mm Hg with a pulse of 86 beats/min is within normal limits.

Test-Taking Strategy: Use the process of elimination, noting the strategy words *indicate an evolving complication*. Eliminate each of the incorrect options because they are normal expected findings. If you had difficulty with this question, review the normal expected postoperative findings and the signs and symptoms of postoperative complications.

Level of Cognitive Ability: Analysis
Client Needs: Physiological Integrity
Integrated Process: Nursing Process—analysis
Content Area: Fundamental skills
Reference: Ignatavicius, D., & Workman, M. (2006). *Medical-surgical nursing: Critical thinking for collaborative care* (5th ed., p. 353). Philadelphia: W.B. Saunders.

4. **2**

Rationale: Prednisone is a corticosteroid. With prolonged use, corticosteroids cause adrenal atrophy, which reduces the ability of the body to withstand stress. When stress is severe, corticosteroids are essential to life. Before and during surgery, dosages may be increased temporarily. Ferrous sulfate is an oral iron preparation used to treat iron deficiency anemia. Cyclobenzaprine (Flexeril) is a skeletal muscle relaxant. Conjugated estrogen (Premarin) is an estrogen used for hormone replacement therapy in postmenopausal women. These other three medications may be withheld before surgery without undue effects on the client.

Test-Taking Strategy: Use the process of elimination and knowledge about medications that may have special implications for the surgical client. Remember that when stress is severe, corticosteroids are essential to life. Review the effects of corticosteroids if you had difficulty with this question.

Level of Cognitive Ability: Analysis
Client Needs: Physiological Integrity
Integrated Process: Nursing Process—analysis
Content Area: Pharmacology
Reference: Ignatavicius, D., & Workman, M. (2006). *Medical-surgical nursing: Critical thinking for collaborative care* (5th ed., p. 297). Philadelphia: W.B. Saunders.

5. **2**
Rationale: Routine screening tests include a complete blood count, serum electrolyte analysis, coagulation studies, and serum creatinine tests. The complete blood count includes the hemoglobin analysis. All these values are within normal range, except the hemoglobin. If a client has a low hemoglobin level, the surgery likely could be postponed by the surgeon.
Test-Taking Strategy: Use the process of elimination and knowledge of the normal laboratory values. The only option that identifies an abnormal laboratory value is option 2. Review these laboratory values if you had difficulty answering this question.
Level of Cognitive Ability: Analysis
Client Needs: Physiological Integrity
Integrated Process: Nursing Process—analysis
Content Area: Fundamental skills
References: Chernecky, C., & Berger, B. (2004). *Laboratory tests and diagnostic procedures* (4th ed., p. 637). Philadelphia: W.B. Saunders.
Ignatavicius, D., & Workman, M. (2006). *Medical-surgical nursing: Critical thinking for collaborative care* (5th ed., p. 301). Philadelphia: W.B. Saunders.

6. **3**
Rationale: When the postoperative client arrives from the postanesthesia care unit, the nurse performs an initial assessment. Common time frames for continuing postoperative assessment activities are every 15 minutes the first hour, every 30 minutes for 2 hours, every hour for 4 hours, and then every 4 hours as needed. Options 1 and 2 identify time frames that are too infrequent and will not provide adequate assessment of the postoperative client. Option 4 identifies close time frames that are unnecessary.
Test-Taking Strategy: Use the process of elimination. Eliminate option 4 first because the time frames are so close. By the time that the nurse completed the assessment, the 5 minutes would have lapsed and the nurse would immediately have to perform the assessment again. This is unnecessary and unreasonable. Eliminate options 1 and 2 because they identify time frames that are too infrequent and will not provide adequate assessment of the postoperative client. Review postoperative assessment procedures if you had difficulty with this question.
Level of Cognitive Ability: Application
Client Needs: Physiological Integrity
Integrated Process: Nursing Process—planning
Content Area: Fundamental skills
Reference: Ignatavicius, D., & Workman, M. (2006). *Medical-surgical nursing: Critical thinking for collaborative care* (5th ed., p. 348). Philadelphia: W.B. Saunders.

7. **1**
Rationale: The first action of the nurse is to assess the patency of the airway and respiratory function. The nurse then takes vital signs followed by checking the dressing and the tubes or drains. If the airway is not patent, the nurse must take immediate measures for the survival of the client. Options 2, 3, and 4 are all nursing actions that should be performed after a patent airway has been established.
Test-Taking Strategy: Use the principles of prioritization when answering this question. Remember the ABCs—airway, breathing, and circulation. Ensuring airway patency is the first action to be taken; therefore, option 1 is correct. Review the initial care of the post-operative client if you had difficulty with this question.

Level of Cognitive Ability: Application
Client Needs: Physiological Integrity
Integrated Process: Nursing Process—planning
Content Area: Delegating/Prioritizing
Reference: Ignatavicius, D., & Workman, M. (2006). *Medical-surgical nursing: Critical thinking for collaborative care* (5th ed., pp. 341-343, 348). Philadelphia: W.B. Saunders.

8. **1**
Rationale: Urine output should be maintained at a minimum of 30 mL/hr for an adult. An output of less than 30 mL for each of 2 consecutive hours should be reported to the physician. A temperature higher than 37.7° C (100° F) or lower than 36.1° C (97° F) and a falling systolic blood pressure, lower than 90 mm Hg, are usually considered reportable immediately. The client's preoperative or baseline blood pressure is used to make informed postoperative comparisons. Moderate or light serous drainage from the surgical site is considered normal.
Test-Taking Strategy: To answer this question correctly, you must know the normal ranges for temperature, blood pressure, urinary output, and wound drainage. Through the process of elimination, you then can determine that the urinary output is the only observation that is not within the normal range. Review these basic postoperative assessment findings if you had difficulty with this question.
Level of Cognitive Ability: Analysis
Client Needs: Physiological Integrity
Integrated Process: Nursing Process—planning
Content Area: Fundamental skills
Reference: Ignatavicius, D., & Workman, M. (2006). *Medical-surgical nursing: Critical thinking for collaborative care* (5th ed., pp. 344, 348). Philadelphia: W.B. Saunders.

9. **1**
Rationale: The most common postoperative respiratory problems are atelectasis, pneumonia, and pulmonary emboli. Pneumonia is the inflammation of lung tissue that causes productive cough, dyspnea, and lung crackles. Fluid imbalance can be a deficit or excess related to fluid loss or overload. Pulmonary edema usually results from failure of the left side of the heart and can be caused by medications or fluid overload. Carbon dioxide retention results from an inability to exhale carbon dioxide in conditions such as chronic obstructive pulmonary disease.
Test-Taking Strategy: Use the process of elimination. Focus on the relationship between the words *deep-breathe and cough* in the question and *pneumonia* in the correct option. Review the common postoperative complications if you had difficulty with this question.
Level of Cognitive Ability: Comprehension
Client Needs: Physiological Integrity
Integrated Process: Teaching and Learning
Content Area: Fundamental skills
Reference: Ignatavicius, D., & Workman, M. (2006). *Medical-surgical nursing: Critical thinking for collaborative care* (5th ed., pp. 248-349). Philadelphia: W.B. Saunders.

10. **3**
Rationale: A postoperative drain should not be curled tightly or obstructed in any way. This could prevent the drain from functioning properly. The nurse should check the tube or drain for

patency to provide an exit for the fluid or blood to promote healing. The nurse must use aseptic technique for emptying the drainage container or changing the dressing to avoid contamination of the wound. The nurse should monitor the drainage characteristics. Usually, the drainage from the wound is pale, red, and watery. Active bleeding will be bright red.

Test-Taking Strategy: Use the process of elimination, noting the strategy word *avoid*. Remember that surgical drains need to remain patent so that accumulated secretions can escape from the wound bed. If you had difficulty with this question, review nursing care for the client with a surgical drain.

Level of Cognitive Ability: Application
Client Needs: Physiological Integrity
Integrated Process: Nursing Process—implementation
Content Area: Fundamental skills
Reference: Ignatavicius, D., & Workman, M. (2006). *Medical-surgical nursing: Critical thinking for collaborative care* (5th ed., p. 346). Philadelphia: W.B. Saunders.

11. **4**

Rationale: If a client has a latex allergy, a cloth barrier should be applied to the client's arm under a blood pressure cuff to prevent skin contact with the cuff. Medications from glass ampules are safe to use, and medications from ampules with rubber stoppers are unsafe to use. Latex-safe intravenous tubing made of polyvinyl chloride should be used for the client with a latex allergy. Additionally, agency procedures should be followed for a client with a latex allergy; usually, a latex allergy cart containing latex-free supplies is kept in the client's room.

Test-Taking Strategy: Use the process of elimination, focusing on the subject of the question, latex allergy. Recalling the causes of a latex allergy will direct you easily to option 4. Review nursing interventions for the client with a latex allergy if you had difficulty with this question.

Level of Cognitive Ability: Application
Client Needs: Safe and Effective Care Environment
Integrated Process: Nursing Process—planning
Content Area: Fundamental skills
Reference: Lewis, S., Heitkemper, M., & Dirksen, S. (2004). *Medical-surgical nursing: Assessment and management of clinical problems* (6th ed., p. 253). St. Louis: Mosby.

12. **1**

Rationale: The nurse would assist the client to void immediately before surgery so that the bladder will be empty. A slight increase in blood pressure and pulse is common during the preoperative period and is usually the result of anxiety. The client usually has a restriction of food and fluids for 6 to 8 hours before surgery instead of 24 hours. Oral hygiene is allowed, but the client should not swallow any water.

Test-Taking Strategy: Use the process of elimination, and read each option carefully. Eliminate option 4 because of the words *immediately* and *slight*. Eliminate option 3, knowing that the client should be NPO for 6 to 8 hours before surgery. There is no useful reason for option 2; in fact, oral hygiene may make the client feel more comfortable. Review general preoperative care if you had difficulty with this question.

Level of Cognitive Ability: Application
Client Needs: Physiological Integrity
Integrated Process: Nursing Process—planning
Content Area: Fundamental skills

Reference: Ignatavicius, D., & Workman, M. (2006). *Medical-surgical nursing: Critical thinking for collaborative care* (5th ed., p. 313). Philadelphia: W.B. Saunders.

13. **4**

Rationale: The type of planning and instruction required varies with each individual and the type of surgery. Specific instructions that the client needs to receive before discharge should include wound care, activity restrictions, dietary instructions, postoperative medication instructions, personal hygiene, and follow-up appointments. Deep-breathing exercises are taught in the preoperative period.

Test-Taking Strategy: Use the process of elimination, noting the strategy words *least appropriate*. Options 1, 2, and 3 are comparative or alike and refer to information that needs to be taught postoperatively. Option 4 refers to information that should be taught preoperatively. Review the client education points related to discharge teaching preoperatively and postoperatively if you had difficulty with this question.

Level of Cognitive Ability: Application
Client Needs: Health Promotion and Maintenance
Integrated Process: Teaching and Learning
Content Area: Fundamental skills
Reference: Ignatavicius, D., & Workman, M. (2006). *Medical-surgical nursing: Critical thinking for collaborative care* (5th ed., pp. 354-355). Philadelphia: W.B. Saunders.

14. **3**

Rationale: To elicit Homans' sign, the nurse would dorsiflex the client's foot and assess the client for pain in the calf area. If pain is present, a positive Homans' sign is present, which is an indication of thrombophlebitis. Incisional pain is an expected occurrence after abdominal surgery. Absent bowel sounds may occur in the immediate postoperative period. Crackles on auscultation of the lungs may indicate a respiratory complication.

Test-Taking Strategy: Use the process of elimination and knowledge of the significance of a positive Homans' sign. Recalling that a positive Homans' sign indicates thrombophlebitis will direct you to option 3. Review this assessment technique if you had difficulty with this question.

Level of Cognitive Ability: Analysis
Client Needs: Physiological Integrity
Integrated Process: Nursing Process—assessment
Content Area: Fundamental skills
Reference: Potter, P., & Perry, A. (2005). *Fundamentals of nursing* (6th ed., p. 1442). St. Louis: Mosby.

15. **3**

Rationale: The client's extremities should not be allowed to dangle over the sides of the table because this may impair circulation to the local area or cause nerve and muscle damage. Part of the operating room nurse's role is to ensure that the safety needs of the client are met, which includes proper positioning.

Test-Taking Strategy: Use the process of elimination and knowledge regarding the basic principles related to positioning. Recalling that the client is anesthetized will direct you to option 3. Review the nurse's role during surgery if you had difficulty with this question.

Level of Cognitive Ability: Application
Client Needs: Physiological Integrity

Integrated Process: Teaching and Learning
Content Area: Fundamental skills
Reference: Potter, P., & Perry, A. (2005). *Fundamentals of nursing* (6th ed., p. 1627). St. Louis: Mosby.

16. **4**

Rationale: Every effort must be made to obtain permission from a responsible family member to perform surgery if the client is unable to sign the consent form. A telephone consent must be witnessed by two persons who hear the family member's oral consent. The two witnesses then sign the consent with the name of the family member, noting that an oral consent was obtained. Consent is not informed if it is obtained from a client who is confused, unconscious, mentally incompetent, or under the influence of sedatives. In an emergency, a client may be unable to sign and family members may not be available. In this situation, a physician is permitted legally to perform surgery without consent. Options 1 and 3 are not appropriate in this situation.
Test-Taking Strategy: Use the process of elimination. Note the strategy word *appropriate* in the question. Eliminate options 1 and 3 first. Option 1 will delay necessary surgery, and option 3 is inappropriate. Select option 4 over option 2 because it is the most appropriate of the options presented and it is legally acceptable to obtain a telephone permission from a family member if it is witnessed by two persons. Review the implications surrounding informed consent if you had difficulty with this question.
Level of Cognitive Ability: Application
Client Needs: Safe and Effective Care Environment
Integrated Process: Nursing Process—implementation
Content Area: Fundamental skills
Reference: Ignatavicius, D., & Workman, M. (2006). *Medical-surgical nursing: Critical thinking for collaborative care* (5th ed., p. 304). Philadelphia: W.B. Saunders.

17. **3**

Rationale: Explanations should begin with the information that the client knows. By providing the client with individualized explanations of care and procedures, the nurse can assist the client in handling anxiety and fear for a smooth preoperative experience. Clients who are calm and emotionally prepared for surgery withstand anesthesia better and experience fewer postoperative complications. Options 1, 2, and 4 will produce anxiety in the client.
Test-Taking Strategy: Use the process of elimination. Note that the question contains the strategy words *most likely* and *stimulate further discussion*. Use the steps of the nursing process and therapeutic communication techniques. Option 3 addresses assessment and is the only therapeutic response. If this question was difficult, review the fundamental principles of therapeutic communication.
Level of Cognitive Ability: Application
Client Needs: Psychosocial Integrity
Integrated Process: Communication and Documentation
Content Area: Fundamental skills
References: Ignatavicius, D., & Workman, M. (2006). *Medical-surgical nursing: Critical thinking for collaborative care* (5th ed., p. 312). Philadelphia: W.B. Saunders.
Potter, P., & Perry, A. (2005). *Fundamentals of nursing* (6th ed., p. 435). St. Louis: Mosby.

18. **4**

Rationale: For optimal lung expansion with the incentive spirometer, the client should assume the semi-Fowler's or high Fowler's position. The mouthpiece should be covered completely and tightly while the client inhales slowly, with a constant flow through the unit. The breath should be held for 5 seconds before exhaling slowly.
Test-Taking Strategy: Use the process of elimination and visualize the procedure for using the incentive spirometer. Options 1, 2, and 3 are incorrect steps regarding incentive spirometer use. If you had difficulty with this question, review the correct procedure related to the use of an incentive spirometer.
Level of Cognitive Ability: Application
Client Needs: Physiological Integrity
Integrated Process: Teaching and Learning
Content Area: Fundamental skills
Reference: Ignatavicius, D. & Workman, M. (2006). *Medical-surgical nursing: Critical thinking for collaborative care* (5th ed., p. 309). Philadelphia: W.B. Saunders.

19. **4**

Rationale: Anticoagulants alter normal clotting factors and increase the risk of bleeding after surgery. Aspirin has properties that can alter the clotting mechanism and should be discontinued at least 48 hours before surgery. Options 1, 2, and 3 are accurate client statements.
Test-Taking Strategy: Note the strategy words *the client needs additional teaching*. These words indicate a negative event query and you need to select the incorrect client statement. Eliminate options 1 and 2 first because they are comparative or alike. From the remaining options, recalling that aspirin has properties that can alter the clotting mechanism will direct you to option 4. If you had difficulty with this question, review medications that affect the client preparing for surgery.
Level of Cognitive Ability: Analysis
Client Needs: Physiological Integrity
Integrated Process: Teaching and Learning
Content Area: Pharmacology
Reference: Ignatavicius, D., & Workman, M. (2006). *Medical-surgical nursing: Critical thinking for collaborative care* (5th ed., p. 398). Philadelphia: W.B. Saunders.

20. **1**

Rationale: The nurse should ensure that the client has voided if a Foley catheter is not in place. The nurse does not administer all daily medications just before sending a client to the operating room. Rather, the physician writes a specific order outlining which medications may be given with a sip of water. The time of transfer to the operating room is not the time to practice breathing exercises. This should have been done earlier. The client has nothing by mouth for 6 to 8 hours before surgery, not 24 hours.
Test-Taking Strategy: Note that the question contains the strategic words *at this time*. This tells you that you must prioritize your answer according to a time line. With this in mind, eliminate options 2 and 4 first because they are incorrect. Choose correctly between the remaining options by knowing that the client must empty his or her bladder or by knowing that the client is likely to be anxious at this time, making it inappropriate to practice breathing exercises. Re-

view preoperative nursing interventions if you had difficulty with this question.

Level of Cognitive Ability: Application
Client Needs: Physiological Integrity
Integrated Process: Nursing Process—implementation
Content Area: Fundamental skills
Reference: Ignatavicius, D. & Workman, M. (2006). *Medical-surgical nursing: Critical thinking for collaborative care* (5th ed., p. 313). Philadelphia: W.B. Saunders.

ALTERNATE ITEM FORMAT: MULTIPLE RESPONSE

Answer: 1, 2, 3, 4
Rationale: Wound dehiscence is the separation of the wound edges. Wound evisceration is protrusion of the internal organs through an incision. If wound dehiscence or evisceration occurs, the surgeon is notified immediately. The client is placed in a low Fowler's position, kept quiet, and instructed not to cough. Protruding organs are covered with a sterile saline dressing. Ice is not applied because of its vasoconstrictive effect. The treatment for evisceration is immediate wound closure under local or general anesthesia. The nurse also documents the findings and actions taken.

Test-Taking Strategy: Focus on the information in the question to determine that the client is experiencing wound evisceration. Visualizing this occurrence will assist you in determining that the client would not be placed supine and that ice packs would not be placed on the incision. Review this surgical complication if you had difficulty with this question.

Level of Cognitive Ability: Application
Client Needs: Physiological Integrity
Integrated Process: Nursing Process—implementation
Content Area: Fundamental skills
Reference: Ignatavicius, D., & Workman, M. (2006). *Medical-surgical nursing: Critical thinking for collaborative care* (5th ed., pp. 346, 350-351). Philadelphia: W.B. Saunders.

REFERENCES

Black, J., & Hawks, J. (2005). *Medical-surgical nursing: Clinical management for positive outcomes* (7th ed.). Philadelphia: W.B. Saunders.

Chernecky, C., & Berger, B. (2004). *Laboratory tests and diagnostic procedures* (4th ed.). Philadelphia: W.B. Saunders.

Elkin, M., Perry, A., & Potter, P. (2004). *Nursing interventions and clinical skills* (3rd ed.). St. Louis: Mosby.

Ignatavicius, D., & Workman, M. (2006). *Medical-surgical nursing: Critical thinking for collaborative care* (5th ed.). Philadelphia: W.B. Saunders.

Lewis, S., Heitkemper, M., & Dirksen, S. (2004). *Medical-surgical nursing: Assessment and management of clinical problems* (6th ed.). St. Louis: Mosby.

National Council of State Boards of Nursing (Eds.). (2007). *2007 NCLEX-RN® detailed test plan.* Chicago: Author.

Phipps, W., Monahan, F., Sands, J. et al. (2003). *Medical-surgical nursing: Health and illness perspectives* (7th ed.). St. Louis: Mosby.

Potter, P., & Perry, A. (2005). *Fundamentals of nursing* (6th ed.). St. Louis: Mosby.

Positioning Clients

PYRAMID TERMS

body mechanics The coordinated efforts of the musculo-skeletal and nervous systems to maintain balance, posture, and body alignment during lifting, bending, and moving to perform activities safely.

ergonomic principles The anatomical, physiological, psychological, and mechanical principles affecting the efficient and safe use of an individual's energy.

Fowler's position The client is supine and the head of the bed is elevated to 45 to 60 degrees.

high Fowler's position The client is supine and the head of the bed is elevated to 90 degrees.

lateral (side-lying) position The client is lying on the side and the head and shoulders are aligned with the hips and the spine and are parallel to the edge of the mattress. The head, neck, and upper arm are supported by a pillow. The lower shoulder is pulled forward slightly and, along with the elbow, flexed at 90 degrees. The legs are flexed or extended. A pillow is placed to support the back.

lithotomy position The client is lying on the back with the hips and knees flexed at right angles and the feet in stirrups.

prone position The client is lying on the abdomen with head turned to the side.

reverse Trendelenburg's position The bed is tilted so that the client's foot of the bed is down.

semi-Fowler's position (low Fowler's) The client is supine and the head of the bed is elevated about 30 degrees.

Sims' position The client is lying on the side with the body turned prone at 45 degrees. The lower leg is extended, with the upper leg flexed at the hip and knee to a 45- to 90-degree angle.

supine position The client is lying on the back. The head and shoulders usually are elevated slightly with a small pillow. The arms and legs are extended, and the legs are slightly abducted.

Trendelenburg's position The bed is tilted so that the client's head of the bed is down. This position is contraindicated in clients with head injuries, increased intracranial pressure, spinal cord injuries, and certain respiratory and cardiac disorders.

THE PYRAMID TO SUCCESS

Nursing responsibility includes positioning clients safely and appropriately to provide safety and comfort. Knowledge regarding the client position required for a certain procedure or condition is expected. The nurse has the responsibility to reduce the likelihood and prevent the development of complications related to an existing condition, prescribed treatment, or medical or surgical procedure. The nurse must review the physician's orders after treatments or procedures and take note of instructions regarding positioning and mobility (Figs. 20-1 and 20-2). The nurse must also be aware of various body pressure points when clients are positioned in the lying or sitting position (Fig. 20-3). The Integrated Processes addressed in this chapter include Caring, Communication and Documentation, Nursing Process, and Teaching/Learning.

CLIENT NEEDS

Safe and Effective Care Environment

Establishing priorities
Ensuring environmental and personal safety
Ensuring home safety
Positioning the client appropriately and safely
Preventing accidents and injuries
Providing protective measures
Using equipment safely
Using ergonomic principles and body mechanics when moving a client

Health Promotion and Maintenance

Information regarding the need for prescribed therapies
Performing the techniques of physical assessment

Psychosocial Integrity

Assisting the client to use coping mechanisms
Keeping the family informed of client progress
Providing support to the client

Physiological Integrity

Assessing the mobility and immobility level of the client
Preventing the complications of immobility
Providing comfort measures for rest and sleep
Providing nutrition and oral intake
Providing personal hygiene as needed
Using assistive devices

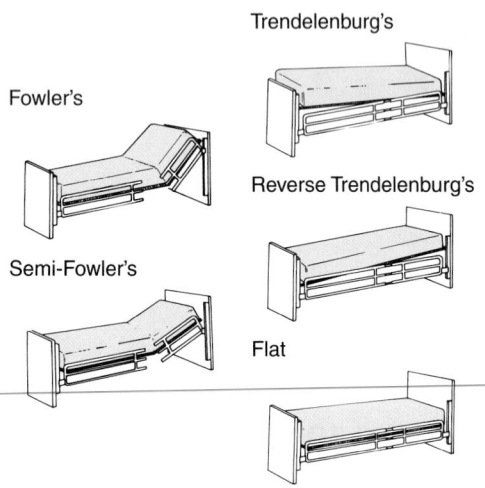

FIG. 20-1 Common bed positions. (Potter, P., & Perry, A. [2005]. *Fundamentals of nursing* [6th ed.]. St. Louis: Mosby.)

I. GUIDELINES FOR POSITIONING
A. Client safety and comfort
  1. Position in a safe and appropriate manner to provide safety and comfort
  2. Review the physician's orders, especially after treatments or procedures, and take note of instructions regarding positioning and mobility
  3. Select a position that will prevent the development of complications related to an existing condition, prescribed treatment, or medical or surgical procedure
B. **Ergonomic principles** related to **body mechanics** (Box 20-1)

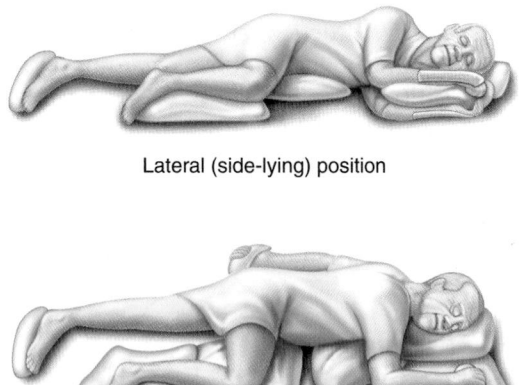

Semiprone (Sims' or forward side-lying) position

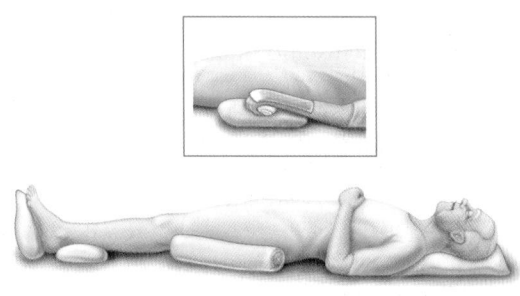

Supine position

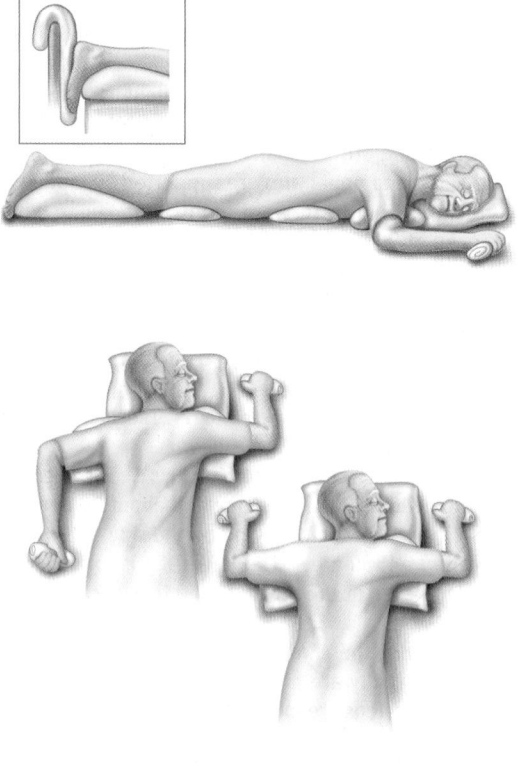

Prone position. The client's arms and shoulders may be positioned in internal or external rotation.

Lateral (side-lying) position

FIG. 20-2 Common client positions. (From Harkreader, H. & Hogan, M.A. [2004]. *Fundamentals of nursing: Caring and clinical judgment* [2nd ed.]. Philadelphia: W.B. Saunders.

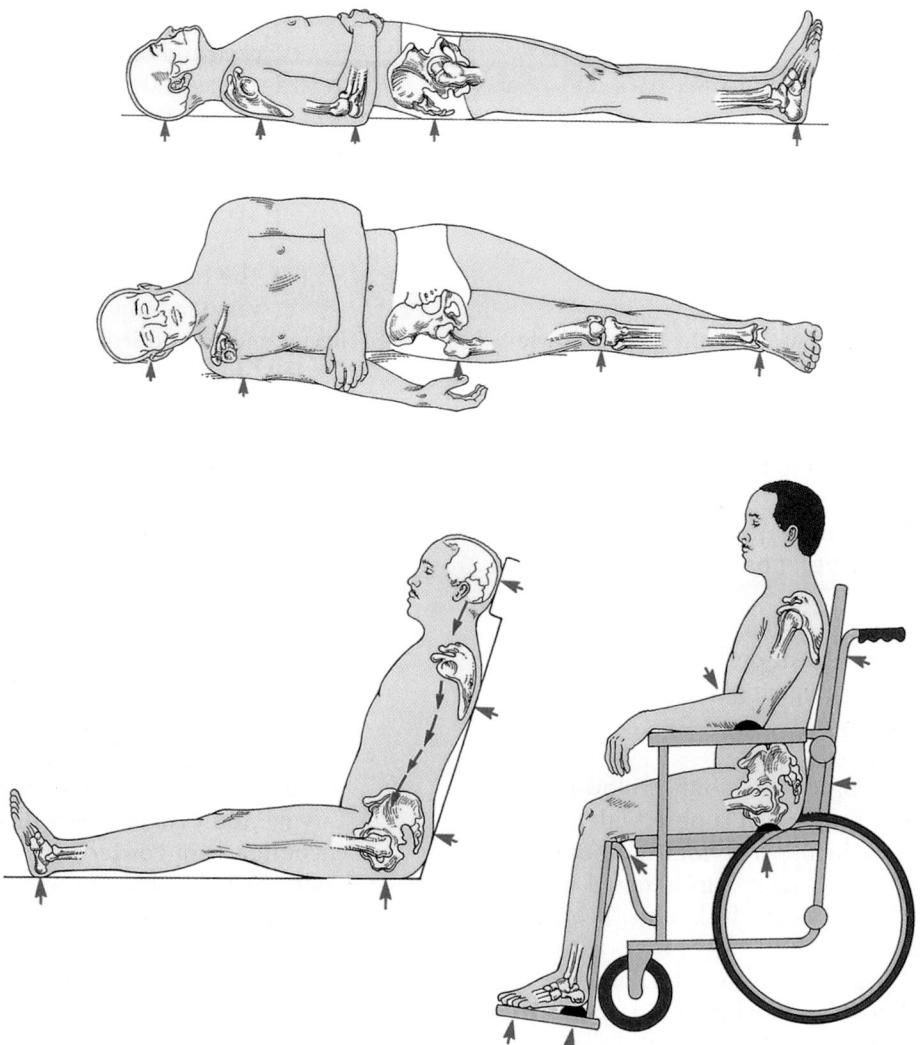

FIG. 20-3 Pressure points in lying and sitting position. (From Elkin, M., Perry, A., & Potter, P. [2004]. *Nursing interventions and clinical skills* [3rd ed]. St. Louis: Mosby)

II. POSITIONS TO ENSURE SAFETY AND COMFORT

A. Integumentary system

1. Autograft: After surgery, the site is immobilized for 3 to 7 days to provide the time needed for the graft to adhere and attach to the wound bed.

2. Burns of the face and head: Elevate the head of the bed to prevent or reduce facial, head, and tracheal edema.

3. Circumferential burns of the extremities: Elevate the extremities above the level of the heart to prevent or reduce dependent edema.

4. Skin graft: Elevate and immobilize the graft site to prevent movement and shearing of the graft and disruption of tissue; avoid weight-bearing.

B. Reproductive system

1. Mastectomy

a. Position the client with the head of the bed elevated at least 30 degrees (**semi-Fowler's position**), with the affected arm elevated on

a pillow to promote lymphatic fluid return after the removal of axillary lymph nodes.
  b. Turn the client only to the back and unaffected side.
  2. Perineal and vaginal procedures: Place the client in the **lithotomy position** (Fig. 20-4).
C. Endocrine system
  1. Hypophysectomy: Elevate the head of the bed to prevent increased intracranial pressure.
  2. Thyroidectomy
    a. Place the client in the **semi-Fowler's position** to reduce swelling and edema in the neck area.
    b. Sandbags or pillows may be used to support the client's head or neck.
D. Gastrointestinal system
  1. Hemorrhoidectomy: Assist the client to a **lateral (side-lying) position** to prevent pain and bleeding.
  2. Gastroesophageal reflux disease: **Reverse Trendelenburg's position** may be prescribed to promote gastric emptying and prevent esophageal reflux.
  3. Liver biopsy
    a. During the procedure, do the following:
      (1) Position the client **supine**, with the right side of the upper abdomen exposed.
      (2) The client's right arm is raised and extended over the left shoulder behind the head.
      (3) The liver is located on the right side, and this position provides for maximal exposure of the right intercostal space.
    b. After the procedure: do the following:
      (1) Assist the client into a right **lateral (side-lying) position**.
      (2) Place a small pillow or folded towel under the puncture site for at least 3 hours to provide pressure to the site and prevent bleeding.
  4. Nasogastric tube
    a. Insertion
      (1) Position the client in a **high Fowler's position** with the head tilted forward.

Lithotomy

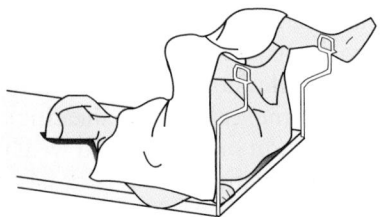

FIG. 20-4 Lithotomy position for examination. (From Potter, P., & Perry, A. [2005]. *Fundamentals of nursing* [6th ed.]. St. Louis: Mosby.)

      (2) This position will assist to close the trachea and open the esophagus.
    b. Irrigations and tube feedings
      (1) Elevate the head of the bed 30 degrees (**semi-Fowler's position**) to prevent aspiration.
      (2) Maintain head elevation for 1 hour after an intermittent feeding.
      (3) The head of the bed should remain elevated for continuous feedings.
  5. Rectal enema and irrigations: Place the client in the left **Sims' position** to allow the solution to flow by gravity in the natural direction of the colon.
  6. Sengstaken-Blakemore and Minnesota tubes: Maintain elevation of the head of the bed to enhance lung expansion and reduce portal blood flow, permitting effective compression of the esophageal varices.
E. Respiratory system
  1. Chronic obstructive pulmonary disease: In advanced disease, place the client in a sitting position, leaning forward, with the client's arms over several pillows or an overbed table; this position will assist the client to breathe easier.
  2. Laryngectomy (radical neck dissection): Place the client in a **semi-Fowler's** or **Fowler's position** to maintain a patent airway and minimize edema.
  3. Bronchoscopy postprocedure: Place the client in a **semi-Fowler's position** to prevent choking or aspiration resulting from an impaired ability to swallow.
  4. Postural drainage: The lung segment to be drained should be in the uppermost position; **Trendelenburg's position** may be used.
  5. Thoracentesis
    a. During the procedure, to facilitate removal of fluid from the chest wall, position the client sitting on the edge of the bed and leaning over the bedside table, with the feet supported on a stool, or lying in bed on the unaffected side with the head of the bed elevated about 45 degrees (**Fowler's position**).
    b. After the procedure, assist the client to a position of comfort.
  6. Thoracotomy: Check physician's orders regarding positioning.
F. Cardiovascular system
  1. Abdominal aneurysm resection
    a. After surgery, limit elevation of the head of the bed to 45 degrees (**Fowler's position**) to avoid flexion of the graft.
    b. The client may be turned from side to side.
  2. Amputation of the lower extremity
    a. During the first 24 hours after amputation, elevate the foot of the bed (the stump is sup-

ported with pillows but not elevated because of the risk of flexion contractures) to reduce edema.

b. Consult with the physician and, if prescribed, position the client in a **prone position** twice a day for a 20- to 30-minute period to stretch muscles and prevent flexion contractures of the hip.

3. Arterial vascular grafting of an extremity
   a. To promote graft patency after the procedure, bed rest usually is maintained for about 24 hours and the affected extremity is kept straight.
   b. Limit movement and avoid flexion of the hip and knee.

4. Cardiac catheterization
   a. If the femoral artery was accessed for the procedure, the client is maintained on bed rest for 3 to 4 hours; the client may turn from side to side.
   b. The affected extremity is kept straight and the head is elevated no more than 30 degrees until hemostasis is adequately achieved.

5. Congestive heart failure and pulmonary edema: Position the client upright, preferably with the legs dangling over the side of the bed, to decrease venous return and lung congestion.

6. Peripheral arterial disease
   a. Obtain the physician's order for positioning.
   b. Because swelling can prevent arterial blood flow, clients may be advised to elevate their feet at rest, but they should not raise their legs above the level of the heart because extreme elevation slows arterial blood flow; some clients may be advised to maintain a slightly dependent position to promote perfusion.

7. Deep vein thrombosis
   a. If the extremity is red, edematous, and painful, and traditional heparin sodium therapy is initiated, bed rest with leg elevation may be prescribed for the client.
   b. Clients receiving low-molecular-weight heparin usually can be out of bed after 24 hours if pain level permits.

8. Varicose veins: Leg elevation above heart level usually is prescribed; the client also is advised to minimize prolonged sitting or standing during daily activities.

9. Venous insufficiency and leg ulcers: Leg elevation usually is prescribed.

G. Sensory system
   1. Cataract surgery: Postoperatively, elevate the head of the bed (**semi-Fowler's** to **Fowler's position**) and position the client on the back or the non-operative side to prevent the development of edema at the operative site.

   2. Retinal detachment
      a. If the detachment is large, bed rest and bilateral eye patching may be prescribed to minimize eye movement and prevent extension of the detachment.
      b. Restrictions in activity and positioning following repair of the detachment depends on the physician's preference and the surgical procedure performed.

H. Neurological system
   1. Autonomic dysreflexia: Elevate the head of the bed to a **high Fowler's position** to assist with adequate ventilation and assist in the prevention of hypertensive stroke.

   2. Cerebral aneurysm: Bed rest is maintained with the head of the bed elevated 30 to 45 degrees (**semi-Fowler's** to **Fowler's position**) to prevent pressure on the aneurysm site.

   3. Cerebral angiography
      a. Maintain bed rest for 12 to 24 hours as prescribed.
      b. The extremity into which the contrast medium was injected is kept straight and immobilized for about 8 hours.

   4. Brain attack (stroke)
      a. In clients with hemorrhagic strokes, the head of the bed is elevated to 30 degrees to reduce intracranial pressure and to facilitate venous drainage.
      b. For clients with ischemic strokes, the head of the bed is kept flat.
      c. Maintain the head in a midline, neutral position to facilitate venous drainage from the head.
      d. Avoid extreme hip and neck flexion; extreme hip flexion may increase intrathoracic pressure, whereas extreme neck flexion prohibits venous drainage from the brain.

   5. Craniotomy
      a. The client should not be positioned on the site that was operated on, especially if the bone flap has been removed, because the brain has no bony covering on the affected site.
      b. Elevate the head of the bed 30 to 45 degrees (**semi-Fowler's** to **Fowler's position**) and maintain the head in a midline, neutral position to facilitate venous drainage from the head.
      c. Avoid extreme hip and neck flexion.

   6. Laminectomy
      a. Logroll the client.
      b. When the client is out of bed, the client's back is kept straight (the client is placed in a

straight-backed chair) with the feet resting comfortably on the floor.

7. Increased intracranial pressure
   a. Elevate the head of the bed 30 to 45 degrees (**semi-Fowler's** to **Fowler's position**) and maintain the head in a midline, neutral position to facilitate venous drainage from the head.
   b. Avoid extreme hip and neck flexion.

8. Lumbar puncture
   a. During the procedure, assist the client to the **lateral (side-lying) position**, with the back bowed at the edge of the examining table, the knees flexed up to the abdomen, and the neck flexed so that the chin is resting on the chest.
   b. After the procedure, place the client in the **supine position** for 4 to 12 hours, as prescribed.

9. Myelogram postprocedure
   a. The head position varies according to the dye used.
   b. The head is usually elevated if an oil-based or water-soluble contrast agent is used and the head is usually positioned lower than the trunk if air contrast is used.

10. Spinal cord injury
    a. Immobilize the client on a spinal backboard, with the head in a neutral position, to prevent incomplete injury from becoming complete.
    b. Prevent head flexion, rotation, or extension; the head is immobilized with a firm, padded cervical collar.
    c. Logroll the client; no part of the body should be twisted or turned, nor should the client be allowed to assume a sitting position.

I. Musculoskeletal system
   1. Total hip replacement
      a. Positioning depends on the surgical techniques used, the method of implantation, and the prosthesis.
      b. Avoid extreme internal and external rotation.
      c. Avoid adduction; side-lying on the operative side is not allowed (unless specifically prescribed by the physician).
      d. Maintain abduction when the client is in a **supine position** or positioned on the nonoperative side.
      e. Place a pillow between the client's legs to maintain abduction; instruct the client not to cross the legs (see Box 20-2).

BOX 20-2
Devices Used for Proper Positioning

PILLOWS
Pillows provide support, elevate body parts, splint incisional areas, and reduce postoperative pain during activity, coughing, or deep-breathing. They should be of the appropriate size for the body part to be positioned.

FOOT BOOTS
Foot boots are made of rigid plastic or heavy foam and keep the foot flexed at the proper angle. They should be removed two or three times a day to assess skin integrity and joint mobility.

TROCHANTER ROLL
These rolls prevent external rotation of the legs when the client is in the supine position. To form a roll, use a cotton bath blanket or a sheet folded lengthwise to a width extending from the greater trochanter of the femur to the lower border of the popliteal space.

SANDBAGS
Sandbags are filled plastic tubes that can be shaped to body contours to provide support. They immobilize extremities and maintain specific body alignment.

HAND ROLLS
Hand rolls maintain the fingers in a slightly flexed and functional position and keep the thumb slightly adducted in opposition to the fingers.

HAND-WRIST SPLINTS
These splints are individually molded for the client to maintain proper alignment of the thumb in slight adduction and the wrist in slight dorsiflexion.

TRAPEZE BAR
This bar descends from a securely fastened overhead bar attached to the bed frame. It allows the client to use the upper extremities to raise the trunk off the bed, assists in transfer from the bed to a wheelchair, and helps the client perform upper arm strengthening exercises.

SIDE RAILS
These bars, positioned along the sides of the length of the bed, ensure client safety and are useful for increasing mobility. They also provide assistance in rolling from side to side or sitting up in bed.

BED BOARDS
These plywood boards are placed under the entire surface area of the mattress and are useful for increasing back support and body alignment.

WEDGE PILLOW
This triangular pillow is made of heavy foam and is used to maintain the legs in abduction following total hip replacement surgery.

Modified from Potter, P., & Perry, A. (2001). *Fundamentals of nursing* (5th ed.). St. Louis: Mosby.

f. Check the physician's orders regarding elevation of the head of the bed; flexion usually is limited to 60 degrees during the first postoperative week (usually 90 degrees for 2 to 3 months thereafter).

2. Devices used for proper positioning (Box 20-2)

PRACTICE QUESTIONS

1. The nurse is caring for a client who is 1 day postoperative for a total hip replacement. Which is the best position in which the nurse should place the client?
   1. Side-lying on the operative side
   2. On the nonoperative side with the legs abducted.
   3. Side-lying with the affected leg internally rotated
   4. Side-lying with the affected leg externally rotated

2. A nurse is providing instructions to a client and the family regarding home care after right eye cataract removal. Which statement by the client would indicate an understanding of the instructions?
   1. "I will not sleep on my left side."
   2. "I will not sleep on my right side."
   3. "I will not sleep with my head elevated."
   4. "I will not wear my glasses until my physician says it is okay."

3. A nurse assists a physician in performing a liver biopsy. After the biopsy, the nurse places the client in which position?
   1. Prone
   2. Supine
   3. A left side-lying position with a small pillow or folded towel under the puncture site
   4. A right side-lying position with a small pillow or folded towel under the puncture site

4. A nurse is administering a cleansing enema to a client with a fecal impaction. Before administering the enema, the nurse places the client in which position?
   1. Left Sims' position
   2. Right Sims' position
   3. On the left side of the body, with the head of the bed elevated 45 degrees
   4. On the right side of the body, with the head of the bed elevated 45 degrees

5. A client is being prepared for a thoracentesis. A nurse assists the client to which position for the procedure?
   1. Lying in bed on the affected side
   2. Lying in bed on the unaffected side
   3. Sims' position with the head of the bed flat
   4. Prone with the head turned to the side and supported by a pillow

6. A nurse is preparing to insert a nasogastric tube into a client. The nurse places the client in which position for insertion?
   1. Right side
   2. Low Fowler's
   3. High Fowler's
   4. Supine with the head flat

7. A client is diagnosed with deep vein thrombophlebitis. A nurse develops a plan of care for the client and includes which client position or activity in the plan?
   1. Out-of-bed activities as desired
   2. Bed rest with the affected extremity kept flat
   3. Bed rest with elevation of the affected extremity
   4. Bed rest with the affected extremity in a dependent position

8. A client has just returned to a nursing unit after an above-knee amputation of the right leg. A nurse places the client in which position?
   1. Prone
   2. Reverse Trendelenburg's
   3. Supine, with the amputated limb flat on the bed
   4. Supine, with the amputated limb supported with pillows

9. A nurse is caring for a client with a severe burn who is scheduled for an autograft to be placed on the lower extremity. The nurse develops a postoperative plan of care for the client and includes which of the following in the plan?
   1. Maintain the client in a prone position.
   2. Elevate and immobilize the grafted extremity.
   3. Maintain the surgical extremity in a flat position.
   4. Keep the surgical extremity covered with a blanket.

10. A nurse is preparing to care for a client who has returned to the nursing unit following cardiac catheterization performed through the femoral artery. The nurse plans to allow which client position or activity following the procedure?
   1. Bed rest in high Fowler's position
   2. Bed rest with bathroom privileges only
   3. Bed rest with head elevation at 60 degrees
   4. Bed rest with head elevation no greater than 30 degrees

ALTERNATE ITEM FORMAT: MULTIPLE RESPONSE

The nurse is caring for a client following a supratentorial craniotomy in which a large tumor was removed from the left side. Select the positions in which the nurse can safely place the client.

❏ 1. On the left side
❏ 2. With the neck flexed
❏ 3. Supine on the left side
❏ 4. With extreme hip flexion
❏ 5. In a semi-Fowler's position
❏ 6. With the head in a midline position

ANSWERS

1. **2**

Rationale: Positioning following a total hip replacement depends on the surgical techniques used, the method of implantation, the prosthesis, and physician's preference. Abduction is maintained when the client is in a supine position or positioned on the nonoperative side. Internal and external rotation, adduction, or side-lying on the operative side (unless specifically prescribed by the physician) is avoided. Options 1, 3, and 4 are incorrect positions for this client.

Test-Taking Strategy: Use the process of elimination and knowledge regarding care of clients following total hip replacement to answer this question. Options 3 and 4 can be eliminated first because of the words *internally rotated* and *externally rotated*. From the remaining options, eliminate option 1 because lying on the operative side can disrupt the replacement. Review positioning after total hip replacement if you had difficulty with this question.

Level of Cognitive Ability: Application
Client Needs: Physiological Integrity
Integrated Process: Nursing Process—planning
Content Area: Fundamental skills
Reference: Ignatavicius, D., & Workman, M. (2006). *Medical surgical nursing: Critical thinking for collaborative care* (5th ed., p. 387). Philadelphia: W.B. Saunders.

2. **2**

Rationale: After cataract surgery, the client should not sleep on the side of the body that was operated on. The client also should be placed in a semi-Fowler's position to assist in minimizing edema and intraocular pressure. During the day, the client may wear glasses or a protective shield; at night, the protective shield alone is sufficient.

Test-Taking Strategy: Use the process of elimination. Remember to instruct the client to remain off the operative side and to rest with the head elevated to minimize edema formation. This will assist you when answering questions related to cataract surgery. Review postoperative instructions for the client following cataract surgery if you had difficulty with this question.

Level of Cognitive Ability: Analysis
Client Needs: Physiological Integrity
Integrated Process: Nursing Process—evaluation
Content Area: Fundamental skills
Reference: Ignatavicius, D., & Workman, M. (2006). *Medical-surgical nursing: Critical thinking for collaborative care* (5th ed., p. 1951). Philadelphia: W.B. Saunders.

3. **4**

Rationale: After a liver biopsy, the client is assisted to assume a right side-lying position with a small pillow or folded towel under the puncture site for 3 hours. This position compresses the liver against the chest wall at the biopsy site. Therefore, options 1, 2, and 3 are incorrect.

Test-Taking Strategy: Use the process of elimination and knowledge regarding the anatomy of the body to answer this question. Remember that the liver is on the right side of the body, and that the application of pressure on the right side will minimize the escape of blood or bile through the punc-

ture site. Review care for the client following a liver biopsy if you had difficulty with this question.

Level of Cognitive Ability: Application
Client Needs: Physiological Integrity
Integrated Process: Nursing Process—implementation
Content Area: Fundamental skills
Reference: Pagana, K., & Pagana, T. (2005). *Mosby's diagnostic and laboratory test reference* (7th ed., p. 597). St. Louis: Mosby.

4. **1**

Rationale: For administering an enema, the client is placed in a left Sims' position so that the enema solution can flow by gravity in the natural direction of the colon. The head of the bed is not elevated in the Sims' position.

Test-Taking Strategy: Use the process of elimination and knowledge regarding the anatomy of the bowel to answer the question. This will assist in eliminating options 2 and 4. Visualize the procedure for administering an enema and eliminate option 3 because the head of the bed should be flat during enema administration. Review the procedure for administering an enema if you had difficulty with this question.

Level of Cognitive Ability: Application
Client Needs: Physiological Integrity
Integrated Process: Nursing Process—implementation
Content Area: Fundamental skills
Reference: Potter, P., & Perry, A. (2005). *Fundamentals of nursing* (6th ed., p. 1339). St. Louis: Mosby.

5. **2**

Rationale: To facilitate removal of fluid from the chest wall, the client is positioned sitting at the edge of the bed leaning over the bedside table, with the feet supported on a stool or lying in bed on the unaffected side with the head of the bed elevated 30 to 45 degrees. The prone and Sims' positions are inappropriate positions for this procedure.

Test-Taking Strategy: Use the process of elimination. Eliminate option 1 first because, if the client were lying on the affected side, it would be difficult to perform the procedure. Option 3 can be eliminated next because the Sims' position is used primarily for rectal enemas or irrigations. Next, visualize the prone position. In the prone position, the client is lying on the abdomen, which is not an appropriate position for this procedure. Review the procedure for a thoracentesis if you had difficulty with this question.

Level of Cognitive Ability: Application
Client Needs: Physiological Integrity
Integrated Process: Nursing Process—implementation
Content Area: Fundamental skills
References: Chernecky, C., & Berger, B. (2004). *Laboratory tests and diagnostic procedures* (4th ed., p. 1043). Philadelphia: W.B. Saunders.
Potter, P., & Perry, A. (2005). *Fundamentals of nursing* (6th ed., p. 1090). St. Louis: Mosby.

6. **3**

Rationale: During insertion of a nasogastric tube, the client is placed in a sitting or high Fowler's position to reduce the risk of pulmonary aspiration if the client should vomit. Options 1, 2, and 4 will not facilitate insertion of the tube or prevent aspiration.

Test-Taking Strategy: Use the process of elimination. Recalling that a concern with insertion of a nasogastric tube is pulmonary aspiration will direct you to option 3. Review the procedure for inserting a nasogastric tube if you had difficulty with this question.

Level of Cognitive Ability: Application
Client Needs: Physiological Integrity
Integrated Process: Nursing Process—implementation
Content Area: Fundamental skills
Reference: Potter, P., & Perry, A. (2005). *Fundamentals of nursing* (6th ed., p. 1043). St. Louis: Mosby.

7. **3**

Rationale: Elevation of the affected leg facilitates blood flow by the force of gravity and also decreases venous pressure, which in turn relieves edema and pain. Bed rest is indicated to prevent emboli and to prevent pressure fluctuations in the venous system that occur with walking.

Test-Taking Strategy: Use the process of elimination. Focus on the client's diagnosis and think about the principles related to gravity flow and edema to answer the question. If you had difficulty with this question, review nursing care for clients with a venous disorder.

Level of Cognitive Ability: Application
Client Needs: Physiological Integrity
Integrated Process: Nursing Process—planning
Content Area: Fundamental skills
Reference: Ignatavicius, D., & Workman, M. (2006). *Medical-surgical nursing: Critical thinking for collaborative care* (5th ed., p. 813). Philadelphia: W.B. Saunders.

8. **4**

Rationale: The amputated limb is supported on pillows for the first 24 hours following surgery to promote venous return and decrease edema. After the first 24 hours, the amputated limb usually is placed flat on the bed to reduce hip contracture. Edema also is controlled by limb-wrapping techniques. Options 1, 2, and 3 are inappropriate positions for the client immediately after surgery.

Test-Taking Strategy: Use the process of elimination. The subject of this question is that the client has just returned from surgery. Using basic principles related to immediate postoperative care will assist in directing you to option 4. If you had difficulty with this question, review postoperative positioning following amputation.

Level of Cognitive Ability: Application
Client Needs: Physiological Integrity
Integrated Process: Nursing Process—implementation
Content Area: Fundamental skills
References: Black, J., & Hawks, J. (2005). *Medical-surgical nursing: Clinical management for positive outcomes* (7th ed., p. 1524). Philadelphia: W.B. Saunders.
Ignatavicius, D., & Workman, M. (2006). *Medical-surgical nursing: Critical thinking for collaborative care* (5th ed., p. 1221). Philadelphia: W.B. Saunders.

9. **2**

Rationale: Autografts placed over joints or on lower extremities are elevated and immobilized following surgery for 3 to 7 days, depending on the surgeon's preference. This period of immobilization allows the autograft time to adhere and attach to the wound bed, and the elevation minimizes edema. Keeping the client in a prone position and covering the extremity with a blanket can disrupt the graft site.

Test-Taking Strategy: Use the process of elimination. Options 1 and 4 can be eliminated first because a prone position and a blanket can disrupt a graft easily. From the remaining options, recall the principles related to gravity and edema to assist in directing you to option 2. Review care for the client following an autograft if you had difficulty with this question.

Level of Cognitive Ability: Application
Client Needs: Physiological Integrity
Integrated Process: Nursing Process—planning
Content Area: Fundamental skills
Reference: Ignatavicius, D., & Workman, M. (2006). *Medical-surgical nursing: Critical thinking for collaborative care* (5th ed., p. 1646). Philadelphia: W.B. Saunders.

10. **4**

Rationale: After cardiac catheterization, the extremity into which the catheter was inserted is kept straight for 4 to 6 hours. If the femoral artery was used, bed rest is enforced for 3 to 4 hours (or as prescribed by the physician). The client may turn from side to side. The affected leg is kept straight and the head is elevated no more than 30 degrees until hemostasis is adequately achieved.

Test-Taking Strategy: Use the process of elimination. Knowing that the head of the bed should not be elevated more than 30 degrees will assist in eliminating options 1 and 3. Remembering that bathroom privileges are not allowed in the immediate postcatheterization period will assist in eliminating option 2. If you had difficulty with this question, review care after cardiac catheterization.

Level of Cognitive Ability: Application
Client Needs: Physiological Integrity
Integrated Process: Nursing Process—planning
Content Area: Fundamental skills
Reference: Ignatavicius, D., & Workman, M. (2006). *Medical-surgical nursing: Critical thinking for collaborative care* (5th ed., p. 698). Philadelphia: W.B. Saunders.

ALTERNATE ITEM FORMAT: MULTIPLE RESPONSE

Answer: 5, 6
Rationale: Clients who have undergone supratentorial surgery should have the head of the bed elevated 30 degrees to promote venous drainage from the head. The client is positioned to avoid extreme hip or neck flexion and the head is maintained in a midline neutral position. If a large tumor has been removed, the client should be placed on the nonoperative side to prevent displacement of the cranial contents.

Test-Taking Strategy: Focus on the data in the question. Remember that a primary concern is the risk for increased intra-

cranial pressure. Therefore, use concepts related to preventing increased intracranial pressure to answer this question. Also remember that with "supra"tentorial surgery the head is kept "up" and that the client is placed on the nonoperative side. Review positioning for a client after craniotomy if you had difficulty with this question.
Level of Cognitive Ability: Application
Client Needs: Physiological Integrity

Integrated Process: Nursing Process—implementation
Content Area: Adult health—neurological
Reference: Ignatavicius, D., & Workman, M. (2006). *Medical-surgical nursing: Critical thinking for collaborative care* (4th ed., p. 1058). Philadelphia: W.B. Saunders.

REFERENCES

Black, J., & Hawks, J. (2005). *Medical-surgical nursing: Clinical management for positive outcomes.* (7th ed.). Philadelphia: W.B. Saunders.

Chernecky, C., & Berger, B. (2004). *Laboratory tests and diagnostic procedures* (4th ed.). Philadelphia: W.B. Saunders.

Elkin, M., Perry, A., & Potter, P. (2004). *Nursing interventions and clinical skills* (3rd ed.). St. Louis: Mosby.

Harkreader, H., & Hogan, M.A. (2004). *Fundamentals of nursing: Caring and clinical judgment* (2nd ed.). Philadelphia: W.B. Saunders.

Ignatavicius, D., & Workman, M. (2006). *Medical-surgical nursing: Critical thinking for collaborative care* (5th ed.). Philadelphia: W.B. Saunders.

National Council of State Boards of Nursing (Eds.). (2007). *2007 NCLEX-RN® detailed test plan.* Chicago: Author.

Pagana, K., & Pagana, T. (2005). *Mosby's diagnostic and laboratory test reference* (7th ed.). St. Louis: Mosby.

Potter, P., & Perry, A. (2005). *Fundamentals of nursing* (6th ed.). St. Louis: Mosby.

Care of a Client With a Tube

PYRAMID TERMS

chest tube Tube that returns negative pressure to the intra-pleural space; used to remove abnormal accumulations of air and fluid from the pleural space.

endotracheal tube Tube used to maintain a patent airway; indicated when a client needs mechanical ventilation.

gastrointestinal intubation Insertion of a tube into the stomach or intestine.

intestinal tube Tube passed nasally and designed so that it enters the small intestine through the pyloric sphincter because of the weight of a small bag filled with a special substance at the end of the tube; used to decompress the bowel or to remove intestinal contents.

Sengstaken-Blakemore tube Triple-lumen gastric tube with an inflatable esophageal balloon, an inflatable gastric balloon, and a gastric aspiration lumen; used as a treatment modality for a client with esophageal varices.

tracheostomy Artificial opening created into the trachea to establish an airway.

▲ THE PYRAMID TO SUCCESS

The Pyramid to Success focuses on the common types of tubes used in the clinical setting. The NCLEX-RN examination is likely to address content areas related to the appropriate care of certain tubes and the immediate interventions required if a complication arises. Focus on the specific assessment points related to the specific type of tube. Review procedures for inserting a particular tube, verifying correct placement, and administering medications or feedings, if appropriate. Pyramid Points also focus on interventions associated with complications or emergencies that may occur. The Integrated Processes addressed in this chapter include Caring, Communication and Documentation, Nursing Process, and Teaching/Learning.

CLIENT NEEDS ▲

Safe and Effective Care Environment

Acting as a client advocate
Collaborating with members of the health care team
Ensuring that advance directives are in the client's medical record
Ensuring client's rights
Establishing priorities
Handling of infectious materials
Maintaining medical and surgical asepsis
Maintaining standard and other precautions
Obtaining informed consent for invasive procedures

Health Promotion and Maintenance

Assisting the client to accept lifestyle changes
Preventing disease
Providing client and family education regarding care at home
Performing the techniques of physical assessment

Psychosocial Integrity

Discussing situational role changes
Discussing unexpected body image changes
Identifying support systems
Monitoring for sensory and perceptual alterations
Providing home care services

Physiological Integrity

Administering medications
Initiating emergency interventions for complications
Implementing measures to ensure basic care and comfort
Monitoring for potential complications associated with the tube

Monitoring laboratory values

Preparing for diagnostic tests to confirm accurate placement of tube

Providing nutrition and oral hydration

Providing respiratory care

I. NASOGASTRIC TUBES

A. Description
   1. These are short tubes used to intubate the stomach.
   2. The tube is inserted from the nose to the stomach.

B. Purpose
   1. To decompress the stomach by removing fluids and/or gas to promote abdominal comfort
   2. To allow surgical anastomoses to heal without distention
   3. To decrease the risk of aspiration
   4. To administer medications to clients who are unable to swallow
   5. To provide nutrition by acting as a temporary feeding tube
   6. To irrigate the stomach and remove toxic substances, such as in poisoning

C. Types of tubes
   1. Levin tube (Fig. 21-1)
      a. Single-lumen nasogastric tube
      b. Used to remove gastric contents via intermittent suction or to provide tube feedings
   2. Salem sump tube (see Fig. 21-1)
      a. A Salem sump is a double-lumen nasogastric tube with an air vent (pigtail) used for decompression with continuous suction.
      b. The air vent is not to be clamped and is to be kept above the level of the stomach.
      c. If leakage occurs through the air vent, instill 30 mL of air into the air vent and irrigate the main lumen with normal saline (NS).

D. Intubation procedures (Box 21-1)

E. Irrigation
   1. Assess placement before irrigating.
   2. Perform irrigation every 4 hours to assess and maintain the patency of the tube.
   3. Gently instill 30 to 50 mL of water or NS (depending on agency policy) with an irrigation syringe.
   4. Pull back on the syringe plunger to withdraw the fluid to check patency; repeat if the tube flow is sluggish.

F. Removal of a nasogastric tube: Ask the client to take a deep breath and hold; remove the tube slowly and evenly over the course of 3 to 6 seconds (coil the tube around the hand while removing it).

II. GASTROINTESTINAL TUBE FEEDINGS

A. Types of tubes and anatomical placement
   1. Nasogastric: Nose to stomach
   2. Nasoduodenal-nasojejunal: Nose to duodenum or jejunum
   3. Gastrostomy: Stomach
   4. Jejunostomy: Jejunum

B. Types of administration
   1. Bolus
      a. A bolus resembles normal meal feeding patterns.
      b. Administration consists of 300 to 400 mL of formula given over a 30- to 60-minute period every 3 to 6 hours.
   2. Continuous
      a. Feeding is administered continually for 24 hours.
      b. An infusion pump regulates the flow.
   3. Cyclical
      a. Feeding is administered in the daytime or nighttime for 8 to 16 hours.
      b. An infusion pump regulates the flow.
      c. Feedings at night allow for more freedom during the day.

C. Administration of feedings
   1. Check the physician's order and agency policy regarding residual amounts; usually, if the residual is less than 100 mL, feeding is administered; large-volume aspirates indicate delayed gastric emptying and place the client at risk for aspiration.
   2. Assess bowel sounds; hold the feeding and notify the physician if bowel sounds are absent.
   3. Position the client in a high Fowler's position and on the right side if comatose.
   4. Assess tube placement by aspirating gastric contents and measuring the pH (should be 3.5 or lower).
   5. Aspirate all stomach contents (residual), measure the amount, and return the contents to the stomach to prevent electrolyte imbalances.
   6. Warm the feeding to room temperature to prevent diarrhea and cramps.
   7. Use a feeding pump for continuous or cyclic feedings.
   8. For bolus feeding, maintain the client in a high Fowler's position for 30 minutes after the feeding.
   9. For a continuous feeding, keep the client in a semi-Fowler's position at all times.

D. Precautions
   1. Always assess placement of the tube before feeding.
   2. Change the feeding container and tubing every 24 hours.
   3. Do not hang more solution than will be required for a 4-hour period to prevent bacterial growth.

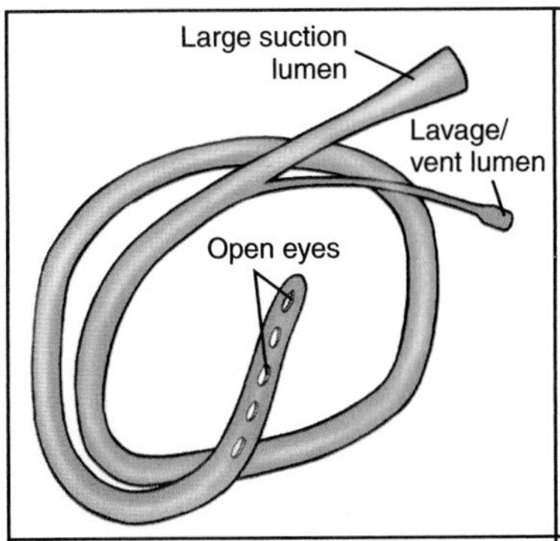

Large suction lumen / Lavage/ vent lumen / Open eyes	**Lavacuator tube** An orogastric tube with a large suction lumen and a smaller lavage/vent lumen that provides continuous suction because irrigating solution enters the lavage lumen while stomach contents are removed through the suction lumen. Used to remove toxic substances from the stomach.
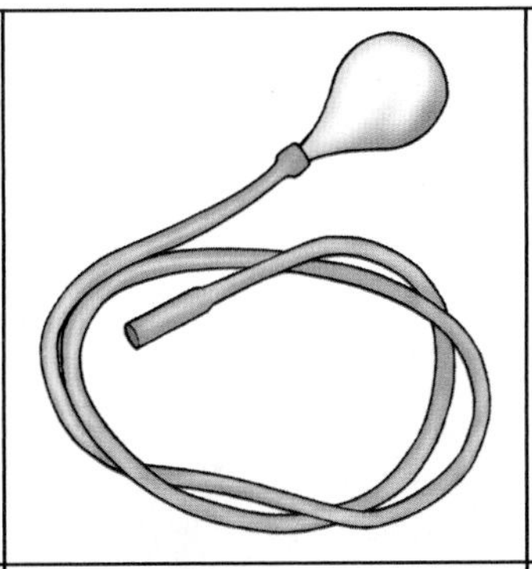	**Cantor tube** A single-lumen long tube with a small inflatable bag at the distal end. A special substance is injected with a needle (gauge 21 or smaller or balloon may leak) and syringe into the bag of the tube.
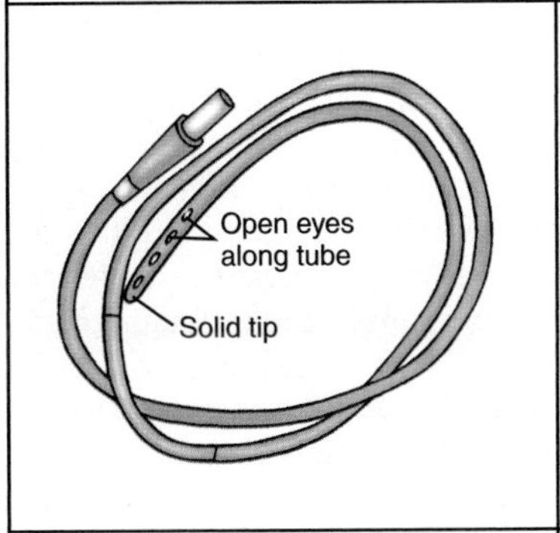 Open eyes along tube / Solid tip	**Levin tube** A plastic or rubber single-lumen tube with a solid tip that may be inserted into the stomach via the nose or mouth. Used to drain fluid and gas from the stomach. Single lumen must be used for irrigation and drainage, so continuous irrigation is not possible.
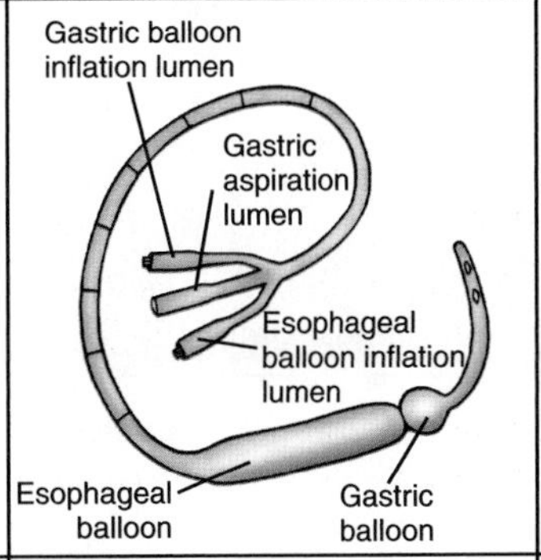 Gastric balloon inflation lumen / Gastric aspiration lumen / Esophageal balloon inflation lumen / Esophageal balloon / Gastric balloon	**Sengstaken-Blakemore tube** A three-lumen tube. Two ports inflate an esophageal and a gastric balloon for tamponade, and the third is used for nasogastric suction. This tube does not provide esophageal suction, but a nasogastric tube may be inserted in the opposite naris or the mouth and allowed to rest on top of the esophageal balloon. Esophageal suction is then possible, reducing the risk of aspiration.
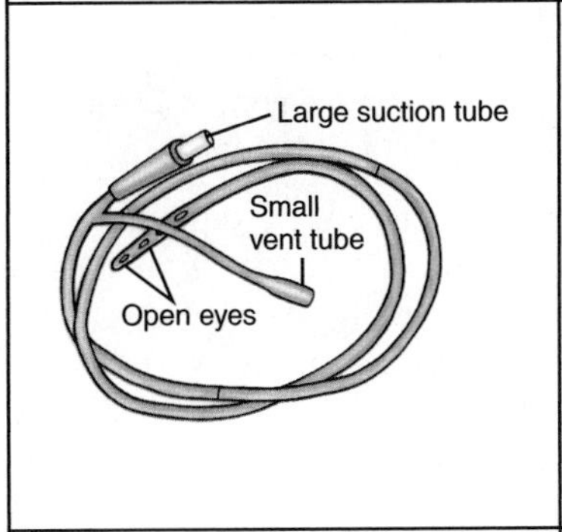 Large suction tube / Small vent tube / Open eyes	**Salem sump tube** A short double-lumen tube. The small vent tube within the large suction tube prevents mucosal suction damage by maintaining the pressure in open eyes at the distal end of the tube at less than 25 mm Hg.
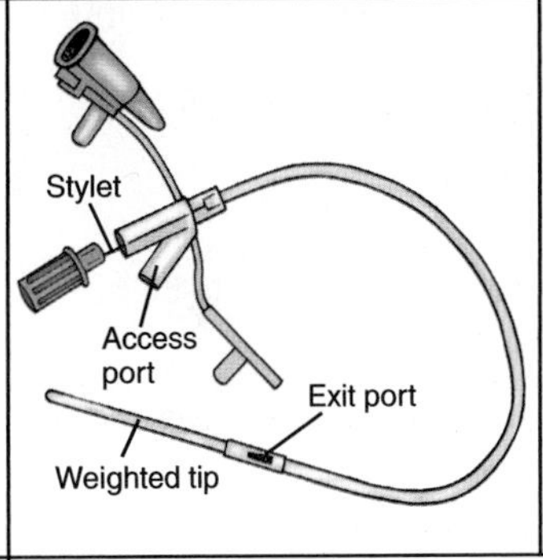 Stylet / Access port / Exit port / Weighted tip	**Weighted flexible feeding tube with stylet** Access port with irrigation adaptor allows maintenance of the tube without disconnecting the feeding set.
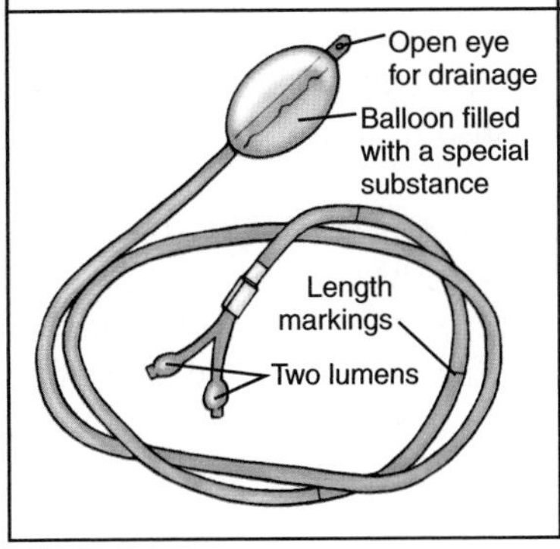 Open eye for drainage / Balloon filled with a special substance / Length markings / Two lumens	**Miller-Abbott tube** A long double-lumen tube used to drain and decompress the small intestine. One lumen leads to a balloon that is filled with a special substance once it is in the stomach; the second is for irrigation and drainage.

FIG. 21-1 Comparison of design and function of selected gastrointestinal tubes. (From Monahan, F., & Neighbors, M. [1998]. *Medical-surgical nursing* [2nd ed.]. Philadelphia: W.B. Saunders.)

4. Check the expiration date on the formula before administering.
5. Shake the formula well before pouring it into the container (feeding bag).
6. Always assess bowel sounds; do not administer any feedings if bowel sounds are absent.
7. Administer the feeding at the prescribed rate or via gravity flow (intermittent bolus feedings) with a 60-mL syringe with the plunger removed.

8. Gently flush with 30 to 50 mL of water or normal saline (depending on agency policy) with the irrigation syringe after the feeding.
E. Prevention of complications
   1. Diarrhea
      a. Use fiber-containing feedings.
      b. Administer feeding slowly and at room temperature.
   2. Aspiration
      a. Verify tube placement.

BOX 21-1
Nasogastric Tubes: Intubation Procedures

1. Follow agency procedures.
2. Explain the procedure and its potential discomfort to the client.
3. Position the client with pillows behind the shoulders.
4. Determine which nostril is more patent.
5. Measure the length of the tube from the bridge of the nose to the earlobe to the xiphoid process and indicate this length with a piece of tape on the tube.
6. If the client is conscious and alert, have him or her swallow or drink water (follow agency procedure).
7. Lubricate the tip of the tube with water-soluble lubricant.
8. Gently insert the tube into the nasopharynx and advance the tube.
9. When the tube nears the back of the throat (first black measurement on the tube) instruct the client to swallow or drink sips of water (unless contraindicated). If resistance is met, then slowly rotate and aim the tube downward and toward the closer ear; in the intubated or semiconscious client, flex the head toward the chest while passing the tube.
10. Immediately withdraw the tube if any change is noted in the client's respiratory status.
11. Test for tube placement by one of the following techniques:
    a. Obtain a sample of the gastric contents by aspirating with a 50-mL catheter-tipped syringe.
    b. Test the pH of the gastric contents (should be between 1 and 3.5).
    c. Obtain an order for an x-ray study to confirm placement.
12. Connect the tube to suction at low pressure.
    a. The Levin tube is usually connected to intermittent low suction.
    b. The Salem sump tube is usually connected to continuous low suction.
13. Secure the tube to the client's nose with adhesive tape and to the client's gown (follow agency procedure).
14. Observe the client for nausea, vomiting, abdominal fullness, or distention and monitor output.
15. Check residual volumes every 4 hours, before each feeding, and before giving medications. Aspirate all stomach contents (residual) and measure the amount. Reinstill residual feeding to prevent excessive fluid and electrolyte losses, unless the residual volume appears abnormal. Withhold the feeding if the amount is more than 100 mL or according to agency or nutritional consult recommendations.
16. If irrigation is indicated, use normal saline solution (check agency procedure).
17. Observe the client for fluid and electrolyte balance.
18. Instruct the client about movement to prevent nasal irritation and dislodgment of the tube.
19. On a daily basis, remove the adhesive tape securing the tube to the nose and clean and dry the skin; then, reapply the tape.

Modified from Ignatavicius, D., & Workman, M. (2002). *Medical-surgical nursing: Critical thinking for collaborative care* (4th ed.). Philadelphia: W.B. Saunders).

   b. Do not administer the feeding if residual is more than 100 mL (check physician's order and agency policy).
   c. Keep the head of the bed elevated.
   d. If aspiration occurs, suction as needed, assess respiratory rate, auscultate lung sounds, monitor temperature for aspiration pneumonia, and prepare to obtain chest radiograph.
3. Clogged tube
   a. Use liquid forms of medication, if possible.
   b. Flush the tube with 30 to 50 mL of water or NS (depending on agency policy) before and after medication administration and before and after bolus feeding.
   c. Flush with water every 4 hours for continuous feeding.
4. Vomiting
   a. Administer feedings slowly and, for bolus feedings, make the feeding last for 30 minutes.
   b. Measure abdominal girth.
   c. Do not allow the feeding bag to empty.
   d. Do not allow air to enter the tubing.
   e. Administer the feeding at room temperature.
   f. Elevate the head of the bed.
   g. Administer antiemetics as prescribed.
   h. If the client vomits, place the client in a side-lying position.

III. MEDICATIONS VIA NASOGASTRIC OR GASTROSTOMY TUBE
A. Ensure that the medication prescribed can be crushed or that the capsule can be opened.
B. Crush medications or use elixir forms of medications.
C. Dissolve crushed medication or capsule contents in 5 to 10 mL of water.
D. Check placement and residual before instilling medications.
E. Draw up the medication into a catheter tip syringe, clear excess air, and insert the medication into the tube.
F. Flush with 30 to 50 mL of water or NS (depending on agency policy).
G. Clamp the tube for 30 to 60 minutes (depending on medication and agency policy).

IV. INTESTINAL TUBES
A. Description
   1. The **intestinal tube** is passed nasally into the small intestine.

2. The tube may be used to decompress the bowel or to remove intestinal contents.
3. The tube enters the small intestine through the pyloric sphincter because of the weight of a small bag containing a special substance at the end.

B. Types of tubes (see Fig. 21-1)
   1. Cantor or Harris tube (single lumen)
   2. Miller-Abbott tube (double lumen)

▲ C. Interventions
   1. Assess the physician's orders and agency policy for advancement and removal of tube.
   2. Position the client on the right side to facilitate passage of the weighted bag in the tube through the pylorus of the stomach and into the small intestine.
   3. Do not secure the tube to the face with tape until it has reached final placement (may take several hours) in the intestines.
   4. Radiography is performed to verify desired placement.
   5. Monitor drainage from the tube.
   6. If the tube becomes blocked, notify the physician. A small amount of air injected into the lumen may be prescribed to clear the tube; do not irrigate the tube with air or fluid without an order from the physician.
   7. Assess the abdomen and measure abdominal girth.
   8. To remove the tube, the substance and air are removed from the balloon portion of the tube with a 5-mL syringe; the tube is removed gradually (6 inches every hour) as prescribed by the physician.
   9. Dispose of the tube in the appropriate manner as per agency policy.

V. ESOPHAGEAL AND GASTRIC TUBES
A. Description
   1. Used to apply pressure against esophageal veins to control bleeding
   2. Not used if the client has ulceration or necrosis of the esophagus or has had previous esophageal surgery

▲ B. **Sengstaken-Blakemore tube** (see Fig. 21-1)
   1. The **Sengstaken-Blakemore tube** is a triple-lumen gastric tube with an inflatable esophageal balloon, an inflatable gastric balloon, and a gastric aspiration lumen.
   2. The gastric balloon applies pressure at the cardioesophageal junction to compress gastric varices directly and to decrease blood flow to esophageal varices; traction is applied to maintain the gastric balloon in place.
   3. The esophageal balloon directly compresses esophageal varices.
   4. If bleeding is not stopped with inflation of the gastric balloon, the esophageal balloon is inflated to 25 to 45 mm Hg.

5. A radiograph of the upper abdomen and chest confirms placement.
6. Gastric contents are aspirated by gastric lavage or intermittent suction via the gastric aspiration port.
7. With the **Sengstaken-Blakemore tube**, a nasogastric tube also is inserted in the opposite naris to collect secretions that accumulate above the esophageal balloon.

C. Minnesota tube
   1. Four-lumen gastric tube
   2. Modified **Sengstaken-Blakemore tube** with an additional lumen for aspirating esophagopharyngeal secretions

D. Interventions
   1. Check patency and integrity of all balloons before insertion.
   2. Label each lumen.
   3. Place the client in the upright or Fowler's position for insertion.
   4. Immediately after insertion, prepare for radiography to verify placement.
   5. Maintain head elevation once the tube is in place.
   6. Double-clamp the balloon ports to prevent air leaks.
   7. Keep scissors at the bedside at all times; monitor for respiratory distress, and if it occurs, cut the tubes to deflate balloons.
   8. To prevent ulceration or necrosis of the esophagus, release esophageal pressure as prescribed and per agency policy.
   9. Monitor for increased bloody drainage, which may indicate persistent bleeding.
   10. Monitor for signs of esophageal rupture, which includes a drop in blood pressure, increased heart rate, and back and upper abdominal pain. (esophageal rupture is an emergency and signs of esophageal rupture must be reported to the physician immediately).

VI. LAVAGE TUBES
A. Description: Used to remove toxic substances from the stomach
B. Types of tubes
   1. Lavacuator
      a. The Lavacuator is an orogastric tube with a large suction lumen and a smaller lavage–vent lumen that provides continuous suction.
      b. Irrigation solution enters the lavage lumen while stomach contents are removed through the suction lumen.
   2. Ewald tube: A single-lumen large tube used for rapid one-time irrigation and evacuation

VII. URINARY AND RENAL TUBES
A. Types of urinary catheters (Fig. 21-2)
   1. Single lumen
   2. Double lumen
   3. Triple lumen

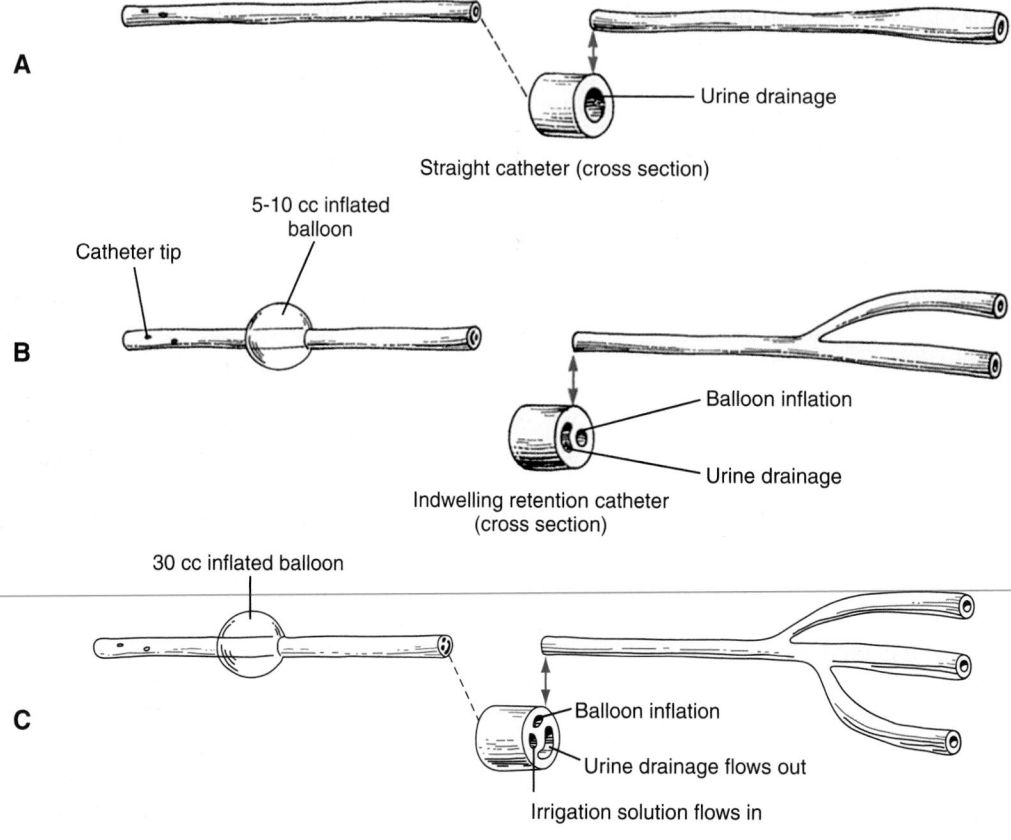

FIG. 21-2   Types of urinary catheters. **A,** Straight catheter (cross section). **B,** Indwelling retention catheter (cross section). **C,** Triple-lumen catheter (cross section). (From Elkin, M., Perry, A., & Potter, P. [2004]. *Nursing interventions and clinical skills* [3rd ed.]. St. Louis: Mosby.)

B. Routine urinary catheter care
  1. Use gloves and wash the perineal area with warm soapy water.
  2. With the nondominant hand, pull back the labia or foreskin to expose the meatus (in the adult male, return the foreskin to its normal position).
  3. Cleanse along the catheter with soap and water.
  4. Anchor the catheter to the thigh.
  5. Maintain the catheter bag below the level of the bladder.
C. Ureteral and nephrostomy tubes
  1. Never clamp the tube.
  2. Maintain patency.
  3. Monitor output closely; urine output of less than 30 mL/hr or lack of output for more than 15 minutes should be reported to the physician immediately.
  4. Irrigate only if prescribed by a physician, using strict aseptic technique; a maximum of 5 mL of sterile normal saline is instilled slowly and gently.
  5. If patency cannot be established with the prescribed irrigation, notify the physician immediately.

VIII. **RESPIRATORY SYSTEM TUBES**
A. **Endotracheal tubes** (Fig. 21-3)
  1. Description
    a. The **endotracheal tube** is used to maintain a patent airway.
    b. **Endotracheal tubes** are indicated when the client needs mechanical ventilation.
    c. If the client requires an artificial airway for longer than 10 to 14 days, a **tracheostomy** may be created to avoid mucosal and vocal cord damage that can be caused by the **endotracheal tube**.
    d. The cuff (located at the distal end of the tube), when inflated, produces a seal between the trachea and the cuff to prevent aspiration and ensure delivery of a set tidal volume when mechanical ventilation is used; an inflated cuff also prevents air from passing to the vocal cords, nose, or mouth.
    e. The pilot balloon permits air to be inserted into the cuff, prevents air from escaping, and is used as a guideline for determining the presence or absence of air in the cuff.

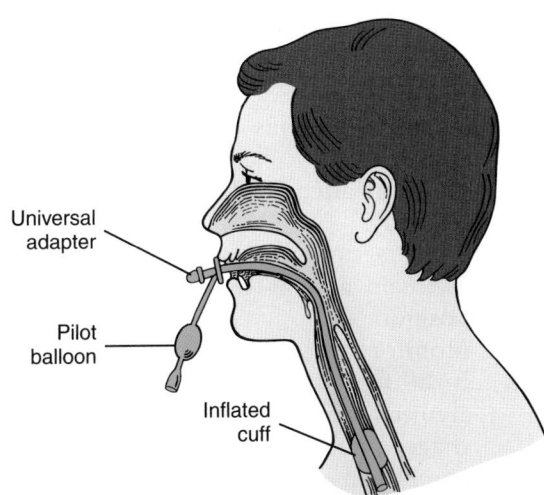

FIG. 21-3 Endotracheal tube with inflated cuff. (Modified from Perry, A., & Potter, P. [2002]. *Clinical nursing skills & techniques* [5th ed.]. St. Louis: Mosby.)

    f. The universal adapter enables attachment of the tube to mechanical ventilation tubing or other types of oxygen delivery systems.

    g. Types of tubes: Orotracheal and nasotracheal

2. Orotracheal tubes

    a. Allows use of a larger diameter tube and reduces the work of breathing.

    b. Indicated when the client has a nasal obstruction or a predisposition to epistaxis.

    c. Uncomfortable and can be manipulated by the tongue, causing airway obstruction; an oral airway may be needed to keep the client from biting on the tube.

3. Nasotracheal tubes

    a. This smaller tube increases resistance and the client's work of breathing.

    b. Its use is avoided in clients with bleeding disorders.

    c. It is more comfortable for the client, and the client is unable to manipulate the tube with the tongue.

4. Interventions

    a. Placement is confirmed by chest x-ray film (correct placement is 1 to 2 cm above the carina).

    b. Assess placement by auscultating both sides of chest while manually ventilating with a resuscitation (Ambu) bag (if breath sounds and chest wall movement are absent in the left side, the tube may be in the right main stem bronchus).

    c. Perform auscultation over the stomach to rule out esophageal intubation.

    d. If the tube is in the stomach, louder breath sounds will be heard over the stomach than over the chest, and abdominal distention will be present.

    e. Secure the tube with adhesive tape immediately after intubation.

    f. Monitor the position of the tube at the lip or nose.

    g. Monitor skin and mucous membranes.

    h. Suction the tube only when needed.

    i. The oral tube needs to be moved to the opposite side of the mouth daily to prevent pressure and necrosis of the lip and mouth area, prevent nerve damage, and facilitate inspection and cleaning of the mouth; moving the tube to the opposite side of the mouth should be done by two health care providers.

    j. Prevent dislodgment and pulling or tugging on the tube; suction, coughing, and speaking attempts by the client place extra stress on the tube and can cause dislodgment.

    k. Keep a resuscitation (Ambu) bag at the bedside at all times.

    l. Assess the pilot balloon to ensure that the cuff is inflated; maintain cuff inflation, which creates a seal and allows complete mechanical control of respiration.

    m. Monitor cuff pressures at least every 8 hours per agency procedure to ensure that they do not exceed 20 mm Hg (an aneroid pressure manometer is used to measure cuff pressures); minimal leak and occlusive techniques are used for cuff inflation to check cuff pressures.

5. Minimal leak technique

    a. This is used for cuff inflation and checking cuff pressures for cuffs without pressure relief valves.

    b. Inflate the cuff until a seal is established; no harsh sound should be heard through a stethoscope placed over the trachea when the client breathes in, but a slight air leak on peak inspiration is present and can be heard.

    c. The client cannot make verbal sounds, and no air is felt coming out of the client's mouth.

6. Occlusive technique

    a. For cuff inflation and checking cuff pressures for cuffs with pressure relief valves

    b. Provides an adequate seal in the trachea at the lowest possible cuff pressure

    c. Uses same procedure as minimal leak technique, without an air leak

7. Extubation

    a. Hyperoxygenate the client and suction the **endotracheal tube** and the oral cavity.

    b. Place the client in a semi-Fowler's position.

    c. Deflate the cuff; have the client inhale and, at peak inspiration, remove the tube, suctioning the airway through the tube while pulling it out.

d. After removal, instruct the client to cough and deep-breathe to assist in removing accumulated secretions in the throat.

e. Apply oxygen therapy, as prescribed.

f. Monitor for respiratory difficulty; contact the physician if respiratory difficulty occurs.

g. Inform the client that hoarseness or a sore throat is normal and that the client should limit talking if it occurs.

B. **Tracheostomy**

1. Description

a. A tracheotomy is a surgical incision into the trachea for the purpose of establishing an airway.

b. A **tracheostomy** is the stoma or opening that results from the tracheotomy (Box 21-2).

c. The **tracheostomy** can be temporary or permanent.

2. Interventions

a. Assess respirations and for bilateral breath sounds.

b. Monitor arterial blood gases and pulse oximetry.

c. Encourage coughing and deep breathing.

d. Maintain a semi-Fowler's to high Fowler's position.

e. Monitor for bleeding, difficulty with breathing, absence of breath sounds, and crepitus, which are indications of hemorrhage, pneumothorax, and subcutaneous emphysema.

f. Provide respiratory treatments as prescribed.

BOX 21-2

Types of Tracheostomy Tubes

DOUBLE-LUMEN TUBE

The double-lumen tube has three major parts:

Outer cannula—fits into the stoma and keeps the airway open. The face plate indicates the size and type of tube and has small holes on both sides for securing the tube with tracheostomy ties.

Inner cannula—fits snugly into the outer cannula and locks into place. It provides the universal adaptor for use with the ventilator and other respiratory therapy equipment. Some may be removed, cleaned, and reused; others are disposable.

Obturator—a stylet with a smooth end used to facilitate the direction of the tube when inserting or changing a tracheostomy tube. The obturator is removed immediately after tube placement and is always kept with the client and at the bedside in case of accidental decannulation.

SINGLE-LUMEN TUBE

The single-lumen tube is a long tube used for clients with long or extra thick necks. The tube often is called a "bull neck trach" because of the long distance from the skin to the trachea or the longer length of the trachea in larger individuals. More intensive nursing care is required with this tube because there is no inner cannula to ensure a patent lumen.

CUFFED TUBE

A cuff, when inflated, seals the airway. The cuffed tube is used for mechanical ventilation, preventing aspiration of oral or gastric secretions, or for the client receiving a tube feeding to prevent aspiration. A pilot balloon attached to the outside of the tube indicates the presence or absence of air in the cuff.

CUFFLESS TUBE

The cuffless tube is a plastic silicone-like (Silastic) or metal tube, usually with a double lumen. The tube is used for long-term airway management in those clients who require a tracheostomy, who can protect themselves from aspiration, and who do not require mechanical ventilation. Many persons can speak with this tube in place.

FENESTRATED TUBE

The fenestrated tube has a precut opening (fenestration) in the upper posterior wall of the outer cannula. The tube is used to wean the client from a tracheostomy by ensuring that the client can tolerate breathing through his or her natural airway before the entire tube is removed. This tube allows the client to speak.

CUFFED FENESTRATED TUBE

The cuffed fenestrated tube facilitates mechanical ventilation and speech and often is used for clients with spinal cord paralysis or neuromuscular disease who do not require ventilation at all times. When not on the ventilator, the client can have the cuff deflated and the tube capped for speech. A cuffed fenestrated tube is never used in weaning from a tracheostomy because the cuff, even fully deflated, may partially obstruct the airway.

METAL TRACHEOSTOMY TUBE

The metal tracheostomy tube is used for permanent tracheostomy. It is a cuffless double-lumen tube and the inner cannula can be cleaned and reused indefinitely. A special adaptor attaches a manual resuscitation bag. Popular types are the Jackson and Holinger tubes.

TALKING TRACHEOSTOMY TUBE

The talking tracheostomy tube provides a means of communication for the client who is using a ventilator on a long-term basis. An extra air channel allows air to flow up through the vocal cords so that the client can speak with the cuff inflated. The air can cause drying of the vocal cords from constant dry airflow.

Modified from Ignatavicius, D., & Workman, M. (2006). *Medical-surgical nursing: Critical thinking for collaborative care* (5th ed.). Philadelphia: W.B. Saunders.

g. Suction fluids as needed; hyperoxygenate the client before suctioning.

h. If the client is allowed to eat, sit the client up for meals and ensure that the cuff is inflated (if the tube is not capped) for meals and for 1 hour after meals.

i. Monitor cuff pressures as prescribed.

j. Assess the stoma and secretions for blood or purulent drainage.

k. Follow the physician's orders and agency policy for cleaning the **tracheostomy** site and inner cannula; usually, half-strength hydrogen peroxide is used.

l. Administer humidified oxygen as prescribed, because the normal humidification process is bypassed in a client with a **tracheostomy**.

m. Obtain assistance in changing **tracheostomy** ties; after placing the new ties, cut and remove the old ties holding the **tracheostomy** in place.

n. Never insert a decannulation plug into a **tracheostomy** tube until the cuff is deflated and the inner cannula is removed; prior insertion prevents airflow to the client (Fig. 21-4).

o. Keep a resuscitation (Ambu) bag, obturator, clamps, and a tracheotomy set at the bedside.

3. Complications of a **tracheostomy** (Box 21-3; Table 21-1)

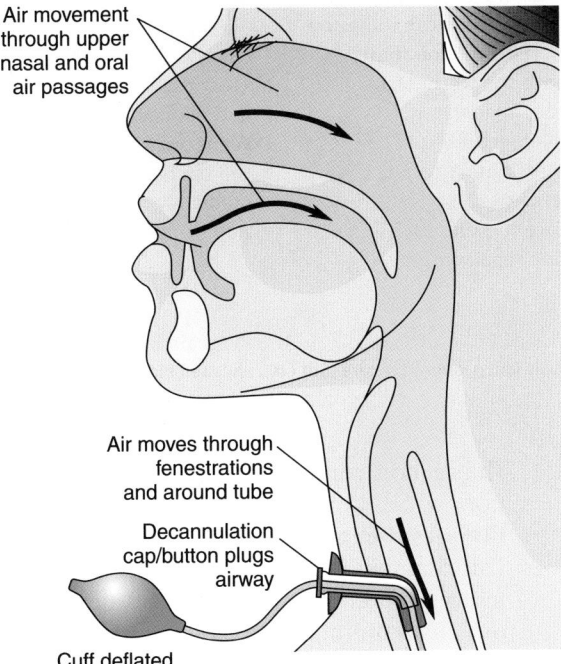

Air movement through upper nasal and oral air passages

Air moves through fenestrations and around tube

Decannulation cap/button plugs airway

Cuff deflated

FIG. 21-4 Breathing through a fenestrated tracheostomy tube with a cap in place and the cuff deflated. (From Ignatavicius, D., & Workman, M. [2006]. *Medical-surgical nursing: Critical thinking for collaborative care* [5th ed.]. Philadelphia: W.B. Saunders.)

▲ IX. CHEST TUBE DRAINAGE SYSTEM

A. Description

1. The **chest tube** drainage system returns negative pressure to the intrapleural space.

2. The system is used to remove abnormal accumulations of air and fluids from the pleural space (Fig. 21-5).

B. Collection chamber (Fig. 21-6)

1. The collection chamber is located where the **chest tube** from the client connects to the system.

BOX 21-3
Complications of a Tracheostomy

TUBE OBSTRUCTION
Assessment
Difficulty in breathing
Noisy respirations
Difficulty in inserting the suction catheter
Thick, dry secretions
Unexplained peak pressures if client is on a mechanical ventilator
Prevention and Interventions
Assist the client to cough and deep-breathe.
Provide humidification and suctioning.
Clean the inner cannula regularly.
The physician repositions or replaces the tube if obstruction occurs as a result of cuff prolapse over the end of the tube.

TUBE DISLODGMENT
Prevention and Interventions
Secure the tube in place. Minimize manipulation and traction on the tube. Ensure that the client does not pull on the tube. Ensure that a tracheostomy tube of the same type and size is at the client's bedside.
Be familiar with institutional policy regarding replacement of a tracheostomy tube as a nursing procedure.
During the first 72 hours following surgical placement of the tracheostomy:
  The nurse manually ventilates the client by using a manual resuscitation (Ambu) bag while another nurse calls the resuscitation team for help.
After 72 hours following surgical placement of the tracheostomy:
  Extend the client's neck and open the tissues of the stoma to secure the airway.
  Grasp the retention sutures (if they are present) to spread the opening.
  Use a tracheal dilator (curved clamp) to hold the stoma open.
  Prepare to insert tracheostomy tube; place obturator into tracheostomy tube, replace the tube, and remove the obturator.
Maintain ventilation by resuscitation (Ambu) bag.
Assess airflow and bilateral breath sounds.
If unable to secure an airway, call the resuscitation team and the anesthesiologist.

TABLE 21-1

Complications of a Tracheostomy

Complications and Description	Manifestations	Management	Prevention
Tracheomalacia: Constant pressure exerted by the cuff causes tracheal dilation and erosion of cartilage.	An increased amount of air is required in the cuff to maintain the seal. A larger tracheostomy tube is required to prevent an air leak at the stoma. Food particles are seen in tracheal secretions. The client does not receive the set tidal volume on the ventilator.	No special management is needed unless bleeding occurs.	Use an uncuffed tube as soon as possible. Monitor cuff pressure and air volume closely and detect changes.
Tracheal stenosis: Narrowed tracheal lumen is the result of scar formation from irritation of tracheal mucosa by the cuff.	Stenosis is usually seen after the cuff is deflated or the tracheostomy tube is removed. The client has increased coughing, inability to expectorate secretions, or difficulty in breathing and talking.	Tracheal dilation or surgical intervention is used.	Prevent pulling of and traction on the tracheostomy tube. Properly secure the tube in the midline position. Maintain cuff pressure. Minimize oronasal intubation time.
Tracheoesophageal fistula (TEF): Excessive cuff pressure causes erosion of the posterior wall of the trachea. A hole is created between the trachea and the anterior esophagus. The client at highest risk also has a nasogastric tube present.	Similar to tracheomalacia: 1. Food particles are seen in tracheal secretions. 2. Increased air in cuff is needed to achieve a seal. 3. The client has increased coughing and choking while eating. 4. The client does not receive the set tidal volume on the ventilator.	Manually administer oxygen by mask to prevent hypoxemia. Use a small soft feeding tube instead of a nasogastric tube for tube feedings. A gastrostomy or jejunostomy may be performed. Monitor the client with a nasogastric tube closely; assess for TEF and aspiration.	Maintain cuff pressure. Monitor the amount of air needed for inflation and detect changes. Progress to a deflated or cuffless tube as soon as possible.
Trachea-innominate artery fistula: A malpositioned tube causes its distal tip to push against the lateral wall of the tracheostomy. Continued pressure causes necrosis and erosion of the innominate artery. *This is a medical emergency.*	The tracheostomy tube pulsates in synchrony with the heartbeat. There is heavy bleeding from the stoma. *This is a life-threatening complication.*	Remove the tracheostomy tube immediately. Apply direct pressure to the innominate artery at the stoma site. Prepare the client for immediate repair surgery.	Correct the tube size, length, and midline position. Prevent pulling or tugging of the tracheostomy tube. Immediately notify the physician of the pulsating tube.

From Ignatavicius, D., & Workman, M. (2006). *Medical-surgical nursing: Critical thinking for collaborative care* (5th ed.). Philadelphia: W.B. Saunders.

2. Drainage from the tube drains into and collects in a series of calibrated columns in this chamber.

C. Water seal chamber (see Fig. 21-6)

1. The tip of the tube is underwater, allowing fluid and air to drain from the pleural space and preventing air from entering the pleural space.

2. Water oscillates (moves up as the client inhales and moves down as the client exhales).

3. Excessive bubbling indicates an air leak in the **chest tube** system.

D. Suction control chamber (see Fig. 21-6)

1. The suction control chamber provides the suction, which can be controlled to provide negative pressure to the chest.

2. This chamber is filled with various levels of water to achieve the desired level of suction; without this control, lung tissue could be sucked into the **chest tube**.

3. Gentle bubbling in this chamber indicates that there is suction and does not indicate that air is escaping from the pleural space.

E. Dry suction system

1. Because this is a dry suction system, absence of bubbling is noted in the suction control chamber.

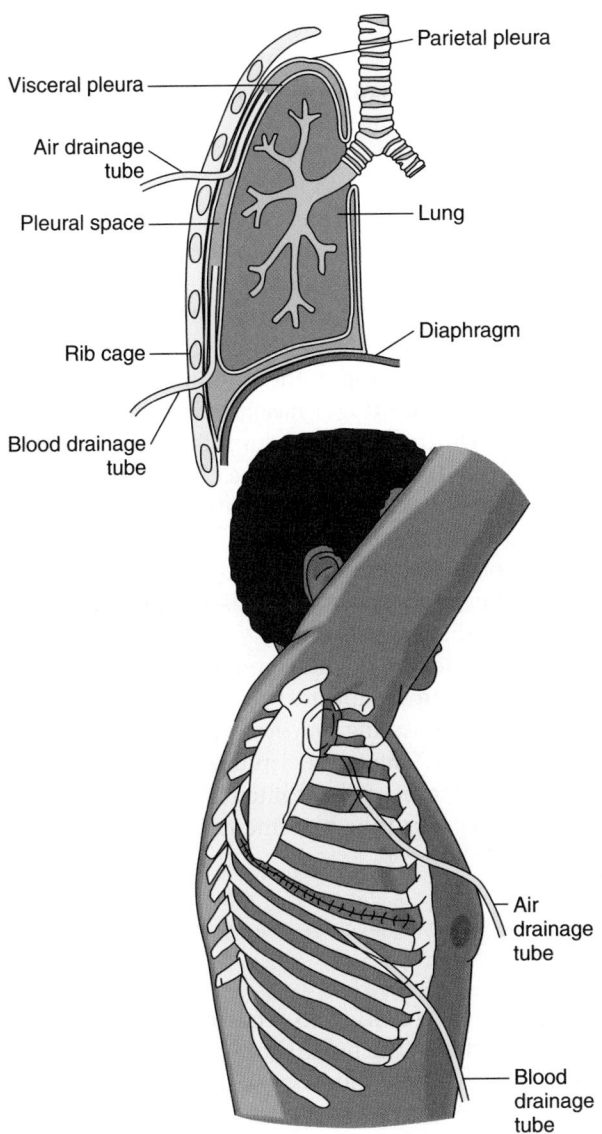

FIG. 21-5   Chest tube placement. (From Ignatavicius, D., & Workman, M. [2006]. *Medical-surgical nursing: Critical thinking for collaborative care* [5th ed.]. Philadelphia: W.B. Saunders.)

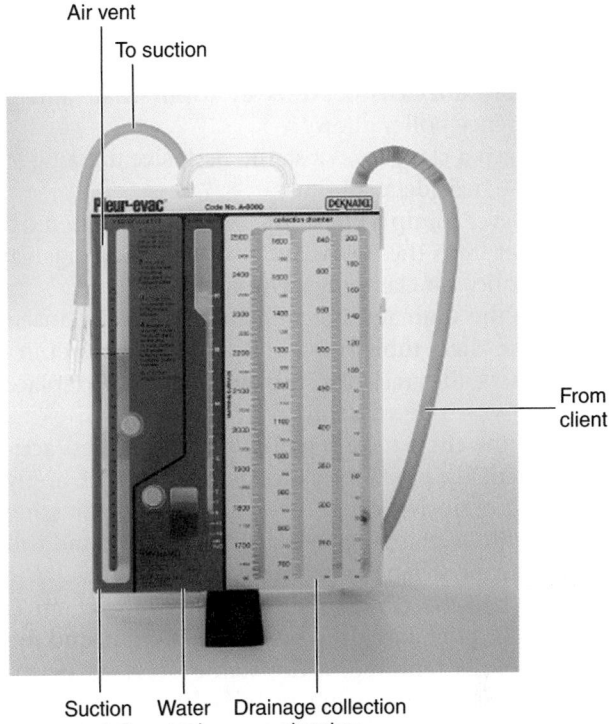

FIG. 21-6   The Pleur-Evac drainage system, a commercial three-bottle chest drainage device. (From Ignatavicius, D., & Workman, M. [2006]. *Medical-surgical nursing: Critical thinking for collaborative care* [5th ed.]. Philadelphia: W.B. Saunders.)

2. A knob on the collection device is used to set the prescribed amount of suction; then the wall suction source dial is turned until a small orange floater valve appears in the window on the device (when the orange floater valve is in the window, the correct amount of suction is applied).

F. Interventions
 1. Collection chamber
   a. Monitor drainage; notify the physician if drainage is more than 100 mL/hr or if drainage becomes bright red or increases suddenly.
   b. Mark the **chest tube** drainage in the collection chamber at 1- to 4-hour intervals, using a piece of tape.
 2. Water seal chamber
   a. Monitor for fluctuation of the fluid level in the water seal chamber.

   b. Fluctuation in the water seal chamber stops if the tube is obstructed, if a dependent loop exists, if the suction is not working properly, or if the lung has reexpanded.
   c. If the client has a known pneumothorax, intermittent bubbling in the water seal chamber is expected as air is drained from the chest, but continuous bubbling indicates an air leak in the system.
   d. Notify the physician if there is continuous bubbling in the water seal chamber.
 3. Suction control chamber: Gentle (not vigorous) bubbling should be noted in the suction control chamber.
 4. An occlusive sterile dressing is maintained at the insertion site.
 5. A chest radiograph assesses the position of the tube and determines whether the lung has reexpanded.
 6. Assess respiratory status and auscultate lung-sounds.
 7. Monitor for signs of extended pneumothorax or hemothorax.
 8. Keep the drainage system below the level of the chest and the tubes free of kinks, dependent loops, or other obstructions.
 9. Ensure that all connections are secure.
10. Encourage coughing and deep breathing.

11. Change the client's position frequently to promote drainage and ventilation.

12. Do not strip or milk a **chest tube** unless specifically directed to do so by a physician and if agency policy allows it.

13. Keep a clamp and a sterile occlusive dressing at the bedside at all times.

14. Never clamp a **chest tube** without a written order from the physician; also, determine agency policy for clamping a **chest tube**.

15. If the drainage system cracks or breaks, insert the **chest tube** into a bottle of sterile water, remove the cracked or broken system, and replace it with a new system.

16. If the **chest tube** is pulled out of the chest accidentally, pinch the skin opening together, apply an occlusive sterile dressing, cover the dressing with overlapping pieces of 2-inch tape, and call the physician immediately.

17. When the **chest tube** is removed, the client is asked to take a deep breath and hold it, and the tube is removed; a dry sterile dressing, petroleum gauze dressing, or Telfa dressing (depending on the physician's preference) is taped in place after removal of the **chest tube**.

18. Depending on the physician's preference, when the **chest tube** is removed, the client may be asked to take a deep breath, exhale, and bear down (Valsalva's maneuver).

PRACTICE QUESTIONS

1. The nurse checks for residual before administering a bolus tube feeding to a client with a nasogastric tube and obtains a residual amount of 150 mL. What is the appropriate action for the nurse to take?
   1. Hold the feeding.
   2. Reinstill the amount and continue with administering the feeding
   3. Elevate the client's head at least 45 degrees and administer the feeding.
   4. Discard the residual amount and proceed with administering the feeding.

2. A nurse caring for a client with a pneumothorax and who has had a chest tube inserted notes continuous gentle bubbling in the suction control chamber. What action is appropriate?
   1. Do nothing, because this is an expected finding.
   2. Immediately clamp the chest tube and notify the physician.
   3. Check for an air leak because the bubbling should be intermittent.
   4. Increase the suction pressure so that the bubbling becomes vigorous.

3. A registered nurse is preparing to insert a nasogastric tube in an adult client. To determine the accurate measurement of the length of the tube to be inserted, the nurse should:
   1. Mark the tube at 10 inches.
   2. Mark the tube at 32 inches.
   3. Place the tube at the tip of the nose and measure by extending the tube to the earlobe and then down to the xiphoid process.
   4. Place the tube at the tip of the nose and measure by extending the tube to the earlobe and then down to the top of the sternum.

4. A nurse is inserting a nasogastric tube in an adult client. During the procedure, the client begins to cough and has difficulty breathing. Which of the following is the appropriate nursing action?
   1. Quickly insert the tube.
   2. Notify the physician immediately.
   3. Remove the tube and reinsert when the respiratory distress subsides.
   4. Pull back on the tube and wait until the respiratory distress subsides.

5. A nurse is assessing for correct placement of a nasogastric tube. The nurse aspirates the stomach contents and checks the contents for pH. The nurse verifies correct tube placement if which pH value is noted?
   1. 3.5
   2. 7.0
   3. 7.35
   4. 7.5

6. A nurse is preparing to remove a nasogastric tube from a client. The nurse should instruct the client to do which of the following just before the nurse removes the tube?
   1. Exhale.
   2. Inhale and exhale quickly.
   3. Take and hold a deep breath.
   4. Perform a Valsalva maneuver.

7. A nurse is preparing to administer medication through a nasogastric tube that is connected to suction. To administer the medication, the nurse would:
   1. Position the client supine to assist in medication absorption.
   2. Aspirate the nasogastric tube after medication administration to maintain patency.
   3. Clamp the nasogastric tube for 30 minutes following administration of the medication.
   4. Change the suction setting to low intermittent suction for 30 minutes after medication administration.

8. A nurse is preparing to care for a client with esophageal varices who has just had a Sengstaken-Blakemore tube inserted. The nurse gathers sup-

plies, knowing that which of the following items must be kept at the bedside at all times?

1. An obturator
2. A Kelly clamp
3. An irrigation set
4. A pair of scissors

9. A nurse is inserting an indwelling urinary catheter into the urethra of a male client. As the nurse inflates the balloon, the client complains of discomfort. The appropriate nursing action is to:

1. Aspirate the fluid, remove the catheter and insert a new catheter.
2. Aspirate the fluid, advance the catheter farther, and reinflate the balloon.
3. Remove the syringe from the balloon; discomfort is normal and temporary.
4. Aspirate the fluid, withdraw the catheter slightly, and reinflate the balloon.

10. A nurse is inserting an indwelling urinary catheter into a male client. As the catheter is inserted into the urethra, urine begins to flow into the tubing. At this point, the nurse:

1. Immediately inflates the balloon.
2. Inserts the catheter 2.5 to 5 cm and inflates the balloon.
3. Withdraws the catheter about 1 inch and inflates the balloon.
4. Inserts the catheter until resistance is met and inflates the balloon.

11. A nurse has assisted a physician with the insertion of a chest tube. The nurse monitors the client and notes fluctuation of the fluid level in the water seal chamber after the tube is inserted. Based on this assessment, which action would be appropriate?

1. Inform the physician.
2. Continue to monitor the client.
3. Reinforce the occlusive dressing.
4. Encourage the client to deep-breathe.

12. A nurse caring for a client with a chest tube turns the client to the side, and the chest tube accidentally disconnects. The initial nursing action is to:

1. Call the physician.
2. Place the tube in a bottle of sterile water.
3. Immediately replace the chest tube system.
4. Place a sterile dressing over the disconnection site.

13. A nurse is assisting a physician with the removal of a chest tube. The nurse should instruct the client to:

1. Exhale slowly.
2. Stay very still.
3. Inhale and exhale quickly.
4. Perform the Valsalva maneuver.

14. While changing the tapes on a tracheostomy tube, the client coughs and the tube is dislodged. The initial nursing action is to:

1. Call the physician to reinsert the tube.
2. Grasp the retention sutures to spread the opening.
3. Call the respiratory therapy department to reinsert the tracheotomy.
4. Cover the tracheostomy site with a sterile dressing to prevent infection.

15. A nurse is caring for a client immediately after removal of the endotracheal tube. The nurse reports which of the following signs immediately if experienced by the client?

1. Stridor
2. Occasional pink-tinged sputum
3. A few basilar lung crackles on the right
4. Respiratory rate of 24 breaths/min

ALTERNATE ITEM FORMAT: MULTIPLE RESPONSE

A nurse is assessing the functioning of a chest tube drainage system in a client who has just returned from the recovery room following a thoracotomy with wedge resection. Select all expected assessment findings.

❏ 1. Excessive bubbling in the water seal chamber
❏ 2. Vigorous bubbling in the suction control chamber
❏ 3. 50 mL of drainage in the drainage collection chamber
❏ 4. Drainage system maintained below the client's chest
❏ 5. Occlusive dressing in place over the chest tube insertion site
❏ 6. Fluctuation of water in the tube in the water seal chamber during inhalation and exhalation

ANSWERS

1. 1
Rationale: Unless specifically indicated, residual amounts more than 100 mL require holding the feeding. Therefore options 2, 3, and 4 are incorrect. Additionally, the feeding is not discarded unless its contents are abnormal in color or characteristics.
Test Taking Strategy: Use the process of elimination and note that the residual amount is 150 mL. Also, note that options 2, 3, and 4 are comparative or alike and indicate administering the feeding. If you had difficulty with this question, review nursing interventions for clients with nasogastric tubes.
Level of Cognitive Ability: Application
Client Needs: Physiological Integrity
Integrated Process: Nursing Process—implementation
Content Area: Adult health—gastrointestinal
Reference: Ignatavicius, D., & Workman, M. (2006). *Medical-surgical nursing: Critical thinking for collaborative care* (5th ed., p. 1431). Philadelphia: W.B. Saunders.

2. 1
Rationale: Continuous gentle bubbling should be noted in the suction control chamber. Option 2 is incorrect. Chest tubes should only be clamped to check for an air leak or when changing drainage devices (according to agency policy). Option 3 is incorrect. Bubbling should be continuous and not intermittent. Option 4 is incorrect because bubbling should be gentle. Increasing the suction pressure only increases the rate of evaporation of water in the drainage system.
Test Taking Strategy: Use the process of elimination and think about the physiology associated with each chamber of the chest tube drainage system. Remember that continuous gentle bubbling in the suction control chamber is expected. If you had difficulty with this question, review nursing interventions for clients with chest tubes.
Level of Cognitive Ability: Application
Client Needs: Physiological Integrity
Integrated Process: Nursing Process—implementation
Content Area: Adult health—respiratory
Reference: Potter, P., & Perry, A. (2005). *Fundamentals of nursing* (6th ed., pp. 1118-1121). St. Louis: Mosby.

3. 3
Rationale: Measuring the length of tube needed is done by placing the tube at the tip of the client's nose and extending the tube to the earlobe and then down to the xiphoid process. The average length for an adult is about 22 to 26 inches.
Test-Taking Strategy: Use the process of elimination and visualize this procedure. Eliminate options 1 and 2 first because 10 inches is short and 32 inches is too long. Remember the abbreviation *NEX*, which stands for *nose, earlobe,* and *xiphoid* process, to assist in answering questions similar to this one. Review the procedure for measuring the length of a nasogastric tube for insertion if you had difficulty with this question.
Level of Cognitive Ability: Application
Client Needs: Physiological Integrity

Integrated Process: Nursing Process—implementation
Content Area: Adult health—gastrointestinal
Reference: Potter, P., & Perry, A. (2005). *Fundamentals of nursing* (6th ed., p. 1404). St. Louis: Mosby).

4. 4
Rationale: During the insertion of a nasogastric tube, if the client experiences difficulty breathing or any respiratory distress, withdraw the tube slightly, stop the tube advancement, and wait until the distress subsides. Options 2 and 3 are unnecessary. Quickly inserting the tube is not an appropriate action because, in this situation, it may be likely that the tube has entered the bronchus.
Test-Taking Strategy: Use the process of elimination. Option 1 can be eliminated first. Visualizing the procedure and anticipating potential complications will assist in eliminating options 2 and 3 as unnecessary actions. Review the cautions related to inserting a nasogastric tube if you had difficulty with this question.
Level of Cognitive Ability: Application
Client Needs: Physiological Integrity
Integrated Process: Nursing Process—implementation
Content Area: Adult health—gastrointestinal
Reference: Potter, P., & Perry, A. (2005). *Fundamentals of nursing* (6th ed., p. 1405). St. Louis: Mosby.

5. 1
Rationale: If the nasogastric tube is in the stomach, the pH of the contents will be acidic. Gastric aspirates have acidic pH values and should be 3.5 or lower. Option 2 indicates a slightly acidic pH. Option 3 indicates a neutral pH. Option 4 indicates an alkaline pH.
Test-Taking Strategy: Use the process of elimination and note the strategic word *verifies*. Recalling that gastric contents are acidic will direct you to option 1. If you had difficulty with this question, review the procedure for assessing nasogastric tube placement.
Level of Cognitive Ability: Analysis
Client Needs: Physiological Integrity
Integrated Process: Nursing Process—analysis
Content Area: Adult health—gastrointestinal
Reference: Perry, A., & Potter, P. (2006). *Clinical nursing skills & techniques* (6th ed., pp. 644, 1021). St. Louis: Mosby.

6. 3
Rationale: When the nurse removes a nasogastric tube, the client is instructed to take and hold a deep breath. This will close the epiglottis. This allows for easy withdrawal through the esophagus into the nose. The nurse removes the tube with one smooth, continuous pull.
Test-Taking Strategy: Use the process of elimination and focus on the subject, removing a nasogastric tube. Visualize the procedure as a guide, considering what each action identified in the options would produce. Review the procedure for removing a nasogastric tube if you had difficulty with this question.
Level of Cognitive Ability: Application
Client Needs: Physiological Integrity

Integrated Process: Nursing Process—implementation
Content Area: Adult health—gastrointestinal
Reference: Potter, P., & Perry, A. (2005). *Fundamentals of nursing* (6th ed., p. 1407). St. Louis: Mosby.

7. **3**
Rationale: If a client has a nasogastric tube connected to suction, the nurse should wait up to 30 minutes before reconnecting the tube to the suction apparatus to allow adequate time for medication absorption. Aspirating the nasogastric tube will remove the medication just administered. Low intermittent suction also will remove the medication just administered. The client should not be placed in the supine position because of the risk for aspiration.
Test-Taking Strategy: Use the process of elimination. Eliminate options 2 and 4 first because these actions are comparative or alike and will produce the same effect. Recalling that the client should not be placed in a supine position will assist in eliminating option 1. If you had difficulty with this question, review the procedure for administering medications through a nasogastric tube.
Level of Cognitive Ability: Application
Client Needs: Physiological Integrity
Integrated Process: Nursing Process—implementation
Content Area: Adult health—gastrointestinal
Reference: Perry, A., & Potter, P. (2006). *Clinical nursing skills & techniques* (6th ed., p. 645). St. Louis: Mosby.

8. **4**
Rationale: When the client has a Sengstaken-Blakemore tube, a pair of scissors must be kept at the client's bedside at all times. The client needs to be observed for sudden respiratory distress, which occurs if the gastric balloon ruptures and the entire tube moves upward. If this occurs, the nurse immediately cuts all balloon lumens and removes the tube. An obturator and a Kelly clamp are kept at the bedside of a client with a tracheostomy. An irrigation set may be kept at the bedside, but it is not the priority item.
Test-Taking Strategy: Use the process of elimination and knowledge regarding the structure, function, and placement of a Sengstaken-Blakemore tube to answer this question. Note the strategic word *must* in the question. This should assist in eliminating options 1, 2, and 3. If you had difficulty with this question, review nursing care for a client with a Sengstaken-Blakemore tube.
Level of Cognitive Ability: Application
Client Needs: Physiological Integrity
Integrated Process: Nursing Process—planning
Content Area: Adult health—gastrointestinal
Reference: Ignatavicius, D., & Workman, M. (2006). *Medical-surgical nursing: Critical thinking for collaborative care* (5th ed., p. 1379). Philadelphia: W.B. Saunders.

9. **2**
Rationale: If the balloon is positioned in the urethra, inflating the balloon could produce trauma, and pain will occur. If pain occurs, the fluid should be aspirated and the catheter inserted

a little further into the bladder to provide sufficient space to inflate the balloon. The balloon of the catheter is behind the opening at the insertion tip. Inserting the catheter the extra distance will ensure that the balloon is inflated inside the bladder and not in the urethra. There is no need to remove the catheter and insert a new one. Pain when the balloon is inflated is not normal.
Test-Taking Strategy: Use the process of elimination, noting the subject of the question, the client's complaint of discomfort. Visualize this procedure and the anatomy of the urinary system to direct you to the correct option. If you had difficulty with this question, review the procedure for inserting a urinary catheter.
Level of Cognitive Ability: Application
Client Needs: Physiological Integrity
Integrated Process: Nursing Process—implementation
Content Area: Adult health—renal
Reference: Potter, P., & Perry, A. (2005). *Fundamentals of nursing* (6th ed., p. 1356). St. Louis: Mosby.

10. **2**
Rationale: The balloon of the catheter is behind the opening at the insertion tip. The catheter is inserted 2.5 to 5 cm after urine begins to flow to provide sufficient space to inflate the balloon. Inserting the catheter the extra distance will ensure that the balloon is inflated inside the bladder and not in the urethra. Inflating the balloon in the urethra could produce trauma.
Test-Taking Strategy: Visualizing the proper procedure for inserting an indwelling urinary catheter will assist you in answering this question. Note the strategic words *urine begins to flow*. Options 3 and 4 can be eliminated easily. Eliminate option 1 next because of the word *immediately*. If you had difficulty with this question, review the procedure for bladder catheterization.
Level of Cognitive Ability: Application
Client Needs: Physiological Integrity
Integrated Process: Nursing Process—implementation
Content Area: Adult health—renal
Reference: Potter, P., & Perry, A. (2005). *Fundamentals of nursing* (6th ed., p. 1355). St. Louis: Mosby.

11. **2**
Rationale: The presence of fluctuation of the fluid level in the water seal chamber indicates a patent drainage system. With normal breathing, the water level rises with inspiration and falls with expiration. Fluctuation stops if the tube is obstructed, if a dependent loop exists, if the suction is not working properly, or if the lung has reexpanded. Options 1, 3, and 4 are incorrect.
Test-Taking Strategy: Use the process of elimination and focus on the subject, fluctuation of the fluid level in the water seal chamber. Recalling that this is an expected finding will direct you to the correct option. Review the expected and unexpected assessment findings in the care of a client with a chest tube if you had difficulty with this question.
Level of Cognitive Ability: Analysis

Client Needs: Physiological Integrity
Integrated Process: Nursing Process—implementation
Content Area: Adult health—respiratory
Reference: Potter, P., & Perry, A. (2005). *Fundamentals of nursing* (6th ed., p. 1118). St. Louis: Mosby.

12. **2**

Rationale: If the chest drainage system is disconnected, the end of the tube is placed in a bottle of sterile water held below the level of the chest. The system is replaced if it breaks or cracks or if the collection chamber is full. Placing a sterile dressing over the disconnection site will not prevent complications resulting from the disconnection. The physician may need to be notified, but this is not the initial action.
Test-Taking Strategy: Use the process of elimination and note the strategic word *initial* in the question. This indicates that a nursing action is required that will prevent a serious complication as a result of the disconnection. Eliminate options 1 and 3 because these actions delay required and immediate intervention. From the remaining options, recalling the complications that can occur from a disconnection will direct you to option 2. Review interventions related to the complications of a chest tube if you had difficulty with this question.
Level of Cognitive Ability: Application
Client Needs: Physiological Integrity
Integrated Process: Nursing Process—implementation
Content Area: Adult health—respiratory
References: Perry, A.. & Potter, P. (2006). *Clinical nursing skills & techniques* (6th ed., p. 874). St. Louis: Mosby.
Potter, P., & Perry, A. (2005). *Fundamentals of nursing* (6th ed., p. 1119). St. Louis: Mosby.

13. **4**

Rationale: When the chest tube is removed, the client is asked to perform the Valsalva maneuver (take a deep breath, exhale, and bear down). The tube is quickly withdrawn, and an airtight dressing is taped in place. An alternative instruction is to ask the client to take a deep breath and hold the breath while the tube is removed. Options 1, 2, and 3 are incorrect client instructions.
Test-Taking Strategy: Use the process of elimination and focus on the subject. Visualize the procedure and the client instructions as you select an option. If you had difficulty with this question, review the procedure for removal of a chest tube.
Level of Cognitive Ability: Application
Client Needs: Physiological Integrity
Integrated Process: Nursing Process—implementation
Content Area: Adult health—respiratory
Reference: Perry, A., & Potter, P. (2006). *Clinical nursing skills & techniques* (6th ed., pp. 869-870). St. Louis: Mosby.

14. **2**

Rationale: If the tube is dislodged accidentally, the initial nursing action is to grasp the retention sutures and spread the opening. If agency policy permits, the nurse then attempts immediately to replace the tube. Covering the tracheostomy site will block the airway. Options 1 and 3 will delay treatment in this emergency situation.

Test-Taking Strategy: Use the process of elimination. Eliminate options 1 and 3 first because they are comparative or alike and will delay the immediate intervention needed. Eliminate option 4 because this action will block the airway. If you had difficulty with this question, review the intervention required if a tracheostomy tube dislodges.
Level of Cognitive Ability: Application
Client Needs: Physiological Integrity
Integrated Process: Nursing Process—implementation
Content Area: Adult health—respiratory
Reference: Lewis, S., Heitkemper, M., & Dirksen, S. (2004). *Medical-surgical nursing: Assessment and management of clinical problems* (6th ed., p. 582). St. Louis: Mosby.

15. **1**

Rationale: The nurse reports stridor to the physician immediately. This is a high-pitched, coarse sound that is heard with the stethoscope over the trachea. Stridor indicates airway edema and places the client at risk for airway obstruction. Options 2, 3, and 4 are not signs that require immediate notification of the physician.
Test Taking Strategy: Use the process of elimination. Recall that the prime danger after removal of an artificial airway is the client's ability to maintain a patent airway and breathe independently. In comparing each of the options with this risk in mind, eliminate options 2, 3, and 4. Because stridor indicates laryngeal edema and possible airway obstruction, it is the symptom that must be reported immediately. Review care to the client following removal of an endotracheal tube if you had difficulty with this question.
Level of Cognitive Ability: Analysis
Client Needs: Physiological Integrity
Integrated Process: Nursing Process—implementation
Content Area: Adult health—respiratory
Reference: Ignatavicius, D., & Workman, M. (2006). *Medical-surgical nursing: Critical thinking for collaborative care* (5th ed., p. 669). Philadelphia: W.B. Saunders.

ALTERNATE ITEM FORMAT: MULTIPLE RESPONSE

Answer: 3, 4, 5, 6
Rationale: The bubbling of water in the water seal chamber indicates air drainage from the client and usually is seen when intrathoracic pressure is higher than atmospheric pressure, and may occur during exhalation, coughing, or sneezing. Excessive bubbling in the water seal chamber may indicate an air leak, an unexpected finding. Fluctuation of water in the tube in the water seal chamber during inhalation and exhalation is expected. An absence of fluctuation may indicate that the chest tube is obstructed or that the lung has reexpanded and that no more air is leaking into the pleural space.

Gentle (not vigorous) bubbling should be noted in the suction control chamber. A total of 50 mL of drainage is not excessive in a client returning to the nursing unit from the recovery room. Drainage that is more that 100 mL/hr is considered excessive and requires physician notification. The chest tube insertion site is covered with an occlusive (airtight) dressing to prevent air from entering the pleural space. Positioning the drainage system below the client's chest allows gravity to drain the pleural space.

Test-Taking Strategy: Thinking about the physiology associated with the functioning of a chest tube drainage system will assist in answering this question. The words *excessive bubbling* and *vigorous bubbling* will assist in eliminating these assessment findings. Review care for the client with a chest tube drainage system if you had difficulty with this question.

Level of Cognitive Ability: Analysis

Client Needs: Physiological Integrity
Integrated Process: Nursing Process—assessment
Content Area: Adult health—respiratory
References: Ignatavicius, D., & Workman, M. (2006). *Medical-surgical nursing: Critical thinking for collaborative care* (5th ed., pp. 623-625). Philadelphia: W.B. Saunders.
Potter, P., & Perry, A. (2005). *Fundamentals of nursing* (6th ed., pp. 1118-1121). St. Louis: Mosby.

REFERENCES

Elkin, M., Perry, A., & Potter, P. (2004). *Nursing interventions and clinical skills* (3rd ed.). St. Louis: Mosby.

Ignatavicius, D., & Workman, M. (2006). *Medical-surgical nursing: Critical thinking for collaborative care* (5th ed.). Philadelphia: W.B. Saunders.

Lewis, S., Heitkemper, M., & Dirksen, S. (2004). *Medical-surgical nursing: Assessment and management of clinical problems* (6th ed.). St. Louis: Mosby.

National Council of State Boards of Nursing (Eds.). (2007). *2007 NCLEX-RN® detailed test plan*. Chicago: Author.

Perry, A., & Potter, P. (2006). *Clinical nursing skills & techniques* (6th ed.). St. Louis: Mosby.

Potter, P., & Perry, A. (2005). *Fundamentals of nursing* (6th ed.). St. Louis: Mosby.

Maternity Nursing

PYRAMID TERMS

amniotic fluid The pale, straw-colored fluid in which the fetus floats. It serves as a cushion against injury from sudden blows or movements and helps maintain a constant body temperature for the fetus. The fetus modifies the amniotic fluid through the processes of swallowing, urinating, and movement through the respiratory tract.

ballottement Rebounding of the fetus against the examiner's finger on palpation. When the examiner taps the cervix, the fetus floats upward in the amniotic fluid. The examiner feels a rebound when the fetus falls back.

Chadwick's sign Bluish coloration of the mucous membranes of the cervix, vagina, and vulva that occurs at about 6 weeks of pregnancy and is a probable sign of pregnancy.

delivery Actual event of birth; the expulsion or extraction of the neonate.

embryo Stage of fetal development that lasts from day 15 until approximately 8 weeks after conception or until the embryo measures 3 cm from crown to rump.

fertilization Uniting of the sperm and ovum, which occurs within 12 hours of ovulation and within 2 to 3 days of insemination, the average duration of viability for the ovum and sperm.

Goodell's sign Softening of the cervix that occurs at the beginning of the second month of gestation and is a probable sign of pregnancy.

gravida A pregnant woman; called gravida I (primigravida) during the first pregnancy, gravida II during the second, and so on.

Hegar's sign Compressibility and softening of the lower uterine segment that occurs at about week 6 of gestation; a probable sign of pregnancy.

implantation Attachment of the zygote to the uterine wall 6 to 10 days after conception.

infant A baby born alive; also, a baby from 28 days of age until the first birthday.

labor Coordinated sequence of involuntary uterine contractions resulting in effacement and dilation of cervix, followed by expulsion of the products of conception.

lecithin (L)-to-sphingomyelin (S) ratio The ratio of two components of amniotic fluid, used for predicting fetal lung maturity; the normal L/S ratio in amniotic fluid is 2:1 or higher when the fetal lungs are mature.

lochia Discharge from the uterus that consists of blood from the vessels of the placental site and debris from the decidua; lasts for 2 to 3 weeks after delivery.

Nägele's rule Determines the estimated date of confinement and works on the premise that the woman has a 28-day menstrual cycle. Add 7 days to the first day of the last menstrual period. Subtract 3 months and add 1 year. Alternatively, add 7 days to the last menstrual period and count forward 9 months.

neonate A human offspring from the time of birth to the twenty-eighth day of life; also called newborn.

newborn A human offspring from the time of birth to the twenty-eighth day of life; also called neonate.

oligohydramnios An abnormally small amount or absence of amniotic fluid; associated with fetal renal abnormalities.

parity The number of pregnancies that have been carried to viability.

placenta The organ that provides for the exchange of nutrients and waste products between the fetus and the mother, produces hormones to maintain pregnancy, and develops by the third month of gestation; also called afterbirth.

quickening First perception of fetal movement, appearing usually in the sixteenth to twentieth week of pregnancy.

surfactant Phospholipid that is necessary to keep the fetal lung alveoli from collapsing; amount is usually sufficient after 32 weeks' gestation.

uterus Located behind the symphysis pubis, between the bladder and the rectum. It is comprised of four parts—fundus (upper part), corpus (body), isthmus (lower segment), and cervix.

vagina A tubular structure located behind the bladder and in front of the rectum; extends from the cervix to the vaginal opening in the perineum. It functions as the outflow tract for menstrual fluid and for vaginal and cervical secretions, the birth canal, and the organ for coitus.

viability The capability of the fetus to survive outside the uterus; about 22 to 24 weeks after the last menstrual period, or fetal weight more than 500 g.

THE PYRAMID TO SUCCESS

The Pyramid to Success focuses on the physiological and psychosocial aspects related to the experience of pregnancy, delivery, and postpartum period. Pyramid Points begin with the assessment and knowledge of expected findings of the pregnant client and fetus during the antepartum period. Instructing the pregnant client in measures that will promote a healthy environment for the mother and the fetus is included. The focus is on the importance of antepartum follow-up, nutrition, and interventions for common discomforts that occur during pregnancy. Knowledge of the purpose of the commonly prescribed diagnostic tests and procedures in the antepartum period is also part of the Pyramid to Success. The focus is on disorders that can occur during pregnancy, particularly gestational hypertension and diabetes mellitus. Review of the labor and delivery process and the immediate interventions for conditions in which the mother or fetal status is compromised, such as prolapsed cord or altered fetal heart rate, is part of the Pyramid to Success for the labor and delivery area. Review of the fetus from the mother with human immunodeficiency virus or acquired immunodeficiency syndrome or the substance-abusing mother is recommended. The Pyramid to Success also includes a focus on the normal expectations of the postpartum period and the complications that can occur during this time. The next Pyramid Point focuses on the normal physical assessment findings and early identification of disorders in the neonate. The last Pyramid Point in this unit is on maternity and newborn medications. Integrated Processes addressed in this unit include Caring, Communication and Documentation, Nursing Process, and Teaching/Learning.

▲ CLIENT NEEDS

Safe and Effective Care Environment

Consulting with other health care team members
Delegating client care activities
Establishing priorities of care
Handling hazardous and infectious materials safely
Maintaining confidentiality
Managing the health care environment
Obtaining informed consent for diagnostic tests and procedures
Providing continuity of client care
Upholding client's rights
Using medical and surgical asepsis when providing care
Using standard, transmission-based, and other precautions when providing care

Health Promotion and Maintenance

Assessing for growth and development
Discussing expected body image changes with the client
Discussing family planning and birthing and parenting issues
Discussing reproductive and human sexuality issues
Identifying health and wellness concepts and providing health care screening
Identifying high-risk behaviors
Identifying lifestyle choices
Performing techniques of physical assessment
Providing antepartum, intrapartum, postpartum, and newborn care
Teaching regarding antepartum, intrapartum, and postpartum care
Teaching regarding care to the newborn

Psychosocial Integrity

Considering cultural, religious, and spiritual influences regarding birth and motherhood
Discussing situational role changes in the family
Ensuring therapeutic interactions within the family
Identifying available support systems
Identifying coping mechanisms

Physiological Integrity

Providing nonpharmacological comfort interventions during labor
Identifying the action and contraindications for prescribed pharmacological agents
Monitoring for side effects and adverse effects related to prescribed pharmacological and parenteral therapies
Calculating medication dosages and administering medications safely
Monitoring for expected outcomes and effects related to pharmacological and parenteral therapies
Providing pharmacological pain management during labor
Instructing the client about prescribed diagnostic tests and procedures
Providing interventions for unexpected events during pregnancy
Monitoring the client during the labor and delivery process
Monitoring for normal expectations during pregnancy
Teaching the client about nutrition during pregnancy and in the postpartum period
Teaching the client about the physiological changes that occur during pregnancy
Identifying at-risk clients during pregnancy

REFERENCES

Chernecky, C., & Berger, B. (2004). *Laboratory tests and diagnostic procedures* (4th ed.). Philadelphia: W.B. Saunders.
Hockenberry, M., Wilson, D., & Winkelstein, M. (2005). *Wong's essentials of pediatric nursing* (7th ed.). St. Louis: Mosby.
Lowdermilk, D., & Perry, S. (2006). *Maternity nursing* (7th ed.). St. Louis: Mosby.
Mattson, S., & Smith, J. (2004). *Core curriculum for maternal-newborn nursing* (3rd ed.). St. Louis: W.B. Saunders.
McKinney, E., James, S., Murray, S., & Ashwill, J. (2005). *Maternal-child nursing* (2nd ed.). St. Louis: W.B. Saunders.
Murray, S., & McKinney, E., (2006). *Foundations of maternal-newborn nursing* (4th ed.). Philadelphia: W.B. Saunders.
National Council of State Boards of Nursing (2007). *2007 NCLEX-RN© detailed test plan*. Chicago: Author.
Potter, P., & Perry, A. (2005). *Fundamentals of nursing* (6th ed.). St. Louis: Mosby.
Varcarolis, E., Carson, V., & Shoemaker, N. (2006). *Foundations of psychiatric mental health nursing: A clinical approach* (5th ed.). Philadelphia: W.B. Saunders.
Wong, D., Hockenberry, M., Perry, S., et al. (2006). *Maternal-child nursing care* (3rd ed.). St. Louis: Mosby.

Female Reproductive System

I. REPRODUCTIVE STRUCTURES (Fig. 22-1)

A. Ovaries
 1. Form and expel ova
 2. Secrete estrogen and progesterone
B. Fallopian tubes
 1. Muscular tubes (oviducts) approximate to the ovaries and connect to the **uterus**
 2. Tubes that propel the ova from the ovaries to the **uterus**
C. **Uterus**
 1. A muscular, pear-shaped cavity in which the fetus develops
 2. The cavity from which menstruation occurs
D. Cervix
 1. The internal os of the cervix opens into the body of the uterine cavity.
 2. The cervical canal is located between the internal os and the external os.
 3. The external cervical os opens into the **vagina**.
E. **Vagina**
 1. A muscular tube that extends from the cervix to the vaginal opening in the perineum
 2. Known as the birth canal
 3. Passage between the cervical os and the external environment
   a. Passageway for menstrual blood flow
   b. Passageway for fetus
   c. Passageway for penis for intercourse

II. MENSTRUAL CYCLE (Box 22-1)

A. Ovarian hormones
 1. Ovarian hormones include the follicle-stimulating hormone (FSH) and luteinizing hormone (LH).
 2. The hormones are released by the anterior pituitary gland.
 3. The hormones produce changes in the ovaries.
 4. Secretion of ovarian hormones leads to changes in the endometrium.
 5. The menstrual cycle, the regularly recurring physiological changes in the endometrium that culminate in its shedding, may vary in length, with the average length being about 28 days.
B. Ovarian changes
 1. Preovulatory phase
 2. Luteal phase
C. Uterine changes
 1. Menstrual phase
 2. Proliferative phase
 3. Secretory phase

III. FEMALE PELVIS AND MEASUREMENTS

A. True pelvis
 1. Lies below the pelvic brim
 2. Consists of the pelvic inlet, midpelvis, and pelvic outlet
B. False pelvis
 1. Is the shallow portion above the pelvic brim
 2. Supports the abdominal viscera
C. Types of pelvis
 1. Gynecoid
   a. Normal female pelvis
   b. Transversely rounded or blunt
   c. Most favorable for successful **labor** and birth
 2. Anthropoid
   a. Oval shape
   b. Adequate outlet, with a normal or moderately narrow pubic arch
 3. Android
   a. Wedge-shaped or angulated
   b. Seen in males
   c. Not favorable for **labor**

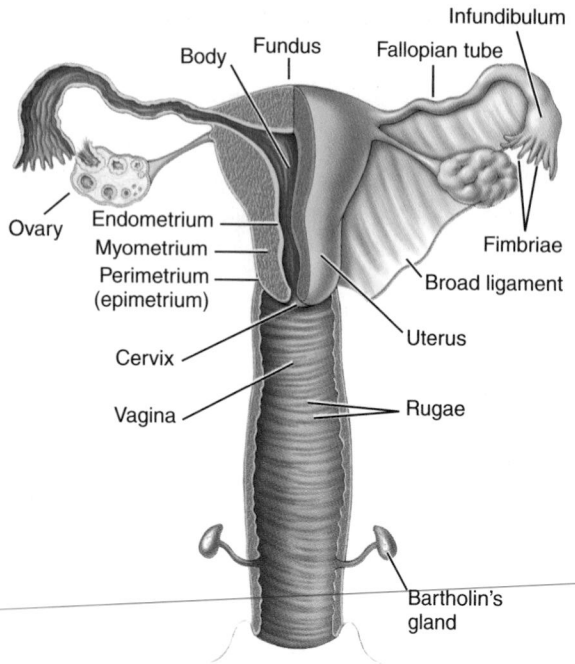

Labels on figure: Body, Fundus, Infundibulum, Fallopian tube, Ovary, Endometrium, Myometrium, Perimetrium (epimetrium), Cervix, Vagina, Fimbriae, Broad ligament, Uterus, Rugae, Bartholin's gland

FIG. 22-1 Female reproductive organs. (From Herlihy, B., & Maebius, N. [2003]. *The human body in health and illness* [2nd ed.] Philadelphia: W.B. Saunders.)

d. Narrow pelvic planes can cause slow descent and midpelvic arrest.
4. Platypelloid
  a. Flat with an oval inlet
  b. Wide transverse diameter but short anteroposterior diameter, making the outlet inadequate
D. Pelvic inlet diameters
  1. Anteroposterior diameters
    a. Diagonal conjugate: Distance from the lower margin of the symphysis pubis to the sacral promontory
    b. True conjugate or conjugate vera: Distance from the upper margin of the symphysis pubis to the sacral promontory
    c. Obstetric conjugate: The smallest front-to-back distance through which the fetal head must pass in moving through the pelvic inlet
  2. Transverse diameter: The largest of the pelvic inlet diameters; located at right angles to the true conjugate
  3. Oblique (diagonal) diameter: Not clinically measurable
  4. Posterior sagittal diameter: Distance from the point where the anteroposterior and transverse

---

BOX 22-1

Menstrual Cycle

OVARIAN CHANGES

Preovulatory Phase

The hypothalamus releases gonadotropin-releasing hormone through the portal system to the anterior pituitary system.

Secretion of follicle-stimulating hormone (FSH) by the anterior lobe of the pituitary gland stimulates growth of follicles.

Most follicles die, leaving one to mature into a large graafian follicle.

Estrogen produced by the follicle stimulates increased secretions of luteinizing hormone (LH) by the anterior lobe of the pituitary gland.

The follicle ruptures and releases an ovum into the peritoneal cavity.

Luteal Phase

The luteal phase begins with ovulation.

Body temperature drops and then rises by 0.5° to 1° F around the time of ovulation.

Corpus luteum is formed from follicle cells that remain in the ovary following ovulation.

Corpus luteum secretes estrogen and progesterone during the remaining 14 days of the cycle.

Corpus luteum degenerates if the ovum is not fertilized, and secretion of estrogen and progesterone declines.

The decline of estrogen and progesterone stimulates the anterior pituitary to secrete more FSH and LH, initiating a new reproductive cycle.

UTERINE CHANGES

Menstrual Phase

The menstrual phase consists of 4 to 6 days of bleeding as the endometrium breaks down because of the decreased levels of estrogen and progesterone.

The level of FSH increases, enabling the beginning of a new cycle.

Proliferative Phase

The proliferative phase lasts about 9 days.

Estrogen stimulates proliferation and growth of the endometrium.

As estrogen increases, it suppresses secretion of FSH and increases secretion of LH.

Secretion of LH stimulates ovulation and the development of the corpus luteum.

Ovulation occurs between days 12 and 16.

The estrogen level is high and the progesterone level is low.

Secretory Phase

The secretory phase lasts about 12 days and follows ovulation.

This phase is initiated in response to the increase in LH level.

The graafian follicle is replaced by the corpus luteum.

The corpus luteum secretes progesterone and estrogen.

Progesterone prepares the endometrium for pregnancy if a fertilized ovum is implanted.

diameters cross each other to the middle of the sacral promontory
E. Pelvic midplane diameters
1. Transverse diameter (interspinous diameter)
2. Midplane normally is the largest plane and has the longest diameter
F. Pelvic outlet diameters
1. Transverse (intertuberous diameter)
2. Outlet presents the smallest plane of the pelvic canal

IV. FERTILIZATION AND IMPLANTATION
A. **Fertilization**
1. Fertilization occurs in the upper region of the fallopian tubes
2. It occurs within 12 hours of ovulation and within 2 to 3 days of insemination, the average durations of **viability** for the ovum and sperm.
3. It takes place when sperm and ovum unite.
4. Once fertilized, the membrane of the ovum undergoes changes that prevent entry of other sperm.
5. Each reproductive cell carries 23 chromosomes.
6. Sperm carry an X or a Y chromosome—XY, male; XX, female.
B. **Implantation**
1. Zygote is propelled toward the **uterus**.
2. Zygote implants 6 to 8 days after ovulation.
3. Blastocyst secretes chorionic gonadotropin to ensure that the corpus luteum remains viable and secretes estrogen and progesterone for the first 2 to 3 months of gestation.

V. FETAL DEVELOPMENT (Box 22-2)
A. Preembryonic period: First 2 weeks after conception
B. Embryonic period: Beginning of the third through the eighth week after conception
C. Fetal period: Beginning of the ninth week after conception and ending with birth

VI. FETAL ENVIRONMENT
A. Amnion
1. Encloses the amniotic cavity.
2. Is the inner membrane that forms about the second week of embryonic development
3. Forms a fluid-filled sac that surrounds the **embryo** and later the fetus
B. Chorion
1. Is the outer membrane
2. Becomes vascularized and forms the fetal part of the **placenta**
C. **Amniotic fluid**
1. Consists of 800 to 1200 mL by the end of pregnancy

2. Surrounds, cushions, and protects the fetus and allows for fetal movement
3. Maintains the body temperature of the fetus
4. Consists largely of fetal urine and is therefore a measure of fetal kidney function
5. The fetus modifies the **amniotic fluid** through the processes of swallowing, urinating, and movement through the respiratory tract.
D. Placenta
1. The placenta provides for exchange of nutrients and waste products between the fetus and mother
2. It develops by the third month.
3. It depends on maternal circulation.
4. It produces hormones to maintain pregnancy and assumes full responsibility for the production of these hormones by the twelfth week of gestation.
5. Large particles such as bacteria cannot pass through the **placenta**.
6. Nutrients, drugs, antibodies, and viruses can pass through the **placenta**.
7. In the third trimester, transfer of maternal immunoglobulin provides the fetus with passive immunity to certain diseases for the first few months after birth.
8. By week 8, genetic testing can be done.

VII. FETAL CIRCULATION
A. Umbilical cord
1. It contains two arteries and one vein.
2. The arteries carry deoxygenated blood and waste products from the fetus.
3. The vein carries oxygenated blood and provides oxygen and nutrients to the fetus.
B. Fetal heart rate
1. The fetal heart rate (FHR) depends on gestational age; the fetal heart rate is 160 to 170 beats/min in the first trimester but slows with fetal growth to 120 to 160 beats/min near or at term.
2. The fetal heart rate is about twice the maternal heart rate.
C. Fetal circulation bypass (Fig. 22-2)
1. Fetal circulation bypass is present because of nonfunctioning lungs.
2. Bypasses must close following birth to allow blood to flow through the lungs and the liver.
3. The ductus arteriosus connects the pulmonary artery to the aorta, bypassing the lungs.
4. The ductus venosus connects the umbilical vein and the inferior vena cava, bypassing the liver.
5. The foramen ovale is the opening between the right and left atria of the heart, bypassing the lungs.

BOX 22-2
Fetal Development

EMBRYONIC PERIOD (weeks 3 through 8)
Week 1
Blastocyst is free-floating.
Weeks 2 to 3
Embryo is 2 mm in length.
Groove forms along middle of back.
Blood circulation begins.
Heart is tubular.
Week 5
Embryo is 4 to 6 mm in length.
Embryo is 0.4 g.
Double heart chambers are visible.
Heart begins to beat.
Limb buds form.
Week 8
Embryo is 3 cm in length.
Embryo is 2 g.
Eyelids begin to fuse.
Circulatory system through umbilical cord is well
  established.
Every organ system is present.

FETAL PERIOD (week 9 to birth)
Week 12
Fetus is 8 cm in length.
Fetus is 45 g.
Face is well formed
Limbs are long and slender.
Kidneys begin to form urine.
Spontaneous movements occur.
Heartbeat is detected by Doppler transducer between 10
  and 12 weeks.
Sex is visually recognizable.
Week 16
Active movements are present.
Fetal skin is transparent.
Lanugo hair begins to develop.
Skeletal ossification occurs.
Week 20
Fetus is 19 cm in length.
Fetus is 465 g.
Lanugo covers the entire body.
Fetus has nails.
Muscles are developed.

Enamel and dentin are depositing.
Heartbeat is detected by regular (nonelectronic) feto-
  scope.
Week 24
Fetus is 28 cm in length.
Fetus is 780 g.
Hair on head is well formed.
Skin is reddish and wrinkled.
Reflex hand grasp functions.
Vernix caseosa covers entire body.
Fetus has ability to hear.
Week 28
Fetus is 38 cm in length.
Fetus is 1200 g.
Limbs are well flexed.
Brain is developing rapidly.
Eyelids open and close.
Lungs are developed sufficiently to provide gas exchange
  (lecithin forming).
If born, neonate can breathe at this time.
Week 32
Fetus is 40 cm in length.
Fetus is 2000 g.
Bones are fully developed.
Subcutaneous fat has collected.
The L/S (lecithin-to-sphingomyelin) ratio is 1.2:1.
Week 36
The fetus is 42 to 48 cm in length.
The fetus is 2500 g.
The skin is pink and the body is rounded.
The skin is less wrinkled.
Lanugo is disappearing.
The L/S ratio is higher than 2:1.
Week 40
The fetus is 48 to 52 cm in length.
The fetus is 3000 to 3600 g.
The skin is pinkish and smooth.
Lanugo is present on upper arms and shoulders.
Vernix caseosa decreases
Fingernails extend beyond fingertips.
Sole (plantar) creases run down to the heel.
The testes are in the scrotum.
The labia majora are well developed.

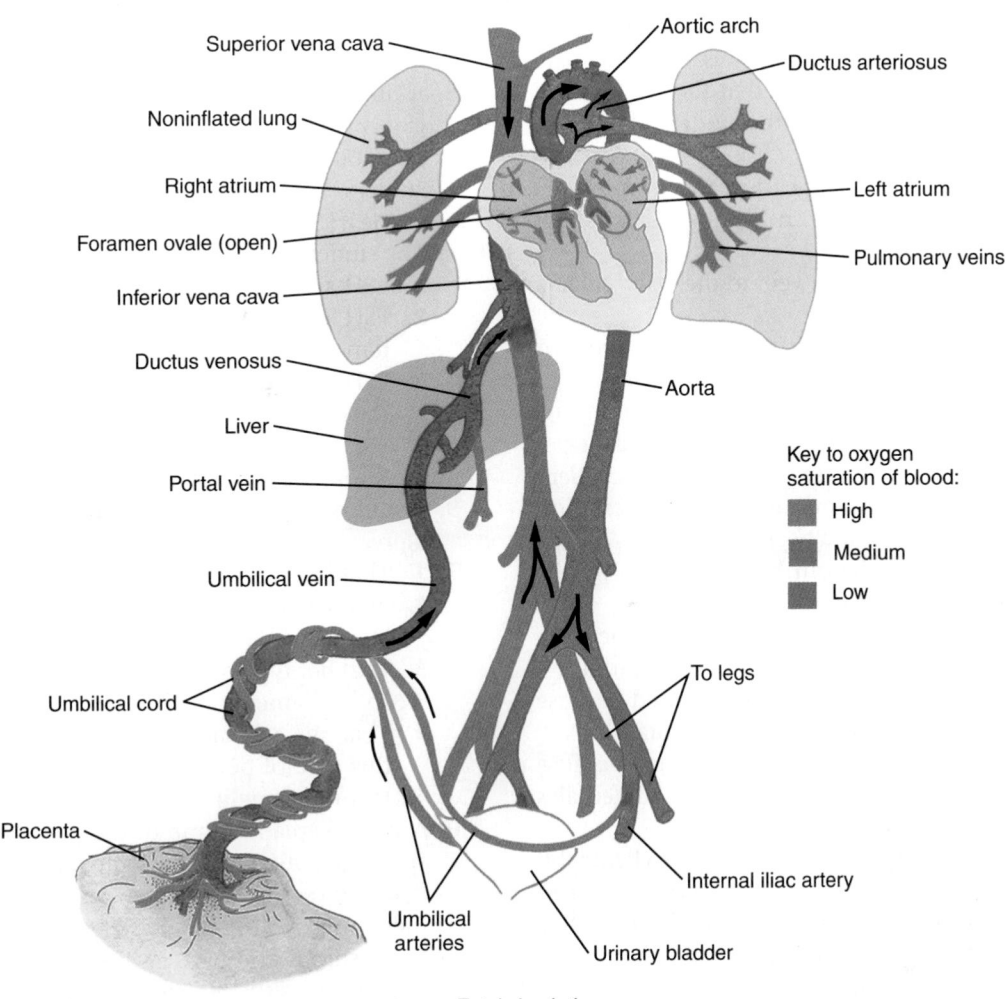

FIG. 22-2 Fetal circulation. Three shunts allow most blood from the placenta to by-pass the fetal lungs and liver: ductus venosus, ductus arteriosus, and foramen ovale. (From Murray, S., & McKinney, E., [2006]. *Foundations of maternal-newborn nursing* [4th ed.]. Philadelphia: W.B. Saunders.)

PRACTICE QUESTIONS

1. A nurse is providing information to a client on the female reproductive system. While discussing the uterus and its different layers, the nurse understands that the myometrium has unique muscle fibers that make it ideally suited for the birth process. The nurse would describe this layer to the client as:
   1. The inner layer of muscle that is in the uterus
   2. The middle layer of thick muscle in the uterus
   3. The outer layer of muscle that covers most of the uterus
   4. The functional layer that lies above the basal layer of the uterus

2. A nursing student is preparing a prenatal class on the process of fetal circulation. The nursing instructor asks the student to specifically describe the process through the umbilical cord. The best response from the student is which of the following?
   1. "The one artery carries freshly oxygenated blood and nutrient-rich blood back from the placenta to the fetus."
   2. "The two arteries carry freshly oxygenated blood and nutrient-rich blood back from the placenta to the fetus.
   3. "The two arteries in the umbilical cord carry blood that is high in carbon dioxide and other waste products away from the fetus to the placenta."
   4. "The two veins in the umbilical cord carry blood that is high in carbon dioxide and other waste products away from the fetus to the placenta."

3. A nursing student is assigned to a client in labor. A nursing instructor asks the student to describe fetal circulation, specifically the ductus venosus. The nursing instructor determines that the student understands fetal circulation if the student states that the ductus venosus:
   1. Connects the pulmonary artery to the aorta
   2. Is an opening between the right and left atria
   3. Connects the umbilical vein to the inferior vena cava
   4. Connects the umbilical artery to the inferior vena cava

4. A pregnant client tells the clinic nurse that she wants to know the sex of the baby as soon as it can be determined. The nurse knows that the client should be able to find out at 12 weeks' gestation because by the end of the twelfth week:
   1. The sex of the baby can be determined by the appearance of the external genitalia.
   2. The sex of the baby can be determined because the external genitalia begins to differentiate.
   3. The sex of the baby can be determined because the testes are descended into the scrotal sac.
   4. The sex of the baby can be determined because the internal differences in males and females become apparent.

5. A nurse is performing an assessment on a client who is at 38 weeks' gestation and notes that the fetal heart rate (FHR) is 174 beats/min. On the basis of this finding, the appropriate nursing action is to:
   1. Notify the physician.
   2. Document the finding.
   3. Check the mother's heart rate.
   4. Tell the client that the fetal heart rate is normal.

6. A pregnant adolescent client asks the nurse about the menstrual cycle. The nurse describes the cycle and tells the adolescent that its normal duration is about how many days?
   1. 14
   2. 28
   3. 30
   4. 45

7. A nurse is conducting a prenatal class on the female reproductive system. When a client in the class asks why the fertilized ovum stays in the fallopian tube for 3 days, the nurse responds that the reason for this is that it:
   1. Promotes the fertilized ovum's chances of survival
   2. Promotes the fertilized ovum's exposure to estrogen and progesterone
   3. Promotes the fertilized ovum's normal implantation in the top portion of the uterus
   4. Promotes the fertilized ovum's exposure to luteinizing hormone (LH) and follicle-stimulating hormone (FSH)

8. A nursing instructor is reviewing the menstrual cycle with a nursing student who will be conducting a prenatal teaching session. The instructor asks the student to describe the follicle-stimulating hormone (FSH) and the luteinizing hormone (LH). The student accurately responds by stating that:
   1. FSH and LH are secreted by the adrenal glands.
   2. FSH and LH are released from the anterior pituitary gland.
   3. FSH and LH are secreted by the corpus luteum of the ovary.
   4. FSH and LH stimulate the formation of milk during pregnancy.

9. The nurse should explain which of the following to a pregnant client found to have a gynecoid pelvis?
   1. That her type of pelvis has a narrow pubic arch
   2. That her type of pelvis is the most favorable for labor and birth
   3. That her type of pelvis is a wide pelvis, but has a short diameter
   4. That she will need a cesarean section because this type of pelvis is not favorable for a normal labor and vaginal delivery

10. A nurse explains some of the purposes of the placenta to a client during a prenatal visit. The nurse determines that the client understands some of these purposes when she states that the placenta:
    1. Cushions and protects the baby.
    2. Maintains the temperature of the baby.
    3. Is the way the baby gets food and oxygen.
    4. Prevents all antibodies and viruses from passing to the baby.

ALTERNATE ITEM FORMAT: MULTIPLE RESPONSE

A nursing instructor asks a nursing student to list the functions of the amniotic fluid. The student responds correctly by stating that which of the following are functions of amniotic fluid? Select all that apply.

1. Allows for fetal movement
2. Is a measure of kidney function
3. Surrounds, cushions, and protects the fetus
4. Maintains the body temperature of the fetus
5. Prevents large particles such as bacteria from passing to the fetus
6. Provides an exchange of nutrients and waste products between the mother and the fetus

ANSWERS

1. **2**
Rationale: The myometrium is the middle layer of thick muscle in the uterus. These muscles assist the birth process by expelling the fetus, ligating blood vessels after birth, and controlling the opening of the cervical os. Options 1, 3, and 4 describe the other layers of the uterus.
Test-Taking Strategy: Use the process of elimination and knowledge of the anatomy and physiology of the uterus. Focus on the strategic word *myometrium* and use medical terminology skills to direct you to option 2. If you had difficulty with this question, review anatomy and physiology of the female reproductive system.
Level of Cognitive Ability: Application
Client Needs: Physiological Integrity
Integrated Process: Teaching and Learning
Content Area: Maternity—antepartum
Reference: Wong, D., Perry, S., Hockenberry, M., et al. (2006). *Maternal child nursing care* (3rd ed., p. 85). St. Louis: Mosby.

2. **3**
Rationale: Blood pumped by the embryo's heart leaves the embryo through two umbilical arteries. Once oxygenated, the blood then is returned by one umbilical vein. Arteries carry deoxygenated blood and waste products from the fetus, and veins carry oxygenated blood and provide oxygen and nutrients to the fetus.
Test-Taking Strategy: Use the process of elimination. Recall that three umbilical vessels are within the umbilical cord (two arteries and one vein) and that the veins carry oxygenated blood and the arteries carry deoxygenated blood. If you had difficulty with this question, review fetal circulation.
Level of Cognitive Ability: Application
Client Needs: Physiological Integrity
Integrated Process: Teaching and Learning
Content Area: Maternity—antepartum
References: Lowdermilk, D., & Perry, A. (2004). *Maternity and women's health care* (8th ed., p. 337). St. Louis: Mosby.
Wong, D., Perry, S., Hockenberry, M., et al. (2006). *Maternal child nursing care* (3rd ed., pp. 201-202). St. Louis: Mosby.

3. **3**
Rationale: The ductus venosus connects the umbilical vein to the inferior vena cava. Options 1, 2, and 4 are incorrect. The foramen ovale is a temporary opening between the right and left atria. The ductus arteriosus joins the aorta and the pulmonary artery.
Test-Taking Strategy: Use the process of elimination and knowledge regarding fetal circulation to answer this question. Remember that the ductus venosus connects the umbilical vein to the inferior vena cava. Review fetal circulation if you had difficulty with this question.
Level of Cognitive Ability: Analysis
Client Needs: Physiological Integrity
Integrated Process: Nursing Process—evaluation
Content Area: Maternity—intrapartum
References: Lowdermilk, D., & Perry, A. (2004). *Maternity and women's health care* (8th ed., p. 337). St. Louis: Mosby.
Wong, D., Perry, S., Hockenberry, M., et al. (2006). *Maternal child nursing care* (3rd ed., p. 337). St. Louis: Mosby.

4. **1**
Rationale: By the end of the twelfth week, the external genitalia of the fetus have developed to such a degree that the sex of the fetus can be determined visually. Option 2 occurs at the end of the ninth week. Option 3 occurs at the end of the thirty-eighth week. Option 4 occurs at the end of the seventh week.
Test-Taking Strategy: Use knowledge regarding fetal development to answer this question. Remember that the sex of the fetus can be recognizable visually by the appearance of the external genitalia by gestational week 12. If you had difficulty with this question, review fetal development.
Level of Cognitive Ability: Application
Client Needs: Health Promotion and Maintenance
Integrated Process: Teaching and Learning
Content Area: Maternity—antepartum
Reference: McKinney, E., James, S., Murray, S., & Ashwill, J. (2005). *Maternal-child nursing* (2nd ed., p. 242). St. Louis: W.B. Saunders.

5. **1**
Rationale: The fetal heart rate depends on gestational age and ranges from 160 to 170 beats/min in the first trimester but slows with fetal growth to 120 to 160 beats/min near or at term. At or near term, if the fetal heart rate is less than 120 or more than 160 beats/min with the uterus at rest, the fetus may be in distress. Because the FHR is increased from the reference range, the nurse should notify the physician. Options 3 and 4 are inappropriate actions based on the information in the question. Although the nurse documents the findings, based on the information in the question, the physician needs to be notified.
Test-Taking Strategy: Use the process of elimination and note the fetal heart rate and that the client is at 38 weeks of gestation. Remember that the normal fetal heart rate at or near term is 120 to 160 beats/min. Review fetal heart rate if you had difficulty with this question.
Level of Cognitive Ability: Application
Client Needs: Physiological Integrity
Integrated Process: Nursing Process—implementation
Content Area: Maternity—antepartum
References: McKinney, E., James, S., Murray, S., & Ashwill, J. (2005). *Maternal-child nursing* (2nd ed., p. 399). St. Louis: W.B. Saunders.
Murray, S., & McKinney, E. (2006). *Foundations of maternal-newborn nursing* (4th ed., p. 317). Philadelphia: W.B. Saunders.

6. **2**
Rationale: The normal duration of the menstrual cycle is about 28 days, although it may range from 20 to 45 days. Significant deviations from the 28-day cycle may be associated with reduced fertility. The first day of the menstrual period is counted as day 1 of the woman's cycle.
Test-Taking Strategy: Use the process of elimination and note the strategic words *normal duration* in the question. Recalling the duration of the menstrual cycle will assist in eliminating options 1, 3, and 4. If you had difficulty with this question, review the menstrual cycle.
Level of Cognitive Ability: Application
Client Needs: Physiological Integrity
Integrated Process: Teaching and Learning
Content Area: Maternity—antepartum

Reference: McKinney, E., James, S., Murray, S., & Ashwill, J. (2005). *Maternal-child nursing* (2nd ed., p. 224). St. Louis: W.B. Saunders.

7. 3

Rationale: The tubal isthmus remains contracted until 3 days after conception to allow the fertilized ovum to develop within the tube. This initial growth of the fertilized ovum promotes its normal implantation in the fundal portion of the uterine corpus. Estrogen is a hormone produced by the ovarian follicles, corpus luteum, adrenal cortex, and placenta during pregnancy. Progesterone is a hormone secreted by the corpus luteum of the ovary, adrenal glands, and placenta during pregnancy. Luteinizing hormone and follicle-stimulating hormone are excreted by the anterior pituitary gland. The survival of the fertilized ovum does not depend on it staying in the fallopian tubes for 3 days.

Test-Taking Strategy: Use knowledge of the anatomy and physiology of the female reproductive system. Remember that fertilization occurs in the fallopian tubes and the fertilized ovum remains in the fallopian tube for about 3 days. This promotes its normal implantation. If you had difficulty with this question, review anatomy and physiology of the reproductive system.

Level of Cognitive Ability: Application
Client Needs: Physiological Integrity
Integrated Process: Teaching and Learning
Content Area: Maternity—antepartum
Reference: Murray, S., & McKinney, E., (2006). *Foundations of maternal-newborn nursing* (4th ed., pp. 55, 58). Philadelphia: W.B. Saunders.

8. 2

Rationale: FSH and LH, when stimulated by gonadotropin-releasing hormone (GnRH) from the hypothalamus, are released from the anterior pituitary gland to stimulate follicular growth and development, growth of the graafian follicle, and production of progesterone. Options 1, 3, and 4 are incorrect.

Test-Taking Strategy: Use the process of elimination, recalling that FSH and LH are released from the anterior pituitary gland. If you had difficulty with this question, review the menstrual cycle.

Level of Cognitive Ability: Comprehension
Client Needs: Physiological Integrity
Integrated Process: Nursing Process—evaluation
Content Area: Maternity—antepartum
Reference: Wong, D., Perry, S., Hockenberry, M., et al. (2006). *Maternal child nursing care* (3rd ed., p. 91). St. Louis: Mosby.

9. 2

Rationale: A gynecoid pelvis is a normal female pelvis and is the most favorable for successful labor and birth. An android pelvis (resembling a male pelvis) would not be favorable for labor because of the narrow pelvic planes. An anthropoid pelvis has an outlet that is adequate, with a normal or moder-

ately narrow pubic arch. The platypelloid pelvis (flat pelvis) has a wide transverse diameter, but the anteroposterior diameter is short, making the outlet inadequate.

Test-Taking Strategy: Use the process of elimination. Recalling that the gynecoid pelvis is the normal female pelvis will direct you to the correct option. Review pelvic types if you had difficulty with this question.

Level of Cognitive Ability: Comprehension
Client Needs: Health Promotion and Maintenance
Integrated Process: Teaching and Learning
Content Area: Maternity—antepartum
Reference: Wong, D., Perry, S., Hockenberry, M., et al. (2006). *Maternal child nursing care* (3rd ed., p. 422). St. Louis: Mosby.

10. 3

Rationale: The placenta provides an exchange of oxygen, nutrients, and waste products between the mother and the fetus. The amniotic fluid surrounds, cushions, and protects the fetus and maintains the body temperature of the fetus. Nutrients, drugs, antibodies, and viruses can pass through the placenta.

Test-Taking Strategy: Use the process of elimination and recall that the placenta provides oxygen and nutrients. If you had difficulty with this question, review the structure and function of the placenta and amniotic fluid.

Level of Cognitive Ability: Application
Client Needs: Health Promotion and Maintenance
Integrated Process: Teaching and Learning
Content Area: Maternity—antepartum
Reference: Murray, S., & McKinney, E. (2006). *Foundations of maternal-newborn nursing* (4th ed., pp. 100-101). Philadelphia: W.B. Saunders.

ALTERNATE ITEM FORMAT: MULTIPLE RESPONSE

Answer: 1, 2, 3, 4

Rationale: The amniotic fluid surrounds, cushions, and protects the fetus. It allows the fetus to move freely, maintains the body temperature of the fetus, and helps measure kidney function, because the amount of fluid is based on the amount of urination from the fetus. The placenta prevents large particles such as bacteria from passing to the fetus and provides an exchange of nutrients and waste products between the mother and the fetus.

Test-Taking Strategy: Focus on the subject of the question, the functions of amniotic fluid. Visualizing the location of the amniotic fluid will assist in answering this question. If you had difficulty with this question, review the function of the amniotic fluid.

Level of Cognitive Ability: Comprehension
Client Needs: Physiological Integrity
Integrated Process: Nursing Process—evaluation
Content Area: Maternity—antepartum
Reference: Wong, D., Perry, S., Hockenberry, M., et al. (2006). *Maternal child nursing care.* (3rd ed., p. 197). St. Louis: Mosby.

REFERENCES

Lowdermilk, D., & Perry, A. (2004). *Maternity and women's health care* (8 ed.). St. Louis: Mosby.

McKinney, E., James, S., Murray, S., & Ashwill, J. (2005). *Maternal-child nursing* (2nd ed.). St. Louis: W.B. Saunders.

Murray, S., & McKinney, E. (2006). *Foundations of maternal-newborn nursing* (4 ed.). Philadelphia: W.B. Saunders.

National Council of State Boards of Nursing. (2007). *2007 NCLEX-RN® detailed test plan.* Chicago: Author.

Wong, D., Perry, S., Hockenberry, M., et al. (2006). *Maternal child nursing care* (3rd ed.). St. Louis: Mosby.

Obstetrical Assessment

I. GESTATION
A. Time from **fertilization** of the ovum until the estimated date of confinement or estimated date of delivery.
B. About 280 days
C. **Nägele's rule** for estimating the date of confinement (Box 23-1)
  1. Use of **Nägele's rule** requires that the woman have a regular 28-day menstrual cycle.
  2. Add 7 days to the first day of the last menstrual period, subtract 3 months, and then add 1 year to that date; alternatively, add 7 days to the date of the last menstrual period and count forward 9 months.

II. GRAVIDITY AND PARITY
A. Gravidity
  1. Gravida refers to a pregnant woman.
  2. Gravidity refers to the number of pregnancies.
  3. Nulligravida is a woman who has never been pregnant.
  4. Primigravida is a woman who is pregnant for the first time.
  5. Multigravida is a woman in at least her second pregnancy.
B. **Parity**
  1. **Parity** is the number of births (not the number of fetuses—e.g., twins) carried past 20 weeks' gestation, whether or not the fetus was born alive.
  2. Nullipara is a woman who has not had a birth at more than 20 weeks of gestation.
  3. Primipara is a woman who has had one birth that occurred after the twentieth week of gestation.
  4. Multipara is a woman who has had two or more pregnancies resulting in viable offspring.

> **BOX 23-1**
> Nägele's Rule for Estimating the Date of Confinement
>
> First day of last menstrual period: September 12, 2008
> Add 7 days: September 19, 2008
> Subtract 3 months: June 19, 2008
> Add 1 year: June 19, 2009
> Estimated date of confinement: June 19, 2009

C. Use of GTPAL: Pregnancy outcomes can be described with the acronym *GTPAL* (Box 23-2).
  1. *G* is gravidity, the number of pregnancies, including the present one.
  2. *T* is term births, the number born at term (longer than 37 weeks' gestation).
  3. *P* is preterm births, the number born before 37 weeks' gestation.
  4. *A* is abortions and/or miscarriages, the number of abortions and/or miscarriages (included in gravida if before 20 weeks' gestation; included in *parity* if past 20 weeks' gestation). Note that a termination of the pregnancy after 20 weeks is referred to as a "therapeutic termination."
  5. *L* is the number of current living children.

III. PREGNANCY SIGNS
A. Presumptive signs
  1. Amenorrhea
  2. Nausea and vomiting
  3. Increased size and increased feeling of fullness in breasts
  4. Pronounced nipples
  5. Urinary frequency
  6. **Quickening:** The first perception of fetal movement may occur as early as the sixteenth to twentieth week of gestation.

G, gravidity
T, term births
P, preterm births
A, abortions or miscarriages
L, current living children
Example: A woman is pregnant for the fourth time. She had one elective abortion in the first trimester, a daughter who was born at 40 weeks' gestation, and a son who was born at 36 weeks' gestation. Therefore, she is gravida (G) 4, parity 2, and term (T) 1 (the daughter born at 40 weeks); preterm (P), 1 (the son born at 36 weeks); abortion (A), 1 (the abortion is counted in the gravida but is not included in the para because it occurred before 20 weeks); living children (L), 2.
   GTPAL = 4, 1, 1, 1, 2

1. Place the client in the supine position.
2. Place the end of the tape measure at the level of the symphysis pubis.
3. Stretch the tape to the top of the uterine fundus.
4. Note and record the measurement.

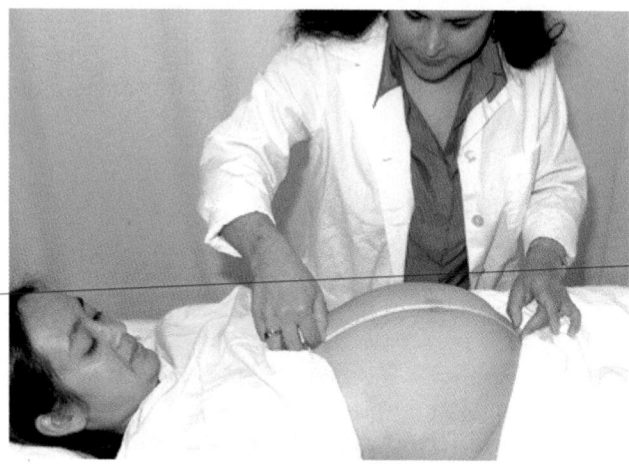

FIG. 23-1 Measurement of fundal height. (From Wong, D., Hockenberry, M., Perry, S., et al. [2006]. *Maternal child nursing care* [3rd ed.]. St. Louis: Mosby.)

   7. Fatigue
   8. Discoloration of the vaginal mucosa
 B. Probable signs
   1. Uterine enlargement
   2. **Hegar's sign:** Softening and thinning of the lower uterine segment that occurs at about week 6
   3. **Goodell's sign:** Softening of the cervix that occurs at the beginning of the second month
   4. **Chadwick's sign:** Bluish coloration of the mucous membranes of the cervix, **vagina,** and vulva that occurs at about week 6
   5. **Ballottement:** Rebounding of the fetus against the examiner's fingers on palpation
   6. Braxton Hicks contractions
   7. Positive pregnancy test for determination of the presence of human chorionic gonadotropin
 C. Positive signs (diagnostic)
   1. Fetal heart rate detected by electronic device (Doppler transducer) at 10 to 12 weeks and by nonelectronic device (fetoscope) at 20 weeks of gestation
   2. Active fetal movements palpable by examiner
   3. Outline of fetus via radiography or ultrasonography

IV. FUNDAL HEIGHT (Box 23-3)
 A. Fundal height is measured to evaluate the gestational age of the fetus (Fig. 23-1).
 B. During the second and third trimesters (weeks 18 to 30), fundal height in centimeters approximately equals fetal age in weeks ± 2 cm (Fig. 23-2).
 C. At 16 weeks, the fundus can be found approximately halfway between the symphysis pubis and the umbilicus.
 D. At 20 to 22 weeks, the fundus is approximately at the location of the umbilicus.
 E. At 36 weeks, the fundus is at the xiphoid process.

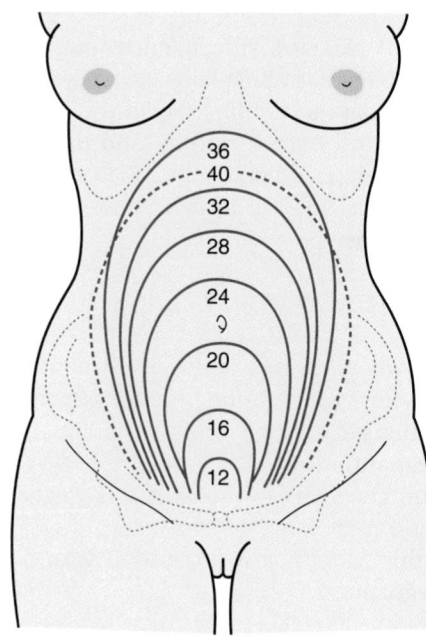

FIG. 23-2 Height of fundus by weeks of normal gestation with a single fetus. (From Wong, D., Hockenberry, M., Perry, S., et al. [2006]. *Maternal child nursing care* [3rd ed.]. St. Louis: Mosby.)

V. MATERNAL RISK FACTORS
 A. German measles (rubella)
   1. The risk of maternal and fetal or congenital infection is related to the trimester of placental infection.

2. Maternal infection during the first 8 weeks of gestation carries the highest rate of fetal infection.

B. Sexually transmitted infections
   1. Syphilis
      a. Organism may cross the **placenta.**
      b. Infection usually leads to spontaneous abortions.
      c. Infection increases the incidence of mental subnormality and physical deformities.
   2. Genital herpes
      a. Organism may cross the **placenta.**
      b. Fetus is contaminated after membranes rupture or with vaginal **delivery.**
   3. Gonorrhea
      a. Fetus is contaminated at the time of **delivery.**
      b. Maternal infection may result in postpartum infection of the **neonate.**
      c. Risks to the **neonate** include ophthalmia neonatorum, pneumonia, and sepsis.

C. Human immunodeficiency virus (HIV)
   1. The virus is transmitted through blood, blood products, and other bodily fluids, such as urine, semen, and vaginal secretions.
   2. Repeated exposure to the virus during pregnancy through unsafe sex practices or intravenous drug use can increase the risk of transmission to the fetus.
   3. Perinatal administration of zidovudine (ZDV) may be recommended to decrease the transmission of HIV virus from mother to fetus.

D. Substance abuse
   1. Many substances cross the **placenta;** therefore, no drugs, including over-the-counter medications, should be taken unless prescribed by a health care provider.
   2. Substances commonly abused include alcohol, cocaine, crack, marijuana, amphetamines, barbiturates, and heroin.
   3. Substance abuse threatens normal fetal growth and successful term completion of the pregnancy.
   4. Substance abuse places the pregnancy at risk for fetal growth restriction, abruptio placentae, and fetal bradycardia.
   5. Physical signs of drug abuse may include dilated or contracted pupils, fatigue, track (needle) marks, skin abscesses, inflamed nasal mucosa, and inappropriate behavior by the mother.
   6. Consumption of alcohol during pregnancy may lead to fetal alcohol syndrome (FAS) and can cause jitteriness, physical abnormalities, congenital anomalies, and growth deficits.
   7. Smoking can result in low birth weight, a higher incidence of birth defects, and stillbirths.

E. Viral hepatitis (see Chap. 25 for information regarding hepatitis B infection)

F. Adolescent pregnancy

1. Factors that result in adolescent pregnancy include the early onset of menarche, changing sexual behaviors in this age group, problems with family relationships, poverty, and the lack of knowledge of reproduction and birth control.
2. The major concerns related to adolescent pregnancy include poor nutritional status, emotional and behavioral difficulties, lack of support systems, increased risk of stillbirth, low-birth-weight **infants,** fetal mortality, cephalopelvic disproportion, and increased risk of maternal complications, such as hypertension, anemia, prolonged **labor,** and infections.
3. The role of the nurse in reducing risks and consequences of adolescent pregnancy is twofold—first, to encourage early and continued prenatal care; and second, to refer the adolescent, if necessary, for appropriate assistance, which can help counter the effects of a negative socioeconomic environment.

PRACTICE QUESTIONS

1. A nurse midwife is assessing a pregnant client for the presence of ballottement. To make this determination, the nurse-midwife does which of the following?
   1. Assesses the cervix for thinning
   2. Auscultates for fetal heart sounds
   3. Palpates the abdomen for fetal movement
   4. Initiates a gentle upward tap on the cervix

2. A pregnant client asks the nurse in the clinic when she will be able to begin to feel the fetus move. The nurse responds by telling the mother that fetal movements will be noted between which of the following weeks of gestation?
   1. 6 and 8
   2. 8 and 10
   3. 10 and 12
   4. 16 and 20

3. A nurse is performing an assessment of a primipara who is being evaluated in a clinic during her second trimester of pregnancy. Which of the following indicates an abnormal physical finding that necessitates further testing?
   1. Quickening
   2. Braxton Hicks contractions
   3. Consistent increase in fundal height
   4. Fetal heart rate of 180 beats/min

4. A nurse is providing instructions to a pregnant client with genital herpes about the measures that are needed to protect the fetus. The nurse tells the client that:
   1. Total abstinence from sexual intercourse is necessary during the entire pregnancy.

2. A cesarean section will be necessary if vaginal lesions are present at the time of labor.

3. Sitz baths need to be taken every 4 hours while awake if vaginal lesions are present.

4. Daily administration of acyclovir (Zovirax) is necessary during the entire pregnancy.

5. A nurse is performing an assessment of a pregnant client who is at 28 weeks of gestation. The nurse measures the fundal height in centimeters and expects the finding to be which of the following?
   1. 22 cm
   2. 30 cm
   3. 36 cm
   4. 40 cm

6. A nurse is collecting data during an admission assessment of a client who is pregnant with twins. The client has a healthy 5-year-old child that was delivered at 38 weeks and tells the nurse that she does not have a history of any type of abortion or fetal demise. The nurse would document the GTPAL for this client as
   1. G = 3, T = 2, P = 0, A = 0, L = 1
   2. G = 2, T = 1, P = 0, A = 0, L = 1
   3. G = 1, T = 1, P = 1, A = 0, L = 1
   4. G = 2, T = 0, P = 0, A = 0, L = 1

7. A pregnant client is seen in a health care clinic for a regular prenatal visit. The client tells the nurse that she is experiencing irregular contractions, and the nurse determines that she is experiencing Braxton Hicks contractions. Based on this finding, which nursing action is appropriate?
   1. Contact the physician.
   2. Instruct the client to maintain bed rest for the remainder of the pregnancy.
   3. Inform the client that these are common and may occur throughout the pregnancy.
   4. Call the maternity unit and inform them that the client will be admitted in a prelabor condition.

8. A nurse is reviewing the record of a client who has just been told that a pregnancy test is positive. The physician has documented the presence of Goodell's sign. The nurse determines that this sign indicates:
   1. A softening of the cervix
   2. The presence of fetal movement
   3. The presence of human chorionic gonadotropin in the urine
   4. A soft blowing sound that corresponds to the maternal pulse during auscultation of the uterus

9. A client arrives at the clinic for the first prenatal assessment. The client tells a nurse that the first day of her last menstrual period was October 19, 2008. Using Nägele's rule, the nurse determines the estimated date of confinement as:
   1. July 12, 2008
   2. July 26, 2009
   3. August 12, 2009
   4. August 26, 2009

ALTERNATE ITEM FORMAT: MULTIPLE RESPONSE

A nurse is assisting in performing an assessment on a client who suspects that she is pregnant and is checking the client for probable signs of pregnancy. Select all probable signs of pregnancy.
1. Ballottement
2. Chadwick's sign
3. Uterine enlargement
4. Braxton Hicks contractions
5. Outline of fetus via radiography or ultrasonography
6. Fetal heart rate detected by a nonelectronic device

ALTERNATE ITEM FORMAT: FIGURE WITH A FILL IN THE BLANK

The nurse is performing an assessment on a client who is at 20 weeks' gestation. The nurse expects to note uterine height to be at which location (Fig. 23-3)?
Answer: _____

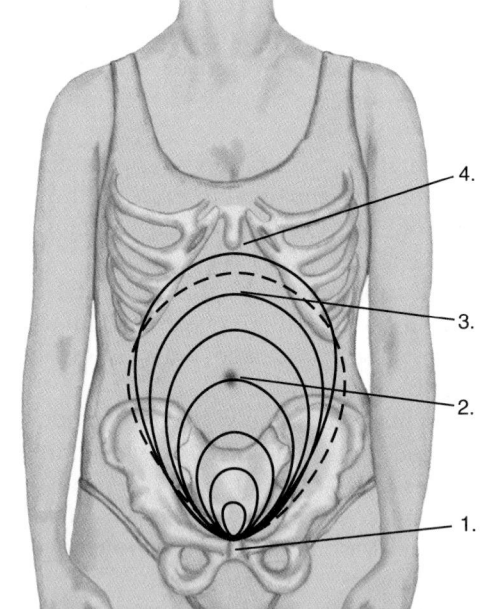

FIG. 23-3 (From McKinney, E., James, S., Murray, S., & Ashwill, J. [2005]. *Maternal-child nursing* [2nd ed.]. St. Louis: W.B. Saunders.)

ANSWERS

1. **4**

Rationale: Ballottement is a technique of palpating a floating structure by bouncing it gently and feeling it rebound. In the technique used to palpate the fetus, the examiner places a finger in the vagina and taps gently upward, causing the fetus to rise. The fetus then sinks, and the examiner feels a gentle tap on the finger. Options 1, 2, and 3 are incorrect.

Test-Taking Strategy: Use the process of elimination. Recalling that ballottement is a technique of palpating a floating structure by bouncing it gently and feeling it rebound will direct you to option 4. Review this assessment technique if you had difficulty with this question.

Level of Cognitive Ability: Application
Client Needs: Health Promotion and Maintenance
Integrated Process: Nursing Process—assessment
Content Area: Maternity—antepartum
References: Murray, S., & McKinney, E. (2006). *Foundations of maternal-newborn nursing* (4th ed., p. 126). Philadelphia: W.B. Saunders.
Wong, D., Perry, S., Hockenberry, M., et al. (2006). *Maternal child nursing care.* (3rd ed., p. 241). St. Louis: Mosby.

2. **4**

Rationale: Quickening is fetal movement and may occur as early as the sixteenth to twentieth week of gestation. The expectant mother first notices subtle fetal movements during this time, which gradually increase in intensity. Options 1, 2, and 3 are incorrect.

Test-Taking Strategy: Use the process of elimination and knowledge regarding the occurrence of quickening. In this situation, selecting the option that indicates the greatest length of gestational time is best. Review the process of quickening if you had difficulty with this question.

Level of Cognitive Ability: Application
Client Needs: Health Promotion and Maintenance
Integrated Process: Nursing Process—implementation
Content Area: Maternity—antepartum
Reference: Murray, S., & McKinney, E., (2006). *Foundations of maternal-newborn nursing* (4th ed., pp. 125, 203). Philadelphia: W.B. Saunders.

3. **4**

Rationale: The normal range of the fetal heart rate depends on gestational age. The heart rate is usually 160 to 170 beats/min in the first trimester and slows with fetal growth. Near and at term, the fetal heart rate ranges from 120 to 160 beats/min. Options 1, 2, and 3 are normal expected findings.

Test-Taking Strategy: Note the strategic words *indicates an abnormal physical finding* and note that the client is in the second trimester of pregnancy. Recalling the normal fetal heart rate will direct you to option 4. Review normal assessment findings in pregnancy if you had difficulty with this question.

Level of Cognitive Ability: Analysis
Client Needs: Physiological Integrity
Integrated Process: Nursing Process—assessment
Content Area: Maternity—antepartum
Reference: McKinney, E., James, S., Murray, S., & Ashwill, J. (2005). *Maternal-child nursing* (2nd ed., pp. 398-399). St. Louis: W.B. Saunders.

4. **2**

Rationale: For women with active lesions, either recurrent or primary at the time of labor, delivery should be by cesarean section to prevent the fetus from being in contact with the genital herpes. The safety of acyclovir has not been established during pregnancy, and it should be used only when a life-threatening infection is present. Clients should be advised to abstain from sexual contact while the lesions are present. If this is an initial infection, clients should continue to abstain until they become culture-negative, because prolonged viral shedding may occur in such cases. Keeping the genital area clean and dry will promote healing.

Test-Taking Strategy: Use the process of elimination. Eliminate options 1 and 4 first because of the close-ended word *entire* in these options. From the remaining options, recalling that the lesions should be kept clean and dry to promote healing will assist in eliminating option 3. If you had difficulty with this question, review the content related to genital herpes as a maternal risk factor.

Level of Cognitive Ability: Application
Client Needs: Physiological Integrity
Integrated Process: Teaching and Learning
Content Area: Maternity—antepartum
Reference: Wong, D., Perry, S., Hockenberry, M., et al. (2006). *Maternal child nursing care* (3rd ed., p. 129). St. Louis: Mosby.

5. **2**

Rationale: During the second and third trimesters (weeks 18 to 30), fundal height in centimeters approximately equals the fetus's age in weeks ± 2 cm. At 16 weeks, the fundus can be located halfway between the symphysis pubis and the umbilicus. At 20 to 22 weeks, the fundus is at the umbilicus, and at 36 weeks the fundus is at the xiphoid process.

Test-Taking Strategy: Use the process of elimination. Remember that during the second and third trimesters (weeks 18 to 30), fundal height in centimeters approximately equals the fetus's age in weeks ± 2 cm. If you are unfamiliar with this assessment technique, review this content area.

Level of Cognitive Ability: Analysis
Client Needs: Health Promotion and Maintenance
Integrated Process: Nursing Process—assessment
Content Area: Maternity—antepartum
References: McKinney, E., James, S., Murray, S., & Ashwill, J. (2005). *Maternal-child Nursing* (2nd ed., p. 261). St. Louis: W.B. Saunders.
Wong, D., Perry, S., Hockenberry, M., et al. (2006). *Maternal child nursing care.* (3rd ed., p. 273). St. Louis: Mosby.

6. **2**

Rationale: Pregnancy outcomes can be described with the acronym *GTPAL*. G is gravidity, the number of pregnancies. *T* is term births, the number born at term (longer than 37 weeks), *P* is preterm births, the number born before 37 weeks' gestation, A is abortions or miscarriages, the number of abortions or miscarriages (included in gravida if before 20 weeks' gestation; included in parity if past 20 weeks' gestation), and *L* is the number of current living children. Therefore, a woman who is pregnant with twins and has a child has a gravida of 2. Because the child was delivered at 38 weeks, the number of term births is 1 and the number of preterm births is 0. The number of abortions is 0 and the number of living children is 1.

Test-Taking Strategy: Focus on the data in the question. Recalling the meaning of the acronym *GTPAL* will direct you to option 2. If you had difficulty answering this question, review this method of describing pregnancy outcomes.

Level of Cognitive Ability: Application
Client Needs: Health Promotion and Maintenance
Integrated Process: Nursing Process—assessment
Content Area: Maternity—antepartum
Reference: Wong, D., Perry, S., Hockenberry, M., et al. (2006). *Maternal child nursing care* (3rd ed., p. 236). St. Louis: Mosby.

7. **3**

Rationale: Braxton Hicks contractions are irregular, painless contractions that may occur intermittently throughout pregnancy. Because Braxton Hicks contractions may occur and are normal in some pregnant women during pregnancy, options 1, 2, and 4 are unnecessary and inappropriate actions.

Test-Taking Strategy: Use the process of elimination. Options 1 and 4 are comparative or alike and can be eliminated first. From the remaining options, knowing that Braxton Hicks contractions are common and can occur throughout pregnancy will assist in directing you to option 3. Review the physiology associated with Braxton Hicks contractions if you had difficulty with this question.

Level of Cognitive Ability: Application
Client Needs: Health Promotion and Maintenance
Integrated Process: Nursing Process—implementation
Content Area: Maternity—antepartum
References: Murray, S., & McKinney, E., (2006). *Foundations of maternal-newborn nursing* (4th ed., p. 126). Philadelphia: W.B. Saunders.
Wong, D., Perry, S., Hockenberry, M., et al. (2006). *Maternal child nursing care* (3rd ed., p. 239). St. Louis: Mosby.

8. **1**

Rationale: In the early weeks of pregnancy, the cervix becomes softer as a result of increased vascularity and hyperplasia, which cause Goodell's sign. Cervical softening is noted by the examiner during pelvic examination. A soft blowing sound that corresponds to the maternal pulse may be auscultated over the uterus and is caused by blood circulating through the placenta. Human chorionic gonadotropin is noted in maternal urine in a positive urine pregnancy test. Goodell's sign does not indicate the presence of fetal movement.

Test-Taking Strategy: Use the process of elimination and knowledge regarding the physiological findings in Goodell's sign to answer this question. Remember that Goodell's sign refers to a softening of the cervix. If you had difficulty with this question, review the changes in the cervix that occur during pregnancy.

Level of Cognitive Ability: Analysis
Client Needs: Health Promotion and Maintenance
Integrated Process: Nursing Process—analysis
Content Area: Maternity—antepartum
Reference: Wong, D., Perry, S., Hockenberry, M., et al. (2006). *Maternal child nursing care.* (3rd ed., p. 240). St. Louis: Mosby.

9. **2**

Rationale: Accurate use of Nägele's rule requires that the woman have a regular 28-day menstrual cycle. Add 7 days to the first day of the last menstrual period, subtract 3 months, and then add 1 year to that date. First day of the last menstrual period, October 19, 2008; add 7 days, October 26, 2008; subtract 3 months, July 26, 2008; add 1 year, July 26, 2009.

Test-Taking Strategy: Use knowledge regarding the use of Nägele's rule to answer this question. Read all the options carefully, noting the dates and years in the options, before selecting an answer. Review Nägele's rule if you had difficulty with this question.

Level of Cognitive Ability: Comprehension
Client Needs: Health Promotion and Maintenance
Integrated Process: Nursing Process—assessment
Content Area: Maternity—antepartum
Reference: Wong, D., Perry, S., Hockenberry, M., et al. (2006). *Maternal child nursing care.* (3rd ed., p. 256). St. Louis: Mosby.

ALTERNATE ITEM FORMAT: MULTIPLE RESPONSE

Answer: 1, 2, 3, 4
Rationale: The probable signs of pregnancy include uterine enlargement, Hegar's sign (softening and thinning of the lower uterine segment that occurs at about week 6), Goodell's sign (softening of the cervix that occurs at the beginning of the second month), Chadwick's sign (bluish coloration of the mucous membranes of the cervix, vagina, and vulva that occurs at about week 6), ballottement (rebounding of the fetus against the examiner's fingers on palpation), Braxton Hicks contractions, and a positive pregnancy test for the presence of human chorionic gonadotropin (hCG). Positive signs of pregnancy include fetal heart rate detected by electronic device (Doppler transducer) at 10 to 12 weeks and by a nonelectronic device (fetoscope) at 20 weeks of gestation, active fetal movements palpable by the examiner, and an outline of the fetus by radiography or ultrasonography.

Test-Taking Strategy: Focusing on the subject, probable signs of pregnancy, will assist in answering this question. Remember that detection of the fetal heart rate and an outline of the fetus via radiography or ultrasonography are positive signs of pregnancy. Review the probable signs of pregnancy if you had difficulty with this question.

Level of Cognitive Ability: Analysis
Client Needs: Health Promotion and Maintenance
Integrated Process: Nursing Process—assessment
Content Area: Maternity—antepartum
Reference: McKinney, E., James, S., Murray, S., & Ashwill, J. (2005). *Maternal-child nursing* (2nd ed., p. 263). St. Louis: Mosby.

ALTERNATE ITEM FORMAT: FIGURE WITH A FILL IN THE BLANK

Answer: 2
Rationale: By the twentieth week of gestation, the fundal height should be at the umbilicus. Option 1 identifies the symphysis pubis area, prepregnancy location. Option 3 identi-

fies the height of the uterus at 32 weeks of gestation. Option 4 identifies the height of the uterus at 36 weeks' gestation. *Test-Taking Strategy:* Focus on the data in the question and note that it asks about the height of the uterus at 20 weeks' gestation. Remember that by the twentieth week of gestation the fundal height should be at the umbilicus. Review normal antenatal findings if you had difficulty with this question. *Level of Cognitive Ability:* Analysis

Client Needs: Health Promotion and Maintenance
Integrated Process: Nursing Process—assessment
Content Area: Maternity—antepartum
References: McKinney, E., James, S., Murray, S., Ashwill, J. (2005). *Maternal-child nursing.* (2nd ed., p. 252). St. Louis: W.B. Saunders.
Wong, D., Perry, S., Hockenberry, M., et al. (2006). *Maternal child nursing care* (3rd ed, p. 239.). St. Louis: Mosby.

REFERENCES

Murray, S., & McKinney, E., (2006). *Foundations of maternal-newborn nursing* (4 ed.). Philadelphia: W.B. Saunders.

McKinney, E., James, S., Murray, S., & Ashwill, J. (2005). *Maternal-child nursing* (2nd ed.). St. Louis: W.B. Saunders.

National Council of State Boards of Nursing (2007). *2007 NCLEX-RN® detailed test plan.* Chicago: Author.

Wong, D., Perry, S., Hockenberry, M., et al. (2006). *Maternal child nursing care* (3rd ed.). St. Louis: Mosby.

24

Prenatal Period

I. PHYSIOLOGICAL MATERNAL CHANGES

A. Cardiovascular system
1. Circulating blood volume increases, plasma increases, and total red blood cell volume increases (total volume increases by 40% to 50%).
2. Physiological anemia occurs as the plasma increase exceeds the increase in red blood cell production.
3. Iron requirements are increased.
4. Heart size increases and is elevated upward and to the left because of displacement of the diaphragm as the **uterus** enlarges.
5. Pulse may increase about 10 beats/min.
6. Blood pressure slightly decreases in the second trimester.
7. Retention of sodium and water may occur.

B. Respiratory system
1. Oxygen consumption increases by 15% to 20%.
2. Diaphragm is elevated because of the enlarged **uterus.**
3. Respiratory rate remains unchanged or slightly increases.
4. Shortness of breath may be experienced.

C. Gastrointestinal system
1. Nausea and vomiting may occur as a result of the secretion of human chorionic gonadotropin and subside by the third month.
2. Poor appetite may occur because of decreased gastric motility.
3. Alterations in taste and smell may occur.
4. Constipation may occur as a result of an increase in progesterone production or pressure of the **uterus,** resulting in decreased gastrointestinal motility.
5. Flatulence and heartburn may occur because of decreased gastrointestinal motility and slowed emptying of the stomach caused by an increase in progesterone production.
6. Hemorrhoids may occur as a result of increased venous pressure.
7. Gum tissue may become swollen and easily bleed due to rising levels of estrogen.
8. Ptyalism (excessive secretion of saliva) may occur because of rising levels of estrogen.

D. Renal system
1. Frequency of urination occurs in the first and third trimesters as a result of pressure of the enlarging **uterus** on the bladder.
2. Decreased bladder tone may occur and is caused by an increase in progesterone and estrogen levels; bladder capacity increases in response to increasing levels of progesterone.
3. Renal threshold for glucose may be reduced.

E. Endocrine system
1. The basal metabolic rate rises.
2. The anterior lobe of the pituitary gland enlarges.
3. The thyroid enlarges slightly, and thyroid activity increases.
4. The parathyroid increases in size.
5. Aldosterone levels gradually increase.

F. Reproductive system
1. **Uterus**
   a. The **uterus** enlarges, increasing in mass from 60 to 1000 g as a result of both hyperplasia (influence of estrogen) and hypertrophy.
   b. Size and number of blood vessels and lymphatics increase.
   c. Irregular contractions occur.
2. Cervix
   a. The cervix becomes shorter, more elastic, and larger in diameter.

b. Endocervical glands secrete a thick mucous plug, which is expelled from the canal when dilation begins.

c. Increased vascularization and an increase in estrogen causes softening and a blue-purple discoloration known as **Chadwick's sign,** which occurs at about 6 weeks of gestational age.

3. Ovaries
  a. A major function of the ovaries is to secrete progesterone for the first 6 to 7 weeks of pregnancy.
  b. The maturation of new follicles is blocked.
  c. The ovaries cease ovum production.

4. **Vagina**
  a. Hypertrophy and thickening of the muscle occur.
  b. An increase in vaginal secretions is experienced; secretions are usually thick, white, and acidic.

5. Breasts: Breast changes occur because of the increasing effects of estrogen and progesterone (Fig 24-1).
  a. Breast size increases.
  b. Nipples become more pronounced.
  c. The areola becomes darker in color.
  d. Superficial veins become prominent.
  e. Hypertrophy of Montgomery's follicles occurs.
  f. Colostrum may leak from the breast.

G. Skin
  1. Some changes occur because the levels of melanocyte-stimulating hormone (MSH) elevate as a result of an increase in estrogen and progesterone levels; these changes include the following:
    a. Increased pigmentation

b. A dark streak down the midline of the abdomen (linea nigra).

c. Chloasma (mask of pregnancy), a blotchy brownish hyperpigmentation, over the forehead, cheeks, and nose

d. Reddish-purple stretch marks (striae) on the abdomen, breasts, thighs, and upper arms (Fig. 24-2)

2. Vascular spider nevi may occur on the neck, chest, face, arms, and legs.

3. Rate of hair growth may increase.

H. Skeletal system (Fig. 24-3)
  1. Center of gravity changes begin in the second trimester and are caused by the hormones relaxin and progesterone.
  2. Postural changes occur as the increased weight of the **uterus** causes a forward pull of the bony pelvis.

I. Metabolism
  1. Metabolic function increases.
  2. Body weight increases.
  3. Water retention is increased, which can contribute to weight gain.

II. PSYCHOLOGICAL MATERNAL CHANGES

A. Ambivalence
  1. Ambivalence occurs early in pregnancy, even when the pregnancy is planned.
  2. The mother may experience a dependence-independence conflict and ambivalence related to role changes.
  3. The father may experience ambivalence related to the new role that he is assuming, increased financial responsibilities, and sharing the wife's attention with the child.

B. Acceptance: Factors that may be related to acceptance of the pregnancy are the woman's readiness

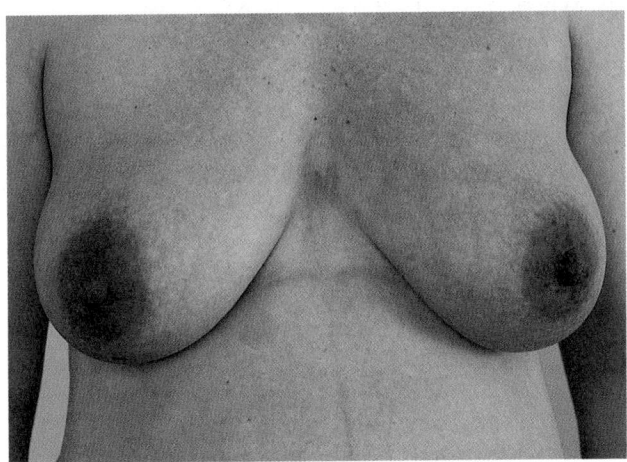

FIG. 24-1 Enlarged breasts in pregnancy with venous network and darkened areolae and nipples. (From Wong, D., Perry, S., Hockenberry, M., et al. [2006]. *Maternal child nursing care* [3rd ed.]. St. Louis: Mosby.)

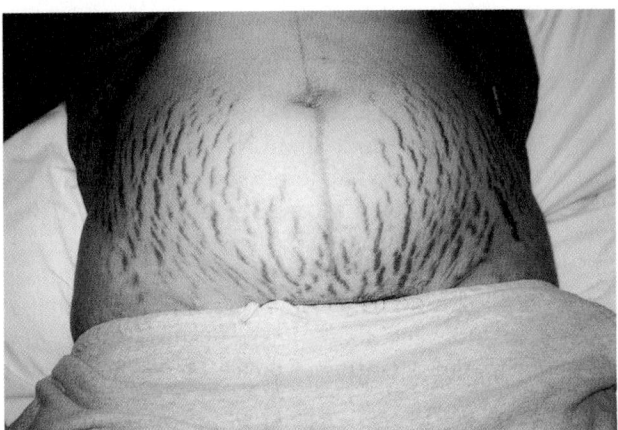

FIG. 24-2 Striae gravidarum and linea nigra in a dark-skinned woman. (From Wong, D., Perry, S., Hockenberry, M., et al. [2006]. *Maternal child nursing care* [3rd ed.]. St. Louis: Mosby.)

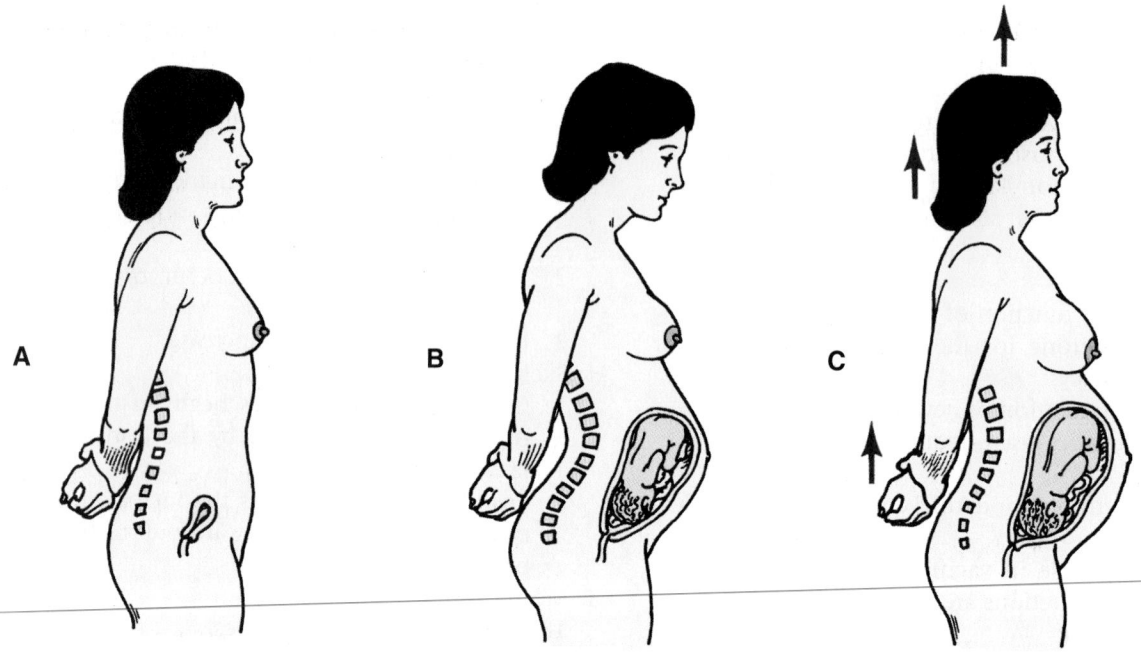

FIG. 24-3   Postural changes during pregnancy. **A,** Nonpregnant. **B,** Incorrect posture during pregnancy. **C,** Correct posture during pregnancy. (From Wong, D., Perry, S., Hockenberry, M., et al. [2006]. *Maternal child nursing care* [3rd ed.]. St. Louis: Mosby.)

for the experience and her identification with the motherhood role.

C. Emotional lability
1. Emotional lability may be manifested by frequent changes of emotional states or extremes in emotional states.
2. These emotional changes are common, but the mother may think that these changes are abnormal.

D. Body image changes
1. The changes in a woman's perception of her image during pregnancy occurs gradually and may be positive or negative.
2. The physical changes and symptoms that the woman experiences during pregnancy contribute to her body image.

E. Relationship with the fetus
1. The woman may daydream to prepare for motherhood and think about the maternal qualities that she would like to possess.
2. The woman first accepts the biological fact that she is pregnant.
3. The woman next accepts the growing fetus as distinct from herself and a person to nurture.
4. Finally, the woman prepares realistically for the birth and parenting of the child.

III. DISCOMFORTS OF PREGNANCY
A. Nausea and vomiting
1. Occurs in the first trimester
2. Caused by elevated levels of human chorionic gonadotropin and changes in carbohydrate metabolism

3. Interventions
a. Eating dry crackers before arising
b. Avoiding brushing teeth immediately after arising
c. Eating small, frequent, low-fat meals during the day
d. Drinking liquids between meals rather than at meals
e. Avoiding fried foods and spicy foods
f. Acupressure (some types may require a prescription)
g. Herbal remedies, but only if approved by a physician or nurse-midwife

B. Syncope
1. Usually occurs in the first trimester; supine hypotension occurs particularly in the second and third trimesters
2. May be triggered hormonally or caused by the increased blood volume, anemia, fatigue, sudden position changes, or lying supine
3. Interventions
a. Sitting with the feet elevated
b. Changing positions slowly
c. Changing the position to the lateral recumbent to relieve the pressure of the **uterus** on the inferior vena cava

C. Urinary urgency and frequency
1. Usually occurs in the first and third trimesters
2. Caused by pressure of the **uterus** on the bladder
3. Interventions
a. Drinking adequate amounts of fluid during the day
b. Limiting fluid intake in the evening

c. Voiding at regular intervals

d. Sleeping side lying at night

e. Wearing perineal pads, if necessary

f. Performing Kegel exercises

D. Breast tenderness

1. Can occur from the first through the third trimesters.

2. Caused by increased levels of estrogen and progesterone.

3. Interventions

a. Encouragement for wearing a supportive bra

b. Avoiding the use of soap on the nipples and areola area to prevent drying

E. Increased vaginal discharge

1. Can occur from the first through the third trimesters.

2. Caused by hyperplasia of vaginal mucosa and increased mucus production.

3. Interventions

a. Proper cleansing and hygiene

b. Wearing cotton underwear

c. Avoiding douching

d. Advising the client to consult the physician or nurse-midwife if infection is suspected

F. Nasal stuffiness

1. Occurs during the first through third trimesters

2. Results from increased estrogen, which causes swelling of the nasal tissues and dryness

3. Interventions

a. Encouraging the use of a humidifier

b. Avoiding the use of nasal sprays or antihistamines

G. Fatigue

1. Occurs usually in the first and third trimesters

2. Usually results from hormonal changes

3. Interventions

a. Arranging frequent rest periods throughout the day

b. Using correct body mechanics

c. Obtaining regular exercise

d. Performing muscle relaxation and strengthening exercises for the legs and hip joints

e. Avoiding eating and drinking foods containing stimulants throughout the entire pregnancy

H. Heartburn

1. Occurs in the second and the third trimesters.

2. Results from increased progesterone levels, decreased gastrointestinal motility, and esophageal reflux, and displacement of the stomach by the enlarging **uterus**

3. Interventions

a. Eating small, frequent meals

b. Sitting upright for 30 minutes following a meal

c. Drinking milk between meals

d. Avoiding fatty and spicy food

e. Performing tailor-sitting exercises

f. Taking antacids only if recommended by the physician or nurse-midwife

I. Ankle edema

1. Usually occurs in the second and the third trimesters

2. Results from vasodilation, venous stasis, and increased venous pressure below the **uterus**

3. Interventions

a. Elevating the legs at least twice a day

b. Sleeping on the side

c. Wearing supportive stockings

d. Avoiding sitting or standing in one position for long periods of time

J. Varicose veins

1. Usually occur in the second and third trimesters

2. Result from weakening walls of the veins or valves and venous congestion

3. Interventions

a. Wearing support hose

b. Elevating the feet when sitting

c. Lying with the feet and hips elevated

d. Avoiding long periods of standing or sitting

e. Moving about while standing to improve circulation

f. Avoiding leg crossing

g. Avoiding constricting articles of clothing

K. Headaches

1. Usually occur in the second and third trimesters.

2. Result from changes in blood volume and vascular tone.

3. Interventions

a. Changing position slowly

b. Applying a cool cloth to the forehead

c. Eating a small snack

d. Using acetaminophen (Tylenol) only if prescribed by the physician or nurse-midwife

L. Hemorrhoids

1. Usually occur in the second and third trimesters

2. Result from increased venous pressure and constipation

3. Interventions

a. Soaking in a warm sitz bath

b. Sitting on a soft pillow

c. Eating high-fiber foods and avoiding constipation

d. Drinking sufficient fluids

e. Increasing exercise, such as walking

f. Applying ointments, suppositories, or compresses as prescribed by the physician or nurse-midwife

M. Constipation

1. Usually occurs in the second and third trimesters

2. Results from decreased intestinal motility, displacement of the intestines, and taking iron supplements

3. Interventions
   a. Eating high-fiber foods
   b. Drinking sufficient fluids
   c. Exercising regularly
   d. Avoiding laxatives or enemas and consulting with the physician or nurse-midwife about their use

N. Backache
   1. Usually occurs in the second and third trimesters
   2. Caused by an exaggerated lumbosacral curve resulting from the enlarged **uterus**
   3. Interventions
      a. Encouraging rest
      b. Using correct body mechanics and improving posture
      c. Wearing low-heeled shoes
      d. Performing pelvic rocking and abdominal breathing exercises
      e. Sleeping on a firm mattress

O. Leg cramps
   1. Usually occur in the second and third trimesters
   2. Result from an altered calcium-phosphorus balance and pressure of the **uterus** on nerves or from fatigue
   3. Interventions
      a. Getting regular exercise, especially walking
      b. Dorsiflexing the foot of the affected leg
      c. Increasing calcium intake

P. Shortness of breath and dyspnea
   1. Can occur in the second and third trimesters
   2. Results from pressure on the diaphragm
   3. Interventions
      a. Allowing frequent rest periods
      b. Sleeping with the head elevated or on the side
      c. Avoiding overexertion
      d. Performing tailor-sitting exercises

IV. **LABORATORY TESTS** (Box 24-1)
A. Blood type and Rh factor
   1. ABO typing is performed to determine the woman's blood type in the ABO antigen system.
   2. Rh typing is done to determine the woman's blood type in the rhesus antigen system. (Rh positive indicates the presence of the antigen; Rh negative indicates the absence of the antigen.)
   3. If the client is Rh negative and has a negative antibody screen, she will need repeat antibody screens and should receive Rh immune globulin at 28 weeks' gestation.

BOX 24-1

Usual Schedule for Prenatal Visits

Every 4 weeks for the first 28 to 32 weeks
Every 2 weeks from 32 to 36 weeks
Every week from 36 to 40 weeks

B. Rubella titer
   1. If the client has a negative titer (lower than 1:8), indicating susceptibility to the rubella virus, she should receive the appropriate immunization postpartum.
   2. The client must be using effective birth control at the time of the immunization and must be counseled not to become pregnant for 1 to 3 months following immunization (as specified by health care provider) and to avoid contact with anyone who is immunocompromised.
   3. If the rubella vaccine is administered at the same time as Rh immune globulin, it may not be effective.

C. Hemoglobin and hematocrit levels
   1. Hemoglobin and hematocrit levels will drop during gestation as a result of increased plasma volume.
   2. A decrease in the hemoglobin level to lower than 10 g/dL or in the hematocrit level to lower than 30% indicates anemia.

D. Papanicolaou's smear is done during the initial prenatal examination to screen for cervical neoplasia.

E. Sexually transmitted infections (Table 24-1)

F. Sickle cell screening
   1. Screening is indicated for clients at risk for sickle cell disease.

TABLE 24-1

Monitoring for Sexually Transmitted Infections

Disease	Laboratory Test
Gonorrhea	A vaginal culture is done during the initial prenatal examination to screen for gonorrhea. The culture may be repeated during the third trimester in high-risk clients.
Syphilis	A culture is done of the lesions (if present) during the initial prenatal examination to screen for syphilis. Diagnosis is dependent on microscopic examination of primary and secondary lesion tissue and serology (Venereal Disease Research Laboratory [VDRL] or rapid plasma reagin [RPR] test) during latency and late infection. The culture may be repeated during the third trimester in high-risk clients.
Herpes virus	A culture is indicated for clients with a positive history or those with active lesions. The test is performed to determine the route of delivery. Weekly cultures may be done at week 35 or 36 of pregnancy until delivery.
Chlamydia	A vaginal culture is indicated for all pregnant clients, if the client is in a high-risk group, or if infants from previous pregnancies have developed neonatal conjunctivitis or pneumonia.

2. A positive test may indicate a need for further screening.

▲ G. Tuberculin skin test
   1. The health care provider may prefer to perform this skin test after **delivery.**
   ▲ 2. A positive skin test indicates the need for a chest radiograph (using an abdominal lead shield) to rule out active disease; in a pregnant client, chest radiography will not be performed until after 20 weeks of gestation (after the fetal organs are formed).
   3. Converters to positive may be referred for treatment with medication following **delivery.**

▲ H. Hepatitis B surface antigens
   1. Testing for hepatitis antigens is recommended for all women because of the prevalence of the disease in the general population.
   2. Vaccination for hepatitis B antigen may be specifically indicated for the following:
      a. Health care workers
      b. Intravenous drug users
      c. Clients born in Asia, Africa, Haiti, or the Pacific islands
      d. Clients with previously undiagnosed jaundice or chronic liver disease
      e. Clients with tattoos
      f. Clients with histories of blood transfusions
      g. Clients with histories of multiple episodes of sexually transmitted infections
      h. Clients who have been rejected previously as blood donors
      i. Clients with histories of dialysis or renal transplantation
      j. Clients from households having hepatitis B–infected members or hemodialysis clients
   3. See Chapter 55 for additional information about hepatitis.

I. Urinalysis and urine culture
   1. A urine specimen for glucose and protein determinations should be obtained at every prenatal visit.
   2. Glycosuria is a common result of decreased renal threshold that occurs during pregnancy.
   3. If glycosuria persists, it may indicate diabetes.
   4. White blood cells in the urine may indicate infection.
   5. Ketonuria may result from insufficient food intake or vomiting.
   ▲ 6. Levels of 2+ to 4+ protein in the urine may indicate infection or preeclampsia

▲ **V. DIAGNOSTIC TESTS**
▲ A. Ultrasonography
   1. Outlines and identifies fetal and maternal structures
   2. Assists in confirming gestational age and estimated date of **delivery**

   3. May be done abdominally or transvaginally during pregnancy
   4. Interventions
      a. If an abdominal ultrasound is being performed, the woman may need to drink water to fill the bladder before the procedure to obtain a better image of the fetus.
      b. If a transvaginal ultrasound is being performed, a lubricated probe is inserted into the **vagina.**
      c. Inform the client that the test presents no known risks to the client or the fetus.

B. Alpha-fetoprotein screening
   1. Assesses the quantity of fetal serum proteins; elevated levels of protein are associated with open neural tube and abdominal wall defects
   2. Can detect spina bifida and Down syndrome
   3. Interventions
      a. Explain that the level is determined by a maternal blood sample drawn at 15 to 18 weeks' gestation.
      b. If the level is elevated and the gestation is less than 18 weeks, a second sample is drawn.
      c. An ultrasound is performed for elevated levels to rule out fetal abnormalities or multiple gestation.

C. Chorionic villus sampling
   1. The physician aspirates a small sample of chorionic villus tissue at 8 to 12 weeks' gestation.
   2. The test is performed for the purpose of detecting genetic abnormalities.
   3. Interventions
      a. Obtain informed consent.
      b. Instruct the client to drink water to fill the bladder before the procedure to aid in the visualization of the **uterus** for catheter insertion.
      c. Instruct the client to report bleeding, infection, or leakage of fluid at insertion site after the procedure.
      d. Rh-negative women may be given $Rh_o(D)$ immune globulin (RhoGAM), since chorionic villus sampling increases the risk of Rh sensitization.

D. Kick counts (fetal movement counting)
   1. Mother sits quietly or lies down on her side and counts fetal kicks for a period of time, as instructed.
   2. Instruct the client to notify the physician or nurse-midwife if there are fewer than 10 kicks in a 12-hour period or as instructed by the physician or nurse-midwife.

E. Amniocentesis
   1. Aspiration of **amniotic fluid;** may be done after 13 to 14 weeks of pregnancy
   2. Performed to determine genetic disorders, metabolic defects, and fetal lung maturity

3. Risks
   a. Maternal hemorrhage
   b. Infection
   c. Rh isoimmunization
   d. Abruptio placentae
   e. **Amniotic fluid** emboli
   f. Premature rupture of the membranes
4. Interventions
   a. Obtain informed consent.
   b. Instruct the client to empty the bladder before the procedure.
   c. Prepare the client for ultrasonography, which is performed to locate the **placenta.**
   d. Obtain baseline vital signs and fetal heart rate, and monitor every 15 minutes.
   e. Position the client supine.
   f. Instruct the client that if chills, fever, leakage of fluid at the needle insertion site, decreased fetal movement, or uterine contractions occur, she is to notify the physician or nurse-midwife.
F. Fern test
1. The fern test is a microscopic slide test to determine the presence of **amniotic fluid** leakage.
2. Using sterile technique, a specimen is obtained from the external os of the cervix and vaginal pool and is examined on a slide under a microscope.
3. A fern-like pattern produced by the effects of salts of the **amniotic fluid** indicates the presence of **amniotic fluid.**
4. Interventions
   a. Position the client in the dorsal lithotomy position.
   b. Instruct the client to cough, which will cause the fluid to leak from the **uterus** if the membranes are ruptured.
▲ G. Nitrazine test
1. A nitrazine test strip is used to detect the presence of **amniotic fluid** in vaginal secretions.
2. Vaginal secretions have a pH of 4.5 to 5.5 and do not affect the nitrazine strip or swab.
3. **Amniotic fluid** has a pH of 7.0 to 7.5 and turns the nitrazine strip or swab blue.
4. Interventions
   a. Position the client in the dorsal lithotomy position.
   b. Touch the test tape to the fluid.
   c. Assess the test tape for a blue-green, blue-gray, or deep blue color, which indicates that the membranes are probably ruptured.
H. Nonstress test (Box 24-2)
I. Contraction stress test (Box 24-3)

▲ VI. NUTRITION
▲ A. General guidelines
1. The average expected weight gain during pregnancy is 25 to 35 lb for women with a normal prepregnancy weight.

BOX 24-2
Nonstress Test

DESCRIPTION
The test is performed to assess placental function and oxygenation.
The test determines fetal well-being.
The test evaluates fetal heart rate (FHR) response to fetal movement.

INTERVENTIONS
An external ultrasound transducer and the tocodynamometer are applied to the client, and a tracing of at least 20 minutes' duration is obtained so that the FHR and the uterine activity can be observed.
Obtain baseline blood pressure and monitor blood pressure frequently.
Position the client in the left lateral position to avoid vena cava compression.
The client may be asked to press a button every time she feels fetal movement; the monitor records a mark at each point of fetal movement, which is used as a reference point to assess FHR response.

RESULTS
Reactive Nonstress Test (Normal, Negative)
"Reactive" indicates a healthy fetus.
The result requires two or more FHR accelerations of at least 15 beats/min, lasting at least 15 seconds from the beginning of the acceleration to the end, in association with fetal movement, during a 20-minute period.
Nonreactive Nonstress Test (Abnormal)
No accelerations or accelerations of less than 15 beats/min or lasting less than 15 seconds in duration occur during a 40-minute observation.
Unsatisfactory
The result cannot be interpreted because of the poor quality of the FHR tracing.

---

2. An increase of about 300 cal/day is needed during pregnancy.
3. Calorie needs are greater in the last two trimesters than in the first.
4. An increase of about 500 cal/day is needed during lactation.
5. Encourage a diet high in folic acid with folic acid supplements.
6. A diet high in folic acid is necessary for all women of childbearing age to prevent neural tube defects in the fetus during the first trimester of pregnancy.
7. At least 8 to 10 (8-oz) glasses of fluid are needed each day, of which 4 to 6 glasses are water.
8. Sodium is not restricted unless specifically prescribed by the physician or nurse-midwife.
B. Vegetarian diet (Box 24-4)
1. Ensure that the client eats a sufficient amount of varied foods to meet normal nutrient and energy needs.

DESCRIPTION
The test assesses placental oxygenation and function.
The test determines fetal ability to tolerate labor and determines fetal well-being.
The fetus is exposed to the stress of contractions to assess the adequacy of placental perfusion under simulated labor conditions.
The test is performed if the nonstress test is abnormal.

INTERVENTIONS
The external fetal monitor is applied to the client, and a 20- to 30-minute baseline strip is recorded.
The uterus is stimulated to contract by the administration of a dilute dose of oxytocin (Pitocin) or by having the client use nipple stimulation until three palpable contractions with a duration of 40 seconds or more in a 10-minute period have been achieved.
Frequent maternal blood pressure readings are done, and the mother is monitored closely while increasing doses of oxytocin are given.

RESULTS
Negative Contraction Stress Test (Normal)
A negative result is represented by no late decelerations of the fetal heart rate.
Positive Contraction Stress Test (Abnormal)
A positive result is represented by late decelerations of the fetal heart rate, with 50% or more of the contractions in the absence of hyperstimulation of the uterus.
Equivocal
An equivocal result contains decelerations but with less than 50% of the contractions, or the uterine activity shows a hyperstimulated uterus.
Unsatisfactory
An unsatisfactory result means that adequate uterine contractions cannot be achieved, or the fetal heart rate tracing is not of sufficient quality for adequate interpretation.

LACTO-OVO VEGETARIAN
Consumes eggs and dairy products, but excludes meat, poultry, and seafood.

LACTO VEGETARIAN
Consumes dairy products, but excludes eggs, meat, poultry, and seafood.

VEGAN
Refrains from eating animal products.

PESCO VEGETARIAN
Consumes seafood, but excludes meat, poultry, eggs, and dairy products.

5. To enhance absorption of iron, vegetarians should include a good source of iron and vitamin C with each meal.
6. Foods commonly eaten include tofu, tempeh, soy milk and soy products, meat analogues, legumes, nuts and seeds, sprouts, and a variety of fruits and vegetables.
7. Soy protein is considered equivalent in quality to animal proteins.

C. Lactose intolerance
   1. Lactose consumed by an individual with an intolerance can cause abdominal distention, discomfort, nausea, vomiting, cramps, and loose stools.
   2. Clients experiencing lactose intolerance need to incorporate sources of calcium other than dairy products into their dietary patterns regularly.
   3. Milk may be tolerated in cooked form, such as in custards or fermented dairy products.
   4. Cheese and yogurt sometimes are tolerated.
   5. Lactase, an enzyme, may be prescribed and is taken before ingesting milk or milk products.
   6. Lactase-treated milk or lactose-free products are also available commercially.

D. Pica
   1. Pica is the eating of nonfood substances such as dirt, clay, starch, and freezer frost.
   2. The cause is unknown; cultural values, such as beliefs regarding the effect of a material on the mother or fetus, may make pica a common practice.
   3. Iron deficiency anemia may occur as a result of pica.

E. Cultural considerations: See Chapter 6 for information on cultural considerations in nutrition.

2. Clients should be educated about consuming complementary proteins over the course of each day to ensure that all essential amino acids are provided.
3. Potential deficiencies in vegetarian diets include energy, protein, vitamin B_{12}, zinc, iron, calcium, omega-3 fatty acids, and vitamin D (if limited exposure to sunlight).
4. Protein consumption can be increased by consumption of a variety of vegetable protein sources based on whole grains, legumes, seeds, nuts, and vegetables combined to provide all essential amino acids.

PRACTICE QUESTIONS

1. A nurse is instructing a pregnant client regarding measures to increase iron in the diet. The nurse tells the client to consume which food that contains the highest source of dietary iron?
   1. Milk
   2. Potatoes
   3. Cantaloupe
   4. Dark green, leafy vegetables

2. A nurse is providing instructions regarding treatment of hemorrhoids to a client who is in the second trimester of pregnancy. Which statement by the client indicates a need for further instruction?
   1. "I should avoid straining during bowel movements."
   2. "I can gently replace the hemorrhoids into the rectum."
   3. "I can apply ice packs to the hemorrhoids to reduce the swelling."
   4. "I should apply heat packs to the hemorrhoids to help the hemorrhoids shrink."

3. A nurse is providing instructions to a client in the first trimester of pregnancy regarding measures to assist in reducing breast tenderness. The nurse tells the client to:
   1. Avoid wearing a bra.
   2. Wash the breasts with warm water and keep them dry.
   3. Wear tight-fitting blouses or dresses to provide support.
   4. Wash the nipples and areola area daily with soap, and massage the breasts with lotion.

4. A nonstress test is prescribed for a pregnant client and the client asks the nurse about the procedure. The nurse tells the client that:
   1. The test is a procedure that will require an informed consent to be signed.
   2. The test will take about 2 hours and will require close monitoring for 2 hours after the procedure is completed.
   3. The test is done to see if the baby can handle the stress of labor and that medicine is given to make the uterus contract.
   4. A round, hard, plastic disk called an ultrasound transducer picks up and marks the fetal heart activity on the paper and is secured over the abdomen.

5. A nurse is describing cardiovascular system changes that occur during pregnancy to a client and understands that which finding would be normal for a client in the second trimester?
   1. Increase in pulse rate
   2. Increase in blood pressure
   3. Frequent bowel elimination
   4. Decrease in red blood cell (RBC) production

6. A nurse has performed a nonstress test on a pregnant client and is reviewing the fetal monitor strip. The nurse interprets the test as reactive and understands that this indicates:
   1. Normal findings
   2. Abnormal findings
   3. The need for further evaluation
   4. That the findings on the monitor were difficult to interpret

7. A nonstress test is performed on a client who is pregnant and the results of the test indicate nonreactive findings. The physician orders a contraction stress test to be done and the results are documented as negative. The nurse interprets this finding as indicating:
   1. A normal test result
   2. An abnormal test result
   3. A high risk for fetal demise
   4. The need for a cesarean delivery

8. A nurse is reviewing a nutritional plan of care with a pregnant client and is identifying the food items highest in folic acid. The nurse determines that the client understands the foods that supply the highest amounts of folic acid if the client states that she will include which of the following in the daily diet?
   1. Milk
   2. Yogurt
   3. Bananas
   4. Leafy, green vegetables

9. A pregnant client tells a nurse that she has been craving "unusual foods." The nurse gathers additional assessment data from the client and discovers that the client has been ingesting daily amounts of white clay dirt from her backyard. Laboratory studies are performed on the client. The nurse reviews the laboratory results and determines that which of the following indicates a physiological consequence of this client's practice?
   1. Hematocrit, 38%
   2. Glucose, 86 mg/dL
   3. Hemoglobin, 9.1 g/dL
   4. White blood cell count, 12,400/mm^3

10. A pregnant client who is at 30 weeks' gestation comes to the clinic for a routine visit, and the nurse performs an assessment on the client. Which observation made by the nurse during the assessment indicates a need for teaching?
    1. The client is wearing sneakers.
    2. The client is wearing knee-high hose.
    3. The client is wearing flat shoes with rubber soles.
    4. The client is wearing pants with an elastic waistband.

11. A nurse is developing a plan of care for a pregnant client who is complaining of intermittent episodes

of constipation. To help alleviate this problem, the nurse instructs the client to:

1. Consume a low-roughage diet.
2. Drink 6 glasses of water per day.
3. Use a Fleet enema when the episodes occur.
4. Take a mild stool softener daily in the evening.

12. A pregnant client visits a clinic for a scheduled prenatal appointment. The client tells the nurse that she frequently has a backache, and the nurse provides instructions regarding measures that will assist in relieving the backache. Which statement by the client indicates a need for further instructions?

1. "I should wear flat-heeled shoes."
2. "I should sleep on a firm mattress."
3. "I should try to maintain good posture."
4. "I should do more exercises to strengthen my back muscles."

13. A nurse is providing instructions to a pregnant client who is scheduled for an amniocentesis. The nurse tells the client that:

1. Strict bed rest is required following the procedure.
2. An informed consent will need to be signed before the procedure.
3. Hospitalization is necessary for 24 hours following the procedure.
4. A fever is expected following the procedure because of the trauma to the abdomen.

14. A pregnant client in the first trimester calls a nurse at a health care clinic and reports that she has noticed a thin, colorless, vaginal drainage. The nurse should make which statement to the client?

1. "Come to the clinic immediately."
2. "Report to the emergency room at the maternity center immediately."
3. "The vaginal discharge may be bothersome but is a normal occurrence."
4. "Use tampons if the discharge is bothersome but to be sure to change the tampons every 2 hours."

15. A pregnant client asks a nurse about the types of exercises that are allowable during the pregnancy. The nurse should instruct the client that the safest exercise to engage in is which of the following?

1. Swimming
2. Scuba diving
3. Low-impact gymnastics
4. Bicycling with the legs in the air

16. A physician has prescribed transvaginal ultrasonography for a client in the first trimester of pregnancy and the client asks the nurse about the procedure. The nurse tells the client that:

1. The procedure takes about 2 hours.

2. It will be necessary to drink 1 to 2 quarts of water before the examination.
3. Gel is spread over the abdomen, and a round disk transducer will be moved over the abdomen to obtain the picture.
4. The probe that will be inserted into the vagina will be covered with a disposable cover and coated with a gel.

17. A clinic nurse has instructed a pregnant client in measures to prevent varicose veins during pregnancy. Which statement by the client indicates a need for further instructions?

1. "I should wear panty hose."
2. "I should wear support hose."
3. "I should be wearing flat nonslip shoes that have good support."
4. "I should wear knee-high hose as long as I don't leave them on longer than 8 hours."

18. A pregnant client calls a clinic and tells the nurse that she is experiencing leg cramps that awaken her at night. To provide relief from the leg cramps, the nurse tells the client to:

1. Bend her foot toward her body while flexing the knee when the cramps occur.
2. Bend her foot toward her body while extending the knee when the cramps occur.
3. Point her foot away from her body while flexing the knee when the cramps occur.
4. Point her foot away from her body while extending the knee when the cramps occur.

19. A clinic nurse is providing instructions to a pregnant client regarding measures that will assist in alleviating heartburn. Which statement by the client indicates an understanding of the instructions?:

1. "I should avoid between-meal snacks."
2. "I should lie down for an hour after eating."
3. "I should use spices for cooking rather than using salt."
4. "I should avoid eating foods that produce gas, such as beans, vegetables, and fatty foods like deep fried chicken. "

20. A nurse in a health care clinic is instructing a pregnant client about how to perform "kick counts." Which statement by the client indicates a need for further instructions?

1. "I will record the number of movements or kicks."
2. "I need to lie flat on my back to perform the procedure."
3. "A count of fewer than 10 kicks in a 12-hour period indicates the need to contact the physician."
4. "I should place my hands on the largest part of my abdomen and concentrate on the fetal movements to count the kicks."

ALTERNATE ITEM FORMAT: MULTIPLE RESPONSE

A 1-day postpartum client's rubella titer result is lower than 1:8 and a rubella virus vaccine is prescribed to be administered before discharge. The nurse provides which information to the client about the vaccine? Select all that apply.

1. Pregnancy needs to be avoided for 1 to 3 months.
2. Breast-feeding needs to be stopped for 3 months.
3. The vaccine is administered by the subcutaneous route.
4. A hypersensitivity reaction can occur if the client has an allergy to eggs.
5. Exposure to other people who are immunosuppressed needs to be avoided.
6. The area of the injection needs to be covered with a sterile gauze for 1 week.

ANSWERS

1. **4**

Rationale: Dietary sources of iron include lean meats, liver, shellfish, dark green leafy vegetables, legumes, whole grains, and enriched grains, cereals, and molasses. Milk is high in calcium and also contains phosphorus. Cantaloupe and potatoes are high in vitamin C.

Test-Taking Strategy: Use the process of elimination and knowledge of the dietary sources of iron to assist in answering the question. Remember that dark green, leafy vegetables are high in iron. If you had difficulty with this question, review food items high in iron.

Level of Cognitive Ability: Application
Client Needs: Physiological Integrity
Integrated Process: Teaching and Learning
Content Area: Maternity—antepartum
Reference: Murray, S., & McKinney, E. (2006). *Foundations of maternal-newborn nursing* (4th ed., p. 180). Philadelphia: W.B. Saunders.

2. **4**

Rationale: Measures that provide relief from hemorrhoids include avoiding constipation and straining during bowel movements; applying ice packs to reduce the hemorrhoidal swelling; gently replacing the hemorrhoids into the rectum; using stool softeners, ointments, or sprays as prescribed; and assuming certain positions to relieve pressure on the hemorrhoids. Heat packs will increase the blood flow to the area and worsen the discomfort from hemorrhoids.

Test-Taking Strategy: Use the process of elimination, noting the strategic words *need for further instruction*. These words indicate a negative event query and ask you to select an option that is an incorrect statement. Recalling the principles regarding heat and cold will assist in directing you to option 4. If you had difficulty with this question, review the measures for the treatment of hemorrhoids.

Level of Cognitive Ability: Analysis
Client Needs: Physiological Integrity
Integrated Process: Teaching and Learning
Content Area: Maternity—antepartum
Reference: Murray, S., & McKinney, E. (2006). *Foundations of maternal-newborn nursing* (4th ed., p. 137). Philadelphia: W.B. Saunders.

3. **2**

Rationale: The pregnant client should be instructed to wash the breasts with warm water and keep them dry. The client should be instructed to avoid using soap on the nipples and areola area to prevent the drying of tissues. Wearing a supportive bra with wide adjustable straps can decrease breast tenderness. Tight-fitting blouses or dresses will cause discomfort. The client is instructed to wear soft-textured clothing to decrease nipple tenderness and to use breast pads inside the bra to prevent leakage if colostrum is a problem.

Test-Taking Strategy: Use the process of elimination. Focusing on the subject of the question, reducing breast tenderness, and visualizing each of the measures identified in the options will direct you to option 2. If you had difficulty with this question, review treatment measures for the client with breast tenderness.

Level of Cognitive Ability: Application
Client Needs: Health Promotion and Maintenance
Integrated Process: Teaching and Learning
Content Area: Maternity—antepartum
Reference: McKinney, E., James, S., Murray, S., & Ashwill, J. (2005). *Maternal-child nursing* (2nd ed., p. 276). St. Louis: W.B. Saunders.

4. **4**

Rationale: The nonstress test takes about 20 to 30 minutes. The test is termed *nonstress* because it consists of monitoring only; the fetus is not challenged or stressed by uterine contractions (medication is not given) to obtain the necessary data. The test is noninvasive (an informed consent is not required), and an ultrasound transducer that records fetal heart activity is secured over the maternal abdomen, where the fetal heart is heard most clearly. A tocotransducer that detects uterine activity and fetal movement also is secured to the maternal abdomen. Fetal heart activity and movements are recorded.

Test-Taking Strategy: Use the process of elimination. Focus on the name of the test and the procedure for this test to eliminate options 1, 2, and 3. If you are unfamiliar with this test or had difficulty answering this question, review this procedure.

Level of Cognitive Ability: Application
Client Needs: Physiological Integrity
Integrated Process: Teaching and Learning
Content Area: Maternity—antepartum
Reference: Murray, S., & McKinney, E. (2006). *Foundations of maternal-newborn nursing* (4th ed., pp. 213-214) Philadelphia: W.B. Saunders.

5. **1**

Rationale: Between 14 and 20 weeks' gestation, the pulse increases about 10 to 15 beats/min, which then persists to term. Options 2, 3, and 4 are incorrect. During pregnancy, the blood

pressure usually remains the same as the prepregnancy level, but then gradually decreases up to about 20 weeks of gestation. During the second trimester, both systolic and diastolic pressures decrease by about 5 to 10 mm Hg. Constipation may occur as a result of decreased gastrointestinal motility or pressure of the uterus. During pregnancy, there is an accelerated production of RBCs.
Test-Taking Strategy: Focus on the subject of the question, the findings that would be considered normal for a client in her second trimester. Think about the physiological occurrences during pregnancy and remember that between 14 and 20 weeks' gestation, the pulse increases about 10 to 15 beats/min. If you had difficulty with this question, review normal physiological changes during the second trimester of pregnancy.
Level of Cognitive Ability: Comprehension
Client Needs: Physiological Integrity
Integrated Process: Teaching and Learning
Content Area: Maternity—antepartum
Reference: Wong, D., Perry, S., Hockenberry, M., et al. (2006). *Maternal child nursing care* (3rd ed., p. 242). St. Louis: Mosby.

6. 1
Rationale: A reactive nonstress test is a normal result. To be considered reactive, the baseline fetal heart rate must be within normal range (120 to 160 beats/min) with good long-term variability. In addition, two or more fetal heart rate accelerations of at least 15 beats/min must occur, each with a duration of at least 15 seconds, in a 20-minute interval.
Test-Taking Strategy: Use the process of elimination. Eliminate options 2, 3, and 4 because they are comparative or alike. If you had difficulty with this question and are unfamiliar with the interpretation of the results of a nonstress test, review this content.
Level of Cognitive Ability: Analysis
Client Needs: Physiological Integrity
Integrated Process: Nursing Process—analysis
Content Area: Maternity—antepartum
References: Murray, S., & McKinney, E. (2006). *Foundations of maternal-newborn nursing* (4th ed., p. 214). Philadelphia: W.B. Saunders.
Wong, D., Perry, S., Hockenberry, M., et al. (2006). *Maternal child nursing care* (3rd ed., p. 231). St. Louis: Mosby.

7. 1
Rationale: Contraction stress test results may be interpreted as negative (normal), positive (abnormal), or equivocal. A negative test result indicates that no late decelerations occurred in the fetal heart rate, although the fetus was stressed by three contractions of at least 40 seconds' duration in a 10-minute period. Therefore, options 2, 3, and 4 are incorrect interpretations.
Test-Taking Strategy: Use the process of elimination, noting that options 2, 3, and 4 are comparative or alike in that they indicate an abnormal test result finding. If you had difficulty with this question and are unfamiliar with the interpretation of the results of a contraction stress test, review this content.
Level of Cognitive Ability: Analysis
Client Needs: Physiological Integrity

Integrated Process: Nursing Process—analysis
Content Area: Maternity—antepartum
References: Murray, S., & McKinney, E. (2006). *Foundations of maternal-newborn nursing* (4th ed., p. 214). Philadelphia: W.B. Saunders, p. 214.
Wong, D., Perry, S., Hockenberry, M., et al. (2006). *Maternal child nursing care* (3rd ed., p. 231). St. Louis: Mosby.

8. 4
Rationale: Leafy green vegetables are rich in folate (folic acid). Bananas provide potassium; milk and yogurt supply calcium.
Test-Taking Strategy: Use the process of elimination. Eliminate options 1 and 2 first because they are comparative or alike. From the remaining options, recalling that leafy green vegetables are high in folic acid will direct you to option 4. Review these foods if you had difficulty with this question.
Level of Cognitive Ability: Analysis
Client Needs: Physiological Integrity
Integrated Process: Nursing Process—evaluation
Content Area: Maternity—antepartum
Reference: Wong, D., Perry, S., Hockenberry, M., et al. (2006). *Maternal child nursing care* (3rd ed., p. 316). St. Louis: Mosby.

9. 3
Rationale: Pica cravings often lead to iron deficiency anemia, resulting in a lowered hemoglobin level. The laboratory values in options 1, 2, and 4 are within normal limits for the pregnant client.
Test-Taking Strategy: Use the process of elimination, recalling that pica results in anemia. This will assist in eliminating options 2 and 4. From the remaining options, recall the normal laboratory values in a pregnant client to assist in directing you to option 3. Review the physiological effects of pica and the normal laboratory values in a pregnant client if you had difficulty with this question.
Level of Cognitive Ability: Analysis
Client Needs: Physiological Integrity
Integrated Process: Nursing Process—analysis
Content Area: Maternity—antepartum
Reference: Wong, D., Perry, S., Hockenberry, M., et al. (2006). *Maternal child nursing care* (3rd ed., p. 316). St. Louis: Mosby.

10. 2
Rationale: Varicose veins often develop in the lower extremities during pregnancy. Any constricting clothing such as knee-high hose impede venous return from the lower legs and thus place the client at higher risk for developing varicosities. Clients should be encouraged to wear panty hose or support hose. Flat nonslip shoes with proper support are important to assist the pregnant woman to maintain proper posture and balance and minimize the risk for falls. Pants with an elastic waistband are comfortable and are not constricting.
Test-Taking Strategy: Use the process of elimination, noting the strategic words *indicates a need for teaching*. These words indicate a negative event query and ask you to select an option that is an incorrect statement. Remembering that the pregnant client is at risk for developing varicosities and recalling the measures to prevent their occurrence will direct you to option 2. Review the measures that will assist in preventing varicosities if you had difficulty with this question.

Level of Cognitive Ability: Analysis
Client Needs: Physiological Integrity
Integrated Process: Teaching and Learning
Content Area: Maternity—antepartum
Reference: Wong, D., Perry, S., Hockenberry, M., et al. (2006). *Maternal child nursing care* (3rd ed., p. 280). St. Louis: Mosby.

11. **2**
Rationale: The nurse should instruct the client to drink 6 glasses of water per day and to consume a diet that includes roughage to prevent the constipation. The client should not take stool softeners, laxatives, mineral oil, other medications, or enemas without first consulting with the physician or nurse-midwife.
Test-Taking Strategy: Use the process of elimination and recall the basic principles related to the prevention of constipation. Eliminate option 1 because of the word *low*. Next, eliminate options 3 and 4 because they are invasive measures. Review measures to prevent constipation in the pregnant client if you had difficulty with this question.
Level of Cognitive Ability: Application
Client Needs: Health Promotion and Maintenance
Integrated Process: Teaching and Learning
Content Area: Maternity—antepartum
Reference: Wong, D., Perry, S., Hockenberry, M., et al. (2006). *Maternal child nursing care* (3rd ed., p. 287). St. Louis: Mosby.

12. **4**
Rationale: Some measures that will assist in relieving a backache include maintaining good posture and body mechanics, resting and avoiding fatigue, wearing flat-heeled shoes, and sleeping on a firm mattress. The back discomfort that occurs in a pregnant client is often caused by the exaggerated lumbar and cervicothoracic curves resulting from a change in the center of gravity because of the enlarged uterus. Performing more exercises to strengthen the back muscles could be harmful to a pregnant client.
Test-Taking Strategy: Use the process of elimination, focusing on the strategic words *need for further instructions*. These words indicate a negative event query and ask you to select an option that is an incorrect statement. Recalling the principles related to relieving a backache will assist in directing you to the correct option. Review these measures if you had difficulty with this question.
Level of Cognitive Ability: Analysis
Client Needs: Health Promotion and Maintenance
Integrated Process: Teaching and Learning
Content Area: Maternity—antepartum
Reference: Wong, D., Perry, S., Hockenberry, M., et al. (2006). *Maternal child nursing care* (3rd ed., p. 287). St. Louis: Mosby.

13. **2**
Rationale: Because amniocentesis is an invasive procedure, informed consent will need to be obtained before the procedure. After the procedure, the client is instructed to rest but may resume light activity after the cramping subsides. The client is instructed to keep the puncture site clean and to report any complications such as vaginal discharge, severe, persistent cramping, or onset of fever. Amniocentesis is an outpatient procedure and may be done in a physician's private office or

in a special prenatal testing unit. Hospitalization is not necessary following the procedure.
Test-Taking Strategy: Use the process of elimination. Simply recalling that this procedure is invasive will direct you to option 2. If you had difficulty with this question, review the procedure related to amniocentesis.
Level of Cognitive Ability: Application
Client Needs: Physiological Integrity
Integrated Process: Teaching and Learning
Content Area: Maternity—antepartum
Reference: Chernecky, C., & Berger, B. (2004). *Laboratory tests and diagnostic procedures* (4th ed., p. 167). Philadelphia: W.B. Saunders.

14. **3**
Rationale: Leukorrhea begins during the first trimester. Many clients notice a thin colorless or yellow vaginal discharge throughout pregnancy. Some clients become distressed about this condition, but it does not require that the client report to the health care clinic or the emergency room immediately. If vaginal discharge is profuse, the client may use panty liners but should not wear tampons because of the risk of infection. If the client uses panty liners, she should change them frequently.
Test-Taking Strategy: Use the process of elimination. Eliminate options 1 and 2 first because they are comparative or alike. From the remaining options, recalling that this manifestation is a normal physiological occurrence or that tampons should be avoided will assist in directing you to the correct option. Review the normal occurrences related to vaginal discharge in a pregnant client if you had difficulty with this question.
Level of Cognitive Ability: Application
Client Needs: Health Promotion and Maintenance
Integrated Process: Nursing Process—implementation
Content Area: Maternity—antepartum
Reference: Wong, D., Perry, S., Hockenberry, M., et al. (2006). *Maternal child nursing care* (3rd ed., p. 241). St. Louis: Mosby.

15. **1**
Rationale: Non–weight-bearing exercises are preferable to weight-bearing exercises during pregnancy. Exercises to avoid are shoulder standing and bicycling with the legs in the air because the knee-chest position should be avoided. Competitive or high-risk sports such as scuba diving, water skiing, downhill skiing, horseback riding, basketball, volleyball, and gymnastics should be avoided. Non–weight-bearing exercises such as swimming are allowable.
Test-Taking Strategy: Use the process of elimination. Identify those activities or exercises that could cause an injury to the fetus. This should direct you to option 1. If you had difficulty with this question, review the teaching points related to exercising for a client who is pregnant.
Level of Cognitive Ability: Application
Client Needs: Health Promotion and Maintenance
Integrated Process: Teaching and Learning
Content Area: Maternity—antepartum
References: McKinney, E., James, S., Murray, S., & Ashwill, J. (2005). *Maternal-child nursing* (2nd ed., p. 278). St. Louis: W.B. Saunders.

Wong, D., Perry, S., Hockenberry, M., et al. (2006). *Maternal child nursing care* (3rd ed., p. 316). St. Louis: Mosby.

16. 4

Rationale: Transvaginal ultrasonography allows clear visibility of the uterus, gestational sac, embryo, and deep pelvic structures, such as the ovaries and fallopian tubes. The client is placed in a lithotomy position and a transvaginal probe, encased in a disposable cover and coated with a gel that provides lubrication and promotes conductivity, is inserted into the vagina. The client may feel more comfortable if she is allowed to insert the probe. The procedure takes about 10 to 15 minutes. Options 2 and 3 identify components of the abdominal ultrasound.

Test-Taking Strategy: Use the process of elimination. Note the strategic words *transvaginal ultrasonography*. Also, note the relationship of the name of the test and the description in the correct option. If you had difficulty with this question, review the procedure for transvaginal ultrasonography.

Level of Cognitive Ability: Application
Client Needs: Physiological Integrity
Integrated Process: Teaching and Learning
Content Area: Maternity—antepartum
References: McKinney, E., James, S., Murray, S., & Ashwill, J. (2005). *Maternal-child nursing* (2nd ed., p. 325). St. Louis: W.B. Saunders.
Murray, S., & McKinney, E. (2006). *Foundations of maternal-newborn nursing* (4th ed., p. 2205). Philadelphia: W.B. Saunders.

17. 4

Rationale: Varicose veins often develop in the lower extremities during pregnancy. Any constrictive clothing, such as knee-high hose, impedes venous return from the lower legs and places the client at risk for developing varicosities. The client should be encouraged to wear support hose or panty hose. Flat nonslip shoes with proper support are important to assist the pregnant woman to maintain proper posture and balance and minimize falls.

Test-Taking Strategy: Use the process of elimination and note the strategic words *a need for further instructions*. These words indicate a negative event query and ask you to select an option that is an incorrect statement. Focus on the subject of the question as it relates to preventing varicose veins. Recall that anything that constricts the lower vessels and impedes venous return from the lower legs will place the client at risk for varicosities. If you had difficulty with this question, review measures to prevent varicose veins.

Level of Cognitive Ability: Analysis
Client Needs: Health Promotion and Maintenance
Integrated Process: Teaching and Learning
Content Area: Maternity—antepartum
Reference: Murray, S., & McKinney, E. (2006). *Foundations of maternal-newborn nursing* (4th ed., p. 137). Philadelphia: W.B. Saunders.

18. 2

Rationale: Leg cramps occur when the pregnant client stretches her leg and plantar flexes her foot. Dorsiflexion of the foot while extending the knee stretches the affected muscle, pre-

vents the muscle from contracting, and stops the cramping. Options 1, 3, and 4 are not measures that will provide relief from the leg cramps.

Test-Taking Strategy: Use the process of elimination and focus on the subject of the question, to provide relief from the leg cramps. Visualize each of the descriptions in the options to assist in directing you to option 2. If you had difficulty with this question, review measures that assist in alleviating muscle cramps.

Level of Cognitive Ability: Application
Client Needs: Health Promotion and Maintenance
Integrated Process: Teaching and Learning
Content Area: Maternity—antepartum
Reference: Murray, S., & McKinney, E. (2006). *Foundations of maternal-newborn nursing* (4th ed., p. 138). Philadelphia: W.B. Saunders.

19. 4

Rationale: Lying down is likely to lead to reflux of stomach contents, especially immediately following a meal. The client should be instructed to avoid spices, along with salt, because spices will trigger heartburn. Salt will produce edema. The client should be encouraged to eat between-meal snacks and should be instructed that to control heartburn, eating smaller, more frequent portions is preferred over eating three large meals. The client also should limit or avoid gas-producing and fatty foods.

Test-Taking Strategy: Use the process of elimination and note the strategic words *indicates an understanding of the instructions*. Recalling that the client needs to limit or avoid gas-producing and fatty foods will assist in directing you to option 4. Review the measures that will alleviate heartburn in the pregnant client if you had difficulty with this question.

Level of Cognitive Ability: Analysis
Client Needs: Health Promotion and Maintenance
Integrated Process: Nursing Process—evaluation
Content Area: Maternity—antepartum
Reference: Murray, S., & McKinney, E. (2006). *Foundations of maternal-newborn nursing* (4th ed., p. 137). Philadelphia: W.B. Saunders.

20. 2

Rationale: The client should sit or lie quietly on her side to perform kick counts. Lying flat on the back is not necessary to perform this procedure, can cause discomfort, and presents a risk of vena cava (hypotensive) syndrome. The client is instructed to place her hands on the largest part of the abdomen and concentrate on the fetal movements. The client records the number of movements felt during a specified time period. The client needs to notify the physician or nurse-midwife if there are fewer than 10 kicks in a 12-hour period or as instructed by the physician or nurse-midwife.

Test-Taking Strategy: Use the process of elimination, noting the strategic words *a need for further instructions*. These words indicate a negative event query and ask you to select an option that is an incorrect statement. If you are unfamiliar with this procedure, recalling that the risk of vena cava (hypotensive) syndrome exists when the client lies on her back will direct you to option 2. Review the procedure for kick counts if you had difficulty with this question.

Level of Cognitive Ability: Analysis
Client Needs: Health Promotion and Maintenance
Integrated Process: Teaching and Learning
Content Area: Maternity—antepartum
Reference: Murray, S., & McKinney, E. (2006). *Foundations of maternal-newborn nursing* (4th ed., p. 218). Philadelphia: W.B. Saunders.

ALTERNATE ITEM FORMAT: MULTIPLE RESPONSE

Answer: 1, 3, 4, 5
Rationale: Rubella vaccine is administered to women who have not had rubella or women who are not serologically immune. The vaccine may be administered in the immediate postpartum period to prevent the possibility of contracting rubella in future pregnancies. The live attenuated rubella virus is not communicable in breast milk; therefore, breast-feeding does not need to be stopped. The client is counseled not to become pregnant for 1 to 3 months following immunization as specified by the health care provider because of a possible risk to a fetus from the live virus vaccine; the client must be using effective birth control at the time of the immunization. The client should avoid contact with immunosuppressed individuals because of their low immunity toward live viruses, because the virus is shed in the urine and other body fluids. The vaccine is administered by the subcutaneous route. A hypersensitivity reaction can occur if the client has an allergy to eggs because the vaccine is made from duck eggs. There is no useful or necessary reason for covering the area of the injection with a sterile gauze.

Test-Taking Strategy: Focus on the subject, client instructions regarding the rubella vaccine. Recalling that the rubella vaccine is a live virus vaccine will assist in selecting options 1 and 5. Next, recalling the route of administration and the contraindications associated with its use will assist in selecting options 3 and 4. Review client instructions following this immunization if you had difficulty with this question.

Level of Cognitive Ability: Application
Client Needs: Health Promotion and Maintenance
Integrated Process: Teaching and Learning
Content Area: Maternity—postpartum
References: Murray, S., McKinney, E. (2006). *Foundations of maternal-newborn nursing* (4th ed., p. 684). Philadelphia: W.B. Saunders.

Wong, D., Perry, S., Hockenberry, M., Lowdermilk, D., & Wilson, D. (2006). *Maternal-child nursing care* (3rd ed., p. 410). St. Louis: Mosby.

REFERENCES

Chernecky, C., & Berger, B. (2004). *Laboratory tests and diagnostic procedures* (4 ed.). Philadelphia: W.B. Saunders.

Lowdermilk, D., & Perry, A. (2004). *Maternity and women's health care* (8 ed.). St. Louis: Mosby.

McKinney, E., James, S., Murray, S., & Ashwill, J. (2005). *Maternal-child nursing* (2nd ed.). St. Louis: W.B. Saunders.

Murray, S., & McKinney, E. (2006). *Foundations of maternal-newborn nursing* (4th ed.). Philadelphia: W.B. Saunders.

National Council of State Boards of Nursing (2007). *2007 NCLEX-RN® detailed test plan.* Chicago: Author.

Wong, D., Perry, S., Hockenberry, M., et al. (2006). *Maternal child nursing care* (3rd ed.). St. Louis: Mosby.

Risk Conditions Related to Pregnancy

I. ABORTION

A. Description: A pregnancy that ends before 20 weeks' gestation, spontaneously or electively

B. Types (Box 25-1)

C. Assessment
1. Spontaneous vaginal bleeding occurs.
2. Passage of clots or tissue through the **vagina** may occur.
3. Low uterine cramping or contractions occur.
4. Hemorrhage and shock can result.

D. Interventions
1. Maintain bed rest as prescribed.
2. Monitor vital signs.
3. Monitor for cramping and bleeding.
4. Count perineal pads to evaluate blood loss, and save expelled tissues and clots.
5. Maintain intravenous fluids as prescribed; monitor for signs of hemorrhage or shock.

BOX 25-1
Types of Abortions

Spontaneous: Pregnancy ends because of natural causes.
Induced: Therapeutic or elective reasons exist for terminating the pregnancy.
Threatened: Spotting and cramping without cervical change occur.
Inevitable: Spotting and cramping occur and the cervix begins to dilate and efface.
Incomplete: Loss of some of the products of conception occurs, with part of the products retained (most often the placenta is retained).
Complete: Loss of all products of conception occurs.
Missed: The products of conception are retained in utero after fetal death.
Habitual: This is characterized by spontaneous abortions in three or more successive pregnancies.

---

6. Prepare the client for dilatation and curettage as prescribed for incomplete abortion.
7. Rh immune globulin is prescribed for an Rh-negative woman.

II. HUMAN IMMUNODEFICIENCY VIRUS AND ACQUIRED IMMUNODEFICIENCY SYNDROME

A. Description
1. The human immunodeficiency virus (HIV) is a causative agent of acquired immunodeficiency syndrome (AIDS).
2. Women infected with HIV first may demonstrate symptoms at the time of pregnancy or possibly develop life-threatening infections because normal pregnancy involves some suppression of the maternal immune system.
3. Zidovudine (ZDV) is recommended for the prevention of maternal-fetal HIV transmission and is administered orally beginning after 14 weeks' gestation, intravenously during **labor,** and in the form of syrup to the **neonate** for 6 weeks after birth.

B. Transmission
1. Sexual exposure to genital secretions of an infected person
2. Parenteral exposure to infected blood and tissue
3. Perinatal exposure of an **infant** to infected maternal secretions through birth or breast-feeding

C. Risks to the mother: The mother with HIV is managed as high risk because she is vulnerable to infections.

D. Diagnosis
1. Tests used to determine the presence of antibodies to HIV include the enzyme-linked immunosorbent assay (ELISA), Western blot, and immunofluorescence assay (IFA).
2. A single reactive ELISA test by itself cannot be used to diagnose HIV and should be repeated

with the same blood sample; if the result is again reactive, follow-up tests using the Western blot or IFA should be done.

3. A positive Western blot or IFA is considered confirmatory for HIV.

4. A positive ELISA that fails to be confirmed by Western blot or IFA should not be considered negative, and repeat testing should take place in 3 to 6 months.

5. See Chapter 11 for additional laboratory tests.

E. Assessment (Box 25-2)

▲ F. Interventions

▲ 1. Prenatal period

 a. Prevent opportunistic infections.

 b. Avoid procedures that increase the risk of perinatal transmission, such as amniocentesis and fetal scalp sampling.

▲ 2. Intrapartum period

 a. If the fetus has not been exposed to HIV in utero, the highest risk exists during **delivery** through the birth canal.

 b. Avoid the use of internal scalp electrodes for monitoring of the fetus.

 c. Avoid episiotomy to decrease the amount of maternal blood in and around the birth canal.

 d. Avoid the administration of oxytocin (Pitocin), because contractions induced by oxytocin can be strong, causing vaginal tears or necessitating an episiotomy.

 e. Place heavy absorbent pads under the mother's hips to absorb **amniotic fluid** and maternal blood.

 f. Minimize the **neonate's** exposure to maternal blood and body fluids; promptly remove the **neonate** from the mother's blood following **delivery.**

 g. Suction fluids from the **neonate** promptly.

 h. Prepare to administer ZDV as prescribed to the mother during **labor** and **delivery.**

▲ 3. Postpartum period

 a. Monitor for signs of infection.

 b. Place the mother in protective isolation if the mother is immunosuppressed.

 c. Restrict breast-feeding.

 d. Instruct the mother to monitor for signs of infection and report any signs if they occur.

G. The **neonate** and HIV

 1. Description

 a. **Neonates** born to HIV-positive clients may test positive because antibodies received from the mother may persist for as long as 18 months after birth; all **neonates** acquire maternal antibody to HIV infection, but not all acquire infection.

 b. The use of antiviral medication, reduction of **neonate** exposure to maternal blood and

body fluids, and early identification of HIV in pregnancy reduce the risk of transmission to the **neonate.**

 2. Interventions

 a. Bathe the **neonate** carefully before any invasive procedure, such as the administration of vitamin K, heel sticks, or venipunctures; clean the umbilical cord stump meticulously every day until healed.

 b. **Neonate** can room with mother.

 c. Administer ZDV to the **newborn infant** as prescribed for the first 6 weeks of life.

 d. All HIV-exposed **newborn infants** should be treated with medication to prevent infection by *Pneumocystis jiroveci.*

 e. Note that an HIV culture is recommended at 1 and 4 months after birth; **infants** at risk for HIV infection should be seen by the physician at birth, 1 week, 2 weeks, 1 month, 2 months, and 4 months of age.

 f. **Infants** at risk for HIV infection need to receive all recommended immunizations at the regular schedule; no live vaccines should be administered.

 g. The **neonate** may be asymptomatic for the first several years of life and should be monitored for early signs of immunodeficiency

---

BOX 25-2

Stages of Acquired Immunodeficiency Syndrome (AIDS)

STAGE 1
Fever
Headache
Lymphadenopathy
Myalgia

STAGE 2
Infection is active but asymptomatic and may remain so for years.
Client may experience an outbreak of herpes zoster (shingles).
Client may experience a transient thrombocytopenia.

STAGE 3
Client is symptomatic.
Immune dysfunction is evident.
All body systems can show signs of immune dysfunction.
Integumentary and gynecological problems are common.

STAGE 4
Advanced human immunodeficiency virus infection
Client vulnerable to common bacterial infections
Development of opportunistic infections
Serious immune compromise

III. ANEMIA
  A. Description
    1. Iron deficiency anemia is a condition that develops as a result of an inadequate amount of serum iron.
    2. Anemia predisposes the client to postpartum infection.
  B. Assessment
    1. Fatigue
    2. Headache
    3. Pallor
    4. Tachycardia
    5. Hemoglobin value usually lower than 10 g/dL; hematocrit value usually lower than 30%.
  C. Interventions
    1. Monitor hemoglobin and hematocrit levels every 2 weeks.
    2. Administer and instruct the client about iron and folic acid supplements.
    3. Instruct the client to take iron with a source of vitamin C and to avoid taking iron with tea.
    4. Instruct the client to eat foods high in iron, folic acid, and protein.
    5. Teach the client to monitor for signs and symptoms of infection.
    6. Prepare to administer parenteral iron; this may be prescribed for severe anemia.
    7. Prepare to administer blood transfusions for severe anemia, if prescribed.
    8. Prepare for the administration of oxytocic medications in the postpartum period to prevent hemorrhage.

IV. CARDIAC DISEASE
  A. Description: The pregnant client with cardiac disease may be unable physiologically to cope with the added plasma volume and increased cardiac output that occur during pregnancy. Blood volume is at a maximum during the last weeks of the second trimester.
  B. Maternal cardiac disease risk groups (Box 25-3)
  C. Functional classification of heart disease (Box 25-4)
  D. Assessment
    1. Signs and symptoms of cardiac decompensation
    2. Cough
    3. Dyspnea and fatigue
    4. Palpitations and tachycardia
    5. Peripheral edema
    6. Chest pain
    7. Signs of respiratory infection
    8. Signs of congestive heart failure and pulmonary edema
  E. Interventions
    1. Monitor vital signs, fetal heart rate, and condition of the fetus.
    2. Limit physical activities and stress the need for sufficient rest.

BOX 25-3
Maternal Cardiac Disease Risk Groups

GROUP I (mortality rate, 1%)
Corrected tetralogy of Fallot
Pulmonic or tricuspid disease
Mitral stenosis (Classes I and II)
Patent ductus arteriosus
Ventricular septal defect
Atrial septal defect
Porcine valve

GROUP II (mortality rate, 5%-15%)
Mitral stenosis with atrial fibrillation
Artificial heart valves
Mitral stenosis (Classes III and IV)
Uncorrected tetralogy
Aortic coarctation (uncomplicated)
Aortic stenosis

GROUP III (mortality rate, 25%-50%)
Aortic coarctation (complicated)
Myocardial infarction
Marfan syndrome
True cardiomyopathy
Pulmonary hypertension

Modified from Lowdermilk, D., & Perry, S. (2006): *Maternity nursing* (7th ed.). St. Louis: Mosby.

BOX 25-4
New York Heart Association Functional Classification of Heart Disease

Class I: Uncompromised. No limitation of physical activity. Asymptomatic with ordinary activity.
Class II: Slightly compromised, requiring slight limitation of physical activity. Patient is comfortable at rest, but ordinary physical activity causes fatigue, dyspnea, palpitations, or anginal pain.
Class III: Markedly compromised. Marked limitation of physical activity. Patient is comfortable at rest, but less than ordinary activity causes excessive fatigue, palpitation, dyspnea, or anginal pain.
Class IV: Inability to perform any physical activity without discomfort. Symptoms of cardiac insufficiency even at rest. In general, maternal and fetal risks for Classes I and II disease are small but are greatly increased with Classes III and IV.

From Murray, S., & McKinney, E. (2005). *Foundations of maternal-newborn nursing* (4th ed.). Philadelphia: W.B. Saunders.

    3. Monitor for signs of cardiac stress such as cough, fatigue, dyspnea, chest pain, and tachycardia
    4. Encourage adequate nutrition to prevent anemia; additionally, a low-sodium diet may be prescribed to prevent congestive heart failure
    5. Avoid excessive weight gain

6. Monitor for signs of congestive heart failure, pulmonary edema, and cardiac decompensation
7. During **labor,** prepare to do the following:
   a. Monitor vital signs frequently.
   b. Place the client on a cardiac monitor and on an external fetal monitor.
   c. Maintain bed rest, with mother lying on her side with her head and shoulders elevated.
   d. Administer oxygen as prescribed.

V. CHORIOAMNIONITIS
A. Description
   1. A bacterial infection of the amniotic cavity; can result from premature rupture of the membrane, vaginitis, amniocentesis, or intrauterine procedures
   2. May result in the development of postpartum endometritis
B. Assessment
   1. Uterine tenderness and contractions
   2. Elevated temperature
   3. Maternal or fetal tachycardia
   4. Foul odor to **amniotic fluid**
   5. Leukocytosis
C. Interventions
   1. Monitor maternal vital signs and fetal heart rate.
   2. Monitor for uterine tenderness, contractions, and fetal activity.
   3. Monitor results of blood cultures.
   4. Prepare for amniocentesis to obtain **amniotic fluid** for Gram stain and leukocyte count.
   5. Administer antibiotics as prescribed after cultures are obtained.
   6. Administer oxytocic medications as prescribed to increase uterine tone.
   7. Obtain neonatal cultures after **delivery.**

VI. DIABETES MELLITUS
A. Description
   1. Pregnancy places demands on carbohydrate metabolism and causes insulin requirements to change.
   2. Maternal glucose crosses the **placenta** but insulin does not.
   3. During the first trimester, maternal insulin needs decrease.
   4. During the second and third trimesters, increases in placental hormones cause an insulin-resistant state, requiring an increase in the client's insulin dose.
   5. After placental **delivery,** placental hormone levels drop abruptly and insulin requirements decrease.
   6. The fetus produces its own insulin and pulls glucose from the mother, which predisposes the mother to hypoglycemic reactions.
   7. The **newborn infant** of a diabetic mother may be large in size but will have functions related to gestational age rather than size.

8. The **newborn infant** of a diabetic mother is at risk for hypoglycemia, hyperbilirubinemia, respiratory distress syndrome, hypocalcemia, and congenital anomalies.
B. Gestational diabetes mellitus
   1. Gestational diabetes occurs in pregnancy (during the second or third trimester) in clients not previously diagnosed as diabetic, and occurs when the pancreas cannot respond to the demand for more insulin.
   2. Pregnant women should be screened for gestational diabetes between 24 and 28 weeks of pregnancy.
   3. A 3-hour oral glucose tolerance test (GTT) will be performed to confirm gestational diabetes mellitus.
   4. Gestational diabetes frequently can be treated by diet alone; however, some clients may need insulin (oral hypoglycemic agents are never used during pregnancy).
   5. Most women with gestational diabetes return to a euglycemia state after **delivery;** however, these individuals have an increased risk of developing diabetes mellitus in their lifetimes.
C. Predisposing conditions to gestational diabetes
   1. Older than 35 years
   2. Obesity
   3. Multiple gestation
   4. Family history of diabetes mellitus
D. Assessment
   1. Excessive thirst
   2. Hunger
   3. Weight loss
   4. Frequent urination
   5. Blurred vision
   6. Recurrent urinary tract infections and vaginal yeast infections
   7. Glycosuria and ketonuria
   8. Signs of gestational hypertension
   9. Polyhydramnios
   10. Large fetus for gestational age (LGA)
E. Interventions
   1. Include diet, insulin (if diet cannot control blood glucose levels), exercise, and blood glucose determinations to maintain blood glucose levels between 65 and 130 mg/dL.
   2. Observe for signs of hyperglycemia, glycosuria and ketonuria, and hypoglycemia.
   3. Monitor weight.
   4. Increase calorie intake as prescribed, with adequate insulin therapy so that glucose will move into the cells.
   5. Assess for signs of maternal complications such as preeclampsia (hypertension, proteinuria, and edema).
   6. Monitor for signs of infection.
   7. Instruct the client to report burning and pain on urination, vaginal discharge or itching, or any

other signs of infection to the health care provider.

8. Assess fetal status and monitor for signs of fetal compromise.

F. Interventions during **labor**
1. Monitor fetal status continuously for signs of distress and, if noted, prepare the client for immediate cesarean section.
2. Carefully regulate insulin and provide glucose intravenously as prescribed, because **labor** depletes glycogen.

G. Interventions during the postpartum period
1. Observe the mother closely for a hypoglycemic reaction, because a precipitous drop in insulin requirements normally occurs (the mother may not require insulin for the first 24 hours).
2. Reregulate insulin needs as prescribed after the first day, according to blood glucose testing.
3. Assess dietary needs based on blood glucose testing and insulin requirements.
4. Monitor for signs of infection or postpartum hemorrhage.

VII. DISSEMINATED INTRAVASCULAR COAGULATION (DIC)

A. Description
1. DIC is a maternal condition in which the clotting cascade is activated, resulting in the formation of clots in the microcirculation.
2. Thromboplastin from placental tissue and clots enter the bloodstream through open vessels at the placental site and initiate an exaggeration of the normal clotting process.
3. The rapid and extensive formation of clots causes the platelets and clotting factors to be depleted; this results in bleeding and the potential vascular occlusion of organs from thromboembolus formation.

B. Predisposing conditions (Box 25-5)
C. Assessment
1. Uncontrolled bleeding
2. Bruising, purpura, petechiae, and ecchymosis
3. Presence of occult blood in excretions such as stool.
4. Hematuria, hematemesis, or vaginal bleeding
5. Signs of shock

6. Decreased fibrinogen level, platelet count, and hematocrit level
7. Increased prothrombin time (PT) and partial thromboplastin time (PTT), clotting time, and fibrin degradation products (FDPs).

D. Interventions
1. Remove the underlying cause.
2. Monitor vital signs; assess for bleeding and signs of shock.
3. Prepare for oxygen therapy, volume replacement, blood component therapy, and possibly heparin therapy.
4. Monitor for complications associated with fluid and blood replacement and heparin therapy.
5. Monitor urine output and maintain at 30 mL/hr (renal failure is a complication of DIC).

VIII. ECTOPIC PREGNANCY

A. Description: **Implantation** of the fertilized ovum outside of the uterine cavity; most common location is the ampulla of the fallopian tube (Fig. 25-1)
B. Assessment
1. Missed menstrual period
2. Abdominal pain
3. Vaginal spotting to bleeding that is dark red or brown
4. Rupture: Increased pain, referred shoulder pain, signs of shock
C. Interventions
1. Obtain assessment data and vital signs.
2. Monitor bleeding and initiate measures to prevent rupture and shock.
3. Methotrexate (a folic acid antagonist) may be prescribed to inhibit cell division in the developing **embryo.**
4. Prepare the client for laparotomy and removal of the pregnancy and tube, if necessary, or repair of the tube.

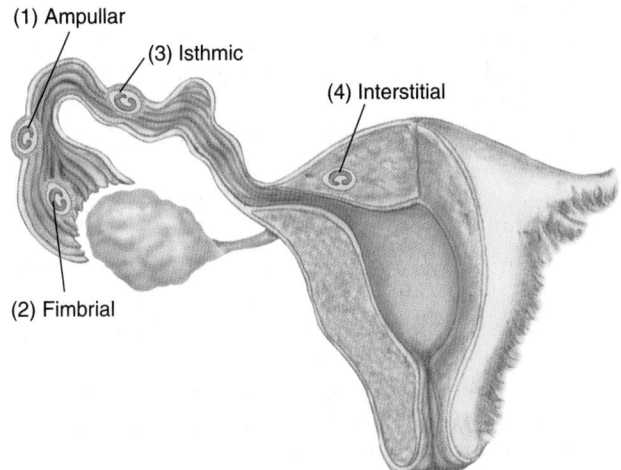

FIG. 25-1   Sites of tubal ectopic pregnancy. Numbers indicate the order of prevalence. (From Murray, S., & McKinney, E. [2005]. *Foundations of maternal-newborn nursing* [4th ed.]. Philadelphia: W.B. Saunders.)

BOX 25-5

Predisposing Conditions for Disseminated Intravascular Coagulation (DIC)

Abruptio placentae
Amniotic fluid embolism
Gestational hypertension
Intrauterine fetal death
Liver disease
Sepsis

5. Administer antibiotics; Rh immune globulin is prescribed for Rh-negative women.

IX. ENDOMETRITIS

A. Description
  1. Endometritis is an infection of the lining of the **uterus** occurring in the postpartum period and caused by bacteria that invade the **uterus** at the placental site.
  2. The infection may spread and involve the entire endometrium and cause peritonitis or pelvic thrombophlebitis.

▲ B. Assessment
  1. Chills and fever
  2. Increased pulse
  3. Decreased appetite
  4. Headache
  5. Backache
  6. Prolonged, severe afterpains
  7. Tender, large **uterus**
  8. Foul odor to **lochia** or reddish-brown **lochia**
  9. Ileus
  10. Elevated white blood cell count, with a left shift of immature cells

C. Interventions
  1. Monitor vital signs.
▲   2. Position the client in Fowler's position to facilitate drainage of **lochia.**
  3. Provide a private room for the mother; inform the mother that isolation of the **newborn infant** from the mother is not necessary.
  4. Instruct the mother in proper hand washing techniques.
  5. Initiate wound and skin precautions as necessary.
  6. Monitor intake and output and encourage fluid intake.
  7. Administer antibiotics as prescribed.
  8. Administer comfort measures such as back rubs and position changes and pain medications as prescribed.
  9. Administer oxytocic medications as prescribed to improve uterine tone.

▲ X. FETAL DEATH IN UTERO

A. Description
  1. The death of a fetus after the twentieth week of gestation and before birth
  2. Client can develop DIC if the dead fetus is retained in the **uterus** for 3 to 4 weeks or longer

B. Assessment
  1. Absence of fetal movement
  2. Absence of fetal heart tones
  3. Maternal weight loss
  4. Lack of fetal growth or decrease in fundal height

5. No evidence of fetal cardiac activity and other characteristics suggestive of fetal death noted on ultrasound

C. Interventions
  1. Prepare for the **delivery** of the fetus.
  2. Support the client's decision about **labor**, birth, and the postpartum period.
  3. Facilitate the grieving process.
  4. Allow the parents to hold the **infant** after birth.
  5. Allow the parents to name the **infant.**
  6. Accept behaviors such as anger and hostility from the parents.
  7. Refer the parents to an appropriate support group.

XI. HEPATITIS B ▲

A. Description
  1. The risks of prematurity, low birth weight, and neonatal death increase if the mother has hepatitis B infection.
  2. Hepatitis is transmitted through blood, saliva, vaginal secretions, semen, and breast milk and across the placental barrier.

B. Interventions ▲
  1. Minimize the risk for intrapartum ascending infections (limit the number of vaginal examinations).
  2. Remove maternal blood from the **neonate** immediately after birth.
  3. Suction the fluids from the **neonate** immediately after birth.
  4. Bathe the **neonate** before any invasive procedures.
  5. Clean and dry the face and eyes of the **neonate** before instilling eye prophylaxis.
  6. Infection of the **neonate** can be prevented by the administration of hepatitis B immune globulin and hepatitis B vaccine soon after birth.
  7. Discourage the mother from kissing the **neonate** until the **neonate** has received the vaccine.
  8. Support breast-feeding after neonatal treatment; breast-feeding is not contraindicated if the **neonate** has been vaccinated.
  9. Inform the mother that the hepatitis B vaccine will be administered to the **neonate** and that a second dose should be administered at 1 month after birth and a third dose at 6 months after birth.

XII. HEMATOMA

A. Description
  1. Hematoma occurs following the escape of blood into the maternal tissue after the **delivery.**
  2. Predisposing conditions include operative **delivery** with forceps or injury to a blood vessel.

B. Assessment (Box 25-6)

Abnormal, severe pain
Pressure in the perineal area (client states that she feels like she has to have a bowel movement)
Palpable, sensitive swelling in the perineal area, with discolored skin
Inability to void
Decreased hemoglobin and hematocrit levels
Signs of shock, such as pallor, tachycardia, and hypotension, if significant blood loss has occurred

C. Interventions
1. Monitor vital signs.
2. Monitor client for abnormal pain, especially when forceps **delivery** has been performed.
3. Apply ice to the hematoma site.
4. Administer analgesics as prescribed.
5. Monitor intake and output.
6. Encourage fluids and voiding; prepare for urinary catheterization if the client is unable to void.
7. Administer blood replacements as prescribed.
8. Monitor for signs of infection, such as increased temperature, pulse rate, and white blood cell count.
9. Administer antibiotics as prescribed, because infection is common following hematoma formation.
10. Prepare for incision and evacuation of the hematoma if necessary.

XIII. HYDATIDIFORM MOLE
A. Description (Fig. 25-2)
1. This is a form of gestational trophoblastic disease that occurs when the trophoblasts, which are the peripheral cells that attach the fertilized ovum to the uterine wall, develop abnormally.
2. The mole presents as an edematous grape-like cluster that may be nonmalignant or may develop into choriocarcinoma.
B. Assessment
1. Fetal heart rate not detectable
2. Vaginal bleeding, which may occur as early as the fourth week or as late as the second trimester; may be bright red or dark brown in color and may be slight, profuse, or intermittent
3. Symptoms of gestational hypertension, such as elevated blood pressure, edema, and proteinuria, before the twentieth week of gestation
4. Fundal height greater than expected for gestational date
5. Elevated human chorionic gonadotropin (hCG) levels
6. Ultrasound showing a characteristic snowstorm pattern

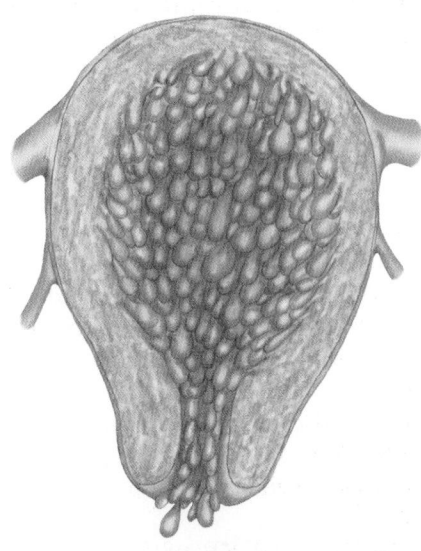

FIG. 25-2 Gestational trophoblastic disease, also called hydatidiform mole. (From Murray, S., & McKinney, E. [2005]. *Foundations of maternal-newborn nursing* [4th ed.]. Philadelphia: W.B. Saunders.)

C. Interventions
1. Prepare the mother for uterine evacuation (before evacuation, diagnostic tests are done to detect metastatic disease).
2. Evacuation of the mole is done by vacuum aspiration; oxytocin is administered after evacuation to contract the **uterus.**
3. Monitor for postprocedure hemorrhage and infection.
4. Tissue is sent to the laboratory for evaluation, and follow-up is important to detect changes suggestive of malignancy.
5. Human chorionic gonadotropin levels are monitored every 1 to 2 weeks until normal prepregnancy levels are attained; then the levels are checked every 1 to 2 months for 1 year.
6. Instruct the client and significant other about birth control measures so that pregnancy can be prevented during the 1-year follow-up.

XIV. HYPEREMESIS GRAVIDARUM
A. Description: Intractable nausea and vomiting during the first trimester that causes disturbances in nutrition and fluid and electrolyte balance
B. Assessment
1. Nausea most pronounced on arising; may occur at other times during the day
2. Persistent vomiting
3. Weight loss
4. Signs of dehydration
5. Fluid and electrolyte imbalances
C. Interventions
1. Initiate measures to alleviate nausea, including medication therapy; if unsuccessful and weight

loss and fluid and electrolyte imbalances occur, intravenously administered fluid and electrolyte replacement or parenteral nutrition may be necessary.

2. Monitor vital signs, intake and output, weight, and calorie count.
3. Monitor laboratory data and for signs of dehydration and electrolyte imbalances.
4. Monitor urine for ketones.
5. Monitor fetal heart rate, activity, and growth.
6. Encourage intake of small portions of food (low-fat, easily digestible carbohydrates, such as cereals, rice, and pasta).
7. Liquids should be taken between meals to avoid distending the stomach and triggering vomiting.
8. Encourage the client to sit upright after meals.

XV. GESTATIONAL HYPERTENSION
A. Description and types (Table 25-1)
1. Hypertension can be mild or severe, leading to preeclampsia and then eclampsia (seizures).
2. Signs of preeclampsia are hypertension, generalized edema, and proteinuria.

TABLE 25-1

Classification of Hypertensive Stages of Pregnancy

Type	Description
GESTATIONAL HYPERTENSIVE DISORDERS	
Gestational hypertension	Development of mild hypertension during pregnancy in previously normotensive woman without proteinuria or pathological edema
Gestational proteinuria	Development of proteinuria after 20 weeks of gestation in previously nonproteinuric woman without hypertension
Preeclampsia	Development of hypertension and proteinuria in previously normotensive woman after 20 weeks of gestation or in early postpartum period; in presence of trophoblastic disease, can develop before 20 weeks of gestation
Eclampsia	Development of convulsions or coma in preeclamptic woman
CHRONIC HYPERTENSIVE DISORDERS	
Chronic hypertension	Hypertension and/or proteinuria in pregnant woman with chronic hypertension prior to 20 weeks of gestation and persistent after 12 weeks postpartum
Superimposed pre-eclampsia or eclampsia	Development of preeclampsia or eclampsia in woman with chronic hypertension prior to 20 weeks of gestation

From Lowdermilk, D., & Perry, S. (2006). *Maternity nursing* (7th ed.). St. Louis: Mosby.

B. Assessment (Table 25-2)
C. Predisposing conditions
1. Primigravida
2. Women younger than 19 years or older than 40 years
3. Chronic renal disease
4. Chronic hypertension
5. Diabetes mellitus
6. Rh incompatibility
7. History of or family history of gestational hypertension (GH)
D. Complications of GH
1. Abruptio placentae
2. Disseminated intravascular coagulation
3. Thrombocytopenia
4. Placental insufficiency
5. Intrauterine growth restriction (IUGR)
6. Intrauterine fetal death
E. Interventions for mild hypertension
1. Monitor blood pressure.
2. Monitor fetal activity and fetal growth.
3. Encourage frequent rest periods, instructing the client to lie in the lateral position.
4. Administer antihypertensive medications as prescribed; teach client about the importance of the medications.
5. Monitor intake and output.
6. Evaluate renal function through prescribed studies such as blood urea nitrogen, serum creatinine, and 24-hour urine levels for creatinine clearance and protein.
F. Interventions for mild preeclampsia
1. Provide bed rest and place the client in lateral position.
2. Monitor blood pressure and weight.
3. Monitor neurological status, because changes can indicate cerebral hypoxia or impending seizure.
4. Monitor deep tendon reflexes and for the presence of clonus, because hyperreflexia indicates increased central nervous system irritability (Box 25-7).
5. Provide adequate fluids.
6. Monitor intake and output; a urinary output of 30 mL/hr indicates adequate renal perfusion.
7. Increase dietary protein and carbohydrates with no added salt.
8. Administer medications as prescribed to lower the blood pressure; blood pressure should not be lowered drastically because placental perfusion can be compromised.
9. Monitor for HELLP syndrome, a laboratory diagnosis for severe preeclampsia characterized by *h*emolysis, *e*levated *l*iver enzyme *l*evels, and *l*ow *p*latelet count.
G. Interventions for severe preeclampsia
1. Maintain bed rest.
2. Administer magnesium sulfate (use a controlled infusion device) as prescribed to prevent sei-

TABLE 25-2

Mild Versus Severe Preeclampsia

Parameter Evaluated	Mild	Severe
Systolic blood pressure	≥140 but <160 mm Hg	≥160 mm Hg (two readings, 6 hours apart, while on bed rest)
Diastolic blood pressure	≥90 but <110 mm Hg	≥110 mm Hg
Proteinuria (24-hr specimen is preferred to eliminate hour-to-hour variations)	≥0.3 but <2 g in 24-hr specimen (1+ on random dipstick)	≥5 g in 24-hr specimen (3+ or higher random dipstick sample)
Creatinine, serum (renal function)	Normal	Elevated (>1.2 mg/dL)
Platelets	Normal	Decreased (<100,00 cells/mm^3)
Liver enzymes (alanine aminotransferase [ALT] or aspartate aminotransferase [AST])	Normal or minimal increase in levels	Elevated levels
Urine output	Normal	Oliguria common, often <500 mL/day
Severe, unrelenting headache not attributable to other cause; mental confusion (cerebral edema)	Absent	Often present
Persistent right upper quadrant or epigastric pain or pain penetrating to the back (distention of the liver capsule); nausea and vomiting	Absent	May be present and often precedes seizure
Visual disturbances (spots or "sparkles"; temporary blindness; photophobia)	Absent to minimal	Common
Pulmonary edema; heart failure; cyanosis	Absent	May be present
Fetal growth restriction	Normal growth	Growth restriction; reduced amniotic fluid volume

From Murray, S., & McKinney, E. (2005). *Foundations of maternal-newborn nursing* (4th ed.). Philadelphia: W.B. Saunders.

BOX 25-7

Assessment of Reflexes

BICEPS

Position thumb over the client's biceps tendon, supporting the client's elbow with the palm of the hand.

Strike a downward blow over the thumb with the percussion hammer.

Normal response: Flexion of the arm at the elbow

PATELLAR

Position the client with her legs dangling over the edge of the examining table or lying on her back with her legs slightly flexed.

Strike the patellar tendon just below the kneecap with the percussion hammer.

Normal response: Extension or kicking out of the leg

CLONUS

Position the client with her legs dangling over the edge of the examining table.

Support the leg with one hand and sharply dorsiflex the client's foot with the other hand.

Maintain the dorsiflexed position for a few seconds and then release the foot.

Normal response (negative clonus response):

Foot will remain steady in the dorsiflexed position.

No rhythmic oscillations or jerking of the foot will be felt.

When released, the foot will drop to a plantar flexed position with no oscillations.

Abnormal response (positive clonus response):

Rhythmic oscillations occur when the foot is dorsiflexed.

Similar oscillations will be noted when the foot drops to the plantar-flexed position.

GRADING THE RESPONSE

0, Reflex absent

1+, Reflex present but hypoactive

2+, Normal reflex

3+, Hyperactive reflex

4+, Hyperactive reflex with clonus present

zures; may be continued for 24 to 48 hours postpartum.

3. Monitor for signs of magnesium toxicity, including flushing, sweating, hypotension, depressed deep tendon reflexes, and central nervous system depression, including respiratory depression; keep antidote (calcium gluconate) at the client's bedside.

4. Administer antihypertensives, as prescribed.

5. Prepare for the induction of **labor.**

BOX 25-8
Eclampsia

Seizure typically begins with twitching around the mouth.
The body then becomes rigid in a state of tonic muscular contractions that last 15 to 20 seconds.
The facial muscles and then all body muscles alternately contract and relax in rapid succession (clonic phase may last about 1 minute).
Respiration ceases during the seizure because the diaphragm tends to remain fixed (breathing resumes shortly after the seizure).
Postictal sleep occurs.

H. Eclampsia
1. Assessment: Characterized by generalized seizures (Box 25-8)
2. Interventions
   a. Maintain a patent airway and administer oxygen.
   b. Protect the client from injury.
   c. Monitor fetal heart rate and contractions.
   d. Administer medications to control the seizures (magnesium sulfate may be prescribed).
   e. Prepare for **delivery** of the fetus after stabilization of the client.

XVI. INCOMPETENT CERVIX
A. Description
1. This premature dilation of the cervix, which occurs most often in the fourth or fifth month of pregnancy, is associated with structural or functional defects of the cervix.
2. Treatment involves surgical placement of a cervical cerclage.
B. Assessment
1. Vaginal bleeding
2. Fetal membranes visible through the cervix
C. Interventions
1. Provide bed rest, hydration, and tocolysis, as prescribed, to inhibit uterine contractions.
2. Prepare for cervical cerclage (at 10 to 14 weeks' gestation) in which a band of fascia or nonabsorbable ribbon is placed around the cervix beneath the mucosa to constrict the internal os.
3. Following cervical cerclage, the woman is told to refrain from intercourse and to avoid prolonged standing and heavy lifting.
4. The cervical cerclage is removed at 37 weeks' gestation or left in place and a cesarean birth is performed; if removed, cerclage must be repeated with each successive pregnancy.
5. Following placement of the cervical cerclage, monitor for contractions, rupture of the membranes, and signs of infection.
6. Instruct the woman to report to the health care provider immediately any postprocedure vaginal bleeding or increased uterine contractions.

XVII. INFECTIONS
A. Toxoplasmosis
1. Caused by infection with the intracellular protozoan parasite *Toxoplasma gondii*
2. Produces a rash and symptoms of acute, flu-like infection in the mother.
3. Transmitted to the mother through raw meat or handling of cat litter of infected cats
4. Organism transmitted to the fetus across the **placenta**
5. Can cause spontaneous abortion in the first trimester
B. Rubella (German measles)
1. Teratogenic in the first trimester
2. Organism transmitted to the fetus across the **placenta**
3. Causes congenital defects of the eyes, heart, ears, and brain
4. If not immune (titer of 1:8 or less), mother should be vaccinated in postpartum period; must wait 1 to 3 months (as specified by health care provider) before becoming pregnant
C. Cytomegalovirus
1. Organism is transmitted through close personal contact, across the **placenta** to the fetus, or the fetus may be infected through the birth canal.
2. The mother may be asymptomatic; most **infants** are asymptomatic at birth.
3. Cytomegalovirus causes low birth weight, intrauterine growth retardation, enlarged liver and spleen, jaundice, mental restriction, blindness, hearing loss, and seizures.
4. Antiviral medications may be prescribed for severe infections in the mother but these medications are toxic and may only temporarily suppress shedding of the virus.
D. Genital herpes
1. This affects the external genitalia, **vagina**, and cervix and causes draining, painful vesicles.
2. Virus usually is transmitted to the fetus during birth through the infected **vagina** or via an ascending infection after rupture of the membranes.
3. No vaginal examinations are done in the presence of active vaginal herpetic lesions.
4. Herpes can cause death or severe neurological impairment in the **newborn.**
5. **Delivery** of the fetus is usually by cesarean section if active lesions are present in the **vagina; delivery** may be performed vaginally if the lesions are in the anal, perineal, or inner thigh area (strict precautions are necessary to protect the fetus during **delivery**).
6. Maintain contact precautions.
E. Group B *Streptococcus* (GBS)
1. GBS is a leading cause of life-threatening perinatal infections.

2. The gram-positive bacterium colonizes the rectum, **vagina**, cervix, and urethra of pregnant and nonpregnant women.
3. Meningitis, fasciitis, and intraabdominal abscess can occur in the pregnant client if she is infected at the time of birth.
4. Transmission occurs during vaginal **delivery.**
5. Early-onset **newborn** GBS occurs within the first week after birth, usually within 48 hours, and can include infections such as sepsis, pneumonia, or meningitis; permanent neurological disability can result.
6. Diagnosis of the mother is done via vaginal and rectal cultures between 35 and 37 weeks' gestation.
7. Antibiotics such as penicillin may be prescribed for the mother during **labor** and birth; intravenous antibiotics may be prescribed for infected infants.

XVIII. MULTIPLE GESTATION
A. Description
 1. Multiple gestation results from **fertilization** of two ova (fraternal or dizygotic) or a splitting of one fertilized ovum (identical or monozygotic).
 2. Complications include spontaneous abortion, anemia, congenital anomalies, hyperemesis gravidarum, intrauterine growth restriction , gestational hypertension, polyhydramnios, postpartum hemorrhage, premature rupture of membranes, and preterm **labor** and **delivery.**
B. Assessment
 1. Excessive fetal activity
 2. **Uterus** large for gestational age
 3. Palpation of three or four large parts in the **uterus**
 4. Auscultation of more than one fetal heart rate
 5. Excessive weight gain
C. Interventions
 1. Monitor vital signs.
 2. Monitor fetal heart rates, activity, and growth.
 3. Monitor for cervical changes.
 4. Prepare the client for ultrasound, as prescribed.
 5. Monitor for anemia; administer supplemental vitamins as prescribed.
 6. Monitor for preterm **labor,** and treat preterm **labor** promptly.
 7. Prepare for cesarean section for abnormal presentations.
 8. Prepare to administer oxytocic medications after **delivery** to prevent postpartum hemorrhage from uterine overdistention.

XIX. PYELONEPHRITIS
A. Description
 1. Results from bacterial infections that extend upward from the bladder through the blood vessels and lymphatics

2. Frequently follows untreated urinary tract infections and is associated with increased incidence of anemia, low birth weight, GH, premature **labor** and **delivery,** and premature rupture of the membranes
B. Assessment
 1. Flank pain
 2. Burning or painful urination
 3. Increased frequency of urination
 4. Chills, malaise, nausea
 5. Increased temperature, pulse rate, and fetal heart rate
 6. Vomiting
 7. Uterine contractions
 8. Elevated white blood cell count
C. Interventions
 1. Monitor vital signs.
 2. Monitor fetal heart rate.
 3. Monitor for uterine contractions.
 4. Encourage fluids; monitor intake and output.
 5. Monitor renal function.
 6. Administer antibiotics as prescribed.
 7. Administer antipyretics such as acetaminophen (Tylenol) as prescribed.
 8. Obtain urine cultures every 2 to 4 weeks after resolution of infection.

XX. SEXUALLY TRANSMITTED DISEASES
A. Chlamydia
 1. Description
    a. A common sexually transmitted pathogen associated with an increased risk for premature births, stillbirths, neonatal conjunctivitis, and **newborn** chlamydial pneumonia
    b. Can cause salpingitis, pelvic abscesses, ectopic pregnancy, chronic pelvic pain, and infertility
    c. Diagnostic test is culture for *Chlamydia trachomatis*
 2. Assessment
    a. Usually asymptomatic
    b. Bleeding between periods or after coitus
    c. Mucoid or purulent cervical discharge
    d. Dysuria and pelvic pain
 3. Interventions
    a. Screen the client to determine whether the client is high risk.
    b. Instruct the client in the importance of rescreening because reinfection can occur as the client nears term.
    c. Ensure that the sexual partner is treated.
B. Syphilis
 1. Description
    a. Syphilis is a chronic infectious disease caused by the organism *Treponema pallidum.*
    b. Transmission is by physical contact with syphilitic lesions, which usually are found on the skin, mucous membranes of the mouth, or genitals.

BOX 25-9
Stages of Syphilis

PRIMARY STAGE
Most infectious stage
Appearance of ulcerative, painless lesions produced by
  spirochetes at the point of entry into the body

SECONDARY STAGE
Highly infectious stage
Appearance of lesions about 6 weeks to 6 months after
  the primary stage located anywhere on the skin and
  mucous membranes
Generalized lymphadenopathy

TERTIARY STAGE
Entrance of spirochetes into the internal organs, causing
  permanent damage; symptoms occur 10 to 30 years
  following the untreated primary lesion
Invasion of the central nervous system, causing meningitis, ataxia, general paresis, and progressive mental
  deterioration
Deleterious effects on the aortic valve and aorta

c. The infection may cause abortion or premature **labor** and is passed to the fetus after the
  fourth month of pregnancy as congenital
  syphilis.
2. Assessment (Box 25-9)
3. Interventions
  a. Obtain a serum test (Venereal Disease Re-
    search Laboratory [VDRL] or rapid plasma
    reagin [RPR]) for syphilis on the first prenatal
    visit; prepare to repeat the test at 36 weeks'
    gestation because the disease may be ac-
    quired after the initial visit.
  b. If the test result is positive, treatment with an
    antibiotic such as penicillin may be necessary.
  c. Instruct the client that treatment of her part-
    ner is necessary if infection is present.
C. Gonorrhea
  1. Description
    a. This infection, caused by *Neisseria gonor-
      rhoeae*, causes inflammation of the mucous
      membranes of the genital and urinary tracts.
    b. Transmission of the organism is by sexual
      intercourse.
    c. Infection may be transmitted to the new-
      born's eyes during **delivery**, causing blind-
      ness (ophthalmia neonatorum).
  2. Assessment: Usually asymptomatic; vaginal dis-
    charge, urinary frequency, and lower abdominal
    pain possible
  3. Interventions
    a. Obtain culture for gonorrhea on the first pre-
      natal visit; prepare to repeat culture because
      infection may occur during pregnancy.

    b. Instruct the client that treatment of her part-
      ner is necessary if infection is present.
D. Condylomata acuminata (venereal warts)
  1. Description
    a. Caused by human papillomavirus (HPV);
      infection affects cervix, urethra, anus, penis,
      and scrotum
    b. Transmitted through sexual contact
  2. Assessment
    a. Infection produces small to large wart-like
      growths on the genitals.
    b. Cervical cell changes may be noted because
      human papillomavirus is associated with cer-
      vical malignancies.
  3. Interventions
    a. Lesions are removed by the use of cytotoxic
      agents, cryotherapy, electrocautery, and la-
      ser.
    b. Encourage annual Papanicolaou's smear.
    c. Avoid sexual contact until the lesions are
      healed (condoms reduce transmission).
E. Bacterial vaginosis
  1. Description
    a. Caused by *Haemophilus vaginalis* (*Gardnerella
      vaginalis*); transmitted via sexual contact
    b. Associated with premature **labor** and birth
  2. Assessment
    a. Client complains of "fishy odor" to vaginal
      secretions and increased odor after inter-
      course.
    b. Microscopic examination of vaginal secre-
      tions identifies the infection.
  3. Interventions
    a. Oral metronidazole (Flagyl) may be pre-
      scribed.
    b. Sexual partner may need to be treated.
F. Vaginal candidiasis
  1. Description
    a. *Candida albicans* most common causative or-
      ganism
    b. Predisposing factors include use of antibiot-
      ics, diabetes mellitus, and obesity
    c. Diagnosed by identifying spores of *Candida
      albicans*
  2. Assessment
    a. Vulvar and vaginal pruritus
    b. White, lumpy, and cottage cheese–like dis-
      charge from **vagina**
  3. Interventions
    a. An antifungal vaginal preparation such as
      miconazole (Monistat) may be prescribed.
    b. For extensive irritation and swelling, sitz
      baths may be prescribed.
    c. Sexual partner may need to be treated.
G. Trichomoniasis
  1. Description: Caused by *trichomonas vaginalis* and
    is transmitted via sexual contact.

2. Assessment
   a. Yellowish to greenish, frothy, mucopurulent, copious, malodorous vaginal discharge
   b. May be inflammation of vulva, **vagina,** or both
3. Interventions
   a. Metronidazole (Flagyl) may be prescribed.
   b. Sexual partner may need to be treated.

XXI. TUBERCULOSIS

A. Description
   1. Highly communicable disease caused by *Mycobacterium tuberculosis*
   2. Transmitted by airborne route
   3. Multidrug-resistant strain of tuberculosis can exist as result of improper compliance, noncompliance with treatment programs, or development of mutations in tubercle bacillus
B. Transmission
   1. Transplacental transmission is rare.
   2. Transmission can occur during birth through aspiration of infected **amniotic fluid.**
   3. **Neonate** can become infected from contact with infected individuals.
C. Risk to mother: Active disease during pregnancy has been associated with an increase in hypertensive disorders of pregnancy.
D. Diagnosis
   1. If a chest radiograph is required for the mother, it is done only after 20 weeks of gestation, and a lead shield for the abdomen is required.
   2. Tuberculin skin testing is safe during pregnancy.
E. Assessment
   1. Mother
      a. Possibly asymptomatic
      b. Fever and chills
      c. Night sweats
      d. Weight loss
      e. Fatigue
      f. Cough, hemoptysis, or green or yellow sputum
      g. Dyspnea
      h. Pleural pain
   2. **Neonate**
      a. Fever
      b. Lethargy
      c. Poor feeding
      d. Failure to thrive
      e. Respiratory distress
      f. Hepatosplenomegaly
      g. Meningitis
      h. Disease may spread to all major organs
F. Interventions
   1. Pregnant client
      a. Administration of isoniazid (INH), pyrazinamide, and rifampin (Rifadin) daily for

9 months; ethambutol (Myambutol) is added if medication resistance is likely.
      b. Pyridoxine (vitamin B$_6$) should be administered with isoniazid to pregnant client to prevent fetal neurotoxicity caused by the isoniazid.
      c. Promote breast-feeding only if the client is noninfectious.
   2. **Newborn infant**
      a. Management focuses on preventing disease and treating early infection.
      b. The **infant** is skin tested at birth and may be placed on INH therapy; the skin test is repeated in 3 to 4 months and INH may be stopped if the skin test results remain negative.
      c. If the skin test result is positive, the **infant** should receive INH for at least 6 months.
      d. If the mother's sputum is free of organisms, the **infant** does not need to be isolated from the mother while in the hospital.

XXII. URINARY TRACT INFECTION

A. Description: A urinary tract infection can occur during pregnancy; if untreated, the client can develop pyelonephritis.
B. Predisposing conditions
   1. History of urinary tract infections
   2. Sickle cell trait
   3. Poor hygiene
   4. Anemia
   5. Diabetes mellitus
   6. Pregnancy
C. Assessment
   1. Possibly asymptomatic during pregnancy
   2. Burning and pain on urination
   3. Increased frequency of urination
   4. Lower abdominal pain and costovertebral angle (CVA) tenderness
   5. Fever
   6. Proteinuria, hematuria, bacteruria, and white blood cells in urine
D. Interventions
   1. Monitor vital signs.
   2. Monitor fetal heart rate.
   3. Increase fluid intake.
   4. Monitor intake and output.
   5. Monitor urine for consistency and odor.
   6. Monitor for signs and symptoms of pyelonephritis (dip test urine for increase in protein, glucose, and ketone levels with each prenatal visit).
   7. Obtain urine for culture and sensitivity.
   8. Provide heat to lower abdomen or back.
   9. Administer antibiotics as prescribed.
   10. Instruct the client to complete the course of antibiotics if prescribed.
   11. Instruct the client regarding the need to repeat the culture after treatment is completed.

PRACTICE QUESTIONS

1. A pregnant client reports to a health care clinic, complaining of loss of appetite, weight loss, and fatigue. Following assessment of the client, tuberculosis is suspected. A sputum culture is obtained and identifies *Mycobacterium tuberculosis*. The nurse provides instructions to the client regarding therapeutic management of the tuberculosis and the nurse tells the client that:
   1. Therapeutic abortion is required.
   2. She will have to stay at home until treatment is completed.
   3. Medication will not be started until after delivery of the fetus.
   4. Isoniazid (INH) plus rifampin (Rifadin) will be required for a total of 9 months.

2. During a prenatal visit, the nurse is explaining dietary management to a client with diabetes mellitus. The nurse determines that teaching has been effective if the client makes which statement?
   1. "Diet and insulin needs change during pregnancy."
   2. "I will plan my diet based on the results of urine glucose testing."
   3. "I will need to eat 600 more calories every day since I am pregnant."
   4. "I can continue with the same diet as before pregnancy, as long as it is well-balanced."

3. A clinic nurse has provided home care instructions to a client with a history of cardiac disease who has just been told that she is pregnant. Which statement, if made by the client, indicates a need for further instructions?
   1. "It is best that I rest lying on my side to promote blood return to the heart."
   2. "I need to avoid excessive weight gain to prevent increased demands on my heart."
   3. "I need to try to avoid stressful situations because stress increases the workload on the heart."
   4. "During the pregnancy, I need to avoid contact with other individuals as much as possible to prevent infection."

4. A nurse is providing instructions to a maternity client with a history of cardiac disease regarding appropriate dietary measures. Which statement, if made by the client, indicates an understanding of the information provided by the nurse?
   1. "I should drink adequate fluids and increase my intake of high-fiber foods."
   2. "I should maintain a low-calorie diet to prevent any weight gain."
   3. "I should lower my blood volume by limiting my fluids."
   4. "I should increase my sodium intake during pregnancy."

5. A clinic nurse is performing a psychosocial assessment of a client who has been told that she is pregnant. Which assessment finding indicates to the nurse that the client is at high risk for contracting human immunodeficiency virus (HIV)?
   1. A client who has a history of intravenous drug use
   2. A client who has a significant other who is heterosexual
   3. A client who has a history of sexually transmitted diseases
   4. A client who has had one sexual partner for the past 10 years

6. A nurse in a maternity unit is providing emotional support to a client and her husband who are preparing to be discharged from the hospital after the birth of a dead fetus. Which statement, if made by the client, indicates a component of the normal grieving process?
   1. "We want to attend a support group."
   2. "We never want to try to have a baby again."
   3. "We are going to try to adopt a child immediately."
   4. "We are okay, and we are going to try to have another baby immediately."

7. A nurse assists a pregnant client with cardiac disease to identify resources to help her care for her 18-month-old child during the last trimester of pregnancy. The nurse encourages the pregnant client to use these resources primarily to:
   1. Reduce excessive maternal stress and fatigue.
   2. Help the mother prepare for labor and delivery.
   3. Avoid exposure to potential pathogens and resulting infections.
   4. Prepare the 18-month-old child for maternal separation during hospitalization.

8. A nurse evaluates a hepatitis B–positive mother's ability for safe bottle-feeding of her infant during postpartum hospitalization. Which maternal action best exemplifies the mother's knowledge of potential disease transmission to the infant?
   1. The mother requests that the window be closed before feeding.
   2. The mother holds the infant properly during feeding and burping.
   3. The mother tests the temperature of the formula before initiating feeding.
   4. The mother washes and dries her hands before and following self-care of the perineum and asks for a pair of gloves before feeding.

9. A nurse is providing instructions to a pregnant client with human immunodeficiency virus (HIV) infection regarding care to the newborn infant following delivery. The client asks the nurse about the feeding options that are available. The best response by the nurse is:

1. "You will need to bottle-feed the newborn infant."
2. "You will need to feed the newborn infant by nasogastric tube feeding."
3. "You will be able to breast-feed for 6 months and then will need to switch to bottle-feeding."
4. "You will be able to breast-feed for 9 months and then will need to switch to bottle-feeding."

10. During the intrapartum period, a nurse is caring for a client with sickle cell disease. The nurse ensures that the client receives adequate intravenous fluid intake and oxygen consumption primarily to:
    1. Stimulate the labor process.
    2. Prevent dehydration and hypoxemia.
    3. Avoid the necessity of a cesarean delivery.
    4. Eliminate the need for analgesic administration.

11. A home care nurse visits a pregnant client who has a diagnosis of mild preeclampsia and who is being monitored for gestational hypertension. Which assessment finding indicates a worsening of the preeclampsia and the need to notify the physician?
    1. Urinary output has increased.
    2. Dependent edema has resolved.
    3. Blood pressure reading is at the prenatal baseline.
    4. The client complaints of a headache and blurred vision.

12. A client with a 38-week twin gestation is admitted to a birthing center in early labor. One of the fetuses is a breech presentation. Of the following interventions, which is the lowest priority in planning the nursing care of this client?
    1. Measure fundal height.
    2. Attach electronic fetal monitoring.
    3. Prepare the client for a possible cesarean section.
    4. Visually examine the perineum and vaginal opening.

13. A stillborn infant was delivered in the birthing suite a few hours ago. After the delivery, the family remained together, holding and touching the baby. Which statement by the nurse would further assist the family in their initial period of grief?
    1. "What have you named your baby?"
    2. "We need to take the baby from you now so that you can get some sleep."
    3. "Don't worry, there is nothing you could have done to prevent this from happening."
    4. "We will see to it that you have an early discharge so that you don't have to be reminded of this experience."

14. A nurse implements a teaching plan for a pregnant client who is newly diagnosed with gestational diabetes mellitus. Which statement, if made by the client, indicates a need for further teaching?

1. "I should stay on the diabetic diet."
2. "I should perform glucose monitoring at home."
3. "I should avoid exercise because of the negative effects on insulin production."
4. "I should be aware of any infections and report signs of infection immediately to my health care provider."

15. A nurse is caring for a pregnant client with preeclampsia. The nurse prepares a plan of care for the client and documents in the plan that if the client progresses from preeclampsia to eclampsia, the nurse's first action should be to:
    1. Administer oxygen by face mask.
    2. Clear and maintain an open airway.
    3. Administer magnesium sulfate intravenously
    4. Assess the blood pressure and fetal heart rate.

16. A client has just had surgery to deliver a nonviable fetus resulting from abruptio placentae. As a result of the abruptio placentae, the client develops disseminated intravascular coagulation (DIC) and is told about the complication. The client begins to cry and screams, "God, just let me die now!" Which nursing diagnosis should direct care for this client at this time?
    1. Grieving related to the loss of the baby
    2. Situational low self-esteem related to being ill
    3. Deficient knowledge related to the disease process
    4. Hopelessness related to the loss of the baby and personal health

17. A pregnant client in the last trimester has been admitted to the hospital with a diagnosis of severe preeclampsia. A nurse monitors for complications associated with the diagnosis and assesses the client for:
    1. Enlargement of the breasts
    2. Complaints of feeling hot when the room is cool
    3. Periods of fetal movement followed by quiet periods
    4. Evidence of bleeding, such as in the gums, petechiae, and purpura

18. A nurse in a maternity unit is reviewing the records of the clients on the unit. Which client would the nurse identify as being at the greatest risk for developing disseminated intravascular coagulation (DIC)?
    1. A primigravida with mild preeclampsia
    2. A primigravida who delivered a 10-lb baby 3 hours ago
    3. A gravida II who has just been diagnosed with dead fetus syndrome
    4. A gravida IV who delivered 8 hours ago and has lost 500 mL of blood

19. A client in the first trimester of pregnancy arrives at a health care clinic and reports that she has been experiencing vaginal bleeding. A threatened abortion is suspected, and the nurse instructs the client regarding management of care. Which statement, if made by the client, indicates a need for further instructions?
    1. "I will watch for the evidence of the passage of tissue."
    2. "I will maintain strict bed rest throughout the remainder of the pregnancy."
    3. "I will count the number of perineal pads used on a daily basis and note the amount and color of blood on the pad."
    4. "I will avoid sexual intercourse until the bleeding has stopped, and for 2 weeks following the last evidence of bleeding."

20. The nurse is assessing a pregnant client with type 1 diabetes mellitus about her understanding regarding changing insulin needs during pregnancy. The nurse determines that teaching is needed if the client makes which statement?
    1. "I will need to increase my insulin dosage during the first 3 months of pregnancy."
    2. "My insulin dose will likely need to be increased during the second and third trimesters."
    3. "Episodes of hypoglycemia are more likely to occur during the first 3 months of pregnancy."
    4. "My insulin needs should return to normal within 7 to 10 days after birth if I am bottle-feeding."

ALTERNATE ITEM FORMAT: MULTIPLE RESPONSE

A home care nurse is monitoring a pregnant client with gestational hypertension who is at risk for preeclampsia. At each home care visit, the nurse assesses the client for which classic signs of preeclampsia?

❏ 1. Proteinuria
❏ 2. Hypertension
❏ 3. Low-grade fever
❏ 4. Generalized edema
❏ 5. Increased pulse rate
❏ 6. Increased respiratory rate

ANSWERS

1. **4**

Rationale: More than one medication may be used to prevent the growth of resistant organisms in the pregnant client with tuberculosis. Treatment must continue for a prolonged period of time. The preferred treatment for the pregnant client is isoniazid (INH) plus rifampin (Rifadin) daily for a total of 9 months. Ethambutol is added initially if medication resistance is suspected. Pyridoxine (Vitamin B_6) often is administered with isoniazid to prevent fetal neurotoxicity. It is not necessary for the client to stay at home during treatment and therapeutic abortion is not required.

Test-Taking Strategy: Focus on the subject, the therapeutic management for the client with tuberculosis. Recalling the pathophysiology associated with tuberculosis will assist in eliminating options 1, 2, and 3. If you had difficulty with this question, review treatment measures for the client with tuberculosis.

Level of Cognitive Ability: Application
Client Needs: Physiological Integrity
Integrated Process: Teaching and Learning
Content Area: Maternity—antepartum
Reference: Murray, S., & McKinney, E. (2005). *Foundations of maternal-newborn nursing* (4th ed., p. 691). Philadelphia: W.B. Saunders.

2. **1**

Rationale: The diet for a pregnant client with diabetes mellitus is individualized to allow for increased fetal and metabolic requirements, with consideration of such factors as prepregnancy weight and dietary habits, overall health, ethnic background, lifestyle, stage of pregnancy, knowledge of nutrition, and insulin therapy. An increase of 600 additional calories a day is not required. Diet and insulin needs change during the pregnancy in direct correlation to hormonal changes and energy needs. In the third trimester, insulin needs increase. Dietary management during diabetic pregnancy must be based on blood, not urine, glucose changes.

Test-Taking Strategy: Use the process of elimination and knowledge regarding the dietary needs and management of a pregnant client with diabetes mellitus. Note that option 1 is the umbrella option and is a general statement. If you had difficulty with this question, review dietary management of a pregnant client with diabetes mellitus.

Level of Cognitive Ability: Analysis
Client Needs: Health Promotion and Maintenance
Integrated Process: Nursing Process—evaluation
Content Area: Maternity—antepartum
Reference: Wong, D., Perry, S., Hockenberry, M., et al. (2006). *Maternal child nursing care* (3rd ed., p. 335). St. Louis: Mosby.

3. **4**

Rationale: To avoid infections, visitors with active infections should not be allowed to visit the client; otherwise, restrictions are not required. Stress causes increased heart workload, and the client should be instructed to avoid stress. Too much weight gain can place further demands on the heart. Resting should be done by lying on the side to promote blood return.

Test-Taking Strategy: Use the process of elimination and note the strategic words *cardiac disease* and *need for further instructions* in the question. These words indicate a negative event query and the need to select an incorrect client statement. Using principles related to the therapeutic management of cardiac disease in general will assist in directing you to option 4. If you had difficulty with this question, review the measures for the pregnant client with cardiac disease.
Level of Cognitive Ability: Analysis
Client Needs: Health Promotion and Maintenance
Integrated Process: Teaching and Learning
Content Area: Maternity—antepartum
Reference: Murray, S., & McKinney, E., (2006). *Foundations of maternal-newborn nursing* (4th ed., p. 694). Philadelphia: W.B. Saunders.

4. **1**
Rationale: Constipation can cause the client to use Valsalva's maneuver. This maneuver can cause blood to rush to the heart and overload the cardiac system. Therefore, high-fiber foods are important. A low-calorie diet is not recommended during pregnancy and could be harmful to the fetus. Diets low in fluid can cause a decrease in blood volume, which could deprive the fetus of nutrients, so adequate fluid intake and high-fiber foods are important. Sodium should be restricted somewhat, as prescribed by the physician, because excess sodium will cause an overload to the circulating blood volume and contribute to cardiac complications.
Test-Taking Strategy: Use the process of elimination. Think about the physiology of the cardiac system, maternal and fetal needs, and the factors that increase the workload on the heart to answer the question. This will direct you to option 1. If you had difficulty with this question, review nursing measures for the pregnant client with cardiac disease.
Level of Cognitive Ability: Analysis
Client Needs: Physiological Integrity
Integrated Process: Nursing Process—evaluation
Content Area: Maternity—antepartum
References: Murray, S., & McKinney, E., (2006). *Foundations of maternal-newborn nursing* (4th ed., p. 674). Philadelphia: W.B. Saunders.
Wong, D., Perry, S., Hockenberry, M., et al. (2006). *Maternal child nursing care* (3rd ed., p. 350). St. Louis: Mosby.

5. **1**
Rationale: Human immunodeficiency virus (HIV) is transmitted by intimate sexual contact and the exchange of body fluids, exposure to infected blood, and passing from an infected woman to her fetus. Clients who fall into the high-risk category for HIV infection include those with persistent and recurrent sexually transmitted diseases, a history of multiple sexual partners, or have used intravenous drugs. A heterosexual partner, particularly a partner who has had only one sexual partner in 10 years, does not have a high risk for contracting HIV.
Test-Taking Strategy: Use the process of elimination, recalling that exchange of blood and body fluids places the client at high risk for HIV infection. This will assist in directing you to the correct option. If you had difficulty with this question, review the risk factors for HIV.

Level of Cognitive Ability: Analysis
Client Needs: Safe and Effective Care Environment
Integrated Process: Nursing Process—assessment
Content Area: Maternity—antepartum
Reference: Wong, D., Perry, S., Hockenberry, M., et al. (2006). *Maternal child nursing care* (3rd ed., p. 131). St. Louis: Mosby.

6. **1**
Rationale: A support group can help the parents work through their pain by nonjudgmental sharing of feelings. Option 1 identifies a statement that would indicate positive, normal grieving. Although the other options may indicate reactions of the client and significant other, they are not specifically a part of the normal grieving process.
Test-Taking Strategy: Use the process of elimination. Read all the options carefully before selecting an answer and focus on the subject of the question, the normal grieving process. Note that options 2, 3, and 4 are comparative or alike in that they relate to childbearing. If you had difficulty with this question, review the components of the normal grieving process.
Level of Cognitive Ability: Analysis
Client Needs: Psychosocial Integrity
Integrated Process: Caring
Content Area: Maternity—postpartum
Reference: Wong, D., Perry, S., Hockenberry, M., et al. (2006). *Maternal child nursing care* (3rd ed., p. 681). St. Louis: Mosby.

7. **1**
Rationale: A variety of factors can cause increased emotional stress during pregnancy, resulting in further cardiac complications. The client with known cardiac disease is at greater risk for such complications. The use of resources will assist the client to avoid emotional stress, thus reducing additional cardiac compromise during the last trimester. These resources are not intended to minimize potential risk of maternal infection or prepare the client and family for the subsequent labor, delivery, and hospitalization.
Test-Taking Strategy: Focus on the subject of the question, noting the client's diagnosis. Also note the strategic word *primarily* in the question. Use Maslow's Hierarchy of Needs theory and focus on the client's condition to assist in directing you to option 1. Review considerations of caring for the pregnant client with cardiac disease if you had difficulty with this question.
Level of Cognitive Ability: Application
Client Needs: Health Promotion and Maintenance
Integrated Process: Nursing Process—implementation
Content Area: Maternity—antepartum
Reference: McKinney, E., James, S., Murray, S., & Ashwill, J. (2005). *Maternal-child nursing* (2nd ed., p. 657). St. Louis: W.B. Saunders.

8. **4**
Rationale: Hepatitis B virus is highly contagious and is transmitted by direct contact with blood and body fluids of infected persons. The rationale for identifying childbearing clients with this disease is to provide adequate protection of the fetus and the newborn infant, to minimize transmission to other human beings, and to reduce maternal complications. Option 4 provides the best evaluation of maternal under-

standing of disease transmission. Option 1 will not affect disease transmission. Options 2 and 3 are appropriate feeding techniques for bottle-feeding but do not minimize disease transmission for hepatitis B.

Test-Taking Strategy: Focus on the subject of the question, "disease transmission to the infant." This focus and the process of elimination will easily direct you to option 4. Review measures to prevent transmission of hepatitis if you had difficulty with this question.

Level of Cognitive Ability: Analysis
Client Needs: Safe and Effective Care Environment
Integrated Process: Nursing Process—evaluation
Content Area: Maternity—postpartum
Reference: McKinney, E., James, S., Murray, S., & Ashwill, J. (2005). *Maternal-child nursing* (2nd ed., p. 664). St. Louis: W.B. Saunders.

9. 1
Rationale: Perinatal transmission of HIV can occur during the antepartal period, during labor and birth, or in the postpartum period if the mother is breast-feeding. Clients who carry HIV are advised not to breast-feed. There is no physiological reason why the newborn infant needs to be fed by nasogastric tube.

Test-Taking Strategy: Use the process of elimination and knowledge regarding the transmission of HIV to assist in answering the question. Eliminate options 3 and 4 first because these options are comparative or alike in that they both address breast-feeding. From the remaining options, select option 1, knowing that it is not necessary to feed the infant by nasogastric tube. Review feeding options for the newborn infant of an HIV client if you had difficulty with this question.

Level of Cognitive Ability: Application
Client Needs: Safe and Effective Care Environment
Integrated Process: Teaching and Learning
Content Area: Maternity—postpartum
Reference: McKinney, E., James, S., Murray, S., & Ashwill, J. (2005). *Maternal-child nursing* (2nd ed., p. 666). St. Louis: W.B. Saunders.

10. 2
Rationale: A variety of conditions, including dehydration, hypoxemia, infection, and exertion, can stimulate the sickling process during the intrapartum period. Maintaining adequate intravenous fluid intake and the administration of oxygen via face mask will help to ensure a safe environment for maternal and fetal health during labor. These measures will not stimulate the labor process, avoid the need for a cesarean delivery, or eliminate the need for analgesic administration.

Test-Taking Strategy: Note the relationship between "adequate intravenous fluid intake and oxygen consumption" in the question and "prevent dehydration and hypoxemia" in the correct option. This relationship and knowledge regarding the care measures for sickle cell anemia will direct you easily to option 2. Review these care measures if you had difficulty with this question.

Level of Cognitive Ability: Application
Client Needs: Physiological Integrity
Integrated Process: Nursing Process—implementation
Content Area: Maternity—intrapartum

Reference: Murray, S., & McKinney, E., (2006). *Foundations of maternal-newborn nursing* (4th ed., p. 678). Philadelphia: W.B. Saunders.

11. 4
Rationale: If the client complains of a headache and blurred vision, the physician should be notified because these are signs of worsening preeclampsia. Options 1, 2, and 3 are normal signs.

Test-Taking Strategy: Use the process of elimination, noting the strategic word *worsening* in the question. Eliminate options 1, 2, and 3 because these options indicate normal findings. Review the signs that indicate a worsening of preeclampsia if you had difficulty with this question.

Level of Cognitive Ability: Analysis
Client Needs: Physiological Integrity
Integrated Process: Nursing Process—assessment
Content Area: Maternity—antepartum
Reference: Lowdermilk, D., & Perry, A. (2004). *Maternity and women's health care* (8th ed., pp. 838-839, 850). St. Louis: Mosby.

12. 1
Rationale: Option 1 is a low priority because fundal height should be measured at each antepartum clinic visit, not in the intrapartum period. Options 2, 3, and 4 are high priorities. Intrapartum management and assessment require careful attention to maternal and fetal status. The fetuses should be monitored by dual electronic fetal monitoring, and any signs of distress need to be reported to the physician or health care provider. A cesarean section may be necessary if a fetus is breech. The nurse should examine the perineum and vaginal opening visually for signs of the cord, which sometimes will prolapse through the cervix.

Test-Taking Strategy: Use the process of elimination and note the strategic words *lowest priority*. Also, note that the client is in early labor. With this in mind, think about the nursing interventions associated with early labor. Review care for the pregnant client with a twin pregnancy and a breech presentation if you had difficulty with this question.

Level of Cognitive Ability: Analysis
Client Needs: Physiological Integrity
Integrated Process: Nursing Process—planning
Content Area: Maternity—intrapartum
References: McKinney, E., James, S., Murray, S., & Ashwill, J. (2005). *Maternal-child nursing* (2nd ed., pp. 348-349). St. Louis: W.B. Saunders.
Murray, S., & McKinney, E., (2006). *Foundations of maternal-newborn nursing* (4th ed., pp. 702-703). Philadelphia: W.B. Saunders.

13. 1
Rationale: Nurses should be able to explore measures that help the family create memories of the newborn infant so that the existence of the child is confirmed and the parents can complete the grieving process. Option 1 provides this support and demonstrates a caring and empathetic response. Options 2, 3, and 4 are blocks to communication and devalue the parents' feelings.

Test-Taking Strategy: Use the process of elimination and therapeutic communication techniques to answer the question.

Option 1 is the only option that reflects use of therapeutic communication techniques. Review these techniques and the nursing strategies for caring for parents who experience perinatal death if you had difficulty with this question.
Level of Cognitive Ability: Application
Client Needs: Psychosocial Integrity
Integrated Process: Caring
Content Area: Maternity—postpartum
Reference: Wong, D., Perry, S., Hockenberry, M., et al. (2006) *Maternal child nursing care* (3rd ed., pp. 681-683). St. Louis: Mosby.

14. **3**
Rationale: Exercise is safe for the client with gestational diabetes mellitus and is helpful in lowering the blood glucose level. Dietary modifications are the mainstay of treatment, and the client is placed on a standard diabetic diet. Many clients are taught to perform blood glucose monitoring. If the client is not performing the blood glucose monitoring at home, then it will be performed at the clinic or health care provider's office. Signs of infection need to be reported to the health care provider.
Test-Taking Strategy: Use the process of elimination, noting the strategic words *need for further teaching*. These words indicate a negative event query and the need to select an incorrect client statement. Noting these strategic words and the close-ended word *avoid* in option 3 will assist in answering the question. If you had difficulty with this question, review the teaching points for a client with gestational diabetes mellitus.
Level of Cognitive Ability: Analysis
Client Needs: Physiological Integrity
Integrated Process: Teaching and Learning
Content Area: Maternity—antepartum
Reference: Wong, D., Perry, S., Hockenberry, M., et al. (2006). *Maternal child nursing care* (3rd ed., p. 668). St. Louis: Mosby.

15. **2**
Rationale: The immediate care during a seizure (eclampsia) is to ensure a patent airway. Options 1, 3, and 4 are actions that follow or are implemented after the seizure has ceased.
Test-Taking Strategy: Note the strategic words *first action* in the question. Use the ABCs—airway, breathing, and circulation—to answer the question. Remember that the airway is always the first priority. Review care for the client with eclampsia if you had difficulty with this question.
Level of Cognitive Ability: Application
Client Needs: Physiological Integrity
Integrated Process: Nursing Process—implementation
Content Area: Delegating/Prioritizing
Reference: Wong, D., Perry, S., Hockenberry, M., et al. (2006). *Maternal child nursing care* (3rd ed., p. 385). St. Louis: Mosby.

16. **4**
Rationale: By seeing no way out of the situation except for death, the client meets the criteria for hopelessness. A person who lacks hope thinks that life is too much to handle. Option 1 is a possible nursing diagnosis at a later time; however, at this time, the diagnosis of hopelessness should take precedence. Option 3 is a possible nursing diagnosis later, but not enough data support it at this point. The data given do not support the nursing diagnosis of situational low self-esteem.

Test-Taking Strategy: Use the process of elimination. When answering a question regarding a nursing diagnosis, focus on the subject of the question and only on the data in the question. No data support options 1, 2, or 3. Review the defining characteristics of hopelessness if you had difficulty with this question.
Level of Cognitive Ability: Analysis
Client Needs: Psychosocial Integrity
Integrated Process: Nursing Process—analysis
Content Area: Maternity—postpartum
References: Lowdermilk, D., & Perry, A. (2004). *Maternity and women's health care* (8th ed., p. 877). St. Louis: Mosby.
Murray, S., & McKinney, E., (2006). *Foundations of maternal-newborn nursing* (4th ed., pp. 634-636). Philadelphia: W.B. Saunders.

17. **4**
Rationale: Severe preeclampsia can trigger disseminated intravascular coagulation (DIC) because of the widespread damage to vascular integrity. Bleeding is an early sign of DIC and should be reported to the health care provider if noted on assessment. Options 1, 2, and 3 are normal occurrences in the last trimester of pregnancy.
Test-Taking Strategy: Use the process of elimination and knowledge regarding the normal physiological occurrences in pregnancy to answer the question. Eliminate options 1, 2, and 3 because they are normal occurrences in the last trimester of pregnancy. Review the assessment findings in DIC if you had difficulty with this question.
Level of Cognitive Ability: Analysis
Client Needs: Physiological Integrity
Integrated Process: Nursing Process—assessment
Content Area: Maternity—antepartum
References: Lowdermilk, D., & Perry, A. (2004). *Maternity and women's health care* (8th ed., pp. 852, 878). St. Louis: Mosby.
Wong, D., Perry, S., Hockenberry, M., et al. (2006). *Maternal child nursing care* (3rd ed., p. 406). St. Louis: Mosby.

18. **3**
Rationale: Dead fetus syndrome is considered a risk factor for DIC. Severe preeclampsia is considered a risk factor for DIC; a mild case is not. Delivering a large baby is not considered a risk factor for DIC. Hemorrhage is a risk factor with DIC; however, a loss of 500 mL is not considered hemorrhage.
Test-Taking Strategy: Use the process of elimination and knowledge regarding the risk factors associated with DIC to answer this question. Recalling that dead fetus syndrome is a risk factor for DIC will assist in directing you to option 3. If you had difficulty answering this question, review these risk factors.
Level of Cognitive Ability: Analysis
Client Needs: Physiological Integrity
Integrated Process: Nursing Process—analysis
Content Area: Maternity—intrapartum
Reference: Lowdermilk, D., & Perry, A. (2004). *Maternity and women's health care* (8th ed., pp. 876-877). St. Louis: Mosby.

19. **2**
Rationale: Strict bed rest throughout the remainder of the pregnancy is not required. The client is advised to curtail sexual activities until bleeding has ceased, and for 2 weeks fol-

lowing the last evidence of bleeding or as recommended by the physician or other health care provider. The client is instructed to count the number of perineal pads used daily and to note the quantity and color of blood on the pad. The client also should watch for the evidence of the passage of tissue.
Test-Taking Strategy: Use the process of elimination to assist in answering the question. Note the strategic words *need for further instructions* in the question. These words indicate a negative event query and the need to select an incorrect client statement. Noting the word *strict* in option 2 will assist in directing you to this option. Review therapeutic management for a threatened abortion if you had difficulty with this question.
Level of Cognitive Ability: Analysis
Client Needs: Physiological Integrity
Integrated Process: Teaching and Learning
Content Area: Maternity—antepartum
References: Murray, S., & McKinney, E., (2006). *Foundations of maternal-newborn nursing* (4th ed., pp. 623-624) Philadelphia: W.B. Saunders.
Wong, D., Perry, S., Hockenberry, M., et al. (2006). *Maternal child nursing care* (3rd ed., p. 394). St. Louis: Mosby.

20. 1
Rationale: Insulin needs decrease in the first trimester because of increased insulin production by the pancreas and increased peripheral sensitivity to insulin. The statements in options 2, 3, and 4 are accurate and signify that the client understands control of her diabetes during pregnancy.
Test-Taking Strategy: Note the strategic words *teaching is needed*. These words indicate a negative event query and the need to select an incorrect client statement. Eliminate options 2, 3, and 4 because they are accurate statements. Remember that insulin needs decrease in the first trimester of pregnancy. Review the insulin needs of the pregnant client with diabetes mellitus if you had difficulty with this question.
Level of Cognitive Ability: Analysis
Client Needs: Physiological Integrity
Integrated Process: Teaching and Learning
Content Area: Maternity—antepartum
Reference: Wong, D., Perry, S., Hockenberry, M., et al. (2006). *Maternal child nursing care* (3rd ed., p. 331). St. Louis: Mosby.

ALTERNATE ITEM FORMAT: MULTIPLE RESPONSE

Answer: 1, 2, 4
Rationale: The three classic signs of preeclampsia are hypertension, generalized edema, and proteinuria. A low-grade fever, increased pulse rate, or increased respiratory rate is not associated with preeclampsia.
Test-Taking Strategy: Focus on the subject, the classic signs of preeclampsia. Thinking about the pathophysiology associated with preeclampsia will direct you to the correct options. Remember that the three classic signs of preeclampsia are hypertension, generalized edema, and proteinuria. Review these signs if you had difficulty with this question.
Level of Cognitive Ability: Application
Client Needs: Physiological Integrity
Integrated Process: Nursing Process—assessment
Content Area: Maternity—antepartum
Reference: Lowdermilk, D., & Perry, A. (2004). *Maternity and women's health care* (8th ed., pp. 838-839, 850). St. Louis: Mosby.

REFERENCES

Lowdermilk, D., & Perry, S. (2003). *Maternity nursing* (6 ed.). St. Louis: Mosby.

Murray, S., & McKinney, E. (2005). *Foundations of maternal-newborn nursing* (4 ed.). Philadelphia: W.B. Saunders.

McKinney, E., James, S., Murray, S., & Ashwill, J.W. (2005). *Maternal-child nursing* (2nd ed.). St. Louis: W.B. Saunders.

National Council of State Boards of Nursing (2007). *2007 NCLEX-RN® detailed test plan.* Chicago: Author.

Wong, D., Perry, S., Hockenberry, M., et al. (2006). *Maternal child nursing care* (3rd ed.). St. Louis: Mosby.

Labor and Delivery

I. THE PROCESS OF LABOR—FOUR *P*'s

A. Description
1. **Labor:** Coordinated sequence of involuntary, intermittent uterine contractions
2. **Delivery:** Actual event of birth

B. Four major factors (four *P*'s) interact during normal childbirth; the four *P*'s are interrelated and depend on each other for a safe **delivery** (Box 26-1).

C. Powers: Uterine contractions
1. The forces acting to expel the fetus
2. Effacement: Shortening and thinning of the cervix during the first stage of **labor**
3. Dilation: Enlargement of cervical os and cervical canal during the first stage of **labor**
4. Pushing efforts of mother during second stage

D. Passageway: The mother's rigid bony pelvis and the soft tissues of the cervix, pelvic floor, **vagina,** and introitus (external opening to the **vagina**).

E. Passenger: The fetus, membranes, and **placenta**

F. Psyche: A woman's emotional system that can determine her total response to **labor** and influence both physiological and psychological functioning; the mother may experience anxiety or fear.

G. Attitude
1. Attitude is the relationship of the fetal body parts to one another.
2. Normal intrauterine attitude is flexion, in which the fetal back is rounded, the head is forward on the chest, and the arms and legs are folded in against the body. The other attitude, extension, tends to present larger fetal diameters.

H. Lie
1. Relationship of the spine of the fetus to the spine of the mother
2. Longitudinal or vertical (Fig. 26-1)
   a. Fetal spine is parallel to the mother's spine.
   b. Fetus is in cephalic or breech presentation.

BOX 26-1
Four P's

Powers
Passageway
Passenger
Psyche

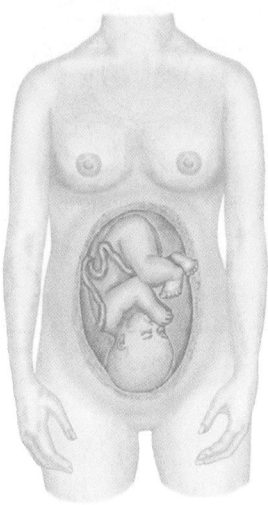

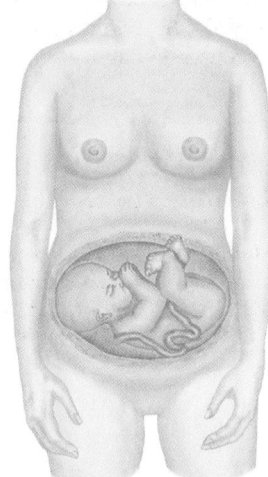

A Longitudinal lie   **B** Transverse lie

FIG. 26-1   Fetal lie. **A,** In a longitudinal lie, the long axis of the fetus is parallel to the long axis of the woman. **B,** In a transverse lie, the long axis of the fetus is at a right angle to the long axis of the mother. The women's abdomen has a wide, short appearance. (From Murray, S., & McKinney, E. [2006]. *Foundations of maternal-newborn nursing* [4th ed.]. St. Louis: W.B. Saunders.)

3. Transverse or horizontal (see Fig. 26-1)
   a. Fetal spine is at a right angle, or perpendicular, to the mother's spine.
   b. Presenting part is the shoulder.
   c. **Delivery** by cesarean section is necessary.

I. Presentation
1. Portion of the fetus that enters the pelvic inlet first
2. Cephalic: Head first
   a. Cephalic is the most common presentation.
   b. Cephalic presentation has four variations, vertex, military, brow and face.

BOX 26-2

Fetal Positions

ROA: Right occipitoanterior
LOA: Left occipitoanterior
ROP: Right occipitoposterior
LOP: Left occipitoposterior
ROT: Right occipitotransverse
LOT: Left occipitotransverse
RMA: Right mentum anterior
LMA: Left mentum anterior
RMP: Right mentum posterior
LSA: Left sacrum anterior
LSP: Left sacrum posterior

---

3. Breech: Buttocks present first.
   a. **Delivery** by cesarean section may be required, although vaginal birth is often possible.
   b. Breech presentation has three variations: frank, full (complete), and footling
4. Shoulder
   a. Fetus is in a transverse lie, or the arm, back, abdomen, or side could present.
   b. If the fetus does not spontaneously rotate, or if it is not possible to turn the fetus manually, a cesarean section may be performed.
J. Presenting part: The specific fetal structure lying nearest to the cervix
K. Position: Relationship of assigned area of the presenting part or landmark to the maternal pelvis (Box 26-2, Fig. 26-2)
L. Station
1. The measurement of the progress of descent in centimeters above or below the midplane from the presenting part to the ischial spine
2. Station 0: At ischial spine

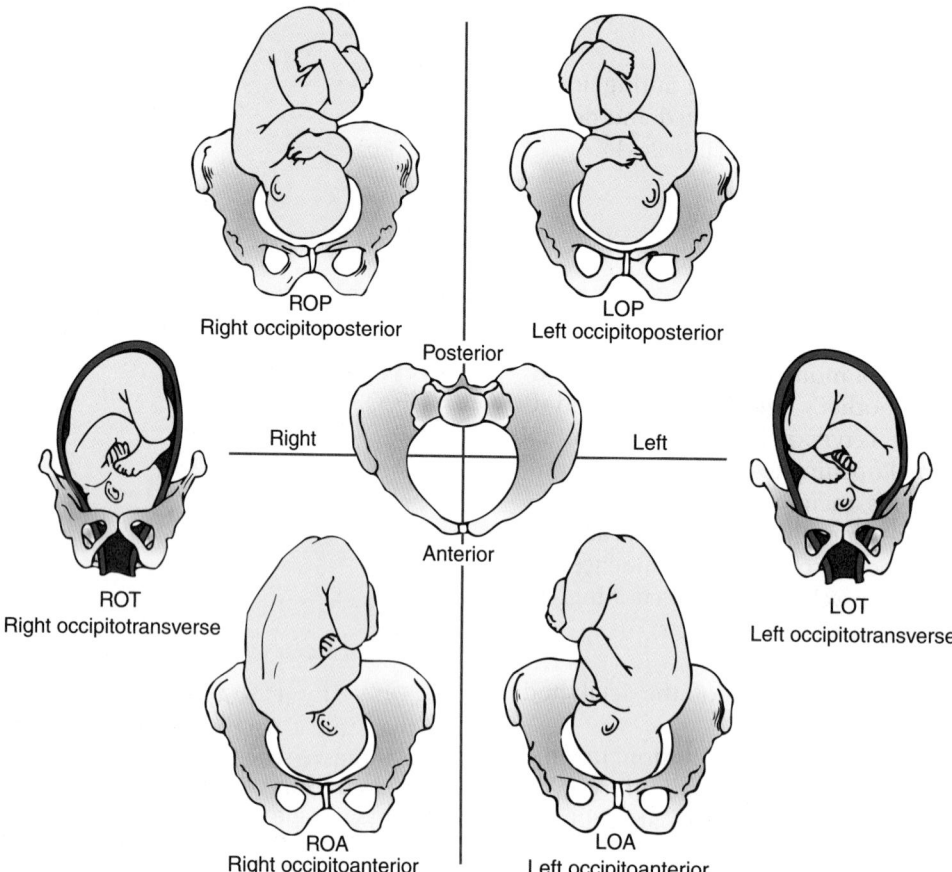

ROP
Right occipitoposterior

LOP
Left occipitoposterior

Posterior

Right   Left

Anterior

ROT
Right occipitotransverse

LOT
Left occipitotransverse

ROA
Right occipitoanterior

LOA
Left occipitoanterior

Lie: Longitudinal or vertical
Presentation: Vertex
Reference point: Occiput
Attitude: Complete flexion

FIG. 26-2 Examples of fetal vertex (occiput) presentations in relation to the front, back, or side of the maternal pelvis. (From Lowdermilk, D., & Perry, S. [2004]. *Maternity and women's health care* [8th ed.]. St. Louis: Mosby.)

3. Minus station: Above ischial spine
4. Plus station: Below ischial spine
5. Engagement: When the widest diameter of the presenting part has passed the inlet; usually corresponds to a 0 station

II. MECHANISMS OF LABOR (Box 26-3)
A. Assessment
1. Lightening or dropping: Fetus descends into the pelvis about 2 weeks before **delivery** for a primipara; the fetus may engage into the pelvis after **labor** commences for a multipara.
2. Braxton Hicks contractions increase.
3. The vaginal mucosa is congested and vaginal discharge increases.

BOX 26-3
Mechanisms of Labor

ENGAGEMENT
Engagement is the mechanism whereby the fetus nestles into the pelvis.
Engagement also is termed *lightening* or *dropping*.

DESCENT
Descent is the process that the fetal head undergoes as it begins its journey through the pelvis.
Descent is a continuous process from the time of engagement until birth and is assessed by the measurement called station.

FLEXION
Flexion is a process of the fetal head's nodding forward toward the fetal chest.

INTERNAL ROTATION
Internal rotation of the fetus occurs most commonly from the occiput transverse position, assumed at engagement into the pelvis, to the occipitoanterior position while continuously descending.

EXTENSION
Extension enables the head to emerge when the fetus is in a cephalic position.
Extension begins after the head crowns.
Extension is complete when the head passes under the symphysis pubis and occiput and the anterior fontanel, brow, face, and chin pass over the sacrum and coccyx and are over the perineum.

RESTITUTION
Restitution is realignment of the fetal head with the body after the head emerges.

EXTERNAL ROTATION
The shoulders externally rotate after the head emerges and restitution occurs, so that the shoulders are in the anteroposterior diameter of the pelvis.

EXPULSION
Expulsion is the birth of the entire body.

---

4. Brownish or blood-tinged cervical mucus is passed.
5. Cervix ripens, becomes soft, partly effaced, and may begin to dilate.
6. Mother has a sudden burst of energy, also known as "nesting," often 24 to 48 hours before onset of labor.
7. Weight loss of 1 to 3 lb resulting from fluid shifts produced by the changes in progesterone and estrogen levels 24 to 48 hours before the onset of **labor.**
8. Spontaneous rupture of membranes occurs.

B. True **labor** (Box 26-4)
1. Contractions may present as back pain in some women; often resembles menstrual cramps during early **labor.**
2. Contractions increase in duration and intensity

C. False **labor** (see Box 26-4)
1. Prodromal **labor:** contractions are felt in the abdomen and groin and may be more annoying than painful.
2. Contractions are irregular, and do not produce dilation, effacement, or descent.

III. LEOPOLD'S MANEUVER
A. Description: Method to determine presentation and position of the fetus and aid in location of fetal heart sounds
B. If the head is in the fundus a hard, round, movable object is felt. The buttocks will feel soft and have an irregular shape and are more difficult to move.
C. The fetus's back, which is a smooth, hard surface, should be felt on one side of the abdomen.
D. Irregular knobs and lumps, which may be the hands, feet, elbows, and knees, will be felt on the opposite side of the abdomen.

BOX 26-4
True Labor and False Labor

TRUE LABOR
Contractions occur regularly, become stronger, last longer, and occur closer together. Cervical dilation and effacement are progressive.
The fetus usually becomes engaged in the pelvis and begins to descend.

FALSE LABOR
False labor does not produce dilation, effacement, or descent.
Contractions are irregular, without progression.
Activity, like walking, often relieves false labor.
Example: If a woman has been sleeping and wakes up with contractions, gets up, and moves around, and her contractions become stronger and closer together, this is true labor. If the contractions go away, this is false labor.

▲ IV. BREATHING TECHNIQUES (Box 26-5)
  A. Provide a focus during contractions, interfering with pain sensory transmission
  B. Promote relaxation and oxygenation
  C. Begin with simple breathing patterns and progress to more complex ones as needed.

▲ V. FETAL MONITORING
  A. Description
    1. The fetal monitor displays the fetal heart rate (FHR).
    2. The device monitors uterine activity.
    3. The monitor assesses frequency, duration, and intensity of contractions.
    4. The monitor assesses FHR in relation to maternal contractions.
    5. Baseline FHR is measured between contractions; the normal FHR at term is 120 to 160 beats/min.
  B. External fetal monitoring
    1. External fetal monitoring is noninvasive and is performed using a tocotransducer or Doppler ultrasonic transducer.
    2. Leopold's maneuver is performed to determine on which side the fetal back is located, and the ultrasound transducer is placed over this area (fasten with a belt).
    3. The tocotransducer is placed over the fundus of the uterus where contractions feel the strongest (fasten with a belt).
    4. Allow the client to assume a comfortable position, avoiding vena cava compression (maternal supine hypotensive syndrome).
    5. The preferred maternal position is to have her lie on her side to increase perfusion.
  C. Internal fetal monitoring
    1. Internal fetal monitoring is invasive and requires rupturing of the membranes and attaching an electrode to the presenting part of the fetus.
    2. Mother must be dilated 2 to 3 cm to perform internal monitoring.
  D. Periodic patterns in the FHR
    1. Fetal bradycardia and tachycardia
      a. Bradycardia: The FHR is less than 120 beats/min for 10 minutes or longer.
      b. Tachycardia: The FHR is more than 160 beats/min for 10 minutes or longer.
      c. Change position of the mother and administer oxygen.
      d. Assess mother's vital signs.
      e. Notify the physician.
    2. Variability (Box 26-6)
      a. Fluctuations in the baseline FHR may include irregular fluctuations of two or more cycles/min.
      b. Decreased variability can result from fetal hypoxemia, acidosis, or certain medications.
      c. A temporary decrease in variability can occur when the fetus is in a sleep state (sleep states do not usually last longer than 30 minutes).
      d. External Doppler ultrasound can only detect long-term variability. Internal monitoring of the FHR can detect long-term and short-term variability.
    3. Accelerations
      a. Accelerations are brief, temporary increases in the FHR of at least 15 beats more than the baseline and lasting at least 15 seconds.
      b. Accelerations usually are a reassuring sign, reflecting a responsive, nonacidotic fetus.

BOX 26-5

Breathing Techniques

FIRST-STAGE BREATHING
Cleansing Breath
Each contraction begins and ends with a deep inspiration and expiration.
Slow-Paced Breathing
Slow-paced breathing promotes relaxation.
Slow-paced breathing is used as long as possible during labor.
Modified-Paced Breathing
Modified-paced breathing is used when slow-paced breathing is no longer effective.
Breathing is shallow and fast.
Pattern-Paced Breathing
Pattern-paced breathing sometimes is referred to as pant-blow.
After a certain number of breaths (modified-paced breathing), the woman exhales with a slight blow, and then begins modified-paced breathing again.
Breathing to Prevent Pushing
The woman blows repeatedly using short puffs when the urge to push is strong.

SECOND-STAGE BREATHING
Several variations of breathing can be used in the pushing stage of labor and the woman may grunt, groan, sigh, or moan as she pushes. Prolonged breath-holding while pushing with a closed glottis may result in a decrease in cardiac output. Therefore, if breath-holding while pushing is used, the open glottis method or limiting breath-holding to less than 6 to 8 seconds should be done.

BOX 26-6

Variability in the Fetal Heart Rate

Absent variability: Undetected variability
Minimal variability: Greater than undetected but not more than 5 beats/min
Moderate variability: Fetal heart rate fluctuations from 6 to 25 beats/min
Marked variability: Fetal heart rate fluctuations greater than 25 beats/min

c. Accelerations usually occur with fetal movement.

d. Acclerations may be nonperiodic (having no relation to contractions) or periodic.

e. Accelerations may occur with uterine contractions, vaginal examinations, or mild cord compression, or when the fetus is in a breech presentation.

4. Early decelerations (Fig. 26-3)

a. Early decelerations are decreases in FHR below baseline; the rate at the lowest point of the deceleration usually remains greater than 100 beats/min.

b. Early decelerations occur during contractions as the fetal head is pressed against the woman's pelvis or soft tissues, such as the cervix, and return to the baseline FHR by the end of the contraction.

c. Tracing shows a uniform shape and mirror image of uterine contractions.

d. Early decelerations are not associated with fetal compromise and require no intervention.

5. Late decelerations (see Fig. 26-3)

a. Late decelerations are nonreassuring patterns that reflect impaired placental exchange or uteroplacental insufficiency.

b. The patterns look similar to early decelerations but begin well after the contraction begins and return to baseline after the contraction ends.

c. The degree of fall in the heart rate from baseline is not related to the amount of uteroplacental insufficiency.

d. Interventions include improving placental blood flow and fetal oxygenation.

6. Variable decelerations (see Fig. 26-3)

a. Variable decelerations are caused by conditions that restrict flow through the umbilical cord.

b. Variable decelerations do not have the uniform appearance of early and late decelerations.

c. The shape, duration, and degree of fall below baseline heart rate are variable; these fall and rise abruptly with the onset and relief of cord compression.

d. Variable decelerations also may be nonperiodic, occurring at times unrelated to contractions.

e. Baseline rate and variability are considered when evaluating variable decelerations.

f. Variable decelerations are significant when the FHR repeatedly decreases to less than 70 beats/min and persists at that level for at least 60 seconds before returning to baseline.

7. Hypertonic uterine activity

a. Assessment of uterine activity includes frequency, duration, intensity of the contractions, and uterine resting tone.

b. The **uterus** should relax between contractions for 60 seconds or longer.

c. Uterine contraction intensity is about 50 to 75 mm Hg (with the intrauterine uterine catheter) during **labor** and may reach 110 mm Hg with pushing during the second stage.

d. The average resting tone is 5 to 15 mm Hg.

e. In hypertonic uterine activity, the uterine resting tone between contractions is high,

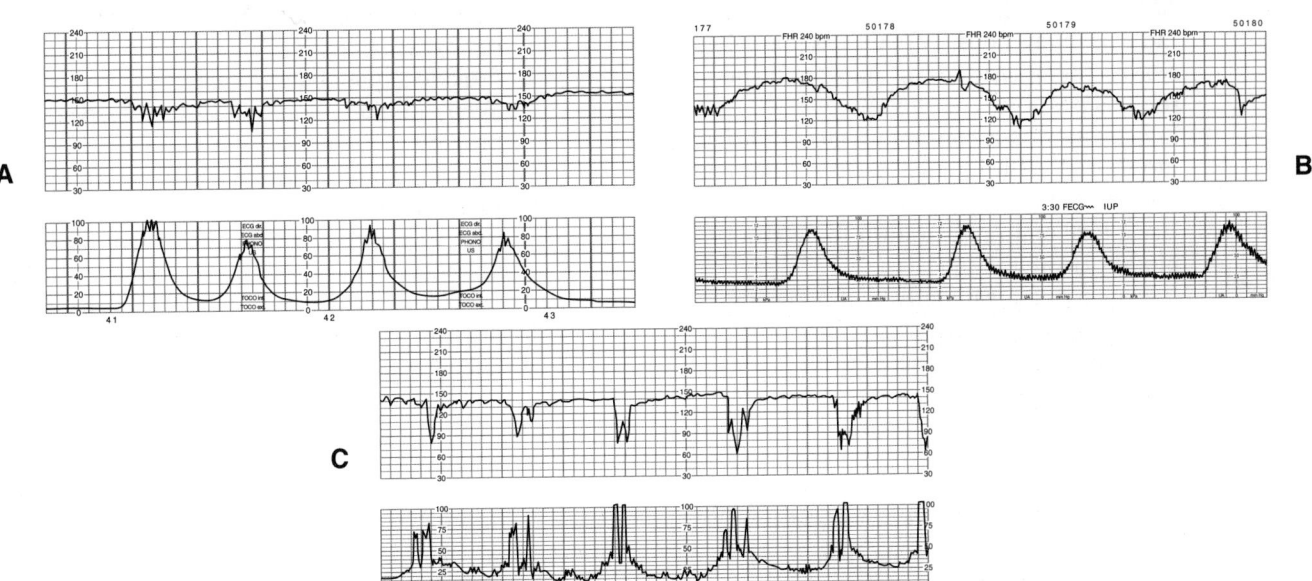

FIG. 26-3 Deceleration patterns. **A,** Early decelerations caused by head compression. **B,** Late decelerations caused by uteroplacental insufficiency. **C,** Variable decelerations caused by cord compression. (From Wong, D., Perry, S., Hockenberry, M., et al. [2006]. *Maternal child nursing care* [3rd ed.]. St. Louis: Mosby.)

TABLE 26-1

Four Stages of Labor

First Stage	Second Stage	Third Stage	Fourth Stage
Effacement and dilation of cervix	Expulsion of fetus	Separation of placenta	Physical recovery
Three stages—latent, active, and transition	Pushing stage	Expulsion of placenta	1-4 hr after expulsion of placenta
Woman is sociable and excited in latent phase, becoming more inwardly focused as labor intensifies	Woman has intense concentration on pushing with contractions; may doze between contractions	Woman is excited and relieved after baby's birth; usually very tired	Tired, but may find it difficult to rest because of excitement; eager to become acquainted with newborn

---

BOX 26-7

Nonreassuring Patterns

Bradycardia
Tachycardia
Late decelerations
Prolonged decelerations
Hypertonic uterine activity
Decreased or absent variability
Variable decelerations falling to less than 70 beats/min for longer than 60 seconds

---

reducing uterine blood flow and decreasing fetal oxygen supply.

8. Interventions for nonreassuring patterns (Box 26-7)
   a. Identify the cause (assess for cord prolapse).
   b. Discontinue oxytocin (Pitocin) if infusing
   c. Change the mother's position
   d. Administer oxygen by face mask at 8 to 10 L/min.
   e. Increase intravenous (IV) fluids as prescribed.
   f. Notify the physician or nurse-midwife as soon as possible.
   g. Prepare to initiate continuous electronic fetal monitoring with internal devices if not contraindicated.
   h. Use a fetal scalp pH monitor to determine a blood pH value.
   i. Prepare for cesarean **delivery** if necessary.

▲ VI. **FOUR STAGES OF LABOR** (Table 26-1)
   A. Stage 1: Latent phase
      1. Description: Stage 1 is the longest for both nulliparous and multiparous women. A **labor** curve, often called a Friedman curve, may be used to identify whether a woman's cervical dilation is progressing at the expected rate (Fig. 26-4).
      2. Assessment
         a. Cervical dilation is 1 to 4 cm.
         b. Uterine contractions occur every 15 to 30 minutes, are 15 to 30 seconds in duration, and are of mild intensity.
         c. Mother is talkative and eager to be in **labor.**

3. Interventions
   a. Encourage mother and partner to participate in care.
   b. Assist with comfort measures, changes of position, and ambulation.
   c. Keep mother and partner informed of progress.
   d. Offer fluids and ice chips.
   e. Encourage voiding every 1 to 2 hours.
B. Stage 1: Active phase
   1. Assessment
      a. Cervical dilation is 4 to 7 cm.
      b. Uterine contractions occur every 3 to 5 minutes, are 30 to 60 seconds in duration, and are of moderate intensity.
      c. Mother may experience feelings of helplessness.
      d. Mother becomes restless and anxious as contractions become stronger.
   2. Interventions
      a. Encourage maintenance of effective breathing patterns.
      b. Provide a quiet environment.
      c. Keep mother and partner informed of progress.
      d. Promote comfort with back rubs, sacral pressure, pillow support, and position changes.
      e. Instruct partner in effleurage (light stroking of abdomen).
      f. Offer fluids and ice chips and ointment for dry lips.
      g. Encourage voiding every 1 to 2 hours.
C. Stage 1: Transition phase
   1. Assessment
      a. Cervical dilation is 8 to 10 cm.
      b. Uterine contractions occur every 2 to 3 minutes, are 45 to 90 seconds in duration, and are of strong intensity.
      c. Mother becomes tired, is restless and irritable, and feels out of control.
   2. Interventions
      a. Encourage rest between contractions.
      b. Wake mother at beginning of contraction so she can begin breathing pattern.

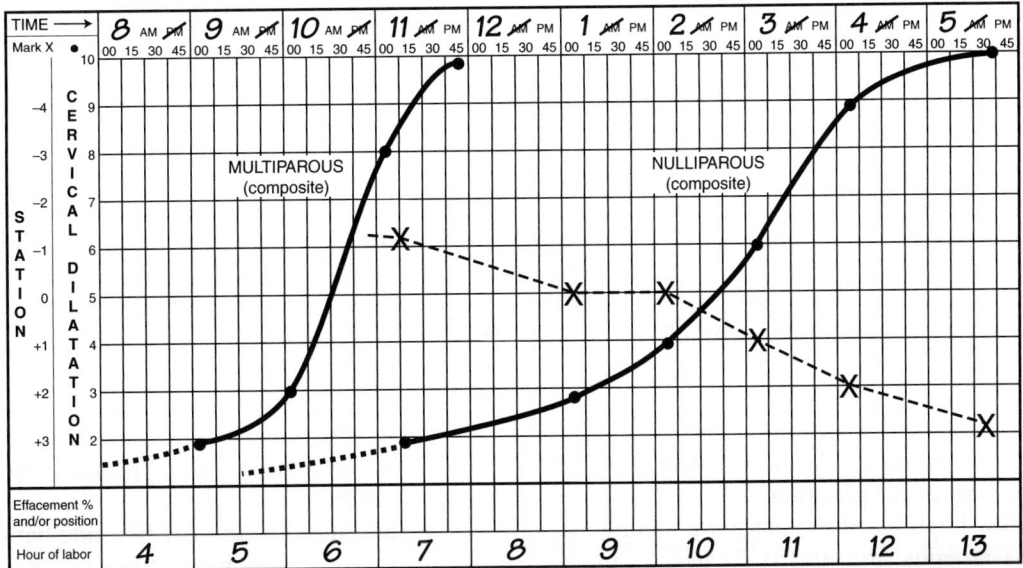

Composite normal dilation curves

FIG. 26-4 A labor curve, often called a Friedman curve, may be used to identify whether a woman's cervical dilation is progressing at the expected rate. The symbol for station (X) may be added to the labor curve. Typical labor curves for a multiparous woman and a nulliparous woman are illustrated for comparison of patterns. (From Murray, S., & McKinney, E. [2006]. *Foundations of maternal-newborn nursing* [4th ed.]. St. Louis: W.B. Saunders.)

c. Keep mother and partner informed of progress.

d. Provide privacy.

e. Offer fluids and ice chips and ointment for dry lips.

f. Encourage voiding every 1 to 2 hours.

D. Interventions throughout stage 1
1. Monitor maternal vital signs.
2. Monitor FHR via ultrasound Doppler, fetoscope, or electronic fetal monitor.
3. Assess FHR before, during, and after a contraction, noting that the normal FHR is 120 to 160 beats/min.
4. Monitor uterine contractions by palpation or monitor, determining frequency, duration, and intensity.
5. Assess status of cervical dilation and effacement.
6. Assess fetal station presentation and position by Leopold's maneuver.
7. Assist with pelvic examination and prepare for a fern test.
8. Assess the color of the **amniotic fluid** if the membranes have ruptured, because meconium-stained fluid can indicate fetal distress.

E. Stage 2
1. Assessment
   a. Cervical dilation is complete.
   b. Progress of **labor** is measured by descent of fetal head through the birth canal (change in fetal station).

c. Uterine contractions occur every 2 to 3 minutes, lasting 60 to 75 seconds, and are of strong intensity.

d. Increase in bloody show occurs.

e. Mother feels urge to bear down; assist mother in pushing efforts.

2. Interventions
   a. Perform assessments every 5 minutes.
   b. Monitor maternal vital signs.
   c. Monitor FHR via ultrasound Doppler, fetoscope, or electronic fetal monitor.
   d. Assess FHR before, during, and after a contraction, noting that the normal fetal heart rate is 120 to 160 beats/min.
   e. Monitor uterine contractions by palpation or monitor, determining frequency, duration, and intensity.
   f. Provide mother with encouragement and praise and provide for rest between contractions.
   g. Keep mother and partner informed of progress.
   h. Maintain privacy.
   i. Provide ice chips and ointment for dry lips.
   j. Assist mother into a position that promotes comfort and assists pushing efforts, such as lithotomy, semisitting, kneeling, side-lying, or squatting.
   k. Monitor for signs of approaching birth, such as perineal bulging or visualization of the fetal head.
   l. Prepare for birth.

F. Stage 3
1. Assessment
   a. Contractions occur until the **placenta** is born.
   b. Placental separation and expulsion occur.
   c. Birth of **placenta** occurs 5 to 30 minutes after birth of the baby.
   d. Schultze mechanism: Center portion of **placenta** separates first, and its shiny fetal surface emerges from the **vagina.**
   e. Duncan mechanism: Margin of **placenta** separates, and the dull, red, rough maternal surface emerges from the **vagina** first.
2. Interventions
   a. Assess maternal vital signs.
   b. Assess uterine status.
   c. Provide parents with an explanation regarding birth of the **placenta.**
   d. Following birth of the **placenta,** uterine fundus remains firm and is located 2 fingerbreadths below the umbilicus.
   e. Examine **placenta** for cotyledons and membranes to verify that it is intact.
   f. Assess mother for shivering and provide warmth.
   g. Promote parental-neonatal attachment.
G. Stage 4
1. Description: Period of time from 1 to 4 hours after **delivery**
2. Assessment
   a. Blood pressure returns to prelabor level.
   b. Pulse is slightly lower than during **labor.**
   c. Fundus remains contracted, in the midline, 1 or 2 fingerbreadths below the umbilicus.
   d. **Lochia** is moderate or scant and red.
3. Interventions
   a. Perform maternal assessments every 15 minutes for 1 hour, every 30 minutes for 1 hour, and hourly for 2 hours.
   b. Provide warm blankets.
   c. Apply ice packs to the perineum.
   d. Massage the **uterus** if needed and teach the mother to massage the **uterus.**
   e. Provide breast-feeding support as needed.
   f. See Chapter 30 for information on caring for the **newborn.**

VII. ANESTHESIA
A. Local anesthesia
1. Local anesthesia is used for blocking pain during episiotomy.
2. Local anesthesia is administered just before the birth of the baby.
3. The anesthetic has no effect on the fetus.
B. Pudendal block
1. A pudendal block is administered just before the birth of the baby.
2. Injection site is at the pudendal nerve through a transvaginal route.

3. Anesthetic blocks the perineal area for episiotomy.
4. Its effect lasts about 30 minutes.
5. Anesthetic has no effect on contractions or the fetus.
C. Lumbar epidural block
1. Injection site is in epidural space at L3 to L4.
2. The block is administered after **labor** is established or just before a scheduled cesarean birth.
3. The anesthetic relieves pain from contractions and numbs the **vagina** and perineum.
4. The block may cause hypotension, bladder distention, and a prolonged second stage.
5. The anesthetic does not cause headache because the dura mater is not penetrated.
6. Assess maternal blood pressure and assess bladder frequently.
7. Maintain the mother in a side-lying position or place a rolled blanket beneath the right hip to displace the **uterus** from the vena cava.
8. Administer IV fluids as prescribed.
9. Increase fluids as prescribed if hypotension occurs.
10. Observe for any adverse effects from opioid epidurals—nausea and vomiting, pruritis, or respiratory depression.
D. Intrathecal opioid analgesics
1. The medication is injected into the subarachnoid space and has a rapid onset of action.
2. It may be used in combination with a lumbar epidural block.
E. Subarachnoid (spinal) block
1. Injection site is in the spinal subarachnoid space at L3 to L5.
2. The block is administered just before birth.
3. The anesthetic relieves uterine and perineal pain and numbs the vagina, perineum, and lower extremities.
4. The anesthetic may cause maternal hypotension.
5. The anesthetic may cause postpartum headache.
6. The mother must lie flat for 8 to 12 hours following spinal injection.
7. Administer IV fluids as prescribed.
F. General anesthesia
1. General anesthesia may be used for some surgical interventions.
2. The mother is not awake.
3. General anesthesia presents a danger of respiratory depression and vomiting.

VIII. OBSTETRICAL PROCEDURES
A. Bishop score (Table 26-2)
1. The Bishop score is used to determine maternal readiness for **labor.**
2. The Bishop score evaluates cervical status and fetal position.
3. The Bishop score is indicated before the induction of **labor.**

TABLE 26-2

Factors of the Bishop Score

Score	0	1	2	3
Dilation of cervix	0	1-2 cm	3-4 cm	>5 cm
Effacement of cervix	0%-30%	40%-50%	60%-70%	>80%
Consistency of cervix	Firm	Medium	Soft	—
Position of cervix	Posterior	Midposition	Anterior	—
Station of presenting part	−3	−2	−1	+1, +2

4. The five factors are assigned a score of 0 to 3, and the total score is calculated.
5. A score of 6 or more indicates a readiness for **labor** induction.

B. Cervical ripening
   1. Procedures to ripen (soften) the cervix and make it more likely to dilate with the forces of **labor** may be performed as an adjunct to induction.
   2. Prostaglandin is a medication that may be used to cause cervical ripening
   3. An adverse reaction to prostaglandin is hyperstimulation of uterine contractions.

▲ C. Induction
   1. This is a deliberate initiation of uterine contractions that stimulates **labor.**
   2. Elective induction may be accomplished by oxytocin (Pitocin) infusion.
   3. Obtain baseline tracing of uterine contractions and FHR.
   4. Increase IV dosage of oxytocin as prescribed only after assessing contractions, FHR, and maternal blood pressure and pulse.
   5. Do not increase rate of oxytocin once the desired contraction pattern is obtained (contraction frequency of 2 to 3 minutes and lasting 60 seconds).
   6. Discontinue oxytocin as prescribed if contraction frequency is less than 2 minutes or duration is longer than 90 seconds, or if fetal distress is noted.

▲ D. Amniotomy
   1. Artificial rupture of membranes is performed by the physician or nurse-midwife to stimulate **labor.**
   2. Amniotomy is performed if the fetus is at 0 or a plus station.
   3. Amniotomy increases risk of prolapsed cord and infection.
   4. Monitor FHR before and after amniotomy.
   5. Record time of amniotomy, FHR, and characteristics of the fluid.
   6. Meconium-stained **amniotic fluid** may be associated with fetal distress.

7. Bloody **amniotic fluid** may indicate abruptio placentae or fetal trauma.
8. An unpleasant odor to **amniotic fluid** is associated with infection.
9. Polyhydramnios is associated with maternal diabetes and certain congenital disorders.
10. **Oligohydramnios** is associated with intrauterine growth restriction and congenital disorders.
11. Expect more variable decelerations after rupture of the membranes as a result of possible cord compression during contractions.
12. Limit client activity if prescribed.

E. External version
   1. External version is manipulation of the fetus from an abnormal position into a normal presentation.
   2. External version is indicated for an abnormal presentation that exists after the thirty-fourth week.
   3. Monitor vital signs.
   4. If the mother is Rh-negative, ensure that Rh immune globulin was given at 28 weeks' gestation.
   5. Prepare for nonstress test to evaluate fetal well-being.
   6. Intravenous fluids and tocolytic therapy may be administered to relax the uterus and permit easier manipulation of fetus.
   7. Ultrasound is used during the procedure to evaluate fetal position and placental placement and guide direction of the fetus.
   8. Abdominal wall is manipulated to direct fetus into a cephalic presentation if possible.
   9. Monitor blood pressure to identify vena cava compression.
   10. Monitor for unusual pain.
   11. After the procedure, do the following:
      a. Perform nonstress test to evaluate fetal well-being.
      b. Monitor for uterine activity, bleeding, ruptured membranes, and decreased fetal activity.
      c. With Rh-negative clients, perform Kleihauer-Betke test as prescribed to detect the presence and amount of fetal blood in the maternal circulation and to identify clients who need additional Rh immune globulin.

F. Episiotomy
   1. An episiotomy is an incision made into the perineum to enlarge the vaginal outlet and facilitate **delivery.**
   2. Check episiotomy site.
   3. Institute measures to relieve pain.
   4. Provide ice packs during the first 24 hours.
   5. Instruct the client in the use of sitz baths.
   6. Apply analgesic spray or ointment as prescribed.
   7. Provide perineal care, using clean technique.
   8. Instruct the client in the proper care of the incision. ●

9. Instruct the client to dry the perineal area from front to back and to blot the area rather than wipe it.
10. Instruct the client to shower rather than bathe in a tub.
11. Apply a perineal pad without touching the inside surface of the pad.
12. Report any bleeding or discharge to the physician.

G. Forceps **delivery**
1. Two double-crossed, spoon-like articulated blades are used to assist in the **delivery** of the fetal head.
2. Reassure the mother and explain the need for forceps.
3. Monitor mother and fetus during **delivery.**
4. Check neonate and mother after **delivery** for any possible injury.
5. Assist with repair of any lacerations.

H. Vacuum extraction
1. A cap-like suction device is applied to the fetal head to facilitate extraction.
2. Suction is used to assist in **delivery** of the fetal head.
3. Traction is applied during uterine contractions until descent of the fetal head is achieved.
4. The suction device should not be kept in place any longer than 25 minutes.
5. Monitor FHR every 5 minutes if external fetal monitoring is not used.
6. Assess **newborn infant** at birth and throughout postpartum period for signs of cerebral trauma.
7. Monitor for developing cephalohematoma.
8. Caput succedaneum is normal and will resolve in 24 hours.

I. Cesarean **delivery**
1. Cesarean section is **delivery** of the fetus usually through a transabdominal, low-segment incision of the **uterus.**
2. Preoperative
   a. If planned, prepare the mother and partner.
   b. If an emergency, quickly explain the need and procedure to the mother and partner.
   c. Obtain informed consent.
   d. Make sure that the preoperative diagnostic tests are done, including Rh factor determination.
   e. Prepare to insert an IV line and a Foley catheter.
   f. Prepare the abdomen as prescribed.
   g. Monitor the mother and fetus continuously for signs of **labor**.
   h. Provide emotional support.
   i. Administer preoperative medications as prescribed.

3. Postoperative
   a. Monitor vital signs.
   b. Provide pain relief.
   c. Encourage turning, coughing, and deep breathing.
   d. Encourage ambulation.
   e. Monitor for signs of infection and bleeding.
   f. Burning and pain on urination may indicate a bladder infection.
   g. A tender uterus and foul-smelling **lochia** may indicate endometritis.
   h. A productive cough or chills may indicate pneumonia.
   i. A positive Homans' sign, pain, or edema of an extremity may indicate thrombophlebitis.

PRACTICE QUESTIONS

1. A nurse is reviewing true and false labor signs with a multiparous client. The nurse determines that the client understands the signs of true labor if she makes which statement?
   1. "I won't be in labor until the baby engages."
   2. "My contractions will be felt in the abdominal area."
   3. "My contractions will not be as painful if I walk around."
   4. "My contractions will increase in duration and intensity."

2. Immediately after an amniotomy has been performed, the nurse should first assess:
   1. For bladder distention
   2. For cervical dilation
   3. The maternal blood pressure
   4. The fetal heart rate (FHR) pattern

3. A nurse explains the purpose of effleurage to a client in early labor. The nurse tells the client that effleurage is:
   1. The application of pressure to the sacrum to relieve a backache
   2. A form of biofeedback to enhance bearing-down efforts during delivery
   3. Light stroking of the abdomen to facilitate relaxation during labor and provide tactile stimulation to the fetus
   4. Performed to stimulate uterine activity by contracting a specific muscle group while other parts of the body rest

4. A client in labor has been pushing effectively for 1 hour. A nurse determines that the client's primary physiological need at this time is to:
   1. Ambulate.
   2. Rest between contractions.
   3. Change positions frequently.
   4. Consume oral food and fluids.

5. A client in labor is dilated 10 cm. At this point of the labor process, the nurse would plan to assess and document the fetal heart rate at least:
   1. Hourly
   2. Every 15 minutes
   3. Every 30 minutes
   4. Before each contraction

6. A nurse is caring for a client in labor. The nurse determines that the client is beginning the second stage of labor when which of the following assessments is noted?
   1. The contractions are regular.
   2. The membranes have ruptured.
   3. The cervix is dilated completely.
   4. The client begins to expel clear vaginal fluid.

7. A nurse in the labor room is caring for a client in the active stage of labor. The nurse is assessing the fetal patterns and notes a late deceleration on the monitor strip. The appropriate nursing action is to:
   1. Administer oxygen via face mask.
   2. Place the mother in a supine position.
   3. Increase the rate of the oxytocin (Pitocin) IV infusion.
   4. Document the findings and continue to monitor the fetal patterns.

8. A nurse is performing an assessment of a client who is scheduled for a cesarean delivery. Which assessment finding would indicate a need to contact the physician?
   1. Hemoglobin of 11.0 g/dL
   2. Fetal heart rate of 180 beats/min
   3. Maternal pulse rate of 85 beats/min
   4. White blood cell count of 12,000/mm³

9. A client in labor is transported to the delivery room and prepared for a cesarean delivery. After the client is transferred to the delivery room table, the nurse places her in:
   1. Supine position with a wedge under the right hip
   2. Trendelenburg's position with the legs in stirrups
   3. Prone position with the legs separated and elevated
   4. Semi-Fowler's position with a pillow under the knees

10. A nurse has provided discharge instructions to a client who delivered a healthy newborn infant by cesarean delivery. Which statement, if made by the client, indicates a need for further instructions?
    1. "I will begin abdominal exercises immediately."
    2. "I will notify the physician if I develop a fever."
    3. "I will turn on my side and push up with my arms to get out of bed."
    4. "I will lift nothing heavier than the newborn infant for at least 2 weeks."

11. A nurse is caring for a client in labor and prepares to auscultate the fetal heart rate by using a Doppler ultrasound device. The nurse accurately determines that the fetal heart sounds are heard by:
    1. Noting whether the heart rate is greater than 140 beats/min
    2. Placing the diaphragm of the Doppler on the mother's abdomen
    3. Palpating the maternal radial pulse while listening to the fetal heart rate
    4. Performing Leopold's maneuver first to determine the location of the fetal heart

12. A nurse is caring for a client in labor who is receiving oxytocin (Pitocin) by intravenous infusion to stimulate uterine contractions. Which assessment finding would indicate to the nurse that the infusion needs to be discontinued?
    1. Increased urinary output
    2. A fetal heart rate of 90 beats/min.
    3. Three contractions occurring within a 10-minute period.
    4. Adequate resting tone of the uterus palpated between contractions.

13. A nurse is preparing to care for a client in labor. The physician has prescribed an intravenous infusion of oxytocin (Pitocin). The nurse ensures that which of the following is implemented before initiating the infusion?
    1. An intravenous infusion of antibiotics
    2. Placing the client on complete bed rest
    3. Continuous electronic fetal monitoring
    4. Placing a code cart at the client's bedside

14. A nurse is monitoring a client in active labor and notes that the client is having contractions every 3 minutes that last 45 seconds. The nurse notes that the fetal heart rate between contractions is 100 beats/min. Which of the following nursing actions is appropriate?
    1. Notify the physician or nurse-midwife.
    2. Continue monitoring the fetal heart rate.
    3. Encourage the client to continue pushing with each contraction.
    4. Instruct the client's coach to continue to encourage breathing techniques.

15. A nurse is caring for a client in labor and is monitoring the fetal heart rate patterns. The nurse notes the presence of episodic accelerations on the electronic fetal monitor tracing. Which of the following actions is appropriate?
    1. Notify the physician or nurse-midwife of the findings.
    2. Reposition the mother and check the monitor for changes in the fetal tracing.
    3. Document the findings and tell the mother that the monitor indicates fetal well-being.
    4. Take the mother's vital signs and tell the mother that bed rest is required to conserve oxygen.

16. A nurse is admitting a pregnant client to the labor room and attaches an external electronic fetal monitor to the client's abdomen. After attachment of the

electronic fetal monitor, the initial nursing assessment is which of the following?
1. Identify the types of accelerations.
2. Assess the baseline fetal heart rate.
3. Determine the frequency of the contractions.
4. Determine the intensity of the contractions.

17. A nurse is reviewing the record of a client in the labor room and notes that the nurse-midwife has documented that the fetus is at negative 1 (−1) station. The nurse determines that the fetal presenting part is:
1. 1 inch below the coccyx.
2. 1 inch below the iliac crest.
3. 1 cm above the ischial spine.
4. 1 fingerbreadth below the symphysis pubis.

18. A nurse assists in the vaginal delivery of a newborn infant. After the delivery, the nurse observes the umbilical cord lengthen and a spurt of blood from the vagina. The nurse documents these observations as signs of:
1. Hematoma
2. Uterine atony
3. Placenta previa
4. Placental separation

19. A client arrives at a birthing center in active labor. Her membranes are still intact, and the nurse-midwife prepares to perform an amniotomy. A nurse who is assisting the nurse-midwife explains to the client that after this procedure, she will most likely have:
1. Less pressure on her cervix
2. Decreased number of contractions

3. Increased efficiency of contractions
4. The need for increased maternal blood pressure monitoring

20. A nurse is monitoring a client in labor. The nurse suspects umbilical cord compression if which of the following is noted on the external monitor tracing during a contraction?
1. Late decelerations
2. Early decelerations
3. Short-term variability
4. Variable decelerations

ALTERNATE ITEM FORMAT: PRIORITIZING (ORDERED RESPONSE)

A nurse is monitoring a client in labor who is receiving oxytocin (Pitocin) and notes that the client is experiencing hypertonic uterine contractions. List in order of priority the actions that the nurse takes. (Number 1 is the first action and number 6 is the last action.)

_____ Reposition the client.
_____ Stop the oxytocin infusion.
_____ Perform a vaginal examination.
_____ Check the client's blood pressure.
_____ Administer oxygen by face mask at 8 to 10 L/min.
_____ Administer medication as prescribed to reduce uterine activity

ANSWERS

1. **4**

Rationale: True labor for a multiparous client is present when the contractions increase in duration and intensity. A multiparous client experiences true labor before the fetus engages. Contractions felt in the abdominal area and contractions that ease with walking are signs of false labor.

Test-Taking Strategy: Focus on the subject, understanding the signs of true labor. Use the process of elimination and eliminate 2 and 3 because they are signs of false labor. Eliminate option 1 because labor occurs before engagement. Review the signs of true and false labor if you had difficulty with this question.

Level of Cognitive Ability: Analysis
Client Needs: Health Promotion and Maintenance
Integrated Process: Nursing Process—evaluation
Content Area: Maternity—intrapartum
Reference: Lowdermilk, D., & Perry, S. (2004). *Maternity and women's health care* (8th ed., p. 542). St. Louis: Mosby.

2. **4**

Rationale: The FHR is assessed immediately after amniotomy to detect any changes that may indicate cord compression or prolapse. Bladder distention or maternal blood pressure would not be the first things to check after an amniotomy. Once the membranes are ruptured, minimal vaginal examinations will be done because of the risk of infection.

Test-Taking Strategy: Note the strategic word *first*. Because of the risk of a prolapsed cord after an amniotomy, the first action is to check the FHR for signs of bradycardia or variable decelerations. Review care after an amniotomy if you had difficulty with this question.

Level of Cognitive Ability: Application
Client Needs: Physiological integrity
Integrated Process: Nursing Process—assessment
Content Area: Maternity—intrapartum
Reference: Lowdermilk, D., & Perry, S. (2004). *Maternity and women's health care* (8th ed., p. 1009). St. Louis: Mosby.

3. **3**

Rationale: Effleurage is a specific type of cutaneous stimulation involving light stroking of the abdomen and is used before transition to promote relaxation and relieve mild to moderate pain. Effleurage provides tactile stimulation to the fetus. Options 1, 2, and 4 are inaccurate descriptions of effleurage.

Test-Taking Strategy: Use the process of elimination. Focus on the strategic words *in early labor* to eliminate option 2. Eliminate option 1 because not all clients in labor experience backache. Eliminate option 4 because it focuses on stimulation of uterine activity rather than relaxation. Review the components of effleurage if you had difficulty with this question.

Level of Cognitive Ability: Application
Client Needs: Psychosocial Integrity

Integrated Process: Teaching and Learning
Content Area: Maternity—intrapartum
References: Lowdermilk, D., & Perry, S. (2006). *Maternity nursing* (7th ed.). St. Louis: Mosby, p. 344.
McKinney, E., James, S., Murray, S., & Ashwill, J. (2005). *Maternal-child nursing* (2nd ed., p. 417). St. Louis: W.B. Saunders.
Wong, D., Perry, S., Hockenberry, M., et al. (2006). *Maternal child nursing care* (3rd ed., pp. 231-232). St. Louis: Mosby.

4. 2
Rationale: The birth process expends a great deal of energy. Encouraging rest between contractions conserves maternal energy, facilitating voluntary pushing efforts with contractions. Uteroplacental perfusion also is enhanced, which promotes fetal tolerance of the stress of labor. Changing positions frequently is not the primary physiological need. Ambulation is encouraged during early labor. Ice chips should be provided. Food and fluids likely are to be withheld at this time.
Test-Taking Strategy: Use the process of elimination. Focusing on the strategic words *pushing effectively* will assist in directing you to option 2. Review care for the client in the transition stage of labor if you had difficulty with this question.
Level of Cognitive Ability: Analysis
Client Needs: Physiological Integrity
Integrated Process: Nursing Process—analysis
Content Area: Maternity—intrapartum
References: Lowdermilk, D., & Perry, S. (2006). *Maternity nursing* (7th ed., p. 347). St. Louis: Mosby.
Murray, S., & McKinney, E. (2006). *Foundations of maternal-newborn nursing* (4th ed., p. 258). Philadelphia: W.B. Saunders.
Wong, D., Perry, S., Hockenberry, M., et al. (2006). *Maternal child nursing care* (3rd ed., p. 514). St. Louis: Mosby.

5. 2
Rationale: The second stage of labor begins when the cervix is dilated completely (10 cm). Maternal pulse, blood pressure, and fetal heart rate are assessed every 5 to 15 minutes; some agency protocols recommend assessment after each contraction. Options 1 and 3 represent lengthy time intervals for assessment in this stage of labor.
Test-Taking Strategy: Use the process of elimination and focus on the data in the question, dilated 10 cm. Noting the strategic words *at least* will assist in directing you to the option that identifies the most frequent time frame. Review care for the client in the second stage of labor if you had difficulty with this question.
Level of Cognitive Ability: Application
Client Needs: Physiological Integrity
Integrated Process: Nursing Process—planning
Content Area: Maternity—intrapartum
References: Lowdermilk, D., & Perry, S. (2006). *Maternity nursing* (7th ed., p. 437). St. Louis: Mosby.
Lowdermilk, D., & Perry, A. (2004). *Maternity and women's health care* (8th ed., p. 584). St. Louis: Mosby.

6. 3
Rationale: The second stage of labor begins when the cervix is dilated completely and ends with birth of the neonate. Options 1, 2, and 4 are not specific assessment findings of the second stage of labor.

Test-Taking Strategy: Use the process of elimination. Eliminate options 2 and 4 first because they are comparative or alike. From the remaining options, recalling that regular contractions occur before the second stage of labor will direct you easily to option 3. Review the stages of labor if you had difficulty with this question.
Level of Cognitive Ability: Analysis
Client Needs: Health Promotion and Maintenance
Integrated Process: Nursing Process—assessment
Content Area: Maternity—intrapartum
References: McKinney, E., James, S., Murray, S., & Ashwill, J. (2005). *Maternal-child nursing* (2nd ed., p. 355). St. Louis: W.B. Saunders.
Wong, D., Perry, S., Hockenberry, M., et al. (2006). *Maternal child nursing care* (3rd ed., p. 521). St. Louis: Mosby.

7. 1
Rationale: Late decelerations are the result of uteroplacental insufficiency as the result of decreased blood flow and oxygen to the fetus during the uterine contractions. This causes hypoxemia; therefore, oxygen is necessary. The supine position is avoided because it decreases uterine blood flow to the fetus. The client should be turned onto her side to displace pressure of the gravid uterus on the inferior vena cava. An intravenous oxytocin infusion is discontinued when a late deceleration is noted. The oxytocin would cause further hypoxemia because of increased uteroplacental insufficiency resulting from stimulation of contractions by this medication. Option 4 would delay necessary treatment.
Test-Taking Strategy: Use the ABCs—airway, breathing, and circulation—and knowledge related to the significance of a late deceleration to answer this question. Review content related to late decelerations if you had difficulty with this question.
Level of Cognitive Ability: Application
Client Needs: Physiological Integrity
Integrated Process: Nursing Process—implementation
Content Area: Maternity—intrapartum
References: Lowdermilk, D., & Perry, S. (2006). *Maternity nursing* (7th ed., p. 386). St. Louis: Mosby.
Murray, S., & McKinney, E. (2006). *Foundations of maternal-newborn nursing* (4th ed., p. 325). Philadelphia: W.B. Saunders.

8. 2
Rationale: A normal fetal heart rate is 120 to 160 beats/min. A count of 180 beats/min could indicate fetal distress and would warrant physician notification. White blood cell counts in a normal pregnancy begin to rise in the second trimester and peak in the third trimester, with a normal range of 11,000 to 15,000/mm^3, up to 18,000/mm^3. During the immediate postpartum period, the count may be as high as 25,000 to 30,000/mm^3 as a result of increased leukocytosis during delivery. By full term, a normal maternal hemoglobin range is 11 to 13 g/dL as a result of the hemodilution caused by an increase in plasma volume during pregnancy. The maternal pulse rate during pregnancy increases 10 to 15 beats/min over prepregnancy readings to facilitate increased cardiac output, oxygen transport, and kidney filtration.
Test-Taking Strategy: Use the process of elimination, noting the strategic words *indicate a need to contact the physician*.

Knowledge regarding the normal and abnormal findings in the pregnant client and fetus will direct you to option 2. If you are unfamiliar with these normal and abnormal findings, review this content.

Level of Cognitive Ability: Analysis
Client Needs: Physiological Integrity
Integrated Process: Nursing Process—analysis
Content Area: Maternity—intrapartum
References: Lowdermilk, D., & Perry, S. (2004). *Maternity and women's health care* (8th ed., pp. 356, 358, 518). St. Louis: Mosby.
McKinney, E., James, S., Murray, S., & Ashwill, J. (2005). *Maternal-child nursing* (2nd ed., p. 399). St. Louis: W.B. Saunders.
Murray, S., & McKinney, E. (2006). *Foundations of maternal-newborn nursing* (4th ed., pp. 379, 385). Philadelphia: W.B. Saunders.

9. **1**
Rationale: Vena cava and descending aorta compression by the pregnant uterus impedes blood return from the lower trunk and extremities. This leads to decreasing cardiac return, cardiac output, and blood flow to the uterus and subsequently the fetus. The best position to prevent this would be side-lying, with the uterus displaced off the abdominal vessels. Positioning for abdominal surgery necessitates a supine position; however, a wedge placed under the right hip provides displacement of the uterus. Trendelenburg's position places pressure from the pregnant uterus on the diaphragm and lungs, decreasing respiratory capacity and oxygenation. A semi-Fowler's or prone position is not practical for this type of abdominal surgery.
Test-Taking Strategy: Knowledge regarding vena cava syndrome and the appropriate position to prevent this syndrome is required to answer this question. Use the process of elimination, visualizing each of the positions identified in the options and considering the effect that the position may have on the mother and the fetus. If you had difficulty with this question, review care for the mother requiring cesarean delivery.
Level of Cognitive Ability: Application
Client Needs: Physiological Integrity
Integrated Process: Nursing Process—implementation
Content Area: Maternity—intrapartum
References: Lowdermilk, D., & Perry, S. (2006). *Maternity nursing* (7th ed., p. 803). St. Louis: Mosby.
Murray, S., & McKinney, E. (2006). *Foundations of maternal-newborn nursing* (4th ed., p. 382). Philadelphia: W.B. Saunders.
Wong, D., Perry, S., Hockenberry, M., et al. (2006). *Maternal child nursing care* (3rd ed., p. 575). St. Louis: Mosby.

10. **1**
Rationale: Abdominal exercises should not start immediately following abdominal surgery, and the client should wait at least 3 to 4 weeks postoperatively to allow for healing of the incision. Options 2, 3, and 4 are appropriate instructions for the client following a cesarean delivery.
Test-Taking Strategy: Use the process of elimination. Note the strategic words *indicates a need for further instructions*. These words indicate a negative event query and ask you to select an

option that is an incorrect statement. Keeping in mind that the client had a cesarean delivery and noting the word *immediately* in option 1 will assist in directing you to this option. Review home care instructions for the client following cesarean delivery if you had difficulty with this question.
Level of Cognitive Ability: Analysis
Client Needs: Health Promotion and Maintenance
Integrated Process: Teaching and Learning
Content Area: Maternity—postpartum
References: Lowdermilk, D., & Perry, S. (2006). *Maternity nursing* (7th ed., p. 804). St. Louis: Mosby.
Lowdermilk, D. & Perry, S. (2004). *Maternity and women's health care* (8th ed., p. 1021). St. Louis: Mosby.

11. **3**
Rationale: The nurse should simultaneously palpate the maternal radial or carotid pulse and auscultate the fetal heart rate (FHR) to differentiate the two. If the fetal and maternal heart rates are similar, the nurse may mistake the maternal heart rate for the FHR. Noting whether the heart rate is more than 140 beats/min or placing the diaphragm of the Doppler on the mother's abdomen will not ensure accuracy in obtaining the FHR. Leopold's maneuver may help the examiner locate the position of the fetus but will not ensure a distinction between the two heart rates.
Test-Taking Strategy: Use the process of elimination and focus on the strategic words *accurately determines*. Option 3 is the only option that identifies an action that will directly distinguish the maternal heart rate from the FHR. Review FHR monitoring if you had difficulty with this question.
Level of Cognitive Ability: Analysis
Client Needs: Physiological Integrity
Integrated Process: Nursing Process—assessment
Content Area: Maternity—intrapartum
References: Lowdermilk, D., & Perry, S. (2006). *Maternity nursing* (7th ed., p. 413). St. Louis: Mosby.
McKinney, E., James, S., Murray, S., & Ashwill, J. (2005). *Maternal-child nursing* (2nd ed., p. 394). St. Louis: W.B. Saunders.

12. **2**
Rationale: A normal fetal heart rate is 120 to 160 beats/min. Bradycardia or late or variable decelerations indicate fetal distress and the need to discontinue the oxytocin. The goal of labor augmentation is to achieve three good-quality contractions (appropriate intensity and duration) in a 10-minute period. The uterus should return to resting tone between contractions, and there should be no evidence of fetal distress. Increased urinary output is unrelated to the use of oxytocin.
Test-Taking Strategy: Use the process of elimination and note the strategic words *infusion needs to be discontinued*. Eliminate option 1 first because it is unrelated to the use of oxytocin. Next, eliminate option 4 because of the words *adequate resting tone*. From the remaining options, knowing that the normal fetal heart rate is 120 to 160 beats/min will direct you easily to option 2. Review monitoring of the client receiving an oxytocin infusion if you had difficulty with this question.
Level of Cognitive Ability: Analysis
Client Needs: Physiological Integrity
Integrated Process: Nursing Process—assessment

Content Area: Maternity—intrapartum
References: McKinney, E., James, S., Murray, S., & Ashwill, J. (2005). *Maternal-child nursing* (2nd ed., p. 448). St. Louis: W.B. Saunders.
Murray, S., & McKinney, E. (2006). *Foundations of maternal-newborn nursing* (4th ed., p. 371). St. Louis: W.B. Saunders.

13. 3
Rationale: Continuous electronic fetal monitoring should be implemented during an intravenous infusion of oxytocin. No data in the question indicate the need for complete bed rest or the need for antibiotics. Placing a code cart at the bedside of a client receiving an oxytocin infusion is not necessary.
Test-Taking Strategy: Use the process of elimination and the ABCs—airway, breathing, and circulation—to assist in answering the question. Option 3 is the only option that addresses oxygenation and circulation. If you had difficulty with this question, review the nursing considerations related to the administration of oxytocin.
Level of Cognitive Ability: Application
Client Needs: Physiological Integrity
Integrated Process: Nursing Process—planning
Content Area: Maternity—intrapartum
Reference: Murray, S., & McKinney, E. (2006). *Foundations of maternal-newborn nursing* (4th ed., pp. 369, 371). St. Louis: W.B. Saunders.

14. 1
Rationale: A normal fetal heart rate is 120 to 160 beats/min. Fetal bradycardia between contractions may indicate the need for immediate medical management, and the physician or nurse-midwife needs to be notified. Options 2, 3, and 4 are not appropriate nursing actions in this situation.
Test-Taking Strategy: Use the process of elimination. Knowledge that the normal fetal heart rate is 120 to 160 beats/min will assist you easily to recognize that fetal bradycardia is present. If you had difficulty with this question, review the expected and unexpected findings during the labor process.
Level of Cognitive Ability: Application
Client Needs: Physiological Integrity
Integrated Process: Nursing Process—implementation
Content Area: Maternity—intrapartum
Reference: Murray, S., & McKinney, E. (2006). *Foundations of maternal-newborn nursing* (4th ed., pp. 317, 323). St. Louis: W.B. Saunders.

15. 3
Rationale: Accelerations are transient increases in the fetal heart rate that often accompany contractions or are caused by fetal movement. Episodic accelerations are thought to be a sign of fetal well-being and adequate oxygen reserve. Options 1, 2, and 4 are inaccurate nursing actions and are unnecessary.
Test-Taking Strategy: Use the process of elimination. Note that options 1, 2, and 4 are comparative or alike in that they indicate the need for further intervention. Knowing that accelerations indicate fetal well-being will direct you easily to option 3. Review the significance of episodic accelerations if you had difficulty with this question.
Level of Cognitive Ability: Application
Client Needs: Physiological Integrity

Integrated Process: Nursing Process—implementation
Content Area: Maternity—intrapartum
References: Lowdermilk, D., & Perry, S. (2006). *Maternity nursing* (7th ed., p. 380). St. Louis: Mosby.
Wong, D., Perry, S., Hockenberry, M., et al. (2006). *Maternal child nursing care* (3rd ed., p. 474). St. Louis: Mosby.

16. 2
Rationale: Assessing the baseline fetal heart rate is important so that abnormal variations of the baseline rate can be identified if they occur. The intensity of contractions is assessed by an internal fetal monitor, not an external fetal monitor. Options 1 and 3 are important to assess, but not as the first priority. Fetal heart rate is evaluated by assessing baseline and periodic changes. Periodic changes occur in response to the intermittent stress of uterine contractions and the baseline beat-to-beat variability of the fetal heart rate.
Test-Taking Strategy: Use the process of elimination. Note the strategic word *initial* in the event query of the question. Use the ABCs—airway, breathing, and circulation. Fetal heart rate reflects the ABCs. Review the concepts related to external fetal monitoring if you had difficulty with this question.
Level of Cognitive Ability: Application
Client Needs: Physiological Integrity
Integrated Process: Nursing Process—assessment
Content Area: Maternity—intrapartum
Reference: Lowdermilk, D., & Perry, S. (2006). *Maternity nursing* (7th ed., p. 374). St. Louis: Mosby.

17. 3
Rationale: Station is the relationship of the presenting part to an imaginary line drawn between the ischial spines, measured in centimeters, and noted as a negative number above the line and a positive number below the line. At negative 1 (−1) station, the fetal presenting part is 1 cm above the ischial spines.
Test-Taking Strategy: Use the process of elimination. Knowledge that station is measured in centimeters and uses the ischial spines as a reference point will assist in answering this question. Note that options 1, 2, and 4 are comparative or alike in the use of the word *below*, which would be represented by a positive measurement in determining station. Review stations of the presenting part if you had difficulty with this question.
Level of Cognitive Ability: Analysis
Client Needs: Health Promotion and Maintenance
Integrated Process: Nursing Process—analysis
Content Area: Maternity—intrapartum
References: Lowdermilk, D., & Perry, S. (2006). *Maternity nursing* (7th ed., p. 316). St. Louis: Mosby.
Wong, D., Perry, S., Hockenberry, M., et al. (2006). *Maternal child nursing care* (3rd ed., pp. 420, 422). St. Louis: Mosby.

18. 4
Rationale: As the placenta separates, it settles downward into the lower uterine segment. The umbilical cord lengthens, and a sudden trickle or spurt of blood appears. Options 1, 2, and 3 are incorrect interpretations.
Test-Taking Strategy: Use the process of elimination. Options 1, 2, and 3 are comparative or alike in that they identify complications of pregnancy. Option 4 indicates a normal finding

following vaginal delivery of the newborn infant. Review this stage of labor if you had difficulty with this question.
Level of Cognitive Ability: Application
Client Needs: Physiological Integrity
Integrated Process: Communication and Documentation
Content Area: Maternity—intrapartum
References: Lowdermilk, D., & Perry, S. (2006). *Maternity nursing* (7th ed., p. 446). St. Louis: Mosby.
Lowdermilk, D., & Perry, S. (2004). *Maternity and women's health care* (8th ed., p. 596). St. Louis: Mosby.

19. **3**
Rationale: Amniotomy (artificial rupture of the membranes) can be used to induce labor when the condition of the cervix is favorable (ripe) or to augment labor if the progress begins to slow. Rupturing of membranes allows the fetal head to contact the cervix more directly and may increase the efficiency of contractions. Increased monitoring of maternal blood pressure is not necessary following this procedure. The fetal heart rate, however, needs to be monitored frequently.
Test-Taking Strategy: Use the process of elimination. Recalling that amniotomy is performed to augment labor if the progress begins to slow will direct you easily to option 3. Review the purpose of amniotomy if you had difficulty with this question.
Level of Cognitive Ability: Application
Client Needs: Physiological Integrity
Integrated Process: Nursing Process—implementation
Content Area: Maternity—intrapartum
References: Lowdermilk, D., & Perry, S. (2006). *Maternity nursing* (7th ed., p. 792). St. Louis: Mosby.
Lowdermilk, D., & Perry, S. (2004). *Maternity and women's health care* (8th ed., p. 1009). St. Louis: Mosby.

20. **4**
Rationale: Variable decelerations occur if the umbilical cord becomes compressed, thus reducing blood flow between the placenta and the fetus. Early decelerations result from pressure on the fetal head during a contraction. Late decelerations are an ominous pattern in labor because they suggest uteroplacental insufficiency during a contraction. Short-term variability refers to the beat-to-beat range in the fetal heart rate.
Test-Taking Strategy: Use the process of elimination, focusing on the subject, umbilical cord compression. Recalling that variable decelerations occur if the umbilical cord becomes compressed will direct you easily to option 4. Review the findings in umbilical cord compression if you had difficulty with this question.

Level of Cognitive Ability: Analysis
Client Needs: Physiological Integrity
Integrated Process: Nursing Process—assessment
Content Area: Maternity—intrapartum
References: Lowdermilk, D., & Perry, S. (2006). *Maternity nursing* (7th ed., p. 378). St. Louis: Mosby.
Lowdermilk, D., & Perry, S. (2004). *Maternity and women's health care* (8th ed.). St. Louis: Mosby.

ALTERNATE ITEM FORMAT: PRIORITIZING (ORDERED RESPONSE)

Answer: 2, 1, 4, 5, 3, 6
Rationale: If uterine hypertonicity occurs, the nurse would immediately intervene to reduce uterine activity and increase fetal oxygenation. The nurse would stop the oxytocin infusion and increase the rate of the nonadditive solution, position the woman in a side-lying position, and administer oxygen by a snug face mask at 8 to 10 L/min. The nurse then would attempt to determine the cause of the uterine hypertonicity and perform a vaginal examination to check for a prolapsed cord. The nurse would check maternal blood pressure for the presence of hypertension or hypotension. The nurse also contacts the physician and then implements prescribed orders, including the administration of medications to reduce uterine activity.
Test-Taking Strategy: Noting that the client is experiencing uterine hypertonicity will assist in determining that the first action would be to stop the oxytocin infusion. The mother's position would then be changed because this would immediately provide oxygen to the fetus. Because fetal oxygenation is a concern, oxygen would be administered next. The nurse then would determine the cause of the uterine hypertonicity by performing a vaginal examination and checking the client's blood pressure. Medications cannot be administered without a physician's order; therefore, medication administration would be the last action in this situation. Review care for the client experiencing hypertonic uterine contractions if you had difficulty with this question.
Level of Cognitive Ability: Application
Client Needs: Physiological Integrity
Integrated Process: Nursing Process—implementation
Content Area: Maternity—intrapartum
References: Lowdermilk, D., & Perry, S. (2004). *Maternity and women's health care* (8th ed., pp. 1040, 1043). St. Louis: Mosby.
Murray, S., & McKinney, E. *(2006). Foundations of maternal-newborn nursing* (4th ed.. pp. 371, 698-699). Philadelphia: W.B. Saunders.

REFERENCES

Lowdermilk, D., & Perry, S. (2006). *Maternity nursing* (7 ed.). St. Louis: Mosby.
Lowdermilk, D., & Perry, S. (2004). *Maternity and women's health care* (8 ed.). St. Louis: Mosby.
McKinney, E., James, S., Murray, S., & Ashwill, J. (2005). *Maternal-child nursing* (2nd ed.). St. Louis: W.B. Saunders.

Murray, S., & McKinney, E. (2006). *Foundations of maternal-newborn nursing* (4 ed.). St. Louis: W.B. Saunders.
National Council of State Boards of Nursing (2007). *2007 NCLEX-RN® detailed test plan.* Chicago: Author.
Wong, D., Perry, S., Hockenberry, M., et al. (2006). *Maternal child nursing care* (3rd ed.). St. Louis: Mosby.

Problems With Labor and Delivery

I. DYSTOCIA

A. Description
1. Dystocia is difficult **labor** that is prolonged or more painful.
2. Dystocia occurs because of problems caused by uterine contractions, the fetus, or the bones and tissues of the maternal pelvis.
3. Contractions may be hypotonic or hypertonic.
4. Fetus may be excessively large, malpositioned, or in an abnormal presentation.
5. Dystocia can result in maternal dehydration, infection, fetal injury, or death.

B. Assessment
1. Excessive abdominal pain
2. Abnormal contraction pattern
3. Fetal distress
4. Maternal or fetal tachycardia
5. Lack of progress in **labor**

C. Interventions
1. Assess fetal heart rate; monitor for fetal distress.
2. Monitor uterine contractions.
3. Monitor maternal temperature and heart rate.
4. Assist with pelvic examination, measurements, ultrasound, and other procedures.
5. Administer prophylactic antibiotics as prescribed to prevent infection.
6. Administer intravenous (IV) fluids as prescribed.
7. Monitor intake and output.
8. Assess for dehydration.
9. Instruct the mother in breathing techniques and relaxation exercises.
10. Perform fetal monitoring if oxytocin (Pitocin) is prescribed.
11. Monitor color of **amniotic fluid**.
12. Provide rest and comfort as with a normal **delivery**, such as back rubs and position changes.
13. Assess mother's fatigue and pain, and administer sedatives and pain medications as prescribed.
14. Assess for prolapse of the cord after rupture of the membranes.

II. PROLAPSED CORD

A. Description: The umbilical cord is displaced, between the presenting part and the amnion or protruding through the cervix, causing compression of the cord and compromising fetal circulation (Fig. 27-1).

B. Assessment
1. Mother has a feeling that something is coming through the **vagina**.
2. Umbilical cord is visible or palpable.
3. The fetal heart rate is irregular and slow.
4. Fetal heart monitor will show variable deceleration or bradycardia after rupture of the membranes.
5. If fetal hypoxia is severe, violent fetal activity may occur and then cease.

C. Interventions (Box 27-1)

III. PRECIPITOUS LABOR AND DELIVERY

A. Description: **Labor** lasting less than 3 hours
B. Interventions
1. Have a precipitous **delivery** tray available (hemostats, scissors, and a cord clamp).
2. Stay with the mother at all times.
3. Provide emotional support and keep the mother calm.
4. Encourage the mother to pant between contractions.
5. Prepare for rupturing membranes when the head crowns, if they are not already ruptured.

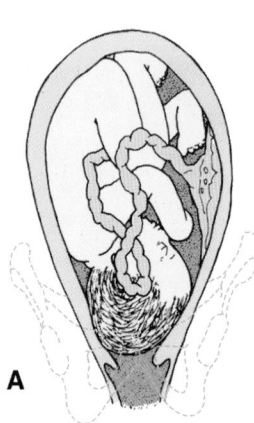 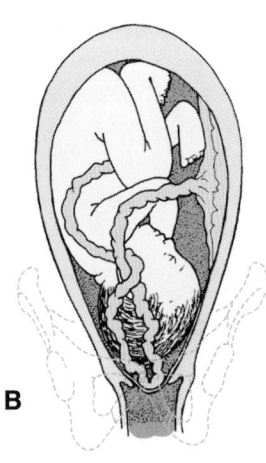 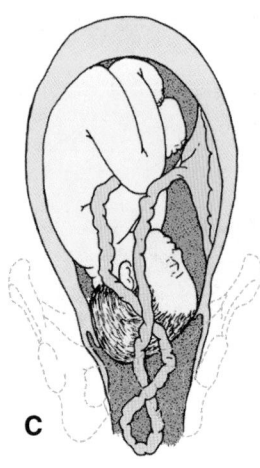 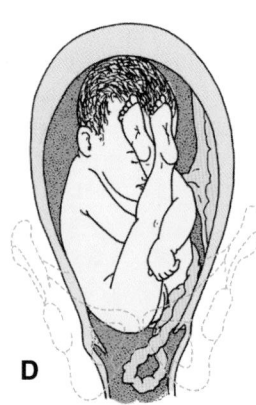

A **B** **C** **D**

FIG. 27-1 Prolapse of umbilical cord. Note the pressure of the presenting part on the umbilical cord, which endangers fetal circulation. **A,** Occult (hidden) prolapse of cord. **B,** Complete prolapse of cord. Note that membranes are intact. **C,** Cord presenting in front of the fetal head may be seen in the vagina. **D,** Frank breech presentation with prolapsed cord. (From Lowdermilk, D., & Perry, S. [2004]. *Maternity and women's health care* [8th ed.]. St. Louis: Mosby.)

BOX 27-1

Interventions: Cord Prolapse

Relieve cord pressure immediately.
Place the woman into the extreme Trendelenburg or a modified Sims' position, or a knee-chest position.
Elevate the fetal presenting part that is lying on the cord by applying finger pressure with a sterile gloved hand.
Do not attempt to push the cord into the uterus.
Monitor the fetal heart rate.
Assess the fetus for hypoxia.
Administer oxygen by face mask to the mother.
Prepare for emergency cesarean birth.

---

6. Do not try to keep the fetus from being delivered.
7. If **delivery** is necessary before the arrival of the health care provider, do the following:
   a. Apply gentle pressure to the fetal head upward toward the **vagina** to prevent damage to the fetal head and vaginal lacerations.
   b. Support the **infant's** body during **delivery**.
   c. Deliver the **infant** between contractions, checking for the cord around the neck.
   d. Use restitution to deliver the posterior shoulder.
   e. Use gentle downward pressure to move the anterior shoulder under the pubic symphysis.
   f. Clear the **infant's** mouth.
   g. Dry and cover the **infant** to keep the body warm.
   h. Allow the **placenta** to separate naturally.
   i. Place the **infant** on the mother's abdomen or breast to induce uterine contractions.

IV. PRETERM LABOR
A. Description
   1. Preterm **labor** occurs after the twentieth week but before the thirty-seventh week of gestation.
   2. Contractions occur more frequent than every 10 minutes, last 30 seconds or longer, and persist.
   3. Preterm **labor** may be associated with infection, such as a urinary tract infection (UTI).
B. Assessment
   1. Uterine contractions (painful or painless)
   2. Abdominal cramping (may be accompanied by diarrhea)
   3. Low back pain
   4. Pelvic pressure or heaviness
   5. Change in the character and amount of usual discharge; may be thicker or thinner, bloody, brown or colorless, odorous
   6. Rupture of amniotic membranes
C. Interventions
   1. Focus on stopping the **labor**: Identify and treat infection, restrict activity, and ensure hydration.
   2. Maintain bed rest and a lateral position.
   3. Monitor fetal status.
   4. Administer fluids.
   5. Administer medications as prescribed and monitor for side effects of tocolytics (see Table 31-1 for a description of medications used to treat preterm labor).

V. PREMATURE RUPTURE OF MEMBRANES
A. Description
   1. Premature rupture of the membranes (PROM) refers to the spontaneous rupture of the amniotic membrane before the onset of **labor**.

2. Gestational age usually determines the plan and intervention.
3. When the rupture of membranes is before term and **delivery** will be delayed, infection becomes a risk.
B. Assessment
   1. Evidence of fluid pooling in vaginal vault; nitrazine test positive
   2. Amount, color, consistency and odor of fluid
   3. Vital signs; elevated temperature may indicate presence of infection.
   4. Fetal monitoring; tachycardia may indicate infection.
C. Interventions
   1. Assist with tests to assess gestational age.
   2. Monitor maternal and fetus status for signs of compromise or infection.
   3. Administer antibiotics as ordered.

VI. RUPTURE OF UTERUS
A. Description
   1. Complete or incomplete separation of the uterine tissue as a result of a tear in the wall of the **uterus** from the stress of **labor**
   2. Complete: Direct communication between the uterine and peritoneal cavities
   3. Incomplete: Rupture into the peritoneum covering the **uterus** but not into the peritoneal cavity
   4. Manifestations vary with the degree of rupture.
B. Assessment
   1. Abdominal pain or tenderness
   2. Chest pain
   3. Contractions may stop or fail to progress

4. Rigid abdomen
5. Absent fetal heart rate
6. Signs of maternal shock
7. Fetus palpated outside the **uterus** (complete rupture)
C. Interventions
   1. Monitor for and treat signs of shock (administer oxygen, IV fluids, and blood products).
   2. Prepare client for cesarean section or hysterotomy with hysterectomy.
   3. Provide emotional support for the client and partner.

VII. PLACENTA PREVIA
A. Description
   1. **Placenta** previa is an improperly implanted **placenta** in the lower uterine segment near or over the internal cervical os (Fig. 27-2).
   2. Total: The internal cervical os is covered entirely by the **placenta** when the cervix is dilated fully.
   3. Partial: The lower border of the **placenta** is within 3 cm of the internal cervical os but does not fully cover it.
   4. Marginal: The **placenta** is implanted in the lower **uterus** but its lower border is greater than 3 cm from the internal cervical os.
   5. Management depends on the classification of the previa and gestational age of the fetus.
B. Assessment
   1. Sudden onset of painless, bright red vaginal bleeding occurs in the last half of pregnancy.
   2. **Uterus** is soft, relaxed, and nontender.
   3. Fundal height may be more than expected for gestational age.

Marginal   Partial   Total

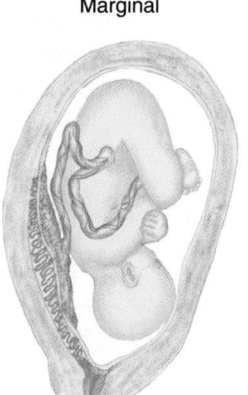 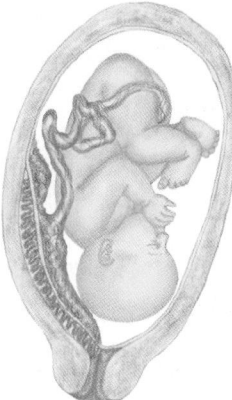 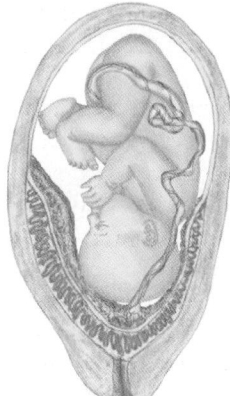

Placenta is implanted in lower uterus but its lower border is >3 cm from internal cervical os.

Lower border of placenta is within 3 cm of internal cervical os but does not fully cover it.

Placenta completely covers internal cervical os.

FIG. 27-2 The three classifications of placenta previa. (From Murray, S. & McKinney, E. [2006]. *Foundations of maternal-newborn nursing* [4th ed.]. Philadelphia: W.B. Saunders.)

▲ C. Interventions
1. Monitor maternal vital signs, fetal heart rate, and fetal activity.
2. Prepare for ultrasound to confirm diagnosis.
3. Vaginal examinations or any other actions that would stimulate uterine activity are avoided.
4. Maintain bed rest in a side-lying position as prescribed.
5. Monitor amount of bleeding (treat signs of shock).
6. Administer IV fluids, blood products, or tocolytic medications as prescribed.
7. If bleeding is heavy, a cesarean section may be performed.

▲ VIII. ABRUPTIO PLACENTAE
A. Description: Premature separation of the **placenta** from the uterine wall after the twentieth week of gestation and before the fetus is delivered (Fig. 27-3)
▲ B. Assessment
1. Dark red vaginal bleeding; however, if the bleed is high in the **uterus** or minimal, there can be an absence of visible blood.
2. Uterine pain and/or tenderness
3. Uterine rigidity
4. Severe abdominal pain
5. Signs of fetal distress
6. Signs of maternal shock if bleeding is excessive
▲ C. Interventions
1. Monitor maternal vital signs and fetal heart rate.
2. Assess for excessive vaginal bleeding, abdominal pain, and increase in fundal height.
3. Maintain bed rest; administer oxygen, IV fluids, and blood products as prescribed.
4. Place in Trendelenburg's position if indicated to decrease the pressure of the fetus on the **placenta**, or place in the lateral position with

the head of the bed flat if hypovolemic shock occurs.
5. Monitor and report any uterine activity.
6. Prepare for the **delivery** of the fetus as quickly as possible, with vaginal **delivery** preferable if the fetus is healthy and stable and the presenting part is in the pelvis; emergency cesarean section is performed if the fetus is alive but shows signs of distress.
7. Monitor for signs of disseminated intravascular coagulation in the postpartum period.

IX. PLACENTAL ABNORMALITIES
A. Description: **Placenta** accreta is an abnormally adherent **placenta**; **placenta** increta occurs when the **placenta** penetrates the uterine muscle itself; **placenta** percreta occurs when the **placenta** goes all the way through the **uterus**.
B. Assessment: May cause hemorrhage immediately after birth because the **placenta** does not separate cleanly
C. Intervention
1. Monitor for hemorrhage and shock.
2. Prepare client for a hysterectomy if a large portion of the **placenta** is abnormally adherent. ▲

X. UTERINE INVERSION
A. Description
1. **Uterus** completely or partly turns inside out.
2. This usually occurs during **delivery** or after **delivery** of the **placenta**.
B. Assessment
1. A depression in the fundal area of the **uterus** is noted.
2. The interior of the **uterus** may be seen through the cervix or protruding through the **vagina**.
3. The woman has severe pain.

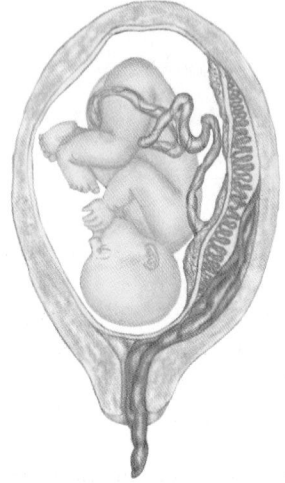 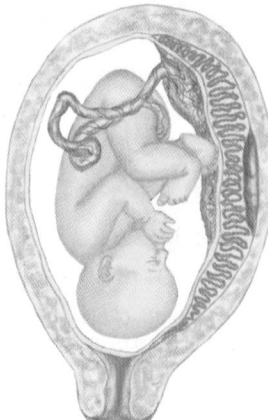 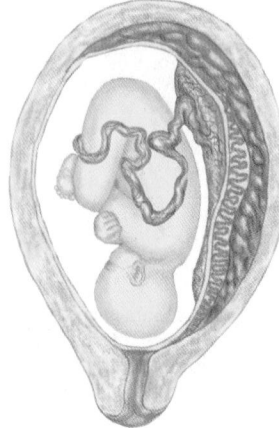

Marginal abruption with external bleeding

Partial abruption with concealed bleeding

Complete abruption with concealed bleeding

FIG. 27-3 Types of abruptio placentae. (From Murray, S. & McKinney, E. [2006]. *Foundations of maternal-newborn nursing* [4th ed.]. Philadelphia: W.B. Saunders.)

4. Hemorrhage is evident.

5. The woman shows signs of shock.

C. Interventions

1. Monitor for hemorrhage and signs of shock and treat shock.

2. Prepare the client for a return of the **uterus** to the correct position via the **vagina**; if unsuccessful, laparotomy with replacement is done.

XI. AMNIOTIC FLUID EMBOLISM

A. Description

1. **Amniotic fluid** embolism is the escape of **amniotic fluid** into the maternal circulation.

2. The debris-containing **amniotic fluid** deposits in the pulmonary arterioles and is usually fatal to the mother.

B. Assessment

1. Abrupt onset of respiratory distress and chest pain

2. Cyanosis

3. Seizures

4. Heart failure and pulmonary edema

5. Fetal bradycardia and distress if **delivery** has not occurred at the time of the embolism

C. Interventions

1. Institute emergency measures to maintain life.

2. Administer oxygen at 8 to 10 L/min by face mask or resuscitation bag delivering 100% oxygen.

3. Prepare for intubation and mechanical ventilation.

4. Position the woman on her side.

5. Administer IV fluids, blood products, and medications to correct coagulation failure.

6. Monitor fetal status.

7. Prepare for emergency **delivery** once the woman is stabilized.

8. Provide emotional support to the woman, partner, and family.

XII. SUPINE HYPOTENSIVE SYNDROME (VENA CAVA SYNDROME)

A. Description

1. Supine hypotensive syndrome (also known as vena cava syndrome) occurs when the venous return to the heart is impaired by the weight of the **uterus**.

2. The syndrome results in partial occlusion of the vena cava and descending aorta and in reduced cardiac return, cardiac output, and blood pressure.

B. Assessment

1. Faintness, light-headedness, dizziness

2. Hypotension

3. Fetal distress

C. Interventions

1. Position the client in a left lateral recumbent position to shift the weight of the fetus off the inferior vena cava.

2. Monitor vital signs and fetal heart rate.

XIII. FETAL DISTRESS

A. Assessment

1. Fetal heart rate less than 120 or greater than 160 beats/min

2. Meconium-stained **amniotic fluid**

3. Fetal hyperactivity

4. Progressive decrease in baseline variability

5. Severe variable decelerations

6. Late decelerations

B. Interventions

1. Place the mother in a lateral position as indicated.

2. Administer oxygen at 8 to 10 L/min via face mask.

3. Discontinue oxytocin (Pitocin) if infusing.

4. Monitor maternal and fetal status.

5. Prepare for emergency cesarean section.

XIV. INTRAUTERINE FETAL DEMISE

A. Assessment

1. Loss of fetal movement

2. Absence of fetal heart tones

3. Disseminated intravascular coagulopathy (DIC) screen (monitor for coagulation abnormalities because DIC is a complication related to intrauterine fetal demise)

4. Low hemoglobin and hematocrit; low platelet count; prolonged bleeding and clotting time

5. Bleeding from puncture sites (could be indicative of DIC)

B. Interventions

1. Encourage client and her family to verbalize feelings; provide emotional support.

2. Allow client choices relating to **labor** and **delivery.**

3. Administer blood and blood products as ordered if DIC occurs.

PRACTICE QUESTIONS

1. A labor and delivery room nurse has just received report on four clients. The nurse should assess which client first?

   1. A primiparous client in the active stage of labor

   2. A multiparous client who was admitted for induction of labor

   3. A client who is not contracting, but has suspected premature rupture of the membranes

   4. A client who has just received an IV loading dose of magnesium sulfate to stop preterm labor

2. A nurse is reviewing the physician's orders for a client admitted for premature rupture of the membranes. Gestational age of the fetus is determined to be 37 weeks. Which physician's order should the nurse question?

1. Perform a vaginal examination every shift.
2. Monitor maternal vital signs every 4 hours.
3. Monitor fetal heart rate (FHR) continuously.
4. Administer ampicillin 1 gm as an intravenous piggyback (IVPB) every 6 hours.

3. A nurse is providing emergency measures to a client in labor who has been diagnosed with a prolapsed cord. The mother becomes anxious and frightened and says to the nurse, "Why are all of these people in here? Is my baby going to be all right?" Which of the following nursing diagnoses would be most appropriate for this client at this time?
   1. Fear
   2. Fatigue
   3. Powerlessness
   4. Ineffective coping

4. A nurse has developed a plan of care for a client experiencing dystocia and includes several nursing interventions in the plan of care. The nurse prioritizes the plan of care and selects which intervention as the highest priority?
   1. Providing comfort measures
   2. Monitoring the fetal heart rate
   3. Changing the client's position frequently
   4. Keeping the significant other informed of the progress of the labor

5. Fetal distress is occurring with a laboring client. As the nurse prepares the client for a cesarean birth, what other intervention should be done?
   1. Slow the intravenous (IV) flow rate.
   2. Place the client in a high Fowler's position.
   3. Continue the oxytocin (Pitocin) drip if infusing.
   4. Administer oxygen at 8 to 10 L/min via face mask.

6. A nurse in the postpartum unit is caring for a client who has just delivered a newborn infant following a pregnancy with a placenta previa. The nurse reviews the plan of care and prepares to monitor the client for which of the following risks associated with placenta previa?
   1. Infection
   2. Hemorrhage
   3. Chronic hypertension
   4. Disseminated intravascular coagulation

7. A nurse in a labor room is performing a vaginal assessment on a pregnant client in labor. The nurse notes the presence of the umbilical cord protruding from the vagina. Which of the following is the initial nursing action?
   1. Gently push the cord into the vagina.
   2. Place the client in Trendelenburg's position.
   3. Find the closest telephone and page the physician stat.
   4. Call the delivery room to notify the staff that the client will be transported immediately.

8. A maternity nurse is caring for a client with abruptio placentae and is monitoring the client for disseminated intravascular coagulopathy. Which assessment finding is least likely to be associated with disseminated intravascular coagulation?
   1. Prolonged clotting times
   2. Decreased platelet count
   3. Swelling of the calf of one leg
   4. Petechiae, oozing from injection sites, and hematuria

9. A nurse is assessing a pregnant client in the second trimester of pregnancy who was admitted to the maternity unit with a suspected diagnosis of abruptio placentae. Which of the following assessment findings would the nurse expect to note if this condition is present?
   1. A soft abdomen
   2. Uterine tenderness
   3. Absence of abdominal pain
   4. Painless, bright red vaginal bleeding

10. A maternity nurse is preparing for the admission of a client in the third trimester of pregnancy who is experiencing vaginal bleeding and has a suspected diagnosis of placenta previa. The nurse reviews the physician's orders and would question which order?
    1. Prepare the client for an ultrasound.
    2. Obtain equipment for a manual pelvic examination.
    3. Prepare to draw a hemoglobin and hematocrit blood sample.
    4. Obtain equipment for external electronic fetal heart rate monitoring.

11. An ultrasound is performed on a client at term gestation who is experiencing moderate vaginal bleeding. The results of the ultrasound indicate that abruptio placentae is present. Based on these findings, the nurse would prepare the client for:
    1. Delivery of the fetus
    2. Strict monitoring of intake and output
    3. Complete bed rest for the remainder of the pregnancy
    4. The need for weekly monitoring of coagulation studies until the time of delivery

12. A nurse in a labor room is assisting with the vaginal delivery of a newborn infant. The nurse would monitor the client closely for the risk of uterine rupture if which of the following occurred?
    1. Forceps delivery
    2. Schultz presentation
    3. Hypotonic contractions
    4. Weak bearing-down efforts

13. A clinic nurse is performing a prenatal assessment on a pregnant client. The nurse would implement teaching related to the risk of abruptio placentae if which of the following information was obtained on assessment?
    1. The client is 28 years of age.
    2. This is the second pregnancy.

3. The client has a history of hypertension.
4. The client performs moderate exercise on a regular daily schedule.

14. A nurse is performing an initial assessment on a client who has just been told that a pregnancy test is positive. Which assessment finding would indicate that the client is at risk for preterm labor?
    1. The client is a 35-year-old primigravida.
    2. The client has a history of cardiac disease.
    3. The client's hemoglobin level is 13.5 g/dL.
    4. The client is a 20-year-old primigravida of average weight and height.

15. A nurse is monitoring a client who is in the active stage of labor. The client has been experiencing contractions that are short, irregular, and weak. The nurse documents that the client is experiencing which type of labor dystocia?
    1. Hypotonic
    2. Precipitous
    3. Hypertonic
    4. Preterm labor

16. A nurse is caring for a client who is experiencing a precipitous birth. The nurse is waiting for the physician to arrive. When the infant's head crowns, the nurse would instruct the client to:
    1. Bear down.
    2. Hold her breath.
    3. Breathe rapidly (pant).
    4. Push with each contraction.

17. After a precipitous delivery, a nurse notes that the new mother is passive and only touches her newborn infant briefly with her fingertips. The nurse should do which of the following to help the woman process what has happened?
    1. Encourage the mother to breast-feed soon after birth.
    2. Support the mother in her reaction to the newborn infant.
    3. Tell the mother that it is important to hold the newborn infant.
    4. Document a complete account of the mother's reaction on the birth record.

18. A nurse in a labor room is monitoring a client with dysfunctional labor for signs of fetal or maternal compromise. Which of the following assessment findings would alert the nurse to a compromise?
    1. Maternal fatigue
    2. Coordinated uterine contractions
    3. Progressive changes in the cervix
    4. Persistent nonreassuring fetal heart rate

19. A nurse is assigned to care for a client with hypotonic uterine dysfunction and signs of a slowing labor. The nurse is reviewing the physician's orders and would expect to note which of the following prescribed treatments for this condition?
    1. Increased hydration
    2. Oxytocin (Pitocin) infusion
    3. Medication that will provide sedation
    4. Administration of a tocolytic medication

20. A nurse in a labor room is preparing to care for a client with hypertonic uterine dysfunction. The nurse is told that the client is experiencing uncoordinated contractions that are erratic in their frequency, duration, and intensity. The priority nursing intervention in caring for the client is to:
    1. Provide pain relief measures.
    2. Prepare the client for an amniotomy.
    3. Promote ambulation every 30 minutes.
    4. Monitor the oxytocin (Pitocin) infusion closely.

ALTERNATE ITEM FORMAT: MULTIPLE RESPONSE

A nurse is performing an assessment on a client diagnosed with placenta previa. Which of these assessment findings would the nurse expect to note? Select all that apply.
❑ 1. Uterine rigidity
❑ 2. Uterine tenderness
❑ 3. Severe abdominal pain
❑ 4. Bright red vaginal bleeding
❑ 5. Soft, relaxed, nontender uterus
❑ 6. Fundal height may be greater than expected for gestational age

ANSWERS

1. **4**
Rationale: Magnesium sulfate is a central nervous system (CNS) depressant and the client could experience adverse effects that includes depressed respiratory rate (below 12 breaths/min), severe hypotension, and absent deep tendon reflexes (DTRs). This client should be seen before the clients in options 1, 2, and 3 because these clients conditions represent stable ones.
Test-Taking Strategy: Note the strategic word *first.* The client receiving a loading dose of magnesium sulfate should be seen first because of the adverse effects associated with this medication. The primiparous client in active labor, the client who may have premature rupture of the membranes, and the multiparous client admitted for an induction are stable clients and can be assessed after the client receiving the loading dose of magnesium sulfate has been assessed. Review the adverse effects of magnesium sulfate if you had difficulty with this question.
Level of Cognitive Ability: Analysis
Client Needs: Safe and Effective Care Environment
Integrated Process: Nursing Process—assessment
Content Area: Delegating/Prioritizing

Reference: Lowdermilk, D., & Perry, S. (2006). *Maternity nursing* (7th ed., p. 778). St. Louis: Mosby.

2. 1
Rationale: Vaginal examinations should not be done routinely on a client with premature rupture of the membranes because of the risk of infection. The nurse would expect to administer an antibiotic, monitor maternal vital signs, and monitor the FHR.
Test-Taking Strategy: Note the strategic word *question*. This word indicates the activity that the nurse should not implement without clarification. Options 2, 3, and 4 are expected activities for the nurse to perform for a client with premature rupture of the membranes. Performing a vaginal examination every shift should not be done on a client with premature rupture of the membranes, so the nurse would question this order. Review care for the client with premature rupture of the membranes if you had difficulty with this question.
Level of Cognitive Ability: Analysis
Client Needs: Physiological Integrity
Integrated Process: Nursing Process—implementation
Content Area: Maternity—intrapartum
Reference: Lowdermilk, D., & Perry, S. (2006). *Maternity nursing* (7th ed., p. 782). St. Louis: Mosby.

3. 1
Rationale: The mother is anxious and frightened, and the most appropriate nursing diagnosis for the client at this time is fear. No data in the question support a nursing diagnosis of powerlessness, ineffective coping, or fatigue, although these nursing diagnoses may be considered for this client at some point during the hospitalization experience.
Test-Taking Strategy: When answering questions related to nursing diagnosis, focus specifically on the data provided in the question. Note the relationship between the words *frightened* in the question and *fear* in the correct option. Review maternal psychosocial responses when a prolapsed cord occurs if you had difficulty with this question.
Level of Cognitive Ability: Analysis
Client Needs: Psychosocial Integrity
Integrated Process: Nursing Process—analysis
Content Area: Maternity—intrapartum
References: Lowdermilk, D., & Perry, S. (2006). *Maternity nursing* (7th ed., p. 811). St. Louis: Mosby.
Murray, S., & McKinney, E. (2006). *Foundations of maternal-newborn nursing* (4th ed., pp. 340, 724-726). Philadelphia: W.B. Saunders.

4. 2
Rationale: The priority is to monitor the fetal heart rate. Although providing comfort measures, changing the client's position frequently, and keeping the significant other informed of the progress of the labor are components of the plan of care, the fetal status would be the priority.
Test-Taking Strategy: Note the strategic words *highest priority*. Use Maslow's Hierarchy of Needs theory and the ABCs—airway, breathing, and circulation—to assist in answering the question. Review priority nursing interventions for the client with dystocia if you had difficulty with this question.
Level of Cognitive Ability: Application
Client Needs: Physiological Integrity

Integrated Process: Nursing Process—planning
Content Area: Maternity—intrapartum
References: Murray, S., & McKinney, E. (2006). *Foundations of maternal-newborn nursing* (4th ed., p. 698). Philadelphia: W.B. Saunders.
Wong, D., Perry, S., Hockenberry, M., et al. (2006). *Maternal child nursing care* (3rd ed., p. 467). St. Louis: Mosby.

5. 4
Rationale: Oxygen is administered at 8 to 10 L/min via face mask to optimize oxygenation of the circulating blood. Option 1 is incorrect because the IV infusion should be increased to increase the maternal blood volume. Option 2 is incorrect because the client is placed in the lateral position with her legs raised to increase maternal blood volume and improve fetal perfusion. Option 3 is incorrect because the oxytocin stimulation of the uterus is discontinued if fetal heart rate patterns change for any reason.
Test-Taking Strategy: Use the ABCs, airway, breathing, and circulation. Oxygen is the only option that will improve cardiac output, thus improving perfusion to the fetus. The other options will not improve perfusion to the fetus. Review care for the laboring client experiencing fetal distress if you had difficulty with this question.
Level of Cognitive Ability: Application
Client Needs: Physiological Integrity
Integrated Process: Nursing Process—implementation
Content Area: Maternity—intrapartum
Reference: Lowdermilk, D., & Perry, S. (2006). *Maternity nursing* (7th ed., p. 386). St. Louis: Mosby.

6. 2
Rationale: Because the placenta is implanted in the lower uterine segment, which does not contain the same intertwining musculature as the fundus of the uterus, this site is more prone to bleeding. Options 1, 3, and 4 are not risks that are related specifically to placenta previa.
Test-Taking Strategy: Use the process of elimination, focusing on the subject of the question, placenta previa. Recalling that bleeding is a primary concern in this client will direct you easily to option 2. Review the complications associated with placenta previa if you had difficulty with this question.
Level of Cognitive Ability: Analysis
Client Needs: Physiological Integrity
Integrated Process: Nursing Process—assessment
Content Area: Maternity—postpartum
References: Murray, S., & McKinney, E. (2006). *Foundations of maternal-newborn nursing* (4th ed., p. 634). Philadelphia: W.B. Saunders.
Wong, D., Perry, S., Hockenberry, M., et al. (2006). *Maternal child nursing care.* (3rd ed., p. 402). St. Louis: Mosby.

7. 2
Rationale: When cord prolapse occurs, prompt actions are taken to relieve cord compression and increase fetal oxygenation. The client should be positioned with the hips higher than the head to shift the fetal presenting part toward the diaphragm. The nurse should push the call light to summon help, and other staff members should call the physician and notify the delivery room. If the cord is protruding from the

vagina, no attempt should be made to replace it because to do so could traumatize it and further reduce blood flow. The examiner, however, may place a gloved hand into the vagina and hold the presenting part off the umbilical cord. Oxygen at 8 to 10 L/min by face mask is administered to the client to increase fetal oxygenation.

Test-Taking Strategy: Use the process of elimination, noting the strategic words *umbilical cord protruding from the vagina.* Options 3 and 4 can be eliminated first because these actions delay necessary and immediate treatment. Knowledge that the cord should not be pushed back into the vagina will easily direct you to option 2. Review priority nursing measures for prolapsed cord if you had difficulty with this question.

Level of Cognitive Ability: Application
Client Needs: Physiological Integrity
Integrated Process: Nursing Process—implementation
Content Area: Maternity—intrapartum
References: Lowdermilk, D., & Perry, S. (2006). *Maternity nursing* (7th ed., p. 811). St. Louis: Mosby.
Murray, S., & McKinney, E. (2006). *Foundations of maternal-newborn nursing* (4th ed., p. 725). Philadelphia: W.B. Saunders.

8. **3**

Rationale: Disseminated intravascular coagulation (DIC) is a state of diffuse clotting in which clotting factors are consumed, leading to widespread bleeding. Platelets are decreased because they are consumed by the process, coagulation studies show no clot formation (and are thus normal to prolonged), and fibrin plugs may clog the microvasculature diffusely, rather than in an isolated area. The presence of petechiae, oozing from injection sites, and hematuria are signs associated with DIC. Swelling and pain in the calf of one leg are more likely to be associated with thrombophlebitis.

Test-Taking Strategy: Use the process of elimination. Note the strategic words *least likely* in the event query. Knowledge that DIC is a widespread problem rather than a localized one will direct you easily to option 3. Review the signs related to DIC if you had difficulty with this question.

Level of Cognitive Ability: Analysis
Client Needs: Physiological Integrity
Integrated Process: Nursing Process—assessment
Content Area: Maternity—intrapartum
References: Mattson, S., & Smith, J. (2004). *Core curriculum for maternal-newborn nursing* (4th ed., p. 838). Philadelphia: W.B. Saunders.
Murray, S., & McKinney, E. (2006). *Foundations of maternal-newborn nursing* (4th ed., p. 626). Philadelphia: W.B. Saunders.

9. **2**

Rationale: Painless, bright red vaginal bleeding in the second or third trimester of pregnancy is a sign of placenta previa. In abruptio placentae, acute abdominal pain is present. Uterine tenderness accompanies placental abruption, especially with a central abruption and trapped blood behind the placenta. The abdomen will feel hard and board-like on palpation as the blood penetrates the myometrium and causes uterine irritability. Observation of the fetal monitor often reveals increased uterine resting tone, caused by failure of the uterus to relax in an attempt to constrict blood vessels and control bleeding.

Test-Taking Strategy: Use the process of elimination. Remember that the difference between placenta previa and abruptio placentae involves the presence of uterine pain and tenderness with an abruption, as opposed to painless bleeding with a previa. Review the signs of abruptio placentae if you had difficulty with this question.

Level of Cognitive Ability: Analysis
Client Needs: Physiological Integrity
Integrated Process: Nursing Process—assessment
Content Area: Maternity—intrapartum
References: Lowdermilk, D., & Perry, S. (2006). *Maternity nursing* (7th ed., p. 753). St. Louis: Mosby.
Lowdermilk, D., & Perry, S. (2004). *Maternity and women's health care* (8th ed., p. 876). St. Louis: Mosby.

10. **2**

Rationale: Manual pelvic examinations are contraindicated when vaginal bleeding is apparent in the third trimester until a diagnosis is made and placenta previa is ruled out. Digital examination of the cervix can lead to maternal and fetal hemorrhage. A diagnosis of placenta previa is made by ultrasound. The hemoglobin and hematocrit levels are monitored, and external electronic fetal heart rate monitoring is initiated. Electronic fetal monitoring (external) is crucial in evaluating the status of the fetus who is at risk for severe hypoxia.

Test-Taking Strategy: Use the process of elimination and knowledge of the pathophysiology associated with placenta previa. Note the strategic words *would question which order* in the event query. Also, note that option 2 is the only procedure that is invasive to the pregnancy and endangers the physiological safety of the client and the fetus. Review care for the client with placenta previa if you had difficulty with this question.

Level of Cognitive Ability: Application
Client Needs: Physiological Integrity
Integrated Process: Nursing Process—implementation
Content Area: Maternity—intrapartum
References: Lowdermilk, D., & Perry, S. (2004). *Maternity and women's health care* (8th ed., pp. 872, 874-875). St. Louis: Mosby.
Wong, D., Perry, S., Hockenberry, M., et al. (2006). *Maternal child nursing care* (3rd ed., p. 402). St. Louis: Mosby.

11. **1**

Rationale: The goal of management in abruptio placentae is to control the hemorrhage and deliver the fetus as soon as possible. Delivery is the treatment of choice if the fetus is at term gestation or if the bleeding is moderate to severe and the mother or fetus is in jeopardy. Because delivery of the fetus is necessary, options 2, 3, and 4 are incorrect regarding management of the client with abruptio placentae.

Test-Taking Strategy: Use the process of elimination and knowledge regarding the management of abruptio placentae to answer the question. Note the strategic words *term gestation* and *moderate vaginal bleeding*. Knowing that the goal is to deliver the fetus will direct you easily to option 1. If you had difficulty with this question or are unfamiliar with the management of abruptio placentae, review this content.

Level of Cognitive Ability: Application

Client Needs: Physiological Integrity
Integrated Process: Nursing Process—planning
Content Area: Maternity—intrapartum
References: Lowdermilk, D., & Perry, S. (2004). *Maternity and women's health care* (8th ed., p. 877). St. Louis: Mosby.
Murray, S., & McKinney, E. (2006). *Foundations of maternal-newborn nursing* (4th ed., pp. 638-639). Philadelphia: W.B. Saunders.
Wong, D., Perry, S., Hockenberry, M., et al. (2006). *Maternal child nursing care* (3rd ed., p. 405). St. Louis: Mosby.

12. **1**
Rationale: Excessive fundal pressure, forceps delivery, violent bearing-down efforts, tumultuous labor, and shoulder dystocia can place a client at risk for traumatic uterine rupture. Hypotonic contractions and weak bearing-down efforts do not add to the risk of rupture because they do not add to the stress on the uterine wall. Schultz presentation is the expulsion of the placenta with the fetal side presenting first and is not associated with uterine rupture.
Test-Taking Strategy: Use the process of elimination. Read each option carefully, and select the option that provides an additional source of pressure to the uterus and would be most likely to add to the risk of rupturing or "tearing" the uterus. Option 1 is the only option that would provide an additional source of pressure to the uterus. Review the risks associated with uterine rupture if you had difficulty with this question.
Level of Cognitive Ability: Analysis
Client Needs: Physiological Integrity
Integrated Process: Nursing Process—assessment
Content Area: Maternity—intrapartum
References: Lowdermilk, D., & Perry, S. (2006). *Maternity nursing* (7th ed., p. 812). St. Louis: Mosby.
McKinney, E., James, S., Murray, S., & Ashwill, J. (2005). *Maternal-child nursing* (2nd ed., p. 697). St. Louis: W.B. Saunders.

13. **3**
Rationale: Abruptio placentae is associated with conditions characterized by poor uteroplacental circulation, such as hypertension, smoking, and alcohol or cocaine abuse. The condition also is associated with physical and mechanical factors, such as overdistention of the uterus, which occurs with multiple gestation or polyhydramnios. In addition, a short umbilical cord, physical trauma, and increased maternal age and parity are risk factors.
Test-Taking Strategy: Use the process of elimination, focusing on the risk factors associated with abruptio placentae. Eliminate options 1, 2, and 4 because they are not situations that would present a risk for this condition. Review the risk factors associated with abruptio placentae if you had difficulty with this question.
Level of Cognitive Ability: Analysis
Client Needs: Health Promotion and Maintenance
Integrated Process: Nursing Process—assessment
Content Area: Maternity—antepartum
Reference: Wong, D., Perry, S., Hockenberry, M., et al. (2006). *Maternal child nursing care.* (3rd ed., p. 404). St. Louis: Mosby.

14. **2**
Rationale: Several factors are associated with preterm labor. These include a history of medical conditions, present and past obstetric problems, social and environmental factors, and demographic factors such as race and age. Other risk factors include a multifetal pregnancy, which contributes to overdistention of the uterus, anemia, which decreases oxygen supply to the uterus, and age younger 18 years or first pregnancy older than the age of 40.
Test-Taking Strategy: Use the process of elimination and note that option 2 is the only option that identifies an abnormal condition. Options 1, 3, and 4 are average and normal findings. Review the risk factors for preterm labor if you had difficulty with this question.
Level of Cognitive Ability: Analysis
Client Needs: Physiological Integrity
Integrated Process: Nursing Process—assessment
Content Area: Maternity—antepartum
References: Murray, S., & McKinney, E. (2006). *Foundations of maternal-newborn nursing* (4th ed., pp. 710-711). Philadelphia: W.B. Saunders.
Wong, D., Perry, S., Hockenberry, M., et al. (2006). *Maternal child nursing care* (3rd ed., p. 216). St. Louis: Mosby.

15. **1**
Rationale: Hypotonic labor contractions are short, irregular, and weak and usually occur during the active phase of labor. Hypertonic dystocia usually occurs during the latent phase of labor and contractions would be painful, frequent, and usually uncoordinated. Precipitous labor is that which lasts in its entirety for 3 hours or less. Preterm labor is the onset of labor after 20 weeks of gestation and before the thirty-seventh week of gestation.
Test-Taking Strategy: Use the process of elimination. Note the relationship between the words *short, irregular, and weak* in the question and *hypotonic* in the correct option. If you are unfamiliar with dysfunctional labor (dystocia), review this content.
Level of Cognitive Ability: Application
Client Needs: Physiological Integrity
Integrated Process: Communication and Documentation
Content Area: Maternity—intrapartum
Reference: Murray, S., & McKinney, E. (2006). *Foundations of maternal-newborn nursing* (4th ed., pp. 698-699). Philadelphia: W.B. Saunders.

16. **3**
Rationale: During a precipitous birth, when the infant's head crowns, the nurse instructs the client to breathe rapidly to decrease the urge to push. The client is not instructed to push or bear down. Holding the breath decreases the amount of oxygen to the mother and to the fetus.
Test-Taking Strategy: Use the process of elimination, focusing on the strategic words *precipitous birth*. Option 2 can be eliminated first because this action decreases the amount of oxygen to the mother and to the fetus. Next, eliminate options 1 and 4 because they are comparative or alike. Review the nursing interventions in the care of a client experiencing a precipitous birth if you had difficulty with this question.

Level of Cognitive Ability: Application
Client Needs: Physiological Integrity
Integrated Process: Nursing Process—implementation
Content Area: Maternity—intrapartum
Reference: Murray, S., & McKinney, E. (2006). *Foundations of maternal-newborn nursing* (4th ed., p. 706). Philadelphia: W.B. Saunders.

17. 2
Rationale: Women who have experienced precipitous labor and delivery often describe feelings of disbelief that their labor progressed so rapidly. To assist the client to process what has happened, the best option is to support the client in her reaction to the newborn infant. Options 1, 3, and 4 do not acknowledge the client's feelings.
Test-Taking Strategy: Use therapeutic communication techniques. Option 2 is the only option that acknowledges the mother's feelings. If you had difficulty with this question, review these techniques and care to the mother following a precipitous birth.
Level of Cognitive Ability: Application
Client Needs: Psychosocial Integrity
Integrated Process: Caring
Content Area: Maternity—postpartum
References: Lowdermilk, D., & Perry, S. (2006). *Maternity nursing* (7th ed., p. 784). St. Louis: Mosby.
Wong, D., Perry, S., Hockenberry, M., et al. (2006). *Maternal child nursing care.* (3rd ed., p. 563). St. Louis: Mosby.

18. 4
Rationale: Signs of a fetal or maternal compromise include a persistent, nonreassuring fetal heart rate, fetal acidosis, and the passage of meconium. Maternal exhaustion and infection can occur if the labor is prolonged but do not indicate fetal or maternal compromise. Progressive changes in the cervix and coordinated uterine contractions are a reassuring pattern in labor.
Test-Taking Strategy: Focus on the subject of the question, signs of fetal or maternal compromise. Use the process of elimination, noting that options 1, 2, and 3 are normal expectations during labor. Review the assessment findings that indicate fetal or maternal compromise if you had difficulty with this question.
Level of Cognitive Ability: Analysis
Client Needs: Physiological Integrity
Integrated Process: Nursing Process—assessment
Content Area: Maternity—intrapartum
Reference: Murray, S., & McKinney, E. (2006). *Foundations of maternal-newborn nursing* (4th ed., pp. 285, 325). Philadelphia: W.B. Saunders.

19. 2
Rationale: Therapeutic management for hypotonic uterine dysfunction includes oxytocin augmentation and amniotomy to stimulate a labor that slows. A cesarean birth will be performed if no progress in labor occurs. Options 1, 3, and 4 identify therapeutic measures for a client with hypertonic dysfunction.
Test-Taking Strategy: Focus on the strategic word *hypotonic* to assist in answering the question. Use the process of elimination and identify the option that will assist to stimulate labor. This should direct you easily to option 2. If you had difficulty

with this question, review the therapeutic management for hypotonic uterine dysfunction.
Level of Cognitive Ability: Analysis
Client Needs: Physiological Integrity
Integrated Process: Nursing Process—analysis
Content Area: Maternity—intrapartum
Reference: Murray, S., & McKinney, E. (2006). *Foundations of maternal-newborn nursing* (4th ed., p. 698-699). Philadelphia: W.B. Saunders.

20. 1
Rationale: Management of hypertonic labor depends on the cause. Relief of pain is the primary intervention to promote a normal labor pattern. An amniotomy and oxytocin infusion are not treatment measures for hypertonic dysfunction; however, these treatments may be used in clients with hypotonic dysfunction. The client with hypertonic uterine dysfunction would not be encouraged to ambulate every 30 minutes but would be encouraged to rest.
Test-Taking Strategy: Use the process of elimination, focusing on the strategic word *hypertonic*. This strategic word and knowledge of the therapeutic management for this condition will assist in directing you to option 1. Options 2, 3, and 4 are therapeutic measures for hypotonic dysfunction. If you had difficulty with this question, review the therapeutic management for hypertonic uterine dysfunction.
Level of Cognitive Ability: Application
Client Needs: Physiological Integrity
Integrated Process: Nursing Process—implementation
Content Area: Maternity—intrapartum
Reference: Murray, S., & McKinney, E. (2006). *Foundations of maternal-newborn nursing* (4th ed., p. 699). Philadelphia: W.B. Saunders.

ALTERNATE ITEM FORMAT: MULTIPLE RESPONSE

Answer: **4, 5, 6**
Rationale: Painless, bright red vaginal bleeding in the second or third trimester of pregnancy is a sign of placenta previa. The client will have a soft, relaxed, nontender uterus, and fundal height may be more than expected for gestational age. In abruptio placentae, severe abdominal pain is present. Uterine tenderness accompanies placental abruption. Additionally, in abruptio placentae, the abdomen will feel hard and board-like on palpation as the blood penetrates the myometrium and causes uterine irritability.
Test-Taking Strategy: Remember that the difference between placenta previa and abruptio placentae involves the presence of uterine pain and tenderness with an abruption, as opposed to painless bleeding with placenta previa. Review the signs of placenta previa and abruptio placentae if you had difficulty with this question.
Level of Cognitive Ability: Analysis
Client Needs: Physiological Integrity
Integrated Process: Nursing Process—assessment
Content Area: Maternity—intrapartum
Reference: Murray, S., & McKinney, E. (2006). *Foundations of maternal-newborn nursing* (4th ed., pp. 632-634). Philadelphia: W.B. Saunders.

REFERENCES

Lowdermilk, D., & Perry, S. (2006). *Maternity nursing* (7 ed.). St. Louis: Mosby.

Lowdermilk, D., & Perry, S. (2004). *Maternity and women's health care* (8th ed.). St. Louis: Mosby.

Mattson, S., & Smith, J. (2004). *Core curriculum for maternal-newborn nursing* (4th ed.). Philadelphia: W.B. Saunders.

McKinney, E., James, S., Murray, S., & Ashwill, J. (2005). *Maternal-child nursing* (2nd ed.). St. Louis: W.B. Saunders.

Murray, S., & McKinney, E. (2006). *Foundations of maternal-newborn nursing* (4th ed.). Philadelphia: W.B. Saunders.

National Council of State Boards of Nursing (2007). *2007 NCLEX-RN® detailed test plan.* Chicago: Author.

Wong, D., Perry, S., Hockenberry, M., et al. (2006). *Maternal child nursing care* (3rd ed.). St. Louis: Mosby.

The Postpartum Period

I. POSTPARTUM
A. Description: Period when the reproductive tract returns to the normal, nonpregnant state
B. The postpartum period starts immediately after **delivery** and is usually completed by week 6 following **delivery**.

II. PHYSIOLOGICAL MATERNAL CHANGES
A. Involution
   1. Description
      a. Involution is the rapid decrease in the size of the **uterus** as it returns to the nonpregnant state.
      b. Clients who breast-feed may experience a more rapid involution because of the release of oxytocin during breast-feeding.
   2. Assessment
      a. The weight of the **uterus** decreases from 2 lb to 2 oz in 6 weeks.
      b. The endometrium regenerates.
      c. The fundus steadily descends into the pelvis.
      d. Fundal height decreases about 1 fingerbreadth (1 cm) per day (Fig. 28-1).
      e. By 10 days postpartum, the **uterus** cannot be palpated abdominally.
      f. Note that a flaccid fundus indicates uterine atony and should be massaged until firm; a tender fundus indicates an infection (Fig. 28-2).
      g. Afterpains decrease in frequency after the first few days.

B. **Lochia**
   1. Description: Discharge from the **uterus** that consists of blood from the vessels of the placental site and debris from the decidua
   2. Assessment
      a. Rubra is bright red discharge that occurs from **delivery** day to day 3.
      b. Serosa is brownish-pink discharge that occurs from days 4 to 10.
      c. Alba is white discharge that occurs from days 10 to 14.
      d. The discharge should smell like normal menstrual flow.
      e. Discharge decreases daily in amount.
      f. Discharge may increase with ambulation.
      g. Weigh the perineal pad before and after use and identify the amount of time between pad changes to determine most accurately the amount of lochial flow (Box 28-1).

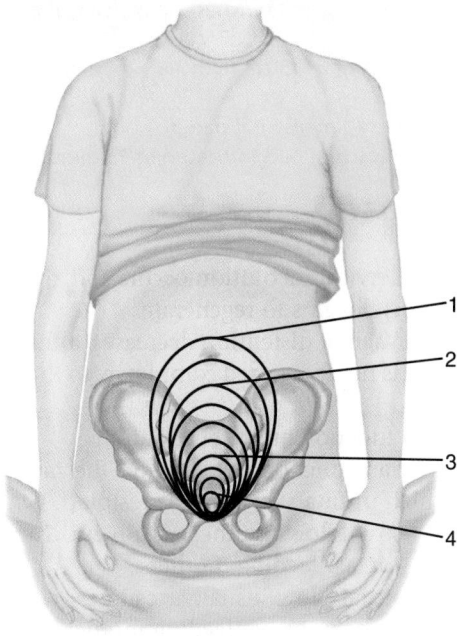

FIG. 28-1 Involution of the uterus. The height of the uterine fundus decreases by approximately 1 cm/day. (From Murray, S., & McKinney, E. [2006]. *Foundations of maternal-newborn nursing* [4th ed.]. Philadelphia: W.B. Saunders.)

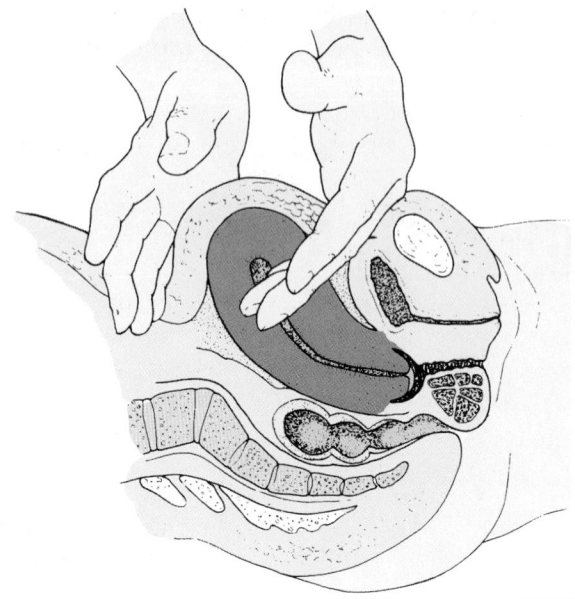

FIG. 28-2 Palpating fundus of uterus during fourth stage of labor. Note that the upper hand is cupped over the fundus; the lower hand dips in above the symphysis pubis and supports the uterus while it is massaged gently. (From Lowdermilk, D., & Perry, S. [2006]. *Maternity nursing* [7th ed.]. St. Louis: Mosby.)

BOX 28-1

Amount of Lochia

Scant: Less than 2.5 cm (1 inch) on menstrual pad in 1 hour
Light: Less than 10 cm (4 inches) on menstrual pad in 1 hour
Moderate: Less than 15 cm (6 inches) on menstrual pad in 1 hour
Heavy: Saturated menstrual pad in 1 hour
Excessive: Menstrual pad saturated in 15 minutes

C. Cervix: Cervical involution occurs and, after 1 week, the muscle begins to regenerate.
D. **Vagina:** Vaginal distention decreases, although muscle tone is never restored completely to the pregravid state.
E. Ovarian function and menstruation
   1. Ovarian function depends on the rapidity with which pituitary function is restored.
   2. Menstrual flow resumes within 1 to 2 months in non–breast-feeding mothers.
   3. Menstrual flow usually resumes within 3 to 6 months in breast-feeding mothers.
   4. Breast-feeding mothers may experience amenorrhea during the entire period of lactation.
   5. Women may ovulate without menstruating, so breast-feeding should not be considered a form of birth control.

BOX 28-2

Care of Breasts for Non–Breast-feeding Mothers

Avoid nipple stimulation.
The mother can apply a breast binder, wear a tight-fitting bra, apply ice packs, or take a mild analgesic.
Engorgement usually resolves within 24 to 36 hours after it begins.

F. Breasts
   1. Breasts continue to secrete colostrum for the first 48 to 72 hours after **delivery.**
   2. A decrease in estrogen and progesterone levels after **delivery** stimulates increased prolactin levels, which promote breast milk production.
   3. Breasts become distended with milk on the third day.
   4. Engorgement occurs on approximately day 4 in non–breast-feeding mothers (Box 28-2 summarizes care of breasts for non–breast-feeding mothers).
   5. Breast-feeding will relieve engorgement.
G. Urinary tract
   1. Woman may have urinary retention as a result of loss of elasticity and tone, loss of sensation in the bladder from trauma, medications, anesthesia, and lack of privacy.
   2. Diuresis usually begins within the first 12 hours after **delivery.**
H. Gastrointestinal tract
   1. Women are usually hungry after **delivery.**
   2. Constipation can occur, with bowel movement (soft, formed stool) by second or third postpartum day.
   3. Hemorrhoids are common.
I. Vital signs (Table 28-1)
   1. Temperature may be elevated during the first 24 hours because of dehydration.
   2. Bradycardia is common during the first week, with a range of 50 to 70 beats/min.
   3. Blood pressure remains unchanged.

III. POSTPARTUM INTERVENTIONS
A. Assessment
   1. Monitor vital signs.
   2. Assess pain level.
   3. Assess height, consistency, and location of the fundus (see Fig. 28-1).
   4. Monitor color, amount, and odor of **lochia.**
   5. Assess breasts for engorgement.
   6. Monitor perineum for swelling or discoloration.
   7. Monitor episiotomy for healing.
   8. Assess incisions or dressings of cesarean birth client.
   9. Monitor bowel status.
   10. Monitor intake and output.

TABLE 28-1

Normal Postpartum Vital Signs

Vital Sign	Description
Temperature	May rise to 100.4° F because of dehydrating effects of labor. Any higher elevation may be caused by infection and must be reported.
Pulse	May decrease to 50 beats/min (normal puerperal bradycardia). Pulse > 100 beats/min may indicate excessive blood loss or infection.
Blood pressure	Should be normal; suspect hypovolemia if it decreases.
Respirations	Rarely change; if respirations increase significantly, suspect pulmonary embolism, uterine atony, and/or hemorrhage.

11. Encourage frequent voiding.
12. Encourage ambulation.
13. Assess extremities for thrombophlebitis (calf pain on passive dorsiflexion of the foot or any redness, tenderness, or warmth of the leg).
14. Administer Rh$_o$(D) immune globulin (Rho-GAM) as prescribed within 72 hours postpartum to the Rh-negative client who has given birth to an Rh-positive **newborn.**
15. Assess bonding with the **newborn infant.**
16. Assess emotional status.
B. Client teaching
1. Demonstrate **newborn** care skills as necessary.
2. Provide the opportunity for the mother to bathe the **newborn infant.**
3. Instruct in feeding technique.
4. Instruct the mother to avoid heavy lifting for at least 3 weeks.
5. Instruct the mother to plan at least one rest period per day.
6. Instruct the mother that contraception should begin after **delivery** or with the initiation of intercourse (intercourse should be postponed at least until the **lochia** ceases).
7. Instruct the mother in the importance of follow-up, which should be scheduled at 4 to 6 weeks.
8. Instruct the mother to report any signs of chills, fever, increased **lochia,** or depressed feelings to the physician immediately.

IV. POSTPARTUM DISCOMFORTS
A. Afterbirth pains
1. Afterbirth pains occur as a result of contractions of the **uterus.**
2. Afterbirth pains are more common in multiparas, breast-feeding mothers, clients treated with oxytocin (Pitocin), and clients who had an overdistended **uterus** during pregnancy, such as with carrying twins.
B. Perineal discomfort
1. Apply ice packs to the perineum during the first 24 hours to reduce swelling.
2. After the first 24 hours, apply warmth by sitz baths.
C. Episiotomy
1. Instruct the client to administer perineal care after each voiding.
2. Encourage the use of an analgesic spray as prescribed.
3. Administer analgesics as prescribed if comfort measures are unsuccessful.
D. Perineal lacerations
1. Care as for an episiotomy; administer perineal care and use analgesic spray and analgesics for comfort.
2. Rectal suppositories and enemas may be contraindicated (to avoid injury to sutures).
E. Breast discomfort from engorgement
1. Encourage wearing a support bra at all times, even while the client is sleeping.
2. Encourage the use of ice packs between feedings if the client is breast-feeding.
3. Encourage the use of warm soaks or a warm shower before feeding for the breast-feeding mother.
4. Administer analgesics as prescribed if comfort measures are unsuccessful.
F. Constipation
1. Encourage adequate intake of fluids (maximum intake of 2000 mL/day).
2. Encourage diet high in fiber.
3. Encourage ambulation.
4. Administer stool softener, laxative, enema, or suppository if needed.
G. Postpartum blues (Box 28-3)
1. The postpartum blues is a condition caused by physiological and emotional stress.
2. The mother may feel upset and depressed at times.
3. Verbalization should be encouraged.
4. Postpartum blues may progress to postpartum depression if unresolved.

V. NUTRITIONAL COUNSELING
A. Discuss caloric intake with breast-feeding and non–breast-feeding mothers.
B. Nutritional needs depend on prepregnancy weight, ideal weight for height, and whether the mother is breast-feeding.
C. If the mother is breast-feeding, calorie needs increase by 200 to 500 cal/day, and the mother may require increased fluids and the continuance of prenatal vitamins and minerals.

BOX 28-3	BOX 28-4
Rubin's Postpartum Phases of Regeneration	Breastfeeding Procedure for Mother

TAKING-IN PHASE: FIRST 3 DAYS

Mother focuses on her own primary needs, such as sleep and food.

For the nurse to listen and help the mother interpret the events of delivery to make them more meaningful is important.

This phase is not an optimum time to teach the mother about baby care.

TAKING HOLD PHASE: DAYS 3 TO 10

The woman is more in control of independence.

The woman begins to assume the tasks of mothering.

This phase is an optimum time to teach the mother about baby care.

LETTING GO PHASE

Mother may feel deep loss over separation of the baby from part of the body and may grieve over the loss.

Mother may be caught in a dependent-independent role, wanting to feel safe and secure yet wanting to make decisions.

Teenage mothers need special consideration because of the conflict taking place within them as part of adolescence.

Wash hands and assume a comfortable position.

Start with the breast with which the last feeding ended.

Brush the newborn infant's lower lip with nipple.

Tickle the lips to have the infant open the mouth wide.

Guide the nipple and surrounding areola into the infant's mouth.

Encourage the infant to nurse on each breast for 15 to 20 minutes

After the baby has nursed, release suction by depressing the infant's chin or inserting a clean finger into the infant's mouth.

Burp the infant after the first breast.

Repeat the procedure on the second breast until the infant stops nursing.

Burp the infant again.

Instruct the mother to listen for audible sucking and swallowing.

▲ VI. BREAST-FEEDING

A. Interventions

1. Put the baby to the mother's breast as soon as the mother's and baby's conditions are stable (on **delivery** table, if possible).

2. Stay with the mother each time she nurses until she feels secure and confident with the baby and her feelings.

3. Assess *LATCH*. (*l*atch achieved by **infant**; *a*udible swallowing; *t*ype of nipple; *c*omfort of mother; *h*elp given to mother with nursing).

4. Uterine cramping may occur the first day after **delivery** while the mother is nursing, when oxytocin stimulation causes the **uterus** to contract.

5. Use general hygiene and wash the breasts once daily.

6. If engorgement occurs, breast-feed frequently, apply warm packs before feeding, apply ice packs between feedings, and massage the breasts.

7. Do not use soap on the breasts because it tends to remove natural oils, which increases the chance of cracked nipples.

8. If cracked nipples develop, expose the nipples to air for 10 to 20 minutes after feeding, rotate the position of the baby for each feeding, and be sure that the baby is latched on to the areola, not just the nipple.

9. The bra should be well-fitted and supporting.

10. Breasts may leak between feedings or during coitus; place breast pad in bra.

11. Calories should be increased by 200 to 500 cal/day, and the diet should include additional fluids; prenatal vitamins should be taken as prescribed.

12. Baby's stools will be light yellow, seedy, watery, and frequent.

13. Medications should be avoided unless prescribed.

14. Gas-producing foods and caffeine should be avoided.

15. Hormonal contraceptives may cause a decrease in the milk supply and are best avoided during the first 6 weeks after birth.

16. Oral contraceptives containing estrogen are not recommended for breast-feeding mothers; progestin-only birth control pills are less likely to interfere with the milk supply.

17. The baby will develop his or her own feeding schedule.

B. Breast-feeding procedure for mother (Box 28-4)

C. Engorgement

1. Breast-feed frequently.

2. Apply warm packs before feeding.

3. Apply ice packs between feedings.

D. Cracked nipples

1. Expose nipples to air for 10 to 20 minutes after feeding.

2. Rotate the position of the baby for each feeding.

3. Be sure that the baby is latched on to the areola, not just the nipple.

PRACTICE QUESTIONS

1. A nurse is preparing to perform a fundal assessment on a postpartum client. The initial nursing action in performing this assessment is which of the following?
   1. Ask the client to turn on her side.
   2. Ask the client to urinate and empty her bladder.
   3. Massage the fundus gently before determining the level of the fundus.
   4. Ask the client to lie flat on her back with the knees and legs flat and straight.

2. A nurse is caring for four 1-day postpartum clients. Which client has an abnormal finding that would require further intervention?
   1. The client with mild afterpains
   2. The client with a pulse rate of 60 beats/min
   3. The client with colostrum discharge from both breasts
   4. The client with lochia that is red and has a foul-smelling odor

3. When performing a postpartum assessment on a client, a nurse notes the presence of clots in the lochia. The nurse examines the clots and notes that they are larger than 1 cm. Which nursing action is appropriate?
   1. Notify the physician.
   2. Document the findings.
   3. Reassess the client in 2 hours.
   4. Encourage increased oral intake of fluids.

4. A postpartum nurse is taking the vital signs of a client who delivered a healthy newborn infant 4 hours ago. The nurse notes that the client's temperature is 100.2° F. Which of the following actions would be appropriate?
   1. Notify the physician.
   2. Document the findings.
   3. Retake the temperature in 15 minutes.
   4. Increase hydration by encouraging oral fluids.

5. A nurse is assessing a client who is 6 hours postpartum after delivering a full-term healthy newborn infant. The client complains to the nurse of feelings of faintness and dizziness. Which of the following nursing actions would be most appropriate?
   1. Elevate the client's legs.
   2. Determine hemoglobin and hematocrit levels.
   3. Instruct the client to request help when getting out of bed.
   4. Inform the nursery room nurse to avoid bringing the newborn infant to the client until the feelings of light-headedness and dizziness have subsided.

6. A postpartum nurse is providing instructions to a client after delivery of a healthy newborn infant. The nurse instructs the client that she should expect normal bowel elimination to return:
   1. 3 days postpartum
   2. 7 days postpartum
   3. On the day of delivery
   4. Within 2 weeks postpartum

7. A nursing student is preparing to perform a cardiovascular assessment on a postpartum client. A nursing instructor asks the student about the procedure to elicit Homans' sign. Which response by the nursing student would indicate an understanding of this assessment technique?
   1. "I will ask the client to raise her legs up to her waist and then to lower her legs slowly."
   2. "I will ask the client to raise her legs and to try to lower them against pressure from my hand."
   3. "I will ask the client to extend her legs flat on the bed, and I will grasp her foot and gently dorsiflex it forward."
   4. "I will ask the client to extend her legs flat on the bed, and I will grasp her foot and sharply extend it backward."

8. A nurse is planning care for a postpartum client who had a vaginal delivery 2 hours ago. The client had a midline episiotomy and has several hemorrhoids. What is the priority nursing diagnosis for this client?
   1. Acute pain
   2. Disturbed body image
   3. Impaired urinary elimination
   4. Risk for imbalanced fluid volume

9. A nurse on a postpartum unit is instructing a client regarding lochia and the amount of expected lochia drainage. The nurse instructs the client that the normal amount of lochia may vary but should never exceed the need for:
   1. One peripad a day
   2. Two peripads a day
   3. Eight peripads a day
   4. Three peripads a day

10. A nurse is teaching a postpartum client about breast-feeding. Which of the following instructions should the nurse include?
    1. The diet should include additional fluids.
    2. Prenatal vitamins should be discontinued.
    3. Soap should be used to cleanse the breasts.
    4. Birth control measures are not necessary while breastfeeding.

ALTERNATE ITEM FORMAT: MULTIPLE RESPONSE

A nurse is providing postpartum instructions to a client who will be breast-feeding her newborn. The nurse determines that the client has understood the instructions if she makes which of the following statements? Select all that apply.

❏ 1. "I will use soap to wash my breasts often."
❏ 2. "Drinking alcohol can affect my milk supply."
❏ 3. "The use of caffeine can decrease my milk supply."
❏ 4. "I will start my estrogen birth control pills again as soon as I get home."
❏ 5. "I know if my breasts get engorged I will limit my breast-feeding and supplement the baby."
❏ 6. "I plan on having bottled water available in the refrigerator so I can get additional fluids easily."

ANSWERS

1. **2**

Rationale: Before starting the fundal assessment, the nurse should ask the client to empty her bladder so that an accurate assessment can be done. When the nurse is performing fundal assessment, the nurse asks the client to lie flat on her back with the knees flexed. Massaging the fundus is not appropriate unless the fundus is boggy or soft, and then it should be massaged gently until firm.

Test-Taking Strategy: Use the process of elimination. Note the strategic words *initial nursing action* in the event query. Attempt to visualize the procedure when answering the question. This should direct you easily to option 2. If you had difficulty with this question, review fundal assessment in the postpartum period.

Level of Cognitive Ability: Application
Client Needs: Health Promotion and Maintenance
Integrated Process: Nursing Process—implementation
Content Area: Maternity—postpartum
Reference: Murray, S., & McKinney, E. (2006). *Foundations of maternal-newborn nursing* (4th ed., p. 410). Philadelphia: W.B. Saunders.

2. **4**

Rationale: Lochia, the discharge present after birth, is red for the first 1 to 3 days and gradually decreases in amount. Normal lochia has a fleshy odor or an odor similar to menstrual flow. Foul-smelling or purulent lochia usually indicates infection, and these findings are not normal. The other options are normal findings for a 1-day postpartum client.

Test-Taking Strategy: Note the strategic words *abnormal finding*. Options 1, 2, and 3 are normal for 1-day postpartum clients. This should direct you to option 4. If you had difficulty with this question, review normal assessment findings in the postpartum client.

Level of Cognitive Ability: Analysis
Client Needs: Physiological Integrity
Integrated Process: Nursing Process—analysis
Content Area: Maternity—postpartum
References: Lowdermilk, D., & Perry, S. (2004). *Maternity and women's health care* (8th ed., p. 627). St. Louis: Mosby.
Wong, D., Perry, S., Hockenberry, M., et al. (2006). *Maternal child nursing care* (3rd ed., p. 608). St. Louis: Mosby.

3. **1**

Rationale: Normally, a few small clots may be found in the first 1 to 2 days after birth from pooling of the blood in the vagina. Clots larger than 1 cm are considered abnormal. The cause of these clots, such as uterine atony or retained placental fragments, needs to be determined and treated to prevent further blood loss. Although the findings would be documented, the appropriate action is to notify the physician. Reassessing the client in 2 hours would delay necessary treatment. Increasing oral intake of fluids would not be an appropriate action in this situation.

Test-Taking Strategy: Use the process of elimination, focusing on the strategic words *larger than 1 cm*. Knowledge regarding the presence of clots in the postpartum period and their significance will direct you to option 1. If you had difficulty with this question, review normal postpartum findings in the woman.

Level of Cognitive Ability: Application
Client Needs: Physiological Integrity
Integrated Process: Nursing Process—implementation
Content Area: Maternity—postpartum
References: Lowdermilk, D., & Perry, S. (2006). *Maternity nursing* (7th ed., p. 479). St. Louis: Mosby.
Murray, S., & McKinney, E. (2006). *Foundations of maternal-newborn nursing* (4th ed., p. 395). Philadelphia: W.B. Saunders.
Wong, D., Perry, S., Hockenberry, M., et al. (2006). *Maternal child nursing care* (3rd ed., pp. 591-592). St. Louis: Mosby.

4. **4**

Rationale: The client's temperature should be taken every 4 hours while she is awake. Temperatures up to 100.4° F (38.0° C) in the first 24 hours after birth often are related to the dehydrating effects of labor. The appropriate action is to increase hydration by encouraging oral fluids, which should bring the temperature to a normal reading. Although the nurse also would document the findings, the appropriate action would be to increase the hydration. Contacting the physician is not necessary. Taking the temperature in another 15 minutes is not a necessary action.

Test-Taking Strategy: Use the process of elimination and knowledge regarding the physiological findings in the immediate postpartum period to assist in answering this question. Recalling that a temperature elevation often is related to the dehydrating effects of labor will direct you to the correct option. Review normal postpartum assessment findings if you had difficulty with this question.

Level of Cognitive Ability: Application
Client Needs: Physiological Integrity
Integrated Process: Nursing Process—implementation
Content Area: Maternity—postpartum
Reference: Murray, S., & McKinney, E. (2006). *Foundations of maternal-newborn nursing* (4th ed, pp. 405, 409, 419). Philadelphia: W.B. Saunders.
Wong, D., Perry, S., Hockenberry, M., et al. (2006). *Maternal child nursing care* (3rd ed., p. 610). St. Louis: Mosby.

5. 3
Rationale: Orthostatic hypotension may be evident during the first 8 hours after birth. Feelings of faintness or dizziness are signs that caution the nurse to beware for the client's safety. The nurse should advise the client to get help the first few times the mother gets out of bed. Option 1 is not the most appropriate or helpful action in this situation. Option 2 requires a physician's order. Option 4 is unnecessary.
Test-Taking Strategy: Use the process of elimination and focus on the subject of the question, client safety. Option 4 is inappropriate and should be eliminated first. Elevating the client's legs is not an appropriate or helpful nursing intervention. From the remaining options, recall that safety is a primary issue. This should assist in directing you to the correct option. If you had difficulty with this question, review postpartum nursing interventions.
Level of Cognitive Ability: Application
Client Needs: Safe and Effective Care Environment
Integrated Process: Nursing Process—implementation
Content Area: Maternity—postpartum
Reference: Murray, S. & McKinney, E. (2006). *Foundations of maternal-newborn nursing* (4th ed., p. 407). Philadelphia: W.B. Saunders.

6. 1
Rationale: After birth, the nurse should auscultate the client's abdomen in all four quadrants to determine the return of bowel sounds. Normal bowel elimination usually returns 2 to 3 days postpartum. Surgery, anesthesia, and the use of opioids and pain control agents also contribute to the longer period of altered bowel functions. Options 2, 3, and 4 are incorrect.
Test-Taking Strategy: Use the process of elimination and general principles related to postpartum care to assist in answering this question. Eliminate options 2 and 4 first because of the length of time stated in these options. From the remaining options, eliminate option 3 because it would seem unreasonable that bowel function would return that quickly in the postpartum woman. Review normal gastrointestinal functions in the postpartum client if you had difficulty with this question.
Level of Cognitive Ability: Application
Client Needs: Physiological Integrity
Integrated Process: Teaching and Learning
Content Area: Maternity—postpartum
References: Murray, S., & McKinney, E. (2006). *Foundations of maternal-newborn nursing* (4th ed., p. 389). Philadelphia: W.B. Saunders.
Wong, D., Perry, S., Hockenberry, M., et al. (2006). *Maternal child nursing care* (3rd ed., p. 616). St. Louis: Mosby.

7. 3
Rationale: To elicit Homans' sign, the nurse asks the client to extend her legs flat on the bed. The nurse grasps the foot and dorsiflexes it forward. If this causes any discomfort or resistance, the nurse should notify the physician or midwife that Homans' sign is present. Options 1, 2, and 4 are incorrect descriptions of this assessment technique.
Test-Taking Strategy: Knowledge regarding the assessment technique to elicit Homans' sign is required to answer this question. Use the process of elimination and visualize this technique to assist in directing you to option 3. If you had

difficulty with this question, review the technique to elicit Homans' sign.
Level of Cognitive Ability: Analysis
Client Needs: Health Promotion and Maintenance
Integrated Process: Teaching and Learning
Content Area: Maternity—postpartum
Reference: Murray, S., & McKinney, E. (2006). *Foundations of maternal-newborn nursing* (4th ed., p. 413). Philadelphia: W.B. Saunders.

8. 1
Rationale: The priority nursing diagnosis for a client who delivered 2 hours ago and who has a midline episiotomy and hemorrhoids is acute pain. Most clients have some degree of discomfort during the immediate postpartum period. There is no data in the question that indicate the presence of Body image, disturbed, Urinary elimination, impaired, or Fluid volume, imbalanced, risk for.
Test-Taking Strategy: Note the strategic word *priority*. Use Maslow's Hierarchy of Needs theory to eliminate option 2 because this is a psychosocial, not a physiological, need. From the remaining options, focus on the data in the question to direct you to option 1. Review care for the postpartum client if you had difficulty with this question.
Level of Cognitive Ability: Analysis
Client Needs: Physiological Integrity
Integrated Process: Nursing Process—analysis
Content Area: Maternity—postpartum
References: Lowdermilk, D., & Perry, S. (2004). *Maternity and women's health care* (8th ed., p. 632). St. Louis: Mosby.

9. 3
Rationale: The normal amount of lochia may vary with the individual but should never exceed 4 to 8 peripads a day. The average number of peripads used is 6 per day.
Test-Taking Strategy: Use the process of elimination and knowledge regarding the normal amount of lochia drainage in the postpartum period to answer the question. Noting the strategic words *should never exceed* will assist in directing you to option 3. If you had difficulty with this question, review postpartum assessment.
Level of Cognitive Ability: Application
Client Needs: Health Promotion and Maintenance
Integrated Process: Teaching and Learning
Content Area: Maternity—postpartum
References: Lowdermilk, D., & Perry, S. (2006). *Maternity nursing* (7th ed., p. 477). St. Louis: Mosby.
McKinney, E., James, S., Murray, S., & Ashwill, J. (2005). *Maternal-child nursing* (2nd ed. p. 396). St. Louis: W.B. Saunders,.

10. 1
Rationale: The diet for a breast-feeding client should include additional fluids. Prenatal vitamins should be taken as prescribed, and soap should not be used on the breast because it tends to remove natural oils, which increases the chance of cracked nipples. Breast-feeding is not a method of contraception, so birth control measures should be resumed.
Test-Taking Strategy: Use the process of elimination, noting the subject of the question, teaching for the breast-feeding client. Remember that fluids, as well as calories, should be in-

creased when the client is breast-feeding. If you had difficulty with this question, review breast-feeding interventions.
Level of Cognitive Ability: Application
Client Needs: Physiological Integrity
Integrated Process: Teaching and Learning
Content Area: Maternity—postpartum
Reference: Wong, D., Perry, S., Hockenberry, M., et al. (2006). *Maternal child nursing care* (3rd ed., p. 781). St. Louis: W.B. Saunders.

ALTERNATE ITEM FORMAT: MULTIPLE RESPONSE

Answer: 2, 3, 6
Rationale: Breast-feeding clients should increase their daily fluid intake; therefore, having bottled water available indicates that the postpartum client understands the importance of increasing fluids. If engorgement occurs, the client should not limit breast-feeding, but should breast-feed frequently. Oral contraceptives containing estrogen are not recommended for breast-feeding mothers and soap should not be used on the breasts because it tends to remove natural oils, which increases the chance of cracked nipples. Common causes of decreased milk supply include formula use, inadequate rest or diet, smoking by the mother or others in the home, and use of caffeine, alcohol, or other medications.
Test-Taking Strategy: Note the strategic words *understood the instructions*. Think about the physiology associated with milk production and the complications of breast-feeding. This will direct you to the correct options. Review postpartum instructions for a breast-feeding client if you had difficulty with this question.
Level of Cognitive Ability: Analysis
Client Needs: Health Promotion and Maintenance
Integrated Process: Nursing Process/Evaluation
Reference: Lowdermilk, D., & Perry, S. (2006). *Maternity nursing* (7th ed., p. 635). St. Louis: Mosby.

REFERENCES

Lowdermilk, D., & Perry, S. (2006). *Maternity nursing* (7th ed.). St. Louis: Mosby.

Lowdermilk, D., & Perry, S. (2004). *Maternity and women's health care* (8th ed.). St. Louis: Mosby.

McKinney, E., James, S., Murray, S., & Ashwill, J. (2005). *Maternal-child nursing* (2nd ed.). St. Louis: W.B. Saunders.

Murray, S., & McKinney, E. (2006). *Foundations of maternal-newborn nursing* (4th ed.). Philadelphia: W.B. Saunders.

National Council of State Boards of Nursing (2007). *2007 NCLEX-RN® detailed test plan.* Chicago: Author.

Wong, D., Perry, S., Hockenberry, M., et al. (2006). *Maternal child nursing care* (3rd ed.). St. Louis: Mosby.

Postpartum Complications

I. CYSTITIS

A. Description: An infection of the bladder

B. Assessment
1. Burning and pain on urination
2. Lower abdominal pain
3. Increased frequency of urination
4. Costovertebral angle tenderness
5. Fever
6. Proteinuria, hematuria, bacteriuria, white blood cells in the urine

C. Interventions
1. Palpate bladder for distention.
2. Palpate fundus.
3. Obtain urine specimen for culture and sensitivity if prescribed.
4. Institute measures to assist the client to void.
5. Encourage frequent and complete emptying of the bladder.
6. Encourage fluids to 3000 mL/day.
7. Administer antibiotics as prescribed after the urine culture is obtained.
8. Instruct the client in the methods of prevention and treatment of cystitis.

II. HEMATOMA

A. Description
1. Hematoma is a localized collection of blood into the tissues of the reproductive sac after the **delivery**; vulvar hematomas are the most common (Fig. 29-1).
2. Predisposing conditions include operative **delivery** with forceps and injury to a blood vessel.
3. Hematoma can be a life-threatening condition.

B. Assessment
1. Abnormal severe pain
2. Pressure in the perineal area

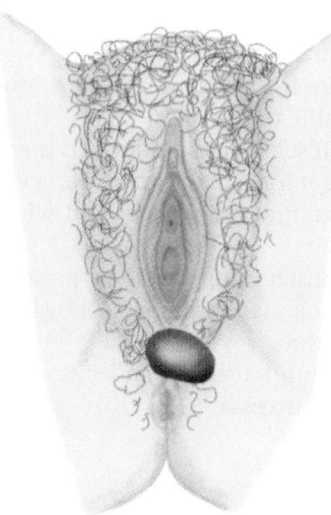

FIG. 29-1 A vulvar hematoma is caused by rapid bleeding into soft tissue, and it causes severe pain and feelings of pressure. (From Murray, S., & McKinney, E., [2006] *Foundations of maternal-newborn nursing* [4th ed.]. St. Louis: W.B. Saunders.)

3. Sensitive, bulging mass in the perineal area with discolored skin
4. Inability to void
5. Decreased hemoglobin and hematocrit levels
6. Signs of shock, such as pallor, tachycardia, and hypotension, if significant blood loss has occurred

C. Interventions
1. Monitor vital signs.
2. Monitor client for abnormal pain, especially when forceps **delivery** has occurred.
3. Place ice at the hematoma site.
4. Administer analgesics as prescribed.
5. Monitor intake and output.

CAUSES

Uterine atony (poor muscle tone)
Laceration of the vagina
Cervix, perineum, or labia hematoma development
Retained placental fragments

PREDISPOSING FACTORS

High parity
Dystocia, prolonged labor
Operative delivery—cesarean or forceps delivery, intra-uterine manipulation
Overdistention of the uterus—polyhydramnios, multiple gestation, large neonate
Abruptio placentae
Previous history of postpartum hemorrhage
Infection
Placenta previa

6. Encourage fluids and voiding.
7. Prepare for urinary catheterization if the client is unable to void.
8. Administer blood products as prescribed.
9. Monitor for signs of infection, such as increased temperature, pulse rate, and white blood cell count.
10. Administer antibiotics as prescribed because infection is common following hematoma formation.
11. Prepare for incision and evacuation of hematoma if necessary.

▲ III. HEMORRHAGE

A. Description
   1. Bleeding of 500 mL or more following **delivery**
   2. A leading cause of maternal mortality that demands prompt recognition and intervention

▲ B. Assessment (Box 29-1)
   1. Early: Hemorrhage occurs during the first 24 hours after **delivery**.
   2. Late: Hemorrhage occurs after the first 24 hours following **delivery**.

▲ C. Interventions for signs of bleeding or shock
   1. Massage fundus for uterine atony, with care not to overmassage.
   2. Notify physician or health care provider
   3. Monitor vital signs and fundus every 5 to 15 minutes.
   4. Remain with the client.
   5. Assess and estimate blood loss by pad count.
   6. Turn client to assess for pooled blood underneath her.
   7. Assess level of consciousness.
   8. Administer fluids and monitor intake and output.
   9. Monitor hemoglobin and hematocrit levels.

10. Maintain asepsis because hemorrhage predisposes to infection.
11. Prepare for the administration of oxytocin (Pitocin) if prescribed.
12. Prepare for the administration of blood transfusions if prescribed.

IV. INFECTION ▲

A. Description: Any infection of the reproductive organs that occurs within 28 days of **delivery** or abortion

B. Assessment
   1. Temperature of 100.4° F is normal during the first 24 hours postpartum because of dehydration; a temperature of 100.4° F or higher after 24 hours postpartum indicates infection
   2. Chills
   3. Anorexia
   4. Pelvic discomfort or pain
   5. Vaginal discharge that is malodorous; normal vaginal discharge has a fleshy odor or the odor similar to that which occurs with a menstrual period.
   6. Elevated white blood cell count

C. Interventions
   1. Monitor vital signs and temperature every 2 to 4 hours.
   2. Make the mother as comfortable as possible; position the mother to promote drainage.
   3. Keep the mother warmed if chilled.
   4. Isolate the baby from the mother only if the mother can infect the baby.
   5. Provide nutritious, high-calorie, high-protein diet.
   6. Encourage fluids to 3000 to 4000 mL/day, if not contraindicated.
   7. Encourage frequent voiding and monitor intake and output.
   8. Monitor culture results if cultures were prescribed.
   9. Administer antibiotics according to identified organism, as prescribed.

V. MASTITIS ▲

A. Description
   1. Mastitis is the inflammation of the breast as a result of infection.
   2. Mastitis primarily occurs in breast-feeding mothers 2 to 3 weeks after **delivery** but may occur at any time during lactation.

B. Assessment (Fig. 29-2)
   1. Localized heat and swelling
   2. Pain; tender axillary lymph nodes
   3. Elevated temperature
   4. Complaints of flu-like symptoms

C. Interventions
   1. Instruct the mother in good hand washing and breast hygiene techniques.

Early mastitis

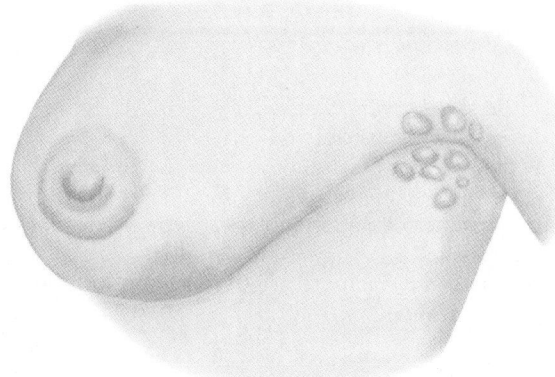

Enlarged, tender axillary lymph nodes.
Tender "flush" without swelling.

Acute mastitis

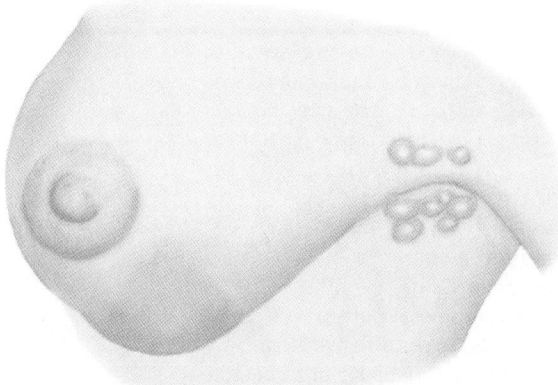

Enlarged, tender axillary lymph nodes.
Area of inflammation is red, swollen, hot,
and tender.

FIG. 29-2 Mastitis typically occurs 2 to 3 weeks following birth in the breast of a woman who breast-feeds. (From Murray, S., & McKinney, E. [2006] *Foundations of maternal-newborn nursing* [4th ed.]. St. Louis: W.B. Saunders.)

2. Promote comfort.
3. Apply heat or cold to the site as prescribed.
4. Maintain lactation in breast-feeding mothers.
5. Encourage manual expression of breast milk or use of a breast pump every 4 hours.
6. Encourage the mother to support the breasts by wearing a supportive bra.
7. Administer analgesics as prescribed.
8. Administer antibiotics as prescribed.

VI. PULMONARY EMBOLISM
A. Description: Passage of thrombus, often originating in a uterine or other pelvic vein, into the lungs, where it disrupts the circulation of the blood
B. Assessment
   1. Dyspnea, tachypnea, and tachycardia
   2. Cough and lung crackles
   3. Hemoptysis
   4. Pleuritic chest pain
   5. Feeling of impending doom
C. Interventions
   1. Administer oxygen.
   2. Position client with the head of the bed elevated.
   3. Monitor vital signs frequently especially respiratory rate and breath sounds.
   4. Monitor for signs of respiratory distress and for signs of increasing hypoxemia.
   5. Administer intravenous fluids as prescribed.
   6. Administer anticoagulants as prescribed.
   7. Prepare to assist physician to administer streptokinase (Streptase) to dissolve the clot if prescribed.

VII. SUBINVOLUTION
A. Description: Incomplete involution or failure of the **uterus** to return to its normal size and condition

B. Assessment
   1. Uterine pain on palpation
   2. **Uterus** larger than expected
   3. More than normal vaginal bleeding
C. Interventions
   1. Assess vital signs.
   2. Assess **uterus** and fundus.
   3. Monitor for vaginal bleeding.
   4. Elevate the legs to promote venous return.
   5. Encourage frequent voiding.
   6. Monitor hemoglobin and hematocrit.
   7. Prepare to administer methylergonovine maleate (Methergine) as prescribed.

VIII. THROMBOPHLEBITIS
A. Description
   1. In this condition, a clot forms in a vessel wall as a result of the inflammation of the vessel wall.
   2. A partial obstruction of the vessel can occur.
   3. Increased blood-clotting factors in the postpartum period place the client at risk.
B. Types
   1. Superficial thrombophlebitis
   2. Femoral thrombophlebitis
   3. Pelvic thrombophlebitis
C. Assessment (Box 29-2)
D. Interventions
   1. Assess the lower extremities for edema, tenderness, varices, and increased skin temperature (Fig. 29-3)
   2. Maintain bed rest.
   3. Elevate the affected leg.
   4. Apply a bed cradle and keep bedclothes off affected leg.
   5. Never massage the leg.

BOX 29-2
Assessment of Types of Thrombophlebitis

SUPERFICIAL
Palpable thrombus that feels bumpy and hard
Tenderness and pain in the affected lower extremity
Warm and pinkish-red color over the thrombus area

FEMORAL
Malaise
Chills and fever
Positive Homans' sign
Diminished peripheral pulses
Shiny white skin over affected area
Pain, stiffness, and swelling of affected leg

PELVIC
Severe chills
Dramatic body temperature changes
Pulmonary embolism may be first sign

BOX 29-3
Client Education for Thrombophlebitis

Never massage the leg.
Avoid crossing the legs.
Avoid prolonged sitting.
Avoid constrictive clothing.
Avoid pressure behind the knees.
Know how to apply support hose if prescribed.
Understand the importance of anticoagulant therapy if prescribed.
Understand the importance of follow-up with the health care provider.

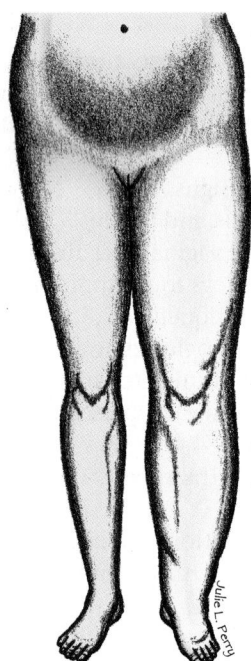

FIG. 29-3 Deep vein thrombophlebitis. (From Lowdermilk, D., & Perry, S. [2006]. *Maternity nursing* [7th ed.]. St. Louis: Mosby.)

6. Monitor for manifestations of pulmonary embolism.
7. Superficial thrombophlebitis
   a. Provide bed rest.
   b. Apply hot packs to the affected site as prescribed.
   c. Apply elastic stockings (support hose).
   d. Administer analgesics as prescribed.

8. Femoral thrombophlebitis
   a. Provide bed rest.
   b. Elevate affected leg.
   c. Apply moist heat continuously to affected area if prescribed to alleviate discomfort.
   d. Administer analgesics as prescribed.
   e. Administer antibiotics if prescribed.
   f. Prepare to administer heparin sodium intravenously to prevent further thrombus formation if prescribed.
9. Pelvic thrombophlebitis
   a. Provide bed rest.
   b. Administer analgesics as prescribed.
   c. Administer antibiotics if prescribed.
   d. Prepare to administer heparin sodium intravenously.
E. Client education (Box 29-3)

IX. PERINATAL LOSS
A. Description
   1. Perinatal loss is associated with miscarriage, neonatal death, stillbirth, and therapeutic abortion.
   2. Loss, and hence grief, may also coincide with the birth of a preterm infant, an infant who has suffered complications, or an infant with congenital anomalies; it may also occur in a family who is giving up a child for adoption.
B. Interventions
   1. Communicate therapeutically and actively listen, providing parents time to grieve.
   2. Notify the hospital chaplain.
   3. Inform parents about options such as seeing, holding, bathing, and/or dressing the deceased infant, visitation by other family members or friends, religious rituals, and funeral arrangements.
   4. Prepare a special memories box with keepsakes such as footprints, handprints, locks of hair, and pictures.
   5. Admit the mother to a private room; if possible, mark the door to the room with a special card (per agency procedure) that denotes to hospital staff that this family has experienced a loss.

PRACTICE QUESTIONS

1. A nurse is preparing staff assignments for the postpartum unit and has two licensed practical nurses (LPNs) and one registered nurse (RN) to care for clients. Which client should be assigned to the RN?
   1. A primiparous client who delivered 4 hours ago
   2. A multiparous client who delivered 6 hours ago
   3. A primiparous client who delivered 6 hours ago and had epidural anesthesia
   4. A multiparous client who delivered a large fetus after oxytocin (Pitocin) induction

2. A postpartum client is diagnosed with cystitis. The nurse plans for which priority nursing intervention in the care of the client?
   1. Providing sitz baths
   2. Encouraging fluid intake
   3. Placing ice on the perineum
   4. Monitoring hemoglobin and hematocrit levels

3. A nurse is monitoring a postpartum client who received epidural anesthesia for the presence of a vulvar hematoma. Which of the following assessment findings would best indicate the presence of a hematoma?
   1. Changes in vital signs
   2. Signs of heavy bruising
   3. Complaints of intense pain
   4. Complaints of a tearing sensation

4. A nurse is developing a plan of care for a postpartum woman with a small vulvar hematoma. The nurse includes which specific intervention in the plan during the first 12 hours following delivery?
   1. Assess vital signs every 4 hours.
   2. Measure fundal height every 4 hours.
   3. Prepare an ice pack for application to the area.
   4. Inform health care provider of assessment findings.

5. A new mother is seen in a health care clinic 2 weeks after giving birth to a healthy newborn infant. The mother is complaining that she feels as though she has the flu and complains of fatigue and aching muscles. On further assessment, the nurse notes a localized area of redness on the left breast, and the mother is diagnosed with mastitis. The mother asks the nurse about the condition. The appropriate nursing response is which of the following?
   1. "The infection usually involves both breasts."
   2. "The infection can occur at any time during breast-feeding."
   3. "The infection usually is caused by wearing a supportive bra."
   4. "The infection is most common for women who have breast-fed in the past."

6. A nurse is providing instructions about measures to prevent postpartum mastitis to a client who is breast-feeding her newborn. Which of the following, if stated by the client, would indicate a need for further instructions?

   1. "I should breast-feed every 2 to 3 hours."
   2. "I should change the breast pads frequently."
   3. "I should wash my hands well before breast-feeding."
   4. "I should wash my nipples daily with soap and water."

7. A home care nurse visits a client who has delivered a healthy newborn infant via vaginal delivery. An episiotomy was performed, and the woman has developed a wound infection at the episiotomy site. The nurse provides instructions to the client regarding care related to the infection. Which of the following statements, if made by the mother, would indicate a need for further instructions?
   1. "I need to take the antibiotics as prescribed."
   2. "I need to take warm sitz baths to promote healing."
   3. "I need to apply warm compresses to provide comfort."
   4. "I need to isolate the infant for 48 hours after beginning the antibiotics."

8. A new mother received epidural anesthesia during labor and had a forceps delivery after pushing for 2 hours. At 6 hours postpartum, her systolic blood pressure has dropped 20 points, her diastolic blood pressure has dropped 10 points, and her pulse is 120 beats/min. The client is anxious and restless. On further assessment, a vulvar hematoma is verified. After notifying the health care provider, the nurse immediately plans to:
   1. Reassure the client.
   2. Monitor fundal height.
   3. Apply perineal pressure.
   4. Prepare the client for surgery.

9. After surgical evacuation and repair of a paravaginal hematoma, a client is discharged 3 days postpartum. The nurse determines that the client needs further discharge instructions when she states:
   1. "I will probably need my mother to help me with housekeeping."
   2. "Because I am so sore, I will nurse the baby while lying on my side."
   3. "My husband and I will not have intercourse until the stitches are healed."
   4. "The only medications I will take are prenatal vitamins and stool softeners."

10. A nurse is monitoring a client in the immediate postpartum period for signs of hemorrhage. Which of the following signs, if noted, would be an early sign of excessive blood loss?
    1. A temperature of 100.4° F
    2. A blood pressure change from 130/88 to 124/80 mm Hg
    3. An increase in the pulse rate from 88 to 102 beats/min
    4. An increase in the respiratory rate from 18 to 22 breaths/min

11. A nurse is preparing to assess the uterine fundus of a client in the immediate postpartum period. When the nurse locates the fundus, she notes that the uterus feels soft and boggy. Which nursing intervention would be appropriate initially?
    1. Elevate the mother's legs.
    2. Encourage the mother to void.
    3. Massage the fundus until it is firm.
    4. Push on the uterus to assist in expressing clots.

12. A postpartum nurse is assessing a client who delivered a healthy newborn infant by cesarean section for signs and symptoms of superficial venous thrombosis. Which of the following signs or symptoms would the nurse note if superficial venous thrombosis were present?
    1. Paleness of the calf area
    2. Coolness of the calf area
    3. Enlarged, hardened veins
    4. Palpable dorsalis pedis pulses

13. A nurse is developing a plan of care for a postpartum client who was diagnosed with superficial venous thrombosis. Which of the following interventions would be a component of the plan of care?
    1. Ambulation four to six times daily
    2. Administration of anticoagulants
    3. Elevation of the affected extremity
    4. Application of ice packs to the affected area

14. A client in a postpartum unit complains of sudden sharp chest pain. The nurse notes that the client is tachycardic and the respiratory rate is elevated. The nurse suspects a pulmonary embolism. The initial nursing action is which of the following?
    1. Initiate an intravenous line.
    2. Assess the client's blood pressure.
    3. Prepare to administer morphine sulfate.
    4. Administer oxygen at 8 to 10 L/min by face mask.

15. A nurse is providing instructions to a client who has been diagnosed with mastitis. Which of the following statements, if made by the client, indicates a need for further instructions?
    1. "I need to wear a supportive bra to relieve the discomfort."
    2. "I need to stop breast-feeding until this condition resolves."
    3. "I can use analgesics to assist in alleviating some of the discomfort."
    4. "I need to take antibiotics, and I should begin to feel better in 24 to 48 hours."

16. A nurse is monitoring a postpartum client in the fourth stage of labor. Which of the following findings, if noted by the nurse, would indicate a complication related to a laceration of the birth canal?
    1. Presence of dark red lochia
    2. Palpation of the uterus as a firm contracted ball
    3. The saturation of more than one peripad per hour
    4. Palpation of the fundus at the level of the umbilicus

17. A nurse is developing a plan of care for a client recovering from a cesarean delivery. To prevent thrombophlebitis, the nurse plans to encourage the woman to:
    1. Elevate her legs.
    2. Remain on bed rest.
    3. Ambulate frequently.
    4. Apply warm moist packs to the legs.

18. A postpartum client is being treated for deep venous thrombophlebitis. A nurse understands that the client's response to treatment will be evaluated by regularly assessing the client for:
    1. Dysuria, ecchymosis, and vertigo
    2. Epistaxis, hematuria, and dysuria
    3. Hematuria, ecchymosis, and vertigo
    4. Hematuria, ecchymosis, and epistaxis

19. A nurse performs an assessment on a client who is 4 hours postpartum. The nurse notes that the client has cool, clammy skin and is restless and excessively thirsty. The nurse prepares immediately to:
    1. Begin hourly pad counts and reassure the client.
    2. Begin fundal massage and start oxygen by mask.
    3. Elevate the head of the bed and assess vital signs.
    4. Assess for hypovolemia and notify the health care provider.

20. A nurse is assessing a client in the fourth stage of labor and notes that the fundus is firm but that bleeding is excessive. The initial nursing action would be which of the following?
    1. Record the findings.
    2. Notify the physician.
    3. Massage the fundus.
    4. Place the client in Trendelenburg's position.

ALTERNATE ITEM FORMAT: MULTIPLE RESPONSE

A nurse is preparing a list of self-care instructions for a postpartum client who was diagnosed with mastitis. Which of the following instructions would be included on the list? Select all that apply.

❏ 1. Wear a supportive bra.
❏ 2. Rest during the acute phase.
❏ 3. Maintain a fluid intake of at least 3000 mL.
❏ 4. Continue to breast-feed if the breasts are not too sore.
❏ 5. Take the prescribed antibiotics until the soreness subsides.
❏ 6. Avoid decompression of the breasts by breast-feeding or breast pump.

ANSWERS

1. 4

Rationale: The client at highest risk for hemorrhage should be assigned to a registered nurse. In this case, the multiparous client who delivered a large fetus after oxytocin induction has more risk factors associated with postpartum hemorrhage than the other clients.

Test-Taking Strategy: Focus on the subject, assignment to the RN. Read the client description in each option. Noting the words *large* and *oxytocin* in option 4 will direct you to this option. Review delegating and assignment-making guidelines if you had difficulty with this question.

Level of Cognitive Ability: Analysis
Client Needs: Safe and Effective Care Environment
Integrated Process: Nursing Process—planning
Content Area: Delegating/Prioritizing
Reference: Lowdermilk, D., & Perry, S. (2004). *Maternity and women's health care* (8th ed., p. 1037). St. Louis: Mosby.

2. 2

Rationale: Cystitis is an infection of the bladder. The client should consume 3000 mL of fluids per day. Sitz baths and ice would be appropriate interventions for perineal discomfort. Hemoglobin and hematocrit levels would be monitored with hemorrhage.

Test-Taking Strategy: Focus on the subject, priority intervention for the client with cystitis. Remember that increased fluids is a priority intervention for the client with cystitis. Review these interventions if you had difficulty with this question.

Level of Cognitive Ability: Application
Client Needs: Physiological Integrity
Integrated Process: Nursing Process—implementation
Content Area: Maternity—postpartum
Reference: Murray, S., & McKinney, E. (2006). *Foundations of maternal-newborn nursing* (4th ed., p. 749). St. Louis: W.B. Saunders.

3. 1

Rationale: Because the client has had epidural anesthesia and is anesthetized, she cannot feel pain, pressure, or a tearing sensation. Changes in vital signs indicate hypovolemia in the anesthetized postpartum woman with vulvar hematoma. Option 2 (heavy bruising) may be visualized, but vital sign changes indicate hematoma caused by blood collection in the perineal tissues.

Test-Taking Strategy: Use the process of elimination, noting the strategic words *epidural anesthesia*. With this in mind, eliminate options 3 and 4. From the remaining options, use the ABCs—airway, breathing, and circulation—to direct you to option 1. Review the signs of a vulvar hematoma in a client who had epidural anesthesia if you had difficulty with this question.

Level of Cognitive Ability: Analysis
Client Needs: Physiological Integrity
Integrated Process: Nursing Process—assessment
Content Area: Maternity—postpartum
References: Lowdermilk, D., & Perry, S. (2004). *Maternity and women's health care* (8th ed., p. 1037). St. Louis: Mosby.
Murray, S., & McKinney, E. (2006). *Foundations of maternal-newborn nursing* (4th ed., pp. 348, 737). Philadelphia: W.B. Saunders.

Wong, D., Perry, S., Hockenberry, M., et al. (2006). *Maternal child nursing care* (3rd ed., pp. 456-457). St. Louis: Mosby.

4. 3

Rationale: Application of ice will reduce swelling caused by hematoma formation in the vulvar area. Options 1, 2, and 4 are not interventions that are specific to the plan of care for a client with a small vulvar hematoma.

Test-Taking Strategy: Use the process of elimination, noting the strategic words *small* and *specific intervention* in the question. This focus will assist in directing you to option 3. Review nursing care of the client with a hematoma if you had difficulty with this question.

Level of Cognitive Ability: Application
Client Needs: Physiological Integrity
Integrated Process: Nursing Process—planning
Content Area: Maternity—postpartum
References: McKinney, E., James, S., Murray, S., & Ashwill, J. (2005). *Maternal-child nursing* (2nd ed., p. 386). St. Louis: W.B. Saunders.
Murray, S., & McKinney, E. (2006). *Foundations of maternal-newborn nursing* (4th ed., pp. 259, 737). Philadelphia: W.B. Saunders.
Wong, D., Perry, S., Hockenberry, M., et al. (2006). *Maternal child nursing care* (3rd ed., p. 660). St. Louis: Mosby.

5. 2

Rationale: Mastitis is an infection of the lactating breasts and occurs most often during the second and third weeks after birth, although it may develop at any time during breast-feeding. Mastitis is more common in mothers nursing for the first time and usually affects one breast. A supportive bra will not cause mastitis; however, constriction of the breasts from a bra that is too tight may interfere with emptying of all the ducts and may lead to infection.

Test-Taking Strategy: Use the process of elimination and focus on the diagnosis presented in the question. Remember that mastitis can occur at any time during breast-feeding. If you are unfamiliar with the cause and characteristics associated with mastitis, review this content.

Level of Cognitive Ability: Application
Client Needs: Physiological Integrity
Integrated Process: Teaching and Learning
Content Area: Maternity—postpartum
References: Lowdermilk, D., & Perry, S. (2006). *Maternity nursing* (7th ed., p. 831). St. Louis: Mosby.
Murray, S., & McKinney, E. (2006). *Foundations of maternal-newborn nursing* (4th ed., p. 750). Philadelphia: W.B. Saunders.
Wong, D., Perry, S., Hockenberry, M., et al. (2006). *Maternal child nursing care* (3rd ed., p. 669). St. Louis: Mosby.

6. 4

Rationale: Mastitis generally is caused by an organism that enters through an injured area of the nipples, such as a crack or blister. Measures to prevent the development of mastitis include changing nursing pads when they are wet and avoiding continuous pressure on the breasts. Soap is drying and could lead to cracking of the nipples, and the mother should be instructed to avoid the use of soap on the nipples during breast-feeding.

The mother is taught about the importance of hand washing and that she should breast-feed every 2 to 3 hours.

Test-Taking Strategy: Use the process of elimination and note the strategic words *a need for further instructions*. Recalling that the use of soap is drying to the skin, could cause cracking, and thus provide an entry point for organisms will direct you easily to option 4. Review these measures if you had difficulty with this question.

Level of Cognitive Ability: Analysis
Client Needs: Health Promotion and Maintenance
Integrated Process: Teaching and Learning
Content Area: Maternity—postpartum
Reference: Murray, S., & Gorrie, T. (2006). *Foundations of maternal-newborn nursing* (4th ed., p. 750). Philadelphia: W.B. Saunders.

7. 4
Rationale: Broad-spectrum antibiotics will be prescribed for the mother, and the mother should be instructed to take the antibiotics as prescribed. Analgesics are often necessary, and warm compresses or sitz baths may be used to provide comfort in the area. The infant is not isolated routinely from the mother with a wound infection, but the mother must be taught how to protect the infant from contact with contaminated articles.

Test-Taking Strategy: Use the process of elimination, noting the strategic words *need for further instructions*. Eliminate options 2 and 3 first because they are comparative or alike. Knowing that the infant does not need to be isolated from the mother will assist in directing you to the correct option. Review care for the client with a wound infection from an episiotomy site if you had difficulty with this question.

Level of Cognitive Ability: Analysis
Client Needs: Physiological Integrity
Integrated Process: Teaching and Learning
Content Area: Maternity—postpartum
References: Murray, S., & Gorrie, T. (2006). *Foundations of maternal-newborn nursing* (4th ed., p. 752). Philadelphia: W.B. Saunders.
Wong, D., Perry, S., Hockenberry, M., et al. (2006). *Maternal child nursing care* (3rd ed., p. 611). St. Louis: Mosby.

8. 4
Rationale: The use of an epidural, prolonged second-stage labor, and forceps delivery are predisposing factors for hematoma formation, and a collection of up to 500 mL of blood can occur in the vaginal area. Although the other options may be implemented, the immediate action would be to prepare the client for surgery to stop the bleeding.

Test-Taking Strategy: Use the process of elimination and note the strategic word *immediately*. Focus on the clinical manifestations identified in the question to direct you to option 4. Review nursing content related to vulvar hematomas if you had difficulty with this question.

Level of Cognitive Ability: Application
Client Needs: Physiological Integrity
Integrated Process: Nursing Process—planning
Content Area: Maternity—postpartum
Reference: Murray, S., & Gorrie, T. (2006). *Foundations of maternal-newborn nursing* (4th ed., pp. 737, 740). Philadelphia: W.B. Saunders.

9. 4
Rationale: The postoperative client will need an antibiotic because she is at increased risk for infection as a result of the break in skin integrity and collection of blood at the hematoma site. Options 1, 2, and 3 indicate that the mother understands the home care measures following surgical evacuation and repair of a paravaginal hematoma.

Test-Taking Strategy: Use the process of elimination, noting the strategic words *needs further discharge instructions*. These words indicate a negative event query and ask you to select an option that is an incorrect statement. Recalling that the client is at increased risk for infection because of the break in skin integrity and collection of blood at the hematoma site will direct you easily to option 4. Review treatment plans associated with hematoma if you had difficulty with this question.

Level of Cognitive Ability: Analysis
Client Needs: Health Promotion and Maintenance
Integrated Process: Teaching and Learning
Content Area: Maternity—postpartum
References: Lowdermilk, D., & Perry, S. (2004). *Maternity and women's health care* (8th ed., p. 1042). St. Louis: Mosby.
Mattson, S., & Smith, J. (2004). *Core curriculum for maternal-newborn nursing* (3rd ed., p. 853). St. Louis: W.B. Saunders.

10. 3
Rationale: During the fourth stage of labor, the maternal blood pressure, pulse, and respiration should be checked every 15 minutes during the first hour. A rising pulse is an early sign of excessive blood loss because the heart pumps faster to compensate for reduced blood volume. The blood pressure will fall as the blood volume diminishes, but a decreased blood pressure would not be the earliest sign of hemorrhage. A slight rise in temperature is normal. The respiratory rate is increased slightly.

Test-Taking Strategy: Use the process of elimination, noting the strategic word *early* in the question. Think about the physiological occurrences of shock and the expected findings in the postpartum period. This should assist in directing you to option 3. Review signs of early hemorrhage if you had difficulty with this question.

Level of Cognitive Ability: Analysis
Client Needs: Physiological Integrity
Integrated Process: Nursing Process—analysis
Content Area: Maternity—postpartum
References: Lowdermilk, D., & Perry, S. (2004). *Maternity and women's health care* (8th ed., p. 1042). St. Louis: Mosby.
Murray, S., & Gorrie, T. (2006). *Foundations of maternal-newborn nursing* (4th ed., pp. 738-739). Philadelphia: W.B. Saunders.

11. 3
Rationale: If the uterus is not contracted firmly, the initial intervention is to massage the fundus until it is firm and to express clots that may have accumulated in the uterus. Pushing on an uncontracted uterus can invert the uterus and cause massive hemorrhage. Elevating the client's legs and encouraging the client to void will not assist in managing uterine atony. If the uterus does not remain contracted as a result of the uterine massage, the problem may be a distended bladder and the nurse should assist the mother to urinate, but this would not be the initial action.

Test-Taking Strategy: Use the process of elimination. Note the strategic word *initially* in the question. Focus on the subject of the question and knowledge regarding the therapeutic management for uterine atony to assist in directing you to the correct option. If you had difficulty with this question, review therapeutic management for the client with uterine atony.
Level of Cognitive Ability: Application
Client Needs: Physiological Integrity
Integrated Process: Nursing Process—implementation
Content Area: Maternity—postpartum
Reference: Murray, S., & Gorrie, T. (2006). *Foundations of maternal-newborn nursing* (4th ed., pp. 734-735). Philadelphia: W.B. Saunders.

12. **3**
Rationale: Thrombosis of superficial veins usually is accompanied by signs and symptoms of inflammation. These include swelling of the involved extremity and redness, tenderness, and warmth. It also may be possible to palpate the enlarged, hard vein. Clients sometimes experience pain when they walk.
Test-Taking Strategy: Use the process of elimination, eliminating option 4 first because this is a normal and expected finding. Next eliminate options 1 and 2 because they are comparative or alike. If you had difficulty with this question, review the clinical manifestations associated with venous thrombosis.
Level of Cognitive Ability: Analysis
Client Needs: Physiological Integrity
Integrated Process: Nursing Process—assessment
Content Area: Maternity—postpartum
Reference: Murray, S., & Gorrie, T. (2006). *Foundations of maternal-newborn nursing* (4th ed., pp. 742-743). Philadelphia: W.B. Saunders.

13. **3**
Rationale: Thrombosis that is limited to the superficial veins of the saphenous system is treated with analgesics, rest, and elastic support stockings. Elevation of the affected lower extremity to improve venous return also may be recommended. Warm packs may be applied to the affected area to promote healing. There is no need for anticoagulants or antiinflammatory agents unless the condition persists. After 5 to 7 days of bed rest, and when symptoms disappear, the woman may ambulate gradually.
Test-Taking Strategy: Use the process of elimination, focusing on the diagnosis of superficial venous thrombosis. Recalling that anticoagulants are not used in this disorder will assist in eliminating option 2. From the remaining options, eliminate options 1 and 4, recalling that rest and warmth are prescribed to treat this complication. Review therapeutic management of superficial venous thrombosis if you had difficulty with this question.
Level of Cognitive Ability: Application
Client Needs: Physiological Integrity
Integrated Process: Nursing Process—planning
Content Area: Maternity—postpartum
Reference: Murray, S., & Gorrie, T. (200). *Foundations of maternal-newborn nursing* (4th ed., pp. 742-743). Philadelphia: W.B. Saunders.

14. **4**
Rationale: If pulmonary embolism is suspected, oxygen should be administered at 8 to 10 L/min by face mask. Oxygen is used to decrease hypoxia. The woman also is kept on bed rest with the head of the bed slightly elevated to reduce dyspnea. Morphine sulfate may be prescribed for the client, but this action would not be the initial nursing action. An intravenous line also will be required, and vital signs need to be monitored, but these actions would follow the administration of the oxygen.
Test-Taking Strategy: Use the process of elimination, noting the strategic word *initial* in the event query. Use the ABCs—airway, breathing, and circulation—to assist in directing you to option 4. If you had difficulty with this question, review therapeutic management of the client with pulmonary embolism.
Level of Cognitive Ability: Application
Client Needs: Physiological Integrity
Integrated Process: Nursing Process—implementation
Content Area: Maternity—postpartum
Reference: Murray, S., & Gorrie, T. (2006). *Foundations of maternal-newborn nursing* (4th ed., p. 746). Philadelphia: W.B. Saunders.

15. **2**
Rationale: In most cases, the mother can continue to breast-feed with both breasts. If the affected breast is too sore, the mother can pump the breast gently. Regular emptying of the breast is important to prevent abscess formation. Antibiotic therapy assists in resolving the mastitis within 24 to 48 hours. Additional supportive measures include ice packs, breast supports, and analgesics.
Test-Taking Strategy: Use the process of elimination, noting the strategic words *need for further instructions*. These words indicate a negative event query and ask you to select an option that is an incorrect statement. Knowledge regarding the therapeutic management associated with mastitis will assist in eliminating options 1, 3, and 4. Review measures for the client with mastitis if you had difficulty with this question.
Level of Cognitive Ability: Analysis
Client Needs: Physiological Integrity
Integrated Process: Teaching and Learning
Content Area: Maternity—postpartum
Reference: Murray, S., & Gorrie, T. (2006). *Foundations of maternal-newborn nursing* (4th ed., p. 750). Philadelphia: W.B. Saunders.

16. **3**
Rationale: In the first 24 hours after birth, the uterus will feel like a firmly contracted ball, roughly the size of a large grapefruit. One easily can locate the uterus at the level of the umbilicus. Lochia should be dark red and moderate in amount. Saturation of more than one peripad per hour is considered excessive even in the early postpartum period.
Test-Taking Strategy: Use the process of elimination, focusing on the subject of the question. Eliminate those options that indicate normal physiological findings in the fourth stage of labor. Noting the strategic word *saturation* in option 3 will assist in directing you to this option. Review the normal findings in the fourth stage of labor if you had difficulty with this question.
Level of Cognitive Ability: Analysis
Client Needs: Physiological Integrity

Integrated Process: Nursing Process—assessment
Content Area: Maternity—postpartum
References: Lowdermilk, D., & Perry, S. (2006). *Maternity nursing* (7th ed., p. 821). St. Louis: Mosby.
Lowdermilk, D., & Perry, S. (2004). *Maternity and women's health care* (8th ed., pp. 628-629). St. Louis: Mosby.

17. **3**

Rationale: Stasis is believed to be a predisposing factor in the development of thrombophlebitis. Because cesarean delivery is also a risk factor for thrombophlebitis, new mothers should ambulate early and frequently to promote circulation and prevent stasis. Options 1, 2, and 4 are interventions for the client diagnosed with thrombophlebitis.
Test-Taking Strategy: Use the process of elimination, noting the strategic words *prevent thrombophlebitis*. Eliminate options 1, 2, and 4 because they are comparative or alike and are interventions for the client who has been diagnosed with thrombophlebitis. Review content related to the prevention of thrombophlebitis in the postoperative period if you had difficulty with this question.
Level of Cognitive Ability: Application
Client Needs: Health Promotion and Maintenance
Integrated Process: Teaching and Learning
Content Area: Maternity—postpartum
References: Lowdermilk, D., & Perry, S. (2006). *Maternity nursing* (7th ed., p. 829). St. Louis: Mosby.
Murray, S., & Gorrie, T. (2006). *Foundations of maternal-newborn nursing* (4th ed., p. 744). Philadelphia: W.B. Saunders.

18. **4**

Rationale: The treatment for deep venous thrombophlebitis is anticoagulant therapy. The nurse assesses for bleeding, which is an adverse effect of anticoagulants. This includes hematuria, ecchymosis, and epistaxis. Dysuria and vertigo (options 1, 2, and 3) are not associated specifically with bleeding.
Test-Taking Strategy: Use the process of elimination. Recall that deep venous thrombophlebitis is treated with anticoagulant therapy and that bleeding is an adverse effect. Eliminate options 1, 2, and 3 because dysuria and vertigo are not associated specifically with bleeding. Review the treatment for deep venous thrombophlebitis and the adverse effects of treatment if you had difficulty with this question.
Level of Cognitive Ability: Analysis
Client Needs: Physiological Integrity
Integrated Process: Nursing Process—evaluation
Content Area: Maternity—postpartum
References: Lowdermilk, D., & Perry, S. (2006). *Maternity nursing* (7th ed., p. 829). St. Louis: Mosby.
Murray, S., & McKinney, E. (2006). *Foundations of maternal-newborn nursing* (4th ed., pp. 743-745). Philadelphia: W.B. Saunders.

19. **4**

Rationale: Symptoms of hypovolemia include cool, clammy, pale skin, sensations of anxiety or impending doom, restlessness, and thirst. When these symptoms are present, the nurse should further assess for hypovolemia and notify the health care provider. Option 1 will delay necessary treatment. The question gives no indication of the cause of the hypovolemia or that the client is hemorrhaging and that fundal massage is needed. The head of the bed is not elevated in a hypovolemic condition.
Test-Taking Strategy: Use the process of elimination and focus on the data provided in the question. Note the strategic word *immediately*. Use the steps of the nursing process to select the correct option. Option 4 is the only option that addresses assessment. Review the interventions for the client experiencing hypovolemia if you had difficulty with this question.
Level of Cognitive Ability: Application
Client Needs: Physiological Integrity
Integrated Process: Nursing Process—implementation
Content Area: Maternity—postpartum
References: Murray, S., & McKinney, E. (2006). *Foundations of maternal-newborn nursing* (4th ed., pp. 740-741). Philadelphia: W.B. Saunders.
Wong, D., Perry, S., Hockenberry, M., et al. (2006). *Maternal child nursing care* (3rd ed., p. 664). St. Louis: Mosby.

20. **2**

Rationale: If bleeding is excessive, the cause may be laceration of the cervix or birth canal. Massaging the fundus if it is firm will not assist in controlling the bleeding. Trendelenburg's position is to be avoided because it may interfere with cardiac function. Although the nurse would record the findings, the initial nursing action would be to notify the physician.
Test-Taking Strategy: Read the question carefully, noting the subject of the question and the clinical manifestations identified in the question. Use the process of elimination and eliminate option 3 first because, if the uterus is firm, it would not be necessary to perform fundal massage. Knowing that Trendelenburg's position is not advised will assist in eliminating this option. From the remaining options, noting the strategic words *bleeding is excessive* will assist in directing you to option 2. Review the interventions related to a client who is hemorrhaging if you had difficulty with this question.
Level of Cognitive Ability: Application
Client Needs: Physiological Integrity
Integrated Process: Nursing Process—implementation
Content Area: Maternity—postpartum
Reference: Murray, S., & Gorrie, T. (2006). *Foundations of maternal-newborn nursing* (4th ed., pp. 739-740). Philadelphia: W.B. Saunders.

ALTERNATE ITEM FORMAT: MULTIPLE RESPONSE

Answer: 1, 2, 3, 4
Rationale: Mastitis is an infection of the lactating breast. Client instructions include resting during the acute phase, maintaining a fluid intake of at least 3000 mL/day, and taking analgesics to relieve discomfort. Antibiotics may be prescribed and are taken until the complete prescribed course is finished. They are not stopped when the soreness subsides. Additional supportive measures include the use of moist heat or ice packs and wearing a supportive bra. Continued decompression of the breast by breast-feeding or breast pump is important to empty the breast and prevent the formation of an abscess.

Test-Taking Strategy: Think about the pathophysiology associated with mastitis. Recalling that supportive measures include rest, moist heat or ice packs, antibiotics, analgesics, increased fluid intake, breast support, and decompression of the breasts will assist in answering the question. Review the measures to treat mastitis if you had difficulty with this question.
Level of Cognitive Ability: Application

Client Needs: Physiological Integrity
Integrated Process: Teaching and Learning
Content Area: Maternity—postpartum
Reference: Murray, S., & McKinney, E. (2006). *Foundations of maternal-newborn nursing* (4th ed., p. 750). Philadelphia: W.B. Saunders.

REFERENCES

Lowdermilk, D., & Perry, S. (2006). *Maternity nursing* (7th ed.). St. Louis: Mosby.

Lowdermilk, D. & Perry, S. (2004). *Maternity and women's health care* (8th ed.). St. Louis: Mosby.

Mattson, S., & Smith, J. (2004). *Core curriculum for maternal-newborn nursing* (3rd ed.). St. Louis: W.B. Saunders.

Murray, S., & McKinney, E. (2006). *Foundations of maternal-newborn nursing* (4th ed.). Philadelphia: W.B. Saunders.

National Council of State Boards of Nursing (2007). *2007 NCLEX-RN® detailed test plan*. Chicago: Author.

Wong, D., Perry, S., Hockenberry, M., et al. (2006). *Maternal child nursing care* (3rd ed.). St. Louis: Mosby.

Care of the Newborn

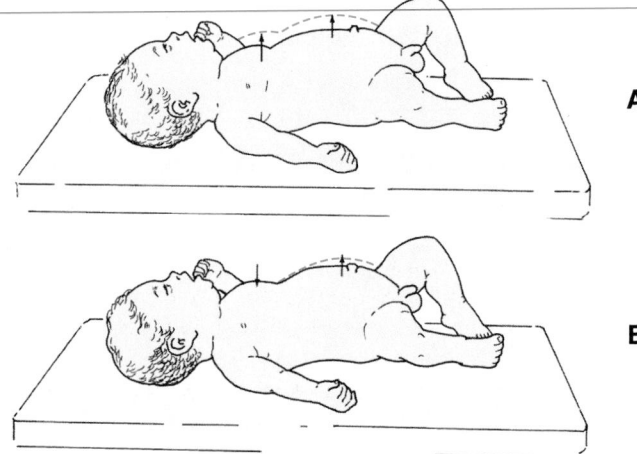

FIG. 30-1 Comparison of normal and seesaw respirations. **A,** Normal respiration. Chest and abdomen rise with inspiration. **B,** Seesaw respiration. Chest wall retracts and abdomen rises with inspiration. (From Lowdermilk, D., & Perry, S. [2006]. *Maternity nursing* [7th ed.]. St. Louis: Mosby. Courtesy of Mead Johnson, Evansville, IN.)

I. INITIAL CARE OF THE NEWBORN

A. Assessment
1. Observe or assist with initiation of respirations.
2. Assess Apgar score.
3. Note characteristics of cry.
4. Monitor for nasal flaring, grunting, retractions, and abnormal respirations, such as a seesaw respiratory pattern (the rise and fall of the chest and abdomen do not occur together) (Fig. 30-1).
5. Assess for cyanosis.
6. Obtain vital signs.
7. Observe **newborn** for signs of hypothermia or hyperthermia.
8. Assess for gross anomalies.

B. Interventions
1. Suction mouth, then nares, with a bulb syringe.
2. Dry **newborn** and stimulate crying by rubbing.
3. Maintain temperature stability; wrap **newborn** in warm blankets and place a stockinette cap on **newborn's** head.
4. Keep **newborn** with mother to facilitate bonding.
5. Place **newborn** at mother's breast if breast-feeding is planned, or place on mother's abdomen.
6. Place **newborn** in radiant warmer.
7. Position **newborn** on side with a rolled blanket at the back to facilitate drainage of mucus.
8. Ensure **newborn's** proper identification.
9. Footprint **newborn** and fingerprint mother on identification sheet per agency policies and procedures.
10. Place matching identification bracelets on mother and **newborn**.

C. Apgar scoring system
1. Perform and record the Apgar score at 1 minute and at 5 minutes.
2. Assess each of five items to be scored, and assign value of 0 (very poor) to 2 (excellent) for each item.
3. Add the points to determine the **newborn's** total score.
4. Five vital indicators (Table 30-1)
5. Interventions: Apgar score (Table 30-2)

II. INITIAL PHYSICAL EXAMINATION

A. General guidelines
1. Keep **newborn** warm during the examination.
2. Begin with general observations and then perform assessments that are least disturbing to the **newborn** first.
3. Initiate nursing interventions for abnormal findings.
4. Document all abnormal findings.

TABLE 30-1

Five Vital Indicators of Apgar Scoring

Indicator	0 Points	1 Point	2 Points
Heart rate	Absent	Less than 100 beats/min	More than 100 beats/min
Respiratory rate	Absent	Slow, irregular, weak cry	Good, vigorous cry
Muscle tone	Flaccid, limp	Minimal flexion of extremities	Good flexion, active motion
Reflex irritability	No response	Minimal response (grimace) to suction or to gentle slap on soles	Responds promptly with a cry or active movement
Skin color	Pallor or cyanosis	Body skin normal, extremities blue	Body and extremity skin color normal

TABLE 30-2

Apgar Score Interventions

Score	Intervention
8-10	No intervention is required except to support the infant's spontaneous efforts.
4-7	Gently stimulate. Rub infant's back. Administer oxygen to infant.
0-3	Infant requires resuscitation.

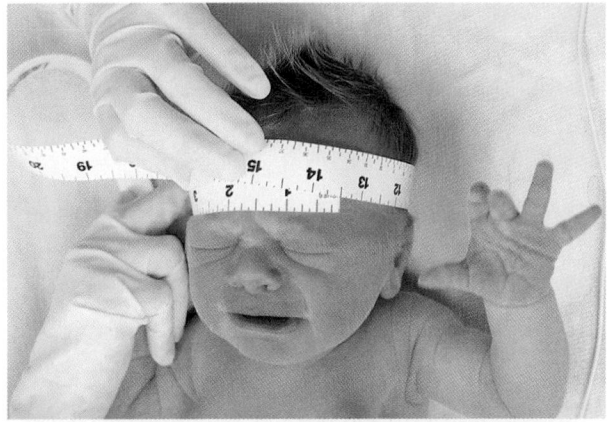
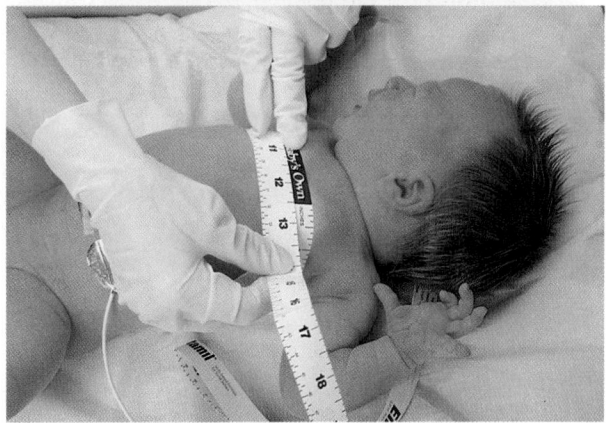

FIG. 30-2 Circumference of head and chest. (From Murray, S., & McKinney, E. [2006]. *Foundations of maternal-newborn nursing* [4th ed.]. Philadelphia: W.B. Saunders.)

 B. Vital signs
   1. Heart rate (resting): 100 to 160 beats/min (apical); auscultate at the fourth intercostal space for 1 full minute to detect abnormalities
   2. Respirations: 30 to 60 breaths/min; assess for 1 full minute
   3. Assess heart rate and respiratory rate first while **infant** is resting or sleeping.
   4. Axillary temperature: 96.8° to 99° F
   5. Blood pressure: 73/55 mm Hg
C. Body measurements
   1. Length: 45 to 55 cm (18 to 22 inches)
   2. Weight: 2500 to 4300 g (5.5 to 9.5 lb)
   3. Head and chest circumference (Fig. 30-2)
D. Head
   1. Head should be 25% of the body length (cephalocaudal development).
   2. Bones of the skull are not fused.
   3. Sutures (connective tissue between the skull bones) are palpable and may be overlapping because of head molding but should not be widened.
   4. Fontanels are unossified membranous tissue at the junction of the sutures (Table 30-3).
   5. Molding is asymmetry of the head resulting from pressure in the birth canal; molding disappears in about 72 hours (Fig. 30-3)
   6. Masses from birth trauma
     a. Caput succedaneum is edema of the soft tissue over bone (crosses over suture line); it subsides within a few days.
     b. Cephalhematoma is swelling caused by bleeding into an area between the bone and

its periosteum (does not cross over suture line); it usually is absorbed within 6 weeks with no treatment.
   7. Head lag
     a. Common when pulling **newborn** to a sitting position
     b. When prone, **newborn** should be able to lift the head slightly and turn the head from side to side
E. Eyes
   1. Slate gray (light skin), dark blue, or brown-gray (dark skin)
   2. Symmetrical and clear

TABLE 30-3

Fontanels

Fontanel	Characteristics	Closure
Anterior	Soft, flat, diamond-shaped, 3-4 cm wide by 2-3 cm long	Between 12 and 18 months of age
Posterior	Triangular, 0.5-1 cm wide Located between occipital and parietal bones	Between birth and 2-3 months of age

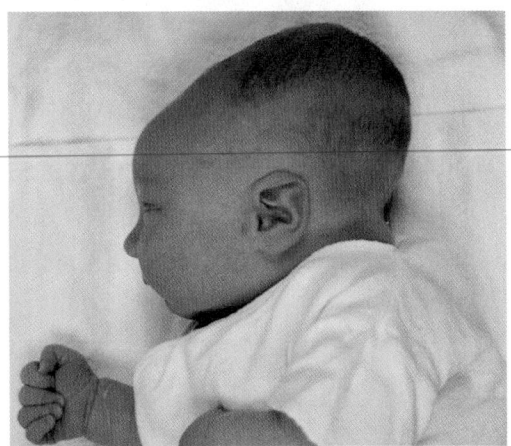

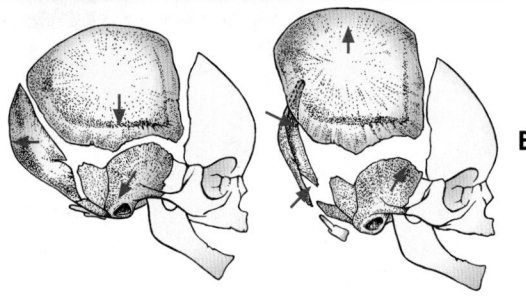

FIG. 30-3 Molding. **A,** Significant molding, soon after birth. **B,** Schematic of bones of skull when molding is present. (From Lowdermilk, D., & Perry, S. [2006]. *Maternity nursing* [7th ed.]. St. Louis: Mosby. Courtesy of Kim Molloy, Knoxville, IA.)

3. Pupils equal, round, react to light and by accommodation
4. Blink reflex present
5. Eyes cross because of weak extraocular muscles
6. Ability to track and fixate momentarily
7. Red reflex present
8. Eyelids often edematous as a result of pressure during the birth process and effects of eye medication

F. Ears
1. Symmetrical
2. Firm cartilage with recoil
3. Top of pinna on or above line drawn from outer canthus of eye
4. Low-set ears associated with Down syndrome

G. Nose
1. Flat, broad, in center of face
2. Obligatory nose breathing
3. Occasional sneezing to remove obstructions
4. Nares are patent and should not flare (flaring is indication of respiratory distress)

H. Mouth
1. Pink, moist gums
2. Soft and hard palates intact
3. Epstein's pearls (small, white cysts) may be present on hard palate
4. Uvula in midline
5. Freely moving tongue, symmetrical, has short frenulum
6. Sucking and crying movements symmetrical
7. Able to swallow
8. Root and gag reflexes present
9. Assess for thrush *(Candida albicans);* white patchy areas evident on tongue or gums that cannot be removed with a washcloth (may be painful)

I. Neck
1. Short and thick
2. Head held in midline
3. Trachea on midline
4. Good range of motion and ability to flex and extend
5. Assess for torticollis (head inclined to one side as a result of contraction of muscles on that side of the neck)

J. Chest
1. Circular appearance because anteroposterior and lateral diameters are about equal
2. Diaphragmatic respirations—chest and abdomen should rise and fall in synchrony, not in seesaw pattern
3. Bronchial sounds heard on auscultation
4. Nipples prominent and often edematous; milky secretion (witch's milk) common
5. Breast tissue present
6. Clavicles need to be palpated to assess for fractures.

K. Skin
1. Pinkish-red (light-skinned **newborn**) to pinkish-brown or pinkish-yellow (dark-skinned **newborn**)
2. Vernix caseosa, cheesy white substance, can be found on entire body but more intense between folds
3. Lanugo, fine hair, might be seen, especially on back
4. Milia, small white sebaceous glands, appearing on forehead, nose and chin

5. Dry, peeling skin
6. Dark red color common in premature **newborns**
7. Cyanosis common with hypothermia, infection, and hypoglycemia and with cardiac, respiratory, or neurological abnormalities
8. Acrocyanosis (peripheral cyanosis) normal in first few hours after birth and then may be noted intermittently for next 7 to 10 days
9. Assessment for ecchymosis and petechiae resulting from trauma of birth
10. Assessment of skin turgor over the abdomen to determine hydration status
11. Observation for forceps marks
12. Harlequin sign
    a. Deep pink or red color develops over one side of **newborn's** body while other side remains pale or of normal color.
    b. Harlequin sign may indicate shunting of blood with a cardiac problem or may indicate sepsis.
13. Birthmarks (Table 30-4)
L. Abdomen
1. Umbilical cord
    a. Umbilical cord should have three vessels: two arteries and one vein; if fewer than three vessels are noted, notify the physician.
    b. Small, thin cord may be associated with poor fetal growth.
    c. Assess for intact cord, and ensure that the cord clamp is secured.
    d. Cord should be clamped for at least the first 24 hours after birth; clamp can be removed when the cord is dried and occluded.
    e. Note any bleeding or drainage from the cord.
    f. Hospital protocol and physician's preference determine the technique for cord care; an antibiotic ointment or triple dye may be prescribed, or cleansing with sterile water or soap and water.
    g. If symptoms of infection, such as moistness, oozing, discharge, and a reddened base occur, antibiotic treatment is prescribed.
2. Gastrointestinal
    a. Monitor cord for meconium staining.
    b. Assess for umbilical hernia.
    c. Assess for abdominal depression associated with diaphragmatic hernia.
    d. Assess for abdominal distention associated with obstruction, mass, or sepsis.
    e. Monitor bowel sounds, which should occur within 1 to 2 hours after birth.
3. Anus
    a. Ensure that anal opening is patent.
    b. First stool meconium should pass within first 24 hours.

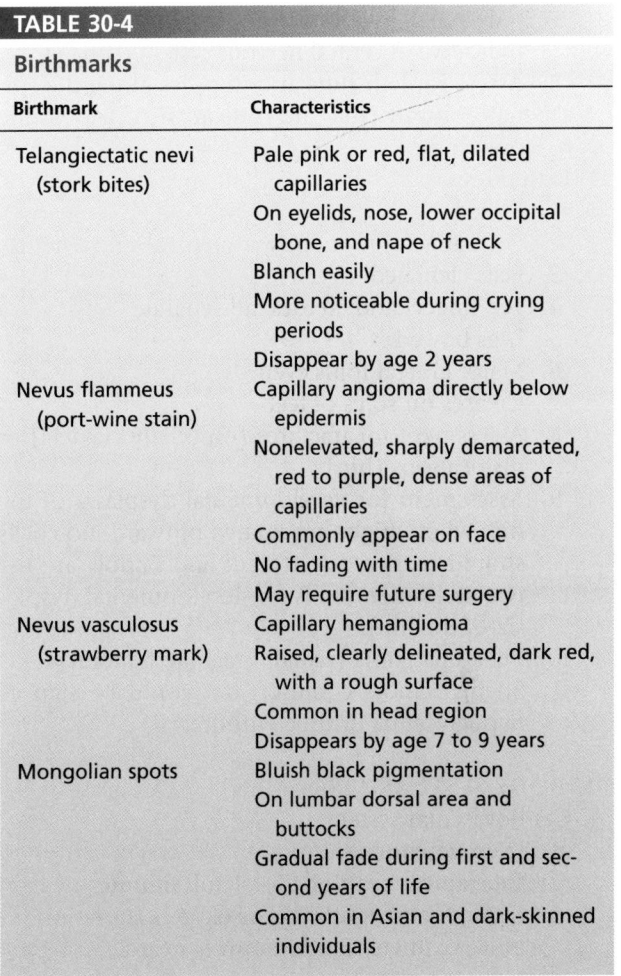

TABLE 30-4

Birthmarks

Birthmark	Characteristics
Telangiectatic nevi (stork bites)	Pale pink or red, flat, dilated capillaries
	On eyelids, nose, lower occipital bone, and nape of neck
	Blanch easily
	More noticeable during crying periods
	Disappear by age 2 years
Nevus flammeus (port-wine stain)	Capillary angioma directly below epidermis
	Nonelevated, sharply demarcated, red to purple, dense areas of capillaries
	Commonly appear on face
	No fading with time
	May require future surgery
Nevus vasculosus (strawberry mark)	Capillary hemangioma
	Raised, clearly delineated, dark red, with a rough surface
	Common in head region
	Disappears by age 7 to 9 years
Mongolian spots	Bluish black pigmentation
	On lumbar dorsal area and buttocks
	Gradual fade during first and second years of life
	Common in Asian and dark-skinned individuals

M. Genitals
1. Female
    a. Labia are edematous; clitoris is enlarged.
    b. Smegma may be present (thick, white mucous discharge).
    c. Pseudomenstruation, caused from the withdrawal of the maternal hormone estrogen, is possible (blood-tinged mucus).
    d. Hymen tag may be visible.
    e. First voiding should occur within 24 hours.
2. Male
    a. Prepuce (foreskin) covers glans penis.
    b. Scrotum is edematous.
    c. Verify meatus at tip of penis.
    d. Testes descended but may retract with cold.
    e. Assess for hernia or hydrocele.
    f. First voiding should occur within 24 hours.
N. Spine
1. Straight
2. Posture flexed
3. Supportive of head momentarily when prone
4. Arms and legs flexed
5. Chin flexed on upper chest
6. Well-coordinated, sporadic movements

7. A degree of hypotonicity or hypertonicity may be indicative of central nervous system damage.
8. Assess for hair tufts and dimples along the spinal column (may be indicative of a possible opening).

O. Extremities
1. Flexed
2. Full range of motion; symmetrical movements
3. Fists clenched
4. Ten fingers and 10 toes, all separate
5. Legs bowed
6. Major gluteal folds even
7. Creases on soles of feet
8. Assessment for fractures (especially clavicle) or dislocations (hip)
9. Assessment for developmental dysplasia of the hip; when thighs are rotated outward, no clicks should be heard (Ortolani and Barlow are the two assessment tools for developmental dysplasia of the hip).
10. Pulses palpable (radial, brachial, femoral)
11. Slight tremors common but could be sign of hypoglycemia or drug withdrawal

III. BODY SYSTEMS ASSESSMENT

A. Cardiovascular system
1. Keep **newborn** warm.
2. Take apical heart rate for 1 full minute.
3. Listen for murmurs; assess oxygen saturation via pulse oximetry if a murmur is heard.
4. Palpate pulses.
5. Assess for cyanosis; blanch skin on trunk and extremities to assess circulation.
6. Observe for cardiac distress when **newborn** is feeding.

B. Respiratory system
1. Position **newborn** on side.
2. Suction airway as necessary: use a bulb syringe for upper airway suctioning (compress bulb before insertion) and a French catheter for deeper suctioning.
3. Observe for respiratory distress and hypoxemia.
   a. Nasal flaring
   b. Increasingly severe retractions
   c. Grunting
   d. Cyanosis
   e. Bradycardia and periods of apnea lasting longer than 15 seconds
4. Administer oxygen via hood if necessary and as prescribed.

C. Hepatic system
1. Normal or physiological jaundice appears after the first 24 hours in full-term **neonates** and after the first 48 hours in premature **neonates;** jaundice occurring before this time (pathological jaundice) may indicate early hemolysis of red blood cells and must be reported to the physician.
2. Physiological jaundice peaks about the fifth day of life (indirect bilirubin levels, 6 to 7 mg/dL).
3. Monitor serum bilirubin levels.
4. Feed early to stimulate intestinal activity and to keep the bilirubin level low.
5. Prevent chilling, because hypothermia can cause acidosis that interferes with bilirubin conjugation and excretion.
6. Liver stores iron passed from the mother for 5 to 6 months.
7. Glycogen storage occurs in the liver.
8. **Neonate** is at risk for hemorrhagic disorders; coagulation factors synthesized in the liver depend on vitamin K, which is not synthesized until intestinal bacteria are present.
9. Handle **neonate** carefully and monitor for any bruising or bleeding episodes.
10. Watch for meconium stool and subsequent stools.
11. Administer intramuscular vitamin K (Aqua-MEPHYTON) to the **neonate** as prescribed to prevent hemorrhagic disorders (usually, a dose of 0.5 to 1.0 mg is prescribed); administer in the lateral aspect of the middle third of the vastus lateralis muscle.
12. Assess **newborn's** hemoglobin and blood glucose levels.

D. Renal system
1. The immature kidneys are unable to concentrate urine.
2. A weight loss of 5% to 15% during the first week of life occurs as a result of voiding and limited intake; birth weight should be regained by 10 to 14 days after birth.
3. Weigh **newborn** daily.
4. Monitor intake and output; weigh diapers if necessary (1 g of diaper weight equals 1 mL of urine).
5. If the diaper requires weighing, record the weight before putting it on the **infant;** after the **infant** voids, reweigh the diaper and subtract the prevoided weight.
6. Measure specific gravity of urine if necessary.
7. Assess for signs of dehydration (dry mucous membranes, sunken eyeballs, poor skin turgor, sunken fontanels).

E. Immune system
1. **Newborn** receives passive immunity via the **placenta** (immunoglobulin G).
2. **Newborn** receives passive immunity from colostrum (immunoglobulin A).
3. Elevations in immunoglobulin M indicate infection in utero.
4. Use aseptic technique when caring for the **newborn.**
5. Observe standard precautions when handling the **newborn.**
6. Ensure meticulous hand washing.

7. Ensure that an infection-free staff cares for the **newborn.**
8. Monitor **newborn's** temperature.
9. Observe for any cracks or openings in the skin.
10. Administer eye medication within 1 hour after birth to prevent ophthalmia neonatorum.
    a. Erythromycin (0.5%) and tetracycline (1%) ophthalmic ointment or drops are bacteriostatic and bactericidal and provide prophylaxis against *Neisseria gonorrhoeae* and *Chlamydia trachomatis.*
    b. Silver nitrate (1%) solution may be prescribed, but its use is minimal because it does not protect against chlamydial infection and can cause chemical conjunctivitis.
11. Provide cord care.
    a. Umbilical clamp can be removed after 24 hours.
    b. Teach mother how to perform cord care.
    c. Keep the cord clean and dry; soap and water may be prescribed for cleansing the cord.
    d. Keep diaper from covering cord; fold diaper below cord.
    e. Assess cord for odor, swelling, or discharge.
    f. The **newborn** is cleaned via a sponge bath until the cord falls off (within 2 weeks).
12. Provide circumcision care.
    a. Apply petroleum jelly gauze to the penis except when a PlastiBell is used (Fig. 30-4).
    b. Remove petroleum jelly gauze, if applied, after first voiding following circumcision.
    c. Observe for swelling, infection, or bleeding from the circumcision site.
    d. Teach mother care of circumcision site.
    e. Cleanse the penis after each voiding by squeezing warm water over the penis.

f. A milky covering over the glans penis is normal and should not be disrupted.
g. Monitor for urinary retention.

F. Metabolic system and gastrointestinal system
1. **Newborns** are able to digest simple carbohydrates but are unable to digest fats because of the lack of lipase.
2. Proteins may be broken down only partially, so they may serve as antigens and provoke an allergic reaction.
3. The **newborn** has a small stomach capacity (about 90 mL), with rapid intestinal peristalsis (bowel emptying time is 2.5 to 3 hours).
4. Breast-feeding usually can begin immediately after birth; bottle-fed **newborns** may be offered a few milliliters of sterile water or 5% dextrose 1 to 4 hours after birth before a feeding with formula.
5. Observe feeding reflexes, such as rooting, sucking, and swallowing.
6. Assist mother with breast-feeding or formula feeding; breast-feeding should be done every 2 to 3 hours and formula feeding (minimum of 30 mL, or 1 oz) should be done every 3 to 4 hours.
7. Burp **newborn** during and after feeding.
8. Assess for regurgitation or vomiting.
9. Position **newborn** on right side after feeding.
10. Observe for normal stool and the passage of meconium.
    a. Meconium stool, which is greenish-black with a thick, sticky, tar-like consistency, usually is passed within the first 24 hours of life.
    b. Transitional stool, the second type of stool excreted by the **newborn,** is greenish-

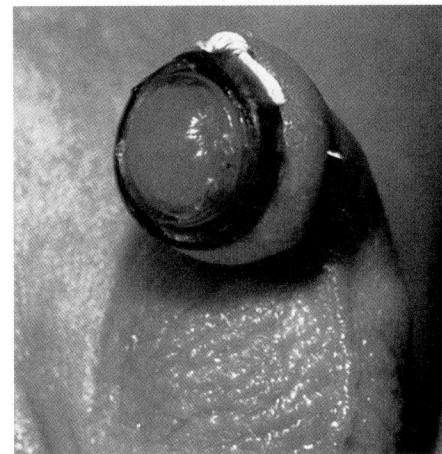
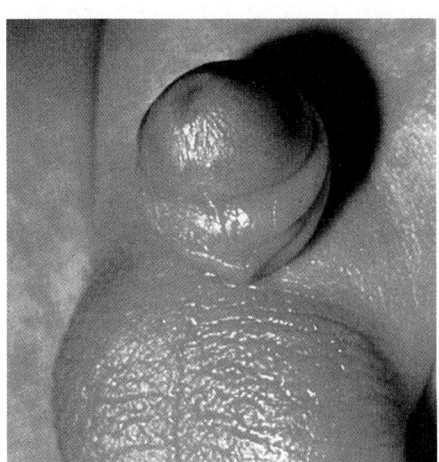

FIG. 30-4 Circumcision by using the Hollister PlastiBell. **A,** Suture around rim of PlastiBell controls bleeding. **B,** Plastic rim and suture drop off in 7 to 10 days. (From Lowdermilk, D., & Perry, S. [2006]. *Maternity nursing* [7th ed.]. St. Louis: Mosby. Courtesy of Hollister Incorporated, Libertyville, IL.)

brown and of looser consistency than meconium.

c. Seedy, yellow stools are noted in breast-fed **newborns;** pale yellow to light brown stools are seen in formula-fed **newborns.**

11. Perform **newborn** screening test (including the test for phenylketonuria) before discharge after sufficient protein intake occurs; the **newborn** should be on formula or breast milk for 24 hours before screening.

▲ G. Neurological system

1. **Newborn** head size is proportionally larger than that of an adult because of cephalocaudal development.
2. Myelinization of nerve fibers is incomplete, so primitive reflexes are present.
3. Fontanels are open to allow for brain growth.
4. Assess for an abnormal head size and a bulging or depressed anterior fontanel.
5. Measure and graph head circumference in relation to chest circumference and length.
6. Assess **newborn's** movements, noting symmetry, posture, and abnormal movements.
7. Observe for jitteriness, marked tremors, and seizures.
8. Test **newborn's** reflexes.
9. Assess for lethargy.
10. Assess pitch of cry.

▲ H. Thermal regulatory system

1. **Newborns** do not shiver to produce heat.
2. **Newborns** have brown fat deposits, which produce heat.
3. Heat is dissipated through vasodilation.
4. Prevent heat loss resulting from evaporation by keeping **newborn** dry and well wrapped with a blanket.
5. Prevent heat loss resulting from radiation by keeping **newborn** away from cold objects and outside walls.
6. Prevent heat loss resulting from convection by shielding the **newborn** from drafts.
7. Prevent heat loss resulting from conduction by performing all treatments on a warm, padded surface.
8. Keep temperature in room warm.
9. Take **newborn's** axillary temperature every hour for the first 4 hours of life, every 4 hours for the remainder of the first 24 hours, and then every shift.

▲ I. Reflexes

1. Sucking and rooting
   a. Touch the **newborn's** lip, cheek, or corner of the mouth with a nipple.
   b. Newborn turns head toward the nipple, opens the mouth, takes hold of the nipple, and sucks.
   c. Rooting reflex usually disappears after 3 to 4 months but may persist for up to 1 year.

2. Swallowing reflex
   a. Swallowing reflex occurs spontaneously after sucking and obtaining fluids.
   b. **Newborn** swallows in coordination with sucking without gagging, coughing, or vomiting.

3. Tonic neck or fencing
   a. While the **newborn** is falling asleep or sleeping, gently and quickly turn the head to one side.
   b. As the **newborn** faces the left side, the left arm and leg extend outward while the right arm and leg flex.
   c. When the head is turned to the right side, the right arm and leg extend outward while the left arm and leg flex.
   d. Response usually disappears within 3 to 4 months.

4. Palmar-plantar grasp
   a. Place a finger in the palm of the **newborn's** hand and then place a finger at the base of the toes.
   b. The **newborn's** fingers curl around the examiner's fingers, and the **newborn's** toes curl downward.
   c. Palmar response lessens within 3 to 4 months.
   d. Plantar response lessens within 8 months.

5. Moro reflex
   a. Place the **newborn** on a flat surface and strike the surface or make a loud abrupt noise to startle the **newborn.**
   b. The **newborn** symmetrically abducts and extends the arms.
   c. The **newborn** fans the fingers out and forms a "C" with the thumb and the forefinger.
   d. The **newborn** adducts the arms to an embracing position and returns to a relaxed flexion state.
   e. The Moro reflex is present at birth; a complete response may occur up to 8 weeks.
   f. A body jerk motion occurs from 8 to 18 weeks.
   g. No response may be noted by 6 months as long as neurological maturation has not been delayed.
   h. A persistent response lasting more than 6 months may indicate the occurrence of brain damage during pregnancy.

6. Startle reflex
   a. The response is best elicited if the **newborn** is a least 24 hours old.
   b. The examiner makes a loud noise or claps hands to elicit the response.
   c. The **newborn's** arms adduct while the elbows flex.
   d. The hands stay clenched.
   e. The reflex should disappear within 4 months.

7. Pull-to-sit response
    a. Pull the **newborn** up from the wrist while the **newborn** is in the supine position.
    b. The head will lag until the **newborn** is in an upright position, and then the head will be level with the chest and shoulders momentarily before falling forward.
    c. The head will then lift for a few minutes.
    d. The response depends on the **newborn's** general muscle tone and condition and on maturity level.
8. Babinski sign: Plantar reflex
    a. Beginning at the heel of the foot, gently stroke upward along the lateral aspect of the sole, and then move the finger along the ball of the foot.
    b. The **newborn's** toes hyperextend while the big toe dorsiflexes.
    c. The reflex disappears after the **newborn** is 1 year old.
    d. Absence of this reflex indicates the need for a neurological examination.
9. Stepping or walking
    a. Hold the **newborn** in a vertical position, allowing one foot to touch a table surface.
    b. The **newborn** simulates walking, alternately flexing and extending the feet.
    c. The reflex is usually present for 3 to 4 months.
10. Crawling
    a. Place the **newborn** on the abdomen
    b. The **newborn** begins making crawling movements with the arms and legs.
    c. The reflex usually disappears after about 6 weeks.

▲ IV. NEWBORN SAFETY
A. **Infant** identification
1. Information bracelets are applied to mother and **newborn** immediately after birth and before the mother and **newborn** are separated.
2. The bracelets include name, sex, date, time of birth, and identification numbers.
B. **Infant** abduction
1. Mother is taught to check identification of any person who comes to remove the baby from her room and is taught other precautions to prevent **infant** abduction (Box 30-1**)**.
2. Closed-circuit televisions, code-alert bands, or computer monitoring systems may be used on some units (Fig. 30-5).
3. The **newborn** is wheeled in a bassinette, not carried in a staff member's arms.

▲ V. PARENT TEACHING
A. Formula feeding
1. Teach sterilization techniques if the water supply is located in areas where the purification process of the water is questionable.

BOX 30-1
Precautions to Prevent Infant Abduction

All personnel must wear identification that is easily visible at all times.
Teach parents only to allow hospital staff with proper identification to take their infants from them.
Question anyone with a newborn near an exit or in an unusual part of the facility.
Never leave infants unattended.
Teach parents that infants must be observed at all times.
When infant is in the mother's room, position the crib away from the doorway.
Suggest that parents not place announcements in the paper or signs in their yard that might alert an abductor that a new baby is in the home.

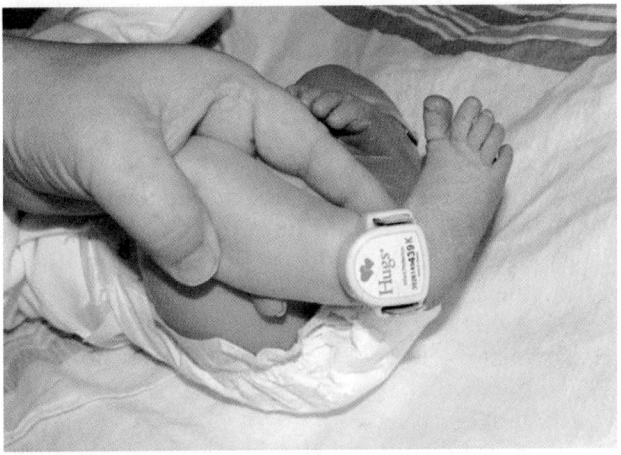

FIG. 30-5 Neonatal safety device. (From Lowdermilk, D., & Perry, S. [2006]. *Maternity nursing* [7th ed.]. St. Louis: Mosby. Courtesy of Shannon Perry, Phoenix, AZ.)

2. Remind the mother not to heat the bottle of formula in a microwave oven.
3. Inform the mother that formula is a sufficient diet for the first 4 to 6 months.
4. Assess the mother's ability to burp the **newborn.**
B. Breast-feeding
1. Assess the **newborn's** ability to attach to the mother's breast and suck (Fig. 30-6).
2. Teach the mother about engorgement.
3. Teach the mother how to pump her breasts and how to store breast milk properly.
4. Inform the mother that breast milk is a sufficient and superior diet for the first 4 to 6 months.
5. Give the mother the phone numbers of the local organizations that offer support to breast-feeding mothers.
C. Bathing
1. Bathe the **newborn** in a warm room before feeding.
2. Have all equipment for bathing available.
3. Use a mild soap (not on the face).

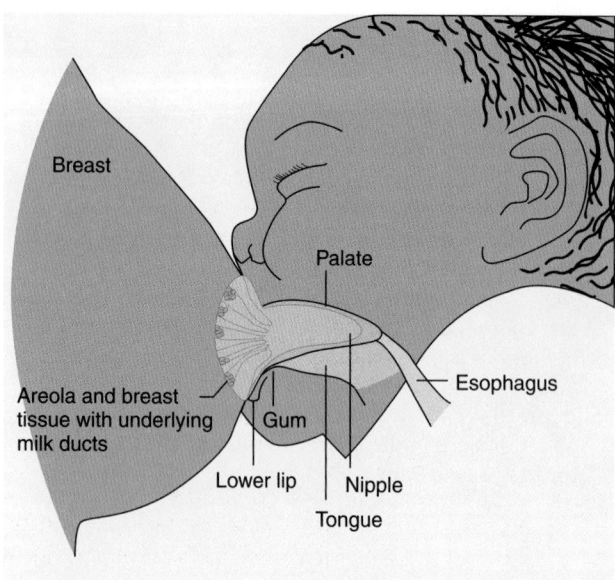

FIG. 30-6 Correct attachment (latch-on) of infant at breast. (From Lowdermilk, D., & Perry, S. [2006]. *Maternity nursing* [7th ed.]. St. Louis: Mosby.)

4. Proceed from the cleanest area to the dirtiest.
5. Clean eyes from the inner canthus outward.
6. Special care should be taken to clean under the folds of the neck, underarms, groin, and genitals.
7. Make bath time enjoyable for the **newborn** and the mother.

D. Clothing
1. Assess diaper and clothing needs for the **newborn** with the mother.
2. Instruct the mother that the **newborn's** head should be covered in cold weather to prevent heat loss.
3. Instruct the mother to layer the **newborn's** clothing in cooler weather.
4. As a rule, to be comfortable, the **infant** should be dressed in one more layer of clothing than what the parents are wearing.

E. Cord care: See earlier for cord care, "Body Systems Assessment."

F. Circumcision: See earlier for circumcision care, "Body Systems Assessment."

G. Uncircumcised **newborn**
1. Inform the mother that the foreskin and glans are two similar layers of cells that separate from each other and that the separation process normally is complete by 3 years of age, but can remain adhered until puberty.
2. Instruct the mother not to pull back the foreskin but to allow for the natural separation to occur.
3. Inform the mother that as the process of separation occurs, sloughed cells build up between the layers of the foreskin and the glans, and that

when retraction occurs, daily gentle washing of the glans with soap and water is sufficient to maintain adequate cleanliness.

VI. PRETERM NEWBORN
A. Description
1. A **neonate** born before 37 weeks of gestation
2. Primary concern relates to immaturity of all body systems

B. Assessment
1. Respirations are irregular with periods of apnea.
2. Body temperature is below normal.
3. **Newborn** has poor suck and swallow reflexes.
4. Bowel sounds are diminished.
5. Urinary output is increased or decreased.
6. Extremities are thin, with minimal creasing on soles and palms.
7. **Newborn** extends extremities and does not maintain flexion.
8. Lanugo, on skin and in the hair on the **newborn's** head, is present in woolly patches.
9. Skin is thin, with visible blood vessels and minimal subcutaneous fat pads.
10. Skin may appear jaundiced.
11. Testes are undescended in boys.
12. Labia are narrow in girls.

C. Interventions
1. Monitor vital signs every 2 to 4 hours.
2. Maintain cardiopulmonary functions.
3. Administer oxygen and humidification as prescribed.
4. Monitor intake and output and electrolyte balance.
5. Monitor daily weight.
6. Maintain **newborn** in a warming device.
7. Reposition every 1 to 2 hours, and handle **newborn** carefully.
8. Avoid exposure to infections.
9. Provide **newborn** with appropriate stimulation, such as touch.

VII. POST-TERM NEWBORN
A. Description: N**eonate** born after 42 weeks of gestation
B. Assessment
1. Hypoglycemia
2. Parchment-like skin (dry and cracked) without lanugo
3. Fingernails long and extended over ends of fingers
4. Profuse scalp hair
5. Long and thin body
6. Wasting of fat and muscle in extremities
7. Meconium staining possibly present on nails and umbilical cord

C. Interventions
1. Provide normal **newborn** care.
2. Monitor for hypoglycemia.
3. Maintain **newborn's** temperature.
4. Monitor for meconium aspiration.

VIII. SMALL FOR GESTATIONAL AGE
A. Description: **Neonate** who is plotted at or below the 10th percentile on the intrauterine growth curve
B. Assessment
1. Fetal distress
2. Gestational age and physical maturity
3. Lowered or elevated body temperature
4. Physical abnormalities
5. Hypoglycemia
6. Signs of polycythemia
   a. Ruddy appearance
   b. Cyanosis
   c. Jaundice
7. Signs of infection
8. Signs of aspiration of meconium
C. Interventions
1. Maintain airway.
2. Maintain body temperature.
3. Observe for signs of respiratory distress.
4. Monitor for infection and initiate measures to prevent sepsis.
5. Monitor blood glucose levels and for signs of hypoglycemia.
6. Initiate early feedings and monitor for signs of aspiration.
7. Provide stimulation, such as touch and cuddling.

IX. LARGE FOR GESTATIONAL AGE
A. Description: **Neonate** who is plotted at or above the 90th percentile on the intrauterine growth curve
B. Assessment
1. Gestational age
2. Birth trauma or injury
3. Respiratory distress
4. Hypoglycemia
C. Interventions
1. Monitor vital signs.
2. Monitor blood glucose levels and for signs of hypoglycemia.
3. Initiate early feedings.
4. Monitor for infection and initiate measures to prevent sepsis.
5. Provide stimulation, such as touch and cuddling.

X. RESPIRATORY DISTRESS SYNDROME (RDS)
A. Description: Serious lung disorder caused by immaturity and inability to produce **surfactant**, resulting in hypoxia and acidosis

B. Assessment
1. Tachypnea
2. Flaring nares
3. Expiratory grunting
4. Retractions
5. Seesaw respirations
6. Decreased breath sounds
7. Apnea
8. Pallor and cyanosis
9. Hypothermia
10. Poor muscle tone
C. Interventions
1. Monitor color, respiratory rate, and degree of effort in breathing.
2. Support respirations as prescribed.
3. Monitor arterial blood gases and oxygen saturation levels (arterial blood gases from umbilical artery).
4. Monitor arterial blood gases so that oxygen administered to the **newborn** is at the lowest possible concentration necessary to maintain adequate arterial oxygenation.
5. Any premature **newborn** who required oxygen support should be scheduled for an eye examination before discharge to assess for retinal damage.
6. Suction every 2 hours or more often as necessary.
7. Position **newborn** on side or back, with neck slightly extended.
8. Prepare to administer **surfactant** replacement therapy (instilled into the endotracheal tube).
9. Administer respiratory therapy (percussion and vibration) as prescribed; use padded small plastic cup or small oxygen mask for percussion; use padded electric toothbrush for vibration.
10. Provide nutrition.
11. Support bonding.
12. Prepare parents for short- to long-term period of oxygen dependency if necessary.
13. Encourage mother to pump breasts for future breast-feeding if she so desires.
14. Encourage as much parental participation in **newborn's** care as condition allows.

XI. MECONIUM ASPIRATION SYNDROME
A. Description
1. Occurs in term or post-term **infants**
2. Fetal distress increases intestinal peristalsis, relaxing the anal sphincter and releasing meconium into the **amniotic fluid.**
3. Aspiration can occur in utero or with the first breath.
B. Assessment
1. Respiratory distress is present at birth; tachypnea, cyanosis, retractions, nasal flaring, grunting, crackles, and rhonchi may be present.

2. The **infant's** nails, skin, and umbilical cord may be stained a yellow-green color.

C. Interventions

1. Suctioning must be done immediately after the head is delivered before the first breath is taken; vocal cords should be viewed to see if the airway is clear before stimulation and crying.

2. **Infants** with severe meconium aspiration syndrome may benefit from extracorporeal membrane oxygenation (ECMO).

XII. BRONCHOPULMONARY DYSPLASIA

A. Description

1. This chronic pulmonary condition affects **infants** who have experienced respiratory failure or have been oxygen-dependent for more than 28 days.

2. X-ray findings are abnormal, indicating areas of overinflation and atelectasis.

3. Neonate may exhibit respiratory symptoms.

B. Assessment

1. Tachypnea

2. Tachycardia

3. Retractions

4. Nasal flaring

5. Labored breathing

6. Crackles and decreased air movement

7. Occasional expiratory wheezing

C. Interventions

1. Oxygen therapy

2. Fluid restriction may be prescribed

3. Medications may include **surfactant,** diuretics, corticosteroids, bronchodilators

XIII. TRANSIENT TACHYPNEA OF THE NEWBORN (TTN)

A. Description

1. Respiratory condition that results from incomplete evacuation of fetal lung fluid in full-term **infants**

2. Usually disappears within 24 to 48 hours

B. Assessment

1. Tachypnea

2. Expiratory grunting

3. Retractions

4. Cyanosis that responds to minimal oxygen

5. Nasal flaring

6. Wet lung sounds per auscultation

C. Interventions

1. Supportive care

2. Oxygen administration

XIV. INTRAVENTRICULAR HEMORRHAGE

A. Description

1. Bleeding within the ventricles of the brain

2. Risk factors include prematurity, RDS, trauma, or asphyxia.

B. Assessment: Diminished or absent Moro reflex, lethargy, apnea, poor feeding, high-pitched shrill cry, seizure activity

C. Interventions: Supportive treatment

XV. RETINOPATHY OF PREMATURITY

A. Description

1. Vascular disorder involving gradual replacement of retina by fibrous tissue and blood vessels

2. Primarily caused by prematurity and use of supplemental oxygen (longer than 30 days)

B. Assessment: Leukoria (white tissue on the retrolental space), vitreous hemorrhage, myopia, strabismus, cataracts (check for red reflex)

C. Interventions: Laser photocoagulation surgery

XVI. NECROTIZING ENTEROCOLITIS

A. Description

1. Acute inflammatory disease of the gastrointestinal tract

2. Usually occurs 4 to 10 days after birth in a term baby

B. Assessment: Increased abdominal girth, decreased or absent bowel sounds, bowel loop distension, vomiting, bile-stained emesis, abdominal tenderness, occult blood in stool

C. Interventions

1. Hold oral feedings.

2. Insert oral gastric tube to decompress abdomen.

3. Intravenous antibiotics

4. Intravenous fluids to correct fluid, electrolyte, and acid-base imbalances

5. Surgery if indicated

XVII. HYPERBILIRUBINEMIA

A. Description

1. At any serum bilirubin level, the appearance of jaundice during the first day of life indicates a pathological process.

2. Evaluation is indicated when serum levels are higher than 12 mg/dL in the term **newborn.**

3. Therapy is aimed at preventing kernicterus, which results in permanent neurological damage resulting from the deposition of bilirubin in the brain cells.

B. Assessment

1. Jaundice

2. Elevated serum bilirubin levels

3. Enlarged liver

4. Poor muscle tone

5. Lethargy

6. Poor sucking reflex

C. Interventions

1. Monitor for the presence of jaundice; assess skin and sclera for jaundice.

a. Examine the **newborn's** skin color in natural light.

b. Press finger over a bony prominence or tip of the **newborn's** nose to press out capillary blood from the tissues.

c. Note that jaundice starts at the head first, spreads to the chest, abdomen, and then the arms and legs, followed by the hands and feet, which are the last to be jaundiced.

2. Keep **newborn** well hydrated to maintain blood volume.

3. Facilitate early, frequent feeding to hasten passage of meconium and encourage excretion of bilirubin.

4. Report to the physician any signs of jaundice in the first 24 hours of life and any abnormal signs and symptoms.

5. Prepare for phototherapy, and monitor the **newborn** closely during the treatment.

D. Phototherapy

1. Description

a. Phototherapy is use of intense florescent lights to reduce serum bilirubin levels in the **newborn.**

b. Injury from treatment, such as eye damage, dehydration, or sensory deprivation, can occur.

2. Interventions

a. Expose as much of the **newborn's** skin as possible.

b. Cover the genital area, and monitor the genital area for skin irritation or breakdown.

c. Cover the **newborn's** eyes with eye shields or patches; make sure that eyelids are closed when shields or patches are applied.

d. Remove the shields or patches at least once per shift (during a feeding time) to inspect the eyes for infection or irritation and to allow eye contact and bonding with parents.

e. Measure the quantity of light every 8 hours.

f. Monitor skin temperature closely.

g. Increase fluids to compensate for water loss.

h. Expect loose green stools and green urine.

i. Monitor the **newborn's** skin color with the fluorescent light turned off, every 4 to 8 hours.

j. Monitor the skin for bronze baby syndrome, a grayish-brown discoloration of the skin.

k. Reposition **newborn** every 2 hours.

l. Provide stimulation.

m. After treatment, continue monitoring for signs of hyperbilirubinemia, because rebound elevations are normal after therapy is discontinued.

n. Turn off phototherapy lights before drawing blood specimen for serum bilirubin levels and avoid allowing blood specimen to remain uncovered under fluorescent lights (to prevent the breakdown of bilirubin in the blood specimen).

XVIII. ERYTHROBLASTOSIS FETALIS

A. Description

1. Erythroblastosis fetalis is destruction of red blood cells that results from an antigen-antibody reaction.

2. The disorder is characterized by hemolytic anemia or hyperbilirubinemia.

3. Exchange of fetal and maternal blood takes place primarily when the **placenta** separates at birth.

4. Rh antigens from the baby's blood enter the maternal bloodstream.

5. The mother produces anti-Rh antibodies against the fetal blood cells.

6. Antibodies are harmless to the mother but attach to the erythrocytes in the fetus and cause hemolysis.

7. Sensitization is rare with the first pregnancy.

8. ABO incompatibility is usually less severe.

B. Assessment

1. Anemia

2. Jaundice that develops rapidly after birth and before 24 hours

3. Edema

C. Interventions

1. Administer Rho(D) immune globulin to the mother during the first 72 hours after **delivery** if the Rh-negative mother delivers an Rh-positive fetus but remains unsensitized.

2. Assist with exchange transfusion after birth or intrauterine transfusion as prescribed.

3. The baby's blood is replaced with Rh-negative blood to stop the destruction of the baby's red blood cells; the Rh-negative blood is replaced with the baby's own blood gradually.

4. Reassure the mother that the **newborn** will suffer no untoward effects from the condition.

XIX. SEPSIS

A. Description: Generalized infection resulting from the presence of bacteria in the blood

B. Assessment

1. Pallor

2. Tachypnea, tachycardia

3. Poor feeding

4. Abdominal distention

5. Temperature instability

C. Interventions

1. Assess for periods of apnea or irregular respirations.

2. If apnea is present, stimulate by gently rubbing chest or foot.

3. Administer oxygen as prescribed

4. Monitor vital signs.

5. Maintain warmth in a radiant warmer.

6. Provide isolation as necessary.

7. Assess for a fever.
8. Monitor intake and output and obtain daily weight.
9. Monitor for diarrhea.
10. Assess feeding and sucking reflex, which may be poor.
11. Assess for jaundice.
12. Assess for irritability and lethargy.
13. Administer antibiotics as prescribed and observe carefully for toxicity because a **newborn's** liver and kidneys are immature.

XX. TORCH SYNDROME

A. Description
1. TORCH syndrome refers to infections of the fetus or **newborn.**

2. The syndrome is caused by one of the following:
   a. *Toxoplasmosis*
   b. *Other* infections such as gonorrhea, syphilis, varicella, hepatitis B, and human immunodeficiency virus (HIV)
   c. *Rubella*
   d. *Cytomegalovirus*
   e. *Herpes simplex*
B. Infections (Table 30-5)

XXI. SYPHILIS

A. Description
1. Syphilis is a sexually transmitted disease.
2. Congenital syphilis can result in premature **delivery,** skin lesions, abnormal skeletal development
3. The causative organism, *Treponema pallidum,* a spirochete, is able to cross the **placenta** throughout pregnancy and infect the fetus, usually after 18 weeks' gestation.
4. Risks include preterm birth, stillbirth, and low birth weight.
5. Congenital effects are irreversible and may include central nervous system damage and hearing loss.
B. Assessment
1. Hepatosplenomegaly
2. Joint swelling
3. Palmar rash and lesions (Fig. 30-7)
4. Anemia
5. Jaundice
6. Snuffles
7. Ascites
8. Pneumonitis
9. Cerebrospinal fluid changes
C. Interventions
1. Monitor **newborn** for signs of syphilis.
2. Monitor for palmar rash and snuffles.
3. Prepare **newborn** for serological testing if prescribed.
4. Administer antibiotic therapy as prescribed.

TABLE 30-5

Infections Included in TORCH Syndrome

Infection	Characteristics and Description
*T*oxoplasmosis	Caused by protozoan infection
	Produces no serious effects in mother
	Organism can be transmitted to fetus
	Infection can result in severe physical, developmental abnormalities
	Common carriers include cat feces, raw beef
*O*ther infections	Can include syphilis, gonorrhea, varicella, hepatitis B, HIV
*R*ubella	Systemic viral infection
	Rubella causes congenital rubella syndrome—includes congenital heart disease, cataracts, growth retardation, and pneumonia if mother becomes infected within first trimester
	Deafness and some learning disabilities can occur if mother becomes infected during first trimester
*C*ytomegalovirus	Viral infection that persists in the body indefinitely; has periods of reactivation without symptoms
	Can infect fetus or infant during delivery or after birth through breast milk, blood transfusions, or contact with infected secretions
	May cause microcephaly, blindness, deafness, mental and motor retardation
*H*erpes simplex virus	Sexually transmitted disease
	Has periods of reactivation
	Neonate commonly infected during delivery by direct contact with lesions in genital tract
	Can cause neurological impairment or death

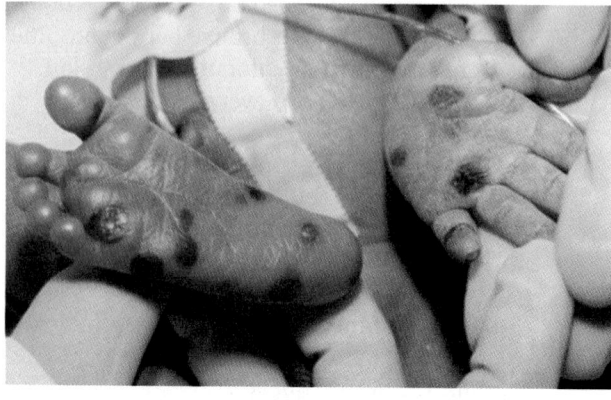

FIG. 30-7 Neonatal syphilitic lesions on hands and feet. (From Lowdermilk, D., & Perry, S. [2006]. *Maternity nursing* [7th ed.]. St. Louis: Mosby. Courtesy of Mahesh Kotwal, Phoenix, AZ.)

5. Use standard precautions and drainage and secretion (contact) precautions with suspected congenital syphilis.
6. Wear gloves when handling **neonate** until antibiotic therapy has been administered for 24 hours.
7. Provide psychological support to the mother, and provide instructions regarding follow-up care to the **newborn**.

XXII. THE ADDICTED NEWBORN

A. Description: **Newborn** who has become passively addicted to drugs that have passed through the **placenta**
B. Addicting drugs
   1. Heroin
      a. **Newborn** may appear normal at birth, with a low birth weight.
      b. Withdrawal occurs within 12 to 24 hours and may last 5 to 7 days.
   2. Methadone
      a. Withdrawal occurs within 1 to 2 days to 1 week or more, is most evident at 48 to 72 hours, and may last 6 days to 8 weeks.
      b. **Newborn** appears very ill.
      c. **Newborn** may develop jaundice as a result of prematurity.
   3. Cocaine
      a. Cocaine addiction causes decreased interactive behavior.
      b. Feeding problems are present.
      c. Irregular sleep patterns and diarrhea occur.
C. Assessment
   1. Irritability
   2. Tremors
   3. Hyperactivity and hypertonicity
   4. Respiratory distress
   5. Vomiting
   6. High-pitched cry
   7. Sneezing
   8. Fever
   9. Diarrhea
   10. Excessive sweating
   11. Poor feeding
   12. Extreme sucking of fists
   13. Convulsions
D. Interventions
   1. Monitor respiratory and cardiac status frequently.
   2. Monitor temperature and vital signs.
   3. Hold **newborn** firmly and close to the body during feeding and when giving care.
   4. Initiate seizure precautions (pad sides of crib).
   5. Provide small frequent feedings and allow a longer period for feeding.
   6. Monitor intake and output.
   7. Administer intravenous hydration if prescribed.
   8. Protect **neonate's** skin from injury that can be caused by the constant rubbing from hyperactive jitters.

9. Swaddle **newborn**.
10. Place **newborn** in a quiet room and reduce stimulation.
11. Allow mother to ventilate feelings of anxiety and guilt.
12. Refer mother for treatment of substance abuse problem.

XXIII. FETAL ALCOHOL SYNDROME

A. Description
   1. Fetal alcohol syndrome is caused by maternal alcohol use during pregnancy.
   2. The syndrome is a cause of teratogenesis.
   3. The syndrome causes mental and physical retardation.
B. Assessment
   1. Facial changes (Fig. 30-8)
      a. Short palpebral fissures
      b. Hypoplastic philtrum
      c. Short, upturned nose
      d. Flat midface
      e. Thin upper lip
      f. Low nasal bridge
   2. Abnormal palmar creases
   3. Respiratory distress (apnea, cyanosis)
   4. Congenital heart disorders
   5. Irritability, hypersensitivity to stimuli
   6. Tremors
   7. Poor feeding
   8. Seizures
C. Interventions
   1. Monitor for respiratory distress.
   2. Position **newborn** on side to facilitate drainage of secretions.
   3. Keep resuscitation equipment at the bedside.

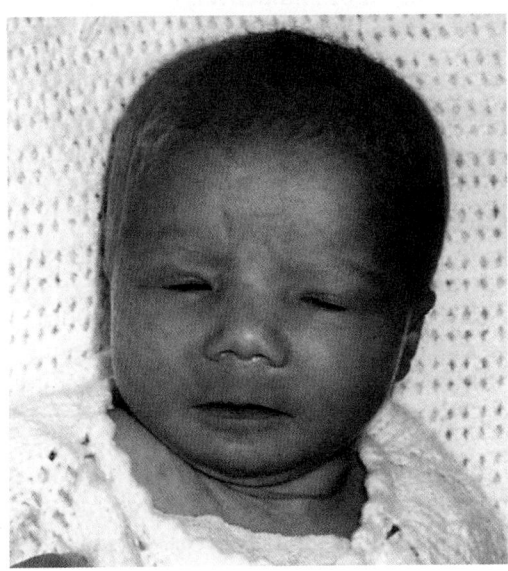

FIG. 30-8 Infant with alcohol-related birth defects. (From Lowdermilk, D., & Perry, S. [2006]. *Maternity nursing* [7th ed.]. St. Louis: Mosby.)

4. Monitor for hypoglycemia.
5. Assess suck and swallow reflex.
6. Administer small feedings and burp well.
7. Suction as necessary.
8. Monitor intake and output.
9. Monitor weight and head circumference.
10. Decrease environmental stimuli.

▲ XXIV. NEWBORN WITH ACQUIRED IMMUNODEFICIENCY SYNDROME

A. Description
1. The fetus of a human immunodeficiency virus (HIV) antibody–positive woman should be monitored closely throughout the pregnancy.
2. Serial ultrasound screenings should be done during pregnancy to identify intrauterine growth restriction.
3. Weekly nonstress testing after 32 weeks of gestation, and biophysical profiles may be necessary during pregnancy.
4. **Neonates** born to HIV-positive clients may test positive because the mother's antibodies may persist in the **newborn** for as long as 18 months after birth.
5. The use of antiviral medication, the reduction of **neonate** exposure to maternal blood and body fluids, and the early identification of HIV in pregnancy reduce the risk of transmission to the **newborn.**
6. All **neonates** born to HIV-positive mothers acquire maternal antibody to HIV infection, but not all acquire the infection.
7. The **neonate** may be asymptomatic for the first several months to years of life.

B. Transmission
1. Across placental barrier
2. During **labor** and **delivery**
3. Breast milk

C. Assessment
1. Possibly no outward signs at birth
2. Signs of immune deficiency
3. Hepatomegaly
4. Splenomegaly
5. Lymphadenopathy
6. Impairment in growth and development

D. Interventions
1. Cleanse **newborn's** skin carefully before any invasive procedure, such as the administration of vitamin K, heel sticks, or venipunctures.
2. Circumcisions are not done on **newborns** with HIV-positive mothers until the **newborn's** status is determined.
3. **Newborn** can room with mother.
4. All HIV-exposed **newborns** should be treated with medication to prevent infection by *Pneumocystis jiroveci.*
5. Antiretroviral medications may be administered as prescribed for the first 6 weeks of life.

6. Monitor for early signs of immune deficiency, such as enlarged spleen or liver, lymphadenopathy, and impairment in growth and development.
7. **Newborns** at risk for HIV infection should be seen by the physician at birth and at 1 week, 2 weeks, 1 month, and 2 months of age.
8. Inform the mother that an HIV culture is recommended at 1 month and after 4 months of age.

E. Immunizations
1. **Newborns** at risk for HIV infection need to receive all recommended immunizations at the regular schedule.
2. Immunizations with live vaccines, such as measles-mumps-rubella and varicella, should not be done until the **newborn's**, **infant's**, or child's status is confirmed.
3. If a child is infected, live vaccine will not be given.

XXV. NEWBORN OF A DIABETIC MOTHER ▲

A. Description
1. **Neonate** born to an insulin-dependent mother or gestational diabetic mother
2. Hypoglycemia, hyperbilirubinemia, respiratory distress syndrome, hypocalcemia, birth trauma, and congenital anomalies may be present.

B. Assessment
1. Excessive size and weight as a result of excess fat and glycogen in tissues
2. Edema or puffiness in the face and cheeks
3. Signs of hypoglycemia, such as twitching, difficulty in feeding, lethargy, apnea, seizures, and cyanosis
4. Hyperbilirubinemia
5. Signs of respiratory distress, such as tachypnea, cyanosis, retractions, grunting, and nasal flaring

C. Interventions
1. Monitor for signs of respiratory distress, birth trauma, and congenital anomalies.
2. Monitor bilirubin and blood glucose levels.
3. Monitor weight.
4. Feed the **infant** soon after birth with glucose in water, breast milk, or formula as prescribed.
5. Administer glucose intravenously to treat hypoglycemia if necessary and as prescribed.
6. Monitor for edema.
7. Monitor for apnea, tremors, and seizures.

XXVI. HYPOGLYCEMIA ▲

A. Description
1. Hypoglycemia is an abnormally low level of glucose in the blood (lower than 40 mg/dL in the first 72 hours or lower than 45 mg/dL after the first 3 days of life).
2. Normal blood glucose level is 40 to 60 mg/dL in a 1-day-old **neonate** and 50 to 90 mg/dL in a **neonate** older than 1 day.

B. Assessment
1. Increased respiratory rate
2. Twitching, nervousness, or tremors

3. Unstable temperature
4. Lethargy, apnea, seizures, cyanosis
C. Interventions
   1. Prevent low blood glucose level through early feedings.
   2. Administer glucose orally or intravenously as prescribed.
   3. Monitor blood glucose levels as prescribed.
   4. Monitor for feeding problems.
   5. Monitor for apneic periods.
   6. Assess for shrill or intermittent cries.
   7. Evaluate lethargy and poor muscle tone.

PRACTICE QUESTIONS

1. A nurse is assessing a newborn infant following circumcision and notes that the circumcised area is red with a small amount of bloody drainage. Which of the following nursing actions would be appropriate?
   1. Contact the physician.
   2. Apply gentle pressure.
   3. Reinforce the dressing.
   4. Document the findings.

2. A nurse has provided instructions to a mother of a male newborn infant who is not circumcised about measures to clean the penis. Which statement, if made by the mother, indicates an understanding of how to clean the newborn infant's penis?
   1. "I should retract the foreskin and clean the penis every time I change the diaper."
   2. "I need to retract the foreskin and clean the penis every time I give my infant a bath."
   3. "I need to avoid pulling back the foreskin to clean the penis because this may cause adhesions."
   4. "I should gently retract the foreskin as far as it will go on the penis and then pull the skin back over the penis after cleaning."

3. A nurse in a newborn nursery is monitoring a preterm newborn infant for respiratory distress syndrome. Which assessment signs, if noted in the newborn infant, would alert the nurse to the possibility of this syndrome?
   1. Tachypnea and retractions ✓
   2. Acrocyanosis and grunting
   3. Hypotension and bradycardia
   4. Presence of a barrel chest with acrocyanosis

4. A nurse is assessing the reflexes of a newborn infant. In eliciting the Moro reflex, the nurse would perform which of the following?
   1. Clap the hand or slap on the newborn infant's mattress.
   2. Stimulate the ball of the foot of the newborn by firm pressure.
   3. Stimulate the perioral cavity of the newborn infant with a finger.
   4. Stimulate the pads of the newborn infant's hands by firm pressure.

5. A postpartum nurse is providing instructions to a client of a newborn infant with hyperbilirubinemia who is being breast-fed. The nurse provides which appropriate instruction to the client?
   1. Feed the newborn infant less frequently.
   2. Continue to breast-feed every 2 to 4 hours.
   3. Switch to bottle-feeding the baby for 2 weeks.
   4. Stop the breast-feedings and switch to bottle-feeding permanently.

6. A nurse in the newborn nursery is caring for a neonate. On assessment, the infant is exhibiting signs of cyanosis, tachypnea, nasal flaring, and grunting. Respiratory distress syndrome is diagnosed, and the physician prescribes surfactant replacement therapy. The nurse prepares to administer this therapy by:
   1. Intravenous injection
   2. Subcutaneous injection
   3. Intramuscular injection
   4. Instillation of the preparation into the lungs through an endotracheal tube

7. A nurse is assessing a newborn infant who was born to a mother who is addicted to drugs. Which of the following assessment findings would the nurse expect to note during the assessment of this newborn?
   1. Lethargy
   2. Sleepiness
   3. Incessant crying
   4. Cuddles when being held

8. A nurse is preparing to administer an injection of vitamin K to a newborn. In preparing to administer the injection, the nurse should select which of the following injection sites?
   1. The gluteal muscle
   2. The lower aspect of the rectus femoris muscle
   3. The medial aspect of the upper third of the vastus lateralis muscle
   4. The lateral aspect of the middle third of the vastus lateralis muscle

9. A 4-day-old newborn infant is receiving phototherapy at home for a bilirubin level of 14 mg/dL. The nurse should plan to include which of the following in the plan of care during the home visit to the mother of the newborn infant?
   1. Applying lotions to exposed newborn infant's skin
   2. Assessing skin integrity and fluid status of the newborn infant
   3. Having minimal contact with the newborn infant to prevent stimulation
   4. Advising the mother to limit newborn infant oral intake during phototherapy

10. A nurse notes hypotonia, irritability, and a poor sucking reflex in a full-term newborn infant on admission to the nursery. The nurse suspects fetal alcohol syndrome and is aware that which additional

sign would be consistent with fetal alcohol syndrome?

1. Length of 19 inches
2. Abnormal palmar creases
3. Birth weight of 6 lb, 14 oz
4. Head circumference appropriate for gestational age

11. A nurse is preparing a plan of care for a newborn infant with fetal alcohol syndrome. The nurse should include which of the following priority interventions in the plan of care?
    1. Allow the newborn infant to establish own sleep-rest pattern.
    2. Maintain the newborn infant in a brightly lighted area of the nursery.
    3. Encourage frequent handling of the newborn infant by staff and parents.
    4. Monitor the newborn infant's response to feedings and weight gain pattern.

12. A nurse administers erythromycin ointment (0.5%) to the eyes of a newborn infant and the mother asks the nurse why this is performed. The nurse explains to the mother that this is routinely done to:
    1. Prevent cataracts in the newborn infant born to a woman who is susceptible to rubella.
    2. Protect the newborn infant's eyes from possible infections acquired while hospitalized.
    3. Minimize the spread of microorganisms to the newborn infant from invasive procedures during labor.
    4. Prevent ophthalmia neonatorum from occurring after delivery in a newborn infant born to a woman with an untreated gonococcal infection.

13. A nurse prepares to administer a vitamin K injection to a newborn and the mother asks the nurse why her newborn infant needs the injection. The best response by the nurse would be:
    1. "Your infant needs vitamin K to develop immunity."
    2. "The vitamin K will protect your infant from being jaundiced."
    3. "Newborn infants have sterile bowels, and vitamin K promotes the growth of bacteria in the bowel."
    4. "Newborn infants are deficient in vitamin K, and this injection prevents your infant from abnormal bleeding."

14. A nurse develops a plan of care for a human immunodeficiency virus–infected client and her newborn infant. The nurse includes which intervention in the plan of care?
    1. Monitoring the newborn infant's vital signs routinely
    2. Maintaining standard precautions at all times while caring for the newborn
    3. Initiating referral to evaluate for blindness, deafness, learning, or behavioral problems

4. Instructing the breast-feeding mother regarding the treatment of the nipples with nystatin ointment

15. A nurse instructs a client in how to bathe a newborn infant. The nurse tells the client to:
    1. Begin with the eyes and face.
    2. Begin with the feet and work upward.
    3. Do the back side first, and then the front side.
    4. Start with the chest, move to the face, and then finish the rest of the body.

16. A nurse in a delivery room is assisting with the delivery of a newborn infant. After delivery, the nurse prepares to prevent heat loss in the newborn infant resulting from evaporation by:
    1. Warming the crib pad
    2. Closing the doors to the room
    3. Drying the infant with a warm blanket
    4. Turning on the overhead radiant warmer

17. The mother of a newborn infant calls a clinic and reports to a nurse that when cleansing the umbilical cord, the mother noticed that the cord was moist and that discharge was present. The appropriate nursing instruction to the mother is which of the following?
    1. Bring the infant to the clinic.
    2. This is a normal occurrence.
    3. Increase the number of times that the cord is cleansed per day.
    4. Monitor the cord for another 24 to 48 hours and call the clinic if the discharge continues.

18. A nurse in a newborn nursery receives a telephone call to prepare for the admission of a 43-week gestation newborn infant with Apgar scores of 1 and 4. In planning for admission of this infant, the nurse's highest priority should be to:
    1. Turn on the apnea and cardiorespiratory monitors.
    2. Connect the resuscitation bag to the oxygen outlet.
    3. Set up the intravenous line with 5% dextrose in water.
    4. Set the radiant warmer control temperature at 36.5° C (97.6° F).

19. A nurse is planning care for a newborn of a diabetic mother. A priority nursing diagnosis for this infant is:
    1. Hyperthermia related to excess fat and glycogen
    2. Risk for injury related to low blood glucose levels
    3. Risk for delayed development related to excessive size
    4. Risk for aspiration related to impaired suck and swallow

20. The nurse determines that a new mother understands the teaching about prevention of newborn abduction if she states:
    1. "I will place my baby's crib close to the door."
    2. "Some health care personnel won't have name badges."

3. "It's OK to allow the nurse assistant to carry my newborn to the nursery."

4. "I will ask the nurse to attend to the infant if I am napping and my husband is not here."

ALTERNATE ITEM FORMAT: MULTIPLE RESPONSE

The nurse is preparing to care for a newborn receiving phototherapy. Select all interventions that apply.

❏ 1. Avoid stimulation.
❏ 2. Decrease fluid intake.
❏ 3. Expose all of the newborn's skin.
❏ 4. Monitor skin temperature closely.
❏ 5. Reposition newborn every 2 hours.
❏ 6. Cover the newborn's eyes with eye shields or patches.

ANSWERS

1. **4**

Rationale: The penis is normally red during the healing process. A yellow exudate may be noted in 24 hours, and this is part of normal healing. The nurse would expect that the area would be red with a small amount of bloody drainage. Only if the bleeding were excessive would the nurse apply gentle pressure with a sterile gauze. If bleeding is not controlled, then the blood vessel may need to be ligated, and the nurse would notify the physician. Because the findings identified in the question are normal, the nurse would document the assessment.

Test-Taking Strategy: Use the process of elimination. Note the strategic words *small amount of bloody drainage*. This should assist in directing you to option 4 because this is a normal occurrence following circumcision. If you had difficulty with this question, review the expected findings following this procedure.

Level of Cognitive Ability: Application
Client Needs: Physiological Integrity
Integrated Process: Nursing Process—implementation
Content Area: Maternity—postpartum
References: Lowdermilk, D., & Perry, S. (2004). *Maternity and women's health care* (8th ed., p. 793). St. Louis: Mosby.
Murray, S., & McKinney, E., (2006). *Foundations of maternal-newborn nursing* (4th ed., p. 527). Philadelphia: W.B. Saunders.

2. **3**

Rationale: In male newborn infants, the prepuce is continuous with the epidermis of the glans and is not retractable. If retraction is forced, this may cause adhesions to develop. The mother should be told to allow separation to occur naturally, which usually occurs between 3 years and puberty. Most foreskins are retractable by 3 years of age and should be pushed back gently at this time for cleaning. Options 1, 2, and 4 identify an action that addresses retraction of the foreskin.

Test-Taking Strategy: Use the process of elimination. Note that options 1, 2, and 4 are comparative or alike in that they all identify retracting the foreskin. Option 3 is the option that is different. If you had difficulty with this question, review teaching points related to cleaning the penis of a newborn male infant who is uncircumcised.

Level of Cognitive Ability: Analysis
Client Needs: Health Promotion and Maintenance
Integrated Process: Nursing Process—evaluation
Content Area: Maternity—postpartum
Reference: Murray, S., & McKinney, E. (2006). *Foundations of maternal-newborn nursing* (4th ed., p. 526). Philadelphia: W.B. Saunders.

3. **1**

Rationale: The newborn infant with respiratory distress syndrome may present with clinical signs of cyanosis, tachypnea or apnea, nasal flaring, chest wall retractions, or audible grunts. Acrocyanosis is the bluish discoloration of the hands and feet, is associated with immature peripheral circulation, and is not uncommon in the first few hours of life. Options 2, 3, and 4 do not indicate clinical signs of respiratory distress syndrome.

Test-Taking Strategy: Use the process of elimination. Recalling that acrocyanosis may be a normal sign in a newborn infant will assist in eliminating options 2 and 4. From the remaining options, you must be familiar with the signs of respiratory distress syndrome. Also, note the relationship between the diagnosis and the signs noted in option 1. If you had difficulty with this question, review the signs of respiratory distress syndrome.

Level of Cognitive Ability: Analysis
Client Needs: Physiological Integrity
Integrated Process: Nursing Process—assessment
Content Area: Maternity—postpartum
References: Murray, S., & McKinney, E. (2006). *Foundations of maternal-newborn nursing* (4th ed., p. 789). Philadelphia: W.B. Saunders.
Wong, D., Perry, S., Hockenberry, M., et al. (2006). *Maternal child nursing care* (3rd ed., p. 814). St. Louis: Mosby.

4. **1**

Rationale: The Moro reflex is elicited by a loud noise such as a hand clap or slap on the mattress to startle the newborn infant. Symmetrical extension and abduction of the arms are seen, fingers fan out and form a "C" with the thumb and forefinger, a slight tremor may be noted, and the arms are adducted in an embracing motion and then return to a relaxed flexion state. Legs may follow a similar pattern of response. This reflex disappears at 6 months of age. The rooting reflex is elicited by stimulating the perioral area with the finger. The palmar grasp reflex is elicited by stimulating the palm of the hand by firm pressure, and the plantar grasp reflex is elicited by stimulating the ball of the foot by firm pressure.

Test-Taking Strategy: Use the process of elimination. Options 2 and 4 are comparative or alike and should be eliminated first. Focusing on the subject of the question, the Moro reflex, will assist in directing you to option 1. Review assessment of neonatal reflexes if you had difficulty with this question.

Level of Cognitive Ability: Application
Client Needs: Health Promotion and Maintenance
Integrated Process: Nursing Process—assessment
Content Area: Maternity—postpartum

References: Lowdermilk, D., & Perry, S. (2006). *Maternity nursing* (7th ed., p. 551). St. Louis: Mosby.
Murray, S., & McKinney, E. (2006). *Foundations of maternal-newborn nursing* (4th ed., pp. 484, 486). Philadelphia: W.B. Saunders.
Wong, D., Perry, S., Hockenberry, M., et al. (2006). *Maternal child nursing care* (3rd ed., p. 704). St. Louis: Mosby.

5. **2**

Rationale: Breast-feeding should be initiated within 2 hours after birth and every 2 to 4 hours thereafter. The infant should not be fed less frequently. Switching to bottle-feeding for 2 weeks or stopping breast-feeding permanently is not necessary.
Test-Taking Strategy: Use the process of elimination. Note that options 3 and 4 are comparative or alike. These options discourage the continuation of breast-feeding. From the remaining options, recalling the pathophysiology associated with hyperbilirubinemia will assist you in eliminating option 1. Review client instructions related to hyperbilirubinemia in the newborn infant if you had difficulty with this question.
Level of Cognitive Ability: Application
Client Needs: Physiological Integrity
Integrated Process: Teaching and Learning
Content Area: Maternity—postpartum
References: Lowdermilk, D., & Perry, S. (2006). *Maternity nursing* (7th ed., p. 630). St. Louis: Mosby.
Murray, S., & McKinney, E. (2006). *Foundations of maternal-newborn nursing* (4th ed., pp. 554-555). Philadelphia: W.B. Saunders.
Wong, D., Perry, S., Hockenberry, M., et al. (2006). *Maternal child nursing care* (3rd ed., pp. 740; 778). St. Louis: Mosby.

6. **4**

Rationale: The aim of therapy in respiratory distress syndrome is to support the disease until the disease runs its course, with the subsequent development of surfactant. The infant may benefit from surfactant replacement therapy. In surfactant replacement, an exogenous surfactant preparation is instilled into the lungs through an endotracheal tube. Options 1, 2, and 3 identify incorrect methods of administering surfactant.
Test-Taking Strategy: Knowledge regarding surfactant replacement therapy is required to answer this question. Remember that surfactant preparation is instilled into the lungs. If you are unfamiliar with the administration of this therapy, review this procedure.
Level of Cognitive Ability: Analysis
Client Needs: Physiological Integrity
Integrated Process: Nursing Process—planning
Content Area: Maternity—postpartum
Reference: Murray, S., & McKinney, E. (2006). *Foundations of maternal-newborn nursing* (4th ed., p. 790). Philadelphia: W.B. Saunders.

7. **3**

Rationale: A newborn infant born to a woman using drugs is irritable. The infant is overloaded easily by sensory stimulation. The infant may cry incessantly and be difficult to console. The infant would hyperextend and posture rather than cuddle when being held.

Test-Taking Strategy: Use the process of elimination. Note that options 1 and 2 are comparative or alike in that they indicate hypoactivity of the newborn. From the remaining options, recalling the pathophysiology associated with a newborn infant born to a drug-addicted mother will assist you in eliminating option 4. Review assessment findings for the newborn infant born to a drug-addicted mother if you had difficulty with this question.
Level of Cognitive Ability: Analysis
Client Needs: Physiological Integrity
Integrated Process: Nursing Process—assessment
Content Area: Maternity—postpartum
Reference: Murray, S., & McKinney, E. (2006). *Foundations of maternal-newborn nursing* (4th ed., p. 817). Philadelphia: W.B. Saunders.

8. **4**

Rationale: The preferred injection site for vitamin K in the newborn infant is the lateral aspect of the middle third of the vastus lateralis muscle in the infant's thigh. This muscle is the preferred injection site because it is free of major blood vessels and nerves and is large enough to absorb the medication.
Test-Taking Strategy: Use the process of elimination and knowledge regarding the preferred injection site for a newborn infant. Remember that the preferred site is the lateral aspect of the middle third of the vastus lateralis muscle. If you had difficulty with this question, review the procedure for administering vitamin K to the newborn infant.
Level of Cognitive Ability: Application
Client Needs: Physiological Integrity
Integrated Process: Nursing Process—planning
Content Area: Maternity—postpartum
References: Lowdermilk, D., & Perry, S. (2006). *Maternity nursing* (7th ed., p. 579). St. Louis: Mosby.
Murray, S., & McKinney, E. (2006). *Foundations of maternal-newborn nursing* (4th ed., pp. 512-513). Philadelphia: W.B. Saunders.

9. **2**

Rationale: Assessing skin integrity and fluid status of the newborn infant is an essential component of phototherapy. Contact with the newborn infant is important. Lotions are not used to minimize skin breakdown and to ensure the therapeutic effect of light exposure in subcutaneous tissue. Adequate oral fluids are essential to prevent dehydration, because diarrhea is a common side effect of therapy. In addition, safe care for the newborn infant during phototherapy requires shielding the eyes with a soft eye shield to prevent retinal damage, keeping the newborn's skin exposed except for a diaper, and changing the newborn's position frequently.
Test-Taking Strategy: Use the process of elimination and knowledge regarding phototherapy. Note that option 2 addresses the first step of the nursing process, assessment. If you had difficulty with this question, review care of the newborn infant receiving phototherapy.
Level of Cognitive Ability: Application
Client Needs: Physiological Integrity
Integrated Process: Teaching/Learning
Content Area: Maternity—postpartum

References: Murray, S., & McKinney, E. (2006). *Foundations of maternal-newborn nursing* (4th ed., pp. 807-809). Philadelphia: W.B. Saunders.
Wong, D., Perry, S., Hockenberry, M., et al. (2006). *Maternal child nursing care* (3rd ed., p. 752). St. Louis: Mosby.

10. **2**
Rationale: Features of newborn infants diagnosed with fetal alcohol syndrome include craniofacial abnormalities, intrauterine growth retardation, cardiac abnormalities, abnormal palmar creases, and respiratory distress. Options 1, 3, and 4 are normal assessment findings in the full-term newborn infant.
Test-Taking Strategy: Use the process of elimination and knowledge regarding normal assessment findings in the full-term newborn infant to answer this question. Note that options 1, 3, and 4 are comparative or alike and represent normal assessment findings in the full-term newborn infant. If you had difficulty with this question, review the content related to normal newborn infant assessment findings and fetal alcohol syndrome.
Level of Cognitive Ability: Analysis
Client Needs: Physiological Integrity
Integrated Process: Nursing Process—assessment
Content Area: Maternity—postpartum
References: Lowdermilk, D., & Perry, S. (2006). *Maternity nursing* (7th ed., p. 902). St. Louis: Mosby.
McKinney, E., James, S., Murray, S., & Ashwill, J. (2005). *Maternal-child nursing* (2nd ed., p. 602). St. Louis: W.B. Saunders.

11. **4**
Rationale: A primary nursing goal for the newborn infant diagnosed with fetal alcohol syndrome is to establish nutritional balance following delivery. These newborn infants may exhibit hyperirritability, vomiting, diarrhea, or an uncoordinated sucking and swallowing ability. A quiet environment with minimal stimuli and handling will help establish appropriate sleep-rest cycles in the newborn infant as well. Options 1, 2, and 3 are inappropriate interventions.
Test-Taking Strategy: Use the process of elimination. Recalling that these newborn infants may exhibit hyperirritability, vomiting, diarrhea, or an uncoordinated sucking and swallowing ability will direct you easily to option 4. Review care of the newborn infant with fetal alcohol syndrome if you had difficulty with this question.
Level of Cognitive Ability: Application
Client Needs: Physiological Integrity
Integrated Process: Nursing Process—planning
Content Area: Maternity—postpartum
References: Lowdermilk, D., & Perry, S. (2004). *Maternity and women's health care* (8th ed., p. 1072). St. Louis: Mosby.
Wong, D., Perry, S., Hockenberry, M., et al. (2006). *Maternal child nursing care* (3rd ed., pp. 844, 850). St. Louis: Mosby.

12. **4**
Rationale: Erythromycin ophthalmic ointment (Ilotycin ophthalmic) 0.5% is used as a prophylactic treatment for ophthalmia neonatorum, which is caused by the bacterium *Neisseria gonorrhoeae.* Preventive treatment of gonorrhea is required by

law. Options 1, 2, and 3 are not the purposes for administering this medication to the newborn infant.
Test-Taking Strategy: Use the process of elimination and knowledge of the purpose of administering erythromycin ophthalmic ointment to the newborn infant. Remember that this is done to prevent ophthalmia neonatorum. If you had difficulty with this question, review initial care for the newborn infant.
Level of Cognitive Ability: Application
Client Needs: Health Promotion and Maintenance
Integrated Process: Teaching and Learning
Content Area: Maternity—postpartum
Reference: Murray, S., & McKinney, E. (2006). *Foundations of maternal-newborn nursing* (4th ed., p. 513). Philadelphia: W.B. Saunders.

13. **4**
Rationale: Vitamin K is necessary for the body to synthesize coagulation factors. Vitamin K is administered to the newborn infant to prevent abnormal bleeding. Vitamin K promotes liver formation of the clotting factors II, VII, IX, and X. Newborn infants are vitamin K–deficient because the bowel does not have the bacteria necessary for synthesizing fat-soluble vitamin K. The normal flora in the intestinal tract produces vitamin K. The newborn infant's bowel does not support the normal production of vitamin K until bacteria adequately colonize it. The bowel becomes colonized by bacteria as food is ingested. Vitamin K does not promote the development of immunity or prevent the infant from becoming jaundiced.
Test-Taking Strategy: Use the process of elimination. Note the strategic word *best.* Because jaundice and immunity are not related to the action of vitamin K, eliminate options 1 and 2. From the remaining options, recall the action of vitamin K to direct you to option 4. If you had difficulty with this question, review the purpose of vitamin K injection.
Level of Cognitive Ability: Application
Client Needs: Physiological Integrity
Integrated Process: Teaching and Learning
Content Area: Maternity—postpartum
Reference: Murray, S., & McKinney, E. (2006). *Foundations of maternal-newborn nursing* (4th ed., p. 513). Philadelphia: W.B. Saunders.

14. **2**
Rationale: The newborn infant born to a mother infected with human immunodeficiency virus (HIV) must be cared for with strict attention to standard precautions. This prevents the transmission of HIV from the newborn infant, if infected, to others, and prevents transmission of other infectious agents to the possibly immunocompromised newborn infant. Mothers infected with HIV should not breast-feed. Options 1 and 3 are not associated specifically with the care of a potentially HIV-infected newborn infant.
Test-Taking Strategy: Use the process of elimination and knowledge regarding care of a newborn infant born to an HIV-infected woman. Eliminate options 1 and 3 first because they are not associated specifically with the care of a potentially HIV-infected newborn infant. Recalling that HIV-infected mothers should not breast-feed will direct you easily to

option 2. Review care of an infant born to an HIV-infected woman if you had difficulty with this question.
Level of Cognitive Ability: Application
Client Needs: Safe and Effective Care Environment
Integrated Process: Nursing Process—planning
Content Area: Maternity—postpartum
References: Lowdermilk, D., & Perry, S. (2004). *Maternity and women's health care* (8th ed., p. 216). St. Louis: Mosby.
Murray, S., & McKinney, E. (2006). *Foundations of maternal-newborn nursing* (4th ed., pp. 812-813). Philadelphia: W.B. Saunders.

15. **1**
Rationale: Bathing should start at the eyes and face, usually the cleanest area. Next, the external ear and the area behind the ears are cleansed. The infant's neck should be washed because formula, lint, or breast milk will often accumulate in the folds of the neck. Hands and arms are then washed. The infants legs are washed next and the diaper area is washed last.
Test-Taking Strategy: Use the process of elimination. Remember the basic techniques of bathing a client to assist in answering this question. Always start with the cleanest area of the body first and proceed to the dirtiest area. Use techniques related to washing an adult to assist in answering this question. If you had difficulty with this question, review home care measures related to the care of the newborn infant.
Level of Cognitive Ability: Application
Client Needs: Physiological Integrity
Integrated Process: Teaching and Learning
Content Area: Maternity—postpartum
Reference: Wong, D., Perry, S., Hockenberry, M., et al. (2006). *Maternal child nursing care* (3rd ed., p. 763). St. Louis: Mosby.

16. **3**
Rationale: Evaporation of moisture from a wet body dissipates heat along with the moisture. Keeping the newborn infant dry by drying the wet newborn infant at birth will prevent hypothermia via evaporation. Hypothermia caused by conduction occurs when the newborn infant is on a cold surface, such as a cold pad or mattress, and heat from the newborn infant's body is transferred to the colder object (direct contact). Warming the crib pad will assist in preventing hypothermia by conduction. Convection occurs as air moves across the newborn infant's skin from an open door and heat is transferred to the air. Radiation occurs when heat from the newborn infant radiates to a colder surface (indirect contact).
Test-Taking Strategy: Use the process of elimination. Note the strategic word *evaporation* in the question to assist in selecting the correct option. Knowledge that evaporation of moisture from a wet body dissipates heat along with the moisture will assist in directing you to option 3. Review these heat loss concepts if you had difficulty with this question.
Level of Cognitive Ability: Application
Client Needs: Physiological Integrity
Integrated Process: Nursing Process—planning
Content Area: Maternity—postpartum
References: Lowdermilk, D., & Perry, S. (2006). *Maternity nursing* (7th ed., p. 537). St. Louis: Mosby.
Wong, D., Perry, S., Hockenberry, M., et al. (2006). *Maternal child nursing care* (3rd ed., pp. 694, 732). St. Louis: Mosby.

17. **1**
Rationale: Symptoms of infection are moistness, oozing, discharge, and a reddened base around the cord. If symptoms of infection occur, the mother should be instructed to notify a health care provider. If these symptoms occur, antibiotics are necessary. Options 2, 3, and 4 are inappropriate nursing interventions for the description given in the question.
Test-Taking Strategy: Use the process of elimination. Focus on the clinical manifestations provided in the question to assist in directing you to the correct option. Noting the strategic word *discharge* in the question will assist in directing you to the option that indicates that the newborn needs to be seen by the health care provider. Review interventions related to cord care if you had difficulty with this question.
Level of Cognitive Ability: Application
Client Needs: Physiological Integrity
Integrated Process: Nursing Process—implementation
Content Area: Maternity—postpartum
Reference: Murray, S., & McKinney, E. (2006). *Foundations of maternal-newborn nursing* (4th ed., pp. 520-521). Philadelphia: W.B. Saunders.

18. **2**
Rationale: The highest priority on admission to the nursery for a newborn with a low Apgar scores is the airway, which would involve preparing respiratory resuscitation equipment. The remaining options are also important, although they are of lower priority. The newborn infant will be placed on an apnea and cardiorespiratory monitor. Setting up an intravenous line with 5% dextrose in water would provide circulatory support. The radiant warmer will provide an external heat source, which is necessary to prevent further respiratory distress.
Test-Taking Strategy: Use the process of elimination and note the strategic words *highest priority*. This question asks you to prioritize care on the basis of information about a newborn infant's condition. Use the ABCs—airway, breathing, and circulation. A method of planning for airway support is to have the resuscitation bag connected to an oxygen source. Review care to the newborn infant with low Apgar scores if you had difficulty with this question.
Level of Cognitive Ability: Application
Client Needs: Physiological Integrity
Integrated Process: Nursing Process—planning
Content Area: Delegating/Prioritizing
References: Mattson, S., & Smith, J. (2004). *Core curriculum for maternal-newborn nursing* (3rd ed., p. 428). Philadelphia: W.B. Saunders.
McKinney, E., James, S., Murray, S., & Ashwill, J. (2005). *Maternal-child nursing* (2nd ed., p. 377). St. Louis: W.B. Saunders.

19. **2**
Rationale: The neonate born to a diabetic mother is at risk for hypoglycemia so risk for injury related to low blood glucose levels would be a priority nursing diagnosis. The infant would also be at risk for hyperbilirubinemia, respiratory distress, hypocalcemia, and congenital anomalies. Hyperthermia, risk for delayed development, and risk for aspiration are not expected problems.

Test-Taking Strategy: Note the strategic word *priority*. Read each option thoroughly and eliminate options 1, 3, and 4 because newborns of diabetic mothers are not at risk for these problems. Review nursing interventions for newborns of diabetic mothers if you had difficulty with this question.
Level of Cognitive Ability: Analysis
Client Needs: Physiological Integrity
Integrated Process: Nursing Process—planning
Content Area: Delegating/Prioritizing
References: Murray, S., & McKinney, E. (2006). *Foundations of maternal-newborn nursing* (4th ed., p. 815). Philadelphia: W.B. Saunders.

20 **4**
Rationale: Precautions to prevent infant abduction include placing a newborn's crib away from the door, transporting an infant only in the crib and never carrying the infant, expecting health care personnel to wear identification that is easily visible at all times, and asking a nurse to attend to the infant if the mother is napping and no family member is available to watch the infant (the infant is never left unattended). Therefore, if the client states that she will ask the nurse to watch the infant while she is sleeping, she has understood the teaching. Options 1, 2, and 3 are incorrect and would indicate that the client needs further teaching.
Test-Taking Strategy: Focus on the subject, that the client understands precautions to prevent infant abduction. Read each option carefully and select the option that provides protection to the infant. This will direct you to option 4. Review precautions to prevent infant abduction if you had difficulty with this question.
Level of Cognitive Ability: Analysis
Client Needs: Safe and Effective Care Environment
Integrated Process: Nursing Process—evaluation
Content Area: Maternity—postpartum
Reference: Murray, S., & McKinney, E. (2006). *Foundations of maternal-newborn nursing* (4th ed., p. 523). Philadelphia: W.B. Saunders.

ALTERNATE ITEM FORMAT: MULTIPLE RESPONSE

Answer: 4, 5, 6
Rationale: Phototherapy is the use of intense fluorescent lights to reduce serum bilirubin levels in the newborn. Injury from treatment, such as eye damage, dehydration, or sensory deprivation, can occur. Interventions include exposing as much of the newborn's skin as possible; however, the genital area is covered. The newborn's eyes are also covered with eye shields or patches, ensuring that the eyelids are closed when shields or patches are applied. The shields or patches are removed at least once per shift to inspect the eyes for infection or irritation and to allow eye contact. The nurse measures the quantity of light every 8 hours, monitors skin temperature closely, and increases fluids to compensate for water loss. The newborn will have loose green stools and green-colored urine. The newborn's skin color is monitored with the fluorescent light turned off every 4 to 8 hours and is monitored for bronze baby syndrome, a grayish-brown discoloration of the skin. The newborn is repositioned every 2 hours and stimulation is provided. After treatment, the newborn is monitored for signs of hyperbilirubinemia, because rebound elevations are normal after therapy is discontinued.
Test-Taking Strategy: Focus on the subject, phototherapy. Recalling that injury from treatment, such as eye damage, dehydration, or sensory deprivation, can occur will assist in determining the correct interventions. Review the interventions for the newborn receiving phototherapy if you had difficulty with this question.
Level of Cognitive Ability: Application
Client Needs: Safe and Effective Care Environment
Integrated Process: Nursing Process—implementation
Content Area: Maternity—postpartum
Reference: Murray, S., & McKinney, E. (2006). *Foundations of maternal-newborn nursing* (4th ed., pp. 793-794). Philadelphia: W.B. Saunders.

REFERENCES

Lowdermilk, D., & Perry, S. (2006). *Maternity nursing* (7th ed.). St. Louis: Mosby.
Lowdermilk, D., & Perry, S. (2004). *Maternity and women's health care* (8th ed.). St. Louis: Mosby.
Mattson, S., & Smith, J. (2004). *Core curriculum for maternal-newborn nursing* (3rd ed.). Philadelphia: W.B. Saunders.
Murray, S., & McKinney, E. (2006). *Foundations of maternal-newborn nursing* (4th ed.). Philadelphia: W.B. Saunders.

McKinney, E., James, S., Murray, S., & Ashwill, J. (2005). *Maternal-child nursing* (2nd ed., p. 602). St. Louis: W.B. Saunders.
National Council of State Boards of Nursing (Eds.). (2007). *2007 NCLEX-RN® detailed test plan.* Chicago: Author.
Wong, D., Perry, S., Hockenberry, M., et al. (2006). *Maternal child nursing care* (3rd ed.). St. Louis: Mosby.

Maternity and Newborn Medications

31

I. OXYTOCIC MEDICATION: OXYTOCIN (PITOCIN)

A. Description
1. Oxytocin stimulates the smooth muscle of the uterus and induces contraction of the myocardium.
2. Oxytocin promotes milk letdown.
3. Routes of administration include intranasal, intramuscular, and intravenous (IV).
4. Minimal cervical change usually is noted until the active phase of **labor** is achieved.

B. Uses
1. Induces or augments **labor**
2. Controls postpartum bleeding
3. Promotes milk letdown and facilitates breast-feeding (intranasal route)
4. Induces or completes an abortion

C. Adverse reactions and contraindications
1. Adverse reactions are rare but may include allergies, dysrhythmias, changes in blood pressure, uterine rupture, and water intoxication; intranasal administration may cause nasal vasoconstriction.
2. Oxytocin may produce uterine hypertonicity, resulting in fetal or maternal injury.
3. High doses may cause hypotension, with rebound hypertension.
4. Postpartum hemorrhage can occur because the uterus may become atonic when the medication wears off.
5. Oxytocin should not be used in a client who cannot deliver vaginally or in a client with hypertonic uterine contractions.

D. Interventions
1. Monitor maternal vital signs (every 15 minutes), especially the blood pressure and heart rate, weight, intake and output, level of consciousness, and lung sounds.
2. Monitor frequency, duration, force of contractions, and resting uterine tone every 15 minutes.
3. Monitor fetal heart rate every 15 minutes, and notify the health care provider if significant changes occur; an internal fetal scalp electrode should be used if possible.
4. Administered by IV infusion via an infusion monitoring device (Y setup or stopcock is used with normal saline in the primary line); carefully monitor the dose being administered.
5. Do not leave the client unattended while the oxytocin is infusing.
6. Administer oxygen if prescribed.
7. Monitor for hypertonic contractions.
8. Stop the medication if uterine hyperstimulation or a nonreassuring fetal heart rate occurs; turn the client on her side, increase the IV rate of the normal saline, and administer oxygen via face mask.
9. Notify the health care provider if uterine hyperstimulation or a nonreassuring fetal heart rate occurs.
10. Monitor for signs of water intoxication.
11. Have emergency equipment available.
12. Document the dose of the medication and the time the medication was started, increased, maintained, and discontinued.
13. Keep the family informed of the client's progress.

II. MEDICATIONS USED TO MANAGE POSTPARTUM HEMORRHAGE (Box 31-1)

A. Ergot alkaloids
1. Description
   a. Ergonovine maleate (Ergotrate, Ergometrine) and methylergonovine maleate (Methergine) are ergot alkaloids.
   b. Directly stimulate uterine muscle, increase the force and frequency of contractions, and produce a firm tetanic contraction of the uterus

BOX 31-1
Medications Used to Manage Postpartum Bleeding

Ergonovine maleate (Ergotrate, Ergometrine)
Methylergonovine maleate (Methergine)
Oxytocin (Pitocin)
Prostaglandin $F_{2\alpha}$ (Carboprost tromethamine, Hemabate)

BOX 31-2
Medications Used To Stop Preterm Labor Contractions

Indomethacin
Magnesium sulfate
Nifedipine (Procardia, Adalat)
Ritodrine hydrochloride
Terbutaline (Brethine)

c. Can produce arterial vasoconstriction and vasospasm of the coronary arteries

d. Ergot alkaloids are not administered before the **delivery** of the **placenta.**

2. Uses
   a. Postpartum hemorrhage
   b. Postabortal hemorrhage resulting from atony or involution

3. Adverse reactions and contraindications
   a. Can cause nausea, uterine cramping, bradycardia, dysrhythmias, myocardial infarction, and severe hypertension
   b. High doses associated with peripheral vasospasm or vasoconstriction, angina, miosis, confusion, respiratory depression, seizures, or unconsciousness; uterine tetany can occur
   c. Contraindicated during pregnancy and in clients with significant cardiovascular disease, peripheral vascular disease, or hypertension

4. Interventions
   a. Monitor maternal vital signs, weight, intake and output, level of consciousness, and lung sounds.
   b. Monitor the blood pressure closely; the medication produces vasoconstriction and, if a rise in blood pressure is noted, withhold the medication and notify the health care provider.
   c. Monitor uterine contractions (frequency, strength, and duration).
   d. Assess for chest pain, headache, shortness of breath, itching, pale or cold hands or feet, nausea, diarrhea, or dizziness.
   e. Notify the health care provider if chest pain occurs.
   f. Assess the extremities for color, warmth, movement, and pain.
   g. Assess vaginal bleeding.
   h. Administer analgesics as prescribed; they may be required because the medication produces painful uterine contractions.

B. Prostaglandin $F_{2\alpha}$ (carboprost tromethamine, Hemabate)
   1. Description: Contracts the uterus
   2. Uses: Postpartum hemorrhage
   3. Adverse reactions and contraindications
      a. Can cause headache, nausea, vomiting, fever
      b. Contraindicated if the client has asthma

4. Interventions
   a. Check temperature every 1 to 2 hours.
   b. Auscultate breath sounds frequently.

III. **MEDICATIONS TO STOP PRETERM LABOR CONTRACTIONS**
A. Description: Tocolytics are medications that produce uterine relaxation and suppress uterine activity in an attempt to prevent preterm birth (Box 31-2 and Table 31-1).
B. Uses: To prevent preterm birth
C. Adverse reactions and contraindications
   1. See Table 31-1 for a description of adverse reactions
   2. Maternal contraindications include severe preeclampsia and eclampsia, active vaginal bleeding, intrauterine infection, cardiac disease, and a medical or obstetric condition that contraindicates continuation of pregnancy.
   3. Fetal contraindications include estimated gestational age over 37 weeks, cervical dilation over 4 cm, fetal demise, lethal fetal anomaly, chorioamnionitis, acute fetal distress, and chronic intrauterine growth restriction.
D. Interventions for the client receiving tocolytic therapy
   1. Position the client on her side to enhance **placental** perfusion and reduce pressure on the cervix.
   2. Monitor maternal vital signs, fetal status, and **labor** status frequently according to agency protocol.
   3. Monitor for signs of adverse reactions to the medication.
   4. Monitor daily weight and input and output (I&O) status and limit fluid intake as prescribed.
   5. Offer comfort measures and provide psychosocial support to the client and family.
   6. See Table 31-1 for interventions specific to each tocolytic medication.

IV. PROSTAGLANDINS (Box 31-3)
A. Description
   1. Ripen the cervix, making it softer and causing it to begin to dilate and efface
   2. Stimulate uterine contractions
   3. Administered vaginally

TABLE 31-1

Medications Used in Preterm Labor

Medication, Classification, and Actions	Adverse Reactions	Nursing Interventions
Magnesium sulfate—central nervous system (CNS) depressant; relaxes smooth muscle, including the uterus; used to halt preterm labor contractions; used for preeclamptic clients to prevent seizures	Depressed respirations Depressed deep tendon reflexes (DTRs) Hypotension Extreme muscle weakness Flushing Decreased urine output Pulmonary edema Serum magnesium levels > 9 mg/dL	Use controller pump for administration. Follow agency protocol for administration. Discontinue infusion and notify physician if adverse reactions occur. Monitor for respirations < 12/min, urine output < 100 mL/4 hr (25-30 mL/hr). Monitor DTRs. Monitor magnesium levels and report values outside therapeutic range (4 to 7.5 mEq/L or 5 to 8 mg/dL). Keep calcium gluconate at bedside (antidote).
Ritodrine—β-adrenergic agonist; relaxes smooth muscles, inhibiting uterine activity and causing bronchodilation	Shortness of breath, coughing, tachypnea, pulmonary edema Tachycardia, palpitations, chest pain, hypotension Fluid retention and decreased urine production Tremors, dizziness, muscle cramps and weakness Headache Hypokalemia, hyperglycemia, hypocalcemia	Discontinue infusion and notify physician if the following occur—maternal heart rate > 120-140 beats/min, dysrhythmias, chest pain, blood pressure < 90/60 mm Hg, signs of pulmonary edema, fetal heart rate > 180 beats/min. Ensure that a beta-blocking agent such as propranolol (Inderal) is available to reverse cardiovascular adverse reactions.
Terbutaline (Brethine)—β-adrenergic agonist; relaxes smooth muscles, inhibiting uterine activity and causing bronchodilation	Similar to ritodrine but limited and less severe	Monitor for adverse reactions and notify the physician if they occur. Teach woman and family to monitor for adverse reactions and when to notify the physician.
Nifedipine (Procardia, Adalat)—calcium channel blocker; relaxes smooth muscles, including the uterus, by blocking calcium entry	Transient tachycardia Palpitations Hypotension Dizziness, headache, nervousness Facial flushing Fatigue, nausea	Follow agency protocol for administration. Avoid use or use cautiously with magnesium sulfate because severe hypotension can occur. Monitor for adverse reactions.
Indomethacin—prostaglandin inhibitor; relaxes uterine smooth muscle	Maternal—nausea and vomiting, dyspepsia, dizziness Fetal—premature closure of ductus arteriosus Neonatal—bronchopulmonary dysplasia, respiratory distress syndrome, intracranial pressure, necrotizing enterocolitis, hyperbilirubinemia	Used only when other methods fail only if gestational age is < 32 weeks. Not used in women with bleeding potential, peptic ulcer disease, or oligohydramnios. Follow agency protocol for administration. Prepare to determine amniotic fluid volume and function of ductus arteriosus before therapy and within 48 hours of discontinuing therapy.

Modified from Wong, D., Perry, S., Hockenberry, M., et al. (2006). *Maternal child nursing care* (3rd ed.). St. Louis: Mosby.

B. Uses
   1. Preinduction cervical ripening (ripening of the cervix before the induction of **labor**)
   2. Induction of **labor**
   3. Induction of abortion (abortifacient agent)
▲ C. Adverse reactions and contraindications
   1. Significant gastrointestinal side effects, including diarrhea, nausea, vomiting, and stomach cramps
   2. Fever, chills, flushing, headache, hypotension
   3. Tachysystole (12 or more uterine contractions in 20 minutes without an alteration in the fetal heart rate pattern)

Prostaglandin E$_1$ (PGE$_1$): Misoprostol (Cytotec)
Prostaglandin E$_2$ (PGE$_2$): Dinoprostone (Cervidil vaginal insert, Prepidil gel)

Active cardiac, hepatic, pulmonary, or renal disease
Acute pelvic inflammatory disease
Clients whom vaginal delivery is not indicated
Fetal malpresentation
History of cesarean section or major uterine surgery
History of difficult labor or traumatic labor
Hypersensitivity to prostaglandins
Maternal fever or infection
Nonreassuring fetal heart rate pattern
Placenta previa or unexplained vaginal bleeding
Regular progressive uterine contractions
Significant cephalopelvic disproportion

4. Hyperstimulation of the uterus
5. Fetal passage of meconium
6. Contraindications (Box 31-4)

D. Interventions
1. Monitor maternal vital signs, fetal heart rate pattern, and status of pregnancy, including indications for cervical ripening or the induction of **labor**, signs of **labor** or impending **labor**, and Bishop score (see Table 26-2 for information about the Bishop score).
2. Monitor for adverse reactions to the medication
3. Have woman void before administration of medication and then have her maintain a supine with lateral tilt or side-lying position for 30 to 40 minutes after administration.
4. Follow agency protocol for the induction of **labor** if cervical ripening has occurred and **labor** has not begun.

V. MAGNESIUM SULFATE
A. Description (see Table 31-1)
1. Magnesium sulfate is a central nervous system depressant and anticonvulsant.
2. The medication causes smooth muscle relaxation.
3. The antidote is calcium gluconate.
B. Uses
1. Stopping preterm **labor**
2. Preventing and controlling seizures in preeclamptic and eclamptic clients

C. Adverse reactions and contraindications
1. Magnesium sulfate can cause respiratory depression, depressed reflexes, flushing, hypotension, extreme muscle weakness, decreased urine output, pulmonary edema, and elevated serum magnesium levels.
2. Continuous IV infusion increases the risk of magnesium toxicity in the **neonate.**
3. Intravenous administration should not be used for 2 hours preceding **delivery.**
4. Magnesium sulfate is usually continued for the first 12 to 24 hours postpartum if it is used for preeclampsia.
5. High doses can cause loss of deep tendon reflexes, heart block, respiratory paralysis, and cardiac arrest.
6. The medication is contraindicated in the client with heart block, myocardial damage, or renal failure.
7. The medication is used with caution in the client with severe renal impairment.

D. Interventions
1. Monitor maternal vital signs, especially respirations, every 30 to 60 minutes.
2. Call the health care provider if respirations are less than 12 breaths/min, indicating respiratory depression, or if any other adverse reactions occur.
3. Assess renal function and electrocardiogram for cardiac function.
4. Monitor magnesium levels—the target range is 4 to 7.5 mEq/L (5 to 8 mg/dL); if a rise in the magnesium level occurs, notify the health care provider.
5. Administered by IV infusion via an infusion monitoring device such as a controller pump; carefully monitor the dose being administered and follow agency protocol for administration.
6. Keep calcium gluconate on hand in case of a magnesium sulfate overdose, because calcium gluconate antagonizes the effect of magnesium sulfate.
7. Monitor deep tendon reflexes hourly for signs of developing toxicity.
8. Test the patellar reflex or knee jerk reflex before administering repeat parenteral doses (used as an indicator of central nervous system depression; suppressed reflex may be a sign of impending respiratory arrest); Fig. 31-1 and Table 31-2).
9. Patellar reflex must be present and respiratory rate must be greater than 16 breaths/min (or as designated by agency protocol) before each parenteral dose.
10. Monitor I&O hourly; output should be maintained at 30 mL/hr because the medication is eliminated through the kidneys.

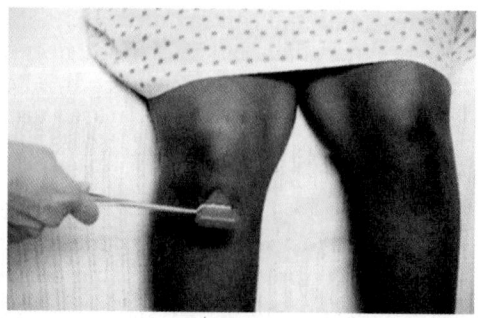

FIG. 31-1 Patellar reflex, with woman's legs hanging freely over end of examining table. (From Wong, D., Perry, S., Hockenberry, M., et al. [2006]. *Maternal child nursing care* [3rd ed.]. St. Louis: Mosby.)

TABLE 31-2	

Assessing Deep Tendon Reflexes

Grade	Deep Tendon Reflex Response
0	No response
1	Sluggish or diminished
2	Active or expected response
3	More brisk than expected, slightly hyperactive
4	Brisk, hyperactive, with intermittent or transient clonus

From Seidel, H.M., Ball, J.W., Dains, J.E., & Benedict, G.W. (2006). *Mosby's guide to physical examination* (5th ed.). St. Louis, Mosby.

VI. OPIOID ANALGESICS

A. Description: Opioid analgesic
   1. Used to relieve moderate to severe pain associated with **labor**
   2. Administered by intramuscular or intravenous (IV) route
   3. Regular use of opioids during pregnancy may produce withdrawal symptoms in the **neonate** (irritability, excessive crying, tremors, hyperactive reflexes, fever, vomiting, diarrhea, yawning, sneezing, and seizures).
   4. Antidote for opioids: Naloxone (Narcan)
B. Meperidine hydrochloride (Demerol)
   1. Can cause dizziness, nausea, vomiting, sedation, decreased blood pressure, decreased respirations, diaphoresis, flushed face, urinary retention
   2. May be prescribed to be administered with promethazine (Phenergan) to prevent nausea
   3. High dosages may result in respiratory depression, skeletal muscle flaccidity, cold clammy skin, cyanosis, extreme somnolence progressing to convulsions, stupor, and coma.
   4. Used cautiously in clients delivering preterm infants
   5. Not administered in early **labor** because it may slow the **labor** process
   6. Not administered in advanced **labor** (within 1 hour of **delivery**) if the **neonate** is to be deliv-

ered before the medication is removed adequately from the fetal circulation (may cause respiratory depression)
C. Morphine sulfate, fentanyl (Sublimaze): Can cause respiratory depression, fetal narcosis and distress, hypotension, urinary retention
D. Butorphanol tartrate (Stadol), nalbuphine (Nubain)
   1. Cause less respiratory depression than the agonists (morphine sulfate)
   2. Use with caution in a client with preexisting narcotic dependency because withdrawal symptoms will occur immediately.
E. Interventions
   1. Obtain a drug history before administration (butorphanol is contraindicated if the client has a history of opioid dependency).
   2. Monitor vital signs, particularly respiratory status; if respirations are 12 breaths/min or fewer, withhold medication and contact the health care provider.
   3. Monitor the fetal heart rate and characteristics of uterine contractions.
   4. Monitor for blood pressure changes (hypotension); maintain client in a recumbent position.
   5. Record the client's response and level of pain relief.
   6. Monitor bladder for distention and retention.
   7. Have antidote naloxone (Narcan) available, especially if **delivery** is going to occur during peak drug absorption time.

VII. BETAMETHASONE

A. Description: Corticosteroid that increases the production of surfactant
B. Use: For client in preterm **labor** between 28 and 32 weeks' gestation whose **labor** can be inhibited for 48 hours without jeopardizing the mother or fetus
C. Adverse reactions and contraindications
   1. May decrease mother's resistance to infection
   2. Pulmonary edema secondary to sodium and fluid retention can occur
   3. Elevated blood glucose levels in client with diabetes mellitus can occur
D. Interventions
   1. Monitor maternal vital signs, lung sounds, and for edema.
   2. Monitor mother for signs of infection.
   3. Monitor white blood cell count.
   4. Monitor blood glucose levels.

VIII. LUNG SURFACTANTS (Box 31-5)

A. Description
   1. Lung surfactants replenish surfactant and restore surface activity to the lungs.
   2. Lung surfactants are administered by the intratracheal route.
B. Use: To prevent or treat respiratory distress syndrome (hyaline membrane disease) in premature infants

BOX 31-5
Lung Surfactant Replacement Therapy

Beractant (Survanta)
Colfosceril palmitate (Exosurf)

C. Adverse reactions and contraindications
   1. Side effects include transient bradycardia and oxygen desaturation.
   2. Surfactants are administered with caution in those at risk for circulatory overload.
D. Interventions
   1. Instill surfactant through catheter inserted into infant's endotracheal tube; avoid suctioning for at least 2 hours after administration.
   2. Monitor for bradycardia and decreased oxygen saturation during administration.
   3. Assess lung sounds for crackles and moist breath sounds.

IX. Rh$_o$(D) IMMUNE GLOBULIN (RhoGAM)
A. Description
   1. Prevention of anti-Rh$_o$(D) antibody formation is most successful if the medication is administered twice, at 28 weeks of gestation and again within 72 hours after **delivery.**
   2. The immune globulin also should be administered within 72 hours after potential or actual exposure to Rh-positive blood and must be given with each subsequent exposure or potential exposure to Rh-positive blood.
   3. The immune globulin is of no benefit once the client has developed a positive antibody titer to the Rh antigen.
B. Use: To prevent isoimmunization in Rh-negative clients who are exposed or potentially exposed to Rh-positive red blood cells by transfusion, termination of pregnancy, amniocentesis, chorionic villus sampling (CVS), abdominal trauma, or bleeding during pregnancy or birth process
C. Adverse reactions and contraindications
   1. Elevated temperature
   2. Tenderness at the injection site
   3. Contraindicated for Rh-positive women
   4. Contraindicated in clients with a history of systemic allergic reactions to preparations containing human immunoglobulins
   5. Not administered to a **newborn** infant
D. Interventions
   1. Administer to mother by intramuscular injection at 28 weeks' gestation and within 72 hours after **delivery.**
   2. Never administer by the IV route.
   3. Monitor for temperature elevation.
   4. Monitor injection site for tenderness.

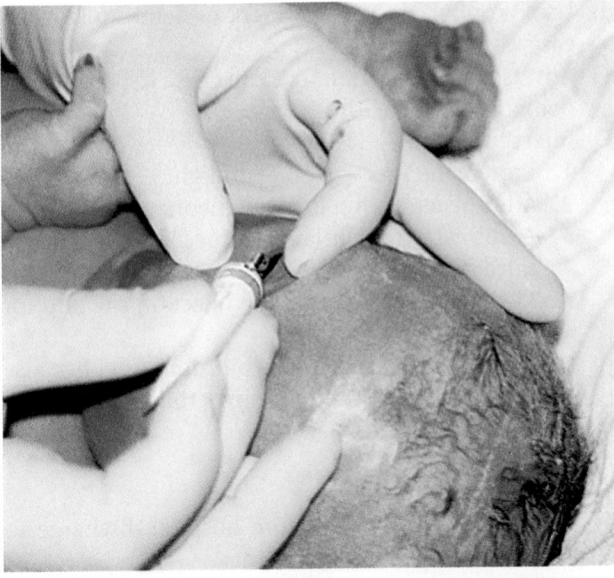

FIG. 31-2 Instillation of medication into eye of newborn. The thumb and forefinger are used to open the eye; medication is placed into the lower conjunctiva from the inner to the outer canthus. (From Lowdermilk, D., & Perry, S. [2006]. *Maternity nursing* [7th ed.]. St. Louis: Mosby.)

X. EYE PROPHYLAXIS FOR THE NEONATE
A. Description
   1. Erythromycin (0.5% Ilotycin) and tetracycline (1%) ophthalmic ointment or drops are bacteriostatic and bactericidal and provide prophylaxis against infection by *Neisseria gonorrhoeae* and *Chlamydia trachomatis*.
   2. Silver nitrate (1%) solution may be prescribed, but its use is minimal because it does not protect against chlamydial infection and can cause chemical conjunctivitis.
   3. Preventive treatment of gonorrhea is required by law.
B. Use: As prophylactic measure to protect against *Neisseria gonorrhoeae* and *Chlamydia trachomatis*
C. Adverse reaction: Silver nitrate (1%) solution can cause chemical conjunctivitis.
D. Interventions
   1. Cleanse the **neonate**'s eyes before instilling drops or ointment.
   2. Instill into each of the **neonate**'s conjunctival sacs within 1 hour after **delivery** (Fig. 31-2).
   3. Do not flush the eyes after instillation.

XI. VITAMIN K
A. Description
   1. Vitamin K (AquaMEPHYTON) is necessary to assist in the production of active prothrombin.
   2. **Newborns** are deficient in vitamin K for the first 5 to 8 days of life because of the lack of intestinal flora necessary to absorb vitamin K.

▲ B. Use: Prophylaxis and treatment of hemorrhagic disease of the **newborn**

▲ C. Adverse reaction: Vitamin K can cause hyperbilirubinemia in the **newborn.**

▲ D. Interventions

1. Protect the medication from light.

2. Administer during the early neonatal period.

▲ 3. Administer in the lateral aspect of the middle third of the vastus lateralis muscle of the thigh.

4. Monitor for bruising at the injection site and for bleeding from the cord.

5. Monitor for jaundice and bilirubin level because the medication can cause hyperbilirubinemia in the **newborn.**

▲ **XII. RUBELLA VACCINE**

A. Given subcutaneously before hospital discharge to nonimmune postpartum clients

▲ B. Administered if rubella titer is lower than 1:8

C. Adverse reaction: Transient rash, hypersensitivity

▲ D. Interventions

1. Do not give if client or other family members are immunocompromised.

▲ 2. Teach about contraception; client should avoid pregnancy for 1 to 3 months after immunization.

▲ **XIII. HEPATITIS B VACCINE (HBV)**

A. Description: Given IM to the **newborn** before discharge

▲ B. Use: Recommended for all infants to prevent hepatitis B

C. Adverse reaction: Rash, fever, erythema and pain at injection site

▲ D. Interventions

1. Parental consent must be obtained.

2. Administer in the lateral aspect of the middle third of the vastus lateralis muscle IM.

3. If the infant was born to a HBsAg-positive mother, hepatitis B immune globulin (HBIG) should be given within 12 hours of birth in addition to the hepatitis B vaccine. Then follow the regularly scheduled HBV vaccination schedule.

PRACTICE QUESTIONS

1. Methylergonovine (Methergine) is prescribed for a woman to treat postpartum hemorrhage. Before administration of methylergonovine, the priority nursing assessment is to check the:
   1. Uterine tone
   2. Blood pressure
   3. Amount of lochia
   4. Deep tendon reflexes

2. A nurse is preparing to administer beractant (Survanta) to a premature infant who has respiratory distress syndrome. The nurse plans to administer the medication by which of the following routes?
   1. Intradermal
   2. Intratracheal
   3. Subcutaneous
   4. Intramuscular

3. A nurse is caring for a client who is receiving oxytocin (Pitocin) to induce labor. The nurse discontinues the oxytocin infusion if which of the following is noted on assessment of the client?
   1. Fatigue
   2. Drowsiness
   3. Uterine hyperstimulation
   4. Early decelerations of the fetal heart rate

4. A pregnant client is receiving magnesium sulfate for the management of preeclampsia. A nurse determines that the client is experiencing toxicity from the medication if which of the following is noted on assessment?
   1. Proteinuria of +3
   2. Presence of deep tendon reflexes
   3. Serum magnesium level of 6 mEq/L
   4. Respirations of 10 breaths/min

5. Epidural analgesia is administered to a woman for pain relief following a cesarean birth. The nurse assigned to care for the woman ensures that which medication is readily available if respiratory depression occurs?
   1. Morphine sulfate
   2. Naloxone (Narcan)
   3. Betamethasone (Celestone)
   4. Meperidine hydrochloride (Demerol)

6. Rho(D) immune globulin (RhoGAM) is prescribed for a woman following delivery of a newborn infant and the nurse provides information to the woman about the purpose of the medication. The nurse determines that the woman understands the purpose of the medication if the woman states that it will protect her next baby from which of the following?
   1. Having Rh-positive blood
   2. Developing a rubella infection
   3. Developing physiological jaundice
   4. Being affected by Rh incompatibility

7. A woman with preeclampsia is receiving magnesium sulfate. The nurse assigned to care for the client determines that the magnesium sulfate therapy is effective if:
   1. Scotomas are present.
   2. Seizures do not occur.
   3. Ankle clonus is noted.
   4. The blood pressure decreases.

8. Methylergonovine (Methergine) is prescribed for a client with postpartum hemorrhage. Before administering the medication, a nurse contacts the health care provider who prescribed the medication if which of the following conditions is documented in the client's medical history?

1. Hypotension
2. Hypothyroidism
3. Diabetes mellitus
4. Peripheral vascular disease

9. A nursing instructor asks a nursing student to describe the procedure for administering erythromycin (0.5% Ilotycin) ointment to the eyes of a neonate. The instructor determines that the student needs to research this procedure further if the student states that:
   1. "I will flush the eyes after instilling the ointment."
   2. "I will cleanse the neonate's eyes before instilling ointment."
   3. "Administration of the eye ointment is within 1 hour after delivery."
   4. "I will instill the eye ointment into each of the neonate's conjunctival sacs."

10. A 31-week preterm labor client dilated to 4 cm has been started on magnesium sulfate and contractions have stopped. If the client's labor can be inhibited for the next 48 hours, what medication does the nurse anticipate will be prescribed?
    1. Nalbuphine (Nubain)
    2. Misoprostol (Cytotec)
    3. Betamethasone (Celestone)
    4. $Rh_o(D)$ immune globulin (RhoGAM)

ALTERNATE ITEM FORMAT: MULTIPLE RESPONSE

A nurse is monitoring a preterm **labor** client who is receiving intravenous (IV) magnesium sulfate. The nurse monitors for which adverse reactions of this medication? Select all that apply.

❏ 1. Flushing
❏ 2. Hypertension
❏ 3. Increased urine output
❏ 4. Depressed respirations
❏ 5. Extreme muscle weakness
❏ 6. Hyperactive deep tendon reflexes

ANSWERS

1. **2**

Rationale: Methylergonovine, an ergot alkaloid, is an agent that is used to prevent or control postpartum hemorrhage by contracting the uterus. Methylergonovine causes continuous uterine contractions and may elevate blood pressure. A priority assessment before the administration of the medication is to check the blood pressure. The physician should be notified if hypertension is present. Although options 1, 3, and 4 may be components of the postpartum assessment, option 2, blood pressure, is related specifically to the administration of this medication.
Test-Taking Strategy: Use the process of elimination. Eliminate options 1 and 3 first because they are comparative or alike and related to one another. From the remaining options, use the ABCs—airway, breathing, and circulation. Blood pressure is a method of assessing circulation. Review the adverse effects of this medication if you had difficulty with this question.
Level of Cognitive Ability: Analysis
Client Needs: Physiological Integrity
Integrated Process: Nursing Process—assessment
Content Area: Maternity—postpartum
References: Lilley, L., Harrington, S., & Snyder, J. (2005). *Pharmacology and the nursing process* (4th ed., p. 59). St. Louis: Mosby.
Murray, S., & McKinney, E. (2006). *Foundations of maternal-newborn nursing* (4th ed., p. 662). Philadelphia: W.B. Saunders.

2. **2**

Rationale: Respiratory distress is common in premature neonates and may be due to lung immaturity as a result of surfactant deficiency. The mainstay of treatment is the administration of exogenous surfactant, which is administered by the intratracheal route. Options 1, 3, and 4 are not routes of administration for this medication.
Test-Taking Strategy: Use the process of elimination. Note the relationship between the diagnosis *respiratory distress syndrome* and the correct option, *intratracheal*. Review this medication if you had difficulty with this question.
Level of Cognitive Ability: Analysis
Client Needs: Physiological Integrity
Integrated Process: Nursing Process—planning
Content Area: Maternity—postpartum
References: Lowdermilk, D. & Perry, S. (2004). *Maternity and women's health care* (8th ed., p. 1120). St. Louis: Mosby.
McKinney, E., James, S., Murray, S., & Ashwill, J. (2005). *Maternal-child nursing* (2nd ed., pp. 722-723). St. Louis: W.B. Saunders.

3. **3**

Rationale: Oxytocin stimulates uterine contractions and is a common pharmacological method to induce labor. An adverse reaction associated with administration of the medication is hyperstimulation of uterine contractions. Therefore, oxytocin infusion must be stopped when any signs of uterine hyperstimulation are present. Drowsiness and fatigue may be caused by the labor experience. Early decelerations of the fetal heart rate are a reassuring sign and do not indicate fetal distress.
Test-Taking Strategy: Use the process of elimination, focusing on the subject, an adverse reaction to oxytocin. Options 1 and 2 can be eliminated first. From the remaining options, recalling that early decelerations of the fetal heart rate are a reassuring sign will direct you to option 3. Review the nursing responsibilities associated with this medication if you had difficulty with this question.
Level of Cognitive Ability: Analysis

Client Needs: Physiological Integrity
Integrated Process: Nursing Process—implementation
Content Area: Maternity—intrapartum
References: Hodgson, B., & Kizior, R. (2007). *Saunders nursing drug handbook 2007.* St. Louis: W.B. Saunders, p. 885.
Wong, D., Perry, S., Hockenberry, M., et al. (2006). *Maternal child nursing care* (3rd ed., p. 567). St. Louis: Mosby.

4. **4**
Rationale: Magnesium toxicity can occur from magnesium sulfate therapy. Signs of magnesium sulfate toxicity relate to central nervous system depressant effects of the medication and include respiratory depression, loss of deep tendon reflexes, and a sudden drop in fetal heart rate and maternal heart rate and blood pressure. Therapeutic serum levels of magnesium are 4 to 7.5 mEq/L. Proteinuria of 3+ is likely to be noted in a client with preeclampsia.
Test-Taking Strategy: Use the process of elimination and eliminate option 2 first because it is a normal finding. Next, eliminate option 3, knowing that the therapeutic serum level of magnesium is between 4 and 7.5 mEq/L. From the remaining options, recalling that proteinuria of 3+ would be noted in a client with preeclampsia will direct you to the correct option. Review the adverse effects of magnesium sulfate if you had difficulty with this question.
Level of Cognitive Ability: Analysis
Client Needs: Physiological Integrity
Integrated Process: Nursing Process—assessment
Content Area: Maternity—intrapartum
References: Hodgson, B., & Kizior, R. (2007). *W.B. Saunders nursing drug handbook 2007.* St. Louis: W.B. Saunders, pp. 717-720.
McKinney, E., James, S., Murray, S., & Ashwill, J. (2005). *Maternal-child nursing* (2nd ed., pp. 637, 640-641). St. Louis: W.B. Saunders.

5. **2**
Rationale: Opioids (narcotics) are used for epidural analgesia. An adverse reaction of epidural analgesia is a delayed respiratory depression. Naloxone (Narcan) is a opioid antagonist, which reverses the effects of opioids and is given for respiratory depression. Morphine sulfate and meperidine hydrochloride are opioid analgesics. Betamethasone is a corticosteroid administered to enhance fetal lung maturity.
Test-Taking Strategy: Use the process of elimination, focusing on the subject of the question, the antidote for respiratory depression. Eliminate options 1 and 4 first, knowing that these medications are opioid analgesics. Next, eliminate option 3, knowing that this medication is a corticosteroid. Review the purpose and actions of these medications if you had difficulty with this question.
Level of Cognitive Ability: Application
Client Needs: Physiological Integrity
Integrated Process: Nursing Process—planning
Content Area: Maternity—postpartum
References: Lilley, L., Harrington, S., & Snyder, J. (2005). *Pharmacology and the nursing process* (4th ed., p. 154). St. Louis: Mosby.
Murray, S., & McKinney, E. (2006). *Foundations of maternal-newborn nursing* (4th ed., pp. 348, 351). Philadelphia: W.B. Saunders.

6. **4**
Rationale: Rh incompatibility can occur when an Rh-negative mother becomes sensitized to the Rh antigen. Sensitization may develop when an Rh-negative woman becomes pregnant with a fetus who is Rh positive. During pregnancy and at delivery, some of the baby's Rh-positive blood can enter the maternal circulation, causing the woman's immune system to form antibodies against Rh-positive blood. Administration of $Rh_o(D)$ immune globulin prevents the woman from developing antibodies against Rh-positive blood by providing passive antibody protection against the Rh antigen.
Test-Taking Strategy: Use the process of elimination. Options 2 and 3 can be eliminated first. From the remaining options, note the relationship between the name of the medication, $Rh_o(D)$ immune globulin, and the word *incompatibility* in the correct option. Review the purpose of this medication if you had difficulty with this question.
Level of Cognitive Ability: Analysis
Client Needs: Physiological Integrity
Integrated Process: Nursing Process—evaluation
Content Area: Maternity—postpartum
References: Hodgson, B., & Kizior, R. (2007). *Saunders nursing drug handbook 2007.* St. Louis: W.B. Saunders, pp. 1014-1016.
Murray, S., & McKinney, E. (2006). *Foundations of maternal-newborn nursing* (4th ed., p. 411). Philadelphia: W.B. Saunders.

7. **2**
Rationale: For a client with preeclampsia, the goal of care is directed at preventing eclampsia (seizures). Magnesium sulfate is an anticonvulsant, not an antihypertensive agent. Although a decrease in blood pressure may be noted initially, this effect is usually transient. Ankle clonus indicates hyperreflexia and may precede the onset of eclampsia. Scotomas are areas of complete or partial blindness. Visual disturbances, such as scotomas, often precede an eclamptic seizure.
Test-Taking Strategy: Use the process of elimination. Knowing that magnesium sulfate is an anticonvulsant will direct you to option 2. Review this medication if you had difficulty with this question.
Level of Cognitive Ability: Analysis
Client Needs: Physiological Integrity
Integrated Process: Nursing Process—evaluation
Content Area: Maternity—intrapartum
References: Lilley, L., Harrington, S., & Snyder, J. (2005). *Pharmacology and the nursing process* (4th ed., p. 906). St. Louis: Mosby.
McKinney, E., James, S., Murray, S., & Ashwill, J. (2005). *Maternal-child nursing* (2nd ed., p. 638). St. Louis: W.B. Saunders.

8. **4**
Rationale: Methylergonovine is an ergot alkaloid used for postpartum hemorrhage. Ergot alkaloids are avoided in clients with significant cardiovascular disease, peripheral disease, hypertension, eclampsia, or preeclampsia. These conditions are worsened by the vasoconstrictive effects of the ergot alkaloids. Options 1, 2, and 3 are not contraindications related to the use of ergot alkaloids.

Test-Taking Strategy: Use the process of elimination. Recalling that ergot alkaloids produce vasoconstriction will direct you to option 4. Review the effects of this medication and the associated contraindications if you had difficulty with this question.
Level of Cognitive Ability: Analysis
Client Needs: Physiological Integrity
Integrated Process: Nursing Process—implementation
Content Area: Maternity—postpartum
References: Hodgson, B., & Kizior, R. (2007). *Saunders nursing drug handbook 2007.* St. Louis: W.B. Saunders, pp. 754-756. McKinney, E., James, S., Murray, S., & Ashwill, J. (2005). *Maternal-child nursing* (2nd ed., p. 704). St. Louis: W.B. Saunders.

9. 1
Rationale: Eye prophylaxis protects the neonate against *Neisseria gonorrhoeae* and *Chlamydia trachomatis.* The eyes are not flushed after instillation of the medication because the flush will wash away the administered medication. Options 2, 3, and 4 are correct statements regarding the procedure for administering eye medication to the neonate.
Test-Taking Strategy: Use the process of elimination, noting the strategic words *needs to research.* These words indicate a negative event query and ask you to select an option that is an incorrect statement. Eliminate options 3 and 4 first because they are comparative or alike. From the remaining options, visualize the effect of each. This will direct you to option 1. Review the procedure for administering eye medication to the neonate if you had difficulty with this question.
Level of Cognitive Ability: Analysis
Client Needs: Health Promotion and Maintenance
Integrated Process: Teaching and Learning
Content Area: Maternity—postpartum
Reference: Murray, S., & McKinney, E. (2006). *Foundations of maternal-newborn nursing* (4th ed., p. 513). Philadelphia: W.B. Saunders.

10. 3
Rationale: Betamethasone (Celestone), a glucocorticoid, is given to stimulate fetal lung maturation. It is used for clients in preterm labor between 28 to 32 weeks if the labor can be inhibited for 48 hours. Nalbuphine (Nubain) is an opioid analgesic. Misoprostol (Cytotec) is a prostaglandin given to ripen and soften the cervix and to stimulate uterine contractions. Rh_o(D) immune globulin (RhoGAM) is given to Rh-negative clients to prevent sensitization.
Test-Taking Strategy: Use the process of elimination. Noting the strategic words *31-week preterm labor client* and recalling that betamethasone is used to stimulate surfactant release will direct you to option 3. Review the purpose and actions of the medications in the options if you had difficulty with this question.
Level of Cognitive Ability: Analysis
Client Needs: Physiological Integrity
Integrated Process: Nursing Process—analysis
Content Area: Maternity—intrapartum
Reference: Lowdermilk, D., & Perry, S. (2006). *Maternity nursing* (7th ed., p. 780). St. Louis: Mosby.

ALTERNATE ITEM FORMAT: MULTIPLE RESPONSE

Answer: 1, 4, 5
Rationale: Magnesium sulfate is a central nervous system depressant and relaxes smooth muscle, including the uterus. It is used to halt preterm labor contractions and is used for preeclamptic clients to prevent seizures. Adverse effects include flushing, depressed respirations, depressed deep tendon reflexes, hypotension, extreme muscle weakness, decreased urine output, pulmonary edema, and elevated serum magnesium levels.
Test-Taking Strategy: Focus on the subject, adverse effects of magnesium sulfate. Recalling that this medication is a central nervous system depressant will assist in answering correctly. Review the adverse effects of this medication if you had difficulty with this question.
Level of Cognitive Ability: Analysis
Client Needs: Physiological Integrity
Integrated Process: Nursing Process—assessment
Content Area: Maternity—intrapartum
Reference: Hodgson, B., & Kizior, R. (2007). *Saunders nursing drug book 2007.* St. Louis: W.B. Saunders, pp. 717-720.

REFERENCES

Hodgson, B., & Kizior, R. (2007). *Saunders nursing drug handbook 2007.* St. Louis: W.B. Saunders.

Kee, J., Hayes, E., & McCuistion, L. (2006). *Pharmacology: A nursing process approach* (5th ed.). St. Louis: W.B. Saunders.

Lilley, L., Harrington, S., & Snyder, J. (2005). *Pharmacology and the nursing process* (4th ed.). St. Louis: Mosby.

Lowdermilk, D., & Perry, S. (2006). *Maternity nursing* (7th ed.). St. Louis: Mosby.

Lowdermilk, D., & Perry, S. (2004). *Maternity and women's health care* (8th ed.). St. Louis: Mosby.

McKinney, E., James, S., Murray, S., & Ashwill, J. (2005). *Maternal-child nursing* (2nd ed.). St. Louis: W.B. Saunders.

Murray, S., & McKinney, E. (2006). *Foundations of maternal-newborn nursing* (4th ed.). Philadelphia: W.B. Saunders.

National Council of State Boards of Nursing (Eds.). (2007). *2007 NCLEX-RN® detailed test plan.* Chicago: Author.

Wong, D., Perry, S., Hockenberry, M., et al. (2006). *Maternal-child nursing care* (3rd ed.). St. Louis: Mosby.

Growth and Development Across the Life Span

PYRAMID TERMS

abuse The willful infliction of pain, injury, mental anguish, or unreasonable confinement. Abuse can include verbal assaults, the demand to perform demeaning tasks, theft, or mismanagement of personal belongings. Abuse inflicted can be physical, emotional, or sexual.

accommodation The ability to change a schema (an individual's cognitive structure or framework of thought) to introduce new ideas, objects, or experiences.

aging The biopsychosocial process of change occurring between birth and death.

assimilation The ability to incorporate new ideas, objects, and experiences into the framework of one's thoughts.

conscious All experiences that are part of an individual's awareness and that the individual is able to control.

dementia An organic syndrome identified by gradual and progressive deterioration in intellectual functioning. Long- and short-term memory loss occur with impairment in judgment, abstract thinking, problem-solving ability, and behavior, resulting in a self-care deficit. A common type of dementia is Alzheimer's disease.

depression A mood disorder that can be identified by feelings of sadness, hopelessness, and worthlessness, and a decreased interest in activities.

ego One's "sense of self"; provides functions such as problem solving, mobilization of defense mechanisms, reality testing, and the capability of functioning independently; the mediator between the id and the superego.

exploitation Illegal or improper use of the individual's resources.

gerontology The study of the process of aging.

id Source of all primitive drives and instincts; considered to be the reservoir of all psychic energy.

neglect The lack of providing services necessary for physical or mental health; includes failure to prevent injury.

polypharmacy Taking multiple prescription and/or over-the-counter medications together.

schema An individual's cognitive structure or framework of thought.

schemata Categories that an individual forms in his or her mind to organize and understand the world.

self-neglect The choice to avoid medical care or other services that could improve optimal function. Unless declared legally incompetent, an individual has the right to refuse care.

subconscious Often called the preconscious; includes experiences, thoughts, feelings, or desires that might not be in immediate awareness but can be recalled to consciousness; helps repress unpleasant thoughts or feelings.

superego The moral component of personality, including internalization of the values, ideals, and moral standards of society.

unconscious Memories, feelings, thoughts, or wishes that are repressed and are not available to the conscious mind.

THE PYRAMID TO SUCCESS

Normal growth and development proceed in an orderly, systematic, and predictable pattern, which provides a basis for identifying and assessing an individual's abilities. Understanding the path of growth and development across the life span assists the nurse in identifying appropriate and expected human behavior. The Pyramid to Success focuses on Sigmund Freud's theory of psychosexual development, Jean Piaget's theory of cognitive development, Erik Erikson's psychosocial theory, and Lawrence Kohlberg's theory of moral development. Growth and development concepts focus on the aging process and on physical characteristics, nutritional behaviors, skills, play, and specific safety measures relevant to a particular age group that will ensure a safe and hazard-free environment. When a question is presented on the NCLEX-RN examination, if an age is identified in the question, note the age and think about the associated growth and developmental concepts. The Integrated Processes addressed in this unit include Caring, Communication and Documentation, Nursing Process, and Teaching/Learning.

▲ CLIENT NEEDS

Safe and Effective Care Environment

Acting as a client advocate
Consulting with members of the health care team
Establishing priorities
Maintaining confidentiality
Preventing accidents
Providing care following ethical and legal standards
Respecting client and family needs based on their preferences
Upholding client's rights

Health Promotion and Maintenance

Assisting with family planning
Discussing lifestyle choices
Identifying changes that occur as a result of the aging process
Identifying developmental stages and transitions
Identifying expected body image changes
Maintaining health and wellness
Monitoring growth and development
Providing client and family education
Respecting health care beliefs and preferences

Psychosocial Integrity

Assessing for abuse and neglect
Considering grief and loss issues with the older client
Identifying coping mechanisms
Identifying loss of quantity and quality of relationships with the older client
Identifying support systems
Monitoring for adjustment to potential deterioration in physical and mental health and well-being in the older client

Monitoring for changes and adjustment in role function in the older client (threat to independent functioning)
Monitoring for sensory and perceptual alterations
Providing resources for the client and family

Physiological Integrity

Administering medication safely
Identifying health care preferences
Identifying practices or restrictions related to procedures and treatments
Monitoring for alterations in body systems and the related risks from the aging process
Providing basic care and comfort needs
Providing care using a nonjudgmental approach
Providing interventions compatible with the client's age, cultural, religious, and health care beliefs, education level, and language.

REFERENCES

Black, J., & Hawks, J. (2005). *Medical-surgical nursing: Clinical management for positive outcomes* (7th ed.). Philadelphia: W.B. Saunders.

Burke, M., & Laramie, J. (2004). *Primary care of the older adults: A multidisciplinary approach* (2nd ed.). St. Louis: Mosby.

Ebersole, P., Hess, P., & Luggan, A. (2004). *Toward healthy aging: Human needs and nursing response* (6th ed.) St. Louis: Mosby.

Hockenberry, M., Wilson, D., & Winkelstein, M. (2005). *Wong's essentials of pediatric nursing* (7th ed.). St. Louis: Mosby.

Ignatavicius, D., & Workman, M. (2006). *Medical-surgical nursing: Critical thinking for collaborative care* (5th ed.). Philadelphia: W.B. Saunders.

Murray, S., & McKinney, E. (2006). *Foundations of maternal-newborn nursing* (4th ed.). Philadelphia: W.B. Saunders.

Meiner, S. & Leuckenotte, A. (2006). *Gerontologic nursing* (3rd ed.). St. Louis: Mosby.

National Council of State Boards of Nursing (Eds.). (2007). *2007 NCLEX-RN® detailed test plan*. Chicago: Author.

Potter, P., & Perry, A. (2005) *Fundamentals of nursing* (6th ed.). St. Louis: Mosby.

Stuart, G., & Laraia, M. (2005). *Principles and practice of psychiatric nursing* (8th ed.). St. Louis: Mosby.

Varcarolis, E., Carson, V., & Shoemaker, N. (2006). *Foundations of psychiatric mental health nursing: A clinical approach* (5th ed.). Philadelphia: W.B. Saunders.

Wong, D., Hockenberry, M., Perry, S., et al. (2006). *Maternal-child nursing care* (3rd ed.). St. Louis: Mosby.

Theories of Growth and Development

32

I. PSYCHOSOCIAL DEVELOPMENT AND ERIK ERIKSON

A. The theory
1. Erikson's theory of psychosocial development describes the human life cycle as a series of eight **ego** developmental stages from birth to death.
2. Each stage presents a psychosocial crisis, the goal of which is to integrate physical, maturation, and societal demands.
3. The result of one stage may not be permanent, but can be changed by experience(s) later in life.
4. The theory focuses on psychosocial tasks that are accomplished throughout the life cycle.

B. Psychosocial development
1. Occurs through a lifelong series of conflicts affected by social and cultural factors
2. Each conflict must be resolved for the child or adult to progress emotionally.
3. Unsuccessful resolution leaves the individual emotionally handicapped.

C. Stages of psychosocial development (Table 32-1)

II. COGNITIVE DEVELOPMENT AND JEAN PIAGET

A. The theory
1. Piaget's theory of cognitive development defines cognitive acts as ways in which the mind organizes and adapts to its environment (i.e., "mental mapping").
2. **Schema** refers to an individual's cognitive structure or framework of thought.
3. **Schemata**
   a. **Schemata** are categories that an individual forms in his or her mind to organize and understand the world.
   b. A young child has only a few **schemata** with which to understand the world, and gradually these are increased.
   c. Adults use a wide variety of **schemata** to understand the world.
4. **Assimilation**
   a. **Assimilation** is the ability to incorporate new ideas, objects, and experiences into the framework of one's thoughts.
   b. The growing child will perceive and give meaning to new information according to what is already known and understood.
5. **Accommodation**
   a. **Accommodation** is the ability to change a **schema** to introduce new ideas, objects, or experiences.
   b. **Accommodation** changes the mental structure so that new experiences can be added.

B. Stages of cognitive development
1. Sensorimotor stage
   a. Birth to 2 years
   b. Development proceeds from reflex activity to imagining and solving problems through the senses and movement.
   c. The infant or toddler learns about reality and how it works.
   d. The infant or toddler does not recognize that objects continue to be in existence, even if out of their visual field.
2. Preoperational stage
   a. 2 to 7 years
   b. The child learns to think in terms of past, present, and future.
   c. The child moves from knowing the world through sensation and movement to prelogical thinking and finding solutions to problems.
   d. The child is egocentric.

403

TABLE 32-1

Erik Erikson's Stages of Psychosocial Development

Age	Psychosocial Crisis	Task	Resolution of Crisis	
			Successful	**Unsuccessful**
Infancy (birth to 18 months)	Trust versus mistrust	Attachment to the mother	Trust in persons; faith and hope about the environment and future	General difficulties relating to persons effectively; suspicion; trust-fear conflict, fear of the future
Early childhood (18 months to 3 years)	Autonomy versus shame and doubt	Gaining some basic control over self and environment	Sense of self-control and adequacy; will power	Independence-fear conflict; severe feelings of self-doubt
Late childhood (3-6 years)	Initiative versus guilt	Becoming purposeful and directive	Ability to initiate one's own activities; sense of purpose	Aggression-fear conflict; sense of inadequacy or guilt
School age (6-12 years)	Industry versus inferiority	Developing social, physical, and learning skills	Competence; ability to learn and work	Sense of inferiority; difficulty learning and working
Adolescence (12-20 years)	Identity versus role confusion	Developing sense of identity	Sense of personal identity	Confusion about who one is; identity submerged in relationships or group memberships
Early adulthood (20-35 years)	Intimacy versus isolation	Establishing intimate bonds of love and friendship	Ability to love deeply and commit oneself	Emotional isolation, ego-centricity
Middle adulthood (35-65 years)	Generativity versus stagnation	Fulfilling life goals that involve family, career, and society	Ability to give and care for others	Self-absorption; inability to grow as a person
Later adulthood (65 years to death)	Integrity versus despair	Looking back over one's life and accepting its meaning	Sense of integrity and fulfillment	Dissatisfaction with life

Modified from Varcarolis, E. (2006). *Foundations of psychiatric mental health nursing* (5th ed.). Philadelphia: W.B. Saunders.

e. The child is unable to conceptualize and requires concrete examples.
3. Concrete operational
   a. 7 to 11 years
   b. The child is able to classify, order, and sort facts.
   c. The child moves from prelogical thought to solving concrete problems through logic.
   d. The child begins to develop abstract thinking.
4. Formal operations
   a. 11 years to adulthood
   b. The person is able to think abstractly and logically.
   c. Logical thinking is expanded to include solving abstract and concrete problems.

III. MORAL DEVELOPMENT AND LAWRENCE KOHLBERG
A. Moral development
   1. Moral development is a complicated process involving the acceptance of the values and rules of society in a way that shapes behavior.

2. Moral development is classified in a series of levels and behaviors.
3. Moral development is sequential but people do not automatically go from one stage or level to the next as they mature.
4. Stages or levels of moral development cannot be skipped.
B. Levels of moral development (Box 32-1)

IV. PSYCHOSEXUAL DEVELOPMENT AND SIGMUND FREUD
A. Components of the theory (Box 32-2)
B. Levels of awareness
   1. **Conscious** level of awareness
      a. The **conscious** mind is logical and is regulated by the Reality Principle.
      b. Consciousness includes all experiences that are within an individual's awareness and that the individual is able to control.
      c. Consciousness includes all information that is remembered easily and is immediately available to an individual.

BOX 32-1
Moral Development and Lawrence Kohlberg

LEVEL ONE: PRECONVENTIONAL MORALITY

Stage 0 (Birth to 2 years): Egocentric Judgment

The infant has no awareness of right or wrong.

Stage 1 (2-3 years): Punishment-Obedience Orientation

At this stage, children cannot reason as mature members of society.

Children view the world in a selfish way, with no real understanding of right or wrong.

The child obeys rules and demonstrates acceptable behavior to avoid punishment and to avoid displeasing those who are in power, and because the child fears punishment from a superior force, such as a parent.

A toddler typically is at the first substage of the preconventional stage, involving punishment and obedience orientation, in which the toddler makes judgments based on avoiding punishment or obtaining a reward.

Physical punishment and withholding privileges tend to give the toddler a negative view of morals.

Withdrawing love and affection as punishment leads to feelings of guilt in the toddler.

Appropriate discipline includes providing simple explanations why certain behaviors are unacceptable, praising appropriate behavior, and using distractions when the toddler is headed for an unsafe action.

Stage 2 (4-7 years): Instrumental Relativist Orientation

The child conforms to rules to obtain rewards or have favors returned.

The child's moral standards are those of others, and the child observes them either to avoid punishment or obtain rewards.

A preschooler is in the preconventional stage of moral development.

In this stage, conscience emerges and the emphasis is on external control.

LEVEL TWO: CONVENTIONAL MORALITY

The child conforms to rules to please others.

The child has increased awareness of others' feelings.

A concern for social order begins to emerge.

A child views good behavior as that which those in authority will approve.

If the behavior is not acceptable, the child feels guilty.

Stage 3 (7-10 years): Good Boy–Nice Girl Orientation

Conformity occurs to avoid disapproval or dislike by others.

This stage involves living up to what is expected by individuals close to the child or what individuals generally expect of others in their roles such as daughter, son, brother, sister, and friend.

Being good is important and is interpreted as having good motives and showing concern about others.

Being good also means maintaining mutual relationships, such as trust, loyalty, respect, and gratitude.

Stage 4 (10-12 years): Law and Order Orientation

The child has more concern with society as a whole.

Emphasis is on obeying laws to maintain social order.

Moral reasoning develops as the child shifts the focus of living to society.

The school-age child is at the conventional level of the conformity stage and has an increased desire to please others.

The child observes and to some extent internalizes the standards of others.

The child wants to be considered "good" by those individuals whose opinions matter to her or him.

LEVEL THREE: POSTCONVENTIONAL MORALITY

The individual focuses on individual rights and principles of conscience.

The focus is on concerns regarding what is best for all.

Stage 5: Social Contract and Legalistic Orientation

The person is aware that others hold a variety of values and opinions and that most values and rules are relative to the group.

The adolescent in this stage gives and takes and does not expect to get something without paying for it.

Stage 6: Universal Ethical Principles Orientation

Conformity is based on universal principles of justice and occurs to avoid self-condemnation.

This stage involves following self-chosen ethical principles.

The development of the postconventional level of morality occurs in the adolescent at about age 13 years, marked by the development of an individual conscience and a defined set of moral values.

The adolescent can now acknowledge a conflict between two socially accepted standards and try to decide between them.

Control of conduct is now internal in standards observed and in reasoning about right and wrong.

BOX 32-2
Psychosexual Development and Sigmund Freud: Components of the Theory

Levels of awareness

Agencies of the mind (id, ego, superego)

Concept of anxiety and defense mechanisms

Psychosexual stages of development

2. Preconscious level of awareness
   a. The preconscious is called the **subconscious.**
   b. The preconscious includes experiences, thoughts, feelings, or desires that might not be in immediate awareness but can be recalled to consciousness.
   c. The **subconscious** can help repress unpleasant thoughts or feelings and can examine and censor certain wishes and thinking.

3. **Unconscious** level of awareness
   a. The **unconscious** is not logical and is governed by the Pleasure Principle, which refers to seeking immediate tension reduction.
   b. Memories, feelings, thoughts, or wishes are repressed and are not available to the **conscious** mind.
   c. These repressed memories, thoughts, or feelings, if made prematurely **conscious**, can cause anxiety.

C. Agencies of the mind
   1. **Id, ego,** and **superego**
      a. The **id, ego,** and **superego** are the three systems of personality.
      b. These psychological processes follow different operating principles.
      c. In a mature and well-adjusted personality, they work together as a team under the leadership of the **ego**.
   2. The **id**
      a. Source of all drives
      b. Present at birth
      c. Includes genetic inheritance, reflexes, capacities to respond, instincts, basic drives, needs, and wishes that motivate an individual
      d. Operates according to the Pleasure Principle
      e. Does not tolerate uncomfortable states and seeks to discharge the tension and return to a more comfortable, constant level of energy
      f. Acts immediately in an impulsive, irrational way and pays no attention to the consequences of its actions; therefore, often behaves in ways harmful to self and others
      g. The primary process is a psychological activity in which the **id** attempts to reduce tension.
      h. The primary process can include hallucinating or forming an image of the object that will satisfy its needs and remove the tension.
      i. The primary process by itself is not capable of reducing tension; therefore, a secondary psychological process must develop if the individual is to survive. When this occurs, the structure of the second system of the personality, the **ego**, begins to take form.
   3. The **ego**
      a. Functions include reality testing and problem solving
      b. Begins its development during the fourth or fifth month of life
      c. Emerges out of the **id** and acts as an intermediary between the **id** and the external world
      d. Emerges because the needs, wishes, and demands of the **id** require appropriate exchanges with the outside world of reality
      e. The **ego** distinguishes between things in the mind and things in the external world.

   f. Reality testing is a function of the **ego**, and the **ego** uses realistic thinking.
   g. The **ego** follows the Reality Principle and operates by means of the secondary process—that is, realistic thinking.
   h. The aim of the Reality Principle is to satisfy the **id's** impulses in the external world with an object that is suitable; the Reality Principle determines whether an experience is true or false and whether it has external existence.
   i. The **ego** devises a plan and tests the plan by some type of action to see whether it will work.

   4. The **superego**
      a. Necessary part of socialization that develops during the phallic stage at 3 to 6 years of age
      b. Develops from interactions with the child's parents during the extended period of childhood dependency
      c. Includes internalization of the values, ideals, and moral standards of society
      d. Child internalizes moral standards of parents and society
      e. **Superego** consists of the conscience and the **ego** ideal
      f. Conscience refers to capacity for self-evaluation and criticism
      g. When moral codes are violated, the conscience punishes the individual by instilling guilt.
      h. What parents approve of and what they reward the child for doing become incorporated as the **ego** ideal by the mechanism of introjection.
      i. The **superego** strives for perfection rather than pleasure and represents the ideal rather than the real.
      j. Living up to one's **ego** ideal results in the individual feeling proud and increases self-esteem.

D. Anxiety and defense mechanisms
   1. The **ego** develops defenses or defense mechanisms to fight off anxiety.
   2. Defense mechanisms operate on an **unconscious** level, except for suppression, so the individual is not aware of their operation.
   3. Defense mechanisms deny, falsify, or distort reality to make it less threatening.
   4. An individual cannot survive without defense mechanisms; however, if they become too extreme in distorting reality, then interference in healthy adjustment and personal growth may occur.

E. Psychosexual stages of development (Box 32-3)
   1. Human development proceeds through a series of stages from infancy to adulthood.

BOX 32-3

Freud's Psychosexual Stages of Development

ORAL STAGE (BIRTH TO 1 YEAR)

During this stage, the infant is concerned with self-gratification.

The infant is all id, operating on the Pleasure Principle and striving for immediate gratification of needs.

When the infant experiences gratification of basic needs, a sense of trust and security begins.

The ego begins to emerge as the infant begins to see self as separate from the mother; this marks the beginning of the development of a sense of self.

ANAL STAGE (1-3 YEARS)

Toilet training occurs during this period, and the child gains pleasure from the elimination of the feces and from their retention.

The conflict of this stage is between those demands from society and the parents and the sensations of pleasure associated with the anus.

The child begins to gain a sense of control over instinctive drives and learns to delay immediate gratification to gain a future goal.

PHALLIC STAGE (3-6 YEARS)

The child experiences pleasurable and conflicting feelings associated with the genital organs.

The pleasures of masturbation and the fantasy life of children set the stage for the Oedipus complex.

The child's unconscious sexual attraction to and wish to possess the parent of the opposite gender, the hostility and desire to remove the parent of the same gender, and the subsequent guilt about these wishes is the conflict the child faces.

The conflict is resolved when the child identifies with the parent of the same gender.

The emergence of the superego is the solution to and the result of these intense impulses.

LATENCY STAGE (6-12 YEARS)

The latency stage is a tapering off of conscious biological and sexual urges.

The sexual impulses are channeled and elevated into a more culturally accepted level of activity.

Growth of ego functions and the ability to care about and relate to others outside the home is the task of this stage of development.

GENITAL STAGE (12 YEARS AND BEYOND)

The genital stage emerges at adolescence with the onset of puberty, when the genital organs mature.

The individual gains gratification from his or her own body.

During this stage, the individual develops satisfying sexual and emotional relationships with members of the opposite gender.

The individual plans life goals and gains a strong sense of personal identity.

---

2. Each stage is characterized by the inborn tendency of all individuals to reduce tension and seek pleasure.

3. Each stage is associated with a particular conflict that must be resolved before the child can move successfully to the next stage.

4. Experiences during the early stages determine an individual's adjustment patterns and the personality traits that the individual has as an adult.

PRACTICE QUESTIONS

1. The mother of an 8-year-old child tells the clinic nurse that she is concerned about the child because the child seems to be more attentive to friends than anything else. Using Erikson's psychosocial development theory, the appropriate nursing response is which of the following?
   1. "You need to be concerned."
   2. "You need to monitor the child's behavior closely."
   3. "At this age, the child is developing his own personality."
   4. "You need to provide more praise to the child to stop this behavior."

2. The mother of a 4-year-old child calls the clinic nurse and expresses concern because the child has been masturbating. Using Erikson's psychosocial development theory, the appropriate response by the nurse is which of the following?
   1. "This is a normal behavior at this age."
   2. "Children usually begin this behavior at age 8 years."
   3. "This is not normal behavior, and the child should be seen by the physician."
   4. "The child is very young to begin this behavior and should be brought to the clinic."

3. A nursing instructor asks a nursing student to present a clinical conference to peers regarding Freud's psychosexual stages of development, specifically the anal stage. The student plans the conference, knowing that which of the following most appropriately relates to this stage of development?
   1. This stage is associated with toilet training.
   2. This stage is characterized by the gratification of self.
   3. This stage is characterized by a tapering off of conscious biological and sexual urges.
   4. This stage is associated with pleasurable and conflicting feelings about the genital organs.

4. Which statement would indicate the "law and order orientation" found in level two of Kohlberg's theory of moral development?
   1. "If I skip down the hall, will the teacher be mad at me?"
   2. "We will spend time talking about the activities for the week."
   3. "I don't like it when you yell while I am talking to my friend. Here are some activities to do until I am finished talking."
   4. "If you do all of your class work today without bothering others in the class, you will get an extra 'seed' for your good behavior garden."

5. A nursing instructor asks a nursing student to describe the formal operations stage of Piaget's cognitive developmental theory. The appropriate response by the nursing student is:
   1. "The child has the ability to think abstractly."
   2. "The child develops logical thought patterns."
   3. "The child begins to understand the environment."
   4. "The child has difficulty separating fantasy from reality."

6. A clinic nurse is preparing to discuss the concepts of moral development with a mother. The nurse understands that according to Kohlberg's theory of moral development, in the preconventional level, moral development is thought to be motivated by which of the following?
   1. Peer pressure
   2. Social pressures
   3. Parents' behavior
   4. Punishment and reward

7. A maternity nurse is providing instructions to a new mother regarding the psychosocial development of the newborn infant. Using Erikson's psychosocial development theory, the nurse instructs the mother to:
   1. Allow the newborn infant to signal a need.
   2. Anticipate all the needs of the newborn infant.
   3. Attend to the newborn infant immediately when crying.
   4. Avoid the newborn infant during the first 10 minutes of crying.

8. A mother of a 3-year-old tells a clinic nurse that the child is rebelling constantly and having temper tantrums. Using Erikson's psychosocial development theory, the nurse tells the mother to:
   1. Set limits on the child's behavior.
   2. Ignore the child when this behavior occurs.
   3. Allow the behavior, because this is normal at this age period.
   4. Punish the child every time the child says "no" to change the behavior.

ALTERNATE ITEM FORMAT: MULTIPLE RESPONSE

A nurse educator is preparing to conduct a session to the nursing staff regarding the theories of growth and development and plans to discuss Kohlberg's theory of moral development. Which of the following should the nurse include in the session? Select all that apply.

❏ 1. Individuals move through all six stages in a sequential fashion.
❏ 2. Moral development progresses in relationship to cognitive development.
❏ 3. A person's ability to make moral judgments develops over a period of time.
❏ 4. The theory provides a framework for understanding how individuals determine a moral code to guide their behavior.
❏ 5. In stage 1 (punishment-obedience orientation), children are expected to reason as mature members of society.
❏ 6. In stage 3 (instrumental relativist orientation), the child conforms to rules to obtain rewards or have favors returned.

ANSWERS

1. **3**
Rationale: According to Erikson, during school-age years (6 to 12 years of age), the child begins to move toward peers and friends and away from the parents for support. The child also begins to develop special interests that reflect his or her own developing personality instead of the parents. Therefore, options 1, 2, and 4 are incorrect.
Test-Taking Strategy: Use the process of elimination and knowledge of Erikson's psychosocial development theory related to middle childhood. Options 1 and 2 can be eliminated easily first. Eliminate option 4 next because, although praising the child for accomplishments is important at this age, the behavior that the child is exhibiting is normal. Review psycho-

social development related to this age group according to Erikson if you had difficulty with this question.
Level of Cognitive Ability: Application
Client Needs: Psychosocial Integrity
Integrated Process: Nursing Process—implementation
Content Area: Child health
Reference: McKinney, E., James, S., Murray, S., & Ashwill, J. (2005). *Maternal-child nursing* (2nd ed., p. 58). St. Louis: W.B. Saunders.

2. **1**
Rationale: According to Freud's psychosexual stages of development, between the ages of 3 and 6 the child is in the phallic stage. At this time, the child devotes much energy to examining

his or her genitalia, masturbating, and expressing interest in sexual concerns. Therefore, options 2, 3, and 4 are incorrect.
Test-Taking Strategy: Use the process of elimination. Eliminate options 3 and 4 first because they are comparative or alike. Focus on the subject of the question and note the words *age 8 years* in option 2 to assist in eliminating this option. If you had difficulty with this question, review Freud's psychosocial stages of development.
Level of Cognitive Ability: Application
Client Needs: Psychosocial Integrity
Integrated Process: Nursing Process—implementation
Content Area: Child health
Reference: McKinney, E., James, S., Murray, S., & Ashwill, J. (2005). *Maternal-child nursing* (2nd ed., p. 59). St. Louis: W.B. Saunders.

3. **1**
Rationale: Generally, toilet training occurs during this period. According to Freud, the child gains pleasure from the elimination of feces and from their retention. Option 2 relates to the oral stage. Option 3 relates to the latency period. Option 4 relates to the phallic stage.
Test-Taking Strategy: Use the process of elimination. Note the relationship between the words *anal* in the question and *toilet training* in the correct option. If you had difficulty with this question, review Freud's psychosocial stages of development.
Level of Cognitive Ability: Comprehension
Client Needs: Psychosocial Integrity
Integrated Process: Nursing Process—planning
Content Area: Child health
Reference: McKinney, E., James, S., Murray, S., & Ashwill, J. (2005). *Maternal-child nursing* (2nd ed., p. 58). St. Louis: W.B. Saunders.

4. **1**
Rationale: In the law and order orientation of Kohlberg's theory, the child has more concern with society as a whole and emphasis is on obeying laws to maintain social order. The child wants to be considered "good" by persons whose opinions matter to them. Option 1 is the only option that reflects this criteria. Options 2, 3, and 4 are unrelated to the law and order orientation.
Test-Taking Strategy: Focus on the subject of the question, law and order orientation. Look for the option that indicates the child wants to be considered "good" by a person in authority. This will direct you to option 1. Review Kohlberg's theory of moral development if you had difficulty with this question.
Level of Cognitive Ability: Analysis
Client Needs: Health Promotion and Maintenance
Integrative Process: Nursing process—evaluation
Content Area: Fundamental skills
Reference: Hockenberry, M., Wilson, D., & Winkelstein, M. (2005). *Wong's essentials of pediatric nursing* (7th ed., pp. 89-90). St. Louis: Mosby.

5. **1**
Rationale: In the formal operations stage, the child has the ability to think abstractly and logically. Option 2 identifies the concrete operations stage. Option 3 identifies the sensorimotor stage. Option 4 identifies the preoperational stage.

Test-Taking Strategy: Use the process of elimination and knowledge regarding the characteristics of Piaget's cognitive developmental theory to answer this question. Remember that in the formal operations stage, the child has the ability to think abstractly and logically. If you had difficulty with this question, review these concepts.
Level of Cognitive Ability: Comprehension
Client Needs: Psychosocial Integrity
Integrated Process: Teaching and Learning
Content Area: Child health
References: Hockenberry, M., Wilson, D., & Winkelstein, M. (2005). *Wong's essentials of pediatric nursing* (7th ed., pp. 88-89). St. Louis: Mosby.
McKinney, E., James, S., Murray, S., & Ashwill, J. (2005). *Maternal-child nursing* (2nd ed., p. 944). St. Louis: W.B. Saunders.

6. **4**
Rationale: In the preconventional stage, morals are thought to be motivated by punishment and reward. If the child is obedient and is not punished, then the child is being moral. The child sees actions as good or bad. If the child's actions are good, the child is praised. If the child's actions are bad, the child is punished. Options 1, 2, and 3 are incorrect.
Test-Taking Strategy: Use the process of elimination. Eliminate options 1 and 2 because they are comparative or alike. Knowledge that the preconventional stage occurs between birth and 7 years will assist in directing you to option 4 from the remaining options. If you had difficulty with this question, review Kohlberg's theory of moral development.
Level of Cognitive Ability: Comprehension
Client Needs: Psychosocial Integrity
Integrated Process: Nursing Process—planning
Content Area: Child health
Reference: Hockenberry, M., Wilson, D., & Winkelstein, M. (2005). *Wong's essentials of pediatric nursing* (7th ed., pp. 89-90). St. Louis: Mosby.

7. **1**
Rationale: According to Erikson, the caregiver should not try to anticipate the newborn infant's needs at all times but must allow the newborn infant to signal needs. If a newborn infant is not allowed to signal a need, the newborn will not learn how to control the environment. Erikson believed that a delayed or prolonged response to a newborn infant's signal would inhibit the development of trust and lead to mistrust of others.
Test-Taking Strategy: Use the process of elimination. Eliminate options 2, 3, and 4 because of the close-ended words *all, immediately,* and *avoid* in these options. Review Erikson's stages of psychosocial development if you had difficulty with this question.
Level of Cognitive Ability: Application
Client Needs: Psychosocial Integrity
Integrated Process: Teaching and Learning
Content Area: Child health
Reference: Wong, D., Perry, S., Hockenberry, M., et al. (2006). *Maternal child nursing care* (3rd ed., pp. 943-944). St. Louis: Mosby.

8. **1**
Rationale: According to Erikson, the child focuses on independence between ages 1 and 3 years. Gaining independence often

means that the child has to rebel against the parents' wishes. Saying things like *no* or *mine* and having temper tantrums are common during this period of development. Being consistent and setting limits on the child's behavior are necessary elements.

Test-Taking Strategy: Use the process of elimination. Options 2 and 3 can be eliminated first because they are comparative or alike. Next, eliminate option 4 because this action is likely to produce a negative response during this normal developmental pattern. Review psychosocial development of the toddler according the Erikson if you had difficulty with this question.

Level of Cognitive Ability: Application
Client Needs: Psychosocial Integrity
Integrated Process: Teaching and Learning
Content Area: Child health
Reference: Wong, D., Perry, S., Hockenberry, M., et al. (2006). *Maternal child nursing care* (3rd ed., pp. 1091, 1097). St. Louis: Mosby.

ALTERNATE ITEM FORMAT: MULTIPLE RESPONSE

Answer: 2, 3, 4, 6
Rationale: Kohlberg's theory states that individuals move through the six stages of development in a sequential fashion but that not everyone reaches stages 5 and 6 in his or her development of personal morality. The theory provides a framework for understanding how individuals determine a moral code to guide their behavior. It states that moral development progresses in relationship to cognitive development and that a person's ability to make moral judgments develops over a period of time. In stage 1, ages 2 to 3 years (punishment-obedience orientation), children cannot reason as mature members of society. In stage 3, ages 4 to 7 years, (instrumental relativist orientation), the child conforms to rules to obtain rewards or have favors returned.

Test-Taking Strategy: Read each option carefully. Recalling that the theory provides a framework for understanding how individuals determine a moral code to guide their behavior and recalling the ages associated with each stage will assist in answering the question. If you had difficulty with this question, review Kohlberg's theory.

Level of Cognitive Ability: Comprehension
Client Needs: Psychosocial Integrity
Integrated Process: Nursing Process—planning
Content Area: Fundamental skills
Reference: Hockenberry, M., Wilson, D., & Winkelstein, M. (2005). *Wong's essentials of pediatric nursing* (7th ed., pp. 89-90). St. Louis: Mosby.

REFERENCES

Hockenberry, M., Wilson, D., & Winkelstein, M. (2005). *Wong's essentials of pediatric nursing* (7th ed.). St. Louis: Mosby.

Lowdermilk, D., & Perry, S. (2006). *Maternity nursing* (7th ed.). St. Louis: Mosby.

McKinney, E., James, S., Murray, S., & Ashwill, J. (2005). *Maternal-child nursing* (2nd ed.). St. Louis: W.B. Saunders.

Murray, S., & McKinney, E. (2006). *Foundations of maternal-newborn nursing* (4th ed.). Philadelphia: W.B. Saunders.

National Council of State Boards of Nursing (Eds.). (2007). *2007 NCLEX-RN® detailed test plan.* Chicago: Author.

Wong, D., Perry, S., Hockenberry, M., et al. (2006). *Maternal child nursing care* (3rd ed.). St. Louis: Mosby.

Developmental Stages

I. THE HOSPITALIZED INFANT AND TODDLER

A. Separation anxiety
1. Protest
   a. Crying, screaming, searching for a parent; avoidance and rejection of contact with strangers
   b. Verbal attacks on others
   c. Physical fighting; kicking, fighting, biting, hitting, pinching
2. Despair
   a. Withdrawn, depressed, uninterested in the environment
   b. Loss of newly learned skills
3. Detachment
   a. Detachment is uncommon and occurs only after lengthy separations from the parent.
   b. Superficially, the toddler appears to have adjusted to the loss.
   c. During this phase, the toddler again becomes more interested in the environment, plays with others, and seems to form new relationships; this behavior is a form of resignation and is not a sign of contentment.
   d. The toddler detaches from the parents in an effort to escape the emotional pain of desiring the parent's presence.
   e. The toddler copes by forming shallow relationships with others, becoming increasingly self-centered, and attaching primary importance to material objects.
   f. This is the most serious phase because reversal of the potential adverse effects is less likely to occur once detachment is established. In most situations, the temporary separation imposed by hospitalization does not cause such prolonged parental absence that the toddler enters into detachment.
B. Fear of injury and pain: Affected by previous experiences, separation from parents, and preparation for the experience
C. Loss of control
1. Hospitalization, with its own set of rituals and routines, can severely disrupt the life of a toddler.
2. The lack of control often is exhibited in behaviors related to feeding, toileting, playing, and bedtime.
3. The toddler may demonstrate regression.
D. Interventions
1. Provide swaddling and talk softly to the infant.
2. Provide opportunities for sucking and oral stimulation for the infant using a pacifier if the infant is not to receive anything by mouth.
3. Provide stimulation, if appropriate, for the infant, using objects of contrasting colors and textures.
4. Provide routines and rituals as close as possible to what the toddler is used to at home.
5. Provide choices as much as possible to the toddler to enable him or her to have some control.
6. Approach the toddler with a positive attitude.
7. Allow the toddler to express feelings of protest.
8. Encourage the toddler to talk about parents or others in their lives.
9. Accept regressive behavior without ridiculing the toddler.
10. Provide the toddler with favorite and comforting objects.
11. Allow the toddler as much mobility as possible.
12. Anticipate temper tantrums from the toddler, and maintain a safe environment for physical acting out.

▲ 13. Employ pain reduction techniques, as appropriate.

▲ II. THE HOSPITALIZED PRESCHOOLER
  A. Separation anxiety
    1. Separation anxiety is generally less obvious and less serious than in the toddler.
    2. As stress increases, the preschooler's ability to separate from the parents decreases.
    3. Protest
      a. Protest is less direct and aggressive than in the toddler.
      b. The preschooler may displace feelings onto others.
    4. Despair
      a. The preschooler reacts in a manner similar to that of the toddler.
      b. The preschooler is quietly withdrawn, depressed, and uninterested in the environment.
      c. The child exhibits loss of newly learned skills.
      d. The preschooler becomes generally uncooperative, refusing to eat or take medication.
      e. The preschooler repeatedly asks when the parents will be visiting.
    5. Detachment: Similar to the toddler
▲ B. Fear of injury and pain
    1. The preschooler has a general lack of understanding of body integrity.
    2. The child fears invasive procedures and mutilation.
    3. The child imagines things to be much worse than they are.
    4. Preschoolers believe that they are ill because of something they did or thought.
  C. Loss of control
    1. The preschooler likes familiar routines and rituals and may show regression if not allowed to maintain some control.
    2. The child has attained a good deal of independence and self-care at home and may expect that to continue in the hospital.
▲ D. Interventions
    1. Provide a safe and secure environment.
    2. Take time for communication.
    3. Allow the preschooler to express anger.
    4. Acknowledge fears and anxieties.
    5. Accept regressive behavior; assist the preschooler in moving from regressive to appropriate behaviors according to age.
    6. Encourage rooming-in or leaving a favorite toy.
    7. Allow mobility and provide play and diversional activities.
    8. Place the preschooler with other children of the same age if possible.
    9. Encourage the preschooler to be independent.

    10. Explain procedures simply, on the preschooler's level.
    11. Avoid intrusive procedures when possible. ▲
    12. Allow wearing of underpants. ▲

III. THE HOSPITALIZED SCHOOL-AGE CHILD ▲
  A. Separation anxiety
    1. The school-age child is accustomed to periods of separation from the parents, but as stressors are added, the separation becomes more difficult.
    2. The child is more concerned with missing school and the fear that friends will forget her or him.
    3. Usually, the stages of behavior of protest, despair, and detachment do not occur with school-age children.
  B. Fear of injury and pain ▲
    1. The school-age child fears bodily injury and pain.
    2. The child fears illness itself, disability, death, and intrusive procedures in genital areas.
    3. The child is uncomfortable with any type of sexual examination.
    4. The child groans or whines, holds rigidly still, and communicates about pain.
  C. Loss of control
    1. The child is usually highly social, independent, and involved with activities.
    2. The child seeks information and asks relevant questions about tests and procedures and the illness.
    3. The child associates his or her actions with the cause of the illness.
    4. The child may feel helpless and dependent if physical limitations occur.
  D. Interventions ▲
    1. Encourage rooming-in.
    2. Focus on the school-age child's abilities and needs.
    3. Encourage the school-age child to become involved with his or her own care.
    4. Accept regression but encourage independence.
    5. Provide choices to the school-age child.
    6. Allow expression of feelings verbally and nonverbally.
    7. Acknowledge fears and concerns and allow for discussion.
    8. Explain all procedures, using body diagrams or outlines.
    9. Provide privacy.
    10. Avoid intrusive procedures if possible. ▲
    11. Allow the school-age child to wear underpants. ▲
    12. Involve the school-age child in activities appropriate to developmental level and illness.
    13. Encourage the school-age child to contact friends.
    14. Provide for educational needs.
    15. Use appropriate interventions to relieve pain.

IV. THE HOSPITALIZED ADOLESCENT
A. Separation anxiety
1. Adolescents are not sure whether they want their parents with them when they are hospitalized.
2. Separation from friends is a source of anxiety.
3. Adolescents become upset if friends go on with their lives, excluding them.

B. Fear of injury and pain
1. Adolescents fear being different from others and their peers.
2. Adolescents may give the impression that they are not afraid, even though they are terrified.
3. Adolescents become guarded when any areas related to sexual development are examined.

C. Loss of control
1. Behaviors exhibited include anger, withdrawal, and uncooperativeness.
2. Adolescents seek help and then reject it.

D. Interventions
1. Encourage questions about appearance and effects of the illness on the future.
2. Explore feelings about the hospital and the significance that the illness might have for relationships.
3. Encourage adolescents to wear their own clothes and carry out normal grooming activities.
4. Allow favorite foods to be brought in to the hospital if possible.
5. Provide privacy.
6. Use body diagrams to prepare for procedures.
7. Introduce them to other adolescents in the nursing unit.
8. Encourage maintaining contact with peer groups.
9. Provide for educational needs.
10. Identify formation of future plans.
11. Help develop positive coping mechanisms.

V. COMMUNICATION APPROACHES
A. General guidelines
1. Allow the child to feel comfortable with the nurse.
2. Communicate through the use of objects.
3. Allow the child to express fears and concerns.
4. Speak clearly and in a quiet, unhurried voice.
5. Offer choices when possible.
6. Be honest with the child.
7. Set limits with the child as appropriate.

B. Infant
1. Infants respond to nonverbal communication behaviors of adults, such as holding, rocking, patting, and touching.
2. Use a slow approach and allow the infant to get to know the nurse.
3. Use a calm, soft, soothing voice.
4. Be responsive to cries.
5. Talk and read to infants.
6. Allow security objects such as blankets and pacifiers if the infant has them.

C. Toddler
1. Approach the toddler cautiously.
2. Remember that toddlers accept verbal communications of others literally.
3. Learn the toddler's words for common items and use them in conversations.
4. Use short, concrete terms.
5. Prepare the toddler for procedures immediately before the event.
6. Repeat explanations and descriptions.
7. Use play for demonstrations.
8. Use visual aids such as picture books, puppets, and dolls.
9. Allow the toddler to handle the equipment or instruments; explain what the equipment or instrument does and how it feels.
10. Encourage the use of comfort objects.

D. Preschooler
1. Seek opportunities to offer choices.
2. Speak in simple sentences.
3. Be concise and limit the length of explanations.
4. Allow asking questions.
5. Describe procedures as they are about to be performed.
6. Use play to explain procedures and activities.
7. Allow handling the equipment or instruments, which will ease fear and help answer questions.

E. School-age child
1. Establish limits.
2. Provide reassurance to help in alleviating fears and anxieties.
3. Engage in conversations that encourage thinking.
4. Use medical play techniques.
5. Use photographs, books, dolls, and videos to explain procedures.
6. Explain in clear terms.
7. Allow time for composure and privacy.

F. Adolescent
1. Remember that the adolescent may be preoccupied with body image.
2. Encourage and support independence.
3. Provide privacy.
4. Use photographs, books, and videos to explain procedures.
5. Engage in conversations about adolescent's interests.
6. Avoid becoming too abstract, too detailed, and too technical.
7. Avoid responding to less than desirable social behaviors by prying, confrontation, or judgmental attitudes.

VI. DEVELOPMENTAL CHARACTERISTICS
A. Infant
1. Physical
   a. Height increases by $^3/_4$ inch per month.
   b. Weight is doubled at 5 to 6 months and tripled at 12 months.
   c. At birth, head circumference is 2 to 3 cm more than chest circumference.
   d. By 1 to 2 years of age, head circumference and chest circumference are equal.
   e. Anterior fontanel (soft and flat in a normal infant) closes by 12 to 18 months of age.
   f. Posterior fontanel (soft and flat in a normal infant) closes by end of the second month.
   g. Infant has 10 upper and 10 lower deciduous teeth by 2$^1/_2$ years of age.
   h. Lower central incisors are present by 6 to 8 months.
   i. Sleep patterns vary among infants; generally, by 3 to 4 months of age, most infants have developed a nocturnal pattern of sleep that lasts 9 to 11 hours.
2. Vital signs (Box 33-1)
3. Nutrition
   a. The infant may breast-feed or bottle-feed, depending on the mother's choice; however, human milk is the preferred form of nutrition for all infants, especially during the first 6 months.
   b. Infants should remain on human milk or iron-fortified formula for the first year of life.
   c. Iron stores from birth are depleted by 4 months of age.
   d. Whole milk should not be introduced to infants until after 1 year of age.
   e. Skim and low-fat milk should not be given prior to age 2 years because the essential fatty acids are inadequate and the solute concentrations of protein and electrolytes are too high.
   f. Fluoride supplementation may be needed at about 6 months of age, depending on the infant's intake of fluoridated tap water.
   g. Solid foods are introduced at 5 to 6 months of age; introduce solid foods one at a time, usually at intervals of 4 to 5 days, to identify food allergens.
   h. Sequence of introduction of solid foods is as follows: rice cereal; fruits and vegetables, starting with yellow and then green; meats; and then egg yolks, avoiding egg whites (introduce egg white toward the end of the first year); cheese may be used as a substitute for meat and as a finger food.
   i. Avoid solid foods that place the infant at risk for choking, such as nuts, foods with seeds, raisins, popcorn, grapes, and hot dog pieces.

BOX 33-1

Vital Signs: Newborn and 1-Year-Old Infant

NEWBORN
Temperature: Axillary, 97.9° to 98° F
Apical rate: 120 to 140 beats/min
Respirations: 30 to 60 (average 40) breaths/min
Blood pressure: 73/55 mm Hg

1-YEAR-OLD INFANT
Temperature: Axillary, 97° to 99° F
Apical rate: 90 to 130 beats/min
Respirations: 20 to 40 breaths/min
Blood pressure: 90/56 mm Hg

   j. Avoid microwaving baby bottles and baby food.
   k. Never mix food or medications with formula.
   l. Avoid adding honey to formula, water, or other fluid to prevent botulism.
   m. Offer fruit juice from a cup (12 to 13 months or at a prescribed age) rather than a bottle to prevent nursing (bottle-mouth) caries; fruit juice is limited because of its high sugar content.
4. Skills (Box 33-2)
5. Play
   a. Solitary
   b. Birth to 3 months: Verbal, visual, and tactile stimuli
   c. 4 to 6 months: Initiation of actions and recognition of new experiences
   d. 6 to 12 months: Awareness of self, imitation, repetition of pleasurable actions
   e. Enjoyment of soft stuffed animals, crib mobiles with contrasting colors, squeeze toys, rattles, musical toys, water toys during the bath, large picture books, and push toys after he or she begins to walk
6. Safety
   a. Parents must baby-proof the home.
   b. Guard the infant when on a bed or changing table.
   c. Use gates to protect the infant from stairs.
   d. Never shake an infant.
   e. Be sure that bath water is not hot; do not leave the infant unattended in the bath.
   f. Do not hold the infant while drinking or working near hot liquids.
   g. Cool vaporizers should be used if needed, instead of steam, to prevent burn injuries.
   h. Avoid offering food that is round and similar to the size of the airway to prevent choking.
   i. Be sure toys have no small pieces.
   j. Toys or mobiles hanging over the crib should be well out of reach to prevent strangulation.

BOX 33-2
Infant Skills

2-3 MONTHS
Smiles
Turns head side to side
Cries
Follows objects
Holds head in midline

4-5 MONTHS
Grasps objects
Switches objects from hands
Rolls over for the first time
Enjoys social interaction
Begins to show memory
Aware of unfamiliar surroundings

6-7 MONTHS
Creeps
Sits with support
Imitates
Exhibits fear of strangers
Holds arms out
Frequent mood swings
Waves bye-bye

8-9 MONTHS
Sits steadily unsupported
Crawls
May stand while holding on
Begins to stand without help

10-11 MONTHS
Can change from prone to sitting position
Walks while holding on to furniture
Stands securely
Entertains self for periods of time

12-13 MONTHS
Walks with one hand held
Can take a few steps without falling
Can drink from a cup

14-15 MONTHS
Walks alone
Can crawl upstairs
Shows emotions such as anger and affection
Will explore away from mother in familiar surroundings

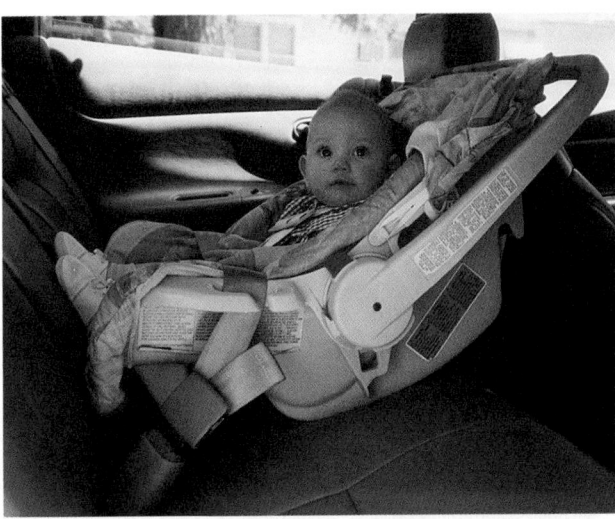

FIG. 33-1 The infant rides facing the rear of the vehicle, ideally in the middle of the back seat. The infant seat is secured to the vehicle with the seat belt(s), and straps on the car seat adjust to accommodate the growing baby. The smaller infant will need a rolled blanket to prevent excess head movement. (From McKinney, E., James, S., Murray, S., & Ashwill, J. [2005]. *Maternal-child nursing* [2nd ed.]. St. Louis: W.B. Saunders.)

    p. Keep the poison control number available.
    q. Infants should ride in a car in a semireclined, rear-facing position in an infant-only seat or a convertible seat until they weigh at least 20 lb and have reached at least 1 year of age (convertible seats can be used rear-facing for infants and then converted to a forward-facing position once the child is old enough and big enough to do so safely; Fig. 33-1).
    r. Infants are placed in the back seat of the car in their safety seat; the infant could be seriously injured if the air bag is released in the passenger side of the front seat because rear-facing safety seats extend close to the dashboard.

B. Toddler
  1. Physical
    a. Height and weight increase in a step-like fashion, reflecting growth spurts and lags.
    b. Head circumference increases about 1 inch between ages 1 and 2; thereafter, head circumference increases about $1/2$ inch per year until age 5.
    c. Anterior fontanel closes between ages 12 to 18 months.
    d. Weight gain is slower than in infancy; by age 2, the average weight is 22 to 27 lb.
    e. Normal height changes include a growth of about 3 inches per year; the average height of the toddler is 34 inches at age 2 years.
    f. Lordosis (pot belly) is evident.
    g. The toddler should see a dentist soon after the first teeth erupt, usually around 1 year of

    k. Avoid placing large toys in the crib because an older infant may use them as steps to climb.
    l. Cribs should be positioned away from curtains and blind cords.
    m. Cover electrical outlets.
    n. Remove hazardous objects from low, reachable places.
    o. Remove chemicals, medications, poisons, and plants from the infant's reach.

BOX 33-3
The Toddler's Vital Signs

Temperature: Axillary, 97.5° to 98.6° F
Apical rate: 80 to 120 beats/min
Respirations: 20 to 30 breaths/min
Blood pressure: Average, 92/55 mm Hg

BOX 33-4
Signs of Readiness for Toilet Training

Child is able to stay dry for 2 hours.
Child is waking up dry from a nap.
Child is able to sit, squat, and walk.
Child is able to remove clothing.
Child recognizes urge to defecate or urinate.
Child expresses willingness to please parent.
Child is able to sit on toilet for 5 to 10 minutes without fussing or getting off.

age; fluoride supplements may be necessary if the water is not fluoridated.

  h. A toddler should never be allowed to fall asleep with a bottle containing milk, juice, soda pop, or sweetened water because of the risk of nursing (bottle-mouth) caries.

  i. Typically, the toddler sleeps through the night and has one daytime nap; the daytime nap is normally discontinued at about age 3.

  j. A consistent bedtime ritual helps prepare the toddler for sleep.

  k. Security objects at bedtime may assist in sleep.

2. Vital signs (Box 33-3)
3. Nutrition
  a. Most toddlers prefer to feed themselves.
  b. The toddler generally does best by eating several small nutritious meals each day rather than three large meals.
  c. Offer a limited number of foods at any one time.
  d. Offer finger foods and avoid concentrated sweets and empty calories.
  e. The toddler is at risk for aspiration of small foods that are not chewed easily, such as nuts, foods with seeds, raisins, popcorn, grapes, and hot dog pieces.
  f. Physiological anorexia is normal because of the alternating stages of fast and slow growth.
  g. Sit the toddler in a high chair at the family table for meals.
  h. Allow sufficient time to eat, but remove food when the toddler begins to play with it.
  i. The toddler drinks well from a cup held with both hands.
  j. Avoid using food as a reward or punishment.

4. Skills
  a. The toddler begins to walk with one hand held by age 12 to 13 months.
  b. The toddler runs by age 2 years and walks backward and hops on one foot by age 3 years.
  c. The toddler usually cannot alternate feet when climbing stairs.
  d. The toddler begins to master fine motor skills for building, undressing, and drawing lines.

  e. The young toddler often uses *no* even when he or she means *yes* to assert independence.
  f. The toddler begins to use short sentences and has a vocabulary of about 300 words by age 2.

5. Bowel and bladder control
  a. Certain signs indicate that a toddler is ready for toilet training (Box 33-4).
  b. Bowel control develops before bladder control.
  c. By age 3, the toddler achieves fairly good bowel and bladder control.
  d. The toddler may stay dry during the day but may need a diaper at night until about age 4.

6. Play
  a. The major socializing mechanism is parallel play, and therapeutic play can begin at this age.
  b. The toddler has a short attention span, causing the toddler to change toys often.
  c. The toddler explores body parts of self and others.
  d. Typical toys include push-pull toys, blocks, sand, finger paints and bubbles, large balls, crayons, trucks and dolls, containers, Play-Doh, toy telephones, cloth books, and wooden puzzles.

7. Safety
  a. Toddlers are eager to explore the world around them.
  b. The toddler should be supervised at play.
  c. The toddler can be placed in an upright forward-facing position in a car safety seat (convertible restraint); the transition point for switching to a forward-facing position is defined by the manufacturer of the car seat but is generally at a body weight of at least 20 lb and 1 year of age.
  d. Convertible restraints (car safety seats) are used until the child weighs at least 40 lb (Fig. 33-2)
  e. Booster seats are used for children shorter than 4 feet, 9 inches tall and weigh more than 40 lb (typically between 4 and 8 years of age); a booster seat is used until the child can

FIG. 33-2 When the child reaches 1 year of age and 20 lb, the car safety seat can be adjusted to a forward-facing, upright position. The seat is appropriate for the toddler until the child weighs about 40 lb. The safety straps should be adjusted to provide a snug fit, and the seat should be placed in the back seat of the car, ideally in the middle. (From McKinney, E., James, S., Murray, S., & Ashwill, J. [2005]. *Maternal-child nursing* [2nd ed.]. St. Louis: W.B. Saunders.)

sit against the back of the seat with feet hanging down and legs bent at the knees.
f. Children should use specially designed car restraints until they weigh at least 60 lb or are 8 years old.
g. Lock the car doors.
h. Four-door cars should be equipped with child safety locks on the back doors.
i. Use back burners on the stove to prepare a meal, and turn pot handles inward and toward the middle of the stove.
j. Keep dangling cords from small appliances away from the toddler.
k. Place inaccessible locks on windows and doors, and keep furniture away from windows.
l. Secure screens on all windows.
m. Place gates at stairways.
n. Do not allow the toddler to sleep or play in an upper bunk bed.
o. Never leave the toddler alone near a bathtub, pail of water, swimming pool, or any other body of water.
p. Keep toilet lids closed.
q. Keep all medicines, poisons, household plants, and toxic products high and locked out of reach.
r. Keep the poison control number available.

C. Preschooler
1. Physical
a. The preschooler grows $2\frac{1}{2}$ to 3 inches per year.
b. Average height is 37 inches at age 3, $40\frac{1}{2}$ inches at age 4, and 43 inches at age 5.
c. The preschooler gains approximately 5 lb per year; average weight of 35 to 40 lb at age 5.
d. The preschooler requires about 12 hours of sleep each day.
e. A security object and a nightlight help with sleeping.
f. At the beginning of the preschool period, the eruption of the deciduous (primary) teeth is complete.
g. Regular dental care is essential, and the preschooler requires assistance with brushing and flossing of teeth; fluoride supplements may be necessary if the water is not fluoridated.
2. Vital signs (Box 33-5)
3. Nutrition
a. The preschooler exhibits food fads and strong taste preferences.
b. By 5 years old, the child tends to focus on social aspects of eating, table conversations, manners, and willingness to try new foods.
4. Skills
a. The preschooler has good posture.
b. The child develops fine motor coordination.
c. The child can hop, skip, and run more smoothly.
d. Athletic abilities begin to develop.
e. The preschooler demonstrates increased skills in balancing.
f. The child alternates feet when climbing stairs.
g. The child can tie shoelaces by age 6.
h. The child may talk continuously and ask many *why* questions.
i. Vocabulary increases to about 900 words by age 3 and to 2100 words by age 5.
j. By age 3, the preschooler usually talks in three- or four-word sentences and speaks in short phrases.
k. By age 4, the preschooler speaks five- or six-word sentences and, by age 5, speaks in longer sentences that contain all parts of speech.
l. The child can be understood readily by others and can understand clearly what others are saying.

5. Bowel and bladder control
   a. By age 4, the preschooler has daytime control of bowel and bladder but may experience bed-wetting accidents at night.
   b. By age 5, the preschooler achieves bowel and bladder control, although accidents may occur in stressful situations.
6. Play
   a. The preschooler is cooperative.
   b. The preschooler has imaginary playmates.
   c. The child likes to build and create things, and play is simple and imaginative.
   d. The child understands sharing and is able to interact with peers.
   e. The child requires regular socialization with mates of similar age.
   f. Play activities include a large space for running and jumping.
   g. The preschooler likes dress-up clothes, paints, paper, and crayons for creative expression.
   h. Swimming and sports aid in growth development.
   i. Puzzles and toys aid with fine motor development.
7. Safety
   a. Preschoolers are active and inquisitive.
   b. Because of their magical thinking, they may believe that daring feats seen in cartoons are possible and may attempt them.
   c. The preschooler can learn simple safety practices because they can follow simple verbal directions and their attention span is longer.
   d. Once the child has outgrown the convertible restraint car safety seat (weight more than 40 lb), the preschooler should be placed and restrained in a booster seat.
   e. Booster seats are used for children shorter than 4 feet, 9 inches tall and weight more than 40 lb (typically between 4 and 8 years of age); a booster seat is used until the child can sit against the back of the seat with feet hanging down and legs bent at the knees (Fig. 33-3).
   f. Children should use specially designed car restraints until they weigh at least 60 lb or are 8 years old.
   g. Teach the preschooler basic safety rules to ensure safety when playing in a playground near swings and ladders.
   h. Teach the preschooler never to play with matches or lighters.
   i. The preschooler should be taught what to do in the event of a fire or if clothes catch fire; fire drills should be practiced with the preschooler.
   j. Guns should be stored unloaded and secured under lock and key (ammunition should be locked in a separate place); the preschooler

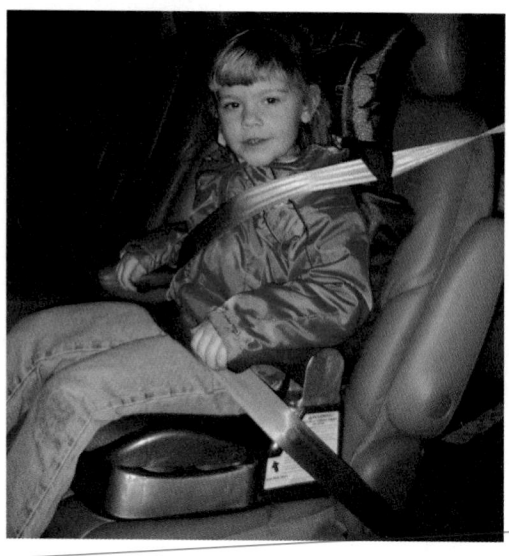

FIG. 33-3   A high-backed booster seat designed to hold car lap and shoulder belts properly is strongly recommended for children who have outgrown a child safety seat. Booster seats raise the young child high enough to allow the car seat belt to be positioned correctly over the child's chest and pelvis. (From McKinney, E., James, S., Murray, S., & Ashwill, J. [2005]. *Maternal-child nursing* [2nd ed.]. St. Louis: W.B. Saunders. Photo courtesy of Michele M. Hayden.)

should be taught to leave an area immediately if a gun is visible and to tell an adult.
   k. The preschooler should be taught never to point a toy gun at another person.
   l. Teach the preschooler that if another person touches his or her body in an inappropriate way, an adult should be told.
   m. Teach the preschooler to avoid speaking to strangers and never to accept a ride, toys, or gifts from a stranger.
   n. Teach the preschooler his or her full name, address, parents' names, and telephone number.
   o. Teach the preschooler how to dial 911 in an emergency situation.
   p. Keep the poison control number available.
D. School-age child
   1. Physical
      a. Girls usually grow faster than boys.
      b. Growth is about 2 inches per year between ages 6 and 12.
      c. Height ranges from 45 inches at age 6 to 59 inches at age 12.
      d. School-age children gain weight at a rate of about $4\frac{1}{2}$ to $6\frac{1}{2}$ lb per year.
      e. Average weight is 46 lb at age 6 and 88 lb at age 12.
      f. The first permanent (secondary) teeth erupt around age 6, and deciduous teeth are lost gradually.

g. Regular dentist visits are necessary, and the school-age child needs to be supervised with brushing and flossing teeth; fluoride supplements may be necessary if the water is not fluoridated.

h. For school-age children with primary and permanent dentition, the best toothbrush is one with soft nylon bristles and an overall length of about 6 inches.

i. Sleep requirements range from 10 to 12 hours a night.

2. Vital signs (Box 33-6)

3. Nutrition

a. School-age children have increased growth needs.

b. Children require a balanced diet from foods in the MyPyramid Food Guide; healthy snacks should be emphasized to prevent childhood obesity.

c. Children still may be picky eaters but are willing to try new foods.

4. Skills

a. School-age children exhibit refinement of fine motor skills.

b. Development of gross motor skills continues.

c. Strength and endurance increase.

5. Play

a. Play is more competitive.

b. Rules and rituals are important aspects of play and games.

c. The school-aged child enjoys drawing, collecting items, dolls, pets, guessing games, board games, listening to the radio, TV, reading, watching videos or DVDs, and computer games.

d. The child participates in team sports.

e. The child may participate in secret clubs, group peer activities, and scout organizations.

6. Safety

a. The school-age child experiences less fear in play activities and frequently imitates real life by using tools and household items.

b. School-age children are ready to transition from booster seats when the adult seat belts fit correctly (the shoulder belt fits across the chest and shoulder, the lap belt fits across the thighs, and the child is tall enough to sit comfortably against the seat back with the knees bent, without slouching, for the length of the trip). This typically occurs when the child is at least 4 feet 9 inches tall and is between 8 and 12 years of age.

c. Car safety belts should be worn across the thighs; the shoulder belt is used only if it does not cross over the child's neck and face.

d. Major causes of injuries include bicycles, skateboards, and team sports as the child

BOX 33-6
The School-age Child's Vital Signs

Temperature: Oral, 97.5° to 98.6° F
Apical rate: 60 to 100 beats/min
Respirations: 18 to 20 breaths/min
Blood pressure: Average, 107/64 mm Hg

increases in motor abilities and independence.

e. Children should always wear a helmet when riding a bike or using in-line skates or skateboards.

f. Teach the child water safety rules.

g. Instruct the child to avoid teasing or playing roughly with animals.

h. Teach the child never to play with matches or lighters.

i. The child should be taught what to do in the event of a fire or if clothes catch fire; fire drills should be practiced with the child.

j. Guns should be stored unloaded and secured under lock and key (ammunition should be locked in a separate place); the school-age child should be taught to leave an area immediately if a gun is visible and to tell an adult.

k. Teach the school-age child that if another person touches his or her body in an inappropriate way, an adult should be told.

l. Teach the school-age child to avoid speaking to strangers and never to accept a ride, toys, or gifts from a stranger.

m. Teach the child traffic safety rules.

n. Teach the child how to dial 911 in an emergency situation.

o. Keep the poison control number available.

E. Adolescent

1. Physical

a. Puberty is the maturational, hormonal, and growth process that occurs when the reproductive organs begin to function and the secondary sex characteristics develop.

b. Body mass increases to adult size.

c. Sebaceous and sweat glands become active and fully functional.

d. Body hair distribution occurs.

e. Increases in height, weight, breast development, and pelvic girth occur in girls.

f. Menstrual periods occur about $2\frac{1}{2}$ years after the onset of puberty.

g. In boys, increases in height, weight, muscle mass, and penis and testicle size occur.

h. The voice deepens in boys.

i. Normal weight gain during puberty: girls gain 15 to 55 lb; boys gain 15 to 65 lb.

j. Careful brushing and care of the teeth are important, and many adolescents need to wear braces.

k. Sleep patterns include a tendency to stay up late; therefore, in an attempt to catch up on missed sleep, adolescents sleep late whenever possible; an overall average of 8 hours per night is recommended.

2. Vital signs (Box 33-7)
3. Nutrition
   a. Teaching about the MyPyramid Food Guide is important.
   b. Adolescents typically eat whenever they have a break in activities.
   c. Calcium, zinc, iron, folic acid, and protein are especially important nutritional needs.
   d. Adolescents tend to snack on empty calories.
   e. Body image is important.
4. Skills
   a. Gross and fine motor skills are well developed.
   b. Strength and endurance increase.
5. Play
   a. Games and athletic activities are the most common forms of play.
   b. Competition and strict rules are important.
   c. Adolescents enjoy activities such as sports, videos, movies, reading, parties, dancing, hobbies, computer games, music, and experimenting, such as with makeup and hairstyles.
   d. Friends are important, and adolescents like to gather in small groups.
6. Safety
   a. Adolescents are risk takers.
   b. Adolescents have a natural urge to experiment and to be independent.
   c. Reinforce instructions about the dangers related to cigarette smoking, caffeine ingestion, alcohol, and drugs.
   d. Help adolescents recognize that they have choices when difficult or potentially dangerous situations arise.
   e. Ensure that the adolescent uses a seat belt.
   f. Instruct adolescents in the consequences of injuries that motor vehicle accidents can cause.
   g. Instruct adolescents in water safety and emphasize that they should enter the water feet first as opposed to diving, especially when the depth of the water is unknown.
   h. Instruct adolescents about the dangers associated with guns, violence, and gangs.
   i. Instruct adolescents about the complications associated with body piercing, tattooing, and sun tanning.

BOX 33-7
The Adolescent's Vital Signs

Temperature: Oral, 97.5° to 98.6° F
Apical rate: 55 to 90 beats/min
Respirations: 12 to 20 breaths/min
Blood pressure: Average, 121/70 mm Hg

---

   j. Discuss issues such as date rape, sexual relationships, and transmission of sexually transmitted diseases.

F. Early adulthood
   1. Description: Period between the late teens and mid to late 30s
   2. Physical changes
      a. Person has completed physical growth by the age of 20.
      b. Person is active.
      c. Severe illnesses are less common than in older age groups.
      d. Person tends to ignore physical symptoms and postpone seeking health care.
      e. Lifestyle habits such as smoking, stress, lack of exercise, poor personal hygiene, and family history of disease increase the risk of future illness.
   3. Cognitive changes
      a. Person has rational thinking habits.
      b. Conceptual, problem-solving, and motor skills increase.
      c. Person identifies preferred occupational areas.
   4. Psychosocial changes
      a. Person separates from family of origin.
      b. Person gives much attention to occupational and social pursuits to improve socioeconomic status.
      c. Person makes decisions regarding career, marriage, and parenthood.
      d. Person needs to adapt to new situations.
   5. Sexuality
      a. Person has the emotional maturity to develop mature sexual relationships.
      b. Person is at risk for sexually transmitted diseases.

G. Middle adulthood
   1. Description: Period between the mid to late 30s and mid 60s
   2. Physical changes
      a. Physical changes occur between 40 and 65 years of age.
      b. Individual becomes aware that changes in reproductive and physical abilities signify the beginning of another stage in life.
      c. Menopause occurs in women and climacteric occurs in men.

d. Physiological changes often have an impact on self-concept and body image.

e. Physiological concerns include stress, level of wellness, and the formation of positive health habits.

3. Cognitive changes

a. Person may be interested in learning new skills.

b. Person may become involved in educational or vocational programs for entering the job market or for changing careers.

4. Psychosocial changes

a. Changes may include expected events, such as children moving away from home (post-parental family stage), or unexpected events, such as the death of a close friend.

b. Time and financial demands decrease as children move away from home and the couple faces redefining their relationship.

c. Adults may become grandparents.

d. Adults are achieving generativity.

5. Sexuality

a. Many couples renew their relationships and find increased marital and sexual satisfaction.

b. The onset of menopause and climacteric may affect sexual health.

c. Stress, health, and medications can affect sexuality.

PRACTICE QUESTIONS

1. Which of the following car safety devices should be used for a child who is 8 years old and is 4 feet tall?

1. Seat belt.

2. Booster seat

3. Rear-facing convertible seat

4. Front-facing convertible seat

2. A nurse assesses the vital signs of a 12-month-old infant with a respiratory infection and notes that the respiratory rate is 35 breaths/min. Based on this finding, which action is appropriate?

1. Administer oxygen.

2. Notify the physician.

3. Document the findings.

4. Reassess the respiratory rate in 15 minutes.

3. A nurse provides instructions to the parents of an infant regarding car travel and safety seats. Which of the following is the appropriate information related to the safety of the infant?

1. Restrain in a car seat in the back seat in a semi-reclined, rear-facing position.

2. Restrain in a car seat in the front seat in a semi-reclined, rear-facing position.

3. Restrain in a car seat in the back seat in a semi-reclined, forward-facing position.

4. Restrain in a car seat in the front seat in a semi-reclined, forward-facing position.

4. A nurse is monitoring a 3-month-old infant for signs of increased intracranial pressure. On palpation of the fontanels, the nurse notes that the anterior fontanel is soft and flat. Based on this finding, which nursing action is appropriate?

1. Increase oral fluids.

2. Notify the physician.

3. Document the finding.

4. Elevate the head of the bed to 90 degrees.

5. A nurse is evaluating the developmental level of a 2-year-old. Which of the following does the nurse expect to observe in this child?

1. Uses a fork to eat

2. Uses a cup to drink

3. Pours own milk into a cup

4. Uses a knife for cutting food

6. The parents of a 2-year-old arrive at a hospital to visit their child. The child is in the playroom when the parents arrive. When the parents enter the playroom, the child does not readily approach the parents. The nurse interprets this behavior as indicating that:

1. The child is withdrawn.

2. This is a normal pattern.

3. The child is self-centered.

4. The child has adjusted to the hospital setting.

7. A mother arrives at a clinic with her toddler and tells a nurse that she has a difficult time getting the child to go to bed at night. Which of the following is appropriate for the nurse to suggest to the mother?

1. Avoid a nap during the day.

2. Allow the child to set bedtime limits.

3. Allow the child to have temper tantrums.

4. Inform the child of bedtime a few minutes before it is time for bed.

8. A mother of a 3-year-old asks a clinic nurse about appropriate and safe toys for the child. The nurse tells the mother that the most appropriate toy for a 3-year-old is which of the following?

1. A wagon

2. A golf set

3. A farm set

4. A jack set with marbles

9. A clinic nurse provides information to the mother of a toddler regarding toilet training. Which statement by the mother indicates a need for further information regarding the toilet training?

1. "Bladder control usually is achieved before bowel control."

2. "The child should not be forced to sit on the potty for long periods."

3. "The ability of the child to remove clothing is a sign of physical readiness."

4. "The child will not be ready to toilet train until the age of about 18 to 24 months."

10. The mother of a 3-year-old is concerned because her child still is insisting on a bottle at nap time and at bedtime. Which of the following is the appropriate suggestion to the mother?
    1. Allow the bottle if it contains juice.
    2. Allow the bottle if it contains water.
    3. Do not allow the child to have the bottle.
    4. Allow the bottle during naps but not at bedtime.

11. A nurse is preparing to care for a 5-year-old who has been placed in traction following a fracture of the femur. The nurse plans care, knowing that which of the following is the most appropriate activity for this child?
    1. A radio
    2. A sports video
    3. Large picture books
    4. Crayons and a coloring book

12. The mother of a 16-year-old tells a nurse that she is concerned because the child sleeps about 8 hours every night and until noontime every weekend. The appropriate nursing response is which of the following?
    1. "The child should not be staying up so late at night."
    2. "Adolescents need that amount of sleep every night."
    3. "If the child eats properly, that should not be happening."
    4. "The child probably is anemic and should eat more foods containing iron."

13. A 4-year old child diagnosed with leukemia is hospitalized for chemotherapy. The child is fearful of the hospitalization. Which nursing intervention would be most appropriate to alleviate the child's fears?
    1. Encourage the child's parents to stay with the child.
    2. Encourage play with other children of the same age.
    3. Advise the family to visit only during the scheduled visiting hours.
    4. Provide a private room, allowing the child to bring the favorite toys from home.

14. A 16-year-old is admitted to the hospital for acute appendicitis and an appendectomy is performed. Which nursing intervention is appropriate to facilitate normal growth and development postoperatively?
    1. Encourage the child to rest and read.
    2. Encourage the parents to room in with the child.
    3. Allow the child to interact with others in his or her same age group.
    4. Allow the family to bring in the child's favorite computer games.

15. A clinic nurse assesses the communication patterns of a 5-month-old infant. The nurse determines that the infant is demonstrating the highest level of developmental achievement expected if the infant:
    1. Coos when comforted.
    2. Links syllables together.
    3. Uses monosyllabic babbling.
    4. Uses simple words such as "mama."

16. A nurse prepares to administer digoxin (Lanoxin) to a 3-year-old child with a diagnosis of congestive heart failure and notes that the apical rate is 110 beats/min. Based on this finding, which nursing action is appropriate?
    1. Hold the medication.
    2. Notify the physician.
    3. Administer the digoxin.
    4. Recheck the apical rate in 15 minutes.

17. A 2-year-old child is treated in the emergency room for a burn to the chest and abdomen. The child sustained the burn by grabbing a cup of hot coffee that was left on the kitchen counter. The nurse reviews safety principles with the parents before discharge. Which statement by the parents indicates an understanding of measures to provide safety in the home?
    1. "We will be sure not to leave hot liquids unattended."
    2. "I guess my children need to understand what the word *hot* means."
    3. "We will be sure that the children stay in their rooms when we work in the kitchen."
    4. "We will install a safety gate as soon as we get home so the children cannot get into the kitchen."

18. A mother of a 4-year-old expresses concern because her hospitalized child has begun thumb sucking. The mother states that this behavior began 2 days after hospital admission. The appropriate nursing response is which of the following?
    1. "It is best to ignore the behavior."
    2. "Your child is acting like a baby."
    3. "The doctor will need to notified."
    4. "A 4-year-old is too old for this type of behavior."

ALTERNATE ITEM FORMAT: MULTIPLE RESPONSE

Which interventions are appropriate for the care of an infant? Select all that apply.
- ❏ 1. Provide swaddling.
- ❏ 2. Talk in a loud voice.
- ❏ 3. Provide the infant with a bottle of juice at nap time.
- ❏ 4. Hang mobiles with black and white contrast designs.
- ❏ 5. Caress the infant while bathing or during diaper changes.
- ❏ 6. Allow the infant to cry for at least 10 minutes before responding.

ANSWERS

1. **2**
Rationale: Children should remain in a booster seat until they are 8 to 12 years old and at least 4 feet, 9 inches tall. An infant should ride in a car in a semireclined, rear-facing position in an infant-only seat or a convertible seat until they weigh at least 20 lb and are at least 1 year of age. The transition point for switching to the forward-facing position is defined by the manufacturer of the convertible car safety seat but is generally at a body weight of 9 kg (20 lb) and 1 year of age. Convertible car safety seats are used until the child weighs at least 40 lb.
Test-Taking Strategy: Note the age and height of the child to identity the appropriate safety device. Remember, children should remain in a booster seat until they are 8 to 12 years old and at least 4 feet, 9 inches tall. If you had difficulty with this question, review the physical development requirements for car safety devices.
Level of Cognitive Ability: Analysis
Client Needs: Safe and Effective Care Environment
Integrated Process: Nursing Process—planning
Content Area: Child health
Reference: American Academy of Pediatrics. (2006). *Car safety seats: A guide for families.* http://www.aap.org/family/carseatguide.htm.

2. **3**
Rationale: The normal respiratory rate in a 12-month-old infant is 20 to 40 breaths/min. The normal apical rate is 90 to 130 beats/min, and the average blood pressure is 90/56 mm Hg. The nurse would document the findings.
Test-Taking Strategy: Focus on the data in the question. Recalling the normal vital signs of an infant will direct you to the correct option. If you had difficulty with this question, review these normal parameters.
Level of Cognitive Ability: Application
Client Needs: Health Promotion and Maintenance
Integrated Process: Nursing Process—implementation
Content Area: Child health
Reference: McKinney, E., James, S., Murray, S., & Ashwill, J. (2005). *Maternal-child nursing* (2nd ed.). St. Louis: W.B. Saunders.

3. **1**
Rationale: Infants who weigh up to 20 lb and are at least 1 year of age should be restrained in a car seat (convertible seat) or infant-only seat in a semireclined, rear-facing position in the back seat of the car. Options 2, 3, and 4 are incorrect.
Test-Taking Strategy: Visualize each of the descriptions in the options, with a focus of safety in mind. Eliminate options 2 and 4 because of the words *front seat.* Next, eliminate option 3 because of the words *forward-facing.* If you had difficulty with this question, review the car safety measures for the infant.
Level of Cognitive Ability: Application
Client Needs: Safe and Effective Care Environment
Integrated Process: Teaching and Learning
Content Area: Child health
Reference: Wong, D., Perry, S., Hockenberry, M., et al. (2006). *Maternal child nursing care* (3rd ed., p. 761). St. Louis: Mosby.

4. **3**
Rationale: The anterior fontanel is diamond-shaped and located on the top of the head. The fontanel should be soft and flat in a normal infant, and it normally closes by 12 to 18 months of age. The nurse would document the finding because it is normal.
Test-Taking Strategy: Use the process of elimination and note the strategic words *soft and flat.* This should provide you with the clue that this is a normal finding. A bulging or tense fontanel may result from crying or increased intracranial pressure. If you had difficulty with this question, review normal assessment findings in an infant.
Level of Cognitive Ability: Application
Client Needs: Health Promotion and Maintenance
Integrated Process: Nursing Process—implementation
Content Area: Child health
Reference: McKinney, E., James, S., Murray, S., & Ashwill, J. (2005). *Maternal-child nursing* (2nd ed., p. 521). St. Louis: W.B. Saunders.

5. **2**
Rationale: By age 2 years, the child can use a cup and spoon correctly but with some spilling. By age 3 to 4, the child begins to use a fork. By the end of the preschool period, the child should be able to pour milk into a cup and begin to use a knife for cutting.
Test-Taking Strategy: Note the age of the child and use the process of elimination. Option 4 can be eliminated easily. Next, think about the fine motor skills that need to be developed in selecting the correct option. With this in mind, eliminate options 1 and 3. If you had difficulty with this question, review the developmental skills of a 2-year-old.
Level of Cognitive Ability: Analysis
Client Needs: Health Promotion and Maintenance
Integrated Process: Nursing Process—assessment
Content Area: Child health
Reference: McKinney, E., James, S., Murray, S., & Ashwill, J. (2005). *Maternal-child nursing* (2nd ed., p. 110). St. Louis: W.B. Saunders.

6. **2**
Rationale: The phases through which young children progress when separated from their parents include protest, despair, and denial or detachment. In the stage of protest, when the parents return, the child readily goes to them. In the stage of despair, the child may not approach them readily or may cling to a parent. In denial or detachment, when the parents return, the child becomes cheerful, interested in the environment and new persons (seemingly unaware of the lost parents), friendly with the staff, and interested in developing superficial relationships. Options 1, 3, and 4 are incorrect interpretations of the child's behavior.
Test-Taking Strategy: Use the process of elimination and knowledge regarding the phases of separation anxiety to answer the question. In addition, focusing on the data in the question will assist in eliminating options 1, 3, and 4. Review the concepts related to the hospitalized toddler and separation anxiety if you had difficulty with this question.
Level of Cognitive Ability: Analysis

Client Needs: Psychosocial Integrity
Integrated Process: Nursing Process—analysis
Content Area: Child health
Reference: Hockenberry, M., Wilson, D., & Winkelstein, M. (2005). *Wong's essentials of pediatric nursing* (7th ed., pp. 638-639). St. Louis: Mosby.

7. 4

Rationale: Toddlers often resist going to bed. Bedtime protests may be reduced by establishing a consistent before-bedtime routine and enforcing consistent limits regarding the child's bedtime behavior. Informing the child of bedtime a few minutes before it is time for bed is the most appropriate option. Most toddlers take an afternoon nap and, until their second birthday, also may require a morning nap. Firm, consistent limits are needed for temper tantrums or when toddlers try stalling tactics.

Test-Taking Strategy: Use the process of elimination. Eliminate options 1, 2, and 3 by using concepts related to growth and development. Remember that preparing the toddler for an event will minimize resistive behavior. Review concepts related to sleep patterns and the toddler if you had difficulty with this question.
Level of Cognitive Ability: Application
Client Needs: Physiological Integrity
Integrated Process: Teaching and Learning
Content Area: Child health
Reference: Hockenberry, M., Wilson, D., & Winkelstein, M. (2005). *Wong's essentials of pediatric nursing* (7th ed., p. 403). St. Louis: Mosby.

8. 1

Rationale: Toys for the toddler must be strong, safe, and too large to swallow or place in the ear or nose. Toddlers need supervision at all times. Push-pull toys, large balls, large crayons, trucks, and dolls are some of the appropriate toys. A farm set, a golf set, and jacks with marbles may contain items that the child could swallow.

Test-Taking Strategy: Use the process of elimination and focus on the subject, the appropriate toy for a 3-year-old. Options 2, 3, and 4 can be eliminated easily because they contain items that the child could swallow. Remember that large and strong toys are safest for the toddler. Review the principles related to play activities and the toddler if you had difficulty with this question.
Level of Cognitive Ability: Application
Client Needs: Safe and Effective Care Environment
Integrated Process: Teaching and Learning
Content Area: Child health
Reference: McKinney, E., James, S., Murray, S., & Ashwill, J. (2005). *Maternal-child nursing* (2nd ed., p. 113). St. Louis: W.B. Saunders.

9. 1

Rationale: Bowel control usually is achieved before bladder control. The child should not be forced to sit for long periods. The ability to remove clothing is one of the physical signs of readiness. The physical ability to control the anal and urethral sphincters is achieved some time after the child is walking, probably between the age of 18 and 24 months.

Test-Taking Strategy: Use the process of elimination and knowledge of the concepts related to readiness for toilet training. Note the strategic words *indicates a need for further information*. These words indicate a negative event query and ask you to select an option that is an incorrect statement. Look for the option that indicates that the nurse needs to provide additional information to the mother regarding the toilet training. Review the concepts related to readiness for toilet training if you had difficulty with this question.
Level of Cognitive Ability: Analysis
Client Needs: Health Promotion and Maintenance
Integrated Process: Teaching and Learning
Content Area: Child health
Reference: Hockenberry, M., Wilson, D., & Winkelstein, M. (2005). *Wong's essentials of pediatric nursing* (7th ed., p. 397). St. Louis: Mosby.

10. 2

Rationale: A toddler should never be allowed to fall asleep with a bottle containing milk, juice, soda pop, or sweetened water because of the risk of nursing (bottle-mouth) caries. If a bottle is allowed at nap time or bedtime, it should contain only water.

Test-Taking Strategy: Use the process of elimination. Eliminate options 3 and 4 first because they are comparative or alike. From the remaining options, recalling that nursing (bottle-mouth) caries is a concern in a child will assist in directing you to option 2. Review dental health principles related to children if you had difficulty with this question.
Level of Cognitive Ability: Application
Client Needs: Health Promotion and Maintenance
Integrated Process: Teaching and Learning
Content Area: Child health
Reference: Wong, D., Perry, S., Hockenberry, M., et al. (2006). *Maternal child nursing care* (3rd ed., p. 1104). St. Louis: Mosby.

11. 4

Rationale: In the preschooler, play is simple and imaginative and includes activities such as crayons and coloring books, puppets, felt and magnetic boards, and Play-Doh. A radio or sports video are most appropriate for the adolescent. Large picture books are most appropriate for the infant.

Test-Taking Strategy: Use the process of elimination. Note the age of the child, and think about the age-related activity that would be most appropriate. Eliminate options 1 and 2, knowing that they are most appropriate for the adolescent. From the remaining options, the word *large* in option 3 should provide you with the clue that this activity would be more appropriate for a child younger than age 5. If you had difficulty with this question, review the appropriate activities for a preschooler.
Level of Cognitive Ability: Application
Client Needs: Health Promotion and Maintenance
Integrated Process: Nursing Process—planning
Content Area: Child health
Reference: McKinney, E., James, S., Murray, S., & Ashwill, J. (2005). *Maternal-child nursing* (2nd ed., p. 113). St. Louis: W.B. Saunders.

12. 2

Rationale: The adolescent needs about 8 hours of sleep per night. During this age, with an increase in social activities, school commitments, and possibly work activities, it is important that the adolescent receive enough sleep at night. Options 1, 3, and 4 are inaccurate and inappropriate nursing responses.

Test-Taking Strategy: Use the process of elimination and focus on the subject of the question. The question gives no indication that a physiological alteration is present; therefore, eliminate option 4. From the remaining options, use therapeutic communication techniques to direct you to option 2. Review adolescent sleep patterns if you had difficulty with this question.

Level of Cognitive Ability: Application
Client Needs: Health Promotion and Maintenance
Integrated Process: Communication and Documentation
Content Area: Child health
Reference: McKinney, E., James, S., Murray, S., & Ashwill, J. (2005). *Maternal-child nursing* (2nd ed., p. 113). St. Louis: W.B. Saunders.

13. **1**
Rationale: Although the preschooler already may be spending some time away from parents at a day care center or preschool, illness adds a stressor that makes separation more difficult. The child may ask repeatedly when parents will be coming for a visit or may constantly be wanting to call the parents. Options 3 and 4 will increase stress related to separation anxiety. Option 2 is unrelated to the subject of the question and, in addition, may not be appropriate for a child who is immunocompromised and at risk for infection.

Test-Taking Strategy: Note that the subject relates to the child's fear and use the process of elimination. Options 3 and 4 will increase anxiety and fear further and should be eliminated. Bearing the subject of the question in mind and considering the child's diagnosis will assist you in eliminating option 2. Review interventions to prevent or minimize separation anxiety if you had difficulty with this question.

Level of Cognitive Ability: Application
Client Needs: Psychosocial Integrity
Integrated Process: Caring
Content Area: Child health
Reference: McKinney, E., James, S., Murray, S., & Ashwill, J. (2005). *Maternal-child nursing* (2nd ed., p. 890). St. Louis: W.B. Saunders.

14. **3**
Rationale: Adolescents often are not sure whether they want their parents with them when they are hospitalized. Because of the importance of their peer group, separation from friends is a source of anxiety. Ideally, the members of the peer group will support their ill friend. Options 1, 2, and 4 isolate the child from the peer group.

Test-Taking Strategy: Consider the psychosocial needs of the adolescent when answering the question. Options 1, 2, and 4 are comparative or alike in that they isolate the child from his or her own peer group. If you had difficulty with this question, review the psychosocial needs of the adolescent.

Level of Cognitive Ability: Application
Client Needs: Psychosocial Integrity
Integrated Process: Caring
Content Area: Child health

Reference: McKinney, E., James, S., Murray, S., & Ashwill, J. (2005). *Maternal-child nursing* (2nd ed.). St. Louis: W.B. Saunders.

15. **3**
Rationale: Using monosyllabic babbling occurs between 3 and 6 months of age. Using simple words such as "mama" occurs between 9 and 12 months of age. Linking syllables together when communicating occurs between 6 and 9 months of age. Cooing begins at birth and continues until 2 months of age.

Test-Taking Strategy: Use the process of elimination and knowledge of language and communication developmental milestones to answer the question. Focus on the age of the infant to assist in directing you to the correct option. Review the patterns of infant communication if you had difficulty with this question.

Level of Cognitive Ability: Analysis
Client Needs: Health Promotion and Maintenance
Integrated Process: Nursing Process—assessment
Content Area: Child health
Reference: Hockenberry, M., Wilson, D., & Winkelstein, M. (2005). *Wong's essentials of pediatric nursing* (7th ed., p. 112). St. Louis: Mosby.

16. **3**
Rationale: The normal apical heart rate for a 3-year-old is 80 to 120 beats/min. Because the apical rate is within the normal range, options 1, 2, and 4 are inappropriate.

Test-Taking Strategy: Use the process of elimination and knowledge of the normal apical heart rate for a 3-year-old to answer the question. Recalling that a heart rate of 110 beats/min is within the normal range will direct you to option 3. Review the normal vital signs for a 3-year-old if you had difficulty with this question.

Level of Cognitive Ability: Application
Client Needs: Physiological Integrity
Integrated Process: Nursing Process—implementation
Content Area: Child health
Reference: McKinney, E., James, S., Murray, S., & Ashwill, J. (2005). *Maternal-child nursing* (2nd ed., p. 817). St. Louis: W.B. Saunders.

17. **1**
Rationale: Toddlers, with their increased mobility and development of motor skills, can reach hot water or hot objects placed on counters and stoves and can reach open fires or stove burners above their eye level. The nurse should encourage parents to remain in the kitchen when preparing a meal, use the back burners on the stove, and turn pot handles inward and toward the middle of the stove. Hot liquids should never be left unattended, and the toddler should always be supervised. The statements in options 2, 3, and 4 do not indicate an understanding of the principles of safety.

Test-Taking Strategy: Use the process of elimination, noting the strategic words *indicates an understanding*. Option 2 can be eliminated easily. Options 3 and 4 are comparative or alike in that they isolate the child from the environment. Option 1 is the only option that reflects an understanding of safety principles by the parents. Review these safety principles if you had difficulty with this question.

Level of Cognitive Ability: Analysis
Client Needs: Safe and Effective Care Environment
Integrated Process: Nursing Process—evaluation
Content Area: Child health
Reference: Wong, D., Perry, S., Hockenberry, M., et al. (2006). *Maternal child nursing care* (3rd ed., pp. 1072, 1074). St. Louis: Mosby.

18. **1**
Rationale: In the hospitalized preschooler, the best option is to accept regression if it occurs. Regression is most often a result of the stress of the hospitalization. Parents may be overly concerned about regression and should be told that their child may continue the behavior at home. When regression does occur, the best approach is to ignore it while praising existing patterns of appropriate behavior. Calling the physician is not necessary. Options 2 and 4 are inappropriate.
Test-Taking Strategy: Use the process of elimination. Options 2 and 4 are clearly inappropriate and are eliminated first. Option 3 may cause increased concern in the mother. If you had difficulty with this question, review the psychosocial issues related to the hospitalized preschool child.
Level of Cognitive Ability: Application
Client Needs: Psychosocial Integrity
Integrated Process: Communication and Documentation
Content Area: Child health
Reference: Hockenberry, M., Wilson, D., & Winkelstein, M. (2005). *Wong's essentials of pediatric nursing* (7th ed., p. 401). St. Louis: Mosby.

ALTERNATE ITEM FORMAT: MULTIPLE RESPONSE

Answer: 1, 4, 5
Rationale: Holding, caressing, and swaddling provide warmth and tactile stimulation for the infant. To provide auditory stimulation, the nurse should talk to the infant in a soft voice and should instruct the mother to do so also. Additional interventions include playing a music box, radio, or television, or having a ticking clock or metronome nearby. Hanging a bright shiny object in midline within 20 to 25 cm of the infant's face and hanging mobiles with contrasting colors, such as black and white, provide visual stimulation. Crying is an infant's way of communicating; therefore, the nurse would respond to the infant's crying. The mother is taught to do so also. An infant or child should never be allowed to fall asleep with a bottle containing milk, juice, soda pop, or sweetened water because of the risk of nursing (bottle-mouth) caries.
Test-Taking Strategy: Focus on the subject, care of the infant. Noting the word *loud* and the words *at least 10 minutes before responding* will assist in eliminating these interventions. Also, recalling the concerns related to dental caries will assist in eliminating option 3. Review the guidelines related to the care of an infant if you had difficulty with this question.
Level of Cognitive Ability: Application
Client Needs: Psychosocial Integrity
Integrated Process: Nursing Process—implementation
Content Area: Child health
Reference: Hockenberry, M., Wilson, D., & Winkelstein, M. (2005). *Wong's essentials of pediatric nursing* (7th ed., p. 408). St. Louis: Mosby.

REFERENCES

American Academy of Pediatrics. (2006). *Car safety seats: A guide for families.* http://www.aap.org/family/carseatguide.htm.

Hockenberry, M., & Wilson, D. (2007). *Wong's nursing care of infants and children* (8th ed.). St. Louis: Mosby.

Hockenberry, M., Wilson, D., & Winkelstein, M. (2005). *Wong's essentials of pediatric nursing* (7th ed.). St. Louis: Mosby.

National Council of State Boards of Nursing. (Eds.). (2007). *2007 NCLEX-RN® detailed test plan.* Chicago: Author.

McKinney, E., James, S., Murray, S., & Ashwill, J. (2005). *Maternal-child nursing* (2nd ed.). St. Louis: W.B. Saunders.

Wong, D., Perry, S., Hockenberry, M., et al. (2006). *Maternal child nursing care* (3rd ed.). St. Louis: Mosby.

Care of the Older Client

I. PHYSIOLOGICAL CHANGES
A. Integumentary system
   1. Loss of pigment in hair and skin
   2. Wrinkling of the skin
   3. Thinning of the epidermis and easy bruising and tearing of the skin (Fig. 34-1)
   4. Decreased skin turgor, elasticity, and subcutaneous fat
   5. Increased nail thickness and decreased nail growth
   6. Decreased perspiration
   7. Dry, itchy, scaly skin
   8. Seborrheic dermatitis and keratosis formation
B. Neurological system
   1. Slowed reflexes
   2. Slight tremors and difficulty with fine motor movement
   3. Loss of balance
   4. Increased incidence of awakening after sleep onset
   5. Increased susceptibility to hypothermia and hyperthermia
   6. Short-term memory decline possible
   7. Long-term memory usually maintained
C. Musculoskeletal system
   1. Decreased muscle mass and strength and atrophy of muscles
   2. Decreased mobility, range of motion, flexibility, coordination, and stability
   3. Change of gait, with shortened step and wider base
   4. Posture and stature changes causing a decrease in height (Fig. 34-2)
   5. Increased brittleness of the bones
   6. Deterioration of joint capsule components
   7. Kyphosis of the dorsal spine

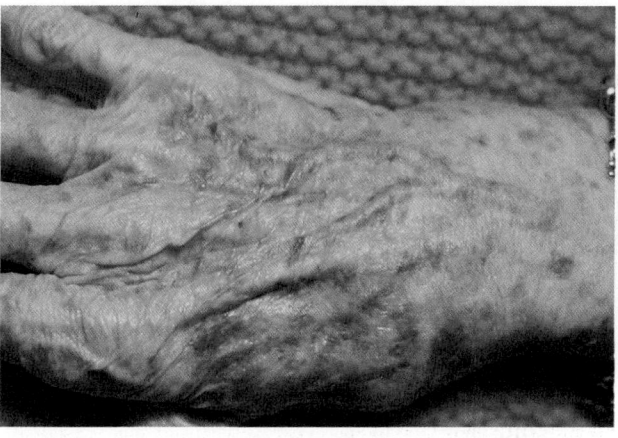

FIG. 34-1   Paper-thin, transparent skin. (From Ignatavicius, D., & Workman, M. [2006]. *Medical surgical nursing: Critical thinking for collaborative care* [5th ed.]. Philadelphia: W.B. Saunders.)

D. Cardiovascular system
   1. Diminished energy and endurance, with lowered tolerance to exercise
   2. Decreased compliance of the heart muscle, with heart valves becoming thicker and more rigid
   3. Decreased cardiac output and decreased efficiency of blood return to the heart
   4. Decreased compensatory response, so less able to respond to increased demands on the cardiovascular system
   5. Decreased resting heart rate
   6. Weak peripheral pulses
   7. Increased blood pressure but susceptibility to postural hypotension
E. Respiratory system
   1. Decreased stretch and compliance of the chest wall

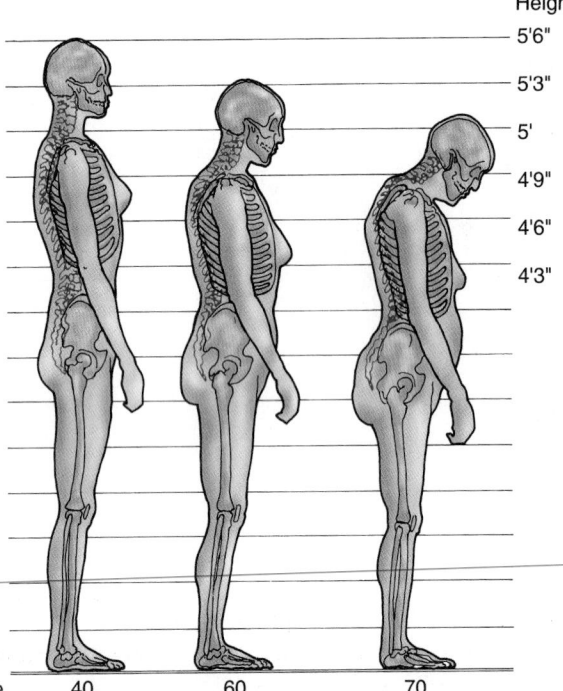

Height
5'6"
5'3"
5'
4'9"
4'6"
4'3"

Age   40   60   70

FIG. 34-2 A normal spine at age 40 years of age and osteoporotic changes at 60 and 70 years of age. These changes can cause a loss of as much as 6 inches in height and can result in the so-called "dowager's hump" *(far right)* in the upper thoracic vertebrae. (From Ignatavicius, D. & Workman, M. [2006]. *Medical-surgical nursing: Critical thinking for collaborative care* [5th ed.]. Philadelphia: W.B. Saunders.)

   2. Decreased strength and function of respiratory muscles
   3. Decreased size and number of alveoli
   4. Increased rate of respirations, generally 16 to 25 breaths/min
   5. Decreased depth of respirations and oxygen intake
   6. Decreased ability to cough and expectorate sputum
 F. Hematological system
   1. Hemoglobin and hematocrit average levels toward the low end of normal
   2. Prone to increased blood clotting
   3. Decreased protein available for protein-bound medications
 G. Immune system
   1. Tendency for lymphocyte counts to be low with altered immunoglobulin production
   2. Decreased resistance to infection and disease
 H. Gastrointestinal system
   1. Decreased need for calories because of lowered basal metabolic rate
   2. Decreased appetite, thirst, and oral intake
   3. Decreased lean body weight
   4. Decreased stomach-emptying time
   5. Increased tendency toward constipation

   6. Increased susceptibility for dehydration
   7. Tooth loss
   8. Difficulty in chewing and swallowing food
 I. Endocrine system
   1. Decreased secretion of hormones, with specific changes related to each hormone's function
   2. Decreased metabolic rate
   3. Decreased glucose tolerance, with resistance to insulin in peripheral tissues
 J. Renal system
   1. Decreased kidney size, function, and ability to concentrate urine
   2. Decreased glomerular filtration rate
   3. Decreased capacity of the bladder
   4. Increased residual urine and increased incidence of infection and incontinence
   5. Impaired medication excretion
 K. Reproductive system
   1. Decreased testosterone production and decreased size of testes
   2. Changes in the prostate gland, leading to urinary problems
   3. Decreased secretion of hormones with the cessation of menses
   4. Vaginal changes, including decreased muscle tone and lubrication
   5. Impotence or sexual dysfunction for both genders; sexual function varies and depends on general physical condition, mental health status, and medications
 L. Special senses
   1. Decreased visual acuity
   2. Decreased **accommodation** in eyes, requiring increased adjustment time to changes in light
   3. Decreased peripheral vision and increased sensitivity to glare
   4. Presbyopia and cataract formation
   5. Possible loss of hearing ability; low-pitched tones are heard more easily
   6. Inability to discern taste of food
   7. Decreased sense of smell
   8. Changes in touch sensation
   9. Decreased pain awareness

II. PSYCHOSOCIAL CONCERNS
A. Adjustment to deterioration in physical and mental health and well-being
B. Threat to independent functioning and fear of becoming a burden to loved ones
C. Adjustment to retirement and loss of income
D. Loss of skills and competencies developed early in life
E. Coping with changes in role function and social life
F. Diminished quantity and quality of relationships and coping with loss
G. Dependence on governmental and social systems
H. Access to social support systems
I. Costs of health care and medications

BOX 34-1
Mental Health Concerns

Depression
Grief
Isolation
Suicide

III. MENTAL HEALTH CONCERNS (Box 34-1)

A. Depression: The increased dependency that older adults may experience can lead to hopelessness, helplessness, lowered sense of self-control, and decreased self-esteem and self-worth; these changes can interfere with daily functioning and lead to **depression.**

B. Grief: Client reacts to the perception of loss, including physical, psychological, social, and spiritual aspects.

C. Isolation: Client is alone and desires contact with others but is unable to make that contact.

D. Suicide: All suicide threats from an older client should be taken seriously.

▲ IV. PAIN

A. Description
   1. Pain can occur from numerous causes and most often occurs from degenerative changes in the musculoskeletal system.
   ▲ 2. The failure to alleviate pain in the older client can lead to functional limitations affecting his or her ability to function independently.
▲ B. Assessment
   1. Agitation
   2. Moaning
   3. Crying
   4. Restlessness
   5. Verbal reporting of pain
▲ C. Interventions
   1. Monitor the client for signs of pain.
   2. Identify the pattern of pain.
   3. Identify the precipitating factor(s) for the pain.
   4. Monitor the impact of the pain on activities of daily living.
   5. Provide pain relief through measures such as distraction, relaxation, massage, and biofeedback.
   6. Administer pain medication as prescribed, and instruct the client in its use.
   7. Evaluate the effects of pain-reducing measures.

▲ V. INFECTION (Box 34-2)

A. Confusion is a common sign of infection in the older adult, especially of the urinary tract.

B. Carefully monitor the older adult with infection because of the diminished and altered immune response.

C. Nonspecific symptoms may indicate illness or infection (see Box 34-2).

Apathy
Anorexia
Changes in functional status
Confusion
Dyspnea
Falling
Fatigue
Incontinence
Self-neglect
Shortness of breath, tachypnea
Vital sign changes

VI. MEDICATIONS ▲

A. Major problems with prescriptive medications include adverse effects, medication interactions, medication errors, noncompliance, and cost.

B. Determine the use of over-the-counter medications. ▲

C. **Polypharmacy**
   1. Routinely monitor the number of prescription and nonprescription medications used and determine whether any can be eliminated or combined.
   2. Keep the use of medications to a minimum.
   3. Overprescribing medications leads to increased problems with more side effects, increased interaction between medications, replication of medication treatment, diminished quality of life, and pointless costs.

D. Medication dosages normally are prescribed at one third to one half of normal adult dosages.

E. Closely monitor client for adverse effects and response to therapy because of the increased risk for medication toxicity. ▲

F. Note that a common sign of an adverse reaction in the older client is an acute change in mental status. ▲

G. Assess for medication interactions in the client taking multiple medications.

H. Advise the client to use one pharmacy and notify the consulting physician(s) of the medications taken. ▲

I. Administration of medications ▲
   1. Place the client in a sitting position when administering medication.
   2. Check for mouth dryness because medication may stick and dissolve in the mouth.
   3. Administer liquid preparations if the client has difficulty swallowing tablets.
   4. Crush tablets if necessary and give with textured food (nectar, applesauce) if not contraindicated.
   5. Do not crush enteric-coated tablets and do not open capsules.
   6. If administering a suppository, do not insert suppository immediately after removing from the refrigerator.

7. A suppository may take longer to dissolve because of decreased body core temperature.

8. When administering parenteral medication, monitor the site, because it may ooze medication or bleed because of decreased tissue elasticity.

9. Do not use an immobile limb for administering parenteral medication.

10. Monitor client compliance with taking prescribed medications.

11. Monitor client for safety in correctly taking medications, including an assessment of their ability to read the instructions and discriminate among the pills and their color and shape.

12. Use a medication cassette to facilitate proper administration of medication.

VII. ABUSE OF THE OLDER ADULT

A. **Abuse** involves physical, emotional, or sexual **abuse** and also can involve **neglect** or economic **exploitation.**

B. Categories of mistreatment to the older client.

1. Domestic mistreatment takes place in the home of the older adult and is usually carried out by a family member or significant other; this can include physical maltreatment, **neglect**, or abandonment.

2. Institutional mistreatment takes place when an older adult experiences **abuse** when hospitalized or living somewhere other than home (e.g., long-term care facility).

3. **Self-neglect** is the lack of caring for oneself by a mentally competent individual who is cognitively competent but engages in actions that negatively affect his or her personal safety.

C. Individuals at most risk for **abuse** include those who are dependent because of their immobility or altered mental status.

D. Factors that contribute to **abuse** and **neglect** include long-standing family violence, caregiver stress, and the individual's increasing dependence on others.

E. Abusers tend to be male, engage in substance **abuse,** have a mental illness or **dementia;** in addition, they tend to depend on the older client for financial assistance or other resources.

F. Victims may attempt to dismiss injuries as accidental, and abusers may prevent victims from receiving proper medical care to avoid discovery.

G. Victims often are isolated socially by their abusers.

H. For additional information on **abuse** of the older client, see Chapter 75.

PRACTICE QUESTIONS

1. The nurse is performing an assessment on an older adult client. Which assessment data would indicate a potential complication associated with the skin of this client?
   1. Crusting
   2. Wrinkling
   3. Deepening of expression lines
   4. Thinning and loss of elasticity in the skin

2. The nurse who volunteers at a senior citizens' center is planning activities for the members who attend the center. Which activity would best promote health and maintenance for these senior citizens?
   1. Gardening every day for an hour
   2. Sculpting once a week for 40 minutes
   3. Cycling three times a week for 20 minutes
   4. Walking three to five times a week for 30 minutes

3. The home health nurse is visiting a client for the first time. While assessing the client's medication, it is noted that there are at least 19 prescription and several over-the-counter medications that the client has been taking. Which intervention should the nurse take first?
   1. Check for drug-drug interactions.
   2. Determine whether there are any adverse side effects.
   3. Determine whether there are medication duplications.
   4. Call the prescribing physician and report any polypharmacy.

4. The nurse is working with older clients in a long-term care facility. Which of the following activities performed by the nurse fosters reminiscence among these clients?
   1. Having storytelling hours
   2. Setting up pet therapy sessions
   3. Displaying calendars and clocks
   4. Encouraging client participation in pottery class

5. The home care nurse is performing an environmental assessment in the home of an older client. Which of the following, if observed by the nurse, requires immediate attention?
   1. Unsecured scatter rugs
   2. Clear exit passageways
   3. An operable smoke detector
   4. A prefilled medication cassette

6. The nurse is teaching an older client about measures to prevent constipation. Which statement, if made by the client, indicates that further teaching about bowel elimination is necessary?
   1. "I walk 1 to 2 miles every day."
   2. "I need to decrease fiber in my diet."
   3. "I have a bowel movement every other day."
   4. "I drink six to eight glasses of water every day."

7. The nurse educator is providing an information session to nursing assistants regarding caring for the older adult. The nurse educator tells the nursing assistants that which of the following situations portrays ageism?
   1. Informing the older adult of their rights
   2. Allowing older adults to make decisions

3. Accepting differences among older adults

4. Advising older adults to forego aggressive treatment

8. The nurse is providing medication instructions to an older client who is taking digoxin (Lanoxin) daily. The nurse notes that which age-related body changes could place the client at risk for digoxin toxicity?
   1. Decreased muscle strength and loss of bone density
   2. Decreased cough efficiency and decreased vital capacity
   3. Decreased salivation and decreased gastrointestinal motility
   4. Decreased lean body mass and decreased glomerular filtration rate

9. The nurse employed in a long-term care facility is caring for an older male client. Which nursing action contributes to encouraging autonomy in the client?
   1. Planning his meals
   2. Decorating his room
   3. Scheduling his barber appointments
   4. Allowing him to choose social activities

10. The home care nurse is visiting an older female client whose husband died 6 months ago. Which behavior by the client indicates ineffective coping?
    1. Neglecting her personal grooming
    2. Looking at old snapshots of her family
    3. Participating in a senior citizens' program
    4. Visiting her husband's grave once a month

11. The nurse is providing instructions to a nursing assistant regarding care of an older client with hearing loss. The nurse tells the assistant that clients with a hearing loss:
    1. Are often distracted.
    2. Have middle ear changes.
    3. Respond to low-pitched tones.
    4. Develop moist cerumen production.

12. The nurse is providing an educational session to new employees, and the topic is abuse of the older client. The nurse helps the employees identify that which client is most typical of a victim of abuse?

   1. A 75-year-old man with moderate hypertension
   2. A 68-year-old man with newly diagnosed cataracts
   3. A 90-year-old woman with advanced Parkinson's disease
   4. A 70-year-old woman with early diagnosed Lyme disease

13. The nurse is performing an assessment on an older client who is having difficulty sleeping at night. Which statement, if made by the client, indicates that teaching about improving sleep is necessary?
    1. "I swim three times a week."
    2. "I have stopped smoking cigars."
    3. "I drink hot chocolate before bedtime."
    4. "I read for 40 minutes before bedtime."

14. The visiting nurse observes that the older male client is confined by his daughter-in-law to his room. When the nurse suggests that he walk to the den and join the family, he says, "I'm in everyone's way; my daughter-in-law needs me to stay here." The most important action for the nurse to take is to:
    1. Say nothing, because it is best for the nurse to remain neutral and wait to be asked for help.
    2. Suggest to the client and daughter-in-law that they consider a nursing home for the client.
    3. Say to the daughter-in-law, "Confining your father-in-law to his room is inhuman."
    4. Suggest appropriate resources to the client and daughter-in-law, such as respite care and a senior citizens' center.

ALTERNATE ITEM FORMAT: MULTIPLE RESPONSE

Select all the normal age-related physiological changes.
- ❏ 1. Increased heart rate
- ☑ 2. Decline in visual acuity
- ❏ 3. Decreased respiratory rate
- ❏ 4. Decline in long-term memory
- ☑ 5. Increased susceptibility to urinary tract infections
- ☑ 6. Increased incidence of awakening after sleep onset

ANSWERS

1. **1**

Rationale: The normal physiological changes that occur in the skin of older adults include thinning of the skin, loss of elasticity, deepening of expression lines, and wrinkling. Crusting noted on the skin would indicate a potential complication.
Test-Taking Strategy: Use the process of elimination and note the strategic words *potential complication*. Think about the normal physiological changes that occur in the aging process to direct you to option 1. Review these age-related skin changes if you had difficulty with this question.

Level of Cognitive Ability: Analysis
Client Needs: Physiological Integrity
Integrated Process: Nursing Process—assessment
Content Area: Fundamental skills
Reference: Meiner, S., & Leuckenotte, A. (2006). *Gerontologic nursing* (3rd ed., p. 896) St. Louis: Mosby.

2. **4**

Rationale: Exercise and activity are essential for health promotion and maintenance in the older adult and to achieve an optimal level of functioning. About half of the physical

deterioration of the older client is caused by disuse rather than by the aging process or disease. One of the best exercises for an older adult is walking, progressing to 30-minute sessions three to five times each week. Swimming and dancing are also beneficial.
Test-Taking Strategy: Use the process of elimination, noting the strategic word *best*. Options 1, 2, and 3, although possible, are not the best activities. Remember, walking is one of the best forms of exercise. Review this content if you had difficulty with this question.
Level of Cognitive Ability: Application
Client Needs: Health Promotion and Maintenance
Integrated Process: Nursing Process—planning
Content Area: Fundamental skills
Reference: Ignatavicius, D., & Workman, M. (2006). *Medical-surgical nursing: Critical thinking for collaborative care* (5th ed., p. 43). Philadelphia: W.B. Saunders.

3. **3**
Rationale: Polypharmacy is a concern in the geriatric population. Duplication of medications needs to be identified before drug-drug interactions or adverse side effects can be determined. The phone call to the health care provider is the intervention after all other information has been collected.
Test-Taking Strategy: Note the strategic word *first*. Note that options 1, 2, and 3 all relate to obtaining data. Therefore, think about the order of action with these options. Options 1, 2, and 4 should be done after possible medication duplication has been identified. Review the interventions related to polypharmacy if you had difficulty with this question.
Level of Cognitive Ability: Application
Client Needs: Physiological Integrity
Integrated Process: Nursing Process—implementation
Content Area: Pharmacology
Reference: Burke, M., & Laramie, J. (2004). *Primary care of older adults: A multidisciplinary approach* (2nd ed., p. 91). St. Louis: Mosby.

4. **1**
Rationale: Clients who like to retell stories or past events need to be provided the opportunity to do so. This phenomenon is called life review, or reminiscence. In a sense, reminiscence is a way for the older client to relive and restructure life experiences and is a part of achieving ego identity. Options 2 and 4 indicate socialization and physical activity. Option 3 indicates reality orientation techniques.
Test-Taking Strategy: Use the process of elimination. Focusing on the strategic word *reminiscence* and recalling the definition of this word will direct you to option 1. Review this form of activity if you had difficulty with this question.
Level of Cognitive Ability: Application
Client Needs: Psychosocial Integrity
Integrated Process: Caring
Content Area: Mental health
Reference: Meiner, S., & Leuckenotte, A. (2006). *Gerontologic nursing* (3rd ed., p. 287) St. Louis: Mosby.

5. **1**
Rationale: Trauma to the older client in the home may be caused by a variety of factors. These include an unsteady gait,

the presence of unsecured scatter rugs, cluttered passageways, inoperable smoke detectors, and a history of previous falls.
Test-Taking Strategy: Use the process of elimination and note the strategic words *requires immediate attention*. Focusing on the subject and looking for the item that identifies an unsafe condition will direct you to option 1. Review the components of an environmental assessment if you had difficulty with this question.
Level of Cognitive Ability: Analysis
Client Needs: Safe and Effective Care Environment
Integrated Process: Nursing Process—assessment
Content Area: Fundamental skills
Reference: Potter, P., & Perry, A. (2005) *Fundamentals of nursing* (6th ed., p. 968). St. Louis: Mosby.

6. **2**
Rationale: Adequate dietary fiber is an important factor in aiding bowel function. Dietary fiber increases fecal weight and water content and accelerates the transit of fecal mass through the gastrointestinal tract. The retention of water by the fiber has the ability to soften stools and promote regularity. Fluid intake and exercise also facilitate bowel elimination.
Test-Taking Strategy: Note the strategic words *further teaching about bowel elimination is necessary*. These words indicate a negative event query and ask you to select an option that is an incorrect statement. Use the process of elimination and basic principles related to preventing constipation. If you had difficulty with this question, review these basic principles.
Level of Cognitive Ability: Analysis
Client Needs: Physiological Integrity
Integrated Process: Teaching and Learning
Content Area: Fundamental skills
Reference: Meiner, S., & Leuckenotte, A. (2006). *Gerontologic nursing* (3rd ed., p. 566). St. Louis: Mosby.

7. **4**
Rationale: Ageism is a form of prejudice in which older adults are stereotyped by characteristics found in only a few members of their group. Fundamental to ageism is the view that older persons are different from "me" and will remain different from "me." Therefore, they are portrayed as not experiencing the same desires, needs, and concerns. Options 1, 2, and 3 identify supportive roles that the nurse engages in when dealing with the older adult. Option 4 suggests that the older adult is not worthy of aggressive treatment and demonstrates ageism.
Test-Taking Strategy: Use the process of elimination and focus on the subject, ageism. Recalling the definition of ageism will direct you to option 4. Review this concept if you had difficulty with this question.
Level of Cognitive Ability: Comprehension
Client Needs: Health Promotion and Maintenance
Integrated Process: Caring
Content Area: Fundamental skills
Reference: Meiner, S., & Leuckenotte, A. (2006). *Gerontologic nursing* (3rd ed., pp. 13-14). St. Louis: Mosby.

8. **4**
Rationale: The older client is at risk for medication toxicity because of decreased lean body mass and an age-associated

decreased glomerular filtration rate. Although options 1, 2, and 3 identify age-related changes that occur in the older client, they are not associated specifically with this risk.
Test-Taking Strategy: Use the process of elimination and focus on the subject, age-related body changes that could place the client at risk for medication toxicity. Note that option 4 is the only option that addresses renal excretion. If you had difficulty with this question, review the physiological changes associated with aging.
Level of Cognitive Ability: Analysis
Client Needs: Physiological Integrity
Integrated Process: Teaching and Learning
Content Area: Fundamental skills
Reference: Meiner, S., & Leuckenotte, A. (2006). *Gerontologic nursing* (3rd ed., pp. 452-453). St. Louis: Mosby.

9. **4**
Rationale: Autonomy is the personal freedom to direct one's own life as long as it does not impinge on the rights of others. An autonomous person is capable of rational thought. This individual can identify problems, search for alternatives, and select solutions that allow continued personal freedom as long as others and their rights and property are not harmed. Loss of autonomy, and therefore independence, is a real fear of older clients. Option 4 is the only option that allows the client to be a decision maker.
Test-Taking Strategy: Use the process of elimination, focusing on the subject, encouraging autonomy. Recalling the definition of autonomy will direct you to the correct option. Remember, giving the client choices is essential to promote independence. Review the concept of autonomy if you had difficulty with this question.
Level of Cognitive Ability: Application
Client Needs: Safe and Effective Care Environment
Integrated Process: Caring
Content Area: Fundamental skills
Reference: Meiner, S., & Leuckenotte, A. (2006). *Gerontologic nursing* (3rd ed., p. 43). St. Louis: Mosby.

10. **1**
Rationale: Coping mechanisms are behaviors used to decrease stress and anxiety. In response to a death, ineffective coping is manifested by an extreme behavior that in some cases may be harmful to the individual physically or psychologically. Option 1 is indicative of a behavior that identifies an ineffective coping behavior in the grieving process.
Test-Taking Strategy: Use the process of elimination and note the subject, an ineffective coping behavior. Eliminate options 2, 3, and 4 because they are comparative or alike and are positive activities in which the individual is engaging to get on with her life. Review coping mechanisms in response to grief and loss if you had difficulty with this question.
Level of Cognitive Ability: Analysis
Client Needs: Psychosocial Integrity
Integrated Process: Nursing Process—assessment
Content Area: Mental health
Reference: Ignatavicius, D., & Workman, M. (2006). *Medical-surgical nursing: Critical thinking for collaborative care* (5th ed., pp. 41-42). Philadelphia: W.B. Saunders.

11. **3**
Rationale: Presbycusis refers to the age-related irreversible degenerative changes of the inner ear that lead to decreased hearing ability. As a result of these changes, the older client has a decreased response to high-frequency sounds. Low-pitched voice tones are heard more easily and can be interpreted by the older client. Options 1, 2, and 4 are not accurate.
Test-Taking Strategy: Use the process of elimination. Recalling that the client with a hearing loss responds to low-pitched tones will direct you to option 3. If you had difficulty with this question, review the characteristics associated with presbycusis and hearing loss.
Level of Cognitive Ability: Application
Client Needs: Physiological Integrity
Integrated Process: Teaching and Learning
Content Area: Adult health—ear
Reference: Meiner, S., & Leuckenotte, A. (2006). *Gerontologic nursing* (3rd ed., pp. 659, 742). St. Louis: Mosby.

12. **3**
Rationale: Elder abuse is widespread and occurs among all subgroups of the population. Elder abuse includes physical and psychological abuse, misuse of property, and violation of rights. The typical abuse victim is a woman of advanced age with few social contacts and at least one physical or mental impairment that limits her ability to perform activities of daily living. In addition, the client usually lives alone or with the abuser and depends on the abuser for care.
Test-Taking Strategy: Use the process of elimination. Read each option carefully and identify the client who is most defenseless as the result of the disease process. This will direct you to option 3. If you had difficulty with this question, review content related to elder abuse.
Level of Cognitive Ability: Application
Client Needs: Psychosocial Integrity
Integrated Process: Teaching and Learning
Content Area: Mental health
Reference: Ignatavicius, D., & Workman, M. (2006). *Medical-surgical nursing: Critical thinking for collaborative care* (5th ed., pp. 48-49). Philadelphia: W.B. Saunders.

13. **3**
Rationale: Many nonpharmacological sleep aids can be used to influence sleep. The client should avoid caffeinated beverages and stimulants such as tea, cola, and chocolate. The client should exercise regularly, because exercise promotes sleep by burning off tension that accumulates during the day. A 20- to 30-minute walk, swim, or bicycle ride three times a week is helpful. The client should sleep on a bed with a firm mattress. Smoking and alcohol should be avoided. The client should avoid large meals, peanuts, beans, fruit and raw vegetables that produce gas, and snacks high in fat that are difficult to digest.
Test-Taking Strategy: Focus on the subject, that teaching is necessary. These words indicate a negative event query and ask you to select an option that is an incorrect statement. Options 1, 2, and 4 are positive statements indicating that the client understands the methods of improving sleep. Review the factors that can interfere with sleep if you had difficulty with this question.

Level of Cognitive Ability: Analysis
Client Needs: Physiological Integrity
Integrated Process: Teaching and Learning
Content Area: Fundamental skills
Reference: Meiner, S., & Leuckenotte, A. (2006). *Gerontologic nursing* (3rd ed., pp. 13-14). St. Louis: Mosby.

14. **4**

Rationale: Assisting clients and families to become aware of available community support systems is a role and responsibility of the nurse. Option 2 suggests committing the client to a nursing home and is a premature action on the nurse's part. Although the data provided tell the nurse that this client requires nursing care, the nurse does not know the extent of the nursing care required. Observing that the client has begun to be confined to his room makes it necessary for the nurse to intervene legally and ethically, so option 1 is not appropriate and is passive in terms of advocacy. Option 3 is incorrect and judgmental.

Test-Taking Strategy: Use the process of elimination and note the strategic words *most important action*. Using principles related to the ethical and legal responsibility of the nurse and knowledge of the nurse's role will direct you to option 4. Review these principles if you had difficulty with this question.

Level of Cognitive Ability: Application
Client Needs: Safe and Effective Care Environment
Integrated Process: Nursing Process—implementation
Content Area: Fundamental skills
Reference: Meiner, S., & Leuckenotte, A. (2006). *Gerontologic nursing* (3rd ed., pp. 125, 354-355). St. Louis: Mosby.

ALTERNATE ITEM FORMAT:
MULTIPLE RESPONSE

Answer: 2, 5, 6

Rationale: Anatomical changes to the eye affect the individual's visual ability, leading to potential problems with activities of daily living. Light adaptation and visual fields are reduced. Respiratory rates are generally higher in older adults, ranging from 16 to 25 breaths/min. Heart rate decreases and heart valves thicken. Age-related changes that affect the urinary tract increase an older client's susceptibility to urinary tract infections. Short-term memory may decline with age, but long-term memory usually is maintained. Change in sleep patterns is a consistent, age-related change. Older persons experience an increased incidence of awakening after sleep onset.

Test-Taking Strategy: Knowledge regarding normal age-related changes is needed to answer this question. Read each characteristic carefully and think about the physiological changes that occur with aging to select the correct items. Review the normal age-related changes if you had difficulty with this question.

Level of Cognitive Ability: Analysis
Client Needs: Health Promotion and Maintenance
Integrated Process: Nursing Process—assessment
Content Area: Fundamental skills
Reference: Black, J., & Hawks, J. (2005). *Medical-surgical nursing: Clinical management for positive outcomes.* (7th ed., pp. 52-53). Philadelphia: W.B. Saunders.

REFERENCES

Black, J., & Hawks, J., (2005). *Medical-surgical nursing: Clinical management for positive outcomes* (7th ed.). Philadelphia: W.B. Saunders.

Burke, M., and Laramie, J. (2004). *Primary care of older adults: A multidisciplinary approach.* (2nd ed.). St. Louis: Mosby.

Ignatavicius, D., & Workman, M. (2006). *Medical-surgical nursing: Critical thinking for collaborative care* (5th ed.). Philadelphia: W.B. Saunders.

Meiner, S., & Leuckenotte, A. (2006). *Gerontologic nursing* (3rd ed.). St. Louis: Mosby.

National Council of State Boards of Nursing (Eds.). (2007). *2007 NCLEX-RN® detailed test plan.* Chicago: Author.

Potter, P., & Perry, A. (2005). *Fundamentals of nursing* (6th ed.). St. Louis: Mosby.

Pediatric Nursing

PYRAMID TERMS

abuse   Nonaccidental physical injury or the nonaccidental act of omission of care by a parent or person responsible for a child; includes neglect, physical, sexual, and emotional maltreatment.

active immunity   A form of long-term acquired antibody protection that develops naturally after an initial infection or exposure to antigens, or artificially after a vaccination.

atresia   Congenital absence or closure of a body orifice.

attenuated vaccines   Vaccines derived from microorganisms or viruses; their virulence has been weakened as a result of passage through another host.

cephalocaudal   Characterized by growth and development that proceeds from head to toe.

crackles   Audible high-pitched crackling or popping sounds heard during lung auscultation; result from fluid in the airways, and are not cleared by coughing (formerly referred to as "rales").

chronological age   Age in years.

cyanosis   The bluish color that results in tissues, nail beds, and mucous membranes when tissues are deprived of adequate amounts of oxygen.

developmental age   Age based on functional behavior and ability to adapt to the environment; does not necessarily correspond with chronological age.

encopresis   Fecal incontinence after age 4.

functional age   The age equivalent at which a child actually is able to perform specific self-care or related tasks.

growth   Measurable physical and physiological body changes that occur over time.

grunting   The sound made by forced expiration, which is the body's attempt to improve oxygenation when hypoxemia is present.

hereditary   Refers to the transmission of genetic characteristics from parent to offspring.

inactivated vaccines   Vaccines that contain killed microorganisms.

intelligence   Measured individual behavior that relates to learning, thinking, and problem solving.

learning   Behavior changes that occur as a result of maturation and experience with the environment.

nasal flaring   A widening of the nares to enable an infant or child to take in more oxygen; a serious indicator of air hunger.

passive immunity   A form of acquired immunity that occurs artificially through injection or is acquired naturally as the result of antibody transfer through the placenta to a fetus or through colostrum to an infant; is not permanent.

prodromal   Pertaining to early symptoms that mark the onset of a disease.

puberty   The period of time during which the adolescent experiences a growth spurt, develops secondary sex characteristics, and achieves reproductive maturity.

regression   Behavior more appropriate to an earlier stage of development; often is used to cope with stress or anxiety.

regurgitation   An abnormal backward flow of body fluid.

retraction   An abnormal movement of the chest wall during inspiration in which the skin appears to be drawn in between the ribs, and above and/or below the clavicle, and scapula; indicates respiratory difficulty.

shunt   Movement of blood or body fluid through an abnormal anatomical or surgically created opening.

stenosis   The narrowing or constriction of an opening.

stridor   A shrill harsh sound heard during inspiration, expiration, or both, produced by the flow of air through a narrowed segment of the respiratory tract.

vaccine   A suspension of attenuated or killed microorganisms administered to induce active immunity to infectious disease.

wheezing   High-pitched musical whistle sounds heard with or without a stethoscope as air is compressed through narrowed or obstructed airways because of swelling, secretions, or tumors.

PYRAMID TO SUCCESS

Pyramid Points focus on growth and development, safety, and age-appropriate measures to ensure a safe and hazard-free environment for the child, and on acute disorders that can occur in children. The focus is on specific feeding techniques, positioning techniques, and interventions that will provide and maintain adequate airway, breathing, and circulation patterns in the child. On the NCLEX-RN examination, be alert to the age of the child if the age is presented in a question. The Integrated Processes addressed in this unit include Caring, Communication and Documentation, Nursing Process, and Teaching/Learning.

▲ **CLIENT NEEDS**
Safe and Effective Care Environment

Considering issues related to informed consent regarding minors
Ensuring environmental and personal safety related to the developmental age of the child
Establishing priorities
Instituting measures related to the spread and control of infectious agents, particularly regarding communicable diseases
Maintaining confidentiality
Preventing accidents
Providing continuity of care
Providing protective measures
Protecting the child and other contacts to prevent illness
Upholding parent and child rights

Health Promotion and Maintenance

Considering concepts of family systems when planning care
Ensuring that immunization schedules are up to date
Focusing on developmental stages when planning care
Preventing disease in the pediatric population
Providing health promotion programs for the pediatric client
Providing instructions to the child and parents regarding care at home

Psychosocial Integrity

Assessment for child abuse and neglect
Communicating with the pediatric client
Considering cultural, religious, and spiritual beliefs when planning care
Considering end-of-life issues and grief and loss in the pediatric population

Identifying family and support systems for the child
Providing play therapies

Physiological Integrity

Following medication administration procedures
Following nutritional guidelines for the pediatric population
Identifying comfort measures appropriate for the child
Maintaining sensitivity for intrusive procedures needed for the pediatric client
Managing childhood illnesses
Monitoring elimination patterns
Monitoring for age-appropriate normal body structure and function
Monitoring for infectious diseases of the pediatric client
Monitoring for potential for alterations in body systems from disease
Monitoring for responses to treatments
Providing for consistent rest and sleep patterns
Responding to medical emergencies

REFERENCES

Behrman, R., Kliegman, R., & Jenson, H. (2004). *Nelson textbook of pediatrics* (17th ed.). Philadelphia: W.B. Saunders.

Betz, C., & Sowden, L. (2004). *Pediatric nursing reference* (5th ed.). St. Louis: Mosby.

Hockenberry, M. (2004). *Wong's clinical manual of pediatric nursing* (6th ed.). St. Louis: Mosby.

Hockenberry, M., & Wilson, D. (2007) *Nursing care of infants and children* (8th ed). St. Louis: Mosby.

Jarvis, C. (2004) *Physical examination and health assessment* (4th ed.). Philadelphia: W.B. Saunders.

McKinney, E., James, S., Murray, S. Ashwill, J., (2005). *Maternal-child nursing* (2nd ed.). St. Louis: W.B. Saunders.

National Council of State Boards of Nursing. (Eds.). (2007). *2007 NCLEX-RN® detailed test plan*. Chicago: Author.

Perry, A., & Potter, P. (2006). *Clinical nursing skills & techniques* (6th ed.). St. Louis: Mosby.

Potter, P., & Perry, A. (2005). *Fundamentals of nursing* (6th ed.). St. Louis: Mosby.

Stuart, G., & Laraia, M. (2005). *Principles and practice of psychiatric nursing* (8th ed.). St. Louis: Mosby.

Varcarolis, E. (2006). *Foundations of psychiatric mental health nursing* (5th ed.). Philadelphia: W.B. Saunders.

Wong, D., Perry, S., & Hockenberry, M. (2006). *Maternal child nursing care* (3rd ed.). St. Louis: Mosby.

Neurological, Cognitive, and Psychosocial Disorders

▲ I. HEAD INJURY

A. Description

1. Head injury is the pathological result of any mechanical force to the skull, scalp, meninges, or brain.
   a. Open head injury occurs when there is a fracture of the skull or penetration of the skull by an object.
   b. Closed head injury is the result of blunt trauma (more serious because of chance of increased intracranial pressure in "closed" vault).
2. Manifestations depend on the type of injury and the subsequent amount of increased intracranial pressure (ICP).

▲ B. Assessment (increased ICP)

1. Early signs
   a. Headache
   b. Visual disturbances, diplopia
   c. Nausea and vomiting
   d. Dizziness or vertigo
   e. Slight change in vital signs
   f. Change in pupillary response and equality
   g. Sunsetting eyes: Sclera visible above the iris
   h. Slight change in level of consciousness
   i. Infant: Bulging fontanel, wide sutures, increased head circumference, dilated scalp veins, high-pitched cry
   j. Child: Headache, nausea, vomiting, ataxia, nystagmus
2. Late signs
   a. Significant decrease in level of consciousness
   b. Bradycardia
   c. Decorticate posturing: Adduction of the arms at the shoulders; arms are flexed on the chest with the wrists flexed and the hands fisted, and the lower extremities are extended and adducted; seen with severe dysfunction of the cerebral cortex (Fig. 35-1)
   d. Decerebrate posturing: Rigid extension and pronation of the arms and the legs; a sign of dysfunction at the level of the midbrain (see Fig. 35-1)
   e. Fixed and dilated pupils

C. Interventions

1. Monitor the airway.
2. Assess injuries; immobilize the neck if a cervical injury is suspected.
3. Monitor vital signs and neurological function.
4. Monitor for decreased responsiveness to pain (a significant sign of altered level of consciousness).
5. Initiate seizure precautions (Box 35-1).
6. Maintain an NPO status or provide clear liquids, if prescribed, until it is determined that vomiting will not occur.
7. Administer oxygen and intravenous fluids as prescribed.
8. Monitor intravenous fluids carefully to avoid aggravating any cerebral edema and to minimize the possibility of overhydration.
9. Elevate the head of the bed 15 to 30 degrees, if not contraindicated, to facilitate venous drainage.
10. Position the client so that the head is maintained midline to avoid jugular vein compression, which can increase ICP.
11. Assess wound dressings for the presence of drainage and monitor for nose or ear drainage, which could indicate leakage of cerebrospinal fluid (CSF); drainage that is positive for glucose (as tested with regent strips) indicates leakage of CSF from a skull fracture.

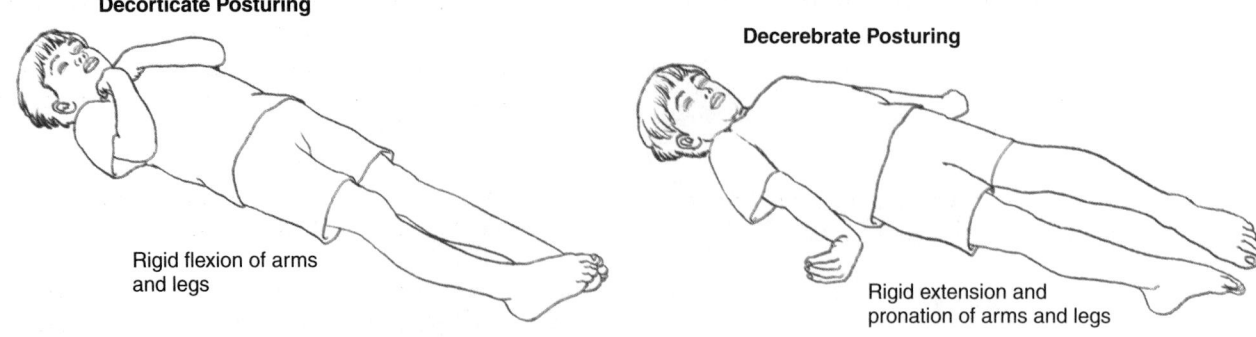

Decorticate Posturing

Rigid flexion of arms
and legs

Decerebrate Posturing

Rigid extension and
pronation of arms and legs

FIG. 35-1   Decorticate and decerebrate posturing. (From McKinney, E., James, S., Murray, S., & Ashwill, J. [2005]. *Maternal-child nursing* [2nd ed.]. St. Louis: W.B. Saunders.)

BOX 35-1
Seizure Precautions

Raise the side rails when the child is sleeping or
resting.
Pad the side rails and other hard objects.
Place a waterproof mattress or pad on the bed or
crib.
Instruct the child to wear or carry medical identification.
Instruct the child in precautions to take during potentially hazardous activities.
Instruct the child to swim with a companion.
Instruct the child to use a protective helmet and padding
when engaged in bicycle riding, skateboarding, and
in-line skating.
Alert caregivers to the need for any special precautions.

---

12. Administer tepid sponge baths or place on a hypothermia blanket if hyperthermia occurs.
13. Avoid suctioning through the nares because of the possibility of the catheter entering the brain through a fracture and placing the child at high risk for a secondary infection.
14. As prescribed, administer acetaminophen (Tylenol) for headache, anticonvulsants for seizures, antibiotics if a laceration is present, an osmotic diuretic (Mannitol) to reduce cerebral edema, corticosteroids such as dexamethasone (Decadron) to reduce brain edema, and tetanus toxoid as appropriate.
15. Withhold sedating medications during the acute phase of the injury so that changes in levels of consciousness can be assessed.
16. Monitor for signs of brainstem involvement (Box 35-2).
17. Monitor for signs of epidural hematoma: Asymmetrical pupils (one dilated, nonreactive pupil) can be a neurosurgical emergency that may require evacuation of the hematoma.
18. Keep stimuli to a minimum; attempt to minimize crying in the infant.

BOX 35-2
Signs of Brainstem Involvement

Deep, rapid, or intermittent and gasping respirations
Wide fluctuations or noticeable slowing of the pulse
Widening pulse pressure or extreme fluctuations in
blood pressure

II. NEAR-DROWNING
A. Description
   1. Survival of at least 24 hours after submersion in a fluid medium
   2. Hypoxia is the primary problem because it results in global cell damage; cerebral cells sustain irreversible damage after 4 to 6 minutes of submersion.
B. Interventions
   1. Monitor respiratory status because respiratory compromise and cerebral edema may occur 24 hours after the incident.
   2. Monitor for aspiration pneumonia.
   3. If child has had a severe cerebral insult, endotracheal intubation and mechanical ventilation may be required.
   4. Teach the parents to provide adequate supervision of infants and small children around water to prevent accidents.

III. HYDROCEPHALUS
A. Description
   1. An imbalance of cerebrospinal fluid (CSF) absorption or production caused by malformations, tumors, hemorrhage, infections, or trauma
   2. Results in head enlargement and increased ICP
B. Types (Box 35-3)
C. Assessment
   1. Infant
      a. Increased head circumference
      b. Thin, widely separated bones of the head that produce a cracked pot sound (Macewen's sign) on percussion

c. Anterior fontanel tense, bulging, and non-pulsating
d. Dilated scalp veins
e. Frontal bossing
f. Sunsetting eyes
2. Child
a. Behavior changes, such as irritability and lethargy
b. Headache on awakening
c. Nausea and vomiting
d. Ataxia
e. Nystagmus
3. Late signs: High, shrill cry and seizures.
D. Surgical interventions
1. The goal of surgical treatment is to prevent further CSF accumulation by bypassing the blockage and draining the fluid from the ventricles to a location where it may be reabsorbed.
2. In a ventriculoperitoneal **shunt,** the CSF drains into the peritoneal cavity from the lateral ventricle (Fig. 35-2).

BOX 35-3
Types of Hydrocephalus

COMMUNICATING
Hydrocephalus occurs as a result of impaired absorption within the subarachnoid space.
Interference of the cerebrospinal fluid in the ventricular system does not occur.

NONCOMMUNICATING
Obstruction of cerebrospinal flow in the ventricular system does occur.

3. In an atrioventricular **shunt,** CSF drains into the right atrium of the heart from the lateral ventricle, bypassing the obstruction (used in older children and in children with pathological conditions of the abdomen).
E. Preoperative interventions
1. Monitor intake and output; give small frequent feedings as tolerated until a preoperative NPO status is prescribed.
2. Reposition head frequently and use an egg crate mattress under the head to prevent pressure sores.
3. Prepare the child and family for diagnostic procedures and surgery
F. Postoperative interventions
1. Monitor vital signs and neurological signs.
2. Position the child on the unoperated side to prevent pressure on the **shunt** valve.
3. Keep the child flat as prescribed to avoid rapid reduction of intracranial fluid.
4. Observe for increased ICP; if increased ICP occurs, elevate the head of the bed to 15 to 30 degrees to enhance gravity flow through the **shunt.**
5. Monitor for signs of infection and assess dressings for drainage.
6. Measure head circumference.
7. Monitor intake and output.
8. Provide comfort measures; administer medications as prescribed, which may include diuretics, antibiotics, or anticonvulsants.
9. Instruct the parents on how to recognize **shunt** infection or malfunction.
10. In an infant, irritability, lethargy, and feeding poorly may indicate **shunt** malfunction or infection.

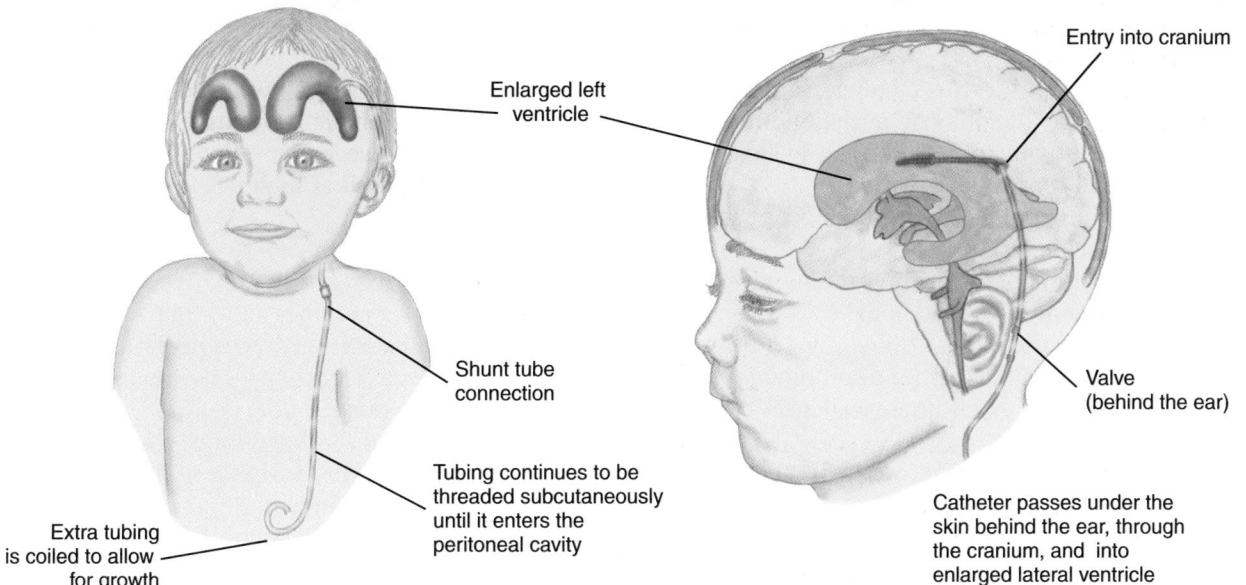

FIG. 35-2 Ventriculoperitoneal shunt. (From McKinney, E., James, S., Murray, S., & Ashwill, J. [2005]. *Maternal-child nursing* [2nd ed.]. St. Louis: W.B. Saunders.)

11. In a toddler, headache and a lack of appetite are the earliest common signs of **shunt** malfunction.
12. In older children, the most valuable indicator of **shunt** malfunction is an alteration in the child's level of consciousness.

IV. SPINA BIFIDA
A. Description
   1. This central nervous system defect results from failure of the neural tube to close during embryonic development.
   2. Associated deficits may include sensorimotor disturbance, dislocated hips, talipes equinovarus (clubfoot), and hydrocephalus.
   3. Defect closure is done immediately after birth.
B. Types
   1. Spina bifida occulta
      a. Posterior vertebral arches fail to close in the lumbosacral area.
      b. Spinal cord remains intact and usually is not visible.
      c. Meninges are not exposed on the skin surface.
      d. Neurological deficits are not usually present.
   2. Spina bifida cystica
      a. Protrusion of the spinal cord and/or its meninges occurs.
      b. Defect results in incomplete closure of the vertebral and neural tubes, resulting in a sac-like protrusion in the lumbar or sacral area, with varying degrees of nervous tissue involvement.
      c. Defect can include meningocele, myelomeningocele, lipomeningocele, and lipomeningomyelocele.
   3. Meningocele
      a. Protrusion involves meninges and a sac-like cyst that contains CSF in the midline of the back, usually in the lumbosacral area.
      b. Spinal cord is not involved.
      c. Neurological deficits are usually not present.
   4. Myelomeningocele
      a. Protrusion of the meninges, CSF, nerve roots, and a portion of the spinal cord occurs.
      b. The sac (defect) is covered by a thin membrane prone to leakage or rupture.
      c. Neurological deficits are evident.
C. Assessment
   1. Depends on the spinal cord involvement
   2. Visible spinal defect
   3. Flaccid paralysis of the legs
   4. Altered bladder and bowel function
   5. Hip and joint deformities
   6. Hydrocephalus

D. Interventions
   1. Evaluate the sac and measure the lesion.
   2. Perform neurological assessment.
   3. Monitor for increased ICP, which might indicate developing hydrocephalus.
   4. Measure head circumference; assess the anterior fontanel for fullness.
   5. Protect the sac; cover with a sterile, moist (normal saline), nonadherent dressing to maintain the moisture of the sac and contents, and change the dressing every 2 to 4 hours as prescribed.
   6. Place in a prone position to minimize tension on the sac and the risk of trauma; the head is turned to one side for feeding.
   7. Change the dressing covering the sac whenever it becomes soiled because of the risk of infection; diapering may be contraindicated until the defect has been repaired.
   8. Use aseptic technique to prevent infection.
   9. Assess the sac for redness, clear or purulent drainage, abrasions, irritation, and signs of infection.
   10. Early signs of infection include elevated temperature (axillary), irritability, lethargy, and nuchal rigidity.
   11. Assess for physical impairments such as hip and joint deformities.
   12. Prepare the child and family for surgery.
   13. Administer antibiotics preoperatively, as prescribed, to prevent infection.
   14. Teach the parents and eventually the child about long-term home care
      a. Positioning, feeding, skin care, and range-of-motion exercises.
      b. Performing clean intermittent catheterization technique.
      c. Administer propantheline (Pro-Banthine) as prescribed to improve continence.
      d. Implement a bowel program including a high-fiber diet, increased fluids, suppositories, as needed.
      e. The child is at high risk for latex allergy.

V. REYE'S SYNDROME
A. Description
   1. This acute encephalopathy follows a viral illness and is characterized pathologically by cerebral edema and fatty changes in the liver.
   2. The exact cause is not clear.
   3. Administration of aspirin is not recommended for children with varicella or influenza because of its association with Reye's syndrome.
   4. Acetaminophen (Tylenol) is considered the medication of choice for pediatric clients.
   5. The goal of treatment is to maintain effective cerebral perfusion and control increasing ICP.

▲ B. Assessment
1. History of systemic viral illness 4 to 7 days before the onset of symptoms
2. Malaise
3. Nausea and vomiting
4. Progressive neurological deterioration

▲ C. Interventions
1. Assess neurological status.
2. Monitor for altered level of consciousness and signs of increased ICP.
3. Monitor intake and output.
4. Provide rest and decrease stimulation in the environment.
5. Monitor for signs of bleeding and signs of impaired coagulation, such as a prolonged bleeding time.
6. Monitor liver function studies.

▲ VI. MENINGITIS
A. Description
1. Meningitis is an infectious process of the central nervous system caused by bacteria and viruses that may be acquired as a primary disease or as a result of complications of neurosurgery, trauma, infection of the sinus or ears, or systemic infections.
▲ 2. Diagnosis of bacterial meningitis is made by testing CSF obtained by lumbar puncture; the fluid is cloudy with increased pressure, increased white blood cell (WBC) count, and elevated protein and decreased glucose levels.
3. Bacterial meningitis (*Haemophilus influenza* type B, *Streptococcus pneumoniae*, or *Neisseria meningitidis*) occurs in epidemic form and can be transmitted by droplets from nasopharyngeal secretions.
4. Viral meningitis is associated with viruses such as mumps, paramyxovirus, herpesvirus, and enterovirus.

▲ B. Assessment
1. Signs and symptoms vary, depending on the type, the age of the child, and the duration of the preceding illness; there is no one classic sign or symptom.
2. Fever, chills, headache
3. Vomiting, diarrhea
4. Poor feeding or anorexia
5. Nuchal rigidity
6. Poor or high-pitched cry
7. Altered level of consciousness, such as lethargy or irritability
8. Bulging anterior fontanel in the infant
9. Positive Kernig sign (inability to extend the leg when the thigh is flexed anteriorly at the hip) and Brudzinski sign (neck flexion causes adduction and flexion movements of the lower extremities) in children and adolescents

10. Muscle or joint pain
11. Petechial or purpuric rashes (meningococcal infection)

C. Interventions
1. Provide isolation and maintain it for at least 24 hours after antibiotics are initiated.
2. Administer antibiotics and antipyretics as prescribed.
3. Perform neurological assessment and monitor for seizures; assess for the complication of inappropriate antidiuretic hormone (ADH) secretion, causing fluid retention (cerebral edema) and dilutional hyponatremia.
4. Assess for changes in level of consciousness and irritability.
5. Monitor intake and output.
6. Assess nutritional status.
7. Determine close contacts of the child with meningitis because the contacts will need prophylactic treatment.
8. Meningococcal **vaccine** is recommended to protect against meningitis (see Chap. 47 for information on vaccines).

VII. SEIZURE DISORDERS
A. Description
1. Sudden, transient alterations in brain function resulting from excessive levels of electrical activity in the brain
2. Classified as generalized, partial, or unclassified, depending on the area of the brain involved
3. Generalized seizures
   a. Tonic-clonic (grand mal); consciousness is lost.
   b. Absence (petit mal); momentary loss of consciousness, posture is maintained; has minor face, eye, and hand movements.
4. Partial seizures arise from a specific area in the brain and cause limited symptoms; examples include focal and psychomotor seizures.

B. Assessment
1. Obtain information from the parents about the time of onset, precipitating events, and behavior before and after the seizure.
2. Determine the child's history related to seizures.
3. Aura (a warning sign of impending seizure).
4. Apnea, **cyanosis**
5. Postseizure: Disoriented, sleepy.
6. Absence seizures: Occur in children between 4 to 12 years of age, last 5 to 10 seconds, and the child appears inattentive.
C. Seizure precautions (see Box 35-1)
D. Interventions (Box 35-4)
E. Anticonvulsant medications (see Chap. 66 for information on medications)

BOX 35-4
Emergency Treatment for Seizures

Ensure airway patency.
Have suction equipment and oxygen available.
Time the seizure episode.
If the child is standing or sitting, ease the child down to the floor, placing the child in a side-lying position.
Place a pillow or folded blanket under the child's head; if no bedding is available, place your own hands under the child's head or place the child's head in your own lap.
Loosen restrictive clothing.
Remove eyeglasses from the child if present.
Clear the area of any hazards or hard objects.
Allow the seizure to proceed and end without interference.
If vomiting occurs, turn the child to one side as a unit.
Do not restrain the child, place anything in the child's mouth, or give any food or liquids to the child.
Prepare to administer medications as prescribed.
Remain with the child until the child fully recovers.
Observe for incontinence, which may have occurred during the seizure.
Document the occurrence.

VIII. CEREBRAL PALSY

A. Description
   1. Disorder characterized by impaired movement and posture resulting from an abnormality in the extrapyramidal or pyramidal motor system
   2. The most common clinical type is spastic cerebral palsy, which represents an upper motor neuron–type of muscle weakness.
   3. Less common types of cerebral palsy are athetoid, ataxic, and mixed.

B. Assessment
   1. Extreme irritability and crying
   2. Feeding difficulties
   3. Stiff and rigid arms or legs
   4. Delayed developmental milestones
   5. Abnormal motor performance
   6. Alterations of muscle tone
   7. Abnormal posturing, such as opisthotonos (exaggerated arching of the back)
   8. Persistence of primitive infantile reflexes (Moro, tonic neck) after 6 months
   9. Seizures

C. Interventions
   1. The goal of management is early recognition and interventions to maximize the child's abilities.
   2. A multidisciplinary team approach is implemented to meet the many needs of the child.
   3. Therapeutic management includes physical therapy, occupational therapy, speech therapy, education, and recreation.
   4. Assess the child's developmental level and **intelligence.**
   5. Encourage early intervention and participation in school programs.
   6. Prepare for using mobilizing devices to help prevent or reduce deformities.
   7. Encourage communication and interaction with the child on his or her developmental level rather than **chronological age** level.
   8. Provide a safe environment such as removing sharp objects, using a protective helmet if the child falls frequently, and implementing seizure precautions if necessary.
   9. Provide safe appropriate toys for the child's age and developmental level.
   10. Position the child upright after meals.
   11. Administer medications as prescribed to decrease spasticity.
   12. Surgical interventions are reserved for the child who does not respond to more conservative measures or for the child whose spasticity causes progressive deformity.
   13. Intrathecal baclofen (Lioresal) may be used to provide relief of spasticity.

IX. MENTAL RETARDATION

A. Description
   1. In mental retardation, the child manifests subaverage intellectual functioning along with deficits in adaptive skills.
   2. Down syndrome is a congenital condition that results in moderate to severe retardation and has been linked to an extra group G chromosome, chromosome 21 (trisomy 21).

B. Assessment
   1. Deficits in cognitive skills and level of adaptive functioning
   2. Delays in fine and gross motor skills
   3. Speech delays
   4. Decreased spontaneous activity
   5. Nonresponsiveness
   6. Irritability
   7. Poor eye contact during feeding

C. Interventions
   1. Medical strategies are focused at correcting structural deformities and treating associated behaviors.
   2. Implement community and educational services using a multidisciplinary approach.
   3. Promote care skills as much as possible.
   4. Assist with communication and socialization skills.
   5. Facilitate appropriate play time.
   6. Initiate safety precautions as necessary.
   7. Assist the family with decisions regarding care.
   8. Provide information regarding support services and community agencies.

X. AUTISM

A. Description
1. Severe mental disorder beginning in infancy or toddlerhood
2. Disorder apparent to the parents before the child is 3 years old.
3. Autism is characterized by impairment in reciprocal social interaction and in verbal and nonverbal communication.
4. The cause is unknown and the prognosis may be poor.
5. Diagnosis is established based on symptoms and the use of specialized autism assessment tools.
6. The disorder also is called infantile autism.

B. Assessment
1. The child experiences a disturbance in the rate and appearance of physical, social, and language skills.
2. The child experiences abnormal responses of body sensations.
3. The child has abnormal ways of relating to persons, objects, and events; the child is self-absorbed and unable to relate to others.
4. The child has no delusions, hallucinations, or incoherence, and the facies is intelligent and responsive.
5. The child may play happily alone for hours but have temper tantrums if interrupted.
6. Language disturbance often includes repetition of previously heard speech (echolalia) and reversal of the pronouns *I* and *you*.
7. If the child can talk, he or she uses speech not for communication but to repeat words or phrases meaninglessly.
8. The child may develop an unusual attachment to a significant object and display frequent rocking, spinning, twirling, or other bizarre behaviors.

C. Interventions
1. Determine the child's routines, habits, and preferences and maintain consistency as much as possible.
2. Determine the specific ways in which the child communicates.
3. Facilitate communication through the use of picture boards.
4. Evaluate the child for safety.
5. Implement safety precautions as necessary for self-injurious behaviors such as head banging.
6. Monitor for stress and anxiety.
7. Avoid placing demands on the child.
8. Initiate referrals to special programs as required.
9. Provide support to parents.

XI. ATTENTION-DEFICIT/HYPERACTIVITY DISORDER

A. Description
1. Developmental disorder characterized by inappropriate degrees of inattention, overactivity, and impulsivity

2. One of the most common reasons for referral of children to mental health services
3. Childhood problems include lowered intellectual development, some minor physical abnormalities, sleeping disturbances, behavioral or emotional disorders, and difficulty in social relationships.
4. Diagnosis is established based on self-reports, parent and teacher reports, and psychological assessments.

B. Assessment
1. Fidgets with hands or feet or squirms in the seat
2. Easily distracted with external or internal stimuli
3. Difficulty with following through on instructions
4. Poor attention span
5. Shifting from one uncompleted activity to another
6. Talking excessively
7. Interrupting or intruding on others
8. Engaging in physically dangerous activities without considering the possible consequences

C. Interventions
1. Provide environmental and physical safety measures.
2. Enhance capabilities and self-esteem.
3. Encourage support groups for parents.
4. Administer prescribed medication; some commonly prescribed medications include methylphenidate hydrochloride (Ritalin), pemoline (Cylert), and dextroamphetamine sulfate (Dexedrine).
5. Instruct the child and parents regarding medication administration.
6. Inform the child and parents that positive effects of the medication may be seen within 1 to 2 weeks if taken as prescribed.

XII. CHILD ABUSE

A. Description: Child **abuse** involves emotional or physical **abuse** or neglect, as well as sexual exploitation or molestation by caretakers or other individuals.

B. Assessment
1. Physical **abuse**
   a. Unexplained bruises, burns, or fractures
   b. Bald spots on the scalp
   c. Apprehensive child
   d. Extreme aggressiveness or withdrawal
   e. Fear of parents
   f. Lack of crying (older infant, toddler, or young preschool child) when approached by a stranger
2. Physical neglect
   a. Inadequate weight gain
   b. Poor hygiene
   c. Consistent hunger

d. Inconsistent school attendance

e. Constant fatigue

f. Reports of lack of child supervision

g. Delinquency

3. Emotional **abuse**

a. Speech disorders

b. Habit disorders such as sucking, biting, and rocking

c. Psychoneurotic reactions

d. **Learning** disorders

e. Suicide attempts

4. Sexual **abuse**

a. Difficulty walking or sitting

b. Torn, stained, or bloody underclothing

c. Pain, swelling, or itching of the genitals

d. Bruises, bleeding, or lacerations in the genital or anal area

e. Unwillingness to change clothes or unwillingness to participate in gym activities

f. Poor peer relations

5. Shaken baby syndrome: Intracranial (usually subdural hemorrhage) trauma caused by violent shaking of a child younger than 1 year

a. Ophthalmoscopic assessment reveals retinal hemorrhages; external signs of trauma are usually absent.

b. Can cause intracranial hemorrhage, leading to cerebral edema and death

c. Full bulging fontanels and head circumference greater than expected are noted.

C. Interventions

1. Support the child during a thorough physical assessment.

2. Assess injuries.

3. Report case of suspected **abuse**; nurses are legally required to report all cases of suspected **abuse** to the appropriate local/state agency.

4. Place the child in an environment that is safe, thereby preventing further injury.

5. Document information related to the suspected **abuse** in an objective manner.

6. Assess parents' strengths and weaknesses, normal coping mechanisms, and presence or absence of support systems.

7. Assist the family in identifying stressors, support systems, and resources.

8. Refer the family to appropriate support groups.

9. If shaken baby syndrome is suspected, monitor the infant's level of consciousness.

XIII. CHILD ABDUCTION

A. Description

1. Child abduction is the kidnapping of a child (or baby) by an older person.

a. A stranger removes a child for criminal or mischievous purposes.

b. A stranger removes a child (usually a baby) to bring up him or her as that person's own child.

c. A parent removes or retains a child from the other parent's care (often in the course of or after divorce proceedings).

2. Around the preschool age, parents are less able to provide the constant protection they once did.

B. Interventions

1. Instruct parents to teach a child basic guidelines about personal safety that include the following:

a. The child is not to go anywhere alone.

b. Always tell an adult where he or she is going and when he or she will return.

c. Say *no* if he or she feels uncomfortable with a situation.

d. Do not give directions to a stranger.

e. Do not talk with strangers or get into their cars.

f. Do not help anyone look for a lost dog or cat and do not accept candy from a stranger.

g. If lost in a store, do not wander around looking for the parent; go at once to a clerk or guard.

2. Children need to learn their full name, address, and parent's name.

3. Watch for posttraumatic stress disorder (PTSD) in any child who has experienced an abduction.

PRACTICE QUESTIONS

1. A child is diagnosed with Reye's syndrome. A nurse develops a nursing care plan for the child and includes which intervention in the plan?

1. Assessing hearing loss

2. Monitoring urine output

3. Changing body position every 2 hours

4. Providing a quiet atmosphere with dimmed lighting

2. A nurse develops a plan of care for a child at risk for generalized tonic-clonic seizures. In the plan of care, the nurse identifies seizure precautions and documents that which items need to be placed at the child's bedside?

1. Emergency cart

2. Airway and a tracheotomy set

3. Oxygen with a tracheotomy set

4. Suctioning equipment and an airway

3. A nurse is caring for a child recently diagnosed with cerebral palsy and the parents of the child ask the nurse about the disorder. The nurse bases her response on the understanding that cerebral palsy is:

1. An infectious disease of the central nervous system.

2. An inflammation of the brain as a result of a viral illness.

3. A congenital condition that results in moderate to severe retardation.
4. A chronic disability characterized by impaired muscle movement and posture.

4. A child with autism is being admitted to the hospital for diagnostic tests. The nurse should assign this child to a:
   1. Private room.
   2. Semiprivate room.
   3. Four-bed ward room.
   4. Contact isolation room.

5. A nurse is assigned to care for an 8-year-old child with a diagnosis of a basilar skull fracture. The nurse reviews the physician's orders and contacts the physician to question which order?
   1. Obtain daily weight.
   2. Suction as needed.
   3. Provide clear liquid intake.
   4. Maintain a patent intravenous line.

6. A lumbar puncture is performed on a child suspected of having bacterial meningitis and cerebrospinal fluid (CSF) is obtained for analysis. A nurse reviews the results of the CSF analysis and determines that which of the following results would verify the diagnosis?
   1. Clear CSF, elevated protein and decreased glucose levels
   2. Clear CSF, decreased pressure, and elevated protein level
   3. Cloudy CSF, elevated protein and decreased glucose levels
   4. Cloudy CSF, decreased protein and decreased glucose levels

7. A nurse is planning care for a child with acute bacterial meningitis. Based on the mode of transmission of this infection, which of the following should be included in the plan of care?
   1. Maintain enteric precautions.
   2. Maintain neutropenic precautions.
   3. No precautions are required as long as antibiotics have been started.
   4. Maintain respiratory isolation precautions for at least 24 hours after the initiation of antibiotics.

8. An emergency room nurse is performing an assessment on a child suspected of being sexually abused. Which assessment data obtained by the nurse most likely support this suspicion?
   1. Poor hygiene
   2. Fear of the parents
   3. Difficulty walking
   4. Bald spots on the scalp

9. A nurse performs an admission assessment on a child and suspects physical abuse. Based on this suspicion, the primary legal nursing responsibility is which of the following?

1. Refer the family to the appropriate support groups.
2. Assist the family in identifying resources and support systems.
3. Report the case in which the abuse is suspected to the local authorities.
4. Document the child's physical assessment findings accurately and thoroughly.

10. A nurse employed in a neonatal intensive care nursery receives a telephone call from the delivery room and is told that a newborn with spina bifida (myelomeningocele type) will be transported to the nursery. The maternity nurse prepares for the arrival of the newborn and places which of the following priority items at the newborn's bedside?
    1. A rectal thermometer
    2. A blood pressure cuff
    3. A specific gravity urinometer
    4. A bottle of sterile normal saline

11. A nurse is performing an assessment of a 7-year-old child who is suspected of having episodes of absence seizures. Which assessment question to the mother will assist in providing information that will identify the symptoms associated with this type of seizure?
    1. "Does twitching occur in the face and neck?"
    2. "Does the muscle twitching occur on one side of the body?"
    3. "Does the muscle twitching occur on both sides of the body?"
    4. "Does the child have a blank expression during these episodes?"

12. A nurse is reviewing the record of a child with increased intracranial pressure and notes that the child has exhibited signs of decerebrate posturing. On assessment of the child, the nurse expects to note which of the following if this type of posturing is present?
    1. Rigid pronation of all extremities
    2. Flaccid paralysis of all extremities
    3. Rigid extension and pronation of the arms and legs
    4. Abnormal flexion of the upper extremities and extension of the lower extremities

13. A nurse is caring for an infant with a diagnosis of hydrocephalus. Preoperatively, a priority nursing intervention is to:
    1. Test the urine for protein.
    2. Reposition the infant frequently.
    3. Provide a stimulating environment.
    4. Obtain blood pressures every 30 minutes.

14. A mother arrives at an emergency room with her 5-year-old child and the mother states that the child fell off a bunk bed. A head injury is suspected, and a nurse is assessing the child continuously for signs of increased intracranial pressure (ICP). Which of

the following is a late sign of increased ICP in this child?

1. Nausea
2. Bradycardia
3. Bulging fontanel
4. Dilated scalp veins

15. A nurse is caring for a newborn infant with spina bifida (myelomeningocele) who is scheduled for surgical closure of the sac. In the preoperative period, the priority nursing diagnosis would be:

1. Risk for infection.
2. Risk for aspiration.
3. Risk for activity intolerance.
4. Risk for altered growth and development.

ALTERNATE ITEM FORMAT: MULTIPLE RESPONSE

A nurse is developing a plan of care for a child who is at risk for seizures. Select all the interventions that apply if the child has a seizure.

❑ 1. Time the seizure.
❑ 2. Restrain the child.
❑ 3. Stay with the child.
❑ 4. Place the child in a prone position.
❑ 5. Move furniture away from the child.
❑ 6. Insert a padded tongue blade in the child's mouth.

ANSWERS

1. 4

Rationale: In Reye's syndrome, supportive care is directed toward monitoring and managing cerebral edema. Decreasing stimuli in the environment by providing a quiet environment with dimmed lighting would decrease the stress on the cerebral tissue and neuron responses. Hearing loss and urine output are not affected. Changing the body position every 2 hours would not affect the cerebral edema directly. The child should be in a head-elevated position to decrease the progression of the cerebral edema and promote drainage of cerebrospinal fluid.

Test-Taking Strategy: Use the process of elimination. Recalling that cerebral edema is a concern for the child with Reye's syndrome will direct you to option 4. If you had difficulty with this question, review the appropriate plan of nursing care for the child with Reye's syndrome.

Level of Cognitive Ability: Application
Client Needs: Physiological Integrity
Integrated Process: Nursing Process—planning
Content Area: Child health
Reference: Wong, D., Hockenberry, M. Wilson, D., et al. (2006). *Maternal child nursing care.* (3rd ed., p. 1702). St. Louis: Mosby.

2. 4

Rationale: Generalized tonic-clonic seizures cause rigidity of all body muscles, followed by intense jerking movements. Because airway obstruction and increased oral secretions can occur during and after the seizure, airway and suctioning equipment are placed at the bedside. A tracheotomy is not performed during a seizure. An emergency cart would not be left at the bedside but would be available in the treatment room or nearby on the nursing unit.

Test-Taking Strategy: Use the process of elimination and note the strategic words *need to be placed at the child's bedside.* Remember that when an option contains two parts, both parts of the option must be correct for the option to be the correct one. Eliminate options 2 and 3 first, knowing that a tracheotomy is not performed. From the remaining options, focusing on the primary concern during seizure activity will direct you to option 4. If you had difficulty with this question, review the plan of care associated with seizure precautions.

Level of Cognitive Ability: Application
Client Needs: Physiological Integrity
Integrated Process: Nursing Process—planning
Content Area: Child health
Reference: Wong, D., Hockenberry, M. Wilson, D., et al. (2006). *Maternal child nursing care.* (3rd ed., p. 1708). St. Louis: Mosby.

3. 4

Rationale: Cerebral palsy is a chronic disability characterized by impaired movement and posture resulting from an abnormality in the extrapyramidal or pyramidal motor system. Meningitis is an infectious process of the central nervous system. Encephalitis is an inflammation of the brain that occurs as a result of viral illness or central nervous system infection. Down syndrome is an example of a congenital condition that results in moderate to severe retardation.

Test-Taking Strategy: Use the process of elimination. Eliminate options 1 and 2 first, noting that they are comparative or alike. Next, note the relationship between the words *palsy* in the question and *impaired muscle movement* in option 4. If you had difficulty with this question, review the characteristics associated with cerebral palsy.

Level of Cognitive Ability: Comprehension
Client Needs: Physiological Integrity
Integrated Process: Teaching and Learning
Content Area: Child health
Reference: Wong, D., Perry, S., Hockenberry, M., et al. (2006). *Maternal child nursing care.* (3rd ed., p. 1842). St. Louis: Mosby.

4. 1

Rationale: Autistic disorder is a complex childhood disorder that involves abnormalities in behavior, social interactions, and communication. Autistic children are unable to relate to persons or to respond to social and emotional cues. Characteristically, these children engage in repetitive behaviors, including head banging, twirling in circles, biting themselves, and flapping their hands or arms. Abnormal communication patterns include verbal and nonverbal communication. A child with autism needs decreased stimulation, with limited visual and auditory distractions. A private room would be the

best environment, allowing for control of visual and auditory distractions. The semiprivate and four-bed ward rooms would be too stimulating for the child with autism. Autism is not a disorder that requires contact isolation.
Test-Taking Strategy: Focus on the child's diagnosis and recall the characteristics associated with this disorder. Providing a structured routine for the child is a priority in the management of autism. A semiprivate room and a four-bed ward room would not allow for a consistent structured routine. The disorder does not require a contact isolation room because it is not contagious. Review the characteristics of autism if you had difficulty with this question.
Level of Cognitive Ability: Analysis
Client Needs: Safe and Effective Care Environment
Integrated Process: Nursing Process—planning
Content Area: Child health
Reference: Wong, D., Hockenberry, M. Wilson, D., et al. (2006). *Maternal-child nursing care* (3rd ed., p. 1279). St. Louis: Mosby.

5. **2**
Rationale: Nasotracheal suctioning is contraindicated in a child with a basilar skull fracture. Because of the nature of the injury, there is a high risk of secondary infection and the probability of the catheter entering the brain through the fracture. Fluid balance is monitored closely by daily weight, intake and output measurement, and serum osmolality determination to detect early signs of water retention, excessive dehydration, and states of hypertonicity or hypotonicity. The child is maintained on an NPO status or restricted to clear liquids until it is determined that vomiting will not occur. An intravenous line is maintained to administer fluids or medications if necessary.
Test-Taking Strategy: Note the strategic words *question which order*. Eliminate options 1, 3, and 4 because they are comparative or alike in that they address the subject of fluids. Remember that nasotracheal suctioning is contraindicated in a child with a skull fracture. If you had difficulty with this question, review the care of a child with this type of a skull fracture.
Level of Cognitive Ability: Analysis
Client Needs: Physiological Integrity
Integrated Process: Nursing Process—implementation
Content Area: Child health
Reference: Hockenberry, M., Wilson, D., & Winkelstein, M. (2005). *Wong's essentials of pediatric nursing* (7th ed., p. 1032). St. Louis: Mosby.

6. **3**
Rationale: Meningitis is an infectious process of the central nervous system caused by bacteria and viruses; it may be acquired as a primary disease or as a result of complications of neurosurgery, trauma, infection of the sinus or ears, or systemic infections. Meningitis is diagnosed by testing cerebrospinal fluid obtained by lumbar puncture. In the case of bacterial meningitis, findings usually include an elevated pressure, turbid or cloudy cerebrospinal fluid, and elevated leukocyte, elevated protein, and decreased glucose levels.
Test-Taking Strategy: Use the process of elimination and knowledge regarding the diagnostic findings in meningitis. Eliminate options 1 and 2 first because clear cerebrospinal fluid is not likely to be found in an infectious process such as

meningitis. From this point, recall that an elevated protein level indicates a possible diagnosis of meningitis to direct you to the correct option. If you had difficulty with this question, review this diagnostic test.
Level of Cognitive Ability: Analysis
Client Needs: Physiological Integrity
Integrated Process: Nursing Process—analysis
Content Area: Child health
Reference: Hockenberry, M., Wilson, D., & Winkelstein, M. (2005). *Wong's essentials of pediatric nursing* (7th ed., p. 1042). St. Louis: Mosby.

7. **4**
Rationale: Meningitis is an infectious process of the central nervous system caused by bacteria and viruses; it may be acquired as a primary disease or as a result of complications of neurosurgery, trauma, infection of the sinus or ears, or systemic infections. A major priority of nursing care for a child suspected of having meningitis is to administer the prescribed antibiotic as soon as it is ordered. The child also is placed on respiratory isolation for at least 24 hours while culture results are obtained and the antibiotic is having an effect. Enteric precautions and neutropenic precautions are not associated with the mode of transmission of meningitis. Enteric precautions are instituted when the mode of transmission is through the gastrointestinal tract. Neutropenic precautions are instituted when a child has a low neutrophil count.
Test-Taking Strategy: Use the process of elimination and knowledge regarding the mode of transmission of meningitis. Eliminate options 1 and 2 first because both enteric and neutropenic precautions are unrelated to the mode of transmission. Recalling that it takes about 24 hours for antibiotics to reach a therapeutic blood level will assist in directing you to option 4. If you had difficulty with this question, review the mode of transmission of meningitis.
Level of Cognitive Ability: Application
Client Needs: Safe and Effective Care Environment
Integrated Process: Nursing Process—planning
Content Area: Child health
Reference: Hockenberry, M., Wilson, D., & Winkelstein, M. (2005). *Wong's essentials of pediatric nursing* (7th ed., p. 1042). St. Louis: Mosby.

8. **3**
Rationale: The most likely assessment findings in sexual abuse include difficulty walking or sitting; torn, stained, or bloody underclothing; pain, swelling, or itching of the genitals; and bruises, bleeding, or lacerations in the genital or anal area. Poor hygiene may indicate physical neglect. Bald spots on the scalp and fear of the parents most likely are associated with physical abuse.
Test-Taking Strategy: Use the process of elimination, noting the strategic words *sexually abused*. The only option that specifically addresses an assessment finding related to sexual abuse is option 3. If you had difficulty with this question, review the assessment findings in a child suspected of being abused.
Level of Cognitive Ability: Analysis
Client Needs: Psychosocial Integrity
Integrated Process: Nursing Process—assessment

Content Area: Child health
Reference: Hockenberry, M., Wilson, D., & Winkelstein, M. (2005). *Wong's essentials of pediatric nursing* (7th ed., pp. 463, 465). St. Louis: Mosby.

9. **3**
Rationale: The primary legal nursing responsibility when child abuse is suspected is to report the case. All states and provinces in North America have laws for mandatory reporting of child maltreatment. Suspected child abuse should be reported to the local authorities. Although documentation of assessment findings, assisting the family, and referring the family to appropriate resources and support groups are important, the primary legal responsibility is to report the suspected case.
Test-Taking Strategy: Use the process of elimination, noting the strategic words *primary* and *legal*. In addition to the many implications associated with child abuse, abuse is a crime. With this in mind, option 3, reporting the case of abuse, is the primary responsibility. If you had difficulty with this question, review the responsibilities of the nurse when child abuse is suspected.
Level of Cognitive Ability: Application
Client Needs: Psychosocial Integrity
Integrated Process: Nursing Process—implementation
Content Area: Child health
Reference: Hockenberry, M., Wilson, D., & Winkelstein, M. (2005). *Wong's essentials of pediatric nursing* (7th ed., p. 466). St. Louis: Mosby.

10. **4**
Rationale: The newborn with spina bifida is at risk for infection before the closure of the sac. A sterile normal saline dressing is placed over the sac to maintain moisture of the sac and its contents. This prevents tearing or breakdown of the skin integrity at the site. Blood pressure may be difficult to assess during the newborn period and is not the best indicator of infection. Urine concentration is not well developed in the newborn stage of development. A thermometer will be needed to assess temperature, but in this newborn the priority is to maintain sterile normal saline dressings over the sac.
Test-Taking Strategy: Focus on the characteristics of spina bifida, the care involved, and the potential complications. Eliminate options 2 and 3 first as unlikely needed items. Recalling that this newborn will have a sac and is at risk for infection will direct you to the correct option from those remaining. Review care of the newborn with spina bifida if you had difficulty with this question.
Level of Cognitive Ability: Application
Client Needs: Physiological Integrity
Integrated Process: Nursing Process—planning
Content Area: Child health
Reference: Wong, D., Hockenberry, M. Wilson, D., et al. (2006). *Maternal-child nursing care* (3rd ed., p. 855). St. Louis: Mosby.

11. **4**
Rationale: Absence seizures are brief episodes of altered awareness. No muscle activity occurs except eyelid fluttering or twitching. The child has a blank facial expression. These seizures last only 5 to 10 seconds, but they may occur one after

another several times a day. Myoclonic seizures are brief random contractions of a muscle group that can occur on one or both sides of the body. Simple partial seizures consist of twitching of an extremity, face, or neck, or the sensation of twitching or numbness in an extremity or face or neck.
Test-Taking Strategy: Focus on the type of seizure identified in the question. Note the relationship between the words *absence seizures* in the question and *blank expression* in the correct option. Review the characteristics of the various types of seizures if you had difficulty with this question.
Level of Cognitive Ability: Analysis
Client Needs: Physiological Integrity
Integrated Process: Nursing Process—assessment
Content Area: Child health
Reference: Hockenberry, M., Wilson, D., & Winkelstein, M. (2005). *Wong's Essentials of pediatric nursing* (7th ed., p. 1048). St. Louis: Mosby.

12. **3**
Rationale: Decerebrate posturing is characterized by the rigid extension and pronation of the arms and legs. Options 1 and 2 are incorrect. Option 4 describes decorticate posturing.
Test-Taking Strategy: Focus on the data in the question. Recalling the clinical manifestations associated with decerebrate posturing will direct you to the correct option. Remember that decerebrate posturing is characterized by the rigid extension and pronation of the arms and legs. Review the characteristics of posturing if you had difficulty with this question.
Level of Cognitive Ability: Analysis
Client Needs: Physiological Integrity
Integrated Process: Nursing Process—assessment
Content Area: Child health
Reference: Hockenberry, M., & Wilson, D. (2007). *Nursing care of infants and children* (8th ed., p. 1622). St. Louis: Mosby.

13. **2**
Rationale: In infants with hydrocephalus, the head grows at an abnormal rate and if the infant is not repositioned frequently, pressure ulcers can occur on the back and side of the head. An egg crate mattress under the head is also a nursing intervention that can help prevent skin breakdown. Proteinuria is not specific to hydrocephalus. Stimulus should be kept at a minimum because of the increase in intracranial pressure. It is not necessary to check the blood pressure every 30 minutes.
Test-Taking Strategy: Focus on the client's diagnosis. Eliminate option 4 because of the words *30 minutes*. From the remaining options, recall that because of the severe head enlargement, the nursing intervention that has priority is to reposition the infant frequently to prevent development of pressure areas. Review the complications associated with hydrocephalus if you had difficulty with this question.
Level of Cognitive Ability: Application
Client Needs: Physiological Integrity
Integrated Process: Nursing Process—implementation
Content Area: Child health
Reference: Hockenberry, M., Wilson, D., & Winkelstein, M. (2005). *Wong's essentials of pediatric nursing* (7th ed., p. 1059). St. Louis: Mosby.

14. 2

Rationale: Late signs of increased intracranial pressure (ICP) include a significant decrease in level of consciousness, bradycardia, and fixed and dilated pupils. A bulging fontanel and dilated scalp veins are early signs of increased ICP and would be noted in an infant, not a 5-year-old child. Nausea is an early sign of increased ICP.

Test-Taking Strategy: Use the process of elimination and note the age of the child and the strategic word *late*. Options 3 and 4 can be eliminated first because these signs would be noted in an infant, not a 5-year-old child. Focusing on the strategic word *late* will direct you to option 2. If you had difficulty with this question, review the early and late signs of increased ICP in an infant and in a child.

Level of Cognitive Ability: Analysis
Client Needs: Physiological Integrity
Integrated Process: Nursing Process—assessment
Content Area: Child health
Reference: Hockenberry, M., Wilson, D., & Winkelstein, M. (2005). *Wong's essentials of pediatric nursing* (7th ed., p. 1013). St. Louis: Mosby.

15. 1

Rationale: Initial care of the newborn with myelomeningocele involves prevention of infection. A sterile normal saline dressing is placed over the sac to maintain moisture of the sac and its contents and to prevent tearing or breakdown of the skin integrity at the site. Any opening in the sac greatly increases the risk of infection of the central nervous system. Activity intolerance and risk for aspiration would not be priority problems with this defect. Risk for altered growth and development is a problem for the infant with myelomeningocele, but preventing infection has priority in the preoperative period.

Test-Taking Strategy: Note the strategic words *preoperative period* and *priority nursing diagnosis*. Use the process of elimination, recalling the importance of prevention of infection in the preoperative period. Eliminate options 2 and 3 first because they would not be risks with this type of disorder. Option 4,

risk for altered growth and development, would be a potential problem for this infant, but it would not be a priority problem over risk for infection. Review preoperative care for the infant with a meningomyelocele if you had difficulty with this question.

Level of Cognitive Ability: Application
Client Needs: Physiological Integrity
Integrated Process: Nursing Process—planning
Content Area: Delegating/Prioritizing
Reference: Hockenberry, M., Wilson, D., & Winkelstein, M. (2005). *Wong's essentials of pediatric nursing* (7th ed., pp. 1197, 1199-1200). St. Louis: Mosby.

ALTERNATE ITEM FORMAT: MULTIPLE RESPONSE

Answer: 1, 3, 5

Rationale: During a seizure, the child is placed on his or her side in a lateral position. Positioning on the side will prevent aspiration because saliva will drain out the corner of the child's mouth. The child is not restrained because this could cause injury to the child. The nurse would loosen clothing around the child's neck and ensure a patent airway. Nothing is placed into the child's mouth during a seizure because this action may cause injury to the child's mouth, gums, or teeth. The nurse would stay with the child to reduce the risk of injury and allow for observation and timing of the seizure.

Test-Taking Strategy: Visualize this clinical situation. Recalling that airway patency and safety is the priority will assist in determining the appropriate interventions. Review care of the child experiencing a seizure if you had difficulty with this question.

Level of Cognitive Ability: Application
Client Needs: Physiological Integrity
Integrated Process: Nursing Process—implementation
Content Area: Child health
Reference: Hockenberry, M., Wilson, D., & Winkelstein, M. (2005). *Wong's essentials of pediatric nursing* (7th ed., p. 1052). St. Louis: Mosby.

REFERENCES

Hockenberry, M. Wilson, D., & Winkelstein, M. (2005). *Wong's essentials of pediatric nursing* (7th ed.). St. Louis: Mosby.

Hockenberry, M., & Wilson, D. (2007). *Nursing care of infants and children* (8th ed.). St. Louis: Mosby.

Kliegman, R., Marcdante, K., Jenson, H., & Behrman, R. (2006). *Nelson essentials of pediatrics* (5th ed.). St. Louis: W.B. Saunders.

McKinney, E., James, S., Murray, S., & Ashwill, J. (2005). *Maternal-child nursing* (2nd ed.). St. Louis: W.B. Saunders.

National Council of State Boards of Nursing (Eds.). (2007). *2007 NCLEX-RN® detailed test plan.* Chicago: Author.

Wong, D., Hockenberry, M, Wilson, D., et al. (2006). *Maternal child nursing care* (3rd ed.). St. Louis: Mosby.

Eye, Ear, and Throat Disorders

I. STRABISMUS

A. Description
1. Called "squint" or "lazy eye"
2. Condition in which the eyes are not aligned because of lack of coordination of the extraocular muscles
3. Most often results from muscle imbalance or paralysis of extraocular muscles but also may result from conditions such as a brain tumor, myasthenia gravis, or infection
4. Normal in the young infant but should not be present after about age 4 months

B. Assessment
1. Amblyopia (reduced visual acuity) if not treated early
2. Permanent loss of vision if not treated early
3. Loss of binocular vision
4. Impairment of depth perception
5. Frequent headaches
6. Squinting or tilting of the head to see

C. Interventions
1. Corrective lenses may be indicated.
2. Instruct the parents regarding patching (occlusion therapy) of the "good" eye to strengthen the weak eye.
3. Injection of botulinum toxin (Botox) may be prescribed (injected into the eye muscle) as a nonsurgical intervention (treatment produces temporary paralysis to allow the muscles opposite the paralyzed muscle to straighten the eye).
4. Inform the parents that the injection of botulinum toxin wears off in about 2 months and, if successful, correction will occur.
5. Prepare for surgery to realign the weak muscles as prescribed if nonsurgical interventions are unsuccessful; this is performed before the age of 2 years.
6. Instruct the parents about the need for follow-up visits.

II. CONJUNCTIVITIS

A. Description
1. Also is known as "pinkeye"; is an inflammation of the conjunctiva
2. Conjunctivitis usually is caused by allergy, infection, or trauma.
3. Bacterial or viral conjunctivitis is extremely contagious.
4. Chlamydial conjunctivitis is rare in older children and, if diagnosed in a child who is not sexually active, the child should be assessed for possible sexual **abuse.**

B. Assessment
1. Itching, burning, or scratchy eyelids
2. Redness
3. Edema
4. Discharge

C. Interventions
1. Instruct in infection control measures such as good hand washing and not sharing towels and washcloths.
2. Administer antibiotic or antiviral eye drops or ointment as prescribed if infection is present.
3. Administer antihistamines as prescribed if an allergy is present.
4. Instruct the child and parents about the administration of the prescribed medications.
5. Instruct the parents that the child should be kept home from school or day care until antibiotic eye drops have been administered for 24 hours.
6. Instruct about the use of cool compresses to lessen irritation and wearing dark glasses for photophobia.
7. Instruct the child to avoid rubbing the eye to prevent injury.

8. Instruct the child who is wearing contact lenses to discontinue wearing them and to obtain new lenses to eliminate the chance of reinfection.
9. Instruct the adolescent that eye makeup should be discarded and replaced.

III. OTITIS MEDIA

A. Description
1. Otitis media is an inflammatory disorder usually caused by an infection of the middle ear occurring as a result of a blocked eustachian tube, which prevents normal drainage.
2. Otitis media is a common complication of an acute respiratory infection.
3. Infants and children are more prone to otitis media because their eustachian tubes are shorter, wider, and straighter.

B. Assessment
1. Fever
2. Irritability and restlessness
3. Loss of appetite
4. Rolling of head from side to side
5. Pulling on or rubbing the ear
6. Earache or pain
7. Signs of hearing loss
8. Purulent ear drainage
9. Red, opaque, bulging, or retracting tympanic membrane

C. Interventions
1. Encourage fluid intake.
2. Teach the parents to feed infants in upright position, to prevent reflux.
3. Instruct the child to avoid chewing as much as possible during the acute period because chewing increases pain.
4. Provide local heat and have the child lie with the affected ear down.
5. Instruct the parents in the appropriate procedure to clean drainage from the ear with sterile cotton swabs.
6. Instruct the parents in the administration of analgesics or antipyretics such as acetaminophen (Tylenol) to decrease fever and pain.
7. Instruct the parents in the administration of the prescribed antibiotics, emphasizing that the 10- to 14-day period is necessary to eradicate infective organisms.
8. Instruct the parents that screening for hearing loss may be necessary.
9. Instruct the parents about the procedure for administering ear medications (Box 36-1; Fig. 36-1).

D. Myringotomy
1. Description: Insertion of tympanoplasty tubes into the middle ear to equalize pressure and keep the ear aerated

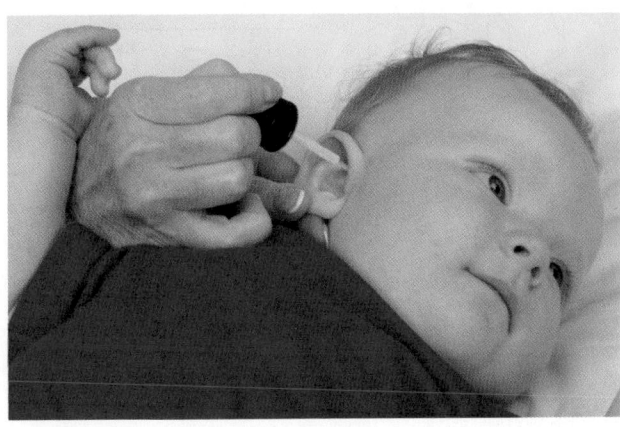

FIG. 36-1 For infants and children younger than 3 years, pull the lobe back and down. (From Lilley, L., Harrington, S., & Snyder, J. [2004]. *Pharmacology and the nursing process* [4th ed.]. St. Louis: Mosby.)

2. Postoperative interventions
   a. Instruct the parents and child to keep the ears dry.
   b. The client should wear earplugs while bathing, shampooing, and swimming,
   c. Diving and submerging under water are not allowed.
   d. Instruct the parents that if the tubes fall out, it is not an emergency, but the physician should be notified.
   e. Parents can administer an analgesic such as acetaminophen (Tylenol) to relieve discomfort following insertion of tympanoplasty tubes.
   f. Parents should be taught that the child should not blow his or her nose for 7 to 10 days after surgery.

IV. TONSILLECTOMY AND ADENOIDECTOMY

A. Description
1. Tonsillitis refers to inflammation and infection of the tonsils (Fig. 36-2).
2. Adenoiditis refers to inflammation and infection of the adenoids.

B. Assessment
1. Persistent or recurrent sore throat
2. Enlarged, bright red tonsils that may be covered with white exudate
3. Difficulty in swallowing
4. Mouth breathing and an unpleasant mouth odor

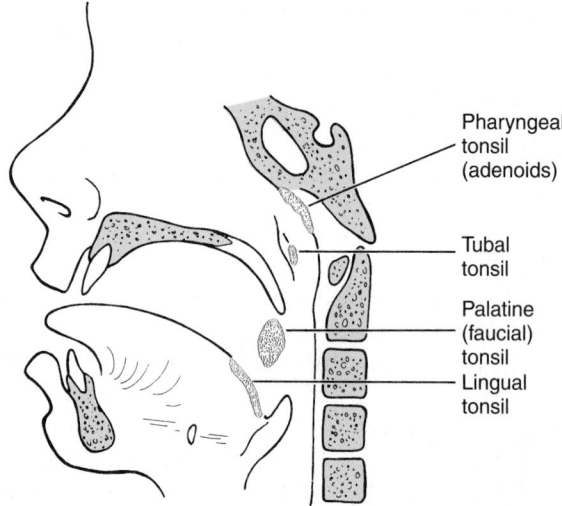

FIG. 36-2 Location of various tonsillar masses. (From Hockenberry, M., Wilson, D., & Winkelstein, M. [2005]. *Wong's essentials of pediatric nursing* [7th ed.]. St. Louis: Mosby.)

Pharyngeal tonsil (adenoids)

Tubal tonsil

Palatine (faucial) tonsil

Lingual tonsil

5. Fever
6. Cough
7. Enlarged adenoids may cause nasal quality of speech, mouth breathing, hearing difficulty, snoring, and/or obstructive sleep apnea.

C. Preoperative interventions
1. Assess for signs of active infection.
2. Assess bleeding and clotting studies because the throat is vascular.
3. Prepare the child for a sore throat postoperatively, and inform the child that he or she will need to drink liquids.
4. Assess for any loose teeth to decrease the risk of aspiration during surgery.

D. Interventions postoperatively
1. Position the child prone or side-lying to facilitate drainage.
2. Have suction equipment available, but do not suction unless there is an airway obstruction.
3. Monitor for signs of hemorrhage (frequent swallowing may indicate hemorrhage); if hemorrhage occurs, turn the child to the side and notify the physician.
4. Discourage coughing or clearing the throat.
5. Provide clear, cool, noncitrus and noncarbonated fluids.
6. Avoid milk products initially because they will coat the throat.
7. Avoid red liquids, which simulate the appearance of blood if the child vomits.
8. Do not give the child any straws, forks, or sharp objects that can be put into the mouth.
9. Administer acetaminophen (Tylenol) for sore throat as prescribed.

10. Instruct the parents to notify the physician if bleeding, persistent earache, or fever occurs.
11. Instruct the parents to keep the child away from crowds until healing has occurred.

V. EPISTAXIS (NOSEBLEEDS)
A. Description
1. The nose, especially the septum, is a highly vascular structure, and bleeding usually results from direct trauma, foreign bodies, and nose picking, or from mucosal inflammation.
2. Recurrent epistaxis and severe bleeding may indicate an underlying disease.

B. Interventions
1. Have the child sit up and lean forward (not lying down).
2. Apply continuous pressure to nose with the thumb and forefinger for at least 10 minutes.
3. Insert cotton or wadded tissue into each nostril, and apply ice or a cold cloth to the bridge of the nose if bleeding persists.
4. Keep the child calm and quiet.
5. If bleeding cannot be controlled, packing or cauterization of the bleeding vessel may be prescribed.

PRACTICE QUESTIONS

1. After a tonsillectomy, a child begins to vomit bright red blood. The initial nursing action is to:
   1. Notify the physician.
   2. Turn the child to the side.
   3. Maintain an NPO status.
   4. Administer the prescribed antiemetic.

2. A day care nurse is observing a 2-year-old child and suspects that the child may have strabismus. Which observation made by the nurse might indicate this condition?
   1. The child has difficulty hearing.
   2. The child consistently tilts the head to see.
   3. The child consistently turns the head to see.
   4. The child does not respond when spoken to.

3. The mother of a 6-year-old child arrives at a clinic because the child has been experiencing scratchy, red, and swollen eyes. The nurse notes a discharge from the eyes and sends a culture to the laboratory for analysis. Chlamydial conjunctivitis is diagnosed. Based on this diagnosis, the nurse determines that which of the following requires further investigation?
   1. Possible trauma
   2. Possible sexual abuse
   3. Presence of an allergy
   4. Presence of a respiratory infection

4. A nurse prepares a teaching plan for a mother of a child diagnosed with bacterial conjunctivitis. Which

of the following, if stated by the mother, indicates a need for further teaching?
1. "I need to wash my hands frequently."
2. "I need to clean the eye as prescribed."
3. "It is okay to share towels and washcloths."
4. "I need to give the eye drops as prescribed."

5. A nurse is reviewing the laboratory results for a child scheduled for tonsillectomy. The nurse determines that which laboratory value is most significant to review?
1. Creatinine level
2. Prothrombin time
3. Sedimentation rate
4. Blood urea nitrogen level

6. A child is scheduled for a tonsillectomy. A nurse plans care, knowing that which of the following would present the highest risk of aspiration during surgery?
1. Difficulty in swallowing
2. Bleeding during surgery
3. Exudate in the throat area
4. Presence of loose teeth

7. A nurse is preparing to care for a child after a tonsillectomy. The nurse documents on the plan of care to place the child in which appropriate position?
1. Supine
2. Side-lying
3. High Fowler's
4. Trendelenburg's

8. After a tonsillectomy, a nurse reviews the physician's postoperative orders. Which of the following physician's orders does the nurse question?
1. Monitor for bleeding.
2. Suction every 2 hours.
3. Give no milk or milk products.
4. Give clear, cool liquids when awake.

9. A nurse is caring for a child after a tonsillectomy. The nurse monitors the child, knowing that which of the following indicates that the child is bleeding?
1. Frequent swallowing
2. A decreased pulse rate
3. Complaints of discomfort
4. An elevation in blood pressure

10. Antibiotics are prescribed for a child after a myringotomy with insertion of tympanostomy tubes and the nurse provides discharge instructions to the parents regarding the administration of the antibiotics. Which statement, if made by the parents, indicates that they understood the instructions?
1. "Administer the antibiotics until they are gone."
2. "Administer the antibiotics if the child has a fever."
3. "Administer the antibiotics until the child feels better."
4. "Begin to taper the antibiotics after 3 days of a full course."

11. A child is scheduled for a tonsillectomy in a day surgical unit. On the day following surgery, the mother calls the surgical unit and expresses concern because the child has a bad mouth odor. Which response is appropriate?
1. "The child probably has an infection."
2. "You need to contact the physician immediately."
3. "Have the child gargle with mouthwash every 4 hours."
4. "Bad mouth odor is normal and may be relieved by drinking more liquids."

ALTERNATE ITEM FORMAT: MULTIPLE RESPONSE

A child has been diagnosed with acute otitis media of the right ear. Which interventions should the nurse include in the plan of care? Select all that apply.
❏ 1. Provide a soft diet.
❏ 2. Position the child on the left side.
❏ 3. Administer an antihistamine twice daily
❏ 4. Irrigate the right ear with normal saline every 8 hours.
❏ 5. Administer acetaminophen (Tylenol) for fever every 4 hours as needed.
❏ 6. Instruct the parents about the need to administer the antibiotics for the full 14-day prescribed course.

ANSWERS

1. **2**
Rationale: After tonsillectomy, if bleeding occurs, the nurse turns the child to the side and then notifies the physician. An NPO status would be maintained, and an antiemetic may be prescribed; however, the initial nursing action would be to turn the child to the side.
Test-Taking Strategy: Use the process of elimination and note the strategic word *initial* in the question. Although all the options may be appropriate to maintain physiological integrity, the initial action is to turn the child to the side. Review care of the postoperative child who vomits if you had difficulty with this question.
Level of Cognitive Ability: Application
Client Needs: Physiological Integrity
Integrated Process: Nursing Process—implementation
Content Area: Delegating/Prioritizing
Reference: McKinney, E., James, S., Murray, S., & Ashwill, J. (2005). *Maternal-child nursing* (2nd ed., p. 1202). St. Louis: W.B. Saunders.

2. **2**

Rationale: Strabismus is a condition in which the eyes are not aligned because of lack of coordination of the extraocular muscles. The nurse may suspect strabismus in a child when the child complains of frequent headaches, squints, or tilts the head to see. Options 1, 3, and 4 are not indicative of this condition.

Test-Taking Strategy: Use the process of elimination. Eliminate options 1 and 4 first because they are comparative or alike. From the remaining options, recall that the child may tilt the head to see to direct you to option 2. Review the signs of strabismus if you had difficulty with this question.

Level of Cognitive Ability: Analysis
Client Needs: Physiological Integrity
Integrated Process: Nursing Process—assessment
Content Area: Child health
Reference: Hockenberry, M., Wilson, D., & Winkelstein, M. (2005). *Wong's essentials of pediatric nursing* (7th ed., p. 611). St. Louis: Mosby.

3. **2**

Rationale: Conjunctivitis is an inflammation of the conjunctiva. A diagnosis of chlamydial conjunctivitis in a child who is not sexually active should signal the health care provider to assess the child for possible sexual abuse. Allergy, infection, and trauma can cause conjunctivitis, but the causative organism is not likely to be chlamydia.

Test-Taking Strategy: Use the process of elimination and note the age of the child and the organism that is identified in the question. This will assist in directing you to option 2. Options 1, 3, and 4 can be recognized as the common causes of conjunctivitis. These options are comparative or alike in that they relate to a physiological problem. Review content related to chlamydial conjunctivitis if you had difficulty with this question.

Level of Cognitive Ability: Analysis
Client Needs: Psychosocial Integrity
Integrated Process: Nursing Process—assessment
Content Area: Child health
Reference: McKinney, E., James, S., Murray, S., & Ashwill, J. (2005). *Maternal-child nursing* (2nd ed., p. 1041). St. Louis: W.B. Saunders.

4. **3**

Rationale: Conjunctivitis is an inflammation of the conjunctiva. Bacterial conjunctivitis is highly contagious, and the nurse should teach infection control measures. These include good hand washing and not sharing towels and washcloths. Options 1, 2, and 4 are correct treatment measures.

Test-Taking Strategy: Use the process of elimination and note the strategic words *need for further teaching*. These words indicate a negative event query and ask you to select an option that is an incorrect statement. Options 1, 2, and 4 can be eliminated by recalling that bacterial conjunctivitis is highly contagious. If you had difficulty with this question, review infection control measures for bacterial conjunctivitis.

Level of Cognitive Ability: Analysis
Client Needs: Safe and Effective Care Environment
Integrated Process: Teaching and Learning
Content Area: Child health

Reference: Hockenberry, M., Wilson, D., & Winkelstein, M. (2005). *Wong's essentials of pediatric nursing* (7th ed., pp. 444-445). St. Louis: Mosby.

5. **2**

Rationale: Because the tonsillar area is so vascular, postoperative bleeding is a concern. The prothrombin time, partial thromboplastin time, platelet count, hemoglobin and hematocrit, white blood cell count, and urinalysis are performed preoperatively. The prothrombin time results would identify a potential for bleeding. The creatinine level, sedimentation rate, and blood urea nitrogen would not determine the potential for bleeding.

Test-Taking Strategy: Focus on the subject of the question. The subject of the question relates to the potential for bleeding. Options 1 and 4 can be eliminated because they relate to kidney function. Similarly, option 3 can be eliminated because it is unrelated to the subject of the question. Review preoperative care of the child scheduled for tonsillectomy if you had difficulty with this question.

Level of Cognitive Ability: Analysis
Client Needs: Physiological Integrity
Integrated Process: Nursing Process—assessment
Content Area: Child health
Reference: McKinney, E., James, S., Murray, S., & Ashwill, J. (2005). *Maternal-child nursing* (2nd ed., p. 1202). St. Louis: W.B. Saunders.

6. **4**

Rationale: In the preoperative period, the child should be observed for the presence of loose teeth to decrease the risk of aspiration during surgery. Options 1 and 3 are incorrect because these are characteristics that may indicate the need for the surgery. Bleeding during surgery will be controlled via packing and suction as needed.

Test-Taking Strategy: Use the process of elimination, noting that the child is scheduled for surgery. The subject of the question relates to aspiration, and note the strategic words *highest risk* in the question. Options 1 and 3 can be eliminated easily because these are characteristics that may indicate the need for the surgery. Recall that the tonsillar area is vascular; bleeding during surgery is expected and would be controlled. Therefore, eliminate option 2. Review preoperative assessment procedures related to tonsillectomy if you had difficulty with this question.

Level of Cognitive Ability: Analysis
Client Needs: Physiological Integrity
Integrated Process: Nursing Process—planning
Content Area: Child health
Reference: Wong, D., Hockenberry, M., Wilson, D., et al. (2006). *Maternal-child nursing care* (3rd ed., p. 1433). St. Louis: Mosby.

7. **2**

Rationale: The child should be placed in a prone or side-lying position following tonsillectomy to facilitate drainage. Options 1, 3, and 4 will not achieve this goal.

Test-Taking Strategy: Use the process of elimination and visualize each of the positions described in the options. Keeping in mind that the goal is to facilitate drainage will direct you to option 2. Review positioning procedures following tonsillectomy if you had difficulty with this question.

Level of Cognitive Ability: Application
Client Needs: Physiological Integrity
Integrated Process: Nursing Process—planning
Content Area: Child health
References: McKinney, E., James, S., Murray, S., & Ashwill, J. (2005). *Maternal-child nursing* (2nd ed., p. 1202). St. Louis: W.B. Saunders.
Wong, D., Hockenberry, M., Wilson, D., et al. (2006). *Maternal-child nursing care* (3rd ed., p. 1433). St. Louis: Mosby.

8. **2**
Rationale: After tonsillectomy, suction equipment should be available, but suctioning is not performed unless there is an airway obstruction because of the risk of trauma to the oropharynx. Monitoring for bleeding is an important nursing intervention following any type of surgery. Milk and milk products are avoided initially because they coat the throat, cause the child to clear the throat, and increase the risk of bleeding. Clear, cool liquids are encouraged.
Test-Taking Strategy: Focus on the subject, the order that the nurse questions. Option 1 can be eliminated first because this is a nursing action, not a medical order. From the remaining options, consider the anatomical location of the surgery. This should direct you to option 2. Review postoperative care following tonsillectomy if you had difficulty with this question.
Level of Cognitive Ability: Analysis
Client Needs: Physiological Integrity
Integrated Process: Nursing Process—implementation
Content Area: Child health
Reference: Hockenberry, M., & Wilson, D. (2007). *Nursing care of infants and children* (8th ed., pp. 1322-1323). St. Louis: Mosby.

9. **1**
Rationale: Frequent swallowing, restlessness, a fast and thready pulse, and vomiting bright red blood are signs of bleeding. An elevated blood pressure and complaints of discomfort are not indications of bleeding.
Test-Taking Strategy: Use the concepts related to the signs of shock to assist in answering the question. These concepts should assist in eliminating options 2 and 4. From the remaining options, recalling that discomfort does not indicate bleeding will direct you to option 1. Review the signs of bleeding after tonsillectomy if you had difficulty with this question.
Level of Cognitive Ability: Analysis
Client Needs: Physiological Integrity
Integrated Process: Nursing Process—assessment
Content Area: Child health
Reference: McKinney, E., James, S., Murray, S., & Ashwill, J. (2005). *Maternal-child nursing* (2nd ed., p. 1202). St. Louis: W.B. Saunders.

10. **1**
Rationale: A myringotomy is the insertion of tympanoplasty tubes into the middle ear to equalize pressure and keep the ear aerated. The nurse must instruct parents regarding the administration of antibiotics. Antibiotics need to be taken as prescribed, and the full course needs to be completed. Options 2, 3, and 4 are incorrect. Antibiotics are not tapered but are administered for the full course of therapy.

Test-Taking Strategy: Use the process of elimination and recall that antibiotics must be taken for the full course, regardless of whether the child is feeling better. Noting the strategic words *understood the instructions* will assist in directing you to option 1. Review concepts related to the administration of antibiotics if you had difficulty with this question.
Level of Cognitive Ability: Analysis
Client Needs: Physiological Integrity
Integrated Process: Nursing Process—evaluation
Content Area: Child health
Reference: Wong, D., Hockenberry, M., Wilson, D., et al. (2006). *Maternal child nursing care* (3rd ed., p. 1435). St. Louis: Mosby.

11. **4**
Rationale: Bad mouth odor is normal following tonsillectomy and may be relieved by drinking more liquids. Options 1, 2, and 3 are incorrect. In addition, mouthwash gargles (option 3) will irritate the throat.
Test-Taking Strategy: Use the process of elimination. Eliminate option 3 first, knowing that mouthwash gargles will irritate the surgical site. Options 1 and 2 are comparative or alike and will cause additional concern in the mother. Review postoperative expectations following tonsillectomy if you had difficulty with this question.
Level of Cognitive Ability: Application
Client Needs: Health Promotion and Maintenance
Integrated Process: Nursing Process—implementation
Content Area: Child health
Reference: Hockenberry, M., Wilson, D., & Winkelstein, M. (2005). *Wong's essentials of pediatric nursing* (7th ed., p. 637). St. Louis: Mosby.

ALTERNATE ITEM FORMAT: MULTIPLE RESPONSE

Answer: 1, 5, 6
Rationale: Acute otitis media is usually an infectious inflammation of the middle ear. The child will often have fever, pain, loss of appetite, and possible ear drainage. The child's fever should be treated with acetaminophen (Tylenol). The child is positioned on his or her affected side to facilitate drainage. A soft diet is recommended during the acute stage to avoid pain that can occur with chewing. Antibiotics are prescribed to treat the bacterial infection and should be administered for the full 10- to 14-day prescribed course. The ear should not be irrigated with normal saline because it can further exacerbate the inflammation. Antihistamines are not recommended.
Test-Taking Strategy: Focus on the child's diagnosis. Think about the pathophysiology associated with the disorder and the associated manifestations to select the correct options. Review the nursing interventions for acute otitis media if you had difficulty with this question.
Level of Cognitive Ability: Application
Client Needs: Physiological Integrity
Integrated Process: Nursing Process—planning
Content Area: Child health
Reference: Hockenberry, M., & Wilson, D. (2007). *Wong's nursing care of infants and children* (8th ed., p. 1328). St. Louis: Mosby.

REFERENCES

Hockenberry, M. Wilson, D., & Winkelstein, M. (2005). *Wong's essentials of pediatric nursing* (7th ed.). St. Louis: Mosby.

Hockenberry, M., & Wilson, D. (2007). *Nursing care of infants and children* (8th ed.). St. Louis: Mosby.

Kliegman, R., Marcdante, K., Jenson, H., Behrman, R. (2006). *Nelson essentials of pediatrics* (5th ed.). St. Louis: W.B. Saunders.

McKinney, E., James, S., Murray, S., & Ashwill, J. (2005). *Maternal-child nursing* (2nd ed.). St. Louis: W.B. Saunders.

National Council of State Boards of Nursing (Eds.). (2007). *2007 NCLEX-RN® detailed test plan.* Chicago: Author.

Wong, D., Hockenberry, M. Wilson, D., et al. (2006). *Maternal-child nursing care* (3rd ed.). St. Louis: Mosby.

Respiratory Disorders

I. EPIGLOTTITIS

A. Description
1. Bacterial form of croup.
2. Inflammation of the epiglottis occurs, which may be caused by *Haemophilus influenzae* type b or *Streptococcus pneumoniae*
3. Occurs most frequently between 2 to 5 years of age
4. The onset is abrupt, and the condition occurs most often in the winter.
5. Considered an emergency situation

B. Assessment
1. High fever
2. Sore, red, and inflamed throat (large, cherry red, edematous epiglottis) (Fig. 37-1)
3. Absence of spontaneous cough
4. Drooling
5. Difficulty in swallowing
6. Muffled voice
7. Inspiratory **stridor** aggravated by the supine position
8. Tachycardia
9. Tachypnea progressing to more severe respiratory distress
   a. Hypoxia
   b. Hypercapnia
   c. Respiratory acidosis
   d. Decreased level of consciousness
   e. Decreased muscle tone
   f. Sudden death
10. Agitation
11. Tripod positioning: while supporting the body with the hands, the child thrusts the chin forward and opens the mouth in an attempt to widen the airway.

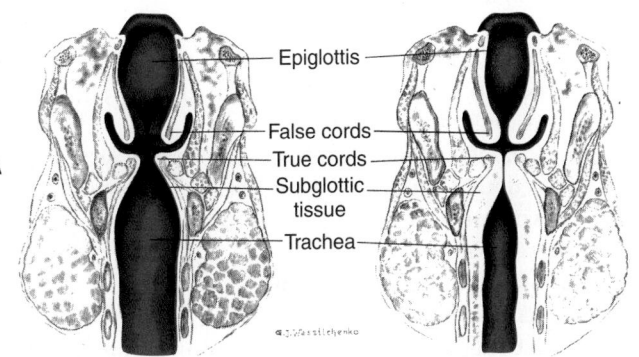

FIG. 37-1   A, Normal larynx. **B,** Obstruction and narrowing resulting from edema of croup. (From Hockenberry, M., & Wilson, D. [2007]. *Wong's nursing care of infants and children* [8th ed.]. St. Louis: Mosby.)

C. Interventions
1. Maintain a patent airway.
2. Assess respiratory status and breath sounds, noting **nasal flaring,** the use of accessory muscles, and the presence of **stridor.**
3. Assess temperature by the axillary route, not the oral route.
4. To prevent spasm of the epiglottis and airway occlusion, no attempts should be made to visualize the posterior pharynx, obtain a throat culture, or take an oral temperature.
5. Prepare the child for lateral neck films to confirm the diagnosis.
6. Maintain an NPO status.
7. Do not leave the child unattended.
8. Do not force the child to lie down.
9. Do not restrain the child.
10. Administer intravenous fluids as prescribed.

11. Administer intravenous antibiotics as prescribed; these are usually followed by oral antibiotics to complete a 7 to 10 day course.
12. Administer analgesics and antipyretics (acetaminophen [Tylenol]) to reduce fever and throat pain as prescribed.
13. Administer corticosteroids (prednisone [Deltasone]) to decrease inflammation as prescribed.
14. Provide cool mist oxygen therapy as prescribed.
15. Provide high humidification to cool the airway and decrease swelling.
16. Have resuscitation equipment available, and prepare for endotracheal intubation or tracheotomy for severe respiratory distress.
17. Ensure that the child is up to date with the immunization schedule, including *Haemophilus influenzae* type b (Hib) conjugate **vaccine**.

II. LARYNGOTRACHEOBRONCHITIS

A. Description
1. Inflammation of the larynx, trachea, and bronchi
2. Most common type of croup; may be viral or bacterial; most frequently occurs in children younger than 5 years
3. Characterized by gradual onset that may be preceded by an upper respiratory infection
B. Assessment (Box 37-1)
C. Interventions
1. Maintain a patent airway.
2. Assess respiratory status, monitoring for **nasal flaring**, sternal **retraction**, and inspiratory **stridor** (Fig. 37-2)
3. Monitor oxygen saturation as prescribed.
4. Monitor for pallor or **cyanosis.**
5. Elevate the head of the bed and provide bed rest.
6. Provide humidified oxygen via a cool mist tent for the hospitalized child.
7. Instruct the parents to use a cool air vaporizer or humidifier at home; other measures include having the child breathe in the cool night air or the air from an open freezer, or taking the child to a cool basement or garage.
8. Provide and encourage fluid intake; intravenous fluids may be prescribed to maintain hydration status if the child is unable to take fluids orally.
9. Administer acetaminophen (Tylenol) as prescribed to reduce fever.
10. Avoid cough syrups, such as guaifenesin (Robitussin) and cold medicines, which may dry and thicken secretions.
11. Administer bronchodilators if prescribed to relax smooth muscle and relieve **stridor.**
12. Administer corticosteroids such as prednisone (Deltasone) if prescribed for the anti-inflammatory effect.

BOX 37-1

Progression of Symptoms in Laryngotracheobronchitis

STAGE I
Low-grade fever
Fear
Seal bark and brassy cough
Inspiratory stridor
Irritability and restlessness

STAGE II
Continuous respiratory stridor
Retractions
Use of accessory muscles
Crackles and wheezing
Labored respirations

STAGE III
Restlessness
Anxiety
Pallor
Diaphoresis
Tachypnea
Signs of anoxia and hypercapnia

STAGE IV
Intermittent cyanosis progressing to permanent cyanosis
Apneic episodes progressing to cessation of breathing

Modified from Hockenberry, M., & Wilson, D. (2007). *Wong's nursing care of infants and children.* (8th ed.). St. Louis: Mosby.

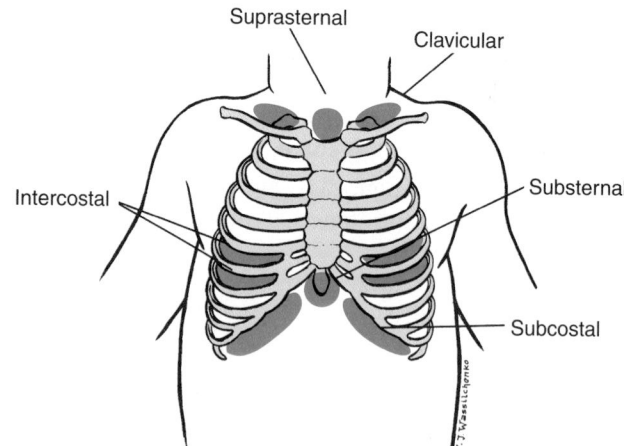

FIG. 37-2 Location of retractions. (From Hockenberry, M., & Wilson, D. [2007]. *Wong's nursing care of infants and children* [8th ed.]. St. Louis: Mosby.)

13. Administer nebulized epinephrine (racemic epinephrine) as prescribed; may be prescribed for children with severe disease, **stridor** at rest, **retractions,** or difficulty breathing.
14. Administer antibiotics as prescribed, noting that they are not indicated unless a bacterial infection is present.

15. Have resuscitation equipment available.
16. Provide appropriate reassurance and education to the parents or caregivers.

III. BRONCHITIS

A. Description
1. Infection of the major bronchi; may be referred to as tracheobronchitis
2. Usually occurs in association with an upper respiratory infection (URI)
3. Mild, self-limiting disorder; causative agent most often viral
B. Assessment
1. Fever
2. Dry, hacking, and nonproductive cough that is worse at night and becomes productive in 2 to 3 days
C. Interventions
1. Treat the symptoms as needed
2. Monitor for respiratory distress.
3. Provide cool, humidified air.
4. Monitor for signs of dehydration, such as a sunken fontanel, nonelastic skin turgor, decreased and concentrated urinary output, dry mucous membranes, and decreased tear production.
5. Encourage increased fluid intake.
6. Administer acetaminophen (Tylenol) for fever as prescribed.
7. Administer cough suppressants such as guaifenesin (Robitussin) as prescribed.

IV. BRONCHIOLITIS AND RESPIRATORY SYNCYTIAL VIRUS (RSV)

A. Description
1. This is an inflammation of the bronchioles that causes a production of thick mucus that occludes bronchiole tubes and small bronchi.
2. Respiratory syncytial virus is a common cause of bronchiolitis.
3. Respiratory syncytial virus, although not airborne, is highly communicable and is usually transferred by direct contact with respiratory secretions.
4. Occurs primarily in the winter and spring
5. Rare in children older than 2 years, with a peak incidence at approximately 6 months of age
B. Assessment (Box 37-2)
C. Interventions
1. Maintain a patent airway.
2. Position the child at a 30- to 40-degree angle with the neck slightly extended to maintain an open airway and decrease pressure on the diaphragm.
3. Provide cool, humidified oxygen.
4. Monitor oxygen saturation as prescribed.
5. Encourage fluids; fluids administered intravenously may be necessary until the acute stage has passed.

BOX 37-2

Assessment: Respiratory Syncytial Virus

INITIAL MANIFESTATIONS
Rhinorrhea
Pharyngitis
Coughing
Wheezing
Intermittent fever

MANIFESTATIONS AS THE DISEASE PROGRESSES
Increased coughing and wheezing
Signs of air hunger
Tachypnea and retractions
Periods of cyanosis

MANIFESTATIONS IN SEVERE ILLNESS
Tachypnea more than 70 breaths/min
Decreased breath sounds and poor air exchange
Listlessness
Apneic episodes

Modified from Hockenberry, M., & Wilson, D. (2007). *Wong's nursing care of infants and children* (8th ed.). St. Louis: Mosby.

---

6. Assess for signs of dehydration, such as a sunken fontanel, nonelastic skin turgor, decreased and concentrated urinary output, dry mucous membranes, and decreased tear production.
D. The child with RSV
1. Isolate the child in a single room or place in a room with another child with RSV.
2. Maintain effective hand-washing procedures.
3. Ensure that nurses caring for these children do not care for other high-risk children.
4. Wear gowns when soiling of clothing may occur during care.
5. Administer ribavirin (Virazole), an antiviral medication, if prescribed (Box 37-3).
6. Prepare for the administration of respiratory syncytial virus immune globulin (RSV-IG or RespiGam) or palivizumab (Synagis).
   a. Used prophylactically to prevent RSV in high-risk infants
   b. Not administered to infants or children with congenital heart disease or cyanotic heart disease

V. PNEUMONIA

A. Description
1. Inflammation of the pulmonary parenchyma and/or alveoli caused by a virus, mycoplasmal agents, bacteria, or aspiration of foreign substances
2. The causative agent usually is introduced into the lungs through inhalation or from the bloodstream.
3. Viral pneumonia occurs more frequently than bacterial pneumonia and often is associated with a viral upper respiratory infection.

4. Primary atypical pneumonia *(Mycoplasma pneumoniae)* is a common cause of pneumonia in children between the ages of 5 and 12 years.
   a. Occurs primarily in the fall and winter months
   b. More prevalent in crowded living conditions
5. Bacterial pneumonia is often a serious infection requiring hospitalization when pleural effusion or empyema accompanies the disease; hospitalization is also necessary for children with staphylococcal pneumonia.
6. Aspiration pneumonia occurs when food, secretions, liquids, or other materials enter the lung and cause inflammation and a chemical pneumonitis. Classic symptoms include an increasing cough or fever with foul-smelling sputum, deteriorating results on chest x-rays, and other signs of airway involvement.

B. Viral pneumonia
   1. Assessment
      a. Acute or insidious onset
      b. Symptoms range from mild fever, slight cough, and malaise to high fever, severe cough, and diaphoresis
      c. Nonproductive or productive cough of small amounts of whitish sputum
      d. Wheezes or fine **crackles**
   2. Interventions
      a. Treatment is symptomatic.
      b. Administer oxygen with cool mist as prescribed.
      c. Increase fluid intake.
      d. Administer antipyretics (acetaminophen [Tylenol]) for fever as prescribed.
      e. Administer chest physiotherapy and postural drainage as prescribed.

C. Primary atypical pneumonia
   1. Assessment
      a. Acute or insidious onset
      b. Fever (lasting several days to 2 weeks), chills, anorexia, headache, malaise, and myalgia (muscle pain)
      c. Rhinitis, sore throat, and dry, hacking cough
      d. Nonproductive cough initially progressing to

the production of seromucoid sputum that becomes mucopurulent or blood-streaked
   2. Interventions
      a. Treatment is symptomatic.
      b. Recovery generally occurs in 7 to 10 days.

D. Bacterial pneumonia
   1. Assessment
      a. Acute onset
      b. Infant: Irritability, lethargy, poor feeding; abrupt fever (may be accompanied by seizures); respiratory distress (air hunger, tachypnea, and circumoral **cyanosis**)
      c. Older child: Headache, chills, abdominal pain, chest pain, meningeal symptoms (meningism)
      d. Hacking, nonproductive cough
      e. Diminished breath sounds or scattered **crackles**
      f. With consolidation, decreased breath sounds are more pronounced.
      g. As the infection resolves, the cough becomes productive and the child expectorates purulent sputum; coarse **crackles** and **wheezing** are noted.
   2. Interventions
      a. Antimicrobial therapy is initiated as soon as the diagnosis is suspected; in the hospitalized infant or child, intravenous antibiotics are usually prescribed.
      b. Administer oxygen for respiratory distress as prescribed and monitor oxygen saturation (Table 37-1).
      c. Place the child in a cool mist tent as prescribed; cool humidification moistens the airways and assists in temperature reduction.
      d. Suction mucus from the infant to maintain a patent airway if the infant is unable to handle secretions.
      e. Administer chest physiotherapy and postural drainage every 4 hours as prescribed (Fig. 37-3).
      f. Promote bed rest to conserve energy.
      g. Encourage the child to lie on the affected side (if pneumonia is unilateral) to splint the chest and reduce the discomfort caused by pleural rubbing.
      h. Encourage fluid intake (administer cautiously to prevent aspiration); intravenously administered fluids may be necessary.
      i. Administer antipyretics (acetaminophen [Tylenol]) for fever as prescribed.
      j. Monitor temperature frequently because of the risk for febrile seizures.
      k. Institute isolation precautions with pneumococcal or staphylococcal pneumonia (according to agency policy).

TABLE 37-1

Advantages and Disadvantages of Various Oxygen Delivery Systems

Systems	Advantages	Disadvantages
Oxygen mask	Various sizes available; delivers higher O_2 concentration than cannula Able to provide a predictable concentration of oxygen (with Venturi mask) whether child breathes through nose or mouth	Skin irritation Fear of suffocation Accumulation of moisture on face Possibility of aspiration of vomitus Difficulty in controlling O_2 concentrations (except with Venturi mask)
Nasal cannula	Provides low-moderate O_2 concentration (22%-40%) Child able to eat and talk while getting O_2 Possibility of more complete observation of child because nose and mouth remain unobstructed	Must have patent nasal passages May cause abdominal distention and discomfort or vomiting Difficulty controlling O_2 concentrations if child breathes through mouth Inability to provide mist if desired
Oxygen tent	Provides lower O_2 concentrations (Fio_2 up to 0.3-0.5) Child able to receive desired inspired O_2 concentrations, even while eating	Necessity for tight fit around bed to prevent leakage of oxygen Cool and wet tent environment Poor access to child; inspired O_2 levels fall when tent is entered
Oxygen hood, face tent	Provides high O_2 concentrations (Fio_2 up to 1.00) Free access to patient's chest for assessment	High-humidity environment Need to remove child for feeding and care

From Hockenberry, M., & Wilson, D. (2007). *Wong's nursing care of infants and children* (8th ed.). St. Louis: Mosby.

l. Administer antitussives such as guaifenesin (Robitussin) as prescribed before rest times and meals if the cough is disturbing.

m. Continuous closed chest drainage may be instituted if purulent fluid is present (usually noted in *Staphylococcus* infections).

n. Fluid accumulation in the pleural cavity may be removed by thoracentesis; thoracentesis also provides a means for obtaining fluid for culture and for instilling antibiotics directly into the pleural cavity.

VI. ASTHMA

A. Description
1. Asthma is a chronic inflammatory disease of the airways (see Chap. 57 for additional information about this disorder).
2. Asthma commonly is caused by physical and chemical irritants such as foods, pollens, dust mites, cockroaches, smoke, animal dander, temperature changes, respiratory infection, activity, and stress.
3. The allergic reaction in the airways can cause an immediate reaction, with obstruction occurring, and it can precipitate a late bronchial obstructive reaction several hours after the initial exposure.
4. Mast cell release of histamine leads to a bronchoconstrictive process.
5. A common symptom is coughing in the absence of respiratory infection, especially at night.

6. Status asthmaticus
   a. Child displays respiratory distress despite vigorous treatment measures.
   b. Status asthmaticus is a medical emergency that can result in respiratory failure and death if left untreated.
B. Assessment
1. Child has episodes of **wheezing,** breathlessness, dyspnea, chest tightness, and cough, particularly at night and/or in the early morning.
2. Child may present with **prodromal** itching localized at the front of the neck or over the upper part of the back.
3. Exacerbations are episodes of progressively worsening shortness of breath, cough, **wheezing,** chest tightness, decreases in expiratory airflow secondary to bronchospasm, mucosal edema, and mucous plugging; air is trapped behind occluded or narrow airways, and hypoxemia can occur.
4. Asthmatic episode
   a. The episode begins with irritability, restlessness, headache, feeling tired, and/or chest tightness.
   b. Respiratory symptoms include a hacking, irritable, nonproductive cough caused by bronchial edema.
   c. Accumulated secretions stimulate the cough; the cough becomes rattling and there is production of frothy, clear, gelatinous sputum.
   d. The child experiences **retractions.**
   e. Hyperresonance on percussion of the chest is noted.

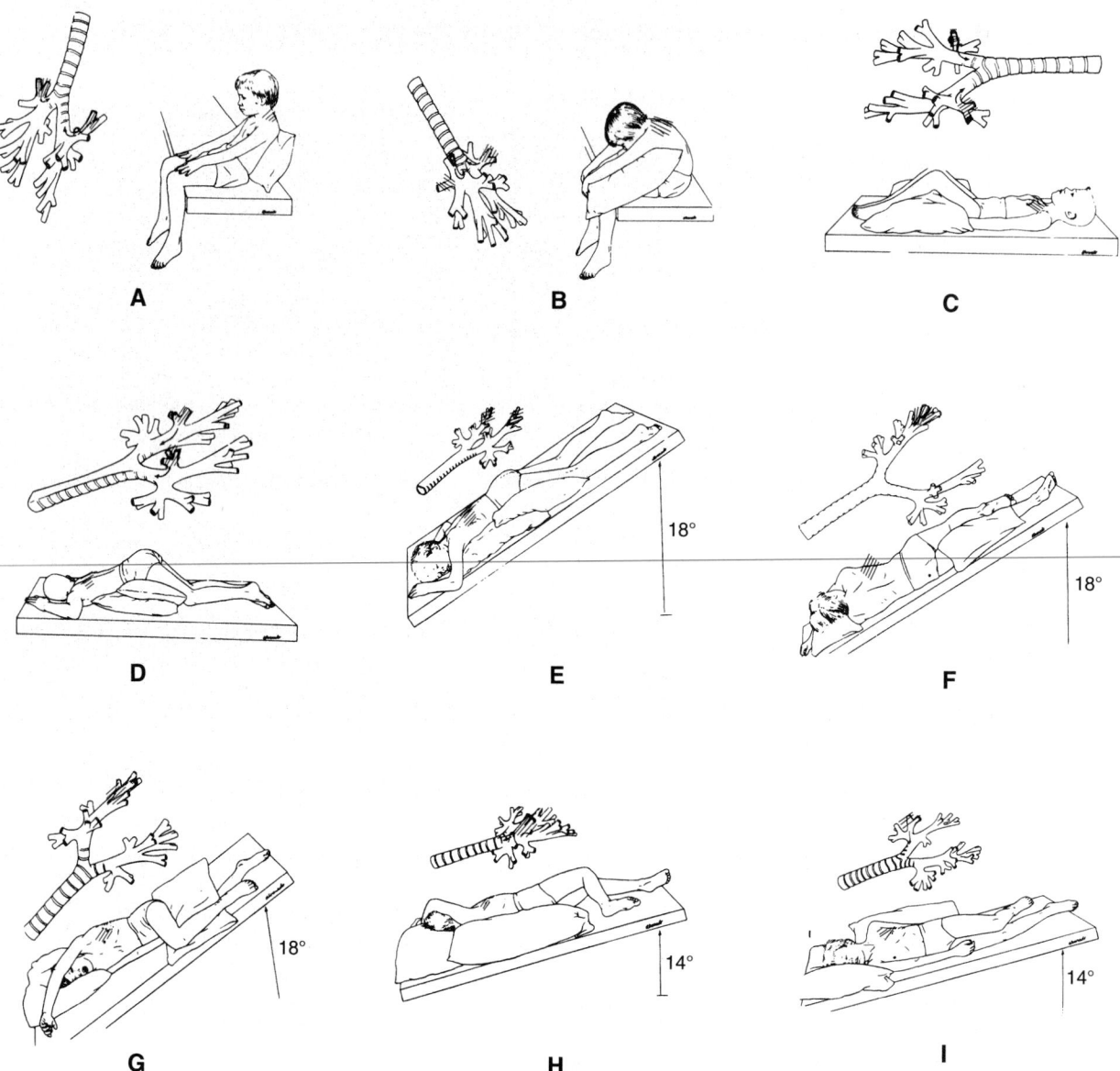

FIG. 37-3 Bronchial drainage positions for all major child lung segments. For each position, model of bronchial tree is projected beside child to show segmental bronchus *(striped)* being drained and pathway of secretions out of bronchus. Drainage platform is horizontal unless otherwise noted. *Striped area* on child's chest indicates area to be cupped or vibrated by therapist. **A,** Apical segment of right upper lobe and apical subsegment of apical-posterior segment of left upper lobe. **B,** Posterior segment of right upper lobe and posterior subsegment of apical-posterior segment of left upper lobe. **C,** Anterior segments of both upper lobes; child should be rotated slightly away from side being drained. **D,** Superior segments of both lower lobes. **E,** Posterior basal segments of both lower lobes. **F,** Lateral basal segments of right lower lobe; right anterior basal segment would be drained by mirror image of this position (left side down). **G,** Anterior basal segment of left lower lobe; right anterior basal segment would be drained by mirror image of this position (left side down). **H,** Medial and lateral segments of right middle lobe. **I,** Lingular segments (superior and inferior) of left upper lobe (homologue of right middle lobe). (From Hockenberry, M., & Wilson, D. [2007]. *Wong's nursing care of infants and children* [8th ed.]. St. Louis: Mosby, p. 1290.)

f. Breath sounds are coarse and loud, with **crackles,** coarse rhonchi, and inspiratory and expiratory **wheezing;** expiration is prolonged.

g. Exercise-induced bronchospasm—cough, shortness of breath, chest pain or tightness, **wheezing,** and endurance problems occur during exercise.

h. Severe spasm or obstruction—breath sounds and **crackles** may become inaudible, and the cough is ineffective (represents a lack of air movement).

i. Ventilatory failure and asphyxia—shortness of breath, with air movement in the chest restricted to the point of absent breath sounds accompanied by a sudden rise in the respiratory rate.

j. Child may be pale or flushed, and the lips may have a deep, dark red color that may progress to **cyanosis** observed in the nail beds and skin, especially around the mouth.

k. Restlessness, apprehension, and diaphoresis occur.

l. Younger children assume the tripod sitting position; older children sit upright, with the shoulders in a hunched-over position, the hands on the bed or a chair, and the arms braced to facilitate the use of the accessory muscles of breathing (child refuses to lie down).

m. Child speaks in short, broken phrases.

C. Interventions: Acute episode (Box 37-4)

D. Medications

1. Quick-relief (rescue medications): To treat symptoms and exacerbations (Box 37-5)

2. Long-term control (preventer medications): To achieve and maintain control of inflammation (Box 37-6)

3. Nebulizer, metered-dose inhaler (MDI) or peak expiratory flowmeters may be used to administer medications; if the child has difficulty using the MDI, medication can be administered by nebulization (medication is mixed with saline and then nebulized with compressed air by a machine).

E. Chest physiotherapy (see Fig. 37-3)

1. Chest physiotherapy includes clapping, vibration, postural drainage, suctioning, and breathing exercises.

2. Chest physiotherapy is not recommended during an acute exacerbation.

F. Allergen control

1. Prevention and reduction of exposure to airborne and environmental allergens

2. Skin testing to identify allergens; immunotherapy (hyposensitization) is not recommended for allergens that can be eliminated effectively.

BOX 37-4

Interventions in the Event of an Acute Asthma Attack

Assess airway patency.
Administer humidified oxygen by nasal prongs or face mask.
Administer quick relief (rescue) medications.
Continuously monitor respiratory status, pulse oximetry, and color; be alert to decreased wheezing or a silent chest, which may signal the inability to move air.
Initiate an intravenous line and prepare to correct dehydration, acidosis, and/or electrolyte imbalances.
Prepare the child for a chest radiograph.
Prepare to obtain samples for determining arterial blood gas and serum electrolyte levels.

BOX 37-5

Quick Relief (Rescue Medications)

Short-acting β_2 agonists
Anticholinergics (for relief of acute bronchospasm)
Systemic corticosteroid(s) (for its anti-inflammatory action to treat reversible airflow obstruction)

BOX 37-6

Long-Term Control (Preventer Medications)

Corticosteroids
Antiallergic medications
Nonsteroidal anti-inflammatory drugs
Long-acting β_2 agonists
Leukotriene modifiers to prevent bronchospasm and inflammatory cell infiltration
Long-acting bronchodilators

G. Home care measures

1. Instruct the family in measures to eliminate allergens.

2. Avoid extremes of environmental temperature; in cold temperatures, instruct the child to breathe through the nose, not the mouth, and to cover the nose and mouth with a scarf.

3. Avoid exposure to individuals with a respiratory infection.

4. Instruct the child and family in how to recognize early symptoms of an asthma attack.

5. Instruct the child and family how to administer medications as prescribed.

6. Instruct the child and family how to use a nebulizer, MDI, or peak expiratory flowmeter.

7. Instruct the child and family about the importance of home monitoring of the peak expiratory flow rate; a decrease in the expiratory flow rate may indicate impending infection or exacerbation.

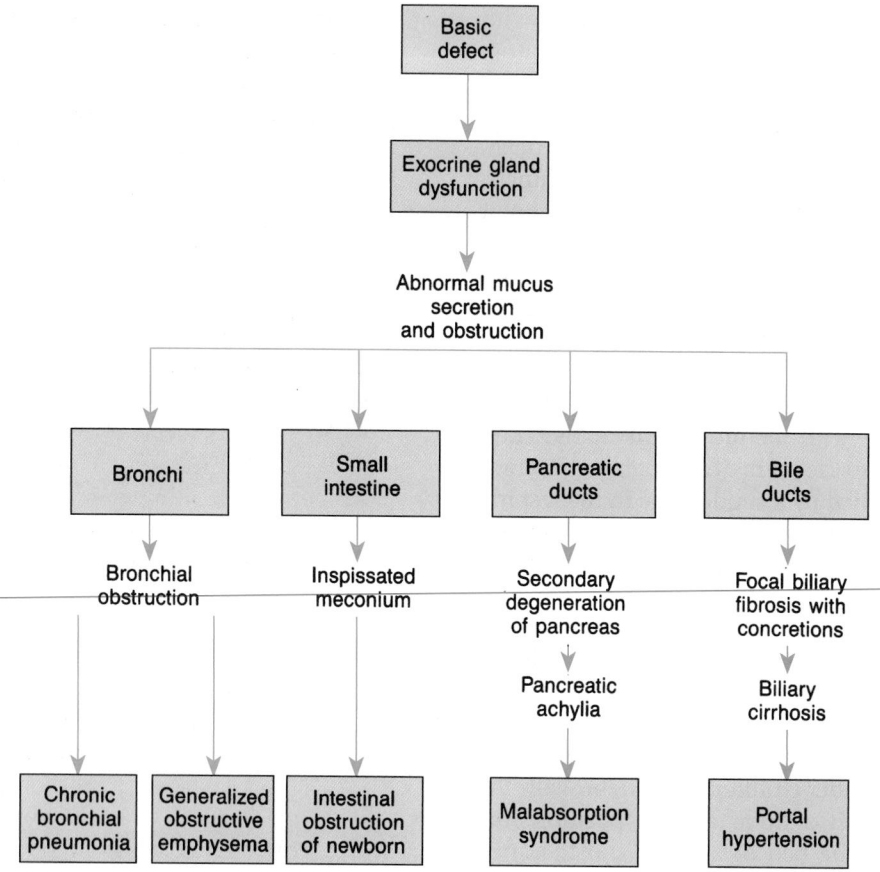

FIG. 37-4 Various effects of exocrine gland dysfunction in cystic fibrosis. (From Hockenberry, M., & Wilson, D. [2007]. *Wong's nursing care of infants and children* [8th ed.]. St. Louis: Mosby.)

8. Instruct the child in the cleaning of devices used for inhaled medications (oral candidiasis can occur with the use of aerosolized steroids).
9. Encourage adequate rest, sleep, and a well-balanced diet.
10. Instruct the child in the importance of adequate fluid intake to liquefy secretions.
11. Assist in developing an exercise program.
12. Instruct the child in the procedure for respiratory treatments and exercises as prescribed.
13. Encourage the child to cough effectively.
14. Encourage the parents to keep immunizations up to date; annual influenza vaccinations may also be recommended.
15. Inform other health care providers and school personnel of the asthma condition.
16. Allow the child to take control of self-care measures based on age appropriateness.

VII. CYSTIC FIBROSIS (CF)
A. Description (Fig. 37-4)
1. This is a chronic multisystem disorder (autosomal recessive trait disorder) characterized by exocrine gland dysfunction.

2. The mucus produced by the exocrine glands is abnormally thick, tenacious, and copious, causing obstruction of the small passageways of the affected organs, particularly in the respiratory, gastrointestinal, and reproductive systems.
3. The most common symptoms are pancreatic enzyme deficiency caused by duct blockage, progressive chronic lung disease associated with infection, and sweat gland dysfunction resulting in increased sodium and chloride sweat concentrations.
4. An increase in sodium and chloride in sweat and saliva forms the basis for the most reliable diagnostic test, the sweat chloride test (Box 37-7).
5. CF is a fatal genetic disorder and respiratory failure is the most common cause of death.

B. Respiratory system
1. Symptoms are produced by the stagnation of mucus in the airway, leading to bacterial colonization and destruction of lung tissue.
2. Emphysema and atelectasis occur as the airways become increasingly obstructed.
3. Chronic hypoxemia causes contraction and hypertrophy of the muscle fibers in pulmonary ar-

The production of sweat is stimulated (pilocarpine ionto-phoresis), the sweat is collected, and the sweat electrolytes are measured (a minimum of 50 mg of sweat is needed).

Normally, sweat chloride concentration is lower than 40 mEq/L.

A chloride concentration higher than 60 mEq/L is a positive test result.

Chloride concentrations of 40 to 60 mEq/L are highly suggestive of cystic fibrosis and require a repeat test.

teries and arterioles, leading to pulmonary hypertension and eventual cor pulmonale.
4. Pneumothorax from ruptured bullae and hemoptysis from erosion of the bronchial wall occur as the disease progresses.
5. Other respiratory symptoms
   a. **Wheezing** and dry nonproductive cough
   b. Dyspnea
   c. **Cyanosis**
   d. Clubbing of the fingers and toes
   e. Barrel chest
   f. Repeated episodes of bronchitis and pneumonia

C. Gastrointestinal system
1. Meconium ileus in the neonate
2. Intestinal obstruction (distal intestinal obstructive syndrome) caused by thick intestinal secretions; signs include pain, abdominal distention, nausea, and vomiting.
3. Steatorrhea (frothy, foul-smelling stools)
4. Deficiency of the fat-soluble vitamins A, D, E, and K, which causes easy bruising and anemia
5. Malnutrition and failure to thrive
6. Demonstration of hypoalbuminemia from diminished absorption of protein, resulting in generalized edema
7. Rectal prolapse that can result from the large, bulky stools and lack of the supportive fat pads around the rectum

D. Integumentary system
1. Abnormally high concentrations of sodium and chloride in sweat
2. Parents reporting that the infant tastes "salty" when kissed
3. Dehydration and electrolyte imbalances, especially during hyperthermic conditions

E. Reproductive system
1. Cystic fibrosis can delay **puberty** in girls.
2. Fertility can be inhibited by the highly viscous cervical secretions, which act as a plug and block sperm entry.
3. Males are usually sterile, caused by the blockage of the vas deferens by abnormal secretions

or by failure of normal development of duct structures.

F. Diagnostic tests
1. Quantitative sweat chloride test (see Box 37-7)
2. Chest x-ray film reveals atelectasis and obstructive emphysema.
3. Pulmonary function tests provide evidence of abnormal small airway function.
4. Stool, fat, enzyme analysis: A 72-hour stool sample is collected to check the fat and/or enzyme (trypsin) content (food intake is recorded during the collection).

G. Interventions
1. Respiratory system
   a. Goals of treatment include preventing and treating pulmonary infection by improving aeration, removing secretions, and administering antimicrobial medications.
   b. Chest physiotherapy (percussion and postural drainage) on awakening and in the evening (more frequently during pulmonary infection).
   c. Chest physiotherapy should not be performed before or immediately after a meal.
   d. Bronchodilator medication by aerosol opens the bronchi for easier expectoration (administered before the chest physiotherapy when the child has reactive airway disease or is **wheezing**).
   e. Use of a Flutter Mucus Clearance Device (a small, hand-held plastic pipe with a stainless steel ball on the inside) that facilitates removal of mucus; store away from small children because if the device separates, the steel ball poses a choking hazard.
   f. Use of a ThAIRapy vest device that provides high-frequency chest wall oscillation to help loosen secretions
   g. Administering medications as prescribed to decrease the viscosity of mucus
   h. Instruct the parents not to give cough suppressants such as guaifenesin (Robitussin) because they will inhibit expectoration of secretions and promote infection.
   i. Teach the child forced expiratory technique (huffing) to mobilize secretions.
   j. Develop a physical exercise program with the aim of establishing an effective habitual breathing pattern.
   k. Administer antibiotics as prescribed, which may be prescribed prophylactically or when pulmonary symptoms develop.
   l. Aerosolized antibiotics may be prescribed and are administered after chest physiotherapy is performed, or antibiotics may be prescribed and administered intravenously at home through a central venous access device.

m. Administer oxygen as prescribed during acute episodes; monitor closely for oxygen narcosis (signs include nausea and vomiting, malaise, fatigue, numbness and tingling of extremities, substernal distress).

n. Monitor for hemoptysis; more than 300 mL in 24 hours for the older child (less for a younger child) needs to be treated immediately.

o. Hemoptysis may be controlled by bed rest, cough suppressants, antibiotics, and vitamin K; if hemoptysis persists, the site of bleeding may be cauterized or embolized.

p. Lung transplantation is a final therapeutic option for the child with end-stage disorder.

2. Gastrointestinal system

a. The goal of treatment for pancreatic insufficiency is to replace pancreatic enzymes; this is administered with all meals and all snacks to ensure that digestive enzymes are mixed with food in the duodenum.

b. The amount of pancreatic enzymes administered is adjusted to achieve normal **growth** and a decrease in the number of stools to two or three daily.

c. Enteric-coated pancreatic enzymes should not be crushed or chewed.

d. Pancreatic enzymes should not be given if the child is NPO.

e. Encourage a well-balanced, high-protein, high-calorie diet; multivitamins and vitamins A, D, E, and K are also administered.

f. Assess weight and monitor for failure to thrive.

g. Monitor for constipation and intestinal obstruction.

h. Ensure adequate salt intake and fluids that provide an adequate supply of electrolytes during extremely hot weather and if the child has a fever.

H. Home care

1. Instruct the child and family about the prescribed treatment measures and their importance.

2. Instruct the parents and caregivers to be sure immunizations are up to date.

3. Inform the parents and caregivers that the child should be vaccinated yearly for influenza; pneumococcus **vaccine** may also be prescribed.

4. Inform the child and family about the Cystic Fibrosis Foundation.

▲ VIII. SUDDEN INFANT DEATH SYNDROME
A. Description

1. Unexpected death of an apparently healthy infant younger than 1 year for whom a thorough autopsy fails to demonstrate an adequate cause of death

2. Unknown cause that may be related to a brainstem abnormality in the neurological regulation of cardiorespiratory control

3. Most frequently occurs during winter months

4. Death usually occurs during sleep periods, but not necessarily at night.

5. Most frequently affects infants from 2 months to 4 months of age

6. Incidence is higher in males

7. Incidence is higher in Native Americans, African Americans, and Hispanics

8. High-risk sleep behaviors
   a. Prone position
   b. Use of soft bedding
   c. Overheating (thermal stress)
   d. Possibly sleeping with an adult

B. Assessment

1. Child is apneic, blue, and lifeless.

2. Frothy blood-tinged fluid is in the nose and mouth

3. Child may be found in any position, but typically is found in a disheveled bed, with blankets over the head, and huddled in a corner.

4. Child may appear to have been clutching bedding.

5. Diaper may be wet and full of stool.

C. Prevention ▲

1. Infants should be placed in the supine position for sleep.

2. Soft moldable mattresses and bedding, such as pillows or quilts, should not be used for bedding.

3. Stuffed animals should be removed from the crib while the infant is sleeping.

4. Discourage bed sharing (sleeping with an adult).

5. Avoid overheating during sleep.

IX. FOREIGN BODY ASPIRATION ▲
A. Description (Fig. 37-5)

1. Swallowing and aspiration of a foreign body(ies) into the air passages

2. Most inhaled foreign bodies lodge in the main stem or lobar bronchus.

3. Most common offending foods are round in ▲ shape and include hot dogs, candy, peanuts, and grapes.

B. Assessment ▲

1. Initially, choking, gagging, coughing, and retractions are general findings.

2. If the condition worsens, **cyanosis** may occur.

3. Laryngotracheal obstruction leads to dyspnea, **stridor,** cough, and hoarseness.

4. Bronchial obstruction produces paroxysmal cough, **wheezing,** asymmetrical breath sounds, and dyspnea.

5. If any obstruction progresses, unconsciousness and asphyxiation may occur.

FIRST-DEGREE OBSTRUCTION

SECOND-DEGREE OBSTRUCTION

COMPLETE OBSTRUCTION

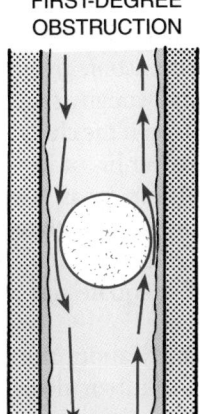

Obstruction allows passage of air in both directions

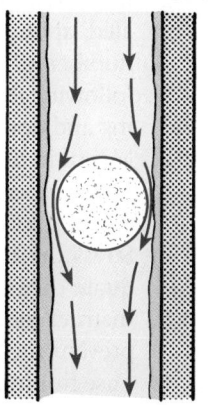

Inhalation

Expiration

Air able to move past the obstruction in one direction only. Air passages enlarge during inspiration and diminish during expiration.

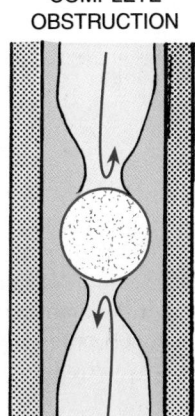

Air unable to move in either direction. FB and edematous mucosa obliterate passage.

FIG. 37-5 Mechanisms of airway obstruction by a foreign body (FB). (From Hockenberry, M., & Wilson, D. [2007]. *Wong's nursing care of infants and children* [8th ed.]. St. Louis: Mosby.)

6. Partial obstructions may occur without symptoms.
7. Distressed child cannot speak, becomes cyanotic, and collapses.

C. Interventions
1. Emergency care (see Chapter 18)
   a. Abdominal thrusts in children over 1 year of age (Heimlich maneuver) to remove the foreign body
   b. Back blows and chest thrusts in children younger than 1 year of age to remove the foreign body
2. Nonemergency management entails removal by endoscopy.
   a. Postprocedure, the child receives high-humidity air.
   b. Observe for signs and symptoms of airway edema.
3. Prevention
   a. Keep small objects out of reach of small children.
   b. Keep rubber balloons out of reach of small children.
   c. Avoid giving small children small, round, food items.
4. Parent, day care provider, babysitter education
   a. Teach about the hazards of aspiration.
   b. Discuss potential situations in which small items may be aspirated.
   c. Teach about the symptoms of aspiration.
   d. Teach the Heimlich maneuver and emergency care measures.

X. TUBERCULOSIS
A. Description
1. Tuberculosis (TB) is a contagious disease caused by *Mycobacterium tuberculosis*, an acid-fast bacillus (see Chap. 57 for additional information about TB).
2. Multidrug-resistant strains of *Mycobacterium tuberculosis* occur because of child or family noncompliance with therapeutic regimens.
3. The route of transmission of *M. tuberculosis* is through inhalation of droplets from an individual with active tuberculosis.
4. There is an increased incidence in urban low-income areas, nonwhite racial or ethnic groups, and first-generation immigrants from endemic countries.
5. Most children are infected by a family member or by another individual with whom they have frequent contact, such as a babysitter.
B. Assessment
1. Client may be asymptomatic or develop symptoms such as malaise, fever, cough, weight loss, anorexia, and lymphadenopathy.
2. Specific symptoms related to the site of infection, such as the lungs, brain, or bone, may be present.
3. With increased time, asymmetrical expansion of the lungs, decreased breath sounds, **crackles**, and dullness to percussion develop.
C. Mantoux test (Box 37-8)
1. The test will produce a positive reaction 2 to 10 weeks after the initial infection.

BOX 37-8

Mantoux Test Interpretation

Induration measuring 15 mm or more is considered to be a positive reaction in children 4 years of age or older who do not have any risk factors.

Induration measuring 10 mm or more is considered to be a positive reaction in children younger than 4 years of age and in those with chronic illness or at high risk for exposure to tuberculosis.

Induration measuring 5 mm or more is considered to be positive for the highest risk groups, such as children with immunosuppressive conditions or human immunodeficiency virus infection.

2. The test determines whether the child has been infected and has developed a sensitivity to the protein of the tubercle bacillus; a positive reaction does not confirm the presence of active disease (exposure versus presence).

3. Once the child reacts positively, the child will always react positively; a positive reaction in a previously negative child indicates that the child has been infected since the last test.

4. Tuberculosis testing should not be done at the same time as measles immunization (viral interference from the measles **vaccine** may cause a false-negative result).

▲ D. Sputum culture

1. A definitive diagnosis is made by demonstrating the presence of mycobacteria in a culture.

2. Chest x-rays are supplemental to sputum cultures and are not definitive alone.

3. Because an infant or young child often swallows sputum rather than expectorates it, gastric washings (aspiration of lavaged contents from the fasting stomach) may be done to obtain a specimen; the specimen is obtained in the early morning before breakfast.

▲ E. Interventions

1. Medications

a. A 9-month course of isoniazid (INH) may be prescribed to prevent a latent infection from progressing to clinically active TB and to prevent initial infection in children in high-risk situations; a 12-month course may be prescribed for the child infected with human immunodeficiency virus.

b. Recommendation for the child with clinically active tuberculosis may include combination administration of isoniazid (INH), rifampin (Rifadin), and pyrazinamide daily for 2 months, and then isoniazid and rifampin twice weekly for 4 months.

c. Inform the parents and child that bodily fluids may turn orange with isoniazid and the urine may turn orange-red with rifampin.

2. Place children with infectious disease on respiratory isolation until medications have been initiated, sputum cultures demonstrate a diminished number of organisms, and cough is improving; following this, a mask is worn if the child is coughing and does not reliably cover his or her mouth.

3. Maintain airborne precautions (mask) with family members until they are demonstrated not to have infectious tuberculosis.

4. Stress the importance of adequate rest and adequate diet.

5. Instruct the child and family about measures to prevent the transmission of tuberculosis.

6. Case finding and follow-up with known contacts is critical to decrease the number of cases of individuals with active TB.

PRACTICE QUESTIONS

1. An emergency room nurse is caring for a child diagnosed with epiglottitis. Assessing the child, the nurse monitors for which indication that the child may be experiencing airway obstruction?
   1. The child exhibits nasal flaring and bradycardia.
   2. The child is leaning forward, with the chin thrust out.
   3. The child has a low-grade fever and complains of a sore throat.
   4. The child is leaning backward, supporting himself or herself with the hands and arms.

2. A nurse is caring for an infant with bronchiolitis and diagnostic tests have confirmed respiratory syncytial virus. Based on this finding, which of the following is the appropriate nursing action?
   1. Initiate strict enteric precautions.
   2. Move the infant to a room with another child with RSV.
   3. Leave the infant in the present room because RSV is not contagious.
   4. Inform the staff that they must wear a gown and gloves when caring for the child.

3. Ribavirin (Virazole) is prescribed for a hospitalized child with respiratory syncytial virus. The nurse prepares to administer this medication via which of the following routes?
   1. Oral
   2. Oxygen tent
   3. Intramuscular
   4. Subcutaneous

4. A 10-year-old child with asthma is treated for acute exacerbation in the emergency room. A nurse reports which of the following, knowing that it indicates a worsening of the condition?
   1. Warm, dry skin
   2. Decreased wheezing
   3. Pulse rate of 90 beats/min
   4. Respirations of 18 breaths/min

5. The mother of an 8-year-old child being treated for right lower lobe pneumonia at home calls the clinic nurse. The mother tells the nurse that the child complains of discomfort on the right side and that the acetaminophen (Tylenol) is not effective. The nurse should tell the mother to:
   1. Increase the dose of the acetaminophen.
   2. Encourage the child to lie on the left side.
   3. Encourage the child to lie on the right side.
   4. Increase the frequency of the acetaminophen.
6. A new mother expresses concern to a nurse regarding sudden infant death syndrome. She asks the nurse how to position her new infant for sleep. The nurse appropriately tells the mother that the infant should be placed on the:
   1. Side or prone.
   2. Back or prone.
   3. Stomach with the face turned.
   4. Back rather than on the stomach.
7. A clinic nurse is providing instructions to a mother of a child with cystic fibrosis regarding the immunization schedule for the child. Which statement would the nurse make to the mother?
   1. "The immunization schedule will need to be altered."
   2. "The child should not receive any hepatitis vaccines."
   3. "The child will receive all the immunizations except for the polio series."
   4. "The child will receive the recommended basic series of immunizations along with a yearly pneumococcal and influenza vaccination."
8. A clinic nurse reads the results of a Mantoux test on a 3-year-old child. The results indicate an area of induration measuring 10 mm. The nurse would interpret these results as:
   1. Positive.
   2. Negative.
   3. Inconclusive.
   4. Definitive and requiring a repeat test.
9. Isoniazid (INH) is prescribed for a child with human immunodeficiency virus infection who has a positive Mantoux test result. The mother of the child asks the nurse how long the child will need to take the medication. The nurse tells the mother that the medication will need to be taken for:

   1. 4 months.
   2. 6 months.
   3. 9 months.
   4. 12 months.
10. A hospitalized 2-year-old child with croup is receiving corticosteroid therapy and the mother asks a nurse why the physician did not prescribe antibiotics. The appropriate response is:
    1. "The child may be allergic to antibiotics."
    2. "The child is too young to receive antibiotics."
    3. "Antibiotics are not indicated unless a bacterial infection is present."
    4. "The child still has the maternal antibodies from birth and does not need antibiotics."
11. A child with croup is placed in a cool mist tent. The mother becomes concerned because the child is frightened, consistently crying, and trying to climb out of the tent. The appropriate nursing action is to:
    1. Tell the mother that the child must stay in the tent.
    2. Call the physician and obtain an order for a mild sedative.
    3. Place a toy in the tent to make the child feel more comfortable.
    4. Let the mother hold the child and direct the cool mist over the child's face.

ALTERNATE ITEM FORMAT: MULTIPLE RESPONSE

A nurse is preparing for the admission of an infant with a diagnosis of bronchiolitis caused by the respiratory syncytial virus. Select all interventions that would be included in the plan of care.
❏ 1. Place the infant in a private room.
❏ 2. Place the infant in a room near the nurse's station.
❏ 3. Ensure that the infant's head is in a flexed position.
❏ 4. Wear a mask at all times when in contact with the infant.
❏ 5. Place the child in a tent that delivers warm humidified air.
❏ 6. Position the infant side-lying, with the head lower than the chest.

ANSWERS

1. **2**
Rationale: Clinical manifestations suggestive of airway obstruction include tripod positioning (leaning forward while supported by arms, chin thrust out, mouth open), nasal flaring, tachycardia, a high fever, and a sore throat. Option 4 is an incorrect position. Options 1 and 3 are incorrect because epiglottitis causes a high fever and tachycardia.

Test-Taking Strategy: Use the process of elimination. Eliminate option 1 first because tachycardia rather than bradycardia will occur in a child experiencing respiratory distress. Eliminate option 3 next, knowing that a high fever occurs with epiglottitis. From the remaining options, visualize the descriptions in each and determine which position would best assist a child experiencing respiratory distress. Review

the indications of airway obstruction if you had difficulty with this question.
Level of Cognitive Ability: Analysis
Client Needs: Physiological Integrity
Integrated Process: Nursing Process—assessment
Content Area: Child health
Reference: Hockenberry, M., Wilson, D., & Winkelstein, M. (2005). *Wong's essentials of pediatric nursing* (7th ed., p. 802). St. Louis: Mosby.

2. **2**
Rationale: Respiratory syncytial virus (RSV) is a highly communicable disorder and is not transmitted via the airborne route. The virus usually is transferred by the hands, and meticulous hand washing is necessary to decrease the spread of organisms. The infant with RSV is isolated in a single room or placed in a room with another child with RSV. Enteric precautions are not necessary.
Test-Taking Strategy: Use the process of elimination, recalling the method of viral transmission. Remember that the infant with RSV is isolated in a single room or placed in a room with another child with RSV. Review care of the infant with RSV if you had difficulty with this question.
Level of Cognitive Ability: Application
Client Needs: Safe and Effective Care Environment
Integrated Process: Nursing Process—implementation
Content Area: Child health
Reference: Hockenberry, M., Wilson, D., & Winkelstein, M. (2005). *Wong's essentials of pediatric nursing* (7th ed., p. 805). St. Louis: Mosby.

3. **2**
Rationale: Ribavirin (Virazole) is an antiviral respiratory medication used mainly for hospitalized children with severe RSV. Administration is via hood, face mask, or oxygen tent. Ribavirin is not administered orally, intramuscularly, or subcutaneously.
Test-Taking Strategy: Use the process of eliminating. Recalling that this medication is aerosolized will direct you to option 2. If you are unfamiliar with this medication, review its method of administration.
Level of Cognitive Ability: Application
Client Needs: Physiological Integrity
Integrated Process: Nursing Process—planning
Content Area: Child health
Reference: Hockenberry, M., Wilson, D., & Winkelstein, M. (2005). *Wong's essentials of pediatric nursing* (7th ed., p. 804). St. Louis: Mosby.

4. **2**
Rationale: Decreased wheezing in a child with asthma may be interpreted incorrectly as a positive sign when it may actually signal an inability to move air. A "silent chest" is an ominous sign during an asthma episode. With treatment, increased wheezing actually may signal that the child's condition is improving. Warm, dry skin indicates an improvement in condition, because the child is normally diaphoretic during exacerbation. The normal pulse rate in a 10-year-old is 70 to 110 beats/min. The normal respiratory rate in a 10-year-old is 16 to 20 breaths/min.

Test-Taking Strategy: Use the process of elimination and note the strategic word *worsening* in the question. Options 1 and 4 can be eliminated easily because they are normal findings. From the remaining options, recall that a "silent chest" is an ominous sign during an asthma episode. Review these clinical manifestations if you had difficulty with this question.
Level of Cognitive Ability: Application
Client Needs: Physiological Integrity
Integrated Process: Nursing Process—implementation
Content Area: Child health
Reference: McKinney, E., James, S., Murray, S., & Ashwill, J. (2005). *Maternal-child nursing* (2nd ed., p. 1225). St. Louis: W.B. Saunders.

5. **3**
Rationale: Splinting of the affected side by lying on that side may decrease discomfort. To advise the mother to increase the dose or frequency of the acetaminophen is inappropriate. Lying on the left side will not be helpful in alleviating discomfort.
Test-Taking Strategy: Use the process of elimination. Options 1 and 4 can be eliminated easily because the nurse does not adjust the dose or frequency of medications. Recalling the principles related to splinting an incision in the postoperative client will assist in directing you to option 3 because these principles can be applied in this situation. Review care of the child with pneumonia if you had difficulty with this question.
Level of Cognitive Ability: Application
Client Needs: Physiological Integrity
Integrated Process: Nursing Process—implementation
Content Area: Child health
Reference: Hockenberry, M., Wilson, D., & Winkelstein, M. (2005). *Wong's essentials of pediatric nursing* (7th ed., p. 807). St. Louis: Mosby.

6. **4**
Rationale: Nurses should encourage parents to place the infant on the back (supine) for sleep. The infant may have the ability to turn to a prone position from the side-lying position. Infants in the prone position (on the stomach) may be unable to move their heads to the side, thus increasing the risk of suffocation.
Test-Taking Strategy: Use the process of elimination. Eliminate options 1, 2, and 3 because they are comparative or alike. Remember that the infant needs to be placed on his or her back. Review positioning of the healthy infant for sleep if you had difficulty with this question.
Level of Cognitive Ability: Application
Client Needs: Safe and Effective Care Environment
Integrated Process: Teaching and Learning
Content Area: Child health
Reference: Hockenberry, M., Wilson, D., & Winkelstein, M. (2005). *Wong's essentials of pediatric nursing* (7th ed., p. 383). St. Louis: Mosby.

7. **4**
Rationale: Adequately protecting children with cystic fibrosis from communicable diseases by immunization is essential. In addition to the basic series of immunizations, a yearly influ-

enza and possibly a pneumococcal vaccine also are recommended for children with cystic fibrosis. Therefore, options 1, 2, and 3 are incorrect.

Test-Taking Strategy: Use the process of elimination. Eliminate options 1, 2, and 3 because they are comparative or alike. Recalling the importance of protection from communicable diseases, particularly in children with a disorder such as cystic fibrosis, will assist in directing you to option 4. Review the immunization schedule for the child with cystic fibrosis if you had difficulty with this question.

Level of Cognitive Ability: Application
Client Needs: Health Promotion and Maintenance
Integrated Process: Teaching and Learning
Content Area: Child health
References: Hockenberry, M., & Wilson, D. (2007). *Nursing care of infants and children* (8th ed., p. 1381). St. Louis: Mosby.
McKinney, E., James, S., Murray, S., & Ashwill, J. (2005). *Maternal-child nursing* (2nd ed., p. 1244). St. Louis: W.B. Saunders.

8. **1**
Rationale: Induration measuring 10 mm or more is considered to be a positive result in children younger than 4 years of age and in those with chronic illness or at high risk for environmental exposure to tuberculosis. A reaction of 5 mm or more is considered to be a positive result for the highest risk groups, such as the child with an immunosuppressive condition or the child with human immunodeficiency virus infection. A reaction of 15 mm or more is positive in children 4 years of age or older without any risk factors.

Test-Taking Strategy: Use the process of elimination. Options 3 and 4 are comparative or alike and can be eliminated first. From the remaining options, note the child's age to assist in directing you to option 1. If you had difficulty with this question, review the analysis of the Mantoux test in children.

Level of Cognitive Ability: Analysis
Client Needs: Physiological Integrity
Integrated Process: Nursing Process—analysis
Content Area: Child health
Reference: McKinney, E., James, S., Murray, S., & Ashwill, J. (2005). *Maternal-child nursing* (2nd ed., p. 1246). St. Louis: W.B. Saunders.

9. **4**
Rationale: For children with human immunodeficiency virus infection, a minimum of 12 months of treatment with isoniazid is recommended.

Test-Taking Strategy: Focus on the child's diagnosis. Noting that the child has human immunodeficiency virus infection will direct you to option 4, the longest length of treatment time. Review the treatment plans for tuberculosis in children if you had difficulty with this question.

Level of Cognitive Ability: Application
Client Needs: Physiological Integrity
Integrated Process: Nursing Process—implementation
Content Area: Child health
Reference: McKinney, E., James, S., Murray, S., & Ashwill, J. (2005). *Maternal-child nursing* (2nd ed., p. 1246). St. Louis: W.B. Saunders.

10. **3**
Rationale: Antibiotics are not indicated in the treatment of croup unless a bacterial infection is present. Options 1, 2, and 4 are incorrect. In addition, no supporting data in the question indicate that the child may be allergic to antibiotics.

Test-Taking Strategy: Use the process of elimination. Eliminate option 1 because no supporting data are in the question regarding the potential for allergies. Noting the age of the child will assist in eliminating options 2 and 4. In addition, recalling the general principles related to the use of antibiotics will direct you to the correct option. Review the indications for the use of antibiotics if you had difficulty with this question.

Level of Cognitive Ability: Application
Client Needs: Physiological Integrity
Integrated Process: Teaching and Learning
Content Area: Child health
References: Hockenberry, M., Wilson, D., & Winkelstein, M. (2005). *Wong's essentials of pediatric nursing* (7th ed., p. 801). St. Louis: Mosby.
McKinney, E., James, S., Murray, S., & Ashwill, J. (2005). *Maternal-child nursing* (2nd ed., p. 1210). St. Louis: W.B. Saunders.

11. **4**
Rationale: If the use of a tent or hood is causing distress, treatment may be more effective if the child is held by the parent and a cool mist is directed toward the child's face. A mild sedative would not be administered to the child. Crying will aggravate laryngospasm and increase hypoxia, which may cause airway obstruction. Options 1 and 3 will not alleviate the child's fear.

Test-Taking Strategy: Focus on the subject of the question. Options 1, 2, and 3 will not alleviate the child's fear and are comparative or alike in that they do not address the fear. Option 4 is the option that addresses the subject of the question. Review care of the child in a mist tent if you had difficulty with this question.

Level of Cognitive Ability: Application
Client Needs: Psychosocial Integrity
Integrated Process: Caring
Content Area: Child health
References: Hockenberry, M., Wilson, D., & Winkelstein, M. (2005). *Wong's essentials of pediatric nursing* (7th ed., pp. 801-802). St. Louis: Mosby.
McKinney, E., James, S., Murray, S., & Ashwill, J. (2005). *Maternal-child nursing* (2nd ed., pp. 1206, 1209). St. Louis: W.B. Saunders.

ALTERNATE ITEM FORMAT: MULTIPLE RESPONSE

Answer: **1, 2**
Rationale: The infant with RSV should be isolated in a private room or in a room with another infant with RSV infection. The infant should be placed in a room near the nurses' station for easy observation. The infant should be positioned with the head and chest at a 30- to 40-degree angle and the neck slightly extended to maintain an open airway and decrease pressure on the diaphragm. Cool humidified oxygen is delivered to relieve dyspnea, hypoxemia, and insensible water loss

from tachypnea. Contact precautions (wearing gloves and a gown) reduce nosocomial transmission of RSV.
Test-Taking Strategy: Recalling the mode of transmission of RSV will assist in determining that the infant needs to be placed in a private room or in a room with another infant with RSV infection, and that contact precautions need to be maintained. Recalling the need to maintain a patent airway (edema and the accumulation of mucus obstruct the bronchioles) will assist in determining that the infant needs to be observed closely, the infant's head should be elevated, and the infant should receive cool humidified oxygen. Review care of the child with bronchiolitis and RSV if you had difficulty with this question.
Level of Cognitive Ability: Application
Client Needs: Physiological Integrity
Integrated Process: Nursing Process—planning
Content Area: Child health
Reference: McKinney, E., James, S., Murray, S., & Ashwill, J. (2005). *Maternal-child nursing* (2nd ed., pp. 1214-1215). St. Louis: W.B. Saunders.

REFERENCES

American Lung Association. http://www.lungusa.org.

American SIDS Institute. http://www.sids.org.

Asthma and Allergy Foundation of America. http://www.aafa.org.

Cystic Fibrosis Foundation. http://www.CFF.org.

Hockenberry, M., Wilson, D., & Winkelstein, M. (2005). *Wong's essentials of pediatric nursing* (7th ed.). St. Louis: Mosby.

Hockenberry, M., & Wilson, D. (2007). *Nursing care of infants and children* (8th ed.). St. Louis: Mosby.

Kliegman, R., Marcdante, K., Jenson, H., & Behrman, R. (2006). *Nelson essentials of pediatrics* (5th ed.). St. Louis: W.B. Saunders.

McKinney, E., James, S., Murray, S., & Ashwill, J. (2005). *Maternal-child nursing* (2nd ed.). St. Louis: W.B. Saunders.

National Council of State Boards of Nursing (Eds.). (2007). *2007 NCLEX-RN® detailed test plan*. Chicago: Author.

Wong, D., Perry, S., Hockenberry, M., et al. (2006). *Maternal child nursing care* (3rd ed.). St. Louis: Mosby.

Cardiovascular Disorders

▲ I. CONGESTIVE HEART FAILURE (CHF)

A. Description

1. Congestive heart failure (Box 38-1) is the inability of the heart to pump a sufficient amount of oxygen to meet the metabolic needs of the body.
2. In infants and children, inadequate cardiac output most commonly is caused by congenital heart defects (**shunt,** obstruction, or a combination of both) that produce an excessive volume or pressure load on the myocardium.
3. In infants and children, a combination of left-sided and right-sided heart failure is usually present.
4. The goals of treatment are to improve cardiac function, remove accumulated fluid and sodium, decrease cardiac demands, improve tissue oxygenation, and decrease oxygen consumption.

B. Assessment of early signs

1. Tachycardia, especially during rest and slight exertion
2. Tachypnea
3. Profuse scalp diaphoresis, especially in infants
4. Fatigue and irritability
5. Sudden weight gain
6. Respiratory distress

C. Interventions

1. Monitor for early signs of CHF.
2. Monitor for respiratory distress (count respirations for 1 minute).
3. Monitor apical pulse (count pulse for 1 minute) and monitor for dysrhythmias.
4. Monitor temperature for hyperthermia and for other signs of infection, particularly respiratory infection.
5. Monitor strict intake and output.

BOX 38-1

Signs and Symptoms of Congestive Heart Failure

LEFT-SIDED FAILURE
Crackles and wheezes
Cough
Dyspnea
Grunting (infants)
Head bobbing (infants)
Nasal flaring
Orthopnea
Periods of cyanosis
Retractions
Tachypnea

RIGHT-SIDED FAILURE
Ascites
Hepatosplenomegaly
Jugular vein distention
Oliguria
Peripheral edema, especially dependent and periorbital edema
Weight gain

---

6. Weigh diapers as appropriate.
7. Monitor daily weight to assess for fluid retention; a weight gain of 0.5 kg (1 lb) in 1 day is caused by the accumulation of fluid.
8. Monitor for facial or peripheral dependent edema, auscultate lung sounds, and report abnormal findings indicating excessive fluid in the body.
9. Elevate the head of the bed in a semi-Fowler's position.
10. Maintain a neutral thermal environment to prevent cold stress in infants.
11. Provide rest and decrease environmental stimuli.

12. Administer cool humidified oxygen as prescribed, using an oxygen hood for young infants and a nasal cannula or face mask for older infants and children.
13. Organize nursing activities to allow for uninterrupted sleep.
14. Maintain adequate nutritional status.
15. Feed when hungry and soon after awakening, conserving energy and oxygen supply.
16. Provide small, frequent feedings, conserving energy and oxygen supply.
17. Administer sedation as prescribed during the acute stage to promote rest.
18. Administer digoxin (Lanoxin) as prescribed
    a. Assess apical heart rate for 1 minute before administration
    b. Hold digoxin if pulse is less than 90 beats/min in infants and young children and less than 70 beats/min in older children, as prescribed
    c. Be aware that infants rarely receive more than 1 mL (50 mcg or 0.05 mg) of digoxin in one dose
19. Monitor digoxin levels and for signs of digoxin toxicity, including bradycardia, headache, and vomiting.
    a. Normal digoxin level is 0.5 to 2.0 mg/dL
    b. Digoxin toxicity occurs when level is above 2.0 mg/dL
20. Administer angiotensin-converting enzyme inhibitors (captopril [Capoten] or enalapril [Vasotec]) as prescribed.
    a. Monitor for hypotension, renal dysfunction, and cough when angiotensin-converting enzyme inhibitors are administered.
    b. Assess the blood pressure, serum protein, albumin, blood urea nitrogen, and creatinine levels, white blood cell count, urine output, urinary specific gravity, and urinary protein level.
21. Administer diuretics (furosemide [Lasix]) as prescribed
    a. Monitor for signs and symptoms of hypokalemia (serum potassium level less than 3.5 mEq/L), including muscle weakness and cramping, confusion, irritability, restlessness, and inverted T wave on the electrocardiogram (ECG).
    b. If signs and symptoms of hypokalemia are present and the child is also being administered digoxin, then monitor closely for digoxin toxicity because hypokalemia potentiates digoxin toxicity.
22. Administer potassium supplements and provide dietary sources of potassium as prescribed.
    a. Supplemental potassium should only be given if indicated by serum potassium levels and if adequate renal function is evident,

---

BOX 38-2

Home Care Instructions for Administering Digoxin (Lanoxin)

Administer as prescribed.
Administer 1 hour before or 2 hours after feedings.
Use a calendar to mark off the dose administered.
Do not mix the medication with foods or fluid.
If a dose is missed and more than 4 hours has elapsed, withhold the dose and give the next dose at the scheduled time; if less than 4 hours has elapsed, administer the missed dose.
If the child vomits, do not administer a second dose.
If more than two consecutive doses have been missed, notify the physician; do not increase or double the dose for missed doses.
If the child has teeth, give water after the medication; if possible, brush the teeth to prevent tooth decay from the sweetened liquid.
If the child becomes ill, notify the physician.
Keep the medication in a locked cabinet.
Call the poison control center immediately if accidental overdose occurs.

---

and is usually necessary when administering a non–potassium-sparing diuretic such as furosemide (Lasix).
    b. Encourage foods that the child will eat that are high in potassium, as appropriate, such as bananas, baked potato skins, and peanut butter.
23. Monitor serum electrolyte levels, particularly the potassium level (normal level is 3.5 to 5.1 mEq/L).
24. Restrict fluid as prescribed in the acute stage.
25. Monitor for signs and symptoms of dehydration, including sunken fontanel, nonelastic skin turgor, dry mucous membranes, decreased tear production, decreased urine output, and concentrated urine.
26. Monitor sodium levels as prescribed.
    a. Normal level is 135 to 145 mEq/L.
    b. Many infant formulas have slightly more sodium than breast milk.
27. Instruct the parents regarding the description of the diagnosis and administration of medications (Box 38-2).
28. Instruct the parents in cardiopulmonary resuscitation (CPR); see Chapter 18 for information on CPR.

II. DEFECTS WITH INCREASED PULMONARY BLOOD FLOW (Box 38-3)
A. Description
    1. Intracardiac communication along the septum or an abnormal connection between the great arteries allows blood to flow from the high-pressure left side of the heart to the low-pressure right side of the heart.

2. The infant typically demonstrates signs and symptoms of CHF.

B. Atrial septal defect (ASD)
  1. Atrial septal defect is an abnormal opening between the atria that causes an increased flow of oxygenated blood into the right side of the heart.
  2. Right atrial and ventricular enlargement occur.
  3. Infant may be asymptomatic or may develop CHF.
  4. Signs and symptoms of decreased cardiac output may be present (Box 38-4).
  5. Types
    a. ASD 1 (ostium primum): Opening is at the lower end of the septum.
    b. ASD 2 (ostium secundum): Opening is n ear the center of the septum.
    c. ASD 3 (sinus venosus defect): Opening is near the junction of the superior vena cava and the right atrium.
  6. Nonsurgical treatment: The defect may be closed during a cardiac catheterization.
  7. Surgical treatment: Open repair with cardiopulmonary bypass usually is performed before school age.

C. Atrioventricular canal defect
  1. The defect results from incomplete fusion of the endocardial cushions.
  2. The defect is the most common cardiac defect in Down syndrome.
  3. A characteristic murmur is present.
  4. The infant usually has mild to moderate CHF, with **cyanosis** increasing with crying.
  5. Signs and symptoms of decreased cardiac output may be present.
  6. Surgical treatment can include pulmonary artery banding for infants with severe symptoms (palliative) or complete repair via cardiopulmonary bypass.

D. Patent ductus arteriosus
  1. Patent ductus arteriosus is failure of the fetal ductus arteriosus (artery connecting the aorta and the pulmonary artery) to close within the first weeks of life.
  2. A characteristic machinery-like murmur is present.
  3. Infant may be asymptomatic or may show signs of CHF.
  4. A widened pulse pressure and bounding pulses are present.
  5. Signs and symptoms of decreased cardiac output may be present.
  6. Medical management: Indomethacin (Indocin), a prostaglandin inhibitor, may be administered to close a patent ductus in premature infants and some newborns.
  7. Management: The defect may be closed during cardiac catheterization or the defect may require surgical management.

E. Ventricular septal defect (VSD)
  1. A VSD is an abnormal opening between the right and left ventricles.
  2. Many VSDs close spontaneously during the first year of life in children having small or moderate defects.
  3. A characteristic murmur is present.
  4. Signs and symptoms of CHF are commonly present.
  5. Signs and symptoms of decreased cardiac output may be present.
  6. Nonsurgical treatment: Closure during cardiac catheterization may be possible.
  7. Surgical treatment: Open repair is done with cardiopulmonary bypass.

III. **OBSTRUCTIVE DEFECTS** (Box 38-5)
A. Description
  1. Blood exiting a portion of the heart meets an area of anatomical narrowing **(stenosis)**, causing obstruction to blood flow.
  2. The location of narrowing is usually near the valve of the obstructive defect.
  3. Infants and children exhibit signs of CHF.
  4. Children with mild obstruction may be asymptomatic.

B. Aortic **stenosis**
  1. Aortic **stenosis** is narrowing or stricture of the aortic valve, causing resistance to blood flow in the left ventricle, decreased cardiac output, left

ventricular hypertrophy, and pulmonary vascular congestion.

2. Valvular **stenosis** is the most common type and usually is caused by malformed cusps, resulting in a bicuspid rather than a tricuspid valve, or fusion of the cusps.

▲ 3. A characteristic murmur is present.

4. Infants with severe defects demonstrate signs of decreased cardiac output.

▲ 5. Children show signs of exercise intolerance, chest pain, and dizziness when standing for long periods of time.

6. Nonsurgical treatment for valvular aortic **stenosis** is done during cardiac catheterization to dilate the narrowed valve.

7. Surgical treatment for valvular aortic **stenosis** is aortic valvotomy (palliative); a valve replacement may be required at a second procedure.

C. Coarctation of the aorta

1. Coarctation of the aorta is localized narrowing near the insertion of the ductus arteriosus.

▲ 2. The blood pressure is higher in the upper extremities than the lower extremities; bounding pulses in the arms, weak or absent femoral pulses, and cool lower extremities may be present.

▲ 3. Signs of CHF may occur in infants.

4. Signs and symptoms of decreased cardiac output may be present.

▲ 5. Children may experience headaches, dizziness, fainting, and epistaxis resulting from hypertension.

6. Nonsurgical treatment is balloon angioplasty in children; restenosis can occur.

7. Surgical management

a. Mechanical ventilation and medications to improve cardiac output are often necessary before surgery.

b. Resection of the coarcted portion with end-to-end anastomosis of the aorta or enlargement of the constricted section using a graft may be required.

c. Because the defect is outside the heart, cardiopulmonary bypass is not required and a thoracotomy incision is used.

D. Pulmonary **stenosis**

1. Pulmonary **stenosis** is narrowing at the entrance to the pulmonary artery.

2. Resistance to blood flow causes right ventricular hypertrophy and decreased pulmonary blood flow; the right ventricle may be hypoplastic.

3. Pulmonary **atresia** is the extreme form of pulmonary **stenosis** in that there is total fusion of the commissures and no blood flows to the lungs.

▲ 4. A characteristic murmur is present.

5. The infant or child may be asymptomatic.

▲ 6. Newborns with severe narrowing will be cyanotic.

> **BOX 38-6**
> Defects With Decreased Pulmonary Blood Flow
>
> Tetralogy of Fallot
> Tricuspid atresia

7. If pulmonary **stenosis** is severe, CHF occurs.

8. Signs and symptoms of decreased cardiac output may occur.

9. Nonsurgical treatment is done during cardiac catheterization to dilate the narrowed valve.

10. Surgical treatment

a. In infants, transventricular (closed) valvotomy procedure.

b. In children, pulmonary valvotomy with cardiopulmonary bypass.

IV. **DEFECTS WITH DECREASED PULMONARY BLOOD FLOW** (Box 38-6)

A. Description

1. Obstructed pulmonary blood flow and an anatomical defect (ASD or VSD) between the right and left sides of the heart are present.

2. Pressure on the right side of the heart increases, exceeding pressure on the left side, which allows desaturated blood to **shunt** right to left, causing desaturation in the left side of the heart and in the systemic circulation.

3. Typically hypoxemia and **cyanosis** appear.

B. Tetralogy of Fallot ▲

1. The tetralogy of Fallot includes four defects—VSD, pulmonary **stenosis**, overriding aorta, and right ventricular hypertrophy.

2. If pulmonary vascular resistance is higher than systemic resistance, the **shunt** is from right to left; if systemic resistance is higher than pulmonary resistance, the **shunt** is left to right.

3. Infants

a. The infant may be acutely cyanotic at birth or may have mild **cyanosis** that progresses over the first year of life as the pulmonic **stenosis** worsens.

b. A characteristic murmur is present.

c. Acute episodes of **cyanosis** and hypoxia ▲ (hypercyanotic spells), called blue spells or tet spells, occur when the infant's oxygen requirements exceed the blood supply, such as during periods of crying, feeding, or defecating.

4. Children: With increasing **cyanosis**, squatting, ▲ clubbing of the fingers, and poor growth may occur.

a. Squatting is a compensatory mechanism to facilitate increased return of blood flow to the heart for oxygenation.

b. Clubbing (an abnormal enlargement in the distal phalanges seen in the fingers) is symptomatic of chronic hypoxia as peripheral circulation is diminished to allow oxygenation of vital organs and tissues.
5. Surgical treatment: Palliative **shunt**
   a. The **shunt** increases pulmonary blood flow and increases oxygen saturation in infants who cannot undergo primary repair.
   b. The **shunt** provides blood flow to the pulmonary arteries from the left or right subclavian artery.
6. Surgical treatment: Complete repair
   a. Complete repair usually is performed in the first year of life.
   b. The repair requires a median sternotomy and cardiopulmonary bypass.
C. Tricuspid **atresia**
   1. Tricuspid **atresia** is failure of the tricuspid valve to develop.
   2. No communication exists from the right atrium to the right ventricle.
   3. Blood flows through an ASD or a patent foramen ovale to the left side of the heart and through a VSD to the right ventricle and out to the lungs.
   4. The defect often is associated with pulmonic **stenosis** and transposition of the great arteries.
   5. The defect results in complete mixing of unoxygenated and oxygenated blood in the left side of the heart, resulting in systemic desaturation, pulmonary obstruction, and decreased pulmonary blood flow.
   6. **Cyanosis**, tachycardia, and dyspnea are seen in the newborn.
   7. Older children exhibit signs of chronic hypoxemia and clubbing.
   8. Surgical treatment
      a. If the ASD is small, the defect may be closed during cardiac catheterization; otherwise, surgery is needed.
      b. For the neonate whose pulmonary blood flow depends on the patency of the ductus arteriosus, a continuous infusion of prostaglandin E_1 is initiated until surgery.

V. MIXED DEFECTS (Box 38-7)
A. Description
   1. Fully saturated systemic blood flow mixes with the desaturated blood flow, causing a desaturation of the systemic blood flow.
   2. Pulmonary congestion occurs and cardiac output decreases.
   3. Signs of CHF are present; symptoms vary with the degree of desaturation.

BOX 38-7
Mixed Defects

Hypoplastic left heart syndrome
Total anomalous pulmonary venous connection
Transposition of the great arteries or transposition of the great vessels
Truncus arteriosus

B. Hypoplastic left heart syndrome
   1. Underdevelopment of the left side of the heart occurs, resulting in a hypoplastic left ventricle and aortic **atresia.**
   2. Mild **cyanosis** and signs of CHF occur until the ductus arteriosus closes; then progressive deterioration with **cyanosis** and decreased cardiac output are seen, leading to cardiovascular collapse.
   3. The defect is fatal in the first few months of life without intervention.
   4. Surgical treatment
      a. Surgical treatment is necessary; transplantation in the newborn period may be considered.
      b. In the preoperative period, the neonate requires mechanical ventilation and a continuous infusion of prostaglandin E_1 to maintain ductal patency, ensuring adequate systemic blood flow.
C. Transposition of the great arteries or transposition of the great vessels.
   1. The pulmonary artery leaves the left ventricle, and the aorta exits from the right ventricle.
   2. No communication exists between the systemic and pulmonary circulation.
   3. Infants with minimal communication are severely cyanotic and depressed at birth.
   4. Infants with large septal defects or a patent ductus arteriosus may be less severely cyanotic, but may have symptoms of CHF.
   5. Cardiomegaly is evident a few weeks after birth.
   6. Nonsurgical treatment
      a. Prostaglandin E_1 may be initiated to increase blood mixing temporarily if systemic and pulmonary mixing are inadequate.
      b. Balloon atrial septostomy during cardiac catheterization may be performed to increase mixing and to maintain cardiac output over a longer period.
   7. Surgical treatment: The arterial switch procedure reestablishes normal circulation with the left ventricle acting as the systemic pump and creation of a new aorta.
D. Total anomalous pulmonary venous connection
   1. The defect is a failure of the pulmonary veins to join the left atrium.

2. The defect results in mixed blood being returned to the right atrium and shunted from the right to the left through an ASD.

3. The right side of the heart hypertrophies, whereas the left side of the heart may remain small.

4. Signs and symptoms of CHF develop

5. **Cyanosis** worsens with pulmonary vein obstruction; once obstruction occurs, the infant's condition deteriorates rapidly.

6. Surgical treatment
   a. Corrective repair is performed in early infancy.
   b. The pulmonary vein is anastomosed to the left atrium, the ASD is closed, and the anomalous pulmonary venous connection is ligated.

E. Truncus arteriosus
   1. Truncus arteriosus is failure of normal septation and division of the embryonic bulbar trunk into the pulmonary artery and the aorta, resulting in a single vessel that overrides both ventricles.
   2. Blood from both ventricles mixes in the common great artery, causing desaturation and hypoxemia.
   3. A characteristic murmur is present.
   4. The infant exhibits moderate to severe CHF and variable **cyanosis**, poor growth, and activity intolerance.
   5. Surgical treatment: Corrective surgical repair is performed in the first few months of life.

VI. INTERVENTIONS: CARDIOVASCULAR DEFECTS

A. Monitor for signs of a defect in the infant or child (as described with defects above).

B. Monitor vital signs closely.

C. Monitor respiratory status for the presence of **nasal flaring,** use of accessory muscles, and other signs of impending respiratory distress and notify the physician if any changes occur.

D. Auscultate breath sounds for **crackles,** rhonchi, or wheezes.

E. If respiratory effort is increased, place the child in a reverse Trendelenburg position, elevating the head and upper body, to decrease the work of breathing.

F. Administer humidified oxygen as prescribed.

G. Provide endotracheal tube and ventilator care as prescribed.

H. Monitor for hypercyanotic spells (Box 38-8).

I. Assess for signs of CHF, such as periorbital edema or dependent edema in the hands and feet.

J. Assess peripheral pulses.

K. Maintain strict fluid restriction if prescribed.

L. Monitor intake and output, and notify the physician if a decrease in urine output occurs.

M. Obtain daily weight.

N. Provide adequate nutrition (high calorie requirements) as prescribed.

BOX 38-8

Treatment for Hypercyanotic Spells

Place the infant in a knee-chest position.
Administer 100% oxygen by face mask.
Administer morphine sulfate as prescribed.
Administer fluids intravenously as prescribed.

O. Administer medications as prescribed.

P. Keep the child as stress-free as possible.

Q. Plan interventions to allow maximal rest for the child.

R. Prepare the child and parents for cardiac catheterization, if appropriate.

VII. CARDIAC CATHETERIZATION

A. Description
   1. The most invasive diagnostic procedure to determine cardiac defects
   2. Provides information about oxygenation saturation of blood in great vessels and heart chambers
   3. May be done for diagnostic, interventional, or electrophysiological reasons
   4. May be carried out on an outpatient basis
   5. Risks include hemorrhage from the entry site, clot formation and subsequent blockage distally, transient dysrhythmias
   6. General anesthesia is usually unnecessary.
   7. See Chapter 59 for additional information regarding cardiac catheterization.

B. Preprocedure nursing interventions
   1. Assess accurate height and weight, because this helps with the selection of the correct catheter size.
   2. Obtain a history of the presence of allergic reactions to iodine.
   3. Assess for symptoms of infection, including a diaper rash.
   4. Assess and mark bilateral pulses, such as the dorsalis pedis and posterior tibial.
   5. Assess baseline oxygen saturation.
   6. Familiarize the parents and child with hospital procedures and equipment.
   7. Educate child, if of an appropriate age, and parents about the procedure.
   8. Allow the parents and child to verbalize feelings and concerns regarding the procedure and the disorder.

C. Postprocedure nursing interventions
   1. Assess findings on the cardiac monitor/oxygen saturation for up to 4 hours following procedure.
   2. Assess pulses below the catheter site for equality and symmetry.
   3. Assess the temperature and color of the affected extremity and report coolness, which may indicate arterial obstruction.

4. Monitor vital signs every 15 minutes four times, every half-hour four times, and then every hour four times.
5. Assess the pressure dressing for intactness and signs of hemorrhage.
6. Assess for signs of bleeding under the extremity on the bed sheets.
7. If bleeding is present, apply continuous, direct pressure at the cardiac catheter entry site and report immediately.
8. Immobilize the affected extremity for at least 4 to 6 hours for venous entry site and 6 to 8 hours for arterial entry site.
9. Hydrate the child via the oral or intravenous route, or both routes as prescribed.
10. Administer acetaminophen (Tylenol) or ibuprofen (Advil, Motrin) for pain or discomfort as prescribed.
11. Prepare the parents and child, if appropriate, for surgery.

▲ D. Discharge teaching for the child and parents
1. Remove the dressing on the day after the procedure and cover it with a Band-Aid for 2 or 3 days.
2. Keep the site clean and dry.
3. Avoid tub baths for 2 to 3 days.
4. Observe for redness, edema, drainage, bleeding, fever and report any of these signs immediately.
5. Avoid strenuous activity, if applicable.
6. The child may return to school, if appropriate.
7. Provide a diet as tolerated.
8. Administer acetaminophen (Tylenol) or ibuprofen (Advil, Motrin) for pain, discomfort, or fever.
9. Keep follow-up appointment with primary care provider.

VIII. CARDIAC SURGERY
▲ A. Postoperative interventions
1. Monitor vital signs frequently, especially the temperature, and notify the physician if fever occurs.
2. Monitor for signs of sepsis, such as fever, chills, diaphoresis, lethargy, and altered levels of consciousness.
3. Maintain strict aseptic technique.
4. Monitor lines, tubes, or catheters that are in place and monitor for signs and symptoms of infection.
5. Assess for signs of discomfort, such as irritability, restlessness, changes in heart rate, respiratory rate, and blood pressure.
6. Administer pain medications as prescribed.
7. Administer antibiotics and antipyretics as prescribed.
8. Encourage rest periods.
9. Facilitate parent-child contact as soon as possible.
▲ B. Postoperative home care (Box 38-9)

BOX 38-9

Home Care After Cardiac Surgery

Omit play outside for several weeks.
Avoid activities in which the child could fall, such as bike riding, for 2 to 4 weeks.
Avoid crowds for 2 weeks after discharge.
Follow a no-added salt diet if prescribed.
Do not add any new foods to the infant's diet.
Do not place creams, lotions, or powders on the incision until completely healed.
The child may return to school the third week after discharge, starting with half-days.
The child should not participate in physical education for 2 months.
Instruct the parents to discipline the child normally.
Instruct the parents about the importance of the 2-week follow-up.
Avoid immunizations, invasive procedures, and dental visits for 2 months.
Advise the parents regarding the importance of a dental visit every 6 months after age 3 years and to inform the dentist of the cardiac problem so that antibiotics can be prescribed if necessary.
Instruct the parents to call the physician if coughing, tachypnea, cyanosis, vomiting, diarrhea, anorexia, pain, or fever occur, or any swelling, redness, or drainage occurs at the site of the incision.

IX. RHEUMATIC FEVER
A. Description
1. Rheumatic fever is an inflammatory autoimmune disease that affects the connective tissues of the heart, joints, subcutaneous tissues, and blood vessels of the central nervous system.
2. The most serious complication is rheumatic heart disease, which affects the cardiac valves, particularly the mitral valve.
3. Rheumatic fever presents 2 to 6 weeks following an untreated or partially treated group A beta-hemolytic streptococcal infection of the upper respiratory tract.
4. Jones criteria are used to determine the diagnosis (Box 38-10).
B. Assessment (Fig. 38-1)
1. Fever: Low-grade fever that spikes in the late afternoon
2. Elevated antistreptolysin O titer
3. Elevated sedimentation rate
4. Elevated C-reactive protein level
5. Aschoff bodies (lesions): Found in the heart, blood vessels, brain, and serous surfaces of the joints and pleura
C. Interventions
1. Assess vital signs.
2. Control joint pain and inflammation with massage and alternating hot and cold applications as prescribed.

Jones Criteria for Diagnosis of Rheumatic Fever

MAJOR MANIFESTATIONS
Carditis
Polyarthritis
Chorea
Erythema marginatum
Subcutaneous nodules

MINOR MANIFESTATIONS
Fever
Arthralgia
Elevated erythrocyte sedimentation rate (ESR) or positive
  C-reactive protein (CRP) level
Prolonged P-R interval

OTHER CRITERIA
Supporting evidence of preceding streptococcal
  infection—history of recent scarlet fever, positive
  throat culture for group A streptococcus, increased
  antistreptolysin O (ASO) titer, or presence of other
  streptococcal antibodies

From McKinney, E., James, S., Murray, S., & Ashwill, J. (2005). *Maternal-child nursing* (2nd ed.). St. Louis: W.B. Saunders.

3. Provide bed rest during acute febrile phase.
4. Limit physical exercise in the child with carditis.
5. Administer antibiotics (penicillin) as prescribed.
6. Administer salicylates and anti-inflammatory agents (prednisone [Deltasone]) as prescribed; these medications should not be administered before the diagnosis is confirmed, because these medications mask the polyarthritis).
7. Initiate seizure precautions if the child is experiencing chorea.
8. Instruct the parents about the importance of follow-up and the need for antibiotic prophylaxis for dental work, infection, and invasive procedures.
9. Advise the child to inform the parents if anyone in school develops a streptococcal throat infection.

X. KAWASAKI DISEASE

A. Description
   1. Kawasaki disease is known as mucocutaneous lymph node syndrome and is an acute systemic inflammatory illness.
   2. The cause is unknown but may be associated with an infection from an organism or toxin.
   3. Cardiac involvement is the most serious complication; aneurysms can develop.
B. Assessment
   1. Acute stage
      a. Fever
      b. Conjunctival hyperemia

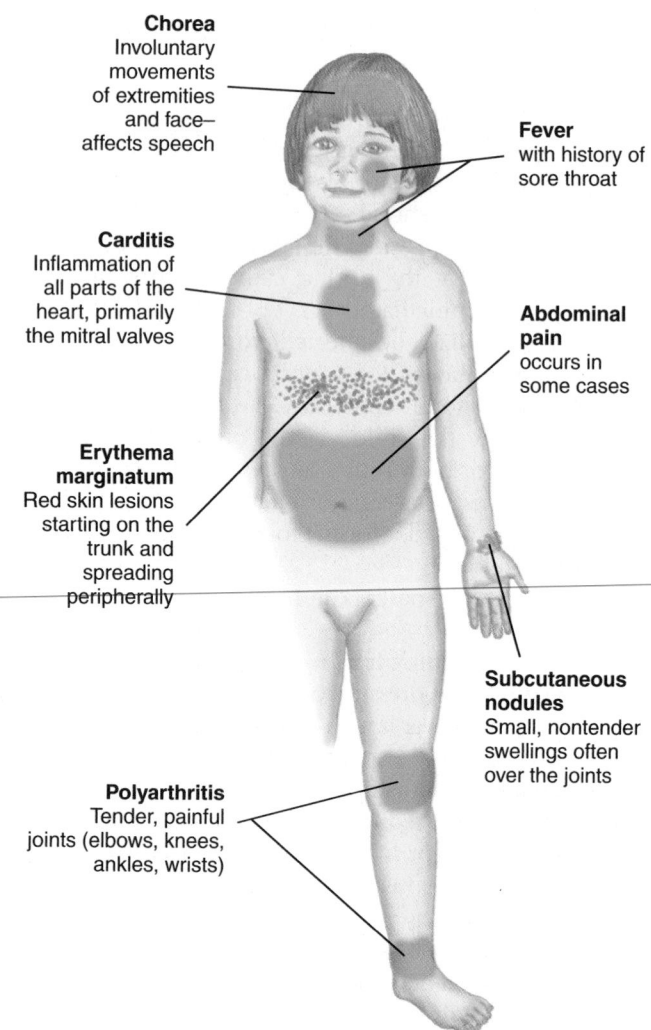

Chorea
Involuntary movements of extremities and face—affects speech

Fever
with history of sore throat

Carditis
Inflammation of all parts of the heart, primarily the mitral valves

Abdominal pain
occurs in some cases

Erythema marginatum
Red skin lesions starting on the trunk and spreading peripherally

Subcutaneous nodules
Small, nontender swellings often over the joints

Polyarthritis
Tender, painful joints (elbows, knees, ankles, wrists)

FIG. 38-1 Clinical manifestations of rheumatic fever. (From McKinney, E., James, S., Murray, S., & Ashwill, J. [2005]. *Maternal-child nursing* [2nd ed.]. St. Louis: W.B. Saunders.)

      c. Red throat
      d. Swollen hands, rash, and enlargement of the cervical lymph nodes
   2. Subacute stage
      a. Cracking lips and fissures
      b. Desquamation of the skin on the tips of the fingers and toes
      c. Joint pain
      d. Cardiac manifestations
      e. Thrombocytosis
   3. Convalescent stage: Child appears normal but signs of inflammation may be present.
C. Interventions
   1. Monitor temperature frequently.
   2. Assess heart sounds, rate, and rhythm.
   3. Assess extremities for edema, redness, and desquamation.
   4. Examine eyes for conjunctivitis.

BOX 38-11
Parent Education for Kawasaki Disease

Follow-up care is essential to recovery.
The signs and symptoms of Kawasaki disease include the following:
   Irritability may last up for up to 2 months after the onset of symptoms.
   Peeling of the hands and feet may occur.
   Pain in the joints may persist for several weeks.
   Stiffness in the morning, after naps, and in cold temperatures may occur.
Record the temperature (because fever is expected) until child has been afebrile for several days.
Notify the physician if the temperature is 101° F or higher.
Salicylates such as acetylsalicylic acid (aspirin) may be given.
Signs of aspirin toxicity include tinnitus, headache, vertigo, bruising; do not administer aspirin or aspirin-containing products if child has been exposed to chickenpox or the flu.
Signs and symptoms of bleeding include epistaxis (nose bleeds), hemoptysis (coughing up blood), hematemesis (vomiting up blood), hematuria (blood in urine), melena (blood in stool), and bruises on body.
Signs and symptoms of cardiac complications include chest pain or tightness (older children), cool and pale extremities, abdominal pain, nausea and vomiting, irritability, restlessness, and uncontrollable crying.
Child should avoid contact sports, if age appropriate, if taking aspirin or anticoagulants.
Avoid administration of MMR or varicella vaccine to the child for 11 months post–intravenous immune globulin therapy, if appropriate.

5. Monitor mucous membranes for inflammation.
6. Monitor strict intake and output.
7. Administer soft foods and liquids that are neither too hot nor too cold.
8. Weigh the child daily.
9. Provide passive range-of-motion exercises to facilitate joint movement.
10. Administer acetylsalicylic acid (aspirin) as prescribed for its antipyretic and antiplatelet effects.
11. Administer immune globulin intravenously as prescribed to reduce the duration of the fever and the incidence of coronary artery lesions and aneurysms; IV immune globulin (IVIG) is a blood product, so blood precautions when administering it are warranted.
12. Parent education (Box 38-11)

PRACTICE QUESTIONS

1. A clinic nurse reviews the record of a child just seen by a physician and diagnosed with suspected aortic stenosis. The nurse expects to note documentation of which clinical manifestation specifically found in this disorder?
   1. Pallor
   2. Hyperactivity
   3. Exercise intolerance
   4. Gastrointestinal disturbances

2. A nurse has provided home care instructions to the mother of a child who is being discharged following cardiac surgery. Which statement made by the mother indicates a need for further instructions?
   1. "A balance of rest and exercise is important."
   2. "I can apply lotion or powder to the incision if it is itchy."
   3. "Activities in which my child could fall need to be avoided for 2 to 4 weeks."
   4. "Large crowds of people need to be avoided for at least 2 weeks following surgery."

3. A nurse receives a telephone call from the admitting office and is told that a child with rheumatic fever will be arriving in the nursing unit for admission. On admission, the nurse prepares to ask the mother which question to elicit assessment information specific to the development of rheumatic fever?
   1. "Has the child complained of back pain?"
   2. "Has the child complained of headaches?"
   3. "Has the child had any nausea or vomiting?"
   4. "Did the child have a sore throat or fever within the last 2 months?"

4. A nurse is caring for a child with a suspected diagnosis of rheumatic fever. The nurse reviews the laboratory results, knowing that which laboratory study would assist in confirming the diagnosis?
   1. Immunoglobulin
   2. Red blood cell count
   3. White blood cell count
   4. Antistreptolysin O titer

5. A nurse is preparing for the admission of a child with a diagnosis of acute-stage Kawasaki disease. On assessment of the child, the nurse expects to note which clinical manifestation of the acute stage of the disease?
   1. Cracked lips
   2. A normal appearance
   3. Conjunctival hyperemia
   4. Desquamation of the skin

6. A nurse provides home care instructions to the parents of a child with congestive heart failure (CHF) regarding the procedure for the administration of digoxin (Lanoxin). Which statement, if made by the parent, indicates the need for further instructions?
   1. "I will not mix the medication with food."
   2. "If more than one dose is missed, I will call the physician."
   3. "I will take the child's pulse before administering the medication."
   4. "If the child vomits after medication administration, I will repeat the dose."

7. A nurse is caring for an infant with a diagnosis of tetralogy of Fallot. The infant suddenly becomes cyanotic, and the nurse recognizes that the infant is experiencing a hypercyanotic spell (blue or tet spell). The nurse immediately places the infant in what position?
   1. Prone position
   2. Knee-chest position
   3. High Fowler's position
   4. Reverse Trendelenburg position

8. A nurse caring for an infant with congenital heart disease is monitoring the infant closely for signs of congestive heart failure (CHF). The nurse assesses the infant for which early sign of CHF?
   1. Cough
   2. Pallor
   3. Tachycardia
   4. Slow and shallow breathing

9. A physician has prescribed oxygen as needed for an infant with congestive heart failure (CHF). In which situation should the nurse administer the oxygen to the infant?
   1. During sleep
   2. When changing the infant's diapers
   3. When the mother is holding the infant
   4. When drawing blood for electrolyte level testing

10. An infant with congestive heart failure (CHF) is receiving diuretic therapy, and a nurse is closely monitoring the intake and output. The nurse uses which most appropriate method to assess the urine output?
    1. Weighing the diapers
    2. Inserting a Foley catheter
    3. Comparing intake with output
    4. Measuring the amount of water added to formula

11. A nurse is monitoring an infant with congestive heart failure (CHF). Which of the following alerts

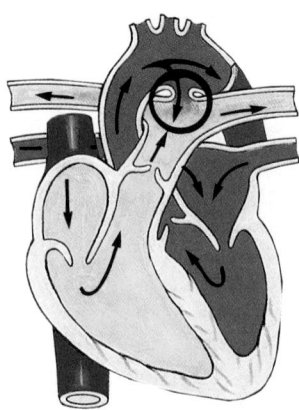

FIG. 38-2 (From Hockenberry, M., & Wilson, D. [2007]. *Wong's nursing care of infants and children* [8th ed.]. St. Louis: W.B. Saunders.)

the nurse to suspect fluid accumulation and the need to call the physician?
   1. Bradypnea
   2. Diaphoresis
   3. Decreased blood pressure
   4. A weight gain of 1 lb in 1 day

ALTERNATE ITEM FORMAT: FIGURE/ILLUSTRATION

Assessment findings of an infant admitted to the hospital reveal a machinery-like murmur on auscultation of the heart and signs of congestive heart failure. The nurse reviews congenital cardiac anomalies and identifies the infant's condition as which of the following? Refer to the circled area in Figure 38-2 to determine the condition.
   ❑ 1. Aortic stenosis
   ❑ 2. Atrial septal defect
   ❑ 3. Ventricular septal defect
   ❑ 4. Patent ductus arteriosus

ANSWERS

1. **3**
Rationale: The child with aortic stenosis shows signs of exercise intolerance, chest pain, and dizziness when standing for long periods of time. Pallor may be noted but is not specific to this type of disorder alone. Options 2 and 4 are not related to this disorder.
Test-Taking Strategy: Use the process of elimination, focusing on the disorder. Options 2 and 4 can be easily eliminated first because they are not associated with a cardiac disorder. From the remaining options, noting the word *specifically* in the question will direct you to option 3. Review the manifestations associated with aortic stenosis if you had difficulty with this question.
Level of Cognitive Ability: Analysis
Client Needs: Physiological Integrity
Integrated Process: Communication and Documentation

Content Area: Child health
References: Hockenberry, M. & Wilson, D. (2007). *Nursing care of infants and children* (8th ed., p. 1464). St. Louis: Mosby. Wong, D., Perry, S., Hockenberry, M., et al. (2006). *Maternal child nursing care* (3rd ed., p. 1563). St. Louis: Mosby.

2. **2**
Rationale: The mother should be instructed that lotions and powders should not be applied to the incision site. Lotions and powders can irritate the surrounding skin, which could lead to skin breakdown and subsequent infection of the incision site. Options 1, 3, and 4 are accurate instructions regarding home care after cardiac surgery.
Test-Taking Strategy: Use the process of elimination and note the strategic words *indicates a need for further instructions*. These words indicate a negative event query and ask you to select an

option that is an incorrect statement. Using general principles related to postoperative incisional site care will direct you to option 2. Review home care instructions following cardiac surgery if you had difficulty with this question.
Level of Cognitive Ability: Analysis
Client Needs: Physiological Integrity
Integrated Process: Teaching and Learning
Content Area: Child health
Reference: McKinney, E., James, S., Murray, S., & Ashwill, J. (2005). *Maternal-child nursing* (2nd ed., p. 1283). St. Louis: W.B. Saunders.

3. 4
Rationale: Rheumatic fever characteristically presents 2 to 6 weeks after an untreated or partially treated group A beta-hemolytic streptococcal infection of the upper respiratory tract. Initially, the nurse determines whether the child had a sore throat or an unexplained fever within the past 2 months. Options 1, 2, and 3 are unrelated to rheumatic fever.
Test-Taking Strategy: Use the process of elimination and note the similarity between rheumatic *fever* in the question and the word *fever* in the correct option. If you had difficulty with this question, review the etiology related to rheumatic fever.
Level of Cognitive Ability: Analysis
Client Needs: Physiological Integrity
Integrated Process: Nursing Process—assessment
Content Area: Child health
Reference: Hockenberry, M., Wilson, D., & Winkelstein, M. (2005). *Wong's essentials of pediatric nursing* (7th ed., p. 923). St. Louis: Mosby.

4. 4
Rationale: A diagnosis of rheumatic fever is confirmed by the presence of two major manifestations or one major and two minor manifestations from the Jones criteria. In addition, evidence of a recent streptococcal infection is confirmed by a positive antistreptolysin O titer, Streptozyme assay, or an anti-DNase B assay. Options 1, 2, and 3 will not help to confirm the diagnosis of rheumatic fever.
Test-Taking Strategy: Use the process of elimination. Recalling that rheumatic fever characteristically is associated with streptococcal infection will direct you to option 4. If you had difficulty with this question, review the Jones criteria and diagnostic tests for rheumatic fever.
Level of Cognitive Ability: Analysis
Client Needs: Physiological Integrity
Integrated Process: Nursing Process—analysis
Content Area: Child health
References: McKinney, E., James, S., Murray, S., & Ashwill, J. (2005). *Maternal-child nursing* (2nd ed., p. 1288). St. Louis: W.B. Saunders.
Wong, D., Perry, S., Hockenberry, M., et al. (2006). *Maternal child nursing care* (3rd ed., p. 1585). St. Louis: Mosby.

5. 3
Rationale: In the acute stage, the child has a fever, conjunctival hyperemia, red throat, swollen hands, rash, and enlargement of the cervical lymph nodes. In the subacute stage, cracking lips and fissures, desquamation of the skin on the tips of the

fingers and toes, joint pain, cardiac manifestations, and thrombocytosis occur. In the convalescent stage, the child appears normal, but signs of inflammation may be present.
Test-Taking Strategy: Use the process of elimination. Noting the strategic words *acute stage* in the question will assist in directing you to option 3. Review the clinical manifestations associated with each stage of Kawasaki disease if you had difficulty with this question.
Level of Cognitive Ability: Analysis
Client Needs: Physiological Integrity
Integrated Process: Nursing Process—assessment
Content Area: Child health
Reference: McKinney, E., James, S., Murray, S., & Ashwill, J. (2005). *Maternal-child nursing* (2nd ed., p. 1289). St. Louis: W.B. Saunders.

6. 4
Rationale: The parents need to be instructed that if the child vomits after the digoxin is administered, they are not to repeat the dose. Options 1, 2, and 3 are accurate instructions regarding the administration of this medication. In addition, the parents should be instructed that if a dose is missed and is not identified until 4 hours later, the dose should not be administered.
Test-Taking Strategy: Use the process of elimination and note the strategic words *need for further instructions*. These words indicate a negative event query and ask you to select an option that is an incorrect statement. General knowledge regarding digoxin administration will assist in eliminating option 3. Principles related to administering medications to children will assist in eliminating option 1. From the remaining options, select option 4 because if the child vomits, it would be difficult to determine whether the medication also was vomited or was absorbed by the body. Review home care instructions regarding the administration of digoxin if you had difficulty with this question.
Level of Cognitive Ability: Analysis
Client Needs: Physiological Integrity
Integrated Process: Teaching and Learning
Content Area: Child health
Reference: Hockenberry, M., Wilson, D., & Winkelstein, M. (2005). *Wong's essentials of pediatric nursing* (7th ed., p. 910). St. Louis: Mosby.

7. 2
Rationale: If a hypercyanotic spell occurs, the nurse immediately places the infant in a knee-chest position. This position improves systemic arterial oxygen saturation. Therefore, options 1, 3, and 4 are incorrect and will not improve systemic arterial oxygen saturation.
Test-Taking Strategy: Focus on the subject of the question, a hypercyanotic spell. Think about the position that will improve oxygenation. This will direct you to option 2. Review the interventions if a hypercyanotic spell occurs in an infant if you had difficulty with this question.
Level of Cognitive Ability: Application
Client Needs: Physiological Integrity
Integrated Process: Nursing Process—implementation
Content Area: Child health

Reference: McKinney, E., James, S., Murray, S., & Ashwill, J. (2005). *Maternal-child nursing* (2nd ed., p. 1267). St. Louis: W.B. Saunders.

8. 3

Rationale: The early signs of congestive heart failure (CHF) include tachycardia, tachypnea, profuse scalp sweating, fatigue and irritability, sudden weight gain, and respiratory distress. A cough may occur in CHF as a result of mucosal swelling and irritation but is not an early sign. Pallor may be noted in the infant with CHF but is also not an early sign.

Test-Taking Strategy: Use the process of elimination and note the strategic word *early*. Think about the physiology and the effects on the heart when fluid overload occurs. These concepts will assist in directing you to option 3. If you had difficulty with this question, review the early signs of CHF in an infant.

Level of Cognitive Ability: Analysis
Client Needs: Physiological Integrity
Integrated Process: Nursing Process—assessment
Content Area: Child health
References: Hockenberry, M., Wilson, D., & Winkelstein, M. (2005). *Wong's essentials of pediatric nursing* (7th ed., p. 907). St. Louis: Mosby.
Hockenberry, M., & Wilson, D. (2007). *Nursing care of infants and children* (8th ed., p. 1448). St. Louis: Mosby.

9. 4

Rationale: Crying exhausts the limited energy supply, increases the workload of the heart, and increases the oxygen demands. Oxygen administration may be prescribed for stressful periods, especially during bouts of crying or invasive procedures. Options 1, 2, and 3 are not likely to produce crying in the infant.

Test-Taking Strategy: Use the process of elimination. Recall the situations that would place stress and an increased workload on the heart. This concept should direct you to option 4. Drawing blood is an invasive procedure, which would likely cause the child to cry. Review care of the child with CHF if you had difficulty with this question.

Level of Cognitive Ability: Analysis
Client Needs: Physiological Integrity
Integrated Process: Nursing Process—implementation
Content Area: Child health
References: Hockenberry, M., Wilson, D., & Winkelstein, M. (2005). *Wong's essentials of pediatric nursing* (7th ed., p. 909). St. Louis: Mosby.
McKinney, E., James, S., Murray, S., & Ashwill, J. (2005). *Maternal-child nursing* (2nd ed., p. 1265). St. Louis: W.B. Saunders.

10. 1

Rationale: The most appropriate method for assessing urine output in an infant receiving diuretic therapy is to weigh the diapers. Comparing intake with output would not provide an accurate measure of urine output. Measuring the amount of water added to formula is unrelated to the amount of output. Although Foley catheter drainage is most accurate in determining output, it is not the most appropriate method in an infant and places the infant at risk for infection.

Test-Taking Strategy: Use the process of elimination. Eliminate options 3 and 4 first because they will not provide an indication of urine output. From the remaining options, note the words *most appropriate* in the question. These words will direct you to option 1. Review care of the infant receiving diuretic therapy if you had difficulty with this question.

Level of Cognitive Ability: Application
Client Needs: Physiological Integrity
Integrated Process: Nursing Process—assessment
Content Area: Child health
References: Hockenberry, M., Wilson, D., & Winkelstein, M. (2005). *Wong's essentials of pediatric nursing* (7th ed., p. 913). St. Louis: Mosby.
McKinney, E., James, S., Murray, S., & Ashwill, J. (2005). *Maternal-child nursing* (2nd ed., p. 1264). St. Louis: W.B. Saunders.

11. 4

Rationale: A weight gain of 0.5 kg (1 lb) in 1 day is caused by the accumulation of fluid. The nurse should assess urine output, assess for evidence of facial or peripheral edema, auscultate lung sounds, and report the weight gain to the physician. Tachypnea and an increased blood pressure would occur with fluid accumulation. Diaphoresis is a sign of CHF but is not specific to fluid accumulation, and usually occurs with exertional activities.

Test-Taking Strategy: Use the process of elimination and focus on the subject, fluid accumulation. Note the relationship between *fluid accumulation* in the question and *weight gain* in the correct option. Review the indications of fluid accumulation in an infant with CHF if you had difficulty with this question.

Level of Cognitive Ability: Analysis
Client Needs: Physiological Integrity
Integrated Process: Nursing Process—analysis
Content Area: Child health
Reference: McKinney, E., James, S., Murray, S., & Ashwill, J. (2005). *Maternal-child nursing* (2nd ed., p. 1264). St. Louis: W.B. Saunders.

ALTERNATE ITEM FORMAT: FIGURE

Answer: 4

Rationale: A patent ductus arteriosus is failure of the fetal ductus arteriosus (artery connecting the aorta and the pulmonary artery) to close. A characteristic machinery-like murmur is present and the infant may show signs of congestive heart failure. Aortic stenosis is a narrowing or stricture of the aortic valve. Atrial septal defect is an abnormal opening between the atria. Ventricular septal defect is an abnormal opening between the right and left ventricles.

Test-Taking Strategy: Focus on the figure and the location of the defect. Recalling the anatomical locations in the heart will direct you to option 4. Review congenital heart defects if you had difficulty with this question.

Level of Cognitive Ability: Analysis
Client Needs: Physiological Integrity
Integrated Process: Nursing Process—assessment
Content Area: Child health
Reference: Hockenberry, M., & Wilson, D. (2007). *Wong's nursing care of infants and children* (8th ed., p. 1463). St. Louis: Mosby.

REFERENCES

Hockenberry, M. Wilson, D., & Winkelstein, M. (2005). *Wong's essentials of pediatric nursing* (7th ed.). St. Louis: Mosby.

Hockenberry, M., & Wilson, D. (2007). *Nursing care of infants and children* (8th ed.). St. Louis: Mosby.

Kliegman, R., Marcdante, K., Jenson, H., & Behrman, R. (2006). *Nelson essentials of pediatrics* (5th ed.). St. Louis: W.B. Saunders.

McKinney, E., James, S., Murray, S., & Ashwill, J. (2005). *Maternal-child nursing* (2nd ed.). St. Louis: W.B. Saunders.

National Council of State Boards of Nursing (Eds.). (2007). *2007 NCLEX-RN® detailed test plan.* Chicago: Author.

Wong, D., Perry, S., Hockenberry, M., et al. (2006). *Maternal child nursing care* (3rd ed.). St. Louis: Mosby.

Gastrointestinal Disorders

I. VOMITING

A. Description
1. The major concerns when a child is vomiting are the risk of dehydration, the loss of fluid and electrolytes, and the development of metabolic alkalosis.
2. Additional concerns include aspiration, atelectasis, and the development of pneumonia.
3. Causes include acute infectious diseases, increased intracranial pressure, toxic ingestions, food intolerance, mechanical obstruction of gastrointestinal tract, metabolic disorders, and psychogenic disorders.

B. Assessment
1. Signs of aspiration
2. Character of vomitus
3. Pain and abdominal cramping
4. Dehydration
5. Fluid and electrolyte imbalances
6. Metabolic alkalosis

C. Interventions
1. Maintain a patent airway.
2. Position the child on the side to prevent aspiration.
3. Monitor vital signs.
4. Monitor the character, amount, and frequency of vomiting.
5. Assess the force of the vomiting; projectile vomiting indicates pyloric **stenosis** or increased intracranial pressure.
6. Monitor strict intake and output
7. Monitor for signs and symptoms of dehydration, such as sunken fontanel (age-appropriate), nonelastic skin turgor, dry mucous membranes, decreased tear production, and oliguria.
8. Monitor electrolyte levels.

9. Provide oral rehydration therapy as tolerated and as prescribed; begin feeding slowly, with small amounts of fluid at frequent intervals.
10. Assess for diarrhea or abdominal pain.
11. Advise the parents to inform the physician when signs of dehydration, blood in vomitus, forceful vomiting, or abdominal pain are present.

II. DIARRHEA

A. Description
1. The major concerns when a child is having diarrhea are the risk of dehydration, the loss of fluid and electrolytes, and the development of metabolic acidosis.
2. Acute diarrhea is a cause of dehydration particularly in children younger than 5 years.
3. Some causes of acute diarrhea include parasitic infestation, acute infectious disorders of the gastrointestinal tract, and antibiotic therapy.
4. Some causes of chronic diarrhea include malabsorption syndromes, inflammatory bowel disease, immune deficiencies, food intolerances, and nonspecific factors.

B. Assessment
1. Character of stools
2. Pain and abdominal cramping
3. Dehydration
4. Fluid and electrolyte imbalances
5. Metabolic acidosis

C. Interventions
1. Monitor vital signs.
2. Monitor the character, amount, and frequency of diarrhea.
3. Provide enteric isolation as required; instruct the parents in effective hand-washing technique.
4. Monitor skin integrity.
5. Monitor strict intake and output.

6. Monitor electrolyte levels.
7. Monitor for signs and symptoms of dehydration
8. For mild to moderate dehydration, provide oral rehydration therapy with Pedialyte or a similar rehydration solution as prescribed; avoid carbonated beverages because they can contain high amounts of sugar.
9. For severe dehydration, maintain an NPO status to place the bowel at rest and provide fluid and electrolyte replacement by the intravenous (IV) route as prescribed; if potassium is prescribed for IV administration, ensure that the child has voided before administering.
10. Reintroduce a normal diet once rehydration is achieved.

III. CLEFT LIP AND CLEFT PALATE
A. Description
   1. Cleft lip and/or cleft palate are congenital anomalies that occur as a result of failure of soft tissue or bony structure to fuse during embryonic development.
   2. The defects involve abnormal openings in the lip and/or palate that may occur unilaterally or bilaterally and are readily apparent at birth.

3. Causes include genetic, **hereditary,** and environmental factors, exposure to radiation or rubella virus, chromosome abnormalities, and teratogenic factors.
4. Closure of cleft lip defect precedes that of the cleft palate and is usually performed during the first weeks of life.
5. Cleft palate repair is performed sometime between 12 and 18 months of age to allow for the palatal changes that take place with normal growth; a cleft palate is closed before the child develops faulty speech habits.
B. Assessment (Fig. 39-1)
   1. Cleft lip can range from a slight notch to a complete separation from the floor of the nose.
   2. Cleft palate can include nasal distortion, midline or bilateral cleft, and variable extension from the uvula and soft and hard palate.
C. Interventions
   1. Assess the ability to suck, swallow, handle normal secretions, and breathe without distress.
   2. Assess fluid and calorie intake daily
   3. Monitor daily weight.
   4. Modify feeding techniques; plan to use specialized feeding techniques, obturators, and special nipples and feeders.

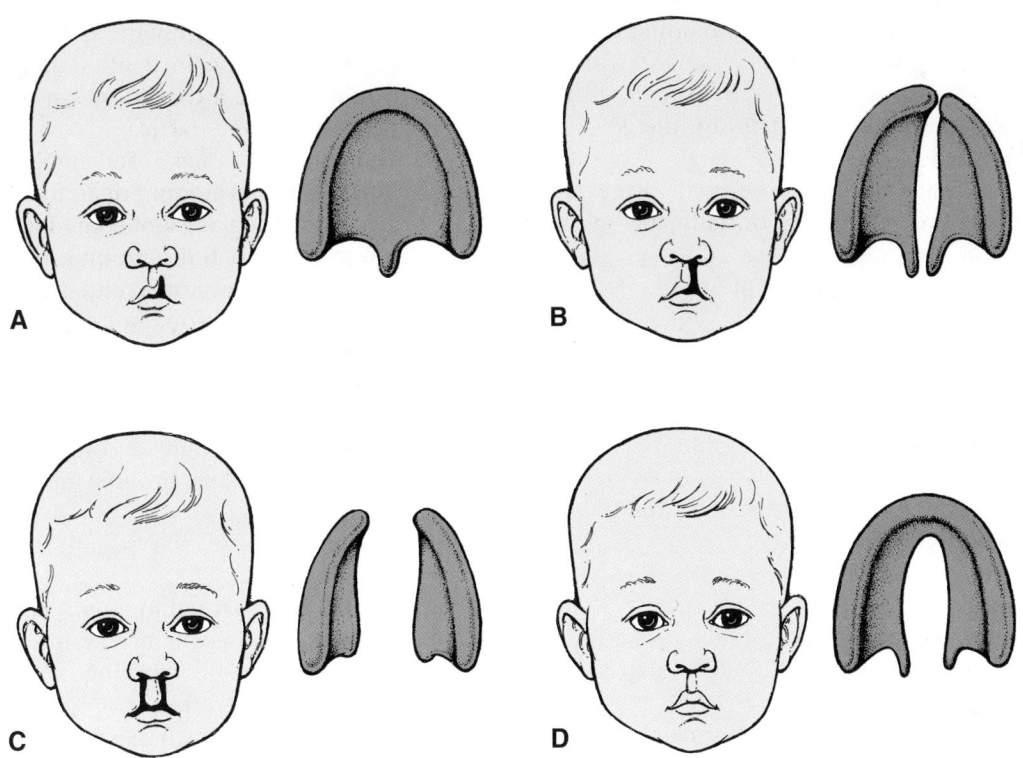

FIG. 39-1 Variations in clefts of lip and palate at birth. **A,** Notch in vermilion border. **B,** Unilateral cleft lip and palate. **C,** Bilateral cleft lip and palate. **D,** Cleft palate. (From Hockenberry, M., Wilson, D., & Winkelstein, M. [2005]. *Wong's essentials of pediatric nursing* [7th ed.]. St. Louis: Mosby.)

5. Hold the child in an upright position and direct the formula to the side and back of the mouth to prevent aspiration.

6. Feed small amounts gradually and burp frequently.

7. Position on the side after feeding.

8. Keep suction equipment and a bulb syringe at the bedside.

9. Teach the parents special feeding or suctioning techniques.

10. Teach the parents the *ESSR* (*e*nlarge, *s*timulate sucking, *s*wallow, *r*est) method of feeding (Box 39-1).

11. Encourage the parents to express their feelings about the disorder.

12. Encourage parental bonding with the child, including holding the child and calling the child by name.

D. Postoperative interventions

1. Cleft lip repair

a. A lip protector device or Logan bar may be taped securely to the cheeks to prevent trauma to the suture line.

b. Position the child on the side lateral to the repair or on the back (position to prevent airway obstruction by secretions, blood, or the tongue).

c. Avoid the prone position to prevent rubbing of the surgical site on the mattress.

d. After feeding, cleanse the suture line of formula or serosanguineous drainage with a cotton-tipped swab dipped in normal saline.

e. Apply antibiotic ointment to the site as prescribed.

f. Elbow restraints should be used to prevent the infant from injuring or traumatizing the surgical site.

g. Monitor for signs and symptoms of infection at the surgical site.

h. Keep the surgical site clean and dry.

2. Cleft palate repair

a. The child is allowed to lie on the abdomen.

b. Feedings are resumed by bottle, breast, or cup.

c. Oral packing may be secured to the palate (removed in 2 to 3 days).

d. Do not allow the child to brush his or her teeth.

e. Instruct the parents to avoid offering hard food items to the child, such as toast or cookies.

3. Soft elbow or jacket restraints may be used (check agency policies and procedures) to keep the child from touching the repair site; remove restraints at least every 2 hours to assess skin integrity and to allow for exercising the arms.

BOX 39-1
ESSR Method of Feeding

*E*nlarge the nipple.
*S*timulate the suck reflex.
*S*wallow.
*R*est to allow the child to finish swallowing what has been placed in the mouth.

---

4. Avoid contact with sharp objects near the surgical site.

5. Avoid the use of oral suction or placing objects in the mouth such as a tongue depressor, thermometer, straws, spoons, forks, or pacifiers.

6. Provide analgesics for pain.

7. Instruct the parents in feeding techniques and in the care of the surgical site.

8. Instruct the parents to monitor for signs of infection at the surgical site, such as redness, swelling, or drainage.

9. Encourage the parents to hold the child.

10. Initiate appropriate referrals for speech impairment or language-based learning difficulties.

IV. **ESOPHAGEAL ATRESIA AND TRACHEOESOPHAGEAL FISTULA** (Fig. 39-2)

A. Description

1. The esophagus terminates before it reaches the stomach, ending in a blind pouch, and/or a fistula is present that forms an unnatural connection with the trachea.

2. The condition causes oral intake to enter the lungs or a large amount of air to enter the stomach, presenting a risk of coughing and choking; severe abdominal distention can occur.

3. Aspiration pneumonia and severe respiratory distress may develop, and death is likely to occur without surgical intervention.

4. Treatment includes maintenance of a patent airway, prevention of aspiration pneumonia, gastric or blind pouch decompression, supportive therapy, and surgical repair.

B. Assessment

1. Frothy saliva in the mouth and nose and drooling

2. The "3 C's"—*c*oughing and *c*hoking during feedings and unexplained *c*yanosis

3. **Regurgitation** and vomiting

4. Abdominal distention

5. Inability to pass a small-gauge (such as a No. 5 French) orogastric feeding tube via the mouth into the stomach

C. Preoperative interventions

1. The infant may be placed in an incubator or radiant warmer in which humidified oxygen is admin-

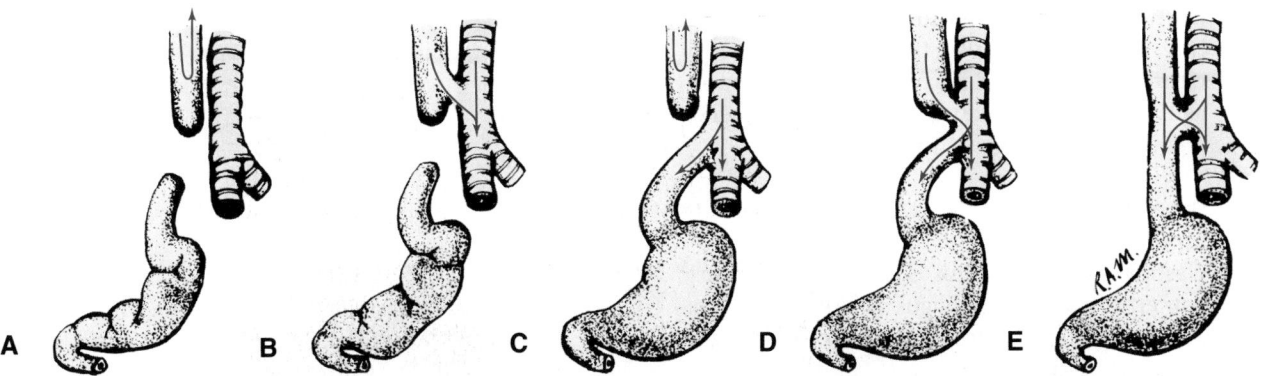

FIG. 39-2 Congenital atresia of esophagus and tracheoesophageal fistula. **A,** Upper and lower segments of esophagus end in blind sac (occurring in 5% to 8% of such infants). **B,** Upper segment of esophagus ends in atresia and connects to trachea by fistulous tract (occurring rarely). **C,** Upper segment of esophagus ends in blind pouch; lower segment connects with trachea by small fistulous tract (occurring in 80% to 95% of such infants). **D,** Both segments of esophagus connect by fistulous tracts to trachea (occurring in less than 1% of such infants). Infant may aspirate with first feeding. **E,** Esophagus is continuous but connects by fistulous tract to trachea; known as H-type. (From Hockenberry, M. & Wilson, D. [2007]. *Wong's nursing care of infants and children* [8th ed.]. St. Louis: Mosby.)

istered (intubation and mechanical ventilation may be necessary if respiratory distress occurs).

2. Maintain an NPO status.

3. Maintain IV fluids as prescribed.

4. Monitor respiratory status closely.

5. Suction accumulated secretions from the mouth and pharynx.

6. Maintain in an upright position to facilitate drainage and prevent aspiration of gastric secretions.

7. Maintain a double-lumen catheter, which is placed into the upper esophageal pouch and attached to intermittent or continuous low suction to keep the pouch empty of secretions; monitor its patency and irrigate with normal saline as prescribed to prevent clogging.

8. Maintain the gastrostomy tube, which may be left open so that air entering the stomach through the fistula can escape, minimizing the danger of **regurgitation.**

9. Administer broad-spectrum antibiotics as prescribed because of the high risk for aspiration pneumonia.

▲ D. Postoperative interventions

1. Monitor respiratory status.

2. Maintain IV fluids, antibiotics, and parenteral nutrition as prescribed.

3. Monitor strict intake and output.

4. Monitor daily weight.

5. Inspect the surgical site for signs and symptoms of infection.

6. Maintain the chest tube if present.

7. Assess for signs of pain.

8. Assess for dehydration and possible fluid overload.

9. Monitor for anastomotic leaks as evidenced by purulent drainage from the chest tube, increased temperature, and increased white blood cell count.

10. Maintain the double-lumen catheter at low suction as prescribed.

11. If a gastrostomy tube is present, attach it to gravity drainage until the infant can tolerate feedings (usually the fifth to seventh day postoperatively) as prescribed.

12. Before oral feedings and removal of the chest tube, prepare for a barium swallow as prescribed to verify the integrity of the esophageal anastomosis.

13. Before feeding, elevate the gastrostomy tube and secure it above the level of the stomach to allow gastric secretions to pass to the duodenum and swallowed air to escape through the open gastrostomy tube.

14. Administer gastrostomy tube feedings as prescribed until the anastomosis is healed.

15. Administer oral feedings with sterile water, followed by frequent small feedings of formula as prescribed.

16. Assess cervical esophagostomy site, if appropriate, for redness, breakdown, or exudate; remove accumulated drainage frequently and apply protective ointment, barrier dressing, and/or collection device as prescribed.

17. Provide non-nutritive sucking using a pacifier for infants who remain NPO for extended periods.

18. Instruct the parents in the techniques of suctioning, gastrostomy tube care and feedings, and skin site care as appropriate.

19. Instruct the parents to identify behaviors that indicate the need for suctioning, signs of respiratory distress, and signs of a constricted esophagus (e.g., poor feeding, dysphagia, drooling, regurgitated undigested food).

V. GASTROESOPHAGEAL REFLUX

A. Description

1. Gastroesophageal reflux is backflow of gastric contents into the esophagus as a result of relaxation or incompetence of the lower esophageal or cardiac sphincter.
2. Complications include esophagitis, esophageal strictures, aspiration of gastric contents, and aspiration pneumonia.
3. Most infants with gastroesophageal reflux have a mild problem that improves in about 1 year and requires only medical therapy.
4. Gastroesophageal reflux disease (GERD) occurs when gastric contents reflux into the esophagus or oropharynx and produce symptoms.
5. Treatment (Box 39-2)

B. Assessment

1. Passive **regurgitation** or emesis
2. Poor weight gain
3. Hematemesis
4. Melena
5. Irritability
6. Heartburn (in older children)
7. Anemia from blood loss

C. Interventions

1. Assess amount and characteristics of emesis.
2. Assess the relation of vomiting to the times of feedings and infant activity.
3. Monitor breath sounds before and after feedings.
4. Assess for signs of aspiration, such as drooling, coughing, or dyspnea following feeding.
5. Place suction equipment at the bedside.
6. Monitor intake and output.
7. Monitor for signs and symptoms of dehydration.
8. Maintain IV fluids as prescribed.

D. Positioning

1. In infants, the nonprone position during sleep (to reduce the incidence of sudden infant death syndrome); prone position is only acceptable while the infant is awake.
2. In children older than 1 year, position on the left side with the head of the bed elevated.

E. Diet

1. Provide small, frequent feedings to decrease the amount of **regurgitation.**
2. Provide nasogastric tube feedings if severe **regurgitation** and poor growth are present as prescribed.
3. For infants, thicken formula by adding 1 tablespoon of rice cereal per 6 oz of formula and cross-cut the nipple.

BOX 39-2

Treatment for Gastroesophageal Reflux

Diet
Positioning
Medications
Surgery: Performed when severe complications occur

---

4. Breast-feeding may continue, and the mother may provide more frequent feeding times or express milk for thickening with rice cereal.
5. Burp the infant frequently when feeding and handle the infant minimally after feedings; monitor for coughing during feeding and other signs of aspiration.
6. For toddlers, feed solids first, followed by liquids.
7. Instruct the parents to avoid feeding the child fatty foods, chocolate, tomato products, carbonated liquids, fruit juices, citrus products, and spicy foods.
8. Instruct the parents that the child should avoid vigorous play after feeding and avoid feeding just before bedtime.

F. Medications

1. Administer histamine 2 (H_2) antagonists (famotidine [Pepcid]) as prescribed.
2. Administer acetaminophen (Tylenol) as prescribed to relieve reflux pain.

G. Surgery

1. Fundoplication, in which a wrap to the stomach fundus is made around the distal esophagus (restores the competence of the lower esophageal sphincter)
2. A gastrostomy may be performed at the same time as the fundoplication for decompression of the stomach postoperatively.
3. Fundoplication may be combined with pyloroplasty in children with gastroesophageal reflux who also have delayed gastric emptying.
4. Postoperative care is similar to that for other types of abdominal surgery.
5. Instruct the parents about the potential postoperative problems, such as bloating symptoms or discomfort after consuming large, solid meals.

VI. HYPERTROPHIC PYLORIC STENOSIS (Fig. 39-3)

A. Description

1. Hypertrophy of the circular muscles of the pylorus causes narrowing of the pyloric canal between the stomach and the duodenum.
2. The **stenosis** usually develops in the first few weeks of life, causing projectile vomiting, dehydration, metabolic alkalosis, and failure to thrive.

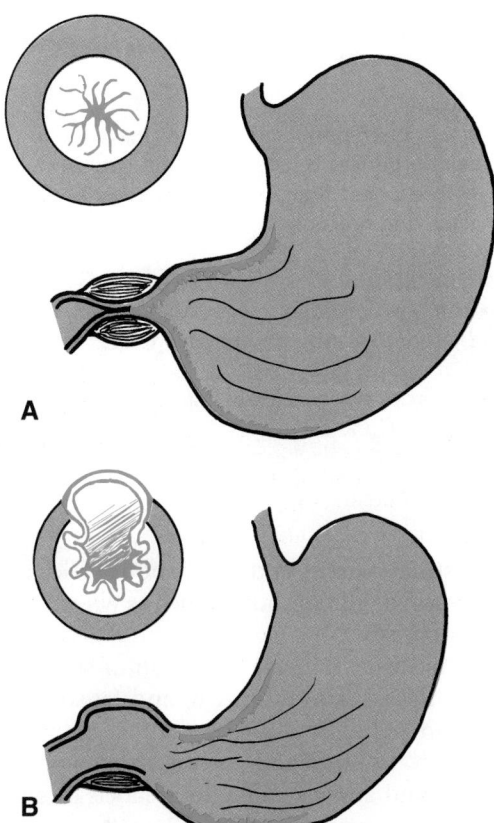

FIG. 39-3 Hypertrophic pyloric stenosis. **A,** Enlarged muscular area nearly obliterates pyloric channel. **B,** Longitudinal surgical division of muscle down to submucosa establishes adequate passageway. (From Hockenberry, M., Wilson, D., & Winkelstein, M. [2005]. *Wong's essentials of pediatric nursing* [7th ed.]. St. Louis: Mosby.)

B. Assessment
  1. Vomiting that progresses from mild **regurgitation** to forceful and projectile vomiting; it usually occurs after a feeding.
  2. Vomitus contains gastric contents such as milk or formula, may contain mucus, may be blood-tinged, and does not usually contain bile.
  3. The child exhibits hunger and irritability.
  4. Peristaltic waves are visible from left to right across the epigastrium during or immediately following a feeding.
  5. Olive-shaped mass is in the epigastrium just right of the umbilicus.
  6. Dehydration and malnutrition can occur.
  7. Electrolyte imbalances can occur.
  8. Metabolic alkalosis can occur.
C. Interventions
  1. Monitor vital signs.
  2. Monitor strict intake and output.
  3. Obtain daily weights.
  4. Monitor for signs of dehydration and electrolyte imbalances.

  5. Prepare the child and parents for pyloromyotomy if prescribed.
D. Pyloromyotomy
  1. Description: An incision through the muscle fibers of the pylorus that may be performed by laparoscopy
  2. Preoperative interventions
    a. Monitor hydration status by daily weights, intake and output, and urine for specific gravity.
    b. Correct fluid and electrolyte imbalances; administer fluids intravenously as prescribed for rehydration.
    c. Maintain an NPO status as prescribed.
    d. Monitor the number and character of stools.
    e. Maintain patency of the nasogastric tube placed for stomach decompression.
  3. Postoperative interventions
    a. Monitor intake and output.
    b. Begin small, frequent feedings of glucose, water, or electrolyte solution 4 to 6 hours postoperatively as prescribed, advancing the diet to formula 24 hours postoperatively as prescribed.
    c. Gradually increase amount and interval between feedings until a full feeding schedule has been reinstated, usually by 48 hours postoperatively.
    d. Feed the infant slowly, burping frequently and handle the infant minimally after feedings.
    e. Monitor for abdominal distention.
    f. Monitor the surgical wound and for signs of infection.
    g. Instruct the parents about wound care and feeding.

VII. LACTOSE INTOLERANCE
A. Description: Inability to tolerate lactose as a result of an absence or deficiency of lactase, an enzyme found in the secretions of the small intestine that is required for the digestion of lactose
B. Assessment
  1. Symptoms occur after the ingestion of milk products.
  2. Abdominal distention
  3. Crampy, abdominal pain; colic
  4. Diarrhea and excessive flatus
C. Interventions
  1. Eliminate the offending dairy product or administer an enzyme replacement such as LactAid, Lactrase, or Dairy Ease.
  2. Provide information to the parents about enzyme tablets that predigest the lactose in milk or supplement the body's own lactase.
  3. Substitute soy-based formulas for cow's milk formula or human milk.

4. Provide calcium and vitamin D supplements to prevent deficiency.
5. Limit milk consumption to one glass at a time.
6. Instruct the child and family that the child should drink milk with other foods rather than by itself.
7. Encourage consumption of hard cheese, cottage cheese, or yogurt, which contains the inactive lactase enzyme.
8. Encourage consumption of small amounts of dairy foods daily to help colonic bacteria adapt to ingested lactose.
9. Instruct the parents about the importance of calcium and vitamin D supplements.
10. Instruct the parents about the foods that contain lactose, including hidden sources.

VIII. CELIAC DISEASE
A. Description
1. Celiac disease also is known as gluten enteropathy or celiac sprue.
2. Intolerance to gluten, the protein component of wheat, barley, rye, and oats, is characteristic.
3. Celiac disease results in the accumulation of the amino acid glutamine, which is toxic to intestinal mucosal cells.
4. Intestinal villi atrophy occurs, which affects absorption of ingested nutrients.
5. Symptoms of the disorder occur most often between the ages of 1 and 5 years
6. There is usually an interval of 3 to 6 months between the introduction of gluten in the diet and the onset of symptoms.
7. Strict dietary avoidance of gluten minimizes the risk of developing malignant lymphoma of the small intestine and other gastrointestinal malignancies.
B. Assessment
1. Acute or insidious diarrhea
2. Steatorrhea
3. Anorexia
4. Abdominal pain and distention
5. Muscle wasting, particularly in the buttocks and extremities
6. Vomiting
7. Anemia
8. Irritability
C. Celiac crisis
1. Precipitated by infection, fasting, ingestion of gluten
2. Can lead to electrolyte imbalance, rapid dehydration, severe acidosis
3. Causes profuse watery diarrhea and vomiting
D. Interventions
1. Maintain a gluten-free diet, substituting corn, rice, and millet as grain sources.

BOX 39-3
Basics of a Gluten-Free Diet

FOODS ALLOWED
Meat such as beef, pork, and poultry and fish, eggs, milk and dairy products, vegetables, fruits, rice, corn, gluten-free wheat flour, puffed rice, cornflakes, cornmeal, and precooked gluten-free cereals

FOODS PROHIBITED
Commercially prepared ice cream, malted milk, prepared puddings, grains, including anything made from wheat, rye, oats, or barley, such as breads, rolls, cookies, cakes, crackers, cereal, spaghetti, macaroni noodles, beer, and ale

---

2. Instruct parents and child about lifelong elimination of gluten sources such as wheat, rye, oats, and barley.
3. Administer mineral and vitamin supplements, including iron, folic acid, and fat-soluble supplements A, D, E, and K
4. Teach the child and parents about a gluten-free diet and about reading food labels carefully for hidden sources of gluten (Box 39-3).
5. Instruct the parents in measures to prevent celiac crisis.
6. Inform the parents about the Celiac Sprue Association.

IX. APPENDICITIS
A. Description
1. Inflammation of the appendix
2. When the appendix becomes inflamed or infected, perforation may occur within a matter of hours, leading to peritonitis, sepsis, septic shock, and potential death.
3. Treatment is surgical removal of the appendix before perforation occurs.
B. Assessment
1. Pain in periumbilical area that descends to the right lower quadrant
2. Abdominal pain that is most intense at McBurney's point
3. Referred pain indicating the presence of peritoneal irritation
4. Rebound tenderness and abdominal rigidity
5. Elevated white blood cell count
6. Side-lying position with abdominal guarding (legs flexed) to relieve pain
7. Difficulty walking and pain in the right hip
8. Low-grade fever
9. Anorexia, nausea, and vomiting after the pain develops
10. Diarrhea

C. Peritonitis
1. Description: Results from a perforated appendix
2. Assessment
   a. Increased fever
   b. Sudden relief of pain after the perforation and then a subsequent increase in pain accompanied by right guarding of the abdomen
   c. Progressive abdominal distention
   d. Tachycardia and tachypnea
   e. Pallor
   f. Chills
   g. Restlessness and irritability
D. Appendectomy
1. Description: Surgical removal of the appendix
2. Interventions preoperatively
   a. Maintain an NPO status.
   b. Administer fluids and electrolytes intravenously as prescribed to prevent dehydration and correct electrolyte imbalances.
   c. Monitor for signs of a ruptured appendix and peritonitis.
   d. Administer antibiotics as prescribed.
   e. Monitor for changes in the level of pain.
   f. Avoid the use of pain medications so as not to mask pain changes associated with perforation.
   g. Monitor bowel sounds.
   h. Position in a right side-lying or low to semi-Fowler's position to promote comfort.
   i. Apply ice packs to the abdomen for 20 to 30 minutes every hour if prescribed.
   j. Avoid the application of heat to the abdomen.
   k. Avoid laxatives or enemas.
3. Postoperative interventions
   a. Monitor vital signs, particularly the temperature
   b. Maintain an NPO status until bowel function has returned, advancing diet gradually as tolerated and as prescribed when bowel sounds return.
   c. Assess the incision for signs of infection, such as redness, swelling, drainage, and pain.
   d. Monitor Penrose drain drainage, inserted if perforation occurred, as prescribed.
   e. Position in a right side-lying or low to semi-Fowler's position with legs flexed to facilitate drainage.
   f. Change the dressing as prescribed, and record the type and amount of drainage.
   g. Perform wound irrigations if prescribed.
   h. Maintain nasogastric tube suction and patency of the tube if present.
   i. Administer antibiotics and analgesics as prescribed.

X. HIRSCHSPRUNG'S DISEASE (Fig. 39-4)
A. Description
1. Congenital anomaly also known as congenital aganglionosis or aganglionic megacolon
2. The disease occurs as the result of an absence of ganglion cells in the rectum and other areas of the affected intestine.
3. The disease results in mechanical obstruction because of inadequate motility in an intestinal segment.
4. The disease may be a familial congenital defect or may be associated with other anomalies, such as Down syndrome and genitourinary abnormalities.
5. A rectal biopsy demonstrates histological evidence of the absence of ganglionic cells.
6. The most serious complication is enterocolitis; signs include fever, severe prostration, gastrointestinal bleeding, and explosive watery diarrhea.
7. Treatment for mild or moderate disease is based on relieving the chronic constipation with stool softeners and rectal irrigations; however, most children require surgery.
8. Treatment for moderate to severe disease involves a two-step surgical procedure.
   a. Initially, in the neonatal period, a temporary colostomy is created to relieve obstruction and allow the normally innervated, dilated bowel to return to its normal size.
   b. A complete surgical repair is performed when the child weighs about 9 kg (20 lb) via a pull-through procedure to excise portions of the bowel; at this time, the colostomy is closed.

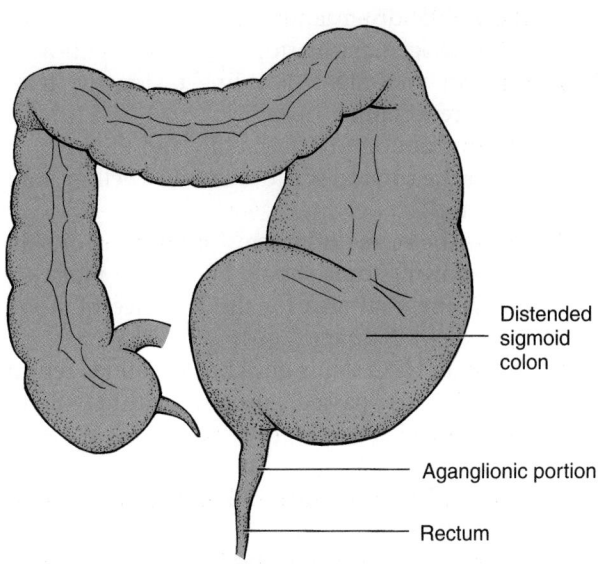

Distended sigmoid colon

Aganglionic portion

Rectum

FIG. 39-4   Hirschsprung's disease. (From Wong, D., Perry, S., & Hockenberry, M. [2002]. *Maternal child nursing care* [2nd ed.]. St. Louis: Mosby.)

B. Assessment
1. Newborn infants
   a. Failure to pass meconium stool
   b. Refusal to suck
   c. Abdominal distention
   d. Bile-stained vomitus
2. Children
   a. Failure to gain weight and delayed growth
   b. Abdominal distention
   c. Vomiting
   d. Constipation alternating with diarrhea
   e. Ribbon-like and foul-smelling stools
C. Interventions: Medical management
1. Maintain low-fiber, high-calorie, high-protein diet; parenteral nutrition may be necessary in extreme situations.
2. Administer stool softeners as prescribed.
3. Administer daily rectal irrigations with normal saline to promote adequate elimination and prevent obstruction as prescribed.
D. Surgical management: Preoperative interventions
1. Assess bowel function.
2. Administer bowel preparation as prescribed.
3. Maintain an NPO status.
4. Monitor hydration and fluid and electrolyte status; provide fluids intravenously as prescribed for hydration.
5. Administer antibiotics such as metronidazole (Flagyl) as prescribed to clear the bowel of bacteria.
6. Monitor strict intake and output.
7. Obtain daily weight.
8. Measure abdominal girth daily
9. Avoid taking the temperature rectally.
10. Monitor for respiratory distress associated with abdominal distention.
E. Surgical management: Postoperative interventions
1. Monitor vital signs, avoiding taking the temperature rectally.
2. Measure abdominal girth daily and PRN.
3. Assess the surgical site for redness, swelling, and drainage.
4. Assess the stoma if present for bleeding or skin breakdown (stoma should be red and moist).
5. Assess the anal area for the presence of stool, redness, or discharge.
6. Maintain NPO status until bowel sounds return or flatus is passed, usually within 48 to 72 hours
7. Maintain the nasogastric tube to allow intermittent suction until peristalsis returns.
8. Maintain IV fluids until the child tolerates appropriate oral intake, advancing the diet from clear liquids to regular as tolerated and as prescribed.
9. Assess for dehydration and fluid overload.
10. Monitor strict intake and output.
11. Obtain daily weight.
12. Assess for pain and provide comfort measures as required.
13. Provide the parents with instructions regarding colostomy care and skin care.
14. Teach the parents about the appropriate diet and the need for adequate fluid intake.

XI. INTUSSUSCEPTION (Fig. 39-5)
A. Description
1. Telescoping of one portion of the bowel into another portion
2. The condition results in an obstruction to the passage of intestinal contents.
B. Assessment
1. Colicky abdominal pain that causes the child to scream and draw the knees to the abdomen, similar to the fetal position
2. Vomiting of gastric contents
3. Bile-stained fecal emesis
4. Currant jelly–like stools containing blood and mucus
5. Hypoactive or hyperactive bowel sounds
6. Tender distended abdomen, possibly with a palpable sausage-shaped mass in the upper right quadrant
C. Interventions
1. Monitor for signs of perforation and shock as evidenced by fever, increased heart rate, changes in level of consciousness or blood

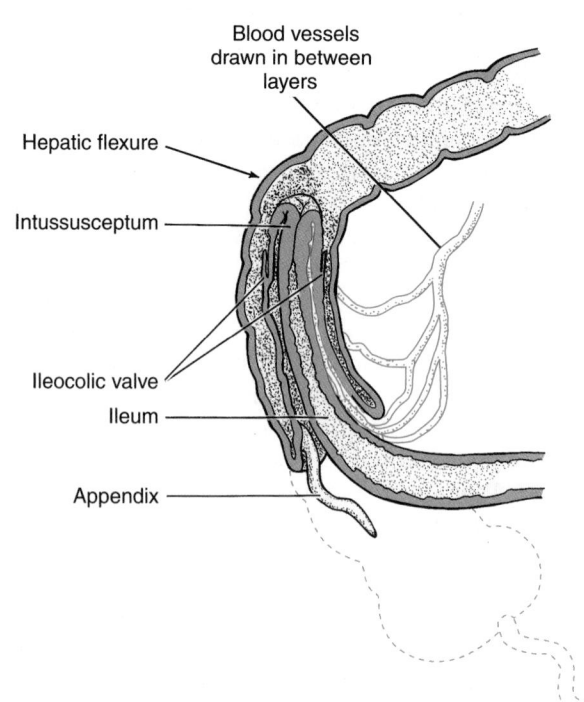

FIG. 39-5 Ileocolic intussusception. (From Hockenberry, M., Wilson, D., Winkelstein, M. [2005]. *Wong's essentials of pediatric nursing* [7th ed.]. St. Louis: Mosby.)

pressure, and respiratory distress, and report immediately.

2. Antibiotics, IV fluids, and decompression via nasogastric tube may be prescribed.

3. Monitor for the passage of normal, brown stool, which indicates that the intussusception has reduced itself.

4. Prepare for hydrostatic reduction as prescribed, if no signs of perforation or shock occur (in hydrostatic reduction, fluid is used to exert pressure on area involved to lessen, diminish, or rid the intestine of prolapse).

5. Posthydrostatic reduction
   a. Monitor for the return of normal bowel sounds, for the passage of barium, and the characteristics of stool.
   b. Administer clear fluids and advance the diet gradually as prescribed.

6. If surgery is required, postoperative care is similar to that following any abdominal surgery.

XII. ABDOMINAL WALL DEFECTS

A. Omphalocele
   1. Herniation of the abdominal contents through the umbilical ring, usually with an intact peritoneal sac
   2. The protrusion is covered by a translucent sac that may contain bowel or other abdominal organs.
   3. Rupture of the sac results in evisceration of the abdominal contents.
   4. Immediately after birth, the sac is covered with sterile gauze soaked in normal saline to prevent drying of abdominal contents; a layer of plastic wrap is placed over the gauze to provide additional protection against moisture loss.
   5. Monitor vital signs every 2 to 4 hours, particularly the temperature, because the infant can lose heat through the sac.
   6. Preoperatively: Maintain NPO status, administer IV fluids as prescribed to maintain hydration and electrolyte balance, monitor for signs of infection, and handle the infant carefully to prevent rupture of the sac.
   7. Postoperatively: Control pain, prevent infection, maintain fluid and electrolyte balance, and ensure adequate nutrition.

B. Gastroschisis
   1. Occurs when the herniation of the intestine is lateral to the umbilical ring
   2. No membrane covers the exposed bowel.
   3. The exposed bowel is covered loosely in saline-soaked pads, and the abdomen is loosely wrapped in a plastic drape; wrapping directly around the exposed bowel is contraindicated because if the exposed bowel expands, wrapping could cause pressure and necrosis.

4. Preoperatively: Care is similar to that for omphalocele; surgery is performed within several hours after birth because no membrane is covering the sac.

5. Postoperatively: Most infants have a prolonged ileus and require mechanical ventilation and parenteral nutrition; otherwise, care is similar to that for omphalocele.

XIII. UMBILICAL HERNIA

A. Description
   1. A hernia is a protrusion of the bowel through an abnormal opening in the abdominal wall.
   2. In children, hernias most commonly occur at the umbilicus and through the inguinal canal.
   3. A hydrocele is the presence of abdominal fluid in the scrotal sac.

B. Assessment
   1. Umbilical hernia: Soft swelling or protrusion around the umbilicus that is usually reducible with the finger
   2. Inguinal hernia
      a. Painless inguinal swelling that is reducible
      b. Swelling may disappear during periods of rest and is most noticeable when the infant cries or coughs.
   3. Incarcerated hernia
      a. Occurs when the descended portion of the bowel becomes tightly caught in the hernial sac, compromising blood supply
      b. Represents a medical emergency requiring surgical repair
      c. Assessment findings—include irritability, tenderness at site, anorexia, abdominal distention, difficulty defecating
      d. May lead to complete intestinal obstruction and gangrene
   4. Noncommunicating hydrocele
      a. Occurs when residual peritoneal fluid is trapped with no communication to the peritoneal cavity
      b. Usually disappears by age 1 year
   5. Communicating hydrocele
      a. Associated with a hernia that remains open from the scrotum to the abdominal cavity
      b. Assessment includes a bulge in the inguinal area or the scrotum that increases with crying or straining and decreases when the child is at rest

C. Postoperative interventions (hernia)
   1. Monitor vital signs.
   2. Assess for wound infection.
   3. Monitor for redness or drainage.
   4. Monitor input and output (I&O) and hydration status.
   5. Advance the diet as tolerated.
   6. Administer analgesics as prescribed.

▲ D. Postoperative interventions (hydrocele)
   1. Provide ice bags and a scrotal support to relieve pain and swelling.
   2. Instruct the child and parents to avoid tub bathing until the incision heals.
   3. Instruct the child and parents to avoid strenuous physical activities.

XIV. CONSTIPATION AND ENCOPRESIS
A. Description
   1. Constipation is the infrequent and difficult passage of dry, hard stools.
   2. **Encopresis** is constipation with fecal incontinence; children often complain that soiling is involuntary and occurs without warning.
   3. If the child does not have a neurological or anatomical disorder, **encopresis** is usually the result of fecal impaction and an enlarged rectum caused by chronic constipation.
B. Assessment
   1. Constipation
      a. Abdominal pain and cramping without distention
      b. Palpable movable fecal masses
      c. Normal or decreased bowel sounds
      d. Malaise and headache
      e. Anorexia, nausea, and vomiting
   2. **Encopresis**
      a. Evidence of soiling of clothing
      b. Scratching or rubbing of the anal area
      c. Fecal odor
      d. Social withdrawal
C. Interventions
   1. Maintain a diet high in fiber and fluids for simple constipation (Box 39-4).
   2. Monitor treatment regimen for severe encopresis for 3 to 6 months
   3. Decrease sugar and milk intake.
   4. Administer enemas as prescribed until the impaction is cleared.
   5. Monitor for hypernatremia or hyperphosphatemia when administering repeated enemas.
      a. Signs of hypernatremia include increased thirst, dry, sticky mucous membranes, flushed skin, increased temperature, nausea and vomiting, oliguria, and lethargy.
      b. Signs of hyperphosphatemia include tetany, muscle weakness, dysrhythmias, and hypotension.
   6. Administer stool softeners or laxatives as prescribed; if mineral oil is prescribed, administer chilled or mixed with cold drinks to disguise taste.
   7. Administer fat-soluble vitamins while mineral oil is used because the oil can interfere with vitamin absorption in the small intestine.
   8. Encourage the child to sit on the toilet for 5 to

BOX 39-4

High-Fiber Foods

Bread, grains
Whole-grain bread or rolls
Whole-grain cereals
Bran
Pancakes, waffles, and muffins with fruit or bran
Unrefined (brown) rice
Vegetables
Raw vegetables, especially broccoli, cabbage, carrots, cauliflower, celery, lettuce, and spinach
Cooked vegetables such as those listed above, and asparagus, beans, Brussels sprouts, corn, potatoes, rhubarb, squash, string beans, and turnips
Fruits
   Prunes, raisins, or other dried fruits
   Raw fruits, especially those with skins or seeds, other than ripe banana or avocado
Miscellaneous
   Legumes (beans), popcorn, nuts, and seeds
   High-fiber snack bars

From Hockenberry, M., & Wilson, D. (2007) *Wong's nursing care of infants and children* (8th ed.). St. Louis: Mosby.

10 minutes approximately 20 to 30 minutes after breakfast and dinner to assist with defecation.

XV. IRRITABLE BOWEL SYNDROME
A. Description
   1. Results from increased motility, which can lead to spasm and pain
   2. The diagnosis is based on the elimination of pathological conditions.
   3. The syndrome is a self-limiting, intermittent problem with no definitive treatment.
   4. Stress and emotional factors may contribute to its occurrence.
B. Assessment
   1. Diffuse abdominal pain unrelated to meals or activity.
   2. Alternating constipation and diarrhea with the presence of undigested food and mucus in the stool.
C. Interventions
   1. Reassure the parents and child that the problem is self-limiting and intermittent and will resolve
   2. Medication, such as psyllium (Metamucil), antidiarrheals (loperamide hydrochloride [Imodium]), antispasmodics (propantheline bromide [Pro-Banthine]), or simethicone (Mylicon) may be prescribed.
   3. Encourage the maintenance of a healthy, well-balanced, moderate-fiber diet.
   4. Encourage health promotion activities such as exercise and school activities.
   5. Inform the parents of psychosocial resources if required.

XVI. IMPERFORATE ANUS

A. Description: Incomplete development or absence of the anus in its normal position in the perineum

B. Types
1. Membrane noted over the anal opening, with a normal anus just above the membrane
2. Complete absence of the anus (anal agenesis) with a rectal pouch ending some distance above
3. Rectum ends blindly or has a fistula connection to the perineum, urethra, bladder, or vagina

C. Assessment (Box 39-5)

D. Preoperative interventions
1. Determine patency of the anus.
2. Monitor for the presence of stool in the urine and vagina (indicates a fistula) and report immediately.
3. Administer IV fluids as prescribed
4. Prepare the child and parents for the surgical procedures, including the potential for colostomy.

E. Postoperative interventions
1. Monitor the skin for signs of infection.
2. Position side-lying with the legs flexed or in a prone position to keep the hips elevated to reduce edema and pressure on the surgical site.
3. Keep the anal surgical incision clean and dry, and monitor for redness, swelling, or drainage.
4. Maintain an NPO status and nasogastric tube if in place.
5. Maintain IV fluids until gastrointestinal motility returns.
6. Provide colostomy care, if present, as prescribed.
7. A new colostomy stoma will be red and edematous, but this should decrease with time.
8. Instruct the parents to perform anal dilation if prescribed to achieve and maintain bowel patency.
9. Instruct the parents to use only dilators supplied by the physician and a water-soluble lubricant and to insert the dilator no more than 1 to 2 cm into the anus to prevent damage to the mucosa.

XVII. HEPATITIS

A. This section contains specific information regarding hepatitis as it relates to infants and children; see Chapters 25 and 55 for additional information on hepatitis

B. Description: An acute or chronic inflammation of the liver that may be caused by a virus, a medication reaction, or another disease process

C. Hepatitis A (HAV)
1. Highest incidence of HAV infection occurs among preschool or school-age children younger than 15 years
2. Many affected children are asymptomatic, but mild nausea, vomiting, and diarrhea may occur.

BOX 39-5
Assessment Findings: Imperforate Anus

Failure to pass meconium stool
Absence or stenosis of the anal rectal canal
Presence of an anal membrane
External fistula to the perineum

---

3. Infected children who are asymptomatic still can spread HAV to others.

D. Hepatitis B (HBV)
1. Most HBV infection in children is acquired perinatally.
2. Newborn infants are at risk if the mother is infected with HBV or was a carrier of HBV during pregnancy.
3. Possible routes of maternal-fetal (infant) transmission include leakage of the virus across the placenta late in pregnancy or during labor, ingestion of amniotic fluid or maternal blood, and breast-feeding, especially if the mother has cracked nipples
4. The severity in the infant varies from no liver disease to fulminant (severe acute course) or chronic active disease.
5. In children and adolescents, HBV occurs in specific high-risk groups, including children with hemophilia or other disorders requiring multiple blood transfusions, children or adolescents involved in drug abuse, institutionalized children, and preschool children in endemic areas, and if involvement with heterosexual activity or sexual activity with homosexual males occurs.
6. Infection with HBV can cause a carrier state and lead to eventual cirrhosis or hepatocellular carcinoma in adulthood.

E. Hepatitis C (HCV)
1. Transmission is primarily by the parenteral route.
2. Some children may be asymptomatic, but HCV often becomes a chronic condition and can cause cirrhosis and hepatocellular carcinoma.

F. Hepatitis D
1. Infection occurs in children already infected with HBV.
2. Acute and chronic forms tend to be more severe than HBV and can lead to cirrhosis.
3. Children with hemophilia are more likely to be infected, as are children who are IV drug users.

G. Hepatitis E
1. Infection is uncommon in children.
2. Infection is not a chronic condition, does not cause chronic liver disease, and has no carrier state.

H. Hepatitis G
1. Hepatitis G virus is bloodborne and is similar to HCV.

2. High-risk groups include transfusion recipients, IV drug users, and individuals infected with HCV.

3. Individuals are often asymptomatic, and most infections are chronic.

▲ I. Assessment (Box 39-6)

J. Diagnostic evaluation: See Chapter 11 for laboratory tests used to diagnose hepatitis.

▲ K. Prevention

1. Proper hand washing and standard precautions can prevent the spread of viral hepatitis.

2. Prophylactic use of standard immune globulin to prevent HAV infection in case of preexposure, such as anticipated travel to areas where HAV is prevalent, or within 2 weeks of exposure

3. Hepatitis B immune globulin is effective in preventing infection following a one-time exposure, such as an accidental needle puncture or other contact of contaminated material with mucous membranes, and should be given to newborns whose mothers are HBsAg-positive and within 72 hours of exposure.

4. Hepatitis A **vaccine** is recommended for children 2 to 18 years of age who reside in communities with high endemic rates and for preexposure prophylaxis.

5. Hepatitis B **vaccine**: See Chapter 47 for the immunization schedule.

▲ L. Interventions

1. Strict hand washing is required.

2. Hospitalization is required in the event of coagulopathy or fulminant hepatitis.

3. Standard precautions and enteric precautions are followed during hospitalization.

4. Provide enteric precautions for at least 1 week after the onset of jaundice with HAV.

5. The hospitalized child usually is not isolated in a separate room unless he or she is fecally incontinent and items are likely to become contaminated with feces.

6. Children are discouraged from sharing toys.

7. Instruct the child and parents in effective hand-washing techniques.

8. Instruct the parents to disinfect diaper-changing surfaces thoroughly with a solution of $^1/_4$ cup bleach in a gallon of water.

9. Maintain comfort and provide adequate rest and sleep.

10. Provide a low-fat, balanced diet.

11. Inform the parents that because HAV is not infectious 1 week after the onset of jaundice, the child may return to school at that time if he or she feels well enough.

12. Inform the parents that jaundice may get worse before it resolves.

13. Caution the parents about administering any medications to the child, explaining the role of

---

BOX 39-6
Assessment Findings: Hepatitis

PRODROMAL OR ANICTERIC PHASE
Lasts 5 to 7 days
Absence of jaundice
Anorexia, malaise, lethargy, easy fatigability
Fever (especially in adolescents)
Nausea and vomiting
Epigastric or right upper quadrant abdominal pain
Arthralgia and rashes (more likely with hepatitis B virus)
Hepatomegaly

ICTERIC PHASE
Jaundice, which is best assessed in the sclera, nail beds, and mucous membranes
Dark urine and pale stools
Pruritus

---

the liver in detoxification and excretion of medications in understandable terms.

14. Instruct the parents about the signs of the child's condition worsening, such as changes in neurological status, bleeding, and fluid retention.

XVIII. INGESTION OF POISONS

A. Lead poisoning ▲

1. Description: Excessive accumulation of lead in the blood

2. Causes ▲

a. The pathway for exposure may be food, air, or water.

b. Dust and soil contaminated with lead may be a source of exposure.

c. Lead enters the child's body through ingestion or inhalation or through placental transmission to an unborn child when the mother is exposed; the most common route is hand to mouth from contaminated objects or from eating loose paint chips, crayons, or pottery that contains lead.

d. When lead enters the body, it affects the erythrocytes, bones and teeth, and organs and tissues, including the brain and nervous system; the most serious consequences are the effects on the central nervous system.

3. Universal screening ▲

a. Screening is recommended in high-risk areas for children 1 to 2 years of age; children at high risk should be screened earlier.

b. Any child between the ages of 3 and 6 years who has not been screened should be tested.

4. Targeted screening ▲

a. Targeted screening is acceptable in low-risk areas.

b. A child at the age of 1 to 2 years (or a child between the ages of 3 and 6 years who has not been screened) may be targeted for screening if determined to be at risk.

5. Blood lead level test: Used for screening and diagnosis (Table 39-1)

6. Erythrocyte protoporphyrin test
   a. Indicator of anemia
   b. Normal value for a child is 35 mcg/100 mL of whole blood or lower

7. Chelation therapy
   a. Chelation therapy removes lead from the circulating blood and from some organs and tissues.
   b. Therapy does not counteract any effects of the lead.
   c. Medications include dimercaprol in peanut oil (BAL in Oil), calcium disodium edetate (CaNa$_2$EDTA), and succimer (Chemet).
   d. Dimercaprol (BAL) is contraindicated in children with an allergy to peanuts because the medication is prepared in a peanut oil solution.
   e. Ensure adequate urinary output before administering the medication.
   f. Provide adequate hydration and monitor kidney function for nephrotoxicity when the medication is given because the medication is excreted via the kidneys.
   g. Follow-up of lead levels to monitor progress are essential.
   h. Provide instructions to parents about safety from lead hazards, medication administration, and the need for follow-up.
   i. Confirm that the child will be discharged to home without lead hazards.

B. Acetaminophen (Tylenol)
   1. Description
      a. Seriousness of ingestion is determined by the amount ingested and the length of time before intervention
      b. Toxic dose is 150 mg/kg or higher in children.
   2. Assessment
      a. First 2 to 4 hours: Malaise, nausea, vomiting, sweating, pallor, weakness
      b. Latent period: 24 to 36 hours; child improves
      c. Hepatic involvement: May last up to 7 days and may be permanent; right upper quadrant pain, jaundice, confusion, stupor, elevated liver enzyme and bilirubin levels, prolonged prothrombin time
   3. Interventions
      a. Administer antidote: *N*-Acetylcysteine (Mucomyst)
      b. Dilute antidote in juice or soda because of its offensive odor.
      c. Loading dose is followed by maintenance doses.

TABLE 39-1	
Blood Lead Level Test	
Level	**Intervention**
Less than 10 mcg/dL	Reassess or rescreen in 1 year or sooner if exposure status changes.
10 to 14 mcg/dL	Provide family lead education, follow-up testing, and social service referral if necessary.
15 to 19 mcg/dL	Provide family lead education, follow-up testing, and social service referral if necessary; on follow-up testing, initiate actions for blood lead level of 20 to 44 mcg/dL.
20 to 69 mcg/dL	A blood lead level greater than 20 mcg/dL is considered acute; provide coordination of care, clinical management, including treatment, environmental investigation, and lead-hazard control (the child must not remain in a lead-hazardous environment if resolution is necessary).
70 mcg/dL or greater	Medical treatment is provided immediately, including coordination of care, clinical management, environmental investigation, and lead-hazard control.

   d. In unconscious child, prepare to administer gastric lavage with activated charcoal to decrease absorption of acetaminophen
   e. If using activated charcoal with lavage, do not also use *N*-acetylcysteine because activated charcoal will inactivate antidote.

C. Acetylsalicylic acid (aspirin)
   1. Description
      a. Overdose may be caused by acute ingestion or chronic ingestion.
      b. Acute: Severe toxicity with 300 to 500 mg/kg
      c. Chronic: Ingestion of more than 100 mg/kg per day for 2 days or more, which can be more serious than acute ingestion
   2. Assessment
      a. Gastrointestinal effects: Nausea, vomiting, and thirst from dehydration
      b. Central nervous system effects: Hyperpnea, confusion, tinnitus, convulsions, coma, respiratory failure, circulatory collapse
      c. Renal effects: Oliguria
      d. Hematopoietic effects: Bleeding tendencies
      e. Metabolic effects: Diaphoresis, fever, hyponatremia, hypokalemia, dehydration, hypoglycemia, metabolic acidosis

3. Interventions
   a. Prepare to administer activated charcoal to decrease the absorption of salicylate.
   b. Administer IV fluids, sodium bicarbonate, electrolytes, or volume expanders as prescribed.
   c. Administer vitamin K for bleeding tendencies as prescribed.
   d. Administer glucose for hypoglycemia as prescribed.
   e. Prepare the child for dialysis as prescribed if the child is unresponsive to the therapy.

XIX. INTESTINAL PARASITES

A. Description: Common infections in children are giardiasis and pinworm infestation.
   1. Giardiasis is caused by protozoa and is prevalent among children in crowded environments, such as classrooms or daycare centers.
   2. Pinworms (enterobiasis) are universally present in temperate climate zones and are easily transmitted in crowded environments.
B. Assessment
   1. Giardiasis
      a. Diarrhea and vomiting
      b. Anorexia
      c. Failure to thrive
      d. Abdominal cramps with intermittent loose stools and constipation
      e. Steatorrhea
      f. Resolves in 4 to 6 weeks spontaneously
      g. Stool specimens from three or more collections are used for diagnosis.
   2. Pinworms
      a. Intense perianal itching
      b. Irritability, restlessness
      c. Poor sleeping
      d. Bed wetting
C. Interventions
   1. Giardiasis
      a. Administer metronidazole (Flagyl) as prescribed.
      b. Caregivers should wash hands meticulously.
      c. Provide education to family and caregivers regarding sanitary practices.
   2. Pinworms
      a. Perform a visual inspection of the anus with a flashlight 2 to 3 hours after sleep.
      b. The tape test is the most common diagnostic test.
      c. Educate the family and caregivers regarding the tape test. A loop of transparent tape is placed firmly against the child's perianal area; it is removed in the morning and placed in a glass jar or plastic bag and transported to the primary care provider for analysis.

d. Mebendazole (Vermox) may be prescribed for children over age 2 years.
e. Piperazine phosphate may be prescribed for children younger than 2 years.
f. The medication regimen may be repeated in 2 weeks to prevent reinfection
g. All members of the family are treated for the infection.
h. Teach the family and caregivers about the importance of meticulous hand washing and about washing all clothes and bed linens in hot water.

PRACTICE QUESTIONS

1. An infant has just returned to the nursing unit following a surgical repair of a cleft lip located on the right side of the lip. The nurse places the infant in which best position?
   1. Prone position
   2. Supine position
   3. Left lateral position
   4. Right lateral position

2. A nurse reviews the record of a newborn infant and notes that a diagnosis of esophageal atresia with tracheoesophageal fistula is suspected. The nurse expects to note which most likely sign of this condition documented in the record?
   1. Incessant crying
   2. Coughing at nighttime
   3. Choking with feedings
   4. Severe projectile vomiting

3. A nurse provides feeding instructions to a mother of an infant diagnosed with gastroesophageal reflux. To assist in reducing the episodes of emesis, the nurse tells the mother to:
   1. Provide less frequent, larger feedings.
   2. Burp the infant less frequently during feedings.
   3. Thin the feedings by adding water to the formula.
   4. Thicken the feedings by adding rice cereal to the formula.

4. A nurse admits a child to the hospital with a diagnosis of pyloric stenosis. On admission assessment, which data would the nurse expect to obtain when asking the mother about the child's symptoms?
   1. Watery diarrhea
   2. Projectile vomiting
   3. Increased urine output
   4. Vomiting large amounts of bile

5. A home care nurse instructs the mother about dietary measures for a 5-year-old child with lactose intolerance. The nurse tells the mother that it is necessary to provide which dietary supplement in the child's diet?

1. Fats
2. Zinc
3. Protein
4. Calcium

6. A nurse provides home care instructions to the parents of a child with celiac disease. The nurse teaches the parents to include which food item in the child's diet?
   1. Rice
   2. Oatmeal
   3. Rye toast
   4. Wheat bread

7. A nurse is preparing to care for a child with a diagnosis of intussusception. The nurse reviews the child's record and expects to note which symptom of this disorder documented?
   1. Watery diarrhea
   2. Ribbon-like stools
   3. Profuse projectile vomiting
   4. Bright red blood and mucus in the stools

8. A child is receiving succimer (Chemet) for the treatment of lead poisoning. A nurse monitors which of the following most important laboratory results?
   1. Potassium level
   2. Blood urea nitrogen level
   3. Red blood cell count
   4. White blood cell count

9. A clinic nurse reviews the record of a 3-week-old infant and notes that the physician has documented a diagnosis of suspected Hirschsprung's disease. The nurse reviews the assessment findings documented in the record, knowing that which symptom most likely led the mother to seek health care for the infant?
   1. Diarrhea
   2. Projectile vomiting
   3. Regurgitation of feedings
   4. Foul-smelling ribbon-like stools

10. A child is hospitalized because of persistent vomiting and the nurse monitors the child closely for:
    1. Diarrhea.
    2. Metabolic acidosis.
    3. Metabolic alkalosis.
    4. Hyperactive bowel sounds.

11. A nurse is caring for a newborn infant with a suspected diagnosis of imperforate anus. The nurse monitors the infant, knowing that which of the following is a clinical manifestation associated with this disorder?
    1. Bile-stained fecal emesis
    2. The passage of currant jelly–like stools
    3. Failure to pass meconium stool in the first 24 hours after birth
    4. Sausage-shaped mass palpated in the upper right abdominal quadrant

12. A nurse has been assigned to care for a neonate just delivered who has gastroschisis. Which nursing diagnosis would have the highest priority at this time?
    1. Risk of infection
    2. Risk for impaired parenting
    3. Risk for disorganized infant behavior
    4. Risk for impaired urinary elimination

ALTERNATE ITEM FORMAT: MULTIPLE RESPONSE (1)

A nurse is assigned to care for a child who is scheduled for an appendectomy. Select the orders that the nurse anticipates will be prescribed.
- ❏ 1. Initiate an IV line.
- ❏ 2. Maintain an NPO status.
- ❏ 3. Administer a Fleet enema.
- ❏ 4. Administer preoperative medications.
- ❏ 5. Administer intravenous antibiotics.
- ❏ 6. Place a heating pad on the abdomen to decrease pain.

ALTERNATE ITEM FORMAT: MULTIPLE RESPONSE (2)

Which interventions would a nurse include when writing a care plan for a child with hepatitis? Select all that apply.
- ❏ 1. Notifying physician if jaundice is present
- ❏ 2. Providing a low-fat, well-balanced diet
- ❏ 3. Teaching child effective hand-washing techniques
- ❏ 4. Scheduling playtime in the playroom with other children
- ❏ 5. Instructing the parents about caution when administering medications
- ❏ 6. Arranging for indefinite home schooling because the child will not be able to return to school

ANSWERS

1. **3**

Rationale: After cleft lip repair, the infant should be positioned supine or on the side lateral to the repair to prevent contact of the suture lines with the bed linens. Placing the infant on the left side rather than supine immediately after surgery is best to prevent the risk of aspiration if the infant vomits.

Test-Taking Strategy: Use the process of elimination and note the strategic words *right side*. Consider the anatomical location of the surgical site and the strategic words to direct you to the correct option. Review postoperative positioning techniques if you had difficulty with this question.
Level of Cognitive Ability: Application
Client Needs: Physiological Integrity

Integrated Process: Nursing Process—implementation
Content Area: Child health
References: Hockenberry, M., Wilson, D., & Winkelstein, M. (2005). *Wong's essentials of pediatric nursing* (7th ed., p. 876). St. Louis: Mosby.
Wong, D., Perry, S., Hockenberry, M., et al. (2006). *Maternal child nursing care* (3rd ed., p. 1527). St. Louis: Mosby.

2. 3
Rationale: Any child who exhibits the "3 C's"—coughing and choking with feedings and unexplained cyanosis—should be suspected of tracheoesophageal fistula. Options 1, 2, and 4 are not specifically associated with tracheoesophageal fistula.
Test-Taking Strategy: Use the process of elimination, focusing on the diagnosis. Recalling the "3 C's" associated with this disorder will assist in directing you to the correct option. Review the clinical manifestations associated with this disorder if you had difficulty with this question.
Level of Cognitive Ability: Analysis
Client Needs: Physiological Integrity
Integrated Process: Nursing Process—assessment
Content Area: Child health
Reference: McKinney, E., James, S., Murray, S., & Ashwill, J. (2005). *Maternal-child nursing* (2nd ed., p. 1113). St. Louis: W.B. Saunders.

3. 4
Rationale: Small, more frequent feedings with frequent burping often are prescribed in the treatment of gastroesophageal reflux. Feedings thickened with rice cereal may reduce episodes of emesis. If thickened formula is used, cross-cutting of the nipple may be required.
Test-Taking Strategy: Use the process of elimination and basic principles related to feeding an infant to assist in eliminating options 1 and 2. Noting the strategic words *reducing the episodes of emesis* will assist in directing you to select option 4 over option 3. Review therapeutic interventions associated with this disorder if you had difficulty with this question.
Level of Cognitive Ability: Application
Client Needs: Physiological Integrity
Integrated Process: Teaching and Learning
Content Area: Child health
Reference: McKinney, E., James, S., Murray, S., & Ashwill, J. (2005). *Maternal-child nursing* (2nd ed., p. 1122). St. Louis: W.B. Saunders.

4. 2
Rationale: Clinical manifestations of pyloric stenosis include projectile vomiting, irritability, hunger and crying, constipation, and signs of dehydration, including a decrease in urine output.
Test-Taking Strategy: Use the process of elimination. Considering the anatomical location of this disorder and its potential effects will assist in eliminating options 1 and 3. Recalling that a major clinical manifestation is projectile vomiting will assist in directing you to option 4 from the remaining options. Review these clinical manifestations if you had difficulty with this question.
Level of Cognitive Ability: Analysis
Client Needs: Physiological Integrity

Integrated Process: Nursing Process—assessment
Content Area: Child health
Reference: Wong, D., Perry, S., Hockenberry, M., et al. (2006). *Maternal child nursing care* (3rd ed., p. 1533). St. Louis: Mosby.

5. 4
Rationale: Lactose intolerance is the inability to tolerate lactose, the sugar found in dairy products. Removing milk and other dairy products from the diet can provide adequate relief from symptoms. Additional dietary changes may be required to provide adequate sources of calcium and, in the infant, protein and calories.
Test-Taking Strategy: Use the process of elimination. Knowledge that lactose is the sugar found in dairy products will easily direct you to option 4, because dairy products contain high levels of calcium. Review the dietary management for lactose intolerance if you had difficulty with this question.
Level of Cognitive Ability: Application
Client Needs: Physiological Integrity
Integrated Process: Teaching and Learning
Content Area: Child health
Reference: Hockenberry, M., Wilson, D., & Winkelstein, M. (2005). *Wong's essentials of pediatric nursing* (7th ed., pp. 376-377). St. Louis: Mosby.

6. 1
Rationale: Dietary management is the mainstay of treatment in celiac disease. All wheat, rye, barley, and oats should be eliminated from the diet and replaced with corn, rice, or millet. Vitamin supplements—especially the fat-soluble vitamins, iron, and folic acid—may be needed in the early period of treatment to correct deficiencies. Dietary restrictions are likely to be lifelong, although small amounts of grains may be tolerated after ulcerations have healed.
Test-Taking Strategy: Use the process of elimination. Recalling that corn, rice, and millet are substitute food replacements in this disease will direct you to option 1. Review the dietary management in this disorder if you had difficulty with this question.
Level of Cognitive Ability: Application
Client Needs: Health Promotion and Maintenance
Integrated Process: Teaching and Learning
Content Area: Child health
Reference: Hockenberry, M., Wilson, D., & Winkelstein, M. (2005). *Wong's essentials of pediatric nursing* (7th ed., p. 886). St. Louis: Mosby.

7. 4
Rationale: Intussusception is a telescoping of one portion of the bowel into another. The condition results in an obstruction to the passage of intestinal contents. The child with intussusception typically has severe abdominal pain that is crampy and intermittent, causing the child to draw in the knees to the chest. Vomiting may be present but is not projectile. Bright red blood and mucus are passed through the rectum and commonly are described as currant jelly–like stools. Watery diarrhea and ribbon-like stools are not manifestations of this disorder.
Test-Taking Strategy: Use the process of elimination. Recalling that a classic manifestation is currant jelly–like stools will as-

sist in directing you to option 4. Review this disorder if you had difficulty with this question.
Level of Cognitive Ability: Analysis
Client Needs: Physiological Integrity
Integrated Process: Nursing Process—assessment
Content Area: Child health
Reference: Hockenberry, M., Wilson, D., & Winkelstein, M. (2005). *Wong's essentials of pediatric nursing* (7th ed., p. 882). St. Louis: Mosby.

8. 2
Rationale: Renal function is monitored closely during the administration of chelation therapy because the medications are excreted via the kidneys. Although it is important to monitor the red blood cell count for the presence of anemia in a child with lead poisoning, this laboratory result is not specific to chelation therapy. Options 1 and 4 are unrelated to the administration of chelation therapy.
Test-Taking Strategy: Use the process of elimination. Recalling that the medications used in chelation therapy are excreted via the kidneys will direct you to option 2. Review this treatment for lead poisoning if you had difficulty with this question.
Level of Cognitive Ability: Analysis
Client Needs: Physiological Integrity
Integrated Process: Nursing Process—assessment
Content Area: Child health
References: Hockenberry, M. & Wilson, D. (2007). *Nursing care of infants and children* (8th ed., pp. 694-695). St. Louis: Mosby. McKinney, E., James, S., Murray, S., & Ashwill, J. (2005). *Maternal-child nursing* (2nd ed., p. 873). St. Louis: W.B. Saunders.

9. 4
Rationale: Hirschsprung's disease is a congenital anomaly also known as congenital aganglionosis or aganglionic megacolon. It occurs as the result of an absence of ganglion cells in the rectum and other areas of the affected intestine. Chronic constipation beginning in the first month of life and resulting in pellet-like or ribbon-like stools that are foul-smelling is a clinical manifestation of this disorder. Delayed passage or absence of meconium stool in the neonatal period is also a sign. Bowel obstruction, especially in the neonatal period, abdominal pain and distention, and failure to thrive are also clinical manifestations. Options 1, 2, and 3 are not associated specifically with this disorder.
Test-Taking Strategy: Use the process of elimination and knowledge regarding the pathophysiology associated with Hirschsprung's disease to direct you to option 4. Remember that chronic constipation beginning in the first month of life and resulting in pellet-like or ribbon-like foul-smelling stools is a clinical manifestation of this disorder. If you are unfamiliar with this disorder, review the assessment findings associated with it.
Level of Cognitive Ability: Analysis
Client Needs: Physiological Integrity
Integrated Process: Nursing Process—assessment
Content Area: Child health
Reference: Hockenberry, M., Wilson, D., & Winkelstein, M. (2005). *Wong's Essentials of pediatric nursing* (7th ed., p. 854). St. Louis: Mosby.

10. 3
Rationale: Vomiting will cause the loss of hydrochloric acid and subsequent metabolic alkalosis. Metabolic acidosis would occur in a child experiencing diarrhea because of the loss of bicarbonate. Diarrhea might or might not accompany vomiting. Hyperactive bowel sounds are not necessarily associated with vomiting.
Test-Taking Strategy: Use the process of elimination. Recalling that gastric fluids are acidic and that the loss of these fluids will lead to alkalosis will assist in answering the question. No data in the question support options 1 and 4. Review the manifestations that occur with vomiting if you had difficulty with this question.
Level of Cognitive Ability: Analysis
Client Needs: Physiological Integrity
Integrated Process: Nursing Process—assessment
Content Area: Child health
Reference: Wong, D., Perry, S., Hockenberry, M., et al. (2006). *Maternal child nursing care* (3rd ed., pp. 1506-1507). St. Louis: Mosby.

11. 3
Rationale: During the newborn assessment, this defect should be identified easily on sight. However, a rectal thermometer or tube may be necessary to determine patency if meconium is not passed in the first 24 hours after birth. Other assessment findings include absence or stenosis of the anal rectal canal, presence of an anal membrane, and an external fistula to the perineum. Options 1, 2, and 4 are findings noted in intussusception.
Test-Taking Strategy: Focus on the newborn's diagnosis. Use the process of elimination and the definition of the word *imperforate* to assist in answering this question. This should direct you to option 3. Review the assessment findings associated with this disorder if you had difficulty with this question.
Level of Cognitive Ability: Analysis
Client Needs: Physiological Integrity
Integrated Process: Nursing Process—assessment
Content Area: Child health
Reference: Hockenberry, M., Wilson, D., & Winkelstein, M. (2005). *Wong's essentials of pediatric nursing* (7th ed., p. 884). St. Louis: Mosby.

12. 1
Rationale: Gastroschisis occurs when the bowel herniates through a defect in the abdominal wall to the right of the umbilical cord. There is no membrane covering the exposed bowel. Surgical repair will be done as soon as possible because of the risk of infection in the unprotected bowel. Therefore, the highest risk immediately after delivery would be infection. Risk for impaired parenting and risk for disorganized infant behavior are possible later nursing problems, but they would not have priority. Risk for impaired urinary elimination is unlikely because the gastrointestinal tract is affected, not the genitourinary system.
Test-Taking Strategy: Recall that gastroschisis is a defect that has no protective membrane covering the bowel. Infection would be the priority problem in the immediate period just after delivery and before corrective surgery. Eliminate options

2 and 3 as problems that could occur later. Eliminate option 4 as a problem that would be unlikely to occur with this defect. Review the characteristics of gastroschisis if you had difficulty with this question.

Level of Cognitive Ability: Analysis
Client Needs: Physiological Integrity
Integrated Process: Nursing Process—analysis
Content Area: Child health
Reference: Hockenberry, M., & Wilson, D. (2007). *Wong's nursing care of infants and children* (8th ed., pp. 479-480). St. Louis: Mosby.

ALTERNATE ITEM FORMAT:
MULTIPLE RESPONSE (1)

Answer: 1, 2, 4, 5
Rationale: In the preoperative period, enemas or laxatives should not be administered. Additionally, heat is not applied to the abdomen. Any of these interventions can cause rupture of the appendix and resultant peritonitis. IV fluids would be started, and the child would be NPO while awaiting surgery. Usually, antibiotics are administered because of the risk of perforation. Prescribed preoperative medications most likely would be administered on call to the operating room.
Test-Taking Strategy: Consider the anatomical location of appendicitis and think about the concern of rupture in this disorder. This will assist in determining the correct interventions. Review preoperative care of the child with appendicitis if you had difficulty with this question.
Level of Cognitive Ability: Analysis
Client Needs: Physiological Integrity
Integrated Process: Nursing Process—analysis
Content Area: Child health
Reference: Hockenberry, M., & Wilson, D. (2007). *Wong's nursing care of infants and children* (8th ed., p. 1405). St. Louis: Mosby.

ALTERNATE ITEM FORMAT:
MULTIPLE RESPONSE (2)

Answer: 2, 3, 5
Rationale: Because hepatitis can be viral, standard precautions should be instituted in the hospital. The child should be discouraged from sharing toys, so playtime in the playroom with other children is not part of the plan of care. The child will be allowed to return to school 1 week after the onset of jaundice, so indefinite home schooling would not need to be arranged. Jaundice is an expected finding with hepatitis and would not warrant notification of the physician. Provision of a low-fat, well-balanced diet is recommended. Parents are cautioned about administering any medication to the child, because normal doses of many medications may become dangerous because of the liver's inability to detoxify and excrete them. Hand washing is the single most effective measure in control of hepatitis in any setting and effective hand washing can prevent the compromised child from picking up an opportunistic type of infection.
Test-Taking Strategy: Use the process of elimination and eliminate any intervention that would be inappropriate for a child with hepatitis. Thinking about the pathophysiology associated with hepatitis and the method of transmission will assist in answering the question. Playing with other children in the playroom, planning for an indefinite period of home schooling, and notifying the physician of jaundice would not be appropriate interventions. Review hepatitis if you had difficulty with this question.
Level of Cognitive Ability: Application
Client Needs: Physiological Integrity
Integrated Process: Nursing Process—planning
Content Area: Child health
Reference: Swearingen, P. (2004). *All-in-one care planning resource: Medical-surgical, pediatric, maternity, and psychiatric nursing care plans.* St. Louis: Mosby, pp. 483-487.

REFERENCES

Celiac Sprue Association. http://www.csaceliacs.org.

Hockenberry, M. Wilson, D., & Winkelstein, M. (2005). *Wong's essentials of pediatric nursing* (7th ed.). St. Louis: Mosby.

Hockenberry, M., & Wilson, D. (2007). *Wong's nursing care of infants and children* (8th ed.). St. Louis: Mosby.

McKinney, E., James, S., Murray, S., & Ashwill, J. (2005). *Maternal-child nursing* (2nd ed.). St. Louis: W.B. Saunders.

National Council of State Boards of Nursing (Eds.). (2007). *2007 NCLEX-RN® detailed test plan.* Chicago: Author.

Swearingen, P. (2004). *All-in-one care planning resource: Medical-surgical, pediatric, maternity, and psychiatric nursing care plans.* St. Louis: Mosby.

Wong, D., Perry, S., Hockenberry, M, Wilson, D., et al. (2006). *Maternal child nursing care* (3rd ed.). St. Louis: Mosby.

Metabolic and Endocrine Disorders

I. FEVER

A. Description
1. Fever is an abnormal body temperature elevation.
2. A child's temperature can vary depending on activity, emotional stress, disease processes, medications, the type of clothing the child is wearing, and the temperature of the environment.
3. Assessment findings associated with the fever provide important indications of the seriousness of the fever.

B. Assessment
1. Temperature elevation: Normal temperature range for a child is 97.5° to 98.6° F (36.4° to 37° C); 100.4° F (38° C) is considered to be fever for an infant and 102° F (38.8° C) for a child.
2. Flushed skin, warm to touch
3. Diaphoresis
4. Chills
5. Restlessness or lethargy

C. Interventions
1. Monitor vital signs; take the temperature via the tympanic or axillary route.
2. Remove excess clothing and blankets
3. Administer a sponge bath with lukewarm water for 20 to 30 minutes; do not use alcohol because it can cause peripheral vasoconstriction.
4. Administer antipyretics such as acetaminophen (Tylenol) as prescribed.
5. Do not administer aspirin (acetylsalicylic acid) because of the risk of Reye's syndrome.
6. Retake the temperature 30 to 60 minutes after the antipyretic is administered.
7. Provide adequate fluid intake as tolerated and as prescribed.
8. Monitor for signs and symptoms that indicate dehydration and electrolyte imbalances; monitor laboratory values.
9. Instruct the parents in how to take the temperature, how to medicate their child safely, and when it is necessary to call the physician.

II. DEHYDRATION (Box 40-1)

A. Description
1. Dehydration is a common fluid and electrolyte imbalance in infants and children.
2. Infants and children are more vulnerable to fluid volume deficit because more of their body water is in the extracellular fluid compartment.
3. In infants and children, the organs that conserve water are immature, placing them at risk for fluid volume deficit.
4. The causes can include decreased fluid intake, diaphoresis, vomiting, diarrhea, diabetic ketoacidosis, and extensive burns or other serious injuries.

B. Assessment
1. Tachycardia
2. Dry skin and mucous membranes
3. Sunken eyeballs and fontanels
4. Decreased urine output (less than 1 mL/kg/hr) and increased urine specific gravity (higher than 1.020)

BOX 40-1

Types of Dehydration

ISOTONIC DEHYDRATION
Electrolyte and water deficits occur in approximately balanced proportions.

HYPERTONIC DEHYDRATION
Water loss exceeds electrolyte loss.

HYPOTONIC DEHYDRATION
Electrolyte loss exceeds water loss.

5. Changes in level of consciousness and responses to stimuli
6. Signs of circulatory failure, such as coolness and mottling of the extremities
7. Loss of skin elasticity and turgor
8. Delayed capillary filling time (longer than 3 seconds)
9. Weight loss
10. Decreased blood pressure
11. Thirst
12. Absence of tears

C. Interventions
1. Treat and eliminate the cause of the dehydration.
2. Monitor vital signs.
3. Monitor for signs of dehydration.
4. Monitor weight and monitor for changes, including fluid gains and losses.
5. Monitor intake and output and urine for specific gravity.
6. Monitor level of consciousness.
7. Monitor skin turgor and mucous membranes for dryness.
8. Provide oral rehydration therapy with solutions, such as Pedialyte, as prescribed, if the child is able to take fluids orally.
9. Administer fluids and electrolyte replacements intravenously, such as 0.9% normal saline or lactated Ringer's, as prescribed, if the child is unable to take sufficient fluids orally.
10. Introduce a regular diet as prescribed when the child is rehydrated.
11. Provide instructions to the parents about the types and amounts of fluid to encourage, signs of dehydration, and indications of the need to notify the physician.

III. PHENYLKETONURIA
A. Description
1. A genetic disorder (autosomal recessive disorder) that results in central nervous system damage from toxic levels of phenylalanine in the blood.
2. It is characterized by blood phenylalanine levels higher than 8 mg/dL (normal level is lower than 2 mg/dL 2 to 5 days after birth).
3. All 50 states require routine screening of all newborn infants for phenylketonuria.
B. Assessment
1. In all children
   a. Digestive problems and vomiting
   b. Seizures
   c. Musty odor of the urine
   d. Mental retardation
2. In older children
   a. Eczema
   b. Hypertonia

c. Hypopigmentation of the hair, skin, and irises
d. Hyperactive behavior

C. Interventions
1. Screening of newborn infants for phenylketonuria: the infant should have begun formula or breast milk feeding before specimen collection.
2. If initial screening is positive, a repeat test is performed and further diagnostic evaluation is required to verify the diagnosis.
3. Rescreen infants by 14 days of age if the initial screening was done before 48 hours of age.
4. If phenylketonuria is diagnosed, prepare to implement the following:
   a. Restrict phenylalanine intake; high-protein foods (meats and dairy products) and aspartame are avoided because they contain large amounts of phenylalanine.
   b. Monitor physical, neurological, and intellectual development.
   c. Stress the importance of follow-up treatment.
   d. Encourage the parents to express feelings about the diagnosis and the risk of phenylketonuria in future children.
   e. Educate the parents about use of special preparation formulas.
   f. Consult with social care services to assist the parents with financial burdens of special prepared formulas.

IV. DIABETES MELLITUS
A. Description (Fig. 40-1)
1. Type 1 diabetes mellitus is characterized by the destruction of the pancreatic beta cells, which produce insulin; this results in absolute insulin deficiency.
2. Type 2 diabetes mellitus usually arises because of insulin resistance, in which the body fails to use insulin properly, combined with relative (rather than absolute) insulin deficiency.
3. Complete insulin deficiency requires the use of exogenous insulin to promote appropriate glucose use and to prevent complications related to elevated blood glucose levels, such as hyperglycemia, diabetic ketoacidosis, and death.
4. Diagnosis is based on the presence of classic symptoms and an elevated blood glucose level (normal blood glucose level is 70 to 110 mg/dL).
5. Children may be admitted directly to the Pediatric Intensive Care unit because of the manifestations of diabetic ketoacidosis (DKA), which may be the initial occurrence when diagnosed with diabetes mellitus.
B. Assessment
1. Polyuria, polydipsia, polyphagia
2. Hyperglycemia

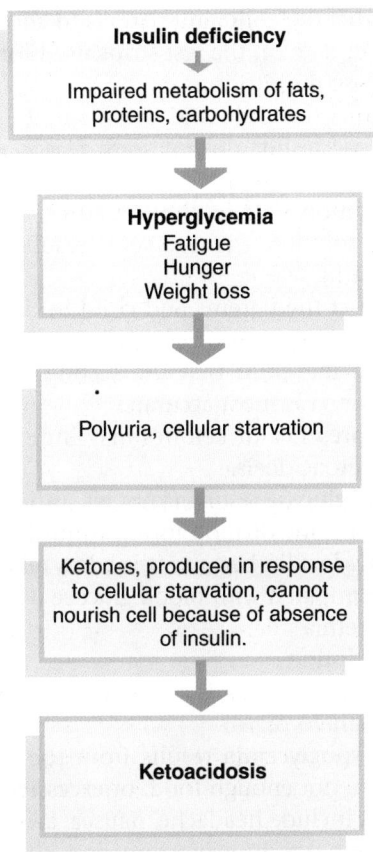

FIG. 40-1 Insulin deficiency leading to ketoacidosis. (From McKinney, E., James, S., Murray, S., & Ashwill, J. [2005]. *Maternal-child nursing* [2nd ed.]. St. Louis: W.B. Saunders.)

3. Weight loss
4. Unexplained fatigue or lethargy
5. Headaches
6. Stomachaches
7. Occasional enuresis in a previously toilet-trained child
8. Vaginitis in adolescent girls (caused by *Candida vaginitis,* which thrives in hyperglycemic tissues)
9. Fruity odor to breath
10. Dehydration
11. Blurred vision
12. Slow wound healing
13. Changes in level of consciousness
C. Long-term effects
1. Failure to grow at a normal rate
2. Delayed maturation
3. Recurrent infections
4. Neuropathy
5. Cardiovascular disease
6. Retinal microvascular disease
7. Renal microvascular disease
D. Complications
1. Hypoglycemia
2. Hyperglycemia

3. Diabetic ketoacidosis
4. Coma
5. Hypokalemia
6. Hyperkalemia
7. Microvascular changes
8. Cardiovascular changes
E. Diet
1. Normal healthy nutrition is encouraged and the total number of calories is individualized based on the child's age and **growth** expectations.
2. As prescribed by the physician, the child may be instructed to follow the food exchange from the American Diabetic Association diet or the dietary guidelines (MyPyramid) issued by the U.S. Departments of Agriculture and Health and Human Services.
3. Dietary intake should include three meals per day, eaten at regular intervals, plus a midafternoon carbohydrate snack and a bedtime snack high in protein; a consistent intake of carbohydrates at each meal and snack is needed.
4. Instruct the child and parents that the child should carry a source of glucose, such as glucose tablets, with him or her at all times to treat hypoglycemia if it occurs.
5. Incorporate the diet into individual child's needs, likes and dislikes, lifestyle, and cultural and socioeconomic patterns.
6. Allow the child to participate in making food choices to provide a sense of control.
F. Exercise
1. Instruct the child in dietary adjustments when exercising.
2. Extra food needs to be consumed for increased activity, usually 10 to 15 g of carbohydrates for every 30 to 45 minutes of activity.
3. Instruct the child to monitor the blood glucose level before exercising.
4. Plan an appropriate exercise regimen with the child, taking the developmental stage into account.
G. Insulin
1. Diluted insulin may be required for some infants to provide small enough doses to avoid hypoglycemia; diluted insulin should be labeled clearly to avoid dosage errors.
2. Laboratory evaluation of glycosylated hemoglobin should be performed every 3 months.
3. Illness, infection, and stress increase the need for insulin, and insulin should not be withheld during illness, infection, or stress, because hyperglycemia and ketoacidosis can result.
4. When the child is not receiving anything by mouth for a special procedure, verify with the physician the need to withhold the morning insulin, and when food, fluids, and insulin are to be resumed.

5. Instruct the child and parents in the administration of the insulin.
6. Instruct the child and parents to recognize symptoms of hypoglycemia and hyperglycemia.
7. Instruct the parents in the administration of glucagon intramuscularly or subcutaneously if the child has a hypoglycemic reaction and is unable to consume sugar-containing items orally.
8. Instruct the child and parents always to have a spare bottle of insulin available.
9. Advise the parents to obtain a Medic-Alert bracelet indicating the type and daily insulin dosage prescribed for the child.
10. See Chapter 54 for information on insulin types, administration sites, and administration procedure.

H. Blood glucose monitoring
1. Results provide information needed to maintain good glycemic control.
2. Blood glucose monitoring is more accurate than urine testing.
3. Monitoring requires that the child prick himself or herself several times a day as prescribed (Box 40-2).
4. Instruct the child and parents about the proper procedure for obtaining the blood glucose level.
5. Inform the child and parents that the procedure must be done precisely to obtain accurate results.
6. Stress the importance of hand washing before and after performing the procedure to prevent infection.
7. Stress the importance of following the manufacturer's instructions for the blood glucose monitoring device.
8. Instruct the child and parents to calibrate the monitor as instructed by the manufacturer.

9. Instruct the child and parents to check the expiration date on the test strips used for the blood glucose monitoring.
10. Instruct the child and parents that if the blood glucose results do not seem reasonable, reread the instructions, reassess technique, check the expiration date of the test strips, and perform the procedure again to verify results.

I. Urine testing
1. Instruct the parents and child in the procedure for testing urine for ketones and glucose.
2. Teach the child that the second voided urine specimen is most accurate.
3. The presence of ketones may indicate impending ketoacidosis.
4. Urine glucose testing is not recommended as the only means of monitoring control in the child taking insulin because it is a less reliable indicator compared with blood glucose monitoring.

J. Hypoglycemia
1. Description
   a. Hypoglycemia is a blood glucose level lower than 70 mg/dL.
   b. Hypoglycemia results from too much insulin, not enough food, or excessive activity.
2. Signs include headache, nausea, sweating, tremors, lethargy, hunger, confusion, slurred speech, tingling around the mouth, and anxiety.
3. Interventions (Boxes 40-3 and 40-4)

K. Hyperglycemia
1. Description: Elevated blood glucose level, higher than 200 mg/dL.
2. Signs include polydipsia, polyuria, polyphagia, blurred vision, weakness, weight loss, and syncope.
3. Interventions (Box 40-5)
4. Sick day rules (Box 40-6)

BOX 40-2

Lessening the Pain of Blood Glucose Monitoring

Hold the finger under warm water for a few seconds before puncture (enhances blood flow to the finger).
Use the ring finger or thumb to obtain a blood sample because blood flows more easily to these areas; puncture the finger just to the side of the finger pad because there are more blood vessels in this area and fewer nerve endings.
Press the lancet device lightly against the skin to prevent a deep puncture.
Use glucose monitors that require very small blood samples for measurement.
Apply an anesthetic cream, such as EMLA (lidocaine, prilocaine), to the site before puncture.

Modified from Hockenberry, M., Wilson, D., Winkelstein, M. (2005). *Wong's essentials of pediatric nursing* (7th ed.). St. Louis: Mosby.

BOX 40-3

Interventions for Hypoglycemia

If possible, the nurse should confirm hypoglycemia with a blood glucose reading.
Administer glucose immediately; the rapid-releasing glucose is followed by a complex carbohydrate and protein, such as a slice of bread or a peanut butter cracker.
Give an extra snack if the next meal is not planned for more than 30 minutes or if activity is planned.
If the child becomes unconscious, squeeze cake frosting or glucose paste onto the gums and retest the blood glucose level if the child does not improve within 15 to 20 minutes; if the reading remains low, administer additional glucose.
If the child remains unconscious, the administration of glucagon may be necessary.
In the hospital setting, prepare to administer dextrose intravenously.

BOX 40-4
Food Items to Treat Hypoglycemia

½ cup orange juice or a sugar-sweetened carbonated
beverage
1 small box of raisins
3 to 4 hard candies
4 sugar cubes
3 to 4 Life Savers
1 candy bar
1 tsp honey
2 or 3 glucose tablets

BOX 40-5
Interventions for Hyperglycemia

Instruct the parents to notify the physician when the
following occur:
Blood glucose results are higher than the targeted range
(usually 200 mg/dL).
Moderate or high ketonuria is present.
The child is unable to take food or fluids.
Illness persists.

L. Diabetic ketoacidosis
   1. Description
      a. Diabetic ketoacidosis is a complication of diabetes mellitus that develops when a severe insulin deficiency occurs.
      b. Diabetic ketoacidosis is a life-threatening condition.
      c. Hyperglycemia that progresses to metabolic acidosis occurs.
      d. Diabetic ketoacidosis develops over a period of several hours to days.
      e. The blood glucose level is higher than 300 mg/dL, and urine and serum ketone tests are positive.
      f. Manifestations include signs of hyperglycemia, Kussmaul's respirations, acetone (fruity) breath odor, increasing lethargy, and decreasing level of consciousness.
   2. Interventions
      a. Restore circulating blood volume and protect against cerebral, coronary, or renal hypoperfusion.
      b. Correct dehydration with intravenous (IV) infusions of 0.9% or 0.45% saline as prescribed.
      c. Correct hyperglycemia with IV regular insulin administration as prescribed.
      d. Monitor vital signs, urine output, and mental status closely.
      e. Correct acidosis and electrolyte imbalances as prescribed.
      f. Administer oxygen as prescribed.
      g. Monitor blood glucose level frequently.

BOX 40-6
Sick Day Rules for the Diabetic Child

Always give insulin, even if the child does not have an appetite, or contact the physician for specific instructions.
Test blood glucose levels at least every 4 hours.
Test for urinary ketones with each voiding.
Notify the physician if moderate or large amounts of urinary ketones are present.
Follow the child's usual meal plan.
Encourage calorie-free liquids to aid in clearing ketones.
Encourage rest, especially if urinary ketones are present.
Notify the physician if vomiting, fruity odor to the breath, deep rapid respirations, decreasing level of consciousness, or persistent hyperglycemia occurs.

---

      h. Monitor potassium level closely because when the child receives insulin to lower the blood glucose level, the serum potassium level will change; if the potassium level decreases, potassium replacement may be required.
      i. The child should be voiding adequately before administering potassium; if the child does not have an adequate output, hyperkalemia may result.
      j. Monitor the child closely for signs of fluid overload.
      k. Intravenously administered dextrose is added as prescribed when the blood glucose reaches an appropriate level.
      l. Treat the cause of hyperglycemia.

PRACTICE QUESTIONS

1. A physician orders an intravenous solution of 5% dextrose and half-normal saline (0.45%) with 40 mEq of potassium chloride (KCl) for a child with hypertonic dehydration. The nurse performs which priority assessment before administering the potassium chloride to the intravenous bag?
   1. Obtains a weight
   2. Takes the temperature
   3. Takes the blood pressure
   4. Checks the amount of urine output
2. An adolescent client with type 1 diabetes mellitus is admitted to the emergency department for treatment of diabetic ketoacidosis. Which assessment findings should the nurse expect to note?
   1. Sweating and tremors
   2. Hunger and hypertension
   3. Cold, clammy skin and irritability
   4. Fruity breath and decreasing level of consciousness
3. A pediatric nurse educator provides a teaching session to the nursing staff regarding phenylketonuria. The nurse educator tells the nursing staff that:

1. Treatment includes dietary restriction of tyramine.
2. Phenylketonuria is an autosomal dominant disorder.
3. Phenylketonuria primarily affects the gastrointestinal system.
4. All 50 states require routine screening of all newborn infants for phenylketonuria.

4. A mother brings her 3-week-old infant to a clinic for a phenylketonuria rescreening blood test. The test indicates a serum phenylalanine level of 1 mg/dL. The nurse interprets this result as:
   1. Positive.
   2. Negative.
   3. Inconclusive.
   4. Requiring rescreening at age 6 weeks.

5. A school-age child with type 1 diabetes mellitus has soccer practice three afternoons a week. The school nurse provides instructions regarding how to prevent hypoglycemia during practice. The school nurse tells the child to:
   1. Eat twice the amount normally eaten at lunchtime.
   2. Take half the amount of prescribed insulin on practice days.
   3. Take the prescribed insulin at noontime rather than in the morning.
   4. Eat six graham crackers or drink a cup of orange juice before soccer practice.

6. A home care nurse is teaching an adolescent with type 1 diabetes mellitus about insulin administration and rotation sites. Which statement, if made by the adolescent, would indicate effective teaching?
   1. "I need to use a different site for each insulin injection."
   2. "I should use only my stomach and my thighs for injections."
   3. "I need to use the same site for 1 month before rotating to another site."
   4. "I need to use one major site for 2 to 3 weeks before changing major sites."

7. The mother of a 6-year-old child who has type 1 diabetes mellitus calls a clinic nurse and tells the nurse that the child has been sick. The mother reports that she checked the child's urine and it was positive for ketones. The nurse instructs the mother to:

1. Come to the clinic immediately.
2. Hold the next dose of insulin.
3. Administer an additional dose of regular insulin.
4. Encourage the child to drink calorie-free liquids.

8. A child with type 1 diabetes mellitus is brought to an emergency room by the mother, who states that the child has been complaining of abdominal pain and has a fruity odor of the breath. Diabetic ketoacidosis is diagnosed. Anticipating the plan of care, the nurse prepares to administer:
   1. Potassium IV infusion.
   2. NPH insulin IV infusion.
   3. 5% dextrose IV infusion.
   4. Normal saline IV infusion.

9. A nurse has just administered acetaminophen (Tylenol) to a child with a temperature of 102° F. The nurse should also take which action?
   1. Withhold oral fluids for 8 hours.
   2. Sponge the child with cold water.
   3. Plan to administer salicylate (aspirin) in 4 hours.
   4. Remove excess blankets and clothing from the child.

10. A child has fluid volume deficit. The nurse performs an assessment and determines that the child is improving and the deficit is resolving if:
   1. The child has no tears.
   2. Urine specific gravity is 1.030.
   3. Urine output is less than 1 mL/kg/hr.
   4. Capillary refill is shorter than 3 seconds.

ALTERNATE ITEM FORMAT: MULTIPLE RESPONSE

Select all interventions for a child older than 2 years with type 1 diabetes mellitus who has a blood glucose level of 60 mg/dL.
❑ 1. Administer regular insulin.
❑ 2. Encourage the child to ambulate.
❑ 3. Give the child a teaspoon of honey.
❑ 4. Provide electrolyte replacement therapy intravenously.
❑ 5. Wait 30 minutes and confirm the blood glucose reading.
❑ 6. Prepare to administer glucagon subcutaneously if unconsciousness occurs.

ANSWERS

1. **4**

Rationale: The priority assessment before administering potassium chloride intravenously would be to assess the status of the urine output. Potassium chloride should never be administered in the presence of oliguria or anuria. If the urine output is less than 1 to 2 mL/kg/hr, potassium chloride should not be administered. Although options 1, 2, and 3 are appropriate assessments for the child with dehydration, these as-

sessments are not related specifically to the intravenous (IV) administration of potassium chloride.

Test-Taking Strategy: Use the process of elimination. Recalling that the kidneys play a key role in the excretion and reabsorption of potassium will direct you to option 4. Review this important medication if you had difficulty with this question.

Level of Cognitive Ability: Analysis
Client Needs: Physiological Integrity

Integrated Process: Nursing Process—assessment
Content Area: Child health
Reference: McKinney, E., James, S., Murray, S., & Ashwill, J. (2005). *Maternal-child nursing* (2nd ed., pp. 1087-1088). St. Louis: W.B. Saunders.

2. **4**
Rationale: Hyperglycemia occurs with diabetic ketoacidosis. Signs of hyperglycemia include fruity breath and a decreasing level of consciousness. Hunger can be a sign of hypoglycemia or hyperglycemia, but hypertension is not a sign of diabetic ketoacidosis. Instead, hypotension occurs because of a decrease in blood volume related to the dehydrated state that occurs during diabetic ketoacidosis. Cold, clammy skin, irritability, sweating, and tremors are all signs of hypoglycemia.
Test-Taking Strategy: Focus on the subject, the signs of diabetic ketoacidosis. Eliminate options 1, 2 and 3 because these signs do not occur with hyperglycemia. Recall that fruity breath and a change in the level of consciousness can occur during diabetic ketoacidosis. Review the signs and symptoms of hypoglycemia and hyperglycemia and the signs of diabetic ketoacidosis if you had difficulty with this question.
Level of Cognitive Ability: Analysis
Client Needs: Physiological Integrity
Integrated Process: Nursing Process—assessment
Content Area: Child health
Reference: Hockenberry, M., & Wilson, D. (2007). *Wong's nursing care of infants and children* (8th ed., p. 1716). St. Louis: Mosby.

3. **4**
Rationale: Phenylketonuria is an autosomal recessive disorder. Treatment includes dietary restriction of phenylalanine intake. Phenylketonuria is a genetic disorder that results in central nervous system damage from toxic levels of phenylalanine in the blood. Option 4 is accurate.
Test-Taking Strategy: Use the process of elimination. Recalling that phenylketonuria is a recessive disorder will assist you in eliminating option 2. Reading option 1 carefully will direct you to eliminate this option because phenylalanine, not tyramine, is restricted. Recalling that phenylketonuria affects the central nervous system will direct you to option 4. Review the characteristics associated with this disorder if you had difficulty with this question.
Level of Cognitive Ability: Application
Client Needs: Physiological Integrity
Integrated Process: Teaching and Learning
Content Area: Child health
References: Hockenberry, M., & Wilson, D. (2007). *Nursing care of infants and children* (8th ed., p. 335). St. Louis: Mosby.
McKinney, E., James, S., Murray, S., & Ashwill, J. (2005). *Maternal-child nursing* (2nd ed., p. 1452). St. Louis: W.B. Saunders.

4. **2**
Rationale: Phenylketonuria is characterized by blood phenylalanine levels higher than 8 mg/dL. A normal level is lower than 2 mg/dL. A result of 1 mg/dL is a negative test result.
Test-Taking Strategy: Use the process of elimination. Eliminate options 3 and 4 first because they are comparative or alike. Note

that the level identified in the question is a low level. This should assist you in directing you to option 2. Review this important screening test if you had difficulty with this question.
Level of Cognitive Ability: Analysis
Client Needs: Physiological Integrity
Integrated Process: Nursing Process—analysis
Content Area: Child health
References: Hockenberry, M., & Wilson, D. (2007). *Nursing care of infants and children* (8th ed., p. 336). St. Louis: Mosby.
McKinney, E., James, S., Murray, S., & Ashwill, J. (2005). *Maternal-child nursing* (2nd ed., p. 1452). St. Louis: W.B. Saunders.

5. **4**
Rationale: An extra snack of 15 to 30 g of carbohydrates eaten before activities such as soccer practice will prevent hypoglycemia. Six graham crackers or a cup of orange juice will provide 15 to 30 g of carbohydrates. The child or parents should not be instructed to adjust the amount or time of insulin administration. Meal amounts should not be doubled.
Test-Taking Strategy: Use the process of elimination. Options 2 and 3 can be eliminated first because insulin doses and times should not be adjusted. From the remaining options, recalling the manifestations and treatment associated with hypoglycemia will direct you to option 4. Review treatment to prevent hypoglycemia if you had difficulty with this question.
Level of Cognitive Ability: Application
Client Needs: Health Promotion and Maintenance
Integrated Process: Teaching and Learning
Content Area: Child health
References: Hockenberry, M., Wilson, D., & Winkelstein, M. (2005). *Wong's essentials of pediatric nursing* (7th ed., p. 1083). St. Louis: Mosby.
McKinney, E., James, S., Murray, S., & Ashwill, J. (2005). *Maternal-child nursing* (2nd ed., p. 1471). St. Louis: W.B. Saunders.

6. **4**
Rationale: To help decrease variations in absorption from day to day, the adolescent should use one major site for injections for 2 to 3 weeks before changing major sites. The injections are rotated to different locations within that major site. Options 1, 2, and 3 are incorrect.
Test-Taking Strategy: Use the process of elimination. Eliminate option 2 first because of the word *only*. From the remaining options, recalling the physiology associated with absorption of insulin will direct you to option 4. If you had difficulty with this question, review insulin administration.
Level of Cognitive Ability: Analysis
Client Needs: Physiological Integrity
Integrated Process: Nursing Process—evaluation
Content Area: Child health
Reference: Hockenberry, M., Wilson, D., & Winkelstein, M. (2005). *Wong's essentials of pediatric nursing* (7th ed., pp. 1085, 1087). St. Louis: Mosby.

7. **4**
Rationale: When the child is sick, the mother should test for urinary ketones with each voiding. If ketones are present, liq-

uids are essential to aid in clearing the ketones. The child should be encouraged to drink calorie-free liquids. Bringing the child to the clinic immediately is not necessary. Insulin doses should not be adjusted or changed.

Test-Taking Strategy: Use the process of elimination. Eliminate options 2 and 3 first because insulin doses should not be adjusted or changed. From the remaining options, note the words *positive for ketones.* Recalling that liquids are essential to aid in clearing the ketones will direct you to the correct option. Review home care instructions for the sick diabetic child if you had difficulty with this question.

Level of Cognitive Ability: Application
Client Needs: Physiological Integrity
Integrated Process: Nursing Process—implementation
Content Area: Child health
Reference: McKinney, E., James, S., Murray, S., & Ashwill, J. (2005). *Maternal-child nursing* (2nd ed., p. 1478). St. Louis: W.B. Saunders.

8. **4**
Rationale: Rehydration is the initial step in resolving diabetic ketoacidosis. Normal saline is the initial IV rehydration fluid. NPH insulin is never administered by the IV route. Dextrose solutions are added to the treatment when the blood glucose level reaches an acceptable level. Intravenously administered potassium may be required, depending on the potassium level, but would not be part of the initial treatment.

Test-Taking Strategy: Use the process of elimination. Eliminate option 3, knowing that dextrose would not be administered in a hyperglycemic state. Eliminate option 2 next, knowing that NPH insulin is never administered by the IV route. Recalling that hydration is the initial treatment in diabetic ketoacidosis will direct you to option 4. Review the treatment for this important condition if you had difficulty with this question.

Level of Cognitive Ability: Analysis
Client Needs: Physiological Integrity
Integrated Process: Nursing Process—planning
Content Area: Child health
Reference: McKinney, E., James, S., Murray, S., & Ashwill, J. (2005). *Maternal-child nursing* (2nd ed., p. 1480). St. Louis: W.B. Saunders.

9. **4**
Rationale: After administering the acetaminophen, excess clothing and blankets should be removed. The child can be sponged with tepid water, but not cold water, because the cold water can cause shivering, which increases metabolic requirements above those already caused by the fever. Aspirin is not administered to a child with fever because of the risk of Reye's syndrome. Fluids should be encouraged to·prevent dehydration, so oral fluids should not be withheld.

Test-Taking Strategy: Use the process of elimination and remember that cooling measures such as wearing minimum clothing should be done when a child has a fever. Options 1, 2, and 3 would not be done if a child has a fever. Review interventions to reduce an elevated temperature if you had difficulty with this question.

Level of Cognitive Ability: Application
Client Needs: Physiological Integrity
Integrated Process: Nursing Process—implementation
Content Area: Child health
Reference: Hockenberry, M., Wilson, D., & Winkelstein, M. (2005). *Wong's essentials of pediatric nursing* (7th ed., p. 732). St. Louis: Mosby.

10. **4**
Rationale: Indicators that fluid volume deficit is resolving would be capillary refill less than 3 seconds, specific gravity of 1.002 to 1.025, urine output of at least 1mL/kg/hour, and adequate tear production. Therefore, a capillary refill time shorter than 3 seconds is the only indicator that the child is improving. Urine output of less than 1 mL/kg/hr, a specific gravity of 1.030 and no tears would indicate that the deficit is not resolving.

Test-Taking Strategy: Use the process of elimination and recall the parameters that indicate adequate hydration status. The only option that indicates a fluid balance is option 4. The other options indicate fluid imbalance. Review normal parameters for fluid balance if you had difficulty with this question.

Level of Cognitive Ability: Analysis
Client Needs: Physiological Integrity
Integrated Process: Nursing Process—evaluation
Content Area: Child health
Reference: Hockenberry, M., Wilson, D., & Winkelstein, M. (2005). *Wong's essentials of pediatric nursing* (7th ed., p. 842). St. Louis: Mosby.

ALTERNATE ITEM FORMAT: MULTIPLE RESPONSE

Answer: 3, 6
Rationale: Hypoglycemia is defined as a blood glucose level lower than 70 mg/dL. Hypoglycemia occurs as a result of too much insulin, not enough food, or excessive activity. If possible, the nurse should confirm hypoglycemia with a blood glucose reading. Glucose is administered orally immediately; the rapid-releasing sugar is followed by a complex carbohydrate and protein, such as a slice of bread or a peanut butter cracker. An extra snack is given if the next meal is not planned for more than 30 minutes or if activity is planned. If the child becomes unconscious, cake frosting or glucose paste is squeezed onto the gums and the blood glucose level is retested if the child does not improve within 15 to 20 minutes; if the reading remains low, additional sugar is administered. If the child remains unconscious, administration of glucagon may be necessary, and the nurse should be prepared for this intervention. Encouraging the child to ambulate and administering regular insulin will result in a lowered blood glucose level. Providing electrolyte replacement therapy intravenously is an intervention to treat diabetic ketoacidosis. Waiting 30 minutes to confirm the blood glucose level delays necessary intervention.

Test-Taking Strategy: Focus on the information in the question. Recalling that a blood glucose level of 60 mg/dL indicates hypoglycemia will assist in determining the correct interventions. Review the interventions for hypoglycemia if you had difficulty with this question.

Level of Cognitive Ability: Application
Client Needs: Physiological Integrity
Integrated Process: Nursing Process—implementation
Content Area: Child health

Reference: Hockenberry, M., Wilson, D., & Winkelstein, M. (2005). *Wong's essentials of pediatric nursing* (7th ed., p. 1083). St. Louis: Mosby.

REFERENCES

Hockenberry, M., Wilson, D., & Winkelstein, M. (2005). *Wong's essentials of pediatric nursing* (7th ed.). St. Louis: Mosby.

Hockenberry, M., & Wilson, D. (2007). *Nursing care of infants and children* (8th ed.). St. Louis: Mosby.

Kliegman, R., Marcdante, K., Jenson, J., & Behrman, R. (2006). *Nelson essentials of pediatrics* (5th ed.). St. Louis: W.B. Saunders.

Lilley, L., Harrington, S., & Snyder, J. (2005). *Pharmacology and the nursing process* (4th ed.). St. Louis: Mosby.

McKinney, E., James, S., Murray, S., & Ashwill, J. (2005). *Maternal-child nursing* (2nd ed.). St. Louis: W.B. Saunders.

National Council of State Boards of Nursing (Eds.). (2007). *2007 NCLEX-RN® detailed test plan.* Chicago: Author.

Swearingen, P. (2004). *All-in-one care planning resource: Medical-surgical, pediatric, maternity, and psychiatric nursing care plans.* St. Louis: Mosby.

Wong, D., Perry, S., Hockenberry, D., et al. (2006). *Maternal child nursing care* (3rd ed.). St. Louis: Mosby.

Renal and Urinary Disorders

I. GLOMERULONEPHRITIS

A. Description

1. Glomerulonephritis is a term that refers to a group of kidney disorders characterized by inflammatory injury in the glomerulus, most of which are caused by an immunological reaction.
2. The disorder results in proliferative and inflammatory changes within the glomerular structure.
3. Destruction, inflammation, and sclerosis of the glomeruli of the kidneys occur.
4. Inflammation of the glomeruli results from an antigen-antibody reaction produced by an infection elsewhere in the body.
5. Loss of kidney function develops.

B. Causes

1. Immunological diseases
2. Autoimmune diseases
3. Antecedent group A beta-hemolytic streptococcal infection of the pharynx or skin
4. History of pharyngitis or tonsillitis 2 to 3 weeks before symptoms

C. Types (Box 41-1)

D. Complications

1. Renal failure
2. Hypertensive encephalopathy
3. Pulmonary edema
4. Heart failure

E. Assessment

1. Periorbital and facial edema that is more prominent in the morning
2. Anorexia
3. Decreased urinary output
4. Cloudy, smoky, brown-colored urine (hematuria)
5. Pallor, irritability, lethargy
6. In the older child, headaches, abdominal or flank pain, dysuria

---

BOX 41-1

Types of Glomerulonephritis

Acute: Occurs 2 to 3 weeks after a streptococcal infection
Chronic: Can occur after the acute phase or slowly over time

---

7. Hypertension
8. Proteinuria that produces a persistent and excessive foam in the urine
9. Azotemia
10. Increased blood urea nitrogen and creatinine levels
11. Increased antistreptolysin O titer (used to diagnose disorders caused by streptococcal infections)

F. Interventions

1. Monitor vital signs, weight, intake and output, and the characteristics of urine.
2. Limit activity; provide safety measures.
3. Provide high-quality nutrient foods.
   a. Restrictions depend on the stage and severity of the disease, especially the extent of the edema.
   b. In uncomplicated cases, a regular diet is permitted but sodium is restricted to a "no added salt to foods" diet.
   c. Moderate sodium restriction is prescribed for the child with hypertension or edema.
   d. Foods high in potassium are restricted during periods of oliguria.
   e. Protein is restricted if the child has severe azotemia resulting from prolonged oliguria.
4. Monitor for complications (e.g., renal failure, hypertensive encephalopathy, seizures, pulmonary edema, heart failure).

5. Administer diuretics (if significant edema and fluid overload are present), antihypertensives (for hypertension), and antibiotics (to the child with evidence of persistent streptococcal infections) as prescribed.
6. Initiate seizure precautions and administer anticonvulsants as prescribed for seizures associated with hypertensive encephalopathy.
7. Instruct the parents to report signs of bloody urine, headache, or edema.
8. Instruct the parents that the child needs to obtain appropriate adequate treatment for infections, specifically for sore throats, upper respiratory infections, and skin infections.

II. NEPHROTIC SYNDROME

A. Description
1. Nephrotic syndrome is a kidney disorder characterized by massive proteinuria, hypoalbuminemia (hypoproteinemia), and edema (Fig. 41-1).
2. The primary objective of therapeutic management is to reduce the excretion of urinary protein and maintain protein-free urine.

B. Assessment (Box 41-2)

C. Interventions
1. Monitor vital signs, intake and output, and daily weights.
2. Monitor urine for specific gravity and albumin.
3. Monitor for edema.
4. Nutrition: A regular diet without added salt is prescribed if the child is in remission; sodium is restricted during periods of massive edema.
5. Corticosteroid therapy is prescribed as soon as the diagnosis has been determined; monitor the child closely for signs of infection (Box 41-3).
6. Immunosuppressant therapy may be prescribed to reduce the relapse rate and induce long-term remission or, if the child is nonresponsive to corticosteroid therapy, therapy may be administered along with the corticosteroid.
7. Diuretics may be prescribed to reduce edema.
8. Plasma expanders such as salt-poor human albumin may be prescribed for the severely edematous child.
9. Instruct the parents about testing the urine for albumin, medication administration, side effects of medications, and general care of the child.

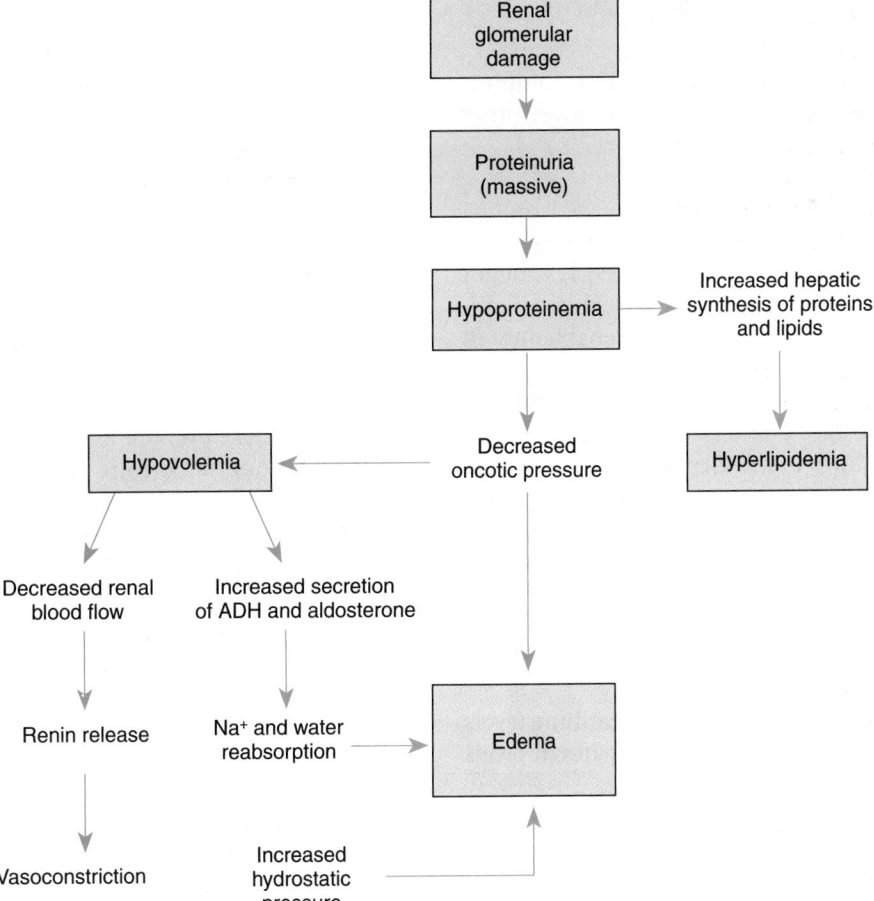

FIG. 41-1 Sequence of events in the nephrotic syndrome. (From Wong, D., Hockenberry, M. Wilson, D., et al. [2006]. *Maternal child nursing care* [3rd ed.]. St. Louis: Mosby.)

BOX 41-2

Assessment Findings in Nephrotic Syndrome

Child gains weight.
Periorbital and facial edema is most prominent in the morning.
Leg, ankle, labial, or scrotal edema occurs.
Urine output decreases; urine is dark and frothy.
Ascites (fluid in the abdominal cavity)
Blood pressure is normal or slightly decreased.
Lethargy, anorexia, and pallor occur.
Massive proteinuria is seen.
Decreased serum protein (hypoproteinemia) and elevated serum lipid levels occur.

BOX 41-3

Adverse Reactions to Corticosteroid Therapy

Impaired wound healing
Hyperglycemia
Skin fragility
Abnormal fat deposition
Emotional lability
Hirsutism
Moon face
Osteoporosis

10. Instruct the parents regarding the signs of infection and the need to avoid contact with other children who may be infectious.

III. HEMOLYTIC-UREMIC SYNDROME

A. Description
   1. Hemolytic-uremic syndrome (HUS) is thought to be associated with bacterial toxins, chemicals, and viruses that cause acute renal failure in children.
   2. It occurs primarily in infants and small children between the ages of 6 months and 5 years.
   3. Clinical features of the disease include acquired hemolytic anemia, thrombocytopenia, renal injury, and central nervous system symptoms.

B. Assessment
   1. Triad of anemia, thrombocytopenia, and renal failure is diagnostic (Box 41-4).
   2. Proteinuria, hematuria, and presence of urinary casts
   3. Blood urea nitrogen and serum creatinine levels are elevated; hemoglobin and hematocrit levels are decreased.

C. Interventions
   1. Hemodialysis or peritoneal dialysis may be prescribed if the child is anuric
      a. Hemodialysis requires venous access (arteriovenous [AV] **shunt**, fistula, or graft) and treatment is usually 3 to 8 hours in length (three times per week); peritoneal dialysis

BOX 41-4

Manifestations of Hemolytic-Uremic Syndrome

Vomiting
Irritability
Lethargy
Marked pallor
Hemorrhagic manifestations such as bruising, petechiae, jaundice, bloody diarrhea
Oliguria or anuria
Central nervous system involvement such as seizures, stupor, coma

requires surgical placement of an abdominal catheter (correction of fluid and electrolyte imbalance is slower than hemodialysis).
      b. Dialysate solution is prescribed to meet the child's electrolyte needs.
   2. Strict monitoring of fluid balance is necessary; fluid restrictions may be prescribed if the child is anuric.
   3. Institute measures to prevent infection.
   4. Provide adequate nutrition.

IV. ENURESIS

A. Description
   1. Enuresis refers to a condition in which the child is unable to control bladder function, even though the child has reached an age at which control of voiding is expected or the child has successfully completed a bladder control program.
   2. By age 5, most children are aware of bladder fullness and are able to control voiding.

B. Primary nocturnal enuresis
   1. Primary nocturnal enuresis is bed-wetting in a child who has never been dry for extended periods.
   2. The condition is common in children, and most children eventually will outgrow bed-wetting without therapeutic intervention.
   3. The child is not able to sense a full bladder and does not awaken to void.
   4. The child may have delayed maturation of the central nervous system.
   5. The child should be evaluated for any pathological causes before the diagnosis of primary nocturnal enuresis is made.

C. Secondary or acquired enuresis
   1. The onset of wetting occurs after a period of established urinary continence.
   2. Secondary enuresis may occur during nighttime sleep (nocturnal), only during the waking hours (diurnal), or during both day and nighttime.
   3. The child may complain of dysuria, urgency, or frequency.
   4. The child should be assessed for urinary tract infections.

D. Assessment: History of bed-wetting with no extended period of dryness in a child older than age 5 years

E. Interventions
1. Perform urinalysis and urine culture as prescribed to rule out infection or an existing disorder.
2. Assist the family with identifying a treatment plan that will best fit the needs of the child.
3. Limit fluid intake at night and encourage the child to void just before going to bed.
4. Involve the child in caring for the wet sheets and changing the bed to assist the child to take ownership of the problem.
5. Provide reward systems as appropriate for the child.
6. Incorporate behavioral conditioning techniques.
7. Encourage follow-up to determine the effectiveness of the treatment.

V. CRYPTORCHIDISM

A. Description: Cryptorchidism occurs when one or both testes fail to descend through the inguinal canal into the scrotal sac.

B. Assessment: Testes are not palpable or easily guided into the scrotum.

C. Interventions
1. Monitor during the first 12 months of life to determine whether spontaneous descent occurs.
2. After age 1 year, medical or surgical treatment may be instituted.
3. Human chorionic gonadotropin, a pituitary hormone that stimulates the production of testosterone, may be prescribed.
4. Surgical correction, if needed, is done by orchiopexy before the child's second birthday (preferably between 1 and 2 years of age) if the testes do not descend spontaneously.
5. Monitor for bleeding and infection postoperatively.
6. Instruct the parents in postoperative home care measures, including preventing infection, pain control, and activity restrictions.
7. Provide an opportunity for parental counseling if the parents are concerned about the future fertility of the child.

VI. EPISPADIAS AND HYPOSPADIAS (Fig. 41-2)

A. Description
1. Congenital defects involving abnormal placement of the urethral orifice of the penis
2. These anatomical defects can lead to the easy entry of bacteria into the urine.

B. Assessment
1. Epispadias: Urethral orifice is located on the dorsal surface of the penis; the condition often occurs with exstrophy of the bladder.

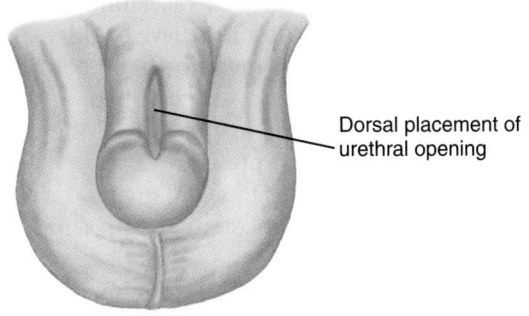

Epispadias

Dorsal placement of urethral opening

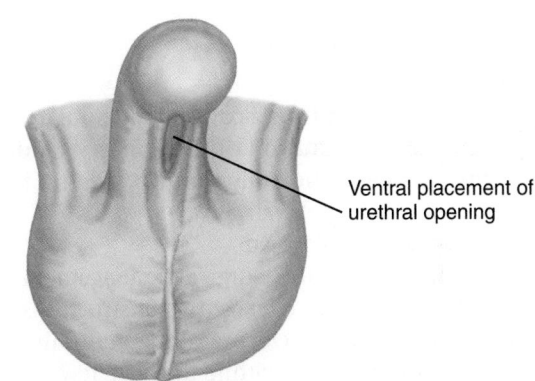

Hypospadias

Ventral placement of urethral opening

FIG. 41-2 Epispadias and hypospadias are genital anomalies in which the urethral opening is above or below its normal location on the glans of the penis. (From James, S., Ashwill, J., & Droske, S. [2002]. *Nursing care of children: Principles and practice* [2nd ed.]. Philadelphia: W.B. Saunders.)

2. Hypospadias: Urethral orifice is located below the glans penis along the ventral surface.

C. Surgical interventions
1. Surgery is done before the age of toilet training, preferably between 16 and 18 months of age.
2. The child should not be circumcised because the foreskin may be used in surgical reconstruction.

D. Postoperative interventions
1. The child will have a pressure dressing and may have some type of urinary diversion or a urinary stent (used to maintain patency of the urethral opening) while the meatus is healing.
2. Monitor vital signs.
3. Encourage fluid intake to maintain adequate urine output and maintain patency of the stent.
4. Monitor intake and output and the urine for cloudiness or a foul odor.
5. Notify the physician if there is no urinary output for 1 hour because this may indicate kinks in the urinary diversion or stent, or obstruction by sediment.

6. Provide pain medication (acetaminophen [Tylenol]) or medication to relieve bladder spasms (anticholinergic) as prescribed.
7. Administer antibiotics as prescribed.
8. Instruct the parents in the care of the urinary diversion or stent if present.
9. Instruct the parents to avoid giving the child a tub bath until the stent, if present, is removed.
10. Instruct the parents about fluid intake, medication administration, signs and symptoms of infection, and need for physician follow-up for dressing removal about 4 days after surgery as prescribed.

VII. BLADDER EXSTROPHY

A. Description
  1. Bladder exstrophy is a congenital anomaly characterized by extrusion of the urinary bladder to the outside of the body through a defect in the lower abdominal wall.
  2. The cause is unknown.
  3. Treatment requires surgical management and occurs in a series of staged reconstructions.
  4. Initial surgery for closure of the abdominal defect should occur within the first few days of life.
  5. The goal of subsequent operations is to reconstruct the bladder and genitalia and enable the child to achieve urinary continence.
B. Assessment
  1. Exposed bladder mucosa
  2. Widened symphysis pubis
  3. Defects of the external genitalia
C. Interventions
  1. Monitor urinary output.
  2. Monitor for signs of urinary tract or wound infection.
  3. Maintain the integrity of the exposed bladder mucosa.
  4. Prevent the bladder tissue from drying, while allowing the drainage of urine, until surgical closure is performed.
    a. The bladder is covered with sterile, nonadherent clear plastic wrap or a sterile thin film dressing without adhesive.
    b. Petroleum jelly is avoided because it tends to dry out, adhere to the bladder mucosa, and damage the delicate tissues when the dressing is removed.
  5. Monitor laboratory values and urinalysis to assess for renal function.
  6. Administer antibiotics as prescribed.
  7. Provide emotional support to the parents, and encourage verbalization of their fears and concerns.

PRACTICE QUESTIONS

1. A nurse is developing a plan of care for a 7-year-old child diagnosed with acute glomerulonephritis. The nurse includes which priority intervention in the plan of care?
  1. Force oral fluids to prevent hypovolemic shock.
  2. Encourage limited activity and provide safety measures.
  3. Catheterize the child to monitor intake and output strictly.
  4. Encourage classmates to visit and to keep the child informed of school events.

2. A nurse is performing an admission assessment on a 2-year-old child who has been diagnosed with nephrotic syndrome. The nurse knows that the most common characteristic associated with nephrotic syndrome is:
  1. Hypertension.
  2. Generalized edema.
  3. Increased urinary output.
  4. Frank, bright red blood in the urine.

3. A nurse is planning care for a child with hemolytic-uremic syndrome. The child has been anuric and will be receiving peritoneal dialysis treatment. The nurse plans to:
  1. Restrict fluids as prescribed.
  2. Encourage foods high in potassium.
  3. Administer analgesics as prescribed.
  4. Care for the arteriovenous (AV) shunt.

4. A 7-year-old child is seen in a clinic, and the primary health care provider documents a diagnosis of primary nocturnal enuresis. When the mother asks a nurse about the diagnosis, the nurse plans to respond knowing that primary nocturnal enuresis:
  1. Does not respond to treatment.
  2. Is caused by a psychiatric problem.
  3. Requires surgical intervention to improve the problem.
  4. Is common, and most children will outgrow the bed-wetting problem without therapeutic intervention.

5. A nurse has provided discharge instructions to the mother of a 2-year-old child who had an orchiopexy to correct cryptorchidism. Which statement by the mother of the child indicates that further teaching is necessary?
  1. "I'll check his temperature."
  2. "I'll give him medication so he'll be comfortable."
  3. "I'll check his voiding to be sure there's no problem."
  4. "I'll let him decide when to return to his play activities."

6. A nurse collects a urine specimen preoperatively from a child with epispadias who is scheduled for surgical repair. When the nurse is analyzing the re-

sults of the urinalysis, which of the following would the nurse most likely expect to note?
1. Hematuria
2. Proteinuria
3. Bacteriuria
4. Glucosuria

7. A priority nursing diagnosis for a child with severe edema caused from nephrotic syndrome would be:
1. Risk for constipation
2. Risk for impaired skin integrity
3. Risk for ineffective thermoregulation
4. Risk for imbalanced nutrition: more than body requirements

8. A 1-year-old child with hypospadias is scheduled for surgery to correct this condition. The nurse prepares a nursing care plan for this child and understands that this surgery is taking place at a time when:
1. Fears of separation are great.
2. Sibling rivalry will cause regression to occur.
3. Concern over size and function of the penis is present.
4. Embarrassment about voiding irregularities is common.

9. A nurse is reviewing a treatment plan with the parents of a newborn infant with hypospadias. Which statement by the parents indicates their understanding of the plan?
1. "Caution should be used when straddling the infant on a hip."
2. "Vital signs should be taken daily to check for bladder infection."
3. "Catheterization will be necessary when the infant does not void."
4. "Circumcision has been delayed to save tissue for surgical repair."

10. After performing an assessment of an infant with bladder exstrophy, a nurse prepares a plan of care. The nurse identifies which nursing diagnosis as the priority for the infant?
1. Infection, risk for
2. Tissue integrity, impaired
3. Incontinence, urinary, total
4. Knowledge, deficient (parental)

11. A nurse is caring for an infant with a diagnosis of bladder exstrophy. To protect the exposed bladder tissue, the nurse plans to:
1. Cover the bladder with petroleum jelly gauze.
2. Cover the bladder with a nonadhering plastic wrap.
3. Apply sterile distilled water dressings over the bladder mucosa.
4. Keep the bladder tissue dry by covering it with dry sterile gauze.

12. A nurse interviews the parents of a child recently diagnosed with glomerulonephritis. The nurse understands that which information collected during the assessment most often is associated with the diagnosis of glomerulonephritis?
1. Child fell off a bike onto the handlebars
2. Nausea and vomiting for the last 24 hours
3. Urticaria and itching for 1 week before diagnosis
4. Streptococcal throat infection 2 weeks before diagnosis

13. A nurse is assigned to care for a child suspected of having glomerulonephritis. The nurse reviews the child's record and notes that which finding is associated with the diagnosis of glomerulonephritis?
1. Hypotension
2. Red-brown urine
3. Low blood urea nitrogen level
4. Low urinary specific gravity

ALTERNATE ITEM FORMAT: MULTIPLE RESPONSE

A nurse is performing an assessment on a child admitted to the hospital with a probable diagnosis of nephrotic syndrome. What assessment findings would the nurse expect to observe?
❑ 1. Pallor
❑ 2. Edema
❑ 3. Anorexia
❑ 4. Proteinuria
❑ 5. Weight loss
❑ 6. Decreased serum lipids

ANSWERS

1. **2**
Rationale: Glomerulonephritis is a term that refers to a group of kidney disorders characterized by inflammatory injury in the glomerulus. In glomerulonephritis, activity is limited and most children, because of fatigue, voluntarily restrict their activities during the active phase of the disease. Catheterization may cause a risk of infection. Fluids should never be forced. Visitors should be limited to allow for adequate rest.
Test-Taking Strategy: Use the process of elimination. Eliminate option 4 because rest is the priority over socialization. Elimi-

nate option 3 next. Although monitoring intake and output is essential, the risk of infection could occur with catheterization. From the remaining options, eliminate option 1 because of the word *force*. Review the appropriate nursing interventions for the child with glomerulonephritis if you had difficulty with this question.
Level of Cognitive Ability: Application
Client Needs: Physiological Integrity
Integrated Process: Nursing Process—planning
Content Area: Child health

Reference: Hockenberry, M., Wilson, D., & Winkelstein, M. (2005). *Wong's essentials of pediatric nursing* (7th ed., pp. 998-999). St. Louis: Mosby.

2. **2**

Rationale: Nephrotic syndrome is defined as massive protein-uria, hypoalbuminemia, hyperlipemia, and edema. Other manifestations include weight gain, periorbital and facial edema that is most prominent in the morning, leg, ankle, la-bial or scrotal edema, decreased urine output and urine that is dark and frothy, abdominal swelling, and blood pressure that is normal or slightly decreased.

Test-Taking Strategy: Recall the pathophysiology associated with nephrotic syndrome. Associate edema with nephrotic syndrome to help you if you encounter a question similar to this one. If you had difficulty with this question, review the characteristics of nephrotic syndrome.

Level of Cognitive Ability: Analysis
Client Needs: Physiological Integrity
Integrated Process: Nursing Process—assessment
Content Area: Child health

References: Hockenberry, M., Wilson, D., & Winkelstein, M. (2005). *Wong's essentials of pediatric nursing* (7th ed., p. 996). St. Louis: Mosby.

Wong, D., Perry, S., Hockenberry, M., et al. (2006). *Maternal child nursing care* (3rd ed., p. 1653). St. Louis: Mosby.

3. **1**

Rationale: Hemolytic-uremic syndrome (HUS) is thought to be associated with bacterial toxins, chemicals, and viruses that cause acute renal failure in children. Clinical features of the disease include acquired hemolytic anemia, thrombocytope-nia, renal injury, and central nervous system symptoms. A child with hemolytic-uremic syndrome undergoing peritoneal dialysis because of anuria will be on fluid restriction. Pain is not associated with hemolytic-uremic syndrome and potas-sium would be restricted, not encouraged, if the child was anuric. Peritoneal dialysis does not require an AV shunt (only hemodialysis).

Test-Taking Strategy: Focus on the child's diagnosis and recall knowledge about the care of a client for acute renal failure. Also focus on the data in the question. Noting the word *peri-toneal* will assist in eliminating option 4. From the remaining options, remember that because the child is anuric, fluids will be restricted. Review care of the child with hemolytic-uremic syndrome if this question was difficult.

Level of Cognitive Ability: Analysis
Client Needs: Physiological Integrity
Integrated Process: Nursing Process—planning
Content Area: Child health

References: Hockenberry, M., & Wilson, D. (2007). *Nursing care of infants and children* (8th ed., pp. 1252-1253). St. Louis: Mosby.

Wong, D., Perry, S., Hockenberry, M., et al. (2006). *Maternal child nursing care* (3rd ed., p. 1658). St. Louis: Mosby.

4. **4**

Rationale: Primary nocturnal enuresis occurs in a child who has never been dry at night for extended periods. The condi-tion is common in children, and most children eventually will

outgrow bed-wetting without therapeutic intervention. The child is not able to sense a full bladder and does not awaken to void. The child may have delayed maturation of the central nervous system. The condition is not caused by a psychiatric problem.

Test-Taking Strategy: Use the process of elimination, noting the relationship between the words *enuresis* in the question and *bed-wetting* in the correct option. If you had difficulty with this question, review the characteristics associated with enuresis.

Level of Cognitive Ability: Comprehension
Client Needs: Physiological Integrity
Integrated Process: Nursing Process—planning
Content Area: Child health

References: Hockenberry, M., Wilson, D., & Winkelstein, M. (2005). *Wong's essentials of pediatric nursing* (7th ed., pp. 538-539). St. Louis: Mosby.

McKinney, E., James, S., Murray, S., & Ashwill, J. (2005). *Maternal-child nursing* (2nd ed., p. 1163). St. Louis: W.B. Saunders.

5. **4**

Rationale: All vigorous activities should be restricted for 2 weeks following surgery to promote healing and prevent injury. This will prevent dislodging of the suture, which is in-ternal. Normally, 2-year-olds want to be active; therefore, al-lowing the child to decide when to return to his play activities may prevent healing and cause injury. The parent should be taught to monitor the temperature, provide analgesics as needed, and monitor the urine output.

Test-Taking Strategy: Use the process of elimination and note the strategic words *further teaching is necessary*. These words indicate a negative event query and ask you to select an option that is an incorrect statement. Option 1 is an important action to recognize signs of infection. Option 2 is appropriate to keep pain to a minimum. Option 3 monitors voiding pattern, which is also important following this type of surgery. If you had difficulty with this question, review the discharge instruc-tions following surgical correction of cryptorchidism.

Level of Cognitive Ability: Analysis
Client Needs: Health Promotion and Maintenance
Integrated Process: Teaching and Learning
Content Area: Child health

References: Hockenberry, M., Wilson, D., & Winkelstein, M. (2005). *Wong's essentials of pediatric nursing* (7th ed., p. 994). St. Louis: Mosby.

McKinney, E., James, S., Murray, S., & Ashwill, J. (2005). *Maternal-child nursing* (2nd ed., p. 1170). St. Louis: W.B. Saunders.

6. **3**

Rationale: Epispadias is a congenital defect involving abnor-mal placement of the urethral orifice of the penis. The urethral opening is located anywhere on the dorsum of the penis. This anatomical characteristic facilitates entry of bacteria into the urine. Options 1, 2, and 4 are not characteristically noted in this condition.

Test-Taking Strategy: Use knowledge regarding the anatomical characteristic of epispadias and the process of elimination to answer the question. Options 1, 2, and 4 do not relate to the

potential for infection, which can be present in the condition of epispadias. If you had difficulty with this question, review the diagnostic findings associated with epispadias.
Level of Cognitive Ability: Analysis
Client Needs: Physiological Integrity
Integrated Process: Nursing Process—assessment
Content Area: Child health
Reference: Wong, D., Perry, S., Hockenberry, M., et al. (2006). *Maternal child nursing care.* (3rd ed., p. 1648). St. Louis: Mosby.

7. 2
Rationale: Nephrotic syndrome is a kidney disorder characterized by massive proteinuria, hypoalbuminemia (hypoproteinemia), and edema. A child with edema from nephrotic syndrome will be at high risk for skin breakdown. Skin surfaces should be cleaned and separated with clothing to prevent irritation and resultant skin breakdown. The child will be anorexic so a risk for imbalanced nutrition, more than body requirements is not a concern. A risk for constipation or ineffective thermoregulation is not a concern with nephrotic syndrome.
Test-Taking Strategy: Focus on the child's diagnosis and the manifestations associated with nephrotic syndrome. Recalling that nephrotic syndrome is characterized by massive proteinuria, hypoalbuminemia (hypoproteinemia), and edema will direct you to the correct option. Review care of the child with nephrotic syndrome if you had difficulty with this question.
Level of Cognitive Ability: Analysis
Client Needs: Physiological Integrity
Integrated Process: Nursing Process—analysis
Content Area: Child health
References: Hockenberry, M., Wilson, D., & Winkelstein, M. (2005). *Wong's essentials of pediatric nursing* (7th ed., pp. 996-997). St. Louis: Mosby.
Hockenberry, M., & Wilson, D. (2007). *Nursing care of infants and children* (8th ed., pp. 1248, 1250). St. Louis: Mosby.

8. 1
Rationale: At the age of 1 year, a child's fears of separation are great because the child is facing the developmental task of trusting others. Options 3 and 4 may be issues if the child was older. No data in the question allow one to determine that siblings exist.
Test-Taking Strategy: Use the process of elimination and knowledge regarding the stages of growth and development to answer the question. Options 3 and 4 can be eliminated easily. Next, eliminate option 2 because no data in the question allow one to determine that siblings exist. If you had difficulty with this question, review the stages of growth and development.
Level of Cognitive Ability: Analysis
Client Needs: Health Promotion and Maintenance
Integrated Process: Nursing Process—planning
Content Area: Child health
References: Hockenberry, M. Wilson, D., & Winkelstein, M. (2003). *Wong's nursing care of infants and children* (7th ed., p. 481). St. Louis: Mosby.
Wong, D., Perry, S., Hockenberry, M., et al. (2006). *Maternal child nursing care* (3rd ed., p. 1297-1298). St. Louis: Mosby.

9. 4
Rationale: Hypospadias is a congenital defect involving abnormal placement of the urethral orifice of the penis. In hypospadias, the urethral orifice is located below the glans penis along the ventral surface. The infant should not be circumcised because the dorsal foreskin tissue will be used for surgical repair of the hypospadias. Options 1, 2, and 3 are unrelated to this disorder.
Test-Taking Strategy: Use the process of elimination and note the strategic words *indicates their understanding*. Recalling that hypospadias is a congenital defect involving abnormal placement of the urethral orifice of the penis will direct you to option 4. Review the treatment plan related to the repair of the hypospadias if you had difficulty with this question.
Level of Cognitive Ability: Analysis
Client Needs: Physiological Integrity
Integrated Process: Nursing process—evaluation
Content Area: Child health
References: Hockenberry, M., & Wilson, D. (2007). *Nursing care of infants and children* (8th ed., p. 487). St. Louis: Mosby.
McKinney, E., James, S., Murray, S., & Ashwill, J. (2005). *Maternal-child nursing* (2nd ed., p. 1171). St. Louis: W.B. Saunders.

10. 2
Rationale: In bladder exstrophy, the bladder is exposed and external to the body. The highest priority is impaired tissue integrity related to the exposed bladder mucosa. Although the infant needs to be monitored for elimination patterns and kidney function, option 3 is not a concern for this condition. Parental knowledge deficit related to the diagnosis and treatment of the condition will need to be addressed but again is not the priority. Although infection related to the anatomical location of the defect is an appropriate nursing diagnosis, it is a potential problem and not an actual one.
Test-Taking Strategy: Use the process of elimination. Eliminate option 1 first because this addresses a potential problem rather than an actual one. Eliminate option 4 next because physiological needs take precedence over psychosocial needs. From the remaining options, knowledge that the bladder mucosa is exposed in this condition should direct you to the correct option. Review this disorder if you had difficulty with this question.
Level of Cognitive Ability: Analysis
Client Needs: Physiological Integrity
Integrated Process: Nursing Process—analysis
Content Area: Child health
Reference: Wong, D., Perry, S., Hockenberry, M., et al. (2006). *Maternal child nursing care* (3rd ed., p. 863). St. Louis: Mosby.

11. 2
Rationale: In bladder exstrophy, the bladder is exposed and external to the body. In this disorder, one must take care to protect the exposed bladder tissue from drying while allowing the drainage of urine. This is accomplished best by covering the bladder with a nonadhering plastic wrap. The use of petroleum jelly gauze should be avoided because this type of dressing can dry out, adhere to the mucosa, and damage the delicate tissue when removed. Dry sterile dressings and dressings soaked in solutions (that can dry out) also damage the mucosa when removed.

Test-Taking Strategy: Use the process of elimination and focus on the diagnosis. Noting the strategic word *nonadhering* in option 2 will direct you to this option. If you had difficulty with this question, review care of the infant with bladder exstrophy.
Level of Cognitive Ability: Analysis
Client Needs: Physiological Integrity
Integrated Process: Nursing Process—planning
Content Area: Child health
Reference: Hockenberry, M., & Wilson, D. (2007). *Nursing care of infants and children* (8th ed., p. 488). St. Louis: Mosby.

12. **4**
Rationale: Glomerulonephritis is a term that refers to a group of kidney disorders characterized by inflammatory injury in the glomerulus. Group A beta-hemolytic streptococcal infection is a cause of glomerulonephritis. Often, the child becomes ill with streptococcal infection of the upper respiratory tract and then develops symptoms of acute poststreptococcal glomerulonephritis after an interval of 1 to 2 weeks. The assessment data in options 1, 2, and 3 are unrelated to a diagnosis of glomerulonephritis.
Test-Taking Strategy: Use the process of elimination. Option 1 relates to a kidney injury, not an infectious process. From the remaining options, recalling a streptococcal infection 1 to 2 weeks before the development of glomerulonephritis is the classic assessment finding will assist in directing you to option 4. If you had difficulty with this question, review the causes of glomerulonephritis.
Level of Cognitive Ability: Analysis
Client Needs: Physiological Integrity
Integrated Process: Nursing Process—assessment
Content Area: Child health
Reference: Hockenberry, M., Wilson, D., & Winkelstein, M. (2005). *Wong's essentials of pediatric nursing* (7th ed., p. 997). St. Louis: Mosby.

13. **2**
Rationale: Glomerulonephritis is a term that refers to a group of kidney disorders characterized by inflammatory injury in

the glomerulus. Gross hematuria, resulting in dark, smoky, cola-colored or red-brown urine, is a classic symptom of glomerulonephritis. Hypertension is also common. Blood urea nitrogen levels may be elevated. A moderately elevated to high urinary specific gravity is associated with glomerulonephritis.
Test-Taking Strategy: Use the process of elimination. Eliminate options 1 and 4 first because hypertension and a high specific gravity are most likely to occur in this kidney disorder. Knowledge that blood urea nitrogen levels elevate will assist in directing you to option 2. If you had difficulty with this question, review the clinical manifestations associated with glomerulonephritis.
Level of Cognitive Ability: Analysis
Client Needs: Physiological Integrity
Integrated Process: Nursing Process—analysis
Content Area: Child health
Reference: Hockenberry, M., Wilson, D., & Winkelstein, M. (2005). *Wong's essentials of pediatric nursing* (7th ed., p. 998). St. Louis: Mosby.

ALTERNATE ITEM FORMAT: MULTIPLE RESPONSE

Answer: 1, 2, 3, 4
Rationale: Nephrotic syndrome is a kidney disorder characterized by massive proteinuria, hypoalbuminemia, edema, elevated serum lipids, anorexia, and pallor. The child gains weight.
Test-Taking Strategy: Note the child's diagnosis. Recalling the assessment findings for nephrotic syndrome will direct you to the correct options. Review the clinical manifestations associated with nephrotic syndrome if you had difficulty with this question.
Level of Cognitive Ability: Analysis
Client Needs: Physiological Integrity
Integrated Process: Nursing Process—assessment
Content Area: Child health
Reference: McKinney, E., James, S., Murray, S., & Ashwill, J. (2005). *Maternal-child nursing* (2nd ed., p. 1175). St. Louis: W.B. Saunders.

REFERENCES

Ackley, B., & Ladwig, G. (2006). *Nursing diagnosis handbook: a guide to planning* (7th ed.). St. Louis: Mosby.
Hockenberry, M. Wilson, D., & Winkelstein, M. (2005). *Wong's essentials of pediatric nursing* (7th ed.). St. Louis: Mosby.
Hockenberry, M., & Wilson, D. (2007). *Nursing care of infants and children* (8th ed.). St. Louis: Mosby.

McKinney, E., James, S., Murray, S., & Ashwill, J. (2005). *Maternal-child nursing* (2nd ed.). St. Louis: W.B. Saunders.
National Council of State Boards of Nursing (Eds.). (2007). *2007 NCLEX-RN® detailed test plan.* Chicago: Author.
Wong, D., Perry, S., Hockenberry, M., et al. (2006). *Maternal child nursing care* (3rd ed.). St. Louis: Mosby.

Integumentary Disorders

I. ECZEMA (ATOPIC DERMATITIS)

A. Description

1. Superficial inflammatory process involving primarily the epidermis
2. Associated with family history, immunoglobulin E (IgE) level elevations, allergies, and excessive water exposure, as in frequent hand washing
3. The major goals of management are to relieve pruritus, lubricate the skin, reduce inflammation, and prevent or control secondary infections.

B. Forms of eczema (Box 42-1)

C. Assessment

1. Redness
2. Scaliness
3. Itching
4. Minute papules (firm elevated circumscribed lesions smaller than 1 cm in diameter) and vesicles (similar to papules but fluid-filled)
5. Weeping, oozing, and crusting of lesions
6. Adolescent and early adult forms commonly occur in antecubital and popliteal areas.

D. Interventions

1. Avoid exposure to skin irritants such as soaps, detergents, fabric softeners, diaper wipes, and powder.
2. Avoid excessive bathing and washing of affected areas; lubricate skin.
3. Intermittently apply cool, wet compresses for short periods to soothe the skin; pat dry between cooling treatments.
4. Administer antihistamines and topical corticosteroids as prescribed; corticosteroids are applied in a thin layer and are rubbed into the area thoroughly.
5. Administer immunomodulator medications as prescribed.

6. Administer prescribed antibiotics if secondary infections occur.
7. Prevent or minimize scratching; keep the nails short and clean, and place gloves or cotton socks over the hands.
8. Eliminate conditions that increase itching, such as wet diapers, excessive bathing, ambient heat, woolen clothes or blankets, and proximity to rough fabrics or furry stuffed animals.
9. Instruct the parents to wash clothing in a mild detergent and rinse thoroughly; putting the clothes through a second complete wash cycle without detergent will minimize the amount of residue remaining on the fabric.
10. Instruct the parents about measures to prevent skin infections.
11. Instruct the parents to monitor the lesions for signs of infection (honey-colored crusts with surrounding erythema), and to seek immediate medical intervention if such signs are noted.

BOX 42-1
Forms of Eczema

INFANTILE
Usually begins at 2 to 6 months of age and decreases in incidence with aging; spontaneous remission may occur by 3 years of age.

CHILDHOOD
May follow the infantile form; occurs at 2 to 3 years of age.

PREADOLESCENT AND ADOLESCENT
Begins at about 12 years of age and may continue into the early adult years or indefinitely.

II. IMPETIGO

A. Description

1. Highly contagious bacterial infection of the skin caused by beta-hemolytic streptococci or staphylococci, or both

2. Can occur because of poor hygiene; can be a primary infection or occur secondarily at a site that has been injured, or at a site that was originally a rash, such as that caused by exposure to poison ivy or poison oak

3. The most common sites of infection are on the face and around the mouth, and then on the hands, neck, and extremities.

4. The lesions begin as vesicles or pustules surrounded by edema and redness (a pustule is similar to a vesicle except its fluid content is purulent).

5. The lesions progress to an exudative and crusting stage; after the crusting of the lesions, the initially serous vesicular fluid becomes cloudy and the vesicles rupture, leaving honey-colored crusts covering ulcerated bases.

B. Assessment (Fig. 42-1)

1. Lesions
2. Erythema
3. Pruritus
4. Burning
5. Secondary lymph node involvement

C. Interventions

1. Contact isolation; use standard precautions and implement agency-specific isolation procedures for the hospitalized child; strict hygiene practices are important because it is a highly contagious condition.

2. Allow lesions to dry by air exposure.

3. Assist the child with daily bathing with antibacterial soap, as prescribed.

4. Apply warm saline or other prescribed compresses to the lesions two or three times daily, followed by soap and water to remove crusts and allow for healing.

5. Apply topical antibiotic ointments and instruct the parents in their use; the infection is still communicable for 48 hours beyond initiation of antibiotic treatment.

6. Administer oral antibiotics, which may be prescribed if there is no response to topical antibiotic treatment; it is extremely important to comply with the prescribed antibiotic regimen because secondary infections such as glomerulonephritis may result if the infectious agent is of a streptococcal type that can affect the nephrons.

7. Apply and instruct the parents in the use of emollients to prevent skin cracking.

8. Instruct the parents in the methods to prevent the spread of the infection, especially careful hand washing.

9. Inform the parents that the child needs to use separate towels, linens, and dishes.

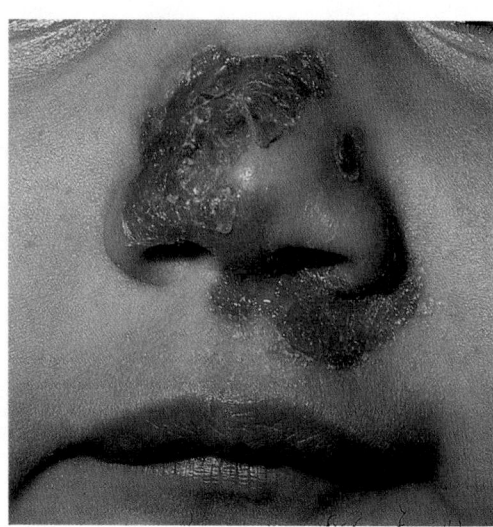

FIG. 42-1 Impetigo contagiosa. (From Hockenberry, M., Wilson, D., Winkelstein, M., & Kline, N. [2003]. *Wong's nursing care of infants and children* [7th ed.]. St. Louis: Mosby.)

10. Inform the parents that all linens and clothing used by the child should be washed with detergent in hot water separately from those of other household members.

III. PEDICULOSIS CAPITIS (LICE)

A. Description

1. An infestation of the hair and scalp with lice

2. The most common sites of involvement are the occipital area, behind the ears at the nape of the neck, and occasionally the eyebrows and eyelashes.

3. The female louse lays her eggs (nits) on the hair shaft, close to the scalp; the incubation period is 7 to 10 days.

4. Head lice live and reproduce only on human beings and are transmitted by direct and indirect contact, such as sharing of brushes, hats, towels, and bedding.

5. All contacts of the infested child, especially siblings, should be examined for lice infestation and referred for treatment as appropriate.

B. Assessment (Box 42-2; Fig. 42-2)

C. Interventions

1. Use a pediculicide shampoo or rinse as prescribed; follow package instructions for timing the application and for contraindications for their use in children.

2. Instruct the parents about the use of shampoo or rinse as prescribed, and that siblings may also need treatment; grooming items are not to be shared and a single comb or brush should be used for each individual child.

3. Instruct the parents that bedding and clothing used by the child should be changed daily, laundered in hot water with detergent, and dried in a

FIG. 42-2 Viable nits. (From Morse, S., Ballard, R., Holmes, K., Moreland, A. [2003]. Atlas of sexually transmitted diseases and AIDS [3rd ed]. London: Mosby.)

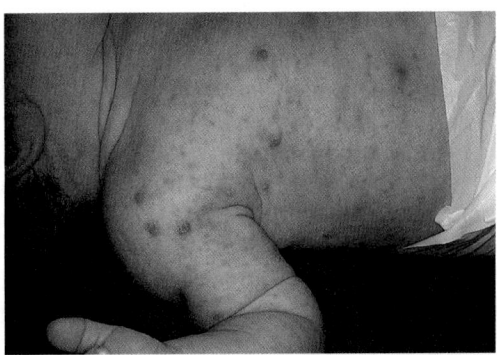

FIG. 42-3 Scabies rash on an infant. (From Mosby. [2006]. *Mosby's dictionary of medical, nursing, and health professions* [7th ed.]. St. Louis: Mosby.)

BOX 42-2

Assessment Findings: Pediculosis Capitis

Pruritis is caused by the crawling insect and insect saliva on the skin

Nits (white eggs) are observable on the hair shaft (it is important to differentiate nits from lint or dandruff, which flakes away easily)

Adult lice are difficult to see and appear as small tan or grayish specks, which may crawl fast.

BOX 42-3

Assessment Findings: Scabies

Pruritic papular rash

Burrows on the skin (fine grayish-red lines that may be difficult to see)

---

hot dryer for 20 minutes; this process should continue for 1 week.

4. Instruct the parents that nonessential bedding and clothing can be stored in a tightly sealed bag for 2 weeks and then washed.

5. Instruct the parents to seal toys that cannot be washed or dry-cleaned in a plastic bag for 2 weeks.

6. Instruct the parents that hairbrushes or combs should be discarded or soaked in boiling water or in a commercially available lice-killing product for 1 hour.

7. Instruct the parents that furniture and carpets need to be vacuumed frequently, and that the dust bag from the vacuum should be discarded after vacuuming.

8. Teach the child not to share clothing, headwear, brushes, and combs.

9. Lice of the eyelashes may be treated by the application of Vaseline twice daily for 1 week to suffocate the lice.

▲ IV. SCABIES

A. Description

1. Scabies is a parasitic skin disorder caused by an infestation of *Sarcoptes scabiei* (itch mite; see Chap. 49 for more information related to scabies)

2. Endemic among schoolchildren and institutionalized populations as a result of close personal contact

3. Incubation period
   a. Female mite burrows into epidermis, lays eggs, and dies in the burrow after 4 to 5 weeks.
   b. The eggs hatch in 3 to 5 days, and larvae mature and complete their life cycle.

4. Infectious period: During the entire course of the infestation

5. Transmission: By close personal contact with infected person

B. Assessment (Box 42-3; Fig. 42-3) ▲

C. Interventions ▲

1. Topical application of a scabicide such as lindane or permethrin (Elimite, Nix, Acticin) kills the mites.

2. Lindane should not be used in children younger than 2 years because of the risk of neurotoxicity and seizures.

3. Instruct the parents in the application of the scabicide.
   a. Application should be preceded by a warm soap and water bath.
   b. Skin must be cool and dry before the application of the lotion.
   c. Lotion is left in place for 8 to 14 hours before it is washed off.

4. When permethrin is used, the cream is massaged thoroughly and gently into all skin surfaces (not just the areas that have the rash) from the head to the soles of the feet; care should be taken to avoid contact with the eyes.

5. Household members and contacts of the infected child need to be treated at the same time.

6. Instruct the parents about the importance of frequent hand washing.

7. Instruct the parents that all clothing, bedding, and pillowcases used by the child need to be changed daily, washed in hot water with detergent, dried in a hot dryer, and ironed before reuse; this process should continue for one week.

8. Instruct the parents that nonwashable toys and other items should be sealed in plastic bags for 4 days.

V. THE BURNED CHILD

A. Pediatric considerations
1. Very young children who have been burned severely have a higher mortality rate than older children and adults with comparable burns (see Chap. 49 for additional information related to burns).
2. Lower burn temperatures and shorter exposure to heat can cause a more severe burn in a child than in an adult because a child's skin is thinner.
3. The degree of pain experienced by the child and the ability to communicate it will be different than in an adult with the same exposure.
4. Severely burned children are at increased risk for fluid and heat loss, dehydration, and metabolic acidosis than an adult.
5. The higher proportion of body fluid to mass in children increases the risk of cardiovascular problems.
6. Burns involving more than 10% of the total body surface area require some form of fluid resuscitation.
7. Infants and children are at increased risk for protein and calorie deficiency because they have smaller muscle mass and less body fat than adults.
8. Scarring is more severe in a child; disturbed body image will be a distinct issue for a child or adolescent, especially as growth continues.
9. An immature immune system presents an increased risk of infection for infants and young children.
10. A delay in growth may occur following a burn.

B. Extent of the burn injury
1. The rule of nines, used for an adult with a burn injury, gives an inaccurate estimate in children because of the difference in body proportions between children and adults.
2. A modified rule of nines may be used for the pediatric population (Fig. 42-4).

C. Fluid replacement therapy
1. Fluid replacement is necessary during the initial 24-hour period following the burn injury be-

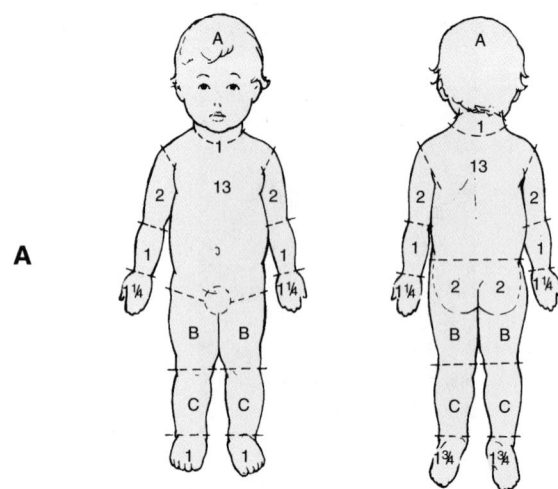

A

RELATIVE PERCENTAGES OF AREAS AFFECTED BY GROWTH

AREA	BIRTH	AGE 1 YR	AGE 5 YR
A = ½ of head	9½	8½	6½
B = ½ of one thigh	2¾	3¼	4
C = ½ of one leg	2½	2½	2¾

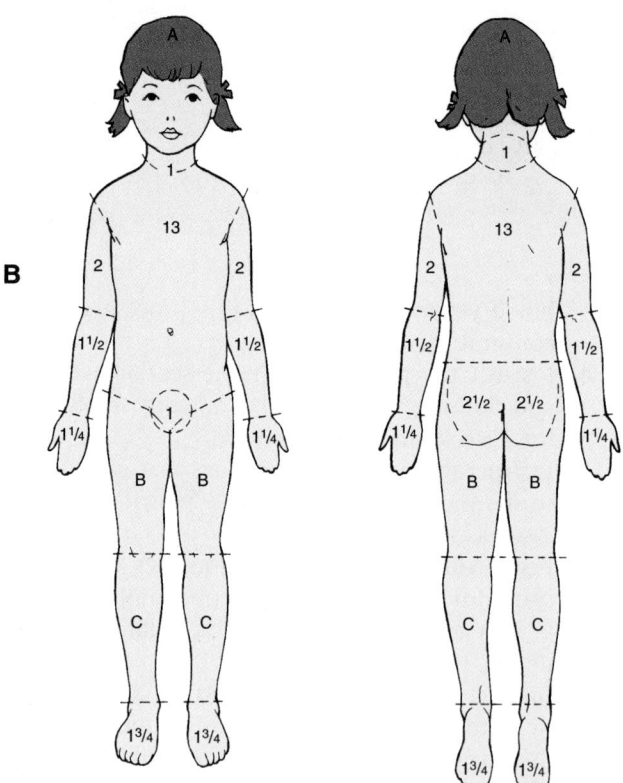

B

RELATIVE PERCENTAGES OF AREAS AFFECTED BY GROWTH

AREA	AGE 10 YR	AGE 15 YR	ADULT
A = ½ of head	5½	4½	3½
B = ½ of one thigh	4½	4½	4¾
C = ½ of one leg	3	3¼	3½

FIG. 42-4 Estimation of distribution of burns in children. **A,** Children from birth to age 5 years. **B,** Older children. (From Wong, D., Perry, S., Hockenberry, M., et al. [2006]. *Maternal child nursing care* [3rd ed.]. St. Louis: Mosby.)

cause of the fluid shifts that occur as a result of the injury.
2. Several formulas are available to calculate the child's fluid needs and the formula used depends on the physician's preference.
3. Crystalloid solutions are used during the initial phase of therapy; colloid solutions such as albumin, Plasma-Lyte (combined electrolyte solution), or fresh-frozen plasma are useful in maintaining plasma volume.
4. Parameters such as vital signs (especially the heart rate), urine output, adequacy of capillary filling, and sensorium status determine adequacy of fluid resuscitation.

PRACTICE QUESTIONS

1. A nurse is monitoring a child with burns during the treatment for burn shock. The nurse understands that which of the following assessments provides the most accurate guide to determining the adequacy of fluid resuscitation?
   1. Skin turgor
   2. Neurological assessment
   3. Level of edema at burn site
   4. Quality of peripheral pulses
2. A school nurse is conducting pediculosis capitis (head lice) assessments. A child with a "positive" head check would have:
   1. Maculopapular lesions behind the ears
   2. Lesions in the scalp that extend to the hairline or neck.
   3. White flaky particles throughout the entire scalp region
   4. White sacs attached to the hair shafts in the occipital area.
3. The nurse is developing a plan of care for a 12-year-old girl with an exacerbation of eczema. Which nursing diagnosis applies to the care for this child?
   1. Risk for infection related to viral lesions
   2. Risk for infection related to scratching of pruritic lesions
   3. Imbalanced nutrition, less than body requirements related to throat edema and mouth ulcers
   4. Disturbed body image related to the presence of thick white crusty plaques over the elbows and knees
4. A school nurse prepares a list of home care instructions for the parents of schoolchildren diagnosed with pediculosis capitis. Which of the following will the nurse include in the list?
   1. Soak combs and brushes in warm water.
   2. Use antilice sprays on all bedding and furniture.
   3. Take all bedding and linens to the cleaners to be dry-cleaned.

4. Vacuum floors, play areas, and furniture to remove any hairs that might carry live nits.
5. A mother of a 3-year-old child arrives at a clinic and tells the nurse that the child has been scratching the skin continuously and has developed a rash. The nurse assesses the child and suspects the presence of scabies. The nurse bases this suspicion on which finding noted on assessment of the child's skin?
   1. Fine grayish-red lines
   2. Purple-colored lesions
   3. Thick, honey-colored crusts
   4. Clusters of fluid-filled vesicles
6. Permethrin (Elimite, Nix, Acticin) is prescribed for a 4-year-old child with a diagnosis of scabies. A clinic nurse instructs the mother regarding the use of this treatment and tells the mother:
   1. To apply the lotion and leave it on for 6 hours.
   2. To avoid putting clothes on the child while the lotion is in place.
   3. That the lotion should be applied to areas of the rash only.
   4. To apply the lotion to cool, dry skin at least 30 minutes after bathing.
7. A clinic nurse is reviewing the physician's orders for a child who has been diagnosed with scabies. Lindane has been prescribed for the child. The nurse questions the order if which of the following is noted in the child's record?
   1. The child is 18 months old.
   2. The child is being bottle-fed.
   3. A sibling is using lindane for the treatment of scabies.
   4. The child has a history of frequent respiratory infections.
8. A topical corticosteroid is prescribed by a physician for a child with atopic dermatitis (eczema). A nurse instructs the mother in how to apply the cream and tells the mother to:
   1. Apply the cream over the entire body.
   2. Apply a thick layer of cream to affected areas only.
   3. Avoid cleansing the area before application of the cream.
   4. Apply a thin layer of cream and rub it into the area thoroughly.
9. A school nurse has provided an instructional session about impetigo to parents of the children attending the school. Which statement, if made by a parent, indicates a need for further instructions?
   1. "It is extremely contagious."
   2. "It is most common in humid weather."
   3. "Lesions most often are located on the arms and chest."
   4. "It might show up in an area of broken skin, such as an insect bite."

ALTERNATE ITEM FORMAT: MULTIPLE RESPONSE

A nurse caring for a child who sustained a burn injury plans care based on which pediatric considerations associated with this injury? Select all that apply.

❏ 1. Scarring is less severe in a child than in an adult.
❏ 2. A delay in growth may occur following a burn injury.
❏ 3. Fluid resuscitation is not necessary unless the burned area is more than 25% of the total body surface area.
❏ 4. An immature immune system presents an increased risk of infection for infants and young children.
❏ 5. The lower proportion of body fluid to mass in a child increases the risk of cardiovascular problems.
❏ 6. Infants and young children are at increased risk for protein and calorie deficiency because they have smaller muscle mass and less body fat than adults.

ANSWERS

1. **2**

Rationale: Sensorium is an accurate guide to determine the adequacy of fluid resuscitation. The burn injury itself does not affect the sensorium, so the child should be alert and oriented. Any alteration in sensorium should be evaluated further. A neurological assessment would determine the level of sensorium in the child. Options 1, 3, and 4 would not provide an accurate assessment of the adequacy of fluid resuscitation.

Test-Taking Strategy: Note the strategic words *most accurate* in the event query. Although options 1, 3, and 4 may provide some information related to fluid volume, in a burn injury, from the options provided, neurological assessment is most accurate. Review assessments during fluid resuscitation and treatment for burn shock if you had difficulty with this question.

Level of Cognitive Ability: Analysis
Client Needs: Physiological Integrity
Integrated Process: Nursing Process—evaluation
Content Area: Child health
Reference: Wong, D., Perry, S., Hockenberry, M., et al. (2006). *Maternal child nursing care* (3rd ed., p. 1788). St. Louis: Mosby.

2. **4**

Rationale: Pediculosis capitis is an infestation of the hair and scalp with lice. The nits are visible and firmly attach to the hair shaft near the scalp. The occiput is an area in which nits can be seen. White flaky particles are indicative of dandruff. Maculopapular lesions behind the ears or lesions that extend to the hairline or neck are indicative of an infectious process, not pediculosis.

Test-Taking Strategy: Use the process of elimination and eliminate options 1, 2, and 3 because these are not signs associated with pediculosis capitis. Option 4 is a common sign associated with pediculosis capitis. Review assessment findings with pediculosis capitis if you had difficulty with this question.

Level of Cognitive Ability: Analysis
Client Needs: Physiological Integrity
Integrated Process: Nursing Process—assessment
Content Area: Child health
Reference: Hockenberry, M., & Wilson, D. (2007). *Wong's nursing care of infants and children* (8th ed., p. 772). St. Louis: Mosby.

3. **2**

Rationale: Eczema is a superficial inflammatory process involving primarily the epidermis. The major goals of management are to relieve pruritus, lubricate the skin, reduce inflammation, and prevent and control secondary infection. Secondary infection can occur when areas affected by eczema are scratched as a result of the itching because open skin is a portal of entry for pathogens. The lesions are not viral and they do not present as thick white crusty plaques. They appear as red and scaly lesions that can weep, ooze, and crust. They commonly occur in the antecubital and popliteal areas. Throat edema and mouth ulcers are not characteristics of this disorder.

Test-Taking Strategy: Use the process of elimination. Eliminate option 1 first because eczema is an inflammatory process, which is not viral in origin. Eliminate option 3 because eczema affects primarily the epidermis, not the oral mucosa or nutrition. Eliminate option 4 because it describes psoriasis, not eczema. Review the characteristics of eczema if you had difficulty with this question.

Level of Cognitive Ability: Analysis
Client Needs: Physiological Integrity
Integrated Process: Nursing Process—planning
Content Area: Child health
Reference: Hockenberry, M. (2005). *Wong's essentials of pediatric nursing and virtual clinical excursions* (7th ed., pp. 578-582). St. Louis: Mosby.

4. **4**

Rationale: Thorough home cleaning is necessary to remove any remaining lice or nits. Antilice sprays are unnecessary. In addition, they should never be used on a child or on bedding or linens. Bedding and linens should be washed with hot water and dried on a hot setting. Items that cannot be washed should be dry-cleaned or sealed in plastic bags in a warm place for 2 weeks. Combs and brushes should be soaked in a scabicide shampoo or hot water for 1 hour.

Test-Taking Strategy: Use the process of elimination. Eliminate option 2 first, knowing that antilice sprays should not be used. Eliminate option 3 next, knowing that bedding and linens can be washed. Also note the close-ended word *all* in this option and in option 2. From the remaining options, eliminate option 1 because of the words *warm water*. If you had difficulty with this question, review these important home care instructions.

Level of Cognitive Ability: Application
Client Needs: Safe and Effective Care Environment
Integrated Process: Teaching and Learning
Content Area: Child health
Reference: McKinney, E., James, S., Murray, S., & Ashwill, J. (2005). *Maternal-child nursing* (2nd ed., p. 1375). St. Louis: W.B. Saunders.

5. 1
Rationale: Scabies appears as burrows or fine, grayish-red, thread-like lines. They may be difficult to see if they are obscured by excoriation and inflammation. Purple-colored lesions may indicate various disorders, including systemic conditions. Thick, honey-colored crusts are characteristic of impetigo or secondary infection in eczema. Clusters of fluid-filled vesicles are seen in herpesvirus infection.
Test-Taking Strategy: Use the process of elimination. Recalling that scabies infestation produces burrows will assist in directing you to option 1. If you are unfamiliar with the clinical manifestations associated with scabies, review this content.
Level of Cognitive Ability: Analysis
Client Needs: Physiological Integrity
Integrated Process: Nursing Process—assessment
Content Area: Child health
Reference: McKinney, E., James, S., Murray, S., & Ashwill, J. (2005). *Maternal-child nursing* (2nd ed., p. 1376). St. Louis: W.B. Saunders.

6. 4
Rationale: Permethrin is massaged thoroughly and gently into all skin surfaces (not just the areas that have the rash) from the head to the soles of the feet. Care should be taken to avoid contact with the eyes. The lotion should not be applied until at least 30 minutes after bathing and should be applied only to cool, dry skin. The lotion should be kept on for 8 to 14 hours, and then the child should be given a bath. The child should be clothed during the 8 to 14 hours of treatment contact time.
Test-Taking Strategy: Use the process of elimination. Options 2 and 3 can be eliminated easily. Also, note the close-ended word *only* in option 3. From the remaining options, recalling the procedure for the application of this lotion will direct you to option 4. Review this treatment if you had difficulty with this question.
Level of Cognitive Ability: Application
Client Needs: Physiological Integrity
Integrated Process: Teaching and Learning
Content Area: Child health
Reference: McKinney, E., James, S., Murray, S., & Ashwill, J. (2005). *Maternal-child nursing* (2nd ed., p. 1377). St. Louis: W.B. Saunders.

7. 1
Rationale: Lindane is contraindicated for children younger than 2 years. These children have more permeable skin and high systemic absorption may occur, placing the child at risk for central nervous system toxicity and seizures. Lindane also is used with caution in children between the ages of 2 and 10 years. Siblings and other household members also should be treated at the same time. Options 2 and 4 are unrelated to the

use of lindane. Lindane is not recommended for use by a breast-feeding woman because the medication is secreted into breast milk.
Test-Taking Strategy: Use the process of elimination and recall the concepts related to the body surface area of children and medication administration. These concepts will direct you easily to option 1. If you are unfamiliar with this medication, review the contraindications associated with its use.
Level of Cognitive Ability: Analysis
Client Needs: Physiological Integrity
Integrated Process: Nursing Process—analysis
Content Area: Child health
Reference: Hockenberry, M., Wilson, D., & Winkelstein, M. (2005). *Wong's essentials of pediatric nursing* (7th ed., pp. 1114-1115). St. Louis: Mosby.

8. 4
Rationale: A topical corticosteroid should be applied sparingly (thin layer) and rubbed into the area thoroughly. The affected area should be cleansed gently before application. A topical corticosteroid should not be applied over extensive areas. Systemic absorption is more likely to occur with extensive application.
Test-Taking Strategy: Use the process of elimination. Eliminate option 3 first because it does not make sense not to cleanse an affected area. Eliminate option 1 because medicated cream should be applied only to areas that are affected. Eliminate option 2 because of the word *thick*. Review the procedure for the application of a topical corticosteroid if you had difficulty with this question.
Level of Cognitive Ability: Application
Client Needs: Physiological Integrity
Integrated Process: Teaching and Learning
Content Area: Pharmacology
Reference: Hockenberry, M., Wilson, D., & Winkelstein, M. (2005). *Wong's essentials of pediatric nursing* (7th ed., p. 1126). St. Louis: Mosby.

9. 3
Rationale: Impetigo is most common during hot, humid summer months. Impetigo may begin in an area of broken skin, such as an insect bite or atopic dermatitis. Infection may be caused by *Staphylococcus aureus*, group A beta-hemolytic streptococci, or a combination of these bacteria. Impetigo is extremely contagious. Lesions usually are located around the mouth and nose but may be present on the hands and extremities.
Test-Taking Strategy: Use the process of elimination, noting the strategic words *need for further instructions*. These words indicate a negative event query and ask you to select an option that is an incorrect statement. Knowledge regarding the cause and manifestations of impetigo will direct you to option 3. If you are unfamiliar with this disorder, review this content.
Level of Cognitive Ability: Analysis
Client Needs: Safe and Effective Care Environment
Integrated Process: Teaching and Learning
Content Area: Child health
Reference: McKinney, E., James, S., Murray, S., & Ashwill, J. (2005). *Maternal-child nursing* (2nd ed., p. 1366). St. Louis: W.B. Saunders.

ALTERNATE FORMAT ITEM:
MULTIPLE RESPONSE

Answer: **2, 4, 6**

Rationale: Some pediatric considerations in the care of a burn victim include the following: scarring is more severe in a child than in an adult; a delay in growth may occur following a burn injury; burns involving more than 10% of total body surface area require some form of fluid resuscitation; an immature immune system presents an increased risk of infection for infants and young children; the higher proportion of body fluid to mass in a child increases the risk of cardiovascular problems; and infants and young children are at increased risk for protein and calorie deficiencies because they have smaller muscle mass and less body fat than adults.

Test-Taking Strategy: Focus on the subject, pediatric considerations in the care of a child who sustained a burn injury. Think about the physiology of a child related to body size to answer correctly. Review these considerations if you had difficulty with this question.

Level of Cognitive Ability: Analysis

Client Needs: Physiological Integrity

Integrated Process: Nursing Process—planning

Content Area: Child health

Reference: McKinney, E., James, S., Murray, S., & Ashwill, J. (2005). *Maternal-child nursing* (2nd ed., p. 1388). St. Louis: W.B. Saunders.

REFERENCES

Hockenberry, M.J. (2004). *Wong's essentials of pediatric nursing and virtual clinical excursions* (7th ed.). St. Louis: Mosby.

Hockenberry, M. & Wilson, D. (2007). *Wong's nursing care of infants and children* (8th ed.). St. Louis: Mosby.

Hodgson, B., & Kizior, R. (2007). *Saunders nursing drug handbook 2007.* Philadelphia: W.B. Saunders.

Jarvis, C.(2004). *Physical examination and health assessment* (4th ed.). St. Louis: W.B. Saunders.

McKinney, E., James, S., Murray S., & Ashwill, J. (2005) *Maternal-child nursing.* (2nd ed.). St. Louis: W.B. Saunders.

National Council of State Boards of Nursing (Eds.). (2007). *2007 NCLEX-RN® detailed test plan.* Chicago: Author.

Wong, D., Perry, S., Hockenberry, M., et al. (2006). *Maternal child nursing care* (3rd ed.). St. Louis: Mosby.

Musculoskeletal Disorders

I. **DEVELOPMENTAL DYSPLASIA OF THE HIP (DDH)**

A. Description

    1. Refers to disorders related to abnormal development of the hip that may develop during fetal life, infancy, or childhood; in these disorders, the head of the femur is seated improperly in the acetabulum or hip socket of the pelvis.

    2. Degrees of DDH (Box 43-1)

B. Assessment (Fig. 43-1)

    1. Neonate: Laxity of the ligaments around the hip

    2. Infant

        a. Shortening of the limb on the affected side (Galeazzi sign, Allis sign)

        b. Restricted abduction of the hip on the affected side when the child is placed supine with the knees and hips flexed

        c. Unequal gluteal folds when the infant is prone and the legs are extended against the examining table

        d. Positive Ortolani test: A click (clunk) or popping sensation is felt by the examiner because the head of the femur moves out of the acetabulum under pressure from the examiner's hands during rotation and abduction of the hip joints.

        e. Positive Barlow test: The femoral head can be displaced from the acetabulum on manipulation and pressure, and then the femoral head repositions correctly when the pressure is released.

    3. Older infant and child

        a. Affected leg is shorter than the other.

        b. The head of the femur can be felt to move up and down in the buttock when the extended thigh is pushed first toward the child's head and then pulled distally.

        c. Trendelenburg's sign: The child stands on one foot and then the other foot, holding onto a support and bearing weight on the affected hip; the pelvis tilts downward on the normal side instead of upward, as it would with normal stability.

        d. Greater trochanter is prominent.

        e. Marked lordosis or waddling gait in noted in bilateral dislocations.

C. Interventions

    1. Birth to 6 months of age: Splinting of the hips with a Pavlik harness to maintain flexion and abduction and external rotation (worn continu-

---

BOX 43-1

Degrees of Developmental Dysplasia of the Hip (DDH)

ACETABULAR DYSPLASIA (PRELUXATION)
Mildest form
Neither subluxation nor dislocation
Delay in acetabular development occurs
Femoral head remains in the acetabulum

SUBLUXATION
Incomplete dislocation of the hip
Femoral head remains in the acetabulum
Stretched capsule and ligamentum teres causes head of the femur to be partially displaced

DISLOCATION
Femoral head loses contact with acetabulum and is displaced posteriorly and superiorly over the fibrocartilaginous rim
Ligamentum teres—elongated and taut

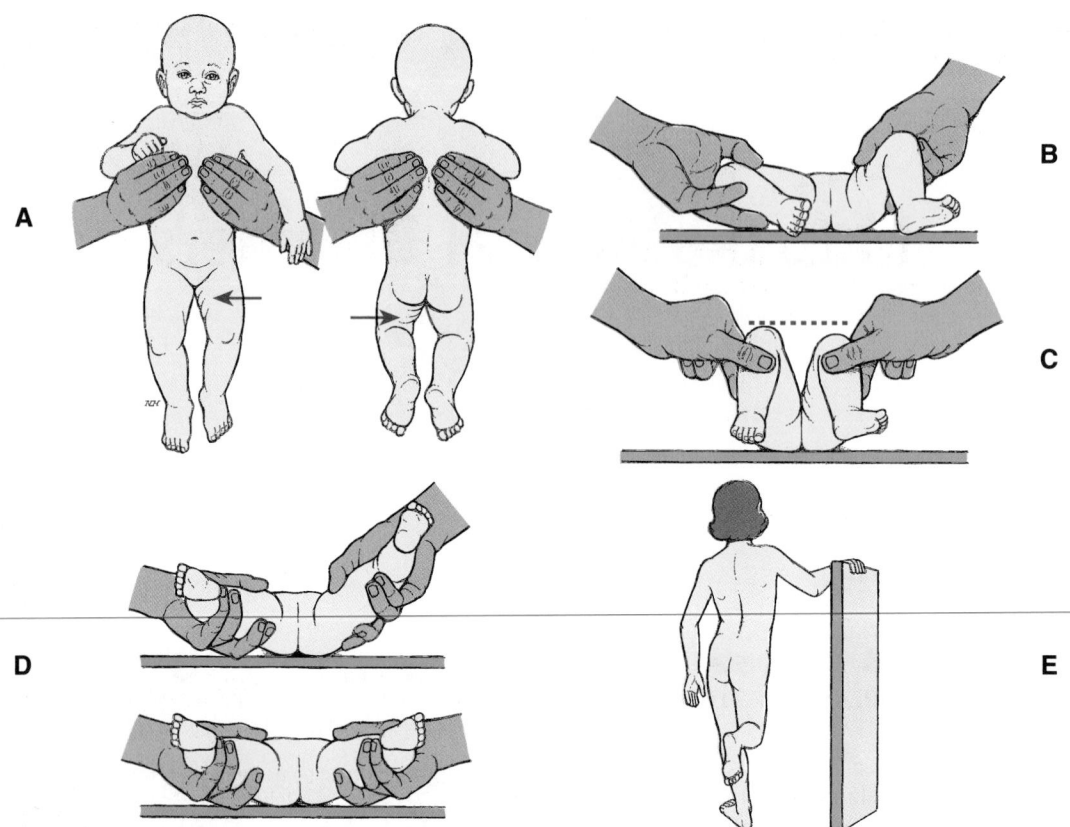

FIG. 43-1 Signs of development dysplasia of the hip. **A,** Asymmetry of gluteal and thigh folds. **B,** Limited hip abduction, as seen in flexion. **C,** Apparent shortening of the femur, as indicated by the level of the knees in flexion. **D,** Ortolani click (if infant is younger than 4 weeks old). **E,** Positive Trendelenburg's sign or gait (if child is weight-bearing). (From Hockenberry, M., Wilson, S., Winkelstein, M. [2005]. *Wong's essentials of pediatric nursing* [7th ed.]. St. Louis: Mosby.)

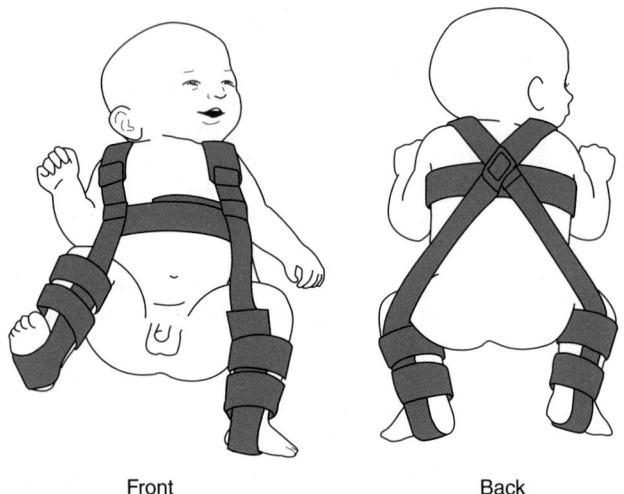

Front   Back

FIG. 43-2 Child in Pavlik harness. (From Hockenberry, M., Wilson, S., Winkelstein, M. [2005] *Wong's essentials of pediatric nursing* [7th ed.]. St. Louis: Mosby.)

ously until the hip is stable in about 3 to 6 months; Fig. 43-2)

2. Ages 6 to 18 months: Gradual reduction by traction followed by closed reduction or open reduction (if necessary) under general anesthesia;

child is then placed in a hip spica cast for 2 to 4 months until the hip is stable, and then a flexion-abduction brace is applied for approximately 3 months.

3. Older child: Operative reduction and reconstruction are usually required.

4. Instruction is given to the parents regarding proper care of a Pavlik harness, spica cast, or abduction brace.

II. CONGENITAL CLUBFOOT

A. Description

1. A complex deformity of the ankle and foot that includes forefoot adduction, midfoot supination, hindfoot varus, and ankle equinus; defect may be unilateral or bilateral.

2. The goal of treatment is to achieve a painless plantigrade (able to walk on the sole of the foot with the heel on the ground) and stable foot.

3. Long-term interval follow-up is required until the child reaches skeletal maturity.

B. Assessment: Deformities are described based on the position of the ankle and foot.

1. Talipes varus: An inversion or bending inward

2. Talipes valgus: An eversion or bending outward

3. Talipes equinus: Plantar flexion in which the toes are lower than the heel
4. Talipes calcaneus: Dorsiflexion in which the toes are higher than the heel

C. Interventions
   1. Treatment begins as soon after birth as possible.
   2. Manipulation and casting are performed weekly for about 8 to 12 weeks to accommodate the rapid **growth** of early infancy; a splint is then applied if casting and manipulation are successful.
   3. Surgical intervention is necessary if normal alignment is not achieved by about 6 to 12 weeks of age.
   4. Monitor for pain and monitor the neurovascular status of the toes.
   5. Instruct the parents in cast and splint care and the signs of neurovascular impairment that require physician notification.

III. IDIOPATHIC SCOLIOSIS

A. Description
   1. Three-dimensional spinal deformity that usually involves lateral curvature, spinal rotation resulting in rib asymmetry, and hypokyphosis of the thorax (Fig. 43-3)
   2. Usually diagnosed during the preadolescent **growth** spurt; screenings are important when **growth** spurts occur.
   3. Surgical (spinal fusion, placement of an instrumentation system) and nonsurgical (bracing) interventions are used; the type of treatment depends on the location and degree of the curvatures, the age of the child, the amount of **growth** that is yet anticipated, and any underlying disease processes.
   4. Long-term monitoring is essential to detect any progression of the curve.

B. Assessment
   1. Asymmetry of the ribs and flanks is noted when the child bends forward at the waist and hangs arms down toward feet (Adams test).
   2. Hip height, rib positioning, and shoulder height are asymmetrical (can be noted when standing behind an undressed child); leg length discrepancy is also apparent.
   3. Radiographs are obtained to confirm the diagnosis.

C. Interventions
   1. Monitor progression of the curvatures.
   2. Prepare the child and parents for the use of a brace if prescribed; the potential for altered role performance, body image disturbance, fear, anger, and isolation exists.
   3. Prepare the child and parents for surgery (spinal fusion, placement of internal instrumentation systems) if prescribed.

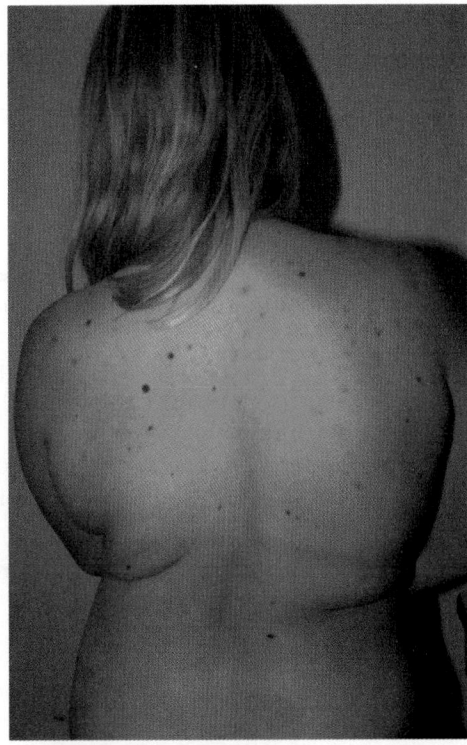

FIG. 43-3 Scoliosis in a standing erect posture. (From Lewis, S., Heitkemper, M., & Dirksen, S. [2004]. *Medical-surgical nursing. Assessment and management of clinical problems* [6th ed.]. St. Louis: Mosby.)

D. Braces
   1. Braces are not curative but may slow the progression of the curvature to allow skeletal **growth** and maturity.
   2. Braces usually are prescribed to be worn from 16 to 23 hours a day.
   3. Inspect the skin for signs of redness or breakdown.
   4. Keep the skin clean and dry, avoiding lotions and powders.
   5. Advise the child to wear soft nonirritating clothing under the brace.
   6. Instruct in prescribed exercises (exercises help maintain and strengthen spinal and abdominal muscles during treatment).
   7. Encourage verbalization about body image and other psychosocial issues.

E. Postoperative interventions
   1. Maintain proper alignment; avoid twisting movements.
   2. Logroll the child when turning to maintain alignment.
   3. Assess extremities for neurovascular status.
   4. Encourage coughing and deep breathing and the use of incentive spirometry.
   5. Assess pain and administer prescribed analgesics.
   6. Monitor for incontinence.
   7. Monitor for signs and symptoms of infection.

8. Monitor for superior mesenteric artery syndrome (caused by mechanical changes in the position of the child's abdominal contents during surgery) and notify the physician if it occurs; symptoms include emesis and abdominal distention similar to what occurs with intestinal obstruction or paralytic ileus.
9. Instruct in activity restrictions.
10. Instruct the child how to roll from a side-lying position to a sitting position, and assist with ambulation.
11. Prepare the child for the use of a molded plastic orthosis (brace) to provide external stability of the spine when resuming activities.
12. Use extreme sensitivity and consider body image disturbance when formulating a plan of nursing care.

IV. JUVENILE IDIOPATHIC ARTHRITIS
A. Description
 1. An autoimmune, inflammatory disease affecting the joints and other tissues, such as articular cartilage, that most often occurs in girls
 2. Treatment is supportive (there is no cure) and directed toward preserving joint function, controlling inflammation, minimizing deformity, and reducing the impact that the disease may have on the development of the child.
 3. Treatment includes medications, physical and occupational therapies, and child and family education.
 4. Surgical intervention may be implemented if the child has problems with joint contractures and unequal **growth** of extremities.
B. Assessment (Box 43-2)
 1. There are no definitive tests to diagnose juvenile idiopathic arthritis.
 2. Some laboratory tests, such as an elevated erythrocyte sedimentation rate or determination of the presence of leukocytosis, may support evidence of the disease.
 3. Radiographs may show soft tissue swelling and joint space widening from increased synovial fluid in the joint.
C. Interventions
 1. Facilitate social and emotional development.
 2. Instruct the parents and child in the administration of medications; medications may be given alone or in combination and are prescribed in a step-like level depending on the disease response to each level (Box 43-3).
 3. Assist the child with range-of-motion exercises and instruct in prescribed exercises.
 4. Encourage normal performance of activities of daily living.
 5. Instruct the parents and child in the use of hot or cold packs, splinting, and positioning the af-

---

BOX 43-2
Assessment Findings: Juvenile Idiopathic Arthritis

Stiffness, swelling, and limited motion occur in the affected joints.
Affected joints are warm to the touch, tender, and painful.
Joint stiffness is present on arising in the morning and after inactivity.
Uveitis (inflammation of structures in the uveal tract) can occur and cause blindness.

BOX 43-3
Medications Used in Juvenile Idiopathic Arthritis

Nonsteroidal Anti-Inflammatory Drugs (NSAIDs)
 First medications used
 May cause gastrointestinal irritation and bruising
Methotrexate (MTX)
 Used if NSAIDs are ineffective
 Complete blood cell counts and liver function studies monitored closely
Corticosteroids
 Potent immunosuppressives used for life-threatening complications, incapacitating arthritis, and uveitis
 Administered at lowest effective dose for briefest period; discontinued on tapering schedule
 Prolonged use—can cause Cushing's syndrome, osteoporosis, increased infection risk, glucose intolerance, cataracts, growth suppression
Tumor necrosis factor receptor inhibitors
 Etanercept (Enbrel)
 Infliximab (Remicade)
 Adverse effects—include allergic reaction at the injection site, increased risk for infection, demyelinating disease, pancytopenia
Slower Acting Antirheumatic Drugs (SAARDs)
 May require months to be effective; usually prescribed in combination with NSAIDs
 Includes medications such as sulfasalazine (Azulfidine), hydroxychloroquine (Plaquenil), gold sodium thiomalate (Myochrysine), and D-penicillamine

---

fected joint in a neutral position during painful episodes.
 6. Encourage and support prescribed physical and occupational therapy.
 7. Instruct in the importance of preventive eye care and reporting visual disturbances.
 8. Assess the child's and family's perceptions regarding the chronic illness; plan to discuss the nature of a chronic illness and the grief associated with the new recognition of life alterations that result from the chronic progression of the disorder.

V. FRACTURES
A. Description
 1. A break in the continuity of the bone as a result of trauma, twisting, or bone decalcification

2. Fractures in children usually occur as a result of increased mobility and inadequate or immature motor and cognitive skills; they may result from trauma or bone diseases such as congenital bone disease or bone tumors.

3. Fractures in infancy are generally rare and warrant further investigation to rule out the possibility of child **abuse** and to recognize bone structure defects.

B. Assessment
   1. Pain or tenderness over the involved area
   2. Loss of function
   3. Obvious deformity
   4. Crepitation
   5. Ecchymosis
   6. Edema
   7. Muscle spasm

C. Initial care of a fracture (Box 43-4)

D. Interventions
   1. Reduction
      a. Restoring the bone to proper alignment
      b. Closed reduction: Accomplished by manual alignment of the fragments, followed by immobilization
      c. Open reduction: Surgical insertion of internal fixation devices, such as rods, wires, or pins, that help maintain alignment while healing occurs
   2. Retention: Application of traction or a cast to maintain alignment until healing occurs

E. Traction (see Chap. 67 for additional information on traction)
   1. Russell skin traction
      a. Used to stabilize a fractured femur before surgery
      b. Similar to Buck's traction but provides a double pull using a knee sling that pulls at the knee and foot
   2. Balanced suspension
      a. Used with skin or skeletal traction to approximate fractures of the femur, tibia, or fibula
      b. Balanced suspension is produced by a counterforce other than the child.
      c. Provide pin care if pins are used with the skeletal traction.
   3. 90-degree–90-degree traction
      a. The lower leg is supported by a boot cast or a calf sling.
      b. A skeletal Steinmann pin or Kirschner wire is placed in the distal fragment of the femur, allowing 90-degree flexion at both the hip and knee.
   4. Interventions
      a. Maintain correct amount of weight as prescribed.
      b. Ensure that weights hang freely.

BOX 43-4

Initial Care of a Fracture

Assess the extent of injury and immobilize the affected extremity.

Observe for the five P's: Pain, pulselessness, pallor, paresthesia, paralysis.

Monitor for compartment syndrome.

If a compound fracture exists, splint the extremity to minimize further soft tissue damage, and cover the wound with a sterile dressing.

---

   c. Check all ropes for fraying and all knots for tightness; be sure that the ropes are appropriately tracking in the grooves of the pulley wheels.
   d. Monitor neurovascular status of the involved extremity.
   e. Protect the skin from breakdown.
   f. Monitor for signs and symptoms of complications of immobilization, such as constipation, skin breakdown, lung congestion, renal complications, and disuse syndrome of unaffected extremities.
   g. Provide therapeutic and diversional play.

F. Casts (see Chap. 67 for additional information on casts)
   1. Description
      a. Made of plaster or fiberglass to provide immobilization of bone and joints after a fracture or injury
      b. Fractures of the hip or knee may require spica cast
   2. Interventions
      a. Examine the cast for pressure areas.
      b. Ensure that no rough casting material remains in contact with the skin; petal the cast edges as necessary (Fig. 43-4).
      c. If a hip spica cast is placed, the cast edges around the perineum and buttocks may need to be taped with waterproof tape.
      d. Monitor the extremity for circulatory impairment, such as pain out of proportion to that expected for the type of injury, edema, rubor, pallor, numbness and tingling, coolness, decreased sensation or mobility, or diminished pulse.
      e. Notify the physician if circulatory impairment occurs.
      f. Prepare for bivalving or cutting the cast if circulatory impairment occurs; prepare for emergency fasciotomy if cast removal does not improve the neurocirculatory compromise.
      g. Instruct the family and child not to stick objects down the cast.

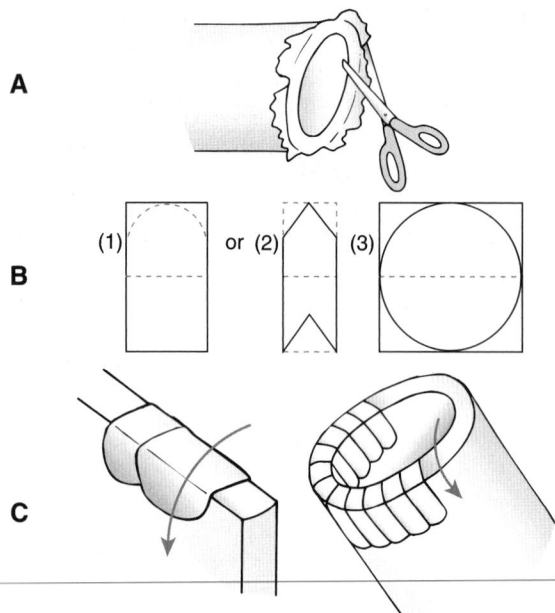

FIG. 43-4 Painting edges of a cast with waterproof adhesive strips. **A,** Cast must be thoroughly dry. The nurse trims the excess sheet wadding and stretches the stockinette over the cast edge (when possible). **B,** Several strips (petals) of waterproof adhesive tape (2-inch–wide strips for small areas, each 1 inch long) are made in advance. **C,** Uncut end of the tape is placed beneath the cast edge. Each succeeding petal overlaps the previous one by ½ inch, ensuring a smooth cast edge. (From Lewis, S., Heitkemper, M., & Dirksen, S. [2004]. *Medical-surgical nursing. Assessment and management of clinical problems* [6th ed.]. St. Louis: Mosby.)

 h. Teach the family and the child to keep the cast clean and dry.

 i. Instruct the family and the child in isometric exercises to prevent muscle atrophy.

PRACTICE QUESTIONS

1. A child has a right femur fracture caused by a motor vehicle accident and is placed in skin traction temporarily until surgery can be performed. During assessment, the nurse notes that the dorsalis pedal pulse is absent on the right foot. What action should the nurse do next?
   1. Notify the physician.
   2. Administer an analgesic.
   3. Release the skin traction.
   4. Apply ice to the extremity.

2. A nurse is caring for a child after spinal fusion for scoliosis treatment. The child complains of abdominal discomfort and begins to have episodes of vomiting. On further assessment, the nurse notes abdominal distention. Based on these findings, the nurse should take which action?
   1. Notify the physician.
   2. Administer an antiemetic.
   3. Increase the intravenous fluids.
   4. Place the child in a Sims' position.

3. A nurse is assisting a physician during the examination of an infant with developmental dysplasia of the hip (DDH). The physician performs an Ortolani maneuver. The nurse is aware that this maneuver is performed to:
   1. Assess for asymmetry on the affected side.
   2. Determine the presence of range of motion.
   3. Push the unstable femoral head out of the acetabulum.
   4. Attempt reduction of the dislocated femoral head back into the acetabulum.

4. A clinic nurse provides instructions to the parents of an infant with developmental dysplasia of the hip (DDH) regarding care of the Pavlik harness. Which of the following should the nurse include in the instructions?
   1. The harness should be worn 12 hours a day.
   2. The infant should not be moved when out of the harness.
   3. The harness needs be removed for diaper changes and for feeding.
   4. The harness should be removed only to check the skin and for bathing.

5. A child is placed in skeletal traction for treatment of a fractured femur. The nurse develops a plan of care for the child and includes which intervention in the plan?
   1. Ensures that all ropes are outside the pulleys
   2. Ensures that the weights are resting lightly on the floor
   3. Checks the physician's orders for the amount of weight to be applied
   4. Restricts diversional and play activities until the child is out of traction

6. A 4-year-old child sustains a fall at home and is brought to the emergency room by the mother. After an x-ray examination, the child is determined to have a fractured arm and a plaster cast is applied. The nurse provides instructions to the mother regarding care for the child's cast. Which statement by the mother indicates a need for further instructions?
   1. "The cast may feel warm as the cast dries."
   2. "I can use lotion or powder around the cast edges to relieve itching."
   3. "A small amount of white shoe polish can touch up a soiled white cast."
   4. "If the cast becomes wet, a blow drier set on the cool setting may be used to dry the cast."

7. A mother brings her 2-week-old infant to a clinic for treatment following a diagnosis of clubfoot made at birth. Which statement by the mother indicates a need for further teaching regarding this disorder?
   1. "Treatment needs to be started as soon as possible."

2. "I realize my infant will require follow-up care until full grown."
3. "I need to bring my infant back to the clinic in 1 month for a new cast."
4. "I need to come to the clinic every week with my infant for the casting."

8. A nurse is providing instructions to the parents of a child with scoliosis regarding the use of a brace. Which statement by the parents indicates a need for further instructions?
   1. "I will encourage my child to perform prescribed exercises."
   2. "I will have my child wear soft fabric clothing under the brace."
   3. "I should apply lotion under the brace to prevent skin breakdown."
   4. "I should avoid the use of powder because it will cake under the brace."

9. A 1-month-old infant is seen in a clinic and is diagnosed with developmental dysplasia of the hip (DDH). The nurse assesses the infant, knowing that which of the following findings would be noted in this condition?
   1. Limited range of motion in the affected hip
   2. An apparent lengthened femur on the affected side
   3. Asymmetrical adduction of the affected hip when the infant is placed supine with the knees and hips flexed
   4. Symmetry of the gluteal skinfolds when the infant is placed prone and the legs are extended against the examining table

10. The mother of a child with juvenile idiopathic arthritis (JIA) calls the clinic nurse because the child is experiencing a painful exacerbation of the disease. The mother asks the nurse if the child can perform range-of-motion exercises at this time. The appropriate nursing response is:
    1. "Avoid all exercise during painful periods."
    2. "Range-of-motion exercises must be performed every day."
    3. "Have the child perform simple isometric exercises during this time."
    4. "Administer additional pain medication before performing range-of-motion exercises."

ALTERNATE ITEM FORMAT: MULTIPLE RESPONSE

A nurse prepares a list of home care instructions for the parents of a child who has a plaster cast applied to the left forearm. Select all instructions that would be included on the list.

❑ 1. Use fingertips to lift the cast while it is drying.
❑ 2. Keep small toys and sharp objects away from the cast.
❑ 3. Use a padded ruler or another padded object to scratch the skin under the cast if it itches.
❑ 4. Contact the physician if the child complains of numbness or tingling in the extremity.
❑ 5. Elevate the extremity on pillows for the first 24 to 48 hours after casting to prevent swelling.
❑ 6. Place a heating pad on the lower end of the cast and over the fingers if the fingers feel cold.

ANSWERS

1. **1**
Rationale: An absent pulse to an extremity of an affected limb could mean that the child is developing or experiencing compartment syndrome. This is an emergency situation and the physician should be notified immediately. Applying ice to an extremity with absent perfusion is incorrect. Ice may be prescribed when perfusion is adequate to decrease swelling. Administering analgesics will not improve circulation. The skin traction should not be released without a physician's order.
Test-Taking Strategy: Use the ABCs airway, breathing, and circulation—to assist in answering the question. Focusing on the data in the question indicates that circulation is impaired. This should direct you to option 1. Review care of the child in traction if you had difficulty with this question.
Level of Cognitive Ability: Application
Client Needs: Physiological Integrity
Integrated Process: Nursing Process—implementation
Content Area: Child health
Reference: Hockenberry, M., & Wilson, D. (2007). *Wong's nursing care of infants and children* (8th ed., pp. 1758-1762). St. Louis: Mosby.

2. **1**
Rationale: A complication after surgical treatment of scoliosis is superior mesenteric artery syndrome. This disorder is caused by mechanical changes in the position of the child's abdominal contents, resulting from lengthening of the child's body. The disorder results in a syndrome of emesis and abdominal distention similar to that which occurs with intestinal obstruction or paralytic ileus. Postoperative vomiting in children with body casts or those who have undergone spinal fusion warrants attention because of the possibility of superior mesenteric artery syndrome. Therefore options 2, 3, and 4 are incorrect.
Test-Taking Strategy: Use the process of elimination. Eliminate option 3 first because it should not be implemented without a prescribed order. Eliminate option 4 next because this child requires logrolling, and Sims' position may cause injury following surgery. From the remaining options, note the assessment signs and symptoms in the question. These should alert you that physician notification is necessary. Review superior mesenteric artery syndrome if you had difficulty with this question.
Level of Cognitive Ability: Application

Client Needs: Physiological Integrity
Integrated Process: Nursing Process—implementation
Content Area: Child health
References: Hockenberry, M., Wilson, D., & Winkelstein, M. (2005). *Wong's essentials of pediatric nursing* (7th ed., p. 1176). St. Louis: Mosby.
McKinney, E., James, S., Murray, S., & Ashwill, J. (2005). *Maternal-child nursing* (2nd ed., p. 1440). St. Louis: W.B. Saunders.

3. **4**
Rationale: In DDH, the head of the femur is seated improperly in the acetabulum or hip socket of the pelvis. In the Ortolani maneuver, the examiner reduces the dislocated femoral head back into the acetabulum. A positive finding is the palpable click or "clunk" on movement of the femoral head over the acetabular ring. This maneuver does not result in permanent relocation. Its purpose is to note the possibility of correction by means of the Pavlik harness or spica casting. In the Barlow maneuver, the examiner pushes the unstable femoral head out of the acetabulum. If it dislocates, it usually relocates immediately. The purpose is to note the presence of instability. Options 1 and 2 are done to assess for the possible presence of DDH.
Test-Taking Strategy: Use the process of elimination. Options 1 and 2 can be eliminated first because they are specific assessments performed to determine the presence of DDH. To select from the remaining options, recall the purpose of the Ortolani maneuver. Review this maneuver if you had difficulty with this question.
Level of Cognitive Ability: Comprehension
Client Needs: Physiological Integrity
Integrated Process: Nursing Process—implementation
Content Area: Child health
References: Hockenberry, M., Wilson, D., & Winkelstein, M. (2005). *Wong's essentials of pediatric nursing* (7th ed., p. 1165). St. Louis: Mosby.
McKinney, E., James, S., Murray, S., & Ashwill, J. (2005). *Maternal-child nursing* (2nd ed., p. 1415). St. Louis: W.B. Saunders.

4. **4**
Rationale: The Pavlik harness should be worn 16 to 23 hours a day and should be removed only to check the skin and for bathing. The infant can be moved when out of the harness, but the hips and buttocks should be supported carefully. The harness does not need to be removed for diaper changes or feedings.
Test-Taking Strategy: Use the process of elimination. Visualize this harness to assist in eliminating options 2 and 3. Select option 4 over option 1 because the time frame in option 1 is short. Review home care instruction regarding this harness if you had difficulty with this question.
Level of Cognitive Ability: Application
Client Needs: Physiological Integrity
Integrated Process: Teaching and Learning
Content Area: Child health
Reference: Hockenberry, M., Wilson, D., & Winkelstein, M. (2005). *Wong's essentials of pediatric nursing* (7th ed., p. 1165). St. Louis: Mosby.

5. **3**
Rationale: When a child is in traction, the nurse would check the physician's orders to verify the prescribed amount of traction weight. The nurse would maintain the correct amount of weight as ordered, ensure that the weights hang freely, check the ropes for fraying and be sure that they are on the pulleys appropriately, monitor the neurovascular status of the involved extremity, and monitor for signs and symptoms of immobilization. The nurse would provide therapeutic and diversional play activities for the child.
Test-Taking Strategy: Use the process of elimination and recall the general principles related to traction. Remember that weights should hang freely and ropes should remain in the pulleys. Review care of the child in traction if you had difficulty with this question.
Level of Cognitive Ability: Application
Client Needs: Physiological Integrity
Integrated Process: Nursing Process—planning
Content Area: Child health
Reference: McKinney, E., James, S., Murray, S., & Ashwill, J. (2005). *Maternal-child nursing* (2nd ed., p. 1412). St. Louis: W.B. Saunders.

6. **2**
Rationale: The mother needs to be instructed not to use lotion or powders on the skin around the cast edges or inside the cast. Lotions or powders can become sticky or caked and cause skin irritation. Options 1, 3, and 4 are appropriate instructions.
Test-Taking Strategy: Use the process of elimination and note the strategic words *indicates a need for further instructions*. These words indicate a negative event query and ask you to select an option that is an incorrect statement. Remember that lotions or powders can become sticky or caked and cause skin irritation. Review home care instructions regarding cast care if you had difficulty with this question.
Level of Cognitive Ability: Analysis
Client Needs: Physiological Integrity
Integrated Process: Teaching and Learning
Content Area: Child health
Reference: McKinney, E., James, S., Murray, S., & Ashwill, J. (2005). *Maternal-child nursing* (2nd ed., p. 1412). St. Louis: W.B. Saunders.

7. **3**
Rationale: Clubfoot is a complex deformity of the ankle and foot that includes forefoot adduction, midfoot supination, hindfoot varus, and ankle equinus; the defect may be unilateral or bilateral. Treatment for clubfoot is started as soon as possible after birth. Serial manipulation and casting are performed at least weekly. If sufficient correction is not achieved in 3 to 6 months, surgery usually is indicated. Because clubfoot can recur, all children with clubfoot require long-term interval follow-up until they reach skeletal maturity to ensure an optimal outcome.
Test-Taking Strategy: Use the process of elimination and note the strategic words *indicates a need for further teaching*. These words indicate a negative event query and ask you to select an option that is an incorrect statement. This will assist you in eliminating options 1 and 2. Recalling that serial manipulations and casting are required weekly will assist in directing

you to option 3. Review these treatment procedures if you had difficulty with this question.
Level of Cognitive Ability: Analysis
Client Needs: Health Promotion and Maintenance
Integrated Process: Teaching and Learning
Content Area: Child health
Reference: Hockenberry, M., Wilson, D., & Winkelstein, M. (2005). *Wong's essentials of pediatric nursing* (7th ed., p. 1168). St. Louis: Mosby.

8. 3
Rationale: The use of lotions or powders under a brace should be avoided because they can become sticky and cake under the brace, causing irritation. Options 1, 2, and 4 are appropriate interventions in the care of a child with a brace.
Test-Taking Strategy: Use the process of elimination and note the strategic words *need for further instructions* in the question. These words indicate a negative event query and ask you to select an option that is an incorrect statement. Careful reading of the options will assist in directing you to option 3. Review home care instructions regarding the care of a child in a brace if you had difficulty with this question.
Level of Cognitive Ability: Analysis
Client Needs: Health Promotion and Maintenance
Integrated Process: Teaching and Learning
Content Area: Child health
Reference: McKinney, E., James, S., Murray, S., & Ashwill, J. (2005). *Maternal-child nursing* (2nd ed., p. 1440). St. Louis: W.B. Saunders.

9. 1
Rationale: In DDH, the head of the femur is seated improperly in the acetabulum or hip socket of the pelvis. Asymmetrical abduction of the affected hip, when the child is placed supine with the knees and hips flexed, would be an assessment finding in DDH in infants beyond the newborn period. Other findings include an apparent short femur on the affected side, asymmetry of the gluteal skinfolds, and limited range of motion in the affected extremity.
Test-Taking Strategy: Note the age of the infant and focus on the infant's diagnosis. Visualizing each of the assessment findings described in the options will direct you to option 1. If you had difficulty with this question, review the assessment findings in hip dysplasia.
Level of Cognitive Ability: Analysis
Client Needs: Physiological Integrity
Integrated Process: Nursing Process—assessment
Content Area: Child health
Reference: McKinney, E., James, S., Murray, S., & Ashwill, J. (2005). *Maternal-child nursing* (2nd ed., p. 1415). St. Louis: W.B. Saunders.

10. 3
Rationale: During painful episodes of juvenile idiopathic arthritis, hot or cold packs and splinting and positioning the affected joint in a neutral position help reduce the pain. Although resting the extremity is appropriate, beginning simple isometric or tensing exercises as soon as the child is able is important. These exercises do not involve joint movement.
Test-Taking Strategy: Use the process of elimination. Eliminate options 1, 2, and 4 because of the words *all*, *must*, and *additional* in these options. Review pain management and care during exacerbations of juvenile idiopathic arthritis if you had difficulty with this question.
Level of Cognitive Ability: Application
Client Needs: Physiological Integrity
Integrated Process: Teaching and Learning
Content Area: Child health
References: Hockenberry, M., Wilson, D., & Winkelstein, M. (2005). *Wong's essentials of pediatric nursing* (7th ed., pp. 1183-1184). St. Louis: Mosby.
McKinney, E., James, S., Murray, S., & Ashwill, J. (2005). *Maternal-child nursing* (2nd ed., p. 1435). St. Louis: W.B. Saunders.

ALTERNATE ITEM FORMAT: MULTIPLE RESPONSE
Answer: 2, 4, 5
Rationale: While the cast is drying, the palms of the hands are used to lift the cast. If the fingertips are used, indentations in the cast could occur and cause constant pressure on the underlying skin. Small toys and sharp objects are kept away from the cast and no objects (including padded objects) are placed inside the cast because of the risk of altered skin integrity. The extremity is elevated to prevent swelling and the physician is notified immediately if any signs of neurovascular impairment develop. A heating pad is not applied to the cast or fingers. Cold fingers could indicate neurovascular impairment and the physician should be notified.
Test-Taking Strategy: Use of the ABCs—airway, breathing, and circulation—and safety principles related to care of the child with a cast will assist in answering the question. Review these general principles if you had difficulty with this question.
Level of Cognitive Ability: Application
Client Needs: Physiological Integrity
Integrated Process: Teaching and Learning
Content Area: Child health
Reference: McKinney, E., James, S., Murray, S., & Ashwill, J. (2005). *Maternal-child nursing* (2nd ed., p. 1411). St. Louis: W.B. Saunders.

REFERENCES

Hockenberry, M., & Wilson, D. (2007). *Wong's nursing care of infants and children* (8th ed.). St. Louis: Mosby.
Hockenberry, M. (2004). *Wong's essentials of pediatric nursing and virtual clinical excursions* (7th ed.). St. Louis: Mosby.
Hodgson, B., & Kizior, R. (2007). *Saunders nursing drug handbook 2007.* Philadelphia: W.B. Saunders.

McKinney, E., James, S., Murray S., & Ashwill, J. (2005). *Maternal-child nursing.* (2nd ed.). St. Louis: W.B. Saunders.
National Council of State Boards of Nursing (Eds.). (2007). *2007 NCLEX-RN® detailed test plan.* Chicago: Author.
Wong, D., Perry, S., Hockenberry, M., et al. (2006). *Maternal child nursing care* (3rd ed.). St. Louis: Mosby.

Hematological Disorders

I. SICKLE CELL ANEMIA

A. Description

1. This constitutes a group of diseases termed *hemoglobinopathies*, in which hemoglobin A is partly or completely replaced by abnormal sickle hemoglobin S.

2. It is caused by the inheritance of a gene for a structurally abnormal portion of the hemoglobin chain.

3. Hemoglobin S is sensitive to changes in the oxygen content of the red blood cell.

4. Insufficient oxygen causes the cells to assume a sickle shape and the cells become rigid and clumped together, obstructing capillary blood flow (Fig. 44-1)

5. Situations that precipitate sickling include fever and emotional or physical stress; any condition that increases the need for oxygen or alters the transport of oxygen can result in sickle cell crisis (acute exacerbation).

6. Risk factors include having parents heterozygous for hemoglobin S or being of African American descent.

7. The sickling response is reversible under conditions of adequate oxygenation and hydration; after repeated sickling, the cell becomes permanently sickled.

8. The clinical manifestations primarily occur as a result of obstruction caused by sickled red blood cells and increased red blood cell destruction.

9. Sickle cell crises are acute exacerbations of the disease, which vary considerably in severity and frequency; these include vaso-occlusive crisis, splenic sequestration, and aplastic crisis.

10. Care focuses on the prevention (preventing exposure to infection and maintaining normal hydration) and treatment (oxygen, hydration, pain management, and bed rest) of the crisis.

B. Assessment of the crisis (Box 44-1)

C. Interventions

1. Maintain adequate hydration and blood flow with intravenously administered normal saline as prescribed, and with oral fluids.

2. Administer oxygen and blood transfusions as prescribed to increase tissue perfusion.

3. Administer analgesics as prescribed (around the clock); administration of meperidine (Demerol) is avoided because of the risk of normeperidine-induced seizures.

4. Assist the child to assume a comfortable position so that the child keeps the extremities extended to promote venous return; elevate the head of the bed no more than 30 degrees, avoid putting strain on painful joints, and do not raise the knee gatch of the bed.

5. Encourage consumption of a high-calorie, high-protein diet, with folic acid supplementation.

6. Administer antibiotics as prescribed to prevent infection.

7. Monitor for signs of complications, including increasing anemia, decreased perfusion, and shock (mental status changes, pallor, vital sign changes).

8. Instruct the child and parents about the early signs and symptoms of crisis and the measures to prevent crisis.

9. Ensure that the child receives pneumococcal, *Haemophilus influenzae* type B, and meningococcal vaccines because of the susceptibility to infection from functional asplenia.

10. Inform the parents of the **hereditary** aspects of the disorder.

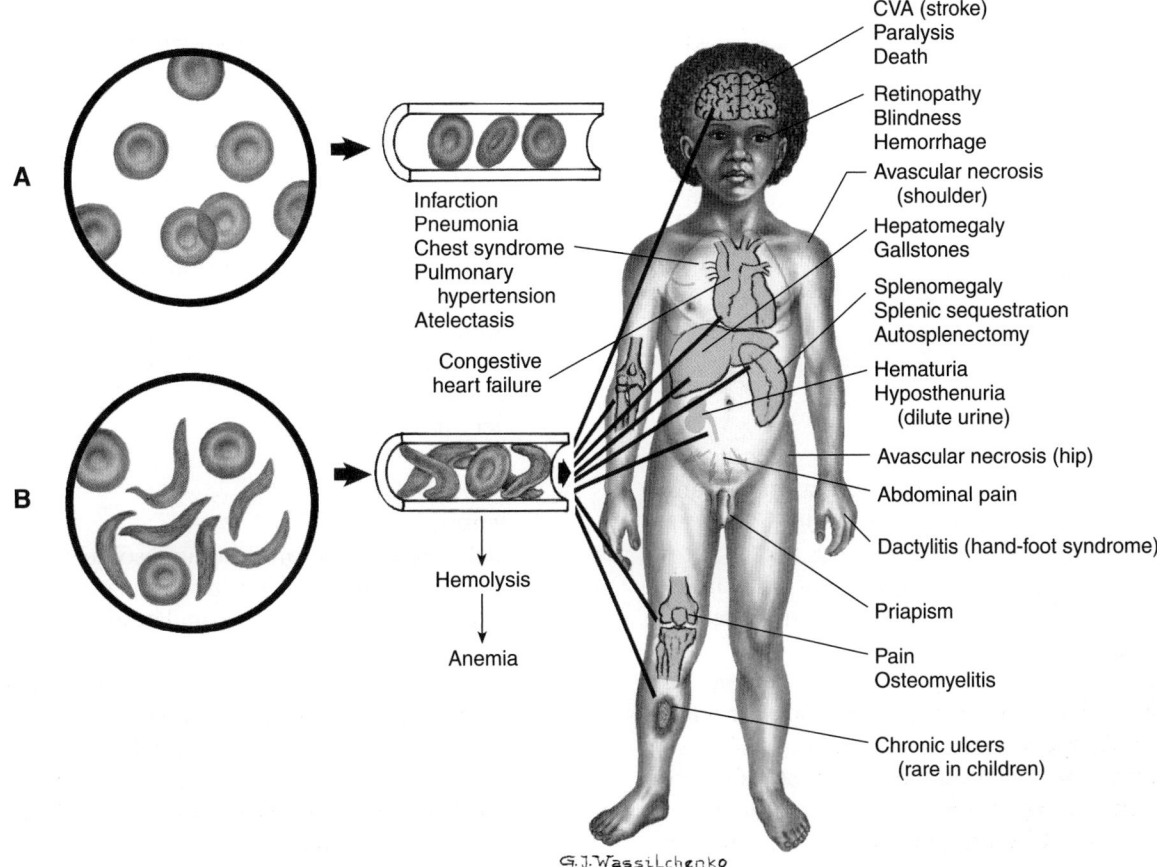

G.J.Wassilchenko

FIG. 44-1 Differences between normal red blood cells **(A)** and sickled red blood cells **(B)** in circulation, with related complications. (Hockenberry, M., & Wilson, D. [2007]. *Nursing care of infants and children* [8th ed.]. St. Louis: Mosby.)

BOX 44-1

Sickle Cell Crisis

VASO-OCCLUSIVE CRISIS

Caused by stasis of blood with clumping of the cells in the microcirculation, ischemia, and infarction. Manifestations include fever, painful swelling of the hands, feet, and joints, and abdominal pain.

SPLENIC SEQUESTRATION

Caused by the pooling and clumping of blood in the spleen (hypersplenism). Manifestations include profound anemia, hypovolemia, and shock.

APLASTIC CRISIS

Caused by the diminished production and increased destruction of red blood cells, triggered by viral infection or the depletion of folic acid. Manifestations include profound anemia and pallor.

II. IRON DEFICIENCY ANEMIA

A. Description

1. Iron stores are depleted, resulting in a decreased supply of iron for the manufacture of hemoglobin in red blood cells.

2. Iron deficiency anemia commonly results from blood loss, increased metabolic demands, syndromes of gastrointestinal malabsorption, and dietary inadequacy.

B. Assessment

1. Pallor

2. Weakness and fatigue

3. Irritability

C. Interventions

1. Increase the oral intake of iron.

2. Instruct the child and parents in food choices that are high in iron (Box 44-2).

3. Administer iron supplements as prescribed.

4. Teach the parents how to administer the iron supplements.

a. Give iron supplements between meals for maximum absorption.

BOX 44-2
Iron-Rich Foods

Breads and cereals	Meats
Dark green, leafy	Molasses
vegetables	Nuts
Dried fruits	Potatoes
Egg yolks	Prune juice
Iron-enriched infant	Raisins
formula and cereal	Seeds
Kidney beans	Shellfish
Legumes	Tofu
Liver	Whole grains

      b. Give iron supplements with a multivitamin or fruit juice because vitamin C increases absorption.

      c. Do not give iron supplements with milk or antacids because these items decrease absorption.

  5. Teach the child and parents that a liquid iron preparation stains the teeth and should be taken through a straw.

  6. Instruct the child and parents about the side effects of iron supplements (black stools, constipation, and foul aftertaste).

III. APLASTIC ANEMIA

A. Description

  1. This is a deficiency of circulating erythrocytes and all other formed elements of blood, resulting from the arrested development of cells within the bone marrow.

  2. Several possible causes exist, including chronic exposure to myelotoxic agents, viruses, infection, autoimmune disorders, and allergic states.

  3. The definitive diagnosis is determined by bone marrow aspiration (demonstrates conversion of red bone marrow to fatty red bone marrow).

  4. Therapeutic management focuses on restoring function to the bone marrow and involves immunosuppressive therapy and bone marrow transplantation (treatment of choice if a suitable donor exists).

  5. If the cause is a myelotoxic medication that is being administered for another purpose, the medication may be discontinued to improve bone marrow function.

B. Assessment

  1. Pancytopenia (a deficiency of erythrocytes, leukocytes, and thrombocytes)

  2. Petechiae, purpura, bleeding, pallor, weakness, tachycardia, and fatigue

C. Interventions

  1. Prepare the child for bone marrow transplantation if planned.

  2. Administer immunosuppressive medications as prescribed; antilymphocyte globulin or antithymocyte globulin may be prescribed to suppress the autoimmune response.

  3. Colony-stimulating factors may be prescribed to enhance bone marrow production.

  4. Corticosteroids and cyclosporine may be prescribed.

  5. Administer blood transfusions if prescribed and monitor for transfusion reactions.

  6. Monitor for signs related to the disease and to the treatments and medications administered.

  7. Advise the parents to obtain a Medic-Alert bracelet for the child.

IV. HEMOPHILIA

A. Description

  1. Refers to a group of bleeding disorders resulting from a deficiency of specific coagulation proteins

  2. Identifying the specific coagulation deficiency is important so that definitive treatment with the specific replacement agent can be implemented; aggressive replacement therapy is initiated to prevent the chronic crippling effects from joint bleeding.

  3. The most common types include factor VIII deficiency (hemophilia A or classic hemophilia) and factor IX deficiency (hemophilia B or Christmas disease; Box 44-3)

  4. Hemophilia is transmitted as an X-linked recessive disorder (it may also occur as a result of a gene mutation).

  5. It is most frequently transmitted by the union of an unaffected male with a trait-carrier female; however, it can result from the union between an affected male and a normal female or a carrier female, leading to offspring such as an affected son, affected daughter, carrier daughter, or normal son.

  6. The primary treatment is replacement of the missing clotting factor; additional medications, such as those to relieve pain, may be prescribed depending on the source of bleeding from the disorder.

B. Assessment

  1. Abnormal bleeding in response to trauma or surgery (sometimes is detected after circumcision)

  2. Epistaxis (nosebleeds)

  3. Joint bleeding causing pain, tenderness, swelling, and limited range of motion

  4. Tendency to bruise easily

  5. Results of tests that measure platelet function are normal; results of tests that measure clotting factor function may be abnormal.

C. Interventions

  1. Monitor for bleeding and maintain bleeding precautions.

BOX 44-3
Hemophilia

HEMOPHILIA A (CLASSIC HEMOPHILIA)
Results from a deficiency of factor VIII

HEMOPHILIA B (CHRISTMAS DISEASE)
Results from a deficiency of factor IX

---

2. Prepare to administer replacement factors as prescribed.
3. Monitor for joint pain; immobilize the affected extremity if joint pain occurs.
4. Assess neurological status (child is at risk for intracranial hemorrhage).
5. Monitor urine for hematuria.
6. Control joint bleeding by immobilization, elevation, and the application of ice; in addition, apply pressure (15 minutes) for superficial bleeding.
7. Instruct the child and parents about the signs of internal bleeding.
8. Instruct the parents in how to control the bleeding.
9. Instruct the parents regarding activities for the child, emphasizing the avoidance of contact sports and the need for protective devices while learning to walk.
10. Instruct the child to wear protective devices such as helmets and knee and elbow pads when participating in sports such as bicycling and skating.
11. Instruct the parents to obtain a Medic-Alert bracelet or medallion for the child.

V. VON WILLEBRAND DISEASE
A. Description
  1. A **hereditary** bleeding disorder characterized by a deficiency of or a defect in a protein termed *von Willebrand factor* (vWF)
  2. The disorder causes platelets to adhere to damaged endothelium; the vWF protein also serves as a carrier protein for factor VIII.
  3. It is characterized by an increased tendency to bleed from mucous membranes.
B. Assessment
  1. Epistaxis
  2. Gum bleeding
  3. Easy bruising
  4. Excessive menstrual bleeding
C. Interventions
  1. Treatment and care are similar to those measures implemented for hemophilia, including the administration of clotting factors.
  2. Provide emotional support to the child and parents, especially if the child is experiencing an episode of bleeding.

BOX 44-4
Types of β-Thalassemia

Thalassemia minor: Asymptomatic silent carrier case
Thalassemia trait: Produces a mild microcytic anemia
Thalassemia intermedia: Manifested as splenomegaly and moderate to severe anemia
Thalassemia major: Results in severe anemia requiring transfusion support to sustain life (also known as Cooley's anemia)

VI. β-THALASSEMIA MAJOR
A. Description (Box 44-4)
  1. Autosomal recessive disorder characterized by the reduced production of one of the globin chains in the synthesis of hemoglobin (both parents must be carriers to produce a child with β-thalassemia major).
  2. The incidence is highest in individuals of Mediterranean descent, such as Italians, Greeks, Syrians, or their offspring.
  3. Treatment is supportive; the goal of therapy is to maintain normal hemoglobin levels by the administration of blood transfusions.
  4. Bone marrow transplantation may be offered as an alternative therapy.
  5. A splenectomy may be performed in a child with severe splenomegaly who requires repeated transfusions (assists in relieving abdominal pressure and may increase the life span of supplemental red blood cells).
B. Assessment
  1. Frontal bossing
  2. Maxillary prominence
  3. Wide-set eyes with a flattened nose
  4. Greenish-yellow skin tone
  5. Hepatosplenomegaly
  6. Severe anemia
  7. Microcytic, hypochromic red blood cells
C. Interventions
  1. Administer blood transfusions as prescribed; monitor for transfusion reactions.
  2. Monitor for iron overload; chelation therapy with deferoxamine (Desferal) may be prescribed to treat iron overload and to prevent organ damage from the elevated levels of iron caused by the multiple transfusion therapy.
  3. If the child has had a splenectomy, instruct the parents to report any signs of infection because of the risk of sepsis.
  4. Provide genetic counseling.

PRACTICE QUESTIONS

1. A clinic nurse instructs the mother of a child with sickle cell anemia about the precipitating factors related to pain crisis. Which of the following, if identified by the mother as a precipitating factor, indicates the need for further instructions?
   1. Stress
   2. Trauma
   3. Infection
   4. Fluid overload

2. A 10-year-old child with hemophilia A has slipped on the ice and bumped his knee. The nurse should prepare to administer an:
   1. Injection of factor X
   2. Intravenous infusion of factor VIII
   3. Intravenous infusion of cryoprecipitate
   4. Intravenous infusion of desmopressin (DDAVP)

3. Laboratory studies are performed for a child suspected of having iron deficiency anemia. The nurse reviews the laboratory results, knowing that which of the following results would indicate this type of anemia?
   1. An elevated hemoglobin level
   2. A decreased reticulocyte count
   3. An elevated red blood cell count
   4. Red blood cells that are microcytic and hypochromic

4. A home care nurse is instructing the parents of a child with iron deficiency anemia regarding the administration of a liquid oral iron supplement. The nurse tells the mother to:
   1. Administer the iron at mealtimes.
   2. Administer the iron through a straw.
   3. Mix the iron with cereal to administer.
   4. Add the iron to formula for easy administration.

5. A nurse analyzes the laboratory results of a child with hemophilia. The nurse understands that which of the following would most likely be abnormal in this child?
   1. Platelet count
   2. Hematocrit level
   3. Hemoglobin level
   4. Partial thromboplastin time

6. A nurse is providing home care instructions to the mother of a 10-year-old child with hemophilia. Which of the following activities should the nurse suggest that the child could participate safely with peers?
   1. Soccer
   2. Basketball
   3. Swimming
   4. Field hockey

7. A nursing student is presenting a clinical conference and discusses the cause of β-thalassemia. The nursing student informs the group that the child at greatest risk of developing this disorder is:
   1. A child of Mexican descent
   2. A child of Mediterranean descent

3. A child whose intake of iron is extremely poor
   4. A breast-fed child of a mother with chronic anemia

8. A child with β-thalassemia is receiving long-term blood transfusion therapy for the treatment of this disorder. Chelation therapy is prescribed to prevent organ damage from the presence of too much iron in the body as a result of the transfusions. Which of the following medications would the nurse anticipate to be prescribed in chelation therapy?
   1. Meropenem (Merrem)
   2. Metoprolol (Toprol-XL)
   3. Deferoxamine (Desferal)
   4. Dalteparin sodium (Fragmin)

9. A pediatric nursing instructor asks a nursing student to describe the cause of the clinical manifestations that occur in sickle cell anemia. The student responds correctly by telling the instructor that:
   1. Bone marrow depression occurs because of the development of sickled cells
   2. Sickled cells increase blood flow through the body and cause a great deal of pain
   3. Sickled cells mix with the unsickled cells and cause the immune system to become depressed
   4. Sickled cells are unable to flow easily through the microvasculature and their clumping obstructs blood flow

ALTERNATE ITEM FORMAT: MULTIPLE RESPONSE (1)

A nurse is reviewing a physician's orders for a child with sickle cell anemia who was admitted to the hospital for the treatment of vaso-occlusive crisis. Which orders documented in the child's record should the nurse question?
   ❑ 1. Restrict fluid intake.
   ❑ 2. Position for comfort.
   ❑ 3. Avoid strain on painful joints.
   ❑ 4. Apply nasal oxygen at 2 L/min
   ❑ 5. Provide a high-calorie, high-protein diet.
   ❑ 6. Give meperidine (Demerol), 25 mg IV, every 4 hours for pain.

ALTERNATE ITEM FORMAT: MULTIPLE RESPONSE (2)

Which of the following are characteristics of von Willebrand disease? Select all that apply.
   ❑ 1. Gum bleeding occurs.
   ❑ 2. Easy bruising occurs.
   ❑ 3. It is a hereditary bleeding disorder.
   ❑ 4. It is characterized by extremely high creatinine levels.
   ❑ 5. The disorder causes platelets to adhere to damaged endothelium.
   ❑ 6. Treatment and care are similar to those implemented for hemophilia.

ANSWERS

1. **4**

Rationale: Pain crisis may be precipitated by infection, dehydration, hypoxia, trauma, or physical or emotional stress. The mother of a child with sickle cell disease should encourage fluid intake of 1½ to 2 times the daily requirement to prevent dehydration.

Test-Taking Strategy: Use the process of elimination and note the strategic words *the need for further instructions*. These words indicate a negative event query and ask you to select an option that is an incorrect statement. Recalling that fluids are a main component of treatment in sickle cell anemia to prevent pain crisis will direct you to option 4. Remember that fluids are required to prevent dehydration. Review the precipitating factors of pain crisis if you had difficulty with this question.

Level of Cognitive Ability: Analysis
Client Needs: Health Promotion and Maintenance
Integrated Process: Teaching and Learning
Content Area: Child health
References: McKinney, E., James, S., Murray, S., & Ashwill, J. (2005). *Maternal-child nursing* (2nd ed., p. 1309). St. Louis: W.B. Saunders.
Wong, D., Perry, S., Hockenberry, M., et al. (2006). *Maternal child nursing care* (3rd ed., p. 1608). St. Louis: Mosby.

2. **2**

Rationale: Hemophilia refers to a group of bleeding disorders resulting from a deficiency of specific coagulation proteins. The primary treatment is replacement of the missing clotting factor; additional medications, such as those to relieve pain, may be prescribed depending on the source of bleeding from the disorder. A child with hemophilia A will be at risk for joint bleeding after a fall. Factor VIII will be prescribed intravenously to replace the missing clotting factor and minimize the bleeding. Desmopressin (DDAVP) is used to stimulate production of factor VIII, but it is not given intravenously. Factor X and cryoprecipitate are not used for clients with hemophilia A.

Test-Taking Strategy: Focus on the child's diagnosis. Recalling that a child with hemophilia A is missing clotting factor VIII will direct you to the correct option. Review treatment of bleeding episodes for children with hemophilia A if you had difficulty with this question.

Level of Cognitive Ability: Analysis
Client Needs: Physiological Integrity
Integrated Process: Nursing Process—analysis
Content Area: Pharmacology
Reference: Ward, K., & Hagemann, T. (2006). *Mosby's pediatric drug consult* (pp. 651-658). St. Louis: Mosby.

3. **4**

Rationale: The results of a complete blood cell count in children with iron deficiency anemia will show decreased hemoglobin levels and microcytic and hypochromic red blood cells. The red blood cell count is decreased. The reticulocyte count is usually normal or slightly elevated.

Test-Taking Strategy: Use the process of elimination. Eliminate options 1 and 3 first, knowing that the hemoglobin and red blood cell counts would be decreased. From the remaining options, select option 4 over option 2 because of the relationship between anemia and red blood cells. Review the laboratory findings in iron deficiency anemia if you had difficulty with this question.

Level of Cognitive Ability: Analysis
Client Needs: Physiological Integrity
Integrated Process: Nursing Process—assessment
Content Area: Child health
Reference: McKinney, E., James, S., Murray, S., & Ashwill, J. (2005). *Maternal-child nursing* (2nd ed., p. 1304). St. Louis: W.B. Saunders.

4. **2**

Rationale: An oral iron supplement should be administered through a straw or medicine dropper placed at the back of the mouth because the iron will stain the teeth. The parents should be instructed to brush or wipe the child's teeth after administration. Iron is administered between meals because absorption is decreased if there is food in the stomach. Iron requires an acid environment to facilitate its absorption in the duodenum. Iron is not added to formula or mixed with cereal or other food items.

Test-Taking Strategy: Use the process of elimination. Eliminate options 3 and 4 first because they are comparative or alike and because medication should not be added to formula and food. Note the strategic word *liquid* in the question. This should assist you in recalling that iron in liquid form stains teeth. Review the teaching points related to this medication if you had difficulty with this question.

Level of Cognitive Ability: Application
Client Needs: Physiological Integrity
Integrated Process: Teaching and Learning
Content Area: Child health
Reference: McKinney, E., James, S., Murray, S., & Ashwill, J. (2005). *Maternal-child nursing* (2nd ed., p. 1305). St. Louis: W.B. Saunders.

5. **4**

Rationale: Hemophilia refers to a group of bleeding disorders resulting from a deficiency of specific coagulation proteins. Results of tests that measure platelet function are normal; results of tests that measure clotting factor function may be abnormal. Therefore, abnormal laboratory results in hemophilia indicate a prolonged partial thromboplastin time. The platelet count, hemoglobin level, and hematocrit level are normal in hemophilia.

Test-Taking Strategy: Use the process of elimination and knowledge regarding the laboratory tests used to monitor hemophilia. Recalling the pathophysiology associated with this disorder will direct you to option 4. Review these laboratory tests if you had difficulty with this question.

Level of Cognitive Ability: Analysis
Client Needs: Physiological Integrity
Integrated Process: Nursing Process—analysis
Content Area: Child health
Reference: McKinney, E., James, S., Murray, S., & Ashwill, J. (2005). *Maternal-child nursing* (2nd ed., pp. 1316, 1320). St. Louis: W.B. Saunders.

6. **3**

Rationale: Hemophilia refers to a group of bleeding disorders resulting from a deficiency of specific coagulation proteins. Children with hemophilia need to avoid contact sports and to take precautions such as wearing elbow and knee pads and helmets with other sports. The safest activity for them is swimming.

Test-Taking Strategy: Use the process of elimination and note the strategic word *safely* in the question. Recalling that bleeding is a major concern in this condition will assist in directing you to option 3. Eliminate options 1, 2, and 4 because these activities present the potential for injury. Review home care instructions for the child with hemophilia if you had difficulty with this question.

Level of Cognitive Ability: Application
Client Needs: Safe and Effective Care Environment
Integrated Process: Teaching and Learning
Content Area: Child health
Reference: Hockenberry, M., Wilson, D., & Winkelstein, M. (2005). *Wong's essentials of pediatric nursing* (7th ed., p. 953). St. Louis: Mosby.

7. **2**

Rationale: β-Thalassemia is an autosomal recessive disorder characterized by the reduced production of one of the globin chains in the synthesis of hemoglobin (both parents must be carriers to produce a child with β-thalassemia major). This disorder is found primarily in individuals of Mediterranean descent. Options 1, 3, and 4 are incorrect.

Test-Taking Strategy: Use the process of elimination. Recalling that this disorder occurs primarily in individuals of Mediterranean descent will direct you to the correct option. If you are unfamiliar with this disorder, review the information associated with its incidence and cause.

Level of Cognitive Ability: Application
Client Needs: Physiological Integrity
Integrated Process: Teaching and Learning
Content Area: Child health
Reference: McKinney, E., James, S., Murray, S., & Ashwill, J. (2005). *Maternal-child nursing* (2nd ed., p. 1313). St. Louis: W.B. Saunders.

8. **3**

Rationale: β-Thalassemia is an autosomal recessive disorder characterized by the reduced production of one of the globin chains in the synthesis of hemoglobin (both parents must be carriers to produce a child with β-thalassemia major). The major complication of chronic transfusion therapy is hemosiderosis. To prevent organ damage from too much iron in the blood, chelation drug therapy with deferoxamine (Desferal) is used. Deferoxamine is classified as an antidote for acute iron toxicity. Dalteparin is an anticoagulant used as prophylaxis for postoperative deep vein thrombosis. Meropenem is an antibiotic. Metoprolol is a β blocker used to treat hypertension.

Test-Taking Strategy: Use the process of elimination and knowledge regarding the antidote for iron toxicity. Remember that deferoxamine is used to prevent iron toxicity. If you had difficulty with this question, review these medications.

Level of Cognitive Ability: Analysis
Client Needs: Physiological Integrity
Integrated Process: Nursing Process—analysis

Content Area: Child health
Reference: McKinney, E., James, S., Murray, S., & Ashwill, J. (2005). *Maternal-child nursing* (2nd ed., p. 1314). St. Louis: W.B. Saunders.

9. **4**

Rationale: Sickle cell anemia is a group of diseases termed hemoglobinopathies, in which hemoglobin A is partly or completely replaced by abnormal sickle hemoglobin S. It is caused by the inheritance of a gene for a structurally abnormal portion of the hemoglobin chain. Hemoglobin S is sensitive to changes in the oxygen content of the red blood cell; insufficient oxygen causes the cells to assume a sickle shape and the cells become rigid and clumped together, obstructing capillary blood flow. All the clinical manifestations of sickle cell anemia result from the sickled cells being unable to flow easily through the microvasculature, and their clumping obstructs blood flow. With reoxygenation, most of the sickled red blood cells resume their normal shape. Options 1, 2, and 3 are incorrect statements.

Test-Taking Strategy: Use the process of elimination. Recalling that sickled cells clump will direct you to the correct option. Review the pathophysiology associated with sickle cell anemia if you had difficulty with this question.

Level of Cognitive Ability: Comprehension
Client Needs: Physiological Integrity
Integrated Process: Teaching and Learning
Content Area: Child health
Reference: McKinney, E., James, S., Murray, S., & Ashwill, J. (2005). *Maternal-child nursing* (2nd ed., p. 1307). St. Louis: W.B. Saunders.

ALTERNATE ITEM FORMAT: MULTIPLE RESPONSE (1)

Answer: 1, 6

Rationale: Sickle cell anemia is a group of diseases termed *hemoglobinopathies*, in which hemoglobin A is partly or completely replaced by abnormal sickle hemoglobin S. It is caused by the inheritance of a gene for a structurally abnormal portion of the hemoglobin chain. Hemoglobin S is sensitive to changes in the oxygen content of the red blood cell; insufficient oxygen causes the cells to assume a sickle shape and the cells become rigid and clumped together, obstructing capillary blood flow. Therefore, oral and intravenous fluids are an important part of treatment. Meperidine (Demerol) is not recommended for the child with sickle cell disease because of the risk for normeperidine-induced seizures. Normeperidine, a metabolite of meperidine, is a central nervous system stimulant that produces anxiety, tremors, myoclonus, and generalized seizures when it accumulates with repetitive dosing. The nurse would thus question the order for restricted fluids and meperidine for pain control. Positioning for comfort, avoiding strain in painful joints, oxygen, and a high-calorie, high-protein diet are also important parts of the treatment plan.

Test-Taking Strategy: Focus on the pathophysiology that occurs in sickle cell disease to assist in identifying the orders that need to be questioned. Recalling that fluids are an important component of the treatment plan will assist in identifying that a fluid restriction order would need to be questioned. Recalling the effects of meperidine will assist in identifying that this order needs to be questioned. Review care of the child with sickle cell anemia experiencing a crisis if you had difficulty with this question.

Level of Cognitive Ability: Analysis
Client Needs: Physiological Integrity
Integrated Process: Nursing Process—analysis
Content Area: Child health
Reference: McKinney, E., James, S., Murray, S., & Ashwill, J. (2005). *Maternal-child nursing* (2nd ed., p. 1314). St. Louis: W.B. Saunders.

ALTERNATE ITEM FORMAT:
MULTIPLE RESPONSE (2)

Answer: 1, 2, 3, 5, 6
Rationale: von Willebrand disease is a hereditary bleeding disorder characterized by a deficiency of or a defect in a protein termed von Willebrand factor (vWF). The disorder causes platelets to adhere to damaged endothelium. It is characterized by an increased tendency to bleed from mucous membranes. Assessment findings include epistaxis, gum bleeding, easy bruising, and excessive menstrual bleeding. An elevated creatinine level is not associated with this disorder.

Test-Taking Strategy: Focus on the child's diagnosis. Recalling that this disorder is characterized by an increased tendency to bleed from mucous membranes will direct you to select the correct options. Review this disorder if you had difficulty with this question.

Level of Cognitive Ability: Analysis
Client Needs: Physiological Integrity
Integrated Process: Nursing Process—analysis
Content Area: Child health
Reference: Hockenberry, M., & Wilson, D. (2007). *Wong's nursing care of infants and children* (8th ed., pp. 1540-1541). St. Louis: Mosby.

REFERENCES

Cooley's Anemia Foundation. http://www.thalassemia.org.

Hockenberry, M. (2004). *Wong's essentials of pediatric nursing and virtual clinical excursions* (7th ed.). St. Louis: Mosby.

Hockenberry, M., & Wilson, D. (2007). *Wong's nursing care of infants and children* (8th ed.). St. Louis: Mosby.

Hodgson, B., & Kizior, R. (2007). *Saunders nursing drug handbook 2007.* Philadelphia: W.B. Saunders.

McKinney, E., James, S., Murray S., & Ashwill, J. (2005). *Maternal-child nursing* (2nd ed). St. Louis: W.B. Saunders.

National Council of State Boards of Nursing (Eds.). (2007). *2007 NCLEX-RN® detailed test plan.* Chicago: Author.

Ward, K., & Hagemann, T. (2006). *Mosby's pediatric drug consult.* St. Louis: Mosby.

Wong, D., Perry, S., Hockenberry, M., et al. (2006). *Maternal child nursing care* (3rd ed.). St. Louis: Mosby.

Oncological Disorders

I. LEUKEMIA

A. Description
1. Leukemia (Box 45-1) is a malignant increase in the number of leukocytes, usually at an immature stage, in the bone marrow.
2. Leukemia affects the bone marrow, causing anemia from decreased erythrocytes, infection from neutropenia, and bleeding from decreased platelet production (thrombocytopenia)
3. The cause is unknown and appears to involve genetic damage of cells, leading to the transformation of cells from a normal state to a malignant state.
4. Risk factors include genetic, viral, immunological, and environmental factors and exposure to radiation, chemicals, and medications.
5. Acute lymphocytic leukemia is the most frequent type of cancer in children; peak onset is age 2 to 6 years.
6. Leukemia is more common in boys than girls after 1 year of age.
7. Treatment involves the use of chemotherapeutic agents, with or without cranial radiation.
8. The phases of treatment include induction, which achieves a complete remission or disappearance of leukemic cells; intensification or consolidation therapy, which further decreases the tumor burden; central nervous system prophylactic therapy, which prevents leukemic cells from invading the central nervous system; and maintenance, which serves to maintain the remission phase.
9. Bone marrow transplantation also may be performed to treat some children with leukemia.

BOX 45-1
Classification of Leukemia

ACUTE LYMPHOCYTIC LEUKEMIA
Mostly lymphoblasts present in bone marrow
Age of onset younger than 15 years

ACUTE MYELOGENOUS LEUKEMIA
Mostly myeloblasts present in bone marrow
Age of onset between 15 and 39 years

B. Assessment
1. Infiltration of the bone marrow by malignant cells causes fever, pallor, fatigue, anorexia, hemorrhage (usually petechiae), and bone and joint pain; pathological fractures can occur as a result of bone marrow invasion with leukemic cells.
2. Signs of infection occur as a result of neutropenia.
3. The child experiences hepatosplenomegaly and lymphadenopathy.
4. The child has normal, elevated, or low white blood cell count, depending on the presence of infection or of immature versus mature white blood cells
5. The child has decreased hemoglobin and hematocrit levels.
6. The child has a decreased platelet count.
7. Positive bone marrow biopsy identifies leukemic blast (immature) phase cells.
8. Signs of increased intracranial pressure, such as severe headache, vomiting, papilledema, irritability, lethargy, and eventually coma, occur as a result of central nervous system involvement.

BOX 45-2

Protecting the Child From Infection

Initiate protective isolation procedures.

Maintain frequent and thorough hand washing.

Maintain the child in a private room and a room with high-efficiency particulate air filtration or laminar air flow system if possible.

Be sure that the child's room is cleaned daily.

Use strict aseptic technique for all nursing procedures.

Limit the number of caregivers entering the child's room, and ensure that anyone entering the child's room is wearing a mask.

Keep supplies for the child separate from supplies for other children.

Reduce exposure to environmental organisms by eliminating raw fruits and vegetables from the diet and not allowing fresh flowers in the child's room, and by not leaving standing water in the child's room.

Assist the child with daily bathing, using antimicrobial soap.

Assist the child to perform oral hygiene frequently.

Assess for signs and symptoms of infection.

Monitor temperature, pulse, and blood pressure.

Change wound dressings daily and inspect wounds for redness, swelling, or drainage.

Assess urine for color and cloudiness.

Assess the skin and oral mucous membranes for signs of infection.

Auscultate lung sounds.

Encourage the child to cough and deep-breathe.

Monitor the white blood cell and neutrophil counts.

Notify the physician if signs of infection are present, and prepare to obtain specimens for culture of open lesions, urine, and sputum.

Initiate a bowel program to prevent constipation and rectal trauma.

Avoid invasive procedures such as injections, rectal temperatures, and urinary catheterization.

Administer antibiotic, antifungal, and antiviral medications as prescribed.

Administer granulocyte colony-stimulating factor as prescribed.

Instruct the parents to keep the child away from crowds and those with infections.

Instruct the parents that the child should not receive immunization with a live virus.

Keep any child with chickenpox or any child who has been exposed to the virus away from the child with leukemia.

Instruct the parents to inform the teacher that they should be notified immediately if a case of chickenpox occurs in another child at school.

---

9. Child shows signs of cranial nerve (cranial nerve VII, or the facial nerve, is most commonly affected) or spinal nerve involvement; clinical manifestations relate to the area involved.

10. Clinical manifestations indicate the invasion of leukemic cells to the kidneys, testes, prostate, ovaries, gastrointestinal tract, and lungs.

C. Infection (Box 45-2)

1. Infection is a major cause of death in the immunosuppressed child.

2. Infection can occur through self-contamination or cross-contamination.

3. Most common sites of infection are the skin (any break in the skin is a potential site of infection), respiratory tract, and gastrointestinal tract.

D. Bleeding (Box 45-3)

1. The child with a platelet count less than 20,000/μL may need a platelet transfusion.

2. For the child with severe blood loss, packed red blood cells may be prescribed.

E. Fatigue and nutrition

1. Assist the parents and child in selecting a well-balanced diet.

2. Provide small meals that require little chewing.

3. If the child cannot take oral feedings, then parenteral nutrition or enteral feedings may be prescribed.

4. Assist the child in self-care and mobility activities.

5. Allow adequate rest periods during care.

6. Do not perform activities unless they are essential.

F. Chemotherapy

1. Monitor for severe bone marrow suppression; during the period of greatest bone marrow suppression (the nadir), blood cell counts will be extremely low.

2. Monitor for infection and bleeding.

3. Protect the child from life-threatening infections.

4. Monitor for nausea, vomiting, and diarrhea.

5. Administer stool softeners as prescribed.

6. Provide rectal hygiene as needed.

7. Administer antiemetics as prescribed.

8. Monitor for signs of dehydration.

9. Monitor for signs of hemorrhagic cystitis.

10. Monitor for signs of peripheral neuropathy.

11. Assess oral mucous membranes for mucositis; administer frequent mouth rinses (normal saline with or without sodium bicarbonate solution and/or chlorhexidine [Peridex]) to promote healing and/or prevent infection as prescribed.

12. Instruct the parents and child in signs and symptoms to watch for after chemotherapy and when to notify the physician.

BOX 45-3

Protecting the Child From Bleeding

Examine the child for signs and symptoms of bleeding.

Handle the child gently.

Measure abdominal girth; an increase can indicate internal hemorrhage.

Instruct the child to use a soft toothbrush and avoid dental floss.

Provide soft foods that are cool to warm in temperature.

Avoid injections, if possible, to prevent trauma to the skin and bleeding.

Apply firm and gentle pressure to a needlestick site for at least 10 minutes.

Pad side rails and sharp corners of the bed and furniture.

Discourage the child from engaging in activities involving the use of sharp objects.

Instruct the child to avoid constrictive or tight clothing.

Use caution when taking the blood pressure to prevent skin injury.

Instruct the child to avoid blowing his or her nose.

Avoid rectal suppositories, enemas, and rectal thermometers.

Examine all body fluids and excrement for the presence of blood.

Count the number of pads or tampons used if the female adolescent is menstruating.

Instruct the child about the signs and symptoms of bleeding.

Instruct the parents to avoid administering nonsteroidal anti-inflammatory drugs and products that contain aspirin to the child.

BOX 45-4

Central Venous Access Devices

PERIPHERALLY INSERTED CENTRAL CATHETERS (PICC LINES)

Inserted into the antecubital fossa and passed through the basilic or cephalic vein into the superior vena cava (SVC)

Can be inserted by a specially trained registered nurse

General anesthesia is not required for insertion

Associated with low sepsis rates

Not suitable for rapid fluid replacement because of its small lumen size

TUNNELED CATHETERS (HICKMAN OR BROVIAC CATHETER)

One or two Dacron cuffs or Vitacuffs on the catheter to enhance tissue ingrowth

May have one or more lumen

Reduced risk of bacterial migration after tissue adherence to Dacron cuff or Vitacuff occurs

Easy to use for self-administered infusions

Requires daily heparin flushes

Must keep clamped at all times when not in use

Necessary to keep exit site dry

Activity restrictions needed until tissue adheres to cuff

Protrudes outside the body and is therefore susceptible to damage; may affect body image

Family teaching about catheter care essential

GROSHONG CATHETER

Dacron cuff or Vitacuff on catheter—enhances tissue ingrowth

May have one or more lumen

Minimal maintenance required

No heparin flushes required

No clamping required because of two-way valve

Easy to use for self-administered infusions

Requires weekly irrigation with normal saline

Necessary to keep exit site dry

Activity restrictions necessary until tissue adheres to cuff

Protrudes outside body, therefore susceptible to damage; may affect body image

Family teaching about catheter care essential

IMPLANTED PORTS

Include Port-A-Cath, Infus-A-Port, Mediport, Norport, Groshong port

Totally implantable device; consists of self-sealing injection port

Associated with reduced risk of infection

Placed completely under the skin, so no risk of external damage

No maintenance care required

Heparinized monthly and after each infusion

No activity restrictions

Dressing only required when port accessed with Huber needle and left in place

No change or only slight change in body appearance

Must pierce the skin for access, leading to pain with insertion; can use EMLA cream (eutectic mixture of local anesthetics [lidocaine, prilocaine])

Skin preparation required before injection

Difficult to manipulate for self-administered infusions

Vigorous contact sports prohibited

Modified from Hockenberry, M., Wilson, D., & Winkelstein, M. (2005). *Wong's essentials of pediatric nursing* (7th ed.). St. Louis: Mosby.

13. Inform the parents and child that hair loss may occur from chemotherapy (hair will regrow in 3 to 6 months and may be a slightly different color or texture).

14. Instruct the parents and child about the care of a central venous access device, as necessary (Box 45-4)

15. Listen to the child and family, and encourage them to verbalize their feelings and express their concerns.

16. Introduce the family to other families of children with cancer.

17. Consult social services and chaplains as necessary.

BOX 45-5
Staging of Hodgkin's Disease

STAGE I
Involvement of a single lymph node region or an extralymphatic organ or site

STAGE II
Involvement of two or more lymph node regions on the same side of the diaphragm or localized involvement of an extralymphatic organ or site

STAGE III
Involvement of lymph node regions on both sides of the diaphragm

STAGE IV
Diffuse or disseminated involvement of one or more extralymphatic organs, with or without associated lymph node involvement

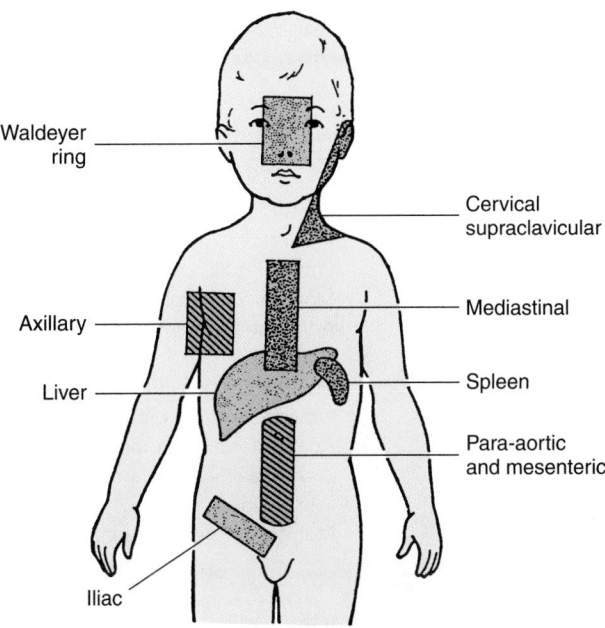

FIG. 45-1 Main areas of lymphadenopathy and organ involvement in Hodgkin's disease. (From Hockenberry, M., Wilson, D., & Winkelstein, M. [2003]. *Wong's essentials of pediatric nursing* [7th ed.]. St. Louis: Mosby.)

II. HODGKIN'S DISEASE

A. Description

1. Hodgkin's disease (a type of lymphoma) is a malignancy of the lymph nodes that originates in a single lymph node or a single chain of nodes (Box 45-5; Fig. 45-1).

2. The disease predictably metastasizes to non-nodal or extralymphatic sites, especially the spleen, liver, bone marrow, lungs, and mediastinum.

3. Hodgkin's disease is characterized by the presence of Reed-Sternberg cells in the lymph nodes.

4. Peak incidence is in midadolescence.

5. Possible causes include viral infections and previous exposure to alkylating chemical agents.

6. The prognosis depends on the stage of the disease; the prognosis is excellent in the child with localized disease.

7. The primary treatment modalities are radiation and chemotherapy; each may be used alone or in combination, depending on the clinical stage of the disease.

8. Bone marrow transplantation may be a consideration in treating Hodgkin's disease.

B. Assessment

1. Painless enlargement of lymph nodes

2. Enlarged, firm, nontender, movable nodes in the supraclavicular area; in children, the "sentinel" node located near the left clavicle may be the first enlarged node

3. Nonproductive cough as a result of mediastinal lymphadenopathy

4. Abdominal pain as a result of enlarged retroperitoneal nodes

5. Advanced lymph node and extralymphatic involvement that may cause systemic symptoms, such as low-grade or intermittent fever, anorexia, nausea, weight loss, night sweats, and pruritus

6. Positive biopsy of lymph node (presence of Reed-Sternberg cells) and positive bone marrow biopsy

7. Computed tomography scan of the liver, spleen, and bone marrow to detect metastasis

C. Interventions

1. For stages I and II without mediastinal node involvement, the treatment of choice is extensive external radiation of the involved lymph node regions.

2. With more extensive disease, radiation and multidrug chemotherapy are used.

3. Monitor for drug-induced pancytopenia, an abnormal depression of all the cellular components of the blood, which increases the risk for infection, bleeding, and anemia.

4. Monitor for signs of infection and bleeding.

5. Protect the child from infection.

6. Provide a safe, hazard-free environment.

7. Monitor for side effects related to chemotherapy or radiation; the most common side effect of extensive irradiation is malaise, which can be difficult for older children and adolescents to tolerate both physically and psychologically (Table 45-1)

8. Monitor for nausea and vomiting, and administer antiemetics as prescribed.

9. Monitor for skin irritation and breakdown as a result of radiation therapy.

TABLE 45-1

Side Effects of Radiation Therapy and Nursing Interventions

Body Area and Side Effects	Interventions
GASTROINTESTINAL TRACT	
Anorexia	Encourage fluids and foods best tolerated.
	Provide small, frequent meals.
	Monitor for weight loss.
Nausea, vomiting	Administer antiemetics around the clock.
	Monitor for dehydration.
Mucosal ulceration	Provide soothing oral hygiene
Diarrhea	Administer antispasmodics and antidiarrheal preparations as prescribed
	Monitor for dehydration.
SKIN	
Alopecia	Introduce idea of wig.
	Provide scalp hygiene.
	Stress need for head covering in cold weather.
Dry or moist desquamation	Keep skin clean.
	Wash skin daily, using mild soap sparingly.
	Do not remove skin markings for radiation.
	Avoid exposure to sun and other extreme temperature changes.
	For dryness, apply lubricant as prescribed.
URINARY BLADDER	
Cystitis	Encourage fluid intake and frequent voiding.
	Monitor for hematuria.
BONE MARROW	
Myelosuppression	Monitor for fever.
	Administer antibiotics as prescribed.
	Avoid use of suppositories and rectal temperatures.
	Institute bleeding precautions.
	Monitor for signs of anemia.

Modified from Hockenberry, M. (2003). *Wong's nursing care of infants and children* (7th ed.). St. Louis: Mosby.

III. NEPHROBLASTOMA (WILMS' TUMOR)

A. Description
  1. Wilms' tumor is the most common intraabdominal and kidney tumor of childhood; it may present unilaterally and localized or bilaterally, sometimes with metastasis to other organs (Box 45-6; Fig. 45-2).
  2. The peak incidence is at 3 years of age.
  3. The occurrence is associated with a genetic inheritance and with several congenital anomalies.

BOX 45-6

Staging of Wilms' Tumor

Stage I: Tumor is limited to kidney and completely resected

Stage II: Tumor extends beyond kidney but is completely resected

Stage III: Residual nonhematogenous tumor is confined to abdomen

Stage IV: Hematogenous metastases; deposits are beyond stage III—to lung, bone and brain

Stage V: Bilateral renal involvement present at diagnosis

From Hockenberry, M., Wilson, D., & Winkelstein, M. (2005). *Wong's essentials of pediatric nursing* (7th ed.). St. Louis: Mosby.

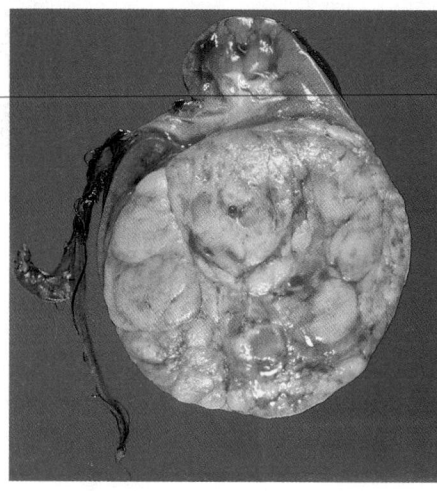

FIG. 45-2   Wilms' tumor. (From Mosby. [2006]. *Mosby's dictionary of medicine, nursing and health professions* [7th ed.]. St. Louis: Mosby.)

  4. Therapeutic management includes a combined treatment of surgery (partial to total nephrectomy) and chemotherapy with or without radiation, depending on the clinical stage and histological pattern of tumor.
B. Assessment
  1. Swelling or mass within the abdomen (mass is characteristically firm, nontender, confined to one side, and deep within the flank)
  2. Abdominal pain
  3. Urinary retention and/or hematuria
  4. Anemia (caused by hemorrhage within the tumor)
  5. Pallor, anorexia, lethargy (resulting from anemia)
  6. Hypertension (caused by secretion of excess amounts of renin by the tumor)
  7. Weight loss and fever
  8. Symptoms of lung involvement such as dyspnea, shortness of breath, and pain in the chest, if metastasis has occurred

C. Preoperative interventions
1. Monitor vital signs, particularly blood pressure.

2. Avoid palpation of the abdomen.

3. Place a sign at the bedside, "Do Not Palpate Abdomen."
4. Measure abdominal girth at least once daily.
D. Postoperative interventions
1. Monitor temperature and blood pressure closely.
2. Monitor for signs of hemorrhage and infection.
3. Monitor strict intake and urine output closely.
4. Monitor for abdominal distention; monitor bowel sounds and other signs of gastrointestinal activity because of the risk for intestinal obstruction.

IV. NEUROBLASTOMA

A. Description
1. Neuroblastoma is a tumor that originates from the embryonic neural crest cells that normally give rise to the adrenal medulla and the sympathetic ganglia (Box 45-7)
2. Most tumors develop in the adrenal gland or the retroperitoneal sympathetic chain; other sites may be within the head, neck, chest, or pelvis.
3. Most children present with the tumor before 10 years of age.

4. Most presenting signs are caused by the tumor compressing adjacent normal tissue and organs.
5. Diagnostic evaluation is aimed at locating the primary site of the tumor.
6. The prognosis is poor because of the frequency of invasiveness of the tumor and because, in most cases, a diagnosis is not made until after metastasis has occurred.
7. Therapeutic management
   a. Surgery is performed to remove as much of the tumor as possible and to obtain biopsies; in stages I and II, complete surgical removal of the tumor is the treatment of choice.
   b. Surgery usually is limited to biopsy in stages III and IV because of extensive metastasis.
   c. Radiation is used commonly with stage III disease and provides palliation for metastatic lesions in bones, lungs, liver, and brain.
   d. Chemotherapy is the mainstay of treatment for extensive local or disseminated disease.
B. Assessment
1. Firm, nontender, irregular mass in the abdomen that crosses the midline
2. Urinary frequency or retention from compression of the kidney, ureter, or bladder
3. Lymphadenopathy, especially in the cervical and supraclavicular areas
4. Bone pain if skeletal involvement occurs
5. Supraorbital ecchymosis, periorbital edema, and exophthalmos as a result of invasion of retrobulbar soft tissue

---

BOX 45-7
Staging of Neuroblastoma

Stage I: Localized tumor confined to the area of origin; local excision with or without microscopic disease; negative lymph nodes
Stage II: Unilateral tumor with incomplete gross excision; lymph nodes negative
Stage III: Tumor infiltrating across the midline, with or without regional lymph node involvement; unilateral tumor with regional involvement; midline tumor with bilateral regional lymph node involvement
Stage IV: Dissemination of tumor to distant lymph nodes, bone, bone marrow, liver, or other organs

Modified Hockenberry, M., Wilson, D., & Winkelstein, M. (2005). *Wong's nursing care of infants and children* (7th ed.). St. Louis: Mosby.

---

6. Pallor, weakness, irritability, anorexia, weight loss
7. Signs of respiratory impairment (thoracic lesion)
8. Signs of neurological impairment (intracranial lesion)
9. Paralysis from compression of the spinal cord
C. Preoperative interventions
1. Monitor for signs and symptoms related to the location of the tumor.
2. Provide emotional support to the child and parents.
D. Postoperative interventions
1. Monitor for postoperative complications related to the location (organ) of the surgery.
2. Monitor for complications related to chemotherapy or radiation if prescribed.
3. Provide support to the parents and encourage them to express their feelings; many parents suffer from guilt for not having recognized signs in the child earlier.
4. Refer the parents to appropriate community services.

V. OSTEOGENIC SARCOMA

A. Description
1. This is the most common bone cancer in children; it is also known as osteosarcoma (Fig. 45-3).
2. Cancer usually is found in the metaphysis of long bones, especially in the lower extremities, with most tumors occurring in the femur.
3. The peak age of incidence is between 10 and 25 years.
4. Symptoms in the earliest stage are almost always attributed to extremity injury or normal growing pains.
5. Treatment may include surgical resection to save a limb or remove affected tissue, or amputation.
6. Chemotherapy plays a vital role in treatment and may be used before and after surgery.
B. Assessment
1. Localized pain at the affected site (may be severe or dull) that may be attributed to trauma or the

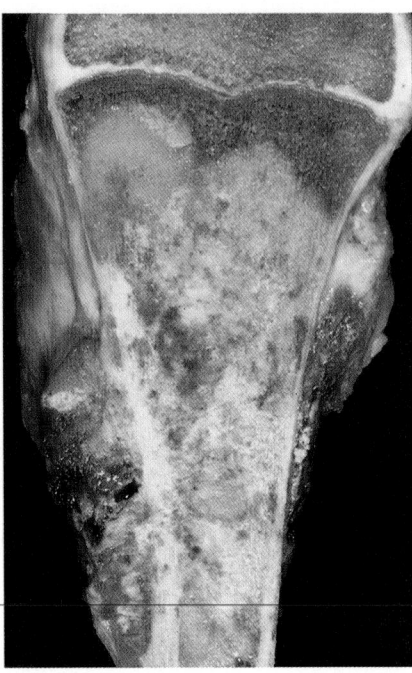

FIG. 45-3 Osteosarcoma. (From Mosby. [2006]. *Mosby's dictionary of medicine, nursing and health professions* [7th ed.]. St. Louis: Mosby.)

vague complaint of "growing pains"; pain often is relieved by a flexed position.
2. Palpable mass
3. Limping if weight-bearing limb is affected
4. Progressive limited range of motion and the child's curtailing of physical activity
5. Child may be unable to hold heavy objects because of their weight and resultant pain in the affected extremity.
6. Pathological fractures at the tumor site

C. Interventions
1. Prepare the child and family for prescribed treatment modalities, which may include surgical resection by limb salvage to remove affected tissue, amputation, and chemotherapy.
2. Provide honesty and support for the child and family.
3. Prepare for prosthetic fitting as necessary.
4. Assist the child in dealing with problems of self-image.
5. Instruct child and parents about the potential development of phantom limb pain that may occur after amputation, characterized by tingling, itching, and a painful sensation in the area where the limb was amputated.

VI. BRAIN TUMORS

A. Description
1. An infratentorial (below the tentorium cerebelli) tumor, the most common of brain tu-

mors, is located in the posterior third of the brain (primarily in the cerebellum or brainstem) and accounts for the frequency of symptoms resulting from increased intracranial pressure (ICP).
2. A supratentorial tumor is located within the anterior two thirds of the brain, mainly the cerebrum.
3. The signs and symptoms of a brain tumor depend on its anatomical location and size and, to some extent, the age of the child.
4. Therapeutic management includes surgery, radiation, and chemotherapy; the treatment of choice is total removal of the tumor without residual neurological damage.

B. Assessment
1. Headache that is worse on awakening and improves during the day
2. Vomiting that is unrelated to feeding or eating
3. Ataxia
4. Seizures
5. Behavioral changes
6. Clumsiness; awkward gait or difficulty walking
7. Diplopia
8. Facial weakness

C. Preoperative interventions
1. Perform a neurological assessment at least every 4 hours.
2. Institute seizure precautions and safety measures.
3. Assess weight loss and nutritional status.
4. Shave the child's head as prescribed (provide a favorite cap or hat for the child).
5. Prepare the child as much as possible; tell the child that he or she will wake up with a large head dressing.

D. Postoperative interventions
1. Assess neurological and motor function and level of consciousness.
2. Monitor temperature closely, which may be elevated because of hypothalamus or brainstem involvement during surgery; maintain a cooling blanket by the bedside.
3. Monitor for signs of respiratory infection.
4. Monitor for signs of meningitis (opisthotonos, Kernig's and Brudzinski's signs).
5. Monitor for signs of increased ICP (Box 45-8)
6. Monitor for hemorrhage, checking the back of the head dressing for posterior pooling of blood.
7. Assess pupillary response; sluggish, dilated, or unequal pupils are reported immediately because they may indicate increased ICP and potential brainstem herniation.
8. Monitor for colorless drainage on the dressing or from the ears or nose, which indicates cerebrospinal fluid and should be reported immedi-

BOX 45-8

Manifestations of Increased Intracranial Pressure in Infants and Children

INFANTS
Tense, bulging fontanel
Separated cranial sutures
Macewen's sign (cracked pot sound on percussion)
Irritability
High-pitched cry
Increased head circumference
Distended scalp veins
Poor feeding
Crying when disturbed
Setting sun sign (eyes appear to look only downward, with the sclera prominent over the iris)

CHILDREN
Headache
Nausea
Forceful vomiting
Diplopia; blurred vision
Seizures

PERSONALITY AND BEHAVIOR SIGNS
Irritability, restlessness
Indifference, drowsiness
Decline in school performance
Diminished physical activity and motor performance
Increased sleeping
Inability to follow simple commands
Lethargy

LATE SIGNS
Bradycardia
Decreased motor response to command
Decreased sensory response to painful stimuli
Alterations in pupil size and reaction
Decerebrate or decorticate posturing
Cheyne-Stokes respirations
Papilledema
Decreased consciousness
Coma

From Hockenberry, M., Wilson, D., & Winkelstein, M. (2005). *Wong's nursing care of infants and children* (7th ed.). St. Louis: Mosby.

BOX 45-9

Positioning Following Craniotomy

Assess the physician's order for positioning, including the degree of neck flexion.
If a large tumor has been removed, the child is not placed on the operative side because the brain may shift suddenly to that cavity.
In an infratentorial procedure, the child usually is positioned flat and on either side.
In a supratentorial procedure, the head usually is elevated above the heart level to facilitate cerebrospinal fluid drainage and to decrease excessive blood flow to the brain to prevent hemorrhage.
Never place the child in Trendelenburg's position because it increases intracranial pressure and the risk of hemorrhage.

ately; assess for the presence of glucose in the drainage (dipstick).
9. Assess the physician's order for positioning, including the degree of neck flexion (Box 45-9).
10. Monitor intravenous fluids closely.
11. Promote measures that prevent vomiting (vomiting increases intracranial pressure and the risk for incisional rupture).
12. Provide a quiet environment.
13. Administer analgesics as prescribed.
14. Provide emotional support to the child and parents, and promote optimal **growth** and development.

PRACTICE QUESTIONS

1. A 9-year-old child with leukemia is in remission and has returned to school. The school nurse calls the mother of the child and tells the mother that a classmate has just been diagnosed with chickenpox. The mother immediately calls the clinic nurse because the leukemic child has never had chickenpox. The appropriate response by the clinic nurse to the mother is:
    1. "There is no need to be concerned."
    2. "Bring the child into the clinic for a vaccine."
    3. "Keep the child out of school for a 2-week period."
    4. "Monitor the child for an elevated temperature, and call the clinic if this happens."
2. The nurse analyzes the laboratory values of a child with leukemia who is receiving chemotherapy. The nurse notes that the platelet count is 20,000/μL. Based on this laboratory result, which intervention will the nurse document in the plan of care?
    1. Monitor closely for signs of infection.
    2. Monitor the temperature every 4 hours.
    3. Initiate protective isolation precautions.
    4. Use a soft small toothbrush for mouth care.
3. A nurse is monitoring a 3-year-old child for signs and symptoms of increased intracranial pressure (ICP) following a craniotomy. The nurse plans to monitor for which early sign or symptom of increased ICP?
    1. Excessive vomiting
    2. Bulging anterior fontanel

3. Increasing head circumference
4. Complaints of a frontal headache

4. A 4-year-old child is admitted to the hospital for abdominal pain. The mother reports that the child has been pale and excessively tired and is bruising easily. On physical examination, lymphadenopathy and hepatosplenomegaly are noted. Diagnostic studies are being performed on the child because acute lymphocytic leukemia is suspected. The nurse understands that which diagnostic study will confirm this diagnosis?
   1. A platelet count
   2. A lumbar puncture
   3. Bone marrow biopsy
   4. White blood cell count

5. A nurse instructs the parents of a child with leukemia regarding measures related to monitoring for infection. Which statement, if made by the parent, indicates a need for further instructions?
   1. "I will take a rectal temperature daily."
   2. "I will inspect the skin daily for redness."
   3. "I will inspect the mouth daily for lesions."
   4. "I will perform proper hand washing techniques."

6. A 6-year-old child with leukemia is hospitalized and is receiving combination chemotherapy. Laboratory results indicate that the child is neutropenic, and protective isolation procedures are initiated. The grandmother of the child visits and brings a fresh bouquet of flowers picked from her garden and asks the nurse for a vase for the flowers. The nurse responds to the grandmother by telling her:
   1. "I have a vase in the utility room, and I will get it for you."
   2. "I will get the vase and wash it well before you put the flowers in it."
   3. "The flowers from your garden are beautiful but should not be placed in the child's room at this time."
   4. "When you bring the flowers into the room, place them on the bedside stand as far away from the child as possible."

7. A child with leukemia is complaining of nausea. A nurse suspects that the nausea is related to the chemotherapy regimen. The nurse, concerned about the child's nutritional status, most appropriately would offer which of the following during this episode of nausea?
   1. Cool, clear liquids
   2. Low-protein foods
   3. Low-calorie foods
   4. The child's favorite foods

8. A 12-year-old child is seen in a clinic, and a diagnosis of Hodgkin's disease is suspected. Several diagnostic studies are performed to determine the presence of this disease. Which diagnostic test results confirm the diagnosis of Hodgkin's disease?

1. Elevated vanillylmandelic acid urinary levels
2. The presence of blast cells in the bone marrow
3. The presence of Epstein-Barr virus in the blood
4. The presence of Reed-Sternberg cells in the lymph nodes

9. A nurse is performing an assessment on a 10-year-old child suspected of having Hodgkin's disease. The nurse understands that which of the following assessment findings is characteristic of this disease?
   1. Fever and malaise
   2. Anorexia and weight loss
   3. Painful, enlarged inguinal lymph nodes
   4. Painless, firm, and movable adenopathy in the cervical area

10. A nurse is monitoring a child for bleeding following surgery for removal of a brain tumor. The nurse checks the head dressing for the presence of blood and notes a colorless drainage on the back of the dressing. Which of the following is the appropriate nursing intervention?
    1. Notify the physician.
    2. Reinforce the dressing.
    3. Document the findings and continue to monitor.
    4. Circle the area of drainage and continue to monitor.

11. After surgical removal of a brain tumor, the physician writes an order to maintain the child in a flat position. During the postoperative period, a nurse is monitoring the child and notes that the child is restless, the pulse rate is elevated, and the blood pressure has dropped significantly from the baseline value. The nurse suspects that the child is in shock. Which of the following would be the appropriate nursing action?
    1. Notify the physician.
    2. Elevate the head of the bed.
    3. Increase the intravenous fluids.
    4. Place the child in Trendelenburg's position.

12. The mother of a 4-year-old child brings the child to a clinic and tells a pediatric nurse specialist that the child's abdomen seems to be swollen. During further assessment of subjective data, the mother tells the nurse that the child is eating well and that the activity level of the child is unchanged. The nurse, suspecting the possibility of Wilms' tumor, would avoid which of the following during the physical assessment?
    1. Palpating the abdomen for a mass
    2. Assessing the urine for the presence of hematuria
    3. Monitoring the temperature for the presence of fever
    4. Monitoring the blood pressure for the presence of hypertension

13. A pediatric nurse specialist provides a teaching session to the nursing staff regarding osteogenic sarcoma. Which statement by a member of the nursing

staff indicates a need for clarification of the information presented?

1. "The femur is the most common site of this sarcoma."
2. "The child does not experience pain at the primary tumor site."
3. "Limping, if a weight-bearing limb is affected, is a clinical manifestation."
4. "The symptoms of the disease in the early stage are almost always attributed to normal growing pains."

14. A nurse is caring for a child after surgical removal of a brain tumor. The nurse assesses the child for which of the following signs that would indicate that brainstem involvement occurred during the surgical procedure?

1. Inability to swallow
2. Elevated temperature
3. Altered hearing ability
4. Orthostatic hypotension

ALTERNATE ITEM FORMAT: MULTIPLE RESPONSE

Select the specific nursing interventions that are implemented in the care of a child with leukemia who is at risk for infection.

❑ 1. Maintain the child in a private room.
❑ 2. Reduce exposure to environmental organisms.
❑ 3. Use strict aseptic technique for all procedures.
❑ 4. Ensure that anyone entering the child's room wears a mask.
❑ 5. Apply firm pressure to a needlestick area for at least 10 minutes.
❑ 6. Avoid rectal suppositories, enemas, and the use of rectal thermometers.

ANSWERS

1. **2**

Rationale: Immunocompromised children are unable to fight varicella adequately. Chickenpox can be deadly to the immunocompromised child. If an immunocompromised child who has not had chickenpox is exposed to someone with varicella, the child should receive varicella zoster immune globulin within 96 hours of exposure. Options 1, 3, and 4 are incorrect because they do nothing to minimize the chances of developing the disease.

Test-Taking Strategy: Use the process of elimination and note the strategic words *never had chickenpox* in the question. Recall that a child with leukemia is immunocompromised and is unable to fight infection. This should assist you in eliminating options 1, 3, and 4. Review protective procedures for the immunocompromised child if you had difficulty with this question.

Level of Cognitive Ability: Application
Client Needs: Health Promotion and Maintenance
Integrated Process: Nursing Process—implementation
Content Area: Child health
Reference: McKinney, E., James, S., Murray, S., & Ashwill, J. (2005). *Maternal-child nursing* (2nd ed., p. 1340). St. Louis: W.B. Saunders.

2. **4**

Rationale: If a child is severely thrombocytopenic and has a platelet count less than 20,000/μL, bleeding precautions need to be initiated because of the increased risk of bleeding or hemorrhage. The precautions include limiting activity that could result in head injury, using soft toothbrushes or Toothettes, checking urine and stools for blood, and administering stool softeners to prevent straining with constipation. In addition, suppositories and rectal temperatures are avoided.

Options 1, 2, and 3 are related to the prevention of infection rather than bleeding.

Test-Taking Strategy: Use the process of elimination. Noting that the platelet count is low and that a low platelet count places the child at risk for bleeding will assist in directing you to option 4. In addition, note that options 1, 2, and 3 are comparative or alike because they relate to prevention of and monitoring for infection. Review interventions for the child who is at risk for bleeding if you had difficulty with this question.

Level of Cognitive Ability: Analysis
Client Needs: Safe and Effective Care Environment
Integrated Process: Nursing Process—implementation
Content Area: Child health
Reference: McKinney, E., James, S., Murray, S., & Ashwill, J. (2005). *Maternal-child nursing* (2nd ed., p. 1341). St. Louis: W.B. Saunders.

3. **1**

Rationale: The brain, while well protected by the solid bony cranium, is highly susceptible to pressure that may accumulate within the enclosure. Volume and pressure must remain constant within the brain. A change in the size of the brain, such as occurs with edema, or increased volume of intracranial blood or cerebrospinal fluid without a compensatory change, will lead to an increase in intracranial pressure, which may be life-threatening. An early sign of increased intracranial pressure, vomiting, can become excessive as pressure builds up and stimulates the medulla in the brainstem, which houses the vomit center. Children with open fontanels (posterior closes at 2 to 3 months; anterior closes at 12 to 18 months) compensate for intracranial pressure changes by skull expansion and subsequent bulging fontanels. Once the fontanels have closed, nausea, excessive vomiting, diplopia, and head-

aches become pronounced, with headaches becoming more prevalent in older children.
Test-Taking Strategy: Note the strategic word *early* and use age as key to principles of growth and development. Knowing when the fontanels close and focusing on the child's age as 3 years eliminates options 2 and 3. The subjective symptom of headache in option 4 is not reliable in a 3-year-old; therefore, eliminate this option. Review the pathophysiology of increased intracranial pressure if you had difficulty with this question.
Level of Cognitive Ability: Analysis
Client Needs: Physiological Integrity
Integrated Process: Nursing Process—analysis
Content Area: Child health
Reference: McKinney, E., James, S., Murray, S., & Ashwill, J. (2005). *Maternal-child nursing* (2nd ed., p. 1497). St. Louis: W.B. Saunders.

4. 3
Rationale: The confirmatory test for leukemia is microscopic examination of bone marrow obtained by bone marrow aspirate and biopsy. A lumbar puncture may be done to look for blast cells in the spinal fluid that indicate central nervous system disease. The white blood cell count may be normal, high, or low in leukemia. An altered platelet count occurs as a result of the disease but also may occur as a result of chemotherapy and does not confirm the diagnosis.
Test-Taking Strategy: Use the process of elimination and note the strategic word *confirm* in the question. This strategic word and knowledge that the bone marrow is affected in leukemia will direct you to option 3. If you had difficulty with this question, review the significance of the bone marrow biopsy.
Level of Cognitive Ability: Comprehension
Client Needs: Physiological Integrity
Integrated Process: Nursing Process—assessment
Content Area: Child health
Reference: Hockenberry, M., Wilson, D., & Winkelstein, M. (2005). *Wong's essentials of pediatric nursing* (7th ed., p. 958). St. Louis: Mosby.

5. 1
Rationale: The risk of injury to fragile mucous membranes is so high in the child with leukemia that oral, tympanic, or axillary temperature should be taken. Rectal abscesses can occur easily to damaged rectal tissue. No rectal temperatures should be taken. In addition, oral temperature taking should be avoided if the child has oral ulcers. Options 2, 3, and 4 are appropriate measures to prevent infection.
Test-Taking Strategy: Use the process of elimination and note the strategic words *a need for further instructions*. These words indicate a negative event query and ask you to select an option that is an incorrect statement. Options 2 and 4 can be eliminated easily first. From the remaining options, note the word *rectal* in option 1. Recalling that rectal temperature should be avoided will direct you to this option. Review home care instructions related to infection in the child with leukemia if you had difficulty with this question.
Level of Cognitive Ability: Analysis
Client Needs: Safe and Effective Care Environment
Integrated Process: Teaching and Learning
Content Area: Child health

Reference: Hockenberry, M., Wilson, D., & Winkelstein, M. (2005). *Wong's essentials of pediatric nursing* (7th ed., p. 961). St. Louis: Mosby.

6. 3
Rationale: For the hospitalized neutropenic child, flowers or plants should not be kept in the room because standing water and damp soil harbor *Aspergillus* and *Pseudomonas aeruginosa*, to which these children are susceptible. In addition, fresh fruits and vegetables harbor molds and should be avoided until the white blood cell count rises.
Test-Taking Strategy: Use the process of elimination. Note that options 1 and 2 are comparative or alike and should be eliminated first. From the remaining options, select option 3 over option 4 because this nursing response maintains the protective isolation procedures required. Review protective isolation procedures for the neutropenic child if you had difficulty with this question.
Level of Cognitive Ability: Application
Client Needs: Safe and Effective Care Environment
Integrated Process: Nursing Process—implementation
Content Area: Child health
Reference: McKinney, E., James, S., Murray, S., & Ashwill, J. (2005). *Maternal-child nursing* (2nd ed., p. 1340). St. Louis: W.B. Saunders.

7. 1
Rationale: When the child is nauseated, offering cool, clear liquids is best because they are soothing and better tolerated. One should not offer favorite foods when the child is nauseated because foods eaten during times of nausea will be associated with being sick. Supportive nutritional measures should include oral supplements with high-protein and high-calorie foods.
Test-Taking Strategy: The subject of the question relates to the nutritional status in a child with nausea. Focusing on this subject will assist in eliminating options 2 and 3. From the remaining options, you may be tempted to select option 4. Remember that it is best not to offer favorite foods when the child is nauseated because foods eaten during times of nausea will be associated with being sick. Review these interventions related to nutrition if you had difficulty with this question.
Level of Cognitive Ability: Application
Client Needs: Physiological Integrity
Integrated Process: Nursing Process—implementation
Content Area: Child health
Reference: McKinney, E., James, S., Murray, S., & Ashwill, J. (2005). *Maternal-child nursing* (2nd ed., p. 1341). St. Louis: W.B. Saunders.

8. 4
Rationale: Hodgkin's disease is a neoplasm of lymphatic tissue. The presence of giant, multinucleated cells (Reed-Sternberg cells) is the hallmark of this disease. The presence of blast cells in the bone marrow indicates leukemia. The Epstein-Barr virus is associated with infectious mononucleosis. Elevated levels of vanillylmandelic acid in the urine may be found in children with neuroblastoma.
Test-Taking Strategy: Use the process of elimination. Recalling that the Reed-Sternberg cell is characteristic of Hodgkin's disease will direct you easily to option 4. Review the clinical

manifestations associated with Hodgkin's disease if you had difficulty with this question.
Level of Cognitive Ability: Comprehension
Client Needs: Physiological Integrity
Integrated Process: Nursing Process—assessment
Content Area: Child health
Reference: Hockenberry, M., Wilson, D., & Winkelstein, M. (2005). *Wong's essentials of pediatric nursing* (7th ed., pp. 970-971). St. Louis: Mosby.

9. **4**
Rationale: Clinical manifestations specifically associated with Hodgkin's disease include painless, firm, and movable adenopathy in the cervical and supraclavicular areas. Hepatosplenomegaly also is noted. Although fever, malaise, anorexia, and weight loss are associated with Hodgkin's disease, these manifestations are seen in many disorders.
Test-Taking Strategy: Use the process of elimination and note the strategic word *characteristic* in the question. Eliminate options 1 and 2 first because these symptoms are general and vague. Recalling that painless adenopathy is associated with Hodgkin's disease will direct you to option 4. Review the clinical manifestations related to Hodgkin's disease if you had difficulty with this question.
Level of Cognitive Ability: Analysis
Client Needs: Physiological Integrity
Integrated Process: Nursing Process—assessment
Content Area: Child health
Reference: Hockenberry, M., Wilson, D., & Winkelstein, M. (2005). *Wong's essentials of pediatric nursing* (7th ed., p. 971). St. Louis: Mosby.

10. **1**
Rationale: Colorless drainage on the dressing indicates the presence of cerebrospinal fluid and should be reported to the physician immediately. Options 2, 3, and 4 are inaccurate nursing interventions, because they do not address the need for immediate intervention to prevent complications.
Test-Taking Strategy: Use the process of elimination. Eliminate options 3 and 4 first because they are comparative or alike. Note the strategic words *colorless drainage*. This should alert you quickly to the possibility of the presence of cerebrospinal fluid and direct you to option 1. If you had difficulty with this question, review the significance of the presence of colorless drainage following cranial surgery.
Level of Cognitive Ability: Application
Client Needs: Physiological Integrity
Integrated Process: Nursing Process—implementation
Content Area: Child health
References: Hockenberry, M., Wilson, D., & Winkelstein, M. (2005). *Wong's essentials of pediatric nursing* (7th ed., p. 1038). St. Louis: Mosby.
McKinney, E., James, S., Murray, S., & Ashwill, J. (2005). *Maternal-child nursing* (2nd ed., p. 1348). St. Louis: W.B. Saunders.

11. **1**
Rationale: The child is never placed in Trendelenburg's position because it increases intracranial pressure (ICP) and the risk of bleeding. In the event of shock, the physician is notified

immediately before changing the child's position or increasing intravenous fluids. Increasing intravenous fluids can cause an increase in ICP.
Test-Taking Strategy: Recall the complications associated with cranial surgery to answer this question. Eliminate option 2 because this intervention will not assist in alleviating shock. In fact, this action could cause harm to the child. Eliminate option 3 because this action could increase ICP. In addition, the nurse should not increase intravenous fluids without a physician's order. Eliminate option 4 because this position increases ICP. Review care of the child after surgical removal of a brain tumor if you had difficulty with this question.
Level of Cognitive Ability: Application
Client Needs: Physiological Integrity
Integrated Process: Nursing Process—implementation
Content Area: Child health
Reference: McKinney, E., James, S., Murray, S., & Ashwill, J. (2005). *Maternal-child nursing* (2nd ed., p. 1348). St. Louis: W.B. Saunders.

12. **1**
Rationale: If Wilms' tumor is suspected, the tumor mass should not be palpated by the nurse. Excessive manipulation can cause seeding of the tumor and spread of the cancerous cells. Fever, hematuria, and hypertension are clinical manifestations associated with Wilms' tumor.
Test-Taking Strategy: Use the process of elimination and note the strategic word *avoid*. This word indicates a negative event query and asks you to select an option that is an incorrect action. Knowledge that this tumor is located in the kidney will assist in eliminating options 2, 3, and 4 because of the relationship of these options to renal function. Review the significant assessment procedures in the child with Wilms' tumor if you had difficulty with this question.
Level of Cognitive Ability: Application
Client Needs: Physiological Integrity
Integrated Process: Nursing Process—implementation
Content Area: Child health
Reference: Hockenberry, M., Wilson, D., & Winkelstein, M. (2005). *Wong's essentials of pediatric nursing* (7th ed., p. 1000). St. Louis: Mosby.

13. **2**
Rationale: A clinical manifestation of osteogenic sarcoma is progressive, insidious, and intermittent pain at the tumor site. By the time these children receive medical attention, they may be in considerable pain from the tumor. Options 1, 3, and 4 are accurate regarding osteogenic sarcoma.
Test-Taking Strategy: Use the process of elimination and note the strategic words *need for clarification of the information presented* in the question. These words indicate a negative event query and ask you to select an option that is an incorrect statement. Knowledge that osteogenic sarcoma is a malignant tumor of the bone will direct you to option 2. Review the clinical manifestations associated with osteogenic sarcoma if you had difficulty with this question.
Level of Cognitive Ability: Analysis
Client Needs: Physiological Integrity
Integrated Process: Teaching and Learning
Content Area: Child health

Reference: McKinney, E., James, S., Murray, S., & Ashwill, J. (2005). *Maternal-child nursing* (2nd ed., p. 1353). St. Louis: W.B. Saunders.

14. **2**

Rationale: Vital signs and neurological status are assessed frequently. Special attention is given to the child's temperature, which may be elevated because of hypothalamic or brainstem involvement during surgery. A cooling blanket should be in place on the bed or readily available if the child becomes hyperthermic. Options 1 and 3 are related to functional deficits following surgery. Orthostatic hypotension is not a common clinical manifestation following brain surgery. An elevated blood pressure and widened pulse pressure may be associated with increased intracranial pressure, which is a complication following brain surgery.

Test-Taking Strategy: Use the process of elimination and focus on the subject, brainstem involvement. Recalling the functions of the hypothalamus and the brainstem will direct you easily to option 2. If you had difficulty with this question, review the complications that can occur following surgical removal of a brain tumor.

Level of Cognitive Ability: Analysis
Client Needs: Physiological Integrity
Integrated Process: Nursing Process—assessment
Content Area: Child health
References: Hockenberry, M., Wilson, D., & Winkelstein, M. (2005). *Wong's essentials of pediatric nursing* (7th ed., pp. 1036-1037). St. Louis: Mosby.
McKinney, E., James, S., Murray, S., & Ashwill, J. (2005). *Maternal-child nursing* (2nd ed., p. 1348). St. Louis: W.B. Saunders.

ALTERNATE ITEM FORMAT: MULTIPLE RESPONSE

Answer: 1, 2, 3, 4

Rationale: A common complication of treatment for leukemia is overwhelming infection secondary to neutropenia. Measures to prevent infection include the use of a private room, strict aseptic technique, restriction of visitors and health care personnel with active infection, strict hand washing, ensuring that anyone entering the child's room wears a mask, and reducing exposure to environmental organisms by eliminating raw fruits and vegetables from the diet and fresh flowers from the child's room and by not leaving standing water in the child's room. The other interventions listed are measures to prevent bleeding.

Test-Taking Strategy: Focus on the subject, preventing infection. Reading each intervention carefully and keeping this subject in mind will assist in answering the question. Applying firm pressure to a needlestick area for at least 10 minutes, and avoiding the use of rectal suppositories, enemas, and rectal thermometers, are related to preventing bleeding. Review interventions for the child at risk for infection if you had difficulty with this question.

Level of Cognitive Ability: Application
Client Needs: Physiological Integrity
Integrated Process: Nursing Process—implementation
Content Area: Child health
References: Hockenberry, M., Wilson, D., & Winkelstein, M. (2005). *Wong's essentials of pediatric nursing* (7th ed., pp. 960, 966). St. Louis: Mosby.
McKinney, E., James, S., Murray, S., & Ashwill, J. (2005). *Maternal-child nursing* (2nd ed., pp. 1339-1340). St. Louis: W.B. Saunders.

REFERENCES

American Cancer Society. http://www.cancer.org.
Hockenberry, M., Wilson, D., & Winkelstein, M. (2005). *Wong's essentials of pediatric nursing* (7th ed.). St. Louis: Mosby.
Hockenberry, M., & Wilson, D. (2007). *Wong's nursing care of infants and children* (8th ed.). St. Louis: Mosby.
McKinney, E., James, S., Murray, S., & Ashwill, J. (2005). *Maternal-child nursing* (2nd ed.). St. Louis: W.B. Saunders.

Mosby. (2006). *Mosby's dictionary of medicine, nursing and health professions* (7th ed.). St. Louis: Mosby.
National Brain Tumor Foundation. http://www.braintumor.org.
National Council of State Boards of Nursing (Eds.). (2007). *NCLEX-RN® detailed test plan.* Chicago: Author.

Acquired Immunodeficiency Syndrome

I. ACQUIRED IMMUNODEFICIENCY SYNDROME (AIDS)

A. Description
   1. Acquired immunodeficiency syndrome is a disorder caused by the human immunodeficiency virus (HIV) and characterized by generalized dysfunction of the immune system (Fig. 46-1).
   2. HIV virus infects the CD4$^+$ T cells, causing a gradual decrease in the cell count and leading to progressive immune deficiency; the risk for opportunistic infections is present.
   3. HIV is found in blood, semen, vaginal secretions, and breast milk and the retrovirus has an incubation period of months to years,
   4. Horizontal transmission of HIV occurs through intimate sexual contact or parenteral exposure to blood or body fluids containing visible blood.
   5. Vertical (perinatal) transmission of HIV occurs when an HIV-infected pregnant woman passes the infection to her fetus.
   6. Routine HIV counseling and voluntary testing for pregnant women is recommended and zidovudine (ZDV, AZT, Retrovir) therapy is recommended for HIV-infected pregnant women (and subsequently the newborn infant) to prevent transmission.
   7. The most common opportunistic infection of children infected with HIV is *Pneumocystis jiroveci* pneumonia (formerly known as *Pneumocystis carinii* pneumonia [PCP]), which occurs most frequently between the ages of 3 and 6 months, when HIV status may be indeterminate.

B. Assessment (Boxes 46-1 and 46-2)

C. Diagnostic tests: Before testing, counseling should be provided to parent, guardian, and caregiver regarding the cause of HIV, reason for testing, implications of positive test results, confidentiality issues, risk reduction, and beneficial effects of early intervention (Table 46-1).

II. CARE OF THE CHILD WITH HIV INFECTION OR AIDS

A. The goals of therapy include slowing the growth of the virus, preventing and treating opportunistic infections, and providing nutritional support and treatment of symptoms.

B. Prophylaxis (*P. jiroveci* pneumonia and other opportunistic infections)
   1. Provide prophylaxis as prescribed against *P. jiroveci* pneumonia and other opportunistic infections, particularly during the first year of life of the infant born to an HIV-infected mother.
   2. After 1 year of age, the need for prophylaxis is determined by the presence of severe immunosuppression or a history of *P. jiroveci* pneumonia.
   3. Continuing prophylaxis is based on HIV status, past history of opportunistic infections, and CD4$^+$ counts.

C. Antiretroviral therapy (ART; Box 46-3)
   1. The goal of ART is to suppress viral replication to slow the decline in the number of CD4$^+$ cells, preserve immune function, reduce the incidence and severity of opportunistic infections, and delay disease progression.
   2. ART works at various stages of the HIV life cycle to prevent reproduction of new functional virus particles.
   3. Classes of medications include reverse transcriptase (RT) inhibitors and protease inhibitors; RT inhibitors are divided into nucleoside analogues and non-nucleoside analogues (see Box 46-3).

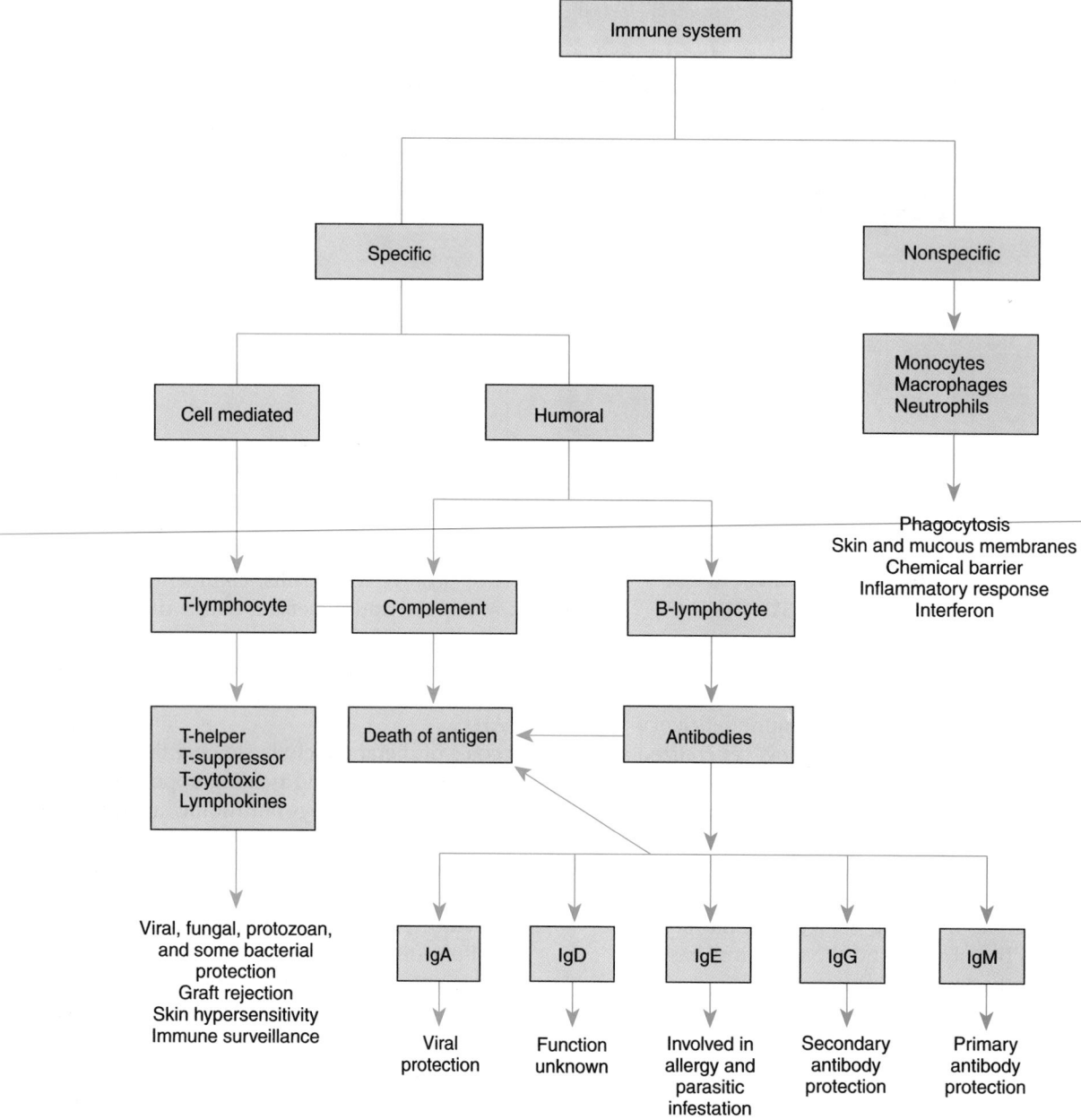

FIG. 46-1 Components of the immune system. (From Hockenberry, M. [2003]. *Wong's nursing care of infants and children* [7th ed.]. St. Louis: Mosby.)

BOX 46-1
Common Manifestations of HIV Infection in Children

Chronic cough	Hepatosplenomegaly
Chronic or recurrent	Lymphadenopathy
diarrhea	Malaise and fatigue
Developmental delay or	Night sweats
regression of develop-	Oral candidiasis
mental milestones	Parotitis
Failure to thrive	Weight loss

Modified from Hockenberry, M., Wilson, D., & Winkelstein, M. (2005). *Wong's essentials of pediatric nursing*. St. Louis: Mosby.

BOX 46-2
AIDS-Defining Conditions in Children

Candidal esophagitis	*Pneumocystis jiroveci*
Cryptosporidiosis	pneumonia
Cytomegalovirus disease	Pulmonary candidiasis
Herpes simplex disease	Recurrent bacterial
HIV encephalopathy	infections
Lymphoid interstitial	Wasting syndrome
pneumonitis	
Mycobacterium avium-	
intracellulare infection	

From Hockenberry, M., Wilson, D., & Winkelstein, M. (2005). *Wong's essentials of pediatric nursing*. St. Louis: Mosby.

TABLE 46-1

Diagnostic Tests for HIV

Test	Age-Appropriate Use	Test Determines	Special Considerations
Enzyme-linked immunosorbent assay (ELISA)	18 mo or older	Response of antibodies to HIV virus	If used and found to be positive in infants younger than 18 mo, indicates only that the mother is infected, because maternal antibodies are transmitted transplacentally; use another diagnostic test.
Western blot	18 mo or older	Presence of HIV antibodies	Same as above
Polymerase chain reaction (PCR)	Younger than 18 mo	Presence of proviral DNA	95% accuracy in infants 1-3 mo of age
p24 antigen	Younger than 18 mo	HIV antigen specific	95% accuracy in infants 1-3 mo of age
CD4$^+$ lymphocyte count, T-lymphocyte count	Infant up to 13 yr	Immune system status related specifically to suppression	Age adjustment is essential, because normal counts are relatively high in infants and steadily decline until 6 yr of age. Severe suppression in all age groups is <15% total lymphocytes (less than 750/μL in an infant younger than 12 mo, less than 500/μL in a child 1-5 yr, less than 200/μL in a child 6-12 yr).

BOX 46-3

Antiretroviral Therapy

REVERSE TRANSCRIPTASE INHIBITORS (RT INHIBITORS)
Nucleoside Analogues
Abacavir (Ziagen)
Didanosine (Videx)
Lamivudine (Epivir)
Stavudine (d4T, Zerit XR)
Zidovudine (ZDV, AZT, Retrovir)
Non-nucleoside Analogues
Delavirdine (Rescriptor)
Efavirenz (Sustiva)
Nevirapine (Viramune)

PROTEASE INHIBITORS
Amprenavir (Agenerase)
Indinavir (Crixivan)
Nelfinavir (Viracept)
Ritonavir (Norvir)
Saquinavir (Invirase)

D. Highly active antiretroviral therapy (HAART)
   1. Combination therapy usually includes two nucleoside analogues and a protease inhibitor.
   2. HAART may be prescribed for an HIV-infected infant, child who exhibits clinical signs of infection or whose immune status is depressed, or HIV-infected infant younger than 1 year of age when the diagnosis is confirmed.
   3. Substantial decreases in mortality and morbidity, including opportunistic infections, have been observed in children receiving HAART.
E. Immunizations
   1. Immunization against childhood diseases is recommended for all children exposed to and infected with HIV.

2. The pneumococcal and influenza **vaccines** are recommended.
3. Because they are live **vaccines,** measles, mumps, rubella (MMR) and varicella (chickenpox) **vaccines** are administered if the child is not severely immunocompromised.
4. The child receiving intravenous gamma globulin prophylaxis against opportunistic infections may not respond to the MMR **vaccine.**
5. See Chapter 47 for additional information regarding immunizations.
F. Caretaker instructions
   1. Wash hands frequently.
   2. Assess for fever, malaise, fatigue, weight loss, vomiting and diarrhea, altered activity level, and oral lesions; notify the physician if any of these occur.
   3. Assess for the signs and symptoms of opportunistic infections, such as pneumonia.
   4. Administer antiretroviral medications and other medications as prescribed.
   5. Restrict contact with persons who have infections or other contagious or potentially contagious illnesses.
   6. Keep immunizations up to date.
   7. Keep the child home when sick.
   8. Avoid direct unprotected contact with body fluids.
   9. Monitor the child's weight.
   10. Provide a high-calorie and high-protein diet.
   11. Administer appetite stimulants as needed.
   12. Do not share eating utensils.
   13. Wash eating utensils in the dishwasher.
   14. Cover unused food and formula and refrigerate.
   15. Discard unused refrigerated formula and food after 24 hours.

Sexual transmission of the infection
Risks of perinatal infection
Dangers of promiscuity
Abstinence from sexual contact, such as intercourse
Use of condoms
Avoidance of high-risk behaviors
Coping behaviors

16. Avoid fresh fruits or vegetables, or raw fish (neutropenic diet if immunosuppressed).
17. Wear gloves for care, especially when in contact with body fluids and changing diapers.
18. Change diapers frequently, away from food areas.
19. Fold soiled disposable diapers inward, close with tabs, and dispose in a tightly covered plastic-lined container.
20. Dispose of trash daily.
21. Clean up body fluid spills with a bleach solution (10:1 ratio of water to bleach).
22. See Box 46-4 for teaching points to address for an adolescent infected with HIV.

PRACTICE QUESTIONS

1. A mother with human immunodeficiency virus (HIV) infection brings her 10-month-old infant to the clinic for a routine checkup. The physician has documented that the infant is asymptomatic for HIV infection. After the checkup, the mother tells the nurse that she is so pleased that the infant will not get HIV. The appropriate nursing response to the mother is:
   1. "I am so pleased also that everything has turned out fine."
   2. "Since symptoms have not developed, it is unlikely that your infant will develop HIV infection."
   3. "Everything looks great, but be sure that you return with your infant next month for the scheduled visit."
   4. "Most children infected with HIV develop symptoms within the first 9 months of life, and some become symptomatic sometime before they are 3 years old."

2. A 6-year-old child diagnosed with human immunodeficiency virus (HIV) has been admitted to the hospital for pain management. The child asks the nurse if the pain will ever go away. The nurse should make which best response to the child?
   1. "The pain will go away if you lie still and let the medicine work."
   2. "Try not to think about it. The more you think it hurts, the more it will hurt."
   3. "I know it must hurt, but if you tell me when it does, I will try and make it hurt a little less."
   4. "Every time it hurts, press on the call button and I will give you something to make the pain go all away."

3. An infant of a mother infected with human immunodeficiency virus (HIV) is seen in the clinic each month and is being monitored for symptoms indicative of HIV infection. The nurse assesses the infant, knowing that the most common opportunistic infection of children infected with HIV is:
   1. Meningitis
   2. Gastroenteritis
   3. Cytomegalovirus infection
   4. *Pneumocystis jiroveci* pneumonia

4. The nurse provides home care instructions to the parent of a child with acquired immunodeficiency syndrome (AIDS). Which statement by the parent indicates the need for further teaching?
   1. "I will wash my hands frequently."
   2. "I will keep my child's immunizations up to date."
   3. "I can send my child to day care with a low-grade fever."
   4. "I will avoid direct unprotected contact with my child's body fluids."

5. A clinic nurse is instructing the mother of a child with human immunodeficiency virus (HIV) infection regarding immunizations. The nurse tells the mother that:
   1. The hepatitis B vaccine will not be given to the child
   2. Pneumococcal and influenza vaccines are recommended
   3. Household members need to avoid receiving the varicella vaccine
   4. A Western blot test needs to be performed and the results evaluated before immunizations

6. A nurse is caring for a 4-year-old child with a diagnosis of human immunodeficiency virus (HIV) infection. In planning care to address the child's psychosocial needs, the nurse expects that this child:
   1. Will express fear, withdrawal, and denial
   2. Begins to understand that something is wrong
   3. Is unable to grasp the concept of illness and death
   4. Begins to conceptualize the death process as involving physical harm

7. A home care nurse provides instructions regarding basic infection control to the mother of an infant with human immunodeficiency virus (HIV) infection. Which statement, if made by the mother, indicates the need for further instructions?
   1. "I will carefully wash all fresh fruits and vegetables."

2. "I will wash baby bottles, nipples, and pacifiers in the dishwasher."

3. "I will clean up any spills from the diaper with full-strength alcohol."

4. "I will rub the inside of the nipple with salt and rinse well if it becomes slimy."

8. A newborn infant of a mother who has human immunodeficiency virus (HIV) infection is tested for the presence of HIV antibodies. An enzyme-linked immunosorbent assay (ELISA) is performed, and the results are positive. The nurse interprets these results as:

1. Positive for HIV

2. Negative for HIV

3. Indicating the absence of maternal infection

4. Indicating the presence of maternal infection

9. A physician orders laboratory studies for an infant of a woman positive for human immunodeficiency virus (HIV) to determine the presence of HIV antigen in the infant. The nurse anticipates that which laboratory study will be prescribed for the infant?

1. CD4$^+$ cell count

2. Chest x-ray

3. Western blot

4. p24 antigen assay

ALTERNATE ITEM FORMAT: MULTIPLE RESPONSE

Select the home care instructions that the nurse would provide to the mother of a child with acquired immunodeficiency syndrome (AIDS). Select all that apply.

❑ 1. Frequent hand washing is important.

❑ 2. The child should avoid exposure to other illnesses.

❑ 3. The child's immunization schedule will need revision.

❑ 4. Kissing the child on the mouth will never transmit the virus.

❑ 5. Clean up body fluid spills with bleach solution (10:1 ratio of water to bleach).

❑ 6. Fever, malaise, fatigue, weight loss, vomiting, and diarrhea are expected to occur and do not require special intervention.

ANSWERS

1. 4

Rationale: Most children infected with HIV develop symptoms within the first 9 months of life. The remainder of these infected children become symptomatic sometime before the age of 3 years. Children, with their immature immune systems, have a much shorter incubation period than adults. Options 1, 2, and 3 are incorrect.

Test-Taking Strategy: Use the process of elimination. Eliminate options 1, 2, and 3 because they are comparative or alike in content. Option 4 is the only option that provides specific and accurate data regarding HIV infection in the infant. Review assessment findings associated with HIV infection if you had difficulty with this question.

Level of Cognitive Ability: Application

Client Needs: Psychosocial Integrity

Integrated Process: Nursing Process—implementation

Content Area: Child health

References: Hockenberry, M., Wilson, D., & Winkelstein, M. (2005). *Wong's essentials of pediatric nursing* (7th ed., p. 975). St. Louis: Mosby.

McKinney, E., James, S., Murray, S., & Ashwill, J. (2005). *Maternal-child nursing* (2nd ed., pp. 1055-1056). St. Louis: W.B. Saunders.

2. 3

Rationale: The multiple complications associated with HIV are accompanied by a high level of pain. Aggressive pain management is essential for the child to have an acceptable quality of

life. A nurse must acknowledge the child's pain and let the child know that everything will be done to decrease the pain. Telling the child that movement or lack thereof will eliminate the pain is not accurate. Allowing a child to think that he or she can control the pain simply by thinking or not thinking about it oversimplifies the pain cycle associated with HIV. Giving false hope by telling the child that the pain will be taken "all away" is neither truthful nor realistic.

Test-Taking Strategy: Recall the general concept of pain as well as growth and development concepts of a 6-year-old child. Giving the child information about the pain in words that he or she can understand, but without providing false hope or not telling the truth, should guide you to option 3. Option 1 provides inaccurate information about pain management, as does option 2. Option 4 provides false hope that the pain can be alleviated completely. Review the concepts associated with pain management in a child if you had difficulty with this question.

Level of Cognitive Ability: Application

Client Needs: Physiological Integrity

Integrated Process: Nursing Process—implementation

Content Area: Child health

Reference: McKinney, E., James, S., Murray, S., & Ashwill, J. (2005). *Maternal-child nursing* (2nd ed., p. 1064). St. Louis: W.B. Saunders.

3. 4

Rationale: The most common opportunistic infection of children infected with HIV is *Pneumocystis jiroveci* pneumonia, which occurs most frequently between the ages of 3 and

6 months, when HIV status may be indeterminate. Cytomegalovirus infection is also characteristic of HIV infection; however, it is not the most common opportunistic infection. Although gastrointestinal disturbances and neurological abnormalities may occur in the child with HIV infection, options 1 and 2 are not specific opportunistic infections noted in the HIV-infected child.

Test-Taking Strategy: Use the process of elimination and note the strategic words *most common opportunistic infection.* This focus will direct you to option 4. Review the common manifestations associated with HIV if you had difficulty with this question.

Level of Cognitive Ability: Analysis
Client Needs: Physiological Integrity
Integrated Process: Nursing Process—assessment
Content Area: Child health
Reference: Hockenberry, M., Wilson, D., & Winkelstein, M. (2005). *Wong's essentials of pediatric nursing* (7th ed., p. 974). St. Louis: Mosby.

---

4. **3**
Rationale: A child with AIDS who is sick or has a fever should be kept home and not brought to a day care center or other environment. Options 1, 2, and 4 are correct statements and would be actions a caretaker should take when the child has AIDS.

Test-Taking Strategy: Use the process of elimination and note the strategic words *indicates the need for further teaching,* which indicate a negative event query and ask you to select an option that is an incorrect statement. Noting the word *fever* in option 3 will direct you to this option. Review teaching related to the care of a child with AIDS if you had difficulty with this question.

Level of Cognitive Ability: Analysis
Client Needs: Physiological Integrity
Integrated Process: Teaching and Learning
Content Area: Child health
Reference: Hockenberry, M., & Wilson, D. (2007). *Wong's nursing care of infants and children* (8th ed., p. 1551). St. Louis: Mosby.

5. **2**
Rationale: Immunizations against common childhood illnesses are recommended for all children exposed to or infected with HIV. Pneumococcal and influenza vaccines also are recommended. The varicella (chickenpox) vaccine is avoided in the child who is HIV-infected and severely immunocompromised. The hepatitis B vaccine is administered according to the recommended immunization schedule. Option 4 is not necessary and is inaccurate.

Test-Taking Strategy: Use the process of elimination. Option 4 can be eliminated first. From the remaining options, recalling that the child infected with HIV is at risk for opportunistic infections will assist in directing you to option 2. Review immunizations in the immunodeficient child if you had difficulty with this question.

Level of Cognitive Ability: Application
Client Needs: Health Promotion and Maintenance
Integrated Process: Teaching and Learning
Content Area: Child health
Reference: Hockenberry, M., Wilson, D., & Winkelstein, M. (2005). *Wong's essentials of pediatric nursing* (7th ed., pp. 975-976). St. Louis: Mosby.

6. **4**
Rationale: The preschool child will begin to conceptualize the death process as involving physical harm. A child from birth to 2 years of age will be unable to grasp the concept of illness and death. A school-age child will begin to understand that something is wrong. An adolescent will express fear, withdrawal, and denial.

Test-Taking Strategy: Use concepts of growth and development and the related psychosocial issues to answer the question. Noting the age of the child will assist in directing you to the correct option. Review these concepts if you had difficulty with this question.

Level of Cognitive Ability: Analysis
Client Needs: Psychosocial Integrity
Integrated Process: Nursing Process—analysis
Content Area: Child health
Reference: McKinney, E., James, S., Murray, S., & Ashwill, J. (2005). *Maternal-child nursing* (2nd ed., p. 1063). St. Louis: W.B. Saunders.

7. **3**
Rationale: The mother should be instructed to use a bleach solution for disinfecting contaminated objects or cleaning up spills from the child's diaper. Options 1, 2, and 4 are accurate instructions related to basic infection control.

Test-Taking Strategy: Use the process of elimination and note the strategic words *need for further instructions.* These words indicate a negative event query and ask you to select an option that is an incorrect statement. Knowledge regarding basic infection control measures will direct you easily to option 3. Review these measures if you had difficulty with this question.

Level of Cognitive Ability: Analysis
Client Needs: Safe and Effective Care Environment
Integrated Process: Teaching and Learning
Content Area: Child health
Reference: McKinney, E., James, S., Murray, S., & Ashwill, J. (2005). *Maternal-child nursing* (2nd ed., p. 1058). St. Louis: W.B. Saunders.

8. **4**
Rationale: A positive antibody test in a child younger than 18 months of age indicates only that the mother is infected, because maternal immunoglobulin G antibodies persist in infants for 6 to 9 months and, in some cases, as long as 18 months. A positive enzyme-linked immunosorbent assay (ELISA) does not indicate true HIV infection.

Test-Taking Strategy: Use the process of elimination. Noting the strategic words *newborn infant* in the question, and recalling that a positive antibody test in a child younger than 18 months indicates only that the mother is infected will assist in directing you to the correct option. Review tests associated with HIV infection if you had difficulty with this question.

Level of Cognitive Ability: Analysis
Client Needs: Physiological Integrity
Integrated Process: Nursing Process—analysis
Content Area: Child health
Reference: Hockenberry, M., Wilson, D., & Winkelstein, M. (2005). *Wong's essentials of pediatric nursing* (7th ed., p. 973). St. Louis: Mosby.

9. **4**
Rationale: The detection of HIV in infants is confirmed by a p24 antigen assay, virus culture of HIV, or polymerase chain reaction. A Western blot test confirms the presence of HIV antibodies. The CD4$^+$ cell count indicates how well the immune system is working. A chest x-ray evaluates the presence of other manifestations of HIV infection, such as pneumonia.
Test-Taking Strategy: Note the strategic word *infant*. Recalling the laboratory tests used to determine the presence of HIV infection is needed to answer this question. If you are unfamiliar with these laboratory tests, review them. Specific laboratory tests to review include ELISA, Western blot, CD4$^+$ cell count, and p24 antigen assay.
Level of Cognitive Ability: Analysis
Client Needs: Physiological Integrity
Integrated Process: Nursing Process—analysis
Content Area: Child health
Reference: McKinney, E., James, S., Murray, S., & Ashwill, J. (2005). *Maternal-child nursing* (2nd ed., pp. 1053, 1055). St. Louis: W.B. Saunders.

ALTERNATE ITEM FORMAT: MULTIPLE RESPONSE

Answer: 1, 2, 5
Rationale: AIDS is a disorder caused by the human immunodeficiency virus (HIV) and is characterized by a generalized dysfunction of the immune system. Home care instructions include the following: frequent hand washing; monitoring for fever, malaise, fatigue, weight loss, vomiting and diarrhea, and notifying the physician if these occur; monitoring for signs and symptoms of opportunistic infections; administering antiretroviral medications and other medications as prescribed; avoiding exposure to other illnesses; keeping immunizations up to date; avoiding kissing the child on the mouth; and monitoring weight and providing a high-calorie, high-protein diet; washing eating utensils in the dishwasher; and avoiding sharing eating utensils. Gloves are worn for care, especially when in contact with body fluids and changing diapers (diapers are changed frequently and away from food areas) and soiled disposable diapers are folded inward, tabbed, and disposed in a tightly covered plastic-lined container. Any body fluid spills are cleaned with a bleach solution (10:1 ratio of water to bleach).
Test-Taking Strategy: Focus on the subject, care of the child with AIDS. Recalling that this disorder is characterized by a generalized dysfunction of the immune system and recalling the modes of transmission of the virus will assist in selecting the home care instructions. Review these instructions if you had difficulty with this question.
Level of Cognitive Ability: Application
Client Needs: Safe and Effective Care Environment
Integrated Process: Teaching and Learning
Content Area: Child health
References: Hockenberry, M., Wilson, D., & Winkelstein, M. (2005). *Wong's essentials of pediatric nursing* (7th ed., pp. 976-977). St. Louis: Mosby.
McKinney, E., James, S., Murray, S., & Ashwill, J. (2005). *Maternal-child nursing* (2nd ed., pp. 1058, 1068). St. Louis: W.B. Saunders.

REFERENCES

Chernecky, C., & Berger, B. (2004). *Laboratory tests and diagnostic procedures* (4th ed.). Philadelphia: W.B. Saunders.
Hockenberry, M., Wilson, D., & Winkelstein, M. (2005). *Wong's essentials of pediatric nursing* (7th ed.). St. Louis: Mosby.
Hockenberry, M., & Wilson, D. (2007). *Wong's nursing care of infants and children* (8th ed.). St. Louis: Mosby.

Hodgson, B., & Kizior, R. (2007). *Saunders nursing drug handbook 2003*. Philadelphia: W.B. Saunders.
McKinney, E., James, S., Murray, S., & Ashwill, J. (2005). *Maternal-child nursing* (2nd ed.). St. Louis: W.B. Saunders.
National Council of State Boards of Nursing (Eds.). (2007). *2007 NCLEX-RN® detailed test plan.* Chicago: Author.

Infectious and Communicable Diseases

I. RUBEOLA (MEASLES)

A. Description
1. Agent: Paramyxovirus
2. Incubation period: 10 to 20 days
3. Communicable period: From 4 days before to 5 days after the rash appears, mainly during prodromal stage (pertaining to early symptoms that may mark the onset of disease)
4. Source: Respiratory tract secretions, blood, or urine of infected person
5. Transmission: Airborne particles or direct contact with infectious droplets; transplacental

B. Assessment (Fig. 47-1)
1. Fever
2. Malaise
3. The three C's: Coryza, cough, conjunctivitis
4. Rash appears as red, erythematous maculopapular eruption starting on the face and spreading downward to the feet; blanches easily with pressure and gradually turns a brownish color (lasts 6 to 7 days); may have desquamation.
5. Koplik's spots: Small red spots with a bluish white center and a red base; located on the buccal mucosa and last 3 days

C. Interventions
1. Use airborne droplet precautions if the child is hospitalized.
2. Restrict child to quiet activities and bed rest.
3. Use a cool mist vaporizer for cough and coryza.
4. Dim lights if photophobia is present.
5. Administer antipyretics for fever.

II. ROSEOLA (EXANTHEMA SUBITUM)

A. Description
1. Agent: Human herpesvirus type 6 (HHV-6)
2. Incubation period: 5 to 15 days

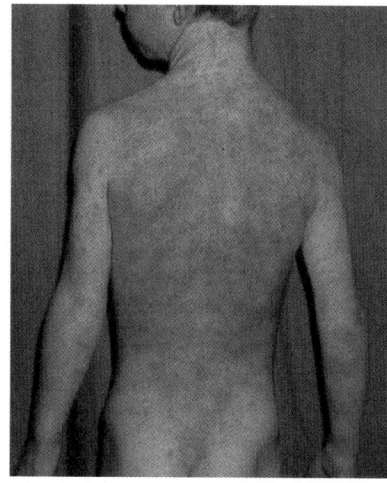

FIG. 47-1 Rubeola (measles). (From Hockenberry, M., & Wilson, D. [2007]. *Wong's nursing care of infants and children* [8th ed.]. St. Louis: Mosby.)

3. Communicable period: Unknown but thought to extend from the febrile stage to the time the rash first appears
4. Source: Unknown
5. Transmission: Unknown

B. Assessment (Fig. 47-2)
1. Sudden high (higher than 102° F) fever of 3 to 5 days' duration in a child who appears well, followed by a rash (rose-pink macules that blanch with pressure)
2. The rash appears several hours to 2 days after the fever subsides and lasts 1 to 2 days.

C. Interventions: Supportive

III. RUBELLA (GERMAN MEASLES)

A. Description
1. Agent: Rubella virus
2. Incubation period: 14 to 21 days

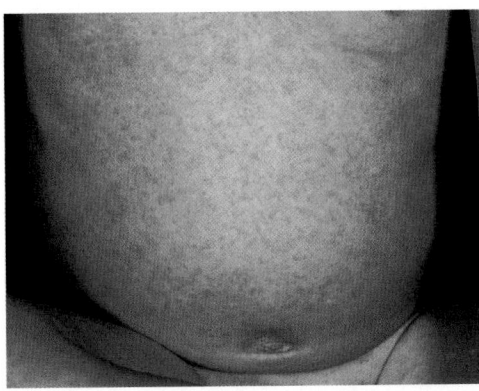

FIG. 47-2   Roseola (exanthema subitum). (From Hocken-berry, M., & Wilson, D. [2007]. *Wong's nursing care of infants and children* [8th ed.]. St. Louis: Mosby.)

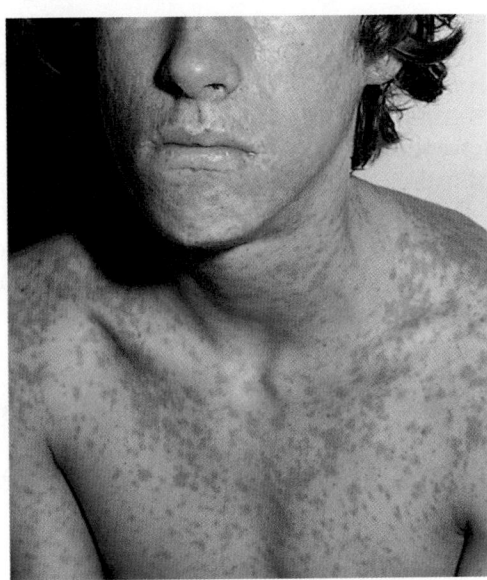

FIG. 47-3   Rubella (German measles). (From Hocken-berry, M., & Wilson, D. [2007]. *Wong's nursing care of infants and children* [8th ed.]. St. Louis: Mosby.)

3. Communicable period: 7 days before to about 5 days after the rash appears
4. Source: Nasopharyngeal secretions; virus is also present in blood, stool, and urine
5. Transmission
   a. Airborne or direct contact with infectious droplets
   b. Indirectly via articles freshly contaminated with nasopharyngeal secretions, feces, or urine
   c. Transplacental
B. Assessment (Fig. 47-3)
   1. Low-grade fever
   2. Malaise
   3. Pinkish-red maculopapular rash that begins on the face and spreads to the entire body within 1 to 3 days

4. Petechial red, pinpoint spots may occur on the soft palate.
C. Interventions
   1. Provide supportive treatment.
   2. Isolate the infected child from pregnant women.

IV. MUMPS
A. Description
   1. Agent: paramyxovirus
   2. Incubation period: 14 to 21 days
   3. Communicable period: Immediately before and after parotid gland swelling begins
   4. Source: Saliva of infected person and possibly urine
   5. Transmission: Direct contact or droplet spread from an infected person
B. Assessment
   1. Fever
   2. Headache and malaise
   3. Anorexia
   4. Jaw or ear pain aggravated by chewing, followed by parotid glandular swelling
   5. Orchitis may occur
C. Interventions
   1. Institute droplet precautions.
   2. Provide bed rest until the parotid gland swelling subsides.
   3. Avoid foods that require chewing.
   4. Apply hot or cold compresses as prescribed to the neck.
   5. Apply warmth and local support with tight-fitting underpants to relieve orchitis.

V. CHICKENPOX (VARICELLA)
A. Description
   1. Agent: Varicella-zoster virus (VZV)
   2. Incubation period: 13 to 17 days
   3. Communicable period: 1 to 2 days before the onset of the rash to 6 days after the first crop of vesicles, when crusts have formed
   4. Source: Respiratory tract secretions of infected person; skin lesions
   5. Transmission: Direct contact, droplet (airborne) spread, and contaminated objects
B. Assessment (Fig. 47-4)
   1. Slight fever, malaise, and anorexia are followed by a macular rash that first appears on the trunk and scalp and moves to the face and extremities.
   2. Lesions become pustules, begin to dry, and develop a crust.
   3. Lesions may appear on the mucous membranes of the mouth, the genital area, and the rectal area.
C. Interventions
   1. In the hospital setting, ensure strict isolation (contact and droplet precautions).

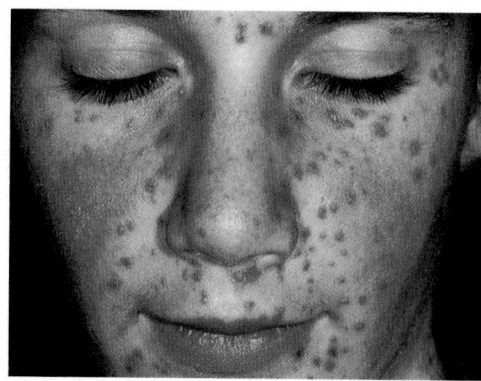

FIG. 47-4 Chickenpox (varicella). (From Hockenberry, M., & Wilson, D. [2007]. *Wong's nursing care of infants and children* [8th ed.]. St. Louis: Mosby.)

2. In the home setting, isolate the infected child until the vesicles have dried; isolate high-risk children from the infected child.

3. Supportive care

VI. PERTUSSIS (WHOOPING COUGH)

A. Description
1. Agent: *Bordetella pertussis*
2. Incubation period: 5 to 21 days (usually 10 days)
3. Communicable period: Greatest during the catarrhal stage (when discharge from respiratory secretions occurs)
4. Source: Discharge from the respiratory tract of the infected person
5. Transmission: Direct contact or droplet spread from infected person; indirect contact with freshly contaminated articles

B. Assessment
1. Symptoms of respiratory infection followed by increased severity of cough, with a loud whooping inspiration
2. May experience cyanosis, respiratory distress, and tongue protrusion
3. Listlessness, irritability, anorexia

C. Interventions
1. Isolate child during the catarrhal stage; if the child is hospitalized, institute droplet precautions.
2. Administer antimicrobial therapy as prescribed.
3. Administer pertussis immune globulin as prescribed.
4. Reduce environmental factors that cause coughing spasms, such as dust, smoke, and sudden changes in temperature.
5. Ensure adequate hydration and nutrition.
6. Provide suction and humidified oxygen if needed.
7. Monitor cardiopulmonary status (via monitor as prescribed) and pulse oximetry.
8. Infants do not receive maternal immunity to pertussis.

VII. DIPHTHERIA

A. Description
1. Agent: *Corynebacterium diphtheriae*
2. Incubation period: 2 to 5 days
3. Communicable period: Variable, until virulent bacilli are no longer present (three negative cultures of discharge from the nose and nasopharynx, skin, and other lesions); usually 2 weeks but can be as long as 4 weeks
4. Source: Discharge from the mucous membrane of the nose and nasopharynx, skin, and other lesions of the infected person
5. Transmission: Direct contact with infected person, carrier, or contaminated articles

B. Assessment
1. Low-grade fever, malaise, sore throat
2. Foul-smelling, mucopurulent nasal discharge
3. Dense pseudomembrane formation of the throat that may interfere with eating, drinking, and breathing
4. Lymphadenitis, neck edema, "bull neck"

C. Interventions
1. Ensure strict isolation for the hospitalized child.
2. Administer diphtheria antitoxin as prescribed (after a skin or conjunctival test to rule out sensitivity to horse serum).
3. Provide bed rest.
4. Administer antibiotics as prescribed.
5. Provide suction and humidified oxygen as needed.
6. Provide tracheostomy care if a tracheostomy is necessary.

VIII. POLIOMYELITIS

A. Description
1. Agent: Enteroviruses
2. Incubation period: 7 to 14 days
3. Communicable period: Unknown; the virus is present in the throat and feces shortly after infection and persists for about 1 week in the throat and 4 to 6 weeks in the feces
4. Source: Oropharyngeal secretions and feces of the infected person
5. Transmission: Direct contact with infected person; fecal-oral and oropharyngeal routes

B. Assessment
1. Fever, malaise, anorexia, nausea, headache, sore throat
2. Abdominal pain followed by soreness and stiffness of the trunk, neck, and limbs that may progress to central nervous system paralysis

C. Interventions
1. Enteric precautions
2. Supportive treatment
3. Bed rest

4. Monitoring for respiratory paralysis
5. Physical therapy

IX. SCARLET FEVER

A. Description
   1. Agent: group A beta-hemolytic streptococci
   2. Incubation period: 1 to 7 days
   3. Communicable period: During the incubation period and clinical illness, about 10 days; during the first 2 weeks of the carrier stage, although may persist for months
   4. Source: nasopharyngeal secretions of infected person and carriers
   5. Transmission: Direct contact with infected person or droplet spread; indirectly by contact with contaminated articles, ingestion of contaminated milk, or other foods

B. Assessment (Fig. 47-5)
   1. Abrupt high fever, flushed cheeks, vomiting, headache, enlarged lymph nodes in the neck, malaise, and abdominal pain
   2. Red, fine sandpaper-like rash develops in the axilla, groin, and neck that spreads to cover the entire body, except the face
   3. The rash blanches with pressure (Schultz-Charlton reaction), except in areas of deep creases and folds of the joints (Pastia's sign).
   4. Desquamation, sheet-like sloughing of the skin on palms and soles, appears by weeks 1 to 3.
   5. The tongue is initially coated with a white, furry covering with red projecting papillae (white strawberry tongue); by the third to fifth day, the white coat sloughs off, leaving a red swollen tongue (red strawberry tongue).
   6. Tonsils are reddened, edematous, and covered with exudate.
   7. Pharynx is edematous and beefy red.

C. Interventions
   1. Institute respiratory precautions until 24 hours after the initiation of antibiotic therapy.
   2. Provide supportive therapy.
   3. Provide bed rest.
   4. Encourage fluid intake

X. ERYTHEMA INFECTIOSUM (FIFTH DISEASE)

A. Description
   1. Agent: Human parvovirus B19
   2. Incubation period: 4 to 14 days; may be as long as 20 days
   3. Communicable period: Uncertain but before the onset of symptoms in most children
   4. Source: Infected person
   5. Transmission: Unknown; possibly respiratory secretions and blood

B. Assessment
   1. Prior to rash, asymptomatic or mild fever, malaise, headache, runny nose

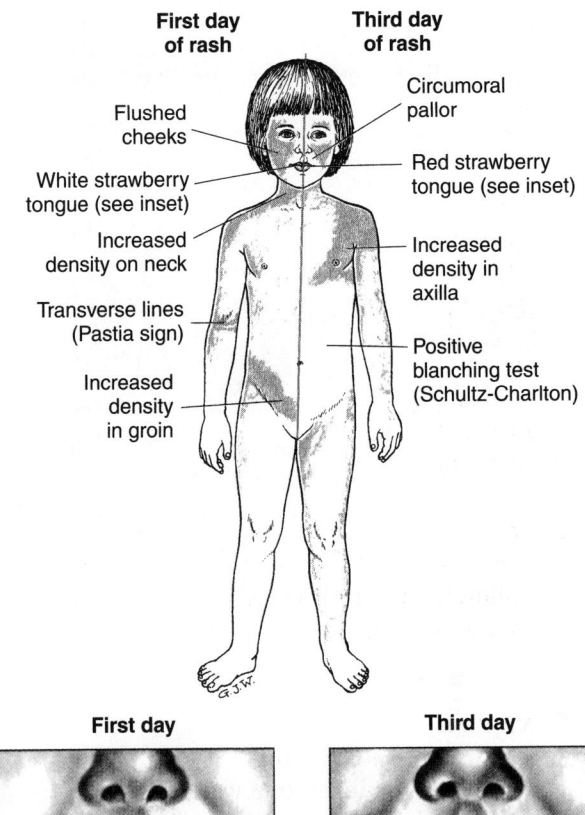

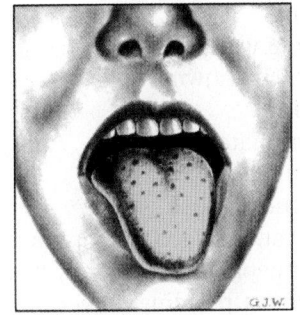

White strawberry tongue

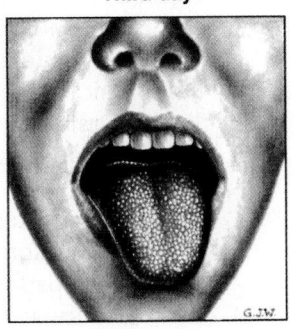

Red strawberry tongue

FIG. 47-5 Scarlet fever. (From Hockenberry, M., & Wilson, D. [2007]. *Wong's nursing care of infants and children* [8th ed.]. St. Louis: Mosby.)

2. Stages of the rash
   a. Erythema of the face (slapped-cheek appearance) develops and disappears by 1 to 4 days (Fig. 47-6).
   b. About 1 day after the rash appears on the face, maculopapular red spots appear, symmetrically distributed on the extremities; rash progresses from proximal to distal surfaces and may last a week or more.
   c. The rash subsides but may reappear if the skin becomes irritated by the sun, heat, cold, exercise, or friction.

C. Interventions
   1. Child is not usually hospitalized.
   2. Pregnant women should avoid the infected individual.
   3. Provide supportive care.

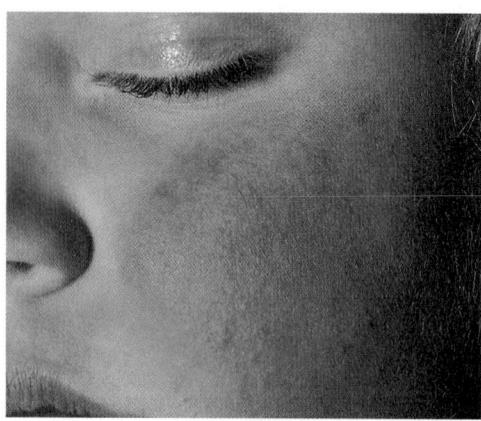

FIG. 47-6 Erythema infectiosum [fifth disease]: Slapped-face appearance. (From Hockenberry, M., & Wilson, D. [2007]. *Wong's nursing care of infants and children* [8th ed.]. St. Louis: Mosby.)

4. Administer antipyretics, analgesics, and anti-inflammatory medications as prescribed.

XI. INFECTIOUS MONONUCLEOSIS
A. Description
1. Agent: Epstein-Barr virus
2. Incubation period: 4 to 6 weeks
3. Communicable period: Unknown
4. Source: Oral secretions
5. Transmission: Direct intimate contact
B. Assessment
1. Fever, malaise, headache, fatigue, nausea, abdominal pain, sore throat, enlarged red tonsils
2. Lymphadenopathy and hepatosplenomegaly
3. Discrete macular rash most prominent over the trunk may occur.
C. Interventions
1. Provide supportive care.
2. Monitor for signs of splenic rupture, which include abdominal pain, left upper quadrant pain, and left shoulder pain.

XII. ROCKY MOUNTAIN SPOTTED FEVER
A. Description
1. Agent: *Rickettsia rickettsii*
2. Incubation period: 2 to 14 days
3. Source: Tick from a mammal, most often from wild rodents and dogs
4. Transmission: Bite of infected tick
B. Assessment
1. Fever, malaise, anorexia, vomiting, headache, myalgia
2. Maculopapular or petechial rash primarily on the extremities (ankles and wrists) but may spread to other areas, characteristically on the palms and soles
C. Interventions
1. Provide vigorous supportive care.
2. Administer antibiotics as prescribed.

BOX 47-1
Protection From Tick Bites

Wear long-sleeved shirts, long pants tucked into long socks, and a hat when walking in tick-infested areas.
Wear light-colored clothing to make ticks more visible.
Avoid walking in tall grass and shrubs; follow paths.
Apply insect repellents containing diethyltoluamide (DEET) and permethrin before possible exposure (use with caution in infants and small children).
Keep yards trimmed and free of brush.
Apply tick repellent to dogs.
Check children for the presence of ticks after being in high-risk or tick-infested areas.
Save the tick for later identification if it is removed from the body.

3. Teach the child and parents about protection from tick bites (Box 47-1)

XIII. ENTEROBIASIS (PINWORM)
A. Description
1. Agent: *Enterobius vermicularis*
2. Source: Common pinworm
   a. The nematode is universally present in temperate climate zones.
   b. Eggs are ingested or inhaled (transferred from the hands to the mouth); the worms infect the large intestine, females then mate, deposit eggs in the perianal area, and migrate out through the anus.
3. Transmission
   a. Occurs most frequently in crowded conditions (classrooms, day care centers)
   b. Ingestion or inhalation of eggs
   c. Hands to mouth or fecal-oral route
   d. Contaminated items (pinworm eggs remain viable for several days)
B. Assessment: Intense perianal itching, irritability, restlessness, poor sleep, bed-wetting, distractibility, short attention span; in girls, the worm may migrate to the vagina and urethra and cause infection.
C. Interventions
1. Identify the worms.
   a. Use a flashlight to inspect the anal area 2 to 3 hours after the child is asleep.
   b. Tape test: Lightly press transparent sticky tape against the child's perianal skin. The tape is then examined for eggs microscopically; the specimen should be collected in the morning as soon as the child awakens and before a bowel movement or a bath.
2. Use enteric precautions.
3. Administer anthelmintic medications (all household members are treated) as prescribed; course of medication is repeated in 2 weeks following the first course to prevent reinfection.

BOX 47-2
General Contraindications and Precautions to Immunizations

CONTRAINDICATIONS
Anaphylactic reaction to a previously administered vaccine or a component in the vaccine
Live virus vaccines generally not administered to individuals with severely deficient immune system, marked sensitivity to gelatin, or pregnant women

PRECAUTIONS
Moderate or severe acute illness, with or without fever

From Centers for Disease Control and Prevention (CDC), National Immunization Program, Contraindications to Vaccines Chart. (2006). *Guide to contraindications and precautions to commonly used vaccines.* http://www.cdc.gov/nip/recs/contraindications_vacc.htm.

4. Teach home care measures to prevent reinfection.

▲ XIV. IMMUNIZATIONS
  A. Guidelines
    1. In the United States, the recommended age for beginning primary immunizations of infants is at birth.
    2. Children born prematurely should receive the full dose of each vaccine at the appropriate chronological age.
    3. Children who began primary immunizations at the recommended age but fail to receive all the required doses do not need to begin the series again but instead receive only the missed doses.
    4. If there is suspicion that the parent will not bring the child to the pediatrician or health care clinic for follow-up immunizations according to the optimal immunization schedule, any of the recommended vaccines can be administered simultaneously.
  B. General contraindications and precautions (Box 47-2)
  C. Guidelines for administration (Box 47-3)

▲ XV. RECOMMENDED CHILDHOOD AND ADOLESCENT IMMUNIZATIONS (Box 47-4)
  A. Hepatitis B vaccine (HepB)
    1. Protects against hepatitis B
    2. Administered by the intramuscular route
    3. First dose of hepatitis B vaccine (monovalent) should be administered soon after birth and before hospital discharge (the birth dose can be delayed in rare circumstances if the infant's mother tests negative for hepatitis B surface antigen [HBsAg]).
    4. Monovalent HepB or a combination vaccine containing hepatitis B may be used to complete the series.

BOX 47-3
Guidelines for Administration of Vaccines

Follow manufacturer's recommendations for route of administration, storage, and reconstitution of the vaccine.
If refrigeration is necessary, store on a center shelf and not on the door; frequent temperature increases from opening the refrigerator door can alter the vaccine's potency.
A vaccine information statement needs to be given to the parents or individual, and informed consent for administration needs to be obtained.
Check the expiration date on the vaccine bottle.
Parenteral vaccines are given in separate syringes in different injection sites.
Vaccines administered intramuscularly are given in the vastus lateralis muscle (best site) or ventrogluteal muscle (the deltoid can be used for children 36 months and older); the dorsogluteal site (buttocks) is avoided.
Vaccines administered subcutaneously are given into the fatty areas in the lateral upper arms and anterior thighs.
Adequate needle length and gauge are as follows: intramuscular, 1 inch, 23-25 gauge; subcutaneous, ⅝ inch, 25 gauge.
Mild side effects may include fever, soreness, swelling, or redness at the injection site.
A topical anesthetic may be applied to injection site before the injection.
For painful or red injection sites, advise the parent to apply cool compresses for the first 24 hours, and then use warm or cold compresses as long as needed.
An age-appropriate dose of acetaminophen (Tylenol) may be administered every 4 to 6 hours for vaccine-associated discomfort.
Maintain an immunization record—document day, month, year of administration; manufacturer and lot number of vaccine; name, address, title of person administering the vaccine; and site and route of administration.
A Vaccine Adverse Event Report needs to be filed and the health department needs to be notified if an adverse reaction to an immunization occurs.

    5. The second dose is administered at age 1 to 2 months.
    6. The final dose should be given at 24 weeks or older (6 to 18 months).
    7. Contraindications: Severe allergic reaction to previous dose or vaccine component (components include aluminum hydroxide, yeast protein)
    8. Precautions: Infant weighing less than 2000 g—moderate or severe acute illness with or without fever
    9. HBsAg-positive mothers
      a. Infant should receive HepB vaccine and hepatitis B immune globulin (HBIG) within 12 hours of birth.

Birth: Hepatitis B vaccine (HepB)
1 month: HepB
2 months: Inactivated poliovirus vaccine (IPV); diphtheria, tetanus, acellular pertussis (DTaP) vaccine; *Haemophilus influenzae* type b conjugate vaccine (Hib); pneumococcal conjugate vaccine (PCV)
4 months: DTaP, Hib, IPV, PCV
6 months: DTaP, Hib, HepB, IPV, PCV
12-15 months: Hib; measles, mumps, rubella (MMR) vaccine; PCV; hepatitis A, first dose (second dose is given 6 months after the first dose)
12-18 months: Varicella vaccine
15-18 months: DTaP
18-21 months: Hepatitis A, second dose (given 6 months after the first dose)
4-6 years: DTaP, IPV, MMR
11-12 years: MMR (if not administered at 4-6 years); Tdap (diphtheria, tetanus, acellular pertussis adolescent preparation); meningococcal vaccine (MCV4)
9-26 years: Gardasil (quadrivalent human papillomavirus types 6, 11, 16, and 18 recombinant vaccine) series may be recommended; administered as three injections over 6 months—first dose, second dose 2 months after the first dose, and third dose 6 months after the first dose

   b. Infant should be tested for HBsAg and antibody to hepatitis B surface antigen after completion of the HepB series (between 9 to 18 months of age).
   10. Mother whose HBsAg status is unknown
      a. Infant should receive the first dose of hepatitis vaccine series within 12 hours of birth.
      b. Maternal blood should be drawn as soon as possible to determine the mother's HBsAg status.
      c. If the mother's HBsAg test result is positive, the infant should receive HBIG as soon as possible (no later than age 1 week).
B. Diphtheria, tetanus, acellular pertussis (DTaP); tetanus toxoid; reduced diphtheria toxoid and acellular pertussis vaccine (Tdap adolescent preparation)
   1. Protect against diphtheria, tetanus, and pertussis
   2. Administered by the intramuscular route
   3. DTaP is administered at 2, 4, 6, and between 15 and 18 months, and between 4 and 6 years of age.
   4. Fourth dose of DTaP can be given at 12 months of age if 6 months have elapsed since the third dose and the child might not return for follow-up at 12 to 18 months of age.
   5. The fifth (final) dose is administered at age 4 years or older.

   6. The Tdap (adolescent preparation) is recommended at 11 to 12 years of age for those who have completed the recommended childhood DTaP series but have not received a tetanus and diphtheria toxoid (Td) booster dose.
   7. Subsequent routine Td boosters are recommended every 10 years.
   8. Encephalopathy within 7 days of administration of previous dose of DTaP is a complication
   9. Contraindication: Severe allergic reaction to a previous dose or to a vaccine component
C. *Haemophilus influenzae* type b conjugate vaccine (Hib)
   1. Protects against a number of serious infections caused by *H. influenzae* type b, such as bacterial meningitis, epiglottitis, bacterial pneumonia, septic arthritis, and sepsis
   2. Administered by the intramuscular route
   3. Hib is administered at 2, 4, 6, and between 12 and 15 months of age.
   4. Depending on the brand of Hib vaccine used for the first and second doses, a dose at 6 months of age may not be needed.
   5. DTaP–Hib combination products should not be used for primary immunization in infants at 2, 4, or 6 months of age but can be used as boosters following any Hib vaccine.
   6. Contraindications: Severe allergic reaction to a previous dose or vaccine component
D. Influenza vaccine
   1. Vaccine is recommended annually for children from age 6 months with certain risk factors such as asthma, cardiac disease, sickle cell disease, human immunodeficiency virus, diabetes mellitus, and conditions that can compromise respiratory function; health care workers; and others in close contact with those in high-risk groups.
   2. Healthy children age 6 to 23 months are encouraged to receive influenza vaccine because of their increased risk for influenza-related hospitalization.
E. Inactivated poliovirus vaccine (IPV)
   1. IPV protects against polio.
   2. Administered by the subcutaneous route (may also be given by the intramuscular route)
   3. IPV is administered at 2, 4, and 6 to 18 months, and between 4 and 6 years of age.
   4. Contraindications: Severe allergic reaction to a previous dose or vaccine component; components may include formalin, neomycin, streptomycin, polymyxin B
F. Measles, mumps, rubella (MMR) vaccine
   1. MMR protects against measles, mumps, and rubella.
   2. Administered by the subcutaneous route
   3. First dose of MMR is administered between 12 and 15 months of age; the second dose is

recommended at 4 to 6 years of age (the second dose may be administered during any visit as long as at least 4 weeks have elapsed since the first dose).

4. Those who have not received the second dose previously should complete the schedule at the 11- to 12-year-old pediatric or health care clinic visit.

▲ 5. Contraindications: Severe allergic reaction to a previous dose or vaccine component (gelatin, neomycin, sorbitol), pregnancy, known immunodeficiency

G. Varicella vaccine
1. Vaccine protects against chickenpox.
2. Administered by the subcutaneous route
3. Varicella vaccine is administered between 12 and 18 months of age.
4. Susceptible children 13 years of age and older (who have not had chickenpox or have not been previously vaccinated) need two doses given at least 4 weeks apart.
5. Vaccine should be kept frozen and used within 30 minutes of reconstitution to ensure maximum potency.
▲ 6. Contraindications: Severe allergic reaction to a previous dose or vaccine component (gelatin, bovine albumin, neomycin, and others), substantial suppression of cellular immunity, pregnancy.

H. Pneumococcal conjugate vaccine (PCV)
1. Vaccine prevents infection with *Streptococcus pneumoniae*, which may cause meningitis, pneumonia, septicemia, sinusitis, and otitis media.
2. Administered by the intramuscular route
3. Vaccine can be given concurrently with other childhood vaccines at 2, 4, 6, and 12 to 15 months of age (the final dose in the series is to be given at age 12 months or older).
4. Pneumococcal polysaccharide vaccine (PPV) is recommended in addition to pneumococcal conjugate vaccine (PCV) for certain high-risk groups, such as children with chronic illness specifically associated with increased risk of pneumococcal disease or its complications; anatomical or functional asplenia; hemoglobinopathies; nephrotic syndrome; cerebrospinal fluid leaks; and conditions associated with immunosuppression (PPV is given at least 8 weeks after the last dose of PCV).
5. Contraindications: Severe allergic reaction to a previous dose or vaccine component

I. Hepatitis A vaccine
1. Vaccine protects against hepatitis A.
2. Vaccine is recommended for all children at age 1 year (12 to 23 months); the two doses should be administered at least 6 months apart.
3. Administered by the intramuscular route

4. Contraindications: Severe allergic reaction to a previous dose or vaccine component (e.g., aluminum hydroxide, bovine albumin or serum, formalin)

J. Meningococcal vaccine
1. Vaccine protects against Neisseria meningitis.
2. Meningococcal polysaccharide (MPSV4) vaccination is given subcutaneously; meningococcal (MCV4) is given intramuscularly (MPSV4 is used for children age 2 to 10 years and MCV4 is used for older children).
3. MCV4 should be administered to all children at age 11 to 12 years and to unvaccinated adolescents at high school entry (age 15 years); all college freshman living in dormitories should be vaccinated.
4. Safety in pregnancy has not been established.

K. Gardasil (quadrivalent human papillomavirus types 6, 11, 16, and 18 recombinant vaccine)
1. Guards against diseases that are caused by the human papillomavirus (HPV) types 6, 11, 16, and 18, such as cervical cancer, cervical abnormalities that can lead to cervical cancer, and genital warts
2. May be recommended for girls and women ages 9 to 26 years
3. Administered as three injections over 6 months— first dose, second dose 2 months after the first dose, and third dose 6 months after the first dose
4. Can cause pain, swelling, itching, and redness at the injection site, fever, nausea, and dizziness
5. Contraindicated in those with a reaction to a previous injection and in pregnant women

L. Vaccines for adults and selected populations; see Chapter 69 for information about these vaccines

XVI. REACTIONS TO A VACCINE
A. Local reactions
1. Tenderness, erythema, and swelling at the injection site
2. Low-grade fever
3. Behavioral changes such as drowsiness, unusual crying, decreased appetite

B. Minimizing local reactions
1. Select a needle of adequate length to deposit the vaccine deep into the muscle or subcutaneous mass.
2. Inject into the appropriate recommended site.

C. Anaphylactic reactions ▲
1. Goals of treatment are to secure and protect the airway, restore adequate circulation, and prevent further exposure to the antigen.
2. For a mild reaction with no evidence of respiratory distress or cardiovascular compromise, a subcutaneous injection of an antihistamine such as diphenhydramine (Benadryl) and epinephrine (Adrenalin) may be administered.

3. For moderate or severe distress, establish an airway; provide cardiopulmonary resuscitation if the child is not breathing; elevate the head; administer epinephrine, fluids, and vasopressors as prescribed; monitor vital signs; and monitor urine output.

PRACTICE QUESTIONS

1. A nurse provides instructions to the mother of a child with mumps regarding respiratory precautions and the mother asks the nurse about the length of time required for the respiratory precautions. The nurse should make which statement to the mother?
   1. "Droplet precautions are not necessary once the swelling appears."
   2. "Droplet precautions are not necessary before the swelling begins."
   3. "Droplet precautions are indicated during the period of communicability."
   4. "Droplet precautions are indicated for 18 days following the onset of parotid swelling."

2. A mother brings her 6-year-old child to the clinic because the child has developed a rash on the trunk and on the scalp. The mother reports that the child has had a low-grade fever, has not felt like eating, and has been tired. The child is diagnosed with chickenpox. The mother inquires about the communicable period associated with chickenpox and the nurse bases the response on which of the following?
   1. The communicable period is unknown.
   2. The communicable period ranges from 2 weeks or less to 4 weeks.
   3. The communicable period is 10 days before the onset of symptoms to 15 days after the rash appears.
   4. The communicable period is 1 to 2 days before the onset of the rash to 6 days after the first crop of vesicles, when crusts have formed.

3. A nurse provides home care instructions to the parents of a child hospitalized with pertussis. The child is in the convalescent stage and is being prepared for discharge. Which statement by a parent indicates a need for further instructions?
   1. "We need to encourage our child to drink fluids."
   2. "Coughing spells may be triggered by dust or smoke."
   3. "Vomiting may occur when our child has coughing episodes."
   4. "We need to maintain droplet precautions and a quiet environment for at least 2 weeks."

4. A 6-month-old infant receives a diphtheria, tetanus, and acellular pertussis (DTaP) immunization at a well-baby clinic. The mother returns home and calls the clinic to report that the infant has developed swelling and redness at the site of injection. The nurse tells the mother to:
   1. Monitor the infant for a fever.
   2. Bring the infant back to the clinic.
   3. Apply an ice pack to the injection site.
   4. Apply a warm pack to the injection site.

5. A home health nurse visits a child with infectious mononucleosis and provides home care instructions to the parents about the care of the child. The nurse tells the parents to:
   1. Maintain the child on bed rest for 2 weeks.
   2. Maintain respiratory precautions for 1 week.
   3. Notify the physician if the child develops a fever.
   4. Notify the physician if the child develops abdominal pain or left shoulder pain.

6. The mother of a preschooler who attends day care calls a clinic nurse and tells the nurse that the child is constantly scratching the perianal area and that the area is irritated. The nurse suspects the possibility of pinworm infection (enterobiasis). The nurse instructs the mother to obtain a rectal specimen by a tape test and tells the mother to obtain the specimen:
   1. After bathing
   2. After toileting
   3. When the child is put to bed
   4. In the morning, when the child awakens

7. A mother brings her 4-month-old infant to a well-baby clinic for immunizations. The child has already received two doses of Hepatitis B (HepB). A nurse would prepare to administer which of the following immunizations to this infant?
   1. DtaP (diphtheria, tetanus, acellular pertussis), Hib (*Haemophilus influenzae* type b), IPV (inactivated poliovirus vaccine), PCV (pneumococcal vaccine)
   2. Varicella, HepB
   3. MMR (measles, mumps, rubella), Hib, DTaP
   4. DTaP, MMR, IPV

8. A clinic nurse prepares to administer a measles, mumps, rubella (MMR) vaccine to a 5-year-old child. The nurse administers this vaccine
   1. Intramuscularly in the deltoid muscle
   2. Subcutaneously in the gluteal muscle
   3. Subcutaneously in the outer aspect of the upper arm
   4. Intramuscularly in the anterolateral aspect of the thigh

9. A child is scheduled to receive inactivated polio (IPV) vaccine and the nurse preparing to administer the vaccine reviews the child's record. The nurse

questions the administration of IPV if which of the following is documented in the child's record?

1. Recent recovery from a cold
2. A history of frequent respiratory infections
3. A history of an anaphylactic reaction to neomycin
4. A local reaction at the site of injection of a previous IPV vaccine

10. A 12-year-old child is scheduled to receive a series of the hepatitis B vaccine. The child arrives at a clinic for the second dose. Before administering the vaccine, a nurse performs an assessment on the child and asks the child and parent about a history of a severe allergy to:

1. Eggs
2. Penicillin
3. Sulfonamides
4. A previous dose of hepatitis B vaccine or component

11. A child with rubeola (measles) is being admitted to the hospital. In preparing for the admission of the child, a nurse plans to place the child on which precautions?

1. Contact
2. Enteric
3. Airborne
4. Protective

12. Several children have contracted rubeola (measles) in a local school and the school nurse conducts a teaching session for the mothers of the school children. Which statement made by a mother indicates a need for further teaching regarding this communicable disease?

1. "Small blue-white spots with a red base may appear in the mouth."
2. "The rash usually begins on the face and spreads downward toward the feet."
3. "The communicable period ranges from 10 days before the onset of symptoms to 15 days after the rash appears."
4. "Respiratory symptoms such as a profuse runny nose, cough, and fever occur before the development of a rash."

ALTERNATE ITEM FORMAT: MULTIPLE RESPONSE (1)

The clinic nurse is assessing a child who is scheduled to receive a vaccine (immunization). Select all that apply of the following general contraindications associated with receiving a vaccine.

❑ 1. Symptoms of a cold
❑ 2. Previous anaphylactic reaction to the vaccine
❑ 3. Mother reports anaphylaxis to a vaccine component.
❑ 4. Mother reports that the child is having episodes of diarrhea.
❑ 5. Mother reports that the child has not had an appetite and has been fussy.
❑ 6. Mother reports that the child has recently been exposed to an infectious disease.

ALTERNATE ITEM FORMAT: MULTIPLE RESPONSE (2)

A child diagnosed with scarlet fever is being cared for at home. A home health nurse performs an assessment on the child and checks for which clinical manifestations of this disease? Select all that apply.

❑ 1. Pastia's sign
❑ 2. White strawberry tongue
❑ 3. Edematous and beefy-red pharynx
❑ 4. Koplik's spots
❑ 5. Petechial red, pinpoint spots on the soft palate
❑ 6. Small red spots with a bluish white center and a red base located on the buccal mucosa

ALTERNATE ITEM FORMAT: PRIORITIZING (ORDERED RESPONSE)

A nurse is preparing to administer a measles, mumps, rubella (MMR) vaccination to a 1-year-old child. List the steps that the nurse should take when administering this vaccination. (Number 1 is the first step and number 6 is the last step.)

_____ Obtain parental consent.
_____ Select the appropriate site.
_____ Administer the vaccination.
_____ Verify the order for immunization.
_____ Document the lot number of the vaccination.
_____ Provide a vaccination record for parents to keep.

ANSWERS

1. **3**

Rationale: Mumps is transmitted via direct contact with or droplet spread from an infected person. Droplet precautions are indicated during the period of communicability (immediately before and after swelling begins).

Test-Taking Strategy: Use the process of elimination. Options 1 and 2 can be eliminated because they are comparative or alike and not accurate. From the remaining options, select option 3 because it is the umbrella option and addresses communicability. Also, the time frame indicated in option 4 seems rather long. Review the infectious period related to mumps if you had difficulty with this question.

Level of Cognitive Ability: Application
Client Needs: Safe and Effective Care Environment
Integrated Process: Teaching and Learning
Content Area: Child health
Reference: Hockenberry, M., Wilson, D., & Winkelstein, M. (2005). *Wong's essentials of pediatric nursing* (7th ed., p. 441). St. Louis: Mosby.

2. **4**

Rationale: The communicable period for chickenpox is 1 to 2 days before the onset of the rash to 6 days after the first crop of vesicles, when crusts have formed. In roseola, the communicable period is unknown. Option 2 describes diphtheria. Option 3 describes rubella.

Test-Taking Strategy: Use the process of elimination. Option 1 can be eliminated easily. Eliminate options 2 and 3 next because the time frames in these two options seem rather long and are comparative or alike. If you had difficulty with this question, review the communicable period for chickenpox.

Level of Cognitive Ability: Application
Client Needs: Safe and Effective Care Environment
Integrated Process: Teaching and Learning
Content Area: Child health
Reference: Hockenberry, M., Wilson, D., & Winkelstein, M. (2005). *Wong's essentials of pediatric nursing* (7th ed., p. 436). St. Louis: Mosby.

3. **4**

Rationale: Pertussis is transmitted by direct contact or respiratory droplets from coughing. The communicable period occurs primarily during the catarrhal stage. Respiratory precautions are not required during the convalescent phase. Options 1, 2, and 3 are components of home care instructions.

Test-Taking Strategy: Use the process of elimination and note the strategic words *convalescent* in the question. Also, note the words *need for further instructions*. These words indicate a negative event query and ask you to select an option that is an incorrect statement. Options 1 and 3 can be eliminated because they are generally associated with convalescence. Knowing that 2 weeks of respiratory precautions is not required will direct you to option 4. If you had difficulty with this question, review home care instructions for the child with pertussis.

Level of Cognitive Ability: Analysis
Client Needs: Health Promotion and Maintenance
Integrated Process: Teaching and Learning
Content Area: Child health

References: Hockenberry, M., Wilson, D., & Winkelstein, M. (2005). *Wong's essentials of pediatric nursing* (7th ed., p. 443). St. Louis: Mosby.
McKinney, E., James, S., Murray, S., & Ashwill, J. (2005). *Maternal-child nursing* (2nd ed., p. 1035). St. Louis: W.B. Saunders.

4. **3**

Rationale: Occasionally, tenderness, redness, or swelling may occur at the site of the DTaP injection. This can be relieved with ice packs for the first 24 hours, followed by warm or cold compresses if the inflammation persists. Bringing the infant back to the clinic is not necessary. Option 1 may be an appropriate intervention but is not specific to the subject of the question.

Test-Taking Strategy: Use the process of elimination. Option 1 can be eliminated first because it does not relate specifically to the subject of the question. Eliminate option 2 next as an unnecessary intervention. From the remaining options, general principles related to the effects of heat and cold will direct you to option 3. Review interventions following immunizations and injections if you had difficulty with this question.

Level of Cognitive Ability: Application
Client Needs: Health Promotion and Maintenance
Integrated Process: Nursing Process—implementation
Content Area: Child health
Reference: McKinney, E., James, S , Murray, S.,& Ashwill, J. (2005). *Maternal-child nursing* (2nd ed., p. 71). Philadelphia: W.B. Saunders.

5. **4**

Rationale: The parents need to be instructed to notify the physician if abdominal pain, especially in the left upper quadrant, or left shoulder pain occurs because this may indicate splenic rupture. Children with enlarged spleens also are instructed to avoid contact sports until splenomegaly resolves. Bed rest is not necessary, and children usually self-limit their activity. Respiratory precautions are not required, although transmission can occur via direct intimate contact or contact with infected blood. Fever is treated with acetaminophen (Tylenol).

Test-Taking Strategy: Use the process of elimination and knowledge regarding the organs affected in mononucleosis. Options 1 and 2 can be eliminated first because they are unnecessary interventions in this disease. From the remaining options, recalling that splenic rupture is a concern will direct you to option 4. Review the complications associated with mononucleosis if you had difficulty with this question.

Level of Cognitive Ability: Application
Client Needs: Physiological Integrity
Integrated Process: Teaching and Learning
Content Area: Child health
References: Hockenberry, M., Wilson, D., & Winkelstein, M. (2005). *Wong's essentials of pediatric nursing* (7th ed., p. 517). St. Louis: Mosby.
McKinney, E., James, S., Murray, S., & Ashwill, J. (2005). *Maternal-child nursing* (2nd ed., p. 1031). St. Louis: W.B. Saunders.

6. 4

Rationale: Diagnosis of pinworm infection is confirmed by direct visualization of the worms. Parents can view the sleeping child's anus with a flashlight. The worm is white, thin, about ½-inch long, and moves. A simple technique, the tape test, is used to capture worms and eggs. Transparent tape is lightly touched to the anus and then applied to a slide for microscopic examination. The best specimens are obtained as the child awakens, before toileting or bathing.

Test-Taking Strategy: Use the process of elimination. Thinking about the test and the purpose of the test (to obtain a specimen that contains worms and eggs) will direct you to option 4. Review the procedure for this test if you are unfamiliar with it.

Level of Cognitive Ability: Application
Client Needs: Physiological Integrity
Integrated Process: Nursing Process—implementation
Content Area: Child health
Reference: Hockenberry, M., Wilson, D., & Winkelstein, M. (2005). *Wong's essentials of pediatric nursing* (7th ed., pp. 450-451). St. Louis: Mosby.

7. 1

Rationale: Diphtheria, tetanus, acellular pertussis vaccine (DTaP), *Haemophilus influenzae* type b conjugate vaccine (Hib), inactivated poliovirus vaccine (IPV), and pneumococcal vaccine (PCV) are administered at 4 months of age. DTaP is administered at 2, 4, 6, and between 15 and 18 months of age, and between 4 and 6 years of age. Hib is administered at 2, 4, 6, and between 12 and 15 months of age. IPV is administered at 2, 4, and 6 months and between 4 and 6 years of age. PCV is administered at 2, 4, 6, and between 12 and 15 months. The first dose of measles, mumps, rubella vaccine (MMR) is administered between 12 and 15 months of age; the second dose is administered at 4 to 6 years of age (if the second dose was not given by 4 to 6 years of age, it should be given at the next visit). The first dose of hepatitis B vaccine is administered at birth, the second dose is administered at 1 to 2 months, and the third dose is administered between the ages of 6 and 18 months. Varicella-zoster vaccine is administered between 12 and 18 months of age.

Test-Taking Strategy: Knowledge regarding the immunization schedule for infants and children is required to answer this question. Noting the age of the infant in the question will assist in directing you to option 1. Learn the immunization schedule if you are unfamiliar with it.

Level of Cognitive Ability: Application
Client Needs: Health Promotion and Maintenance
Integrated Process: Nursing Process—implementation
Content Area: Child health
References: Centers for Disease Control and Prevention (CDC). (2006). *Childhood and adolescent immunization schedule—United States, 2006*, http://www.cdc.gov/nip; American Academy of Pediatrics, http://www.aap.org; American Academy of Family Physicians, http://www.aafp.org.
McKinney, E., James, S., Murray, S., & Ashwill, J. (2005). *Maternal-child nursing* (2nd ed., p. 70). St. Louis: W.B. Saunders.

8. 3

Rationale: MMR vaccine is administered subcutaneously in the outer aspect of the upper arm. The gluteal muscle is not recommended for injections. It is not administered by the intramuscular route.

Test-Taking Strategy: Use the process of elimination. Recalling that MMR vaccine is administered subcutaneously will assist you in eliminating options 1 and 4. From the remaining options, recalling that the gluteal muscle is not used for injections will assist in directing you to option 3. Review the procedures related to the administration of MMR vaccine if you had difficulty with this question.

Level of Cognitive Ability: Application
Client Needs: Physiological Integrity
Integrated Process: Nursing Process—implementation
Content Area: Child health
References: Hockenberry, M., Wilson, D., & Winkelstein, M. (2005). *Wong's essentials of pediatric nursing* (7th ed., pp. 340, 344-345). St. Louis: Mosby.
McKinney, E., James, S., Murray, S., & Ashwill, J. (2005). *Maternal-child nursing* (2nd ed., p. 69). St. Louis: W.B. Saunders.

9. 3

Rationale: IPV contains neomycin. A history of an anaphylactic reaction to neomycin is considered a contraindication to IPV. The presence of a minor illness such as the common cold is not a contraindication. In addition, a history of frequent respiratory infections is not a contraindication to receiving a vaccine. A local reaction to an immunization is not a contraindication to receiving a vaccine.

Test-Taking Strategy: Use the process of elimination. Recalling that a general contraindication to all immunizations is a severe illness will assist you in eliminating options 1 and 2. From the remaining options, note that option 4 identifies a local reaction. This will direct you to option 3, the systemic reaction, and a potential life-threatening condition. Review the contraindications to receiving immunizations if you had difficulty with this question.

Level of Cognitive Ability: Analysis
Client Needs: Physiological Integrity
Integrated Process: Nursing Process—analysis
Content Area: Child health
Reference: Hockenberry, M., Wilson, D., & Winkelstein, M. (2005). *Wong's essentials of pediatric nursing* (7th ed., pp. 340, 342-343). St. Louis: Mosby.

10. 4

Rationale: A contraindication to receiving the hepatitis B vaccine is a previous anaphylactic reaction to a previous dose of hepatitis B vaccine or to a component of the vaccine. An allergy to eggs, penicillin, and sulfonamides is unrelated to the contraindication to receiving this vaccine.

Test-Taking Strategy: Use the process of elimination and knowledge regarding the contraindications associated with the administration of vaccines. Note the relationship to the words *hepatitis B vaccine* in the question and option 4. Review the contraindications to receiving the hepatitis B vaccine if you had difficulty with this question.

Level of Cognitive Ability: Analysis

Client Needs: Physiological Integrity
Integrated Process: Nursing Process—assessment
Content Area: Child health
Reference: Centers for Disease Control, National Immunization Program, Contraindications to Vaccines Chart. (2006). *Guide to contraindications and precautions to commonly used vaccines.* http://www.cdc.gov/nip/recs/contraindications_vacc.htm.

11. **3**

Rationale: Rubeola is transmitted via airborne particles or direct contact with infectious droplets. Airborne droplet precautions are required, and those in contact with the child should wear masks. The child is placed in a private room with negative air pressure. Doors remain closed. Gowns and gloves are not necessary, but standard precautions are used. Articles that are contaminated should be bagged and labeled. Special enteric precautions and protective isolation are not indicated in rubeola.
Test-Taking Strategy: Use the process of elimination and focus on the communicable disease. Remember that rubeola is transmitted via the airborne route. This will direct you to option 3. Review the route of transmission and therapeutic management of rubeola if you had difficulty with this question.
Level of Cognitive Ability: Application
Client Needs: Safe and Effective Care Environment
Integrated Process: Nursing Process—planning
Content Area: Child health
Reference: Hockenberry, M., Wilson, D., & Winkelstein, M. (2005). *Wong's essentials of pediatric nursing* (7th ed., p. 441). St. Louis: Mosby.

12. **3**

Rationale: The communicable period for rubeola ranges from 4 days before to 5 days after the rash appears, mainly during the prodromal stage. Options 1, 2, and 4 are accurate descriptions of rubeola. The small blue-white spots found in this communicable disease are called Koplik's spots. Option 3, the incorrect option, describes the incubation period for rubella, not rubeola.
Test-Taking Strategy: Focus on the communicable disease and note the strategic words *need for further teaching* in the question. These words indicate a negative event query and ask you to select an option that is an incorrect statement. Recall that the communicable period for rubeola ranges from 4 days before to 5 days after the rash appears. This will direct you to option 3. Review the clinical manifestations associated with rubeola if you had difficulty with this question.
Level of Cognitive Ability: Analysis
Client Needs: Safe and Effective Care Environment
Integrated Process: Teaching and Learning
Content Area: Child health
Reference: Hockenberry, M., Wilson, D., & Winkelstein, M. (2005). *Wong's essentials of pediatric nursing* (7th ed., p. 441). St. Louis: Mosby.

ALTERNATE ITEM FORMAT:
MULTIPLE RESPONSE (1)

Answer: 2, 3
Rationale: The general contraindications for vaccines include a previous anaphylactic reaction to a vaccine or a component

of a vaccine or the presence of a severe illness. The other items listed are not contraindications to receiving a vaccine.
Test-Taking Strategy: Focus on the subject, contraindications associated with receiving a vaccine. Remember that previous anaphylactic reactions and a severe illness are the general contraindications to all vaccines. Review these contraindications if you had difficulty with this question.
Level of Cognitive Ability: Analysis
Client Needs: Physiological Integrity
Integrated Process: Nursing Process—assessment
Content Area: Child health
Reference: Centers for Disease Control, National Immunization Program, Contraindications to Vaccines Chart. (2006). *Guide to contraindications and precautions to commonly used vaccines.* http://www.cdc.gov/nip/recs/contraindications_vacc.htm.

ALTERNATE ITEM FORMAT:
MULTIPLE RESPONSE (2)

Answer: 1, 2, 3
Rationale: Pastia's sign describes a rash seen in scarlet fever that will blanch with pressure except in areas of deep creases and the folds of joints. The tongue initially is coated with a white furry covering, with red projecting papillae (white strawberry tongue). By the fourth to fifth day, the white strawberry tongue sloughs off, leaving a red swollen tongue (strawberry tongue). The pharynx is edematous and beefy red. Koplik's spots are associated with rubeola (measles). These are small red spots with a bluish white center and a red base located on the buccal mucosa. Petechial red, pinpoint spots occurring on the soft palate are characteristic of rubella (German measles).
Test-Taking Strategy: Focus on the child's diagnosis. Eliminate options 4 and 5 because they are comparative or alike in that Koplik's spots are small red spots with a bluish white center and a red base located on the buccal mucosa. Next, recall that petechial red, pinpoint spots on the soft palate are characteristic of rubella (German measles). Review the clinical manifestations associated with scarlet fever if you had difficulty with this question.
Level of Cognitive Ability: Analysis
Client Needs: Physiological Integrity
Integrated Process: Nursing Process—assessment
Content Area: Child health
References: Hockenberry, M., Wilson, D., & Winkelstein, M. (2005). *Wong's essentials of pediatric nursing* (7th ed., pp. 444-445). St. Louis: Mosby.
McKinney, E., James, S., Murray, S., & Ashwill, J. (2005). *Maternal-child nursing* (2nd ed., p. 1035). St. Louis: W.B. Saunders.

ALTERNATE ITEM FORMAT:
PRIORITIZING (ORDERED RESPONSE)

Answer: 2, 4, 5, 1, 3, 6
Rationale: The nurse should first verify the order and then obtain parental consent. The nurse should also question the parents about the presence of any allergies in the child. The nurse should next prepare the injection and document the lot number (located on the medication vial) of the vaccination. The nurse then selects an appropriate site and administers the

vaccination. The nurse then documents that the vaccination has been administered and provides an updated immunization record to the parents.

Test-Taking Strategy: Focus on the information in the question and note that it requires you to list, in order of priority, the steps for administering an immunization. Visualize this procedure to answer correctly. Review the procedure for the administration of immunizations if you had difficulty with this question.

Level of Cognitive Ability: Application
Client Needs: Health Promotion and Maintenance
Integrated Process: Nursing Process—implementation
Content Area: Delegating/Prioritizing
Reference: Hockenberry, M., & Wilson, D. (2007). *Wong's nursing care of infants and children* (8th ed., p. 548). St. Louis: Mosby.

REFERENCES

Centers for Disease Control and Prevention (CDC). (2006). *Childhood and adolescent immunization schedule—United States, 2006,* http://www.cdc.gov/nip; American Academy of Pediatrics, http://www.aap.org; American Academy of Family Physicians, http://www.aafp.org.

Centers for Disease Control and Prevention (CDC), National Immunization Program, Contraindications to Vaccines Chart. (2006). *Guide to contraindications and precautions to commonly used vaccines.* http://www.cdc.gov/nip/recs/contraindications_vacc.htm.

Centers for Disease Control and Prevention. (2006). *Recommended childhood and adolescent immunization schedule.* http://www.cdc.gov/nip.

Hockenberry, M., & Wilson, D. (2007). *Wong's nursing care of infants and children* (8th ed.). St. Louis: Mosby.

Hockenberry, M., Wilson, D., & Winkelstein, M. (2005). *Wong's essentials of pediatric nursing* (7th ed.). St. Louis: Mosby.

McKinney, E., James, S., Murray, S., & Ashwill, J. (2005). *Maternal-child nursing* (2nd ed.). St. Louis: W.B. Saunders.

National Council of State Boards of Nursing (Eds.). (2007). *2007 NCLEX-RN® detailed test plan.* Chicago: Author.

Pediatric Medication Administration and Calculations

I. ORAL MEDICATIONS

A. Most oral pediatric medications are in liquid or suspension form because children usually are not able to swallow a tablet.

B. Solutions may be measured by using an oral syringe or other acceptable measurement or administration device (Fig. 48-1).

C. Medications in suspension settle to the bottom of the bottle between uses, and thorough mixing is required before pouring the medication.

D. Suspensions must be administered immediately after measurement to prevent settling and administration of an incomplete dose.

E. Administer oral medications with the child sitting in an upright position and with the head elevated to prevent aspiration if the child cries or resists.

F. Never pinch the infant or child's nostrils when administering medication.

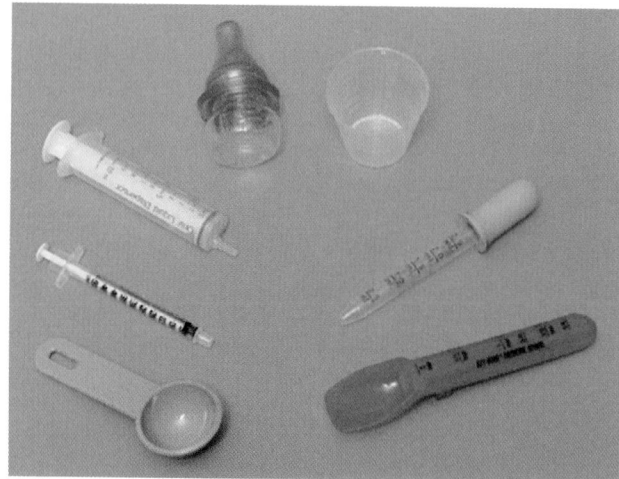

FIG. 48-1 Acceptable devices for measuring and administering oral medication to children (clockwise from bottom left): measuring spoon, plastic syringes, calibrated nipple, plastic medicine cup, calibrated dropper, hollow-handled medicine spoon. (From Hockenberry, M., Wilson, D., & Winkelstein, M. [2005]. *Wong's essentials of pediatric nursing.* (7th ed.) St. Louis: Mosby.)

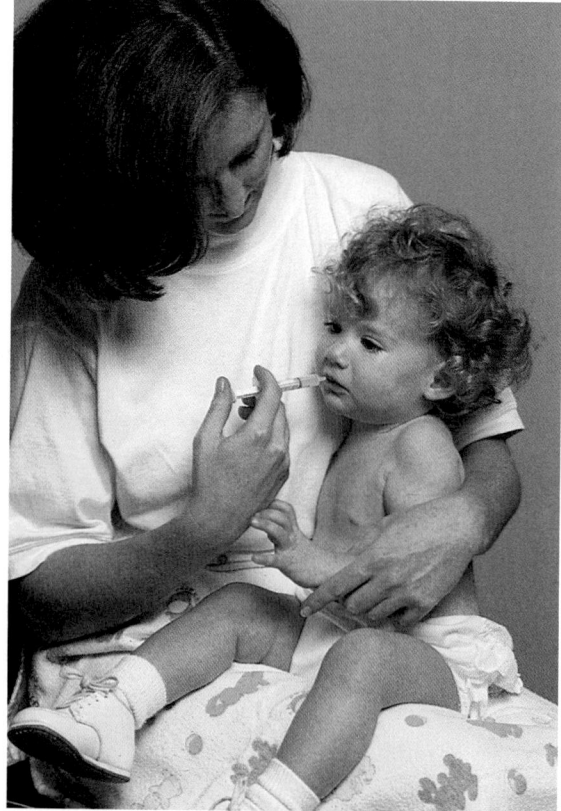

FIG. 48-2 Nurse partially restrains child for easy and comfortable administration of oral medication. (From Hockenberry, M., Wilson, D., & Winkelstein, M. [2005]. *Wong's essentials of pediatric nursing.* (7th ed.) St. Louis: Mosby.)

Consult with parents, because parents are often good sources of information about successful methods for administering medications to their children.

Try to avoid putting medications in essential foods, such as milk, cereal, baby food, bottles, or orange juice, because the child may refuse to accept that same food in the future.

The taste of the medication may or may not need to be disguised.

Sugarless items should be used to disguise the taste of medications given to children who have diabetes mellitus or are following a ketogenic diet.

A sip of cold fruit juice, ice chips, a frozen fruit bar, or a mint-flavored substance before and after the administration of an unpalatable medicine may effectively dull its taste.

Jam and syrup are ideal for suspending medications that do not dissolve easily in water.

Because fruit syrups are usually acidic, they should not be used for medications that react in an acid medium, such as sodium bicarbonate, soluble barbiturates, and penicillin.

Elixirs have an alcohol base that, when undiluted, may cause the child to refuse them or to cough and choke; small amounts of water added to elixirs may help.

Nursing time can be saved by recording the most successful method of administering medications and pertinent nursing orders on the child's care plan; this notation also saves the child frustration, fear, and anxiety.

From McKenry, L., and Salerno, E. (2003). *Mosby's pharmacology in nursing.* St. Louis: Mosby.

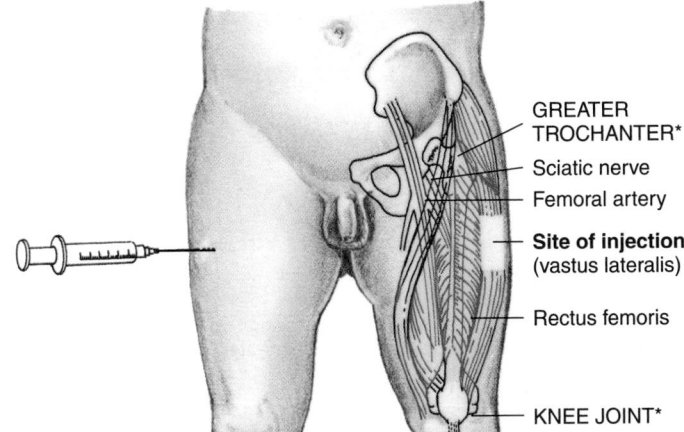

FIG. 48-3 Intramuscular injection site—vastus lateralis. Landmarks are indicated by asterisks. (From Hockenberry, M., Wilson, D., & Winkelstein, M. [2005]. *Wong's essentials of pediatric nursing.* (7th ed.) St. Louis: Mosby.)

1. Medications most often given via the subcutaneous route are insulin and most immunizations.
2. Any site with sufficient subcutaneous tissue may be used for subcutaneous injections; common sites include the central third of the lateral aspect of the upper arm, the abdomen, and the center third of the anterior thigh.
3. The safe use of all injection sites is based on normal muscle development and the size of the child; the preferred site for intramuscular injections in infants is the vastus lateralis (Fig. 48-3).
4. Usually not more than 0.5 mL (infant) to 2 mL (child) is injected per intramuscular or subcutaneous site, and the site of injection is rotated if frequent injections are necessary.
5. The usual needle length and gauge for pediatric clients are 1/2 to 1 inch and 22 to 25 gauge.
6. Needle length also can be estimated by grasping the muscle for injection between the thumb and forefinger; half the resulting distance between the thumb and forefinger would be the needle length.
7. Pediatric dosages for subcutaneous and intramuscular administration are calculated to the nearest hundredth and measured by using a tuberculin syringe.
8. For the toddler or preschooler, place an adhesive bandage or decorated Band-Aid over the puncture site.
B. Intravenously administered medications
1. Intravenous (IV) medications are diluted for administration.
2. When an infant or child is receiving an IV medication, the IV site needs to be assessed for signs of inflammation and infiltration or extravasation immediately before, during, and after completion of each medication (Box 48-2).

G. Draw the required dose of an unpleasant medication into a small syringe, and place the syringe into the side and toward the back of the infant's mouth; administer the medication slowly, allowing the infant to swallow.
H. Place the small child sideways on the lap; the child's closest arm should be placed under the adult's arm and behind the adult's back; cradle the child's head and hold the child's hand, and administer the medication slowly with a plastic spoon, small plastic cup, or syringe (Fig. 48-2).
I. If a tablet or capsule has been administered, check the child's mouth to ensure that it has been swallowed; if swallowing is a problem, some tablets can be crushed and given in small amounts of puréed food or flavored syrup (enteric-coated tablets, timed-release tablets, and capsules should not be crushed).
J. Follow generally accepted medication administration guidelines for children (Box 48-1).

II. PARENTERAL MEDICATIONS
A. Subcutaneously and intramuscularly administered medications

INFLAMMATION
Redness, heat, swelling, and tenderness

INFILTRATION OR EXTRAVASATION
Erythema, pain, edema, blanching, streaking on the skin
along the vein, darkened area at insertion site

Note: If inflammation, infiltration, or extravasation occurs, the intravenous line is discontinued, the extremity is elevated and the IV line is restarted at a new site; the physician may need to be notified, depending
on agency protocol.

a. Infiltration is defined as inadvertent administration of a nonvesicant solution or medication into surrounding tissue.
b. Extravasation is defined as inadvertent administration of a vesicant solution or medication into surrounding tissue.
3. Intravenous medication may be administered
continuously by adding the medication to an IV
solution bag and infusing it through a primary
infusion line.
4. Intravenous medications may be administered
intermittently; several doses may be administered in a 24-hour period.
5. Medications for IV administration are diluted
according to the directions accompanying the
medication and according to the physician's orders and agency procedures.
6. Infusion time for IV medications is determined
based on the directions accompanying the medication, the physician's orders, and agency procedures.
7. Determine agency procedures related to the volume of flush for peripheral IV lines and for central lines.
8. The flush volume (3 to 20 mL) must be included
in the child's intake; the flush is usually administered before administering an IV medication
and after the IV medication is completed and is
infused at the same rate as the medication.
C. Intermittent IV medication administration
1. Children receiving IV medications intermittently
may or may not have a primary IV solution
infusing.
2. If a primary IV solution is infusing, the medication may be administered by IV piggyback via a
secondary line.
3. If a primary IV solution does not exist, an indwelling infusion catheter is used for medication administration.
4. All intermittent medication administrations are
preceded and followed by a flush to ensure that
the medication has cleared the IV tubing and
that the total dose has been administered.

5. Electronic controllers and pumps are used to
regulate and administer IV fluids and intermittent IV medications.
D. Special IV administration sets
1. Special IV administration sets, referred to by
their trade names (Buretrol, Soluset, Volutrol),
may be used for medication preparation and
administration.
2. These special sets are all microdrip sets calibrated to deliver 60 gtt/mL.
3. The total capacity of these special IV administration sets is between 100 and 150 mL, calibrated
in 1-mL increments so that exact measurements
of small volumes are possible.
4. The medication is mixed with the appropriate
amount of diluent, added to the special IV administration set, and allowed to infuse at the
prescribed rate.
5. Label the special IV administration set so as to
identify the medication and fluid dosage
added.
6. Attach a label that states "medication infusing"
during the medication infusion time.
7. Attach a label that states "flush infusing" during
the flush infusion time.
E. Retrograde IV injection
1. The medication is mixed with the appropriate
amount of diluent in a syringe.
2. The IV tubing is clamped close to the child, the
medication is injected through the port in the
direction of the burette, the tubing is un-
clamped, the prescribed rate is set, and the
medication is allowed to infuse over the prescribed time.
F. Syringe pump for IV medication administration
1. A syringe containing the medication is fitted into
a pump that is connected to the IV tubing
through a Y connector.
2. The medication is administered over the prescribed time.

III. CALCULATION OF MEDICATION DOSAGE
BY BODY WEIGHT
A. Conversion of body weight (Box 48-3)
B. Calculation of daily dosages
1. Abbreviations (Box 48-4)
2. Dosages are expressed in terms of milligrams per
kilogram per day, milligrams per pound per day,
or milligrams per kilogram per dose.
3. The total daily dosage usually is administered in
divided (more than one) doses per day.
4. Express the child's body weight in kilograms
or pounds to correlate with the dosage specifi-
cations.
5. Calculate the total daily dosage.
6. Divide the total daily dosage by the number of
doses to be administered in 1 day.

MEASUREMENTS
1 lb = 16 oz
0.5 lb = 8 oz
1 kg = 2.2 lb

POUNDS TO KILOGRAMS
1 kg = 2.2 lb
When converting from pounds to kilograms, divide by 2.2. Kilograms are expressed to the nearest tenth.

KILOGRAMS TO POUNDS
1 kg = 2.2 lb
When converting from kilograms to pounds, multiply by 2.2. Pounds are expressed to the nearest tenth.

BSA, body surface area
g, gram(s)
gr, grain(s)
kg, kilogram(s)
lb, pound(s)
m^2, square meters
mcg, microgram(s)
mg, milligram(s)
mL, milliliter(s)
SA, surface area

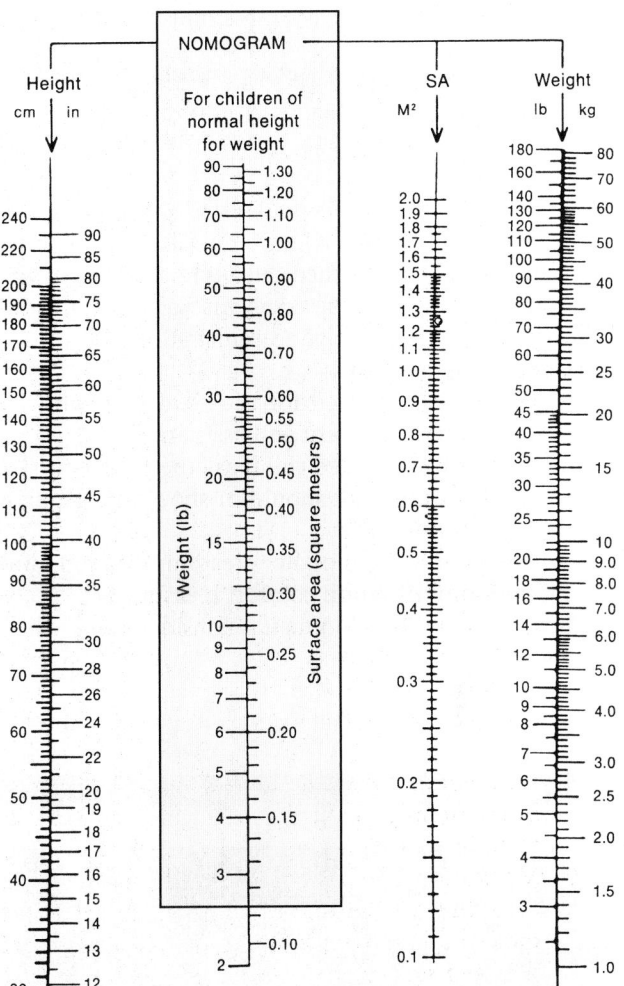

FIG. 48-4 West nomogram for estimation of surface areas in infants and children. First, find height; next, find weight; finally, draw a straight line connecting the height and weight. The body surface area (in square meters, m^2) is indicated where a straight line connecting the height and weight intersects the surface area (SA) column or, if patient is approximately of normal proportion, from weight alone (yellow area). (From Hockenberry, M., Wilson, D., & Winkelstein, M. [2005]. *Wong's essentials of pediatric nursing.* (7th ed.) St. Louis: Mosby.)

IV. CALCULATION OF BODY SURFACE AREA

A. The body surface area (BSA) is determined by comparing body weight and height with averages or norms on a graph called a nomogram.

B. Not all children are the same size at the same age; therefore, the nomogram is used to determine the BSA of a child.

C. Look at the nomogram (Fig. 48-4), and note that the height is on the left-hand side of the chart and the weight is on the right-hand side of the chart.

D. Place a ruler across the chart.

E. Line up the left side of the ruler on the height and the right side of the ruler on the weight; read the BSA at the point where the straight edge of the ruler intersects the surface area (SA) column.

F. The estimated surface area is given in square meters (m^2).

G. Box 48-5 gives a sample practice question using the nomogram.

V. CALCULATION BASED ON BODY SURFACE AREA

A. When dosage recommendations for children specify milligrams, micrograms, or units per square meter,

Example: Use the nomogram (see Fig. 48-4) and calculate the body surface area for a child whose height is 58 inches and weight is 12 kg.
Look at the nomogram chart and note that the height is on the left-hand side of the chart and the weight is on the right-hand side.
Place a ruler on the chart and line up the left side of the ruler on the height and the right side of the ruler on the weight; read the body surface area at the point where the straight edge of the ruler intersects the surface area (SA) column.
The estimated surface area is given in squares meters.
Answer: 0.66 m^2

calculating the dosage is simple multiplication (Box 48-6).

B. When dosages are specified only for adults, a formula is used to calculate a child's dosage from the adult dosage (Box 48-7).

▲ VI. DEVELOPMENTAL CONSIDERATIONS FOR ADMINISTERING MEDICATIONS

A. When administering medications to children, **developmental age** must be taken into consideration to ensure safe and effective administration.

B. General interventions
1. Always be prepared for the procedure with all necessary equipment and assistance.
2. For the hospitalized child, ask the parent and/or child if the parent should or should not remain for the procedure.
3. Determine appropriate preadministration and postadministration comfort measures.

C. Box 48-8 lists developmental considerations when giving medications.

BOX 48-6

Calculating Medication Dosage

When dosage recommendations for children specify milligrams, micrograms, or units per square meter, calculating the dosage is simple multiplication.

Example: The dosage recommendation is 4 mg/m². The child has a body surface area of 1.1 m². What is the dosage to be administered?

Answer: 1.1 × 4 mg = 4.4 mg

BOX 48-7

Calculating a Child's Dosage From the Adult Dosage

When dosages are specified only for adults, a formula is used to calculate a child's dosage from the adult dosage. The adult dosage is based on a standardized body surface area of 1.73 m².

Example: A physician has prescribed an antibiotic for a child. The average adult dose is 250 mg. The child has a body surface area (BSA) of 0.41 m². What is the dose for the child?

Answer: 59.24 mg

Formula:

$$\frac{\text{BSA of child (m}^2)}{1.73 \text{ m}^2} \times \text{adult dose} = \text{child's dose}$$

$$\frac{0.41}{1.73} \times 250 \text{ mg} = 59.24 \text{ mg}$$

BOX 48-8

Developmental Considerations for Administering Medications

INFANTS

Perform the procedure quickly; then offer comfort measures, such as parent holding, rocking, cuddling, and soothing.

Allow self-comforting measures, such as the use of a pacifier, placing fingers in the mouth, and self-movement.

TODDLERS

Offer a brief, concrete explanation of the procedure, and then perform it.

Accept aggressive behavior, within reasonable limits, as a healthy response, and provide outlets for the toddler.

Provide comfort measures immediately after the procedure, such as touch, holding, providing a favorite toy.

PRESCHOOLERS

Offer a brief, concrete explanation of the procedure and then perform it.

Provide comfort measures after the procedure, such as touch, holding, or providing a favorite toy.

Accept aggressive behavior, within reasonable limits, as a healthy response, and provide outlets for the child.

Make use of magical thinking; use "ointments" or "special medicines" to make discomfort go away.

The role of the parents is very important for comfort and understanding.

SCHOOL-AGE CHILDREN

Explain the procedure, allowing for some control over the body and situation.

Explore feelings and concepts through therapeutic play, drawings of own body and self in the hospital, and the use of books and realistic hospital equipment.

Set appropriate behavior limits, such as it is all right to cry or scream, but not to bite.

Provide activities for releasing aggression and anger.

Use the opportunity to teach about the relationship between the medication and body function and structure—for example, what the child's disorder is and how medication helps the disorder.

ADOLESCENTS

Explain the procedure, allowing for some control over body and situation.

Explore concepts of self, hospitalization, and illness, and correct any misconceptions.

Encourage self-expression, individuality, and self-care needs.

Encourage participation in the procedure.

Modified from McKenry, L., and Salerno, E. (2003). *Mosby's pharmacology in nursing.* St. Louis: Mosby.

PRACTICE QUESTIONS

1. A physician's order reads "ampicillin sodium 125 mg intravenous (IV) every 6 hours." The medication label reads "1 g and reconstitute with 7.4 mL of bacteriostatic water." A nurse prepares to draw up how many milliliters to administer one dose?
   1. 0.54 mL
   2. 0.92 mL
   3. 1.1 mL
   4. 7.4 mL

2. A pediatric client with ventricular septal defect repair is placed on a maintenance dosage of digoxin (Lanoxin) elixir. The dosage is 0.07 mg/kg/day, and the client's weight is 7.2 kg. The physician orders the digoxin to be given twice daily. A nurse prepares how much digoxin to administer to the client at each dose?
   1. 0.25 mg
   2. 0.37 mg
   3. 0.5 mg
   4. 2.5 mg

3. Cloxacillin, 200 mg orally every 8 hours, is prescribed for a child with an elevated temperature who is suspected of having a respiratory tract infection. The child weighs 17 lb. The safe pediatric dosage is 50 mg/kg/day. The nurse determines that:
   1. The dose prescribed is safe.
   2. The dose prescribed is too low.
   3. The dose prescribed is too high.
   4. There is not enough information to determine the safe dose.

4. Sulfisoxazole (Gantrisin), 1 g orally four times daily, is prescribed for an adolescent with a urinary tract infection. The medication label reads "500-mg tablets." A nurse has determined that the dosage prescribed is safe. The nurse administers how many tablets per dose to the adolescent?
   1. ½ tablet
   2. 1 tablet
   3. 2 tablets
   4. 3 tablets

5. Diphenhydramine hydrochloride (Benadryl), 25 mg orally every 6 hours, is prescribed for a child with an allergic reaction. The child weighs 25 kg. The safe pediatric dosage is 5 mg/kg/day. The nurse determines that:
   1. The dose prescribed is safe.
   2. The dose prescribed is too low.
   3. The dose prescribed is too high.
   4. There is not enough information to determine the safe dose.

6. Penicillin G procaine (Wycillin), 1,000,000 units IM (intramuscularly), is prescribed for a child with an infection. The medication label reads "1,200,000 units per 2 mL." A nurse has determined that the dose prescribed is safe. The nurse administers how many milliliters per dose to the child?
   1. 0.8 mL
   2. 1.2 mL
   3. 1.44 mL
   4. 1.66 mL

7. Morphine sulfate, 2.5 mg, intravenous (IV) piggyback, is prescribed for a child with cancer. The safe pediatric dose is 0.05 to 0.1 mg/kg per dose. The child weighs 50 kg. The nurse determines that:
   1. The dose prescribed is too low.
   2. The dose prescribed is too high.
   3. The dose prescribed is within the safe dosage range.
   4. There is not enough information to determine the safe dosage range.

8. Morphine sulfate, 2.5 mg, IV piggyback, in 10 mL of normal saline, is prescribed for a child postoperatively. The medication label reads "¹⁄₁₅ gr per mL." The nurse has determined that the dosage is safe. The nurse adds how many milliliters of morphine sulfate to the 10 mL of normal saline solution?
   1. 0.62 mL
   2. 0.82 mL
   3. 1.35 mL
   4. 1.62 mL

ALTERNATE ITEM FORMAT: FILL IN THE BLANK

Atropine sulfate, 0.6 mg IM (intramuscularly), is prescribed for a child preoperatively. The medication label reads "0.8 mg per 2 mL." A nurse has determined that the dose prescribed is safe. The nurse prepares to administer how many milliliters to the child?

_____ mL

ANSWERS

1. **2**

Rationale: Convert 1 g to milligrams. In the metric system, to convert larger to smaller, multiply by 1000 or move the decimal point three places to the right.

1 g = 1000 mg

Formula:

$$\frac{\text{Desired}}{\text{Available}} \times \text{volume} = \frac{125 \text{ mg}}{1000 \text{ mg}} \times 7.4 \text{ mL} =$$

$$0.925 \text{ mL} = 0.92 \text{ mL per dose}$$

Test-Taking Strategy: Focus on the subject, milliliters per dose. Convert grams to milligrams first. Next, use the formula to determine the correct dose, knowing that 1000 mg = 7.4 mL. Verify the answer using a calculator. Review this formula if you had difficulty with this question.
Level of Cognitive Ability: Application
Client Needs: Physiological Integrity
Integrated Process: Nursing Process—implementation
Content Area: Fundamental skills
Reference: Macklin, D., Chernecky, C., & Infortuna, H. (2005). *Math for clinical practice* (p. 119). St. Louis: Mosby.

2. **1**

Rationale:

Calculate the dosage by weight first:

0.07 mg/day × 7.2 kg = 0.5 mg/day

The physician orders digoxin twice daily; therefore, two doses in 24 hours will be administered:

$$\frac{0.5 \text{ mg/day}}{2 \text{ doses}} = 0.25 \text{ mg for each dose}$$

Test-Taking Strategy: Read the question carefully, noting that the question states *twice daily* and *each dose*. Calculate the dosage by weight first, and then determine the milligrams per each dose. Verify the answer using a calculator. Review this formula if you had difficulty with this question.
Level of Cognitive Ability: Application
Client Needs: Physiological Integrity
Integrated Process: Nursing Process—implementation
Content Area: Child health
Reference: Kee, J., & Marshall, S. (2004). *Clinical calculations: With applications to general and specialty areas* (5th ed., p. 80). Philadelphia: W.B. Saunders.

3. **3**

Rationale: Convert pounds to kilograms by dividing by 2.2.

Pounds to kilograms:

$$\frac{17 \text{ lb}}{2.2 \text{ lb/kg}} = 7.72 \text{ kg}$$

Dosage parameters:

50 mg/kg per day × 7.72 kg = 386 mg/day

Dosage frequency:

200 mg × 3 doses (every 8 hours) = 600 mg/day

The dose is unsafe because it is higher than the safe dosage parameters of 386 mg/day.

Test-Taking Strategy: Focus on the subject, the safe dose of the medication. Convert pounds to kilograms and then calculate the dose by using the safe dosage identified in the question and the child's weight in kilograms. Verify the answer using a calculator. Remember to determine the total daily dosage be-fore selecting an option. Review this formula if you had difficulty with this question.
Level of Cognitive Ability: Analysis
Client Needs: Physiological Integrity
Integrated Process: Nursing Process—analysis
Content Area: Child health
Reference: Kee, J., & Marshall, S. (2004). *Clinical calculations: With applications to general and specialty areas* (5th ed., p. 235). Philadelphia: W.B. Saunders.

4. **3**

Rationale: Change 1 g to milligrams, knowing that 1000 mg = 1 g. Also, when converting from grams to milligrams (larger to smaller), move the decimal point three places to the right. Therefore, 1 g = 1000 mg. Next, use the formula for calculating the correct dose.

Formula:

$$\frac{\text{Desired}}{\text{Available}} \times \text{tablet} = \frac{1000 \text{ mg}}{500 \text{ mg}} \times \text{tablet} = 2 \text{ tablets}$$

Test-Taking Strategy: Focus on the subject, tablets per dose. Convert grams to milligrams first. Then, use the formula to determine the correct dose and verify the answer using a calculator. Review this formula if you had difficulty with this question.
Level of Cognitive Ability: Application
Client Needs: Physiological Integrity
Integrated Process: Nursing Process—implementation
Content Area: Child health
Reference: Macklin, D., Chernecky, C., & Infortuna, H. (2005). *Math for clinical practice* (p. 119). St. Louis: Mosby.

5. **1**

Rationale: Use the formula for calculating dosage parameters and dosage frequency.

Dosage parameters:

5 mg/kg per day × 25 kg = 125 mg/day

Dosage frequency:

25 mg × 4 doses (every 6 hours) = 100 mg/day

The dose is within the safe dosage range.

Test-Taking Strategy: Focus on the subject, the safe dose of the medication. Calculate the dosage parameters by using the safe dosage identified in the question and the child's weight in kilograms and use a calculator to verify the answer. Remember to determine the total daily dosage before selecting an option. Review this formula if you had difficulty with this question.
Level of Cognitive Ability: Analysis
Client Needs: Physiological Integrity
Integrated Process: Nursing Process—analysis
Content Area: Child health
Reference: Kee, J., & Marshall, S. (2004). *Clinical calculations: With applications to general and specialty areas* (5th ed., p. 235). Philadelphia: W.B. Saunders.

6. **4**

Rationale: Use the medication calculation formula.

Formula:

$$\frac{\text{Desired}}{\text{Available}} \times \text{volume} = \frac{1,000,000}{1,200,000} \times 2 \text{ mL} = 1.66 \text{ mL per dose}$$

Test-Taking Strategy: Focus on the subject, milliliters per dose. Use the formula to determine the correct dose and verify the answer using a calculator. Review this formula if you had difficulty with this question.
Level of Cognitive Ability: Application
Client Needs: Physiological Integrity
Integrated Process: Nursing Process—implementation
Content Area: Child health
Reference: Macklin, D., Chernecky, C., & Infortuna, H. (2005). *Math for clinical practice* (p. 119). St. Louis: Mosby.

7. 3
Rationale: Determine the dosage parameters.
Dosage parameters:
0.05 mg/kg per dose × 50 kg = 2.5 mg/dose
0.1 mg/kg per dose × 50 kg = 5 mg/dose
The dose is within the safe dosage range.
Test-Taking Strategy: Focus on the subject, the safe dose of the medication. Calculate the dosage parameters, using the safe dosage range identified in the question and the child's weight in kilograms. Verify the answer using a calculator. Review this formula if you had difficulty with this question.
Level of Cognitive Ability: Analysis
Client Needs: Physiological Integrity
Integrated Process: Nursing Process—analysis
Content Area: Child health
Reference: Kee, J., & Marshall, S. (2004). *Clinical calculations: With applications to general and specialty areas* (5th ed., p. 235). Philadelphia: W.B. Saunders.

8. 1
Rationale: Convert grains to milligrams.
60 mg = 1 gr
$\frac{1}{15}$ gr × 60 mg = 4 mg
Formula:
$$\frac{Desired}{Available} \times volume = \frac{2.5\ mg}{4\ mg} \times 1\ mL = 0.62\ mL$$

Test-Taking Strategy: Focus on the subject, milliliters per dose. Begin by converting grains to milligrams and then use the formula to determine the correct dose. Remember to verify the answer using a calculator. Review this formula if you had difficulty with this question.
Level of Cognitive Ability: Application
Client Needs: Physiological Integrity
Integrated Process: Nursing Process—implementation
Content Area: Child health
Reference: Kee, J., & Marshall, S. (2004). *Clinical calculations: With applications to general and specialty areas* (5th ed., p. 80). Philadelphia: W.B. Saunders.

ALTERNATE ITEM FORMAT: FILL IN THE BLANK
Answer: 1.5 mL
Rationale: Use the formula for calculating the medication dose.
Formula:
$$\frac{Desired}{Available} \times volume = \frac{0.6\ mg}{0.8\ mg} \times 2\ mL = 1.5\ mL$$

Test-Taking Strategy: Focus on the subject, the milliliters to be administered. Use the formula to determine the correct dose and verify the answer using a calculator. Review this formula if you had difficulty with this question.
Level of Cognitive Ability: Application
Client Needs: Physiological Integrity
Integrated Process: Nursing Process—implementation
Content Area: Child health
Reference: Kee, J., & Marshall, S. (2004). *Clinical calculations: With applications to general and specialty areas* (5th ed., p. 80). Philadelphia: W.B. Saunders.

REFERENCES

Hockenberry, M., & Wilson, D. (2007). *Wong's nursing care of infants and children* (8th ed.). St. Louis: Mosby.
Hockenberry, M., Wilson, D., & Winkelstein, M. (2005). *Wong's essentials of pediatric nursing.* (7th ed.). St. Louis: Mosby.
Hodgson, B., & Kizior, R. (2007). *Saunders nursing drug handbook 2007.* Philadelphia: W.B. Saunders.
The Joint Commission. (2004). *The official "do not use" list [of abbreviations].* http://www.jointcommission.org.

Kee, J., & Marshall, S. (2004). *Clinical calculations: With applications to general and specialty areas* (5th ed.). Philadelphia: W.B. Saunders.
Macklin, D., Chernecky, C., & Infortuna, H. (2005). *Math for clinical practice.* St. Louis: Mosby.
National Council of State Boards of Nursing (Eds.). (2007). *2007 NCLEX-RN® detailed test plan.* Chicago: Author.
Wong, D., Perry, S., & Hockenberry, M. (2006). *Maternal child nursing care* (3rd ed.). St. Louis: Mosby.

The Adult Client With an Integumentary Disorder

PYRAMID TERMS

burn Cell destruction of the layers of the skin and the resultant depletion of fluid and electrolytes.

carbon monoxide poisoning Carbon monoxide is a colorless, odorless, and tasteless gas that has an affinity for hemoglobin 200 times greater than that of oxygen. Oxygen molecules are displaced, and carbon monoxide reversibly binds to hemoglobin to form carboxyhemoglobin. Tissue hypoxia occurs.

chemical burn Tissue injury caused by tissue contact with strong acids, alkalis, or organic compounds. Systemic toxicity from cutaneous absorption can occur.

deep full-thickness burn Involves injury to the muscle, bone, and tendons. Injured area appears black and eschar is hard and inelastic.

deep partial-thickness burn Injury extends into the skin dermis and the wound is red and dry, with white areas in deeper parts; can convert to full-thickness burn when tissue damage increases with infection, hypoxia, or ischemia.

electrical burn Tissue injury caused by heat generated from electrical energy as it passes through the body; results in internal tissue damage.

full-thickness burn The injured area appears waxy white, deep red, yellow, brown, or black; injured surface appears dry. Edema is present under eschar.

herpes zoster (shingles) An acute viral infection of the nerve structure caused by varicella-zoster. Herpes zoster is contagious to individuals who have not had chickenpox.

pressure ulcer Area of tissue damage that occurs as a result of skin and underlying soft tissue compression from pressure between a surface and a bony prominence; formerly referred to as a decubitus or decubitus ulcer.

skin cancer A malignant lesion of the skin that may or may not metastasize. Causes include chronic friction and irritation to a skin area and exposure to ultraviolet rays. Diagnosis is confirmed by a skin biopsy that is positive for cancer cells.

smoke inhalation injury Respiratory injury resulting when the victim is trapped in an enclosed, smoke-filled space.

superficial-thickness burn Involves injury to the upper third of the dermis. Mild to severe erythema is noted, and the skin blanches with pressure. The burn is painful.

superficial partial-thickness burn A mottled red base and broken epidermis and a wet shiny and weeping surface are present. Large blisters can be seen covering an extensive area. Skin is edematous and painful.

thermal burn Tissue injury caused by exposure to flames, hot liquids, steam, or hot objects.

PYRAMID TO SUCCESS

The Pyramid to Success focuses on the concept that the integumentary system provides the first line of defense against infections. Focus on the protective measures necessary to prevent infection. Pyramid Points address the risk factors related to the development of integumentary disorders, and the preventive measures related to skin cancer. Focus on the emergency measures related to a client with a burn, fluid resuscitation, monitoring for complications, and skin grafting. Psychosocial issues relate to the body image disturbances that can occur as a result of the integumentary disorder. The Integrated Processes addressed in this unit include Caring, Communication and Documentation, Nursing Process, and Teaching/Learning.

CLIENT NEEDS
Safe and Effective Care Environment

Consulting with members of the health care team regarding treatments

Establishing priorities of care

Handling of hazardous and infectious materials

Instituting standard and other precautions

Maintaining confidentiality related to the disorder

Making referrals to appropriate care providers

Obtaining informed consent for treatments and procedures

Practicing medical and surgical asepsis and preventing infection

Health Promotion and Maintenance

Implementing disease prevention measures

Performing a physical assessment of the integumentary system

Promoting health screening and health promotion programs to prevent skin disorders

Providing instructions to the client regarding care of integumentary disorder

Psychosocial Integrity

Addressing end-of-life issues

Discussing unexpected body image changes

Identifying coping mechanisms

Identifying situational role changes

Using support systems

Physiological Integrity

Assessing for alterations in body systems

Providing adequate nutrition for healing

Providing basic care and comfort

Providing emergency care

Monitoring for expected effects of treatments

Monitoring for fluid and electrolyte imbalances and other complications

Monitoring laboratory values

REFERENCES

Chernecky, C., & Berger, B. (2004). *Laboratory tests and diagnostic procedures* (4th ed.). Philadelphia: W.B. Saunders.

Harkreader, H., & Hogan, M. A. (2004). *Fundamentals of nursing: caring and clinical judgment* (2nd ed.). Philadelphia: W.B. Saunders.

Ignatavicius, D. & Workman, M. (2005). *Medical-surgical nursing: Critical thinking for collaborative care* (5th ed.). St. Louis: W.B. Saunders.

Jarvis, C. (2004). *Physical examination & health assessment* (4th ed.). St. Louis: W.B. Saunders.

Lewis, S., Heitkemper, M., & Dirksen, S. (2004). *Medical-surgical nursing: Assessment and management of clinical problems* (6th ed.). St. Louis: Mosby.

National Council of State Boards of Nursing (Eds.). (2007). *2007 NCLEX-RN® detailed test plan.* Chicago: Author.

Potter, P., & Perry, A. (2005). *Fundamentals of nursing* (6th ed.). St. Louis: Mosby.

Varcarolis, E., Carson, V., & Shoemaker, N. (2006). *Foundations of psychiatric mental health nursing: A clinical approach* (5th ed.). Philadelphia: W.B. Saunders.

Integumentary System

I. ANATOMY AND PHYSIOLOGY
A. The skin is the largest sensory organ of the body, with a surface area of 15 to 20 square feet and a weight of about 9 lb.
B. Functions
   1. The skin is the first line of defense against infections.
   2. The skin protects underlying tissues and organs from injury.
   3. The skin receives stimuli from the external environment; detects touch, pressure, pain, and temperature stimuli; and relays that information to the nervous system.
   4. The skin maintains normal body temperature.
   5. The skin excretes salts, water, and organic wastes.
   6. The skin protects the body from excessive water loss.
   7. The skin synthesizes vitamin D_3, which converts to calcitriol, for normal calcium metabolism.
   8. The skin stores nutrients.
C. Layers
   1. Epidermis
   2. Dermis
   3. Hypodermis (subcutaneous fat)
D. Epidermal appendages
   1. Nails
   2. Hair
   3. Glands
      a. Sebaceous
      b. Sweat
E. Normal bacterial flora
   1. Types of normal bacterial flora include the following:
      a. Gram-positive and gram-negative staphylococci
      b. *Pseudomonas* sp.
      c. *Streptococcus* sp.
   2. Organisms are shed with normal exfoliation.
   3. A pH of 4.2 to 5.6 halts the growth of bacteria.

II. RISK FACTORS FOR INTEGUMENTARY DISORDERS
A. Exposure to chemical and environmental pollutants
B. Exposure to radiation
C. Exposure to the sun
D. Lack of personal hygiene habits
E. Use of cosmetics and harsh soaps
F. Medications, such as long-term corticosteroid and anticoagulant therapy
G. Nutritional deficiencies
H. Moderate to severe emotional stress
I. Infection, with injured areas as the potential entry points for infection
J. Changes associated with developmental stages and aging

III. PSYCHOSOCIAL IMPACT
A. Change in body image and decreased self-esteem
B. Social isolation and fear of rejection (because of embarrassment about changes in skin appearance)
C. Restrictions in physical activity
D. Pain
E. Disruption or loss of employment
F. Cost of medications, hospitalizations, and follow-up care including dressing supplies

IV. DIAGNOSTIC TESTS
A. Skin biopsy
   1. Description
      a. Skin biopsy is the collection of a small piece of skin tissue for histopathological study.

b. Methods include punch, excisional, incisional, and shave.

2. Preprocedure interventions
   a. Obtain informed consent.
   b. Cleanse site as prescribed.

3. Postprocedure interventions
   a. Place specimen when obtained by physician in the appropriate container and send to pathology laboratory for analysis.
   b. Use surgically aseptic technique for biopsy site dressings.
   c. Assess the biopsy site for bleeding and infection.
   d. Instruct the client to keep dressing in place for at least 8 hours, and then clean daily and use antibiotic ointment as prescribed.

B. Skin cultures
   1. Description
      a. Noninvasive procedure
      b. A small skin culture sample is obtained using a sterile applicator and appropriate type of culture tube (e.g., bacterial or viral).
      c. Viral culture is placed immediately on ice.
      d. Sample is sent to laboratory to identify an existing organism.
   2. Preprocedure intervention: Obtain skin culture samples before instituting antibiotic therapy.
   3. Postprocedure intervention: Send skin culture sample to the laboratory.

C. Wood's light examination
   1. Description: Skin is viewed under ultraviolet light through a special glass (Wood's glass) to identify superficial infections of the skin.
   2. Preprocedure intervention: Darken the room before the examination.
   3. Postprocedure intervention: Assist the client during adjustment from the darkened room.

V. SKIN DISORDERS

A. **Skin cancer**
   1. Description
      a. **Skin cancer** is a malignant lesion of the skin, which may or may not metastasize.
      b. **Skin cancer** causes include chronic friction and irritation to a skin area and exposure to ultraviolet rays.
      c. Diagnosis is confirmed by a skin biopsy that is positive for cancer cells.
   2. Types
      a. Basal cell: The most common type, basal cell cancer arises from the basal cells contained in the epidermis.
      b. Squamous cell: The second most common type of **skin cancer** in whites; squamous cell cancer is a tumor of the epidermal keratino-

cytes and can infiltrate surrounding structures, metastasize to lymph nodes, and subsequently be fatal.
      c. Malignant melanoma: May occur any place on the body, especially where birthmarks or new moles are apparent. Cancer of the melanocytes can metastasize to the brain, lungs, bone, liver, and skin and is ultimately fatal.
   3. Assessment (Box 49-1)
      a. Change in color, size, or shape of preexisting lesion
      b. Pruritus
      c. Local soreness
   4. Interventions
      a. Instruct the client regarding preventive measures.
      b. Instruct the client to monitor for lesions that do not heal or that change characteristics.
      c. Instruct the client to have moles or lesions removed that are subject to chronic irritation.
      d. Instruct the client to avoid contact with chemical irritants.
      e. Instruct the client to wear layered clothing and use sunscreen lotions with an appropriate skin protection factor when outdoors.
      f. Instruct the client to avoid sun exposure between 11 AM and 3 PM.
      g. Assist with surgical excision of the lesion as prescribed.

B. Contact dermatitis
   1. Description: An inflammatory response of the skin that produces skin changes after contact with a specific antigen
   2. Assessment
      a. Pruritus and burning
      b. Edema
      c. Erythema at the point of contact
      d. Signs of infection
      e. Vesicles with drainage
   3. Interventions
      a. Elevate the extremity to reduce edema.
      b. Apply cool, wet dressings and tepid baths as prescribed.
      c. Maintain a cool environment.
      d. Protect the affected area from trauma.
      e. Prevent scratching and rubbing of the affected area.
      f. Assist with skin testing as prescribed to determine allergen(s).
      g. Instruct the client to avoid contact with the allergen when determined.
      h. Instruct the client to avoid harsh soaps.
      i. Instruct the client to avoid using heating pads or blankets.

BASAL CELL CARCINOMA

Waxy border
Papule, red, central crater
Metastasis is rare

SQUAMOUS CELL CARCINOMA

Oozing, bleeding, crusting lesion
Potentially metastatic
Larger tumors associated with a higher risk for metastasis

MELANOMA

Irregular, circular, bordered lesion with hues of tan,
  black, or blue
Rapid infiltration into tissue, rapid metastasis, significant
  rate of morbidity and mortality

    j. Administer antibiotic for infection, antipru-
ritic or antihistamine for itching, and corticosteroids for inflammation as prescribed.
C. Poison ivy, poison oak, and poison sumac
  1. Description: A dermatitis that develops from
contact with urushiol from poison ivy, oak, or
sumac plants

  2. Assessment
    a. Papulovesicular lesions
    b. Severe itching
  3. Interventions
    a. Cleanse the skin of the plant oils immedi-
ately.
    b. Apply cool, wet dressings with Burow's solu-
tion, as prescribed, to relieve the itching.
    c. Apply lotion or topical corticosteroids as
prescribed.
    d. Administer oral corticosteroids as prescribed
for severe reaction.
D. Erysipelas and cellulitis
  1. Description
    a. Erysipelas is an acute, superficial, rapidly
spreading inflammation of the dermis and
lymphatics caused by *Streptococcus* group A
that enters the tissue via an abrasion, bite,
trauma, or wound.
    b. Cellulitis is a skin infection into the deeper
dermis and subcutaneous fat, and the causative organism is usually *Streptococcus
pyogenes*.
  2. Assessment
    a. Pain
    b. Itching
    c. Swelling
    d. Redness and warmth
  3. Interventions
    a. Promote rest.
    b. Apply warm compresses as prescribed (usu-
ally twice daily) to promote circulation
and to decrease discomfort, erythema, and
edema.
    c. Administer antibiotics as prescribed for in-
fection following a culture of the area.
    d. Clean skin daily with an antibacterial type of
soap as prescribed.
E. Psoriasis
  1. Description
    a. Psoriasis is a chronic, noninfectious skin in-
flammation involving keratin synthesis that
results in psoriatic patches.
    b. Various forms exist, with psoriasis vulgaris
being the most common.
    c. Possible causes of the disorder include stress,
trauma, infection, and changes in climate.
    d. The disorder also may be exacerbated by the
use of certain medications.
    e. Koebner phenomenon is the development of
psoriatic lesions at a site of injury, such as a
scratched or sunburned area.
  2. Assessment
    a. Pruritus
    b. Shedding, silvery, white scales on a raised,
reddened, round plaque that usually affects

the scalp, knees, elbows, extensor surfaces of arms and legs, and sacral regions

c. A yellow discoloration, pitting, and thickening of the nails, if they are affected

d. Joint inflammation with psoriatic arthritis

3. Interventions

a. Administer daily soaks and tepid, wet compresses to the affected areas to remove scales; oils or coal tar preparations may be added to the bath water.

b. Assist the client to remove the scales during the soak, using a soft washcloth and gentle, circular motions; emollient creams or salicylic acid may be applied to affected areas after the bath to continue to soften thick scales.

4. Topical pharmacological therapy

a. Pharmacological therapy includes tar preparations, anthralin, salicylic acid, and corticosteroids; vitamin D preparation, calcipotriene (Dovonex), and a retinoid compound, tazarotene (Tazorac), suppress epidermopoiesis and cause sloughing of the rapidly growing epidermal cells

b. Occlusive dressings may be applied following application of the corticosteroid to increase its effectiveness.

c. Use plastic wrap or bags as the occlusive dressing, and use rubber gloves on the client's hands, plastic bags on the feet, and a shower cap on the head, if affected; a plastic vinyl jogging suit may be used for the client being treated at home.

5. Intralesional therapy involves injections of triamcinolone acetonide (Aristocort, Kenalog-10) into highly visible or isolated patches of psoriasis that are resistant to other forms of therapy.

6. Systemic therapy

a. Systemic medications may be prescribed to treat extensive psoriasis that does not respond to other forms of therapy.

b. Prescribed medications may include methotrexate, hydroxyurea (Hydrea), and cyclosporine.

7. Photochemotherapy

a. Combination of psoralens and ultraviolet A light therapy decreases cellular proliferation.

b. The client takes a photosensitizing medication (8-methoxypsoralen) and subsequently is exposed to long-wave ultraviolet light.

8. Client education

a. Instruct the client not to scratch the affected areas and to keep the skin lubricated to minimize itching.

b. Monitor for and instruct the client to recognize the signs and symptoms of infection.

c. Instruct the client to wear light cotton clothing over affected areas.

d. Instruct the client regarding prescribed treatments and medications and to avoid over-the-counter medications.

e. Assist the client to identify ways to reduce stress.

F. **Herpes zoster (shingles)**

1. Description

a. With a history of chickenpox, shingles is caused by the reactivation of the varicella-zoster virus; shingles can occur during any immunocompromised state in a client with a history of chickenpox.

b. The dormant virus is located in the dorsal nerve root ganglion of the sensory cranial and spinal nerves.

c. Diagnosis is determined by visual examination, skin cultures, and skin stains that identify the organism and by an antinuclear antibody blood test that produces a positive result.

d. A culture provides the definitive diagnosis.

e. **Herpes zoster** is contagious to individuals who have not had chickenpox.

2. Assessment

a. Unilaterally clustered skin vesicles along peripheral sensory nerves on the trunk, thorax, or face

b. Fever

c. Burning and neuralgia

d. Pruritus

e. Paresthesia

3. Interventions

a. Isolate the client because exudate from the lesions contains the virus (maintain standard and other precautions, such as contact precautions).

b. Assess neurovascular status and seventh cranial nerve function.

c. Assess for signs and symptoms of infection.

d. Keep blisters intact if formed.

e. Assist the client with acetic acid compresses, cool, wet compresses, and tepid baths as prescribed.

f. Prepare to assist physician with a nerve block using lidocaine (Xylocaine) if prescribed.

g. Administer antiviral agents, analgesics, antianxiety agents, antipruritics, and corticosteroids as prescribed.

h. Use an air mattress and bed cradle on the client's bed and keep the environment cool; warmth and touch aggravate pain.

i. Prevent the client from scratching and rubbing the affected area.

j. Instruct the client to wear lightweight, loose cotton clothing and to avoid wool and synthetic clothing

G. Paronychia
1. Description: An infection of the tissue around the nail plate that most commonly occurs in middle-aged women and in the client with diabetes mellitus
2. Assessment
   a. Redness and swelling around the nail bed
   b. Soreness at the nail bed
3. Interventions
   a. Monitor temperature.
   b. Monitor for infection around the nails.
   c. Monitor for cellulitis in the affected area.
   d. Assist the client with warm soaks as prescribed.
   e. Prepare to assist with incision and drainage of infected area if prescribed.
   f. Administer antibiotic or fungicidal ointments as prescribed.
H. Impetigo: See Chapter 42 for information on this disorder.
I. Frostbite
1. Description
   a. Frostbite is damage to tissues and blood vessels as a result of prolonged exposure to cold.
   b. Fingers, toes, nose, and ears often are affected.
2. Assessment
   a. Numbness
   b. Paresthesia
   c. Pallor
   d. Severe pain, swelling, erythema, and blistering that occur once the client is in a warm environment
   e. Necrosis and gangrene may develop in severe cases
3. Interventions
   a. Handle the tissues gently.
   b. Rewarm the affected part rapidly and continuously with a warm water bath (90° to 107° F) for 15 to 20 minutes or until skin flushing occurs.
   c. Avoid slow thawing, interrupted periods of warmth, or massage (may result in further tissue damage).
   d. Do not débride blisters.
   e. Leave area exposed initially for continued assessment, and then apply bulky dressings as prescribed to provide protection.
J. Scabies
1. Description
   a. Scabies is a parasitic skin disorder caused by an infestation by *Sarcoptes scabiei* (itch mite).
   b. Scabies is endemic among schoolchildren and institutionalized populations because of close personal contact.

c. Risk factors include close personal contact with an infected person or contaminated article.
   d. Usually a 1-month delay occurs between the initial infestation and onset of pruritus in the host.
2. Assessment
   a. Erythematous papules and pustules
   b. Thread-like, brownish, linear burrows up to 1 cm long
   c. Burrows are most common between fingers, on the palms, and the inner aspect of the wrist.
   d. Secondary lesions consist of vesicles, crusts, reddish-brown nodules, and excoriations.
   e. Intense pruritus that worsens at night
3. Interventions
   a. Administer antihistamines or topical steroids to relieve itching as prescribed.
   b. Apply topical antiscabies creams or lotions such as lindane, crotamiton (Eurax), or permethrin (Elimite, Nix) as prescribed.
   c. Lindane should not be used in children younger than age 2 years because of the risk of neurotoxicity and seizures.
   d. Instruct the client to apply the antiscabies preparation thinly to the entire skin from the neck down (face and scalp are not affected in scabies) and to leave on for 12 to 24 hours, as prescribed.
   e. Instruct the client to apply antiscabies preparations to dry skin, because moist skin increases absorption and the potential for central nervous system side effects, such as seizures.
   f. Following treatment with antiscabies preparations, instruct the client to remove the medication by thoroughly washing with soap and water.
   g. Contact precautions need to be maintained and all family members and close contacts should be treated simultaneously.
   h. Instruct the client that all bedding and clothing should be washed in hot water and dried with the drier set at "hot" or dry-cleaned (mites can survive up to 36 hours on linen).
K. Acne vulgaris
1. Description
   a. Acne is a common, self-limiting, multifactorial disorder.
   b. Acne requires active treatment for control until it spontaneously resolves.
   c. The types of lesions include comedones (open and closed), pustules, papules, and nodules.
   d. The exact cause is unknown but may include androgenic influence on sebaceous glands, in-

creased sebum production, and proliferation of *Propionibacterium acnes* (the enzymes of which reduce lipids to irritating fatty acids).

    e. Exacerbations coincide with the menstrual cycle because of hormonal activity.

    f. Heat, humidity, and excessive perspiration have a role in increased acne.

2. Assessment

    a. Closed comedones are whiteheads and non-inflamed lesions that develop as follicles and enlarge, with the retention of horny cells.

    b. Open comedones are blackheads that result from continuing accumulation of horny cells and sebum, which dilates the follicles.

    c. Pustules and papules result as the inflammatory process progresses.

    d. Nodules result from total disintegration of a comedone and subsequent collapse of the follicle.

    e. Deep scarring can result from nodules.

3. Interventions

    a. Instruct the client in the administration (provide written instructions) of topical or oral antibiotics as prescribed.

    b. Instruct the client in the use of isotretinoin (Accutane) or other medications, if prescribed, to inhibit sebum production and reduce sebaceous gland size.

    c. Instruct the client about the adverse effects of isotretinoin, which include cheilitis (lip inflammation), skin dryness, elevated triglyceride levels, eye discomfort, and depression in some cases.

    d. Instruct the client to stop taking vitamin A supplements during treatment with isotretinoin.

    e. Inform the client that improvement may not be apparent for 4 to 6 weeks.

    f. Instruct the client in appropriate skin-cleansing methods, with emphasis on not scrubbing the face and using only the prescribed topical agents.

    g. Instruct the client not to squeeze, prick, or pick at lesions.

    h. Instruct the client to use products labeled noncomedogenic and cosmetics that are water-based and to avoid contact with excessively oil-based products.

    i. Instruct the client on the importance of follow-up treatment.

L. **Pressure ulcer**

1. Description

    a. **Pressure ulcer** is an impairment of skin integrity.

    b. Localized areas of necrosis of the skin and subcutaneous tissue are caused by pressure.

    c. Prevention of skin breakdown is a major role of the nurse, particularly in caring for the bedridden or immobile client.

2. Risk factors

    a. Malnutrition

    b. Incontinence

    c. Immobility

    d. Skin shearing

    e. Decreased sensory perception

3. Assessment and staging (Box 49-2)

4. Interventions

    a. Institute measures to prevent **pressure ulcers.**

    b. Assess the nutritional status of the client.

    c. Provide adequate nutritional intake to promote tissue integrity.

    d. Monitor for an alteration in skin integrity.

    e. Relieve or remove pressure on the skin.

    f. Turn and reposition the immobile client every 2 hours or more frequently if necessary.

    g. Help the client ambulate.

    h. Provide active and passive exercises every 8 hours.

    i. Keep the skin clean and dry and the sheets wrinkle-free.

    j. Apply moisture barrier as prescribed to protect the skin.

    k. Use pressure reduction or relief devices to prevent pressure, such as a special mattress (alternating air pressure mattress), mattress overlay, or wheelchair cushions

    l. Apply medications or dressings to the wound as prescribed.

VI. BURN INJURIES

A. Description: Cell destruction of the layers of the skin and the resultant depletion of fluid and electrolytes

B. Burn size

1. Small **burns:** The response of the body to injury is localized to the injured area.

2. Large or extensive **burns**

    a. Large **burns** consist of 25% or more of the total body surface area

    b. The response of the body to the injury is systemic.

    c. The burn affects all of the major systems of the body.

C. Estimating the extent of injury (Box 49-3; Fig. 49-1)

D. Burn depth

1. **Superficial-thickness burn** (Fig. 49-2)

    a. Involves injury to the upper third of the dermis; the blood supply to dermis is still intact.

    b. Mild to severe erythema (pink to red) is present, but no blisters.

    c. Skin blanches with pressure.

BOX 49-2
Stages of Pressure Ulcers

STAGE I

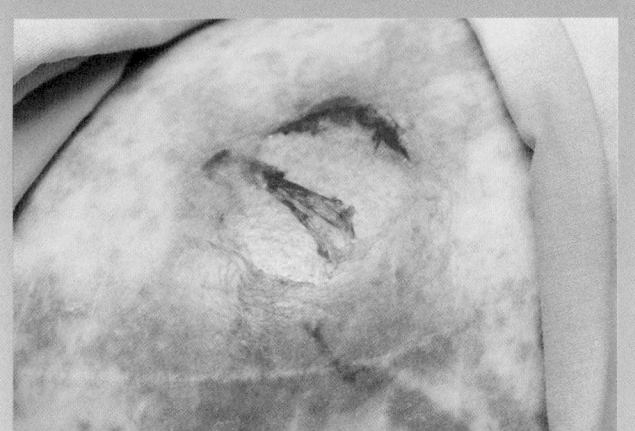

Skin is intact.
Area is red and does not blanch with external pressure.
Area may be painful, firm, soft, warmer or cooler compared with adjacent tissue.

STAGE II

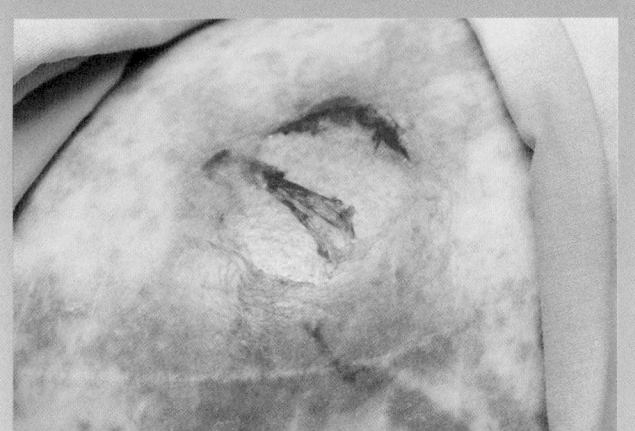

Skin is not intact.
Partial-thickness skin loss of the dermis occurs.
Presents as a shallow open ulcer with a red-pink wound bed or as intact or open/ruptured serum–filled blister.

STAGE III

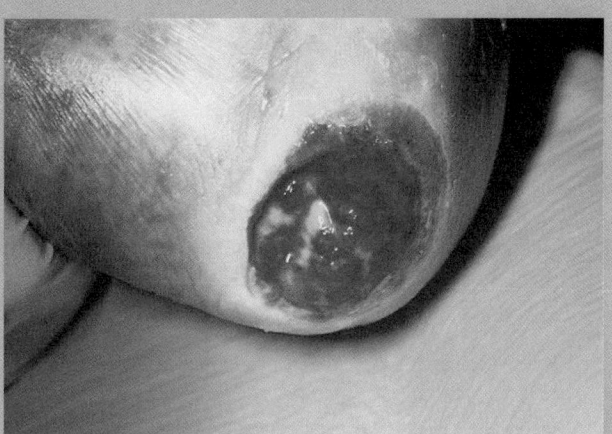

Full-thickness skin loss extends into the dermis and subcutaneous tissues, and slough may be present.
Subcutaneous tissue may be visible.
Undermining and tunneling may or may not be present.

STAGE IV

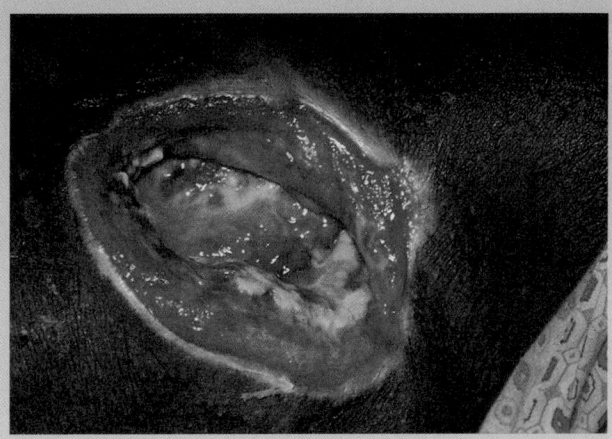

Full-thickness skin loss is present with exposed bone, tendon or muscle.
Slough or escar may be present.
Undermining and tunneling may develop.

d. Burn is painful, with tingling sensation, and pain is eased by cooling.
e. Discomfort lasts about 48 hours; healing occurs in about 3 to 5 days.
f. No scarring and skin grafts are not required.
2. **Superficial partial-thickness burn** (Fig. 49-3)
   a. Involves injury deeper into the dermis; the blood supply is reduced.
   b. Large blisters may cover an extensive area.
   c. Edema is present.

d. Mottled pink to red base and broken epidermis, with a wet, shiny, and weeping surface, is characteristic.
e. Burn is painful and sensitive to cold air.
f. Heals in 10 to 21 days with no scarring, but some minor pigment changes may occur.
g. Grafts may be used if the healing process is prolonged.
3. **Deep partial-thickness burn** (Fig. 49-4)
   a. Extends into the skin dermis

BOX 49-3
Methods to Estimate Extent of Burn Injury

RULE OF NINES (ADULT)
Head: 9%
Anterior trunk: 18%
Posterior trunk: 18%
Arms (9% each): 18%
Legs (9% each): 18%
Perineum: 1%

LUND-BROWDER AND BERKOW CLASSIFICATION
Modifies percentages for body segments according to age
Provides a more accurate estimate of the burn size
Uses a diagram of the body divided into sections, with the representative percentage of the total body surface area from birth throughout adulthood
Should be reevaluated after initial wound débridement

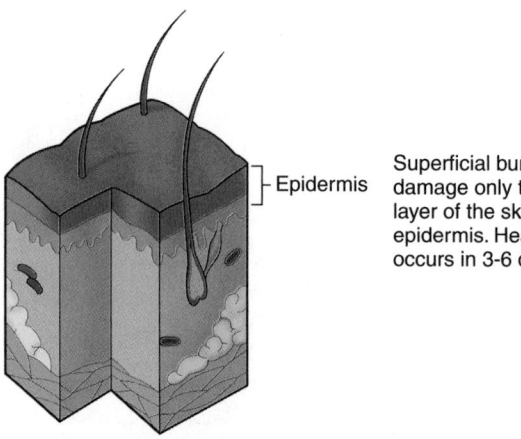

FIG. 49-2 Tissues involved in superficial burns. (From Ignatavicius, D., & Workman, M. [2006]. *Medical surgical nursing: Critical thinking for collaborative care* [5th ed.]. Philadelphia: W.B. Saunders.)

Superficial burns damage only the top layer of the skin—the epidermis. Healing occurs in 3-6 days.

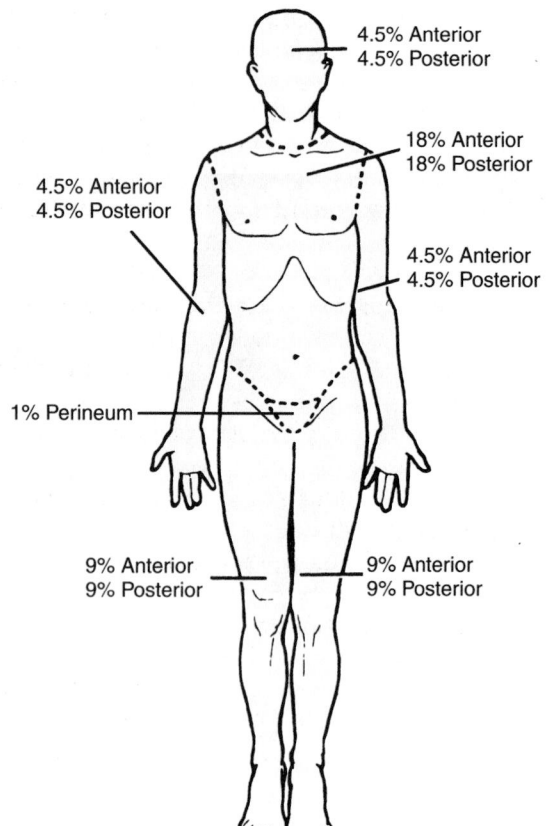

4.5% Anterior
4.5% Posterior

18% Anterior
18% Posterior

4.5% Anterior
4.5% Posterior

4.5% Anterior
4.5% Posterior

1% Perineum

9% Anterior
9% Posterior

9% Anterior
9% Posterior

FIG. 49-1 The rule of nines for estimating burn percentage. (From Ignatavicius, D., & Workman, M. [2006]. *Medical-surgical nursing: Critical thinking for collaborative care* [5th ed.]. Philadelphia: W.B. Saunders.)

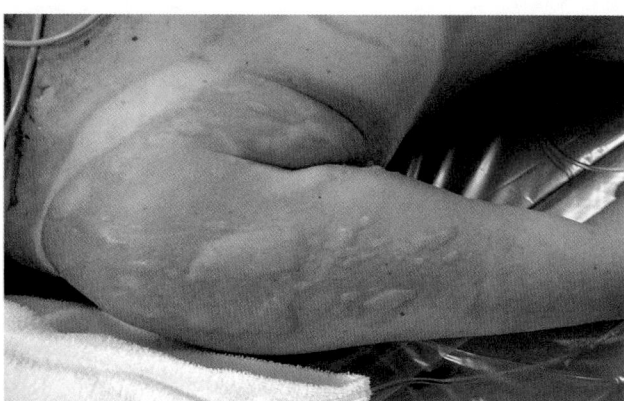

FIG. 49-3 Typical appearance of superficial partial-thickness burn injury. (From Ignatavicius, D., & Workman, M. [2006]. *Medical surgical nursing: Critical thinking for collaborative care* [5th ed.]. Philadelphia: W.B. Saunders.)

b. Blister formation usually does not occur because the dead tissue layer is thick and sticks to underlying viable dermis.
c. Wound surface is red and dry with white areas in deeper parts.

d. May or may not blanch and edema is moderate
e. Can convert to **full-thickness** when tissue damage increases with infection, hypoxia, or ischemia
f. Generally heals in 3 to 6 weeks, but scar formation results, and skin grafting may be necessary
4. **Full-thickness burn** (Fig. 49-5)
a. Involves injury and destruction of the epidermis and the dermis; the wound will not heal by re-epithelialization and grafting may be required.
b. Appears as a dry, hard, leathery eschar (burn crust or dead tissue that must slough off or be removed from the wound before healing can occur)
c. Appears as a waxy white, deep red, yellow, brown, or black

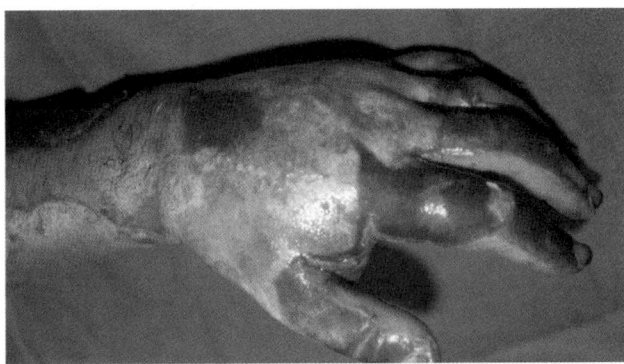

FIG. 49-4 Typical appearance of deep partial-thickness burn injury. (From Ignatavicius, D., & Workman, M. [2006]. *Medical-surgical nursing: Critical thinking for collaborative care* [5th ed.]. Philadelphia: W.B. Saunders.)

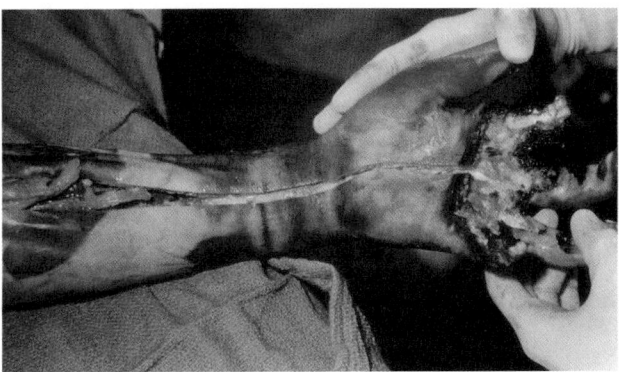

FIG. 49-6 Typical appearance of deep full-thickness burn injury. (From Ignatavicius, D., & Workman, M. [2006]. *Medical-surgical nursing: Critical thinking for collaborative care* [5th ed.]. Philadelphia: W.B. Saunders.)

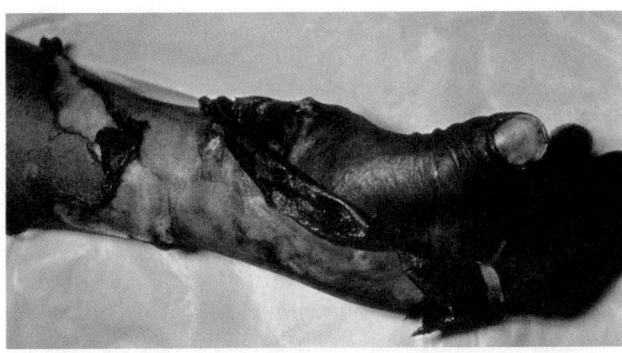

FIG. 49-5 Typical appearance of full-thickness burn injury. (From Ignatavicius, D., & Workman, M. [2006]. *Medical-surgical-nursing: Critical thinking for collaborative care* [5th ed.]. Philadelphia: W.B. Saunders.)

    d. Injured surface appears dry.
    e. Edema is present under the eschar.
    f. Sensation is reduced or absent because of nerve ending destruction.
    g. Healing may take weeks to months and depends on establishing an adequate blood supply.
    h. Burn requires removal of eschar and split- or **full-thickness** skin grafting.
    i. Scarring and wound contractures are likely to develop without preventive measures.
  5. **Deep full-thickness burn** (Fig. 49-6)
    a. Extends beyond the skin into underlying fascia and tissues and damage to the muscle, bone, and tendons occurs.
    b. Injured area appears black and sensation is completely absent.
    c. Eschar is hard and inelastic.
    d. Healing time takes months and grafts are required.
E. Age and general health

1. Mortality rates are higher for children younger than 4 years of age, particularly from birth to 1 year of age, and for clients older than 65 years.
2. Debilitating disorders, such as cardiac, respiratory, endocrine, and renal disorders, negatively influence the client's response to injury and treatment.
3. Mortality rate is higher when the client has a preexisting disorder at the time of the burn injury.
F. Burn location
  1. **Burns** of the head, neck, and chest are associated with pulmonary complications.
  2. **Burns** of the face are associated with corneal abrasion.
  3. **Burns** of the ear are associated with auricular chondritis.
  4. Hands and joints require intensive therapy to prevent disability.
  5. The perineal area is prone to autocontamination by urine and feces.
  6. Circumferential **burns** of the extremities can produce a tourniquet-like effect and lead to vascular compromise (compartment syndrome).
  7. Circumferential thorax **burns** lead to inadequate chest wall expansion and pulmonary insufficiency.

VII. TYPES OF BURNS
A. **Thermal burns** are caused by exposure to flames, hot liquids, steam, or hot objects.
B. **Chemical burns**
  1. **Burns** are caused by tissue contact with strong acids, alkalis, or organic compounds.
  2. Systemic toxicity from cutaneous absorption can occur.
C. **Electrical burns**
  1. **Burns** are caused by heat generated by electrical energy as it passes through the body.

2. **Electrical burns** result in internal tissue damage.
3. Cutaneous **burns** cause muscle and soft tissue damage that may be extensive, particularly in high-voltage electrical injuries.
4. The voltage, type of current, contact site, and duration of contact are important to identify.
5. Alternating current is more dangerous than direct current because it is associated with cardiopulmonary arrest, ventricular fibrillation, tetanic muscle contractions, and long bone or vertebral fractures.

D. Radiation **burns** are caused by exposure to ultraviolet light, x-rays, or radioactivity.

VIII. INHALATION INJURIES

▲ A. **Smoke inhalation injury**
   1. Description: Injury results when the victim is trapped in an enclosed, hot, smoke-filled space.
   2. Assessment
      a. Facial **burns**
      b. Erythema
      c. Swelling of oropharynx and nasopharynx
      d. Singed nasal hairs
      e. Flaring nostrils
      f. Stridor, wheezing, and dyspnea
      g. Hoarse voice
      h. Sooty (carbonaceous) sputum and cough
      i. Tachycardia
      j. Agitation and anxiety

▲ B. **Carbon monoxide poisoning**
   1. Description
      a. Carbon monoxide is a colorless, odorless, and tasteless gas that has an affinity for hemoglobin 200 times greater than that of oxygen.
      b. Oxygen molecules are displaced and carbon monoxide reversibly binds to hemoglobin to form carboxyhemoglobin.
      c. Tissue hypoxia occurs.
   2. Assessment (Table 49-1)

▲ C. Smoke poisoning
   1. Description
      a. Smoke poisoning is caused by the inhalation of the by-products of combustion.
      b. A localized inflammatory reaction occurs, causing a decrease in bronchial ciliary action and a decrease in surfactant.
   2. Assessment
      a. Mucosal edema occurs in the airways.
      b. Wheezing is evident on auscultation.
      c. After several hours, sloughing of the tracheobronchial epithelium may occur, and hemorrhagic bronchitis may develop.
      d. Acute respiratory distress syndrome can result.

▲ D. Direct thermal heat injury

1. Description
   a. Thermal heat injury can occur to the lower airways by the inhalation of steam or explosive gases or the aspiration of scalding liquids.
   b. Injury can occur to the upper airways, which appear erythematous and edematous, with mucosal blisters and ulcerations.
   c. Mucosal edema can lead to upper airway obstruction, especially during the first 24 to 48 hours.
   d. All clients with head or neck **burns** should be monitored closely for the development of airway obstruction and are considered immediately for endotracheal intubation if obstruction occurs.
2. Assessment
   a. Erythema and edema of the upper airways
   b. Mucosal blisters and ulcerations

IX. PATHOPHYSIOLOGY OF BURNS

A. Following the burn, vasoactive substances are released from the injured tissue, and these substances cause an increase in capillary permeability, allowing the plasma to seep into the surrounding tissues.
B. The direct injury to the vessels increases capillary permeability (capillary permeability decreases 18 to 26 hours after the burn, but does not normalize until 2 to 3 weeks following injury).
C. Extensive **burns** result in generalized body edema and a decrease in circulating intravascular blood volume. ▲

TABLE 49-1

Carbon Monoxide Poisoning

Blood Level (%)	Clinical Manifestations
1-10	Normal level
11-20 (mild poisoning)	Headache
	Flushing
	Decreased visual acuity
	Decreased cerebral functioning
	Slight breathlessness
21-40 (moderate poisoning)	Headache
	Nausea and vomiting
	Drowsiness
	Tinnitus and vertigo
	Confusion and stupor
	Pale to reddish-purple skin
	Decreased blood pressure
	Increased and irregular heart rate
41-60 (severe poisoning)	Coma
	Seizures
61-80 (fatal poisoning)	Death

Modified from Ignatavicius, D., & Workman, M. (2006). *Medical-surgical nursing: Critical thinking for collaborative care* (5th ed.). Philadelphia: W.B. Saunders.

D. The fluid losses result in a decrease in organ perfusion.

E. The heart rate increases, cardiac output decreases, and blood pressure drops.

F. Initially, hyponatremia and hyperkalemia occur.

G. The hematocrit level increases as a result of plasma loss; this initial increase falls to below normal at the third to fourth day after the burn as a result of red blood cell damage and loss at the time of injury.

H. Initially, the body shunts blood from the kidneys, causing oliguria; then the body begins to reabsorb fluid, and diuresis of the excess fluid occurs over the next days to weeks.

I. Blood flow to the gastrointestinal tract is diminished, leading to intestinal ileus and gastrointestinal dysfunction.

J. Immune system function is depressed, resulting in immunosuppression and thus increasing the risk of infection and sepsis.

K. Pulmonary hypertension can develop, resulting in a decrease in the arterial oxygen tension level and a decrease in lung compliance.

L. Evaporative fluid losses through the burn wound are greater than normal, and the losses continue until complete wound closure occurs.

M. If the intravascular space is not replenished with intravenously administered fluids, hypovolemic shock and ultimately death will occur.

X. MANAGEMENT OF THE BURN INJURY

A. Emergent phase (Table 49-2)
  1. Description
     a. The emergent phase begins at the time of injury and ends with the restoration of normal capillary permeability (fluid resuscitation), usually at 48 to 72 hours following injury; this phase includes prehospital and emergency room care.
     b. The primary goal is to prevent hypovolemic shock and preserve vital organ functioning.
  2. Prehospital care
     a. Prehospital care begins at the scene of the accident and ends when emergency care is obtained.
     b. Remove the victim from the source of the burn.
     c. Remove the source of heat.
     d. Assess the ABCs—airway, breathing, and circulation.
     e. Assess for associated trauma.
     f. Conserve body heat.
     g. Cover **burns** with sterile or clean cloths.
     h. Remove constricting jewelry and clothing.
     i. Assess the need for intravenous fluids.
     j. Transport.
  3. Emergency room care is a continuation of care administered at the scene of the injury.

TABLE 49-2

Phases of Management of the Burn Injury

Phase	Goal
EMERGENT PHASE Begins at the time of injury Ends with the restoration of normal capillary permeability Duration usually 48 to 72 hr Includes prehospital care and emergency room care	The primary goal is to prevent hypovolemic shock and preserve vital organ functioning.
RESUSCITATIVE PHASE Begins with the initiation of fluids Ends when capillary integrity returns to near-normal levels and large fluid shifts have decreased Amount of fluid administered based on client's weight and extent of injury (*Note:* Most fluid replacement formulas are calculated from the time of injury and not from the time of arrival at the hospital.)	The goal is to prevent shock by maintaining adequate circulating blood volume and maintaining vital organ perfusion.
ACUTE PHASE Begins when the client is hemodynamically stable, capillary permeability is restored, and diuresis has begun Usually begins 48 to 72 hr after time of injury Focus is on infection control, wound care, wound closure, nutritional support, pain management, physical therapy	The goal during this phase is placed on restorative therapy, and the phase continues until wound closure is achieved.
REHABILITATIVE PHASE Overlaps acute phase of care Extends beyond hospitalization	The goals of this phase are designed so that the client can gain independence and achieve maximal function

4. Major **burns**
   a. Evaluate the degree and extent of the burn and treat life-threatening conditions.
   b. Ensure a patent airway and administer 100% oxygen as prescribed if the burn occurred in an enclosed area.
   c. Monitor for respiratory distress and assess the need for intubation.
   d. Assess oropharynx for blisters and erythema.
   e. Monitor arterial blood gases and carboxyhemoglobin levels.
   f. For an inhalation injury, administer 100% oxygen via a tight-fitting nonrebreather face mask as prescribed until the carboxyhemoglobin level falls below 15%.
   g. Initiate peripheral intravenous (IV) access to nonburned skin proximal to any extremity burn, or prepare for the insertion of a central venous line as prescribed.
   h. Assess for hypovolemia and prepare to administer fluids intravenously to maintain fluid balance.
   i. Monitor vital signs closely.
   j. Insert a Foley catheter as prescribed, and maintain urine output at 30 to 50 mL/hr.
   k. Maintain NPO status.
   l. Insert a nasogastric tube as prescribed to remove gastric secretions and prevent aspiration.
   m. Administer tetanus prophylaxis as prescribed.
   n. Administer pain medication, as prescribed, by the IV route.
   o. Prepare the client for an escharotomy or fasciotomy as prescribed.

5. Minor **burns**
   a. Administer pain medication with small doses of morphine sulfate or meperidine (Demerol) as prescribed.
   b. Instruct the client in the use of oral analgesics as prescribed.
   c. Administer tetanus prophylaxis as prescribed.
   d. Administer wound care as prescribed, which may include cleansing, débriding loose tissue, and removing any damaging agents, followed by the application of topical antimicrobial cream and a sterile dressing.
   e. Instruct the client in follow-up care, including active range-of-motion exercises and wound care treatments.

B. Resuscitative phase (see Table 49-2)
   1. Description
      a. The resuscitative phase begins with the initiation of fluids and ends when capillary integrity returns to near-normal levels and the large fluid shifts have decreased.
      b. The amount of fluid administered is based on client's weight and extent of injury.
      c. Most fluid replacement formulas are calculated from the time of injury and not from the time of arrival at the hospital.
      d. The goal is to prevent shock by maintaining adequate circulating blood volume and maintaining vital organ perfusion.
   2. Fluid resuscitation (Table 49-3)

TABLE 49-3

Common Fluid Resuscitation Formulas for First 24 Hours After a Burn Injury

Formula	Solution	Rate of Administration
MODIFIED BROOKE		
0.5 mL/kg/% TBSA burn	Protenate or 5% albumin in isotonic saline	Half given in first 8 hr
1.5 mL/kg/% TBSA burn	Lactated Ringer's without dextrose	Half given in next 16 hr
PARKLAND (BAXTER)		
4 mL/kg/% TBSA burn for 24-hr period	Crystalloid only (lactated Ringer's)	Half given in first 8 hr, half given in next 16 hr
MONAFO	Crystalloid (hypertonic saline, sodium = 250 mEq/L)	Adjust to maintain urine output of 30 mL/hr
MODIFIED PARKLAND		
4 mL/kg/% TBSA burn = 15 mL/m² of TBSA	Crystalloid only (lactated Ringer's)	Half given in first 8 hr, half given in next 16 hr
WINSKI		
2 mL/kg/% burn + maintenance fluid	Crystalloid only (lactated Ringer's)	Half given in first 8 hr, half given in next 16 hr

TBSA, Total body surface area.
From Ignatavicius, D., & Workman, M. (2006). *Medical-surgical nursing: Critical thinking for collaborative care* (5th ed.). Philadelphia: W.B. Saunders.

a. The amount of fluid administered depends on how much intravenous fluid per hour is required to maintain a urinary output of 30 to 50 mL/hr.

b. Successful fluid resuscitation is evaluated by stable vital signs, an adequate urine output, palpable peripheral pulses, and a clear sensorium.

c. Urinary output is the most common and most sensitive noninvasive assessment parameter for cardiac output and tissue perfusion.

d. Intravenous fluid replacement may be titrated (adjusted) based on urinary output plus serum electrolyte levels to meet the perfusion needs of the client with **burns.**

e. If the hemoglobin and hematocrit levels decrease or if the urinary output exceeds 50 mL/hr, the rate of IV fluid administration may be decreased.

3. Interventions

a. Monitor for tracheal or laryngeal edema and administer respiratory treatments as prescribed.

b. Monitor pulse oximetry and prepare for arterial blood gases and carboxyhemoglobin levels if inhalation injury is suspected.

c. Elevate the head of the bed to 30 degrees or more for **burns** of the face and head.

d. Initiate electrocardiographic monitoring.

e. Monitor temperature and assess for infection.

f. Initiate protective isolation techniques; maintain strict hand washing; use sterile sheets and linens when caring for the client; and use gloves, cap, masks, shoe covers, scrub clothes, and plastic aprons.

g. Shave or cut body hair around wound margins.

h. Monitor daily weights, expecting a weight gain of 15 to 20 lb in the first 72 hours.

i. Monitor gastric output and pH levels and for gastric discomfort and bleeding, indicating a stress ulcer.

j. Administer antacids, H_2 receptor antagonists, and antiulcer medications such as sucralfate (Carafate) as prescribed.

k. Auscultate bowel sounds for ileus and monitor for abdominal distention and gastrointestinal dysfunction.

l. Monitor stools for occult blood.

m. Obtain urine specimen for myoglobin and hemoglobin levels.

n. Monitor IV fluids and hourly intake and output to determine the adequacy of fluid replacement therapy; notify the physician if urine output is less than 30 or greater than 50 mL/hr.

o. Elevate circumferential **burns** of the extremities on pillows above the level of the heart to reduce dependent edema if no obvious fractures are present; diuretics increase the risk of hypovolemia and are generally avoided as a means of decreasing edema.

p. Monitor pulses and capillary refill of the affected extremities and assess perfusion of the distal extremity with a circumferential burn.

q. Prepare to obtain chest x-rays and other radiographs to rule out fractures or associated trauma.

r. Keep the room temperature warm.

s. Place the client on an air-fluidized bed (FluidAir Elite) and use a bed cradle to keep sheets off the client's skin.

4. Pain management

a. Administer morphine sulfate or meperidine (Demerol) as prescribed by the IV route.

b. Avoid intramuscular or subcutaneous medication routes because absorption through the soft tissue is unreliable when hypovolemia and large fluid shifts are occurring.

c. Avoid administering medication by the oral route because of the possibility of gastrointestinal dysfunction.

d. Medicate the client before painful procedures.

5. Nutrition

a. Proper nutrition is essential to promote wound healing and prevent infection.

b. The basal metabolic rate is 40 to 100 times higher than normal with a burn injury.

c. Maintain NPO status until the bowel sounds are heard, and then advance to clear liquids as prescribed.

d. Nutrition may be provided via enteral tube feeding or parenteral nutrition

e. Provide a diet high in protein, carbohydrates, fats, and vitamins.

f. Monitor calorie intake.

6. Escharotomy

a. A lengthwise incision is made through the burn eschar to relieve constriction and pressure and to improve circulation.

b. Escharotomy is performed for circulatory compromise caused by circumferential **burns.**

c. Escharotomy is performed at the bedside without anesthesia because nerve endings have been destroyed by the burn injury.

d. Escharotomy can be performed on the thorax to improve ventilation.

e. Following the escharotomy, assess pulses, color, movement, and sensation of affected extremity and control any bleeding with pressure.

f. Pack incision gently with fine mesh gauze for 24 hours after escharotomy as prescribed.

g. Apply topical antimicrobial agents to the area as prescribed following the procedure.

7. Fasciotomy

a. An incision is made extending through the subcutaneous tissue and fascia.

b. The procedure is performed if adequate tissue perfusion does not return following an escharotomy.

c. Fasciotomy is performed in the operating room with the client under general anesthesia.

d. Following the procedure, assess pulses, color, movement, and sensation of affected extremity and control any bleeding with pressure.

e. Apply topical antimicrobial agents and dressings to the area, as prescribed, following the procedure.

C. Acute phase (see Table 49-2)

1. Description

a. The acute phase begins when the client is hemodynamically stable, capillary permeability is restored, and diuresis has begun.

b. The acute phase usually begins 48 to 72 hours after the time of injury.

c. Emphasis during this phase is placed on restorative therapy, and the phase continues until wound closure is achieved.

d. The focus is on infection control, wound care, wound closure, nutritional support, pain management, and physical therapy.

2. Interventions

a. Continue with protective isolation techniques.

b. Provide wound care as prescribed and prepare for wound closure.

c. Provide pain management.

d. Provide adequate nutrition as prescribed.

e. Prepare client for rehabilitation.

D. Wound care (Table 49-4)

1. Description: Cleansing, débridement, and dressing of burn wounds

2. Hydrotherapy

a. Wounds are cleansed by immersion, showering, or spraying.

b. Hydrotherapy occurs for 30 minutes or less to prevent increased sodium loss through the burn wound, heat loss, pain, and stress.

c. Client should be premedicated before procedure.

d. Hydrotherapy generally is not used for clients who are hemodynamically unstable or those with new skin grafts.

e. Care is taken to minimize bleeding and maintain body temperature during the procedure.

f. If hydrotherapy is not used, wounds are washed and rinsed with the client in bed before the application of antimicrobial agents.

3. Débridement (Box 49-4)

a. Débridement is removal of eschar or necrotic tissue to prevent bacterial proliferation under the eschar and to promote wound healing.

b. Débridement may be mechanical, enzymatic, or surgical.

c. **Deep partial-** or **full-thickness burns:** Wound is cleansed and débrided, and topical antimicrobial agents are applied once or twice daily.

E. Wound closure

1. Description

a. Wound closure prevents infection and loss of fluid.

b. Closure promotes healing.

c. Closure prevents contractures.

d. Wound closure is performed on day 5 to 21, depending on the extent of the burn.

TABLE 49-4

Open Method Versus Closed Method of Wound Care

Method	Advantages	Disadvantages
OPEN Antimicrobial cream is applied, and wound is left open to the air without a dressing. Antimicrobial cream may be prescribed every 12 hr.	Visualization of the wound Easier mobility and joint range of motion Simplicity in wound care	Increased chance of hypothermia from exposure
CLOSED Gauze dressings are carefully wrapped from the distal to the proximal area of the extremity to ensure that circulation is not compromised. No two burn surfaces should be allowed to touch; touching can promote webbing of digits, contractures, and poor cosmetic outcome. Dressings are changed usually every 8-12 hr.	Decreases evaporative fluid and heat loss Aids in débridement	Mobility limitations Prevents effective range-of-motion exercises Wound assessment limited

BOX 49-4
Débridement

MECHANICAL

Performed during hydrotherapy; involves use of washcloths or sponges to débride eschar and scissors and forceps to lift and trim away loose eschar

May include wet-to-dry or wet-to-wet dressing changes

Painful procedure; may cause bleeding

ENZYMATIC

Application of topical enzyme agents directly to the wound; digest collagen necrotic tissue

SURGICAL

Excision of eschar or necrotic tissue via surgical procedure in the operating room

Tangential Technique

Very thin layers of the necrotic burn surface are excised until bleeding occurs (bleeding indicates that a healthy dermis or subcutaneous fat has been reached).

Fascial Technique

The burn wound is excised to the level of superficial fascia; is usually reserved for very deep and extensive burns.

2. Wound coverings (Box 49-5)
3. Autografting (see Box 49-5)
   a. Autografting provides permanent wound coverage.
   b. Autografting is surgical removal of a thin layer of the client's own unburned skin, which then is applied to the excised burn wound.
   c. Autografting is performed in the operating room under anesthesia.
   d. Monitor for bleeding following the graft because bleeding beneath an autograft can prevent adherence.
   e. If prescribed, small amounts of blood or serum can be removed by gently rolling the fluid from the center of the graft to the periphery with a sterile gauze pad, where it can be absorbed.
   f. For large accumulations of blood, the physician will aspirate the blood using a small-gauge needle and syringe.
   g. Autografts are immobilized following surgery for 3 to 7 days to allow time to adhere and attach to the wound bed.

BOX 49-5
Wound Coverings

BIOLOGICAL

Amnion

Amniotic membranes from human placenta used; adheres to the wound

Effective as a dressing until epithelial cell regrowth occurs

Requires frequent changes because it does not develop a blood supply and disintegrates in about 48 hours

Allograft or Homograft (Human Tissue)

Donated human cadaver skin provided through a skin bank

Monitor for wound exudate and signs of infection

Rejection—can occur within 24 hours

Risk of transmitting bloodborne infection exists when used

Xenograft or Heterograft (Animal Tissue)

Pigskin harvested after slaughter, preserved for storage.

Monitor for infection and wound adherence

Placed over granulation tissue; replaced every 2 to 5 days until wound heals naturally or until closure with autograft is complete.

Cultured Skin

Grown in laboratory from small specimen of epidermal cells from unburned portion of client's body

Cell sheets grafted on the client to generate permanent skin surface

Cell sheets are not durable; care must be taken when applying to ensure adherence, prevent sloughing

Artificial Skin

Consists of two layers—Silastic epidermis and porous dermis made from bovine hide collagen and shark cartilage

After application, fibroblasts move into collagen part of artificial skin and create structure similar to normal dermis

Artificial dermis then dissolves; replaced with normal blood vessels and connective tissue called *neodermis*

Neodermis supports standard autograph placed over it when Silastic layer removed

BIOSYNTHETIC

Combination of biosynthetic and synthetic materials

Placed in contact with the wound surface; forms an adherent bond until epithelialization occurs

Porous substance allows exudate to pass through

Monitor for wound exudate and signs of infection

SYNTHETIC

Applied directly to surface of clean or surgically prepared wound; remains in place until falling off or removed

Covering is transparent or translucent; therefore, wound can be inspected without removing dressing

Pain at wound site reduced because covering prevents contact of wound with air

AUTOGRAFT

Skin taken from a remote unburned area of client's own body; transplanted to cover burn wound

Graft placed on clean granulated bed or over surgically excised area of the burn

Provides for permanent skin coverage

h. Position the client for immobilization and elevation of the graft site to prevent movement and shearing of the graft.

4. Care of the graft site
   a. Elevate and immobilize the graft site.
   b. Keep the site free from pressure.
   c. Avoid weight-bearing.
   d. When the graft takes, roll a cotton-tipped applicator over the graft to remove exudate, because exudate can lead to infection and prevent graft adherence.
   e. Monitor for foul-smelling drainage, increased temperature, increased white blood cell count, hematoma, and fluid accumulation.
   f. Instruct the client to avoid using fabric softeners and harsh detergents in the laundry.
   g. Instruct the client to lubricate healing skin with prescribed agents.
   h. Instruct the client to protect the affected area from sunlight.
   i. Instruct the client to use splints and support garments as prescribed.

5. Care of the donor site
   a. Method of care varies, depending on physician's preference
   b. A moist gauze dressing is applied at the time of the surgery to maintain pressure and stop any oozing.
   c. The physician may prescribe site treatment with single-layer gauze impregnated with petrolatum or with a biosynthetic dressing such as Biobrane.
   d. Keep the donor site clean, dry, and free from pressure.
   e. Prevent the client from scratching the donor site.
   f. Apply lubricating lotions to soften the area and reduce the itching after the donor site is healed.
   g. Donor site can be reused once healing has occurred (heals spontaneously within 7 to 14 days with proper care).

F. Physical therapy
   1. An individualized program of splinting, positioning, exercises, ambulation, and activities of daily living is implemented early in the acute phase of recovery to maximize functional and cosmetic outcomes.
   2. Perform range-of-motion exercises as prescribed to reduce edema and maintain strength and joint function.
   3. Ambulate the client as prescribed to maintain the strength of the lower extremities.
   4. Apply splints as prescribed to maintain proper joint position and prevent contractures.
      a. Static splints immobilize the joint and are applied for periods of immobilization, during sleeping, and for clients who cannot maintain proper positioning.
      b. Dynamic splints exercise the affected joint.
      c. Avoid pressure to skin areas when applying splints, which could lead to further tissue and nerve damage.
   5. Scarring is controlled by elastic wraps and bandages that apply continuous pressure to the healing skin while the skin is vulnerable to shearing.
   6. Anti-burn scar support garments are usually worn 23 hours a day until the burn scar tissue has matured, which takes 18 to 24 months.
G. Rehabilitative phase (see Table 49-2)
   1. Description
      a. Rehabilitation is the final phase of burn care.
      b. Rehabilitation overlaps the acute-care phase and goes well beyond hospitalization.
      c. Goals of this phase are designed so that the client can gain independence and achieve maximal function.
   2. Goals
      a. Promote wound healing.
      b. Minimize deformities.
      c. Increase strength and function.
      d. Provide emotional support.

PRACTICE QUESTIONS

1. Which of the following individuals is least likely to be at risk of developing psoriasis?
   1. A 32-year-old African American
   2. A woman experiencing menopause
   3. A client with a family history of the disorder
   4. An individual who has experienced a significant amount of emotional distress

2. A male client calls the emergency room and tells the nurse that he had been cleaning a wooded area in the backyard and came directly into contact with poison ivy shrubs. The client tells the nurse that he cannot see anything on the skin and asks the nurse what to do. Which of the following is the appropriate nursing response?
   1. "Come to the emergency room."
   2. "Apply calamine lotion immediately to the exposed skin areas."
   3. "Take a shower immediately, lathering and rinsing several times."
   4. "It is not necessary to do anything if you cannot see anything on your skin."

3. The client is being admitted to the hospital for treatment of acute cellulitis of the lower left leg. The client asks the admitting nurse to explain what cellulitis means. The nurse bases the response on

the understanding that the characteristics of cellulitis include:

1. An inflammation of the epidermis only
2. A skin infection into the dermis and subcutaneous tissue
3. An acute superficial infection of the dermis and lymphatics
4. An epidermal and lymphatic infection caused by *Staphylococcus*

4. The nurse prepares to care for a client with acute cellulitis of the lower leg. The nurse anticipates that which of the following will be prescribed for the client?

1. Cold compresses to the affected area
2. Warm compresses to the affected area
3. Intermittent heat lamp treatments four times daily
4. Alternating hot and cold compresses continuously

5. The clinic nurse assesses the skin of a white client with a diagnosis of psoriasis. The nurse understands that which characteristic is associated with this skin disorder?

1. Clear, thin nail beds
2. Red-purplish scaly lesions
3. Oily skin and no episodes of pruritus
4. Silvery-white scaly patches on the scalp, elbows, knees, and sacral regions

6. Ultraviolet light therapy is prescribed as a component of the treatment plan for a client with psoriasis and the nurse provides instructions to the client regarding the treatment. Which statement by the client indicates a need for further instructions?

1. "Treatments are limited to two or three times a week."
2. "The ultraviolet light treatments are given on consecutive days."
3. "Eye goggles need to be worn to prevent exposure to ultraviolet light."
4. "Just the area requiring treatment should be exposed to the ultraviolet light."

7. The clinic nurse notes that the physician has documented a diagnosis of herpes zoster (shingles) in the client's chart. Based on an understanding of the cause of this disorder, the nurse determines that this definitive diagnosis was made following which diagnostic test?

1. Patch test
2. Skin biopsy
3. Culture of the lesion
4. Wood's light examination

8. The nurse is assigned to care for a client with herpes zoster (shingles). Which of the following characteristics would the nurse expect to note when assessing the lesions of this infection?

1. Clustered skin vesicles
2. A generalized body rash

3. Small blue-white spots with a red base
4. A fiery red, edematous rash on the cheeks

9. The nurse manager is planning the clinical assignments for the day and avoids assigning which staff member to the client with herpes zoster?

1. The nurse who never had roseola
2. The nurse who never had mumps
3. The nurse who never had chickenpox
4. The nurse who never had German measles

10. A client returns to the clinic for follow-up treatment following a skin biopsy of a suspicious lesion performed 1 week ago. The biopsy report indicates that the lesion is a melanoma. The nurse understands that which of the following describes a characteristic of this type of a lesion?

1. Metastasis is rare.
2. Melanoma is encapsulated.
3. Melanoma is highly metastatic.
4. Melanoma is characterized by local invasion.

11. When assessing a lesion diagnosed as malignant melanoma, the nurse most likely expects to note which of the following?

1. An irregularly shaped lesion
2. A small papule with a dry, rough scale
3. A firm, nodular lesion topped with crust
4. A pearly papule with a central crater and a waxy border

12. The nurse prepares discharge instructions for a client following cryosurgery for the treatment of a malignant skin lesion. Which of the following should the nurse include in the instructions?

1. Avoid showering for 7 to 10 days.
2. Apply ice to the site to prevent discomfort.
3. Apply alcohol-soaked dressings twice a day.
4. Clean the site with hydrogen peroxide to prevent infection.

13. The health education nurse provides instructions to a group of clients regarding measures that will assist in preventing skin cancer. Which statement by a client indicates a need for further instructions?

1. "I will avoid sun exposure after 3 PM."
2. "I will use sunscreen when participating in outdoor activities."
3. "I will wear a hat, opaque clothing, and sunglasses when in the sun."
4. "I will examine my body monthly for any lesions that may be suspicious."

14. The client arrives at the emergency room and has experienced frostbite to the right hand. Which of the following would the nurse note on assessment of the client's hand?

1. A pink, edematous hand
2. A fiery red skin with edema in the nail beds
3. Black fingertips surrounded by an erythematous rash
4. A white color to the skin, which is insensitive to touch

15. The nurse prepares to treat a client with frostbite of the toes. Which of the following does the nurse anticipate to be prescribed for this condition?
    1. Rapid and continuous rewarming of the toes after flushing returns
    2. Rapid and continuous rewarming of the toes in cold water for 45 minutes
    3. Rapid and continuous rewarming of the toes in hot water for 15 to 20 minutes
    4. Rapid and continuous rewarming of the toes in a warm water bath until flushing of the skin occurs

16. The evening nurse reviews the nursing documentation in the client's chart and notes that the day nurse has documented that the client has a stage II pressure ulcer in the sacral area. Which of the following would the nurse expect to note on assessment of the client's sacral area?
    1. Intact skin
    2. Full-thickness skin loss
    3. Exposed bone, tendon, or muscle
    4. Partial-thickness skin loss of the dermis

17. The nurse is implementing a teaching plan to a group of adolescents regarding the causes of acne. Which of the following is an appropriate nursing statement regarding the cause of this disorder?
    1. "Acne is caused by oily skin."
    2. "The actual cause is not known."
    3. "Acne is caused by eating chocolate."
    4. "Acne is caused as a result of exposure to heat and humidity."

18. The nurse is reviewing the health care record of the clients scheduled to be seen at the health care clinic. The nurse determines that which of the following individuals is at the greatest risk for development of an integumentary disorder?
    1. An adolescent
    2. An older female
    3. A physical education teacher
    4. An outdoor construction worker

19. The client scheduled for a skin biopsy is concerned and asks the nurse how painful the procedure is. The appropriate response by the nurse is:
    1. "There is no pain associated with this procedure."
    2. "The local anesthetic may cause a burning or stinging sensation."
    3. "A preoperative medication will be given so you will be sleeping and will not feel any pain."
    4. "There is some pain, but the physician will prescribe an opioid analgesic following the procedure."

20. The nurse is reviewing the discharge instructions for the client who had a skin biopsy. Which statement by the client indicates a need for further instruction?
    1. "I will use the antibiotic ointment as prescribed."
    2. "I will return in 7 days to have the sutures removed."
    3. "I will call the physician if I see any drainage from the wound."
    4. "I will remove the dressing as soon as I get home and wash it with tap water."

21. The nurse prepares to assist the physician to examine the client's skin with a Wood's light. The nurse includes which of the following in the plan for this procedure?
    1. Prepare a local anesthetic.
    2. Obtain an informed consent.
    3. Darken the room for the examination.
    4. Shave the skin and scrub with povidone-iodine solution.

22. Isotretinoin (Accutane) is prescribed for a client with severe cystic acne. The nurse provides instructions to the client regarding administration of the medication. Which of the following if stated by the client indicates a need for further teaching regarding this medication?
    1. "I need to continue to take my vitamin A supplements."
    2. "The medication may cause dryness and burning in my eyes."
    3. "I need to use emollients and lip balms for my dry skin and lips."
    4. "I will need to return for a blood test to check my triglyceride level."

23. The clinic nurse inspects the skin of a client suspected of having scabies. Which assessment finding would the nurse note if this disorder was present?
    1. Patchy hair loss and round red macules with scales
    2. The presence of white patches scattered about the trunk
    3. Multiple straight or wavy, thread-like lines beneath the skin
    4. The appearance of vesicles or pustules with a thick honey-colored crust

24. The home health nurse visits a client suspected of having scabies. Which of the following precautions will the nurse institute during the assessment of the client?
    1. Wear gloves only.
    2. Wear a mask and gloves.
    3. Wear a gown and gloves.
    4. Avoid touching the client's home furnishings.

25. The nurse is preparing to care for a burn client scheduled for an escharotomy procedure being performed for a third-degree circumferential arm burn. The nurse understands that the anticipated therapeutic outcome of the escharotomy is:
    1. Return of distal pulses
    2. Brisk bleeding from the site
    3. Decreasing edema formation
    4. Formation of granulation tissue

26. A client is undergoing fluid replacement after being burned on 20% of her body 12 hours ago. The

nursing assessment reveals a blood pressure of 90/50 mm Hg, a pulse rate of 110 beats/min, and a urine output of 20 mL over the past hour. The nurse reports the findings to the physician and anticipates which of the following orders to be prescribed?
1. Transfusing 1 unit of packed red blood cells
2. Administering a diuretic to increase urine output
3. Changing the IV lactated Ringer's solution to one that contains dextrose in water
4. Increasing the amount of IV lactated Ringer's solution administered per hour

27. When caring for a client with extensive burns, the nurse anticipates that pain medication will be administered via which route?
1. Oral
2. Intravenous
3. Intramuscular
4. Subcutaneous

28. The nurse is caring for a client who sustained superficial partial-thickness burns on the anterior lower legs and anterior thorax. Which of the following does the nurse expect to note during the emergent phase of the burn injury?
1. Decreased heart rate
2. Increased urinary output
3. Increased blood pressure
4. Elevated hematocrit levels

29. The nurse is caring for a client who suffered an inhalation injury from a wood stove. The carbon monoxide blood report reveals a level of 12%. Based on this level, the nurse would anticipate which of the following signs in the client?
1. Coma
2. Flushing
3. Dizziness
4. Tachycardia

30. The client arrives at the emergency room following a burn injury that occurred in the basement at home and an inhalation injury is suspected. Which of the following would the nurse anticipate to be prescribed for the client?
1. 100% oxygen via an aerosol mask
2. Oxygen via nasal cannula at 15 L/min
3. Oxygen via nasal cannula at 10 L/min
4. 100% oxygen via a tight-fitting, nonrebreather face mask

31. The nurse is administering fluids intravenously as prescribed to a client who sustained superficial partial-thickness burn injuries of the back and legs. In evaluating the adequacy of fluid resuscitation, the nurse understands that which of the following would provide the most reliable indicator for determining the adequacy?
1. Vital signs
2. Urine output
3. Mental status
4. Peripheral pulses

32. The nurse manager is observing a new nursing graduate caring for a burn client in protective isolation. The nurse manager intervenes if the new nursing graduate planned to implement which incorrect component of protective isolation technique?
1. Using sterile sheets and linens
2. Performing strict hand-washing technique
3. Wearing gloves and a gown only when giving direct care to the client
4. Wearing protective garb, including a mask, gloves, cap, shoe covers, gowns, and plastic apron

33. The nurse is caring for a client following an autograft and grafting to a burn wound on the right knee. Which of the following would the nurse anticipate to be prescribed for the client?
1. Out of bed
2. Bathroom privileges
3. Immobilization of the affected leg
4. Placing the affected leg in a dependent position

ALTERNATE ITEM FORMAT: FILL IN THE BLANK

The adult client was burned as a result of an explosion. The burn initially affected the client's entire face (anterior half of the head) and the upper half of the anterior torso, and there were circumferential burns to the lower half of both arms. The client's clothes caught on fire, and the client ran, causing subsequent burn injuries to the posterior surface of the head and the upper half of the posterior torso. Using the rule of nines, what would be the extent of the burn injury?

Answer: _____%

ANSWERS

1. 1
Rationale: Psoriasis occurs equally among women and men, although the incidence is lower in darker skinned races and ethnic groups. A genetic predisposition has been recognized in some cases. Emotional distress, trauma, systemic illness, seasonal changes, and hormonal changes are linked to exacerbations.
Test-Taking Strategy: Note the strategic words *least likely*. Use the process of elimination and knowledge regarding the description of psoriasis and the risk factors associated with the disorder to answer the question. If you had difficulty with the question, review the risk factors of the disorder and the factors that affect exacerbations.
Level of Cognitive Ability: Analysis
Client Needs: Health Promotion and Maintenance
Integrated Process: Nursing Process—assessment
Content Area: Adult health—integumentary
Reference: Huether, S., & McCance, K. (2004). *Understanding pathophysiology* (3rd ed., p. 1144). St. Louis: Mosby.

2. 3
Rationale: When an individual comes in contact with a poison ivy plant, the sap from the plant forms an invisible film on the human skin. The client should be instructed to shower immediately and to lather the skin several times and rinse each time in running water. Calamine lotion is a treatment used if dermatitis develops. The client does not need to be seen in the emergency room at this time.
Test-Taking Strategy: Use the process of elimination. Recalling that dermatitis can develop from contact with an allergen and that contact with poison ivy results in an invisible film will assist in directing you to option 3. Review the immediate treatment for contact with poison ivy if you had difficulty with this question.
Level of Cognitive Ability: Application
Client Needs: Physiological Integrity
Integrated Process: Nursing Process—implementation
Content Area: Adult health—integumentary
References: Phipps, W., Monahan, F., Sands, J., et al. (2003). *Medical-surgical nursing: Health and illness perspectives* (7th ed., p. 1957). St. Louis: Mosby.
Wong, D., Hockenberry, M., Perry, S., et al. (2006). *Maternal-child nursing care* (3rd ed., p. 1766). St. Louis: Mosby.

3. 2
Rationale: Cellulitis is a skin infection into deeper dermal and subcutaneous tissues that results in a deep red erythema without sharp borders and spreads widely throughout tissue spaces. The skin is erythematous, edematous, tender, and sometimes nodular. Erysipelas is an acute, superficial, rapidly spreading inflammation of the dermis and lymphatics.
Test-Taking Strategy: Use the process of elimination. Eliminate options 3 and 4 because they are comparative or alike. Eliminate option 1 because of the close-ended word *only*. If you had difficulty with this question, review the characteristics of cellulitis and erysipelas.
Level of Cognitive Ability: Comprehension
Client Needs: Physiological Integrity
Integrated Process: Teaching and Learning
Content Area: Adult health—integumentary

Reference: Ignatavicius, D., & Workman, M. (2006). *Medical-surgical nursing: Critical thinking for collaborative care* (5th ed., p. 1595). Philadelphia: W.B. Saunders.

4. 2
Rationale: Cellulitis is a skin infection into deeper dermal and subcutaneous tissues that results in a deep red erythema without sharp borders and spreads widely throughout tissue spaces. Warm compresses may be used to decrease the discomfort, erythema, and edema. After tissue and blood cultures are obtained, antibiotics will be initiated. The nurse should provide supportive care as prescribed to manage symptoms such as fatigue, fever, chills, headache, and myalgia. Heat lamps can cause more disruption to already inflamed tissue. Cold compresses and alternating cold and hot compresses are not the best measures.
Test-Taking Strategy: Use the process of elimination, noting that option 2 is different from the other options. The words *cold*, *heat*, and *hot* identify extremes in temperature. If you had difficulty with this question, review the treatment associated with cellulitis.
Level of Cognitive Ability: Analysis
Client Needs: Physiological Integrity
Integrated Process: Nursing Process—planning
Content Area: Adult health—integumentary
Reference: Lewis, S., Heitkemper, M., & Dirksen, S. (2004). *Medical-surgical nursing: Assessment and management of clinical problems* (6th ed., p. 494). St. Louis: Mosby.

5. 4
Rationale: Psoriatic patches are covered with silvery white scales. Affected areas include the scalp, elbows, knees, shins, sacral area, and trunk. Thickening, pitting, and discoloration of the nails occur. Pruritus may occur. The lesions in psoriasis are not red-purplish scaly lesions.
Test-Taking Strategy: Use the process of elimination. Recalling that psoriasis is associated with the presence of silvery white scaly patches will direct you to option 4. If you had difficulty with this question, review the manifestations associated with psoriasis.
Level of Cognitive Ability: Comprehension
Client Needs: Physiological Integrity
Integrated Process: Nursing Process—assessment
Content Area: Adult health—integumentary
References: Ignatavicius, D., & Workman, M. (2006). *Medical-surgical nursing: Critical thinking for collaborative care* (5th ed., p. 1604). Philadelphia: W.B. Saunders.
Lewis, S., Heitkemper, M., & Dirksen, S. (2004). *Medical-surgical nursing: Assessment and management of clinical problems* (6th ed., p. 506). St. Louis: Mosby.

6. 2
Rationale: Ultraviolet light (UVL) treatments are limited to two or three times a week and are not given on consecutive days. Safety precautions are required during UVL therapy. Exposure of only those areas requiring treatment to the UVL is best. Protective wraparound goggles prevent exposure of the eyes to UVL. The face should be shielded with a loosely applied pillow case if it is unaffected. Direct contact with the light bulbs of the treatment unit should be avoided to prevent burning of the skin.

Test-Taking Strategy: Use the process of elimination and note the strategic words *indicates a need for further instructions.* These words indicate a negative event query and ask you to select an option that is an incorrect statement. Recalling that safety precautions are necessary for this treatment and noting the words *given on consecutive days* will direct you to this option. If you had difficulty with this question, review client education for UVL treatment.
Level of Cognitive Ability: Analysis
Client Needs: Safe and Effective Care Environment
Integrated Process: Teaching and Learning
Content Area: Adult health—integumentary
Reference: Ignatavicius, D., & Workman, M. (2006). *Medical-surgical nursing: Critical thinking for collaborative care* (5th ed., p. 1605). Philadelphia: W.B. Saunders.

7. 3
Rationale: With the classic presentation of herpes zoster, the clinical examination is diagnostic. A viral culture of the lesion provides the definitive diagnosis. Herpes zoster (shingles) is caused by a reactivation of the varicella-zoster virus, the virus that causes chickenpox. A patch test is a skin test that involves the administration of an allergen to the surface of the skin to identify specific allergies. A biopsy would provide a cytological examination of tissue. In a Wood's light examination, the skin is viewed under ultraviolet light to identify superficial infections of the skin.
Test-Taking Strategy: Use the process of elimination. Recalling that herpes zoster is caused by a virus will assist in directing you to the correct option. Remember that a biopsy will determine tissue type, whereas a culture will identify an organism. Review the diagnostic measures for herpes zoster (shingles) if you had difficulty with this question.
Level of Cognitive Ability: Comprehension
Client Needs: Physiological Integrity
Integrated Process: Nursing Process—assessment
Content Area: Adult health—integumentary
Reference: Black, J., & Hawks, J. (2005). *Medical-surgical nursing: Clinical management for positive outcomes* (7th ed., p. 1421). Philadelphia: W.B. Saunders.

8. 1
Rationale: The primary lesion of herpes zoster is a vesicle. The classic presentation is grouped vesicles on an erythematous base along a dermatome. Because the lesions follow nerve pathways, they do not cross the midline of the body. Options 2, 3, and 4 are incorrect descriptions of herpes zoster.
Test-Taking Strategy: Use the process of elimination. Remembering that these lesions occur as grouped vesicles along a nerve pathway will assist in answering the question. If you had difficulty with this question, review the characteristics of herpes zoster lesions.
Level of Cognitive Ability: Analysis
Client Needs: Physiological Integrity
Integrated Process: Nursing Process—assessment
Content Area: Adult health—integumentary
Reference: Black, J., & Hawks, J. (2005). *Medical-surgical nursing: Clinical management for positive outcomes* (7th ed., p. 1421). Philadelphia: W.B. Saunders.

9. 3
Rationale: Herpes zoster (shingles) is caused by a reactivation of the varicella-zoster virus, the causative virus of chickenpox. Individuals who have not been exposed to the varicella-zoster virus are susceptible to chickenpox. Health care workers who are unsure of their immune status should have varicella titers done before exposure to a person with herpes zoster. Options 1, 2, and 4 are unrelated to the herpes zoster virus.
Test-Taking Strategy: Use the process of elimination. Recalling that herpes zoster is caused by a reactivation of the varicella-zoster virus, the causative virus of chickenpox, will direct you to the correct option. Review the relationship between herpes zoster virus and chickenpox if you had difficulty with this question.
Level of Cognitive Ability: Application
Client Needs: Safe and Effective Care Environment
Integrated Process: Nursing Process—planning
Content Area: Delegating/Prioritizing
Reference: Black, J., & Hawks, J. (2005). *Medical-surgical nursing: Clinical management for positive outcomes* (7th ed., p. 1421). Philadelphia: W.B. Saunders.

10. 3
Rationale: Melanomas are pigmented malignant lesions originating in the melanin-producing cells of the epidermis. This skin cancer is highly metastatic, and a person's survival depends on early diagnosis and treatment. Options 1, 2, and 4 are not characteristics of a melanoma.
Test-Taking Strategy: Use the process of elimination. Note that options 1, 2, and 4 are comparative or alike. Also, recalling that melanomas are highly metastatic will assist in directing you to the correct option. If you had difficulty with this question, review the characteristics of skin cancers.
Level of Cognitive Ability: Comprehension
Client Needs: Physiological Integrity
Integrated Process: Nursing Process—assessment
Content Area: Adult health—integumentary
Reference: Ignatavicius, D., & Workman, M. (2006). *Medical-surgical nursing: Critical thinking for collaborative care* (5th ed., p. 1608). Philadelphia: W.B. Saunders.

11. 1
Rationale: A melanoma is an irregularly shaped pigmented papule or plaque with a red-, white-, or blue-toned color. Basal cell carcinoma appears as a pearly papule with a central crater and rolled waxy border. Squamous cell carcinoma is a firm, nodular lesion topped with a crust or a central area of ulceration. Actinic keratosis, a premalignant lesion, appears as a small macule or papule with a dry, rough, adherent yellow or brown scale.
Test-Taking Strategy: Use the process of elimination. Remembering that irregularly shaped lesions are a cause for concern will assist in directing you to option 1. If you had difficulty with this question, review the characteristics of malignant skin lesions.
Level of Cognitive Ability: Comprehension
Client Needs: Physiological Integrity
Integrated Process: Nursing Process—assessment
Content Area: Adult health—integumentary
Reference: Lewis, S., Heitkemper, M., & Dirksen, S. (2004). *Medical-surgical nursing: Assessment and management of clinical problems* (6th ed., p. 492). St. Louis: Mosby.

12. **4**

Rationale: Cryosurgery involves the local application of liquid nitrogen to isolated lesions and causes cell death and tissue destruction. The nurse informs the client that swelling and increased tenderness of the treated area can occur when the skin thaws. Tissue freezing is followed by hemorrhagic blister formation in 1 to 2 days. The nurse instructs the client to clean the treatment site with hydrogen peroxide to prevent secondary infection. A topical antibiotic also may be prescribed. Application of a warm, damp washcloth intermittently to the site will provide relief from any discomfort. Alcohol-soaked dressings will cause irritation. The client does not need to avoid showering.

Test-Taking Strategy: Use the process of elimination. Eliminate option 1 first because there is no reason for the client to avoid showers. Eliminate option 3 next because alcohol-soaked dressings will cause irritation. From the remaining options, note that option 4 addresses the prevention of infection. Therefore, this is the best option. If you had difficulty with this question, review client education following cryosurgery.

Level of Cognitive Ability: Application
Client Needs: Physiological Integrity
Integrated Process: Teaching and Learning
Content Area: Adult health—integumentary
Reference: Ignatavicius, D., & Workman, M. (2006). *Medical-surgical nursing: Critical thinking for collaborative care* (5th ed., p. 1610). Philadelphia: W.B. Saunders.

13. **1**

Rationale: The client should be instructed to avoid sun exposure between the hours of 11 AM and 3 PM. Sunscreen, a hat, opaque clothing, and sunglasses should be worn for outdoor activities. The client should be instructed to examine the body monthly for the appearance of any possible cancerous or any precancerous lesions.

Test-Taking Strategy: Use the process of elimination and note the strategic words *a need for further instructions*. These words indicate a negative event query and ask you to select an option that is an incorrect statement. Note the strategic word *avoid* in option 1 to help direct you to this option. Review client teaching points for the prevention of skin cancer if you had difficulty with this question.

Level of Cognitive Ability: Analysis
Client Needs: Health Promotion and Maintenance
Integrated Process: Teaching and Learning
Content Area: Adult health—integumentary
Reference: Ignatavicius, D., & Workman, M. (2006). *Medical-surgical nursing: Critical thinking for collaborative care* (5th ed., p. 1609). Philadelphia: W.B. Saunders.

14. **4**

Rationale: Assessment findings in frostbite include a white or blue color; the skin will be hard, cold, and insensitive to touch. As thawing occurs, flushing of the skin, the development of blisters or blebs, or tissue edema appears. Options 1, 2, and 3 are incorrect.

Test-Taking Strategy: Use the process of elimination. Noting the strategic words *insensitive to touch* in option 4 should direct you to this option. If you had difficulty with this question, review the characteristics associated with frostbite.

Level of Cognitive Ability: Analysis
Client Needs: Physiological Integrity
Integrated Process: Nursing Process—assessment
Content Area: Adult health—integumentary
References: Ignatavicius, D., & Workman, M. (2006). *Medical-surgical nursing: Critical thinking for collaborative care* (5th ed., pp. 186-187, 1614). Philadelphia: W.B. Saunders.
Lewis, S., Heitkemper, M., & Dirksen, S. (2004). *Medical-surgical nursing: Assessment and management of clinical problems* (6th ed., p. 1854). St. Louis: Mosby.

15. **4**

Rationale: Acute frostbite is treated ideally with rapid and continuous rewarming of the tissue in a warm water bath for 15 to 20 minutes or until flushing of the skin occurs. Slow thawing or interrupted periods of warmth are avoided, because this can contribute to increased cellular damage. Cold or hot water is not used. Thawing can cause considerable pain, and the nurse administers analgesics as prescribed.

Test-Taking Strategy: Use the process of elimination. Eliminate options 2 and 3 because of the words *cold* and *hot*. Eliminate option 1 because intervention would begin immediately. If you had difficulty with this question, review the interventions associated with frostbite.

Level of Cognitive Ability: Analysis
Client Needs: Physiological Integrity
Integrated Process: Nursing Process—planning
Content Area: Adult health—integumentary
Reference: Lewis, S., Heitkemper, M., & Dirksen, S. (2004). *Medical-surgical nursing: Assessment and management of clinical problems* (6th ed., p. 1854). St. Louis: Mosby.

16. **4**

Rationale: In a stage II pressure ulcer, the skin is not intact. Partial-thickness skin loss of the dermis has occurred. It presents as a shallow open ulcer with a red-pink wound bed, without slough. It may also present as an intact, open or ruptured, serum-filled blister. The skin is intact in stage I. Full-thickness skin loss occurs in stage III. Exposed bone, tendon, or muscle is present in stage IV.

Test-Taking Strategy: Use the process of elimination. Focus on the strategic words *stage II* to direct you to option 4. If you had difficulty with this question, review the characteristics associated with each stage of pressure ulcers.

Level of Cognitive Ability: Comprehension
Client Needs: Physiological Integrity
Integrated Process: Nursing Process—assessment
Content Area: Adult health—integumentary
References: Ignatavicius, D., & Workman, M. (2006). *Medical-surgical nursing: Critical thinking for collaborative care* (5th ed., p. 1586). Philadelphia: W.B. Saunders.
Lewis, S., Heitkemper, M., & Dirksen, S. (2004). *Medical-surgical nursing: Assessment and management of clinical problems* (6th ed., p. 226). St. Louis: Mosby.

17. **2**

Rationale: The actual cause of acne is unknown. Oily skin or the consumption of foods such as chocolate, nuts, or fatty foods are not causes of acne. Exacerbations that coincide with the menstrual cycle result from hormonal activity. Heat, humidity, and excessive perspiration may play a role in exacerbating acne but does not cause it.

Test-Taking Strategy: Use the process of elimination. Note that the question asks for the *cause* of acne. Options 1, 3, and 4 relate specifically to factors that exacerbate acne. Review the cause of acne and factors that exacerbate acne if you had difficulty with this question.

Level of Cognitive Ability: Comprehension
Client Needs: Health Promotion and Maintenance
Integrated Process: Teaching and Learning
Content Area: Adult health—integumentary
References: Black, J., & Hawks, J. (2005). *Medical-surgical nursing: Clinical management for positive outcomes* (7th ed., p. 1401). Philadelphia: W.B. Saunders.
Huether, S., & McCance, K. (2004). *Understanding pathophysiology* (3rd ed., p. 1171). St. Louis: Mosby.
Ignatavicius, D., & Workman, M. (2006). *Medical-surgical nursing: Critical thinking for collaborative care* (5th ed., p. 1612). Philadelphia: W.B. Saunders.

18. **4**
Rationale: Prolonged exposure to the sun, unusual cold, or other conditions can damage the skin. The outdoor construction worker would fit into a high-risk category for the development of an integumentary disorder. An adolescent may be prone to the development of acne, but this does not occur in all adolescents. Immobility and lack of nutrition would increase the older person's risk but the older client is not at as high a risk as the outdoor construction worker. The physical education teacher is at low or no risk of developing an integumentary problem.

Test-Taking Strategy: Use the process of elimination and note the strategic words *greatest risk*. Eliminate option 3 first. Eliminate options 1 and 2 next because not all older clients or adolescents are at risk for the development of integumentary disorders. Noting the strategic word *outdoor* in option 4 should direct you to this option. If you had difficulty with this question, review the risk factors associated with integumentary disorders.

Level of Cognitive Ability: Analysis
Client Needs: Health Promotion and Maintenance
Integrated Process: Nursing Process—assessment
Content Area: Adult health—integumentary
Reference: Ignatavicius, D., & Workman, M. (2006). *Medical-surgical nursing: Critical thinking for collaborative care* (5th ed., pp. 1562-1563). Philadelphia: W.B. Saunders.

19. **2**
Rationale: Depending on the size and location of the lesion, a biopsy is usually a quick and almost painless procedure. The most common source of pain is the initial local anesthetic, which can produce a burning or stinging sensation. Preoperative medication is not necessary with this procedure.

Test-Taking Strategy: Use the process of elimination. Eliminate option 1 first because of the words *no pain*. Eliminate option 4 because this option addresses postprocedure, which is not the subject of the client's question to the nurse. Also, an opioid analgesic is not necessary. Eliminate option 3 because a preoperative medication that puts the client to sleep is not part of the procedure for a skin biopsy. If you had difficulty with this question, review the procedure related to a skin biopsy.

Level of Cognitive Ability: Application
Client Needs: Psychosocial Integrity
Integrated Process: Caring
Content Area: Adult health—integumentary
Reference: Ignatavicius, D., & Workman, M. (2006). *Medical-surgical nursing: Critical thinking for collaborative care* (5th ed., p. 1573). Philadelphia: W.B. Saunders.

20. **4**
Rationale: Following a skin biopsy, the nurse instructs the client to keep the dressing dry and in place for a minimum of 8 hours. After the dressing is removed, the site is cleaned once daily with tap water or saline to remove any dry blood or crusts. The physician may prescribe an antibiotic ointment to minimize local bacterial colonization. The nurse instructs the client to report any redness or excessive drainage at the site. Sutures usually are removed 7 to 10 days after biopsy.

Test-Taking Strategy: Use the process of elimination. Note the strategic words *indicate a need for further instruction*. These words indicate a negative event query and ask you to select an option that is an incorrect statement. Eliminate option 1 first because of the words *as prescribed*. Eliminate options 2 and 3 next. A client needs to report signs of drainage and needs to return to the physician for follow-up and suture removal. Consider the alteration in skin integrity that occurs with a skin biopsy. This should assist in directing you to option 4. Review care of the client following this procedure if you had difficulty with this question.

Level of Cognitive Ability: Analysis
Client Needs: Physiological Integrity
Integrated Process: Teaching and Learning
Content Area: Adult health—integumentary
Reference: Ignatavicius, D., & Workman, M. (2006). *Medical-surgical nursing: Critical thinking for collaborative care* (5th ed., p. 1573). Philadelphia: W.B. Saunders.

21. **3**
Rationale: Examination of the skin under a Wood's light is always carried out in a darkened room. This is a noninvasive examination; therefore, an informed consent is not required. A hand-held long-wavelength ultraviolet light or Wood's light is used. The skin does not need to be shaved, and a local anesthetic is not necessary. Areas of blue-green or red fluorescence are associated with certain skin infections. The procedure is painless.

Test-Taking Strategy: Use the process of elimination. Knowing that this is a noninvasive procedure will assist in eliminating options 1, 2, and 4. Review this procedure if you had difficulty answering this question.

Level of Cognitive Ability: Application
Client Needs: Physiological Integrity
Integrated Process: Nursing Process—planning
Content Area: Adult health—integumentary
Reference: Ignatavicius, D., & Workman, M. (2006). *Medical-surgical nursing: Critical thinking for collaborative care* (5th ed., p. 1573). Philadelphia: W.B. Saunders.

22. **1**
Rationale: In severe cystic acne, isotretinoin (Accutane) is used to inhibit inflammation. Adverse effects include elevated tri-

glyceride levels, skin dryness, eye discomfort such as dryness and burning, and cheilitis (lip inflammation). Close medical follow-up is required, and dry skin and cheilitis can be decreased by the use of emollients and lip balms. Vitamin A supplements are stopped during this treatment.

Test-Taking Strategy: Use the process of elimination and note the strategic words *a need for further teaching*. Recalling that vitamin A supplements need to be discontinued during this treatment will direct you to the correct option. If you had difficulty with this question, review the mechanism of action, side effects, and adverse effects related to this medication.

Level of Cognitive Ability: Analysis
Client Needs: Physiological Integrity
Integrated Process: Teaching and Learning
Content Area: Pharmacology
Reference: Kee, J., & Hayes, E., & McCuistion, L. (2006). *Pharmacology: A nursing process approach* (5th ed., p. 742). Philadelphia: W.B. Saunders.

---

23. 3
Rationale: Scabies can be identified by the multiple straight or wavy, thread-like lines noted beneath the skin. The skin lesions are caused by the female mite, which burrows beneath the skin and lays her eggs. The eggs hatch in a few days, and the baby mites find their way to the skin surface, where they mate and complete the life cycle. Options 1, 2, and 4 are not characteristics of scabies.

Test-Taking Strategy: Use the process of elimination. Recalling that scabies burrows beneath the skin surface will direct you to the correct option. If you had difficulty with this question, review the characteristics associated with scabies.

Level of Cognitive Ability: Analysis
Client Needs: Physiological Integrity
Integrated Process: Nursing Process—assessment
Content Area: Adult health—integumentary
Reference: Black, J., & Hawks, J. (2005). *Medical-surgical nursing: Clinical management for positive outcomes* (7th ed., p. 1419). Philadelphia: W.B. Saunders.

24. 3
Rationale: The Centers for Disease Control and Prevention (CDC) recommends wearing gowns and gloves for close contact with a person infested with scabies. Masks are not necessary. Transmission via clothing and other inanimate objects is uncommon. Scabies usually is transmitted from person to person by direct skin contact. All contacts that the client has had should be treated at the same time.

Test-Taking Strategy: Consider the mode of transmission of scabies and use the process of elimination. Because scabies is transmitted by direct skin contact, eliminate options 1, 2, and 4. If you had difficulty with question, review standard precautions and the transmission mode of scabies.

Level of Cognitive Ability: Application
Client Needs: Safe and Effective Care Environment
Integrated Process: Nursing Process—implementation
Content Area: Adult health—integumentary
References: Black, J., & Hawks, J. (2005). *Medical-surgical nursing: Clinical management for positive outcomes* (7th ed., p. 1419). Philadelphia: W.B. Saunders.
Potter, P., & Perry, A. (2005). *Fundamentals of nursing* (6th ed., p. 797). St. Louis: Mosby.

---

25. 1
Rationale: Escharotomies are performed to relieve the compartment syndrome that can occur when edema forms under nondistensible eschar in a circumferential third-degree burn. Escharotomies are performed through avascular eschar to subcutaneous fat. Although bleeding may occur from the site, it is considered a complication rather than an anticipated therapeutic outcome. Usually, direct pressure with a bulky dressing and elevation will control the bleeding, but occasionally an artery is damaged and may require ligation. Formation of granulation tissue is not the intent of an escharotomy. Escharotomy will not affect the formation of edema.

Test-Taking Strategy: Use the ABCs—airway, breathing, and circulation—to answer the question. The only option that addresses circulation is option 1. If you had difficulty with this question, review the purpose of an escharotomy.

Level of Cognitive Ability: Analysis
Client Needs: Physiological Integrity
Integrated Process: Nursing Process—evaluation
Content Area: Adult health—integumentary
Reference: Ignatavicius, D., & Workman, M. (2006). *Medical-surgical nursing: Critical thinking for collaborative care* (5th ed., pp. 1634-1635). Philadelphia: W.B. Saunders.

26. 4
Rationale: Fluid management during the first 24 hours following a burn injury generally includes the infusion of a balanced salt solution, usually lactated Ringer's solution. Fluid resuscitation is determined by urine output and hourly urine output should be at least 30 mL/hr. The client's urine output is indicative of insufficient fluid resuscitation, which places the client at risk for inadequate perfusion of the brain, heart, kidneys, and other body organs. Therefore, the physician would prescribe an increase in the amount of IV lactated Ringer's solution administered per hour. Administering a diuretic would not correct the problem because it would not replace needed fluid. Diuretics promote the removal of the circulating volume, thereby further compromising the inadequate tissue perfusion. Dextrose in water is an isotonic solution and an isotonic solution maintains fluid balance. This type of solution may be administered after the first 24 hours following the burn injury, depending on the client's physiological needs. Blood replacement is not consistent with fluid therapy for burn injuries.

Test-Taking Strategy: Focus on the data in the question and think about the pathophysiology that occurs in a burn injury. Noting that the burn injury occurred 12 hours ago and that the client's urine output is 20 mL and is indicative of insufficient fluid resuscitation will direct you to the correct option. Review fluid resuscitation in a client with a burn injury if you had difficulty with this question.

Level of Cognitive Ability: Analysis
Client Needs: Physiological Integrity
Integrated Process: Nursing Process—analysis
Content Area: Adult health—integumentary
Reference: Ignatavicius, D., & Workman, M. (2006). *Medical-surgical nursing: Critical thinking for collaborative care* (5th ed., pp. 220, 1633, 1643). St. Louis: W.B. Saunders.

27. 2
Rationale: An extensive burn injury causes impairment of muscle and subcutaneous tissue. Additionally, the gastrointes-

tinal tract has decreased perfusion related to the burn injury. Medications administered by mouth, intramuscularly, or subcutaneously are not absorbed consistently as a result of the burn injury. The client may not experience pain relief from these routes of administration and may also receive a sudden bolus of medication at some point after administration, when fluid shifts occur. Therefore, options 1, 3, and 4 are incorrect.
Test-Taking Strategy: Focus on the data in the question. Noting the word *extensive* in the question will assist in directing you to option 2. Review pain management techniques in a client with a burn injury if you had difficulty with this question.
Level of Cognitive Ability: Application
Client Needs: Physiological Integrity
Integrated Process: Nursing Process—planning
Content Area: Adult health—integumentary
Reference: Ignatavicius, D., & Workman, M. (2006). *Medical-surgical nursing: Critical thinking for collaborative care* (5th ed., p. 1636). St. Louis: W.B. Saunders.

28. **4**
Rationale: The emergent phase begins at the time of injury and ends with the restoration of capillary permeability, usually at 48 to 72 hours following the injury. During the emergent phase, the hematocrit level increases to above normal because of hemoconcentration from the large fluid shifts. Hematocrit levels of 50% to 55% are expected during the first 24 hours after injury, with return to normal by 36 hours after injury. Initially, blood is shunted away from the kidneys, and renal perfusion and glomerular filtration are decreased, resulting in low urine output. Pulse rates are typically higher than normal, and the blood pressure is decreased as a result of the large fluid shifts.
Test-Taking Strategy: Use the process of elimination and think about how the body would react in such a traumatizing event. Eliminate options 1 and 2 first. Knowledge that the blood pressure would decrease as a result of the decrease in circulating blood volume will direct you to option 4. Review pathophysiology related to burn injuries if you had difficulty with this question.
Level of Cognitive Ability: Analysis
Client Needs: Physiological Integrity
Integrated Process: Nursing Process—analysis
Content Area: Adult health—integumentary
References: Ignatavicius, D., & Workman, M. (2006). *Medical-surgical nursing: Critical thinking for collaborative care* (5th ed., p. 1632). Philadelphia: W.B. Saunders.
Lewis, S., Heitkemper, M., & Dirksen, S. (2004). *Medical-surgical nursing: Assessment and management of clinical problems* (6th ed., p. 522). St. Louis: Mosby.

29. **2**
Rationale: Carbon monoxide levels between levels of 11% to 20% result in flushing, headache, decreased visual activity, decreased cerebral functioning, and slight breathlessness; levels of 21% to 40% result in nausea, vomiting, dizziness, tinnitus, vertigo, confusion, drowsiness, pale to reddish-purple skin, tachycardia; levels of 41% to 60% result in seizure and coma; and levels higher than 61% result in death.
Test-Taking Strategy: Use the process of elimination and focus on the carbon monoxide level presented in the question.

Remember flushing occurs with levels between 11% to 20%. If you had difficulty with this question, review these clinical manifestations.
Level of Cognitive Ability: Analysis
Client Needs: Physiological Integrity
Integrated Process: Nursing Process—assessment
Content Area: Adult health—integumentary
Reference: Ignatavicius, D., & Workman, M. (2006). *Medical-surgical nursing: Critical thinking for collaborative care* (5th ed., pp. 1628-1629). Philadelphia: W.B. Saunders.

30. **4**
Rationale: If an inhalation injury is suspected, administration of 100% oxygen via a tight-fitting nonrebreather face mask is prescribed until carboxyhemoglobin levels fall (usually below 15%). In inhalation injuries, the oropharynx is inspected for evidence of erythema, blisters, or ulcerations. The need for endotracheal intubation also is assessed. Options 1, 2, and 3 are incorrect.
Test-Taking Strategy: Use the process of elimination. Recalling that 100% oxygen is required following an inhalation injury will assist you in eliminating options 2 and 3. From the remaining options, recall that a tight-fitting nonrebreather mask is preferred so that the client will not rebreathe exhaled air. If you had difficulty with this question, review care to the client following an inhalation injury.
Level of Cognitive Ability: Analysis
Client Needs: Physiological Integrity
Integrated Process: Nursing Process—analysis
Content Area: Adult health—integumentary
References: Ignatavicius, D., & Workman, M. (2006). *Medical-surgical nursing: Critical thinking for collaborative care* (5th ed., p. 1627). Philadelphia: W.B. Saunders.
Lewis, S., Heitkemper, M., & Dirksen, S. (2004). *Medical-surgical nursing: Assessment and management of clinical problems* (6th ed., pp. 516-517). St. Louis: Mosby.

31. **2**
Rationale: Successful or adequate fluid resuscitation in the client is signaled by stable vital signs, adequate urine output, palpable peripheral pulses, and clear sensorium. The most reliable indicator for determining adequacy of fluid resuscitation is the urine output. For an adult, the hourly urine volume should be 30 to 50 mL.
Test-Taking Strategy: Use the process of elimination and note the strategic words *most reliable*. Note the subject of the question, fluid resuscitation. Urine output is most similar to the subject of administering fluids. Review care of the burn client during fluid resuscitation if you had difficulty with this question.
Level of Cognitive Ability: Analysis
Client Needs: Physiological Integrity
Integrated Process: Nursing Process—evaluation
Content Area: Adult health—integumentary
Reference: Ignatavicius, D., & Workman, M. (2006). *Medical-surgical nursing: Critical thinking for collaborative care* (5th ed., pp. 1630, 1634). Philadelphia: W.B. Saunders.

32. **3**
Rationale: Thorough hand washing should be done before and after each contact with the burn-injured client. Sterile

sheets and linens are used. Protective garb, including gloves, cap, masks, shoe covers, gowns, and plastic apron need to be worn when in the client's room and when directly caring for the client.

Test-Taking Strategy: Use the process of elimination, noting the strategic word *incorrect* in the question. Options 1 and 2 can be eliminated easily. Note the close-ended word *only* in option 3. Also, option 3 identifies the least thorough technique to prevent infection. If you had difficulty with this question, review protective isolation techniques when caring for a burn client.

Level of Cognitive Ability: Analysis
Client Needs: Safe and Effective Care Environment
Integrated Process: Nursing Process—implementation
Content Area: Leadership/Management
References: Lewis, S., Heitkemper, M., & Dirksen, S. (2004). *Medical-surgical nursing: Assessment and management of clinical problems* (6th ed., p. 526). St. Louis: Mosby.
Potter, P., & Perry, A. (2005). *Fundamentals of nursing* (6th ed., p. 798). St. Louis: Mosby.

33. 3
Rationale: Autografts placed over joints or on the lower extremities often are elevated and immobilized following surgery for 3 to 7 days. This period of immobilization allows the autograft time to adhere and attach to the wound bed. Options 1, 2, and 4 are incorrect.

Test-Taking Strategy: Use the process of elimination. Eliminate options 1 and 2 first because they are comparative or alike. From the remaining options, note that the autograft was placed over a joint. This should direct you to option 3. If you had difficulty with this question, review care of an autograft placed over a joint.

Level of Cognitive Ability: Analysis

Client Needs: Physiological Integrity
Integrated Process: Nursing Process—analysis
Content Area: Adult health—integumentary
References: Black, J., & Hawks, J. (2005). *Medical-surgical nursing: Clinical management for positive outcomes* (7th ed., p. 1460). Philadelphia: W.B. Saunders.
Lewis, S., Heitkemper, M., & Dirksen, S. (2004). *Medical-surgical nursing: Assessment and management of clinical problems* (6th ed., pp. 533-534). St. Louis: Mosby.

ALTERNATE ITEM FORMAT: FILL IN THE BLANK
Answer: 36
Rationale: According to the rule of nines, with the initial burn, the anterior half of the head equals 4.5%, the upper half of the anterior torso equals 9%, and the lower half of both arms equals 9%. The subsequent burn included the posterior half of head, equaling 4.5%, and the upper half of posterior torso, equaling 9%. This totals 36%.

Test-Taking Strategy: Knowledge regarding the rule of nines is required to answer this question. The entire head equals 9%, each arm equals 9% (both arms equal 18%), anterior or posterior torso each equals 18% (36% for entire torso), each leg equals 18% (both legs equal 36%), and the perineum equals 1%. Remember, 9 (head), 18 (arms), 36 (torso), 36 (legs), and 1 (perineum) equals 100. If you had difficulty with this question, learn the rule of nines.

Level of Cognitive Ability: Analysis
Client Needs: Physiological Integrity
Integrated Process: Nursing Process—assessment
Content Area: Adult health—integumentary
Reference: Lewis, S., Heitkemper, M., & Dirksen, S. (2004). *Medical-surgical nursing: Assessment and management of clinical problems* (6th ed., p. 519). St. Louis: Mosby.

REFERENCES

Black, J., & Hawks, J. (2005). *Medical-surgical nursing: Clinical management for positive outcomes* (7th ed.). Philadelphia: W.B. Saunders.

Huether, S., & McCance, K. (2004). *Understanding pathophysiology* (3rd ed.). St. Louis: Mosby.

Ignatavicius, D., & Workman, M. (2006). *Medical-surgical nursing: Critical thinking for collaborative care* (5th ed.). Philadelphia: W.B. Saunders.

Kee, J., Hayes, E., & McCuistion, L. (2006). *Pharmacology: A nursing process approach* (5th ed.). Philadelphia: W.B. Saunders.

Phipps, W., Monahan, F., Sands, J., et al. (2003). *Medical-surgical nursing: Health and illness perspectives* (7th ed.). St. Louis: Mosby.

Potter, P., & Perry, A. (2005). *Fundamentals of nursing* (6th ed.). St. Louis: Mosby.

Wong, D., Perry, S., Hockenberry, M., et al. (2006). *Maternal child nursing care* (3rd ed.). St. Louis: Mosby.

Integumentary Medications

I. EMOLLIENTS AND LOTIONS

A. Emollients (Box 50-1)
   1. Oily or fatty substances that soften and soothe irritated skin by allowing the skin to retain water
   2. Available as creams or ointments
   3. Used for dry, scaly, itchy inflammatory conditions

B. Solutions and lotions (Box 50-2)
   1. Solutions and lotions are liquid suspensions or dispersions.
   2. Solutions and lotions require shaking before application.
   3. Although lotions are predominantly water, they have a drying effect on the skin when the water evaporates.
   4. Solutions and lotions are used as a wash for the skin, as soaks, or as wet dressings on ulcers or **burns.**
   5. Solutions and lotions are used for subacute inflammatory lesions after the severe exudative phase has ceased.
   6. Medicated lotions are often used as anti-inflammatory agents because they provide a drying, protective, and cooling effect.

C. Therapeutic baths (Box 50-3)
   1. Relieve itching
   2. Soothe and lubricate
   3. Reduce skin bacteria
   4. Clean skin and add moisture
   5. Loosen scaled skin
   6. Support ultraviolet A or B light therapy

II. RUBS AND LINIMENTS (Box 50-4)

A. Rubs and liniments are used for the temporary relief of muscular aches, rheumatism, arthritis, sprains, and neuralgia.

BOX 50-1
Emollients

Cold cream
Glycerin
Lanolin
Lubriderm
Petrolatum
Vitamin A and D ointment
Zinc ointment

BOX 50-2
Solutions and Lotions

Aluminum acetate solution (Burow's solution)
Calamine lotion (Caladryl lotion)

BOX 50-3
Therapeutic Baths

ANTIPRURITICS (relieve itching)
Colloidal oatmeal (Aveeno Regular Bath)
Colloidal oatmeal, mineral oil (Aveeno Oilated Bath)
Starch and baking soda

ANTIBACTERIAL BATHS (reduce skin bacteria)
Potassium permanganate

EMOLLIENT BATHS (clean skin and add moisture)
Bath emollient (Alpha Keri Therapeutic Bath Oil)
Bath oils
Mineral oil

TAR BATHS (loosen scaled skin, support ultraviolet A or B light therapy)
Coal tar (Balnetar)
Coal tar (Zetar shampoo)
Coal tar solution (Polytar soap, shampoo)
Other coal tar preparations

BOX 50-4
Rubs and Liniments

Methyl salicylate; menthol (Ben-Gay, Icy Hot)
Trolamine salicylate (Aspercreme, Myoflex Creme)

B. Over-the-counter products contain combinations of antiseptics, local anesthetics, analgesics, and counterirritants.

C. Some products contain salicylates and, if used over a large area of the skin, may cause salicylate side effects, such as tinnitus, nausea, or vomiting.

▲ D. A heating pad is not used with these products because irritation or burning of the skin may occur.

III. ANTI-INFECTIVE AGENTS

A. Description
   1. Anti-infective agents include antiseptics and antibacterial, antifungal, antiviral, and antiparasitic medications.
   2. Topical antibiotics are safe and effective for certain conditions; extensive use may encourage the emergence of resistant bacteria.

B. Antiseptics: These substances pose a risk for caustic adverse effects; care should be taken to prevent irritation and injury.
   ▲ 1. Sodium hypochlorite (Dakin's solution)
      a. Dakin's solution is a diluted 0.5% sodium hypochlorite solution that loosens, dissolves, and deodorizes necrotic tissue and blood clots.
      b. The solution kills most common bacteria including spores, amebas, protozoa, viruses, and yeast.
      c. The solution is used for irrigating, cleaning, and deodorizing necrotic or purulent wounds.
      ▲ d. The solution loses its potency during storage, so fresh solution is prepared frequently.
      ▲ e. The solution should not be in contact with healing or normal tissue, because its mechanism of action results in clotting delays.
      ▲ f. To keep tissue irritation to a minimum, the solution should be rinsed off immediately following irrigation.
   2. Chlorhexidine gluconate (Hibiclens)
      a. Effective for cleaning wounds caused by most gram-positive bacteria
      ▲ b. Used for irrigating and cleansing wounds but not for packing wounds because it may cause contact dermatitis
      c. Effectiveness of chlorhexidine is decreased in wounds where soap, blood, or pus is present
   3. Acetic acid preparations
      a. Acetic acid is effective for irrigating, cleansing, and packing wounds infected by *Pseudomonas aeruginosa*.

   ▲ b. Healthy skin surrounding the wound must be protected with a petroleum barrier because acetic acid excoriates the skin.
   4. Hydrogen peroxide
      a. As a 3% solution, hydrogen peroxide has effervescent action that releases gas and breaks up necrotic tissue.
      b. Used to irrigate and clean necrotic tissue and pus from open wounds
      c. Not used to pack wounds because it decomposes too rapidly
      ▲ d. When epithelial tissue begins to form, use of hydrogen peroxide is discontinued because it inhibits tissue formation.
   5. Hexachlorophene (pHisoHex, Septisol)
      a. Combination of hexachlorophene and alcohol
      b. Bacteriostatic agent with activity against staphylococci and other gram-positive bacteria
      ▲ c. Absorbs through broken skin and can cause neurotoxicity; it should not be used on wounds.
      d. The alcohol component dries and irritates tissue, is not an effective germicide, and forms a film that actually can promote infection.
      ▲ e. All hexachlorophene products should be rinsed well from the skin after their use to prevent systemic absorption.

C. Antibacterials (Box 50-5)
   1. Description: Used for superficial skin infections
   ▲ 2. Mupirocin calcium (Bactroban)
      a. Topical antibacterial active against *Staphylococcus aureus*, beta-hemolytic streptococci, and *Streptococcus pyogenes*
      b. Usually applied three times daily; if improvement is not observed within 3 to 5 days, mupirocin calcium is discontinued.

D. Antifungals
   1. Antifungal agents may cause erythema, stinging, blistering, peeling, pruritis, urticaria, and general skin irritation.
   2. Client is reevaluated if no results are obtained after 4 weeks of treatment.

E. Antiviral: Acyclovir (Zovirax)   ▲
   1. Inhibits DNA replication in the virus
   2. Used for herpes simplex types 1 and 2, varicella-zoster, Epstein-Barr, and cytomegalovirus
   3. Can cause mild pain and transient burning and stinging
   4. Applied completely over the lesion usually every 3 hours six times daily for 1 week
   ▲ 5. Rubber gloves are used to apply the ointment to prevent the spread of infection.

F. Antiparasitics   ▲
   1. Used to treat scabies (mites) and pediculosis (lice)

BOX 50-5
Antibacterials, Antifungals, and Antiparasitics

ANTIBACTERIALS
Bacitracin preparations
Chloramphenicol
Chlortetracycline
Erythromycin
Gentamicin sulfate
Mupirocin calcium (Bactroban)
Neomycin preparations

ANTIFUNGALS
Amphotericin B (Fungizone, intravenous preparation)
Betamethasone dipropionate; clotrimazole (Lotrisone)
Ciclopirox olamine (Loprox)
Clotrimazole (Lotrimin AF, Desenex cream)
Clotrimazole (Mycelex troches)
Econazole nitrate (Spectazole)
Haloprogin
Ketoconazole (Ketoderm)
Miconazole nitrate (Micatin)
Nystatin (Mycostatin)
Tolnaftate (Tinactin)
Triacetin
Undecylenic acid (Desenex foam, soap, powder)

ANTIVIRAL
Acyclovir (Zovirax)

ANTIPARASITICS
Crotamiton (Eurax)
Ivermectin
Lindane
Malathion (Ovide)
Permethrin (Elimite, Nix, Acticin)

BOX 50-6
Antipruritics

Calamine lotion (Caladryl lotion)
Colloidal oatmeal (Aveeno)
Colloidal oatmeal; mineral oil (Aveeno Oilated Bath)
Starch and baking soda

BOX 50-7
Keratolytics

Cantharidin
Imiquimod (Aldara)
Masoprocol
Podophyllum resin
Podofilox (Condylox)
Salicylic acid

---

2. May be harmful during pregnancy and in young children
3. May irritate the skin, eyes, and mucous membranes
4. May cause allergic reactions
5. Antiparasitic agents such as permethrin (Elimite, Nix, Acticin), used in the treatment of pediculosis capitis, are removed with a warm water rinse 10 minutes after application.
6. Antiparasitic agents such as malathion (Ovide), used in the treatment of pediculosis capitis, is washed off with shampoo 8 to 12 hours after application.
7. Antiparasitic agents such as lindane, used in the treatment of scabies, are washed off the affected areas 8 to 12 hours after application.

IV. ANTIPRURITICS (Box 50-6)
A. Used to allay itching
B. Applied as wet dressings, pastes, lotions, creams, or ointments, or are used in a bath

C. Persons with dry skin should be instructed to bathe less frequently.

V. KERATOLYTICS (Box 50-7)
A. Description
1. Preparations that dissolve keratin
2. Soften scales and loosen the horny layer of the skin, resulting in minimal peeling or extensive desquamation
3. For treatment of superficial fungal infections, dermatitis, psoriasis, and localized dermatitis
B. Salicylic acid
1. Used to treat seborrheic dermatitis, acne, and psoriasis and to thin and remove calluses
2. Can be absorbed systematically and can cause salicylism, which is characterized by dizziness and tinnitus; salicylic acid is not applied to large surface areas or open wounds.
C. Podophyllum resin, imiquimod (Aldara)
1. Used for various types of **skin cancer**
2. Causes lesions to slough off, leaving a superficial ulcer and moderate dermatitis
3. After the therapy is discontinued, the lesions are treated with a mild antiseptic ointment; healing usually occurs within a few days.
D. Cantharidin, podofilox (Condylox), imiquimod (Aldara)
1. Used to treat warts
2. Have an exfoliation effect only on epidermal cells
3. May cause tingling, itching, and burning
4. Site may be tender for 2 to 6 days
E. Masoprocol
1. Has antiproliferative activity against keratinocytes and is used to treat keratosis
2. Occlusive dressings are not to be used with masoprocol.
3. Client may experience transient burning after administration.

BOX 50-8

Stimulants and Irritants

Benzoin compound
Coal tar

BOX 50-9

Protectives

TRANSPARENTS
Bio-occlusive membrane dressing
OpSite
Tegaderm

HYDROCOLLOIDS
DuoDerm
Tegasorb

ALGINATES
Alginate
Algosteril
Comfeel

BIOLOGICALS
Alloderm
Allograft
Xenograft

VI. **STIMULANTS AND IRRITANTS** (Box 50-8)
  A. Description: Stimulants and irritants produce a mild irritation to the surface of the skin, causing hyperemia and inflammation that promote the healing process.
  B. Coal tar
    1. Used to treat psoriasis, seborrheic dermatitis, and atopic dermatitis
    2. Has an unpleasant odor and frequently stains the skin and hair
    3. Can cause phototoxicity
  C. Benzoin compound
    1. Protects the skin when the client has sores, cracked nipples, and fissures of any orifice
    2. Causes a mild irritation that produces increased blood flow and healing

VII. **PROTECTIVES** (Box 50-9)
  A. Description
    1. Preparations that provide a film on the skin to protect it from irritations such as light, moisture, air, and dust
    2. Promote natural healing without the usual formation of dry crust over the wound
    3. Allow exudate to collect beneath the dressing, forming an artificial blister
    4. Transparents and hydrocolloidal protectives are designed to be left in place for up to 7 days or until leakage around the dressing occurs.
    5. Transparent protectives provide visualization of the wound; they can be difficult to apply and are nonabsorbent.
    6. Hydrocolloidal protectives provide wound protection for the wound bed and protection from bacterial contamination as well as wound débridement by autolysis; these protectives can soften and lose shape with heat, friction, and pressure and wound visualization is not possible.
    7. Alginates absorb heavy drainage and provide protection for the wound bed; the advantages of alginates include high absorbency and easy application; however, wound visualization is not possible.
    8. Biological dressings provide protection for the wound bed and conform to uneven surfaces within the wound.
  B. Sunscreens
    1. Sunscreens act by absorbing ultraviolet rays.
    2. Sunscreens are most effective when applied about 30 to 60 minutes before exposure to the sun and should be reapplied every 2 to 3 hours and after swimming or sweating.
    3. Sunscreens can cause contact dermatitis and photosensitivity reactions.
  C. Nonadherent dressings
    1. Woven or nonwoven dressings may be impregnated with saline, petrolatum, or antimicrobials.
    2. Some nonadherent dressings include Telfa, Vaseline gauze, and Xeroform.

VIII. **ENZYMES**
  A. Description
    1. Enzymes are used to promote healing of wounds and débride necrotic tissue.
    2. Enzymes reduce inflammation resulting from trauma and infection.
    3. Enzymes dissolve fibrin clots, which helps reduce the size of surface hematomas.
    4. To be effective, enzymes must be in contact with affected tissue in adequate concentrations for a sufficient length of time.
    5. Uninfected wounds with necrotic tissue may be débrided by enzymes over the course of 2 to 3 days, liquefying necrotic tissue.
  B. Enzymes to débride and remove exudates (Box 50-10)
    1. Description
      a. Enzymes digest or alter the thick purulent drainage to a thin liquid that can be wiped or irrigated easily off the wound.
      b. Enzyme contact with necrotic tissue in the wound is necessary.
      c. Enzymes to débride wounds are discontinued when bleeding occurs or granulation tissue is apparent.

BOX 50-10

Enzymes to Débride and Remove Exudates

Collagenase (Santyl)
Dextranomer (Debrisan)
Fibrinolysin and desoxyribonuclease (Elase)
Papain (Accuzyme)
Sutilains (Travase)

2. Sutilains (Travase)
   a. Proteolytic enzymes used to remove nonviable or necrotic tissue and purulent enzymes from **burns,** ulcers, traumatic injury, and peripheral vascular disease wounds
   b. Inactive on viable tissue.
3. Collagenase (Santyl)
   a. Used as a topical débriding agent
   b. Provides effective débridement of the collagen tissue at the wound edges where necrotic tissue is anchored
   c. Encourages the formation of granulation tissue at the wound edges and quicker epithelialization of wounds
   d. Apply with a tongue depressor directly into deep wounds.
   e. Before application, cleanse wound of debris by gently rubbing with a gauze pad with sterile water or Dakin's solution, followed by sterile normal saline.
   f. Remove all excess ointment each time dressing is changed.
   g. Apply only to injured area; collagenase causes erythema in healthy tissues.
   h. Protect healthy tissue by applying zinc oxide paste.
   i. Use is discontinued when necrotic tissue is gone
4. Fibrinolysin and desoxyribonuclease (Elase)
   a. Elase is used to débride wounds, including **burns, pressure ulcers,** and inflamed or infected lesions.
   b. Clean wound with sterile normal saline to flush away necrotic debris and pat dry; then apply a thin layer of fibrinolysin and desoxyribonuclease and cover with petrolatum gauze.
5. Dextranomer (Debrisan)
   a. Not a débriding agent but a cleansing agent that actually absorbs peptides and proteins
   b. Effective in wet wounds only
   c. Not packed tightly into the wound because maceration of surrounding tissue may occur from contact with the agent
6. Papain (Accuzyme)
   a. Does not injure or affect healthy tissue or cells

   b. Must be in immediate contact with the purulent wound material
   c. Dressings are changed once a day.

IX. **CORTICOSTEROIDS**
A. Topical corticosteroids have anti-inflammatory, antipruritic, and vasoconstrictive actions.
B. Contraindications
   1. Clients demonstrating previous sensitivity to corticosteroids
   2. Clients with current systemic fungal, viral, or bacterial infections
   3. Clients with current complications related to corticosteroid therapy
C. Local adverse effects
   1. Hypopigmentation
   2. Acneiform eruptions
   3. Contact dermatitis
   4. Burning, dryness, irritation, itching
   5. Overgrowth of bacteria, fungi, and viruses
   6. Skin atrophy
D. Systemic adverse effects
   1. Rare occurrence
   2. Adrenal suppression
   3. Cushing's syndrome
   4. Striae, skin atrophy
   5. Ocular effects (glaucoma and cataracts)
E. Interventions
   1. Monitor plasma cortisol levels if prolonged therapy is necessary.
   2. Wash area just before application to increase medication penetration.
   3. Apply sparingly in a thin film, rubbing gently.
   4. May apply to the skin alone or with a dry occlusive dressing only if prescribed by the physician
   5. Instruct the client to report burning, irritation, or signs of infection to the physician.

X. **ACNE PRODUCTS** (Box 50-11; Fig. 50-1)
A. Description
   1. Mild acne can be treated with bar soaps, soap-free cakes, liquid cleansers, lotions, gels, and creams.
   2. For moderate acne, topical anti-inflammatory medication such as benzoyl peroxide, tretinoin (Retin-A), isotretinoin (Accutane), azelaic acid (Azelex), and adapalene (Differin) may be prescribed; antibiotics also may be prescribed.
   3. Side effects can include excessive redness, extreme dryness of the skin leading to blistering and crusting, temporary pigmentation changes, and peeling of the skin.
   4. All products are kept away from the eyes, inside the nose, mucous membranes, and hair.
B. Benzoyl peroxide is a keratolytic agent that is bacteriostatic and may decrease the production of irritant free fatty acids in the follicle.

BOX 50-11
Acne Products

CLEANSERS
Aluminum oxide (Brasivol)
Salicylic acid; alcohol (Clearasil Acne-Fighting Pads, Stri-Dex pads)

DRYING AGENTS
Benzalkonium chloride (Ionax)
Sulfur; resorcinol; alcohol (Acnomel)

MISCELLANEOUS
Adapalene (Differin)
Antibiotics
Azelaic acid (Azelex)
Benzoyl peroxide wash, gel
Colloidal sulfur; resorcinol; alcohol (Bensulfoid cream)
Erythromycin; benzoyl peroxide; alcohol (Benzamycin gel)
Isotretinoin (Accutane)
Resorcinol (as an ingredient in other preparations)
Salicylic acid (as an ingredient in other preparations)
Tazarotene
Tretinoin (Retin-A)

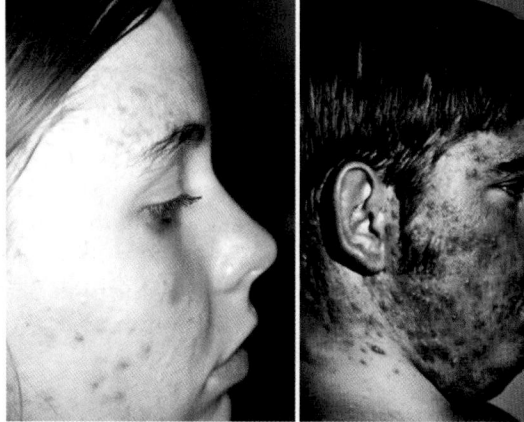

A **B**

FIG. 50-1 Acne vulgaris. **A,** Comedones with a few inflammatory pustules. **B,** Papulopustular acne. (From Wong, D., Hockenberry, M., Wilson, S., et al. [2006]. *Maternal child nursing care* [3rd ed.]. St. Louis: Mosby.)

C. Tretinoin and adapalene are acids of vitamin A used to treat acne vulgaris and also may be used to treat **skin cancer** and aging of the skin.

D. Tretinoin (Retin-A)
   1. Decreases cohesiveness of the epithelial cells, increasing cell mitosis and turnover; tretinoin is potentially irritating, and mild redness and skin peeling are expected with topical use.
   2. Within 48 hours of use, the skin generally becomes red and begins to peel.
   3. Temporary hyperpigmentation and hypopigmentation can occur.

4. Client should avoid sun exposure because photosensitivity may occur.
5. Applied liberally to the skin; the hands should be washed thoroughly immediately after applying tretinoin.
6. Therapeutic results should be seen after 2 to 3 weeks but may not be optimal until after 6 weeks.
7. Client may use cosmetics, but the skin needs to be cleaned thoroughly before applying the cosmetics.

E. Isotretinoin (Accutane)
   1. Metabolite of vitamin A
   2. Used to treat severe cystic acne; its use is reserved for persons who have not responded to other therapies, including systemic antibiotics.
   3. Can cause xerosis and facial desquamation, palmoplantar desquamation, pruritus, brittle nails, and hair loss.
   4. Administered with meals twice daily for a 15- to 20-week course; if needed, another course of therapy should not be carried out for 8 weeks.
   5. Photosensitivity may occur, so the client needs to be instructed to decrease sun exposure.
   6. May cause depression in some clients
   7. Alcohol consumption should be eliminated during therapy because alcohol could potentiate elevation of serum triglyceride levels.

F. Local antibiotics
   1. Antibiotics may be used to treat acne
   2. Therapeutic response generally requires 6 to 12 weeks of therapy.
   3. Side effects include acute contact dermatitis, transient stinging or burning, staining of the skin, erythema, and skin tenderness.

XI. POISON IVY TREATMENT (Box 50-12; Fig. 50-2)
A. Treatment of lesions includes calamine lotion and other products that soothe lesions, Burow's solution compresses, and/or Aveeno baths to relieve discomfort
B. Topical corticosteroids are effective to prevent or relieve inflammation, especially when used before blisters form.
C. Oral corticosteroids may be prescribed for severe reactions and a sedative such as diphenhydramine (Benadryl) may be prescribed.

XII. BURN PRODUCTS (Box 50-13)
A. Nitrofurazone (Furacin)
   1. Applied topically to the burn as a solution, ointment, or cream
   2. Has a broad spectrum of antibacterial activity
   3. Used for **burns** when bacterial resistance to other agents is a problem
   4. Topical: Apply $\frac{1}{16}$-inch film directly to burn.
   5. Side effects: Contact dermatitis, rash
   6. Less common side effects: Pruritus, local edema

Bentoquatam—for preventive use (Ivy Block)
Calamine lotion (Caladryl lotion)
Hydrocortisone (Ivy Soothe, Ivy Stat)
Isopropanol; cetyl alcohol (Ivy Cleanse)
Zinc acetate; isopropanol (Ivy Dry)
Zinc acetate; isopropanol; benzyl alcohol (Ivy Super Dry)

Mafenide acetate (Sulfamylon)
Nitrofurazone (Furacin)
Silver nitrate
Silver sulfadiazine (Silvadene)

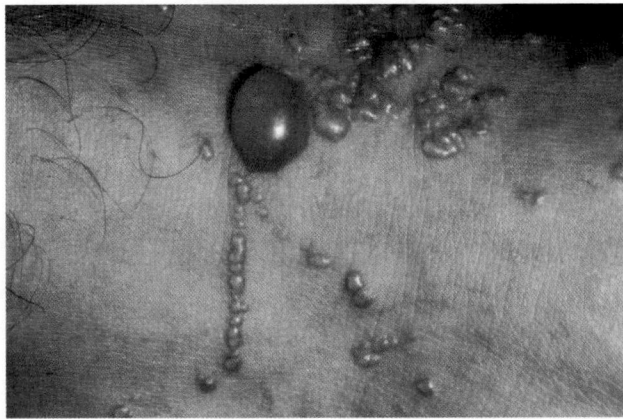

FIG. 50-2 Poison ivy. Note "streaked" blisters surrounding one large blister. (From Wong, D., Hockenberry, M., Wilson, S., et al. [2006]. *Maternal child nursing care* [3rd ed.]. St. Louis: Mosby.)

5. Apply $^1/_{16}$-inch film (keep burn covered at all times with silver sulfadiazine).
6. Side effects include rash and itching.
7. Systemic effects include leukopenia and interstitial nephritis.
8. Monitor complete blood cell count, particularly the white blood cells, frequently; if leukopenia develops, the medication is discontinued.

D. Silver nitrate
1. Antiseptic solution active against gram-negative bacteria
2. Dressings are applied to the burn and then are kept moist with silver nitrate, which stains anything with which it comes in contact; this discoloration is usually not permanent.
3. May be prescribed for use on extensive **burns** that may precipitate fluid and electrolyte imbalances
4. Apply silver nitrate to the dressing; do not apply directly to wounds, cuts, or broken skin.

PRACTICE QUESTIONS

1. Salicylic acid is prescribed for a client with a diagnosis of psoriasis. The nurse monitors the client, knowing that which of the following would indicate the presence of systemic toxicity from this medication?
   1. Tinnitus
   2. Diarrhea
   3. Constipation
   4. Decreased respirations

2. The client is diagnosed with herpes simplex type 1. The physician prescribes a topical medication for treatment. The nurse anticipates that which of the following medications will be prescribed?
   1. Salicylic acid
   2. Gentamicin sulfate
   3. Acyclovir (Zovirax)
   4. Mupirocin calcium (Bactroban)

3. The physician has prescribed coal tar treatments for the client with psoriasis, and the nurse provides information to the client about the treatments. Which statement made by the client indicates a lack of understanding about the treatments?
   1. "The medication has an unpleasant odor."
   2. "The medication can cause phototoxicity."
   3. "The medication can stain the skin and hair."
   4. "The medication always causes systemic toxicity."

B. Mafenide acetate (Sulfamylon)
1. Water-soluble cream that is bacteriostatic for gram-negative and gram-positive organisms
2. Used to treat **burns** to reduce the bacteria present in avascular tissues
3. Diffuses through the devascularized areas of the skin and may precipitate metabolic acidosis (usually compensated for by hyperventilation)
4. Apply $^1/_{16}$-inch film directly to the burn.
5. Side effects can include local pain and rash.
6. Systemic effects include bone marrow depression, hemolytic anemia, and metabolic acidosis.
7. Keep burn covered with mafenide acetate at all times.
8. Notify physician if hyperventilation occurs; if acidosis develops, mafenide acetate is washed off the skin.

C. Silver sulfadiazine (Silvadene)
1. Has broad spectrum of activity against gram-negative bacteria, gram-positive bacteria, and yeast
2. Released slowly from the cream, which is selectively toxic to bacteria
3. Used primarily to prevent sepsis in clients with **burns**
4. Not a carbonic anhydrase inhibitor; therefore, does not cause acidosis

4. The camp nurse asks the children preparing to swim in the lake if they have applied sunscreen. The nurse reminds the children that chemical sunscreens are most effective when applied:
   1. Immediately before swimming
   2. 15 minutes before exposure to the sun
   3. Immediately before exposure to the sun
   4. 30 to 60 minutes before exposure to the sun

5. Mafenide acetate (Sulfamylon) is prescribed for the client with a burn injury. When applying the medication, the client complains of local discomfort and burning. Which of the following is the most appropriate nursing action?
   1. Notify the physician.
   2. Discontinue the medication.
   3. Inform the client that this is normal.
   4. Apply a thinner film than prescribed to the burn site.

6. The burn client is receiving treatments of topical mafenide acetate (Sulfamylon) to the site of injury. The nurse monitors the client, knowing that which of the following indicates that a systemic effect has occurred?
   1. Hyperventilation
   2. Elevated blood pressure
   3. Local pain at the burn site
   4. Local rash at the burn site

7. Sodium hypochlorite (Dakin's solution) is prescribed for a client with a leg wound that is draining purulent material and the home health nurse teaches a family member how to perform wound treatments. Which statement, if made by the family member, indicates a need for further teaching?
   1. "A fresh solution needs to be prepared frequently."
   2. "The solution should not come in contact with normal skin tissue."
   3. "I should rinse the solution off immediately following the irrigation."
   4. "I will soak a sterile dressing with solution and pack it into the wound."

8. The nurse has provided instructions to a client regarding the use of tretinoin (Retin-A). Which statement, if made by the client, indicates the need for further instructions?
   1. "I must apply a very thin layer to the skin."
   2. "Optimal results will be seen after 6 weeks."
   3. "I will wash my hands thoroughly after applying the medication."
   4. "I will cleanse the skin thoroughly before applying the medication."

9. Isotretinoin (Accutane) is prescribed for a client with severe acne. Before the administration of this medication, the nurse anticipates that which laboratory test will be prescribed?
   1. Platelet count
   2. Triglyceride level
   3. Complete blood count
   4. White blood cell count

10. A client with severe acne is seen in the clinic and the physician prescribes isotretinoin (Accutane). The nurse reviews the client's medication record and would contact the physician if the client is taking which medication?
    1. Vitamin A
    2. Digoxin (Lanoxin)
    3. Furosemide (Lasix)
    4. Phenytoin (Dilantin)

11. An outbreak of pediculosis capitus has occurred at the local school. The school nurse is providing instructions to the parents of the children attending the school regarding the application of permethrin (Elimite, Nix, Acticin). The nurse tells the parents to:
    1. Apply before washing the hair.
    2. Apply at bedtime and rinse off in the morning.
    3. Avoid saturating the hair and scalp when applying.
    4. Allow to remain on the hair 10 minutes and then rinse with water.

12. A client is seen in the clinic for complaints of skin itchiness that has persisted over the past several weeks. Following an assessment, the client has been determined to have scabies. Lindane is prescribed, and the nurse provides instructions to the client regarding the use of the medication. The nurse tells the client to:
    1. Apply the cream for 2 days in a row.
    2. Apply a thick layer of cream to the entire body.
    3. Apply to the entire body and scalp, excluding the face.
    4. Leave the cream on for 8 to 12 hours and then remove by washing.

13. A topical corticosteroid is prescribed for the client with dermatitis. The nurse provides instructions to the client regarding the use of the medication. Which of the following, if stated by the client, would indicate a need for further instruction?
    1. "I need to apply the medication in a thin film."
    2. "I should gently rub the medication into the skin."
    3. "The medication will help relieve the inflammation and itching."
    4. "I should place a bandage over the site after applying the medication."

14. The nurse is applying a topical corticosteroid to a client with eczema. The nurse would be concerned about the potential for increased systemic absorption of the medication if the medication were being applied to which of the following body areas?
    1. Back
    2. Axilla
    3. Soles of the feet
    4. Palms of the hands

15. The registered nurse is observing a newly hired nurse perform a dressing change on a client with a leg ulcer. Sutilains (Travase) is being used to treat the ulcer. Which observation by the registered nurse would indicate an inaccurate action by the newly hired nurse when performing the dressing change?
    1. The nurse cleans the wound with a sterile solution.
    2. The nurse places the sutilains in the refrigerator following use.
    3. The nurse dries the wound and covers the sutilains application with a dry sterile dressing.
    4. The nurse moistens the wound with sterile normal saline and then applies the sutilains.

16. Dextranomer (Debrisan) is prescribed for a client with a pressure ulcer. The nursing instructor asks the nursing student preparing to perform the treatment about the medication and procedure. Which statement, if made by the student, indicates a need for further research?
    1. "It is effective in wet wounds only."
    2. "It should be packed lightly into the wound."
    3. "The wound bed must be dried thoroughly before applying the medication."
    4. "Maceration of tissue surrounding the wound can occur from the medication."

17. Fibrinolysin and desoxyribonuclease (Elase) is prescribed to treat a skin ulcer, and the nurse is observing a nursing student perform the treatment. The nurse intervenes if the nursing student is observed doing which of the following?
    1. Applies a thin layer of medication
    2. Cleans the wound with a sterile solution
    3. Places petrolatum gauze over the fibrinolysin and desoxyribonuclease
    4. Applies a thick layer of medication and covers with a dry sterile dressing

18. The clinic nurse is performing an admission assessment on a client. The nurse notes that the client is taking azelaic acid (Azelex). Because of the medication prescription, the nurse would suspect that the client is being treated for:
    1. Acne
    2. Eczema
    3. Hair loss
    4. Herpes simplex

19. The physician has prescribed silver sulfadiazine (Silvadene) for the client with a partial-thickness burn, which has cultured positive for gram-negative bacteria, and the nurse provides information to the client about the medication. Which statement made by the client indicates a lack of understanding about the treatments?
    1. "The medication is an antibacterial."
    2. "The medication will help heal the burn."
    3. "The medication will permanently stain my skin."
    4. "The medication should be applied directly to the wound."

20. The nurse notes necrotic tissue present in the wound bed of a client and reports the findings to the physician. The nurse anticipates that which medication will be prescribed to treat the wound?
    1. Dextranomer (Debrisan)
    2. Nitrofurazone (Furacin)
    3. Silver sulfadiazine (Silvadene)
    4. Fibrinolysin and desoxyribonuclease (Elase)

ALTERNATE ITEM FORMAT: FILL IN THE BLANK

The home health care nurse makes a home visit to a client who has an ulcer on the medial aspect of the left ankle. The wound is being treated with DuoDerm (a hydrocolloid). The nurse removes the DuoDerm, cleanses the wound as prescribed, and reapplies the DuoDerm. The nurse schedules the next visit for wound care and for changing the DuoDerm in how many days?

Answer: _____ days

ANSWERS

1. **1**
Rationale: Salicylic acid is absorbed readily through the skin, and systemic toxicity (salicylism) can result. Symptoms include tinnitus, dizziness, hyperpnea, and psychological disturbances. Constipation and diarrhea are not associated with salicylism.
Test-Taking Strategy: Use the process of elimination. Noting the name of the medication will assist in directing you to the correct option if you can recall the toxic effects that occur with acetylsalicylic acid (aspirin). Review the toxic effects of salicylic acid if you are unfamiliar with them.
Level of Cognitive Ability: Analysis

Client Needs: Physiological Integrity
Integrated Process: Nursing Process—assessment
Content Area: Pharmacology
References: Lilley, L., Harrington, S., & Snyder, J. (2005). *Pharmacology and the nursing process* (4th ed., pp. 732-733). St. Louis: Mosby.
Skidmore-Roth, L. (2005). *Mosby's nursing drug reference 2005* (p. 150). St. Louis: Mosby.

2. **3**
Rationale: Acyclovir is a topical antiviral agent that inhibits DNA replication in the virus. Acyclovir has activity against herpes simplex virus types 1 and 2, varicella-zoster virus,

Epstein-Barr virus, and cytomegalovirus. Gentamicin sulfate is an antibacterial and would not be effective in treating herpesvirus. Mupirocin calcium is a topical antibacterial active against *Staphylococcus aureus*, beta-hemolytic streptococci, or *Streptococcus pyogenes*. Salicylic acid is a keratolytic.

Test-Taking Strategy: Use the process of elimination. Recalling that herpes simplex is a virus will direct you to the option that identifies an antiviral medication (Acyclo*vir*). Review these medications if you are unfamiliar with them.

Level of Cognitive Ability: Analysis
Client Needs: Physiological Integrity
Integrated Process: Nursing Process—analysis
Content Area: Pharmacology
Reference: Kee, J., Hayes, E., & McCuistion, L. (2006). *Pharmacology: A nursing process approach* (5th ed., pp. 474-475). Philadelphia: W.B. Saunders.

3. **4**

Rationale: Coal tar is used to treat psoriasis and other chronic disorders of the skin. Coal tar suppresses DNA synthesis, mitotic activity, and cell proliferation. Coal tar has an unpleasant odor, frequently stains the skin and hair, and can cause phototoxicity. Systemic toxicity does not occur.

Test-Taking Strategy: Use the process of elimination and note the strategic words *lack of understanding*. These words indicate a negative event query and ask you to select an option that is an incorrect statement. The name of the medication will assist in eliminating options 1 and 3. From the remaining options, note the close-ended word *always* in option 4 to direct you to this option. If you had difficulty with this question, review this treatment.

Level of Cognitive Ability: Analysis
Client Needs: Physiological Integrity
Integrated Process: Teaching and Learning
Content Area: Pharmacology
References: Ignatavicius, D., & Workman, M. (2005). *Medical-surgical nursing: Critical thinking for collaborative care* (5th ed., p. 1604). St. Louis: W.B. Saunders.
Kee, J., Hayes, E., & McCuistion, L. (2006). *Pharmacology: A nursing process approach* (5th ed., p. 743). Philadelphia: W.B. Saunders.
Lehne, R. (2004). *Pharmacology for nursing care* (5th ed., p. 1116). St. Louis: W.B. Saunders.

4. **4**

Rationale: Sunscreens are most effective when applied about 30 to 60 minutes before exposure to the sun so that they can penetrate the skin. All sunscreens should be reapplied after swimming or sweating.

Test-Taking Strategy: Use the process of elimination. Knowledge that sunscreens need to penetrate the skin will assist in eliminating options 2 and 3. Noting the strategic words *most effective* will assist in directing you to option 4. Review protective skin measures if you had difficulty with this question.

Level of Cognitive Ability: Application
Client Needs: Physiological Integrity
Integrated Process: Teaching and Learning
Content Area: Pharmacology

References: Kee, J., Hayes, E., & McCuistion, L. (2006). *Pharmacology: A nursing process approach* (5th ed., pp. 747-748). Philadelphia: W.B. Saunders.
Lehne, R. (2004). *Pharmacology for nursing care* (5th ed., p. 1115). St. Louis: W.B. Saunders.

5. **3**

Rationale: Mafenide acetate is bacteriostatic for gram-negative and gram-positive organisms and is used to treat burns to reduce bacteria present in avascular tissues. The client should be informed that the medication will cause local discomfort and burning.

Test-Taking Strategy: Use the process of elimination. Eliminate options 2 and 4 because it is not within the scope of nursing practice to alter or discontinue a medication therapy. Recalling that this is a normal expected occurrence will direct you to option 3. If you had difficulty with this question, review the effects of this medication.

Level of Cognitive Ability: Application
Client Needs: Physiological Integrity
Integrated Process: Nursing Process—implementation
Content Area: Pharmacology
References: Kee, J., Hayes, E., & McCuistion, L. (2006). *Pharmacology: A nursing process approach* (5th ed., pp. 748-749). Philadelphia: W.B. Saunders.
Skidmore-Roth, L. (2005). *Mosby's nursing drug reference 2005* (p. 1120). St. Louis: Mosby,

6. **1**

Rationale: Mafenide acetate is a carbonic anhydrase inhibitor and can suppress renal excretion of acid, thereby causing acidosis. Clients receiving this treatment should be monitored for signs of an acid-base imbalance (hyperventilation). If this occurs, the medication should be discontinued for 1 to 2 days. Options 3 and 4 describe local rather than systemic effects. An elevated blood pressure may be expected from the pain that occurs with a burn injury.

Test-Taking Strategy: Use the process of elimination. Note the strategic words *systemic effect*. Options 3 and 4 can be eliminated because these are local rather than systemic effects. From the remaining options, recall that the client in pain would likely have an elevated blood pressure. This should direct you to option 1. Review the systemic effects of this medication if you had difficulty with this question.

Level of Cognitive Ability: Analysis
Client Needs: Physiological Integrity
Integrated Process: Nursing Process—assessment
Content Area: Pharmacology
References: Kee, J., Hayes, E., & McCuistion, L. (2006). *Pharmacology: A nursing process approach* (5th ed., pp. 748-749). Philadelphia: W.B. Saunders.
McKenry, L., Tessier, E., & Hogan, M. (2006) *Mosby's pharmacology in nursing* (22nd ed., p. 1188). St Louis: Mosby.

7. **4**

Rationale: Sodium hypochlorite is a solution used for irrigating and cleaning necrotic or purulent wounds. It cannot be used to pack purulent wounds because the solution is inactivated by copious pus. The solution should not come into contact with healing or normal tissue and should be rinsed off immediately

following irrigation. The solution loses its potency during storage, so fresh solution should be prepared frequently.
Test-Taking Strategy: Use the process of elimination and note the strategic words *need for further teaching*. These words indicate a negative event query and ask you to select an option that is an incorrect statement. Eliminate options 2 and 3 first because they are comparative or alike and indicate avoiding healthy tissue. Preparing the solution frequently makes sense; therefore, eliminate option 1. If you are unfamiliar with the use of this solution, review these concepts.
Level of Cognitive Ability: Analysis
Client Needs: Physiological Integrity
Integrated Process: Teaching and Learning
Content Area: Pharmacology
References: Lehne, R. (2004). *Pharmacology for nursing care* (5th ed., p. 1033). St. Louis: W.B. Saunders.
Lilley, L., Harrington, S., & Snyder, J. (2005). *Pharmacology and the nursing process* (4th ed., pp. 721-722). St. Louis: Mosby.

8. 1
Rationale: Tretinoin is applied liberally to the skin. The hands are washed thoroughly immediately after applying. Therapeutic results should be seen after 2 to 3 weeks but may not be optimal until after 6 weeks. The skin needs to be cleansed thoroughly before applying the medication.
Test-Taking Strategy: Use the process of elimination and note the strategic words *need for further instructions*. These words indicate a negative event query and ask you to select an option that is an incorrect statement. Eliminate options 3 and 4 first using the principles of asepsis. Recalling that the medication is applied liberally to the skin and noting the close-ended word *must* in option 1 will direct you to this option. Review this medication if you had difficulty with this question.
Level of Cognitive Ability: Analysis
Client Needs: Physiological Integrity
Integrated Process: Teaching and Learning
Content Area: Pharmacology
Reference: Lilley, L., Harrington, S. & Snyder, J. (2005). *Pharmacology and the nursing process* (4th ed., p. 938). St. Louis: Mosby.

9. 2
Rationale: Isotretinoin can elevate triglyceride levels. Blood triglyceride levels should be measured before treatment and periodically thereafter until the effect on the triglycerides has been evaluated. Options 1, 3, and 4 do not need to be monitored specifically during this treatment.
Test-Taking Strategy: Use the process of elimination. Eliminate options 3 and 4 first because a complete blood count also will measure the white blood cell count. From the remaining options, recall that the medication can affect triglyceride levels in the client. Review this medication if you had difficulty with this question
Level of Cognitive Ability: Analysis
Client Needs: Physiological Integrity
Integrated Process: Nursing Process—analysis
Content Area: Pharmacology
References: Ignatavicius, D., & Workman, M. (2006). *Medical-surgical nursing: Critical thinking for collaborative care* (5th ed., p. 1613). Philadelphia: W.B. Saunders.

Kee, J., Hayes, E., & McCuistion, L. (2006). *Pharmacology: A nursing process approach* (5th ed., p. 742). Philadelphia: W.B. Saunders.

10. 1
Rationale: Isotretinoin is a metabolite of vitamin A and can produce generalized intensification of isotretinoin toxicity. Because of the potential for increased toxicity, vitamin A supplements should be discontinued before isotretinoin therapy. Options 2, 3, and 4 are not contraindicated with the use of isotretinoin.
Test-Taking Strategy: Use the process of elimination. Recalling that isotretinoin is a metabolite of vitamin A will direct you to the correct option. If you are unfamiliar with this medication, review the contraindications associated with its use.
Level of Cognitive Ability: Analysis
Client Needs: Physiological Integrity
Integrated Process: Nursing Process—analysis
Content Area: Pharmacology
Reference: Kee, J., Hayes, E., & McCuistion, L. (2006). *Pharmacology: A nursing process approach* (5th ed., p. 742). Philadelphia: W.B. Saunders.

11. 4
Rationale: The instructions for the use of permethrin include wash, rinse, and towel-dry hair, apply sufficient volume to saturate hair and scalp, allow to remain on hair 10 minutes, and then rinse with water. Options 1, 2, and 3 are incorrect instructions.
Test-Taking Strategy: Use the process of elimination. Note that options 2 and 4 address a time frame for allowing the medication to remain on the hair. Recognizing this may provide you with the clue that one of these options is correct. Remember that permethrin remains on the head for 10 minutes and then is rinsed off. Review this treatment if you are unfamiliar with it.
Level of Cognitive Ability: Application
Client Needs: Physiological Integrity
Integrated Process: Teaching and Learning
Content Area: Pharmacology
Reference: Kee, J., Hayes, E., & McCuistion, L. (2006). *Pharmacology: A nursing process approach* (5th ed., p. 901). Philadelphia: W.B. Saunders.

12. 4
Rationale: Lindane is applied in a thin layer to the body below the head. No more than 30 g (1 oz) should be used. The medication is removed by washing 8 to 12 hours later. In most cases, only one application is required.
Test-Taking Strategy: Use the process of elimination. Eliminate option 2 because of the word *thick*. Eliminate option 3 because of the word *entire*. From the remaining options, eliminate option 1, knowing that only one application is required. Review this medication if you are unfamiliar with it.
Level of Cognitive Ability: Application
Client Needs: Physiological Integrity
Integrated Process: Teaching and Learning
Content Area: Pharmacology
Reference: Skidmore-Roth, L. (2005). *Mosby's nursing drug reference 2005* (6th ed., p. 497). St. Louis: Mosby.

13. 4

Rationale: Clients should be advised not to use occlusive dressings (bandages or plastic wraps) to cover the affected site following the application of the topical corticosteroid, unless the physician specifically prescribes wound coverage. Options 1, 2, and 3 are accurate statements related to the use of this medication.

Test-Taking Strategy: Use the process of elimination. Note the strategic words *need for further instruction*. These words indicate a negative event query and ask you to select an option that is an incorrect statement. Eliminate option 3, knowing that this is the action of a corticosteroid. The words *thin* in option 1 and *gently* in option 2 should assist you in eliminating these options. If you had difficulty with this question, review this medication.

Level of Cognitive Ability: Analysis
Client Needs: Physiological Integrity
Integrated Process: Teaching and Learning
Content Area: Pharmacology

References: Lehne, R. (2004). *Pharmacology for nursing care* (5th ed., p.1108) St. Louis: W.B. Saunders.
Lilley, L., Harrington, S., & Snyder, J. (2005). *Pharmacology and the nursing process* (4th ed., p. 945). St. Louis: Mosby.
Skidmore-Roth, L. (2005). *Mosby's nursing drug reference 2005* (p. 1118). St. Louis: Mosby.

14. 2

Rationale: Topical corticosteroids can be absorbed into the systemic circulation. Absorption is higher from regions where the skin is especially permeable (scalp, axilla, face, eyelids, neck, perineum, genitalia), and lower from regions where permeability is poor (back, palms, soles).

Test-Taking Strategy: Use the process of elimination. Focus on the subject of the question, permeability and the potential for increased systemic absorption. Eliminate options 3 and 4 because these body areas are similar or alike in terms of skin substance. From the remaining options, think about permeability of the skin area. This should direct you to option 2. Review the principles related to the administration of topical corticosteroids if you had difficulty with this question.

Level of Cognitive Ability: Analysis
Client Needs: Physiological Integrity
Integrated Process: Nursing Process—analysis
Content Area: Pharmacology

Reference: Black, J., & Hawks, J. (2005). *Medical-surgical nursing: Clinical management for positive outcomes* (7th ed., p. 1399). Philadelphia: W.B. Saunders.

15. 3

Rationale: The wound should be cleansed with a sterile solution before treatment. The nurse then thoroughly moistens the wound with normal saline or sterile water, applies a thin film of sutilains extending ¼ to ½ inch beyond the area to be débrided, and then applies a loose thin dressing. The ointment should be refrigerated.

Test-Taking Strategy: Use the process of elimination. Note the strategic word *inaccurate*. This word indicates a negative event query and asks you to select an option that is an incorrection action. Recalling that the wound is moistened before applying the sutilains will direct you to the correct option. Review the

method of application of sutilains if you had difficulty with this question.

Level of Cognitive Ability: Analysis
Client Needs: Physiological Integrity
Integrated Process: Teaching and Learning
Content Area: Leadership/Management

References: McKenry, L. Tessier, E., & Hogan, M. (2006). *Mosby's pharmacology in nursing* (22nd ed., pp. 1202-1203). St Louis: Mosby.
Potter, P., & Perry, A. (2005). *Fundamentals of nursing* (6th ed., p. 1520). St. Louis: Mosby.

16. 3

Rationale: Dextranomer is a cleansing rather than a débriding agent that is effective for wet wounds only. Dextranomer is not packed tightly into the wound because maceration of surrounding tissue may result.

Test-Taking Strategy: Use the process of elimination and note the strategic words *indicates a need for further research*. These words indicate a negative event query and ask you to select an option that is an incorrect statement. Noting that option 1 indicates that the wound should be wet and option 3 indicates that the wound should be dry provides the clue that one of these options is correct. If you are unfamiliar with the use of dextranomer, review the procedure associated with its use.

Level of Cognitive Ability: Analysis
Client Needs: Physiological Integrity
Integrated Process: Teaching and Learning
Content Area: Pharmacology

Reference: Ignatavicius, D., & Workman, M. (2006). *Medical-surgical nursing: Critical thinking for collaborative care* (5th ed., pp. 1588-1590). St. Louis: W.B. Saunders.

17. 4

Rationale: The wound should be cleansed with a sterile solution and gently patted dry. A thin layer of fibrinolysin and desoxyribonuclease (Elase) is applied and covered with a petrolatum gauze. If a dry powder preparation is used, for best effects, the solution should be prepared just before use.

Test-Taking Strategy: Use the process of elimination and note the strategic word *intervenes*. This word indicates a negative event query and asks you to select an option that is an incorrect action. Also, noting the strategic word *thick* in option 4 will direct you to this option. Review the method of application of fibrinolysin and desoxyribonuclease (Elase) if you had difficulty with this question.

Level of Cognitive Ability: Application
Client Needs: Physiological Integrity
Integrated Process: Nursing Process—implementation
Content Area: Leadership/Management

Reference: McKenry, L., Tessier, E., & Hogan, M. (2006). *Mosby's pharmacology in nursing* (22nd ed., p. 1204). St Louis: Mosby.

18. 1

Rationale: Azelaic acid is a topical medication used to treat mild to moderate acne. The acid appears to work by suppressing the growth of *Propionibacterium acnes* and by decreasing the proliferation of keratinocytes. Options 2, 3, and 4 are incorrect.

Test-Taking Strategy: Use the process of elimination. Focusing on the name of the medication, azelaic acid, will direct you to the correct option. Review this medication if you are unfamiliar with it.
Level of Cognitive Ability: Analysis
Client Needs: Physiological Integrity
Integrated Process: Nursing Process—analysis
Content Area: Pharmacology
Reference: Kee, J., Hayes, E., & McCuistion, L. (2006). *Pharmacology: A nursing process approach* (5th ed., p. 742). Philadelphia: W.B. Saunders.

19. **3**
Rationale: Silver sulfadiazine (Silvadene) is an antibacterial that has a broad spectrum of activity against gram-negative bacteria, gram-positive bacteria, and yeast. It is applied directly to the wound to assist in healing. It does not stain the skin.
Test-Taking Strategy: Note the strategic words *lack of understanding*. These words indicate a negative event query and ask you to select an option that is an incorrect statement. Recall the characteristics of this medication. Noting the words *permanently stain* in option 3 will direct you to this option. Review this medication if you had difficulty with this question.
Level of Cognitive Ability: Analysis
Client Needs: Physiological Integrity
Integrated Process: Teaching and Learning
Content Area: Pharmacology
References: Skidmore-Roth, L. (2005). *Mosby's nursing drug reference 2005* (p. 583). St. Louis: Mosby.
Lehne, R. (2004). *Pharmacology for nursing care* (5th ed., p. 929). St. Louis: W.B. Saunders.

20. **4**
Rationale: Fibrinolysin and desoxyribonuclease (Elase) is used to débride wounds, including burns, pressure ulcers, and inflamed or infected lesions. Dextranomer (Debrisan) is not a débriding agent but is a cleansing agent that actually absorbs peptides and proteins. Nitrofurazone (Furacin) and silver sulfadiazine (Silvadene) are antibacterials and are not used for wound débridement.
Test-Taking Strategy: Focus on the strategic words *necrotic tissue present in the wound bed*. Recall the action of each medication in the options to answer correctly. Remember that fibrinolysin and desoxyribonuclease (Elase) is used to débride wounds. Review the actions of these medications if you had difficulty with this question.
Level of Cognitive Ability: Analysis
Client Needs: Physiological Integrity
Integrated Process: Nursing Process—analysis
Content Area: Pharmacology
Reference: Skidmore-Roth, L. (2005). *Mosby's nursing drug reference 2005* (p. 459). St. Louis: Mosby.

ALTERNATE ITEM FORMAT: FILL IN THE BLANK

Answer: 7
Rationale: The nurse would schedule the next home care visit in 7 days. Protective hydrocolloid dressings such as DuoDerm are designed to be left in place for 7 days unless leakage occurs around the dressing.
Test-Taking Strategy: Focus on the name of the protective dressing. Recalling that hydrocolloid protective dressings are designed to be left in place for 7 days will assist you in answering this question. Review the purpose and procedure for using protective dressings if you had difficulty with this question.
Level of Cognitive Ability: Application
Client Needs: Physiological Integrity
Integrated Process: Nursing Process—planning
Content Area: Pharmacology
References: Potter, P., & Perry, A. (2005). *Fundamentals of nursing* (6th ed., p. 1534). St. Louis: Mosby.
Lewis, S., Heitkemper, M., & Dirksen, S. (2004). *Medical-surgical nursing: Assessment and management of clinical problems* (6th ed., p. 220). St. Louis: Mosby.

REFERENCES

Hodgson, B., & Kizior, R. (2007). *Saunders nursing drug handbook 2007.* Philadelphia: W.B. Saunders.

Ignatavicius, D., & Workman, M. (2005). *Medical-surgical nursing: Critical thinking for collaborative care* (5th ed.). St. Louis: W.B. Saunders.

Lehne, R. (2004). *Pharmacology for nursing care* (5th ed.). St. Louis: W.B. Saunders.

McKenry, L., Tessier, E., & Hogan, M. (2006). *Mosby's pharmacology in nursing* (22nd ed.). St Louis: Mosby.

Potter, P., & Perry, A. (2005). *Fundamentals of nursing* (6th ed.). St. Louis: Mosby.

Skidmore-Roth, L. (2005). *Mosby's nursing drug reference 2005.* St. Louis: Mosby.

The Adult Client With an Oncological Disorder

PYRAMID TERMS

benign Usually a reference to growths that are encapsulated, remain localized, and are slow-growing.

cancer A neoplastic disorder that can involve all body organs. Cells lose their normal growth-controlling mechanism, and the growth of cells is uncontrolled.

carcinogen A physical, chemical, or biological stressor that causes neoplastic changes in normal cells.

carcinoma A new growth or malignant tumor that originates from epithelial cells, the skin, gastrointestinal tract, lungs, uterus, breast, or other organ.

carcinoma in situ A lesion with all the histological characteristics of malignancies, except invasion.

hospice A concept of care for terminally ill clients that includes the idea of intensive caring rather than intensive care. The client and the family are the focus of nursing care, and the goal is to relieve pain and facilitate the optimal quality of life.

lymphoma Neoplasm that originates from lymphoid tissue.

leukemia or myeloma Neoplasm that originates from a blood-forming organ.

malignant Term for growths that are not encapsulated but metastasize and grow. These growths are cancerous lesions having the characteristics of disorderly, uncontrolled, and chaotically proliferating cells.

metastasis The transfer of disease from one organ or part to another not directly connected with it. Secondary malignant lesions, originating from the primary tumor, are located in anatomically distant places.

nadir The period of time during which an antineoplastic medication has its most profound effects on the bone marrow.

neoplasm A new growth, which may be benign or malignant.

sarcoma Neoplasm that originates from muscle, bone, fat, the lymph system, or connective tissue.

staging A method of classifying malignancies based on the presence and extent of the tumor within the body.

tumor marker Specific bodily substances that seem to indicate tumor progression or regression.

undifferentiated cells Cells that have lost the capacity for specialized functions.

PYRAMID TO SUCCESS

Pyramid Points focus on treatment modalities related to an oncological disorder, such as pain management, internal and external radiation, and chemotherapy, and on oncological disorders, such as skin cancer, leukemia, breast cancer, and lung cancer. Specific focus relates to the nursing care related to these treatment modalities and disorders, client adaptation, and the impact of the treatment or the disorder. Specifically, focus on the complications related to chemotherapy and the nursing measures required in monitoring for these complications and preventing life-threatening conditions, such as infection and bleeding. Specific laboratory values include the white blood cell count and the platelet count. The Integrated Processes addressed in this unit include Caring, Communication and Documentation, Nursing Process, and Teaching/Learning.

CLIENT NEEDS

Safe and Effective Care Environment

Discussing oncology-related consultations and referrals

Ensuring advocacy related to client's decisions

Ensuring ethical practice

Ensuring that advance directives are in the client's medical record

Establishing priorities

Handling hazardous and infectious materials related to radiation and chemotherapy safely

Implementing protective, standard, and other precautions

Maintaining medical and surgical asepsis

Preventing disease related to infection

Providing confidentiality regarding diagnosis

Providing informed consent for treatments and procedures

Upholding the client's rights

Health Promotion and Maintenance

Discussing expected body image changes related to chemotherapy and treatments

Providing client and family instructions regarding home care

Providing instructions regarding monthly breast or testicular self-examinations

Respecting client lifestyle choices

Teaching about health promotion programs regarding risks for cancer

Teaching about health screening measures for cancer

Psychosocial Integrity

Assessing the client's ability to cope, adapt, and/or solve problems during illness or stressful events

Assisting the client and family to cope with the alteration in body image

Discussing end-of-life and grief and loss issues related to death and the dying process

Mobilizing appropriate support and resource systems

Promoting a positive environment to maintain optimal quality of life

Respecting religious and cultural preferences

Physiological Integrity

Administering blood and blood products

Caring for central venous access devices

Caring for the client receiving chemotherapy

Caring for the client receiving radiation therapy

Managing pain

Monitoring diagnostic tests and laboratory values, such as white blood cell and platelet counts

Monitoring for expected and unexpected responses to radiation and chemotherapy

Protecting the client from the life-threatening side effects of treatments

Providing basic care and comfort

Providing nutrition

REFERENCES

Chernecky, C., & Berger, B. (2004). *Laboratory tests & diagnostic procedures* (4th ed.). Philadelphia: W.B. Saunders.

Harkreader, H., & Hogan, M. A. (2004). *Fundamentals of nursing: Caring and clinical judgment* (2nd ed.). St. Louis: W.B. Saunders.

Ignatavicius, D., & Workman, M. (2005). *Medical-surgical nursing: Critical thinking for collaborative care* (5th ed.). St. Louis: W.B. Saunders.

Jarvis, C. (2004). *Physical examination and health assessment* (4th ed.). St. Louis: W.B. Saunders.

Lewis, S., Heitkemper, M., & Dirksen, S. (2004). *Medical-surgical nursing: Assessment and management of clinical problems* (6th ed.). St. Louis: Mosby.

National Council of State Boards of Nursing (Eds.). (2007). *2007 NCLEX-RN® detailed test plan.* Chicago: Author.

Potter, P., & Perry, A. (2005). *Fundamentals of nursing* (6th ed.). St. Louis: Mosby.

Varcarolis, E., Carson, V., & Shoemaker, N. (2006). *Foundations of psychiatric mental health nursing: A clinical approach* (5th ed.). Philadelphia: W.B. Saunders.

Oncological Disorders

I. CANCER

A. Description

1. **Cancer** is a neoplastic disorder that can involve all body organs with manifestations that vary according to the body system affected and type of tumor cells.
2. Cells lose their normal growth-controlling mechanism, and the growth of cells is uncontrolled.
3. **Cancer** produces serious health problems such as impaired immune and hematopoietic (blood-producing) function, altered gastrointestinal tract structure and function, motor and sensory deficits, and decreased respiratory function.

B. **Metastasis** (Box 51-1)

1. **Cancer** cells move from their original location to other sites.
2. Routes of **metastasis**
   a. Local seeding: Distribution of shed **cancer** cells occurs in the local area of the primary tumor.
   b. Bloodborne **metastasis**: Tumor cells enter the blood, which is the most common cause of **cancer** spread.
   c. Lymphatic spread: Primary sites rich in lymphatics are more susceptible to early metastatic spread.

C. **Cancer** classification

1. Solid tumors: Associated with the organs from which they develop, such as breast **cancer** or lung **cancer**
2. Hematological **cancer**s: Originate from blood cell–forming tissues, such as leukemias, **lymphomas,** and multiple myeloma

D. Grading and **staging** (Box 51-2)

1. Grading and **staging** are methods used to describe the tumor.

BOX 51-1
Common Sites of Metastasis

BREAST CANCER
Bone
Lung

LUNG CANCER
Brain

COLORECTAL CANCER
Liver

PROSTATE CANCER
Bone
Spine and legs

BRAIN TUMORS
Central nervous system

---

2. These methods describe the extent of the tumor, the extent to which malignancy has increased in size, the involvement of regional nodes, and metastatic development.
3. Grading a tumor classifies the cellular aspects of the **cancer.**
4. **Staging** classifies the clinical aspects of the **cancer** and degree of **metastasis** at diagnosis.

E. Factors that influence **cancer** development

1. Environmental factors
   a. Chemical **carcinogen**: Factors include industrial chemicals, drugs, and tobacco.
   b. Physical **carcinogen**: Factors include ionizing radiation (diagnostic and therapeutic x-rays) and ultraviolet radiation (sun, tanning beds, and germicidal lights), chronic irritation, and tissue trauma.
   c. Viral **carcinogen**: Viruses capable of causing **cancer** are known as oncoviruses, such as

---

BOX 51-2
Grading and Staging

GRADING
Grade I: Cells differ slightly from normal cells and are well differentiated (mild dysplasia).
Grade II: Cells are more abnormal and are moderately differentiated (moderate dysplasia).
Grade III: Cells are very abnormal and are poorly differentiated (severe dysplasia).
Grade IV: Cells are immature (anaplasia) and undifferentiated; cell of origin is difficult to determine.

STAGING
Stage 0: Carcinoma in situ
Stage I: Tumor limited to the tissue of origin; localized tumor growth
Stage II: Limited local spread
Stage III: Extensive local and regional spread
Stage IV: Distant metastasis

BOX 51-3
Warning Signs of Cancer

Any sore that does not heal
Change in bowel or bladder habits
Indigestion
Nagging cough or hoarseness
Obvious change in wart or mole
Thickening or lump in breast or elsewhere
Unusual bleeding or discharge

Epstein-Barr virus, hepatitis B virus, and human papillomavirus.

    d. *Helicobacter pylori* infection is associated with an increased risk of gastric **cancer.**

2. Obesity and dietary factors including preservatives, contaminants, additives, and nitrates.
3. Genetic predisposition: Factors include an inherited predisposition to specific **cancers,** inherited conditions associated with **cancer,** familial clustering, and chromosomal aberrations.
4. Age: Advancing age is a significant risk factor for the development of **cancer.**
5. Immune function: The incidence of **cancer** is higher in immunosuppressed individuals, such as those with acquired immunodeficiency syndrome and organ transplant recipients who are taking immunosuppressive medications.

F. Prevention: Avoidance of known or potential **carcinogens** and avoidance or modification of the factors associated with the development of **cancer** cells

G. Early detection (Box 51-3)
1. Mammography
2. Papanicolaou's (Pap) test
3. Stools for occult blood
4. Sigmoidoscopy, colonoscopy
5. Breast self-examination and clinical breast examination
6. Testicular self-examination
7. Skin inspection

▲ II. BREAST SELF-EXAMINATION
A. Performing breast self-examination (BSE)
1. Perform 7 to 10 days after menses.
2. Postmenopausal clients or clients who have had a hysterectomy should select a specific day of the month and perform BSE monthly on that day.
B. Client instructions (Fig. 51-1)

III. TESTICULAR SELF-EXAMINATION ▲
A. Performing testicular self-examination: A day of the month is selected and the examination is performed on the same day each month.
B. Client instructions (Fig. 51-2)

IV. DIAGNOSTIC TESTS
A. Diagnostic tests to be performed depend on the suspected primary or metastatic site(s) of the **cancer** (Box 51-4).
B. Biopsy ▲
1. Description
    a. Biopsy is the definitive means of diagnosing **cancer** and provides histological proof of malignancy.
    b. Biopsy involves the surgical incision of a small piece of tissue for microscopic examination.
2. Types
    a. Needle: Aspiration of cells
    b. Incisional: Removal of a wedge of suspected tissue from a larger mass
    c. Excisional: Complete removal of the entire lesion
    d. **Staging:** Multiple needle or incisional biopsies in tissues where **metastasis** is suspected or likely (see Boxes 51-1 and 51-2.)
3. Tissue examination
    a. Following excision, a frozen section or a permanent paraffin section is prepared to examine the specimen.
    b. The advantage of the frozen section is the speed with which the section can be prepared and the diagnosis made, because only minutes are required for this test.
    c. Permanent paraffin section takes about 24 hours; however, it provides clearer details than the frozen section.
4. Interventions
    a. The procedure usually is performed in an outpatient surgical setting.
    b. Prepare the client for the diagnostic procedure, and provide postprocedure instructions.
    c. Obtain an informed consent.

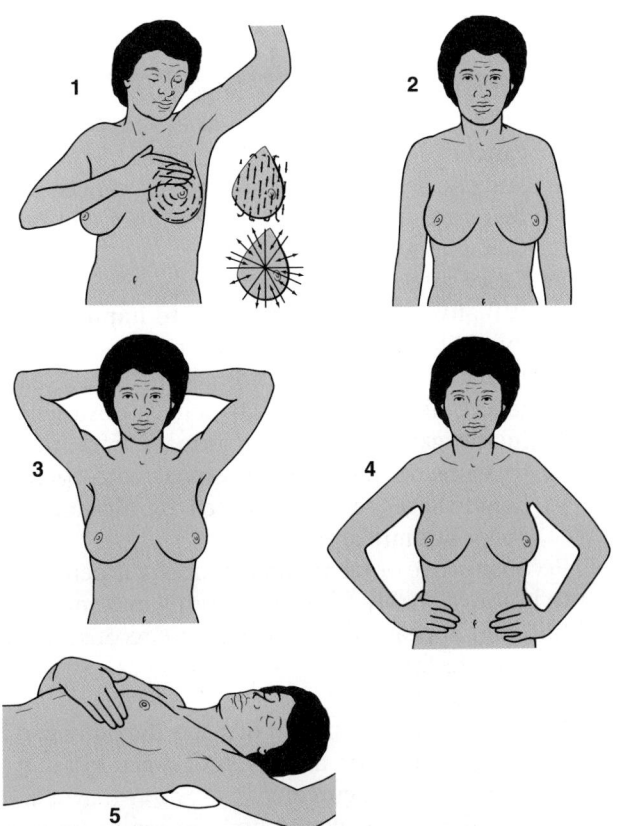

FIG. 51-1 Breast self-examination and patient instruction. **1,** While in the shower or bath, when the skin is slippery with soap and water, examine your breasts. Use the pads of your second, third, and fourth fingers to press every part of the breast firmly. Use your right hand to examine your left breast, and use your left hand to examine your right breast. Using the pads of the fingers on your left hand, examine the entire right breast using small circular motions in a spiral or up-and-down motion so that the entire breast area is examined. Repeat the procedure using your right hand to examine your left breast. Repeat the pattern of palpation under the arm. Check for any lump, hard knot, or thickening of the tissue. **2,** Look at your breasts in a mirror. Stand with your arms at your side. **3,** Raise your arms overhead and check for any changes in the shape of your breasts, dimpling of the skin, or any changes in the nipple. **4,** Next, place your hands on your hips and press down firmly, tightening the pectoral muscles. Observe for asymmetry or changes, keeping in mind that your breasts probably do not match exactly. **5,** While lying down, feel your breasts as described in **1.** When examining your right breast, place a folded towel under your right shoulder and put your right hand behind your head. Repeat the procedure while examining your left breast. Mark your calendar that you have completed your breast-self-examination; note any changes or unique characteristics you want to check with your health care provider. (From Lewis, S., Heitkemper, M., & Dirksen, S. [2004]. *Medical-surgical nursing: Assessment and management of clinical problems* [6th ed.]. St. Louis: Mosby.)

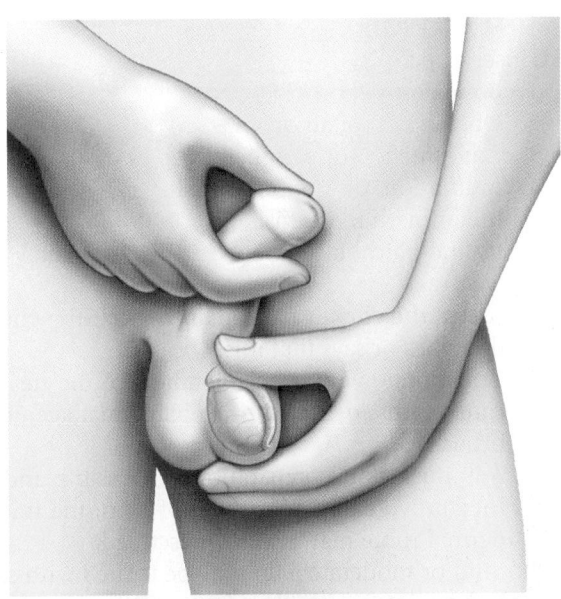

FIG. 51-2 Testicular self-examination. The best time to perform this examination is right after a shower when your scrotal skin is moist and relaxed, making the testicles easy to feel. First, gently lift each testicle. Each one should feel like an egg, firm but not hard, and smooth with no lumps. Then, using both hands, place your middle fingers on the underside of each testicle and your thumbs on top. Gently roll the testicle between the thumb and fingers to feel for any lumps, swelling, or mass. If you notice any changes from one month to the next, notify your physician or nurse practitioner. (From Harkreader, H., & Hogan, M. A. [2004]. *Fundamentals of nursing: Caring and clinical judgment* [2nd ed.]. Philadelphia: W.B. Saunders.)

BOX 51-4

Diagnostic Tests

Biopsy
Bone marrow examination (particularly if a hematolymphoid malignancy is suspected)
Chest radiograph
Complete blood count (CBC)
Computed tomography (CT)
Cytological studies (Papanicolaou's smear)
Liver function studies
Magnetic resonance imaging (MRI)
Evaluation of serum tumor markers (e.g., carcinoembryonic antigen and alpha-fetoprotein)
Proctoscopic examination (including guaiac for occult blood)
Radiographic studies (mammography)
Radioisotope scanning (liver, brain, bone, lung)

▲ V. PAIN CONTROL
A. Causes of pain
1. Bone destruction
2. Obstruction of an organ
3. Compression of peripheral nerves
4. Infiltration, distention of tissue
5. Inflammation, necrosis
6. Psychological factors, such as fear or anxiety
▲ B. Interventions
1. Assess the client's pain; pain is what the client describes or says that it is.
2. Collaborate with other members of the health care team to develop a pain management program.
3. Administer oral preparations if possible and if they provide adequate relief of pain; the transdermal route may also be prescribed.
4. Mild or moderate pain may be treated with salicylates, acetaminophen (Tylenol), and nonsteroidal anti-inflammatory drugs (NSAIDs); drug-drug interactions occur with NSAIDs and anticoagulants, oral hypoglycemics, and antihypertensives.
5. Severe pain is treated with opioids, such as codeine sulfate, morphine sulfate, methadone, and hydromorphone hydrochloride (Dilaudid). Neuropathic pain is treated with a variety of anticonvulsants and antidepressants, as well as opioids.
6. Subcutaneous injections and continuous intravenous (IV) infusions of opioids provide rapid pain control; equianalgesic comparison charts should be used when switching routes of administration of opioids.
7. Monitor vital signs and for side effects of medications.
8. Monitor for effectiveness of medications.
9. Provide nonpharmacological techniques of pain control, such as relaxation, guided imagery, biofeedback, massage, and heat-cold application.
10. Do not undermedicate the **cancer** client who is in pain.

VI. SURGERY
A. Description: Surgery is indicated to diagnose, stage, and treat **cancer.**
B. Prophylactic surgery
1. Prophylactic surgery is performed in clients with an existing premalignant condition or a known family history that strongly predisposes the person to the development of **cancer.**
2. An attempt is made to remove the tissue or organ at risk and thus prevent the development of **cancer.**
C. Curative surgery: All gross and microscopic tumor is removed or destroyed.

D. Control (cytoreductive or "debulking") surgery
1. Control surgery is a debulking procedure that consists of removing a large portion of a locally invasive tumor, such as advanced ovarian **cancer.**
2. Surgery decreases the number of **cancer** cells; therefore, it may increase the chance that other therapies will be successful.
E. Palliative surgery
1. Palliative surgery is performed to improve quality of life during the survival time.
2. Palliative surgery is performed to reduce pain, relieve airway obstruction, relieve obstructions in the gastrointestinal or urinary tract, relieve pressure on the brain or spinal cord, prevent hemorrhage, remove infected or ulcerated tumors, or drain abscesses.
F. Reconstructive or rehabilitative surgery is performed to improve quality of life by restoring maximal function and appearance, such as breast reconstruction after mastectomy.
G. Side effects of surgery
1. Loss or loss of function of a specific body part
2. Reduced function as a result of organ loss
3. Scarring or disfigurement
4. Grieving about altered body image or imposed change in lifestyle

VII. CHEMOTHERAPY
A. Description
1. Chemotherapy kills or inhibits the reproduction of neoplastic cells and kills normal cells.
2. The effects are systemic because chemotherapy is usually administered systemically.
3. Normal cells most profoundly affected include those of the skin, hair, and lining of the gastrointestinal tract, spermatocytes, and hematopoietic cells.
4. Cell cycle phase-specific medications affect cells only during a certain phase of the reproductive cycle, and cell cycle phase-nonspecific medications affect cells in any phase of the reproductive cycle.
5. Usually, several chemotherapy and biotherapy agents are used in combination (combination therapy) to increase the therapeutic response.
6. Combination chemotherapy is planned to avoid prescribing medications with overlapping toxicities and **nadirs** (the time during which bone marrow activity and white blood cell counts are at their lowest) at or near the same time to minimize immunosuppression.
7. Chemotherapy may be combined with other treatments, such as surgery and radiation.
8. The preferred route of administration is intravenously.
9. Common side effects include fatigue, alopecia, nausea and vomiting, mucositis, skin changes,

and myelosuppression (neutropenia anemia, and thrombocytopenia).

10. See Chapter 52 for information regarding the care of the client receiving chemotherapy.

VIII. RADIATION THERAPY

A. Description
   1. Radiation therapy destroys **cancer** cells, with minimal exposure of normal cells to the damaging effects of radiation; the damaged cells die or become unable to divide.
   2. Radiation therapy is effective on tissues directly within the path of the radiation beam.
   3. Side effects include local skin changes and irritation, alopecia (hair loss), fatigue (most common side effect of radiation), and altered taste sensation; the effects vary according to the site of treatment.
   4. External beam radiation (also called teletherapy) and brachytherapy are the types of radiation therapy most commonly used to treat **cancer.**
B. External beam radiation (teletherapy): the actual radiation source is external to the client.
   1. Instruct the client regarding self-care of the skin (Box 51-5).
   2. The client does not emit radiation and does not pose a hazard to anyone else.
C. Brachytherapy
   1. The radiation source comes into direct, continuous contact with tumor tissues for a specific time.
   2. The radiation source is within the client; for a period of time, the client emits radiation and can pose a hazard to others.

3. Brachytherapy includes an unsealed source or a sealed source of radiation.
4. Unsealed radiation source
   a. Administration is via the oral or IV route or by instillation into body cavities.
   b. The source is not confined completely to one body area, and it enters body fluids and eventually is eliminated via various excreta, which are radioactive and harmful to others. Most of the source is eliminated from the body within 48 hours; then neither the client nor the excreta is radioactive or harmful.
5. Sealed radiation source (Boxes 51-6 and 51-7)
   a. A sealed, temporary or permanent radiation source (solid implant) is implanted within the tumor target tissues.
   b. The client emits radiation while the implant is in place, but the excreta are not radioactive.

BOX 51-5

Client Education Guide: Radiation Therapy for Cancer

Wash the irradiated area gently each day with warm water alone or with mild soap and water.
Use your hand rather than a washcloth to be more gentle.
Rinse soap thoroughly from your skin.
Take care not to remove the markings that indicate exactly where the beam of radiation is to be focused.
Dry the irradiated area with patting motions rather than rubbing motions; use a clean, soft towel or cloth.
Use no powders, ointments, lotions, or creams on your skin at the radiation site unless they are prescribed by your radiologist.
Wear soft clothing over the skin at the radiation site.
Avoid wearing belts, buckles, straps or any type of clothing that binds or rubs the skin at the radiation site.
Avoid exposure of the irradiated area to the sun.
Avoid heat exposure.

From Ignatavicius, D., & Workman, M. (2006). *Medical-surgical nursing: Critical thinking for collaborative care* (5th ed.). Philadelphia: W.B. Saunders.

BOX 51-6

Care of the Client With a Sealed Radiation Source

Place the client in a private room with a private bath.
Place a caution sign on the client's door.
Organize nursing tasks to minimize exposure to the radiation source.
Nursing assignments to a client with a radiation implant should be rotated.
Limit time to 30 minutes per care provider per shift.
Wear a dosimeter film badge to measure radiation exposure.
Wear a lead shield to reduce the transmission of radiation.
A nurse should never care for more than one client with a radiation implant at one time.
Do not allow a pregnant nurse to care for the client.
Do not allow children younger than 16 years or a pregnant woman to visit the client.
Limit visitors to 30 minutes per day; visitors should be at least 6 feet from the source.
Save bed linens and dressings until the source is removed; then dispose of in the usual manner.
Other equipment can be removed from the room at any time.

BOX 51-7

Dislodged Radiation Source

Do not touch a dislodged radiation source with bare hands.
If the radiation source dislodges, use long-handled forceps to place the source in the lead container kept in the client's room, and call the physician.
If unable to locate the radiation source, prohibit visitors and notify the physician.

6. Removal of sealed radiation sources
   a. The client is no longer radioactive.
   b. Inform the client that sexual partners cannot "catch" **cancer.**
   c. Inform the female client that she may resume sexual intercourse after 7 to 10 days if the implant was cervical or vaginal.
   d. Provide a povidone-iodine douche, if prescribed, if the implant was placed into the cervix.
   e. Administer a Fleet enema if prescribed.
   f. Advise the client who had a cervical or vaginal implant to notify the physician if nausea, vomiting, diarrhea, frequent urination, vaginal or rectal bleeding, hematuria, foul-smelling vaginal discharge, abdominal pain or distention, or fever occurs.

IX. BONE MARROW TRANSPLANTATION

A. Description
   1. Bone marrow transplantation (BMT) and peripheral blood stem cell transplantation (PBSCT) are procedures that replace stem cells that have been destroyed by high doses of chemotherapy and/or radiation therapy.
   2. BMT and PBSCT are most commonly used in the treatment of leukemia and **lymphoma,** but are also used to treat other **cancers,** such as neuroblastoma and multiple myeloma.
   3. The goal of treatment is to rid the client of all leukemic or other **malignant** cells through treatment with high doses of chemotherapy and whole-body irradiation.
   4. Because these treatments are damaging to bone marrow cells, without the replacement of blood-forming stem cell function through transplantation, the client would die of infection or hemorrhage.

B. Types of donor stem cells
   1. Allogeneic: Stem cell donor is usually a sibling, parent with a similar tissue type, or a person who is not related to the client (unrelated donor).
   2. Syngeneic: Stem cell is from an identical twin.
   3. Autologous
      a. Autologous donation is the most common type.
      b. The client receives his or her own stem cells.
      c. Stem cells are harvested during disease remission and are stored frozen to be reinfused later.

C. Procedure
   1. Harvest
      a. The stem cells used in PBSCT come from the bloodstream in a 4- to 6-hour process call apheresis or leukapheresis (the blood is removed through a central venous catheter and an apheresis machine removes the stem cells

and returns the remainder of the blood to the donor).
      b. In BMT, marrow is harvested through multiple aspirations from the iliac crest to retrieve sufficient bone marrow for the transplant.
      c. Marrow is filtered for residual **cancer** cells.
      d. Allogeneic marrow is transfused immediately; autologous marrow is frozen for later use (cryopreservation).
      e. Harvesting is done before the initiation of the conditioning regimen.
   2. Conditioning refers to an immunosuppression therapy regimen used to eradicate all **malignant** cells, provide a state of immunosuppression, and create space in the bone marrow for the engraftment of the new marrow.
   3. Transplantation
      a. Stem cells are administered through the client's central line in a manner similar to that for a blood transfusion.
      b. Stem cells may be administered by IV infusion or by IV push directly into the central line.
   4. Engraftment
      a. The transfused stem cells move to the marrow-forming sites of the recipient's bones.
      b. Engraftment occurs when the white blood cell, erythrocyte, and platelet counts begin to rise.
      c. When successful, the engraftment process takes 2 to 5 weeks.

D. Post-transplantation period
   1. The client remains without any natural immunity until the donor stem cells begin to proliferate and engraftment occurs.
   2. Infection, bleeding, or neutropenia and thrombocytopenia are major concerns until engraftment occurs.

E. Complications
   1. Failure to engraft: If the transplanted stem cells fail to engraft, the client will die unless another transplantation is attempted and is successful.
   2. Graft-versus-host disease in allogeneic transplants
      a. Although the recipient cannot recognize the donated stem cells as foreign or non-self because of the total immunosuppression, the immune competent cells of the donor recognize the recipient's cells as foreign and mount an immune offense against them.
      b. Graft-versus-host disease is managed with immunosuppressive agents cautiously to avoid suppressing the new immune system to the extent that the client becomes more susceptible to infection, or the transplanted cells stop engrafting.

3. Veno-occlusive disease
   a. The disease involves occlusion of the hepatic venules by thrombosis or phlebitis.
   b. Signs include right upper quadrant abdominal pain, jaundice, ascites, weight gain, and hepatomegaly.
   c. Early detection is critical because there is no known way to open the hepatic vessels.
   d. The client will be treated with fluids and supportive therapy.

X. SKIN CANCER (see Chap. 49)

XI. LEUKEMIA (Box 51-8)
A. Description
   1. Leukemias are a group of hematological malignancies involving abnormal overproduction of leukocytes, usually at an immature stage, in the bone marrow.
   2. The two major types of leukemia are lymphocytic (involving abnormal cells from the lymphoid pathway) and myelocytic or myelogenous (involving abnormal cells from the myeloid pathways).
   3. Leukemia may be acute, with a sudden onset, or chronic, with a slow onset and persistent symptoms over a period of years.
   4. Leukemia affects the bone marrow, causing anemia, leukopenia, the production of immature cells, thrombocytopenia, and a decline in immunity.
   5. The cause is unknown and appears to involve gene damage of cells, leading to the transformation of cells from a normal state to a **malignant** state.
   6. Risk factors include genetic, viral, immunological, and environmental factors and exposure to radiation, chemicals, and medications, such as previous chemotherapy.

BOX 51-8

Classification of Leukemia

ACUTE LYMPHOCYTIC LEUKEMIA
Mostly lymphoblasts present in bone marrow
Age of onset is younger than 15 years.

ACUTE MYELOGENOUS LEUKEMIA
Mostly myeloblasts present in bone marrow
Age of onset is between 15 and 39 years

CHRONIC MYELOGENOUS LEUKEMIA
Mostly granulocytes present in bone marrow
Age of onset is in the fourth decade

CHRONIC LYMPHOCYTIC LEUKEMIA
Mostly lymphocytes present in bone marrow
Age of onset is after 50 years

B. Assessment
   1. Anorexia, fatigue, weakness, weight loss
   2. Anemia
   3. Overt bleeding (nosebleeds, gum bleeding, rectal bleeding, hematuria, increased menstrual flow) and occult bleeding (e.g., as detected in a fecal occult blood test)
   4. Ecchymosis, petechiae
   5. Prolonged bleeding after minor abrasions or lacerations
   6. Elevated temperature
   7. Enlarged lymph nodes, spleen, liver
   8. Palpitations, tachycardia, orthostatic hypotension
   9. Pallor and dyspnea on exertion
   10. Headache
   11. Bone pain and joint swelling
   12. Normal, elevated, or reduced white blood cell count
   13. Decreased hemoglobin and hematocrit levels
   14. Decreased platelet count
   15. Positive bone marrow biopsy identifying leukemic blast phase cells

C. Infection
   1. Infection is a major cause of death in the immunosuppressed client.
   2. Infection can occur through autocontamination or cross-contamination.
   3. Common sites of infection are the skin, respiratory tract, and gastrointestinal tract.
   4. Initiate protective isolation procedures.
   5. Ensure frequent and thorough hand hygiene by the client, family, and health care providers.
   6. Staff and visitors with known infections or exposure to communicable diseases should avoid contact with the client until risk of infectious spread has passed.
   7. Use strict aseptic technique for all procedures.
   8. Keep supplies for the client separate from supplies for other clients; keep frequently used equipment in the room for the client's use only.
   9. Limit the number of staff entering the client's room; reducing the number of staff who come into contact with the client reduces the risk of cross-infection.
   10. Maintain the client in a private room with door closed.
   11. Place the client in a room with high-efficiency particulate air filtration or a laminar airflow system if possible.
   12. Reduce exposure to environmental organisms by thoroughly washing or eliminating fresh or raw fruits and vegetables (low-bacteria diet) from the diet; eliminate fresh flowers and live plants from the client's room and avoid leaving standing water in the client's room.
   13. Be sure that the client's room is cleaned daily.

14. Assist the client with daily bathing, using an antimicrobial soap.
15. Assist the client to perform oral hygiene frequently.
16. Initiate a bowel program to prevent constipation and prevent rectal trauma.
17. Avoid invasive procedures such as injections, rectal temperatures, and urinary catheterization.
18. Change wound dressings daily, and inspect the wounds for redness, swelling, or drainage.
19. Assess the urine for color and cloudiness.
20. Assess skin and oral mucous membranes for signs of infection (Box 51-9).
21. Auscultate lung sounds, and encourage the client to cough and deep-breathe.
22. Monitor temperature, pulse, and blood pressure.
23. Monitor white blood cell and neutrophil counts.
24. Notify the physician if signs of infection are present, and prepare to obtain specimens for culture of open lesions, urine, and sputum.
25. Anticipate and administer prescribed antibiotic, antifungal, and antiviral medications.
26. Instruct the client to avoid crowds and those with infections.
27. Instruct the client about a low-bacteria diet.
28. Instruct the client to avoid activities that expose the client to infection, such as changing a pet's litter box or working with house plants or in the garden.
29. Instruct the client that neither they nor their household contacts should receive immunization with a live virus.

▲ D. Bleeding
1. During the period of greatest bone marrow suppression (the **nadir**), the platelet count may be extremely low.
2. The client is at risk for bleeding when the platelet count falls below 50,000/mm^3, and spontaneous bleeding frequently occurs when the platelet count is fewer than 20,000/mm^3.
3. Clients with platelet counts lower than 20,000/mm^3 may need a platelet transfusion.
4. For clients with anemia and fatigue, packed red blood cells may be prescribed.
5. Monitor laboratory values.
6. Examine the client for signs and symptoms of bleeding; examine all body fluids and excrement for the presence of blood.
7. Handle the client gently; use caution when taking blood pressures to prevent skin injury.
8. Monitor for signs of internal hemorrhage (e.g., pain, rapid and weak pulse, increased abdominal girth, and "guarding" of the abdomen).
9. Provide soft foods that are cool to warm to avoid oral mucosa damage.
10. Avoid injections, if possible, to prevent trauma to the skin and bleeding; apply firm and gentle

---

BOX 51-9
Mouth Care for the Client With Mucositis

Inspect mouth daily.
Offer complete mouth care before and after every meal and at bedtime.
Brush teeth and tongue with a soft-bristled toothbrush or sponges.
Provide mouth rinses every 12 hours (saline or sodium bicarbonate and water, as prescribed).
Administer topical anesthetic agents to the mouth sores as prescribed.
Avoid the use of alcohol- or glycerin-based mouthwashes or swabs.
Avoid foods that are hard or spicy.

---

pressure to a needlestick site for at least 5 minutes, longer if needed.
11. Pad side rails and sharp corners of the bed and furniture.
12. Avoid rectal suppositories, enemas, and thermometers.
13. If the female client is menstruating, count the number of pads or tampons used.
14. Administer blood products as prescribed.
15. Instruct the client to use a soft toothbrush and avoid dental floss.
16. Instruct the client to use only an electric razor for shaving.
17. Instruct the client to avoid blowing the nose.
18. Discourage the client from engaging in activities involving the use of sharp objects.
19. Instruct the client to avoid using nonsteroidal anti-inflammatory drugs and products that contain aspirin.

E. Fatigue and nutrition ▲
1. Assist the client in selecting a well-balanced diet.
2. Provide small, frequent meals (high calorie, high protein, high carbohydrate) that require little chewing to reduce energy expenditure at mealtimes.
3. Assist the client in self-care and mobility activities.
4. Allow adequate rest periods during care.
5. Do not perform activities unless they are essential; assist the client in scheduling important or pleasurable activities during periods of highest energy.
6. Administer blood products for anemia as prescribed.

F. Additional interventions
1. Chemotherapy
   a. Induction therapy is aimed at achieving a rapid, complete remission of all manifestations of the disease.

b. Consolidation therapy is administered early in remission with the aim of cure.

c. Maintenance therapy may be prescribed for months or years following successful induction and consolidation therapy; the aim is to maintain remission.

2. Administer antibiotic, antibacterial, antiviral, and antifungal medications as prescribed.
3. Administer blood replacements as prescribed.
4. Prepare the client for transplantation if indicated.
5. Administer colony-stimulating factors as prescribed.
6. Maintain infection and bleeding precautions.
7. Provide an adequate diet.
8. Provide an activity schedule that will conserve energy.
9. Instruct the client in appropriate home care measures.
10. Provide psychosocial support and support services for home care.

XII. LYMPHOMA: HODGKIN'S DISEASE

A. Description
1. **Lymphomas,** classified as Hodgkin's and non-Hodgkin's depending on the cell type, are characterized by abnormal proliferation of lymphocytes.
2. Hodgkin's disease is a malignancy of the lymph nodes that originates in a single lymph node or a chain of nodes.
3. **Metastasis** occurs to other adjacent lymph structures and eventually invades nonlymphoid tissue.
4. The disease usually involves lymph nodes, tonsils, spleen, and bone marrow and is characterized by the presence of Reed-Sternberg cells in the nodes.
5. Possible causes include viral infections; clients treated with combination chemotherapy for Hodgkin's disease have a greater risk of developing acute leukemia and non-Hodgkin's **lymphoma,** among other secondary malignancies.
6. Prognosis depends on the stage of the disease (Box 51-10).

B. Assessment
1. Fever
2. Malaise, fatigue, and weakness
3. Night sweats
4. Loss of appetite and significant weight loss
5. Anemia and thrombocytopenia
6. Enlarged lymph nodes, spleen, and liver
7. Positive biopsy of lymph nodes, with cervical nodes most often affected first
8. Presence of Reed-Sternberg cells in nodes
9. Positive computed tomography (CT) scan of the liver and spleen

---

BOX 51-10

Staging in Hodgkin's Disease

STAGE I
Involvement of a single lymph node region or an extra-lymphatic organ or site

STAGE II
Involvement of two or more lymph node regions on the same side of the diaphragm or localized involvement of an extralymphatic organ or site

STAGE III
Involvement of lymph node regions on both sides of the diaphragm

STAGE IV
Diffuse or disseminated involvement of one or more extralymphatic organs with or without associated lymph node involvement

---

C. Interventions
1. For stages I and II, without mediastinal node involvement, the treatment of choice is extensive external radiation of the involved lymph node regions.
2. With more extensive disease, radiation and multiagent chemotherapy are used.
3. Monitor for side effects related to chemotherapy or radiation therapy.
4. Monitor for signs of infection and bleeding.
5. Maintain infection and bleeding precautions.
6. Discuss the possibility of sterility with the male client receiving radiation, and inform the client of fertility options such as sperm banking.

XIII. MULTIPLE MYELOMA

A. Description
1. A **malignant** proliferation of plasma cells within the bone
2. An excessive number of abnormal plasma cells invade the bone marrow and ultimately destroy bone; invasion of the lymph nodes, spleen, and liver occurs.
3. The abnormal plasma cells produce an abnormal antibody (myeloma protein or the Bence Jones protein) found in the blood and urine.
4. Multiple myeloma causes decreased production of immunoglobulin and antibodies and increased levels of uric acid and calcium, which can lead to renal failure.
5. The disease typically develops slowly and the cause is unknown.

B. Assessment
1. Bone (skeletal) pain, especially in the ribs, spine, and pelvis

2. Weakness and fatigue
3. Recurrent infections
4. Anemia
5. Urinalysis shows Bence Jones proteinuria and elevated total serum protein level.
6. Osteoporosis (bone loss and the development of pathological fractures)
7. Thrombocytopenia and leukopenia
8. Elevated calcium and uric acid levels
9. Renal failure
10. Spinal cord compression and paraplegia
11. Bone marrow aspiration shows an abnormal number of immature plasma cells.

C. Interventions
1. Administer chemotherapy as prescribed.
2. Provide supportive care to control symptoms and prevent complications, especially bone fractures, hypercalcemia, renal failure, and infections.
3. Maintain neutropenic and bleeding precautions as necessary.
4. Monitor for signs of bleeding, infection, and skeletal fractures.
5. Encourage at least 2 L of fluids per day to offset potential problems associated with hypercalcemia, hyperuricemia, and proteinuria, and encourage additional fluid as indicated and tolerated.
6. Monitor for signs of renal failure.
7. Encourage ambulation to prevent renal problems and to slow down bone resorption.
8. Provide skeletal support during moving, turning, and ambulating to prevent pathological fractures; provide a hazard-free environment.
9. Administer IV fluids and diuretics as prescribed to increase renal excretion of calcium.
10. Administer blood transfusions as prescribed for anemia.
11. Administer analgesics as prescribed and provide nonpharmacological therapies to control pain.
12. Administer antibiotics as prescribed for infection.
13. Prepare the client for local radiation therapy if prescribed.
14. Instruct the client in home care measures and the signs and symptoms of infection.
15. Administer bisphosphonate medications such as pamidronate disodium (Aredia) and zoledronic acid (Zometa) as prescribed to slow bone damage and reduce pain and risk of fractures.

XIV. TESTICULAR CANCER

A. Description
1. Testicular **cancer** arises from germinal epithelium from the sperm-producing germ cells or from nongerminal epithelium from other structures in the testicles (Box 51-11).

BOX 51-11
Types of Testicular Cancer

GERMINAL TUMORS
Seminomas
Nonseminomas

NONGERMINAL TUMORS
Interstitial cell tumors
Androblastoma

---

2. Testicular **cancer** most often occurs between the ages of 15 and 40 years.
3. The cause of testicular **cancer** is unknown, but a history of undescended testicle (cryptorchidism) and genetic predisposition have been associated with testicular tumor development.
4. **Metastasis** occurs to the lung, liver, bone, and adrenal glands via the blood, and to the retroperitoneal lymph nodes via lymphatic channels.

B. Early detection: Perform monthly testicular self-examination

C. Assessment
1. Painless testicular swelling occurs.
2. "Dragging" or "pulling" sensation is experienced in the scrotum.
3. Palpable lymphadenopathy, abdominal masses, and gynecomastia may indicate **metastasis**.
4. Late signs include back or bone pain and respiratory symptoms.

D. Interventions
1. Administer chemotherapy as prescribed.
2. Prepare the client for radiation therapy as prescribed.
3. Prepare the client for unilateral orchiectomy, if prescribed, for diagnosis and primary surgical management or radical orchiectomy (surgical removal of the affected testis, spermatic cord, and regional lymph nodes).
4. Prepare the client for retroperitoneal lymph node dissection, if prescribed, to stage the disease and reduce tumor volume so that chemotherapy and radiation therapy are more effective.
5. Discuss reproduction, sexuality, and fertility information and options with the client.
6. Identify reproductive options such as sperm storage, donor insemination, and adoption.

E. Postoperative interventions
1. Monitor for signs of bleeding and wound infection; antibiotic ointment may be administered to prevent wound infection.
2. Monitor intake and output.
3. Provide and explain pain management methods; to reduce swelling in the first 48 hours, apply an ice pack with an intervening protective layer of cloth.

4. Notify the physician if chills, fever, increasing pain or tenderness at the incision site, or drainage of the incision occurs.
5. After the orchiectomy, instruct the client to avoid heavy lifting and strenuous activity for the length of time prescribed by the physician.
6. Instruct the client to perform a monthly testicular self-examination on the remaining testicle.
7. Inform the client that sutures will be removed 7 to 10 days after surgery.

XV. CERVICAL CANCER

A. Description
   1. Preinvasive **cancer** is limited to the cervix (Box 51-12).
   2. Invasive **cancer** is in the cervix and other pelvic structures.
   3. **Metastasis** usually is confined to the pelvis, but distant **metastasis** occurs through lymphatic spread.
   4. Premalignant changes are described on a continuum from dysplasia, which is the earliest premalignancy change, to **carcinoma in situ**, the most advanced premalignant change.
B. Risk factors
   1. Human papillomavirus (HPV) infection (vaccination against HPV is effective to avoid HPV infection, and thus cervical **cancer**)
   2. Cigarette smoking, both active and passive
   3. Reproductive behavior including early first intercourse (before age 17), multiple sex partners, or male partners with multiple sex partners.
   4. Screening via regular gynecological examinations and Papanicolaou smear (Pap test), with treatment of precancerous abnormalities, decreases the incidence and mortality of cervical **cancer.**
C. Assessment
   1. Painless vaginal postmenstrual and postcoital bleeding
   2. Foul-smelling or serosanguineous vaginal discharge
   3. Pelvic, lower back, leg, or groin pain
   4. Anorexia and weight loss
   5. Leakage of urine and feces from the vagina
   6. Dysuria
   7. Hematuria
   8. Cytological changes on Pap test
D. Interventions (Box 51-13)
E. Laser therapy
   1. Laser therapy is used when all boundaries of the lesion are visible during colposcopic examination.
   2. Energy from the beam is absorbed by fluid in the tissues, causing them to vaporize.
   3. Minimal bleeding is associated with the procedure.

BOX 51-12
Preinvasive Cancers: Cervical Intraepithelial Neoplasia

Stage I: Mild dysplasia
Stage II: Moderate dysplasia
Stage III: Severe dysplasia to carcinoma in situ

BOX 51-13
Treatment for Cervical Cancer

NONSURGICAL
Chemotherapy
Cryosurgery
External radiation
Internal radiation implants (intracavitary)
Laser therapy

SURGICAL
Conization
Hysterectomy
Pelvic exenteration

---

   4. Slight vaginal discharge is expected following the procedure, and healing occurs in 6 to 12 weeks.
F. Cryosurgery
   1. Cryosurgery involves freezing of the tissues using a probe, with subsequent necrosis and sloughing.
   2. No anesthesia is required, although cramping may occur during the procedure.
   3. A heavy watery discharge will occur for several weeks following the procedure.
   4. Instruct the client to avoid intercourse and the use of tampons while the discharge is present.
G. Conization
   1. A cone-shaped area of the cervix is removed.
   2. Conization allows the woman to retain reproductive capacity.
   3. Long-term follow-up care is needed because new lesions can develop.
   4. The risks of the procedure include hemorrhage, uterine perforation, incompetent cervix, cervical stenosis, and preterm labor in future pregnancies.
H. Hysterectomy
   1. Description
      a. Hysterectomy is performed for microinvasive **cancer** if childbearing is not desired.
      b. A vaginal approach is most commonly used.
      c. A radical hysterectomy and bilateral lymph node dissection may be performed for **cancer** that has spread beyond the cervix but not to the pelvic wall.
   2. Postoperative interventions
      a. Monitor vital signs
      b. Assist with coughing and deep-breathing exercises.
      c. Assist with range-of-motion exercises and provide early ambulation.

d. Apply antiembolism stockings as prescribed.

e. Monitor intake and output, Foley catheter drainage, and hydration status.

f. Monitor bowel sounds.

g. Monitor vaginal bleeding; more than one saturated pad per hour may indicate excessive bleeding.

h. Assess incision site for signs of infection.

i. Administer pain medication as prescribed.

j. Instruct the client to avoid stair climbing for 1 month as prescribed and to avoid tub baths and sitting for long periods.

k. Avoid strenuous activity or lifting anything weighing more than 20 lb.

l. Instruct the client to consume foods that promote tissue healing.

m. Instruct the client to avoid sexual intercourse for 3 to 6 weeks as prescribed.

n. Instruct the client in the signs associated with complications.

I. Pelvic exenteration (Box 51-14)

1. Description

a. Pelvic exenteration, the removal of all pelvic contents, including bowel, vagina, and bladder, is a radical surgical procedure performed for recurrent **cancer** if no evidence of tumor outside the pelvis and no lymph node involvement exist.

b. When the bladder is removed, an ileal conduit is created and located on the right side of the abdomen to divert urine.

c. A colostomy may need to be created on the left side of the abdomen for the passage of feces.

2. Postoperative interventions

a. Monitor for atelectasis and pneumonia.

b. Assist with coughing and deep-breathing exercises.

c. Monitor for hemorrhage, shock, and deep vein thrombosis.

d. Apply antiembolism stockings or sequential compression devices as prescribed.

e. Administer prophylactic heparin as prescribed.

f. Monitor bowel sounds.

BOX 51-14

Types of Pelvic Exenteration

ANTERIOR
Removal of the uterus, ovaries, fallopian tubes, vagina, bladder, urethra, and pelvic lymph nodes

POSTERIOR
Removal of the uterus, ovaries, fallopian tubes, descending colon, rectum, and anal canal

TOTAL
Combination of anterior and posterior

---

g. Monitor intake and output and for signs of dehydration.

h. Monitor incision site for infection.

i. Administer perineal irrigations and sitz baths as prescribed.

j. Administer analgesics as prescribed for pain and instruct the client regarding pain management.

k. Instruct the client to avoid strenuous activity for 6 months.

l. Instruct the client that the perineal opening, if present, may drain for several months.

m. Instruct the client in the care of the ileal conduit and colostomy, if created.

n. Provide sexual counseling because vaginal intercourse is not possible after anterior and total pelvic exenteration.

XVI. OVARIAN CANCER

A. Description

1. Ovarian **cancer** grows rapidly, spreads fast, and is often bilateral.

2. **Metastasis** occurs by direct spread to the organs in the pelvis, by distal spread through lymphatic drainage, or by peritoneal seeding.

3. In its early stages, ovarian **cancer** is often asymptomatic; because most women are diagnosed in advanced stages, ovarian **cancer** has more deaths than any other **cancer** of the female reproductive system, particularly white women between 55 and 65 years of age of North American or European descent.

4. An exploratory laparotomy is performed to diagnose and stage the tumor.

B. Assessment

1. Abdominal discomfort or swelling

2. Gastrointestinal disturbances

3. Dysfunctional vaginal bleeding

4. Abdominal mass

5. Elevated **tumor marker**

C. Interventions

1. External radiation may be used if the tumor has invaded other organs; intraperitoneal radioisotopes may be instilled for stage I disease.

2. Chemotherapy is used postoperatively for most stages of ovarian **cancer**.

3. Intraperitoneal chemotherapy involves the instillation of chemotherapy into the abdominal cavity.

4. Total abdominal hysterectomy and bilateral salpingo-oophorectomy with tumor debulking may be necessary.

XVII. ENDOMETRIAL CANCER

A. Description

1. Endometrial **cancer** is a slow-growing tumor arising from the endometrial mucosa of the uterus, associated with the menopausal years.

2. **Metastasis** occurs through the lymphatic system to the ovaries and pelvis, via the blood to the lungs, liver, and bone, or intraabdominally to the peritoneal cavity.

B. Risk factors
   1. Use of estrogen replacement therapy (ERT)
   2. Nulliparity
   3. Polycystic ovary disease
   4. Increased age
   5. Late menopause
   6. Family history of uterine **cancer** or hereditary nonpolyposis colorectal **cancer**
   7. Obesity
   8. Hypertension
   9. Diabetes mellitus

C. Assessment
   1. Abnormal bleeding, especially in postmenopausal women
   2. Vaginal discharge
   3. Low back, pelvic, or abdominal pain (pain occurs late in the disease process)
   4. Enlarged uterus (in advanced stages)

D. Nonsurgical interventions
   1. External or internal radiation is used alone or in combination with surgery, depending on the stage of **cancer.**
   2. Chemotherapy is used to treat advanced or recurrent disease.
   3. Progestational therapy with medication such as medroxyprogesterone (Depo-Provera) or megestrol acetate (Megace) is used for estrogen-dependent tumors.
   4. Tamoxifen (Nolvadex), an antiestrogen, also may be prescribed.

E. Surgical interventions: Total abdominal hysterectomy and bilateral salpingo-oophorectomy

 XVIII. BREAST CANCER

A. Description
   1. Breast **cancer** is classified as invasive when it penetrates the tissue surrounding the mammary duct and grows in an irregular pattern.
   2. **Metastasis** occurs via lymph nodes.
   3. Common sites of **metastasis** are the bone, lungs, brain, liver, and skin.
   4. Diagnosis is made by breast biopsy through a needle aspiration or by surgical removal of the tumor with microscopic examination for **malignant** cells.

B. Risk factors
   1. Age
   2. Family history of breast **cancer**
   3. Early menarche and late menopause
   4. Previous **cancer** of the breast, uterus, or ovaries
   5. Nulliparity, late first birth
   6. Obesity
   7. High-dose radiation exposure to chest

C. Assessment
   1. Mass felt during breast self-examination (BSE)
   2. Mass usually felt in the upper outer quadrant, beneath the nipple, or in axilla
   3. A fixed, irregular nonencapsulated mass; typically painless except in the late stages
   4. Nipple retraction or elevation
   5. Asymmetry, with the affected breast being higher
   6. Bloody or clear nipple discharge
   7. Skin dimpling, retraction, or ulceration
   8. Skin edema or peau d'orange skin
   9. Axillary lymphadenopathy
   10. Lymphedema of the affected arm
   11. Symptoms of bone or lung **metastasis** in late stage
   12. Presence of the lesion on mammography

D. Early detection: Monthly BSE

E. Nonsurgical interventions
   1. Chemotherapy
   2. Radiation therapy
   3. Hormonal manipulation via the use of medication in postmenopausal women or other medications such as tamoxifen (Nolvadex) for estrogen receptor–positive tumors

F. Surgical interventions: Surgical breast procedures, with possible breast reconstruction (Box 51-15)

G. Postoperative interventions
   1. Monitor vital signs.
   2. Position the client in a semi-Fowler's position; turn from the back to the unaffected side, with the affected arm elevated above the level of the heart to promote drainage and prevent lymphedema.
   3. Encourage coughing and deep breathing.
   4. If a drain (usually a Jackson-Pratt) is in place, maintain suction and record the amount of drainage and drainage characteristics (Fig. 51-3).

BOX 51-15
Surgical Breast Procedures

LUMPECTOMY
Tumor is excised and removed.
Lymph node dissection may also be performed.

SIMPLE MASTECTOMY
Breast tissue and the nipple are removed.
Lymph nodes are left intact.

MODIFIED RADICAL MASTECTOMY
Breast tissue, nipple, and lymph nodes are removed.
Muscles are left intact.

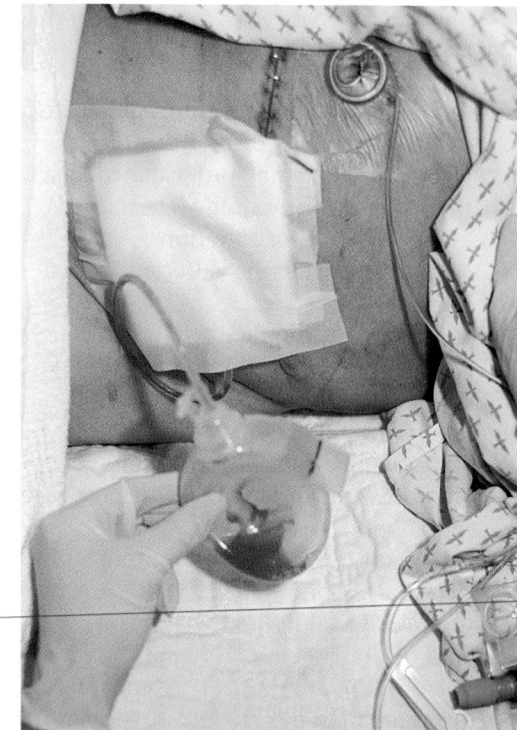

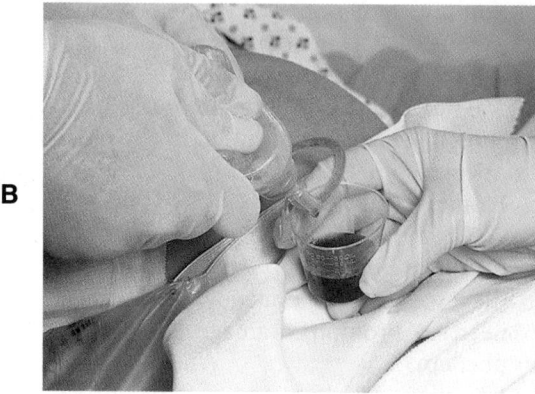

FIG. 51-3 Jackson-Pratt device. **A,** Drainage tubes and reservoir. **B,** Emptying drainage reservoir. (From Potter, P., & Perry, A. [2001]. *Fundamentals of nursing* [5th ed.]. St. Louis: Mosby.)

5. Assess operative site for infection, swelling, or the presence of fluid collection under the skin flaps or in the arm.
6. Monitor incision site for restriction of dressing, impaired sensation, or color changes of the skin.
7. If breast reconstruction was performed, the client will return from surgery with a surgical brassiere and the temporary prosthesis in place.
8. Place a sign above the bed stating *No IVs, No Injections, No BPs, No Venipunctures in Affected Arm;* the affected arm is protected and any intervention that could traumatize the affected arm is avoided.
9. Provide the use of a pressure sleeve as prescribed if edema is severe

10. Maintain fluid and electrolyte balance; administer diuretics and provide a low-salt diet as prescribed for severe lymphedema.
11. Consult with the physician and physical therapist regarding the appropriate exercise program and assist client with prescribed exercise.
12. Instruct the client about home care measures (Box 51-16).

XIX. GASTRIC CANCER
  A. Description
    1. Gastric **cancer** is a **malignant** growth of the mucosal cells in the inner lining of the stomach, with invasion to the muscle and beyond in advanced disease.
    2. No single causative agent has been identified but it is believed that *Helicobacter pylori* infection and a diet of smoked, highly salted, processed, or spiced foods have carcinogenic effects; other risk factors include smoking, alcohol and nitrate ingestion, and a history of gastric ulcers.
    3. Complications include hemorrhage, obstruction, **metastasis,** and dumping syndrome.
    4. The goal of treatment is to remove the tumor and provide a nutritional program.
  B. Assessment
    1. Early symptoms of gastric **cancer**
      a. Indigestion
      b. Abdominal discomfort
      c. Full feeling
      d. Epigastric, back, or retrosternal pain
    2. Late symptoms of gastric **cancer**
      a. Weakness and fatigue
      b. Anorexia and weight loss
      c. Nausea and vomiting
      d. A sensation of pressure in the stomach
      e. Dysphagia and obstructive symptoms
      f. Iron deficiency anemia
      g. Ascites
      h. Palpable epigastric mass
  C. Interventions
    1. Monitor vital signs.
    2. Monitor hemoglobin and hematocrit and administer blood transfusions as prescribed.
    3. Monitor weight.
    4. Assess nutritional status; encourage small, bland, easily digestible meals with vitamin and mineral supplements.
    5. Administer pain medication as prescribed.
    6. Prepare the client for chemotherapy or radiation therapy as prescribed.
    7. Prepare the client for surgical resection of the tumor as prescribed (Box 51-17).
  D. Postoperative interventions
    1. Monitor vital signs.
    2. Place in Fowler's position for comfort.

BOX 51-16
Client Instructions Following Mastectomy

Avoid overuse of the arm during the first few months.

To prevent lymphedema, keep the affected arm elevated.

Provide incision care with lanolin to soften and prevent wound contracture.

Encourage use of Reach for Recovery volunteers.

Encourage the client to perform breast self-examination on the remaining breast.

Protect the affected hand and arm.

Avoid strong sunlight on the affected arm.

Do not let the affected arm hang dependent.

Do not carry a pocketbook or anything heavy over the affected arm.

Avoid trauma, cuts, bruises, or burns to the affected side.

Avoid wearing constricting clothing or jewelry on the affected side.

Wear gloves when gardening.

Use thick oven mitts when cooking.

Use a thimble when sewing.

Apply lanolin hand cream several times daily.

Use cream cuticle remover.

Call the physician if signs of inflammation occur in the affected arm.

Wear a Medic-Alert bracelet stating which arm is lymphedematous.

---

3. Administer analgesics, antiemetics, as prescribed.
4. Monitor intake and output; administer fluids and electrolyte replacement by IV as prescribed; administer parenteral nutrition as indicated.
5. Maintain NPO status as prescribed for 1 to 3 days until peristalsis returns.
6. Monitor nasogastric suction.
7. Do not irrigate or remove the nasogastric tube; assist the physician with irrigation or removal.
8. Assess for bowel sounds.
9. Advance the diet from NPO to sips of clear water to six small bland meals a day, as prescribed.
10. Monitor for complications such as hemorrhage, dumping syndrome, diarrhea, hypoglycemia, and vitamin B$_{12}$ deficiency.

XX. PANCREATIC CANCER

A. Description
1. Most pancreatic tumors are highly **malignant,** rapidly growing adenocarcinomas originating from the epithelium of the ductal system.
2. Pancreatic **cancer** is associated with increased age, a history of diabetes mellitus, alcohol use, history of previous pancreatitis, smoking, ingestion of a high-fat diet, and exposure to environmental chemicals.

BOX 51-17
Surgical Interventions for Gastric Cancer

SUBTOTAL GASTRECTOMY
Billroth I
Also called gastroduodenostomy
Partial gastrectomy, with remaining segment anastomosed to the duodenum
Billroth II
Also called gastrojejunostomy
Partial gastrectomy, with remaining segment anastomosed to the jejunum

TOTAL GASTRECTOMY
Also called esophagojejunostomy
Removal of the stomach, with attachment of the esophagus to the jejunum or duodenum

---

3. Symptoms usually do not occur until the tumor is large; therefore, the prognosis is poor.
B. Assessment
1. Nausea and vomiting
2. Jaundice
3. Unexplained weight loss
4. Clay-colored stools
5. Glucose intolerance
6. Abdominal pain
7. Endoscopic retrograde cholangiopancreatography (ERCP) for visualization of the pancreatic duct and biliary system and collection of tissue and secretions
C. Interventions
1. Radiation
2. Chemotherapy
3. Whipple procedure, which involves a pancreaticoduodenectomy with removal of the distal third of the stomach, pancreaticojejunostomy, gastrojejunostomy, and choledochojejunostomy (Fig. 51-4)
4. Postoperative care measures are similar to those for the care of a client with pancreatitis and the client following gastric surgery; monitor blood glucose levels for transient hyperglycemia or hypoglycemia resulting from surgical manipulation of the pancreas.

XXI. INTESTINAL TUMORS

A. Description
1. Intestinal tumors are **malignant** lesions that develop in the cells lining the bowel wall or develop as adenomatous polyps in the colon or rectum.
2. Tumors spread is by direct invasion and through the lymphatic and circulatory systems.
3. Complications include bowel perforation with peritonitis, abscess and fistula formation, hemorrhage, and complete intestinal obstruction.

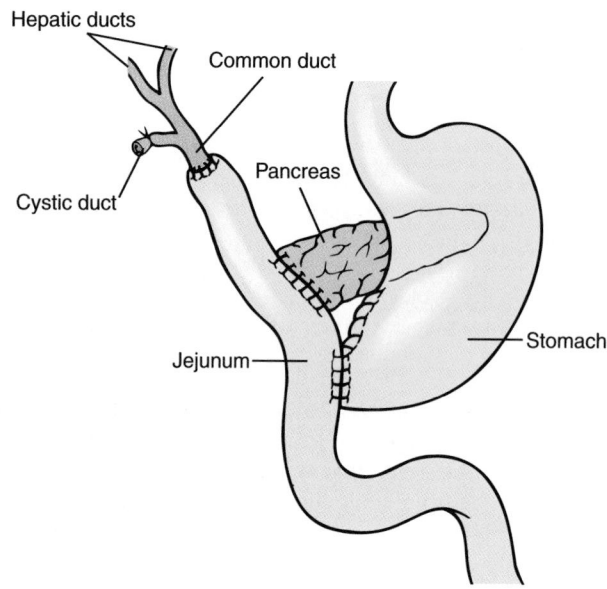

FIG. 51-4 Whipple procedure, or radical pancreaticoduodenectomy. (From Lewis, S., Heitkemper, M., & Dirksen, S. [2004]. *Medical-surgical nursing: Assessment and management of clinical problems* [6th ed.]. St. Louis: Mosby.)

B. Risk factors for colorectal **cancer**
  1. Age older than 50 years
  2. Familial polyposis, family history of colorectal **cancer**
  3. Previous colorectal polyps, history of colorectal **cancer**
  4. History of chronic inflammatory bowel disease
  5. History of ovarian or breast **cancer**
C. Assessment
  1. Blood in stool (most common manifestation)
  2. Anorexia, vomiting, and weight loss
  3. Anemia
  4. Abnormal stools
    a. Ascending colon tumor: Diarrhea
    b. Descending colon tumor: Constipation or some diarrhea, or flat, ribbon-like stool caused by a partial obstruction
    c. Rectal tumor: Alternating constipation and diarrhea
  5. Guarding or abdominal distention, abdominal mass (late sign)
  6. Cachexia (late sign)
  7. Masses noted on barium enema, colonoscopy, CT scan, sigmoidoscopy.
D. General interventions
  1. Monitor for signs of complications, which include bowel perforation with peritonitis, abscess or fistula formation (fever associated with pain), hemorrhage (signs of shock), and complete intestinal obstruction.
  2. Monitor for signs of bowel perforation, which include low blood pressure, rapid and weak pulse, distended abdomen, and elevated temperature.
  3. Monitor for signs of intestinal obstruction, which include vomiting (may be fecal contents), pain, constipation, and abdominal distention; provide comfort measures.
  4. Note that an early sign of intestinal obstruction is increased peristaltic activity, which produces an increase in bowel sounds; as the obstruction progresses, hypoactive bowel sounds may be heard.
  5. Prepare for radiation preoperatively to facilitate surgical resection, and postoperatively to decrease the risk of recurrence or to reduce pain, hemorrhage, bowel obstruction, or **metastasis.**
E. Nonsurgical interventions
  1. Preoperative radiation for local control, postoperative radiation for palliation may be prescribed.
  2. Postoperative chemotherapy to control symptoms and the spread of disease
F. Surgical interventions: Bowel, local lymph node resection and creation of a colostomy or ileostomy
G. Colostomy, ileostomy
  1. Preoperative interventions
    a. Consult with the enterostomal therapist to assist in identifying optimal placement of ostomy.
    b. Instruct the client to eat a low-residue diet for 1 to 2 days before surgery and administer bowel preparation (laxatives and enemas), as prescribed.
    c. Administer intestinal antiseptics and antibiotics, as prescribed, to decrease the bacterial content of the colon and to reduce the risk of infection from the surgical procedure.
  2. Postoperative: Colostomy
    a. If a pouch system is not in place, apply a petroleum jelly gauze over the stoma to keep it moist, covered with a dry sterile dressing; place a pouch system on the stoma as soon as possible.
    b. Monitor the stoma for size, unusual bleeding, color changes, or necrotic tissue.
    c. Note that the normal stoma color is red or pink, indicating high vascularity.
    d. Note that a pale pink stoma indicates low hemoglobin and hematocrit levels, and a purple-black stoma indicates compromised circulation, requiring physician notification.
    e. Monitor the pouch system for proper fit and signs of leakage.
    f. Assess the functioning of the colostomy.
    g. Expect that stool will be liquid postoperatively but will become more solid, depending on the area of the colostomy.
    h. Expect liquid stool from an ascending colon colostomy, loose to semiformed stool from a transverse colon colostomy, or close to normal stool from a descending colon colostomy

i. Fecal matter should not be allowed to remain on the skin.

j. Empty the pouch when one-third full.

k. Administer analgesics and antibiotics as prescribed.

l. Irrigate perineal wound if present and if prescribed, and monitor for signs of infection; provide comfort measures for perineal itching and pain.

m. Instruct the client to avoid foods that cause excessive gas formation and odor.

n. Instruct the client in stoma care and irrigations as prescribed.

o. Instruct the client on how to resume normal activities, including work, travel, and sexual intercourse, as prescribed; provide psychosocial support.

3. Postoperative: Ileostomy

a. Healthy stoma is red; a color change to dark blue or black should be reported to the physician.

b. Postoperative drainage will be dark green and progress to yellow as the client begins to eat.

c. Stool is liquid.

d. Risk for dehydration and electrolyte imbalance exists.

e. Note that suppositories are not administered through an ileostomy.

XXII. LUNG CANCER

A. Description

1. Lung **cancer, malignant** tumor of the bronchi and peripheral lung tissue, is a leading cause of **cancer**-related deaths in men and women in the United States.

2. The lungs are a common target for **metastasis** from other organs.

3. Bronchogenic **cancer** (tumors originate in the epithelium of the bronchus) spreads through direct extension and lymphatic dissemination.

4. Classified according to histological cell type, there are two main types of lung **cancer,** small cell lung cancer (SCLC) and non–small cell lung **cancer** (NSCLC); epidermal (squamous cell), adenocarcinoma, and large cell anaplastic **carcinoma** are classified as NSCLC because of their similar responses to treatment.

5. Diagnosis is made by a chest x-ray, CT scan, or magnetic resonance imaging (MRI), which will show a lesion or mass, and by bronchoscopy and sputum studies, which will demonstrate a positive cytological study for **cancer** cells.

B. Causes

1. Cigarette smoking, exposure to "passive" tobacco smoke

2. Exposure to environmental and occupational pollutants

C. Assessment

1. Cough

2. Wheezing, dyspnea

3. Hoarseness

4. Hemoptysis, blood-tinged or purulent sputum

5. Chest pain

6. Anorexia and weight loss

7. Weakness

8. Diminished or absent breath sounds, respiratory changes

D. Interventions

1. Monitor vital signs.

2. Monitor breathing patterns and breath sounds and for signs of respiratory impairment.

3. Assess for tracheal deviation.

4. Administer analgesics as prescribed for pain management.

5. Place in a Fowler's position to help ease breathing.

6. Administer oxygen as prescribed and humidification to moisten and loosen secretions.

7. Monitor pulse oximetry.

8. Provide respiratory treatments as prescribed.

9. Administer bronchodilators and corticosteroids as prescribed to decrease bronchospasm, inflammation, and edema.

10. Provide a high-calorie, high-protein, high-vitamin diet.

11. Provide activity as tolerated, rest periods, and active and passive range-of-motion exercises.

12. Monitor for bleeding, infection, and electrolyte imbalances.

E. Nonsurgical interventions

1. Radiation therapy may be prescribed for localized intrathoracic lung **cancers** and for palliation of hemoptysis, obstructions, dysphagia, superior vena cava syndrome, and pain.

2. Chemotherapy may be prescribed for treatment of nonresectable tumors or as adjuvant therapy.

F. Surgical interventions

1. Laser therapy: To relieve endobronchial obstruction

2. Thoracentesis and pleurodesis: To remove pleural fluid and relieve hypoxia

3. Thoracotomy (opening into the thoracic cavity) with pneumonectomy: Surgical removal of one entire lung

4. Thoracotomy with lobectomy: Surgical removal of one lobe of the lung for tumors confined to a single lobe

5. Thoracotomy with segmental resection: Surgical removal of a lobe segment

G. Preoperative interventions

1. Explain the potential postoperative need for chest tubes.

2. Note that closed chest drainage usually is not used for a pneumonectomy and the serous

fluid that accumulates in the empty thoracic cavity eventually consolidates, preventing shifts of the mediastinum, heart, and remaining lung.

H. Postoperative interventions
1. Monitor vital signs.
2. Assess cardiac and respiratory status; monitor for the absence and presence of lung sounds.
3. Maintain the chest tube drainage system, which will drain air and blood that accumulates in the pleural space; monitor for excess bleeding.
4. Assess chest tube insertion site for crepitus (subcutaneous emphysema) and drainage.
5. Administer oxygen as prescribed.
6. Check the physician's orders regarding client positioning; avoid complete lateral turning.
7. Monitor pulse oximetry.
8. Provide activity as tolerated.
9. Encourage active range-of-motion exercises of the operative shoulder as prescribed.
10. See Chapter 21 for care of the client with a chest tube.

XXIII. LARYNGEAL CANCER

A. Description
1. Laryngeal **cancer** is a **malignant** tumor of the larynx (Fig. 51-5).
2. Laryngeal **cancer** presents as **malignant** ulcerations with underlying infiltration and is spread by local extension to adjacent structures in the throat and neck, and by the lymphatic system.
3. Diagnosis is made by laryngoscopy and biopsy showing a positive cytological study for **cancer** cells.

B. Risk factors
1. Cigarette smoking
2. Heavy alcohol use and the combined use of tobacco and alcohol
3. Exposure to environmental pollutants (e.g., asbestos, wood dust)
4. Exposure to radiation

C. Assessment
1. Persistent hoarseness or sore throat
2. Painless neck mass
3. Feeling of a lump in the throat
4. Burning sensation in the throat
5. Dysphagia
6. Change in voice quality
7. Dyspnea
8. Weakness and weight loss
9. Hemoptysis
10. Foul breath odor
11. Laryngoscopy allows for evaluation of the throat and biopsy of tissues; chest radiography, CT, and MRI are used for **staging**.

D. Interventions
1. Place in Fowler's position to promote optimal air exchange.
2. Monitor respiratory status.
3. Monitor for signs of aspiration of food and fluid.
4. Administer oxygen as prescribed.
5. Provide respiratory treatments as prescribed.
6. Provide activity as tolerated.
7. Provide a high-calorie and high-protein diet.
8. Provide nutritional support via parenteral nutrition, nasogastric tube feedings, or gastrostomy or jejunostomy tube, as prescribed.
9. Administer analgesics as prescribed for pain.

E. Nonsurgical interventions
1. Radiation therapy if the **cancer** is limited to a small area in one vocal cord
2. Chemotherapy, which may be given in combination with radiation and surgery

F. Surgical interventions
1. The goal is to remove the **cancer** while preserving as much normal function as possible.
2. Surgical intervention depends on the tumor size, location, and amount of tissue to be resected.
3. Types of resection include cordal stripping, cordectomy, partial laryngectomy, and total laryngectomy.
4. A tracheostomy is performed with a total laryngectomy; this airway opening is permanent and is referred to as a laryngectomy stoma.

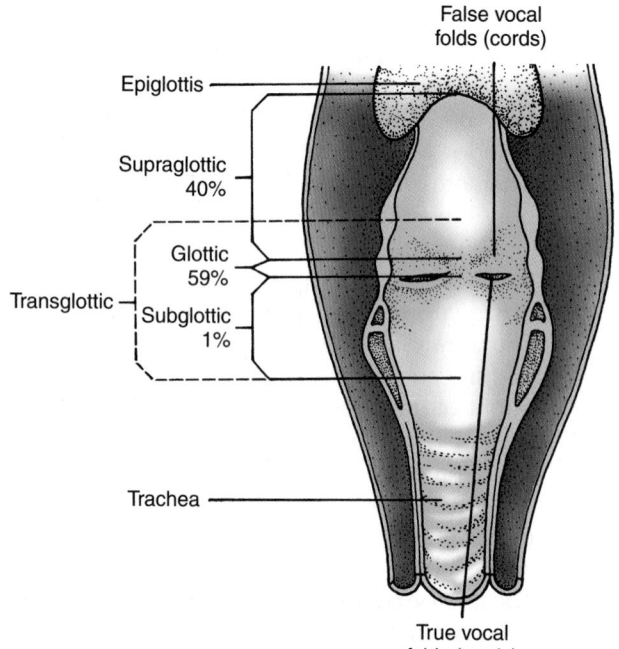

FIG. 51-5 Sites and incidence of primary laryngeal tumors. (From Ignatavicius, D., & Workman, M. [2006]. *Medical-surgical nursing: Critical thinking for collaborative care* [5th ed.]. Philadelphia: W.B. Saunders.)

Figure labels: Epiglottis; False vocal folds (cords); Supraglottic 40%; Glottic 59%; Transglottic; Subglottic 1%; Trachea; True vocal folds (cords)

G. Preoperative interventions

1. Discuss self-care of the airway, alternate methods of communication, suctioning, pain control methods, the critical care environment, and nutritional support.
2. Encourage the client to express feelings about changes in body image and loss of voice.
3. Describe the rehabilitation program and information about the tracheostomy and suctioning.

H. Postoperative interventions

1. Monitor vital signs.
2. Monitor respiratory status; monitor airway patency and provide frequent suctioning to remove bloody secretions.
3. Place the client in a high Fowler's position.
4. Maintain mechanical ventilator support or a tracheostomy collar with humidification, as prescribed.
5. Monitor pulse oximetry.
6. Maintain surgical drains in the neck area if present.
7. Observe for hemorrhage and edema in the neck
8. Monitor IV fluids or parenteral nutrition until nutrition is administered via a nasogastric, gastrostomy, or jejunostomy tube.
9. Provide oral hygiene.
10. Assess gag and cough reflexes and the ability to swallow.
11. Increase activity as tolerated.
12. Assess the color, amount, and consistency of sputum.
13. Provide stoma and laryngectomy care (Box 51-18).
14. Provide consultation with speech and language pathologist as prescribed.
15. Reinforce method of communication established preoperatively.
16. Prepare the client for rehabilitation and speech therapy (Box 51-19).

XXIV. PROSTATE CANCER

A. Description

1. Prostate **cancer,** a slow-growing malignancy of the prostate gland, is a common **cancer** in American men; most prostate tumors are adenocarcinomas arising from androgen-dependent epithelial cells.
2. The risk increases in men with each decade after the age of 50 years.
3. Prostate **cancer** can spread via direct invasion of surrounding tissues or by **metastasis,** through the bloodstream and lymphatics, to the bony pelvis and spine.
4. Bone **metastasis** is a concern, as is spread to the lungs, liver, and kidneys.
5. The cause of prostate **cancer** is unclear, but advancing age, heavy metal exposure, smoking,

---

BOX 51-18

Stoma Care Following Laryngectomy

Teach the client clean suctioning technique.
Instruct the client in how to clean the incision and provide stoma care.
Protect the neck from injury.
Instruct the client to wear a stoma guard to shield the stoma.
Avoid swimming, showering, and using aerosol sprays.
Demonstrate ways to prevent debris from entering the stoma.
Advise the client to wear loose-fitting, high-collared clothing to cover the stoma.
Advise the client to increase humidity in the home.
Instruct the client in range-of-motion exercises for the arms, shoulders, and neck as prescribed.
Avoid exposure to persons with infections.
Alternate rest periods with activity.
Increase fluid intake to 3000 mL/day as prescribed.
Advise the client to wear a Medic-Alert bracelet.

BOX 51-19

Speech Rehabilitation Following Laryngectomy

ESOPHAGEAL SPEECH
The client produces esophageal speech by "burping" the air swallowed.
The voice produced is monotone, cannot be raised or lowered, and carries no pitch.
The client must have adequate hearing because his or her mouth shapes words as they are heard.

MECHANICAL DEVICES
The devices are known as an electrolarynx.
The device is placed against the side of the neck; the air inside the neck and pharynx is vibrated, and the client articulates.
A Cooper-Rand device consists of a plastic tube placed inside the client's mouth that vibrates on articulation.

TRACHEOESOPHAGEAL FISTULA
A fistula is created surgically between the trachea and the esophagus, with eventual placement of a prosthesis to produce speech.
The prosthesis provides the client with a means to divert air from the trachea into the esophagus, and out of the mouth.
Lip and tongue movement produce the speech.

---

and history of sexually transmitted disease are contributing factors.

B. Assessment

1. Asymptomatic in early stages
2. Hard, pea-sized nodule or irregularities palpated on rectal examination
3. Gross, painless hematuria

4. Late symptoms such as weight loss, urinary obstruction, and bone pain radiating from the lumbosacral area down the leg
5. The prostate-specific antigen (PSA) level is elevated in various noncancerous conditions; therefore, it should not be used as a screening test without a digital rectal examination. It is routinely used to monitor response to therapy.
6. Diagnosis is made through biopsy of the prostate gland.

C. Nonsurgical interventions
  1. Prepare the client for hormone manipulation therapy as prescribed.
  2. Administer luteinizing hormone, such as leuprolide acetate (Lupron), flutamide (Eulexin), or estrogens such as diethylstilbestrol (DES), as prescribed, to slow the rate of growth of the tumor.
  3. Pain medication, radiation therapy, corticosteroids, and bisphosphonates may be prescribed for palliation of advanced prostate **cancer.**
  4. Prepare the client for external beam radiation or brachytherapy, which may be prescribed alone or with surgery, preoperatively or postoperatively, to reduce the lesion and limit **metastasis.**
  5. Prepare the client for the administration of chemotherapy in cases of hormone-resistant tumors.

D. Surgical interventions
  1. Prepare the client for orchiectomy (palliative), if prescribed, which will limit the production of testosterone.
  2. Prepare the client for prostatectomy, if prescribed.
  3. The radical prostatectomy can be performed via a retropubic, perineal, or suprapubic approach.
  4. Cryosurgical ablation is a minimally invasive procedure that may be an alternative to radical prostatectomy; liquid nitrogen freezes the gland, and the dead cells are absorbed by the body.

E. Transurethral resection of the prostate (TURP) may be performed for palliation in prostate **cancer** clients.
  1. The procedure involves insertion of a scope into the urethra to excise prostatic tissue.
  2. Monitor for hemorrhage; bleeding is common following TURP.
  3. Postoperative continuous bladder irrigation (CBI) may be prescribed, which prevents catheter obstruction.
  4. Assess for signs of transurethral resection syndrome, which include signs of cerebral edema and increased intracranial pressure, such as increased blood pressure, bradycardia, confusion, disorientation, muscle twitching, visual disturbances, and nausea and vomiting.
  5. Antispasmodics may be prescribed for bladder spasm.
  6. Instruct the client to monitor and report dribbling or incontinence postoperatively and teach perineal exercises.

7. Sterility is possible following the surgical procedure.

F. Suprapubic prostatectomy
  1. Suprapubic prostatectomy is removal of the prostate gland by an abdominal incision with a bladder incision.
  2. The client will have an abdominal dressing that may drain copious amounts of urine, and the abdominal dressing will need to be changed frequently.
  3. Severe hemorrhage is possible, and monitoring for blood loss is an important nursing intervention.
  4. Antispasmodics may be prescribed for bladder spasms.
  5. Continuous bladder irrigation (CBI) is prescribed and carried out to keep the urine pink.
  6. Sterility occurs with this procedure.

G. Retropubic prostatectomy
  1. Retropubic prostatectomy is removal of the prostate gland by a low abdominal incision without opening the bladder.
  2. Less bleeding occurs with this procedure compared with the suprapubic procedure, and the client experiences fewer bladder spasms.
  3. Abdominal drainage is minimal.
  4. CBI may be used.
  5. Sterility occurs with this procedure.

H. Perineal prostatectomy
  1. The prostate gland is removed through an incision made between the scrotum and anus.
  2. Minimal bleeding occurs with this procedure.
  3. The client needs to be monitored closely for infection, because the risk of infection is increased with this type of prostatectomy.
  4. Urinary incontinence is common.
  5. The procedure causes sterility.
  6. Teach the client how to perform perineal exercises.

I. Postoperative interventions
  1. Monitor vital signs.
  2. Monitor urinary output and urine for hemorrhage or clots.
  3. Increase fluids to 2400 to 3000 mL/day, unless contraindicated.
  4. Monitor for arterial bleeding as evidenced by bright red urine with numerous clots; if it occurs, increase CBI and notify the physician immediately.
  5. Monitor for venous bleeding as evidenced by burgundy-colored urine output; if it occurs, inform the physician, who may apply traction on the catheter.
  6. Monitor hemoglobin and hematocrit levels.
  7. Expect red to light pink urine for 24 hours, turning to amber in 3 days.
  8. Ambulate the client as early as possible and as soon as urine begins to clear in color.

9. Inform the client that a continuous feeling of an urge to void is normal.

10. Instruct the client to avoid attempts to void around the catheter because this will cause bladder spasms.

11. Administer antibiotics, analgesics, stool softeners, and antispasmodics as prescribed.

12. Monitor the three-way Foley catheter, which will have a 30- to 45-mL retention balloon.

13. Maintain CBI with sterile bladder irrigation solution as prescribed to keep the catheter free of obstruction and maintain the urine pink in color (Box 51-20).

J. Postoperative interventions: Suprapubic prostatectomy
   1. Monitor suprapubic and Foley catheter drainage.
   2. Monitor CBI if prescribed.
   3. Note that the Foley catheter will be removed 2 to 4 days postoperatively if the client has a suprapubic catheter.
   4. If prescribed, clamp the suprapubic catheter after the Foley catheter is removed, and instruct the client to attempt to void; after the client has voided, assess the residual urine in the bladder by unclamping the suprapubic catheter and measuring the output.

5. Prepare for removal of the suprapubic catheter when the client consistently empties the bladder and residual urine is 75 mL or less.

6. Monitor the suprapubic incision dressing, which may become saturated with urine, until the incision heals.

K. Postoperative interventions: Retropubic prostatectomy
   1. Note that because the bladder is not entered, there is no urinary drainage on the abdominal dressing.
   2. Assess for urinary or purulent drainage on the dressing; if this occurs, notify the physician.
   3. Monitor for fever and increased pain, which may indicate an infection.

L. Postoperative interventions: Perineal prostatectomy
   1. Note that the client will have an incision, which may or may not have a drain.
   2. Avoid the use of rectal thermometers, rectal tubes, and enemas because they may cause trauma and bleeding.

XXV. BLADDER CANCER
A. Description
   1. Bladder **cancer** is papillomatous growths in the bladder urothelium that undergo **malignant** changes and that may infiltrate the bladder wall.

BOX 51-20

Postoperative Care Following Transurethral Resection of the Prostate*

CONTINUOUS BLADDER IRRIGATION (CBI): DESCRIPTION
A three-way (lumen) irrigation is used to decrease bleeding and to keep the bladder free from clots—one lumen is for inflating the balloon (30 mL); one lumen is for instillation (inflow); one lumen is for outflow.

INTERVENTIONS
Maintain traction on the catheter, if applied, to prevent bleeding by pulling the catheter taut and taping it to the abdomen or thigh.
Instruct the client to keep the leg straight if traction is applied to the catheter and it is taped to the thigh.
Catheter traction is not released without a physician's order; it usually is released after any bright red drainage has diminished.
Use only normal saline or prescribed solution to prevent water intoxication.
Run the solution at a rate, as prescribed, to keep the urine pink. Run the solution rapidly if bright red drainage or clots are present. Run the solution at about 40 gtt/min when the bright red drainage clears.
If the urinary catheter becomes obstructed, turn off the CBI and irrigate the catheter with 30 to 50 mL of normal saline, if prescribed; notify the physician if obstruction does not resolve.
Monitor for transurethral resection syndrome or severe hyponatremia (water intoxication) caused by the

excessive absorption of bladder irrigation during surgery (altered mental status, bradycardia, increased blood pressure, and confusion).
Discontinue CBI and the Foley catheter as prescribed, usually 24 to 48 hours after surgery.
Monitor for continence and urinary retention when the catheter is removed. Inform the client that some burning, frequency, and dribbling may occur following catheter removal.
Inform the client that he should be voiding 150 to 200 mL of clear yellow urine every 3 to 4 hours by 3 days after surgery.
Inform the client that he may pass small clots and tissue debris for several days.
Teach the client to avoid heavy lifting, stressful exercise, driving, Valsalva's maneuver, and sexual intercourse for 2 to 6 weeks to prevent strain, and to call the physician if bleeding occurs or if there is a decrease in urinary stream.
Instruct the client to drink 2400 to 3000 mL of fluid each day, preferably before 8 PM.
Instruct the client to avoid alcohol, caffeinated beverages, and spicy foods, and overstimulation of the bladder.
Instruct the client that if the urine becomes bloody, to rest and increase fluid intake and, if the bleeding does not subside, to notify the physician.

*For palliation in prostate cancer.

2. Predisposing factors include cigarette smoking, exposure to industrial chemicals, and exposure to radiation.
3. Common sites of **metastasis** include the liver, bones, and lungs.
4. As the tumor progresses, it can extend into the rectum, vagina, other pelvic soft tissues, and retroperitoneal structures.

B. Assessment
1. Gross or microscopic, painless hematuria
2. Frequency, urgency, dysuria
3. Clot-induced obstruction
4. Bladder wash specimens and biopsy confirms diagnosis

C. Radiation
1. Radiation therapy is indicated for advanced disease that cannot be eradicated by surgery; palliative radiation may be used to relieve pain and bowel obstruction and control potential hemorrhage and leg edema caused by venous or lymphatic obstruction.
2. Intracavitary radiation may be prescribed, which protects adjacent tissue.
3. External beam radiation combined with chemotherapy or surgery may be prescribed to improve survival.
4. Complications of radiation
   a. Abacterial cystitis
   b. Proctitis
   c. Fistula formation
   d. Ileitis or colitis
   e. Bladder ulceration and hemorrhage

D. Chemotherapy
1. Intravesical instillation
   a. An alkylating chemotherapeutic agent is instilled into the bladder.
   b. This method provides a concentrated topical treatment with little systemic absorption.
   c. Chemotherapeutic agents used may include thiotepa, mitomycin (Mutamycin), doxorubicin (Adriamycin), cyclophosphamide (Cytoxan), or immunotherapy with instillation of bacille Calmette-Guérin (BCG).
   d. The medication is injected into a urethral catheter and retained for 2 hours.
   e. Following instillation, the client's position is rotated every 15 to 30 minutes, starting in the supine position, to avoid lying on a full bladder.
   f. After 2 hours, the client voids in a sitting position and is instructed to increase fluids to flush the bladder.
   g. Treat the urine as a biohazard and send to the radioisotope laboratory for monitoring.
   h. For 6 hours following intravesical chemotherapy, disinfect the toilet with household bleach after the client has voided.

2. Systemic chemotherapy
   a. Systemic chemotherapy is used to treat inoperable tumors or distant **metastasis.**
   b. Agents used may include cisplatin (Platinol), doxorubicin (Adriamycin), cyclophosphamide (Cytoxan), and methotrexate (Folex).
3. Complications of chemotherapy
   a. Bladder irritation
   b. Hemorrhagic cystitis

E. Surgical interventions
1. Transurethral resection of bladder tumor
   a. Local resection and fulguration (destruction of tissue by electrical current through electrodes placed in direct contact with the tissue)
   b. Performed for early tumors for cure or for inoperable tumors for palliation
2. Partial cystectomy
   a. Partial cystectomy is the removal of up to half the bladder.
   b. The procedure is done for early-stage tumors and for clients who cannot tolerate a radical cystectomy.
   c. During the initial postoperative period, bladder capacity is reduced greatly to about 60 mL; however, as the bladder tissue expands, the capacity increases to 200 to 400 mL.
   d. Maintenance of a continuous output of urine following surgery is critical to prevent bladder distention and stress on the suture line.
   e. A urethral catheter and a suprapubic catheter may be in place, and the suprapubic catheter may be left in place for 2 weeks until healing occurs.
3. Cystectomy and urinary diversion (Fig. 51-6)
   a. Various surgical procedures performed to create alternate pathways for urine collection and excretion
   b. Urinary diversion may be performed with or without cystectomy (bladder removal).
   c. The surgery may be performed in two stages if the tumor is extensive, with the creation of the urinary diversion first and the cystectomy several weeks later.
   d. If a radical cystectomy is performed, lower extremity lymphedema may occur as a result of lymph node dissection, and male impotence may occur.
4. Ileal conduit
   a. The ileal conduit also is called ureteroileostomy, or Bricker's procedure.
   b. Ureters are implanted into a segment of the ileum, with the formation of an abdominal stoma.
   c. The urine flows into the conduit and is propelled continuously out through the stoma by peristalsis.

Ureterostomies divert urine directly to the skin surface through a ureteral-skin opening (stoma). After ureterostomy, the client must wear a pouch.

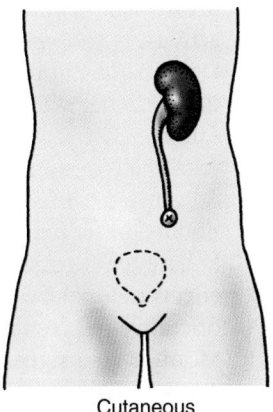

Cutaneous ureterostomy

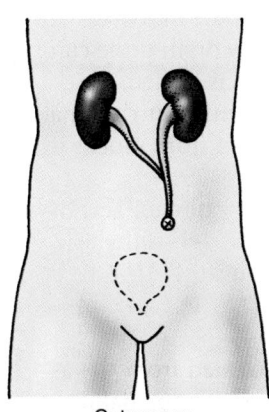

Cutaneous istomy

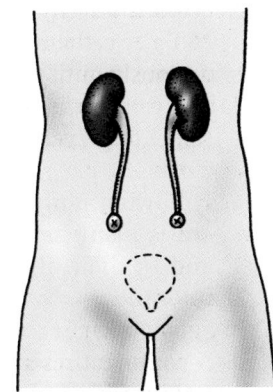

Bilateral cutaneous ureterostomy

Conduits collect urine in a portion of the intestine, which is then opened onto the skin surface as a stoma. After the creation of a conduit, the client must wear a pouch.

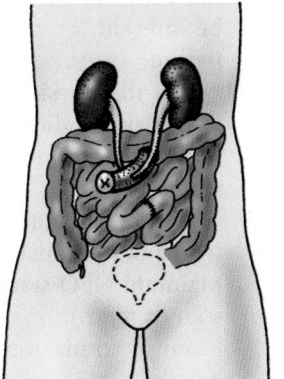

Ileal (Bricker's) conduit

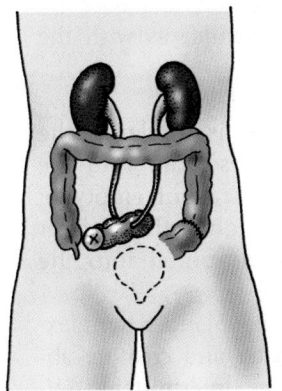

Colon conduit

Ileal reservoirs divert urine into a surgically created pouch, or pocket, that functions as a bladder. The stoma is continent, and the client removes urine by regular self-catheterization.

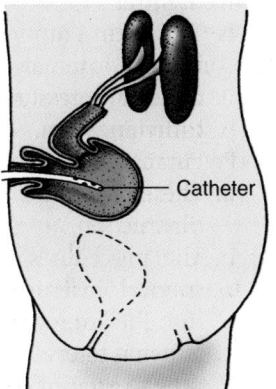

Catheter

Continent internal ileal reservoir (Kock's pouch)

Sigmoidostomies divert urine to the large intestine, so no stoma is required. The client excretes urine with bowel movements, and bowel incontinence may result.

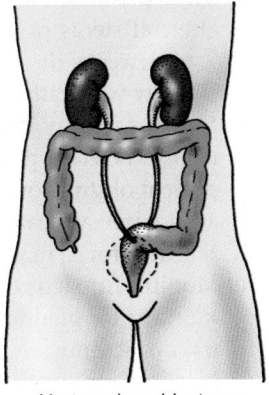

Ureterosigmoidostomy

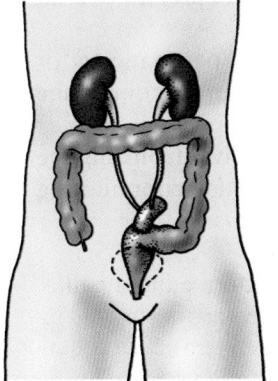

Ureteroiliosigmoidostomy

FIG. 51-6 Urinary diversion procedures used in the treatment of bladder cancer. (From Ignatavicius, D., & Workman, M. [2006]. *Medical-surgical nursing: Critical thinking for collaborative care* [5th ed.]. Philadelphia: W.B. Saunders.)

d. The client is required to wear an appliance over the stoma to collect the urine.
e. Complications include obstruction, pyelonephritis, leakage at the anastomosis site, stenosis, hydronephrosis, calculi, skin irritation and ulceration, and stomal defects.
5. Kock pouch

a. The Kock pouch is a continent internal ileal reservoir created from a segment of the ileum and ascending colon.
b. The ureters are implanted into the side of the reservoir, and a special nipple valve is constructed to attach the reservoir to the skin.

c. Postoperatively, the client will have a 24 to 26 Foley catheter in place to drain urine continuously until the pouch has healed.

d. The catheter is irrigated gently with normal saline to prevent obstruction from mucus or clots.

e. Following removal of the catheter, the client is instructed in how to self-catheterize and to drain the reservoir at 4- to 6-hour intervals.

6. Indiana pouch
   a. A continent reservoir is created from the ascending colon and terminal ileum, making a pouch larger than the Kock pouch (additional continent reservoirs include the Mainz and Florida pouch systems)
   b. Postoperatively, care is similar as with the Koch pouch.

7. Creation of a neobladder
   a. Creation of a neobladder is similar to the creation of an internal reservoir, with the difference being that instead of emptying through an abdominal stoma, the bladder empties through a pelvic outlet into the urethra.
   b. The client empties the neobladder by relaxing the external sphincter and creating abdominal pressure or by intermittent self-catheterization.

8. Percutaneous nephrostomy or pyelostomy
   a. These procedures are used to prevent or treat obstruction.
   b. The procedures involve a percutaneous or surgical insertion of a nephrostomy tube into the kidney for drainage.
   c. Nursing interventions involve stabilizing the tube to prevent dislodgment and monitoring output.

9. Ureterostomy
   a. Ureterostomy may be performed as a palliative procedure if the ureters are obstructed by the tumor.
   b. The ureters are attached to the surface of the abdomen, where the urine flows directly into a drainage appliance without a conduit.
   c. Potential problems include infection, skin irritation, and obstruction to urinary flow as a result of strictures at the opening.

10. Vesicostomy
    a. The bladder is sutured to the abdomen, and a stoma is created in the bladder wall.
    b. The bladder empties through the stoma.

F. Preoperative interventions
   1. Instruct the client in preoperative, operative, and postoperative management including diet, medications, nasogastric tube placement, IVs, NPO status, pain control, coughing and deep breathing, leg exercises, and postoperative activity.
   2. Demonstrate appliance application and use for those clients who will have a stoma.
   3. Arrange an enterostomal nurse consult and for a visit with a person who has had urinary diversion.
   4. Administer antimicrobials for bowel preparation as prescribed.
   5. Encourage discussion of feelings including the effects on sexual activities.

G. Postoperative interventions
   1. Monitor vital signs.
   2. Assess incision site.
   3. Assess stoma (should be red and moist) every hour for the first 24 hours (Box 51-21).
   4. Monitor for edema in the stoma, which may be present in the immediate postoperative period.
   5. Notify the physician if the stoma appears dark and dusky (indicates necrosis).
   6. Monitor for prolapse or retraction of the stoma.
   7. Assess bowel function; monitor for expected return of peristalsis in 3 to 4 days.
   8. Maintain NPO status as prescribed until bowel sounds return.
   9. Monitor continuous urine flow (30 to 60 mL/hr).
   10. Notify the physician if the urine output is less than 30 mL/hr or if no urine output occurs for more than 15 minutes.
   11. Ureteral stents or catheters may be in place for 2 to 3 weeks or until healing occurs; maintain stability with catheters to prevent dislodgment.
   12. Monitor urinary output closely and irrigate ureteral catheter (if present), if prescribed, gently to prevent obstruction; follow physician's orders and agency policy regarding irrigation (Box 51-22).
   13. Monitor for hematuria.
   14. Monitor for signs of peritonitis.
   15. Monitor for bladder distention following a partial cystectomy.
   16. Monitor for shock, hemorrhage, thrombophlebitis, and lower extremity lymphedema after a radical cystectomy.
   17. Monitor the urinary drainage pouch for leaks, and check skin integrity.
   18. Monitor the pH of the urine (do not place the dipstick in the stoma) because strongly alkaline urine can cause skin irritation and facilitate crystal formation.
   19. Instruct the client regarding the potential for urinary tract infection or the development of calculi.
   20. Instruct the client to assess the skin for irritation, monitor the urinary drainage pouch, and report any leakage.

BOX 51-21
Urinary Stoma Care

Instruct the client to change the appliance in the morning, when urinary production is slowest.

Collect equipment, remove collection bag, and use water or commercial solvent to loosen adhesive.

Hold a rolled gauze pad against the stoma to collect and absorb urine during the procedure.

Cleanse the skin around stoma and under the drainage bag with mild nonresidue soap and water.

Inspect the skin for excoriation, and instruct the client to prevent urine from coming into contact with the skin.

After the skin is dry, apply skin adhesive around the appliance.

Instruct the client to cut the stoma opening of the skin barrier just large enough to fit over the stoma (no more that 3 mm larger than the stoma).

Instruct the client that the stoma will begin to shrink, requiring a smaller stoma opening on the skin barrier.

Apply skin barrier before attaching the pouch or face plate.

Place the appliance over the stoma and secure in place.

Encourage self-care; teach the client to use a mirror.

Instruct the client that the pouch may be drained by a bedside bag or leg bag, especially at night.

Instruct the client to empty the urinary collection bag when it is one-third to one-half full to prevent pulling of the appliance and leakage.

Instruct the client to check the appliance seal if perspiring occurs.

Instruct the client to leave the urinary pouch in place as long as it is not leaking and to change it every 5 to 7 days.

During appliance changes, leave the skin open to air as long as possible.

Use a nonkaraya gum product, because urine erodes karaya gum.

To control odor, instruct the client to drink adequate fluids, wash the appliance thoroughly with soap and lukewarm water, and soak the collection pouch in dilute white vinegar for 20 to 30 minutes; a special deodorant tablet can also be placed into the pouch while it is being worn.

Instruct the client who takes baths to keep the level of the water below the stoma and to avoid oily soaps.

If the client plans to shower, instruct the client to direct the flow of water away from the stoma.

BOX 51-22
Self-Irrigation and Catheterization of Stoma

IRRIGATION

Instruct the client to wash hands and use clean technique.

Instruct the client to use a catheter and syringe, instill 60 mL of normal saline or water into the reservoir, and aspirate gently or allow to drain.

Instruct the client to irrigate until the drainage remains free of mucus but to be careful not to overirrigate.

CATHETERIZATION

Instruct the client to wash hands and use clean technique.

Initially, instruct the client to insert a catheter every 2 to 3 hours to drain the reservoir; during each week thereafter, increase the interval by 1 hour until catheterization is done every 4 to 6 hours.

Lubricate the catheter well with water-soluble lubricant, and instruct the client never to force the catheter into the reservoir.

If resistance is met, instruct the client to pause, rotate the catheter, and apply gentle pressure to insert.

Instruct the client to notify the physician if the client is unable to insert the catheter.

When urine has stopped, instruct the client to take several deep breaths and move the catheter in and out 2 to 3 inches to ensure that the pouch is empty.

Instruct the client to withdraw the catheter slowly and pinch the catheter when withdrawn so that it does not leak urine.

Instruct the client to carry catheterization supplies with him or her.

---

21. Encourage the client to express feelings about changes in body image, embarrassment, and sexual dysfunction.

XXVI. ONCOLOGICAL EMERGENCIES

A. Sepsis and disseminated intravascular coagulation (DIC)
   1. Description: The client with **cancer** is at increased risk for infection, particularly gram-negative organisms in the bloodstream (sepsis or septicemia) and DIC, a life-threatening problem frequently associated with sepsis.
   2. Interventions
      a. Prevent complication through early identification of clients at high risk for sepsis and DIC.
      b. Maintain strict aseptic technique with the immunocompromised client and monitor closely for infection.
      c. Administer antibiotics intravenously as prescribed.
      d. Administer anticoagulants as prescribed during the early phase of DIC.
      e. Administer cryoprecipitated clotting factors, as prescribed, when DIC progresses and hemorrhage is the primary problem.

B. Syndrome of inappropriate antidiuretic hormone (SIADH)
   1. Description
      a. Tumors can produce, secrete, or stimulate substances that mimic antidiuretic hormone.
      b. Mild symptoms include weakness, muscle cramps, loss of appetite, and fatigue; serum sodium levels range from 115 to 120 mEq/L.

c. More serious signs and symptoms relate to water intoxication and include weight gain, personality changes, confusion, and extreme muscle weakness.

d. As the serum sodium level approaches 110 mEq/L, seizures, coma, and eventually death will occur, unless the condition is treated rapidly.

2. Interventions

a. Initiate fluid restriction and increased sodium intake as prescribed.

b. Administer demeclocycline (Declomycin) as prescribed, an antagonist to antidiuretic hormone.

c. Monitor serum sodium levels.

d. Treat the underlying cause with chemotherapy or radiation to reduce the tumor.

C. Spinal cord compression

1. Description

a. Spinal cord compression occurs when a tumor directly enters the spinal cord or when the vertebral column collapses from tumor entry, impinging on the spinal cord.

b. Spinal cord compression causes back pain, usually before neurological deficits occur.

c. Neurological deficits relate to the spinal level of compression and include numbness, tingling, loss of urethral, vaginal, and rectal sensation, and muscle weakness.

2. Interventions

a. Early recognition of treatment; assess for back pain and neurological deficits.

b. Administer high-dose corticosteroids to reduce swelling around the spinal cord and relieve symptoms.

c. Prepare the client for immediate radiation and/or chemotherapy to reduce the size of the tumor and relieve compression.

d. Surgery may need to be performed to remove the tumor and relieve the pressure on the spinal cord.

e. Instruct the client in the use of neck or back braces if they are prescribed.

D. Hypercalcemia

1. Description

a. Hypercalcemia is a late manifestation of extensive malignancy that occurs most often with bone **metastasis,** when the bone releases calcium into the bloodstream.

b. Decreased physical mobility contributes to or worsens hypercalcemia.

c. Early signs include fatigue, anorexia, nausea, vomiting, constipation, and polyuria.

d. More serious signs and symptoms include severe muscle weakness, diminished deep tendon reflexes, paralytic ileus, dehydration, and changes in the electrocardiogram (ECG).

2. Interventions

a. Monitor serum calcium level and electrocardiographic changes

b. Administer oral or parenteral fluids as prescribed.

c. Administer medications that lower the calcium level as prescribed.

d. Prepare the client for dialysis if the condition becomes life-threatening or is accompanied by renal impairment.

E. Superior vena cava syndrome

1. Description

a. Superior vena cava (SVC) syndrome occurs when the SVC is compressed or obstructed by tumor growth (commonly associated with lung **cancer** and **lymphoma**).

b. Signs and symptoms result from blockage of blood flow in the venous system of the head, neck, and upper trunk.

c. Early signs and symptoms generally occur in the morning and include edema of the face, especially around the eyes, and tightness of the shirt or blouse collar (Stokes' sign).

d. As the condition worsens, edema in the arms and hands, dyspnea, erythema of the upper body, and epistaxis occur.

e. Life-threatening signs and symptoms include airway obstruction, hemorrhage, cyanosis, mental status changes, decreased cardiac output, and hypotension.

2. Interventions

a. Assess for early signs and symptoms of superior vena cava syndrome.

b. Prepare the client for high-dose radiation therapy to the mediastinal area, and possible surgery to insert a metal stent in the vena cava.

F. Tumor lysis syndrome

1. Description

a. Tumor lysis syndrome occurs when large quantities of tumor cells are destroyed rapidly and intracellular components such as potassium and uric acid are released into the bloodstream faster than the body can eliminate them.

b. Tumor lysis syndrome can indicate that **cancer** treatment is destroying tumor cells; however, if left untreated, it can cause severe tissue damage and death.

c. Hyperkalemia, hyperphosphatemia with resultant hypocalcemia, and hyperuricemia occur; hyperuricemia can lead to acute renal failure.

2. Interventions

a. Encourage oral hydration; IV hydration may be prescribed for the client experiencing nausea; monitor renal function.

b. Administer diuretics to increase the urine flow through the kidneys as prescribed.

c. Administer medications that increase the excretion of purines, such as allopurinol (Aloprim, Zyloprim), as prescribed.

d. Prepare to administer IV infusion of glucose and insulin to treat hyperkalemia.

e. Prepare the client for dialysis if hyperkalemia and hyperuricemia persist despite treatment.

PRACTICE QUESTIONS

1. The nurse is instructing the client to perform a testicular self-examination. The nurse tells the client:
   1. To examine the testicles while lying down
   2. That the best time for the examination is after a shower
   3. To gently feel the testicle with one finger to feel for a growth
   4. That testicular self-examinations should be done at least every 6 months

2. The community nurse is conducting a health promotion program at a local school and is discussing the risk factors associated with cervical cancer. Which of the following, if identified by the client as a risk factor for cervical cancer, indicates a need for further teaching?
   1. Smoking
   2. Multiple sex partners
   3. First intercourse after age 20
   4. Annual gynecological examinations

3. The community health nurse is instructing a group of female clients about breast self-examination. The nurse instructs the clients to perform the examination:
   1. At the onset of menstruation
   2. Every month during ovulation
   3. Weekly at the same time of day
   4. 1 week after menstruation begins

4. The nurse is caring for a client who has undergone a vaginal hysterectomy. The nurse avoids which of the following in the care of this client?
   1. Elevating the knee gatch on the bed
   2. Assisting with range-of-motion leg exercises
   3. Removal of antiembolism stockings twice daily
   4. Checking placement of pneumatic compression boots

5. The client is diagnosed as having a bowel tumor and several diagnostic tests are prescribed. The nurse understands that which test will confirm the diagnosis of malignancy?
   1. Biopsy of the tumor
   2. Abdominal ultrasound
   3. Magnetic resonance imaging
   4. Computed tomography scan

6. A client is diagnosed with multiple myeloma and the client asks the nurse about the diagnosis. The nurse bases the response on which description of this disorder?
   1. Altered red blood cell production
   2. Altered production of lymph nodes
   3. Malignant exacerbation in the number of leukocytes
   4. Malignant proliferation of plasma cells within the bone

7. The nurse is reviewing the laboratory results of a client diagnosed with multiple myeloma. Which of the following would the nurse expect to note specifically in this disorder?
   1. Increased calcium level
   2. Increased white blood cells
   3. Decreased blood urea nitrogen level
   4. Decreased number of plasma cells in the bone marrow

8. The nurse is developing a plan of care for the client with multiple myeloma and includes which priority intervention in the plan?
   1. Encouraging fluids
   2. Providing frequent oral care
   3. Coughing and deep breathing
   4. Monitoring the red blood cell count

9. The oncology nurse specialist provides an educational session to nursing staff regarding the characteristics of Hodgkin's disease. The nurse determines that further teaching is needed if a nursing staff member states that which of the following is a characteristic of the disease?
   1. Presence of Reed-Sternberg cells
   2. Occurs most often in the older client
   3. Prognosis depending on the stage of the disease
   4. Involvement of lymph nodes, spleen, and liver

10. The community health nurse conducts a health promotion program regarding testicular cancer to community members. The nurse determines that further information needs to be provided if a community member states that which of the following is a sign of testicular cancer?
    1. Alopecia
    2. Back pain
    3. Painless testicular swelling
    4. Heavy sensation in the scrotum

11. The client is receiving external radiation to the neck for cancer of the larynx. The most likely side effect to be expected is:
    1. Dyspnea
    2. Diarrhea
    3. Sore throat
    4. Constipation

12. The nurse is caring for a client with an internal radiation implant. When caring for the client, the nurse should observe which of the following principles?

1. Limit the time with the client to 1 hour per shift.
2. Do not allow pregnant women into the client's room.
3. Remove the dosimeter badge when entering the client's room.
4. Individuals younger than 16 years old may be allowed to go in the room as long as they are 6 feet away from the client.

13. A cervical radiation implant is placed in the client for treatment of cervical cancer. The nurse initiates what most appropriate activity order for this client?
    1. Bed rest
    2. Out of bed ad lib
    3. Out of bed in a chair only
    4. Ambulation to the bathroom only

14. The client is hospitalized for insertion of an internal cervical radiation implant. While giving care, the nurse finds the radiation implant in the bed. The initial action by the nurse is to:
    1. Call the physician.
    2. Reinsert the implant into the vagina immediately.
    3. Pick up the implant with gloved hands and flush it down the toilet.
    4. Pick up the implant with long-handled forceps and place it in a lead container.

15. The nurse is caring for a client experiencing neutropenia as a result of chemotherapy and develops a plan of care for the client. The nurse plans to:
    1. Restrict all visitors.
    2. Restrict fluid intake.
    3. Teach the client and family about the need for hand hygiene.
    4. Insert an indwelling urinary catheter to prevent skin breakdown.

16. The home health care nurse is caring for a client with cancer and the client is complaining of acute pain. The appropriate nursing assessment of the client's pain would include which of the following?
    1. The client's pain rating
    2. Nonverbal cues from the client
    3. The nurse's impression of the client's pain
    4. Pain relief after appropriate nursing intervention

17. The nurse is caring for a client who is postoperative following a pelvic exenteration and the physician changes the client's diet from NPO status to clear liquids. The nurse makes which priority assessment before administering the diet?
    1. Bowel sounds
    2. Ability to ambulate
    3. Incision appearance
    4. Urine specific gravity

18. The client is admitted to the hospital with a suspected diagnosis of Hodgkin's disease. Which assessment finding would the nurse expect to note specifically in the client?

1. Fatigue
2. Weakness
3. Weight gain
4. Enlarged lymph nodes

19. During the admission assessment of a client with advanced ovarian cancer, the nurse recognizes which symptom as typical of the disease?
    1. Diarrhea
    2. Hypermenorrhea
    3. Abnormal bleeding
    4. Abdominal distention

20. When assessing the laboratory results of the client with bladder cancer and bone metastasis, the nurse notes a calcium level of 12 mg/dL. The nurse recognizes that this is consistent with which oncological emergency?
    1. Hyperkalemia
    2. Hypercalcemia
    3. Spinal cord compression
    4. Superior vena cava syndrome

21. The client reports to the nurse that when performing testicular self-examination, he found a lump the size and shape of a pea. The appropriate response to the client is which of the following?
    1. "Lumps like that are normal; don't worry."
    2. "Let me know if it gets bigger next month."
    3. "That could be cancer. I'll ask the doctor to examine you."
    4. "That's important to report even though it might not be serious."

22. The hospice nurse visits a client dying of ovarian cancer. During the visit, the client expresses that "If I can just live long enough to attend my daughter's graduation, I'll be ready to die." Which phase of coping is this client experiencing?
    1. Anger
    2. Denial
    3. Bargaining
    4. Depression

23. The nurse is caring for a client following a mastectomy. Which assessment finding indicates that the client is experiencing a complication related to the surgery?
    1. Pain at the incisional site
    2. Arm edema on the operative side
    3. Sanguineous drainage in the Jackson-Pratt drain
    4. Complaints of decreased sensation near the operative site

24. The nurse is admitting a client with laryngeal cancer to the nursing unit. The nurse assesses for which most common risk factor for this type of cancer?
    1. Alcohol abuse
    2. Cigarette smoking
    3. Use of chewing tobacco
    4. Exposure to air pollutants

25. The female client who has been receiving radiation therapy for bladder cancer tells the nurse that it feels

as if she is voiding through the vagina. The nurse interprets that the client may be experiencing:
1. Rupture of the bladder
2. The development of a vesicovaginal fistula
3. Extreme stress caused by the diagnosis of cancer
4. Altered perineal sensation as a side effect of radiation therapy

26. The client with leukemia is receiving busulfan (Myleran) and allopurinol (Zyloprim) is prescribed for the client. The nurse tells the client that the purpose of the allopurinol is to:
1. Prevent nausea
2. Prevent alopecia
3. Prevent vomiting
4. Prevent hyperuricemia

27. The client receiving chemotherapy is experiencing mucositis. The nurse advises the client to use which of the following as the best substance to rinse the mouth?
1. Alcohol-based mouthwash
2. Hydrogen peroxide mixture
3. Lemon-flavored mouthwash
4. Weak salt and bicarbonate mouth rinse

28. The community nurse is conducting a health promotion program and the topic of the discussion relates to the risk factors for gastric cancer. Which risk factor, if identified by a client, indicates a need for further discussion?
1. Smoking
2. A high-fat diet
3. Foods containing nitrates
4. A diet of smoked, highly salted, and spiced food

29. A gastrectomy is performed on a client with gastric cancer. In the immediate postoperative period, the nurse notes bloody drainage from the nasogastric tube. Which of the following is the appropriate nursing intervention?
1. Notify the physician.
2. Measure abdominal girth.
3. Irrigate the nasogastric tube.
4. Continue to monitor the drainage.

30. The nurse is teaching a client about the risk factors associated with colorectal cancer. The nurse determines that further teaching related to colorectal cancer is necessary if the client identifies which of the following as an associated risk factor?
1. Age younger than 50 years
2. History of colorectal polyps
3. Family history of colorectal cancer
4. Chronic inflammatory bowel disease

31. The nurse is reviewing the preoperative orders of a client with a colon tumor who is scheduled for abdominal perineal resection and notes that the physician has prescribed neomycin (Mycifradin) for the client. The nurse determines that this medication has been prescribed primarily:

1. To prevent an immune dysfunction
2. Because the client has an infection
3. To decrease the bacteria in the bowel
4. Because the client is allergic to penicillin

32. The nurse is assessing the perineal wound in a client who has returned from the operating room following an abdominal perineal resection and notes serosanguineous drainage from the wound. Which nursing intervention is appropriate?
1. Notify the physician.
2. Clamp the Penrose drain.
3. Change the dressing as prescribed.
4. Remove and replace the perineal packing.

33. The nurse is assessing the colostomy of a client who has had an abdominal perineal resection for a bowel tumor. Which of the following assessment findings indicates that the colostomy is beginning to function?
1. Absent bowel sounds
2. The passage of flatus
3. The client's ability to tolerate food
4. Bloody drainage from the colostomy

34. The nurse is caring for a client following a radical neck dissection and creation of a tracheostomy performed for laryngeal cancer and is providing discharge instructions to the client. Which statement by the client indicates a need for further instructions?
1. "I will protect the stoma from water."
2. "I need to keep powders and sprays away from the stoma site."
3. "I need to use an air conditioner to provide cool air to assist in breathing."
4. "I need to apply a thin layer of petrolatum to the skin around the stoma to prevent cracking."

35. What is the purpose of cytoreductive ("debulking") surgery for ovarian cancer?
1. Cancer control by reducing the size of the tumor
2. Cancer prevention by removal of precancerous tissue
3. Cancer cure by removing all gross and microscopic tumor cells
4. Cancer rehabilitation by improving the appearance of a previously treated body part

36. Hormone therapy is prescribed as the mode of treatment for a client with prostate cancer. The nurse understands that the goal of this form of treatment is to:
1. Increase testosterone levels.
2. Increase prostaglandin levels.
3. Limit the amount of circulating androgens.
4. Increase the amount of circulating androgens.

37. The nurse is caring for a client with cancer of the prostate following a prostatectomy. The nurse provides discharge instructions to the client and tells the client to:

1. Avoid driving the car for 1 week.
2. Restrict fluid intake to prevent incontinence.
3. Avoid lifting objects heavier than 20 lb for at least 6 weeks.
4. Notify the physician if small blood clots are noticed during urination.

38. The oncology nurse is providing a teaching session to a group of nursing students regarding the risks and causes of bladder cancer. Which statement by a student indicates a need for further teaching?
    1. "Bladder cancer most often occurs in women."
    2. "Using cigarettes and coffee drinking can increase the risk."
    3. "Bladder cancer generally is seen in clients older than age 40."
    4. "Environmental health hazards have been attributed as a cause."

39. The nurse is reviewing the history of a client with bladder cancer. The nurse expects to note documentation of which most common symptom of this type of cancer?
    1. Dysuria
    2. Hematuria
    3. Urgency on urination
    4. Frequency of urination

40. The nurse is caring for a client following intravesical instillation of an alkylating chemotherapeutic agent into the bladder for the treatment of bladder cancer. Following the instillation, the nurse should instruct the client to:
    1. Urinate immediately.
    2. Maintain strict bed rest.
    3. Change position every 15 minutes.
    4. Retain the instillation fluid for 30 minutes.

41. The nurse is assessing the stoma of a client following a ureterostomy. Which of the following should the nurse expect to note?
    1. A dry stoma
    2. A pale stoma
    3. A dark-colored stoma
    4. A red and moist stoma

42. The nurse is caring for a client following a mastectomy. Which nursing intervention would assist in preventing lymphedema of the affected arm?
    1. Placing cool compresses on the affected arm
    2. Elevating the affected arm on a pillow above heart level
    3. Avoiding arm exercises in the immediate postoperative period
    4. Maintaining an intravenous site below the antecubital area on the affected side

43. A nurse is monitoring a client for signs and symptoms related to superior vena cava syndrome. Which of the following is an early sign of this oncological emergency?
    1. Cyanosis
    2. Arm edema
    3. Periorbital edema
    4. Mental status changes

44. A nurse manager is teaching the nursing staff about signs and symptoms related to hypercalcemia in a client with metastatic prostate cancer and tells the staff that which of the following is a serious late sign of this oncological emergency?
    1. Headache
    2. Dysphagia
    3. Constipation
    4. Electrocardiographic changes

45. As part of chemotherapy education, the nurse teaches a female client about the risk for bleeding and self-care during the period of the greatest bone marrow suppression (the nadir). The nurse understands that further teaching is needed when the client states:
    1. "I should avoid blowing my nose."
    2. "I may need a platelet transfusion if my platelet count is too low."
    3. "I'm going to take aspirin for my headache as soon as I get home."
    4. "I will count the number of pads and tampons I use when menstruating."

ALTERNATE ITEM FORMAT: MULTIPLE RESPONSE

A client with carcinoma of the lung develops syndrome of inappropriate antidiuretic hormone (SIADH) as a complication of the cancer. The nurse anticipates that which of the following may be prescribed?

❑ 1. Radiation
❑ 2. Chemotherapy
❑ 3. Increased fluid intake
❑ 4. Serum sodium levels
❑ 5. Decreased oral sodium intake
❑ 6. Medication that is antagonistic to antidiuretic hormone

ANSWERS

1. 2

Rationale: The testicular-self examination is recommended monthly after a warm bath or shower when the scrotal skin is relaxed. The client should stand to examine the testicles. Using both hands, with fingers under the scrotum and thumbs on top, the client should gently roll the testicles, feeling for any lumps.

Test-Taking Strategy: Use the process of elimination. Eliminate option 4 first because of the words *6 months*. Next, eliminate option 3 because of the word *one*. From the remaining options, eliminate option 1 by trying to visualize the process of the self-examination. If you had difficulty with this question, review the procedure for this self-examination.

Level of Cognitive Ability: Application
Client Needs: Health Promotion and Maintenance
Integrated Process: Teaching and Learning
Content Area: Adult health—oncology
Reference: Ignatavicius, D., & Workman, M. (2006). *Medical-surgical nursing: Critical thinking for collaborative care* (5th ed., p. 1871). Philadelphia: W.B. Saunders.

2. 3

Rationale: Risk factors for cervical cancer include human papillomavirus (HPV) infection, active and passive cigarette smoking, certain high-risk sexual activities (first intercourse before 17 years of age, multiple sex partners, or male partners with multiple sex partners). Screening via regular gynecological exams and Papanicolaou smear (Pap test) with treatment of precancerous abnormalities decrease the incidence and mortality of cervical cancer.

Test-Taking Strategy: Use the process of elimination and note the strategic words *indicates a need for further teaching* in the question. These words indicate a negative event query and ask you to select an option that is an incorrect statement. Reading carefully and familiarity with the risk factors related to cervical cancer will direct you to option 3. Review these risk factors if you had difficulty with this question.

Level of Cognitive Ability: Analysis
Client Needs: Health Promotion and Maintenance
Integrated Process: Teaching and Learning
Content Area: Adult health—oncology
Reference: Ignatavicius, D., & Workman, M. (2006). *Medical-surgical nursing: Critical thinking for collaborative care* (5th ed., p. 478). Philadelphia: W.B. Saunders.

3. 4

Rationale: The breast self-examination should be performed monthly 7 days after the onset of the menstrual period. Performing the examination weekly is not recommended. At the onset of menstruation and during ovulation, hormonal changes occur that may alter breast tissue.

Test-Taking Strategy: Use the process of elimination. Option 3 can be eliminated easily because of the word *weekly*. Eliminate options 1 and 2 next because of the similarity that exists regarding the hormonal changes that occur during these times. Review the procedure for performing breast self-examination if you had difficulty with this question.

Level of Cognitive Ability: Application
Client Needs: Health Promotion and Maintenance

Integrated Process: Teaching and Learning
Content Area: Adult health—oncology
Reference: Ignatavicius, D., & Workman, M. (2006). *Medical-surgical nursing: Critical thinking for collaborative care* (5th ed., p. 1797). Philadelphia: W.B. Saunders.

4. 1

Rationale: The client is at risk of deep vein thrombosis or thrombophlebitis after this surgery, as for any other major surgery. For this reason, the nurse implements measures that will prevent this complication. Range-of-motion exercises, antiembolism stockings, and pneumatic compression boots are helpful. The nurse should avoid using the knee gatch in the bed, which inhibits venous return, thus placing the client more at risk for deep vein thrombosis or thrombophlebitis.

Test-Taking Strategy: Use the process of elimination and note the strategic word *avoids*. This tells you that the correct option is an incorrect nursing action. Recalling that the client is at risk for deep vein thrombosis or thrombophlebitis will direct you to option 1. Review postoperative nursing interventions following vaginal hysterectomy if you had difficulty with this question.

Level of Cognitive Ability: Application
Client Needs: Physiological Integrity
Integrated Process: Nursing Process—implementation
Content Area: Adult health—oncology
Reference: Black, J., & Hawks, J. (2005). *Medical-surgical nursing: Clinical management for positive outcomes* (7th ed., p. 1536). Philadelphia: W.B. Saunders.

5. 1

Rationale: A biopsy is done to determine whether a tumor is malignant or benign. Magnetic resonance imaging, computed tomography scan, and ultrasound will visualize the presence of a mass but will not confirm a diagnosis of malignancy.

Test-Taking Strategy: Use the process of elimination and note the strategic word *confirm*. This strategic word should direct you easily to option 1. Review the purpose of the tests identified in the options if you had difficulty with this question.

Level of Cognitive Ability: Analysis
Client Needs: Physiological Integrity
Integrated Process: Nursing Process—analysis
Content Area: Adult health—oncology
Reference: Ignatavicius, D., & Workman, M. (2006). *Medical-surgical nursing: Critical thinking for collaborative care* (5th ed., p. 487). Philadelphia: W.B. Saunders.

6. 4

Rationale: Multiple myeloma is a B-cell neoplastic condition characterized by abnormal malignant proliferation of plasma cells and the accumulation of mature plasma cells in the bone marrow. Options 1 and 2 are not characteristics of multiple myeloma. Option 3 describes the leukemic process.

Test-Taking Strategy: Use the process of elimination. Focusing on the name of the disorder, *multiple myeloma*, will direct you to option 4. Review this information if you are unfamiliar with this oncological disorder.

Level of Cognitive Ability: Comprehension
Client Needs: Physiological Integrity

Integrated Process: Teaching and Learning
Content Area: Adult health—oncology
References: Ignatavicius, D., & Workman, M. (2006). *Medical-surgical nursing: Critical thinking for collaborative care* (5th ed., p. 910). Philadelphia: W.B. Saunders.
Lewis, S., Heitkemper, M., & Dirksen, S. (2004). *Medical-surgical nursing: Assessment and management of clinical problems* (6th ed., p. 744). St. Louis: Mosby.

7. **1**
Rationale: Findings indicative of multiple myeloma are an increased number of plasma cells in the bone marrow, anemia, hypercalcemia caused by the release of calcium from the deteriorating bone tissue, and an elevated blood urea nitrogen level. An increased white blood cell count may or may not be present and is not related specifically to multiple myeloma.
Test-Taking Strategy: Use the process of elimination. Noting the name of the disorder and recalling the pathophysiology of the disease will direct you to option 1. Review this information if you are unfamiliar with this oncological disorder.
Level of Cognitive Ability: Analysis
Client Needs: Physiological Integrity
Integrated Process: Nursing Process—assessment
Content Area: Adult health—oncology
References: Black, J., & Hawks, J. (2005). *Medical-surgical nursing: Clinical management for positive outcomes* (7th ed., pp. 2302-2303). Philadelphia: W.B. Saunders.
Ignatavicius, D., & Workman, M. (2006). *Medical-surgical nursing: Critical thinking for collaborative care* (5th ed., p. 910). Philadelphia: W.B. Saunders.

8. **1**
Rationale: Hypercalcemia caused by bone destruction is a priority concern in the client with multiple myeloma. The nurse should administer fluids in adequate amounts to maintain a urine output of 1.5 to 2 L/day; this requires about 3 L of fluid intake per day. The fluid is needed not only to dilute the calcium overload but also to prevent protein from precipitating in the renal tubules. Options 2, 3, and 4 may be components of the plan of care but are not the priority in this client.
Test-Taking Strategy: Use the process of elimination. Recalling the pathophysiology of this disorder and that encouraging fluids is specific to the care of a client with this disorder will direct you to option 1. Review the specific manifestations of this disorder if you had difficulty with this question.
Level of Cognitive Ability: Application
Client Needs: Physiological Integrity
Integrated Process: Nursing Process—planning
Content Area: Delegating/Prioritizing
References: Black, J., & Hawks, J. (2005). *Medical-surgical nursing: Clinical management for positive outcomes* (7th ed., p. 2303). Philadelphia: W.B. Saunders.
Lewis, S., Heitkemper, M., & Dirksen, S. (2004). *Medical-surgical nursing: Assessment and management of clinical problems* (6th ed., p. 746). St. Louis: Mosby.

9. **2**
Rationale: Hodgkin's disease is a disorder of young adults. Options 1, 3, and 4 are characteristics of this disease.

Test-Taking Strategy: Use the process of elimination and note the strategic words *further teaching is needed* in the question. These words indicate a negative event query and ask you to select an option that is an incorrect statement. Recalling that Hodgkin's disease occurs in the young adult will direct you to option 2. Review the characteristics of this disorder if you had difficulty with this question.
Level of Cognitive Ability: Analysis
Client Needs: Physiological Integrity
Integrated Process: Teaching and Learning
Content Area: Adult health—oncology
Reference: Ignatavicius, D., & Workman, M. (2006). *Medical-surgical nursing: Critical thinking for collaborative care* (5th ed., p. 909). Philadelphia: W.B. Saunders.

10. **1**
Rationale: Alopecia is not an assessment finding in testicular cancer. Alopecia may occur, however, as a result of radiation or chemotherapy. Options 2, 3, and 4 are assessment findings in testicular cancer. Back pain may indicate metastasis to the retroperitoneal lymph nodes.
Test-Taking Strategy: Note the strategic words *further information needs to be provided* in the question. These words indicate a negative event query and ask you to select an option that is an incorrect statement. Use the process of elimination, remembering that alopecia occurs as a result of chemotherapy rather than as a result of the disease. Review the manifestations associated with testicular cancer if you had difficulty with this question.
Level of Cognitive Ability: Analysis
Client Needs: Health Promotion and Maintenance
Integrated Process: Teaching and Learning
Content Area: Adult health—oncology
Reference: Lewis, S., Heitkemper, M., & Dirksen, S. (2004). *Medical-surgical nursing: Assessment and management of clinical problems* (6th ed., p. 1454). St. Louis: Mosby.

11. **3**
Rationale: In general, only the area in the treatment field is affected by the radiation. Skin reactions, fatigue, nausea, and anorexia may occur with radiation to any site, whereas other side effects occur only when specific areas are involved in treatment. A client receiving radiation to the larynx is most likely to experience a sore throat. Options 2 and 4 may occur with radiation to the gastrointestinal tract. Dyspnea may occur with lung involvement.
Test-Taking Strategy: Use the process of elimination. Eliminate options 2 and 4 first because they are comparative or alike and are gastrointestinal related. Consider the anatomical location of the radiation therapy to assist you in selecting option 3. Review the effects of radiation therapy if you had difficulty with this question.
Level of Cognitive Ability: Analysis
Client Needs: Physiological Integrity
Integrated Process: Nursing Process—assessment
Content Area: Adult health—oncology
References: Black, J., & Hawks, J. (2005). *Medical-surgical nursing: Clinical management for positive outcomes* (7th ed., p. 365). Philadelphia: W.B. Saunders.
Ignatavicius, D., & Workman, M. (2006). *Medical-surgical*

nursing: Critical thinking for collaborative care (5th ed., pp. 495, 1276-1277). Philadelphia: W.B. Saunders.

12. 2
Rationale: The time that the nurse spends in a room of a client with an internal radiation implant is 30 minutes per 8-hour shift. The dosimeter badge must be worn when in the client's room. Children younger than 16 years of age and pregnant women are not allowed in the client's room.
Test-Taking Strategy: Use the process of elimination. Option 3 can be eliminated first. Recalling the time frame related to exposure to the client will assist in eliminating option 1. From the remaining options, select option 2 because of the possible risks associated with exposure to the mother and fetus. Review these principles if you had difficulty with this question.
Level of Cognitive Ability: Application
Client Needs: Safe and Effective Care Environment
Integrated Process: Nursing Process—implementation
Content Area: Adult health—oncology
Reference: Ignatavicius, D., & Workman, M. (2006). *Medical-surgical nursing: Critical thinking for collaborative care* (5th ed., p. 490). Philadelphia: W.B. Saunders.

13. 1
Rationale: The client with a cervical radiation implant should be maintained on bed rest in the dorsal position to prevent movement of the radiation source. The head of the bed is elevated to a maximum of 10 to 15 degrees for comfort. The nurse avoids turning the client on the side. If turning is absolutely necessary, a pillow is placed between the knees and, with the body in straight alignment, the client is logrolled.
Test-Taking Strategy: Use the process of elimination. Consider the anatomical location of the implant and the risk of dislodgment to answer the question. Additionally, note that options 2, 3, and 4 are comparative or alike. If you had difficulty with this question, review care of the client with a radiation implant.
Level of Cognitive Ability: Application
Client Needs: Physiological Integrity
Integrated Process: Nursing Process—implementation
Content Area: Adult health—oncology
Reference: Ignatavicius, D., & Workman, M. (2006). *Medical-surgical nursing: Critical thinking for collaborative care* (5th ed., p. 490). Philadelphia: W.B. Saunders.

14. 4
Rationale: A lead container and long-handled forceps should be kept in the client's room at all times during internal radiation therapy. If the implant becomes dislodged, the nurse should pick up the implant with long-handled forceps and place it in the lead container. Options 1, 2, and 3 are inaccurate interventions.
Test-Taking Strategy: Use the process of elimination and note the strategic word *initial* in the question. Option 2 is not an appropriate action. Eliminate option 3 next because the implant would not be discarded. Although the physician would be notified, the initial action is option 4. Review the initial measures related to a dislodged implant if you had difficulty with this question.

Level of Cognitive Ability: Application
Client Needs: Safe and Effective Care Environment
Integrated Process: Nursing Process—implementation
Content Area: Adult health—oncology
Reference: Ignatavicius, D., & Workman, M. (2006). *Medical-surgical nursing: Critical thinking for collaborative care* (5th ed., p. 490). Philadelphia: W.B. Saunders.

15. 3
Rationale: In the neutropenic client, meticulous hand hygiene education is implemented for the client, family, visitors, and staff. Not all visitors are restricted, but the client is protected from persons with known infections. Fluids should be encouraged. Invasive measures such as an indwelling urinary catheter should be avoided to prevent infections.
Test-Taking Strategy: Use the process of elimination. Eliminate option 1 because of the word *all*. Next, eliminate option 2 because it is not reasonable to eliminate fluids in a client receiving chemotherapy who is at risk for fluid and electrolyte imbalances. Eliminate option 4 because of the risk of infection that exists with this measure. Review interventions for the client with hematologic toxicity if you had difficulty with this question.
Level of Cognitive Ability: Application
Client Needs: Physiological Integrity
Integrated Process: Nursing Process—planning
Content Area: Adult health—oncology
Reference: Ignatavicius, D., & Workman, M. (2006). *Medical-surgical nursing: Critical thinking for collaborative care* (5th ed., p. 497). Philadelphia: W.B. Saunders.

16. 1
Rationale: The client's self-report is a critical component of pain assessment. The nurse should ask the client about the description of the pain and listen carefully to the client's words used to describe the pain. The nurse's impression of the client's pain is not appropriate in determining the client's level of pain. Nonverbal cues from the client are important but are not the most appropriate pain assessment measure. Assessing pain relief is an important measure, but this option is not related to the subject of the question.
Test-Taking Strategy: Use the process of elimination. Noting the subject of the question will assist in eliminating option 4. Eliminate option 3 because the nurse is not the client of the question. From the remaining options, the subjective data from the client will provide the most accurate description of the pain. Review pain assessment techniques if the question was difficult.
Level of Cognitive Ability: Analysis
Client Needs: Physiological Integrity
Integrated Process: Caring
Content Area: Adult health—oncology
Reference: Ignatavicius, D., & Workman, M. (2006). *Medical-surgical nursing: Critical thinking for collaborative care* (5th ed., pp. 68, 72). Philadelphia: W.B. Saunders.

17. 1
Rationale: The client is kept NPO until peristalsis returns, usually in 4 to 6 days. When signs of bowel function return, clear fluids are given to the client. If no distention occurs, the diet is advanced as tolerated. The most important assessment is to

assess bowel sounds before feeding the client. Options 2, 3, and 4 are unrelated to the subject of the question.
Test-Taking Strategy: Use the process of elimination and note the strategic word *priority* and the strategic words *NPO to clear liquids* in the question. Option 1 is the only option that relates to gastrointestinal function, which is the subject of the question. Review care of the client following pelvic exenteration if you had difficulty with this question.
Level of Cognitive Ability: Analysis
Client Needs: Physiological Integrity
Integrated Process: Nursing Process—assessment
Content Area: Adult health—oncology
Reference: Ignatavicius, D., & Workman, M. (2006). *Medical-surgical nursing: Critical thinking for collaborative care* (5th ed., p. 345). Philadelphia: W.B. Saunders.

18. **4**
Rationale: Hodgkin's disease is a chronic progressive neoplastic disorder of lymphoid tissue characterized by the painless enlargement of lymph nodes with progression to extralymphatic sites, such as the spleen and liver. Weight loss is most likely to be noted. Fatigue and weakness may occur but are not related significantly to the disease.
Test-Taking Strategy: Use the process of elimination. Recalling that Hodgkin's disease affects the lymph nodes will direct you to option 4. Option 3 easily can be eliminated because, in such a disorder, weight loss is most likely to occur. Options 1 and 2 are comparative or alike and are rather vague symptoms that can occur in many disorders. Review the manifestations associated with Hodgkin's disease if you had difficulty with this question.
Level of Cognitive Ability: Analysis
Client Needs: Physiological Integrity
Integrated Process: Nursing Process—assessment
Content Area: Adult health—oncology
Reference: Black, J., & Hawks, J. (2005). *Medical-surgical nursing: Clinical management for positive outcomes* (7th ed., p. 2412). Philadelphia: W.B. Saunders.

19. **4**
Rationale: Clinical manifestations of ovarian cancer include abdominal distention, urinary frequency and urgency, pleural effusion, malnutrition, pain from pressure caused by the growing tumor and the effects of urinary or bowel obstruction, constipation, ascites with dyspnea, and ultimately general severe pain. Abnormal bleeding, often resulting in hypermenorrhea, is associated with uterine cancer.
Test-Taking Strategy: Use the process of elimination. Eliminate options 2 and 3 first because they are comparative or alike. From the remaining options, consider the anatomical location of the cancer. This will assist in directing you to option 4. Review the manifestations associated with ovarian cancer if you had difficulty with this question.
Level of Cognitive Ability: Analysis
Client Needs: Physiological Integrity
Integrated Process: Nursing Process—assessment
Content Area: Adult health—oncology
Reference: Ignatavicius, D., & Workman, M. (2006). *Medical-surgical nursing: Critical thinking for collaborative care* (5th ed., p. 1849). Philadelphia: W.B. Saunders.

20. **2**
Rationale: Hypercalcemia is a serum calcium level higher than 10 mg/dL, most often occurs in clients who have bone metastasis, and is a late manifestation of extensive malignancy. The presence of cancer in the bone causes the bone to release calcium into the bloodstream.
Test-Taking Strategy: Use the process of elimination. Recalling the normal calcium level will direct you easily to option 2. Also note the relationship of *calcium level* in the question and *hypercalcemia* in the correct option. Review oncological emergencies if you had difficulty with this question.
Level of Cognitive Ability: Analysis
Client Needs: Physiological Integrity
Integrated Process: Nursing Process—assessment
Content Area: Adult health—oncology
Reference: Ignatavicius, D., & Workman, M. (2006). *Medical-surgical nursing: Critical thinking for collaborative care* (5th ed., p. 502). Philadelphia: W.B. Saunders.

21. **4**
Rationale: Testicular cancer almost always occurs in only one testicle and is usually a pea-sized painless lump. The cancer is highly curable when found early. The finding should be reported to the physician.
Test-Taking Strategy: Use the process of elimination. Eliminate option 1 because it does not address the client's concern and is a block to communication. Option 2 places the client's concern on hold and is an inappropriate and inaccurate response. Option 3 is nontherapeutic and may cause concern in the client. Review testicular self-examination and therapeutic communication techniques if you had difficulty with this question.
Level of Cognitive Ability: Application
Client Needs: Psychosocial Integrity
Integrated Process: Caring
Content Area: Adult health—oncology
Reference: Ignatavicius, D., & Workman, M. (2006). *Medical-surgical nursing: Critical thinking for collaborative care* (5th ed., p. 1873). Philadelphia: W.B. Saunders.

22. **3**
Rationale: Denial, bargaining, anger, depression, and acceptance are recognized stages that a person facing a life-threatening illness experiences. Bargaining identifies a behavior in which the individual is willing to do anything to avoid loss or change prognosis or fate. Denial is expressed as shock and disbelief and may be the first response to hearing bad news. Depression may be manifested by hopelessness, weeping openly, or remaining quiet or withdrawn. Anger also may be a first response to upsetting news and the predominant theme is "why me?" or the blaming of others.
Test-Taking Strategy: Use the process of elimination. Focus on the client's statement as identified in the question to assist in selecting the correct option. From this point, you should easily be able to eliminate options 1, 2, and 4. Review these stages if you had difficulty with this question.
Level of Cognitive Ability: Analysis
Client Needs: Psychosocial Integrity
Integrated Process: Nursing Process—assessment
Content Area: Adult health—oncology

Reference: Black, J., & Hawks, J. (2005). *Medical-surgical nursing: Clinical management for positive outcomes* (7th ed., pp. 488, 526). Philadelphia: W.B. Saunders.

23. **2**

Rationale: Arm edema on the operative side (lymphedema) is a complication following mastectomy and can occur immediately postoperatively or may occur months or even years after surgery. Options 1, 3, and 4 are expected occurrences following mastectomy and do not indicate a complication.

Test-Taking Strategy: Use the process of elimination, considering the normally expected occurrences following a mastectomy. You should be able to eliminate options 1, 3, and 4 easily. If you had difficulty with this question, review the complications following mastectomy.

Level of Cognitive Ability: Analysis
Client Needs: Physiological Integrity
Integrated Process: Nursing Process—assessment
Content Area: Adult health—oncology
Reference: Lewis, S., Heitkemper, M., & Dirksen, S. (2004). *Medical-surgical nursing: Assessment and management of clinical problems* (6th ed., p. 1376). St. Louis: Mosby.

24. **2**

Rationale: The most common risk factor associated with laryngeal cancer is cigarette smoking. Heavy alcohol use and the combined use of tobacco increases the risk. Another risk factor is exposure to environmental pollutants.

Test-Taking Strategy: Note the strategic words *most common* in the question. Begin to answer this question by eliminating options 1 and 4, because cancer of the upper and lower airway most often is related to tobacco. To select between the remaining options, recall that cigarettes are more harmful than chewing tobacco. Review the causes of lung cancer if this question was difficult.

Level of Cognitive Ability: Analysis
Client Needs: Physiological Integrity
Integrated Process: Nursing Process—analysis
Content Area: Adult health—oncology
Reference: Lewis, S., Heitkemper, M., & Dirksen, S. (2004). *Medical-surgical nursing: Assessment and management of clinical problems* (6th ed., pp. 586-587). St. Louis: Mosby.

25. **2**

Rationale: A vesicovaginal fistula is a genital fistula that occurs between the bladder and vagina. The fistula is an abnormal opening between these two body parts and, if this occurs, the client may experience drainage of urine through the vagina. The client's complaint is not associated with options 1, 3, and 4.

Test-Taking Strategy: Use the process of elimination. Noting the strategic words *voiding through the vagina* should direct you to option 2. Review the symptoms associated with vesicovaginal fistula if you had difficulty with this question.

Level of Cognitive Ability: Analysis
Client Needs: Physiological Integrity
Integrated Process: Nursing Process—analysis
Content Area: Adult health—oncology
Reference: Ignatavicius, D., & Workman, M. (2006). *Medical-surgical nursing: Critical thinking for collaborative care* (5th ed., p. 1836). Philadelphia: W.B. Saunders.

26. **4**

Rationale: Allopurinol decreases uric acid production and reduces uric acid concentrations in serum and urine. In the client receiving chemotherapy, uric acid levels increase as a result of the massive cell destruction that occurs from the chemotherapy. This medication prevents or treats hyperuricemia caused by chemotherapy. Allopurinol is not used to prevent alopecia, nausea, or vomiting.

Test-Taking Strategy: Use the process of elimination. Recalling that hyperuricemia occurs as a result of chemotherapy will assist in directing you to option 4. If you had difficulty with this question or are unfamiliar with this medication, review its action in the client receiving chemotherapy.

Level of Cognitive Ability: Application
Client Needs: Physiological Integrity
Integrated Process: Nursing Process—implementation
Content Area: Adult health—oncology
Reference: Ignatavicius, D., & Workman, M. (2006). *Medical-surgical nursing: Critical thinking for collaborative care* (5th ed., p. 416). Philadelphia: W.B. Saunders.

27. **4**

Rationale: An acidic environment in the mouth is favorable for bacterial growth, particularly in an area already compromised from chemotherapy. Therefore, the client is advised to rinse the mouth before every meal and at bedtime with a weak salt and sodium bicarbonate mouth rinse. This lessens the growth of bacteria and limits plaque formation. The other substances are irritating to oral tissue. If hydrogen peroxide must be used because of severe plaque, it should be a weak solution because it dries the mucous membranes.

Test-Taking Strategy: Use the process of elimination. Options 1 and 3 can be eliminated first because of the irritating effects of these solutions. From the remaining options, note the word *weak* in the correct option. Review the treatment measures for mucositis if you had difficulty with this question.

Level of Cognitive Ability: Application
Client Needs: Physiological Integrity
Integrated Process: Nursing Process—implementation
Content Area: Adult health—oncology
Reference: Ignatavicius, D., & Workman, M. (2006). *Medical-surgical nursing: Critical thinking for collaborative care* (5th ed., pp. 496, 1250). Philadelphia: W.B. Saunders.

28. **2**

Rationale: A high-fat diet plays a role in the development of cancer of the pancreas. Options 1, 3, and 4 are risk factors related to gastric cancer.

Test-Taking Strategy: Use the process of elimination and note that the question asks about the risk factors associated with gastric cancer. Note the strategic words *indicates a need for further discussion.* These words indicate a negative event query and ask you to select an option that is an incorrect statement. Option 1 can be easily eliminated. Next, focus on the subject, gastric cancer. This will assist in eliminating options 3 and 4. Review the risk factors associated with gastric cancer if you had difficulty with this question.

Level of Cognitive Ability: Analysis
Client Needs: Health Promotion and Maintenance
Integrated Process: Teaching and Learning

Content Area: Adult health—oncology
Reference: Ignatavicius, D., & Workman, M. (2006). *Medical-surgical nursing: Critical thinking for collaborative care* (5th ed., p. 1318). Philadelphia: W.B. Saunders.

29. 4
Rationale: Following gastrectomy, drainage from the nasogastric tube is normally bloody for 24 hours postoperatively, changes to brown-tinged, and is then to yellow or clear. Because bloody drainage is expected in the immediate postoperative period, the nurse should continue to monitor the drainage. The nurse does not need to notify the physician at this time. Measuring abdominal girth is performed to detect the development of distention. Following gastrectomy, a nasogastric tube should not be irrigated unless there are specific physician orders to do so.
Test-Taking Strategy: Use the process of elimination and note the strategic word *appropriate*. This should direct you to option 4. Remember that drainage from the nasogastric tube is normally bloody for 24 hours postoperatively, changes to brown-tinged and then to yellow or clear. If you had difficulty with this question, review the postoperative expected findings following gastrectomy.
Level of Cognitive Ability: Application
Client Needs: Physiological Integrity
Integrated Process: Nursing Process—implementation
Content Area: Adult health—oncology
Reference: Ignatavicius, D., & Workman, M. (2006). *Medical-surgical nursing: Critical thinking for collaborative care* (5th ed., pp. 1298, 1303). Philadelphia: W.B. Saunders.

30. 1
Rationale: Colorectal cancer risk factors include age older than 50 years, a family history of the disease, colorectal polyps, and chronic inflammatory bowel disease.
Test-Taking Strategy: Use the process of elimination and note the strategic words *further teaching is necessary*. These words indicate a negative event query and ask you to select an option that is an incorrect statement. Noting the words *younger than* in option 1 will direct you to this option. Review the risk factors associated with colorectal cancer if you had difficulty with this question.
Level of Cognitive Ability: Analysis
Client Needs: Health Promotion and Maintenance
Integrated Process: Teaching and Learning
Content Area: Adult health—oncology
Reference: Lewis, S., Heitkemper, M., & Dirksen, S. (2004). *Medical-surgical nursing: Assessment and management of clinical problems* (6th ed., p. 1082). St. Louis: Mosby.

31. 3
Rationale: To reduce the risk of contamination at the time of surgery, the bowel is emptied and cleansed. Laxatives and enemas are given to empty the bowel. Intestinal anti-infectives such as neomycin or kanamycin (Kantrex) are administered to decrease the bacteria in the bowel.
Test-Taking Strategy: Use the process of elimination. Eliminate options 2 and 4 first because no reference is made to this information in the question. Recalling the concepts related to the flora of the intestinal tract will assist in directing you to

option 3 as the primary purpose of this medication. Review this important preoperative intervention if you had difficulty with this question.
Level of Cognitive Ability: Analysis
Client Needs: Physiological Integrity
Integrated Process: Nursing Process—analysis
Content Area: Adult health—oncology
Reference: Ignatavicius, D., & Workman, M. (2006). *Medical-surgical nursing: Critical thinking for collaborative care* (5th ed., p. 1380). Philadelphia: W.B. Saunders.

32. 3
Rationale: Immediately after surgery, profuse serosanguineous drainage from the perineal wound is expected. The nurse does not need to notify the physician at this time. A Penrose drain should not be clamped because this action will cause the accumulation of drainage within the tissue. Penrose drains and packing are removed gradually over a period of 5 to 7 days as prescribed. The nurse should not remove the perineal packing.
Test-Taking Strategy: Use the process of elimination. Eliminate options 2 and 4, knowing that these are inappropriate interventions. Recalling that serosanguineous drainage is expected following this type of surgery will assist in directing you to option 3. Review postoperative nursing care following abdominal perineal resection if you had difficulty with this question.
Level of Cognitive Ability: Application
Client Needs: Physiological Integrity
Integrated Process: Nursing Process—implementation
Content Area: Adult health—oncology
Reference: Lewis, S., Heitkemper, M., & Dirksen, S. (2004). *Medical-surgical nursing: Assessment and management of clinical problems* (6th ed., p. 1087). St. Louis: Mosby.

33. 2
Rationale: Following abdominal perineal resection, the nurse would expect the colostomy to begin to function within 72 hours after surgery, although it may take up to 5 days. The nurse should assess for a return of peristalsis, listen for bowel sounds, and check for the passage of flatus. Absent bowel sounds would not indicate the return of peristalsis. The client would remain NPO until bowel sounds return and the colostomy is functioning. Bloody drainage is not expected from a colostomy.
Test-Taking Strategy: Use the process of elimination and note the strategic words *beginning to function*. These should assist in eliminating option 1. Knowledge of general postoperative measures will assist in eliminating option 3. Focus on the subject of the question to assist in eliminating option 4 as a correct option. Review postoperative care of a client following abdominal perineal resection if you had difficulty with this question.
Level of Cognitive Ability: Analysis
Client Needs: Physiological Integrity
Integrated Process: Nursing Process—assessment
Content Area: Adult health—oncology
Reference: Black, J., & Hawks, J. (2005). *Medical-surgical nursing: Clinical management for positive outcomes* (7th ed., pp. 836, 838). Philadelphia: W.B. Saunders.

34. 3

Rationale: Air conditioners need to be avoided to protect from excessive coldness. A humidifier in the home should be used if excessive dryness is a problem. Options 1, 2, and 4 are appropriate interventions regarding stoma care following radical neck dissection and creation of a tracheotomy.

Test-Taking Strategy: Use the process of elimination and note the strategic words *need for further instructions*. These words indicate a negative event query and ask you to select an option that is an incorrect statement. You should easily be able to eliminate options 1 and 2. From the remaining options, recalling that a humidifier rather than an air conditioner is recommended will assist you in selecting the correct option. If you had difficulty with this question, review discharge instructions following radical neck dissection.
Level of Cognitive Ability: Analysis
Client Needs: Physiological Integrity
Integrated Process: Teaching and Learning
Content Area: Adult health—oncology
Reference: Black, J., & Hawks, J. (2005). *Medical-surgical nursing: Clinical management for positive outcomes* (7th ed., p. 1794). Philadelphia: W.B. Saunders.

35. 1

Rationale: Cytoreductive or "debulking" surgery may be used if a large tumor cannot be completely removed as is often the case with late-stage ovarian cancer (e.g., the tumor is attached to a vital organ or spread throughout the abdomen). When this occurs, as much tumor as possible is removed and adjuvant chemotherapy or radiation may be prescribed.

Test-Taking Strategy: Use the process of elimination. Option 3 can be eliminated first, knowing that cytoreductive surgery does not remove all tumor cells for a curative intent. From the remaining options, select option 1 because it is the most accurate description of cytoreductive surgery. Review the purpose of surgical interventions for cancer if you had difficulty with this question.
Level of Cognitive Ability: Comprehension
Client Needs: Physiological Integrity
Integrated Process: Nursing Process—planning
Content Area: Adult health—oncology
References: Ignatavicius, D., & Workman, M. (2006). *Medical-surgical nursing: Critical thinking for collaborative care* (5th ed., p. 1866). Philadelphia: W.B. Saunders.
Lewis, S., Heitkemper, M., & Dirksen, S. (2004). *Medical-surgical nursing: Assessment and management of clinical problems* (6th ed., p. 1445). St. Louis: Mosby.

36. 3

Rationale: Hormone therapy (androgen deprivation) is a mode of treatment for prostatic cancer. The goal is to limit the amount of circulating androgens because prostate cells depend on androgen for cellular maintenance. Deprivation of androgen often can lead to regression of disease and improvement of symptoms.

Test-Taking Strategy: Use the process of elimination. Note that options 1, 2, and 4 indicate an *increase*. Review the goal of this form of therapy if you had difficulty with this question.
Level of Cognitive Ability: Comprehension

Client Needs: Physiological Integrity
Integrated Process: Nursing Process—planning
Content Area: Adult health—oncology
Reference: Ignatavicius, D., & Workman, M. (2006). *Medical-surgical nursing: Critical thinking for collaborative care* (5th ed., p. 1869). Philadelphia: W.B. Saunders.

37. 4 3

Rationale: Small pieces of tissue or blood clots can be passed during urination for up to 2 weeks after surgery. Driving a car and sitting for long periods of time are restricted for at least 3 weeks. A high daily fluid intake should be maintained to limit clot formation and prevent infection. Option 3 is an accurate discharge instruction following prostatectomy.

Test-Taking Strategy: Use the process of elimination. Option 2 easily can be eliminated first. Eliminate option 1 next, because 1 week is a rather short time. Recalling that blood clots are expected following this type of surgery will assist in directing you to option 3. Review client teaching points following prostatectomy if you had difficulty with this question.
Level of Cognitive Ability: Application
Client Needs: Health Promotion and Maintenance
Integrated Process: Teaching and Learning
Content Area: Adult health—oncology
Reference: Black, J., & Hawks, J. (2005). *Medical-surgical nursing: Clinical management for positive outcomes.* (7th ed., p. 1025). Philadelphia: W.B. Saunders.

38. 1

Rationale: The incidence of bladder cancer is greater in men than in women and affects the white population twice as often as blacks. Options 2, 3, and 4 are associated with the incidence of bladder cancer.

Test-Taking Strategy: Use the process of elimination and note the strategic words *need for further teaching*. These words indicate a negative event query and ask you to select an option that is an incorrect statement. Basic information regarding the risks associated with cancer will assist in eliminating options 2, 3, and 4. If you had difficulty with this question, review these risks.
Level of Cognitive Ability: Analysis
Client Needs: Physiological Integrity
Integrated Process: Teaching and Learning
Content Area: Adult health—oncology
References: Black, J., & Hawks, J. (2005). *Medical-surgical nursing: Clinical management for positive outcomes* (7th ed., p. 866). Philadelphia: W.B. Saunders.
Lewis, S., Heitkemper, M., & Dirksen, S. (2004). *Medical-surgical nursing: Assessment and management of clinical problems* (6th ed., p. 1194). St. Louis: Mosby.

39. 2

Rationale: The most common symptom in clients with cancer of the bladder is hematuria. The client also may experience irritative voiding symptoms such as frequency, urgency, and dysuria, and these symptoms often are associated with carcinoma in situ.

Test-Taking Strategy: Use the process of elimination and note the strategic words *most common* in the question. Options 1, 3,

and 4 are symptoms that are associated most often with bladder infection. Review the clinical manifestations associated with bladder cancer if you had difficulty with this question.
Level of Cognitive Ability: Analysis
Client Needs: Physiological Integrity
Integrated Process: Nursing Process—assessment
Content Area: Adult health—oncology
Reference: Black, J., & Hawks, J. (2005). *Medical-surgical nursing: Clinical management for positive outcomes* (7th ed., p. 869). Philadelphia: W.B. Saunders.

40. **3**
Rationale: Normally, the medication is injected into the bladder through a urethral catheter, the catheter is clamped or removed, and the client is asked to retain the fluid for 2 hours. The client changes position every 15 to 30 minutes from side to side and from supine to prone or resumes all activity immediately. The client then voids and is instructed to drink water to flush the bladder.
Test-Taking Strategy: Use the process of elimination and note the strategic words *intravesical instillation*. Remembering the purpose of this treatment will direct you to option 3. If you are unfamiliar with this treatment measure, review the nursing interventions.
Level of Cognitive Ability: Application
Client Needs: Physiological Integrity
Integrated Process: Nursing Process—implementation
Content Area: Adult health—oncology
Reference: Lewis, S., Heitkemper, M., & Dirksen, S. (2004). *Medical-surgical nursing: Assessment and management of clinical problems* (6th ed., p. 1195). St. Louis: Mosby.

41. **4**
Rationale: Following ureterostomy, the stoma should be red and moist. A pale stoma may indicate an inadequate amount of vascular supply. A dry stoma may indicate a body fluid deficit. Any sign of darkness or duskiness in the stoma may indicate a loss of vascular supply and must be reported immediately or necrosis can occur.
Test-Taking Strategy: Use the process of elimination. You should be able to eliminate options 2 and 3 easily. From the remaining options, note the strategic word *moist* in option 4. This should indicate that this is an expected and positive assessment. If you had difficulty with this question, review expected and unexpected findings following ureterostomy.
Level of Cognitive Ability: Analysis
Client Needs: Physiological Integrity
Integrated Process: Nursing Process—assessment
Content Area: Adult health—oncology
Reference: Black, J., & Hawks, J. (2005). *Medical-surgical nursing: Clinical management for positive outcomes* (7th ed., p. 877). Philadelphia: W.B. Saunders.

42. **2**
Rationale: Following mastectomy, the arm should be elevated above the level of the heart. Simple arm exercises should be encouraged. No blood pressure readings, injections, intravenous lines, or blood draws should be performed on the affected arm. Cool compresses are not a suggested measure to prevent lymphedema from occurring.

Test-Taking Strategy: Note the strategic words *assist in preventing*. Use the process of elimination and note the relationship between lymph*edema* in the question and *elevating* in the correct option. Review these important measures if you had difficulty with this question.
Level of Cognitive Ability: Application
Client Needs: Physiological Integrity
Integrated Process: Nursing Process—implementation
Content Area: Adult health—oncology
Reference: Black, J., & Hawks, J. (2005). *Medical-surgical nursing: Clinical management for positive outcomes* (7th ed., p. 1108). Philadelphia: W.B. Saunders.

43. **3**
Rationale: Superior vena cava syndrome occurs when the superior vena cava is compressed or obstructed by tumor growth. Early signs and symptoms generally occur in the morning and include edema of the face, especially around the eyes, and client complaints of tightness of a shirt or blouse collar. As the compression worsens, the client experiences edema of the hands and arms. Mental status changes and cyanosis are late signs.
Test-Taking Strategy: Use the process of elimination and note the strategic word *early* in the question. This strategic word should assist in eliminating options 1, 2, and 4. If you are unfamiliar with vena cava syndrome, review this oncological emergency.
Level of Cognitive Ability: Analysis
Client Needs: Physiological Integrity
Integrated Process: Nursing Process—assessment
Content Area: Adult health—oncology
Reference: Black, J., & Hawks, J. (2005). *Medical-surgical nursing: Clinical management for positive outcomes* (7th ed., p. 389). Philadelphia: W.B. Saunders.

44. **4**
Rationale: Hypercalcemia is a late manifestation of bone metastasis in late-stage cancer. Headache and dysphagia are not associated with hypercalcemia. Constipation may occur early in the process. Electrocardiogram changes include shortened ST segment and a widened T wave.
Test-Taking Strategy: Use the process of elimination. Focus on the name of the oncological emergency, *hypercalcemia*, to direct you to option 4. Eliminate options 1 and 2 because they are not signs of hypercalcemia. Eliminate option 3 because it is an early sign of hypercalcemia. Also, noting the strategic word *serious* will direct you to option 4. Review this information if you are unfamiliar with this oncological disorder.
Level of Cognitive Ability: Analysis
Client Needs: Physiological Integrity
Integrated Process: Teaching and Learning
Content Area: Adult health—oncology
Reference: Ignatavicius, D., & Workman, M. (2006). *Medical-surgical nursing: Critical thinking for collaborative care* (5th ed., p. 502). Philadelphia: W.B. Saunders.

45. **3**
Rationale: During the period of greatest bone marrow suppression (the nadir), the platelet count may be low, less than 20,000 cells/mm³. Option 3 describes an incorrect statement

by the client. Aspirin and nonsteroidal anti-inflammatory drugs and product that contain aspirin should be avoided because of their antiplatelet activity, thus further teaching is needed. Options 1, 2 and 4 are correct statements by the client to prevent and monitor bleeding.

Test-Taking Strategy: Use the process of elimination and note the strategic word *nadir*. Focus on the causes of thrombocytopenia to direct you to option 3. Review this information if you are unfamiliar with thrombocytopenia precautions.

Level of Cognitive Ability: Analysis
Client Needs: Physiological Integrity
Integrated Process: Teaching and Learning
Content Area: Adult health—oncology
Reference: Ignatavicius, D., & Workman, M. (2006). *Medical-surgical nursing: Critical thinking for collaborative care* (5th ed., p. 497). Philadelphia: W.B. Saunders.

ALTERNATE ITEM FORMAT: MULTIPLE RESPONSE

Answer: 1, 2, 4, 6
Rationale: Cancer is a common cause of syndrome of inappropriate antidiuretic hormone (SIADH). In SIADH, excessive amounts of water are reabsorbed by the kidney and put into the systemic circulation. The increased water causes hyponatremia (decreased serum sodium levels) and some degree of fluid retention. The syndrome is managed by treating the condition and cause and usually includes fluid restriction, increased sodium intake, and medication with a mechanism of action that is antagonistic to antidiuretic hormone. Sodium levels are monitored closely because hypernatremia can develop suddenly as a result of treatment. The immediate institution of appropriate cancer therapy, usually radiation or chemotherapy, can cause tumor regression so that antidiuretic hormone synthesis and release processes return to normal.

Test-Taking Strategy: Focusing on the client's diagnosis and recalling that in SIADH excessive amounts of water are reabsorbed by the kidney and put into the systemic circulation will assist in answering this question. Review the treatment for SIADH if you had difficulty with this question.

Level of Cognitive Ability: Analysis
Client Needs: Physiological Integrity
Integrated Process: Nursing Process—analysis
Content Area: Adult health—oncology
Reference: Ignatavicius, D., & Workman, M. (2006). *Medical-surgical nursing: Critical thinking for collaborative care* (5th ed., pp. 501-502, 1469). Philadelphia: W.B. Saunders.

REFERENCES

Black, J., & Hawks, J. (2005). *Medical-surgical nursing: Clinical management for positive outcomes* (7th ed.). Philadelphia: W.B. Saunders.

Harkreader, H., & Hogan, M.A. (2004) *Fundamentals of nursing: Caring and clinical judgment* (2nd ed.). Philadelphia: W.B. Saunders.

Huether, S., & McCance, K. (2004). *Understanding pathophysiology* (3rd ed.). St. Louis: Mosby.

Ignatavicius, D., & Workman, M. (2006). *Medical-surgical nursing: Critical thinking for collaborative care* (5th ed.). Philadelphia: W.B. Saunders.

Kee, J., Hayes, E., & McCuistion, L. (2006). *Pharmacology: A nursing process approach* (5th ed.). Philadelphia: W.B. Saunders.

Lewis, S., Heitkemper, M., & Dirksen, S. (2004). *Medical-surgical nursing: Assessment and management of clinical problems* (6th ed.). St. Louis: Mosby.

Pagana, K., & Pagana, T. (2005). *Mosby's diagnostic and laboratory test reference* (7th ed.). St. Louis: Mosby.

Potter, P., & Perry, A. (2005). *Fundamentals of nursing* (6th ed.). St. Louis: Mosby.

Antineoplastic Medications

I. ANTINEOPLASTIC MEDICATIONS

A. Description

1. Antineoplastic medications kill or inhibit the reproduction of neoplastic cells.

2. Antineoplastic medications are used to cure, increase survival time, and decrease life-threatening complications.

3. The effect of antineoplastic medications may not be limited to neoplastic cells; normal cells also are affected by the medication.

4. Cell cycle phase-specific medications affect cells only during a certain phase of the reproductive cycle (Fig. 52-1).

5. Cell cycle phase-nonspecific medications affect cells in any phase of the reproductive cycle (see Fig. 52-1).

6. Usually, several medications are used in combination to increase the therapeutic response.

7. Antineoplastic medications may be combined with other treatments, such as surgery and radiation.

8. Although the intravenous (IV) route is most common for administration, antineoplastic medication may be given by the oral, intra-arterial, isolated limb perfusion, or intracavitary route; dosing is usually based on the client's body surface area and type of **cancer**.

9. Chemotherapy dosing is usually based on total body surface area (BSA), which requires a current, accurate height and weight for BSA calculation (before each medication administration) to ensure that the client receives optimal doses of chemotherapy medications.

10. Side effects result from the effects of the antineoplastic medication on normal cells.

B. Side effects

1. Mucositis

2. Alopecia

3. Anorexia, nausea, and vomiting

4. Diarrhea

5. Anemia

6. Low white blood cell count (neutropenia)

7. Thrombocytopenia

8. Infertility, sexual alterations

C. Interventions

1. Physiological integrity

a. Monitor complete blood count (CBC), white blood cell count, platelet count, and electrolytes.

b. Initiate bleeding precautions if thrombocytopenia occurs.

c. When the platelet count is less than 50,000 cells/mm^3, minor trauma can lead to episodes of prolonged bleeding; when less than 20,000 cells/mm^3, spontaneous and uncontrollable bleeding can occur.

d. Monitor for petechiae, ecchymosis, bleeding of the gums, and nosebleeds because the decreased platelet count can precipitate bleeding tendencies.

e. Avoid intramuscular injections and venipunctures as much as possible to prevent bleeding.

f. Initiate neutropenic precautions if the white blood cell count decreases.

g. Monitor for fever, sore throat, unusual bleeding, or signs and symptoms of infection.

h. Inform the client that loss of appetite also may be the result of taste changes or a bitter taste in the mouth from the medications.

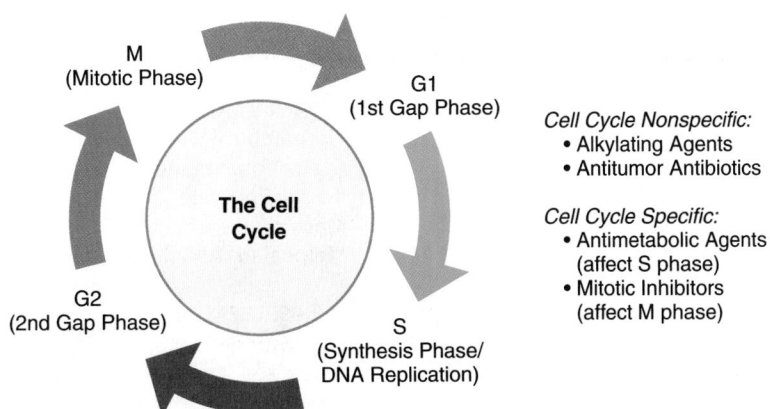

FIG. 52-1 The cell cycle. G1, The cell is preparing for division; *S* (synthesis phase, DNA replication), the cell doubles its DNA content through DNA synthesis; *G2*, the cell produces proteins to be used in cell division and in normal physiological function after cell division is complete; *M* (mitotic phase), the single cell splits apart into two cells.

i. Monitor for nausea and vomiting and provide a high-calorie diet with protein supplements.

j. Administer antiemetics several hours before chemotherapy and for 12 to 48 hours after as prescribed, because antineoplastic medications stimulate the vomiting center in the brain; delayed nausea and vomiting can continue as long as 7 days.

k. Encourage hydration; IV fluids will be administered before and during therapy.

l. Promote a fluid intake of at least 2000 mL/day to maintain adequate renal function.

m. Administer allopurinol (Zyloprim) as prescribed to lower the serum uric acid level that results from the rapid destruction of cells by the antineoplastic medication.

2. Safe and effective care environment
   a. Prepare IV chemotherapy in an air-vented space (biohazard cabinet area).
   b. Wear gloves, gown, eye protectors, and mask when handling IV medications.
   c. Nurses who are pregnant should consider avoiding chemotherapy preparation or the administration of chemotherapy.
   d. Discard IV equipment in designated (biohazard) containers.
   e. Administer antineoplastic medication precisely as prescribed to maximize antineoplastic effects while allowing normal cells to recover.
   f. Monitor for phlebitis with IV administration because these medications may irritate the veins.
   g. Monitor for extravasation (leakage of medication into surrounding skin and subcutaneous tissue, which causes tissue necrosis) and notify the physician if this occurs; heat or ice

is applied depending on the medication, and an antidote may be injected into the site.

3. Psychosocial integrity
   a. Instruct the client about the possibility of hair loss and that varying degrees of hair loss may occur after the first or second treatment.
   b. Discuss the purchase of a wig before treatment starts.
   c. Inform the client that new hair growth will occur several months after the final treatment.
   d. Instruct the client about the need for contraception because these medications have teratogenic effects.
   e. Discuss the potential effect of infertility, which may be irreversible.
   f. Encourage pretreatment counseling.

4. Health promotion and maintenance
   a. Instruct the client that if diarrhea is a problem, avoid hot foods and high-fiber foods, which increase peristalsis.
   b. Instruct the client to inspect the oral mucosa frequently for erythema and ulcers, rinse the mouth after meals, and carry out good oral hygiene.
   c. Instruct the client to use saline sodium bicarbonate mouth rinses for mouth sores if necessary.
   d. Instruct the client in the use of antifungal agents for mouth sores, if prescribed, for the development of a fungal infection.
   e. Instruct the client to avoid crowds and persons with infections and to report signs of infection such as a low-grade fever, chills, or sore throat.
   f. Instruct individuals with colds or infections to wear a mask when visiting or to avoid visiting the client.

g. Instruct the client to use a soft toothbrush and electric razor to minimize the risk of bleeding.

h. Instruct the client to avoid aspirin-containing products to minimize the risk of bleeding.

i. Instruct the client to consult the physician before receiving vaccinations (live vaccines should not be administered).

D. Anaphylactic reactions

1. Precautions
   a. Obtain an allergy history.
   b. Administer a test dose when prescribed by the physician.
   c. Stay with the client during the administration of medication.
   d. Monitor vital signs.
   e. Have emergency equipment and medications readily available.
   f. Provide an IV line for the administration of emergency medications if needed.

2. Signs of anaphylactic reaction
   a. Dyspnea
   b. Chest tightness or pain
   c. Pruritis or urticaria
   d. Tachycardia
   e. Dizziness
   f. Anxiety or agitation
   g. Flushed appearance
   h. Hypotension
   i. Decreased sensorium
   j. Cyanosis

3. Interventions for anaphylactic reaction
   a. Stop the medication.
   b. Maintain the airway.
   c. Notify the physician.
   d. Maintain the IV access with 0.9% normal saline.
   e. Place the client in a supine position with the legs elevated if not contraindicated.
   f. Monitor vital signs.
   g. Administer prescribed emergency medications.

II. ALKYLATING MEDICATIONS (Box 52-1)

A. Description
1. Breaks DNA helix, thereby interfering with DNA replication
2. Cell cycle phase-nonspecific medications

B. Side effects
1. Anorexia, nausea, and vomiting may occur.
2. Stomatitis may occur.
3. Rash may occur.
4. Client may feel IV site pain during IV administration.
5. Busulfan (Myleran, Busulfex) may cause hyperuricemia.

BOX 52-1
Alkylating Medications

NITROGEN MUSTARDS
Chlorambucil (Leukeran)
Cyclophosphamide (Cytoxan, Neosar)
Ifosfamide (Ifex)
Mechlorethamine (Mustargen)
Melphalan (Alkeran)

NITROSOUREAS
Carmustine (BiCNU, Gliadel)
Lomustine (CeeNu)
Streptozocin (Zanosar)

ALKYLATING-LIKE MEDICATIONS
Altretamine (Hexalen)
Busulfan (Myleran, Busulfex)
Carboplatin (Paraplatin)
Cisplatin (Platinol)
Dacarbazine (DTIC-Dome)
Oxaliplatin (Eloxatin)
Temozolomide (Temodar)
Thiotepa (Thioplex)

---

6. Chlorambucil (Leukeran) and mechlorethamine (Mustargen) may cause gonadal suppression and hyperuricemia.

7. Cisplatin may cause ototoxicity, tinnitus, hypokalemia, hypocalcemia, hypomagnesemia, and nephrotoxicity .

8. Cyclophosphamide (Cytoxan, Neosar) may cause alopecia, gonadal suppression, hemorrhagic cystitis, and hematuria.

C. Interventions
1. Assess vital signs and the temperature for signs of infection.
2. Monitor CBC, white blood cell and platelet counts, and uric acid and electrolyte levels.
3. Withhold medication if the platelet count is lower than 75,000/mm³ or the neutrophil count is lower than 2,000/mm³, and notify the physician (this may vary depending on alkylating agent and agency policy).
4. Assess results of pulmonary function tests.
5. Assess results of chest radiography and renal and liver function studies.
6. Hydrate the client with IV and/or oral fluids before administering the antineoplastic medication as prescribed.
7. Administer antiemetic 30 to 60 minutes before the antineoplastic medication as prescribed.
8. As prescribed, reduce IV site pain by altering IV rates or warming the injection site to distend vein and increase blood flow.
9. Monitor IV site for irritation and phlebitis, change site as needed.

10. When administering cisplatin assess the client for dizziness, tinnitus, hearing loss, incoordination, and numbness or tingling of extremities.
11. Monitor for signs of hemorrhagic cystitis, such as hematuria or dysuria, during cyclophosphamide or ifosfamide (Ifex) therapy, and encourage the client to drink increased fluids (2 to 3 L per day).
12. Mesna (Mesnex) may be administered with ifosfamide to reduce the potential of ifosfamide-induced cystitis.
13. Instruct the client that cyclophosphamide, when prescribed orally, is administered without food.
14. Instruct the client to follow a diet low in purines to alkalinize the urine and lower uric acid blood levels.
15. Instruct the client how to avoid infection.
16. Instruct the client to report signs of infection or bleeding.
17. Instruct the client about good oral hygiene and use of a soft toothbrush.

III. **ANTITUMOR ANTIBIOTIC MEDICATIONS** (Box 52-2)
A. Description
   1. Interfere with DNA and RNA synthesis
   2. Cell cycle phase-nonspecific medications
B. Side effects
   1. Nausea and vomiting
   2. Fever
   3. Bone marrow depression
   4. Rash
   5. Alopecia
   6. Stomatitis
   7. Gonadal suppression
   8. Hyperuricemia
   9. Vesication (blistering of tissue at IV site)
   10. Daunorubicin (DaunoXome) may cause congestive heart failure and dysrhythmias.
   11. Doxorubicin (Adriamycin, Doxil) and idarubicin may cause cardiotoxicity, cardiomyopathy, and electrocardiographic changes (Dexrazoxane [Zinecard] may be administered with doxorubicin to reduce cardiomyopathy).
   12. Pulmonary toxicity can occur with bleomycin (Blenoxane).
C. Interventions
   1. Assess vital signs and temperature for signs of infection.
   2. Monitor CBC, white blood cell and platelet counts, and uric acid, bleeding time, and electrolytes.
   3. Withhold medication if the platelets are lower than 75,000/mm³ or the neutrophil count is lower than 2,000/mm³, and notify physician (this may vary depending on alkylating agent and agency policy).

BOX 52-2
Antitumor Antibiotic Medications

Bleomycin sulfate (Blenoxane)
Dactinomycin (Cosmegen)
Daunorubicin (DaunoXome)
Doxorubicin (Adriamycin, Doxil)
Epirubicin (Ellence)
Idarubicin
Mitomycin (Mutamycin)
Mitoxantrone (Novantrone)

---

   4. Assess results of pulmonary function tests.
   5. Monitor for electrocardiographic changes.
   6. Assess lung sounds for crackles.
   7. Assess for signs of congestive heart failure, including dyspnea, crackles, peripheral edema, and weight gain.
   8. Assess results of chest radiography and renal and liver function studies.
   9. Hydrate the client with IV and/or oral fluids before the antineoplastic medication.
   10. Administer antiemetic 30 to 60 minutes before the antineoplastic medication.
   11. As prescribed, reduce IV site pain by altering IV rates or warming injection site to distend vein and increase blood flow.
   12. Monitor IV site for irritation, phlebitis, and vesication, change site as needed.
   13. Assess for myocardial toxicity, dyspnea, dysrhythmias, hypotension, and weight gain when administering doxorubicin (Adriamycin, Doxil) or idarubicin
   14. Monitor pulmonary status when administering bleomycin (Blenoxane).

IV. **ANTIMETABOLITE MEDICATIONS** (Box 52-3)
A. Description
   1. Antimetabolite medications halt the synthesis of cell protein; as "counterfeit" metabolites, their presence impairs cell division
   2. Antimetabolite medications are cell cycle phase-specific and affect the S phase.
B. Side effects
   1. Anorexia, nausea, and vomiting
   2. Diarrhea
   3. Alopecia
   4. Stomatitis
   5. Depression of bone marrow
   6. Cytarabine (DepoCyt, Tarabine PFS) may cause alopecia, stomatitis, hyperuricemia, and hepatotoxicity.
   7. Fluorouracil (Adrucil) may cause alopecia, stomatitis, diarrhea, phototoxicity reactions, and cerebellar dysfunction.

BOX 52-3
Antimetabolite Medications

Capecitabine (Xeloda)
Cladribine (Leustatin)
Cytarabine (DepoCyt, Tarabine PFS)
Floxuridine (FUDR)
Fludarabine (Fludara)
Fluorouracil (Adrucil)
Gemcitabine (Gemzar)
Hydroxyurea (Hydrea, Mylocel)
Mercaptopurine (Purinethol)
Methotrexate (Rheumatrex, Trexall)
Pentostatin (Nipent)
Thioguanine (Tabloid)

---

8. Mercaptopurine (Purinethol) may cause hyperuricemia and hepatotoxicity.
9. Methotrexate may cause alopecia, stomatitis, hyperuricemia, photosensitivity, hepatotoxicity, and hematological, gastrointestinal, and skin toxicity.

C. Interventions
1. Monitor vital signs and temperature for signs of infection.
2. Assess CBC, white blood cell count, uric acid, and platelet count.
3. Hold medication if the neutrophil count is lower than 2000 cells/mm³ or the platelet count is lower than 75,000 cells/mm³, and notify the physician (this may vary depending on alkylating agent and agency policy).
4. Monitor renal function studies.
5. Monitor for cerebellar dysfunction.
6. Assess for photosensitivity.
7. Administer antiemetics 30 to 60 minutes before the antineoplastic medication as prescribed.
8. Monitor IV site for extravasation.
9. Encourage fluid intake of 2 to 3 L/day.
10. Encourage good oral hygiene.
11. Instruct the client how to avoid infections and bleeding.
12. When administering fluorouracil, assess for signs of cerebellar dysfunction, such as dizziness, weakness, and ataxia, and assess for stomatitis and diarrhea, which may necessitate medication discontinuation.
13. When administering methotrexate in large doses, prepare to administer leucovorin (folinic acid or citrovorum factor) as prescribed to prevent toxicity (known as leucovorin rescue).
14. When administering fluorouracil or methotrexate, instruct the client to use sunscreen and wear protective clothing to prevent photosensitivity reactions.

BOX 52-4
Miotic Inhibitors

VINCA ALKALOIDS
Vinblastine sulfate (Velban)
Vincristine sulfate (Oncovin, Vincasar PFS)
Vinorelbine (Navelbine)

TAXANES
Docetaxel (Taxotere)
Paclitaxel (Abraxane, Taxol, Onxol)

V. ANTIMITOTIC MEDICATIONS (VINCA ALKALOIDS) (Box 52-4)
A. Description
1. Mitotic inhibitors prevent mitosis, causing cell death; mitotic inhibitors prevent cell division.
2. Mitotic inhibitors are cell cycle phase-specific and act on the M phase.
B. Side effects
1. Leukopenia
2. Neurotoxicity with vincristine (Oncovin, Vincasar PFS) manifested as numbness and tingling in the fingers and toes, constipation, paralytic ileus.
3. Ptosis
4. Hoarseness
5. Motor instability
6. Anorexia, nausea, and vomiting
7. Peripheral neuropathy
8. Alopecia
9. Stomatitis
10. Hyperuricemia
11. Phlebitis at IV site
C. Interventions
1. Monitor vital signs.
2. Monitor white blood cell count, CBC, uric acid, and platelet count.
3. Monitor for hoarseness.
4. Assess eyes for ptosis.
5. Assess motor stability and initiate safety precautions as necessary.
6. Monitor for neurotoxicity with vincristine sulfate manifested as numbness and tingling in the fingers and toes.
7. Monitor for constipation and paralytic ileus.

VI. TOPOISOMERASE INHIBITORS (Box 52-5)
A. Description
1. Block the enzyme needed for DNA synthesis and cell division
2. Cell cycle phase-specific; act on the G2 and S phases
B. Side effects
1. Leukopenia, thrombocytopenia, anemia
2. Anorexia, nausea, and vomiting

Etoposide (VePesid, Toposar, Etopophos)
Irinotecan (Camptosar)
Teniposide (Vumon)
Topotecan (Hycamtin)

3. Diarrhea
4. Alopecia
5. Orthostatic hypotension
6. Hypersensitivity reaction
C. Interventions
1. Monitor vital signs.
2. Monitor white blood cell count, CBC, and platelet count.

VII. HORMONAL MEDICATIONS AND ENZYMES
(Box 52-6)
A. Description
1. Suppress the immune system and block normal hormones in hormone-sensitive tumors
2. Change the hormonal balance and slow the growth rates of certain tumors
B. Side effects
1. Anorexia, nausea, and vomiting
2. Leukopenia
3. Impaired pancreatic function with asparaginase (Elspar)
4. Sex characteristic alterations
   a. Masculinizing effect in women: Chest and facial hair, menses stops (androgens, antiestrogen receptor drugs)
   b. Feminine manifestations in men: Gynecomastia (estrogens, progestins, antiestrogen receptors)
5. Breast swelling
6. Hot flashes
7. Weight gain
8. Hemorrhagic cystitis, hypouricemia, and hypercholesterolemia, with mitotane (Lysodren)
9. Hypertension
10. Thromboembolic disorders
11. Edema
12. Electrolyte imbalances
13. Tamoxifen citrate (Nolvadex) may cause edema, hypercalcemia, and elevated cholesterol and triglyceride levels.
14. Tamoxifen citrate decreases the effects of estrogen.
15. Diethylstilbestrol may cause impotence and gynecomastia in men.
16. Diethylstilbestrol may alter effects of insulin, orally administered anticoagulants, and orally administered hypoglycemic agents.

ESTROGENS
Diethylstilbestrol
Estramustine (Emcyt)
Ethinyl estradiol (Estinyl)

ANTIESTROGENS
Anastrozole (Arimidex)
Exemestane (Aromasin)
Fulvestrant (Faslodex)
Letrozole (Femara)
Raloxifene (Evista)
Tamoxifen citrate (Nolvadex)
Testolactone (Teslac)
Toremifene (Fareston)

ANDROGENS
Fluoxymesterone
Testosterone

ANTIANDROGENS
Bicalutamide (Casodex)
Flutamide (Eulexin)
Goserelin acetate (Zoladex)
Nilutamide (Nilandron)
Triptorelin (Trelstar)

PROGESTINS
Medroxyprogesterone (Depo-Provera)
Megestrol acetate (Megace)

OTHER HORMONAL ANTAGONISTS AND ENZYMES
Aminoglutethimide (Cytadren)
Asparaginase (Elspar)
Leuprolide acetate (Lupron)
Mitotane (Lysodren)

C. Interventions
1. Monitor vital signs.
2. Assess medications that the client is taking currently.
3. Monitor serum calcium levels with androgens.
4. Monitor for signs of alterations in sexual characteristics.
5. Monitor pancreatic function with asparaginase
6. Encourage an oral intake of 2 to 3 L of fluids per day.
7. Monitor uric acid and cholesterol levels.
8. Monitor for signs of hemorrhagic cystitis.

VIII. IMMUNOMODULATOR AGENTS: BIOLOGICAL RESPONSE MODIFIERS (Box 52-7)
A. Description
1. Immunomodulators stimulate the immune system to recognize **cancer** cells and take action to eliminate or destroy them.

BOX 52-7
Immunomodulator Agents

Aldesleukin (Proleukin, interleukin-2)
Interferon alfa-2a
Interferon alfa-2b
Interferon alfa-n3 (Alferon N)
Levamisole (Ergamisole)
Recombinant interferon alfa-2a (Intron A)
Recombinant interferon alfa-2b (Roferon-A)

COMMON MONOCLONAL ANTIBODIES
Alemtuzumab (Campath)
Gemtuzumab ozogamicin (Mylotarg)
Ibritumomab (Zevalin)
Rituximab (Rituxan)
Trastuzumab (Herceptin)

BOX 52-8
Colony-Stimulating Factors

GRANULOCYTE-MACROPHAGE COLONY-STIMULATING FACTOR
Sargramostim (Leukine)

GRANULOCYTE COLONY-STIMULATING FACTOR
Filgrastim (Neupogen)

ERYTHROPOIETIN
Epoetin alfa (Epogen)
Darbepoetin alfa (Aranesp)

BOX 52-9
Other Antineoplastic Medications

Asparaginase (Elspar)
Arsenic trioxide (Trisenox)
Bexarotene (Targretin)
Bortezomib (Velcade)
Imatinib (Gleevec)
Procarbazine (Natulan)
Temozolomide (Temodar)

---

2. Interleukins help different immune system cells recognize and destroy abnormal body cells.
3. Interferons slow down tumor cell division, stimulate proliferation, and cause **cancer** cells to differentiate into nonproliferative forms.

B. Colony-stimulating factors induce more rapid bone marrow recovery after suppression by chemotherapy (Box 52-8).

IX. GENE THERAPY

A. Gene therapy is experimental but early response rates indicate a potential for this therapy.

B. Gene therapy is used to render tumor cells more susceptible to damage by other treatments and make the client's immune system better able to recognize **cancer** cells as non-self.

X. TARGETED THERAPY

A. Description
 1. Medications used as targeted therapies are monoclonal antibodies that target a cellular element of the **cancer** cell or antisense medications that work at the gene level.
 2. Some examples of monoclonal antibodies are rituximab (Rituxan), tositumomab (Bexxar), trastuzumab (Herceptin), alemtuzumab (Campath), and cetuximab (Erbitux).

B. Side effects: Allergic reactions (monoclonal antibodies)

XI. OTHER ANTINEOPLASTIC MEDICATIONS
 (Box 52-9)

A. Altretamine (Hexalen): Cytotoxic agent used to treat ovarian **cancer**

B. Denileukin diftitox (Ontak): Recombinant DNA-derived medication used to treat cutaneous T-cell **lymphoma**

C. Gemcitabine (Gemzar): FDA-approved to treat non–small cell lung **cancer** and adenocarcinoma

of the pancreas and metastatic breast **cancer,** and lung **cancer** (in combination with paclitaxel [Abraxane, Taxol, Onxol]).

D. Irinotecan (Camptosar): Used to treat colorectal or rectal **cancer**

E. Paclitaxel (Abraxane, Taxol, Onxol): Used to treat ovarian or metastatic breast **cancer**

F. Pegaspargase (Oncaspar): Used in combination chemotherapies for acute lymphoblastic leukemia in clients unable to take asparaginase (Elspar)

G. Topotecan (Hycamtin): Indicated for the treatment of relapsed or refractory metastatic ovarian **cancer** after other therapies have failed

H. Trastuzumab (Herceptin): Used in combination chemotherapy to treat breast **cancer**

I. Bexarotene (Targretin): Use to treat advanced stage cutaneous T-cell **lymphoma**

PRACTICE QUESTIONS

1. The nurse is monitoring the laboratory results of a client receiving an antineoplastic medication by the intravenous route. The nurse plans to initiate bleeding precautions if which laboratory result is noted?
 1. A clotting time of 10 minutes
 2. An ammonia level of 20 mcg/dL
 3. A platelet count of 50,000/mm^3
 4. A white blood cell count of 5,000/mm^3

2. The nurse is analyzing the laboratory results of a client with leukemia who has received a regimen of chemotherapy. Which of the following laboratory values would the nurse specifically note as a result

of the massive cell destruction that occurred from the chemotherapy?
1. Anemia
2. Decreased platelets
3. Increased uric acid level
4. Decreased leukocyte count

3. The nurse is providing medication instructions to a client with breast cancer who is receiving cyclophosphamide (Cytoxan, Neosar). The nurse tells the client to:
   1. Take the medication with food.
   2. Increase fluid intake to 2000 to 3000 mL daily.
   3. Decrease sodium intake while taking the medication.
   4. Increase potassium intake while taking the medication.

4. The client with non–Hodgkin's lymphoma is receiving daunorubicin (DaunoXome). Which of the following would indicate to the nurse that the client is experiencing a toxic effect related to the medication?
   1. Fever
   2. Diarrhea
   3. Complaints of nausea and vomiting
   4. Crackles on auscultation of the lungs

5. Chemotherapy dosage is frequently based on total body surface area (BSA), so it is important for the nurse to do which of the following before administering chemotherapy?
   1. Measure abdominal girth.
   2. Calculate body mass index.
   3. Ask the client about his or her height and weight.
   4. Weigh and measure the client on the day of drug administration.

6. The client with squamous cell carcinoma of the larynx is receiving bleomycin (Blenoxane) intravenously. The nurse caring for the client anticipates that which diagnostic study will be prescribed?
   1. Echocardiography
   2. Electrocardiography
   3. Cervical radiographphy
   4. Pulmonary function studies

7. Each chemotherapeutic agent has a specific nadir. The nurse administering a combination chemotherapy regimen understands the importance of:
   1. Giving two agents from the same medication class
   2. Giving two agents with like nadirs at the same time
   3. Testing the client's knowledge about each agent's nadir
   4. Avoid giving agents with the same nadirs and toxicities at the same time

8. The clinic nurse prepares a teaching plan for the client receiving an antineoplastic medication. When implementing the plan, the nurse tells the client:
   1. To take aspirin (acetylsalicylic acid) as needed for headache

   2. Drink beverages containing alcohol in moderate amounts each evening
   3. Consult with health care providers before receiving immunizations
   4. That it is not necessary to consult health care providers before receiving a flu vaccine at the local health fair

9. The client with bladder cancer is receiving cisplatin (Platinol) and vincristine (Oncovin, Vincasar PFS). The nurse preparing to give the medication understands that the purpose of administering both these medications is to:
   1. Prevent alopecia
   2. Decrease the destruction of cells
   3. Increase the therapeutic response
   4. Prevent gastrointestinal side effects

10. The client with lung cancer is receiving a high dose of methotrexate (Rheumatrex, Trexall). Leucovorin (citrovorum factor, folic acid) is also prescribed. The nurse caring for the client understands that the purpose of administering the leucovorin is to:
    1. Preserve normal cells.
    2. Promote DNA synthesis.
    3. Promote medication excretion.
    4. Promote the synthesis of nucleic acids.

11. The client with ovarian cancer is being treated with vincristine (Oncovin, Vincasar PFS). The nurse monitors the client, knowing that which of the following indicates a side effect specific to this medication?
    1. Diarrhea
    2. Hair loss
    3. Chest pain
    4. Numbness and tingling in the fingers and toes

12. The nurse is reviewing the history and physical examination of a client who will be receiving asparaginase (Elspar), an antineoplastic agent. The nurse contacts the physician before administering the medication if which of the following is documented in the client's history?
    1. Pancreatitis
    2. Diabetes mellitus
    3. Myocardial infarction
    4. Chronic obstructive pulmonary disease

13. Tamoxifen (Nolvadex) is prescribed for the client with metastatic breast carcinoma. The nurse administering the medication understands that the primary action of this medication is to:
    1. Increase DNA and RNA synthesis.
    2. Promote the biosynthesis of nucleic acids.
    3. Increase estrogen concentration and estrogen response.
    4. Compete with estradiol for binding to estrogen in tissues containing high concentrations of receptors.

14. The client with metastatic breast cancer is receiving tamoxifen (Nolvadex). The nurse specifically moni-

tors which laboratory value while the client is taking this medication?
1. Glucose level
2. Calcium level
3. Potassium level
4. Prothrombin time

15. Megestrol acetate (Megace), an antineoplastic medication, is prescribed for the client with metastatic endometrial carcinoma. The nurse reviews the client's history and contacts the physician if which of the following is documented in the client's history?
1. Gout
2. Asthma
3. Thrombophlebitis
4. Myocardial infarction

16. A female client with carcinoma of the breast is admitted to the hospital for treatment with intravenously administered doxorubicin (Adriamycin). The client tells the nurse that she has been told by her friends that she is going to lose all her hair. The appropriate nursing response is which of the following?
1. "Your friends are correct."
2. "You will not lose your hair."
3. "Hair loss may occur, but it will grow back just as it is now."
4. "Hair loss may occur, and it will grow back, but it may have a different color or texture."

17. The clinic nurse prepares instructions for a client who developed stomatitis following the administration of a course of antineoplastic medications. The nurse tells the client to:
1. Rinse the mouth with baking soda or saline.
2. Avoid foods and fluids for the next 24 hours.
3. Swab the mouth daily with lemon and glycerin pads.
4. Brush the teeth and use waxed dental floss three times a day.

18. The client with acute myelocytic leukemia is being treated with busulfan (Myleran, Busulfex). Which of the following laboratory values would the nurse specifically monitor during treatment with this medication?

1. Clotting time
2. Blood glucose level
3. Uric acid level
4. Potassium level

19. The client with small cell lung cancer is being treated with etoposide (VePesid). The nurse monitors the client during administration, knowing that which of the following indicates a side effect specific to this medication?
1. Alopecia
2. Chest pain
3. Pulmonary fibrosis
4. Orthostatic hypotension

20. The nurse is assigned to care for several male and female clients who take estrogen or progestins. The nurse knows that this group of clients is a increased risk for which complication of the medication?
1. Sepsis
2. Dehydration
3. Deep vein thrombosis
4. Electrocardiographic changes

ALTERNATE ITEM FORMAT: MULTIPLE RESPONSE

The nurse is monitoring the intravenous infusion of an antineoplastic medication. During the infusion, the client complains of pain at the insertion site. On inspection of the site, the nurse notes redness and swelling and that the infusion of the medication has slowed in rate. Select all the following actions taken by the nurse that apply.
❏ 1. Stop the infusion.
❏ 2. Notify the physician.
❏ 3. Prepare to apply ice or heat to the site.
❏ 4. Restart the IV at a distal part of the same vein.
❏ 5. Prepare to administer a prescribed antidote into the site.
❏ 6. Increase the flow rate of the solution to flush the skin and subcutaneous tissue.

ANSWERS

1. **3**

Rationale: Bleeding precautions need to be initiated when the platelet count decreases. The normal platelet count is 150,000 to 450,000/mm³. When the platelets are lower than 50,000 / mm³, any small trauma can lead to episodes of prolonged bleeding. The normal white blood cell count is 5,000 to 10,000/mm³. When the white blood cell count drops, neutropenic precautions need to be implemented. The normal clot-

ting time is 8 to 15 minutes. The normal ammonia value is 15 to 45 mcg/dL.
Test-Taking Strategy: Use the process of elimination and knowledge regarding normal laboratory values. Options 1, 2, and 4 identify normal laboratory values. Remember, correlate a low platelet count with the need for bleeding precautions and a low white blood cell count with the need for neutropenic precaution. Review the indications to implement bleeding precau-

tions in a client receiving chemotherapy if you had difficulty with this question.
Level of Cognitive Ability: Analysis
Client Needs: Physiological Integrity
Integrated Process: Nursing Process—planning
Content Area: Pharmacology
Reference: Kee, J., Hayes, E., & McCuistion, L. (2006). *Pharmacology: A nursing process approach* (5th ed., pp. 535, 537). Philadelphia: W.B. Saunders.

2. 3
Rationale: Hyperuricemia is especially common following treatment for leukemias and lymphomas because chemotherapy results in massive cell kill. Although options 1, 2, and 4 also may be noted, an increased uric acid level is related specifically to cell destruction.
Test-Taking Strategy: Note the strategic words *massive cell destruction* in the question. Recalling the cell response to destruction will assist in directing you to option 3. Review this concept if you had difficulty with this question.
Level of Cognitive Ability: Analysis
Client Needs: Physiological Integrity
Integrated Process: Nursing Process—assessment
Content Area: Pharmacology
References: Huether, S., & McCance, K. (2004). *Understanding pathophysiology* (3rd ed., pp. 90, 556). St. Louis: Mosby.
Lehne, R. (2007). *Pharmacology for nursing care* (6th ed., p. 1153). Philadelphia: W.B. Saunders.

3. 2
Rationale: Hemorrhagic cystitis is a toxic effect that can occur with the use of cyclophosphamide (Cytoxan, Neosar). The client needs to be instructed to drink copious amounts of fluid during the administration of this medication. Clients also should monitor urine output for hematuria. The medication should be taken on an empty stomach, unless gastrointestinal upset occurs. Hyperkalemia can result from the use of the medication; therefore, the client would not be told to increase potassium intake. The client would not be instructed to alter sodium intake.
Test-Taking Strategy: Use the process of elimination. Recalling that cyclophosphamide can cause hemorrhagic cystitis will direct you easily to option 2. If you had difficulty with this question, review the toxic effects associated with this medication.
Level of Cognitive Ability: Application
Client Needs: Health Promotion and Maintenance
Integrated Process: Teaching and Learning
Content Area: Pharmacology
Reference: Hodgson, B., & Kizior, R. (2007). *Saunders nursing drug handbook 2007* (p. 300). Philadelphia: W.B. Saunders.

4. 4
Rationale: Cardiotoxicity noted by abnormal electrocardiographic findings or cardiomyopathy manifested as congestive heart failure is a toxic effect of daunorubicin. Bone marrow depression is also a toxic effect. Nausea and vomiting is a frequent side effect associated with the medication that begins a few hours after administration and lasts 24 to 48 hours. Fever is a frequent side effect and diarrhea can occur occasionally. Options 1, 2, and 3, however, are not toxic effects.

Test-Taking Strategy: Use the process of elimination, keeping in mind that the question is asking about a toxic effect. Use of the ABCs—airway, breathing, and circulation—will direct you easily to option 4. If you had difficulty with this question, review the toxic effects associated with daunorubicin.
Level of Cognitive Ability: Analysis
Client Needs: Physiological Integrity
Integrated Process: Nursing Process—analysis
Content Area: Pharmacology
Reference: Mosby (2007). *2007 Mosby's nursing drug reference* (20th ed., p. 331). St. Louis: Mosby.

5. 4
Rationale: To ensure that the client receives optimal doses of chemotherapy, dosing is usually based on the total body surface area (BSA), which requires a current accurate height and weight for BSA calculation (before each medication administration). Asking the client about his or her height and weight may lead to inaccuracies in determining a true BSA and dosage. Calculating body mass index and measuring abdominal girth will not provide the data needed.
Test-Taking Strategy: Use the process of elimination, recalling the basis for dosing chemotherapy. Recalling that a current accurate height and weight need to be obtained for BSA calculation and chemotherapy dosing will direct you to option 4. Eliminate option 3 because it is an unreliable way of obtaining the information, and options 1 and 2 do not relate to chemotherapy dosing. If you are unfamiliar with BSA and chemotherapy dosing, review these concepts.
Level of Cognitive Ability: Analysis
Client Needs: Physiological Integrity
Integrated Process: Nursing Process—implementation
Content Area: Pharmacology
References: Ignatavicius, D., & Workman, M. (2006). *Medical-surgical nursing: Critical thinking for collaborative care* (5th ed., pp. 491, 493). Philadelphia: W.B. Saunders.
Kee, J., Hayes, E., & McCuistion, L. (2006). *Pharmacology: A nursing process approach* (5th ed., pp. 536-537). Philadelphia: W.B. W.B. Saunders.

6. 4
Rationale: Bleomycin (Blenoxane) is an antineoplastic medication that can cause interstitial pneumonitis, which can progress to pulmonary fibrosis. Pulmonary function studies along with hematological, hepatic, and renal function tests need to be monitored. The nurse needs to monitor lung sounds for dyspnea and crackles, which indicate pulmonary toxicity. The medication needs to be discontinued immediately if pulmonary toxicity occurs. Options 1, 2, and 3 are unrelated to the specific use of this medication.
Test-Taking Strategy: Use the process of elimination. Eliminate options 1 and 2 first because they are cardiac-related and are therefore comparative or alike. From the remaining options, use the ABCs—airway, breathing, and circulation—to direct you to option 4. If you had difficulty with this question, review the toxic effects of this medication.
Level of Cognitive Ability: Analysis
Client Needs: Physiological Integrity
Integrated Process: Nursing Process—analysis
Content Area: Pharmacology

Reference: Gahart, B., & Nazareno, A. (2006). *2006 intravenous medications* (22nd ed., p. 185). St. Louis: Mosby.

7. 4

Rationale: Chemotherapy agents are usually given in combinations (also called regimens or protocols). The goal of administering combination chemotherapy in cycles or specific sequences is to produce additive or synergistic therapeutic effects. Administering combination therapy by administering several medications with different mechanisms of action and differents onsets of nadirs and toxicities enhances tumor cell destruction while minimizing medication resistance and overlapping toxicities.

Test-Taking Strategy: Use the process of elimination. Eliminate options 1 and 2 first because they are comparative or alike. From this point, knowledge regarding combination chemotherapy is required to answer the question. Review the purpose of chemotherapy combinations if you had difficulty with this question.

Level of Cognitive Ability: Comprehension
Client Needs: Physiological Integrity
Integrated Process: Nursing Process—implementation
Content Area: Pharmacology
Reference: Lehne, R. (2007). *Pharmacology for nursing care* (6th ed., pp. 958-959). Philadelphia: W.B. Saunders.

8. 3

Rationale: Because antineoplastic medications lower the resistance of the body, clients must be informed not to receive immunizations without a physician's or health care provider's approval. Clients also need to avoid contact with individuals who have recently received a live virus vaccine. Clients need to avoid aspirin and aspirin-containing products to minimize the risk of bleeding, and they need to avoid alcohol to minimize the risk of toxicity and side effects.

Test-Taking Strategy: Use the process of elimination. Recalling that antineoplastic medications lower the resistance of the body will direct you to option 3. Review the client teaching points regarding these medications if you had difficulty with this question.

Level of Cognitive Ability: Application
Client Needs: Health Promotion and Maintenance
Integrated Process: Teaching and Learning
Content Area: Pharmacology
Reference: Lilley, L., Harrington, S., & Snyder, J. (2005). *Pharmacology and the nursing process* (4th ed., p. 805). St. Louis: Mosby.

9. 3

Rationale: Cisplatin (Platinol) is an alkylating type of medication and vincristine (Oncovin, Vincasar PFS) is a vinca (plant) alkaloid. Alkylating medications are cell cycle phase-nonspecific. Vinca alkaloids are cell cycle phase-specific and act on the M phase. Combinations of medications are used to enhance tumoricidal effects and increase the therapeutic response.

Test-Taking Strategy: Use the process of elimination. Option 2 easily can be eliminated first. Eliminate options 1 and 4 next. It may be possible, with some specific interventions, to reduce gastrointestinal effects and alopecia, but these occur-

rences are unlikely be prevented. Review the purpose of combination medication therapy if you had difficulty with this question.

Level of Cognitive Ability: Analysis
Client Needs: Physiological Integrity
Integrated Process: Nursing Process—planning
Content Area: Pharmacology
Reference: Hodgson, B., & Kizior, R. (2007). *Saunders nursing drug handbook 2007* (pp. 255, 1208). Philadelphia: W.B. Saunders.

10. 1

Rationale: High concentrations of methotrexate harm and damage normal cells. To save normal cells, leucovorin is given, which is known as leucovorin rescue. Leucovorin bypasses the metabolic block caused by methotrexate, thereby permitting normal cells to synthesize. Note that leucovorin rescue is potentially hazardous. Failure to administer leucovorin in the right dose at the right time can be fatal.

Test-Taking Strategy: Use the process of elimination. Eliminate options 2 and 4 first because they are comparative or alike. Nucleic acids include RNA and DNA. Eliminate option 3 because increased fluids and diuretics normally are administered to promote medication excretion. This leaves option 1 as the correct answer. If you had difficulty with this question, review the purpose of leucovorin rescue.

Level of Cognitive Ability: Analysis
Client Needs: Physiological Integrity
Integrated Process: Nursing Process—analysis
Content Area: Pharmacology
References: Hodgson, B., & Kizior, R. (2007). *Saunders nursing drug handbook 2007* (p. 677). Philadelphia: W.B. Saunders.
Lehne, R. (2007). *Pharmacology for nursing care* (6th ed., p. 633). Philadelphia: W.B. Saunders.

11. 4

Rationale: A side effect specific to vincristine is peripheral neuropathy, which occurs in almost every client. Peripheral neuropathy can be manifested as numbness and tingling in the fingers and toes. Depression of the Achilles tendon reflex may be the first clinical sign indicating peripheral neuropathy. Constipation rather than diarrhea is most likely to occur with this medication, although diarrhea may occur occasionally. Hair loss occurs with nearly all the antineoplastic medications. Chest pain is unrelated to this medication.

Test-Taking Strategy: Use the process of elimination. Eliminate options 1 and 2 first because these side effects are associated with many of the antineoplastic agents. Note that the question asks for the side effect "specific" to this medication. Correlate peripheral neuropathy with vincristine. Review the side effects of this medication if you had difficulty with this question.

Level of Cognitive Ability: Analysis
Client Needs: Physiological Integrity
Integrated Process: Nursing Process—assessment
Content Area: Pharmacology
References: Gahart, B., & Nazareno, A. (2006). *2006 intravenous medications* (22nd ed., p. 1238). St. Louis: Mosby.
Hodgson, B., & Kizior, R. (2007). *Saunders nursing drug handbook 2007* (p. 1209). Philadelphia: W.B. Saunders.

12. 1
Rationale: Asparaginase (Elspar) is contraindicated if hypersensitivity exists, in pancreatitis, or if the client has a history of pancreatitis. The medication impairs pancreatic function and pancreatic function tests should be performed before therapy begins and when a week or more has elapsed between administration of the doses. The client needs to be monitored for signs of pancreatitis, which include nausea, vomiting, and abdominal pain. The conditions noted in options 2, 3, and 4 are not contraindicated with this medication.
Test-Taking Strategy: Use the process of elimination. Recalling that this medication affects pancreatic function will direct you to option 1. Review this medication if you had difficulty answering this question.
Level of Cognitive Ability: Analysis
Client Needs: Physiological Integrity
Integrated Process: Nursing Process—assessment
Content Area: Pharmacology
Reference: Hodgson, B., & Kizior, R. (2007). *Saunders nursing drug handbook 2007* (p. 93). Philadelphia: W.B. Saunders.

13. 4
Rationale: Tamoxifen (Nolvadex) is an antineoplastic medication that competes with estradiol for binding to estrogen in tissues containing high concentrations of receptors. Tamoxifen is used to treat metastatic breast carcinoma in women and men. Tamoxifen is also effective in delaying the recurrence of cancer following mastectomy. Tamoxifen reduces DNA synthesis and estrogen response.
Test-Taking Strategy: Use the process of elimination. Eliminate options 1 and 2 first because they are comparative or alike. Nucleic acids include DNA and RNA. From this point, select option 4, because it is unlikely that treatment of metastatic breast carcinoma would focus on increasing estrogen concentration and estrogen response. If you had difficulty with this question, review the action of this medication.
Level of Cognitive Ability: Analysis
Client Needs: Physiological Integrity
Integrated Process: Nursing Process—implementation
Content Area: Pharmacology
Reference: Hodgson, B., & Kizior, R. (2007). *Saunders nursing drug handbook 2007* (p. 1095). Philadelphia: W.B. Saunders.

14. 2
Rationale: Tamoxifen (Nolvadex) may increase calcium, cholesterol, and triglyceride levels. Before the initiation of therapy, a complete blood count, platelet count, and serum calcium levels should be assessed. These blood levels, along with cholesterol and triglyceride levels, should be monitored periodically during therapy. The nurse should assess for hypercalcemia while the client is taking this medication. Signs of hypercalcemia include increased urine volume, excessive thirst, nausea, vomiting, constipation, hypotonicity of muscles, deep bone, and flank pain.
Test-Taking Strategy: Use the process of elimination. Recalling that this medication causes hypercalcemia will direct you to option 2. Review this medication if you had difficulty answering this question.
Level of Cognitive Ability: Analysis
Client Needs: Physiological Integrity

Integrated Process: Nursing Process—assessment
Content Area: Pharmacology
Reference: Hodgson, B., & Kizior, R. (2007). *Saunders nursing drug handbook 2007* (p. 1096). Philadelphia: W.B. Saunders.

15. 3
Rationale: Megestrol acetate (Megace) suppresses the release of luteinizing hormone from the anterior pituitary by inhibiting pituitary function and regressing tumor size. Megestrol is used with caution if the client has a history of thrombophlebitis. Options 1, 2, and 4 are not contraindications for this medication.
Test-Taking Strategy: Use the process of elimination. Recalling that megestrol acetate is a hormonal antagonist enzyme and that a side effect is thrombotic disorders will direct you to option 3. Review this medication if you had difficulty answering this question.
Level of Cognitive Ability: Analysis
Client Needs: Physiological Integrity
Integrated Process: Nursing Process—implementation
Content Area: Pharmacology
Reference: Hodgson, B., & Kizior, R. (2007). *Saunders nursing drug handbook 2007* (pp. 727-728). Philadelphia: W.B. Saunders.

16. 4
Rationale: Alopecia (hair loss) can occur following the administration of many antineoplastic medications. Alopecia is reversible, but new hair growth may have a different color and texture.
Test-Taking Strategy: Use the process of elimination. Eliminate option 1 because it is a nontherapeutic response. Next, eliminate options 2 and 3 because they are incorrect. Review content related to hair loss and antineoplastic medications if you had difficulty with this question.
Level of Cognitive Ability: Application
Client Needs: Psychosocial Integrity
Integrated Process: Caring
Content Area: Pharmacology
Reference: Lehne, R. (2007). *Pharmacology for nursing care* (6th ed., p. 1168). Philadelphia: W.B. Saunders.

17. 1
Rationale: Stomatitis (ulceration in the mouth) can result from the administration of antineoplastic medications. The client should be instructed to examine her or his mouth daily and to report any signs of ulceration. If stomatitis occurs, the client should be instructed to rinse the mouth with baking soda or saline. Food and fluid is important and should not be restricted. If chewing and swallowing are painful, the client may switch to a liquid diet that includes milk shakes and ice cream. Instruct the client to avoid spicy foods and foods with hard crusts or edges. The client should avoid toothbrushing and flossing when stomatitis is severe. Lemon and glycerin swabs may cause pain and further irritation.
Test-Taking Strategy: Knowing that stomatitis involves ulcerations in the mucous membrane of the mouth will assist you in the process of eliminating the incorrect options. Eliminate option 2 first because foods and fluids would not be restricted in a client who has received antineoplastic medication. Eliminate option 3 because lemon can be irritating to ulcer-

ated lesions. Eliminate option 4 because a toothbrush and floss also will irritate ulcerations and may cause bleeding. If you had difficulty with this question, review the client teaching points related to stomatitis.
Level of Cognitive Ability: Application
Client Needs: Physiological Integrity
Integrated Process: Teaching and Learning
Content Area: Pharmacology
Reference: Kee, J., Hayes, E., & McCuistion, L. (2006). *Pharmacology: A nursing process approach* (5th ed., p. 541). Philadelphia: W.B. Saunders.

18. **3**
Rationale: Busulfan (Myleran, Busufex) can cause an increase in the uric acid level. Hyperuricemia can produce uric acid nephropathy, renal stones, and acute renal failure. Options 1, 2, and 4 are not specifically related to this medication.
Test-Taking Strategy: Use the process of elimination. Recalling that busulfan increases the uric acid level will direct you to the correct option. If you had difficulty with this question, review the effects of busulfan.
Level of Cognitive Ability: Analysis
Client Needs: Physiological Integrity
Integrated Process: Nursing Process—assessment
Content Area: Pharmacology
Reference: Hodgson, B., & Kizior, R. (2007). *Saunders nursing drug handbook 2007* (p. 166). Philadelphia: W.B. Saunders.

19. **4**
Rationale: A side effect specific to etoposide is orthostatic hypotension. Etoposide should be administered slowly over 30 to 60 minutes to avoid hypotension. The client's blood pressure is monitored during the infusion. Hair loss occurs with nearly all the antineoplastic medications. Chest pain and pulmonary fibrosis are unrelated to this medication.
Test-Taking Strategy: Use the process of elimination. Eliminate option 1 first because this side effect is associated with many of the antineoplastic agents. Eliminate options 2 and 3 next because they are unrelated to etoposide. Note that the question asks for the side effect *specific* to this medication. Correlate hypotension with etoposide. Review the side effects of this medication if you had difficulty with this question.
Level of Cognitive Ability: Analysis
Client Needs: Physiological Integrity
Integrated Process: Nursing Process—assessment
Content Area: Pharmacology
Reference: Lehne, R. (2007). *Pharmacology for nursing care* (6th ed., p. 1170). Philadelphia: W.B. Saunders.

20. **3**
Rationale: Male and female clients who take estrogen or progestins are at increased risk for deep vein thrombosis (DVT). Women receiving estrogens or progestins have irregular but heavy menses, fluid retention, and breast tenderness. Options 1, 2, and 4 are not specifically associated with these type of medications.
Test-Taking Strategy: Use the process of elimination, recalling the side effects of the hormone treatments. Recalling that estrogen and progestins increase the risk of DVT will direct you to option 3. If you are unfamiliar with these medications, review their classifications and purposes for their use.
Level of Cognitive Ability: Analysis
Client Needs: Physiological Integrity
Integrated Process: Nursing Process—assessment
Content Area: Pharmacology
References: Ignatavicius, D., & Workman, M. (2006). *Medical-surgical nursing: Critical thinking for collaborative care* (5th ed., p. 498) Philadelphia: W.B. Saunders.
Lehne, R. (2007). *Pharmacology for nursing care* (6th ed., pp. 712-718). Philadelphia: W.B. Saunders.

ALTERNATE ITEM FORMAT:
MULTIPLE RESPONSE
Answer: **1, 2, 3, 5**
Rationale: Redness and swelling and a slowed infusion indicate signs of extravasation. If extravasation occurs during the intravenous administration of an antineoplastic medication, the infusion is stopped and the physician is notified. Ice or heat may be prescribed for application to the site and an antidote may be prescribed to be administered into the site. Increasing the flow rate can increase damage to the tissues. Restarting an IV in the same vein can increase damage to the site and vein.
Test-Taking Strategy: Focus on the assessment signs in the question. Visualize the situation to identify the nursing actions. Think about the actions that will cause further damage. This will assist in eliminating options 4 and 6. Review nursing actions if extravasation occurs if you had difficulty with this question.
Level of Cognitive Ability: Application
Client Needs: Physiological Integrity
Integrated Process: Nursing Process—implementation
Content Area: Pharmacology
Reference: Kee, J., Hayes, E., & McCuistion, L. (2006). *Pharmacology: A nursing process approach* (5th ed., p. 541). Philadelphia: W.B. Saunders.

REFERENCES

Gahart, B., & Nazareno, A. (2006). *Intravenous medications 2006* (22nd ed.). St. Louis: Mosby.

Hodgson, B., & Kizior, R. (2007). *Saunders nursing drug handbook 2007.* Philadelphia: W.B. Saunders.

Huether, S., & McCance, K. (2004). *Understanding pathophysiology* (3rd ed.). St. Louis: Mosby.

Ignatavicius, D., & Workman, M. (2006). *Medical-surgical nursing: Critical thinking for collaborative care* (5th ed.). Philadelphia: W.B. Saunders.

Kee, J., Hayes, E., & McCuistion, L. (2006). *Pharmacology: A nursing process approach* (5th ed.). Philadelphia: W.B. Saunders

Lehne, R. (2007). *Pharmacology for nursing care* (6th ed.). Philadelphia: W.B. Saunders.

Lilley, L., Harrington, S., & Snyder, J. (2005). *Pharmacology and the nursing process* (4th ed.). St. Louis: Mosby.

Mosby. (2007). *Mosby's 2007 nursing drug reference* (20th ed.). St. Louis: Mosby.

Skidmore-Roth, L. (2005). *Mosby's drug reference.* St. Louis: Mosby.

The Adult Client With an Endocrine Disorder

PYRAMID TERMS

addisonian crisis A life-threatening disorder caused by adrenal hormone insufficiency. Crisis is precipitated by infection, trauma, stress, or surgery. Death can occur from shock, vascular collapse, or hyperkalemia.

Addison's disease Hyposecretion of adrenal cortex hormones (glucocorticoids and mineralocorticoids) from the adrenal gland, resulting in deficiency of the corticosteroid hormones. The condition is fatal if left untreated.

adrenalectomy The surgical removal of an adrenal gland. Lifelong replacement of glucocorticoids and mineralocorticoids is necessary with a bilateral adrenalectomy. Temporary replacement may be necessary for up to 2 years for a unilateral adrenalectomy.

Chvostek's sign A spasm of the facial muscles elicited by tapping the facial nerve just anterior to the ear. The sign is noted in hypocalcemia.

Cushing's disease A metabolic disorder characterized by abnormally increased secretion (endogenous) of cortisol, caused by increased amounts of adrenocorticotropic hormone (ACTH) secreted by the pituitary gland.

Cushing's syndrome A metabolic disorder resulting from the chronic and excessive production of cortisol by the adrenal cortex or by the administration of glucocorticoids in large doses for several weeks or longer (exogenous or iatrogenic).

dawn phenomenon A nocturnal release of growth hormone, which may cause blood glucose level elevations before breakfast in the client with diabetes mellitus. Treatment includes administering an evening dose of intermediate-acting insulin at 10 PM.

diabetes insipidus The hyposecretion of antidiuretic hormone from the posterior pituitary gland, resulting in failure of tubular reabsorption of water in the kidneys and diuresis.

diabetic ketoacidosis A life-threatening complication of diabetes mellitus that develops when a severe insulin deficiency occurs. Hyperglycemia progresses to ketoacidosis over a period of several hours to several days. Acidosis occurs in clients with type 1 diabetes mellitus, persons with undiagnosed diabetes, and persons who stop prescribed treatment for diabetes.

diabetes mellitus A chronic disorder of glucose intolerance and impaired carbohydrate, protein, and lipid metabolism caused by a deficiency of insulin or resistance to the action of insulin. A deficiency of effective insulin results in hyperglycemia.

hypercortisolism A condition resulting from the hypersecretion of glucocorticoids from the adrenal cortex.

hyperglycemia Elevated blood glucose level.

hyperglycemic hyperosmolar nonketotic syndrome Extreme hyperglycemia without acidosis. A complication of type 2 diabetes mellitus, which may result in dehydration or vascular collapse but does not include the acidosis component of diabetic ketoacidosis. Onset is usually slow, taking from hours to days.

hyperthyroidism A condition that occurs as a result of excessive thyroid hormone secretion.

hypoglycemia Low blood glucose level (lower than 60 mg/dL) that results from too much insulin, not enough food, or excess activity.

hypophysectomy The removal of the pituitary gland.

hypothyroidism A hypothyroid state resulting from a hyposecretion of thyroid hormone. The condition occurs in adulthood.

myxedema The most severe form of hypothyroidism characterized by swelling of the hands, face, feet, and periorbital tissues. At this stage, the disease may lead to coma and death.

myxedema coma A rare but serious disorder that results from persistently low thyroid production. Coma can be precipitated by acute illness, rapid withdrawal of thyroid medication, anesthesia and surgery, hypothermia, and the use of sedatives and opioid analgesics.

Somogyi phenomenon A rebound phenomenon that occurs in clients with type 1 diabetes mellitus. Normal or elevated blood glucose levels are present at bedtime; hypoglycemia occurs at about 2 to 3 AM. Counterregulatory hormones, produced to prevent further hypoglycemia, result in hyperglycemia (evident in the prebreakfast blood glucose level). Treatment includes decreasing the evening (predinner or bedtime) dose of intermediate-acting insulin or increasing the bedtime snack.

thyroidectomy Surgical removal of the thyroid gland to treat persistent hyperthyroidism or thyroid tumors.

thyroid storm An acute, potentially fatal exacerbation of hyperthyroidism that may result from manipulation of the thyroid gland during surgery, severe infection, or stress.

Trousseau's sign A sign of hypocalcemia. Carpal spasm can be elicited by compressing the brachial artery with a blood pressure cuff for 3 minutes.

▲ PYRAMID TO SUCCESS

The endocrine system is made up of organs or glands that secrete hormones and release them directly into the circulation. The endocrine system can be understood easily if you remember that basically one of two situations can occur—hypersecretion or hyposecretion of hormones from the organ or gland. When an excess of the hormone occurs, treatment is aimed at blocking the hormone release through medication or surgery. When a deficit of the hormone exists, treatment is aimed at replacement therapy. Pyramid Points focus on diabetes mellitus, including the prevention and treatment of complications, insulin therapy, hypoglycemic and hyperglycemic reactions, and diabetic ketoacidosis; Addison's disease and addisonian crisis; Cushing's disease or Cushing's syndrome; thyroid disorders and thyroid storm; and care of the client after thyroidectomy or adrenalectomy. The Integrated Processes addressed in this unit include Caring, Communication and Documentation, Nursing Process, and Teaching/Learning.

▲ CLIENT NEEDS

Safe and Effective Care Environment

Acting as a client advocate
Collaborating with multidisciplinary team regarding treatment
Consulting with appropriate care providers
Delegating care activities to others
Establishing priorities of care
Handling hazardous and infectious materials
Informed consent for treatments and procedures
Maintaining confidentiality related to the disorder
Preventing accidents and client injury
Using medical and surgical asepsis to prevent infection

Health Promotion and Maintenance

Discussing expected body image changes
Identifying lifestyle choices related to treatment
Performing physical assessment of the endocrine system
Preventing disease
Providing health screening
Teaching about self-care measures

Psychosocial Integrity

Discussing grief and loss issues related to complications of the disorder
Discussing situational role changes related to the disorder

Discussing unexpected body image changes
Identifying coping mechanisms
Monitoring for sensory and perceptual alterations as a result of the disorder
Using support systems

Physiological Integrity

Administering medications safely
Monitoring for alterations in body systems as a result of the disorder
Monitoring for expected outcomes and effects of pharmacological therapy
Monitoring for fluid and electrolyte imbalances that can occur
Monitoring laboratory values
Monitoring for potential for complications of diagnostic tests, treatments, procedures
Monitoring for potential for complications from surgical procedures and health alterations
Monitoring for problems with elimination as a result of the disorder
Monitoring for unexpected response to therapies
Performing dosage calculation related to medication administration
Preparing the client for diagnostic tests
Providing nonpharmacological comfort interventions
Providing nutrition and oral hydration measures
Providing emergency care to the client

REFERENCES

Chernecky, C., & Berger, B. (2004). *Laboratory tests and diagnostic procedures* (4th ed.). Philadelphia: W.B. Saunders.

Cherry, B., & Jacob, S. (2005). *Contemporary nursing: Issues, trends, and management* (3rd ed.). St. Louis: Mosby.

Harkreader, H., & Hogan, M. (2004). *Fundamentals of nursing: caring and clinical judgment* (2nd ed.). Philadelphia: W.B. Saunders.

Ignatavicius, D., & Workman, M. (2006). *Medical-surgical nursing: Critical thinking for collaborative care* (5th ed.). Philadelphia: W.B. Saunders.

Jarvis, C. ((2004). *Physical examination and health assessment* (4th ed.). St. Louis: W.B. Saunders.

Lewis, S., Heitkemper, M., & Dirksen, S. (2004). *Medical-surgical nursing: Assessment and management of clinical problems* (6th ed.). St. Louis: Mosby.

Lilley, L., Harrington, S., & Snyder, J. (2005). *Pharmacology and the nursing process* (4th ed.). St. Louis: Mosby.

National Council of State Boards of Nursing (Eds.). (2007). *2007 NCLEX-RN® detailed test plan*. Chicago: Author.

Potter, P., & Perry, A. (2005) *Fundamentals of nursing* (6th ed.). St. Louis: Mosby.

Varcarolis, E., Carson, V., & Shoemaker, N. (2006). *Foundations of psychiatric mental health nursing: A clinical approach* (5th ed.). Philadelphia: W.B. Saunders.

Endocrine System

I. ANATOMY AND PHYSIOLOGY OF ENDOCRINE GLANDS (Box 53-1)

A. Functions
1. Maintenance and regulation of vital functions (Box 53-2)
2. Response to stress and injury
3. Growth and development
4. Energy metabolism
5. Reproduction
6. Fluid, electrolyte, and acid-base balance

B. Hypothalamus (Box 53-3)
1. Portion of the diencephalon of the brain, forming the floor and part of the lateral wall of the third ventricle
2. Activates, controls, and integrates the peripheral autonomic nervous system, endocrine processes, and many somatic functions, such as body temperature, sleep, and appetite

C. Pituitary gland (Box 53-4; Fig. 53-1)
1. The master gland; located at the base of the brain
2. Influenced by the hypothalamus; directly affects the function of the other endocrine glands
3. Promotes growth of body tissue, influences water absorption by the kidney, and controls sexual development and function

D. Adrenal gland
1. One adrenal gland is on top of each kidney.
2. Regulates sodium and electrolyte balance; affects carbohydrate, fat, and protein metabolism; influences the development of sexual characteristics; and sustains the fight-or-flight response
3. Adrenal cortex
   a. The cortex is the outer shell of the adrenal gland.
   b. The cortex synthesizes glucocorticoids and mineralocorticoids and secretes small

amounts of sex hormones (androgens, estrogens; Box 53-5).
4. Adrenal medulla
   a. The medulla is the inner core of the adrenal gland.
   b. The medulla works as part of the sympathetic nervous system and produces epinephrine and norepinephrine.

BOX 53-1
Endocrine Glands

Adrenal	Parathyroid
Hypothalamus	Pituitary
Ovaries	Testes
Pancreas	Thyroid

BOX 53-2
Risk Factors for Endocrine Disorders

Age
Heredity
Congenital factors
Trauma
Environmental factors
Consequence of other disorders

BOX 53-3
Hypothalamus Hormones

Corticotropin-releasing hormone (CRH)
Gonadotropin-releasing hormone (GnRH)
Growth hormone-inhibiting hormone (GHIH)
Growth hormone-releasing hormone (GHRH)
Melanocyte-inhibiting hormone (MIH)
Prolactin-inhibiting hormone (PIH)
Thyrotropin-releasing hormone (TRH)

E. Thyroid gland
1. Located in the anterior part of the neck
▲ 2. Controls the rate of body metabolism and growth and produces thyroxine (T_4), triiodothyronine (T_3), and thyrocalcitonin
F. Parathyroid glands
1. Located on the thyroid gland
▲ 2. Control calcium and phosphorus metabolism; produce parathyroid hormone
G. Pancreas
1. Located posteriorly to the stomach
▲ 2. Influences carbohydrate metabolism, indirectly influences fat and protein metabolism, and produces insulin and glucagon
H. Ovaries and testes
1. The ovaries are located in the pelvic cavity and produce estrogen and progesterone.
2. The testes are located in the scrotum, control the development of the secondary sex characteristics, and produce testosterone.
I. Negative feedback loop
1. Regulates hormone secretion by the hypothalamus and pituitary gland

2. Increased amounts of target gland hormones in the bloodstream decrease secretion of the same hormone and other hormones that stimulate its release.

BOX 53-4
Pituitary Gland Hormones

ANTERIOR LOBE PRODUCTION
Adrenocorticotropic hormone (ACTH)
Follicle-stimulating hormone (FSH)
Growth hormone (GH)
Luteinizing hormone (LH)
Melanocyte-stimulating hormone (MSH)
Prolactin (PRL)
Somatotrophic growth-stimulating hormone
Thyroid-stimulating hormone (TSH)

POSTERIOR LOBE
These hormones are produced by the hypothalamus, stored in the posterior lobe, and secreted into the blood when needed.
Oxytocin
Vasopressin, antidiuretic hormone (ADH)

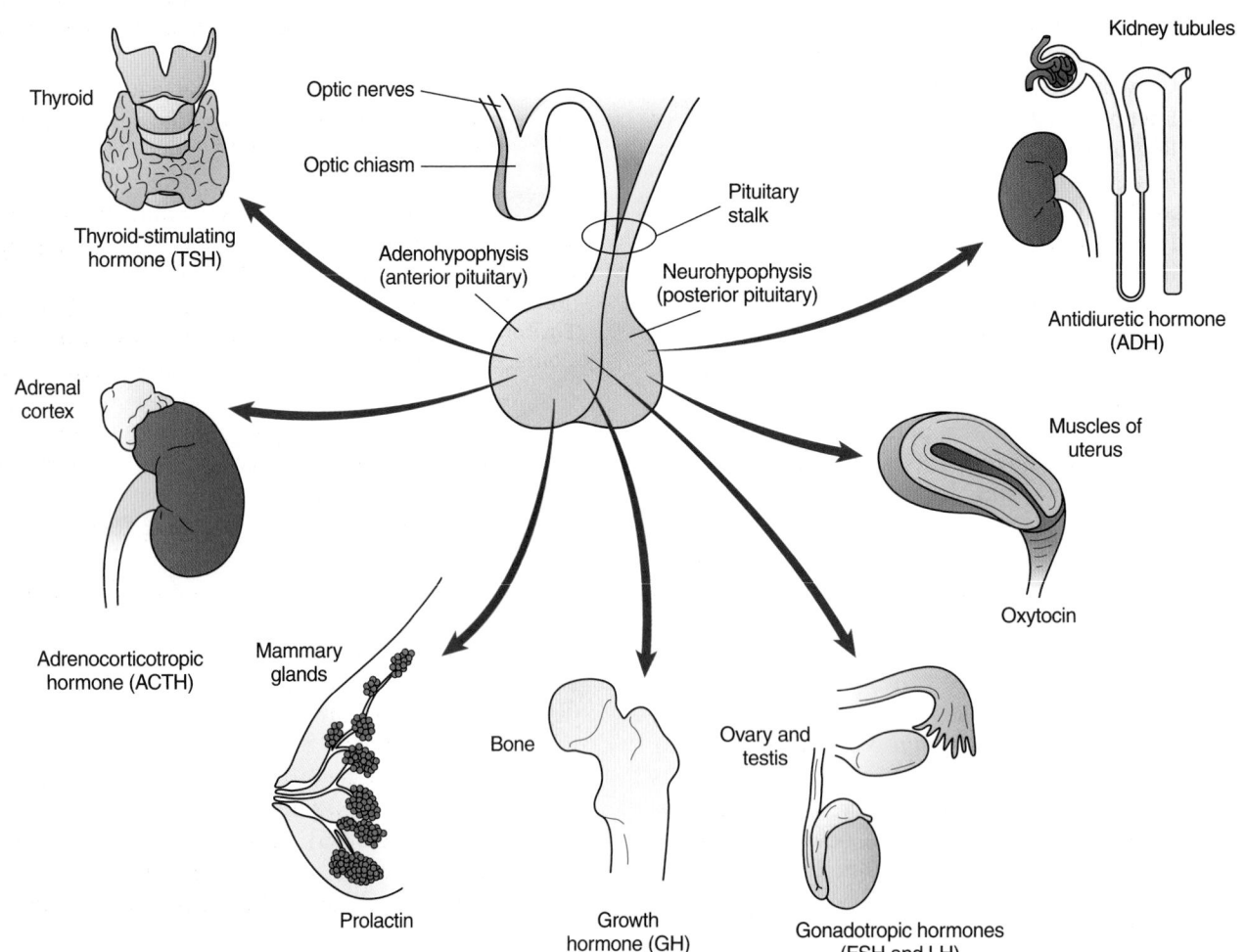

FIG. 53-1 Pituitary hormones. (From Lilley, L., Harrington, S., & Snyder, J. [2005]. *Pharmacology and the nursing process* [4th ed.]. St. Louis: Mosby.)

BOX 53-5
Adrenal Cortex

GLUCOCORTICOIDS: CORTISOL, CORTISONE, CORTICOSTERONE
Responsible for glucose metabolism, protein metabolism, fluid and electrolyte balance, suppression of the inflammatory response to injury, protective immune response to invasion by infectious agents, and resistance to stress
MINERALOCORTICOIDS: ALDOSTERONE
Regulation of electrolyte balance by promoting sodium retention and potassium excretion

II. DIAGNOSTIC TESTS
A. Stimulation and suppression tests
  1. Stimulation testing
    a. In the client with suspected underactivity of an endocrine gland, a stimulus may be provided to determine whether the gland is capable of normal hormone production.
    b. Measured amounts of selected hormones or substances are administered to stimulate the target gland to produce its hormone.
    c. Hormone levels produced by the target gland are measured.
    d. Failure of the hormone level to increase with stimulation indicates hypofunction.
  2. Suppression tests
    a. Suppression tests are used when hormone levels are high or in the upper range of normal.
    b. Agents that normally induce a suppressed response are administered to determine whether normal negative feedback is intact.
    c. Failure of hormone production to be suppressed during standardized testing indicates hyperfunction.
B. Radioactive iodine uptake
  1. This thyroid function test measures the absorption of the iodine isotope to determine how the thyroid gland is functioning.
  2. A small dose of radioactive iodine is given by mouth or intravenously; the amount of radioactivity is measured in 2 to 4 hours and again at 24 hours.
  3. Normal values are 3% to 10% at 2 to 4 hours, and 5% to 30% in 24 hours.
  4. Elevated values indicate **hyperthyroidism,** decreased iodine intake, or increased iodine excretion.
  5. Decreased values indicate a low T_4 level, the use of antithyroid medications, thyroiditis, **myxedema,** or **hypothyroidism.**
  6. The test is contraindicated in pregnancy.
C. T_3 and T_4 resin uptake test
  1. Blood tests are used to diagnose thyroid disorders.
  2. T_3 and T_4 regulate thyroid-stimulating hormone.

  3. Normal values (normal findings vary between laboratory settings)
    a. T_3: 80 to 230 ng/dL
    b. T_4: 5 to 12 mcg/dL
    c. Thyroxine, free (FT_4): 0.8 to 2.4 ng/dL
  4. The T_3 level is elevated in **hyperthyroidism,** decreases with the aging process, and may be decreased in **hypothyroidism.**
  5. The T_4 level is elevated in **hyperthyroidism** and decreased in **hypothyroidism.**
D. Thyroid-stimulating hormone
  1. Blood test is used to differentiate the diagnosis of primary **hypothyroidism**
  2. Normal value is 0.2 to 5.4 microunits/mL (normal findings vary among laboratories).
  3. Elevated values indicate primary **hypothyroidism.**
  4. Decreased values indicate **hyperthyroidism** or secondary **hypothyroidism.**
E. Thyroid scan
  1. A thyroid scan is performed to identify nodules or growths in the thyroid gland.
  2. A radioisotope of iodine or technetium is administered before scanning the thyroid gland.
  3. Reassure clients that the level of radioactive medication is not dangerous to themselves or others.
  4. Determine whether the client has received radiographic contrast agents within the past 3 months, because these may invalidate the scan.
  5. Check with the physician regarding discontinuing medications containing iodine for 14 days before the test and the need to discontinue thyroid medication before the test.
  6. Instruct the client to maintain an NPO status after midnight on the day before the test; if iodine is used, the client will fast for an additional 45 minutes after ingestion of the oral isotope and the scan will be performed in 24 hours.
  7. If technetium is used, it is administered by the intravenous (IV) route 30 minutes before the scan.
  8. The test is contraindicated in pregnancy.
F. Needle aspiration of thyroid tissue
  1. Aspiration of thyroid tissue is done for cytological examination.
  2. No client preparation is necessary.
  3. Light pressure is applied to the aspiration site after the procedure.
G. Glucose tolerance test
  1. The glucose tolerance test aids in the diagnosis of **diabetes mellitus.**
  2. A 2-hour postload glucose level (2 hours after injection or ingestion of glucose) higher than 200 mg/dL confirms the diagnosis of **diabetes mellitus.**
  3. Client preparation (Box 53-6)
  4. Many factors can alter the results and therefore it is not always a reliable test.

BOX 53-6

Client Preparation: Glucose Tolerance Test

Eat a diet with at least 150 g of carbohydrates for 3 days before the test.

Avoid alcohol, coffee, and smoking for 36 hours before testing.

Fast for 10 to 12 hours before the test.

Avoid strenuous exercise for 8 hours before and after the test.

Withhold morning insulin or oral hypoglycemic medication (client with diabetes mellitus).

A sample is drawn for determination of the fasting blood glucose level and then the client will be given a high-glucose drink.

Blood samples will be drawn at 30-minute intervals for a minimum of 2 hours.

H. Glycosylated hemoglobin
   1. Description
      a. Glycosylated hemoglobin is blood glucose bound to hemoglobin.
      b. Glycosylated hemoglobin A_{1c} (HbA_{1c}) indicates how well blood glucose levels have been controlled for the prior 3 to 4 months.
      c. **Hyperglycemia** in a client with **diabetes mellitus** is usually the cause of an increase in the HbA_{1c} value.
   2. Values
      a. Values are expressed as a percentage of the total hemoglobin.
      b. The goal for clients with **diabetes mellitus** is 7% or lower.
      c. For clients without **diabetes mellitus**, the normal range is 4% to 6%.
   3. Nursing consideration: Fasting is not required.
I. Glycosylated serum albumin (fructosamine)
   1. Reflects average serum glucose levels over a period of 2 to 3 weeks
   2. More sensitive to recent changes than the HbA_{1c} value
   3. Normal ranges vary according to method of testing used; nondiabetic client, 1.5 to 2.7 mmol/L; diabetic client, 2.0 to 5.0 mmol/L

III. **PITUITARY GLAND DISORDERS** (Box 53-7)
A. Hypopituitarism
   1. Description: Hyposecretion of one or more of the pituitary hormones caused by tumors, trauma, encephalitis, autoimmunity, or stroke.
   2. Hormones most often affected are growth hormone (GH) and gonadotropic hormones (luteinizing hormone, follicle-stimulating hormone), but thyroid-stimulating hormone (TSH), adrenocorticotropic hormone (ACTH), or antidiuretic hormone (ADH) may be involved.
   3. Assessment
      a. Mild to moderate obesity (GH, TSH)
      b. Reduced cardiac output (GH, ADH)

BOX 53-7

Pituitary Gland Disorders

ANTERIOR PITUITARY
Hyperpituitarism
Hypopituitarism

POSTERIOR PITUITARY
These disorders can be caused by damage to the posterior pituitary or hypothalamus.
Diabetes insipidus
Syndrome of inappropriate antidiuretic hormone (SIADH)

---

      c. Infertility, sexual dysfunction (gonadotropins, ACTH)
      d. Fatigue, low blood pressure (TSH, ADH, ACTH, GH)
      e. Tumors of the pituitary also may cause headaches and visual defects (pituitary is located near the optic nerve).
   4. Interventions
      a. Provide emotional support to client and family.
      b. Encourage client and family to express feelings related to disturbed body image or sexual dysfunction.
      c. Client may need hormone replacement for specific deficient hormones.
      d. Client education needed regarding signs and symptoms of hypofunction and hyperfunction related to insufficient or excess hormone replacement
B. Hyperpituitarism
   1. Description
      a. Hypersecretion of growth hormone by the anterior pituitary gland in an adult; caused primarily by pituitary tumors.
      b. Leads to conditions such as acromegaly and **Cushing's disease**
   2. Assessment
      a. Large hands and feet
      b. Thickening and protrusion of the jaw
      c. Arthritic changes
      d. Visual disturbances
      e. Diaphoresis
      f. Oily, rough skin
      g. Organomegaly
      h. Hypertension
      i. Dysphagia
      j. Deepening of the voice
   3. Interventions
      a. Provide emotional support to client and family, and encourage client and family to express feelings related to disturbed body image.
      b. Provide frequent skin care.
      c. Provide pharmacological and nonpharmacological interventions for joint pain.

d. Prepare the client for radiation of the pituitary gland if prescribed.

e. Prepare the client for **hypophysectomy** if planned.

C. **Hypophysectomy** (pituitary adenectomy, transsphenoidal pituitary surgery)

1. Description
   a. Removal of pituitary tumor via craniotomy or transsphenoidal (endoscopic transnasal) approach (latter approach is preferred because it is associated with fewer complications)
   b. Complications for craniotomy include increased intracranial pressure, bleeding, meningitis, and hypopituitarism.
   c. Complications for the transsphenoidal surgery include cerebrospinal fluid leak, infection, and hypopituitarism.

2. Postoperative interventions
   a. Initiate postoperative care similar to craniotomy care.
   b. Monitor vital signs, neurological status, and level of consciousness.
   c. Elevate the head of the bed.
   d. Monitor for increased intracranial pressure.
   e. Monitor for bleeding.
   f. Monitor for any postnasal drip or nasal drainage, which might indicate leakage of cerebrospinal fluid in the transsphenoidal approach (check the nasal drainage for glucose).
   g. Instruct the client to avoid sneezing, coughing, and blowing the nose.
   h. Monitor electrolyte values for temporary **diabetes insipidus** or syndrome of inappropriate diuretic hormone resulting from ADH disturbances.
   i. Monitor intake and output, and avoid water intoxication.
   j. Administer glucocorticoids and other hormone replacements as prescribed.
   k. Administer antibiotics, analgesics, and antipyretics as prescribed.
   l. Instruct the client in the administration of prescribed medications, which may include vasopressin (synthetic ADH), levothyroxine (Synthroid), gonadotropic hormones, growth hormone (somatotropin), and glucocorticoids if the entire gland has been removed.

D. **Diabetes insipidus**

1. Description
   a. Hyposecretion of ADH caused by strokes or trauma, or may be idiopathic
   b. Kidney tubules fail to reabsorb water.

2. Assessment
   a. Polyuria of 4 to 24 L/day
   b. Polydipsia
   c. Dehydration such as decreased skin turgor and dry mucous membranes
   d. Inability to concentrate urine
   e. Low urinary specific gravity, 1.006 or lower
   f. Fatigue
   g. Muscle pain and weakness
   h. Headache
   i. Postural hypotension that may progress to vascular collapse without rehydration
   j. Tachycardia

3. Interventions
   a. Monitor vital signs and neurological and cardiovascular status.
   b. Provide a safe environment, particularly for the client with postural hypotension.
   c. Monitor electrolyte values and for signs of dehydration.
   d. Maintain the intake of adequate fluids.
   e. Monitor intake and output, weight, serum osmolality, and specific gravity of urine.
   f. Instruct the client to avoid foods or liquids that produce diuresis.
   g. Chlorpropamide (Diabinese) may be prescribed for mild **diabetes insipidus.**
   h. Vasopressin tannate (Pitressin) or desmopressin acetate (DDAVP, Stimate) may be prescribed; these are used when the ADH deficiency is severe or chronic.
   i. Instruct the client in the administration of medications as prescribed; DDAVP may be administered by injection, intranasally, or orally.
   j. Instruct the client to wear a Medic-Alert bracelet.

E. Syndrome of inappropriate antidiuretic hormone (SIADH)

1. Description
   a. Excess ADH is released, but not in response to the body's need for it.
   b. Causes include trauma, stroke, malignancies (often in the lungs or pancreas), medications, and stress.
   c. The syndrome results in water intoxication and hyponatremia.

2. Assessment
   a. Signs of fluid volume overload
   b. Changes in level of consciousness and mental status changes
   c. Weight gain
   d. Hypertension
   e. Tachycardia
   f. Anorexia, nausea, and vomiting
   g. Hyponatremia

3. Interventions
   a. Monitor vital signs and cardiac and neurological status.
   b. Provide a safe environment, particularly for the client with changes in level of consciousness or mental status.
   c. Monitor intake and output and obtain weight daily.

d. Monitor fluid and electrolyte balance.
e. Monitor serum and urine osmolality
f. Restrict fluid intake as prescribed.
g. Administer diuretics and IV fluids (normal saline or hypertonic saline) as prescribed; monitor IV fluids carefully because of the risk for fluid volume overload (IV solutions containing water are contraindicated because of the risk of water intoxication)
h. Demeclocycline (Declomycin) may be prescribed (inhibits ADH-induced water reabsorption and produces water diuresis).

IV. ADRENAL GLAND DISORDERS (Box 53-8)
▲ A. **Addison's disease**
  1. Description
    a. Hyposecretion of adrenal cortex hormones (glucocorticoids and mineralocorticoids)
    b. Can be primary or secondary
    c. The condition is fatal if left untreated.
▲ 2. Assessment (Table 53-1)
  3. Interventions
    a. Monitor vital signs, particularly blood pressure, weight, and intake and output.
    b. Monitor blood glucose and potassium levels.
    c. Administer glucocorticoid or mineralocorticoid medications as prescribed.
▲ d. Observe for **addisonian crisis** caused by stress, infection, trauma, or surgery.
▲ 4. Client education
    a. Avoid individuals with an infection.
    b. Diet: High protein and high carbohydrate, normal sodium intake
    c. Avoid strenuous exercise and stressful situations.
    d. Need for lifelong glucocorticoid therapy
    e. Avoid over-the-counter medications.
▲ f. Wear a Medic-Alert bracelet.
    g. Signs and symptoms related to underreplacement and overreplacement of hormones
  B. **Addisonian crisis**
    1. Description (Box 53-9)
▲ 2. Assessment
    a. Severe headache
    b. Severe abdominal, leg, and lower back pain
    c. Generalized weakness
    d. Irritability and confusion
    e. Severe hypotension
    f. Shock
    3. Interventions
    a. Prepare to administer glucocorticoids intravenously as prescribed; hydrocortisone sodium succinate (Solu-Cortef) usually is prescribed initially.

BOX 53-8
Adrenal Gland Disorders

ADRENAL CORTEX
Addison's disease
Primary hyperaldosteronism (Conn's syndrome)
Cushing's disease
Cushing's syndrome

ADRENAL MEDULLA
Pheochromocytoma

TABLE 53-1

Assessment: Addison's Disease and Cushing's Disease (Cushing's Syndrome)

Addison's Disease	Cushing's Disease and Syndrome
Lethargy, fatigue, and muscle weakness	Generalized muscle wasting and weakness
Gastrointestinal disturbances	Moon face, buffalo hump
Weight loss	Truncal obesity with thin extremities, supraclavicular fat pads; weight gain
Menstrual changes in women; impotence in men	Hirsutism (masculine characteristics in female)
Hypoglycemia, hyponatremia	Hyperglycemia, hypernatremia
Hyperkalemia, hypercalcemia	Hypokalemia, hypocalcemia
Postural hypotension	Hypertension
Hyperpigmentation of skin (bronzed) with primary disease	Fragile skin that easily bruises
	Reddish-purple striae on the abdomen and upper thighs

BOX 53-9
Addisonian Crisis

A life-threatening disorder caused by acute adrenal insufficiency
Precipitated by stress, infection, trauma, surgery, or abrupt withdrawal of exogenous corticosteroid use
Can cause hyponatremia, hyperkalemia, hypoglycemia, and shock

---

b. Following resolution of the crisis, administer glucocorticoid and mineralocorticoid orally as prescribed.
c. Monitor vital signs, particularly blood pressure.
d. Monitor neurological status, noting irritability and confusion.
e. Monitor intake and output.
f. Monitor laboratory values, particularly the sodium, potassium, and blood glucose levels.

g. Administer IV fluids as prescribed to restore electrolyte balance.

h. Protect the client from infection.

i. Maintain bed rest and provide a quiet environment.

C. **Cushing's disease** and **Cushing's syndrome (hypercortisolism)**

1. Description

a. Characterized by a hypersecretion of glucocorticoids from the adrenal cortex

b. **Cushing's disease** is a metabolic disorder characterized by abnormally increased secretion (endogenous) of cortisol, caused by increased amounts of ACTH secreted by the pituitary gland.

c. **Cushing's syndrome** is a metabolic disorder resulting from the chronic and excessive production of cortisol by the adrenal cortex or by the administration of glucocorticoids in large doses for several weeks or longer (exogenous or iatrogenic).

2. Assessment (Fig. 53-2; see Table 53-1)

3. Interventions

a. Monitor vital signs, particularly blood pressure.

b. Monitor intake and output and weight

c. Monitory laboratory values, particularly the white blood cell count, and serum glucose, sodium, potassium, and calcium levels.

d. Provide meticulous skin care.

e. Allow the client to discuss feelings related to body appearance.

f. Administer chemotherapeutic agents as prescribed for inoperable adrenal tumors.

g. Prepare the client for radiation as prescribed if the condition results from a pituitary adenoma.

h. Prepare the client for removal of pituitary tumor (**hypophysectomy**, transsphenoidal adenectomy) if the condition results from increased pituitary secretion of ACTH.

i. Prepare the client for **adrenalectomy** if the condition results from an adrenal adenoma; glucocorticoid replacement may be required following **adrenalectomy**.

D. Primary hyperaldosteronism (Conn's syndrome)

1. Description

a. Hypersecretion of mineralocorticoids (aldosterone) from the adrenal cortex of the adrenal gland

b. Most commonly caused by an adenoma

2. Assessment

a. Symptoms related to hypokalemia, hypernatremia, and hypertension

b. Headache, fatigue, muscle weakness, nocturia

c. Polydipsia and polyuria

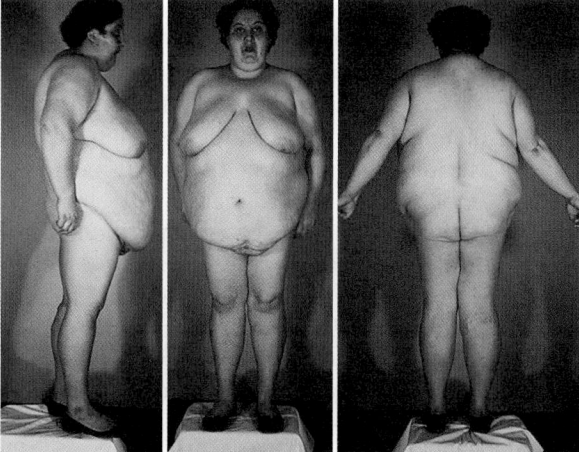

FIG. 53-2 Typical appearance of a client with Cushing's syndrome. Note truncal obesity, moon face, buffalo hump, thinner arms and legs, and abdominal striae. (From Ignatavicius, D., & Workman, M. [2006]. *Medical-surgical nursing: Critical thinking for collaborative care* [5th ed.]. Philadelphia: W.B. Saunders.)

d. Paresthesias

e. Visual changes

f. Low urine specific gravity and increased urinary aldosterone level

g. Elevated serum aldosterone levels

h. Metabolic alkalosis

3. Interventions

a. Monitor vital signs, particularly blood pressure.

b. Monitor for signs of hypokalemia and hypernatremia.

c. Monitor intake and output and urine for specific gravity.

d. Spironolactone (Aldactone) may be prescribed to promote fluid balance and control hypertension; this is a potassium-sparing diuretic and aldosterone antagonist, and clients need to be monitored for hyperkalemia, particularly those with impaired renal function or excessive potassium intake.

e. Administer potassium supplements as prescribed.

f. Prepare the client for **adrenalectomy.**

g. Maintain sodium restriction, if prescribed, preoperatively.

h. Administer glucocorticoids preoperatively, as prescribed, to prevent adrenal hypofunction.

i. Monitor the client for adrenal insufficiency postoperatively.

j. Instruct the client regarding the need for glucocorticoid therapy following **adrenalectomy.**

k. Instruct the client about the need to wear a Medic-Alert bracelet.

▲ E. Pheochromocytoma
  1. Description
     a. Catecholamine-producing tumor usually found in the adrenal medulla, but extra-adrenal locations include the chest, bladder, abdomen, and brain; typically a benign tumor but can be malignant
     b. Excessive amounts of epinephrine and norepinephrine are secreted.
     c. Diagnostic tests include a 24-hour urine collection for vanillylmandelic acid (VMA), a product of catecholamine metabolism, metanephrine, and catecholamines, all of which are elevated in the presence of pheochromocytoma; the normal range of urinary catecholamines is up to 14 mcg/100 mL of urine, with higher levels occurring in pheochromocytoma.
     d. Surgical removal of the adrenal gland is the primary treatment.
     e. Symptomatic treatment is initiated if surgical removal is not possible.
     f. The complications associated with pheochromocytoma include hypertensive crisis, including hypertensive retinopathy and nephropathy, cardiac enlargement, and dysrhythmias, congestive heart failure, myocardial infarction, increased platelet aggregation, and stroke.
     g. Death can occur from shock, stroke, renal failure, dysrhythmias, or dissecting aortic aneurysm.
  ▲ 2. Assessment
     a. Paroxysmal or sustained hypertension
     b. Severe headaches
     c. Palpitations
     d. Flushing and profuse diaphoresis
     e. Pain in the chest or abdomen with nausea and vomiting
     f. Heat intolerance
     g. Weight loss
     h. Tremors
     i. **Hyperglycemia**
  ▲ 3. Interventions
     a. Monitor vital signs, particularly the blood pressure and heart rate.
     b. Monitor for hypertensive crisis; monitor for complications that can occur with hypertensive crisis, such as stroke, cardiac dysrhythmias, myocardial infarction.
     c. Be alert to stimuli that can precipitate a hypertensive crisis, such as increased abdominal pressure, urination, and vigorous abdominal palpation (avoid these stimuli).
     d. Instruct the client not to smoke, drink caffeine-containing beverages, or change position suddenly.
     e. Prepare to administer a β-adrenergic blocking agent, such as phenoxybenzamine (Dibenzyline) as prescribed to control hypertension.
     f. Monitor serum glucose level.
     g. Promote rest and a nonstressful environment.
     h. Provide a diet high in calories, vitamins, and minerals.
     i. Prepare the client for **adrenalectomy.**
F. **Adrenalectomy** ▲
  1. Description (Box 53-10)
  2. Preoperative interventions
     a. Monitor electrolyte levels and correct electrolyte imbalances.
     b. Assess for dysrhythmias.
     c. Monitor for **hyperglycemia.**
     d. Protect the client from infections.
     e. Administer glucocorticoids as prescribed.
  3. Postoperative interventions
     a. Monitor vital signs.
     b. Monitor intake and output; if the urinary ▲ output is lower that 30 mL/hr, notify the physician, because this may indicate renal failure and impending shock.
     c. Monitor weight daily.
     d. Monitor electrolyte and serum glucose levels.
     e. Monitor for signs of shock and hemorrhage, ▲ particularly during the first 24 to 48 hours.
     f. Monitor for manifestations of adrenal insufficiency.
     g. Assess the dressing for drainage.
     h. Monitor for paralytic ileus, as manifested by abdominal distention and pain, nausea, vomiting, and diminished or absent bowel sounds (paralytic ileus can develop from internal bleeding, anesthesia effects, and bowel manipulation).
     i. Administer IV fluids as prescribed to maintain blood volume.
     j. Administer glucocorticoids and mineralocorticoids as prescribed. ▲
     k. Administer pain medication as prescribed.

BOX 53-10

Adrenalectomy

Surgical removal of an adrenal gland.
Lifelong glucocorticoid and mineralocorticoid replacement are necessary with bilateral adrenalectomy
Temporary glucocorticoid replacement, up to 2 years, is necessary after a unilateral adrenalectomy.
Catecholamine levels drop as a result of surgery, which can result in cardiovascular collapse, hypotension, and shock, and the client needs to be monitored closely.
Hemorrhage also can occur because of the high vascularity of the adrenal glands.

l. Provide pulmonary interventions to prevent atelectasis (cough and deep breathing, incentive spirometry, splinting of incision)

m. Instruct the client in the importance of hormone replacement therapy following surgery.

n. Instruct the client regarding signs and symptoms of underreplacement and overreplacement of hormones.

o. Instruct the client regarding the need to wear a Medic-Alert bracelet.

V. THYROID GLAND DISORDERS (Box 53-11)

A. **Hypothyroidism**

1. Description
   a. Hypothyroid state resulting from hyposecretion of thyroid hormones T_3 and T_4.
   b. Characterized by a decreased rate of body metabolism

2. Assessment
   a. Lethargy and fatigue
   b. Weakness, muscle aches, paresthesias
   c. Intolerance to cold
   d. Weight gain
   e. Dry skin and hair and loss of body hair
   f. Bradycardia
   g. Constipation
   h. Generalized puffiness and edema around the eyes and face (**myxedema**)
   i. Forgetfulness and loss of memory
   j. Menstrual disturbances
   k. Cardiac enlargement, tendency to develop congestive heart failure
   l. Goiter may or may not be present.

3. Interventions
   a. Monitor vital signs, including heart rate and rhythm.
   b. Administer thyroid replacement; levothyroxine sodium (Synthroid) is most commonly prescribed.
   c. Instruct the client about thyroid replacement therapy and about the clinical manifestations of both hypothyroidism and **hyperthyroidism** related to underreplacement or overreplacement of the hormone.
   d. Instruct the client in low-calorie, low-cholesterol, low–saturated fat diet.
   e. Assess the client for constipation; provide roughage and fluids to prevent constipation.
   f. Provide a warm environment for the client.
   g. Avoid sedatives and opioid analgesics be-

cause of increased sensitivity to these medications.

   h. Monitor for overdose of thyroid medications, characterized by tachycardia, chest pain, restlessness, nervousness, and insomnia.
   i. Instruct the client to report episodes of chest pain or other signs of overdose immediately.

B. **Myxedema coma**

1. Description (Box 53-12)

2. Assessment
   a. Hypotension
   b. Bradycardia
   c. Hypothermia
   d. Hyponatremia
   e. **Hypoglycemia**
   f. Generalized edema
   g. Respiratory failure
   h. Coma

3. Interventions
   a. Maintain a patent airway.
   b. Administer IV fluids (normal or hypertonic saline) as prescribed.
   c. Administer levothyroxine sodium intravenously as prescribed.
   d. Administer glucose intravenously as prescribed.
   e. Administer corticosteroids as prescribed.
   f. Assess client's temperature hourly.
   g. Monitor blood pressure frequently.
   h. Keep client warm.
   i. Monitor for changes in mental status.
   j. Monitor electrolyte and glucose levels.
   k. Institute aspiration precautions.

C. **Hyperthyroidism**

1. Description
   a. Hyperthyroid state resulting from hypersecretion of thyroid hormones (T_3 and T_4)
   b. Characterized by an increased rate of body metabolism
   c. A common cause is Graves' disease, also known as toxic diffuse goiter.
   d. Clinical manifestations are referred to as thyrotoxicosis.

2. Assessment for **hyperthyroidism** caused by Graves' disease
   a. Enlarged thyroid gland (goiter)

BOX 53-11

Thyroid Gland Disorders

Hyperthyroidism
Hypothyroidism

BOX 53-12

Myxedema Coma

This rare but serious disorder results from persistently low thyroid production.

Coma can be precipitated by acute illness, rapid withdrawal of thyroid medication, anesthesia and surgery, hypothermia, or the use of sedatives and opioid analgesics.

b. Palpitations, cardiac dysrhythmias, such as tachycardia or atrial fibrillation
c. Protruding eyeballs (exophthalmos) may be present (Fig. 53-3)
d. Hypertension
e. Heat intolerance
f. Diaphoresis
g. Weight loss
h. Diarrhea
i. Smooth, soft skin and hair
j. Nervousness and fine tremors of hands
k. Personality changes such as irritability, agitation and mood swings

3. Interventions
a. Provide adequate rest.
b. Administer sedatives as prescribed.
c. Provide a cool and quiet environment.
d. Obtain weight daily.
e. Provide a high-calorie diet.
f. Avoid the administration of stimulants.
g. Administer antithyroid medications (propylthiouracil, PTU) that block thyroid synthesis as prescribed.
h. Administer iodine preparations that inhibit the release of thyroid hormone as prescribed.
i. Administer propranolol (Inderal) for tachycardia as prescribed.
j. Prepare the client for radioactive iodine therapy, as prescribed, to destroy thyroid cells.
k. Prepare the client for **thyroidectomy** if prescribed.

D. **Thyroid storm**
1. Description (Box 53-13)
2. Assessment
a. Elevated temperature (fever)
b. Tachycardia

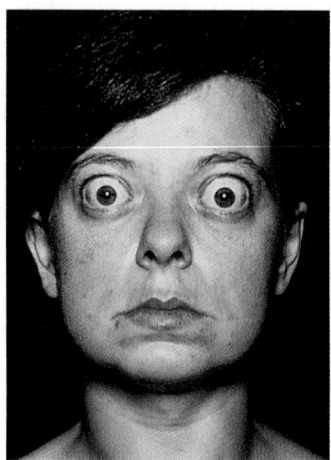

FIG. 53-3 Exophthalmos. (From Ignatavicius, D., & Workman, M. [2006]. *Medical-surgical nursing: Critical thinking for collaborative care* [5th ed.]. Philadelphia: W.B. Saunders.)

c. Systolic hypertension
d. Nausea, vomiting, and diarrhea
e. Agitation, tremors, anxiety
f. Irritability, agitation, restlessness, confusion, and seizures as the condition progresses
g. Delirium and coma
3. Interventions
a. Maintain a patent airway and adequate ventilation.
b. Administer antithyroid medications, sodium iodide solution, propranolol, and glucocorticoids as prescribed.
c. Monitor vital signs.
d. Monitor continually for cardiac dysrhythmias.
e. Administer nonsalicylate antipyretics as prescribed (salicylates increase free thyroid hormone levels).
f. Use a cooling blanket to decrease temperature as prescribed.

E. **Thyroidectomy**
1. Description
a. Removal of the thyroid gland
b. Performed when persistent **hyperthyroidism** exists
2. Preoperative interventions
a. Obtain vital signs and weight.
b. Assess electrolyte levels.
c. Assess for **hyperglycemia.**
d. Instruct the client in how to perform coughing and deep-breathing exercises and how to support the neck in the postoperative period when coughing and moving.
e. Administer antithyroid medications, sodium iodide solution, propranolol, and glucocorticoids as prescribed to prevent the occurrence of **thyroid storm.**
3. Postoperative interventions
a. Monitor for respiratory distress.
b. Have a tracheotomy set, oxygen, and suction at the bedside.
c. Maintain client in a semi-Fowler's position.
d. Monitor surgical site for edema and for signs of bleeding; check dressing anteriorly and at the back of the neck.

BOX 53-13

Thyroid Storm

This acute and life-threatening condition occurs in a client with uncontrollable hyperthyroidism.
It can be caused by manipulation of the thyroid gland during surgery and the release of thyroid hormone into the bloodstream; it also can occur from severe infection and stress.
Antithyroid medications, β-blockers, glucocorticoids, and iodides are administered to the client before thyroid surgery to prevent its occurrence.

e. Limit client talking, and assess level of hoarseness.

f. Monitor for laryngeal nerve damage, as evidenced by respiratory obstruction, dysphonia, high-pitched voice, stridor, dysphagia, and restlessness.

g. Monitor for signs of hypocalcemia and tetany, which can be caused by trauma to the parathyroid gland (Box 53-14).

h. Prepare to administer calcium gluconate as prescribed for tetany.

i. Monitor for **thyroid storm.**

VI. PARATHYROID GLAND DISORDERS (Box 53-15)

A. Hypoparathyroidism

1. Description
   a. Condition caused by hyposecretion of parathyroid hormone by the parathyroid gland
   b. Can occur following **thyroidectomy** because of removal of parathyroid tissue

2. Assessment
   a. Hypocalcemia and hyperphosphatemia
   b. Numbness and tingling in the face
   c. Muscle cramps and cramps in the abdomen or in the extremities
   d. Positive **Trousseau's sign** or **Chvostek's sign**
   e. Signs of overt tetany, such as bronchospasm, laryngospasm, carpopedal spasm, dysphagia, photophobia, cardiac dysrhythmias, seizures
   f. Hypotension
   g. Anxiety, irritability, depression

3. Interventions
   a. Monitor vital signs.
   b. Monitor for signs of hypocalcemia and tetany.
   c. Initiate seizure precautions.
   d. Place a tracheotomy set, oxygen, and suctioning at the bedside.
   e. Prepare to administer calcium gluconate intravenously for hypocalcemia.
   f. Provide a high-calcium, low-phosphorus diet.
   g. Instruct the client in the administration of calcium supplements as prescribed.

h. Instruct the client in the administration of vitamin D supplements as prescribed; vitamin D enhances the absorption of calcium from the gastrointestinal tract.

i. Instruct the client in the administration of phosphate binders as prescribed to promote the excretion of phosphate through the gastrointestinal tract.

j. Instruct the client to wear a Medic-Alert bracelet.

B. Hyperparathyroidism

1. Description: Condition caused by hypersecretion of parathyroid hormone by the parathyroid gland

2. Assessment
   a. Hypercalcemia and hypophosphatemia
   b. Fatigue and muscle weakness
   c. Skeletal pain and tenderness
   d. Bone deformities that result in pathological fractures
   e. Anorexia, nausea, vomiting, epigastric pain
   f. Weight loss
   g. Constipation
   h. Hypertension
   i. Cardiac dysrhythmias
   j. Renal stones

3. Interventions
   a. Monitor vital signs, particularly the blood pressure.
   b. Monitor for cardiac dysrhythmias.
   c. Monitor intake and output and for signs of renal stones.
   d. Monitor for skeletal pain; move client slowly and carefully.
   e. Encourage fluid intake.
   f. Administer furosemide (Lasix) as prescribed to lower calcium levels.
   g. Administer normal saline intravenously as prescribed to maintain hydration.
   h. Administer phosphates as prescribed, which interfere with calcium resorption.
   i. Administer calcitonin (Calcimar) as prescribed to decrease skeletal calcium release and increase renal clearance of calcium.
   j. Monitor calcium and phosphorus levels.
   k. Notify the physician immediately if a precipitous drop in the calcium level occurs; assess for tingling and numbness in the face and extremities and for other signs of hypocalcemia.

BOX 53-14

Signs of Tetany

Cardiac dysrhythmias
Carpopedal spasm
Dysphagia
Muscle and abdominal cramps
Numbness and tingling of the face and extremities
Positive Chvostek's sign
Positive Trousseau's sign
Visual disturbances (photophobia)
Wheezing and dyspnea (bronchospasm, laryngospasm)
Seizures

BOX 53-15

Parathyroid Gland Disorders

Hyperparathyroidism
Hypoparathyroidism

l. Prepare the client for parathyroidectomy as prescribed.

C. Parathyroidectomy

1. Description: Removal of one or more of the parathyroid glands

2. Preoperative interventions
   a. Monitor electrolytes, calcium, phosphate, and magnesium levels.
   b. Ensure that calcium levels are decreased to near-normal values.
   c. Inform the client that talking may be painful for the first day or two after surgery.

3. Postoperative interventions
   a. Monitor for respiratory distress.
   b. Place a tracheotomy set, oxygen, and suctioning at the bedside.
   c. Monitor vital signs.
   d. Position the client in a semi-Fowler's position.
   e. Assess neck dressing for bleeding.
   f. Monitor for hypocalcemic crisis, as evidenced by tingling and twitching in the extremities and face.
   g. Assess for positive **Trousseau's** or **Chvostek's sign,** which signals the potential for tetany.
   h. Monitor for changes in voice pattern and hoarseness.
   i. Monitor for laryngeal nerve damage.
   j. Instruct the client in the administration of calcium and vitamin D supplements as prescribed.

VII. DISORDERS OF THE PANCREAS

A. **Diabetes mellitus** (Box 53-16)

1. Description
   a. Chronic disorder of impaired carbohydrate, protein, and lipid metabolism caused by a deficiency of insulin
   b. An absolute or relative deficiency of insulin results in **hyperglycemia.**
   c. Type 1 **diabetes mellitus** is a nearly absolute deficiency of insulin; if insulin is not given, fats are metabolized for energy, resulting in ketonemia (acidosis).
   d. Type 2 **diabetes mellitus** is a relative lack of insulin or resistance to the action of insulin; usually, insulin is sufficient to stabilize fat

and protein metabolism but not to deal with carbohydrate metabolism (obesity is a major risk factor for type 2 **diabetes mellitus**).

   e. Macrovascular complications include coronary artery disease, cardiomyopathy, hypertension, cerebrovascular disease, peripheral vascular disease, and infection.
   f. Microvascular complications include retinopathy, nephropathy, and neuropathy.

2. Assessment
   a. Polyuria, polydipsia, polyphagia (more common in type 1 **diabetes mellitus**)
   b. **Hyperglycemia**
   c. Weight loss (common in type 1 **diabetes mellitus,** rare in type 2 **diabetes mellitus**)
   d. Blurred vision
   e. Slow wound healing
   f. Vaginal infections
   g. Weakness and paresthesias
   h. Signs of inadequate circulation to the feet
   i. Signs of accelerated atherosclerosis (renal, cerebral, cardiac, peripheral)

3. Diet
   a. The total number of calories is individualized based on the client's current or desired weight and the presence of other existing health problems.
   b. Day to day consistency in timing and amount of food intake helps control the blood glucose level.
   c. As prescribed by the physician, the client may be advised to follow the food exchange recommendations of the American Diabetic Association diet or U.S. dietary guidelines (My-Pyramid) issued by the U.S. Departments of Agriculture and Health and Human Services.
   d. Carbohydrate counting may be a simpler approach; it focuses on the total grams of carbohydrates eaten per meal. The client may be more compliant with carbohydrate counting, resulting in better glycemic control; it is usually necessary for clients undergoing intense insulin therapy.
   e. Incorporate diet into individual client needs, lifestyle, and cultural and socioeconomic patterns.

4. Exercise
   a. Exercise lowers the blood glucose level, encourages weight loss, reduces cardiovascular risks, improves circulation and muscle tone, decreases total cholesterol and triglyceride levels, and decreases insulin resistance and glucose intolerance.
   b. Instruct the client in dietary adjustments when exercising; dietary adjustments are individualized.

BOX 53-16

Major Types of Diabetes Mellitus

Type 1: Primary beta cell destruction leading to absolute insulin deficiency

Type 2: Ranges from insulin resistance with an insulin deficiency to secretory deficit with insulin resistance

c. Instruct the client to monitor the blood glucose level before exercising; if the client plans to participate in extended periods of exercise, blood glucose levels should be checked before, during, and after the exercise period.

d. If the client requires extra food during exercise to prevent **hypoglycemia,** it need not be deducted from the regular meal plan.

e. If the blood glucose level is higher than 250 mg/dL and urinary ketones (type 1 **diabetes mellitus**) are present, the client is instructed not to exercise until the blood glucose level is closer to normal and urinary ketones are absent.

5. Oral hypoglycemic medications

a. Oral medications are prescribed for clients with **diabetes mellitus** type 2 when diet and weight control therapy have failed to maintain satisfactory blood glucose levels.

b. Assess the client's knowledge of **diabetes mellitus** and the use of oral hypoglycemic agents.

c. Assess vital signs and blood glucose levels.

d. Assess the medications that the client is currently taking.

e. Aspirin, alcohol, sulfonamides, oral contraceptives, and monoamine oxidase inhibitors increase the hypoglycemic effect, causing a decrease in blood glucose levels.

f. Glucocorticoids, thiazide diuretics, and estrogen increase blood glucose levels.

g. Teach the client to recognize symptoms of **hypoglycemia** and **hyperglycemia.**

h. Teach the client to avoid over-the-counter medications unless prescribed by the physician.

i. Teach the client to avoid alcohol if taking sulfonylureas.

j. Inform the client with type 2 **diabetes mellitus** that insulin may be needed during stress, surgery, or infection.

k. Teach the client about the importance of compliance with the prescribed medication.

l. Advise the client to wear a Medic-Alert bracelet.

6. Insulin

a. Insulin is used to treat types 1 and 2 **diabetes mellitus** when diet, weight control therapy, and oral hypoglycemic agents have failed to maintain satisfactory blood glucose levels.

b. Regular insulin is the only insulin that can be administered intravenously (used in the emergency treatment of **diabetic ketoacidosis**).

c. Aspirin, alcohol, oral anticoagulants, oral hypoglycemic medications β-blockers, tricyclic antidepressants, tetracycline, and mono-amine oxidase inhibitors increase the hypoglycemic effect of insulin, causing a further decrease in the blood glucose level.

d. Glucocorticoids, thiazide diuretics, thyroid agents, oral contraceptives, and estrogen increase the blood glucose level.

e. Illness, infection, and stress increase the blood glucose level and the need for insulin; insulin should not be withheld during illness, infection, or stress because **hyperglycemia** and ketoacidosis can result.

f. Instruct the client to recognize symptoms of **hypoglycemia** and **hyperglycemia.**

g. The peak action time of insulin is important because of the possibility of hypoglycemic reactions occurring during that time.

B. Complications of insulin therapy

1. Local allergic reactions

a. Redness, swelling, tenderness, and induration or a wheal at the site of injection may occur 1 to 2 hours after administration.

b. Reactions usually occur during the early stages of insulin therapy.

c. Instruct the client to cleanse the skin with alcohol before injection.

2. Insulin lipodystrophy

a. Lipoatrophy is loss of subcutaneous fat and appears as slight dimpling or more serious pitting of subcutaneous fat; the use of human insulin helps prevent this complication (Fig. 53-4).

b. Lipohypertrophy is the development of fibrous fatty masses at the injection site and is caused by repeated use of an injection site (Fig. 53-5).

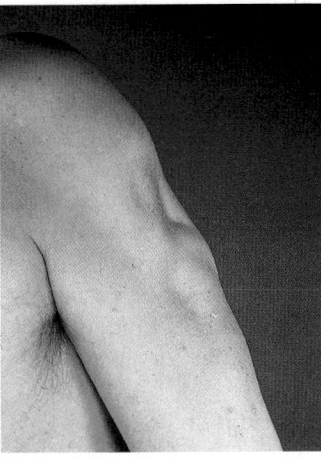

FIG. 53-4 Lipoatrophy at insulin injection site. (From Mosby. [2005]. *Mosby's dictionary of medicine, nursing, and health professions* [7th ed.]. St. Louis: Mosby.)

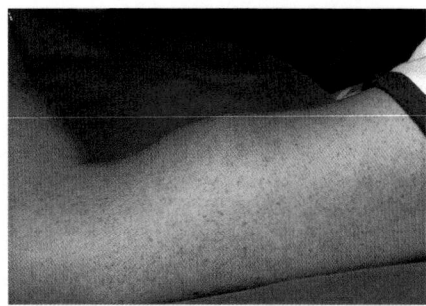

FIG. 53-5 Lipohypertrophy at insulin injection site. (From Mosby. [2005]. *Mosby's dictionary of medicine, nursing, and health professions* [7th ed.]. St. Louis: Mosby.)

    c. Instruct the client to avoid injecting insulin into affected sites.

    d. Instruct the client about the importance of rotating insulin injection at one anatomical site.

  3. Insulin resistance

    a. The client receiving insulin develops immune antibodies that bind the insulin, thereby decreasing the insulin available for use in the body.

    b. Treatment consists of administering a purer insulin preparation.

    c. Insulin resistance is also the term used for lack of tissue sensitivity to the insulin from the body, which results in **hyperglycemia.**

  4. **Dawn phenomenon**

    a. **Dawn phenomenon** results from reduced tissue sensitivity to insulin that develops between 5 and 8 AM (prebreakfast **hyperglycemia** occurs); it may be caused by nocturnal release of growth hormone.

    b. Treatment includes administering an evening dose (or increasing the amount of a current dose) of intermediate-acting insulin at 10 PM.

  5. **Somogyi phenomenon**

    a. Normal or elevated blood glucose levels are present at bedtime; **hypoglycemia** occurs at 2 to 3 AM, which causes an increase in the production of counterregulatory hormones.

    b. By 7 AM, in response to the counterregulatory hormones, the blood glucose rebounds significantly to the hyperglycemic range.

    c. Treatment includes decreasing the evening (predinner or bedtime) dose of intermediate-acting insulin or increasing the bedtime snack.

▲ C. Insulin administration

  1. Subcutaneous injections and mixing insulin: See Chapter 54.

  2. Insulin pens

    a. An insulin pen is a device that uses a small, prefilled insulin cartridge loaded into a pen-like holder; a disposable needle is attached to the device for injection and the dosage is selected by dialing in the desired amount.

    b. The client inserts the needle for injection, and the insulin is delivered by pushing a button.

  3. Jet injectors

    a. A jet injector is a device that delivers insulin through the skin under pressure in an extremely fine stream.

    b. Insulin administered by this device usually absorbs faster.

    c. The injector can cause bruising at the site of insulin delivery.

  4. Insulin pumps

    a. Continuous subcutaneous insulin infusion is administered by an externally worn device that contains a syringe attached to a long, thin, narrow-lumen tube with a needle or Teflon catheter attached to the end.

    b. The client inserts the needle or Teflon catheter into the subcutaneous tissue (usually on the abdomen) and secures it with tape or a transparent dressing; the pump is worn on a belt or in a pocket; the needle or Teflon catheter is changed at least every 3 days.

    c. A continuous basal rate of insulin infuses; in addition, based on the blood glucose level, the anticipated food intake, and the activity level, the client delivers a bolus of insulin before each meal.

    d. Both rapid-acting and regular insulin (buffered to prevent the precipitation of insulin crystals within the catheter) are appropriate for use in these pumps.

  5. Implantable insulin delivery

    a. An insulin pump is implanted in the peritoneal cavity, where insulin can be absorbed in a more physiological manner.

    b. Implants are not widely used because of mechanical problems associated with the pump, the catheter, and the insulin delivery.

  6. Newer methods of insulin administration

    a. Inhaled insulin: Insulin contained in a pellet is vaporized in an inhaler or delivered as a dry powder inhaled through a mouthpiece; insulin particles quickly dissolve in the alveoli and pass into the circulation.

    b. Transdermal insulin: Insulin is administered via the skin through a patch (currently being tested).

  7. Pancreas transplants

    a. The goal of pancreatic transplantation is to halt or reverse the complications of **diabetes mellitus.**

    b. Transplantations are performed on a limited number of clients (generally, these are clients

Use the proper procedure for obtaining the sample for determining the blood glucose level.
Perform the procedure precisely to obtain accurate results.
Follow the manufacturer's instructions for the glucometer.
Wash hands before and after performing the procedure to prevent infection.
Calibrate the monitor as instructed by the manufacturer.
Check the expiration date on the test strips.
If the blood glucose level results do not seem reasonable, reread the instructions, reassess technique, check the expiration date of the test strips, and perform the procedure again to verify results.

BOX 53-18
Assessment of Hypoglycemia

MILD
Hunger
Nervousness
Palpitations
Sweating
Tachycardia
Tremor

MODERATE
Confusion
Double vision
Drowsiness
Emotional changes
Headache
Impaired coordination
Inability to concentrate
Irrational or combative behavior
Light-headedness
Numbness of the lips and tongue
Slurred speech

SEVERE
Difficulty arousing
Disoriented behavior
Loss of consciousness
Seizures

who are undergoing kidney transplantation simultaneously).
   c. Immunosuppressive therapy is prescribed to prevent and treat rejection.
D. Self-monitoring of blood glucose level
   1. Self-monitoring provides the client with the current blood glucose level and information to maintain good glycemic control.
   2. Monitoring requires a finger prick to obtain a drop of blood for testing.
   3. Alternative site testing (obtaining blood from the forearm, upper arm, abdomen, thigh, or calf) is now available using specific measurement devices.
   4. Tests must be used with caution in clients with diabetic neuropathy.
   5. Client instructions (Box 53-17)
E. Urine testing
   1. Urine testing for glucose is not a reliable indicator of the blood glucose level and is therefore no longer used for monitoring purposes
   2. Instruct the client in the procedure for testing urine ketones
   3. The presence of ketones may indicate impending ketoacidosis.
   4. Urine ketone testing should be performed during illness and whenever the client with type 1 **diabetes mellitus** has persistently elevated blood glucose levels (higher than 240 mg/dL for two consecutive testing periods).

VIII. ACUTE COMPLICATIONS OF DIABETES MELLITUS
A. **Hypoglycemia**
   1. Description
     a. **Hypoglycemia** occurs when the blood glucose level falls below 60 mg/dL or when the blood glucose level drops rapidly from an elevated level.

     b. **Hypoglycemia** is caused by too much insulin or oral hypoglycemic agents, too little food, or excessive activity.
     c. The client needs to be instructed always to carry some form of fast-acting simple carbohydrate with him or her.
     d. If the client has a hypoglycemic reaction and does not have any of the recommended emergency foods available, any available food should be eaten; high-fat foods slow the absorption of glucose and the hypoglycemic symptoms may not resolve quickly.
   2. Assessment (Box 53-18)
     a. Mild **hypoglycemia:** The client remains fully awake but displays adrenergic symptoms; the blood glucose level is usually lower than 60 mg/dL.
     b. Moderate **hypoglycemia:** The client displays symptoms of worsening hypoglycemia; the blood glucose level is usually lower than 40 mg/dL.
     c. Severe **hypoglycemia:** The client displays severe neuroglycopenic symptoms; the blood glucose level is usually lower than 20 mg/dL.
   3. Interventions: Mild **hypoglycemia**
     a. Give 10 to 15 g of a fast-acting simple carbohydrate (Box 53-19).

b. Retest the blood glucose level in 15 minutes and repeat the treatment if symptoms do not resolve.

c. Once symptoms resolve, a snack containing protein and carbohydrates, such as milk or cheese and crackers, is recommended unless the client plans to eat a regular meal within 60 minutes.

4. Interventions: Moderate **hypoglycemia**
   a. Administer 15 to 30 g of a fast-acting simple carbohydrate.
   b. Administer additional food such as low-fat milk or cheese after 10 to 15 minutes.

BOX 53-19

Simple Carbohydrates to Treat Hypoglycemia

Commercially prepared glucose tablets
6 to 10 Life Savers or hard candy
4 tsp of sugar
4 sugar cubes
1 Tbsp of honey or syrup
½ cup of fruit juice or regular (nondiet) soft drink
8 oz low-fat milk
6 saltine crackers
3 graham crackers

---

5. Interventions for severe **hypoglycemia**
   a. If the client is unconscious and cannot swallow, an injection of glucagon is administered subcutaneously or intramuscularly.
   b. Administer a second dose in 10 minutes if the client remains unconscious.
   c. A small meal is given to the client when the client awakens as long as the client is not nauseated.
   d. The physician is notified if a severe hypoglycemic reaction occurs.
   e. In the hospital or emergency department, the client may be treated with an IV injection of 25 to 50 mL of 50% dextrose in water.
   f. Family members need to be instructed about the administration of glucagon.

B. **Diabetic ketoacidosis** (DKA)
   1. Description (Fig. 53-6)
      a. **Diabetic ketoacidosis** is a life-threatening complication of type 1 **diabetes mellitus** that develops when a severe insulin deficiency occurs.
      b. The main clinical manifestations include **hyperglycemia,** dehydration, ketosis, and acidosis.
   2. Assessment (Table 53-2)

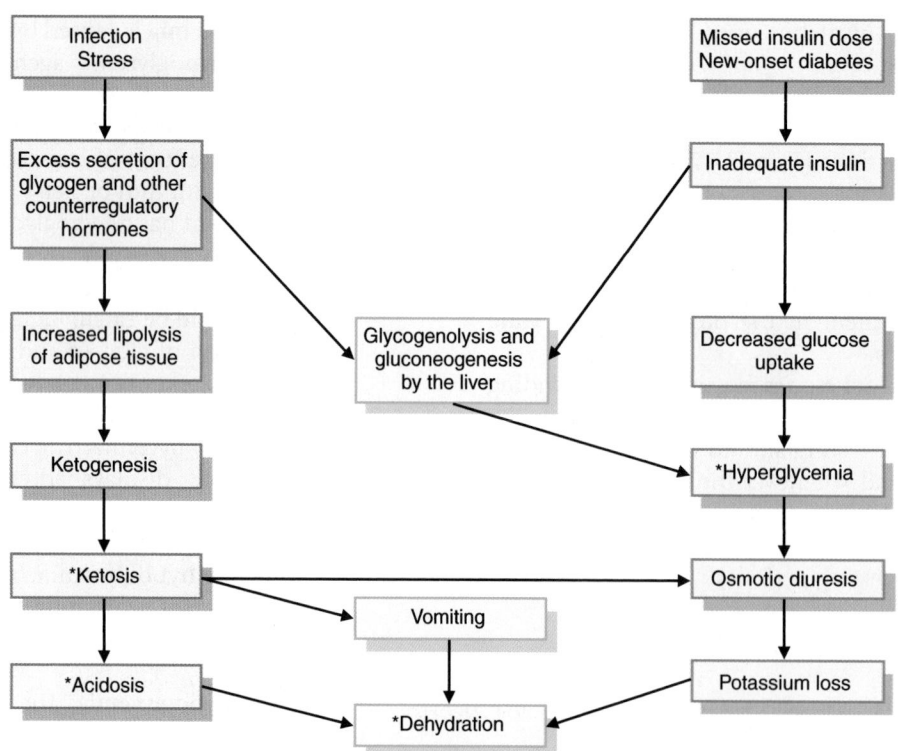

*Hallmarks of DKA

FIG. 53-6 Pathophysiology of diabetic ketoacidosis (DKA). (From Black, J., & Hawks, J., [2005]. *Medical-surgical nursing: Clinical management for positive outcomes* [7th ed.]. Philadelphia: W.B. Saunders.)

3. Interventions
   a. Restore circulating blood volume and protect against cerebral, coronary, or renal hypoperfusion.
   b. Treat dehydration with rapid IV infusions of 0.9% or 0.45% normal saline (NS) as prescribed; dextrose is added to IV fluids (D₅NS, or 5% dextrose in 0.45% saline) when the blood glucose level reaches 250 to 300 mg/dL.
   c. Treat **hyperglycemia** with regular insulin administered intravenously as prescribed.
   d. Correct electrolyte imbalances (potassium level may be elevated as a result of dehydration and acidosis).
   e. Monitor potassium level closely because when the client receives treatment for the dehydration and acidosis, the serum potassium level will decrease and potassium replacement may be required.
4. Insulin IV administration
   a. Use regular insulin only.
   b. A dose of 5 to 10 units of regular insulin by IV bolus may be prescribed before a continuous infusion is begun.
   c. Mix the prescribed IV dose of regular insulin for continuous infusion in 0.9% or 0.45% NS as prescribed.
   d. Flush the insulin solution through the entire intravenous infusion set and discard the first 50 to 100 mL of solution before connecting and administering to the client; insulin molecules adhere to the plastic of IV infusion sets.
   e. Always place the insulin infusion on an IV infusion controller.
   f. Insulin is infused continuously until subcutaneous administration resumes.
   g. Monitor vital signs
   h. Monitor urinary output and for signs of fluid overload.
   i. Monitor potassium and glucose levels and for signs of increased intracranial pressure.
   j. If the blood glucose level falls too far or too fast before the brain has time to equilibrate, water is pulled from the blood to the cerebrospinal fluid and the brain, causing cerebral edema and increased intracranial pressure.
   k. The potassium level will fall rapidly within the first hour of treatment as the dehydration and the acidosis are treated.
   l. Potassium is administered intravenously in a diluted solution as prescribed when the potassium reaches a normal level to prevent hypokalemia; ensure adequate renal function before administering potassium.
5. Client education (Box 53-20)
C. **Hyperglycemic hyperosmolar nonketotic syndrome** (HHNS)
   1. Description
      a. Extreme **hyperglycemia** occurs without ketosis or acidosis.

TABLE 53-2

Differences Between Diabetic Ketoacidosis and Hyperglycemic-Hyperosmolar Nonketotic Syndrome

	Diabetic Ketoacidosis (DKA)	Hyperglycemic-Hyperosmolar Nonketotic Syndrome (HHNS)
Onset	Sudden	Gradual
Precipitating factors	Infection	Infection
	Other stressors	Other stressors
	Inadequate insulin dose	Poor fluid intake
Manifestations	Ketosis: Kussmaul respiration, "fruity" breath, nausea, abdominal pain	Altered central nervous system function with neurologic symptoms
	Dehydration or electrolyte loss: polyuria, polydipsia, weight loss, dry skin, sunken eyes, soft eyeballs, lethargy, coma	Dehydration or electrolyte loss: same as for DKA
LABORATORY FINDINGS		
Serum glucose	>300 mg/dL (16.7 mmol/L)	>800 mg/dL (44.5 mmol/L)
Osmolarity	Variable	>350 mOsm/L
Serum ketones	Positive at 1:2 dilutions	Negative
Serum pH	<7.35	>7.4
Serum HCO₃	<15 mEq/L	>20 mEq/L
Serum Na	Low, normal, or high	Normal or low
Serum K	Normal; elevated with acidosis, low following dehydration	Normal or low
BUN	>20 mg/dL; elevated because of dehydration	Elevated
Creatinine	>1.5 mg/dL; elevated because of dehydration	Elevated
Urine ketones	Positive	Negative

BUN, Blood urea nitrogen; *HCO₃,* bicarbonate.
From Ignatavicius, D., & Workman, M. (2006). *Medical-surgical nursing: Critical thinking for collaborative care* (5th ed.). Philadelphia: W.B. Saunders.

BOX 53-20

Client Education: Guidelines During Illness

Take insulin or oral antidiabetic medications as prescribed.

Test blood glucose level and test the urine for ketones every 3 to 4 hours.

If the usual meal plan cannot be followed, substitute soft foods six to eight times a day.

If vomiting, diarrhea, or fever occurs, consume liquids every 30 to 60 minutes to prevent dehydration and to provide calories.

Notify the physician if vomiting, diarrhea, or fever persists, if blood glucose levels are higher than 250 to 300 mg/dL, when ketonuria is present for more than 24 hours, when unable to take food or fluids for a period of 4 hours, or when illness persists for more than 2 days.

    b. The syndrome occurs most often in individuals with type 2 **diabetes mellitus.**

    c. The major difference between HHNS and DKA is that ketosis and acidosis do not occur with HHNS; enough insulin is present with HHNS to prevent breakdown of fats for energy, thus preventing ketosis.

2. Assessment (see Table 53-2)

3. Interventions

    a. Treatment is similar to that for DKA.

    b. Treatment includes fluid replacement, correction of electrolyte imbalances, and insulin administration.

    c. Fluid replacement in the older client must be done very carefully secondary to potential for heart failure.

    d. Insulin plays a less critical role in the treatment of HHNS than it does for the treatment of DKA because ketosis and acidosis do not occur; rehydration alone may decrease glucose levels.

IX. **CHRONIC COMPLICATIONS OF DIABETES MELLITUS**

A. Diabetic retinopathy

1. Description

    a. Chronic and progressive impairment of the retinal circulation that eventually causes hemorrhage

    b. Permanent vision changes and blindness can occur.

    c. The client has difficulty with carrying out the daily tasks of blood glucose testing and insulin injections.

2. Assessment

    a. A change in vision is caused by the rupture of small microaneurysms in retinal blood vessels.

    b. Blurred vision results from macular edema.

    c. Sudden loss of vision results from retinal detachment.

    d. Cataracts result from lens opacity.

3. Interventions

    a. Maintain safety.

    b. Early prevention via the control of hypertension and blood glucose levels

    c. Photocoagulation (laser therapy) removes hemorrhagic tissue to decrease scarring and prevent progression of the disease process.

    d. Vitrectomy removes vitreous hemorrhages and thus decreases tension on the retina, preventing detachment.

    e. Cataract removal with lens implantation improves vision.

B. Diabetic nephropathy

1. Description: Progressive decrease in kidney function

2. Assessment

    a. Microalbuminuria

    b. Thirst

    c. Fatigue

    d. Anemia

    e. Weight loss

    f. Signs of malnutrition

    g. Frequent urinary tract infections

    h. Signs of a neurogenic bladder

3. Interventions

    a. Early prevention measures include the control of hypertension and blood glucose levels.

    b. Assess vital signs.

    c. Monitor intake and output.

    d. Monitor serum blood urea nitrogen and creatinine and urine albumin levels.

    e. Restrict dietary protein, sodium, and potassium intake as prescribed.

    f. Avoid nephrotoxic medications.

    g. Prepare the client for dialysis procedures as prescribed.

    h. Prepare the client for kidney transplant as prescribed.

    i. Prepare the client for pancreas transplant as prescribed.

C. Diabetic neuropathy

1. Description

    a. General deterioration of the nervous system throughout the body

    b. Complications include the development of nonhealing ulcers of the feet, gastric paresis, and erectile dysfunction.

2. Classifications

    a. Focal neuropathy or mononeuropathy: Involves a single nerve or group of nerves, most frequently cranial nerves III (oculomotor) and VI (abducens), resulting in diplopia; usually resolves spontaneously

    b. Sensory or peripheral neuropathy: Affects distal portion of nerves, most frequently in the lower extremities

    c. Autonomic neuropathy: Symptoms vary according to organ system involved

d. Cardiovascular: Cardiac denervation syndrome (heart rate does not respond to changes in oxygenation needs) and orthostatic hypotension occur.

e. Pupillary: Pupil does not dilate in response to decreased light.

f. Gastric: Decreased gastric emptying (gastroparesis)

g. Urinary: Neurogenic bladder

h. Sudomotor: Decreased sweating

i. Adrenal: Hypoglycemic unawareness

j. Reproductive: Impotence (male), painful intercourse (female)

3. Assessment
   a. Paresthesias
   b. Decreased or absent reflexes
   c. Decreased sensation to vibration or light touch
   d. Pain, aching, and burning in the lower extremities
   e. Poor peripheral pulses
   f. Skin breakdown and signs of infection
   g. Weakness or loss of sensation in cranial nerves III (oculomotor), IV (trochlear), V (trigeminal), VI (abducens)
   h. Dizziness and postural hypotension
   i. Nausea and vomiting
   j. Diarrhea or constipation
   k. Incontinence
   l. Dyspareunia
   m. Impotence
   n. Hypoglycemic unawareness

4. Interventions
   a. Early prevention measures include the control of hypertension and blood glucose levels.
   b. Careful foot care is required to prevent trauma (Box 53-21).
   c. Administer medications as prescribed for pain relief.
   d. Initiate bladder training programs.
   e. Instruct in the use of estrogen-containing lubricants for women with dyspareunia.
   f. Prepare the male client with impotence for penile injections or implantable devices as prescribed.
   g. Prepare for surgical decompression of compression lesions related to the cranial nerves as prescribed.

X. CARE OF THE DIABETIC CLIENT UNDERGOING SURGERY

A. Preoperative care
   1. Check with physician regarding withholding oral hypoglycemic medications or insulin.
   2. Some long-acting oral antidiabetic medications are discontinued 24 to 48 hours before surgery.
   3. Metformin (Glucophage) may need to be discontinued 48 hours before surgery and may not

---

BOX 53-21
Preventive Foot Care Instructions

Provide meticulous skin care and proper foot care.

Inspect feet daily and monitor feet for redness, swelling, or break in skin integrity.

Notify the physician if redness or a break in the skin occurs.

Avoid thermal injuries from hot water, heating pads, and baths.

Wash feet with warm (not hot) water and dry thoroughly (avoid foot soaks).

Do not treat corns, blisters, or ingrown toenails.

Do not cross legs or wear tight garments that may constrict blood flow.

Apply moisturizing lotion to the feet but not between the toes.

Prevent moisture from accumulating between the toes.

Wear loose socks and well-fitting (not tight) shoes, and instruct the client not to go barefoot.

Wear clean cotton socks to keep the feet warm and change the socks daily.

Do not wear the same pair of shoes 2 days in a row.

Do not wear open-toed shoes or shoes with a strap that goes between the toes.

Check shoes for cracks or tears in the lining and for foreign objects before putting them on.

Break in new shoes gradually.

Cut toenails straight across and smooth nails with an emery board.

Do not smoke.

---

be restarted until renal function is normal postoperatively.

4. All other oral antidiabetic medications are stopped the day of surgery.

5. Insulin dose may be adjusted or withheld if IV insulin administration during surgery is planned.

6. Monitor blood glucose level.

7. Administer IV fluids as prescribed.

B. Intraoperative care
   1. Monitor blood glucose levels frequently
   2. Administer IV short- or rapid-acting insulin as prescribed to maintain the blood glucose level lower than 200 mg/dL.

C. Postoperative care
   1. Administer IV glucose and regular insulin infusions as prescribed until the client can tolerate oral feedings.
   2. Administer supplemental short-acting insulin as prescribed based on blood glucose results.
   3. Monitor blood glucose levels frequently if the client is receiving parenteral nutrition.
   4. When the client is tolerating food, ensure that the client receives an adequate amount of carbohydrates daily to prevent **hypoglycemia** and ketosis.
   5. Client is at higher risk for cardiovascular and renal complications postoperatively.
   6. Client is also at risk for impaired wound healing.

PRACTICE QUESTIONS

1. A nurse is preparing a teaching plan for a client with diabetes mellitus regarding proper foot care. Which instruction is included in the plan?
   1. Soak feet in hot water.
   2. Avoid using a mild soap on the feet.
   3. Apply a moisturizing lotion to dry feet but not between the toes.
   4. Always have a podiatrist cut your toenails; never cut them yourself.

2. A client is brought to the emergency room in an unresponsive state, and a diagnosis of hyperglycemic hyperosmolar nonketotic syndrome is made. The nurse would immediately prepare to initiate which of the following anticipated physician's orders?
   1. Endotracheal intubation
   2. 100 units of NPH insulin
   3. Intravenous infusion of normal saline
   4. Intravenous infusion of sodium bicarbonate

3. An external insulin pump is prescribed for a client with diabetes mellitus and the client asks the nurse about the functioning of the pump. The nurse bases the response on the information that the pump:
   1. Is timed to release programmed doses of regular or NPH insulin into the bloodstream at specific intervals
   2. Continuously infuses small amounts of NPH insulin into the bloodstream while regularly monitoring blood glucose levels
   3. Is surgically attached to the pancreas and infuses regular insulin into the pancreas, which in turn releases the insulin into the bloodstream
   4. Gives a small continuous dose of regular insulin subcutaneously, and the client can self-administer a bolus with an additional dose from the pump before each meal

4. A client newly diagnosed with diabetes mellitus has been stabilized with daily insulin injections. A nurse prepares a discharge teaching plan regarding the insulin and plans to reinforce which of the following concepts?
   1. Always keep insulin vials refrigerated.
   2. Ketones in the urine signify a need for less insulin.
   3. Increase the amount of insulin before unusual exercise.
   4. Systematically rotate insulin injections within one anatomic site.

5. A client with a diagnosis of diabetic ketoacidosis (DKA) is being treated in an emergency room. Which finding would a nurse expect to note as confirming this diagnosis?
   1. Comatose state
   2. Decreased urine output
   3. Increased respirations and an increase in pH

4. Elevated blood glucose level and low plasma bicarbonate level

6. A nurse teaches a client with diabetes mellitus about differentiating between hypoglycemia and ketoacidosis. The client demonstrates an understanding of the teaching by stating that glucose will be taken if which of the following symptoms develops?
   1. Polyuria
   2. Shakiness
   3. Blurred vision
   4. Fruity breath odor

7. A client with diabetes mellitus demonstrates acute anxiety when first admitted for the treatment of hyperglycemia. The appropriate intervention to decrease the client's anxiety is to:
   1. Administer a sedative.
   2. Convey empathy, trust, and respect toward the client.
   3. Ignore the signs and symptoms of anxiety so that they will soon disappear.
   4. Make sure that the client knows all the correct medical terms to understand what is happening.

8. A nurse provides instructions to a client newly diagnosed with type 1 diabetes mellitus. The nurse recognizes accurate understanding of measures to prevent diabetic ketoacidosis when the client states:
   1. "I will stop taking my insulin if I'm too sick to eat."
   2. "I will decrease my insulin dose during times of illness."
   3. "I will adjust my insulin dose according to the level of glucose in my urine."
   4. "I will notify my physician if my blood glucose level is higher than 250 mg/dL."

9. A client is admitted to a hospital with a diagnosis of diabetic ketoacidosis (DKA). The initial blood glucose level was 950 mg/dL. A continuous intravenous infusion of regular insulin is initiated, along with intravenous rehydration with normal saline. The serum glucose level is now 240 mg/dL. The nurse would next prepare to administer which of the following?
   1. Ampule of 50% dextrose
   2. NPH insulin subcutaneously
   3. Intravenous fluids containing 5% dextrose
   4. Phenytoin (Dilantin) for the prevention of seizures

10. A physician has prescribed propylthiouracil (PTU) for a client with hyperthyroidism and the nurse develops a plan of care for the client. A priority nursing assessment to be included in the plan regarding this medication is to assess for:
    1. Relief of pain
    2. Signs of renal toxicity
    3. Signs and symptoms of hyperglycemia
    4. Signs and symptoms of hypothyroidism

11. A nurse is monitoring a client newly diagnosed with diabetes mellitus for signs of complications. Which of the following, if exhibited in the client, would indicate hyperglycemia and warrant physician notification?
    1. Polyuria
    2. Diaphoresis
    3. Hypertension
    4. Increased pulse rate
12. A nurse is preparing a plan of care for a client with diabetes mellitus who has hyperglycemia. The priority nursing diagnosis would be:
    1. Fluid volume, deficient.
    2. Family processes, dysfunctional.
    3. Nutrition: less than body requirements, imbalanced.
    4. Knowledge, deficient: disease process and treatment.
13. A home health nurse visits a client with a diagnosis of type 1 diabetes mellitus. The client relates a history of vomiting and diarrhea and tells the nurse that no food has been consumed for 36 hours. Which additional statement by the client indicates a need for further teaching?
    1. "I need to stop my insulin."
    2. "I need to increase my fluid intake."
    3. "I need to monitor my blood glucose every 3 to 4 hours."
    4. "I need to call the physician because of these symptoms."
14. After hypophysectomy, a client complains of being thirsty and having to urinate frequently. The initial nursing action is to:
    1. Increase fluid intake.
    2. Document the complaints.
    3. Assess for urinary glucose.
    4. Assess urine specific gravity.
15. A nurse is caring for a client after hypophysectomy. The nurse notices clear nasal drainage from the client's nostril. The initial nursing action would be to:
    1. Lower the head of the bed.
    2. Test the drainage for glucose.
    3. Obtain a culture of the drainage.
    4. Continue to observe the drainage.
16. After several diagnostic tests, a client is diagnosed with diabetes insipidus. A nurse performs an assessment on the client, knowing that which symptom is most indicative of this disorder?
    1. Fatigue
    2. Diarrhea
    3. Polydipsia
    4. Weight gain
17. A nurse is performing an assessment on a client following a thyroidectomy and notes that the client has developed hoarseness and a weak voice. Which nursing action is appropriate?

    1. Check for signs of bleeding.
    2. Administer calcium gluconate.
    3. Notify the physician immediately.
    4. Reassure the client that this is usually a temporary condition.
18. A client is admitted to an emergency room, and a diagnosis of myxedema coma is made. Which action would the nurse prepare to carry out initially?
    1. Warm the client.
    2. Maintain a patent airway.
    3. Administer thyroid hormone.
    4. Administer fluid replacement.
19. A nurse is assisting a client with diabetes mellitus who is recovering from diabetic ketoacidosis (DKA) to develop a plan to prevent a recurrence. Which of the following is most important to include in the plan of care?
    1. Test urine for ketone levels.
    2. Eat six small meals per day.
    3. Monitor blood glucose levels frequently.
    4. Receive appropriate follow-up health care.
20. A nurse is caring for a client admitted to the emergency room with diabetic ketoacidosis (DKA). In the acute phase, the priority nursing action is to prepare to:
    1. Correct the acidosis.
    2. Apply a monitor for an electrocardiogram.
    3. Administer 5% dextrose intravenously.
    4. Administer regular insulin intravenously.
21. A client with type 2 diabetes mellitus has a blood glucose level higher than 600 mg/dL and is complaining of polydipsia, polyuria, weight loss, and weakness. A nurse reviews the physician's documentation and would expect to note which of the following diagnoses?
    1. Hypoglycemia
    2. Pheochromocytoma
    3. Diabetic ketoacidosis (DKA)
    4. Hyperglycemic hyperosmolar nonketotic syndrome (HHNS)
22. The family of a bedridden client with type 2 diabetes mellitus and chronic renal failure calls a nurse to report the following symptoms: headache, polydipsia, and increased lethargy. To determine a possible diagnosis, the nurse asks the family which most important question?
    1. "What is the client's urine output?"
    2. "What is the client's capillary blood glucose level?"
    3. "Has there been any change in the dietary intake?"
    4. "Have you increased the amount of fluids provided?"
23. A client with type 1 diabetes mellitus calls the nurse to report recurrent episodes of hypoglycemia with exercising. Which statement by the client indicates

an inadequate understanding of the peak action of NPH insulin and exercise?

1. "The best time for me to exercise is after I eat."
2. "The best time for me to exercise is after breakfast."
3. "The best time for me to exercise is mid- to late afternoon."
4. "The best time for me to exercise is after my morning snack."

24. A nurse is completing an assessment on a client who is being admitted for a diagnostic workup for primary hyperparathyroidism. Which client complaint would be characteristic of this disorder?
    1. Diarrhea
    2. Polyuria
    3. Polyphagia
    4. Weight gain

25. A nurse is caring for a postoperative parathyroidectomy client. Which client complaint would indicate that a serious, life-threatening complication may be developing, requiring immediate notification of the physician?
    1. Laryngeal stridor
    2. Abdominal cramps
    3. Difficulty in voiding
    4. Mild to moderate incisional pain

26. A nurse notes that a client with type 1 diabetes mellitus has lipodystrophy on both upper thighs. The nurse would appropriately inquire whether the client:
    1. Rotates sites for injection
    2. Administers the insulin at a 45-degree angle
    3. Cleanses the skin with alcohol before each injection
    4. Aspirates for blood before injection into the subcutaneous tissue

27. A nurse is caring for a client with type 1 diabetes mellitus. Which client complaint would alert the nurse to the presence of a possible hypoglycemic reaction?
    1. Tremors
    2. Anorexia
    3. Hot, dry skin
    4. Muscle cramps

28. A nurse needs to maintain food and fluid intake to minimize the risk of dehydration in a client with diabetes mellitus who has gastroenteritis. The appropriate nursing intervention is to:
    1. Offer water only until the client is able to tolerate solid foods.
    2. Withhold all fluids until vomiting has ceased for at least 4 hours.
    3. Encourage the client to take 8 to 12 oz of fluid every hour while awake.
    4. Maintain a clear liquid diet for at least 5 days before advancing to solids to allow inflammation of the stomach and bowel to dissipate.

29. A client is diagnosed with pheochromocytoma. A nurse prepares a plan of care for the client; while planning, the nurse understands that pheochromocytoma is a condition that:
    1. Causes profound hypotension
    2. Is manifested by severe hypoglycemia
    3. Is not curable and is treated symptomatically
    4. Causes the release of excessive amounts of catecholamines

30. A nurse is performing an admission assessment on a client admitted with a diagnosis of pheochromocytoma. The nurse assesses for the major symptom associated with pheochromocytoma when the nurse:
    1. Obtains the client's weight
    2. Takes the client's blood pressure
    3. Tests the client's urine for glucose
    4. Palpates the skin for its temperature

31. A nurse collects urine specimens for catecholamine testing from a client with suspected pheochromocytoma. The results of the catecholamine test are reported as 20 mcg/100 mL urine. The nurse analyzes these results as:
    1. Normal
    2. Insignificant and unrelated to pheochromocytoma
    3. Lower than normal, ruling out pheochromocytoma
    4. Higher than normal, indicating pheochromocytoma

32. A nurse is caring for a client with pheochromocytoma who is scheduled for adrenalectomy. In the preoperative period, the priority nursing action would be to monitor:
    1. Vital signs
    2. Intake and output
    3. Blood urea nitrogen results
    4. Urine for glucose and ketones

33. A nurse is caring for a client with pheochromocytoma. The client asks for a snack and something warm to drink. The most appropriate choice for this client to meet nutritional needs would be which of the following?
    1. Crackers with cheese and tea
    2. Graham crackers and warm milk
    3. Toast with peanut butter and cocoa
    4. Vanilla wafers and coffee with cream and sugar

34. A nurse is performing an assessment on a client with pheochromocytoma. Which of the following assessment data would indicate a potential complication associated with this disorder?
    1. A coagulation time of 5 minutes
    2. A blood urea nitrogen level of 20 mg/dL
    3. A urinary output of 50 mL per hour
    4. A heart rate that is 90 beats/min and irregular

35. A nurse is preparing to provide instructions to a client with Addison's disease regarding diet therapy.

The nurse knows that which of the following diets most likely would be prescribed for this client?
1. High-fat intake
2. Low-protein intake
3. Normal sodium intake
4. Low-carbohydrate intake

36. A nursing instructor asks a student to describe the pathophysiology that occurs in Cushing's disease. Which statement by the student indicates an accurate understanding of this disorder?
1. "Cushing's disease results from an oversecretion of insulin."
2. "Cushing's disease results from an undersecretion of corticotropic hormones."
3. "Cushing's disease results from an undersecretion of mineralocorticoid hormones."
4. "Cushing's disease results from an increased pituitary secretion of adrenocorticotropic hormone."

37. A nurse performs a physical assessment on a client with type 2 diabetes mellitus. Findings include a fasting blood glucose of 120 mg/dL, temperature of 101° F, pulse of 88 beats/min, respirations of 22 breaths/min, and blood pressure of 100/72 mm Hg. Which finding would be of most concern to the nurse?
1. Pulse
2. Respiration
3. Temperature
4. Blood pressure

38. A nurse is interviewing a client with type 2 diabetes mellitus. Which statement by the client indicates an understanding of the treatment for this disorder?
1. "I take oral insulin instead of shots."
2. "By taking these medications, I am able to eat more."
3. "When I become ill, I need to increase the number of pills I take."
4. "The medications I'm taking help release the insulin I already make."

39. A nurse is providing discharge instructions to a client who has Cushing's syndrome. Which client statement indicates that instructions related to dietary management are understood?
1. "I can eat foods that have a lot of potassium in them."
2. "I will need to limit the amount of protein in my diet."
3. "I am fortunate that I can eat all the salty foods I enjoy."
4. "I am fortunate that I do not need to follow any special diet."

40. The nurse is caring for a client who is 2 days postoperative following an abdominal hysterectomy. The client has a history of diabetes mellitus and has been receiving regular insulin according to capillary blood glucose testing four times a day. A carbohydrate-controlled diet has been prescribed but the client has been complaining of nausea and is not eating. On entering the client's room, the nurse finds the client to be confused and diaphoretic. Which action is appropriate at this time?
1. Call a code to obtain needed assistance immediately.
2. Obtain a capillary blood glucose level and perform a focused assessment.
3. Stay with the client and ask the nursing assistant to call the physician for an order for intravenous 50% dextrose.
4. Ask the nursing assistant to stay with the client while obtaining 15 to 30 g of a carbohydrate snack for the client to eat.

ALTERNATE ITEM FORMAT: PRIORITIZING (ORDERED RESPONSE)

A hospitalized client with type 1 diabetes mellitus received NPH and regular insulin 2 hours ago (at 7:30 AM). The client calls the nurse and reports that he is feeling hungry, shaky, and weak. The client ate breakfast at 8 AM and is due to eat lunch at noon. List in order of priority the actions that the nurse would take. (Number 1 is the first action.)

_____ Take the client's vital signs.
_____ Retest the blood glucose level
_____ Check the client's blood glucose level.
_____ Give the client ½ cup of fruit juice to drink.
_____ Give the client a small snack of carbohydrate and protein.
_____ Document the client's complaints, actions taken, and outcome.

ANSWERS

1. 3

Rationale: The client is instructed to use a moisturizing lotion on the feet and to avoid applying the lotion between the toes. The client should be instructed not to soak the feet and should avoid hot water to prevent burns. The client may cut the toenails straight across and even with the toe itself and would consult a podiatrist if the toenails were thick or hard to cut or if vision were poor. The client should be instructed to wash the feet daily with a mild soap.

Test-Taking Strategy: Use the process of elimination. Eliminate option 4 because of the words *always* and *never* and option 1 because of the word *hot*. Eliminate option 2 next because of the words *avoid* and *mild*. Review diabetic foot care instructions if you had difficulty with this question.

Level of Cognitive Ability: Application
Client Needs: Health Promotion and Maintenance
Integrated Process: Nursing Process—planning
Content Area: Adult health—endocrine
Reference: Ignatavicius, D., & Workman, M. (2006). *Medical-surgical nursing: Critical thinking for collaborative care* (5th ed., p. 1537). Philadelphia: W.B. Saunders.

2. 3

Rationale: The primary goal of treatment in hyperglycemic hyperosmolar nonketotic syndrome (HHNS) is to rehydrate the client to restore fluid volume and to correct electrolyte deficiency. Intravenous fluid replacement is similar to that administered in diabetic ketoacidosis (DKA) and begins with IV infusion of normal saline. Regular insulin, not NPH insulin, would be administered. The use of sodium bicarbonate to correct acidosis is avoided because it can precipitate a further drop in serum potassium levels. Intubation and mechanical ventilation are not required to treat HHNS.

Test-Taking Strategy: Use the process of elimination. If you can recall the treatment for DKA, you will be able to answer this question easily. Treatment for HHNS is similar to the treatment for DKA and begins with rehydration. Review the treatment for HHNS if you had difficulty with this question.

Level of Cognitive Ability: Analysis
Client Needs: Physiological Integrity
Integrated Process: Nursing Process—planning
Content Area: Adult health—endocrine
Reference: Black, J., & Hawks, J. (2005). *Medical-surgical nursing: Clinical management for positive outcomes* (7th ed., p. 1273). Philadelphia: W.B. Saunders.

3. 4

Rationale: An insulin pump provides a small continuous dose of regular insulin subcutaneously throughout the day and night, and the client can self-administer a bolus with an additional dose from the pump before each meal as needed. Regular insulin is used in an insulin pump. An external pump is not attached surgically to the pancreas.

Test-Taking Strategy: Use the process of elimination. Recalling that regular insulin is used in an insulin pump will assist in eliminating options 1 and 2. Noting the word *external* in the question will assist in eliminating option 3. Review the use of the insulin pump if you are unfamiliar with it.

Level of Cognitive Ability: Application
Client Needs: Physiological Integrity
Integrated Process: Teaching and Learning
Content Area: Adult health—endocrine
Reference: Black, J., & Hawks, J. (2005). *Medical-surgical nursing: Clinical management for positive outcomes* (7th ed., pp. 1255-1256). Philadelphia: W.B. Saunders.

4. 4

Rationale: Insulin doses should not be adjusted nor increased before unusual exercise. If ketones are found in the urine, it possibly may indicate the need for additional insulin. To minimize the discomfort associated with insulin injections, insulin should be administered at room temperature. Injection sites should be rotated systematically within one anatomic site.

Test-Taking Strategy: Use the process of elimination. Eliminate option 1 first because of the close-ended word *always*. Knowledge regarding insulin administration and the significance of ketones in the urine will assist in eliminating options 2 and 3. If you had difficulty with this question, review the components of insulin management.

Level of Cognitive Ability: Application
Client Needs: Physiological Integrity
Integrated Process: Teaching and Learning
Content Area: Adult health—endocrine
Reference: Ignatavicius, D., & Workman, M. (2006). *Medical-surgical nursing: Critical thinking for collaborative care* (5th ed., p. 1519). Philadelphia: W.B. Saunders.

5. 4

Rationale: In DKA, the arterial pH is lower than 7.35, plasma bicarbonate is lower than 15 mEq/L, the blood glucose level is higher than 250 mg/dL, and ketones are present in the blood and urine. The client would be experiencing polyuria, and Kussmaul's respirations would be present. A comatose state may occur if DKA is not treated, but coma would not confirm the diagnosis.

Test-Taking Strategy: Use the process of elimination and note the strategic word *confirming* in the question. Eliminate option 1 because a comatose state can exist in many conditions. Eliminate option 3 because in acidosis the pH would be low. Remember that polyuria exists in DKA. Review the clinical manifestations of DKA if you had difficulty with this question.

Level of Cognitive Ability: Analysis
Client Needs: Physiological Integrity
Integrated Process: Nursing Process—assessment
Content Area: Adult health—endocrine
Reference: Lewis, S., Heitkemper, M., & Dirksen, S. (2004). *Medical-surgical nursing: Assessment and management of clinical problems* (6th ed., p. 1293). St. Louis: Mosby.

6. 2

Rationale: Shakiness is a sign of hypoglycemia and would indicate the need for food or glucose. A fruity breath odor, blurred vision, and polyuria are signs of hyperglycemia.

Test-Taking Strategy: Focus on the subject of the question, the treatment of hypoglycemia. Recalling the signs of hypoglycemia will direct you to option 2. Review these signs if you had difficulty with this question.

Level of Cognitive Ability: Analysis
Client Needs: Physiological Integrity
Integrated Process: Nursing Process—evaluation
Content Area: Adult health—endocrine
Reference: Ignatavicius, D., & Workman, M. (2006). *Medical-surgical nursing: Critical thinking for collaborative care* (5th ed., p. 1541). Philadelphia: W.B. Saunders.

7. 2
Rationale: The appropriate intervention is to address the client's feelings related to the anxiety. Administering a sedative is not the most appropriate intervention. The nurse should not ignore the client's anxious feelings. A client will not relate to medical terms, particularly when anxiety exists.
Test-Taking Strategy: Use therapeutic communication techniques to answer the question. Remember that the client's feelings are the priority. Keeping this in mind will direct you easily to option 2. Review therapeutic communication techniques if you had difficulty with this question.
Level of Cognitive Ability: Application
Client Needs: Psychosocial Integrity
Integrated Process: Caring
Content Area: Adult health—endocrine
References: Black, J., & Hawks, J. (2005). *Medical-surgical nursing: Clinical management for positive outcomes* (7th ed., p. 526). Philadelphia: W.B. Saunders.
Ignatavicius, D., & Workman, M. (2006). *Medical-surgical nursing: Critical thinking for collaborative care* (5th ed., pp. 1509, 1547). Philadelphia: W.B. Saunders.

8. 4
Rationale: During illness, the client should monitor blood glucose levels and should notify the physician if the level is higher than 250 mg/dL. Insulin should never be stopped. In fact, insulin may need to be increased during times of illness. Doses should not be adjusted without the physician's advice and are usually adjusted based on blood glucose levels, not urinary glucose readings.
Test-Taking Strategy: Use the process of elimination. Note that options 1, 2, and 3 are comparative or alike and all relate to adjustment of insulin doses. Review diabetic management during illness if you had difficulty with this question.
Level of Cognitive Ability: Analysis
Client Needs: Physiological Integrity
Integrated Process: Nursing Process—evaluation
Content Area: Adult health—endocrine
References: Black, J., & Hawks, J. (2005). *Medical-surgical nursing: Clinical management for positive outcomes* (7th ed., p. 1286). Philadelphia: W.B. Saunders.
Ignatavicius, D., & Workman, M. (2006). *Medical-surgical nursing: Critical thinking for collaborative care* (5th ed., p. 1545). Philadelphia: W.B. Saunders.

9. 3
Rationale: During management of DKA, when the blood glucose level falls to 250 to 300 mg/dL, the infusion rate is reduced and 5% dextrose is added to maintain a blood glucose level of about 250 mg/dL, or until the client recovers from ketosis. NPH insulin is not used to treat DKA. Fifty percent dextrose is used to treat hypoglycemia. Phenytoin (Dilantin) is not a usual treatment measure for DKA.
Test-Taking Strategy: Use the process of elimination. Eliminate option 2 first, knowing that regular insulin is used in the management of DKA. Eliminate option 1 next, knowing that this is the treatment for hypoglycemia. Note the strategic words *the serum glucose level is now 240 mg/dL*. This should indicate that the IV solution of 5% dextrose is the next step in the management of care. Review care of the client with DKA if you had difficulty with this question.
Level of Cognitive Ability: Analysis
Client Needs: Physiological Integrity
Integrated Process: Nursing Process—planning
Content Area: Adult health—endocrine
Reference: Black, J., & Hawks, J. (2005). *Medical-surgical nursing: Clinical management for positive outcomes* (7th ed., pp. 1271-1272). Philadelphia: W.B. Saunders.

10. 4
Rationale: Excessive dosing with propylthiouracil (PTU) may convert the client from a hyperthyroid state to a hypothyroid state. If this occurs, the dosage should be reduced. Temporary administration of thyroid hormone may be required. Propylthiouracil is not used for pain and does not cause hyperglycemia or renal toxicity.
Test-Taking Strategy: Read the question carefully, noting the client's diagnosis. Noting that propylthiouracil is used to treat hyperthyroidism should direct you easily to option 4. If you had difficulty with this question, review the side effects and adverse effects of this medication.
Level of Cognitive Ability: Analysis
Client Needs: Physiological Integrity
Integrated Process: Nursing Process—assessment
Content Area: Adult health—endocrine
References: Black, J., & Hawks, J. (2005). *Medical-surgical nursing: Clinical management for positive outcomes* (7th ed., p. 1196). Philadelphia: W.B. Saunders.
Ignatavicius, D., & Workman, M. (2006). *Medical-surgical nursing: Critical thinking for collaborative care* (5th ed., p. 1485). Philadelphia: W.B. Saunders.

11. 1
Rationale: Classic symptoms of hyperglycemia include polydipsia, polyuria, and polyphagia. Options 2, 3, and 4 are not signs of hyperglycemia.
Test-Taking Strategy: Use the process of elimination. Remember the three P's associated with hyperglycemia—polyuria, polydipsia, polyphagia. Learn the signs of hyperglycemia if you had difficulty with this question.
Level of Cognitive Ability: Analysis
Client Needs: Physiological Integrity
Integrated Process: Nursing Process—assessment
Content Area: Adult health—endocrine
References: Ignatavicius, D., & Workman, M. (2006). *Medical-surgical nursing: Critical thinking for collaborative care* (5th ed., p. 1500). Philadelphia: W.B. Saunders.

Lewis, S., Heitkemper, M., & Dirksen, S. (2004). *Medical-surgical nursing: Assessment and management of clinical problems* (6th ed., p. 1272). St. Louis: Mosby.

12. **1**

Rationale: An increased blood glucose level will cause the kidneys to excrete the glucose in the urine. This glucose is accompanied by fluids and electrolytes, causing an osmotic diuresis leading to dehydration. This fluid loss must be replaced when it becomes severe. Options 2, 3, and 4 are not related specifically to the subject of the question.
Test-Taking Strategy: Use Maslow's Hierarchy of Needs theory to answer this question. Option 1 indicates a physiological need and is the priority. Options 2, 3, and 4 are nursing diagnoses that may need to be addressed after providing for the high-priority physiological needs. Review the priority concerns for the client with hyperglycemia if you had difficulty with this question.
Level of Cognitive Ability: Analysis
Client Needs: Physiological Integrity
Integrated Process: Nursing Process—analysis
Content Area: Delegating/Prioritizing
Reference: Lewis, S., Heitkemper, M., & Dirksen, S. (2004). *Medical-surgical nursing: Assessment and management of clinical problems* (6th ed., p. 1291). St. Louis: Mosby.

13. **1**

Rationale: When a client with diabetes mellitus is unable to eat normally because of illness, the client still should take the prescribed insulin or oral medication. The client should consume additional fluids and should notify the physician. The client should monitor the blood glucose level every 3 to 4 hours.
Test-Taking Strategy: Use the process of elimination and knowledge regarding the guidelines related to illness in the diabetic client to answer this question. Remembering that the client needs to take insulin will direct you easily to option 1. Review these guidelines if you had difficulty with this question.
Level of Cognitive Ability: Analysis
Client Needs: Physiological Integrity
Integrated Process: Teaching and Learning
Content Area: Adult health—endocrine
Reference: Black, J., & Hawks, J. (2005). *Medical-surgical nursing: Clinical management for positive outcomes* (7th ed., p. 1286). Philadelphia: W.B. Saunders.

14. **4**

Rationale: After hypophysectomy, diabetes insipidus can occur temporarily because of antidiuretic hormone deficiency. This deficiency is related to surgical manipulation. The nurse should assess the specific gravity of the urine and notify the physician if the result is lower than 1.006. Although options 1 and 2 may be components of the plan of care, they are not initial actions. Additionally, the physician will prescribe increased fluids. Option 3 is unrelated to the client's condition.
Test-Taking Strategy: Use the process of elimination. Recalling that diabetes insipidus is a complication of this type of surgery will assist in eliminating option 3. Note the strategic word *initial*. Knowledge of the nursing assessment measures in diabetes insipidus will easily direct you to option 4. Review the complications of hypophysectomy if you had difficulty with this question.

Level of Cognitive Ability: Application
Client Needs: Physiological Integrity
Integrated Process: Nursing Process—implementation
Content Area: Adult health—endocrine
Reference: Ignatavicius, D., & Workman, M. (2006). *Medical-surgical nursing: Critical thinking for collaborative care* (5th ed., pp. 1466-1467, 1459). Philadelphia: W.B. Saunders.

15. **2**

Rationale: After hypophysectomy, the client should be monitored for rhinorrhea, which could indicate a cerebrospinal fluid leak. If this occurs, the drainage should be collected and tested for the presence of cerebrospinal fluid. The head of the bed should not be lowered to prevent increased intracranial pressure. Clear nasal drainage would not indicate the need for a culture. Continuing to observe the drainage without taking action could result in a serious complication.
Test-Taking Strategy: Use the process of elimination and note the strategic word *initial*. This indicates that an action is required. Option 1 can be eliminated easily. Option 3 can be eliminated also because the drainage is clear. Because an action is required, eliminate option 4. Review the complications following hypophysectomy if you had difficulty with this question.
Level of Cognitive Ability: Application
Client Needs: Physiological Integrity
Integrated Process: Nursing Process—implementation
Content Area: Adult health—endocrine
Reference: Ignatavicius, D., & Workman, M. (2006). *Medical-surgical nursing: Critical thinking for collaborative care* (5th ed., p. 1464). Philadelphia: W.B. Saunders.

16. **3**

Rationale: Polydipsia and polyuria are classic symptoms of diabetes insipidus. The urine is pale, and the specific gravity is low. Anorexia and weight loss occur. Option 1 is a vague symptom. Options 2 and 4 are not specific to this disorder.
Test-Taking Strategy: Note the strategic words *most indicative*. Eliminate option 1 first because this symptom is rather vague and occurs in many conditions. Knowledge of the manifestations of diabetes insipidus will assist you in eliminating options 2 and 4. If you had difficulty with this question, review the clinical manifestations associated with diabetes insipidus.
Level of Cognitive Ability: Analysis
Client Needs: Physiological Integrity
Integrated Process: Nursing Process—assessment
Content Area: Adult health—endocrine
References: Black, J., & Hawks, J. (2005). *Medical-surgical nursing: Clinical management for positive outcomes* (7th ed., p. 1237). Philadelphia: W.B. Saunders.
Ignatavicius, D., & Workman, M. (2006). *Medical-surgical nursing: Critical thinking for collaborative care* (5th ed., p. 1466). Philadelphia: W.B. Saunders.

17. **4**

Rationale: Following thyroidectomy, weakness and hoarseness of the voice can occur as a result of trauma from the surgery. If this develops, the client should be reassured that the problem will subside in a few days. Unnecessary talking should be discouraged. The nurse does not need to notify the physician immediately. These signs do not indicate bleeding or the need to administer calcium gluconate.

Test-Taking Strategy: Use the process of elimination. Options 1 and 2 can be eliminated easily because they are unrelated to the signs presented in the question. No data are presented requiring immediate physician notification. Review care of the client following thyroidectomy if you had difficulty with this question.

Level of Cognitive Ability: Application
Client Needs: Physiological Integrity
Integrated Process: Nursing Process—implementation
Content Area: Adult health—endocrine
Reference: Ignatavicius, D., & Workman, M. (2006). *Medical-surgical nursing: Critical thinking for collaborative care* (5th ed., p. 1487). Philadelphia: W.B. Saunders.

18. 2
Rationale: The initial nursing action would be to maintain a patent airway. Oxygen would be administered, followed by fluid replacement, keeping the client warm, monitoring vital signs, and administering thyroid hormones by the intravenous (IV) route.

Test-Taking Strategy: Use the process of elimination and note the strategic word *initially*. All the options are appropriate interventions, but use the ABCs—airway, breathing, and circulation—in selecting the correct option. Review the initial interventions for myxedema coma if you had difficulty with this question.

Level of Cognitive Ability: Application
Client Needs: Physiological Integrity
Integrated Process: Nursing Process—implementation
Content Area: Delegating/Prioritizing
Reference: Black, J., & Hawks, J. (2005). *Medical-surgical nursing: Clinical management for positive outcomes* (7th ed., p. 1196). Philadelphia: W.B. Saunders.

19. 3
Rationale: Client education following DKA should emphasize the need for home glucose monitoring two to four times per day. Instructing the client to notify the health care provider when illness occurs is also important. The presence of urine ketones indicates that DKA has occurred already. The client should eat well-balanced meals with snacks as prescribed.

Test-Taking Strategy: Note the strategic words *most important* and focus on the subject, prevent a recurrence. Option 1 does not prevent DKA but actually confirms the diagnosis. Option 2 is not an accurate component of the dietary measures for a client with diabetes mellitus and option 4 will not prevent DKA. Review the measures to prevent DKA if you had difficulty with this question.

Level of Cognitive Ability: Analysis
Client Needs: Health Promotion and Maintenance
Integrated Process: Nursing Process—planning
Content Area: Adult health—endocrine
Reference: Ignatavicius, D., & Workman, M. (2006). *Medical-surgical nursing: Critical thinking for collaborative care* (5th ed., p. 1542). Philadelphia: W.B. Saunders.

20. 4
Rationale: Lack (absolute or relative) of insulin is the primary cause of DKA. Treatment consists of insulin administration

(regular insulin), IV fluid administration (normal saline initially), and potassium replacement, followed by correcting acidosis. Applying an electrocardiogram monitor is not a priority action.

Test-Taking Strategy: Use the process of elimination and focus on the client's diagnosis. Note the strategic word *priority*. Remember that in DKA, the initial treatment is regular insulin. Normal saline is administered initially; therefore, option 3 is incorrect. Options 1 and 2 may be components of the treatment plan but are not the priority. Review the initial treatment for DKA if you had difficulty with this question.

Level of Cognitive Ability: Application
Client Needs: Physiological Integrity
Integrated Process: Nursing Process—implementation
Content Area: Adult health—endocrine
Reference: Black, J., & Hawks, J. (2005). *Medical-surgical nursing: Clinical management for positive outcomes* (7th ed., p. 1269). Philadelphia: W.B. Saunders.

21. 4
Rationale: Hyperglycemic hyperosmolar nonketotic syndrome occurs in clients with type 2 diabetes mellitus. The onset of symptoms may be gradual. The symptoms may include polyuria, polydipsia, dehydration, mental status alterations, weight loss, and weakness. Options 1, 2, and 3 are incorrect interpretations of the client's symptoms.

Test-Taking Strategy: Use the process of elimination and note the strategic words *a blood glucose level higher than 600 mg/dL*. This will assist you in eliminating options 1 and 2. Recalling that HHNS most commonly occurs in type 2 diabetes mellitus will direct you easily to option 4. Review the clinical manifestations of HHNS if you had difficulty with this question.

Level of Cognitive Ability: Analysis
Client Needs: Physiological Integrity
Integrated Process: Nursing Process—analysis
Content Area: Adult health—endocrine
Reference: Ignatavicius, D., & Workman, M. (2006). *Medical-surgical nursing: Critical thinking for collaborative care* (5th ed., pp. 1545-1546). Philadelphia: W.B. Saunders.

22. 2
Rationale: Hyperglycemic hyperosmolar nonketotic syndrome (HHNS) is an acute complication of type 2 diabetes, leading to hyperglycemia and dehydration. Headache and polydipsia and increasing lethargy can be caused by the dehydration. Options 1, 3, and 4 will not assist in determining a possible diagnosis.

Test-Taking Strategy: Use the process of elimination and the strategic words *most important*. Knowing that the client has chronic renal failure eliminates option 1 because urine output would not be a reliable indicator of fluid status. From the remaining options, option 2 is related most specifically to a client with diabetes mellitus. Review the manifestations of HHNS if you had difficulty with this question.

Level of Cognitive Ability: Analysis
Client Needs: Physiological Integrity
Integrated Process: Nursing Process—assessment
Content Area: Adult health—endocrine
Reference: Ignatavicius, D., & Workman, M. (2006). *Medical-surgical nursing: Critical thinking for collaborative care* (5th ed., pp. 1545-1546). Philadelphia: W.B. Saunders.

23. **3**

Rationale: A hypoglycemic reaction may occur in response to increased exercise. Clients should avoid exercise during the peak time of insulin. NPH insulin peaks at 4 to 12 hours; therefore, afternoon exercise takes place during the peak of the medication. Options 1, 2, and 4 do not address peak action times.

Test-Taking Strategy: Use the process of elimination and note the strategic words *inadequate understanding*. Focus on the subject, peak action of NPH. Recalling that NPH peaks at 4 to 12 hours will direct you to option 3. Review the peak action time of NPH insulin if you had difficulty with this question.

Level of Cognitive Ability: Analysis
Client Needs: Physiological Integrity
Integrated Process: Teaching and Learning
Content Area: Adult health—endocrine
Reference: Lewis, S., Heitkemper, M., & Dirksen, S. (2004). *Medical-surgical nursing: Assessment and management of clinical problems* (6th ed., p. 1282-1283). St. Louis: Mosby.

24. **2**

Rationale: Hypercalcemia is the hallmark of hyperparathyroidism. Elevated serum calcium levels produce osmotic diuresis and thus polyuria. This diuresis leads to dehydration (weight loss rather than weight gain). Options 1, 3, and 4 are gastrointestinal symptoms and are not associated with the common gastrointestinal symptoms typical of hyperparathyroidism (nausea, vomiting, anorexia, constipation).

Test-Taking Strategy: Use the process of elimination. Note that options 1, 3, and 4 are gastrointestinal symptoms and are comparative or alike. Review the clinical manifestations of hyperparathyroidism if you had difficulty with this question.

Level of Cognitive Ability: Analysis
Client Needs: Physiological Integrity
Integrated Process: Nursing Process—assessment
Content Area: Adult health—endocrine
Reference: Black, J., & Hawks, J. (2005). *Medical-surgical nursing: Clinical management for positive outcomes* (7th ed., pp. 1209-1210). Philadelphia: W.B. Saunders.

25. **1**

Rationale: During the postoperative period, the nurse carefully observes the client for signs of hemorrhage, which causes swelling and compression of adjacent tissue. Laryngeal stridor is a harsh, high-pitched sound heard on inspiration and expiration; stridor is caused by compression of the trachea, leading to respiratory distress. Stridor is an acute emergency situation that requires immediate attention to avoid complete obstruction of the airway. Options 2, 3, and 4 do not identify signs of a life-threatening complication.

Test-Taking Strategy: Consider the anatomical location of the surgical procedure and use the ABCs—airway, breathing, and circulation—to select the correct option. Options 2, 3, and 4 are usual postoperative findings that are not life-threatening. Option 1 addresses the airway. Review postoperative care of the parathyroidectomy client if you had difficulty with this question.

Level of Cognitive Ability: Analysis
Client Needs: Physiological Integrity
Integrated Process: Nursing Process—assessment

Content Area: Adult health—endocrine
References: Black, J., & Hawks, J. (2005). *Medical-surgical nursing: Clinical management for positive outcomes* (7th ed., p. 1213). Philadelphia: W.B. Saunders.
Ignatavicius, D., & Workman, M. (2006). *Medical surgical nursing: Critical thinking for collaborative care* (5th ed., p. 1487). Philadelphia: W.B. Saunders.

26. **1**

Rationale: Lipodystrophy (hypertrophy of subcutaneous tissue at the injection site) occurs in some clients with diabetes mellitus when injection sites are used for a prolonged period of time. Thus, clients are instructed to adhere to a plan of rotating injection sites to avoid tissue changes. Cleansing with alcohol, aspiration, and angle of insulin administration do not produce this complication.

Test-Taking Strategy: Use the process of elimination and knowledge of the definition of lipodystrophy to answer this question. This will direct you easily to option 1. Review this complication of insulin therapy if you had difficulty with this question.

Level of Cognitive Ability: Analysis
Client Needs: Physiological Integrity
Integrated Process: Nursing Process—assessment
Content Area: Adult health—endocrine
Reference: Ignatavicius, D., & Workman, M. (2006). *Medical-surgical nursing: Critical thinking for collaborative care* (5th ed., p. 1519-1520). Philadelphia: W.B. Saunders.

27. **1**

Rationale: Decreased blood glucose levels produce autonomic nervous system symptoms, which are manifested classically as nervousness, irritability, and tremors. Option 3 is more likely to occur with hyperglycemia. Options 2 and 4 are unrelated to the signs of hypoglycemia.

Test-Taking Strategy: Use the process of elimination and focus on the subject, a hypoglycemic reaction. Recalling the signs of this type of reaction will direct you easily to option 1. Review the signs of hypoglycemia if you had difficulty with this question.

Level of Cognitive Ability: Analysis
Client Needs: Physiological Integrity
Integrated Process: Nursing Process—assessment
Content Area: Adult health—endocrine
Reference: Ignatavicius, D., & Workman, M. (2006). *Medical-surgical nursing: Critical thinking for collaborative care* (5th ed., p. 1540). Philadelphia: W.B. Saunders.

28. **3**

Rationale: Small amounts of fluid may be tolerated, even when vomiting is present. The nurse should encourage liquids containing glucose and electrolytes every hour. Options 1, 2, and 4 will not provide the adequate intake needed by the client with diabetes mellitus.

Test-Taking Strategy: Use the process of elimination. Eliminate options 1 and 2 because of the close-ended words *only* and *all*. The time frame in option 4 (5 days) is unreasonable; therefore, select option 3. Review care of the client with diabetes mellitus during times of illness if you had difficulty with this question.

Level of Cognitive Ability: Application

Client Needs: Physiological Integrity
Integrated Process: Nursing Process—implementation
Content Area: Adult health—endocrine
Reference: Ignatavicius, D., & Workman, M. (2006). *Medical-surgical nursing: Critical thinking for collaborative care* (5th ed., p. 1545). Philadelphia: W.B. Saunders.

29. **4**
Rationale: Pheochromocytoma is a catecholamine-producing tumor and causes secretion of excessive amounts of epinephrine and norepinephrine. Hypertension is the principal manifestation, and the client has episodes of high blood pressure accompanied by pounding headaches. The excessive release of catecholamine also results in excessive conversion of glycogen into glucose in the liver. Consequently, hyperglycemia and glucosuria occur during attacks. Pheochromocytoma is curable. The primary treatment is surgical removal of one or both of the adrenal glands, depending on whether the tumor is unilateral or bilateral.
Test-Taking Strategy: Use the process of elimination and knowledge of the manifestations of pheochromocytoma to answer this question. Remember that pheochromocytoma is a catecholamine-producing tumor. If you are unfamiliar with this disorder, review this content.
Level of Cognitive Ability: Comprehension
Client Needs: Physiological Integrity
Integrated Process: Nursing Process—planning
Content Area: Adult health—endocrine
Reference: Black, J., & Hawks, J. (2005). *Medical-surgical nursing: Clinical management for positive outcomes.* (7th ed., pp. 1231-1232). Philadelphia: W.B. Saunders.

30. **2**
Rationale: Pheochromocytoma is a catecholamine-producing tumor. Hypertension is the major symptom associated with pheochromocytoma. Taking the client's blood pressure would assess the blood pressure status. Glycosuria, weight loss, and diaphoresis are also clinical manifestations of pheochromocytoma, yet hypertension is the major symptom.
Test-Taking Strategy: Use the process of elimination, noting the strategic words *major symptom.* Use the ABCs—airway, breathing, and circulation. A method of assessing circulation is to take the blood pressure. Review the clinical manifestations of pheochromocytoma if you had difficulty with this question.
Level of Cognitive Ability: Analysis
Client Needs: Physiological Integrity
Integrated Process: Nursing Process—assessment
Content Area: Delegating/Prioritizing
Reference: Black, J., & Hawks, J. (2005). *Medical-surgical nursing: Clinical management for positive outcomes* (7th ed., p. 1231). Philadelphia: W.B. Saunders.

31. **4**
Rationale: Assays of catecholamines are performed on single-voided urine specimens, 2- to 4-hour specimens, and 24-hour urine specimens. The normal range of urinary catecholamines is up to 14 mcg/100 mL of urine, with higher levels occurring in pheochromocytoma.
Test-Taking Strategy: Recall that pheochromocytoma is a catecholamine-producing tumor. Because the question ad-dresses urine specimens for catecholamine testing, expect the results to indicate higher than normal amounts of catecholamine. In addition, the question indicates that the client is suspected of having pheochromocytoma, so if you need to select an answer and you are not sure, select the option that is comparative to a concept in the question. In this case, suspected pheochromocytoma is comparative to *indicating pheochromocytoma* in option 4. Review diagnostic tests for pheochromocytoma if you had difficulty with this question.
Level of Cognitive Ability: Analysis
Client Needs: Physiological Integrity
Integrated Process: Nursing Process—analysis
Content Area: Adult health—endocrine
Reference: Black, J., & Hawks, J. (2005). *Medical-surgical nursing: Clinical management for positive outcomes* (7th ed., p. 1231). Philadelphia: W.B. Saunders.

32. **1**
Rationale: Pheochromocytoma is a catecholamine-producing tumor. Hypertension is the hallmark of pheochromocytoma. Severe hypertension can precipitate a stroke or sudden blindness. Although all the options are accurate nursing interventions for the client with pheochromocytoma, the priority nursing action is to monitor the vital signs, particularly the blood pressure.
Test-Taking Strategy: Use the process of elimination and note the strategic words *priority nursing action.* Use the ABCs—airway, breathing, and circulation. Monitoring vital signs is the nursing action that would assess airway, breathing, and circulation. Also, options 2, 3, and 4 refer to the assessment of the renal system, whereas option 1 does not. Review preoperative care of the client with pheochromocytoma if you had difficulty with this question.
Level of Cognitive Ability: Application
Client Needs: Physiological Integrity
Integrated Process: Nursing Process—implementation
Content Area: Delegating/Prioritizing
Reference: Black, J., & Hawks, J. (2005). *Medical-surgical nursing: Clinical management for positive outcomes* (7th ed., pp. 1232-1233). Philadelphia: W.B. Saunders.

33. **2**
Rationale: The client with pheochromocytoma needs to be provided with a diet high in vitamins, minerals, and calories. Of particular importance are the foods or beverages that contain caffeine, such as cocoa, coffee, tea, or colas. These foods are prohibited because they can precipitate a hypertensive crisis.
Test-Taking Strategy: Use the process of elimination. Note that options 1, 3, and 4 are comparative or alike in that they include a drink that contains caffeine; therefore, eliminate these options. Review dietary measures for the client with pheochromocytoma if you had difficulty with this question.
Level of Cognitive Ability: Application
Client Needs: Physiological Integrity
Integrated Process: Nursing Process—implementation
Content Area: Adult health—endocrine
Reference: Ignatavicius, D., & Workman, M. (2006). *Medical-surgical nursing: Critical thinking for collaborative care* (5th ed., pp. 1476-1478). Philadelphia: W.B. Saunders.

34. **4**

Rationale: The complications associated with pheochromocytoma include hypertensive retinopathy and nephropathy, myocarditis, increased platelet aggregation, and stroke. Death can occur from shock, stroke, renal failure, dysrhythmias, or dissecting aortic aneurysm. An irregular heart rate indicates the presence of a dysrhythmia. A urinary output of 50 mL/hr is an adequate output. A blood urea nitrogen level of 20 mg/dL is a normal finding. A coagulation time of 5 minutes is normal.

Test-Taking Strategy: Use the process of elimination and the ABCs—airway, breathing, and circulation. An irregular heart rate is associated with circulation. In addition, if you knew the normal hourly expectations associated with urinary output and the normal laboratory values for coagulation time and blood urea nitrogen level, you would be easily directed to option 4. Review the complications associated with pheochromocytoma if you had difficulty with this question.

Level of Cognitive Ability: Analysis
Client Needs: Physiological Integrity
Integrated Process: Nursing Process—analysis
Content Area: Adult health—endocrine
References: Black, J., & Hawks, J. (2005). *Medical-surgical nursing: Clinical management for positive outcomes* (7th ed., pp. 1478-1479). Philadelphia: W.B. Saunders.
Ignatavicius, D., & Workman, M. (2006). *Medical-surgical nursing: Critical thinking for collaborative care* (5th ed., pp. 1231-1232). Philadelphia: W.B. Saunders.

35. **3**

Rationale: A high–complex carbohydrate and high-protein diet will be prescribed for the client with Addison's disease. To prevent excess fluid and sodium loss, the client is instructed to maintain a normal salt intake daily (3 g) and to increase salt intake during hot weather, before strenuous exercise, and in response to fever, vomiting, or diarrhea. A high fat diet is not prescribed.

Test-Taking Strategy: Use the process of elimination and knowledge regarding the pathophysiology associated with Addison's disease to answer this question. Remember that a high–complex carbohydrate, high-protein diet with normal sodium intake is prescribed for the client with Addison's disease. If you are unfamiliar with this disorder, review the pathophysiology and dietary measures associated with Addison's disease.

Level of Cognitive Ability: Comprehension
Client Needs: Physiological Integrity
Integrated Process: Nursing Process—planning
Content Area: Adult health—endocrine
References: Ignatavicius, D., & Workman, M. (2006). *Medical-surgical nursing: Critical thinking for collaborative care* (5th ed., p. 1230). Philadelphia: W.B. Saunders.
Lewis, S., Heitkemper, M., & Dirksen, S. (2004). *Medical-surgical nursing: Assessment and management of clinical problems* (6th ed., p. 1334). St. Louis: Mosby.

36. **4**

Rationale: Cushing's disease is a metabolic disorder characterized by abnormally increased secretion (endogenous) of corti-

sol, caused by increased amounts of adrenocorticotropic hormone (ACTH) secreted by the pituitary gland. Addison's disease is characterized by the hyposecretion of adrenal cortex hormones (glucocorticoids and mineralocorticoids) from the adrenal gland, resulting in deficiency of the corticosteroid hormones. Options 1, 2, and 3 are inaccurate regarding Cushing's disease.

Test-Taking Strategy: Use the process of elimination. Options 2 and 3 can be eliminated easily if you remember that in Cushing's (*up*) disease there is an oversecretion and in Addison's disease there is an undersecretion. Next, eliminate option 1 because this disease is unrelated to insulin. Review the pathophysiology associated with Cushing's disease if you had difficulty with this question.

Level of Cognitive Ability: Comprehension
Client Needs: Physiological Integrity
Integrated Process: Teaching and Learning
Content Area: Adult health—endocrine
Reference: Huether, S., & McCance, K. (2004). *Understanding pathophysiology* (3rd ed., p. 497). St. Louis: Mosby.

37. **3**

Rationale: An elevated temperature may indicate infection. Infection is a leading cause of hyperglycemic hyperosmolar nonketotic syndrome or diabetic ketoacidosis. The other findings noted in the question are within normal limits.

Test-Taking Strategy: Use the process of elimination and knowledge of the normal values of vital signs to direct you to option 3. The client's temperature is the only abnormal value. Remember that an elevated temperature can indicate an infectious process that can lead to complications in the client with diabetes mellitus. Review normal and abnormal findings in the client with diabetes mellitus if you had difficulty with this question.

Level of Cognitive Ability: Analysis
Client Needs: Physiological Integrity
Integrated Process: Nursing Process—analysis
Content Area: Adult health—endocrine
References: Black, J., & Hawks, J. (2005). *Medical-surgical nursing: Clinical management for positive outcomes* (7th ed., p. 1273, 1281). Philadelphia: W.B. Saunders.
Ignatavicius, D., & Workman, M. (2006). *Medical-surgical nursing: Critical thinking for collaborative care* (5th ed., pp. 1504-1505). Philadelphia: W.B. Saunders.

38. **4**

Rationale: Clients with type 2 diabetes mellitus have decreased or impaired insulin secretion. Oral hypoglycemic agents are given to these clients to facilitate glucose uptake. Insulin injections may be given during times of stress-induced hyperglycemia. Oral insulin is not available because of the breakdown of the insulin by digestion. Options 1, 2, and 3 are incorrect.

Test-Taking Strategy: Use the process of elimination, focusing on the subject, type 2 diabetes mellitus. Eliminate option 1 because *oral insulin* is not available. Treatment with medication does not mean that the client can eat more; therefore, eliminate option 2. Recalling that during times of illness insulin may be required will eliminate option 3. Review treatment measures for type 2 diabetes mellitus if you had difficulty with this question.

Level of Cognitive Ability: Analysis
Client Needs: Physiological Integrity
Integrated Process: Nursing Process—evaluation
Content Area: Adult health—endocrine
Reference: Lewis, S., Heitkemper, M., & Dirksen, S. (2004). *Medical-surgical nursing: Assessment and management of clinical problems* (6th ed., p. 1271). St. Louis: Mosby.

39. **1**
Rationale: A diet low in carbohydrates and sodium but ample in protein and potassium is encouraged for a client with Cushing's syndrome. Such a diet promotes weight loss, reduction of edema and hypertension, control of hypokalemia, and rebuilding of wasted tissue.
Test-Taking Strategy: Use the process of elimination. Eliminate option 4 because it reflects that no dietary change is necessary. Eliminate option 2 next because protein most likely is limited in liver or renal disorders (not in Cushing's syndrome). From the remaining options, eliminate option 3 because excess sodium is not normally healthy. Review dietary management in Cushing's syndrome if you had difficulty with this question.
Level of Cognitive Ability: Analysis
Client Needs: Health Promotion and Maintenance
Integrated Process: Nursing Process—evaluation
Content Area: Adult health—endocrine
References: Black, J., & Hawks, J. (2005). *Medical-surgical nursing: Clinical management for positive outcomes* (7th ed., pp. 1229, 1230). Philadelphia: W.B. Saunders.
Ignatavicius, D., & Workman, M. (2006). *Medical-surgical nursing: Critical thinking for collaborative care* (5th ed., pp. 1476-1477). Philadelphia: W.B. Saunders.

40. **2**
Rationale: Diaphoresis and confusion are signs of moderate hypoglycemia. A likely cause of the client's change in condition could be related to the administration of insulin without the client eating enough food. However, an assessment is necessary to confirm the presence of hypoglycemia. The nurse would obtain a capillary blood glucose level to confirm the hypoglycemia and perform a focused assessment to determine the extent and cause of the client's condition. Once hypoglycemia is confirmed, the nurse stays with the client and asks the nursing assistant to obtain the appropriate carbohydrate snack. A code is called if the client is not breathing or if the heart is not beating.
Test-Taking Strategy: Focus on the data in the question and note the strategic words *at this time*. Eliminate option 1 because there are no data in the question indicating the need to call a code. Eliminate option 3 next because it is inappropriate to ask a nursing assistant to call a physician for an order. To

select from the remaining options, use the steps of the nursing process, recalling that assessment is the first step. Review care of the client experiencing a hypoglycemic reaction if you had difficulty with this question.
Level of Cognitive Ability: Application
Client Needs: Physiological Integrity
Integrated Process: Nursing Process—implementation
Content Area: Adult health—endocrine
References: Cherry, B., & Jacob, S.R. (2005). *Contemporary nursing: Issues, trends, and management* (3rd ed., p. 430). St. Louis: Mosby.

**ALTERNATE ITEM FORMAT:
PRIORITIZING (ORDERED RESPONSE)**

Answer: 3, 4, 1, 2, 5, 6
Rationale: The client is experiencing symptoms of mild hypoglycemia. If symptoms such as hunger, irritability, shakiness, or weakness occur, the nurse first would check the client's blood glucose level to verify that the client is experiencing hypoglycemia. Once this is verified, the nurse would give the client 10 to 15 g of carbohydrates. The nurse would retest the blood glucose level in 15 minutes. In the meantime, the nurse would check the client's vital signs. The nurse would give the client another 10- to 15-g carbohydrate food item if the client's symptoms do not resolve. Otherwise, the nurse would provide a small snack of carbohydrates and protein if the client's next scheduled meal is more than an hour away from the time of the occurrence. Following treatment and resolution of the hypoglycemic event, the nurse would document the occurrence, actions taken, and outcome.
Test-Taking Strategy: Focus on the client's symptoms. Noting that the client is hospitalized will assist you in determining that the first action would be to check the client's blood glucose level. Once this has been done, treating the hypoglycemia is necessary. Recalling that an outcome cannot be determined until treatment has been instituted will assist you in selecting the documentation action as the last action. From the remaining three actions, select taking the vital signs as the third action. The nurse would not give the client a carbohydrate and protein item immediately after giving the client a 10- to 15-g carbohydrate item or before retesting the blood glucose level. Review management of hypoglycemia if you had difficulty with this question.
Level of Cognitive Ability: Application
Client Needs: Physiological Integrity
Integrated Process: Nursing Process—implementation
Content Area: Delegating/Prioritizing
Reference: Ignatavicius, D., & Workman, M. (2006). *Medical-surgical nursing: Critical thinking for collaborative care* (5th ed., pp. 1540-1541). Philadelphia: W.B. Saunders.

REFERENCES

Black, J., Hawks, J., & Keene, A. (2005). *Medical-surgical nursing: Clinical management for positive outcomes* (7th ed.). Philadelphia: W.B. Saunders.

Brown, M., & Mulholland., J. (2004). *Drug calculations: Process and problems for clinical practice* (7th ed.). St. Louis: Mosby.

Chernecky, C., & Berger, B. (2004). *Laboratory tests and diagnostic procedures* (4th ed.). Philadelphia: W.B. Saunders.

Cherry, B., & Jacob, S. (2005). *Contemporary nursing: Issues, trends, and management* (3rd ed.). St. Louis: Mosby.

Hodgson, B., & Kizior, R. (2007). *Saunders nursing drug handbook 2007.* Philadelphia: W.B. Saunders.

Huether, S., & McCance, K. (2004). *Understanding pathophysiology* (3rd ed.). St. Louis: Mosby.

Ignatavicius, D., & Workman, M. (2006). *Medical-surgical nursing: Critical thinking for collaborative care* (5th ed.). Philadelphia: W.B. Saunders.

Lewis, S., Heitkemper, M., & Dirksen, S. (2004). *Medical-surgical nursing: Assessment and management of clinical problems* (6th ed.). St. Louis: Mosby.

Phipps, W., Monahan, F., Sands, J., et al. (2003). *Medical-surgical nursing: Health and illness perspectives* (7th ed.). St. Louis: Mosby.

Skidmore-Roth, L. (2005). *Mosby's drug guide for nurses* (6th ed.). St. Louis: Mosby.

Endocrine Medications

I. PITUITARY MEDICATIONS

A. Description

   1. The anterior pituitary gland secretes growth hormone (GH), thyroid-stimulating hormone (TSH), adrenocorticotropic hormone (ACTH), prolactin, melanocyte-stimulating hormone (MSH), and gonadotropins (follicle-stimulating hormone [FSH] and luteinizing hormone [LH]).

   2. The posterior pituitary gland secretes antidiuretic hormone (vasopressin) and oxytocin.

B. Growth hormones and related medications

   1. Uses and side effects (Table 54-1)

   2. Interventions

     a. Assess child's physical growth and compare growth with standards.

     b. Recommend annual bone age determinations for children receiving growth hormones.

     c. Monitor blood glucose levels and thyroid function tests.

     d. Teach the client and family about the clinical manifestations of **hyperglycemia** and the importance of follow-up regarding periodic blood tests.

II. ANTIDIURETIC HORMONES (Box 54-1)

A. Description

   1. Antidiuretic hormones enhance reabsorption of water in the kidneys, promoting an antidiuretic effect and regulating fluid balance.

   2. Antidiuretic hormones are used in **diabetes insipidus.**

B. Side effects

   1. Flushing

   2. Headache

   3. Nausea and abdominal cramps

   4. Water intoxication

   5. Hypertension with water intoxication

   6. Nasal congestion with nasal administration

C. Interventions

   1. Monitor weight.

   2. Monitor intake and output and urine osmolality.

   3. Monitor electrolyte levels.

   4. Monitor for signs of dehydration, indicating need to increase dosage.

   5. Monitor for signs of water intoxication (drowsiness, listlessness, shortness of breath, and headache), indicating need to decrease dosage.

   6. Monitor blood pressure.

   7. Instruct the client in how to use the intranasal medication.

   8. Instruct the client to weigh themselves daily to identify weight gain

   9. Instruct the client to report signs of water intoxication or symptoms of headache or shortness of breath.

III. THYROID HORMONES (Box 54-2)

A. Description

   1. Thyroid hormones control the metabolic rate of tissues and accelerate heat production and oxygen consumption.

   2. Thyroid hormones are used to replace the thyroid hormone deficit in conditions such as **hypothyroidism** and **myxedema.**

   3. Thyroid hormones enhance the action of oral anticoagulants, sympathomimetics, and antidepressants and decrease the action of insulin, oral hypoglycemics, and digitalis preparations; the action of thyroid hormones is decreased by phenytoin (Dilantin) and carbamazepine (Tegretol).

   4. Thyroid hormones should be given at least 4 hours apart from multivitamins, aluminum hydroxide and magnesium hydroxide, simethi-

TABLE 54-1

Growth Hormones and Related Medications

Medication(s)	Use	Side Effects
Somatrem (Protropin)	Growth failure (children)	Development of antibodies to growth hormone
Somatropin (Humatrope)	Growth failure (children and adults)	Headache, muscle pain, weakness, mild hyperglycemia, hypertension, allergic reaction (rash, swelling), pain at injection site
Bromocriptine mesylate (Parlodel)	Acromegaly	Nausea, headache, dizziness
Octreotide acetate (Sandostatin)	Acromegaly	Diarrhea, nausea, abdominal discomfort, increased or decreased glucose level
Cabergoline (Dostinex)	Acromegaly	Abdominal pain, vertigo
Pegvisomant (Somavert)	Acromegaly	AST and ALT elevations, injection site reactions, flu syndrome, weight gain, infection, dizziness, peripheral edema, sinusitis, nausea, diarrhea, pain

ALT, Alanine aminotransferase; *AST,* aspartate aminotransferase.

BOX 54-1

Antidiuretic Hormones

Desmopressin acetate (DDAVP)
Lypressin
Vasopressin (Pitressin)

BOX 54-2

Thyroid Hormones

Levothyroxine sodium (Synthroid, Levothroid, Levoxyl)
Liothyronine sodium (Cytomel)
Liotrix (Thyrolar)

cone, calcium carbonate, bile acid sequestrants, iron, and sucralfate (Carafate) because these medications decrease the absorption of thyroid replacements.

B. Side effects
1. Nausea and decreased appetite
2. Abdominal cramps and diarrhea
3. Weight loss
4. Nervousness and tremors
5. Insomnia
6. Sweating and heat intolerance
7. Tachycardia, dysrhythmias, palpitations, chest pain
8. Hypertension
9. Headache
10. Toxicity: **Hyperthyroidism**
C. Interventions
1. Assess client for history of medications currently being taken.
2. Monitor vital signs.
3. Monitor weight.
4. Monitor triiodothyronine, thyroxine, and thyroid-stimulating hormone levels.
5. Instruct the client to take the medication at the same time each day, preferably in the morning without food.

BOX 54-3

Antithyroid Medications

Methimazole (Tapazole)
Propylthiouracil (PTU)
Potassium iodide (Lugol's solution)
Radioactive iodine (sodium iodide, ^{131}I)

6. Instruct the client in how to monitor pulse rate.
7. Advise the client to report symptoms of **hyperthyroidism,** such as tachycardia, chest pain, palpitations, and excessive sweating.
8. Instruct the client to avoid foods that can inhibit thyroid secretion, such as strawberries, peaches, pears, cabbage, turnips, spinach, kale, Brussels sprouts, cauliflower, radishes, and peas.
9. Advise the client to avoid over-the counter-medications.
10. Instruct the client to wear a Medic-Alert bracelet.

IV. **ANTITHYROID MEDICATIONS** (Box 54-3)
A. Description
1. Antithyroid medications inhibit the synthesis of thyroid hormone.
2. Antithyroid medications are used for **hyperthyroidism,** or Graves' disease.
B. Side effects
1. Nausea and vomiting
2. Diarrhea
3. Drowsiness, headache, fever
4. Hypersensitivity with skin rash
5. Agranulocytosis with leukopenia and thrombocytopenia
6. Alopecia and hyperpigmentation
7. Toxicity: **Hypothyroidism**
8. Iodism: Characterized by vomiting, abdominal pain, metallic or brassy taste in the mouth, rash, and sore gums and salivary glands

C. Interventions
1. Monitor vital signs.
2. Monitor triiodothyronine, thyroxine, and thyroid-stimulating hormone levels.
3. Monitor weight.
4. Instruct the client to take medication with meals to avoid gastrointestinal upset.
5. Instruct the client in how to monitor the pulse rate.
6. Inform the client of side effects and when to notify the physician.
7. Advise the client to contact the physician if a fever or sore throat develops.
8. Instruct the client in the signs of **hypothyroidism.**
9. Instruct the client regarding the importance of medication compliance and that abruptly stopping the medication could cause **thyroid storm.**
10. Instruct the client to monitor for signs and symptoms of **thyroid storm** (fever, flushed skin, confusion and behavioral changes, tachycardia, dysrhythmias, and signs of heart failure).
11. Instruct the client to monitor for signs of iodism.
12. Advise the client to consult physician before eating iodized salt and iodine-rich foods.
13. Instruct the client to avoid acetylsalicylic acid (aspirin) and medications containing iodine.

V. PARATHYROID MEDICATIONS (Box 54-4)
A. Description
1. Parathyroid hormone regulates serum calcium levels.
2. Low serum levels of calcium stimulate parathyroid hormone release.
3. Hyperparathyroidism results in a high serum calcium level and bone demineralization; medication is used to lower the serum calcium level.
4. Hypoparathyroidism results in a low serum calcium level, which increases neuromuscular excitability; treatment includes calcium and vitamin D supplements.
5. Calcium salts administered with digoxin (Lanoxin) increases the risk of digoxin toxicity.
6. Oral calcium salts reduce the absorption of tetracycline hydrochloride.
B. Interventions
1. Monitor electrolyte and calcium levels.
2. Assess for signs and symptoms of hypocalcemia and hypercalcemia.
3. Assess for symptoms of tetany in the client with hypocalcemia.
4. Assess for renal calculi in the client with hypercalcemia
5. Instruct the client in the signs and symptoms of hypercalcemia and hypocalcemia.

BOX 54-4
Medications to Treat Calcium Disorders

CALCIUM SUPPLEMENTS
Calcium carbonate (Caltrate 600, Rolaids, Tums)
Calcium carbonate (Os-Cal, Oysco, Oyst-Cal)
Calcium citrate (Citracal)
Calcium glubionate (Calcionate)
Calcium gluconate
Calcium lactate
Dibasic calcium phosphate
Tribasic calcium phosphate (Posture)

VITAMIN D SUPPLEMENTS
Calcitriol (Calcijex, Rocaltrol)
Ergocalciferol (Calciferol, Drisdol)

CALCIUM REGULATORS
Alendronate sodium (Fosamax)
Calcitonin human (Cibacalcin)
Calcitonin salmon (Miacalcin)
Etidronate disodium (Didronel)
Pamidronate disodium (Aredia)
Risedronate sodium (Actonel)
Tiludronate disodium (Skelid)

ANTIHYPERCALCEMICS
Cinacalcet hydrochloride (Sensipar)
Doxercalciferol (Hectorol)
Gallium nitrate (Ganite)
Paricalcitol (Zemplar)

---

6. Instruct the client to check over-the-counter medication labels for the possibility of calcium content.
7. Instruct the client receiving oral calcium supplements to maintain an adequate intake of vitamin D because vitamin D enhances absorption of calcium.
8. Instruct the client receiving calcium regulators such as alendronate sodium (Fosamax) to swallow the tablet whole with water at least 30 minutes before breakfast and not to lie down for at least 30 minutes.
9. Instruct the client using nasal spray of calcitonin (Miacalcin) to alternate nares.
10. Instruct the client using antihypercalcemic agents to avoid foods rich in calcium such as green, leafy vegetables, dairy products, shellfish, and soy.
11. Instruct the client not to take other medications within 1 hour of taking a calcium salt.
12. Instruct the client to increase fluid and fiber in diet to prevent constipation associated with calcium supplements.

BOX 54-5
Corticosteroid: Mineralocorticoid

Fludrocortisone acetate (Florinef Acetate)

BOX 54-6
Corticosteroids: Glucocorticoids

Dexamethasone (Decadron)
Hydrocortisone (Cortef)
Methylprednisolone (Medrol dose pack, Depo-Medrol, Solu-Medrol)
Prednisolone (Prelone, Orapred, Pediapred)
Prednisone (Orasone, Deltasone, Meticorten)
Triamcinolone (Aristocort)

VI. CORTICOSTEROIDS (MINERALOCORTICOIDS) (Box 54-5)

A. Description
1. Mineralocorticoids are steroid hormones that enhance the reabsorption of sodium and chloride and promote the excretion of potassium and hydrogen from the renal tubules, thereby helping maintain fluid and electrolyte balance.
2. Mineralocorticoids are used for replacement therapy in primary and secondary adrenal insufficiency in **Addison's disease.**

B. Side effects
1. Sodium and water retention (hypernatremia and edema), hypertension
2. Hypokalemia
3. Hypocalcemia
4. Osteoporosis, compression fractures
5. Weight gain
6. Heart failure

C. Interventions
1. Monitor vital signs.
2. Monitor intake and output and weight and for edema.
3. Monitor electrolyte and calcium levels.
4. Instruct the client to take medication with food or milk.
5. Instruct the client to consume a high-potassium diet.
6. Instruct the client not to stop the medication abruptly.
7. Instruct the client to report illness, such as severe diarrhea, vomiting, and fever.
8. Instruct the client to notify physician if low blood pressure, weakness, cramping, palpitations, or changes in mental status occur.
9. Instruct the client to wear a Medic-Alert bracelet.

VII. CORTICOSTEROIDS (GLUCOCORTICOIDS) (Box 54-6)

A. Description
1. Glucocorticoids affect glucose, protein, and bone metabolism, alter the normal immune response and suppress inflammation, and produce anti-inflammatory, antiallergic, and antistress effects.
2. Glucocorticoids may be used as a replacement for adrenocortical insufficiency.

B. Side effects
1. **Hyperglycemia**
2. Hypokalemia

3. Hypocalcemia, osteoporosis
4. Sodium and fluid retention
5. Weight gain
6. Mood swings
7. Moon face, buffalo hump, truncal obesity
8. Increased susceptibility to infection and masking of the signs and symptoms of infection
9. Cataracts
10. Hirsutism, acne, fragile skin, bruising
11. Growth retardation in children
12. Gastrointestinal (GI) irritation, peptic ulcer, pancreatitis
13. Seizures, psychosis

C. Contraindications and cautions
1. Contraindicated in clients with hypersensitivity, psychosis, and fungal infections
2. Should be used with caution in clients with **diabetes mellitus**
3. Used with extreme caution in clients with infections because they mask the signs and symptoms of an infection
4. Increase the potency of medications taken concurrently, such as aspirin, and nonsteroidal anti-inflammatory drugs, thus increasing the risk of gastrointestinal bleeding and ulceration.
5. Use of potassium-wasting diuretics increases potassium loss, resulting in hypokalemia.
6. Dexamethasone (Decadron) decreases the effects of orally administered anticoagulants and antidiabetic agents.
7. Barbiturates, phenytoin (Dilantin), and rifampin (Rifadin) decrease the effect of prednisone.

D. Interventions
1. Monitor vital signs.
2. Monitor serum electrolyte and blood glucose levels.
3. Monitor for hypokalemia and **hyperglycemia.**
4. Monitor intake and output and weight and for edema.
5. Monitor for hypertension.
6. Assess medical history for glaucoma, cataracts, peptic ulcer, mental health disorders, or **diabetes mellitus.**
7. Monitor the older client for signs and symptoms of increased osteoporosis.

8. Assess for changes in muscle strength.
9. Prepare a schedule for the client with information on short-term tapered doses.
10. Instruct the client that it is best to take medication in the early morning.
11. Advise the client to eat foods high in potassium.
12. Instruct the client to avoid individuals with respiratory infections.
13. Advise the client to inform all health care providers of the medication regimen.
14. Instruct the client to report signs and symptoms of a medication overdose or **Cushing's syndrome,** including a moon face, puffy eyelids, edema in the feet, increased bruising, dizziness, bleeding, and menstrual irregularities.
15. Note that the client may need additional doses during periods of stress, such as surgery.
16. Instruct the client not to stop the medication abruptly because abrupt withdrawal can result in severe adrenal insufficiency.
17. Advise the client to consult with the physician before receiving vaccinations.
18. Advise the client to wear a Medic-Alert bracelet.

VIII. ANDROGENS (Box 54-7)
A. Description
1. Used to replace deficient hormones or to treat hormone-sensitive disorders
2. Can cause bleeding if the client is taking oral anticoagulants (increase the effect of anticoagulants)
3. Can cause decreased serum glucose concentration, thereby reducing insulin requirements in the client with **diabetes mellitus**
4. Hepatotoxic medications are avoided with the use of androgens because of the risk of additive damage to the liver.
5. Androgens usually are avoided in men with known prostate or breast carcinoma because androgens often stimulate growth of these tumors.
B. Side effects
1. Masculine secondary sexual characteristics (body hair growth, lowered voice, muscle growth)
2. Bladder irritation and urinary tract infections
3. Breast tenderness
4. Gynecomastia
5. Priapism
6. Menstrual irregularities
7. Virilism
8. Sodium and water retention with edema
9. Nausea, vomiting, or diarrhea
10. Acne
11. Changes in libido
12. Hepatotoxicity, jaundice
13. Hypercalcemia

BOX 54-7
Androgens

Fluoxymesterone
Methyltestosterone (Testred, Virilon)
Testosterone preparations
   Testosterone, pellets (Testopel)
   Testosterone, transdermal (Androderm)
   Testosterone cypionate (Depo-Testosterone)
   Testosterone enanthate (Delatestryl)

C. Interventions
1. Monitor vital signs.
2. Monitor for edema, weight gain, and skin changes.
3. Assess mental status and neurological function.
4. Assess for signs of liver dysfunction, including right upper quadrant abdominal pain, malaise, fever, jaundice, and pruritus.
5. Assess for the development of secondary sexual characteristics.
6. Instruct the client to take medication with meals or a snack.
7. Instruct the client to notify the physician if priapism develops.
8. Instruct the client to notify the physician if fluid retention occurs.
9. Instruct women to use a nonhormonal contraceptive while on therapy.
10. For women, monitor for menstrual irregularities and decreased breast size.

IX. ESTROGENS AND PROGESTINS
A. Description
1. Estrogens are steroids that stimulate female reproductive tissue.
2. Progestins are steroids that specifically stimulate the uterine lining.
3. Estrogen and progestin preparations may be used to stimulate the endogenous hormones to restore hormonal balance or to treat hormone-sensitive tumors (suppress tumor growth) or for contraception (Boxes 54-8 and 54-9).
B. Contraindications and cautions
1. Estrogens
   a. Estrogens are contraindicated in clients with breast cancer, endometrial hyperplasia, endometrial cancer, history of thromboembolism, known or suspected pregnancy, or lactation.
   b. Use estrogens with caution in clients with hypertension, gallbladder disease, or liver or kidney dysfunction.
   c. Estrogens increase the risk of toxicity when used with hepatotoxic medications.
   d. Barbiturates, phenytoin (Dilantin), and rifampin (Rifadin) decrease the effectiveness of estrogen.

BOX 54-8

Estrogens

Diethylstilbestrol (DES)
Estradiol (Estrace, Climara, Estraderm, Vivelle)
Estradiol cypionate (Depo-Estradiol)
Estradiol hemihydrate (Estrasorb)
Estradiol valerate (Delestrogen)
Estrogens, conjugated (Premarin)
Estrone (from estropipate; Ogen)
Ethinyl estradiol
Norgestrel; ethinyl estradiol (Ogestrel 0.5/50)

BOX 54-9

Progestins

Hydroxyprogesterone
Levonorgestrel
Medroxyprogesterone acetate (Depo-Provera, Provera)
Medroxyprogesterone and conjugated estrogens (Premphase, Prempro)
Megestrol acetate (Megace)
Norethindrone acetate (Aygestin)
Progesterone (Crinone, Progestasert, Prometrium)

---

2. Progestins are contraindicated in clients with thromboembolic disorders and should be avoided in clients with breast tumors or hepatic disease.

C. Side effects
   1. Breast tenderness, menstrual changes
   2. Nausea, vomiting, and diarrhea
   3. Malaise, depression, excessive irritability
   4. Weight gain
   5. Edema and fluid retention
   6. Atherosclerosis
   7. Hypertension, stroke, myocardial infarction
   8. Thromboembolism (estrogen)
   9. Migraine headaches and vomiting (estrogen)

D. Interventions
   1. Monitor vital signs.
   2. Monitor for hypertension.
   3. Assess for edema and weight gain.
   4. Advise the client not to smoke.
   5. Advise the client to undergo routine breast and pelvic examinations.

X. CONTRACEPTIVES

A. Description
   1. These medications contain a combination of estrogen and a progestin or a progestin alone.
   2. Estrogen-progestin combinations suppress ovulation and change the cervical mucus, making it difficult for sperm to enter.
   3. Medications that contain only progestins are less effective than the combined medications.

   4. Contraceptives usually are taken for 21 consecutive days and stopped for 7 days; the administration cycle is then repeated.
   5. Contraceptives provide reversible prevention of pregnancy.
   6. Contraceptives are useful in controlling irregular or excessive menstrual cycles.
   7. Risk factors associated with the development of complications related to the use of contraceptives include smoking, obesity, and hypertension.
   8. Contraceptives are contraindicated in women with hypertension, thromboembolic disease, cerebrovascular or coronary artery disease, estrogen-dependent cancers, and pregnancy.
   9. Contraceptives should be avoided with the use of hepatotoxic medications.
   10. Contraceptives interfere with the activity of bromocriptine mesylate (Parlodel) and anticoagulants and increase the toxicity of tricyclic antidepressants.
   11. Contraceptives may alter blood glucose levels.
   12. Antibiotics may decrease the absorption and effectiveness of oral contraceptives.

B. Side effects
   1. Breakthrough bleeding
   2. Excessive cervical mucus formation
   3. Breast tenderness
   4. Hypertension
   5. Nausea, vomiting

C. Interventions
   1. Monitor vital signs and weight.
   2. Instruct the client in the administration of the medication (it may take up to 1 week for full contraceptive effect to occur when the medication is begun).
   3. Instruct the client with **diabetes mellitus** to monitor blood glucose levels carefully.
   4. Instruct the client to report signs of thromboembolic complications.
   5. Instruct the client to notify the physician if vaginal bleeding or menstrual irregularities occur or if pregnancy is suspected.
   6. Advise the client to use an alternate method of birth control when taking antibiotics because these may decrease absorption of the oral contraceptive.
   7. Instruct the client to perform breast self-examination monthly and about the importance of annual physical examinations.
   8. If the client decides to discontinue the contraceptive to become pregnant, recommend that the client use an alternative form of birth control for 2 months after discontinuation to ensure more complete excretion of hormonal agents before conception.

9. Contraceptive patches
   a. Designed to be worn for 3 weeks and removed for a 1-week period
   b. Applied on clean, dry, intact skin on the buttocks, abdomen, upper outer arm, or upper torso
   c. Instruct the client to peel away half of backing on patch, apply the sticky surface to the skin, remove the other half of the backing, and then press down on the patch with the palm for 10 seconds.
   d. Instruct the client to change the patch weekly, using a new location for each patch.
   e. If the patch falls off and remains off for less than 24 hours (such as when the client is sleeping or is unaware that it has fallen off), it can be reapplied if still sticky, or it can be replaced with a new patch.
   f. If the patch is off for more than 24 hours, a new 4-week cycle must be started immediately.
10. Vaginal ring
    a. Inserted into the vagina by the client, left in place for 3 weeks, and removed for 1 week
    b. The medication is absorbed through mucous membranes of the vagina.
    c. Removed rings should be wrapped in a foil pouch and discarded, not flushed down the toilet.
11. Implants and depot injections provide long-acting forms of birth control, from 3 months to 5 years in duration.

XI. FERTILITY MEDICATIONS (Box 54-10)

A. Description
   1. Fertility medications act to stimulate follicle development and ovulation in functioning ovaries and are combined with human chorionic gonadotropin to maintain the follicles once ovulation has occurred.
   2. Fertility medications are contraindicated in the presence of primary ovarian dysfunction, thyroid or adrenal dysfunction, ovarian cysts, pregnancy, or idiopathic uterine bleeding.
   3. Fertility medications should be used with caution in clients with thromboembolic or respiratory disease.
B. Side effects
   1. Risk of multiple births and birth defects
   2. Ovarian overstimulation (abdominal pain, distention, ascites, pleural effusion)
   3. Headache, irritability
   4. Fluid retention and bloating
   5. Nausea, vomiting
   6. Uterine bleeding
   7. Ovarian enlargement
   8. Gynecomastia

BOX 54-10
Fertility Medications

Bromocriptine mesylate (Parlodel)
Chorionic gonadotropin (Profasi)
Clomiphene citrate (Clomid)
Follitropin alfa (Gonal-f)
Follitropin beta (Follistim AQ)
Menotropins

---

   9. Rash
   10. Orthostatic hypotension
   11. Febrile reactions
C. Interventions
   1. Instruct the client regarding administration of the medication.
   2. Provide a calendar of treatment days and instructions on when intercourse should occur to increase therapeutic effectiveness of the medication.
   3. Provide information about the risks and hazards of multiple births.
   4. Instruct the client to notify the physician if signs of ovarian stimulation occur.
   5. Inform the client about the need for regular follow-up for evaluation.

XII. MEDICATIONS FOR ERECTILE DYSFUNCTION

A. Description
   1. Alprostadil (Caverject, Muse) is a prostaglandin that relaxes smooth muscle and promotes blood flow into the corpus cavernosum.
   2. Sildenafil (Viagra), tadalafil (Cialis), and vardenafil (Levitra) cause smooth muscle relaxation and allow blood flow into the corpus cavernosum.
   3. Erectile dysfunction medications are contraindicated in the presence of any anatomical obstruction or condition that might predispose to priapism and in clients with penile implants.
   4. Caution should be used in clients with bleeding disorders.
   5. Sildenafil, tadalafil, and vardenafil are used cautiously in clients with coronary artery disease, active peptic ulcer disease, bleeding disorders, or retinitis pigmentosa.
   6. Sildenafil, tadalafil, and vardenafil cannot be administered to clients taking nitrates, nitroprusside, or β-blockers.
B. Side effects
   1. Alprostadil: Pain at the injection site, infection, priapism, fibrosis, rash, hypertension
   2. Sildenafil, tadalafil, and vardenafil: Headache, flushing, dyspepsia, urinary tract infection, diarrhea, hypotension, dizziness, rash, neuralgia, insomnia
   3. Blurred vision and changes in color vision

C. Interventions
1. Perform a thorough assessment of health and medication history.
2. Instruct the client regarding administration of the medication; alprostadil is injected intracavernously or inserted urogenitally as a suppository; sildenafil, tadalafil, and vardenafil are taken orally.
▲ 3. Inform the client of side effects necessitating the need to notify the physician.

XIII. MEDICATIONS FOR DIABETES MELLITUS

▲ A. Insulin and oral hypoglycemic medications
1. Description
   a. Insulin increases glucose transport into cells and promotes conversion of glucose to glycogen, decreasing serum glucose levels.
   b. Oral hypoglycemic agents stimulate the pancreas to produce more insulin, increase the sensitivity of peripheral receptors to insulin, decrease hepatic glucose output, or delay intestinal absorption of glucose, thus decreasing serum glucose levels.
2. Contraindications and concerns
   a. Insulin is contraindicated in clients with hypersensitivity.
   b. Oral hypoglycemic agents are contraindicated in type 1 **diabetes mellitus**.
   ▲ c. β-Adrenergic blocking agents may mask signs and symptoms of **hypoglycemia** associated with hypoglycemic medications.
   d. Anticoagulants, chloramphenicol (Chloromycetin), salicylates, propranolol (Inderal), monoamine oxidase inhibitors, pentamidine (Pentam 300), and sulfonamides may cause **hypoglycemia**.
   ▲ e. Corticosteroids, sympathomimetics, thiazide diuretics, phenytoin (Dilantin), thyroid preparations, oral contraceptives, and estrogen compounds may cause **hyperglycemia**.
   ▲ f. Side effects of the sulfonylureas include gastrointestinal symptoms and dermatological reactions; **hypoglycemia** can occur when an excessive dose is administered or when meals are omitted or delayed, food intake is decreased, or activity is increased.
   ▲ g. Sulfonylureas, such as chlorpropamide (Diabinese), can cause a disulfiram (Antabuse) type of reaction when alcohol is ingested.
B. Oral hypoglycemic medications
1. Prescribed for clients with type 2 **diabetes mellitus**
2. Sulfonylureas (Box 54-11)
   a. Sulfonylureas may be classified as first- or second-generation sulfonylureas.
   b. Sulfonylureas stimulate the beta cells to produce more insulin.

BOX 54-11

Sulfonylureas and Nonsulfonylureas

SULFONYLUREAS
Acetohexamide
Chlorpropamide (Diabinese)
Glimepiride (Amaryl)
Glipizide (Glucotrol)
Glyburide (DiaBeta, Micronase)
Tolazamide
Tolbutamide (Orinase)

BIGUANIDE
Metformin (Glucophage)

ALPHA GLUCOSIDASE INHIBITORS
Acarbose (Precose)
Miglitol (Glyset)

THIAZOLIDINEDIONES
Pioglitazone (Actos)
Rosiglitazone (Avandia)

MEGLITINIDES
Nateglinide (Starlix)
Repaglinide (Prandin)

---

3. Biguanides (see Box 54-11)
   a. May be used alone or in combination with a sulfonylurea
   b. Suppresses hepatic production of glucose and increases insulin sensitivity
   c. Side effects: Diarrhea (most common), lactic acidosis (most serious)
4. Alpha-glucosidase inhibitors (see Box 54-11)
   a. Delay absorption of ingested carbohydrates (sucrose and complex carbohydrates), resulting in smaller increase in blood glucose level after meals.
   b. Do not increase insulin production
   c. Can be given alone or in combination with sulfonylureas
   d. Will not cause **hypoglycemia** when given alone
   e. Given with first bite of meal
5. Thiazolidinediones (see Box 54-11)
   a. Insulin-sensitizing agents that lower blood glucose by decreasing hepatic glucose production and improving target cell response to insulin
   b. May cause liver toxicity
6. Meglitinides (see Box 54-11)
   a. Stimulate pancreatic insulin secretion
   b. Quicker and shorter duration of action; therefore, less chance of **hypoglycemia** because blood glucose–lowering effect wears off quickly

c. Very fast onset of action allows client to take the medication with meals and skip a dose when a meal is skipped

7. Interventions
   a. Assess the client's knowledge of **diabetes mellitus** and the use of oral antidiabetic agents.
   b. Obtain a medication history regarding the medications that the client is taking currently.
   c. Assess vital signs and blood glucose levels.
   d. Instruct the client to recognize the signs and symptoms of **hypoglycemia** and **hyperglycemia**.
   e. Instruct the client to avoid over-the-counter medications unless prescribed by the health care provider.
   f. Instruct the client not to ingest alcohol with sulfonylureas.
   g. Inform the client that insulin may be needed during stress, surgery, or infection.
   h. Instruct the client in the necessity of compliance with prescribed medication.
   i. Instruct the client on how to take each specific medication, such as with the first bite of the meal for meglitinides and alpha-glucosidase inhibitors.
   j. Advise the client to wear a Medic-Alert bracelet.

C. Insulin
   1. Insulin primarily acts in the liver, muscle, and adipose tissue by attaching to receptors on cellular membranes and facilitating the passage of glucose, potassium, and magnesium.
   2. Insulin is prescribed for clients with type 1 **diabetes mellitus** and type 2 **diabetes mellitus** in clients whose blood glucose level is not controlled with oral hypoglycemic agents.
   3. The onset, peak, and duration of action depends on the insulin type (Table 54-2).
   4. Storing of insulin (Box 54-12)
   5. Insulin injection sites
      a. The main areas for injections are the abdomen, arms (posterior surface), thighs (anterior surface), and hips (Fig. 54-1).
      b. Insulin injected into the abdomen may absorb more evenly and rapidly than at other sites.
      c. Systematic rotation within one anatomical area is recommended to prevent lipodystrophy; client should be instructed not to use the same site more than once in a 2- to 3-week period.

TABLE 54-2

Activity of Subcutaneous Human Insulin

Preparation	Onset (hr)	Peak (hr)	Duration (hr)
RAPID-ACTING INSULIN			
Human insulin aspart (rDNA) injection (NovoLog)	0.25	1-3	3-5
Insulin lispro, human (rDNA) injection (Humalog)	0.25	0.5-1.5	3-4
Insulin glulisine (rDNA) injection (Apidra)	0.3	0.5-1.5	5
SHORT-ACTING INSULIN			
Regular human insulin (rDNA) injection			
Humulin R	0.5	2-4	6-8
Novolin R	0.5	2.5-5	8
Buffered regular human insulin injection	0.5	1-3	8
INTERMEDIATE-ACTING INSULIN			
Insulin, human, isophane suspension (NPH)	1.5	4-12	24
Insulin, human, zinc suspension	2.5	7-15	22
LONG-ACTING INSULIN			
Insulin, human, extended zinc suspension	4-6	8-20	28
Insulin, human, glargine injection (Lantus)	2-4	None	24
COMBINATION INSULIN			
Insulin aspart protamine 70%; insulin aspart 30% injection (Novolog Mix 70/30)	0.25	1-4	24
Insulin lispro protamine 75%; insulin lispro, human (rDNA) 25% (Humalog Mix 75/25)	0.25	1-2	24
Isophane human insulin suspension 70% (NPH); human insulin injection (regular) 30% (Humulin 70/30, Novolin 70/30)	0.5	2-12	24
Isophane human insulin suspension (NPH) 50%; human insulin injection (regular) 50% (Humulin 50/50)	0.5	3-5	24

From Ignatavicius, D., & Workman, M. (2006). *Medical surgical nursing: Critical thinking for collaborative care* (5th ed.). Philadelphia: W.B. Saunders.

BOX 54-12

Storing Insulin

Avoid exposing insulin to extremes in temperature.
Insulin should not be frozen or kept in direct sunlight or
  a hot car.
Before injection, insulin should be at room temperature.
If a vial of insulin will be used up in 1 month, it may be
  kept at room temperature; otherwise, the vial should
  be refrigerated.

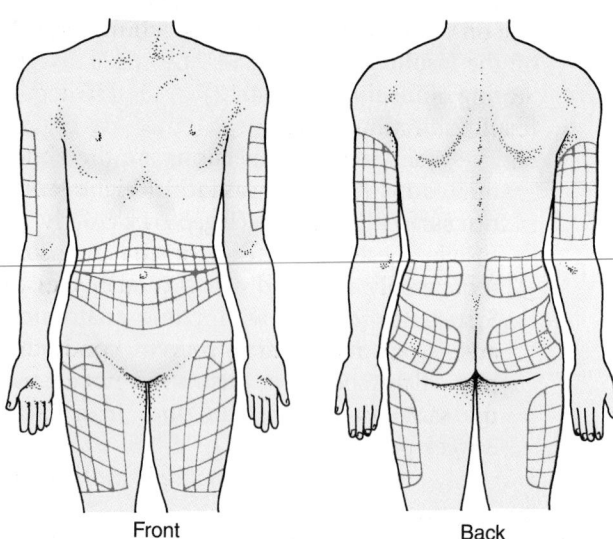

FIG. 54-1 Common insulin injection sites. (From Ignata-vicius, D., & Workman, M. [2006]. *Medical surgical nursing: Critical thinking for collaborative care* [5th ed.]. Philadelphia: W.B. Saunders.)

1 Wash hands.
2 Gently rotate NPH insulin bottle.
3 Wipe off tops of insulin vials with alcohol sponge.
4 Draw back amount of air into the syringe that equals total dose.

5 Inject air equal to NPH dose into NPH vial. Remove syringe from vial.   6 Inject air equal to regular dose into regular vial.

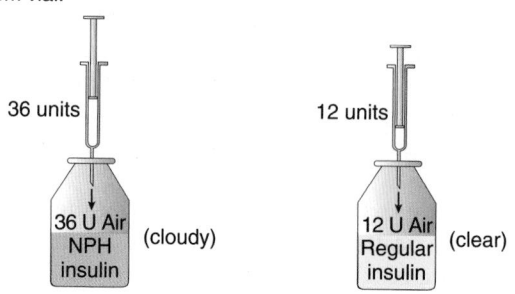

7 Invert regular insulin bottle and withdraw regular insulin dose.   8 Without adding more air to NPH vial, carefully withdraw NPH dose.

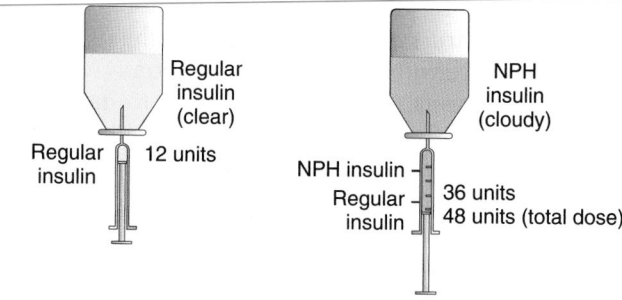

FIG. 54-2 Mixing insulins. (From Lewis, S., Heitkemper, M., & Dirksen, S. [2004]. *Medical-surgical nursing: Assessment and management of clinical problems* [6th ed.]. St. Louis: Mosby.)

d. Injections should be 1½ inches apart within the anatomical area.
e. Heat, massage, and exercise of the injected area can increase absorption rates and may result in **hypoglycemia.**
f. Injection into scar tissue may delay absorption of insulin.

6. Administering insulin
  a. To prevent dosage errors, be certain that there is a match between the insulin concentration noted on the vial and the calibration of units on the insulin syringe; the usual concentration of insulin is U 100 (100 units/mL).
  b. Most insulin syringes have a 27- to 29-gauge needle that is about ½-inch long.
  c. Before use, swirl insulin vial gently or rotate between palms to ensure that the insulin and ingredients are mixed well; otherwise, an inaccurate dose will be drawn; vigorously shaking the bottle will cause bubbles to form.

d. Premixed insulins (NPH and regular insulin) are available as 70/30 (most commonly used) and 50/50 (premixed insulin lispro protamine and insulin lispro 75/25 are also available).
e. Inject air into the insulin bottle (a vacuum makes it difficult to draw up the insulin).
f. When mixing insulins, draw up the regular (shorter acting) insulin first (Fig. 54-2).
g. Regular insulin may be mixed with NPH or Lente insulin.
h. Lispro insulin may be mixed with Humulin N or Humulin-U (Ultralente)
i. Insulin aspart protamine may be mixed with NPH insulin only.
j. Insulin zinc suspensions may be mixed only with each other and regular insulin, not with other types of insulin.
k. Insulin glargine *cannot* be mixed with any other types of insulin.
l. Administer a mixed dose of insulin within 5 to 15 minutes of preparation; after this

time, the regular insulin binds with the NPH insulin and its action is reduced.

    m. Aspiration generally is not recommended with self-injection of insulin.

    n. Administer insulin at a 45- to 90-degree angle in normal clients and at a 45- to 60-degree angle in thin persons.

    o. Remember: Regular insulin is the only type of insulin that can be administered intravenously.

D. Exubera (insulin, human [rDNA origin]) inhalation powder

  1. Short-acting inhaled insulin indicated for treatment of types 1 and 2 diabetes

  2. Consists of a fine dry powder insulin that enters the bloodstream more rapidly than by subcutaneous injection

  3. Inhaled 10 minutes before meals

  4. Causes a decrease in pulmonary function; pulmonary function studies are done before treatment starts and periodically during treatment

  5. Contraindicated in the client who smokes, starts smoking, or quits smoking less than 6 months prior to initiation of treatment; in the client with unstable or poorly controlled lung disease such as asthma, emphysema, or chronic obstructive pulmonary disease; in the pregnant client; and in individuals younger than 18 years.

  6. Side effects include cough, dry mouth, chest discomfort, **hypoglycemia.**

  7. Teach the client about the side effects of the medication, how and when to use the inhaler, and how to care for the inhaler.

E. Exenatide (Byetta)

  1. A synthetic hormone classified as an incretin mimetic that is administered subcutaneously.

  2. Used for clients with type 2 **diabetes mellitus** (not recommended for clients taking insulin nor should clients be taken off of insulin and given exenatide)

  3. Restores first-phase insulin response (first 10 minutes after food ingestion), lowers the production of glucagon after meals, slows gastric emptying (which limits the rise in the blood glucose level after a meal), reduces fasting and postprandial blood glucose levels, and reduces caloric intake, resulting in weight loss

  4. Packaged in premeasured doses (pen) that require refrigeration (cannot be frozen)

  5. Administered as a subcutaneous injection in the thigh, abdomen, or upper arm within 60 minutes before morning and evening meals; not taken after meals; if a dose is missed, the treatment regimen is resumed as prescribed with the next scheduled dose.

  6. Can cause mild to moderate nausea that abates with use.

F. Pramlintide (Symlin)

  1. Synthetic form of amylin, a naturally occurring hormone secreted by the pancreas

  2. Used for clients with types 1 and 2 **diabetes mellitus** who use insulin; given before meals to lower blood glucose level after meals, leading to less fluctuation during the day and better long-term glucose control

  3. Associated with an increased risk of insulin-induced severe **hypoglycemia,** particularly in clients with type 1 **diabetes mellitus**

  4. Gastrointestinal side effects including nausea can occur.

  5. Unopened vials are refrigerated; opened vials can be refrigerated or kept at room temperature for up to 28 days.

G. Glucagon

  1. Hormone secreted by the alpha cells of the islets of Langerhans in the pancreas

  2. Increases blood glucose level by stimulating glycogenolysis in the liver

  3. Can be administered subcutaneously, intramuscularly, or intravenously

  4. Used to treat insulin-induced **hypoglycemia** when the client is semiconscious or unconscious and is unable to ingest liquids

  5. The blood glucose level begins to increase within 5 to 20 minutes after administration.

  6. Instruct the family in the procedure for administration.

  7. See Chapter 53 for additional information regarding interventions for severe **hypoglycemia.**

H. Diazoxide (Proglycem)

  1. Increases blood glucose level by inhibiting insulin release from the beta cells and stimulating the release of epinephrine from the adrenal medulla

  2. Used to treat chronic **hypoglycemia** caused by hyperinsulinism resulting from islet cell cancer or hyperplasia

  3. Not used for hypoglycemic reactions from insulin

PRACTICE QUESTIONS

1. A client is taking NPH insulin daily every morning. The nurse instructs the client that the most likely time for a hypoglycemic reaction to occur is:
   1. 2 to 4 hours after administration
   2. 4 to 12 hours after administration
   3. 16 to 18 hours after administration
   4. 18 to 24 hours after administration

2. A client with diabetes mellitus visits a health care clinic. The client's diabetes mellitus previously had been well controlled with glyburide (DiaBeta), 5 mg orally daily, but recently the fasting blood glucose level has been 180 to 200 mg/dL. Which medication, if added to the client's regimen, may have contributed to the hyperglycemia?
   1. Phenelzine (Nardil)
   2. Atenolol (Tenormin)
   3. Prednisone (Deltasone)
   4. Allopurinol (Zyloprim)

3. A community health nurse visits a client at home. Prednisone (Deltasone), 10 mg orally daily, has been prescribed for the client and the nurse teaches the client about the medication. Which statement, if made by the client, indicates that further teaching is necessary?
   1. "I can take aspirin or my antihistamine if I need it."
   2. "I need to take the medication every day at the same time."
   3. "I need to avoid coffee, tea, cola, and chocolate in my diet."
   4. "If I gain more than 5 pounds a week, I will call my doctor."

4. Somatrem (Protropin) is administered to a client with growth failure. A nurse monitors the client, knowing that the expected therapeutic effect of this medication is to:
   1. Promote weight gain.
   2. Increase bone density.
   3. Stimulate linear growth.
   4. Decrease the mobilization of fats.

5. Desmopressin acetate (DDAVP) is prescribed for the treatment of diabetes insipidus. The nurse administering the medication monitors the client for which therapeutic response?
   1. Decreased blood glucose level
   2. Decreased urinary output
   3. Decreased blood pressure
   4. Decreased peripheral edema

6. A nurse is monitoring a client receiving desmopressin acetate (DDAVP) for adverse effects to the medication. Which of the following indicates the presence of an adverse effect?
   1. Insomnia
   2. Drowsiness

3. Weight loss
4. Increased urination

7. Vasopressin (Pitressin) is prescribed for a client with diabetes insipidus. A nurse is particularly cautious in monitoring the client receiving this medication if the client has which of the following preexisting conditions?
   1. Depression
   2. Endometriosis
   3. Pheochromocytoma
   4. Coronary artery disease

8. A nurse provides instructions to a client who is taking levothyroxine (Synthroid). The nurse tells the client to take the medication:
   1. With food
   2. At lunchtime
   3. On an empty stomach
   4. At bedtime with a snack

9. A nurse provides medication instructions to a client who is taking levothyroxine (Synthroid). The nurse instructs the client to notify the physician if which of the following occurs?
   1. Fatigue
   2. Tremors
   3. Cold intolerance
   4. Excessively dry skin

10. A nurse performs an admission assessment on a client who visits a health care clinic for the first time. The client tells the nurse that propylthiouracil (PTU) is taken daily. The nurse continues to collect data from the client, suspecting that the client has a history of:
    1. Myxedema
    2. Graves' disease
    3. Addison's disease
    4. Cushing's syndrome

11. A nurse is instructing a client regarding intranasal desmopressin (DDAVP). The nurse tells the client that which of the following is a side effect of the medication?
    1. Headache
    2. Vulval pain
    3. Runny nose
    4. Flushed skin

12. A client is receiving somatropin (Humatrope). The nurse monitors which most significant laboratory study during therapy with this medication?
    1. Lipase level
    2. Amylase level
    3. Blood urea nitrogen level
    4. Thyroid-stimulating hormone level

13. A client is scheduled for a subtotal thyroidectomy and potassium iodide (Lugol's solution) is prescribed. A nurse prepares to administer the medication, knowing that the therapeutic effect of this medication is to:
    1. Replace thyroid hormone.
    2. Prevent the oxidation of iodide.

3. Increase thyroid hormone production.

4. Suppress thyroid hormone production.

14. Potassium iodide (Lugol's solution) is prescribed for a client with thyrotoxic crisis. The client calls a clinic nurse and complains of a brassy taste in the mouth. The appropriate instruction to the client is which of the following?

   1. Continue with the medication.

   2. Withhold the medication and notify the physician.

   3. Take half of the prescribed dose for the next 24 hours.

   4. Withhold the medication for the next 24 hours and then continue as prescribed.

15. A nurse provides instructions to a client taking fludrocortisone acetate (Florinef Acetate). The nurse instructs the client to notify the physician if which of the following occurs?

   1. Nausea

   2. Fatigue

   3. Weight loss

   4. Swelling of the feet

16. Calcium carbonate (Os-Cal) is prescribed for a client with hypocalcemia. A nurse instructs the client to take the medication:

   1. With meals

   2. Every 4 hours

   3. Just before meals

   4. 1 hour after meals

17. A daily dose of prednisone (Deltasone) is prescribed for a client. A nurse provides instructions to the client regarding administration of the medication and instructs the client that the best time to take this medication is:

   1. At noon

   2. At bedtime

   3. Early morning

   4. Any time, at the same time, each day

18. Acarbose (Precose) is prescribed to treat a client with type 2 diabetes mellitus. Which instruction should the nurse include when teaching the client about this medication?

   1. Take the medication at bedtime.

   2. Take the medication with the first bite of each regular meal.

   3. The medication will be used to treat symptoms of hypoglycemia.

   4. Headache and dizziness are the most common side effects of this medication.

19. The nurse is caring for a 23-year-old client newly diagnosed with type 1 diabetes mellitus and teaches the client insulin administration. Which statement by the client indicates a need for further teaching?

   1. "It is not necessary for me to aspirate before injecting my insulin."

   2. "I will rotate my insulin injection between my arms, thighs, and abdomen on a daily basis."

   3. "I will perform a capillary blood glucose measurement before I administer my insulin regimen."

   4. "My glargine insulin is long-acting and should be administered once a day, but lispro insulin is given just before I eat."

20. Prednisone (Deltasone) is prescribed for a client with diabetes mellitus who is taking NPH insulin daily. Which of the following prescription changes does the nurse anticipate during therapy with the prednisone?

   1. An additional dose of prednisone daily

   2. A decreased amount of daily NPH insulin

   3. An increased amount of daily NPH insulin

   4. The addition of an oral hypoglycemic medication daily

21. A nurse is teaching a client how to mix regular insulin and NPH insulin in the same syringe. Which of the following actions, if performed by the client, indicates the need for further teaching?

   1. Withdraws the NPH insulin first

   2. Withdraws the regular insulin first

   3. Injects air into NPH insulin vial first

   4. Injects an amount of air equal to the desired dose of insulin into the vial

22. A home care nurse visits a client recently diagnosed with diabetes mellitus who is taking NPH insulin daily. The client asks the nurse how to store the unopened vials of insulin. The nurse tells the client to:

   1. Freeze the insulin.

   2. Refrigerate the insulin.

   3. Store the insulin in a dark, dry place.

   4. Keep the insulin at room temperature.

23. Glimepiride (Amaryl) is prescribed for a client with diabetes mellitus. A nurse instructs the client to avoid which of the following while taking this medication?

   1. Alcohol

   2. Organ meats

   3. Whole-grain cereals

   4. Carbonated beverages

24. Sildenafil (Viagra) is prescribed to treat a client with erectile dysfunction. A nurse reviews the client's medical record and would question the prescription if which of the following is noted in the client's history?

   1. Neuralgia

   2. Insomnia

   3. Use of nitroglycerin

   4. Use of multivitamins

25. The health care provider orders exenatide (Byetta) for a client with type 1 diabetes mellitus who takes insulin. The nurse plans to take which appropriate intervention?

   1. Administer the medication within 60 minutes before the morning and evening meal.

2. Hold the medication and call the health care provider, questioning the order for the client.

3. Monitor the client for gastrointestinal side effects after administering the medication.

4. Withdraw the insulin from the penlet into an insulin syringe to prepare for administration.

ALTERNATE ITEM FORMAT: MULTIPLE RESPONSE

The home health care nurse is visiting a client who was recently diagnosed with type 2 diabetes mellitus. The client is prescribed repaglinide (Prandin) and metformin (Glucophage) and asks the nurse to explain these medications. The nurse should provide which instructions to the client? Select all that apply.

❑ 1. Diarrhea can occur secondary to the metformin.

❑ 2. The repaglinide is not taken if a meal is skipped.

❑ 3. The repaglinide is taken 30 minutes before eating.

❑ 4. Candy or another simple sugar is carried and used to treat mild hypoglycemia episodes.

❑ 5. Metformin increases hepatic glucose production to prevent hypoglycemia associated with repaglinide.

❑ 6. Muscle pain is an expected side effect of metformin and may be treated with acetaminophen (Tylenol).

ALTERNATE ITEM FORMAT: FILL IN THE BLANK

A client with type 1 diabetes mellitus is admitted to the hospital with diabetic ketoacidosis and a serum glucose level of 789 mg/dL. The physician prescribes 10 units of regular insulin by intravenous (IV) bolus, followed by a continuous insulin infusion to infuse at 5 units/hr. The pharmacy sends 500 mL of normal saline solution containing 50 units of regular insulin. After administering the IV bolus of 10 units of regular insulin, the nurse sets the flow rate of the normal saline solution to infuse at how many milliliters per hour to deliver 5 units/hr?

_____ mL

ANSWERS

1. 2

Rationale: NPH is an intermediate-acting insulin. The onset of action is 1.5 hours, it peaks in 4 to 12 hours, and its duration of action is 24 hours. Hypoglycemic reactions most likely occur during peak time.

Test-Taking Strategy: Use the process of elimination and knowledge regarding the onset, peak, and duration of action for NPH insulin. Remember that NPH peaks in 4 to 12 hours. If you had difficulty with this question, review the characteristics of NPH insulin.

Level of Cognitive Ability: Application
Client Needs: Physiological Integrity
Integrated Process: Teaching and Learning
Content Area: Adult health—endocrine
Reference: Ignatavicius, D., & Workman, M. (2006). *Medical-surgical nursing: Critical thinking for collaborative care* (5th ed., p. 1518). Philadelphia: W.B. Saunders.

2. 3

Rationale: Prednisone may decrease the effect of oral hypoglycemics, insulin, diuretics, and potassium supplements. Option 1, a monoamine oxidase inhibitor, and option 2, a β-blocker, have their own intrinsic hypoglycemic activity. Option 4 decreases urinary excretion of sulfonylurea agents, causing increased levels of the oral agents, which can lead to hypoglycemia.

Test-Taking Strategy: Use the process of elimination and focus on the subject, an increase in the blood glucose level. Recalling that prednisone decreases the effects of oral hypoglycemics will direct you to the correct option. Review medication interactions with hypoglycemics if you had difficulty with this question.

Level of Cognitive Ability: Analysis

Client Needs: Physiological Integrity
Integrated Process: Nursing Process—analysis
Content Area: Adult health—endocrine
References: Ignatavicius, D., & Workman, M. (2006). *Medical-surgical nursing: Critical thinking for collaborative care* (5th ed., p. 1493). Philadelphia: W.B. Saunders.
Skidmore-Roth, L. (2005). *Mosby's drug guide for nurses* (6th ed., p. 714). St. Louis: Mosby.

3. 1

Rationale: Aspirin and other over-the-counter medications should not be taken unless the client consults with the physician. The client needs to take the medication at the same time every day and should be instructed not to stop the medication. A slight weight gain as a result of an improved appetite is expected, but after the dosage is stabilized, a weight gain of 5 lb or more weekly should be reported to the physician. Caffeine-containing foods and fluids need to be avoided because they may contribute to steroid-ulcer development.

Test-Taking Strategy: Use the process of elimination, noting the strategic words *further teaching is necessary*. These words indicate a negative event query and ask you to select an option that is an incorrect statement. Remember that a client should not take other medications, especially over-the-counter medications, without first consulting with his or her physician. Review teaching points for the client taking prednisone if you had difficulty with this question.

Level of Cognitive Ability: Analysis
Client Needs: Physiological Integrity
Integrated Process: Teaching and Learning
Content Area: Adult health—endocrine
Reference: Skidmore-Roth, L. (2005). *Mosby's drug guide for nurses* (6th ed., p. 714). St. Louis: Mosby.

4. 3

Rationale: Somatrem (Protropin) is a growth stimulator used in the long-term treatment of growth failure resulting from endogenous growth hormone deficiency. Somatrem stimulates linear growth and increases the number and size of muscle cells and increases red cell mass. Somatrem affects carbohydrate metabolism by antagonizing the action of insulin, increases mobilization of fats, and increases cellular protein synthesis. Options 1, 2, and 4 are not actions of this medication.

Test-Taking Strategy: Focus on the client's diagnosis to assist in the process of elimination. Note the relationship between the diagnosis and option 3. Review the action of this medication if you had difficulty with this question.

Level of Cognitive Ability: Analysis
Client Needs: Physiological Integrity
Integrated Process: Nursing Process—evaluation
Content Area: Pharmacology
Reference: Hodgson, B., & Kizior, R. (2007). *Saunders nursing drug handbook 2007* (p. 1068). Philadelphia: W.B. Saunders.

5. 2

Rationale: Desmopressin promotes renal conservation of water. The hormone carries out this action by acting on the collecting ducts of the kidney to increase their permeability to water, which results in increased water reabsorption. The therapeutic effect of this medication would be manifested by a decreased urine output. Options 1, 3, and 4 are unrelated to the effects of this medication.

Test-Taking Strategy: Use the process of elimination. Focus on the diagnosis in the question to assist in answering the question. Recalling the manifestations related to the loss of large volumes of urine in this disorder will help direct you to option 2. Review diabetes insipidus and the action of desmopressin if you had difficulty with this question.

Level of Cognitive Ability: Analysis
Client Needs: Physiological Integrity
Integrated Process: Nursing Process—evaluation
Content Area: Pharmacology
Reference: Hodgson, B., & Kizior, R. (2007). *Saunders nursing drug handbook 2007* (p. 331). Philadelphia: W.B. Saunders.

6. 2

Rationale: Water intoxication (overhydration) or hyponatremia is an adverse reaction to desmopressin. Early signs include drowsiness, listlessness, and headache. Decreased urination, rapid weight gain, confusion, seizures, and coma also may occur in overhydration.

Test-Taking Strategy: Use the process of elimination. Recalling that this medication is used to treat diabetes insipidus will assist you in eliminating options 3 and 4. Also, recalling the action of the medication will assist you in determining that water intoxication is an adverse reaction. This will direct you to option 2. Review the adverse effects related to this medication if you had difficulty with this question.

Level of Cognitive Ability: Analysis
Client Needs: Physiological Integrity
Integrated Process: Nursing Process—assessment
Content Area: Pharmacology
Reference: Skidmore-Roth, L. (2005). *Mosby's drug guide for nurses* (6th ed., p. 249). St. Louis: Mosby.

7. 4

Rationale: Because of its powerful vasoconstrictor actions, vasopressin can cause adverse cardiovascular effects. By constricting arteries of the heart, vasopressin can cause angina pectoris and even myocardial infarction, especially if administered to clients with coronary artery disease. In addition, vasopressin may cause vascular problems by decreasing blood flow in the periphery. Options 1, 2, and 3 are incorrect.

Test-Taking Strategy: Use the process of elimination. Note the relationship between the name of the medication, vasopressin, and coronary artery disease, the correct option. Review the cautions associated with the administration of this medication if you had difficulty with this question.

Level of Cognitive Ability: Analysis
Client Needs: Physiological Integrity
Integrated Process: Nursing Process—analysis
Content Area: Pharmacology
Reference: Hodgson, B. & Kizior, R. (2007). *Saunders nursing drug handbook 2007* (p. 1200). Philadelphia: Saunders.

8. 3

Rationale: Oral doses of levothyroxine (Synthroid) should be taken on an empty stomach to enhance absorption. Dosing should be done in the morning before breakfast.

Test-Taking Strategy: Use the process of elimination. Note that options 1, 2, and 4 are comparative or alike in that these options address administering the medication with food. Review client teaching points regarding the administration of levothyroxine if you had difficulty with this question.

Level of Cognitive Ability: Application
Client Needs: Physiological Integrity
Integrated Process: Teaching and Learning
Content Area: Pharmacology
Reference: Hodgson, B., & Kizior, R. (2007). *Saunders nursing drug handbook 2007* (p. 687). Philadelphia: Saunders.

9. 2

Rationale: Excessive doses of levothyroxine (Synthroid) can produce signs and symptoms of hyperthyroidism. These include tachycardia, chest pain, tremors, nervousness, insomnia, hyperthermia, heat intolerance, and sweating. The client should be instructed to notify the physician if these occur. Options 1, 3, and 4 are signs of hypothyroidism.

Test-Taking Strategy: Use the process of elimination, recalling the symptoms associated with hypothyroidism, the purpose of administering levothyroxine, and the effects of the medication. Options 1, 3, and 4 are symptoms related to hypothyroidism. Review the adverse effects of this medication if you are unfamiliar with them.

Level of Cognitive Ability: Application
Client Needs: Physiological Integrity
Integrated Process: Teaching and Learning
Content Area: Pharmacology
Reference: Hodgson, B., & Kizior, R. (2007). *Saunders nursing drug handbook 2007* (p. 688). Philadelphia: W.B. Saunders.

10. 2

Rationale: Propylthiouracil (PTU) inhibits thyroid hormone synthesis and is used to treat hyperthyroidism, or Graves' disease. Myxedema indicates hypothyroidism. Cushing's syndrome and Addison's disease are disorders related to adrenal function.

Test-Taking Strategy: Use the process of elimination and knowledge regarding the action of the medication and treatment measures for Graves' disease to answer the question. Remember that propylthiouracil is used to treat Graves' disease. Review this medication and Graves' disease if you had difficulty with this question.

Level of Cognitive Ability: Analysis
Client Needs: Physiological Integrity
Integrated Process: Nursing Process—assessment
Content Area: Pharmacology
References: Hodgson, B., & Kizior, R. (2007). *Saunders nursing drug handbook 2007* (pp. 982-983). Philadelphia: W.B. Saunders.
Skidmore-Roth, L. (2005). *Mosby's drug guide for nurses* (6th ed., pp. 730-731). St. Louis: Mosby.

11. **3**

Rationale: Desmopressin administered by the intranasal route can cause a runny or stuffy nose. Options 1, 2, and 4 are side effects if the medication is administered by the intravenous route.

Test-Taking Strategy: Note the relationship between the words *intranasal* in the question and *runny nose* in option 3. Review this medication if you are unfamiliar with it.

Level of Cognitive Ability: Application
Client Needs: Physiological Integrity
Integrated Process: Teaching and Learning
Content Area: Pharmacology
Reference: Skidmore-Roth, L. (2005). *Mosby's drug guide for nurses* (6th ed., pp. 248-249). St. Louis: Mosby.

12. **4**

Rationale: An adverse effect of somatropin (Humatrope) is hypothyroidism. Thyroid function is monitored throughout therapy. Options 1 and 2 would evaluate pancreatic function, and option 3 evaluates renal function.

Test-Taking Strategy: Use the process of elimination. Eliminate options 1 and 2 first because both evaluate pancreatic function and therefore are comparative or alike. Next, eliminate option 3 because it evaluates renal function. Recalling that somatropin is a growth hormone will assist in directing you to option 4. If you had difficulty with this question, review interventions associated with the administration of somatropin.

Level of Cognitive Ability: Analysis
Client Needs: Physiological Integrity
Integrated Process: Nursing Process—assessment
Content Area: Pharmacology
Reference: Hodgson, B., & Kizior, R. (2007). *Saunders nursing drug handbook 2007* (p. 1068). Philadelphia: W.B. Saunders.
Skidmore-Roth, L. (2005). *Mosby's drug guide for nurses* (6th ed., p. 790). St. Louis: Mosby.

13. **4**

Rationale: Lugol's solution is administered to hyperthyroid individuals in preparation for thyroidectomy to suppress thyroid function. Initial effects develop within 24 hours; peak effects develop in 10 to 15 days. In most cases, plasma levels of thyroid hormone are reduced with propylthiouracil (PTU) before Lugol's solution therapy is initiated. Then, Lugol's solu-

tion along with propylthiouracil, is administered for the last 10 days before surgery.

Test-Taking Strategy: Use the process of elimination. Eliminate options 1 and 3 first because they are comparative or alike. From the remaining options, select option 4 because of its relationship to the subject of the question. If you had difficulty with this question, review the purpose of this medication for the client scheduled for subtotal thyroidectomy.

Level of Cognitive Ability: Comprehension
Client Needs: Physiological Integrity
Integrated Process: Nursing Process—planning
Content Area: Pharmacology
References: Kee, J., Hayes, E., & McCuistion, L. (2006). *Pharmacology: A nursing process approach* (5th ed., p. 764). Philadelphia: W.B. Saunders.
Mosby. (2007). 2007 *Mosby's nursing drug reference* (20th ed., p. 821). St. Louis: Mosby.

14. **2**

Rationale: Chronic ingestion of iodine can produce iodism. The client needs to be instructed about the symptoms of iodism, which include a brassy taste, soreness of gums and teeth, vomiting, and abdominal pain. The client needs to be instructed to notify the physician if these symptoms occur.

Test-Taking Strategy: Use the process of elimination. Eliminate options 3 and 4 first because the nurse cannot legally alter medication prescriptions without a physician's order. Considering the client symptoms presented in the question will eliminate option 1. Review the adverse effects of iodine solution if you had difficulty with this question.

Level of Cognitive Ability: Application
Client Needs: Physiological Integrity
Integrated Process: Nursing Process—implementation
Content Area: Pharmacology
Reference: Mosby. (2007). 2007 *Mosby's nursing drug reference* (20th ed., p. 822). St. Louis: Mosby.

15. **4**

Rationale: Excessive levels of fludrocortisone acetate (Florinef) cause retention of sodium and water and excessive excretion of potassium, resulting in expansion of blood volume, hypertension, cardiac enlargement, edema, and hypokalemia. The client needs to be informed about the signs of sodium and water retention, such as unusual weight gain or swelling of the feet or lower legs. If these signs occur, the physician needs to be notified.

Test-Taking Strategy: Use the process of elimination. Recalling that fludrocortisone acetate can cause water retention will direct you to option 4. Review client teaching points related to this medication if you had difficulty with this question.

Level of Cognitive Ability: Application
Client Needs: Physiological Integrity
Integrated Process: Teaching and Learning
Content Area: Pharmacology
Reference: Hodgson, B., & Kizior, R. (2007). *Saunders nursing drug handbook 2007* (pp. 418, 489). Philadelphia: W.B. Saunders.

16. **4**

Rationale: Calcium carbonate tablets should be taken with a full glass of water 30 to 60 minutes after meals. Therefore, options 1, 2, and 3 are incorrect.

Test-Taking Strategy: Use the process of elimination. Option 2 easily can be eliminated first. From the remaining options, eliminate options 1 and 3 because they are comparative or alike. If you are unfamiliar with the administration of calcium supplements, review this information.
Level of Cognitive Ability: Application
Client Needs: Physiological Integrity
Integrated Process: Teaching and Learning
Content Area: Pharmacology
Reference: Hodgson, B., & Kizior, R. (2007). *Saunders nursing drug handbook 2007* (p. 173). Philadelphia: W.B. Saunders.

17. 3
Rationale: Corticosteroids (glucocorticoids) should be administered before 9 AM. Administration at this time helps minimize adrenal insufficiency and mimics the burst of glucocorticoids released naturally by the adrenal glands each morning. Options 1, 2, and 4 are incorrect.
Test-Taking Strategy: Use the process of elimination. Note the suffix -*sone* and recall that medication names that end with these letters are corticosteroids. This will direct you to option 3. If you had difficulty with this question, review the administration of glucocorticoids.
Level of Cognitive Ability: Application
Client Needs: Physiological Integrity
Integrated Process: Teaching and Learning
Content Area: Pharmacology
Reference: Hodgson, B., & Kizior, R. (2007). *Saunders nursing drug handbook 2007* (p. 958). Philadelphia: W.B. Saunders.

18. 2
Rationale: Acarbose (Precose) is an alpha-glucosidase inhibitor. Taken with the first bite of each major meal, acarbose delays absorption of ingested carbohydrates, decreasing postprandial hyperglycemia. Abdominal pain and flatulence are the most common side effects of this medication. It is not taken at bedtime.
Test-Taking Strategy: Focus on the medication and the client's diagnosis. Recalling that the medication is an antihyperglycemic will direct you to the correct option. Review this medication if you had difficulty with this question.
Level of Cognitive Ability: Application
Client Needs: Physiological Integrity
Integrated Process: Teaching and Learning
Content Area: Pharmacology
Reference: Lilley, L., Harrington, S., & Snyder, J. (2005). *Pharmacology and the nursing process* (4th ed., p. 525). St. Louis: Mosby.

19. 2
Rationale: Rotation of insulin injections should be done within one anatomical site to maintain consistent absorption of insulin. Options 1, 3, and 4 are correct statements regarding insulin administration and thus do not indicate a need for additional client teaching.
Test-Taking Strategy: Note the strategic words *need for further teaching*. These indicate a negative event query and ask you to select an option that is incorrect. Remember that insulin injections should be rotated within one anatomical site to maintain consistent absorption of insulin. Review informa-

tion related to insulin administration if you had difficulty with this question.
Level of Cognitive Ability: Analysis
Client Needs: Physiological Integrity
Integrated Process: Teaching and Learning
Content Area: Pharmacology
References: Lewis, S., Heitkemper, M., & Dirksen, S. (2004). *Medical-surgical nursing: Assessment and management of clinical problems* (6th ed., pp. 1275-1276). St. Louis: Mosby.
Lilley, L., Harrington, S., & Snyder, J. (2005). *Pharmacology and the nursing process* (4th ed., pp. 521-522, 530). St. Louis: Mosby.

20. 3
Rationale: Glucocorticoids can elevate blood glucose levels. Clients with diabetes mellitus may need their dosages of insulin or oral hypoglycemic medications increased during glucocorticoid therapy. Therefore, options 1, 2, and 4 are incorrect.
Test-Taking Strategy: Use the process of elimination. Recalling that glucocorticoids can increase blood glucose levels will direct you to option 3. Review the effects of glucocorticoids if you had difficulty with this question.
Level of Cognitive Ability: Analysis
Client Needs: Physiological Integrity
Integrated Process: Nursing Process—analysis
Content Area: Pharmacology
Reference: Hodgson, B., & Kizior, R. (2006). *Saunders nursing drug handbook 2006* (p. 959). Philadelphia: Saunders.

21. 1
Rationale: When preparing a mixture of regular insulin with another insulin preparation, the regular insulin is drawn into the syringe first. This sequence will avoid contaminating the vial of regular insulin with insulin of another type. Options 2, 3, and 4 identify the correct actions for preparing NPH and regular insulin.
Test-Taking Strategy: Use the process of elimination, noting the strategic words *need for further teaching*. These words indicate a negative event query and ask you to select an option that is an incorrect action. Remember *RN*—draw up the *R*egular insulin before the *N*PH insulin. Review the procedure for preparing NPH and regular insulin if you had difficulty with this question.
Level of Cognitive Ability: Analysis
Client Needs: Physiological Integrity
Integrated Process: Teaching and Learning
Content Area: Pharmacology
Reference: Hodgson, B., & Kizior, R. (2007). *Saunders nursing drug handbook 2007* (p. 621). Philadelphia: W.B. Saunders.

22. 2
Rationale: Insulin in unopened vials should be stored under refrigeration until needed. Vials should not be frozen. When stored unopened under refrigeration, insulin can be used up to the expiration date on the vial. Options 1, 3, and 4 are incorrect.
Test-Taking Strategy: Use the process of elimination and note the strategic words *store the unopened vials* in the question. Remembering that insulin should not be frozen will assist in eliminating option 1. Options 3 and 4 are comparative or alike and should be eliminated. Review client teaching points

related to insulin if you had difficulty with this question.
Level of Cognitive Ability: Application
Client Needs: Physiological Integrity
Integrated Process: Teaching and Learning
Content Area: Pharmacology
Reference: Hodgson, B., & Kizior, R. (2007). *Saunders nursing drug handbook 2007* (p. 621). Philadelphia: W.B. Saunders.

23. **1**
Rationale: When alcohol is combined with glimepiride (Amaryl), a disulfiram-like reaction may occur. This syndrome includes flushing, palpitations, and nausea. Alcohol can also potentiate the hypoglycemic effects of the medication. Clients need to be instructed to avoid alcohol consumption while taking this medication. The items in options 2, 3, and 4 do not need to be avoided.
Test-Taking Strategy: Use the process of elimination. Eliminate options 2, 3, and 4 because these food items are allowed in a diabetic diet. Remembering that alcohol can affect the action of many medications will assist in directing you to option 1. Review this medication if you had difficulty with this question.
Level of Cognitive Ability: Application
Client Needs: Physiological Integrity
Integrated Process: Teaching and Learning
Content Area: Pharmacology
Reference: Kee, J., & Hayes, E., McCuistion, L. (2006). *Pharmacology: A nursing process approach* (5th ed., p. 789). Philadelphia: W.B. Saunders.

24. **3**
Rationale: Sildenafil (Viagra) enhances the vasodilating effect of nitric oxide in the corpus cavernosum of the penis, thus sustaining an erection. Because of the effect of the medication, it is contraindicated with concurrent use of organic nitrates and nitroglycerin. Sildenafil is not contraindicated with the use of vitamins. Neuralgia and insomnia are side effects of the medication.
Test-Taking Strategy: Use the process of elimination, noting the strategic words *would question the prescription*. Recalling the action of the medication will direct you to option 3. If you had difficulty with this question, review the contraindications associated with the use of this medication.
Level of Cognitive Ability: Analysis
Client Needs: Physiological Integrity
Integrated Process: Nursing Process—analysis
Content Area: Pharmacology
Reference: Hodgson, B., & Kizior, R. (2007). *Saunders nursing drug handbook 2007* (p. 1053). Philadelphia: W.B. Saunders.

25. **2**
Rationale: Exenatide (Byetta) is an incretin mimetic used for type 2 diabetes mellitus only. It is not recommended for clients taking insulin. Hence, the nurse should hold the medication and question the health care provider regarding this order. Although options 1 and 3 are correct statements about the medication, in this situation the medication should not be administered. The medication is packaged in prefilled pens ready for injection without the need for drawing it up into another syringe.

Test-Taking Strategy: Use the process of elimination. Eliminate option 4 because the medication is packaged in prefilled pens ready for injection without the need for drawing it up into another syringe. From the remaining options, focus on the data in the question. Although options 1 and 3 are appropriate when administering this medication, this client should not receive the medication. Review this medication if you had difficulty with this question.
Level of Cognitive Ability: Application
Client Needs: Physiological Integrity
Integrated Process: Nursing Process—planning
Content Area: Pharmacology
Reference: The Diabetes Monitor. (2007). Exenatide (Byetta). http://www.diabetesmonitor.com/byetta.htm.

ALTERNATE ITEM FORMAT: MULTIPLE RESPONSE
Answer: 1, 2, 3, 4
Rationale: Repaglinide is a rapid-acting oral hypoglycemic agent that stimulates pancreatic insulin secretion that should be taken before meals, and that should be held if the client does not eat. Hypoglycemia is a side effect of repaglinide and the client should always be prepared by carrying a simple sugar with her or him at all times. Metformin is an oral hypoglycemic given in combination with repaglinide and works by decreasing hepatic glucose production. A common side effect of metformin is diarrhea. Muscle pain may occur as an adverse effect from metformin but it might signify a more serious condition that warrants physician notification, not the use of acetaminophen.
Test-Taking Strategy: Focus on the data in the question and the client's diagnosis to assist in answering the question. Also, recalling the actions and effects of these medications will assist in answering correctly. Review these medications if you are not familiar with them.
Level of Cognitive Ability: Application
Client Needs: Physiological Integrity
Integrated Process: Nursing Process—implementation
Content Area: Pharmacology
Reference: Hodgson, B., & Kizior, R. (2007). *Saunders nursing drug handbook 2007* (pp. 744, 1010). Philadelphia: W.B. Saunders.

ALTERNATE ITEM FORMAT: FILL IN THE BLANK
Answer: 50
Rationale: This is a dosage calculation problem. Because the physician does not order a specific intravenous rate (mL/hr), the nurse needs to determine how many milliliters of the normal saline solution contains 5 units of insulin. Using the ratio and proportion method for dosage calculation and the information contained in the question, the calculation is as follows:
5 units:X mL::50 units:500 mL
Then, cross-multiply the extremes (outside numbers) (5 units × 500 mL) and the means (inside numbers) (X mL × 50 units) to obtain 2500 = 50X.
The next step is dividing both sides by 50 to solve for X:
X = 50 mL

Therefore, 50 mL = 5 units and the infusion rate is 50 mL/hr to administer 5 units/hr.

Test-Taking Strategy: Focus on the subject of the question, the infusion rate to infuse 5 units per hour. Recall the ratio and proportion method to calculate correct dosages and focus on the data in the question to perform the calculation. Use a calculator to verify the answer. Review dosage calculation by the ratio and proportion method if you have difficulty with this question.

Level of Cognitive Ability: Application
Client Needs: Physiological Integrity
Integrated Process: Nursing Process—implementation
Content Area: Adult health—endocrine
Reference: Brown, M., & Mulholland, J. (2004). *Drug calculations: Process and problems for clinical practice* (7th ed., p. 165). St. Louis: Mosby.

REFERENCES

The Diabetes Monitor. (2007). Exenatide (Byetta). http://www. diabetesmonitor.com/byetta.htm.

Exubera (insulin human [rDNA origin]) Inhalation Powder. (2007). http://www.exubera.com/ content/con.

Hodgson, B., & Kizior, R. (2007). *Saunders nursing drug handbook 2007.* Philadelphia: W.B. Saunders.

Ignatavicius, D. & Workman, M. (2006). *Medical-surgical nursing: Critical thinking for collaborative care* (5th ed.). Philadelphia: W.B. Saunders.

Kee, J., Hayes, E., & McCuistion, L. (2006). *Pharmacology: A nursing process approach* (5th ed.). Philadelphia: W.B. Saunders.

Lilley, L., Harrington, S., & Snyder, J. (2005). *Pharmacology and the nursing process* (4th ed.). St. Louis: Mosby.

Mosby. (2007). *2007 Mosby's nursing drug reference* (20th ed.). St. Louis: Mosby.

Skidmore-Roth, L. (2005). *Mosby's drug guide for nurses* (6th ed.). St. Louis: Mosby.

The Adult Client With a Gastrointestinal Disorder

PYRAMID TERMS

ascites The accumulation of fluid within the peritoneal cavity that results from venous congestion of the hepatic capillaries, which leads to plasma leaking directly from the liver surface and portal vein.

asterixis A coarse tremor characterized by rapid, nonrhythmic extensions and flexions in the wrist and fingers; also termed *liver flap*.

Billroth I Partial gastrectomy with the remaining segment being anastomosed to duodenum; also termed *gastroduodenostomy*.

Billroth II Partial gastrectomy with the remaining segment being anastomosed to the jejunum; also termed *gastrojejunostomy*.

cholecystectomy Removal of the gallbladder.

cholecystitis An inflammation of the gallbladder that may occur as an acute or chronic process. Acute inflammation is associated with gallstones (cholelithiasis). Chronic cholecystitis results when inefficient bile emptying and gallbladder muscle wall disease causes a fibrotic and contracted gallbladder.

choledocholithotomy Incision into the common bile duct to remove a gallstone.

cirrhosis A chronic progressive disease of the liver characterized by diffuse degeneration and destruction of hepatocytes. Repeated destruction of hepatic cells causes the formation of scar tissue.

Crohn's disease An inflammatory disease that can occur anywhere in the gastrointestinal tract but most often affects the terminal ileum; leads to thickening and scarring, narrowed lumen, fistulas, ulcerations, and abscesses. The disease is characterized by remissions and exacerbations.

Cullen's sign Bluish discoloration of the abdomen and periumbilical area seen in acute hemorrhagic pancreatitis.

diverticulitis Inflammation of one or more diverticula from penetration of fecal matter through the thin-walled diverticula, resulting in local abscess formation. A perforated diverticulum can progress to intraabdominal perforation with generalized peritonitis.

diverticulosis Outpouching or herniations of the intestinal mucosa that can occur in any part of the intestine but is most common in the sigmoid colon.

dumping syndrome Rapid emptying of the gastric contents into the small intestine, which occurs following gastric resection.

esophageal varices Dilated and tortuous veins in the submucosa of the esophagus caused by portal hypertension, often associated with liver cirrhosis; at high risk for rupture if portal circulation pressure rises.

fetor hepaticus The fruity, musty breath odor associated with severe chronic liver disease.

gastrectomy Removal of the stomach with attachment of the esophagus to the jejunum or duodenum; also termed *esophagojejunostomy* or *esophagoduodenostomy*.

gastric resection Removal of the lower half of the stomach, usually including a vagotomy; also termed *antrectomy*.

hiatal hernia A portion of the stomach that herniates through the diaphragm and into the thorax. Herniation results from weakening of the muscles of the diaphragm and is aggravated by factors that increase abdominal pressure, such as pregnancy, ascites, obesity, tumors, and heavy lifting; also termed *esophageal* or *diaphragmatic hernia*.

Kock ileostomy (continent ileostomy) An intraabdominal pouch constructed from the terminal ileum. The pouch is connected to the stoma with a nipple-like valve constructed from a portion of the ileum. The stoma is flush with the skin.

Murphy's sign A sign of gallbladder disease consisting of pain on taking a deep breath when the examiner's fingers are on the approximate location of the gallbladder.

pancreatitis An acute or chronic inflammation of the pancreas, with associated escape of pancreatic enzymes into surrounding tissue. Acute pancreatitis can occur suddenly as one attack or can be recurrent with resolution. Chronic pancreatitis is a continual inflammation and destruction of the pancreas, with scar tissue replacing pancreatic tissue.

peristalsis Wave-like rhythmic contractions that propel material through the gastrointestinal tract.

portal hypertension A persistent increase in pressure within the portal vein that develops as a result of obstruction to flow.

pyloroplasty Enlarging the pylorus to prevent or decrease pyloric obstruction, thereby enhancing gastric emptying.

Turner's sign A gray-blue discoloration of the flanks seen in acute hemorrhagic pancreatitis.

Ulcerative colitis Ulcerative and inflammatory disease of the bowel that results in poor absorption of nutrients. Acute ulcerative colitis results in vascular congestion, hemorrhage, edema, and ulceration of the bowel mucosa. Chronic ulcerative colitis causes muscular hypertrophy, fat deposits, and fibrous tissue with bowel thickening, shortening, and narrowing.

vagotomy Surgical division of the vagus nerve to eliminate the vagal impulses that stimulate hydrochloric acid secretion in the stomach.

▲ PYRAMID TO SUCCESS

Pyramid Points focus on diagnostic tests and nursing care related to the various gastric or intestinal tubes, gastric surgery, cirrhosis, hepatitis, pancreatitis, and colostomy care. Focus on preprocedure and postprocedure care of the client undergoing a gastrointestinal diagnostic test. Remember that an informed consent is required for any invasive procedure. Focus on diet restrictions before and after the diagnostic test and remember that the gag reflex or bowel sounds must return before allowing a client to consume food or fluids. Pyramid Points include instructions to the client and family regarding the prevention of gastrointestinal disorders and the complications associated with the disorder. Focus on teaching the client and family about diet and nutrition specific to the disorder, tube and wound care, preventing the transmission of infection, and care of a colostomy or ileostomy. Remember that body image disturbances can occur in clients with a gastrointestinal disorder. Specific focus relates to the client with a diversion, such as an ileostomy or colostomy, the social isolation issues that can occur and effective coping strategies. The Integrated Processes addressed in this unit include Caring, Communication and Documentation, Nursing Process, and Teaching/Learning.

▲ CLIENT NEEDS

Safe and Effective Care Environment

Consulting with other health care professionals regarding the client's nutritional status
Ensuring that confidentiality issues related to the gastrointestinal disorder are maintained
Establishing priorities of care
Handling infectious drainage and secretions safely
Maintaining standard precautions and other precautions as appropriate
Obtaining informed consent for treatments and surgical procedures
Obtaining referrals for home care and community services
Preventing disease transmission

Health Promotion and Maintenance

Performing physical assessment techniques of the gastrointestinal system
Preventing disease related to the gastrointestinal system
Providing health screening and health promotion programs related to gastrointestinal disorders
Teaching related to colostomy or ileostomy care
Teaching related to preventing the transmission of disease
Teaching related to prescribed dietary and other treatment measures

Psychosocial Integrity

Assessing coping mechanisms
Considering end-of-life and grief and loss issues
Identifying available support systems
Monitoring for expected body image changes related to colostomy or ileostomy

Physiological Integrity

Administering medications as prescribed specific to the gastrointestinal disorder
Assessing for signs and symptoms of infectious diseases of the gastrointestinal tract
Assisting with personal hygiene
Monitoring elimination patterns
Monitoring for complications related to tests, procedures, and surgical interventions
Monitoring for fluid and electrolyte imbalances
Monitoring laboratory values related to gastrointestinal disorders
Monitoring parenterally administered fluids, including parenteral nutrition
Providing adequate nutrition and oral hydration
Providing care for gastrointestinal tubes
Providing nonpharmacological and pharmacological comfort measures
Providing preprocedure and postprocedure care for diagnostic tests related to the gastrointestinal system

REFERENCES

Chernecky, C., & Berger, B. (2004). *Laboratory tests and diagnostic procedures* (4th ed.). Philadelphia: W.B. Saunders.
Harkreader, H., & Hogan, M. A. (2004). *Fundamentals of nursing: Caring and clinical judgment* (2nd ed.). Philadelphia: W.B. Saunders.
Ignatavicius, D., & Workman, M. (2006). *Medical-surgical nursing: Critical thinking for collaborative care* (5th ed.). Philadelphia: W.B. Saunders.
Jarvis, C. (2004). *Physical examination and health assessment* (4th ed.). St. Louis: W.B. Saunders.
Lewis, S., Heitkemper, M., & Dirksen, S. (2004). *Medical-surgical nursing: Assessment and management of clinical problems* (6th ed.). St. Louis: Mosby.
Lilley, L., Harrington, S., & Snyder, J. (2005). *Pharmacology and the nursing process* (4th ed.). St. Louis: Mosby.
Mosby. (2006). *Mosby's dictionary of medicine, nursing and health professions* (7th ed.). St. Louis: Mosby.
National Council of State Boards of Nursing (Eds.) (2007). *2007 NCLEX-RN® detailed test plan.* Chicago: Author.
Potter, P., & Perry, A. (2005) *Fundamentals of nursing* (6th ed.). St. Louis: Mosby.
Varcarolis, E., Carson, V., & Shoemaker, N. (2006). *Foundations of psychiatric mental health nursing: A clinical approach* (5th ed.). Philadelphia: W.B. Saunders.

Gastrointestinal System

I. ANATOMY AND PHYSIOLOGY

A. Functions of the gastrointestinal system
1. Process food substances.
2. Absorb the products of digestion into the blood.
3. Excrete unabsorbed materials.
4. Provide an environment for microorganisms to synthesize nutrients, such as vitamin K.
5. For risk factors associated with the gastrointestinal system, see Box 55-1.

B. Mouth
1. Contains the lips, cheeks, palate, tongue, teeth, salivary glands, muscles, and maxillary bones
2. Saliva contains the amylase enzyme (ptyalin) that aids in digestion.

C. Esophagus
1. Collapsible muscular tube about 10 inches long
2. Carries food from the pharynx to the stomach

D. The stomach
1. Contains the cardia, fundus, the body, and the pylorus
2. Mucous glands are located in the mucosa and prevent autodigestion by providing an alkaline protective covering.
3. The lower esophageal (cardiac) sphincter prevents reflux of gastric contents into the esophagus.
4. The pyloric sphincter regulates the rate of stomach emptying into the small intestine.
5. Hydrochloric acid kills microorganisms, breaks food into small particles, and provides a chemical environment that facilitates gastric enzyme activation.
6. Pepsin is the chief coenzyme of gastric juice, which converts proteins into proteases and peptones.

7. Intrinsic factor is necessary for the absorption of vitamin B_{12}.
8. Gastrin controls gastric acidity.

E. Small intestine
1. The duodenum contains the openings of the bile and pancreatic ducts.
2. The jejunum is about 8 feet long.
3. The ileum is about 12 feet long.
4. The small intestine terminates in the cecum.

F. Pancreatic intestinal juice enzymes
1. Amylase digests starch to maltose.
2. Maltase reduces maltose to monosaccharide glucose.
3. Lactase splits lactose into galactose and glucose.
4. Sucrase reduces sucrose to fructose and glucose.

5. Nucleases split nucleic acids to nucleotides.
6. Enterokinase activates trypsinogen to trypsin.

G. Large intestine
1. About 5 feet long
2. Absorbs water and eliminates wastes
3. Intestinal bacteria play a vital role in the synthesis of some B vitamins and vitamin K.
4. Colon: Includes the ascending, transverse, descending, and sigmoid colons and rectum
5. The ileocecal valve prevents contents of the large intestine from entering the ileum.
6. The anal sphincters control the anal canal.

H. Peritoneum: Lines the abdominal cavity and forms the mesentery that supports the intestines and blood supply

I. Liver
1. The largest gland in the body, weighing 3 to 4 lb.
2. Contains Kupffer's cells, which remove bacteria in the portal venous blood
3. Removes excess glucose and amino acids from the portal blood
4. Synthesizes glucose, amino acids, and fats
5. Aids in the digestion of fats, carbohydrates, and proteins
6. Stores and filters blood (200 to 400 mL of blood stored)
7. Stores vitamins A, D, and B and iron
8. The liver secretes bile to emulsify fats (500 to 1000 mL of bile/day).
9. Hepatic ducts
   a. Deliver bile to the gallbladder via the cystic duct and to the duodenum via the common bile duct.
   b. The common bile duct opens into the duodenum, with the pancreatic duct at the ampulla of Vater.
   c. The sphincter prevents the reflux of intestinal contents into the common bile duct and pancreatic duct.

J. Gallbladder
1. Stores and concentrates bile and contracts to force bile into the duodenum during the digestion of fats
2. The cystic duct joins the hepatic duct to form the common bile duct.
3. The sphincter of Oddi is located at the entrance to the duodenum.
4. The presence of fatty materials in the duodenum stimulates the liberation of cholecystokinin, which causes contraction of the gallbladder and relaxation of the sphincter of Oddi.

K. Pancreas
1. Exocrine gland
   a. Secretes sodium bicarbonate to neutralize the acidity of the stomach contents that enter the duodenum
   b. Pancreatic juices contain enzymes for digesting carbohydrates, fats, and proteins.
2. Endocrine gland
   a. Secretes glucagon to raise blood glucose levels and secretes somatostatin to exert a hypoglycemic effect
   b. The islets of Langerhans secrete insulin.
   c. Insulin is secreted into the bloodstream and is important for carbohydrate metabolism.

II. DIAGNOSTIC PROCEDURES (Box 55-2)

A. Upper gastrointestinal tract study (barium swallow)
1. Description: Examination of the upper gastrointestinal tract under fluoroscopy after the client drinks barium sulfate
2. Preprocedure: NPO after midnight the day of the test
3. Postprocedure
   a. A laxative may be prescribed.
   b. Instruct the client to increase oral fluid intake to help pass the barium.
   c. Monitor stools for the passage of barium (stools will appear chalky white) because barium can cause a bowel obstruction.

B. Lower gastrointestinal tract study (barium enema)
1. Description
   a. A fluoroscopic and radiographic examination of the large intestine is performed after rectal instillation of barium sulfate.
   b. The study may be done with or without air.
2. Preprocedure
   a. A low-residue diet is given for 1 to 2 days before the test.

BOX 55-2

Gastrointestinal System Diagnostic Studies*

Anoscopy, proctoscopy, and sigmoidoscopy
Cholecystography
Defecography
Endoscopic retrograde cholangiopancreatography (ERCP)
Fiberoptic colonoscopy
Gastric analysis
Gastrointestinal motility studies
Hydrogen and urea breath test
Laparoscopy (peritoneoscopy)
Liver and pancreas laboratory studies
Liver biopsy
Lower gastrointestinal tract study (barium enema)
Paracentesis
Percutaneous transhepatic cholangiography
Stool specimens
Upper gastrointestinal fiberoscopy or esophagogastroduodenoscopy (EGD)
Upper gastrointestinal tract study (barium swallow)

*Note: Informed consent is obtained for a diagnostic study that is invasive.

b. A clear liquid diet and laxative are given the evening before the test.

c. NPO after midnight the day of the test

d. Cleansing enemas on the morning of the test

3. Postprocedure

a. Instruct the client to increase oral fluid intake to help pass the barium.

b. Administer a mild laxative as prescribed to facilitate emptying of the barium.

c. Monitor stools for the passage of barium.

d. Notify the physician if a bowel movement does not occur within 2 days.

C. Gastric analysis

1. Description

a. Gastric analysis requires the passage of a nasogastric tube into the stomach to aspirate gastric contents for the analysis of acidity (pH), appearance, and volume; the entire gastric contents are aspirated, and then specimens are collected every 15 minutes for 1 hour.

b. Histamine or pentagastrin may be administered subcutaneously to stimulate gastric secretions; these medications may produce a flushed feeling.

c. Esophageal reflux of gastric acid may be performed by ambulatory pH monitoring; a probe is placed just above the lower esophageal sphincter and connected to an external recording device. It provides a computer analysis and graphic display of results.

2. Preprocedure

a. Fasting for 8 to 12 hours is required before the test.

b. Tobacco and chewing gum are avoided for 6 hours before the test.

c. Medications that stimulate gastric secretions are withheld for 24 to 48 hours.

3. Postprocedure

a. Client may resume normal activities.

b. Refrigerate gastric samples if not tested within 4 hours.

D. Upper gastrointestinal fiberoscopy

1. Description

a. Also known as esophagogastroduodenoscopy

b. Following sedation, an endoscope is passed down the esophagus to view the gastric wall, sphincters, and duodenum; tissue specimens can be obtained.

2. Preprocedure

a. The client must be NPO for 6 to 12 hours before the test.

b. A local anesthetic (spray or gargle) is administered along with medication that provides

conscious sedation and relieves anxiety, such as IV midazolam (Versed), just before the scope is inserted.

c. Atropine sulfate may be administered to reduce secretions, and glucagon may be administered to relax smooth muscle.

d. Client is positioned on the left side to facilitate saliva drainage and to provide easy access of the endoscope.

e. Airway patency is monitored during the test and pulse oximetry is used to monitor oxygen saturation; emergency equipment should be readily available.

3. Postprocedure

a. Client must be NPO until the gag reflex returns (1 to 2 hours).

b. Monitor for signs of perforation (pain, bleeding, unusual difficulty swallowing, elevated temperature).

c. Maintain bed rest for the sedated client until alert.

d. Lozenges, saline gargles, or oral analgesics can relieve a minor sore throat (not given to the client until the gag reflex returns).

E. Anoscopy, proctoscopy, and sigmoidoscopy

1. Description

a. Anoscopy requires the use of a rigid scope to examine the anal canal; the client is placed in the knee-chest or left lateral position.

b. Proctoscopy and sigmoidoscopy require the use of a flexible scope to examine the rectum and sigmoid colon; the client is placed on the left side with the right leg bent and placed anteriorly.

c. Biopsies and polypectomies can be performed.

2. Preprocedure: Enemas are given until the returns are clear.

3. Postprocedure: Monitor for rectal bleeding and signs of perforation and peritonitis (Box 55-3).

F. Fiberoptic colonoscopy

1. Description

a. Colonoscopy is a fiberoptic endoscopy study in which the lining of the large intestine is

---

BOX 55-3

Signs of Bowel Perforation and Peritonitis

Guarding of the abdomen
Increased fever and chills
Pallor
Progressive abdominal distention and abdominal pain
Restlessness
Tachycardia and tachypnea

visually examined; biopsies and polypectomies can be performed.

b. Cardiac and respiratory function are monitored continuously during the test.

c. Colonoscopy is performed with the client lying on the left side with the knees drawn up to the chest; position may be changed during the test to facilitate passing of the scope.

2. Preprocedure

a. Adequate cleansing of the colon is necessary, as prescribed by the physician.

b. A clear liquid diet is started at noon on the day before the test.

c. Consult with the physician regarding medications that must be withheld before the test.

d. Client is NPO after midnight on the day of the test.

e. Midazolam (Versed) is administered intravenously to provide sedation.

f. Glucagon may be administered to relax smooth muscle.

3. Postprocedure

a. Provide bed rest until alert.

b. Monitor for signs of bowel perforation and peritonitis (see Box 55-3).

c. Instruct the client to report any bleeding to the physician.

G. Laparoscopy (peritoneoscopy) is performed with a fiberoscopic laparoscope that allows direct visualization of organs and structures within the abdomen; biopsies may be obtained.

H. Cholecystography

1. Description: Performed to detect gallstones and assess the ability of the gallbladder to fill, concentrate its contents, contract, and empty

2. Preprocedure

a. Assess for allergies to iodine or seafood.

b. Contrast agents such as iopanoic acid, iodipamide meglumine (Cholografin Meglumine), or sodium ipodate (Oragrafin) may be administered 10 to 12 hours (evening before) before the test.

c. Client is NPO after the contrast agent is administered.

d. Instruct the client that if a rash, itching, hives, or difficulty in breathing occurs after taking the contrast agent to report to the emergency room.

3. Postprocedure

a. Inform the client that dysuria is common because the contrast agent is excreted in the urine.

b. A normal diet may be resumed (a fatty meal may enhance excretion of the contrast agent).

I. Endoscopic retrograde cholangiopancreatography (ERCP)

1. Description

a. Examination of the hepatobiliary system is performed via a flexible endoscope inserted into the esophagus to the descending duodenum; multiple positions are required during the procedure to pass the endoscope.

b. If medication is administered before the procedure, the client is monitored closely for signs of respiratory and central nervous system depression, hypotension, oversedation, and vomiting.

2. Preprocedure

a. Client is NPO for several hours before the procedure.

b. Sedation is administered before the procedure.

3. Postprocedure

a. Monitor vital signs.

b. Monitor for the return of the gag reflex.

c. Monitor for signs of perforation (see Box 55-3) or peritonitis.

J. Percutaneous transhepatic cholangiography

1. Description

a. The examination involves the injection of dye directly into the biliary tree.

b. The hepatic ducts within the liver, the entire length of the common bile duct, the cystic duct, and the gallbladder are outlined clearly.

2. Preprocedure

a. Client is NPO.

b. Sedating medication is administered.

3. Postprocedure

a. Monitor vital signs.

b. Monitor for signs of bleeding, peritonitis (see Box 55-3), and septicemia; report the presence of pain immediately.

c. Administer antibiotics as prescribed to reduce the risk of sepsis.

K. Paracentesis

1. Description: Transabdominal removal of fluid from the peritoneal cavity for analysis

2. Preprocedure

a. Have client void before the start of procedure to empty the bladder and to move the bladder out of the way of the paracentesis needle.

b. Measure abdominal girth, weight, and baseline vital signs.

c. Note that the client is positioned upright on the edge of the bed, with the back supported and the feet resting on a stool (Fowler's position is used for the client confined to bed).

3. Postprocedure

a. Monitor vital signs.

b. Measure fluid collected, describe, and record.

c. Label fluid samples and send to the laboratory for analysis.

d. Apply a dry sterile dressing to the insertion site; monitor site for bleeding.

e. Measure abdominal girth and weight.

f. Monitor for hypovolemia, electrolyte loss, mental status changes, or encephalopathy.

g. Monitor for hematuria caused by bladder trauma.

h. Instruct the client to notify the physician if the urine becomes bloody, pink, or red.

L. Liver biopsy

1. Description: A needle is inserted through the abdominal wall to the liver to obtain a tissue sample for biopsy and microscopic examination.

2. Preprocedure

a. Assess results of coagulation tests (prothrombin time, partial thromboplastin time, platelet count).

b. Administer a sedative as prescribed.

c. Note that the client is placed in the supine or left lateral position during the procedure to expose the right side of the upper abdomen.

3. Postprocedure

a. Assess vital signs.

b. Assess biopsy site for bleeding.

c. Monitor for peritonitis (see Box 55-3).

d. Maintain bed rest for several hours.

e. Place the client on the right side with a pillow under the costal margin to decrease the risk of hemorrhage, and instruct the client to avoid coughing and straining.

f. Instruct the client to avoid heavy lifting and strenuous exercise for 1 week.

M. Stool specimens

1. Testing of stool specimens includes inspecting the specimen for consistency and color and testing for occult blood.

2. Tests for fecal urobilinogen, fat, nitrogen, parasites, pathogens, food substances, and other substances may be performed; these tests require that the specimen be sent to the laboratory.

3. Random specimens are sent promptly to the laboratory.

4. Quantitative 24- to 72- hour collections must be kept refrigerated until they are taken to the laboratory.

5. Some specimens require that a certain diet be followed or that certain medications be withheld; check agency guidelines regarding specific procedures.

N. Urea breath test

1. The urea breath test detects the presence of *Helicobacter pylori*, the bacteria that cause peptic ulcer disease.

2. The client consumes a capsule of carbon-labeled urea and provides a breath sample 10 to 20 minutes later.

3. Certain medications may need to be avoided before testing; these may include antibiotics or bismuth subsalicylate (Pepto-Bismol) for 1 month before the test; sucralfate (Carafate) and omeprazole (Prilosec) for 1 week before the test; and cimetidine (Tagamet), famotidine (Pepcid), ranitidine (Zantac), or nizatidine (Axid) for 24 hours before breath testing.

4. *H. pylori* can also be detected by assessing serum antibody levels.

O. Liver and pancreas laboratory studies (see Chap. 11)

1. Alkaline phosphatase is released during liver damage or biliary obstruction.

2. Prothrombin time is prolonged with liver damage.

3. The serum ammonia level assesses the ability of the liver to deaminate protein by-products.

4. Liver enzyme levels (transaminase studies) are elevated with liver damage.

5. An increase in cholesterol level indicates **pancreatitis** or biliary obstruction.

6. An increase in bilirubin level indicates liver damage or biliary obstruction.

7. Increased values for amylase and lipase levels indicate **pancreatitis.**

III. ASSESSMENT

A. Abdominal assessment (Box 55-4)

1. Inspect the skin for color, abnormalities, contour, and tautness, and inspect the abdomen for distention.

2. Auscultate for bowel sounds

3. Percuss for air or solids.

4. Palpate for tenderness.

B. Bowel sounds

1. Auscultate bowel sounds before percussion and palpation.

2. Normal bowel sounds occur 5 to 30 times a minute, or every 5 to 15 seconds.

3. Auscultate in all abdominal quadrants.

4. Listen at least 5 minutes in each quadrant before assuming sounds are absent.

IV. GASTROINTESTINAL TUBES

A. See Chapter 21 for information regarding care of the client with these tubes.

BOX 55-4

Order for Performing the Abdominal Assessment

1. Inspect
2. Auscultate
3. Percuss
4. Palpate

V. GASTROESOPHAGEAL REFLUX DISEASE
A. Description
   1. Gastroesophageal reflux is the backflow of gastric and duodenal contents into the esophagus.
   2. The reflux is caused by an incompetent lower esophageal sphincter, pyloric stenosis, or motility disorder.
B. Assessment
   1. Pyrosis
   2. Dyspepsia
   3. Regurgitation
   4. Pain and difficulty with swallowing
   5. Hypersalivation
C. Interventions
   1. Instruct the client to avoid factors that decrease lower esophageal sphincter pressure or cause esophageal irritation.
   2. Instruct the client to eat a low-fat, high-fiber diet and to avoid caffeine, tobacco, and carbonated beverages, eating and drinking 2 hours before bedtime, and wearing tight clothes; also, elevate the head of the bed on 6- to 8-inch blocks.
   3. Avoid the use of anticholinergics, which delay stomach emptying.
   4. Instruct the client regarding prescribed medications, such as antacids, H_2-receptor antagonists, or proton pump inhibitors.
   5. Instruct the client regarding the administration of prokinetic medications, if prescribed, which accelerate gastric emptying.
   6. If medical management is unsuccessful, surgery may be required; this involves a fundoplication (wrapping a portion of the gastric fundus around the sphincter area of the esophagus); surgery may be performed by laparoscopy.

VI. HIATAL HERNIA
A. Description
   1. A **hiatal hernia** is also known as esophageal or diaphragmatic hernia.
   2. A portion of the stomach herniates through the diaphragm and into the thorax.
   3. Herniation results from weakening of the muscles of the diaphragm and is aggravated by factors that increase abdominal pressure such as pregnancy, **ascites,** obesity, tumors, and heavy lifting.
   4. Complications include ulceration, hemorrhage, regurgitation and aspiration of stomach contents, strangulation, and incarceration of the stomach in the chest with possible necrosis, peritonitis, and mediastinitis.
B. Assessment
   1. Heartburn
   2. Regurgitation or vomiting
   3. Dysphagia
   4. Feeling of fullness

C. Interventions
   1. Medical and surgical management are similar to those for gastroesophageal reflux disease.
   2. Provide small frequent meals and limit the amount of liquids taken with meals.
   3. Advise the client not to recline for 1 hour after eating.
   4. Avoid anticholinergics, which delay stomach emptying.

VII. GASTRITIS
A. Description
   1. Inflammation of the stomach or gastric mucosa
   2. Acute gastritis is caused by the ingestion of food contaminated with disease-causing microorganisms or food that is irritating or too highly seasoned, the overuse of aspirin or other nonsteroidal anti-inflammatory drugs (NSAIDs), excessive alcohol intake, bile reflux, or radiation therapy.
   3. Chronic gastritis is caused by benign or malignant ulcers or by the bacteria *H. pylori*, and also may be caused by autoimmune diseases, dietary factors, medications, alcohol, smoking, or reflux.
B. Assessment (Box 55-5)
C. Interventions
   1. Acute gastritis: Food and fluids may be withheld until symptoms subside; afterward, ice chips can be given, followed by clear liquids, and then solid food.
   2. Monitor for signs of hemorrhagic gastritis such as hematemesis, tachycardia, and hypotension, and notify the physician if these signs occur.
   3. Instruct the client to avoid irritating foods, fluids, and other substances, such as spicy and highly seasoned foods, caffeine, alcohol, and nicotine.
   4. Instruct the client in the use of prescribed medications, such as antibiotics and bismuth salts (Pepto-Bismol).
   5. Provide the client with information about the importance of vitamin B_{12} injections if a deficiency is present.

BOX 55-5

Assessment Findings in Acute and Chronic Gastritis

ACUTE
Abdominal discomfort
Anorexia, nausea, and vomiting
Headache
Hiccupping

CHRONIC
Anorexia, nausea, and vomiting
Belching
Heartburn after eating
Sour taste in the mouth
Vitamin B_{12} deficiency

VIII. PEPTIC ULCER DISEASE

A. Description
1. A peptic ulcer is an ulceration in the mucosal wall of the stomach, pylorus, duodenum, or esophagus in portions accessible to gastric secretions; erosion may extend through the muscle.
2. The ulcer may be referred to as gastric, duodenal, or esophageal, depending on its location.
3. The most common peptic ulcers are gastric ulcers and duodenal ulcers.

B. Gastric ulcers
1. Description
   a. A gastric ulcer involves ulceration of the mucosal lining that extends to the submucosal layer of the stomach.
   b. Predisposing factors include stress, smoking, the use of corticosteroids, NSAIDs, alcohol, history of gastritis, family history of gastric ulcers, or infection with *H. pylori.*
   c. Complications include hemorrhage, perforation, and pyloric obstruction.
2. Assessment (Box 55-6)
3. Interventions
   a. Monitor vital signs and for signs of bleeding.
   b. Administer small, frequent bland feedings during the active phase.
   c. Administer H_2-receptor antagonists as prescribed to decrease the secretion of gastric acid.
   d. Administer antacids as prescribed to neutralize gastric secretions.
   e. Administer anticholinergics as prescribed to reduce gastric motility.
   f. Administer mucosal barrier protectants as prescribed 1 hour before each meal.
   g. Administer prostaglandins as prescribed for their protective and antisecretory actions.
4. Client education
   a. Avoid consuming alcohol and substances that contain caffeine or chocolate.
   b. Avoid smoking.

BOX 55-6

Assessment: Gastric and Duodenal Ulcers

GASTRIC

Gnawing, sharp pain in or left of the midepigastric region occurs 30 to 60 minutes after a meal (food ingestion accentuates the pain).
Hematemesis is more common than melena.

DUODENAL

Burning pain occurs in the midepigastric area 1½ to 3 hours after a meal and during the night (often awakens the client).
Melena is more common than hematemesis.
Pain is often relieved by the ingestion of food.

---

   c. Avoid aspirin or NSAIDs.
   d. Obtain adequate rest and reduce stress.
5. Interventions during active bleeding
   a. Monitor vital signs closely.
   b. Assess for signs of dehydration, hypovolemic shock, sepsis, and respiratory insufficiency.
   c. Maintain NPO status and administer intravenous (IV) fluid replacement as prescribed; monitor intake and output.
   d. Monitor hemoglobin and hematocrit.
   e. Administer blood transfusions as prescribed.
   f. Assist with the insertion of a nasogastric tube for decompression and for lavage access.
   g. Assist with normal saline or tap water lavage at room temperature to reduce active bleeding.
   h. Prepare to assist with administering vasopressin (Pitressin) intravenously as prescribed to induce vasoconstriction and reduce bleeding.
6. Surgical interventions
   a. Total **gastrectomy**: Removal of the stomach with attachment of the esophagus to the jejunum or duodenum; also called esophagojejunostomy or esophagoduodenostomy
   b. **Vagotomy**: Surgical division of the vagus nerve to eliminate the vagal impulses that stimulate hydrochloric acid secretion in the stomach
   c. **Gastric resection**: Removal of the lower half of the stomach and usually includes a **vagotomy**; also called antrectomy
   d. **Billroth I**: Partial **gastrectomy**, with the remaining segment anastomosed to the duodenum; also called gastroduodenostomy (Fig. 55-1).
   e. **Billroth II**: Partial **gastrectomy**, with the remaining segment anastomosed to the jejunum; also called gastrojejunostomy (Fig. 55-2)
   f. **Pyloroplasty**: Enlargement of the pylorus to prevent or decrease pyloric obstruction, thereby enhancing gastric emptying
7. Postoperative interventions
   a. Monitor vital signs.
   b. Place in a Fowler's position for comfort and to promote drainage.
   c. Administer fluids and electrolyte replacements intravenously as prescribed; monitor intake and output.
   d. Assess bowel sounds.
   e. Monitor nasogastric suction as prescribed.
   f. Do not irrigate or remove the nasogastric tube; assist the physician with nasogastric tube irrigation or removal.
   g. Maintain NPO status as prescribed for 1 to 3 days until **peristalsis** returns.

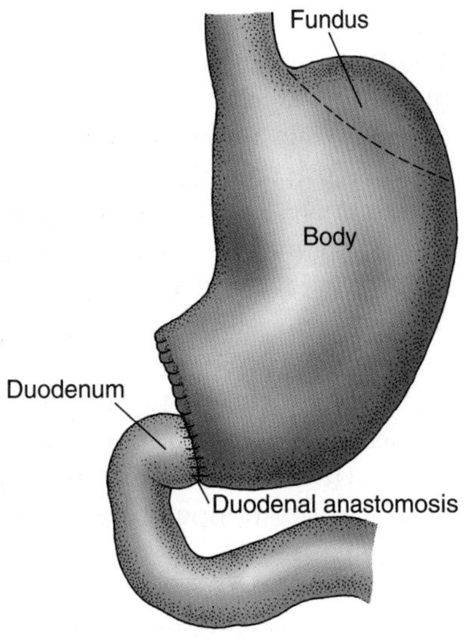

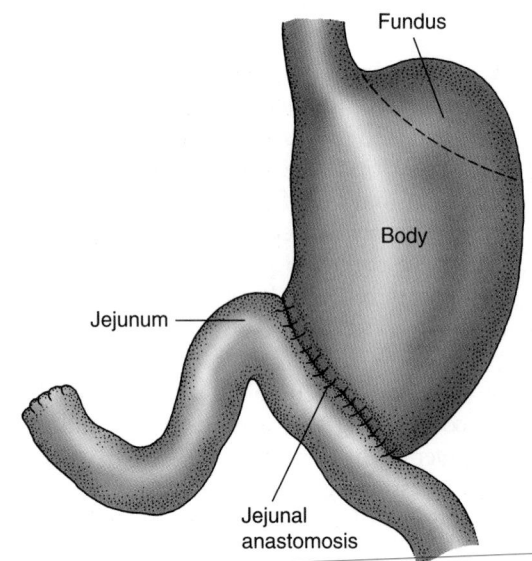

FIG. 55-1 The Billroth I procedure (gastroduodenostomy). The distal portion of the stomach is removed, and the remainder is anastomosed to the duodenum. (From Ignatavicius, D., & Workman, M. [2006]. *Medical-surgical nursing: Critical thinking for collaborative care* [5th ed.]. St. Louis: W.B. Saunders.)

FIG. 55-2 The Billroth II procedure (gastrojejunostomy). The lower portion of the stomach is removed, and the remainder is anastomosed to the jejunum. (From Ignatavicius, D., & Workman, M. [2006]. *Medical-surgical nursing: Critical thinking for collaborative care* [5th ed.]. St. Louis: W.B. Saunders.)

h. Progress the diet from NPO to sips of clear water to six small bland meals a day, as prescribed when bowel sounds return.

i. Monitor for postoperative complications of hemorrhage, **dumping syndrome**, diarrhea, hypoglycemia, and vitamin B$_{12}$ deficiency.

C. Duodenal ulcers
1. Description
   a. A duodenal ulcer is a break in the mucosa of the duodenum.
   b. Risk factors and causes include alcohol intake; smoking; stress; caffeine; the use of aspirin, corticosteroids, and NSAIDs; and infection with *H. pylori*.
   c. Complications include bleeding, perforation, gastric outlet obstruction, and intractable disease.
2. Assessment (see Box 55-6)
3. Interventions
   a. Monitor vital signs.
   b. Instruct the client about a bland diet, with small frequent meals.
   c. Provide for adequate rest.
   d. Encourage the cessation of smoking.
   e. Instruct the client to avoid alcohol intake, caffeine, the use of aspirin, corticosteroids, and NSAIDs.
   f. Administer antacids as prescribed to neutralize acid secretions.

g. Administer H$_2$-receptor antagonists as prescribed to block the secretion of acid.
4. Surgical interventions: Surgery is performed only if the ulcer is unresponsive to medications or if hemorrhage, obstruction, or perforation occurs.

D. **Dumping syndrome**
1. Description: The rapid emptying of the gastric contents into the small intestine that occurs following **gastric resection**
2. Assessment
   a. Symptoms occurring 30 minutes after eating
   b. Nausea and vomiting
   c. Feelings of abdominal fullness and abdominal cramping
   d. Diarrhea
   e. Palpitations and tachycardia
   f. Perspiration
   g. Weakness and dizziness
   h. Borborygmi (loud gurgles indicating hyperperistalsis)
3. Client education (Box 55-7)

BOX 55-7

Client Education: Preventing Dumping Syndrome

Avoid sugar, salt, and milk.
Eat a high-protein, high-fat, low-carbohydrate diet.
Eat small meals and avoid consuming fluids with meals.
Lie down after meals.
Take antispasmodic medications as prescribed to delay gastric emptying.

IX. VITAMIN B$_{12}$ DEFICIENCY

A. Description
1. Vitamin B$_{12}$ deficiency results from an inadequate intake of vitamin B$_{12}$ or a lack of absorption of ingested vitamin B$_{12}$ from the intestinal tract.
2. Pernicious anemia results from a deficiency of intrinsic factor, necessary for intestinal absorption of vitamin B$_{12}$; gastric disease or surgery can result in a lack of intrinsic factor.

B. Assessment
1. Severe pallor
2. Fatigue
3. Weight loss
4. Smooth, beefy red tongue
5. Slight jaundice
6. Paresthesias of the hands and feet
7. Disturbances with gait and balance

C. Interventions
1. Increase dietary intake of foods rich in vitamin B$_{12}$ if the anemia is the result of a dietary deficiency (Box 55-8).
2. Administer vitamin B$_{12}$ injections as prescribed weekly initially and then monthly for maintenance (lifelong) if the anemia is the result of a deficiency of intrinsic factor or disease or surgery of the ileum.

X. BARIATRIC SURGERY

A. Description
1. Surgical reduction of gastric capacity that may be performed on a client with morbid obesity to produce permanent weight loss
2. Surgery may be performed by laparoscope; the decision is based on the client's weight, body build, history of abdominal surgery, and current medical disorders.
3. Obese clients are at increased postoperative risk for pulmonary and thromboembolic complications and death.
4. Surgery can prevent the complications of obesity, such as diabetes mellitus, hypertension and other cardiovascular disorders, depression, or sleep apnea.
5. The client needs to agree to modify his or her lifestyle, lose weight and keep the weight off,

and obtain support from available community resources (Box 55-9).

B. Types (Fig. 55-3)
1. Gastric restrictive surgery
   a. Allows for normal digestion without the risk of nutritional deficiency
   b. A vertical banded gastroplasty may be performed; the surgeon places a vertical line of staples to create a small stomach pouch to which the band is connected to provide an outlet to the small intestine.
   c. A circumgastric banding may be performed; an inflatable band is placed around the stomach to limit stomach size; the band can be inflated or deflated through a subcutaneous port to change the size of the stomach as the client loses weight.
2. Gastric restriction combined with malabsorption surgery
   a. Known as a gastric bypass or Roux-en-Y gastric bypass
   b. In addition to stapling, the stomach, duodenum, and part of the ileum are bypassed so that fewer calories can be absorbed.

C. Postoperative interventions
1. Care is similar to that for the client undergoing abdominal surgery.
2. Clear liquids are introduced slowly once bowel sounds have returned and the client passes flatus (1-oz cups are used for each serving).
3. Clear fluids are followed by puréed foods, juices, thin soups, and milk 24 to 48 hours after clear fluids are tolerated (the diet is limited to liquids or puréed foods for 6 weeks); then, the diet is progressed to nutrient-dense regular food.

D. Client teaching points about diet (Box 55-10)

XI. GASTRIC CANCER (see Chapter 51)

XII. ESOPHAGEAL VARICES

A. Description
1. Dilated and tortuous veins in the submucosa of the esophagus.
2. Caused by **portal hypertension,** often associated with liver **cirrhosis;** are at high risk for rupture if portal circulation pressure rises
3. Bleeding varices are an emergency.
4. The goal of treatment is to control bleeding, prevent complications, and prevent the recurrence of bleeding.

BOX 55-8

Foods Rich in Vitamin B$_{12}$

Brewer's yeast
Citrus fruits
Dried beans
Green, leafy vegetables
Liver
Nuts
Organ meats

BOX 55-9

Community Resources Following Bariatric Surgery

American Obesity Association
American Society of Bariatric Surgery
Overeaters Anonymous

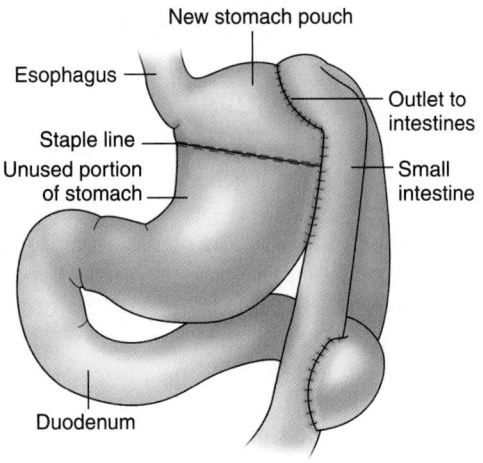

New stomach pouch

Esophagus

Outlet to intestines

Staple line

Unused portion of stomach

Small intestine

Duodenum

Gastric Bypass

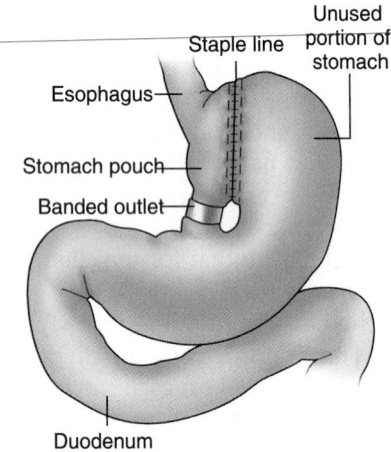

Unused portion of stomach

Staple line

Esophagus

Stomach pouch

Banded outlet

Duodenum

Vertical Banded Gastroplasty

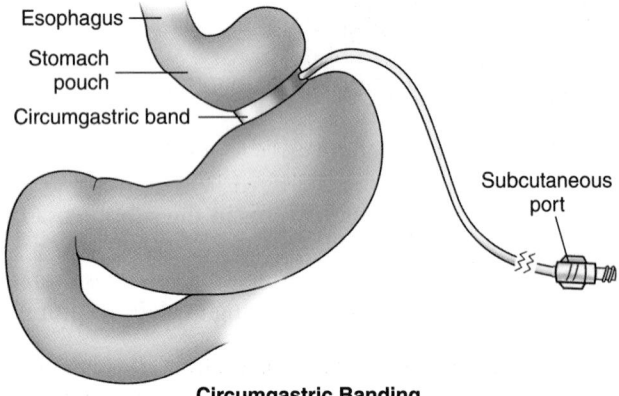

Esophagus

Stomach pouch

Circumgastric band

Subcutaneous port

Circumgastric Banding

FIG. 55-3 Bariatric surgical procedures. (From Ignatavicius, D., & Workman, M. [2006]. *Medical-surgical nursing: Critical thinking for collaborative care* [5th ed.]. St. Louis: W.B. Saunders.)

B. Assessment
1. Hematemesis
2. Melena
3. Tarry stools

BOX 55-10

Dietary Measures for the Client Following Bariatric Surgery

Avoid alcohol, high-protein foods, and foods high in sugar and fat.

Eat slowly and chew food well.

Progress food types and amounts as prescribed.

Take nutritional supplements as prescribed, which may include calcium, iron, multivitamins, and vitamin B_{12}.

Monitor and report signs and symptoms of complications, such as dehydration.

---

4. **Ascites**
5. Jaundice
6. Hepatomegaly and splenomegaly
7. Dilated abdominal veins
8. Signs of shock

C. Interventions
1. Monitor vital signs.
2. Elevate the head of the bed.
3. Monitor for orthostatic hypotension.
4. Monitor lung sounds and for the presence of respiratory distress.
5. Administer oxygen as prescribed to prevent tissue hypoxia.
6. Monitor level of consciousness.
7. Maintain NPO status.
8. Administer fluids intravenously as prescribed to restore fluid volume and electrolyte imbalances; monitor intake and output.
9. Monitor hemoglobin and hematocrit values and coagulation factors.
10. Administer blood transfusions or clotting factors as prescribed.
11. Assist in inserting a nasogastric tube or a balloon tamponade as prescribed.
12. Assist with the administration of iced saline irrigations to achieve vasoconstriction of the varices.
13. Prepare to assist with administering vasopressin (Pitressin) by IV or intraarterial infusion as prescribed to induce vasoconstriction and reduce bleeding.
14. Prepare to assist with administering nitroglycerin with the vasopressin if prescribed to prevent vasoconstriction of the coronary arteries.
15. Instruct the client to avoid activities that will initiate vasovagal responses.
16. Prepare the client for endoscopic procedures or surgical procedures as prescribed.

D. Endoscopic injection (sclerotherapy)
1. The procedure involves the injection of a sclerosing agent into and around bleeding varices.
2. Complications include chest pain, pleural effusion, aspiration pneumonia, esophageal stricture, and perforation of the esophagus.

NORMAL HEPATIC CIRCULATION PORTACAVAL (END-TO-SIDE) SHUNT SPLENORENAL (END-TO-SIDE) SHUNT

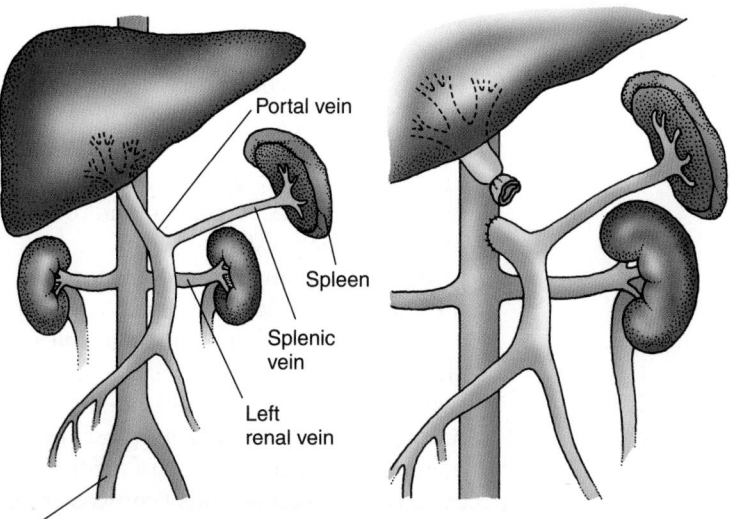
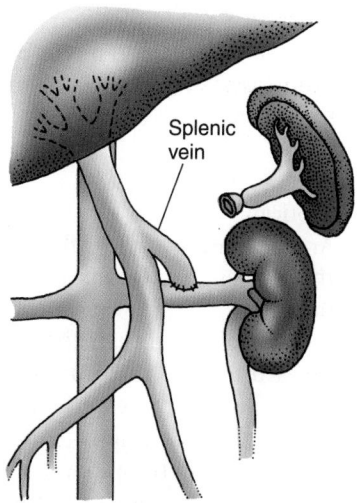

Portal vein

Spleen

Splenic vein

Left renal vein

Inferior vena cava

Splenic vein

FIG. 55-4 Surgical shunting diverts portal venous blood flow from the liver to decrease portal and esophageal pressure. (From Ignatavicius, D., & Workman, M. [2006]. *Medical-surgical nursing: Critical thinking for collaborative care* [5th ed.]. St. Louis: W.B. Saunders.)

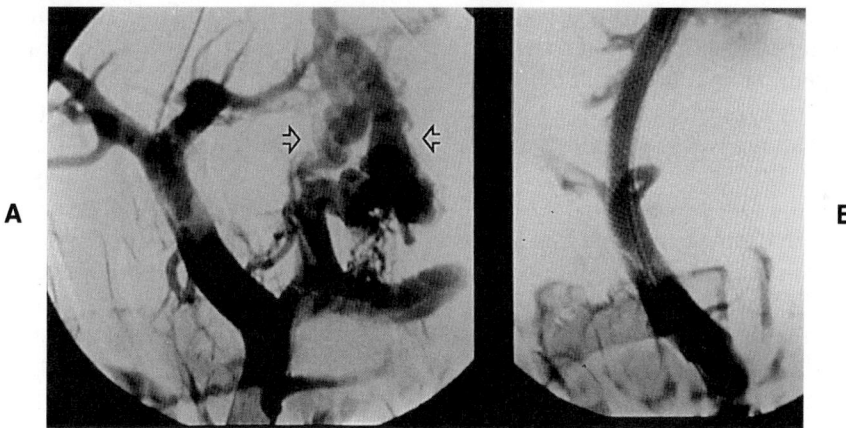

A   B

FIG. 55-5 Total portal diversion after transjugular intrahepatic portosystemic shunt (TIPS). **A,** Portal venogram before TIPS shows filling of large esophageal varices (arrows). **B,** After insertion of a TIPS, flow to varices is eliminated. Intrahepatic portal vein flow is now reversed, with the direction of intrahepatic flow toward the TIPS. (From Lewis, S., Heitkemper, M., & Dirksen, S. [2004]. *Medical-surgical nursing: Assessment and management of clinical problems* [3rd ed.]. St. Louis: Mosby.)

E. Endoscopic variceal ligation
 1. The procedure involves ligation of the varices with an elastic rubber band.
 2. Sloughing, followed by superficial ulceration, occurs in the area of ligation within 3 to 7 days.
F. Shunting procedures
 1. Description: Shunt blood away from the **esophageal varices**
 2. Distal splenorenal shunt (Fig. 55-4)
  a. The shunt involves anastomosis of the splenic vein to the left renal vein.

 b. The spleen conducts blood from the high pressure varices to the low pressure renal vein.
 3. Portacaval shunt involves anastomosis of the portal vein to the inferior vena cava, diverting blood from the portal system to the systemic circulation (see Fig. 55-4)
 4. Mesocaval shunting involves a side anastomosis of the superior mesenteric vein to the proximal end of the inferior vena cava.
 5. Transjugular intrahepatic portosystemic shunt (TIPS; Fig. 55-5)

6. The nonsurgical procedure uses the normal vascular anatomy of the liver to create a shunt with the use of a metallic stent.
7. The shunt is between the portal and systemic venous system in the liver and is aimed at relieving **portal hypertension.**

XIII. ULCERATIVE COLITIS

A. Description
   1. An ulcerative and inflammatory disease of the bowel that results in poor absorption of nutrients.
   2. Commonly begins in the rectum and spreads upward toward the cecum
   3. The colon becomes edematous and may develop bleeding lesions and ulcers; the ulcers may lead to perforation.
   4. Scar tissue develops and causes loss of elasticity and loss of the ability to absorb nutrients.
   5. Colitis is characterized by various periods of remissions and exacerbations.
   6. Acute **ulcerative colitis** results in vascular congestion, hemorrhage, edema, and ulceration of the bowel mucosa.
   7. Chronic **ulcerative colitis** causes muscular hypertrophy, fat deposits, and fibrous tissue, with bowel thickening, shortening, and narrowing.
   8. Surgical intervention involves creation of an ostomy; the ostomy can be created within the ileum or at various sites within the large bowel.
   9. An ileostomy is the surgical creation of an opening into the ileum or small intestine that allows for drainage of fecal matter from the ileum to the outside of the body.
   10. A colostomy is the surgical creation of an opening into the colon that allows for drainage of fecal matter from the colon to the outside of the body.
B. Assessment
   1. Anorexia
   2. Weight loss
   3. Malaise
   4. Abdominal tenderness and cramping
   ▲ 5. Severe diarrhea that may contain blood and mucus
   ▲ 6. Dehydration and electrolyte imbalances
   7. Anemia
   8. Vitamin K deficiency
▲ C. Interventions
   1. Acute phase: Maintain NPO status and administer fluids and electrolytes intravenously or via parenteral nutrition as prescribed.
   2. Restrict the client's activity to reduce intestinal activity.
   3. Monitor bowel sounds and for abdominal tenderness and cramping.

4. Monitor stools, noting color, consistency, and the presence or absence of blood.
5. Monitor for bowel perforation, peritonitis (see Box 55-3), and hemorrhage.
6. Following the acute phase, the diet progresses from clear liquids to a low-residue diet as tolerated.
7. Instruct the client to consume a low-residue, high-protein diet; vitamins and iron supplements may be prescribed.
8. Instruct the client to avoid gas-forming foods, milk products, and foods such as whole wheat grains, nuts, raw fruits and vegetables, pepper, alcohol, and caffeine-containing products.
9. Instruct the client to avoid smoking.
10. Administer medications as prescribed, which may include a combination of medications such as salicylate compounds, corticosteroids, immunosuppressants, and antidiarrheals.

D. Surgical interventions
   1. Total proctocolectomy with permanent ileostomy
      a. The procedure is curative and involves the removal of the entire colon (colon, rectum, and anus, with anal closure).
      b. The end of the terminal ileum forms the stoma, which is located in the right lower quadrant.
   2. **Kock ileostomy (continent ileostomy)** (Fig. 55-6)
      a. The **Kock ileostomy** is an intraabdominal pouch that stores the feces and is constructed from the terminal ileum.
      b. The pouch is connected to the stoma with a nipple-like valve constructed from a portion of the ileum; the stoma is flush with the skin.
      c. A catheter is used to empty the pouch, and a small dressing or adhesive bandage is worn over the stoma between emptyings.
   3. Ileoanal reservoir (Fig. 55-7)
      a. Creation of an ileoanal reservoir is a two-stage procedure that involves the excision of the rectal mucosa, an abdominal colectomy, construction of a reservoir to the anal canal, and a temporary loop ileostomy.
      b. The ileostomy is closed in 3 to 4 months after the capacity of the reservoir is increased and has had time to heal.
   4. Ileoanal anastomosis (ileorectostomy)
      a. Ileorectostomy does not require an ileostomy.
      b. A 12- to 15-cm rectal stump is left after the colon is removed, and the small intestine is inserted into this rectal sleeve and anastomosed.
      c. Ileorectostomy requires a large, compliant rectum.

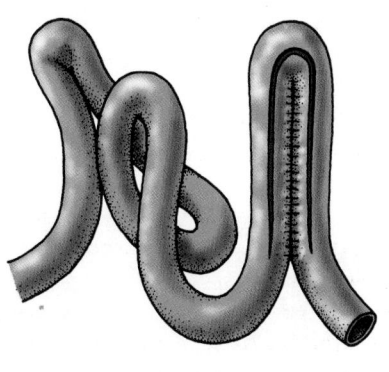 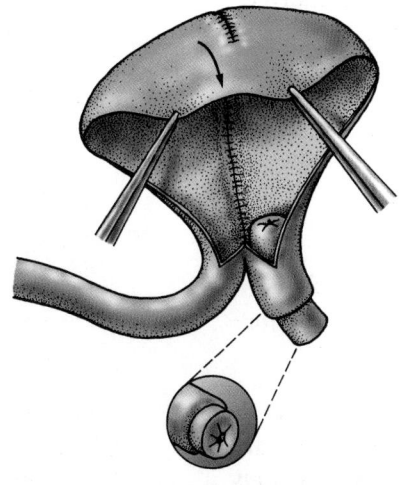 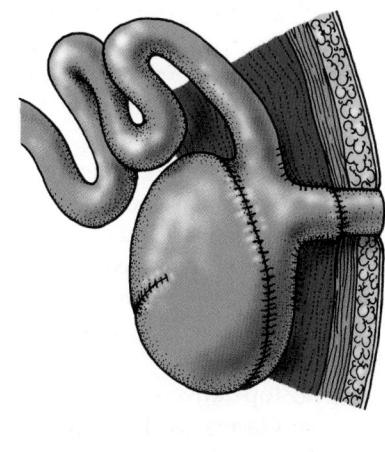

1. A reservoir, in which the client will retain stool until draining it, is constructed from a loop of ileum folded and sutured together, then cut.

2. A portion of the ileum is intussuscepted to form a nipple valve, and the upper part of the stitched and cut ileum is pulled down and sutured to form a pouch.

3. The nipple valve, which shuts tight against pressure from a filled pouch, is pulled through the stoma and sutured flush with the abdomen.

FIG. 55-6 Creation of a Kock (continent) ileostomy. (From Ignatavicius, D., & Workman, M. [2006]. *Medical-surgical nursing: Critical thinking for collaborative care* [5th ed.]. St. Louis: W.B. Saunders.)

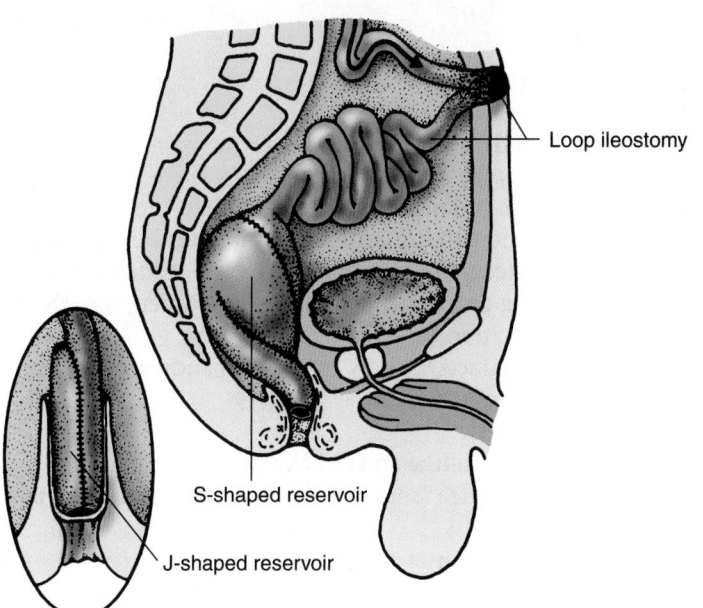 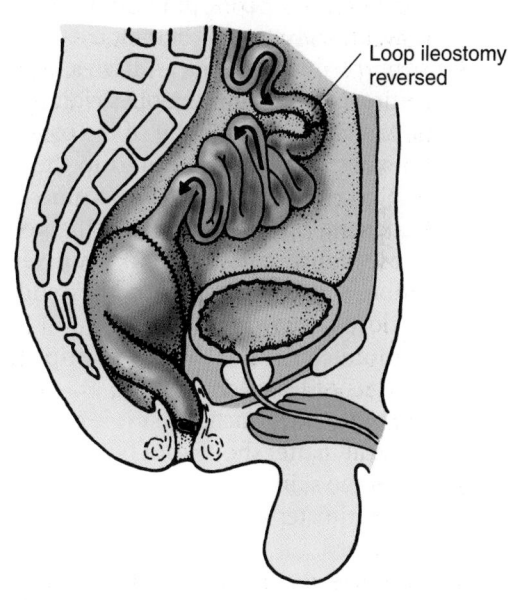

Loop ileostomy

S-shaped reservoir

J-shaped reservoir

Loop ileostomy reversed

Stage 1.
After removal of the colon, a temporary loop ileostomy is created and an ileoanal reservoir is formed. The reservoir is created in an S-shaped reservoir (using three loops of ileum) or a J-shaped reservoir (suturing a portion of ileum to the rectal cuff, with an upward loop).

Stage 2.
After the reservoir has had time to heal—usually several months—the temporary loop ileostomy is reversed, and stool is allowed to drain into the reservoir.

FIG. 55-7 Creation of an ileoanal reservoir. (From Ignatavicius, D., & Workman, M. [2006]. *Medical-surgical nursing: Critical thinking for collaborative care* [5th ed.]. St. Louis: W.B. Saunders.)

5. Preoperative colostomy and ileostomy interventions
    a. Consult with the enterostomal therapist to help identify optimal placement of the ostomy.
    b. Instruct the client to eat a low-residue diet for 1 to 2 days before surgery as prescribed.
    c. Administer intestinal antiseptics and antibiotics as prescribed to cleanse the bowel and to decrease the bacterial content of the colon.
    d. Administer laxatives and enemas as prescribed.
6. Postoperative colostomy interventions
    a. Place a petrolatum gauze over the stoma as prescribed to keep it moist, followed by a dry sterile dressing if a pouch (external) system is not in place.
    b. Place a pouch system on the stoma as soon as possible.
    c. Monitor the stoma for size, unusual bleeding, or necrotic tissue.
    d. Monitor for color changes in the stoma.
    e. Note that the normal stoma color is pink to bright red and shiny, indicating high vascularity.
    f. Note that a pale pink stoma indicates low hemoglobin and hematocrit levels and a purple-black stoma indicates compromised circulation, requiring physician notification.
    g. Assess the functioning of the colostomy.
    h. Expect that stool is liquid in the immediate postoperative period but becomes more solid depending on the area of the colostomy—ascending colon, liquid; transverse colon, loose to semiformed; and descending colon, close to normal.
    i. Monitor the pouch system for proper fit and signs of leakage.
    j. Empty the pouch when it is one-third full.
    k. Fecal matter should not be allowed to remain on the skin.
    l. Administer analgesics and antibiotics as prescribed.
    m. Irrigate the perineal wound (if present) as prescribed and monitor for signs of infection.
    n. Instruct the client to avoid foods that cause excess gas formation and odor.
    o. Instruct the client about stoma care and irrigations as prescribed (Box 55-11).
    p. Instruct the client that normal activities may be resumed when approved by the physician.
7. Postoperative ileostomy interventions
    a. Note that normal stool is liquid.
    b. Monitor for dehydration and electrolyte imbalance.
    c. Do not give suppositories through an ileostomy.

BOX 55-11

Colostomy Irrigation

PURPOSE
An enema is given through the stoma to stimulate bowel emptying.

DESCRIPTION
Irrigation is performed by instilling 500 to 1000 mL of lukewarm tap water through the stoma and allowing the water and stool to drain into a collection bag.

PROCEDURE
If ambulatory, position the client sitting on toilet.
If on bed rest, position the client on his or her side.
Hang the irrigation bag so that the bottom of the bag is at the level of the client's shoulder or slightly higher.
Insert the irrigation tube carefully without force.
Begin the flow of irrigation.
Clamp the tubing if cramping occurs; release the tubing as cramping subsides.
Avoid frequent irrigations with water, which can lead to loss of fluids and electrolytes.
Perform irrigation at about the same time each day.
Perform irrigation preferably 1 hour after a meal.
To enhance effectiveness of the irrigation, massage the abdomen gently.

XIV. CROHN'S DISEASE

A. Description
1. An inflammatory disease that can occur anywhere in the gastrointestinal tract but most often affects the terminal ileum and leads to thickening and scarring, a narrowed lumen, fistulas, ulcerations, and abscesses
2. Characterized by remissions and exacerbations

B. Assessment
1. Fever
2. Cramp-like and colicky pain after meals
3. Diarrhea (semisolid), which may contain mucus and pus
4. Abdominal distention
5. Anorexia, nausea, and vomiting
6. Weight loss
7. Anemia
8. Dehydration
9. Electrolyte imbalances

C. Interventions: Care is similar to that for the client with **ulcerative colitis;** however, surgery is avoided as much as possible because recurrence of the disease process in the same region is likely to occur.

XV. PANCREATIC TUMORS, INTESTINAL TUMORS, AND BOWEL OBSTRUCTIONS (See Chap. 51)

XVI. DIVERTICULOSIS AND DIVERTICULITIS

A. Description
  1. **Diverticulosis**
     a. **Diverticulosis** is an outpouching or herniation of the intestinal mucosa.
     b. The disorder can occur in any part of the intestine but is most common in the sigmoid colon.
  2. **Diverticulitis**
     a. **Diverticulitis** is the inflammation of one or more diverticula that occurs from penetration of fecal matter through the thin-walled diverticula; it can result in local abscess formation and perforation.
     b. A perforated diverticulum can progress to intraabdominal perforation with generalized peritonitis.

B. Assessment
  1. Left lower quadrant abdominal pain that increases with coughing, straining, or lifting
  2. Elevated temperature
  3. Nausea and vomiting
  4. Flatulence
  5. Cramp-like pain
  6. Abdominal distention and tenderness
  7. Palpable, tender rectal mass
  8. Blood in the stools

C. Interventions
  1. Provide bed rest during the acute phase.
  2. Maintain NPO status or provide clear liquids during the acute phase as prescribed.
  3. Introduce a fiber-containing diet gradually, when the inflammation has resolved.
  4. Administer antibiotics, analgesics, and anticholinergics to reduce bowel spasms as prescribed.
  5. Instruct the client to refrain from lifting, straining, coughing, or bending to avoid increased intraabdominal pressure.
  6. Monitor for perforation (see Box 55-3), hemorrhage, fistulas, and abscesses.
  7. Instruct the client to increase fluid intake to 2500 to 3000 mL daily, unless contraindicated.
  8. Instruct the client to eat soft high-fiber foods, such as whole grains.
  9. Instruct the client to avoid gas-forming foods or foods containing indigestible roughage, seeds, or nuts because these food substances become trapped in diverticula and cause inflammation.
  10. Instruct the client to consume a small amount of bran daily and to take bulk-forming laxatives as prescribed to increase stool mass.
  11. Instruct the client to avoid high-fiber foods when inflammation occurs because these foods will irritate the mucosa further.

D. Surgical interventions
  1. Colon resection with primary anastomosis may be an option.
  2. Temporary or permanent colostomy may be required for increased bowel inflammation.

XVII. HEMORRHOIDS

A. Description
  1. Dilated varicose veins of the anal canal
  2. May be internal, external, or prolapsed
  3. Internal hemorrhoids lie above the anal sphincter and cannot be seen on inspection of the perianal area.
  4. External hemorrhoids lie below the anal sphincter and can be seen on inspection.
  5. Prolapsed hemorrhoids can become thrombosed or inflamed.
  6. Hemorrhoids are caused from **portal hypertension,** straining, irritation, or increased venous or abdominal pressure.

B. Assessment
  1. Bright red bleeding with defecation
  2. Rectal pain
  3. Rectal itching

C. Interventions
  1. Apply cold packs to the anal-rectal area followed by sitz baths as prescribed.
  2. Apply witch hazel soaks and topical anesthetics as prescribed.
  3. Encourage a high-fiber diet and fluids to promote bowel movements without straining.
  4. Administer stool softeners as prescribed.

D. Surgical interventions: May include ultrasound, sclerotherapy, circular stapling, or simple resection of the hemorrhoids (hemorrhoidectomy)

E. Postoperative interventions following hemorrhoidectomy
  1. Assist the client to a prone or side-lying position to prevent bleeding.
  2. Maintain ice packs over the dressing as prescribed until the packing is removed by the physician.
  3. Monitor for urinary retention.
  4. Administer stool softeners as prescribed.
  5. Instruct the client to increase fluids and high-fiber foods.
  6. Instruct the client to limit sitting to short periods of time.
  7. Instruct the client in the use of sitz baths three or four times a day as prescribed.

XVIII. APPENDICITIS

A. Description
  1. Inflammation of the appendix.
  2. When the appendix becomes inflamed or infected, rupture may occur within a matter of hours, leading to peritonitis and sepsis.

B. Assessment
  1. Pain in the periumbilical area that descends to the right lower quadrant

2. Abdominal pain that is most intense at McBurney's point
3. Rebound tenderness and abdominal rigidity
4. Low-grade fever
5. Elevated white blood cell count
6. Anorexia, nausea, and vomiting
7. Client in side-lying position, with abdominal guarding and legs flexed
8. Constipation or diarrhea

C. Peritonitis: Inflammation of the peritoneum (see Box 55-3)
D. Appendectomy: Surgical removal of the appendix
   1. Preoperative interventions
      a. Maintain NPO status.
      b. Administer fluids intravenously to prevent dehydration.
      c. Monitor for changes in level of pain.
      d. Monitor for signs of ruptured appendix and peritonitis (see Box 55-3).
      e. Position the client in a right side-lying or low to semi-Fowler's position to promote comfort.
      f. Monitor bowel sounds.
      g. Avoid the application of heat to the abdomen.
      h. Apply ice packs to the abdomen for 20 to 30 minutes every hour as prescribed.
      i. Administer antibiotics as prescribed.
      j. Avoid laxatives or enemas.
   2. Postoperative interventions
      a. Monitor temperature for signs of infection.
      b. Assess incision for signs of infection such as redness, swelling, and pain.
      c. Maintain NPO status until bowel function has returned.
      d. Advance diet gradually as tolerated and as prescribed, when bowel sounds return.
      e. If rupture of the appendix occurred, expect a Penrose drain to be inserted, or the incision may be left open to heal from the inside out.
      f. Expect that drainage from the Penrose drain may be profuse for the first 12 hours.
      g. Position the client in a right side-lying or low to semi-Fowler's position, with legs flexed, to facilitate drainage.
      h. Change the dressing as prescribed and record the type and amount of drainage.
      i. Perform wound irrigations if prescribed.
      j. Maintain nasogastric suction and patency of the nasogastric tube if present.
      k. Administer antibiotics and analgesics as prescribed.

XIX. CIRRHOSIS (Box 55-12)
A. Description
   1. A chronic, progressive disease of the liver characterized by diffuse degeneration and destruction of hepatocytes

   2. Repeated destruction of hepatic cells causes the formation of scar tissue.
B. Complications
   1. **Portal hypertension:** A persistent increase in pressure in the portal vein that develops as a result of obstruction to flow
   2. **Ascites**
      a. Accumulation of fluid in the peritoneal cavity that results from venous congestion of the hepatic capillaries
      b. Capillary congestion leads to plasma leaking directly from the liver surface and portal vein.
   3. Bleeding **esophageal varices:** Fragile, thin-walled, distended esophageal veins that become irritated and rupture
   4. Coagulation defects
      a. Decreased synthesis of bile fats in the liver prevents the absorption of fat-soluble vitamins.
      b. Without vitamin K and clotting factors II, VII, IX, and X, the client is prone to bleeding.
   5. Jaundice: Occurs because the liver is unable to metabolize bilirubin and because the edema, fibrosis, and scarring of the hepatic bile ducts interfere with normal bile and bilirubin secretion
   6. Portal systemic encephalopathy: End-stage hepatic failure and **cirrhosis** characterized by altered level of consciousness, neurological symptoms, impaired thinking, and neuromuscular disturbances

NEUROLOGIC FINDINGS
Asterixis
Paresthesias of feet
Peripheral nerve degeneration
Portal-systemic encephalopathy
Reversal of sleep-wake pattern
Sensory disturbances

GASTROINTESTINAL (GI)
FINDINGS
Abdominal pain
Anorexia
Ascites
Clay-colored stools
Diarrhea
Esophageal varices
Fetor hepaticus
Gallstones
Gastritis
Gastrointestinal bleeding
Hemorrhoidal varices
Hepatomegaly
Hiatal hernia
Hypersplenism
Malnutrition
Nausea
Small nodular liver
Vomiting

RENAL FINDINGS
Hepatorenal syndrome
Increased urine bilirubin

ENDOCRINE FINDINGS
Increased aldosterone
Increased antidiuretic hormone
Increased circulating estrogens
Increased glucocorticoids
Gynecomastia

IMMUNE SYSTEM DISTURBANCES
Increased susceptibility to infection
Leukopenia

CARDIOVASCULAR FINDINGS
Cardiac dysrhythmias
Development of collateral circulation
Fatigue
Hyperkinetic circulation
Peripheral edema
Portal hypertension
Spider angiomas

PULMONARY FINDINGS
Dyspnea
Hydrothorax
Hyperventilation
Hypoxemia

HEMATOLOGIC FINDINGS
Anemia
Disseminated intravascular
  coagulation
Impaired coagulation
Splenomegaly
Thrombocytopenia

DERMATOLOGIC FINDINGS
Axillary and pubic hair changes
Caput medusae
Ecchymosis
Increased skin pigmentation
Jaundice
Palmar erythema
Pruritus
Spider angiomas

FLUID AND ELECTROLYTE
DISTURBANCES
Ascites
Decreased effective blood volume
Dilutional hyponatremia or
  hypernatremia
Hypocalcemia
Hypokalemia
Peripheral edema
Water retention

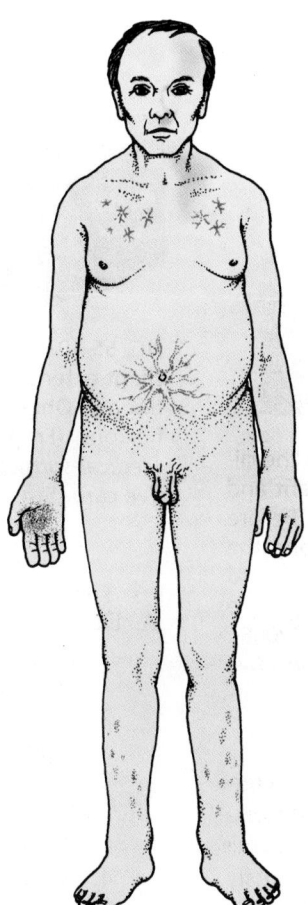

FIG. 55-8 Clinical picture of a client with liver dysfunction. Manifestations vary according to the progression of the disease. Early manifestations are noted in color. (From Ignatavicius, D., & Workman, M. [2006]. *Medical-surgical nursing: Critical thinking for collaborative care* [5th ed.]. St. Louis: W.B. Saunders.)

7. Hepatorenal syndrome
   a. Progressive renal failure associated with hepatic failure
   b. Characterized by a sudden decrease in urinary output, elevated blood urea nitrogen and creatinine levels, decreased urine sodium excretion, and increased urine osmolarity
C. Assessment (Fig. 55-8)
D. Interventions
   1. Elevate the head of the bed to minimize shortness of breath.
   2. If **ascites** and edema are absent and the client does not exhibit signs of impending coma, a high-protein diet supplemented with vitamins is prescribed.
   3. Provide supplemental vitamins (B complex, vitamins A, C, and K, folic acid, and thiamine) as prescribed.
   4. Restrict sodium intake and fluid intake as prescribed.
   5. Initiate enteral feedings or parenteral nutrition as prescribed.
   6. Administer diuretics as prescribed to treat **ascites.**
   7. Monitor intake and output and electrolyte balance.
   8. Weigh client and measure abdominal girth daily (Fig. 55-9).
   9. Monitor level of consciousness; assess for precoma state (tremors, delirium).

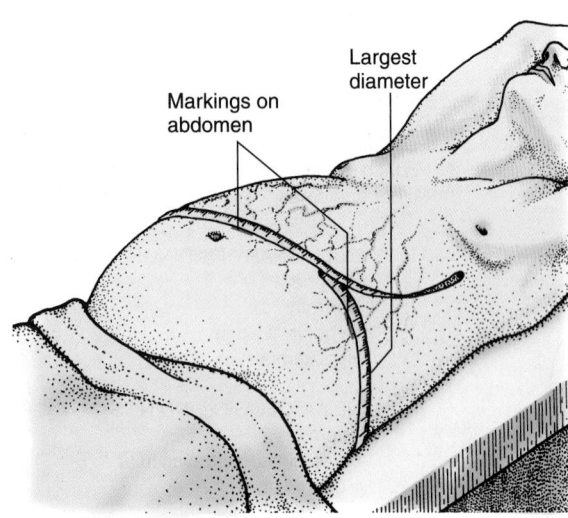

FIG. 55-9 How to measure abdominal girth. With the client supine, bring the tape measure around the client and take a measurement at the level of the umbilicus. Before removing the tape, mark the client's abdomen along the sides of tape on the client's flanks (sides) and midline to ensure that later measurements are taken at the same place. (From Ignatavicius, D., & Workman, M. [2006]. *Medical-surgical nursing: Critical thinking for collaborative care* [5th ed.]. St. Louis: W.B. Saunders.)

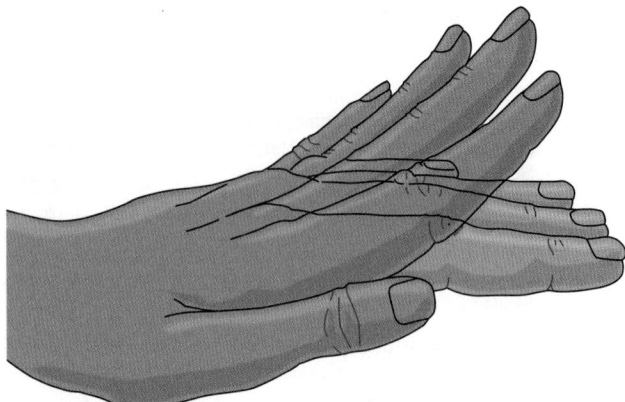

FIG. 55-10 Eliciting asterixis (flapping tremor). Have the client extend the arm, dorsiflex the wrist, and extend the fingers. Observe for rapid, nonrhythmic extensions and flexions. (From Ignatavicius, D., & Workman, M. [2006]. *Medical-surgical nursing: Critical thinking for collaborative care* [5th ed.]. St. Louis: W.B. Saunders.)

10. Monitor for **asterixis,** a coarse tremor characterized by rapid, nonrhythmic extensions and flexions in the wrist and fingers (Fig. 55-10).
11. Monitor for **fetor hepaticus,** the fruity, musty breath odor of severe chronic liver disease.
12. Maintain gastric intubation to assess bleeding or esophagogastric balloon tamponade to control bleeding varices if prescribed.
13. Administer blood products as prescribed.
14. Monitor coagulation laboratory results; administer vitamin K if prescribed.
15. Administer low sodium antacids as prescribed.
16. Administer lactulose (Chronulac) as prescribed, which decreases the pH of the bowel, decreases production of ammonia by bacteria in the bowel, and facilitates the excretion of ammonia.
17. Administer neomycin (Mycifradin) or metronidazole (Flagyl) as prescribed to inhibit protein synthesis in bacteria and decrease the production of ammonia.
18. Avoid medications such as opioids, sedatives, and barbiturates and any hepatotoxic medications or substances.
19. Instruct the client about the restriction of alcohol intake.
20. Prepare the client for paracentesis to remove abdominal fluid.
21. Prepare the client for surgical shunting procedures if prescribed to divert fluid from **ascites** into the venous system.

XX. CHOLECYSTITIS
A. Description
1. Inflammation of the gallbladder that may occur as an acute or chronic process
2. Acute inflammation is associated with gallstones (cholelithiasis).
3. Chronic **cholecystitis** results when inefficient bile emptying and gallbladder muscle wall disease cause a fibrotic and contracted gallbladder.
4. Acalculous **cholecystitis** occurs in the absence of gallstones and is caused by bacterial invasion via the lymphatic or vascular system.
B. Assessment
1. Nausea and vomiting
2. Indigestion
3. Belching
4. Flatulence
5. Epigastric pain that radiates to the scapula 2 to 4 hours after eating fatty foods and may persist for 4 to 6 hours
6. Pain localized in right upper quadrant
7. Guarding, rigidity, and rebound tenderness
8. Mass palpated in the right upper quadrant
9. **Murphy's sign** (cannot take a deep breath when the examiner's fingers are passed below the hepatic margin because of pain)
10. Elevated temperature
11. Tachycardia
12. Signs of dehydration
C. Biliary obstruction
1. Jaundice
2. Dark orange and foamy urine
3. Steatorrhea and clay-colored feces
4. Pruritus
D. Interventions
1. Maintain NPO status during nausea and vomiting episodes.

2. Maintain nasogastric decompression as prescribed for severe vomiting.

3. Administer antiemetics as prescribed for nausea and vomiting.

4. Administer analgesics as prescribed to relieve pain and reduce spasm. (*Note:* Although morphine sulfate or codeine sulfate may be prescribed, they generally are avoided because they can cause spasm of the sphincter of Oddi and increase pain.)

5. Administer antispasmodics (anticholinergics) as prescribed to relax smooth muscle.

6. Instruct the client with chronic **cholecystitis** to eat small, low-fat meals.

7. Instruct the client to avoid gas-forming foods.

8. Prepare the client for nonsurgical and surgical procedures as prescribed.

E. Surgical interventions
1. **Cholecystectomy** is the removal of the gallbladder.
2. **Choledocholithotomy** requires incision into the common bile duct to remove the stone.
3. Surgical procedures may be performed by laparoscopy.

F. Postoperative interventions
1. Monitor for respiratory complications caused by pain at the incisional site.
2. Encourage coughing and deep breathing.
3. Encourage early ambulation.
4. Instruct the client about splinting the abdomen to prevent discomfort during coughing.
5. Administer antiemetics as prescribed for nausea and vomiting.
6. Administer analgesics as prescribed for pain relief.
7. Maintain NPO status and nasogastric tube suction as prescribed.
8. Advance diet from clear liquids to solids when prescribed and as tolerated by the client.
9. Maintain and monitor drainage from the T tube, if present (Box 55-13).

XXI. PANCREATITIS

A. Description
1. Acute or chronic inflammation of the pancreas, with associated escape of pancreatic enzymes into surrounding tissue
2. Acute **pancreatitis** occurs suddenly as one attack or can be recurrent, with resolutions.
3. Chronic **pancreatitis** is a continual inflammation and destruction of the pancreas, with scar tissue replacing pancreatic tissue.
4. Precipitating factors include trauma, the use of alcohol, biliary tract disease, viral or bacterial disease, hyperlipidemia, hypercalcemia, cholelithiasis, hyperparathyroidism, ischemic vascular disease, and peptic ulcer disease.

BOX 55-13
Care of a T Tube

PURPOSE AND DESCRIPTION
A T tube is placed after surgical exploration of the common bile duct. The tube preserves the patency of the duct and ensures drainage of bile until edema resolves and bile is effectively draining into the duodenum. A gravity drainage bag is attached to the T tube to collect the drainage.

INTERVENTIONS
Position the client in a semi-Fowler's position to facilitate drainage.
Monitor the amount, color, consistency, and odor of the drainage.
Report sudden increases in bile output to the physician.
Monitor for inflammation and protect the skin from irritation.
Keep the drainage system below the level of the gallbladder.
Monitor for foul odor and purulent drainage and report its presence to the physician.
Avoid irrigation, aspiration, or clamping of the T tube without a physician's order.
As prescribed, clamp the tube before a meal and observe for abdominal discomfort and distention, nausea, chills, or fever; unclamp the tube if nausea or vomiting occurs.

B. Acute **pancreatitis**
1. Assessment
   a. Abdominal pain, including a sudden onset at a midepigastric or left upper quadrant location with radiation to the back
   b. Pain aggravated by a fatty meal, alcohol, or lying in a recumbent position
   c. Abdominal tenderness and guarding
   d. Nausea and vomiting
   e. Weight loss
   f. **Cullen's sign** (discoloration of the abdomen and periumbilical area)
   g. **Turner's sign** (bluish discoloration of the flanks)
   h. Absent or decreased bowel sounds
   i. Elevated white blood cell count, and glucose, bilirubin, alkaline phosphatase, and urinary amylase levels
   j. Elevated serum lipase and amylase levels
2. Interventions
   a. Maintain NPO status and maintain hydration with IV fluids as prescribed.
   b. Administer parenteral nutrition for severe nutritional depletion.
   c. Administer supplemental preparations and vitamins and minerals to increase caloric intake if prescribed.
   d. Maintain nasogastric tube to decrease gastric distention and suppress pancreatic secretion.

e. Administer meperidine hydrochloride (Demerol) as prescribed for pain because it causes less incidence of smooth muscle spasm of the pancreatic ducts and sphincter of Oddi. (*Note:* Although morphine sulfate or codeine sulfate may be prescribed, they generally are avoided because they can cause spasm of the sphincter of Oddi and increase pain.)

f. Administer antacids as prescribed to neutralize gastric secretions.

g. Administer H_2-receptor antagonists as prescribed to decrease hydrochloric acid production and prevent activation of pancreatic enzymes.

h. Administer anticholinergics as prescribed to decrease vagal stimulation, decrease gastrointestinal motility, and inhibit pancreatic enzyme secretion.

i. Instruct the client in the importance of avoiding alcohol.

j. Instruct the client in the importance of follow-up visits with the physician.

k. Instruct the client to notify the physician if acute abdominal pain, jaundice, clay-colored stools, or dark-colored urine develops.

C. Chronic **pancreatitis**

1. Assessment

a. Abdominal pain and tenderness

b. Left upper quadrant mass

c. Steatorrhea and foul-smelling stools that may increase in volume as pancreatic insufficiency increases

d. Weight loss

e. Muscle wasting

f. Jaundice

g. Signs and symptoms of diabetes mellitus

2. Interventions

a. Instruct the client in the prescribed dietary measures (fat and protein intake may be limited).

b. Instruct the client to avoid heavy meals.

c. Instruct the client about the importance of avoiding alcohol.

d. Provide supplemental preparations and vitamins and minerals to increase caloric intake.

e. Administer pancreatic enzymes as prescribed to aid in the digestion and absorption of fat and protein.

f. Administer insulin or oral hypoglycemic medications as prescribed to control diabetes mellitus, if present.

g. Instruct the client in the use of pancreatic enzyme medications.

h. Instruct the client in the treatment plan for glucose management.

i. Instruct the client to notify the physician if increased steatorrhea, abdominal distention or cramping, or skin breakdown develops.

j. Instruct the client in the importance of follow-up visits.

XXII. HEPATITIS

A. Description

1. Inflammation of the liver caused by a virus, bacteria, or exposure to medications or hepatotoxins

2. The goals of treatment include resting the inflamed liver to reduce metabolic demands and increasing the blood supply, thus promoting cellular regeneration and preventing complications.

B. Types of viral hepatitis

1. Hepatitis A virus (HAV), infectious hepatitis

2. Hepatitis B virus (HBV), serum hepatitis

3. Hepatitis C virus (HCV), non-A, non-B hepatitis or post-transfusion hepatitis

4. Hepatitis D virus (HDV), delta agent hepatitis

5. Hepatitis E virus (HEV), enterically transmitted or epidemic non-A, non-B hepatitis

6. Hepatitis G virus, non-A, non-B, non-C hepatitis

C. Stages of viral hepatitis (Box 55-14)

D. Assessment

1. Preicteric stage

a. Flu-like symptoms—malaise, fatigue

b. Anorexia, nausea, vomiting, diarrhea

c. Pain—headache, muscle aches, polyarthritis

d. Serum bilirubin and enzyme levels are elevated.

2. Icteric stage

a. Jaundice

b. Pruritus

c. Brown-colored urine

d. Lighter colored stools

e. Decrease in preicteric phase symptoms

BOX 55-14

Stages of Viral Hepatitis

PREICTERIC STAGE
The first stage of hepatitis preceding the appearance of jaundice; includes flu-like symptoms

ICTERIC STAGE
The second stage of hepatitis; includes the appearance of jaundice and associated symptoms such as elevated bilirubin levels, dark or tea-colored urine, and clay-colored stools

POSTICTERIC STAGE
The convalescent stage of hepatitis, in which the jaundice decreases and the color of the urine and stool return to normal

3. Posticteric stage
   a. Increased energy levels
   b. Subsiding of pain
   c. Minimal to absent gastrointestinal symptoms
   d. Serum bilirubin and enzyme levels return to normal
E. Laboratory assessment
   1. Alanine aminotransferase level: Elevated into the thousands (normal, 4 to 36 international units/L)
   2. Aspartate aminotransferase level: Elevated into the thousands (normal, 8 to 33 units/L).
   3. Alkaline phosphatase levels: May be normal or mildly elevated (normal, 4.5 to 13 King-Armstrong units/dL).
   4. Total bilirubin levels: Elevated in the serum and urine (normal, lower than 1.5 mg/dL).

XXIII. HEPATITIS A
A. Description
   1. Formerly known as infectious hepatitis
   2. Commonly seen during the fall and early winter
B. Individuals at increased risk
   1. Commonly seen in young children
   2. Individuals in institutionalized settings
   3. Health care personnel
C. Transmission
   1. Fecal-oral route
   2. Person-to-person contact
   3. Parenteral
   4. Contaminated fruits, vegetables, or uncooked shellfish
   5. Contaminated water or milk
   6. Poorly washed utensils
D. Incubation and infectious period
   1. Incubation period is 2 to 6 weeks.
   2. Infectious period is 2 to 3 weeks before and 1 week after development of jaundice.
E. Testing
   1. Infection is established by the presence of HAV antibodies (anti-HAV) in the blood.
   2. Immunoglobulin M (IgM) and IgG are normally present in the blood, and increased levels indicate infection and inflammation.
   3. Ongoing inflammation of the liver is evidenced by the presence of elevated levels of IgM antibodies, which persist in the blood for 4 to 6 weeks.
   4. Previous infection is indicated by the presence of elevated levels of IgG antibodies.
F. Complication: Fulminant (severe acute and often fatal) hepatitis
G. Prevention
   1. Strict hand washing
   2. Stool and needle precautions
   3. Treatment of municipal water supplies
   4. Serological screening of food handlers
   5. Hepatitis A vaccine (Havrix)

6. Immune globulin: For individuals exposed to HAV who have never received the hepatitis A vaccine; administer immune globulin during the period of incubation and within 2 weeks of exposure.
7. Immune globulin and hepatitis A vaccine are recommended for household members and sexual contacts of individuals with hepatitis A.
8. Preexposure prophylaxis with immunoglobulin is recommended to individuals traveling to countries with poor or uncertain sanitation conditions.

XXIV. HEPATITIS B
A. Description
   1. Hepatitis B is nonseasonal.
   2. All age groups are affected.
B. Individuals at increased risk
   1. Drug addicts
   2. Clients undergoing long-term hemodialysis
   3. Health care personnel
C. Transmission
   1. Blood or body fluid contact
   2. Infected blood products
   3. Infected saliva or semen
   4. Contaminated needles
   5. Sexual contact
   6. Parenteral
   7. Perinatal period
   8. Blood or body fluids contact at birth
D. Incubation period: 6 to 24 weeks
E. Testing
   1. Infection is established by the presence of hepatitis B antigen-antibody systems in the blood.
   2. Presence of hepatitis B surface antigen (HBsAg) is the serological marker to establish the diagnosis of hepatitis B.
   3. The client is considered infectious if these antigens are present in the blood.
   4. If the serological marker (HBsAg) is present after 6 months, it indicates a carrier state or chronic hepatitis.
   5. Normally, the serological marker (HBsAg) level declines and disappears after the acute hepatitis B episode.
   6. The presence of antibodies to HBsAg (anti-HBs) indicates recovery and immunity to hepatitis B.
   7. Hepatitis B early antigen (HBeAg) is detected in the blood about 1 week after the appearance of HBsAg and its presence determines the infective state of the client.
F. Complications
   1. Fulminant hepatitis
   2. Chronic liver disease
   3. **Cirrhosis**
   4. Primary hepatocellular carcinoma
G. Prevention
   1. Strict hand washing
   2. Screening blood donors

3. Testing of all pregnant women
4. Needle precautions
5. Avoiding intimate sexual contact if test for hepatitis B surface antigen (HBsAg) is positive.
6. Hepatitis B vaccine: Engerix-B, Recombivax HB
7. Hepatitis B immune globulin is for individuals exposed to HBV through sexual contact or through the percutaneous or transmucosal routes who have never had hepatitis B and have never received hepatitis B vaccine.

XXV. HEPATITIS C

A. Description
  1. Hepatitis C virus infection occurs year-round.
  2. Infection can occur in any age group.
  3. Infection with HCV is common among drug abusers and is the major cause of post-transfusion hepatitis.
  4. Risk factors are similar to those for HBV because hepatitis C is also transmitted parenterally.
B. Individuals at increased risk
  1. Parenteral drug users
  2. Clients receiving frequent transfusions
  3. Health care personnel
C. Transmission: Same as for HBV, primarily through blood
D. Incubation period: 5 to 10 weeks
E. Testing: Anti-HCV is the antibody to HCV and is most accurate in detecting chronic states of hepatitis C.
F. Complications
  1. Chronic liver disease
  2. **Cirrhosis**
  3. Primary hepatocellular carcinoma
G. Prevention
  1. Strict hand washing
  2. Needle precautions
  3. Screening of blood donors

XXVI. HEPATITIS D

A. Description
  1. Hepatitis D is common in the Mediterranean and Middle Eastern areas.
  2. Hepatitis D occurs with hepatitis B and causes infection only in the presence of active HBV infection.
  3. Coinfection with the delta agent (HDV) intensifies the acute symptoms of hepatitis B.
  4. Transmission and risk of infection are the same as for HBV via contact with blood and blood products.
  5. Prevention of HBV infection with vaccine also prevents HDV infection, because HDV depends on HBV for replication.
B. High-risk individuals
  1. Drug users
  2. Clients receiving hemodialysis
  3. Clients receiving frequent blood transfusions

C. Transmission: Same as for HBV
D. Incubation period: 7 to 8 weeks
E. Testing: Serological HDV determination is made by detection of the hepatitis D antigen (HDAg) early in the course of the infection and by detection of anti-HDV antibody in the later disease stages.
F. Complications
  1. Chronic liver disease
  2. Fulminant hepatitis
G. Prevention: Because hepatitis D must coexist with hepatitis B, the precautions that help prevent hepatitis B are also useful in preventing delta hepatitis.

XXVII. HEPATITIS E

A. Description
  1. Hepatitis E is a waterborne virus.
  2. Hepatitis E is prevalent in areas where sewage disposal is inadequate or where communal bathing in contaminated rivers is practiced.
  3. Risk of infection is the same as for HAV.
  4. Infection with HEV presents as a mild disease except in infected women in the third trimester of pregnancy, who have a high mortality rate.
B. Individuals with increased risk
  1. Travelers to countries that have a high incidence of hepatitis E such as India, Burma (Myanmar), Afghanistan, Algeria, and Mexico
  2. Eating or drinking of food or water contaminated with the virus
C. Transmission: Same as for HAV
D. Incubation period: 2 to 9 weeks
E. Testing: Specific serological tests for HEV include detection of IgM and IgG antibodies to hepatitis E (anti-HEV).
F. Complications
  1. High mortality rate in pregnant women
  2. Fetal demise
G. Prevention
  1. Strict hand washing
  2. Treatment of water supplies and sanitation measures

XXVIII. HEPATITIS G

A. Hepatitis G is non-A, non-B, non-C hepatitis.
B. Autoantibodies are absent.
C. Risk factors are similar to those for hepatitis C.
D. Hepatitis G virus has been found in some blood donors, IV drug users, hemodialysis clients, and clients with hemophilia; however, hepatitis G virus does not appear to cause significant liver disease.

XXIX. CLIENT AND FAMILY HOME CARE INSTRUCTIONS FOR HEPATITIS (Box 55-15)

BOX 55-15

Home Care Instructions About Hepatitis

Hand washing must be strict and frequent.

Do not share bathrooms unless the client strictly adheres to personal hygiene measures.

Individual washcloths, towels, drinking and eating utensils, and toothbrushes and razors must be labeled and identified.

The client must not prepare food for other family members.

The client should avoid alcohol and over-the-counter medications, particularly acetaminophen (Tylenol) and sedatives, because these medications are hepatotoxic.

The client should increase activity gradually to prevent fatigue.

The client should consume small, frequent meals consisting of high-carbohydrate, low-fat foods.

The client is not to donate blood.

The client may maintain normal contact with persons as long as proper personal hygiene is maintained.

Close personal contact such as kissing should be discouraged until hepatitis B surface antigen test results are negative.

The client is to avoid sexual activity until hepatitis B surface antigen results are negative.

The client needs to carry a Medic-Alert card noting the date of hepatitis onset.

The client needs to inform other health professionals, such as medical or dental personnel, of the onset of hepatitis.

The client needs to keep follow-up appointments with the health care provider.

PRACTICE QUESTIONS

1. The physician has determined that the client with hepatitis has contracted the infection from contaminated food. The nurse understands that this client is most likely experiencing what type of hepatitis?
   1. Hepatitis A
   2. Hepatitis B
   3. Hepatitis C
   4. Hepatitis D

2. A client is suspected of having hepatitis. Which diagnostic test result will assist in confirming this diagnosis?
   1. Elevated hemoglobin level
   2. Elevated serum bilirubin level
   3. Elevated blood urea nitrogen level
   4. Decreased erythrocyte sedimentation rate

3. The nurse is reviewing the physician's orders written for a client admitted to the hospital with acute pancreatitis. Which physician order should the nurse question if noted on the client's chart?
   1. NPO status
   2. Nasogastric tube insertion
   3. Morphine sulfate for pain
   4. An anticholinergic medication

4. The nurse has given postprocedure instructions to a client who has undergone a colonoscopy. Which statement by the client indicates the need for further teaching?
   1. "It is normal to feel gassy or bloated after the procedure."
   2. "The abdominal muscles may be tender from the procedure."

   3. "It is all right to drive once I've been home for an hour or so."
   4. "Intake should be light at first and then progress to regular intake."

5. The nurse is performing an abdominal assessment and inspects the skin on the abdomen. The nurse performs which assessment technique next?
   1. Palpates the abdomen for size
   2. Palpates the liver at the right rib margin
   3. Listens to bowel sounds in all four quadrants
   4. Percusses the right lower abdominal quadrant

6. The nurse is caring for a client with a diagnosis of chronic gastritis. The nurse monitors the client knowing that this client is at risk for which vitamin deficiency?
   1. Vitamin A
   2. Vitamin B_{12}
   3. Vitamin C
   4. Vitamin E

7. The nurse is reviewing the medication record of a client with acute gastritis. Which medication, if noted on the client's record, would the nurse question?
   1. Digoxin (Lanoxin)
   2. Furosemide (Lasix)
   3. Indomethacin (Indocin)
   4. Propranolol hydrochloride (Inderal)

8. The nurse is assessing a client 24 hours following a cholecystectomy. The nurse notes that the T tube has drained 750 mL of green-brown drainage since the surgery. Which nursing intervention is appropriate?
   1. Clamp the T tube.
   2. Irrigate the T tube.
   3. Notify the physician.
   4. Document the findings.

9. The nurse is monitoring a client with a diagnosis of peptic ulcer. Which assessment finding would most likely indicate perforation of the ulcer?
   1. Bradycardia
   2. Numbness in the legs
   3. Nausea and vomiting
   4. A rigid, board-like abdomen

10. The nurse is caring for a client following a Billroth II procedure. Which postoperative order should the nurse question and verify?
   1. Leg exercises
   2. Early ambulation
   3. Irrigating the nasogastric tube
   4. Coughing and deep-breathing exercises

11. The nurse is providing discharge instructions to a client following gastrectomy and instructs the client to take which measure to assist in preventing dumping syndrome?
   1. Ambulate following a meal.
   2. Eat high carbohydrate foods.
   3. Limit the fluids taken with meals.
   4. Sit in a high Fowler's position during meals.

12. The nurse is monitoring a client for the early signs and symptoms of dumping syndrome. Which of the following indicate this occurrence?
   1. Sweating and pallor
   2. Bradycardia and indigestion
   3. Double vision and chest pain
   4. Abdominal cramping and pain

13. The nurse is caring for a hospitalized client with a diagnosis of ulcerative colitis. Which finding, if noted on assessment of the client, would the nurse report to the physician?
   1. Hypotension
   2. Bloody diarrhea
   3. Rebound tenderness
   4. A hemoglobin level of 12 mg/dL

14. The nurse is caring for a client postoperatively following creation of a colostomy. Which nursing diagnosis should the nurse include in the plan of care?
   1. Sexual dysfunction
   2. Body image, disturbed
   3. Fear related to poor prognosis
   4. Nutrition: more than body requirements, imbalanced

15. The nurse is reviewing the record of a client with Crohn's disease. Which stool characteristic should the nurse expect to note documented in the client's record?
   1. Diarrhea
   2. Chronic constipation
   3. Constipation alternating with diarrhea
   4. Stool constantly oozing from the rectum

16. The nurse is performing a colostomy irrigation on a client. During the irrigation, the client begins to complain of abdominal cramps. What is the appropriate nursing action?
   1. Notify the physician.
   2. Stop the irrigation temporarily.
   3. Increase the height of the irrigation.
   4. Medicate for pain and resume the irrigation.

17. The nurse is reviewing the record of a client with a diagnosis of cirrhosis and notes that there is documentation of the presence of asterixis. How should the nurse assess for its presence?
   1. Dorsiflex the client's foot.
   2. Measure the abdominal girth.
   3. Ask the client to extend the arms.
   4. Instruct the client to lean forward.

18. The nurse is reviewing the laboratory results in a client with cirrhosis and notes that the ammonia level is elevated. Which diet does the nurse anticipate to be prescribed for this client?
   1. Low-protein diet
   2. High-protein diet
   3. Moderate-fat diet
   4. High-carbohydrate diet

19. The nurse is doing an admission assessment on a client with a history of duodenal ulcer. To determine whether the problem is currently active, the nurse should assess the client for which symptom(s) of duodenal ulcer?
   1. Weight loss
   2. Nausea and vomiting
   3. Pain relieved by food intake
   4. Pain radiating down the right arm

20. The medication history of a client with peptic ulcer disease reveals intermittent use of several medications. The nurse would teach the client to avoid which of these medications because of the irritating effects on the lining of the gastrointestinal tract?
   1. Nizatidine (Axid)
   2. Ibuprofen (Motrin)
   3. Sucralfate (Carafate)
   4. Omeprazole (Prilosec)

21. The nurse instructs the ileostomy client to include which action as part of essential care of the stoma?
   1. Massage the area below the stoma.
   2. Limit fluid intake to prevent diarrhea.
   3. Take in high-fiber foods such as nuts.
   4. Cleanse the peristomal skin meticulously.

22. The client with hiatal hernia chronically experiences heartburn following meals. The nurse plans to teach the client to avoid which action because it is contraindicated with a hiatal hernia?
   1. Lying recumbent following meals
   2. Taking in small, frequent, bland meals
   3. Raising the head of bed on 6-inch blocks
   4. Taking H$_2$-receptor antagonist medication

23. The client who has undergone creation of a colostomy has a nursing diagnosis of body image, dis-

turbed. What action by the client indicates the most significant progress toward identified goals?
1. Looking at the ostomy site
2. Reading the ostomy product literature
3. Watching the nurse empty the ostomy bag
4. Practicing proper cutting of the ostomy appliance

24. The nurse is assessing for stoma prolapse in a client with a colostomy. What should the nurse observe if stoma prolapse occurs?
1. Protruding stoma
2. Sunken and hidden stoma
3. Narrowed and flattened stoma
4. Dark- and bluish-colored stoma

25. The client had a new colostomy created 2 days earlier and is beginning to pass malodorous flatus from the stoma. What is the correct interpretation by the nurse?
1. This is a normal, expected event.
2. The client is experiencing early signs of ischemic bowel.
3. The client should not have the nasogastric tube removed.
4. This indicates inadequate preoperative bowel preparation.

26. The client with a new colostomy is concerned about the odor from stool in the ostomy drainage bag. The nurse teaches the client to include which food in the diet to reduce odor?
1. Eggs
2. Yogurt
3. Broccoli
4. Cucumbers

27. The client has just had surgery to create an ileostomy. The nurse assesses the client in the immediate postoperative period for which most frequent complication of this type of surgery?
1. Folate deficiency
2. Malabsorption of fat
3. Intestinal obstruction
4. Fluid and electrolyte imbalance

28. The nurse is doing preoperative teaching with the client who is about to undergo creation of a Kock pouch. The nurse interprets that the client has the best understanding of the nature of the surgery if the client makes which statement?
1. "I will be able to pass stool by the rectum eventually."
2. "The drainage from this type of ostomy will be formed."
3. "I will need to drain the pouch regularly with a catheter."
4. "I will need to wear a drainage bag for the rest of my life."

29. The client with a colostomy has an order for irrigation of the colostomy. The nurse uses which solution for the irrigation?

1. Tap water
2. Sterile water
3. Sterile distilled water
4. Sterile lactated Ringer's

30. The nurse is monitoring a client admitted to the hospital with a diagnosis of appendicitis who is scheduled for surgery in 2 hours. The client begins to complain of increased abdominal pain and begins to vomit. On assessment, the nurse notes that the abdomen is distended and bowel sounds are diminished. Which is the appropriate nursing intervention?
1. Notify the physician.
2. Administer the prescribed pain medication.
3. Call and ask the operating room team to perform the surgery as soon as possible.
4. Reposition the client and apply a heating pad on warm setting to the client's abdomen.

31. The client has been admitted to the hospital with a diagnosis of acute pancreatitis and the nurse is assessing the client's pain. What type of pain is consistent with this diagnosis?
1. Burning and aching, located in the left lower quadrant and radiating to the hip
2. Severe and unrelenting, located in the epigastric area and radiating to the back
3. Burning and aching, located in the epigastric area and radiating to the umbilicus
4. Severe and unrelenting, located in the left lower quadrant and radiating to the groin

32. The client with chronic pancreatitis needs information on dietary modification to manage the health problem. The nurse teaches the client to limit which item in the diet?
1. Fat
2. Protein
3. Carbohydrate
4. Water-soluble vitamins

33. The nurse has taught the client with chronic pancreatitis about risk factor modification to reduce the incidence of recurrences. The nurse determines that the client has understood the information if the client states that it will be necessary to control which factor?
1. Alcohol intake
2. Duodenal ulcer
3. Crohn's disease
4. Diabetes mellitus

34. The nurse is evaluating the effect of dietary counseling on the client with cholecystitis. The nurse evaluates that the client understands the instructions given if the client states that which food item(s) is (are) acceptable in the diet?
1. Baked fish
2. Fried chicken
3. Sauces and gravies
4. Fresh whipped cream

35. The nurse is assessing a client who is experiencing an acute episode of cholecystitis. Where should the nurse anticipate the location of the pain?
    1. Right lower quadrant, radiating to the back
    2. Right lower quadrant, radiating to the umbilicus
    3. Right upper quadrant, radiating to the left scapula and shoulder
    4. Right upper quadrant, radiating to the right scapula and shoulder

36. The client with cirrhosis is beginning to show signs of hepatic encephalopathy. The nurse would plan a dietary consult to limit the amount of which ingredient in the client's diet?
    1. Fat
    2. Protein
    3. Minerals
    4. Carbohydrate

37. The client with cirrhosis complicated by ascites is admitted to the hospital. The client has stated a 10-lb weight gain over the last 1½ weeks. The client has edema of the feet and ankles and his abdomen is distended, taut, and shiny with striae. The nurse selects which nursing diagnosis as the most appropriate for this client?
    1. Fluid volume, excess
    2. Gas exchange, impaired
    3. Skin integrity, impaired, risk for
    4. Nutrition: more than body requirements, imbalanced

38. The client with Crohn's disease has a nursing diagnosis of pain, acute. The nurse should teach the client to avoid which action in managing this problem?
    1. Massaging the abdomen
    2. Using relaxation techniques
    3. Using antispasmodic medication
    4. Lying supine with the legs straight

39. The client with ulcerative colitis has an order to begin a salicylate medication to reduce inflammation. What instruction should the nurse give the client regarding when to take this medication?
    1. On arising
    2. After meals
    3. On an empty stomach
    4. 30 minutes before meals

40. The client is admitted to the hospital with viral hepatitis, complaining of "no appetite" and "losing my taste for food." What instruction should the nurse give the client to provide adequate nutrition?
    1. Select foods high in fat.
    2. Increase intake of fluids, including juices.
    3. Eat a good supper when anorexia is not as severe.
    4. Eat less often, preferably only three large meals daily.

41. A client has developed hepatitis A after eating contaminated oysters. The nurse assesses the client for which of the following?
    1. Malaise
    2. Dark stools
    3. Weight gain
    4. Left upper quadrant discomfort

42. A client is admitted with a diagnosis of acute diverticulitis. What nursing intervention is appropriate for this client?
    1. Instruct the client to remain NPO.
    2. Encourage ambulation at least four times daily.
    3. Administer cholinergic medications to reduce pain.
    4. Encourage coughing and deep breathing every 2 hours.

43. A client has just had a hemorrhoidectomy. What nursing intervention is appropriate for this client?
    1. Instruct the client to limit fluid intake to avoid urinary retention.
    2. Instruct the client to eat low-fiber foods to decrease the bulk of the stool.
    3. Apply and maintain ice packs over the dressing until the packing is removed.
    4. Help the client to a Fowler's position to place pressure on the rectal area and decrease bleeding.

44. The nurse is participating in a health screening clinic and is preparing teaching materials about colorectal cancer. Which risk factor for colorectal cancer should the nurse include?
    1. Age older than 30 years
    2. High-fiber, low-fat diet
    3. Distant relative with colorectal cancer
    4. Personal history of ulcerative colitis or gastrointestinal polyps

45. The nurse is planning to teach the client with gastroesophageal reflux disease about substances that will increase the lower esophageal sphincter pressure. Which item should the nurse include on this list?
    1. Coffee
    2. Chocolate
    3. Fatty foods
    4. Nonfat milk

46. The client has undergone esophagogastroduodenoscopy. The nurse places highest priority on which item as part of the client's care plan?
    1. Monitoring the temperature
    2. Monitoring complaints of heartburn
    3. Giving warm gargles for a sore throat
    4. Assessing for the return of the gag reflex

47. The nurse has taught the client about an upcoming endoscopic retrograde cholangiopancreatography procedure. The nurse determines that the client needs further information if the client makes which statement?

1. "I know I must sign the consent form."
2. "I hope the throat spray keeps me from gagging."
3. "I'm glad I don't have to lie still for this procedure."
4. "I'm glad some IV medication will be given to relax me."

ALTERNATE ITEM FORMAT: MULTIPLE RESPONSE

A nurse is reviewing the orders of a client admitted to the hospital with a diagnosis of acute pancreatitis.

Which of the following interventions would the nurse expect to be prescribed for the client? Select all that apply.

❏ 1. Administer antacids as prescribed.
❏ 2. Give small, frequent high-calorie feedings.
❏ 3. Encourage coughing and deep breathing.
❏ 4. Administer anticholinergics as prescribed.
❏ 5. Give Meperidine (Demerol) as prescribed for pain.
❏ 6. Maintain the client in a supine and flat position.

ANSWERS

1. **1**
Rationale: Hepatitis A is transmitted by the fecal-oral route via contaminated food or infected food handlers. Hepatitis B, C, and D are transmitted most commonly via infected blood or body fluids.
Test-Taking Strategy: Knowledge regarding the modes of transmission of the various types of hepatitis is required to answer this question. Remember that hepatitis A is transmitted by the fecal-oral route. Review this content if you are unfamiliar with it.
Level of Cognitive Ability: Comprehension
Client Needs: Safe and Effective Care Environment
Integrated Process: Nursing Process—assessment
Content Area: Adult health—gastrointestinal
Reference: Ignatavicius, D., & Workman, M. (2006). *Medical-surgical nursing: Critical thinking for collaborative care* (5th ed., p. 1382). Philadelphia: W.B. Saunders.

2. **2**
Rationale: Laboratory indicators of hepatitis include elevated liver enzyme levels, elevated serum bilirubin levels, elevated erythrocyte sedimentation rates, and leukopenia. An elevated blood urea nitrogen level may indicate renal dysfunction. A hemoglobin level is unrelated to this diagnosis.
Test-Taking Strategy: Use the process of elimination. Eliminate option 3 because blood urea nitrogen identifies renal rather than hepatic dysfunction. Thinking about the organ that is involved in hepatitis should assist in directing you to option 2, the liver function test. Review diagnostic tests for hepatitis if you had difficulty with this question.
Level of Cognitive Ability: Analysis
Client Needs: Physiological Integrity
Integrated Process: Nursing Process—assessment
Content Area: Adult health—gastrointestinal
References: Ignatavicius, D., & Workman, M. (2006). *Medical-surgical nursing: Critical thinking for collaborative care* (5th ed., pp. 1385-1386). Philadelphia: W.B. Saunders.
Lewis, S., Heitkemper, M., & Dirksen, S. (2004). *Medical-surgical nursing: Assessment and management of clinical problems* (6th ed., p. 1110). St. Louis: Mosby.

3. **3**
Rationale: Meperidine (Demerol) rather than morphine sulfate is the medication of choice to treat pain because morphine sulfate can cause spasms in the sphincter of Oddi. Options 1, 2, and 4 are appropriate interventions for the client with acute pancreatitis.
Test-Taking Strategy: Note the strategic word *acute* in the question. Recalling the pathophysiology associated with this disorder will direct you to option 3. Review the treatment for acute pancreatitis if you had difficulty with this question.
Level of Cognitive Ability: Analysis
Client Needs: Physiological Integrity
Integrated Process: Nursing Process—analysis
Content Area: Adult health—gastrointestinal
References: Ignatavicius, D., & Workman, M. (2006). *Medical-surgical nursing: Critical thinking for collaborative care* (5th ed., pp. 1407-1408). Philadelphia: W.B. Saunders.
Lewis, S., Heitkemper, M., & Dirksen, S. (2004). *Medical-surgical nursing: Assessment and management of clinical problems* (6th ed., p. 1135). St. Louis: Mosby.

4. **3**
Rationale: The client should not drive for several hours after discharge because the client would have received sedative medications during the procedure. Important decisions also should be delayed for at least 24 hours for the same reason. The client should resume intake slowly and progress as tolerated. The client may experience gas, bloating, or abdominal tenderness for a short while after the procedure, and this is normal.
Test-Taking Strategy: Note the strategic words *need for further teaching*. These words indicate a negative event query and ask you to select an option that is an incorrect statement. Recalling that sedating medications are administered will direct you to option 3. Review postprocedure instructions following colonoscopy if you had difficulty with this question.
Level of Cognitive Ability: Analysis
Client Needs: Physiological Integrity
Integrated Process: Teaching and Learning
Content Area: Adult health—gastrointestinal

Reference: Ignatavicius, D., & Workman, M. (2006). *Medical-surgical nursing: Critical thinking for collaborative care* (5th ed., p. 1245). Philadelphia: W.B. Saunders.

5. 3

Rationale: The appropriate sequence for abdominal examination is inspection, auscultation, percussion, and palpation. Auscultation is performed after inspection to ensure that the motility of the bowel and bowel sounds are not altered by percussion or palpation. Therefore, after inspecting the skin on the abdomen, the nurse should listen for bowel sounds.

Test-Taking Strategy: Use the process of elimination and visualize this procedure. Remember that the sequence for abdominal assessment is different than the usual systematic assessment approach and that auscultation is done following inspection. Review this technique if you had difficulty with this question.

Level of Cognitive Ability: Application
Client Needs: Health Promotion and Maintenance
Integrated Process: Nursing Process—assessment
Content Area: Adult health—gastrointestinal
Reference: Potter, P., & Perry, A. (2005). *Fundamentals of nursing* (6th ed., pp. 743-745). St. Louis: Mosby.

6. 2

Rationale: Chronic gastritis causes deterioration and atrophy of the lining of the stomach, leading to the loss of the function of the parietal cells. The source of the intrinsic factor is lost, which results in the inability to absorb vitamin B_{12}. This leads to the development of pernicious anemia. The client is not at risk for vitamin A, C, or E deficiency.

Test-Taking Strategy: Recalling the pathophysiology related to pernicious anemia and vitamin B_{12} deficiency will direct you to option 2. If you are unfamiliar with vitamin B_{12} deficiency and its relationship to gastric disorders, review this content.

Level of Cognitive Ability: Analysis
Client Needs: Physiological Integrity
Integrated Process: Nursing Process—assessment
Content Area: Adult health—gastrointestinal
Reference: Ignatavicius, D., & Workman, M. (2006). *Medical-surgical nursing: Critical thinking for collaborative care* (5th ed., p. 1283). Philadelphia: W.B. Saunders.

7. 3

Rationale: Indomethacin (Indocin) is a nonsteroidal anti-inflammatory drug and can cause ulceration of the esophagus, stomach, or small intestine. Indomethacin is contraindicated in a client with gastrointestinal disorders. Furosemide (Lasix) is a loop diuretic. Digoxin is a cardiac medication. Propranolol (Inderal) is a β-adrenergic blocker. Furosemide, digoxin, and propranolol are not contraindicated in clients with gastric disorders.

Test-Taking Strategy: Identify the classification of each of the medications listed. Use the process of elimination, selecting option 3 because this medication is the one that would affect the gastrointestinal tract. Review these medications if you are unfamiliar with them.

Level of Cognitive Ability: Analysis
Client Needs: Physiological Integrity
Integrated Process: Nursing Process—analysis
Content Area: Adult health—gastrointestinal

Reference: Ignatavicius, D., & Workman, M. (2006). *Medical-surgical nursing: Critical thinking for collaborative care* (5th ed., pp. 1285-1286). Philadelphia: W.B. Saunders.
Skidmore-Roth, L. (2005). *Mosby's drug guide for nurses* (6th ed., pp. 446-447). St. Louis: Mosby.

8. 4

Rationale: Following cholecystectomy, drainage from the T tube is initially bloody and then turns to a greenish-brown color. The drainage is measured as output. The amount of expected drainage will range from 500 to 1000 mL/day. The nurse would document the output.

Test-Taking Strategy: Use the process of elimination. Options 1 and 2 can be eliminated because a T tube is not irrigated and would not be clamped with this amount of drainage. From the remaining options, you must know normal expected findings following this surgical procedure. Review postoperative assessment findings following cholecystectomy if you had difficulty with this question.

Level of Cognitive Ability: Application
Client Needs: Physiological Integrity
Integrated Process: Nursing Process—implementation
Content Area: Adult health—gastrointestinal
Reference: Ignatavicius, D., & Workman, M. (2006). *Medical-surgical nursing: Critical thinking for collaborative care* (5th ed., p. 1401). Philadelphia: W.B. Saunders.

9. 4

Rationale: Perforation of an ulcer is a surgical emergency and is characterized by sudden, sharp, intolerable severe pain beginning in the midepigastric area and spreading over the abdomen, which becomes rigid and board-like. Nausea and vomiting may occur. Tachycardia may occur as hypovolemic shock develops. Numbness in the legs is not an associated finding.

Test-Taking Strategy: Use the process of elimination and note the strategic words *most likely*. Option 2 can be eliminated easily because it is not related to perforation. Eliminate option 1 next because tachycardia rather than bradycardia would develop if perforation occurs. From the remaining options, focusing on the strategic words will help direct you to option 4. Review the signs of a perforated ulcer if you had difficulty with this question.

Level of Cognitive Ability: Analysis
Client Needs: Physiological Integrity
Integrated Process: Nursing Process—assessment
Content Area: Adult health—gastrointestinal
Reference: Black, J., & Hawks, J. (2005). *Medical-surgical nursing: Clinical management for positive outcomes* (7th ed., p. 754). Philadelphia: W.B. Saunders.

10. 3

Rationale: In a Billroth II procedure, the proximal remnant of the stomach is anastomosed to the proximal jejunum. Patency of the nasogastric tube is critical for preventing the retention of gastric secretions. The nurse should never irrigate or reposition the gastric tube after gastric surgery, unless specifically ordered by the physician. In this situation, the nurse should clarify the order. Options 1, 2, and 4 are appropriate postoperative interventions.

Test-Taking Strategy: Note the strategic words *question and verify*. Eliminate options 1, 2, and 4 because they are general postoperative measures. Consider the anatomical location of

the surgical procedure to assist in directing you to option 3. Review postoperative measures following a Billroth II procedure if you had difficulty with this question.
Level of Cognitive Ability: Analysis
Client Needs: Physiological Integrity
Integrated Process: Nursing Process—analysis
Content Area: Adult health—gastrointestinal
Reference: Ignatavicius, D., & Workman, M. (2006). *Medical-surgical nursing: Critical thinking for collaborative care* (5th ed., pp. 1298, 1303). Philadelphia: W.B. Saunders.

11. **3**
Rationale: Dumping syndrome is a term that refers to a constellation of vasomotor symptoms that occurs after eating, especially following a Billroth II procedure. Early manifestations usually occur within 30 minutes of eating and include vertigo, tachycardia, syncope, sweating, pallor, palpitations, and the desire to lie down. The nurse should instruct the client to decrease the amount of fluid taken at meals and to avoid high-carbohydrate foods, including fluids such as fruit nectars; to assume a low Fowler's position during meals; to lie down for 30 minutes after eating to delay gastric emptying; and to take antispasmodics as prescribed.
Test-Taking Strategy: Use the process of elimination. Eliminate options 1 and 4 first because these measures will promote gastric emptying. From the remaining options, select option 3 because this measure will delay gastric emptying. If you are unfamiliar with this syndrome, review the important client teaching points.
Level of Cognitive Ability: Application
Client Needs: Physiological Integrity
Integrated Process: Teaching and Learning
Content Area: Adult health—gastrointestinal
Reference: Ignatavicius, D., & Workman, M. (2006). *Medical-surgical nursing: Critical thinking for collaborative care* (5th ed., p. 1303). Philadelphia: W.B. Saunders.

12. **1**
Rationale: Early manifestations of dumping syndrome occur 5 to 30 minutes after eating. Symptoms include vertigo, tachycardia, syncope, sweating, pallor, palpitations, and the desire to lie down.
Test-Taking Strategy: Use the process of elimination and recall the pathophysiology associated with dumping syndrome. Focus on the strategic word *early* to direct you to option 1. Review the early manifestations of this syndrome if you had difficulty with this question.
Level of Cognitive Ability: Analysis
Client Needs: Physiological Integrity
Integrated Process: Nursing Process—assessment
Content Area: Adult health—gastrointestinal
Reference: Ignatavicius, D., & Workman, M. (2006). *Medical-surgical nursing: Critical thinking for collaborative care* (5th ed., p. 1303). Philadelphia: W.B. Saunders.

13. **3**
Rationale: Rebound tenderness may indicate peritonitis. Bloody diarrhea is expected to occur in ulcerative colitis. Because of the blood loss, the client may be hypotensive and the

hemoglobin level may be lower than normal. Signs of peritonitis must be reported to the physician.
Test-Taking Strategy: Use the process of elimination. Consider the expected manifestations that would occur in ulcerative colitis. This will assist in eliminating option 2. Recalling that bleeding would cause a lowered hemoglobin and hypotension will assist you in eliminating options 1 and 4. Review the normal assessment findings in ulcerative colitis if you had difficulty with this question.
Level of Cognitive Ability: Analysis
Client Needs: Physiological Integrity
Integrated Process: Nursing Process—analysis
Content Area: Adult health—gastrointestinal
Reference: Ignatavicius, D., & Workman, M. (2006). *Medical-surgical nursing: Critical thinking for collaborative care* (5th ed., p. 1347). Philadelphia: W.B. Saunders.

14. **2**
Rationale: Body image, disturbed relates to loss of bowel control, the presence of a stoma, the release of fecal material onto the abdomen, the passage of flatus, odor, and the need for an appliance (external pouch). No data in the question support options 1 and 3. Nutrition: less than body requirements, imbalanced is the more likely nursing diagnosis.
Test-Taking Strategy: Use the process of elimination and the data presented in the question to assist you in selecting the correct option. No data in the question support options 1 and 3. Reading option 4 carefully will assist you in eliminating this option. Review care of the client following a colostomy if you had difficulty with this question.
Level of Cognitive Ability: Analysis
Client Needs: Psychosocial Integrity
Integrated Process: Nursing Process—analysis
Content Area: Adult health—gastrointestinal
Reference: Ignatavicius, D., & Workman, M. (2006). *Medical-surgical nursing: Critical thinking for collaborative care* (5th ed., p. 1325). Philadelphia: W.B. Saunders.

15. **1**
Rationale: Crohn's disease is characterized by nonbloody diarrhea of usually not more than four to five stools daily. Over time, the diarrhea episodes increase in frequency, duration, and severity. Options 2, 3, and 4 are not characteristics of Crohn's disease.
Test-Taking Strategy: Use the process of elimination. Eliminate option 4 first as the most unlikely occurrence. From the remaining options, think about the pathophysiology associated with Crohn's disease to direct you to option 1. If you are unfamiliar with this disorder, review this content.
Level of Cognitive Ability: Analysis
Client Needs: Physiological Integrity
Integrated Process: Nursing Process—assessment
Content Area: Adult health—gastrointestinal
References: Ignatavicius, D., & Workman, M. (2006). *Medical-surgical nursing: Critical thinking for collaborative care* (5th ed., p. 1355). Philadelphia: W.B. Saunders.
Lewis, S., Heitkemper, M., & Dirksen, S. (2004). *Medical-surgical nursing: Assessment and management of clinical problems* (6th ed., p. 1067). St. Louis: Mosby.

16. **2**

Rationale: If cramping occurs during a colostomy irrigation, the irrigation flow is stopped temporarily and the client is allowed to rest. Cramping may occur from an infusion that is too rapid or is causing too much pressure. The physician does not need to be notified. Increasing the height of the irrigation will cause further discomfort. Medicating the client for pain is not the appropriate action in this situation.

Test-Taking Strategy: Focus on the subject, abdominal cramping during irrigation. This will assist in eliminating options 1, 3, and 4. If you had difficulty answering this question, review the procedure for colostomy irrigation.

Level of Cognitive Ability: Application
Client Needs: Physiological Integrity
Integrated Process: Nursing Process—implementation
Content Area: Adult health—gastrointestinal
References: Black, J., & Hawks, J. (2005). *Medical-surgical nursing: Clinical management for positive outcomes* (7th ed., p. 838). Philadelphia: W.B. Saunders.
Lewis, S., Heitkemper, M., & Dirksen, S. (2004). *Medical-surgical nursing: Assessment and management of clinical problems* (6th ed., p. 1092). St. Louis: Mosby.

17. **3**

Rationale: Asterixis is irregular flapping movements of the fingers and wrists when the hands and arms are outstretched, with the palms down, wrists bent up, and fingers spread. Asterixis is the most common and reliable sign that hepatic encephalopathy is developing. Options 1, 2, and 4 are incorrect.

Test-Taking Strategy: Use the process of elimination and knowledge regarding the procedure for this assessment to answer this question. Remember that asterixis is irregular flapping movements of the fingers and wrists. This will direct you to the correct option. Review this assessment procedure if you had difficulty with this question.

Level of Cognitive Ability: Application
Client Needs: Health Promotion and Maintenance
Integrated Process: Nursing Process—assessment
Content Area: Adult health—gastrointestinal
Reference: Ignatavicius, D., & Workman, M. (2006). *Medical-surgical nursing: Critical thinking for collaborative care* (5th ed., p. 1373). Philadelphia: W.B. Saunders.

18. **1**

Rationale: Cirrhosis is a chronic, progressive disease of the liver characterized by diffuse degeneration and destruction of hepatocytes. Most of the ammonia in the body is found in the gastrointestinal tract. Protein provided by the diet is transported to the liver by the portal vein. The liver breaks down protein, and this results in the formation of ammonia. If the client has hepatic encephalopathy, a low-protein diet would be prescribed.

Test-Taking Strategy: Recall the physiology of the liver in answering this question. You should be directed easily to option 1. Also, note that options 1 and 2 are opposite, which should provide you with the clue that one of these options is correct. Review dietary measures for the client with a high ammonia level if you had difficulty with this question.

Level of Cognitive Ability: Analysis
Client Needs: Physiological Integrity

Integrated Process: Nursing Process—analysis
Content Area: Adult health—gastrointestinal
References: Ignatavicius, D., & Workman, M. (2006). *Medical-surgical nursing: Critical thinking for collaborative care* (5th ed., pp. 1369, 1380). Philadelphia: W.B. Saunders.
Lewis, S., Heitkemper, M., & Dirksen, S. (2004). *Medical-surgical nursing: Assessment and management of clinical problems* (6th ed., p. 1125). St. Louis: Mosby.

19. **3**

Rationale: A frequent symptom of duodenal ulcer is pain that is relieved by food intake. These clients generally describe the pain as a burning, heavy, sharp, or "hungry" pain that often localizes in the midepigastric area. The client with duodenal ulcer usually does not experience weight loss or nausea and vomiting. These symptoms are more typical in the client with a gastric ulcer.

Test-Taking Strategy: Use the process of elimination. To answer this question accurately, you must be able to discriminate between symptoms of duodenal and gastric ulcer. This will allow you to eliminate options 1 and 2 first. Choose option 3 over option 4, knowing that the pain does not radiate down the right arm and that a pattern of pain-food-relief occurs with duodenal ulcer. Review the clinical manifestations of a duodenal ulcer if you had difficulty with this question.

Level of Cognitive Ability: Analysis
Client Needs: Physiological Integrity
Integrated Process: Nursing Process—assessment
Content Area: Adult health—gastrointestinal
References: Black, J., & Hawks, J. (2005). *Medical-surgical nursing: Clinical management for positive outcomes* (7th ed., p. 750). Philadelphia: W.B. Saunders.
Ignatavicius, D., & Workman, M. (2006). *Medical-surgical nursing: Critical thinking for collaborative care* (5th ed., pp. 1288-1289). Philadelphia: W.B. Saunders.

20. **2**

Rationale: Ibuprofen is a nonsteroidal anti-inflammatory drug that typically is irritating to the lining of the gastrointestinal tract and should be avoided by clients with a history of peptic ulcer disease. The other medications listed are frequently used to treat peptic ulcer disease. Nizatidine is an H_2-receptor antagonist that reduces the secretion of gastric acid. Sucralfate coats the surface of an ulcer to promote healing. Omeprazole is a proton pump inhibitor, which blocks transport of hydrogen ions into the lumen of the gastrointestinal tract.

Test-Taking Strategy: Focus on the medication classification. Recalling the types of medications irritating to the gastrointestinal tract and which medications are used to treat peptic ulcer disease will direct you to option 2. Review the pharmacological treatment measures for peptic ulcer disease if you had difficulty with this question.

Level of Cognitive Ability: Application
Client Needs: Physiological Integrity
Integrated Process: Teaching and Learning
Content Area: Adult health—gastrointestinal
Reference: Ignatavicius, D., & Workman, M. (2006). *Medical-surgical nursing: Critical thinking for collaborative care* (5th ed., p. 1290). Philadelphia: W.B. Saunders.

21. 4

Rationale: The peristomal skin must receive meticulous cleansing because ileostomy drainage has more enzymes and is more caustic to the skin than colostomy drainage. Foods such as nuts and those with seeds will pass through the ileostomy. The client should be taught that these foods will remain undigested. The area below the ileostomy may be massaged if needed if the ileostomy becomes blocked by high-fiber foods. Fluid intake should be at least six to eight glasses of water per day to prevent dehydration.

Test-Taking Strategy: Focus on the subject and note the strategic words *essential care* and *stoma*. This tells you that the correct option deals with the stoma directly. This will direct you to option 4. Review client instructions regarding ileostomy care if you had difficulty with this question.

Level of Cognitive Ability: Application
Client Needs: Physiological Integrity
Integrated Process: Teaching and Learning
Content Area: Adult health—gastrointestinal
References: Ignatavicius, D., & Workman, M. (2006). *Medical-surgical nursing: Critical thinking for collaborative care* (5th ed., p. 1326). Philadelphia: W.B. Saunders.
Perry, A., & Potter, P. (2006). *Clinical nursing skills and techniques* (6th ed., pp. 1157, 1160). St. Louis: Mosby.

22. 1

Rationale: Hiatal hernia is caused by a protrusion of a portion of the stomach above the diaphragm where the esophagus usually is positioned. The client usually experiences pain from reflux caused by ingestion of irritating foods, lying flat following meals or at night, and eating large or fatty meals. Relief is obtained with the intake of small, frequent, and bland meals, use of H_2-receptor antagonists and antacids, and elevation of the thorax following meals and during sleep.

Test-Taking Strategy: Use the process of elimination noting the strategic word *contraindicated*. Thinking about the pathophysiology that occurs in hiatal hernia will direct you to option 1. Review this pathophysiology if you had difficulty with this question.

Level of Cognitive Ability: Application
Client Needs: Physiological Integrity
Integrated Process: Teaching and Learning
Content Area: Adult health—gastrointestinal
References: Black, J., & Hawks, J. (2005). *Medical-surgical nursing: Clinical management for positive outcomes* (7th ed., pp. 726-727). Philadelphia: W.B. Saunders.
Ignatavicius, D., & Workman, M. (2006). *Medical-surgical nursing: Critical thinking for collaborative care* (5th ed., pp. 1270, 1273). Philadelphia: W.B. Saunders.

23. 4

Rationale: The client is expected to have a body image disturbance after colostomy. The client progresses through normal grieving stages to adjust to this change. The client demonstrates the greatest deal of acceptance when the client participates in the actual colostomy care. Each incorrect option represents an interest in colostomy care but is a passive activity. The correct option shows the client participating in self-care.

Test-Taking Strategy: Note the strategic words *colostomy* and *most significant progress*. Eliminate options 1, 2, and 3 because

they are similar or alike and indicate passive activities. Review psychosocial adjustment in a client with a colostomy if you had difficulty with this question.

Level of Cognitive Ability: Analysis
Client Needs: Psychosocial Integrity
Integrated Process: Nursing Process—evaluation
Content Area: Adult health—gastrointestinal
References: Black, J., & Hawks, J. (2005). *Medical-surgical nursing: Clinical management for positive outcomes* (7th ed., p. 837). Philadelphia: W.B. Saunders.
Ignatavicius, D., & Workman, M. (2006). *Medical-surgical nursing: Critical thinking for collaborative care* (5th ed., pp. 1325-1326). Philadelphia: W.B. Saunders.

24. 1

Rationale: A prolapsed stoma is one in which the bowel protrudes through the stoma. A stoma retraction is characterized by sinking of the stoma. Ischemia of the stoma would be associated with a dusky or bluish color. A stoma with a narrowed opening at the level of the skin or fascia is said to be stenosed.

Test-Taking Strategy: Focus on the subject and the strategic word *prolapse*. This will direct you to option 1. If this question was difficult, review the complications associated with a colostomy stoma.

Level of Cognitive Ability: Analysis
Client Needs: Physiological Integrity
Integrated Process: Nursing Process—assessment
Content Area: Adult health—gastrointestinal
References: Ignatavicius, D., & Workman, M. (2006). *Medical-surgical nursing: Critical thinking for collaborative care* (5th ed., p. 1324). Philadelphia: W.B. Saunders.
Lewis, S., Heitkemper, M., & Dirksen, S. (2004). *Medical-surgical nursing: Assessment and management of clinical problems* (6th ed., p. 1089). St. Louis: Mosby.

25. 1

Rationale: As peristalsis returns following creation of a colostomy, the client begins to pass malodorous flatus. This indicates returning bowel function and is an expected event. Within 72 hours of surgery, the client should begin passing stool via the colostomy. Options 2, 3, and 4 are incorrect.

Test-Taking Strategy: Use the process of elimination. Recalling the normal progression of bowel activity following ostomy formation will direct you to option 1. Review the expected findings following creation of a colostomy if you had difficulty with this question.

Level of Cognitive Ability: Analysis
Client Needs: Physiological Integrity
Integrated Process: Nursing Process—analysis
Content Area: Adult health—gastrointestinal
References: Black, J., & Hawks, J. (2005). *Medical-surgical nursing: Clinical management for positive outcomes* (7th ed., p. 836). Philadelphia: W.B. Saunders.
Ignatavicius, D., & Workman, M. (2006). *Medical-surgical nursing: Critical thinking for collaborative care* (5th ed., pp. 1324-1325). Philadelphia: W.B. Saunders.

26. 2

Rationale: The client should be taught to include deodorizing foods in the diet, such as beet greens, parsley, buttermilk, and

yogurt. Spinach also reduces odor but is a gas-forming food as well. Broccoli, cucumbers, and eggs are gas-forming foods.
Test-Taking Strategy: Use the process of elimination. Recalling the effect of various foods on the gastrointestinal tract of the client with an ostomy will direct you to option 2. If this question was difficult, review which foods cause odor or gas and those that have a deodorizing effect.
Level of Cognitive Ability: Application
Client Needs: Physiological Integrity
Integrated Process: Teaching and Learning
Content Area: Adult health—gastrointestinal
Reference: Ignatavicius, D., & Workman, M. (2006). *Medical-surgical nursing: Critical thinking for collaborative care* (5th ed., p. 1325). Philadelphia: W.B. Saunders.

27. 4
Rationale: A frequent complication that occurs following ileostomy is fluid and electrolyte imbalance. The client requires constant monitoring of intake and output to prevent this from occurring. Losses require replacement by intravenous infusion until the client can tolerate a diet orally. Intestinal obstruction is a less frequent complication. Fat malabsorption and folate deficiency are complications that could occur later in the postoperative period.
Test-Taking Strategy: Use the process of elimination and note the strategic words *ileostomy, immediate postoperative period,* and *complication.* This tells you that the correct option occurs early in the postoperative course, with relative frequency. Remember that ileostomy drainage is liquid, placing the client at risk for fluid and electrolyte imbalance. If you had difficulty with this question, review the postoperative complications following this surgical procedure.
Level of Cognitive Ability: Analysis
Client Needs: Physiological Integrity
Integrated Process: Nursing Process—assessment
Content Area: Adult health—gastrointestinal
Reference: Ignatavicius, D., & Workman, M. (2006). *Medical-surgical nursing: Critical thinking for collaborative care* (5th ed., p. 1324). Philadelphia: W.B. Saunders.

28. 3
Rationale: A Kock pouch is a continent ileostomy. As the ileostomy begins to function, the client drains it every 3 to 4 hours and then decreases the draining to about three times a day, or as needed when full. The client does not need to wear a drainage bag but should wear an absorbent dressing to absorb mucous drainage from the stoma. Ileostomy drainage is liquid. The client would be able to pass stool only from the rectum if an ileal-anal pouch or anastomosis were created. This type of operation is a two-stage procedure.
Test-Taking Strategy: Use the process of elimination. Focusing on the strategic word *pouch* will assist in directing you to option 3. If this question was difficult, review this content.
Level of Cognitive Ability: Analysis
Client Needs: Physiological Integrity
Integrated Process: Nursing Process—evaluation
Content Area: Adult health—gastrointestinal
Reference: Ignatavicius, D., & Workman, M. (2006). *Medical-surgical nursing: Critical thinking for collaborative care* (5th ed., p. 1704). Philadelphia: W.B. Saunders.

29. 1
Rationale: Warm tap water or saline solution is used to irrigate a colostomy. If the tap water is not suitable for drinking, then bottled water should be used. Options 2, 3, and 4 are incorrect solutions.
Test-Taking Strategy: Use the process of elimination. Recalling that the irrigation involves the gastrointestinal tract and that the gastrointestinal tract is not a sterile organ will direct you to option 1. Review the procedure for performing colostomy irrigation if you had difficulty with this question.
Level of Cognitive Ability: Application
Client Needs: Physiological Integrity
Integrated Process: Nursing Process—implementation
Content Area: Adult health—gastrointestinal
References: Lewis, S., Heitkemper, M., & Dirksen, S. (2004). *Medical-surgical nursing: Assessment and management of clinical problems* (6th ed., p. 1092). St. Louis: Mosby.
Perry, A., & Potter, P. (2006). *Clinical nursing skills and techniques* (6th ed., p. 1162). St. Louis: Mosby.

30. 1
Rationale: Based on the signs and symptoms presented in the question, the nurse should suspect peritonitis and notify the physician. Administering pain medication is not an appropriate intervention. Heat should never be applied to the abdomen of a client with suspected appendicitis because of the risk of rupture. Scheduling surgical time is not within the scope of nursing practice, although the physician probably would perform the surgery earlier than the prescheduled time.
Test-Taking Strategy: Use the process of elimination. Focus on the signs and symptoms in the question and consider the complications that can occur with appendicitis. Options 3 and 4 can be eliminated easily. Noting that the signs presented in the question indicate a complication will assist in directing you to option 1. Review care of the client with appendicitis if you had difficulty with this question.
Level of Cognitive Ability: Application
Client Needs: Physiological Integrity
Integrated Process: Nursing Process—implementation
Content Area: Adult health—gastrointestinal
Reference: Ignatavicius, D., & Workman, M. (2006). *Medical-surgical nursing: Critical thinking for collaborative care* (5th ed., pp. 1339-1340). Philadelphia: W.B. Saunders.

31. 2
Rationale: The pain associated with acute pancreatitis is often severe and unrelenting, is located in the epigastric region, and radiates to the back. The other options are incorrect.
Test-Taking Strategy: Use the process of elimination. Noting the strategic word *acute* will assist in eliminating options 1 and 3. From the remaining options, recalling the anatomical location of the pancreas will direct you to option 2. Review the manifestations in acute pancreatitis if you had difficulty with this question.
Level of Cognitive Ability: Analysis
Client Needs: Physiological Integrity
Integrated Process: Nursing Process—assessment
Content Area: Adult health—gastrointestinal

Reference: Ignatavicius, D., & Workman, M. (2006). *Medical-surgical nursing: Critical thinking for collaborative care* (5th ed., p. 1405). Philadelphia: W.B. Saunders.

32. 1
Rationale: The client with chronic pancreatitis should limit fat in the diet and also take in small meals, which will reduce the amount of carbohydrates and protein that the client must digest at any one time. The client does not need to limit water-soluble vitamins in the diet.
Test-Taking Strategy: Use the process of elimination and note the strategic word *limit*. Recalling the function of the pancreas will direct you to option 1. Review dietary measures for the client with chronic pancreatitis if you had difficulty with this question.
Level of Cognitive Ability: Application
Client Needs: Physiological Integrity
Integrated Process: Teaching and Learning
Content Area: Adult health—gastrointestinal
Reference: Ignatavicius, D., & Workman, M. (2006). *Medical-surgical nursing: Critical thinking for collaborative care* (5th ed., p. 1411). Philadelphia: W.B. Saunders.

33. 1
Rationale: Chronic pancreatitis is aggravated by continued alcohol intake. Each of the other options is not associated with pancreatitis.
Test-Taking Strategy: Use the process of elimination. Remember that options that are comparative or alike are not likely to be correct. In this question, two of the incorrect options (2 and 3) represent other disorders of the digestive system. Choose option 1 over option 4 by recalling that diabetes mellitus is an endocrine disorder of the pancreas, whereas pancreatitis is an exocrine disorder. Review the factors that contribute to a recurrence of pancreatitis if you had difficulty with this question.
Level of Cognitive Ability: Analysis
Client Needs: Physiological Integrity
Integrated Process: Nursing Process—evaluation
Content Area: Adult health—gastrointestinal
Reference: Ignatavicius, D., & Workman, M. (2006). *Medical-surgical nursing: Critical thinking for collaborative care* (5th ed., p. 1412). Philadelphia: W.B. Saunders.

34. 1
Rationale: The client with cholecystitis should decrease overall intake of dietary fat. Foods that should be avoided include sauces and gravies, fatty meats, fried foods, products made with cream, and heavy desserts. The correct option is baked fish, which is low in fat.
Test-Taking Strategy: Use the process of elimination. Recalling the function of the gallbladder and knowledge of the foods that are low in fat will direct you to option 1. Review dietary measures for the client with cholecystitis if you had difficulty with this question.
Level of Cognitive Ability: Analysis
Client Needs: Physiological Integrity
Integrated Process: Nursing Process—evaluation
Content Area: Adult health—gastrointestinal
Reference: Ignatavicius, D., & Workman, M. (2006). *Medical-surgical nursing: Critical thinking for collaborative care* (5th ed., pp. 1399, 1401). Philadelphia: W.B. Saunders.

35. 4
Rationale: During an acute episode of cholecystitis, the client may complain of severe right upper quadrant pain that radiates to the right scapula and shoulder. This is determined by the pattern of dermatomes in the body. The other options are incorrect.
Test-Taking Strategy: Use the process of elimination. Recalling the anatomical location of the gallbladder will direct you to option 4. Review the characteristics of the pain associated with cholecystitis if you had difficulty with this question.
Level of Cognitive Ability: Analysis
Client Needs: Physiological Integrity
Integrated Process: Nursing Process—assessment
Content Area: Adult health—gastrointestinal
Reference: Ignatavicius, D., & Workman, M. (2006). *Medical-surgical nursing: Critical thinking for collaborative care* (5th ed., p. 1398). Philadelphia: W.B. Saunders.

36. 2
Rationale: Ammonia is formed as a product of protein metabolism. Clients with hepatic encephalopathy have high serum ammonia levels, which are responsible for the symptoms of encephalopathy. Limiting protein intake will prevent further elevation in the serum ammonia level and prevent further deterioration of the client's mental status.
Test-Taking Strategy: Recall the function of the liver and the pathophysiology associated with cirrhosis. This will direct you to option 2. Review this content if you had difficulty with this question.
Level of Cognitive Ability: Application
Client Needs: Physiological Integrity
Integrated Process: Nursing Process—planning
Content Area: Adult health—gastrointestinal
Reference: Ignatavicius, D., & Workman, M. (2006). *Medical-surgical nursing: Critical thinking for collaborative care* (5th ed., p. 1370). Philadelphia: W.B. Saunders.

37. 1
Rationale: The client with weight gain who also has cirrhosis complicated by ascites most often is retaining fluid. This is especially true when the client has not demonstrated an appreciable increase in food intake or when the weight gain is massive in relation to the time frame given. Therefore, Fluid volume, excess is the most appropriate nursing diagnosis. The client does not have Nutrition: more than body requirements, imbalanced; in fact, this client is most likely malnourished as part of the overall clinical picture. No data are given to support Gas exchange, impaired, although in some clients, upward pressure on the diaphragm from ascites does impair respiration. Skin integrity, impaired, risk for assumes a lower priority than actual diagnoses.
Test-Taking Strategy: Focus on the data provided in the question and note the strategic words *most appropriate*. Begin to answer this question by eliminating option 3 because it is not an actual nursing diagnosis. Eliminate option 2 next because there are no supportive data. Choose correctly between the remaining options, knowing that the weight gain is because of fluid retention. Review the complications associated with cirrhosis if you had difficulty with this question.

Level of Cognitive Ability: Analysis
Client Needs: Physiological Integrity
Integrated Process: Nursing Process—analysis
Content Area: Adult health—gastrointestinal
Reference: Ignatavicius, D., & Workman, M. (2006). *Medical-surgical nursing: Critical thinking for collaborative care* (5th ed., p. 1375). Philadelphia: W.B. Saunders.

38. 4
Rationale: Pain associated with Crohn's disease is alleviated by the use of analgesics and antispasmodics and also by having the client practice relaxation techniques, applying local cold or heat to the abdomen, massaging the abdomen, and lying with the legs flexed. Lying with the legs extended is not useful because it increases the muscle tension in the abdomen, which could aggravate inflamed intestinal tissues as the abdominal muscles are stretched.
Test-Taking Strategy: Note the strategic word *avoid*. This word indicates a negative event query and asks you to select an option that is an incorrect action. Use the process of elimination and use general knowledge of pain management strategies, application of cold or heat, and client positioning to answer this question. If this question was difficult, review pain management techniques for the client with Crohn's disease.
Level of Cognitive Ability: Application
Client Needs: Physiological Integrity
Integrated Process: Teaching and Learning
Content Area: Adult health—gastrointestinal
References: Black, J., & Hawks, J. (2005). *Medical-surgical nursing: Clinical management for positive outcomes* (7th ed., p. 870). Philadelphia: W.B. Saunders.
Ignatavicius, D., & Workman, M. (2006). *Medical-surgical nursing: Critical thinking for collaborative care* (5th ed., p. 818). Philadelphia: W.B. Saunders.

39. 2
Rationale: Salicylate compounds such as sulfasalazine (Azulfidine) act by inhibiting prostaglandin synthesis and reducing inflammation. The nurse teaches the client to take the medication with a full glass of water and to increase fluid intake throughout the day. The medication needs to be taken after meals to reduce gastrointestinal irritation. The other options are incorrect.
Test-Taking Strategy: Use the process of elimination. Eliminate options 1, 3, and 4 because they are comparative or alike and indicate taking the medication on an empty stomach. Review the administration of salicylate medications if you had difficulty with this question.
Level of Cognitive Ability: Application
Client Needs: Physiological Integrity
Integrated Process: Teaching and Learning
Content Area: Adult health—gastrointestinal
Reference: Ignatavicius, D., & Workman, M. (2006). *Medical-surgical nursing: Critical thinking for collaborative care* (5th ed., p. 1348). Philadelphia: W.B. Saunders.

40. 2
Rationale: Although no special diet is required to treat viral hepatitis, it is generally recommended that clients consume a low-fat diet because fat may be tolerated poorly because of decreased bile production. Small frequent meals are preferable and may even prevent nausea. Frequently, appetite is better in the morning, so it is easier to eat a good breakfast. An adequate fluid intake of 2500 to 3000 mL/day that includes nutritional juices is also important.
Test-Taking Strategy: Use the process of elimination. Knowledge regarding the nutritional problems associated with hepatitis and focusing on the client's complaints will assist in directing you to the correct option. Review measures to provide adequate nutrition in the client with hepatitis if you had difficulty with this question.
Level of Cognitive Ability: Application
Client Needs: Physiological Integrity
Integrated Process: Teaching and Learning
Content Area: Adult health—gastrointestinal
References: Ignatavicius, D., & Workman, M. (2006). *Medical-surgical nursing: Critical thinking for collaborative care* (5th ed., p. 1386). Philadelphia: W.B. Saunders.
Lewis, S., Heitkemper, M., & Dirksen, S. (2004). *Medical-surgical nursing: Assessment and management of clinical problems* (6th ed., p. 1113). St. Louis: Mosby.

41. 1
Rationale: Hepatitis causes gastrointestinal symptoms such as anorexia, nausea, right upper quadrant discomfort, and weight loss. Fatigue and malaise are common. Stools will be light- or clay-colored if conjugated bilirubin is unable to flow out of the liver because of inflammation or obstruction of the bile ducts.
Test-Taking Strategy: Use the process of elimination. Recalling the function of the liver will easily direct you to option 1. Remember that fatigue and malaise are common. If you had difficulty with this question, review the signs and symptoms of hepatitis.
Level of Cognitive Ability: Analysis
Client Needs: Physiological Integrity
Integrated Process: Nursing Process—assessment
Content Area: Adult health—gastrointestinal
Reference: Ignatavicius, D., & Workman, M. (2006). *Medical-surgical nursing: Critical thinking for collaborative care* (5th ed., p. 1383). Philadelphia: W.B. Saunders.

42. 1
Rationale: During the acute phase of diverticulitis, the goal of treatment is to rest the bowel and allow the inflammation to subside. The client remains NPO and is placed on bed rest. Pain occurs from bowel spasms and increased intraabdominal pressure may precipitate an attack. Options 2, 3, and 4 are not interventions for the client with acute diverticulitis.
Test-Taking Strategy: Use the process of elimination. Ambulation and cholinergics will increase peristalsis eliminating options 2 and 3. Coughing and deep breathing will increase intraabdominal pressure, eliminating option 4. Knowing that NPO status allows the bowel to rest directs you to option 1. Review care of the client with acute diverticulitis if you had difficulty with this question.
Level of Cognitive Ability: Application
Client Needs: Physiological Integrity

Integrated Process: Nursing Process—implementation
Content Area: Adult health—gastrointestinal
Reference: Lewis, S., Heitkemper, M., & Dirksen, S. (2004). *Medical-surgical nursing: Assessment and management of clinical problems* (6th ed., p. 1095). St. Louis, Mosby.

43. **3**
Rationale: Nursing interventions after a hemorrhoidectomy are aimed at management of pain and avoidance of bleeding. An ice pack will increase comfort and decrease bleeding. Options 1, 2, and 4 are incorrect interventions.
Test-Taking Strategy: Use the process of elimination. Decreasing fluid intake and avoiding high-fiber foods will cause difficulty with defecation because of hard stool, eliminating options 1 and 2. Fowler's position will increase pressure in the rectal area, causing increased bleeding and increased pain, eliminating option 4. Knowing that an ice pack will decrease swelling and cause vasoconstriction leads you to option 3. Review care of the client following hemorrhoidectomy if you had difficulty with this question.
Level of Cognitive Ability: Application
Client Needs: Physiological Integrity
Integrated Process: Nursing Process—Implementation
Content Area: Adult health—gastrointestinal
Reference: Lewis, S., Heitkemper, M., & Dirksen, S. (2004). *Medical-surgical nursing: Assessment and management of clinical problems* (6th ed., p. 1100). St. Louis: Mosby.

44. **4.**
Rationale: Common risk factors for colorectal cancer include age older than 40 years, first-degree relative with colorectal cancer, high-fat, low-fiber diet, and history of bowel problems, such as ulcerative colitis or familial polyposis.
Test-Taking Strategy: Use the process of elimination, reading each option carefully. Eliminate option 1 because of the age. Eliminate option 2 because this diet is healthful. Eliminate option 3 because of the word *distant*. Review risk factors for colorectal cancer if you had difficulty with this question.
Level of Cognitive Ability: Application
Client Needs: Health Promotion and Maintenance
Integrated Process: Teaching and Learning
Content Area: Adult health—gastrointestinal
References: Black, J., & Hawks, J. (2005). *Medical-surgical nursing: Clinical management for positive outcomes* (7th ed., pp. 830-831). Philadelphia: W.B. Saunders.
Ignatavicius, D., & Workman, M. (2006). *Medical-surgical nursing: Critical thinking for collaborative care* (5th ed., p. 1318). Philadelphia: W.B. Saunders.

45. **4**
Rationale: Foods that increase lower esophageal sphincter (LES) pressure will decrease reflux and lessen the symptoms of gastroesophageal reflux disease (GERD). The food that will increase LES pressure is nonfat milk. The other substances listed decrease LES pressure, thus increasing reflux symptoms. Aggravating substances include chocolate, coffee, fatty foods, and alcohol.
Test-Taking Strategy: Use the process of elimination and knowledge of the effect of various foods on LES pressure and GERD. However, if you were unsure, select the option that

identifies the most healthful food item. Review the dietary regimen for a client with GERD if you had difficulty with this question.
Level of Cognitive Ability: Application
Client Needs: Physiological Integrity
Integrated Process: Teaching and Learning
Content Area: Adult health—gastrointestinal
Reference: Ignatavicius, D., & Workman, M. (2006). *Medical-surgical nursing: Critical thinking for collaborative care* (5th ed., p. 1263). Philadelphia: W.B. Saunders.

46. **4**
Rationale: The nurse places highest priority on assessing for return of the gag reflex. This assessment addresses the client's airway. The nurse also monitors the client's vital signs and for a sudden increase in temperature, which could indicate perforation of the gastrointestinal tract. This complication would be accompanied by other signs as well, such as pain. Monitoring for sore throat and heartburn are also important; however, the client's airway is the priority.
Test-Taking Strategy: Use the ABCs—airway, breathing, and circulation. Note the strategic words *highest priority*. Option 4 addresses the airway. Review care of the client following esophagogastroduodenoscopy if you had difficulty with this question.
Level of Cognitive Ability: Application
Client Needs: Physiological Integrity
Integrated Process: Nursing Process—planning
Content Area: Delegating/Prioritizing
References: Ignatavicius, D., & Workman, M. (2006). *Medical-surgical nursing: Critical thinking for collaborative care* (5th ed., p. 1244). Philadelphia: W.B. Saunders.
Lewis, S., Heitkemper, M., & Dirksen, S. (2004). *Medical-surgical nursing: Assessment and management of clinical problems* (6th ed., p. 963). St. Louis: Mosby.

47. **3**
Rationale: The client does have to lie still for endoscopic retrograde cholangiopancreatography (ERCP), which takes about 1 hour to perform. The client also has to sign a consent form. Intravenous sedation is given to relax the client, and an anesthetic spray is used to help keep the client from gagging as the endoscope is passed.
Test-Taking Strategy: Note the strategic words *needs further information*. These words indicate a negative event query and ask you to select an option that is incorrect. Invasive procedures require consent, so option 1 can be eliminated. Noting the name of the procedure and considering the anatomical location will assist you in eliminating options 2 and 4. Review this procedure if you had difficulty with this question.
Level of Cognitive Ability: Analysis
Client Needs: Physiological Integrity
Integrated Process: Teaching and Learning
Content Area: Adult health—gastrointestinal
References: Chernecky, C., & Berger, B. (2004). *Laboratory tests and diagnostic procedures* (4th ed., p. 501). Philadelphia: W.B. Saunders.
Ignatavicius, D., & Workman, M. (2006). *Medical-surgical nursing: Critical thinking for collaborative care* (5th ed., pp. 1244-1245). Philadelphia: W.B. Saunders.

ALTERNATE ITEM FORMAT: MULTIPLE RESPONSE

Answer: 1, 3, 4, 5

Rationale: The client with acute pancreatitis normally is placed on NPO status to rest the pancreas and suppress gastrointestinal secretions. Because abdominal pain is a prominent symptom of pancreatitis, pain medication such as meperidine will be prescribed. Some clients experience lessened pain by assuming positions that flex the trunk, with the knees drawn up to the chest. A side-lying position with the head elevated 45 degrees decreases tension on the abdomen and also may help ease the pain. The client is susceptible to respiratory infections because the retroperitoneal fluid raises the diaphragm, which causes the client to take shallow, guarded abdominal breaths. Therefore, measures such as turning, coughing, and deep breathing are instituted. Antacids and anticholinergics may be prescribed to suppress gastrointestinal secretions.

Test-Taking Strategy: Focus on the pathophysiology associated with pancreatitis and note the strategic word *acute*. This will assist in answering the question. Review treatment measures for acute pancreatitis if you had difficulty with this question.

Level of Cognitive Ability: Analysis

Client Needs: Physiological Integrity

Integrated Process: Nursing Process—analysis

Content Area: Adult health—gastrointestinal

Reference: Lewis, S., Heitkemper, M., & Dirksen, S. (2004). *Medical-surgical nursing: Assessment and management of clinical problems* (6th ed., p. 1138). St. Louis: Mosby.

REFERENCES

Chernecky, C., & Berger, B. (2004). *Laboratory tests and diagnostic procedures* (4th ed.). Philadelphia: W.B. Saunders.

Black, J., & Hawks, J. (2005). *Medical-surgical nursing: Clinical management for positive outcomes* (7th ed.). Philadelphia: W.B. Saunders.

Grodner, M., Long, S., & DeYoung, S. (2004). *Foundations and clinical applications of nutrition: A nursing approach.* (3rd ed.). St. Louis: Mosby.

Harkreader, H., & Hogan, M.A. (2004) *Fundamentals of nursing: Caring and clinical judgment.* (2nd ed.). Philadelphia: W.B. Saunders.

Ignatavicius, D., & Workman, M. (2006). *Medical-surgical nursing: Critical thinking for collaborative care* (5th ed.). Philadelphia: W.B. Saunders.

Kee, J., Hayes, E., & McCuistion, L. (2006). *Pharmacology: A nursing process approach* (5th ed.). Philadelphia: W.B. Saunders.

Lewis, S., Heitkemper, M., & Dirksen, S. (2004). *Medical-surgical nursing: Assessment and management of clinical problems* (6th ed.). St. Louis: Mosby.

Perry, A., & Potter, P. (2006). *Clinical nursing skills and techniques* (6th ed.). St. Louis: Mosby.

Potter, P., & Perry, A. (2005). *Fundamentals of nursing* (6th ed.). St. Louis: Mosby.

Skidmore-Roth, L. (2005). *Mosby's drug guide for nurses* (6th ed.). St. Louis: Mosby.

Gastrointestinal Medications

I. ANTACIDS (Box 56-1; Fig. 56-1)

A. Description
1. React with gastric acid to produce neutral salts or salts of low acidity
2. Inactivate pepsin and enhance mucosal protection but do not coat the ulcer crater to protect it from the acid and pepsin
3. These medications are used for peptic ulcer disease and gastroesophageal reflux disease.
4. These medications should be taken on a regular schedule; some are prescribed to be taken 1 and 3 hours after each meal and at bedtime.
5. To provide maximum benefit, treatment should elevate the gastric pH above 5.
6. Antacid tablets should be chewed thoroughly and followed with a glass of water or milk.
7. Liquid preparations should be shaken before dispensing.
8. To prevent interactions with other medications and interference with the action of other medications, allow 1 hour between antacid administration and the administration of other medications.

B. Aluminum hydroxide preparations
1. Slow-acting.
2. Contain significant amounts of sodium; should be used with caution in clients with hypertension and heart failure.
3. The most common side effect is constipation.
4. Aluminum hydroxide can reduce the effects of tetracyclines, warfarin sodium (Coumadin), and digoxin (Lanoxin) and can reduce phosphate absorption and thereby cause hypophosphatemia.

C. Calcium carbonate preparations
1. Rapid-acting; release carbon dioxide in the stomach, causing belching and flatulence

2. A common side effect is constipation; milk-alkali syndrome (headache, urinary frequency, anorexia, nausea/vomiting, fatigue) can occur (the client should avoid milk products and vitamin D supplements).

D. Magnesium hydroxide preparations
1. Rapid-acting
2. Magnesium hydroxide is also a saline laxative and the most prominent side effect is diarrhea; it is usually administered in combination with aluminum hydroxide, an antacid that assists in preventing diarrhea.
3. Contraindicated in clients with intestinal obstruction, appendicitis, or undiagnosed abdominal pain.
4. In clients with renal impairment, magnesium can accumulate to high levels, causing signs of toxicity.

E. Sodium bicarbonate
1. Has a rapid onset and liberates carbon dioxide, increases intraabdominal pressure, and promotes flatulence
2. Should be used with caution in clients with hypertension and heart failure
3. Can cause systemic alkalosis in clients with renal impairment

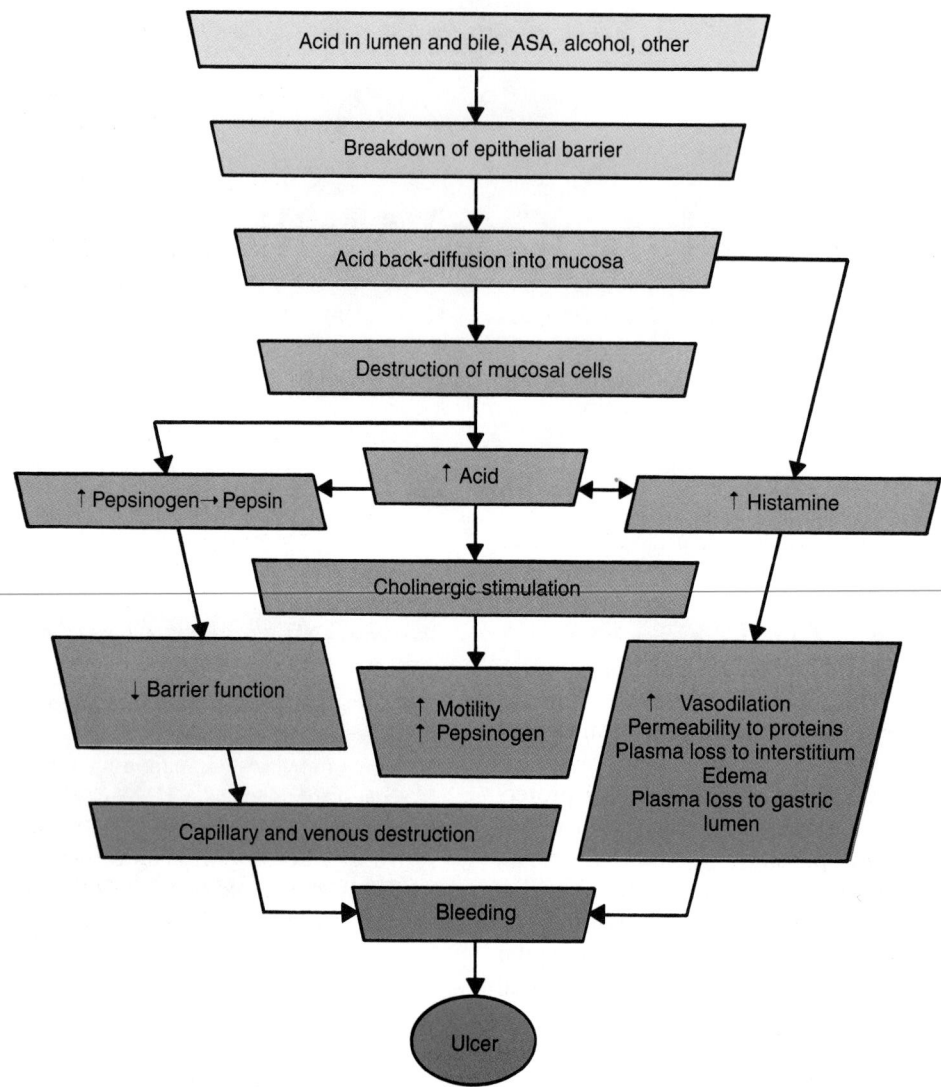

FIG. 56-1 Pathophysiological consequences of back-diffusion of acid through the damaged mucosal barrier. (From Price, S., & Wilson, L. [2003] *Pathophysiology: Clinical concepts of disease processes* [6th ed.]. St. Louis: Mosby.)

4. Useful for treating acidosis and elevating urinary pH to promote excretion of acidic medications following overdose

II. GASTRIC PROTECTANTS (Box 56-2)

A. Misoprostol (Cytotec)
   1. Suppresses secretion of gastric acid
   2. Promotes secretion of bicarbonate and cytoprotective mucus
   3. Maintains submucosal blood flow by promoting vasodilation
   4. Used to prevent gastric ulcers caused by long-term therapy with nonsteroidal anti-inflammatory drugs

   5. Administered with meals
   6. Causes diarrhea and abdominal pain
   7. Contraindicated for use in pregnancy

BOX 56-2

Gastric Protectants

Misoprostol (Cytotec)
Sucralfate (Carafate)

B. Sucralfate (Carafate)
   1. Creates a protective barrier against acid and pepsin.
   2. Administered orally; should be taken on an empty stomach
   3. May cause constipation
   4. May impede absorption of warfarin sodium (Coumadin), phenytoin (Dilantin), theophylline, digoxin (Lanoxin), and some antibiotics;

Cimetidine (Tagamet)
Famotidine (Pepcid)
Nizatidine (Axid)
Ranitidine (Zantac)

should be administered at least 2 hours apart from these medication.

III. **HISTAMINE 2 (H₂)-RECEPTOR ANTAGONISTS** (Box 56-3)
A. Description
   1. Suppress secretion of gastric acid
   2. Alleviate symptoms of heartburn and assist in preventing complications of peptic ulcer disease
   3. Prevent stress ulcers and reduce the recurrence of all ulcers
   4. Promote healing in gastroesophageal reflux disease
   5. Are contraindicated in hypersensitive clients
   6. Should be used with caution in clients with impaired renal or hepatic function
B. Cimetidine (Tagamet)
   1. Can be administered orally, intramuscularly, or intravenously
   2. Food reduces the rate of absorption; if taken with meals, absorption will be slowed
   3. By the intravenous route, a 300-mg dose can be diluted in a total volume of 20 mL and injected slowly over not less than 2 minutes, or it may be diluted in 100 mL and infused over 15 to 20 minutes (always follow agency guidelines for its administration).
   4. Antacids can decrease the absorption of oral cimetidine.
   5. Cimetidine and antacids should be administered at least 1 hour apart from each other.
   6. Cimetidine passes the blood-brain barrier, and central nervous system side effects can occur; it may cause mental confusion, agitation, psychosis, depression, anxiety, and disorientation.
   7. Dosage should be reduced in clients with renal impairment.
   8. Intravenous administration can cause hypotension and dysrhythmias.
   9. If cimetidine is administered with warfarin sodium (Coumadin), phenytoin (Dilantin), theophylline, or lidocaine, the dosages of these medications should be reduced.
C. Ranitidine (Zantac)
   1. Can be administered orally, intramuscularly, or intravenously
   2. Side effects are uncommon and does not penetrate the blood-brain barrier as cimetidine does.

   3. Ranitidine is not affected by food.
   4. For intravenous injection, ranitidine should be diluted with 20 mL and administered slowly over 5 minutes or more, or diluted in 100 mL and administered over 15 to 20 minutes (always follow agency guidelines for its administration).
D. Famotidine (Pepcid) and nizatidine (Axid)
   1. Famotidine and nizatidine are similar to ranitidine and cimetidine.
   2. These medications do not need to be administered with food.

IV. **PROTON PUMP INHIBITORS** (Box 56-4)
A. Suppress gastric acid secretion
B. Used to treat active ulcer disease, erosive esophagitis, and pathological hypersecretory conditions
C. Contraindicated in hypersensitivity
D. Common side effects include headache, diarrhea, abdominal pain, and nausea

V. **MEDICATION REGIMENS TO TREAT *HELICOBACTER PYLORI* INFECTIONS** (Box 56-5)
A. An antibacterial agent alone is not effective for eradicating *Helicobacter pylori* because the bacterium readily becomes resistant to the agent.
B. Dual, triple, and quadruple therapy with a variety of medication combinations is used.

Esomeprazole (Nexium)
Lansoprazole (Prevacid)
Omeprazole (Prilosec)
Pantoprazole (Protonix)
Rabeprazole (Aciphex)

DUAL THERAPY
Ranitidine bismuth citrate plus clarithromycin (Biaxin)
Omeprazole (Prilosec) plus clarithromycin (Biaxin)

TRIPLE THERAPY
Metronidazole (Flagyl), omeprazole (Prilosec), plus clarithromycin (Biaxin)
Amoxicillin (Amoxil), lansoprazole (Prevacid), plus clarithromycin (Biaxin)

QUADRUPLE THERAPY
Colloidal bismuth subnitrate, tetracycline (Achromycin), metronidazole (Flagyl), plus omeprazole (Prilosec)

Note: Other combinations may be prescribed for each level of therapy.

Bethanechol chloride (Urecholine, Duvoid)
Dexpanthenol (Ilopan)
Metoclopramide (Reglan)
Neostigmine methylsulfate (Prostigmin)

C. The combinations can include antibacterial agents, proton pump inhibitors, H$_2$-receptor antagonists, and antacids.
D. A common treatment protocol is triple therapy with two antibacterial agents and a proton pump inhibitor.
E. If triple therapy fails, quadruple therapy is recommended with two antibacterial agents, a proton pump inhibitor, and a bismuth or H$_2$-receptor antagonist

BOX 56-7
Bile Acid Sequestrants

Cholestyramine (Questran, Prevalite)
Colestipol (Colestid)

BOX 56-8
Medications to Treat Hepatic Encephalopathy

Lactulose (Cholac, Chronulac, Duphalac)
Neomycin (Mycifradin)

BOX 56-9
Pancreatic Enzyme Replacements

Pancreatin
Pancrelipase (Pancrease, Viokase)

VI. GASTROINTESTINAL STIMULANTS (Box 56-6)
A. These medications stimulate motility of the upper gastrointestinal tract and increase the rate of gastric emptying without stimulating gastric, biliary, or pancreatic secretions.
B. Used to treat gastroesophageal reflux and paralytic ileus
C. May cause restlessness, drowsiness, extrapyramidal reactions, dizziness, insomnia, and headache
D. Usually administered 30 minutes before meals and at bedtime
E. Contraindicated in clients with sensitivity and in clients with mechanical obstruction, perforation, or gastrointestinal hemorrhage
F. Can precipitate hypertensive crisis in clients with pheochromocytoma
G. Safety in pregnancy is not established
H. Metoclopramide (Reglan) can cause parkinsonian reactions; if this occurs, the medication will be discontinued by the physician.
I. Anticholinergics and opioid analgesics antagonize the effects of metoclopramide.
J. Alcohol, sedatives, cyclosporine (Sandimmune), and tranquilizers produce an additive effect.

VII. BILE ACID SEQUESTRANTS (Box 56-7)
A. Description
B. Act by absorbing and combining with intestinal bile salts, which then are secreted in the feces, preventing intestinal reabsorption
C. Used to treat hypercholesterolemia in adults, biliary obstruction, and pruritis associated with biliary disease
D. Taste and palatability are often reasons for noncompliance and can be improved by the use of flavored products or mixing the medication with various juices.

E. Should be used cautiously in clients with bowel obstruction or severe constipation because of adverse gastrointestinal effects
F. Side effects include nausea, bloating, and constipation; fecal impaction and intestinal obstruction can result.
G. Stool softeners and other sources of fiber can be used to abate the gastrointestinal side effects.

VIII. MEDICATIONS TO TREAT HEPATIC ENCEPHALOPATHY (Box 56-8)
A. Lactulose (Cholac, Chronulac, Duphalac)
1. Reduces ammonia levels; lowers the colonic pH from 7 to 5; this acidification pulls ammonia into the bowel to be excreted in the feces, thus lowering the ammonia level.
2. Improves protein tolerance in clients with advanced hepatic **cirrhosis**
3. Administered orally in the form of a syrup or rectally
B. Neomycin (Mycifradin)
1. Reduces the number of colonic bacteria that normally convert urea and amino acids into ammonia
2. Administered orally or via nasogastric tube
3. Used with caution in clients with kidney impairment

IX. PANCREATIC ENZYME REPLACEMENTS (Box 56-9)
A. Used to supplement or replace pancreatic enzymes, improve nutritional status, and reduce the amount of fatty stools.
B. They should be taken with meals or a snack (food helps buffer the stomach acid).
C. A high-fiber diet may increase the efficacy of the medication.

BOX 56-10
Medications to Treat Inflammatory Bowel Disease

ANTIMICROBIAL
Metronidazole (Flagyl)

5-AMINOSALICYLATES
Sulfasalazine (Azulfidine)
Mesalamine (Rowasa, Asacol, Pentasa, Canasa)
Olsalazine (Dipentum)

CORTICOSTEROIDS
Cortisone
Prednisone (Deltasone)
Budesonide (Entocort-EC)
Hydrocortisone

IMMUNOSUPPRESSANTS
Azathioprine (Imuran)
Cyclosporine (Neoral)
Mercaptopurine (6-MP)

IMMUNOMODULATOR
Infliximab (Remicade)
Natalizumab (Tysabri)

BOX 56-11
Commonly Administered Antiemetics

Diphenidol
Dolasetron (Anzemet)
Dronabinol (Marinol)
Granisetron (Kytril)
Hydroxyzine pamoate (Vistaril)
Meclizine hydrochloride (Antivert)
Metoclopramide (Reglan)
Ondansetron (Zofran)
Prochlorperazine (Compazine)
Promethazine hydrochloride (Phenergan)
Scopolamine transdermal (Transderm Scōp)
Thiethylperazine maleate (Torecan)
Trimethobenzamide hydrochloride (Tigan)

BOX 56-12
Laxatives

BULK-FORMING LAXATIVES
Calcium polycarbophil (FiberCon)
Methylcellulose (Citrucel)
Psyllium hydrophilic mucilloid (Metamucil, Fiberall, Konsyl, Serutan)

STIMULANT CATHARTICS
Bisacodyl (Modane)
Cascara sagrada
Castor oil (Neoloid)
Docusate sodium, sennosides (Ex-Lax)
Sennosides (Senexon, Senna-Gen, Senokot)

SALINE (OSMOTIC) CATHARTICS
Lactulose (Constilac)
Magnesium citrate (citrate of magnesia)
Magnesium hydroxide (Milk of Magnesia)
Polyethylene glycol and electrolytes (GoLYTELY)
Sodium phosphates (Fleet enema, Fleet Phospho-Soda)

STOOL SOFTENERS
Docusate calcium (Surfak)
Docusate sodium (Colace, Peri-Colace)

LUBRICANT
Mineral oil (Kondremul Plain)

D. Side effects include abdominal cramps or pain, nausea, and diarrhea.
E. Products that contain calcium carbonate or magnesium hydroxide interfere with the action of the medication.

X. **TREATMENT OF INFLAMMATORY BOWEL DISEASE** (Box 56-10)
A. Antimicrobials: Prevent or treat secondary infection
B. 5-Aminosalicylates (5-ASA): Decrease gastrointestinal inflammation
C. Corticosteroids: Decrease gastrointestinal inflammation
D. Immunosuppressants: Suppress the immune system
E. Immunomodulators
  1. Inhibit cytokine tumor necrosis factor α, which reduces the degree of inflammation (infliximab [Remicade])
  2. Interrupt the movement of leukocytes, which reduces the inflammatory process (natalizumab [Tysabri])

XI. **ANTIEMETICS** (Box 56-11)
A. Medications used to control vomiting and motion sickness
B. The choice of the antiemetic is determined by the cause of the nausea and vomiting.
C. Monitor for drowsiness and protect the client from injury.
D. Monitor vital signs and intake and output.
E. Limit odors in the client's room when the client is nauseated or vomiting.
F. Limit oral intake to clear liquids when the client is nauseated or vomiting.

XII. **LAXATIVES** (Box 56-12)
A. Bulk-forming laxatives
  1. Description
    a. Absorb water into the feces and increase bulk to produce large and soft stools
    b. Contraindicated in bowel obstruction
    c. Dependency can occur with chronic use.
  2. Side effects include gastrointestinal disturbances, dehydration, and electrolyte imbalances.

BOX 56-13
Medications to Control Diarrhea

OPIOIDS AND RELATED MEDICATIONS
Codeine phosphate; codeine sulfate
Difenoxin with atropine sulfate (Motofen)
Diphenoxylate hydrochloride with atropine sulfate
  (Lomotil)
Loperamide hydrochloride (Imodium)
Tincture of opium

ADSORBENT ANTIDIARRHEALS
Bismuth subsalicylate (Pepto-Bismol, Kaopectate,
  Kapectolin)

BOX 56-14
Antispasmodic

Dicyclomine hydrochloride (Antispas, Bentyl)

B. Stimulant cathartics: Stimulate motility of large intestine
C. Saline (osmotic) cathartics: Attract water into the large intestine to produce bulk and stimulate **peristalsis**
D. Stool softeners
   1. Inhibit absorption of water so fecal mass remains large and soft
   2. Used to avoid straining
E. Lubricants
   1. Act to soften the feces, ease the strain of passing stool, and lessen irritation to hemorrhoids
   2. Mineral oil: Interferes with absorption of the fat-soluble vitamins A, D, E, and K and can cause lipid pneumonia if accidentally aspirated

XIII. **MEDICATIONS TO CONTROL DIARRHEA**
   (Box 56-13)
A. Opioids
   1. Opioids decrease intestinal motility and **peristalsis.**
   2. When poisons, infections, or bacterial toxins are the cause of the diarrhea, opioids worsen the condition by delaying the elimination of toxins.
   3. Tincture of opium has an unpleasant taste and can be diluted with 15 to 30 mL of water for administration.
B. Other antidiarrheals: See Box 56-13.

XIV. **ANTISPASMODICS** (Box 56-14)
A. Description: Relax the smooth muscle of the gastrointestinal tract
B. Side effects include nausea, constipation or diarrhea, headache, drowsiness, weakness, dizziness, rash, and euphoria.

PRACTICE QUESTIONS

1. The client has a new order for metoclopramide (Reglan). On review of the chart, the nurse identifies that this medication can be safely administered with which condition?
   1. Intestinal obstruction
   2. Peptic ulcer with melena
   3. Diverticulitis with perforation
   4. Vomiting following cancer chemotherapy

2. The nurse has given instructions to a client who has just been prescribed cholestyramine (Questran). Which statement by the client indicates a need for further instructions?
   1. I will continue taking vitamin supplements.
   2. This medication will help lower my cholesterol.
   3. This medication should only be taken with water.
   4. A high-fiber diet is important while taking this medication.

3. A client with Crohn's disease is scheduled to receive an infusion of infliximab (Remicade). What intervention by the nurse will determine the effectiveness of treatment?
   1. Carrying out a Hematest on gastric fluids after the infusion is completed
   2. Checking the frequency and consistency of bowel movements
   3. Monitoring the leukocyte count for 2 days after the infusion
   4. Checking serum liver enzyme levels before and after the infusion

4. The client is taking docusate sodium (Colace). The nurse monitors for which sign or symptom to determine whether the client is having a therapeutic effect from this medication?
   1. Reduction in steatorrhea
   2. Hematest-negative stools
   3. Regular bowel movements
   4. Absence of abdominal pain

5. The client is taking cascara sagrada and develops abdominal cramps. What interpretation by the nurse is most likely correct?
   1. The client has peptic ulcer disease.
   2. The client is experiencing a case of influenza.
   3. The client may have a partial bowel obstruction.
   4. This is a common side effect of this medication.

6. The client taking bisacodyl (Dulcolax) wants to obtain a rapid effect from the medication. How should the nurse instruct the client to take the medication?
   1. At bedtime
   2. With a large meal
   3. On an empty stomach
   4. With two glasses of juice

7. The client has a PRN order for loperamide hydro-chloride (Imodium). For which condition should the nurse plan to administer this medication?
   1. Constipation
   2. Abdominal pain
   3. An episode of diarrhea
   4. Hematest-positive nasogastric tube drainage

8. The nurse teaches the client taking metoclopramide (Reglan) to withhold the medication immediately and call the physician if which sign or symptom occurs with long-term use?
   1. Anxiety or irritability
   2. Excessive drowsiness or excitability
   3. Uncontrolled rhythmic movements of the face or limbs
   4. Dry mouth not relieved by sugar-free hard candy

9. The client has just taken a dose of trimethobenza-mide hydrochloride (Tigan). What indicates that this client has had a therapeutic response to the medication?
   1. Relief of constipation
   2. Decrease in heartburn
   3. Absence of abdominal pain
   4. Relief of nausea and vomiting

10. The client has a PRN order for ondansetron (Zofran). For which condition should the nurse administer this medication to the postoperative client?
   1. Paralytic ileus
   2. Incisional pain
   3. Urinary retention
   4. Nausea and vomiting

11. The client has begun medication therapy with pan-crelipase (Pancrease). The nurse evaluates that the medication is having the optimal intended benefit if which effect is observed?
   1. Weight loss
   2. Relief of heartburn
   3. Reduction of steatorrhea
   4. Absence of abdominal pain

12. A calcium carbonate antacid has been prescribed for a client and the nurse provides instructions to the client about the medication. The nurse tells the client that it is best to take the antacid with which of the following?
   1. Milk
   2. Water
   3. Yogurt
   4. A vitamin D supplement

13. The nurse is giving the client directions for proper use of aluminum hydroxide tablets (Alu-Tabs). What should the nurse tell the client?
   1. Swallow the tablets whole with a full glass of water.
   2. Take the tablets at the same time as other medi-cations.

3. Take each dose with a laxative to prevent consti-pation.
4. Chew the tablets thoroughly and follow with 4 oz of water.

14. The client with a history of duodenal ulcer is taking calcium carbonate chewable tablets. Which finding indicates that the client is experiencing optimal effects of the medication?
   1. Heartburn is relieved.
   2. Muscle twitching stops.
   3. The serum calcium level increases.
   4. The serum phosphorus level decreases.

15. The hospitalized client asks the nurse for sodium bicarbonate to relieve heartburn following a meal. The nurse reviews the client's medical record, knowing that the medication is contraindicated in which condition?
   1. Urinary calculi
   2. Chronic bronchitis
   3. Metabolic alkalosis
   4. Respiratory acidosis

16. An older client recently has been taking cimetidine (Tagamet). The nurse monitors the client for which most frequent central nervous system side effect of this medication?
   1. Tremors
   2. Dizziness
   3. Confusion
   4. Hallucinations

17. The client with a gastric ulcer has an order for su-cralfate (Carafate), 1 g by mouth four times daily. The nurse schedules the medication for which times?
   1. With meals and at bedtime
   2. Every 6 hours around the clock
   3. One hour after meals and at bedtime
   4. One hour before meals and at bedtime

18. The client who chronically uses nonsteroidal anti-inflammatory drugs has been taking misoprostol (Cytotec). The nurse determines that the medication is having the intended therapeutic effect if the client does not experience which sign or symptom?
   1. Diarrhea
   2. Epigastric pain
   3. Decreased platelet count
   4. Decreased white blood cell count

19. The physician has written an order for ranitidine (Zantac), 300 mg once daily. The nurse schedules the medication for which time?
   1. At bedtime
   2. After lunch
   3. With supper
   4. Before breakfast

20. The client is taking lansoprazole (Prevacid) for the chronic management of peptic ulcer disease. The nurse advises the client to take which product if needed for a headache?

1. Naproxen (Aleve)
2. Ibuprofen (Motrin)
3. Acetaminophen (Tylenol)
4. Acetylsalicylic acid (aspirin)

21. The client has been taking omeprazole (Prilosec) for 4 weeks. The ambulatory care nurse evaluates that the client is receiving optimal intended effect of the medication if the client reports the absence of which symptom?
    1. Diarrhea
    2. Heartburn
    3. Flatulence
    4. Constipation

22. A client with a peptic ulcer is diagnosed with a *Helicobacter pylori* infection. The nurse is teaching the client about the medications prescribed, including metronidazole (Flagyl), omeprazole (Prilosec), and clarithromycin (Biaxin). Which statement by the client indicates the best understanding of the medication regimen?

1. "My ulcer will heal because these medications will kill the bacteria."
2. "These medications are only taken when I have pain from my ulcer."
3. "The medications will kill the bacteria and stop the acid production."
4. "These medications will coat the ulcer and decrease the acid production in my stomach."

ALTERNATE ITEM FORMAT: MULTIPLE RESPONSE

A histamine (H_2)-receptor antagonist will be prescribed for a client. The nurse understands that which medications are H_2-receptor antagonists? Select all that apply.

1. Nizatidine (Axid)
2. Ranitidine (Zantac)
3. Famotidine (Pepcid)
4. Cimetidine (Tagamet)
5. Esomeprazole (Nexium)
6. Lansoprazole (Prevacid)

ANSWERS

1. **4**

Rationale: Metoclopramide is a gastrointestinal stimulant and antiemetic. Because it is a gastrointestinal stimulant, it is contraindicated with gastrointestinal obstruction, hemorrhage, or perforation. It is used in the treatment of emesis after surgery, chemotherapy, and radiation.

Test-Taking Strategy: Use the process of elimination. Recalling the classification and action of this medication and that it is an antiemetic will direct you to option 4. Review the action of this medication if you had difficulty with this question.

Level of Cognitive Ability: Analysis

Client Needs: Physiological Integrity

Integrated Process: Nursing Process—analysis

Content Area: Pharmacology

Reference: Kee, J., Hayes, E., & McCuistion, L. (2006). *Pharmacology: A nursing process approach* (5th ed., pp. 690-691). St. Louis: W.B. Saunders.

2. **3**

Rationale: Cholestyramine (Questran) is a bile acid sequestrant used to lower the cholesterol level and client compliance is a problem because of its taste and palatability. The use of flavored products or fruit juices can improve the taste. Some side effects of bile acid sequestrants include constipation and decreased vitamin absorption.

Test-Taking Strategy: Use the process of elimination and note the strategic words *need for further instructions*. These words indicate a negative event query and ask you to select an option that is an incorrect statement. Noting the close-ended word *only* in option 3 will direct you to this option. Review the action and side effects of this class of medications if you had difficulty with this question.

Level of Cognitive Ability: Analysis

Client Needs: Physiological Integrity

Integrated Process: Teaching and Learning

Content Area: Pharmacology

Reference: Kee, J., Hayes, E., & McCuistion, L. (2006). *Pharmacology: A nursing process approach* (5th ed., pp. 675-678). St. Louis: W.B. Saunders.

3. **2**

Rationale: The principle manifestations of Crohn's disease are diarrhea and abdominal pain. Infliximab (Remicade) is an immunomodulator that reduces the degree of inflammation in the colon, thereby reducing the diarrhea. Options 1, 3, and 4 are unrelated to this medication.

Test-Taking Strategy: Focus on the client's diagnosis, Crohn's disease. Eliminate option 1 because gastric bleeding is not a characteristic of Crohn's disease. Monitoring the leukocyte count and liver enzyme levels is appropriate when infliximab (Remicade) is given but not to evaluate the effectiveness of treatment, eliminating options 3 and 4. Review the manifestations of Crohn's disease and the actions of this medication if you had difficulty with this question.

Level of Cognitive Ability: Analysis

Client Needs: Physiological Integrity

Integrated Process: Nursing Process—evaluation

Content Area: Pharmacology

Reference: Hodgson, B., & Kizior, R. (2007). *Saunders nursing drug handbook 2007* (pp. 618-619). St. Louis: W.B. Saunders.

4. **3**

Rationale: Docusate sodium is a stool softener that promotes absorption of water into the stool, producing a softer consistency of stool. The intended effect is relief or prevention of constipation. The medication does not decrease the amount of fat in the stools, stop gastrointestinal bleeding, or relieve abdominal pain.

Test-Taking Strategy: Use the process of elimination. Recalling that docusate sodium is used to soften the stool will direct you

to option 3. Review the expected effects of this medication if you had difficulty with this question.
Level of Cognitive Ability: Analysis
Client Needs: Physiological Integrity
Integrated Process: Nursing Process—analysis
Content Area: Pharmacology
Reference: Hodgson, B., & Kizior, R. (2007). *Saunders nursing drug handbook 2007* (p. 372). Philadelphia: W.B. Saunders.

5. 4
Rationale: Cascara sagrada is a laxative that causes nausea and abdominal cramps as the most frequent side effects. Other health problems (options 1, 2, and 3) are not determined based on a single symptom.
Test-Taking Strategy: Use the process of elimination. Remember that options that are comparative or alike are not likely to be correct. This will allow you to eliminate the two gastrointestinal disorders (options 1 and 3). From the remaining options, choose option 4 over option 2, knowing that laxatives can cause abdominal cramping. Review the effects of this medication if you had difficulty with this question.
Level of Cognitive Ability: Analysis
Client Needs: Physiological Integrity
Integrated Process: Nursing Process—analysis
Content Area: Pharmacology
Reference: Hodgson, B., & Kizior, R. (2007). *Saunders nursing drug handbook 2007* (p. 193). Philadelphia: W.B. Saunders.

6. 3
Rationale: Most rapid results from bisacodyl occur when it is taken on an empty stomach. Bisacodyl will not have a rapid effect if taken with a large meal. If bisacodyl is taken at bedtime, the client will have a bowel movement in the morning. Taking the medication with two glasses of juice will not add to its effect.
Test-Taking Strategy: Use the process of elimination, noting the strategic words *rapid effect*. Remember that the most rapid results occur when taken on an empty stomach. Review the administration of this medication if you had difficulty with this question.
Level of Cognitive Ability: Application
Client Needs: Physiological Integrity
Integrated Process: Nursing Process—implementation
Content Area: Pharmacology
Reference: Hodgson, B., & Kizior, R. (2007). *Saunders nursing drug handbook 2007* (p. 140). Philadelphia: W.B. Saunders.

7. 3
Rationale: Loperamide is an antidiarrheal agent. It is used to manage acute and also chronic diarrhea in conditions such as inflammatory bowel disease. Loperamide also can be used to reduce the volume of drainage from an ileostomy. It is not used for the conditions in options 1, 2, and 4.
Test-Taking Strategy: Focus on the name of the medication. Recalling that this medication is an antidiarrheal agent will direct you to option 3. Review the action of this medication if you had difficulty with this question.
Level of Cognitive Ability: Application
Client Needs: Physiological Integrity
Integrated Process: Nursing Process—planning
Content Area: Pharmacology

Reference: Hodgson, B., & Kizior, R. (2007). *Saunders nursing drug handbook 2007* (pp. 703-704). Philadelphia: W.B. Saunders.

8. 3
Rationale: If the client experiences tardive dyskinesia (rhythmic movements of the face or limbs), the client should stop the medication and call the physician. These side effects may be irreversible. Excitability is not a side effect of this medication. Anxiety, irritability, and dry mouth are side effects that are not so harmful to the client.
Test-Taking Strategy: Use the process of elimination, focusing on the strategic words *withhold the medication immediately*. Select option 3 because these effects are most harmful to the client. Review the side effects and adverse effects of this medication if you had difficulty with this question.
Level of Cognitive Ability: Application
Client Needs: Physiological Integrity
Integrated Process: Teaching and Learning
Content Area: Pharmacology
Reference: Hodgson, B., & Kizior, R. (2007). *Saunders nursing drug handbook 2007* (p. 762). Philadelphia: W.B. Saunders.

9. 4
Rationale: Trimethobenzamide (Tigan) is an antiemetic agent used to treat nausea and vomiting. The other options are incorrect.
Test-Taking Strategy: Use the process of elimination. Recalling that this medication is an antiemetic will direct you to option 4. Review this medication if you had difficulty with this question.
Level of Cognitive Ability: Analysis
Client Needs: Physiological Integrity
Integrated Process: Nursing Process—evaluation
Content Area: Pharmacology
Reference: Hodgson, B., & Kizior, R. (2007). *Saunders nursing drug handbook 2007* (p. 1179). Philadelphia: W.B. Saunders.

10. 4
Rationale: Ondansetron is an antiemetic used to treat postoperative nausea and vomiting, as well as nausea and vomiting associated with chemotherapy. The other options are incorrect.
Test-Taking Strategy: Use the process of elimination. Recalling that this medication is an antiemetic will direct you to option 4. Review this medication if you had difficulty with this question.
Level of Cognitive Ability: Application
Client Needs: Physiological Integrity
Integrated Process: Nursing Process—implementation
Content Area: Pharmacology
Reference: Hodgson, B., & Kizior, R. (2007). *Saunders nursing drug handbook 2007* (p. 869). Philadelphia: W.B. Saunders.

11. 3
Rationale: Pancrelipase (Pancrease) is a pancreatic enzyme used in clients with pancreatitis as a digestive aid. The medication should reduce the amount of fatty stools (steatorrhea). Another intended effect could be improved nutritional status. It is not used to treat abdominal pain or heartburn. Its use could result in weight gain but should not result in weight loss if it is aiding in digestion.

Test-Taking Strategy: Use the process of elimination and focus on the name of the medication. Use knowledge of physiology of the pancreas to assist in directing you to the correct option. Review this medication if you had difficulty with this question.
Level of Cognitive Ability: Analysis
Client Needs: Physiological Integrity
Integrated Process: Nursing Process—evaluation
Content Area: Pharmacology
Reference: Hodgson, B., & Kizior, R. (2007). *Saunders nursing drug handbook 2007* (p. 894). Philadelphia: W.B. Saunders.

12. **2**
Rationale: Calcium carbonate antacids should not be taken with milk, milk products, or foods or supplements high in vitamin D because milk-alkali syndrome (headache, urinary frequency, anorexia, nausea, vomiting, fatigue) can occur. The best item to consume when taking calcium carbonate is water.
Test-Taking Strategy: Use the process of elimination. Recalling that antacids should not be taken with food will direct you to option 2. Review this antacid if you had difficulty with this question.
Level of Cognitive Ability: Application
Client Needs: Physiological Integrity
Integrated Process: Teaching and Learning
Content Area: Pharmacology
Reference: Hodgson, B., & Kizior, R. (2007). *Saunders nursing drug handbook 2007* (p. 173). Philadelphia: W.B. Saunders.

13. **4**
Rationale: Aluminum hydroxide tablets should be chewed thoroughly before swallowing. This prevents them from entering the small intestine undissolved. They should not be swallowed whole. Antacids should be taken at least 1 hour apart from other medications to prevent interactive effects. Constipation is a side effect of the use of aluminum products, but it is not correct for the client to take a laxative with each dose. This promotes laxative abuse; the client should first try other means to prevent constipation.
Test-Taking Strategy: Use the process of elimination. Eliminate option 3 first because this action does not promote healthy bowel function. Next, eliminate option 2, using general knowledge of antacid interactive effects. From the remaining options, use principles of digestion and medication use to direct you to option 4. Review this medication if you had difficulty with this question.
Level of Cognitive Ability: Application
Client Needs: Physiological Integrity
Integrated Process: Teaching and Learning
Content Area: Pharmacology
Reference: Hodgson, B., & Kizior, R. (2007). *Saunders nursing drug handbook 2007* (p. 46). Philadelphia: W.B. Saunders.

14. **1**
Rationale: Calcium carbonate can be used as an antacid for the relief of heartburn and indigestion. Calcium carbonate also can be used as a calcium supplement (option 3) or to bind phosphorus in the gastrointestinal tract with renal failure (option 4). Option 2 is incorrect, although adequate

calcium levels are needed for proper neurological function.
Test-Taking Strategy: Note the strategic word *optimal*. Focusing on the client's diagnosis will direct you to option 1. Review this medication if you had difficulty with this question.
Level of Cognitive Ability: Analysis
Client Needs: Physiological Integrity
Integrated Process: Nursing Process—evaluation
Content Area: Pharmacology
Reference: Skidmore-Roth, L. (2005). *Mosby's drug guide for nurses* (6th ed., p. 128). St. Louis: Mosby.

15. **3**
Rationale: Sodium bicarbonate is an electrolyte modifier and antacid, and it would aggravate metabolic alkalosis, which is a difficult acid-base imbalance to correct. The other options are incorrect.
Test-Taking Strategy: Use the process of elimination. Focusing on the name of the medication, sodium bicarbonate, will direct you to option 3, metabolic alkalosis. Review the contraindications associated with the use of sodium bicarbonate if you had difficulty with this question.
Level of Cognitive Ability: Analysis
Client Needs: Physiological Integrity
Integrated Process: Nursing Process—analysis
Content Area: Pharmacology
Reference: Hodgson, B., & Kizior, R. (2007). *Saunders nursing drug handbook 2007* (p. 1059). Philadelphia: W.B. Saunders.

16. **3**
Rationale: Cimetidine is a histamine 2 (H$_2$)-receptor antagonist. Older clients are especially susceptible to central nervous system side effects of cimetidine. The most frequent of these is confusion. Less common central nervous system side effects include headache, dizziness, drowsiness, and hallucinations.
Test-Taking Strategy: Use the process of elimination and note the strategic words *most frequent*. Use knowledge of the older client and medication effects to direct you to option 3. Review the side effects of cimetidine if you had difficulty with this question.
Level of Cognitive Ability: Application
Client Needs: Physiological Integrity
Integrated Process: Nursing Process—assessment
Content Area: Pharmacology
Reference: Hodgson, B., & Kizior, R. (2007). *Saunders nursing drug handbook 2007* (p. 250). Philadelphia: W.B. Saunders.

17. **4**
Rationale: Sucralfate is a gastric protectant. The medication should be scheduled for administration 1 hour before meals and at bedtime. The medication is timed to allow it to form a protective coating over the ulcer before food intake stimulates gastric acid production and mechanical irritation. The other options are incorrect.
Test-Taking Strategy: Use the process of elimination. Focusing on the client's diagnosis will assist in directing you to option 4. Review the administration of this medication if you had difficulty with this question.
Level of Cognitive Ability: Application

Client Needs: Physiological Integrity
Integrated Process: Nursing Process—implementation
Content Area: Pharmacology
Reference: Hodgson, B., & Kizior, R. (2007). *Saunders nursing drug handbook 2007* (p. 1082). Philadelphia: W.B. Saunders.

18. **2**
Rationale: The client who chronically uses nonsteroidal anti-inflammatory drugs (NSAIDs) is prone to gastric mucosal injury. Misoprostol is a gastric protectant and is given specifically to prevent this occurrence. Diarrhea can be a side effect of the medication but is not an intended effect. Options 3 and 4 are incorrect.
Test-Taking Strategy: The strategic words in this question are *intended therapeutic effect* and *does not experience*. This tells you that the medication is being given to prevent the occurrence of specific symptoms. Recalling that NSAIDs can cause gastric mucosal injury will direct you to option 2. Review this medication and the side effects of NSAIDs if you had difficulty with this question.
Level of Cognitive Ability: Analysis
Client Needs: Physiological Integrity
Integrated Process: Nursing Process—evaluation
Content Area: Pharmacology
Reference: Hodgson, B., & Kizior, R. (2007). *Saunders nursing drug handbook 2007* (p. 783). Philadelphia: W.B. Saunders.

19. **1**
Rationale: Ranitidine is a histamine 2 (H_2)-receptor antagonist. A single daily dose of ranitidine is scheduled to be given at bedtime. This allows for a prolonged effect, and the greatest protection of the gastric mucosa. The other options are incorrect.
Test-Taking Strategy: Use the process of elimination. Recalling the action of the medication and focusing on the strategic words *once daily* will direct you to option 1. Review this medication if you had difficulty with this question.
Level of Cognitive Ability: Application
Client Needs: Physiological Integrity
Integrated Process: Nursing Process—planning
Content Area: Pharmacology
Reference: Hodgson, B., & Kizior, R. (2007). *Saunders nursing drug handbook 2007* (p. 2008). Philadelphia: W.B. Saunders.

20. **3**
Rationale: The client with peptic ulcer disease should avoid taking medications that are irritating to the stomach lining. Irritants would include aspirin and nonsteroidal anti-inflammatory drugs (NSAIDs). The client should be advised to take acetaminophen for a headache.
Test-Taking Strategy: Use the process of elimination. Remember that options that are comparative or alike are not likely to be correct. With this in mind, eliminate options 1 and 2 first because both medications are NSAIDs. From the remaining options, choose acetaminophen over aspirin because it is least irritating to the stomach. Review this condition and this medication if you had difficulty with this question.
Level of Cognitive Ability: Application
Client Needs: Physiological Integrity
Integrated Process: Teaching and Learning

Content Area: Pharmacology
References: Hodgson, B., & Kizior, R. (2007). *Saunders nursing drug handbook 2007* (p. 669). Philadelphia: W.B. Saunders. Ignatavicius, D., & Workman, M. (2006). *Medical-surgical nursing: Critical thinking for collaborative care* (5th ed., pp. 1290, 1305). Philadelphia: W.B. Saunders.

21. **2**
Rationale: Omeprazole is a proton pump inhibitor classified as an antiulcer agent. The intended effect of the medication is relief of pain from gastric irritation, often called heartburn by clients. Omeprazole is not used to treat the conditions identified in options 1, 3, and 4.
Test-Taking Strategy: Use the process of elimination. Recalling that this medication is a proton pump inhibitor will direct you to option 2. Review the action of this medication if you had difficulty with this question.
Level of Cognitive Ability: Analysis
Client Needs: Physiological Integrity
Integrated Process: Nursing Process—evaluation
Content Area: Pharmacology
Reference: Hodgson, B., & Kizior, R. (2007). *Saunders nursing drug handbook 2007* (p. 868). Philadelphia: W.B. Saunders.

22. **3**
Rationale: Triple therapy for *Helicobacter pylori* infection usually includes two antibacterial drugs and a proton pump inhibitor. Metronidazole and clarithromycin are antibacterials. Omeprazole is a proton pump inhibitor. These medications will kill the bacteria and decrease acid production.
Test-Taking Strategy: Focus on the name of the medications and their actions. Eliminate option 1 because the medications do more than kill the bacteria. These medications are taken not only when there is pain but continually until gone, usually for 1 to 2 weeks. This will eliminate option 2. These medications do not coat the ulcer, eliminating option 4. Review the medication regimens for treatment of *H. pylori* and their actions if you had difficulty with this question.
Level of Cognitive Ability: Analysis
Client Needs: Physiological Integrity
Integrated Process: Nursing Process—evaluation
Content Area: Pharmacology
Reference: Kee, J., Hayes, E., & McCuistion, L. (2006). *Pharmacology: A nursing process approach* (5th ed., pp. 708-709). St. Louis: W.B. Saunders.

ALTERNATE ITEM FORMAT: MULTIPLE RESPONSE

Answer: 1, 2, 3, 4
Rationale: H_2-receptor antagonists suppress secretion of gastric acid, alleviate symptoms of heartburn, and assist in preventing complications of peptic ulcer disease. These medications also suppress gastric acid secretions and are used in active ulcer disease, erosive esophagitis, and pathological hypersecretory conditions. The other medications listed are proton pump inhibitors.
Test-Taking Strategy: Focus on the subject, H_2-receptor antagonists. Recalling that these medication names end with *-dine*

will assist in answering this question. Also, recall that proton pump inhibitors medication names end with *-zole*. Review the H$_2$-receptor antagonists if you had difficulty with this question.

Level of Cognitive Ability: Analysis

Client Needs: Physiological Integrity
Integrated Process: Nursing Process—analysis
Content Area: Pharmacology
Reference: Mosby. (2005). *Mosby's 2005 drug consult for nurses* (pp. 931, 935, 937, 939). St. Louis: Mosby.

REFERENCES

Hodgson, B., & Kizior, R. (2007). *Saunders nursing drug handbook 2007*. Philadelphia: W.B. Saunders.

Ignatavicius, D., & Workman, M. (2006). *Medical-surgical nursing: Critical thinking for collaborative care* (5th ed.). Philadelphia: W.B. Saunders.

Kee, J., Hayes, E., & McCuistion, L. (2006). *Pharmacology: A nursing process approach* (5th ed.). St. Louis: W.B. Saunders.

Lehne, R. (2007). *Pharmacology for nursing care* (6th ed.). Philadelphia: W.B. Saunders.

Mosby. (2007). *2007 Mosby's nursing drug reference* (20th ed.). St. Louis: Mosby.

Skidmore-Roth, L. (2005). *Mosby's drug guide for nurses* (6th ed.). St. Louis: Mosby.

The Adult Client With a Respiratory Disorder

PYRAMID TERMS

asthma A chronic inflammatory disorder of the airways marked by airway hyperresponsiveness. Asthma causes recurrent episodes of wheezing, breathlessness, chest tightness, and coughing associated with airflow obstruction that is often reversible with treatment.

bacille Calmette-Guérin vaccine A vaccine containing attenuated tubercle bacilli that may be given to persons in foreign countries or to those traveling to foreign countries to produce increased resistance to tuberculosis.

chronic obstructive pulmonary disease A disease state characterized by pulmonary airflow obstruction that is usually progressive, not fully reversible, and sometimes accompanied by airway hyperreactivity. Airflow obstruction may be caused by chronic bronchitis and/or emphysema. In chronic hypercapnia, the stimulus to breathe is a low Po_2 instead of an increased Pco_2.

emphysema Abnormal permanent enlargement of air spaces distal to the terminal bronchioles, with destruction of alveolar walls without obvious fibrosis.

mantoux test The most reliable determinant of infection with tuberculosis. A small amount (0.1 mL) of intermediate-strength purified protein derivative containing 5 tuberculin units is given intradermally in the forearm. An area of induration measuring 10 mm or more in diameter, 48 to 72 hours after injection, indicates that the individual has been exposed to tuberculosis.

mechanical ventilation The use of a ventilator to move room air or oxygen enriched air into and out of the lungs mechanically to maintain proper levels of oxygen and carbon dioxide in the blood. Types of ventilators include negative-pressure and positive-pressure ventilators. Various ventilator modes are adjusted to the client's individual needs.

multidrug-resistant strain A multidrug-resistant strain of tuberculosis (MDR-TB) can occur as a result of improper or noncompliant use of treatment programs and the development of mutations in the tubercle bacilli.

Mycobacterium tuberculosis The causative organism (bacillus) of tuberculosis; an aerobic bacterium that is a nonmotile, nonsporulating, acid-fast rod that secrets niacin.

pneumothorax The accumulation of atmospheric air in the pleural space caused by a rupture in the visceral or parietal pleura. The loss of negative intrapleural pressure results in collapse of the lung. Diagnosis of pneumothorax is made by chest radiography.

suctioning A sterile procedure involving the removal of respiratory secretions that accumulate in the tracheobronchial airway when the client is unable to expectorate secretions; performed to maintain a patent airway.

tuberculosis A highly communicable disease caused by *Mycobacterium tuberculosis*. Tuberculosis is transmitted by the airborne route via droplet infection.

PYRAMID TO SUCCESS

The Pyramid to Success focuses on respiratory acid-base imbalances and reading arterial blood gas results, infectious diseases, particularly tuberculosis, and respiratory care in relation to oxygen delivery systems and mechanical ventilation. Pyramid Points focus on the client with pneumonia, respiratory failure, chronic obstructive pulmonary disease, pneumothorax, and tuberculosis. The Pyramid to Success includes the care of the client with tuberculosis, especially regarding the importance of the medication regimen, providing adequate nutrition and adequate rest to promote the healing process, and prevention of the progression of the disease. Focus on assisting the client to cope with the social isolation issues that exist during the period of illness and on teaching the client and family the critical measures of screening and of preventing respiratory disease and the transmission of disease. The Integrated Processes addressed in this unit include Caring, Communication and Documentation, Nursing Process, and Teaching/Learning.

CLIENT NEEDS

Safe and Effective Care Environment

Collaborating with multidisciplinary team in the management of the respiratory disorder

Discussing consultations and referrals related to the respiratory disorder

Establishing priorities

Handling infectious materials such as sputum or body fluids safely

Maintaining asepsis when caring for wounds or tracheostomy sites and during mechanical ventilation or suctioning

Maintaining confidentiality related to the respiratory disorder

Maintaining respiratory precautions, standard precautions, and other precautions

Obtaining informed consent related to diagnostic and surgical procedures

Upholding client rights

Health Promotion and Maintenance

Educating the client about adequate fluid and nutritional intake

Educating the client about breathing exercises and respiratory therapy and care

Educating the client about medication administration

Educating the client about the need for follow-up care

Educating the client about the prevention of transmission of infection

Informing the client about health promotion programs

Performing respiratory assessment techniques

Preventing respiratory disorders and infectious diseases

Providing health screening related to risks for respiratory disorders

Psychosocial Integrity

Considering religious, cultural, and spiritual influences when providing care

Discussing body image changes related to tracheostomy if performed

Discussing end-of-life and grief and loss issues

Discussing situational role changes

Identifying coping mechanisms

Identifying support systems

Informing the client about community resources

Physiological Integrity

Administering medications

Caring for the client on mechanical ventilation

Caring for the client receiving respiratory care and oxygen

Managing illnesses

Monitoring for acid-base imbalances

Monitoring for alterations in body systems

Monitoring for infectious diseases

Providing comfort

Providing nutrition and oral hygiene

Providing personal hygiene and promoting rest and sleep

Reading arterial blood gas results

REFERENCES

Black, J., & Hawks, J. (2005). *Medical-surgical nursing: Clinical management for positive outcomes* (7th ed.). Philadelphia: W.B. Saunders.

Chernecky, C., & Berger, B. (2004). *Laboratory tests and diagnostic procedures* (4th ed.). Philadelphia: W.B. Saunders.

Harkreader, H., & Hogan, M. (2004). *Fundamentals of nursing: Caring and clinical judgment* (2nd ed.). Philadelphia: W.B. Saunders.

Ignatavicius, D., & Workman, M. (2005). *Medical-surgical nursing: Critical thinking for collaborative care* (5th ed.). St. Louis: W.B. Saunders.

Jarvis, C. (2004). *Physical examination and health assessment* (4th ed.). St. Louis: W.B. Saunders.

Lewis, S., Heitkemper, M., & Dirksen, S. (2004). *Medical-surgical nursing: Assessment and management of clinical problems* (6th ed.). St. Louis: Mosby.

National Council of State Boards of Nursing (Eds.) (2007). *2007 NCLEX-RN® detailed test plan.* Chicago: Author.

Potter, P., & Perry, A. (2005). *Fundamentals of nursing* (6th ed.). St. Louis: Mosby.

Varcarolis, E., Carson, V., & Shoemaker, N. (2006). *Foundations of psychiatric mental health nursing: A clinical approach* (5th ed.). Philadelphia: W.B. Saunders.

Respiratory System

I. ANATOMY AND PHYSIOLOGY

A. Primary functions of the respiratory system
1. Provides oxygen for metabolism in the tissues
2. Removes carbon dioxide, the waste product of metabolism

B. Secondary functions of the respiratory system
1. Facilitates sense of smell
2. Produces speech
3. Maintains acid-base balance
4. Maintains body water levels
5. Maintains heat balance

C. Upper respiratory tract
1. Nose: Humidifies, warms, and filters inspired air
2. Sinuses: Air-filled cavities within the hollow bones that surround the nasal passages and provide resonance during speech
3. Pharynx
   a. Passageway for the respiratory and digestive tracts located behind the oral and nasal cavities
   b. Divided into the nasopharynx, oropharynx, and laryngopharynx
4. Larynx
   a. Located above the trachea, just below the pharynx at the root of the tongue; commonly called the voice box
   b. Contains two pairs of vocal cords, the false and true cords
   c. The opening between the true vocal cords is the glottis.
   d. The glottis plays an important role in coughing, which is the most fundamental defense mechanism of the lungs.

5. Epiglottis
   a. Leaf-shaped elastic structure attached along one end to the top of the larynx
   b. Prevents food from entering the tracheobronchial tree by closing over the glottis during swallowing

D. Lower respiratory tract
1. Trachea: Located in front of the esophagus; branches into the right and left main stem bronchi at the carina
2. Main stem bronchi
   a. Begin at the carina
   b. The right bronchus is slightly wider, shorter, and more vertical than the left bronchus.
   c. The mainstem bronchi divide into secondary or lobar bronchi that enter each of the five lobes of the lung.
   d. The bronchi are lined with cilia, which propel mucus up and away from the lower airway to the trachea, where it can be expectorated or swallowed.
3. Bronchioles
   a. Branch from the secondary bronchi and subdivide into the small terminal and respiratory bronchioles
   b. The bronchioles contain no cartilage and depend on the elastic recoil of the lung for patency.
   c. The terminal bronchioles contain no cilia and do not participate in gas exchange.
4. Alveolar ducts and alveoli
   a. Acinus (plural acini) is a term used to indicate all structures distal to the terminal bronchiole.

b. Alveolar ducts branch from the respiratory bronchioles.

c. Alveolar sacs, which arise from the ducts, contain clusters of alveoli, which are the basic units of gas exchange.

d. Type II alveolar cells in the walls of the alveoli secrete surfactant, a phospholipid protein that reduces the surface tension in the alveoli; without surfactant, the alveoli would collapse.

5. Lungs

a. Located in the pleural cavity in the thorax

b. Extend from just above the clavicles to the diaphragm, the major muscle of inspiration

c. The right lung, which is larger than the left, is divided into three lobes, the upper, middle, and lower lobes.

d. The left lung, which is narrower than the right lung to accommodate the heart, is divided into two lobes.

e. The respiratory structures are innervated by the phrenic nerve, the vagus nerve, and the thoracic nerves.

f. The parietal pleura lines the inside of the thoracic cavity, including the upper surface of the diaphragm.

g. The visceral pleura covers the pulmonary surfaces.

h. A thin fluid layer, which is produced by the cells lining the pleura, lubricates the visceral pleura and the parietal pleura, allowing them to glide smoothly and painlessly during respiration.

i. Blood flows through the lungs via the pulmonary system and the bronchial system.

6. Accessory muscles of respiration include the scalene muscles, which elevate the first two ribs, the sternocleidomastoid muscles, which raise the sternum, and the trapezius and pectoralis muscles, which fix the shoulders.

7. The respiratory process

a. The diaphragm descends into the abdominal cavity during inspiration, causing negative pressure in the lungs.

b. The negative pressure draws air from the area of greater pressure, the atmosphere, into the area of lesser pressure, the lungs.

c. In the lungs, air passes through the terminal bronchioles into the alveoli to oxygenate the body tissues.

d. At the end of inspiration, the diaphragm and intercostal muscles relax and the lungs recoil.

e. As the lungs recoil, pressure within the lungs becomes higher than atmospheric pressure, causing the air, which now contains the cel-

lular waste products carbon dioxide and water, to move from the alveoli in the lungs to the atmosphere.

f. Effective gas exchange depends on distribution of gas (ventilation) and blood (perfusion) in all portions of the lungs.

II. DIAGNOSTIC TESTS

A. Risk factors for respiratory disorders (Box 57-1)

B. Chest x-ray film (radiograph)

1. Description: Provides information regarding the anatomical location and appearance of the lungs

2. Preprocedure

a. Remove all jewelry and other metal objects from the chest area.

b. Assess the client's ability to inhale and hold his or her breath.

c. Question women regarding pregnancy or the possibility of pregnancy.

3. Postprocedure: Help the client get dressed.

C. Sputum specimen

1. Description: Specimen obtained by expectoration or tracheal **suctioning** to assist in the identification of organisms or abnormal cells (Box 57-2)

BOX 57-1

Risk Factors for Respiratory Disorders

Allergies
Chest injury
Crowded living conditions
Exposure to chemicals and environmental pollutants
Family history of infectious disease
Frequent respiratory illnesses
Geographic residence and travel to foreign countries
Smoking
Surgery
Use of chewing tobacco

BOX 57-2

Suctioning Procedure

Use aseptic technique.
Hyperoxygenate the client by a resuscitation bag, increasing the oxygen flow rate, or asking the client to take deep breaths.
Lubricate the catheter with sterile water.
Tracheal suctioning: Insert the catheter 4 inches.
Nasotracheal suctioning: Insert the catheter to induce cough reflex.
Do not apply suction while inserting the catheter.
Apply suction intermittently for 10 seconds; rotate the catheter and withdraw.
Hyperoxygenate the client and encourage deep breaths.

2. Preprocedure
   a. Determine specific purpose of collection and check with institutional policy for appropriate method for collection of a specimen.
   b. Obtain an early morning sterile specimen from **suctioning** or expectoration after a respiratory treatment if a treatment is prescribed.
   c. Instruct the client to rinse the mouth with water before collection.
   d. Obtain 15 mL of sputum.
   e. Instruct the client to take several deep breaths and then cough deeply to obtain sputum.
   f. Always collect the specimen before the client begins antibiotic therapy.

3. Postprocedure
   a. If a culture of sputum is prescribed, transport the specimen to the laboratory immediately.
   b. Assist the client with mouth care.

D. Bronchoscopy
  1. Description: Direct visual examination of the larynx, trachea, and bronchi with a fiberoptic bronchoscope
  2. Preprocedure
   a. Obtain informed consent.
   b. Maintain NPO status for the client from midnight before the procedure.
   c. Obtain vital signs.
   d. Assess the results of coagulation studies.
   e. Remove dentures or eyeglasses.
   f. Prepare suction equipment.
   g. Establish an intravenous (IV) access as necessary and administer medication for sedation as prescribed.
   h. Have emergency resuscitation equipment readily available.
  3. Postprocedure
   a. Monitor vital signs.
   b. Maintain the client in a semi-Fowler's position.
   c. Assess for the return of the gag reflex.
   d. Maintain NPO status until the gag reflex returns.
   e. Have an emesis basin readily available for the client to expectorate sputum.
   f. Monitor for bloody sputum.
   g. Monitor respiratory status, particularly if sedation has been administered.
   h. Monitor for complications, such as bronchospasm or bronchial perforation, indicated by facial or neck crepitus, dysrhythmias, fever, bacteremia, hemorrhage, hypoxemia, and **pneumothorax.**
   i. Notify the physician if fever, difficulty in breathing, or other signs of complications occur following the procedure.

E. Pulmonary angiography
  1. Description
   a. An invasive fluoroscopic procedure in which a catheter is inserted through the antecubital or femoral vein into the pulmonary artery or one of its branches
   b. Involves an injection of iodine or radiopaque contrast material
  2. Preprocedure
   a. Obtain informed consent.
   b. Assess for allergies to iodine, seafood, or other radiopaque dyes.
   c. Maintain NPO status of the client for 8 hours before the procedure.
   d. Monitor vital signs.
   e. Assess results of coagulation studies.
   f. Establish an intravenous access.
   g. Administer sedation as prescribed.
   h. Instruct the client to lie still during the procedure.
   i. Instruct the client that he or she may feel an urge to cough, flushing, nausea, or a salty taste following injection of the dye.
   j. Have emergency resuscitation equipment available.
  3. Postprocedure
   a. Monitor vital signs.
   b. Avoid taking blood pressures for 24 hours in the extremity used for the injection.
   c. Monitor peripheral neurovascular status of the affected extremity.
   d. Assess insertion site for bleeding.
   e. Monitor for delayed reaction to the dye.

F. Thoracentesis
  1. Description: Removal of fluid or air from the pleural space via a transthoracic aspiration
  2. Preprocedure
   a. Obtain informed consent.
   b. Obtain vital signs.
   c. Prepare the client for ultrasound or chest radiograph, if prescribed, before procedure.
   d. Assess results of coagulation studies.
   e. Note that the client is positioned sitting upright, with the arms and shoulders supported by a table at the bedside during the procedure (Fig. 57-1).
   f. If the client cannot sit up, the client is placed lying in bed toward the unaffected side, with the head of the bed elevated.
   g. Instruct the client not to cough, breath deeply, or move during the procedure.
  3. Postprocedure
   a. Monitor vital signs.
   b. Monitor respiratory status.
   c. Apply a pressure dressing, and assess the puncture site for bleeding and crepitus.

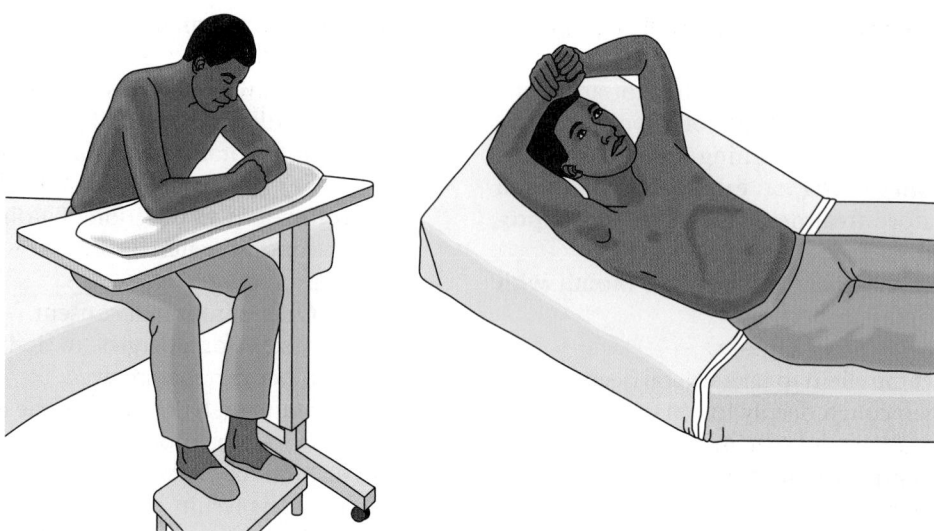

FIG. 57-1 Positions for thoracentesis. (From Ignatavicius, D., & Workman, M. [2006]. *Medical-surgical nursing: Critical thinking for collaborative care* [5th ed.]. Philadelphia: W.B. Saunders.)

d. Monitor for signs of **pneumothorax**, air embolism, and pulmonary edema.

G. Pulmonary function tests
  1. Description: Tests used to evaluate lung mechanics, gas exchange, and acid-base disturbance through spirometric measurements, lung volumes, and arterial blood gas levels.
  2. Preprocedure
    a. Determine whether an analgesic that may depress the respiratory function is being administered.
    b. Consult with the physician regarding holding bronchodilators before testing.
    c. Instruct the client to void before the procedure and to wear loose clothing.
    d. Remove dentures.
    e. Instruct the client to refrain from smoking or eating a heavy meal for 4 to 6 hours before the test.
  3. Postprocedure: Client may resume normal diet and any bronchodilators and respiratory treatments that were held before the procedure.

H. Lung biopsy
  1. Description
    a. A percutaneous lung biopsy is performed to obtain tissue for analysis by culture or cytological examination.
    b. A needle biopsy is done to identify pulmonary lesions, changes in lung tissue, and the cause of pleural effusion.
  2. Preprocedure
    a. Obtain informed consent.
    b. Maintain NPO status of the client before the procedure.

c. Inform the client that a local anesthetic will be used but a sensation of pressure during needle insertion and aspiration may be felt.
    d. Administer analgesics and sedatives as prescribed.
  3. Postprocedure
    a. Monitor vital signs.
    b. Apply a dressing to the biopsy site and monitor for drainage or bleeding.
    c. Monitor for signs of respiratory distress, and notify the physician if they occur.
    d. Monitor for signs of **pneumothorax** and air emboli, and notify the physician if they occur.
    e. Prepare the client for chest radiography if prescribed.

I. Ventilation-perfusion lung scan
  1. Description
    a. The perfusion scan evaluates blood flow to the lungs.
    b. The ventilation scan determines the patency of the pulmonary airways and detects abnormalities in ventilation.
    c. A radionuclide may be injected for the procedure.
  2. Preprocedure
    a. Obtain informed consent.
    b. Assess the client for allergies to dye, iodine, or seafood.
    c. Remove jewelry around the chest area.
    d. Review breathing methods that may be required during testing.
    e. Establish an intravenous access.
    f. Administer sedation if prescribed.

g. Have emergency resuscitation equipment available.
3. Postprocedure
   a. Monitor client for reaction to the radionuclide.
   b. Instruct the client that the radionuclide clears from the body in about 8 hours.
J. Skin tests: A skin test uses an intradermal injection to help diagnose various infectious diseases (Box 57-3)
K. Arterial blood gases (ABGs) (Box 57-4)
   1. Description: Measurement of the dissolved oxygen and carbon dioxide in the arterial blood helps indicate the acid-base state and how well oxygen is being carried to the body.
   2. Preprocedure
      a. Perform Allen's test before drawing radial artery specimens.
      b. Have the client rest for 30 minutes before specimen collection to ensure accurate measurement of body oxygenation.
      c. Avoid **suctioning** before drawing the ABG sample.
      d. Do not turn off oxygen unless the ABG sample is ordered to be drawn with the client breathing room air.

BOX 57-3

Skin Test Procedure

Determine hypersensitivity or previous reactions to skin tests.
Use a skin site that is free of excessive body hair, dermatitis, and blemishes.
Apply the injection at the upper third of the inner surface of the left arm.
Circle and mark the injection test site.
Document the date, time, and test site.
Advise the client not to scratch the test site to prevent infection and possible abscess formation.
Instruct the client to avoid washing the test site.
Interpret the reaction at the injection site 24 to 72 hours after administration of the test antigen.
Assess the test site for the amount of induration (hard swelling) in millimeters and for the presence of erythema and vesiculation (small blister-like elevations).

BOX 57-4

Normal Arterial Blood Gas Values

pH: 7.35 to 7.45
Pco_2: 35 to 45 mm Hg
HCO_3: 22 to 27 mEq/L
Po_2: 80 to 100 mm Hg
O_2 saturation: 96% to 100%
Oxyhemoglobin dissociation curve: No shift

---

3. Postprocedure
   a. Place the specimen on ice.
   b. Note the client's temperature on the laboratory form.
   c. Note the oxygen and type of ventilation that the client is receiving on the laboratory form.
   d. Apply pressure to the puncture site for 5 to 10 minutes or longer if the client is taking anticoagulant therapy or has a bleeding disorder.
   e. Transport the specimen to the laboratory within 15 minutes.
   f. See Chapter 10 for discussion of the analysis of ABG results.
L. Pulse oximetry
   1. Description
      a. Pulse oximetry is a noninvasive test that registers the oxygen saturation of the client's hemoglobin.
      b. The capillary oxygen saturation (SaO_2) is recorded as a percentage.
      c. The normal value is 96% to 100%.
      d. After a hypoxic client uses up the readily available oxygen (measured as the arterial oxygen pressure, Pao_2, on ABG testing), the reserve oxygen, that oxygen attached to the hemoglobin (SaO_2), is drawn on to provide oxygen to the tissues.
      e. A pulse oximeter reading can alert the nurse to hypoxemia before clinical signs occur.
   2. Procedure
      a. A sensor is placed on the client's finger, toe, nose, ear lobe, or forehead to measure oxygen saturation, which then is displayed on a monitor.
      b. Maintain the transducer at heart level.
      c. Do not select an extremity with an impediment to blood flow.
      d. Results lower than 91% necessitate immediate treatment.
      e. If the SaO_2 is lower than 85%, oxygenation to body tissues is compromised; an SaO_2 lower than 70% is life-threatening.

III. **RESPIRATORY TREATMENTS**
   A. Breathing retraining (Box 57-5)
   B. Chest physiotherapy (CPT) (Fig. 57-2)
      1. Description: Percussion, vibration, and postural drainage techniques are performed over the thorax to loosen secretions in the affected area of the lungs and move them into more central airways.
      2. Interventions (Box 57-6)
      3. Contraindications
         a. Unstable vital signs
         b. Increased intracranial pressure

BOX 57-5

Client Education: Breathing Retraining and Huff Coughing

BREATHING RETRAINING

This includes exercises to decrease the use of accessory muscles of breathing to decrease fatigue and to promote CO_2 elimination.

The main types of exercises include pursed-lip breathing and diaphragmatic breathing.

The client should inhale slowly through the nose.

The client should place the hand over the abdomen while inhaling; the abdomen should expand with inhalation and contract during exhalation.

The client should exhale three times longer than inhalation by blowing through pursed lips.

HUFF COUGHING

This is an effective coughing technique that conserves energy, reduces fatigue, and facilitates mobilization of secretions.

The client should take three or four deep breaths using pursed-lip and diaphragmatic breathing. Leaning slightly forward, the client should cough three to four times during exhalation.

The client may need to splint the thorax or abdomen to achieve a maximum cough.

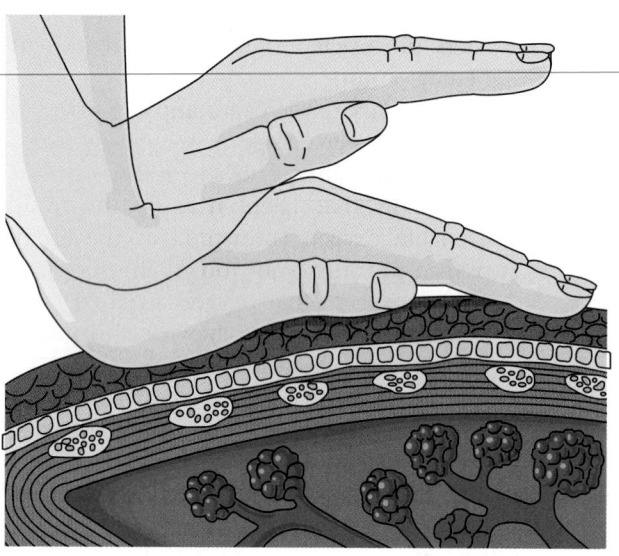
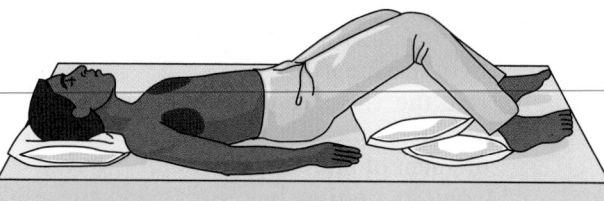
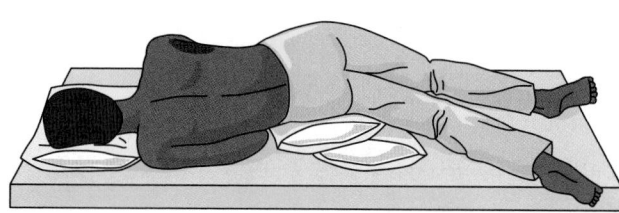
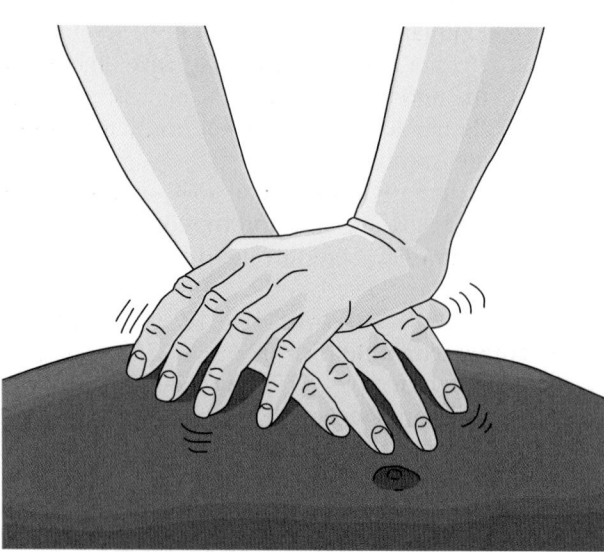

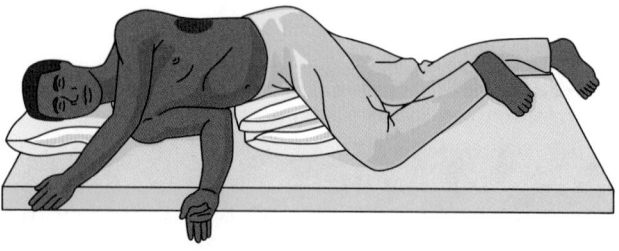

FIG. 57-2 Chest physiotherapy (CPT) and postural drainage. **Left,** Percussion and vibration techniques. The nurse may use one or two hands with vibration, which is performed when the client exhales or coughs. **Right,** Positions for postural drainage of respiratory secretions. (From Ignatavicius, D., & Workman, M. [2006]. *Medical-surgical nursing: Critical thinking for collaborative care* [5th ed.]. Philadelphia: W.B. Saunders.)

BOX 57-6
Chest Physiotherapy (CPT) Procedure

Perform CPT in the morning on arising, 1 hour before meals, or 2 to 3 hours after meals.

Stop CPT if pain occurs.

If the client is receiving a tube feeding, stop the feeding and aspirate the residual before beginning CPT.

Administer the bronchodilator (if prescribed) 15 minutes before the procedure.

Place a layer of material (gown or pajamas) between the hands or percussion device and the client's skin.

Position the client for postural drainage based on assessment.

Percuss the area for 1 to 2 minutes.

Vibrate the same area while the client exhales four or five deep breaths.

Monitor for respiratory tolerance to the procedure.

Stop the procedure if cyanosis or exhaustion occurs.

Maintain the position for 5 to 20 minutes after the procedure.

Repeat in all necessary positions until the client no longer expectorates mucus.

Dispose of sputum properly.

Provide mouth care after the procedure.

BOX 57-7
Client Instructions for Incentive Spirometry

Instruct the client to assume a sitting or upright position.

Instruct the client to place the mouth tightly around the mouthpiece of the device.

Instruct the client to inhale slowly to raise and maintain the flow rate indicator between the 600 and 900 marks.

Instruct the client to hold the breath for 5 seconds and then to exhale through pursed lips.

Instruct the client to repeat this process 10 times every hour.

c. Increase in bronchospasm from CPT
d. History of pathological fractures
e. Rib fractures
f. Chest incisions

C. Incentive spirometry (Box 57-7)

IV. OXYGEN

A. Interventions
1. Assess color and vital signs before and during treatment.
2. Place an *Oxygen in Use* sign at the client's bedside.
3. Assess for the presence of chronic lung problems.
4. Humidify the oxygen if indicated.

B. Nasal cannula (nasal prongs) (Box 57-8 and Fig. 57-3)

BOX 57-8
Fraction of Inspired Oxygen Delivered via Nasal Cannula

24% at 1 L/min
28% at 2 L/min
32% at 3 L/min
36% at 4 L/min
40% at 5 L/min
44% at 6 L/min

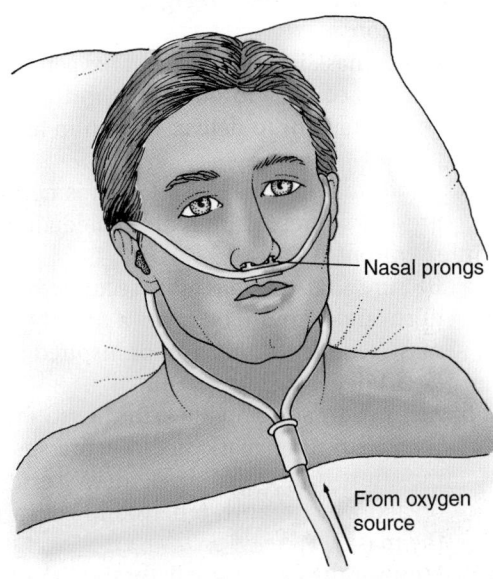

FIG. 57-3 A nasal cannula (prongs). (From Ignatavicius, D., & Workman, M. [2006]. *Medical-surgical nursing: Critical thinking for collaborative care* [5th ed.]. Philadelphia: W.B. Saunders.)

1. Description
   a. A nasal cannula is used at a flow rate of 1 to 6 L/min, providing approximate oxygen concentrations of 24% (at 1 L/min) to 44% (at 6 L/min).
   b. Flow rates higher than 6 L/min do not significantly increase oxygenation because the anatomical reserve or dead space (oral and nasal cavities) is full.
   c. A nasal cannula is used for the client with chronic airflow limitation and for long-term oxygen use.
   d. A client who is hypoxemic and has chronic hypercapnia requires low levels of oxygen delivery at 1 to 2 L/min; a low arterial oxygen level is the client's primary drive for breathing.
   e. Effective oxygen concentration can be delivered to nose breathers and mouth breathers with the use of a nasal cannula.

2. Interventions
   a. Place the nasal prongs in the nostrils, with the openings facing the client.

b. Add humidification as prescribed when a flow rate higher than 2 L/min is prescribed.

c. Check the water level and change the humidifier as needed.

d. Assess the client for changes in respiratory rate or depth.

e. Assess the nasal mucosa because high flow rates have a drying effect and increase mucosal irritation.

f. Assess skin integrity because the oxygen tubing can irritate the skin.

C. Simple face mask (Box 57-9; Fig. 57-4)

1. Description

a. A face mask is used to deliver oxygen concentrations of 40% to 60% for short-term oxygen therapy or to deliver oxygen in an emergency.

b. A minimal flow rate of 5 L/min is needed to prevent the rebreathing of exhaled air.

2. Interventions

a. Be sure that the mask fits securely over the nose and mouth because a poorly fitting mask reduces the fraction of inspired oxygen (FIO₂) delivered.

b. Assess skin and provide skin care to the area covered by the mask because pressure and moisture under the mask may cause skin breakdown (remove mucus and saliva from the mask).

c. Monitor the client closely for the risk of aspiration because the mask limits the client's ability to clear the mouth, especially if vomiting occurs.

d. Provide emotional support to decrease anxiety in the client who feels claustrophobic.

e. Consult with the physician regarding switching the client from a mask to a nasal cannula during eating.

D. Partial rebreather mask (Box 57-10; Fig. 57-5)

1. Description

a. A partial rebreather mask consists of a mask with a reservoir bag that provides an oxygen concentration of 70% to 90% with flow rates of 6 to 15 L/ min.

b. The client rebreathes one third of the exhaled tidal volume, which is high in oxygen, thus providing a high FIO₂.

2. Interventions

a. Make sure that the reservoir does not twist, kink, or become deflated.

b. Adjust the flow rate to keep the reservoir bag inflated two-thirds full during inspiration because deflation results in decreased oxygen delivered and rebreathing of exhaled air.

E. Nonrebreather mask (Fig. 57-6)

1. Description

a. Of the low-flow systems, a nonrebreather mask provides the highest concentration of

---

BOX 57-9

Fraction of Inspired Oxygen Delivered via Simple Face Mask

40% at 5 L/min
45% to 50% at 6 L/min
55% to 60% at 8 L/min

Pyramid Point: Flow rate must be set to at least 5 L/min to flush the mask of carbon dioxide.

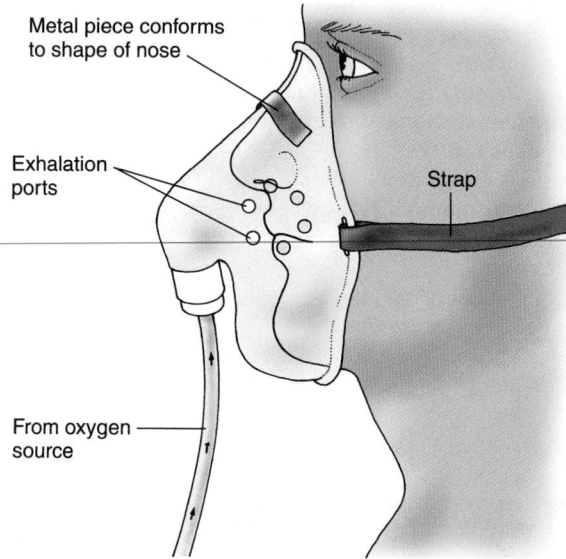

FIG. 57-4   A simple face mask used to deliver oxygen. (From Ignatavicius, D., & Workman, M. [2006]. *Medical-surgical nursing: Critical thinking for collaborative care* [5th ed.]. Philadelphia: W.B. Saunders.)

oxygen and can deliver an FIO₂ higher than 90%, depending on the client's ventilatory pattern.

b. A nonrebreather mask most frequently is used in the client with a deteriorating respiratory status who might require intubation.

c. The nonrebreather mask has a one-way valve between the mask and the reservoir and two flaps over the exhalation ports.

d. The valve allows the client to draw the entire quantity of oxygen from the reservoir bag.

e. The flaps prevent room air from entering through the exhalation ports.

f. During exhalation, air leaves through these exhalation ports while the one-way valve prevents exhaled air from reentering the reservoir bag.

2. FIO₂ delivered: 60% to 100% FIO₂ at a rate of flow that maintains the bag two-thirds full

3. Interventions

a. Remove mucus or saliva from the mask.

b. Assess the client closely.

c. Ensure that the valve and flaps are intact and functional during each breath.

BOX 57-10
Fraction of Inspired Oxygen Delivered via Partial
Rebreather Mask

70% to 90% FIO_2 delivered at 6 to 15 L/min
Pyramid Point: A flow rate high enough to maintain the
bag two-thirds full during inspiration is needed.

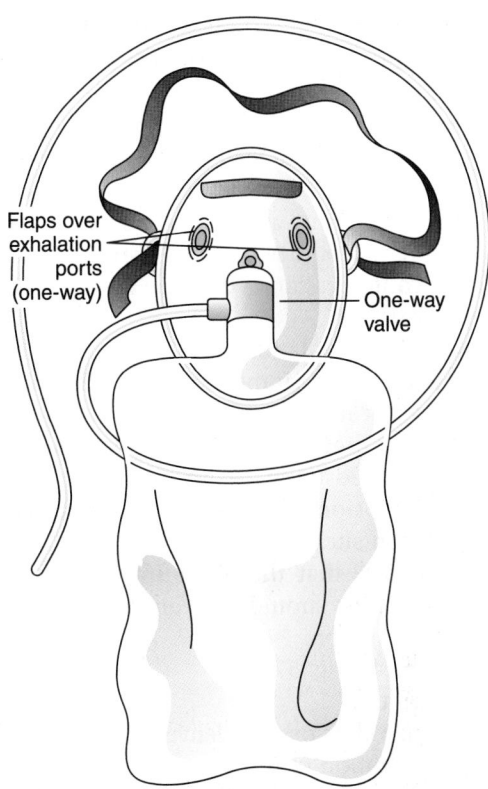

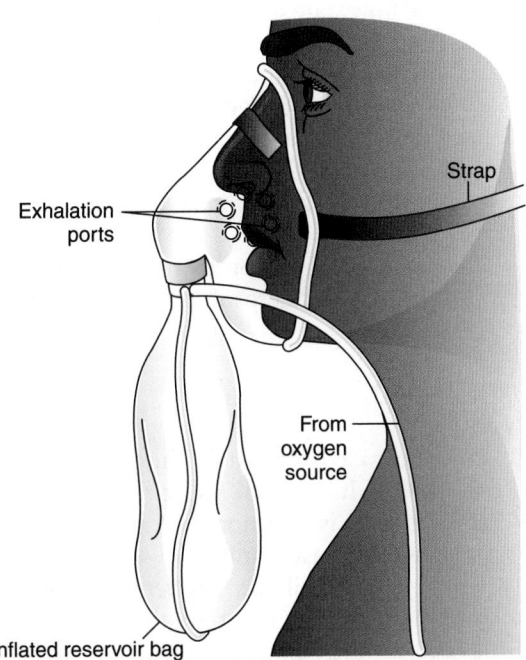

FIG. 57-5   A partial rebreather mask. (From Ignatavicius,
D., & Workman, M. [2006]. *Medical-surgical nursing: Criti-
cal thinking for collaborative care* [5th ed.]. Philadelphia:
W.B. Saunders.)

FIG. 57-6   A nonrebreather mask. (From Ignatavicius, D.,
& Workman, M. [2006]. *Medical-surgical nursing: Critical
thinking for collaborative care* [5th ed.]. Philadelphia: W.
B. Saunders.)

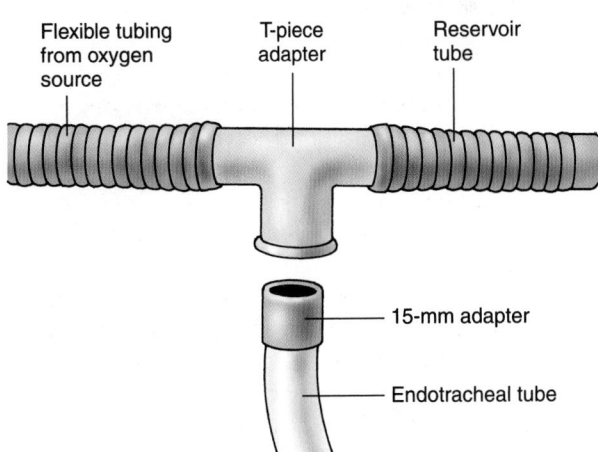

FIG. 57-7   A T-piece apparatus for attachment to an endotracheal tube or tracheostomy tube. (From Ignatavicius, D., & Workman, M. [2006]. *Medical-surgical nursing:
Critical thinking for collaborative care* [5th ed.]. Philadelphia: W.B. Saunders.)

d. Valves should open during expiration and
close during inhalation.
e. Suffocation can occur if the reservoir bag
kinks or if the oxygen source disconnects.
F. Face tent
1. A face tent fits over the client's chin, with the top
extending halfway across the face.
2. The oxygen concentration varies, but the face
tent is useful instead of a tight-fitting mask for
the client who has facial trauma or burns.
G. Aerosol mask: Used for the client who requires high
humidity after extubation or upper airway surgery,
or for the client who has thick secretions
H. Tracheostomy collar and T piece (Fig. 57-7)
1. The tracheostomy collar can be used to deliver
high humidity and the desired oxygen to the client with a tracheostomy.
2. A special adapter, called the T piece, can be used
to deliver any desired FIO_2 to the client with a
tracheostomy, laryngectomy, or endotracheal
tube.
3. See Chap. 21 for information on endotracheal
and tracheostomy tubes.

I. Interventions for face tent, aerosol mask, tracheostomy collar, and T piece
1. Change delivery system to a nasal cannula during mealtime if indicated for the client with a
face mask or aerosol mask.

2. Assess that the aerosol mist escapes from the vents of the delivery system during inspiration and expiration.
3. Empty condensation from the tubing to prevent the client from being lavaged with water and to promote an adequate flow rate; remove and clean the tubing at least every 4 hours.
4. Ensure that sufficient water is in the aerosol water container and change the container as needed.
5. Keep the exhalation port on the T piece open and uncovered (if the port is occluded, the client can suffocate).
6. Position the T piece so that it does not pull on the tracheostomy or endotracheal tube and cause erosion of the skin at the tracheostomy insertion site.
7. Make sure that the humidifier creates enough mist; a mist should be seen during inspiration and expiration.

J. Venturi mask (Fig. 57-8)
   1. Description
      a. High-flow oxygen delivery system
      b. Operation of the Venturi mask is based on a mechanism that pulls in a specific proportional amount of room air for each liter of oxygen delivered.
      c. An adapter is located between the bottom of the mask and the oxygen source; the adapter contains holes of different sizes that allow

only specific amounts of air to mix with the oxygen.
      d. The adapter allows selection of the amount of oxygen desired.
   2. FIO_2 delivered: 24% to 55% FIO_2, with flow rates of 4 to 10 L/min
   3. Interventions
      a. Monitor the client closely to ensure an accurate flow rate for a specific FIO_2.
      b. Keep the air entrapment port for the Venturi adapter open and uncovered to ensure adequate oxygen delivery.
      c. Ensure that the mask fits snugly and that the tubing is free of kinks, because the FIO_2 is altered if kinking occurs or if the mask fits poorly.
      d. Assess the client for dry mucous membranes; humidity or aerosol can be added to the system.

V. MECHANICAL VENTILATION

A. Types
   1. Pressure-cycled ventilator: The ventilator pushes air into the lungs until a specific airway pressure is reached; it is used for short periods, as in the postanesthesia care unit.
   2. Time-cycled ventilator: The ventilator pushes air into the lungs until a preset time has elapsed; it is used for the pediatric or neonatal client.
   3. Volume-cycled ventilator
      a. The ventilator pushes air into the lungs until a preset volume is delivered.
      b. A constant tidal volume is delivered regardless of the changing compliance of the lungs and chest wall or the airway resistance in the client or ventilator.
   4. Microprocessor ventilator
      a. A computer or microprocessor is built into the ventilator to allow continuous monitoring of ventilatory functions, alarms, and client parameters.
      b. This type of ventilator is more responsive to clients who have severe lung disease or require prolonged weaning.

B. Modes of ventilation (Box 57-11)
   1. Controlled
      a. The client receives a set tidal volume at a set rate.
      b. Used for clients who cannot initiate respiratory effort.

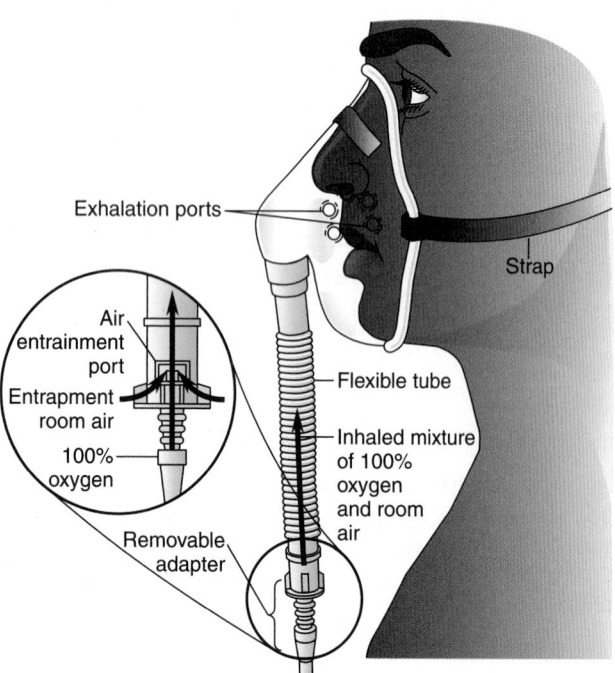

FIG. 57-8 A Venturi mask for precise oxygen delivery. (From Ignatavicius, D., & Workman, M. [2006]. *Medical-surgical nursing: Critical thinking for collaborative care* [5th ed.]. Philadelphia: W.B. Saunders.)

BOX 57-11

Modes of Ventilation

Controlled
Assist-control
Synchronized intermittent mandatory ventilation

c. Least used mode; if the client attempts to initiate a breath, the ventilator blocks the effort.

2. Assist-control
   a. Most commonly used mode
   b. Tidal volume and ventilatory rate are preset on the ventilator.
   c. The ventilator takes over the work of breathing for the client.
   d. The ventilator is programmed to respond to the client's inspiratory effort if the client does initiate a breath.
   e. The ventilator delivers the preset tidal volume when the client initiates a breath while allowing the client to control the rate of breathing.
   f. If the client's spontaneous ventilatory rate increases, the ventilator continues to deliver a preset tidal volume with each breath, which may cause hyperventilation and respiratory alkalosis.

3. Synchronized intermittent mandatory ventilation (SIMV)
   a. Similar to assist-control ventilation in that the tidal volume and ventilatory rate are preset on the ventilator.
   b. Allows clients to breath spontaneously at her or his own rate and tidal volume between the ventilator breaths
   c. Can be used as a primary ventilatory mode or as a weaning mode.
   d. When SIMV is used as a weaning mode, the number of SIMV breaths is decreased gradually, and the client gradually resumes spontaneous breathing.

C. Ventilator controls and settings (Box 57-12)
   1. Tidal volume: The volume of air that the client receives with each breath
   2. Rate: The number of ventilator breaths delivered per minute
   3. Fraction of inspired oxygen (FiO_2): The oxygen concentration delivered to the client; determined by the client's condition and ABG levels

4. Sighs: The volumes of air that are 1.5 to 2 times the set tidal volume, delivered 6 to 10 times per hour; may be used to prevent atelectasis

5. Peak airway inspiratory pressure
   a. The pressure needed by the ventilator to deliver a set tidal volume at a given compliance
   b. Monitoring peak airway inspiratory pressure reflects changes in compliance of the lungs and resistance in the ventilator or client.

6. Continuous positive airway pressure
   a. The application of positive airway pressure throughout the entire respiratory cycle for spontaneously breathing clients.
   b. Keeps the alveoli open during inspiration and prevents alveolar collapse; used primarily as a weaning modality
   c. No ventilator breaths are delivered, but the ventilator delivers oxygen and provides monitoring and an alarm system; the respiratory pattern is determined by the client's efforts.

7. Positive end-expiratory pressure (PEEP)
   a. Positive pressure is exerted during the expiratory phase of ventilation, which improves oxygenation by enhancing gas exchange and preventing atelectasis.
   b. The need for PEEP indicates a severe gas exchange disturbance.
   c. Higher amounts of PEEP (more than 15) increase the chance of complications, such as barotrauma tension pneumothorax.

8. Pressure support
   a. The application of positive pressure on inspiration that eases the workload of breathing
   b. May be used in combination with PEEP as a weaning method
   c. As the weaning process continues, the amount of pressure applied to inspiration is gradually decreased.

9. Interventions
   a. Assess the client first and then assess the ventilator.
   b. Assess vital signs, lung sounds, respiratory status, and breathing patterns (the client will never breathe at a rate lower than the rate set on the ventilator).
   c. Monitor skin color, particularly in the lips and nail beds.
   d. Monitor the chest for bilateral expansion.
   e. Obtain pulse oximetry readings.
   f. Monitor ABG results.
   g. Assess the need for **suctioning** and observe the type, color, and amount of secretions.
   h. Assess ventilator settings.
   i. Assess the level of water in the humidifier and the temperature of the humidification

---

BOX 57-12

Ventilator Controls and Settings

Continuous positive airway pressure
Fraction of inspired oxygen (FiO_2)
Peak airway inspiratory pressure
Positive end-expiratory pressure (PEEP)
Pressure support
Rate
Sighs
Tidal volume

system because extremes in temperature can damage the mucosa in the airway.

   j. Ensure that the alarms are set.

   k. If a cause for an alarm cannot be determined, ventilate the client manually with a resuscitation bag until the problem is corrected.

   l. Empty the ventilator tubing when moisture collects.

   m. Turn the client at least every 2 hours or get the client out of bed, as prescribed, to prevent complications of immobility.

   n. Have resuscitation equipment available at the bedside.

▲ D. Causes of alarms (Box 57-13)

  E. Complications

   1. Hypotension caused by the application of positive pressure, which increases intrathoracic pressure and inhibits blood return to the heart

   2. Respiratory complications such as **pneumothorax** or subcutaneous **emphysema** as a result of positive pressure

   3. Gastrointestinal alterations such as stress ulcers

   4. Malnutrition if nutrition is not maintained

   5. Infections

   6. Muscular deconditioning

   7. Ventilator dependence or inability to wean

▲ F. Weaning: Process of going from ventilator dependence to spontaneous breathing

   1. SIMV

    a. The client breathes between the preset breaths per minute rate of the ventilator.

    b. The SIMV rate is decreased gradually until the client is breathing on his or her own without the use of the ventilator.

   2. T piece

    a. The client is taken off the ventilator and the ventilator is replaced with a T piece or continuous positive airway pressure, which delivers humidified oxygen.

BOX 57-13

Causes of Ventilator Alarms

HIGH-PRESSURE ALARM

Increased secretions are in the airway.

Wheezing or bronchospasm causes decreased airway size.

The endotracheal tube is displaced.

The ventilator tube is obstructed because of water or a kink in the tubing.

Client coughs, gags, or bites on the oral endotracheal tube.

Client is anxious or fights the ventilator.

LOW-PRESSURE ALARM

Disconnection or leak in the ventilator or in the client's airway cuff occurs.

The client stops spontaneous breathing.

---

    b. The client is taken off the ventilator for short periods initially and allowed to breathe spontaneously.

    c. Weaning progresses as the client is able to tolerate progressively longer periods off the ventilator.

   3. Pressure support

    a. Pressure support is a predetermined pressure set on the ventilator to assist the client in respiratory effort.

    b. As weaning continues, the amount of pressure is decreased gradually.

    c. With pressure support, pressure may be maintained while the preset breaths per minute of the ventilator gradually are decreased.

VI. CHEST INJURIES

  A. Rib fracture

   1. Description

    a. Results from direct blunt chest trauma and causes a potential for intrathoracic injury, such as **pneumothorax** or pulmonary contusion

    b. Pain with movement and chest splinting result in impaired ventilation and inadequate clearance of secretions.

   2. Assessment

    a. Pain at the injury site that increases with inspiration ▲

    b. Tenderness at the site

    c. Shallow respirations

    d. Client splints chest ▲

    e. Fractures noted on chest x-ray

   3. Interventions

    a. Note that the ribs usually unite spontaneously.

    b. Place the client in a high Fowler's position. ▲

    c. Administer pain medication as prescribed to maintain adequate ventilatory status.

    d. Monitor for increased respiratory distress. ▲

    e. Instruct the client to self-splint with hands and arms. ▲

    f. Prepare the client for an intercostal nerve block as prescribed if the pain is severe.

  B. Flail chest

   1. Description

    a. Occurs from blunt chest trauma associated with accidents, which may result in hemothorax and rib fractures.

    b. The loose segment of the chest wall becomes ▲ paradoxical to the expansion and contraction of the rest of the chest wall.

   2. Assessment

    a. Paradoxical respirations (inward movement ▲ of a segment of the thorax during inspiration with outward movement during expiration)

    b. Severe pain in the chest

c. Dyspnea
d. Cyanosis
e. Tachycardia
f. Hypotension
g. Tachypnea, shallow respirations
h. Diminished breath sounds

3. Interventions
   a. Place the client in a high Fowler's position.
   b. Administer humidified oxygen as prescribed.
   c. Monitor for increased respiratory distress.
   d. Encourage coughing and deep breathing.
   e. Administer pain medication as prescribed.
   f. Maintain bed rest and limit activity to reduce oxygen demands.
   g. Prepare for intubation with **mechanical ventilation**, with PEEP for severe flail chest associated with respiratory failure and shock.

C. Pulmonary contusion
1. Description
   a. Characterized by interstitial hemorrhage associated with intraalveolar hemorrhage, resulting in decreased pulmonary compliance
   b. The major complication is acute respiratory distress syndrome.

2. Assessment
   a. Dyspnea
   b. Hypoxemia
   c. Increased bronchial secretions
   d. Hemoptysis
   e. Restlessness
   f. Decreased breath sounds
   g. Crackles and wheezes

3. Interventions
   a. Maintain a patent airway and adequate ventilation.
   b. Place the client in a high Fowler's position.
   c. Administer oxygen as prescribed.
   d. Monitor for increased respiratory distress.
   e. Maintain bed rest and limit activity to reduce oxygen demands.
   f. Prepare for **mechanical ventilation** with PEEP if required.

D. **Pneumothorax** (Fig. 57-9)
1. Description
   a. Accumulation of atmospheric air in the pleural space, which results in a rise in intrathoracic pressure and reduced vital capacity
   b. The loss of negative intrapleural pressure results in collapse of the lung.
   c. A spontaneous **pneumothorax** occurs with the rupture of a pulmonary bleb.
   d. An open **pneumothorax** occurs when an opening through the chest wall allows the entrance of positive atmospheric air pressure into the pleural space.

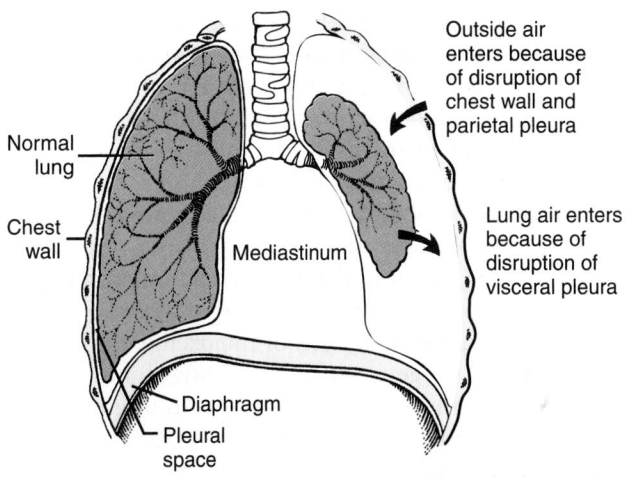

FIG. 57-9 Pneumothorax. Air in the pleural space causes the lungs to collapse around the hilus and may push the mediastinal contents (heart and great vessels) toward the other lung. (From McCance, K., & Huether, S. [2006]. *Pathophysiology: The biologic basis for disease in adults and children* [5th ed.]. St. Louis: Mosby.)

BOX 57-14

Assessment Findings: Pneumothorax

Absent breath sounds on affected side
Cyanosis
Decreased chest expansion unilaterally
Dyspnea
Hypotension
Sharp chest pain
Subcutaneous emphysema as evidenced by crepitus on palpation
Sucking sound with open chest wound
Tachycardia
Tachypnea
Tracheal deviation to the unaffected side with tension pneumothorax

---

   e. A tension **pneumothorax** occurs from a blunt chest injury or from **mechanical ventilation** with PEEP when a buildup of positive pressure occurs in the pleural space.
   f. Diagnosis of **pneumothorax** is made by chest x-ray.

2. Assessment (Box 57-14)

3. Interventions
   a. Apply a dressing over an open chest wound.
   b. Administer oxygen as prescribed.
   c. Place the client in a high Fowler's position.
   d. Prepare for chest tube placement until the lung has expanded fully.
   e. Monitor the chest tube drainage system.
   f. Monitor for subcutaneous **emphysema.**
   g. See Chap. 21 for information on chest tubes.

VII. ACUTE RESPIRATORY FAILURE

A. Description
  1. Occurs when insufficient oxygen is transported to the blood or inadequate carbon dioxide is removed from the lungs and the client's compensatory mechanisms fail
  2. Causes include a mechanical abnormality of the lungs or chest wall, a defect in the respiratory control center in the brain, or an impairment in the function of the respiratory muscles.
  3. In oxygenation failure, or hypoxemic respiratory failure, oxygen may reach the alveoli but cannot be absorbed or used properly, resulting in a PaO_2 lower than 60 mm Hg, arterial oxygen saturation (SaO_2) lower than 90%, or partial pressure of arterial carbon dioxide ($PaCO_2$) greater than 50 mm Hg occurring with acidemia.
  4. Many clients experience both hypoxemic and hypercapnic respiratory failure and retained carbon dioxide in the alveoli displaces oxygen, contributing to the hypoxemia.
  5. Manifestations of respiratory failure are related to the extent and rapidity of change in PaO_2 and $PaCO_2$.

B. Assessment
  1. Dyspnea
  2. Headache
  3. Restlessness
  4. Confusion
  5. Tachycardia
  6. Hypertension
  7. Dysrhythmias
  8. Decreased level of consciousness
  9. Alterations in respirations and breath sounds

C. Interventions
  1. Identify and treat the cause of the respiratory failure
  2. Administer oxygen to maintain the PaO_2 level higher than 60 to 70 mm Hg.
  3. Place the client in a high Fowler's position.
  4. Encourage deep breathing.
  5. Administer bronchodilators as prescribed.
  6. Prepare the client for **mechanical ventilation** if supplemental oxygen cannot maintain acceptable PaO_2 and $PaCO_2$ levels.

VIII. ACUTE RESPIRATORY DISTRESS SYNDROME

A. Description
  1. A form of acute respiratory failure that occurs as a complication of some other condition; it is caused by a diffuse lung injury and leads to extravascular lung fluid.
  2. The major site of injury is the alveolar capillary membrane.
  3. The interstitial edema causes compression and obliteration of the terminal airways and leads to reduced lung volume and compliance.
  4. The ABG levels identify respiratory acidosis and hypoxemia that do not respond to an increased percentage of oxygen.
  5. The chest x-ray shows bilateral interstitial and alveolar infiltrates; interstitial edema may not be noted until there is a 30% increase in fluid content.
  6. Causes include sepsis, fluid overload, shock, trauma, neurological injuries, burns, disseminated intravascular coagulation, drug ingestion, aspiration, and inhalation of toxic substances.

B. Assessment
  1. Tachypnea
  2. Dyspnea
  3. Decreased breath sounds
  4. Deteriorating ABG levels
  5. Hypoxemia despite high concentrations of delivered oxygen
  6. Decreased pulmonary compliance
  7. Pulmonary infiltrates

C. Interventions
  1. Identify and treat the cause of the acute respiratory distress syndrome.
  2. Administer oxygen as prescribed.
  3. Place the client in a high Fowler's position.
  4. Restrict fluid intake as prescribed.
  5. Provide respiratory treatments as prescribed.
  6. Administer diuretics, anticoagulants, or corticosteroids as prescribed.
  7. Prepare the client for intubation and **mechanical ventilation** using PEEP.

IX. ASTHMA (Fig. 57-10)

A. Description
  1. Chronic inflammatory disorder of the airways that causes varying degrees of obstruction in the airways
  2. **Asthma** is marked by airway inflammation and hyperresponsiveness to a variety of stimuli or triggers (Box 57-15)
  3. **Asthma** causes recurrent episodes of wheezing, breathlessness, chest tightness, and coughing associated with airflow obstruction that may resolve spontaneously; it is often reversible with treatment
  4. **Asthma** severity is classified based on the clinical features before treatment (Box 57-16).
  5. Status asthmaticus is a severe life-threatening **asthma** episode that is refractory to treatment and may result in **pneumothorax**, acute cor pulmonale, or respiratory arrest.

B. Assessment
  1. Restlessness
  2. Wheezing or crackles
  3. Absent or diminished lung sounds.
  4. Hyperresonance
  5. Use of accessory muscles for breathing

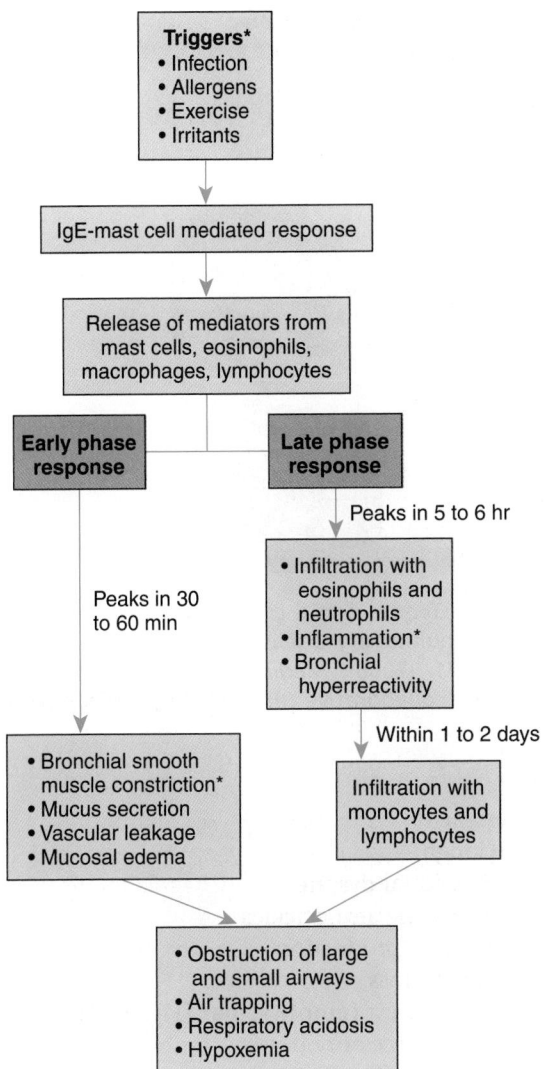

FIG. 57-10 Pathophysiology in asthma. *Primary process. (From Lewis, S., Heitkemper, M., & Dirksen, S. [2004]. *Medical-surgical nursing: Assessment and management of clinical problems* [6th ed.]. St. Louis: Mosby.)

BOX 57-15
Asthma Triggers

ENVIRONMENTAL FACTORS
Animal dander
Cockroaches
Dust
Exhaust fumes
Fireplaces
Molds
Perfumes or other products with aerosol sprays
Pollen
Smoke, including cigarette or cigar smoke
Sudden weather changes

PHYSIOLOGICAL FACTORS
Gastroesophageal reflux disease (GERD)
Hormonal changes
Sinusitis
Stress
Viral upper respiratory infection

MEDICATIONS
Acetylsalicylic acid (Aspirin)
β-Adrenergic blockers
Nonsteroidal anti-inflammatory drugs

OCCUPATIONAL EXPOSURE FACTORS
Metal salts
Wood and vegetable dusts
Industrial chemicals and plastics

FOOD ADDITIVES
Sulfites (bisulfites and metabisulfites)
Beer, wine, dried fruit, shrimp, processed potatoes
Monosodium glutamate

Modified from Lewis, S., Heitkemper, M., & Dirksen, S. (2004). *Medical-surgical nursing: Assessment and management of clinical problems* (6th ed.). St. Louis: Mosby.

---

6. Tachypnea with hyperventilation
7. Prolonged exhalation
8. Tachycardia
9. Pulsus paradoxus
10. Diaphoresis
11. Cyanosis
12. Decreased oxygen saturation
13. Pulmonary function test results that demonstrate decreased air flow rates

C. Interventions
1. Monitor vital signs.
2. Monitor pulse oximetry.
3. Monitor peak flow.
4. During an acute **asthma** episode, provide interventions to assist with breathing (Box 57-17).

D. Client education
1. Instruct the client on the intermittent nature of symptoms and need for long-term management.
2. Instruct the client to identify possible triggers and measures to prevent episodes.
3. Instruct the client on the management of medication and proper administration.
4. Instruct the client on the correct use of a peak flowmeter.
5. Help the client develop an **asthma** action plan with the primary provider and teach the client what to do if an **asthma** episode occurs.

X. CHRONIC OBSTRUCTIVE PULMONARY DISEASE
A. Description
1. Also known as chronic obstructive lung disease and chronic airflow limitation

BOX 57-16
Classification of Asthma Severity

SEVERE PERSISTENT
Symptoms are continuous.
Physical activity requires limitations.
Frequent exacerbations occur.
Nocturnal symptoms occur frequently.

MODERATE PERSISTENT
Daily symptoms occur.
Daily use of inhaled short-acting β agonist is needed.
Exacerbations affect activity.
Exacerbations occur at least twice weekly and may last
  for days.
Nocturnal symptoms occur more frequently than once
  weekly.

MILD PERSISTENT
Symptoms occur more frequently than twice weekly but
  less often than once daily.
Exacerbations may affect activity.
Nocturnal symptoms occur more frequently than twice a
  month.

MILD INTERMITTENT
Symptoms occur twice weekly or less.
Client is asymptomatic between exacerbations.
Exacerbations are brief (hours to days).
Intensity of exacerbations vary.
Nocturnal symptoms occur twice a month or less.

Modified from Ignatavicius, D., & Workman, M. (2006). *Medical-surgical nursing: Critical thinking for collaborative care* (5th ed.). Philadelphia: W.B. Saunders.

BOX 57-17
Nursing Interventions During an Acute Asthma Episode

Position the client in a high Fowler's position or sitting
  to aid in breathing.
Administer oxygen as prescribed.
Stay with the client to decrease anxiety.
Administer bronchodilators as prescribed.
Record the color, amount, and consistency of sputum,
  if any.
Administer corticosteroids as prescribed.
Auscultate lung sounds before, during, and after
  treatments.

2. **Chronic obstructive pulmonary disease** is a disease state characterized by airflow obstruction caused by **emphysema** or chronic bronchitis.
3. Progressive airflow limitation occurs, associated with an abnormal inflammatory response of the lungs that is not completely reversible.
4. **Chronic obstructive pulmonary disease** leads to pulmonary insufficiency, pulmonary hypertension, and cor pulmonale.

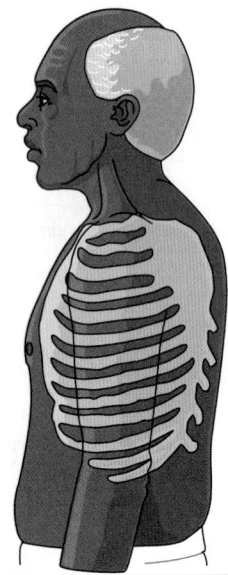

FIG. 57-11 Typical barrel chest in a client with chronic obstructive pulmonary disease. (From Ignatavicius, D., & Workman, M. [2006]. *Medical-surgical nursing: Critical thinking for collaborative care* [5th ed.]. Philadelphia: W. B. Saunders.)

B. Assessment
  1. Cough
  2. Exertional dyspnea
  3. Wheezing and crackles
  4. Sputum production
  5. Weight loss
  6. Barrel chest (**emphysema**) (Fig. 57-11)
  7. Use of accessory muscles for breathing
  8. Prolonged expiration
  9. Orthopnea
  10. Cardiac dysrhythmias
  11. Congestion and hyperinflation seen on chest x-ray (Fig. 57-12)
  12. ABG levels that indicate respiratory acidosis and hypoxemia
  13. Pulmonary function tests that demonstrate decreased vital capacity
C. Interventions
  1. Monitor vital signs.
  2. Administer a low concentration of oxygen (1 to 2 L/min) as prescribed; the stimulus to breathe is a low arterial P_{O_2} instead of an increased P_{CO_2}.
  3. Monitor pulse oximetry.
  4. Provide respiratory treatments and CPT.
  5. Instruct the client in diaphragmatic or abdominal techniques and pursed-lip breathing techniques.
  6. Record the color, amount, and consistency of sputum.
  7. Suction fluids from the client's lungs, if necessary, to clear the airway and prevent infection.

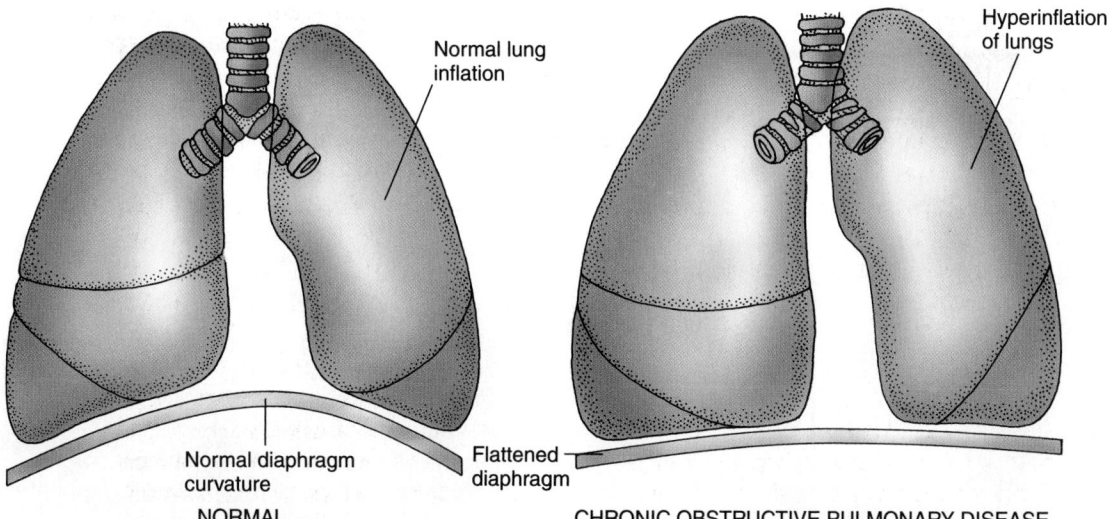

FIG. 57-12 Diaphragm shape and lung inflation in the normal client and in the client with chronic obstructive pulmonary disease. (From Ignatavicius, D., & Workman, M. [2006]. *Medical-surgical nursing: Critical thinking for collaborative care* [5th ed.]. Philadelphia: W.B. Saunders.)

8. Monitor weight.
9. Encourage small frequent meals to maintain nutrition and prevent dyspnea.
10. Provide a high-calorie, high-protein diet with supplements.
11. Encourage fluid intake up to 3000 mL/day to keep secretions thin, unless contraindicated.
12. Place the client in a high Fowler's position and leaning forward to aid in breathing (Fig. 57-13).
13. Allow activity as tolerated.
14. Administer bronchodilators as prescribed, and instruct the client in the use of oral and inhalant medications.
15. Administer corticosteroids, if indicated, as prescribed.
16. Administer mucolytics as prescribed to thin secretions.
17. Administer antibiotics for infection if prescribed.
D. Client education (Box 57-18)

XI. SEVERE ACUTE RESPIRATORY SYNDROME (SARS)
A. Respiratory illness caused by the coronavirus, called SARS-associated coronavirus
B. The syndrome begins with a fever, an overall feeling of discomfort, body aches, and mild respiratory symptoms.
C. After 2 to 7 days, the client may develop a dry cough and dyspnea.
D. Infection is spread by close person-to-person contact by direct contact with infectious material (respiratory secretions or contact with persons or objects infected with infectious droplets)

E. Prevention includes avoiding contact with those suspected of having SARS, avoiding travel to countries where an outbreak of SARS exists, avoiding close contact with crowds in areas where SARS exists, and frequent hand washing if in an area where SARS exists.

XII. PNEUMONIA
A. Description
1. Infection of the pulmonary tissue, including the interstitial spaces, the alveoli, and the bronchioles.
2. The edema associated with inflammation stiffens the lung, decreases lung compliance and vital capacity, and causes hypoxemia.
3. Pneumonia can be community-acquired or hospital-acquired.
4. The chest x-ray film shows lobar or segmental consolidation, pulmonary infiltrates, or pleural effusions.
5. A sputum culture identifies the organism.
6. The white blood cell count and the erythrocyte sedimentation rate are elevated.
B. Assessment
1. Chills
2. Elevated temperature
3. Pleuritic pain
4. Tachypnea
5. Rhonchi and wheezes
6. Use of accessory muscles for breathing
7. Mental status changes
8. Sputum production
C. Interventions
1. Administer oxygen as prescribed.
2. Monitor respiratory status.

Sitting on the edge of a bed with the arms folded and placed on two or three pillows positioned over a nightstand.

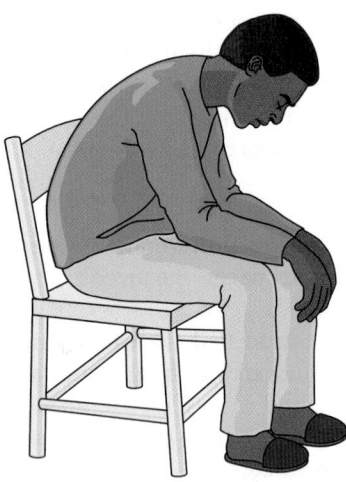

Sitting in a chair with the feet spread shoulder-width apart and leaning forward with the elbows on the knees. Arms and hands are relaxed.

FIG. 57-13 Orthopnea positions that clients with chronic obstructive pulmonary disease can assume to ease the work of breathing. (From Ignatavicius, D., & Workman, M. [2006]. *Medical-surgical nursing: Critical thinking for collaborative care* [5th ed.]. Philadelphia: W.B. Saunders.)

3. Monitor for labored respirations, cyanosis, and cold and clammy skin.
4. Encourage coughing and deep breathing and use of the incentive spirometer.
5. Place the client in a semi-Fowler's position to facilitate breathing and lung expansion.
6. Change the client's position frequently and ambulate as tolerated to mobilize secretions.
7. Provide CPT.

BOX 57-18

Client Education: Chronic Obstructive Pulmonary Disease

Adhere to activity limitations, alternating rest periods with activity.
Avoid eating gas-producing foods, spicy foods, and extremely hot or cold foods.
Avoid exposure to individuals with infections and avoid crowds.
Avoid extremes in temperature.
Avoid fireplaces, pets, feather pillows, and other environmental allergens.
Avoid powerful odors.
Meet nutritional requirements.
Receive immunizations as recommended.
Recognize the signs and symptoms of respiratory infection and hypoxia.
Stop smoking.
Use medications and inhalers as prescribed.
Use oxygen therapy as prescribed.
Use pursed-lip and diaphragmatic or abdominal breathing.
When dusting, use a wet cloth.

8. Perform nasotracheal **suctioning** if the client is unable to clear secretions.
9. Monitor pulse oximetry.
10. Monitor and record color, consistency, and amount of sputum.
11. Provide a high-calorie, high-protein diet with small frequent meals.
12. Encourage fluids, up to 3 L/day, to thin secretions unless contraindicated.
13. Provide a balance of rest and activity, increasing activity gradually.
14. Administer antibiotics as prescribed.
15. Administer antipyretics, bronchodilators, cough suppressants, mucolytic agents, and expectorants as prescribed.
16. Prevent the spread of infection by hand washing and the proper disposal of secretions.

D. Client education
1. Instruct the client about the importance of rest, proper nutrition, and adequate fluid intake.
2. Avoid chilling and exposure to individuals with respiratory infections or viruses.
3. Instruct the client regarding medications and the use of inhalants as prescribed.
4. Instruct the client to notify the physician if chills, fever, dyspnea, hemoptysis, or increased fatigue occurs.
5. Instruct the client in the importance of receiving immunizations as recommended.

XIII. INFLUENZA

A. Description
1. Also known as the flu; highly contagious acute viral respiratory infection

2. May be caused by several viruses, usually known as types A, B, and C

3. Yearly vaccination is recommended to prevent the disease, especially for those older than 50 years of age, individuals with chronic illness or who are immunocompromised, those living in institutions, and health care personnel providing direct care to clients (the vaccination is contraindicated in the individual with egg allergies).

4. Additional prevention measures include avoiding those who developed influenza, frequent and proper hand washing, and cleaning and disinfecting surfaces that have become contaminated with secretions.

5. Avian influenza A (H5N1)
   a. Affects birds; does not usually affect humans; however, human cases have been reported in some countries.
   b. An H5N1 vaccine has been developed for use if a pandemic virus were to emerge.
   c. Reported symptoms are similar to those associated with influenza types A, B, and C.
   d. Prevention measures include thorough cooking of poultry products, avoiding contact with wild animals, frequent and proper hand washing and cleaning and disinfecting surfaces that have become contaminated with secretions.

B. Assessment
   1. Acute onset of fever and muscle aches
   2. Headache
   3. Fatigue, weakness, anorexia
   4. Sore throat, cough, and rhinorrhea

C. Interventions
   1. Encourage rest.
   2. Encourage fluids to prevent pulmonary complications (unless contraindicated).
   3. Monitor lung sounds.
   4. Provide supportive therapy such as antipyretics or antitussives as indicated.
   5. Administer antiviral medications as prescribed for current strain of influenza (see Chap. 58).

XIV. LEGIONNAIRE'S DISEASE

A. Description
   1. Acute bacterial infection caused by *Legionella pneumophila*
   2. Sources of the organism include contaminated cooling tower water and warm stagnant water supplies, including water vaporizers, water sonicators, whirlpool spas, and showers.
   3. Person-to-person contact does not occur; the risk for infection is increased by the presence of other conditions.

B. Assessment: Influenza-like symptoms with a high fever, chills, muscle aches, and headache that may progress to dry cough, pleurisy, and sometimes diarrhea.

C. Interventions: Treatment is supportive and antibiotics may be prescribed.

XV. PLEURAL EFFUSION

A. Description
   1. Pleural effusion is the collection of fluid in the pleural space.
   2. Any condition that interferes with secretion or drainage of this fluid will lead to pleural effusion.

B. Assessment
   1. Pleuritic pain that is sharp and increases with inspiration
   2. Progressive dyspnea with decreased movement of the chest wall on the affected side
   3. Dry, nonproductive cough caused by bronchial irritation or mediastinal shift
   4. Tachycardia
   5. Elevated temperature
   6. Decreased breath sounds over affected area
   7. Chest x-ray film that shows pleural effusion and a mediastinal shift away from the fluid if the effusion is more than 250 mL

C. Interventions
   1. Identify and treat the underlying cause.
   2. Monitor breath sounds.
   3. Place the client in a high Fowler's position.
   4. Encourage coughing and deep breathing.
   5. Prepare the client for thoracentesis.
   6. If pleural effusion is recurrent, prepare the client for pleurectomy or pleurodesis as prescribed.

D. Pleurectomy
   1. Consists of surgically stripping the parietal pleura away from the visceral pleura
   2. This produces an intense inflammatory reaction that promotes adhesion formation between the two layers during healing.

E. Pleurodesis
   1. Involves the instillation of a sclerosing substance into the pleural space via a thoracotomy tube
   2. The substance creates an inflammatory response that scleroses tissues together.

XVI. EMPYEMA

A. Description
   1. Collection of pus within the pleural cavity
   2. The fluid is thick, opaque, and foul-smelling.
   3. The most common cause is pulmonary infection and lung abscess caused by thoracic surgery or chest trauma, in which bacteria are introduced directly into the pleural space.
   4. Treatment focuses on treating the infection, emptying the empyema cavity, reexpanding the lung, and controlling the infection.

B. Assessment
   1. Recent febrile illness or trauma
   2. Chest pain
   3. Cough
   4. Dyspnea

5. Anorexia and weight loss
6. Malaise
7. Elevated temperature and chills
8. Night sweats
9. Pleural exudate on chest x-ray
C. Interventions
1. Monitor breath sounds.
2. Place the client in a semi-Fowler's or high Fowler's position.
3. Encourage coughing and deep breathing.
4. Administer antibiotics as prescribed.
5. Instruct the client to splint the chest as necessary.
6. Assist with thoracentesis or chest tube insertion to promote drainage and lung expansion.
7. If marked pleural thickening occurs, prepare the client for decortication, if prescribed; this surgical procedure involves removal of the restrictive mass of fibrin and inflammatory cells.

XVII. PLEURISY

A. Description
1. Inflammation of the visceral and parietal membranes; may be caused by pulmonary infarction or pneumonia
2. The visceral and parietal membranes rub together during respiration and cause pain.
3. Pleurisy usually occurs on one side of the chest, usually in the lower lateral portions in the chest wall.
B. Assessment
1. Knife-like pain aggravated on deep breathing and coughing
2. Dyspnea
3. Pleural friction rub heard on auscultation
4. Apprehension
C. Interventions
1. Identify and treat the cause.
2. Monitor lung sounds.
3. Administer analgesics as prescribed.
4. Apply hot or cold applications as prescribed.
5. Encourage coughing and deep breathing.
6. Instruct the client to lie on the affected side to splint chest.

XVIII. PULMONARY EMBOLISM

A. Description
1. Occurs when a thrombus forms (most commonly in a deep vein) detaches, travels to the right side of the heart, and then lodges in a branch of the pulmonary artery
2. Clients prone to pulmonary embolism are those at risk for deep vein thrombosis, including those with prolonged immobilization, surgery, obesity, pregnancy, congestive heart failure, advanced age, or a history of thromboembolism.

BOX 57-19

Assessment Findings: Pulmonary Embolism

Blood-tinged sputum
Chest pain
Cough
Cyanosis
Distended neck veins
Dyspnea accompanied by anginal and pleuritic pain, exacerbated by inspiration
Hypotension
Shallow respirations
Tachypnea and tachycardia
Wheezes on auscultation

---

3. Fat emboli can occur as a complication following fracture of a long bone and can cause pulmonary emboli.
4. Treatment is aimed at prevention through risk factor recognition and elimination.
B. Assessment (Box 57-19)
C. Interventions
1. Administer oxygen as prescribed.
2. Place the client in a high Fowler's position.
3. Monitor lung sounds.
4. Maintain bed rest and active and passive range-of-motion exercises as prescribed.
5. Encourage the use of incentive spirometry as prescribed.
6. Monitor pulse oximetry.
7. Prepare for intubation and **mechanical ventilation** for severe hypoxemia.
8. Administer anticoagulation therapy (heparin) intravenously as prescribed
9. Administer warfarin (Coumadin) orally, as prescribed, when heparin infusion is discontinued.
10. Monitor prothrombin time, international normalized ratio (INR), and partial thromboplastin time closely.
11. Prepare the client for embolectomy, vein ligation, or insertion of an umbrella filter, as prescribed.

XIX. LUNG CANCER AND LARYNGEAL CANCER (see Chap. 51)

XX. CARBON MONOXIDE POISONING (Refer to Chap. 49 for information on carbon monoxide poisoning.)

XXI. HISTOPLASMOSIS

A. Description
1. Pulmonary fungal infection caused by spores of *Histoplasma capsulatum*

2. Transmission occurs by the inhalation of spores, which commonly are found in contaminated soil.
3. Spores also are usually found in bird droppings.
B. Assessment
1. Similar to pneumonia
2. Positive skin test for histoplasmosis
3. Positive agglutination test
4. Splenomegaly, hepatomegaly
C. Interventions
1. Administer oxygen as prescribed.
2. Monitor breath sounds.
3. Administer antiemetics, antihistamines, antipyretics, and corticosteroids as prescribed.
4. Administer fungicidal medications as prescribed.
5. Encourage coughing and deep breathing.
6. Place the client in a semi-Fowler's position.
7. Monitor vital signs.
8. Monitor for nephrotoxicity from fungicidal medications.
9. Instruct the client to spray the floor with water before sweeping barn and chicken coops.

XXII. SARCOIDOSIS

A. Description
1. Presence of epithelioid cell tubercles in the lung
2. The cause is unknown, but a high titer of Epstein-Barr virus may be noted.
3. Viral incidence is highest in Blacks and young adults.
B. Assessment
1. Night sweats
2. Fever
3. Weight loss
4. Cough
5. Skin nodules
6. Polyarthritis
7. Kveim test: Sarcoid node antigen is injected intradermally and causes a local nodular lesion in about 1 month.
C. Interventions
1. Administer corticosteroids to control symptoms.
2. Monitor temperature.
3. Increase fluid intake.
4. Provide frequent periods of rest.
5. Encourage small, nutritious meals.

XXIII. OCCUPATIONAL LUNG DISEASE

A. Description
1. Caused by exposure to environmental or occupational fumes, dust, vapors, gases, bacterial or fungal antigens, and allergens; can result in acute reversible effects or chronic lung disease
2. Common disease classifications include occupational **asthmas,** pneumoconiosis (silicosis or coal miner's [black lung] disease), diffuse interstitial fibrosis (asbestosis, talcosis, berylliosis), or extrinsic allergic alveolitis (farmer's lung, bird fancier's lung, or machine operator's lung)
B. Assessment: Manifestations depend on the type of disease and respiratory symptoms.
C. Interventions
1. Prevention through the use of respiratory protective devices
2. Treatment is based on the symptoms experienced by the client.

XXIV. TUBERCULOSIS

A. Description
1. Highly communicable disease caused by *Mycobacterium tuberculosis*
2. *M. tuberculosis* is a nonmotile, nonsporulating, acid-fast rod that secrets niacin; when the bacillus reaches a susceptible site, it multiplies freely.
3. Because *M. tuberculosis* is an aerobic bacterium, it primarily affects the pulmonary system, especially the upper lobes, where the oxygen content is highest, but also can affect other areas of the body, such as the brain, intestines, peritoneum, kidney, joints, and liver.
4. An exudative response causes a nonspecific pneumonitis and the development of granulomas in the lung tissue.
5. **Tuberculosis** has an insidious onset, and many clients are not aware of symptoms until the disease is well advanced.
6. Improper or noncompliant use of treatment programs may cause the development of mutations in the tubercle bacilli, resulting in a **multidrug-resistant strain of tuberculosis (MDR-TB).**
7. The goal of treatment is to prevent transmission, control symptoms, and prevent progression of the disease.
B. Risk factors (Box 57-20)
C. Transmission
1. Transmission of **tuberculosis** is via the airborne route by droplet infection.
2. When an infected individual coughs, laughs, sneezes, or sings, droplet nuclei containing **tuberculosis** bacteria enter the air and may be inhaled by others.
3. Identification of those in close contact with the infected individual is important so that they can be tested and treated as necessary.
4. When contacts have been identified, these persons are assessed with a tuberculin skin test and chest x-rays to determine infection with **tuberculosis.**
5. After the infected individual has received **tuberculosis** medication for 2 to 3 weeks, the risk of transmission is reduced greatly.

BOX 57-20
Risk Factors for Tuberculosis

Child younger than 5 years of age
Drinking unpasteurized milk if the cow is infected with bovine tuberculosis
Homeless individuals or those from a lower socioeconomic group, minority group, or refugee group
Individuals in constant, frequent contact with an untreated or undiagnosed individual
Individuals living in crowded areas, such as long-term care facilities, prisons, and mental health facilities
Older client
Individuals with malnutrition, infection, immune dysfunction or human immunodeficiency virus infection, or immunosuppressed as a result of medication therapy
Individual who abuses alcohol or is an intravenous drug user

D. Disease progression
　1. Droplets enter the lungs, and the bacteria form a tubercle lesion.
　2. The defense systems of the body encapsulate the tubercle, leaving a scar.
　3. If encapsulation does not occur, bacteria may enter the lymph system, travel to the lymph nodes, and cause an inflammatory response termed *granulomatous inflammation*.
　4. Primary lesions form; the primary lesions may become dormant but can be reactivated and become a secondary infection when reexposed to the bacterium.
　5. In an active phase, **tuberculosis** can cause necrosis and cavitation in the lesions, leading to rupture, the spread of necrotic tissue, and damage to various parts of the body.
E. Client history
　1. Past exposure to **tuberculosis**
　2. Client's country of origin and travel to foreign countries in which the incidence of **tuberculosis** is high
　3. Recent history of influenza, pneumonia, febrile illness, cough, or foul-smelling sputum production
　4. Previous tests for **tuberculosis**; results of the testing
　5. Recent **bacille Calmette-Guérin vaccine** (a vaccine containing attenuated tubercle bacilli that may be given to persons in foreign countries or to persons traveling to foreign countries to produce increased resistance to **tuberculosis**)
　6. An individual who has received a **bacille Calmette-Guérin vaccine** will have a positive skin test result and should be evaluated for **tuberculosis** with a chest x-ray.

F. Clinical manifestations
　1. May be asymptomatic in primary infection
　2. Fatigue
　3. Lethargy
　4. Anorexia
　5. Weight loss
　6. Low-grade fever
　7. Chills
　8. Night sweats
　9. Persistent cough and the production of mucoid and mucopurulent sputum, which is occasionally streaked with blood
　10. Chest tightness and a dull, aching chest pain may accompany the cough.
G. Chest assessment
　1. A physical examination of the chest does not provide conclusive evidence of **tuberculosis**.
　2. A chest x-ray is not definitive, but the presence of multinodular infiltrates with calcification in the upper lobes suggests **tuberculosis**.
　3. If the disease is active, caseation and inflammation may be seen on the chest x-ray.
　4. Advanced disease
　　a. Dullness with percussion over involved parenchymal areas, bronchial breath sounds, rhonchi, and crackles indicate advanced disease.
　　b. Partial obstruction of a bronchus caused by endobronchial disease or compression by lymph nodes may produce localized wheezing and dyspnea.
H. Sputum cultures
　1. Sputum specimens are obtained for an acid-fast smear.
　2. A sputum culture identifying *M. tuberculosis* confirms the diagnosis.
　3. After medications are started, sputum samples are obtained again to determine the effectiveness of therapy.
　4. Most clients have negative cultures after 3 months of treatment.
I. **Mantoux skin test**
　1. A positive Mantoux reaction does not mean that active disease is present but indicates previous exposure to **tuberculosis** or the presence of inactive (dormant) disease.
　2. Once the test result is positive, it will be positive in any future tests.
　3. Purified protein derivative containing 5 tuberculin units is administered intradermally in the forearm.
　4. An area of induration measuring 10 mm or more in diameter, 48 to 72 hours after injection, indicates that the individual has been exposed to **tuberculosis**.

BOX 57-21

Client Education: Tuberculosis

Provide the client and family with information about tuberculosis and allay concerns about the contagious aspect of the infection.

Instruct the client to follow the medication regimen exactly as prescribed and always to have a supply of the medication on hand.

Advise the client of the side effects of the medication and ways of minimizing them to ensure compliance.

Reassure the client that after 2 to 3 weeks of medication therapy, it is unlikely that the client will infect anyone.

Inform the client to resume activities gradually.

Instruct the client about the need for adequate nutrition and a well-balanced diet to promote healing and to prevent recurrence of the infection.

Instruct the client to increase intake of foods rich in iron, protein, and vitamin C.

Inform the client and family that respiratory isolation is not necessary because family members already have been exposed.

Instruct the client to cover the mouth and nose when coughing or sneezing and to put used tissues into plastic bags.

Instruct the client and family about thorough hand washing.

Inform the client that a sputum culture is needed every 2 to 4 weeks once medication therapy is initiated.

Inform the client that when the results of three sputum cultures are negative, the client is no longer considered infectious and usually can return to former employment.

Advise the client to avoid excessive exposure to silicone or dust because these substances can cause further lung damage.

Instruct the client regarding the importance of compliance with treatment, follow-up care, and sputum cultures, as prescribed.

---

5. For individuals with human immunodeficiency virus infection or who are immunosuppressed, a reaction of 5 mm or more is considered positive.

6. Once an individual's skin test is positive, a chest x-ray is necessary to rule out active **tuberculosis** or to detect old healed lesions.

J. The hospitalized client

1. The client with active **tuberculosis** is placed in respiratory isolation precautions in a negative-pressure room; to maintain negative pressure, the door of the room must be tightly closed.

2. The room should have at least six exchanges of fresh air per hour and should be ventilated to the outside environment, if possible.

3. The nurse wears a particulate respirator (a special individually fitted mask) when caring for the client and a gown when the possibility of clothing contamination exists.

4. Always thoroughly wash hands before and after caring for the client.

5. If the client needs to leave the room for a test or procedure, the client is required to wear a mask.

6. Respiratory isolation is discontinued when the client is no longer considered infectious.

7. After the infected individual has received **tuberculosis** medication for 2 to 3 weeks, the risk of transmission is reduced greatly.

K. Client education (Box 57-21)

L. Medications (see Chap. 58)

PRACTICE QUESTIONS

1. An emergency room nurse is assessing a client who has sustained a blunt injury to the chest wall. Which of these signs would indicate the presence of a pneumothorax in this client?
   1. A low respiratory rate
   2. Diminished breath sounds
   3. The presence of a barrel chest
   4. A sucking sound at the site of injury

2. A nurse is caring for a client hospitalized with acute exacerbation of chronic obstructive pulmonary disease. Which of the following would the nurse expect to note on assessment of this client?
   1. Hypocapnia
   2. A hyperinflated chest noted on the chest x-ray
   3. Increased oxygen saturation with exercise
   4. A widened diaphragm noted on the chest x-ray

3. An oxygen delivery system is prescribed for a client with chronic obstructive pulmonary disease to deliver a precise oxygen concentration. Which of the following types of oxygen delivery systems would the nurse anticipate to be prescribed?
   1. Face tent
   2. Venturi mask
   3. Aerosol mask
   4. Tracheostomy collar

4. A nurse is instructing a hospitalized client with a diagnosis of emphysema about measures that will enhance the effectiveness of breathing during dyspneic periods. Which of the following posi-

tions will the nurse instruct the client to assume?
1. Sitting up in bed
2. Side-lying in bed
3. Sitting in a recliner chair
4. Sitting on the side of the bed and leaning on an overbed table

5. A community health nurse is conducting an educational session with community members regarding tuberculosis. The nurse tells the group that one of the first symptoms associated with tuberculosis is:
1. Dyspnea
2. Chest pain
3. A bloody, productive cough
4. A cough with the expectoration of mucoid sputum

6. A nurse performs an admission assessment on a client with a diagnosis of tuberculosis. The nurse reviews the results of which diagnostic test that will confirm this diagnosis?
1. Bronchoscopy
2. Sputum culture
3. Chest x-ray
4. Tuberculin skin test

7. A nursing instructor asks a nursing student to describe the route of transmission of tuberculosis. The instructor concludes that the student understands this information if the student states that tuberculosis is transmitted by:
1. Hand to mouth
2. The airborne route
3. The fecal-oral route
4. Blood and body fluids

8. A nurse is caring for a client with emphysema who is receiving oxygen. The nurse assesses the oxygen flow rate to ensure that it does not exceed:
1. 1 L/min
2. 2 L/min
3. 6 L/min
4. 10 L/min

9. A nurse instructs a client to use the pursed-lip method of breathing and the client asks the nurse about the purpose of this type of breathing. The nurse responds, knowing that the primary purpose of pursed-lip breathing is to:
1. Promote oxygen intake.
2. Strengthen the diaphragm.
3. Strengthen the intercostal muscles.
4. Promote carbon dioxide elimination.

10. The low-pressure alarm sounds on a ventilator. A nurse assesses the client and then attempts to determine the cause of the alarm. The nurse is unsuccessful in determining the cause of the alarm and takes what initial action?
1. Administers oxygen
2. Checks the client's vital signs
3. Ventilates the client manually
4. Starts cardiopulmonary resuscitation

11. A nurse reviews the arterial blood gas values and notes a pH of 7.50, a P_{CO_2} of 30 mm Hg, and an HCO_3 of 25 mEq/L. The nurse interprets these values as indicating:
1. Metabolic acidosis, uncompensated
2. Respiratory acidosis, uncompensated
3. Respiratory alkalosis, uncompensated
4. Metabolic acidosis, partially compensated

12. A nurse is caring for a client with acute respiratory distress syndrome. Which of the following would the nurse expect to note in the client?
1. Pallor
2. Low arterial Pa_{O_2}
3. Elevated arterial Pa_{O_2}
4. Decreased respiratory rate

13. A nurse is preparing to obtain a sputum specimen from a client. Which of the following nursing actions will facilitate obtaining the specimen?
1. Limiting fluids
2. Having the client take three deep breaths
3. Asking the client to spit into the collection container
4. Asking the client to obtain the specimen after eating

14. A nurse is caring for a client after a bronchoscopy and biopsy. Which of the following signs, if noted in the client, should be reported immediately to the physician?
1. Dry cough
2. Hematuria
3. Bronchospasm
4. Blood-streaked sputum

15. A nurse is suctioning fluids from a client via a tracheostomy tube. When suctioning, the nurse must limit the suctioning time to a maximum of:
1. 1 minute
2. 5 seconds
3. 10 seconds
4. 30 seconds

16. A nurse is suctioning fluids from a client through an endotracheal tube. During the suctioning procedure, the nurse notes on the monitor that the heart rate is decreasing. Which of the following is the appropriate nursing intervention?
1. Continue to suction.
2. Notify the physician immediately.
3. Stop the procedure and reoxygenate the client.
4. Ensure that the suction is limited to 15 seconds.

17. A client is suspected of having a pulmonary embolus. A nurse assesses the client, knowing that which of the following is a common clinical manifestation of pulmonary embolism?
1. Dyspnea
2. Bradypnea
3. Bradycardia
4. Decreased respirations

18. A female client is scheduled to have a chest radiograph. Which of the following questions is of most

importance to the nurse assessing this client?
1. "Can you hold your breath easily?"
2. "Are you wearing any metal chains or jewelry?"
3. "Are you able to hold your arms above your head?"
4. "Is there any possibility that you could be pregnant?"

19. A client has just returned to a nursing unit following bronchoscopy. A nurse would implement which of the following nursing interventions for this client?
1. Administering atropine intravenously
2. Administering small doses of midazolam (Versed)
3. Encouraging additional fluids for the next 24 hours
4. Ensuring the return of the gag reflex before offering food or fluids

20. A nurse is assessing the respiratory status of a client who has suffered a fractured rib. The nurse would expect to note which of the following?
1. Slow deep respirations
2. Rapid deep respirations
3. Paradoxical respirations
4. Pain, especially with inspiration

21. A client with chest injury has suffered flail chest. A nurse assesses the client for which most distinctive sign of flail chest?
1. Cyanosis
2. Hypotension
3. Paradoxical chest movement
4. Dyspnea, especially on exhalation

22. A client has been admitted with chest trauma after a motor vehicle accident and has undergone subsequent intubation. A nurse checks the client when the high-pressure alarm on the ventilator sounds, and notes that the client has absence of breath sounds in the right upper lobe of the lung. The nurse immediately assesses for other signs of:
1. Right pneumothorax
2. Pulmonary embolism
3. Displaced endotracheal tube
4. Acute respiratory distress syndrome

23. A client with no history of respiratory disease is admitted with respiratory failure. A nurse assesses the arterial blood gas report for which of the following results that are consistent with this disorder?
1. Pao_2 58 mm Hg, $Paco_2$ 32 mm Hg
2. Pao_2 60 mm Hg, $Paco_2$ 45 mm Hg
3. Pao_2 49 mm Hg, $Paco_2$ 52 mm Hg
4. Pao_2 73 mm Hg, $Paco_2$ 62 mm Hg

24. A nurse is assessing a client with multiple trauma who is at risk for developing acute respiratory distress syndrome. The nurse assesses for which earliest sign of acute respiratory distress syndrome?
1. Bilateral wheezing
2. Inspiratory crackles
3. Intercostal retractions
4. Increased respiratory rate

25. A nurse is assessing a client with chronic airflow limitation and notes that the client has a "barrel chest." The nurse interprets that this client has which of the following forms of chronic airflow limitation?
1. Emphysema
2. Bronchial asthma
3. Chronic obstructive bronchitis
4. Bronchial asthma and bronchitis

26. A nurse is caring for a client diagnosed with tuberculosis. Which assessment, if made by the nurse, is inconsistent with the usual clinical presentation of tuberculosis and may indicate the development of a concurrent problem?
1. Cough
2. High-grade fever
3. Chills and night sweats
4. Anorexia and weight loss

27. A nurse is teaching a client with tuberculosis about dietary elements that should be increased in the diet. The nurse suggests that the client increase intake of:
1. Potatoes and fish
2. Eggs and spinach
3. Grains and broccoli
4. Meats and citrus fruits

28. A nurse has conducted discharge teaching with a client diagnosed with tuberculosis. The client has been taking medication for $1\frac{1}{2}$ weeks. The nurse evaluates that the client has understood the information if the client makes which of the following statements?
1. "I need to continue drug therapy for 2 months."
2. "I can't shop at the mall for the next 6 months."
3. "I can return to work if a sputum culture comes back negative."
4. "I should not be contagious after 2 to 3 weeks of medication therapy."

29. A nurse is preparing to give a bed bath to an immobilized client with tuberculosis. The nurse should wear which of the following items when performing this care?
1. Surgical mask and gloves
2. Particulate respirator, gown, and gloves
3. Particulate respirator and protective eyewear
4. Surgical mask, gown, and protective eyewear

30. A client has experienced pulmonary embolism. A nurse assesses for which symptom, which is most commonly reported?
1. Hot, flushed feeling
2. Sudden chills and fever
3. Chest pain that occurs suddenly
4. Dyspnea when deep breaths are taken

31. A client who is human immunodeficiency virus–positive has had a Mantoux skin test. The nurse

notes a 7-mm area of induration at the site of the skin test. The nurse interprets the results as:
1. Positive
2. Negative
3. Inconclusive
4. Indicating the need for repeat testing

32. A client with uncomplicated or simple silicosis is being monitored yearly at the health care clinic. In this type of silicosis, the nurse expects that the client would:
   1. Be asymptomatic
   2. Complain of severe dyspnea
   3. Experience malaise and fatigue
   4. Experience anorexia and weight loss

33. A client with acquired immunodeficiency syndrome has histoplasmosis. A nurse assesses the client for which of the following signs and symptoms?
   1. Dyspnea
   2. Headache
   3. Weight gain
   4. Hypothermia

34. A nurse is giving discharge instructions to a client with pulmonary sarcoidosis. The nurse concludes that the client understands the information if the client reports which of the following early signs of exacerbation?
   1. Fever
   2. Fatigue
   3. Weight loss
   4. Shortness of breath

35. A nurse is taking the history of a client with silicosis. The nurse assesses whether the client wears which of the following items during periods of exposure to silica particles?
   1. Mask
   2. Gown
   3. Gloves
   4. Eye protection

36. A client tells a nurse that a physician has stated a diagnosis of uncomplicated or simple silicosis and asks the nurse exactly what this means. In formulating a response, the nurse incorporates the knowledge that:
   1. There is evidence of silica in the bloodstream but no clinical symptoms.
   2. The client has normal pulmonary function studies but has shortness of breath.
   3. The client has mild ventilation restriction and has fibrosis on chest x-ray.
   4. Massive pulmonary fibrosis is visible on chest x-ray, but no extrapulmonary symptoms are apparent.

37. A client has been taking pyrazinamide for 1 month. The client asks a nurse if the therapy is due to be terminated soon. The nurse evaluates that the medication probably will be continued based on a positive finding in which of the following reports?

1. Blood culture
2. Urine culture
3. Sputum culture
4. Wound culture

38. A nurse working on a medical respiratory nursing unit is caring for several clients with respiratory disorders. The nurse would determine that which of the following clients on the nursing unit is at the lowest risk for infection with tuberculosis?
   1. An uninsured man who is homeless
   2. A newly immigrated woman from Korea
   3. A man who is an inspector for the U.S. Postal Service
   4. An older woman admitted from a long-term care facility

39. A client has an order to receive purified protein derivative, 0.1 mL, intradermally. A nurse administers the medication by using a tuberculin syringe with a:
   1. 20-gauge, 1-inch needle inserted at a 30-degree angle, with the bevel side down
   2. 26-gauge, $\frac{5}{8}$-inch needle inserted at a 45-degree angle, with the bevel side down
   3. 20-gauge, 1-inch needle inserted almost parallel to the skin, with the bevel side up
   4. 26-gauge, $\frac{5}{8}$-inch needle inserted almost parallel to the skin, with the bevel side up

40. A nurse is reading a Mantoux skin test for a client with no documented health problems. The site has no induration and a 1-mm area of ecchymosis. The nurse interprets that the result is:
   1. Positive
   2. Negative
   3. Uncertain
   4. Borderline

ALTERNATE ITEM FORMAT: MULTIPLE RESPONSE

The nurse is preparing a list of home care instructions for the client who has been hospitalized and treated for tuberculosis. Of the following instructions, which will the nurse include on the list? Select all that apply.

❏ 1. Activities should be resumed gradually.
❏ 2. Avoid contact with other individuals, except family members, for at least 6 months.
❏ 3. A sputum culture is needed every 2 to 4 weeks once medication therapy is initiated.
❏ 4. Respiratory isolation is not necessary because family members already have been exposed.
❏ 5. Cover the mouth and nose when coughing or sneezing and put used tissues in plastic bags.
❏ 6. When one sputum culture is negative, the client is no longer considered infectious and usually can return to former employment.

ANSWERS

1. 2

Rationale: This client has sustained a blunt or a closed chest injury. Basic symptoms of a closed pneumothorax are shortness of breath and chest pain. A larger pneumothorax may cause tachypnea, cyanosis, diminished breath sounds, and subcutaneous emphysema. Hyperresonance also may occur on the affected side. A sucking sound at the site of injury would be noted with a open chest injury.

Test-Taking Strategy: Use the process of elimination and note the strategic word *blunt* in the question. This will assist in eliminating option 4, sucking chest wound injury. Knowing that in a respiratory injury increased respirations will occur will assist you in eliminating option 1. Option 3 can be eliminated because a barrel chest is a characteristic finding in a client with chronic obstructive pulmonary disease. Review the signs of pneumothorax if you had difficulty with this question.

Level of Cognitive Ability: Analysis
Client Needs: Physiological Integrity
Integrated Process: Nursing Process—assessment
Content Area: Adult health—respiratory
Reference: Ignatavicius, D., & Workman, M. (2006). *Medical-surgical nursing: Critical thinking for collaborative care* (5th ed., pp. 670-671). Philadelphia: W.B. Saunders.

2. 2

Rationale: Clinical manifestations of chronic obstructive pulmonary disease (COPD) include hypoxemia, hypercapnia, dyspnea on exertion and at rest, oxygen desaturation with exercise, and the use of accessory muscles of respiration. Chest x-rays reveal a hyperinflated chest and a flattened diaphragm if the disease is advanced.

Test-Taking Strategy: Use the process of elimination. Eliminate option 1 because in the client with COPD, hypercapnia would be noted. Next, eliminate option 3 because oxygen desaturation rather than saturation would occur. From the remaining options, reading carefully will assist in directing you to option 2. If you are unfamiliar with the manifestations associated with COPD, review this content.

Level of Cognitive Ability: Analysis
Client Needs: Physiological Integrity
Integrated Process: Nursing Process—assessment
Content Area: Adult health—respiratory
Reference: Ignatavicius, D., & Workman, M. (2006). *Medical-surgical nursing: Critical thinking for collaborative care* (5th ed., p. 559). Philadelphia: W.B. Saunders.

3. 2

Rationale: The Venturi mask delivers the most accurate oxygen concentration. It is the best oxygen delivery system for the client with chronic airflow limitation because it delivers a precise oxygen concentration. The face tent, aerosol mask, and tracheostomy collar are also high-flow oxygen delivery systems but most often are used to administer high humidity.

Test-Taking Strategy: Use the process of elimination and note the strategic words *precise oxygen concentration*. Eliminate options 1, 3, and 4 because they are comparative or alike in that they are used to provide high humidity. Review the various types of oxygen delivery systems if you had difficulty with this question.

Level of Cognitive Ability: Analysis
Client Needs: Physiological Integrity
Integrated Process: Nursing Process—analysis
Content Area: Adult health—respiratory
References: Ignatavicius, D., & Workman, M. (2006). *Medical-surgical nursing: Critical thinking for collaborative care* (5th ed., p. 600). Philadelphia: W.B. Saunders.
Perry, A., & Potter, P. (2006). *Clinical nursing skills and techniques* (6th ed., pp. 766-768). St. Louis: Mosby.

4. 4

Rationale: Positions that will assist the client with emphysema with breathing include sitting up and leaning on an overbed table, sitting up and resting the elbows on the knees, and standing and leaning against the wall.

Test-Taking Strategy: Use the process of elimination. Eliminate options 1 and 3 first because they are comparative or alike. Next, eliminate option 2 because this position will not enhance breathing. If you had difficulty with this question, review the positions that will decrease the work of breathing in a client with emphysema.

Level of Cognitive Ability: Application
Client Needs: Physiological Integrity
Integrated Process: Teaching and Learning
Content Area: Adult health—respiratory
References: Ignatavicius, D., & Workman, M. (2006). *Medical-surgical nursing: Critical thinking for collaborative care* (5th ed., p. 597). Philadelphia: W.B. Saunders.
Lewis, S., Heitkemper, M., & Dirksen, S. (2004). *Medical-surgical nursing: Assessment and management of clinical problems* (6th ed., p. 675). St. Louis: Mosby.

5. 4

Rationale: One of the first pulmonary symptoms is a slight cough with the expectoration of mucoid sputum. Options 1, 2, and 3 are late symptoms and signify cavitation and extensive lung involvement.

Test-Taking Strategy: Use the process of elimination and note the strategic word *first* in the question. This should direct you easily to option 4. If you are unfamiliar with the signs associated with tuberculosis, review this content.

Level of Cognitive Ability: Application
Client Needs: Physiological Integrity
Integrated Process: Teaching and Learning
Content Area: Adult health—respiratory
Reference: Ignatavicius, D., & Workman, M. (2006). *Medical-surgical nursing: Critical thinking for collaborative care* (5th ed., p. 641). Philadelphia: W.B. Saunders.

6. 2

Rationale: Tuberculosis is definitively diagnosed through culture and isolation of *Mycobacterium tuberculosis*. A presumptive diagnosis is made based on a tuberculin skin test, a sputum smear that is positive for acid-fast bacteria, a chest x-ray, and histological evidence of granulomatous disease on biopsy.

Test-Taking Strategy: Note the strategic word *confirm* in the question. Confirmation is made by identifying *M. tuberculosis*. If you had difficulty with this question, review the diagnostic procedures related to tuberculosis.

Level of Cognitive Ability: Analysis
Client Needs: Physiological Integrity
Integrated Process: Nursing Process—assessment
Content Area: Adult health—respiratory
Reference: Ignatavicius, D., & Workman, M. (2006). *Medical-surgical nursing: Critical thinking for collaborative care* (5th ed., pp. 641-642) Philadelphia: W.B. Saunders.

7. 2
Rationale: Tuberculosis is an infectious disease caused by the bacillus *Mycobacterium tuberculosis* and is spread primarily by the airborne route. Options 1, 3, and 4 are incorrect.
Test-Taking Strategy: Focus on the disorder. Recalling that tuberculosis is a respiratory disease will direct you easily to option 2. If you had difficulty with this question, review the transmission of this disease.
Level of Cognitive Ability: Analysis
Client Needs: Safe and Effective Care Environment
Integrated Process: Teaching and Learning
Content Area: Adult health—respiratory
Reference: Ignatavicius, D., & Workman, M. (2006). *Medical-surgical nursing: Critical thinking for collaborative care* (5th ed., p. 644). Philadelphia: W.B. Saunders.

8. 2
Rationale: Oxygen is used cautiously and should not exceed 2 L/min. Because of the long-standing hypercapnia that occurs in emphysema, the respiratory drive is triggered by low oxygen levels rather than increased carbon dioxide levels, as is the case in a normal respiratory system.
Test-Taking Strategy: Use the process of elimination, focusing on the client's diagnosis. Recalling that in the client with emphysema, respiratory drive is triggered by low oxygen levels will direct you to option 2. If you are unfamiliar with this important concept, review this content.
Level of Cognitive Ability: Analysis
Client Needs: Physiological Integrity
Integrated Process: Nursing Process—assessment
Content Area: Adult health—respiratory
Reference: Ignatavicius, D., & Workman, M. (2006). *Medical-surgical nursing: Critical thinking for collaborative care* (5th ed., p. 600). Philadelphia: W.B. Saunders.

9. 4
Rationale: Pursed-lip breathing facilitates maximal expiration for clients with obstructive lung disease. This type of breathing allows better expiration by increasing airway pressure that keeps air passages open during exhalation. Options 1, 2, and 3 are not the purposes of this type of breathing.
Test-Taking Strategy: Visualize the use of this procedure to assist you in answering correctly. Knowledge regarding the respiratory conditions in which this type of breathing is helpful also will assist in directing you to option 4. Review the purpose of this breathing technique, if you had difficulty with this question.
Level of Cognitive Ability: Comprehension
Client Needs: Physiological Integrity
Integrated Process: Teaching and Learning
Content Area: Adult health—respiratory
References: Lewis, S., Heitkemper, M., & Dirksen, S. (2004). *Medical-surgical nursing: Assessment and management of clinical problems* (6th ed., pp. 557, 672). St. Louis: Mosby. Potter, P., & Perry, A. (2005). *Fundamentals of nursing* (6th ed., p. 1130). St. Louis: Mosby.

10. 3
Rationale: If at any time an alarm is sounding and the nurse cannot quickly ascertain the problem, the client is disconnected from the ventilator and manual resuscitation is used to support respirations until the problem can be corrected. No reason is given to begin cardiopulmonary resuscitation. Checking vital signs is not the initial action. Although oxygen is helpful, it will not provide ventilation to the client.
Test-Taking Strategy: Use the process of elimination. Read the question carefully, and note that the subject relates to adequate ventilation of the client. Focusing on this subject will direct you easily to option 3. If you are unfamiliar with the management of ventilators and alarms, review this content.
Level of Cognitive Ability: Application
Client Needs: Physiological Integrity
Integrated Process: Nursing Process—implementation
Content Area: Delegating and Prioritizing
Reference: Ignatavicius, D., & Workman, M. (2006). *Medical-surgical nursing: Critical thinking for collaborative care* (5th ed., pp. 666-667). Philadelphia: W.B. Saunders.

11. 3
Rationale: In respiratory alkalosis, the pH will be higher than normal and the Pco_2 will be low. The normal pH is 7.35 to 7.45. The normal Pco_2 is 35 to 45 mm Hg. The only option that reflects these conditions is option 3.
Test-Taking Strategy: Remember that when an alkalotic condition exists, the pH will be high. Next, recall that in a respiratory alkalotic condition, the Pco_2 will move in the opposite direction from the pH. The only option that represents these conditions is option 3. Compensation can be identified if the pH is within normal limits. Review the process of blood gas analysis if you had difficulty with this question.
Level of Cognitive Ability: Analysis
Client Needs: Physiological Integrity
Integrated Process: Nursing Process—analysis
Content Area: Adult health—respiratory
Reference: Ignatavicius, D., & Workman, M. (2006). *Medical-surgical nursing: Critical thinking for collaborative care* (5th ed., p. 290). Philadelphia: W.B. Saunders.

12. 2
Rationale: The earliest clinical sign of acute respiratory distress syndrome is an increased respiratory rate. Breathing becomes labored, and the client may exhibit air hunger, retractions, and cyanosis. Arterial blood gas analysis reveals increasing hypoxemia, with a Pao_2 lower than 60 mm Hg.
Test-Taking Strategy: Use the process of elimination. Note that options 2 and 3 relate to the same subject but present opposite conditions. This may provide you with the clue that one of these options is correct. Considering the diagnosis of the client, the best choice is option 2. Review the clinical manifestations associated with acute respiratory distress syndrome if you had difficulty with this question.
Level of Cognitive Ability: Analysis
Client Needs: Physiological Integrity

Integrated Process: Nursing Process—assessment
Content Area: Adult health—respiratory
Reference: Ignatavicius, D., & Workman, M. (2006). *Medical-surgical nursing: Critical thinking for collaborative care* (5th ed., pp. 655, 2183). Philadelphia: W.B. Saunders.

13. **2**
Rationale: To obtain a sputum specimen, the client should rinse the mouth to reduce contamination, breathe deeply, and then cough into a sputum specimen container. The client should be encouraged to cough and not spit so as to obtain sputum. Sputum can be thinned by fluids or by a respiratory treatment such as inhalation of nebulized saline or water. The optimal time to obtain a specimen is on arising in the morning.
Test-Taking Strategy: Use the process of elimination. Option 1 can be eliminated first because general principles indicate that fluids assist in loosening or thinning secretions. Eliminate option 3 because of the word *spit*. Spit is different from sputum. Next, eliminate option 4 because of the words *after eating*. Review this procedure if you had difficulty with this question.
Level of Cognitive Ability: Application
Client Needs: Physiological Integrity
Integrated Process: Nursing Process—implementation
Content Area: Adult health—respiratory
Reference: Chernecky, C., & Berger, B. (2004). *Laboratory tests and diagnostic procedures* (4th ed., pp. 1018-1019). Philadelphia: W.B. Saunders.

14. **3**
Rationale: If a biopsy was performed during a bronchoscopy, blood-streaked sputum is expected for several hours. Frank blood indicates hemorrhage. A dry cough may be expected. The client should be assessed for signs of complications, which would include cyanosis, dyspnea, stridor, bronchospasm, hemoptysis, hypotension, tachycardia, and dysrhythmias. Hematuria is unrelated to this procedure.
Test-Taking Strategy: Use the process of elimination. Eliminate option 2 first because it is unrelated to the procedure. Next, eliminate option 1 because a dry cough may be expected. Noting that a biopsy has been performed will assist in eliminating option 4, because blood-streaked sputum would be expected. Note that option 3, the correct option, relates to the airway. If you had difficulty with this question, review postprocedure care following bronchoscopy with biopsy.
Level of Cognitive Ability: Analysis
Client Needs: Physiological Integrity
Integrated Process: Nursing Process—implementation
Content Area: Adult health—respiratory
Reference: Chernecky, C., & Berger, B. (2004). *Laboratory tests and diagnostic procedures* (4th ed., p. 297). Philadelphia: W.B. Saunders.

15. **3**
Rationale: Hypoxemia can be caused by prolonged suctioning, which stimulates the pacemaker cells in the heart. A vasovagal response may occur, causing bradycardia. The nurse must preoxygenate the client before suctioning and limit the suctioning pass to 10 seconds.
Test-Taking Strategy: Use the process of elimination. Recall that during suctioning, the client's airway is blocked; there-

fore, you should be able to eliminate options 1 and 4 easily. From the remaining options, eliminate option 2 because of the short time frame. Five seconds does not seem reasonable to achieve removal of secretions. Review the procedure for suctioning if you had difficulty with this question.
Level of Cognitive Ability: Application
Client Needs: Physiological Integrity
Integrated Process: Nursing Process—implementation
Content Area: Adult health—respiratory
References: Ignatavicius, D., & Workman, M. (2006). *Medical-surgical nursing: Critical thinking for collaborative care* (5th ed., p. 557). Philadelphia: W.B. Saunders.
Lewis, S., Heitkemper, M., & Dirksen, S. (2004). *Medical-surgical nursing: Assessment and management of clinical problems* (6th ed., p. 579). St. Louis: Mosby.

16. **3**
Rationale: During suctioning, the nurse should monitor the client closely for side effects, including hypoxemia, cardiac irregularities such as a decrease in heart rate resulting from vagal stimulation, mucosal trauma, hypotension, and paroxysmal coughing. If side effects develop, especially cardiac irregularities, the procedure is stopped and the client is reoxygenated.
Test-Taking Strategy: Use the process of elimination, recalling that suctioning can cause cardiac irregularities. Noting the strategic words *heart rate is decreasing* should direct you to option 3. If you had difficulty with this question, review the complications and interventions associated with suctioning procedures.
Level of Cognitive Ability: Application
Client Needs: Physiological Integrity
Integrated Process: Nursing Process—implementation
Content Area: Adult health—respiratory
References: Black, J., & Hawks, J. (2005). *Medical-surgical nursing: Clinical management for positive outcomes* (7th ed., pp. 1888, 1890). Philadelphia: W.B. Saunders.
Lewis, S., Heitkemper, M., & Dirksen, S. (2004). *Medical-surgical nursing: Assessment and management of clinical problems* (6th ed., p. 1779). St. Louis: Mosby.

17. **1**
Rationale: The common clinical manifestations of pulmonary embolism are tachypnea, tachycardia, dyspnea, and chest pain.
Test-Taking Strategy: Use the process of elimination. Eliminate options 2, 3, and 4 because they are comparative or alike. Review the clinical manifestations of pulmonary embolism if you had difficulty with this question.
Level of Cognitive Ability: Analysis
Client Needs: Physiological Integrity
Integrated Process: Nursing Process—assessment
Content Area: Adult health—respiratory
Reference: Ignatavicius, D., & Workman, M. (2006). *Medical-surgical nursing: Critical thinking for collaborative care* (5th ed., p. 650). Philadelphia: W.B. Saunders.

18. **4**
Rationale: The most important item to ask about is the client's pregnancy status because pregnant women should not be ex-

posed to radiation. Clients also are asked to remove any chains or metal objects that could interfere with obtaining an adequate film. A chest radiograph most often is obtained at full inspiration, which gives optimal lung expansion. If a lateral view of the chest is ordered, the client is asked to raise the arms above the head. Most films are done in a posterior-anterior view.

Test-Taking Strategy: Note the strategic words *most important.* Eliminate options 1 and 3 first, because they can be determined by the radiological technologist. Option 4 is a higher priority than option 2 because of potential negative teratogenic consequences to the fetus. Review client preparation for a chest radiograph if you had difficulty with this question.

Level of Cognitive Ability: Analysis
Client Needs: Physiological Integrity
Integrated Process: Nursing Process—assessment
Content Area: Delegating/Prioritizing
Reference: Chernecky, C., & Berger, B. (2004). *Laboratory tests and diagnostic procedures* (4th ed., p. 360). Philadelphia: W.B. Saunders.

19. **4**
Rationale: After bronchoscopy, the nurse keeps the client on NPO status until the gag reflex returns because the preoperative sedation and local anesthesia impair swallowing and the protective laryngeal reflexes for a number of hours. Additional fluids are unnecessary because no contrast dye is used that would need flushing from the system. Atropine and midazolam would be administered before the procedure, not after.

Test-Taking Strategy: Use the process of elimination. Recall that the client has lost the protective cough, gag, and swallow reflexes during this procedure. Knowledge of this implication helps you choose option 4 as the only possible answer. Review nursing care measures following a bronchoscopy if you had difficulty with this question.

Level of Cognitive Ability: Application
Client Needs: Physiological Integrity
Integrated Process: Nursing Process—implementation
Content Area: Adult health—respiratory
Reference: Chernecky, C., & Berger, B. (2004). *Laboratory tests and diagnostic procedures* (4th ed., p. 297). Philadelphia: W.B. Saunders.

20. **4**
Rationale: Rib fractures are a common injury, especially in the older client, and result from a blunt injury or a fall. Typical signs and symptoms include pain and tenderness localized at the fracture site and exacerbated by inspiration and palpation, shallow respirations, splinting or guarding the chest protectively to minimize chest movement, and possible bruising at the fracture site. Paradoxical respirations are seen with flail chest.

Test-Taking Strategy: Use the process of elimination. Focusing on the anatomical location of the injury will direct you to option 4. Review the assessment findings in rib fractures if you had difficulty with this question.

Level of Cognitive Ability: Analysis
Client Needs: Physiological Integrity
Integrated Process: Nursing Process—assessment
Content Area: Adult health—respiratory

Reference: Black, J., & Hawks, J. (2005). *Medical-surgical nursing: Clinical management for positive outcomes* (7th ed., p. 1901). Philadelphia: W.B. Saunders.

21. **3**
Rationale: Flail chest results from fracture of two or more ribs in at least two places each. This results in a "floating" section of ribs. Because this section is unattached to the rest of the bony rib cage, this segment results in paradoxical chest movement. This means that the force of inspiration pulls the fractured segment inward, while the rest of the chest expands. Similarly, during exhalation, the segment balloons outward while the rest of the chest moves inward. This is a telltale sign of flail chest.

Test-Taking Strategy: Use the process of elimination, focusing on the strategic words *most distinctive.* Cyanosis and hypotension occur with many different disorders, so eliminate options 1 and 2 first. From the remaining options, choose paradoxical chest movement over dyspnea on exhalation by remembering that a flail chest has broken rib segments that move independently of the rest of the rib cage. Review the assessment findings in flail chest if you had difficulty with this question.

Level of Cognitive Ability: Application
Client Needs: Physiological Integrity
Integrated Process: Nursing Process—assessment
Content Area: Adult health—respiratory
References: Black, J., & Hawks, J. (2005). *Medical-surgical nursing: Clinical management for positive outcomes* (7th ed., p. 1901-1902). Philadelphia: W.B. Saunders.
Ignatavicius, D., & Workman, M. (2006). *Medical-surgical nursing: Critical thinking for collaborative care* (5th ed., p. 670). Philadelphia: W.B. Saunders.

22. **1**
Rationale: Pneumothorax is characterized by restlessness, tachycardia, dyspnea, pain with respiration, asymmetrical chest expansion, and diminished or absent breath sounds on the affected side. Pneumothorax can cause increased airway pressure because of resistance to lung inflation. Acute respiratory distress syndrome and pulmonary embolism are not characterized by absent breath sounds. An endotracheal tube that is inserted too far can cause absent breath sounds, but the lack of breath sounds most likely would be on the left side because of the degree of curvature of the right and left main stem bronchi.

Test-Taking Strategy: Use the process of elimination. Focus on the symptoms presented in the question and note the relationship between *right* upper lobe and *right* pneumothorax in option 1. Review the manifestations associated with pneumothorax if you had difficulty with this question.

Level of Cognitive Ability: Analysis
Client Needs: Physiological Integrity
Integrated Process: Nursing Process—assessment
Content Area: Adult health—respiratory
References: Ignatavicius, D., & Workman, M. (2006). *Medical-surgical nursing: Critical thinking for collaborative care* (5th ed., p. 671). Philadelphia: W.B. Saunders.
Lewis, S., Heitkemper, M., & Dirksen, S. (2004). *Medical-surgical nursing: Assessment and management of clinical problems* (6th ed., pp. 621-622). St. Louis: Mosby.

23. 3

Rationale: Respiratory failure is described as a PaO_2 of 60 mm Hg or lower and a $PaCO_2$ of 50 mm Hg or higher in a client with no history of respiratory disease. In a client with a history of a respiratory disorder with hypercapnia, increases of 5 mm Hg or more ($PaCO_2$) from the client's baseline are considered diagnostic.

Test-Taking Strategy: Use the process of elimination. Focusing on the client's diagnosis will direct you to option 3, the option with the lowest PaO_2 level. Review the blood gas findings in a client with respiratory failure if you had difficulty with this question.

Level of Cognitive Ability: Analysis
Client Needs: Physiological Integrity
Integrated Process: Nursing Process—analysis
Content Area: Adult health—respiratory
Reference: Ignatavicius, D., & Workman, M. (2006). *Medical-surgical nursing: Critical thinking for collaborative care* (5th ed., pp. 652-657). Philadelphia: W.B. Saunders.

24. 4

Rationale: The earliest detectable sign of acute respiratory distress syndrome is an increased respiratory rate, which can begin from 1 to 96 hours after the initial insult to the body. This is followed by increasing dyspnea, air hunger, retraction of accessory muscles, and cyanosis. Breath sounds may be clear or consist of fine inspiratory crackles or diffuse coarse crackles.

Test-Taking Strategy: Use the process of elimination, noting the strategic word *earliest*. Eliminate option 3 first because intercostal retraction is a later sign of respiratory distress. Of the remaining options, recall that adventitious breath sounds (options 1 and 2) would occur later than an increased respiratory rate. Review the early signs of acute respiratory distress syndrome if you had difficulty with this question.

Level of Cognitive Ability: Analysis
Client Needs: Physiological Integrity
Integrated Process: Nursing Process—assessment
Content Area: Adult health—respiratory
Reference: Lewis, S., Heitkemper, M., & Dirksen, S. (2004). *Medical-surgical nursing: Assessment and management of clinical problems* (6th ed., pp. 1839-1840). St. Louis: Mosby.

25. 1

Rationale: The client with emphysema has hyperinflation of the alveoli and flattening of the diaphragm. These lead to increased anteroposterior diameter, referred to as "barrel chest." The client also has dyspnea with prolonged expiration and has hyperresonant lungs to percussion.

Test-Taking Strategy: Use the process of elimination. Recall that the barrel chest is a result of long-term hyperinflation of the lungs and air trapping. Knowing that emphysema is the only type of chronic airflow limitation in which this occurs will enable you to eliminate each of the other, incorrect options. Review the characteristics of emphysema if you had difficulty with this question.

Level of Cognitive Ability: Analysis
Client Needs: Physiological Integrity
Integrated Process: Nursing Process—assessment
Content Area: Adult health—respiratory

References: Ignatavicius, D., & Workman, M. (2006). *Medical-surgical nursing: Critical thinking for collaborative care* (5th ed., p. 598). Philadelphia: W.B. Saunders.
Lewis, S., Heitkemper, M., & Dirksen, S. (2004). *Medical-surgical nursing: Assessment and management of clinical problems* (6th ed., p. 558). St. Louis: Mosby.

26. 2

Rationale: The client with tuberculosis usually experiences cough (productive or nonproductive), fatigue, anorexia, weight loss, dyspnea, hemoptysis, chest discomfort or pain, chills and sweats (which may occur at night), and a low-grade fever.

Test-Taking Strategy: Use the process of elimination. Eliminate options 1 and 4 first because they are symptoms that are common in the client with tuberculosis. From the remaining options, you need to know that the client may get night sweats or that the fever is low grade. Review the clinical manifestations associated with tuberculosis if you had difficulty with this question.

Level of Cognitive Ability: Analysis
Client Needs: Physiological Integrity
Integrated Process: Nursing Process—assessment
Content Area: Adult health—respiratory
Reference: Huether, S., & McCance, K. (2004). *Understanding pathophysiology* (3rd ed., p. 774). St. Louis: Mosby.

27. 4

Rationale: The nurse teaches the client with tuberculosis to increase intake of protein, iron, and vitamin C. Foods rich in vitamin C include citrus fruits, berries, melons, pineapple, broccoli, cabbage, green peppers, tomatoes, potatoes, chard, kale, asparagus, and turnip greens. Food sources that are rich in iron include liver and other meats. Less than 10% of iron is absorbed from eggs, and less than 5% is absorbed from grains and vegetables.

Test-Taking Strategy: Use the process of elimination. Recall that the diet in tuberculosis should be high in protein, vitamin C, and iron. Knowing which types of foods contain these various nutrients will direct you to option 4. If you had difficulty with this question, review these nutritional concepts.

Level of Cognitive Ability: Application
Client Needs: Physiological Integrity
Integrated Process: Teaching and Learning
Content Area: Adult health—respiratory
Reference: Ignatavicius, D., & Workman, M. (2006). *Medical-surgical nursing: Critical thinking for collaborative care* (5th ed., p. 644). Philadelphia: W.B. Saunders.

28. 4

Rationale: The client is continued on medication therapy for 6 to 12 months, depending on the situation. The client generally is considered not to be contagious after 2 to 3 weeks of medication therapy. The client is instructed to wear a mask if there will be exposure to crowds until the medication is effective in preventing transmission. The client is allowed to return to work when the results of three sputum cultures are negative.

Test-Taking Strategy: Use the process of elimination. Knowing that the medication therapy lasts for at least 6 months helps you eliminate option 1 first. Knowing that three sputum cul-

tures must be negative helps you to eliminate option 3 next. From the remaining options, recalling that the client is not contagious after 2 to 3 weeks of therapy will direct you to option 4. If you had difficulty with this question, review the infectious period of tuberculosis.
Level of Cognitive Ability: Analysis
Client Needs: Physiological Integrity
Integrated Process: Nursing Process—evaluation
Content Area: Adult health—respiratory
References: Black, J., & Hawks, J. (2005). *Medical-surgical nursing: Clinical management for positive outcomes* (7th ed., pp. 1847-1848). Philadelphia: W.B. Saunders.
Ignatavicius, D., & Workman, M. (2006). *Medical-surgical nursing: Critical thinking for collaborative care* (5th ed., p. 644). Philadelphia: W.B. Saunders.

29. 2
Rationale: The nurse who is in contact with a client with tuberculosis should wear an individually fitted particulate respirator. The nurse also would wear gloves as per standard precautions. The nurse wears a gown when the possibility exists that the clothing could become contaminated, such as when giving a bed bath.
Test-Taking Strategy: Use the process of elimination. Knowing that the nurse should wear a particulate respirator eliminates options 1 and 4. Knowledge of basic standard precautions directs you to option 2 from the remaining options. Review precautions related to the care of a client with tuberculosis if you had difficulty with this question.
Level of Cognitive Ability: Application
Client Needs: Safe and Effective Care Environment
Integrated Process: Nursing Process—implementation
Content Area: Adult health—respiratory
Reference: Ignatavicius, D., & Workman, M. (2006). *Medical-surgical nursing: Critical thinking for collaborative care* (5th ed., p. 644). Philadelphia: W.B. Saunders.

30. 3
Rationale: The most common initial symptom in pulmonary embolism is chest pain that is sudden in onset. The next most commonly reported symptom is dyspnea, which is accompanied by an increased respiratory rate. Other typical symptoms of pulmonary embolism include tachycardia, fever, diaphoresis, cough, anxiety, and possibly syncope.
Test-Taking Strategy: Use the process of elimination. Because pulmonary embolism does not result from an infectious process or an allergic reaction, eliminate options 1 and 2 first. To select between options 3 and 4, look at them closely. Option 4 states dyspnea when deep breaths are taken. Although dyspnea commonly occurs with pulmonary embolism, dyspnea is not associated only with deep breathing. Therefore, eliminate option 4. Review the signs of pulmonary embolism if you had difficulty with this question.
Level of Cognitive Ability: Analysis
Client Needs: Physiological Integrity
Integrated Process: Nursing Process—assessment
Content Area: Adult health—respiratory
Reference: Ignatavicius, D., & Workman, M. (2006). *Medical-surgical nursing: Critical thinking for collaborative care* (5th ed., p. 650). Philadelphia: W.B. Saunders.

31. 1
Rationale: The client with human immunodeficiency virus (HIV) infection is considered to have positive results on Mantoux skin testing with an area larger than 5 mm of induration. The client without HIV is positive with an induration larger than 10 mm. The client with HIV is immunosuppressed, making a smaller area of induration positive for this type of client. It is possible for the client infected with HIV to have false-negative readings because of the immunosuppression factor. Options 2, 3, and 4 are incorrect interpretations.
Test-Taking Strategy: Use the process of elimination. Eliminate options 3 and 4 first because they are comparative or alike. From the remaining options, recalling that the client with HIV is immunosuppressed will assist in determining the interpretation of the area of induration. Review results of tuberculosis skin testing in an immunosuppressed client if you had difficulty with this question.
Level of Cognitive Ability: Analysis
Client Needs: Physiological Integrity
Integrated Process: Nursing Process—analysis
Content Area: Adult health—respiratory
Reference: Ignatavicius, D., & Workman, M. (2006). *Medical-surgical nursing: Critical thinking for collaborative care* (5th ed., p. 642). Philadelphia: W.B. Saunders.

32. 1
Rationale: In uncomplicated or simple silicosis, the client would be asymptomatic, although evidence of fibrosis on an x-ray would be present. Malaise, anorexia, weight loss, and severe dyspnea on exertion would occur in a client with chronic complicated silicosis.
Test-Taking Strategy: Use the process of elimination. Noting the words *uncomplicated or simple* will direct you to option 1. Review the manifestations associated with silicosis if you had difficulty with this question.
Level of Cognitive Ability: Analysis
Client Needs: Physiological Integrity
Integrated Process: Nursing Process—assessment
Content Area: Adult health—respiratory
Reference: Lewis, S., Heitkemper, M., & Dirksen, S. (2004). *Medical-surgical nursing: Assessment and management of clinical problems* (6th ed., p. 612). St. Louis: Mosby.

33. 1
Rationale: Histoplasmosis is an opportunistic fungal infection that can occur in the client with acquired immunodeficiency syndrome (AIDS). The infection begins as a respiratory infection and can progress to disseminated infection. Typical signs and symptoms include fever, dyspnea, cough, and weight loss. Enlargement of the client's lymph nodes, liver, and spleen may occur as well.
Test-Taking Strategy: Use the process of elimination. Recalling that histoplasmosis is an infectious process will help you eliminate option 4. Because the client has AIDS and another infection, weight gain is an unlikely symptom and can be eliminated next. Knowing that histoplasmosis begins as a respiratory infection helps you choose dyspnea over headache as the correct option. Review the signs of histoplasmosis if you had difficulty with this question.
Level of Cognitive Ability: Application

Client Needs: Physiological Integrity
Integrated Process: Nursing Process—assessment
Content Area: Adult health—respiratory
Reference: Ignatavicius, D., & Workman, M. (2006). *Medical-surgical nursing: Critical thinking for collaborative care* (5th ed., p. 434). Philadelphia: W.B. Saunders.

34. **4**

Rationale: Dry cough and dyspnea are typical signs and symptoms of pulmonary sarcoidosis. Others include chest pain, hemoptysis, and pneumothorax. Systemic signs and symptoms include weakness and fatigue, malaise, fever, and weight loss.
Test-Taking Strategy: Use the process of elimination and note the strategic word *early*. Because sarcoidosis is a pulmonary problem, eliminate options 1 and 3 first. Select option 4 over option 2 because the shortness of breath (and impaired ventilation) appears first and would cause the fatigue as a secondary symptom. Review the early signs of exacerbation in sarcoidosis if you had difficulty with this question.
Level of Cognitive Ability: Analysis
Client Needs: Physiological Integrity
Integrated Process: Nursing Process—evaluation
Content Area: Adult health—respiratory
Reference: Black, J., & Hawks, J. (2005). *Medical-surgical nursing: Clinical management for positive outcomes* (7th ed., p. 1871). Philadelphia: W.B. Saunders.

35. **1**

Rationale: Silicosis results from chronic, excessive inhalation of particles of free crystalline silica dust. The client should wear a mask to limit inhalation of this substance, which can cause restrictive lung disease after years of exposure. Options 2, 3, and 4 are not necessary.
Test-Taking Strategy: Use the process of elimination. Recalling that exposure to silica dust causes the illness and that the dust is inhaled into the respiratory tract will direct you to option 1. If you had difficulty with this question, review the protective measures associated with silicosis.
Level of Cognitive Ability: Analysis
Client Needs: Safe and Effective Care Environment
Integrated Process: Nursing Process—assessment
Content Area: Adult health—respiratory
References: Lewis, S., Heitkemper, M., & Dirksen, S. (2004). *Medical-surgical nursing: Assessment and management of clinical problems* (6th ed., p. 612). St. Louis: Mosby.
Potter, P., & Perry, A. (2005). *Fundamentals of nursing* (6th ed., pp. 795, 798-799). St. Louis: Mosby.

36. **3**

Rationale: The client with simple silicosis may be asymptomatic or have mild ventilatory restriction and has evidence of fibrosis on chest x-ray. Pulmonary function studies reveal some decreases in vital capacity and total lung volume. Massive fibrosis is not evident at this stage. This disease is restricted to the respiratory system only.
Test-Taking Strategy: Use the process of elimination. Option 4 has the least amount of fit with a disorder that is described as simple or uncomplicated and therefore is eliminated first. Because silicosis is a pulmonary disease, option 1 is elimi-

nated. Option 2 is incongruent; it would be difficult for a person to have shortness of breath and have normal pulmonary function tests. Review the pathophysiology associated with simple silicosis if you had difficulty with this question.
Level of Cognitive Ability: Analysis
Client Needs: Physiological Integrity
Integrated Process: Nursing Process—analysis
Content Area: Adult health—respiratory
Reference: Lewis, S., Heitkemper, M., & Dirksen, S. (2004). *Medical-surgical nursing: Assessment and management of clinical problems* (6th ed., p. 612). St. Louis: Mosby.

37. **3**

Rationale: Pyrazinamide is an antitubercular medication given with other antitubercular medications. Pyrazinamide might not be discontinued if sputum cultures continue to be positive. Options 1, 2, and 4 are not related directly to the use of this medication.
Test-Taking Strategy: Focus on the name of the medication. Recalling that this medication is an antitubercular medication will direct you to option 3. If this question was difficult, review this medication.
Level of Cognitive Ability: Analysis
Client Needs: Physiological Integrity
Integrated Process: Nursing Process—evaluation
Content Area: Pharmacology
Reference: Skidmore-Roth, L. (2005). *Mosby's drug guide for nurses* (6th ed., p. 735). St. Louis: Mosby.

38. **3**

Rationale: Persons at high risk for acquiring tuberculosis include immigrants from Asia, Africa, Latin America, and Oceania, medically underserved populations (ethnic minorities, homeless), those with human immunodeficiency virus infection or other immunosuppressive disorders, residents in group settings (long-term care, correctional facilities), and health care workers.
Test-Taking Strategy: Use the process of elimination, noting the strategic words *lowest risk*. Begin to answer this question by eliminating options 1 and 2 because immigrants and the medically underserved more frequently are affected by the disease. From the remaining options, the postal inspector may or may not come into contact with many persons, depending on the job description. The client from the long-term care facility, however, lives in a group setting where a large number of persons share a common environment 24 hours a day. Review the risk factors associated with tuberculosis if you had difficulty with this question.
Level of Cognitive Ability: Analysis
Client Needs: Health Promotion and Maintenance
Integrated Process: Nursing Process—assessment
Content Area: Adult health—respiratory
Reference: Huether, S., & McCance, K. (2004). *Understanding pathophysiology* (3rd ed., p. 773). St. Louis: Mosby.

39. **4**

Rationale: A Mantoux skin test is administered by giving 0.1 mL of purified protein derivative (PPD) intradermally. Administration involves drawing the medication into a tuberculin syringe with a 25- to 27-gauge, $5/8$-inch needle. The injec-

tion is given by inserting the needle as close as possible to a parallel position with the skin and with the needle bevel facing up. This results in formation of a wheal when the PPD is administered correctly.
Test-Taking Strategy: Remember that a tuberculin syringe is small and measures small amounts of medication dosages. Use the process of elimination, eliminating options 1 and 3 first because these options indicate the use of larger syringes and needles. Remembering that the bevel side is up during administration of PPD will assist in directing you to the correct option from the remaining choices. If this question was difficult, review the basics of this injection technique.
Level of Cognitive Ability: Application
Client Needs: Physiological Integrity
Integrated Process: Nursing Process—implementation
Content Area: Adult health—respiratory
Reference: Chernecky, C., & Berger, B. (2004). *Laboratory tests and diagnostic procedures* (4th ed., p. 766). Philadelphia: W.B. Saunders.

40. **2**
Rationale: A positive reading has an induration measuring 10 mm or larger and is considered abnormal. A small area of ecchymosis is insignificant and probably is related to injection technique. Options 1, 3, and 4 are incorrect interpretations.
Test-Taking Strategy: Recall that induration is necessary for a positive response. Because the client in this question has no induration, the result can only be negative. Review Mantoux skin test results if you had difficulty with this question.
Level of Cognitive Ability: Analysis
Client Needs: Physiological Integrity
Integrated Process: Nursing Process—analysis
Content Area: Adult health—respiratory
Reference: Huether, S., & McCance, K. (2004). *Understanding pathophysiology* (3rd ed., p. 773). St. Louis: Mosby.

ALTERNATE ITEM FORMAT: MULTIPLE RESPONSE
Answer: **1, 3, 4, 5**
Rationale: The nurse should provide the client and family with information about tuberculosis and allay concerns about the contagious aspect of the infection. Instruct the client to follow the medication regimen exactly as prescribed and always to have a supply of the medication on hand. Advise the client of the side effects of the medication and ways of minimizing them to ensure compliance. Reassure the client that after 2 to 3 weeks of medication therapy, it is unlikely that the client will infect anyone. Inform the client that activities should be resumed gradually and about the need for adequate nutrition and a well-balanced diet that is rich in iron, protein, and vitamin C to promote healing and prevent recurrence of infection. Inform the client and family that respiratory isolation is not necessary because family members already have been exposed. Instruct the client about thorough hand washing and to cover the mouth and nose when coughing or sneezing and to put used tissues into plastic bags. Inform the client that a sputum culture is needed every 2 to 4 weeks once medication therapy is initiated. When the results of three sputum cultures are negative, the client is no longer considered infectious and can usually return to former employment.
Test-Taking Strategy: Knowledge regarding the pathophysiology, transmission, and treatment of tuberculosis is needed to answer this question. Read each option carefully to answer correctly. Review home care instructions for the client with tuberculosis if you had difficulty with this question.
Level of Cognitive Ability: Application
Client Needs: Health Promotion and Maintenance
Integrated Process: Teaching and Learning
Content Area: Adult health—respiratory
Reference: Black, J., & Hawks, J. (2005). *Medical-surgical nursing: Clinical management for positive outcomes* (7th ed., pp. 1847-1850). Philadelphia: W.B. Saunders.

REFERENCES

Black, J., & Hawks, J., (2005). *Medical-surgical nursing: Clinical management for positive outcomes* (7th ed.). Philadelphia: W.B. Saunders.

Chernecky, C., & Berger, B. (2004). *Laboratory tests and diagnostic procedures* (4th ed.). Philadelphia: W.B. Saunders.

Harkreader, H., & Hogan, M. A. (2004). *Fundamentals of nursing: Caring and clinical judgment* (2nd ed.). Philadelphia: W.B. Saunders.

Hodgson, B., & Kizior, R. (2007). *Saunders nursing drug handbook 2007.* Philadelphia: W.B. Saunders.

Ignatavicius, D., & Workman, M. (2006). *Medical-surgical nursing: Critical thinking for collaborative care* (5th ed.). Philadelphia: W.B. Saunders.

Kee, J., Hayes, E., & McCuistion, L. (2006). *Pharmacology: A nursing process approach* (5th ed.). Philadelphia: W.B. Saunders.

Lewis, S., Heitkemper, M., & Dirksen, S. (2004). *Medical-surgical nursing: Assessment and management of clinical problems* (6th ed.). St. Louis: Mosby.

Lilly, L., Harrington, S., & Snyder, J. (2005) *Pharmacology and the nursing process* (4th ed.). St. Louis: Mosby.

McCance, K., & Huether, S. (2006). *Pathophysiology: The biologic basis for disease in adults and children* (5th ed.). St. Louis: Mosby.

Perry, A., & Potter, P. (2006). *Clinical nursing skills and techniques* (6th ed.). St. Louis: Mosby.

Potter, P., & Perry, A. (2005). *Fundamentals of nursing* (6th ed.). St. Louis: Mosby.

Skidmore-Roth, L. (2005). *Mosby's drug guide for nurses* (6th ed.). St. Louis: Mosby.

Respiratory Medications

I. BRONCHODILATORS

A. Description

1. Sympathomimetic bronchodilators dilate the airways of the respiratory tree, making air exchange and respiration easier for the client, and relax the smooth muscle of the bronchi (Box 58-1).
2. Methylxanthine bronchodilators stimulate the central nervous system and respiration, dilate coronary and pulmonary vessels, cause diuresis, and relax smooth muscle (Box 58-2).
3. Bronchodilators are used to treat allergic rhinitis and sinusitis, acute bronchospasm, acute and chronic asthma, bronchitis, chronic obstructive pulmonary disease, and emphysema.
4. Bronchodilators are contraindicated in individuals with hypersensitivity, peptic ulcer disease, severe cardiac disease and cardiac dysrhythmias, hyperthyroidism, or uncontrolled seizure disorders.
5. Bronchodilators should be used with caution in clients with hypertension, diabetes mellitus, or narrow-angle glaucoma.
6. Theophylline increases the risk of digoxin toxicity and decreases the effects of lithium and phenytoin (Dilantin).
7. If theophylline and a β_2-adrenergic agonist are administered together, cardiac dysrhythmias may result.
8. β-Blockers, cimetidine (Tagamet), and erythromycin increase the effects of theophylline.
9. Barbiturates and carbamazepine (Tegretol) decrease the effects of theophylline.

B. Side effects

1. Palpitations and tachycardia
2. Dysrhythmias
3. Restlessness, nervousness, tremors
4. Anorexia, nausea, and vomiting
5. Headaches and dizziness
6. Hyperglycemia
7. Decreased clotting time
8. Mouth dryness and throat irritation with inhalers
9. Tolerance and paradoxical bronchoconstriction with inhalers

C. Interventions

1. Assess vital signs.
2. Monitor for cardiac dysrhythmias.
3. Assess for cough, wheezing, decreased breath sounds, and sputum production.
4. Monitor for restlessness and confusion.
5. Provide adequate hydration.

BOX 58-1

Bronchodilators: Sympathomimetics

β_2-ADRENERGIC AGONISTS
Inhaled
Albuterol (Proventil, Proventil HFA)
Bitolterol
Formoterol (Foradil Aerolizer)
Levalbuterol (Xopenex)
Pirbuterol (Maxair Autohaler)
Salmeterol (Serevent Diskus)
Oral
Albuterol (Proventil, Volmax)
Terbutaline (Brethine)

ANTICHOLINERGICS
Ipratropium inhaled (Atrovent HFA)
Tiotropium, inhaled (Spiriva)

BOX 58-2

Bronchodilators: Methylxanthines

Theophylline, oral (Theolair-SR, Theo-24, Uniphyl)

---

6. Administer the medication at regular intervals around the clock to maintain a sustained therapeutic level.
7. Administer oral medications with or after meals to decrease gastrointestinal irritation.
8. Instruct the client not to crush enteric-coated or sustained-release tablets or capsules.
9. Instruct the client to avoid caffeine-containing products such as coffee, tea, cola, and chocolate.
10. Instruct the client in the side effects of bronchodilators.

11. Instruct the client in how to monitor the pulse and to report any abnormalities to the physician.
12. Instruct the client in how to use an inhaler or nebulizer and how to monitor the amount of medication remaining in an inhaler canister; how to use a spacer (a device that enhances the delivery of medication) is also taught (Figs. 58-1 and 58-2)
13. Instruct the client to avoid over-the-counter medications.

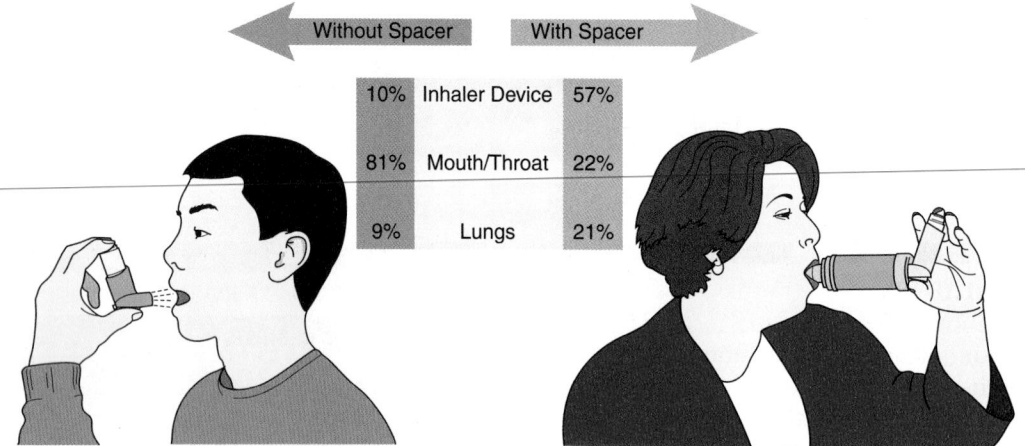

FIG. 58-1 Distribution of medication with and without a spacer. (From Kee, J., & Marshall, S. [2004]. *Clinical calculations: With applications to general and specialty areas* [5th ed.]. Philadelphia: W.B. Saunders.)

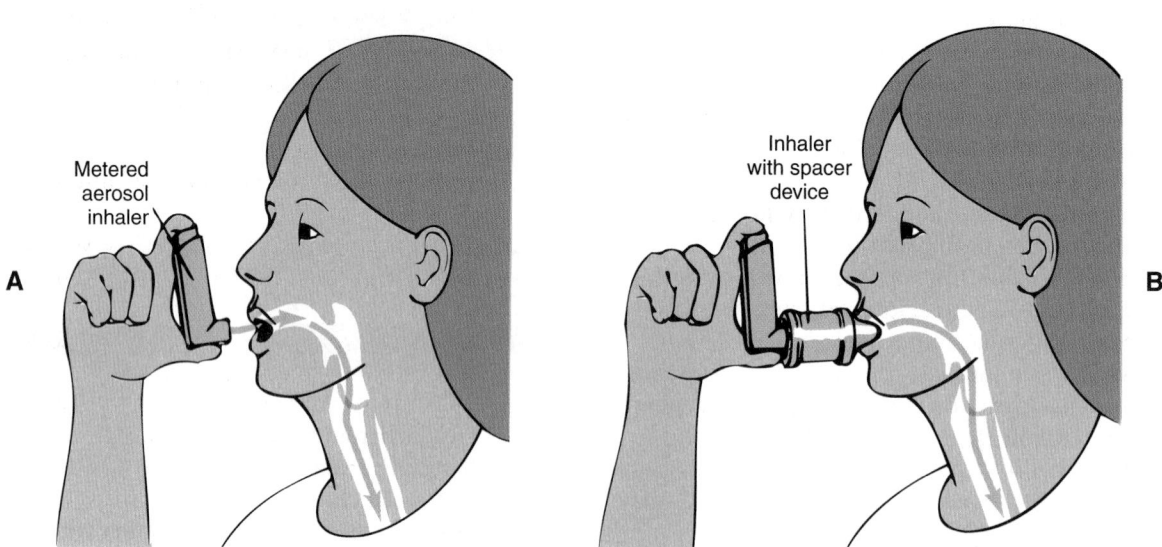

FIG. 58-2 Inhaled drugs commonly used in asthma treatment include β-adrenergic bronchodilators, cromolyn sodium, and aerosol glucocorticoids. **A,** The metered-dose inhaler should not be put in the mouth but held about two fingerwidths (1½ inches) in front of the mouth. **B,** Alternatively, an inhaler with a spacer device can be used. Patients should breathe deeply once before activating the inhaler and then continue breathing in for about 5 seconds. Patients then should hold their breath for 10 to 15 seconds before breathing out slowly. If a second dose is needed, patients should wait 1 to 2 minutes before taking another dose. (From Clark, J., Queener, S., & Karb, V. [2000]. *Pharmacologic basis of nursing practice* [6th ed.]. St. Louis: Mosby.)

BOX 58-3
Glucocorticoids (Corticosteroids)

INHALED
Beclomethasone dipropionate (Qvar)
Budesonide (Pulmicort Turbohaler, Pulmicort Respules)
Flunisolide (AeroBid)
Fluticasone propionate (Flovent HFA, Flovent Rotadisk, Flovent Diskus)
Mometasone furoate (Asmanex Twisthaler)
Triamcinolone (Azmacort)

ORAL
Prednisone
Prednisolone

BOX 58-4
Inhaled Nonsteroidal Antiallergy Agents:
Mast Cell Stabilizers

Cromolyn sodium, inhaled (Intal)
Nedocromil, inhaled (Tilade)

BOX 58-5
Treatment for Asthma

QUICK RELIEF MEDICATIONS
Bronchodilators
 Short-acting inhaled bronchodilators
 Anticholinergics
Anti-inflammatory medications
 Systemic glucocorticoids

LONG-TERM CONTROL MEDICATIONS
Anti-inflammatory medications
Inhaled or oral glucocorticoids
 Cromolyn (Intal); nedocromil (Tilade)
 Leukotriene modifiers
 Omalizumab (Xolair)
Oral and inhaled bronchodilators
 Theophylline

14. Instruct the client to stop smoking and provide information regarding support resources.
15. Instruct the client with diabetes mellitus to monitor blood glucose levels.
16. Instruct the client with asthma to wear a Medic-Alert bracelet.
17. Monitor for a therapeutic serum theophylline level of 10 to 20 mcg/mL.
18. Note that toxicity is likely to occur when the serum level is higher than 20 mcg/mL.
19. Intravenously administered aminophylline or theophylline preparations should be administered slowly and always via an infusion pump.

II. GLUCOCORTICOIDS (CORTICOSTEROIDS) (Box 58-3)
A. Glucocorticoids act as anti-inflammatory agents and reduce edema of the airways.
B. See Chap. 54 for information on glucocorticoids.

III. USE OF AN INHALER
A. Client instructions for use of a metered-dose inhaler (MDI; see Figs. 58-1 and 58-2)
B. If two different inhaled medications are prescribed and one of the medications contains a glucocorticoid (corticosteroid), administer the bronchodilator first and the corticosteroid second.
C. Wait 5 minutes following the bronchodilator before inhaling the corticosteroid.

IV. INHALED NONSTEROIDAL ANTIALLERGY AGENTS (Box 58-4)
A. Description
 1. Antiasthmatic, antiallergic, and mast cell stabilizers inhibit mast cell release after exposure to antigens.
 2. These medications are used to treat allergic rhinitis, bronchial asthma, and exercise-induced bronchospasm (Box 58-5).
 3. These medications are contraindicated in clients with known hypersensitivity.

 4. Orally administered cromolyn sodium (Intal) is used with caution in clients with impaired hepatic or renal function.
B. Side effects
 1. Cough or bronchospasm following inhalation
 2. Nasal sting or sneezing following inhalation
 3. Unpleasant taste in the mouth
C. Interventions
 1. Monitor vital signs.
 2. Monitor respirations and assess lung sounds for rhonchi or wheezing.
 3. Instruct the client to drink a few sips of water before and after inhalation to prevent a cough and an unpleasant taste in the mouth.
 4. Administer oral capsules (cromolyn sodium) at least 30 minutes before meals.
 5. Instruct the client not to discontinue the medication abruptly because a rebound asthmatic attack can occur.

V. LEUKOTRIENE MODIFIERS (Box 58-6)
A. Description
 1. Used in the prophylaxis and treatment of chronic bronchial asthma (not used for acute asthma episodes)
 2. Inhibit bronchoconstriction caused by specific antigens and reduce airway edema and smooth muscle constriction
 3. Contraindicated in clients with hypersensitivity and in breast-feeding mothers

BOX 58-6
Leukotriene Modifiers

LEUKOTRIENE RECEPTOR ANTAGONISTS
Montelukast, oral (Singulair)
Zafirlukast, oral (Accolate)

LEUKOTRIENE INHIBITOR
Zileuton, oral (Zyflo)

---

4. Should be used with caution in clients with impaired hepatic function
5. Coadministration of inhaled glucocorticoids increases the risk of upper respiratory infection.
B. Side effects
   1. Headache
   2. Nausea and vomiting
   3. Dyspepsia
   4. Diarrhea
   5. Generalized pain, myalgia
   6. Fever
   7. Dizziness
C. Interventions
   1. Monitor vital signs.
   2. Assess lung sounds for rhonchi and wheezing.
   3. Assess liver function laboratory values.
   4. Monitor for cyanosis.
   5. Instruct the client to take medication 1 hour before or 2 hours after meals.
   6. Instruct the client to increase fluid intake.
   7. Instruct the client not to discontinue the medication and to take as prescribed, even during symptom-free periods.

VI. MONOCLONAL ANTIBODIES
A. Description
   1. Omalizumab (Xolair) is a recombinant DNA-derived humanized immunoglobulin G (IgG) murine monoclonal antibody that selectively binds to IgE to limit the release of mediators in the allergic response.
   2. Used to treat allergy-related asthma; administered subcutaneously every 2 to 4 weeks
   3. Dose is titrated based on the serum IgE level and body weight.
   4. Contraindicated in those with hypersensitivity to the medication
B. Side effects
   1. Injection site reactions
   2. Viral infections
   3. Upper respiratory infections
   4. Sinusitis
   5. Headache
   6. Pharyngitis
   7. Anaphylaxis
   8. Malignancies

BOX 58-7
Antihistamines

Acrivastine/pseudoephedrine (Semprex-D)
Azelastine hydrochloride (Astelin Ready-Spray)
Brompheniramine (BrōveX)
Cetirizine hydrochloride (Zyrtec)
Chlorpheniramine maleate (Aller-Chlor; Chlor-Trimeton Allergy 8 Hour, 12 Hour)
Chlorpheniramine; pseudoephedrine (Allerest)
Clemastine fumarate (Tavist)
Desloratidine (Clarinex)
Dexchlorpheniramine maleate
Dimenhydrinate (Dramamine)
Diphenhydramine (Benadryl)
Doxylamine succinate (Unisom Nighttime Sleep-Aid)
Fexofenadine (Allegra)
Fexofenadine; pseudoephedrine (Allegra-D)
Loratadine (Claritin)
Loratadine; pseudoephedrine (Claritin-D 12 Hour, 24 Hour)
Triprolidine; pseudoephedrine (Actifed Cold & Allergy)

C. Interventions
   1. Assess respiratory rate, rhythm, and depth and auscultate lung fields bilaterally.
   2. Assess for allergies and/or allergic reaction symptoms such as rash or urticaria.
   3. Instruct the client that respiratory improvement will not be immediate.
   4. Instruct the client not to stop taking or decrease the currently prescribed asthma medications unless instructed.
   5. Avoid live virus vaccines for the duration of treatment.
   6. Have medications for the treatment of severe hypersensitivity reactions available during initial administration in case anaphylaxis occurs.

VII. ANTIHISTAMINES (Box 58-7)
A. Description
   1. Antihistamines are called histamine antagonists or H_1 blockers; these medications compete with histamine for receptor sites, thus preventing a histamine response.
   2. When the H_1 receptor is stimulated, the extravascular smooth muscles, including those lining the nasal cavity, are constricted.
   3. Antihistamines decrease nasopharyngeal, gastrointestinal, and bronchial secretions by blocking the H_1 receptor.
   4. Antihistamines are used for the common cold, rhinitis, nausea and vomiting, motion sickness, urticaria, and as a sleep aid.
   5. Can cause central nervous system (CNS) depression if taken with alcohol, opioids, hypnotics, or barbiturates

6. Should be used with caution in clients with chronic obstructive pulmonary disease because of their drying effect
7. Diphenhydramine (Benadryl) has an anticholinergic effect and should be avoided in clients with narrow-angle glaucoma.
B. Side effects
1. Drowsiness and fatigue
2. Dizziness
3. Urinary retention
4. Blurred vision
5. Wheezing
6. Constipation
7. Dry mouth
8. Gastrointestinal irritation
9. Hypotension
10. Hearing disturbances
11. Photosensitivity
12. Nervousness and irritability
13. Confusion
14. Nightmares
C. Interventions
1. Monitor vital signs.
2. Monitor for signs of urinary dysfunction.
3. Administer with food or milk.
4. Avoid subcutaneous injection, and administer by intramuscular injection in a large muscle if the intramuscular route is prescribed.
5. Instruct the client to avoid hazardous activities, alcohol, and other CNS depressants.
6. Instruct the client taking the medication for motion sickness to take it 30 minutes before the event and then before meals and at bedtime during the event.
7. Instruct the client to suck on hard candy or ice chips for dry mouth.

VIII. NASAL DECONGESTANTS (Box 58-8)
A. Description
1. Nasal decongestants include adrenergic, anticholinergic, and corticosteroid medications.
2. These medications shrink nasal mucosal membranes and reduce fluid secretion.
3. Are used for allergic rhinitis, hay fever, and acute coryza (profuse nasal discharge).
4. Contraindicated or used with extreme caution in clients with hypertension, cardiac disease, hyperthyroidism, or diabetes mellitus
5. Can cause tolerance and rebound nasal congestion (vasodilation) caused by irritation of the nasal mucosa and should not be used for longer than 48 hours
B. Side effects
1. Frequent use of decongestants, especially nasal sprays or drops, can result in tolerance and rebound nasal congestion (vasodilation) caused by irritation of the nasal mucosa.

BOX 58-8

Nasal Decongestants

INTRANASAL NONGLUCOCORTICOSTEROIDS
Naphazoline (Privine)
Oxymetazoline hydrochloride (Afrin 12-Hour Original)
Phenylephrine hydrochloride (Neo-Synephrine)
Pseudoephedrine hydrochloride (Sudafed)
Tetrahydrozoline (Tyzine)
Xylometazoline (Natru-Vent, Otrivin)

INTRANASAL GLUCOSTEROIDS
Beclomethasone dipropionate (Beconase AQ)
Budesonide (Rhinocort Aqua)
Flunisolide (Nasarel)
Fluticasone (Flonase)
Mometasone (Nasonex)
Triamcinolone (Nasacort AQ)

BOX 58-9

Expectorants and Mucolytic Agents

EXPECTORANTS
Dornase alfa (Pulmozyme)
Guaifenesin (Humibid, Robitussin)

MUCOLYTIC
Acetylcysteine (Mucomyst)

---

2. Nervousness
3. Restlessness, insomnia
4. Hypertension
5. Hyperglycemia
C. Interventions
1. Assess the client for existing medical disorders.
2. Monitor for cardiac dysrhythmias.
3. Monitor blood glucose levels.
4. Instruct the client to avoid consuming caffeine in large amounts because it can increase restlessness and palpitations.
5. Instruct the client in the importance of limiting the use of nasal sprays and drops.

IX. EXPECTORANTS AND MUCOLYTIC AGENTS (Box 58-9)
A. Description
1. Expectorants loosen bronchial secretions so that they can be eliminated with coughing; they are used for dry unproductive cough and to stimulate bronchial secretions.
2. Mucolytic agents thin mucous secretions to help make the cough more productive.
3. Mucolytic agents with dextromethorphan should not be used by clients with chronic obstructive pulmonary disease because they suppress the cough.

BOX 58-10
Antitussives

OPIOIDS
Codeine, codeine phosphate, codeine sulfate
Hydrocodone; homatotropine (Hycodan)

NONOPIOIDS
Diphenhydramine hydrochloride (Benadryl)

BOX 58-11
Narcotic Antagonists

Nalmefene (Revex)
Naloxone hydrochloride (Narcan)
Naltrexone (ReVia)

---

4. Acetylcysteine (Mucomyst) can increase airway resistance and should not be used in clients with asthma.
B. Side effects
  1. Gastrointestinal irritation
  2. Skin rash
  3. Oropharyngeal irritation
C. Interventions
  1. Instruct the client to take the medication with a full glass of water to loosen mucus.
  2. Instruct the client to maintain an adequate fluid intake.
  3. Encourage the client to cough and deep breathe.
  4. Acetylcysteine (Mucomyst), administered by nebulization, should not be mixed with another medication.
  5. If acetylcysteine is administered with a bronchodilator, the bronchodilator should be administered 5 minutes before the acetylcysteine.
  6. Monitor for side effects of acetylcysteine such as nausea and vomiting, stomatitis, and runny nose.

X. ANTITUSSIVES (Box 58-10)
A. Description: Act on the cough control center in the medulla to suppress the cough reflex; used for a cough that is nonproductive and irritating
B. Side effects
  1. Dizziness, drowsiness, sedation
  2. Gastrointestinal irritation, nausea
  3. Dry mouth
  4. Constipation
  5. Respiratory depression
C. Interventions
  1. Instruct the client that if the cough lasts longer than 1 week and a fever or rash occurs to notify the physician.
  2. Encourage the client to take adequate fluids with the medication.
  3. Encourage the client to sleep with the head of the bed elevated.
  4. Instruct the client to avoid hazardous activities.
  5. Note that drug dependency can occur.
  6. Avoid administration to the client with a head injury or a postoperative cranial surgery client.

7. Avoid administration to the client using opioids, sedative-hypnotics, barbiturates, or antidepressants because CNS depression can occur.
8. Instruct the client to avoid the use of alcohol.

XI. OPIOID ANTAGONISTS (Box 58-11)
A. Description
  1. An opioid antagonist reverses respiratory depression in opioid overdose.
  2. Avoid its use for non-opioid respiratory depression.
B. Side effects
  1. CNS depression
  2. Nausea, vomiting
  3. Tremors
  4. Sweating
  5. Increased blood pressure
  6. Tachycardia
C. Interventions
  1. Assess vital signs, especially respirations.
  2. For intravenous administration, the dose is titrated every 2 to 5 minutes as prescribed.
  3. Have oxygen and resuscitative equipment available during administration.

XII. TUBERCULOSIS MEDICATIONS
A. Description
  1. Tuberculosis medications offer the most effective method for treating the disease and preventing transmission.
  2. Treatment of identified lesions depends on whether the individual has active disease or has been exposed to the disease.
  3. Treatment is difficult because the bacterium has a waxy substance on the capsule that makes penetration and destruction difficult.
  4. The use of a multidrug regimen destroys organisms as quickly as possible and minimizes the emergence of drug-resistant organisms.
  5. Active tuberculosis is treated with a combination of medications to which the organism is susceptible.
  6. Individuals with active tuberculosis are treated for 6 to 9 months; however, clients with human immunodeficiency virus (HIV) infection are treated for a longer period of time.
  7. After the infected individual has received medication for 2 to 3 weeks, the risk of transmission is greatly reduced.

8. Most clients have negative sputum cultures after 3 months of compliance with medication therapy.
9. Individuals who have been exposed to active tuberculosis are treated with preventive isoniazid (INH) for 9 to 12 months.

B. First-line or second-line medications
   1. First-line medications provide the most effective antituberculosis activity.
   2. Second-line medications are used in combination with first-line medications but are more toxic.
   3. Current infecting organisms are proving resistant to standard first-line medications; the resistant organisms develop because individuals with the disease fail to complete the course of treatment, so surviving bacteria adapt to the medication and become resistant.
   4. Multidrug therapies are instituted because of the resistant organisms.

C. Multidrug-resistant strain of tuberculosis (MDR-TB)
   1. Resistance occurs when a client receiving two medications (first-line and second-line medications) discontinues one of the medications.
   2. The client briefly experiences some response from the single medication but then large numbers of resistant organisms begin to grow.
   3. The client, infectious again, transmits the drug-resistant organism to other individuals.
   4. As this event is repeated, an organism develops that is resistant to many of the first-line tuberculosis medications.

XIII. **FIRST-LINE MEDICATIONS FOR TUBERCULOSIS (Box 58-12)**

A. Isoniazid (INH, Nydrazid)
   1. Description
      a. Isoniazid is bactericidal.
      b. It inhibits the synthesis of mycolic acids and acts to kill actively growing organisms in the extracellular environment.
      c. It inhibits the growth of dormant organisms in the macrophages and caseating granulomas.
      d. It is active only during cell division and is used in combination with other antitubercular medications.
   2. Contraindications and cautions
      a. Isoniazid is contraindicated in clients with hypersensitivity or with acute liver disease.
      b. Use with caution in clients with chronic liver disease, alcoholism, or renal impairment.
      c. Use with caution in clients taking nicotinic acid (niacin).
      d. Use with caution in clients taking hepatotoxic medications because the risk for hepatotoxicity increases.
      e. Alcohol increases the risk of hepatotoxicity.

BOX 58-12

First-Line and Second-Line Medications for Tuberculosis

FIRST-LINE AGENTS
Ethambutol (Myambutol)
Isoniazid (INH, Nydrazid)
Pyrazinamide (PZA)
Rifampin (Rifadin)
Rifapentine (Priftin)
Rifabutin (Mycobutin)

SECOND-LINE AGENTS
Amikacin (Amikin)
Aminosalicylic acid (Paser)
Capreomycin sulfate (Capastat Sulfate)
Cycloserine (Seromycin)
Ethionamide (Trecator)
Gatifloxacin (Tequin)
Kanamycin (Kantrex)
Levofloxacin (Levaquin)
Moxifloxacin (Avelox)
Streptomycin

---

   f. Isoniazid may increase the risk of toxicity of carbamazepine (Tegretol) and phenytoin (Dilantin).
   g. Isoniazid may decrease ketoconazole (Nizoral) concentrations.
   3. Side effects
      a. Hypersensitivity reactions
      b. Peripheral neuritis
      c. Neurotoxicity
      d. Hepatotoxicity; increased liver function test levels
      e. Pyridoxine (vitamin B_6) deficiency
      f. Irritation at injection site with intramuscular administration
      g. Nausea and vomiting
      h. Dry mouth
      i. Dizziness
      j. Hyperglycemia
      k. Vision changes
      l. Hepatitis
   4. Interventions
      a. Assess for hypersensitivity.
      b. Assess for hepatic dysfunction.
      c. Assess for sensitivity to nicotinic acid.
      d. Monitor liver function test results.
      e. Monitor for signs of hepatitis, such as anorexia, nausea, vomiting, weakness, fatigue, dark urine, or jaundice; if these symptoms occur, withhold the medication and notify the physician.
      f. Monitor for tingling, numbness, or burning of the extremities.
      g. Assess mental status.

h. Monitor for visual changes, and notify the physician if they occur.

i. Assess for dizziness and initiate safety precautions.

j. Monitor complete blood count (CBC) and blood glucose levels.

k. Administer isoniazid 1 hour before or 2 hours after a meal because food may delay absorption.

l. Administer isoniazid at least 1 hour before antacids, especially those antacids that contain aluminum.

m. Administer pyridoxine as prescribed to reduce the risk of neurotoxicity.

5. Client education
   a. Instruct the client not to skip doses and to take the medication for the full length of the prescribed therapy.
   b. Instruct the client not to take any other medication without consulting the physician.
   c. Advise the client of the importance of follow-up physician visits, vision testing, and laboratory tests.
   d. Instruct the client to avoid alcohol.
   e. Advise the client to take medication on an empty stomach with 8 oz of water 1 hour before or 2 hours after meals and to avoid taking antacids with the medication.
   f. Instruct the client to avoid tyramine-containing foods because they may cause a reaction such as red and itching skin, a pounding heartbeat, lightheadedness, a hot or clammy feeling, or a headache; if this does occur, the client should notify the physician.
   g. Instruct the client in the signs of neurotoxicity, hepatitis, and hepatotoxicity.
   h. Instruct the client to notify the physician if signs of neurotoxicity, hepatitis and hepatotoxicity, or visual changes occur.

B. Rifampin (Rifadin)
   1. Description
      a. Rifampin inhibits bacterial RNA synthesis.
      b. It binds to DNA-dependent RNA polymerase and blocks RNA transcription.
      c. It is used with at least one other antitubercular medication.
   2. Contraindications and cautions
      a. Rifampin is contraindicated in clients with hypersensitivity.
      b. It should be used with caution in clients with hepatic dysfunction or alcoholism.
      c. Use of alcohol or hepatotoxic medications may increase the risk of hepatotoxicity.
      d. Rifampin decreases the effects of several medications, including oral anticoagulants, oral hypoglycemics, chloramphenicol (Chlo-

romycetin), digoxin (Lanoxin), disopyramide phosphate (Norpace), mexiletine (Mexitil), quinidine polygalacturonate, tocainide hydrochloride, fluconazole (Diflucan), methadone hydrochloride (Dolophine), phenytoin (Dilantin), and verapamil hydrochloride (Calan).
   3. Side effects
      a. Hypersensitivity reaction, including fever, chills, shivering, headache, muscle and bone pain, and dyspnea
      b. Heartburn, nausea, vomiting, diarrhea
      c. Red-orange–colored body secretions
      d. Vision changes
      e. Hepatotoxicity and hepatitis
      f. Increased uric acid levels
      g. Blood dyscrasias
      h. Colitis
   4. Interventions
      a. Assess for hypersensitivity.
      b. Evaluate CBC, uric acid, and liver function test results.
      c. Assess for signs of hepatitis; if they occur, withhold the medication and notify the physician.
      d. Monitor stools for signs of colitis.
      e. Monitor mental status.
      f. Assess for visual changes.
   5. Client education
      a. Instruct the client not to skip doses and to take medication for the full length of the prescribed therapy.
      b. Instruct the client not to take any other medication without consulting the physician.
      c. Advise the client of the importance of follow-up physician visits and laboratory tests.
      d. Instruct the client to avoid alcohol.
      e. Advise the client to take medication on an empty stomach with 8 oz of water 1 hour before or 2 hours after meals and to avoid taking antacids with the medication.
      f. Instruct the client that urine, feces, sweat, and tears will be red-orange and that soft contact lens can become permanently discolored.
      g. Instruct the client to notify the physician if jaundice (yellow eyes or skin) develops or if weakness, fatigue, nausea, vomiting, sore throat, fever, or unusual bleeding occurs.

C. Ethambutol (Myambutol)
   1. Description
      a. Ethambutol is bacteriostatic.
      b. It interferes with cell metabolism and multiplication by inhibiting one or more metabolites in susceptible organisms.
      c. It inhibits bacterial RNA synthesis and is active only during cell division.

d. Ethambutol is slow-acting and must be used with other bactericidal agents.

2. Contraindications and cautions
   a. Ethambutol is contraindicated in clients with hypersensitivity or optic neuritis and in children younger than 13 years.
   b. Use with caution in clients with renal dysfunction, gout, ocular defects, diabetic retinopathy, cataracts, or ocular inflammatory conditions.
   c. Use with caution in clients taking neurotoxic medications because the risk for neurotoxicity increases.

3. Side effects
   a. Hypersensitivity reactions
   b. Anorexia, nausea, vomiting
   c. Dizziness
   d. Malaise
   e. Mental confusion
   f. Joint pain
   g. Dermatitis
   h. Optic neuritis
   i. Peripheral neuritis
   j. Thrombocytopenia
   k. Increased uric acid levels
   l. Anaphylactoid reaction

4. Interventions
   a. Assess the client for hypersensitivity.
   b. Evaluate results of CBC, uric acid, and renal and liver function tests.
   c. Obtain baseline visual acuity and color discrimination, especially to green.
   d. Monitor for visual changes such as altered color perception and decreased visual acuity; if changes occur, withhold the medication and notify the physician.
   e. Administer once every 24 hours and administer with food to decrease gastrointestinal upset.
   f. Monitor uric acid concentration and assess for painful or swollen joints or signs of gout.
   g. Monitor intake and output and for adequate renal function.
   h. Assess mental status.
   i. Monitor for dizziness and initiate safety precautions.
   j. Assess for peripheral neuritis (numbness, tingling or burning of the extremities); if it occurs, notify the physician.

5. Client education
   a. Inform the client that he or she can prevent nausea related to the medication by taking the daily dose at bedtime or by taking the prescribed antinausea medications.
   b. Instruct the client not to skip doses and to take the medication for the full length of the prescribed therapy.

c. Instruct the client not to take any other medication without consulting the physician.
   d. Advise the client of the importance of follow-up physician visits, vision testing, and laboratory tests.
   e. Instruct the client to notify the physician immediately if any visual problems occur or a rash, swelling and pain in the joints, or numbness, tingling, or burning in the hands or feet occurs.

D. Pyrazinamide (PZA)
1. Description
   a. The exact mechanism of action of pyrazinamide is unknown.
   b. Pyrazinamide may be bacteriostatic or bactericidal, depending on its concentration at the infection site and susceptibility of infecting organism.
   c. It is used with at least one other antitubercular medication after failure or ineffectiveness of the primary medication(s).

2. Contraindications and cautions
   a. Pyrazinamide is contraindicated in clients with hypersensitivity.
   b. Use pyrazinamide with caution in clients with diabetes mellitus, renal impairment, or gout, and in children.
   c. Pyrazinamide may decrease the effects of allopurinol (Zyloprim), colchicine, probenecid (Benemid), and sulfinpyrazone (Anturane).
   d. Cross-sensitivity is possible with isoniazid (INH), ethionamide (Trecator-SC), or nicotinic acid.

3. Side effects
   a. Increases liver function tests and uric acid levels
   b. Arthralgia, myalgia
   c. Photosensitivity
   d. Hepatotoxicity
   e. Thrombocytopenia

4. Interventions
   a. Assess for hypersensitivity.
   b. Evaluate CBC, liver function test results, and uric acid levels.
   c. Observe for hepatotoxic effects; if they occur, withhold the medication and notify the physician.
   d. Assess for painful or swollen joints.
   e. Evaluate blood glucose level because diabetes mellitus may be difficult to control while client is taking the medication.

5. Client education
   a. Instruct the client to take the medication with food to reduce gastrointestinal distress.
   b. Instruct the client to avoid sunlight or ultraviolet light until photosensitivity is determined.

    c. Instruct the client to notify the physician if any side effects occur.

    d. Instruct the client not to skip doses and to take the medication for the full length of the prescribed therapy.

    e. Instruct the client not to take any other medication without consulting the physician.

    f. Advise the client of the importance of follow-up physician visits and laboratory tests.

E. Rifabutin (Mycobutin)

  1. Description

    a. Inhibits mycobacterial DNA-dependent RNA polymerase and suppresses protein synthesis

    b. Used to prevent disseminated *Mycobacterium avium* complex (MAC) disease in clients with advanced HIV infection

    c. Used to treat active MAC disease and tuberculosis in clients with HIV infection

  2. Cautions

    a. Can affect blood levels of some medications, including oral contraceptives and some medications used to treat HIV infection

    b. A nonhormonal method of birth control should be used instead of an oral contraceptive.

  3. Side effects

    a. Rash

    b. GI disturbances

    c. Neutropenia

    d. Red-orange–colored body secretions

    e. Uveitis

    f. Myositis

    g. Arthralgia

    h. Hepatitis

    i. Chest pain with dyspnea

    j. Flu-like syndrome

  4. Interventions

    a. Assess medication history of the client.

    b. Observe for hepatotoxic effects; if they occur, withhold the medication and notify the physician.

    c. Assess for painful or swollen joints.

    d. Assess for ocular pain or blurred vision.

  5. Client education

    a. Instruct the client that the medication can be taken without regard to food.

    b. Instruct the client to notify the physician if any side effects occur.

    c. Instruct the client not to skip doses and to take the medication for the full length of the prescribed therapy.

    d. Instruct the client not to take any other medication without consulting the physician.

    e. Advise the client of the importance of follow-up physician visits and laboratory tests.

F. Rifapentine (Priftin)

  1. Description: Used only for pulmonary tuberculosis

  2. Cautions: Can affect blood levels of some medications, including oral contraceptives and warfarin (Coumadin), and some medications used to treat HIV infection

  3. Side effects

    a. Red-orange–colored body secretions

    b. Hepatotoxicity

  4. Interventions

    a. Assess medication history of the client.

    b. Obtain baseline liver function studies and assess throughout therapy.

    c. Observe for hepatotoxic effects; if they occur, withhold the medication and notify the physician.

  5. Client education

    a. Instruct the client that the medication can be taken without regard to food.

    b. Instruct the client to avoid sunlight or ultraviolet light until photosensitivity is determined.

    c. Instruct the client to notify the physician if any side effects occur

    d. Instruct the client not to skip doses and to take the medication for the full length of the prescribed therapy.

    e. Instruct the client not to take any other medication without consulting the physician.

    f. Advise the client of the importance of follow-up physician visits and laboratory tests.

XIV. SECOND-LINE MEDICATIONS FOR TUBERCULOSIS (see Box 58-12)

A. Capreomycin sulfate (Capastat Sulfate)

  1. Description

    a. Mechanism of action for capreomycin is unknown.

    b. Used to treat MDR-TB when significant resistance to other medications is expected

    c. Capreomycin must be given intramuscularly.

  2. Contraindications and cautions

    a. The risk of nephrotoxicity, ototoxicity, and neuromuscular blockade is increased with the use of aminoglycosides or loop diuretics.

    b. Use capreomycin with caution in clients with renal insufficiency, acoustic nerve impairment, hepatic disorder, myasthenia gravis, or parkinsonism.

    c. Do not administer to clients receiving streptomycin.

  3. Side effects

    a. Nephrotoxicity

    b. Ototoxicity

    c. Neuromuscular blockade

4. Interventions
   a. Perform baseline audiometric testing.
   b. Assess renal, hepatic, and electrolyte levels before administration.
   c. Monitor intake and output.
   d. Reconstituted medication may be stored for 48 hours at room temperature.
   e. Administer intramuscularly deep into a large muscle mass.
   f. Rotate injection sites.
   g. Observe injection site for redness, excessive bleeding, and inflammation.
5. Client education
   a. Instruct the client not to perform tasks that require mental alertness.
   b. Instruct the client to report any hearing loss, balance disturbances, respiratory difficulty, weakness, or signs of hypersensitivity reactions.

B. Kanamycin (Kantrex) and amikacin (Amikin)
1. Description
   a. Aminoglycoside antibiotics are given with at least one other antitubercular medication.
   b. These medications are bactericidal because of receptor-binding action interfering with protein synthesis in susceptible microorganisms.
2. Contraindications and cautions
   a. Contraindicated in clients with hypersensitivity, neuromuscular disorders, or eighth cranial nerve damage
   b. Used with caution in the older client, in neonates because of renal insufficiency and immaturity, and in young infants because it may cause CNS depression.
   c. The risk of toxicity increases if taken with other aminoglycosides or nephrotoxicity- or ototoxicity-producing medications.
3. Side effects
   a. Hypersensitivity
   b. Pain and irritation at the injection site
   c. Nephrotoxicity is indicated by increased blood urea nitrogen and serum creatinine levels.
   d. Ototoxicity is indicated by tinnitus, dizziness, ringing or roaring in the ears, and reduced hearing.
   e. Neurotoxicity is indicated by headache, dizziness, lethargy, tremors, and visual disturbances.
   f. Superinfections
4. Interventions
   a. Assess for hypersensitivity.
   b. Monitor for ototoxic, neurotoxic, and nephrotoxic reactions.
   c. Monitor liver and renal function test results.

d. Obtain baseline audiometric test and repeat every 1 to 2 months because the medication impairs the eighth cranial nerve.
   e. Assess acuteness of hearing.
   f. Monitor for visual changes.
   g. Assess hydration status and maintain adequate hydration during therapy.
   h. Monitor intake and output.
   i. Assess urinalysis.
   j. Monitor for superinfection.
5. Client education
   a. Instruct the client not to skip doses and to take the medication for the full length of the prescribed therapy.
   b. Instruct the client not to take any other medication without consulting the physician.
   c. Advise the client of the importance of follow-up physician visits and laboratory tests.
   d. Instruct the client to notify the physician if hearing loss, changes in vision, or urinary problems occur.

C. Ethionamide (Trecator)
1. Description
   a. Mechanism of action of ethionamide is unknown.
   b. Ethionamide is used to treat MDR-TB when significant resistance to other medications is expected.
2. Contraindications and cautions
   a. Ethionamide is contraindicated in clients with hypersensitivity.
   b. Use ethionamide with caution in clients with diabetes mellitus or renal dysfunction.
3. Side effects
   a. Anorexia, nausea, vomiting
   b. Metallic taste in the mouth
   c. Orthostatic hypotension
   d. Jaundice
   e. Mental changes
   f. Peripheral neuritis
   g. Rash
4. Interventions
   a. Assess liver and renal function test results.
   b. Monitor glucose levels in the client with diabetes mellitus.
   c. Administer pyridoxine as prescribed to reduce the risk of neurotoxicity.
5. Client education
   a. Instruct the client to take medication with food or meals to minimize gastrointestinal irritation.
   b. Instruct the client to change positions slowly.
   c. Instruct the client to report signs of a rash, which can progress to exfoliative dermatitis if the medication is not discontinued.
   d. Instruct the client to avoid alcohol.

e. Instruct the client to report signs of jaundice and other side effects of the medication if they occur.

D. Aminosalicylic acid (Paser)
   1. Description
      a. Aminosalicylic acid inhibits folic acid metabolism in mycobacteria.
      b. It is used to treat MDR-TB when significant resistance to other medications is expected.
   2. Contraindications and cautions
      a. Contraindicated with hypersensitivity to aminosalicylates, salicylates, or compounds containing the para-aminophenol group.
      b. Aminobenzoates block the absorption of aminosalicylate sodium.
   3. Side effects
      a. Hypersensitivity
      b. Bitter taste in the mouth
      c. Gastrointestinal tract irritation
      d. Exfoliative dermatitis
      e. Blood dyscrasias
      f. Crystalluria
      g. Changes in thyroid function
   4. Interventions
      a. Assess for hypersensitivity.
      b. Offer clear water to rinse the mouth and chewing gum or hard candy to alleviate the bitter taste.
      c. Encourage fluid intake to prevent crystalluria.
      d. Monitor intake and output.
   5. Client education
      a. Instruct the client to discard the medication and obtain a new supply if a purplish-brown discoloration occurs.
      b. Instruct the client to take the medication with food.
      c. Inform the client that urine may turn red on contact with hypochlorite bleach if bleach was used to clean a toilet.
      d. Instruct the client not to take aspirin or over-the-counter medications without the physician's approval.
      e. Instruct the client to report signs of a blood dyscrasia, such as sore throat or mouth, malaise, fatigue, bruising, or bleeding.

E. Cycloserine (Seromycin)
   1. Description
      a. Cycloserine interferes with cell wall biosynthesis.
      b. It is used to treat MDR-TB when significant resistance to other medications is expected.
   2. Contraindications and cautions
      a. Use of alcohol or ethionamide increases the risk of seizures.
      b. Use cycloserine with caution in clients with epilepsy, depression, severe anxiety, psychosis, or renal insufficiency, or the client who uses alcohol.

   3. Side effects
      a. Hypersensitivity
      b. CNS reactions
      c. Neurotoxicity
      d. Seizures
      e. Congestive heart failure
      f. Headache
      g. Vertigo
      h. Altered level of consciousness
      i. Irritability, nervousness, anxiety
      j. Confusion
      k. Mood changes, depression, thoughts of suicide
   4. Interventions
      a. Monitor level of consciousness.
      b. Monitor for changes in mental status and thought processes.
      c. Monitor renal and hepatic function tests.
      d. Monitor serum drug level to avoid the risk of neurotoxicity; the peak concentration, measured 2 hours after dosing, should be 25 to 35 mcg/mL.
   5. Client education
      a. Instruct the client to take the medication after meals to prevent gastrointestinal upset.
      b. Instruct the client to avoid alcohol.
      c. Instruct the client to report signs of a rash or signs of CNS toxicity.
      d. Instruct the client to avoid driving or performing tasks that require alertness until the reaction to the medication has been determined.
      e. Advise the client of the need for monitoring serum drug levels weekly, as prescribed.

F. Streptomycin
   1. Description
      a. Streptomycin is an aminoglycoside antibiotic used with at least one other antitubercular medication.
      b. It is bactericidal because of receptor-binding action that interferes with protein synthesis in susceptible organisms.
   2. Contraindications and cautions
      a. Streptomycin is contraindicated in clients with hypersensitivity, myasthenia gravis, parkinsonism, or eighth cranial nerve damage.
      b. Use streptomycin with caution in the older client, in neonates because of renal insufficiency and immaturity, and in young infants because the medication may cause CNS depression.
      c. The risk of toxicity increases when streptomycin is taken with other aminoglycosides or nephrotoxicity- or ototoxicity-producing medications.
   3. Side effects (Box 58-13)
      a. Hypersensitivity
      b. Visual changes
      c. Increased liver and renal function studies

BOX 58-13
Side Effects of Streptomycin

NEPHROTOXICITY
Changes in urine output
Decreased appetite
Increased thirst
Nausea, vomiting

NEUROTOXICITY
Muscle numbness
Seizures
Tingling
Twitching

VESTIBULAR OTOTOXICITY
Clumsiness
Dizziness
Unsteadiness

AUDITORY OTOTOXICITY
A full feeling in the ears
Ringing in the ears
Loss of hearing

BOX 58-14
Influenza Vaccines

INACTIVATED (INTRAMUSCULAR ADMINISTRATION)
Fluarix
Fluvirin
Fluzone

LIVE, ATTENUATED (NASAL ADMINISTRATION)
FluMist

d. Peripheral neuritis, such as burning of the face or mouth

4. Interventions
   a. Assess for hypersensitivity.
   b. Monitor liver and renal function test results.
   c. Monitor for ototoxic, neurotoxic, and nephrotoxic reactions.
   d. Perform baseline audiometric testing and repeat every 1 to 2 months because the medication impairs the eighth cranial nerve.
   e. Assess hearing acuity.
   f. Monitor for visual changes.
   g. Assess hydration status and maintain adequate hydration during therapy.
   h. Monitor intake and output.
   i. Assess urinalysis results.
   j. Monitor for signs of peripheral neuritis.

5. Client education
   a. Instruct the client not to skip doses and to take medication for the full length of the prescribed therapy.
   b. Instruct the client not to take any other medication without consulting the physician.
   c. Advise the client of the importance of follow-up physician visits and laboratory tests.
   d. Instruct the client to notify the physician if hearing loss, changes in vision, or urinary problems occur.

G. Fluoroquinolones
   1. Fluoroquinolones (levofloxacin [Levaquin], moxifloxacin [Avelox], gatifloxacin [Tequin]) are used for a wide variety of infections and are active against *Mycobacterium tuberculosis*.

2. Used for infections caused by multidrug-resistant organisms
3. Gastrointestinal disturbances are the most common side effect.
4. Not recommended for use in children

XV. INFLUENZA MEDICATIONS

   A. Vaccines (Box 58-14)
      1. Description
         a. Because the strain of influenza virus is different every year, annual vaccination is recommended (usually in October or November).
         b. Vaccine is available as inactivated influenza vaccine administered intramuscularly or as a live attenuated influenza vaccine, which is administered nasally.
      2. Contraindications and cautions
         a. Contraindications of the inactivated vaccine include hypersensitivity, chicken egg allergy, active infection, Guillain-Barré syndrome, active febrile illness, and children younger than 6 months.
         b. Contraindications of the live attenuated vaccine include age younger than 5 years or older than 50 years, pregnant women, children or adolescents on long-term aspirin therapy, and those with severe nasal congestion or long-term conditions such as asthma, diabetes mellitus, anemia or blood disorders, or heart, kidney, or lung disease.
      3. Side effects
         a. Side effects of the inactivated vaccine include localized pain and swelling at the injection site, general body aches and pains, malaise, fever.
         b. Side effects of the attenuated vaccine include runny nose or nasal congestion, cough, headache, and sore throat.
      4. Interventions
         a. The intramuscular route is recommended for the inactivated vaccine; adults and older children should be vaccinated in the deltoid muscle.
         b. Monitor for side effects of the vaccine.

BOX 58-15
Antiviral Influenza Medications

Amantadine (Symmetrel)
Oseltamivir (Tamiflu)
Rimantadine (Flumadine)
Zanamivir (Relenza)

TABLE 58-1

Side Effects of Antiviral Influenza Medications

Antiviral Medications	Side Effects
Amantadine (Symmetrel)	Drowsiness, anxiety, psychosis, depression, hallucinations, tremors, confusion, insomnia, orthostatic hypotension, heart failure, blurred vision, constipation, dry mouth, urinary frequency and retention, leukopenia, photosensitivity, dermatitis
Oseltamivir (Tamiflu)	Insomnia, diarrhea, abdominal pain cough
Rimantadine (Flumadine)	Depression, hallucinations, tremors, seizures, insomnia, poor concentration, asthenia, gait abnormalities, anxiety, confusion, pallor, palpitations, hypotension, edema, tinnitus, eye pain, constipation, dry mouth, anorexia, abdominal pain, diarrhea, dyspepsia, rash
Zanamivir (Relenza Rotadisks)	Ear, nose, throat infections, diarrhea, nasal symptoms, cough, sinusitis, bronchitis

c. Monitor for hypersensitivity reactions in clients receiving vaccination for the first time.

5. Client education
   a. Instruct the client about the importance of an annual vaccination.
   b. Instruct the client that the inactivated vaccine contains noninfectious killed viruses and cannot cause influenza.
   c. Instruct the client that any respiratory disease unrelated to influenza can occur after the vaccination.
   d. Instruct the client who has received the attenuated vaccine that the virus may be shed up to 2 days after vaccination.
   e. Instruct the client that development of antibodies in adults takes approximately 2 weeks.

B. Antiviral medications (Box 58-15)
   1. Description
      a. Antiviral medication use during outbreaks of influenza depends on the current strain of influenza.
      b. Diagnosis of influenza should include rapid diagnostic tests because symptoms of infection from other pathogens may cause symptoms similar to those of influenza infection.
      c. Influenza antivirals may also be administered as prophylaxis against infection but should not replace vaccination.
   2. Contraindication and cautions: Antiviral medications are contraindicated in hypersensitive clients.
   3. Side effects
      a. Common side effects include headache, dizziness, fatigue, nausea and vomiting.
      b. Some side effects depend on the medication (Table 58-1)
   4. Interventions
      a. Administer within 2 days of onset of symptoms and continue for the entire prescription.
      b. Monitor for side effects of specific medications.
   5. Client education
      a. Teach the client that the medication may not prevent the transmission of influenza to others.
      b. Adjust activities if dizziness or fatigue occur.
      c. Instruct the client about management of side effects of various medications.

   d. Instruct the client to take medication exactly as prescribed and for the duration of prescription.

XVI. PNEUMOCOCCAL CONJUGATE VACCINE

A. Pneumococcal conjugate vaccine (PCV, Prevnar) is used for the prevention of invasive pneumococcal disease in infants and children
B. Pneumococcal polysaccharide vaccine (PPV, Pneumovax) is used for adults and high-risk children older than 2 years.
C. Side effects may include erythema, swelling, pain, and tenderness at the injection site, fever, irritability, drowsiness, and reduced appetite.
D. See Chap. 47 for additional information about vaccines for pneumonia.

PRACTICE QUESTIONS

1. A nurse has an order to give a client salmeterol (Serevent), two puffs, and beclomethasone dipropionate (Qvar), two puffs, by metered-dose inhaler. The nurse administers the medication by giving the:
   1. Beclomethasone first and then the salmeterol
   2. Salmeterol first and then the beclomethasone
   3. Alternating a single puff of each, beginning with the salmeterol
   4. Alternating a single puff of each, beginning with the beclomethasone

2. A client receiving oral theophylline is due to have a theophylline level drawn. A nurse questions the client to ensure that the client has not ingested which of the following substances before the blood sample is drawn?
   1. Glucose
   2. Caffeine
   3. Sedatives
   4. Opioids

3. The nurse is caring for a client with a diagnosis of influenza who first began to experience symptoms yesterday. Antiviral therapy is prescribed and the nurse provides instructions to the client about the therapy. Which statement by the client indicates an understanding of the instructions?
   1. "I must take the medication exactly as prescribed."
   2. "Once I start the medication, I will no longer be contagious."
   3. "I will not get any colds or infections while taking this medication."
   4. "This medication has minimal side effects and I can return to normal activities."

4. A client has begun therapy with theophylline (Theo-24). A nurse plans to teach the client to limit the intake of which of the following while taking this medication?
   1. Coffee, cola, and chocolate
   2. Oysters, lobster, and shrimp
   3. Melons, oranges, and pineapple
   4. Cottage cheese, cream cheese, and dairy creamers

5. A nurse has administered a dose of salmeterol (Serevent Diskus) to a client. The client develops a generalized rash and urticaria, and the eyelids begin to swell. The nurse should:
   1. Call the physician immediately.
   2. Apply a lanolin-based cream to the rash.
   3. Encourage the client to drink fluids quickly.
   4. Assess the client's vision with a Snellen chart.

6. The nurse is preparing to administer the first dose of omalizumab (Xolair) to a client. The nurse should have which of the following items available for possible use during the administration of this medication?
   1. Emesis basin
   2. Nasogastric tube
   3. Suction equipment
   4. Medications for severe anaphylactic reactions

7. A client has an order to take guaifenesin (Humibid). A nurse concludes that the client understands the most effective use of this medication if the client states that he or she will:
   1. Watch for irritability as a side effect.
   2. Take the tablet with a full glass of water.
   3. Take an extra dose if the cough is accompanied by fever.

   4. Crush the sustained-release tablet if immediate relief is needed.

8. A nurse is preparing to administer a dose of naloxone hydrochloride (Narcan) intravenously to a client with an intravenous opioid overdose. The nurse plans to have which of the following available as supportive equipment in case it is needed?
   1. Nasogastric tube
   2. Paracentesis tray
   3. Resuscitation equipment
   4. Central line insertion tray

9. A nurse teaches a client about the effects of diphenhydramine (Benadryl), which has been ordered as a cough suppressant. The nurse determines that the client needs further instructions if the client states that he or she will:
   1. Take the medication on an empty stomach.
   2. Avoid using alcohol while taking this medication.
   3. Use sugarless gum, candy, or oral rinses to decrease dry mouth.
   4. Avoid driving or other activities requiring mental alertness while taking this medication.

10. A client has been prescribed a cough formula containing codeine sulfate. A nurse has given the client instructions for its use. The nurse concludes that the client understands the instructions if the client verbalizes to self-assess for:
    1. Excitability
    2. Rapid pulse
    3. Constipation
    4. Excessive urination

11. A cromolyn sodium (Intal) inhaler is prescribed for a client with allergic asthma. A nurse provides instructions regarding the side effects of this medication. Which of the following undesirable side effects is associated with this medication?
    1. Insomnia
    2. Constipation
    3. Hypotension
    4. Bronchospasm

12. Terbutaline (Brethine) is prescribed for a client with bronchitis. A nurse understands that this medication should be used with caution if which of the following medical conditions is present in the client?
    1. Osteoarthritis
    2. Hypothyroidism
    3. Diabetes mellitus
    4. Polycystic disease

13. Zafirlukast (Accolate) is prescribed for a client with bronchial asthma. Which laboratory test does the nurse expect to be prescribed before the administration of this medication?
    1. Platelet count
    2. Neutrophil count
    3. Liver function tests
    4. Complete blood count

14. A client has been taking isoniazid (INH) for $1\frac{1}{2}$ months. The client complains to a nurse about numbness, paresthesias, and tingling in the extremities. The nurse interprets that the client is experiencing:
    1. Hypercalcemia
    2. Peripheral neuritis
    3. Small blood vessel spasm
    4. Impaired peripheral circulation

15. A client is to begin a 6-month course of therapy with isoniazid (INH). A nurse plans to teach the client to:
    1. Use alcohol in small amounts only.
    2. Report yellow eyes or skin immediately.
    3. Increase intake of Swiss or aged cheeses.
    4. Avoid vitamin supplements during therapy.

16. A client has been started on long-term therapy with rifampin (Rifadin). A nurse teaches the client that the medication:
    1. Should always be taken with food or antacids
    2. Should be double-dosed if one dose is forgotten
    3. Causes orange discoloration of sweat, tears, urine, and feces
    4. May be discontinued independently if symptoms are gone in 3 months

17. A nurse has given a client taking ethambutol (Myambutol) information about the medication. The nurse determines that the client understands the instructions if the client states to report immediately:
    1. Impaired sense of hearing
    2. Gastrointestinal side effects
    3. Orange-red discoloration of body secretions
    4. Difficulty in discriminating the color red from green

18. Cycloserine (Seromycin) is added to the medication regimen for a client with tuberculosis. Which of the following would the nurse include in the client teaching plan regarding this medication?
    1. Take the medication before meals.
    2. Return to the clinic weekly for serum drug level determination.
    3. It is not necessary to call the physician if a skin rash occurs.
    4. It is not necessary to restrict alcohol intake with this medication.

19. A client with tuberculosis is being started on antituberculosis therapy with isoniazid (INH). Before giving the client the first dose, a nurse ensures that which of the following baseline studies has been completed?
    1. Electrolyte levels
    2. Liver enzyme levels
    3. Serum creatinine level
    4. Coagulation times

20. A nurse is preparing to administer albuterol (Proventil) to a client. The nurse assesses which of the following parameters before and during therapy?
    1. Nausea and vomiting
    2. Urine output and blood urea nitrogen level
    3. Headache and level of consciousness
    4. Lung sounds and presence of dyspnea

21. A home care nurse has observed a client self-administer a dose of an adrenergic bronchodilator via metered-dose inhaler. Within a short time, the client begins to wheeze loudly. The nurse interprets that this is the result of:
    1. Insufficient dosage of the medication, which needs to be increased.
    2. Paradoxical bronchospasm, which must be reported to the physician.
    3. Probable interaction of this medication with an over-the-counter cold remedy.
    4. Tolerance to the medication, indicating a need for a stronger type of bronchodilator.

ALTERNATE ITEM FORMAT: MULTIPLE RESPONSE

Rifabutin (Mycobutin) is prescribed for a client with active *Mycobacterium avium* complex (MAC) disease and tuberculosis. For which of the following side effects of the medication should the nurse monitor? Select all that apply.
❏ 1. Signs of hepatitis
❏ 2. Flu-like syndrome
❏ 3. Low neutrophil count
❏ 4. Vitamin B_6 deficiency
❏ 5. Ocular pain or blurred vision
❏ 6. Tingling and numbness of the fingers

ANSWERS

1. **2**

Rationale: Salmeterol (Serevent) is an adrenergic type of bronchodilator and beclomethasone dipropionate is a glucocorticoid. Bronchodilators are always administered before glucocorticoids when both are to be given on the same time schedule. This allows for widening of the air passages by the bronchodilator, which then makes the glucocorticoid more effective.

Test-Taking Strategy: To answer this question correctly, you must know two different things. First, you must know that a bronchodilator is always given before a glucocorticoid. This would allow you to eliminate options 3 and 4 because you would not alternate the medications. To select between options

1 and 2, you must know that salmeterol is a bronchodilator, whereas beclomethasone is a glucocorticoid. Review these medications if you had difficulty with this question.
Level of Cognitive Ability: Application
Client Needs: Physiological Integrity
Integrated Process: Nursing Process—implementation
Content Area: Pharmacology
References: Kee, J., Hayes, E., & McCuistion, L. (2006). *Pharmacology: A nursing process approach* (5th ed., pp. 590-592). Philadelphia: W.B. Saunders.
Mosby. (2007). *2007 Mosby's nursing drug reference* (20th ed., p. 172). St. Louis: Mosby.

2. 2
Rationale: Theophylline is a xanthine bronchodilator. Before drawing of a serum level of the medication, the client should avoid taking foods or beverages that contain xanthine, such as colas, coffee, or chocolate. Thus, the client is told to avoid caffeine intake before the test.
Test-Taking Strategy: Use the process of elimination. Recalling that this medication is a xanthine bronchodilator will direct you to option 2. Review client teaching points related to this medication if you had difficulty with this question.
Level of Cognitive Ability: Application
Client Needs: Physiological Integrity
Integrated Process: Nursing Process—assessment
Content Area: Pharmacology
Reference: Hodgson, B., & Kizior, R. (2007). *Saunders nursing drug handbook 2007* (p. 57). Philadelphia: W.B. Saunders.

3. 1
Rationale: Antiviral medications for influenza must be taken exactly as prescribed. These medications do not prevent the spread of influenza and clients are usually contagious for up to 2 days after the initiation of antiviral medications. Secondary bacterial infections may occur despite antiviral treatment. Side effects occur with these medications and may necessitate change in activities, especially when driving or operating machinery if dizziness occurs.
Test-Taking Strategy: Use process of elimination and note the strategic words *indicates an understanding*. Using general medication guidelines will direct you to option 1. Review these medications if you had difficulty with this question.
Level of Cognitive Ability: Analysis
Client Needs: Physiological Integrity
Integrated Process: Nursing Process—evaluation
Content Area: Pharmacology
Reference: Lehne, R. (2007). *Pharmacology for nursing care* (6th ed., p. 1059). Philadelphia: W.B. Saunders.

4. 1
Rationale: Theophylline (Theo-24) is a methylxanthine bronchodilator. The nurse teaches the client to limit the intake of xanthine-containing foods while taking this medication. These foods include coffee, cola, and chocolate.
Test-Taking Strategy: Use the process of elimination. Recall that oxtriphylline is a xanthine bronchodilator and know that intake of excessive amounts of foods naturally high in xanthines should be curtailed. Review the foods naturally high in xanthines if you had difficulty with this question.

Level of Cognitive Ability: Application
Client Needs: Physiological Integrity
Integrated Process: Teaching and Learning
Content Area: Pharmacology
Reference: Skidmore-Roth, L. (2005). *Mosby's drug guide for nurses* (6th ed., p. 647). St. Louis: Mosby.

5. 1
Rationale: Hypersensitivity reaction can occur in clients taking salmeterol. Signs and symptoms include rash, urticaria, and swelling of the face, lips, or eyelids. The nurse should call the physician immediately if any of these occur. The other options are incorrect.
Test-Taking Strategy: Use the process of elimination. Recognizing that the signs and symptoms listed in the question are typical of a hypersensitivity reaction allows you to eliminate options 2 and 4 first. From the remaining options, recall that the client needs treatment with an antihistamine or epinephrine, not oral fluids. Review this medication if the question was difficult.
Level of Cognitive Ability: Application
Client Needs: Physiological Integrity
Integrated Process: Nursing Process—implementation
Content Area: Pharmacology
References: Lilley, L., Harrington, S. & Snyder, J. (2005). *Pharmacology and the nursing process* (4th ed., p. 302). St. Louis: Mosby.
Skidmore-Roth, L. (2006). *Mosby's drug guide for nurses* (6th ed., p. 772). St. Louis: Mosby.

6. 4
Rationale: Omalizumab is an anti-inflammatory used for long-term control of asthma. Anaphylactic reactions can occur with the administration of omalizumab. The nurse administering the medication should have medications for the treatment of severe hypersensitivity available. Options 1, 2, and 3 are unnecessary.
Test-Taking Strategy: Use the process of elimination. Recall that anaphylactic reactions can occur with the administration of omalizumab and that omalizumab is not associated with gastric side effects or increased mucus production. Review this medication if you had difficulty with this question.
Level of Cognitive Ability: Application
Client Needs: Physiological Integrity
Integrated Process: Nursing Process—implementation
Content Area: Pharmacology
Reference: Skidmore-Roth, L. (2006). *Mosby's 2006 nursing drug reference* (p. 715). St. Louis: Mosby.

7. 2
Rationale: Guaifenesin (Humibid) is an expectorant and should be taken with a full glass of water to decrease the viscosity of secretions. Sustained-release preparations should not be broken open, crushed, or chewed. The medication occasionally may cause dizziness, headache, or drowsiness as side effects. The client should contact the physician if the cough lasts longer than 1 week or is accompanied by fever, rash, sore throat, or persistent headache.
Test-Taking Strategy: Use the process of elimination. Begin to answer this question by eliminating option 4 first. Sustained-

released preparations are not crushed or broken. Option 3 is eliminated next because fever indicates infection, and an "extra dose" of an expectorant is not helpful in treating infection. From the remaining options, knowing that increased fluids helps liquefy secretions for more effective coughing directs you to option 2 as correct. If you had difficulty with this question, review this medication.
Level of Cognitive Ability: Analysis
Client Needs: Physiological Integrity
Integrated Process: Nursing Process—evaluation
Content Area: Pharmacology
Reference: Kee, J., Hayes, E., & McCuistion, L. (2006). *Pharmacology: A nursing process approach* (5th ed., p. 584). Philadelphia: W.B. Saunders.

8. **3**
Rationale: The nurse administering naloxone for suspected opioid overdose should have resuscitation equipment readily available to support naloxone therapy if it is needed. Other adjuncts that may be needed include oxygen, mechanical ventilator, and vasopressors.
Test-Taking Strategy: Use the process of elimination. Note the strategic words *intravenous opioid overdose*. Recalling the effects of these medications will direct you to option 3. Option 3 is also the umbrella response. Review this medication if you had difficulty with this question.
Level of Cognitive Ability: Application
Client Needs: Physiological Integrity
Integrated Process: Nursing Process—planning
Content Area: Pharmacology
Reference: Skidmore-Roth, L. (2005). *Mosby's drug guide for nurses* (6th ed., p. 600). St. Louis: Mosby.

9. **1**
Rationale: Diphenhydramine (Benadryl) has several uses, including antihistamine, antitussive, antidyskinetic, and sedative-hypnotic. Instructions for use include to take with food or milk to decrease gastrointestinal upset and to use oral rinses or sugarless gum or hard candy to minimize dry mouth. Because the medication causes drowsiness, the client should avoid use of alcohol or central nervous system depressants, operating a car, or engaging in other activities requiring mental awareness during use.
Test-Taking Strategy: Use the process of elimination, noting the strategic words *needs further instructions*. These words indicate a negative event query and ask you to select an option that is incorrect. Knowing that the medication has a sedative effect helps you eliminate options 2 and 4 first. Recalling that the medication causes a dry mouth helps you choose option 1 as the answer to the question, according to the way the question is stated. If you had difficulty with this question, review client education related to this medication.
Level of Cognitive Ability: Analysis
Client Needs: Physiological Integrity
Integrated Process: Teaching and Learning
Content Area: Pharmacology
References: Hodgson, B., & Kizior, R. (2007). *Saunders nursing drug handbook 2007* (p. 366). Philadelphia: W.B. Saunders. Skidmore-Roth, L. (2005). *Mosby's drug guide for nurses* (6th ed., p. 276). St. Louis: Mosby.

10. **3**
Rationale: The client is taught about side effects that could occur with the use of codeine sulfate. The most common side effects include drowsiness, confusion, hypotension, nausea and vomiting, and constipation. Others include bradycardia, respiratory depression, and urinary retention.
Test-Taking Strategy: Use the process of elimination. Remember that codeine sulfate causes constipation. Review the side effects of this medication if you had difficulty with this question.
Level of Cognitive Ability: Analysis
Client Needs: Physiological Integrity
Integrated Process: Nursing Process—evaluation
Content Area: Pharmacology
Reference: Hodgson, B., & Kizior, R. (2007). *Saunders nursing drug handbook 2007* (p. 282). Philadelphia: W.B. Saunders.

11. **4**
Rationale: Cromolyn sodium (Intal) is an inhaled nonsteroidal antiallergy agent and a mast cell stabilizer. The most common undesired side effects associated with inhalation therapy of cromolyn sodium are bronchospasm, cough, nasal congestion, throat irritation, and wheezing. Clients receiving this medication orally may experience pruritis, nausea, diarrhea, and myalgia.
Test-Taking Strategy: Use the process of elimination and note the strategic words *undesirable side effects*. This should assist in directing you to option 4. In addition, use the ABCs—airway, breathing, and circulation—to select the correct option. Option 4 addresses the airway. Review the undesirable side effects of this medication if you had difficulty with this question.
Level of Cognitive Ability: Analysis
Client Needs: Physiological Integrity
Integrated Process: Teaching and Learning
Content Area: Pharmacology
Reference: Hodgson, B., & Kizior, R. (2007). *Saunders nursing drug handbook 2007* (p. 295). Philadelphia: W.B. Saunders.

12. **3**
Rationale: Terbutaline (Brethine) is a bronchodilator and is contraindicated in clients with hypersensitivity to sympathomimetics. It should be used with caution in clients with impaired cardiac function, diabetes mellitus, hypertension, or hyperthyroidism, and a history of seizures. The medication may increase blood glucose levels.
Test-Taking Strategy: Knowledge regarding the contraindications and cautions associated with the use of this medication is needed to answer this question. Remember that terbutaline is used with caution in the client with diabetes mellitus. Review the contraindications and cautions associated with this medication if you are unfamiliar with them.
Level of Cognitive Ability: Analysis
Client Needs: Physiological Integrity
Integrated Process: Nursing Process—analysis
Content Area: Pharmacology
Reference: Hodgson, B., & Kizior, R. (2007). *Saunders nursing drug handbook 2007* (p. 1111). Philadelphia: W.B. Saunders.

13. **3**
Rationale: Zafirlukast (Accolate) is a leukotriene receptor antagonist used in the prophylaxis and long-term treatment of bronchial asthma. Zafirlukast is used with caution in cli-

ents with impaired hepatic function. Liver function laboratory tests should be performed to obtain a baseline, and the levels should be monitored during administration of the medication.
Test-Taking Strategy: Use the process of elimination, eliminating options 2 and 4 first because a complete blood count would include a neutrophil count. From the remaining options, you would need to know that this medication would affect hepatic function. If you had difficulty with this question, review this medication.
Level of Cognitive Ability: Analysis
Client Needs: Physiological Integrity
Integrated Process: Nursing Process—analysis
Content Area: Pharmacology
Reference: Hodgson, B., & Kizior, R. (2007). *Saunders nursing drug handbook 2007* (p. 1225). Philadelphia: W.B. Saunders.

14. 2
Rationale: Isoniazid (INH) is an antitubercular medication. A common side effect of isoniazid is peripheral neuritis, manifested by numbness, tingling, and paresthesias in the extremities. This can be minimized with pyridoxine (vitamin B_6) intake. Options 1, 3, and 4 are incorrect.
Test-Taking Strategy: Use the process of elimination. Options 3 and 4 would not cause the symptoms presented in the question but instead would cause pallor and coolness. From the remaining options, you should know that peripheral neuritis is a side effect of the medication or that these signs and symptoms do not correlate with hypercalcemia. Review the side effects associated with isoniazid if you had difficulty with this question.
Level of Cognitive Ability: Analysis
Client Needs: Physiological Integrity
Integrated Process: Nursing Process—analysis
Content Area: Pharmacology
Reference: Hodgson, B. & Kizior, R. (2007). *Saunders nursing drug handbook 2007* (p. 643). Philadelphia: W.B. Saunders.

15. 2
Rationale: Isoniazid (INH) is hepatotoxic, and therefore the client is taught to report signs and symptoms of hepatitis immediately, which include yellow skin and sclera. For the same reason, alcohol should be avoided during therapy. The client should avoid intake of Swiss cheese, fish such as tuna, and foods containing tyramine because they may cause a reaction characterized by redness and itching of the skin, flushing, sweating, tachycardia, headache, or light-headedness. The client can avoid developing peripheral neuritis by increasing the intake of pyridoxine (vitamin B_6) during the course of isoniazid therapy.
Test-Taking Strategy: Use the process of elimination. Because alcohol intake is prohibited with the use of many medications, eliminate option 1 first. Because the client receiving this medication typically is given supplements of vitamin B_6, option 4 is incorrect and is eliminated next. Recalling that the medication is hepatotoxic will direct you to option 2. If you had difficulty with this question, review this medication.
Level of Cognitive Ability: Application
Client Needs: Physiological Integrity
Integrated Process: Teaching and Learning

Content Area: Pharmacology
Reference: Hodgson, B., & Kizior, R. (2007). *Saunders nursing drug handbook 2007* (p. 643). Philadelphia: W.B. Saunders.

16. 3
Rationale: Rifampin should be taken exactly as directed. Doses should not be doubled or skipped. The client should not stop therapy until directed to do so by a physician. The medication should be administered on an empty stomach unless it causes gastrointestinal upset, and then it may be taken with food. Antacids, if prescribed, should be taken at least 1 hour before the medication. Rifampin causes orange-red discoloration of body secretions and will stain soft contact lenses permanently.
Test-Taking Strategy: Use the process of elimination. Options 2 and 4 are inaccurate in general and are eliminated first. Eliminate option 1 next because of the close-ended word *always.* If you had difficulty with this question, review the side effects associated with this medication.
Level of Cognitive Ability: Application
Client Needs: Physiological Integrity
Integrated Process: Teaching and Learning
Content Area: Pharmacology
Reference: Hodgson, B., & Kizior, R. (2007). *Saunders nursing drug handbook 2007* (p. 1021). Philadelphia: W.B. Saunders.

17. 4
Rationale: Ethambutol causes optic neuritis, which decreases visual acuity and the ability to discriminate between the colors red and green. This poses a potential safety hazard when a client is driving a motor vehicle. The client is taught to report this symptom immediately. The client also is taught to take the medication with food if gastrointestinal upset occurs. Impaired hearing results from antitubercular therapy with streptomycin. Orange-red discoloration of secretions occurs with rifampin (Rifadin).
Test-Taking Strategy: Use the process of elimination. Option 2 is the least likely symptom to report; instead, it should be managed by taking the medication with food. To select among the other options, you must know that this medication causes optic neuritis, resulting in difficulty with red-green discrimination. If this question was difficult, review antitubercular medications because the incorrect options for this question are typical side effects of other antitubercular medications.
Level of Cognitive Ability: Analysis
Client Needs: Physiological Integrity
Integrated Process: Nursing Process—evaluation
Content Area: Pharmacology
Reference: Hodgson, B., & Kizior, R. (2007). *Saunders nursing drug handbook 2007* (p. 451). Philadelphia: W.B. Saunders.

18. 2
Rationale: Cycloserine (Seromycin) is an antitubercular medication that requires weekly serum drug level determinations to monitor for the potential of neurotoxicity. Serum drug levels lower than 30 mg/mL reduce the incidence of neurotoxicity. The medication needs to be taken after meals to prevent gastrointestinal irritation. The client needs to be instructed to notify the physician if a skin rash or early signs of central nervous system toxicity are noted. Alcohol needs to be avoided because it increases the risk of seizure activity.

Test-Taking Strategy: Use the process of elimination. Eliminate options 3 and 4 first because they are the least likely correct options. From this point, knowing that the medication level needs to be monitored will assist in selecting the correct option. If you had difficulty with this question, review this medication.
Level of Cognitive Ability: Application
Client Needs: Physiological Integrity
Integrated Process: Teaching and Learning
Content Area: Pharmacology
Reference: Kee, J., Hayes, E., & McCuistion, L. (2006). *Pharmacology: A nursing process approach* (5th ed., pp. 467-468). Philadelphia: W.B. Saunders.

19. **2**
Rationale: Isoniazid (INH) therapy can cause an elevation of hepatic enzyme levels and hepatitis. Therefore, liver enzyme levels are monitored when therapy is initiated and during the first 3 months of therapy. They may be monitored longer in the client who is older than 50 or abuses alcohol. The laboratory tests in options 1, 3, and 4 are not necessary.
Test-Taking Strategy: Use the process of elimination. Recalling that this medication can be toxic to the liver will direct you to the correct option. Review the adverse effects of the various antituberculosis medications if this is an area that is unfamiliar to you.
Level of Cognitive Ability: Application
Client Needs: Physiological Integrity
Integrated Process: Nursing Process—assessment
Content Area: Pharmacology
Reference: Hodgson, B., & Kizior, R. (2007). *Saunders nursing drug handbook 2007* (p. 643). Philadelphia: W.B. Saunders.

20. **4**
Rationale: Albuterol is an adrenergic bronchodilator. The nurse assesses respiratory pattern, lung sounds, pulse, and blood pressure before and during therapy. The nurse also notes the color, character, and amount of sputum.
Test-Taking Strategy: Use the process of elimination. Knowing that this medication is a bronchodilator allows you to eliminate each of the incorrect options. Use the ABCs—airway, breathing, and circulation—to answer the question. Option 4 is the only option that addresses airway. Review this medication if you had difficulty with this question.
Level of Cognitive Ability: Application
Client Needs: Physiological Integrity
Integrated Process: Nursing Process—assessment
Content Area: Pharmacology
Reference: Hodgson, B., & Kizior, R. (2007). *Saunders nursing drug handbook 2004* (p. 27). Philadelphia: W.B. Saunders.

21. **2**
Rationale: The client taking adrenergic bronchodilators may experience paradoxical bronchospasm, which is evidenced by the client's wheezing. This can occur with excessive use of inhalers. Further medication should be withheld, and the physician should be notified. Options 1, 3, and 4 are incorrect interpretations.
Test-Taking Strategy: Use the process of elimination. Eliminate option 1 first because the client began wheezing after the medication was administered and not before. Option 4 may be eliminated next because tolerance generally does not occur. From the remaining options, knowing that wheezing is associated with bronchospasm will direct you to option 2. Review the side effects associated with the use of inhaled bronchodilators if you had difficulty with this question.
Level of Cognitive Ability: Analysis
Client Needs: Physiological Integrity
Integrated Process: Nursing Process—analysis
Content Area: Pharmacology
Reference: Hodgson, B., & Kizior, R. (2007). *Saunders nursing drug handbook 2007* (p. 743). Philadelphia: W.B. Saunders.

ALTERNATE ITEM FORMAT: MULTIPLE RESPONSE
Answer: 1, 2, 3, 5
Rationale: Rifabutin (Mycobutin) may be prescribed for a client with active *Mycobacterium avium* complex (MAC) disease and tuberculosis. It inhibits mycobacterial DNA-dependent RNA polymerase and suppresses protein synthesis. Side effects include rash, gastrointestinal disturbances, neutropenia (low neutrophil count), red-orange–colored body secretions, uveitis (blurred vision and eye pain), myositis, arthralgia, hepatitis, chest pain with dyspnea, and flu-like syndrome. Vitamin B_6 deficiency and numbness and tingling in the extremities is associated with the use of isoniazid (INH). Ethambutol (Myambutol) also causes peripheral neuritis.
Test-Taking Strategy: Focus on the name of the medication to assist in answering the question and use the process of elimination. Recalling that vitamin B_6 deficiency and numbness and tingling in the extremities is associated with the use of isoniazid will assist in answering. Review the side effects associated with rifabutin if you had difficulty with this question.
Level of Cognitive Ability: Analysis
Client Needs: Physiological Integrity
Integrated Process: Nursing Process—assessment
Content Area: Pharmacology
Reference: Lehne, R. (2007). *Pharmacology for nursing care* (6th ed., p. 1022). Philadelphia: W.B. Saunders.

REFERENCES

Harper, S., Fukuda, K., Uyeki, T., Cox, N., & Bridges, C. (2005). Prevention and control of influenza: Recommendations of the Advisory Committee on Immunization Practices. *Morbidity and Mortality Weekly Report MMWR*, 54(RR08), 1-40.

Hodgson, B., & Kizior, R. (2007). *Saunders nursing drug handbook 2007*. Philadelphia: W.B. Saunders.

Kee, J., Hayes, E., & McCuistion, L. (2006). *Pharmacology: A nursing process approach* (5th ed.). Philadelphia: W.B. Saunders.

Lehne, R. (2007). *Pharmacology for nursing care* (6th ed.). Philadelphia: W.B. Saunders.

Lilley, L., Harrington, S., & Snyder, J. (2005). *Pharmacology and the nursing process* (4th ed.). St. Louis: Mosby.

Mosby. 2007 *Mosby's nursing drug reference* (20th ed.). St. Louis: Mosby.

Skidmore-Roth, L. (2005). *Mosby's drug guide for nurses* (4th ed.). St. Louis: Mosby.

The Adult Client With a Cardiovascular Disorder

PYRAMID TERMS

afterload The force against which the heart has to pump (peripheral resistance) to eject blood from the left ventricle. Factors and conditions that would impede blood flow increase left ventricular afterload.

arterial pressure The pressure of the blood against the arterial walls. Pressure can be measured indirectly by sphygmomanometer or directly by arterial catheter. Readings are expressed as systolic over diastolic. Arterial pressure increases when the cardiac output, peripheral resistance, or blood volume increases.

automaticity The ability of cardiac cells to initiate an impulse spontaneously and repetitively without external neurohormonal control. The pacemaker cells have the highest rate of automaticity of all cardiac cells.

baroreceptors Specialized nerve endings located in the walls of the aortic arch and carotid sinuses that are affected by changes in the arterial blood pressure (BP). Increases in arterial pressure stimulate baroreceptors and the heart rate and arterial pressure decrease. Decreases in arterial pressure lead to a lessened stimulation of the baroreceptors, vasoconstriction occurs, and the heart rate increases; also called pressoreceptors.

blood pressure (BP) The force exerted by the blood against the walls of the blood vessels. If the blood pressure falls too low, blood flow to the tissues, heart, brain, and other organs become inadequate. If the blood pressure becomes too high, the risk of vessel rupture and damage increases.

capillary pressure or hydrostatic pressure The pressure exerted by the blood against the capillary wall. Normal capillary pressure is 25 to 30 mm Hg at the arterial end of the capillaries, and 10 to 15 mm Hg at the venous end.

cardiac output The total volume of blood pumped through the heart in 1 minute. The normal cardiac output is 4 to 7 L/min. Cardiac output equals stroke volume multiplied by heart rate. Cardiac output can be calculated via the thermodilution method when the client has a pulmonary artery catheter (Swan-Ganz catheter).

chemoreceptors Nerve endings located in the aortic arch and carotid bodies that are stimulated by hypoxemia and that subsequently transmit impulses to the central nervous system.

conductivity The ability of the heart muscle fibers to propagate electrical impulses along and across cell membranes.

contractility The inherent ability of the myocardium to alter contractile force and velocity. Sympathetic stimulation increases myocardial contractility, so stroke volume increases. Conditions that decrease myocardial contractility reduce stroke volume.

diastole The phase of the cardiac cycle in which the heart relaxes between contractions. Diastole represents the period of time when the two ventricles are dilated by the blood flowing into them.

diastolic pressure The force of the blood exerted against the artery walls when the heart relaxes or fills.

excitability The ability of cardiac muscle cells to depolarize in response to a stimulus. Excitability is influenced by hormones, electrolytes, nutrition, oxygen supply, medication, infections, and nerve characteristics.

mean arterial pressure (MAP) An approximation of the average pressure in the systemic circulation throughout the cardiac cycle; used in hemodynamic monitoring. Mean arterial pressure must be at least 60 mm Hg for adequate organ perfusion.

paradoxical blood pressure An exaggerated decrease in systolic pressure by more than 10 mm Hg during the inspiratory phase of the respiratory cycle. Normal value is 3 to 10 mm Hg.

postural (orthostatic) hypotension A blood pressure decrease of more than 10 to 15 mm Hg of the systolic pressure or a decrease of more than 10 mm Hg of the diastolic pressure and a 10% to 20% increase in heart rate. Postural hypotension occurs when the client's blood pressure is not maintained adequately when moving from a lying to a sitting or standing position.

preload The volume of blood stretching the left ventricle at the end of diastole. Preload is determined by the total circulating blood volume and is increased by an increase in venous return to the heart.

pulmonary capillary wedge pressure (PCWP) The measurement obtained during momentary balloon inflation of a pulmonary artery catheter; it is reflective of left ventricular end-diastolic pressure. The PCWP normally ranges between 6 and 12 mm Hg. Decreased PCWP indicates hypovolemia, whereas increased PCWP indicates hypervolemia, left ventricular failure, or mitral regurgitation.

pulse pressure The difference between the systolic and diastolic pressure. Normal pulse pressure is 30 to 40 mm Hg.

refractoriness The inability of the heart to respond to a new stimulus while still in a state of contraction from an earlier stimulus. Refractoriness prevents uncontrolled rapid cardiac contractions and helps preserve the heart rhythm.

stretch receptors Nerve endings located in the vena cava and the right atrium that respond to pressure changes affecting circulatory blood volume. When the blood pressure decreases because of hypovolemia, a sympathetic response occurs, causing an increased heart rate and blood vessel constriction. When the blood pressure increases because of hypervolemia, an opposite effect occurs.

stroke volume The amount of blood ejected from the left ventricle with each contraction. The normal stroke volume is 70 to 130 mL/heartbeat. The stroke volume can be affected by preload, afterload, contractility, and the Frank-Starling law.

systole The phase of contraction of the heart, especially of the ventricles, during which blood is forced into the aorta and pulmonary artery.

systolic pressure The maximum pressure of blood exerted against the artery walls when the heart contracts.

venous pressure The force exerted by the blood against the vein walls. Normal venous pressures are highest in the extremities (5 to 14 cm H_2O in the arm), and lowest closest to the heart (6 to 8 cm H_2O in the inferior vena cava).

▲ PYRAMID TO SUCCESS

Pyramid Points focus on assessment data related to cardiovascular risks, health screening and promotion, complications of the various cardiovascular disorders, emergency implementation measures, and client education. Focus on the assessment findings in angina, myocardial infarction, congestive heart failure and pulmonary edema, pericarditis, dysrhythmias, pacemakers, aneurysms, hypertension, and arterial and venous disorders. You must be able to identify the most common dysrhythmias and determine the appropriate interventions for these dysrhythmias. Focus also on the care of the client following diagnostic treatments and surgical procedures. Note appropriate and therapeutic client positions, particularly with arterial and venous disorders of the extremities. Focus on treatments and medications prescribed for the various cardiovascular disorders and client teaching related to prescribed treatment plans. Be familiar with the components related to cardiac rehabilitation. The Integrated Processes addressed in this unit include Caring, Communication and Documentation, Nursing Process, and Teaching and Learning.

▲ CLIENT NEEDS

Safe and Effective Care Environment

Consulting with members of the health care team
Establishing priorities
Initiating cardiovascular consultations and referrals
Maintaining medical and surgical asepsis
Maintaining standard and other precautions
Obtaining informed consent related to treatments and procedures
Upholding client rights

Health Promotion and Maintenance

Discussing alterations in lifestyle
Implementing cardiovascular assessment techniques
Mobilizing appropriate community resources

Promoting cardiac rehabilitation
Providing health screening and health promotion programs
Preventing cardiovascular disease
Teaching related to diet therapy, exercise, and medications

Psychosocial Integrity

Assisting the client to accept lifestyle changes
Considering religious, spiritual, and cultural influences on health
Discussing grief and loss and end-of-life issues
Discussing situational role changes
Discussing unexpected body image changes
Identifying coping mechanisms
Identifying fear, anxiety, and denial
Identifying support systems

Physiological Integrity

Administering intravenous medications
Assisting with basic care measures
Discussing activity limitations and promoting rest and sleep
Monitoring hemodynamics
Monitoring for complications related to cardiovascular disorders
Monitoring for therapeutic effects of medications
Monitoring of cardiac enzyme and troponin levels and other laboratory values related to the cardiovascular system
Providing interventions required in emergencies
Providing nonpharmacological and pharmacological comfort interventions
Responding to medical emergencies

REFERENCES

Black, J., & Hawks, J. (2005). *Medical-surgical nursing: Clinical management for positive outcomes* (7th ed.). Philadelphia: W.B. Saunders.

Chernecky, C., & Berger, B. (2004). *Laboratory tests and diagnostic procedures* (4th ed.). Philadelphia: W.B. Saunders.

Harkreader, H., & Hogan, M. (2004). *Fundamentals of nursing: Caring and clinical judgment* (2nd ed.). Philadelphia: W.B. Saunders.

Ignatavicius, D., & Workman, M. (2006). *Medical-surgical nursing: Critical thinking for collaborative care* (5th ed.). Philadelphia: W.B. Saunders.

Jarvis, C. (2004). *Physical examination and health assessment* (4th ed.,) St. Louis: W.B. Saunders.

Lewis, S., Heitkemper, M., & Dirksen, S. (2004). *Medical-surgical nursing: Assessment and management of clinical problems* (6th ed.). St. Louis: Mosby.

National Council of State Boards of Nursing (Eds.). (2007). *2007 NCLEX-RN® detailed test plan.* Chicago: Author.

Potter, P., & Perry, A. (2005). *Fundamentals of nursing* (6th ed.). St. Louis: Mosby.

Varcarolis, E., Carson, V., & Shoemaker, N. (2006). *Foundations of psychiatric mental health nursing: A clinical approach* (5th ed.). Philadelphia: W.B. Saunders.

Cardiovascular Disorders

I. ANATOMY AND PHYSIOLOGY

A. Heart and heart wall layers
1. The heart is located in the left side of the mediastinum.
2. The heart consists of three layers.
   a. The epicardium is the outermost layer of the heart.
   b. The myocardium is the middle layer and is the actual contracting muscle of the heart.
   c. The endocardium is the innermost layer and lines the inner chambers and heart valves.

B. Pericardial sac
1. Encases and protects the heart from trauma and infection
2. Has two layers
   a. The parietal pericardium is the tough, fibrous outer membrane that attaches anteriorly to the lower half of the sternum, posteriorly to the thoracic vertebrae, and inferiorly to the diaphragm.
   b. The visceral pericardium is the thin, inner layer that closely adheres to the heart.
3. The pericardial space is between the parietal and visceral layers; it holds 5 to 20 mL of pericardial fluid, lubricates the pericardial surfaces, and cushions the heart.

C. There are four heart chambers
1. The right atrium receives deoxygenated blood from the body via the superior and inferior vena cava.
2. The right ventricle receives blood from the right atrium and pumps it to the lungs via the pulmonary artery.
3. The left atrium receives oxygenated blood from the lungs via four pulmonary veins.
4. The left ventricle is the largest and most muscular chamber; it receives oxygenated blood from the lungs via the left atrium and pumps blood into the systemic circulation via the aorta.

D. There are four valves in the heart.
1. There are two atrioventricular valves, the tricuspid and the mitral, which lie between the atria and ventricles.
   a. The tricuspid valve is located on the right side of the heart.
   b. The bicuspid (mitral) valve is located on the left side of the heart.
   c. The atrioventricular valves close at the beginning of ventricular contraction and prevent blood from flowing back into the atria from the ventricles; these valves open when the ventricle relaxes.
2. There are two semilunar valves, the pulmonic and the aortic.
   a. The pulmonic semilunar valve lies between the right ventricle and the pulmonary artery.
   b. The aortic semilunar valve lies between the left ventricle and the aorta.
   c. The semilunar valves prevent blood from flowing back into the ventricles during relaxation; they open during ventricular contraction and close when the ventricles begin to relax.

E. Sinoatrial (SA) node
1. The main pacemaker that initiates each heartbeat
2. It is located at the junction of the superior vena cava and the right atrium.
3. The sinoatrial node generates electrical impulses at 60 to 100 times per minute and is controlled by the sympathetic and parasympathetic nervous systems.

F. Atrioventricular (AV) node
1. Located in the lower aspect of the atrial septum
2. Receives electrical impulses from the sinoatrial node

3. If the sinoatrial node fails, the atrioventricular node can initiate and sustain a heart rate of 40 to 60 beats/min.

G. The bundle of His
   1. A continuation of the AV node; located at the interventricular septum
   2. It branches into the right bundle branch, which extends down the right side of the interventricular septum, and the left bundle branch, which extends into the left ventricle.
   3. The right and left bundle branches terminate into Purkinje fibers.

H. Purkinje fibers
   1. Purkinje fibers are a diffuse network of conducting strands located beneath the ventricular endocardium.
   2. These fibers spread the wave of depolarization through the ventricles.
   3. Purkinje fibers can act as the pacemaker with a rate between 20 and 40 beats/min when higher pacemakers fail.

I. Coronary arteries (Fig. 59-1)
   1. The coronary arteries supply the capillaries of the myocardium with blood.
   2. The right coronary artery supplies the right atrium and ventricle, the inferior portion of the left ventricle, the posterior septal wall, and the sinoatrial and atrioventricular nodes.
   3. The left main coronary artery consists of two major branches, the left anterior descending and the circumflex arteries.
   4. The left anterior descending artery supplies blood to the anterior wall of the left ventricle, the anterior ventricular septum, and the apex of the left ventricle.
   5. The circumflex artery supplies blood to the left atrium and the lateral and posterior surfaces of the left ventricle.

J. Heart sounds
   1. The first heart sound (S_1) is heard as the atrioventricular valves close and is heard loudest at the apex of the heart.
   2. The second heart sound (S_2) is heard when the semilunar valves close and is heard loudest at the base of the heart.
   3. A third heart sound (S_3) may be heard if ventricular wall compliance is decreased and structures in the ventricular wall vibrate; this can occur in conditions such as congestive heart failure or valvular regurgitation. However, a third heart sound may be normal in individuals younger than 30 years.
   4. A fourth heart sound (S_4) may be heard on atrial **systole** if resistance to ventricular filling is present; this is an abnormal finding, and the causes include cardiac hypertrophy, disease, or injury to the ventricular wall.

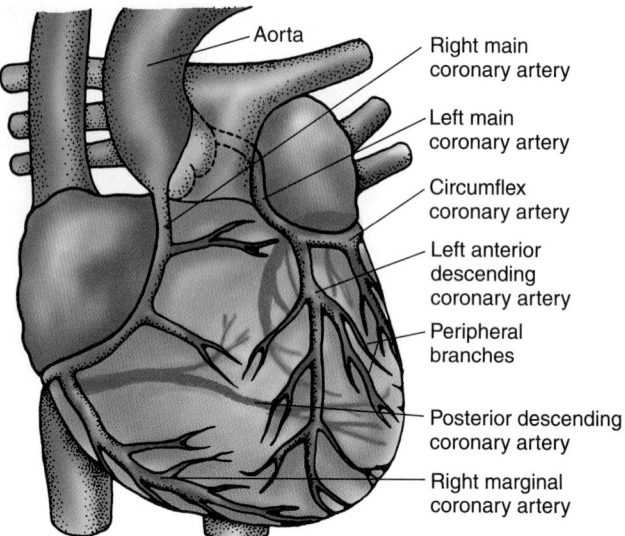

FIG. 59-1 Coronary arterial system. (From Ignatavicius, D., & Workman, M. [2006]. *Medical-surgical nursing: Critical thinking for collaborative care* [5th ed.]. Philadelphia: W.B. Saunders.)

K. Heart rate
   1. The faster the heart rate, the less time the heart has for filling, and the cardiac output decreases.
   2. An increase in heart rate increases oxygen consumption.
   3. The normal sinus heart rate is 60 to 100 beats/min.
   4. Sinus tachycardia is a rate more than 100 beats/min.
   5. Sinus bradycardia is a rate less than 60 beats/min.

L. Autonomic nervous system
   1. Stimulation of sympathetic nerve fibers releases the neurotransmitter norepinephrine, producing an increased heart rate, increased conduction speed through the atrioventricular node, increased atrial and ventricular **contractility**, and peripheral vasoconstriction; stimulation occurs when a decrease in pressure is detected.
   2. Stimulation of the parasympathetic nerve fibers releases the neurotransmitter acetylcholine, which decreases the heart rate and lessens atrial and ventricular **contractility** and **conductivity**. Stimulation occurs when an increase in pressure is detected.

M. **Blood pressure (BP)** control
   1. **Baroreceptors**, also called pressoreceptors, are located in the walls of the aortic arch and carotid sinuses.
   2. **Baroreceptors** are specialized nerve endings affected by changes in the arterial **BP**.
   3. Increases in **arterial pressure** stimulate **baroreceptors**, and the heart rate and **arterial pressure** decrease.

4. Decreases in **arterial pressure** reduce stimulation of the **baroreceptors** and vasoconstriction occurs, as does an increase in heart rate.
5. **Stretch receptors**, located in the vena cava and the right atrium, respond to pressure changes that affect circulatory blood volume.
6. When the **BP** decreases as a result of hypovolemia, a sympathetic response occurs, causing an increased heart rate and blood vessel constriction; when the **BP** increases as a result of hypervolemia, an opposite effect occurs.
7. Antidiuretic hormone (vasopressin) influences **BP** indirectly by regulating vascular volume.
8. Increases in blood volume result in decreased antidiuretic hormone release, increasing diuresis, decreasing blood volume, and thus decreasing **BP**.
9. Decreases in blood volume result in increased antidiuretic hormone release; this promotes an increase in blood volume and therefore **BP**.
10. Renin, a potent vasoconstrictor, causes the **BP** to increase.
11. Renin converts angiotensinogen to angiotensin I; angiotensin I is then converted to angiotensin II in the lungs.
12. Angiotensin II stimulates the release of aldosterone, which promotes water and sodium retention by the kidneys; this action increases blood volume and **BP**.

▲ N. The vascular system
1. Arteries are vessels through which the blood passes away from the heart to various parts of the body; they convey highly oxygenated blood from the left side of heart to the tissues.
2. Arterioles control the blood flow into the capillaries.
3. Capillaries allow the exchange of fluid and nutrients between the blood and the interstitial spaces.
4. Venules receive blood from the capillary bed and move blood into the veins.
5. Veins transport deoxygenated blood from the tissues back to the right heart and then to the lungs for oxygenation.
6. Valves help return blood to the heart against the force of gravity.
7. The lymphatics drain the tissues and return the tissue fluid to the blood.

II. DIAGNOSTIC TESTS AND PROCEDURES

▲ A. Cardiac enzymes
1. CK-MB (creatine kinase, myocardial muscle)
   a. An elevation in value indicates myocardial damage.
   ▲ b. An elevation occurs within 4 to 6 hours and peaks 18 to 24 hours following an acute ischemic attack.
   c. Normal value is 0% to 5% of total; total CK is 26 to 174 units/L.
2. Lactate dehydrogenase (LDH)
   ▲ a. Elevations in LDH levels occur 24 hours following myocardial infarction and peak in 48 to 72 hours.
   ▲ b. Normally, LDH_1 is lower than LDH_2; when the serum concentration of LDH_1 is higher than LDH_2, the pattern is indicated as "flipped," signifying myocardial necrosis.
   c. The normal value of LDH in conventional units is 140 to 280 international units/L.
3. Troponin ▲
   a. Troponin is composed of three proteins—troponin C, cardiac troponin I, and cardiac troponin T.
   b. Troponin I especially has a high affinity for myocardial injury; it rises within 3 hours and persists for up to 7 days.
   c. Normal values are low, with troponin I being lower than 0.6 ng/mL and troponin T normally ranging from 0 to 0.2 ng/mL; thus, any rise can indicate myocardial cell damage.
4. Myoglobin
   a. Myoglobin is an oxygen-binding protein found in cardiac and skeletal muscle.
   b. The level rises within 1 hour after cell death, peaks in 4 to 6 hours, and returns to normal within 24 to 36 hours (even faster in some clients).

B. Complete blood count
1. The red blood cell count decreases in rheumatic heart disease and infective endocarditis and increases in conditions characterized by inadequate tissue oxygenation.
2. The white blood cell count increases in infectious and inflammatory diseases of the heart and after myocardial infarction (MI) because large numbers of white blood cells are needed to dispose of the necrotic tissue resulting from the infarction. ▲
3. An elevated hematocrit level can result from vascular volume depletion.
4. Decreases in hematocrit and hemoglobin levels can indicate anemia.

C. Blood coagulation factors: An increase in coagulation factors can occur during and after MI, which places the client at greater risk of thrombophlebitis and extension of clots in the coronary arteries. ▲

D. Serum lipids
1. The lipid profile measures serum cholesterol, triglyceride, and lipoprotein levels.
2. The lipid profile is used to assess the risk of developing coronary artery disease.

3. The desirable range for serum cholesterol is lower than 200 mg/dL, with low-density lipoprotein cholesterol lower than 130 mg/dL and high-density lipoprotein cholesterol at 30 to 70 mg/dL.

E. Electrolytes
   1. Potassium
      a. Hypokalemia causes increased cardiac electrical instability, ventricular dysrhythmias, and increased risk of digoxin toxicity.
      b. In hypokalemia, the electrocardiogram shows flattening and inversion of the T wave, the appearance of a U wave, and ST depression.
      c. Hyperkalemia causes asystole and ventricular dysrhythmias.
      d. In hyperkalemia, the electrocardiogram may show tall peaked T waves, widened QRS complexes, prolonged PR intervals, or flat P waves.
   2. Sodium
      a. The serum sodium level decreases with the use of diuretics.
      b. The serum sodium level decreases in heart failure, indicating water excess.

F. Calcium
   1. Hypocalcemia can cause ventricular dysrhythmias, prolonged ST and QT intervals, and cardiac arrest.
   2. Hypercalcemia can cause a shortened ST segment and widened T wave, atrioventricular block, tachycardia or bradycardia, digitalis hypersensitivity, and cardiac arrest.

G. Phosphorus level: Phosphorus levels should be interpreted with calcium levels because the kidneys retain or excrete one electrolyte in an inverse relationship to the other.

H. Magnesium
   1. A low magnesium level can cause ventricular tachycardia and fibrillation.
   2. Electrocardiographic changes that may be observed with hypomagnesemia include tall T waves and depressed ST segments.
   3. A high magnesium level can cause muscle weakness, hypotension, and bradycardia.
   4. Electrocardiographic changes that may be observed with hypermagnesemia include a prolonged PR interval and widened QRS complex.

I. Blood urea nitrogen: The blood urea nitrogen level is elevated in heart disorders that adversely affect renal circulation, such as heart failure and cardiogenic shock.

J. Blood glucose: An acute cardiac episode can elevate the blood glucose level.

K. B-type natriuretic peptide (BNP)
   1. BNP is released in response to atrial and ventricular stretch; it serves as a marker for congestive heart failure.

   2. BNP levels should be lower than 100 pg/mL; the higher the level, the more severe the congestive heart failure (CHF).

L. Chest x-ray
   1. Description
      a. Radiography of the chest is done to determine the size, silhouette, and position of the heart.
      b. Specific pathological changes are difficult to determine on x-rays, but anatomical changes can be seen.
   2. Interventions
      a. Prepare the client for radiography, explaining the purpose and procedure.
      b. Remove jewelry.

M. Electrocardiography (Box 59-1)
   1. Description: This common noninvasive diagnostic test records the electrical activity of the heart and is useful for detecting cardiac dysrhythmias, location and extent of myocardial infarction, and cardiac hypertrophy and for evaluation of the effectiveness of cardiac medications.
   2. Interventions
      a. Determine the client's ability to lie still; advise the client to lie still, breathe normally, and refrain from talking during the test.
      b. Reassure the client that an electrical shock will not occur.
      c. Document any cardiac medications the client is taking.

N. Holter monitoring
   1. Description
      a. In this noninvasive test, the client wears a Holter monitor and an electrocardiographic tracing is recorded continuously over a period of 24 hours or more while the client performs his or her activities of daily living.
      b. The Holter monitor identifies dysrhythmias if they occur and evaluates the effectiveness of antidysrhythmics or pacemaker therapy.
   2. Interventions
      a. Instruct the client to resume normal daily activities and to maintain a diary documenting activities and any symptoms that may develop for correlation with the electrocardiographic tracing.
      b. Instruct the client to avoid tub baths or showers because they will interfere with the electrocardiographic recorder device.

O. Echocardiography
   1. Description
      a. This noninvasive procedure is based on the principles of ultrasound and evaluates structural and functional changes in the heart.
      b. Heart chamber size is measured, ejection fraction is calculated, and flow gradient across the valves is determined.

Basics of Electrocardiography

An electrocardiogram (ECG) reflects the electrical activity of cardiac cells and records electrical activity at a speed of 25 mm/sec.

An electrocardiographic strip consists of horizontal lines representing seconds and vertical lines representing voltage.

Each small square represents 0.04 second.

Each large square represents 0.20 second.

The P wave represents atrial depolarization.

The PR interval represents the time it takes an impulse to travel from the atria through the atrioventricular node, bundle of His, and bundle branches to the Purkinje fibers.

Normal PR interval duration ranges from 0.12 to 0.2 second.

The PR interval is measured from the beginning of the P wave to the end of the PR segment.

The QRS complex represents ventricular depolarization.

Normal QRS complex duration ranges from 0.04 to 0.1 second.

The Q wave appears as the first negative deflection in the QRS complex and reflects initial ventricular septal depolarization.

The R wave is the first positive deflection in the QRS complex.

The S wave appears as the second negative deflection in the QRS complex.

The J point marks the end of the QRS complex and the beginning of the ST segment.

The QRS duration is measured from the end of the PR segment to the J point.

The ST segment represents early ventricular repolarization.

The T wave represents ventricular repolarization and ventricular diastole.

The U wave may follow the T wave.

A prominent U wave may indicate an electrolyte abnormality, such as hypokalemia.

The QT interval represents ventricular refractory time or the total time required for ventricular depolarization and repolarization.

The QT interval is measured from the beginning of the QRS complex to the end of the T wave.

The QT interval normally lasts 0.32 to 0.4 second but varies with the client's heart rate, age, and gender.

2. Interventions
   a. Determine the client's ability to lie still, and advise the client to lie still, breathe normally, and refrain from talking during the test.

P. Exercise testing (stress test)
   1. Description
      a. This noninvasive test studies the heart during activity and detects and evaluates coronary artery disease.
      b. Treadmill testing is the most commonly used mode of stress testing.

c. Stress testing may be used with myocardial radionuclide testing (perfusion imaging), at which point the procedure becomes invasive because a radionuclide must be injected.
      d. If the client is unable to tolerate exercise, an intravenous (IV) infusion of dipyridamole (Persantine), dobutamine hydrochloride, or adenosine (Adenocard) is given to dilate the coronary arteries and simulate the effect of exercise.
      e. An informed consent is required if a radionuclide is injected.
   2. Preprocedure interventions
      a. Obtain an informed consent if required.
      b. Provide adequate rest the night before the procedure.
      c. Instruct the client to eat a light meal 1 to 2 hours before the procedure.
      d. Instruct the client to avoid smoking, alcohol, and caffeine before the procedure.
      e. Instruct the client to ask the physician about taking prescribed medication on the day of the procedure; theophylline products are usually held 12 hours before the test and calcium channel blockers and β-blockers are usually held for 24 hours.
      f. Instruct the client to wear nonconstrictive,  comfortable clothing and supportive rubber-soled shoes for the exercise stress test.
      g. Instruct the client to notify the physician if any chest pain, dizziness, or shortness of breath occurs during the procedure.
   3. Postprocedure interventions: Instruct the client to avoid taking a hot bath or shower for at least 1 to 2 hours.

Q. Digital subtraction angiography
   1. Description
      a. This test combines x-ray techniques and a computerized subtraction technique with fluoroscopy for visualization of the cardiovascular system.
      b. A contrast medium (dye) is injected.
   2. Preprocedure interventions
      a. Assess for allergies to seafood, iodine, or radiopaque dyes. If allergic, the client may be premedicated with antihistamines and corticosteroids to prevent a reaction.
      b. Obtain informed consent.
   3. Postprocedure interventions
      a. Monitor vital signs.
      b. Assess injection site for bleeding or discomfort.

R. Nuclear cardiology
   1. Description
      a. Nuclear cardiology is the use of radionuclide techniques and scanning for cardiovascular assessment.

b. The most common tests include technetium pyrophosphate scanning, thallium imaging, and multigated cardiac blood pool imaging.

2. Preprocedure interventions
   a. Obtain informed consent.
   b. Inform the client that a small amount of radioisotope will be injected and that the radiation exposure and risks are minimal.

3. Postprocedure interventions
   a. Assess vital signs.
   b. Assess injection site for bleeding or discomfort.
   c. Inform the client that fatigue is possible.

S. Magnetic resonance imaging (MRI)
   1. Description
      a. This is a noninvasive diagnostic test that produces an image of the heart or great vessels through interaction of magnetic fields, radio waves, and atomic nuclei.
      b. It provides information on chamber size and thickness, valve and ventricular function, and blood flow through the great vessels and coronary arteries.
   2. Preprocedure interventions
      a. Evaluate the client for the presence of a pacemaker or other implanted items that present a contraindication to the test.
      b. Ensure that the client has removed all metallic objects such as watch, jewelry, clothing with metal fasteners, and metal hair fasteners.
      c. Inform the client that she or he may experience claustrophobia while in the scanner.

T. Cardiac catheterization (Fig. 59-2)
   1. Description
      a. An invasive test involving insertion of a catheter into the heart and surrounding vessels
      b. Obtains information about the structure and performance of the heart chambers and valves and the coronary circulation
   2. Preprocedure interventions
      a. Obtain informed consent.
      b. Assess for allergies to seafood, iodine, or radiopaque dyes; if allergic, the client may be premedicated with antihistamines and corticosteroids to prevent a reaction.
      c. Withhold solid food for 6 to 8 hours and liquids for 4 hours as prescribed to prevent vomiting and aspiration during the procedure.
      d. Document the client's height and weight because these data will be needed to determine the amount of dye to be administered.
      e. Document baseline vital signs and note the quality and presence of peripheral pulses for postprocedure comparison.
      f. Inform the client that a local anesthetic will be administered before catheter insertion.

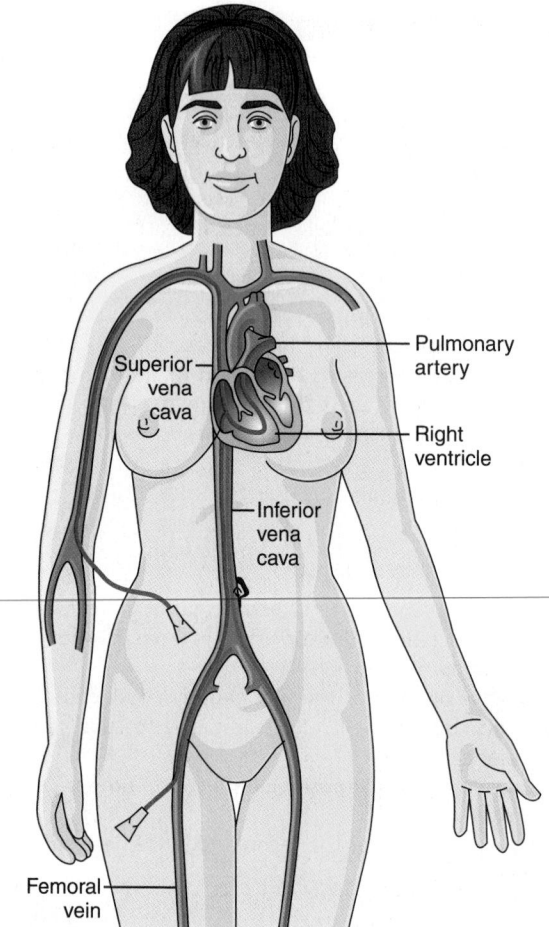

FIG. 59-2 Right-sided heart catheterization. The catheter is inserted into the femoral vein and advanced into the inferior vena cava (or, if into an antecubital or basilic vein, through the superior vena cava), right atrium, and right ventricle and into the pulmonary artery. (From Ignatavicius, D., & Workman, M. [2006]. *Medical-surgical nursing: Critical thinking for collaborative care* [5th ed.]. Philadelphia: W.B. Saunders.)

g. Inform the client that he or she may feel fatigued because of the need to lie still and quiet on a hard table for up to 2 hours.
h. Inform the client that he or she may feel a fluttery feeling as the catheter passes through the heart, a flushed, warm feeling when the dye is injected, a desire to cough, and palpitations caused by heart irritability.
i. If on metformin (Glucophage), the medication is withheld 48 hours prior because of risk of lactic acidosis associated with the iodine dye.
j. Prepare the insertion site by shaving and cleaning with an antiseptic solution if prescribed.
k. Administer preprocedure medications such as sedatives if prescribed.
l. Insert an IV line if prescribed.

3. Postprocedure interventions
   a. Monitor vital signs and cardiac rhythm for dysrhythmias at least every 30 minutes for 2 hours initially.
   b. Assess for chest pain and, if dysrhythmias or chest pain occurs, notify the physician.
   c. Monitor peripheral pulses and the color, warmth, and sensation of the extremity distal to the insertion site at least every 30 minutes for 2 hours initially.
   d. Notify the physician if the client complains of numbness and tingling, if the extremity becomes cool, pale, or cyanotic, or if loss of the peripheral pulses occurs.
   e. Monitor the pressure dressing for bleeding or hematoma formation.
   f. Apply a sandbag or compression device to the insertion site to provide additional pressure if required.
   g. Monitor for bleeding; if bleeding occurs, apply manual pressure immediately and notify the physician.
   h. Monitor for hematoma; if a hematoma develops, notify the physician.
   i. Keep extremity extended for 4 to 6 hours, as prescribed, keeping the leg straight to prevent arterial occlusion.
   j. Maintain strict bed rest for 6 to 12 hours, as prescribed; however, the client may turn from side to side. Do not elevate the head of the bed more than 15 degrees.
   k. If the antecubital vessel was used, immobilize the arm with an armboard.
   l. Encourage fluid intake, if not contraindicated, to promote renal excretion of the dye and to replace fluid loss caused by the osmotic diuretic effect of the dye.
   m. Monitor for nausea, vomiting, rash, or other signs of hypersensitivity to the dye.
   n. Do not resume the administration of metformin until directed by the physician (usually 48 hours postcatheterization).

U. Central **venous pressure** (CVP)
   1. Description
      a. The CVP is the pressure within the superior vena cava; it reflects the pressure under which blood is returned to the superior vena cava and right atrium.
      b. The CVP is measured with a central venous line in the superior vena cava.
      c. Normal CVP pressure is about 3 to 8 mm Hg.
      d. An elevated CVP indicates an increase in blood volume as a result of sodium and water retention, excessive IV fluids, alterations in fluid balance, or renal failure.
      e. A decreased CVP indicates a decrease in circulating blood volume and may be a result of fluid imbalances, hemorrhage, or severe vasodilation, with pooling of blood in the extremities that limits venous return.
   2. Measuring CVP
      a. The right atrium is located at the midaxillary line at the fourth intercostal space; the zero point on the transducer needs to be at the level of the right atrium.
      b. The client needs to be supine, with the head of the bed at 45 degrees.
      c. The client needs to be relaxed; note that activity that increases intrathoracic pressure, such as coughing or straining, will cause false increases in the readings.
      d. If the client is on a ventilator, the reading should be taken at the point of end-expiration.
      e. To maintain patency of the line, a constant small amount of fluid is delivered under pressure.

III. THERAPEUTIC MANAGEMENT
A. Percutaneous transluminal coronary angioplasty (PTCA)
   1. Description (Fig. 59-3)
      a. An invasive, nonsurgical technique in which one or more arteries is (are) dilated with a balloon catheter to open the vessel lumen and improve arterial blood flow
      b. PTCA may be used for clients with an evolving myocardial infarction (MI), alone or in combination with medications to achieve reperfusion.
      c. The client can experience reocclusion after the procedure; thus, the procedure may need to be repeated.
      d. Complications can include arterial dissection or rupture, immobilization of plaque fragments, spasm, and acute MI.
      e. Firm commitment is needed on the client's part to stop smoking, adhere to diet restrictions, lose weight, alter his or her exercise pattern, and stop any behaviors that lead to progression of artery occlusion.
   2. Preprocedure interventions
      a. Maintain NPO status after midnight.
      b. Obtain informed consent, allergy assessment to iodine, and hold metformin (as for cardiac catheterization).
      c. Prepare the groin area with antiseptic soap and shave per institutional procedure and as prescribed.
      d. Assess baseline vital signs and peripheral pulses.
      e. Instruct the client that chest pain may occur during balloon inflation and to report it if it does occur.

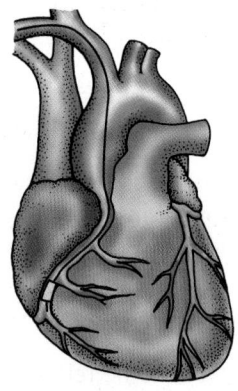 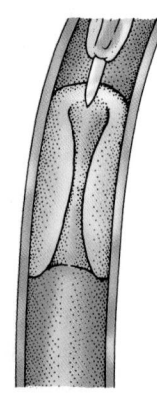 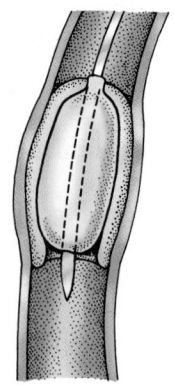 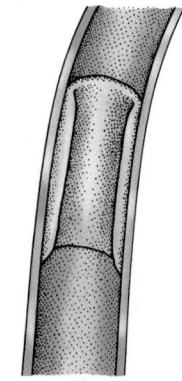

1. The balloon-tipped catheter is positioned in the artery.

2. The uninflated balloon is centered in the obstruction.

3. The balloon is inflated, which flattens plaque against the artery wall.

4. The balloon is removed, and the artery is left unoccluded.

FIG. 59-3 Percutaneous transluminal coronary angioplasty. (From Ignatavicius, D., & Workman, M. [2006]. *Medical-surgical nursing: Critical thinking for collaborative care* [5th ed.]. Philadelphia: W.B. Saunders.)

3. Postprocedure interventions
   a. Monitor vital signs closely.
   b. Assess distal pulses in both extremities.
   c. Maintain bed rest as prescribed, keeping the limb straight for 6 to 8 hours.
   d. Administer anticoagulants such as intravenous heparin and antiplatelet agents as prescribed to prevent thrombus formation.
   e. Intravenous nitroglycerin may be prescribed to prevent coronary artery vasospasm.
   f. Encourage fluids, if not contraindicated, to enhance renal excretion of dye.
   g. Instruct the client in the administration of nitrates, calcium channel blockers, antiplatelet agents, and anticoagulants as prescribed.
   h. Instruct the client to take acetylsalicylic acid (aspirin) daily permanently if prescribed.
   i. Assist the client with planning lifestyle modifications.

B. Laser-assisted angioplasty
   1. Description
      a. A laser probe is advanced through a cannula similar to that used for PTCA.
      b. Laser-assisted angioplasty is used also for clients with small occlusions in the distal superficial femoral, proximal popliteal, and common iliac arteries, and in coronary arteries.
      c. Heat from the laser vaporizes the plaque to open the occluded artery.
   2. Preprocedure and postprocedure interventions
      a. Care is similar to that for PTCA.
      b. Monitor for complications of coronary dissection, acute occlusion, perforation, embolism, and MI.

C. Coronary artery stents
   1. Description
      a. Coronary artery stents are used in conjunction with PTCA to provide a supportive scaf-

fold to eliminate the risk of acute coronary vessel closure and to improve long-term patency of the vessel.
      b. A balloon catheter bearing the stent is inserted into the coronary artery and positioned at the site of occlusion; balloon inflation deploys the stent.
      c. When placed in the coronary artery, the stent reopens the blocked artery.
   2. Preprocedure and postprocedure interventions
      a. Care is similar to that for PTCA.
      b. Acute thrombosis is a major concern following the procedure; the client is placed on antiplatelet therapy such as clopidogrel (Plavix) and acetylsalicylic acid (aspirin) for several months following the procedure.
      c. Monitor for complications of the procedure such as stent migration or occlusion, coronary artery dissection, and bleeding resulting from anticoagulation.

D. Atherectomy
   1. Description
      a. Atherectomy removes plaque from a coronary artery by the use of a cutting chamber on the inserted catheter or a rotating blade that pulverizes the plaque.
      b. Atherectomy is also used to improve blood flow to ischemic limbs in individuals with peripheral arterial disease.
   2. Preprocedure and postprocedure interventions
      a. Care is similar to that for PTCA.
      b. Monitor for complications of perforation, embolus, and reocclusion.

E. Transmyocardial revascularization
   1. Used for clients with widespread atherosclerosis involving vessels that are too small and numerous for replacement or balloon catheterization; performed through a small chest incision

2. Transmyocardial revascularization uses a high-powered laser that creates 20 to 24 channels through the ventricular muscle of the left ventricle; blood enters these small channels, providing the affected region of the heart with oxygenated blood.

3. The opening on the surface of the heart heals; however, the main channels remain and perfuse the myocardium.

F. Arterial revascularization

1. Description

a. Performed to increase arterial blood flow to the affected limb

b. Inflow procedures involve bypassing the arterial occlusion above the superficial femoral arteries

c. Outflow procedures involve bypassing the arterial occlusions at or below the superficial femoral arteries.

d. Graft material is sutured above and below the occlusion to facilitate blood flow around the occlusion.

2. Preoperative interventions

a. Assess baseline vital signs and peripheral pulses.

b. Insert an IV line and urinary catheter as prescribed.

c. Maintain a central venous catheter and/or arterial line if inserted.

3. Postoperative interventions

a. Assess vital signs.

b. Monitor the **BP** and notify the physician if changes occur.

c. Monitor for hypotension, which may indicate hypovolemia.

d. Monitor for hypertension, which may place stress on the graft and facilitate clot formation.

e. Maintain bed rest for 24 hours as prescribed.

f. Instruct the client to keep the affected extremity straight, limit movement, and avoid bending the knee and hip.

g. Monitor for warmth, redness, and edema, which often are expected outcomes because of increased blood flow.

h. Monitor for graft occlusion, which often occurs within the first 24 hours.

i. Assess peripheral pulses and for adverse changes in color and temperature of the extremity.

j. Monitor for a sharp increase in pain because pain is frequently the first indicator of postoperative graft occlusion.

k. If signs of graft occlusion occur, notify the physician immediately.

l. Encourage coughing, deep breathing, and the use of incentive spirometry.

m. Maintain NPO status, with progression to clear liquids as prescribed.

n. Use strict aseptic technique when in contact with the incision.

o. Assess the incision for drainage, warmth, or swelling.

p. Monitor for excessive bleeding (a small amount of bloody drainage is expected).

q. Monitor the area over the graft for hardness, tenderness, and warmth, which may indicate infection; if this occurs, notify the physician immediately.

r. Instruct the client about proper foot care and measures to prevent ulcer formation.

s. Instruct the client to take medications as prescribed.

t. Instruct the client in how to care for incision.

u. Assist the client in modifying lifestyle to prevent further plaque formation.

G. Coronary artery bypass grafting (Fig. 59-4)

1. Description

a. The occluded coronary arteries are bypassed with the client's own venous or arterial blood vessels.

b. The saphenous vein, internal mammary artery, or other arteries may be used to bypass lesions in the coronary arteries.

c. Coronary artery bypass grafting is performed when the client does not respond to medical management of coronary artery disease or when vessels are severely occluded.

2. Preoperative interventions

a. Familiarize the client and family with the cardiac surgical critical care unit.

b. Inform the client to expect a sternal incision, possible arm or leg incision(s), one or two chest tubes, a Foley catheter, and several IV fluid catheters.

c. Inform the client that an endotracheal tube will be in place and that he or she will be unable to speak.

d. Advise the client that he or she will be on mechanical ventilation and to breathe with the ventilator and not fight it.

e. Instruct the client to inform the nurse of any postoperative pain because pain medication will be available.

f. Instruct the client in how to splint the chest incision, cough and deep-breathe, use the incentive spirometer, and perform arm and leg exercises.

g. Encourage the client and family to discuss anxieties and fears related to surgery.

h. Note that prescribed medications may be discontinued preoperatively (usually, diuretics 2 to 3 days before surgery, digoxin

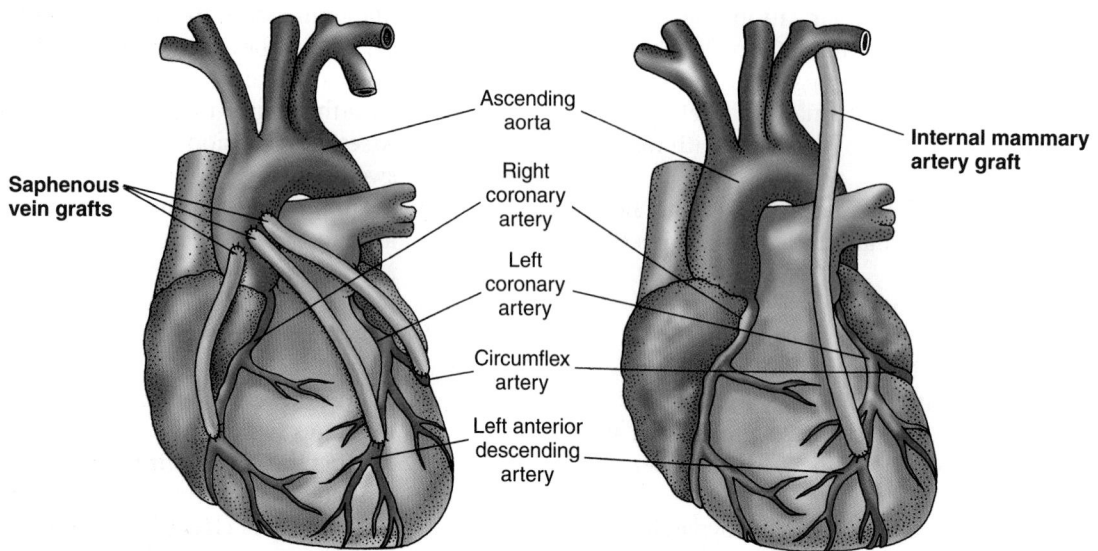

FIG. 59-4 Two methods of coronary artery bypass grafting. The procedure used depends on the nature of the coronary disease, the condition of the vessels available for grafting, and the client's health status. (From Ignatavicius, D., & Workman, M. [2006]. *Medical-surgical nursing: Critical thinking for collaborative care* [5th ed.]. Philadelphia: W.B. Saunders.)

12 hours before surgery, and aspirin and anticoagulants 1 week before surgery).

   i. Administer medications as prescribed, which may include potassium chloride, antihypertensives, antidysrhythmics, and antibiotics.

3. Cardiac surgical unit postoperative interventions

   a. Maintain mechanical ventilation for 6 to 24 hours as prescribed.

   b. Monitor heart rate and rhythm, pulmonary artery and arterial pressures, urinary output, and neurological status.

   c. Maintain mediastinal and pleural chest tubes to the water seal drainage system with ordered suction and report drainage exceeding 100 to 150 mL/hr.

   d. Epicardial pacing wires should be covered by sterile caps or connected to a temporary pacemaker generator; all equipment in use must be properly grounded to prevent microshock.

   e. Assess fluid and electrolyte balance.

   f. Restrict fluids, as prescribed, to 1500 to 2000 mL because the client usually has edema.

   g. Monitor for hypotension, which can cause collapse of a vein graft; determine the cause and provide intervention.

   h. Monitor for hypertension because increased pressure promotes leakage from the suture line and may cause bleeding.

   i. Monitor the temperature and initiate rewarming procedures using warm or thermal blankets if the temperature drops below 96.8° F; rewarm the client no faster than 1.8° F/hr to prevent shivering, and discontinue rewarming procedures when the temperature approaches 98.6° F.

   j. Administer potassium intravenously as prescribed to maintain the potassium level between 4 and 5 mEq/L to prevent dysrhythmias.

   k. Monitor for signs of cardiac tamponade, which will include sudden cessation of previously heavy mediastinal drainage, jugular vein distention with clear lung sounds, equalization of right atrial pressure and pulmonary artery wedge pressure, and pulsus paradoxus.

   l. Monitor pain, differentiating sternotomy pain from anginal pain, which would indicate graft failure.

4. Transfer of the client from the cardiac surgical unit

   a. Monitor vital signs, level of consciousness, and peripheral perfusion.

   b. Monitor for dysrhythmias.

   c. Auscultate lungs and assess respiratory status.

   d. Encourage the client to splint the incision, cough, deep-breathe, and use the incentive spirometer to raise secretions and prevent atelectasis.

   e. Monitor temperature and white blood cell count, which, if elevated after 3 to 4 days, indicate infection.

   f. Provide adequate fluids and hydration as prescribed to liquefy secretions.

BOX 59-2

Home Care Instructions Following Cardiac Surgery

Progressive return to activities at home

Limiting of pushing or pulling activities for 6 weeks following discharge

Maintenance of incisional care and recording signs of redness, swelling, or drainage

Sternotomy incision heals in about 6 to 8 weeks

Avoidance of crossing legs; wearing elastic hose as prescribed until edema subsides, and elevating the surgical limb when sitting in a chair

Use of prescribed medications

Dietary measures, including the avoidance of saturated fats and cholesterol and the use of salt

Resumption of sexual intercourse on the advice of the physician after exercise tolerance is assessed (if client can walk one block or climb two flights of stairs without symptoms, he or she can resume sexual activity safely)

g. Assess suture line and chest tube insertion sites for redness, purulent discharge, and signs of infection.

h. Assess sternal suture line for instability, which may indicate an infection.

i. Guide the client to gradually resume activity.

j. Assess the client for tachycardia, **postural (orthostatic) hypotension**, and fatigue before, during, and after activity.

k. Discontinue activities if the **BP** drops more than 10 to 20 mm Hg or if the pulse increases more than 10 beats/min.

l. Monitor episodes of pain closely.

m. See Box 59-2 for home care instructions.

H. Heart transplantation

1. A donor heart from an individual with a comparable body weight and ABO compatibility is transplanted into a recipient within less than 6 hours of procurement.

2. The surgeon removes the diseased heart, leaving the posterior portion of the atria to serve as an anchor for the new heart.

3. Because a remnant of the client's atria remains, two unrelated P waves are noted on the electrocardiogram.

4. The transplanted heart is denervated and unresponsive to vagal stimulation; because the heart is denervated, clients do not experience angina.

5. Symptoms of heart rejection include hypotension, dysrhythmias, weakness, fatigue, and dizziness.

6. Endomyocardial biopsies are performed at regular scheduled intervals and whenever rejection is suspected.

7. The client requires lifetime immunosuppressive therapy.

8. Strict aseptic technique and vigilant hand washing must be maintained when caring for the post-transplantation client because of increased risk for infection from immunosuppression.

9. The heart rate approximates 100 beats/min and responds slowly to exercise or stress with regard to increases in heart rate, contractility, and cardiac output.

IV. **CARDIAC DYSRHYTHMIAS**

A. Normal sinus rhythm (Fig. 59-5)

1. Rhythm originates from the sinoatrial node.

2. Description

a. Atrial and ventricular rhythms are regular.

b. Atrial and ventricular rates are 60 to 100 beats/min (Fig. 59-6; Box 59-3).

c. PR interval and QRS width are within normal limits.

B. Sinus bradycardia

1. Description

a. Atrial and ventricular rhythms are regular.

b. Atrial and ventricular rates are less than 60 beats/min.

c. PR interval and QRS width are within normal limits.

d. Treatment may be necessary if the client is symptomatic (signs of decreased cardiac output).

e. Note that a low heart rate may be normal for some individuals.

2. Interventions

a. Attempt to determine the cause of sinus bradycardia; if a medication is suspected of causing the bradycardia, hold the medication and notify the physician.

b. Administer oxygen as prescribed.

c. Administer atropine sulfate as prescribed to increase the heart rate to 60 beats/min.

d. Be prepared to apply a noninvasive (transcutaneous) pacemaker initially as prescribed if the atropine sulfate does not increase the heart rate sufficiently.

e. Avoid additional doses of atropine sulfate because this will induce tachycardia.

f. Monitor for hypotension and administer fluids intravenously as prescribed.

g. Depending on the cause of the bradycardia, the client may need a permanent pacemaker.

C. Sinus tachycardia

1. Description

a. Atrial and ventricular rates are 100 to 180 beats/min.

b. Atrial and ventricular rhythms are regular.

c. PR interval and QRS width are within normal limits.

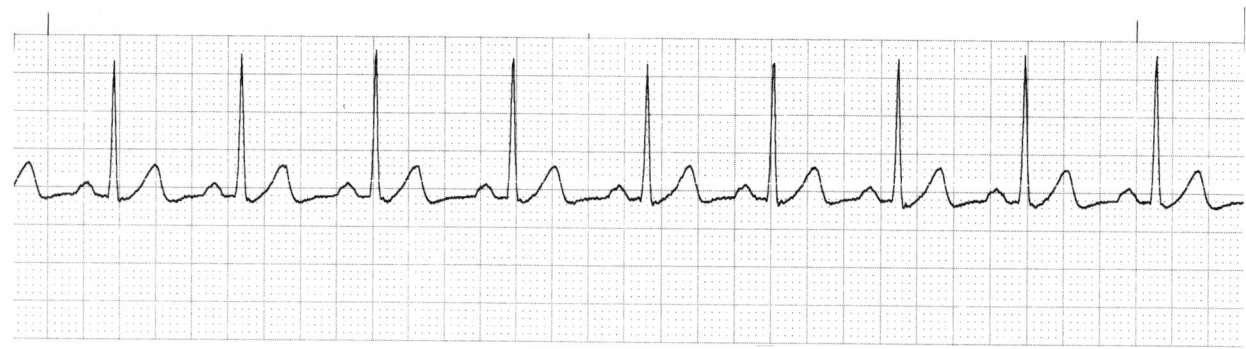

FIG. 59-5 Normal sinus rhythm. Both atrial and ventricular rhythms are essentially regular (a slight variation in rhythm is normal). Atrial and ventricular rates are both 83 beats/min. There is one P wave before each QRS complex, and all the P waves are of a consistent morphology, or shape. The PR interval measures 0.18 second and is constant; the QRS complex measures 0.06 second and is constant. (From Ignatavicius, D., & Workman, M. [2006]. *Medical-surgical nursing: Critical thinking for collaborative care* [5th ed.]. Philadelphia: W.B. Saunders.)

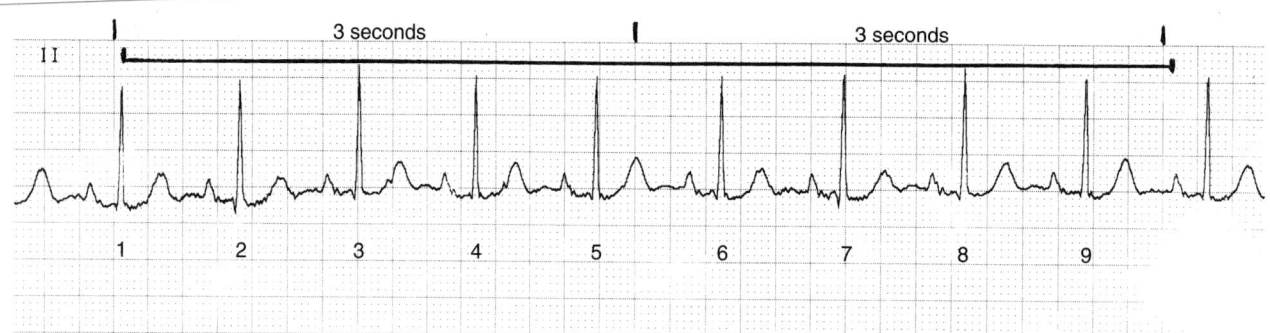

FIG. 59-6 Each segment between the dark lines (above the monitor strip) represents 3 seconds when the monitor is set at a speed of 25 mm/sec. To estimate the ventricular rate, count the QRS complexes in a 6-second strip and then multiply that number by 10 to estimate the heart rate for 1 minute. In this example, there are 9 QRS complexes in 6 seconds. Therefore, the heart rate can be estimated as 90 beats/min. (From Ignatavicius, D., & Workman, M. [2006]. *Medical-surgical nursing: Critical thinking for collaborative care* [5th ed.]. Philadelphia: W.B. Saunders.)

BOX 59-3

**Determination of Heart Rate Using
6-Second Strip Method**

The method can be used to determine heart rate for regular and irregular rhythms.

To determine atrial rate, count the number of P waves in 6 seconds and multiply by 10 to obtain a full minute rate.

To determine ventricular rate, count the number of R waves or QRS complexes in 6 seconds and multiply by 10 to obtain a full minute rate.

For accuracy, timing should begin on the P wave or the QRS complex and end exactly at 30 large blocks later.

---

2. Interventions
   a. Identify the cause of the tachycardia.
   b. Decrease the heart rate to normal by treating the underlying cause.

D. Atrial fibrillation (Fig. 59-7)
   1. Description
      a. Multiple rapid impulses from many foci depolarize in the atria in a totally disorganized manner at a rate of 350 to 600 times/min.
      b. The atria quiver, which can lead to the formation of thrombi.
      c. No definitive P wave can be observed, only fibrillatory waves before each QRS.
   2. Interventions
      a. Administer oxygen.
      b. Administer anticoagulants as prescribed because of the risk of emboli.
      c. Administer cardiac medications as prescribed to control the ventricular rhythm and assist in the maintenance of **cardiac output**.
      d. Prepare the client for cardioversion as prescribed.

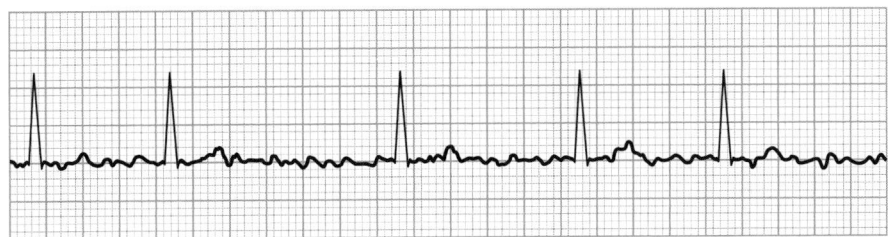

FIG. 59-7 Atrial dysrhythmias—atrial fibrillation. (From Ignatavicius, D., & Workman, M. [2006]. *Medical-surgical nursing: Critical thinking for collaborative care* [5th ed.]. Philadelphia: W.B. Saunders.)

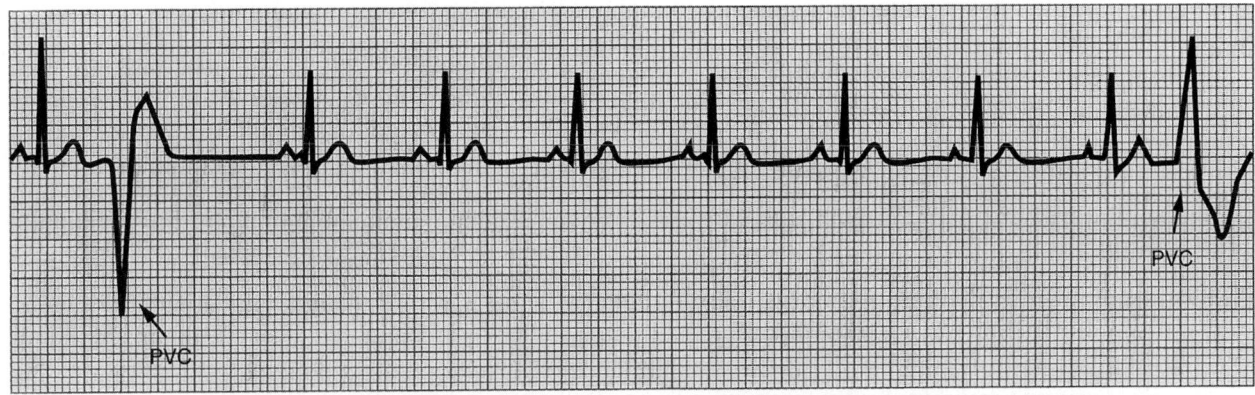

FIG. 59-8 Ventricular dysrhythmias—normal sinus rhythm with multifocal premature ventricular complexes (PVCs; one negative and the other positive). (From Ignatavicius, D., & Workman, M. [2006]. *Medical-surgical nursing: Critical thinking for collaborative care* [5th ed.]. Philadelphia: W.B. Saunders.)

e. Instruct the client in the use of medications as prescribed to control the dysrhythmia.

E. Premature ventricular contractions (PVCs; Fig. 59-8; Box 59-4)
  1. Description
     a. Early ventricular complexes result from increased irritability of the ventricles.
     b. PVCs frequently occur in repetitive patterns such as bigeminy, trigeminy, and quadrigeminy.
     c. The QRS complexes may be unifocal or multifocal.
  2. Interventions
     a. Notify the physician if PVCs occur.
     b. Identify the cause and treat based on the cause.
     c. Evaluate oxygen saturation to assess for hypoxemia, which can cause PVCs.
     d. Administer oxygen as prescribed.
     e. Evaluate electrolytes, particularly the potassium level, because hypokalemia can cause PVCs.
     f. Lidocaine may be prescribed.
     g. Notify the physician if the client complains of chest pain or if PVCs increase in frequency, are multifocal, occur on the T wave (R on T), or occur in runs of ventricular tachycardia.

BOX 59-4

Premature Ventricular Contractions

Bigeminy: Premature ventricular contraction (PVC) every other heartbeat
Trigeminy: PVC every third heartbeat
Quadrigeminy: PVC every fourth heartbeat
Couplet or pair: Two sequential PVCs
Unifocal: Uniform upward or downward deflection, arising from the same ectopic focus
Multifocal: Different shapes, with the impulse generation from different sites
R-on-T phenomenon: PVC falls on the T wave of the preceding beat; may precipitate ventricular fibrillation

---

F. Ventricular tachycardia (VT; Fig. 59-9)
  1. Description
     a. Ventricular tachycardia occurs because of a repetitive firing of an irritable ventricular ectopic focus at a rate of 140 to 250 beats/min or more.
     b. Ventricular tachycardia may present as a paroxysm of three self-limiting beats or more or may be a sustained rhythm.
     c. Ventricular tachycardia can lead to cardiac arrest.

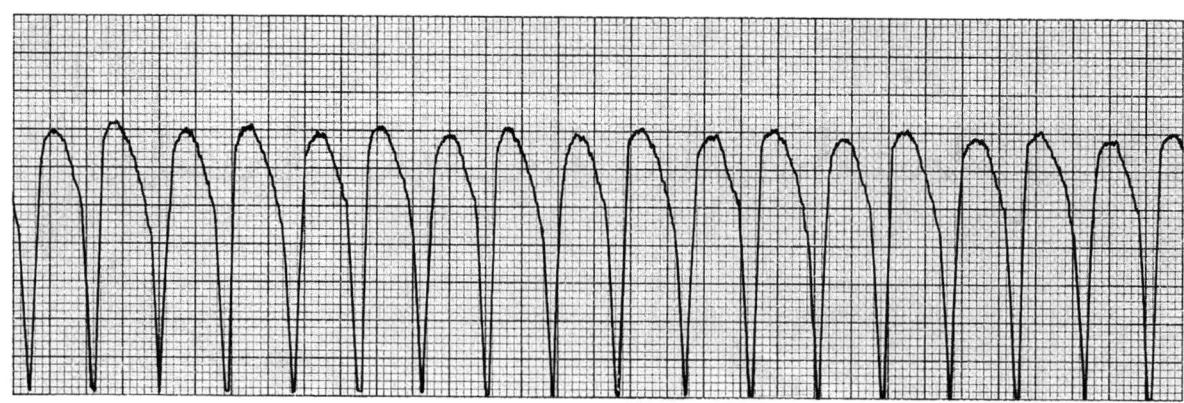

FIG. 59-9   Ventricular dysrhythmias—sustained ventricular tachycardia at a rate of 166 beats/min. (From Ignatavicius, D., & Workman, M. [2006]. *Medical-surgical nursing: Critical thinking for collaborative care* [5th ed.]. Philadelphia: W.B. Saunders.)

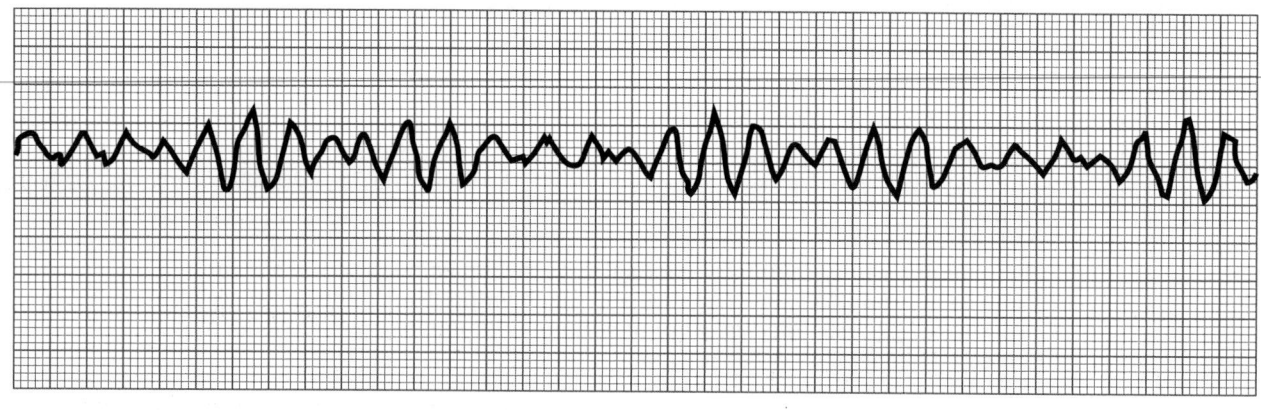

FIG. 59-10   Ventricular dysrhythmias—coarse ventricular fibrillation. (From Ignatavicius, D., & Workman, M. [2006]. *Medical-surgical nursing: Critical thinking for collaborative care* [5th ed.]. Philadelphia: W.B. Saunders.)

2. Stable client with sustained VT (with pulse and no signs or symptoms of decreased cardiac output)
   a. Administer oxygen as prescribed.
   b. Administer antidysrhythmics, such as amiodarone (Cordarone), lidocaine (Xylocaine), or procainamide (Pronestyl) as prescribed.
3. Unstable client with VT (with pulse and signs and symptoms of decreased cardiac output)
   a. Administer oxygen and antidysrhythmic therapy as prescribed.
   b. Prepare for synchronized cardioversion if the client is unstable.
   c. Attempt cough cardiopulmonary resuscitation (CPR) by asking the client to cough hard every 1 to 3 seconds.
4. Pulseless client with ventricular tachycardia: Defibrillation and CPR

G. Ventricular fibrillation (VF; Fig. 59-10)
   1. Description
      a. Impulses from many irritable foci in the ventricles fire in a totally disorganized manner.
      b. VF is a chaotic rapid rhythm in which the ventricles quiver and there is no cardiac output.
      c. VF is fatal if not successfully terminated within 3 to 5 minutes.
      d. Client lacks a pulse, **BP**, respirations, and heart sounds.
   2. Interventions
      a. Defibrillate the client immediately, up to 3 times consecutively at 200, 300, and 360 joules (J).
      b. Initiate CPR.
      c. Administer oxygen as prescribed.
      d. Administer epinephrine or vasopressin and antidysrhythmic therapy with amiodarone or lidocaine as prescribed; other antidysrhythmics also may be prescribed.

V. MANAGEMENT OF DYSRHYTHMIAS
   A. Vagal maneuvers
      1. Description: Vagal maneuvers induce vagal stimulation of the cardiac conduction system and are used to terminate supraventricular tachydysrhythmias.
      2. Carotid sinus massage
         a. The physician instructs the client to turn the head away from the side to be massaged.

b. The physician massages over one carotid artery for a few seconds to determine whether a change in cardiac rhythm occurs.

c. The client should be on a cardiac monitor; an electrocardiographic rhythm strip before, during, and after the procedure should be documented on the chart.

d. Have a defibrillator and resuscitative equipment available.

e. Monitor vital signs, cardiac rhythm, and level of consciousness following the procedure.

3. Valsalva's maneuver

a. The physician instructs the client to bear down or induces a gag reflex in the client to stimulate a vagal response

b. Monitor the heart rate, rhythm, and **BP**.

c. Observe the cardiac monitor for a change in rhythm.

d. Record an electrocardiographic rhythm strip before, during, and after the procedure.

e. Provide an emesis basin if the gag reflex is stimulated, and initiate precautions to prevent aspiration.

f. Have a defibrillator and resuscitative equipment available.

▲ B. Cardioversion

1. Description

a. Cardioversion is synchronized countershock to convert an undesirable rhythm to a stable rhythm.

b. Cardioversion can be an elective procedure performed by the physician for stable tachydysrhythmias resistant to medical therapies or an emergent procedure for hemodynamically unstable ventricular or supraventricular tachydysrhythmias.

c. A lower amount of energy is used than with defibrillation.

▲ d. The defibrillator is synchronized to the client's R wave to avoid discharging the shock during the vulnerable period (T wave).

e. If the defibrillator were not synchronized, it could discharge on the T wave and cause VF.

▲ 2. Preprocedure interventions

a. Obtain an informed consent if an elective procedure.

b. Administer sedation as prescribed.

c. If an elective procedure, hold digoxin (Lanoxin) 48 hours preprocedure as prescribed to prevent postcardioversion ventricular irritability.

d. If an elective procedure for atrial fibrillation or atrial flutter, the client should receive anticoagulant therapy for 4 to 6 weeks preprocedure.

3. During the procedure

a. Ensure that the skin is clean and dry in the area where the electrode paddles will be placed.

b. Stop the oxygen during the procedure to avoid the hazard of fire.

c. Be sure that no one is touching the bed or the client when delivering the countershock.

4. Postprocedure interventions ▲

a. Priority assessment includes ability of the client to maintain the airway and breathing.

b. Resume oxygen administration as prescribed.

c. Assess vital signs.

d. Assess level of consciousness.

e. Monitor cardiac rhythm.

f. Monitor for indications of successful response, such as conversion to sinus rhythm, strong peripheral pulses, an adequate **BP**, and adequate urine output.

g. Assess the skin on the chest for evidence of burns from the edges of the paddles.

C. Defibrillation ▲

1. Description

a. Defibrillation is an asynchronous countershock used to terminate pulseless ventricular tachycardia (VT) or VF.

b. Three rapid consecutive shocks are delivered, with the first at an energy of 200 J.

c. If unsuccessful, the shock is repeated at 200 to 300 J.

d. The third and subsequent shocks will be 360 J.

2. During the procedure

a. Stop the oxygen during the procedure to avoid the hazard of fire.

b. Be sure that no one is touching the bed or the client when delivering the countershock.

D. Use of paddle electrodes

1. Apply conductive pads.

2. One paddle is placed at the third intercostal space to the right of the sternum; the other is placed at the fifth intercostal space on the left midaxillary line.

3. Apply firm pressure of at least 25 lb to each of the paddles.

4. Be sure that no one is touching the bed or the client when delivering the countershock.

E. Automatic external defibrillator ▲

1. An automatic external defibrillator is used by laypersons and emergency medical technicians for prehospital cardiac arrest.

2. Place the client on a firm dry surface.

3. Stop CPR.

4. Ensure that no one is touching the client to avoid motion artifact during rhythm analysis.

5. Place the electrode patches in the correct position on the client's chest.

6. Press the analyzer button to identify the rhythm, which may take 30 seconds; the machine will advise whether a shock is necessary.

7. Shocks are recommended for pulseless VT or VF only.

8. If shock is recommended, the shock initially is delivered at an energy of 200 J.
9. If unsuccessful, the shock is repeated at 200 to 300 J.
10. The third and subsequent shock will be 360 J.
11. If unsuccessful, CPR is continued for 1 minute and then another series of three shocks is delivered, each at 360 J.

▲ F. Implantable cardioverter-defibrillator (ICD)
1. Description
   a. An ICD monitors cardiac rhythm and detects and terminates episodes of VT and VF.
   b. The ICD senses VT or VF and delivers 25 to 30 J up to four times, if necessary.
   c. An ICD is used in clients with episodes of spontaneous sustained VT or VF unrelated to an MI or in clients whose medication therapy has been unsuccessful in controlling life-threatening dysrhythmias.
   d. Transvenous electrode leads are placed in the right atrium and ventricle in contact with the endocardium; leads are used for sensing, pacing, and delivery of cardioversion or defibrillation.
   e. The generator is most commonly implanted in the left pectoral region.

▲ 2. Client education
   a. Instruct the client in the basic functions of the ICD.
   b. Instruct the client in how to perform cough CPR.
   c. Know the rate cutoff of the ICD and the number of consecutive shocks that it will deliver.
   d. Wear loose-fitting clothing over the ICD generator site.
   e. Avoid contact sports to prevent trauma to the ICD generator and lead wires.
   f. Report any fever, redness, swelling, or drainage from the insertion site.
   g. Report symptoms of fainting, nausea, weakness, blackouts, and rapid pulse rates to the physician.
   h. During shock discharge, the client may feel faint or short of breath.
   i. Instruct the client to sit or lie down if he or she feels a shock and to notify the physician.
   j. Advise the client to maintain a log of the date, time, and activity preceding the shock, the symptoms preceding the shock, and post-shock sensations.
   k. Instruct the client and family in how to access emergency medical system.
   l. Encourage the family to learn CPR.
   m. Instruct the client to avoid electromagnetic fields directly over the ICD because they can inactivate the device.
   n. Instruct the client to move away from the magnetic field immediately if beeping tones are heard, and to notify the physician.
   o. Keep an ICD identification card in the wallet and obtain and wear a Medic-Alert bracelet.
   p. Inform all health care providers that an ICD has been inserted; certain diagnostic tests, such as an MRI, and procedures using diathermy or electrocautery interfere with ICD function.
   q. Advise the client of restrictions on activities such as driving and operating dangerous equipment.

VI. PACEMAKERS
A. Description: Temporary or permanent device that provides electrical stimulation and maintains the heart rate when the client's intrinsic pacemaker fails to provide a perfusing rhythm
B. Settings
1. A synchronous (demand) pacemaker senses the client's rhythm and paces only if the client's intrinsic rate falls below the set pacemaker rate to stimulate depolarization.
2. An asynchronous (fixed rate) pacemaker paces at a preset rate regardless of the client's intrinsic rhythm and is used when the client is asystolic or profoundly bradycardic.
3. Overdrive pacing suppresses the underlying rhythm in tachydysrhythmias so that the sinus node will regain control of the heart.
C. Spikes
1. When a pacing stimulus is delivered to the heart, a spike (straight vertical line) is seen on the monitor or electrocardiogram strip.
2. Spikes precede the chamber being paced; a spike preceding a P wave indicates that the atrium is paced and a spike preceding the QRS indicates that the ventricle is being paced.
3. An atrial spike followed by a P wave indicates atrial depolarization and a ventricular spike followed by a QRS represents ventricular depolarization; this is referred to as "capture."
4. If the electrode is in the atrium, the spike is before the P wave; if the electrode is in the ventricle, the spike is before the QRS complex.
D. Temporary pacemakers
1. Noninvasive transcutaneous pacing
   a. Noninvasive transcutaneous pacing is used as a temporary emergency measure in the profoundly bradycardic or asystolic client until invasive pacing can be initiated.
   b. Large electrode pads are placed on the client's chest and back and connected to an external pulse generator.
   c. Wash the skin with soap and water before applying electrodes.

d. It is not necessary to shave the hair or apply alcohol or tinctures to the skin.

e. Place the posterior electrode between the spine and left scapula behind the heart, avoiding placement over bone (Fig. 59-11).

f. Place the anterior electrode between V_2 and V_5 positions over the heart. (Fig. 59-11)

g. Do not place the anterior electrode over female breast tissue; rather, displace breast tissue and place under the breast.

h. Do not take the pulse or **BP** on the left side; the results will not be accurate because of the muscle twitching and electrical current.

i. Ensure that electrodes are in good contact with the skin.

j. Set pacing rate as ordered; establish stimulation threshold to ensure capture.

k. If loss of capture occurs, assess the skin contact of the electrodes and increase the current until capture is regained.

l. Evaluate the client for discomfort from cutaneous and muscle stimulation; administer analgesics as needed.

2. Invasive transvenous pacing

a. Pacing lead wire is placed through the antecubital, femoral, jugular, or subclavian vein into the right atrium for atrial pacing or into the right ventricle; it is positioned in contact with the endocardium.

b. Monitor cardiac rhythm continuously.

c. Monitor vital signs.

d. Monitor the pacemaker insertion site.

e. Restrict client movement to prevent lead wire displacement.

3. Invasive epicardial pacing—applied by using a transthoracic approach; the lead wires are threaded loosely on the epicardial surface of the heart after cardiac surgery

4. Reducing the risk of microshock

a. Use only inspected and approved equipment.

b. Insulate the exposed portion of wires with plastic or rubber material (fingers of rubber gloves) when wires are not attached to the pulse generator; cover with nonconductive tape.

c. Ground all electrical equipment using a three-pronged plug.

d. Wear gloves when handling exposed wires.

e. Keep dressings dry.

E. Permanent pacemakers

1. Pulse generator is internal and surgically implanted in a subcutaneous pocket below the clavicle.

2. The leads are passed transvenously via the cephalic or subclavian vein to the endocardium on the right side of the heart; postoperatively, limitation of arm movement on the operative side is required to prevent lead wire dislodgement.

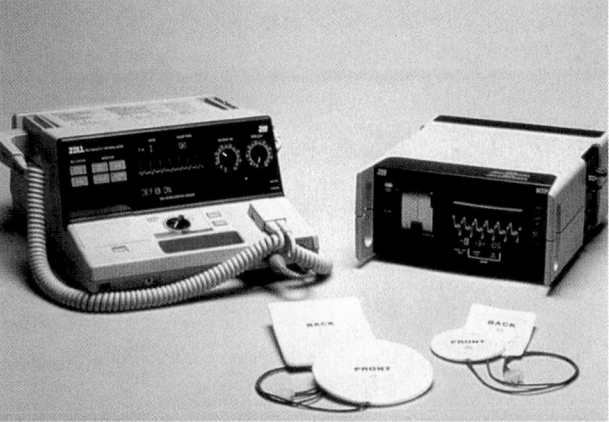

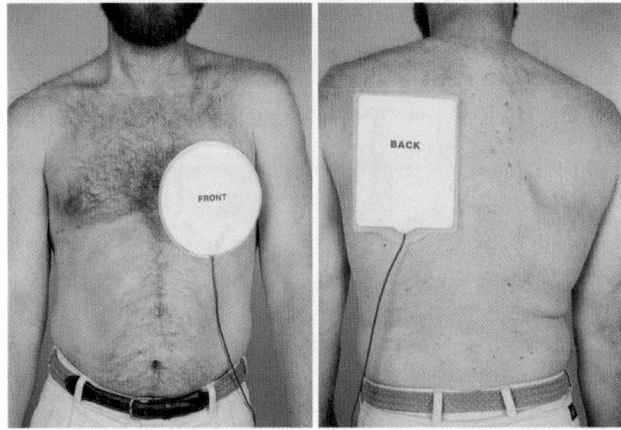

FIG. 59-11 Equipment and electrode placement for transcutaneous external pacing. (From Ignatavicius, D., & Workman, M. [2006]. *Medical-surgical nursing: Critical thinking for collaborative care* [5th ed.]. Philadelphia: W.B. Saunders. Courtesy of Zoll Medical Corporation, Burlington, MA.)

3. Permanent pacemakers may be single-chambered, in which the lead wire is placed in the chamber to be paced, or dual-chambered, with lead wires placed in both the right atrium and ventricle.

4. Biventricular pacing of the ventricles allows for synchronized depolarization and is used for moderate to severe heart failure to improve cardiac output.

5. A permanent pacemaker is programmed when inserted and can be reprogrammed if necessary by noninvasive transmission from an external programmer to the implanted generator.

6. Pacemakers may be powered by a lithium battery with an average life span of 10 years, nuclear-powered with a life span of 20 years or longer, or designed to be recharged externally.

7. Pacemaker function can be checked in the physician's office or clinic by a pacemaker interrogator or programmer or from home using a telephone transmitter device.

BOX 59-5
Pacemakers: Client Education

Instruct the client about the pacemaker, including the programmed rate.
Instruct the client in the signs of battery failure and when to notify the physician.
Instruct the client to report any fever, redness, swelling, or drainage from the insertion site.
Report signs of dizziness, weakness or fatigue, swelling of the ankles or legs, chest pain, or shortness of breath.
Keep a pacemaker identification card in the wallet and obtain and wear a Medic-Alert bracelet.
Instruct the client in how to take the pulse, to take the pulse daily, and to maintain a diary of pulse rates.
Wear loose-fitting clothing over the pulse generator site.
Avoid contact sports.
Inform all health care providers that a pacemaker has been inserted.
Instruct the client to inform airport security that he or she has a pacemaker because the pacemaker may set off the security detector.
Instruct the client that most electrical appliances can be used without any interference with the functioning of the pacemaker; however, advise the client not to operate electrical appliances directly over the pacemaker site.
Avoid transmitter towers and antitheft devices in stores.
Instruct the client that if any unusual feelings occur when near any electrical devices to move 5 to 10 feet away and check the pulse.
Instruct the client about the methods of monitoring the function of the device.
Emphasize the importance of follow-up with the physician.
Use cell phones on the side opposite the pacemaker.

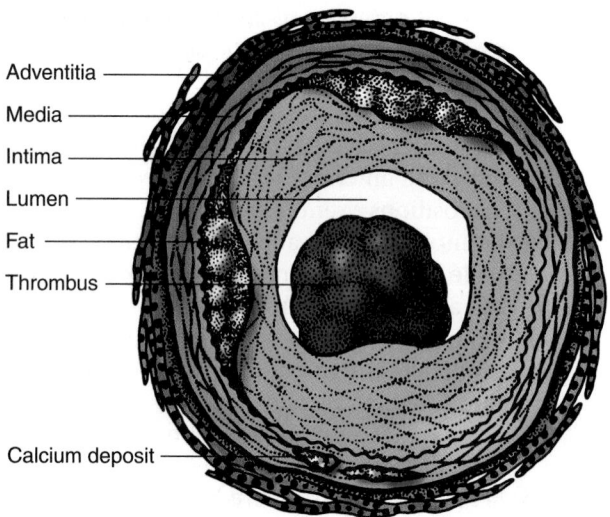

FIG. 59-12 Cross section of an atherosclerotic coronary artery. (From Ignatavicius, D., & Workman, M. [2006]. *Medical-surgical nursing: Critical thinking for collaborative care* [5th ed.]. Philadelphia: W.B. Saunders.)

8. The client may be provided with a device placed over the pacemaker battery generator with an attachment to the telephone; the heart rate then can be transmitted to the clinic.
9. Provide client teaching (Box 59-5).

▲ **VII. CORONARY ARTERY DISEASE**
A. Description
1. Coronary artery disease is a narrowing or obstruction of one or more coronary arteries as a result of atherosclerosis, which is an accumulation of lipid-containing plaque in the arteries (Fig. 59-12).
2. The disease causes decreased perfusion of myocardial tissue and inadequate myocardial oxygen supply leading to hypertension, angina, dysrhythmias, MI, heart failure, and death.
3. Collateral circulation, more than one artery supplying a muscle with blood, is normally present in the coronary arteries, especially in older persons.

4. The development of collateral circulation takes time and develops when chronic ischemia occurs to meet the metabolic demands; therefore, an occlusion of a coronary artery in a younger individual is more likely to be lethal than in an older individual.
5. Symptoms occur when the coronary artery is occluded to the point that inadequate blood supply to the muscle occurs, causing ischemia.
6. Coronary artery narrowing is significant if the lumen diameter of the left main artery is reduced at least 50%, or if any major branch is reduced at least 75%.
7. The goal of treatment is to alter the atherosclerotic progression.
B. Assessment
1. Possibly normal findings during asymptomatic periods
2. Chest pain
3. Palpitations
4. Dyspnea
5. Syncope
6. Cough or hemoptysis
7. Excessive fatigue
C. Diagnostic studies
1. Electrocardiography
a. When blood flow is reduced and ischemia occurs, ST segment depression, T wave inversion, or both is noted; the ST segment returns to normal when the blood flow returns.
b. With infarction, cell injury results in ST segment elevation, followed by T wave inversion and an abnormal Q wave.
2. Cardiac catheterization
a. Cardiac catheterization provides the most definitive source for diagnosis.

b. Cardiac catheterization shows the presence of atherosclerotic lesions.

3. Blood lipid levels
   a. Blood lipid levels may be elevated.
   b. Cholesterol-lowering medications may be prescribed to reduce the development of atherosclerotic plaques.

D. Interventions
   1. Instruct the client regarding the purpose of diagnostic medical and surgical procedures and preprocedure and postprocedure expectations.
   2. Assist the client to identify risk factors that can be modified.
   3. Assist the client to set goals to promote lifestyle changes to reduce the impact of risk factors.
   4. Assist the client to identify barriers to compliance with the therapeutic plan and to identify methods to overcome barriers.
   5. Instruct the client regarding a low-calorie, low-sodium, low-cholesterol, and low-fat diet, with an increase in dietary fiber.
   6. Stress to the client that dietary changes are not temporary and must be maintained for life; instruct the client regarding prescribed medications.
   7. Provide community resources to the client regarding exercise, smoking cessation, and stress reduction as appropriate.

E. Surgical procedures
   1. PTCA to compress the plaque against the walls of the artery and dilate the vessel
   2. Laser angioplasty to vaporize the plaque
   3. Atherectomy to remove the plaque from the artery
   4. Vascular stent to prevent the artery from closing and to prevent restenosis
   5. Coronary artery bypass grafting to improve blood flow to the myocardial tissue at risk for ischemia or infarction because of the occluded artery

F. Medications
   1. Nitrates to dilate the coronary arteries and decrease **preload** and **afterload**
   2. Calcium channel blockers to dilate coronary arteries and reduce vasospasm
   3. Cholesterol-lowering medications to reduce the development of atherosclerotic plaques
   4. β-Blockers to reduce the BP in individuals who are hypertensive

VIII. ANGINA
   A. Description
      1. Angina is chest pain resulting from myocardial ischemia caused by inadequate myocardial blood and oxygen supply.
      2. Angina is caused by an imbalance between oxygen supply and demand.
      3. Causes include obstruction of coronary blood flow resulting from atherosclerosis, coronary artery spasm, or conditions increasing myocardial oxygen consumption.
      4. The goal of treatment is to provide relief of an acute attack, correct the imbalance between myocardial oxygen supply and demand, and prevent the progression of the disease and further attacks to reduce the risk of MI.

   B. Patterns of angina
      1. Stable angina
         a. Also called exertional angina
         b. Occurs with activities that involve exertion or emotional stress; relieved with rest or nitroglycerin
         c. Usually has a stable pattern of onset, duration, severity, and relieving factors
      2. Unstable angina
         a. Also called preinfarction angina
         b. Occurs with an unpredictable degree of exertion or emotion and increases in occurrence, duration, and severity over time
         c. Pain may not be relieved with nitroglycerin.
      3. Variant angina
         a. Also called Prinzmetal's or vasospastic angina
         b. Results from coronary artery spasm
         c. May occur at rest
         d. Attacks may be associated with ST segment elevation noted on the electrocardiogram (ECG).
      4. Intractable angina is a chronic, incapacitating angina unresponsive to interventions.
      5. Preinfarction angina
         a. Associated with acute coronary insufficiency
         b. Lasts longer than 15 minutes
         c. Symptom of worsening cardiac ischemia
         d. Occurs after an MI, when residual ischemia may cause episodes of angina

   C. Assessment
      1. Pain
         a. Pain can develop slowly or quickly.
         b. Pain usually is described as mild or moderate.
         c. Substernal, crushing, squeezing pain may occur.
         d. Pain may radiate to the shoulders, arms, jaw, neck, or back.
         e. Pain intensity is unaffected by inspiration and expiration.
         f. Pain usually lasts less than 5 minutes; however, pain can last up to 15 to 20 minutes.
         g. Pain is relieved by nitroglycerin or rest.
      2. Dyspnea
      3. Pallor
      4. Sweating
      5. Palpitations and tachycardia
      6. Dizziness and faintness
      7. Hypertension
      8. Digestive disturbances

D. Diagnostic studies
1. Electrocardiography: Readings are normal during rest, with ST depression and/or T wave inversion during an episode of pain.
2. Stress testing: Chest pain or changes in the electrocardiogram or vital signs during testing may indicate ischemia.
3. Cardiac enzyme and troponin levels: Findings are normal in angina.
4. Cardiac catheterization: Catheterization provides a definitive diagnosis by providing information about the patency of the coronary arteries.

E. Interventions
1. Immediate management
   a. Assess pain.
   b. Provide bed rest.
   c. Administer oxygen at 3 L/min by nasal cannula as prescribed.
   d. Administer nitroglycerin as prescribed to dilate the coronary arteries, reduce the oxygen requirements of the myocardium, and relieve the chest pain.
   e. Obtain a 12-lead ECG.
   f. Provide continuous cardiac monitoring.
2. Following the acute episode
   a. Instruct the client regarding the purpose of diagnostic medical and surgical procedures and the preprocedure and postprocedure expectations.
   b. Assist the client to identify angina-precipitating events.
   c. Instruct the client to stop activity and rest if chest pain occurs and to take nitroglycerin as prescribed.
   d. Instruct the client to seek medical attention if pain persists.
   e. Instruct the client regarding prescribed medications.
   f. Provide diet instructions to the client, stressing that dietary changes are not temporary and must be maintained for life.
   g. Assist the client to identify risk factors that can be modified.
   h. Assist the client to set goals that will promote changes in lifestyle to reduce the impact of risk factors.
   i. Assist the client to identify barriers to compliance with therapeutic plan and to identify methods to overcome barriers.
   j. Provide community resources to the client regarding exercise, smoking cessation, and stress reduction.

F. Surgical procedures: See Section VII, "Coronary Artery Disease."

G. Medications
1. See Section VII, "Coronary Artery Disease."

2. Antiplatelet therapy may be prescribed; it inhibits platelet aggregation and reduces the risk of developing an acute MI.

IX. MYOCARDIAL INFARCTION

A. Description
1. Myocardial infarction occurs when myocardial tissue is abruptly and severely deprived of oxygen.
2. Ischemia can lead to necrosis of myocardial tissue if blood flow is not restored.
3. Infarction does not occur instantly but evolves over several hours.
4. Obvious physical changes do not occur in the heart until 6 hours after the infarction, when the infarcted area appears blue and swollen.
5. After 48 hours, the infarct turns gray, with yellow streaks developing as neutrophils invade the tissue.
6. By 8 to 10 days after infarction, granulation tissue forms.
7. Over 2 to 3 months, the necrotic area develops into a scar; scar tissue permanently changes the size and shape of the entire left ventricle.
8. Not all clients experience the classic symptoms of an MI.
9. Women may experience atypical discomfort, shortness of breath, or fatigue.
10. An older client may experience shortness of breath, pulmonary edema, dizziness, altered mental status, or a dysrhythmia.

B. Location of MI (see Fig. 59-1)
1. Obstruction of the left anterior descending artery results in anterior wall or septal MI, or both.
2. Obstruction of the circumflex artery results in posterior wall MI or lateral wall MI.
3. Obstruction of the right coronary artery results in inferior wall MI.

C. Risk factors
1. Atherosclerosis
2. Coronary artery disease
3. Elevated cholesterol levels
4. Smoking
5. Hypertension
6. Obesity
7. Physical inactivity
8. Impaired glucose tolerance
9. Stress

D. Diagnostic studies
1. Troponin level
   a. Level rises within 3 hours.
   b. Level remains elevated for up to 7 days.
2. Total creatine kinase level
   a. Level rises within 4 hours after the onset of chest pain.

b. Level peaks within 24 hours after damage and death of cardiac tissue.

3. CK-MB isoenzyme
   a. Peak elevation occurs 18 to 24 hours after the onset of chest pain.
   b. Level returns to normal 48 to 72 hours later.

4. Myoglobin: Level rises within 1 hour after cell death, peaks in 4 to 6 hours, and returns to normal within 24 to 36 hours or less.

5. LDH level
   a. Level rises 24 hours after MI.
   b. Level peaks between 48 and 72 hours and falls to normal in 7 days.
   c. Serum level of LDH_1 isoenzyme rises higher than serum level of LDH_2.

6. White blood cell count: An elevated white blood cell count of 10,000 to 20,000 /mm^3 appears on the second day following the MI and lasts up to 1 week.

7. Electrocardiogram
   a. Electrocardiogram shows ST segment elevation, T wave inversion, and an abnormal Q wave in leads facing the infarct.
   b. Hours to days after the MI, ST and T wave changes will return to normal but the Q wave changes usually remains permanently.

8. Diagnostic tests following the acute stage
   a. Exercise tolerance test or stress test may be prescribed to assess for electrocardiographic changes and ischemia and to evaluate for medical therapy or identify clients who may need invasive therapy.
   b. Thallium scans may be prescribed to assess for ischemia or necrotic muscle tissue.
   c. Multigated cardiac blood pool imaging scans may be used to evaluate left ventricular function.
   d. Cardiac catheterization is performed to determine the extent and location of obstructions of the coronary arteries.

E. Assessment
   1. Pain
      a. Client may experience crushing substernal pain.
      b. Pain may radiate to the jaw, back, and left arm.
      c. Pain may occur without cause, primarily early in the morning.
      d. Pain is unrelieved by rest or nitroglycerin and is relieved only by opioids.
      e. Pain lasts 30 minutes or longer.
   2. Nausea and vomiting
   3. Diaphoresis
   4. Dyspnea
   5. Dysrhythmias
   6. Feelings of fear and anxiety
   7. Pallor, cyanosis, coolness of extremities

F. Complications of MI (Box 59-6)
G. Interventions, acute stage
   1. Obtain a description of the chest discomfort.
   2. Assess vital signs.
   3. Assess cardiovascular status and maintain cardiac monitoring.
   4. Place the client in a semi-Fowler's position to enhance comfort and tissue oxygenation.
   5. Administer oxygen at 2 to 4 L/min by nasal cannula as prescribed.
   6. Establish an IV access route.
   7. Administer nitroglycerin as prescribed.
   8. Administer morphine sulfate as prescribed to relieve chest discomfort that is unresponsive to nitroglycerin.
   9. Obtain a 12-lead ECG.
   10. Administer IV nitroglycerin and antidysrhythmics as prescribed.
   11. Monitor thrombolytic therapy, which may be prescribed within the first 6 hours of the coronary event.
   12. Monitor for signs of bleeding if the client is receiving thrombolytic therapy.
   13. Monitor laboratory values as prescribed.
   14. Administer β-blockers as prescribed to slow the heart rate and increase myocardial perfusion while reducing the force of myocardial contraction.
   15. Monitor for complications related to the MI.
   16. Monitor for cardiac dysrhythmias because tachycardia and PVCs frequently occur in the first few hours after MI.
   17. Assess distal peripheral pulses and skin temperature because poor **cardiac output** may be identified by cool diaphoretic skin and diminished or absent pulses.
   18. Monitor intake and output.
   19. Assess respiratory rate and breath sounds for signs of heart failure, as indicated by the presence of crackles or wheezes or dependent edema.

BOX 59-6

Complications of Myocardial Infarction (MI)

Dysrhythmias
Heart failure
Pulmonary edema
Cardiogenic shock
Thrombophlebitis
Pericarditis
Mitral valve insufficiency
Postinfarction angina
Ventricular rupture
Dressler's syndrome (a combination of pericarditis, pericardial effusion, and pleural effusion, which can occur several weeks to months following an MI)

20. Monitor the **BP** closely after the administration of medications; if the **BP** is lower than 100 mm Hg systolic or 25 mm Hg lower than the previous reading, lower the head of the bed and notify the physician.
21. Provide reassurance to the client and family.

▲ H. Interventions following the acute episode
1. Maintain bed rest for the first 24 to 36 hours as prescribed.
2. Allow the client to stand to void or use a bedside commode if prescribed.
3. Provide range-of-motion exercises to prevent thrombus formation and maintain muscle strength.
4. Progress to dangling legs at the side of the bed or out of bed to the chair for 30 minutes three times a day as prescribed.
5. Progress to ambulation in the client's room and to the bathroom and then in the hallway three times a day.
6. Monitor for complications.
7. Encourage the client to verbalize feelings regarding the MI.

I. Cardiac rehabilitation: Process of actively assisting the client with cardiac disease to achieve and maintain a vital and productive life within the limitations of the heart disease.

▲ X. HEART FAILURE
A. Description
1. Heart failure is the inability of the heart to maintain adequate cardiac output to meet the metabolic needs of the body because of impaired pumping ability.
2. Diminished **cardiac output** results in inadequate peripheral tissue perfusion.
3. Congestion of the lungs and periphery may occur.
B. Classification
1. Acute heart failure occurs suddenly.
2. Chronic heart failure develops over time; however, a client with chronic heart failure can develop an acute episode.
C. Types of heart failure
1. Right ventricular failure, left ventricular failure
   a. Because the two ventricles of the heart represent two separate pumping systems, it is possible for one to fail alone for a short period.
   b. Most heart failure begins with left ventricular failure and progresses to failure of both ventricles.
   c. Acute pulmonary edema, a medical emergency, results from left ventricular failure.
   d. If pulmonary edema is not treated, death will occur from suffocation because the client literally drowns in his or her own fluids.
2. Forward failure, backward failure

a. In forward failure, an inadequate output of the affected ventricle causes decreased perfusion to vital organs.
b. In backward failure, blood backs up behind the affected ventricle, causing increased pressure in the atrium behind the affected ventricle.
3. Low output, high output
   a. In low-output failure, not enough **cardiac output** is available to meet the demands of the body.
   b. High-output failure occurs when a condition causes the heart to work harder to meet the demands of the body.
4. Systolic failure, diastolic failure
   a. Systolic failure leads to problems with contraction and ejection of blood.
   b. Diastolic failure leads to problems with the heart relaxing and filling with blood.
D. Compensatory mechanisms ▲
1. Compensatory mechanisms act to restore **cardiac output** to near-normal levels.
2. Initially, these mechanisms increase **cardiac output**; however, they eventually have a damaging effect on pump action.
3. Compensatory mechanisms contribute to an increase in myocardial oxygen consumption; when this occurs, myocardial reserve is exhausted and clinical manifestations of heart failure develop.
4. Compensatory mechanisms include increased heart rate, improved **stroke volume**, arterial vasoconstriction, sodium and water retention, and myocardial hypertrophy.
E. Assessment ▲
1. Right ventricular failure: Signs of right ventricular failure are evident in the systemic circulation (Table 59-1).
2. Left ventricular failure: Signs of left ventricular failure are evident in the pulmonary system (see Table 59-1).
3. Acute pulmonary edema
   a. Severe dyspnea and orthopnea
   b. Pallor
   c. Tachycardia
   d. Expectoration of large amounts of blood-tinged, frothy sputum
   e. Wheezing and crackles on auscultation
   f. Bubbling respirations
   g. Acute anxiety, apprehension, restlessness
   h. Profuse sweating
   i. Cold, clammy skin
   j. Cyanosis
   k. Nasal flaring
   l. Use of accessory breathing muscles
   m. Tachypnea
   n. Hypocapnia, evidenced by muscle cramps, weakness, dizziness, and paresthesias

TABLE 59-1

Clinical Manifestations of Right-Sided and Left-Sided Heart Failure

Right-Sided Heart Failure	Left-Sided Heart Failure
Dependent edema (legs and sacrum)	Signs of pulmonary congestion
Jugular venous distention	Dyspnea
Abdominal distention	Tachypnea
Hepatomegaly	Crackles in the lungs
Splenomegaly	Dry, hacking cough
Anorexia and nausea	Paroxysmal nocturnal dyspnea
Weight gain	
Nocturnal diuresis	Increased blood pressure (from fluid volume excess) or decreased BP (from pump failure)
Swelling of the fingers and hands	
Increased BP (from fluid volume excess) or decreased BP (from pump failure)	

BP, Blood pressure.

▲ F. Immediate management
1. Place the client in a high Fowler's position, with the legs in a dependent position, to reduce pulmonary congestion and relieve edema.
2. Administer oxygen in high concentrations by mask or cannula as prescribed to improve gas exchange and pulmonary function.
3. Prepare for intubation and ventilator support, if required; monitor lung sounds for crackles and decreased breath sounds.
4. Suction fluids as needed to maintain a patent airway.
5. Assess level of consciousness.
6. Provide reassurance to the client.
7. Monitor vital signs closely, noting tachycardia or pulsus alternans.
8. Monitor for hypotension resulting from decreased tissue perfusion or hypertension resulting from anxiety or history of hypertension.
9. Monitor heart rate and for dysrhythmias by using a cardiac monitor.
10. Assess for edema in dependent areas and in the sacral, lumbar, and posterior thigh regions in the client on bed rest.
11. Insert a Foley catheter as prescribed and monitor urine output closely following administration of a diuretic.
12. Monitor intake and output.
13. Avoid the unnecessary IV administration of fluids.
14. Administer morphine sulfate as prescribed to provide sedation and vasodilation, and monitor for respiratory depression or hypotension after administration.
15. Administer diuretics as prescribed to reduce **preload**, enhance renal excretion of sodium and water, reduce circulating blood volume, and reduce pulmonary congestion.
16. Administer digoxin as prescribed to increase ventricular **contractility** and improve **cardiac output**.
17. Administer bronchodilators as prescribed for severe bronchospasm or bronchoconstriction.
18. Administer medications as prescribed to facilitate myocardial **contractility** and enhance **stroke volume**.
19. Administer vasodilators, such as nitrates as prescribed to reduce **afterload**, increase the capacity of the systemic venous bed, and decrease venous return to the heart.
20. For acute events of heart failure administer nesiritide (Natrecor) as prescribed to increase renal glomerular filtration and lower pulmonary capillary wedge pressure (PCWP).
21. Monitor weight to determine a response to treatment.
22. Assess for hepatomegaly and ascites, and measure and record abdominal girth.
23. Monitor peripheral pulses.
24. Analyze arterial blood gas results and electrolyte levels for imbalances; monitor BNP levels.
25. Monitor potassium level closely, which may decrease as a result of diuretic therapy, and administer potassium supplements as prescribed to prevent digoxin toxicity.

G. Following the acute episode ▲
1. Encourage the client to verbalize feelings about the lifestyle changes required as a result of the heart failure.
2. Assist the client to identify precipitating risk factors of heart failure and methods of eliminating these risk factors.
3. Instruct the client in the prescribed medication regimen, which may include digoxin, a diuretic, angiotensin-converting enzyme (ACE) inhibitors, low-dose β-blockers, and vasodilators.
4. Advise the client to notify the physician if side effects occur from the medications.
5. Advise the client to avoid over-the-counter medications.
6. Instruct the client to contact the physician if he or she is unable to take medications because of illness.
7. Instruct the client to avoid large amounts of caffeine, found in coffee, tea, cocoa, chocolate, and some carbonated beverages.
8. Instruct the client about the prescribed low-sodium, low-fat, and low-cholesterol diet.
9. Provide the client with a list of potassium-rich foods because diuretics can cause hypokalemia (except for potassium-sparing diuretics).
10. Instruct the client regarding fluid restriction, if prescribed, advising the client to spread the

fluid out during the day and to suck on hard candy to reduce thirst.

11. Instruct the client to balance periods of activity and rest.

12. Advise the client to avoid isometric activities, which increase pressure in the heart.

13. Instruct the client to monitor daily weight.

14. Instruct the client to report signs of fluid retention such as edema or weight gain.

▲ XI. CARDIOGENIC SHOCK

A. Description

1. Cardiogenic shock is failure of the heart to pump adequately, thereby reducing **cardiac output** and compromising tissue perfusion.

2. Necrosis of more than 40% of the left ventricle occurs, usually as a result of occlusion of major coronary vessels.

3. The goal of treatment is to maintain tissue oxygenation and perfusion and improve the pumping ability of the heart.

B. Assessment

1. Hypotension: **BP** lower than 90 mm Hg systolic or 30 mm Hg lower than the client's baseline

2. Urine output lower than 30 mL/hr

3. Cold, clammy skin

4. Poor peripheral pulses

5. Tachycardia

6. Pulmonary congestion

7. Tachypnea

8. Disorientation, restlessness, and confusion

9. Continuing chest discomfort

C. Interventions

1. Administer morphine sulfate intravenously as prescribed to decrease pulmonary congestion and relieve pain.

2. Administer oxygen as prescribed.

3. Prepare for intubation and mechanical ventilation.

4. Administer diuretics and nitrates as prescribed while monitoring BP constantly.

5. Administer vasopressors and positive inotropics as prescribed to maintain organ perfusion.

6. Prepare the client for insertion of an intraaortic balloon pump, if prescribed, to improve coronary artery perfusion and improve **cardiac output**.

7. Prepare the client for immediate reperfusion procedures such as PTCA or coronary artery bypass graft.

8. Monitor arterial blood gas levels and prepare to treat imbalances.

9. Monitor urinary output.

10. Assist with the insertion of a pulmonary artery (Swan-Ganz) catheter to assess degree of heart failure; readings obtained from catheter correlating to cardiogenic shock would include an increased PCWP and a decreased cardiac output (Fig. 59-13).

11. Monitor distal pulses and maintain the transducer at the level of the right atrium if the client has a Swan-Ganz catheter.

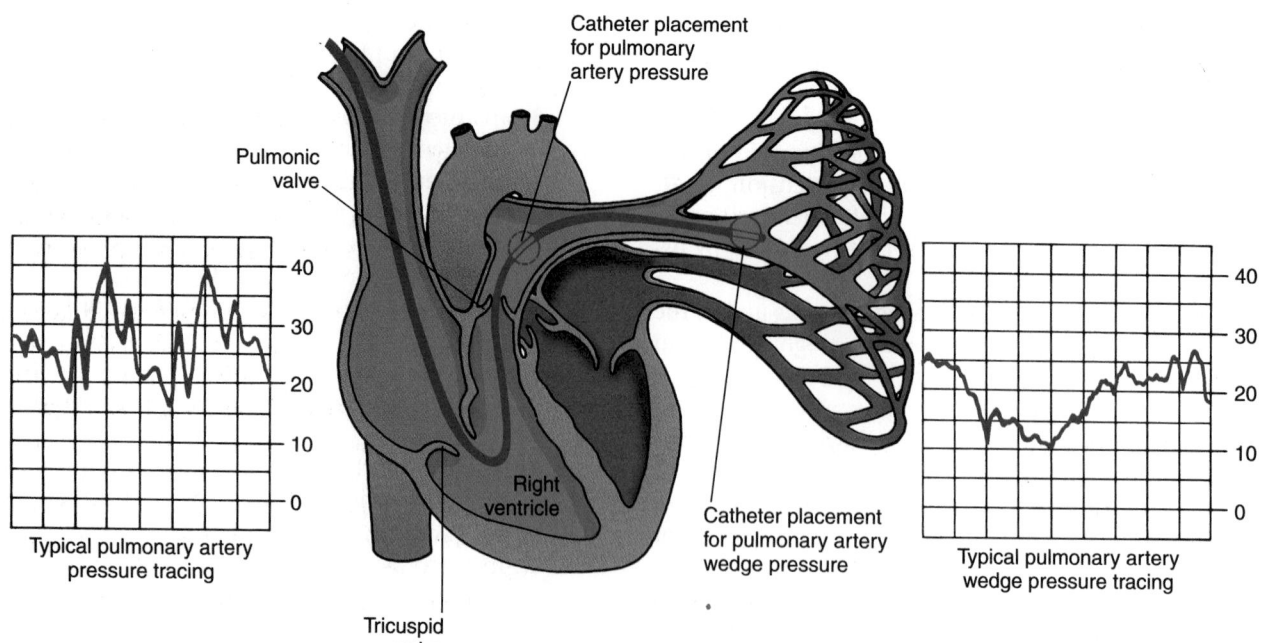

FIG. 59-13 Cardiac pressure waveforms can be visualized on the monitor. (From Ignatavicius, D., & Workman, M. [2006]. *Medical-surgical nursing: Critical thinking for collaborative care* [5th ed.]. Philadelphia: W.B. Saunders.)

XII. INFLAMMATORY DISEASES OF THE HEART

A. Pericarditis
  1. Description
     a. Pericarditis is an acute or chronic inflammation of the pericardium.
     b. Chronic pericarditis, a chronic inflammatory thickening of the pericardium, constricts the heart, causing compression.
     c. The pericardial sac becomes inflamed.
     d. Pericarditis can result in loss of pericardial elasticity or an accumulation of fluid within the sac.
     e. Heart failure or cardiac tamponade may result.
  2. Assessment
     a. Precordial pain in the anterior chest that radiates to the left side of the neck, shoulder, or back
     b. Pain is grating and is aggravated by breathing (particularly inspiration), coughing, and swallowing
     c. Pain is worse when in the supine position and may be relieved by leaning forward.
     d. Pericardial friction rub (scratchy, high-pitched sound) is heard on auscultation and is produced by the rubbing of the inflamed pericardial layers.
     e. Fever and chills
     f. Fatigue and malaise
     g. Elevated white blood cell count
     h. Electrocardiographic changes with acute pericarditis; ST segment elevation with the onset of inflammation; atrial fibrillation is common.
     i. Signs of right ventricular failure in clients with chronic constrictive pericarditis
  3. Interventions
     a. Assess the nature of the pain.
     b. Position the client in a high Fowler's position, or upright and leaning forward.
     c. Administer analgesics, nonsteroidal anti-inflammatory drugs, or corticosteroids for pain as prescribed.
     d. Auscultate for a pericardial friction rub.
     e. Check results of blood culture to identify causative organism.
     f. Administer antibiotics for bacterial infection as prescribed.
     g. Administer diuretics and digoxin as prescribed to the client with chronic constrictive pericarditis; surgical incision of the pericardium (pericardiectomy) may be necessary.
     h. Monitor for signs of cardiac tamponade, including pulsus paradoxus, jugular vein distention with clear lung sounds, muffled heart sounds, narrowed **pulse pressure**, tachycardia, and decreased **cardiac output**.
     i. Notify the physician if signs of cardiac tamponade occur.

B. Myocarditis
  1. Description: Acute or chronic inflammation of the myocardium as a result of pericarditis, systemic infection, or allergic response
  2. Assessment
     a. Fever
     b. Pericardial friction rub
     c. Gallop rhythm
     d. Murmur that sounds like fluid passing an obstruction
     e. Pulsus alternans
     f. Signs of heart failure
     g. Fatigue
     h. Dyspnea
     i. Tachycardia
     j. Chest pain
  3. Interventions
     a. Assist the client to a position of comfort, such as sitting up and leaning forward.
     b. Administer analgesics, salicylates, and nonsteroidal anti-inflammatory drugs as prescribed to reduce fever and pain.
     c. Administer oxygen as prescribed.
     d. Provide adequate rest periods.
     e. Limit activities to avoid overexertion and decrease the workload of the heart.
     f. Administer digoxin as prescribed, and monitor for signs of digoxin toxicity.
     g. Administer antidysrhythmics as prescribed.
     h. Administer antibiotics as prescribed to treat the causative organism.
     i. Monitor for complications, which can include thrombus, heart failure, and cardiomyopathy.

C. Endocarditis
  1. Description
     a. Endocarditis is an inflammation of the inner lining of the heart and valves.
     b. Occurs primarily in clients who are IV drug abusers, have had valve replacements, or have mitral valve prolapse or other structural defects
     c. Ports of entry for the infecting organism include the oral cavity (especially if the client has had a dental procedure in the previous 3 to 6 months), cutaneous invasion, infections, invasive procedures, or surgery.
  2. Assessment
     a. Fever
     b. Anorexia
     c. Weight loss
     d. Fatigue
     e. Cardiac murmurs
     f. Heart failure
     g. Embolic complications from vegetation fragments traveling through the circulation
     h. Petechiae

     i. Splinter hemorrhages in the nail beds

     j. Osler's nodes (reddish tender lesions) on the pads of the fingers, hands, and toes

     k. Janeway lesions (nontender hemorrhagic lesions) on the fingers, toes, nose, or earlobes

     l. Splenomegaly

     m. Clubbing of the fingers

  3. Interventions

     a. Provide adequate rest balanced with activity to prevent thrombus formation.

     b. Maintain antiembolism stockings.

     c. Monitor cardiovascular status.

     d. Monitor for signs of heart failure.

     e. Monitor for signs of emboli.

     f. Monitor for splenic emboli, as evidenced by sudden abdominal pain radiating to the left shoulder and the presence of rebound abdominal tenderness on palpation.

     g. Monitor for renal emboli, as evidenced by flank pain radiating to the groin, hematuria, and pyuria.

     h. Monitor for confusion, aphasia, or dysphasia, which may indicate central nervous system emboli.

     i. Monitor for pulmonary emboli as evidenced by pleuritic chest pain, dyspnea, and cough.

     j. Assess skin, mucous membranes, and conjunctiva for petechiae.

     k. Assess nail beds for splinter hemorrhages.

     l. Assess for Osler's nodes on the pads of the fingers, hands, and toes.

     m. Assess for Janeway lesions on the fingers, toes, nose, or earlobes.

     n. Assess for clubbing of the fingers.

     o. Evaluate blood culture results.

     p. Administer antibiotics intravenously as prescribed.

     q. Plan and arrange for discharge, providing resources required for the continued administration of IV antibiotics.

  4. Client education (Box 59-7)

XIII. CARDIAC TAMPONADE

A. Description

  1. A pericardial effusion occurs when the space between the parietal and visceral layers of the pericardium fills with fluid.

  2. Pericardial effusion places the client at risk for cardiac tamponade, an accumulation of fluid in the pericardial cavity.

  3. Tamponade restricts ventricular filling, and **cardiac output** drops.

  4. Acute tamponade occurs when small volumes (20 to 50 mL) of fluid accumulate rapidly in the pericardium.

B. Assessment

  1. Pulsus paradoxus

BOX 59-7

Home Care Instructions for the Client
With Infective Endocarditis

Teach the client to maintain aseptic technique during setup and administration of intravenous antibiotics.

Instruct the client to administer intravenous antibiotics at scheduled times to maintain the blood level.

Instruct the client to monitor intravenous catheter sites for signs of infection and report this immediately to the physician.

Instruct the client to record the temperature daily for up to 6 weeks and report fever.

Encourage oral hygiene at least twice a day with a soft toothbrush and rinse well with water after brushing.

Client should avoid use of oral irrigation devices and flossing to avoid bacteremia.

Teach the client to cleanse any skin lacerations thoroughly and apply an antibiotic ointment as prescribed.

Client should inform all health care providers of history of endocarditis and request prophylactic antibiotics prior to every invasive procedure, including dentistry.

Teach the client to observe for signs and symptoms of embolic phenomena and heart failure.

---

  2. Increased CVP

  3. Jugular venous distention with clear lungs

  4. Distant, muffled heart sounds

  5. Decreased **cardiac output**

C. Interventions

  1. The client needs to be placed in a critical care unit for hemodynamic monitoring.

  2. Administer fluids intravenously as prescribed to manage decreased **cardiac output**.

  3. Prepare the client for chest x-ray or echocardiography.

  4. Prepare the client for pericardiocentesis to withdraw pericardial fluid if prescribed.

  5. Monitor for recurrence of tamponade following pericardiocentesis.

  6. If the client experiences recurrent tamponade or recurrent effusions or develops adhesions from chronic pericarditis, a portion (pericardial window) or all of the pericardium (pericardiectomy) may be removed to allow adequate ventricular filling and contraction.

XIV. VALVULAR HEART DISEASE

A. Description

  1. Valvular heart disease occurs when the heart valves cannot fully open (stenosis) or close completely (insufficiency or regurgitation).

  2. Valvular heart disease prevents efficient blood flow through the heart.

B. Types

  1. Mitral stenosis: Valvular tissue thickens and narrows the valve opening, preventing blood from flowing from the left atrium to the left ventricle.

2. Mitral insufficiency, regurgitation: Valve is incompetent, preventing complete valve closure during systole.
3. Mitral valve prolapse: Valve leaflets protrude into the left atrium during **systole**.
4. Aortic stenosis: Valvular tissue thickens and narrows the valve opening, preventing blood from flowing from the left ventricle into the aorta.
5. Aortic insufficiency: Valve is incompetent, preventing complete valve closure during diastole.

C. Repair procedures
1. Balloon valvuloplasty
   a. Balloon valvuloplasty is an invasive nonsurgical procedure.
   b. A balloon catheter is passed from the femoral vein through the atrial septum to the mitral valve or through the femoral artery to the aortic valve.
   c. The balloon is inflated to enlarge the orifice.
   d. Institute precautions for arterial puncture if appropriate.
   e. Monitor for bleeding from the catheter insertion site.
   f. Monitor for signs of systemic emboli.
   g. Monitor for signs of a regurgitant valve by monitoring cardiac rhythm, heart sounds, and **cardiac output**.
2. Mitral annuloplasty: Tightening and suturing the malfunctioning valve annulus to eliminate or greatly reduce regurgitation
3. Commissurotomy, valvotomy
   a. The procedure is accomplished with cardiopulmonary bypass during open heart surgery.
   b. The valve is visualized, thrombi are removed from the atria, fused leaflets are incised, and calcium is débrided from the leaflets, thus widening the orifice.

D. Valve replacement procedures
1. Mechanical prosthetic valves
   a. Prosthetic valves are durable.
   b. Thromboembolism is a problem following the valve replacement, and lifetime anticoagulant therapy is required.
2. Bioprosthetic valves
   a. Biological grafts are xenografts (valves from other species)—porcine valves (pig), bovine valves (cow), or homografts (human cadavers).
   b. The risk of clot formation is small; therefore, long-term anticoagulation may not be indicated.
3. Preoperative interventions: Consult with the physician regarding discontinuing anticoagulants 72 hours before surgery.
4. Postoperative interventions
   a. Monitor closely for signs of bleeding.
   b. Monitor **cardiac output** and for signs of heart failure.

BOX 59-8
Client Instructions Following Valve Replacement

Adequate rest is important, and fatigue is usual.
Anticoagulant therapy is necessary if a mechanical prosthetic valve has been inserted.
Instruct the client concerning hazards related to anticoagulant therapy and to notify the physician if bleeding or excessive bruising occurs.
Instruct the client concerning the importance of good oral hygiene to reduce the risk of infective endocarditis.
Brush teeth twice daily with a soft toothbrush, followed by oral rinses.
Avoid irrigation devices, electric toothbrushes, and flossing because these activities can cause the gums to bleed, allowing bacteria to enter the mucous membranes and bloodstream.
Monitor incision and report any drainage or redness.
Avoid any dental procedures for 6 months.
Heavy lifting (more than 10 lb) is to be avoided, and exercise caution when in an automobile to prevent injury to the sternal incision.
If a prosthetic valve was inserted, a soft, audible, clicking sound may be heard.
Instruct the client concerning the importance of prophylactic antibiotics before any invasive procedure and the importance of informing all health care professionals of the valvular disease history.
Obtain and wear a Medic-Alert bracelet.

   c. Administer digoxin as prescribed to maintain **cardiac output** and prevent atrial fibrillation.
   d. Provide client teaching (Box 59-8).
E. Mitral stenosis
1. Assessment
   a. Asymptomatic initially
   b. Symptoms occur when the orifice is reduced by 50%.
   c. Dyspnea
   d. Orthopnea
   e. Paroxysmal nocturnal dyspnea
   f. Dry cough
   g. Rumbling apical diastolic murmur
   h. Right ventricular failure
   i. Hepatomegaly
   j. Neck vein distention
   k. Pitting peripheral edema
   l. Hemoptysis and pulmonary edema as pulmonary hypertension and congestion progress
   m. Development of atrial fibrillation, indicating that the client may decompensate (notify physician immediately)
2. Interventions
   a. Administer prescribed treatment for heart failure.
   b. Administer oxygen as prescribed.
   c. Provide a low-sodium diet.

d. Administer diuretics and digoxin as prescribed.

e. Administer antibiotics as prescribed if infective endocarditis is present.

f. Administer antidysrhythmics and anticoagulants for atrial fibrillation as prescribed.

g. Prepare the client for commissurotomy or valve replacement as indicated.

F. Mitral valve prolapse
1. Assessment
   a. Fatigue
   b. Atypical chest pain
   c. Palpitations
   d. Dizziness and syncope
   e. Tachycardia
   f. Systolic click
2. Interventions
   a. Administer β-blockers for chest pain and antidysrhythmics as prescribed.
   b. Administer prophylactic antibiotics as prescribed prior to invasive procedures.

G. Mitral insufficiency
1. Assessment
   a. Dyspnea
   b. Orthopnea
   c. Fatigue
   d. Dizziness
   e. Palpitations
   f. Signs of right ventricular failure
   g. Atrial fibrillation
   h. Neck vein distention
   i. Pitting peripheral edema
   j. High-pitched systolic murmur
2. Interventions: Refer to interventions for mitral stenosis.

H. Aortic stenosis
1. Assessment
   a. Dyspnea on exertion
   b. Angina
   c. Syncope on exertion
   d. Fatigue
   e. Orthopnea
   f. Paroxysmal nocturnal dyspnea
   g. Harsh systolic crescendo-decrescendo murmur
2. Interventions
   a. Refer to interventions for mitral stenosis.
   b. Prepare the client for valve replacement as indicated.

I. Aortic insufficiency
1. Assessment
   a. Dyspnea
   b. Orthopnea
   c. Paroxysmal nocturnal dyspnea
   d. Fatigue
   e. Angina
   f. Tachycardia
   g. Blowing decrescendo diastolic murmur

2. Interventions
   a. Refer to interventions for mitral stenosis.
   b. Prepare the client for valve replacement as indicated.

J. Tricuspid stenosis
1. Assessment
   a. Easily fatigued
   b. Effort intolerance
   c. Complaints of fluttering sensations in the neck (obstructed venous flow)
   d. Cyanosis
   e. Signs of right ventricular failure
   f. Symptoms of decreased **cardiac output**
   g. Ascites
   h. Hepatomegaly
   i. Peripheral edema
   j. Rumbling diastolic murmur
   k. Jugular vein distention with clear lung fields
2. Interventions
   a. Refer to interventions for mitral stenosis.
   b. Prepare the client for valve replacement as indicated.

K. Tricuspid insufficiency
1. Assessment
   a. Asymptomatic in mild situations
   b. Signs of right ventricular failure
   c. Ascites
   d. Hepatomegaly
   e. Pleural effusion
   f. Peripheral edema
   g. Systolic murmur heard at the left sternal border, fourth intercostal space
2. Interventions
   a. Refer to interventions for mitral stenosis.
   b. Prepare the client for valve replacement as indicated.

L. Pulmonary stenosis
1. Assessment
   a. Asymptomatic in a mild condition
   b. Dyspnea
   c. Fatigue
   d. Syncope
   e. Signs of right ventricular failure
   f. Ascites
   g. Hepatomegaly
   h. Peripheral edema
   i. Systolic thrill heard at left sternal border
2. Interventions
   a. Refer to interventions for mitral stenosis.
   b. Prepare the client for pulmonary valve commissurotomy as indicated.

M. Pulmonary insufficiency
1. Assessment
   a. Asymptomatic in mild condition
   b. Dyspnea
   c. Fatigue
   d. Syncope

e. Signs of right ventricular failure
f. Ascites
g. Hepatomegaly
h. Peripheral edema
i. Systolic thrill heard at the left sternal border
2. Interventions
a. Refer to interventions for mitral stenosis.
b. Prepare the client for valve replacement as indicated.

XV. CARDIOMYOPATHY

A. Description
1. Cardiomyopathy is a subacute or chronic disorder of the heart muscle.
2. Treatment is palliative, not curative, and the client needs to deal with numerous lifestyle changes and a shortened life span.
B. Types, signs and symptoms, and treatment (Table 59-2)

TABLE 59-2

Pathophysiology, Signs and Symptoms, and Treatment of Cardiomyopathies

| Dilated Cardiomyopathy | Hypertrophic Cardiomyopathy | | Restrictive Cardiomyopathy |
	Nonobstructed	Obstructed	
Pathophysiology			
Fibrosis of myocardium and endocardium Dilated chambers Mural wall thrombi prevalent	Hypertrophy of the walls Hypertrophied septum Relatively small chamber size	Same as for nonobstructed except for obstruction of left ventricular outflow tract associated with the hypertrophied septum and mitral valve incompetence	Mimics constrictive pericarditis Fibrosed walls cannot expand or contract Chambers narrowed; emboli common
Signs and Symptoms			
Fatigue and weakness Heart failure (left side) Dysrhythmias or heart block Systemic or pulmonary emboli S_3 and S_4 gallops Moderate to severe cardiomegaly	Dyspnea Angina Fatigue, syncope, palpitations Mild cardiomegaly S_4 gallop Ventricular dysrhythmias Sudden death common Heart failure	Same as for nonobstructed except with mitral regurgitation murmur Atrial fibrillation	Dyspnea and fatigue Heart failure (right sided) Mild to moderate cardiomegaly S_3 and S_4 gallops Heart block Emboli
Treatment			
Symptomatic treatment of heart failure Vasodilators Control of dysrhythmias Surgery: heart transplant	For both: Symptomatic treatment β-Blockers Conversion of atrial fibrillation Surgery: ventriculomyotomy or muscle resection with mitral valve replacement Digitalis, nitrates, and other vasodilators **contraindicated** with the obstructed form		Supportive treatment of symptoms Treatment of hypertension Conversion from dysrhythmias Exercise restrictions Emergency treatment of acute pulmonary edema

From Ignatavicius, D., & Workman, M. (2006). *Medical-surgical nursing: Critical thinking for collaborative care* (5th ed.). Philadelphia: W.B. Saunders.

XVI. VASCULAR DISORDERS
A. Venous thrombosis
1. Description
a. Thrombus can be associated with an inflammatory process.
b. When a thrombus develops, inflammation occurs, thickening the vein wall and leading to embolization.
2. Types
a. Thrombophlebitis: Thrombus associated with inflammation
b. Phlebothrombus: Thrombus without inflammation
c. Phlebitis: Vein inflammation associated with invasive procedures, such as IV lines
d. Deep vein thrombophlebitis: More serious than a superficial thrombophlebitis because of the risk for pulmonary embolism
3. Risks factors for thrombus formation
a. Venous stasis from varicose veins, heart failure, immobility
b. Hypercoagulability disorders
c. Injury to the venous wall from IV injections; administration of vessel irritants (chemotherapy, hypertonic solutions)
d. Following surgery, particularly orthopedic and abdominal surgery
e. Pregnancy
f. Ulcerative colitis
g. Use of oral contraceptives
h. Certain malignancies
i. Fractures or other injuries of the pelvis or lower extremities
▲ B. Phlebitis
▲ 1. Assessment
a. Red, warm area radiating up the vein and extremity
b. Pain and soreness
c. Swelling
2. Interventions
a. Apply warm moist soaks as prescribed to dilate the vein and promote circulation (assess temperature of soak before applying).
b. Assess for signs of complications such as tissue necrosis, infection, or pulmonary embolus.
▲ C. Deep vein thrombophlebitis
▲ 1. Assessment
a. Calf or groin tenderness or pain with or without swelling
b. Positive Homans' sign may be noted; false-positive results are common.
c. Warm skin that is tender to touch
▲ 2. Interventions
a. Provide bed rest as prescribed.
▲ b. Elevate the affected extremity above the level of the heart as prescribed.
▲ c. Avoid using the knee gatch or a pillow under the knees.

d. Do not massage the extremity.
e. Provide thigh-high or knee-high antiembolism stockings as prescribed to reduce venous stasis and assist in the venous return of blood to the heart.
f. Administer intermittent or continuous warm, moist compresses as prescribed.
g. Palpate the site gently, monitoring for warmth and edema.
h. Measure and record the circumferences of the thighs and calves.
i. Monitor for shortness of breath and chest pain, which can indicate pulmonary emboli.
j. Administer thrombolytic therapy (tissue plasminogen activator) if prescribed, which must be initiated within 5 days after the onset of symptoms.
k. Administer heparin therapy as prescribed to prevent enlargement of the existing clot and prevent the formation of new clots.
l. Monitor activated partial thromboplastin time during heparin therapy.
m. Administer warfarin (Coumadin) as prescribed following heparin therapy when the symptoms of deep vein thrombophlebitis have resolved.
n. Monitor prothrombin time and international normalized ratio during warfarin (Coumadin) therapy.
o. Monitor for the hazards and side effects associated with anticoagulant therapy.
p. Administer analgesics as prescribed to reduce pain.
q. Administer diuretics as prescribed to reduce lower extremity edema.
r. Provide client teaching (Box 59-9).

BOX 59-9

Instructions for the Client
With Deep Vein Thrombophlebitis

Instruct the client concerning the hazards of anticoagulation therapy.
Recognize the signs and symptoms of bleeding.
Avoid prolonged sitting or standing, constrictive clothing, or crossing legs when seated.
Elevate the legs for 10 to 20 minutes every few hours each day.
Plan a progressive walking program.
Inspect the legs for edema, and measure the circumference of the legs.
Wear antiembolism stockings as prescribed.
Avoid smoking.
Avoid any medications unless prescribed by the physician.
Instruct the client concerning the importance of follow-up physician visits and laboratory studies.
Obtain and wear a Medic-Alert bracelet.

▲ D. Venous insufficiency
1. Description
   a. Venous insufficiency results from prolonged venous hypertension, which stretches the veins and damages the valves.
   b. The resultant edema and venous stasis cause venous stasis ulcers, swelling, and cellulitis.
   c. Treatment focuses on decreasing edema and promoting venous return from the affected extremity.
   d. Treatment for venous stasis ulcers focuses on healing the ulcer and preventing stasis and ulcer recurrence.
▲ 2. Assessment
   a. Stasis dermatitis or brown discoloration along the ankles, extending up to the calf
   b. Edema
   c. Ulcer formation: Edges are uneven, ulcer bed is pink, and granulation is present.
▲ 3. Interventions
   a. Instruct the client to wear elastic or compression stockings during the day and evening as prescribed (instruct the client to put on elastic stockings on awakening, before getting out of bed).
   b. Advise the client to put on a clean pair of elastic stockings each day; it will probably be necessary to wear the stockings for the remainder of life.
   c. Instruct the client to avoid prolonged sitting or standing, constrictive clothing, or crossing legs when seated.
   d. Instruct the client to elevate the legs for 10 to 20 minutes every few hours each day.
   e. Instruct the client to elevate the legs above the level of the heart when in bed.
   f. Instruct the client in the use of an intermittent sequential pneumatic compression system, if prescribed; instruct the client to apply the compression system twice daily for 1 hour in the morning and evening.
   g. Advise the client with an open ulcer that the compression system is applied over a dressing.
4. Wound care
   a. Provide care to the wound as prescribed by the physician.
   b. Assess the client's ability to care for the wound, and initiate home care resources as necessary.
   c. If an Unna boot (dressing constructed of gauze moistened with zinc oxide) is prescribed, the physician will change it weekly.
   d. The wound is cleansed with normal saline before application of the Unna boot; povidone-iodine (Betadine) and hydrogen peroxide are not used because they destroy granulation tissue.
   e. The Unna boot is covered with an elastic wrap that hardens to promote venous return and prevent stasis.
   f. Monitor for signs of arterial occlusion from an Unna boot that may be too tight.
   g. Keep tape off the client's skin.
   h. Occlusive dressings such as polyethylene film or a hydrocolloid dressing may be used to cover the ulcer.
5. Medications
   a. Apply topical agents to wound as prescribed to débride the ulcer, eliminate necrotic tissue, and promote healing.
   b. When applying topical agents, apply an oil-based agent such as petroleum jelly (Vaseline) on surrounding skin, because débriding agents can injure healthy tissue.
   c. Administer antibiotics as prescribed if infection or cellulitis occurs.
E. Varicose veins
1. Description
   a. Distended, protruding veins that appear darkened and tortuous are evident.
   b. Vein walls weaken and dilate, and valves become incompetent.
2. Assessment
   a. Pain in the legs with dull aching after standing
   b. A feeling of fullness in the legs
   c. Ankle edema
3. Trendelenburg's test
   a. Place the client in a supine position with the legs elevated.
   b. When the client sits up, if varicosities are present, veins fill from the proximal end; veins normally fill from the distal end.
4. Interventions
   a. Assist with Trendelenburg's test.
   b. Emphasize the importance of antiembolism stockings as prescribed.
   c. Instruct the client to elevate the legs as much as possible.
   d. Instruct the client to avoid constrictive clothing and pressure on the legs.
   e. Prepare the client for sclerotherapy or vein stripping as prescribed.
5. Sclerotherapy
   a. A solution is injected into the vein, followed by the application of a pressure dressing.
   b. Incision and drainage of the trapped blood in the sclerosed vein is performed 14 to 21 days after the injection, followed by the application of a pressure dressing for 12 to 18 hours.
6. Vein stripping
   a. Varicose veins are removed if they are larger than 4 mm in diameter or if they are in clusters.
   b. Preoperatively assist the physician with vein marking.

c. Evaluate pulses as a baseline for comparison postoperatively.

d. Maintain elastic (Ace) bandages on the client's legs postoperatively.

e. Monitor the groin and leg for bleeding through the elastic bandages.

f. Monitor the extremity for edema, warmth, color, and pulses.

g. Assess for paresthesias, which could include saphenous nerve damage.

h. Elevate the legs above the level of the heart postoperatively.

i. Encourage range-of-motion exercises of the legs.

j. Instruct the client to avoid leg dangling or chair sitting.

k. Instruct the client to elevate the legs when sitting.

l. Emphasize the importance of wearing elastic  stockings after bandage removal.

7. Laser therapy: A laser fiber is used to heat and close the main vessel contributing to the varicosity.

 XVII. ARTERIAL DISORDERS

A. Peripheral arterial disease

1. Description

a. Chronic disorder in which partial or total arterial occlusion deprives the lower extremities of oxygen and nutrients

b. Tissue damage occurs below the level of the arterial occlusion.

c. Atherosclerosis is the most common cause of peripheral arterial disease.

2. Assessment

a. Intermittent claudication (pain in the muscles resulting from an inadequate blood supply)

b. Rest pain, characterized by numbness, burning, or aching in the distal portion of the lower extremities, which awakens the client at night and is relieved by placing the extremity in a dependent position

c. Lower back or buttock discomfort

d. Loss of hair and dry scaly skin on the lower extremities

e. Thickened toenails

f. Cold and gray-blue color of skin in the lower extremities

g. Elevational pallor and dependent rubor in the lower extremities

 h. Decreased or absent peripheral pulses

i. Signs of arterial ulcer formation occurring on or between the toes or on the upper aspect of the foot that are characterized as painful

j. **BP** measurements at the thigh, calf, and ankle are lower than the brachial pressure (normally, **BP** readings in the thigh and calf are higher than those in the upper extremities).

3. Interventions

a. Assess pain.

b. Monitor the extremities for color, motion and sensation, and pulses.

c. Obtain **BP** measurements.

d. Assess for signs of ulcer formation or signs of gangrene.

e. Assist in developing an individualized exercise program, which is initiated gradually and slowly increased.

f. Encourage prescribed exercise, which will improve arterial flow through the development of collateral circulation.

g. Instruct the client to walk to the point of claudication, stop and rest, and then walk a little farther.

h. Because swelling in the extremities prevents arterial blood flow, instruct the client to elevate the feet at rest but to refrain from elevating them above the level of the heart because extreme elevation slows arterial blood flow to the feet.

i. In severe cases of peripheral arterial disease, clients with edema may sleep with the affected limb hanging from the bed or they may sit upright in a chair for comfort.

j. Instruct the client with peripheral arterial disease to avoid crossing the legs, which interferes with blood flow.

k. Instruct the client to avoid exposure to cold (causes vasoconstriction) to the extremities and to wear socks or insulated shoes for warmth at all times.

l. Instruct the client never to apply direct heat to the limb, such as with a heating pad or hot water, because the decreased sensitivity in the limb will cause burning.

m. Instruct the client to inspect the skin on the extremities daily and to report any signs of skin breakdown.

n. Instruct the client to avoid tobacco and caffeine because of their vasoconstrictive effects.

o. Instruct the client in the use of hemorheological and antiplatelet medications as prescribed.

p. Inform the client of the importance of taking all medications prescribed by the physician.

4. Procedures to improve arterial blood flow

a. Percutaneous transluminal angioplasty, with or without intravascular stent

b. Laser-assisted angioplasty

c. Atherectomy

d. Bypass surgery: Inflow procedures bypass the occlusion above the superficial femoral arteries and include aortoiliac, aortofemoral, and axillofemoral bypasses; outflow procedures bypass the occlusion at or below the superficial femoral arteries and include femoropopliteal and femorotibial bypass (Fig. 59-14).

B. Raynaud's disease
1. Description
   a. Raynaud's disease is vasospasms of the arterioles and arteries of the upper and lower extremities.
   b. Vasospasm causes constriction of the cutaneous vessels.
   c. Attacks are intermittent and occur with exposure to cold or stress.
   d. Affects primarily fingers, toes, ears, and cheeks
2. Assessment
   a. Blanching of the extremity, followed by cyanosis during vasoconstriction
   b. Reddened tissue when the vasospasm is relieved
   c. Numbness, tingling, swelling, and a cold temperature at the affected body part
3. Interventions
   a. Monitor pulses.
   b. Administer vasodilators as prescribed.
   c. Instruct the client regarding medication therapy.
   d. Assist the client to identify and avoid precipitating factors such as cold and stress.
   e. Instruct the client to avoid smoking.

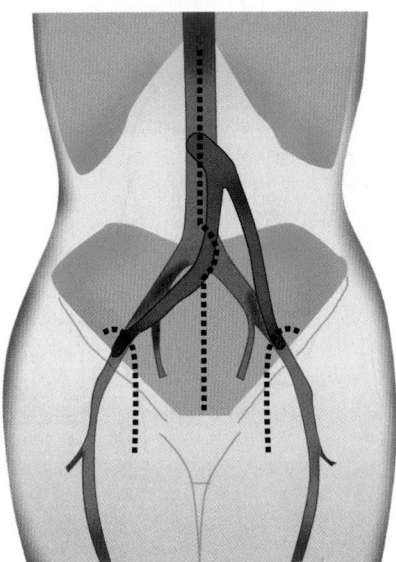

FIG. 59-14 In aortoiliac and aortofemoral bypass surgery, a midline incision into the abdominal cavity is required, with an additional incision in each groin. (From Ignatavicius, D., & Workman, M. [2006]. *Medical-surgical nursing: Critical thinking for collaborative care* [5th ed.]. Philadelphia: W.B. Saunders.)

f. Instruct the client to wear warm clothing, socks, and gloves in cold weather.
g. Advise the client to avoid injuries to fingers and hands.

C. Buerger's disease (thromboangiitis obliterans)
1. Description
   a. Buerger's disease is an occlusive disease of the median and small arteries and veins.
   b. The distal upper and lower limbs are affected most commonly.
2. Assessment
   a. Intermittent claudication
   b. Ischemic pain occurring in the digits while at rest
   c. Aching pain that is more severe at night
   d. Cool, numb, or tingling sensation
   e. Diminished pulses in the distal extremities
   f. Extremities that are cool and red in the dependent position
   g. Development of ulcerations in the extremities
3. Interventions
   a. Instruct the client to stop smoking.
   b. Monitor pulses.
   c. Instruct the client to avoid injury to the upper and lower extremities.
   d. Administer vasodilators as prescribed.
   e. Instruct the client regarding medication therapy.

XVIII. AORTIC ANEURYSMS
A. Description
1. An aortic aneurysm is an abnormal dilation of the arterial wall caused by localized weakness and stretching in the medial layer or wall of an artery.
2. The aneurysm can be located anywhere along the abdominal aorta.
3. The goal of treatment is to limit the progression of the disease by modifying risk factors, controlling the **BP** to prevent strain on the aneurysm, recognizing symptoms early, and preventing rupture.
B. Types of aortic aneurysm
1. Fusiform: Diffuse dilation that involves the entire circumference of the arterial segment
2. Saccular: Distinct localized outpouching of the artery wall
3. Dissecting: Created when blood separates the layers of the artery wall, forming a cavity between them
4. False (pseudoaneurysm)
   a. Pseudoaneurysm occurs when the clot and connective tissue are outside the arterial wall.
   b. Pseudoaneurysm occurs as a result of vessel injury or trauma to all three layers of the arterial wall.

C. Assessment
   1. Thoracic aneurysm
      a. Pain extending to neck, shoulders, lower back, or abdomen
      b. Syncope
      c. Dyspnea
      d. Increased pulse
      e. Cyanosis
      f. Weakness
      g. Hoarseness, difficulty swallowing because of pressure from the aneurysm
   2. Abdominal aneurysm
      a. Prominent, pulsating mass in abdomen, at or above the umbilicus
      b. Systolic bruit over the aorta
      c. Tenderness on deep palpation
      d. Abdominal or lower back pain
   3. Rupturing aneurysm
      a. Severe abdominal or back pain
      b. Lumbar pain radiating to the flank and groin
      c. Hypotension
      d. Increased pulse rate
      e. Signs of shock
      f. Hematoma at flank area
   4. Diagnostic tests
      a. Diagnostic tests are done to confirm the presence, size, and location of the aneurysm.
      b. Tests includes abdominal ultrasound, computed tomography scan, and arteriography.
   5. Interventions
      a. Monitor vital signs.
      b. Assess risk factors for the arterial disease process.
      c. Obtain information regarding back or abdominal pain.
      d. Question the client regarding the sensation of palpation in the abdomen.
      e. Inspect the skin for the presence of vascular disease or breakdown.
      f. Check peripheral circulation, including pulses, temperature, and color.
      g. Observe for signs of rupture.
      h. Note any tenderness over the abdomen.
      i. Monitor for abdominal distention.
   6. Nonsurgical interventions
      a. Modify risk factors.
      b. Instruct the client regarding the procedure for monitoring **BP**.
      c. Instruct the client on the importance of regular physician visits to follow the size of the aneurysm.
      d. Instruct the client that if severe back or abdominal pain or fullness, soreness over the umbilicus, sudden development of discoloration in the extremities, or a persistent elevation of **BP** occurs to notify the physician immediately.

      e. Instruct the client with a thoracic aneurysm to report immediately the occurrence of chest or back pain, shortness of breath, difficulty swallowing, or hoarseness.
D. Pharmacological interventions
   1. Administer antihypertensives to maintain the **BP** within normal limits and to prevent strain on the aneurysm.
   2. Instruct the client about the purpose of the medications.
   3. Instruct the client about the side effects and schedule of the medication.
E. Abdominal aortic aneurysm resection
   1. Description: Surgical resection or excision of the aneurysm; the excised section is replaced with a graft that is sewn end to end (Fig. 59-15).
   2. Preoperative interventions
      a. Assess all peripheral pulses as a baseline for postoperative comparison.
      b. Instruct the client in coughing and deep-breathing exercises.
      c. Administer bowel preparation as prescribed.
   3. Postoperative interventions
      a. Monitor vital signs.
      b. Monitor peripheral pulses distal to the graft site.
      c. Monitor for signs of graft occlusion, including changes in pulses, cool to cold extremities below the graft, white or blue extremities or flanks, severe pain, or abdominal distention.

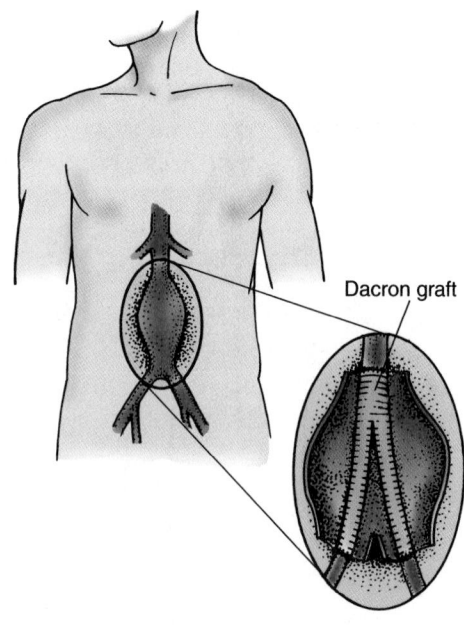

Dacron graft

FIG. 59-15 Surgical repair of an abdominal aortic aneurysm with a woven Dacron graft. (From Ignatavicius, D., & Workman, M. [2006]. *Medical-surgical nursing: Critical thinking for collaborative care* [5th ed.]. Philadelphia: W.B. Saunders.)

d. Limit elevation of the head of the bed to 45 degrees to prevent flexion of the graft.

e. Monitor for hypovolemia and renal failure resulting from significant blood loss during surgery.

f. Monitor urine output hourly, and notify the physician if it is lower than 30 to 50 mL/hr.

g. Monitor serum creatinine and blood urea nitrogen levels daily.

h. Monitor respiratory status and auscultate breath sounds to identify respiratory complications.

i. Encourage turning, coughing and deep breathing, and splinting the incision.

j. Ambulate as prescribed.

k. Maintain nasogastric tube to low suction until bowel sounds return.

l. Assess for bowel sounds and report their return to the physician

m. Monitor for pain and administer medication as prescribed.

n. Assess incision site for bleeding or signs of infection.

o. Prepare the client for discharge by providing instructions regarding pain management, wound care, and activity restrictions.

p. Instruct the client not to lift objects heavier than 15 to 20 lb for 6 to 12 weeks.

q. Advise the client to avoid activities requiring pushing, pulling, or straining.

r. Instruct the client not to drive a vehicle until approved by the physician.

F. Thoracic aneurysm repair

1. Description

a. A thoracotomy or median sternotomy approach is used to enter the thoracic cavity.

b. The aneurysm is exposed and excised, and a graft or prosthesis is sewn onto the aorta.

c. Total cardiopulmonary bypass is necessary for excision of aneurysms in the ascending aorta.

d. Partial cardiopulmonary bypass is used for clients with an aneurysm in the descending aorta.

2. Postoperative interventions

a. Monitor vital signs and neurological and renal status.

b. Monitor for signs of hemorrhage, such as a drop in **BP** and increased pulse rate and respirations, and report to the physician immediately.

c. Monitor chest tubes for an increase in chest drainage, which may indicate bleeding or separation at the graft site.

d. Assess sensation and motion of all extremities and notify the physician if deficits occur, which can occur because of a lack of blood supply to the spinal cord during surgery.

e. Monitor respiratory status and auscultate breath sounds to identify respiratory complications.

f. Encourage turning, coughing, and deep breathing while splinting the incision.

g. Monitor cardiac status for dysrhythmias.

h. Monitor for pain and administer medication as prescribed.

i. Assess the incision site for bleeding or signs of infection.

j. Prepare the client for discharge by providing instructions regarding pain management, wound care, and activity restrictions.

k. Instruct the client not to lift objects heavier than 15 to 20 lb for 6 to 12 weeks.

l. Advise the client to avoid activities requiring pushing, pulling, or straining.

m. Instruct the client not to drive a vehicle until approved by the physician.

XIX. EMBOLECTOMY

A. Description

1. Embolectomy is removal of an embolus from an artery using a catheter.

2. A patch graft may be required to close the artery.

B. Preoperative interventions

1. Obtain a baseline vascular assessment.

2. Administer anticoagulants as prescribed.

3. Administer thrombolytics as prescribed.

4. Place a bed cradle on the bed.

5. Avoid bumping or jarring the bed.

6. Maintain the extremity in slightly dependent position.

C. Postoperative interventions

1. Assess cardiac, respiratory, and neurological status.

2. Monitor affected extremity for color, temperature, and pulse.

3. Assess sensory and motor function of the affected extremity.

4. Monitor for signs and symptoms of new thrombi or emboli.

5. Administer oxygen as prescribed.

6. Monitor pulse oximetry.

7. Monitor for complications caused by reperfusion of the artery, such as spasms and swelling of the skeletal muscles.

8. Monitor for signs of swollen skeletal muscles such as edema, pain on passive movement, poor capillary refill, numbness, and muscle tenseness.

9. Maintain bed rest initially, with the client in a semi-Fowler's position.

10. Place a bed cradle on the bed.

11. Check the incision site for bleeding or hematoma.

12. Administer anticoagulants as prescribed.

13. Monitor laboratory values related to anticoagulant therapy.
14. Instruct the client to recognize the signs and symptoms of infection and edema.
15. Instruct the client to avoid prolonged sitting or crossing the legs when sitting.
16. Instruct the client to elevate the legs when sitting.
17. Instruct the client to wear antiembolism stockings as prescribed and how to remove and reapply the stockings
18. Instruct the client to ambulate daily.
19. Instruct the client about anticoagulant therapy and the hazards associated with anticoagulants.

XX. VENA CAVAL FILTER AND LIGATION OF INFERIOR VENA CAVA

A. Vena caval filter: Insertion of an intracaval filter (umbrella) that partially occludes the inferior vena cava and traps emboli to prevent pulmonary emboli (Fig. 59-16)
B. Ligation: Suturing or placing clips on the inferior vena cava to prevent pulmonary emboli; done via abdominal laparotomy
C. Preoperative interventions: If the client has been taking an anticoagulant, consult with the physician

regarding discontinuation of the medication to prevent hemorrhage.
D. Postoperative interventions
1. Monitor vital signs.
2. Assess cardiac, respiratory, neurological, and renal status.
3. Administer oxygen as prescribed.
4. Monitor pulse oximetry.
5. Maintain a semi-Fowler's position.
6. Avoid hip flexion.
7. Provide activity as prescribed.
8. Check the insertion site for bleeding or hematoma and signs or symptoms of infection.
9. Assess for peripheral edema.
10. Maintain antiembolism stockings as prescribed.
11. Monitor laboratory values related to anticoagulant therapy.
12. Instruct the client to recognize the signs and symptoms of infection and edema.
13. Instruct the client to avoid prolonged sitting or crossing legs when sitting.
14. Instruct the client to elevate the legs when sitting.
15. Instruct the client to wear antiembolism stockings as prescribed and how to remove and reapply the stockings.
16. Instruct the client to ambulate daily.
17. Instruct the client about anticoagulant therapy and the hazards associated with anticoagulants.

XXI. HYPERTENSION

A. Description
1. An individual classified with prehypertension has a systolic **BP** between 120 and 139 mm Hg or a **diastolic pressure** between 80 and 89 mm Hg.
2. In an individual older than 50 years, the **systolic pressure** is a more important value to note than the **diastolic pressure** regarding the need for treatment.
3. Hypertension is a major risk factor for coronary, cerebral, renal, and peripheral vascular disease.
4. The disease is initially asymptomatic.
5. The goals of treatment include reduction of the **BP** and preventing or lessening the extent of organ damage (Table 59-3).

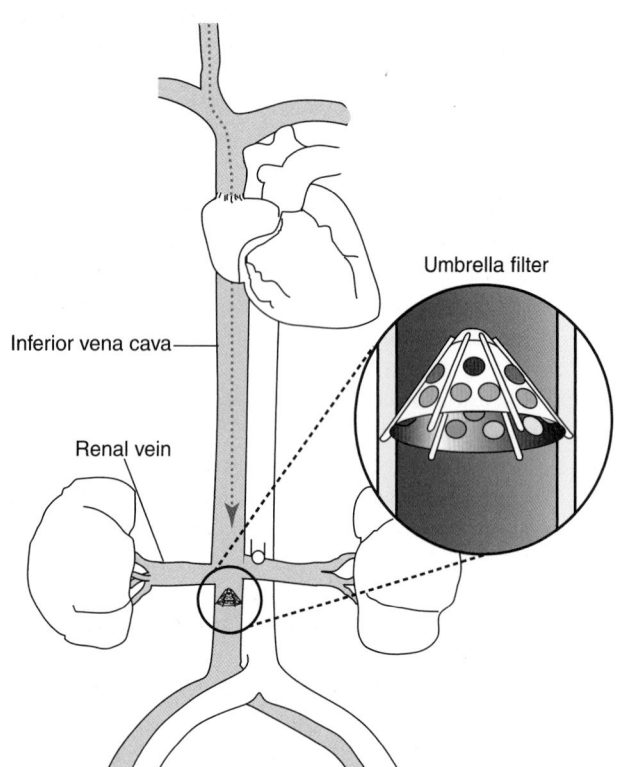

Umbrella filter

Inferior vena cava

Renal vein

FIG. 59-16   An inferior vena caval filter. (From Ignatavicius, D., & Workman, M. [2006]. *Medical-surgical nursing: Critical thinking for collaborative care* [5th ed.]. Philadelphia: W.B. Saunders.)

TABLE 59-3	
Hypertension	
Organ Involvement	**Complications**
Eyes	Visual changes
Brain	Stroke
Cardiovascular system	Heart failure, hypertensive crisis
Kidneys	Renal failure

6. Nonpharmacological approaches, such as lifestyle changes, may be prescribed initially; if the BP cannot be decreased after a reasonable time period (1 to 3 months), the client may require pharmacological treatment.

B. Primary or essential hypertension
1. No known cause
2. Risk factors
   a. Aging
   b. Family history
   c. Black race, with higher prevalence in males
   d. Obesity
   e. Smoking
   f. Stress
   g. Excessive alcohol
   h. Hyperlipidemia
   i. Increased intake of salt or caffeine

C. Secondary hypertension
1. Treatment depends on the cause and the organs involved.
2. Secondary hypertension occurs as a result of other disorders or conditions.
3. Precipitating disorders or conditions
   a. Cardiovascular disorders
   b. Renal disorders
   c. Endocrine system disorders
   d. Pregnancy
   e. Medications (e.g., estrogens, glucocorticoids, mineralocorticoids)

D. Assessment
1. May be asymptomatic
2. Headache
3. Visual disturbances
4. Dizziness
5. Chest pain
6. Tinnitus
7. Flushed face
8. Epistaxis

E. Interventions
1. Goals
   a. One treatment goal is to reduce the **BP**.
   b. Another treatment goal is to prevent or lessen the extent of organ damage.
2. Question the client regarding the signs and symptoms indicative of hypertension.
3. Obtain the **BP** two or more times on both arms, with the client supine and standing.
4. Compare the **BP** with prior documentation.
5. Determine family history of hypertension.
6. Identify current medication therapy.
7. Obtain weight.
8. Evaluate dietary patterns and sodium intake.
9. Assess for visual changes or retinal damage.
10. Assess for cardiovascular changes such as distended neck veins, increased heart rate, and dysrhythmias.
11. Evaluate chest x-ray for heart enlargement.
12. Assess the neurological system.
13. Evaluate renal function.
14. Evaluate results of diagnostic and laboratory studies.

F. Nonpharmacological interventions
1. Weight reduction, if necessary, or maintenance of ideal weight
2. Dietary sodium restriction to 2 g daily as prescribed
3. Moderate intake of alcohol and caffeine-containing products
4. Initiation of a regular exercise program
5. Avoidance of smoking
6. Relaxation techniques and biofeedback therapy
7. Elimination of unnecessary medications that may contribute to the hypertension

G. Stepped-care approach
1. Description
   a. If a pharmacological approach to treating hypertension is required, a single medication is prescribed and monitored for its effectiveness.
   b. Medications are added to the treatment regimen until the BP is controlled.
   c. See Chap. 60 for medications to treat hypertension.
2. Step 1: A single medication is prescribed, which may be a diuretic, β-blocker, calcium channel blocker, angiotensin-converting enzyme inhibitor, or angiotensin II receptor blocker.
3. Step 2
   a. Step 1 therapy is evaluated after 1 to 3 months.
   b. If the response is not adequate, compliance is evaluated.
   c. The medication may be increased or a new medication may be prescribed or a second medication added the treatment plan.
4. Step 3
   a. Compliance is evaluated.
   b. Further evaluation of step 2.
   c. If a therapeutic response is not adequate, a second medication is substituted or a third medication is added to the treatment plan.
5. Step 4
   a. Compliance is evaluated.
   b. Careful assessment of factors limiting the antihypertensive response is done.
   c. A third or fourth medication may be added to the treatment plan.

H. See Box 59-10 for client education.

XXII. HYPERTENSIVE CRISIS
A. Description
1. A hypertensive crisis is any clinical condition requiring immediate reduction in **BP**.

BOX 59-10
Client Education for Hypertension

Describe the importance of compliance with the treatment plan.

Describe the disease process, explaining that symptoms usually do not develop until organs have suffered damage.

Initiate and assist the client in planning a regular exercise program, avoiding heavy weight-lifting and isometric exercises.

Emphasize the importance of beginning the exercise program gradually.

Encourage the client to express feelings about daily stress.

Assist the client to identify ways to reduce stress.

Teach relaxation techniques.

Instruct the client in how to incorporate relaxation techniques into the daily living pattern.

Instruct the client and family in the technique for monitoring blood pressure.

Instruct the client to maintain a diary of blood pressure readings.

Emphasize the importance of lifelong medication and the need for follow-up treatment.

Instruct the client and family about the dietary restrictions, which may include sodium, fat, calories, and cholesterol.

Instruct the client in how to shop for and prepare low-sodium meals.

Provide a list of products that contain sodium.

Instruct the client to read labels of products to determine sodium content, focusing on substances listed as sodium, NaCl, or MSG (monosodium glutamate).

Instruct the client to bake, roast, or boil foods, avoid salt in preparation of foods, and avoid using salt at the table.

Instruct the client that fresh foods are best to consume and to avoid canned foods.

Instruct the client about the actions, side effects, and scheduling of medications.

Advise the client that if uncomfortable side effects occur to contact the physician and not to stop the medication.

Instruct the client to avoid over-the-counter medications.

Stress the importance of follow-up care.

2. A hypertensive crisis is an acute and life-threatening condition.
3. The accelerated hypertension requires emergency treatment because target organ damage (brain, heart, kidneys, retina of the eye) can occur quickly.
4. Death can be caused by stroke, renal failure, or cardiac disease.

B. Assessment
1. An extremely high blood pressure; usually, the **diastolic pressure** is higher than 120 mm Hg
2. Headache
3. Drowsiness and confusion

4. Blurred vision
5. Changes in neurological status
6. Tachycardia and tachypnea
7. Dyspnea
8. Cyanosis
9. Seizures

C. Interventions
1. Maintain a patent airway.
2. Administer antihypertensive medications intravenously as prescribed, which may include nitroprusside (Nitropress), diazoxide (Hyperstat), nicardipine (Cardene), or labetolol (Trandate).
3. Monitor vital signs, assessing the BP every 5 minutes.
4. Assess for hypotension during the administration of antihypertensives; place the client in a supine position if hypotension occurs.
5. Have emergency medications and resuscitation equipment readily available.
6. Maintain bed rest, with the head of the bed elevated at 45 degrees.
7. Monitor IV therapy, assessing for fluid overload.
8. Monitor intake and output.
9. Insert a Foley catheter as prescribed.
10. Monitor urinary output; if oliguria or anuria occurs, notify the physician.

PRACTICE QUESTIONS

1. A client with no history of cardiovascular disease comes to the ambulatory clinic with flu-like symptoms. The client suddenly complains of chest pain. Which of the following questions would best help a nurse discriminate pain caused by a noncardiac problem?
   1. "Can you describe the pain to me?"
   2. "Have you ever had this pain before?"
   3. "Does the pain get worse when you breathe in?"
   4. "Can you rate the pain on a scale of 1 to 10, with 10 being the worst?"

2. A client is admitted to an emergency room with chest pain that is being ruled out for myocardial infarction. Vital signs are as follows: at 11 AM, pulse (P), 92 beats/min, respiratory rate (RR), 24 breaths/min, blood pressure (BP), 140/88 mm Hg; 11:15 AM, P, 96 beats/min, RR, 26 breaths/min, BP, 128/82 mm Hg; 11:30 AM, P, 104 beats/min, RR, 28 breaths/min, BP, 104/68 mm Hg; 11:45 AM, P, 118 beats/min, RR, 32 breaths/min, BP, 88/58 mm Hg. The nurse should alert the physician because these changes are most consistent with which of the following complications?
   1. Cardiogenic shock
   2. Cardiac tamponade
   3. Pulmonary embolism
   4. Dissecting thoracic aortic aneurysm

3. A client with myocardial infarction has been transferred from a coronary care unit to a general medical unit with cardiac monitoring via telemetry. A nurse plans to allow for which of the following client activities?
   1. Strict bed rest for 24 hours after transfer
   2. Bathroom privileges and self-care activities
   3. Ad lib activities because the client is monitored
   4. Unsupervised hallway ambulation with distances under 200 feet

4. A client admitted to the hospital with chest pain and history of type II diabetes mellitus is scheduled for cardiac catheterization. Which of the following medications would need to be held for 48 hours before and after the procedure?
   1. Regular insulin
   2. Glipizide (Glucotrol)
   3. Repaglinide (Prandin)
   4. Metformin (Glucophage)

5. A client is in sinus bradycardia with a heart rate of 45 beats/min, complains of dizziness, and has a blood pressure of 82/60 mmHg. Which of the following should the nurse anticipate will be prescribed?
   1. Defibrillate the client.
   2. Administer digoxin (Lanoxin).
   3. Continue to monitor the client.
   4. Prepare for transcutaneous pacing.

6. A nurse notes bilateral +2 edema in the lower extremities of a client with myocardial infarction who was admitted 2 days ago. The nurse would plan to do which of the following next?
   1. Order daily weights starting on the following morning.
   2. Review the intake and output records for the last 2 days.
   3. Request a sodium restriction of 1 g/day from the physician.
   4. Change the time of diuretic administration from morning to evening.

7. A nurse is conducting a health history of a client with a primary diagnosis of heart failure. Which of the following disorders reported by the client is unlikely to play a role in exacerbating the heart failure?
   1. Atrial fibrillation
   2. Nutritional anemia
   3. Peptic ulcer disease
   4. Recent upper respiratory infection

8. A client with myocardial infarction suddenly becomes tachycardic, shows signs of air hunger, and begins coughing frothy, pink-tinged sputum. Which of the following would the nurse anticipate when auscultating the client's breath sounds?
   1. Stridor
   2. Crackles
   3. Scattered rhonchi
   4. Diminished breath sounds

9. A client who has developed severe pulmonary edema would most likely exhibit which of the following?
   1. Mild anxiety
   2. Slight anxiety
   3. Extreme anxiety
   4. Moderate anxiety

10. A client with pulmonary edema has been on diuretic therapy. The client has an order for additional furosemide (Lasix) in the amount of 40 mg intravenous push. Knowing that the client will also be started on digoxin (Lanoxin), the nurse should review which laboratory result?
    1. Sodium level
    2. Digoxin level
    3. Creatinine level
    4. Potassium level

11. A client with myocardial infarction is going into cardiogenic shock. Because of the risk of myocardial ischemia, for which of the following should the nurse carefully assess the client?
    1. Bradycardia
    2. Ventricular dysrhythmias
    3. Rising diastolic blood pressure
    4. Falling central venous pressure

12. A nurse assesses the sternotomy incision of a client on the third day after cardiac surgery. The incision shows some slight "puffiness" along the edges and is nonreddened, with no apparent drainage. Temperature is 99° F orally. The white blood cell count is 7500 cells/mm³. How should the nurse interpret these findings?
    1. Incision is slightly edematous but shows no active signs of infection.
    2. Incision shows early signs of infection, although the temperature is nearly normal.
    3. Incision shows early signs of infection, supported by an elevated white blood cell count.
    4. Incision shows no sign of infection, although the white blood cell count is elevated.

13. A client who had cardiac surgery 24 hours ago has a urine output averaging 20 mL/hr for 2 hours. The client received a single bolus of 500 mL of intravenous fluid. Urine output for the subsequent hour was 25 mL. Daily laboratory results indicate that the blood urea nitrogen level is 45 mg/dL and the serum creatinine level is 2.2 mg/dL. Based on these findings, the nurse would anticipate that the client is at risk for which of the following?
    1. Hypovolemia
    2. Acute renal failure
    3. Glomerulonephritis
    4. Urinary tract infection

14. A nurse is preparing to ambulate a client on the third day after cardiac surgery. The nurse would plan to do which of the following to enable the client to best tolerate the ambulation?

1. Remove telemetry equipment.
2. Provide the client with a walker.
3. Premedicate the client with an analgesic.
4. Encourage the client to cough and deep breathe.

15. The nurse is reviewing an electrocardiogram rhythm strip. The P waves and QRS complexes are regular. The PR interval is 0.16 second, and QRS complexes measure 0.06 second. The overall heart rate is 64 beats/min. Which of the following would be a correct interpretation based on these characteristics?
    1. Sinus bradycardia
    2. Sick sinus syndrome
    3. Normal sinus rhythm
    4. First-degree heart block

16. A client is wearing a continuous cardiac monitor, which begins to sound its alarm. A nurse sees no electrocardiographic complexes on the screen. Which of the following should be the priority action of the nurse?
    1. Call a code blue.
    2. Call the physician.
    3. Check the client status and lead placement.
    4. Press the recorder button on the electrocardiogram console.

17. A client's electrocardiogram strip shows atrial and ventricular rates of 110 beats/min. The PR interval is 0.14 second, the QRS complex measures 0.08 second, and the PP and RR intervals are regular. How should the nurse correctly interpret this rhythm?
    1. Sinus arrhythmia
    2. Sinus tachycardia
    3. Sinus bradycardia
    4. Normal sinus rhythm

18. A nurse notices frequent artifact on the electrocardiographic monitor for a client whose leads are connected by cable to a console at the bedside. The nurse examines the client to determine the cause. Which of the following items is unlikely to be responsible for the artifact?
    1. Frequent movement of the client
    2. Tightly secured cable connections
    3. Leads applied over hairy areas
    4. Leads applied to the limbs

19. A nurse is watching the cardiac monitor and notices that the rhythm suddenly changes. There are no P waves, the QRS complexes are wide, and the ventricular rate is regular but over 100 beats/min. The nurse determines that the client is experiencing which of the following dysrhythmias?
    1. Sinus tachycardia
    2. Ventricular fibrillation
    3. Ventricular tachycardia
    4. Premature ventricular contractions

20. A client has frequent bursts of ventricular tachycardia on the cardiac monitor. Why should the nurse be most concerned about with this dysrhythmia?

1. It can develop into ventricular fibrillation at any time.
2. It is almost impossible to convert to a normal rhythm.
3. It is uncomfortable for the client, giving a sense of impending doom.
4. It produces a high cardiac output that quickly leads to cerebral and myocardial ischemia.

21. A nurse is caring for a client with unstable ventricular tachycardia. The nurse instructs the client to do which of the following, if prescribed, during an episode of ventricular tachycardia?
    1. Lie down flat in bed.
    2. Remove any metal jewelry.
    3. Breathe deeply, regularly, and easily.
    4. Inhale deeply and cough forcefully every 1 to 3 seconds.

22. A client is having frequent premature ventricular contractions. A nurse would place priority on assessment of which of the following?
    1. Sensation of palpitations
    2. Causative factors, such as caffeine
    3. Precipitating factors, such as infection
    4. Blood pressure and oxygen saturation

23. A client has developed atrial fibrillation, with a ventricular rate of 150 beats/min. The nurse should assess the client for which associated signs or symptoms?
    1. Flat neck veins
    2. Nausea and vomiting
    3. Hypotension and dizziness
    4. Hypertension and headache

24. A nurse is watching the cardiac monitor, and a client's rhythm suddenly changes. There are no P waves; instead, there are fibrillatory waves before each QRS complex. How should the nurse correctly interpret the client's heart rhythm?
    1. Atrial fibrillation
    2. Sinus tachycardia
    3. Ventricular fibrillation
    4. Ventricular tachycardia

25. A client with rapid rate atrial fibrillation asks a nurse why the physician is going to perform carotid sinus massage. Which of the following would be reflective of a correct explanation provided by the nurse?
    1. The vagus nerve slows the heart rate.
    2. The diaphragmatic nerve slows the heart rate.
    3. The diaphragmatic nerve overdrives the rhythm.
    4. The vagus nerve increases the heart rate, overdriving the rhythm.

26. A nurse notes that a client with sinus rhythm has a premature ventricular contraction that falls on the T wave of the preceding beat. The client's rhythm suddenly changes to one with no P waves, no definable QRS complexes, and coarse wavy lines of varying amplitude. How would the nurse correctly interpret this rhythm?

1. Asystole
2. Atrial fibrillation
3. Ventricular fibrillation
4. Ventricular tachycardia

27. A nurse is preparing to defibrillate a client in ventricular fibrillation. After placing the paddles on the client's chest and before discharging them, which of the following should be done?
    1. Ensure that the client has been intubated.
    2. Set the defibrillator to the "synchronize" mode.
    3. Administer lidocaine hydrochloride (Xylocaine).
    4. Confirm that the rhythm is actually ventricular fibrillation.

28. A client in ventricular fibrillation is about to be defibrillated. A nurse knows that to convert this rhythm effectively, the machine should be set at which of the following energy levels (in joules, J) for the first delivery?
    1. 50 J
    2. 100 J
    3. 200 J
    4. 360 J

29. A nurse would evaluate that defibrillation of a client was most successful if which of the following observations was made?
    1. Arousable, sinus rhythm, BP 116/72 mm Hg
    2. Arousable, marked bradycardia, BP 86/54 mm Hg
    3. Nonarousable, supraventricular tachycardia, BP 122/60 mm Hg
    4. Nonarousable, sinus rhythm, BP 88/60 mm Hg

30. A nurse is evaluating a client's response to cardioversion. Which of the following observations would be of highest priority to the nurse?
    1. Blood pressure
    2. Status of airway
    3. Oxygen flow rate
    4. Level of consciousness

31. A nurse is performing cardiopulmonary resuscitation on a client who has had a cardiac arrest. An automatic external defibrillator is available to treat the client. Which of the following activities will allow the nurse to assess the client's cardiac rhythm?
    1. Hold the defibrillator paddles firmly against the chest.
    2. Apply adhesive patch electrodes to the chest and move away from the client.
    3. Apply standard electrocardiographic monitoring leads to the client and observe the rhythm.
    4. Connect standard electrocardiographic electrodes to a transtelephonic monitoring device.

32. A nurse employed in a cardiac unit determines that which of the following clients is the least likely to have implantation of an automatic internal cardioverter-defibrillator (AICD)?
    1. A client with syncopal episodes related to ventricular tachycardia

2. A client with ventricular dysrhythmias despite medication therapy
3. A client with an episode of cardiac arrest related to myocardial infarction
4. A client with three episodes of cardiac arrest unrelated to myocardial infarction

33. A nurse is caring for a client who has just had implantation of an automatic internal cardioverter-defibrillator. The nurse immediately would assess which of the following items based on priority?
    1. Anxiety level of the client and family
    2. Presence of a Medic-Alert card for the client to carry
    3. Knowledge of restrictions of postdischarge physical activity
    4. Activation status of the device, heart rate cutoff, and number of shocks it is programmed to deliver

34. A nurse is caring for a client immediately after insertion of a permanent demand pacemaker via the right subclavian vein. Which of the following activities will assist with preventing dislodgement of the pacing catheter?
    1. Limiting movement and abduction of the left arm
    2. Limiting movement and abduction of the right arm
    3. Assisting the client to get out of bed and ambulate with a walker
    4. Having the physical therapist do active range-of-motion exercises to the right arm

35. A client diagnosed with thrombophlebitis 1 day ago suddenly complains of chest pain and shortness of breath and is visibly anxious. The nurse should immediately assess the client for signs and symptoms of which of the following?
    1. Pneumonia
    2. Pulmonary edema
    3. Pulmonary embolism
    4. Myocardial infarction

36. A client seeks treatment in a physician's office for unsightly varicose veins, and sclerotherapy is recommended. Before leaving the examining room, the client says to the nurse, "Can you tell me again how this sclerotherapy is done?" Which of the following statements would reflect accurate teaching by the nurse?
    1. "The varicosity is surgically removed."
    2. "The vein is tied off at the upper end to prevent stasis from occurring."
    3. "The vein is tied off at the lower end to prevent stasis from occurring."
    4. "An agent is injected into the vein to damage the vein wall and close the vein off."

37. A client is having a follow-up physician office visit after vein ligation and stripping. The client describes

a sensation of "pins and needles" in the affected leg. Which of the following would be an appropriate action by the nurse based on evaluation of the client's comment?

1. Instruct the client to apply warm packs.

2. Report the complaint to the physician.

3. Reassure the client that this is only temporary.

4. Advise the client to take acetaminophen (Tylenol) until it is gone.

38. Postoperatively, a nurse is caring for a client who had a percutaneous insertion of an inferior vena cava filter and was on heparin therapy before surgery. The nurse would inspect the surgical site most closely for evidence of which of the following?

1. Bleeding and infection

2. Thrombosis and infection

3. Bleeding and wound dehiscence

4. Wound dehiscence and evisceration

39. A client with angina has a 12-lead electrocardiogram taken during an episode of chest pain. A nurse examines the tracing for which electrocardiographic change caused by myocardial ischemia?

1. Tall peaked T waves

2. Prolonged PR interval

3. Widened QRS complex

4. ST segment elevation or depression

40. A client is scheduled for a cardiac catheterization using a radiopaque dye. Which of the following assessments is most critical before the procedure?

1. Intake and output

2. Height and weight

3. Allergy to iodine or shellfish

4. Baseline peripheral pulse rates

41. A nurse is assessing the neurovascular status of a client who returned to the surgical nursing unit 4 hours ago after undergoing aortoiliac bypass graft. The affected leg is warm, and the nurse notes redness and edema. The pedal pulse is palpable and unchanged from admission. How would the nurse correctly interpret the client's neurovascular status?

1. The neurovascular status is normal because of increased blood flow through the leg.

2. The neurovascular status is moderately impaired, and the surgeon should be called.

3. The neurovascular status is slightly deteriorating and should be monitored for another hour.

4. The neurovascular status is adequate from an arterial approach, but venous complications are arising.

42. A nurse is evaluating the condition of a client after pericardiocentesis performed to treat cardiac tamponade. Which of the following observations would indicate that the procedure was unsuccessful?

1. Rising blood pressure

2. Clearly audible heart sounds

3. Client expressions of relief

4. Rising central venous pressure

43. A nurse is assessing a client with an abdominal aortic aneurysm. Which of the following assessment findings by the nurse is probably unrelated to the aneurysm?

1. Pulsatile abdominal mass

2. Hyperactive bowel sounds in the area

3. Systolic bruit over the area of the mass

4. Subjective sensation of "heart beating" in the abdomen

44. A nurse is caring for a client who had a resection of an abdominal aortic aneurysm yesterday. The client has an intravenous infusion with a rate of 150 mL/hr, unchanged for the last 10 hours. The client's urine output for the last 3 hours was 90, 50, and 28 mL (28 mL most recent). The client's blood urea nitrogen level is 35 mg/dL and serum creatinine level is 1.8 mg/dL, measured this morning. Which of the following actions should the nurse take next?

1. Call the physician.

2. Check the urine specific gravity.

3. Check to see if the client had a sample for serum albumin level drawn.

4. Put the intravenous line on a pump so that the infusion rate is sure to stay stable.

45. Cardiac magnetic resonance imaging (MRI) is prescribed for a client. The nurse identifies that which of the following is a contraindication for performance of this diagnostic study?

1. Client has a pacemaker.

2. Client is allergic to iodine.

3. Client has diabetes mellitus.

4. Client has a biological porcine valve.

46. A client with angina complains that the anginal pain is prolonged and severe and occurs at the same time each day, most often at rest in the absence of precipitating factors. How would the nurse best describe this type of anginal pain?

1. Stable angina

2. Variant angina

3. Unstable angina

4. Nonanginal pain

ALTERNATE ITEM FORMAT: MULTIPLE RESPONSE

A nurse in a medical unit is caring for a client with heart failure. The client suddenly develops extreme dyspnea, tachycardia, and lung crackles and the nurse suspects pulmonary edema. The nurse immediately asks another nurse to contact the physician and prepares to implement which priority interventions? Select all that apply.

❏ **1.** Administering oxygen

❏ **2.** Inserting a Foley catheter

❏ **3.** Administering furosemide (Lasix)

❏ **4.** Administering morphine sulfate intravenously

❏ **5.** Transporting the client to the coronary care unit

❏ **6.** Placing the client in a low Fowler's side-lying position

ANSWERS

1. 3
Rationale: Chest pain is assessed by using the standard pain assessment parameters (e.g., characteristics, location, intensity, duration, precipitating and alleviating factors, and associated symptoms). Options 1, 2, and 4 may or may not help discriminate the origin of pain. Pain of pleuropulmonary origin usually worsens on inspiration.
Test-Taking Strategy: Use the process of elimination, focusing on the subject, pain resulting from a noncardiac problem. The three incorrect options, although appropriate to use in practice, are general assessment questions only. Option 3 will discriminate between a cardiac and noncardiac cause of pain. Review pain assessment measures for the client with a cardiovascular problem if you had difficulty with this question.
Level of Cognitive Ability: Analysis
Client Needs: Physiological Integrity
Integrated Process: Nursing Process—assessment
Content Area: Adult health—cardiovascular
Reference: Ignatavicius, D., & Workman, M. (2006). *Medical-surgical nursing: Critical thinking for collaborative care* (5th ed., pp. 636, 844, 847). Philadelphia: W.B. Saunders.

2. 1
Rationale: Cardiogenic shock occurs with severe damage (more than 40%) to the left ventricle. Classic signs include hypotension, a rapid pulse that becomes weaker, decreased urine output, and cool, clammy skin. Respiratory rate increases as the body develops metabolic acidosis from shock. Cardiac tamponade is accompanied by distant, muffled heart sounds and prominent neck vessels. Pulmonary embolism presents suddenly with severe dyspnea accompanying the chest pain. Dissecting aortic aneurysms usually are accompanied by back pain.
Test-Taking Strategy: Use the process of elimination. Recalling that the early serious complications of myocardial infarction include dysrhythmias, cardiogenic shock, and sudden death will direct you to option 1. No information in the question would guide you to select options 2, 3, or 4. Review the complications of myocardial infarction if you had difficulty with this question.
Level of Cognitive Ability: Analysis
Client Needs: Physiological Integrity
Integrated Process: Nursing Process—analysis
Content Area: Adult health—cardiovascular
Reference: Ignatavicius, D., & Workman, M. (2006). *Medical-surgical nursing: Critical thinking for collaborative care* (5th ed., p. 854). Philadelphia: W.B. Saunders.

3. 2
Rationale: On transfer from the coronary care unit, the client is allowed self-care activities and bathroom privileges. Supervised ambulation in the hall for brief distances is encouraged, with distances gradually increased (50, 100, 200 feet).
Test-Taking Strategy: Use the process of elimination. Eliminate options 3 and 4 first because they are excessive, given that the client has just been transferred from the coronary care unit. Option 1 is not appropriate because the client would be doing less activity than in the coronary care unit before transfer. Review activity prescriptions for the client with a myocardial infarction if you had difficulty with this question.
Level of Cognitive Ability: Application

Client Needs: Physiological Integrity
Integrated Process: Nursing Process—planning
Content Area: Adult health—cardiovascular
References: Black, J., & Hawks, J. (2005). *Medical-surgical nursing: Clinical management for positive outcomes* (7th ed., p. 178). Philadelphia: W.B. Saunders.
Ignatavicius, D., & Workman, M. (2006). *Medical-surgical nursing: Critical thinking for collaborative care* (5th ed., p. 851). Philadelphia: W.B. Saunders.

4. 4
Rationale: Metformin (Glucophage) needs to be withheld 48 hours before and after cardiac catheterization because of the injection of contrast medium during the procedure. If the contrast medium affects kidney function, with metformin in the system, the client would be at increased risk for lactic acidosis. The medications in options 1, 2, and 3 do not need to be withheld 48 hours before and after cardiac catheterization.
Test-Taking Strategy: Use the process of elimination. Eliminate options 2 and 3 first. Although these medications may be held on the morning of the procedure because of the client's NPO status, there is no indication for withholding the medication the day prior to and the day postprocedure. Regular insulin may be administered if elevated blood glucose levels from infused intravenous solutions occur on the day of the procedure. Review preprocedure and postprocedure interventions if you had difficulty with this question.
Level of Cognitive Ability: Analysis
Client Needs: Physiological integrity
Integrated Process: Nursing Process—planning
Content Area: Adult health—cardiovascular
Reference: Ignativicius, D., & Workman, M. (2006). *Medical-surgical nursing: Critical thinking for collaborative care* (5th ed., p. 1509). Philadelphia: W.B. Saunders.

5. 4
Rationale: Hypotension and dizziness are signs of decreased cardiac output. Transcutaneous pacing provides a temporary measure to increase the heart rate and thus perfusion in the symptomatic client. Digoxin will further decrease the client's heart rate. Defibrillation is used for treatment of pulseless ventricular tachycardia and ventricular fibrillation. Continuing to monitor the client delays necessary intervention.
Test-Taking Strategy: Use the process of elimination. Eliminate option 3 because the client is symptomatic and requires intervention. Option 2 is eliminated because digoxin will further decrease the client's heart rate. Defibrillation is used for treatment of pulseless ventricular tachycardia and ventricular fibrillation; therefore, eliminate option 1. Review the indications for transcutaneous pacing if you had difficulty with this question.
Level of Cognitive Ability: Analysis
Client Needs: Physiological integrity
Integrated Process: Nursing Process—planning
Content Area: Adult health—cardiovascular
Reference: Ignativicius, D., & Workman, M. (2006). *Medical-surgical nursing: Critical thinking for collaborative care* (5th ed., pp. 720, 740). Philadelphia: W.B. Saunders.

6. 2
Rationale: Edema, the accumulation of excess fluid in the interstitial spaces, can be measured by intake greater than out-

put and by a sudden increase in weight. Diuretics should be given in the morning whenever possible to avoid nocturia. Strict sodium restrictions are reserved for clients with severe symptoms.
Test-Taking Strategy: Use the process of elimination, noting the strategic word *next*. Use the steps of the nursing process to prioritize. Option 2 is the only option that addresses assessment of data. Review care of the client with a myocardial infarction if you had difficulty with this question.
Level of Cognitive Ability: Application
Client Needs: Physiological Integrity
Integrated Process: Nursing Process—assessment
Content Area: Adult health—cardiovascular
References: Black, J., & Hawks, J. (2005). *Medical-surgical nursing: Clinical management for positive outcomes* (7th ed., pp. 1656, 1721). Philadelphia: W.B. Saunders.
Ignatavicius, D., & Workman, M. (2006). *Medical-surgical nursing: Critical thinking for collaborative care* (5th ed., pp. 688, 756, 760). Philadelphia: W.B. Saunders.

7. 3
Rationale: Heart failure is precipitated or exacerbated by physical or emotional stress, dysrhythmias, infections, anemia, thyroid disorders, pregnancy, Paget's disease, nutritional deficiencies (thiamine, alcoholism), pulmonary disease, and hypervolemia.
Test-Taking Strategy: Use the process of elimination and note the strategic word *unlikely*. Remembering that heart failure is exacerbated by factors that increase the workload of the heart will assist you in eliminating options 1, 2, and 4. Review the precipitating factors associated with heart failure if you had difficulty with this question.
Level of Cognitive Ability: Analysis
Client Needs: Physiological Integrity
Integrated Process: Nursing Process—assessment
Content Area: Adult health—cardiovascular
Reference: Ignatavicius, D., & Workman, M. (2006). *Medical-surgical nursing: Critical thinking for collaborative care* (5th ed., pp. 752, 754). Philadelphia: W.B. Saunders.

8. 2
Rationale: Pulmonary edema is characterized by extreme breathlessness, dyspnea, air hunger, and the production of frothy, pink-tinged sputum. Auscultation of the lungs reveals crackles. Rhonchi and diminished breath sounds are not associated with pulmonary edema. Stridor is a crowing sound associated with laryngospasm or edema of the upper airway.
Test-Taking Strategy: Use the process of elimination. Recalling that fluid produces sounds that are called crackles will assist you in eliminating options 1, 3, and 4. If you had difficulty with this question, review the manifestations found in pulmonary edema.
Level of Cognitive Ability: Analysis
Client Needs: Physiological Integrity
Integrated Process: Nursing Process—assessment
Content Area: Adult health—cardiovascular
Reference: Ignatavicius, D., & Workman, M. (2006). *Medical-surgical nursing: Critical thinking for collaborative care* (5th ed., pp. 760, 853). Philadelphia: W.B. Saunders.

9. 3
Rationale: Pulmonary edema causes the client to be extremely agitated and anxious. The client may complain of a sense of drowning, suffocation, or smothering.
Test-Taking Strategy: Use the process of elimination. Noting the strategic word *severe* will direct you to option 3. Review the clinical manifestations associated with severe pulmonary edema if you had difficulty with this question.
Level of Cognitive Ability: Analysis
Client Needs: Psychosocial Integrity
Integrated Process: Nursing Process—assessment
Content Area: Adult health—cardiovascular
Reference: Ignatavicius, D., & Workman, M. (2006). *Medical-surgical nursing: Critical thinking for collaborative care* (5th ed., pp. 755, 760). Philadelphia: W.B. Saunders.

10. 4
Rationale: The serum potassium level is measured in the client receiving digoxin and furosemide. Heightened digoxin effect leading to digoxin toxicity can occur in the client with hypokalemia. Hypokalemia also predisposes the client to ventricular dysrhythmias.
Test-Taking Strategy: Use the process of elimination. Eliminate option 2 because the client will just be beginning digoxin therapy. No data indicate the presence of renal insufficiency; therefore, eliminate option 3. Furosemide therapy can cause hyponatremia and hypokalemia, but remember that the risk of hypokalemia has more severe consequences in this situation. Review the nursing considerations related to administering furosemide if you had difficulty with this question.
Level of Cognitive Ability: Analysis
Client Needs: Physiological Integrity
Integrated Process: Nursing Process—assessment
Content Area: Adult health—cardiovascular
References: Black, J., & Hawks, J. (2005). *Medical-surgical nursing: Clinical management for positive outcomes* (7th ed., p. 1658). Philadelphia: W.B. Saunders.
Ignatavicius, D., & Workman, M. (2006). *Medical-surgical nursing: Critical thinking for collaborative care* (5th ed., pp. 227, 762). Philadelphia: W.B. Saunders.

11. 2
Rationale: Classic signs of cardiogenic shock as they relate to this question include low blood pressure and tachycardia. The central venous pressure would rise as the backward effects of the severe left ventricular failure became apparent. Dysrhythmias commonly occur as a result of decreased oxygenation and severe damage to greater than 40% of the myocardium.
Test-Taking Strategy: Use the process of elimination and focus on the strategic words *myocardial ischemia*. Recall that ischemia makes the myocardium irritable, producing dysrhythmias. Also, knowledge of the classic signs of shock helps eliminate the incorrect options. Review the clinical manifestations associated with cardiogenic shock if you had difficulty with this question.
Level of Cognitive Ability: Analysis
Client Needs: Physiological Integrity
Integrated Process: Nursing Process—assessment

Content Area: Adult health—cardiovascular
Reference: Ignatavicius, D., & Workman, M. (2006). *Medical-surgical nursing: Critical thinking for collaborative care* (5th ed., pp. 853-854). Philadelphia: W.B. Saunders.

12. **1**
Rationale: Sternotomy incision sites are assessed for signs and symptoms of infection, such as redness, swelling, induration, and drainage. Elevated temperature and white blood cell count after 3 to 4 days postoperatively usually indicate infection.
Test-Taking Strategy: Use the process of elimination. Eliminate options 3 and 4 because the white blood cell count is within normal range. From the remaining options, focus on the data in the question. A nonreddened incision with no apparent drainage indicates no signs of infection. Review the signs of infection if you had difficulty with this question.
Level of Cognitive Ability: Analysis
Client Needs: Physiological Integrity
Integrated Process: Nursing Process—analysis
Content Area: Adult health—cardiovascular
References: Black, J., & Hawks, J. (2005). *Medical-surgical nursing: Clinical management for positive outcomes* (7th ed., p. 1648). Philadelphia: W.B. Saunders.
Ignatavicius, D., & Workman, M. (2006). *Medical-surgical nursing: Critical thinking for collaborative care* (5th ed., pp. 346, 861, 1587). Philadelphia: W.B. Saunders.

13. **2**
Rationale: The client who undergoes cardiac surgery is at risk for renal injury from poor perfusion, hemolysis, low cardiac output, or vasopressor medication therapy. Renal insult is signaled by decreased urine output and increased blood urea nitrogen and creatinine levels. The client may need medications to increase renal perfusion and possibly could need peritoneal dialysis or hemodialysis. No data in the question indicate the presence of hypovolemia, urinary tract infection, or glomerulonephritis.
Test-Taking Strategy: Use the process of elimination. Eliminate options 3 and 4 first because no data indicate infection or inflammation. Noting that the urine output is inadequate will assist you in eliminating option 1. Review the complications associated with cardiac surgery if you had difficulty with this question.
Level of Cognitive Ability: Analysis
Client Needs: Physiological Integrity
Integrated Process: Nursing Process—analysis
Content Area: Adult health—cardiovascular
References: Black, J., & Hawks, J. (2005). *Medical-surgical nursing: Clinical management for positive outcomes* (7th ed., pp. 914-916, 1642). Philadelphia: W.B. Saunders.
Ignatavicius, D., & Workman, M. (2006). *Medical-surgical nursing: Critical thinking for collaborative care* (5th ed., pp. 860, 1663-1664, 1732). Philadelphia: W.B. Saunders.

14. **3**
Rationale: The nurse should encourage regular use of pain medication for the first 48 to 72 hours after cardiac surgery because analgesia will promote rest, decrease myocardial oxygen consumption resulting from pain, and allow better par-

ticipation in activities such as coughing, deep breathing, and ambulation. Options 2 and 4 will not help in tolerating ambulation. Removal of telemetry equipment is contraindicated unless prescribed.
Test Taking Strategy: Use the process of elimination. Focus on the subject, how best to tolerate the ambulation. Coughing and deep breathing will not actively help endurance, so eliminate option 4. Removal of telemetry equipment is contraindicated unless ordered. From the remaining options, focusing on the subject will direct you to option 3. Review comfort measures for the client following cardiac surgery if you had difficulty with this question.
Level of Cognitive Ability: Application
Client Needs: Physiological Integrity
Integrated Process: Nursing Process—planning
Content Area: Adult health—cardiovascular
References: Black, J., & Hawks, J. (2005). *Medical-surgical nursing: Clinical management for positive outcomes* (7th ed., p. 1645). Philadelphia: W.B. Saunders,.
Ignatavicius, D., & Workman, M. (2006). *Medical-surgical nursing: Critical thinking for collaborative care* (5th ed., pp. 767, 860). Philadelphia: W.B. Saunders.

15. **3**
Rationale: Normal sinus rhythm is defined as a regular rhythm, with an overall rate of 60 to 100 beats/min. The PR and QRS measurements are normal, measuring 0.12 to 0.20 second and 0.04 to 0.10 second, respectively.
Test-Taking Strategy: A baseline knowledge of normal electrocardiographic measurements is needed to answer this question. Focusing on the data in the question and recalling the characteristics of normal sinus rhythm will direct you to option 3. Review this content if you are unfamiliar with it.
Level of Cognitive Ability: Analysis
Client Needs: Physiological Integrity
Integrated Process: Nursing Process—assessment
Content Area: Adult health—cardiovascular
Reference: Ignatavicius, D., & Workman, M. (2006). *Medical-surgical nursing: Critical thinking for collaborative care* (5th ed., p. 716). Philadelphia: W.B. Saunders.

16. **3**
Rationale: Sudden loss of electrocardiographic complexes indicates ventricular asystole or possibly electrode displacement. Accurate assessment of the client and equipment is necessary to determine the cause and identify the appropriate intervention. Options 1, 2, and 4 are unnecessary.
Test-Taking Strategy: Use the steps of the nursing process. Option 3 is the only option that addresses assessment. Review care of the client on a cardiac monitor if you had difficulty with this question. Remember, always assess the client directly before taking any action.
Level of Cognitive Ability: Application
Client Needs: Physiological Integrity
Integrated Process: Nursing Process—implementation
Content Area: Delegating/Prioritizing
References: Black, J., & Hawks, J. (2005). *Medical-surgical nursing: Clinical management for positive outcomes* (7th ed., p. 1583). Philadelphia: W.B. Saunders.

Ignatavicius, D., & Workman, M. (2006). *Medical-surgical nursing: Critical thinking for collaborative care* (5th ed., pp. 711-712, 732). Philadelphia: W.B. Saunders.

17. **2**

Rationale: Sinus tachycardia has the characteristics of normal sinus rhythm, including a regular PP interval and normal width PR and QRS intervals; however, the rate is the differentiating factor. In sinus tachycardia, the atrial and ventricular rates are higher than 100 beats/min.

Test-Taking Strategy: Use the process of elimination. Eliminate options 3 and 4 because they do not meet the rate criteria (ventricular rate is 110 beats/min). Eliminate option 1 because sinus arrhythmia is an irregular rhythm, with changing PP and RR intervals. Review the characteristics of sinus tachycardia if you had difficulty with this question.

Level of Cognitive Ability: Analysis
Client Needs: Physiological Integrity
Integrated Process: Nursing Process—analysis
Content Area: Adult health—cardiovascular
References: Huether, S., & McCance, K. (2004). *Understanding pathophysiology* (3rd ed., p. 680). St. Louis: Mosby.
Ignatavicius, D., & Workman, M. (2006). *Medical-surgical nursing: Critical thinking for collaborative care* (5th ed., pp. 716, 718). Philadelphia: W.B. Saunders.

18. **2**

Rationale: Motion artifact, or "noise," can be caused by frequent client movement, electrode placement on limbs, and insufficient adhesion to the skin, such as placing electrodes over hairy areas of the skin. Electrode placement over bony prominences also should be avoided. Signal interference also can occur with electrode removal and cable disconnection.

Test-Taking Strategy: Use the process of elimination, focusing on the subject, artifact and note the strategic word *unlikely*. Recalling the causes of artifact will direct you to option 2. Review these causes if you had difficulty with this question.

Level of Cognitive Ability: Analysis
Client Needs: Physiological Integrity
Integrated Process: Nursing Process—assessment
Content Area: Adult health—cardiovascular
Reference: Ignatavicius, D., & Workman, M. (2006). *Medical-surgical nursing: Critical thinking for collaborative care* (5th ed., pp. 710-711, 714). Philadelphia: W.B. Saunders.

19. **3**

Rationale: Ventricular tachycardia is characterized by the absence of P waves, wide QRS complexes (longer than 0.12 second), and typically a rate between 140 and 180 impulses/min. The rhythm is regular.

Test-Taking Strategy: Use the process of elimination. Eliminate option 1 first because there are no P waves. Premature ventricular contractions are isolated ectopic beats superimposed on an underlying rhythm, so option 4 is eliminated next. Recalling that there are no true QRS complexes with ventricular fibrillation will direct you to option 3 from the remaining options. Review the characteristics of ventricular tachycardia if you are unfamiliar with it.

Level of Cognitive Ability: Analysis

Client Needs: Physiological Integrity
Integrated Process: Nursing Process—assessment
Content Area: Adult health—cardiovascular
Reference: Ignatavicius, D., & Workman, M. (2006). *Medical-surgical nursing: Critical thinking for collaborative care* (5th ed., pp. 716, 729-731). Philadelphia: W.B. Saunders.

20. **1**

Rationale: Ventricular tachycardia is a life-threatening dysrhythmia that results from an irritable ectopic focus that takes over as the pacemaker for the heart. The low cardiac output that results can lead quickly to cerebral and myocardial ischemia. Clients frequently experience a feeling of impending doom. Ventricular tachycardia is treated with antidysrhythmic medications, cardioversion (client awake), or defibrillation (loss of consciousness). Ventricular tachycardia can deteriorate into ventricular fibrillation at any time.

Test-Taking Strategy: Use the process of elimination and note the strategic words *most concerned*. Option 2 is incorrect and is eliminated first. From the remaining options, focusing on the strategic words will direct you to option 1 because this option identifies the life-threatening condition. Review the concerns associated with ventricular tachycardia if you had difficulty with this question.

Level of Cognitive Ability: Analysis
Client Needs: Physiological Integrity
Integrated Process: Nursing Process—analysis
Content Area: Adult health—cardiovascular
Reference: Ignatavicius, D., & Workman, M. (2006). *Medical-surgical nursing: Critical thinking for collaborative care* (5th ed., pp. 729, 731). Philadelphia: W.B. Saunders.

21. **4**

Rationale: Cough cardiopulmonary resuscitation (CPR) sometimes is used in the client with unstable ventricular tachycardia. The nurse tells the client to use cough CPR, if prescribed, by inhaling deeply and coughing forcefully every 1 to 3 seconds. Cough CPR may terminate the dysrhythmia or sustain the cerebral and coronary circulation for a short time until other measures can be implemented. Options 1, 2, and 3 will not assist in terminating the dysrhythmia.

Test-Taking Strategy: To answer this question, you must be familiar with the treatment for unstable ventricular tachycardia. Remember that cough CPR sometimes is used in the client with unstable ventricular tachycardia. Review the concept of cough CPR if you are not familiar with it.

Level of Cognitive Ability: Application
Client Needs: Physiological Integrity
Integrated Process: Teaching and Learning
Content Area: Adult health—cardiovascular
Reference: Ignatavicius, D., & Workman, M. (2006). *Medical-surgical nursing: Critical thinking for collaborative care* (5th ed., p. 731). Philadelphia: W.B. Saunders.

22. **4**

Rationale: Premature ventricular contractions can cause hemodynamic compromise. The shortened ventricular filling time with the ectopic beat leads to decreased stroke volume and, if frequent enough, to decreased cardiac output. The client may be asymptomatic or may feel palpitations. Premature ventricular contractions can be caused by cardiac disorders, states of hypoxemia or by any number of physiological stressors, such as infection, illness, surgery, or trauma, and by intake of caffeine, nicotine, or alcohol.

Test-Taking Strategy: Note the strategic words *priority on assessment.* Use the ABCs—airway, breathing, and circulation—to direct you to option 4. Review the effects of premature ventricular contractions if you had difficulty with this question.

Level of Cognitive Ability: Analysis
Client Needs: Physiological Integrity
Integrated Process: Nursing Process—assessment
Content Area: Delegating/Prioritizing
References: Huether, S., & McCance, K. (2004). *Understanding pathophysiology* (3rd ed., p. 681). St. Louis: Mosby.
Ignatavicius, D., & Workman, M. (2006). *Medical-surgical nursing: Critical thinking for collaborative care* (5th ed., p. 729). Philadelphia: W.B. Saunders.

23. 3
Rationale: The client with uncontrolled atrial fibrillation with a ventricular rate more than 100 beats/min is at risk for low cardiac output because of loss of atrial kick. The nurse assesses the client for palpitations, chest pain or discomfort, hypotension, pulse deficit, fatigue, weakness, dizziness, syncope, shortness of breath, and distended neck veins.

Test-Taking Strategy: Use the process of elimination. Flat neck veins are normal or indicate hypovolemia, so eliminate option 1. Nausea and vomiting (option 2) are associated with vagus nerve activity and do not correlate with a tachycardic state. From the remaining options, think of the consequences of falling cardiac output to direct you to option 3. Review the effects of atrial fibrillation if you had difficulty with this question.

Level of Cognitive Ability: Analysis
Client Needs: Physiological Integrity
Integrated Process: Nursing Process—assessment
Content Area: Adult health—cardiovascular
Reference: Ignatavicius, D., & Workman, M. (2006). *Medical-surgical nursing: Critical thinking for collaborative care* (5th ed., pp. 727-728). Philadelphia: W.B. Saunders.

24. 1
Rationale: Atrial fibrillation is characterized by a loss of P waves and fibrillatory waves before each QRS complex. The atria quiver, which can lead to thombi formation.

Test-Taking Strategy: Use the process of elimination. Noting the strategic words *there are no P waves* should direct you to option 1. Loss of P waves is characteristic of this dysrhythmia. Review the characteristics of atrial fibrillation if you had difficulty with this question.

Level of Cognitive Ability: Analysis
Client Needs: Physiological Integrity
Integrated Process: Nursing Process—assessment
Content Area: Adult health—cardiovascular
References: Huether, S., & McCance, K. (2004). *Understanding pathophysiology* (3rd ed., p. 680). St. Louis: Mosby.
Lewis, S., Heitkemper, M., & Dirksen, S. (2004). *Medical-surgical nursing: Assessment and management of clinical problems* (6th ed., p. 868). St. Louis: Mosby.

25. 1
Rationale: Carotid sinus massage is one maneuver used for vagal stimulation to decrease a rapid heart rate and possibly terminate a tachydysrhythmia. The others include inducing the gag reflex and asking the client to strain or bear down. Medication therapy often is needed as an adjunct to keep the rate down or maintain the normal rhythm. Options 2, 3, and 4 are incorrect descriptions of this procedure.

Test-Taking Strategy: Knowledge of anatomy and physiology alone may be sufficient to answer this question. Eliminate options 3 and 4 because a rapid rate dysrhythmia would need to be slowed. Recalling the functions of the vagus nerve and the diaphragmatic nerve will direct you to option 1. The vagus nerve affects heart rate. The diaphragmatic nerve affects respiration. If you are unfamiliar with the functions of these nerves, review this content.

Level of Cognitive Ability: Application
Client Needs: Physiological Integrity
Integrated Process: Nursing Process—implementation
Content Area: Adult health—cardiovascular
Reference: Ignatavicius, D., & Workman, M. (2006). *Medical-surgical nursing: Critical thinking for collaborative care* (5th ed., pp. 727, 738).Philadelphia: W.B. Saunders.

26. 3
Rationale: Ventricular fibrillation is characterized by irregular chaotic undulations of varying amplitudes. Ventricular fibrillation has no measurable rate and no visible P waves or QRS complexes and results from electrical chaos in the ventricles.

Test-Taking Strategy: Use the process of elimination and knowledge regarding the characteristics of ventricular fibrillation. The lack of visible QRS complexes eliminates atrial fibrillation and ventricular tachycardia. Recalling that asystole is lack of any electrical activity of the heart will direct you to option 3. Review the characteristics of ventricular fibrillation if you had difficulty with this question.

Level of Cognitive Ability: Analysis
Client Needs: Physiological Integrity
Integrated Process: Nursing Process—assessment
Content Area: Adult health—cardiovascular
References: Huether, S., & McCance, K. (2004). *Understanding pathophysiology* (3rd ed., p. 681). St. Louis: Mosby.
Ignatavicius, D. & Workman, M. (2006). *Medical-surgical nursing: Critical thinking for collaborative care* (5th ed., pp. 731-732). Philadelphia: W.B. Saunders.

27. 4
Rationale: Until the defibrillator is attached and charged, the client is resuscitated by using cardiopulmonary resuscitation. Once the defibrillator has been attached, the electrocardiogram is checked to verify that the rhythm is ventricular fibrillation or pulseless ventricular tachycardia. Leads also are checked for any loose connections. A nitroglycerin patch, if present, is removed. The client does not have to be intubated to be defibrillated. Lidocaine may be given subsequently but is not required before defibrillation. The machine is not set to the synchronous mode because there is no underlying rhythm with which to synchronize.

Test-Taking Strategy: Use the process of elimination, focusing on the subject, ventricular fibrillation. Note that option 4 directly addresses this subject and also addresses assessment of the client. Review the procedure for defibrillation if you had difficulty with this question.

Level of Cognitive Ability: Analysis
Client Needs: Physiological Integrity
Integrated Process: Nursing Process—assessment
Content Area: Adult health—cardiovascular
References: Black, J., & Hawks, J. (2005). *Medical-surgical nursing: Clinical management for positive outcomes* (7th ed., p. 1687). Philadelphia: W.B. Saunders.

Ignatavicius, D., & Workman, M. (2006). *Medical-surgical nursing: Critical thinking for collaborative care* (5th ed., pp. 732, 741-742). Philadelphia: W.B. Saunders.

28. 3
Rationale: The client may be defibrillated up to three times in succession. The energy levels used are 200, 300, and 360 J for the first, second, and third attempts, respectively.
Test-Taking Strategy: Focus on the strategic words *first delivery.* As a general rule, though, remember that lower levels of energy are used for cardioversion. Higher levels are used in defibrillation. Review this procedure if you had difficulty with this question.
Level of Cognitive Ability: Application
Client Needs: Physiological Integrity
Integrated Process: Nursing Process—implementation
Content Area: Adult health—cardiovascular
References: Black, J., & Hawks, J. (2005). *Medical-surgical nursing: Clinical management for positive outcomes* (7th ed., pp. 1685, 1687). Philadelphia: W.B. Saunders.
Ignatavicius, D., & Workman, M. (2006). *Medical-surgical nursing: Critical thinking for collaborative care* (5th ed., p. 742). Philadelphia: W.B. Saunders.

29. 1
Rationale: After defibrillation, the client requires continuous monitoring of electrocardiographic rhythm, hemodynamic status, and neurological status. Respiratory and metabolic acidosis develop during ventricular fibrillation because of lack of respiration and cardiac output. These can cause cerebral and cardiopulmonary complications. Arousable status, adequate blood pressure, and a sinus rhythm indicate successful response to defibrillation.
Test-Taking Strategy: Use the process of elimination and note the strategic words *most successful.* Eliminate options 3 and 4 first because of the word *nonarousable.* From the remaining options, select option 1 because a sinus rhythm is a more successful response compared with marked bradycardia. Review the expected effects of defibrillation if you had difficulty with this question.
Level of Cognitive Ability: Analysis
Client Needs: Physiological Integrity
Integrated Process: Nursing Process—evaluation
Content Area: Adult health—cardiovascular
References: Black, J., & Hawks, J. (2005). *Medical-surgical nursing: Clinical management for positive outcomes* (7th ed., p. 1689). Philadelphia: W.B. Saunders.
Ignatavicius, D., & Workman, M. (2006). *Medical-surgical nursing: Critical thinking for collaborative care* (5th ed., pp. 717, 721). Philadelphia: W.B. Saunders.

30. 2
Rationale: Nursing responsibilities after cardioversion include maintenance first of a patent airway, and then oxygen administration, assessment of vital signs and level of consciousness, and dysrhythmia detection.
Test Taking Strategy: Use the process of elimination, noting the strategic words *highest priority.* Use the ABCs—airway, breathing, and circulation—to direct you to option 2. Review care of the client following cardioversion if you had difficulty with this question.
Level of Cognitive Ability: Analysis
Client Needs: Physiological Integrity
Integrated Process: Nursing Process—evaluation
Content Area: Delegating/Prioritizing
Reference: Ignatavicius, D., & Workman, M. (2006). *Medical-surgical nursing: Critical thinking for collaborative care* (5th ed., p. 742). Philadelphia: W.B. Saunders.

31. 2
Rationale: The nurse or rescuer puts two large adhesive patch electrodes on the client's chest in the usual defibrillator positions. The nurse stops cardiopulmonary resuscitation and orders anyone near the client to move away and not touch the client. The defibrillator then analyzes the rhythm, which may take up to 30 seconds. The machine then indicates if defibrillation is necessary.
Test-Taking Strategy: Use the process of elimination. If you are not familiar with this piece of equipment, look first at the word *automatic* in the name. This implies that a person is not as involved in the process as with a conventional defibrillator and will help eliminate option 1. Because standard electrocardiogram monitoring leads do not play an active role once resuscitation is underway (options 3 and 4), you can eliminate these comparative or alike options. Review the procedure related to the use of an automatic external defibrillator if you had difficulty with this question.
Level of Cognitive Ability: Application
Client Needs: Physiological Integrity
Integrated Process: Nursing Process—implementation
Content Area: Adult health—cardiovascular
Reference: Ignatavicius, D., & Workman, M. (2006). *Medical-surgical nursing: Critical thinking for collaborative care* (5th ed., p. 742). Philadelphia: W.B. Saunders.

32. 3
Rationale: An automatic internal cardioverter-defibrillator (AICD) detects and delivers an electrical shock to terminate life-threatening episodes of ventricular tachycardia and ventricular fibrillation. These devices are implanted in clients who are considered high risk, including those who have survived sudden cardiac death unrelated to myocardial infarction, those who are refractive to medication therapy, and those who have syncopal episodes related to ventricular tachycardia.
Test-Taking Strategy: Use the process of elimination and note the strategic words *least likely.* Ventricular dysrhythmias that induce syncope or occur while the client is on medication are likely to be true indications for the AICD, so eliminate options 1 and 2 first. From the remaining options, the main difference is whether or not the cardiac arrest was related to

myocardial infarction. Of these two, the one most likely to be responsive to AICD would be the client without myocardial infarction because those dysrhythmias are spontaneous. Review the indications for the use of an AICD, if you had difficulty with this question.
Level of Cognitive Ability: Analysis
Client Needs: Physiological Integrity
Integrated Process: Nursing Process—assessment
Content Area: Adult health—cardiovascular
Reference: Ignatavicius, D., & Workman, M. (2006). *Medical-surgical nursing: Critical thinking for collaborative care* (5th ed., p. 743). Philadelphia: W.B. Saunders.

33. 4
Rationale: The nurse who is caring for the client after insertion of an automatic internal cardioverter-defibrillator needs to assess device settings, similar to after insertion of a permanent pacemaker. Specifically, the nurse needs to know whether the device is activated, the heart rate cutoff above which it will fire, and the number of shocks it is programmed to deliver. Options 1, 2, and 3 are also nursing interventions but are not the priority.
Test-Taking Strategy: Use Maslow's Hierarchy of Needs theory. Option 4 is the option that identifies the physiological need. Review care to the client following insertion of an automatic internal cardioverter-defibrillator if you had difficulty with this question.
Level of Cognitive Ability: Application
Client Needs: Physiological Integrity
Integrated Process: Nursing Process—assessment
Content Area: Delegating/Prioritizing
Reference: Ignatavicius, D., & Workman, M. (2006). *Medical-surgical nursing: Critical thinking for collaborative care* (5th ed., pp. 743, 746). Philadelphia: W.B. Saunders.

34. 2
Rationale: In the first several hours after insertion of a permanent or a temporary pacemaker, the most common complication is pacing electrode dislodgment. The nurse helps prevent this complication by limiting the client's activities of the arm on the side of the insertion site.
Test-Taking Strategy: Use the process of elimination. Note that the pacemaker was inserted on the right side. Therefore, to prevent pacing electrode dislodgment, motion must be limited on that side. Options 3 and 4 involve movement of the right arm and are eliminated first. Limiting the movement of the left arm (option 1) is of no benefit to the client. Thus, option 2 is the correct option. Review care of the client following insertion of a pacemaker if you had difficulty with this question.
Level of Cognitive Ability: Application
Client Needs: Physiological Integrity
Integrated Process: Nursing Process—implementation
Content Area: Adult health—cardiovascular
References: Black, J., & Hawks, J. (2005). *Medical-surgical nursing: Clinical management for positive outcomes* (7th ed., p. 1697). Philadelphia: W.B. Saunders.
Ignatavicius, D., & Workman, M. (2006). *Medical-surgical nursing: Critical thinking for collaborative care* (5th ed., pp. 743-745). Philadelphia: W.B. Saunders.

35. 3
Rationale: Pulmonary embolism is a life-threatening complication of deep vein thrombosis and thrombophlebitis. Chest pain is the most common symptom, which is sudden in onset, and may be aggravated by breathing. Other signs and symptoms include dyspnea, cough, diaphoresis, and apprehension.
Test-Taking Strategy: Focus on the client's diagnosis to answer the question. Recalling the complications related to thrombophlebitis will direct you to option 3. Review these complications and the associated signs and symptoms if you had difficulty with this question.
Level of Cognitive Ability: Analysis
Client Needs: Physiological Integrity
Integrated Process: Nursing Process—assessment
Content Area: Adult health—cardiovascular
Reference: Ignatavicius, D., & Workman, M. (2006). *Medical-surgical nursing: Critical thinking for collaborative care* (5th ed., pp. 650-651, 813). Philadelphia: W.B. Saunders.

36. 4
Rationale: Sclerotherapy is the injection of a sclerosing agent into a varicosity. The agent damages the vessel and causes aseptic thrombosis, which results in vein closure. With no blood flow through the vessel, there is no distention. The surgical procedure for varicose veins is vein ligation and stripping. This procedure involves tying off the varicose vein and large tributaries and then removing the vein with hook and wires via multiple small incisions in the leg.
Test-Taking Strategy: Use the process of elimination and note the name of the procedure, *sclerotherapy*. A vessel that is sclerosed is blocked. This will direct you to option 4. Review this procedure if you had difficulty with this question.
Level of Cognitive Ability: Comprehension
Client Needs: Physiological Integrity
Integrated Process: Teaching and Learning
Content Area: Adult health—cardiovascular
Reference: Ignatavicius, D., & Workman, M. (2006). *Medical-surgical nursing: Critical thinking for collaborative care* (5th ed., p. 818). Philadelphia: W.B. Saunders.

37. 2
Rationale: Hypersensitivity or a sensation of "pins and needles" in the surgical limb may indicate temporary or permanent nerve injury following surgery. The saphenous vein and saphenous nerve run close together in the distal third of the leg. Because complications from this surgery are relatively rare, this symptom should be reported.
Test-Taking Strategy: Use the process of elimination. Pins and needles sensations usually indicate nerve irritation or damage. If you know this, you can eliminate options 1 and 4. Reassuring the client about something being "only temporary" is often not an appropriate action, unless this is known to be absolutely true. Review the complications associated with vein ligation and stripping if you had difficulty with this question.
Level of Cognitive Ability: Analysis
Client Needs: Physiological Integrity
Integrated Process: Nursing Process—implementation
Content Area: Adult health—cardiovascular

References: Black, J., & Hawks, J. (2005). *Medical-surgical nursing: Clinical management for positive outcomes* (7th ed., p. 1540). Philadelphia: W.B. Saunders.

Ignatavicius, D., & Workman, M. (2006). *Medical-surgical nursing: Critical thinking for collaborative care* (4th ed., pp. 456, 802). Philadelphia: W.B. Saunders.

38. 1

Rationale: After inferior vena cava filter insertion, the nurse inspects the surgical site for bleeding and signs and symptoms of infection. Otherwise, care is the same as for any other post-operative client.

Test-Taking Strategy: Use the process of elimination. Because inferior vena cava filters are inserted percutaneously through a deep vein, options 3 and 4 are eliminated because no abdominal incision is made. From the remaining options, noting that the client has been on anticoagulant therapy before surgery because of the high risk of pulmonary embolism will direct you to option 1. Review care of the client following insertion of an inferior vena cava filter if you had difficulty with this question.

Level of Cognitive Ability: Analysis
Client Needs: Physiological Integrity
Integrated Process: Nursing Process—assessment
Content Area: Adult health—cardiovascular
Reference: Ignatavicius, D., & Workman, M. (2006). *Medical-surgical nursing: Critical thinking for collaborative care* (5th ed., p. 815). Philadelphia: W.B. Saunders.

39. 4

Rationale: An electrocardiogram taken during a chest pain episode captures ischemic changes, which include ST segment elevation or depression. Tall, peaked T waves may indicate hyperkalemia. A prolonged PR interval indicates first-degree heart block. A widened QRS complex indicates delay in intraventricular conduction, such as a bundle branch block.

Test-Taking Strategy: Use the process of elimination. Recalling that myocardial ischemia causes cellular derangements that alter the processes of depolarization will direct you to option 4. Review the electrocardiographic changes that occur with myocardial ischemia if you had difficulty with this question.

Level of Cognitive Ability: Analysis
Client Needs: Physiological Integrity
Integrated Process: Nursing Process—analysis
Content Area: Adult health—cardiovascular
References: Black, J., & Hawks, J. (2005). *Medical-surgical nursing: Clinical management for positive outcomes* (7th ed., p. 1704). Philadelphia: W.B. Saunders.

Ignatavicius, D., & Workman, M. (2006). *Medical-surgical nursing: Critical thinking for collaborative care* (5th ed., pp. 232, 732, 735, 845-846). Philadelphia: W.B. Saunders.

40. 3

Rationale: A cardiac catheterization requires an informed consent because it involves injection of a radiopaque dye into the blood vessel. The risk of allergic reaction and possible anaphylaxis is a concern and the presence of allergies must be assessed before the procedure. Although options 1, 2, and 4 are accurate, they are not the most critical preprocedure assessments.

Test-Taking Strategy: Use the process of elimination and note the strategic words *most critical*. Recalling the concern related to allergy to the dye and the risk of anaphylaxis makes option 3 correct. Review preprocedure interventions for a cardiac catheterization if you had difficulty with this question.

Level of Cognitive Ability: Analysis
Client Needs: Physiological Integrity
Integrated Process: Nursing Process—assessment
Content Area: Delegating/Prioritizing
References: Black, J., & Hawks, J. (2005). *Medical-surgical nursing: Clinical management for positive outcomes* (7th ed., p. 103). Philadelphia: W.B. Saunders.

Chernecky, C., & Berger, B. (2004). *Laboratory tests and diagnostic procedures* (4th ed., p. 327). Philadelphia: W.B. Saunders.

Ignatavicius, D., & Workman, M. (2006). *Medical-surgical nursing critical thinking for collaborative care* (5th ed., p. 697). Philadelphia: W.B. Saunders.

41. 1

Rationale: An expected outcome of surgery is warmth, redness, and edema in the surgical extremity because of increased blood flow. Therefore, options 2, 3, and 4 are incorrect interpretations.

Test-Taking Strategy: Use the process of elimination. Option 2 can be eliminated because the pedal pulse is unchanged from admission. Venous complications from immobilization resulting from surgery would not be apparent within 4 hours, so eliminate option 4. From the remaining options, think about the effects of sudden reperfusion in an ischemic limb. There would be redness from new blood flow and edema from the sudden change in pressure in the blood vessels. Review the expected assessment findings following this surgical procedure if you had difficulty with this question.

Level of Cognitive Ability: Analysis
Client Needs: Physiological Integrity
Integrated Process: Nursing Process—assessment
Content Area: Adult health—cardiovascular
Reference: Ignatavicius, D., & Workman, M. (2006). *Medical-surgical nursing: Critical thinking for collaborative care* (5th ed., p. 798). Philadelphia: W.B. Saunders.

42. 4

Rationale: Following pericardiocentesis, a rise in blood pressure and a fall in central venous pressure are expected. The client usually expresses immediate relief. Heart sounds are no longer muffled or distant.

Test-Taking Strategy: Use the process of elimination and note the strategic word *unsuccessful*. Successful therapy is measured by the disappearance of the original signs and symptoms of cardiac tamponade. Therefore, look for the option that identifies a sign consistent with continued tamponade. Review signs of cardiac tamponade and the expected effects of pericardiocentesis if you had difficulty with this question.

Level of Cognitive Ability: Analysis
Client Needs: Physiological Integrity
Integrated Process: Nursing Process—evaluation
Content Area: Adult health—cardiovascular
Reference: Ignatavicius, D., & Workman, M. (2006). *Medical-surgical nursing: Critical thinking for collaborative care* (5th ed., p. 771). Philadelphia: W.B. Saunders.

43. 2
Rationale: Not all clients with abdominal aortic aneurysm exhibit symptoms. Those who do may describe a feeling of the "heart beating" in the abdomen when supine or being able to feel the mass throbbing. A pulsatile mass may be palpated in the middle and upper abdomen. A systolic bruit may be auscultated over the mass. Hyperactive bowel sounds are not related specifically to an abdominal aortic aneurysm.
Test-Taking Strategy: Use the process of elimination and note the strategic word *unrelated*. Note that options 1, 3, and 4 are comparative or alike in that they identify a circulatory component. Review the signs of abdominal aortic aneurysm if you had difficulty with this question.
Level of Cognitive Ability: Analysis
Client Needs: Physiological Integrity
Integrated Process: Nursing Process—assessment
Content Area: Adult health—cardiovascular
Reference: Ignatavicius, D. & Workman, M. (2006). *Medical-surgical nursing: Critical thinking for collaborative care* (5th ed., pp. 806-807). Philadelphia: W.B. Saunders.

44. 1
Rationale: Following abdominal aortic aneurysm resection or repair, the nurse monitors the client for signs of renal failure. Renal failure can occur because often much blood is lost during the surgery and, depending on the aneurysm location, the renal arteries may be hypoperfused for a short period during surgery. The nurse monitors hourly intake and output and notes the results of daily blood urea nitrogen and creatinine levels. Urine output lower than 30 to 50 mL/hr is reported to the physician.
Test-Taking Strategy: Focus on the information in the question and the abnormal assessment data. This question indicates elevations in blood urea nitrogen and creatinine levels and a significant drop in hourly urine output. These assessment findings should direct you to option 1. Review the complications associated with this surgical procedure if you had difficulty with this question.
Level of Cognitive Ability: Analysis
Client Needs: Physiological Integrity
Integrated Process: Nursing Process—implementation
Content Area: Adult health—cardiovascular
Reference: Ignatavicius, D., & Workman, M. (2006). *Medical-surgical nursing: Critical thinking for collaborative care* (5th ed., pp. 807-808). Philadelphia: W.B. Saunders.

45. 1
Rationale: The magnetic fields used for magnetic resonance imaging (MRI) can deactivate the pacemaker. Options 2, 3, and 4 are not contraindications for an MRI.
Test-Taking Strategy: Focus on the name of the test and note the strategic word *magnetic*. Remember that the magnetic fields of the MRI can deactivate the pacemaker. Review the contraindications for an MRI if you had difficulty with this question.
Level of Cognitive Ability: Analysis
Client Needs: Safe and Effective Care Environment

Integrated Process: Nursing Process—assessment
Content Area: Adult health—cardiovascular
Reference: Ignativicius, D. & Workman, M. (2006). *Medical-surgical nursing: Critical thinking for collaborative care* (5th ed., p. 703). St. Louis: W.B. Saunders.

46. 2
Rationale: Variant angina, or Prinzmetal's angina, is prolonged and severe and occurs at the same time each day, most often at rest. Stable angina is induced by exercise and relieved by rest or nitroglycerin tablets. Unstable angina occurs at lower and lower levels of activity or at rest, is less predictable, and is often a precursor of myocardial infarction.
Test-Taking Strategy: Use the process of elimination, focusing on the data in the question. Noting the strategic words *at rest* will direct you to option 2. If you had difficulty with this question, review the characteristics of the various types of angina.
Level of Cognitive Ability: Comprehension
Client Needs: Physiological Integrity
Integrated Process: Nursing Process—assessment
Content Area: Adult health—cardiovascular
Reference: Ignatavicius, D., & Workman, M. (2006). *Medical-surgical nursing: critical thinking for collaborative care* (5th ed., p. 840). Philadelphia: W.B. Saunders.

ALTERNATE ITEM FORMAT: MULTIPLE RESPONSE

Answer: 1, 2, 3, 4
Rationale: Pulmonary edema is a life-threatening event that can result from severe heart failure. In pulmonary edema, the left ventricle fails to eject sufficient blood, and pressure increases in the lungs because of the accumulated blood. Oxygen is always prescribed, and the client is placed in a high Fowler's position to ease the work of breathing. Furosemide, a rapid-acting diuretic, will eliminate accumulated fluid. A Foley catheter is inserted to measure output accurately. Intravenously administered morphine sulfate reduces venous return (preload), decreases anxiety, and also reduces the work of breathing. Transporting the client to the coronary care unit is not a priority intervention. In fact, this may not be necessary at all if the client's response to treatment is successful.
Test-Taking Strategy: Note the strategic words *priority interventions* and focus on the client's diagnosis. Recall the pathophysiology associated with pulmonary edema and use the ABCs—airway, breathing, and circulation—to help determine priority interventions. Review priority interventions for the client with pulmonary edema if you had difficulty with this question.
Level of Cognitive Ability: Application
Client Needs: Physiological Integrity
Integrated Process: Nursing Process—implementation
Content Area: Delegating/Prioritizing
Reference: Ignatavicius, D., & Workman, M. (2006). *Medical-surgical nursing: Critical thinking for collaborative care* (5th ed., pp. 760-761). Philadelphia: W.B. Saunders.

REFERENCES

Black, J., & Hawks, J. (2005). *Medical-surgical nursing: Clinical management for positive outcomes* (7th ed.). Philadelphia: W.B. Saunders.

Chernecky, C., & Berger, B. (2004). *Laboratory tests and diagnostic procedures* (4th ed.). Philadelphia: W.B. Saunders.

Hodgson, B., & Kizior, R. (2007). *Saunders nursing drug handbook 2007.* Philadelphia: W.B. Saunders.

Huether, S., & McCance, K. (2004). *Understanding pathophysiology* (3rd ed.). St. Louis: Mosby.

Ignatavicius, D., & Workman, M. (2006). *Medical-surgical nursing: Critical thinking for collaborative care* (5th ed.) Philadelphia: W.B. Saunders.

Lewis, S., Heitkemper, M., & Dirksen, S. (2004). *Medical-surgical nursing: Assessment and management of clinical problems* (6th ed.). St. Louis: Mosby.

Perry, A., & Potter, P. (2006). *Clinical nursing skills and techniques* (6th ed.). St. Louis: Mosby.

Ulrich, S., & Canale, S. (2006). *Nursing care planning guides for adults in acute, extended and home care settings* (6th ed.). St. Louis: W.B. Saunders.

Cardiovascular Medications

I. ANTICOAGULANTS (Box 60-1)

A. Description
1. Anticoagulants prevent the extension and formation of clots by inhibiting factors in the clotting cascade and decreasing blood coagulability.
2. Anticoagulants are administered when there is evidence of or likelihood of clot formation—myocardial infarction, unstable angina, atrial fibrillation, deep vein thrombosis, pulmonary embolism, and the presence of mechanical heart valves.
3. Anticoagulants are contraindicated with active bleeding (except for disseminated intravascular coagulation), bleeding disorders or blood dyscrasias, ulcers, liver and kidney disease, and hemorrhagic brain injuries.

B. Side effects (Box 60-2)
1. Hemorrhage
2. Hematuria
3. Epistaxis
4. Ecchymosis
5. Bleeding gums
6. Thrombocytopenia
7. Hypotension

C. Heparin sodium
1. Description
   a. Heparin prevents thrombin from converting fibrinogen to fibrin.
   b. Heparin prevents thromboembolism.
   c. The therapeutic dose does not dissolve clots but prevents new thrombus formation.
2. Blood levels
   a. The normal activated partial thromboplastin time (aPTT) is 20 to 36 seconds in most laboratories but may be as high as 40 seconds.
   b. To maintain a therapeutic level of anticoagulation when the client is receiving a continuous infusion of heparin, the aPTT should be 1.5 to 2.5 times the normal value.
   c. Activated partial thromboplastin time therapy should be measured every 4 to 6 hours during initial continuous infusion therapy and then daily.

BOX 60-1
Anticoagulants

ORAL
Warfarin sodium (Coumadin)

PARENTERAL
Argatroban (Acova)
Bivalirudin (Angiomax)
Dalteparin (Fragmin)
Desirudin (Iprivask)
Enoxaparin (Lovenox)
Fondaparinux (Arixtra)
Heparin sodium
Tinzaparin (Innohep)
Lepirudin (Refludan)

BOX 60-2
Substances to Avoid with Anticoagulants

Allopurinol (Zyloprim)
Cimetidine (Tagamet)
Corticosteroids
Green leafy vegetables and foods high in vitamin K
Nonsteroidal anti-inflammatory drugs
Oral hypoglycemic agents
Phenytoin (Dilantin)
Salicylates
Sulfonamides
Gingko and ginseng (herbs)

d. If the aPTT is too long, longer than 80 seconds, the dosage should be lowered.

e. If aPTT is too short, less than 60 seconds, the dosage should be increased.

3. Interventions

a. Monitor aPTT.

b. Monitor platelet count.

c. Observe for bleeding gums, bruises, nosebleeds, hematuria, hematemesis, occult blood in the stool, and petechiae.

d. When administering heparin subcutaneously, inject into the abdomen with a ⅝-inch needle (25 to 28 gauge) at a 90-degree angle and do not aspirate or rub the injection site.

e. Continuous infusions must be run on an infusion pump to ensure precise rate of delivery.

f. Instruct the client regarding measures to prevent bleeding.

g. The antidote to heparin is protamine sulfate.

D. Enoxaparin (Lovenox)—low-molecular-weight heparin

1. Description: Enoxaparin has the same mechanism of action and use as heparin but is not interchangeable; has a longer half-life than heparin.

2. Interventions

a. Administer by subcutaneous injection only to the recumbent client in the anterolateral or posterolateral abdominal wall; do not expel the air bubble from the prefilled syringe or aspirate during injection.

b. Monitor the same laboratory values as for heparin and observe for bleeding.

c. The antidote to enoxaparin is protamine sulfate.

E. Warfarin sodium (Coumadin)

1. Description

a. Warfarin suppresses coagulation by acting as an antagonist of vitamin K by inhibiting four dependent clotting factors (X, IX, VII, and II).

b. Warfarin prolongs clotting time and is monitored by the prothrombin time (PT).

c. It is used for long-term anticoagulation and is used mainly to prevent thromboembolic conditions such as thrombophlebitis, pulmonary embolism, and embolism formation caused by atrial fibrillation, thrombosis, myocardial infarction, or heart valve damage.

2. Blood levels

a. The normal PT is 9.6 to 11.8 seconds.

b. Warfarin sodium prolongs the PT; the therapeutic range is 1.5 to 2 times the control value.

3. International normalized ratio (INR)

a. The normal INR is 1.3 to 2.0.

b. The INR is determined by multiplying the observed PT ratio (the ratio of the client's PT to a control PT) by a correction factor specific to a particular thromboplastin preparation used in the testing.

c. The treatment goal is to raise the INR to an appropriate value.

d. An INR of 2 to 3 is appropriate for most clients, although for some clients the target INR is 3 to 4.5.

e. If the INR is below the recommended range, warfarin sodium should be increased.

f. If the INR is above the recommended range, warfarin sodium should be reduced.

4. Interventions

a. Monitor PT and INR.

b. Observe for bleeding gums, bruises, nosebleeds, hematuria, hematemesis, occult blood in the stool, and petechiae.

c. Instruct the client regarding measures to prevent bleeding.

d. The antidote for warfarin is vitamin K (phytonadione, AquaMEPHYTON).

II. THROMBOLYTIC MEDICATIONS (Box 60-3)

A. Description

1. Thrombolytic medications activate plasminogen; plasminogen generates plasmin (the enzyme that dissolves clots).

2. Thrombolytic medications are used early in the course of myocardial infarction (within 4 to 6 hours of the onset of the infarct) to restore blood flow, limit myocardial damage, preserve left ventricular function, and prevent death.

3. Thrombolytics are also used in arterial thrombosis, deep vein thrombosis, occluded shunts or catheters, and pulmonary emboli.

B. Contraindications

1. Active internal bleeding

2. History of hemorrhagic brain attack (stroke)

3. Intracranial problems, including trauma

4. Intracranial or intraspinal surgery within the previous 2 months

5. History of thoracic, pelvic, or abdominal surgery in the previous 10 days

6. History of hepatic or renal disease

7. Uncontrolled hypertension

8. Recently required, prolonged cardiopulmonary resuscitation

---

BOX 60-3

Thrombolytic Medications

Alteplase (Activase, tPA)
Reteplase (Retavase)
Streptokinase (Streptase)
Tenecteplase (TNKase)
Urokinase (Abbokinase)

9. Known allergy to the specific product or any of its preservatives

C. Side effects
   1. Bleeding
   2. Dysrhythmias
   3. Fever
   4. Allergic reactions

D. Interventions
   1. Determine aPTT, PT, fibrinogen level, hematocrit, and platelet count.
   2. Monitor vital signs.
   3. Assess pulses.
   4. Monitor for bleeding.
   5. Monitor all excretions for occult blood.
   6. Monitor for neurological changes such as slurred speech, lethargy, confusion, and hemiparesis.
   7. Monitor for hypotension and tachycardia.
   8. Avoid injections if possible.
   9. Apply direct pressure over a puncture site for 20 to 30 minutes.
   10. Handle the client as little as possible when moving.
   11. Instruct the client to use an electric razor for shaving and to brush teeth gently.
   12. Withhold the medication if bleeding develops, and notify the physician.
   13. Antidote
       a. Aminocaproic acid (Amicar) is the antidote for streptokinase.
       b. Used only in acute, life-threatening conditions

III. ANTIPLATELET MEDICATIONS (Box 60-4)
A. Description
   1. Antiplatelet medications inhibit the aggregation of platelets in the clotting process, thereby prolonging the bleeding time.
   2. Antiplatelet medications may be used with anticoagulants.
   3. Used in the prophylaxis of long-term complications following myocardial infarction, coronary revascularization, stents, and brain attacks (stroke).

4. These medications are contraindicated in those with bleeding disorders and known sensitivity.

B. Side effects
   1. Gastrointestinal bleeding
   2. Bruising
   3. Hematuria
   4. Tarry stools

C. Interventions
   1. Determine sensitivity before administration.
   2. Monitor vital signs.
   3. Instruct the client to take medication with food if gastrointestinal upset occurs.
   4. Monitor bleeding time.
   5. Monitor for side effects related to bleeding.
   6. Instruct the client in the use of the medication.
   7. Instruct the client to monitor for side effects related to bleeding and in the measures to prevent bleeding.

IV. POSITIVE INOTROPIC AND CARDIOTONIC MEDICATIONS (Box 60-5)
A. Description
   1. These medications stimulate myocardial **contractility** and produce a positive inotropic effect.
   2. These are used for short-term management of advanced heart failure; the increase in myocardial **contractility** improves cardiac, peripheral, and kidney function by increasing **cardiac output**, decreasing **preload**, improving blood flow to the periphery and kidneys, decreasing edema, and increasing fluid excretion. As a result, fluid retention in the lungs and extremities is decreased (Fig. 60-1).

BOX 60-4
Antiplatelet Medications

Abciximab (ReoPro)
Aspirin (acetylsalicylic acid, ASA)
Cilostazol (Pletal)
Clopidogrel (Plavix)
Dipyridamole (Persantine)
Dipyridamole; aspirin (Aggrenox)
Eptifibatide (Integrilin)
Ticlopidine (Ticlid)
Tirofiban (Aggrastat)

BOX 60-5
Positive Inotropic/Cardiotonic Medications

DOPAMINE
Used as a short-term rescue measure for clients with severe, acute cardiac failure
Increases myocardial contractility, thereby improving cardiac performance
Dilates renal blood vessels and increases renal blood flow and urine output

DOBUTAMINE
Used for short-term management of heart failure
Increases myocardial contractility, thereby improving cardiac performance

INAMRINONE LACTATE
Used for short-term management of congestive heart failure in those who have not responded adequately to cardiac glycosides, diuretics, and vasodilators

MILRINONE (PRIMACOR)
Used for short-term management of congestive heart failure; may be given before heart transplantation

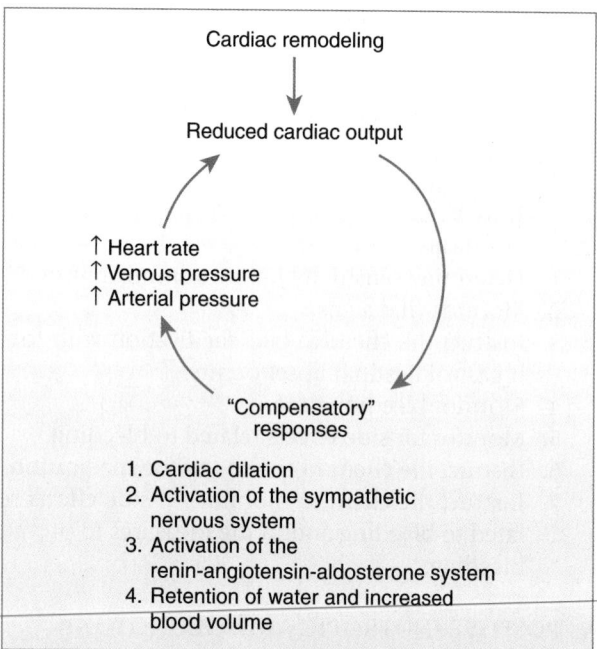

Cardiac remodeling

↓

Reduced cardiac output

↑ Heart rate
↑ Venous pressure
↑ Arterial pressure

"Compensatory" responses

1. Cardiac dilation
2. Activation of the sympathetic nervous system
3. Activation of the renin-angiotensin-aldosterone system
4. Retention of water and increased blood volume

FIG. 60-1 The vicious cycle of maladaptive compensatory responses to a failing heart. (From Lehne, R. [2007]. *Pharmacology for nursing care* [6th ed.]. Philadelphia: W.B. Saunders.)

B. Side effects
   1. Dysrhythmias
   2. Hypotension
   3. Thrombocytopenia
C. Toxic and adverse reactions
   1. Hepatotoxicity manifested by elevated liver enzyme levels
   2. Hypersensitivity manifested by wheezing, shortness of breath, pruritis, urticaria, clammy skin, and flushing
   D. Interventions
   1. Positive inotropic and cardiotonic medications are for intravenous (IV) administration.
     a. Do not dilute with dextrose-containing solutions.
     b. For continuous IV infusion, administer with an infusion pump.
     c. Stop the infusion if the client's **blood pressure (BP)** drops or dysrhythmias occur.
   2. Monitor the apical pulse and **BP**.
   3. Monitor for hypersensitivity.
   4. Assess lung sounds for wheezing and crackles.
   5. Monitor for edema.
   6. Monitor for relief of heart failure as noted by reduction in edema, lessening of dyspnea, orthopnea, and fatigue.
   7. Monitor electrolyte and liver enzyme levels, platelet count, and renal function studies; the medications may decrease potassium and increase liver enzyme levels; continuous electrocar-

BOX 60-6
Cardiac Glycoside

Digoxin (Lanoxicaps, Lanoxin, Digitek)

diographic monitoring is done during administration.
  E. Milrinone (Primacor)
   1. Side effects
     a. Headache
     b. Hypotension
     c. Angina
   2. Toxic and adverse reactions—dysrhythmias
   3. Interventions
     a. For IV injection of a loading dose, administer slowly over 10 minutes.
     b. For continuous IV infusion, administer with an infusion pump.
     c. Monitor the apical pulse and **BP**.
     d. Stop the infusion if the client's **BP** drops or dysrhythmias occur.
     e. Assess lung sounds for wheezing and crackles.
     f. Monitor for edema.
     g. Monitor for relief of heart failure as noted by reduction in edema, lessening of dyspnea, orthopnea, and fatigue.

V. **CARDIAC GLYCOSIDES** (Box 60-6)
  A. Description
   1. Cardiac glycosides inhibit the sodium-potassium pump, thus increasing intracellular calcium, which causes the heart muscle fibers to contract more efficiently.
   2. Cardiac glycosides produce a positive inotropic action, which increases the force of myocardial contractions.
   3. Cardiac glycosides produce a negative chronotropic action, which slows the heart rate.
   4. Cardiac glycosides produce a negative dromotropic action that slows conduction velocity through the atrioventricular (AV) node.
   5. The increase in myocardial **contractility** increases cardiac, peripheral, and kidney function by increasing **cardiac output**, decreasing **preload**, improving blood flow to the periphery and kidneys, decreasing edema, and increasing fluid excretion; as a result, fluid retention in the lungs and extremities is decreased.
   6. Cardiac glycosides are used for heart failure and cardiogenic shock, atrial tachycardia, atrial fibrillation, and atrial flutter.
   7. These medications are contraindicated in those with ventricular dysrhythmias and second- or third-degree heart block and should be used with caution in clients with renal disease, hypothyroidism, and hypokalemia.

B. Side effects and toxic effects
1. Anorexia, nausea, vomiting, diarrhea
2. Headache
3. Visual disturbances: Diplopia, blurred vision, yellow-green halos, photophobia
4. Drowsiness
5. Bradycardia
6. Fatigue, weakness

C. Interventions
1. Monitor for toxicity as evidenced by anorexia, nausea, vomiting, visual disturbances, confusion, bradycardia, heart block, premature ventricular contractions, and tachydysrhythmias.
2. Monitor serum digoxin level, electrolyte levels, and renal function test results.
3. Therapeutic digoxin range is 0.5 to 2 ng/mL; levels above 2 ng/mL are toxic.
4. An increased risk of toxicity exists in clients with hypercalcemia, hypokalemia, hypomagnesemia, or hypothyroidism.
5. Monitor the potassium level; if hypokalemia occurs (potassium lower than 3.5 mEq/L), notify the physician.
6. Instruct the client to avoid over-the-counter medications.
7. Monitor the client taking a potassium-wasting diuretic or corticosteroids closely for hypokalemia because the hypokalemia can cause digoxin toxicity.
8. Note that older clients are more sensitive to digoxin toxicity.
9. Advise the client to eat foods high in potassium, such as fresh and dried fruits, fruit juices, vegetables, and potatoes.
10. Monitor the apical pulse.
11. If the apical pulse rate is lower than 60 beats/min, the medication should be held and the physician notified.
12. Teach the client how to measure pulse.
13. Teach the client to notify physician if the pulse rate is lower than 60 or higher than 100 beats/min.
14. Teach the client the signs and symptoms of toxicity.
15. Antidote: Digoxin immune Fab (Digibind) is used in extreme toxicity.

VI. ANTIHYPERTENSIVE MEDICATIONS
(Box 60-7)
A. Thiazide diuretics (Box 60-8)
1. Description
a. Thiazide diuretics increase sodium and water excretion by inhibiting sodium reabsorption in the distal tubule of the kidney.
b. Used for hypertension and peripheral edema
c. Not effective for immediate diuresis

BOX 60-7
Classifications of Diuretics

Carbonic anhydrase inhibitors
Loop diuretics
Osmotic diuretics
Potassium-sparing diuretics
Thiazide diuretics

BOX 60-8
Thiazide and Thiazide-like Diuretics

Bendroflumethiazide (Naturetin)
Benzthiazide
Chlorothiazide (Diuril)
Chlorthalidone (Hygroton, Thalitone)
Hydrochlorothiazide (HydroDIURIL)
Hydroflumethiazide (Saluron)
Indapamide (Lozol)
Methyclothiazide (Aquatensen, Enduron)
Metolazone (Zaroxolyn)
Polythiazide; reserpine (Renese-R)
Quinethazone
Trichlormethiazide

d. Used in clients with normal renal function (contraindicated in clients with renal failure)
e. Thiazide diuretics should be used with caution in the client taking lithium because lithium toxicity can occur and in the client taking digoxin, corticosteroids, or hypoglycemic medications.
2. Side effects
a. Hypercalcemia, hyperglycemia, hyperuricemia
b. Hypokalemia, hyponatremia
c. Hypovolemia
d. Hypotension
e. Headaches
f. Nausea, vomiting
g. Constipation
h. Rashes
i. Photosensitivity
j. Blood dyscrasias
3. Interventions
a. Monitor vital signs.
b. Monitor weight.
c. Monitor urine output.
d. Monitor electrolyte, glucose, calcium, blood urea nitrogen (BUN), creatinine, and uric acid levels.
e. Check peripheral extremities for edema.
f. Instruct the client to take the medication in the morning to avoid nocturia and sleep interruption.
g. Instruct the client in how to record the **BP**.
h. Instruct the client to eat foods high in potassium.

i. Instruct the client in how to take potassium supplements if prescribed.

j. Instruct the client to take medication with food to avoid gastrointestinal upset.

k. Instruct the client to change positions slowly to prevent **orthostatic hypotension**.

l. Instruct the client to use sunscreen when in direct sunlight because of increased photosensitivity.

m. Instruct the client with diabetes mellitus to have the blood glucose level checked periodically.

B. Loop diuretics (Box 60-9)

1. Description

a. Loop diuretics inhibit sodium and chloride reabsorption from the loop of Henle and the distal tubule.

b. Loop diuretics have little effect on the blood glucose level; however, they cause depletion of water and electrolytes, increased uric acid levels, and the excretion of calcium.

c. Loop diuretics are more potent than thiazide diuretics, causing rapid diuresis, and thus decreasing vascular fluid volume, **cardiac output**, and **BP**.

d. Used for hypertension, pulmonary edema, edema associated with heart failure, hypercalcemia, and renal disease

e. Use loop diuretics with caution in the client taking digoxin or lithium and the client on aminoglycosides, anticoagulants, corticosteroids, or amphotericin B.

2. Side effects

a. Hypokalemia, hyponatremia, hypocalcemia, hypomagnesemia

b. Hypochloremia

c. Thrombocytopenia

d. Hyperuricemia

e. **Orthostatic hypotension**

f. Skin disturbances

g. Ototoxicity and deafness

h. Thiamine deficiency

i. Dehydration

3. Interventions

a. Monitor vital signs.

b. Monitor weight.

c. Monitor urine output.

d. Monitor electrolyte, calcium, magnesium, BUN, creatinine, and uric acid levels.

e. Check the peripheral extremities for edema.

f. Monitor for signs of digoxin or lithium toxicity if the client is on these medications.

g. Instruct the client to take the medication in the morning to avoid nocturia and sleep interruption.

h. Instruct the client in how to record the BP.

i. Instruct the client to eat foods high in potassium.

j. Instruct the client in how to take potassium supplements if prescribed.

k. Instruct the client to take medication with food to avoid gastrointestinal upset.

l. Instruct the client to change positions slowly to prevent **orthostatic hypotension**.

m. Administer IV furosemide (Lasix) slowly because hearing loss can occur if injected rapidly.

C. Osmotic diuretics

1. See Chap. 66 for information regarding osmotic diuretics.

2. Box 60-10 lists osmotic diuretics.

D. Carbonic anhydrase inhibitors (Box 60-11)

1. Description

a. Carbonic anhydrase inhibitors block the action of the enzyme carbonic anhydrase, which is needed to maintain acid-base balance.

b. Inhibition of this enzyme, carbonic anhydrase, causes increased sodium, potassium, and bicarbonate excretion.

c. Metabolic acidosis can occur with prolonged use.

d. Carbonic anhydrase inhibitors are used to decrease intraocular pressure in open-angle (chronic) glaucoma, produce diuresis, manage epilepsy, and treat high-altitude sickness.

e. Carbonic anhydrase inhibitors are used to treat metabolic alkalosis.

f. Carbonic anhydrase inhibitors are contraindicated in narrow-angle or acute glaucoma.

2. Side effects

a. Hyperglycemia, hyperuricemia, hypercalcemia

b. Hypokalemia

c. Anorexia, nausea, vomiting

BOX 60-10

Osmotic Diuretics

Mannitol (Osmitrol)
Urea (Ureaphil)

BOX 60-9

Loop Diuretics

Bumetanide (Bumex)
Ethacrynic acid (Edecrin)
Furosemide (Lasix)
Torsemide (Demadex)

BOX 60-11

Carbonic Anhydrase Inhibitors

Acetazolamide (Diamox)
Methazolamide

d. **Orthostatic hypotension**
e. Renal calculi
f. Hemolytic anemia
3. Interventions
   a. Monitor vital signs.
   b. Monitor weight.
   c. Monitor urine output.
   d. Monitor electrolyte, glucose, calcium, BUN, creatinine, and uric acid levels.
   e. Monitor mental status.
   f. Instruct the client to monitor for signs of renal calculi.

E. Potassium-sparing diuretics (Box 60-12)
   1. Description
      a. Potassium-sparing diuretics act on the distal tubule to promote sodium and water excretion and potassium retention.
      b. Used for edema and hypertension, to increase urine output, and to treat fluid retention and overload associated with heart failure, ascites resulting from cirrhosis or nephrotic syndrome, and diuretic-induced hypokalemia.
      c. Potassium-sparing diuretics are contraindicated in severe kidney or hepatic disease and in severe hyperkalemia.
      d. Potassium-sparing diuretics should be used with caution in the client with diabetes mellitus, taking antihypertensives or lithium, taking angiotensin-converting enzyme inhibitors because hyperkalemia can result, or taking potassium supplements.
   2. Side effects
      a. Hyperkalemia
      b. Nausea, vomiting, diarrhea
      c. Rash
      d. Dizziness, weakness
      e. Headache
      f. Dry mouth
      g. Photosensitivity
      h. Anemia
      i. Thrombocytopenia
   3. Interventions
      a. Monitor vital signs.
      b. Monitor urine output.
      c. Monitor for signs and symptoms of hyperkalemia such as nausea, diarrhea, abdominal cramps, tachycardia followed by bradycardia, tall peaked T wave on the electrocardiogram, and oliguria.
      d. Monitor for a potassium level greater than 5.1 mEq/L, which indicates hyperkalemia.
      e. Instruct the client to avoid foods high in potassium.
      f. Instruct the client to avoid exposure to direct sunlight.
      g. Instruct the client to monitor for signs of hyperkalemia.
      h. Instruct the client to avoid salt substitutes because they contain potassium.
      i. Instruct the client to take with or after meals to decrease gastrointestinal irritation.

VII. **PERIPHERALLY ACTING α-ADRENERGIC BLOCKERS** (Box 60-13)
A. Description
   1. These medications decrease sympathetic vasoconstriction by reducing the effects of norepinephrine at peripheral nerve endings, resulting in vasodilation and decreased **BP**.
   2. These medications are used to maintain renal blood flow.
   3. These medications are used to treat hypertension.
B. Side effects
   1. **Orthostatic hypotension**
   2. Reflex tachycardia
   3. Sodium and water retention
   4. Gastrointestinal disturbances
   5. Nausea
   6. Drowsiness
   7. Nasal congestion
   8. Edema
   9. Weight gain
C. Interventions
   1. Monitor vital signs.
   2. Monitor for fluid retention and edema.
   3. Instruct the client to change positions slowly to prevent **orthostatic hypotension.**
   4. Instruct the client in how to monitor the **BP.**
   5. Instruct the client to monitor for edema.
   6. Instruct the client to decrease salt intake.
   7. Instruct the client to avoid over-the-counter medications.

BOX 60-12
Potassium-Sparing Diuretics

Amiloride (Midamor)
Amiloride hydrochloride; hydrochlorothiazide (Moduretic)
Spironolactone (Aldactone)
Spironolactone; hydrochlorothiazide (Aldactazide)
Triamterene (Dyrenium)

BOX 60-13
Peripherally Acting α-Adrenergic Blockers

Alfuzosin (Uroxatral)
Doxazosin (Cardura)
Phenoxybenzamine (Dibenzyline)
Phentolamine
Prazosin (Minipress)
Tamsulosin (Flomax)
Terazosin (Hytrin)

BOX 60-14
Centrally Acting Sympatholytics

Clonidine (Catapres)
Methyldopa (Aldomet)
Guanabenz acetate

VIII. CENTRALLY ACTING SYMPATHOLYTICS (ADRENERGIC BLOCKERS) (Box 60-14)

A. Description
 1. Centrally acting sympatholytics stimulate alpha receptors in the central nervous system to inhibit vasoconstriction, thus reducing peripheral resistance.
 2. Used to treat hypertension
 3. Contraindicated in impaired liver function
▲ B. Side effects
 1. Sodium and water retention
 2. Drowsiness, dizziness
 3. Dry mouth
 4. Bradycardia
 5. Edema
 6. Impotence
 7. Hypotension
 8. Depression
▲ C. Interventions
 1. Monitor vital signs.
 2. Instruct the client not to discontinue medication because abrupt withdrawal can cause severe rebound hypertension.
 3. Monitor liver function tests.

▲ **IX. ANGIOTENSIN-CONVERTING ENZYME (ACE) INHIBITORS AND ANGIOTENSIN II RECEPTOR BLOCKERS (ARBs) (Box 60-15)**

A. Description
 1. ACE inhibitors prevent peripheral vasoconstriction by blocking conversion of angiotensin I to angiotensin II (AII).
 2. ARBs prevent peripheral vasoconstriction and secretion of aldosterone and block the binding of AII to type 1 AII receptors.
 3. These medications are used to treat hypertension and heart failure; ACE inhibitors are administered for their cardioprotective effect after myocardial infarction.
 4. Avoid use with potassium supplements and potassium-sparing diuretics.
▲ B. Side effects
 1. Nausea, vomiting, diarrhea
 2. Persistent dry cough (ACE inhibitors only)
 3. Hypotension
 4. Hyperkalemia
 5. Tachycardia
 6. Headache
 7. Dizziness, fatigue

BOX 60-15
Angiotensin-Converting Enzyme Inhibitors and Angiotension Receptor Blockers

ANGIOTENSIN-CONVERTING ENZYME INHIBITORS
Benazepril (Lotensin)
Captopril (Capoten)
Enalapril (Vasotec)
Enalaprilat (Vasotec I.V.)
Fosinopril (Monopril)
Lisinopril (Prinivil, Zestril)
Moexipril (Univasc)
Perindopril (Aceon)
Quinapril (Accupril)
Ramipril (Altace)
Trandolapril (Mavik)

ANGIOTENSION II RECEPTOR BLOCKERS
Candesartan (Atacand)
Eprosartan (Teveten)
Irbesartan (Avapro)
Losartan (Cozaar)
Olmesartan (Benicar)
Telmisartan (Micardis)
Valsartan (Diovan)

---

 8. Insomnia
 9. Hypoglycemic reaction in the client with diabetes mellitus
 10. Bruising, petechiae, bleeding
 11. Diminished taste (ACE inhibitors)
C. Interventions
 1. Monitor vital signs.
 2. Monitor white blood cells, and protein, albumin, BUN, creatinine, and potassium levels.
 3. Monitor for hypoglycemic reactions in the client with diabetes mellitus.
 4. Instruct the client to take captopril (Capoten) 20 to 60 minutes before a meal.
 5. Monitor for bruising, petechiae, or bleeding with captopril.
 6. Instruct the client not to discontinue medications because rebound hypertension can occur.
 7. Instruct the client not to take over-the-counter medications.
 8. Instruct the client in how to take the BP.
 9. Instruct the client that if dizziness occurs and persists to notify the physician.
 10. Inform the client that the taste of food may be diminished during the first month of therapy.
 11. Instruct the client to report the side effect of angioedema immediately to the health care provider.

X. ANTIANGINAL MEDICATIONS (Box 60-16)
A. Nitrates
 1. Description
  a. Nitrates produce vasodilation.

Amyl nitrate inhalant
Isosorbide dinitrate (Isordil Titradose)
Isosorbide mononitrate (Imdur, Monoket)
Nitroglycerin, sublingual (Nitrostat, NitroQuick, Nitrotab)
Nitroglycerin, translingual (Nitrolingual Pumpspray)
Nitroglycerin, transmucosal
Nitroglycerin, transdermal patches (Minitran, Nitro-Dur, Nitrek, Transderm-Nitro)
Nitroglycerin ointment (Nitro-Bid)

b. Nitrates decrease **preload** and **afterload** and reduce myocardial oxygen consumption.
c. Contraindicated in the client with significant hypotension, increased intracranial pressure, or severe anemia
d. Should be used with caution with severe renal or hepatic disease
e. Avoid abrupt withdrawal of long-acting preparations to prevent the rebound effect of severe pain from myocardial ischemia.
2. Side effects
   a. Headache
   b. **Orthostatic hypotension**
   c. Dizziness, weakness
   d. Faintness
   e. Nausea, vomiting
   f. Flushing or pallor
   g. Confusion
   h. Rash
   i. Dry mouth
   j. Reflex tachycardia
3. Sublingual medications
   a. Monitor vital signs.
   b. Offer sips of water before giving because dryness may inhibit medication absorption.
   c. Instruct the client to place under the tongue and leave until fully dissolved.
   d. Instruct the client not to swallow the medication.
   e. Instruct the client to take one tablet for pain and repeat every 5 minutes, for a total of three doses.
   f. Instruct the client to seek medical help immediately if pain is not relieved in 15 minutes, following the three doses.
   g. Inform the client that a stinging or burning sensation may indicate that the tablet is fresh.
   h. Instruct the client to store medication in a dark, tightly closed bottle.
   i. Instruct the client to check the expiration date on the medication bottle because expiration may occur within 6 months of obtaining medication.

j. Instruct the client to take acetaminophen (Tylenol) for a headache.
4. Translingual medications (spray)
   a. Instruct the client to direct the spray against the oral mucosa.
   b. Instruct the client to avoid inhaling the spray.
5. Sustained-released medications: Instruct the client to swallow and not to chew or crush the medication.
6. Transmucosal-buccal medications
   a. Instruct the client to place the medication between the upper lip and gum or in the buccal area between the cheek and gum.
   b. Inform the client that the medication will adhere to the oral mucosa and slowly dissolve.
7. Transdermal patch
   a. Instruct the client to apply the patch to a hairless area, using a new patch and different site each day.
   b. As prescribed, instruct the client to remove the patch after 12 to 14 hours, allowing 10 to 12 "patch-free" hours each day to prevent tolerance.
8. Topical ointments
   a. Instruct the client to remove the ointment on the skin from the previous dose.
   b. Instruct the client to squeeze a ribbon of ointment of the prescribed length onto the applicator paper.
   c. Instruct the client to spread the ointment over a 6 × 6-inch area, using the chest, back, abdomen, upper arm, or anterior thigh (avoiding hairy areas), and cover with a plastic wrap.
   d. Instruct the client to rotate sites and to avoid touching the ointment when applying.
9. Patches and ointments
   a. Wear gloves when applying.
   b. Do not apply on the chest in the area of defibrillator-cardioverter paddle placement because skin burns can result if the paddles need to be used.

XI. β-ADRENERGIC BLOCKERS (Box 60-17)
A. Description
1. β-Adrenergic blockers inhibit response to β-adrenergic stimulation, thus decreasing cardiac output.
2. β-Adrenergic blockers block the release of catecholamines, epinephrine, and norepinephrine, thus decreasing the heart rate and **BP**.
3. β-Adrenergic blockers decrease the workload of the heart and decrease oxygen demands.
4. Used for angina, dysrhythmias, hypertension, migraine headaches, prevention of myocardial infarction, and glaucoma

5. β-Adrenergic blockers are contraindicated in the client with asthma, bradycardia, heart failure (with exceptions), severe renal or hepatic disease, hyperthyroidism, or brain attack (stroke); carvedilol, metoprolol and bisoprolol have been approved for use in heart failure once the client has been stabilized with ACE inhibitor and diuretic therapy.

6. β-Adrenergic blockers should be used with caution in the client with diabetes mellitus because the medication may mask symptoms of hypoglycemia.

7. β-Adrenergic blockers should be used with caution in the client taking antihypertensive medications.

▲ B. Side effects
   1. Bradycardia
   2. Bronchospasm
   3. Hypotension
   4. Weakness, fatigue
   5. Nausea, vomiting
   6. Dizziness
   7. Hyperglycemia
   8. Agranulocytosis
   9. Behavioral or psychotic response
   10. Depression
   11. Nightmares

▲ C. Interventions
   1. Monitor vital signs.
   2. Hold the medication if the pulse or **BP** is not within the prescribed parameters.
   3. Monitor for signs of heart failure or worsening heart failure.
   4. Assess for respiratory distress and for signs of wheezing and dyspnea.

5. Instruct the client to report dizziness, light-headedness, or nasal congestion.

6. Instruct the client not to stop the medication because rebound hypertension, rebound tachycardia, or an anginal attack can occur.

7. Advise the client taking insulin that the β-adrenergic blocker can mask early signs of hypoglycemia, such as tachycardia and nervousness.

8. Instruct the client taking insulin to monitor the blood glucose level.

9. Instruct the client in how to take pulse and **BP**.

10. Instruct the client to change positions slowly to prevent **orthostatic hypotension**.

11. Instruct the client to avoid over-the-counter cold medications and nasal decongestants.

XII. CALCIUM CHANNEL BLOCKERS (Box 60-18) ▲

A. Description
   1. Calcium channel blockers decrease cardiac **contractility** (negative inotropic effect by relaxing smooth muscle) and the workload of the heart, thus decreasing the need for oxygen.
   2. Calcium channel blockers promote vasodilation of the coronary and peripheral vessels.
   3. Used for angina, dysrhythmias, or hypertension
   4. Should be used with caution in the client with CHF, bradycardia, or atrioventricular block

B. Side effects ▲
   1. Bradycardia
   2. Hypotension
   3. Reflex tachycardia as a result of hypotension
   4. Headache
   5. Dizziness, light-headedness
   6. Fatigue
   7. Peripheral edema
   8. Constipation
   9. Flushing of the skin
   10. Changes in liver and kidney function

C. Interventions ▲
   1. Monitor vital signs.
   2. Monitor for signs of heart failure.
   3. Monitor liver enzyme levels.
   4. Monitor kidney function tests.

BOX 60-17
β-Adrenergic Blockers

NONSELECTIVE (block β₁ and β₂)
Carteolol (Cartrol Filmtabs)
Carvedilol (Coreg Tiltab)
Labetalol (Trandate)
Nadolol (Corgard)
Penbutolol (Levatol)
Pindolol (Visken)
Propranolol (Inderal)
Sotalol (Betapace)
Timolol (Blocadren)

CARDIOSELECTIVE (block β₁)
Acebutolol (Sectral)
Atenolol (Tenormin)
Betaxolol (Kerlone)
Bisoprolol (Zebeta)
Esmolol (Brevibloc)
Metoprolol (Lopressor, Toprol-XL)

BOX 60-18
Calcium Channel Blockers

Amlodipine (Norvasc, Amvaz)
Diltiazem (Cardizem, Cartia XT, Dilacor XR, Diltia XT, Tiazac)
Felodipine (Plendil)
Isradipine (DynaCirc)
Nicardipine (Cardene)
Nifedipine (Adalat, Nifedical XL, Nifediac CC, Procardia)
Nimodipine (Nimotop)
Nisoldipine (Sular)
Verapamil (Calan, Isoptin SR, Covera-HS, Verelan)

5. Instruct the client not to discontinue the medication.
6. Instruct the client in how to take a pulse.
7. Instruct the client to notify the physician if dizziness or fainting occurs.
8. Instruct the client not to crush or chew sustained-released tablets.

XIII. PERIPHERAL VASODILATORS (Box 60-19)

A. Description
1. Peripheral vasodilators decrease peripheral resistance by exerting a direct action on the arteries or on the arteries and the veins.
2. Peripheral vasodilators increase blood flow to the extremities and are used in peripheral vascular disorders of venous and arterial vessels.
3. Peripheral vasodilators are most effective for disorders resulting from vasospasm (Raynaud's disease).
4. These medications may decrease some symptoms of cerebral vascular insufficiency.

B. Side effects
1. Light-headedness, dizziness
2. **Orthostatic hypotension**
3. Tachycardia
4. Palpitations
5. Flushing
6. Gastrointestinal distress

C. Interventions
1. Monitor vital signs, especially the **BP** and the heart rate.
2. Monitor for **orthostatic hypotension** and tachycardia.
3. Monitor for signs of inadequate blood flow to the extremities, such as pallor, feeling cold, and pain.
4. Instruct the client that it may take up to 3 months for a desired therapeutic response.
5. Advise the client not to smoke because smoking increases vasospasm.

BOX 60-19
Peripheral Vasodilators

α-ADRENERGIC BLOCKERS
Prazosin (Minipress)
Terazosin (Hytrin)

CALCIUM CHANNEL BLOCKERS
Diltiazem (Cardizem, Cartia XT, Dilacor XR, Diltia XT, Tiazac)
Nifedipine (Procardia)
Nimodipine (Nimotop)
Verapamil (Calan, Isoptin SR, Covera-HS, Verelan)

HEMORHEOLOGICAL
Pentoxifylline (Trental; increases microcirculation and tissue perfusion)

---

6. Instruct the client to avoid aspirin or aspirin-like compounds unless approved by the physician.
7. Instruct the client to take the medication with meals if gastrointestinal disturbances occur.
8. Instruct the client to avoid alcohol because it may cause a hypotensive reaction.
9. Encourage the client to change positions slowly to avoid **orthostatic hypotension**.

XIV. DIRECT-ACTING ARTERIOLAR VASODILATORS (Box 60-20)

A. Description
1. Direct-acting vasodilators relax the smooth muscles of the blood vessels, mainly the arteries, causing vasodilation.
2. Direct-acting vasodilators promote an increase in blood flow to the brain and kidneys.
3. With vasodilation, the **blood pressure** drops and sodium and water are retained, resulting in peripheral edema.
4. Diuretics may be given to decrease the edema.
5. Direct-acting vasodilators are used in the client with moderate to severe hypertension.
6. Direct-acting vasodilators are used during acute hypertensive emergencies.

B. Side effects
1. Hypotension
2. Reflex tachycardia caused by vasodilation and the drop in **BP**
3. Palpitations
4. Edema
5. Dizziness
6. Headaches
7. Nasal congestion
8. Gastrointestinal bleeding
9. Neurological symptoms
10. Confusion
11. Excess hair growth with minoxidil (Loniten)
12. With sodium nitroprusside, cyanide toxicity and thiocyanate toxicity can occur.

C. Interventions
1. Monitor vital signs especially **BP**.
2. Sodium nitroprusside
    a. Monitor cyanide and thiocyanate levels.
    b. Protect from light because the medication decomposes.

BOX 60-20
Direct-Acting Vasodilators

Diazoxide (Hyperstat)
Fenoldopam (Corlopam)
Hydralazine (Apresoline)
Minoxidil (Loniten)
Nitroglycerin
Sodium nitroprusside (Nitropress)

c. When administering, solution must be covered by a dark bag provided by the manufacturer and is stable for 24 hours.

d. Discard if the medication is red, green or blue.

XV. MISCELLANEOUS VASODILATOR
A. Description
1. Nesiritide (Natrecor)
a. Recombinant version of human B-type natriuretic peptide that vasodilates arteries and veins
b. Used for the treatment of decompensated heart failure
2. Side effects
a. Hypotension
b. Confusion
c. Dizziness
d. Dysrhythmias
3. Interventions
a. Administer by continuous intravenous infusion via pump
b. Monitor **BP,** cardiac rhythm, urine output, and body weight.
c. Monitor for signs of resolving heart failure

XVI. ANTIDYSRHYTHMIC MEDICATIONS
A. Description: Antidysrhythmic medications suppress dysrhythmias by inhibiting abnormal pathways of electrical conduction through the heart.
B. Class I antidysrhythmics are sodium channel blockers, class II are β-blockers, class III are potassium channel blockers (medications that delay repolarization), and class IV are calcium channel blockers.
C. Class IA antidysrhythmics
1. Disopyramide (Norpace)
2. Procainamide (Procanbid)
3. Quinidine sulfate
D. Class IB antidysrhythmics
1. Lidocaine (Xylocaine)
2. Mexiletine hydrochloride (Mexitil)
3. Phenytoin (Dilantin)
E. Class IC antidysrhythmics
1. Flecainide acetate (Tambocor)
2. Propafenone hydrochloride (Rythmol)
3. Moricizine (Ethmozine)
4. Side effects
a. Hypotension
b. Heart failure
c. Worsened or new dysrhythmias
d. Nausea, vomiting, or diarrhea
F. Class II antidysrhythmics
1. Acebutolol (Sectral)
2. Esmolol (Brevibloc)
3. Propranolol (Inderal)
4. Side effects
a. Dizziness
b. Fatigue

c. Hypotension
d. Bradycardia
e. Heart failure
f. Dysrhythmias
g. Heart block
h. Bronchospasms
i. Gastrointestinal distress
G. Class III antidysrhythmics
1. Amiodarone (Cordarone, Pacerone)
2. Bretylium
3. Dofetilide (Tikosyn)
4. Ibutilide (Corvert)
5. Sotalol (Betapace)
6. Side effects
a. Hypotension
b. Bradycardia
c. Nausea, vomiting
d. Amiodarone hydrochloride may cause pulmonary fibrosis, photosensitivity, bluish skin discoloration, corneal deposits, peripheral neuropathy, tremor, poor coordination, abnormal gait, and hypothyroidism.
e. Bretylium may cause vertigo, syncope, and dizziness.
H. Class IV antidysrhythmics
1. Verapamil (Isoptin SR, Calan, Verelan)
2. Diltiazem (Cardizem)
3. Side effects
a. Dizziness
b. Hypotension
c. Bradycardia
d. Edema
e. Constipation
I. Other antidysrhythmics
1. Adenosine (Adenocard)
2. Digoxin (Lanoxin)
J. Interventions for antidysrhythmics
1. Monitor heart rate, respiratory rate, and **BP.**
2. Monitor electrocardiogram.
3. Provide continuous cardiac monitoring.
4. Maintain therapeutic serum drug levels.
5. Before administering lidocaine, always check the vial label to prevent administering a form that contains epinephrine or preservatives because these solutions are used for local anesthesia only.
6. Do not administer antidysrhythmics with food because food may affect absorption.
7. Mexiletine may be administered with food or antacids to reduce gastrointestinal distress.
8. Always administer IV antidysrhythmics via an infusion pump.
9. Monitor for signs of fluid retention such as weight gain, peripheral edema, or shortness of breath.
10. Advise the client to limit fluid and salt intake to minimize fluid retention.
11. Monitor respiratory, thyroid, and neurological functions.

12. After administering bretylium, keep the client supine and monitor for hypotension.
13. Instruct the client to change positions slowly to minimize **orthostatic hypotension**.
14. Instruct the client taking amiodarone to use sunscreen and protective clothing to prevent photosensitivity reactions.
15. Encourage the client to increase fiber intake to prevent constipation.

XVII. ADRENERGIC AGONISTS (Box 60-21)
A. Dobutamine
   1. Increases myocardial force and **cardiac output** through stimulation of beta receptors
   2. Used in clients with heart failure and for clients undergoing cardiopulmonary bypass surgery
B. Dopamine (Intropin)
   1. Increases **BP** and **cardiac output** through positive inotropic action and increases renal blood flow through its action on alpha and beta receptors
   2. Used to treat mild renal failure caused by low cardiac output.
C. Epinephrine (Adrenalin)
   1. Used for cardiac stimulation in cardiac arrest
   2. Used for bronchodilation in asthma or allergic reactions
   3. Produces mydriasis
   4. Produces local vasoconstriction when combined with local anesthetics and prolongs anesthetic action by decreasing blood flow to the site
D. Isoproterenol (Isuprel)
   1. Stimulates beta receptors
   2. Used for cardiac stimulation and bronchodilation
E. Norepinephrine (Levophed)
   1. Stimulates the heart in cardiac arrest
   2. Vasoconstricts and increases the BP in hypotension and shock
F. Side effects
   1. Dysrhythmias
   2. Tachycardia
   3. Angina
   4. Restlessness
   5. Urgency or urinary incontinence
G. Interventions
   1. Monitor vital signs.
   2. Monitor lung sounds.
   3. Monitor urinary output.

4. Monitor electrocardiogram.
5. Administer the medication through a large vein.

XVIII. ANTILIPEMIC MEDICATIONS
A. Description
   1. Antilipemic medications reduce serum levels of cholesterol, triglycerides, or low-density lipoprotein.
   2. When cholesterol, triglyceride, and low-density lipoprotein levels are elevated, the client is at increased risk for coronary artery disease.
   3. In many cases, diet alone will not lower blood lipid levels; therefore, antilipemic medications will be prescribed.
B. Bile sequestrants (Box 60-22)
   1. Description
      a. Bind with acids in the intestines, which prevents reabsorption of cholesterol
      b. Should not be used as the only therapy in clients with elevated triglyceride levels because they may raise triglyceride levels.
   2. Side effects
      a. Constipation
      b. Gastrointestinal disturbances: Heartburn, nausea, belching, bloating
   3. Interventions
      a. Cholestyramine (Questran) comes in a gritty powder that must be mixed thoroughly in juice or water before administration.
      b. Monitor the client for early signs of peptic ulcer such as nausea and abdominal discomfort followed by abdominal pain and distention.
      c. Instruct the client that the medication must be taken with and followed by sufficient fluids.
C. HMG-CoA reductase inhibitors (Box 60-23)
   1. Description
      a. Lovastatin (Mevacor) is highly protein-bound and should not be administered with anticoagulants.

BOX 60-21
Adrenergic Agonists

Dobutamine
Dopamine
Epinephrine (Adrenalin)
Isoproterenol (Isuprel)
Norepinephrine (Levophed)

BOX 60-22
Bile Acid Sequestrants

Cholestyramine (Questran)
Colesevelam (WelChol)
Colestipol (Colestid)

BOX 60-23
HMG-CoA Reductase Inhibitors

Atorvastatin (Lipitor)
Fluvastatin (Lescol)
Lovastatin (Mevacor)
Pravastatin (Pravachol)
Rosuvastatin (Crestor)
Simvastatin (Zocor)

b. Lovastatin should not be administered with gemfibrozil (Lopid).

c. Administer lovastatin with caution to the client taking immunosuppressive medications.

2. Side effects
   a. Nausea
   b. Diarrhea or constipation
   c. Abdominal pain or cramps
   d. Flatulence
   e. Dizziness
   f. Headache
   g. Blurred vision
   h. Rash
   i. Pruritis
   j. Elevated liver enzyme levels
   k. Muscle cramps and fatigue

3. Interventions
   a. Monitor serum liver enzyme levels.
   b. Instruct the client to receive an annual eye examination because the medications can cause cataract formation.
   c. If lovastatin is not effective in lowering the lipid level after 3 months, it should be discontinued.
   d. Instruct the client to report any unexplained muscular pain to health care provider immediately.

D. Other antilipemic medications (Box 60-24)

1. Description
   a. Gemfibrozil should not be taken with anticoagulants because they compete for protein sites; if the client is taking an anticoagulant, the anticoagulant dose should be reduced during antilipemic therapy and the INR should be monitored closely.
   b. Do not administer gemfibrozil with HMG-CoA reductase inhibitors because it increases the risk for myositis, myalgias, and rhabdomyolysis.

2. Interventions
   a. Monitor vital signs.
   b. Monitor liver enzyme levels.
   c. Monitor serum cholesterol and triglyceride levels.
   d. Instruct the client to restrict intake of fats, cholesterol, carbohydrates, and alcohol.
   e. Instruct the client to follow an exercise program.
   f. Instruct the client that it will take several weeks before the lipid level declines.
   g. Instruct the client to have an annual eye examination and to report any changes in vision.
   h. Instruct the client with diabetes mellitus who is taking gemfibrozil to monitor blood glucose levels regularly.
   i. Instruct the client to increase fluid intake.

BOX 60-24

Other Antilipemic Medications

Ezetimibe (Zetia)
Ezetimibe; simvastatin (Vytorin)
Fenofibrate
Gemfibrozil (Lopid)
Nicotinic acid (Niacin)
Probucol

---

j. Note that nicotinic acid has numerous side effects, including gastrointestinal disturbances, flushing of the skin, elevated liver enzyme levels, hyperglycemia, and hyperuricemia.

k. Instruct the client that aspirin or nonsteroidal anti-inflammatory drugs taken 30 minutes before may assist in reducing the side effect of cutaneous flushing from nicotinic acid.

l. Instruct the client to take nicotinic acid with meals to reduce gastrointestinal discomfort.

PRACTICE QUESTIONS

1. A client with atrial fibrillation is receiving a continuous heparin infusion at 1000 units/hr. The nurse would determine that the client is receiving the therapeutic effect based on which of the following results?
   1. Prothrombin time of 12.5 seconds
   2. Activated partial thromboplastin time of 60 seconds
   3. Activated partial thromboplastin time of 28 seconds
   4. Activated partial thromboplastin time longer than 120 seconds

2. A client develops atrial fibrillation with a ventricular rate of 140 beats/min and signs of decreased cardiac output. Which of the following medications should the nurse first anticipate administering?
   1. Atropine sulfate
   2. Warfarin (Coumadin)
   3. Lidocaine (Xylocaine)
   4. Metoprolol (Lopressor)

3. In reviewing the medication records of the following group of clients, the nurse determines that which client would be at greatest risk for developing hyperkalemia?
   1. Client receiving furosemide (Lasix)
   2. Client receiving bumetanide (Bumex)
   3. Client receiving spironolactone (Aldactone)
   4. Client receiving hydrochlorothiazide (HCTZ)

4. A nurse provides discharge instructions to a postoperative client who is taking warfarin sodium (Coumadin). Which statement, if made by the client, reflects the need for further teaching?

1. "I will take my pills every day at the same time."
2. "I will be certain to limit my alcohol consumption."
3. "I have already called my family to pick up a Medic-Alert bracelet."
4. "I will take Ecotrin (enteric-coated aspirin) for my headaches because it is coated."

5. A client who is receiving digoxin (Lanoxin) daily has a serum potassium level of 3.0 mEq/L and is complaining of anorexia. A physician orders a digoxin level to rule out digoxin toxicity. A nurse checks the results, knowing that which of the following is the therapeutic serum level (range) for digoxin?
   1. 0.5 to 2 ng/mL
   2. 1.2 to 2.8 ng/mL
   3. 3 to 5 ng/mL
   4. 3.5 to 5.5 ng/mL

6. A client is being treated with procainamide (Procanbid) for a cardiac dysrhythmia. Following intravenous administration of the medication, the client complains of dizziness. What intervention should the nurse take first?
   1. Administer ordered nitroglycerin tablets.
   2. Measure the heart rate on the rhythm strip.
   3. Obtain a 12-lead electrocardiogram immediately.
   4. Auscultate the client's apical pulse and obtain a blood pressure.

7. A nurse is monitoring a client who is taking propranolol (Inderal). Which assessment data would indicate a potential serious complication associated with propranolol?
   1. The development of complaints of insomnia
   2. The development of audible expiratory wheezes
   3. A baseline blood pressure of 150/80 mm Hg followed by a blood pressure of 138/72 mm Hg after two doses of the medication
   4. A baseline resting heart rate of 88 beats/min followed by a resting heart rate of 72 beats/min after two doses of the medication

8. A home health care nurse is visiting an older client at home. Furosemide (Lasix) is prescribed for the client and the nurse teaches the client about the medication. Which of the following statements, if made by the client, indicates the need for further teaching?
   1. "I will sit up slowly before standing each morning."
   2. "I will take my medication every morning with breakfast."
   3. "I need to drink lots of coffee and tea to keep myself healthy."
   4. "I will call my doctor if my ankles swell or my rings get tight."

9. A nurse is caring for a client receiving a heparin intravenous (IV) infusion. The nurse anticipates that which laboratory study will be prescribed to monitor the therapeutic effect of heparin?
   1. Hematocrit
   2. Hemoglobin
   3. Prothrombin time
   4. Activated partial thromboplastin time

10. A client is diagnosed with an acute myocardial infarction and is receiving tissue plasminogen activator, alteplase (Activase, tPA). Which of the following is a priority nursing intervention?
    1. Monitor for renal failure.
    2. Monitor psychosocial status.
    3. Monitor for signs of bleeding.
    4. Have heparin sodium available.

11. A home health nurse instructs a client about the use of a nitrate patch. The nurse tells the client that which of the following will prevent client tolerance to nitrates?
    1. "Do not remove the patches."
    2. "Have a 12-hour 'no-nitrate' time."
    3. "Have a 24-hour 'no-nitrate' time."
    4. "Keep nitrates on 24 hours, then off 24 hours."

12. A client is admitted to a medical unit with nausea and bradycardia. The family hands a nurse a small white envelope labeled "heart pill." The envelope is sent to the pharmacy and it is found to be digoxin (Lanoxin). A family member states, "That doctor doesn't know how to take care of my family." Which of the following statements would convey a therapeutic response by the nurse?
    1. "Don't worry about this. I'll take care of everything."
    2. "You are concerned your loved one receives the best care."
    3. "You're right! I've never seen a doctor put pills in an envelope."
    4. "I think you're wrong. That physician has been in practice over 30 years."

13. A nurse is caring for a client receiving dopamine. Which of the following potential nursing diagnoses is appropriate for this client?
    1. Fluid volume, excess
    2. Cardiac output, increased
    3. Tissue perfusion, ineffective
    4. Sensory perception, disturbed

14. A nurse is planning to administer hydrochlorothiazide (HydroDIURIL) to a client. The nurse understands that which of the following are concerns related to the administration of this medication?
    1. Hypouricemia, hyperkalemia
    2. Increased risk of osteoporosis
    3. Hypokalemia, hyperglycemia, sulfa allergy
    4. Hyperkalemia, hypoglycemia, penicillin allergy

15. A home health care nurse is visiting a client with elevated triglyceride levels and a serum cholesterol

level of 398 mg/dL. The client is taking cholestyramine (Questran). Which of the following statements, if made by the client, indicates the need for further education?

1. "Constipation and bloating might be a problem."
2. "I'll continue to watch my diet and reduce my fats."
3. "Walking a mile each day will help the whole process."
4. "I'll continue my nicotinic acid from the health food store."

16. A client is on nicotinic acid (niacin) for hyperlipidemia and the nurse provides instructions to the client about the medication. Which statement by the client would indicate an understanding of the instructions?

1. "It is not necessary to avoid the use of alcohol."
2. "The medication should be taken with meals to decrease flushing."
3. "Clay-colored stools are a common side effect and should not be of concern."
4. "Ibuprofen (Motrin) taken 30 minutes before the nicotinic acid should decrease the flushing."

17. A client has developed paroxysmal nocturnal dyspnea. Which of the following medications does a nurse anticipate will be prescribed by the physician?

1. Propranolol (Inderal)
2. Bumetanide (Bumex)
3. Lidocaine (Xylocaine)
4. Streptokinase (Streptase)

18. A 66-year-old client complaining of not feeling well is seen in a clinic. The client is taking several medications for the control of heart disease and hypertension. These medications include atenolol (Tenormin), digoxin (Lanoxin), and chlorothiazide (Diuril). A tentative diagnosis of digoxin toxicity is made. Which of the following assessment data would support this diagnosis?

1. Dyspnea, edema, and palpitations
2. Chest pain, hypotension, and paresthesia
3. Double vision, loss of appetite, and nausea
4. Constipation, dry mouth, and sleep disorder

19. A client is being treated for acute congestive heart failure with intravenously administered bumetanide (Bumex). The vital signs are as follows: blood pressure, 100/60 mm Hg; pulse, 96 beats/min; and respirations, 24 breaths/min. After the initial dose, which of the following is the priority assessment?

1. Monitoring weight loss
2. Monitoring urine output
3. Monitoring blood pressure
4. Monitoring potassium level

20. Intravenous heparin therapy is ordered for a client. While implementing this order, a nurse ensures that which of the following medications is available on the nursing unit?

1. Protamine sulfate
2. Potassium chloride
3. Aminocaproic acid (Amicar)
4. Vitamin K (AquaMEPHYTON)

21. A client is at risk for pulmonary embolism and is on anticoagulant therapy with warfarin sodium (Coumadin). The client's prothrombin time is 20 seconds, with a control of 11 seconds. How would the nurse interpret these results?

1. Client needs to have test repeated.
2. Client results are within the therapeutic range.
3. Client results are higher than the therapeutic range.
4. Client results are lower than the needed therapeutic level.

22. A client is receiving thrombolytic therapy with a continuous infusion of streptokinase (Streptase). The client suddenly becomes extremely anxious and complains of itching. A nurse hears stridor and on examination of the client notes generalized urticaria and hypotension. Which of the following should be the priority action of the nurse?

1. Administer oxygen and protamine sulfate.
2. Stop the infusion and call the physician.
3. Cut the infusion rate in half and sit the client up in bed.
4. Administer diphenhydramine (Benadryl) and continue the infusion.

23. A client is on enalapril (Vasotec) for the treatment of hypertension. The nurse teaches the client that he should seek emergent care if he experiences which adverse effect?

1. Nausea
2. Insomnia
3. Dry cough
4. Swelling of the tongue

24. Which of the following would be an expected outcome of nesiritide (Natrecor) administration?

1. Client will have an increase in urine output.
2. Client will have an absence of dysrhythmias.
3. Client will have an increase in blood pressure.
4. Client will have an increase in pulmonary capillary wedge pressure.

25. A client is admitted to a hospital with acute myocardial infarction and is started on tissue plasminogen activator (tPA, Activase) by infusion. Of the following parameters, which one would a nurse determine requires the least frequent assessment to detect complications of therapy with tissue plasminogen activator?

1. Neurological signs
2. Presence of bowel sounds
3. Blood pressure and pulse
4. Complaints of abdominal and back pain

26. A client is admitted with pulmonary embolism and is to be treated with streptokinase (Streptase). A nurse would report which of the following as-

sessments to the physician before initiating this therapy?

1. Adventitious breath sounds
2. Temperature of 99.4° F orally
3. Blood pressure of 198/110 mm Hg
4. Respiratory rate of 28 breaths/min

ALTERNATE ITEM FORMAT: MULTIPLE RESPONSE

A client with coronary artery disease complains of substernal chest pain. After assessing the client's heart rate and blood pressure, a nurse administers nitroglycerin, 0.4 mg, sublingually. After 5 minutes, the client states, "My chest still hurts." Select the appropriate actions that the nurse should take. Select all that apply.

1. Call a Code Blue.
2. Contact the physician.
3. Contact the client's family.
4. Assess the client's pain level.
5. Check the client's blood pressure.
6. Administer a second nitroglycerin, 0.4 mg, sublingually.

ANSWERS

1. **2**

Rationale: Common laboratory ranges for activated partial thromboplastin time are 20 to 36 seconds. Because the activated partial thromboplastin time should be 1.5 to 2.5 times the normal value, the client's activated partial thromboplastin time would be considered therapeutic if it were 60 seconds.
Test-Taking Strategy: Use the process of elimination. Option 1 is eliminated because the prothrombin time assesses response to warfarin (Coumadin) therapy. Eliminate option 3 because at 28 seconds the client is receiving no therapeutic effect from the continuous heparin infusion. Eliminate option 4 because this value is beyond the therapeutic range and the client is at risk for bleeding. Review laboratory tests to monitor the effectiveness of heparin therapy if you had difficulty with this question.
Level of Cognitive Ability: Analysis
Client Needs: Physiological Integrity
Integrated Process: Nursing Process—evaluation
Content Area: Pharmacology
Reference: Ignatavicius, D., & Workman, L. (2006). *Medical-surgical nursing: Critical thinking for collaborative care* (5th ed., p. 654). Philadelphia: W.B. Saunders.

2. **4**

Rationale: β-Blockers such as metoprolol slow conduction of impulses through the AV node and decrease the heart rate. In rapid atrial fibrillation, the goal first is to slow the ventricular rate and improve the cardiac output and then attempt to restore normal sinus rhythm.
Test-Taking Strategy: Use the process of elimination. Eliminate option 1 because atropine sulfate will further increase the heart rate and will further decrease the cardiac output. Eliminate option 3 because lidocaine is only useful in suppressing ventricular dysrhythmias. Although warfarin (Coumadin) is administered to clients with atrial fibrillation to prevent clots from forming in the atria it will have no effect in decreasing the ventricular rate or restoring normal sinus rhythm. Review these medications if you had difficulty with this question.
Level of Cognitive Ability: Analysis
Client Needs: Physiological Integrity
Integrated Process: Nursing Process—analysis

Content Area: Pharmacology
References: Ignatavicius, D., & Workman, L. (2006). *Medical-surgical nursing: Critical thinking for collaborative care* (5th ed., pp. 722, 725, 728). Philadelphia: W.B. Saunders.
Skidmore-Roth, L. (2006). *Mosby's 2006 nursing drug reference* (20th ed., p. 641). St. Louis: Mosby.

3. **3**

Rationale: Spironolactone is a potassium-sparing diuretic and competes with aldosterone at receptor sites in the distal tubule, resulting in excretion of sodium, chloride, and water and retention of potassium and phosphate. Use of the medications noted in options 1, 2, and 4 could result in hypokalemia.
Test-Taking Strategy: Use the process of elimination. Eliminate options 1 and 2 because they are both loop diuretics, which lead to the side effect of hypokalemia. Next eliminate option 4 because it is a thiazide diuretic, which acts on the distal tubule and inhibits sodium, chloride, and potassium reabsorption. Review the effects of these medications if you had difficulty with this question.
Level of Cognitive Ability: Analysis
Client Needs: Physiological Integrity
Integrated Process: Nursing Process—assessment
Content Area: Pharmacology
References: Lilley, L., Harrington, S., & Snyder, J. (2005) *Pharmacology and the nursing process* (4th ed., p. 431). St. Louis: Mosby.
Skidmore-Roth, L. (2006). *Mosby's 2006 nursing drug reference* (20th ed., pp. 188, 467, 883, 884). St. Louis: Mosby.

4. **4**

Rationale: Ecotrin is an aspirin-containing product and should be avoided. Excessive alcohol consumption should be avoided by a client taking warfarin sodium. Taking prescribed medication at the same time each day increases client compliance. The Medic-Alert bracelet provides health care personnel emergency information.
Test-Taking Strategy: Use the process of elimination and note the strategic words *need for further teaching*. These words indicate a negative event query and ask you to select an option that is an incorrect statement. Recalling that warfarin (Coumadin) is an anticoagulant and that Ecotrin is an aspirin-

containing product will direct you to option 4. Review client teaching points related to warfarin if you had difficulty with this question.
Level of Cognitive Ability: Analysis
Client Needs: Physiological Integrity
Integrated Process: Teaching and Learning
Content Area: Pharmacology
References: Hodgson, B., & Kizior, R. (2007). *Saunders nursing drug handbook 2007* (p. 1222). Philadelphia: W.B. Saunders. Ignatavicius, D., & Workman, M. (2006). *Medical-surgical nursing: Critical thinking for collaborative care* (5th ed., p. 877). Philadelphia: W.B. Saunders.

5. 1
Rationale: Therapeutic levels for digoxin range from 0.5 to 2 ng/mL. Therefore, options 2, 3, and 4 are incorrect.
Test-Taking Strategy: Knowledge of the therapeutic serum digoxin level will direct you to option 1. If you had difficulty with this question, learn the therapeutic level for digoxin.
Level of Cognitive Ability: Comprehension
Client Needs: Physiological Integrity
Integrated Process: Nursing Process—assessment
Content Area: Pharmacology
Reference: Hodgson, B., & Kizior, R. (2007). *Saunders nursing drug handbook 2007* (p. 358). Philadelphia: W.B. Saunders.

6. 4
Rationale: Signs of toxicity from procainamide include confusion, dizziness, drowsiness, decreased urination, nausea, vomiting, and tachydysrhythmias. If the client complains of dizziness, the nurse should assess the vital signs first. Although options 2 and 3 may be interventions, these would be done after the vital signs are taken. Nitroglycerin is a vasodilator and will lower the blood pressure.
Test-Taking Strategy: Use the steps of the nursing process to eliminate options 1 and 3. From the remaining options, remember always to assess the client first, not the monitoring devices. Therefore, option 4 is correct. Review the signs of toxicity and the nursing interventions if you had difficulty with this question.
Level of Cognitive Ability: Application
Client Needs: Physiological Integrity
Integrated Process: Nursing Process—implementation
Content Area: Pharmacology
Reference: Gahart, B., & Nazareno, A. (2006). *2006 intravenous medications* (22nd ed., p. 1030). St. Louis: Mosby.

7. 2
Rationale: Audible expiratory wheezes may indicate a serious adverse reaction, bronchospasm. β-Blockers may induce this reaction, particularly in clients with chronic obstructive pulmonary disease or asthma. Normal decreases in blood pressure and heart rate are expected. Insomnia is a frequent mild side effect and should be monitored.
Test-Taking Strategy: Use the process of elimination, eliminating options 3 and 4 because these are expected effects from the medication. Note the strategic words *potential serious complication*. These strategic words will direct you to option 2. Review the adverse effects of this medication if you had difficulty with this question.

Level of Cognitive Ability: Analysis
Client Needs: Physiological Integrity
Integrated Process: Nursing Process—assessment
Content Area: Pharmacology
References: Hodgson, B., & Kizior, R. (2007). *Saunders nursing drug handbook 2007* (p. 982). Philadelphia: W.B. Saunders. Skidmore-Roth, L. (2005). *Mosby's drug guide for nurses* (6th ed., p. 730). St. Louis: Mosby.

8. 3
Rationale: Tea and coffee are stimulants and mild diuretics. These are a poor choice for hydration. Taking the medication at the same time each day improves compliance. Because furosemide is a diuretic, the morning is the best time to take the medication so as not to interrupt sleep. Notification of the health care provider is appropriate if edema is noticed in the hands, feet, or face or if the client is short of breath. Sitting up slowly prevents postural hypotension.
Test-Taking Strategy: Use the process of elimination, noting the strategic words *need for further teaching*. These words indicate a negative event query and ask you to select an option that is an incorrect statement. Recalling that tea and coffee are stimulants and that diuretics potentially can worsen dehydration will direct you to option 3. In addition, coffee and tea are not healthy items to consume. Review client teaching points related to this medication if you had difficulty with this question.
Level of Cognitive Ability: Analysis
Client Needs: Physiological Integrity
Integrated Process: Teaching and Learning
Content Area: Pharmacology
References: Hodgson, B., & Kizior, R. (2007). *Saunders nursing drug handbook 2007* (p. 525). Philadelphia: W.B. Saunders. Mosby. (2007). *2007 Mosby's nursing drug reference* (20th ed., p. 492). St. Louis: Mosby.

9. 4
Rationale: The prothrombin time will assess for the therapeutic effect of warfarin sodium (Coumadin), and the activated partial thromboplastin time (aPTT) will assess the therapeutic effect of heparin. Hematocrit and hemoglobin values assess red blood cell concentrations. Baseline assessment, including an aPTT value, should be completed, as well as ongoing daily aPTT values while the client is taking heparin. Heparin doses are determined based on the result of the aPTT.
Test-Taking Strategy: Use the process of elimination. Eliminate options 1 and 2 because they are comparative or alike and are unrelated to heparin therapy. From the remaining options, recall the relationship between the prothrombin time and warfarin and the aPTT and heparin. Review care of a client on heparin infusion if you had difficulty with this question.
Level of Cognitive Ability: Analysis
Client Needs: Physiological Integrity
Integrated Process: Nursing Process—assessment
Content Area: Pharmacology
Reference: Gahart, B., & Nazareno, A. (2006). *2006 intravenous medications* (22nd ed., p. 637). St. Louis: Mosby.

10. 3
Rationale: Tissue plasminogen activator is a thrombolytic. Hemorrhage is a complication of any type of thrombolytic

medication. The client is monitored for bleeding. Monitoring for renal failure and monitoring the client's psychosocial status are important but are not the most critical interventions. Heparin is given after thrombolytic therapy, but the question is not asking about follow-up medications.

Test-Taking Strategy: Use the process of elimination and note the strategic word *priority*. Remember, bleeding is a priority. Review care of the client on tissue plasminogen activator if you had difficulty with this question.

Level of Cognitive Ability: Application
Client Needs: Physiological Integrity
Integrated Process: Nursing Process—implementation
Content Area: Delegating/Prioritizing
Reference: Skidmore-Roth, L. (2005). *Mosby's drug guide for nurses* (6th ed., p. 31). St. Louis: Mosby.

11. 2
Rationale: To help prevent tolerance, clients need a 12-hour "no-nitrate" time, sometimes referred to as a pharmacological vacation away from the medication. Options 1, 3, and 4 are incorrect.

Test-Taking Strategy: Use the process of elimination, focusing on the subject, preventing tolerance to nitrates. This subject and knowledge regarding administering this medication will direct you to option 2. Review the administration of nitrate patches if you had difficulty with this question.

Level of Cognitive Ability: Application
Client Needs: Physiological Integrity
Integrated Process: Teaching and Learning
Content Area: Pharmacology
References: Hodgson, B., & Kizior, R. (2007). *Saunders nursing drug handbook 2007* (p. 842). Philadelphia: W.B. Saunders.
Kee, J., Hayes, E., & McCuistion, L. (2006). *Pharmacology: A nursing process approach* (5th ed., p. 613). Philadelphia: W.B. Saunders.

12. 2
Rationale: This is a therapeutic, nonjudgmental response. The statement reflects the family's concern but remains nonjudgmental. Option 1 dismisses the family's concerns and disempowers the family. Option 3 creates doubt about the physician's practice without actually knowing the circumstances. Option 4 is argumentative and nontherapeutic.

Test-Taking Strategy: Use therapeutic communication techniques. Reflection of the client's or family's concerns is the most therapeutic. Review these techniques if you had difficulty with this question.

Level of Cognitive Ability: Application
Client Needs: Psychosocial Integrity
Integrated Process: Communication and Documentation
Content Area: Pharmacology
References: Hodgson, B., & Kizior, R. (2007). *Saunders nursing drug handbook 2007* (pp. 356-357). Philadelphia: W.B. Saunders.
Potter, P., & Perry, A. (2005). *Fundamentals of nursing* (6th ed., p. 437). St. Louis: Mosby.

13. 3
Rationale: The client receiving dopamine therapy should be assessed for ineffective tissue perfusion related to peripheral

vasoconstriction. Options 1, 2, and 4 are not related directly to this medication therapy.

Test-Taking Strategy: Use the process of elimination. Recalling that dopamine causes peripheral vasoconstriction will direct you to option 3. Review the action of this medication if you had difficulty with this question.

Level of Cognitive Ability: Analysis
Client Needs: Physiological Integrity
Integrated Process: Nursing Process—analysis
Content Area: Pharmacology
Reference: Kee, J., Hayes, E., & McCuistion, L. (2006). *Pharmacology: A nursing process approach* (5th ed., pp. 916-917). Philadelphia: W.B. Saunders.

14. 3
Rationale: Thiazide diuretics such as hydrochlorothiazide are sulfa-based medications, and a client with a sulfa allergy is at risk for an allergic reaction. Also, clients are at risk for hypokalemia, hyperglycemia, hypercalcemia, hyperlipidemia, and hyperuricemia.

Test-Taking Strategy: Use the process of elimination. Recalling that thiazide diuretics carry a sulfa ring will direct you to option 3. Review the nursing considerations related to administering this medication if you had difficulty with this question.

Level of Cognitive Ability: Analysis
Client Needs: Physiological Integrity
Integrated Process: Nursing Process—analysis
Content Area: Pharmacology
References: Hodgson, B., & Kizior, R. (2007). *Saunders nursing drug handbook 2007* (p. 578). Philadelphia: W.B. Saunders.
Skidmore-Roth, L. (2005). *Mosby's drug guide for nurses* (6th ed., p. 419). St. Louis: Mosby.

15. 4
Rationale: Nicotinic acid, even an over-the-counter form, should be avoided because it may lead to liver abnormalities. All lipid-lowering medications also can cause liver abnormalities, so a combination of nicotinic acid and cholestyramine resin is to be avoided. Constipation and bloating are the two most common side effects. Walking and the reduction of fats in the diet are therapeutic measures to reduce cholesterol and triglyceride levels.

Test-Taking Strategy: Use the process of elimination and note the strategic words *need for further education*. These words indicate a negative event query and ask you to select an option that is an incorrect statement. Remembering that over-the-counter medications should be avoided when a client is taking a prescription medication will direct you to option 4. Review client teaching points related to this medication if you had difficulty with this question.

Level of Cognitive Ability: Analysis
Client Needs: Health Promotion and Maintenance
Integrated Process: Teaching and Learning
Content Area: Pharmacology
References: Kee, J., Hayes, E., & McCuistion, L. (2006). *Pharmacology: A nursing process approach* (5th ed., p. 678). Philadelphia: W.B. Saunders.
Lilley, L., Harrington, S., & Snyder, J. (2005). *Pharmacology and the nursing process* (4th ed., pp. 483, 489). St. Louis: Mosby.

16. **4**

Rationale: Flushing is a side effect of this medication. Aspirin or a nonsteroidal anti-inflammatory drug can be taken 30 minutes prior to taking the medication to decrease flushing. Alcohol consumption needs to be avoided because it will enhance this side effect. The medication should be taken with meals but this will decrease gastrointestinal upset; taking the medication with meals has no effect on the flushing. Clay-colored stools are a sign of hepatic dysfunction and should be immediately reported to the physician.

Test-Taking Strategy: Use the process of elimination. Option 1 can be eliminated because alcohol must be abstained from. Option 2 can be eliminated because taking the medication with meals helps decrease the gastrointestinal symptoms. The clay-colored stools in option 3 is a sign of hepatic dysfunction and should be immediately reported to the physician. Review the client teaching points related to this medication if you had difficulty with this question.

Level of Cognitive Ability: Analysis
Client Needs: Physiological Integrity
Integrated Process: Nursing Process—evaluation
Content Area: Pharmacology
Reference: Skidmore-Roth, L. (2006). *Mosby's 2006 nursing drug reference* (20th ed., pp. 689-690). St. Louis: Mosby.

17. **2**

Rationale: Bumetanide (Bumex) is a diuretic. The paroxysmal nocturnal dyspnea may be due to increased venous return when the client is lying in bed, and the client needs diuresis. Propranolol is a β-blocker, lidocaine is an antiarrhythmic, and streptokinase is a thrombolytic.

Test-Taking Strategy: Use the process of elimination. Knowledge of each medication type and that a diuretic will increase urine output will direct you to option 2. Review the actions of the medications identified in the options, if you had difficulty with this question.

Level of Cognitive Ability: Analysis
Client Needs: Physiological Integrity
Integrated Process: Nursing Process—analysis
Content Area: Pharmacology
Reference: Hodgson, B., & Kizior, R. (2007). *Saunders nursing drug handbook 2007* (p. 159). Philadelphia: W.B. Saunders.

18. **3**

Rationale: Double vision, loss of appetite, and nausea are early signs of digoxin toxicity. Additional signs of digoxin toxicity include bradycardia, difficulty reading, visual alterations such as green and yellow vision or seeing spots or halos, confusion, vomiting, diarrhea, decreased libido, and impotence.

Test-Taking Strategy: Use the process of elimination. Recalling that gastrointestinal and visual disturbances occur with digoxin toxicity will direct you to option 3. If you had difficulty with this question, review the signs of digoxin toxicity.

Level of Cognitive Ability: Analysis
Client Needs: Physiological Integrity
Integrated Process: Nursing Process—assessment
Content Area: Pharmacology
Reference: Kee, J., Hayes, E., & McCuistion, L. (2006). *Pharmacology: A nursing process approach* (5th ed., pp. 608-609). Philadelphia: W.B. Saunders.

19. **3**

Rationale: Hypotension is a common side effect associated with the use of this medication. Options 1, 2, and 4 also require assessment but are not the priority.

Test-Taking Strategy: Use the process of elimination and note the strategic word *priority*. Also, note that blood pressure is mentioned in the question and in option 3. Use of the ABCs—airway, breathing, and circulation—also will direct you to option 3. Review care of the client receiving this medication by the intravenous route if you had difficulty with this question.

Level of Cognitive Ability: Application
Client Needs: Physiological Integrity
Integrated Process: Nursing Process—assessment
Content Area: Delegating/Prioritizing
References: Gahart, B., & Nazareno, A. (2006). *2006 intravenous medications* (22nd ed., p. 195). St. Louis: Mosby.
Hodgson, B., & Kizior, R. (2007). *Saunders nursing drug handbook 2007* (p. 160). Philadelphia: W.B. Saunders.

20. **1**

Rationale: The antidote to heparin is protamine sulfate; it should be readily available for use if excessive bleeding or hemorrhage should occur. Vitamin K is an antidote for warfarin sodium. Aminocaproic acid is the antidote for thrombolytic therapy. Potassium chloride is administered for a potassium deficit.

Test-Taking Strategy: Knowledge regarding the various antidotes is needed to answer this question. Remember the antidote to heparin is protamine sulfate. Learn these antidotes if you had difficulty with this question.

Level of Cognitive Ability: Application
Client Needs: Physiological Integrity
Integrated Process: Nursing Process—implementation
Content Area: Adult health—cardiovascular
Reference: Gahart, B., & Nazareno, A. (2006). *2006 intravenous medications* (22nd ed., p. 639). St. Louis: Mosby.

21. **2**

Rationale: The therapeutic range for prothrombin time is 1.5 to 2 times the control for clients at high risk for thrombus. Based on the client's control value, the therapeutic range for this individual would be 16.5 to 22 seconds. Therefore the result is within the therapeutic range.

Test-Taking Strategy: Use the process of elimination. Look at the control value. Remembering that the purpose of anticoagulant therapy is to prolong clotting times will assist in eliminating options 3 and 4. Eliminate option 1, because there is no basis for repeating the test. Because the prothrombin value identified in the question is not even double the control, select option 2 from the remaining options. Review the therapeutic prothrombin level for a client at risk for pulmonary embolism if you had difficulty with this question.

Level of Cognitive Ability: Analysis
Client Needs: Physiological Integrity
Integrated Process: Nursing Process—assessment
Content Area: Adult health—cardiovascular
Reference: Chernecky, C., & Berger, B. (2004). *Laboratory tests and diagnostic procedures* (4th ed., p. 920). Philadelphia: W.B. Saunders.

22. **2**

Rationale: The client is experiencing an anaphylactic reaction to streptokinase, which is allergenic. The infusion should be stopped, the physician notified, and the client treated with epinephrine, antihistamines, and corticosteroids.

Test-Taking Strategy: Recall that an allergic reaction and possible anaphylaxis are risks associated with streptokinase therapy. Also, focusing on the signs and symptoms in the question will assist in answering the question. When a severe allergic reaction occurs, the offending substance should be stopped, and lifesaving treatment should begin. Review the adverse effects of this medication if you had difficulty with this question.

Level of Cognitive Ability: Analysis
Client Needs: Physiological Integrity
Integrated Process: Nursing Process—implementation
Content Area: Adult health—cardiovascular
Reference: Ignatavicius, D., & Workman, M. (2006). *Medical-surgical nursing: Critical thinking for collaborative care* (5th ed., p. 876). Philadelphia: W.B. Saunders.

23. **4**

Rationale: Enalapril (Vasotec) is an angiotensin-converting enzyme inhibitor. Angioedema is an adverse effect. Swelling of the tongue and lips can result in airway occlusion. Nausea, insomnia, and a cough can occur as side (not adverse) effects of the medication.

Test-Taking Strategy: Note the strategic word *adverse*. Use the ABCs—airway, breathing, and circulation—to direct you to option 4. Review the adverse effects of this medication if you had difficulty with this question.

Level of Cognitive Ability: Application
Client Needs: Physiological Integrity
Integrated Process: Teaching and Learning
Content Area: Pharmacology
Reference: Ignatavicius, D., & Workman, L. (2006). *Medical-surgical nursing: Critical thinking for collaborative care* (5th ed., pp. 459, 762). Philadelphia: W.B. Saunders.

24. **1**

Rationale: Nesiritide is a recombinant version of human B-type natriuretic peptide, which vasodilates arteries and veins. It is used for the treatment of decompensated heart failure, increases renal glomerular filtration, and increases urine output. Options 2, 3, and 4 are incorrect.

Test-Taking Strategy: Use the process of elimination. Nesiritide does not have antidysrhythmic properties. Dysrhythmias may be a side effect of the medication, so option 2 should be eliminated. Eliminate option 3 because the medication is a vasodilator and causes a decrease in blood pressure. Eliminate option 4 because the medication decreases pulmonary capillary wedge pressure (PCWP). Review the effects of this medication if you had difficulty with this question.

Level of Cognitive Ability: Analysis
Client Needs: Physiological Integrity
Integrated Process: Nursing Process—evaluation
Content Area: Pharmacology
References: Ignatavicius, D., & Workman, L. (2006). *Medical-surgical nursing: Critical thinking for collaborative care* (5th ed., p. 757). Philadelphia: W.B. Saunders.

25. **2**

Rationale: Thrombolytic agents dissolve existing clots, and bleeding can occur anywhere in the body. The nurse monitors for any obvious signs of bleeding and also for occult signs of bleeding, which would include hemoglobin and hematocrit values, blood pressure and pulse, neurological signs, assessment of abdominal and back pain, and the presence of blood in the urine or stool.

Test-Taking Strategy: Note the strategic words *least frequent assessment*. Remember that bleeding is the primary complication of thrombolytic therapy. Therefore, look for the option that is not related to bleeding. A change in neurological signs could indicate cerebral bleeding, abdominal and back pain could indicate abdominal bleeding, and change in blood pressure and pulse could be general indicators of hemorrhage. The presence of bowel sounds is unrelated to this medication. Review nursing considerations for the client receiving tissue plasminogen activator if you had difficulty with this question.

Level of Cognitive Ability: Analysis
Client Needs: Physiological Integrity
Integrated Process: Nursing Process—assessment
Content Area: Delegating/Prioritizing
Reference: Ignatavicius, D., & Workman, M. (2006). *Medical-surgical nursing: Critical thinking for collaborative care* (5th ed., p. 850). Philadelphia: W.B. Saunders.

26. **3**

Rationale: Thrombolytic therapy is contraindicated in a number of preexisting conditions in which there is a risk of uncontrolled bleeding, similar to the case in anticoagulant therapy. Thrombolytic therapy also is contraindicated in severe uncontrolled hypertension because of the risk of cerebral hemorrhage. Therefore, the nurse would report the results of the blood pressure to the physician before initiating therapy.

Test-Taking Strategy: Use the process of elimination and focus on the client's diagnosis. Options 1, 2, and 4 may be present in the client with pulmonary embolism but are not necessarily signs that warrant reporting before this therapy is initiated. Review the contraindications associated with the administration of this medication if you had difficulty with this question.

Level of Cognitive Ability: Analysis
Client Needs: Physiological Integrity
Integrated Process: Nursing Process—implementation
Content Area: Adult health—cardiovascular
Reference: Hodgson, B., & Kizior, R. (2007). *Saunders nursing drug handbook 2007* (p. 1080). Philadelphia: W.B. Saunders.

ALTERNATE ITEM FORMAT: MULTIPLE RESPONSE

Answer: 4, 5, 6

Rationale: The usual guidelines for administering nitroglycerin tablets for chest pain include administering one tablet every 5 minutes PRN for chest pain, for a total dose of three tablets. If the client does not obtain relief after taking a third dose of nitroglycerin, the physician is notified. Because the client is still complaining of chest pain, the nurse would administer a second nitroglycerin tablet. The nurse would assess the client's pain level and check the client's blood pressure before administering each nitroglycerin dose. There are no data in the question that indicate the need to call a Code Blue. Additionally, it is not necessary to contact the client's family unless the client has requested this.

Test-Taking Strategy: Focus on the data in the question. Use the steps of the nursing process to determine that assessing the client's pain level and checking the client's blood pressure are appropriate actions. Next, recalling the usual guidelines for administering nitroglycerin tablets will assist in determining that an appropriate action is to administer a second nitroglyc-erin tablet, 0.4 mg, sublingually. Review care of the client with chest pain and the guidelines for the administration of nitro-glycerin if you had difficulty with this question.

Level of Cognitive Ability: Application
Client Needs: Physiological Integrity
Integrated Process: Nursing Process—implementation
Content Area: Pharmacology
Reference: Ignatavicius, D., & Workman, M. (2006). *Medical-surgical nursing: Critical thinking for collaborative care* (5th ed., p. 847). Philadelphia: W.B. Saunders.

REFERENCES

Chernecky, C., & Berger, B. (2004). *Laboratory tests and diagnostic proce-dures* (4th ed.). Philadelphia: W.B. Saunders.

Gahart, B., & Nazareno, A. (2006). *2006 intravenous medications* (22nd ed.). St. Louis: Mosby.

Hodgson, B., & Kizior, R. (2007). *Saunders nursing drug handbook 2007.* Philadelphia: W.B. Saunders.

Ignatavicius, D., & Workman, L. (2006). *Medical-surgical nursing: Criti-cal thinking for collaborative care* (5th ed.). Philadelphia: W.B. Saunders.

Kee, J., Hayes, E., & McCuistion, L. (2006). *Pharmacology: A nursing process approach* (5th ed.). Philadelphia: W.B. Saunders.

Kee, J., & Marshall, S. (2004). *Clinical calculations: With applications to general and specialty areas* (5th ed.). Philadelphia: W.B. Saunders.

Lehne, R. (2007). *Pharmacology for nursing care* (6th ed.). Philadelphia: W.B. Saunders.

Lilley, L., Harrington, S., & Snyder, J. (2005) *Pharmacology and the nurs-ing process* (4th ed.). St. Louis: Mosby.

Mosby. (2007). *2007 Mosby's nursing drug reference* (20th ed.). St. Louis: Mosby.

Potter, P., & Perry, A. (2005). *Fundamentals of nursing* (6th ed.). St. Louis: Mosby.

Skidmore-Roth, L. (2006). *Mosby's 2006 nursing drug reference* (20th ed.). St. Louis: Mosby.

The Adult Client With a Renal System Disorder

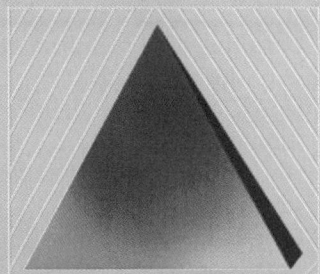

PYRAMID TERMS

acute renal failure The sudden loss of kidney function caused by renal cell damage from ischemia or toxic substances. Acute renal failure occurs abruptly and can be reversible. Acute renal failure leads to hypoperfusion, cell death, and decompensation in renal function. The prognosis depends on the cause and condition of the client. Near-normal or normal kidney function may resume gradually.

anuria Urine output of less than 100 mL/day.

arterial steal syndrome A syndrome that can develop following the insertion of an arteriovenous fistula when too much blood is diverted to the vein and arterial perfusion to the hand is compromised.

azotemia The retention of nitrogenous waste products in the blood.

chronic renal failure The progressive loss and ongoing deterioration in kidney function that occurs slowly over a period of time. Chronic renal failure is irreversible and results in uremia or end-stage renal disease. Chronic renal failure requires dialysis or kidney transplantation to maintain life.

disequilibrium syndrome A rapid change in the composition of the extracellular fluid that occurs during hemodialysis. Solutes are removed from the blood faster than from the cerebrospinal fluid and brain. Fluid is pulled into the brain, causing cerebral edema.

hemodialysis The process of cleansing the client's blood via the movement of dissolved particles from one fluid compartment into another across a semipermeable membrane. The client's blood flows through one fluid compartment, and the dialysate is in another fluid compartment.

internal arteriovenous fistula Surgical creation by anastomosis of an opening, or fistula, between a large artery and a large vein. The flow of arterial blood into the venous system causes the vein to become engorged (maturity). Maturity is necessary so that the engorged vein can be punctured for the dialysis procedure using a large-bore needle.

nephrolithiasis The formation of kidney stones. Kidney stones are formed in the renal parenchyma.

oliguria Urine output of less than 400 mL/day.

peritoneal dialysis The peritoneum is the dialyzing membrane (semipermeable membrane) and substitutes for kidney function during kidney failure. Dialysis works on the principles of diffusion and osmosis; the dialysis occurs via the transfer of fluid and solute from the bloodstream through the peritoneum.

renal failure The loss of kidney function. The types of renal failure include acute renal failure and chronic renal failure. The signs and symptoms of renal failure are caused by the retention of wastes, the retention of fluids, and the inability of the kidneys to regulate electrolytes.

urolithiasis The formation of urinary stones or calculi. Urinary calculi are formed in the ureter.

PYRAMID TO SUCCESS

Pyramid Points focus on acute renal failure and chronic renal failure, dialysis procedures such as hemodialysis and continuous ambulatory peritoneal dialysis, urinary diversions, and postoperative care following urinary or renal surgery. Focus on the major problems associated with renal failure and the rationale for the prescribed treatment modalities. Be familiar with the complications associated with hemodialysis and peritoneal dialysis, the specific assessment data related to complications, and the expected treatment. Focus on the care of a peritoneal catheter and hemodialysis access devices, the complications associated with these access devices, and the appropriate nursing interventions if a complication is suspected. Review preoperative and postoperative care related to renal transplantation and the assessment data indicating rejection. Be familiar with urinary diversions, care to the client following prostatectomy, and treatment measures for the client with urinary or renal calculi. The Integrated Processes addressed in this unit include Caring, Communication and Documentation, Nursing Process, and Teaching/Learning.

▲ CLIENT NEEDS

Safe and Effective Care Environment

Consulting with members of the health care team

Establishing priorities

Identifying the guidelines related to renal organ donation

Maintaining confidentiality related to the renal disorder

Maintaining sepsis related to wound care and dialysis access devices

Obtaining informed consent related to diagnostic and surgical procedures

Preventing injury related to complications associated with disorder

Maintaining standard and other precautions related to care of the client

Upholding client rights

Monitoring for fluid and electrolyte imbalances and acid-base disorders

Obtaining assessment data indicating rejection of renal transplant

Preventing complications arising as a result of dialysis

Providing adequate rest and sleep

Providing care related to dialysis access devices

Providing care related to hemodialysis and peritoneal dialysis

Providing care to the client following prostatectomy

Providing comfort interventions

Providing pharmacological therapy

Providing preoperative and postoperative care related to renal transplantation

Providing treatment measures for the client with urinary or renal calculi or the client with a urinary diversion

Teaching the client about the prescribed nutrition and fluid measures

Health Promotion and Maintenance

Discussing expected body image changes

Performing urinary and renal physical assessment techniques

Providing client instructions regarding care of a urinary diversion, dialysis access device, and dialysis procedures

Providing client instructions regarding postoperative management

Providing client instructions regarding prescribed treatments related to urinary or renal disorder

Providing client instructions regarding the prevention of the recurrence of a urinary or renal disorder

Psychosocial Integrity

Assisting the client to use appropriate coping mechanisms

Discussing body image disturbances

Discussing the loss of function of a body part that occurs in clients with a renal disorder

Identifying appropriate community resources

Identifying grief and loss and end-of-life issues

Identifying religious and spiritual influences on health

Identifying support systems

Physiological Integrity

Ensuring elimination measures

Informing the client about diagnostic tests and laboratory results

REFERENCES

Chernecky, C., & Berger, B. (2004). *Laboratory tests and diagnostic procedures* (4th ed.). Philadelphia: W.B. Saunders.

Harkreader, H., & Hogan, M. (2004). *Fundamentals of nursing: Caring and clinical judgment* (2nd ed.). Philadelphia: W.B. Saunders.

Ignatavicius, D., & Workman, M. (2006). *Medical-surgical nursing: Critical thinking for collaborative care* (5th ed.). Philadelphia: W.B. Saunders.

Jarvis, C. (2004). *Physical examination and health assessment* (4th ed.). St. Louis: W.B. Saunders.

Lewis, S., Heitkemper, M., & Dirksen, S. (2004). *Medical-surgical nursing: Assessment and management of clinical problems* (6th ed.). St. Louis: Mosby.

Lilley, L., Harrington, S., & Snyder, J. (2005). *Pharmacology and the nursing process* (4th ed.). St. Louis: Mosby.

Mosby. (2006). *Mosby's dictionary of medicine, nursing and health professions* (7th ed.). St. Louis: Mosby.

National Council of State Boards of Nursing (Eds.). (2007). *2007 NCLEX-RN® detailed test plan*. Chicago: Author.

Potter, P. & Perry, A. (2005) *Fundamentals of nursing* (6th ed.). St. Louis: Mosby.

Varcarolis, E., Carson, V., & Shoemaker, N. (2006). *Foundations of psychiatric mental health nursing: A clinical approach* (5th ed.). Philadelphia: W.B. Saunders.

61

Renal System

I. ANATOMY AND PHYSIOLOGY

A. Kidney anatomy
   1. Each person has two kidneys; one is attached to the left abdominal wall at the level of the last thoracic and first three lumbar vertebrae and the other is on the right.
   2. The kidneys are enclosed in the renal capsule.
   3. The renal cortex is the outer layer of the renal capsule, which contains blood-filtering mechanisms.
   4. The renal medulla is the inner region, which contains the renal pyramids.
   5. Together the renal cortex, pyramids, and medulla constitute the parenchyma, or functional unit of the kidneys.
   6. Nephrons
      a. The functional unit of the kidney; located within the parenchyma
      b. Composed of glomerulus and tubules
      c. Selectively secretes and reabsorbs ions and filtrates, including fluid, wastes, electrolytes, acids, and bases
   7. Glomerulus
      a. Each nephron contains tufts of capillaries, which filter large plasma proteins and blood cells.
      b. Blood flows into the glomerular capillaries from the afferent arteriole and flows out of the glomerular capillaries into the efferent arteriole.
   8. Bowman's capsule
      a. Thin double-walled capsule that surrounds the glomeruli
      b. Fluid and particles from the blood such as electrolytes, glucose, amino acids, and metabolic waste (glomerular filtrate) are filtered through the glomerular membrane into a fluid-filled space in Bowman's capsule (Bowman's space) and then enters the proximal convoluted tubule (PCT).
   9. Tubules
      a. The tubules include the PCT, Henle's loop, and the distal convoluted tubule (DCT).
      b. The PCT receives filtrate from the glomerular capsule and reabsorbs water and electrolytes through active and passive transport.
      c. The descending loop of Henle passively reabsorbs water from the filtrate.
      d. The ascending loop of Henle passively reabsorbs sodium and chloride from the filtrate and helps maintain osmolality.
      e. The DCT actively and passively removes sodium and water.
      f. The filtered fluid is converted to urine in the tubules, and then the urine moves to the pelvis of the kidney.
      g. The urine flows from the pelvis of the kidneys through the ureters and empties into the bladder.

B. Functions of kidneys
   1. Maintain homeostasis of the blood and acid-base balance
   2. Excrete end products of body metabolism
   3. Control fluid and electrolyte balance
   4. Excrete bacterial toxins, water-soluble drugs, and drug metabolites
   5. Secrete renin and erythropoietin, which play a role in the function of the parathyroid hormones and vitamin D

C. Urine production
   1. As fluid flows through the tubules, water, electrolytes, and solutes are reabsorbed and other solutes such as creatinine, hydrogen ions, and potassium are secreted.

2. Water and solutes that are not reabsorbed become urine.
3. The process of selective reabsorption determines the amount of water and solutes to be secreted.

D. Homeostasis of water
1. Antidiuretic hormone (ADH) is primarily responsible for the reabsorption of water by the kidneys.
2. ADH is produced by the hypothalamus and secreted from the posterior lobe of the pituitary gland.
3. Secretion of ADH is stimulated by dehydration or high sodium intake and by a decrease in blood volume.
4. ADH makes the distal convoluted tubules and collecting duct permeable to water.
5. Water is drawn out of the tubules by osmosis and returns to the blood; concentrated urine remains in the tubule to be excreted.
6. When ADH is lacking, the client develops diabetes insipidus (DI).
7. Clients with DI produce large amounts of dilute urine; treatment is necessary because the client is unable to drink sufficient water to survive.

E. Homeostasis of sodium
1. When the amount of sodium increases, extra water is retained to preserve osmotic pressure.
2. An increase in sodium and water produces an increase in blood volume and blood pressure (BP).
3. When the BP increases, glomerular filtration increases, and extra water and sodium are lost; blood volume is reduced, returning the BP to normal.
4. Reabsorption of sodium in the distal convoluted tubules is controlled by the renin-angiotensin system.
5. Renin, an enzyme, is released from the nephron when the BP or fluid concentration in the distal convoluted tubule is low.
6. Renin catalyzes the splitting of angiotensin I from angiotensinogen; angiotensin I converts to angiotensin II as blood flows through the lung.
7. Angiotensin II, a potent vasoconstrictor, stimulates the secretion of aldosterone.
8. Aldosterone stimulates the distal convoluted tubules to reabsorb sodium and secrete potassium.
9. The additional sodium increases water reabsorption and increases blood volume and BP, returning the BP to normal; the stimulus for the secretion of renin then is removed.

F. Homeostasis of potassium
1. Increases in the serum potassium level stimulate the secretion of aldosterone.
2. Aldosterone stimulates the distal convoluted tubules to secrete potassium; this action returns the serum potassium concentration to normal.

G. Homeostasis of acidity (pH)
1. Blood pH is controlled by maintaining the concentration of buffer systems.
2. Carbonic acid and sodium bicarbonate form the most important buffers for neutralizing acids in the plasma.
3. The concentration of carbonic acid is controlled by the respiratory system.
4. The concentration of sodium bicarbonate is controlled by the kidneys.
5. Normal arterial pH is 7.35 to 7.45, maintained by keeping the ratio of concentrations of sodium bicarbonate to carbon dioxide constant at 20:1.
6. Strong acids are neutralized by sodium bicarbonate to produce carbonic acid and the sodium salts of the strong acid; this process quickly restores the ratio and thus blood pH.
7. The carbonic acid dissociates into carbon dioxide and water; because the concentration of carbon dioxide is maintained at a constant level by the respiratory system, the excess carbonic acid is rapidly excreted.
8. Sodium combined with the strong acid is actively reabsorbed in the distal convoluted tubules in exchange for hydrogen or potassium ions. The strong acid is neutralized by ammonia and is excreted as ammonia or potassium salts.

H. Adrenal glands (see Chap. 53 for information about the adrenal glands)
1. One adrenal gland is on top of each kidney.
2. The adrenal glands influence blood pressure and sodium and water retention.

I. Bladder
1. The bladder detrusor muscle, composed of smooth muscle, distends during bladder filling and contracts during bladder emptying.
2. The ureterovesical sphincter prevents reflux of urine from the bladder to the ureter.
3. The total bladder capacity is 1 L; normal adult urine output is 1500 mL/day.

J. Prostate gland
1. The prostate gland surrounds the male urethra.
2. The prostate gland contains a duct that opens into the prostatic portion of the urethra and secretes the alkaline portion of seminal fluid, which protects passing sperm.

K. Risk factors associated with renal disorders (Box 61-1)

II. DIAGNOSTIC TESTS

A. See Chap. 11 and Box 61-2 for information regarding normal values for renal function studies.
B. Determination of serum creatinine level
1. Description: A test that measures the amount of creatinine in the serum. Creatinine is an end product of protein and muscle metabolism.

BOX 61-1

Risk Factors Associated With Renal Disorders

Chemical or environmental toxin exposure
Contact sports
Diabetes mellitus
Family history of renal disease
Frequent urinary tract infections
Heart failure
High-sodium diet
Hypertension
Medications
Trauma

BOX 61-2

Normal Renal Function Values

Blood urea nitrogen level, 8 to 25 mg/dL
Serum creatinine level, 0.6 to 1.3 mg/dL
Serum uric acid level, 2.5 to 8.0 mg/dL

2. Analysis
   a. Creatinine level reflects glomerular filtration rate.
   b. Renal disease is the only pathological condition that increases the serum creatinine level.
   c. Serum creatinine level increases only when at least 50% of renal function is lost.
C. Determination of blood urea nitrogen (BUN) level
   1. Description: A serum test that measures the amount of nitrogenous urea, a byproduct of protein metabolism in the liver.
   2. Analysis
      a. BUN levels indicate the extent of renal clearance of urea nitrogenous waste products.
      b. An elevation does not always mean that renal disease is present.
      c. Some factors that can elevate the BUN level include dehydration, poor renal perfusion, intake of a high-protein diet, infection, stress, corticosteroid use, and gastrointestinal (GI) bleeding.
      d. When the BUN and serum creatinine levels increase at the same rate the ratio of the BUN to creatinine remains constant, but elevated serum creatinine and BUN levels suggest renal dysfunction.
D. Urinalysis
   1. Description: A urine test for evaluation of the renal system and for determining renal disease
   2. Interventions
      a. Wash perineal area and use a clean container for collection.
      b. Obtain 10 to 15 mL of the first morning voiding.

   c. Refrigerated samples may alter the specific gravity.
   d. If the client is menstruating, note this on the laboratory requisition form.
E. Specific gravity determination
   1. Description: A urine test that measures the ability of the kidneys to concentrate urine
   2. Interventions
      a. Specific gravity can be measured by a multiple-test dipstick method (most common method), refractometer (an instrument used in the laboratory setting), or urinometer (least accurate method).
      b. Factors that interfere with an accurate reading include radiopaque contrast agents, glucose, and proteins.
      c. Cold specimens may produce a false high reading.
      d. Normal value is 1.016 to 1.022 (may vary depending on the laboratory).
      e. An increase in specific gravity (more concentrated urine) occurs with insufficient fluid intake, decreased renal perfusion, or increased ADH.
      f. A decrease in specific gravity (less concentrated urine) occurs with increased fluid intake or DI.
F. Urine culture and sensitivity testing
   1. Description: A urine test that identifies the presence of microorganisms and determines the specific antibiotics to treat the existing microorganism appropriately
   2. Interventions
      a. Clean the perineal area and urinary meatus with a bacteriostatic solution.
      b. Collect the midstream sample in a sterile container.
      c. Send the collected specimen to the laboratory immediately.
      d. Identify any sources of potential contaminants during the collection of the specimen, such as the hands, skin, clothing, hair, or vaginal or rectal secretions.
      e. Urine from the client who drank a very large amount of fluids may be too dilute to provide a positive culture.
G. Creatinine clearance test
   1. Description
      a. The creatinine clearance test evaluates how well the kidneys remove creatinine from the blood.
      b. The test includes obtaining a blood sample and timed urine specimens.
      c. Blood is drawn at the start of the test and when the urine specimen collection is complete.
      d. The urine specimen for the creatinine clearance is usually collected for 24 hours, but

shorter periods such as 8 or 12 hours could be prescribed.

2. Interventions
   a. Encourage fluids before and during the test.
   b. Instruct the client to avoid tea, coffee, and medications as prescribed during testing.
   c. If the client is taking corticosteroids or thyroid medication, check with the physician regarding the administration of these medications during testing.
   d. Instruct the client about the urine collection.
   e. At the start time, ask the client to void (or empty the tubing and drainage bag if the client has a Foley catheter) and discard that sample.
   f. Collect all urine for the prescribed time.
   g. Keep the urine specimen on ice or refrigerated and check with the laboratory regarding adding a preservative to the specimen during collection.
   h. At the end of the prescribed time, ask the client to empty the bladder (or empty the tubing and drainage bag if the client has a Foley catheter) and add that urine to the collection container.
   i. Send the labeled urine specimen to the laboratory in a biohazard bag along with the requisition.
   j. Document specimen collection, time started and completed, and pertinent assessments.

H. Uric acid test
   1. Description: A 24-hour urine collection sample is tested to diagnose gout and kidney disease.
   2. Interventions
      a. Encourage fluid intake and a regular diet during testing.
      b. Follow the same procedure for urine collection as with the creatinine clearance test.

I. Vanillylmandelic acid test
   1. Description
      a. The test is a 24-hour urine collection to diagnose pheochromocytoma, a tumor of the adrenal gland.
      b. The test determines urinary catecholamine levels in the urine.
   2. Interventions
      a. Check with the laboratory regarding medication restrictions.
      b. Instruct the client to avoid foods such as caffeine, cocoa, vanilla, cheese, gelatin, licorice, and fruits for at least 2 days before and during urine collection and to avoid taking medications for 2 to 3 days before the test, as prescribed.
      c. Instruct the client to avoid stress; encourage adequate food and fluid intake during the test.

d. Follow the same procedure for urine collection as for the creatinine clearance test.

J. KUB (kidneys, ureters, and bladder) radiography
   1. Description: An x-ray of the urinary system and adjacent structures is used to detect urinary calculi.
   2. Interventions: No specific preparation is necessary.

K. Bladder ultrasonography (bladder scanning)
   1. Bladder ultrasonography is a noninvasive method for measuring the volume of urine in the bladder.
   2. Bladder ultrasonography may be performed for evaluating urinary frequency, inability to urinate, or amount of residual urine (the amount of urine remaining in the bladder after voiding).

L. Computed tomography (CT) and magnetic resonance imaging (MRI)
   1. Description: These imaging methods provide cross-sectional views of the kidney and urinary tract.
   2. Interventions: See Chap. 65.

M. Intravenous pyelography
   1. Description: An intravenous injection of a radiopaque dye is used to visualize and identify abnormalities in the renal system.
   2. Preprocedure interventions
      a. Obtain an informed consent.
      b. Assess the client for allergies to iodine, seafood, and radiopaque dyes.
      c. Withhold food and fluids after midnight on the night before the test.
      d. Administer laxatives if prescribed.
      e. Inform the client about possible throat irritation, flushing of the face, warmth, or a salty taste during the test.
   3. Postprocedure interventions
      a. Monitor vital signs.
      b. Instruct the client to drink at least 1 L of fluid unless contraindicated.
      c. Assess the venipuncture site for bleeding.
      d. Monitor urinary output.
      e. Monitor for signs of a possible allergic reaction to the dye used during the test and instruct the client to notify the physician if any signs of an allergic reaction occur.

N. Renal angiography
   1. Description: An injection of a radiopaque dye through a catheter inserted into the femoral artery to examine the renal blood vessels and renal arterial supply
   2. Preprocedure interventions
      a. Obtain an informed consent.
      b. Assess the client for allergies to iodine, seafood, and radiopaque dyes.
      c. Inform the client about a possible feeling of burning or heat along the vessel when the dye is injected.

d. Withhold food and fluids after midnight on the night before the test.

e. Instruct the client to void immediately before the procedure.

f. Administer enemas if prescribed.

g. Shave injection sites as prescribed.

h. Assess and mark the peripheral pulses.

3. Postprocedure interventions

a. Assess vital signs and peripheral pulses frequently as prescribed

b. Maintain bed rest and apply a sandbag or other device that will provide pressure to prevent bleeding, if prescribed, at the insertion site for 4 to 8 hours.

c. Assess the temperature, color, sensation, and movement (CMS) of the toes of the involved extremity with each vital sign check.

d. Inspect the catheter insertion site for bleeding or swelling with each vital sign check.

e. Because the dye may be nephrotoxic, encourage increased fluids unless contraindicated and monitor urinary output.

O. Renal scanning

1. Description: An intravenous (IV) injection of a radioisotope for visual imaging of renal blood flow, glomerular filtration, tubular function, and excretion

2. Preprocedure interventions

a. Obtain an informed consent.

b. Assess for allergies.

c. Inform the client that the test requires no dietary or activity restrictions.

d. Assist with administering the radioisotope as necessary.

e. Instruct the client to remain motionless during the test.

f. Instruct the client that imaging may be repeated at various intervals before the test is complete.

3. Postprocedure interventions

a. Encourage fluid intake unless contraindicated.

b. Assess the client for signs of delayed allergic reaction such as itching and hives.

c. The radioactivity is eliminated in 24 hours; wear gloves for excretion precautions.

d. Follow standard precautions when caring for incontinent clients and double-bag client linens per agency policy.

P. Cystoscopy and biopsy

1. Description: The bladder mucosa is examined for inflammation, calculi, or tumors by means of a cystoscope; a sample for biopsy may be obtained.

2. Preprocedure interventions

a. Obtain an informed consent.

b. If a biopsy is planned, withhold food and fluids after midnight the night before the test.

c. If a cystoscopy alone is planned, no special preparation is necessary, and the procedure may be performed in the physician's office; postprocedure interventions include increasing fluid intake.

3. Postprocedure interventions following biopsy

a. Monitor vital signs.

b. Increase fluid intake as prescribed.

c. Monitor intake and output.

d. Encourage deep-breathing exercises to relieve bladder spasms.

e. Administer analgesics as prescribed.

f. Administer sitz or tub baths for back and abdominal pain.

g. Note that leg cramps are common because of the lithotomy position maintained during the procedure.

h. Assess the urine for color and consistency.

i. Inform the client that burning on urination, pink-tinged or tea-colored urine, and urinary frequency are common after cystoscopy and resolve in a few days.

j. Monitor for bright red urine or clots, and notify the physician if this occurs.

Q. Renal biopsy

1. Description: Insertion of a needle into the kidney to obtain a sample of tissue for examination; usually done percutaneously

2. Preprocedure interventions

a. Assess vital signs.

b. Assess baseline coagulation studies; notify the physician if abnormal results are noted.

c. Obtain an informed consent.

d. Withhold food and fluids after midnight the night before the test.

3. Interventions during the procedure: Position the client prone with a pillow under the abdomen and shoulders.

4. Postprocedure interventions

a. Monitor vital signs, especially for hypotension and tachycardia, which could indicate bleeding.

b. Provide pressure to the biopsy site for 30 minutes.

c. Monitor the hemoglobin and hematocrit levels for decreases, which could indicate bleeding.

d. Place the client in the supine position and on bed rest for 8 hours as prescribed.

e. Check the biopsy site and under the client for bleeding.

f. Encourage fluid intake of 1500 to 2000 mL as prescribed.

g. Observe the urine for gross and microscopic bleeding.

h. Instruct the client to avoid heavy lifting and strenuous activity for 2 weeks.

▲ III. **ACUTE RENAL FAILURE**

A. Description
   1. **Acute renal failure** (ARF) is the rapid loss of kidney function from renal cell damage.
   2. Occurs abruptly and can be reversible
   3. Signs and symptoms are primarily caused by the retention of wastes, the retention of fluids, and the inability of the kidneys to regulate electrolytes.
   4. **Acute renal failure** leads to cell hypoperfusion, cell death, and decompensation of renal function.
   5 The prognosis depends on the cause and the condition of the client.
   6. Near-normal or normal kidney function may resume gradually.

B. Causes
   1. Prerenal: Outside the kidney; caused by intravascular volume depletion, dehydration, decreased cardiac output, decreased peripheral vascular resistance, decreased renovascular blood flow, and prerenal infection or obstruction.
   2. Intrarenal: Within the parenchyma of the kidney; caused by tubular necrosis, prolonged prerenal ischemia, intrarenal infection or obstruction, and nephrotoxicity (Box 61-3).
   3. Postrenal: Between the kidney and urethral meatus, such as bladder neck obstruction, bladder cancer, calculi, and postrenal infection

C. Phases of **acute renal failure** and interventions (Box 61-4)
   1. Onset: Begins with precipitating event
   2. Oliguric phase
      a. Duration of 8 to 15 days; the longer the duration, the less chance of recovery.
      ▲ b. Sudden decrease in urine output; urine output is less than 400 mL/day.
      ▲ c. Signs of excess fluid volume: Hypertension, edema, pleural and pericardial effusions, dysrhythmias, congestive heart failure (CHF), and pulmonary edema
      d. Signs of uremia: Anorexia, nausea, vomiting, and pruritus
      e. Signs of metabolic acidosis: Kussmaul respirations
      f. Signs of neurological changes: Tingling of extremities, drowsiness progressing to disorientation, and then coma
      ▲ g. Signs of pericarditis: Friction rub, chest pain with inspiration, and low-grade fever
      ▲ h. Laboratory analysis (see Box 61-4)
      i. Restrict fluid intake; if hypertension is present, daily fluid allowances may be 400 mL to 1000 mL plus the measured urinary output.

j. Administer medications as prescribed such as diuretics (furosemide [Lasix]) to increase renal blood flow and diuresis.
   3. Diuretic phase
      a. Urine output rises slowly, followed by diuresis (4 to 5 L/day). ▲
      b. Excessive urine output indicates that damaged nephrons are recovering their ability to excrete wastes but not to concentrate urine.
      c. Dehydration, hypovolemia, hypotension, and tachycardia can occur.
      d. Level of consciousness improves.
      e. Laboratory analysis (see Box 61-4)
      f. Administer IV fluids as prescribed, which may contain electrolytes to replace losses.
   4. Recovery phase (convalescent)
      a. Recovery is a slow process; complete recovery may take 1 to 2 years.
      b. Urine volume returns to normal.
      c. Memory improves.

BOX 61-3

Potentially Nephrotoxic Substances

DRUGS
Antibiotics–Anti-Infectives
Amphotericin B
Colistimethate
Methicillin
Polymyxin B
Rifampin
Sulfonamides
Tetracycline hydrochloride
Vancomycin
Aminoglycoside Antibiotics
Gentamicin
Kanamycin
Neomycin
Netilmicin sulfate
Tobramycin
Antineoplastics
Cisplatin
Cyclophosphamide
Methotrexate
Nonsteroidal Anti-Inflammatory Drugs (NSAIDs)
Celecoxib
Flurbiprofen
Ibuprofen
Indomethacin
Ketorolac
Meclofenamate
Meloxicam
Nabumetone
Naproxen

Oxaprozin
Rofecoxib
Tolmetin
Other Drugs
Acetaminophen
Captopril
Cyclosporine
Fluorinate anesthetics
D-Penicillamine
Phenazopyridine hydrochloride
Quinine

OTHER SUBSTANCES
Organic Solvents
Carbon tetrachloride
Ethylene glycol
Nonpharmacological Chemical Agents
Radiographic contrast dye
Pesticides
Fungicides
Myoglobin (from breakdown of skeletal muscle)
Heavy Metals and Ions
Arsenic
Bismuth
Copper sulfate
Gold salts
Lead
Mercuric chloride

From Ignatavicius, D., & Workman, M. (2006). *Medical-surgical nursing: Critical thinking for collaborative care* (5th ed., p. 1731). Philadelphia: W.B. Saunders.

Acute Renal Failure Phases and Laboratory Findings

ONSET
Begins with precipitating event

OLIGURIC PHASE
Elevated blood urea nitrogen and serum creatinine levels
Decreased urine specific gravity (prerenal causes) or normal (intrarenal causes)
Decreased glomerular filtration rate
Hyperkalemia
Normal or decreased serum sodium level
Hypervolemia
Hypocalcemia
Hyperphosphatemia

DIURETIC PHASE
Gradual decline in blood urea nitrogen and serum creatinine levels, but still elevated
Low creatinine clearance
Hypokalemia
Hyponatremia
Hypovolemia

RECOVERY PHASE (CONVALESCENT)
Increased glomerular filtration rate
Stabilization or continual decline in blood urea nitrogen and serum creatinine levels toward normal
Complete recovery—may take 1 to 2 years

d. Strength increases.
e. The older adult is less likely than a younger adult to regain full kidney function.
f. Laboratory analysis (see Box 61-4)
g. **Acute renal failure** can progress to **chronic renal failure.**

D. Assessment: Assess objective and subjective data noted in the phases of ARF (see Box 61-4).

E. Other interventions
1. Monitor vital signs, especially for signs of hypertension, tachycardia, tachypnea, and an irregular heart rate.
2. Monitor urine and intake and output (hourly in **acute renal failure**) and urine color and characteristics.
3. Monitor daily weight (same scale, same time of the day), noting that an increase of $\frac{1}{2}$ to 1 lb/day indicates fluid retention.
4. Monitor for changes in the BUN, serum creatinine, and serum electrolyte levels.
5. Monitor for acidosis (may be treated with sodium bicarbonate).
6. Monitor urinalysis for protein level, hematuria, casts, and specific gravity.
7. Monitor for altered level of consciousness caused by uremia.

8. Monitor for signs of infection because the client may not exhibit an elevated temperature or an increased white blood cell count.
9. Monitor the lungs for wheezes and rhonchi and monitor for edema, which can indicate fluid overload.
10. Administer a prescribed diet, which is usually a moderate-protein (to decrease the workload on the kidneys) and high-carbohydrate diet.
11. Restrict potassium and sodium intake as prescribed based on the electrolyte level.
12. Administer medications as prescribed; be alert to the mechanism for metabolism and excretion of all prescribed medications.
13. Be alert to nephrotoxic medications, which may be prescribed (see Box 61-3).
14. Be alert to the health care provider's adjustment of medication dosages for **renal failure.**
15. Prepare the client for dialysis if prescribed; continuous renal replacement therapy may be used in ARF to treat fluid volume overload or rapidly developing **azotemia** and metabolic acidosis.
16. Provide emotional support by allowing opportunities for the client to express concerns and fears and by encouraging family interactions.
17. Promote consistency in caregivers.
18. Also refer to the section in this chapter on special problems in **renal failure** and interventions.

IV. **CHRONIC RENAL FAILURE**
A. Description
1. **Chronic renal failure** (CRF) is a slow, progressive, irreversible loss in kidney function.
2. It occurs in stages and results in uremia or end-stage renal disease (Box 61-5).
3. **Chronic renal failure** affects all major body systems and requires dialysis or kidney transplantation to maintain life.
4. Hypervolemia can occur because of the kidneys' inability to excrete sodium and water; hypovolemia can occur because of the kidneys' inability to conserve sodium and water.

B. Primary causes
1. May follow **acute renal failure**
2. Diabetes mellitus and other metabolic disorders
3. Hypertension
4. Chronic urinary obstruction
5. Recurrent infections
6. Renal artery occlusion
7. Autoimmune disorders

C. Assessment
1. Assess body systems for the manifestations of **chronic renal failure** (Box 61-6).

BOX 61-5
Stages of Chronic Renal Failure

STAGE I: DIMINISHED RENAL RESERVE
Renal function reduced
No accumulation of metabolic wastes
Decreased ability to concentrate urine
Nocturia and polyuria
Healthier kidney compensates

STAGE II: RENAL INSUFFICIENCY
Metabolic wastes begin to accumulate
Decreased responsiveness to diuretics
Decreased ability of the healthier kidney to compensate
Oliguria and edema

STAGE III: END STAGE
Excessive accumulation of metabolic wastes
Kidneys unable to maintain homeostasis
Dialysis or other renal replacement therapy required

BOX 61-6
Key Features of Chronic Renal Failure

NEUROLOGICAL MANIFESTATIONS
Lethargy and daytime drowsiness
Inability to concentrate or decreased attention span
Seizures
Coma
Slurred speech
Asterixis
Tremors, twitching, or jerky movements
Myoclonus
Ataxia (alteration in gait)
Paresthesias

CARDIOVASCULAR MANIFESTATIONS
Cardiomyopathy
Hypertension
Peripheral edema
Heart failure
Uremic pericarditis
Pericardial effusion
Pericardial friction rub
Cardiac tamponade

RESPIRATORY MANIFESTATIONS
Uremic halitosis
Tachypnea
Deep sighing, yawning
Kussmaul's respirations
Uremic pneumonia
Shortness of breath
Pulmonary edema
Pleural effusion
Depressed cough reflex
Crackles

HEMATOLOGICAL MANIFESTATIONS
Anemia
Abnormal bleeding and bruising

GASTROINTESTINAL MANIFESTATIONS
Anorexia
Nausea

Vomiting
Metallic taste in the mouth
Changes in taste acuity and sensation
Uremic colitis (diarrhea)
Constipation
Uremic gastritis (possible GI bleeding)
Uremic fetor
Stomatitis
Diarrhea

URINARY MANIFESTATIONS
Polyuria, nocturia (early)
Oliguria, anuria (later)
Proteinuria
Hematuria
Diluted, straw-like appearance

INTEGUMENTARY MANIFESTATIONS
Decreased skin turgor
Yellow-gray pallor
Dry skin
Pruritus
Ecchymosis
Purpura
Soft tissue calcifications
Uremic frost (late, premorbid)

MUSCULOSKELETAL MANIFESTATIONS
Muscle weakness and cramping
Bone pain
Pathological fractures
Renal osteodystrophy

REPRODUCTIVE MANIFESTATIONS
Decreased fertility
Infrequent or absent menses
Decreased libido
Impotence

From Ignatavicius, D., & Workman, M. (2006). *Medical-surgical nursing: Critical thinking for collaborative care* (5th ed.). Philadelphia: W.B. Saunders.

2. Assess psychological changes, which could include emotional lability, withdrawal, depression, anxiety, suicidal behavior, denial, dependence-independence conflict, and changes in body image.

D. Interventions
   1. Same as the interventions for ARF
   2. Administer a prescribed diet, which is usually a moderate-protein (to decrease the workload on the kidneys) and high-carbohydrate, low-potassium, and low-phosphorus diet.
   3. Provide oral care to prevent stomatitis and reduce discomfort from mouth sores.
   4. Provide skin care to prevent pruritis.
   5. Teach the client about fluid and dietary restrictions and the importance of daily weights.
   6. Provide support to promote acceptance of the chronic illness and prepare the client for long-term dialysis and transplantation, or explain to the client about his or her choice to decline dialysis or transplantation.

E. Special problems in **renal failure** and interventions (Box 61-7)
   1. Activity intolerance and insomnia
      a. Fatigue results from anemia and the buildup of wastes from the diseased kidneys.
      b. Provide adequate rest periods.
      c. Teach the client to plan activities to avoid fatigue.
      d. Administer mild central nervous system depressants as prescribed to promote rest.
   2. Anemia
      a. Anemia results from the decreased secretion of erythropoietin and decreased production of red blood cells as a result of the kidney disease.

Activity intolerance and insomnia
Anemia
Gastrointestinal bleeding
Hyperkalemia
Hypermagnesemia
Hyperphosphatemia
Hypertension
Hypervolemia
Hypocalcemia
Hypovolemia
Infection
Injury
Metabolic acidosis
Muscle cramps
Neurological changes
Ocular irritation
Potential for injury
Pruritis
Psychosocial problems

b. Monitor for decreased hemoglobin and hematocrit levels.
c. Administer epoetin alfa (Epogen, Procrit) or darbepoetin alfa (Aranesp), hematopoietics, as prescribed to stimulate the production of red blood cells.
d. Administer folic acid (vitamin B_9) as prescribed.
e. Administer iron orally as prescribed, but not at the same time as phosphate binders.
f. Administer stool softeners as prescribed because of the constipating effects of iron.
g. Note that oral iron is not well absorbed by the gastrointestinal tract in **chronic renal failure** and causes nausea and vomiting; parenteral iron (iron sucrose [Venofer] or sodium ferric gluconate complex [Ferrlecit]) may be used if iron deficiencies persist despite folic acid or oral iron administration.
h. Administer blood transfusions if prescribed; blood transfusions are prescribed only when necessary (acute blood loss, symptomatic anemia) because they decrease the stimulus to produce red blood cells; note that certain clients' religious beliefs (e.g., Jehovah's Witness) may teach them to refuse blood and blood products.
3. Gastrointestinal bleeding
a. Urea is broken down by the intestinal bacteria to ammonia; ammonia irritates the gastrointestinal mucosa, causing ulceration and bleeding.
b. Monitor for decreasing hemoglobin and hematocrit levels.

c. Monitor stools for occult blood.
d. Instruct the client to use a soft toothbrush.
e. Avoid the administration of acetylsalicylic acid (aspirin) because it is excreted by the kidneys; if administered, aspirin toxicity can occur and prolong the bleeding time.
4. Hyperkalemia
a. Monitor vital signs for hypertension or hypotension and the apical heart rate; an irregular heart rate could indicate dysrhythmias.
b. Monitor the serum potassium level; a serum potassium level above 6 mEq/L can cause tall, peaked T waves, flat P waves, a widened QRS complex, and a prolonged PR interval; decreased cardiac output; heart blocks; fibrillation; or asystole (Fig. 61-1).
c. Place the client on continuous cardiac monitoring because the client is at risk for dysrhythmias.
d. Provide a low-potassium diet, avoiding foods high in potassium (see Chap. 9 for a listing of foods that are high in potassium).

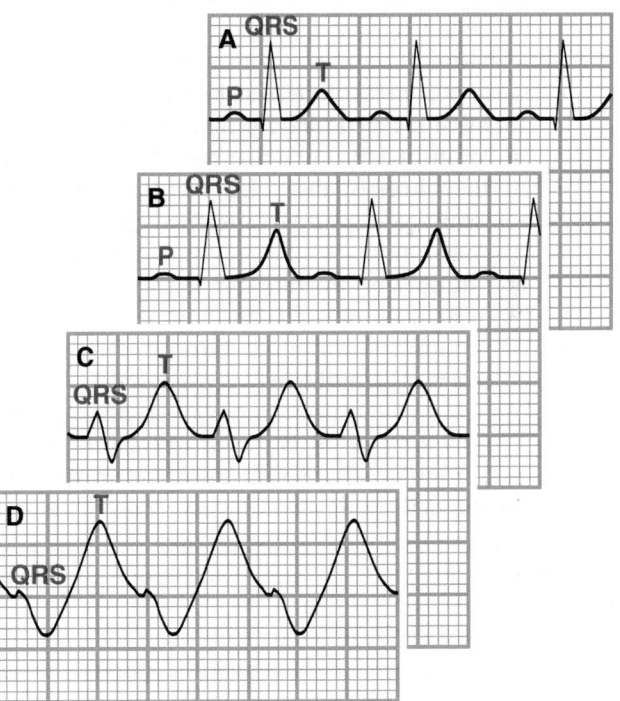

Serum Potassium Levels

A. Normal (3.5-5.1 mEq/L)
B. About 7.0 mEq/L
C. 8.0-9.0 mEq/L
D. >10.0 mEq/L

FIG. 61-1 Cardiac rhythm changes with hyperkalemia. *ECG*, Electrocardiogram. (From Huszar, R. J. [2002]. *Basic dysrhythmias: Interpretation and management* [3rd ed.]. St. Louis: Mosby.) Developed by Kathleen Ohman.

e. Administer electrolyte-binding and electrolyte-excreting medications such as oral or rectal sodium polystyrene sulfonate (Kayexalate) as prescribed to lower the serum potassium level.

f. Administer prescribed medications: 50% dextrose and insulin may be prescribed to shift potassium into the cell; calcium gluconate IV may be prescribed to reduce myocardial irritability from hyperkalemia; and sodium bicarbonate IV may be prescribed to correct acidosis.

g. Administer prescribed loop diuretics to excrete potassium.

h. Avoid potassium-sparing medications such as spironolactone (Aldactone) and triamterene (Dyrenium) because these medications will increase the potassium level.

i. Prepare the client for **peritoneal dialysis or hemodialysis** as prescribed.

5. Hypermagnesemia
   a. Results from decreased renal excretion of magnesium.
   b. Monitor cardiac manifestations of bradycardia, peripheral vasodilation, and hypotension.
   c. Monitor central nervous system (CNS) manifestations of decreased nerve impulse transmission, such as drowsiness or lethargy.
   d. Monitor neuromuscular manifestations, such as reduced or absent deep tendon reflexes or weak or absent voluntary skeletal muscle contractions.
   e. Administer loop diuretics as prescribed, such as furosemide.
   f. Administer calcium as prescribed for resulting cardiac problems.
   g. Avoid medications that contain magnesium, such as antacids, laxatives, or enemas.
   h. During severe elevations, avoid foods that increase magnesium levels (see Chap. 9 for a listing of foods that are high in magnesium).

6. Hyperphosphatemia
   a. As the phosphorus level rises, the calcium level drops; this leads to the stimulation of parathyroid hormone, causing bone demineralization.
   b. Treatment is aimed at lowering the serum phosphorus level.
   c. Administer phosphate binders such as calcium carbonate (TUMS), calcium acetate (PhosLo), or sevelamer (Renagel) as prescribed with meals to lower serum phosphate levels.
   d. Avoid aluminum hydroxide preparations to bind phosphates because they are associated with dementia and osteomalacia.
   e. Administer stools softeners and laxatives as prescribed because phosphate binders are constipating.
   f. Teach the client about the need to limit the intake of foods high in phosphorus (see Chap. 9 for a listing of foods that are high in phosphorus).

7. Hypertension
   a. Caused by failure of the kidneys to maintain BP homeostasis
   b. Monitor vital signs for elevated blood pressure.
   c. Maintain fluid and sodium restrictions as prescribed.
   d. Administer diuretics and antihypertensives as prescribed.
   e. Administer propranolol (Inderal), a β-adrenergic antagonist, as prescribed; propranolol decreases renin release (renin causes vasoconstriction).

8. Hypervolemia
   a. Monitor vital signs for an elevated blood pressure.
   b. Monitor intake and output and daily weight for indications of fluid retention.
   c. Monitor for periorbital, sacral, and peripheral edema.
   d. Monitor the serum electrolyte levels.
   e. Monitor for hypertension and notify the health care provider for sustained elevations.
   f. Monitor for signs of CHF and pulmonary edema, such as restlessness, heightened anxiety, tachycardia, dyspnea, basilar lung crackles, and blood-tinged sputum; notify the physician immediately if signs occur.
   g. Maintain fluid restriction.
   h. Avoid the administration of IV fluids.
   i. Administer diuretics such as furosemide as prescribed.
   j. Teach the client to maintain a low-sodium diet.
   k. Teach the client to avoid antacids or cold remedies containing sodium bicarbonate.

9. Hypocalcemia
   a. Results from the high phosphorus level and the inability of the diseased kidney to activate vitamin D
   b. The absence of vitamin D causes poor calcium absorption from the intestinal tract.
   c. Monitor the serum calcium level.
   d. Administer calcium supplements as prescribed.
   e. Administer activated vitamin D as prescribed.
   f. See Chap. 9 for a listing of foods that are high in calcium.

10. Hypovolemia
    a. Monitor the vital signs for hypotension and tachycardia.

b. Monitor for decreasing intake and output and a reduction in the daily weight.

c. Monitor for dehydration.

d. Monitor electrolyte levels.

e. Provide replacement therapy based on the serum electrolyte level values.

f. Provide sodium supplements as prescribed, based on the serum electrolyte level.

11. Infection

a. The client is at risk for infection caused by a suppressed immune system, dialysis access site, and possible malnutrition.

b. Monitor for signs of infection.

c. Avoid urinary catheters when possible; if used, provide catheter care.

d. Provide strict asepsis during urinary catheter insertion and other invasive procedures.

e. Instruct the client to avoid fatigue, which decreases body resistance.

f. Instruct the client to avoid persons with infections.

g. Administer antibiotics as prescribed, monitoring for nephrotoxic effects.

12. Metabolic acidosis

a. The kidneys are unable to excrete hydrogen ions or manufacture bicarbonate, resulting in acidosis.

b. Administer alkalizers such as sodium bicarbonate as prescribed.

c. Note that clients with **chronic renal failure** adjust to low bicarbonate levels and do not become acutely ill.

13. Muscle cramps

a. Occur from electrolyte imbalances and the effects of uremia on peripheral nerves

b. Monitor serum electrolyte levels.

c. Administer electrolyte replacements and medications to control muscle cramps as prescribed.

d. Administer heat and massage as prescribed.

14. Neurological changes

a. The buildup of active particles and fluids causes changes in the brain cells and leads to confusion and impairment in decision making ability.

b. Peripheral neuropathy results from the effects of uremia on peripheral nerves.

c. Monitor the level of consciousness and for confusion.

15. Ocular irritation

a. Calcium deposits in the conjunctiva cause burning and watering of the eyes.

b. Administer medications to control the calcium and phosphate levels as prescribed.

c. Administer lubricating eye drops.

d. Protect the client from injury.

e. Provide a safe and hazard-free environment.

f. Use side rails as needed.

g. Teach the client to examine areas of decreased sensation for signs of injury.

h. Provide a calm and restful environment.

i. Provide comfort measures and back rubs.

16. Potential for injury

a. The client is at risk for fractures caused by alterations in the absorption of calcium, excretion of phosphate, and vitamin D metabolism.

b. Provide for a safe environment.

c. Avoid injury; tissue breakdown causes increased serum potassium levels.

17. Pruritis

a. To rid the body of excess wastes, urate crystals are excreted through the skin, causing pruritis.

b. The deposit of urate crystals (uremic frost) occurs in advanced stages of **renal failure.**

c. Monitor for skin breakdown, rash, and uremic frost.

d. Provide meticulous skin care and oral hygiene.

e. Avoid the use of soaps.

f. Administer antihistamines and antipruritics as prescribed to relieve itching.

18. Psychosocial problems

a. Listen to the client's concerns to determine how the client is handling the situation.

b. Allow the client time to mourn the loss of kidney function.

c. With client permission, include the family members in discussions of the client's concerns.

d. Offer information about support groups.

e. Provide end-of-life care for the client with end-stage renal disease

V. UREMIC SYNDROME

A. Description

1. Accumulation of nitrogenous waste products in the blood caused by the kidneys' inability to filter out these waste products

2. Uremic syndrome may occur as a result of **acute** or **chronic renal failure.**

B. Assessment

1. **Oliguria**

2. Presence of protein, red blood cells, and casts in the urine

3. Urine specific gravity of 1.010

4. Elevated levels of urea, uric acid, potassium, and magnesium in the urine

5. Hypotension or hypertension

6. Alterations in the level of consciousness

7. Electrolyte imbalances

8. Stomatitis

9. Nausea or vomiting from **azotemia**
10. Diarrhea or constipation

C. Interventions
1. Monitor vital signs for hypertension, tachycardia, and an irregular heart rate.
2. Monitor serum electrolyte levels.
3. Monitor intake and output and for **oliguria.**
4. Provide a limited but high-quality protein diet as prescribed.
5. Provide a limited sodium, nitrogen, potassium, and phosphate diet as prescribed.
6. Assist the client to cope with body image disturbances caused by uremic syndrome.

VI. HEMODIALYSIS

A. Description
1. **Hemodialysis** is the process of cleansing the client's blood
2. It involves the diffusion of dissolved particles from one fluid compartment into another across a semipermeable membrane; the client's blood flows through one fluid compartment, and the dialysate is in another fluid compartment.

B. Functions of **hemodialysis**
1. Cleanses the blood of accumulated waste products
2. Removes the byproducts of protein metabolism such as urea, creatinine, and uric acid from the blood
3. Removes excess body fluids
4. Maintains or restores the buffer system of the body
5. Maintains or restores electrolyte levels in the body

C. Principles of **hemodialysis**
1. The semipermeable membrane is made of a thin, porous cellophane.
2. The pore size of the membrane allows small particles to pass through, such as urea, creatinine, uric acid, and water molecules.
3. Proteins, bacteria, and some blood cells are too large to pass through the membrane.
4. The client's blood flows into the dialyzer; the movement of substances occurs from the blood to the dialysate.
5. Diffusion is the movement of particles from an area of higher concentration to one of lower concentration.
6. Osmosis is the movement of fluids across a semipermeable membrane from an area of lower concentration of particles to an area of higher concentration of particles.
7. Ultrafiltration is the movement of fluid across a semipermeable membrane as a result of an artificially created pressure gradient.

D. Dialysate bath
1. A dialysate bath is composed of water and major electrolytes.

2. The dialysate need not be sterile because bacteria and viruses are too large to pass through the pores of the semipermeable membrane; however, the dialysate must meet specific standards, and water is treated to ensure a safe water supply.

E. Interventions
1. Hold antihypertensives and other medications that can affect the blood pressure or result in hypotension until after the dialysis treatment as prescribed.
2. Hold medications that could be removed by dialysis, such as water-soluble vitamins, certain antibiotics, and digoxin (Lanoxin).
3. Monitor vital signs before, during, and after dialysis; the client's temperature may elevate because of slight warming of the blood from the dialysis machine (notify the physician about excessive temperature elevations because this could indicate sepsis; obtain samples for blood culture as prescribed for excessive temperature elevations).
4. Monitor laboratory values before, during, and after dialysis.
5. Assess the client for fluid overload before dialysis and fluid volume deficit following dialysis.
6. Weigh the client before and after dialysis to determine fluid loss.
7. Assess the patency of the blood access device before, during, and after dialysis.
8. Monitor for bleeding; heparin is added to the dialysis bath to prevent clots from forming in the dialyzer or the blood tubing.
9. Monitor for hypovolemia and shock during dialysis, which can occur from blood loss or excess fluid and electrolyte removal.
10. Provide adequate nutrition; the client may eat before or during dialysis.
11. Identify the client's reactions to the treatment and support coping mechanisms; encourage independence and involvement in care.

VII. ACCESS FOR HEMODIALYSIS

A. Subclavian and femoral catheter (Fig. 61-2)
1. Description
   a. A subclavian (subclavian vein) or femoral (femoral vein) catheter may be inserted for short-term or temporary use in **acute renal failure.**
   b. The catheter is used until a fistula or graft matures or develops or may be required when the client's fistula or graft access has failed because of infection or clotting.
2. Interventions
   a. Assess insertion site for hematoma, bleeding, catheter dislodgement, and infection.
   b. These catheters should only be used for dialysis treatments.

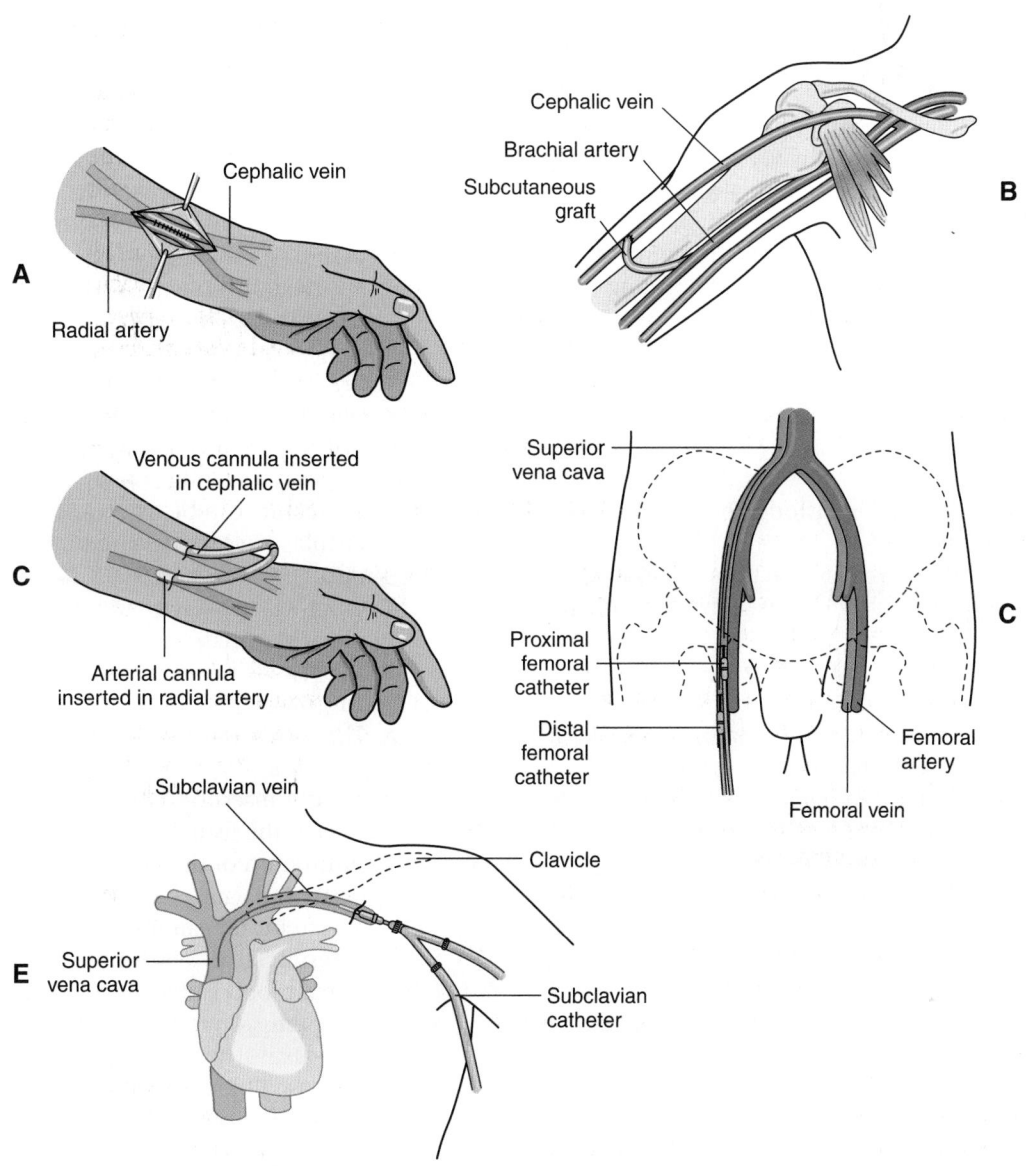

FIG. 61-2 Frequently used means for gaining vascular access for hemodialysis include arteriovenous fistula **(A)**, arteriovenous graft **(B)**, external arteriovenous shunt **(C)**, femoral vein catheterization **(D)**, and subclavian vein catheterization **(E)**. (From Phipps, W., Sands, J., Marek, J. [1999]. *Medical-surgical nursing: Concepts and clinical practice* [6th ed.]. St. Louis: Mosby.)

c. Maintain an occlusive dressing over the catheter insertion site.

3. Subclavian vein catheter
   a. The catheter is usually filled with heparin and capped to maintain patency between dialysis treatments.
   b. The catheter should not be uncapped except for dialysis treatments.
   c. The catheter may be left in place for up to 6 weeks if no complications occur.

4. Femoral vein catheter
   a. The client should not sit up more than 45 degrees or lean forward, because the catheter may kink and occlude.
   b. Assess the extremity for circulation, temperature, and pulses.

c. Prevent pulling or disconnecting of the catheter when giving care.
   d. Because the groin is not a clean site, meticulous perineal care is required.
   e. Use an IV infusion pump or controller with microdrip tubing if a heparin infusion through the catheter to maintain patency is prescribed.

B. External arteriovenous shunt (see Fig. 61-2)
   1. Description
      a. Two Silastic cannulas are surgically inserted into an artery and vein in the forearm or leg to form an external blood path.
      b. The cannulas are connected to form a U shape; blood flows from the client's artery through the shunt into the vein.

c. A tube leading to the membrane compartment of the dialyzer is connected to the arterial cannula.

d. Blood fills the membrane compartment, passes through the dialyzer, and is returned back to the client through a tube connected to the venous cannula.

e. When dialysis is complete, the cannulas are clamped and reattached, reforming the U shape.

2. Advantages
   a. The external arteriovenous shunt can be used immediately following its creation.
   b. No venipuncture is necessary for dialysis.

3. Disadvantages
   a. Disconnection or dislodgment of the external shunt
   b. Risk of hemorrhage, infection, or clotting
   c. Potential for skin erosion around the catheter site

4. Interventions
   a. Avoid getting the shunt wet.
   b. Wrap a dressing completely around the shunt and keep it dry and intact.
   c. Keep cannula clamps at the client's bedside or attached to the arteriovenous dressing for use in case of accidental disconnection.
   d. Teach the client that the shunt extremity should not be used for monitoring BP, drawing blood, placing IV lines, or administering injections.
   e. Fold back the dressing to expose the shunt tubing and assess for signs of hemorrhage, infection, or clotting.
   f. Monitor skin integrity around the insertion site.
   g. Auscultate for a bruit and palpate for a thrill, although a bruit may not be heard with the shunt.
   h. Notify the physician immediately if signs of clotting, hemorrhage, or infection occur.

5. Signs of clotting
   a. Fibrin-white flecks noted in the tubing
   b. Separation of serum and cells
   c. Absence of a previously heard bruit
   d. Coolness of the tubing or extremity
   e. Client complains of a tingling sensation.

C. **Internal arteriovenous fistula** (see Fig. 61-2)
   1. Description
      a. Access of choice for the client with CRF requiring dialysis
      b. The fistula is created surgically by anastomosis of a large artery and large vein in the arm.
      c. The flow of arterial blood into the venous system causes the vein to become engorged (matured or developed).

d. Maturity takes about 1 to 2 weeks, depending on the client's ability to do hand-flexing exercises such as ball squeezing, which help the fistula mature.

e. The fistula is required to be mature before it can be used because the engorged vein is punctured with a large-bore needle for the dialysis procedure.

f. Subclavian or femoral catheters, **peritoneal dialysis,** or an external arteriovenous shunt can be used for dialysis while the fistula is maturing or developing.

2. Advantages
   a. Because the fistula is internal, the risk of clotting and bleeding is low.
   b. The fistula can be used indefinitely.
   c. Fistulas have a decreased incidence of infection.
   d. Once healing has occurred, no external dressing is required.
   e. The fistula allows freedom of movement.

3. Disadvantages
   a. The fistula cannot be used immediately after insertion.
   b. Needle insertions through the skin and tissues to the fistula are required for dialysis.
   c. Infiltration of the needles during dialysis can occur and cause hematomas.
   d. An aneurysm can form in the fistula.
   e. **Arterial steal syndrome** can develop (too much blood is diverted to the vein, and arterial perfusion to the hand is compromised).
   f. Congestive heart failure can occur from the increased blood flow in the venous system.

D. Internal arteriovenous graft (see Fig. 61-2)
   1. Description
      a. The internal graft is used primarily for chronic dialysis clients who do not have adequate blood vessels for the creation of a fistula.
      b. An artificial graft made of Gore-Tex or a bovine (cow) carotid artery is used to create an artificial vein for blood flow.
      c. The procedure involves the anastomosis of the graft to the artery, tunneling under the skin, and anastomosis to a vein.
      d. The graft can be used 2 weeks after insertion.
      e. Complications of the graft include clotting, aneurysms, and infection.

   2. Advantages
      a. Because the graft is internal, the risk of clotting and bleeding is low.
      b. The graft can be used indefinitely.
      c. The graft has a decreased incidence of infection.
      d. Once healing has occurred, no external dressing is required.
      e. The graft allows freedom of movement.

3. Disadvantages
   a. The graft cannot be used immediately after insertion.
   b. Needle insertions through the skin and tissues to the graft are required for dialysis.
   c. Infiltration of the needles during dialysis can occur and cause hematomas.
   d. An aneurysm can form in the graft.
   e. **Arterial steal syndrome** can develop (too much blood is diverted to the vein, and arterial perfusion to the hand is compromised).
   f. Congestive heart failure can occur from the increased blood flow in the venous system.
E. Interventions for an arteriovenous fistula and arteriovenous graft
   1. Teach the client that the extremity should not be used for monitoring blood pressure, drawing blood, placing IV lines, or administering injections.
   2. Teach the client with an arteriovenous fistula hand-flexing exercises such as ball squeezing to promote graft maturity.
   3. Palpate for a thrill or auscultate for a bruit over the fistula or graft.
   4. Palpate pulses below the fistula or graft, and monitor for hand swelling as an indication of ischemia.
   5. Note the temperature and capillary refill of the extremity.
   6. Monitor for clotting.
      a. Complaints of tingling or discomfort in the extremity.
      b. Inability to palpate a thrill or auscultate a bruit over the fistula or graft.
   7. Monitor for **arterial steal syndrome.**
   8. Monitor for infection.
   9. Monitor lung and heart sounds for signs of CHF.
   10. Notify the physician immediately if signs of clotting, infection, or arterial steal syndrome occur.

VIII. COMPLICATIONS OF HEMODIALYSIS
(Box 61-8)
A. Air embolus
   1. Description
      a. Introduction of air into the circulatory system
      b. Results in cardiopulmonary complications
   2. Assessment
      a. Dyspnea and tachypnea
      b. Chest pain
      c. Hypotension
      d. Reduced oxygen saturation
      e. Cyanosis

BOX 61-8

Complications of Hemodialysis

Air embolus
Disequilibrium syndrome
Electrolyte alterations
Encephalopathy
Hemorrhage
Hepatitis
Hypotension
Sepsis
Shock

---

      f. Anxiety
      g. Changes in sensorium
   3. Interventions
      a. Stop dialysis.
      b. Administer oxygen.
      c. Turn the client on the left side, with the head down.
      d. Notify the physician (a medical emergency).
B. **Disequilibrium syndrome**
   1. Description
      a. A rapid change in the composition of the extracellular fluid occurs during **hemodialysis.**
      b. Solutes are removed from the blood faster than from the cerebrospinal fluid and brain; fluid is pulled into the brain, causing cerebral edema.
   2. Assessment
      a. Nausea and vomiting
      b. Headache
      c. Hypertension
      d. Restlessness and agitation
      e. Muscle cramps
      f. Confusion
      g. Seizures
   3. Interventions
      a. Slow or stop the dialysis.
      b. Notify the physician if signs of **disequilibrium syndrome** occur.
      c. Reduce environmental stimuli.
      d. Prepare to administer intravenous hypertonic saline solution, albumin, or mannitol (Osmitrol) if prescribed.
      e. Prepare to dialyze the client for a shorter period of time at reduced flow rates to prevent its occurrence.
C. Dialysis encephalopathy
   1. Description: An aluminum toxicity from dialysate water sources containing aluminum or from ingestion of aluminum-containing antacids (phosphate binders)
   2. Assessment
      a. Progressive neurological impairment

b. Mental cloudiness
c. Speech disturbances
d. Dementia
e. Muscle incoordination
f. Bone pain
g. Seizures
3. Interventions
a. Monitor for the signs of dialysis encephalopathy.
b. Notify the physician if signs of dialysis encephalopathy occur.
c. Administer aluminum-chelating agents as prescribed so that the aluminum is released and dialyzed from the body.

IX. PERITONEAL DIALYSIS
A. Description
1. The peritoneum acts as the dialyzing membrane (semipermeable membrane) and substitutes for kidney function during kidney failure.
2. **Peritoneal dialysis** (PD) works on the principles of osmosis, diffusion and ultrafiltration; PD occurs via the transfer of fluid and solute from the bloodstream through the peritoneum.
3. The peritoneal membrane is large and porous, allowing solutes and fluid to move via osmosis from an area of higher concentration in the body to an area of lower concentration in the dialyzing fluid.
4. The peritoneal cavity is rich in capillaries; therefore, it provides a ready access to the blood supply.
B. Contraindications to **peritoneal dialysis**
1. Peritonitis
2. Recent abdominal surgery
3. Abdominal adhesions
4. Impending renal transplant
C. Access for **peritoneal dialysis** (Fig. 61-3)
1. A siliconized rubber catheter such as a Tenckhoff catheter is surgically inserted into the client's peritoneal cavity to allow infusion of dialysis fluid.
2. The preferred insertion site is 3 to 5 cm below the umbilicus; this area is relatively avascular and has less fascial resistance.
3. The catheter is tunneled under the skin, through the fat and muscle tissue to the peritoneum; it is stabilized with Dacron cuffs in the muscle and under the skin.
4. Over a period of 1 to 2 weeks following insertion, fibroblasts and blood vessels grow into the cuffs, fixing the catheter in place and providing an extra barrier against dialysate leakage and bacterial invasion.
D. Dialysate solution
1. The solution is sterile.
2. The solution contains electrolytes and minerals and has a specific osmolarity, specific glucose concentration, and other medication additives as prescribed.
3. The higher the glucose concentration, the greater the hypertonicity and the amount of fluid removed during an exchange.
4. Increasing the glucose concentration increases the concentration of active particles that cause osmosis, increases the rate of ultrafiltration, and increases the amount of fluid removed.
5. If hyperkalemia is not a problem, potassium may be added to each bag of dialysate solution.

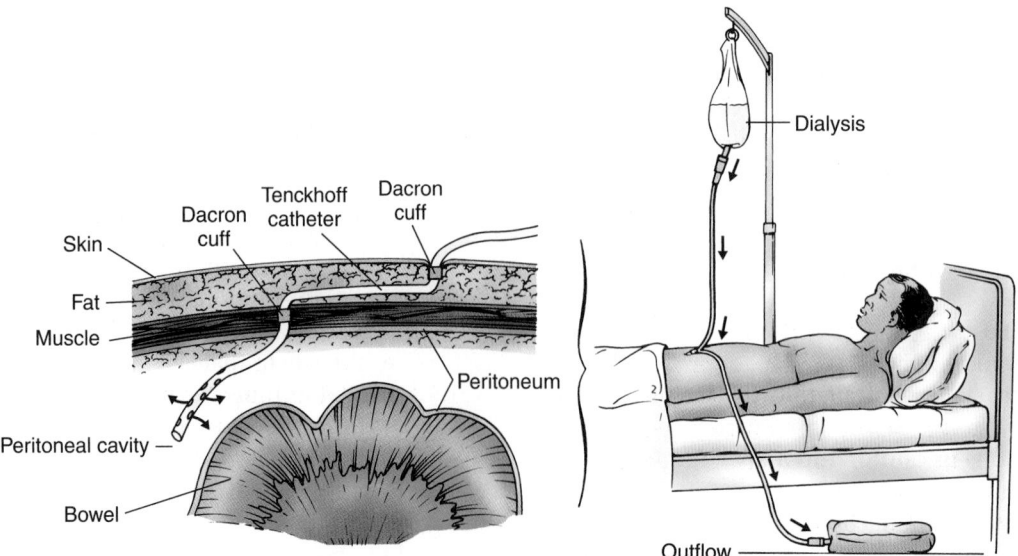

FIG. 61-3 Manual peritoneal dialysis via an implanted abdominal catheter (Tenckhoff catheter). (From Ignatavicius, D., & Workman, M. [2006]. *Medical-surgical nursing across the health care continuum* [5th ed.]. Philadelphia: W.B. Saunders.)

6. Heparin is added to the dialysate solution to prevent clotting of the catheter.
7. Prophylactic antibiotics may be added to the dialysate solution to prevent peritonitis.
8. Insulin may be added to the dialysate solution for the client with diabetes mellitus.

▲ E. **Peritoneal dialysis** infusion
1. Description
    a. One infusion (fill), dwell, and drain is considered one exchange.
    b. Infection is a concern with **peritoneal dialysis.**
    c. Fill: The infusion of 1 to 2 L of dialysate as prescribed is infused by gravity into the peritoneal space, which usually takes 10 to 20 minutes.
    d. Dwell time: The amount of time that the dialysate solution remains in the peritoneal cavity is prescribed by the physician and can last 20 to 30 minutes to 8 or more hours, depending on the type of dialysis used.
    e. Drain (outflow): Fluid drains out of body by gravity into the drainage bag.
2. Interventions before treatment
    a. Monitor vital signs.
    b. Obtain weight.
    c. Have the client void, if possible.
    d. Assess electrolyte and glucose levels.
3. Interventions during treatment
    a. Monitor vital signs.
    b. Monitor for signs of infection.
    c. Monitor for respiratory distress, pain, or discomfort.
    d. Monitor for signs of pulmonary edema.
    e. Monitor for hypotension and hypertension.
    f. Monitor for malaise, nausea, vomiting.
    g. Assess the catheter site dressing for wetness or bleeding.
    h. Monitor dwell time as prescribed by the physician and initiate outflow.
    i. Do not allow dwell time to extend beyond the physician's order because this increases the risk for hyperglycemia.
    j. Turn the client from side to side if the outflow is slow to start.
    k. Monitor outflow, which should be a continuous stream after the clamp is opened.
    l. Monitor outflow for color and clarity.
    m. Monitor intake and output accurately; if outflow is less than inflow, the difference is equal to the amount absorbed or retained by the client during dialysis and should be counted as intake.
F. Types of **peritoneal dialysis**
▲ 1. Continuous ambulatory **peritoneal dialysis** (CAPD)
    a. Closely resembles renal function because it is a continuous process

    b. Does not require a machine for the procedure
    c. Promotes client independence
    d. The client performs self-dialysis 24 hours a day, 7 days a week.
    e. Four dialysis cycles are usually administered in a 24-hour period, including an overnight 8-hour dwell time.
    f. Dialysate, 1½ to 2 L, is instilled into the abdomen four times daily and allowed to dwell as prescribed.
    g. The dialysis bag, attached to the catheter, is folded and carried under the client's clothing until time for outflow.
    h. After dwell, the bag is placed lower than the insertion site so that fluid drains by gravity flow.
    i. When full, the bag is changed, new dialysate is instilled into the abdomen, and the process continues.
2. Automated **peritoneal dialysis** (Box 61-9)
    a. Automated dialysis requires a peritoneal cycling machine.
    b. Automated dialysis can be done as intermittent **peritoneal dialysis,** continuous cycling **peritoneal dialysis,** or nightly **peritoneal dialysis.**

X. COMPLICATIONS OF PERITONEAL DIALYSIS (Box 61-10)
A. Abdominal pain
1. Peritoneal irritation during inflow commonly causes pain during the first few exchanges; the pain usually disappears after 1 to 2 weeks of dialysis treatments.

BOX 61-9

Types of Automated Peritoneal Dialysis

CONTINUOUS CYCLING PERITONEAL DIALYSIS
Dialysis requires a peritoneal cycling machine.
Dialysis usually consists of three cycles done at night and one cycle with an 8-hour dwell done in the morning.
The sterile catheter system is opened only for the on-and-off procedures, which reduces the risk of infection.
The client does not need to do exchanges during the day.

INTERMITTENT PERITONEAL DIALYSIS
Dialysis requires a peritoneal cycling machine.
Dialysis is not a continuous procedure.
Dialysis is performed for 10 to 14 hours, three or four times a week.

NIGHTLY PERITONEAL DIALYSIS
Dialysis is performed 8 to 12 hours each night, with no daytime exchanges or dwells.

BOX 61-10
Complications of Peritoneal Dialysis

Abdominal pain
Bladder or bowel perforation
Insufficient outflow
Leakage around the catheter site
Peritonitis

2. Warm the dialysate before administration using a special dialysate warmer pad, because the cold temperature of the dialysate can cause discomfort.
3. Place a heating pad on the client's abdomen during inflow to relieve discomfort; use a low setting and monitor the client closely.

B. Abnormal outflow characteristics indicative of complications
   1. Bloody outflow after the first few exchanges indicates vascular complications (the outflow should be clear and colorless after the initial exchanges).
   2. Brown outflow indicates bowel perforation.
   3. Urine-colored outflow indicates bladder perforation.
   4. Cloudy outflow indicates peritonitis.

C. Insufficient outflow
   1. The main cause of insufficient outflow is a full colon; encourage a high-fiber diet, because constipation can cause inflow and outflow problems. Administer stool softeners as prescribed.
   2. Insufficient outflow may also be caused by catheter migration out of the peritoneal area; if this occurs, notify the physician to reposition the catheter.
   3. Maintain the drainage bag below the client's abdomen.
   4. Check for kinks in the tubing.
   5. Check for fibrin clots in the tubing and milk the tubing to dislodge the clot as prescribed.
   6. Change the client's outflow position by turning the client to a side-lying position or ambulating the client.

D. Leakage around the catheter site
   1. Clear fluid that leaks from the catheter exit site will be noted.
   2. It takes 1 to 2 weeks following insertion of the catheter before fibroblasts and blood vessels grow into the catheter cuffs, which fix it in place and provide an extra barrier against dialysate leakage and bacterial invasion.
   3. Smaller amounts of dialysate need to be used; it may take up to 2 weeks for the client to tolerate a full 2-L exchange without leaking around the catheter site.

E. Peritonitis
   1. Monitor for symptoms of peritonitis: Fever, cloudy outflow, rebound abdominal tenderness,

abdominal pain, general malaise, nausea, and vomiting
   2. Cloudy or opaque outflow is an early sign of peritonitis.
   3. If peritonitis is suspected, obtain a sample for culture of the outflow to determine the infective organism.
   4. Administer antibiotics as prescribed.
   5. Avoid infections by maintaining meticulous sterile technique when connecting and disconnecting PD solution bags and when caring for the catheter insertion site.
   6. Prevent the catheter insertion site dressing from becoming wet during care of the client or the dialysis procedure; change the dressing if wet or soiled.
   7. Follow institutional procedure for connecting and disconnecting PD solution bags, which may include scrubbing the connection sites with an antiseptic solution.

XI. CONTINUOUS RENAL REPLACEMENT THERAPY
A. Description
   1. Continuous renal replacement therapy (CRRT) provides continuous ultrafiltration of extracellular fluid and clearance of urinary toxins over a period of 8 to 24 hours, primarily for clients in ARF or critically ill clients with CRF.
   2. Water, electrolytes, and other solutes are removed as the client's blood passes through a hemofilter.
   3. Because rapid shifts in fluids and electrolytes typically do not occur, hemofiltration is usually better tolerated by critically ill clients.
   4. There are five variations of CRRT (Box 61-11), some requiring a **hemodialysis** machine and others that rely on the client's blood pressure to power the system.
   5. It CRRT does not require a **hemodialysis** machine, the client's mean arterial blood pressure needs to be maintained above 60 mm Hg and arterial and venous access sites are necessary.

XII. KIDNEY TRANSPLANTATION (Fig. 61-4)
A. Description
   1. A human kidney from a compatible donor is implanted into a recipient.
   2. Kidney transplantation is performed for irreversible kidney failure.
   3. The recipient must take immunosuppressive medications for life.

B. Living related donors
   1. The most desirable source of kidneys for transplantation is living related donors who closely match the client.
   2. Donors are screened for ABO blood group, tissue-specific antigen, human leukocyte antigen suitability, mixed lymphocyte culture index (his-

tocompatibility), and the presence of any communicable diseases.

3. The donor must be in excellent health, with two
properly functioning kidneys.
4. The emotional well-being of the donor is determined.
5. Complete understanding of the donation process and outcome by the donor is necessary.

C. Cadaver donors
1. Cadaver donors must meet the criteria of brain
death.
2. Cadaver donors usually need to be younger than
70 years.
3. Cadaver donors must have normal renal function.
4. No malignant disease outside the central nervous system can be present.
5. No generalized infection or communicable disease can be present.
6. No abdominal or renal trauma can be present.
7. The potential donor must be negative for hepatitis B and C antigens and negative for human
immunodeficiency virus antibody.
8. Once cerebral death has been established for a
potential donor, restoration of intravascular volume, weaning from vasopressors, and establishing diuresis are crucial.
9. Continuous ventilation, and normal blood pressure and heart rate are maintained until the
kidneys are surgically removed.

D. Warm ischemic time
1. Warm ischemic time is the time elapsed between
the cessation of perfusion and cooling of the
kidney and the time required for anastomosis of
the kidney.
2. Maximal allowable warm ischemic time is 30 to
60 minutes.
3. If the kidney has been cooled, the maximum
transplantation time is up to 72 hours.

E. Preoperative interventions
1. Verify histocompatibility tests of identical twin
or family member.
2. Administer immunosuppressive medications to
the recipient as prescribed for 2 days before the
transplantation, if possible.
3. Maintain protective isolation for the recipient.
4. Verify that **hemodialysis** of the recipient was
completed 24 hours before transplantation.

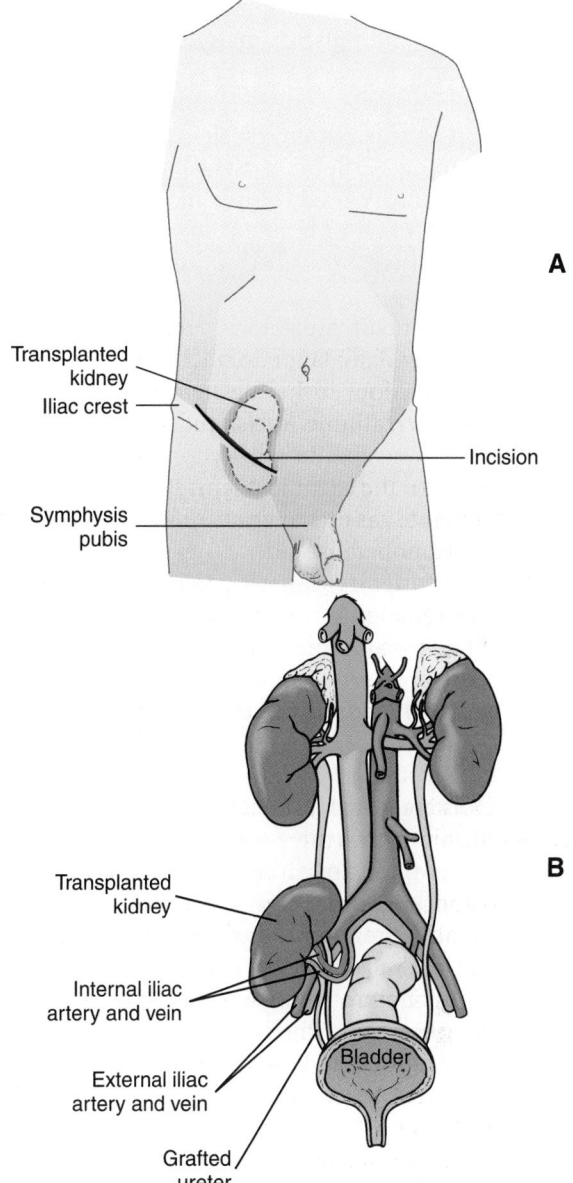

FIG. 61-4   **A,** Surgical incision for renal transplantation.
B, Surgical placement of transplanted kidney. (From
Lewis, S., Heitkemper, M., & Dirksen, S. [2004]. *Medical-
surgical nursing: Assessment and management of clinical
problems* [6th ed]. St. Louis: Mosby.)

5. Ensure that the recipient is free of any infections.
6. Assess renal function studies.
7. Encourage discussion of feelings of the donor
and the recipient.
8. Provide psychological support to the live donor
or cadaver donor family and the recipient.

F. Postoperative interventions for the recipient
1. Urine output usually begins immediately if the
donor was a living donor; it is delayed for a few
days or more with a cadaver kidney.
2. **Hemodialysis** is performed until adequate kidney function is established.

3. Monitor vital signs, central venous pressure (CVP), and pulse oximetry for signs of complications.
4. Monitor urine output hourly; immediately report a urine output less than 100 mL/hr.
5. Monitor IV fluids closely; for the first 12 to 24 hours, IV fluid volume includes replacement per milliliter of hourly urine output.
6. Administer prescribed diuretics and osmotic agents.
7. Monitor daily weight to evaluate fluid status.
8. Monitor daily laboratory results to evaluate renal function, including hematocrit, BUN, and serum creatinine levels, and monitor urine for blood and specific gravity.
9. Position the client in a semi-Fowler's position to promote gas exchange, turning from the back to the nonoperative side.
10. Monitor Foley catheter patency; the Foley catheter remains in the bladder for 3 to 5 days to allow for anastomosis healing.
11. Note that urine is pink and bloody initially but gradually returns to normal within several days to weeks.
12. Notify the physician if gross hematuria and clots are noted in the urine.
13. Monitor the three-way bladder irrigation, if present, for clots, if prescribed; irrigate only if a physician's order is present.
14. Remove the Foley catheter as soon as possible to prevent infection.
15. Maintain protective isolation precautions, including having the client wear a mask when out of the room, and monitor for infection.
16. Maintain strict aseptic technique with wound care.
17. Monitor for bowel sounds and for the passage of flatus; initiate a specific diet and oral fluids as prescribed when flatus and bowel sounds return (usually, fluids, sodium, and potassium are restricted if the client is oliguric).
18. Maintain good oral hygiene, monitoring for stomatitis and bacterial and fungal infections.
19. Encourage coughing and deep-breathing exercises.
20. Administer medications as prescribed, which may include antifungal medications, antibiotics, immunosuppressive agents, and corticosteroids.
21. The client is usually ambulated after 24 hours; avoid the sitting position.
22. Assess for organ rejection.
23. Promote live donor and recipient relationship.
24. Monitor both the donor and recipient for depression.
25. Provide the recipient with instructions following the kidney transplantation (Box 61-12)

BOX 61-12

Client Instructions Following Kidney Transplantation

Avoid prolonged periods of sitting.
Monitor intake and output.
Recognize the signs and symptoms of infection and rejection.
Use medications as prescribed, and maintain immunosuppressive therapy for life.
Avoid contact sports.
Avoid exposure to persons with infections.
Know the signs and symptoms that require the need to contact the physician.
Ensure follow-up care.

---

26. Assist the recipient to cope with the body image disturbances that occur from long-term use of immunosuppressants.
27. Advise the recipient of available support groups.

G. Graft rejection: Except for identical twin donor and recipient, the major postoperative complication is graft rejection.
  1. Assessment (Box 61-13)
  2. Hyperacute rejection
     a. Hyperacute rejection occurs immediately after surgery to 48 hours postoperatively.
     b. Interventions: Removal of rejected kidney
  3. Acute rejection
     a. Most common type; occurs within 6 weeks postoperatively, but can occur as late as 2 years
     b. Interventions: Potentially reversible with increased immunosuppression; administer high doses of corticosteroids, or monoclonal antibodies if corticosteroids are ineffective.
  4. Chronic rejection
     a. Occurs slowly months to years after transplant and mimics CRF.
     b. Interventions: Immunosuppressive medications.

XIII. CYSTITIS–URINARY TRACT INFECTION

A. Description
  1. Cystitis (urinary tract infection, UTI) is an inflammation of the bladder from an infection, obstruction of the urethra, or other irritants (Box 61-14).
  2. The most common causative organisms are *Escherichia coli* and *Enterobacter*, *Pseudomonas*, and *Serratia* species.
  3. Cystitis is more common in women because women have a shorter urethra than men and the urethra in the woman is located close to the rectum.
  4. Sexually active and pregnant women are most vulnerable to cystitis.

BOX 61-13
Clinical Signs of Renal Transplant (Graft) Rejection

Fever higher than 100° F (37.7° C)
Pain or tenderness over the grafted kidney
2- to 3-lb weight gain in 24 hours
Edema
Hypertension
Malaise
Signs of deteriorating renal function
Elevated blood urea nitrogen (BUN) and serum creatinine levels
Decreased creatinine clearance
Elevated white blood cell count (WBC)
Rejection indicated by ultrasound or biopsy

BOX 61-14
Causes of Cystitis

Allergens or irritants, such as soaps, sprays, bubble bath, perfumed sanitary napkins
Bladder distention
Calculus
Hormonal changes, influencing alterations in vaginal flora
Indwelling urethral catheters
Invasive urinary tract procedures
Loss of bactericidal properties of prostatic secretions in the male
Microorganisms
Poor-fitting vaginal diaphragms
Sexual intercourse
Synthetic underwear and pantyhose
Urinary stasis
Use of spermicides
Wet bathing suits

B. Assessment
1. Frequency and urgency
2. Burning on urination
3. Voiding in small amounts
4. Inability to void
5. Incomplete emptying of the bladder
6. Lower abdominal discomfort or back discomfort
7. Cloudy, dark, foul-smelling urine
8. Hematuria
9. Bladder spasms
10. Malaise, chills, fever
11. Nausea and vomiting
12. Altered mentation in older adults; frequency and urgency may not be specific symptoms of UTI in older adults because of urinary elimination changes with aging.

C. Interventions

1. Before administering prescribed antibiotics, obtain a urine specimen for culture and sensitivity, if prescribed, to identify bacterial growth.

2. Encourage the client to increase fluids up to 3000 mL/day, especially if the client is taking a sulfonamide; sulfonamides can form crystals in concentrated urine.
3. Administer prescribed medications, which may include analgesics, antiseptics, antispasmodics, antibiotics, and antimicrobials.
4. Maintain an acid urine pH (5.5); instruct the client about foods to consume to maintain acidic urine.
5. Provide heat to the abdomen or sitz baths for complaints of discomfort.

6. Note that if the client is prescribed an aminoglycoside, sulfonamide, or nitrofurantoin (Macrodantin), the actions of these medications are decreased by acidic urine.
7. Use strict aseptic technique when inserting a urinary catheter.
8. Maintain closed urinary drainage systems for the client with an indwelling catheter and avoid elevating the urinary drainage bag above the level of the bladder.
9. Provide meticulous perineal care for the client ▲ with an indwelling catheter.
10. Discourage caffeine products such as coffee, tea, and cola.
11. Client education
    a. Avoid alcohol.
    b. Take medications as prescribed.
    c. Take antibiotics on schedule and complete ▲ the entire course of medications as prescribed, which may be 10 to 14 days.
    d. Repeat the urine culture following treatment. ▲
    e. Prevent recurrence of cystitis (Box 61-15)

XIV. UROSEPSIS

A. Description
1. Urosepsis is a gram-negative bacteremia originating in the urinary tract.
2. The most common causative organism is *Escherichia coli*.
3. In a client who is immunocompromised, the most common cause is infection from an indwelling urinary catheter or an untreated UTI.
4. The major problem is the ability of this bacterium to develop resistant strains.
5. Urosepsis can lead to septic shock if not treated aggressively.

B. Assessment: Fever is the most common and earliest manifestation.

C. Interventions
1. Obtain a urine specimen for urine culture and sensitivity before administering antibiotics.
2. Administer antibiotics intravenously as prescribed, usually until the client has been afebrile for 3 to 5 days.

BOX 61-15

Teaching for Prevention of Cystitis

Use good perineal care, wiping front to back.
Avoid bubble baths, tub baths, and vaginal deodorants or sprays.
Void every 2 to 3 hours.
Wear cotton pants and avoid wearing tight clothes or pantyhose with slacks.
Avoid sitting in a wet bathing suit for prolonged periods of time.
If pregnant, void every 2 hours.
If menopausal, use estrogen vaginal creams to restore pH.
Use water-soluble lubricants for intercourse, especially after menopause.
Void and drink a glass of water after intercourse.

---

3. Administer oral antibiotics as prescribed after the 3- to 5-day afebrile period.

XV. URETHRITIS

A. Description
1. Inflammation of the urethra commonly associated with a sexually transmitted disease; may occur with cystitis.
2. In men, urethritis most often is caused by gonorrhea or chlamydial infection.
3. In women, urethritis most often is caused by feminine hygiene sprays, perfumed toilet paper or sanitary napkins, spermicidal jelly, UTI, or changes in the vaginal mucosal lining.

B. Assessment
1. Pain or burning on urination
2. Frequency and urgency
3. Nocturia
4. Difficulty voiding
5. Males may have clear to mucopurulent discharge from the penis.
6. Females may have lower abdominal discomfort.

C. Interventions
1. Encourage fluid intake.
2. Prepare the client for testing to determine whether a sexually transmitted disease (STD) is present.
3. Administer antibiotics as prescribed.
4. Instruct the client in the administration of sitz or tub baths.
5. If stricture occurs, prepare the client for dilation of the urethra and instillation of an antiseptic solution.
6. Instruct the female client to avoid the use of perfumed toilet paper or sanitary napkins and feminine hygiene sprays.
7. Instruct the client to avoid intercourse until the symptoms subside or treatment of the STD is complete.

8. Instruct the client about STDs if this is the cause.
   a. Prevent STDs by the use of latex condoms or abstinence.
   b. All sexual partners during the 30 days before diagnosis with chlamydial infection should be notified, examined, and treated if indicated.
   c. Chlamydial infection often coexists with gonorrhea; diagnostic testing is done for both STDs.
   d. Treatment for STDs includes antibiotics as prescribed to treat the causative organism.
   e. The most serious complication of chlamydial infection is sterility.
   f. Follow-up culture may be requested in 4 to 7 days to evaluate the effectiveness of medications.

XVI. URETERITIS

A. Ureteritis
1. Description: An inflammation of the ureter commonly associated with bacterial or viral infections and pyelonephritis
2. Assessment
   a. Dysuria
   b. Frequent urination
   c. Clear to mucopurulent penile discharge in males
3. Interventions
   a. Treatment includes identifying and treating the underlying cause and providing symptomatic relief.
   b. Administer metronidazole (Flagyl) or clotrimazole (Mycelex) as prescribed for treating *Trichomonas* infection.
   c. Administer nystatin (Mycostatin) or fluconazole (Diflucan) as prescribed for treating monilial infections.
   d. Doxycycline (Vibramycin) or azithromycin (Zithromax) may be prescribed for treating chlamydial infections.

XVII. PYELONEPHRITIS

A. Description
1. An inflammation of the renal pelvis and the parenchyma commonly caused by bacterial invasion
2. Acute pyelonephritis often occurs after bacterial contamination of the urethra or following an invasive procedure of the urinary tract.
3. Chronic pyelonephritis most commonly occurs following chronic urinary flow obstruction with reflux.
4. *Escherichia coli* is the most common causative bacterial organism.

B. Acute pyelonephritis
1. Acute pyelonephritis occurs as a new infection or recurs as a relapse of a previous infection.

2. It can progress to bacteremia or chronic pyelonephritis.
3. Assessment
   a. Fever and chills
   b. Nausea
   c. Flank pain on the affected side
   d. Costovertebral angle tenderness
   e. Headache
   f. Dysuria
   g. Frequency and urgency
   h. Cloudy, bloody, or foul-smelling urine
   i. Increased white blood cells in the urine
C. Chronic pyelonephritis
   1. A slow, progressive disease usually associated with recurrent acute attacks
   2. Causes contraction of the kidney and dysfunctioning of the nephrons, which are replaced by scar tissue
   3. Causes the ureter to become fibrotic and narrowed by strictures
   4. Can lead to **renal failure**
   5. Assessment
      a. Frequently diagnosed incidentally when a client is being evaluated for hypertension
      b. Poor urine-concentrating ability
      c. Pyuria
      d. **Azotemia**
      e. Proteinuria
D. Interventions
   1. Monitor vital signs, especially for elevated temperature.
   2. Encourage fluid intake up to 3000 mL/day to reduce fever and prevent dehydration.
   3. Monitor intake and output (ensure that output is a minimum of 1500 mL/24 hr).
   4. Monitor weight.
   5. Encourage adequate rest.
   6. Instruct the client in a high-calorie, low-protein diet.
   7. Provide warm, moist compresses to the flank area to help relieve pain.
   8. Encourage the client to take warm baths for pain relief.
   9. Administer analgesics, antipyretics, antibiotics, urinary antiseptics, and antiemetics as prescribed.
   10. Monitor for signs of **renal failure.**
   11. Encourage follow-up urine culture.

 XVIII. GLOMERULONEPHRITIS
A. Description
   1. Term that includes a variety of disorders, most of which are caused by an immunological reaction
   2. Results in proliferative and inflammatory changes within the glomerular structure
   3. Destruction, inflammation, and sclerosis of the glomeruli of both kidneys occur.
   4. The inflammation of the glomeruli results from an antigen-antibody reaction produced from an infection elsewhere in the body.
   5. Loss of kidney function occurs.
B. Causes
   1. Immunological or autoimmune diseases
   2. Group A beta-hemolytic streptococcal infection ▲
   3. History of pharyngitis or tonsillitis 2 to 3 weeks ▲ before symptoms
C. Types
   1. Acute glomerulonephritis occurs 5 to 21 days ▲ after a streptococcal infection.
   2. Chronic glomerulonephritis can occur after the acute phase or slowly over time.
D. Assessment
   1. Gross hematuria ▲
   2. Dark, smoky, cola-colored or red-brown urine; ▲ smoky urine occurs with bleeding in the upper urinary tract.
   3. Proteinuria that produces a persistent and excessive foam in the urine ▲
   4. Urinary debris
   5. Moderately elevated to high urine specific gravity
   6. Low urinary pH
   7. Urinalysis shows large numbers of erythrocytes
   8. **Oliguria** or **anuria**
   9. Headache
   10. Chills and fever
   11. Fatigue and weakness
   12. Anorexia, nausea, and vomiting
   13. Pallor
   14. Edema in the face, periorbital area, feet, or generalized
   15. Shortness of breath, ascites, pleural effusion, and CHF
   16. Abdominal or flank pain
   17. Hypertension
   18. Reduced visual acuity
   19. Increased blood urea nitrogen and serum creatinine levels
   20. Increased antistreptolysin O titer (used to ▲ diagnose disorders caused by streptococcal infections)
E. Interventions ▲
   1. Monitor vital signs, especially for hypertension and temperature elevations.
   2. Monitor intake and output and urine characteristics closely.
   3. Monitor daily weight.
   4. Monitor for edema.
   5. Monitor for fluid overload, ascites, pulmonary edema, and CHF.
   6. Restrict fluid intake as prescribed.
   7. Provide a high-calorie, low-protein, low-sodium, and low-potassium diet to prevent worsening **azotemia,** fluid retention, and hyperkalemia.
   8. Provide bed rest and limit activity.

9. Administer diuretics, antihypertensives, and antibiotics as prescribed.
10. Monitor for signs of **renal failure,** cardiac failure, and hypertensive encephalopathy.
▲ 11. Instruct the client to report signs of bloody urine, headache, or edema.
▲ 12. Instruct the client to obtain treatment for infections, especially sore throats, skin lesions, and upper respiratory infections.
F. Complications
   1. Heart failure
   2. Hypertensive encephalopathy
   3. Pulmonary edema
   4. Renal failure
   5. Nephrotic syndrome

XIX. NEPHROTIC SYNDROME
A. Description: A set of clinical manifestations arising from protein wasting caused by diffuse glomerular damage
B. Assessment
   1. Proteinuria
   2. Hematuria
▲ 3. Hypoalbuminemia
▲ 4. Edema (generalized periorbital that is most notable in the morning and dependent, such as in the ankles when sitting and in the sacrum or scrotum when lying)
   5. Hyperlipidemia
   6. Anemia
   7. Waxy pallor to the skin
   8. Anorexia
   9. Malaise
   10. Irritability
   11. Amenorrhea or abnormal menses
C. Interventions
   1. Monitor vital signs, especially for signs of hypertension from fluid excess or hypotension from fluid shifting into the tissues.
▲ 2. Monitor intake and output.
▲ 3. Bed rest is necessary if severe edema is present.
▲ 4. Monitor daily weights.
   5. Measure abdominal girth or extremity size.
▲ 6. Provide a low to moderate protein and sodium diet that is adequate in carbohydrates and calories as prescribed to prevent worsening **azotemia** and fluid retention.
   7. Monitor the serum potassium level; potassium may be restricted from the diet if the serum potassium level rises.
   8. Administer antihypertensives, diuretics, and lipid-lowering agents as prescribed.
   9. Administer corticosteroids and cytotoxic medications as prescribed.
   10. Administer plasma volume expanders, such as albumin, plasma, and dextran, to increase the osmotic pressure.

11. Administer anticoagulants as prescribed for clients who develop renal vein thrombosis.
12. Avoid trauma to edematous tissues.

XX. POLYCYSTIC KIDNEY DISEASE
A. Description
   1. A cystic formation and hypertrophy of the kidneys, which leads to cystic rupture, infection, formation of scar tissue, and damaged nephrons
   2. There is no specific treatment to arrest the progress of the destructive cysts.
   3. The ultimate result of this disease is **renal failure.**
B. Types
   1. Infantile polycystic disease: An inherited autosomal recessive trait that results in the death of the infant within a few months after birth
   2. Adult polycystic disease: An autosomal dominant trait that manifests between 30 and 40 years of age and results in end-stage renal disease
C. Assessment
   1. Often asymptomatic during the ages of 30 to 40 years
   2. Flank, lumbar, or abdominal pain that worsens with activity and is relieved when lying
   3. Fever and chills
   4. Urinary tract infections
   5. Hematuria, proteinuria, pyuria
   6. Calculi
   7. Hypertension
   8. Palpable abdominal masses and enlarged kidneys
D. Interventions ▲
   1. Monitor for gross hematuria, which indicates cyst rupture.
   2. Increase sodium and water intake because sodium loss rather than retention occurs.
   3. Provide bed rest if ruptured cysts and bleeding occur.
   4. Prepare the client for percutaneous cyst puncture for relief of obstruction or for draining an abscess.
   5. Administer antihypertensives as prescribed.
   6. Prevent and/or treat urinary tract infections.
   7. Prepare the client for dialysis or renal transplantation.
   8. Encourage the client to seek genetic counseling.
   9. Provide psychological support to the client and family.

XXI. HYDRONEPHROSIS
A. Description
   1. Distention of the renal pelvis and calices caused by an obstruction of normal urine flow
   2. The urine becomes trapped proximal to the obstruction.
   3. The causes include calculus, tumors, scar tissue, ureter obstructions, and hypertrophy of the prostate.
B. Assessment

1. Hypertension
2. Headache
3. Colicky or dull flank pain that radiates to the groin

C. Interventions
1. Monitor vital signs frequently.
2. Monitor for fluid and electrolyte imbalances, including dehydration after the obstruction is relieved.
3. Monitor for diuresis, which can lead to fluid depletion.
4. Monitor weights daily.
5. Monitor urine for specific gravity and albumin and glucose levels.
6. Administer fluid replacement as prescribed.
7. Prepare the client for insertion of a nephrostomy tube or a surgical procedure to relieve the obstruction if prescribed.

XXII. RENAL CALCULI

A. Description
1. Calculi are stones that can form anywhere in the urinary tract; however, the most frequent site is the kidneys.
2. Problems resulting from calculi are pain, obstruction, tissue trauma, secondary hemorrhage, and infection.
3. The stone can be located through radiography of the kidneys, ureters, and bladder, intravenous pyelography, CT scanning, and renal ultrasonography.
4. A stone analysis will be done after passage to determine the type of stone and assist in determining treatment.
5. **Urolithiasis** refers to the formation of urinary calculi; these form in the ureters.
6. **Nephrolithiasis** refers to the formation of kidney calculi; these form in the renal parenchyma.
7. When a calculus occludes the ureter and blocks the flow of urine, the ureter dilates, producing hydroureter (Fig. 61-5).
8. If the obstruction is not removed, urinary stasis results in infection, impairment of renal function on the side of the blockage, hydronephrosis (see Fig. 61-5), and irreversible kidney damage.

B. Causes
1. Family history of stone formation
2. Diet high in calcium, vitamin D, milk, protein, oxalate, purines, or alkali
3. Obstruction and urinary stasis
4. Dehydration
5. Use of diuretics, which can cause volume depletion
6. Urinary tract infections and prolonged urinary catheterization
7. Immobilization

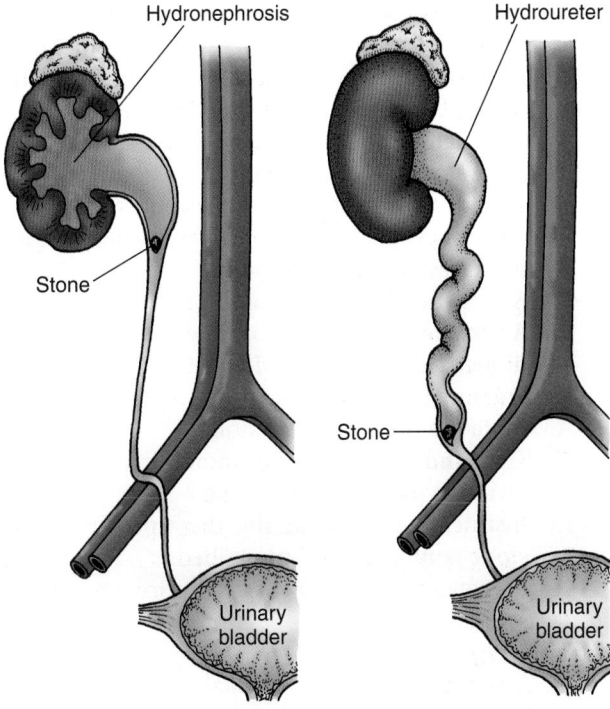

FIG. 61-5 Hydronephrosis and hydroureter. (From Ignatavicius, D., & Workman, M. [2006]. *Medical-surgical nursing across the health care continuum* [5th ed.]. Philadelphia: W.B. Saunders.)

8. Hypercalcemia and hyperparathyroidism
9. Elevated uric acid level, such as in gout

C. Assessment
1. Renal colic, which originates in the lumbar region and radiates around the side and down to the testicles in men and to the bladder in women
2. Ureteral colic, which radiates toward the genitalia and thighs
3. Sharp, severe pain of sudden onset
4. Dull, aching pain in the kidney
5. Nausea and vomiting, pallor, and diaphoresis during acute pain
6. Urinary frequency, with alternating retention
7. Signs of a urinary tract infection
8. Low-grade fever
9. High numbers of red blood cells, white blood cells, and bacteria in the urinalysis
10. Hematuria

D. Interventions
1. Monitor vital signs, especially the temperature, for signs of infection.
2. Monitor intake and output.
3. Assess for fever, chills, and infection.
4. Monitor for nausea, vomiting, and diarrhea.
5. Encourage fluid intake up to 3000 mL/day, unless contraindicated, to facilitate the passage of the stone and prevent infection.

6. Administer fluids intravenously as prescribed if unable to take fluids orally or in adequate amounts to increase the flow of urine and facilitate passage of the stone.
7. Strain all urine for the presence of stones.
8. Send stones to the laboratory for analysis.
9. Provide warm baths and heat to the flank area.
10. Administer analgesics at regularly scheduled intervals as prescribed to relieve pain.
11. Assess the client's response to pain medication.
12. Assist the client in performing relaxation techniques to assist in relieving pain.
13. Encourage client ambulation, if stable, to promote the passage of the stone.
14. Turn and reposition the immobilized client to promote passage of the stone.
15. Instruct the client in the diet specific to the stone composition if prescribed.
16. Prepare the client for surgical procedures if prescribed

E. Stone composition
1. A special diet, such as an alkaline-ash or acid-ash diet, may be prescribed, depending on the physician's preference (Boxes 61-16 and 61-17).
2. Calcium phosphate stones
   a. Caused by supersaturation of urine with calcium and phosphate
   b. Diet includes acid-ash foods because calcium stones are alkaline.
   c. Dietary prescription may include decreasing intake of foods high in calcium and phosphate to reduce urinary calcium content and avoiding excess vitamin D intake to prevent stones from forming.
   d. Medications prescribed for calcium stones may include phosphates, thiazide diuretics, and allopurinol (Zyloprim).
3. Calcium oxalate stones
   a. Caused by supersaturation of urine with calcium and oxalate
   b. Diet includes acid-ash foods because calcium stones are alkaline.
   c. Dietary prescription may include decreasing the intake of foods high in calcium and avoiding oxalate food sources to reduce urinary oxalate content and stone formation.
   d. Oxalate-rich food sources include tea, almonds, cashews, chocolate, cocoa, beans, spinach, and rhubarb.
   e. Allopurinol, pyridoxine (vitamin B_6), or magnesium oxide may be prescribed for clients with oxalate stones.
4. Struvite stones
   a. Also called triple-phosphate stones; composed of magnesium and ammonium phosphate
   b. Struvite stones are caused by urea-splitting bacteria and tend to form in alkaline urine.
   c. Diet includes acid-ash foods and includes limiting high-phosphate foods such as dairy products, red and organ meats, and whole grains to reduce urinary phosphate content.
   d. Treatment includes controlling infection with antibiotics (long-term antibiotic use may be prescribed).
5. Uric acid stones
   a. Caused by excess dietary purine or from gout
   b. Tend to form in acidic urine
   c. Dietary prescription to reduce urinary purine content may include alkaline-ash foods and decreased intake of high-purine foods such as organ meats, gravies, red wines, and sardines.
   d. Allopurinol may be prescribed to lower uric acid levels.
6. Cystine stones
   a. Caused by cystine crystal formation; tend to form in acidic urine
   b. Diet includes alkaline-ash foods; dietary prescription also may include a low intake of methionine, an essential amino acid that forms cystine. The client would be instructed to avoid meat, milk, cheese, and eggs.

BOX 61-16

Alkaline-Ash Diet

OUTCOME
Diet increases the pH of the urine.
Diet reduces the acidity of the urine.

FOODS TO INCLUDE
Fruits, except cranberries, plums, and prunes
Milk
Most vegetables
Rhubarb
Small amounts of beef, halibut, veal, trout, and salmon

BOX 61-17

Acid-Ash Diet

OUTCOME
Diet decreases the pH of the urine.
Diet makes the urine more acidic.

FOODS TO INCLUDE
Bread, cereal, whole grains
Cheese, eggs
Corn and legumes
Cranberries, prunes, plums, tomatoes
Meat, fish, oysters, poultry
Pastries

c. Dietary measures also focus on encouraging fluid intake up to 3 L/day, unless contraindicated, to help dilute the urine and prevent cystine crystals from forming.

d. Long-term antibiotic use may be prescribed for clients with cystine stones.

XXIII. **TREATMENT OPTIONS FOR RENAL CALCULI** (Fig. 61-6)

A. Cystoscopy
1. Cystoscopy may be done for stones in the bladder or lower ureter.
2. No incision is made.
3. One or two ureteral catheters are inserted past the stone; the stone may be manipulated and dislodged by the procedure and the catheters may guide the stones mechanically downward as they are removed.
4. The catheters are left in place for 24 hours to drain the urine trapped proximal to the stone and to dilate the ureter.
5. A continuous chemical irrigation may be prescribed to dissolve the stone.

B. Extracorporeal shock wave lithotripsy (ESWL)
1. A noninvasive mechanical procedure for breaking up stones located in the kidney or upper ureter so that they can pass spontaneously or be removed by other methods
2. No incision is made and no drains are placed; a stent may be placed to facilitate passing stone fragments.
3. Fluoroscopy is used to visualize the stone and ultrasonic waves are delivered to the areas of the stone to disintegrate it.
4. The stones are passed in the urine within a few days.

5. Preprocedure: Maintain the client on an NPO status for 8 hours before the procedure.
6. Postprocedure
   a. Monitor vital signs, especially for hypotension and tachycardia, which could indicate bleeding.
   b. Monitor intake and output.
   c. Monitor for bleeding; hematuria is common after lithotripsy.
   d. Monitor for pain and signs of urinary obstruction.
   e. Instruct the client that the ureteral stent placed to help the stone pass is removed in 1 to 2 weeks.
   f. Instruct the client to increase fluid intake to flush out the stone fragments.
   g. Inform the client that ambulation is important.

C. Percutaneous lithotripsy
1. Performed for stones in the bladder, ureter, or kidney
2. An invasive procedure in which a guide is inserted under fluoroscopy near the area of the stone; an ultrasonic wave is aimed at the stone to break it into fragments.
3. Percutaneous lithotripsy may be performed via cystoscopy or nephroscopy.
4. No incision is required for cystoscopy; a small flank incision is needed for nephroscopy.
5. The client might have an indwelling catheter.
6. A nephrostomy tube may be placed to administer chemical irrigations to break up the stone; the nephrostomy tube may remain in place for 1 to 5 days.
7. Encourage the client to drink 3000 to 4000 mL of fluid/day following the procedure.

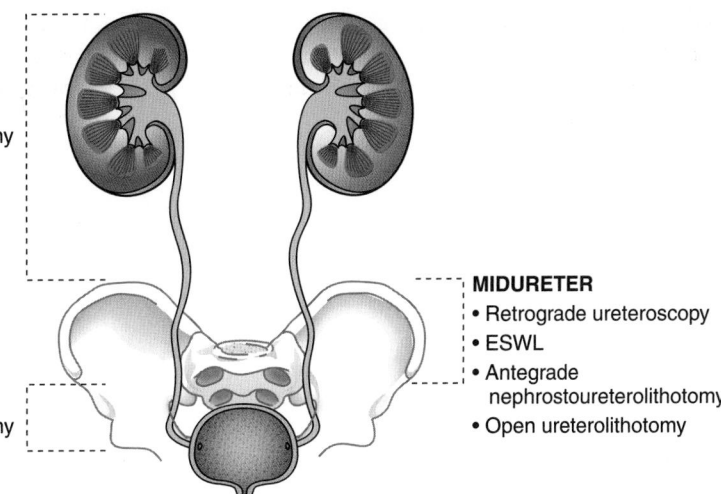

PROXIMAL URETER
- ESWL
- Retrograde ureteroscopy
- Antegrade nephrostoureterolithotomy
- Stenting alone
- Percutaneous ureterolithotomy or nephrolithotomy

DISTAL URETER
- ESWL/ureteroscopy
- Antegrade nephrostoureterolithotomy
- Stenting alone
- Open ureterolithotomy

MIDURETER
- Retrograde ureteroscopy
- ESWL
- Antegrade nephrostoureterolithotomy
- Open ureterolithotomy

FIG. 61-6 Treatment options for ureteral stones. (From Ignatavicius, D., & Workman, M. [2006]. *Medical-surgical nursing across the health care continuum* [5th ed.]. Philadelphia: W.B. Saunders.)

8. Monitor for and instruct the client to monitor for complications of infection, hemorrhage, and extravasation of fluid into the retroperitoneal cavity.

D. Ureterolithotomy
1. An open surgical procedure performed if lithotripsy is not effective for removal of a stone in the ureter
2. An incision is made through the lower abdomen or flank and then into the ureter to remove the stone.
3. The client may have a Penrose drain, ureteral stent catheter, and/or indwelling bladder catheter.

E. Pyelolithotomy and nephrolithotomy
1. Pyelolithotomy is an incision into the renal pelvis to remove a stone; a large flank incision is required and the client may have a Penrose drain and indwelling bladder catheter.
2. Nephrolithotomy is an incision into the kidney made to remove a stone; a large flank incision is required, and the client may have a nephrostomy tube and an indwelling bladder catheter.

F. Partial or total nephrectomy
1. Performed for extensive kidney damage, renal infection, severe obstruction from stones or tumors, and prevention of stone recurrence
2. Postoperative interventions
   a. The plan of care depends on the incision location and the type of drainage tubes present.
   b. Monitor the incision, particularly if a Penrose drain is in place, because it will drain large amounts of urine.
   c. Protect the skin from urinary drainage, changing dressings frequently if necessary.
   d. Place an ostomy pouch over the Penrose drain to protect the skin if urinary drainage is excessive.
   e. Monitor the nephrostomy tube, which may be attached to a drainage bag, for a continuous flow of urine.
   f. Do not irrigate catheters unless specifically prescribed.
   g. Monitor the indwelling bladder (Foley) catheter for drainage.
   h. Encourage fluid intake to ensure a urine output of 2500 to 3000 mL/day or more.
   i. Measure intake and output accurately.
   j. If a stone was removed, determine its composition from laboratory analysis.

XXIV. KIDNEY TUMORS
A. Description
1. Kidney tumors may be benign or malignant, bilateral or unilateral.
2. Common sites of metastasis include bone, lungs, liver, spleen, and other kidney.
3. The exact cause of renal carcinoma is unknown.

B. Assessment of clients with advanced disease
1. Dull flank pain
2. Palpable renal mass
3. Painless gross hematuria

C. Radical nephrectomy
1. Description
   a. Surgical removal of the entire kidney, adjacent adrenal gland, and renal artery and vein
   b. Radiation therapy and possibly chemotherapy may follow radical nephrectomy.
   c. Before surgery, radiation may be used to embolize (occlude) the arteries supplying the kidney to reduce bleeding during nephrectomy.
2. Postoperative interventions
   a. Monitor vital signs for signs of bleeding (hypotension and tachycardia).
   b. Monitor for abdominal distension, decreases in urinary output, and alterations in level of consciousness as signs of bleeding; check the bed linens under the client for bleeding.
   c. Monitor for signs of adrenal insufficiency, which include a large urinary output followed by hypotension and subsequent **oliguria.**
   d. Administer fluids and packed red blood cells intravenously as prescribed.
   e. Monitor intake and output and daily weight.
   f. Monitor for a urinary output of 30 to 50 mL/hr to ensure adequate renal function.
   g. Monitor urine specific gravity.
   h. Maintain the client in a semi-Fowler's position.
   i. Monitor for signs of respiratory complications related to surgery; encourage coughing and deep-breathing exercises.
   j. Monitor for passing of flatus and bowel sounds (lack of flatus and bowel sounds can be indicative of paralytic ileus).
   k. Apply antiembolism stockings as prescribed.
   l. If a nephrostomy tube is in place, do not irrigate (unless specifically prescribed) or manipulate the tube.
   m. Administer pain medications as prescribed.

XXV. EPIDIDYMITIS
A. Description
1. Acute or chronic inflammation of the epididymis that occurs as a result of a UTI, STD, prostatitis, or long-term use of a Foley catheter
2. The infective organism travels upward through the urethra and ejaculatory duct and along the vas deferens to the epididymis.

B. Assessment
1. Scrotal pain
2. Groin pain
3. Swelling in the scrotum and groin
4. Pus and bacteria in the urine

5. Fever and chills
6. Abscess development
C. Interventions
  1. Encourage fluid intake.
  2. Encourage bed rest with the scrotum elevated to prevent traction on the spermatic cord, facilitate drainage, and relieve pain.
  3. Instruct the client in the intermittent application of cold compresses to the scrotum.
  4. Instruct the client in the use of tub or sitz baths.
  5. Instruct the client in the administration of antibiotics for self and sexual partner if the cause is chlamydial or gonorrheal infection.
  6. Instruct the client to avoid lifting, straining, and sexual contact until the infection subsides.
  7. Instruct the client to limit the force of the stream because organisms can be forced into the vas deferens and epididymis from strain or pressure during voiding.
  8. Teach the client that condom use can help prevent urethritis and epididymitis.
  9. Teach the client measures to prevent UTI or STD recurrence.

XXVI. PROSTATITIS

A. Description
  1. Inflammation of the prostate gland commonly caused by an infectious agent (bacterial) or tissue hyperplasia (abacterial).
  2. The bacterial type occurs as a result of the organism reaching the prostate via the urethra, bladder, bloodstream, or lymphatic channels.
  3. The abacterial type usually occurs following a viral illness or a decrease in sexual activity.
B. Assessment
  1. Bacterial prostatitis
    a. Fever and chills
    b. Dysuria
    c. Urethral discharge
    d. Prostate is tender, indurated, and warm to the touch.
    e. Urethral discharge on palpation of prostate
    f. White blood cells are found in prostatic secretions.
  2. Abacterial prostatitis
    a. Backache
    b. Dysuria
    c. Perineal pain
    d. Frequency
    e. Hematuria
    f. Irregularly enlarged, firm, and tender prostate
C. Interventions
  1. Encourage adequate fluid intake.
  2. Instruct the client in the use of tub or sitz baths to promote comfort.
  3. Administer antibiotics, analgesics, antispasmodics, and stool softeners as prescribed.

4. Inform the client of activities to drain the prostate, such as intercourse, masturbation, and prostatic massage.
5. Instruct the client to avoid spicy foods, coffee, alcohol, prolonged automobile rides, and sexual intercourse during an acute inflammation.

XXVII. BENIGN PROSTATIC HYPERTROPHY (HYPERPLASIA) ▲

A. Description
  1. Benign prostatic hypertrophy (benign prostatic hyperplasia; BPH) is a slow enlargement of the prostate gland, with hypertrophy and hyperplasia of normal tissue.
  2. Enlargement compresses the urethra, resulting in partial or complete obstruction.
  3. Usually occurs in men older than 50 years
  4. Possible causes include stimulation from excessive dihydroxytestosterone, estrogen, or local growth hormone.
B. Assessment ▲
  1. Diminished size and force of urinary stream (early sign of BPH)
  2. Urinary urgency and frequency
  3. Nocturia
  4. Inability to start (hesitancy) or continue a urinary stream
  5. Feelings of incomplete bladder emptying
  6. Postvoid dribbling from overflow incontinence (later sign)
  7. Urinary retention and bladder distention
  8. Hematuria
  9. Urinary stasis
  10. Dysuria and bladder pain
  11. UTIs
C. Interventions
  1. Encourage fluid intake of up to 2000 to 3000 mL/day unless contraindicated.
  2. Prepare for urinary catheterization to drain the bladder and prevent distention.
  3. Avoid administering medications that cause urinary retention, such as anticholinergics, antihistamines, decongestants, and antidepressants. ▲
  4. Administer medications as prescribed to shrink the prostate gland and improve urine flow.
  5. Administer medications as prescribed to relax prostatic smooth muscle and improve urine flow.
  6. Instruct the client to decrease intake of caffeine and artificial sweeteners and limit spicy or acidic foods.
  7. Instruct the client to follow a timed voiding schedule.
  8. Prepare the client for surgery or invasive procedures as prescribed (Box 61-18; Figs. 61-7 and 61-8).
D. Surgical interventions and postoperative care (see Chap. 51)

BOX 61-18

Surgical and Invasive Procedures for Prostatic Hyperplasia

Laser prostatectomy: Ablation of the enlarged prostate using laser instead of radiofrequency waves.

Perineal prostatectomy: Removal of prostatic tissue (may be performed for prostatic cancer) low in the pelvic region through an incision between the scrotum and rectum; impotence and incontinence usually result.

Retropubic prostatectomy: Removal of hypertrophied prostatic tissue high in the pelvic region through a low abdominal incision; the bladder is not incised.

Suprapubic prostatectomy: Removal of prostatic tissue mass through a low midline incision; an incision is made into the bladder and urethral mucosa to the anterior aspect of the prostate.

Transurethral electrovaporization of the prostate: Placement of a special metal instrument that emits a high-frequency electrical current that cuts and vaporizes excess tissue and seals the remaining tissue to prevent bleeding; this is especially useful for men on anticoagulants and those at risk for complications.

Transurethral incision of the prostate (TUIP): Removal of prostatic tissue through an incision made in the bladder neck.

Transurethral microwave thermotherapy: Application of heat to destroy the hypertrophied tissue.

Transurethral needle ablation of the prostate (TUNA): Placement of interstitial radiofrequency needles through the urethra and into the lateral lobes of the prostate, causing heat-induced coagulation necrosis of the prostate for treating benign prostatic hypertrophy (BPH).

Transurethral resection of the prostate (TURP): Removal of benign prostatic tissue surrounding the urethra with use of a resectoscope introduced through the urethra; there is little risk of impotence and it is most commonly used for BPH.

Urethral stents: Application of stents or coils in the urethra where it is narrowed by the prostate.

XXVIII. BLADDER TRAUMA

A. Description
   1. Occurs following a blunt or penetrating injury to the lower abdomen
   2. Penetrating wounds occur as a result of a stabbing, gunshot wound, or other objects piercing the abdominal wall.
   3. A fractured pelvis that causes bone fragments to puncture the bladder is a common cause of bladder trauma.
   4. Blunt trauma causes compression of the abdominal wall and bladder.

B. Assessment
   1. **Anuria**
   2. Hematuria
   3. Pain below the level of the umbilicus; can radiate to the shoulders
   4. Nausea and vomiting

C. Interventions
   1. Monitor vital signs.
   2. Monitor for hematuria, bleeding, and signs of shock.
   3. Promote bed rest.
   4. Monitor pain level.
   5. If blood is seen at the meatus, avoid urinary catheterization until a retrograde ureterogram can be obtained.

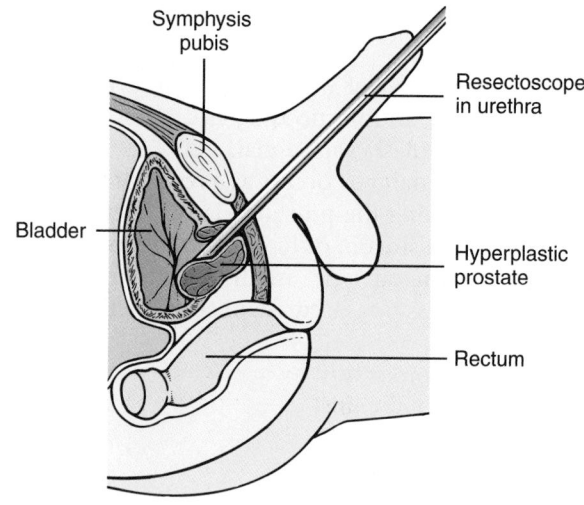

FIG. 61-7   Transurethral resection of the prostate. (From Lewis, S., Heitkemper, M., & Dirksen, S. [2004]. *Medical-surgical nursing: Assessment and management of clinical problems* [6th ed.]. St. Louis: Mosby.)

   6. Prepare the client for insertion of a suprapubic catheter to aid in urinary drainage if prescribed.
   7. Prepare the client for surgical repair of the laceration if prescribed.

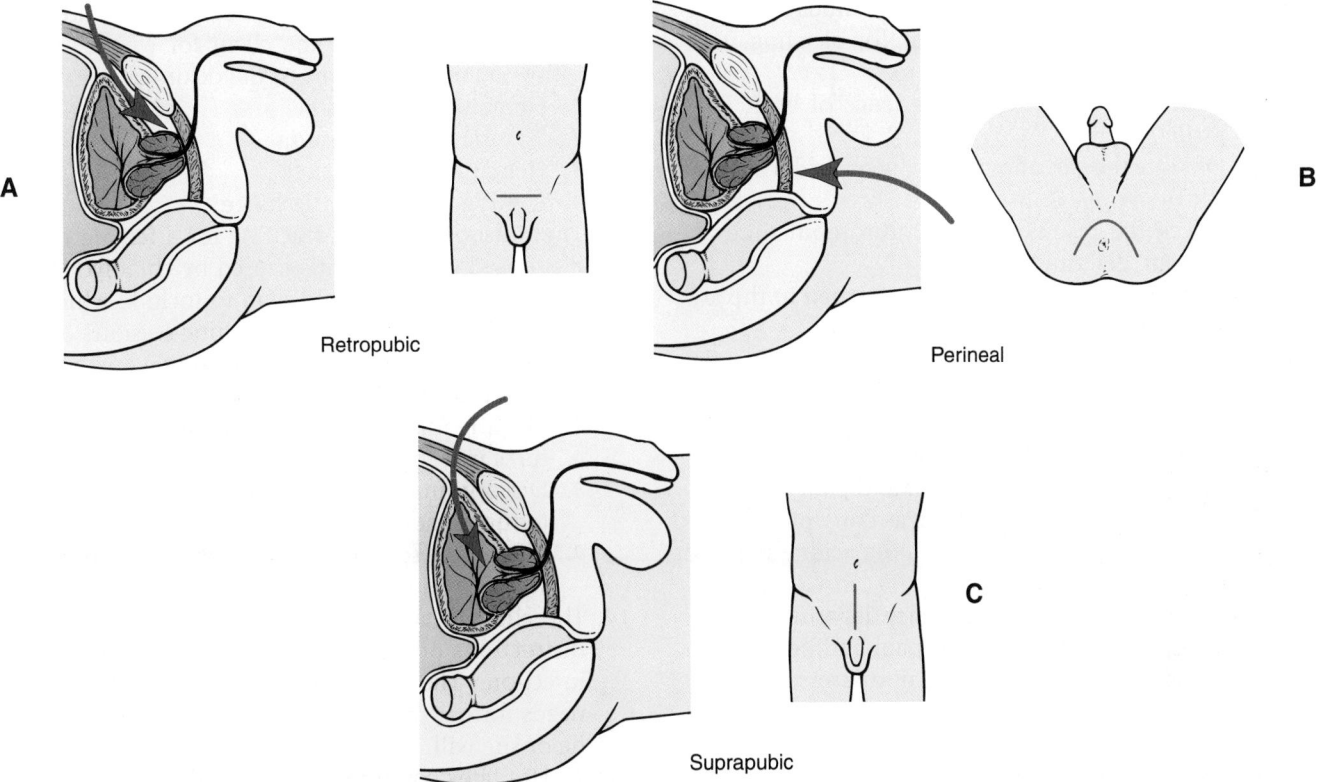

FIG. 61-8 Surgical approaches for prostatectomy. **A,** Retropubic approach involves a midline abdominal incision. **B,** Perineal approach involves an incision between the scrotum and anus. **C,** Suprapubic approach involves an abdomial incision. (From Lewis, S., Heitkemper, M., & Dirksen, S. [2004]. *Medical-surgical nursing: Assessment and management of clinical problems* [6th ed.]. St. Louis: Mosby.)

PRACTICE QUESTIONS

1. The client with acute renal failure has a serum potassium level of 6.0 mEq/L. The nurse would plan which of the following as a priority action?
   1. Check the sodium level.
   2. Place the client on a cardiac monitor.
   3. Encourage increased vegetables in the diet.
   4. Allow an extra 500 mL of fluid intake to dilute the electrolyte concentration.

2. The client with chronic renal failure who is scheduled for hemodialysis this morning is due to receive a daily dose of enalapril (Vasotec). The nurse should plan to administer this medication:
   1. During dialysis
   2. Just before dialysis
   3. The day after dialysis
   4. On return from dialysis

3. The client with chronic renal failure has an indwelling abdominal catheter for peritoneal dialysis. The client spills water on the catheter dressing while bathing. The nurse should immediately:
   1. Change the dressing.
   2. Reinforce the dressing.
   3. Flush the peritoneal dialysis catheter.
   4. Scrub the catheter with povidone-iodine.

4. The client being hemodialyzed suddenly becomes short of breath and complains of chest pain. The client is tachycardic, pale, and anxious. The nurse suspects air embolism. The priority action for the nurse is to:
   1. Discontinue dialysis and notify the physician.
   2. Monitor vital signs every 15 minutes for the next hour.
   3. Continue dialysis at a slower rate after checking the lines for air.
   4. Bolus the client with 500 mL of normal saline to break up the air embolus.

5. The nurse has completed client teaching with the hemodialysis client about self-monitoring between hemodialysis treatments. The nurse determines that the client best understands the information if the client states to record daily the:
   1. Amount of activity
   2. Pulse and respiratory rate
   3. Intake and output and weight
   4. Blood urea nitrogen and creatinine levels

6. The client with an external arteriovenous shunt in place for hemodialysis is at risk for bleeding. The priority nurse action would be to:
   1. Check the shunt for the presence of bruit and thrill.
   2. Observe the site once as time permits during the shift.
   3. Check the results of the prothrombin time as they are determined.
   4. Ensure that small clamps are attached to the arteriovenous shunt dressing.

7. The client with urolithiasis has a history of chronic urinary tract infections. The nurse plans teaching the client to avoid which of the following?
   1. Long-term use of antibiotics
   2. Wearing synthetic underwear and pantyhose
   3. High-phosphate foods, such as dairy products
   4. Foods that make the urine more acidic, such as cranberries.

8. The client arrives at the emergency department with complaints of low abdominal pain and hematuria. The client is afebrile. The nurse next assesses the client to determine a history of:
   1. Pyelonephritis
   2. Glomerulonephritis
   3. Trauma to the bladder or abdomen
   4. Renal cancer in the client's family

9. The client is admitted to the emergency department following a motor vehicle accident. The client was wearing a lap seat belt when the accident occurred and now the client has hematuria and lower abdominal pain. To assess further whether the pain is caused by bladder trauma, the nurse asks the client if the pain is referred to which of the following areas?
   1. Hip
   2. Shoulder
   3. Umbilicus
   4. Costovertebral angle

10. The female client is admitted to the emergency department following a fall from a horse and the physician orders insertion of a Foley catheter. While preparing for the procedure, the nurse notes blood at the urinary meatus. The nurse should:
    1. Notify the physician.
    2. Use a smaller size of catheter.
    3. Administer pain medication before inserting the catheter.
    4. Use extra povidone-iodine solution in cleansing the meatus.

11. A nurse is assessing the patency of a client's left arm arteriovenous fistula prior to initiating hemodialysis. Which finding indicates that the fistula is patent?
    1. Palpation of a thrill over the fistula
    2. Presence of a radial pulse in the left wrist
    3. Absence of a bruit on auscultation of the fistula
    4. Capillary refill less than 3 seconds in the nail beds of the fingers on the left hand

12. The male client has a tentative diagnosis of urethritis. The nurse assesses the client for which of the following manifestations of the disorder?
    1. Hematuria and pyuria
    2. Dysuria and proteinuria
    3. Hematuria and urgency
    4. Dysuria and penile discharge

13. The nurse is planning teaching for a female client diagnosed with urethritis caused by chlamydial infection. The nurse would plan to include which of the following points in the teaching session?
    1. Altering the perineal pH by using a spermicide with a condom
    2. Keeping follow-up appointments for repeat cultures in 4 to 7 days
    3. Discontinuing antibiotics after 3 weeks of uninterrupted administration
    4. Identifying sexual partners for the last 12 months so they can be treated

14. The client with chlamydial infection has received instructions on self-care and prevention of further infection. The nurse determines that the client needs further reinforcement if the client states that he or she will:
    1. Use latex condoms to prevent disease transmission.
    2. Return to the clinic as requested for follow-up culture in 1 week.
    3. Use doxycycline prophylactically to prevent symptoms of chlamydia.
    4. Reduce the chance of reinfection by limiting the number of sexual partners.

15. The nurse is assessing the client with epididymitis. The nurse anticipates which of the following findings on physical examination?
    1. Fever, diarrhea, groin pain, and ecchymosis
    2. Nausea, vomiting, scrotal edema, and ecchymosis
    3. Fever, nausea, vomiting, and painful scrotal edema
    4. Diarrhea, groin pain, testicular torsion, and scrotal edema

16. The client complains of fever, perineal pain, and urinary urgency, frequency, and dysuria. To assess whether the client's problem is related to bacterial prostatitis, the nurse would look at the results of the prostate examination, which should reveal that the prostate gland is:
    1. Soft and swollen
    2. Reddened, swollen, and boggy
    3. Tender and edematous with ecchymosis
    4. Tender, indurated, and warm to the touch

17. The nurse is taking the history of a client who has had benign prostatic hyperplasia in the past. To determine whether the client currently is experiencing difficulty, the nurse asks the client about the presence of which early symptom?

1. Nocturia
2. Urinary retention
3. Urge incontinence
4. Decreased force in the stream of urine

18. The client newly diagnosed with chronic renal failure recently has begun hemodialysis. Knowing that the client is at risk for disequilibrium syndrome, the nurse assesses the client during dialysis for:
    1. Hypertension, tachycardia, and fever
    2. Hypotension, bradycardia, and hypothermia
    3. Restlessness, irritability, and generalized weakness
    4. Headache, deteriorating level of consciousness, and twitching

19. A client with chronic renal failure has completed a hemodialysis treatment. The nurse would use which of the following standard indicators to evaluate the client's status after dialysis?
    1. Vital signs and weight
    2. Potassium level and weight
    3. Vital signs and blood urea nitrogen level
    4. Blood urea nitrogen and creatinine levels

20. The hemodialysis client with a left arm fistula is at risk for arterial steal syndrome. The nurse assesses this client for which of the following manifestations?
    1. Warmth, redness, and pain in the left hand
    2. Pallor, diminished pulse, and pain in the left hand
    3. Edema and reddish discoloration of the left arm
    4. Aching pain, pallor, and edema of the left arm

21. The nurse is reviewing the client's record and notes that the physician has documented that the client has a renal disorder. On review of the laboratory results, the nurse most likely would expect to note which of the following?
    1. Decreased hemoglobin level
    2. Elevated blood urea nitrogen level
    3. Decreased red blood cell count
    4. Decreased white blood cell count

22. The client is scheduled for an intravenous pyelogram. Before the test, the priority nursing action would be to:
    1. Restrict fluids.
    2. Administer a sedative.
    3. Administer an oral preparation of radiopaque dye.
    4. Determine a history of iodine or seafood allergies.

23. The client with chronic renal failure returns to the nursing unit following a hemodialysis treatment. On assessment, the nurse notes that the client's temperature is 100.2° F. Which of the following is the appropriate nursing action?
    1. Encourage fluids.
    2. Notify the physician.
    3. Continue to monitor vital signs.
    4. Monitor the site of the shunt for infection.

24. The nurse is performing an assessment on a client who has returned from the dialysis unit following hemodialysis. The client is complaining of headache and nausea and is extremely restless. Which of the following is the most appropriate nursing action?
    1. Monitor the client.
    2. Notify the physician.
    3. Elevate the head of the bed.
    4. Medicate the client for nausea.

25. The nurse is reviewing the list of components contained in the peritoneal dialysis solution with the client. The client asks the nurse about the purpose of the glucose contained in the solution. The nurse bases the response on knowing that the glucose:
    1. Decreases the risk of peritonitis
    2. Prevents disequilibrium syndrome
    3. Increases osmotic pressure to produce ultrafiltration
    4. Prevents excess glucose from being removed from the client

26. The nurse is preparing to care for a client receiving peritoneal dialysis. Which of the following would be included in the nursing plan of care to prevent the major complication associated with peritoneal dialysis?
    1. Maintain strict aseptic technique.
    2. Add heparin to the dialysate solution.
    3. Change the catheter site dressing daily.
    4. Monitor the client's level of consciousness.

27. A client newly diagnosed with renal failure has just been started on peritoneal dialysis. During the infusion of the dialysate, the client complains of abdominal pain. Which action by the nurse is appropriate?
    1. Stop the dialysis.
    2. Slow the infusion.
    3. Decrease the amount to be infused.
    4. Explain that the pain will subside after the first few exchanges.

28. The nurse is instructing a client with diabetes mellitus about peritoneal dialysis. The nurse tells the client that it is important to maintain the prescribed dwell time for the dialysis because of the risk of:
    1. Infection
    2. Hyperglycemia
    3. Hypophosphatemia
    4. Disequilibrium syndrome

29. The client returns to the nursing unit following a pyelolithotomy for removal of a kidney stone. A Penrose drain is in place. Which of the following actions would the nurse include in the client's postoperative plan of care?
    1. Positioning the client on the affected side
    2. Irrigating the Penrose drain using sterile procedure
    3. Changing dressings frequently around the Penrose drain
    4. Weighing dressings and adding the amount to the output

30. A week after kidney transplantation, the client develops a temperature of 101° F, the blood pressure is elevated, and the kidney is tender. The x-ray indicates that the transplanted kidney is enlarged. Based on these assessment findings, the nurse would suspect which of the following complications?
    1. Acute rejection
    2. Kidney infection
    3. Chronic rejection
    4. Kidney obstruction

31. The client with benign prostatic hyperplasia undergoes a transurethral resection of the prostate. Postoperatively, the client is receiving continuous bladder irrigations. The nurse assesses the client for signs of transurethral resection syndrome. Which of the following assessment data would indicate the onset of this syndrome?
    1. Tachycardia and diarrhea
    2. Bradycardia and confusion
    3. Increased urinary output and anemia
    4. Decreased urinary output and bladder spasms

32. The client is admitted to the hospital with a diagnosis of benign prostatic hyperplasia, and a transurethral resection of the prostate is performed. Four hours after surgery, the nurse takes the client's vital signs and empties the urinary drainage bag. Which of the following assessment findings would indicate the need to notify the physician?
    1. Red bloody urine
    2. Pain related to bladder spasms
    3. Urinary output of 200 mL higher than intake
    4. Blood pressure, 100/50 mm Hg; pulse, 130 beats/min

33. A client diagnosed with polycystic kidney disease has been taught about the treatment plan for this disease. The nurse determines that the client needs additional teaching if the client states that the treatment plan includes:
    1. Genetic counseling
    2. Sodium restriction
    3. Increased water intake
    4. Antihypertensive medications

34. The nurse is caring for the client who has undergone renal angiography using the left femoral artery for access. The nurse determines that the client is experiencing a complication of the procedure if which of the following is observed?
    1. Urine output, 50 mL/hr
    2. Blood pressure, 110/74 mm Hg
    3. Pallor and coolness of the left leg
    4. Absence of hematoma in the left groin

35. The nurse has taught the client with polycystic kidney disease about management of the disorder and prevention and recognition of complications. The nurse determines that the client understands the instructions if the client states that there is no reason to be concerned about:
    1. Burning on urination
    2. A temperature of 100.6° F
    3. New-onset shortness of breath
    4. A blood pressure of 105/68 mm Hg

36. The client with prostatitis following kidney infection has received instructions on management of the condition at home and prevention of recurrence. The nurse determines that the client understands the instructions if the client verbalizes that he will:
    1. Stop antibiotic therapy when pain subsides.
    2. Exercise as much as possible to stimulate circulation.
    3. Use warm tub baths and analgesics to increase comfort.
    4. Keep fluid intake to a minimum to decrease the need to void.

ALTERNATE ITEM FORMAT: MULTIPLE RESPONSE

The nurse monitoring a client receiving peritoneal dialysis notes that the client's outflow is less than the inflow. Select all nursing actions in this situation that apply.

- ❑ 1. Contact the physician.
- ☑ 2. Check the level of the drainage bag.
- ☑ 3. Reposition the client to his or her side.
- ☑ 4. Place the client in good body alignment.
- ☑ 5. Check the peritoneal dialysis system for kinks.
- ❑ 6. Increase the flow rate of the peritoneal dialysis solution.

ANSWERS

1. **2**

Rationale: The client with hyperkalemia is at risk of developing cardiac dysrhythmias and cardiac arrest. Because of this, the client should be placed on a cardiac monitor. Fluid intake is not increased because it contributes to fluid overload and would not affect the serum potassium level significantly. Vegetables are a natural source of potassium in the diet, and their use would not be increased. The nurse also may assess the sodium level because sodium is another electrolyte commonly measured with the potassium level. However, this is not a priority action of the nurse.

Test-Taking Strategy: First, note that the potassium level is elevated. Next, use the ABCs—airway, breathing, and circulation—to direct you to option 2. Review care of the client with hyperkalemia if you had difficulty with this question.

Level of Cognitive Ability: Application
Client Needs: Physiological Integrity
Integrated Process: Nursing Process—planning
Content Area: Adult health—renal

Reference: Ignatavicius, D., & Workman, M. (2006). *Medical-surgical nursing: Critical thinking for collaborative care* (5th ed., pp. 233, 1740). Philadelphia: W.B. Saunders.

2. **4**

Rationale: Antihypertensive medications such as enalapril are given to the client following hemodialysis. This prevents the client from becoming hypotensive during dialysis and also from having the medication removed from the bloodstream by dialysis. No rationale exists for waiting an entire day to resume the medication. This would lead to ineffective control of the blood pressure.

Test-Taking Strategy: Use the process of elimination. Begin to answer this question by thinking about the effects of an antihypertensive medication on the blood pressure when fluid is being removed from the body. Because hypotension is much more likely to occur in this circumstance, eliminate options 1 and 2. Eliminate option 3, because this action would lead to ineffective blood pressure control. Review preprocedure hemodialysis measures if you had difficulty with this question.

Level of Cognitive Ability: Application

Client Needs: Physiological Integrity

Integrated Process: Nursing Process—planning

Content Area: Adult health—renal

Reference: Ignatavicius, D., & Workman, M. (2006). *Medical-surgical nursing: Critical thinking for collaborative care* (5th ed., p. 1755). Philadelphia: W.B. Saunders.

3. **1**

Rationale: Clients with peritoneal dialysis catheters are at high risk for infection. A wet dressing is a conduit for bacteria to reach the catheter insertion site. The nurse ensures that the dressing is kept dry at all times. Reinforcing the dressing is not a safe practice to prevent infection in this circumstance. Flushing the catheter is not indicated. Scrubbing the catheter with povidone-iodine is done at the time of connection or disconnection of peritoneal dialysis.

Test-Taking Strategy: Use the process of elimination. Note the subject of the question, a wet dressing. Recalling that this client is at risk for infection and knowing that it is better to change a wet dressing than reinforce it will direct you to option 1. Review care to the client receiving peritoneal dialysis if you had difficulty with this question.

Level of Cognitive Ability: Application

Client Needs: Safe and Effective Care Environment

Integrated Process: Nursing Process—implementation

Content Area: Adult health—renal

Reference: Ignatavicius, D., & Workman, M. (2006). *Medical-surgical nursing: Critical thinking for collaborative care* (5th ed., p. 1759). Philadelphia: W.B. Saunders.

4. **1**

Rationale: If the client experiences air embolus during hemodialysis, the nurse should terminate dialysis immediately, notify the physician, and administer oxygen as needed. Options 2, 3, and 4 are incorrect.

Test-Taking Strategy: Use the process of elimination. Recalling that air embolism is an emergency situation that affects the cardiopulmonary system suddenly and profoundly will direct you to option 1. Review the emergency care of a client who develops air embolism if you had difficulty with this question.

Level of Cognitive Ability: Application

Client Needs: Physiological Integrity

Integrated Process: Nursing Process—implementation

Content Area: Adult health—renal

Reference: Ignatavicius, D., & Workman, M. (2006). *Medical-surgical nursing: Critical thinking for collaborative care* (5th ed., pp. 264, 1752). Philadelphia: W.B. Saunders.

5. **3**

Rationale: The client on hemodialysis should monitor fluid status between hemodialysis treatments by recording intake and output and measuring weight daily. Ideally, the hemodialysis client should not gain more than 0.5 kg of weight/day.

Test-Taking Strategy: Use the process of elimination. Recalling the pathophysiology of renal failure and the impact on the client's bodily functions will assist in answering the question. Also, note that option 3 relates to monitoring of fluid retention. Review teaching points for the client receiving hemodialysis if you had difficulty with this question.

Level of Cognitive Ability: Analysis

Client Needs: Physiological Integrity

Integrated Process: Teaching and Learning

Content Area: Adult health—renal

Reference: Ignatavicius, D., & Workman, M. (2006). *Medical-surgical nursing: Critical thinking for collaborative care* (5th ed., p. 1755). Philadelphia: W.B. Saunders.

6. **4**

Rationale: An arteriovenous shunt is a less common form of access site but carries a risk for bleeding when it is used because two ends of an external cannula are tunneled subcutaneously into an artery and a vein, and the ends of the cannula are joined. If accidental disconnection occurs, the client could lose blood rapidly. For this reason, small clamps are attached to the dressing that covers the insertion site for use if needed. The shunt site also should be assessed at least every 4 hours.

Test-Taking Strategy: Use the process of elimination. Focus on the subject, preventing bleeding. Visualize this type of access device. Recalling that the risk of disconnection can occur will direct you to option 4. Review care of the client with an arteriovenous shunt if you had difficulty with this question.

Level of Cognitive Ability: Application

Client Needs: Safe and Effective Care Environment

Integrated Process: Nursing Process—implementation

Content Area: Adult health—renal

Reference: Black, J., & Hawks, J. (2005). *Medical-surgical nursing: Clinical management for positive outcomes* (7th ed., pp. 959-960). Philadelphia: W.B. Saunders.

7. **2**

Rationale: Urolithiasis (struvite stones) can result from chronic infections. They form in urine that is alkaline and rich in ammonia, such as with a urinary tract infection. Teaching should focus on prevention of infections and ingesting foods to make the urine more acidic. The client should wear cotton (not synthetic) underclothing to prevent the accumulation of moisture and to prevent irritation of the perineal area, which can lead to infection.

Test-Taking Strategy: Use the process of elimination and note the strategic word *avoid*. Focus on the data in the question. Noting that the client has urolithiasis and a history of chronic urinary tract infections will direct you to option 2, thus eliminating options 1, 3, and 4. Review the causes of the various types of stones and interventions if you had difficulty with this question.
Level of Cognitive Ability: Application
Client Needs: Physiological Integrity
Integrated Process: Teaching and Learning
Content Area: Adult health—renal
Reference: Ignatavicius, D., & Workman, M. (2006). *Medical-surgical nursing: Critical thinking for collaborative care* (5th ed., p. 1696). Philadelphia: W.B. Saunders.

8. **3**
Rationale: Bladder trauma or injury should be considered or suspected in the client with low abdominal pain and hematuria. Glomerulonephritis and pyelonephritis would be accompanied by fever and are thus not applicable to the client in this question. Renal cancer would not cause pain that is felt in the low abdomen; rather pain would be in the flank area.
Test-Taking Strategy: Use the process of elimination. Eliminate options 1 and 2, knowing that any inflammatory disease or infection is accompanied by fever. Because this client is afebrile, these are not possible options. Use knowledge of anatomy and pain assessment to select option 3. Pain from renal cancer is a later finding and is localized in the flank area. Review renal assessment techniques if you had difficulty with this question.
Level of Cognitive Ability: Application
Client Needs: Physiological Integrity
Integrated Process: Nursing Process—assessment
Content Area: Adult health—renal
Reference: Ignatavicius, D., & Workman, M. (2006). *Medical-surgical nursing: Critical thinking for collaborative care* (5th ed., p. 1704). Philadelphia: W.B. Saunders.

9. **2**
Rationale: Bladder trauma or injury is characterized by lower abdominal pain that may radiate to one of the shoulders. Bladder injury pain does not radiate to the umbilicus, costovertebral angle, or hip.
Test-Taking Strategy: Use the process of elimination. Recalling the concepts related to dermatomes of the body and pain characteristics of bladder trauma will direct you to option 2. Review the characteristics of bladder trauma if you had difficulty with this question.
Level of Cognitive Ability: Analysis
Client Needs: Physiological Integrity
Integrated Process: Nursing Process—assessment
Content Area: Adult health—renal
References: Black, J., & Hawks, J. (2005). *Medical-surgical nursing: Clinical management for positive outcomes* (7th ed., p. 790). Philadelphia: W.B. Saunders.
Ignatavicius, D., & Workman, M. (2006). *Medical-surgical nursing: Critical thinking for collaborative care* (5th ed., p. 1704). Philadelphia: W.B. Saunders.

10. **1**
Rationale: The presence of blood at the urinary meatus may indicate urethral trauma or disruption. The nurse notifies the physician, knowing that the client should not be catheterized until the cause of the bleeding is determined by diagnostic testing. Therefore, options 2, 3, and 4 are incorrect.
Test-Taking Strategy: Use the process of elimination. Noting the strategic words *blood at the urinary meatus* will direct you to option 1. Review the assessment findings in a client with trauma to the urinary tract if you had difficulty with this question.
Level of Cognitive Ability: Application
Client Needs: Physiological Integrity
Integrated Process: Nursing Process—implementation
Content Area: Adult health—renal
References: Black, J., & Hawks, J. (2005). *Medical-surgical nursing: Clinical management for positive outcomes* (7th ed., p. 790). Philadelphia: W.B. Saunders.
Ignatavicius, D., & Workman, M. (2006). *Medical-surgical nursing: Critical thinking for collaborative care* (5th ed., p. 790). Philadelphia: W.B. Saunders.

11. **1**
Rationale: The nurse assesses the patency of the fistula by palpating for the presence of a thrill or auscultating for a bruit. The presence of a thrill and bruit indicate patency of the fistula. Although the presence of a radial pulse in the left wrist and capillary refill shorter than 3 seconds in the nail beds of the fingers on the left hand are normal findings, they do not assess fistula patency.
Test-Taking Strategy: Use the process of elimination. Eliminate options 2 and 4 first because they are comparative or alike and assess for adequate circulation in the distal portion of the extremity (not the fistula). From the remaining options, focusing on the subject (patency) and noting the word *absence* in option 3 will assist you in eliminating this option. Review the expected findings when assessing an arteriovenous fistula if you had difficulty with this question.
Level of Cognitive Ability: Analysis
Client Needs: Physiological Integrity
Integrated Process: Nursing Process—analysis
Content Area: Adult health—renal
Reference: Ignatavicius, D., & Workman, M. (2006). *Medical-surgical nursing: Critical thinking for collaborative care* (5th ed., p. 1753). Philadelphia: W.B. Saunders.

12. **4**
Rationale: Urethritis in the male client often results from chlamydial infection and is characterized by dysuria, which is accompanied by a clear to mucopurulent discharge. Because this disorder often coexists with gonorrhea, diagnostic tests are done for both and include culture and rapid assays.
Test-Taking Strategy: Use the process of elimination. Recalling that urethritis generally is accompanied by dysuria in the male client will assist you in eliminating options 1 and 3. Knowing that the problem originates in the urethra, not the kidney, will assist you in eliminating option 2, because proteinuria indicates a problem with kidney function. Review the clinical manifestations of urethritis if you had difficulty with this question.
Level of Cognitive Ability: Application
Client Needs: Physiological Integrity
Integrated Process: Nursing Process—assessment
Content Area: Adult health—renal

Reference: Ignatavicius, D., & Workman, M. (2006). *Medical-surgical nursing: Critical thinking for collaborative care* (5th ed., p. 1685). Philadelphia: W.B. Saunders.

13. 2
Rationale: Follow-up cultures are typically done in 4 to 7 days to evaluate the effectiveness of the medication. Using a spermicide does not change the perineal pH. The infection can be prevented by the use of latex condoms. Chlamydial infection is treated with doxycycline for 7 days or with azithromycin (Zithromax) as a single dose. All sexual partners during the 30 days before diagnosis should be notified, examined, and treated as necessary.
Test-Taking Strategy: Use the process of elimination. Eliminate option 1 first, using principles of infection control. Knowing that most courses of antibiotic therapy generally extend from 7 to 10 days may help eliminate option 3. Eliminate option 4; partners within the last month should be notified and treated as needed. Review the teaching points for the client with chlamydia if you had difficulty with this question.
Level of Cognitive Ability: Application
Client Needs: Physiological Integrity
Integrated Process: Teaching and Learning
Content Area: Adult health—renal
Reference: Ignatavicius, D., & Workman, M. (2006). *Medical-surgical nursing: Critical thinking for collaborative care* (5th ed., p. 1896). Philadelphia: W.B. Saunders.

14. 3
Rationale: Antibiotics are not taken prophylactically to prevent acquisition of urethritis from chlamydial infection. The risk of reinfection can be reduced by limiting the number of sexual partners and by the use of condoms. In some cases, follow-up culture is requested in 4 to 7 days to confirm a cure. Options 1, 2, and 4 are correct measures.
Test-Taking Strategy: Use the process of elimination. Note the strategic words *needs further reinforcement*. These words indicate a negative event query and ask you to select an option that is an incorrect statement. Knowing the basic principles of antibiotic therapy will direct you to option 3 because antibiotics are not used intermittently at will for prophylaxis of this infection. Review client teaching related to chlamydial infection if you had difficulty with this question.
Level of Cognitive Ability: Analysis
Client Needs: Health Promotion and Maintenance
Integrated Process: Teaching and Learning
Content Area: Adult health—renal
Reference: Ignatavicius, D., & Workman, M. (2006). *Medical-surgical nursing: Critical thinking for collaborative care* (5th ed., p. 1896). Philadelphia: W.B. Saunders.

15. 3
Rationale: Typical signs and symptoms of epididymitis include scrotal pain and edema, which often are accompanied by fever, nausea and vomiting, and chills. Epididymitis most often is caused by infection, although sometimes it can be caused by trauma. Epididymitis needs to be distinguished correctly from testicular torsion.
Test-Taking Strategy: Use the process of elimination. Any disorder that ends in *-itis* results from inflammation or infection. Therefore, an expected finding would be elevated temperature. With this in mind, eliminate options 2 and 4 because they do not contain fever as part of the option. Knowing that ecchymosis results from bleeding, which is not part of this clinical picture, directs you to option 3. Review the clinical manifestations of epididymitis if you had difficulty with this question.
Level of Cognitive Ability: Analysis
Client Needs: Physiological Integrity
Integrated Process: Nursing Process—assessment
Content Area: Adult health—renal
References: Black, J., & Hawks, J. (2005). *Medical-surgical nursing: Clinical management for positive outcomes* (7th ed., p. 1039). Philadelphia: W.B. Saunders.
Ignatavicius, D., & Workman, M. (2006). *Medical-surgical nursing: Critical thinking for collaborative care* (5th ed., p. 1880). Philadelphia: W.B. Saunders.

16. 4
Rationale: The client with prostatitis has a swollen and tender prostate gland that is also warm to the touch, firm, and indurated. Systemic symptoms include fever with chills, perineal and low back pain, and signs of urinary tract infection, which often accompany the disorder.
Test-Taking Strategy: Use the process of elimination. Begin to answer this question by reasoning that inflammation of the prostate gland would cause the area to be tender. This would allow you to eliminate options 1 and 2. Recalling that inflammation is accompanied by local warmth will direct you to option 4. Review the signs of prostatitis if you had difficulty with this question.
Level of Cognitive Ability: Analysis
Client Needs: Physiological Integrity
Integrated Process: Nursing process—assessment
Content Area: Adult health—renal
References: Black, J., & Hawks, J. (2005). *Medical-surgical nursing: Clinical management for positive outcomes* (7th ed., p. 1035). Philadelphia: W.B. Saunders.
Ignatavicius, D., & Workman, M. (2006). *Medical-surgical nursing: Critical thinking for collaborative care* (5th ed., pp. 1879-1880). Philadelphia: W.B. Saunders.

17. 4
Rationale: Decreased force in the stream of urine is an early sign of benign prostatic hyperplasia. The stream later becomes weak and dribbling. The client then may develop hematuria, frequency, urgency, urge incontinence, and nocturia. If untreated, complete obstruction and urinary retention can occur.
Test-Taking Strategy: Use the process of elimination and note the strategic word *early*. If you know that benign prostatic hyperplasia can lead to urinary obstruction, look for the option that identifies the least severe symptom. Review early signs of benign prostatic hyperplasia if you had difficulty with this question.
Level of Cognitive Ability: Application
Client Needs: Physiological Integrity
Integrated Process: Nursing Process—assessment
Content Area: Adult health—renal
Reference: Black, J., & Hawks, J. (2005). *Medical-surgical nursing: Clinical management for positive outcomes* (7th ed., pp. 1014-1016). Philadelphia: W.B. Saunders.

18. 4
Rationale: Disequilibrium syndrome is characterized by headache, mental confusion, decreasing level of consciousness,

nausea, vomiting, twitching, and possible seizure activity. Disequilibrium syndrome is caused by rapid removal of solutes from the body during hemodialysis. At the same time, the blood-brain barrier interferes with the efficient removal of wastes from brain tissue. As a result, water goes into cerebral cells because of the osmotic gradient, causing brain swelling and onset of symptoms. The syndrome most often occurs in clients who are new to dialysis and is prevented by dialyzing for shorter times or at reduced blood flow rates.

Test-Taking Strategy: Use the process of elimination. Focus on the name, disequilibrium syndrome, to assist in directing you to option 4. Review the manifestations of this syndrome if you had difficulty with this question.

Level of Cognitive Ability: Analysis
Client Needs: Physiological Integrity
Integrated Process: Nursing Process—assessment
Content Area: Adult health—renal
Reference: Ignatavicius, D., & Workman, M. (2006). *Medical-surgical nursing: Critical thinking for collaborative care* (5th ed., p. 1756). Philadelphia: W.B. Saunders.

19. **1**
Rationale: Following dialysis, the client's vital signs are monitored to determine whether the client is remaining hemodynamically stable. Weight is measured and compared with the client's predialysis weight to determine effectiveness of fluid extraction. Laboratory studies are done as per protocol but are not necessarily done after the hemodialysis treatment has ended.

Test-Taking Strategy: Use the process of elimination. Note the subject, measures to determine the client's status after dialysis. Recalling the purpose of the dialysis will direct you to option 1. Review postdialysis nursing assessments if you had difficulty with this question.

Level of Cognitive Ability: Analysis
Client Needs: Physiological Integrity
Integrated Process: Nursing Process—evaluation
Content Area: Adult health—renal
Reference: Ignatavicius, D., & Workman, M. (2006). *Medical-surgical nursing: Critical thinking for collaborative care* (5th ed., pp. 1756, 1759). Philadelphia: W.B. Saunders.

20. **2**
Rationale: Steal syndrome results from vascular insufficiency after creation of a fistula. The client exhibits pallor and a diminished pulse distal to the fistula. The client also complains of pain distal to the fistula, caused by tissue ischemia. Warmth, redness, and pain probably would characterize a problem with infection. The manifestations described in options 3 and 4 are incorrect.

Test-Taking Strategy: You must understand steal syndrome and know the signs and symptoms to answer this question. Recalling that steal syndrome results from vascular insufficiency after creation of a fistula will direct you to option 2. Review this syndrome and associated signs and symptoms if you had difficulty with this question.

Level of Cognitive Ability: Application
Client Needs: Physiological Integrity
Integrated Process: Nursing Process—assessment
Content Area: Adult health—renal

Reference: Ignatavicius, D., & Workman, M. (2006). *Medical-surgical nursing: Critical thinking for collaborative care* (5th ed., p. 1755). Philadelphia: W.B. Saunders.

21. **2**
Rationale: Measuring the blood urea nitrogen level is a frequently used laboratory test to determine renal function. The blood urea nitrogen level starts to rise when the glomerular filtration rate falls below 40% to 60%. A decreased hemoglobin level and red blood cell count may be noted if bleeding from the urinary tract occurs or if erythropoietic function by the kidney is impaired. An increased white blood cell count is most likely to be noted in renal disease.

Test-Taking Strategy: Use the process of elimination. Recalling the relationship between the blood urea nitrogen level and renal function will direct you to option 2. Review significant laboratory tests related to renal function if you had difficulty with this question.

Level of Cognitive Ability: Analysis
Client Needs: Physiological Integrity
Integrated Process: Nursing Process—assessment
Content Area: Adult health—renal
Reference: Ignatavicius, D., & Workman, M. (2006). *Medical-surgical nursing: Critical thinking for collaborative care* (5th ed., p. 1701). Philadelphia: W.B. Saunders.

22. **4**
Rationale: The iodine-based dye used during intravenous pyelography can cause allergic reactions such as itching, hives, rash, a tight feeling in the throat, shortness of breath, and bronchospasm. Assessing for allergies is the priority.

Test-Taking Strategy: Use the process of elimination and note the strategic word *priority* in the question. Use the steps of the nursing process as a guide. Options 1, 2, and 3 address implementation. Option 4 is the only option that addresses assessment. Review preprocedure care for the client undergoing intravenous pyelography if you had difficulty with this question.

Level of Cognitive Ability: Application
Client Needs: Physiological Integrity
Integrated Process: Nursing Process—assessment
Content Area: Delegating/Prioritizing
Reference: Chernecky, C., & Berger, B. (2004). *Laboratory tests and diagnostic procedures* (4th ed., p. 696). Philadelphia: W.B. Saunders.

23. **3**
Rationale: The client may have an elevated temperature following dialysis because the dialysis machine warms the blood slightly. If the temperature is elevated excessively and remains elevated, sepsis would be suspected and a blood sample would be obtained as prescribed for culture and sensitivity determinations.

Test-Taking Strategy: Use the process of elimination and focus on the data in the question. Recalling that an elevation in temperature is expected following dialysis will direct you to option 3. Review the normal expected findings following dialysis if you had difficulty with this question.

Level of Cognitive Ability: Application
Client Needs: Physiological Integrity

Integrated Process: Nursing Process—implementation
Content Area: Adult health—renal
Reference: Ignatavicius, D., & Workman, M. (2006). *Medical-surgical nursing: Critical thinking for collaborative care* (5th ed., p. 1756). Philadelphia: W.B. Saunders.

24. 2
Rationale: Disequilibrium syndrome may be caused by the rapid decreases in the blood urea nitrogen level during hemodialysis. These changes can cause cerebral edema that leads to increased intracranial pressure. The client is exhibiting early signs of disequilibrium syndrome and appropriate treatments with anticonvulsive medications and barbiturates may be necessary to prevent a life-threatening situation. The physician must be notified.
Test-Taking Strategy: Use the process of elimination and focus on the client's signs and symptoms. Recalling the complications associated with hemodialysis will direct you to option 2. Review the signs and symptoms of disequilibrium syndrome if you had difficulty with this question.
Level of Cognitive Ability: Application
Client Needs: Physiological Integrity
Integrated Process: Nursing Process—implementation
Content Area: Adult health—renal
Reference: Ignatavicius, D., & Workman, M. (2006). *Medical-surgical nursing: Critical thinking for collaborative care* (5th ed., p. 1756). Philadelphia: W.B. Saunders.

25. 3
Rationale: Increasing the glucose concentration makes the solution more hypertonic. The more hypertonic the solution, the higher the osmotic pressure for ultrafiltration and thus the greater the amount of fluid removed from the client during an exchange. Options 1, 2, and 4 do not identify the purpose of the glucose.
Test-Taking Strategy: Use the process of elimination. Knowledge regarding the principles related to ultrafiltration will direct you to option 3. If you had difficulty with this question, review dialysate solutions for peritoneal dialysis.
Level of Cognitive Ability: Application
Client Needs: Physiological Integrity
Integrated Process: Teaching and Learning
Content Area: Adult health—renal
Reference: Ignatavicius, D., & Workman, M. (2006). *Medical-surgical nursing: Critical thinking for collaborative care* (5th ed., p. 1758). Philadelphia: W.B. Saunders.

26. 1
Rationale: The major complication of peritoneal dialysis is peritonitis. Strict aseptic technique is required in caring for the client receiving this treatment. Although option 3 may assist in preventing infection, this option relates to an external site. Options 2 and 4 are unrelated to the major complication of peritoneal dialysis.
Test-Taking Strategy: Use the process of elimination. Visualize this procedure and recall the major concern related to peritonitis. This will direct you to option 1. Review the complications associated with peritoneal dialysis if you had difficulty with this question.
Level of Cognitive Ability: Application
Client Needs: Safe and Effective Care Environment

Integrated Process: Nursing Process—planning
Content Area: Adult health—renal
Reference: Ignatavicius, D., & Workman, M. (2006). *Medical-surgical nursing: Critical thinking for collaborative care* (5th ed., pp. 1755, 1759). Philadelphia: W.B. Saunders.

27. 4
Rationale: Pain during the inflow of dialysate is common during the first few exchanges because of peritoneal irritation; however, the pain usually disappears after 1 to 2 weeks of treatment. The infusion amount should not be decreased, and the infusion should not be slowed or stopped.
Test-Taking Strategy: Use the process of elimination. Eliminate options 1, 2, and 3 because they are comparative or alike actions. Review the complications associated with peritoneal dialysis and the appropriate nursing actions if you had difficulty with this question.
Level of Cognitive Ability: Application
Client Needs: Physiological Integrity
Integrated Process: Nursing Process—implementation
Content Area: Adult health—renal
Reference: Ignatavicius, D., & Workman, M. (2006). *Medical-surgical nursing: Critical thinking for collaborative care* (5th ed., pp. 1758-1759). Philadelphia: W.B. Saunders.

28. 2
Rationale: An extended dwell time increases the risk of hyperglycemia in the client with diabetes mellitus as a result of absorption of glucose from the dialysate and electrolyte changes. Diabetic clients may require extra insulin when receiving peritoneal dialysis.
Test-Taking Strategy: Use the process of elimination. Noting the client's diagnosis and recalling that the dialysate solution contains glucose will direct you to option 2. Review the complications associated with peritoneal dialysis if you had difficulty with this question.
Level of Cognitive Ability: Application
Client Needs: Physiological Integrity
Integrated Process: Teaching and Learning
Content Area: Adult health—renal
Reference: Black, J., & Hawks, J. (2005). *Medical-surgical nursing: Clinical management for positive outcomes* (7th ed., pp. 957-958). Philadelphia: W.B. Saunders.

29. 3
Rationale: Frequent dressing changes around the Penrose drain are required to protect the skin against breakdown from the urinary drainage. If urinary drainage is excessive, an ostomy pouch may be placed over the drain to protect the skin. A Penrose drain is not irrigated. Weighing the dressings is not necessary. Placing the client on the affected side will prevent a free flow of urine through the drain.
Test-Taking Strategy: Use the process of elimination. Identify the subject of the question, which relates to the Penrose drain. This should provide you with the clue that drainage is expected. Eliminate option 4 as the least likely answer. Eliminate option 2 because a Penrose drain is not irrigated. Visualize the effect that positioning on the affected side will have on the client. Review postoperative pyelolithotomy care if you had difficulty with this question.

Level of Cognitive Ability: Application
Client Needs: Physiological Integrity
Integrated Process: Nursing Process—planning
Content Area: Adult health—renal
Reference: Ignatavicius, D., & Workman, M. (2006). *Medical-surgical nursing: Critical thinking for collaborative care* (5th ed., p. 1704). Philadelphia: W.B. Saunders.

30. 1
Rationale: Acute rejection most often occurs in the first 2 weeks after transplantation. Clinical manifestations include fever, malaise, elevated white blood cell count, acute hypertension, graft tenderness, and manifestations of deteriorating renal function. Chronic rejection occurs gradually over a period of months to years. Although kidney infection or obstruction can occur, the symptoms presented in the question do not relate specifically to these disorders.
Test-Taking Strategy: Use the process of elimination and note the strategic words *a week after kidney transplantation.* These words should direct you easily to option 1, *acute* rejection. Review the signs of acute rejection if you had difficulty with this question.
Level of Cognitive Ability: Analysis
Client Needs: Physiological Integrity
Integrated Process: Nursing Process—analysis
Content Area: Adult health—renal
Reference: Ignatavicius, D., & Workman, M. (2006). *Medical-surgical nursing: Critical thinking for collaborative care* (5th ed., p. 1762). Philadelphia: W.B. Saunders.

31. 2
Rationale: Transurethral resection syndrome is caused by increased absorption of nonelectrolyte irrigating fluid used during surgery. The client may show signs of cerebral edema and increased intracranial pressure, such as increased blood pressure, bradycardia, confusion, disorientation, muscle twitching, visual disturbances, and nausea and vomiting.
Test-Taking Strategy: Use the process of elimination. Recalling that increased intracranial pressure is the concern in this syndrome will direct you to option 2. Review the clinical manifestations of this disorder if you had difficulty with this question.
Level of Cognitive Ability: Analysis
Client Needs: Physiological Integrity
Integrated Process: Nursing Process—assessment
Content Area: Adult health—renal
Reference: Black, J., & Hawks, J. (2005). *Medical-surgical nursing: Clinical management for positive outcomes* (7th ed., p. 1020). Philadelphia: W.B. Saunders.

32. 4
Rationale: Frank bleeding (arterial or venous) may occur during the first day after surgery. Some hematuria is usual for several days after surgery. A urinary output of 200 mL more than intake is adequate. Bladder spasms are expected to occur following surgery. A rapid pulse with a low blood pressure is a potential sign of excessive blood loss. The physician should be notified.
Test-Taking Strategy: Use the process of elimination and focus on the subject, need to notify the physician. Think about the expected findings following this procedure and note that the

vital signs noted in option 4 indicate excessive blood loss. Review the expected findings following transurethral resection of the prostate if you had difficulty with this question.
Level of Cognitive Ability: Analysis
Client Needs: Physiological Integrity
Integrated Process: Nursing Process—analysis
Content Area: Adult health—renal
Reference: Black, J., & Hawks, J. (2005). *Medical-surgical nursing: Clinical management for positive outcomes* (7th ed., p. 1024). Philadelphia: W.B. Saunders.

33. 2
Rationale: Individuals with polycystic kidney disease seem to waste rather than retain sodium. Thus, they need increased sodium and water intake. Aggressive control of hypertension is essential. Genetic counseling is advisable because of the hereditary nature of the disease.
Test-Taking Strategy: Use the process of elimination and note the strategic words *needs additional teaching.* These words indicate a negative event query and ask you to select an option that is incorrect. Recalling that sodium wasting occurs in polycystic kidney disease will direct you to option 2. Review the manifestations associated with this disease if you had difficulty with this question.
Level of Cognitive Ability: Analysis
Client Needs: Physiological Integrity
Integrated Process: Teaching and Learning
Content Area: Adult health—renal
Reference: Black, J., & Hawks, J. (2005). *Medical-surgical nursing: Clinical management for positive outcomes* (7th ed., p. 938). Philadelphia: W.B. Saunders.

34. 3
Rationale: Potential complications after renal angiography include allergic reaction to the dye, renal damage from the dye, and vascular complications, which include hemorrhage, thrombosis, or embolism. The nurse detects these complications by noting signs and symptoms of allergic reaction, decreased urine output, hematoma or hemorrhage at the insertion site, and/or signs of decreased circulation to the affected leg.
Test-Taking Strategy: Use the process of elimination, focusing on the subject, a complication. Eliminate options 1 and 2 because they are normal findings. Because a hematoma is abnormal, then "absence of hematoma" is a normal finding, which eliminates option 4 also. Review the signs of a complication following a renal angioplasty if you had difficulty with this question.
Level of Cognitive Ability: Analysis
Client Needs: Physiological Integrity
Integrated Process: Nursing Process—evaluation
Content Area: Adult health—renal
References: Chernecky, C., & Berger, B. (2004). *Laboratory tests and diagnostic procedures* (4th ed, pp. 958-959). Philadelphia: W.B. Saunders.
Pagana, K., & Pagana, T. (2005). *Mosby's diagnostic and laboratory test reference* (7th ed., p. 131). St. Louis: Mosby.

35. 4
Rationale: The client with polycystic kidney disease should report any signs and symptoms of urinary tract infection so

that treatment may begin promptly. Lowered blood pressure is not a complication of polycystic kidney disease, and it is an expected effect of antihypertensive therapy. The client would be concerned about increases in blood pressure because control of hypertension is essential. The client may experience heart failure as a result of hypertension, and thus any symptoms of heart failure, such as shortness of breath, are also a concern.

Test-Taking Strategy: Use the process of elimination and note the strategic words *understands* and *no reason to be concerned.* Recalling that the client with polycystic kidney disease is likely to be hypertensive will direct you to option 4. Also, note that options 1, 2, and 3 identify signs of complications. Review teaching points for the client with polycystic kidney disease if you had difficulty with this question.

Level of Cognitive Ability: Analysis
Client Needs: Physiological Integrity
Integrated Process: Nursing Process—evaluation
Content Area: Adult health—renal
Reference: Ignatavicius, D., & Workman, M. (2006). *Medical-surgical nursing: Critical thinking for collaborative care* (5th ed., p. 1711). Philadelphia: W.B. Saunders.

36. **3**

Rationale: Treatment of prostatitis includes medication with antibiotics, analgesics, and stool softeners. The nurse also teaches the client to rest, increase fluid intake, and use sitz baths for comfort. Antimicrobial therapy is always continued until the prescription is finished.

Test-Taking Strategy: Use the process of elimination. Eliminate option 1 first because stopping medication therapy before the end of the course is contraindicated. Also, eliminate option 4 because fluid intake should be increased. From the remaining options, recall that sitz baths provide comfort and that rest is helpful in the healing process. Review home care instructions for the client with prostatitis if you had difficulty with this question.

Level of Cognitive Ability: Analysis
Client Needs: Health Promotion and Maintenance
Integrated Process: Nursing Process—evaluation
Content Area: Adult health—renal
Reference: Ignatavicius, D., & Workman, M. (2006). *Medical-surgical nursing: Critical thinking for collaborative care* (5th ed., p. 1880). Philadelphia: W.B. Saunders.

ALTERNATE ITEM FORMAT: MULTIPLE RESPONSE

Answer: 2, 3, 4, 5
Rationale: If outflow drainage is inadequate, the nurse attempts to stimulate outflow by changing the client's position. Turning the client to the other side or making sure that the client is in good body alignment may assist with outflow drainage. The drainage bag needs to be lower than the client's abdomen to enhance gravity drainage. The connecting tubing and peritoneal dialysis system are also checked for kinks or twisting and the clamps on the system are checked to ensure that they are open. There is no reason to contact the physician. Increasing the flow rate is an inappropriate action and is not associated with the amount of outflow solution.

Test-Taking Strategy: Use the principles related to gravity flow and preventing obstruction to flow to answer this question. This will assist in determining the correct interventions. Review the nursing interventions related to insufficient flow of dialysate if you had difficulty with this question.

Level of Cognitive Ability: Application
Client Needs: Physiological Integrity
Integrated Process: Nursing Process—Implementation
Content Area: Adult Health—Renal
Reference: Ignatavicius, D., & Workman, M. (2006). *Medical-surgical nursing: Critical thinking for collaborative care* (5th ed., p. 1759). Philadelphia: W.B. Saunders.

REFERENCES

Black, J., & Hawks, J. (2005). *Medical-surgical nursing: Clinical management for positive outcomes* (7th ed.). Philadelphia: W.B. Saunders.

Chernecky, C., & Berger, B. (2004). *Laboratory tests and diagnostic procedures* (4th ed.). Philadelphia: W.B. Saunders.

Ignatavicius, D., & Workman, M. (2006). *Medical-surgical nursing: Critical thinking for collaborative care* (5th ed.). Philadelphia: W.B. Saunders.

Lehne, R. (2007). *Pharmacology for nursing care* (6th ed.). Philadelphia: W.B. Saunders.

Lewis, S., Heitkemper, M., & Dirksen, S. (2004). *Medical-surgical nursing: Assessment and management of clinical problems* (6th ed.). St. Louis: Mosby.

Nix, S. (2005). *Williams basic nutrition and diet therapy* (12th ed.). St. Louis: Mosby.

Pagana, K., & Pagana, T. (2005). *Mosby's diagnostic and laboratory test reference* (7th ed.). St. Louis: Mosby.

Skidmore-Roth, L. (2005). *Mosby's drug guide for nurses* (6th ed.). St. Louis: Mosby.

62

Renal Medications

I. URINARY TRACT ANTISEPTICS

A. Description

1. Urinary tract antiseptics inhibit the growth of bacteria in the urine (Fig. 62-1; Box 62-1).
2. Act as disinfectants within the urinary tract
3. Used to treat acute cystitis or urinary tract infections (UTIs; Table 62-1)
4. Urinary tract antiseptics do not achieve effective antibacterial concentrations in blood or tissues and therefore cannot be used for infections outside the urinary tract.

B. Side effects and nursing considerations

1. Cinoxacin (Cinobac)
   a. Side effects are similar to those of nalidixic acid.
   b. Dosage should be reduced in clients with renal impairment; failure to do so could result in accumulation of the medication to toxic levels.
2. Methenamine (Mandelamine, Hiprex, Urex)
   a. Used to treat chronic UTIs, but not recommended for acute infections
   b. Administer after meals and at bedtime to minimize gastric distress.
   c. Chronic high-dose therapy can cause bladder irritation.
   d. Methenamine can cause crystalluria and should not be used in clients with renal impairment.
   e. Decomposition of the medication generates ammonia; therefore, it should not be used for clients with liver dysfunction.
   f. Methenamine requires acidic urine with a pH of 5.5 or lower.

   g. Forcing fluids reduces antibacterial effects by diluting the medication and raising urine pH.
   h. Methenamine should not be combined with sulfonamides because of the risk of crystalluria and urinary tract injury.
   i. Clients taking this medication should avoid alkalinizing agents, including over-the-counter (OTC) antacids containing sodium bicarbonate or sodium carbonate.
3. Nalidixic acid (NegGram)
   a. Gastrointestinal side effects include anorexia, nausea, vomiting, and diarrhea.
   b. Skin side effects include rash and photosensitivity.
   c. Central nervous system (CNS) side effects include visual disturbances and insomnia.
   d. Nalidixic acid may produce intracranial hypertension in pediatric clients and should not be administered to children younger than 3 months.
   e. When nalidixic acid is used for more than 2 weeks, complete blood cell counts and liver function tests should be performed.
   f. Nalidixic acid can intensify the effects of orally administered anticoagulants.
   g. Nalidixic acid is contraindicated in clients with a history of convulsive disorders.
4. Nitrofurantoin (Furadantin, Macrodantin, Macrobid)
   a. Gastrointestinal side effects include anorexia, nausea, vomiting, and diarrhea; administration with milk or meals minimizes gastrointestinal distress.

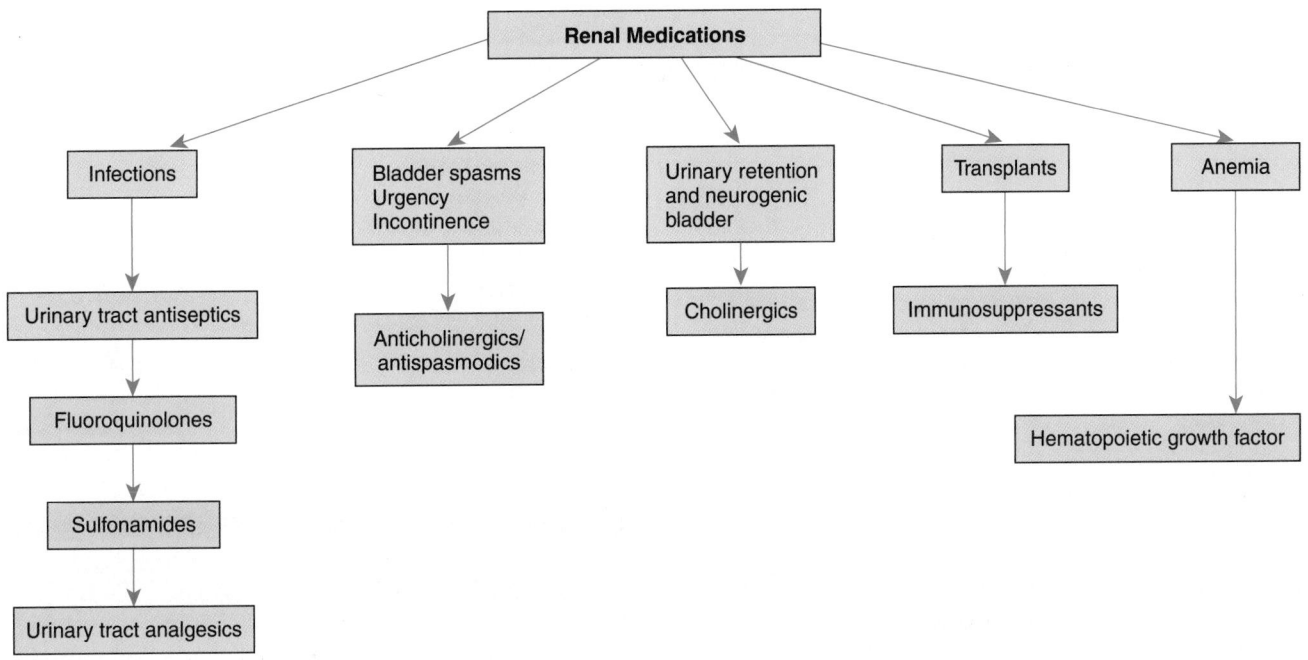

FIG. 62-1 Renal conditions and medications. Developed by Kathleen Ohman.

BOX 62-1

Urinary Tract Antiseptics

Cinoxacin (Cinobac)
Methenamine (Mandelamine, Hiprex, Urex)
Nalidixic acid (NegGram)
Nitrofurantoin (Furadantin, Macrodantin, Macrobid)

b. Pulmonary reactions include dyspnea, chest pain, chills, fever, cough, and alveolar infiltrates; these resolve in 2 to 4 days following cessation of treatment.

c. Hematological side effects include agranulocytosis, leukopenia, thrombocytopenia, and megaloblastic anemia.

d. Peripheral neuropathy side effects include muscle weakness, tingling sensations, and numbness.

e. Neurological side effects include headache, vertigo, drowsiness, and nystagmus.

f. Allergic reactions include anaphylaxis, hives, rash, and tingling sensations around the mouth.

g. Nitrofurantoin may produce a harmless brown color to the urine.

h. Nitrofurantoin is contraindicated in clients with renal impairment.

i. Instruct the client in expected side effects, signs warranting notification of the physician, and not to take nitrofurantoin with antacids.

II. FLUOROQUINOLONES (Box 62-2)

A. Description: Suppress bacterial growth by inhibiting an enzyme necessary for DNA synthesis; active against a broad spectrum of microbes

B. Side effects and nursing considerations

1. Significant side effects include dizziness, drowsiness, gastric distress, diarrhea, vaginitis (trovafloxacin), nausea, and vomiting.

2. Adverse effects include psychoses, hallucinations, confusion, tremors, hypersensitivity, and interstitial nephritis.

3. Fluoroquinolones should be used with caution in clients with hepatic, renal, or central nervous system disorders.

4. Monitor client for side effects or signs of adverse reactions.

5. Administer fluoroquinolones with a full glass of water and ensure that the client maintains a urine output of at least 1200 to 1500 mL daily to minimize the development of crystalluria.

6. Enoxacin and Norfloxacin (Noroxin) are to be taken on an empty stomach.

7. Ciprofloxacin (Cipro), lomefloxacin (Maxaquin), and ofloxacin (Floxin) may be taken with or without food.

8. Intravenously administered ciprofloxacin and ofloxacin are infused slowly over 60 minutes to minimize discomfort and vein irritation.

9. Advise the client to report dizziness, lightheadedness, visual disturbances, increased light sensitivity, and feelings of depression, because these signs could indicate central nervous system toxicity.

TABLE 62-1

Regimens for Oral Therapy of Urinary Tract Infections in Women

Drug	Dose	Duration
ACUTE CYSTITIS		
First-Line Drugs		
Trimethoprim-sulfamethoxazole	160 mg TMP/800 mg SMZ twice daily	3-7 days
Trimethoprim	100 mg twice daily	3-7 days
Norfloxacin	400 mg twice daily	3 days
Ciprofloxacin	250 mg twice daily	3 days
Ofloxacin	400 mg twice daily	3 days
Levofloxacin	400 mg once daily	3 days
Gatifloxacin	200 mg once daily	3 days
Second-Line Drugs		
Nitrofurantoin	500-100 mg four times daily	7 days
Fosfomycin	3 g once	1 day
ACUTE UNCOMPLICATED PYELONEPHRITIS		
First-Line Drugs		
Trimethoprim-sulfamethoxazole	160 mg TMP/800 mg SMZ twice daily	14 days
Trimethoprim	100 mg twice daily	14 days
Ciprofloxacin	250-500 mg twice daily	14 days
Gatifloxacin	400 mg once daily	10-14 days
Levofloxacin	500 mg once daily	10-14 days
Second-Line Drugs		
Amoxicillin (with clavulanic acid)	500 mg three times daily	14 days
Cephalexin	500 mg four times daily	14 days
Cefotaxime	1 g three times daily	14 days
Ceftriaxone	1-2 g once daily	14 days
COMPLICATED URINARY TRACT INFECTIONS		
Trimethoprim-sulfamethoxazole	160 mg TMP/800 mg SMZ twice daily	7-14 days
Norfloxacin	400 mg twice daily	7-14 days
Ciprofloxacin	250-500 mg twice daily	7-14 days
Levofloxacin	400 mg twice daily	7-14 days
Amoxicillin (with clavulanic acid)	500 mg three times daily	7-14 days
Cephalexin	500 mg three times daily	7-14 days
PROPHYLAXIS OF RECURRENT INFECTION		
Trimethoprim-sulfamethoxazole	40 mg TMP/200 mg SMZ at bedtime three times/wk	6 months
Trimethoprim	100 mg at bedtime	6 months
Nitrofurantoin	50-100 mg at bedtime	6 months
Norfloxacin	200 mg at bedtime	6 months

TMP-SMZ, Trimethoprim-sulfamethoxazole.
Modified from Lehne, R. (2007). *Pharmacology for nursing care* (6th ed.). Philadelphia: W.B. Saunders.

BOX 62-2

Fluoroquinolones

Ciprofloxacin (Cipro)
Enoxacin
Gatifloxacin (Tequin)
Gemifloxacin (Factive)
Levofloxacin (Levaquin)
Lomefloxacin (Maxaquin)
Moxifloxacin (Avelox)
Norfloxacin (Noroxin)
Ofloxacin (Floxin)
Sparfloxacin
Trovafloxacin (Trovan)

BOX 62-3

Sulfonamides

Sulfadiazine
Sulfamethizole
Sulfamethoxazole
Sulfisoxazole
Trimethoprim (Proloprim, Trimpex)
Trimethoprim (TMP)-sulfamethoxazole (SMZ) (Bactrim, Cotrim, Septra)

10. Inform the client of signs of hepatic and renal toxicity and the importance of reporting these signs to the physician.

III. **SULFONAMIDES** (Box 62-3)
A. Description: Suppress bacterial growth by inhibiting the synthesis of folic acid; active against a broad spectrum of microbes; used primarily to treat acute urinary tract infections
B. Side effects and nursing considerations
   1. Hypersensitivity reactions include rash, fever, and photosensitivity.
   2. Stevens-Johnson syndrome, the most severe hypersensitivity response, produces symptoms that include widespread lesions of the skin and mucous membranes, fever, malaise, and toxemia.
   3. Sulfonamides should be discontinued if a rash is noted; the physician is notified if a rash appears.
   4. Sulfonamides can cause hemolytic anemia, agranulocytosis, leukopenia, and thrombocytopenia; instruct the client to notify the physician if sore throat or fever occurs.
   5. Administer sulfonamides with caution in clients with renal impairment.
   6. Sulfonamides are contraindicated if a hypersensitivity exists to sulfonamides, sulfonylureas, or thiazide or loop diuretics.
   7. Sulfonamides are contraindicated in infants younger than 2 months and in pregnant women or mothers who are breast-feeding.

BOX 62-4
Urinary Tract Analgesic

Phenazopyridine Hydrochloride (Pyridium, Azo-Standard, Pyridiate, Urogesic)

BOX 62-5
Anticholinergics-Antispasmodics

Oxybutynin chloride (Ditropan, Ditropan XL)
Propantheline bromide (Pro-Banthine)
Tolterodine tartrate (Detrol, Detrol LA)

8. Sulfonamides can potentiate the effects of warfarin sodium (Coumadin), phenytoin (Dilantin), and orally administered hypoglycemics such as tolbutamide (Orinase); when combined with sulfonamides, these medications may require a reduction in dosage.

9. Instruct the client to take the medication on an empty stomach with a full glass of water.

10. Instruct the client to complete the entire course of antibiotics prescribed.

11. Instruct the client to avoid prolonged exposure to sunlight, wear protective clothing, and apply a sunscreen to exposed skin.

12. Adults should maintain a daily urine output of 1200 mL by consuming 8 to 10 glasses of water each day to minimize the risk of renal damage from the medication.

13. Inform the client that some combination medications of sulfonamides can cause the urine to turn dark brown or red.

14. The sulfonamide combination of trimethoprim-sulfamethoxazole (TMP-SMZ; Bactrim, Cotrim, Septra) is more effective than either medication alone because it inhibits the sequential steps in bacterial folic acid synthesis.

15. TMP-SMZ is used cautiously with clients experiencing impaired kidney function, folate deficiency, severe allergy, or bronchial asthma.

16. An intravenous dose of TMP-SMZ is administered over 60 to 90 minutes and is not mixed with other medications.

IV. **URINARY TRACT ANALGESIC** (Box 62-4)
A. Description
  1. Phenazopyridine hydrochloride is a urinary tract analgesic used to treat pain from urinary tract irritation or infection.
  2. A urinary tract analgesic is administered with an antibiotic because the analgesic only treats pain, not the infection.
B. Side effects
  1. Nausea
  2. Headache
  3. Vertigo
C. Nursing considerations
  1. Instruct the client that the urine will turn red or orange and stain clothing.
  2. A urinary tract analgesic is contraindicated in clients with renal or hepatic disease.
  3. The medication interferes with accurate urine testing for glucose and ketones.

V. **ANTICHOLINERGICS-ANTISPASMODICS**
  (Box 62-5)
A. Description
  1. Oxybutynin chloride (Ditropan) relaxes smooth muscles of the urinary tract.
  2. Propantheline bromide (Pro-Banthine) decreases bladder muscle spasms.
  3. Tolterodine tartrate (Detrol, Detrol LA) reduces urinary incontinence, urgency, and frequency by controlling bladder contractions.
B. Side effects
  1. Anorexia, nausea, vomiting, and dry mouth
  2. Blurred vision
  3. Confusion in older clients
  4. Constipation
  5. Decreased sweating
  6. Dizziness
  7. Drowsiness
  8. Dry eyes
  9. Gastric distress
  10. Headache
  11. Tachycardia
  12. Urinary retention
C. Nursing considerations
  1. Extended-release capsules should not be split, chewed, or crushed
  2. Detrol LA should be used cautiously in clients with narrow-angle glaucoma.
  3. Do not administer oxybutynin to clients with known hypersensitivity, gastrointestinal or genitourinary obstruction, glaucoma, severe colitis, or myasthenia gravis.
  4. Do not administer propantheline bromide to clients with narrow-angle glaucoma, obstructive uropathy, gastrointestinal disease, or ulcerative colitis.
  5. Instruct the client to avoid hazardous activities because of the side effects of dizziness and drowsiness.
  6. Monitor intake and output.
  7. Provide gum or hard candy for dry mouth.
  8. Monitor for signs of toxicity (central nervous system stimulation) such as hypotension, hypertension, confusion, tachycardia, flushed or red face, signs of respiratory depression, nervousness, restlessness, hallucinations, and irritability.

VI. **CHOLINERGIC** (Box 62-6)
A. Description: Bethanechol chloride (Urecholine) is a cholinergic used to increase bladder tone and func-

BOX 62-6
Cholinergic

Bethanechol chloride (Urecholine)

tion and to treat nonobstructive urinary retention and neurogenic bladder.

B. Side effects
1. Headache
2. Hypotension
3. Flushing and sweating
4. Increased salivation
5. Abdominal cramps
6. Nausea and vomiting
7. Diarrhea
8. Urinary urgency
9. Bronchoconstriction
10. Transient complete heart block

C. Nursing considerations
1. Do not administer if the client has a urinary stricture or obstruction.
2. Administer on an empty stomach, 1 hour before or 2 hours after meals to lessen nausea and vomiting.
3. Never administer by the intramuscular or intravenous (IV) route.
4. Monitor intake and output.
5. Monitor for increased bladder tone and function.
6. Monitor for cholinergic overdose (excessive salivation, sweating, involuntary urination and defecation, bradycardia, and severe hypotension).
7. Have atropine sulfate (antidote) readily available for IV or subcutaneous administration.

VII. **MEDICATIONS FOR PREVENTING ORGAN REJECTION** (Box 62-7)
A. Medications include immunosuppressants, corticosteroids, cytotoxic medications, and antibodies.
B. Cyclosporine (Sandimmune, Gengraf, Neoral)
1. Cyclosporine inhibits calcineurin and acts on T lymphocytes to suppress the production of interleukin-2, interferon-γ, and other cytokines.
2. Cyclosporine is used to prevent rejection of allogeneic kidney, liver, and heart transplants.
3. Prednisone (Deltasone) is usually administered concurrently.
4. Oral administration of cyclosporine is preferred; intravenous administration is reserved for clients who cannot take the medication orally.
5. Blood levels of the medication should be measured periodically.
6. The most common adverse effects are nephrotoxicity, infection, hypertension, tremor, and hirsutism.
7. Assure the client that hirsutism is reversible; instruct on the use of a depilatory.

BOX 62-7
Preventing Organ Rejection

IMMUNOSUPPRESSANTS
Cyclosporine (Sandimmune, Gengraf, Neoral)
Tacrolimus (Prograf)

GLUCOCORTICOID
Prednisone (Deltasone)

CYTOTOXIC MEDICATIONS
Azathioprine (Imuran)
Mycophenolate mofetil (CellCept)

ANTIBODIES
Basiliximab (Simulect)
Daclizumab (Zenapax)
Antithymocyte globulin, equine (Atgam)
Muromonab-CD3 (Orthoclone OKT3)

8. Other adverse effects include neurotoxicity, gastrointestinal effects, hyperkalemia, and hyperglycemia.
9. The risk of infection and lymphomas is increased with the use of cyclosporine.
10. Cyclosporine is contraindicated in the presence of hypersensitivity, pregnancy and breast-feeding, recent inoculation with live virus vaccines, and recent contact with an active infection such as chickenpox or herpes zoster.
11. Cyclosporine is embryotoxic, and women of childbearing age should use a mechanical form of contraception and avoid oral contraceptives.
12. The client should be informed about the possibility of renal damage and liver damage and the need for periodic liver function tests and determination of coagulation factors and blood urea nitrogen, serum creatinine, serum potassium, and blood glucose levels.
13. The client should be instructed to monitor for early signs of infection and to report these signs immediately.
14. Instruct the client to dispense the oral liquid medication into a glass container by using a specially calibrated pipette, mix well, and drink immediately; rinse the glass container with diluent and drink it to ensure ingestion of the complete dose; dry the outside of the pipette and return to its cover for storage.
15. To promote palatability, instruct the client to mix the medication with milk, chocolate milk, or orange juice just before administration.
16. Consuming grapefruit juice is prohibited because it raises cyclosporine levels and increases the risk of toxicity.
17. Ketoconazole (Nizoral), erythromycin, and amphotericin B deoxycholate (Fungizone) can elevate cyclosporine levels.

18. Phenytoin (Dilantin), phenobarbital, rifampin (Rifadin), and trimethoprim-sulfamethoxazole can decrease cyclosporine levels.
19. Renal damage can be intensified by the concurrent use of other nephrotoxic medications.

C. Sirolimus (Rapamune)
1. Sirolimus is used for the prevention of renal transplant rejection by inhibiting the response of helper T lymphocytes and B lymphocytes to cytokinesis.
2. It is used with cyclosporine and corticosteroids.
3. Increases the risk of infection, increases the risk of renal injury, increases the risk of lymphocele (a complication of renal transplant surgery), and raises cholesterol and triglyceride levels
4. Side effects include rash, acne, anemia, thrombocytopenia, joint pain, diarrhea, and hypokalemia.

D. Tacrolimus (Prograf)
1. Tacrolimus inhibits calcineurin and thereby prevents T cells from producing interleukin-2, interferon-γ, and other cytokines.
2. Tacrolimus is more effective than cyclosporine, but is more toxic.
3. Adverse effects are similar to those of cyclosporine and include nephrotoxicity, infection, hypertension, tremor, hirsutism, neurotoxicity, gastrointestinal effects, hyperkalemia, and hyperglycemia.
4. Tacrolimus should be used cautiously in immunosuppressed clients and those with renal, hepatic, or pancreatic impairment.
5. Tacrolimus is contraindicated for clients hypersensitive to cyclosporine.
6. Concurrent use of glucocorticoids is recommended.
7. Monitor blood glucose levels and administer prescribed insulin or oral hypoglycemics.

E. Prednisone (Deltasone)
1. Prednisone is a glucocorticoid that inhibits accumulation of inflammatory cells at inflammation sites.
2. Hyperglycemia and hypokalemia can occur with prednisone use; monitor glucose and serum potassium levels.
3. See Chap. 54 for additional information about prednisone.

F. Azathioprine (Imuran)
1. Azathioprine suppresses cell-mediated and humoral immune responses by inhibiting the proliferation of B and T lymphocytes.
2. Used as an adjunct to cyclosporine and glucocorticoids to help suppress transplant rejection
3. Can cause neutropenia and thrombocytopenia from bone marrow suppression
4. Contraindicated in pregnancy; associated with an increased incidence of neoplasms

5. Monitor hematocrit, white blood cell count, platelet count, liver enzyme levels, and coagulation factors.

G. Mycophenolate mofetil (CellCept)
1. Mycophenolate mofetil causes selective inhibition of B- and T-lymphocyte proliferation.
2. Used with cyclosporine and glucocorticoids for prophylaxis against organ rejection
3. Major adverse effects include diarrhea, severe neutropenia, vomiting, and sepsis.
4. Mycophenolate mofetil is associated with an increased risk of infection and malignancies.
5. Absorption is decreased by the use of magnesium and aluminum antacids and by cholestyramine (Questran, Prevalite).
6. It is contraindicated in pregnancy and during breast-feeding.
7. Instruct the client to take the medication on an empty stomach and not to open or crush capsules.
8. Instruct the client to contact the physician for unusual bleeding or bruising, sore throat, mouth sores, abdominal pain, or fever.

H. Daclizumab (Zenapax) and basiliximab (Simulect)
1. Daclizumab and basiliximab bind to interleukin-2 receptors on lymphocytes, resulting in diminished cell-mediated immune reactions.
2. Used with other immunosuppressants, such as cyclosporine and glucocorticoids, to prevent acute rejection of transplanted kidneys
3. Administered by the intravenous route
4. Daclizumab (Zenapax)
   a. Initial dose is administered within 24 hours before transplantation.
   b. Side effects include chest pain, gastrointestinal distress, edema, shortness of breath, pain in the joints, and slow wound healing.
5. Basiliximab (Simulect)
   a. Initial dose is administered within 2 hours before transplantation.
   b. Side effects are similar to those for daclizumab; in addition, headache, insomnia, dizziness, and tremors can occur.

I. Antithymocyte globulin, equine (Atgam)
1. Antithymocyte globulin, equine, causes a decrease in the number and activity of thymus-derived lymphocytes and is used to suppress organ rejection following renal, liver, bone marrow, and heart transplantation.
2. Before the first infusion, the client should undergo intradermal skin testing to determine hypersensitivity.
3. Because this product is made using equine and human blood components, it may carry a risk of transmitting infectious agents, such as viruses.
4. Monitor the platelet count and report it if below 100,000/mm³.

5. Arrange for outpatient referral for repeated infusions after discharge.

J. Muromonab-CD3 (Orthoclone OKT3)
1. Blocks all T-cell functions; used to prevent acute allograft rejection of kidney transplants
2. Adverse reactions include fever, chills, dyspnea, chest pain, and nausea and vomiting.
3. Administered via the IV route; the client is pretreated with IV glucocorticoid.

VIII. HEMATOPOIETIC GROWTH FACTORS (Box 62-8)
A. Erythropoietic growth factors
1. Stimulate the production of red blood cells
2. Used to treat anemia of **chronic renal failure**, chemotherapy-induced anemia, anemia caused by zidovudine (AZT), and anemia in clients requiring surgery
3. Initial effects can be seen within 1 to 2 weeks, and the hematocrit reaches normal levels (30% to 33%) in 2 to 3 months.
4. Side effect: Major side effect is hypertension.
5. Other effects can include heart failure, thrombotic effects such as stroke or myocardial infarction, and cardiac arrest.

B. Leukopoietic growth factors
1. Stimulate the production of white blood cells (leukocytes)
2. Used for clients undergoing myelosuppressive chemotherapy or bone marrow transplantation and those with severe chronic neutropenia.
3. Can cause bone pain, leukocytosis, and elevation of plasma uric acid, lactate dehydrogenase, and alkaline phosphatase levels; long-term therapy has caused splenomegaly.

C. Thrombopoietic growth factor
1. Stimulates the production of platelets
2. Used for clients undergoing myelosuppressive chemotherapy to minimize thrombocytopenia and to decrease the need for platelet transfusions
3. Adverse effects include fluid retention, cardiac dysrhythmias, conjunctival infection, visual blurring, and papilledema.

BOX 62-8

Hematopoietic Growth Factors

ERYTHROPOIETIC GROWTH FACTORS
Epoetin alfa (Epogen, Procrit)
Darbepoetin alfa (Aranesp)

LEUKOPOIETIC GROWTH FACTORS
Filgrastim (Neupogen)
Pegfilgrastim (Neulasta)
Sargramostim (Leukine)

THROMBOPOIETIC GROWTH FACTOR
Oprelvekin (Neumega)

PRACTICE QUESTIONS

1. The client who has a cold is seen in the emergency room with an inability to void. Because the client has a history of benign prostatic hyperplasia, the nurse determines that the client should be questioned about the use of which of the following medications?
1. Diuretics
2. Antibiotics
3. Antitussives
4. Decongestants

2. Trimethoprim-sulfamethoxazole (TMP-SMZ; Bactrim) is prescribed to be administered by intravenous infusion to a client with a recurrent urinary tract infection. A nurse would administer this medication:
1. Over 30 minutes
2. Over 60 to 90 minutes
3. Piggybacked into the peripheral line containing parenteral nutrition
4. Piggybacked into the existing infusion of normal saline and potassium chloride

3. Nalidixic acid (NegGram) is prescribed for a client with a urinary tract infection. On review of the client's record, the nurse notes that the client is taking warfarin sodium (Coumadin) daily. Which prescription should the nurse anticipate for this client?
1. Discontinuation of warfarin sodium (Coumadin)
2. A decrease in the warfarin sodium (Coumadin) dosage
3. An increase in the warfarin sodium (Coumadin) dosage
4. A decrease in the usual dose of nalidixic acid (NegGram)

4. A nurse is providing discharge instructions to a client receiving sulfisoxazole. Which of the following would be included in the list of instructions?
1. Restrict fluid intake.
2. Maintain a high fluid intake.
3. If the urine turns dark brown, call the physician immediately.
4. Decrease the dosage when symptoms are improving to prevent an allergic response.

5. Trimethoprim-sulfamethoxazole (TMP-SMZ; Bactrim) is prescribed for a client. A nurse would instruct the client to report which symptom if it developed during the course of this medication therapy?
1. Nausea
2. Diarrhea
3. Headache
4. Sore throat

6. Phenazopyridine hydrochloride (Pyridium) is prescribed for a client for symptomatic relief of pain resulting from a lower urinary tract infection. The nurse teaches the client:
1. To take the medication at bedtime
2. To take the medication before meals

3. To discontinue the medication if a headache occurs

4. That a reddish orange discoloration of the urine may occur

7. Bethanechol chloride (Urecholine) is prescribed for a client with urinary retention. Which disorder would be a contraindication to the administration of this medication?
   1. Gastric atony
   2. Urinary strictures
   3. Neurogenic atony
   4. Gastroesophageal reflux

8. A nurse who is administering bethanechol chloride (Urecholine) is monitoring for acute toxicity associated with the medication. The nurse checks the client for which sign of toxicity?
   1. Dry skin
   2. Dry mouth
   3. Bradycardia
   4. Signs of dehydration

9. Oxybutynin chloride (Ditropan) is prescribed for a client with neurogenic bladder. Which sign would indicate a possible toxic effect related to this medication?
   1. Pallor
   2. Drowsiness
   3. Bradycardia
   4. Restlessness

10. Propantheline bromide (Pro-Banthine) is prescribed for a client with bladder spasms. Which of the following disorders, if noted in the client's record, would alert a nurse to question the prescription for this medication?
    1. Glaucoma
    2. Myxedema
    3. Hypothyroidism
    4. Coronary artery disease

11. Following kidney transplantation, cyclosporine (Sandimmune) is prescribed for a client. Which laboratory result would indicate an adverse effect from the use of this medication?
    1. Decreased creatinine level
    2. Decreased hemoglobin level
    3. Elevated blood urea nitrogen level
    4. Decreased white blood cell count

12. A nurse is providing dietary instructions to a client who has been prescribed cyclosporine (Sandimmune). Which food item would the nurse instruct the client to avoid?
    1. Red meats
    2. Orange juice
    3. Grapefruit juice
    4. Green leafy vegetables

13. A nurse provides instructions to a client who will be taking cyclosporine (Sandimmune) oral solution. The nurse tells the client to:
    1. Mix the concentrate with chocolate milk.
    2. Mix the concentrate with grapefruit juice.

3. Avoid diluting the concentrate for administration.

4. Dilute the concentrate in a Styrofoam cup before administration.

14. A nurse is monitoring a client receiving cyclosporine (Sandimmune). Which sign or symptom would indicate to the nurse that the client is experiencing an adverse effect from this medication?
    1. Nausea
    2. Tremors
    3. Alopecia
    4. Hypotension

15. Tacrolimus (Prograf) is prescribed for a client. Which disorder, if noted in the client's record, would indicate that the medication needs to be administered with caution?
    1. Pancreatitis
    2. Ulcerative colitis
    3. Diabetes insipidus
    4. Coronary artery disease

16. A nurse is reviewing the laboratory results for a client receiving tacrolimus (Prograf). Which laboratory result would indicate to the nurse that the client is experiencing an adverse effect of the medication?
    1. Blood glucose of 200 mg/dL
    2. Potassium level of 3.8 mEq/L
    3. Platelet count of 300,000 cells/mm^3
    4. White blood cell count of 6,000 cells/mm^3

17. Mycophenolate mofetil (CellCept) is prescribed for a client for prophylaxis of organ rejection following allogeneic renal transplantation. Which instruction would a nurse provide to the client regarding administration of this medication?
    1. Administer following meals.
    2. Contact the physician if a sore throat occurs.
    3. Take the medication with a magnesium-type antacid.
    4. Open the capsule and mix with food for administration.

18. The nurse receives a call from a client concerned about eliminating brown-colored urine after taking nitrofurantoin (Furadantin) for a urinary tract infection. Which of the following is the appropriate response from the nurse?
    1. "Discontinue taking the medication and make an appointment for a urine culture."
    2. "Continue taking the medication because the urine is discolored from the medication."
    3. "Decrease your medication to half the dose because your urine is too concentrated."
    4. "Take magnesium hydroxide (Maalox) with your medication to lighten the urine color."

19. A client with chronic renal failure is receiving epoetin alfa (Epogen, Procrit). Which laboratory result would indicate a therapeutic effect of the medication?
    1. Hematocrit of 32%
    2. Platelet count of 400,000 cells/mm^3

3. Blood urea nitrogen level of 15 mg/dL
4. White blood cell count of 6,000 cells/mm³

20. A nurse is instructing a client to administer epoetin alfa (Epogen, Procrit) by the subcutaneous route. The nurse tells the client to:
    1. Shake the vial before use.
    2. Refrigerate the medication.
    3. Freeze the medication before use.
    4. Obtain syringes with 1¹⁄₂-inch needles from the pharmacy.

ALTERNATE ITEM FORMAT: CHART-EXHIBIT

Cinoxacin (Cinobac), a urinary antiseptic, is prescribed for the client. The nurse reviews the client's medical record and would contact the physician regarding which documented finding to verify the prescription?

CHART/EXHIBIT
CLIENT'S MEDICAL RECORD
Laboratory Test Result: Blood glucose, 102 mg/dL
Client's History: Renal insufficiency
Medication History: Folic acid (vitamin B₆) orally daily
Diagnostic Test Result: Chest x-ray: normal

1. Client's history
2. Medication history
3. Diagnostic test result
4. Laboratory test results

ANSWERS

1. **4**

Rationale: In the client with benign prostatic hyperplasia, episodes of urinary retention can be triggered by certain medications, such as decongestants, anticholinergics, and antidepressants. The client should be questioned about the use of these medications if the client has urinary retention. Retention also can be precipitated by other factors, such as alcoholic beverages, infection, bed rest, and becoming chilled.

Test-Taking Strategy: Use the process of elimination. The question is asking about medications that could exacerbate or contribute to urinary retention in the client with benign prostatic hyperplasia. Diuretics should help voiding; therefore, readily eliminate option 1. Antibiotics should have no effect at all, and thus eliminate option 2. From the remaining options, recalling that medications that contain anticholinergics may cause urinary retention will direct you to option 4. Review the factors that can precipitate urinary retention in the client with benign prostatic hyperplasia if you had difficulty with this question.

Level of Cognitive Ability: Analysis
Client Needs: Physiological Integrity
Integrated Process: Nursing Process—assessment
Content Area: Adult health—renal
Reference: Black, J., & Hawks, J. (2005). *Medical-surgical nursing: Clinical management for positive outcomes* (7th ed., pp. 1018-1019). Philadelphia: W.B. Saunders.

2. **2**

Rationale: Trimethoprim (TMP)-sulfamethoxazole (SMX) (Bactrim) may be administered by intravenous infusion but should not be mixed with any other medications or solutions. Trimethoprim-sulfamethoxazole is infused over 60 to 90 minutes, and bolus infusions or rapid infusions must be avoided.

Test-Taking Strategy: Use the process of elimination. Eliminate options 3 and 4 because they address the issue of mixing the trimethoprim-sulfamethoxazole with other solutions. From the remaining options, option 2 identifies the longer time frame and is the safe and correct choice. Review administra-

tion of this medication by intravenous infusion if you had difficulty with this question.
Level of Cognitive Ability: Application
Client Needs: Physiological Integrity
Integrated Process: Nursing Process—implementation
Content Area: Pharmacology
Reference: Gahart, B., & Nazareno, A. (2006). *2006 intravenous medications* (22nd ed., p. 1136). St. Louis: Mosby.

3. **2**

Rationale: Nalidixic acid can intensify the effects of oral anticoagulants by displacing these agents from binding sites on plasma protein. When an oral anticoagulant is combined with nalidixic acid, a decrease in the anticoagulant dosage may be needed.

Test-Taking Strategy: Knowledge about the medication interactions associated with the use of nalidixic acid is needed to answer this question. Remember that nalidixic acid can intensify the effects of oral anticoagulants. Review these interactions if you had difficulty with this question.
Level of Cognitive Ability: Analysis
Client Needs: Physiological Integrity
Integrated Process: Nursing Process—analysis
Content Area: Pharmacology
Reference: Kee, J., Hayes, E., & McCuistion, L. (2006). *Pharmacology: A nursing process approach* (5th ed., p. 488). Philadelphia: W.B. Saunders.

4. **2**

Rationale: Each dose of sulfisoxazole should be administered with a full glass of water, and the client should maintain a high fluid intake. The medication is more soluble in alkaline urine. The client should not be instructed to taper or discontinue the dose. Some forms of sulfisoxazole cause urine to turn dark brown or red. This does not indicate the need to notify the physician.

Test-Taking Strategy: Use the process of elimination. Recalling that this medication is used to treat urinary tract infections

will direct you to option 2. Review client instructions regarding this medication if you had difficulty with this question.
Level of Cognitive Ability: Application
Client Needs: Physiological Integrity
Integrated Process: Teaching and Learning
Content Area: Pharmacology
Reference: Mosby. (2007). *2007 Mosby's nursing drug reference* (20th ed., p. 936). St. Louis: Mosby.

5. **4**
Rationale: Clients taking trimethoprim (TMP)-sulfamethoxazole (SMZ) should be informed about early signs of blood disorders that can occur from this medication. These include sore throat, fever, and pallor, and the client should be instructed to notify the physician if these symptoms occur. The other options do not require physician notification.
Test-Taking Strategy: Use the process of elimination. Knowledge that this medication can cause blood dyscrasias will direct you to option 4. If you are unfamiliar with this medication, review this content.
Level of Cognitive Ability: Application
Client Needs: Physiological Integrity
Integrated Process: Teaching and Learning
Content Area: Pharmacology
Reference: Skidmore-Roth, L. (2005). *Mosby's drug guide for nurses* (6th ed., p. 877). St. Louis: Mosby.

6. **4**
Rationale: The nurse should instruct the client that a reddish-orange discoloration of urine may occur. The nurse also should instruct the client that this discoloration can stain fabric. The medication should be taken after meals to reduce the possibility of gastrointestinal upset. A headache is an occasional side effect of the medication and does not warrant discontinuation of the medication.
Test-Taking Strategy: Use the process of elimination. Eliminate options 1 and 2 first because they are comparative or alike in that they address time schedules for the administration of the medication. From the remaining options, eliminate option 3 because the nurse would not advise the client to discontinue this medication. Review client instructions regarding this medication if you had difficulty with this question.
Level of Cognitive Ability: Application
Client Needs: Physiological Integrity
Integrated Process: Teaching/Learning
Content Area: Pharmacology
Reference: Hodgson, B., & Kizior, R. (2007). *Saunders nursing drug handbook 2007* (p. 919). Philadelphia: W.B. Saunders.

7. **2**
Rationale: Bethanechol chloride (Urecholine) can be hazardous to clients with urinary tract obstruction or weakness of the bladder wall. The medication has the ability to contract the bladder and thereby increase pressure within the urinary tract. Elevation of pressure within the urinary tract could rupture the bladder in clients with these conditions.
Test-Taking Strategy: Use the process of elimination. Noting that the medication is used for urinary retention may assist

in directing you to option 2. Review the contraindications associated with this medication if you had difficulty with this question.
Level of Cognitive Ability: Analysis
Client Needs: Physiological Integrity
Integrated Process: Nursing Process—analysis
Content Area: Pharmacology
Reference: Kee, J., Hayes, E., & McCuistion, L. (2006). *Pharmacology: A nursing process approach* (5th ed., p. 285). Philadelphia: W.B. Saunders.

8. **3**
Rationale: Toxicity (overdose) produces manifestations of excessive muscarinic stimulation such as salivation, sweating, involuntary urination and defecation, bradycardia, and severe hypotension. Treatment includes supportive measures and the administration of atropine sulfate subcutaneously or intravenously.
Test-Taking Strategy: Use the process of elimination. Noting the similarity in options 1, 2, and 4 will assist in eliminating these options. Review these signs if you had difficulty with this question.
Level of Cognitive Ability: Analysis
Client Needs: Physiological Integrity
Integrated Process: Nursing Process—assessment
Content Area: Pharmacology
References: Hodgson, B., & Kizior, R. (2007). *Saunders nursing drug handbook 2007* (p. 135). Philadelphia: W.B. Saunders.
Kee, J., Hayes, E., & McCuistion, L. (2006). *Pharmacology: A nursing process approach* (5th ed., p. 284). Philadelphia: W.B. Saunders.

9. **4**
Rationale: Toxicity (overdosage) of this medication produces central nervous system excitation, such as nervousness, restlessness, hallucinations, and irritability. Other signs of toxicity include hypotension or hypertension, confusion, tachycardia, flushed or red face, and signs of respiratory depression. Drowsiness is a frequent side effect of the medication but does not indicate overdosage.
Test-Taking Strategy: Knowledge regarding the manifestations related to toxicity is required to answer this question. Remember restlessness is a sign of toxicity. Review the signs that indicate toxicity if you had difficulty with this question.
Level of Cognitive Ability: Analysis
Client Needs: Physiological Integrity
Integrated Process: Nursing Process—assessment
Content Area: Pharmacology
Reference: Hodgson, B., & Kizior, R. (2007). *Saunders nursing drug handbook 2007* (p. 882). Philadelphia: W.B. Saunders.

10. **1**
Rationale: Propantheline bromide (Pro-Banthine) is contraindicated in clients with narrow-angle glaucoma, obstructive uropathy, gastrointestinal disease, or ulcerative colitis. The medication decreases bladder muscle spasms.
Test-Taking Strategy: Use the process of elimination. Eliminate options 2 and 3 because they are comparative or alike. From the remaining options, you must know the contraindications

associated with the medication and remember that the medication is contraindicated in glaucoma. Review these contraindications if you had difficulty with this question.
Level of Cognitive Ability: Analysis
Client Needs: Physiological Integrity
Integrated Process: Nursing Process—analysis
Content Area: Pharmacology
Reference: Skidmore-Roth, L. (2005). *Mosby's drug guide for nurses* (6th ed., p. 726). St. Louis: Mosby.

11. **3**
Rationale: Nephrotoxicity can occur from the use of cyclosporine (Sandimmune). Nephrotoxicity is evaluated by monitoring for elevated blood urea nitrogen and serum creatinine levels. Cyclosporine does not depress the bone marrow.
Test-Taking Strategy: Use the process of elimination. Eliminate options 2 and 4 first because they are unrelated to renal function. Next, eliminate option 1 because the creatinine level would be elevated, not decreased. Option 3 is the only option that indicates an increased level of a renal function test. Review the adverse effects related to this medication if you had difficulty with this question.
Level of Cognitive Ability: Analysis
Client Needs: Physiological Integrity
Integrated Process: Nursing Process—analysis
Content Area: Pharmacology
Reference: Hodgson, B., & Kizior, R. (2007). *Saunders nursing drug handbook 2007* (p. 303). Philadelphia: W.B. Saunders.

12. **3**
Rationale: A compound present in grapefruit juice inhibits metabolism of cyclosporine. As a result, consumption of grapefruit juice can raise cyclosporine levels by 50% to 100%, thereby greatly increasing the risk of toxicity.
Test-Taking Strategy: Use the process of elimination, noting the strategic word *avoid*. Use of general pharmacology guidelines will direct you to option 3. If you had difficulty with this question, review this medication and the client instructions regarding its use.
Level of Cognitive Ability: Application
Client Needs: Physiological Integrity
Integrated Process: Teaching/Learning
Content Area: Pharmacology
Reference: Hodgson, B., & Kizior, R. (2007). *Saunders nursing drug handbook 2007* (p. 303). Philadelphia: W.B. Saunders.

13. **1**
Rationale: To improve palatability, the client should be taught to mix the concentrated medication solution with chocolate milk or orange juice just before administration. Grapefruit juice is avoided because it can raise cyclosporine levels. The client is instructed to dilute the concentrate in a glass (not Styrofoam) to ensure ingestion of the complete dose.
Test-Taking Strategy: Knowledge regarding the administration of the oral concentrate of cyclosporine is required to answer this question. Eliminate option 2 using general medication administration guidelines. From the remaining options, remember that the oral solution should be mixed with chocolate milk or orange juice just before administration. Review

the client instructions regarding administering this medication if you had difficulty with this question.
Level of Cognitive Ability: Application
Client Needs: Physiological Integrity
Integrated Process: Teaching/Learning
Content Area: Pharmacology
Reference: Hodgson, B., & Kizior, R. (2007). *Saunders nursing drug handbook 2007* (p. 302). Philadelphia: W.B. Saunders.

14. **2**
Rationale: The most common adverse effects of cyclosporine are nephrotoxicity, infection, hypertension, tremors, and hirsutism. Of these, nephrotoxicity and infection are the most serious.
Test-Taking Strategy: Knowledge regarding the adverse effects associated with cyclosporine is required to answer this question. Remember that tremors are an indication of an adverse effect. If you are unfamiliar with these effects, review this content.
Level of Cognitive Ability: Analysis
Client Needs: Physiological Integrity
Integrated Process: Nursing Process—assessment
Content Area: Pharmacology
Reference: Hodgson, B., & Kizior, R. (2007). *Saunders nursing drug handbook 2007* (p. 303). Philadelphia: W.B. Saunders.

15. **1**
Rationale: Tacrolimus (Prograf) is used with caution in immunosuppressed clients and in clients with renal, hepatic, or pancreatic function impairment. Tacrolimus is contraindicated in clients with hypersensitivity to this medication or hypersensitivity to cyclosporine.
Test-Taking Strategy: Use the process of elimination. Many medications affect renal, hepatic, and pancreatic function. If you had to select an option and were unsure, select the option that addresses these body systems. Review the cautions and contraindications associated with the administration of this medication if you had difficulty with this question.
Level of Cognitive Ability: Analysis
Client Needs: Physiological Integrity
Integrated Process: Nursing Process—analysis
Content Area: Pharmacology
Reference: Hodgson, B., & Kizior, R. (2007). *Saunders nursing drug handbook 2007* (p. 1091). Philadelphia: W.B. Saunders.

16. **1**
Rationale: A blood glucose level of 200 mg/dL is significantly elevated above the normal range of 70 to 110 mg/dL and suggests an adverse reaction. Other adverse reactions include neurotoxicity evidenced by headache, tremor, and insomnia, gastrointestinal effects such as diarrhea, nausea, and vomiting, hypertension, and hyperkalemia.
Test-Taking Strategy: Use the process of elimination, noting that options 2, 3, and 4 represent normal values. Option 1 is the only abnormal value, reflecting an elevation. Review the adverse effects related to this medication and normal laboratory values if you had difficulty with this question.
Level of Cognitive Ability: Analysis
Client Needs: Physiological Integrity
Integrated Process: Nursing Process—analysis
Content Area: Pharmacology

Reference: Hodgson, B., & Kizior, R. (2007). *Saunders nursing drug handbook 2007* (p. 1093). Philadelphia: W.B. Saunders.

17. 2
Rationale: Mycophenolate mofetil (CellCept) should be administered on an empty stomach. The capsules should not be opened or crushed. The client should contact the physician if unusual bleeding or bruising, sore throat, mouth sores, abdominal pain, or fever occurs. Antacids containing magnesium and aluminum may decrease the absorption of the medication and therefore should not be taken with the medication. The medication is given with corticosteroids and cyclosporine.
Test-Taking Strategy: Use the process of elimination. Recalling that neutropenia can occur with the use of this medication will direct you to option 2. Review this medication if you had difficulty with this question.
Level of Cognitive Ability: Application
Client Needs: Physiological Integrity
Integrated Process: Teaching/Learning
Content Area: Pharmacology
Reference: Skidmore-Roth, L. (2005). *Mosby's drug guide for nurses* (6th ed., p. 592). St. Louis: Mosby.

18. 2
Rationale: Nitrofurantoin (Furadantin) produce a harmless brown color to the urine and the medication should not be discontinued until the client's symptoms are alleviated or the prescribed dose is completed. Magnesium hydroxide (Maalox) will not affect urine color. Additionally, antacids should be avoided because they interfere with medication effectiveness.
Test-Taking Strategy: Use the process of elimination. Option 1 can be eliminated because the client should not need a urine culture at this time. These are done before treatment is initiated, if treatment is ineffective, and during follow-up appointment. Option 3 can be eliminated, because the nurse cannot change a medication dosage without a physician's order. Additionally, there is no data in the question to indicate that the urine is concentrated. Option 4 can be eliminated because antacids should be avoided as a result of their interference with the effectiveness of nitrofurantoin. Additionally, magnesium hydroxide will not have an effect on urine color. Review the effects of nitrofurantoin if you had difficulty with this question.
Level of Cognitive Ability: Application
Client Needs: Physiological Integrity
Integrated Process: Nursing Process—implementation
Content Area: Adult health—renal medications
Reference: Lehne, R. (2007). *Pharmacology for nursing care* (6th ed., p. 1012). St. Louis: W.B. Saunders.

19. 1
Rationale: Epoetin alfa is used to reverse anemia associated with chronic renal failure. Therapeutic effect is seen when the hematocrit is between 30% and 33%. Options 2, 3, and 4 are not associated with the action of this medication.

Test-Taking Strategy: Use the process of elimination. Relate the name of the medication, erythropoietin, to the potential action or effect. The only laboratory test that would reflect the effect of this medication is option 1. Review the therapeutic effect of this medication and normal serum laboratory results if you had difficulty with this question.
Level of Cognitive Ability: Analysis
Client Needs: Physiological Integrity
Integrated Process: Nursing Process—evaluation
Content Area: Pharmacology
Reference: Skidmore-Roth, L. (2005). *Mosby's drug guide for nurses* (6th ed., p. 319). St. Louis: Mosby.

20. 2
Rationale: The client should be instructed not to shake the bottle. The medication should be refrigerated at all times. The medication should not be frozen. Syringes with a $5/8$-inch needle are used for subcutaneous injection. A $1^{1}/_{2}$-inch needle may be used for intramuscular injection.
Test-Taking Strategy: Use the process of elimination. Note that options 2 and 3 identify opposite actions. This should provide you with the clue that one of these options may be the correct one. Review the teaching points related to the administration of this medication if you had difficulty with this question.
Level of Cognitive Ability: Application
Client Needs: Physiological Integrity
Integrated Process: Teaching and Learning
Content Area: Pharmacology
Reference: Hodgson, B. & Kizior, R. (2007). *Saunders nursing drug handbook 2007* (p. 423). Philadelphia: W.B. Saunders.

ALTERNATE ITEM FORMAT: CHART-EXHIBIT
Answer: 1
Rationale: Cinoxacin should be administered with caution in clients with renal impairment. The dosage should be reduced, and failure to do so could result in accumulation of cinoxacin to toxic levels. Therefore, the nurse would verify the prescription with the physician if the client had a documented history of renal insufficiency. The laboratory and diagnostic test results are normal findings. Folic acid (vitamin B_6) may be prescribed for a client with renal insufficiency to prevent anemia.
Test-Taking Strategy: Focus on the issue, the need to contact the physician. Eliminate options 3 and 4 because the laboratory and diagnostic test results are normal findings. From the remaining options, note the disorder in the client's history. This directs you to option 1. Review the contraindications associated with this medication if you had difficulty with this question.
Level of Cognitive Ability: Analysis
Client Needs: Physiological Integrity
Integrated Process: Nursing Process—analysis
Content Area: Pharmacology
Reference: Lehne, R. (2007). *Pharmacology for nursing care* (6th ed., p. 1013). Philadelphia: W.B. Saunders.

REFERENCES

Black, J., & Hawks, J. (2005). *Medical-surgical nursing: Clinical management for positive outcomes* (7th ed.). Philadelphia: W.B. Saunders.

Gahart, B., & Nazareno, A. (2006). *2006 Intravenous medications* (22nd ed.). St. Louis: Mosby.

Hodgson, B., & Kizior, R. (2007). *Saunders nursing drug handbook 2007.* Philadelphia: W.B. Saunders.

Kee, J., Hayes, E., & McCuistion, L. (2006). *Pharmacology: A nursing process approach* (5th ed.). Philadelphia: W.B. Saunders.

Lehne, R. (2007). *Pharmacology for nursing care* (6th ed.). Philadelphia: W.B. Saunders.

Mosby. (2007). *2007 Mosby's nursing drug reference* (20th ed.). St. Louis: Mosby.

Skidmore-Roth, L. (2005). *Mosby's drug guide for nurses* (6th ed.). St. Louis: Mosby.

The Adult Client With an Eye or Ear Disorder

PYRAMID TERMS

accommodation Process by which a clear visual image is maintained as the gaze is shifted from a distant to a near point.

astigmatism A condition that results from an uneven curvature of the cornea or lens in which light rays do not focus on a single point on the retina.

cataract An opacity of the lens that distorts the image projected onto the retina and that can progress to blindness.

conductive hearing loss A mechanical dysfunction or blockage of sound waves to the inner ear fibers because of external ear or middle ear disorders. The blockage can be caused by impacted cerumen, foreign bodies, pus, or serum in the middle ear. Disorders often can be corrected with no damage to hearing or minimal permanent hearing loss.

cycloplegia The paralysis of the ciliary muscles by medications that block muscarinic receptors. Cycloplegia causes blurred vision because the shape of the lens can no longer be adjusted to near-vision.

fenestration Removal of the stapes with a small hole drilled in the footplate and connection of a prosthesis between the incus and foot plate. Sounds cause the prosthesis to vibrate in the same manner as the stapes.

glaucoma Increased intraocular pressure as a result of inadequate drainage of aqueous humor from the canal of Schlemm or from overproduction of aqueous humor. The condition damages the optic nerve and can result in blindness.

hyperopia Farsightedness; objects converge to a point behind the retina. Vision beyond 20 feet is normal, but near-vision is poor. The condition is corrected by a convex lens.

legally blind The best visual acuity with corrective lenses in the better eye of 20/200 or less, or visual acuity of less than 20 degrees of the visual field in the better eye.

macular degeneration A blurred central vision caused by progressive degeneration of the center of the retina. The condition may be atrophic or age-related, or dry or exudative (wet).

Menière's syndrome Also called endolymphatic hydrops, this syndrome involves dilation of the endolymphatic system by overproduction or decreased reabsorption of endolymphatic fluid. It is characterized by tinnitus, unilateral sensorineural hearing loss, and vertigo.

miosis A constricted and fixed pupil that occurs primarily by stimulation of the muscarinic receptors of the sphincter muscles. It is seen with the use of pilocarpine drops when treating glaucoma, when using opioids, or when there is brain damage of the pons.

miotic Medication that causes contraction of the pupil.

mydriasis A dilated pupil that occurs because of blockage of the muscarinic receptors of the sphincter muscles or by stimulation of the alpha receptors of the dilator muscles. Enlarged pupils occur with stimulation of the sympathetic nervous system, use of dilating drops, acute glaucoma, or past or recent trauma.

mydriatic Medication that dilates the pupil.

myopia Nearsightedness; rays coming from an object are focused in front of the retina. Near-vision is normal, but distant vision is defective. A biconcave lens is used for correction.

otosclerosis Disease of the labyrinthine capsule of the middle ear that results in a bony overgrowth of tissue surrounding the ossicles. Otosclerosis causes the development of irregular areas of new bone formation and causes fixation of the bones. Stapes fixation leads to a conductive hearing loss.

presbycusis Gradual nerve degeneration associated with aging; a common cause of sensorineural hearing loss.

retinal detachment Separation of the layers of the retina because of the accumulation of fluid between them or because both retinal layers elevate away from the choroid as a result of a tumor. Partial separation becomes complete if untreated. When detachment becomes complete, blindness occurs.

sensorineural hearing loss A pathological process of the inner ear or of the sensory fibers that lead to the cerebral cortex. Such hearing loss often is permanent, and measures must be taken to reduce further damage or to attempt to amplify sound as a means of improving hearing to some degree.

▲ PYRAMID TO SUCCESS

Pyramid Points focus on nursing interventions for clients with impairment of sight or hearing and on the nursing care related to disorders such as cataracts, glaucoma, and retinal detachment. Pyramid Points also focus on emergency interventions for eye and ear disorders and injuries. Review nursing care related to tissue (corneal) donation for the donor and the recipient. Pyramid Points also focus on client instructions related to medication administration, sensory perceptual alterations and safety issues, and available support systems. The Integrated Processes addressed in this unit include Caring, Communication and Documentation, Nursing Process, and Teaching/Learning.

▲ CLIENT NEEDS

Safe and Effective Care Environment

Caring for the recipient of a tissue (corneal) donation
Consulting with members of the health care team
Establishing priorities
Maintaining asepsis with procedures and treatments
Maintaining standard and other precautions
Obtaining informed consent for invasive procedures
Preventing accidents that can occur as a result of sensory impairments
Upholding client rights

Health Promotion and Maintenance

Changes that occur with the aging process
Discussing expected body image changes and self-care deficits
Implementing measures for the prevention and early detection of health problems and diseases related to the eye and the ear
Performing physical assessments of eye and ear disorders
Providing home care instructions following procedures related to the eye and ear
Providing instructions regarding the administration of eye and ear medications
Providing instructions regarding activity limitations or postoperative activities
Teaching regarding the importance of compliance to the prescribed therapy

Psychosocial Integrity

Assessing the client's ability to cope with feelings of isolation, fear or anxiety regarding a possible change in vision and/or hearing status, and loss of independence
Discussing role changes
Identifying family support systems
Informing the client about available community resources
Monitoring for sensory perceptual alterations
Using appropriate communication techniques for impaired vision and hearing

Physiological Integrity

Monitoring for complications related to procedures
Monitoring for expected responses to therapy
Providing care for assistive devices such as eyeglasses, contact lenses, and hearing aids
Taking action in medical emergencies

REFERENCES

Black, J., & Hawks, J., (2005). *Medical-surgical nursing: Clinical management for positive outcomes* (7th ed.). Philadelphia: W.B. Saunders.

Chernecky, C., & Berger, B. (2004). *Laboratory tests and diagnostic procedures* (4th ed.). Philadelphia: W.B. Saunders.

Harkreader, H., & Hogan, M. A. (2004). *Fundamentals of nursing: Caring and clinical judgment* (2nd ed.). Philadelphia: W.B. Saunders.

Ignatavicius, D., & Workman, M. (2005). *Medical-surgical nursing: Critical thinking for collaborative care* (5th ed.). Philadelphia: W.B. Saunders.

Jarvis, C. (2004). *Physical examination and health assessment* (4th ed.). St. Louis: W.B. Saunders.

Lewis, S., Heitkemper, M., & Dirksen, S. (2004). *Medical-surgical nursing: Assessment and management of clinical problems* (6th ed.). St. Louis: Mosby.

National Council of State Boards of Nursing (Eds.). (2007). *2007 NCLEX-RN® detailed test plan.* Chicago: Author.

Potter, P., & Perry, A. (2005). *Fundamentals of nursing* (6th ed.). St. Louis: Mosby.

Varcarolis, E., Carson, V., & Shoemaker, N. (2006). *Foundations of psychiatric mental health nursing: A clinical approach* (5th ed.). Philadelphia: W.B. Saunders.

The Eye and the Ear

I. ANATOMY AND PHYSIOLOGY OF THE EYE
A. The eye
1. The eye is 1 inch in diameter and is located in the anterior portion of the orbit.
2. The orbit is the bony structure of the skull that surrounds the eye and offers protection to the eye.
B. Layers of the eye
1. External layer
   a. The fibrous coat that supports the eye
   b. Contains the sclera, an opaque white tissue
   c. Contains the cornea, a dense transparent layer
2. Middle layer
   a. The second layer of the eyeball
   b. Vascular and heavily pigmented
   c. Consists of the choroid, ciliary body, and iris
   d. The choroid is the dark brown membrane located between the sclera and the retina that has dark pigmentation to prevent light from reflecting internally.
   e. The choroid lines most of the sclera and is attached to the retina but can detach easily from the sclera.
   f. The choroid contains many blood vessels and supplies nutrients to the retina.
   g. The ciliary body connects the choroid with the iris and secretes aqueous humor that helps give the eye its shape; the muscles of the ciliary body control the thickness of the lens.
   h. The iris is the colored portion of the eye, located in front of the lens, and it has a central circular opening called the pupil; the pupil controls the amount of light admitted into the retina (darkness produces dilation and light produces constriction).
3. Internal layer
   a. Consists of the retina, a thin, delicate structure in which the fibers of the optic nerve are distributed
   b. The retina is bordered externally by the choroid and sclera and internally by the vitreous.
   c. The retina is the visual receptive layer of the eye in which light waves are changed into nerve impulses; it contains blood vessels and photoreceptors called rods and cones.
C. Vitreous body
1. Contains a gelatinous substance that occupies the vitreous chamber, the space between the lens and the retina
2. The vitreous body transmits light and gives shape to the posterior eye.
D. Vitreous
1. Gel-like substance that maintains the shape of the eye
2. Provides additional physical support to the retina
E. Rods and cones
1. Rods are responsible for peripheral vision and function at reduced levels of illumination.
2. Cones function at bright levels of illumination and are responsible for color vision and central vision.
F. Optic disk
1. The optic disk is a creamy pink to white depressed area in the retina.
2. The optic nerve enters and exits the eyeball at this area.
3. This area is called the blind spot because it contains only nerve fibers, lacks photoreceptor cells, and is insensitive to light.

G. Macula lutea
1. Small, oval, yellowish-pink area located laterally and temporally to the optic disk
2. The central depressed part of the macula is the fovea centralis, the area of sharpest and keenest vision, where most acute vision occurs.
H. Aqueous humor
1. The aqueous humor is a clear watery fluid that fills the anterior and posterior chambers of the eye.
2. The aqueous humor is produced by the ciliary processes, and the fluid drains into the canal of Schlemm.
3. The anterior chamber lies between the cornea and the iris.
4. The posterior chamber lies between the iris and the lens.
I. Canal of Schlemm: Passageway that extends completely around the eye; it permits fluid to drain out of the eye into the systemic circulation so a constant intraocular pressure is maintained.
J. Lens
1. Transparent convex structure behind the iris and in front of the vitreous body
2. The lens bends rays of light so that the light falls on the retina.
3. The curve of the lens changes to focus on near or distant objects.
K. Conjunctivae: Thin transparent mucous membranes of the eye that line the posterior surface of each eyelid, located over the sclera
L. Lacrimal gland
1. The lacrimal gland produces tears.
2. Tears are drained through the punctum into the lacrimal duct and sac.
M. Eye muscles
1. Muscles do not work independently but work with the muscle that produces the opposite movement.
2. Rectus muscles exert their pull when the eye turns temporally.
3. Oblique muscles exert their pull when the eye turns nasally.
N. Nerves
1. Cranial nerve II: Optic nerve (nerve of sight)
2. Cranial nerve III: Oculomotor
3. Cranial nerve IV: Trochlear
4. Cranial nerve VI: Abducens
O. Blood vessels
1. The ophthalmic artery is the major artery supplying the structures in the eye.
2. The ophthalmic veins drain the blood from the eye.

II. ASSESSMENT OF VISION (Box 63-1)
A. Acuity
1. Visual acuity tests measure the client's distance and near vision

---

BOX 63-1

Assessment of Vision

Color vision
Confrontational test
Extraocular muscle function
Ophthalmoscopy
Snellen chart

---

2. Snellen chart—"eye chart"
a. The chart is a simple tool to measure distance vision.
b. The client stands 20 feet from the chart, covers one eye, and uses the other eye to read the line that appears most clearly.
c. If the client is able to do this accurately, the client reads the next lower line.
d. This sequence is repeated until the client is unable to identify correctly more than half the characters on the line.
e. The procedure is repeated for the other eye, and then both eyes together may be tested.
f. The findings are recorded as a comparison between what the client can read at 20 feet and the distance at which an individual with normal vision can read the same line.
g. A result of 20/50 means that the client is able to read at 20 feet from the chart what a healthy eye can read at 50 feet.
h. Clients who wear corrective lenses other than for reading should have their vision tested with the lens in place.
B. Confrontational test
1. The confrontational test is performed to examine visual fields or peripheral vision.
2. The examiner and the client sit facing each other.
3. The client is asked to look directly into the eyes of the examiner throughout the test.
4. The examiner covers his or her right eye while the client covers his or her left eye (the client covers the eye directly opposite to the examiner's covered eye).
5. The examiner moves a finger from a nonvisible area into the client's line of vision.
6. The examiner and client should see the object at approximately the same time.
7. When the client sees the object coming into the line of vision, the client informs the examiner.
8. The procedure is repeated on the opposite eye.
9. The test assumes that the examiner has normal peripheral vision.
C. Extraocular muscle function (Fig. 63-1)
1. The six muscles that attach the eyeball to its orbit and serve to direct the eye to points of interest are tested.

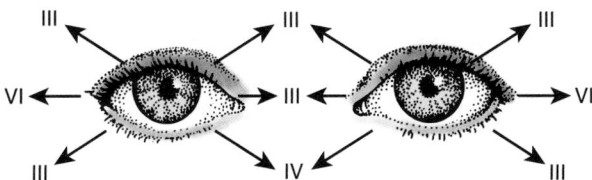

FIG. 63-1   Checking extraocular muscles in the six cardinal positions indicates the functioning of cranial nerves III, IV, and VI. (From Ignatavicius, D., & Workman, M. [2006]. *Medical-surgical nursing: Critical thinking for collaborative care* [5th ed.]. Philadelphia: W.B. Saunders.)

2. Six cardinal positions of gaze include the following:
   a. Client's right (lateral position)
   b. Upward and right (temporal position)
   c. Down and right
   d. Client's left (lateral position)
   e. Upward and left (temporal position)
   f. Down and left
3. Client holds head still and is asked to move his or her eyes and follow a small object.
4. The examiner notes for any parallel movements of the eye or for nystagmus, an involuntary, rhythmic, rapid twitching of the eyeballs.

D. Color vision
1. Tests for color vision involve picking numbers or letters out of a complex and colorful picture.
2. Ishihara chart
   a. The Ishihara chart consists of numbers composed of colored dots located within a circle of colored dots.
   b. The client is asked to read the numbers on the chart.
   c. Each eye is tested separately.
   d. Reading the numbers correctly indicates normal color vision
   e. The test is sensitive for the diagnosis of red-green blindness but cannot detect discrimination of blue.

E. Pupils
1. The pupils are round and of equal size.
2. Increasing light causes pupillary constriction.
3. Decreasing light causes pupillary dilation.
4. Constriction of both pupils is a normal response to direct light.
5. The client is asked to look straight ahead while the examiner quickly brings a beam of light (flashlight) in from the side and directs it onto the eye.
6. The constriction of the eye is a direct response to shining a light into that eye; constriction of the opposite eye is known as a consensual response.

F. Sclera and cornea

BOX 63-2
Diagnostic Tests for the Eye

Computed tomography
Corneal staining
Fluorescein angiography
Slit lamp
Tonometry

1. Normal sclera color is white.
2. A yellow color to the sclera may indicate jaundice or systemic problems.
3. In a dark-skinned person, the sclera may normally appear yellow; pigmented dots may be present.
4. The cornea is transparent, smooth, shiny, and bright.
5. Cloudy areas or specks on the cornea may be the result of an accident or eye injury.

G. Ophthalmoscopy
1. The ophthalmoscope is an instrument used to examine the external structures and the interior of the eye.
2. The room is darkened so that the pupil will dilate.
3. The instrument is held with the right hand when examining the right eye and with the left hand when examining the left eye.
4. The client is asked to look straight ahead at an object on the wall.
5. The examiner should approach the client's eye from about 12 to 15 inches away and 15 degrees lateral to the client's line of vision.
6. As the instrument is directed at the pupil, a red glare (red reflex) is seen in the pupil.
7. The red reflex is the reflection of light on the vascular retina.
8. Absence of the red reflex may indicate opacity of the lens.
9. The retina, optic disk, optic vessels, fundus, and macula can be examined.

III. DIAGNOSTIC TESTS FOR THE EYE (Box 63-2)
A. Fluorescein angiography
1. Description
   a. A detailed imaging and recording of ocular circulation by a series of photographs after the administration of a dye
   b. This test is useful for assessing problems with retinal circulation, such as those that occur in diabetic retinopathy, retinal bleeding, and macular degeneration, or to rule out intraocular tumors.
2. Preprocedure interventions
   a. Assess the client for allergies and previous reactions to dyes.

b. Obtain informed consent.

c. A mydriatic medication, which causes pupil dilation, is instilled into the eye 1 hour before the test.

d. The dye is injected into a vein of the client's arm.

e. Inform the client that the dye may cause the skin to appear yellow for several hours after the test and is eliminated gradually through the urine.

f. The client may experience nausea, vomiting, sneezing, paresthesia of the tongue, or pain at the injection site.

g. If hives appear, orally or intramuscularly administered antihistamines such as diphenhydramine (Benadryl) are given as prescribed.

3. Postprocedure interventions

a. Encourage rest.

b. Encourage fluid intake to assist in eliminating the dye from the client's system.

c. Remind the client that the yellow skin appearance will disappear.

d. Inform the client that the urine will appear bright green until the dye is excreted.

e. Advise the client to avoid direct sunlight for a few hours after the test and to wear sunglasses if staying inside is not possible.

f. Inform the client that the photophobia will continue until pupil size returns to normal.

B. Computed tomography (CT)

1. Description

a. The test is performed to examine the eyes, bony structures around the eye, and extraocular muscles.

b. A beam of x-rays scans the skull and orbits of the eye.

c. A cross-sectional image is formed by the use of a computer.

d. Contrast material may be used unless eye trauma is suspected.

2. Interventions

a. No special client preparation or follow-up care is required.

b. Instruct the client that he or she will be positioned in a confined space and will need to keep the head still during the procedure.

C. Slit lamp

1. Description

a. A slit lamp allows examination of the anterior ocular structures under microscopic magnification.

b. The client leans on a chin rest to stabilize the head while a narrowed beam of light is aimed so that it illuminates only a narrow segment of the eye.

2. Interventions

a. Explain the procedure to the client.

b. Advise the client about the brightness of the light and the need to look forward at a point over the examiner's ear.

D. Corneal staining

1. Description

a. A topical dye is instilled into the conjunctival sac to outline irregularities of the corneal surface that are not easily visible.

b. The eye is viewed through a blue filter, and a bright green color indicates areas of a nonintact corneal epithelium.

2. Interventions

a. If the client wears contact lenses, the lenses must be removed.

b. The client is instructed to blink after the dye has been applied to distribute the dye evenly across the cornea.

E. Tonometry

1. Description

a. The test is used primarily to assess for an increase of intraocular pressure and potential **glaucoma.**

b. Normal intraocular pressure is 10 to 21 mm Hg; intraocular pressure varies throughout the day and is normally higher in the morning (always document the time of intraocular pressure measurement).

2. Noncontact tonometry

a. No direct contact with the client's cornea is needed and no topical eye anesthetic is needed.

b. A puff of air is directed at the cornea to indent the cornea, which can be unpleasant and may startle the client.

c. It is a less accurate method of measurement as compared with contact tonometry.

3. Contact tonometry

a. Requires a topical anesthetic

b. A flattened cone is brought into contact with the cornea and the amount of pressure needed to flatten the cornea is measured.

c. The client must be instructed to avoid rubbing the eye following the examination if the eye has been anesthetized because of the potential for scratching the cornea.

IV. DISORDERS OF THE EYE

A. Risk factors related to eye disorders (Box 63-3)

B. Refractive errors

1. Description

a. Refraction is the bending of light rays; any problem associated with eye length or refraction can lead to refractive errors.

b. Myopia (nearsightedness): Refractive ability of the eye is too strong for the eye length; images are bent and fall in front of, not on, the retina.

  c. Hyperopia (farsightedness): Refractive ability of the eye is too weak; images are focused behind the retina.

  d. Presbyopia: Loss of lens elasticity because of aging; less able to focus the eye for close work and images fall behind the retina.

  e. **Astigmatism:** Occurs because of the irregular curvature of the cornea; image does not focus on the retina.

2. Assessment

  a. Refractive errors are diagnosed through a process called refraction.

  b. The client views an eye chart while various lenses of different strengths are systematically placed in front of the eye and is asked whether the lenses sharpen or worsen the vision.

3. Nonsurgical interventions: Eyeglasses or contact lenses

4. Surgical interventions

  a. Radial keratotomy: Incisions are made through the peripheral cornea to flatten the cornea, which allows the image to be focused closer to the retina; used to treat myopia.

  b. Photorefractive keratotomy: A laser beam is used to remove small portions of the corneal surface to reshape the cornea to focus an image properly on the retina; used to treat myopia and **astigmatism.**

  c. Laser-assisted in-situ keratomileusis (LASIK): The superficial layers of the cornea are lifted as a flap, a laser reshapes the deeper corneal layers, and then the corneal flap is replaced; used to treat hyperopia, myopia, and **astigmatism.**

  d. Intacs corneal ring: The shape of the cornea is changed by placing a flexible ring in the outer edges of the cornea; used to treat myopia.

C. **Legally blind**

1. Description: The best visual acuity with corrective lenses in the better eye of 20/200 or less or visual acuity of less than 20 degrees of the visual field in the better eye

---

BOX 63-3

Risk Factors of Eye Disorders

Aging process
Congenital
Diabetes mellitus
Hereditary
Medications
Trauma

---

2. Interventions

  a. When speaking to the client who has limited sight or is blind, the nurse uses a normal tone of voice.

  b. Alert the client when approaching.

  c. Orient the client to the environment.

  d. Use a focal point and provide further orientation to the environment from that focal point.

  e. Allow the client to touch objects in the room.

  f. Use the clock placement of foods on the meal tray to orient the client.

  g. Promote independence as much as is possible.

  h. Provide radios, televisions, and clocks that give the time orally, or provide a braille watch.

  i. When ambulating, allow the client to grasp the nurse's arm at the elbow; the nurse keeps his or her arm close to the body so that the client can detect the direction of movement.

  j. Instruct the client to remain one step behind the nurse when ambulating.

  k. Instruct the client in the use of the cane for the blind, which is differentiated from other canes by its straight shape and white color with red tip.

  l. Instruct the client that the cane is held in the dominant hand several inches off the floor.

  m. Instruct the client that the cane sweeps the ground where the client's foot will be placed next to determine the presence of obstacles.

D. **Cataracts** (Fig. 63-2)

1. Description

  a. A **cataract** is an opacity of the lens that distorts the image projected onto the retina and that can progress to blindness.

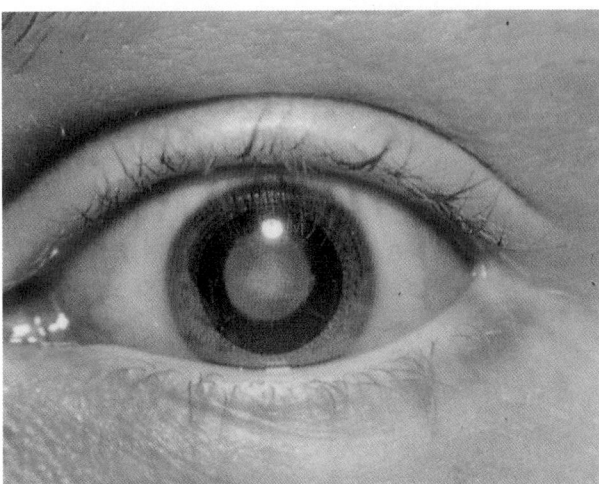

FIG. 63-2 The cloudy appearance of a lens affected by cataract. (From Black, J., & Hawks, J., [2005]. *Medical-surgical nursing: Clinical management for positive outcomes* [7th ed.]. Philadelphia: W.B. Saunders. Courtesy of Ophthalmic Photography at the University of Michigan, W.K. Kellogg Eye Center, Ann Arbor, MI.)

b. Causes include the aging process (senile **cataracts**), inherited (congenital **cataracts**), and injury (traumatic **cataracts**); **cataracts** also can result from another eye disease (secondary **cataracts**).

c. Intervention is indicated when visual acuity has been reduced to a level that the client finds to be unacceptable or adversely affects his or her lifestyle.

2. Assessment
   a. Blurred vision and decreased color perception are early signs
   b. Diplopia, reduced visual acuity, absence of the red reflex, and the presence of a white pupil are late signs. Pain or eye redness is associated with age-related **cataract** formation.
   c. Loss of vision is gradual.

3. Interventions
   a. Surgical removal of the lens, one eye at a time, is performed.
   b. With extracapsular extraction the lens is lifted out without removing the lens capsule; the procedure may be performed by phacoemulsification, in which the lens is broken up by ultrasonic vibrations and extracted.
   c. With intracapsular extraction, the lens and capsule are removed completely.
   d. A partial iridectomy may be performed with the lens extraction to prevent acute secondary **glaucoma**.
   e. A lens implantation may be performed at the time of the surgical procedure.

4. Preoperative interventions
   a. Instruct the client regarding the postoperative measures to prevent or decrease intraocular pressure.
   b. Stress to the client that care after surgery requires instillation of different types of eye drops several times a day for 2 to 4 weeks
   c. Administer eye medications preoperatively, including mydriatics and cycloplegics as prescribed.

5. Postoperative interventions
   a. Elevate the head of the bed 30 to 45 degrees.
   b. Turn the client to the back or nonoperative side.
   c. Maintain an eye patch as prescribed; orient the client to the environment.
   d. Position the client's personal belongings to the nonoperative side.
   e. Use side rails for safety.
   f. Assist with ambulation.

6. Client education (Box 63-4)

E. **Glaucoma**
   1. Description
      a. A group of ocular diseases resulting in increased intraocular pressure

b. Intraocular pressure is the fluid (aqueous humor) pressure within the eye (normal intraocular pressure is 10 to 21 mm Hg).

c. Increased intraocular pressure results from inadequate drainage of aqueous humor from the canal of Schlemm or overproduction of aqueous humor.

d. The condition damages the optic nerve and can result in blindness.

e. The gradual loss of visual fields may go unnoticed because central vision is unaffected.

2. Types
   a. Acute closed-angle or narrow-angle **glaucoma** results from obstruction to outflow of aqueous humor.
   b. Chronic closed-angle **glaucoma** follows an untreated attack of acute closed-angle **glaucoma.**
   c. Chronic open-angle **glaucoma** results from overproduction or obstruction to the outflow of aqueous humor.
   d. Acute **glaucoma** is a rapid onset of intraocular pressure higher than 50 to 70 mm Hg.
   e. Chronic **glaucoma** is a slow, progressive, gradual onset of intraocular pressure higher than 30 to 50 mm Hg.

3. Assessment
   a. Early signs include diminished **accommodation** and increased intraocular pressure.
   b. Late signs include loss of peripheral vision, decreased visual acuity not correctable with

---

BOX 63-4

Client Education Following Cataract Surgery

Avoid eye straining.

Avoid rubbing or placing pressure on the eyes.

Avoid rapid movements, straining, sneezing, coughing, bending, vomiting, or lifting objects heavier than 5 lb.

Take measures to prevent constipation.

Follow instructions for dressing changes and prescribed eye drops and medications.

Wipe excess drainage or tearing with a sterile wet cotton ball from the inner to the outer canthus.

Use an eye shield at bedtime.

If lens implantation is not performed, the eye cannot accommodate and glasses must be worn at all times.

Cataract glasses act as magnifying glasses and replace central vision only.

Because cataract glasses magnify, objects will appear closer; therefore, the client needs to accommodate, judge distance, and climb stairs carefully.

Contact lenses provide sharp visual acuity but dexterity is needed to insert them.

Contact the physician about any decrease in vision, severe eye pain, or increase in eye discharge.

glasses, halos around lights; headache or eye pain occurs with acute closed-angle **glaucoma.**

4. Interventions for acute **glaucoma**
   a. Treat acute **glaucoma** as a medical emergency.
   b. Administer medications as prescribed to lower intraocular pressure.
   c. Prepare the client for peripheral iridectomy, which allows aqueous humor to flow from the posterior to the anterior chamber.

5. Interventions for chronic **glaucoma**
   a. Instruct the client on the importance of medications (**miotics**) to constrict the pupils, (carbonic anhydrase inhibitors) to decrease the production of aqueous humor, and β-blockers to decrease the production of aqueous humor and intraocular pressure.
   b. Instruct the client of the need for lifelong medication use.
   c. Instruct the client to wear a Medic Alert bracelet.
   d. Instruct the client to avoid anticholinergic medications.
   e. Instruct the client to report eye pain, halos around the eyes, and changes in vision to the physician.
   f. Instruct the client that when maximal medical therapy has failed to halt the progression of visual field loss and optic nerve damage, surgery will be recommended.
   g. Prepare the client for trabeculoplasty as prescribed to facilitate aqueous humor drainage.
   h. Prepare the client for trabeculectomy as prescribed, which allows drainage of aqueous humor into the conjunctival spaces by the creation of an opening.

F. **Retinal detachment**
   1. Description
      a. Detachment or separation of the retina from the epithelium
      b. **Retinal detachment** occurs when the layers of the retina separate because of the accumulation of fluid between them, or when both retinal layers elevate away from the choroid as a result of a tumor.
      c. Partial detachment becomes complete if untreated.
      d. When detachment becomes complete, blindness occurs.
   2. Assessment
      a. Flashes of light
      b. Floaters or black spots (signs of bleeding)
      c. Increase in blurred vision
      d. Sense of a curtain being drawn over the eye
      e. Loss of a portion of the visual field

3. Immediate interventions
   a. Provide bed rest.
   b. Cover both eyes with patches as prescribed to prevent further detachment.
   c. Speak to the client before approaching.
   d. Position the client's head as prescribed.
   e. Protect the client from injury.
   f. Avoid jerky head movements.
   g. Minimize eye stress.
   h. Prepare the client for a surgical procedure as prescribed.

4. Surgical procedures
   a. Draining fluid from the subretinal space so that the retina can return to the normal position
   b. Sealing retinal breaks by cryosurgery, a cold probe applied to the sclera, to stimulate an inflammatory response leading to adhesions
   c. Diathermy, the use of an electrode needle and heat through the sclera, to stimulate an inflammatory response
   d. Laser therapy, to stimulate an inflammatory response and seal small retinal tears before the detachment occurs
   e. Scleral buckling, to hold the choroid and retina together with a splint until scar tissue forms, closing the tear (Fig. 63-3)

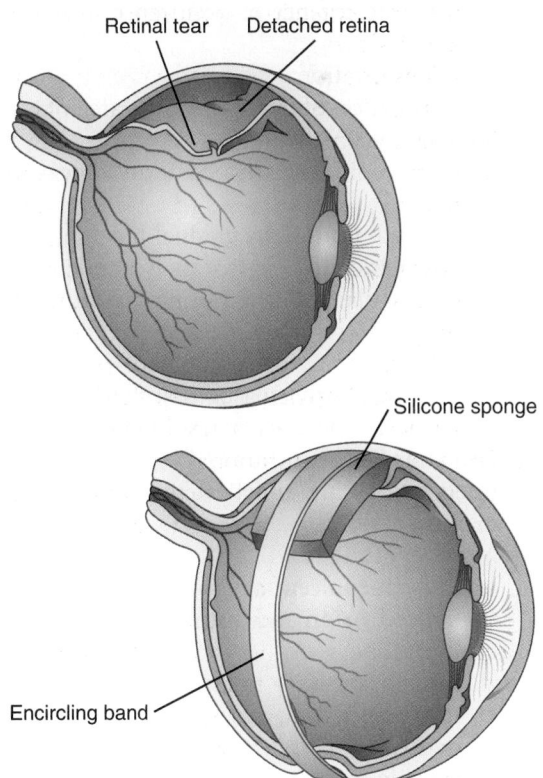

Retinal tear   Detached retina

Silicone sponge

Encircling band

FIG. 63-3 The scleral buckling procedure for repair of retinal detachment. (From Ignatavicius, D., & Workman, M. [2006]. *Medical surgical nursing: Critical thinking for collaborative care* [5th ed.]. Philadelphia: W.B. Saunders.)

f. Insertion of gas or silicone oil to promote reattachment; these agents float against the retina to hold it in place until healing occurs.

5. Postoperative interventions
   a. Maintain eye patches as prescribed.
   b. Monitor for hemorrhage.
   c. Prevent nausea and vomiting and monitor for restlessness, which can cause hemorrhage
   d. Monitor for sudden, sharp eye pain (notify the physician).
   e. Encourage deep breathing but avoid coughing.
   f. Provide bed rest for 1 to 2 days as prescribed.
   g. Position the client as prescribed (positioning depends on the location of the detachment).
   h. Administer eye medications as prescribed.
   i. Assist the client with activities of daily living.
   j. Avoid sudden head movements or anything that increases intraocular pressure.
   k. Instruct the client to limit reading for 3 to 5 weeks.
   l. Instruct the client to avoid squinting, straining and constipation, lifting heavy objects, and bending from the waist.
   m. Instruct the client to wear dark glasses during the day and an eye patch at night.
   n. Encourage follow-up care because of the danger of recurrence or occurrence in the other eye.

G. Macular degeneration
   1. A deterioration of the macula, the area of central vision
   2. Can be atrophic (age-related or dry) or exudative (wet)
   3. Age-related: Caused by gradual blocking of retinal capillaries leading to an ischemic and necrotic macula; rods and cones photoreceptors die.
   4. Exudative: Serous detachment of pigment epithelium in the macula occurs; fluid and blood collect under the macula, resulting in scar formation and visual distortion.
   5. Interventions are aimed at maximizing the remaining vision.
   6. Assessment
      a. A decline in central vision
      b. Blurred vision and distortion
   7. Interventions
      a. Initiate strategies to assist in maximizing remaining vision and maintaining independence.
      b. Provide referrals to community organizations.
      c. Laser therapy or photodynamic therapy may be prescribed to seal the leaking blood vessels in or near the macula.

H. Ocular melanoma
   1. Most common malignant eye tumor in adults
   2. Tumor usually found in the uveal tract and can spread easily because of rich blood supply
   3. Assessment
      a. Tumor can be discovered during routine examination
      b. If macular area is invaded, blurring of vision occurs.
      c. Increased intraocular pressure (IOP) is present if the canal of Schlemm is invaded.
      d. Change of iris color is noted if the tumor invades the iris.
      e. Ultrasonography may be performed to determine tumor size and location.
   4. Interventions
      a. Enucleation: the entire eyeball is removed surgically and a ball implant is inserted to provide a base for a socket prosthesis.
      b. Radiation is given via a radioactive plaque that is sutured to the sclera; the radioactive plaque remains in place until the prescribed radiation dose is delivered.

I. Enucleation and exenteration
   1. Description
      a. Enucleation is the removal of the entire eyeball.
      b. Exenteration is the removal of the eyeball and surrounding tissues and bone.
      c. The procedures are performed for the removal of ocular tumors.
      d. After the eye is removed, a ball implant is inserted to provide a firm base for a socket prosthesis and to facilitate the best cosmetic result.
      e. A prosthesis is fitted about 1 month after surgery.
   2. Preoperative interventions
      a. Provide emotional support to the client.
      b. Encourage the client to verbalize feelings related to loss.
   3. Postoperative interventions
      a. Monitor vital signs.
      b. Assess a pressure patch or dressing as prescribed.
      c. Report changes in vital signs or the presence of bright red drainage on the pressure patch or dressing.

J. Hyphema (Box 63-5)
   1. Description
      a. Presence of blood in the anterior chamber that occurs as a result of an injury
      b. The condition usually resolves in 5 to 7 days.
   2. Interventions
      a. Encourage rest with the client in a semi-Fowler's position.

BOX 63-5
Types of Eye Injuries

Chemical burn
Contusion
Foreign body
Hyphema
Penetrating object

b. Avoid sudden eye movements for 3 to 5 days to decrease the likelihood of bleeding.
c. Administer cycloplegic eye drops as prescribed to relax the eye muscles and place the eye at rest.
d. Instruct the client in the use of eye shields or eye patches as prescribed.
e. Instruct the client to restrict reading and limit watching television.

K. Contusions (see Box 63-5)
1. Description
a. Bleeding into the soft tissue as a result of an injury.
b. A contusion causes a black eye; the discoloration disappears in about 10 days.
c. Pain, photophobia, edema, and diplopia may occur.
2. Interventions
a. Place ice on the eye immediately.
b. Instruct the client to receive a thorough eye examination.

L. Foreign bodies (see Box 63-5)
1. Description: An object such as dust or dirt that enters the eye and causes irritation
2. Interventions
a. Have the client look upward, expose the lower lid, wet a cotton-tipped applicator with sterile normal saline, gently twist the swab over the particle, and remove it.
b. If the particle cannot be seen, have the client look downward, place a cotton applicator horizontally on the outer surface of the upper eye lid, grasp the lashes, and pull the upper lid outward and over the cotton applicator; if the particle is seen, gently twist a swab over it to remove.

M. Penetrating objects (see Box 63-5)
1. Description: An eye injury in which an object penetrates the eye
2. Interventions
a. Never remove the object because it may be holding ocular structures in place; the object must be removed by the physician.
b. Cover the object with a cup.
c. Do not allow the client to bend over.
d. Do not place pressure on the eye.
e. Client is to be seen by a physician immediately.

f. X-rays and CT scans of the orbit are usually obtained.
g. Magnetic resonance imaging (MRI) is contraindicated because of the possibility of metal-containing projectile movement during the procedure.

N. Chemical burns (see Box 63-5)
1. Description: An eye injury in which a caustic substance enters the eye
2. Interventions
a. Treatment should begin immediately.
b. Flush the eyes at the scene of the injury with water for at least 15 to 20 minutes.
c. At the scene of the injury, obtain a sample of the chemical involved.
d. At the emergency room, the eye is irrigated with normal saline solution or an ophthalmic irrigation solution for at least 10 minutes.
e. The solution is directed across the cornea and toward the lateral canthus.
f. Prepare for visual acuity assessment.
g. Apply an antibiotic ointment as prescribed.
h. Cover the eye with a patch as prescribed.

O. Eye (tissue) donation
1. Donor eyes
a. Donor eyes are obtained from cadavers.
b. Donor eyes must be enucleated soon after death because of rapid endothelial cell death.
c. Donor eyes must be stored in a preserving solution.
d. Storage, handling, and coordination of donor tissue with surgeons is provided by a network of state eye bank associations.
2. Care to the deceased client as a potential eye donor
a. Discuss the option of eye donation with the physician and family.
b. Raise the head of the bed 30 degrees.
c. Instill antibiotic eye drops as prescribed.
d. Close the eyes and apply a small ice pack to the closed eyes.
3. Preoperative care to the recipient of the cornea
a. Recipient may be told of the tissue (cornea) availability only several hours to 1 day before the surgery.
b. Assist in alleviating client anxiety.
c. Assess the recipient's eye for signs of infection.
d. Report the presence of any redness, watery or purulent drainage, or edema around the recipient's eye to the physician.
e. Instill antibiotic drops into the recipient's eye as prescribed to reduce the number of microorganisms present.
f. Administer fluids and medications intravenously as prescribed.

4. Postoperative care to the recipient
   a. Eye is covered with a pressure patch and protective shield that is left in place for 1 day.
   b. Do not remove or change the dressing without a physician's order.
   c. Monitor vital signs.
   d. Monitor level of consciousness.
   e. Assess the eye dressing.
   f. Position the client with the head elevated and on the nonoperative side to reduce intraocular pressure.
   g. Orient the client frequently.
   h. Monitor for complications of bleeding, wound leakage, infection, and tissue rejection.
   i. Instruct the client how to apply a patch and eye shield.
   j. Instruct the client to wear the eye shield at night for 1 month and whenever around small children or pets.
   k. Advise the client not to rub the eye.
5. Graft rejection (Box 63-6; Fig. 63-4)
   a. Rejection can occur at any time.
   b. Inform the client of the signs of rejection.
   c. Signs include *r*edness, *s*welling, *d*ecreased vision, and *p*ain (RSVP).

BOX 63-6

Signs of Graft Rejection Following Corneal Transplant: RSVP

*R*edness
*S*welling
*V*isual acuity decreased
*P*ain

---

d. The eye is treated with topical corticosteroids.

V. ANATOMY AND PHYSIOLOGY OF THE EAR

A. Functions
   1. Hearing
   2. Maintenance of balance
B. External ear (pinna)
   1. The external ear is embedded in the temporal bone bilaterally at the level of the eyes.
   2. The external ear extends from the auricle through the external canal to the tympanic membrane or eardrum.
   3. The external ear includes the mastoid process, the bony ridge located over the temporal bone.
C. Middle ear
   1. The middle ear consists of the medial side of the tympanic membrane.
   2. The middle ear contains three bony ossicles.
      a. Malleus
      b. Incus
      c. Stapes
   3. Functions of the middle ear
      a. Conduct sound vibrations from outer ear to the central hearing apparatus in the inner ear
      b. Protect the inner ear by reducing the amplitude of loud sounds
      c. The eustachian tube allows equalization of air pressure on each side of the tympanic membrane so that the membrane does not rupture.
D. Inner ear
   1. The inner ear contains the semicircular canals, cochlea, and distal end of the eighth cranial nerve.

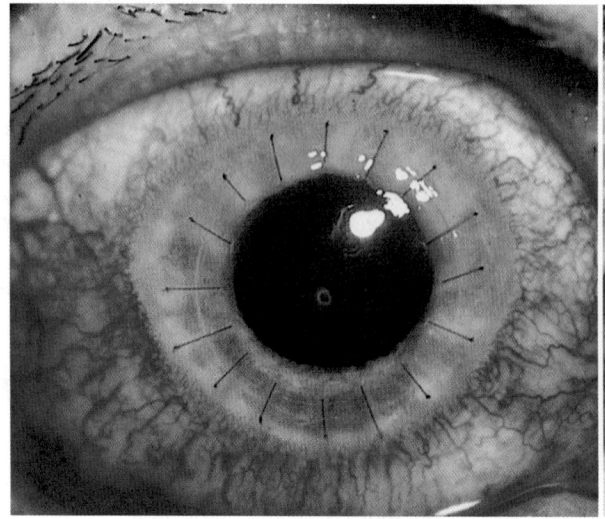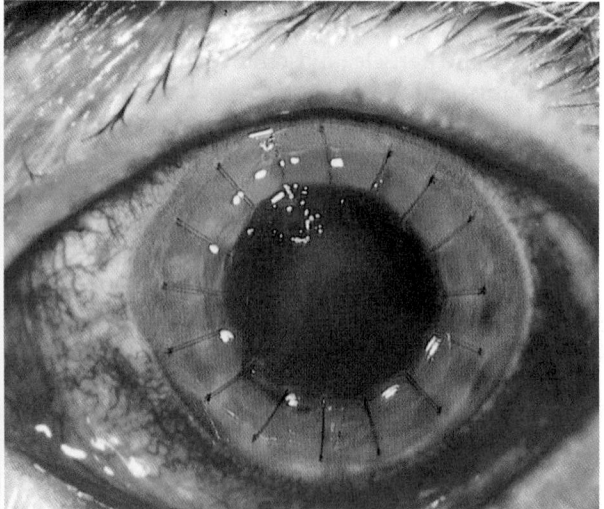

FIG. 63-4 **A,** Clinical appearance of the eye after keratoplasty. **B,** Acute graft rejection. (From Black, J., & Hawks, J., [2005]. *Medical-surgical nursing: Clinical management for positive outcomes* [7th ed.]. Philadelphia: W.B. Saunders. Courtesy of Ophthalmic Photography at the University of Michigan, W.K. Kellogg Eye Center, Ann Arbor, MI.)

2. The semicircular canals contain fluid and hair cells connected to sensory nerve fibers of the vestibular portion of the eighth cranial nerve.
3. The inner ear maintains sense of balance or equilibrium.
4. The cochlea is the spiral-shaped organ of hearing.
5. The organ of Corti (within the cochlea) is the receptor and organ of hearing.
6. Eighth cranial nerve
   a. The cochlear branch of the nerve transmits neuroimpulses from the cochlea to the brain, where they are interpreted as sound.
   b. The vestibular branch maintains balance and equilibrium.
E. Hearing and equilibrium
   1. The external ear conducts sound waves to the middle ear.
   2. The middle ear, also called the tympanic cavity, conducts sound waves to the inner ear.
   3. The middle ear is filled with air, which is kept at atmospheric pressure by the opening of the eustachian tube.
   4. The inner ear contains sensory receptors for sound and for equilibrium.
   5. The receptors in the inner ear transmit sound waves and changes in body position to the nerve impulses.

VI. **ASSESSMENT OF THE EAR** (Box 63-7)
A. Otoscopic examination
   1. The speculum is never introduced blindly into the external canal because of the risk of perforating the tympanic membrane.
   2. The client's head is tilted slightly away and the otoscope is held upside down as if it were a large pen; this permits the examiner's hand to lay against the client's head for support.
   3. Pull the pinna up and back to straighten the external canal in an adult.
   4. Visualize the external canal while slowly inserting the speculum.

BOX 63-7
Assessment of Hearing

Otoscopic examination
Tuning fork tests
    Rinne tuning fork test
    Weber's tuning fork test
Vestibular assessment
    Gaze nystagmus evaluation
    Hallpike's maneuver
    Test for falling
    Test for past pointing
Tests for hearing
    Voice test
    Watch test

---

5. The normal external canal is pink and intact, without lesions and with varying amounts of cerumen and fine little hairs.
6. Assess the tympanic membrane for intactness; the normal tympanic membrane is intact, without perforations, and should be free from lesions.
7. The tympanic membrane is transparent, opaque, pearly gray, and slightly concave.
B. Auditory assessment
   1. Sound is transmitted by air conduction and bone conduction.
   2. Air conduction takes two or three times longer than bone conduction.
   3. **Hearing loss** is categorized as **conductive, sensorineural**, and mixed **conductive** and **sensorineural.**
   4. **Conductive hearing loss** is caused by any physical obstruction to the transmission of sound waves.
   5. **Sensorineural hearing loss** is caused by a defect in the cochlea, eighth cranial nerve, or the brain itself.
   6. A mixed **conductive-sensorineural hearing loss** results in profound hearing loss.
C. Voice test
   1. Ask the client to block one external canal.
   2. The examiner stands 1 to 2 feet away and whispers a statement.
   3. Client is asked to repeat the whispered statement.
   4. Each ear is tested separately.
D. Watch test
   1. A ticking watch is used to test for high-frequency sounds.
   2. The examiner holds a ticking watch about 5 inches from each ear and asks the client if the ticking is heard.
E. Tuning fork tests
   1. Weber's tuning fork test
      a. Place the vibrating tuning fork stem in the middle of the client's head, at the midline of the forehead, or above the upper lip over the teeth.
      b. Hold the fork by the stem only.
      c. The client is asked whether the sound is heard equally in both ears or whether the sound is louder in one ear.
      d. Normal test result is hearing the sound equally in both ears.
      e. If the client hears the sound louder in one ear, the term *lateralization* is applied to the side that hears the loudest.
      f. Such a finding may indicate that the client has a **conductive hearing loss** in the ear to which the sound is lateralized or that **sensorineural hearing loss** has occurred in the opposite ear.

2. Rinne tuning fork test
   a. The test compares the client's hearing by air conduction and bone conduction.
   b. Air conduction is two or three times longer than bone conduction.
   c. The vibrating tuning fork stem is placed on the client's mastoid process and the client is asked to indicate when he or she no longer hears the sound.
   d. The examiner quickly brings the tuning fork in front of the pinna without touching the client and asks the client to indicate whether he or she still hears the sound.
   e. The client normally continues to hear the sound two times longer in front of the pinna; such results are a positive Rinne test.
   f. The examiner records the duration of both phases, bone conduction followed by air conduction, and compares the times.
   g. If the client is unable to hear the sound through the ear in front of the pinna, the client may have a **conductive hearing loss** on the side tested; in this situation, the bone conduction is greater than the air conduction (negative Rinne test).
   h. Both the Rinne test and the Weber tuning fork test are limited in distinguishing between conductive and **sensorineural hearing losses.**

F. Vestibular assessment
   1. Test for falling
      a. The examiner asks the client to stand with the feet together, arms hanging loosely at the side, and eyes closed.
      b. The client normally remains erect with only slight swaying.
      c. A significant sway is a positive Romberg sign.
   2. Test for past pointing
      a. The client sits in front of the examiner.
      b. The client closes the eyes and extends the arms in front, pointing both index fingers at the examiner.
      c. The examiner holds and touches his or her own extended index fingers under the client's extended index fingers to give the client a point of reference.
      d. The client is instructed to raise both arms and then lower them, attempting to return to the examiner's extended index fingers.
      e. The normal test response is that the client can easily return to the point of reference.
      f. The client with a vestibular function problem lacks a normal sense of position and cannot return the extended fingers to the point of reference; instead, the fingers deviate to the right or left of the reference point.

3. Gaze nystagmus evaluation
   a. The client's eyes are examined as the client looks straight ahead, 30 degrees to each side, upward and downward.
   b. Any spontaneous nystagmus—an involuntary, rhythmic, rapid twitching of the eyeballs—represents a problem with the vestibular system.
4. Hallpike's maneuver
   a. Assesses for positional vertigo or induced dizziness.
   b. The client assumes a supine position.
   c. The head is rotated to one side for 1 minute.
   d. A positive test results in nystagmus after 5 to 10 seconds.

VII. **DIAGNOSTIC TESTS FOR THE EAR** (Box 63-8)
A. Tomography
   1. Description
      a. Tomography may be performed with or without contrast medium.
      b. Tomography assesses the mastoid, middle ear, and inner ear structures.
      c. Multiple radiographs of the head are obtained.
      d. Tomography is especially helpful in the diagnosis of acoustic tumors.
   2. Interventions
      a. All jewelry is removed.
      b. Lead eye shields are used to cover the cornea to diminish the radiation dose to the eyes.
      c. The client must remain still in a supine position.
      d. No follow-up care is required.
B. Audiometry
   1. Description
      a. Audiometry measures hearing acuity.
      b. Audiometry uses two types, pure tone audiometry and speech audiometry.
      c. Pure tone audiometry is used to identify problems with hearing, speech, music, and other sounds in the environment.
      d. In speech audiometry, the client's ability to hear spoken words is measured.
      e. After testing, audiographic patterns are depicted on a graph to determine the type and level of the hearing loss.
   2. Interventions
      a. Inform the client regarding the procedure.
      b. Instruct the client to identify the sounds as they are heard.

BOX 63-8
Diagnostic Tests for the Ear

Audiometry
Electronystagmography
Tomography

C. Electronystagmography (ENG)
1. Description
   a. Electronystagmography is a vestibular test that evaluates spontaneous and induced eye movements known as nystagmus.
   b. ENG is used to distinguish between normal nystagmus and medication-induced nystagmus, or nystagmus caused by a lesion in the central or peripheral vestibular pathway.
   c. ENG records changing electrical fields with the movement of the eye, as monitored by electrodes placed on the skin around the eye.
2. Interventions
   a. The client is instructed to remain NPO for 3 hours before testing, avoiding caffeine-containing beverages for 24 to 48 hours before the test.
   b. Unnecessary medications are withheld for 24 hours before testing.
   c. Instruct the client that this is a long and tiring procedure.
   d. The client should bring prescription eyeglasses to the examination.
   e. The client sits and is instructed to gaze at lights, focus on a moving pattern, focus on a moving point, and then close the eyes.
   f. While sitting in a chair, the client may be rotated to provide information about vestibular function.
   g. In addition, the client's ears are irrigated with cool and warm water, which may cause nausea and vomiting.
   h. Following the procedure, the client begins taking clear fluids slowly and cautiously because nausea and vomiting may occur.
   i. Assistance with ambulation may also be necessary following the procedure.

VIII. DISORDERS OF THE EAR

▲ A. Risk factors related to ear disorders (Box 63-9)
B. **Conductive hearing loss**
1. Description
   a. **Conductive hearing loss** occurs when sound waves are blocked to the inner ear fibers because of external or middle ear disorders.

BOX 63-9

Risk Factors for Ear Disorders

Aging process
Infection
Medications
Ototoxicity
Trauma
Tumors

---

   b. Disorders often can be corrected with no damage to hearing or minimal permanent hearing loss.
2. Causes
   a. Any inflammatory process or obstruction of the external or middle ear
   b. Tumors
   c. **Otosclerosis**
   d. A buildup of scar tissue on the ossicles from previous middle ear surgery
C. **Sensorineural hearing loss**
1. Description
   a. **Sensorineural hearing loss** is a pathological process of the inner ear or of the sensory fibers that lead to the cerebral cortex.
   b. **Sensorineural hearing loss** is often permanent, and measures must be taken to reduce further damage or to attempt to amplify sound as a means of improving hearing to some degree.
2. Causes
   a. Damage to the inner ear structures
   b. Damage to the eighth cranial nerve
   c. Prolonged exposure to loud noise
   d. Medications
   e. Trauma
   f. Inherited disorders
   g. Metabolic and circulatory disorders
   h. Infections
   i. Surgery
   j. **Ménière's syndrome**
   k. Diabetes mellitus
   l. Myxedema
D. Mixed hearing loss
1. Mixed hearing loss also is known as **conductive-sensorineural** hearing loss.
2. Client has **sensorineural** and **conductive hearing loss.**
E. Signs of hearing loss and facilitating communication (Boxes 63-10 and 63-11) ▲
F. Cochlear implantation (Fig. 63-5) ▲
1. Cochlear implants are used for **sensorineural hearing loss.**
2. A small computer converts sound waves into electrical impulses.
3. Electrodes are placed by the internal ear with a computer device attached to the external ear.
4. Electronic impulses directly stimulate nerve fibers.
G. Hearing aids ▲
1. Hearing aids are used for the client with **conductive hearing loss.**
2. Hearing aids can help the client with **sensorineural hearing loss,** although they are not as effective.
3. A difficulty that exists in the use of hearing aids is the amplification of background noise and voices.
4. Client education (Box 63-12) ▲

BOX 63-10

Signs of Hearing Loss

Frequently asking others to repeat statements
Straining to hear
Turning head or leaning forward to favor one ear
Shouting in conversation
Ringing in the ears
Failing to respond when not looking in the direction of
  the sound
Answering questions incorrectly
Raising the volume of the television or radio
Avoiding large groups
Better understanding of speech when in small groups
Withdrawing from social interactions

BOX 63-11

Facilitation of Communication

Using written words if the client is able to see, read, and
  write
Providing plenty of light in the room
Getting the attention of the client before beginning
  to speak
Facing the client when speaking
Talking in a room without distracting noises
Moving close to the client and speaking slowly
  and clearly
Keeping hands and other objects away from the mouth
  when talking to the client
Talking in normal volume and at a lower pitch because
  shouting is not helpful and higher frequencies are less
  easily heard
Rephrasing sentences and repeating information
Validating with the client the understanding of state-
  ments made by asking the client to repeat what
  was said
Reading lips
Encouraging the client to wear glasses when talking to
  someone to improve vision for lip reading
Using sign language, which combines speech with hand
  movements that signify letters, words, or phrases
Using telephone amplifiers
Flashing lights that are activated by ringing of the
  telephone or doorbell
Specially trained dogs that help the client be aware of
  sound and alert the client to potential danger

H. Presbycusis
  1. Description
     a. Presbycusis is a **sensorineural hearing loss**
        associated with aging.
     b. Presbycusis leads to degeneration or atrophy
        of the ganglion cells in the cochlea and a loss
        of elasticity of the basilar membranes.
     c. Presbycusis leads to compromise of the vas-
        cular supply to the inner ear, with changes in
        several areas of the ear structure.

  2. Assessment
     a. Hearing loss is gradual and bilateral.
     b. Client states that he or she has no problem
        with hearing but cannot understand what the
        words are.
     c. Client thinks that the speaker is mumbling.
I. External otitis
  1. Description
     a. External otitis is an infective inflammatory or
        allergic response involving the structure of
        the external auditory canal or auricles.
     b. An irritating or infective agent comes into
        contact with the epithelial layer of the exter-
        nal ear.
     c. Contact leads to an allergic response or signs
        and symptoms of an infection.
     d. The skin becomes red, swollen, and tender to
        touch on movement.
     e. The extensive swelling of the canal can lead
        to **conductive hearing loss** because of ob-
        struction.
     f. External otitis is more common in children;
        it is termed *swimmer's ear* and occurs more
        often in hot, humid environments.
     g. Prevention includes the elimination of irri-
        tating or infecting agents.
  2. Assessment
     a. Pain
     b. Itching
     c. Plugged feeling in the ear
     d. Redness and edema
     e. Exudate
     f. Hearing loss
  3. Interventions
     a. Apply heat locally for 20 minutes three times
        a day.
     b. Encourage rest to assist in reducing pain.
     c. Administer antibiotics or corticosteroids as
        prescribed.
     d. Administer analgesics such as aspirin or
        acetaminophen (Tylenol) for the pain as
        prescribed.
     e. Instruct the client that the ears should be
        kept clean and dry.
     f. Instruct the client to use earplugs for
        swimming.
     g. Instruct the client that cotton-tipped appli-
        cators should not be used in dry ears be-
        cause their use can lead to trauma to the
        canal.
     h. Instruct the client that irritating agents such
        as hair products or headphones should be
        discontinued.
J. Otitis media: See Chap. 36.
  1. Myringotomy
     a. See Chap. 36.
     b. Client education (Box 63-13)

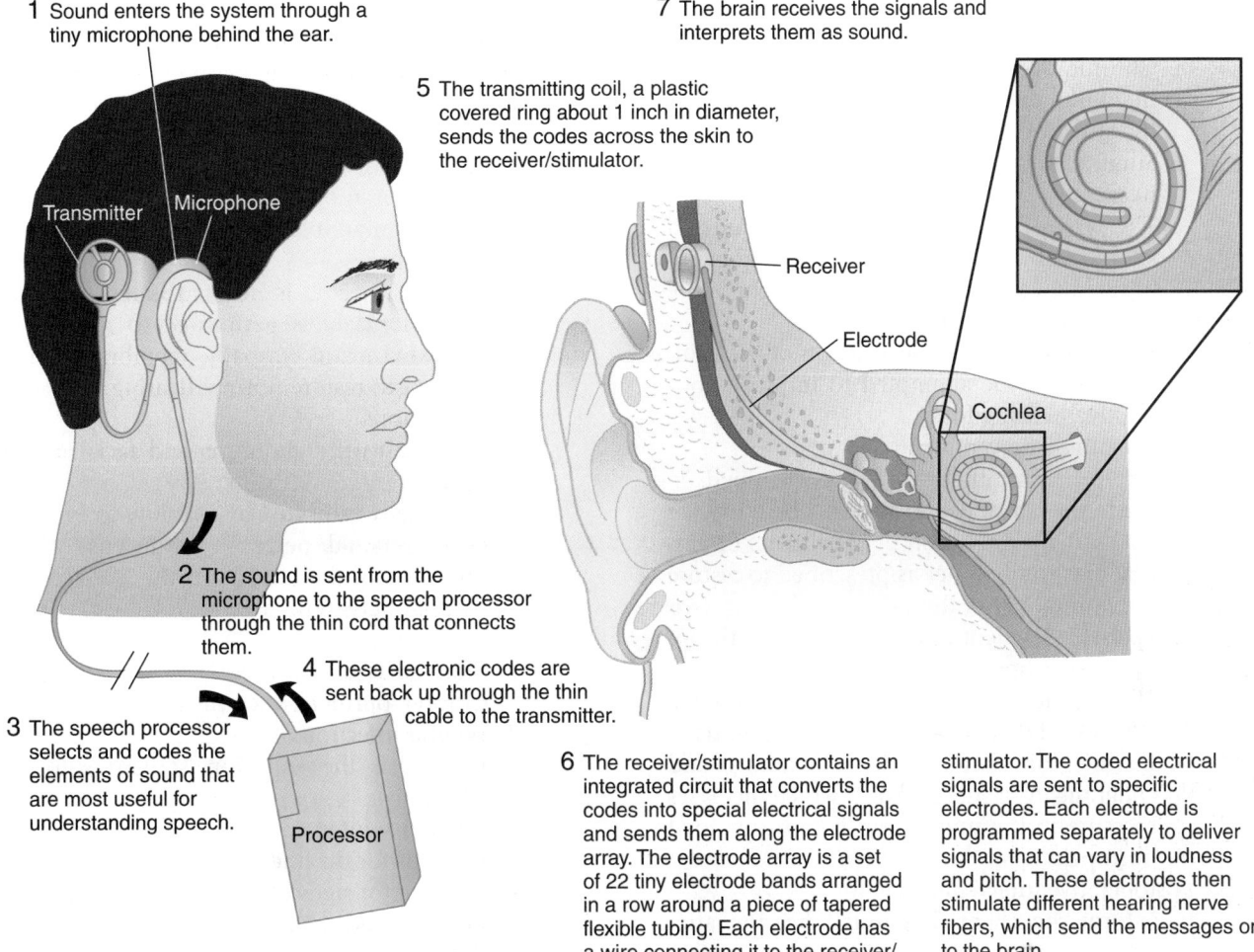

1 Sound enters the system through a tiny microphone behind the ear.

Transmitter   Microphone

2 The sound is sent from the microphone to the speech processor through the thin cord that connects them.

3 The speech processor selects and codes the elements of sound that are most useful for understanding speech.

Processor

4 These electronic codes are sent back up through the thin cable to the transmitter.

5 The transmitting coil, a plastic covered ring about 1 inch in diameter, sends the codes across the skin to the receiver/stimulator.

7 The brain receives the signals and interprets them as sound.

Receiver

Electrode

Cochlea

6 The receiver/stimulator contains an integrated circuit that converts the codes into special electrical signals and sends them along the electrode array. The electrode array is a set of 22 tiny electrode bands arranged in a row around a piece of tapered flexible tubing. Each electrode has a wire connecting it to the receiver/ stimulator. The coded electrical signals are sent to specific electrodes. Each electrode is programmed separately to deliver signals that can vary in loudness and pitch. These electrodes then stimulate different hearing nerve fibers, which send the messages on to the brain.

FIG. 63-5   Cochlear implant to restore hearing. (From Black, J., & Hawks, J., [2005]. *Medical-surgical nursing: Clinical management for positive outcomes* [7th ed.]. Philadelphia: W.B. Saunders.)

BOX 63-12
Client Education Regarding a Hearing Aid

Encourage the client to begin using the hearing aid slowly to adjust to the device.
Adjust the volume to the minimal hearing level to prevent feedback squeaking.
Teach the client to concentrate on the sounds that are to be heard and to filter out background noise.
Instruct the client to clean the ear mold with mild soap and water.
Avoid excessive wetting of the hearing aid and try to keep the hearing aid dry.
Clean the ear cannula of the hearing aid with a toothpick or pipe cleaner.
Turn off the hearing aid and remove the battery when not in use.
Keep extra batteries on hand.
Keep the hearing aid in a safe place.
Prevent hair sprays, oils, or other hair and face products from coming into contact with the receiver of the hearing aid.

BOX 63-13
Client Education Following Myringotomy

Avoid strenuous activities.
Avoid rapid head movements, bouncing, or bending.
Avoid straining on bowel movement.
Avoid drinking through a straw.
Avoid traveling by air.
Avoid forceful coughing.
Avoid contact with persons with colds.
Avoid washing hair, showering, or getting the head wet for 1 week as prescribed.
Instruct the client that if he or she needs to blow the nose, to blow one side at a time with the mouth open.
Instruct the client to keep ears dry by keeping a ball of cotton coated with petroleum jelly in the ear and to change the cotton ball daily.
Instruct the client to report excessive ear drainage to the physician.

K. Chronic otitis media
  1. Description
     a. Chronic otitis media is a chronic infective, inflammatory, or allergic response involving the structure of the middle ear.
     b. Surgical treatment is necessary to restore hearing.
     c. The type of surgery can vary; it includes a simple reconstruction of the tympanic membrane, a myringoplasty, or replacement of the ossicles within the middle ear.
     d. A tympanoplasty, reconstruction of the middle ear, may be attempted to improve **conductive hearing loss.**
  2. Preoperative interventions
     a. Administer antibiotic drops as prescribed.
     b. Clean the ear of debris as prescribed; irrigate the ear with a solution of equal parts of vinegar and sterile water as prescribed to restore the normal pH of the ear.
     c. Instruct the client to avoid persons with upper respiratory infections.
     d. Instruct the client to obtain adequate rest, eat a balanced diet, and drink adequate fluids.
     e. Instruct the client in deep breathing and coughing; forceful coughing, which increases pressure in the middle ear, is to be avoided postoperatively.
  3. Postoperative interventions
     a. Inform the client that initial hearing after surgery is diminished because of the packing in the ear canal; hearing improvement will occur after the ear canal packing is removed.
     b. Keep the dressing clean and dry.
     c. Keep the client flat, with the operative ear up for at least 12 hours.
     d. Administer antibiotics as prescribed.
     e. Instruct the client that he or she may return to work in about 3 weeks postoperatively as prescribed.
L. Mastoiditis
  1. Description
     a. Mastoiditis may be acute or chronic and results from untreated or inadequately treated chronic or acute otitis media.
     b. The pain is not relieved by myringotomy.
  2. Assessment
     a. Swelling behind the ear and pain with minimal movement of the head
     b. Cellulitis on the skin or external scalp over the mastoid process
     c. A reddened, dull, thick, immobile tympanic membrane, with or without perforation
     d. Tender and enlarged postauricular lymph nodes
     e. Low-grade fever
     f. Malaise
     g. Anorexia
  3. Interventions
     a. Prepare the client for surgical removal of infected material.
     b. Monitor for complications.
     c. Simple or modified radical mastoidectomy with tympanoplasty is the most common treatment.
     d. Once tissue that is infected is removed, the tympanoplasty is performed to reconstruct the ossicles and tympanic membranes in an attempt to restore normal hearing.
  4. Complications
     a. Damage to the abducens and facial cranial nerves
     b. Damage is exhibited by inability to look laterally (cranial nerve VI, abducens) and a drooping of the mouth on the affected side (cranial nerve VII, facial).
     c. Meningitis
     d. Brain abscess
     e. Chronic purulent otitis media
     f. Wound infections
     g. Vertigo, if the infection spreads into the labyrinth
  5. Postoperative interventions
     a. Monitor for dizziness.
     b. Monitor for signs of meningitis, as evidenced by a stiff neck and vomiting.
     c. Prepare for a wound dressing change 24 hours postoperatively.
     d. Monitor the surgical incision for edema, drainage, and redness.
     e. Position the client flat with the operative side up.
     f. Restrict the client to bed with bedside commode privileges for 24 hours as prescribed.
     g. Assist the client with getting out of bed to prevent falling or injuries from dizziness.
     h. With reconstruction of the ossicles via a graft, take precautions to prevent dislodging of the graft.
M. **Otosclerosis**
  1. Description
     a. **Otosclerosis** is a disease of the labyrinthine capsule of the middle ear that results in a bony overgrowth of the tissue surrounding the ossicles.
     b. **Otosclerosis** causes the development of irregular areas of new bone formation and causes the fixation of the bones.
     c. Stapes fixation leads to a **conductive hearing loss.**
     d. If the disease involves the inner ear, **sensorineural hearing loss** is present.

e. To have bilateral involvement is not uncommon, although hearing loss may be worse in one ear.

f. The cause is unknown, although it is thought to have a familial tendency.

g. Nonsurgical intervention promotes the improvement of hearing through amplification.

h. Surgical intervention involves removal of the bony growth causing the hearing loss.

i. A partial stapedectomy or complete stapedectomy with prosthesis (**fenestration**) may be performed surgically.

2. Assessment

a. Slowly progressing **conductive hearing loss**

b. Bilateral hearing loss

c. A ringing or roaring type of constant tinnitus

d. Loud sounds heard in the ear when chewing

e. Pinkish discoloration (Schwartze's sign) of the tympanic membrane, which indicates vascular changes within the ear.

f. Negative Rinne test

g. Weber's test shows lateralization of sound to the ear with the most **conductive hearing loss.**

N. Fenestration

1. Description

a. **Fenestration** is removal of the stapes, with a small hole drilled in the footplate; a prosthesis is connected between the incus and footplate.

b. Sounds cause the prosthesis to vibrate in the same manner as the stapes.

c. Complications include complete hearing loss, prolonged vertigo, infection, or facial nerve damage.

2. Preoperative interventions

a. Instruct the client in measures to prevent middle ear or external ear infections.

b. Instruct the client to avoid excessive nose blowing.

c. Instruct the client not to clean the ear canal with cotton-tipped applicators and to avoid trauma or injury to the ear canal.

3. Postoperative interventions

a. Inform the client that hearing is initially worse after the surgical procedure because of swelling and that no noticeable improvement in hearing may occur for as long as 6 weeks.

b. Inform the client that the Gelfoam ear packing interferes with hearing but is used to decrease bleeding.

c. Assist with ambulating during the first 1 to 2 days after surgery.

d. Provide side rails when the client is in bed.

e. Administer antibiotic, antivertiginous, and pain medications as prescribed.

f. Assess for facial nerve damage, weakness, changes in tactile sensation and taste sensation, vertigo, nausea, and vomiting.

g. Instruct the client to move the head slowly when changing positions to prevent vertigo.

h. Instruct the client to avoid persons with upper respiratory tract infections.

i. Instruct the client to avoid showering and getting the head and wound wet.

j. Instruct the client to avoid using small objects (cotton-tipped applicators) to clean the external ear canal.

k. Instruct the client to avoid rapid extreme changes in pressure caused by quick head movements, sneezing, nose blowing, straining, and changes in altitude.

l. Instruct the client to avoid changes in middle ear pressure because they could dislodge the graft or prosthesis.

O. Labyrinthitis

1. Description: Infection of the labyrinth that occurs as a complication of acute or chronic otitis media

2. May result from growth of a cholesteatoma—benign overgrowth of squamous cell epithelium

3. Assessment

a. Hearing loss that may be permanent on the affected side

b. Tinnitus

c. Spontaneous nystagmus to the affected side

d. Vertigo

e. Nausea and vomiting

4. Interventions

a. Monitor for signs of meningitis, the most common complication, as evidenced by headache, stiff neck, and lethargy.

b. Administer systemic antibiotics as prescribed.

c. Advise the client to rest in bed in a darkened room.

d. Administer antiemetics and antivertiginous medications as prescribed.

e. Instruct the client that the vertigo subsides as the inflammation resolves.

f. Instruct the client that balance problems that persist may require gait training through physical therapy.

P. **Menière's syndrome**

1. Description

a. **Menière's syndrome** is also called endolymphatic hydrops; it refers to dilation of the endolymphatic system by overproduction or decreased reabsorption of endolymphatic fluid.

b. The syndrome is characterized by tinnitus, unilateral **sensorineural hearing loss,** and vertigo.

c. Symptoms occur in attacks and last for several days, and the client becomes totally incapacitated during the attacks.

d. Initial hearing loss is reversible but as the frequency of attacks continues, hearing loss becomes permanent.

e. Repeated damage to the cochlea caused by increased fluid pressure leads to permanent hearing loss.

2. Causes
   a. Any factor that increases endolymphatic secretion in the labyrinth
   b. Viral and bacterial infections
   c. Allergic reactions
   d. Biochemical disturbances
   e. Vascular disturbance, producing changes in the microcirculation in the labyrinth
   f. Long-term stress may be a contributing factor.

3. Assessment
   a. Feelings of fullness in the ear
   b. Tinnitus, as a continuous low-pitched roar or humming sound, that is present much of the time but worsens just before and during severe attacks
   c. Hearing loss that is worse during an attack
   d. Vertigo, as periods of whirling, that might cause the client to fall to the ground
   e. Vertigo that is so intense that even while lying down, the client holds the bed or ground in an attempt to prevent the whirling
   f. Nausea and vomiting
   g. Nystagmus
   h. Severe headaches

4. Nonsurgical interventions
   a. Prevent injury during vertigo attacks.
   b. Provide bed rest in a quiet environment.
   c. Provide assistance with walking.
   d. Instruct the client to move the head slowly to prevent worsening of the vertigo.
   e. Initiate sodium and fluid restrictions as prescribed.
   f. Instruct the client to stop smoking.
   g. Administer nicotinic acid (niacin) as prescribed for its vasodilatory effect.
   h. Administer antihistamines as prescribed to reduce the production of histamine and the inflammation.
   i. Administer antiemetics as prescribed.
   j. Administer tranquilizers and sedatives as prescribed to calm the client, allow the client to rest, and control vertigo, nausea, and vomiting.

k. Mild diuretics may be prescribed to decrease endolymph volume

5. Surgical interventions
   a. Surgery is performed when medical therapy is ineffective and the functional level of the client has decreased significantly.
   b. Endolymphatic drainage and insertion of a shunt may be performed early in the course of the disease to assist with the drainage of excess fluids.
   c. A resection of the vestibular nerve or total removal of the labyrinth or a labyrinthectomy may be performed.

6. Postoperative interventions
   a. Assess packing and dressing on the ear.
   b. Speak to the client on the side of the unaffected ear.
   c. Perform neurological assessments.
   d. Maintain side rails.
   e. Assist with ambulating.
   f. Encourage the client to use a bedside commode rather than ambulating to the bathroom.
   g. Administer antivertiginous and antiemetic medications as prescribed.

Q. Acoustic neuroma
   1. Description
      a. Acoustic neuroma is a benign tumor of the vestibular or acoustic nerve.
      b. The tumor may cause damage to hearing and to facial movements and sensations.
      c. Treatment includes surgical removal of the tumor via craniotomy.
      d. Care is taken to preserve the function of the facial nerve.
      e. The tumor rarely recurs after surgical removal.
      f. Postoperative nursing care is similar to postoperative craniotomy care.
   2. Assessment
      a. Symptoms usually begin with tinnitus and progress to gradual **sensorineural hearing loss.**
      b. As the tumor enlarges, damage to adjacent cranial nerves occurs.

R. Trauma
   1. Description
      a. The tympanic membrane has a limited stretching ability and gives way under high pressure.
      b. Foreign objects placed in the external canal may exert pressure on the tympanic membrane and cause perforation.
      c. If the object continues through the canal, the bony structure of the stapes, incus, and malleus may be damaged.

d. A blunt injury to the basal skull and ear can damage the middle ear structures through fractures extending to the middle ear.

e. Excessive nose blowing and rapid changes of pressure that occur with nonpressurized air flights can increase pressure in the middle ear.

f. Depending on the damage to the ossicles, hearing loss may or may not return.

2. Interventions

a. Tympanic membrane perforations usually heal within 24 hours.

b. Surgical reconstruction of the ossicles and tympanic membrane through tympanoplasty or myringoplasty may be performed to improve hearing.

S. Cerumen and foreign bodies

1. Description

a. Cerumen, or wax, is the most common cause of impacted canals.

b. Foreign bodies can include vegetables, beads, pencil erasers, insects, and other objects.

2. Assessment

a. Sensation of fullness in the ear with or without hearing loss

b. Pain, itching, or bleeding

3. Cerumen

a. Removal of wax by irrigation is a slow process.

b. Irrigation is contraindicated in clients with a history of tympanic membrane perforation or otitis media.

c. To soften cerumen, add three drops of glycerin or mineral oil to the ear at bedtime, and three drops of hydrogen peroxide twice daily as prescribed.

d. After several days, irrigate the ear.

e. The maximum amount of solution that should be used for irrigation is 50 to 70 mL.

4. Foreign bodies

a. With a foreign object of vegetable matter, irrigation is used with care because this material expands with hydration.

b. Insects are killed before removal, unless they can be coaxed out by flashlight or a humming noise.

c. Mineral oil or diluted alcohol is instilled to suffocate the insect, which then is removed using ear forceps.

d. Use a small ear forceps to remove the object and avoid pushing the object farther into the canal and damaging the tympanic membrane.

PRACTICE QUESTIONS

1. The nurse is performing an otoscopic examination on a client with mastoiditis. On examination of the tympanic membrane, which of the following would the nurse expect to observe?
   1. A pink-colored tympanic membrane
   2. A pearly colored tympanic membrane
   3. A transparent and clear tympanic membrane
   4. A red, dull, thick and immobile tympanic membrane

2. The client is diagnosed with a disorder involving the inner ear. Which of the following is the most common client complaint associated with a disorder involving this part of the ear?
   1. Pruritus
   2. Tinnitus
   3. Hearing loss
   4. Burning in the ear

3. The nurse is developing a plan of care for the client scheduled for cataract surgery. The nurse documents which most appropriate nursing diagnosis in the plan of care?
   1. Anxiety
   2. Self-care deficit
   3. Nutrition, imbalanced
   4. Sensory perception, disturbed

4. The nurse is performing an assessment on a client with a suspected diagnosis of cataract. The chief clinical manifestation that the nurse would expect to note in the early stages of cataract formation is:
   1. Diplopia
   2. Eye pain
   3. Floating spots
   4. Blurred vision

5. In preparation for cataract surgery, the nurse is to administer prescribed eye drops. The nurse reviews the physician's orders, expecting which type of eye drops to be prescribed?
   1. A miotic agent
   2. A thiazide diuretic
   3. An osmotic diuretic
   4. A mydriatic medication

6. During the early postoperative period, the client who has had a cataract extraction complains of nausea and severe eye pain over the operative site. The initial nursing action is to:
   1. Call the physician.
   2. Reassure the client that this is normal.
   3. Turn the client on his or her operative side.
   4. Administer the ordered pain medication and antiemetic.

7. The client is being discharged from the ambulatory care unit following cataract removal. The nurse provides instructions regarding home care. Which of

the following, if stated by the client, indicates an understanding of the instructions?

1. "I will take aspirin if I have any discomfort."
2. "I will sleep on the side that I was operated on."
3. "I will not lift anything if it weighs more than 10 pounds."
4. "I will wear my eye shield at night and my glasses during the day."

8. The client with glaucoma asks the nurse if complete vision will return. The most appropriate response is:
   1. "Your vision will never return to normal."
   2. "Your vision will return as soon as the medication begins to work."
   3. "Your vision loss is temporary and will return in about 3 to 4 weeks."
   4. "Although some vision has been lost and cannot be restored, further loss may be prevented by adhering to the treatment plan."

9. The nurse is developing a teaching plan for the client with glaucoma. Which of the following instructions would the nurse include in the plan of care?
   1. Avoid overuse of the eyes.
   2. Decrease the amount of salt in the diet.
   3. Eye medications will need to be administered for the client's entire life.
   4. Decrease fluid intake to control the intraocular pressure.

10. The nurse is performing an admission assessment on a client with a diagnosis of detached retina. Which of the following is associated with this eye disorder?
    1. Total loss of vision
    2. Pain in the affected eye
    3. A yellow discoloration of the sclera
    4. A sense of a curtain falling across the field of vision

11. The nurse is caring for a client with a diagnosis of detached retina. Which assessment sign would indicate that bleeding has occurred as a result of the retinal detachment?
    1. Total loss of vision
    2. A reddened conjunctiva
    3. A sudden sharp pain in the eye
    4. Complaints of a burst of black spots or floaters

12. The client arrives in the emergency room following an automobile accident. The client's forehead hit the steering wheel and a hyphema is diagnosed. The nurse places the client in which position?
    1. Flat on bed rest
    2. Semi-Fowler's on bed rest
    3. Lateral on the affected side
    4. Lateral on the unaffected side

13. The client sustains a contusion of the eyeball following a traumatic injury with a blunt object. Which intervention is initiated immediately?

1. Notify the physician.
2. Apply ice to the affected eye.
3. Irrigate the eye with cool water.
4. Accompany the client to the emergency room.

14. The client arrives in the emergency room with a penetrating eye injury from wood chips that occurred while cutting wood. The nurse assesses the eye and notes a piece of wood protruding from the eye. What is the initial nursing action?
    1. Apply an eye patch.
    2. Perform visual acuity tests.
    3. Irrigate the eye with sterile saline.
    4. Remove the piece of wood using a sterile eye clamp.

15. The client arrives in the emergency room after sustaining a chemical eye injury from a splash of battery acid. The initial nursing action is to:
    1. Begin visual acuity testing.
    2. Cover the eye with a pressure patch.
    3. Swab the eye with antibiotic ointment.
    4. Irrigate the eye with sterile normal saline.

16. The nurse is caring for a client following enucleation. The nurse notes the presence of bright red drainage on the dressing. Which nursing action is appropriate?
    1. Notify the physician.
    2. Document the finding.
    3. Continue to monitor the drainage.
    4. Mark the drainage on the dressing and monitor for any increase in bleeding.

17. The nurse is performing a voice test to assess hearing. Which of the following describes the accurate procedure for performing this test?
    1. Whisper a statement while the client blocks both ears.
    2. Whisper a statement with the examiner's back facing the client.
    3. Whisper a statement and ask the client to repeat it while blocking one ear
    4. Stand 4 feet away from the client to ensure that the client can hear at this distance.

18. A 55-year old woman was working in her garden. She accidentally sprayed insecticide into her right eye. She calls the emergency room frantic and screaming for help. The nurse should instruct the woman to take which immediate action?
    1. Call the physician.
    2. Irrigate the eyes with water.
    3. Come to the emergency room.
    4. Irrigate the eyes with diluted hydrogen peroxide.

19. The nurse is caring for a hearing-impaired client. Which of the following approaches will facilitate communication?
    1. Speak loudly.
    2. Speak frequently.
    3. Speak at a normal volume.
    4. Speak directly into the impaired ear.

20. A client arrives at the emergency room with a foreign body in the left ear that has been determined to be an insect. Which intervention would the nurse anticipate to be prescribed initially?
    1. Irrigation of the ear
    2. Instillation of diluted alcohol
    3. Instillation of antibiotic ear drops
    4. Instillation of corticosteroid ointment

21. The nurse notes that the physician has documented a diagnosis of presbycusis on the client's chart. The nurse plans care knowing that the condition is:
    1. Tinnitus that occurs with aging
    2. Nystagmus that occurs with aging
    3. A conductive hearing loss that occurs with aging
    4. A sensorineural hearing loss that occurs with aging

22. The nurse has conducted discharge teaching for a client who has had a fenestration procedure for the treatment of otosclerosis. Which of the following, if stated by the client, would indicate that teaching was effective?
    1. "It is okay to take a shower and wash my hair."
    2. "I can resume my tennis lessons starting next week."
    3. "I will take stool softeners as prescribed by my doctor."
    4. "I should drink liquids through a straw for the next 2 to 3 weeks."

23. A client with Menière's disease is experiencing severe vertigo. Which instruction should the nurse give to the client to assist in controlling the vertigo?
    1. Increase sodium in the diet.
    2. Avoid sudden head movements.
    3. Lie still and watch the television.
    4. Increase fluid intake to 3000 mL a day.

24. The nurse is reviewing the physician's orders for a client with Menière's disease. Which diet most likely would be prescribed for the client?
    1. Low-fat diet
    2. Low-sodium diet
    3. Low-cholesterol diet
    4. Low-carbohydrate diet

25. The clinic nurse is preparing to test the visual acuity of a client using a Snellen chart. Which of the following identifies the accurate procedure for this visual acuity test?
    1. The right eye is tested, followed by the left eye, and then both eyes are tested.
    2. Both eyes are assessed together, followed by the assessment of the right and then the left eyes.
    3. The client is asked to stand at a distance of 40 feet from the chart and is asked to read the largest line on the chart.
    4. The client is asked to stand at a distance of 40 feet from the chart and to read the line that

can be read 200 feet away by an individual with unimpaired vision.

26. The client's vision is tested with a Snellen chart. The results of the tests are documented as 20/60. The nurse interprets this as:
    1. The client is legally blind.
    2. The client's vision is normal.
    3. The client can read at a distance of 60 feet what a client with normal vision can read at 20 feet.
    4. The client can read only at a distance of 20 feet what a client with normal vision can read at 60 feet.

27. The clinic nurse notes that following several eye examinations, the physician has documented a diagnosis of legal blindness in the client's chart. The nurse reviews the results of the Snellen chart test expecting to note which finding?
    1. 20/20 vision
    2. 20/40 vision
    3. 20/60 vision
    4. 20/200 vision

28. Tonometry is performed on the client with a suspected diagnosis of glaucoma. The nurse analyzes the test results as documented in the client's chart and understands that normal intraocular pressure is:
    1. 2 to 7 mm Hg
    2. 10 to 21 mm Hg
    3. 22 to 30 mm Hg
    4. 31 to 35 mm Hg

29. The nurse is caring for a client following craniotomy for removal of an acoustic neuroma. Assessment of which of the following cranial nerves would identify a complication specifically associated with this surgery?
    1. Cranial nerve I, olfactory
    2. Cranial nerve IV, trochlear
    3. Cranial nerve III, oculomotor
    4. Cranial nerve VII, facial nerve

ALTERNATE ITEM FORMAT: MULTIPLE RESPONSE

The nurse is preparing a teaching plan for a client who is undergoing cataract extraction with intraocular implantation. Which home care measures will the nurse include in the plan?

❏ 1. Avoid activities that require bending over.
❏ 2. Contact the surgeon if eye scratchiness occurs.
❏ 3. Place an eye shield on the surgical eye at bedtime.
❏ 4. Episodes of sudden severe pain in the eye are expected.
❏ 5. Contact the surgeon if a decrease in visual acuity occurs.
❏ 6. Take acetaminophen (Tylenol) for minor eye discomfort.

ANSWERS

1. **4**

Rationale: Otoscopic examination in a client with mastoiditis reveals a red, dull, thick, and immobile tympanic membrane, with or without perforation. Postauricular lymph nodes are tender and enlarged. Clients also have a low-grade fever, malaise, anorexia, swelling behind the ear, and pain with minimal movement of the head.

Test-Taking Strategy: Knowledge regarding the pathophysiology associated with mastoiditis is required to answer this question. Remember that mastoiditis reveals a red, dull, thick, and immobile tympanic membrane. If you had difficulty with this question, review the assessment findings associated with this disorder.

Level of Cognitive Ability: Analysis
Client Needs: Physiological Integrity
Integrated Process: Nursing Process—assessment
Content Area: Adult health—ear
Reference: Ignatavicius, D., & Workman, M. (2006). *Medical-surgical nursing: Critical thinking for collaborative care* (5th ed., pp. 1130-1131). Philadelphia: W.B. Saunders.

2. **2**

Rationale: Tinnitus is the most common complaint of clients with otological disorders, especially disorders involving the inner ear. Symptoms of tinnitus range from mild ringing in the ear, which can go unnoticed during the day, to a loud roaring in the ear, which can interfere with the client's thinking process and attention span. Options 1, 3, and 4 are not associated specifically with disorders of the inner ear.

Test-Taking Strategy: Use the process of elimination. Recalling the function of the inner ear will direct you to option 2. Review the manifestations associated with an inner ear disorder if you had difficulty with this question.

Level of Cognitive Ability: Analysis
Client Needs: Physiological Integrity
Integrated Process: Nursing Process—assessment
Content Area: Adult health—ear
Reference: Black, J., & Hawks, J. (2005). *Medical-surgical nursing: Clinical management for positive outcomes* (7th ed., pp. 1973-1974). Philadelphia: W.B. Saunders.

3. **4**

Rationale: The most appropriate nursing diagnosis for the client scheduled for cataract surgery is Sensory perception, disturbed (visual) related to lens extraction and replacement. Although options 1, 2, and 3 identify nursing diagnoses that may be appropriate, they are not related specifically to cataract surgery.

Test-Taking Strategy: Use the process of elimination. When asked questions regarding a nursing diagnosis, use the information presented in the question to select an option. Remember that disorders of the eye or ear relate to sensory perceptual alterations. Review care of the client scheduled for cataract surgery if you had difficulty with this question.

Level of Cognitive Ability: Analysis
Client Needs: Psychosocial Integrity
Integrated Process: Nursing Process—planning
Content Area: Adult health—eye

Reference: Ignatavicius, D., & Workman, M. (2006). *Medical-surgical nursing: Critical thinking for collaborative care* (5th ed., p. 1094). Philadelphia: W.B. Saunders.

4. **4**

Rationale: A gradual, painless blurring of central vision is the chief clinical manifestation of a cataract. Early symptoms include slightly blurred vision and a decrease in color perception. Options 1, 2, and 3 are not signs of a cataract.

Test-Taking Strategy: Use the process of elimination. Remember the pathophysiology related to cataract development. As a cataract develops, the lens of the eye becomes opaque. This description will assist in directing you to the correct option. If you had difficulty with this question, review the assessment signs associated with cataract development.

Level of Cognitive Ability: Analysis
Client Needs: Physiological Integrity
Integrated Process: Nursing Process—assessment
Content Area: Adult health—eye
Reference: Ignatavicius, D., & Workman, M. (2006). *Medical-surgical nursing: Critical thinking for collaborative care* (5th ed., p. 1093). Philadelphia: W.B. Saunders.

5. **4**

Rationale: A mydriatic medication produces mydriasis or dilation of the pupil. Mydriatic medications are used preoperatively in the cataract client. These medications act by dilating the pupils. They also constrict blood vessels. An osmotic diuretic may be used to decrease intraocular pressure. A miotic medication constricts the pupil. A thiazide diuretic is not likely to be prescribed for a client with a cataract.

Test-Taking Strategy: Use the process of elimination. Read the question carefully, noting that the client is being prepared for eye surgery. Dilation of the eye is necessary before cataract extraction. Recalling that a mydriatic dilates will direct you to option 4. Review preoperative care for cataract surgery if you had difficulty with this question.

Level of Cognitive Ability: Analysis
Client Needs: Physiological Integrity
Integrated Process: Nursing Process—analysis
Content Area: Adult health—eye
References: Black, J., & Hawks, J. (2005). *Medical-surgical nursing: Clinical management for positive outcomes* (7th ed., p. 1950). Philadelphia: W.B. Saunders.
Ignatavicius, D., & Workman, M. (2006). *Medical-surgical nursing: Critical thinking for collaborative care* (5th ed., p. 1094). Philadelphia: W.B. Saunders.

6. **1**

Rationale: Severe pain or pain accompanied by nausea is an indicator of increased intraocular pressure and should be reported to the physician immediately. Options 2, 3, and 4 are inappropriate actions.

Test-Taking Strategy: Use the process of elimination. Note the strategic word *severe*. Eliminate option 2 because this is not a normal condition. The client should not be turned to the operative side; therefore, eliminate option 3. From the remaining options, focusing on the strategic word will direct you to option 1. If you had difficulty with this question, review the

postoperative complications of cataract surgery requiring physician notification.
Level of Cognitive Ability: Application
Client Needs: Physiological Integrity
Integrated Process: Nursing Process—implementation
Content Area: Adult health—eye
Reference: Black, J., & Hawks, J. (2005). *Medical-surgical nursing: Clinical management for positive outcomes* (7th ed., p. 1951). Philadelphia: W.B. Saunders.

7. 4
Rationale: The client is instructed to wear a metal or plastic shield to protect the eye from accidental injury and is instructed not to rub the eye. Glasses may be worn during the day. Aspirin or medications containing aspirin are not to be administered or taken by the client and the client is instructed to take acetaminophen (Tylenol) as needed for pain. The client is instructed not to sleep on the side of the body on which the operation occurred. The client is not to lift more than 5 lb.
Test-Taking Strategy: Use the process of elimination, noting the strategic words *understanding of the instructions.* Recalling that the operative site needs to be protected will direct you to option 4. If you had difficulty with this question, review the discharge instructions for the client following cataract extraction.
Level of Cognitive Ability: Analysis
Client Needs: Physiological Integrity
Integrated Process: Nursing Process—evaluation
Content Area: Adult health—eye
Reference: Black, J., & Hawks, J. (2005). *Medical-surgical nursing: Clinical management for positive outcomes* (7th ed., p. 1951). Philadelphia: W.B. Saunders.

8. 4
Rationale: Vision loss to glaucoma is irreparable. The client should be reassured that although some vision has been lost and cannot be restored, further loss may be prevented by adhering to the treatment plan. Option 1 does not provide reassurance to the client.
Test-Taking Strategy: Use the process of elimination and therapeutic communication techniques. Also, note that option 4 is an umbrella option, addressing the importance of compliance with the treatment plan. Review the effects of glaucoma and therapeutic communication techniques if you had difficulty with this question.
Level of Cognitive Ability: Application
Client Needs: Physiological Integrity
Integrated Process: Communication and Documentation
Content Area: Adult health—eye
Reference: Black, J., & Hawks, J. (2005). *Medical-surgical nursing: Clinical management for positive outcomes* (7th ed., pp. 1945-1946). Philadelphia: W.B. Saunders.

9. 3
Rationale: The administration of eye drops is a critical component of the treatment plan for the client with glaucoma. The client needs to be instructed that medications will need to be taken for the rest of his or her life. Options 1, 2, and 4 are not accurate instructions.

Test-Taking Strategy: Use the process of elimination. Recalling that medications are an integral component of the treatment plan will assist in directing you to the correct option. Review the treatment associated with the care of the client with glaucoma if you had difficulty with this question.
Level of Cognitive Ability: Application
Client Needs: Physiological Integrity
Integrated Process: Nursing Process—planning
Content Area: Adult health—eye
References: Black, J., & Hawks, J. (2005). *Medical-surgical nursing: Clinical management for positive outcomes* (7th ed., pp. 1947-1948). Philadelphia: W.B. Saunders.
Ignatavicius, D., & Workman, M. (2006). *Medical-surgical nursing: Critical thinking for collaborative care* (5th ed., p. 298). Philadelphia: W.B. Saunders.

10. 4
Rationale: A characteristic manifestation of retinal detachment described by the client is the feeling that a shadow or curtain is falling across the field of vision. No pain is associated with detachment of the retina. Options 1 and 3 are not characteristics of this disorder. A retinal detachment is an ophthalmic emergency and even more so if visual acuity is still normal.
Test-Taking Strategy: Use the process of elimination, focusing on the diagnosis. Thinking about the pathophysiology associated with this disorder will direct you to option 4. Review the manifestations associated with this condition if you had difficulty with this question.
Level of Cognitive Ability: Analysis
Client Needs: Physiological Integrity
Integrated Process: Nursing Process—assessment
Content Area: Adult health—eye
Reference: Black, J., & Hawks, J. (2005). *Medical-surgical nursing: Clinical management for positive outcomes* (7th ed., p. 1952). Philadelphia: W.B. Saunders.

11. 4
Rationale: Complaints of a sudden burst of black spots or floaters indicates that bleeding has occurred as a result of the detachment. Options 1, 2, and 3 are not signs of bleeding.
Test-Taking Strategy: Focus on the client's diagnosis. Recalling the pathophysiology associated with retinal detachment will direct you to the correct option. Review the manifestations associated with the complications of a detached retina if you had difficulty with this question.
Level of Cognitive Ability: Analysis
Client Needs: Physiological Integrity
Integrated Process: Nursing Process—assessment
Content Area: Adult health—eye
Reference: Black, J., & Hawks, J. (2005). *Medical-surgical nursing: Clinical management for positive outcomes* (7th ed., p. 1952). Philadelphia: W.B. Saunders.

12. 2
Rationale: A hyphema is the presence of blood in the anterior chamber. Hyphema is produced when a force is sufficient to break the integrity of the blood vessels in the eye and can be caused by direct injury, such as a penetrating injury from a BB or pellet, or indirectly, such as from striking the forehead on a

steering wheel during an accident. The client is treated by bed rest in a semi-Fowler's position to assist gravity in keeping the hyphema away from the optical center of the cornea.

Test-Taking Strategy: Use the process of elimination to answer this question. Remember, placing the client flat will produce an increase in pressure at the injured site. Also, note that option 2 is the option that identifies a position different from the other options. Review care of the client with hyphema if you had difficulty with this question.

Level of Cognitive Ability: Application
Client Needs: Physiological Integrity
Integrated Process: Nursing Process—implementation
Content Area: Adult health—eye
Reference: Ignatavicius, D., & Workman, M. (2006). *Medical-surgical nursing: Critical thinking for collaborative care* (5th ed., p. 1105). Philadelphia: W.B. Saunders.

13. **2**
Rationale: Treatment for a contusion begins at the time of injury. Ice is applied immediately. The client then should be seen by a physician and receive a thorough eye examination to rule out the presence of other eye injuries.

Test-Taking Strategy: Use the process of elimination. Focus on the strategic word *immediately*. Recalling the principles related to initial treatment of injuries will direct you to option 2. Review emergency treatment of eye injuries if you had difficulty with this question.

Level of Cognitive Ability: Application
Client Needs: Physiological Integrity
Integrated Process: Nursing Process—implementation
Content Area: Adult health—eye
Reference: Ignatavicius, D., & Workman, M. (2006). *Medical-surgical nursing: Critical thinking for collaborative care* (5th ed., p. 1105). Philadelphia: W.B. Saunders.

14. **2**
Rationale: If the laceration is the result of a penetrating injury, an object may be noted protruding from the eye. This object must never be removed except by the ophthalmologist because it may be holding ocular structures in place. Application of an eye patch or irrigation of the eye may disrupt the foreign body and cause further tearing of the cornea.

Test-Taking Strategy: Use the process of elimination to answer this question. Note the strategic word *penetrating*. This should indicate that a laceration has occurred and that interventions are directed at preventing further disruption of the integrity of the eye. The only option that will prevent further disruption is to assess visual acuity. Review emergency eye care if you had difficulty with this question.

Level of Cognitive Ability: Application
Client Needs: Physiological Integrity
Integrated Process: Nursing Process—implementation
Content Area: Adult health—eye
Reference: Ignatavicius, D., & Workman, M. (2006). *Medical-surgical nursing: Critical thinking for collaborative care* (5th ed., p. 1106). Philadelphia: W.B. Saunders.

15. **4**
Rationale: Emergency care following a chemical burn to the eye includes irrigating the eye immediately with sterile normal

saline or ocular irrigating solution. In the emergency department, the irrigation should be maintained for at least 10 minutes. Following this emergency treatment, visual acuity is assessed. Options 2 and 3 are not a component of initial care.

Test-Taking Strategy: Read the question carefully, noting the type of injury to the eye. Noting the strategic word *splash* will direct you to option 4. Review emergency eye care if you had difficulty with this question.

Level of Cognitive Ability: Application
Client Needs: Physiological Integrity
Integrated Process: Nursing Process—implementation
Content Area: Adult health—eye
References: Black, J., & Hawks, J. (2005). *Medical-surgical nursing: Clinical management for positive outcomes* (7th ed., p. 1446). Philadelphia: W.B. Saunders.
Ignatavicius, D., & Workman, M. (2006). *Medical-surgical nursing: Critical thinking for collaborative care* (5th ed., p. 1106). Philadelphia: W.B. Saunders.

16. **1**
Rationale: If the nurse notes the presence of bright red drainage on the dressing, it must be reported to the physician, because this indicates hemorrhage. Options 2, 3, and 4 are inappropriate.

Test-Taking Strategy: Use the process of elimination and note the strategic words *bright red*. Remember, bright red drainage indicates active bleeding. Review postoperative complications associated with an enucleation if you had difficulty with this question.

Level of Cognitive Ability: Application
Client Needs: Physiological Integrity
Integrated Process: Nursing Process—implementation
Content Area: Adult health—eye
Reference: Ignatavicius, D., & Workman, M. (2006). *Medical-surgical nursing: Critical thinking for collaborative care* (5th ed., pp. 1106-1107). Philadelphia: W.B. Saunders.

17. **3**
Rationale: In the voice test, the examiner stands 1 to 2 feet away from the client and asks the client to block one external ear canal. The nurse whispers a statement and asks the client to repeat it. Each ear is tested separately.

Test-Taking Strategy: Use the process of elimination. Eliminate options 1 and 2 because they are not measures that would assess hearing effectively. Eliminate option 4 because distance hearing is not the subject of the question. Review the procedure for performing a voice test if you had difficulty with this question.

Level of Cognitive Ability: Application
Client Needs: Health Promotion and Maintenance
Integrated Process: Nursing Process—assessment
Content Area: Adult health—ear
Reference: Ignatavicius, D., & Workman, M. (2006). *Medical-surgical nursing: Critical thinking for collaborative care* (5th ed., p 1118). Philadelphia: W.B. Saunders.

18. **2**
Rationale: In this type of accident, the client is instructed to irrigate the eyes immediately with running water for at least 20 minutes or until the emergency medical service personnel arrive. In the emergency department, the cleansing agent of

choice is normal saline. Calling the physician and going to the emergency room delays necessary intervention. Hydrogen peroxide is never placed in the eyes.

Test-Taking Strategy: Use the process of elimination and note the strategic word *immediate*. Focus on the type of injury and eliminate options 1 and 3 because they delay necessary intervention. Next, eliminate option 4 because hydrogen peroxide is never placed in the eyes. Review immediate interventions for a chemical eye injury if you had difficulty with this question.

Level of Cognitive Ability: Application
Client Needs: Physiological Integrity.
Integrated Process: Nursing Process—implementation
Content Area: Adult health—eye
Reference: Ignatavicius, D., & Workman, M. (2006). *Medical-surgical nursing: Critical thinking for collaborative care* (5th ed., p. 1105). St. Louis: W.B. Saunders.

19. **3**
Rationale: Speaking in a normal tone to the client with impaired hearing and not shouting are important. The nurse should talk directly to the client while facing the client and speak clearly. If the client does not seem to understand what is said, the nurse should express it differently. Moving closer to the client and toward the better ear may facilitate communication, but the nurse should avoid talking directly into the impaired ear.

Test-Taking Strategy: Use the process of elimination and knowledge regarding effective communication techniques for the hearing impaired to answer this question. Remember, it is important to speak in a normal tone. If you had difficulty with this question, review these techniques.

Level of Cognitive Ability: Application
Client Needs: Psychosocial Integrity
Integrated Process: Communication and Documentation
Content Area: Adult health—ear
Reference: Ignatavicius, D., & Workman, M. (2006). *Medical-surgical nursing: Critical thinking for collaborative care* (5th ed., p. 1139). Philadelphia: W.B. Saunders.

20. **2**
Rationale: Insects are killed before removal unless they can be coaxed out by a flashlight or a humming noise. Mineral oil or diluted alcohol is instilled into the ear to suffocate the insect, which then is removed using ear forceps. When the foreign object is vegetable matter, irrigation is not used, because this material expands with hydration and the impaction becomes worse.

Test-Taking Strategy: Use the process of elimination. Focusing on the strategic words *foreign body* and *insect* will direct you to option 2. If you had difficulty with this question, review care of the client with a foreign body in the ear.

Level of Cognitive Ability: Analysis
Client Needs: Physiological Integrity
Integrated Process: Nursing Process—planning
Content Area: Adult health—ear
Reference: Ignatavicius, D., & Workman, M. (2006). *Medical-surgical nursing: Critical thinking for collaborative care* (5th ed., p. 1128). Philadelphia: W.B. Saunders.

21. **4**
Rationale: Presbycusis is a type of hearing loss that occurs with aging. Presbycusis is a gradual sensorineural loss caused by

nerve degeneration in the inner ear or auditory nerve. Options 1, 2, and 3 are incorrect.

Test-Taking Strategy: Knowledge regarding the description of presbycusis is required to answer this question. Remember that presbycusis is a gradual sensorineural loss. If you are unfamiliar with this condition, review this age-related disorder.

Level of Cognitive Ability: Comprehension
Client Needs: Physiological Integrity
Integrated Process: Nursing Process—planning
Content Area: Adult health—ear
Reference: Ignatavicius, D., & Workman, M. (2006). *Medical-surgical nursing: Critical thinking for collaborative care* (5th ed., p. 1134). Philadelphia: W.B. Saunders.

22. **3**
Rationale: Following ear surgery, the client needs to avoid straining when having a bowel movement. The client needs to be instructed to avoid drinking with a straw for 2 to 3 weeks, air travel, and coughing excessively. The client needs to avoid getting his or her head wet, washing hair, showering for 1 week, and rapidly moving the head, bouncing, and bending over for 3 weeks.

Test-Taking Strategy: Use the process of elimination and note the strategic words *teaching was effective*. Consider the anatomical area of the client's condition and the surgical procedure in eliminating the incorrect options. If you had difficulty with this question, review client instructions following ear surgery.

Level of Cognitive Ability: Analysis
Client Needs: Physiological Integrity
Integrated Process: Nursing Process—evaluation
Content Area: Adult health—ear
Reference: Ignatavicius, D., & Workman, M. (2006). *Medical-surgical nursing: Critical thinking for collaborative care* (5th ed., p. 1130). Philadelphia: W.B. Saunders.

23. **2**
Rationale: The nurse instructs the client to make slow head movements to prevent worsening of the vertigo. Dietary changes such as salt and fluid restrictions that reduce the amount of endolymphatic fluid are sometimes prescribed. Lying still and watching television will not control vertigo.

Test-Taking Strategy: Use the process of elimination. Identify the subject, vertigo. Note the relationship between vertigo and avoiding sudden head movements in the correct option. If you had difficulty with this question, review the measures that will reduce vertigo in the client with Menière's disease.

Level of Cognitive Ability: Application
Client Needs: Physiological Integrity
Integrated Process: Nursing Process—implementation
Content Area: Adult health—ear
Reference: Ignatavicius, D., & Workman, M. (2006). *Medical-surgical nursing: Critical thinking for collaborative care* (5th ed., pp. 1132-1133). Philadelphia: W.B. Saunders.

24. **2**
Rationale: Dietary changes such as salt and fluid restrictions that reduce the amount of endolymphatic fluid are sometimes prescribed. Options 1, 3, and 4 are not specific to the client with Menière's disease.

Test-Taking Strategy: Use the process of elimination. Recalling the pathophysiology related to Menière's disease will direct you to option 2. Review the pathophysiology related to this condition and the treatment measures if you had difficulty with this question.
Level of Cognitive Ability: Analysis
Client Needs: Physiological Integrity
Integrated Process: Nursing Process—planning
Content Area: Adult health—ear
Reference: Ignatavicius, D., & Workman, M. (2006). *Medical-surgical nursing: Critical thinking for collaborative care* (5th ed., p. 1132). Philadelphia: W.B. Saunders.

25. 1
Rationale: Visual acuity is assessed in one eye at a time, and then in both eyes together, with the client comfortably standing or sitting. The right eye is tested with the left eye covered; then the left eye is tested with the right eye covered. Both eyes are then tested together. Visual acuity is measured with or without corrective lenses and the client stands at a distance of 20 feet from the chart.
Test-Taking Strategy: Use the process of elimination. Remember that normal visual acuity as measured by a Snellen chart is 20/20 vision. This should assist in eliminating options 3 and 4. From the remaining options, remember that it is best to test each eye separately and then test both eyes together. This method assesses visual acuity most accurately. Review the procedure for testing visual acuity with a Snellen chart if you had difficulty with this question.
Level of Cognitive Ability: Application
Client Needs: Health Promotion and Maintenance
Integrated Process: Nursing Process—assessment
Content Area: Adult health—eye
Reference: Ignatavicius, D., & Workman, M. (2006). *Medical-surgical nursing: Critical thinking for collaborative care* (5th ed., p. 1078). Philadelphia: W.B. Saunders.

26. 4
Rationale: Vision that is 20/20 is normal—that is, the client is able to read from 20 feet what a person with normal vision can read from 20 feet. A client with a visual acuity of 20/60 can only read at a distance of 20 feet what a person with normal vision can read at 60 feet.
Test-Taking Strategy: Use the process of elimination. Focus on the test result, 20/60, to direct you to option 4. If you had difficulty with this question, review interpretation of visual acuity test results.
Level of Cognitive Ability: Analysis
Client Needs: Physiological Integrity
Integrated Process: Nursing Process—analysis
Content Area: Adult health—eye
References: Ignatavicius, D., & Workman, M. (2006). *Medical-surgical nursing: Critical thinking for collaborative care* (5th ed., p. 1078). Philadelphia: W.B. Saunders.
Jarvis, C. (2004). *Physical examination and health assessment* (4th ed., pp. 306-307). Philadelphia: W.B. Saunders.

27. 4
Rationale: Legal blindness is defined as 20/200 or less with corrected vision (glasses or contact lenses) or visual acuity of less than 20 degrees of the visual field in the better eye.

Test-Taking Strategy: Knowledge of the definition of legal blindness is required to answer this question. Remember that legal blindness is defined as 20/200 or less with corrected vision. Review this definition if you had difficulty with this question.
Level of Cognitive Ability: Comprehension
Client Needs: Physiological Integrity
Integrated Process: Nursing Process—assessment
Content Area: Adult health—eye
Reference: Ignatavicius, D., & Workman, M. (2006). *Medical-surgical nursing: Critical thinking for collaborative care* (5th ed., pp. 1107-1108). Philadelphia: W.B. Saunders.

28. 2
Rationale: Tonometry is the method of measuring intraocular fluid pressure using a calibrated instrument that indents or flattens the corneal apex. Pressures between 10 and 21 mm Hg are considered within the normal range.
Test-Taking Strategy: Use the process of elimination and knowledge regarding normal intraocular pressure to answer this question. Remember that normal intraocular pressure is between 10 and 21 mm Hg. If you had difficulty with this question, learn this normal value.
Level of Cognitive Ability: Comprehension
Client Needs: Physiological Integrity
Integrated Process: Nursing Process—assessment
Content Area: Adult health—eye
Reference: Ignatavicius, D., & Workman, M. (2006). *Medical-surgical nursing: Critical thinking for collaborative care* (5th ed., pp. 1080-1081). Philadelphia: W.B. Saunders.

29. 4
Rationale: Treatment for acoustic neuroma is surgical removal via a craniotomy. Extreme care is taken to preserve remaining hearing and preserve the function of the facial nerve. Acoustic neuromas rarely recur following surgical removal.
Test-Taking Strategy: Use the process of elimination and knowledge regarding the anatomical location of an acoustic neuroma to direct you to option 4. If you had difficulty with this question, review the complications associated with this surgical procedure.
Level of Cognitive Ability: Analysis
Client Needs: Physiological Integrity
Integrated Process: Nursing Process—assessment
Content Area: Adult health—ear
References: Ignatavicius, D., & Workman, M. (2006). *Medical-surgical nursing: Critical thinking for collaborative care* (5th ed., p. 1133). Philadelphia: W.B. Saunders.
Lewis, S., Heitkemper, M., & Dirksen, S. (2004). *Medical-surgical nursing: Assessment and management of clinical problems* (6th ed., p. 1519). St. Louis: Mosby.

ALTERNATE ITEM FORMAT: MULTIPLE RESPONSE

Answer: 1, 3, 5, 6
Rationale: Following eye surgery, some scratchiness and mild eye discomfort may occur in the operative eye and usually is relieved by mild analgesics. If the eye pain becomes severe, the client should notify the surgeon because this may indicate hemorrhage, infection, or increased intraocular pressure. The nurse also would instruct the client to notify the surgeon of

increased purulent drainage, increased redness, or any decrease in visual acuity. The client is instructed to place an eye shield over the operative eye at bedtime to protect the eye from injury during sleep and to avoid activities that increase intraocular pressure, such as bending over.

Test-Taking Strategy: Note that the client has had eye surgery. Recalling that the eye needs to be protected and that a concern is increased intraocular pressure will assist in determining the home care measures to be included in the plan. Review these measures if you had difficulty with this question.

Level of Cognitive Ability: Application
Client Needs: Physiological Integrity
Integrated Process: Teaching and Learning
Content Area: Adult health—eye
References: Black, J., & Hawks, J. (2005). *Medical-surgical nursing: Clinical management for positive outcomes* (7th ed., p. 1951). Philadelphia: W.B. Saunders.
Lewis, S., Heitkemper, M., & Dirksen, S. (2004). *Medical-surgical nursing: Assessment and management of clinical problems* (6th ed., p. 452). St. Louis: Mosby.

REFERENCES

Black, J., & Hawks, J. (2005). *Medical-surgical nursing: Clinical management for positive outcomes* (7th ed.). Philadelphia: W.B. Saunders.

Ignatavicius, D., & Workman, M. (2006). *Medical-surgical nursing: Critical thinking for collaborative care* (5th ed.). Philadelphia: W.B. Saunders.

Jarvis, C. (2004). *Physical examination and health assessment* (4th ed.). Philadelphia: W.B. Saunders.

Lewis, S., Heitkemper, M., & Dirksen, S. (2004). *Medical-surgical nursing: Assessment and management of clinical problems* (6th ed.). St. Louis: Mosby.

Mosby. (2005). *Mosby's expert 10-minute physical examinations* (2nd ed.). St. Louis: Mosby.

Ophthalmic and Otic Medications

I. OPHTHALMIC MEDICATION ADMINISTRATION

A. Guidelines for the use of eye medications

1. Eye medications are usually in the form of drops or ointments.
2. Because the timing of medication administration is critical, administer medications at frequent, precise intervals; separate the instillation by 3 to 5 minutes if two medications must be administered at the same time.
3. To prevent overflow of medication into the nasal and pharyngeal passages, thus reducing systemic absorption, instruct the client to apply pressure over the inner canthus next to the nose for 30 to 60 seconds following administration of the medication; instruct the client to close the eye gently to help distribute the medication.
4. If both an eye drop and an eye ointment are scheduled to be administered at the same time, administer the eye drop first.
5. Wash hands and don gloves before administering eye medications to avoid contaminating the eye or medication dropper or applicator
6. Use a separate bottle or tube of medication for each client to avoid accidental cross-contamination.
7. Place the prescribed dose of eye medication in the lower conjunctival sac, never directly onto the cornea.
8. Avoid touching any part of the eye with the dropper or applicator.
9. Administer glucocorticoid preparations before other medications.
10. Monitor the pulse of the client receiving an ophthalmic β-blocker, and instruct the client to do the same; if the pulse is less than 50 to 60 beats/min (adult), withhold the next dose of eye medication and notify the physician.
11. Instruct the client how to instill medication correctly and supervise instillation until the client can do it safely.
12. Instruct the client to read the medication labels carefully to ensure administration of the correct medication and correct strength.
13. Remind the client to keep these medications out of the reach of children.
14. Instruct the client to avoid driving or operating hazardous equipment if vision is blurred.
15. Inform the client that he or she may be unable to drive home after eye examinations when a medication to dilate the pupil (**mydriatic**) or to paralyze the ciliary muscle (cycloplegic) is used.
16. If photophobia occurs, instruct the client to wear sunglasses and avoid bright lights.
17. Instruct the client to administer a missed dose of the eye medication as soon as it is remembered, unless the next dose is scheduled to be administered in 1 to 2 hours.
18. Inform the client with **glaucoma** that the disorder cannot be cured, only controlled.
19. Reinforce the importance of using medications to treat **glaucoma** as prescribed and not to discontinue these medications without consulting the physician.
20. Inform the client that medications used to treat **glaucoma** may cause pain and blurred vision, especially when therapy is begun.
21. Instruct the client to report the development of any eye irritation.
22. Inform the client using eye gel to store the gel at room temperature or in the refrigerator, but not to freeze it.

23. Instruct the client to discard unused eye gel kept at room temperature as recommended by the physician and/or the pharmacist.
24. Inform the client that soft contact lenses may absorb certain eye medications and that preservatives in eye medications may discolor the contact lenses.
25. Advise the client wearing contact lenses to question the physician carefully about special precautions to observe with eye medications.
26. In infants, inform the parents that atropine sulfate eye drops may contribute to abdominal distention.
27. Instruct the parents to keep a record of the infant's bowel movements if atropine sulfate eye drops are being administered.
28. Auscultate bowel sounds of the infant or child receiving atropine sulfate eye drops.

B. Instillation of eye medications
1. Drops
   a. Wash hands.
   b. Put gloves on.
   c. Check the name, strength, and expiration date of the medication.
   d. Instruct the client to tilt the head backward, open the eyes, and look up.
   e. Pull the lower lid down against the cheekbone.
   f. Hold the bottle like a pencil, with the tip downward.
   g. Holding the bottle, gently rest the wrist of the hand on the client's cheek.
   h. Squeeze the bottle gently to allow the drop to fall into the conjunctival sac.
   i. Instruct the client to close the eyes gently and not to squeeze the eyes shut.
   j. Wait 3 to 5 minutes before instilling another drop, if more than one drop is prescribed, to promote maximal absorption of the medication.
   k. Do not allow the medication bottle, dropper, or applicator to come into contact with the eyelid or conjunctival sac.
   l. To prevent systemic absorption of the medication, apply gentle pressure with a clean tissue to the client's nasolacrimal duct for 30 to 60 seconds.
2. Ointments
   a. Instruct the client to lie down or tilt head backward and look up.
   b. Hold the ointment tube near, but not touching, the eye or eyelashes.
   c. Squeeze a thin ribbon of ointment along the lining of the lower conjunctival sac from the inner to the outer canthus.
   d. Instruct the client to close the eyes gently, rolling the eyeball in all directions (increases contact area of medication to eye).
   e. Instruct the client that vision may be blurred by the ointment.
   f. If possible, apply ointment just before bedtime.

II. MYDRIATIC-CYCLOPLEGIC AND ANTICHOLINERGIC MEDICATIONS (Box 64-1)
A. Description (Fig. 64-1)
1. **Mydriatics** and cycloplegics dilate the pupils **(mydriasis)** and relax the ciliary muscles **(cycloplegia).**
2. Anticholinergics block responses of the sphincter muscle in the ciliary body, producing **mydriasis** and **cycloplegia.**
3. These medications are used preoperatively or for eye examinations to produce **mydriasis.**

BOX 64-1
Mydriatic and Cycloplegic Medications

Atropine (Isopto Atropine)
Cyclopentolate (AK-Pentolate, Cyclogyl, Pentolair)
Homatropine (Isopto Homatropine)
Scopolamine (Isopto Hyoscine)
Tropicamide (Mydriacyl, Tropicacyl, Opticyl)

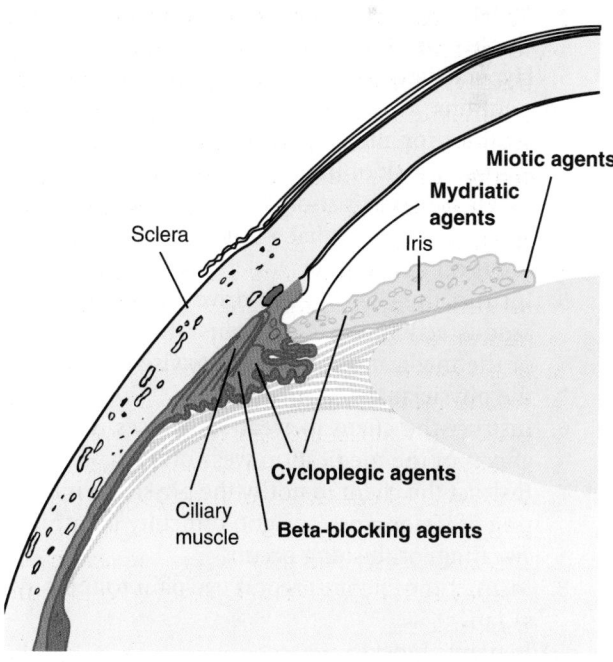

FIG. 64-1 Sites of action of mydriatic, β-blocking, cycloplegic, and miotic agents. (From Black, J., & Hawks, J., [2005]. *Medical-surgical nursing: Clinical management for positive outcomes* [7th ed.]. Philadelphia: W.B. Saunders.)

4. These medications are contraindicated in clients with **glaucoma** because of the risk of increased intraocular pressure.
5. **Mydriatics** are contraindicated in cardiac dysrhythmias and cerebral atherosclerosis and should be used with caution in the older client and in clients with prostatic hypertrophy, diabetes mellitus, or parkinsonism.

▲ B. Side effects
1. Tachycardia
2. Photophobia
3. Conjunctivitis
4. Dermatitis
5. Elevated blood pressure

▲ C. Atropine toxicity
1. Dry mouth
2. Blurred vision
3. Photophobia
4. Tachycardia
5. Fever
6. Urinary retention
7. Constipation
8. Headache, brow pain
9. Confusion
10. Hallucinations, delirium
11. Coma
12. Worsening of narrow-angle **glaucoma**

D. Systemic reactions of anticholinergics
1. Dry mouth and skin
2. Fever
3. Thirst
4. Confusion
5. Hyperactivity

▲ E. Interventions
1. Monitor for allergic response.
2. Assess for risk of injury.
3. Assess for constipation and urinary retention.
4. Instruct the client that a burning sensation may occur on instillation.
5. Instruct the client not to drive or perform hazardous activities for 24 hours after instillation of the medication unless otherwise directed by the physician.
6. Instruct the client to wear sunglasses until the effects of the medication wear off.
7. Instruct the client to notify the physician if blurring of vision, loss of sight, difficulty breathing, sweating, or flushing occurs.
8. Instruct the client to report eye pain to the physician.

F. α-Adrenergic blocker
1. Medication: Dapiprazole hydrochloride (Rev-Eyes)
2. Use: To counteract **mydriasis**

III. **ANTI-INFECTIVE EYE MEDICATIONS** (Box 64-2)
A. Description: Anti-infective medications kill or inhibit the growth of bacteria, fungi, and viruses.

> **BOX 64-2**
> Anti-infective Eye Medications
>
> **ANTIBACTERIAL**
> Chloramphenicol (Chloromycetin powder)
> Erythromycin (Ilotycin)
>
> **AMINOGLYCOSIDES**
> Gentamicin sulfate (Garamycin, Genoptic)
> Tobramycin (Tobrex)
>
> **ANTIFUNGAL**
> Natamycin (Natacyn)
>
> **ANTIVIRAL**
> Idoxuridine
> Trifluridine (Viroptic)
>
> **SULFONAMIDE**
> Sulfacetamide (Bleph-10, Sodium Sulamyd)

B. Side effects
1. Superinfection
2. Global irritation
C. Interventions
1. Assess for risk of injury.
2. Instruct the client how to apply the eye medication; remind the client to clean exudates from the eyes before administering drops.
3. Reinforce the importance of completing the prescribed medication regimen.
4. Instruct the client to wash the hands thoroughly and frequently.
5. Advise the client that if improvement does not occur to notify the physician.

IV. **ANTI-INFLAMMATORY EYE MEDICATIONS** (Box 64-3)
A. Description
1. Anti-inflammatory medications control inflammation, thereby reducing vision loss and scarring.
2. Anti-inflammatory medications are used for uveitis, allergic conditions, and inflammation of the conjunctiva, cornea, and lids.
B. Side effects
1. Cataracts
2. Increased intraocular pressure
3. Impaired healing
4. Masking signs and symptoms of infection
C. Interventions
1. Interventions are the same as for anti-infective medications.
2. Note that dexamethasone (Maxidex) should not be used for eye abrasions and wounds.

V. **TOPICAL EYE ANESTHETICS** (Box 64-4)
A. Description
1. Topical anesthetics produce corneal anesthesia.

ANTIALLERGIC AGENTS
Cromolyn sodium (Crolom, Opticrom)
Ketotifen fumarate (Zaditor)
Levocabastine (Livostin)
Lodoxamide (Alomide)
Nedocromil sodium (Alocril)
Pemirolast potassium (Alamast)

CORTICOSTEROIDS
Dexamethasone (Maxidex)
Fluorometholone; sulfacetamide (FML-S eye drop suspension)
Medrysone (HMS)
Prednisolone; gentamicin (Pred-G, Pred Forte)

NONSTEROIDAL ANTI-INFLAMMATORY AGENTS
Cyclosporine (Restasis)
Diclofenac (Voltaren)
Flurbiprofen sodium (Ocufen)
Ketorolac tromethamine (Acular)

Proparacaine hydrochloride (Ophthetic)
Tetracaine hydrochloride (Pontocaine)

2. Topical anesthetics are used for anesthesia for eye examinations and surgery or to remove foreign bodies from the eye.
3. Do not use discolored solution and store the bottle tightly closed.

B. Side effects
1. Temporary stinging or burning of the eye
2. Temporary loss of corneal reflex

C. Interventions
1. Assess for risk of injury.
2. Note that the medications should not be given to the client for home use and are not to be self-administered by the client.
3. Instruct the client not to rub or touch the eye while it is anesthetized.
4. Note that the blink reflex is lost temporarily and that the corneal epithelium needs to be protected.
5. Provide an eye patch to protect the eye from injury until the corneal reflex returns.

VI. EYE LUBRICANTS (Box 64-5)
A. Description
1. Eye lubricants replace tears or add moisture to the eyes.
2. Eye lubricants moisten contact lenses or an artificial eye and protect the eyes during surgery or diagnostic procedures.

Hydroxypropyl methylcellulose (Lacril, Isopto Plain)
Petroleum-based ointment (Artificial Tears)
Polyvinyl alcohol (Liquifilm Tears)

Carbachol (Carboptic)
Echothiophate
Pilocarpine hydrochloride (Isopto Carpine)

3. Eye lubricants are used for keratitis, during anesthesia, or for a disorder that results in unconsciousness or decreased blinking.
B. Side effects
1. Burning on instillation
2. Discomfort or pain on instillation
C. Interventions
1. Inform the client that burning may occur on instillation.
2. Be alert to allergic responses to the preservatives in the lubricants.

VII. MIOTICS (Box 64-6; see Fig. 64-1)
A. Description
1. **Miotics** reduce intraocular pressure by constricting the pupil and contracting the ciliary muscle, thereby increasing the blood flow to the retina and decreasing retinal damage and loss of vision.
2. **Miotics** open the anterior chamber angle and increase the outflow of aqueous humor.
3. **Miotic** cholinergic medications reduce intraocular pressure by mimicking the action of acetylcholine.
4. **Miotic** acetylcholine inhibitors reduce intraocular pressure by inhibiting the action of cholinesterase.
5. **Miotics** are used for chronic open-angle **glaucoma** or acute and chronic closed-angle **glaucoma.**
6. **Miotics** are used to achieve miosis during eye surgery.
7. **Miotics** are contraindicated in clients with **retinal detachment,** adhesions between the iris and lens, or inflammatory diseases.
8. Use **miotics** with caution in clients with asthma, hypertension, corneal abrasion, hyperthyroidism, coronary vascular disease, urinary tract obstruction, gastrointestinal obstruction, ulcer disease, parkinsonism, and bradycardia.
B. Side effects
1. Myopia
2. Headache
3. Eye pain

4. Decreased vision in poor light
5. Local irritation
6. Systemic effects
   a. Flushing
   b. Diaphoresis
   c. Gastrointestinal upset and diarrhea
   d. Frequent urination
   e. Increased salivation
   f. Muscle weakness
   g. Respiratory difficulty
7. Toxicity
   a. Vertigo and syncope
   b. Bradycardia
   c. Hypotension
   d. Cardiac dysrhythmias
   e. Tremors
   f. Seizures
C. Interventions
   1. Assess vital signs.
   2. Assess for risk of injury.
   3. Assess the client for the degree of diminished vision.
   4. Monitor for side effects and toxic effects.
   5. Monitor for postural hypotension, and instruct the client to change positions slowly.
   6. Assess breath sounds for wheezes and rhonchi because cholinergic medications can cause bronchospasms and increased bronchial secretions.
   7. Maintain oral hygiene because of the increase in salivation.
   8. Have atropine sulfate available as an antidote for pilocarpine.
   9. Instruct the client or family regarding the correct administration of eye medications.
   10. Instruct the client not to stop the medication suddenly.
   11. Instruct the client to avoid activities such as driving while vision is impaired.
   12. Instruct the client with **glaucoma** to read labels on over-the-counter medications and to avoid atropine-like medications because atropine will increase intraocular pressure.

VIII. OCUSERT SYSTEM

A. Description
   1. A thin eye wafer (disk) is impregnated with a time-release dose of pilocarpine (Ocusert Pilo-20, Ocusert Pilo-40).
   2. The Ocusert system was devised to overcome the frequent application of pilocarpine.
   3. It is placed in the upper or lower cul-de-sac of the eye.
   4. The pilocarpine is released over 1 week.
   5. The disk is replaced every 7 days.
   6. Drawbacks of its use include sudden leakage of pilocarpine, migration of the system over the cornea, and unnoticed loss of the system.

B. Interventions
   1. Assess the client's ability to insert the medication disk.
   2. Store the medication in the refrigerator.
   3. Instruct the client to discard damaged or contaminated disks.
   4. Inform the client that temporary stinging is expected but to notify the physician if blurred vision or brow pain occurs.
   5. Instruct the client to check for the presence of the disk in the conjunctival sac daily at bedtime and on arising.
   6. Because vision may change in the first few hours after the eye system is inserted, instruct the client to replace the disk at bedtime.

IX. β-ADRENERGIC BLOCKING EYE MEDICATIONS (Box 64-7)

A. Description (see Fig. 64-1)
   1. These medications reduce intraocular pressure by decreasing sympathetic impulses and decreasing aqueous humor production without affecting **accommodation** or pupil size.
   2. These medications are used to treat chronic open-angle **glaucoma.**
   3. These medications are contraindicated in the client with asthma or chronic obstructive pulmonary disease because systemic absorption can cause increased airway resistance.
   4. Use these medications with caution in the client receiving oral β-blockers.

B. Side effects
   1. Ocular irritation
   2. Visual disturbances
   3. Bradycardia
   4. Hypotension
   5. Bronchospasm

C. Interventions
   1. Monitor vital signs, especially blood pressure and pulse, before administering medication.
   2. If the pulse is 60 beats/min or less or if the systolic blood pressure is less than 90 mm Hg, withhold the medication and contact the physician.
   3. Monitor for shortness of breath.
   4. Assess for risk of injury.
   5. Monitor intake and output.

BOX 64-7
β-Adrenergic Blocking Eye Medications

Betaxolol hydrochloride (Betoptic)
Carteolol hydrochloride (Ocupress)
Levobetaxolol
Levobunolol hydrochloride (Betagan Liquifilm)
Metipranolol (OptiPranolol)
Timolol maleate (Timoptic)

6. Instruct the client to notify the physician if shortness of breath occurs.
7. Instruct the client not to discontinue the medication abruptly.
8. Instruct the client to change positions slowly because of the potential for orthostatic hypotension.
9. Instruct the client to avoid hazardous activities.
10. Instruct the client to avoid over-the-counter medications without the physician's approval.
11. Instruct clients with diabetes mellitus using β-adrenergic blockers to monitor blood glucose levels frequently.
D. Adrenergic medications (Box 64-8)
1. Adrenergic medications decrease the production of aqueous humor and lead to a decrease in intraocular pressure.
2. Adrenergic medications may be used to treat **glaucoma.**

X. CARBONIC ANHYDRASE INHIBITORS (Box 64-9)
A. Description
1. Carbonic anhydrase inhibitors interfere with the production of carbonic acid, which leads to decreased aqueous humor formation and decreased intraocular pressure.
2. These medications are used for long-term treatment of open-angle **glaucoma.**
3. These medications are contraindicated in the client allergic to sulfonamides.
4. Use with caution for clients with severe renal or liver disease.
B. Side effects
1. Appetite loss
2. Gastrointestinal upset
3. Paresthesias in the fingers, toes, and face
4. Polyuria
5. Hypokalemia
6. Renal calculi
7. Photosensitivity

8. Lethargy and drowsiness
9. Depression
C. Interventions
1. Monitor vital signs.
2. Assess visual acuity.
3. Assess for risk of injury.
4. Monitor intake and output.
5. Monitor weight.
6. Maintain oral hygiene.
7. Monitor for side effects such as lethargy, anorexia, drowsiness, polyuria, nausea, and vomiting.
8. Monitor electrolyte levels for hypokalemia.
9. Increase fluid intake unless contraindicated.
10. Advise the client to avoid prolonged exposure to sunlight.
11. Encourage the use of artificial tears for dry eyes.
12. Instruct the client not to discontinue the medication abruptly.
13. Instruct the client to avoid hazardous activities while vision is impaired.
14. Teach the client not to wear contact lenses during or within 15 minutes of instilling these medications.

XI. OSMOTIC MEDICATIONS (Box 64-10)
A. Description
1. Osmotic medications lower intraocular pressure.
2. Osmotic medications are used in emergency treatment of acute closed-angle **glaucoma.**
3. Osmotic medications are used preoperatively and postoperatively to decrease vitreous humor volume.
B. Side effects
1. Headache
2. Nausea, vomiting, diarrhea, dehydration
3. Disorientation
4. Electrolyte imbalances
C. Interventions
1. Assess vital signs.
2. Assess visual acuity.
3. Assess for risk of injury.
4. Monitor intake and output.
5. Monitor weight.
6. Monitor electrolyte imbalances.
7. Increase fluid intake unless contraindicated.
8. Monitor for changes in level of orientation.

XII. OTIC MEDICATION ADMINISTRATION (Box 64-11)
A. Instillation of ear drops
1. In an adult, pull the pinna up and back to straighten the external canal to instill ear drops.

BOX 64-8
Adrenergic Medications

Hydroxyamphetamine (Paredrine)
Naphazoline (Allerest)
Oxymetazoline (OcuClear)
Tetrahydrozoline (Murine Plus, Visine Moisturizing)

BOX 64-9
Carbonic Anhydrase Inhibitor Eye Medications

Acetazolamide (Diamox)
Brinzolamide (Azopt)
Dorzolamide hydrochloride (Trusopt)

BOX 64-10
Osmotic Medications for the Eye

Glycerin (Osmoglyn)
Mannitol (Osmitrol)

BOX 64-11

Medications That Affect Hearing

ANTIBIOTICS
Amikacin (Amikin)
Chloramphenicol
Erythromycin (ERYC, Ery-Tab, PCE Dispertabs, Ilotycin)
Gentamicin (Garamycin)
Streptomycin sulfate
Tobramycin sulfate (Nebcin)
Vancomycin (Vancocin)

DIURETICS
Acetazolamide (Diamox)
Ethacrynic acid (Edecrin)
Furosemide (Lasix)

OTHERS
Cisplatin (Platinol)
Nitrogen mustard
Quinine
Quinidine

BOX 64-12

Anti-infective Ear Medications

Acetic acid; aluminum acetate (Otic Domeboro)
Amoxicillin (Amoxil)
Ampicillin (Principen)
Cefaclor (Ceclor)
Chloramphenicol
Clarithromycin (Biaxin)
Clindamycin hydrochloride (Cleocin)
Erythromycin (Ilotycin)
Gentamicin sulfate otic solution (Garamycin)
Loracarbef (Lorabid)
Penicillin V potassium (Veetids)
Trimethoprim; sulfamethoxazole (Bactrim, Cotrim, Septra)

BOX 64-13

Antihistamines and Decongestants

Cetirizine (Zyrtec)
Chlorpheniramine (Chlor-Trimeton)
Clemastine (Tavist)
Naphazoline hydrochloride (Allerest)
Naphazoline hydrochloride; polyvinyl alcohol (Albalon)

---

2. Tilt the client's head in the opposite direction of the affected ear and apply the drops into the ear.
3. With the head tilted, gently move the head back and forth five times.
4. Pull the pinna down and back for infants and children younger than 3 years, up and back for older children.

▲ B. Irrigation of the ear
1. Irrigation of the ear needs to be prescribed by the physician.
2. Ensure direct visualization of the tympanic membrane.
3. Warm irrigating solution to 98° F because solution temperature not close to the client's body temperature will cause ear injury, nausea, and vertigo.
4. Irrigation must be done gently to avoid damage to the eardrum.
5. When irrigating, do not direct irrigation solution directly toward the eardrum.
6. If a perforation of the eardrum is suspected, do not perform irrigation.

XIII. ANTI-INFECTIVE EAR MEDICATIONS
(Box 64-12)
A. Description
1. Anti-infective medications kill or inhibit the growth of bacteria and are used for otitis media or otitis externa.
2. Anti-infective medications are contraindicated if a prior hypersensitivity exists.
▲ B. Side effects: Overgrowth of nonsusceptible organisms

C. Interventions
1. Monitor vital signs.
2. Assess for allergies.
3. Assess for pain.
4. Monitor for nephrotoxicity.
5. Instruct the client to report dizziness, fatigue, fever, or sore throat, which may indicate a superimposed infection.
6. Instruct the client to complete the entire course of the medication.
7. Instruct the client to keep ear canals dry.

XIV. ANTIHISTAMINES AND DECONGESTANTS
(Box 64-13)
A. Description
1. These medications produce vasoconstriction.
2. These medications stimulate the receptors of the respiratory mucosa.
3. These medications reduce respiratory tissue hyperemia and edema to open obstructed eustachian tubes.
4. These medications are used for acute otitis media.
B. Side effects
1. Drowsiness
2. Blurred vision
3. Dry mucous membranes
C. Interventions
1. Inform the client that drowsiness, blurred vision, and a dry mouth may occur.

2. Instruct the client to increase fluid intake unless contraindicated and to suck on hard candy to alleviate the dry mouth.

3. Instruct the client to avoid hazardous activities if drowsiness occurs.

XV. LOCAL ANESTHETICS

A. Description
  1. Local anesthetics block nerve conduction at or near the application site to control pain.
  2. Local anesthetics are used for pain associated with ear infections.
B. Medication: Benzocaine-antipyrine-phenylephrine (Tympagesic)
C. Side effects
  1. Allergic reaction
  2. Irritation
D. Interventions
  1. Monitor for effectiveness if used for pain relief.
  2. Assess for irritation or allergic reaction.

XVI. CERUMINOLYTIC MEDICATIONS (Box 64-14)

A. Description
  1. Ceruminolytic medications emulsify and loosen cerumen deposits.
  2. Ceruminolytic medications are used to loosen and remove impacted wax from the ear canal.
B. Side effects
  1. Irritation
  2. Redness or swelling of the ear canal
C. Interventions
  1. Instruct the client not to use drops more often than prescribed.
  2. Moisten a cotton plug with medication before insertion.
  3. Keep the container tightly closed and away from moisture.
  4. Avoid touching the ear with the dropper.
  5. Thirty minutes after instillation, gently irrigate the ear as prescribed with warm water, using a soft rubber bulb ear syringe.
  6. Irrigation may be done with hydrogen peroxide solution as prescribed to flush cerumen deposits out of the ear canal.
  7. For a chronic cerumen impaction, one or two drops of mineral oil will soften the wax.
  8. Instruct the client to notify the physician if redness, pain, or swelling persists.

BOX 64-14

Ceruminolytic Medications

Boric acid (Ear-Dry)
Carbamide peroxide (Debrox)
Trolamine polypeptide oleate-condensate (Cerumenex)

PRACTICE QUESTIONS

1. The client is receiving an eye drop and an eye ointment to the right eye. The nurse should:
   1. Administer the eye drop first, followed by the eye ointment.
   2. Administer the eye ointment first, followed by the eye drop.
   3. Administer the eye drop, wait 10 minutes, and administer the eye ointment.
   4. Administer the eye ointment, wait 10 minutes, and administer the eye drop.

2. The nurse is caring for a client with glaucoma. Which of the following medications, if prescribed for the client, would the nurse question?
   1. Carbachol (Carboptic)
   2. Atropine sulfate (Isopto Atropine)
   3. Pilocarpine (Ocusert Pilo-20, Ocusert Pilo-40)
   4. Pilocarpine hydrochloride (Isopto Carpine)

3. A miotic medication has been prescribed for the client with glaucoma. The client asks the nurse about the purpose of the medication. The nurse tells the client that:
   1. "The medication will help dilate the eye to prevent pressure from occurring."
   2. "The medication will relax the muscles of the eyes and prevent blurred vision."
   3. "The medication causes the pupil to constrict and will lower the pressure in the eye."
   4. "The medication will help block the responses that are sent to the muscles in the eye."

4. A client was just admitted to the hospital to rule out a gastrointestinal (GI) bleed. The client has brought several bottles of medications prescribed by different specialists. During the admission assessment, the client states, "Lately, I have been hearing some roaring sounds in my ears, especially when I am alone." Which medication would the nurse determine could be the cause of the client's complaint?
   1. Doxycycline (Vibramycin)
   2. Acetazolamide (Diamox)
   3. Acetylsalicylic acid (aspirin)
   4. Diltiazem hydrochloride (Cardizem)

5. Pilocarpine hydrochloride (Isopto Carpine) is prescribed for the client with glaucoma. Which of the following medications does the nurse plan to have available in case of systemic toxicity?
   1. Atropine sulfate
   2. Pindolol (Visken)
   3. Protamine sulfate
   4. Naloxone hydrochloride (Narcan)

6. Betaxolol hydrochloride (Betoptic) eye drops have been prescribed for the client with glaucoma. Which of the following nursing actions is most appropriate related to monitoring for the side effects of this medication?

   1. Monitoring temperature
   2. Monitoring blood pressure
   3. Assessing peripheral pulses
   4. Assessing blood glucose level

7. The nurse prepares the client for an ear irrigation as prescribed by the physician. In performing the procedure, the nurse
   1. Warms the irrigating solution to 98° F
   2. Positions the client with the affected side up following the irrigation
   3. Directs a slow steady stream of irrigation solution toward the eardrum
   4. Assists the client to turn his or her head so that the ear to be irrigated is facing upward

8. In preparation for cataract surgery, the nurse is to administer cyclopentolate (Cyclogyl) eye drops. The nurse administers the eye drops, knowing that the purpose of this medication is to:
   1. Produce miosis of the operative eye.
   2. Dilate the pupil of the operative eye.
   3. Provide lubrication to the operative eye.
   4. Constrict the pupil of the operative eye.

9. Ear drops are prescribed for an infant with otitis media. The most appropriate method to administer the ear drops to the infant is to:
   1. Pull up and back on the pinna and direct the solution onto the eardrum.
   2. Pull down and back on the pinna and direct the solution onto the eardrum.
   3. Pull down and back on the pinna and direct the solution toward the wall of the canal.
   4. Pull up and back on the ear lobe and direct the solution toward the wall of the canal.

10. The nurse is providing instructions to a client who will be self-administering eye drops. To minimize the systemic effects that eye drops can produce, the nurse instructs the client to:
    1. Eat before instilling the drops.
    2. Swallow several times after instilling the drops.
    3. Blink vigorously to encourage tearing after instilling the drops.
    4. Occlude the nasolacrimal duct with a finger over the inner canthus for 30 to 60 seconds after instilling the drops.

ALTERNATE ITEM FORMAT: MULTIPLE RESPONSE

The nurse is preparing to administer eye drops. Select the interventions that the nurse takes to administer the drops. Select all that apply.
❑ 1. Wash hands.
❑ 2. Put gloves on.
❑ 3. Place the drop in the conjunctival sac.
❑ 4. Pull the lower lid down against the cheek bone.
❑ 5. Instruct the client to squeeze the eyes shut after instilling the eye drop.
❑ 6. Instruct the client to tilt the head forward, open the eyes, and look down.

ANSWERS

1. **1**
Rationale: When an eye drop and an eye ointment are scheduled to be administered at the same time, the eye drop is administered first. Options 2, 3, and 4 are incorrect.
Test-Taking Strategy: Use the process of elimination. Recalling the guidelines for administering eye medications will direct you to option 1. Review these guidelines if you had difficulty with this question.
Level of Cognitive Ability: Application
Client Needs: Physiological Integrity
Integrated Process: Nursing Process—implementation
Content Area: Adult health—eye
References: Ignatavicius, D. & Workman, M. (2006). *Medical-surgical nursing: Critical thinking for collaborative care* (5th ed., p. 1091). Philadelphia: W.B. Saunders.
Kee, J., Hayes, E., & McCuistion, L. (2006). *Pharmacology: A nursing process approach* (5th ed., pp. 34-35). Philadelphia: W.B. Saunders.
Potter, P., & Perry, A. (2005). *Fundamentals of nursing* (6th ed., p. 859). St. Louis: Mosby.

2. **2**
Rationale: Options 1, 3, and 4 are miotic agents used to treat glaucoma. Option 2 is a mydriatic and cycloplegic medication, and its use is contraindicated in clients with glaucoma. Mydriatic medications dilate the pupil and can cause an increase in intraocular pressure in the eye.
Test-Taking Strategy: Use the process of elimination. Knowledge regarding the classifications of the medications identified in the options will assist in answering the question. Remember that mydriatics dilate and that these medications are contraindicated in glaucoma. Review the contraindications related to medications for the client with glaucoma if you had difficulty with this question.
Level of Cognitive Ability: Analysis
Client Needs: Physiological Integrity
Integrated Process: Nursing Process—analysis
Content Area: Adult health—eye
Reference: Kee, J., Hayes, E., & McCuistion, L. (2006). *Pharmacology: A nursing process approach* (5th ed., pp. 734-735). Philadelphia: W.B. Saunders.

3. **3**

Rationale: Miotics cause pupillary constriction and are used to treat glaucoma. They lower the intraocular pressure, thereby increasing blood flow to the retina and decreasing retinal damage and loss of vision. Miotics cause a contraction of the ciliary muscle and a widening of the trabecular meshwork. Options 1, 2, and 4 are incorrect.

Test-Taking Strategy: Use the process of elimination. Note that the client has glaucoma. Recall that prevention of increased intraocular pressure is the goal in the client with glaucoma. Options 1, 2, and 4 describe actions related to mydriatic medications, which primarily dilate the pupils and relax the ciliary muscles. Review the action of a miotic medication if you had difficulty with this question.

Level of Cognitive Ability: Analysis
Client Needs: Physiological Integrity
Integrated Process: Nursing Process—Analysis
Content Area: Adult health—eye
Reference: Kee, J., Hayes, E., & McCuistion, L. (2006). *Pharmacology: A nursing process approach* (5th ed., pp. 728-729). Philadelphia: W.B. Saunders.

4. **3**

Rationale: Aspirin is contraindicated for gastrointestinal bleed and is potentially ototoxic. The client should be advised to notify the prescribing physician so the medication can be discontinued and/or a substitute that is less toxic to the ear can be taken instead. Options 1, 2, and 4 do not have side effects that are potentially associated with hearing difficulties.

Test-Taking Strategy: Focus on the client's complaint. Review the classifications and/or therapeutic effects as well as the side effects of each medication in the options. Of the medications identified, only aspirin can cause ototoxicity. Additionally, it is contraindicated for GI bleed as well. Review medications that can cause ototoxicity if you had difficulty with this question.

Level of Cognitive Ability: Analysis
Client Needs: Physiological Integrity
Integrated Process: Nursing Process—analysis
Content Area: Adult health—ear
Reference: Hodgson, B., & Kizior, R. (2007). *Saunders nursing drug handbook 2007* (p. 95). Philadelphia: W.B. Saunders.

5. **1**

Rationale: Systemic absorption of pilocarpine hydrochloride can produce toxicity and includes manifestations of vertigo, bradycardia, tremors, hypotension, syncope, cardiac dysrhythmias, and seizures. Atropine sulfate must be available in the event of systemic toxicity. Pindolol is a β-blocker. Naloxone hydrochloride is an opioid antagonist used to reverse narcotic-induced respiratory depression. Protamine sulfate is the antidote for heparin.

Test-Taking Strategy: Use the process of elimination and knowledge regarding antidotes related to various medications to answer this question. Remember that atropine sulfate is the antidote for systemic reactions that occur with pilocarpine. Review antidotes if you had difficulty with this question.

Level of Cognitive Ability: Analysis
Client Needs: Physiological Integrity
Integrated Process: Nursing Process—planning
Content Area: Adult health—eye

Reference: Kee, J., Hayes, E., & McCuistion, L. (2006). *Pharmacology: A nursing process approach.* (5th ed., pp. 286-287). Philadelphia: W.B. Saunders.

6. **2**

Rationale: Hypotension, dizziness, nausea, diaphoresis, headache, fatigue, constipation, and diarrhea are systemic effects of the medication. Nursing interventions include monitoring the blood pressure for hypotension and assessing the pulse for strength, weakness, irregular rate, and bradycardia. Options 1, 3, and 4 are not specifically associated with this medication.

Test-Taking Strategy: Use the ABCs—airway, breathing, and circulation—to direct you to option 2. Although option 3, peripheral pulses, also is related to circulation monitoring, the blood pressure is the umbrella option. Review the side effects of this medication if you had difficulty with this question.

Level of Cognitive Ability: Analysis
Client Needs: Physiological Integrity
Integrated Process: Nursing Process—assessment
Content Area: Adult health—eye
Reference: Hodgson, B., & Kizior, R. (2007). *Saunders nursing drug handbook 2007* (p. 133). Philadelphia: W.B. Saunders.

7. **1**

Rationale: Irrigation solutions that are not close to the client's body temperature can be uncomfortable and may cause injury, nausea, and vertigo. The client is positioned so that the ear to be irrigated is facing downward, because this allows gravity to assist in the removal of the ear wax and solution. Following the irrigation, the client is to lie on the affected side to finish draining the irrigating solution. A slow steady stream of solution should be directed toward the upper wall of the ear canal and not toward the eardrum. Too much force could cause the tympanic membrane to rupture.

Test-Taking Strategy: Use the process of elimination. Read each option carefully and remember that the nurse's concern is to prevent damage to the tympanic membrane. Additionally, remember that the client should be positioned with the affected side downward to allow drainage of the irrigation solution. Review the procedure for performing an ear irrigation if you had difficulty with this question.

Level of Cognitive Ability: Application
Client Needs: Physiological Integrity
Integrated Process: Nursing process—implementation
Content Area: Adult health—ear
References: Ignatavicius, D., & Workman, M. (2006). *Medical-surgical nursing: Critical thinking for collaborative care* (5th ed., p. 1128). Philadelphia: W.B. Saunders.
Kee, J., Hayes, E., & McCuistion, L. (2006). *Pharmacology: A nursing process approach* (5th ed., p. 738). Philadelphia: W.B. Saunders.
Potter, P., & Perry, A. (2005). *Fundamentals of nursing* (6th ed., pp. 862-863). St. Louis: Mosby.

8. **2**

Rationale: Cyclopentolate is a rapidly acting mydriatic and cycloplegic medication. Cyclopentolate is effective in 25 to 75 minutes, and accommodation returns in 6 to 24 hours. Cyclopentolate is used for preoperative mydriasis.

Test-Taking Strategy: Use the process of elimination. Options 1

and 4 are comparative or alike and are eliminated first. Miosis refers to a constricted pupil. Note that the question identifies a client being prepared for eye surgery. The pupil would need to be dilated for the surgical procedure. Review the action and purpose of this medication if you had difficulty with this question.
Level of Cognitive Ability: Application
Client Needs: Physiological Integrity
Integrated Process: Nursing Process—implementation
Content Area: Adult health—eye
Reference: Mosby. (2007). *2007 Mosby's nursing drug reference* (20th ed., p. 1084). St. Louis: Mosby.

9. **3**
Rationale: In a child younger than 3 years, the pinna is pulled down and straight back. The infant should be turned on the side with the affected ear uppermost. With the nondominant hand, the pinna is pulled down and back. The medication is administered by aiming it at the wall of the canal rather than directly onto the eardrum. The infant should remain with the affected ear uppermost for 10 to 15 minutes to retain the solution. In the adult or a child older than 3 years, the pinna is pulled up and back to straighten the auditory canal.
Test-Taking Strategy: Use the process of elimination. Eliminate options 1 and 2 because you would not direct ear solution directly onto the eardrum. Remember that in a child younger than 3 years, pulling the pinna down and straight back is the correct procedure for administering ear medications. Review the procedure for the administration of ear medications if you had difficulty with this question.
Level of Cognitive Ability: Application
Client Needs: Physiological Integrity
Integrated Process: Nursing Process—implementation
Content Area: Adult health—ear
Reference: Kee, J., Hayes, E., & McCuistion, L. (2006). *Pharmacology: A nursing process approach* (5th ed., p. 35). Philadelphia: W.B. Saunders.

10. **4**
Rationale: Applying pressure on the nasolacrimal duct prevents systemic absorption of the medication. Options 1, 2, and 3 will not prevent systemic absorption.

Test-Taking Strategy: Use the process of elimination. Eating and swallowing are comparative options and are not related to the systemic absorption of an eye medication. Blinking vigorously to produce tearing may result in the loss of the administered medication. Review the procedure for administering eye drops to prevent systemic absorption if you had difficulty with this question.
Level of Cognitive Ability: Application
Client Needs: Physiological Integrity
Integrated Process: Teaching and Learning
Content Area: Adult health—eye
Reference: Kee, J., Hayes, E., McCuistion, L. (2006). *Pharmacology: A nursing process approach* (5th ed., p. 34). Philadelphia: W.B. Saunders.

ALTERNATE ITEM FORMAT: MULTIPLE RESPONSE
Answer: 1, 2, 3, 4
Rationale: To administer eye medications, the nurse would wash hands and put gloves on. The client is instructed to tilt the head backward, open the eyes, and look up. The nurse pulls the lower lid down against the cheekbone and holds the bottle like a pencil with the tip downward. Holding the bottle, the nurse gently rests the wrist of the hand on the client's cheek and squeezes the bottle gently to allow the drop to fall into the conjunctival sac. The client is instructed to close the eyes gently and not to squeeze the eyes shut to prevent the loss of medication.
Test-Taking Strategy: Use guidelines related to standard precautions and visualize this procedure. This will assist in determining the correct interventions. If you are unfamiliar with the procedure for administering eye medications, review these guidelines.
Level of Cognitive Ability: Application
Client Needs: Physiological Integrity
Integrated Process: Nursing Process—implementation
Content Area: Adult Health—eye
Reference: Kee, J., & Marshall, S. (2004). *Clinical calculations: With applications to general and specialty areas* (5th ed., pp. 73-75). Philadelphia: W.B. Saunders.

REFERENCES

Hodgson, B., & Kizior, R. (2007). *Saunders nursing drug handbook 2007.* Philadelphia: W.B. Saunders.

Ignatavicius, D., & Workman, M. (2006). *Medical-surgical nursing: Critical thinking for collaborative care* (5th ed.). Philadelphia: W.B. Saunders.

Kee, J., Hayes, E., & McCuistion, L. (2006). *Pharmacology: A nursing process approach* (5th ed.). Philadelphia: W.B. Saunders.

Lehne, R. (2007). *Pharmacology for nursing care* (6th ed.). Philadelphia: W.B. Saunders.

Potter, P., & Perry, A. (2005). *Fundamentals of nursing* (6th ed.). St. Louis: Mosby.

Skidmore-Roth, L. (2007). *Mosby's 2007 nursing drug reference* (20th ed.). St. Louis: Mosby.

The Adult Client With a Neurological Disorder

PYRAMID TERMS

agnosia   The inability to use an object correctly.

apraxia   The inability to carry out a purposeful activity.

autonomic dysreflexia   Syndrome characterized by paroxysmal hypertension, bradycardia, excessive sweating, facial flushing, nasal congestion, pilomotor responses, and headache. The syndrome occurs with spinal lesions above T6 after the period of spinal shock is complete. Triggers include visceral distention from a distended bladder or impacted rectum. The syndrome is a neurological emergency and must be treated immediately to prevent a hypertensive stroke. It is also known as hyperreflexia.

Babinski's reflex   Dorsiflexion of the ankle and great toe, with fanning of the other toes; indicates a disruption of the pyramidal tract.

Brudzinski's sign   Flexion of the head that causes flexion of both thighs at the hips and knee flexion; indicates meningeal irritation.

decerebrate posturing   Stiff extension of one or both arms and possibly the legs; indicates a brainstem lesion.

decorticate posturing   Flexure of one or both arms on the chest and possibly stiff extension of the legs; indicates a nonfunctioning cortex.

flaccid posturing   No motor response display in any extremity.

Glasgow Coma Scale   A method of assessing a client's neurological condition; a scoring system based on a scale of 1 to 15 points. A score of less than 8 indicates that coma is present. Eye opening is the most important indicator.

halo traction   Insertion of pins or screws into the client's skull and application of a circular fixation device and halo jacket or cast; used to immobilize the cervical spine.

hemianopsia   Blindness in half the visual field.

homonymous hemianopsia   Blindness in the same visual field of both eyes.

increased intracranial pressure   An increase in intracranial pressure caused by trauma, hemorrhage, growths or tumors, hydrocephalus, edema, or inflammation. Increased pressure can impede circulation to the brain and absorption of cerebrospinal fluid and can affect the functioning of nerve cells, leading to brainstem compression and death.

Kernig's sign   Flexure of the thigh and knee to right angles; when they are extended, if spasm of the hamstring and pain occurs, it indicates meningeal irritation.

nuchal rigidity   Stiff neck; flexion of the neck onto the chest causes intense pain.

skull tongs   Tongs inserted into the outer aspect of the client's skull, just above the ears, with application of traction. Types include Gardner-Wells, Barton, and Crutchfield tongs.

spinal shock   A sudden depression of reflex activity in the spinal cord below the level of injury (areflexia) that occurs within the first hour of injury and lasts days to months. The muscles become completely paralyzed and flaccid, and reflexes are absent; also known as neurogenic shock.

Tensilon test   Test done to diagnose myasthenia gravis and to differentiate between myasthenic crisis and cholinergic crisis.

unconscious client   A state of depressed cerebral functioning with unresponsiveness to sensory and motor function. Causes include head trauma, cerebral toxins, shock, hemorrhage, tumor, and infections.

unilateral neglect   An inability to recognize a physical impairment that occurs most commonly in clients who have had a right cerebral stroke; also known as neglect syndrome.

PYRAMID TO SUCCESS

Pyramid Points related to neurological disorders focus on monitoring for increased intracranial pressure, assessing level of consciousness, positioning clients, head injuries, spinal cord injuries, spinal shock, autonomic dysreflexia, implementation during a seizure, the client with a stroke, Parkinson's disease, myasthenia gravis, and the Tensilon test. Altered body image and psychosocial issues that occur as a result of the neurological disorder are also a focus of the Pyramid to Success. The Integrated Processes addressed in this unit include Caring, Communication and Documentation, Nursing Process, and Teaching/Learning.

▲ CLIENT NEEDS

Safe and Effective Care Environment

Acting as a client advocate

Consulting with members of the health care team

Ensuring that advance directives are in the client's medical record

Establishing priorities

Initiating referrals to appropriate services

Maintaining asepsis with procedures and treatments

Maintaining confidentiality

Maintaining standard and other precautions

Obtaining informed consent for invasive procedures

Preventing accidents that can occur as a result of neurological deficits

Upholding client rights

Health Promotion and Maintenance

Discussing expected and unexpected body image changes resulting from neurological deficits

Performing neurological assessment techniques

Preventing and detecting health problems associated with neurological deficits

Providing home care instructions regarding care related to the neurological disorder

Teaching about the importance of prescribed therapy

Psychosocial Integrity

Acknowledging end-of-life issues and grief and loss issues

Assessing the ability to cope with feelings of isolation and loss of independence

Considering the cultural, religious, and spiritual influences of the client when planning care

Identifying sensory and perceptual alterations

Identifying support systems and encouraging the use of community resources

Mobilizing coping mechanisms

Physiological Integrity

Administering pharmacological therapy

Monitoring for alterations in body systems

Monitoring for complications related to procedures

Monitoring for fluid and electrolyte imbalances

Providing assistive devices for mobility

Providing emergency care

Providing measures to promote comfort

Promoting normal elimination patterns

Promoting self-care measures

REFERENCES

Black, J., & Hawks, J., (2005). *Medical-surgical nursing: Clinical management for positive outcomes* (7th ed.). Philadelphia: W.B. Saunders.

Chernecky, C., & Berger, B. (2004). *Laboratory tests and diagnostic procedures* (4th ed.). Philadelphia: W.B. Saunders.

Harkreader, H., & Hogan, M. A. (2004). *Fundamentals of nursing: Caring and clinical judgment* (2nd ed.). Philadelphia: W.B. Saunders.

Ignatavicius, D., & Workman, M. (2006). *Medical-surgical nursing: Critical thinking for collaborative care* (5th ed.). Philadelphia: W.B. Saunders.

Jarvis, C. (2004). *Physical examination and health assessment* (4th ed.). St. Louis: W.B. Saunders.

Lewis, S., Heitkemper, M., & Dirksen, S. (2004). *Medical-surgical nursing: Assessment and management of clinical problems* (6th ed.). St. Louis: Mosby.

Lilley, L., Harrington, S., & Snyder, J. (2005). *Pharmacology and the nursing process* (4th ed.). St. Louis: Mosby.

Mosby. (2006). *Mosby's dictionary of medicine, nursing and health professions* (7th ed.). St. Louis: Mosby.

National Council of State Boards of Nursing (Eds.). (2007). *2007 NCLEX-RN® detailed test plan*. Chicago: Author.

Potter, P., & Perry, A. (2005). *Fundamentals of nursing* (6th ed.). St. Louis: Mosby.

Varcarolis, E., Carson, V., & Shoemaker, N. (2006). *Foundations of psychiatric mental health nursing: A clinical approach* (5th ed.). Philadelphia: W.B. Saunders.

Neurological System

I. ANATOMY AND PHYSIOLOGY OF THE BRAIN AND SPINAL CORD

A. Cerebrum
1. The cerebrum consists of the right and left hemispheres.
2. Each hemisphere receives sensory information from the opposite side of the body and controls the skeletal muscles of the opposite side.
3. The cerebrum governs sensory and motor activity and thought and learning.

B. Cerebral cortex (Box 65-1)
1. The cerebral cortex is the outer gray layer; it is divided into five lobes.
2. It is responsible for the conscious activities of the cerebrum.

C. Basal ganglia: Cell bodies in white matter that help the cerebral cortex produce smooth voluntary movements

D. Diencephalon
1. Thalamus
   a. Relays sensory impulses to the cortex
   b. Provides a pain gate
   c. Part of the reticular activating system
2. Hypothalamus
   a. Regulates autonomic responses of the sympathetic and parasympathetic nervous systems
   b. Regulates the stress response, sleep, appetite, body temperature, fluid balance, and emotions
   c. Responsible for the production of hormones secreted by the pituitary gland and the hypothalamus

E. Brainstem
1. Midbrain
   a. Responsible for motor coordination
   b. Contains the visual reflex and auditory relay centers

BOX 65-1
Cerebral Cortex

FRONTAL LOBE
Broca's area for speech
Morals, emotions, reasoning and judgment, concentration, and abstraction

PARIETAL LOBE
Interpretation of taste, pain, touch, temperature, and pressure
Spatial perception

TEMPORAL LOBE
Auditory center
Wernicke's area for sensory and speech

OCCIPITAL LOBE
Visual area

LIMBIC LOBE
Emotional and visceral patterns for survival
Learning and memory

---

2. Pons: Contains the respiratory centers and regulates breathing
3. Medulla oblongata
   a. Contains all afferent and efferent tracts and cardiac, respiratory, vomiting, and vasomotor centers
   b. Controls heart rate, respiration, blood vessel diameter, sneezing, swallowing, vomiting, and coughing

F. Cerebellum: Coordinates smooth muscle movement, posture, equilibrium, and muscle tone

G. Spinal cord
1. Provides neuron and synapse networks to produce involuntary responses to sensory stimulation

2. Allows for control of the number of pain impulses that pass through the spinal cord on their way to the brain
3. Carries sensory information to and motor information from the brain
4. Extends from the first cervical to the second lumbar vertebra
5. Protected by the meninges, cerebrospinal fluid, and adipose tissue
6. Horns
   a. Inner column of gray matter; contains two anterior and two posterior horns
   b. Posterior horns connect with afferent (sensory) nerve fibers.
   c. Anterior horns contain efferent (motor) nerve fibers.
7. Nerve tracts
   a. White matter contains the nerve tract.
   b. Ascending tracts (sensory pathway)
   c. Descending tract (motor pathway)

H. Meninges
1. Dura mater is the tough and fibrous membrane.
2. Arachnoid membrane is the delicate membrane and contains subarachnoid fluid.
3. Pia mater is the vascular membrane.
4. Subarachnoid space is formed by the arachnoid membrane and the pia mater.

I. Cerebrospinal fluid
1. Secreted in the ventricles; circulates in the subarachnoid space and through the ventricles to the subarachnoid layer of the meninges, where it is reabsorbed
2. Acts as a protective cushion; aids in the exchange of nutrients and wastes
3. Normal pressure is 50 to 175 mm H_2O.
4. Normal volume is 125 to 150 mL.

J. Ventricles
1. Four ventricles
2. The ventricles communicate between the subarachnoid spaces and produce and circulate cerebrospinal fluid.

K. Blood supply
1. Right and left internal carotid arteries
2. Right and left vertebral arteries
3. These arteries supply the brain via an anastomosis at the base of the brain called the circle of Willis.

L. Neurotransmitters
1. Acetylcholine
2. Norepinephrine
3. Dopamine
4. Serotonin
5. Amino acids
6. Polypeptides

M. Neurons
1. The cell body contains the nucleus.
2. The neuron contains the axons and dendrites.
3. Neurons carrying impulses to the central nervous system (CNS) are called sensory neurons.
4. Neurons carrying impulses away from the CNS are called motor neurons.
5. Synapse is the chemical transmission of impulses from one neuron to another.

N. Axons and dendrites
1. The axon conducts impulses from the cell body.
2. The dendrites receive stimuli from the body and transmit them to the axon.
3. The neurons are protected and insulated by Schwann cells.
4. The Schwann cell sheath is called the neurolemma.
5. Neurons do not reproduce after the neonatal period.
6. If an axon or dendrite is damaged, it will die and be replaced slowly only if the neurolemma is intact and the cell body has not died.

O. Spinal nerves
1. Humans have 31 pairs of spinal nerves.
2. Mixed nerve fibers are formed by the joining of the anterior motor and posterior sensory roots.
3. Posterior roots contain afferent (sensory) nerve fibers.
4. Anterior roots contain efferent (motor) nerve fibers.

P. Autonomic nervous system
1. Sympathetic (adrenergic) fibers dilate pupils, increase heart rate and rhythm, contract blood vessels, and relax smooth muscles of the bronchi.
2. Parasympathetic (cholinergic) fibers produce the opposite effect.

II. DIAGNOSTIC TESTS

A. Skull and spinal radiography
1. Description
   a. Radiographs of the skull reveal the size and shape of the skull bones, suture separation in infants, fractures or bony defects, erosion, and calcification.
   b. Spinal radiographs identify fractures, dislocation, compression, curvature, erosion, narrowed spinal cord, and degenerative processes.
2. Preprocedure interventions
   a. Provide nursing support for the confused, combative, or ventilator-dependent client.
   b. Maintain immobilization of the neck if a spinal fracture is suspected.
   c. Remove metal items from body parts.
   d. If the client has thick and heavy hair, this should be documented, because it could affect interpretation of the x-ray film.
3. Postprocedure intervention: Maintain immobilization until results are known.

B. Computed tomography (CT)
   1. Description
      a. Computed tomography is a type of brain scanning that may or may not require injection of a dye.
      b. It is used to detect intracranial bleeding, space-occupying lesions, cerebral edema, infarctions, hydrocephalus, cerebral atrophy, and shifts of brain structures.
   2. Preprocedure interventions
      a. Obtain an informed consent if a dye is used.
      b. Assess for allergies to iodine, contrast dyes, or shellfish if a dye is used.
      c. Instruct the client of the need to lie still and flat during the test.
      d. Instruct the client to hold his or her breath when requested.
      e. Initiate an intravenous line if prescribed.
      f. Remove objects from the head, such as wigs, barrettes, earrings, and hairpins.
      g. Assess for claustrophobia.
      h. Inform the client of possible mechanical noises as the scanning occurs.
      i. Inform the client that there may be a hot flushed sensation and a metallic taste in the mouth when the dye is injected.
      j. Note that some clients may be given the dye even if they report an allergy; they are treated with an antihistamine and corticosteroids before the injection to reduce the severity of a reaction.
   3. Postprocedure interventions
      a. Provide replacement fluids because diuresis from the dye is expected.
      b. Monitor for an allergic reaction to the dye.
      c. Assess dye injection site for bleeding or hematoma, and monitor the extremity for color, warmth, and the presence of distal pulses.
C. Magnetic resonance imaging (MRI)
   1. Description
      a. Magnetic resonance imaging is a noninvasive procedure that identifies types of tissues, tumors, and vascular abnormalities.
      b. It is similar to CT scanning but provides more detailed pictures.
   2. Preprocedure interventions
      a. Remove all metal objects from the client.
      b. Determine whether the client has a pacemaker, implanted defibrillator, or other metal implants such as a hip prosthesis or vascular clips because these clients cannot have this test performed.
      c. Remove intravenous fluid pumps during the test.
      d. Provide precautions for the client who is attached to a pulse oximeter because it can cause a burn during testing if coiled around the body or a body part.
      e. Provide an assessment of the client with claustrophobia.
      f. Administer medication as prescribed for the client with claustrophobia.
      g. Determine whether a contrast agent is to be used and follow the prescription related to the administration of food, fluids, and medications.
      h. Instruct the client that he or she will need to remain still during the procedure.
   3. Postprocedure interventions
      a. Client may resume normal activities.
      b. Expect diuresis if a contrast agent is used.
D. Lumbar puncture
   1. Description
      a. Insertion of a spinal needle through the L3-L4 interspace into the lumbar subarachnoid space to obtain cerebrospinal fluid (CSF), measure CSF fluid or pressure, or instill air, dye, or medications
      b. The test is contraindicated in clients with increased intracranial pressure because the procedure will cause a rapid decrease in pressure in the CSF around the spinal cord, leading to brain herniation.
   2. Preprocedure interventions
      a. Obtain an informed consent.
      b. Have the client empty the bladder.
   3. Interventions during the procedure
      a. Position the client in a lateral recumbent position and have the client draw the knees up to the abdomen and the chin onto the chest.
      b. Assist with the collection of specimens (label the specimens in sequence).
      c. Maintain strict asepsis.
   4. Postprocedure interventions
      a. Monitor vital signs and neurological signs that may indicate leakage of cerebrospinal fluid.
      b. Position the client flat as prescribed.
      c. Encourage fluids to replace CSF obtained from the specimen collection or from leakage.
      d. Monitor intake and output.
E. Myelography
   1. Description: Injection of dye or air into the subarachnoid space to detect abnormalities of the spinal cord and vertebrae
   2. Preprocedure interventions
      a. Obtain an informed consent.
      b. Provide hydration for at least 12 hours before the test.
      c. Assess for allergies to contrast agents, iodine, or shellfish.

d. If the client is taking a phenothiazine, hold the medication because this medication lowers the seizure threshold.

e. Premedicate for sedation as prescribed.

3. Postprocedure interventions
   a. Assess vital signs and neurological condition frequently as prescribed.
   b. The head position varies according to the dye used; the head is usually elevated if an oil-based or water-soluble contrast agent is used and usually positioned lower than the trunk if air contrast is used.
   c. Administer analgesics for headache or backache as prescribed.
   d. Encourage fluids to help excrete the contrast material.
   e. Monitor intake and output to ensure adequate fluid intake, facilitate excretion of contrast material, and determine adequate urine output of at least 30 mL/hr.

F. Cerebral angiography
   1. Description: Injection of a contrast material through the femoral artery into the carotid arteries to visualize the cerebral arteries and assess for lesions
   2. Preprocedure interventions
      a. Obtain an informed consent.
      b. Assess the client for allergies to iodine and shellfish.
      c. Encourage hydration for 2 days before the test.
      d. Maintain the client on NPO status 4 to 6 hours before the test as prescribed.
      e. Obtain a baseline neurological assessment.
      f. Mark the peripheral pulses.
      g. Remove metal items from the hair.
      h. Administer premedication as prescribed.
   3. Postprocedure interventions
      a. Monitor neurological status and vital signs frequently until stable.
      b. Monitor for swelling in the neck and for difficulty swallowing; notify the physician if these symptoms occur.
      c. Maintain bed rest for 12 hours as prescribed.
      d. Elevate the head of the bed 15 to 30 degrees only if prescribed.
      e. Keep the bed flat if the femoral artery is used, as prescribed.
      f. Assess peripheral pulses.
      g. Apply sandbags or another device to immobilize the limb and a pressure dressing to the injection site to decrease bleeding as prescribed.
      h. Place ice on the puncture site as prescribed.
      i. Encourage fluid intake.

G. Electroencephalography
   1. Description: Graphic recording of the electrical activity of the superficial layers of the cerebral cortex
   2. Preprocedure interventions
      a. Wash the client's hair.
      b. Inform the client that electrodes are attached to the head and that electricity does not enter the head.
      c. Withhold stimulants such as coffee, tea, and caffeine beverages, antidepressants, tranquilizers, and anticonvulsants for 24 to 48 hours before the test as prescribed.
      d. Allow the client to have breakfast if prescribed.
      e. Premedicate for sedation as prescribed.
   3. Postprocedure interventions
      a. Wash the client's hair.
      b. Maintain side rails and safety precautions, if the client was sedated.

H. Caloric testing (oculovestibular reflex)
   1. Description: Caloric testing provides information about the function of the vestibular portion of the eighth cranial nerve and aids in the diagnosis of cerebellar and brainstem lesions.
   2. Procedure
      a. Patency of the external auditory canal is confirmed.
      b. The client is positioned supine with the head of the bed elevated 30 degrees.
      c. Water that is warmer or cooler than body temperature is infused into the ear.
      d. A normal response is the onset of vertigo and nystagmus (involuntary eye movements) within 20 to 30 seconds
      e. Absent or disconjugate eye movements indicate brainstem damage.

III. NEUROLOGICAL ASSESSMENT
A. Assessment of risk factors
   1. Trauma
   2. Hemorrhage
   3. Tumors
   4. Infection
   5. Toxicity
   6. Metabolic disorders
   7. Hypoxic conditions
   8. Hypertension
   9. Cigarette smoking
   10. Stress
   11. Aging process
   12. Chemicals, either ingestion or environmental exposure

B. Assessment of the cranial nerves
   1. Cranial nerve I (olfactory): Sensory, smell
      a. Have the client close the eyes and occlude one nostril with finger.

   b. Ask the client to identify nonirritating odors such as coffee, tea, cloves, toothpaste, orange, and peppermint.
   c. Repeat the test on the other nostril.
2. Cranial nerve II (optic): Sensory, vision
   a. Assess visual acuity with a Snellen chart or newspaper, or ask the client to count how many fingers the examiner is holding up.
   b. Check visual fields by confrontation.
   c. Have the client sit directly in front of the examiner and stare at the examiner's nose.
   d. Examiner slowly moves his or her finger from the periphery toward the center until the client says it can be seen.
   e. Check color vision by asking the client to name the colors of several nearby objects.
3. Cranial nerve III (oculomotor); cranial nerve IV (trochlear); cranial nerve VI (abducens)
   a. The motor functions of these nerves overlap; therefore, they need to be tested together.
   b. First, inspect the eyelids for ptosis (drooping); then assess ocular movements and note any eye deviation.
   c. Test the eyes for size, regularity, equality, direct and consensual light reflexes, and accommodation; May be documented as PERRLA (*p*upils *e*qually *r*ound, *r*eactive to *l*ight and *a*ccommodation).
   d. Test extraocular movements (EOMs) by the cardinal positions of gaze (Fig. 65-1).
   e. Test for nystagmus., by assessing downward and inward eye movements.
4. Cranial nerve V (trigeminal): Sensory, motor
   a. Test assesses sensation to the cornea, nasal and oral mucosa, facial skin, and mastication.
   b. To test motor function, ask the client to close the jaws tightly and then try to separate the clenched jaws.
   c. If decreased level of consciousness is present, test the corneal reflex by lightly touching the client's cornea with a cotton wisp.
   d. Check sensory function by asking the client to close the eyes; then lightly touch the forehead, cheeks, and chin, noting whether the client can feel the touch equally on both sides.
5. Cranial nerve VII (facial): Sensory, motor
   a. Test taste perception on the anterior two thirds of the tongue.
   b. Have the client show the teeth.
   c. Attempt to close the client's eyes against resistance, and ask the client to puff out the cheeks.
   d. Place sugar, salt, or vinegar on the front of the tongue, with an applicator, and have the client identify these substances by their tastes.

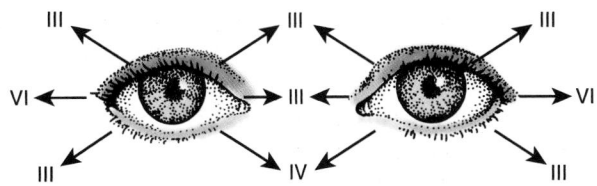

FIG. 65-1 Checking extraocular eye movements. (From Ignatavicius, D., and Workman, M. [2006]. *Medical-surgical nursing: Critical thinking for collaborative care* [5th ed.] Philadelphia: W.B. Saunders.)

6. Cranial nerve VIII (acoustic): Sensory
   a. The ability to hear tests the cochlear portion.
   b. The sense of equilibrium tests the vestibular portion.
   c. Check the client's ability to hear a watch ticking or a whisper.
   d. Observe the client's balance, and observe for swaying when walking or standing.
7. Cranial nerve IX (glossopharyngeal): Sensory, motor
   a. Test assesses swallowing ability.
   b. Test assesses sensation to the pharyngeal soft palate and tonsillar mucosa, taste perception on the posterior third of the tongue, and salivation.
8. Cranial nerve X (vagus): Sensory, motor
   a. Test assesses swallowing and phonation, sensation to the exterior ear's posterior wall, and sensation behind the ear.
   b. Test assesses sensation to the thoracic and abdominal viscera.
9. Cranial nerve IX (glossopharyngeal); cranial nerve X (vagus)
   a. Have the client identify a taste at the back of the tongue.
   b. Inspect the soft palate and observe for symmetrical elevation when the client says "aah."
   c. Touch the posterior pharyngeal wall with a tongue depressor to elicit a gag reflex.
10. Cranial nerve XI (spinal accessory): Motor
   a. Test assesses uvula and soft palate movement and sternocleidomastoid and trapezius muscles.
   b. Test assesses upper portion of the trapezius muscle, which governs shoulder movement and neck rotation.
   c. Palpate and inspect the sternocleidomastoid muscle as the client pushes the chin against the examiner's hand.
   d. Palpate and inspect the trapezius muscle as the client shrugs the shoulders against the examiner's resistance.

11. Cranial nerve XII (hypoglossal): Motor
    a. Test assesses tongue movements involved in swallowing and speech.
    b. Observe the tongue for asymmetry, atrophy, deviation to one side, and fasciculations.
    c. Ask the client to push the tongue against a tongue depressor and then have the client move the tongue rapidly in and out and from side to side.
    d. Ask the client to say "light," "tight," and "dynamite" and observe whether the sounds of the letters *l*, *t*, *d*, and *n* are clear and distinct.

C. Assessment of level of alertness (becomes increasingly invasive as the client is less responsive)
    1. Speak to the client.
    2. Lightly touch the client.
    3. Painful stimuli (sternal rub, supraorbital pressure, trapezius squeeze)

D. Assessment of level of consciousness
    1. Test assesses cerebral function.
    2. Test assesses client behavior to determine level of consciousness, such as confusion, delirium, unconsciousness, stupor, and coma.

E. Assessment of vital signs: Monitor for blood pressure or pulse changes, which may indicate increased intracranial pressure (ICP).

F. Assessment of respirations (Box 65-2)

G. Assessment of temperature
    1. An elevated temperature increases the metabolic rate of the brain.

2. An elevation in temperature may indicate a dysfunction of the hypothalamus or brainstem.
3. A slow rise in temperature may indicate infection.

H. Assessment of pupils (Fig. 65-2)
    1. Size
    2. Equality
    3. Reactions to light: Described as brisk, slow, or fixed
    4. Unusual eye movements
    5. Unilateral pupil dilation indicates compression of the third cranial nerve.
    6. Midposition fixed pupil indicates midbrain injury.
    7. Pinpoint fixed pupil indicates pontine damage.

I. Assessment of motor function
    1. Muscle tone, including strength and equality
    2. Voluntary and involuntary movements
    3. Purposeful and nonpurposeful movements

J. Assessment for posturing (Fig. 65-3)
    1. Posturing indicates a deterioration of the condition.
    2. Flexor **(decorticate posturing)**
        a. Client flexes one or both arms on the chest and may extend the legs stiffly.

BOX 65-2

Assessment of Respirations

CHEYNE-STOKES
Rhythmic, with periods of apnea
Can indicate a metabolic dysfunction or dysfunction in the cerebral hemisphere or basal ganglia

NEUROGENIC HYPERVENTILATION
Regular rapid and deep sustained respirations
Indicates a dysfunction in the low midbrain and middle pons

APNEUSTIC
Irregular respirations, with pauses at the end of inspiration and expiration
Indicates a dysfunction in the middle or caudal pons

ATAXIC
Totally irregular in rhythm and depth
Indicates a dysfunction in the medulla

CLUSTER
Clusters of breaths with irregularly spaced pauses
Indicates a dysfunction in the medulla and pons

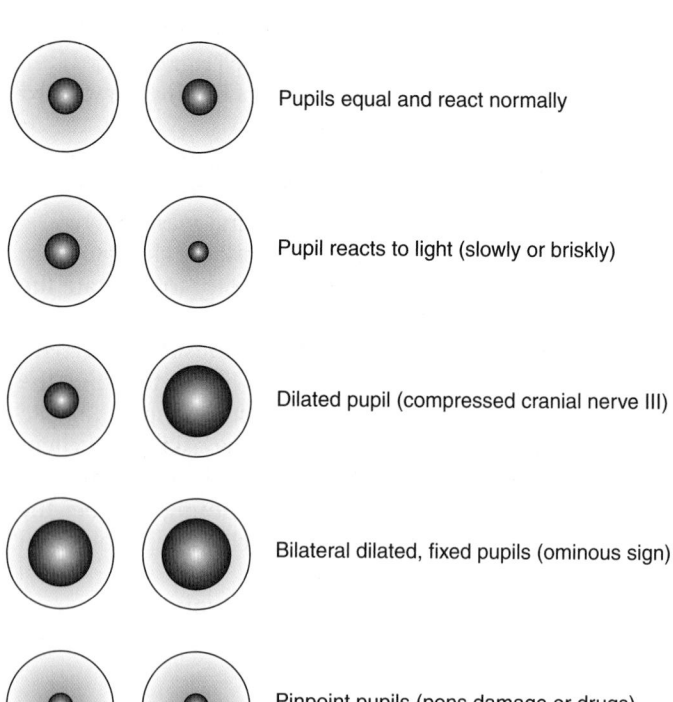

Pupils equal and react normally

Pupil reacts to light (slowly or briskly)

Dilated pupil (compressed cranial nerve III)

Bilateral dilated, fixed pupils (ominous sign)

Pinpoint pupils (pons damage or drugs)

FIG. 65-2 Pupillary check for size and response. (From Lewis, S., Heitkemper, M., & Dirksen, S. [2004]. *Medical-surgical nursing: Assessment and management of clinical problems* [6th ed.]. St. Louis: Mosby.)

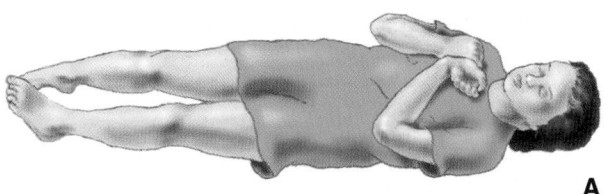

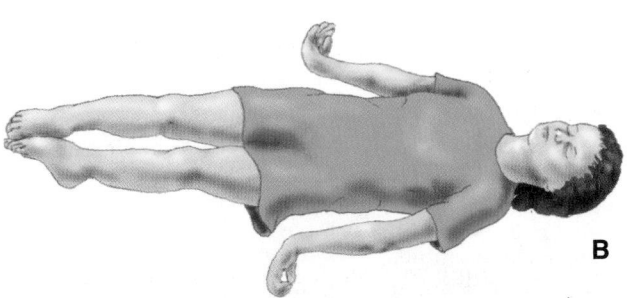

FIG. 65-3 Posturing. **A,** Decorticate posturing. **B,** Decerebrate posturing. (From Ignatavicius, D., and Workman, M. [2006]. *Medical-surgical nursing: Critical thinking for collaborative care* [5th ed.]. Philadelphia: W.B. Saunders.)

b. Flexor posturing indicates a nonfunctioning cortex.
   3. Extensor **(decerebrate posturing)**
      a. Client stiffly extends one or both arms and possibly the legs.
      b. Extensor posturing indicates a brainstem lesion.
   4. **Flaccid posturing:** Client displays no motor response in any extremity.
▲ K. Assessment of reflexes (Box 65-3)
▲ L. Assessment of meningeal irritation (Box 65-4)
▲ M. Assessment of the autonomic system
   1. Sympathetic functions, adrenergic responses
      a. Increased pulse and blood pressure
      b. Dilated pupils
      c. Decreased peristalsis
      d. Increased perspiration
   2. Parasympathetic function, cholinergic responses
      a. Decreased pulse and blood pressure
      b. Constricted pupils
      c. Increased salivation
      d. Increased peristalsis
      e. Dilated blood vessels
      f. Bladder contraction
▲ N. Assessment of sensory function
   1. Touch
   2. Pressure
   3. Pain
   4. Bladder control
   5. Bowel control
▲ O. **Glasgow Coma Scale** (Box 65-5)
   1. The scale is a method of assessing a client's neurological condition.

BOX 65-3
Assessment of Reflexes

BABINSKI'S REFLEX
Dorsiflexion of the ankle and great toe, with fanning of the other toes
Indicates a disruption of the pyramidal tract

CORNEAL REFLEX
Loss of the blink reflex
Indicates a dysfunction of cranial nerve V

GAG REFLEX
Loss of the gag reflex
Indicates a dysfunction of cranial nerves IX and X

BOX 65-4
Assessment of Meningeal Irritation

GENERAL FINDINGS
Irritability
Nuchal rigidity
Severe, unrelenting headaches
Generalized muscle aches and pains
Nausea and vomiting
Fever and chills
Tachycardia
Pupil reaction and eye movements
Photophobia
Nystagmus
Abnormal eye movement

BRUDZINSKI'S SIGN
Flexion of the head causes flexion of both thighs at the hips and knee flexion.

KERNIG'S SIGN
Flexion of the thigh and knee to right angles and when the limbs are extended, it causes spasm of the hamstring and pain.

MOTOR RESPONSE
Hemiparesis, hemiplegia, and decreased muscle tone
Cranial nerve dysfunction, especially cranial nerves III, IV, VI, VII, and VIII

MEMORY CHANGES
Short attention span
Personality and behavioral changes
Bewilderment

   2. The scoring system is based on a scale of 1 to 15 points.
   3. A score lower than 8 indicates that coma is present.
   4. Eye opening is the most important indicator.

BOX 65-5

Glasgow Coma Scale

SCORE
The highest possible score is 15 points.

MOTOR RESPONSE POINTS
Obeys a simple response = 6
Localizes painful stimuli = 5
Normal flexion (withdrawal) = 4
Abnormal flexion (decorticate posturing) = 3
Extensor response (decerebrate posturing) = 2
No motor response to pain = 1

VERBAL RESPONSE POINTS
Oriented = 5
Confused conversation = 4
Inappropriate words = 3
Responds with incomprehensible sounds = 2
No verbal response = 1

EYE-OPENING POINTS
Spontaneous = 4
In response to sound = 3
In response to pain = 2
No response, even to painful stimuli = 1

Modified from Ignatavicius, D., & Workman, M. (2006). *Medical-surgical nursing: Critical thinking for collaborative care* (5th ed.). Philadelphia: W.B. Saunders.

▲ IV. THE UNCONSCIOUS CLIENT
   A. Description
      1. The **unconscious client** is in a state of depressed cerebral functioning with unresponsiveness to sensory and motor function.
      2. Some causes include head trauma, cerebral toxins, shock, hemorrhage, tumor, and infection.
   B. Assessment
      1. Unarousable
      2. Primitive or no response to painful stimuli
      3. Altered respirations
      4. Decreased cranial nerve and reflex activity
▲ C. Interventions (Box 65-6)

▲ V. INCREASED INTRACRANIAL PRESSURE (ICP)
   A. Description
      1. An increase in ICP may be caused by trauma, hemorrhage, growths or tumors, hydrocephalus, edema, or inflammation.
      2. Increased ICP can impede circulation to the brain, impede the absorption of CSF, affect the functioning of nerve cells, and lead to brainstem compression and death.
▲ B. Assessment
      1. Altered level of consciousness, which is the most sensitive and earliest indication of increasing ICP
      2. Headache
      3. Abnormal respirations (see Box 65-2)

BOX 65-6

Care of the Unconscious Client

Assess patency of the airway and keep an airway and emergency equipment at the bedside.
Monitor blood pressure, pulse, and heart sounds.
Assess respiratory and circulatory status.
Maintain a patent airway and ventilation because a high CO$_2$ level increases intracranial pressure.
Assess lung sounds for the accumulation of secretions.
Suction fluids from the airway as needed.
Assess neurological status, including level of consciousness, pupillary reactions, and motor and sensory function, using the Glasgow Coma Scale.
Place the client in a semi-Fowler's position.
Change position of the client every 2 hours, avoiding injury when turning.
Avoid Trendelenburg's position.
Use side rails at all times.
Assess for edema.
Monitor for dehydration.
Monitor intake and output and daily weight.
Maintain NPO status until consciousness returns.
Maintain nutrition as prescribed, and monitor fluid and electrolyte balance.
Check the gag and swallow reflex before resuming a diet, and begin the diet with ice chips and fluids when the client becomes alert.
Provide intravenous or enteral feedings as prescribed.
Assess bowel sounds.
Monitor elimination patterns.
Monitor for constipation, impaction, and paralytic ileus.
Maintain urinary output to prevent stasis, infection, and calculus formation.
Monitor the status of skin integrity.
Initiate measures to prevent skin breakdown.
Provide frequent mouth care.
Remove dentures and contact lenses.
Assess the eyes for the presence of a corneal reflex and irritation, and instill artificial tears or cover the eyes with eye patches.
Monitor drainage from the ears or nose for the presence of cerebrospinal fluid.
Assume that the unconscious client can hear.
Avoid restraints.
Do not leave the client unattended if unstable.
Initiate seizure precautions if necessary.
Provide range-of-motion exercises to prevent contractures.
Use a footboard or high-topped sneakers to prevent footdrop.
Use splints to prevent wrist deformities.
Initiate physical therapy as appropriate.

      4. Rise in blood pressure with widening pulse pressure
      5. Slowing of pulse
      6. Elevated temperature
      7. Vomiting
      8. Pupil changes

9. Changes in motor function from weakness to hemiplegia, a positive **Babinski's reflex,** decorticate or **decerebrate posturing,** and seizures
10. Late signs of increased ICP, including increased systolic blood pressure, widened pulse pressure, and slowed heart rate

C. Interventions
1. Elevate the head of the bed 30 to 40 degrees as prescribed.
2. Avoid Trendelenburg's position.
3. Prevent flexion of the neck and hips.
4. Monitor respiratory status and prevent hypoxia.
5. Avoid the administration of morphine sulfate to prevent the occurrence of hypoxia.
6. Maintain mechanical ventilation as prescribed; maintaining the $PaCO_2$ at 30 to 35 mm Hg will result in vasoconstriction of the cerebral blood vessels, decreased blood flow, and therefore decreased ICP.
7. Maintain body temperature.
8. Prevent shivering, which can increase ICP.
9. Decrease environmental stimuli.
10. Monitor electrolyte levels and acid-base balance.
11. Monitor intake and output.
12. Limit fluid intake to 1200 mL/day.
13. Instruct the client to avoid straining activities, such as coughing and sneezing.
14. Instruct the client to avoid Valsalva's maneuver.

D. Medications (Box 65-7)
E. Surgical intervention (Box 65-8)

VI. HYPERTHERMIA
A. Description
1. Temperature higher than 105° F, which increases the cerebral metabolism and increases the risk of hypoxia
2. Causes include infection, heat stroke, exposure to high environmental temperatures, and dysfunction of the thermoregulatory center.

B. Assessment
1. Temperature higher than 105° F
2. Shivering
3. Nausea and vomiting

C. Interventions
1. Maintain a patent airway.
2. Initiate seizure precautions.
3. Monitor intake and output and assess the skin and mucous membranes for signs of dehydration.
4. Monitor lung sounds.
5. Monitor for dysrhythmias.
6. Assess peripheral pulses for systemic blood flow.
7. Induce normothermia with fluids, cool baths, fans, or a hypothermia blanket.

BOX 65-7
Medications for Increased Intracranial Pressure

ANTICONVULSANTS
Anticonvulsants may be given prophylactically to prevent seizures.
Seizures increase metabolic requirements and cerebral blood flow and volume, thus increasing intracranial pressure.

ANTIPYRETICS AND MUSCLE RELAXANTS
Temperature reduction decreases metabolism, cerebral blood flow, and thus intracranial pressure.
Antipyretics prevent temperature elevations.
Muscle relaxants prevent shivering.

BLOOD PRESSURE MEDICATION
Blood pressure medication may be required to maintain cerebral perfusion at a normal level.
Notify the physician if the blood pressure range is lower than 100 or higher than 150 mm Hg systolic.

CORTICOSTEROIDS
Corticosteroids stabilize the cell membrane and reduce the leakiness in the blood-brain barrier.
Corticosteroids decrease cerebral edema.
A histamine blocker may be administered to counteract the excess gastric secretion that occurs with the corticosteroid.
Clients must be withdrawn slowly from corticosteroid therapy to reduce the risk of adrenal crisis.

INTRAVENOUS FLUIDS
Fluids are administered intravenously via an infusion pump to control the amount administered.
Hypertonic intravenous solutions are avoided because of the risk of promoting additional cerebral edema.

HYPEROSMOTIC AGENT
Mannitol (Osmitrol) is a hyperosmotic agent that increases intravascular pressure by drawing fluid from the interstitial spaces and from the brain cells.
Monitor renal function.
Diuresis is expected.

BOX 65-8
Surgical Intervention for Increased Intracranial Pressure: Ventriculoperitoneal Shunt

DESCRIPTION
A ventriculoperitoneal shunt shunts cerebrospinal fluid from the ventricles into the peritoneum.

POSTPROCEDURE INTERVENTIONS
Position the client supine and turn from the back to the nonoperative side.
Monitor for signs of increasing intracranial pressure resulting from shunt failure.
Monitor for signs of infection.

D. Inducement of normothermia
1. Prevent shivering, which will increase intracranial pressure and oxygen consumption.
2. Administer medications as prescribed to prevent shivering.
3. Monitor neurological status.
4. Monitor for infection and respiratory complications because hypothermia may mask the signs of infection.
5. Monitor for cardiac dysrhythmias.
6. Monitor intake and output.
7. Prevent trauma to the skin and tissues.
8. Apply lotion to the skin frequently.
9. Inspect for frostbite.
E. Medications to prevent shivering (Box 65-9)

▲ VII. HEAD INJURY
A. Description
1. Head injury is trauma to the skull, resulting in mild to extensive damage to the brain.
2. Immediate complications include cerebral bleeding, hematomas, uncontrolled increased ICP, infections, and seizures.
3. Changes in personality or behavior, cranial nerve deficits, and any other residual deficits depend on the area of the brain damage and the extent of the damage.
B. Types of head injuries (Box 65-10)
1. Open
a. Scalp lacerations
b. Fractures in the skull
c. Interruption of the dura mater
2. Closed
a. Concussions
b. Contusions
c. Fractures
C. Hematoma
1. Description: Hematoma can occur as a result of a subarachnoid hemorrhage or an intracerebral hemorrhage.
2. Assessment
a. Assessment findings depend on the injury.
b. Clinical manifestations usually result from increased ICP.

c. Changing neurological signs in the client
d. Changes in level of consciousness
e. Airway and breathing pattern changes
f. Vital signs changes reflecting increasing ICP
g. Headache, nausea, and vomiting
h. Visual disturbances, pupillary changes, and papilledema
i. **Nuchal rigidity** (not tested until spinal cord injury is ruled out)
j. CSF drainage from the ears or nose: When the drainage is placed on a white, sterile background, such as a gauze pad, it can be distinguished from other fluids by the presence of concentric rings (yellowish stain surrounded by bloody fluid); also, CSF tests positive for glucose when tested by a strip test.
k. Weakness and paralysis
l. Posturing
m. Decreased sensation or absence of feeling

BOX 65-10
Types of Head Injuries

CONCUSSION
Concussion is a jarring of the brain within the skull, with temporary loss of consciousness.

CONTUSION
Contusion is a bruising type of injury to the brain.
Contusion may occur with subdural or extradural collections of blood.

SKULL FRACTURES
Linear
Depressed
Compound
Comminuted

EPIDURAL HEMATOMA
The most serious type of hematoma, epidural hematoma forms rapidly and results from arterial bleeding.
Epidural hematoma forms between the dura and skull from a tear in the meningeal artery.
Epidural hematoma is a surgical emergency.

SUBDURAL HEMATOMA
Subdural hematoma forms slowly and results from a venous bleed.
Subdural hematoma occurs under the dura as a result of tears in the veins crossing the subdural space.

INTRACEREBRAL HEMORRHAGE
Multiple hemorrhages occur around a contused area.

SUBARACHNOID HEMORRHAGE
Bleeding occurs directly into the brain, ventricles, or subarachnoid space.

BOX 65-9
Medications to Prevent Shivering

Dantrolene sodium (Dantrium): Dantrium, given intravenously, relaxes skeletal muscle, to reduce shivering.
Chlorpromazine hydrochloride (Thorazine): Chlorpromazine depresses thermoregulation in the hypothalamus and reduces peripheral vasoconstriction, muscle tone, and shivering.
Meperidine hydrochloride (Demerol): Meperidine relaxes smooth muscle and reduces shivering.

n. Reflex activity changes
o. Seizure activity
3. Interventions
a. Monitor respiratory status and maintain a patent airway because increased CO_2 levels increase cerebral edema.
b. Monitor neurological status and vital signs, including temperature.
c. Monitor for increased ICP.
d. Maintain head elevation to reduce venous pressure.
e. Prevent neck flexion.
f. Initiate normothermia measures for increased temperature.
g. Assess cranial nerve function, reflexes, and motor and sensory function.
h. Initiate seizure precautions.
i. Monitor for pain and restlessness.
j. Morphine sulfate may be prescribed to decrease agitation and control restlessness caused by pain for the head injured client on a ventilator; administer with caution because it is a respiratory depressant and may increase ICP.
k. Monitor for drainage from the nose or ears because this fluid may be CSF.
l. Do not attempt to clean the nose, suction, or allow the client to blow his or her nose if drainage occurs.
m. Do not clean the ear if drainage is noted, but apply a loose, dry sterile dressing.
n. Check drainage for the presence of CSF.
o. Notify the physician if drainage from the ears or nose is noted and if the drainage tests positive for CSF.
p. Instruct the client to avoid coughing because this increases ICP.
q. Monitor for signs of infection.
r. Prevent complications of immobility.
D. Craniotomy
1. Description
a. Surgical procedure that involves an incision through the cranium to remove accumulated blood or a tumor
b. Complications of the procedure include increased ICP from cerebral edema, hemorrhage, or obstruction of the normal flow of CSF.
c. Additional complications include hematomas, hypovolemic shock, hydrocephalus, respiratory and neurogenic complications, pulmonary edema, and wound infections.
d. Complications related to fluid and electrolyte imbalances include diabetes insipidus and inappropriate secretion of antidiuretic hormone.

2. Preoperative interventions
a. Explain the procedure to the client and family.
b. Ensure that an informed consent has been obtained.
c. Prepare to shave the client's head as prescribed (usually done in the operating room) and cover the head with an appropriate covering.
d. Stabilize the client before surgery.
3. Postoperative interventions (Box 65-11)
4. Postoperative positioning (Box 65-12)

BOX 65-11
Nursing Care Following Craniotomy

Monitor vital signs and neurological status every 30 to 60 minutes.
Monitor for increased intracranial pressure.
Monitor for decreased level of consciousness, motor weakness or paralysis, aphasia, visual changes, and personality changes.
Maintain mechanical ventilation and slight hyperventilation for the first 24 to 48 hours as prescribed to prevent increased intracranial pressure.
Assess the physician's orders regarding client positioning.
Avoid extreme hip or neck flexion, and maintain the head in a midline neutral position.
Provide a quiet environment.
Monitor the head dressing frequently for signs of drainage.
Mark the area of drainage at least once each nursing shift for baseline comparison.
Monitor the Hemovac or Jackson-Pratt drain, which may be in place for 24 hours.
Maintain suction on the Hemovac or Jackson-Pratt drain.
Measure drainage from the Hemovac or Jackson-Pratt drain every 8 hours, and record the amount and color.
Notify the physician if drainage is more than the normal amount of 30 to 50 mL per shift.
Notify the physician immediately of excessive amounts of drainage or a saturated head dressing.
Record strict measurement of hourly intake and output.
Maintain fluid restriction at 1500 mL/day as prescribed.
Monitor electrolyte levels.
Monitor for dysrhythmias, which may occur as a result of fluid and electrolyte imbalance.
Apply ice packs or cool compresses as prescribed for periorbital edema and ecchymosis of one or both eyes, which is not an unusual occurrence.
Provide range-of-motion exercises every 8 hours.
Place antiembolism stockings on the client as prescribed.
Administer anticonvulsants, antacids, corticosteroids, and antibiotics as prescribed.
Administer analgesics such as codeine sulfate and acetaminophen (Tylenol) as prescribed for pain.

BOX 65-12

Client Positioning Following Craniotomy

Positions prescribed following craniotomy vary with the type of surgery and the specific postoperative physician's orders.
Always check the physician's orders regarding client positioning.
Incorrect positioning may cause serious and possibly fatal complications.

REMOVAL OF A BONE FLAP FOR DECOMPRESSION
To facilitate brain expansion, the client should be turned from the back to the nonoperative side, but not to the side operated on.

POSTERIOR FOSSA SURGERY
To protect the operative site from pressure and minimize tension on the suture line, position the client on the side, with a pillow under the head for support and not on the back.

INFRATENTORIAL SURGERY
Infratentorial surgery involves surgery below the tentorium of the brain.
The physician may order a flat position without head elevation or may order the head of the bed to be elevated at 30 to 45 degrees.
Do not elevate the head of the bed in the acute phase of care following surgery without a physician's order.

SUPRATENTORIAL SURGERY
Supratentorial surgery involves surgery above the tentorium of the brain.
The physician may order the head of the bed to be elevated at 30 degrees to promote venous outflow through the jugular veins.
Do not lower the head of the bed in the acute phase of care following surgery without a physician's order.

▲ VIII. **SPINAL CORD INJURY**
  A. Description
    1. Trauma to the spinal cord causes partial or complete disruption of the nerve tracts and neurons.
    2. The injury can involve contusion, laceration, or compression of the cord.
    3. Spinal cord edema develops; necrosis of the spinal cord can develop as a result of compromised capillary circulation and venous return.
    4. Loss of motor function, sensation, reflex activity, and bowel and bladder control may result.
    5. The most common causes include motor vehicle accidents, falls, sporting and industrial accidents, and gunshot or stab wounds.
    6. Complications related to the injury include respiratory failure, **autonomic dysreflexia, spinal shock,** further cord damage, and death.

  B. Most frequently involved vertebrae
    1. Cervical—C5, C6, and C7
    2. Thoracic—T12
    3. Lumbar—L1
  C. Transection of the cord
    1. Complete transection of the cord
      a. The spinal cord is severed completely, with total loss of sensation, movement, and reflex activity below the level of injury.
      b. If the cord has not suffered irreparable damage, early treatment is needed to prevent partial damage from developing into total and permanent damage.
    2. Partial transection of the cord
      a. The spinal cord is damaged or severed partially.
      b. The symptoms depend on the extent and location of the damage.
  D. Types of injuries (Fig. 65-4)
    1. Central cord syndrome
      a. Central cord syndrome occurs from a lesion in the central portion of the spinal cord.
      b. Loss of motor function is more pronounced in the upper extremities, and varying degrees and patterns of sensation remain intact.
    2. Anterior cord syndrome
      a. Anterior cord syndrome is caused by damage to the anterior portion of the gray and white matter of the spinal cord.
      b. Motor function, pain, and temperature sensation are lost below the level of injury; however, the sensations of position, vibration, and touch remain intact.
    3. Posterior cord syndrome
      a. Posterior cord syndrome is caused by damage to the posterior portion of the gray and white matter of the spinal cord.
      b. Motor function remains intact, but the client experiences a loss of vibratory sense, crude touch, and position sensation.
    4. Brown-Séquard syndrome
      a. Brown-Séquard syndrome results from penetrating injuries that cause hemisection of the spinal cord or injuries that affect half the cord.
      b. Motor function, vibration, proprioception, and deep touch sensations are lost on the same side of the body (ipsilateral) as the lesion or cord damage.
      c. On the opposite side of the body (contralateral) from the lesion or cord damage, the sensations of pain, temperature, and light touch are affected.
    5. Conus medullaris syndrome
      a. Conus medullaris syndrome follows damage to the lumbar nerve roots and conus medullaris in the spinal cord.

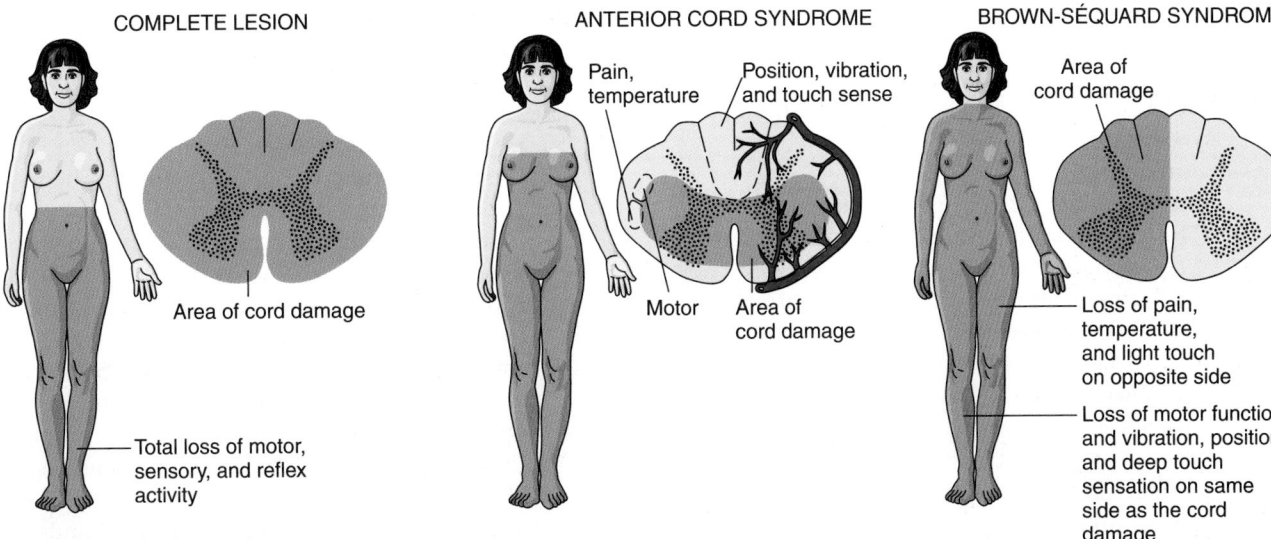

COMPLETE LESION

Area of cord damage

Total loss of motor, sensory, and reflex activity

ANTERIOR CORD SYNDROME

Pain, temperature

Position, vibration, and touch sense

Motor

Area of cord damage

BROWN-SÉQUARD SYNDROME

Area of cord damage

Loss of pain, temperature, and light touch on opposite side

Loss of motor function and vibration, position, and deep touch sensation on same side as the cord damage

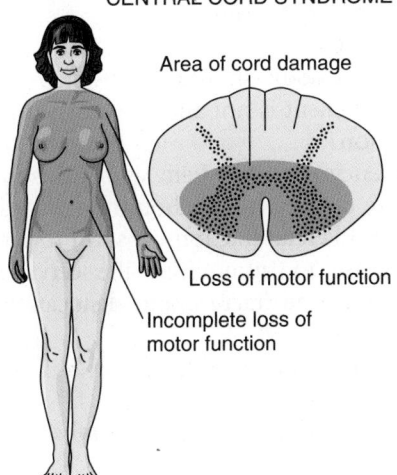

CENTRAL CORD SYNDROME

Area of cord damage

Loss of motor function

Incomplete loss of motor function

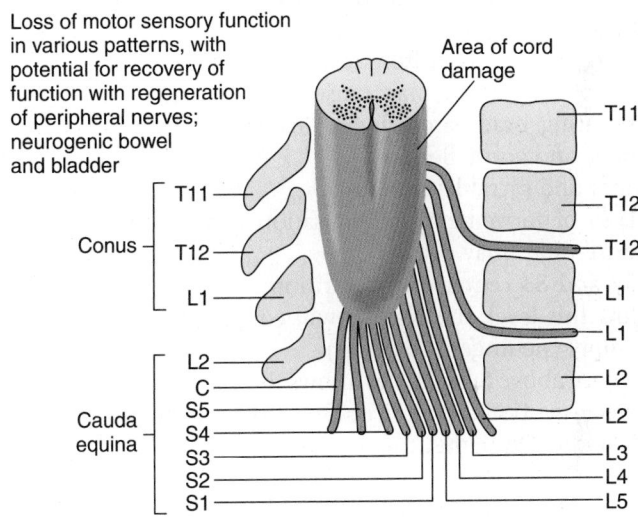

CONUS MEDULLARIS AND CAUDA EQUINA SYNDROMES

Loss of motor sensory function in various patterns, with potential for recovery of function with regeneration of peripheral nerves; neurogenic bowel and bladder

Area of cord damage

Conus — T11, T12, L1

Cauda equina — L2, C, S5, S4, S3, S2, S1

T11, T12, T12, L1, L1, L2, L2, L3, L4, L5

FIG. 65-4 Common spinal cord syndromes. (From Ignatavicius, D., and Workman, M. [2006]. *Medical-surgical nursing: Critical thinking for collaborative care* [5th ed.]. Philadelphia: W.B. Saunders.)

b. Client experiences bowel and bladder areflexia and flaccid lower extremities.
c. If damage is limited to the upper sacral segments of the spinal cord, bulbospongiosus penile (erection) and micturition reflexes will remain.
6. Cauda equina syndrome
   a. Cauda equina syndrome occurs from injury to the lumbosacral nerve roots below the conus medullaris.
   b. The client experiences areflexia of the bowel, bladder, and lower reflexes.
E. Assessment of spinal cord injuries (Box 65-13)
   1. Dependent on the level of the cord injury
   2. Level of spinal cord injury: Lowest spinal cord segment with intact motor and sensory function

BOX 65-13
Effects of Spinal Cord Injury

QUADRIPLEGIA
Injury occurring from C1 through C8
Paralysis involving all four extremities

PARAPLEGIA
Injury occurring from T1 through L4
Paralysis involving only the lower extremities

3. Respiratory status changes
4. Motor and sensory changes below the level of injury
5. Total sensory loss and motor paralysis below the level of injury

6. Loss of reflexes below the level of injury
7. Loss of bladder and bowel control
8. Urinary retention and bladder distention
9. Presence of sweat, which does not occur on paralyzed areas

F. Cervical injuries
1. Injury at C2 to C3 is usually fatal.
2. C4 is the major innervation to the diaphragm by the phrenic nerve.
3. Involvement above C4 causes respiratory difficulty and paralysis of all four extremities.
4. Client may have movement in the shoulder if the injury is at C5 or below.

G. Thoracic level injuries
1. Loss of movement of the chest, trunk, bowel, bladder, and legs may occur, depending on the level of injury.
2. Leg paralysis (paraplegia) may occur.
3. **Autonomic dysreflexia** with lesions or injuries above T6 and in cervical lesions may occur.
4. Visceral distention from a distended bladder or impacted rectum may cause reactions such as sweating, bradycardia, hypertension, nasal stuffiness, and goose flesh.

H. Lumbar and sacral level injuries
1. Loss of movement and sensation of the lower extremities may occur.
2. S2 and S3 center on micturition; therefore, below this level, the bladder will contract but not empty (neurogenic bladder).
3. Injury above S2 in males allows them to have an erection, but they are unable to ejaculate because of sympathetic nerve damage.

4. Injury between S2 and S4 damages the sympathetic and parasympathetic response, preventing erection or ejaculation.

I. Emergency interventions
1. Emergency management is critical because improper movement can cause further damage and loss of neurological function.
2. Assess the respiratory pattern and maintain a patent airway.
3. Always suspect spinal cord injury until this injury is ruled out.
4. Immobilize the client on a spinal backboard with the head in a neutral position to prevent an incomplete injury from becoming complete.
5. Prevent head flexion, rotation, or extension.
6. During immobilization, maintain traction and alignment on the head by placing hands on both sides of the head by the ears.
7. Maintain an extended position.
8. Logroll the client.
9. No part of the body should be twisted or turned, and the client is not allowed to assume a sitting position.
10. In the emergency room, a client who has sustained a severe cervical injury should be placed immediately in skeletal traction via **skull tongs** or **halo traction** to immobilize the cervical spine and reduce the fracture and dislocation (Fig. 65-5)

J. Interventions during hospitalization
1. Respiratory system
   a. Assess respiratory status because paralysis of the intercostal and abdominal muscles occurs with C4 injuries.

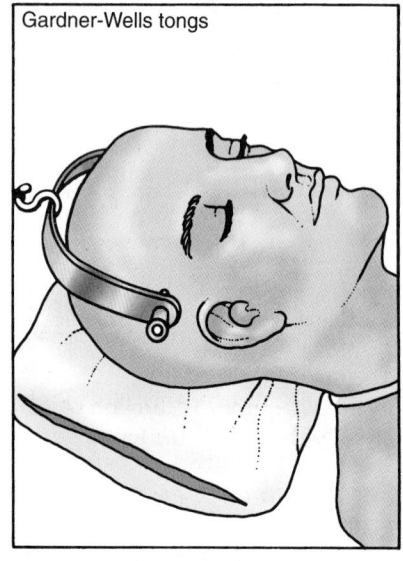

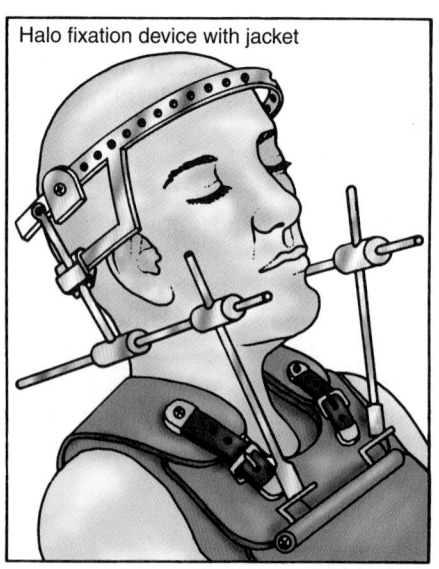

FIG. 65-5 Types of cervical spine traction. (From Ignatavicius, D., and Workman, M. [2006]. *Medical-surgical nursing: Critical thinking for collaborative care* [5th ed.]. Philadelphia: W.B. Saunders.)

b. Monitor arterial blood gas levels and maintain mechanical ventilation if prescribed to prevent respiratory arrest, especially with cervical injuries.

c. Encourage deep breathing and the use of an incentive spirometer.

d. Monitor for signs of infection, particularly pneumonia.

2. Cardiovascular system
   a. Monitor for cardiac dysrhythmias.
   b. Assess for signs of hemorrhage or bleeding around the fracture site.
   c. Assess for signs of shock, such as hypotension, tachycardia, and a weak and thready pulse.
   d. Assess the lower extremities for deep vein thrombosis.
   e. Measure circumferences of the calf and thigh to identify increases in size.
   f. Apply thigh-high antiembolism stockings as prescribed.
   g. Remove antiembolism stockings daily to assess the skin.
   h. Monitor for orthostatic hypotension when repositioning the client.

3. Neuromuscular system
   a. Assess neurological status.
   b. Assess motor and sensory status to determine the level of injury.
   c. Assess motor ability by testing the client's ability to squeeze hands, spread the fingers, move the toes, and turn the feet.
   d. Assess absence of sensation, hyposensation, or hypersensation by pinching the skin or pricking it with a pin, starting at the shoulders and working down the extremities.
   e. Monitor for signs of **autonomic dysreflexia** and **spinal shock.**
   f. Immobilize the client to promote healing and prevent further injury.
   g. Assess pain.
   h. Initiate measures to reduce pain.
   i. Administer analgesics as prescribed.
   j. Monitor for complications of immobility.
   k. Prepare the client for decompression laminectomy, spinal fusion, or insertion of instrumentation or rods if prescribed.
   l. Collaborate with the physical therapist and occupational therapist to determine appropriate exercise techniques, assess the need for hand and wrist splints, and develop an appropriate plan to prevent footdrop.

4. Gastrointestinal system
   a. Assess abdomen for distention and hemorrhage.
   b. Monitor bowel sounds and assess for paralytic ileus.
   c. Prevent bowel retention.
   d. Initiate a bowel control program as appropriate.
   e. Maintain adequate nutrition and a high-fiber diet.

5. Renal system
   a. Prevent urinary retention.
   b. Initiate a bladder control program as appropriate.
   c. Maintain fluid and electrolyte balance.
   d. Maintain adequate fluid intake of 2000 mL/day.
   e. Monitor for urinary tract infection and calculi.

6. Integumentary system
   a. Assess skin integrity.
   b. Turn the client every 2 hours.

7. Psychosocial integrity
   a. Assess psychosocial status.
   b. Encourage the client to express feelings of anger and depression.
   c. Discuss the sexual concerns of the client.
   d. Promote self-care, setting realistic goals based on the client's potential functional level.
   e. Encourage contact with appropriate community resources.

K. **Spinal shock**
   1. Description
      a. **Spinal shock** also is known as neurogenic shock.
      b. A sudden depression of reflex activity in the spinal cord occurs below the level of injury (areflexia).
      c. **Spinal shock** occurs within the first hour of injury and can last days to months.
      d. The muscles become completely paralyzed and flaccid, and reflexes are absent.
      e. **Spinal shock** ends when the reflexes are regained.
   2. Assessment (Box 65-14)
   3. Interventions
      a. Monitor for signs of **spinal shock** following a spinal cord injury.
      b. Monitor for hypotension and bradycardia.
      c. Monitor for reflex activity.
      d. Assess bowel sounds.
      e. Monitor for bowel and urinary retention.
      f. Provide supportive measures as prescribed, based on the presence of symptoms.
      g. Monitor for the return of reflexes.

L. **Autonomic dysreflexia**
   1. Description
      a. **Autonomic dysreflexia** is also known as autonomic hyperreflexia.
      b. **Autonomic dysreflexia** generally occurs after the period of **spinal shock** is resolved and occurs with lesions or injuries above T6 and in cervical lesions.

BOX 65-14
Spinal Shock and Autonomic Dysreflexia

SPINAL SHOCK
Flaccid paralysis
Loss of reflex activity below the level of the lesion
Bradycardia
Paralytic ileus
Hypotension

AUTONOMIC DYSREFLEXIA
Sudden onset, severe, throbbing headache
Severe hypertension
Flushing above the level of the lesion
Pale extremities below the level of the lesion
Nasal stuffiness
Nausea
Dilated pupils or blurred vision
Sweating
Piloerection (goose bumps)
Restlessness and a feeling of apprehension

c. It is commonly caused by visceral distention from a distended bladder or impacted rectum.
d. It is a neurological emergency and must be treated immediately to prevent a hypertensive stroke.

2. Assessment (see Box 65-14)
3. Interventions
   a. Notify the physician if signs of **autonomic dysreflexia** occur.
   b. Assess for the potential cause and remove the stimulus.
   c. Raise the head of the bed to a high Fowler's position.
   d. Loosen tight clothing.
   e. Monitor vital signs, particularly the blood pressure, every 15 minutes.
   f. Assess for bladder distention, and prepare for urinary catheterization.
   g. If a urinary catheter is present, check for kinks in the tubing and for drainage.
   h. Assess for a fecal impaction and disimpact immediately.
   i. Assess the environment to ensure it is not too cool or too drafty.
   j. Administer antihypertensives as prescribed.

M. Cervical spine traction for cervical injuries (see Fig. 65-5)
   1. Description
      a. Skeletal traction is used to stabilize fractures or dislocations of the cervical or upper thoracic spine.
      b. Two types of equipment used for cervical traction are skull (cervical) tongs and **halo traction** (halo fixation device).

2. **Skull tongs**
   a. **Skull tongs** are inserted into the outer aspect of the client's skull, and traction is applied.
   b. Weights are attached to the tongs, and the client is used as countertraction.
   c. Monitor the neurological status of the client.
   d. Determine the amount of weight prescribed to be added to the traction.
   e. Ensure that weights hang securely and freely at all times.
   f. Ensure that the ropes for the traction remain within the pulley.
   g. Maintain body alignment and maintain care of the client on a special bed (such as a RotoRest bed or Stryker or Foster frame) as prescribed.
   h. Turn the client every 2 hours.
   i. Assess insertion site of the tongs for infection.
   j. Provide sterile pin site care as prescribed.

3. **Halo traction**
   a. **Halo traction** is a static traction device that consists of a headpiece with four pins, two anterior and two posterior, inserted into the client's skull.
   b. The metal halo ring may be attached to a vest (jacket) or cast when the spine is stable, allowing increased client mobility.
   c. Monitor the client's neurological status for changes in movement or decreased strength.
   d. Never move or turn the client by holding or pulling on the **halo traction** device.
   e. Assess for tightness of the jacket by ensuring that one finger can be placed under the jacket.
   f. Assess skin integrity to ensure that the jacket or cast is not causing pressure.
   g. Provide sterile pin site care as prescribed.

4. Client education for **halo traction** device (Box 65-15)
5. Initiate interventions in support of the client's self image.
6. Teach the client and family pin care, care of the vest, and signs and symptoms of infection to report to his or her health care provider.

N. Interventions for thoracic, lumbar, and sacral injuries
   1. Bed rest
   2. Immobilization with a body cast
   3. Assess for respiratory impairment and paralytic ileus, possible complications of the body cast.
   4. Use of a brace or corset when the client is out of bed

O. Surgical interventions for thoracic, lumbar, and sacral injuries
   1. Decompressive laminectomy
      a. Removal of one or more laminae

Notify the physician if the halo vest (jacket) or ring bolts loosen.

Use fleece or foam inserts to relieve pressure points.

Keep the vest lining dry.

Clean the pin site daily.

Notify the physician if redness, swelling, drainage, open areas, pain, tenderness, or a clicking sound occurs from the pin site.

A sponge bath or tub bath is allowed; showers are prohibited.

Assess the skin under the vest daily for breakdown, using a flashlight.

Do not use any products other than shampoo on the hair.

When shampooing the hair, cover the vest with plastic.

When getting out of bed, roll onto the side and push on the mattress with the arms.

Never use the metal frame for turning or lifting.

Use a rolled towel or pillowcase between the back of the neck and bed or next to the cheek when lying on the side, and raise the head of the bed to increase sleep comfort.

Adapt clothing to fit over the halo device.

Eat foods high in protein and calcium to promote bone healing.

Have the correct-size wrench available at all times for an emergency.

If cardiopulmonary resuscitation is required, the anterior portion of the vest will be loosened and the posterior portion will remain in place to provide stability.

b. Allows for cord expansion from edema; performed if conventional methods fail to prevent neurological deterioration

2. Spinal fusion
   a. Spinal fusion is used for thoracic spinal injuries.
   b. Bone is grafted between the vertebrae for support and to strengthen the back.

3. Postoperative interventions
   a. Monitor for respiratory impairment.
   b. Monitor vital signs, motor function, sensation, and circulatory status in the lower extremities.
   c. Encourage breathing exercises.
   d. Assess for signs of fluid and electrolyte imbalances.
   e. Observe for complications of immobility.
   f. Keep the client in a flat position as prescribed.
   g. Provide cast care if the client is in a full body cast.
   h. Turn and reposition frequently by logrolling side to back to side, using turning sheets and pillows between the legs to maintain alignment.

i. Administer pain medication as prescribed.
j. Maintain on NPO status until the client is passing flatus.
k. Monitor bowel sounds.
l. Provide the use of a fracture bedpan.
m. Monitor intake and output.
n. Maintain nutritional status.

P. Medications
   1. Dexamethasone (Decadron)
      a. Used for its anti-inflammatory and edema-reducing effects
      b. May interfere with healing
   2. Dextran: Plasma expander used to increase capillary blood flow within the spinal cord and to prevent or treat hypotension
   3. Dantrolene (Dantrium), baclofen (Lioresal): These medications are used for clients with upper motor neuron injuries to control muscle spasticity.

IX. CEREBRAL ANEURYSM
A. Description
   1. Dilation of the walls of a weakened cerebral artery
   2. Aneurysm can lead to rupture.
B. Assessment
   1. Headache and pain
   2. Irritability
   3. Diplopia
   4. Blurred vision
   5. Tinnitus
   6. Hemiparesis
   7. **Nuchal rigidity**
   8. Seizures
C. Interventions
   1. Maintain a patent airway (suction only with a physician's order).
   2. Administer oxygen as prescribed.
   3. Monitor vital signs and for hypertension or dysrhythmias.
   4. Avoid taking temperatures via the rectum.
   5. Initiate aneurysm precautions (Box 65-16)

X. SEIZURES
A. Description
   1. Seizures are an abnormal, sudden, excessive discharge of electrical activity within the brain.
   2. Epilepsy is a disorder characterized by chronic seizure activity and indicates brain or CNS irritation.
   3. Causes include genetic factors, trauma, tumors, circulatory or metabolic disorders, toxicity, and infections.
   4. Status epilepticus involves a rapid succession of epileptic spasms without intervals of consciousness; it is a potential complication that can occur with any type of seizure, and brain damage may result.

BOX 65-16

Aneurysm Precautions

Maintain the client on bed rest in a semi-Fowler's or in a side-lying position.

Maintain a darkened room (subdued lighting and avoid direct, bright, artificial lights) without stimulation (a private room is optimal).

Provide a quiet environment (avoid activities or startling noises); a telephone in the room is not usually allowed.

Reading, watching television, and listening to music are permitted, provided they do not overstimulate the client.

Limit visitors.

Maintain fluid restrictions.

Provide diet as ordered; avoid stimulants in the diet.

Prevent any activities that initiate the Valsalva maneuver (straining at stool, coughing); provide stool softeners to prevent straining.

Administer care gently (such as the bath, back rub, range of motion).

Limit invasive procedures.

Maintain normothermia.

Prevent hypertension.

Provide sedation.

Provide pain control.

Administer prophylactic anticonvulsant medications.

Provide deep vein thrombosis (DVT) prophylaxis as prescribed.

B. Types of seizures (Box 65-17)
1. Generalized seizures
2. Partial seizures

C. Assessment
1. Seizure history
2. Type of seizure
3. Occurrences before, during, and after the seizure
4. Prodromal signs, such as mood changes, irritability, and insomnia
5. Aura: Sensation that warns the client of the impending seizure
6. Loss of motor activity or bowel and bladder function or loss of consciousness during the seizure
7. Occurrences during the postictal state, such as headache, loss of consciousness, sleepiness, and impaired speech or thinking

D. Interventions
1. Note the time and duration of the seizure.
2. Assess behavior at the onset of the seizure: If the client has experienced an aura, if a change in facial expression occurred, or if a sound or cry occurred from the client
3. If the client is standing, place the client on the floor and protect the head and body.
4. Support the ABCs (airway, breathing, and circulation).

BOX 65-17

Types of Seizures

GENERALIZED SEIZURES

Tonic-Clonic

Tonic-clonic seizures may begin with an aura.

The tonic phase involves the stiffening or rigidity of the muscles of the arms and legs and usually lasts 10 to 20 seconds, followed by loss of consciousness.

The clonic phase consists of hyperventilation and jerking of the extremities and usually lasts about 30 seconds.

Full recovery from the seizure may take several hours.

Absence

A brief seizure lasts seconds, and the individual may or may not lose consciousness.

No loss or change in muscle tone occurs.

Seizures may occur several times during a day.

The victim appears to be daydreaming.

This type of seizure is more common in children.

Myoclonic

Myoclonic seizures present as a brief generalized jerking or stiffening of extremities.

The victim may fall to the ground from the seizure.

Atonic or Akinetic (Drop Attacks)

An atonic seizure is a sudden momentary loss of muscle tone.

The victim may fall to the ground as a result of the seizure.

PARTIAL SEIZURES

Simple Partial

The simple partial seizure produces sensory symptoms accompanied by motor symptoms that are localized or confined to a specific area.

The client remains conscious and may report an aura.

Complex Partial

The complex partial seizure is a psychomotor seizure.

The area of the brain most usually involved is the temporal lobe.

The seizure is characterized by periods of altered behavior of which the client is not aware.

The client loses consciousness for a few seconds.

5. Maintain a patent airway (do not force the jaws open or place anything in the client's mouth).
6. Administer oxygen.
7. Prepare to suction secretions from the airway.
8. Turn the client to the side to allow secretions to drain while maintaining the airway.
9. Prevent injury during the seizure.
10. Remain with the client.
11. Do not restrain the client.
12. Loosen restrictive clothing.
13. Note the type, character, and progression of the movements during the seizure.
14. Monitor for incontinence.
15. Administer intravenous medications as prescribed to stop the seizure.

16. Document the characteristics of the seizure
17. Provide privacy, if possible.
18. Monitor behavior following the seizure, such as the state of consciousness, motor ability, and speech ability.
19. Instruct the client about the importance of life-long medication and the need for follow-up medication blood levels.
20. Instruct the client to avoid alcohol, excessive stress, fatigue, and strobe lights.
21. Encourage the client to contact available community resources, such as the Epilepsy Foundation of America.
22. Encourage the client to wear a Medic-Alert bracelet.

▲ XI. STROKE (BRAIN ATTACK)

A. Description
1. A stroke or brain attack, formerly known as a cerebrovascular accident (CVA) is a sudden focal neurological deficit caused by cerebrovascular disease.
2. A stroke is a syndrome in which the cerebral circulation is interrupted, causing neurological deficits.
3. Cerebral anoxia lasting longer than 10 minutes causes cerebral infarction with irreversible change.
4. Cerebral edema and congestion cause further dysfunction.
5. Diagnosis is determined by a CT scan, electroencephalography, cerebral arteriography, and magnetic resonance imaging.
6. The permanent disability cannot be determined until the cerebral edema subsides.
7. The order in which function may return is facial, swallowing, lower limb, speech, and arms.
8. Carotid endarterectomy is a surgical intervention used in stroke management; it is targeted at stroke prevention, especially in clients with symptomatic carotid stenosis.

▲ B. Causes
1. Thrombosis
2. Embolism
3. Hemorrhage from rupture of a vessel
4. Transient ischemic attack

▲ C. Risk factors
1. Atherosclerosis
2. Hypertension
3. Anticoagulation therapy
4. Diabetes mellitus
5. Stress
6. Obesity
7. Oral contraceptives

▲ D. Assessment (Fig. 65-6; Boxes 65-18 and 65-19)
1. Assessment findings depend on the area of the brain affected.

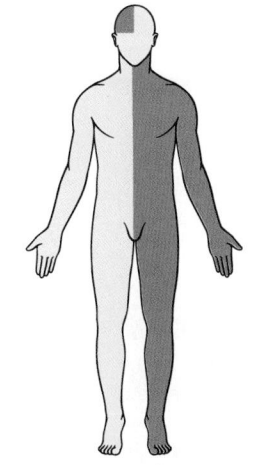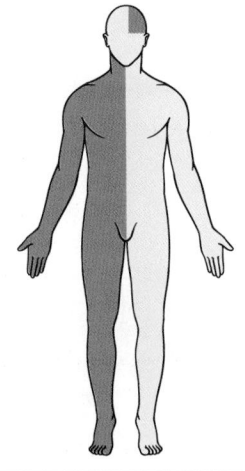

Right-brain damage (stroke on right side of the brain)	**Left-brain damage** (stroke on left side of the brain)
• Paralyzed left side: hemiplegia	• Paralyzed right side: hemiplegia
• Left-sided neglect	• Impaired speech/language aphasias
• Spatial-perceptual deficits	• Impaired right/left discrimination
• Tends to deny or minimize problems	• Slow performance, cautious
• Rapid performance, short attention span	• Aware of deficits: depression, anxiety
• Impulsive, safety problems	• Impaired comprehension related to language, math
• Impaired judgment	
• Impaired time concepts	

FIG. 65-6 Manifestations of right brain and left brain stroke. (From Lewis, S., Heitkemper, M., & Dirksen, S. [2004]. *Medical-surgical nursing: Assessment and management of clinical problems* [6th ed.]. St. Louis: Mosby.)

BOX 65-18
Neurological Assessment in Stroke

Changes in level of consciousness
Signs of increasing intracranial pressure
Assessment of cranial nerves V, VII, IX, X, and XII
  Cranial nerve V: Difficulty with chewing
  Cranial nerve VII: Facial paralysis or paresis
  Cranial nerves IX and X: Dysphagia
  Cranial nerve IX: Absent gag reflex
  Cranial nerve XII: Impaired tongue movement

---

2. Lesions in the cerebral hemisphere result in manifestations on the contralateral side, which is the side of the body opposite the stroke.
3. Airway patency is always a priority.
4. Pulse (may be slow and bounding)
5. Respirations (Cheyne-Stokes)
6. Blood pressure (hypertension)
7. Headache, nausea, and vomiting
8. Facial drooping
9. **Nuchal rigidity**
10. Visual changes

BOX 65-19

Assessment Findings in a Stroke (Brain Attack)

AGNOSIA
Inability to use an object correctly

APRAXIA
Inability to carry out a purposeful activity

HEMIANOPSIA
Blindness in half the visual field

HOMONYMOUS HEMIANOPSIA
Blindness in the same visual field of both eyes

NEGLECT SYNDROME (UNILATERAL NEGLECT)
Client unaware of the existence of his or her
  paralyzed side

PROPRIOCEPTION ALTERATIONS
Altered position sense that places the client at increased
  risk of injury
Pyramid Point: With visual problems, the client must turn
  the head to scan the complete range of vision.

11. Ataxia
12. Dysarthria
13. Dysphagia
14. Speech changes
15. Decreased sensation to pressure, heat, and cold
16. Bowel and bladder dysfunctions
17. Paralysis
E. Aphasia
  1. Expressive
    a. Damage occurs in Broca's area of the frontal brain.
    b. Client understands what is said but is unable to communicate verbally.
  2. Receptive
    a. Injury involves Wernicke's area in the temporoparietal area.
    b. Client is unable to understand the spoken and often the written word.
  3. Global or mixed: Language dysfunction occurs in expression and reception.
  4. Interventions for aphasia
    a. Provide repetitive directions.
    b. Break tasks down to one step at a time.
    c. Repeat names of objects frequently used.
    d. Allow time for the client to communicate.
    e. Use a picture board, communication board, or computer technology.
F. Interventions during the acute phase of stroke
  1. Maintain a patent airway and administer oxygen as prescribed.
  2. Monitor vital signs.
  3. Maintain a blood pressure of 150/100 mm Hg to maintain cerebral perfusion.

4. Suction secretions as prescribed, but never suction nasally or for longer than 10 seconds to prevent increasing ICP.
5. Monitor for increasing ICP because the client is most at risk during the first 72 hours following the stroke.
6. Position the client on the side, with the head of bed elevated 15 to 30 degrees as prescribed.
7. Monitor level of consciousness, pupillary response, motor and sensory response, cranial nerve function, and reflexes.
8. Maintain a quiet environment, and carry out minimal handling of the client to prevent further bleeding.
9. Insert a Foley catheter as prescribed.
10. Administer intravenous fluids as prescribed.
11. Maintain fluid and electrolyte balance.
12. Prepare to administer anticoagulants, antiplatelets, diuretics, antihypertensives, and anticonvulsants as prescribed.
13. Establish a form of communication.
G. Interventions in the postacute phase of a stroke
  1. Continue with interventions from the acute phase.
  2. Position the client 2 hours on the unaffected side and 20 minutes on the affected side.
  3. Position the client in the prone position if prescribed, for 30 minutes three times daily.
  4. Provide skin, mouth, and eye care.
  5. Perform passive range-of-motion exercises to prevent contractures.
  6. Place antiembolism stockings on the client.
  7. Measure thighs and calves for an increase in size.
  8. Monitor gag reflex and ability to swallow.
  9. Provide sips of fluids and slowly advance diet to foods that are easy to chew and swallow.
  10. Provide soft and semisoft foods and flavored, cool or warm, thickened fluids rather than thin liquids because the stroke client can tolerate these types of food better; speech therapists may do swallow studies to recommend consistency of food and fluids.
  11. When the client is eating, position the client sitting in a chair or sitting up in bed, with the head and neck positioned slightly forward and flexed.
  12. Place food in the back of the mouth on the unaffected side to prevent trapping of food in the affected cheek.
H. Interventions in the chronic phase of stroke
  1. Neglect syndrome
    a. Client is unaware of the existence of his or her paralyzed side (**unilateral neglect**), which places the client at risk for injury.
    b. Teach the client to touch and use both sides of the body.

2. **Hemianopsia**
   a. Client has blindness in half the visual field.
   b. **Homonymous hemianopsia** is blindness in the same visual field of both eyes.
   c. Encourage the client to turn the head to scan the complete range of vision; otherwise, he or she does not see half of the visual field.
3. Approach the client from the unaffected side.
4. Place the client's personal objects within the visual field.
5. Provide eye care for visual deficits.
6. Place a patch over the affected eye if the client has diplopia.
7. Increase mobility as tolerated.
8. Encourage fluid intake and a high-fiber diet.
9. Administer stool softeners as prescribed.
10. Encourage the client to express feelings.
11. Encourage independence in activities of daily living
12. Assess the need for assistive devices such as a cane, walker, splint, or braces.
13. Teach transfer technique from bed to chair and from chair to bed.
14. Provide gait training.
15. Initiate physical and occupational therapy.
16. Refer client to a speech and language pathologist as prescribed.
17. Encourage the client and family to contact available community resources.

XII. MULTIPLE SCLEROSIS
A. Description
1. Multiple sclerosis is a chronic, progressive, noncontagious, degenerative disease of the CNS characterized by demyelinization of the neurons.
2. It usually occurs between the ages of 20 and 40 years and consists of periods of remissions and exacerbations.
3. The causes are unknown, but the disease is thought to be the result of an autoimmune response or viral infection.
4. Precipitating factors include pregnancy, fatigue, stress, infection, and trauma.
5. Electroencephalographic findings are abnormal.
6. Assessment of a lumbar puncture indicates an increased gamma globulin level, but the serum globulin level is normal.

B. Assessment
1. Fatigue and weakness
2. Ataxia and vertigo
3. Tremors and spasticity of the lower extremities
4. Parasthesias
5. Blurred vision, diplopia, and transient blindness
6. Nystagmus
7. Dysphasia
8. Decreased perception to pain, touch, and temperature

9. Bladder and bowel disturbances, including urgency, frequency, retention, and incontinence
10. Abnormal reflexes, including hyperreflexia, absent reflexes, and a positive **Babinski's reflex**
11. Emotional changes such as apathy, euphoria, irritability, and depression
12. Memory changes and confusion

C. Interventions
1. Provide bed rest during exacerbation.
2. Protect the client from injury by providing safety measures.
3. Place an eye patch on the eye for diplopia.
4. Monitor for potential complications such as urinary tract infections, calculi, pressure ulcers, respiratory tract infections, and contractures.
5. Promote regular elimination by bladder and bowel training.
6. Encourage independence.
7. Assist the client to establish a regular exercise and rest program.
8. Instruct the client to balance moderate activity with rest periods.
9. Assess the need for and provide assistive devices.
10. Initiate physical and speech therapy.
11. Instruct the client to avoid fatigue, stress, infection, overheating, and chilling.
12. Instruct the client to increase fluid intake and eat a balanced diet, including low-fat, high-fiber foods and foods high in potassium.
13. Instruct the client in safety measures related to sensory loss, such as regulating the temperature of bath water and avoiding heating pads.
14. Instruct the client in safety measures related to motor loss, such as avoiding the use of scatter rugs and using assistive devices.
15. Instruct the client in the self-administration of prescribed medications (Box 65-20).
16. Provide information about the National Multiple Sclerosis Society.

BOX 65-20
Multiple Sclerosis Medications

Baclofen (Lioresal), Dantrolene (Dantrium), Diazepam (Valium): Used to lessen muscle spasticity
Bethanechol: Used to prevent urinary retention
Carbamazepine (Tegretol): Used to treat paresthesia
Corticosteroids: Used to reduce edema and the inflammatory response; used to decrease the length of time the client's symptoms are exacerbated and to improve the degree of recovery
Immunosuppressive medications: Used to treat chronic progressive multiple sclerosis to stabilize the disease process
Oxybutynin chloride (Ditropan): Used to decrease bladder spasms and control urge incontinence and frequency
Propranolol (Inderal), Clonazepam (Klonopin): Used to treat cerebellar ataxia

▲ XIII. MYASTHENIA GRAVIS
A. Description
1. Myasthenia gravis is a neuromuscular disease characterized by considerable weakness and abnormal fatigue of the voluntary muscles.
2. A defect in the transmission of nerve impulses at the myoneural junction occurs.
3. Causes include insufficient secretion of acetylcholine, excessive secretion of cholinesterase, and unresponsiveness of the muscle fibers to acetylcholine.
B. Assessment
1. Weakness and fatigue
▲ 2. Difficulty chewing
3. Dysphagia
4. Ptosis
5. Diplopia
6. Weak, hoarse voice
▲ 7. Difficulty breathing
8. Diminished breath sounds
9. Respiratory paralysis and failure
▲ C. Interventions
1. Monitor respiratory status and ability to cough and deep-breathe adequately.
2. Monitor for respiratory failure.
3. Maintain suctioning and emergency equipment at the bedside.
4. Monitor vital signs.
5. Monitor speech and swallowing abilities to prevent aspiration.
6. Encourage the client to sit up when eating.
7. Assess muscle status.
8. Instruct the client to conserve strength.
9. Plan short activities that coincide with times of maximal muscle strength.
10. Monitor for myasthenic and cholinergic crises.
11. Administer anticholinesterase medications as prescribed.
12. Instruct the client to avoid stress, infection, fatigue, and over-the counter medications.
13. Instruct the client to wear a Medic-Alert bracelet.
14. Inform the client about services from the Myasthenia Gravis Foundation.
D. Anticholinesterase medications
1. Action: Increase levels of acetylcholine at the myoneural junction
2. Medications
a. Neostigmine bromide (Prostigmin)
b. Pyridostigmine bromide (Mestinon)
c. Edrophonium chloride (Tensilon)
3. Side effects
a. Sweating
b. Salivation
c. Nausea
d. Diarrhea and abdominal cramps
e. Bradycardia
f. Hypotension

4. Interventions
a. Administer medications on time. ▲
b. Administer medication 30 minutes before meals with milk and crackers to reduce gastrointestinal upset.
c. Monitor and record muscle strength.
d. Note that excessive doses lead to cholinergic crisis.
e. Have the antidote (atropine sulfate) available.
E. Myasthenic crisis ▲
1. Description
a. Myasthenic crisis is an acute exacerbation of the disease.
b. The crisis is caused by a rapid, unrecognized progression of the disease, inadequate amount of medication, infection, fatigue, or stress.
2. Assessment
a. Increased pulse, respirations, and blood pressure
b. Anoxia and cyanosis
c. Bowel and bladder incontinence
d. Decreased urine output
e. Absent cough and swallow reflex
3. Interventions
a. Assess for signs of myasthenic crisis.
b. Increase anticholinesterase medication, as prescribed.
F. Cholinergic crisis ▲
1. Description
a. Cholinergic crisis results in depolarization of the motor end plates.
b. The crisis is caused by overmedication with anticholinesterase.
2. Assessment
a. Abdominal cramps
b. Nausea, vomiting, and diarrhea
c. Blurred vision
d. Pallor
e. Facial muscle twitching
f. Hypotension
g. Pupillary miosis
3. Interventions
a. Hold anticholinesterase medication.
b. Prepare to administer the antidote, atropine sulfate, if prescribed.
G. **Tensilon test** ▲
1. Description: The **Tensilon test** is performed to diagnose myasthenia gravis and to differentiate between myasthenic crisis and cholinergic crisis.
2. To diagnose myasthenia gravis
a. Edrophonium (Tensilon) injection is administered to the client.
b. Positive for myasthenia gravis: Client shows improvement in muscle strength after the administration of Tensilon.

c. Negative for myasthenia gravis: Client shows no improvement in muscle strength, and strength may even deteriorate after injection of Tensilon.

3. To differentiate crisis
   a. Myasthenic crisis: Tensilon is administered and, if strength improves, the client needs more medication.
   b. Cholinergic crisis: Tensilon is administered and, if weakness is more severe, the client is overmedicated; administer atropine sulfate, the antidote, as prescribed.

▲ XIV. PARKINSON'S DISEASE

A. Description
   1. Parkinson's disease is a degenerative disease caused by the depletion of dopamine, which interferes with the inhibition of excitatory impulses, resulting in a dysfunction of the extrapyramidal system.
   2. It is a slow, progressive disease that results in a crippling disability.
   3. The debilitation can result in falls, self-care deficits, failure of body systems, and depression.
   4. Mental deterioration occurs late in the disease.

▲ B. Assessment
   1. Bradykinesia, abnormal slowness of movement, and sluggishness of physical and mental responses
   2. Akinesia
   3. Monotonous speech
   4. Handwriting that becomes progressively smaller
   5. Tremors in hands and fingers at rest (pill rolling)
   6. Tremors increasing when fatigued and decreasing with purposeful activity or sleep
   7. Rigidity with jerky movements
   8. Restlessness and pacing
   9. Blank facial expression—mask-like facies
   10. Drooling
   11. Difficulty swallowing and speaking
   12. Loss of coordination and balance
   13. Shuffling steps, stooped position, and propulsive gait

▲ C. Interventions
   1. Assess neurological status.
   2. Assess ability to swallow and chew.
   3. Provide high-calorie, high-protein, high-fiber soft diet with small, frequent feedings.
   4. Increase fluid intake to 2000 mL/day.
   5. Monitor for constipation.
   6. Promote independence along with safety measures.
   7. Avoid rushing the client with activities.
   8. Assist with ambulation and provide assistive devices.

9. Instruct the client to rock back and forth to initiate movement.
10. Instruct the client to wear low-heeled shoes.
11. Encourage the client to lift feet when walking and to avoid prolonged sitting.
12. Provide a firm mattress and position the client prone, without a pillow, to facilitate proper posture.
13. Instruct in proper posture by teaching the client to hold the hands behind the back to keep the spine and neck erect.
14. Promote physical therapy and rehabilitation.
15. Administer anticholinergic medications as prescribed to treat tremors and rigidity and to inhibit the action of acetylcholine.
16. Administer antiparkinsonian medications to increase the level of dopamine in the CNS.
17. Instruct the client to avoid foods high in vitamin B_6 because they block the effects of antiparkinsonian medications.
18. Instruct the client to avoid monoamine oxidase inhibitors because they will precipitate hypertensive crisis.
19. See Chap. 66 regarding medication to treat Parkinson's disease.

XV. TRIGEMINAL NEURALGIA

A. Description
   1. Trigeminal neuralgia is a sensory disorder of the trigeminal (fifth cranial) nerve.
   2. It results in severe, recurrent, sharp, facial pain along the trigeminal nerve.

B. Assessment ▲
   1. Client has severe pain on the lips, gums, or nose, or across the cheeks.
   2. Situations that stimulate symptoms include cold, washing the face, chewing, or food or fluids of extreme temperatures.

C. Interventions ▲
   1. Instruct the client to avoid hot or cold foods and fluids.
   2. Provide small feedings of liquid and soft foods.
   3. Instruct the client to chew food on the unaffected side.
   4. Administer medications as prescribed (Box 65-21).

BOX 65-21
Medications to Treat Trigeminal Neuralgia

Amitriptyline
Baclofen (Lioresal)
Carbamazepine (Tegretol)
Diazepam (Valium)
Phenytoin (Dilantin)

D. Surgical interventions
1. Microvascular decompression: Surgical relocation of the artery that compresses the trigeminal nerve as it enters the pons may relieve pain without compromising facial sensation
2. Radiofrequency thermocoagulation: Creates a heat lesion that provides relief of pain without compromising touch or motor function
3. Percutaneous balloon microcompression: Compresses the ganglion and nerve root to control pain
4. Glycerol injection: Destroys the myelinated fibers of the trigeminal nerve (may take up to 3 weeks for pain relief to occur)

XVI. BELL'S PALSY (FACIAL PARALYSIS)
A. Description
1. Bell's palsy is caused by a lower motor neuron lesion of the seventh cranial nerve that may result from infection, trauma, hemorrhage, meningitis, or tumor.
2. It results in paralysis of one side of the face.
3. Recovery usually occurs in a few weeks, without residual effects.
B. Assessment
1. Flaccid facial muscles
2. Inability to raise the eyebrows, frown, smile, close the eyelids, or puff out the cheeks
3. Upward movement of the eye when attempting to close the eyelid
4. Loss of taste
C. Interventions
1. Encourage facial exercises to prevent the loss of muscle tone (a face sling may be prescribed to prevent stretching of weak muscles).
2. Protect the eyes from dryness and prevent injury.
3. Promote frequent oral care.
4. Instruct the client to chew on the unaffected side.

XVII. GUILLAIN-BARRÉ SYNDROME
A. Description
1. Guillain-Barré syndrome is an acute infectious neuronitis of the cranial and peripheral nerves.
2. The immune system overreacts to the infection and destroys the myelin sheath.
3. The syndrome usually is preceded by a mild upper respiratory infection or gastroenteritis.
4. The recovery is a slow process and can take years.
5. The major concern is difficulty breathing.
B. Assessment
1. Paresthesias
2. Weakness of lower extremities
3. Gradual progressive weakness of the upper extremities and facial muscles

4. Possible progression to respiratory failure
5. Cardiac dysrhythmias
6. CSF that reveals an elevated protein level
7. Abnormal electroencephalogram
C. Interventions
1. Care is directed toward the treatment of symptoms.
2. Monitor respiratory status.
3. Provide respiratory treatments.
4. Prepare to initiate respiratory support.
5. Monitor cardiac status.
6. Assess for complications of immobility.
7. Provide the client and family with support.

XVIII. AMYOTROPHIC LATERAL SCLEROSIS
A. Description
1. Amyotrophic lateral sclerosis is also known as Lou Gehrig's disease.
2. It is a progressive degenerative disease involving the motor system.
3. The sensory and autonomic systems are not involved, and mental status changes do not result from the disease.
4. The cause of the disease may be related to an excess of glutamate, a chemical responsible for relaying messages between the motor neurons.
5. As the disease progresses, muscle weakness and atrophy develop until a flaccid quadriplegia develops.
6. Eventually, the respiratory muscles become affected, leading to respiratory compromise, pneumonia, and death.
7. No cure is known, and the treatment is symptomatic.
B. Assessment
1. Fatigue
2. Fatigue while talking
3. Muscle weakness and atrophy
4. Tongue atrophy
5. Dysphagia
6. Weakness of the hands and arms
7. Fasciculations of the face
8. Nasal quality of speech
9. Dysarthria
C. Interventions
1. Care is directed toward the treatment of symptoms.
2. Monitor respiratory status.
3. Provide respiratory treatments.
4. Prepare to initiate respiratory support.
5. Assess for complications of immobility.
6. Provide the client and family with support.

XIX. ENCEPHALITIS
A. Description
1. Encephalitis is an inflammation of the brain parenchyma and often the meninges.

2. It affects the cerebrum, brainstem, and cerebellum.
3. It most often is caused by a viral agent, although bacteria, fungi, or parasites also may be involved.
4. Viral encephalitis is almost always preceded by a viral infection.

▲ B. Transmission
1. Arboviruses can be transmitted to human beings through the bite of an infected mosquito or tick.
2. Echovirus, coxsackievirus, poliovirus, herpes zoster virus, and viruses that cause mumps and chickenpox virus are common enteroviruses associated with encephalitis.
3. Herpes simplex type 1 virus can cause viral encephalitis.
4. The organism that causes amebic meningoencephalitis can enter the nasal mucosa of persons swimming in warm fresh water—for example, in a pond or lake.

▲ C. Assessment
1. Presence of cold sores, lesions, or ulcerations of the oral cavity
2. History of insect bites and swimming in fresh water
3. Exposure to infectious diseases
4. Travel to areas where the disease in prevalent
5. Fever
6. Nausea and vomiting
7. **Nuchal rigidity**
8. Changes in level of consciousness and mental status
9. Signs of increased ICP
10. Motor dysfunction and focal neurological deficits

▲ D. Interventions
1. Monitor vital and neurological signs.
2. Assess level of consciousness using the **Glasgow Coma Scale.**
3. Assess for mental status changes and personality and behavior changes.
4. Assess for signs of increased ICP.
5. Assess for the presence of **nuchal rigidity** and a positive **Kernig's sign** or **Brudzinski's sign,** indicating meningeal irritation.
6. Assist the client to turn, cough, and deep-breathe frequently.
7. Elevate the head of the bed 30 to 45 degrees.
8. Assess for muscle and neurological deficits.
9. Administer acyclovir (Zovirax) as prescribed (medication of choice for herpes encephalitis).
10. Initiate rehabilitation as needed for motor dysfunction or neurological deficits.

▲ XX. WEST NILE VIRUS INFECTION
A. Description
1. West Nile virus infection is a potentially serious illness that affects the CNS.

2. The virus is contracted primarily by the bite of an infected mosquito (mosquitoes become carriers when they feed on infected birds).
3. Symptoms typically develop between 3 and 14 days after being bitten by the infected mosquito.
4. Neurological effects can be permanent.

B. Assessment
1. Many individuals will not experience any symptoms.
2. Mild symptoms include fever, headache and body aches, nausea, vomiting, swollen glands, or a rash on the chest, stomach, or back.
3. Severe symptoms include a high fever, headache, neck stiffness, stupor, disorientation, tremors, muscle weakness, vision loss, numbness, paralysis, seizures, or coma.

C. Interventions are supportive; there is no specific treatment for the virus.

D. Prevention
1. Use insect repellents containing DEET (diethyltoluamide) when outdoors and wear long sleeves and pants and light-colored clothing.
2. Stay indoors at dusk and dawn when mosquitoes are most active.
3. Ensure that mosquito breeding sites are eliminated, such as standing water and water in bird baths, and keep wading pools empty and on their sides when not in use.

XXI. MENINGITIS ▲
A. Description
1. Meningitis is inflammation of the arachnoid and pia mater of the brain and spinal cord.
2. It is caused by bacterial and viral organisms, although fungal and protozoal meningitis also occur.
3. Predisposing factors include skull fractures, brain or spinal surgery, sinus or upper respiratory infections, the use of nasal sprays, and a compromised immune system.
4. Cerebrospinal fluid is analyzed to determine the diagnosis and type of meningitis.

B. Transmission
1. Transmission is by direct contact, including droplet spread.
2. Transmission occurs in areas of high population density, crowded living areas such as college dormitories, and prisons.

C. Assessment (see Box 65-4) ▲
1. Mild lethargy
2. Deterioration in the level of consciousness
3. Signs of meningeal irritation, such as **nuchal rigidity** and a positive **Kernig's sign** and **Brudzinski's sign**
4. Red, macular rash with meningococcal meningitis
5. Abdominal and chest pain with viral meningitis

▲ D. Interventions
1. Monitor vital signs and neurological signs.
2. Assess for signs of increasing ICP.
3. Initiate seizure precautions.
4. Monitor for seizure activity.
5. Monitor for signs of meningeal irritation.
6. Perform cranial nerve assessment.
7. Assess peripheral vascular status.
8. Maintain isolation precautions as necessary with bacterial meningitis.
9. Maintain urine and stool precautions with viral meningitis.
10. Maintain respiratory isolation for the client with pneumococcal meningitis
11. Elevate the head of the bed 30 degrees, and avoid neck flexion and extreme hip flexion.
12. Prevent stimulation and restrict visitors.
13. Administer analgesics as prescribed.
14. Administer antibiotics as prescribed.

PRACTICE QUESTIONS

1. The nurse is assessing the motor function of an unconscious client. The nurse would plan to use which of the following to test the client's peripheral response to pain?
    1. Sternal rub
    2. Nail bed pressure
    3. Pressure on the orbital rim
    4. Squeezing of the sternocleidomastoid muscle
2. The nurse is caring for the client with increased intracranial pressure. The nurse would note which of the following trends in vital signs if the intracranial pressure is rising?
    1. Increasing temperature, increasing pulse, increasing respirations, decreasing blood pressure
    2. Increasing temperature, decreasing pulse, decreasing respirations, increasing blood pressure
    3. Decreasing temperature, decreasing pulse, increasing respirations, decreasing blood pressure
    4. Decreasing temperature, increasing pulse, decreasing respirations, increasing blood pressure
3. The nurse is positioning the client with increased intracranial pressure. Which of the following positions would the nurse avoid?
    1. Head midline
    2. Head turned to the side
    3. Neck in neutral position
    4. Head of bed elevated 30 to 45 degrees
4. The client recovering from a head injury is arousable and participating in care. The nurse determines that the client understands measures to prevent elevations in intracranial pressure if the nurse observes the client doing which of the following activities?
    1. Blowing the nose
    2. Isometric exercises

3. Coughing vigorously
4. Exhaling during repositioning

5. The client has clear fluid leaking from the nose following a basilar skull fracture. The nurse assesses that this is cerebrospinal fluid if the fluid:
    1. Is clear and tests negative for glucose
    2. Is grossly bloody in appearance and has a pH of 6
    3. Clumps together on the dressing and has a pH of 7
    4. Separates into concentric rings and tests positive for glucose
6. The family of a client with a spinal cord injury rushes to the nursing station, saying that the client needs immediate help. On entering the room, the nurse notes that the client is diaphoretic with a flushed face and neck and complains of a severe headache. The pulse rate is 40 beats/min and the blood pressure is 230/100 mm Hg. The nurse acts quickly, suspecting that the client is experiencing:
    1. Spinal shock
    2. Pulmonary embolism
    3. Malignant hyperthermia
    4. Autonomic dysreflexia
7. The client with a spinal cord injury is prone to experiencing autonomic dysreflexia. The nurse would avoid which of the following measures to minimize the risk of recurrence?
    1. Strict adherence to a bowel retraining program
    2. Keeping the linen wrinkle-free under the client
    3. Preventing unnecessary pressure on the lower limbs
    4. Limiting bladder catheterization to once every 12 hours
8. The nurse is evaluating the neurological signs of the male client in spinal shock following spinal cord injury. Which of the following observations by the nurse indicates that spinal shock persists?
    1. Hyperreflexia
    2. Positive reflexes
    3. Reflex emptying of the bladder
    4. Inability to elicit a Babinski's reflex
9. The nurse is planning to institute seizure precautions for a client who is being admitted from the emergency department. Which of the following measures would the nurse avoid in planning for the client's safety?
    1. Padding the side rails of the bed
    2. Putting a padded tongue blade at the head of the bed
    3. Placing an airway, oxygen, and suction equipment at the bedside
    4. Having intravenous equipment ready for insertion of an intravenous catheter
10. The nurse is caring for the client who begins to experience seizure activity while in bed. Which of the following actions by the nurse would be contraindicated?

1. Loosening restrictive clothing
2. Restraining the client's limbs
3. Removing the pillow and raising padded side rails
4. Positioning the client to the side, if possible, with the head flexed forward

11. The nurse is assigned to care for a client with complete right-sided hemiparesis. The nurse plans care knowing that in this condition:
    1. The client has complete bilateral paralysis of the arms and legs.
    2. The client has weakness on the right side of the body, including the face and tongue.
    3. The client has lost the ability to move the right arm but is able to walk independently.
    4. The client has lost the ability to ambulate independently but is able to feed and bathe self without assistance.

12. The client with a brain attack (stroke) has residual dysphagia. When a diet order is initiated, the nurse avoids doing which of the following?
    1. Giving the client thin liquids
    2. Thickening liquids to the consistency of oatmeal
    3. Placing food on the unaffected side of the mouth
    4. Allowing plenty of time for chewing and swallowing

13. The nurse has instructed the family of a client with brain attack (stroke) who has homonymous hemianopsia about measures to help the client overcome the deficit. The nurse determines that the family understands the measures to use if they state that they will:
    1. Place objects in the client's impaired field of vision.
    2. Discourage the client from wearing eyeglasses.
    3. Approach the client from the impaired field of vision.
    4. Remind the client to turn the head to scan the lost visual field.

14. The nurse is assessing the adaptation of the client to changes in functional status after a brain attack (stroke). The nurse assesses that the client is adapting most successfully if the client
    1. Gets angry with family if they interrupt a task
    2. Experiences bouts of depression and irritability
    3. Has difficulty with using modified feeding utensils
    4. Consistently uses adaptive equipment in dressing self

15. A nursing student is caring for a client with a brain attack (stroke) who is experiencing unilateral neglect. The nurse would intervene if the student plans to use which of the following strategies to help the client adapt to this deficit?
    1. Tells the client to scan the environment
    2. Approaches the client from the unaffected side
    3. Places the bedside articles on the affected side

4. Moves the commode and chair to the affected side

16. The nurse is trying to communicate with a client with brain attack (stroke) and aphasia. Which of the following actions by the nurse would be least helpful to the client?
    1. Speaking to the client at a slower rate
    2. Allowing plenty of time for the client to respond
    3. Completing the sentences that the client cannot finish
    4. Looking directly at the client during attempts at speech

17. The client has experienced an episode of myasthenic crisis. The nurse would assess whether the client has precipitating factors such as:
    1. Getting too little exercise
    2. Taking excess medication
    3. Omitting doses of medication
    4. Increasing intake of fatty foods

18. The nurse is teaching the client with myasthenia gravis about the prevention of myasthenic and cholinergic crises. The nurse tells the client that this is most effectively done by:
    1. Eating large, well-balanced meals
    2. Doing muscle-strengthening exercises
    3. Doing all chores early in the day while less fatigued
    4. Taking medications on time to maintain therapeutic blood levels

19. The client with Parkinson's disease has a nursing diagnosis of Falls, Risk for related to an abnormal gait documented in the nursing care plan. The nurse assesses the client, expecting to observe which type of gait?
    1. Unsteady and staggering
    2. Shuffling and propulsive
    3. Broad-based and waddling
    4. Accelerating with walking on the toes

20. The nurse has given instructions to the client with Parkinson's disease about maintaining mobility. The nurse determines that the client understands the directions if the client states that he or she will:
    1. Sit in soft, deep chairs.
    2. Exercise in the evening to combat fatigue.
    3. Rock back and forth to start movement with bradykinesia.
    4. Buy clothes with many buttons to maintain finger dexterity.

21. The nurse has given suggestions to the client with trigeminal neuralgia about strategies to minimize episodes of pain. The nurse determines that the client needs reinforcement of information if the client makes which of the following statements?
    1. "I will wash my face with cotton pads."
    2. "I'll have to start chewing on the unaffected side."

3. "I'll try to eat my food either very warm or very cold."

4. "I should rinse my mouth sometimes if tooth-brushing is painful."

22. The nurse has given the client with Bell's palsy instructions on preserving muscle tone in the face and preventing denervation. The nurse determines that the client needs additional information if the client states that he or she will:

1. Expose the face to cold and drafts.

2. Massage the face with a gentle upward motion.

3. Perform facial exercises.

4. Wrinkle the forehead, blow out the cheeks, and whistle.

23. The client is admitted to the hospital with a diagnosis of Guillain-Barré syndrome. The nurse inquires during the nursing admission interview if the client has a history of:

1. Seizures or trauma to the brain

2. Meningitis during the last 5 years

3. Back injury or trauma to the spinal cord

4. Respiratory or gastrointestinal infection during the previous month

24. The client with Guillain-Barré syndrome has ascending paralysis and is intubated and receiving mechanical ventilation. Which of the following strategies would the nurse incorporate in the plan of care to help the client cope with this illness?

1. Giving client full control over care decisions and restricting visitors

2. Providing positive feedback and encouraging active range of motion

3. Providing information, giving positive feedback, and encouraging relaxation

4. Providing intravenously administered sedatives, reducing distractions, and limiting visitors

25. The client has an impairment of cranial nerve II. Specific to this impairment, the nurse would plan to do which of the following to ensure client safety?

1. Speak loudly to the client.

2. Test the temperature of the shower water.

3. Check the temperature of the food on the dietary tray.

4. Provide a clear path for ambulation without obstacles.

26. The client has a neurological deficit involving the limbic system. Specific to this type of deficit, the nurse would document which of the following information related to the client's behavior?

1. Is disoriented to person, place, and time

2. Affect is flat, with periods of emotional lability

3. Cannot recall what was eaten for breakfast today

4. Demonstrates inability to add and subtract; does not know who is president

27. The nurse is planning to test the function of the trigeminal nerve (cranial nerve V). The nurse would gather which of the following items to perform the test?

1. Tuning fork and audiometer

2. Snellen chart, ophthalmoscope

3. Flashlight, pupil size chart or millimeter ruler

4. Safety pin, hot and cold water in test tubes, cotton wisp

28. The nurse is testing the coordinated functioning of cranial nerves III, IV, and VI. To do this correctly, the nurse would test the:

1. Corneal reflex

2. Pupil response to light

3. Six cardinal fields of gaze

4. Pupil response to light and accommodation

29. The nurse is admitting a client with Guillain-Barré syndrome to the nursing unit. The client has an ascending paralysis to the level of the waist. Knowing the complications of the disorder, the nurse brings which of the following items into the client's room?

1. Nebulizer and pulse oximeter

2. Blood pressure cuff and flashlight

3. Flashlight and incentive spirometer

4. Electrocardiographic monitoring electrodes and intubation tray

30. The nurse is evaluating the respiratory outcomes for the client with Guillain-Barré syndrome. The nurse determines that which of the following is the least optimal outcome for the client?

1. Spontaneous breathing

2. Oxygen saturation of 98%

3. Adventitious breath sounds

4. Vital capacity within normal range

31. The nurse is caring for the client in the emergency department following a head injury. The client momentarily lost consciousness at the time of the injury and then regained it. The client now has lost consciousness again. The nurse takes quick action, knowing that this is compatible with:

1. Concussion

2. Skull fracture

3. Subdural hematoma

4. Epidural hematoma

32. The nurse is evaluating the status of the client who had a craniotomy 3 days ago. The nurse would suspect that the client is developing meningitis as a complication of surgery if the client exhibits:

1. A negative Kernig's sign

2. Absence of nuchal rigidity

3. A positive Brudzinski's sign

4. A Glasgow Coma Scale score of 15

33. The client with a cervical spine injury has Crutchfield (cervical) tongs applied in the emergency department. The nurse would avoid which of the following when planning care for this client?

1. Use of a RotoRest bed

2. Removing the weights to reposition the client

3. Assessment of the integrity of the weights and pulleys

4. Comparing the amount of ordered traction with the amount in use

34. The nurse has completed discharge instructions for the client with application of a halo device. The nurse determines that the client needs further clarification of the instructions if the client states that he or she will:
    1. Use a straw for drinking.
    2. Drive only during the daytime.
    3. Use caution because the device alters balance.
    4. Wash the skin daily under the lamb's wool liner of the vest.
35. The nurse is caring for the client who suffered a spinal cord injury 48 hours ago. The nurse monitors for gastrointestinal complications by assessing for:
    1. A history of diarrhea
    2. A flattened abdomen
    3. Hyperactive bowel sounds
    4. Hematest-positive nasogastric tube drainage

ALTERNATE ITEM FORMAT: PRIORITIZING (ORDERED RESPONSE)

The client with a spinal cord injury suddenly experiences an episode of autonomic dysreflexia. After checking the client's vital signs, number the list in order of priority the nurse's actions, with the first option being of highest and the last of lowest priority. (Number 1 is the first priority and number 6 is the last priority.)

_____ Contact the physician.
_____ Raise the head of the bed.
_____ Check for bladder distention.
_____ Loosen tight clothing on the client.
_____ Administer an antihypertensive medication.
_____ Document the occurrence, treatment, and response.

ANSWERS

1. **2**

Rationale: Motor testing in the unconscious client can be done only by testing response to painful stimuli. Nail bed pressure tests a basic peripheral response. Cerebral responses to pain are tested using sternal rub, placing upward pressure on the orbital rim, or squeezing the clavicle or sternocleidomastoid muscle.

Test-Taking Strategy: Note the strategic words _peripheral response._ The nail beds are the most distal of all the options and are therefore the most peripheral. Each of the other options may elicit a generalized response, but not a localized one. Review the process of peripheral testing if you had difficulty with this question.

Level of Cognitive Ability: Application
Client Needs: Health Promotion and Maintenance
Integrated Process: Nursing Process—assessment
Content Area: Adult health—neurological
References: Black, J., & Hawks, J. (2005). _Medical-surgical nursing: Clinical management for positive outcomes_ (7th ed., pp. 571,2031). Philadelphia: W.B. Saunders.
Ignatavicius, D., & Workman, M. (2006). _Medical-surgical nursing: Critical thinking for collaborative care_ (5th ed., p. 938). Philadelphia: W.B. Saunders.

2. **2**

Rationale: A change in vital signs may be a late sign of increased intracranial pressure. Trends include increasing temperature and blood pressure and decreasing pulse and respirations. Respiratory irregularities also may arise.

Test-Taking Strategy: This question looks complex but can be answered logically. If you remember that the temperature rises, then you are able to eliminate options 3 and 4. If you know that the client becomes bradycardic, or know that the blood pressure rises, you are able to select the correct option. Review the signs of increased intracranial pressure if you had difficulty with this question.

Level of Cognitive Ability: Analysis
Client Needs: Physiological Integrity
Integrated Process: Nursing Process—assessment

Content Area: Adult health—neurological
Reference: Black, J., & Hawks, J. (2005). _Medical-surgical nursing: Clinical management for positive outcomes_ (7th ed., p. 2201). Philadelphia: W.B. Saunders.

3. **2**

Rationale: The head of the client with increased intracranial pressure should be positioned so the head is in a neutral midline position. The nurse should avoid flexing or extending the client's neck or turning the head side to side. The head of the bed should be raised to 30 to 45 degrees. Use of proper positions promotes venous drainage from the cranium to keep intracranial pressure down.

Test-Taking Strategy: Use the process of elimination, noting the strategic word _avoid._ Select the position that interferes with arterial circulation to the brain or with venous drainage from the brain. The only position that meets one of those criteria is option 2. Review positioning of the client with increased intracranial pressure if you had difficulty with this question.

Level of Cognitive Ability: Application
Client Needs: Physiological Integrity
Integrated Process: Nursing Process—implementation
Content Area: Adult health—neurological
References: Black, J., & Hawks, J. (2005). _Medical-surgical nursing: Clinical management for positive outcomes_ (7th ed., p. 2201). Philadelphia: W.B. Saunders.
Ignatavicius, D., & Workman, M. (2006). _Medical-surgical nursing: Critical thinking for collaborative care_ (5th ed., p. 1051). Philadelphia: W.B. Saunders.

4. **4**

Rationale: Activities that increase intrathoracic and intraabdominal pressures cause an indirect elevation of the intracranial pressure. Some of these activities include isometric exercises, Valsalva's maneuver, coughing, sneezing, and blowing the nose. Exhaling during activities such as repositioning or pulling up in bed, opens the glottis, which prevents intrathoracic pressure from rising.

Test-Taking Strategy: Use the process of elimination. Evaluate each option in terms of the tension it puts on the body. Doing so will help you eliminate each incorrect option systematically. Review the measures that will reduce or prevent increased intracranial pressure if you had difficulty with this question.

Level of Cognitive Ability: Analysis
Client Needs: Physiological Integrity
Integrated Process: Nursing Process—evaluation
Content Area: Adult health—neurological
References: Black, J., & Hawks, J. (2005). *Medical-surgical nursing: Clinical management for positive outcomes* (7th ed., pp. 2201, 2293). Philadelphia: W.B. Saunders.
Ignatavicius, D., & Workman, M. (2006). *Medical-surgical nursing: Critical thinking for collaborative care* (5th ed., pp. 1049, 1051). Philadelphia: W.B. Saunders.

5. **4**
Rationale: Leakage of cerebrospinal fluid (CSF) from the ears or nose may accompany basilar skull fracture. CSF can be distinguished from other body fluids because the drainage will separate into bloody and yellow concentric rings on dressing material, called a halo sign. The fluid also tests positive for glucose.
Test-Taking Strategy: Use the process of elimination and knowledge regarding the characteristics of CSF. Recall that CSF contains glucose, whereas other secretions, such as mucus, do not. Knowing that CSF separates into rings also will help you answer this question. Review testing for CSF fluid if you had difficulty with this question.
Level of Cognitive Ability: Analysis
Client Needs: Physiological Integrity
Integrated Process: Nursing Process—assessment
Content Area: Adult health—neurological
Reference: Ignatavicius, D., & Workman, M. (2006). *Medical-surgical nursing: Critical thinking for collaborative care* (5th ed., p. 1050). Philadelphia: W.B. Saunders.

6. **4**
Rationale: The client with a spinal cord injury is at risk for autonomic dysreflexia with an injury above the level of T7. Autonomic dysreflexia is characterized by severe, throbbing headache, flushing of the face and neck, bradycardia, and sudden severe hypertension. Other signs include nasal stuffiness, blurred vision, nausea, and sweating. Autonomic dysreflexia is a life-threatening syndrome triggered by a noxious stimulus below the level of the injury.
Test-Taking Strategy: Use the process of elimination. Begin by eliminating options 1 and 2. The client in spinal shock would be hypotensive (not hypertensive), and the client's clinical picture does not correlate with pulmonary embolism. (Knowing also that autonomic dysreflexia does not occur until spinal shock resolves may be useful.) Recalling that malignant hyperthermia occurs with anesthesia will assist you in eliminating option 3. Review the signs of autonomic dysreflexia if you had difficulty with this question.
Level of Cognitive Ability: Analysis
Client Needs: Physiological Integrity
Integrated Process: Nursing Process—analysis
Content Area: Adult health—neurological
References: Black, J., & Hawks, J. (2005). *Medical-surgical nursing: Clinical management for positive outcomes* (7th ed., p. 2229). Philadelphia: W.B. Saunders.

Ignatavicius, D., & Workman, M. (2006). *Medical-surgical nursing: Critical thinking for collaborative care* (5th ed., pp. 987-988). Philadelphia: W.B. Saunders.

7. **4**
Rationale: The most frequent cause of autonomic dysreflexia is a distended bladder. Straight catheterization should be done every 4 to 6 hours, and Foley catheters should be checked frequently to prevent kinks in the tubing. Constipation and fecal impaction are other causes, so maintaining bowel regularity is important. Other causes include stimulation of the skin from tactile, thermal, or painful stimuli. The nurse administers care to minimize risk in these areas.
Test-Taking Strategy: Use the process of elimination. Remember that autonomic dysreflexia is caused by noxious stimuli to the bowel, bladder, or skin. With this in mind, you can eliminate easily each of the incorrect options. Review the measures to minimize the risk of autonomic dysreflexia if you had difficulty with this question.
Level of Cognitive Ability: Application
Client Needs: Physiological Integrity
Integrated Process: Nursing Process—implementation
Content Area: Adult health—neurological
Reference: Ignatavicius, D., & Workman, M. (2006). *Medical-surgical nursing: Critical thinking for collaborative care* (5th ed., pp. 987-988). Philadelphia: W.B. Saunders.

8. **4**
Rationale: Resolution of spinal shock is occurring when there is return of reflexes (especially flexors to noxious cutaneous stimuli), a state of hyperreflexia rather than flaccidity, reflex emptying of the bladder, and a positive Babinski's reflex.
Test-Taking Strategy: Recall that spinal shock is characterized by the loss of movement of skeletal muscles, bowel or bladder wall, and depressed reflex action. Return of any of these indicates that spinal shock is beginning to resolve. Note that options 1, 2, and 3 are comparative or alike, indicating the presence of reflexes. Review signs of spinal shock if you had difficulty with this question.
Level of Cognitive Ability: Analysis
Client Needs: Physiological Integrity
Integrated Process: Nursing Process—evaluation
Content Area: Adult health—neurological
Reference: Black, J., & Hawks, J. (2005). *Medical-surgical nursing: Clinical management for positive outcomes* (7th ed., pp. 2215, 2218). Philadelphia: W.B. Saunders.

9. **2**
Rationale: Seizure precautions may vary from agency to agency, but they generally have some common features. Usually, an airway, oxygen, and suctioning equipment are kept available at the bedside. The side rails of the bed are padded, and the bed is kept in the lowest position. The client has an intravenous access in place to have a readily accessible route if anticonvulsant medications must be administered. The use of padded tongue blades is highly controversial, and they should not be kept at the bedside. Forcing a tongue blade into the mouth during a seizure more likely will harm the client who bites down during seizure activity. Risks include blocking the airway from improper placement, chipping the client's teeth,

and subsequent risk of aspirating tooth fragments. If the client has an aura before the seizure, it may give the nurse enough time to place an oral airway before seizure activity begins.
Test-Taking Strategy: Use the process of elimination noting the strategic word *avoid*. Evaluate this question from the perspective of causing possible harm. No harm can come to the client from any of the options, except for the tongue blade. Review seizure precautions if you had difficulty with this question.
Level of Cognitive Ability: Application
Client Needs: Safe and Effective Care Environment
Integrated Process: Nursing Process—planning
Content Area: Adult health—neurological
Reference: Ignatavicius, D., & Workman, M. (2006). *Medical-surgical nursing: Critical thinking for collaborative care* (5th ed., p. 953). Philadelphia: W.B. Saunders.

10. **2**
Rationale: Nursing actions during a seizure include providing for privacy, loosening restrictive clothing, removing the pillow and raising side rails in the bed, and placing the client on one side with the head flexed forward, if possible, to allow the tongue to fall forward and facilitate drainage. The limbs are never restrained because the strong muscle contractions could cause the client harm. If the client is not in bed when seizure activity begins, the nurse lowers the client to the floor, if possible, protects the head from injury, and moves furniture that may injure the client. Other aspects of care are as described for the client who is in bed.
Test-Taking Strategy: Use the process of elimination and note the strategic word *contraindicated*. Evaluate this question from the perspective of causing possible harm. No harm can come to the client from any of the options except for restraining the limbs. Remember, avoid restraints. Review care of a client during a seizure if you had difficulty with this question.
Level of Cognitive Ability: Application
Client Needs: Physiological Integrity
Integrated Process: Nursing Process—implementation
Content Area: Adult health—neurological
Reference: Ignatavicius, D., & Workman, M. (2006). *Medical-surgical nursing: Critical thinking for collaborative care* (5th ed., p. 953). Philadelphia: W.B. Saunders.

11. **2**
Rationale: Hemiparesis is a weakness of one side of the body that may occur after a stroke. Complete hemiparesis is weakness of the face and tongue, arm, and leg on one side. Complete bilateral paralysis does not occur in this condition. The client with right-sided hemiparesis has weakness of the right arm and leg and needs assistance with feeding, bathing, and ambulating.
Test-Taking Strategy: Use the process of elimination. Note the strategic words *complete right-sided* and focus on this subject, hemiparesis. Recalling that hemiparesis indicates weakness and focusing on the strategic words will direct you to option 2. Review the description of hemiparesis and care to the client with hemiparesis if you had difficulty with this question.
Level of Cognitive Ability: Comprehension
Client Needs: Physiological Integrity

Integrated Process: Nursing Process—planning
Content Area: Adult Health/Neurological
References: Black, J., & Hawks, J. (2005). *Medical-surgical nursing: Clinical management for positive outcomes* (7th ed., p. 2111). Philadelphia: W.B. Saunders.
Ignatavicius, D., & Workman, M. (2006). *Medical-surgical nursing: Critical thinking for collaborative care* (5th ed., pp. 1034-1035, 1041-1042). Philadelphia: W.B. Saunders.

12. **1**
Rationale: Before the client with dysphagia is started on a diet, the gag and swallow reflexes must have returned. The client is assisted with meals as needed and is given ample time to chew and swallow. Food is placed on the unaffected side of the mouth. Liquids are thickened to avoid aspiration.
Test-Taking Strategy: Use the process of elimination, noting the strategic word *avoids*. Option 4 is generally a good action for all clients. Option 3 is correct because the client has better sensation and motion on the unaffected side of the mouth. Remember that thickened liquids are easier for the client with impaired facial motion and swallowing ability to manage. Knowing this enables you to choose option 1 as the action to avoid. Review care of the client with residual dysphagia if you had difficulty with this question.
Level of Cognitive Ability: Application
Client Needs: Physiological Integrity
Integrated Process: Nursing Process—implementation
Content Area: Adult health—neurological
References: Black, J., & Hawks, J. (2005). *Medical-surgical nursing: Clinical management for positive outcomes* (7th ed., pp. 2114, 2129). Philadelphia: W.B. Saunders.
Ignatavicius, D., & Workman, M. (2006). *Medical-surgical nursing: Critical thinking for collaborative care* (5th ed., pp. 1042-1043). Philadelphia: W.B. Saunders.

13. **4**
Rationale: Homonymous hemianopsia is loss of half of the visual field. The client with homonymous hemianopsia should have objects placed in the intact field of vision, and the nurse also should approach the client from the intact side. The nurse instructs the client to scan the environment to overcome the visual deficit and does client teaching from within the intact field of vision. The nurse encourages the use of personal eyeglasses, if they are available.
Test-Taking Strategy: Use the process of elimination. Recalling the definition of homonymous hemianopsia will direct you easily to option 4. Review the concept of homonymous hemianopsia if you are unfamiliar with it.
Level of Cognitive Ability: Analysis
Client Needs: Safe and Effective Care Environment
Integrated Process: Nursing Process—evaluation
Content Area: Adult health—neurological
References: Black, J., & Hawks, J. (2005). *Medical-surgical nursing: Clinical management for positive outcomes* (7th ed., p. 2114). Philadelphia: W.B. Saunders.
Ignatavicius, D., & Workman, M. (2006). *Medical-surgical nursing: Critical thinking for collaborative care* (5th ed., pp. 1035-1036). Philadelphia: W.B. Saunders.

14. **4**

Rationale: Clients are evaluated as coping successfully with lifestyle changes after a brain attack (stroke) if they make appropriate lifestyle alterations, use the assistance of others, and have appropriate social interactions. Options 1, 2, and 3 are not adaptive behaviors.

Test-Taking Strategy: Use the process of elimination, focusing on the strategic words *adapting most successfully.* Options 1 and 2 are behaviors that may be expected in the client with a brain attack (stroke), but they are not adaptive responses. Instead, they are a result of the insult to the brain. Options 3 and 4 indicate that the client is trying to adapt, but option 4 has the best outcome. Review care of the client with a brain attack (stroke) if you had difficulty with this question.

Level of Cognitive Ability: Analysis
Client Needs: Psychosocial Integrity
Integrated Process: Nursing Process—evaluation
Content Area: Adult health—neurological
References: Black, J., & Hawks, J. (2005). *Medical-surgical nursing: Clinical management for positive outcomes* (7th ed., pp. 2131-2132). Philadelphia: W.B. Saunders.
Ignatavicius, D., & Workman, M. (2006). *Medical-surgical nursing: Critical thinking for collaborative care* (5th ed., p. 1044). Philadelphia: W.B. Saunders.

15. **2**

Rationale: Unilateral neglect is an unawareness of the paralyzed side of the body, which increases the client's risk for injury. The nurse's role is to refocus the client's attention to the affected side. The nurse moves personal care items and belongings to the affected side, as well as the bedside chair and commode. The nurse teaches the client to scan the environment to become aware of that half of the body and approaches the client from the affected side to increase awareness further.

Test-Taking Strategy: Use the process of elimination, noting the strategic word *intervene.* Recall that with unilateral neglect, the client loses awareness of the affected side. If you know that the client needs to be trained to attend to that side, you can eliminate each of the incorrect options. Review care of the client with unilateral neglect if you had difficulty with this question.

Level of Cognitive Ability: Application
Client Needs: Physiological Integrity
Integrated Process: Nursing Process—implementation
Content Area: Leadership/Management
References: Black, J., & Hawks, J. (2005). *Medical-surgical nursing: Clinical management for positive outcomes* (7th ed., p. 2131). Philadelphia: W.B. Saunders.
Ignatavicius, D., & Workman, M. (2006). *Medical-surgical nursing: Critical thinking for collaborative care* (5th ed., pp. 1041-1042). Philadelphia: W.B. Saunders.

16. **3**

Rationale: Clients with aphasia after brain attack (stroke) often fatigue easily and have a short attention span. General guidelines when trying to communicate with the aphasic client include speaking more slowly and allowing adequate response time, listening to and watching attempts to communicate, and trying to put the client at ease with a caring and understanding

manner. The nurse would avoid shouting (because the client is not deaf), appearing rushed for a response, and letting family members provide all the responses for the client.

Test-Taking Strategy: Use the process of elimination, noting the strategic words *least helpful.* These words indicate a negative event query and ask you to select an option that is an incorrect action. This question tests a fundamental concept in communicating with the aphasic client. If this question was difficult, review these communication strategies.

Level of Cognitive Ability: Application
Client Needs: Psychosocial Integrity
Integrated Process: Communication and Documentation
Content Area: Adult health—neurological
References: Black, J., & Hawks, J. (2005). *Medical-surgical nursing: Clinical management for positive outcomes* (7th ed., pp. 2112-2113, 2129-2130). Philadelphia: W.B. Saunders.
Ignatavicius, D., & Workman, M. (2006). *Medical-surgical nursing: Critical thinking for collaborative care* (5th ed., p. 1042). Philadelphia: W.B. Saunders.

17. **3**

Rationale: Myasthenic crisis often is caused by undermedication and responds to the administration of cholinergic medications, such as neostigmine (Prostigmin) and pyridostigmine (Mestinon). Cholinergic crisis (the opposite problem) is caused by excess medication and responds to withholding of medications. Too little exercise and fatty food intake are incorrect. Overexertion and overeating possibly could trigger myasthenic crisis.

Test-Taking Strategy: Use the process of elimination. Recalling that undermedication is a common cause of myasthenic crisis will direct you easily to option 3. Review the causes of myasthenic crisis if you had difficulty with this question.

Level of Cognitive Ability: Analysis
Client Needs: Physiological Integrity
Integrated Process: Nursing Process—assessment
Content Area: Adult health—neurological
Reference: Ignatavicius, D., & Workman, M. (2006). *Medical-surgical nursing: Critical thinking for collaborative care* (5th ed., pp. 1015-1016). Philadelphia: W.B. Saunders.

18. **4**

Rationale: Clients with myasthenia gravis are taught to space out activities over the day to conserve energy and restore muscle strength. Taking medications correctly to maintain blood levels that are not too low or too high is important. Muscle-strengthening exercises are not helpful and can fatigue the client. Overeating is a cause of exacerbation of symptoms, as is exposure to heat, crowds, erratic sleep habits, and emotional stress.

Test-Taking Strategy: Use the process of elimination. Recalling that the common causes of myasthenic and cholinergic crises are undermedication and overmedication, respectively, will assist you in eliminating each of the incorrect options. No other option would prevent both of those complications. Review measures to prevent myasthenic and cholinergic crises if you are unfamiliar with them.

Level of Cognitive Ability: Application
Client Needs: Physiological Integrity
Integrated Process: Teaching and Learning

Content Area: Adult health—neurological
Reference: Ignatavicius, D., & Workman, M. (2006). *Medical-surgical nursing: Critical thinking for collaborative care* (5th ed., pp. 1015-1017). Philadelphia: W.B. Saunders.

19. **2**
Rationale: The parkinsonian gait is characterized by short, accelerating, shuffling steps. The client leans forward with the head, hips, and knees flexed, and has difficulty starting and stopping. A dystrophic gait is broad-based and waddling. A festinating gait is accelerating with walking on the toes. An ataxic gait is staggering and unsteady.
Test-Taking Strategy: Use the process of elimination. Recall that the client has difficulty in initiating movement and bradykinesia. The gait is difficult to start, but it accelerates once it has begun. This will assist in eliminating options 1 and 3. From the remaining options, recall that the client with Parkinson's disease shuffles but does not walk on the toes. Review the characteristics associated with Parkinson's disease if you had difficulty with this question.
Level of Cognitive Ability: Analysis
Client Needs: Physiological Integrity
Integrated Process: Nursing Process—assessment
Content Area: Adult health—neurological
References: Black, J., & Hawks, J. (2005). *Medical-surgical nursing: Clinical management for positive outcomes* (7th ed., p. 2172). Philadelphia: W.B. Saunders.
Ignatavicius, D., & Workman, M. (2006). *Medical-surgical nursing: Critical thinking for collaborative care* (5th ed., p. 960). Philadelphia: W.B. Saunders.

20. **3**
Rationale: The client with Parkinson's disease should exercise in the morning when energy levels are highest. The client should avoid sitting in soft deep chairs because they are difficult to get up from. The client can rock back and forth to initiate movement. The client should buy clothes with Velcro fasteners and slide-locking buckles to support the ability to dress self.
Test-Taking Strategy: Use the process of elimination. Option 2 is not useful to clients with fatigue from any disorder, so eliminate this option first. Knowing that the client with Parkinson's has difficulty with movement and dexterity helps eliminate options 1 and 4 next. Review client teaching points with Parkinson's disease if you had difficulty with this question.
Level of Cognitive Ability: Analysis
Client Needs: Physiological Integrity
Integrated Process: Nursing Process—evaluation
Content Area: Adult health—neurological
References: Black, J., & Hawks, J. (2005). *Medical-surgical nursing: Clinical management for positive outcomes* (7th ed., p. 2174). Philadelphia: W.B. Saunders.
Ignatavicius, D., & Workman, M. (2006). *Medical-surgical nursing: Critical thinking for collaborative care* (5th ed., p. 962). Philadelphia: W.B. Saunders.

21. **3**
Rationale: Facial pain can be minimized by using cotton pads to wash the face and using room temperature water. The client should chew on the unaffected side of the mouth, eat a soft diet, and take in foods and beverages at room temperature. If toothbrushing triggers pain, sometimes an oral rinse after meals is helpful instead.
Test-Taking Strategy: Use the process of elimination, and note the strategic words *needs reinforcement of information*. These words indicate a negative event query and ask you to select an option that is incorrect. Recall that the pain of trigeminal neuralgia is triggered by mechanical or thermal stimuli. Very hot or cold foods are likely to trigger the pain, not relieve it. Review client education points if you had difficulty with this question.
Level of Cognitive Ability: Analysis
Client Needs: Physiological Integrity
Integrated Process: Teaching and Learning
Content Area: Adult health—neurological
References: Black, J., & Hawks, J. (2005). *Medical-surgical nursing: Clinical management for positive outcomes* (7th ed., p. 2154). Philadelphia: W.B. Saunders.
Lewis, S., Heitkemper, M., & Dirksen, S. (2004). *Medical-surgical nursing: Assessment and management of clinical problems* (6th ed., p. 1604). St. Louis: Mosby.

22. **1**
Rationale: Prevention of muscle atrophy with Bell's palsy is accomplished with facial massage, facial exercises, and electrical stimulation of the nerves. Exposure to cold or drafts is avoided. Local application of heat to the face may improve blood flow and provide comfort.
Test-Taking Strategy: Use the process of elimination, noting the strategic words *needs additional information*. These words indicate a negative event query and ask you to select an option that is incorrect. Evaluate each option regarding its effect on preserving muscle tone in the face. Option 1 is unrelated to muscle tone and also is contraindicated in clients with this condition. Review teaching points for the client with Bell's palsy if you had difficulty with this question.
Level of Cognitive Ability: Analysis
Client Needs: Physiological Integrity
Integrated Process: Teaching and Learning
Content Area: Adult health—neurological
Reference: Lewis, S., Heitkemper, M., & Dirksen, S. (2004). *Medical-surgical nursing: Assessment and management of clinical problems* (6th ed., p. 1606). St. Louis: Mosby.

23. **4**
Rationale: Guillain-Barré syndrome is a clinical syndrome of unknown origin that involves cranial and peripheral nerves. Many clients report a history of respiratory or gastrointestinal infection in the 1 to 4 weeks before the onset of neurological deficits. Occasionally, the syndrome can be triggered by vaccination or surgery.
Test-Taking Strategy: Use the process of elimination and knowledge regarding the causes related to this disorder. Remember that a recent history of respiratory or gastrointestinal infection are predisposing factors. If you are unfamiliar with Guillain-Barré syndrome, review this disorder.
Level of Cognitive Ability: Analysis
Client Needs: Physiological Integrity
Integrated Process: Nursing Process—assessment
Content Area: Adult health—neurological

Reference: Ignatavicius, D., & Workman, M. (2006). *Medical-surgical nursing: Critical thinking for collaborative care* (5th ed., pp. 1006-1008). Philadelphia: W.B. Saunders.

24. 3
Rationale: The client with Guillain-Barré syndrome experiences fear and anxiety from the ascending paralysis and sudden onset of the disorder. The nurse can alleviate these fears by providing accurate information about the client's condition, giving expert care and positive feedback to the client, and encouraging relaxation and distraction. The family can become involved with selected care activities and provide diversion for the client as well.
Test-Taking Strategy: Use the process of elimination. Option 1 should be eliminated first because it is not practical to think that the client would be given full control over all care decisions. The client who is paralyzed cannot participate in active range of motion, which eliminates option 2. From the remaining options, option 3 is more beneficial in helping the client cope than option 4. Review care of the client with Guillain-Barré syndrome if you had difficulty with this question.
Level of Cognitive Ability: Application
Client Needs: Psychosocial Integrity
Integrated Process: Caring
Content Area: Adult health—neurological
References: Black, J., & Hawks, J. (2005). *Medical-surgical nursing: Clinical management for positive outcomes* (7th ed., p. 2181). Philadelphia: W.B. Saunders.
Ignatavicius, D., & Workman, M. (2006). *Medical-surgical nursing: Critical thinking for collaborative care* (5th ed., pp. 1009, 1012). Philadelphia: W.B. Saunders.

25. 4
Rationale: Cranial nerve II is the optic nerve, which governs vision. The nurse can provide safety for the visually impaired client by clearing the path of obstacles when ambulating. Testing the shower water temperature would be useful if there were an impairment of peripheral nerves. Speaking loudly may help overcome a deficit of cranial nerve VIII (vestibulocochlear). Cranial nerve VII (facial) and IX (glossopharyngeal) control taste from the anterior two thirds and posterior third of the tongue, respectively.
Test-Taking Strategy: Use the process of elimination. Recalling that cranial nerve II is the optic nerve will direct you to option 4. Review the function of this nerve if you had difficulty with this question.
Level of Cognitive Ability: Application
Client Needs: Safe and Effective Care Environment
Integrated Process: Nursing Process—planning
Content Area: Adult health—neurological
References: Black, J., & Hawks, J. (2005). *Medical-surgical nursing: Clinical management for positive outcomes* (7th ed., p. 2027). Philadelphia: W.B. Saunders.
Ignatavicius, D., & Workman, M. (2006). *Medical-surgical nursing: Critical thinking for collaborative care* (5th ed., p. 1108). Philadelphia: W.B. Saunders.

26. 2
Rationale: The limbic system is responsible for feelings (affect) and emotions. Calculation ability and knowledge of current events relates to function of the frontal lobe. The cerebral hemispheres, with specific regional functions, control orientation. Recall of recent events is controlled by the hippocampus.
Test-Taking Strategy: Use the process of elimination. Recall that the limbic system is responsible for feelings and emotions to direct you to option 2. Review the function of the limbic system if you had difficulty with this question.
Level of Cognitive Ability: Application
Client Needs: Psychosocial Integrity
Integrated Process: Communication and Documentation
Content Area: Adult health—neurological
Reference: Black, J., & Hawks, J. (2005). *Medical-surgical nursing: Clinical management for positive outcomes* (7th ed., p. 2001). Philadelphia: W.B. Saunders.

27. 4
Rationale: The trigeminal nerve has motor and sensory divisions. The motor division innervates the muscles for chewing (mastication). The sensory division innervates the entire face, scalp, cornea, and nasal and oral cavities. The sensations of pain, temperature, and touch can be assessed using each of the respective items noted in option 4. The corneal reflex (motor division) also can be tested using the cotton wisp. The supplies noted in options 1, 2, and 3 are used for testing cranial nerves III, VIII, and II, respectively.
Test-Taking Strategy: Use the process of elimination. Recalling the function of cranial nerve V will direct you to option 4. Review the function of this nerve if you had difficulty with this question.
Level of Cognitive Ability: Application
Client Needs: Health Promotion and Maintenance
Integrated Process: Nursing Process—assessment
Content Area: Adult health—neurological
References: Black, J., & Hawks, J. (2005). *Medical-surgical nursing: Clinical management for positive outcomes* (7th ed., pp. 2012, 2028). Philadelphia: W.B. Saunders.
Perry, A., & Potter, P. (2006). *Clinical nursing skills and techniques* (6th ed., pp. 591-592). St. Louis: Mosby.

28. 3
Rationale: Cranial nerves III (oculomotor), IV (trochlear), and VI (abducens) have only motor components and control, in a coordinated manner, the six cardinal fields of gaze. This is tested by moving an object in six directions (involving horizontal and diagonal movements). Corneal reflex is the function of the trigeminal nerve (cranial nerve V). Pupillary response and accommodation is the function of cranial nerve III (oculomotor) alone.
Test-Taking Strategy: If you look at this question carefully, you will see that each of the incorrect options has to do with pupillary reactions of some type. The correct option is the one that is different from the others. Being able to move the eyes through the six cardinal fields of gaze is a coordinated effort of three cranial nerves. Review cranial nerve testing if you had difficulty with this question.
Level of Cognitive Ability: Application
Client Needs: Health Promotion and Maintenance
Integrated Process: Nursing Process—assessment
Content Area: Adult health—neurological
References: Black, J., & Hawks, J. (2005). *Medical-surgical nursing: Clinical management for positive outcomes* (7th ed., p. 2028). Philadelphia: W.B. Saunders.

Perry, A., & Potter, P. (2006). *Clinical nursing skills and techniques* (6th ed., pp. 591-592). St. Louis: Mosby.

29. **4**

Rationale: The client with Guillain-Barré syndrome is at risk for respiratory failure because of ascending paralysis. An intubation tray should be available for use. Another complication of this syndrome is cardiac dysrhythmias, which necessitates the use of electrocardiographic monitoring. Because the client is immobilized, the nurse should assess for deep vein thrombosis and pulmonary embolism routinely.

Test-Taking Strategy: Use the process of elimination. With an ascending paralysis, the client is at risk for involvement of respiratory muscles and subsequent respiratory failure. Option 4 is the only option that includes an intubation tray, which would be needed if the client's status deteriorated to needing intubation and mechanical ventilation. This option most directly addresses airway. Review care of the client with Guillain-Barré syndrome if you had difficulty with this question.

Level of Cognitive Ability: Application
Client Needs: Physiological Integrity
Integrated Process: Nursing Process—implementation
Content Area: Adult health—neurological
Reference: Ignatavicius, D., & Workman, M. (2006). *Medical-surgical nursing: Critical thinking for collaborative care* (5th ed., pp. 1007, 1010). Philadelphia: W.B. Saunders.

30. **3**

Rationale: Satisfactory respiratory outcomes include clear breath sounds on auscultation, spontaneous breathing, normal vital capacity, and normal arterial blood gas levels and pulse oximetry.

Test-Taking Strategy: Use the process of elimination, noting the strategic words *least optimal*. Only one option does not represent full respiratory function. This should help you eliminate each of the incorrect options. Review care of the client with Guillain-Barré syndrome if you had difficulty with this question.

Level of Cognitive Ability: Analysis
Client Needs: Physiological Integrity
Integrated Process: Nursing Process—evaluation
Content Area: Adult health—neurological
Reference: Ignatavicius, D., & Workman, M. (2006). *Medical-surgical nursing: Critical thinking for collaborative care* (5th ed., pp. 1009, 1012). Philadelphia: W.B. Saunders.

31. **4**

Rationale: The changes in neurological signs from an epidural hematoma begin with loss of consciousness as arterial blood collects in the epidural space and exerts pressure. The client regains consciousness as the cerebrospinal fluid is reabsorbed rapidly to compensate for the rising intracranial pressure. As the compensatory mechanisms fail, even small amounts of additional blood cause the intracranial pressure to rise rapidly, and the client's neurological status deteriorates quickly.

Test-Taking Strategy: Use the process of elimination. Begin to answer this question by ruling out skull fracture and concussion as being responsible for fluctuating neurological signs. Recall that a subdural hematoma is a collection of venous blood, which may accumulate more slowly and cause a steadier deterioration of neurological signs. This will help you discriminate between epidural and subdural hematomas. Review the clinical manifestations associated with the various types of head injury if you had difficulty with this question.

Level of Cognitive Ability: Analysis
Client Needs: Physiological Integrity
Integrated Process: Nursing Process—assessment
Content Area: Adult health—neurological
References: Black, J., & Hawks, J. (2005). *Medical-surgical nursing: Clinical management for positive outcomes* (7th ed., pp. 2204-2205). Philadelphia: W.B. Saunders.
Ignatavicius, D., & Workman, M. (2006). *Medical-surgical nursing: Critical thinking for collaborative care* (5th ed., pp. 1046-1047). Philadelphia: W.B. Saunders.

32. **3**

Rationale: Signs of meningeal irritation compatible with meningitis include nuchal rigidity, positive Brudzinski's sign, and positive Kernig's sign. Nuchal rigidity is characterized by a stiff neck and soreness, which is especially noticeable when the neck is flexed. Kernig's sign is positive when the client feels pain and spasm of the hamstring muscles when the knee and thigh are extended from a flexed, right-angle position. Brudzinski's sign is positive when the client flexes the hips and knees in response to the nurse gently flexing the head and neck onto the chest. A Glasgow Coma Scale score of 15 is a perfect score and indicates that the client is awake and alert, with no neurological deficits.

Test-Taking Strategy: Use the process of elimination, focusing on the client's diagnosis, meningitis. You can eliminate options 1, 2, and 4 because they are normal findings. Review the signs of meningitis if you had difficulty with this question.

Level of Cognitive Ability: Analysis
Client Needs: Physiological Integrity
Integrated Process: Nursing Process—assessment
Content Area: Adult health—neurological
Reference: Black, J., & Hawks, J. (2005). *Medical-surgical nursing: Clinical management for positive outcomes* (7th ed., pp. 2098-2099). Philadelphia: W.B. Saunders.

33. **2**

Rationale: Crutchfield (cervical) tongs are applied after drilling holes in the client's skull under local anesthesia. Weights are attached to the tongs, which exert pulling pressure on the longitudinal axis of the cervical spine. Serial x-rays of the cervical spine are taken, with weights being added gradually until the x-ray reveals that the vertebral column is realigned. After that, weights may be reduced gradually to a point that maintains alignment. The client with Crutchfield tongs is placed on a Stryker frame or RotoRest bed. The nurse ensures that weights hang freely, and the amount of weight matches the current order. The nurse also inspects the integrity and position of the ropes and pulleys. The nurse does not remove the weights to administer care.

Test-Taking Strategy: Use the process of elimination noting the strategic word *avoid*. Recalling the basics related to the care of a client in traction will direct you to option 2. Review nursing care of the client with cervical tongs if you had difficulty with this question.

Level of Cognitive Ability: Application
Client Needs: Physiological Integrity
Integrated Process: Nursing Process—planning
Content Area: Adult health—neurological
References: Black, J., & Hawks, J. (2005). *Medical-surgical nursing: Clinical management for positive outcomes* (7th ed., pp. 2218, 2221). Philadelphia: W.B. Saunders.
Ignatavicius, D., & Workman, M. (2006). *Medical-surgical nursing: Critical thinking for collaborative care* (5th ed., p. 989). Philadelphia: W.B. Saunders.

34. **2**
Rationale: The halo device alters balance and can cause fatigue because of its weight. The client should cleanse the skin daily under the vest to protect the skin from ulceration and should use powder or lotions sparingly, or not at all. The wool liner should be changed if odor becomes a problem. The client should have food cut into small pieces to facilitate chewing and use a straw for drinking. Pin care is done as instructed. The client may not drive because the device impairs the range of vision.
Test-Taking Strategy: Use the process of elimination and note the strategic words *needs further clarification*. These words indicate a negative event query and ask you to select an option that is incorrect. Visualize this device to answer correctly. The inability to turn the head without turning the torso would contraindicate driving. Review client education points related to a halo device if you had difficulty with this question
Level of Cognitive Ability: Analysis
Client Needs: Physiological Integrity
Integrated Process: Teaching and Learning
Content Area: Adult health—neurological
Reference: Ignatavicius, D. & Workman, M. (2006). *Medical-surgical nursing: Critical thinking for collaborative care* (5th ed., p. 994). Philadelphia: W.B. Saunders.

35. **4**
Rationale: After spinal cord injury, the client can develop paralytic ileus, which is characterized by the absence of bowel sounds and abdominal distention. Development of a stress ulcer can be detected by Hematest-positive nasogastric tube aspirate or stool. A history of diarrhea is irrelevant.
Test-Taking Strategy: Use the process of elimination, focusing on the client's diagnosis and the signs of a gastrointestinal complication. This will direct you to option 4. Review this information if you had difficulty with this question.

Level of Cognitive Ability: Application
Client Needs: Physiological Integrity
Integrated Process: Nursing Process—assessment
Content Area: Adult health—neurological
Reference: Black, J., & Hawks, J. (2005). *Medical-surgical nursing: Clinical management for positive outcomes* (7th ed., p. 2148). Philadelphia: W.B. Saunders.

ALTERNATE ITEM FORMAT: PRIORITIZING (ORDERED RESPONSE)
Answer: 4, 1, 3, 2, 5, 6
Rationale: Autonomic dysreflexia is characterized by severe hypertension, bradycardia, severe headache, nasal stuffiness, and flushing. The cause is a noxious stimulus, most often a distended bladder or constipation. Autonomic dysreflexia is a neurological emergency and must be treated promptly to prevent a hypertensive stroke. Immediate nursing actions are to sit the client up in bed in a high Fowler's position and remove the noxious stimulus. The nurse would loosen any tight clothing and then check for bladder distention. If the client has a Foley catheter, the nurse would check for kinks in the tubing. The nurse also would check for a fecal impaction and disimpact the client, if necessary. The physician is contacted, especially if these actions do not relieve the signs and symptoms. Antihypertensive medication may be prescribed by the physician to minimize cerebral hypertension. Finally, the nurse documents the occurrence, treatment, and client response.
Test-Taking Strategy: Recalling that this syndrome causes severe hypertension will assist you in determining that elevating the head of the bed is the first action. Next, recalling that the syndrome is caused by a noxious stimulus will assist you in determining that loosening tight clothing and checking for bladder distention would be the next actions. Because loosening any tight clothing would take less time than checking for bladder distention, this action would be taken next. Antihypertensives require a physician's order; therefore, calling the physician would be the next action. Review immediate nursing interventions for the client experiencing autonomic dysreflexia if you had difficulty with this question.
Level of Cognitive Ability: Application
Client Needs: Physiological Integrity
Integrated Process: Nursing Process—implementation
Content Area: Adult health—neurological
Reference: Black, J., & Hawks, J. (2005). *Medical-surgical nursing: Clinical management for positive outcomes* (7th ed., pp. 2215, 2229). Philadelphia: W.B. Saunders.

REFERENCES

Black, J., & Hawks, J. (2005). *Medical-surgical nursing: Clinical management for positive outcomes* (7th ed.). Philadelphia: W.B. Saunders.

Chernecky, C., & Berger, B. (2004). *Laboratory tests and diagnostic procedures* (4th ed.). Philadelphia: W.B. Saunders.

Harkreader, H., & Hogan, M. A. (2004). *Fundamentals of nursing: Caring and clinical judgment* (2nd ed.). Philadelphia: W.B. Saunders.

Ignatavicius, D., & Workman, M. (2006). *Medical-surgical nursing: Critical thinking for collaborative care* (5th ed.). Philadelphia: W.B. Saunders.

Jarvis, C. (2004). *Physical examination and health assessment* (4th ed.). Philadelphia: W.B. Saunders.

Lehne, R. (2007). *Pharmacology for nursing care* (6th ed.). Philadelphia: W.B. Saunders.

Lewis, S., Heitkemper, M., & Dirksen, S. (2004). *Medical-surgical nursing: Assessment and management of clinical problems* (6th ed.). St. Louis: Mosby.

Perry, A., & Potter, P. (2006). *Clinical nursing skills and techniques* (6th ed.). St. Louis: Mosby.

Skidmore-Roth, L. (2006). *Mosby's 2006 nursing drug reference*. St. Louis: Mosby.

Neurological Medications

I. ANTIMYASTHENIC MEDICATIONS

A. Description

1. Antimyasthenic, also called anticholinesterase, medications relieve muscle weakness associated with myasthenia gravis by blocking acetylcholine breakdown at the neuromuscular junction.
2. Antimyasthenic medications are used to treat or diagnose myasthenia gravis or to distinguish cholinergic crisis from myasthenic crisis.
3. Neostigmine bromide (Prostigmin), pyridostigmine (Mestinon), and ambenonium chloride (Mytelase) are used to control myasthenic symptoms.
4. Edrophonium chloride (Tensilon) is used to diagnose myasthenia gravis and to distinguish cholinergic crisis from myasthenic crisis.

B. Medications (Box 66-1)

C. Side effects: Cholinergic crisis (Box 66-2)

D. Interventions

1. Assess neuromuscular status, including reflexes, muscle strength, and gait.
2. Monitor the client for signs and symptoms of medication overdose (cholinergic crisis) and underdose (myasthenic crisis).
3. Instruct the client to take medications on time to maintain therapeutic blood level, thus preventing weakness, because weakness can impair the client's ability to breathe and swallow.
4. Instruct the client to take the medication with a small amount of food to prevent gastrointestinal symptoms.
5. Instruct the client to eat 45 to 60 minutes after taking medications to decrease the risk for aspiration.
6. Instruct the client to wear a Medic-Alert bracelet.
7. Note that antimyasthenic therapy is lifelong therapy.
8. Evaluate for medication effectiveness, which is based on the improvement of neuromuscular symptoms or strength without cholinergic signs and symptoms.
9. When administering edrophonium chloride, have emergency resuscitation equipment on hand and atropine sulfate available for cholinergic crisis.

E. Tensilon test

1. Edrophonium (Tensilon) is injected intravenously.
2. The Tensilon test can cause bronchospasm, laryngospasm, hypotension, bradycardia, and cardiac arrest.
3. Atropine sulfate is the antidote for overdose.
4. Diagnosis of myasthenia gravis: Most myasthenic clients will show a significant improvement in

---

BOX 66-1
Antimyasthenic Medications

Ambenonium chloride (Mytelase)
Edrophonium chloride (Tensilon, Enlon, Reversol)
Neostigmine bromide (Prostigmin)
Pyridostigmine (Mestinon)

BOX 66-2
Signs of Cholinergic Crisis

Abdominal cramps
Nausea, vomiting, and diarrhea
Pupillary miosis
Hypotension and dizziness
Increased bronchial secretions
Increased tearing and salivation
Increased perspiration
Increased bronchial secretions
Bronchospasm, wheezing, and bradycardia

muscle tone within 30 to 60 seconds after injection, and the muscle improvement lasts 4 to 5 minutes.

5. The Tensilon test is used to diagnose cholinergic crisis (overdose with anticholinesterase) or myasthenic crisis (undermedication).
   a. In cholinergic crisis, muscle tone does not improve after the administration of Tensilon, and muscle twitching may be noted around the eyes and face.
   b. A Tensilon injection makes the client in cholinergic crisis temporarily worse (negative Tensilon test).
   c. A Tensilon injection temporarily improves the condition when the client is in myasthenic crisis (positive Tensilon test).

II. ANTIPARKINSONIAN MEDICATIONS
A. Description
   1. Antiparkinsonian medications restore the balance of the neurotransmitters acetylcholine and dopamine in the central nervous system (CNS), decreasing the signs and symptoms of Parkinson's disease to maximize the client's functional abilities.
   2. These medications include the dopaminergics, which stimulate the dopamine receptors, and the anticholinergics, which block the cholinergic receptors.
   3. Antiparkinsonian medications are used for drug-induced parkinsonism, in which neuroleptic agents block dopamine receptors in the CNS, leading to functional loss of dopamine activity.
   4. Antiparkinsonian medications are used for Parkinson's disease, in which dopamine-containing neurons in the basal ganglia are destroyed or deficient, which causes loss of fine motor control.
B. Dopaminergic medications
   1. Description
      a. Dopaminergic medications stimulate the dopamine receptors and increase the amount of dopamine available in the CNS or enhance neurotransmission of dopamine.
      b. Dopaminergic medications are contraindicated in clients with cardiac, renal, or psychiatric disorders.
      c. Levodopa taken with a monoamine oxidase inhibitor antidepressant can cause a hypertensive crisis.
   2. Medications (Box 66-3; Fig. 66-1)
   3. Side effects
      a. Dyskinesia
      b. Involuntary body movements
      c. Chest pain
      d. Nausea and vomiting
      e. Urinary retention
      f. Constipation

BOX 66-3

Medications to Treat Parkinson's Disease

MEDICATIONS AFFECTING THE AMOUNT OF DOPAMINE
Amantadine (Symmetrel)
Bromocriptine (Parlodel)
Carbidopa; levodopa (Sinemet)
Levodopa (Larodopa, Dopar)
Pramipexole (Mirapex)
Ropinirole (Requip)
Selegiline hydrochloride (Carbex, Eldepryl)

ANTICHOLINERGICS
Benztropine mesylate (Cogentin)
Biperiden hydrochloride (Akineton)
Procyclidine hydrochloride (Kemadrin)
Trihexyphenidyl hydrochloride

CATHECHOL *O*-METHYLTRANSFERASE (COMT) INHIBITORS
Entacapone (Comtan)
Tolcapone (Tasmar)

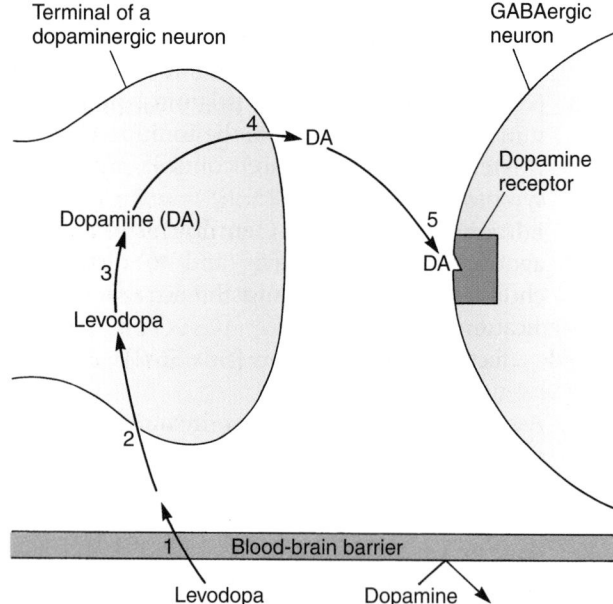

FIG. 66-1 Steps leading to alteration of central nervous system function by levodopa. To produce its beneficial effects in Parkinson's disease (PD), levodopa must be (1) transported across the blood-brain barrier; (2) taken up by dopaminergic nerve terminals in the striatum; (3) converted into dopamine (DA); (4) released into the synaptic space; and (5) bound to DA receptors on striatal GABAergic neurons, causing them to fire at a slower rate. Note that DA itself is unable to cross the blood-brain barrier, and hence cannot be use to treat PD. (From Lehne, R. [2007]. *Pharmacology for nursing care* [6th ed.]. Philadelphia: W. B. Saunders.)

g. Sleep disturbances, insomnia or periods of sedation
h. Orthostatic hypotension and dizziness
i. Confusion
j. Mood changes, especially depression
k. Hallucinations
l. Dry mouth

4. Interventions
   a. Assess vital signs
   b. Assess for risk of injury.
   c. Instruct the client to take the medication with food if nausea and vomiting occur.
   d. Assess for signs and symptoms of parkinsonism such as rigidity, tremors, akinesia, and bradykinesia, a stooped forward posture, shuffling gait, and masked facies.
   e. Monitor for signs of dyskinesia.
   f. Instruct the client to report side effects and symptoms of dyskinesia.
   g. Monitor the client for improvement in signs and symptoms of parkinsonism without the development of severe side effects from the medications.
   h. Instruct the client to change positions slowly to minimize orthostatic hypotension.
   i. Instruct the client not to discontinue the medication abruptly.
   j. Instruct the client to avoid alcohol.
   k. Inform the client that urine or perspiration may be discolored and that this is harmless, but may stain the clothing.
   l. Advise the client with diabetes mellitus that glucose testing should not be done by urine testing because the results will not be reliable.
   m. Instruct the client taking carbidopa-levodopa (Sinemet) to eat low-protein foods because high-protein diets interfere with medication availability to the CNS.
   n. When administering levodopa, instruct the client to avoid excessive vitamin B$_6$ intake to prevent medication reactions.

C. Anticholinergic medications
   1. Description
      a. Anticholinergic medications block the cholinergic receptors in the CNS, thereby suppressing acetylcholine activity.
      b. Anticholinergic medications reduce the tremors and drooling but have a minimal effect on the bradykinesia, rigidity, and balance abnormalities.
      c. Anticholinergic medications are contraindicated in clients with glaucoma.
      d. The client with chronic obstructive lung disease can develop dry, thick mucous secretions.
   2. Medications (see Box 66-3)

3. Side effects
   a. Blurred vision
   b. Dryness of the nose, mouth, throat, and respiratory secretions
   c. Increased pulse rate, palpitations, and arrhythmias
   d. Constipation
   e. Urinary retention
   f. Restlessness, confusion, depression, and hallucinations
   g. Photophobia

4. Interventions
   a. Monitor vital signs.
   b. Assess for risk of injury.
   c. Assess for signs and symptoms of parkinsonism such as rigidity, tremors, akinesia, and bradykinesia, a stooped forward posture, shuffling gait, and masked facies.
   d. Monitor the client for improvement in signs and symptoms.
   e. Assess the client's bowel and urinary function and monitor for urinary retention, constipation, and paralytic ileus.
   f. Monitor for involuntary movements.
   g. Encourage the client to avoid alcohol, smoking, caffeine, and aspirin to decrease gastric acidity.
   h. Instruct the client to consult with the physician before taking any nonprescription medications.
   i. Instruct the client to minimize dry mouth by increasing fluid intake and by using ice chips, hard candy, or gum.
   j. Instruct the client to prevent constipation by increasing fluids and fiber in the diet.
   k. Instruct the client to use sunglasses in direct sunlight because of possible photophobia.
   l. Instruct the client to have routine eye examinations to assess for intraocular pressure.

III. ANTICONVULSANT MEDICATIONS

A. Description
   1. Anticonvulsant medications are used to depress abnormal neuronal discharges and prevent the spread of seizures to adjacent neurons.
   2. Anticonvulsant medications should be used with caution in clients taking anticoagulants, aspirin, sulfonamides, cimetidine (Tagamet), and antipsychotic drugs.
   3. Absorption is decreased with the use of antacids, calcium preparations, and antineoplastic medications.

B. Interventions for clients on anticonvulsants
   1. Initiate seizure precautions.
   2. Monitor urinary output.
   3. Monitor liver and renal function tests and medication blood serum levels (Table 66-1)

TABLE 66-1

Anticonvulsant Medications

Medication	Therapeutic Serum Range
Amobarbital (Amytal)	1-5 mcg/mL
Carbamazepine (Tegretol)	3-14 mcg/mL
Clonazepam (Klonopin)	20-80 ng/mL
Ethosuximide (Zarontin)	40-100 mcg/mL
Ethotoin (Peganone)	10-50 mcg/mL
Lorazepam (Ativan)	50-240 ng/mL
Mephobarbital (Mebaral)	15-40 mcg/mL
Phenobarbital (Luminal)	15-40 mcg/mL
Phenytoin (Dilantin)	10-20 mcg/mL

4. Monitor for signs of medication toxicity, which would include CNS depression, ataxia, nausea, vomiting, drowsiness, dizziness, restlessness, and visual disturbances.
5. If a seizure occurs, assess seizure activity, including location and duration.
6. Protect the client from hazards in the environment during a seizure.

C. Client education (Box 66-4)

D. Hydantoins (Box 66-5)
1. Hydantoins are used to treat partial and generalized tonic-clonic seizures.
2. Phenytoin (Dilantin) also is used to treat dysrhythmias.
3. Phenytoin decreases the effectiveness of some birth control pills and can have teratogenic effects if taken during pregnancy.
4. Side effects
   a. Gingival hyperplasia (reddened gums that bleed easily)
   b. Slurred speech
   c. Confusion
   d. Sedation and drowsiness
   e. Nausea and vomiting
   f. Blurred vision and nystagmus
   g. Headaches
   h. Blood dyscrasias: Decreased platelet count and decreased white blood cell count
   i. Elevated blood glucose level
   j. Alopecia or hirsutism
   k. Skin rash or pruritis
5. Interventions
   a. Oral tube feedings may interfere with the absorption of orally administered phenytoin and diminish the effectiveness of the medication; therefore, feedings should be scheduled as far as possible from the time of phenytoin administration.
   b. Monitor therapeutic serum levels to assess for toxicity.
   c. Monitor for signs of toxicity.

BOX 66-4

Client Education: Anticonvulsants

Take the prescribed medication in the prescribed dose and frequency.
Take anticonvulsants with food to decrease gastrointestinal irritation, but avoid milk and antacids, which impair absorption.
If taking liquid medication, shake well before ingesting.
Do not discontinue the medications.
Avoid alcohol.
Avoid over-the-counter medications.
Wear a Medic-Alert bracelet.
Use caution when driving or performing activities that require alertness.
Maintain good oral hygiene and use a soft toothbrush.
Maintain preventative dental checkups.
Maintain follow-up health care visits with periodic blood studies related to determining toxicity.
Monitor serum glucose levels (diabetes mellitus).
Urine may be a harmless pink-red or red-brown in color.
Report symptoms of sore throat, bruising, and nose-bleeds, which may indicate a blood dyscrasia.
Inform the physician if adverse reactions occur, such as gingivitis, nystagmus, slurred speech, rash, or dizziness.

BOX 66-5

Hydantoins

Ethotoin (Peganone)
Fosphenytoin (Cerebyx)
Phenytoin (Dilantin)

   d. When administering phenytoin intravenously, dilute in normal saline because dextrose causes the medication to precipitate.
   e. When administering phenytoin intravenously to treat status epilepticus, infuse no faster than 25 to 50 mg/min; otherwise, hypotension and cardiac dysrhythmias can occur.
   f. Assess for ataxia (staggering gait).
   g. Instruct the client to consult with the physician before taking other medications to ensure compatibility with anticonvulsants.
E. Barbiturates (Box 66-6)
1. Barbiturates are used for tonic-clonic seizures and acute episodes of seizures caused by status epilepticus.
2. Barbiturates also may be used as adjuncts to anesthesia.
3. Side effects
   a. Sedation, ataxia, and dizziness during initial treatment
   b. Mood changes
   c. Hypotension
   d. Respiratory depression
   e. Tolerance to the medication

BOX 66-6
Barbiturates

Amobarbital (Amytal)
Mephobarbital (Mebaral)
Phenobarbital; alcohol (Luminal)

BOX 66-7
Benzodiazepines

Clonazepam (Klonopin)
Clorazepate (Tranxene)
Diazepam (Valium)
Lorazepam (Ativan)

BOX 66-8
Succinimides

Ethosuximide (Zarontin)
Methsuximide (Celontin)

BOX 66-9
Oxazolidinediones

Paramethadione (Paradione)
Trimethadione (Troxidone)

BOX 66-10
Valproates

Valproic acid (Depakene, Depakote, Depacon)
Divalproex sodium (Depakote ER)

BOX 66-11
Other Anticonvulsants

Carbamazepine (Tegretol)
Gabapentin (Neurontin)
Lamotrigine (Lamictal)
Levetiracetam (Keppra)
Oxcarbazepine (Trileptal)
Pregabalin (Lyrica)
Tiagabine (Gabitril Filmtabs)
Topiramate (Topamax)
Zonisamide (Zonegran)
Vigabatrin (Sabril)

F. Benzodiazepines (Box 66-7)
   1. Benzodiazepines are used to treat absence seizures.
   2. Diazepam (Valium) is used to treat status epilepticus, anxiety, and skeletal muscle spasms.
   3. Clorazepate (Tranxene) is used as adjunctive therapy for partial seizures.
   4. Side effects
      a. Sedation, drowsiness, dizziness, blurred vision
      b. Administer at no more than 5 mg/min intravenously to prevent bradycardia.
      c. Medication tolerance and drug dependency
      d. Blood dyscrasias: Decreased platelet count and decreased white blood cell count
      e. Hepatotoxicity
G. Succinimides (Box 66-8)
   1. Succinimides are used to treat absence seizures.
   2. Side effects
      a. Anorexia, nausea, vomiting
      b. Blood dyscrasias
H. Oxazolidinediones (Box 66-9)
   1. Oxazolidinediones are used for absence seizures.
   2. Side effects
      a. Sedation, drowsiness, fatigue
      b. Headache
      c. Photophobia
      d. Blood dyscrasias
I. Valproates (Box 66-10)
   1. Valproates are used to treat tonic-clonic, partial, myoclonic, and psychomotor seizures.
   2. Side effects
      a. Transient nausea, vomiting, and indigestion
      b. Sedation, drowsiness and dizziness
      c. Pancreatitis
      d. Blood dyscrasias: Decreased platelet count and decreased white blood cell count
      e. Hepatotoxicity
J. Iminostilbenes
   1. Iminostilbenes are used to treat seizure disorders that have not responded to other anticonvulsants (Box 66-11).
   2. Iminostilbenes are used to treat trigeminal neuralgia.
   3. Side effects
      a. Drowsiness
      b. Dizziness
      c. Nausea and vomiting
      d. Constipation or diarrhea
      e. Rash
      f. Visual abnormalities
      g. Dry mouth
      h. Headache

IV. **CENTRAL NERVOUS SYSTEM STIMULANTS**
A. Description
   1. Amphetamines and caffeine stimulate the cerebral cortex of the brain (Box 66-12).
   2. Amphetamines have a high potential for abuse.
   3. Analeptics and caffeine act on the brainstem and medulla to stimulate respiration.
   4. Anorexiants act on the cerebral cortex and hypothalamus to suppress appetite (Box 66-13).
   5. Central nervous system stimulants are used to treat narcolepsy and attention-deficit/hyperactivity disorders.

6. Central nervous system stimulants are used as adjunctive therapy for exogenous obesity.
7. Other central nervous system stimulants (Box 66-14)

B. Side effects
   1. Irritability
   2. Restlessness
   3. Tremors
   4. Insomnia
   5. Heart palpitations
   6. Tachycardia and dysrhythmias
   7. Hypertension
   8. Dry mouth
   9. Anorexia and weight loss
   10. Abdominal cramping
   11. Diarrhea or constipation
   12. Hepatic failure
   13. Psychoses
   14. Impotence
   15. Dependence and tolerance

C. Interventions
   1. Monitor vital signs.
   2. Assess mental status.
   3. Document the degree of inattention, impulsivity, hyperactivity, and periods of sleepiness.
   4. Assess height, weight, and growth of the child.
   5. Monitor complete blood count and white blood cell and platelet counts before and during therapy.
   6. Monitor for side effects.
   7. Monitor sleep patterns.

8. Monitor for withdrawal symptoms such as nausea, vomiting, weakness, and headache.
9. Instruct the client to take the medication before meals.
10. Instruct the client to avoid foods and beverages containing caffeine to prevent additional stimulation.
11. Instruct the client not to chew or crush long-acting forms of the medications.
12. Instruct the client to read labels on over-the-counter products because many contain caffeine.
13. Instruct the client to avoid alcohol.
14. Instruct the client not to discontinue the medication abruptly.
15. Instruct the client to take the last daily dose of the CNS stimulant at least 6 hours before bedtime to prevent insomnia.
16. Monitor for drug dependence and abuse with amphetamines.
17. If a child is taking a CNS stimulant, instruct the parents to notify the school nurse.
18. Monitor for calming effects of CNS stimulants within 3 to 4 weeks on children with attention-deficit/hyperactivity disorder.
19. Monitor growth in the child on long-term therapy with methylphenidate hydrochloride (Ritalin) or other medication to treat attention-deficit/hyperactivity disorder.

V. NONOPIOID ANALGESICS

A. Nonsteroidal anti-inflammatory drugs (NSAIDs; Box 66-15)
   1. Description
      a. NSAIDs are aspirin and aspirin-like medications that inhibit the synthesis of prostaglandins.
      b. The medications act as an analgesic to relieve pain, as an antipyretic to reduce body temperature, and as an anticoagulant to inhibit platelet aggregation.
      c. NSAIDs are used to relieve inflammation and pain and to treat rheumatoid arthritis, bursitis, tendinitis, osteoarthritis, and acute gout.
      d. NSAIDs are contraindicated in clients with hypersensitivity or liver or renal disease.
      e. Children with flu symptoms should not take aspirin because of the risk of Reye's syndrome.
      f. Clients taking anticoagulants should not take aspirin or NSAIDS.
      g. Aspirin and an NSAID should not be taken together because aspirin decreases the blood level and the effectiveness of the NSAID and can increase the risk of bleeding.
      h. NSAIDs can increase the effects of warfarin (Coumadin), sulfonamides, cephalosporins, and phenytoin (Dilantin).

BOX 66-15
Nonopioid Analgesics

ACETAMINOPHEN
Acetaminophen (Tylenol)

ASPIRIN
Aspirin (acetylsalicylic acid) (ASA, Aspergum, Bayer Aspirin, Ecotrin)
Aspirin (acetylsalicylic acid), buffered (Alka-Seltzer, Bufferin)

NONSTEROIDAL ANTI-INFLAMMATORY DRUGS
Fenoprofen (Nalfon)
Flurbiprofen (Ansaid)
Ibuprofen (Motrin, Advil)
Ketoprofen (Orudis, Oruvail)
Naproxen (Advil, Anaprox, Naprosyn, Aleve, Naprelan)
Oxaprozin (Daypro)

CYCLOOXYGENASE-2 (COX-2) INHIBITORS
Celecoxib (Celebrex)

OTHER NONSTEROIDAL ANTI-INFLAMMATORY DRUGS
Diclofenac (Voltaren)
Diflunisal (Dolobid)
Etodolac (Lodine)
Indomethacin (Indocin)
Ketorolac
Meclofenamate
Mefenamic acid (Ponstel)
Meloxicam (Mobic)
Nabumetone (Relafen)
Piroxicam (Feldene)
Sulindac (Clinoril)
Tolmetin (Tolectin)

BOX 66-16
Side Effects of Aspirin and Nonsteroidal Anti-inflammatory Drugs

ASPIRIN
Allergic reactions (anaphylaxis, laryngeal edema)
Bleeding (anemia, hemolysis, increased bleeding time)
Dizziness
Drowsiness
Flushing
Gastrointestinal symptoms (distress, heartburn, nausea, vomiting)
Headaches
Decreased renal function
Tinnitus
Visual changes

NONSTEROIDAL ANTI-INFLAMMATORY DRUGS
Arrhythmias
Blood dyscrasias
Cardiovascular thrombotic events
Dizziness
Gastric irritation
Hepatotoxicity
Hypotension
Pruritus
Decreased renal function
Sodium and water retention
Tinnitus

i. Hypoglycemia can result if ibuprofen (Motrin) is taken with insulin or an oral hypoglycemic medication.
j. A high risk of toxicity exists if ibuprofen is taken concurrently with calcium blockers.

2. Side effects (Box 66-16)
3. Interventions
   a. Assess client for allergies.
   b. Obtain a medication history on the client.
   c. Assess for history of gastric upset or bleeding or liver or renal disease.
   d. Assess the client for gastrointestinal upset during medication administration.
   e. Monitor for edema.
   f. Monitor serum salicylate (aspirin) level when the client is taking high doses.
   g. Monitor for signs of bleeding such as tarry stools, bleeding gums, petechiae, ecchymosis, and purpura.
   h. Instruct the client to take the medication with water, milk, or food.

i. An enteric-coated or buffered form of aspirin can be taken to decrease gastric distress.
j. Instruct the client that enteric-coated tablets cannot be crushed or broken.
k. Advise the client to inform other health care professionals if they are taking high doses of aspirin.
l. Note that aspirin should be discontinued 3 to 7 days before surgery to reduce the risk of bleeding.
m. Instruct the client to avoid alcoholic beverages.

B. Acetaminophen (Tylenol)
   1. Description
      a. Acetaminophen inhibits prostaglandin synthesis.
      b. Acetaminophen is used to decrease pain and fever.
      c. Acetaminophen is contraindicated in clients with hepatic or renal disease, alcoholism, and/or hypersensitivity.
   2. Side effects
      a. Anorexia, nausea, vomiting
      b. Rash
      c. Hypoglycemia
      d. Oliguria
      e. Hepatotoxicity
   3. Interventions

a. Monitor vital signs.

b. Assess client for history of liver and renal dysfunction, alcoholism, and malnutrition.

c. Monitor for hepatic damage, which includes nausea, vomiting, diarrhea, and abdominal pain.

d. Monitor liver enzyme test results.

e. Instruct the client that self-medication should not be used longer than 10 days for an adult and 5 days for a child.

f. Note that the antidote for acetaminophen is acetylcysteine (Mucomyst).

g. Evaluate for the effectiveness of the medication.

VI. OPIOID ANALGESICS

A. Description

1. Opioid analgesics suppress pain impulses but can suppress respiration and coughing by acting on the respiratory and cough center in the medulla of the brainstem.

2. Opioid analgesics can produce euphoria and sedation and can cause physical dependence.

3. Opioid analgesics are used for relief of mild, moderate, or severe pain.

B. Medications (Box 66-17)

1. Codeine sulfate

a. Codeine sulfate also is an effective cough suppressant at low doses.

b. Codeine sulfate can cause constipation.

2. Hydromorphone hydrochloride (Dilaudid)

a. Hydromorphone can decrease respiration.

b. Hydromorphone can cause constipation.

3. Meperidine hydrochloride (Demerol)

a. Meperidine can cause hypotension, dizziness, urinary retention.

b. Meperidine is used for acute pain and as a preoperative medication.

c. Meperidine can increase intracranial pressure in clients with head injuries.

d. Meperidine is contraindicated in clients with head injuries and increased intracranial pressure, respiratory disorders, hypotension, shock, and severe hepatic and renal disease and in clients taking monoamine oxidase inhibitors.

e. Meperidine should not be taken with alcohol or a sedative-hypnotic because it may increase the CNS depression.

4. Morphine sulfate

a. Morphine can cause respiratory depression, orthostatic hypotension, and constipation.

b. Morphine may cause nausea and vomiting because of increased vestibular sensitivity.

c. Morphine is used for acute pain caused by myocardial infarction or cancer, for dyspnea caused by pulmonary edema, surgery, and as a preoperative medication.

BOX 66-17

Opioid Analgesics

Buprenorphine hydrochloride (Buprenex)
Butorphanol tartrate (Stadol)
Codeine sulfate, codeine phosphate
Fentanyl (Duragesic, Sublimaze)
Hydrocodone (Hycodan)
Hydromorphone hydrochloride (Dilaudid)
Levorphanol tartrate (Levo-Dromoran)
Meperidine hydrochloride (Demerol)
Methadone hydrochloride (Dolophine, Methadose)
Morphine sulfate (Duramorph, MS Contin, Kadian, Oramorph SR)
Nalbuphine hydrochloride (Nubain)
Oxycodone (Roxicodone, OxyContin)
Oxycodone hydrochloride; acetaminophen (Percocet)
Oxycodone; aspirin (Percodan)
Oxymorphone hydrochloride (Numorphan)
Pentazocine (Talwin)
Propoxyphene napsylate (Darvon-N)
Remifentanil (Ultiva)
Sufentanil (Sufenta)
Tramadol (Ultram)

---

d. Morphine is contraindicated in clients with severe respiratory disorders, head injuries, increased intracranial pressure, severe renal, hepatic, or pulmonary disease, or seizure activity.

e. Morphine is used with caution in clients with shock or blood loss.

5. Oxycodone with aspirin (Percodan)

a. Percodan should not be taken by a client allergic to aspirin.

b. Percodan can cause gastric irritation and should be taken with food or plenty of liquids.

6. Propoxyphene hydrochloride (Darvon) and propoxyphene napsylate (Darvon-N)

a. Darvon compounds contain aspirin and should not be taken by a client allergic to aspirin.

b. Darvocet-N contains acetaminophen.

7. Nalbuphine hydrochloride (Nubain) is preferable for treating the pain of a myocardial infarction because it reduces the oxygen needs of the heart without reducing blood pressure.

8. Methadone hydrochloride (Dolophine)

a. Dilute doses of oral concentrate with at least 90 mL of water.

b. Dilute dispersible tablets in at least 120 mL of water, orange juice, or acidic fruit beverage.

c. Methadone is used as a replacement medication for opiate dependence and to facilitate withdrawal.

9. Hydrocodone (Hycodan) frequently is used for cough suppression.

C. Interventions for opioid analgesics
1. Monitor vital signs.
2. Assess the client thoroughly before administering pain medication.
3. Initiate nursing measures such as massage, distraction, deep breathing and relaxation exercises, the application of heat or cold as prescribed, and providing care and comfort before administering the opioid analgesic.
4. Administer medications 30 to 60 minutes before painful activities.
5. Monitor respiratory rate and, if the rate is less than 12 breaths/min in an adult, withhold the medication unless ventilatory support is being provided.
6. Monitor pulse and, if bradycardia develops, hold the dose and notify the physician.
7. Monitor blood pressure for hypotension.
8. Auscultate breath sounds because opioid analgesics suppress the cough reflex.
9. Encourage activities such as turning, deep breathing, and incentive spirometry to prevent atelectasis and pneumonia.
10. Monitor level of consciousness.
11. Initiate safety precautions such as side rails, a night light, and supervised ambulation.
12. Monitor intake and output.
13. Assess for urinary retention.
14. Instruct the client to take oral doses with milk or a snack to reduce gastric irritation.
15. Instruct the client to avoid alcohol.
16. Instruct the client to avoid activities that require alertness.
17. Assess bowel function for constipation, abdominal distension, and decreased peristalsis.
18. Evaluate the effectiveness of medication.
19. Have the opioid antagonist, oxygen, and resuscitation equipment available.

D. Morphine sulfate
1. Side effects
   a. Respiratory depression
   b. Orthostatic hypotension
   c. Urinary retention
   d. Nausea and vomiting
   e. Constipation
   f. Sedation, confusion, and hallucinations
   g. Cough suppression
   h. Reduction in pupillary size
   i. Miosis
2. Interventions
   a. Have naloxone (Narcan) available for overdose.
   b. Assess vital signs and level of consciousness.
   c. Compare rate and depth of respirations to baseline.
   d. Withhold the medication if the respiratory rate is less than 12 breaths/min; respirations

of less than 10 breaths/min can indicate respiratory distress.
   e. Monitor urinary output, which should be at least 30 mL/hr.
   f. Monitor bowel sounds for decreased peristalsis because constipation can occur.
   g. Monitor for pupil changes because pinpoint pupils can indicate morphine overdose.
   h. Avoid alcohol or CNS depressants because they can cause respiratory depression.
   i. Instruct the client to report dizziness or difficulty breathing.
   j. If taking sustained-release morphine, the client may need short-acting opioid doses for breakthrough pain.
   k. To administer morphine intravenously, dilute in at least 5 mL of sterile water for injection and administer at a rate of 15 mg or less over 4 to 5 minutes.
   l. Explain to client and family how and when to administer morphine and how to care for infusion equipment.

E. Meperidine hydrochloride (Demerol)
1. Side effects
   a. Respiratory depression
   b. Hypotension
   c. Tachycardia
   d. Drowsiness and confusion
   e. Constipation
   f. Urinary retention
   g. Nausea and vomiting
   h. Seizures
   i. Tremors
2. Interventions
   a. Monitor vital signs.
   b. Monitor for respiratory depression and hypotension.
   c. Have naloxone available for overdose.
   d. Monitor for urinary retention.
   e. Monitor bowel sounds and for constipation.
   f. To administer meperidine intravenously, dilute in at least 5 mL of sterile water or normal saline for injection and administer the dose over 4 to 5 minutes.

VII. OPIOID ANTAGONISTS
A. Opioid antagonists (Box 66-18) are used to treat respiratory depression from opioid overdose.
B. Interventions
1. Monitor blood pressure, pulse, and respiratory rate every 5 minutes initially, tapering to every 15 minutes, and then every 30 minutes until the client is stable.
2. Place the client on a cardiac monitor and monitor cardiac rhythm.
3. Auscultate breath sounds.
4. Have resuscitation equipment available.

BOX 66-18

Opioid Antagonists

Nalmefene (Revex)
Naloxone hydrochloride (Narcan)
Naltrexone (ReVia)

BOX 66-19

Osmotic Diuretics

Mannitol (Osmitrol)
Urea (Ureaphil)

5. Do not leave the client unattended.
6. Monitor the client closely for several hours because when the effects of the antagonist wears off, the client may again display signs of opioid overdose.

VIII. OSMOTIC DIURETICS

A. Description
   1. Osmotic diuretics (Box 66-19) increase osmotic pressure of the glomerular filtrate, inhibiting reabsorption of water and electrolytes.
   2. Osmotic diuretics are used for oliguria and to prevent renal failure, decrease intracranial pressure, and decrease intraocular pressure in clients with narrow-angle glaucoma.
   3. Mannitol is used with chemotherapy to induce diuresis.
B. Side effects
   1. Fluid and electrolyte imbalances
   2. Pulmonary edema from the rapid shifts of fluid
   3. Nausea and vomiting
   4. Headache
   5. Tachycardia from the rapid fluid loss
   6. Hyponatremia and dehydration
C. Interventions
   1. Monitor vital signs.
   2. Monitor weight.
   3. Monitor urine output.
   4. Monitor electrolyte levels.
   5. Monitor lungs and heart sounds for signs of pulmonary edema.
   6. Monitor for signs of dehydration.
   7. Monitor neurological status.
   8. Monitor for increased intraocular pressure.
   9. Assess for signs of decreasing intracranial pressure if appropriate.
   10. Change the client's position slowly to prevent orthostatic hypotension.
   11. Monitor for crystallization in the vial of mannitol before administering the medication; if crystallization is noted, do not administer the medication from that vial.

PRACTICE QUESTIONS

1. The nurse has given medication instructions to the client receiving phenytoin (Dilantin). The nurse determines that the client has an adequate understanding if the client states that:
   1. "Alcohol is not contraindicated while taking this medication."
   2. "Good oral hygiene is needed, including brushing and flossing."
   3. "The medication dose may be self-adjusted, depending on side effects."
   4. "The morning dose of the medication should be taken before a serum drug level is drawn."

2. The client with myasthenia gravis has become increasingly weaker. The physician prepares to identify whether the client is reacting to an overdose of the medication (cholinergic crisis) or an increasing severity of the disease (myasthenic crisis). An injection of edrophonium (Tensilon) is administered. Which of the following would indicate that the client is in cholinergic crisis?
   1. No change in the condition
   2. Complaints of muscle spasms
   3. An improvement of the weakness
   4. A temporary worsening of the condition

3. Carbidopa-levodopa (Sinemet) is prescribed for the client with Parkinson's disease. The nurse monitors the client for adverse reactions to the medication. Which of the following would indicate that the client is experiencing an adverse reaction?
   1. Pruritus
   2. Tachycardia
   3. Hypertension
   4. Impaired voluntary movements

4. The client is taking phenytoin (Dilantin) for seizure control. A sample is drawn to determine the serum drug level, and the nurse reviews the results. Which of the following would indicate a therapeutic serum drug range?
   1. 5 to 10 mcg/mL
   2. 10 to 20 mcg/mL
   3. 20 to 30 mcg/mL
   4. 30 to 40 mcg/mL

5. The nurse is preparing an intravenous infusion of phenytoin (Dilantin) as prescribed by the physician for the client with seizures. Which of the following solutions will the nurse plan to use to dilute this medication?
   1. Dextrose 5%
   2. Normal saline solution
   3. Lactated Ringer's solution
   4. Dextrose 5% and half-normal saline (0.45%)

6. The home health nurse visits a client who is taking phenytoin (Dilantin) for control of seizures. During

the assessment, the nurse notes that the client is taking birth control pills. Which of the following information should the nurse include in the teaching plan?

1. Pregnancy should be avoided while taking phenytoin.
2. The client may stop the medication if it is causing severe gastrointestinal effects.
3. There is the potential of decreased effectiveness of birth control pills while taking phenytoin.
4. There is the increased risk of thrombophlebitis while taking phenytoin and birth control pills together.

7. The nurse is caring for a client in the emergency room diagnosed with Bell's palsy. The client has been taking acetaminophen (Tylenol), and acetaminophen overdose is suspected. The nurse anticipates that the antidote to be prescribed is:
   1. Pentostatin (Nipent)
   2. Auranofin (Ridaura)
   3. Fludarabine (Fludara)
   4. Acetylcysteine (Mucomyst)

8. The client with trigeminal neuralgia tells the nurse that acetaminophen (Tylenol) is taken daily for the relief of generalized discomfort. Which laboratory value would indicate toxicity associated with the medication?
   1. Sodium level of 140 mEq/L
   2. Prothrombin time of 12 seconds
   3. Direct bilirubin level of 2 mg/dL
   4. Platelet count of 400,000/mm³

9. The client is suspected of having myasthenia gravis. Edrophonium (Tensilon) 2 mg is administered intravenously to determine the diagnosis. Which of the following indicates that the client has myasthenia gravis?
   1. Joint pain following administration of the medication
   2. Feelings of faintness, dizziness, hypotension, and signs of flushing in the client
   3. A decrease in muscle strength within 30 to 60 seconds following administration of the medication
   4. An increase in muscle strength within 30 to 60 seconds following administration of the medication

10. The client with epilepsy is taking the prescribed dose of phenytoin (Dilantin) to control seizures. Results of a phenytoin blood level study reveal a level of 35 mcg/mL. Which of the following symptoms would be expected as a result of this laboratory result?
    1. Nystagmus
    2. Tachycardia
    3. Slurred speech
    4. No symptoms, because this is a normal therapeutic level

11. The client arrives at the emergency department complaining of back spasms. The client states, "I have been taking two to three aspirin every 4 hours for the last week, and it hasn't helped my back." Aspirin intoxication is suspected, and the nurse assesses the client for which of the following?
    1. Tinnitus
    2. Diarrhea
    3. Constipation
    4. Photosensitivity

12. A client with trigeminal neuralgia is being treated with carbamazepine (Tegretol), 400 mg PO daily. Which of the following indicates that the client is experiencing an adverse reaction to the medication?
    1. Uric acid level, 5 mg/dL
    2. Sodium level, 140 mEq/L
    3. Blood urea nitrogen level, 15 mg/dL
    4. White blood cell count, 3000/mm³

13. The nurse is caring for a client receiving morphine sulfate 10 mg subcutaneously every 4 hours for pain. Because this medication has been prescribed for this client, which nursing action would be included in the plan of care?
    1. Encourage fluids.
    2. Monitor the client's temperature.
    3. Maintain the client in a supine position.
    4. Encourage the client to cough and deep-breathe.

14. Meperidine hydrochloride (Demerol) is prescribed for the client with pain. For which of the following would the nurse monitor as a side effect of this medication?
    1. Diarrhea
    2. Bradycardia
    3. Hypertension
    4. Urinary retention

15. The nurse is caring for a client with severe back pain. Codeine sulfate has been prescribed for the client. Which of the following does the nurse specifically include in the plan of care while the client is taking this medication?
    1. Monitor fluid balance.
    2. Monitor bowel activity.
    3. Monitor peripheral pulses.
    4. Monitor for hypertension.

ALTERNATE ITEM FORMAT: MULTIPLE RESPONSE

A client is receiving meperidine hydrochloride (Demerol) for pain. Select the side effects of this medication. Select all that apply.

❏ 1. Diarrhea
❏ 2. Tremors
❏ 3. Drowsiness
❏ 4. Hypotension
❏ 5. Urinary frequency
❏ 6. Increased respiratory rate

ANSWERS

1. **2**

Rationale: Typical anticonvulsant medication instructions include taking the prescribed daily dosage to keep the blood level of the drug constant and having a sample drawn for serum drug level before taking the morning dose. The client is taught not to stop the medication abruptly, to avoid alcohol, check with the physician before taking over-the-counter medications, avoid activities where alertness and coordination are required until medication effects are known, provide good oral hygiene, and obtain regular dental care. The client should also wear a Medic-Alert bracelet.

Test-Taking Strategy: Use the process of elimination. Using knowledge of general principles related to the medication administration will assist you in eliminating options 1 and 3. From the remaining options, recall that medications generally are not taken just before drawing therapeutic serum levels because the results would be artificially high. This leaves oral hygiene as the correct option because of the risk of gingival hyperplasia. Review client education related to phenytoin (Dilantin) if you had difficulty with this question.

Level of Cognitive Ability: Analysis
Client Needs: Physiological Integrity
Integrated Process: Nursing Process—evaluation
Content Area: Adult health—neurological
References: Ignatavicius, D., & Workman, M. (2006). *Medical-surgical nursing: Critical thinking for collaborative care* (5th ed., pp. 951-952). Philadelphia: W.B. Saunders.
Skidmore-Roth, L. (2005). *Mosby's drug guide for nurses* (6th ed., p. 691). St. Louis: Mosby.

2. **4**

Rationale: An edrophonium injection makes the client in cholinergic crisis temporarily worse. This in known as a negative Tensilon test.

Test-Taking Strategy: Use the process of elimination. Recalling that a cholinergic crisis indicates an overdose of medication, it seems reasonable that a worsening of the condition will occur when medication is administered. Review cholinergic crisis if you had difficulty with this question.

Level of Cognitive Ability: Analysis
Client Needs: Physiological Integrity
Integrated Process: Nursing Process—analysis
Content Area: Pharmacology
References: Chernecky, C., & Berger, B. (2004). *Laboratory tests and diagnostic procedures* (4th ed., pp. 1035-1036). Philadelphia: W.B. Saunders.
Mosby. (2007). *Mosby's 2007 nursing drug reference* (20th ed., p. 400). St. Louis: Mosby.

3. **4**

Rationale: Dyskinesia and impaired voluntary movement may occur with high levodopa dosages. Nausea, anorexia, dizziness, orthostatic hypotension, bradycardia, and akinesia (the temporary muscle weakness that lasts 1 minute to 1 hour, also known as "on-off phenomenon") is a frequent side effect of the medication.

Test-Taking Strategy: Use the process of elimination. Options 2 and 3 are comparative or alike and are cardiac-related options, so these options can be eliminated first. Note that the question asks for an adverse reaction; therefore, select option 4 over option 1 because it is related neurologically. Review the adverse effects of levodopa if you had difficulty with this question.

Level of Cognitive Ability: Analysis
Client Needs: Physiological Integrity
Integrated Process: Nursing Process—analysis
Content Area: Pharmacology
Reference: Hodgson, B., & Kizior, R. (2007). *Saunders nursing drug handbook 2007* (p. 186). Philadelphia: W.B. Saunders.

4. **2**

Rationale: The therapeutic serum drug level range for phenytoin is 10 to 20 mcg/mL.

Test-Taking Strategy: Use the process of elimination. A helpful Pyramid Point is to remember that the theophylline therapeutic range and the acetaminophen therapeutic range are the same as the phenytoin therapeutic range. Remembering this may assist you when answering questions related to these three medications. Review this medication if you had difficulty with this question.

Level of Cognitive Ability: Analysis
Client Needs: Physiological Integrity
Integrated Process: Nursing Process—analysis
Content Area: Pharmacology
Reference: Hodgson, B., & Kizior, R. (2007). *Saunders nursing drug handbook 2007* (p. 930). Philadelphia: W.B. Saunders.

5. **2**

Rationale: Intravenous infusion of phenytoin should be administered by injection into a large vein. The medication may be diluted in normal saline solution; however, dextrose solution should be avoided because of medication precipitation. The medication is administered as intermittent doses. Continuous intravenous infusions should not be used. Infusion rates of more than 50 mg/min may cause hypotension or cardiac dysrhythmias, especially in older and debilitated clients.

Test-Taking Strategy: Use the process of elimination. In most, but not all, situations, medications can be diluted in normal saline, so this would be the best option to select if you were unfamiliar with the intravenous administration of this medication. Review this procedure if you had difficulty with this question.

Level of Cognitive Ability: Application
Client Needs: Physiological Integrity
Integrated Process: Nursing Process—planning
Content Area: Pharmacology
Reference: Gahart, B., & Nazareno, A. (2006). *2006 intravenous medications* (22nd ed., p. 993). St. Louis: Mosby.

6. **3**

Rationale: Phenytoin enhances the rate of estrogen metabolism, which can decrease the effectiveness of some birth control pills. Options 1, 2, and 4 are inappropriate instructions.

Test-Taking Strategy: Use the process of elimination. Option 4 would cause anxiety in the client. A client should not be instructed to stop anticonvulsant medication, as indicated in option 2. Pregnancy does not need to be "avoided." Review medication interactions related to phenytoin if you had difficulty with this question.

Level of Cognitive Ability: Application
Client Needs: Physiological Integrity
Integrated Process: Teaching and Learning
Content Area: Pharmacology

References: Clayton, B., and Stock, Y. (2004) *Basic pharmacology for nurses* (13th ed., p. 272). St. Louis: Mosby.
Kee, J., Hayes, E., & McCuistion, L. (2006). *Pharmacology: A nursing process approach* (5th ed., p. 347). Philadelphia: W.B. Saunders.

7. 4
Rationale: The antidote for acetaminophen is acetylcysteine (Mucomyst). The normal therapeutic serum level of acetaminophen is 10 to 20 mcg/mL. A toxic level is higher than 50 mcg/mL, and levels higher than 200 mcg/mL could indicate hepatotoxicity. Auranofin (Ridaura) is a gold preparation used to treat rheumatoid arthritis. Fludarabine (Fludara) and pentostatin (Nipent) are antineoplastic agents.
Test-Taking Strategy: Use the process of elimination. Eliminate options 1 and 3 first because they are comparative or alike (antineoplastic agents). Recalling that auranofin is used to treat rheumatoid arthritis will direct you to option 4. Review the antidote for acetaminophen if you had difficulty with this question.
Level of Cognitive Ability: Analysis
Client Needs: Physiological Integrity
Integrated Process: Nursing Process—analysis
Content Area: Pharmacology
Reference: Hodgson, B., & Kizior, R. (2007). *Saunders nursing drug handbook 2007* (p. 13). Philadelphia: W.B. Saunders.

8. 3
Rationale: In adults, overdose of acetaminophen causes liver damage. Option 3 is an indicator of liver function and is the only option that indicates an abnormal laboratory value. The normal direct bilirubin level is 0 to 0.3 mg/dL. The normal platelet count is 150,000 to 400,000/mm³. The normal prothrombin time is 10 to 13 seconds. The normal sodium level is 135 to 145 mEq/L.
Test-Taking Strategy: Use the process of elimination. Knowledge that acetaminophen causes liver damage and knowledge of normal laboratory results will assist you in answering this question. Option 3 is the only abnormal value. Also, of all the options, the bilirubin level is the laboratory value most directly related to liver function. Review the effects of toxicity from acetaminophen and normal laboratory values if you had difficulty with this question.
Level of Cognitive Ability: Analysis
Client Needs: Physiological Integrity
Integrated Process: Nursing Process—analysis
Content Area: Pharmacology
References: Hodgson, B., & Kizior, R. (2007). *Saunders nursing drug handbook 2007* (p. 13). Philadelphia: W.B. Saunders.
Kee, J., Hayes, E., & McCuistion, L. (2006). *Pharmacology: A nursing process approach* (5th ed., pp. 326-327). Philadelphia: W.B. Saunders.
Mosby. (2007). *2007 Mosby's nursing drug reference* (20th ed, p. 76). St. Louis: Mosby.

9. 4
Rationale: Edrophonium is a short-acting acetylcholinesterase inhibitor used as a diagnostic agent. When a client with suspected myasthenia gravis is given 2 mg of the medication intravenously, an increase in muscle strength should be seen in 30 to 60 seconds. If no response occurs, another 4 to 10 mg of edrophonium is given over the next 2 minutes, and muscle strength is tested again. If no increase in muscle strength occurs with this higher dose, the muscle weakness is not caused by myasthenia gravis. Clients receiving injections of this medication commonly demonstrate a drop in blood pressure, feel faint and dizzy, and are flushed.
Test-Taking Strategy: Use the process of elimination. Recalling that the client with myasthenia gravis is treated with medication to improve muscle strength will assist in directing you to option 4. Review this medication as a diagnostic tool for suspected myasthenia gravis if you had difficulty with this question.
Level of Cognitive Ability: Analysis
Client Needs: Physiological Integrity
Integrated Process: Nursing Process—analysis
Content Area: Pharmacology
References: Chernecky, C., & Berger, B. (2004). *Laboratory tests and diagnostic procedures* (4th ed., pp. 1035-1036). Philadelphia: W.B. Saunders.
Gahart, B., & Nazareno, A. (2006). *2006 intravenous medications* (22nd ed., p. 470). St. Louis: Mosby.

10. 3
Rationale: The therapeutic phenytoin level is 10 to 20 mcg/mL. At a level higher than 20 mcg/mL, involuntary movements of the eyeballs (nystagmus) appears. At a level higher than 30 mcg/mL, ataxia and slurred speech occur.
Test-Taking Strategy: Use the process of elimination and knowledge regarding the therapeutic phenytoin level. From this point, you must know the symptoms that would be noted in the client when the phenytoin level is 35 mcg/mL. Remember that ataxia and slurred speech occur with levels higher than 30 mcg/mL. Review therapeutic levels and associated symptoms if you had difficulty with this question.
Level of Cognitive Ability: Analysis
Client Needs: Physiological Integrity
Integrated Process: Nursing Process—assessment
Content Area: Pharmacology
Reference: Hodgson, B., & Kizior, R. (2007). *Saunders nursing drug handbook 2007* (p. 929). Philadelphia: W.B. Saunders.

11. 1
Rationale: Mild intoxication with acetylsalicylic acid (aspirin) is called salicylism and is experienced commonly when the daily dosage is higher than 4 g. Tinnitus (ringing in the ears) is the most frequent effect noted with intoxication. Hyperventilation may occur because salicylate stimulates the respiratory center. Fever may result, because salicylate interferes with the metabolic pathways coupling oxygen consumption and heat production. Options 2, 3, and 4 are not associated specifically with toxicity.
Test-Taking Strategy: Use the process of elimination. Note that the question refers to aspirin intoxication. Options 2 and 3 relate to gastrointestinal symptoms, are comparative or alike, and are eliminated first. From the remaining options, you must know that tinnitus occurs. If you had difficulty with this question, review aspirin intoxication.
Level of Cognitive Ability: Analysis
Client Needs: Physiological Integrity
Integrated Process: Nursing Process—assessment
Content Area: Pharmacology
Reference: Hodgson, B., & Kizior, R. (2007). *Saunders nursing drug handbook 2007* (p. 95). Philadelphia: W.B. Saunders.

12. 4

Rationale: Adverse effects of carbamazepine appear as blood dyscrasias, including aplastic anemia, agranulocytosis, thrombocytopenia, leukopenia, cardiovascular disturbances, thrombophlebitis, dysrhythmias, and dermatological effects.

Test-Taking Strategy: Use the process of elimination. If you are familiar with normal laboratory values, you will note that the only option that indicates an abnormal value is option 4. Review the signs of adverse reactions related to this medication if you had difficulty with this question.

Level of Cognitive Ability: Analysis
Client Needs: Physiological Integrity
Integrated Process: Nursing Process—analysis
Content Area: Pharmacology
References: Mosby. (2007). *2007 Mosby's nursing drug reference* (20th ed., p. 220). St. Louis: Mosby.
Skidmore-Roth, L. (2005). *Mosby's drug guide for nurses* (6th ed., p. 137). St. Louis: Mosby.

13. 4

Rationale: Morphine sulfate suppresses the cough reflex. Clients need to be encouraged to cough and deep-breathe to prevent pneumonia. Options 1, 2, and 3 are not associated specifically with the use of this medication.

Test-Taking Strategy: Use the process of elimination. The question is asking specifically about a nursing action related to this medication. Recalling that morphine sulfate suppresses the cough reflex and the respiratory reflex will direct you to the correct option. Additionally, use the ABCs—airway, breathing, and circulation—when selecting the correct option. Review the nursing considerations when administering this medication if you had difficulty with this question.

Level of Cognitive Ability: Application
Client Needs: Physiological Integrity
Integrated Process: Nursing Process—planning
Content Area: Pharmacology
Reference: Hodgson, B., & Kizior, R. (2007). *Saunders nursing drug handbook 2007* (p. 797). Philadelphia: W.B. Saunders.

14. 4

Rationale: Side effects of meperidine (Demerol) include respiratory depression, orthostatic hypotension, tachycardia, drowsiness and mental clouding, constipation, and urinary retention.

Test-Taking Strategy: Use the process of elimination. Remember that a side effect of meperidine is urinary retention. Review the side effects of this medication if you had difficulty with this question.

Level of Cognitive Ability: Analysis
Client Needs: Physiological Integrity
Integrated Process: Nursing Process—assessment
Content Area: Pharmacology
References: Hodgson, B., & Kizior, R. (2007). *Saunders nursing drug handbook 2007* (p. 735). Philadelphia: W.B. Saunders.
Skidmore-Roth, L. (2005). *Mosby's drug guide for nurses* (6th ed., p. 531). St. Louis: Mosby.

15. 2

Rationale: While the client is taking codeine sulfate, the nurse would monitor vital signs and assess for hypotension. The nurse also should increase fluid intake, palpate the bladder for urinary retention, auscultate bowel sounds, and monitor the pattern of daily bowel activity and stool consistency. The nurse should monitor respiratory status and initiate deep-breathing and coughing exercises. Additionally, the nurse monitors the effectiveness of the pain medication.

Test-Taking Strategy: Use the process of elimination. Note the strategic word *specifically* and recall that codeine sulfate can cause constipation. If you had difficulty with this question, review nursing measures related to the administration of codeine sulfate.

Level of Cognitive Ability: Application
Client Needs: Physiological Integrity
Integrated Process: Nursing Process—planning
Content Area: Pharmacology
Reference: Skidmore-Roth, L. (2005). *Mosby's drug guide for nurses* (6th ed., p. 218). St. Louis: Mosby.

ALTERNATE ITEM FORMAT: MULTIPLE RESPONSE

Answer: 2, 3, 4

Rationale: Meperidine hydrochloride is a opioid analgesic. Side effects include respiratory depression, drowsiness, hypotension, constipation, urinary retention, nausea, vomiting, and tremors.

Test-Taking Strategy: Focus on the name of the medication. Recalling that this medication is an opioid analgesic and recalling the effects of an opioid analgesic will assist in identifying the side effects. Review the side effects of this medication if you had difficulty with this question.

Level of Cognitive Ability: Analysis
Client Needs: Physiological Integrity
Integrated Process: Nursing Process—assessment
Content Area: Pharmacology
Reference: Mosby. (2005). *Mosby's 2005 drug consult for nurses* (p. 812). St. Louis: Mosby.

REFERENCES

Black, J., & Hawks, J., (2005). *Medical-surgical nursing: Clinical management for positive outcomes* (7th ed.). Philadelphia: W.B. Saunders.

Chernecky, C., & Berger, B. (2004). *Laboratory tests and diagnostic procedures* (4th ed.). Philadelphia: W.B. Saunders.

Clayton, B., and Stock, Y. (2004) *Basic pharmacology for nurses* (13th ed.). St. Louis: Mosby.

Hodgson, B., & Kizior, R. (2007). *Saunders nursing drug handbook 2007*. Philadelphia: W.B. Saunders

Ignatavicius, D., & Workman, M. (2006). *Medical-surgical nursing: Critical thinking for collaborative care* (5th ed.). Philadelphia: W.B. Saunders.

Kee, J., Hayes, E., & McCuistion, L. (2006). *Pharmacology: A nursing process approach* (5th ed.). Philadelphia: W.B. Saunders.

McKenry, L., Hogan, M., and Tessier, E. (2005). *Mosby's pharmacology in nursing* (22nd ed.). St. Louis: Mosby.

Mosby. (2005). *Mosby's 2005 drug consult for nurses*. St. Louis: Mosby.

Mosby. (2007). *Mosby's 2007 nursing drug reference* (20th ed.). St. Louis: Mosby.

Skidmore-Roth, L. (2005). *Mosby's drug guide for nurses* (6th ed.). St. Louis: Mosby.

Skidmore-Roth, L. (2006) *Mosby's 2006 drug reference*. St. Louis: Mosby.

The Adult Client With a Musculoskeletal Disorder

PYRAMID TERMS

cast Stiff dressing or casting, made of plaster of Paris or synthetic material, to stabilize a part or parts of the body to encase an unstable or injured bone until healing occurs.

compartment syndrome Condition in which pressure increases in a confined anatomical space that leads to decreased blood flow, ischemia, and dysfunction of these tissues. Initial ischemia with pain, pallor, paresthesia, muscle weakness, and loss of pulses may progress to necrosis and permanent muscle cell dysfunction.

external fixation Stabilization of a fracture by the use of an external frame, with multiple pins applied through the bone.

fat embolism Sudden dislodgment of an embolus that is freed into the circulation, where it can lodge in a blood vessel and obstruct blood flow to tissue distal to the obstruction.

internal fixation Stabilization of a fracture that involves the application of screws, plates, pins, or nails to hold the fragments in alignment.

reduction Correction or realignment of a bone fracture or joint dislocation.

traction Exertion of a pulling force to a fractured bone or dislocated joint to establish and maintain correct alignment for healing and to decrease muscle spasms and pain.

▲ PYRAMID TO SUCCESS

The Pyramid to Success focuses on the emergency care for a client who sustains a fracture or other musculoskeletal injury, monitoring for complications related to fractures, and interventions if complications occur. Nursing care related to casts and traction is emphasized. Skill related to instructing the client in the use of an assistive device such as a cane, walker, or crutches is a Pyramid Point. Pyramid Points also include postopera-

tive care following hip surgery or amputation and care of the client with rheumatoid arthritis or osteoporosis. Focus on the points related to the psychosocial effects as a result of the musculoskeletal disorder, such as unexpected body image changes, and the appropriate and available support services needed for the client. The Integrated Processes addressed in this unit include Caring, Communication and Documentation, Nursing Process, and Teaching and Learning.

CLIENT NEEDS ▲

Safe and Effective Care Environment

Establishing priorities
Handling hazardous and infectious materials safely
Maintaining asepsis related to wounds
Maintaining confidentiality regarding disorder and plan of care
Maintaining standard and other precautions
Preventing accidents and injuries
Providing a dietary consultation
Providing informed consent for diagnostic treatments and surgical procedures
Providing physical therapy and occupational therapy referrals
Upholding client rights

Health Promotion and Maintenance

Discussing expected body image changes
Performing physical assessment related to the musculoskeletal system
Promoting health related to diet and activity
Preventing diseases that occur as a result of the aging process

Providing home care instructions regarding care related to a musculoskeletal disorder

Reinforcing the importance of prescribed therapy

Psychosocial Integrity

Assessing available support systems and use of community resources

Assessing the client's ability to cope with feelings of isolation and loss of independence

Considering cultural, religious, and spiritual influences

Discussing grief and loss related to mobility limitations and restrictions

Discussing situational role changes as a result of musculoskeletal disorder

Identifying unexpected body image changes as a result of injury or disease

Identifying sensory and perceptual alterations

Mobilizing coping mechanisms

Physiological Integrity

Identifying complications of a fracture

Identifying complications related to procedures or injuries

Providing care related to casts and traction

Promoting normal elimination patterns

Promoting self-care measures

Providing emergency care for a fracture or other injury

Providing measures to promote comfort

Teaching about the use of assistive devices for mobility such as canes, walkers, and crutches

Teaching pharmacological therapy

REFERENCES

Black, J., & Hawks, J., (2005). *Medical-surgical nursing: Clinical management for positive outcomes* (7th ed.). Philadelphia: W.B. Saunders.

Chernecky, C., & Berger, B. (2004). *Laboratory tests and diagnostic procedures* (4th ed.). Philadelphia: W.B. Saunders.

Harkreader, H., & Hogan, M. (2004). *Fundamentals of nursing: Caring and clinical judgment* (2nd ed.). Philadelphia: W.B. Saunders.

Ignatavicius, D., & Workman, M. (2006). *Medical-surgical nursing: Critical thinking for collaborative care* (5th ed.). Philadelphia: W.B. Saunders.

Jarvis, C. (2004). *Physical examination and health assessment* (4th ed.). St. Louis: W.B. Saunders.

Lewis, S., Heitkemper, M., & Dirksen, S. (2004). *Medical-surgical nursing: Assessment and management of clinical problems* (6th ed.). St. Louis: Mosby.

Lilley, L., Harrington, S., & Snyder, J. (2005). *Pharmacology and the nursing process* (4th ed.). St. Louis: Mosby.

Mosby. (2006). *Mosby's dictionary of medicine, nursing and health professions* (7th ed.). St. Louis: Mosby.

National Council of State Boards of Nursing (Eds.). (2007). *2007 NCLEX-RN® detailed test plan*. Chicago: Author.

Potter, P., & Perry, A. (2005). *Fundamentals of nursing* (6th ed.). St. Louis: Mosby.

Varcarolis, E., Carson, V., & Shoemaker, N. (2006). *Foundations of psychiatric mental health nursing: A clinical approach* (5th ed.). Philadelphia: W.B. Saunders.

Musculoskeletal System

I. ANATOMY AND PHYSIOLOGY

A. Skeleton
1. Axial portion
   a. Cranium
   b. Vertebrae
   c. Ribs
2. Appendicular portion
   a. Limbs
   b. Shoulders
   c. Hips

B. Types of bones (Box 67-1)
1. Spongy bone
   a. Spongy bone is located in the ends of long bones and the center of flat and irregular bones.
   b. Spongy bone can withstand forces applied in many directions.
2. Dense (compact) bone
   a. Dense bone covers spongy bone.
   b. Forms a cylinder around a central marrow cavity
   c. Can withstand force predominantly in one direction
3. Characteristics of the bones
   a. Support and protect structures of the body
   b. Provide attachments for muscles, tendons, and ligaments
   c. Contain tissue in the central cavities, which aids in the formation of blood cells
   d. Assist in regulating calcium and phosphate concentrations
4. Bone growth
   a. The length of bone growth results from the ossification of the epiphyseal cartilage at the ends of bones, and bone growth stops between the ages of 18 and 25 years.

   b. The width of bone growth results from the activity of osteoblasts; it occurs throughout life but slows down with aging.
   c. As aging occurs, bone resorption accelerates, decreasing bone mass and predisposing the client to injury.

C. Types of joints (Table 67-1)
1. Characteristics of joints
   a. Allow movement between bones
   b. Formed where two bones join
   c. Surfaces are covered with cartilage.
   d. Enclosed in a capsule
   e. Contain a cavity filled with synovial fluid
   f. Ligaments hold the bone and joint in the correct position.

BOX 67-1

Types of Bones

Long
Short
Flat
Irregular

TABLE 67-1

Types of Joints

Type	Description
Amphiarthrosis	Cartilaginous joint
	Slightly movable
Condyloid	Freely movable
	Allows frictionless, painless movement
Diarthrosis	Synovial joint
	Ball-and-socket joint
Synarthrosis	Fibrous or fixed joint
	No movement associated with these joints

---

g. Articulation is the meeting point of two or more bones.

2. Synovial fluid
   a. Found in the joint capsule
   b. Formed by the synovial membrane, which lines the joint capsule
   c. Lubricates the cartilage
   d. Provides a cushion against shocks

D. Muscles
   1. Characteristics of muscles
      a. Made up of bundles of muscle fibers
      b. Provide the force to move bones
      c. Assist in maintaining posture
      d. Assist with heat production
   2. Process of contraction and relaxation
      a. Muscle contraction and relaxation require large amounts of adenosine triphosphate.
      b. Contraction also requires calcium, which functions as a catalyst.
      c. Acetylcholine released by the motor end plate of the motor neuron initiates an action potential.
      d. Acetylcholine is then destroyed by acetylcholinesterase.
      e. Calcium is required to contract muscle fibers and acts as a catalyst for the enzyme needed for the sliding together action of actin and myosin.
      f. Following contraction, adenosine triphosphate transports calcium out to allow actin and myosin to separate and allow the muscle to relax.
   3. Skeletal muscles
      a. Skeletal muscles are attached to two bones and cross at least one joint.
      b. The point of origin is the point of attachment on the bone closest to the trunk.
      c. The point of insertion is the point of attachment on the bone farthest from the trunk.
      d. Skeletal muscles act in groups.
      e. Prime movers contract to produce movement.
      f. Antagonists relax.
      g. Synergists contract to stabilize body movement.
      h. Nerves activate and control the muscles.

E. Bone healing
   1. Description: Bone union or healing is the process that occurs after the integrity of a bone is interrupted.
   2. Three stages
      a. The fracture causes soft tissue edema and bleeding because of the vascularity of the bone; this blood solidifies into a hematoma over 48 to 72 hours.
      b. The postinjury blood supply is interrupted, leading to ischemia and necrosis of the bone around the injury site.
      c. Dead cells promote migration of osteoblasts and fibroblasts to the area and healing starts with the formation of fibrocartilage.
      d. Bone union begins as a callus forms with vascular and cellular proliferation surrounding the fracture site; this loose fibrous tissue, or callus, changes into bone over the next 3 to 6 months.
      e. Remodeling occurs as the excess bone tissue of the callus resorbs as time passes and weight-bearing activities are gradually increased; the time required for complete healing varies and is related to factors such as age, bone type, trauma severity, infection, and blood supply.

II. RISK FACTORS ASSOCIATED WITH MUSCULOSKELETAL DISORDERS (Box 67-2)

III. DIAGNOSTIC TESTS
   A. Radiography
      1. Description: Radiography is a commonly used procedure to diagnose disorders of the musculoskeletal system.
      2. Interventions
         a. Handle injured areas carefully and support ▲ extremities above and below the joint.
         b. Administer analgesics as prescribed before the procedure, particularly if the client is in pain.
         c. Remove any radiopaque objects, such as ▲ jewelry.
         d. Shield client's testes, ovaries, or pregnant ▲ abdomen.
         e. The client must lie still during a radiographic (x-ray) procedure.
         f. Inform the client that exposure to radiation is minimal and not dangerous.
         g. The health care provider is to wear a lead ▲ apron if staying in the room with the client.

BOX 67-2

Risk Factors Associated With Musculoskeletal Disorders

Autoimmune disorders
Calcium deficiency
Degenerative conditions
Falls
Hyperuricemia
Infection
Medications
Metabolic disorders
Neoplastic disorders
Obesity
Postmenopausal states
Trauma and injury

B. Arthrocentesis
1. Description: Arthrocentesis is used to diagnose joint inflammation and infection.
   a. Arthrocentesis involves aspirating synovial fluid, blood, or pus via a needle inserted into a joint cavity.
   b. Medication, such as corticosteroids, may be instilled into the joint if necessary to alleviate inflammation.
2. Interventions
   a. Obtain an informed consent.
   b. Apply an elastic compression bandage postprocedure as prescribed.
   c. Use ice to decrease pain and swelling.
   d. Pain may worsen after aspirating fluid from the joint.
   e. Pain can continue up to 2 days after administration of corticosteroids into a joint.
   f. Instruct the client to rest the joint for 8 to 24 hours postprocedure.
   g. Instruct the client to notify the physician if a fever or swelling of the joint occurs.
C. Arthrography
1. Description: Arthrography is used in unexplained joint pain or inflammation to diagnose trauma to the joint capsule or ligaments.
   a. Arthrography is a radiographic examination of the soft tissues of the joint structures.
   b. A local anesthetic is used for the procedure.
   c. A contrast medium or air is injected into the joint cavity, and the joint is moved through range of motion as a series of x-rays are taken.
2. Interventions
   a. Instruct the client to fast from food and fluids for 8 hours before the procedure as prescribed.
   b. Assess the client for allergies to iodine or shellfish before the procedure.
   c. Obtain an informed consent.
   d. Inform the client of the need to remain as still as possible, except when asked to reposition.
   e. Minimize the use of the joint for 12 hours after the procedure.
   f. Instruct the client that the joint may be edematous and tender for 1 to 2 days after the procedure and may be treated with ice packs and analgesics as prescribed.
   g. Instruct the client that if edema and tenderness last longer than 2 days to notify the physician.
   h. If knee arthrography was performed, an elastic compression wrap over the knee may be prescribed for 3 to 4 days and ice application to decrease pain and swelling.
   i. If air has been used for injection, crepitus may be felt in the joint for up to 2 days.

D. Arthroscopy
1. Description: Arthroscopy is used to diagnose acute and chronic disorders of the joint.
   a. Arthroscopy provides an endoscopic examination of various joints.
   b. Articular cartilage abnormalities can be assessed, loose bodies removed, and the cartilage trimmed.
   c. A biopsy may be performed during the procedure.
2. Interventions
   a. Instruct the client to fast for 8 to 12 hours before the procedure.
   b. Obtain an informed consent.
   c. Administer pain medication as prescribed postprocedure.
   d. Assess the neurovascular status of the affected extremity.
   e. An elastic compression bandage should be worn postprocedure for 2 to 4 days as prescribed.
   f. Instruct the client that walking without weight-bearing usually is permitted after sensation returns but to limit activity for 1 to 4 days as prescribed following the procedure.
   g. Instruct the client to elevate the extremity as often as possible for 2 days following the procedure and to place ice on the site to minimize swelling.
   h. Reinforce instructions regarding the use of crutches, which may be used for 5 to 7 days postprocedure for walking.
   i. Advise the client to notify the physician if fever or increased knee pain occurs or if edema continues for more than 3 days postprocedure.
E. Bone mineral density measurements
1. Dual-energy x-ray absorptiometry
   a. Dual-energy x-ray absorptiometry measures bone mass of the spine, other bones, and the total body.
   b. Radiation exposure is minimal.
   c. Dual-energy x-ray absorptiometry is used to diagnosis metabolic bone disease and to monitor changes in bone density with treatment.
   d. Inform the client that the procedure is painless.
   e. All metallic objects are removed before the test.
2. Quantitative ultrasound
   a. Quantitative ultrasound evaluates strength, density, and elasticity of various bones using ultrasound rather than radiation.
   b. Inform the client that the procedure is painless.

F. Bone scan
1. Description: A bone scan is used to identify, evaluate, and stage bone cancer before and after treatment.
   a. Radioisotope is injected intravenously and will collect in areas that indicate abnormal bone metabolism and some fractures, if they exist.
   b. The isotope is excreted in the urine and feces within 48 hours and is not harmful to others.
2. Interventions
   a. Hold fluids for 4 hours before the procedure.
   b. Obtain an informed consent.
   c. Remove all jewelry and metal objects.
   d. Following the injection of the radioisotope, the client must drink 32 oz of water (if not contraindicated) to promote renal filtering of the excess isotope.
   e. From 1 to 3 hours after the injection, have the client void to clear tracer from the bladder before the scanning procedure is completed.
   f. Inform the client of the need to lie supine during the procedure and that the procedure is not painful.
   g. No special precautions are required after the procedure because a minimal amount of radioactivity exists in the radioisotope.
   h. Monitor the injection site for redness and swelling.
   i. Encourage oral fluid intake following the procedure.
G. Bone or muscle biopsy
1. Description: Biopsy may be done during surgery or through aspiration or punch or needle biopsy.
2. Interventions
   a. Obtain an informed consent.
   b. Monitor for bleeding, swelling, hematoma, or severe pain.
   c. Elevate the site for 24 hours following the procedure to reduce edema.
   d. Apply ice packs as prescribed following the procedure to prevent the development of a hematoma and decrease site discomfort.
   e. Monitor for signs of infection following the procedure.
   f. Inform the client that mild to moderate discomfort is normal following the procedure.
H. Electromyography (EMG)
1. Description: EMG is used to evaluate muscle weakness.
   a. Electromyography measures electrical potential associated with skeletal muscle contractions.
   b. Needles are inserted into the muscle, and recordings of muscular electrical activity are traced on recording paper through an oscilloscope.
2. Interventions
   a. Obtain an informed consent.
   b. Instruct the client that the needle insertion is uncomfortable.
   c. Instruct the client not to take any stimulants or sedatives for 24 hours before the procedure.
   d. Inform the client that slight bruising may occur at the needle insertion sites.
   e. Mild analgesics can be used for the pain.
I. Myelography
1. Description: Myelography requires injection of dye or air into the subarachnoid space followed by radiography to detect abnormalities of the spinal cord and vertebrae.
2. Preprocedure interventions
   a. Obtain an informed consent.
   b. Provide hydration for at least 12 hours before the test.
   c. Assess client for allergies to iodine or seafood (shellfish).
   d. Premedicate for sedation as prescribed.
3. Postprocedure interventions
   a. Obtain vital signs and perform neurological assessment frequently as prescribed.
   b. If a water-base dye is used, elevate the head 15 to 30 degrees for 8 hours as prescribed.
   c. If an oil-based dye is used, the client's head may be kept flat or be elevated for 6 to 8 hours as preferred by the physician.
   d. If air contrast is used, keep the head lower than the trunk, as prescribed by the physician.
   e. Encourage fluids and monitor intake and output to validate dye excretion.

IV. INJURIES
A. Strains
1. Strains are an excessive stretching of a muscle or tendon.
2. Management involves cold and heat applications, exercise with activity limitations, anti-inflammatory medications, and muscle relaxants.
3. Surgical repair may be required for a severe strain (ruptured muscle or tendon).
B. Sprains
1. Sprains are an excessive stretching of a ligament, usually caused by a twisting motion, such as in a fall or step on an uneven surface.
2. Sprains are characterized by pain and swelling.
3. Management involves rest, ice, a compression bandage, and elevation to reduce swelling and provide joint support.

4. Casting may be required for moderate sprains to allow the tear to heal.
5. Surgery may be necessary for severe ligament damage.
C. Rotator cuff injuries
1. Musculotendinous or rotator cuff of the shoulder sustains a tear, usually as a result of trauma.
2. Injury is characterized by shoulder pain and the inability to maintain abduction of the arm at the shoulder (drop arm test).
3. Management involves nonsteroidal anti-inflammatory drugs (NSAIDs), physical therapy, sling support, and ice-heat applications.
4. Surgery may be required if medical management is unsuccessful or for those who have a complete tear.

V. FRACTURES
A. Description: A fracture is a break in the continuity of the bone caused by trauma, twisting as a result of muscle spasm or indirect loss of leverage, or bone decalcification and disease that result in osteopenia.
B. Types of fractures (Box 67-3)
C. Assessment of a fracture of an extremity
1. Pain or tenderness over the involved area
2. Decrease or loss of muscular strength or function
3. Obvious deformity of affected area

BOX 67-3
Types of Fractures

Closed or simple: Skin over the fractured area remains intact.
Comminuted: The bone is splintered or crushed, with three or more fragments.
Complete: The bone is separated completely by a break into two parts.
Compression: A fractured bone is compressed by other bone.
Depressed: Bone fragments are driven inward.
Greenstick: One side of the bone is broken and the other is bent; these fractures occur most commonly in children.
Impacted: A part of the fractured bone is driven into another bone.
Incomplete: The bone is partially broken.
Oblique: The break extends in an oblique direction.
Open or compound: The bone is exposed to air through a break in the skin, and soft tissue injury and infection are common.
Pathological: The fracture results from weakening of the bone structure by pathological processes such as neoplasia or osteomalacia; also called spontaneous fracture.
Spiral: The break partially encircles bone.
Transverse: The bone is fractured straight across.

---

4. Crepitation, erythema, edema, or bruising
5. Muscle spasm and neurovascular impairment
D. Initial care of a fracture of an extremity
1. Immobilize affected extremity with cast or splint.
2. If a compound (open) fracture exists, splint the extremity and cover the wound with a sterile dressing.
3. Assess neurovascular status of the extremity.
4. Interventions for a fracture (Box 67-4)
E. **Reduction** restores the bone to proper alignment.
1. Closed **reduction** is a nonsurgical intervention performed by manual manipulation.
   a. Closed **reduction** may be performed under local or general anesthesia.
   b. A **cast** may be applied following **reduction**.
2. Open **reduction** involves a surgical intervention.
   a. Fracture may be treated with **internal fixation** devices.
   b. The client may be placed in **traction** or a **cast** following the procedure.
F. Fixation
1. **Internal fixation** follows an open **reduction** (Fig. 67-1).
   a. **Internal fixation** involves the application of screws, plates, pins, or intramedullary rods to hold the fragments in alignment.
   b. **Internal fixation** may involve the removal of damaged bone and replacement with a prosthesis.
   c. **Internal fixation** provides immediate bone strength.
2. **External fixation** is the use of an external frame to stabilize a fracture by attaching skeletal pins through bone fragments to a rigid external support (Fig. 67-2)
   a. **External fixation** provides more freedom of movement than with **traction.**
   b. Monitor pin stability and provide pin care to decrease infection risks.
   c. Risk of infection exists with both fixation methods.
   d. **External fixation** is commonly used when massive tissue trauma is present.
G. **Traction** (Fig. 67-3)
1. Description
   a. **Traction** is the exertion of a pulling force applied in two directions to reduce and immobilize a fracture.

BOX 67-4
Interventions for a Fracture

Reduction
Fixation
Traction
Cast

b. **Traction** provides proper bone alignment and reduces muscle spasms.

2. Interventions
   a. Maintain proper body alignment.
   b. Ensure that the weights hang freely and do not touch the floor.

c. Do not remove or lift the weights without a physician's order
d. Ensure that pulleys are not obstructed and that ropes in the pulleys move freely.
e. Place knots in the ropes to prevent slipping.
f. Check the ropes for fraying.

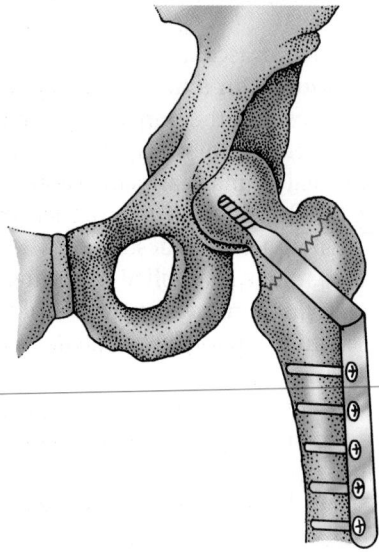

FIG. 67-1   A compression hip screw used for open reduction with internal fixation. (From Ignatavicius, D., & Workman, M. [2006]. *Medical-surgical nursing: Critical thinking for collaborative care* [5th ed.]. Philadelphia: W.B. Saunders.)

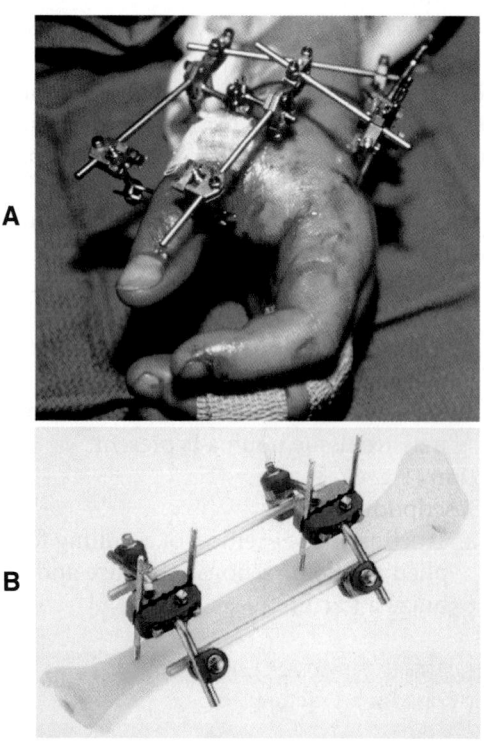

FIG. 67-2   External fixators. **A,** Mini-Hoffman system in use on hand. **B,** Hoffman II on the tibia (standard system). From Lewis, S., Heitkemper, M., & Dirksen, S. [2004]. *Medical-surgical nursing: Assessment and management of clinical problems* [6th ed.]. St. Louis: Mosby.)

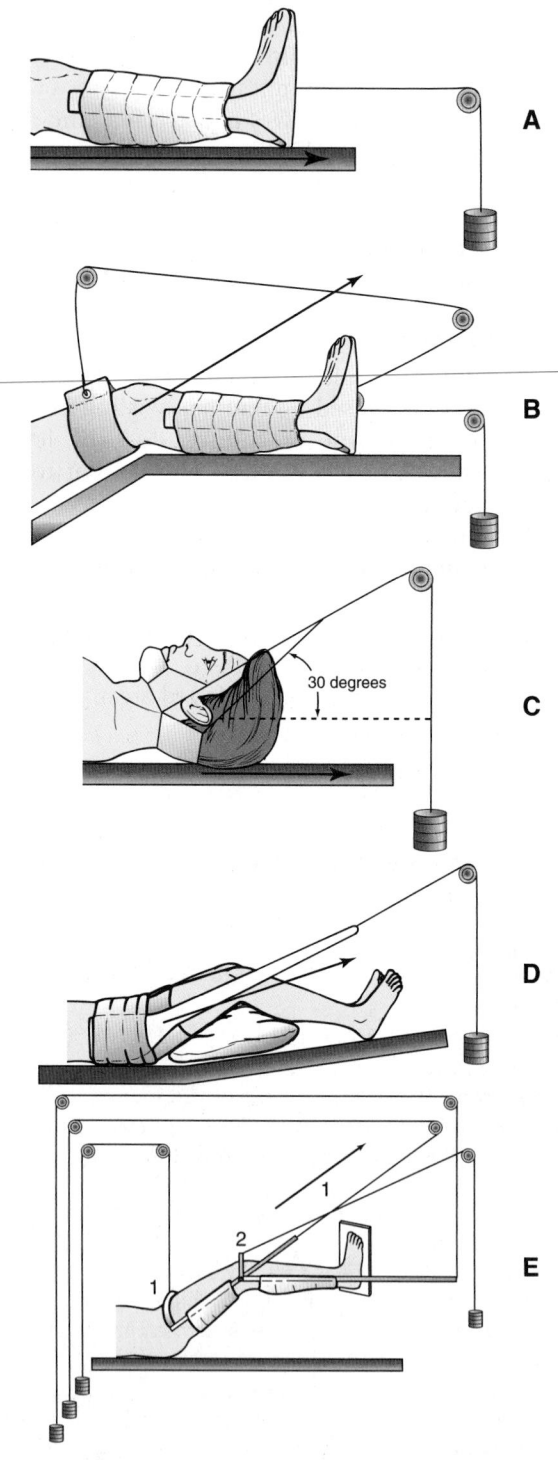

FIG. 67-3   Types of traction. **A,** Buck's traction. **B,** Russell's traction. **C,** Head halter traction. **D,** Pelvic traction. **E,** Balanced suspension traction. (From Lewis, S., Heitkemper, M., & Dirksen, S. [2004]. *Medical-surgical nursing: Assessment and management of clinical problems* [6th ed.]. St. Louis: Mosby.)

H. Skeletal **traction** (Fig. 67-4)
1. Description: **Traction** is applied mechanically to the bone with pins, wires, or tongs.
2. Interventions
   a. Monitor color, motion, and sensation of the affected extremity.
   b. Monitor the insertion sites for redness, swelling, drainage, or increased pain.
   c. Provide insertion site care as prescribed.
3. Cervical tongs and a halo fixation device. See Chap. 65 regarding care of the client with these types of devices.
I. Skin **traction** (Box 67-5)
1. Description: Skin **traction** is applied by using elastic bandages or adhesive.
2. Cervical skin **traction** relieves muscle spasms and compression in the upper extremities and neck (see Fig. 67-3).
   a. Cervical skin **traction** uses a head halter and chin pad to attach the **traction**.
   b. Use powder to protect the ears from friction rub.
   c. Position the client with the head of the bed elevated 30 to 40 degrees, and attach the weights to a pulley system over the head of the bed.
3. Buck's (extension) skin **traction** is used to alleviate muscle spasms and immobilize a lower limb by maintaining a straight pull on the limb with the use of weights (see Fig. 67-3).
   a. A boot appliance is applied to attach to the **traction**.
   b. The weights are attached to a pulley; allow the weights to hang freely over the edge of bed.

c. Not more than 8 to 10 lb of weight should be applied.
d. Elevate the foot of the bed to provide the **traction**.
4. Russell's skin **traction**. See Chap. 43 regarding information related to these types of **traction**.
5. Pelvic skin **traction** is used to relieve low back, hip, or leg pain or to reduce muscle spasm (see Fig. 67-3).
   a. Apply the **traction** snugly over the pelvis and iliac crest and attach to the weights.
   b. Use measures as prescribed to prevent the client from slipping down in bed.
J. Balanced suspension **traction** (see Fig. 67-3)
1. Description
   a. Balanced suspension **traction** is used with skin or skeletal **traction**.
   b. Used to approximate fractures of the femur, tibia, or fibula
   c. Balanced suspension **traction** is produced by a counterforce other than client.
2. Interventions
   a. Position the client in a low Fowler's position on either the side or the back.
   b. Maintain a 20-degree angle from the thigh to the bed.
   c. Protect the skin from breakdown.

BOX 67-5
Types of Skin Traction

Buck's traction
Cervical traction
Pelvic traction
Russell's traction

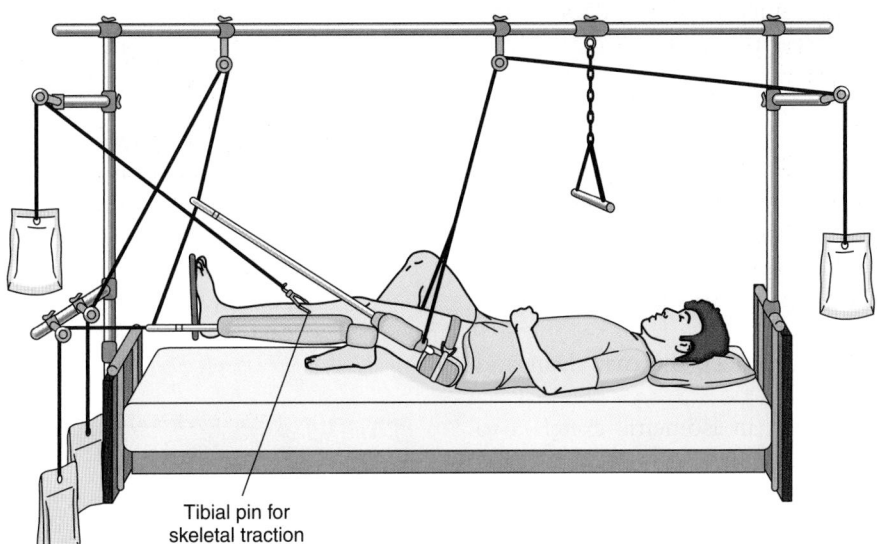

Tibial pin for skeletal traction

FIG. 67-4 Balanced suspension with a Thomas splint and Pearson attachment. The apparatus can be used alone or, as in this case, with skeletal traction. (From Phipps, W., Monahan, F., Sands, J., et al. [2003]. *Medical-surgical nursing: health and illness perspectives* [7th ed.]. St. Louis: Mosby.)

d. Provide pin care if pins are used with the skeletal **traction.**

e. Clean the pin sites with sterile normal saline and hydrogen peroxide or povidone-iodine (Betadine) as prescribed or per agency policy.

K. Dunlop's **traction**

1. Description: Horizontal **traction** is used to align fractures of the humerus; vertical **traction** maintains the forearm in proper alignment.

2. Interventions: Nursing care is similar to that for Buck's skin **traction.**

L. **Casts**

1. Description: Plaster or fiberglass **casts** are used to immobilize bones and joints into correct alignment after a fracture or injury.

2. Interventions

   a. Keep the **cast** and extremity elevated.

   b. Allow a wet **cast** 24 to 72 hours to dry (synthetic **casts** dry in 20 minutes).

   c. Handle a wet **cast** with the palms of the hands until dry.

   d. Turn the extremity every 1 to 2 hours, unless contraindicated, to allow air circulation and promote drying of the **cast.**

   e. A hair dryer can be used on a cool setting to dry a plaster **cast** (heat cannot be used on a plaster **cast** because the **cast** heats up and burns the skin).

   f. Monitor the extremity for circulatory impairment such as pain, swelling, discoloration, tingling, numbness, coolness, or diminished pulse.

   g. Notify the physician immediately if circulatory compromise occurs.

   h. Prepare for bivalving or cutting the **cast** if circulatory impairment occurs.

   i. Petal the **cast**; maintain smooth edges around the **cast** to prevent crumbling of the **cast** material.

   j. Monitor for signs of infection such as temperature, hot spots on the **cast**, foul odor, or changes in pain.

   k. If an open draining area exists on the affected extremity, the physician will make a cutout portion of the **cast** or a window.

   l. Instruct the client not to stick objects inside the **cast.**

   m. Teach the client to keep the **cast** clean and dry.

   n. Instruct the client in isometric exercises to prevent muscle atrophy.

VI. COMPLICATIONS OF FRACTURES (Box 67-6)

A. **Fat embolism**

1. Description: A **fat embolism** originates in the bone marrow and occurs after a fracture when a fat globule is released into the bloodstream.

   a. Clients with long bone fractures are at the greatest risk for the development of a **fat embolism.**

   b. **Fat embolism** can occur within the first 48 to 72 hours following the injury.

2. Assessment: Findings often suggest pulmonary embolism.

   a. Restlessness, hypoxemia, or mental status changes

   b. Tachycardia and hypotension

   c. Dyspnea and tachypnea

   d. Petechial rash over the upper chest and neck

3. Interventions

   a. Notify the physician immediately while initiating emergency care.

   b. Treat symptoms as prescribed to prevent respiratory failure and death.

   c. Corticosteroids may be given to reduce pulmonary injury.

B. **Compartment syndrome**

1. Description

   a. Tough fascia surrounds muscle groups, forming compartments from which arteries, veins, and nerves enter and exit opposite ends.

   b. **Compartment syndrome** occurs when pressure increases within one or more compartments, leading to decreased blood flow, tissue ischemia, and neurovascular impairment.

   c. Within 4 to 6 hours after the onset of **compartment syndrome,** neurovascular damage is irreversible if not treated.

2. Assessment

   a. Unrelieved or increased pain in the limb

   b. Tissue that is distal to the involved area becomes pale, dusky, or edematous.

   c. Pain with passive movement and joint dysfunction

   d. Pulselessness and loss of sensation (paresthesia)

3. Interventions

   a. Notify the physician immediately and prepare to assist physician.

   b. If severe, assist the physician with fasciotomy to relieve pressure and restore tissue perfusion.

   c. Loosen tight dressings or bivalve restrictive **cast** as prescribed.

BOX 67-6

Complications of Fractures

Avascular necrosis
Compartment syndrome
Fat embolism
Infection and osteomyelitis
Pulmonary embolism

C. Infection and osteomyelitis
1. Description: Infection and osteomyelitis can be caused by the introduction of organisms into bones initially leading to localized bone infection.
2. Assessment
   a. Tachycardia and fever (usually above 101° F).
   b. Erythema and pain in the area surrounding the infection
   c. Leukocytosis and elevated erythrocyte sedimentation rate (ESR)
3. Interventions
   a. Notify the physician.
   b. Prepare to initiate aggressive, long-term intravenous antibiotic therapy.
   c. Administer hyperbaric oxygen therapy to promote healing.
   d. Surgery is performed for resistant osteomyelitis with sequestrectomy and/or bone grafts.

D. Avascular necrosis
1. Description: Avascular necrosis occurs when a fracture interrupts the blood supply to a section of bone, leading to bone death.
2. Assessment
   a. Pain
   b. Decreased sensation
3. Interventions
   a. Notify the physician if pain or numbness occurs.
   b. Prepare the client for removal of necrotic tissue because it serves as a focus for infection.

E. Pulmonary embolism
1. Description: Pulmonary embolism is caused by the movement of foreign particles (blood clot, fat, or air) into the pulmonary circulation.
2. Assessment
   a. Restlessness and apprehension
   b. Sudden onset of dyspnea and chest pain
   c. Cough, hemoptysis, hypoxemia, or crackles
3. Interventions
   a. Notify the physician if signs of emboli are present.
   b. Give oxygen and IV anticoagulant therapy if prescribed.

VII. **CRUTCH WALKING**
A. Description
1. An accurate measurement of the client for crutches is important because an incorrect measurement could damage the brachial plexus.
2. The distance between the axillas and the arm pieces on the crutches should be two to three fingerwidths in the axilla space.
3. The elbows should be slightly flexed, 20 to 30 degrees, when the client is walking.
4. When ambulating with the client, stand on the affected side.
5. Instruct the client never to rest the axilla on the axillary bars.
6. Instruct the client to look up and outward when ambulating and to place the crutches 6 to 10 inches diagonally in front of the foot.
7. Instruct the client to stop ambulation if numbness or tingling in the hands or arms occurs.
B. Crutch gaits (Table 67-2)
C. Assisting the client with crutches to sit and stand
1. Place the unaffected leg against the front of the chair.
2. Move the crutches to the affected side, and grasp the arm of the chair with the hand on the unaffected side.

TABLE 67-2

Crutch Gaits

Type of Gait	Use	Procedure
Two-point gait	Used with partial weight-bearing limitations and with bilateral lower extremity prostheses	The crutch on one side and the opposite foot are advanced at the same time.
Three-point gait	Used for partial weight-bearing or no weight-bearing on the affected leg; requires that the client have strength and balance	Both crutches and the foot of the affected extremity are advanced together, followed by the foot of the unaffected extremity.
Four-point gait	Used if weight-bearing is allowed and one foot can be placed in front of the other	The right crutch is advanced, then the left foot, then the left crutch, and then the right foot.
Swing-to gait	Used when there is adequate muscle power and balance in the arms and legs	Both crutches are advanced together, then both legs are lifted and placed down on a spot behind the crutches. The feet and crutches form a tripod.
Swing-through gait	Used when there is adequate muscle power and balance in the arms and legs.	Both crutches are advanced together; then both legs are lifted through and beyond the crutches and placed down again at a point in front of the crutches.

Modified from Linton, A., & Maebius, N. (2003). *Introduction to medical-surgical nursing* (3rd ed.). Philadelphia: W.B. Saunders.

3. Flex the knee of the unaffected leg to lower self into the chair while placing the affected leg straight out in front.
4. Reverse the steps to move from a sitting to standing position.

D. Going up and down stairs
1. Up the stairs
   a. The client moves the unaffected leg up first.
   b. The client moves the affected leg and the crutches up.
2. Down the stairs
   a. The client moves the crutches and the affected leg down.
   b. The client moves the unaffected leg down.

VIII. CANES AND WALKERS

A. Description: Canes and walkers are made of a lightweight material with a rubber tip at the bottom.

B. Interventions
1. Stand at the affected side of the client when ambulating.
2. The handle should be at the level of the client's greater trochanter.
3. The client's elbow should be flexed at a 15- to 30-degree angle.
4. Instruct the client to hold the cane 4 to 6 inches to the side of the foot.
5. Instruct the client to hold the cane in the hand on the unaffected side so that the cane and weaker leg can work together with each step.
6. Instruct the client to move the cane at the same time as the affected leg.
7. Instruct the client to inspect the rubber tips regularly for worn places.

C. Hemicanes or quadripod canes
1. Hemicanes or quadripod canes are used for clients who have the use of only one upper extremity.
2. Hemicanes provide more security than a quadripod cane; however, both types provide more security than a single-tipped cane.
3. Position the cane at the client's unaffected side, with the straight, nonangled side adjacent to the body.
4. Position the cane 6 inches from client's side, with the hand grip level with the greater trochanter.

D. Walker
1. Stand adjacent to the client on the affected side.
2. Instruct the client to put all four points of the walker flat on the floor before putting weight on the hand pieces.
3. Instruct the client to move the walker forward and walk into it.

IX. FRACTURED HIP

A. Types
1. Intracapsular (femoral head is broken within the joint).

a. Femoral head and neck receive decreased blood supply and heal slowly.
b. Skin **traction** is applied preoperatively to reduce fracture and immobilize bone.
c. Treatment includes a total hip replacement or open **reduction internal fixation** with femoral head replacement (Fig. 67-5).
d. To prevent hip displacement postoperatively, avoid extreme hip flexion.

2. Extracapsular
a. Fracture can occur at the greater trochanter or can be an intertrochanteric fracture.
b. Trochanteric fracture is outside the joint.
c. Preoperative treatment includes balanced suspension **traction** or skin **traction** to relieve muscle spasms and reduce pain.
d. Avoid extreme hip flexion to prevent joint displacement.
e. Surgical treatment includes open **reduction internal fixation** with nail plate, screws, pins, or wires

B. Postoperative interventions
1. Maintain leg and hip in proper alignment and prevent internal or external rotation.
2. Turn client to unaffected side and only affected side as prescribed by physician.
3. Elevate the head of the bed 30 to 45 degrees for meals only.
4. Assist the client to ambulate with weight-bearing as prescribed by the physician.
5. Avoid weight-bearing on the affected leg as prescribed; instruct the client in the use of a walker to avoid weight-bearing.
6. Weight-bearing is often restricted after an open **reduction internal fixation** (ORIF) and unre-

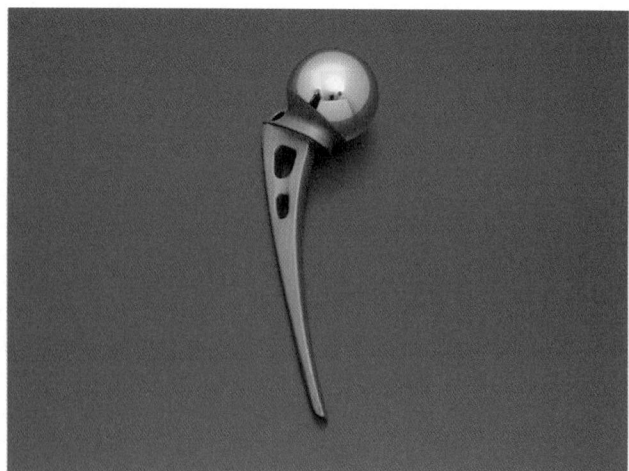

FIG. 67-5 Moore prosthesis, used for hip fractures. (From Ignatavicius, D., & Workman, M. [2006]. *Medical-surgical nursing: Critical thinking for collaborative care* [5th ed.]. Philadelphia: W.B. Saunders. Courtesy of Smith & Nephew, Inc., Orthopaedics Divisions, Memphis, TN.)

stricted after total hip arthroplasty (THA); always refer to physician's orders.

7. Keep the operative leg extended, supported, and elevated when getting client out of bed.
8. Avoid hip flexion greater than 90 degrees and avoid low chairs when out of bed.
9. Monitor for wound infection or hemorrhage.
10. Neurovascular assessment of affected extremity: Check color, pulses, capillary refill, movement, and sensation.
11. Maintain the compression of the Hemovac or Jackson-Pratt drain to facilitate wound drainage.
12. Monitor and record drainage amount, which decreases consistently about 80 mL every 8 hours until 48 hours postoperatively.
13. Carry out postoperative blood salvage to collect, filter, and reinfuse salvaged blood into the client.
14. Use antiembolism stockings or sequential compression stockings; encourage the client to flex and extend the feet to reduce the risk of deep vein thrombosis (DVT).
15. Instruct the client to avoid crossing the legs and activities that require bending over.
16. Physical therapy will be instituted postoperatively with progressive ambulation as prescribed by the physician.

X. TOTAL KNEE REPLACEMENT
A. Description: Total knee replacement is the implantation of a device to substitute for the femoral condyles and the tibial joint surfaces.
B. Postoperative interventions
   1. Monitor surgical incision for drainage and infection.
   2. Maintain the Hemovac or Jackson-Pratt drain if in place.
   3. Begin continuous passive motion 24 to 48 hours postoperatively as prescribed to exercise the knee and provide moderate flexion and extension.
   4. Administer analgesics before continuous passive motion to decrease pain.
   5. The leg should not be dangled to prevent dislocation.
   6. Prepare the client for out of bed activities as prescribed.
   7. Avoid weight-bearing and instruct the client in crutch walking.
   8. Postoperative blood salvage to collect, filter, and reinfuse salvaged blood into client may be prescribed.

XI. JOINT DISLOCATION AND SUBLUXATION
A. Dislocation: Injury of the ligaments surrounding a joint, which leads to displacement or separating of the articular surfaces of the joint

B. Subluxation: Incomplete displacement of joint surfaces when forces disrupt the soft tissue that surrounds the joints
C. Assessment
   1. Asymmetry of the contour of affected body parts
   2. Pain, tenderness, dysfunction, and swelling
   3. Complications include neurovascular compromise, avascular necrosis, and open joint injuries.
   4. X-rays are taken to determine joint shifting.
D. Interventions
   1. Focus of treatment includes pain relief, joint support, and joint protection.
   2. Immediate treatment is done to reduce the dislocation and realign the dislocated joint.
   3. Open or closed **reduction** is done with a post-procedural joint immobilization.
   4. Intravenous conscience sedation, local, or general anesthesia is used during joint manipulation.
   5. Initial activity restriction is followed by gentle range-of-motion activities and a gradual return of activities to normal levels while supporting the affected joint.
   6. A weakened joint is prone to recurrent dislocation and may require extended activity restriction.

XII. HERNIATION: INTERVERTEBRAL DISK
A. Description: Nucleus of the disk protrudes into the annulus, causing nerve compression.
B. Cervical disk herniation occurs at C5 to C6 and C6 to C7 interspaces.
   1. Cervical disk herniation causes pain radiation to shoulders, arms, hands, scapulae, and pectoral muscles.
   2. Motor and sensory deficits can include paresthesia, numbness, and weakness of the upper extremities.
   3. Interventions
      a. Conservative management is used unless client develops signs of neurological deterioration.
      b. Bed rest is prescribed to decrease pressure, inflammation, and pain.
      c. Immobilize the cervical area with cervical collar, **traction,** or brace.
      d. Apply heat to reduce muscle spasms and apply ice to reduce inflammation and swelling.
      e. Maintain the head and spine alignment.
      f. Instruct the client in the use of analgesics, sedatives, anti-inflammatory agents, and corticosteroids as prescribed.
      g. Prepare the client for a corticosteroid injection into the epidural space if prescribed.
      h. Assist and instruct client in the use of cervical collar or cervical **traction** as prescribed.

4. Cervical collar is used for cervical disk herniation.
   a. A cervical collar limits neck movement and holds the head in a neutral or slightly flexed position.
   b. The cervical collar may be worn intermittently or 24 hours daily.
   c. Inspect the skin under the collar for irritation.
   d. When prescribed and after pain decreases, exercises are prescribed to strengthen the muscles.
5. Client education related to cervical disk conditions
   a. Avoid flexing, extending, and rotating neck.
   b. Avoid prone position and maintain neck, spine, and hips in neutral position while sleeping.
   c. Minimize long periods of sitting.
   d. Instruct the client regarding medications such as analgesics, sedatives, anti-inflammatory agents, and corticosteroids.

C. Lumbar disk herniation most often occurs at L4 to L5 or L5 to S1 interspace.
   1. Herniation produces muscle weakness, sensory deficits, and diminished tendon reflexes.
   2. The client experiences pain and muscle spasms in the lower back, with radiation of the pain into one hip and down the leg (sciatica).
   3. Pain is relieved by bed rest and aggravated by movement, lifting, straining, and coughing.
   4. Interventions
      a. Conservative management is indicated unless neurological deterioration or bowel and bladder dysfunction occurs.
      b. Apply moist heat to decrease muscle spasms and apply ice to decrease inflammation.
      c. Instruct the client to sleep on the side, with the knees and hips flexed, and place a pillow between the legs.
      d. Apply pelvic **traction** as prescribed to relieve muscle spasms and decrease pain.
      e. Begin progressive ambulation as inflammation, edema, and pain subside.
   5. Client education related to lumbar disk conditions
      a. Instruct the client in the use of prescribed medications such as analgesics, muscle relaxants, anti-inflammatory agents, or corticosteroids.
      b. Instruct the client about application techniques for corsets or braces to maintain immobilization and proper spine alignment.
      c. Instruct the client in correct posture while sitting, standing, walking, and working.
      d. Instruct the client in the correct technique to use when lifting objects such as bending

knees, maintaining a straight back, and avoiding lifting objects above the elbow.
      e. Instruct in weight control program as prescribed.
      f. Instruct the client in an exercise program to strengthen back and abdominal muscles as prescribed.

D. Disk surgery is used when spinal cord compression is suspected or client's symptoms do not respond to conservative treatment (Box 67-7).
   1. Preoperative interventions
      a. Routine preoperative instructions related to postoperative care.
      b. Instruct the client about logrolling and range-of-motion exercises.
   2. Postoperative interventions: Cervical disk
      a. Monitor for respiratory difficulty from inflammation or hematoma.
      b. Encourage coughing, deep breathing, and early ambulation as prescribed.
      c. Monitor for hoarseness and inability to cough effectively because this may indicate laryngeal nerve damage.
      d. Use throat sprays or lozenges for sore throat, avoiding anesthetic lozenges that may numb the throat and increase choking risks.
      e. Monitor the surgical wound for infection, swelling, redness, drainage, or pain.
      f. Provide a soft diet if the client complains of dysphagia.
      g. Monitor for sudden return of radicular pain, which may indicate cervical spine instability.
   3. Postoperative interventions: Lumbar disk
      a. Monitor for wound hemorrhage.
      b. Monitor lower extremities for sensation, movement, color, temperature, and paresthesia.
      c. Monitor for urinary retention, paralytic ileus, and constipation that can result from decreased movement, narcotic administration, or spinal cord compression.
      d. Prevent constipation by encouraging a high-fiber diet, increased fluid intake, and stool softeners as prescribed.
      e. Administer opioids and sedatives as prescribed to relieve pain and anxiety.

BOX 67-7

Types of Disk Surgery

Diskectomy: Removal of herniated disk tissue and related matter
Diskectomy with fusion: Fusion of vertebrae with bone graft
Laminectomy: Excision of part of the vertebra (lamina) to remove the disk
Laminotomy: Division of the lamina of a vertebra

f. Assist and instruct the client to apply a prescribed back brace or corset with cotton underwear to prevent skin irritation.

4. Postoperative lumbar disk positioning concerns
   a. In the immediate postoperative period, the client may be expected to lie supine or have other activity restrictions depending on specific surgical intervention.
   b. Instruct the client in correct logrolling techniques for turning and to use when getting out of bed.
   c. Instruct the client to avoid spinal flexion or twisting and that the spine should be kept aligned.
   d. Instruct the client to minimize sitting, which may place a strain on the surgical site.
   e. When the client is lying supine, place a pillow under the neck and slightly flex the knees.
   f. Avoid extreme hip flexion when lying on side

XIII. AMPUTATION OF A LOWER EXTREMITY

A. Description: Amputation (Fig. 67-6) is the surgical removal of a lower limb or part of the limb.

B. Postoperative interventions
   1. Monitor vital signs.
   2. Monitor for infection and hemorrhage.
   3. Mark bleeding and drainage on the dressing if it occurs.

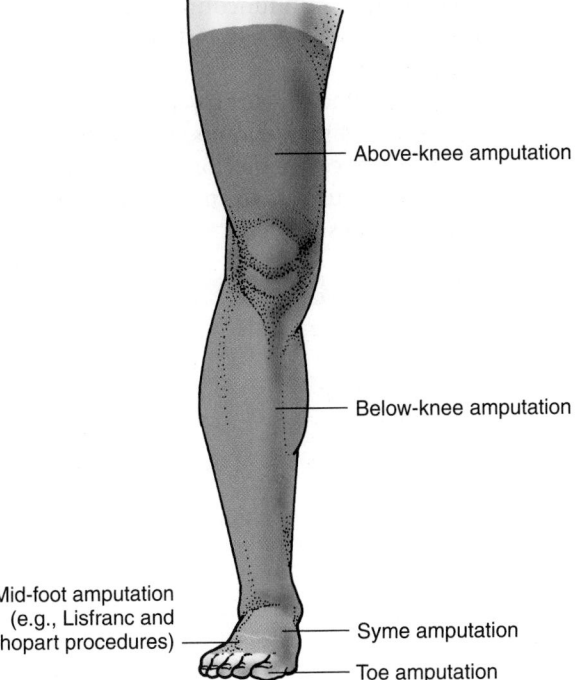

Above-knee amputation

Below-knee amputation

Mid-foot amputation (e.g., Lisfranc and Chopart procedures)

Syme amputation

Toe amputation

FIG. 67-6 Common levels of lower extremity amputation. (From Ignatavicius, D., & Workman, M. [2006]. *Medical-surgical nursing: Critical thinking for collaborative care* [5th ed.]. Philadelphia: W.B. Saunders.)

4. Keep a tourniquet at the bedside.
5. Observe for and prevent contractures, which can result from prolonged residual limb elevation.
6. Monitor for signs of infection, necrosis, and neuroma.
7. Evaluate for phantom limb sensation and pain; explain sensation and pain to the client, and medicate the client as prescribed.
8. First 24 hours: Elevate the foot of the bed to reduce edema; then keep the bed flat to prevent hip flexion contractures, if prescribed by the physician.
9. After 24 to 48 hours postoperatively, position the client prone to stretch the muscles and prevent hip flexion contractures, if prescribed.
10. Do not elevate the residual limb on a pillow, which also prevents hip flexion contractures.
11. Maintain surgical application of dressing, elastic compression wrap, or elastic stump (residual limb) shrinker as prescribed to reduce swelling, minimize pain, and mold the residual limb in preparation for prosthesis.
12. Wash the stump with mild soap and water and dry completely.
13. Massage the skin toward the suture line to mobilize scar and prevent its adherence to underlying bone.
14. Prepare for the prosthesis and instruct client in progressive resistive techniques by gently pushing the residual limb against pillows and progressing to firmer surfaces.
15. Encourage verbalization regarding loss of the body part, and assist the client to identify coping mechanisms to deal with the loss.

C. Interventions for below-knee amputation
   1. Prevent edema.
   2. Do not allow the stump to hang over the edge of the bed.
   3. Discourage long periods of sitting to lessen complications of knee flexion.

D. Interventions for above-knee amputation
   1. Prevent internal or external rotation of the limb.
   2. Place a sandbag, rolled towel, or trochanter roll along the outside of the thigh to prevent external rotation.

E. Rehabilitation
   1. Instruct the client in crutch walking.
   2. Prepare the residual limb for a prosthesis.
   3. Prepare the client for fitting of the residual limb for a prosthesis.
   4. Instruct the client in exercises to maintain range of motion and upper body strengthening.
   5. Provide psychosocial support to the client.

XIV. RHEUMATOID ARTHRITIS

A. Description

1. Rheumatoid arthritis is a chronic systemic inflammatory disease (immune complex disorder); the cause may be related to a combination of environmental and genetic factors.
2. Rheumatoid arthritis leads to destruction of connective tissue and synovial membrane within the joints.
3. Rheumatoid arthritis weakens the joint, leading to dislocation and permanent deformity of the joint.
4. Pannus forms at the junction of synovial tissue and articular cartilage and projects into the joint cavity, causing necrosis.
5. Exacerbations of disease manifestations occur during periods of physical or emotional stress and fatigue.
6. Risk factors include exposure to infectious agents.
7. Vasculitis can impede blood flow, leading to organ or organ system malfunction and failure caused by tissue ischemia.

B. Assessment

1. Inflammation, tenderness, and stiffness of the joints
2. Moderate to severe pain with morning stiffness lasting longer than 30 minutes
3. Joint deformities, muscle atrophy, and decreased range of motion in affected joints
4. Spongy, soft feeling in the joints
5. Low-grade temperature, fatigue, and weakness
6. Anorexia, weight loss, and anemia
7. Elevated ESR and positive rheumatoid factor
8. Radiographic study showing joint deterioration
9. Synovial tissue biopsy reveals inflammation

C. Rheumatoid factor

1. Blood test used to diagnose rheumatoid arthritis
2. Values
   a. Nonreactive: 0 to 39 international units/mL
   b. Weakly reactive: 40 to 79 international units/mL
   c. Reactive: greater than 80 international units/mL

D. Pain relief: Combination of pharmacological therapies includes nonsteroidal anti-inflammatory drugs (NSAIDs), disease-modifying antirheumatic drugs (DMARDs), and glucocorticoids

E. Physical mobility

1. Preserve joint function.
2. Provide range-of-motion exercises to maintain joint motion and muscle strengthening.
3. Balance rest and activity.
4. Splints may be used during acute inflammation to prevent deformity.
5. Prevent flexion contractures.
6. Apply heat or cold therapy as prescribed to joints.

7. Apply paraffin baths and massage as prescribed
8. Encourage consistency with exercise program.
9. Instruct the client to stop exercise if pain increases.
10. Exercise only to the point of pain.
11. Avoid weight-bearing on inflamed joints.

F. Self-care (Box 67-8)

1. Assess the need for assistive devices such as raised toilet seats, self-rising chairs, wheelchairs, and scooters to facilitate mobility.
2. Work with an occupational therapist or health care provider to get assistive or adaptive devices.
3. Instruct the client in alternative strategies for providing activities of daily living.

G. Fatigue

1. Identify factors that may contribute to fatigue.
2. Monitor for signs of anemia and administer iron, folic acid, and vitamins as prescribed.
3. Monitor for medication-related blood loss by testing the stool for occult blood.
4. Instruct the client in measures to conserve energy, such as pacing activities and obtaining assistance when possible.

H. Disturbed body image

1. Assess the client's reaction to the body change.
2. Encourage the client to verbalize feelings.
3. Assist the client with self-care activities and grooming.
4. Encourage the client to wear street clothes.

I. Surgical interventions

1. Synovectomy: Surgical removal of the synovia to help maintain joint function
2. Arthrodesis: Bony fusion of a joint to regain some mobility
3. Joint replacement (arthroplasty): Surgical replacement of diseased joints with artificial joints; performed to restore motion to a joint and function to the muscles, ligaments, and other soft tissue structures that control a joint

---

BOX 67-8

Client Education for Rheumatoid Arthritis and Degenerative Joint Disease

Assist the client to identify and correct safety hazards in the home.
Instruct the client in the correct use of assistive or adaptive devices.
Instruct the client in energy conservation measures.
Review the prescribed exercise program.
Instruct the client to sit in a chair with a high, straight back.
Instruct the client to use only a small pillow when lying down.
Instruct the client in measures to protect the joints.
Instruct the client regarding the prescribed medications.
Stress the importance of follow-up visits with the health care provider.

▲ XV. OSTEOARTHRITIS (DEGENERATIVE JOINT DIS-
EASE)
  A. Description
    1. Osteoarthritis is progressive degeneration of the
       joints as a result of wear and tear.
    2. Osteoarthritis causes bone buildup and the loss
       of articular cartilage in peripheral and axial
       joints.
    3. Osteoarthritis affects the weight-bearing joints
       and joints that receive the greatest stress, such as
       the hips, knees, lower vertebral column, and
       hands.
    4. The cause is unknown but potentially contribut-
       ing factors may include trauma, fractures, infec-
       tions, obesity, and job-related repetitive stress
       activities.
  ▲ B. Assessment
    ▲ 1. Client experiences joint pain that diminishes af-
         ter rest and intensifies after activity, noted early
         in the disease process.
      2. As the disease progresses, pain occurs with slight
         motion or even at rest.
      3. Symptoms are aggravated by temperature change
         and climate humidity.
      4. Presence of Heberden's nodes or Bouchard's nodes
      5. Joint swelling, crepitus, and limited range of
         motion
      6. Difficulty getting up after prolonged sitting
      7. Skeletal muscle disuse atrophy
      8. Inability to perform activities of daily living
      9. Compression of the spine as manifested by radi-
         ating pain, stiffness, and muscle spasms in one
         or both extremities
  ▲ C. Pain
      1. Administer NSAIDs, muscle relaxants, and other
         medications as prescribed.
      2. Prepare the client for corticosteroid injections
         into joints as prescribed.
      3. Position joints in function position and avoid
         flexion of knees and hips.
      4. Immobilize affected joint with a splint or brace
         until inflammation subsides.
      5. Avoid large pillows under the head or knees.
      6. Provide a bed or foot cradle to keep linen off of
         feet.
      7. Instruct the client in the importance of moist
         heat, hot packs or compresses, and paraffin dips
         as prescribed.
      8. Apply cold applications as prescribed when the
         joint is acutely inflamed.
      9. Encourage adequate rest, recommending 10
         hours of sleep at night and a 1- to 2-hour nap
         in the afternoon.
  D. Nutrition
      1. Encourage a well-balanced diet.
      2. Maintain weight within normal range to de-
         crease stress on the joints.

  E. Physical mobility
      1. Instruct the client to balance activity with rest
         and while participating in an exercise program
         that limits stressing affected joints.
      2. Instruct the client that exercises should be active
         rather than passive and to stop exercise if pain
         occurs.
      3. Instruct the client to limit exercise when joint
         inflammation is severe.
  F. Surgical management
      1. Osteotomy: The bone is resected to correct joint
         deformity, promote realignment, and reduce
         joint stress.
      2. Total joint replacement or arthroplasty
         a. Total joint replacement is performed when
            all measures of pain relief have failed.
         b. Hips and knees are replaced most commonly.
         c. Total joint replacement is contraindicated in
            the presence of infection, advanced osteopo-
            rosis, or severe joint inflammation.

XVI. OSTEOPOROSIS   ▲
  A. Description
      1. Osteoporosis is an age-related metabolic disease.
      2. Bone demineralizes, losing calcium and phos-
         phorus salts, leading to fragile bones and subse-
         quent fractures.
      3. Bone resorption accelerates as bone formation
         slows.
      4. Osteoporosis occurs most commonly in the
         wrist, hip, and vertebral column.
      5. Osteoporosis can occur postmenopausally or as
         a result of a metabolic disorder or calcium defi-
         ciency.
      6. Client may be asymptomatic until the bones
         become fragile and a minor injury or movement
         causes a fracture.
      7. Primary osteoporosis
         a. Most often occurs in post menopausal
            women
         b. Risk factors include decreased calcium intake,
            deficient estrogen, and limited exercises.
      8. Secondary osteoporosis
         a. Causes include prolonged therapy with corti-
            costeroids, thyroid-reducing medications,
            aluminum-containing antacid, or anticon-
            vulsants.
         b. Associated with immobility, alcoholism,
            malnutrition, or malabsorption
      9. Risk factors (Box 67-9)
  B. Assessment
      1. Possibly asymptomatic
      2. Back pain occurs after lifting, bending, or stoop-
         ing.
      3. Back pain that increases with palpation
      4. Pelvic or hip pain, especially with weight-bearing
      5. Problems with balance

BOX 67-9
Risk Factors for Osteoporosis

Cigarette smoking
Early menopause
Excessive use of alcohol
Family history
Female gender
Increasing age
Insufficient intake of calcium
Sedentary lifestyle
Thin, small frame
White (European descent) or Asian race

6. Decline in height from vertebral compression
7. Kyphosis of the dorsal spine, also known as "dowager's hump"
8. Pathological fractures
9. Degeneration of lower thorax and lumber vertebrae on radiographic studies

C. Interventions
1. Assess risk for and prevent injury in client's personal environment.
   a. Assist client to identify and correct hazards in his or her environment.
   b. Position household items and furniture for an unobstructed walkway
   c. Use side rails to prevent falls.
   d. Instruct in use of assistive devices such as a cane or walker.
   e. Encourage use of firm mattress.
2. Provide personal care to client to reduce injuries
   a. Move the client gently when turning and repositioning
   b. Assist with ambulation if client is unsteady.
   c. Provide gentle range-of-motion exercises.
   d. Apply a back brace as prescribed during an acute phase to immobilize the spine and provide spinal column support.
3. Provide client instructions to promote optional level of health and function.
   a. Instruct the client in the use of good body mechanics.
   b. Instruct the client in exercises to strengthen abdominal and back muscles to improve posture and provide support for the spine.
   c. Instruct the client to avoid activities that can cause vertebral compression.
   d. Instruct the client to eat a diet high in protein, calcium, vitamins C and D, and iron.
   e. Instruct the client to avoid alcohol and coffee.
   f. Instruct the client to maintain an adequate fluid intake to prevent renal calculi.
4. Administer medication to promote bone strength and decrease pain.

a. Administer calcium, vitamin D, and phosphorus as prescribed for bone metabolism.
b. Administer calcitonin as prescribed to inhibit bone loss.
c. Administer estrogen or androgens to decrease the rate of bone resorption as prescribed.
d. Administer analgesics, muscle relaxants, and anti-inflammatory medications as prescribed.

XVII. GOUT
A. Description
1. Gout is a systemic disease in which urate crystals deposit in joints and other body tissues.
2. Gout results from to abnormal amounts of uric acid in the body.
3. Primary gout results from a disorder of purine metabolism.
4. Secondary gout involves excessive uric acid in the blood caused by another disease.

B. Phases
1. Asymptomatic: Client has no symptoms but serum uric acid level is elevated.
2. Acute: Client has excruciating pain and inflammation of one or more small joints, especially the great toe.
3. Intermittent: Client has intermittent periods without symptoms between acute attacks.
4. Chronic: Results from repeated episodes of acute gout
   a. Chronic gout results in deposits of urate crystals under the skin.
   b. Chronic gout results in deposits of urate crystals within major organs, such as kidneys, leading to organ dysfunction.

C. Assessment
1. Swelling and inflammation of the joints leading to excruciating pain
2. Tophi: Hard, irregular shaped nodules in the skin containing chalky deposits of sodium urate
3. Low-grade fever, malaise and headache
4. Pruritis from urate crystals in the skin
5. Presence of renal stones from elevated uric acid levels

D. Interventions
1. Provide a low-purine diet as prescribed avoiding foods such as organ meats, wines, and aged cheese.
2. Encourage a high fluid intake of 2000 mL/day to prevent stone formation.
3. Encourage weight reduction diet if required.
4. Instruct the client to avoid alcohol and starvation diets because they may precipitate a gout attack.
5. Increase urinary pH (above 6) by eating alkaline ash foods such as citrus fruits and juices, milk, and other dairy products.

6. Provide bed rest during the acute attacks with the affected extremity elevated.
7. Monitor joint range-of-motion ability and appearance of joints.
8. Position the joint in mild flexion during acute attack.
9. Protect the affected joint from excessive movement or direct contact with sheets or blankets.
10. Provide heat or cold for local treatments to affected joint as prescribed.
11. Administer medications such as analgesics, anti-inflammatory, and uricosuric agents as prescribed.

PRACTICE QUESTIONS

1. A client is treated in a physician's office for a sprained ankle after a fall. Radiographic examination has ruled out a fracture. Before sending the client home, the nurse plans to teach the client to avoid which of the following in the next 24 hours?
   1. Resting the foot
   2. Applying a heating pad
   3. Applying an elastic compression bandage
   4. Elevating the ankle on a pillow while sitting or lying down
2. A nurse is conducting health screening for osteoporosis. Which of the following clients is at greatest risk of developing this disorder?
   1. A 25-year-old woman who jogs
   2. A 36-year-old man who has asthma
   3. A 70-year-old man who consumes excess alcohol
   4. A sedentary 65-year-old woman who smokes cigarettes
3. A nurse has given instructions to a client returning home after knee arthroscopy. The nurse determines that the client understands the instructions if the client states that he or she will:
   1. Resume regular exercise the following day.
   2. Stay off the leg entirely for the rest of the day.
   3. Report fever or site inflammation to the physician.
   4. Refrain from eating food for the remainder of the day.
4. A nurse is caring for a client who is going to have arthrography with a contrast medium. Which assessment by the nurse would be of highest priority?
   1. Allergy to iodine or shellfish
   2. Ability of the client to remain still during the procedure
   3. Whether the client wishes to void before the procedure
   4. Whether the client has any remaining questions about the procedure
5. A nurse is one of several persons who witness a vehicle hit a pedestrian at fairly low speed on a small street. The person is dazed and tries to get up. The leg appears fractured. The nurse would plan to:
   1. Try to reduce the fracture manually.
   2. Assist the person to get up and walk to the sidewalk.
   3. Leave the person for a few moments to call an ambulance.
   4. Stay with the person and encourage the person to remain still.
6. A client has a fiberglass (nonplaster) cast applied to the lower leg. The client asks the nurse when the client will be able to walk using the casted leg. The nurse replies that the client will be able to bear weight on the casted leg:
   1. In 48 hours
   2. In 24 hours
   3. In about 8 hours
   4. Within 20 to 30 minutes of application
7. A nurse has given a client with a leg cast instructions on cast care at home. The nurse would evaluate that the client needs further instruction if the client makes which of the following statements?
   1. "I should avoid walking on wet, slippery floors."
   2. "I'm not supposed to scratch the skin underneath the cast."
   3. "It's okay to wipe dirt off the top of the cast with a damp cloth."
   4. "If the cast gets wet, I can dry it with a hair dryer turned to the warmest setting."
8. A client with a hip fracture asks the nurse why Buck's extension traction is being applied before surgery. The nurse's response is based on the understanding that Buck's extension traction primarily:
   1. Allows bony healing to begin before surgery
   2. Provides rigid immobilization of the fracture site
   3. Lengthens the fractured leg to prevent severing of blood vessels
   4. Provides comfort by reducing muscle spasms and provides fracture immobilization
9. A nurse is evaluating the pin sites of a client in skeletal traction. The nurse would be least concerned with which of the following findings?
   1. Inflammation
   2. Serous drainage
   3. Pain at a pin site
   4. Purulent drainage
10. A client has Buck's extension traction applied to the right leg. The nurse would plan which of the following interventions to prevent complications of the device?
    1. Give pin care once a shift.
    2. Massage the skin of the right leg with lotion every 8 hours.
    3. Inspect the skin on the right leg at least once every 8 hours.
    4. Release the weights on the right leg for daily range-of-motion exercises.

11. A nurse is assessing the casted extremity of a client. The nurse would assess for which of the following signs and symptoms indicative of infection?
    1. Dependent edema
    2. Diminished distal pulse
    3. Presence of a "hot spot" on the cast
    4. Coolness and pallor of the extremity

12. A client has sustained a closed fracture and has just had a cast applied to the affected arm. The client is complaining of intense pain. The nurse elevates the limb, applies an ice bag, and administers an analgesic, with little relief. The nurse interprets that this pain may be caused by:
    1. Infection under the cast
    2. The anxiety of the client
    3. Impaired tissue perfusion
    4. The recent occurrence of the fracture

13. A nurse is admitting a client with multiple trauma to the nursing unit. The client has a leg fracture and had a plaster cast applied. In positioning the casted leg, the nurse should:
    1. Keep the leg in a level position.
    2. Elevate the leg for 3 hours and put it flat for 1 hour.
    3. Keep the leg level for 3 hours and elevate it for 1 hour.
    4. Elevate the leg on pillows continuously for 24 to 48 hours.

14. A client is complaining of skin irritation from the edges of a cast applied the previous day. The nurse should take which of the following actions?
    1. Petal the cast edges with adhesive tape.
    2. Massage the skin at the rim of the cast.
    3. Use a rough file to smooth the cast edges.
    4. Apply lotion to the skin at the rim of the cast.

15. A client is being discharged to home after application of a plaster leg cast. The nurse determines that the client understands proper care of the cast if the client states that he or she should:
    1. Avoid getting the cast wet.
    2. Cover the casted leg with warm blankets.
    3. Use the fingertips to lift and move the leg.
    4. Use a padded coat hanger end to scratch under the cast.

16. A client being measured for crutches asks the nurse why the crutches cannot rest up underneath the arm for extra support. The nurse's response is based on the understanding that this could result in:
    1. A fall and further injury
    2. Injury to the brachial plexus nerves
    3. Skin breakdown in the area of the axilla
    4. Impaired range of motion while the client ambulates

17. A nurse has given a client instructions about crutch safety. The nurse determines that the client needs reinforcement of information if the client states:

    1. That he or she will not use someone else's crutches
    2. That crutch tips will not slip even when wet
    3. The need to have spare crutches and tips available
    4. That crutch tips should be inspected periodically for wear

18. A nurse is caring for a client being treated for fat embolus after multiple fractures. Which of the following data would the nurse evaluate as the most favorable indication of resolution of the fat embolus?
    1. Minimal dyspnea
    2. Clear chest radiograph
    3. Oxygen saturation of 85%
    4. Arterial oxygen level of 78 mm Hg

19. A nurse has conducted teaching with a client in an arm cast about signs and symptoms of compartment syndrome. The nurse determines that the client understands the information if the client states that he or she should report which of the following early symptoms of compartment syndrome?
    1. Cold, bluish-colored fingers
    2. Numbness and tingling in the fingers
    3. Pain that increases when the arm is dependent
    4. Pain relieved only by oxycodone and aspirin (Percodan)

20. A client with diabetes mellitus has had a right below-knee amputation. The nurse would assess specifically for which of the following signs and symptoms because of the history of diabetes?
    1. Hemorrhage
    2. Edema of the stump
    3. Slight redness of incision
    4. Separation of wound edges

21. A nurse is caring for a client who had an above-knee amputation 2 days ago. The residual limb was wrapped with an elastic compression bandage, which has come off. The nurse immediately:
    1. Calls the physician
    2. Applies ice to the site
    3. Rewraps the stump with an elastic compression bandage
    4. Applies a dry sterile dressing and elevates it on one pillow

22. A client is complaining of low back pain that radiates down the left posterior thigh. The nurse further assesses the client to see if the pain is worsened or aggravated by:
    1. Bed rest
    2. Bending or lifting
    3. Ibuprofen (Motrin)
    4. Application of heat

23. A nurse is caring for a client who has had spinal fusion, with insertion of hardware. The nurse would be concerned especially with which of the following assessment findings?

1. Temperature of 101.6° F orally
2. Complaints of discomfort during repositioning
3. Old bloody drainage outlined on the surgical dressing
4. Discomfort during coughing and deep-breathing exercises

24. A nurse is caring for a client with a diagnosis of gout. Which of the following laboratory values would the nurse expect to note in the client?
    1. Calcium level of 9.0 mg/dL
    2. Uric acid level of 8.6 mg/dL
    3. Potassium level of 4.1 mEq/L
    4. Phosphorus level of 3.1 mg/dL

25. A nurse is caring for a client with osteoarthritis. The nurse performs an assessment, knowing that which of the following is a clinical manifestation associated with the disorder?
    1. Morning stiffness
    2. A decreased sedimentation rate
    3. Joint pain that diminishes after rest
    4. Elevated antinuclear antibody levels

ALTERNATE ITEM FORMAT: MULTIPLE RESPONSE

A nurse is preparing a list of cast care instructions for a client who just had a plaster cast applied to his right forearm. Select all instructions that the nurse would include on the list.

- ❏ 1. Keep the cast and extremity elevated.
- ❏ 2. The cast needs to be kept clean and dry.
- ❏ 3. Allow the wet cast 24 to 72 hours to dry.
- ❏ 4. Tingling and numbness in the extremity are expected.
- ❏ 5. Use a hair dryer set on a warm to hot setting to dry the cast.
- ❏ 6. Use a soft padded object that will fit under the cast to scratch the skin under the cast.

ANSWERS

1. **2**

Rationale: Soft tissue injuries such as sprains are treated by RICE (*rest, ice, compression,* and *elevation*) for the first 24 hours after the injury. Ice is applied intermittently for 20 to 30 minutes at a time. Heat is not used in the first 24 hours because it could increase venous congestion, which would increase edema and pain.

Test-Taking Strategy: Use the process of elimination. Note the strategic word *avoid*. Sprains should be rested and elevated, so eliminate options 1 and 4. Use of an elastic compression wrap is also helpful in reducing the pain and swelling, so eliminate option 3. Review treatment measures for a sprain if you had difficulty with this question.

Level of Cognitive Ability: Application
Client Needs: Physiological Integrity
Integrated Process: Nursing Process—planning
Content Area: Adult health—musculoskeletal
Reference: Ignatavicius, D., & Workman, M. (2006). *Medical-surgical nursing: Critical thinking for collaborative care* (5th ed., p. 1226). Philadelphia: W.B. Saunders.

2. **4**

Rationale: Risk factors for osteoporosis include female gender, postmenopausal, advanced age, low-calcium diet, excessive alcohol intake, being sedentary, and smoking cigarettes. Long-term use of corticosteroids, anticonvulsants, and/or furosemide (Lasix) also increase risk.

Test-Taking Strategy: Use the process of elimination. Eliminate option 1 first. The 25-year-old woman who jogs (exercises using the long bones) has negligible risk. The 36-year-old man with asthma is eliminated next because his only risk factor might be long-term corticosteroid use. Of the two remaining options, the 65-year-old woman has higher risk (age, gender, postmenopausal, sedentary, smoking) than the 70-year-old

man (age, alcohol consumption). Review the risk factors associated with osteoporosis if you had difficulty with this question.

Level of Cognitive Ability: Analysis
Client Needs: Health Promotion and Maintenance
Integrated Process: Nursing Process—assessment
Content Area: Adult health—musculoskeletal
Reference: Ignatavicius, D., & Workman, M. (2006). *Medical-surgical nursing: Critical thinking for collaborative care* (5th ed., p. 1158). Philadelphia: W.B. Saunders.

3. **3**

Rationale: After arthroscopy, the client usually can walk carefully on the leg once sensation has returned. The client is instructed to avoid strenuous exercise for at least a few days. The client may resume the usual diet. Signs and symptoms of infection should be reported to the physician.

Test-Taking Strategy: Use the process of elimination. Recalling the general client teaching points related to surgical procedures will direct you to option 3. Review client teaching points following arthroscopy if you had difficulty with this question.

Level of Cognitive Ability: Analysis
Client Needs: Physiological Integrity
Integrated Process: Nuring Process—evaluation
Content Area: Adult health—musculoskeletal
Reference: Ignatavicius, D., & Workman, M. (2006). *Medical-surgical nursing: Critical thinking for collaborative care* (5th ed., p. 1153). Philadelphia: W.B. Saunders.

4. **1**

Rationale: Because of the risk of allergy to contrast dye, the nurse places highest priority on assessing whether the client has an allergy to iodine or shellfish. The nurse also reinforces information about the test and tells the client about the need to remain still during the procedure.

Test-Taking Strategy: Use the process of elimination. Note the strategic words *highest priority*. This tells you that more than one or all of the options are correct (in fact, they all are). Use Maslow's Hierarchy of Needs theory. Although options 2, 3, and 4 compete for priority, option 1 (allergy to iodine or shellfish) takes first preference. The consequence of possible anaphylactic shock (physiological risk) makes this the correct option. Review client preparation for arthrography if you had difficulty with this question.
Level of Cognitive Ability: Analysis
Client Needs: Physiological Integrity
Integrated Process: Nursing Process—assessment
Content Area: Delegating/Prioritizing
References: Ignatavicius, D., & Workman, M. (2006). *Medical-surgical nursing: Critical thinking for collaborative care* (5th ed., p. 1153). Philadelphia: W.B. Saunders.
Lewis, S., Heitkemper, M., & Dirksen, S. (2004). *Medical-surgical nursing: Assessment and management of clinical problems* (6th ed., p. 1645). St. Louis: Mosby.

5. **4**
Rationale: With a suspected fracture, the client is not moved unless it is dangerous to remain in that spot. The nurse should remain with the client and have someone else call for emergency help. A fracture is not reduced at the scene. Before the client is moved, the site of fracture is immobilized to prevent further injury.
Test-Taking Strategy: Use the process of elimination. Eliminate options 1 and 2 first because either of these options could result in further injury to the client. Of the remaining options, the more prudent action would be for the nurse to remain with the client and have someone else call for emergency assistance. Review care of the client with a fracture if you had difficulty with this question.
Level of Cognitive Ability: Application
Client Needs: Physiological Integrity
Integrated Process: Nursing Process—implementation
Content Area: Adult health—musculoskeletal
References: Ignatavicius, D., & Workman, M. (2006). *Medical-surgical nursing: Critical thinking for collaborative care* (5th ed., p. 1197). Philadelphia: W.B. Saunders.
Monahan, F., Sands, J., Neighbors, M., et al. (2007). *Phipps' medical-surgical nursing: Health and illness perspectives* (8th ed., p. 1526). St. Louis: Mosby.

6. **4**
Rationale: A fiberglass cast is made of water-activated polyurethane materials that are dry to the touch within minutes and reach full rigid strength in about 20 minutes. Because of this, the client can bear weight on the cast within 20 to 30 minutes.
Test-Taking Strategy: Use the process of elimination. Note the strategic word *nonplaster*. Options 1 and 2 should be eliminated first because these time frames are similar to the drying times for plaster casts. Recalling that the nonplaster type of cast is lighter and dries quickly may help you choose the 20- to 30-minute time frame as correct. Review client teaching points related to a nonplaster cast if you had difficulty with this question.
Level of Cognitive Ability: Application
Client Needs: Physiological Integrity

Integrated Process: Teaching and Learning
Content Area: Adult health—musculoskeletal
Reference: Ignatavicius, D., & Workman, M. (2006). *Medical-surgical nursing: Critical thinking for collaborative care* (5th ed., p. 1198). Philadelphia: W.B. Saunders.

7. **4**
Rationale: Client instructions should include avoiding walking on wet slippery floors to prevent falls. Surface soil on a cast can be removed with a damp cloth. If the cast gets wet, it can be dried with a hair dryer set to a cool setting to prevent skin breakdown. If the skin under the cast itches, cool air from a hair dryer may be used to relieve it. The client should never scratch under a cast because of the risk of skin breakdown and ulcer formation.
Test-Taking Strategy: Use the process of elimination. Note the strategic words *needs further instruction*. These words indicate a negative event query and ask you to select an option that is incorrect. Remember never to use a hair dryer on a cast or on the skin under a cast with the dryer set at the warmest setting; only cool settings are used to prevent burns. Review client teaching points about a cast if you had difficulty with this question.
Level of Cognitive Ability: Analysis
Client Needs: Physiological Integrity
Integrated Process: Teaching and Learning
Content Area: Adult health—musculoskeletal
Reference: Lewis, S., Heitkemper, M., & Dirksen, S. (2004). *Medical-surgical nursing: Assessment and management of clinical problems* (6th ed., p. 1169). St. Louis: Mosby.

8. **4**
Rationale: Buck's extension traction is a type of skin traction often applied after hip fracture before the fracture is reduced in surgery. Traction reduces muscle spasms and helps immobilize the fracture. Traction does not lengthen the leg for the purpose of preventing blood vessel severance. Traction also does not allow for bony healing to begin.
Test-Taking Strategy: Use the process of elimination. Focus on the client's diagnosis, hip fracture. Read each option carefully. Noting the words *provides fracture immobilization* will direct you to option 4. Review the purpose of Buck's traction if you had difficulty with this question.
Level of Cognitive Ability: Application
Client Needs: Physiological Integrity
Integrated Process: Nursing Process—implementation
Content Area: Adult health—musculoskeletal
Reference: Ignatavicius, D., & Workman, M. (2006). *Medical-surgical nursing: Critical thinking for collaborative care* (5th ed., p. 1200). Philadelphia: W.B. Saunders.

9. **2**
Rationale: A small amount of serous oozing is expected at pin insertion sites. Signs of infection such as inflammation, purulent drainage, and pain at the pin site are not expected findings and should be reported to the physician.
Test-Taking Strategy: Use the process of elimination. Note the strategic words *least concerned*. Options 1 and 4 seem to indicate an infectious problem and are eliminated first. From the remaining options, note that the complaint of pain is at "a pin

site." Also, because serous drainage is an expected finding, select option 2. Review expected findings in the client with skeletal traction if you had difficulty with this question.
Level of Cognitive Ability: Analysis
Client Needs: Physiological Integrity
Integrated Process: Nursing Process—evaluation
Content Area: Adult health—musculoskeletal
Reference: Ignatavicius, D., & Workman, M. (2006). *Medical-surgical nursing: Critical thinking for collaborative care* (5th ed., p. 1101). Philadelphia: W.B. Saunders.

10. **3**

Rationale: Buck's extension traction is a type of skin traction. The nurse inspects the skin of the limb in traction at least once every 8 hours for irritation or inflammation. Massaging the skin with lotion is not indicated. The nurse never releases the weights of traction unless specifically ordered by the physician. There are no pins to care for with skin traction.
Test-Taking Strategy: Use the process of elimination and the steps of the nursing process to answer this question. Option 3 is the only option that relates to assessment. Review care of the client in Buck's traction if you had difficulty with this question.
Level of Cognitive Ability: Application
Client Needs: Physiological Integrity
Integrated Process: Nursing Process—planning
Content Area: Adult health—musculoskeletal
Reference: Ignatavicius, D., & Workman, M. (2006). *Medical-surgical nursing: Critical thinking for collaborative care* (5th ed., p. 1201). Philadelphia: W.B. Saunders.

11. **3**

Rationale: Signs and symptoms of infection under a casted area include odor or purulent drainage from the cast or the presence of "hot spots," which are areas of the cast that are warmer than others. The physician should be notified if any of these occur. Signs of impaired circulation in the distal limb include coolness and pallor of the skin, diminished arterial pulse, and edema.
Test-Taking Strategy: Use the process of elimination. Answer this question and think about what you would expect to note with infection—redness, swelling, heat, and purulent drainage. With this in mind, you can eliminate options 2 and 4 easily. From the remaining options, remember that "dependent edema" is not necessarily indicative of infection. Swelling would be continuous. The hot spot on the cast could signify infection underneath that area and is the correct answer to the question. Review signs of infection in an extremity with a cast if you had difficulty with this question.
Level of Cognitive Ability: Analysis
Client Needs: Physiological Integrity
Integrated Process: Nursing Process—assessment
Content Area: Adult health—musculoskeletal
Reference: Ignatavicius, D., & Workman, M. (2006). *Medical-surgical nursing: Critical thinking for collaborative care* (5th ed., p. 1200). Philadelphia: W.B. Saunders.

12. **3**

Rationale: Most pain associated with fractures can be minimized with rest, elevation, application of cold, and adminis-

tration of analgesics. Pain that is not relieved by these measures should be reported to the physician because the pain unrelieved by medications and other measures may indicate neurovascular compromise. Because this is a new closed fracture and cast, infection would not have had time to set in.
Test-Taking Strategy: Use the process of elimination. Focus on the issue, intense pain. Use of the ABCs—airway, breathing, and circulation—will direct you to option 3. Review care of the client with a fracture and new cast if you had difficulty with this question.
Level of Cognitive Ability: Analysis
Client Needs: Physiological Integrity
Integrated Process: Nursing Process—analysis
Content Area: Adult health—musculoskeletal
Reference: Lewis, S., Heitkemper, M., & Dirksen, S. (2004). *Medical-surgical nursing: Assessment and management of clinical problems* (6th ed., p. 1667). St. Louis: Mosby.

13. **4**

Rationale: A casted extremity is elevated continuously for the first 24 to 48 hours to minimize swelling and promote venous drainage. Options 1, 2, and 3 are incorrect.
Test-Taking Strategy: Use the process of elimination. Recalling that edema is a concern and knowledge of the effects of gravity on edema will direct you to option 4. Review care of the client with a new cast if you had difficulty with this question.
Level of Cognitive Ability: Application
Client Needs: Physiological Integrity
Integrated Process: Nursing Process—implementation
Content Area: Adult health—musculoskeletal
References: Lewis, S., Heitkemper, M., & Dirksen, S. (2004). *Medical-surgical nursing: Assessment and management of clinical problems* (6th ed.). St. Louis: Mosby.
Monahan, F., Sands, J., Neighbors, M., et al. (2007). *Phipps' medical-surgical nursing: Health and illness perspectives* (8th ed., p. 1536). St. Louis: Mosby.

14. **1**

Rationale: The nurse petals the edges of the cast with tape to minimize skin irritation. If a client has a cast applied and returns home, the client can be taught to do the same.
Test-Taking Strategy: Use the process of elimination. Options 2 and 4 are comparative or alike and neither helps eliminate the cause of the irritation, so eliminate them first. Imagine the use of a "rough file"—it would create plaster chips and dust that could go underneath the cast. By the process of elimination, the nurse would petal the cast to cushion the skin from the irritating cast material. Review care of the client with a cast if you had difficulty with this question.
Level of Cognitive Ability: Application
Client Needs: Physiological Integrity
Integrated Process: Nursing Process—implementation
Content Area: Adult health—musculoskeletal
Reference: Ignatavicius, D., & Workman, M. (2006). *Medical-surgical nursing: Critical thinking for collaborative care* (5th ed., 1198). Philadelphia: W.B. Saunders.

15. **1**

Rationale: A plaster cast must remain dry to keep its strength. The cast should be handled with the palms of the hands, not the fingertips, until fully dry. Air should circulate freely around the cast to help it dry; the cast also gives off heat as it dries. The client should never scratch under the cast; the client may use a hair dryer on the cool setting to relieve an itch.

Test-Taking Strategy: Use the process of elimination. Knowing that a wet cast can be dented with the fingertips, causing pressure underneath, helps eliminate option 3 first. Knowing that the cast needs to dry helps eliminate option 2 next. Option 4 is dangerous to skin integrity and is also eliminated. Remember that plaster casts, once they have dried after application, should not become wet. Review care of the client with a cast if you had difficulty with this question.

Level of Cognitive Ability: Analysis
Client Needs: Physiological Integrity
Integrated Process: Nursing Process—evaluation
Content Area: Adult health—musculoskeletal
References: Lewis, S., Heitkemper, M., & Dirksen, S. (2004). *Medical-surgical nursing: Assessment and management of clinical problems* (6th ed., pp. 1162, 1169). St. Louis: Mosby.

16. **2**

Rationale: Crutches are measured so that the tops are two to three fingerwidths from the axillae. This ensures that the client's axillae are not resting on the crutch or bearing the weight of the crutch, which could result in injury to the nerves of the brachial plexus.

Test-Taking Strategy: Use the process of elimination. Recalling the risk associated with brachial nerve plexus injury will direct you to option 2. Review the complications associated with the use of crutches if you had difficulty with this question.

Level of Cognitive Ability: Comprehension
Client Needs: Physiological Integrity
Integrated Process: Teaching and Learning
Content Area: Adult health—musculoskeletal
References: Harkreader, H., & Hogan, M. (2004). *Fundamentals of nursing: Caring and clinical judgment* (2nd ed., p. 794). Philadelphia: W.B. Saunders.
Ignatavicius, D., & Workman, M. (2006). *Medical-surgical nursing: Critical thinking for collaborative care* (5th ed., p. 1204). Philadelphia: W.B. Saunders.

17. **2**

Rationale: Crutch tips should remain dry. Water could cause the client to slip by decreasing the surface friction of the rubber tip on the floor. If crutch tips get wet, the client should dry them with a cloth or paper towel. The client should use only crutches measured for the client. The tips should be inspected for wear, and spare crutches and tips should be available if needed.

Test-Taking Strategy: Use the process of elimination. Note the strategic words *needs reinforcement of information*. These words indicate a negative event query and ask you to select an option that is incorrect. Remember that crutch tips can slip when they get wet, posing a possible threat to the unsuspecting client. Review client teaching points related to safety and the use of crutches if you had difficulty with this question.

Level of Cognitive Ability: Analysis
Client Needs: Physiological Integrity
Integrated Process: Teaching and Learning
Content Area: Adult health—musculoskeletal

Reference: Elkin, M., Perry, A., & Potter, P. (2004). *Nursing interventions and clinical skills* (3rd ed., p. 135). St. Louis: Mosby.

18. **2**

Rationale: A clear chest radiograph is a good indicator that a fat embolus is resolving. When fat embolism occurs, the chest radiograph has a "snowstorm" appearance. Eupnea, not minimal dyspnea, is a normal sign. Arterial oxygen levels should be 80 to 100 mm Hg. Oxygen saturation should be higher than 95%.

Test-Taking Strategy: Use the process of elimination. Note the strategic words *most favorable indication*. Knowing that the arterial oxygen and oxygen saturation levels are below normal helps eliminate options 3 and 4. Dyspnea, even at a minimal level, is not normal, so eliminate option 1. Review the expected outcomes in a client being treated for fat embolism if you had difficulty with this question.

Level of Cognitive Ability: Analysis
Client Needs: Physiological Integrity
Integrated Process: Nursing Process—evaluation
Content Area: Adult health—musculoskeletal
References: Lewis, S., Heitkemper, M., & Dirksen, S. (2004). *Medical-surgical nursing: Assessment and management of clinical problems* (6th ed., p. 1673). St. Louis: Mosby.
Monahan, F., Sands, J., Neighbors, M., et al. (2007). *Phipps' medical-surgical nursing: Health and illness perspectives* (8th ed., p. 1538). St. Louis: Mosby.

19. **2**

Rationale: The earliest symptom of compartment syndrome is paresthesia (numbness and tingling in the fingers). Other symptoms include pain unrelieved by narcotics, pain that increases with limb elevation, and pallor and coolness to the distal limb. Cyanosis is a late sign.

Test-Taking Strategy: Use the process of elimination. Note the strategic word *early*. Knowing that compartment syndrome is characterized by insufficient circulation and ischemia caused by pressure will direct you to option 2. Review the early signs of compartment syndrome if you had difficulty with this question.

Level of Cognitive Ability: Analysis
Client Needs: Physiological Integrity
Integrated Process: Nursing Process—evaluation
Content Area: Adult health—musculoskeletal
Reference: Ignatavicius, D., & Workman, M. (2006). *Medical-surgical nursing: Critical thinking for collaborative care* (5th ed., pp. 1191-1192). Philadelphia: W.B. Saunders.

20. **4**

Rationale: Clients with diabetes mellitus are more prone to wound infection and delayed wound healing because of the disease. Postoperative stump edema and hemorrhage are complications in the immediate postoperative period that apply to any client with an amputation. Slight redness of the incision is considered normal, as long as it is dry and intact.

Test-Taking Strategy: Use the process of elimination. Recalling that diabetes mellitus increases the client's chances of developing infection and delayed wound healing will direct you to option 4. Review the complications associated with an ampu-

tation in the client with diabetes mellitus if you had difficulty with this question.
Level of Cognitive Ability: Application
Client Needs: Physiological Integrity
Integrated Process: Nursing Process—assessment
Content Area: Adult health—musculoskeletal
Reference: Lewis, S., Heitkemper, M., & Dirksen, S. (2004). *Medical-surgical nursing: Assessment and management of clinical problems* (6th ed., p. 1299). St. Louis: Mosby.

21. **3**
Rationale: If the client with an amputation has a cast or elastic compression bandage that slips off, the nurse must wrap the stump immediately with another elastic compression bandage. Otherwise, excessive edema will form rapidly, which could cause a significant delay in rehabilitation. If the client had a cast that slipped off, the nurse would have to call the physician so that a new one could be applied. Elevation on one pillow is not going to impede the development of edema greatly once compression is released. Ice would be of limited value in controlling edema from this cause. If the physician were called, the order likely would be to reapply the compression dressing anyway.
Test-Taking Strategy: Use the process of elimination. Recalling that excessive edema can form rapidly will direct you to option 3. Review care of the client after amputation if you had difficulty with this question.
Level of Cognitive Ability: Application
Client Needs: Physiological Integrity
Integrated Process: Nursing Process—implementation
Content Area: Adult health—musculoskeletal
Reference: Ignatavicius, D., & Workman, M. (2006). *Medical-surgical nursing: Critical thinking for collaborative care* (5th ed., p. 1221). Philadelphia: W.B. Saunders.

22. **2**
Rationale: Low back pain that radiates into one leg (sciatica) is consistent with herniated lumbar disk. The nurse assesses the client to see whether the pain is aggravated by events that increase intraspinal pressure, such as bending, lifting, sneezing, and coughing, or by lifting the leg straight up while supine (straight leg raising test).
Test-Taking Strategy: Use the process of elimination. Recall that bed rest, heat (or sometimes ice), and nonsteroidal anti-inflammatory agents usually relieve back pain, whereas bending, lifting, and straining aggravate it. Review the causes of back pain and the factors that alleviate or aggravate pain if you had difficulty with this question.
Level of Cognitive Ability: Application
Client Needs: Physiological Integrity
Integrated Process: Nursing Process—assessment
Content Area: Adult health—musculoskeletal
Reference: Ignatavicius, D., & Workman, M. (2006). *Medical-surgical nursing: Critical thinking for collaborative care* (5th ed., p. 978). Philadelphia: W.B. Saunders.

23. **1**
Rationale: The nursing assessment conducted after spinal surgery is similar to that done after other surgical procedures. For this specific type of surgery, the nurse assesses the neurovascu-

lar status of the lower extremities, watches for signs and symptoms of infection, and inspects the surgical site for evidence of cerebrospinal fluid leakage (drainage is clear and tests positive for glucose). A mild temperature is expected after insertion of hardware, but a temperature of 101.6° F should be reported.
Test-Taking Strategy: Use the process of elimination. Note the strategic words *concerned especially*. Thus, you are looking for the option that has the greatest deviation from normal. Options 2 and 4 are expected after surgery and, although the nurse tries to minimize discomfort, the client is likely to have some discomfort, even with proper analgesic use. The words *old* and *outlined* in option 3 indicate that this is not a new occurrence. This leaves the temperature of 101.6° F, which is excessive and should be reported. Review the signs of complications following this surgical procedure if you had difficulty with this question.
Level of Cognitive Ability: Analysis
Client Needs: Physiological Integrity
Integrated Process: Nursing Process—assessment
Content Area: Adult health—musculoskeletal
References: Ignatavicius, D., & Workman, M. (2006). *Medical-surgical nursing: Critical thinking for collaborative care* (5th ed., p. 980). Philadelphia: W.B. Saunders.
Monahan, F., Sands, J., Neighbors, M., et al. (2007). *Phipps' Medical-surgical nursing: Health and illness perspectives* (8th ed., p. 1599). St. Louis: Mosby.

24. **2**
Rationale: In addition to the presence of clinical manifestations, gout is diagnosed by the presence of persistent hyperuricemia, with a uric acid level higher than 8 mg/dL; a normal value is 4.0 to 8.5 mg/dL. Options 1, 3, and 4 indicate normal laboratory values. Additionally, the presence of uric acid in an aspirated sample of synovial fluid confirms the diagnosis.
Test-Taking Strategy: Use the process of elimination and knowledge of normal laboratory values. Recalling that increased uric acid levels occur in gout and noting that option 2 is the only abnormal value will assist you in answering the question. Review the manifestations of gout and the normal uric acid level if you had difficulty with this question.
Level of Cognitive Ability: Analysis
Client Needs: Physiological Integrity
Integrated Process: Nursing Process—assessment
Content Area: Adult health—musculoskeletal
Reference: Ignatavicius, D., & Workman, M. (2006). *Medical-surgical nursing: Critical thinking for collaborative care* (5th ed., p. 415). Philadelphia: W.B. Saunders.

25. **3**
Rationale: The stiffness and joint pain that occur in osteoarthritis diminish after rest and intensify with activity. No specific laboratory findings are useful in diagnosing osteoarthritis. The client may have a normal or slightly elevated sedimentation rate. Morning stiffness lasting longer than 30 minutes occurs in rheumatoid arthritis. Elevated white blood cell counts, platelet counts, and antinuclear antibody levels occur in rheumatoid arthritis.
Test-Taking Strategy: Use the process of elimination and knowledge about the differences between osteoarthritis and rheumatoid arthritis to answer this question. Review the

characteristics of osteoarthritis if you had difficulty with the question.

Level of Cognitive Ability: Analysis
Client Needs: Physiological Integrity
Integrated Process: Nursing Process—assessment
Content Area: Adult health—musculoskeletal
References: Ignatavicius, D., & Workman, M. (2006). *Medical-surgical nursing: Critical thinking for collaborative care* (5th ed., p. 382). Philadelphia: W.B. Saunders.
Monahan, F., Sands, J., Neighbors, M., et al. (2007). *Phipps' medical-surgical nursing: Health and illness perspectives* (8th ed., p. 1619). St. Louis: Mosby.

ALTERNATE ITEM FORMAT: MULTIPLE RESPONSE

Answer: 1, 2, 3
Rationale: A plaster cast takes 24 to 72 hours to dry (synthetic casts dry in 20 minutes). The cast and extremity may be elevated to reduce edema. However, some authors report that this may impede circulation to the affected limb. A wet cast is handled with the palms of the hand until it is dry, and the extremity is turned (unless contraindicated) so that all sides of the wet cast will dry. A cool setting on the hair dryer can be used to dry a plaster cast (heat cannot be used on a plaster cast because the cast heats up and burns the skin). The cast needs to be kept clean and dry, and the client is instructed not to stick anything under the cast because of the risk of breaking skin integrity. The client is instructed to monitor the extremity for circulatory impairment, such as pain, swelling, discoloration, tingling, numbness, coolness, or diminished pulse. The physician is notified immediately if circulatory impairment occurs.

Test-Taking Strategy: Focus on the issue, a plaster cast. Recalling that edema occurs following a fracture and recalling the complications associated with a cast will assist you in answering the question. Review cast care instructions if you had difficulty with this question.
Level of Cognitive Ability: Application
Client Needs: Physiological Integrity
Integrated Process: Teaching and Learning
Content Area: Adult health—musculoskeletal
Reference: Ignatavicius, D., & Workman, M. (2006). *Medical-surgical nursing: Critical thinking for collaborative care* (5th ed., p. 1199). Philadelphia: W.B. Saunders.

REFERENCES

Black, J., & Hawks, J. (2005). *Medical-surgical nursing: Clinical management for positive outcomes* (7th ed.). Philadelphia: W.B. Saunders.

Elkin, M., Perry, A., & Potter, P. (2004). *Nursing interventions and clinical skills* (3rd ed.). St. Louis: Mosby.

Harkreader, H., & Hogan, M. (2004). *Fundamentals of nursing: Caring and clinical judgment* (2nd ed.). Philadelphia: W.B. Saunders.

Ignatavicius, D., & Workman, M. (2006). *Medical-surgical nursing: Critical thinking for collaborative care* (5th ed.). Philadelphia: W.B. Saunders.

Jarvis, C. (2004). *Physical examination and health assessment* (4th ed.). St. Louis: W.B. Saunders.

Lewis, S., Heitkemper, M., & Dirksen, S. (2004). *Medical-surgical nursing: Assessment and management of clinical problems* (6th ed.). St. Louis: Mosby.

Monahan, F., Sands, J., Neighbors, M., et al. (2007). *Phipps' medical-surgical nursing: Health and illness perspectives* (8th ed.). St. Louis: Mosby.

Sole, M., Klein, D., & Moseley, M. (2005). *Introduction to critical care nursing* (4th ed.). St. Louis: W.B. Saunders.

Musculoskeletal Medications

I. SKELETAL MUSCLE RELAXANTS

A. Description
1. Skeletal muscle relaxants (Box 68-1) act directly on the neuromuscular junction or act indirectly on the central nervous system (CNS).
2. Centrally acting muscle relaxants depress neuron activity in the spinal cord or brain.
3. Peripherally acting muscle relaxants act directly on the skeletal muscles, interfering with calcium release from muscle tubules and thus preventing the fibers from contracting.
4. Skeletal muscle relaxants are used to prevent or relieve muscle spasms and treat spasticity associated with spinal cord disease or lesions, acute painful musculoskeletal conditions, and chronic debilitating disorders such as multiple sclerosis, brain attacks (stroke), or cerebral palsy.
5. Skeletal muscle relaxants are contraindicated in clients with severe liver, renal, or heart disease; these medications are often metabolized in the liver or excreted from the kidney.
6. Skeletal muscle relaxants should not be taken with central nervous system (CNS) depressants, such as barbiturates, narcotics, alcohol, sedatives, hypnotics, or tricyclic antidepressants.

B. Side effects
1. Dizziness and hypotension
2. Drowsiness and muscle weakness
3. Dry mouth
4. Gastrointestinal upset
5. Photosensitivity
6. Liver toxicity

C. Interventions
1. Obtain a medical history.
2. Monitor vital signs.
3. Monitor for CNS side effects.
4. Assess for risk of injury.

BOX 68-1
Skeletal Muscle Relaxants

Baclofen (Lioresal)
Carisoprodol (Soma)
Chlorphenesin carbamate (Maolate)
Chlorzoxazone (Paraflex, Parafon Forte DSC, Remular-S)
Cyclobenzaprine (Flexeril)
Dantrolene (Dantrium)
Diazepam (Valium)
Metaxalone (Skelaxin)
Methocarbamol (Robaxin)
Orphenadrine (Norflex)
Tizanidine (Zanaflex)

5. Assess involved joints and muscles for pain and mobility.
6. Monitor liver function tests because hepatotoxicity can occur.
7. Monitor renal function studies.
8. Instruct the client to take the medication with food to decrease gastrointestinal upset.
9. Instruct the client to report side effects.
10. Instruct the client to avoid alcohol and CNS depressants.
11. Instruct the client to avoid activities requiring alertness such as driving or operating equipment.

D. Nursing considerations
1. Baclofen (Lioresal)
a. Baclofen causes CNS effects such as drowsiness, dizziness, weakness, and fatigue and nausea, constipation, and urinary retention.
b. Administer with caution in the client with renal or hepatic dysfunction or a seizure disorder.
c. Baclofen can be administered by the physician through intrathecal infusion using an

implantable pump or direct intrathecal administration over 1 minute.

  d. Instruct the client with an implantable pump to maintain medication refill appointments to prevent the pump from emptying and experiencing sudden withdrawal symptoms (which could be life threatening).

2. Carisoprodol (Soma)

  a. Advise the client to take the medication with food to prevent gastrointestinal upset.

  b. Instruct the client to report any rash or hypersensitivity to the physician.

3. Chlorzoxazone (Paraflex, Parafon Forte DSC, Remular-S)

  a. Monitor the client for hypersensitivity reactions such as urticaria, redness or itching, and possibly angioedema.

  b. Chlorzoxazone may cause malaise and may cause the urine to turn orange or red.

  c. Can cause hepatitis and hepatic necrosis.

4. Cyclobenzaprine (Flexeril)

  a. Cyclobenzaprine is contraindicated in clients who have received monoamine oxidase inhibitors (MAOIs) within 14 days of initiation of cyclobenzaprine therapy and in clients with cardiac disorders.

  b. Cyclobenzaprine has significant anticholinergic (atropine-like) effects and should be used with caution in clients with a history of urinary retention, angle-closure glaucoma, or increased intraocular pressure.

  c. Cyclobenzaprine should be used only for short-term therapy (2 to 3 weeks).

5. Dantrolene (Dantrium)

  a. Dantrolene acts directly on skeletal muscles to relieve spasticity.

  b. Liver damage is the most serious adverse effect.

  c. Liver function values should be monitored before the initiation of treatment and during treatment.

  d. Dantrolene can cause gastrointestinal bleeding, urinary frequency, impotence, photosensitivity, rash, and muscle weakness.

  e. Instruct the client to wear protective clothing when in the sun.

  f. Instruct the client to notify the physician if rash, bloody or tarry stools, or yellow discoloration of the skin or eyes occurs.

6. Diazepam (Valium)

  a. Acts in the CNS to suppress spasticity; does not affect skeletal muscle directly

  b. Sedation is a common side effect.

7. Methocarbamol (Robaxin)

  a. The parenteral form is contraindicated in clients with renal impairment.

  b. The parenteral form can cause hypotension, bradycardia, anaphylaxis, and seizures, especially when the medication is given too rapidly.

  c. Avoid extravasation, which can result in thrombophlebitis and tissue sloughing.

  d. Methocarbamol may cause the urine to turn brown, black, or green.

  e. Inform the client to notify the physician if blurred vision, nasal congestion, urticaria, or rash occurs.

8. Tizanidine (Zanaflex) and metaxalone (Skelaxin): Can cause liver damage.

9. Orphenadrine (Norflex) has significant anticholinergic (atropine-like) effects and should be used with caution in clients with a history of urinary retention, angle-closure glaucoma, or increased intraocular pressure.

II. ANTIGOUT MEDICATIONS

A. Description

1. Antigout medications (Box 68-2) reduce uric acid production and increase uric acid excretion (uricosuric) to prevent or relieve gout or to manage hyperuricemia.

2. Nonsteroidal anti-inflammatory drugs (NSAIDs) are used for their anti-inflammatory effects and to relieve pain during an acute gouty attack (see Chap. 66 for information on NSAIDs).

3. Glucocorticoids may be prescribed to reduce inflammation during an acute gouty attack (see Chap. 54 for information on glucocorticoids).

4. Antigout medications should be used cautiously in clients with gastrointestinal, renal, cardiac, or hepatic disease.

B. Side effects

1. Headaches

2. Nausea, vomiting, and diarrhea

3. Blood dyscrasias, such as bone marrow depression

4. Flushed skin and rash

5. Uric acid kidney stones

6. Sore gums

7. Metallic taste

C. Interventions

1. Assess serum uric acid levels.

2. Monitor intake and output.

3. Maintain a fluid intake of at least 2000 to 3000 mL/day to avoid kidney stones.

BOX 68-2

Antigout Medications

Allopurinol (Zyloprim)
Colchicine
Probenecid
Sulfinpyrazone (Anturane)

4. Monitor complete blood cell count and renal and liver function.
5. Instruct the client to avoid alcohol and caffeine because these products can increase uric acid levels.
6. Encourage the client to comply with therapy to prevent elevated uric acid levels, which can trigger a gout attack.
7. Instruct the client to avoid foods high in purine as prescribed, such as wine, alcohol, organ meats, sardines, salmon, scallops, and gravy.
8. Instruct the client to take the medication with food to decrease gastric irritation.
9. Instruct the client to report side effects to the physician.
10. Advise the client to minimize exposure to sunlight and have an annual eye examination because visual changes can occur from prolonged use of allopurinol.
11. Caution the client not to take aspirin with these medications because this could trigger a gout attack.
12. Concurrent use of aspirin causes elevated uric acid levels; the client should be instructed to take acetaminophen (Tylenol).

D. Nursing considerations
1. Allopurinol (Zyloprim)
   a. Can increase the effect of warfarin (Coumadin) and oral hypoglycemic agents.
   b. Instruct the client not to take large doses of vitamin C while taking allopurinol because kidney stones may occur.
   c. Hypersensitivity syndrome (rare) can occur, characterized by rash, fever, eosinophilia, and dysfunction of the liver and kidneys (medication is stopped and the physician is notified.
2. Colchicine
   a Used with caution in older clients, debilitated clients, and clients with cardiac, renal, and/or gastrointestinal disease.
   b. If gastrointestinal symptoms occur (nausea, vomiting, diarrhea, and abdominal pain), the medication is stopped and the physician is notified.
3. Probenecid
   a. Mild gastrointestinal effects can occur and can be reduced by taking the medication with food.
   b. Aspirin and other salicylates interfere with the uricosuric action of the medication.
4. Sulfinpyrazone (Anturane)
   a. Contraindicated in clients with active ulcer disease; used with caution in clients with a history of ulcer disease
   b. Salicylates counteract the uricosuric action of the medication

---

BOX 68-3
Antiarthritic Medications

Anakinra (Kineret)
Adalimumab (Humira)
Auranofin (Ridaura)
Aurothioglucose (Solganal)
Azathioprine (Imuran)
Cyclosporine; alcohol (Neoral)
Etanercept (Enbrel)
Gold sodium thiomalate (Aurolate, Myochrysine)
Hydroxychloroquine sulfate (Plaquenil)
Leflunomide (Arava)
Methotrexate (Rheumatrex, Trexall)
Penicillamine (Cuprimine)
Infliximab (Remicade)
Sulfasalazine (Azulfidine)

---

c. Inhibits hepatic metabolism of tolbutamide (Orinase), causing hypoglycemia, and warfarin, causing bleeding tendencies.

III. **ANTIARTHRITIC MEDICATIONS** (Box 68-3)
A. Description (Fig. 68-1)
1. Rheumatoid arthritis occurs as inflammation progresses into the synovia, cartilage and bone; if this inflammation is not controlled, it will lead to joint destruction, thus affecting client mobility and comfort.
2. The focus of treatment is early diagnosis and aggressive treatment in order to preserve joint function.
3. Medication therapy includes NSAIDs, glucocorticoids, and disease-modifying antirheumatic drugs (DMARDs).
4. Gold salts: Use of gold salts has decreased, but their purpose is to reduce the progression of joint damage caused by arthritic processes. Gold toxicity, which includes pruritis, rash, metallic taste, stomatitis, and diarrhea, can occur; if toxicity occurs, dimercaprol (BAL in oil) may be prescribed to enhance gold excretion.
B. NSAIDs may be prescribed for their anti-inflammatory and analgesic effects (see Chap. 66 for information on NSAIDs).
C. Glucocorticoids may be prescribed for their anti-inflammatory effects (see Chap. 54 for information on glucocorticoids).
D. DMARDs
1. Description
   a. DMARDs are effective antirheumatic medications that are used to slow the degenerative effects of the disorder.
   b. DMARDs are usually prescribed secondary to NSAIDs and are often the first choice in the treatment of severe arthritis.
2. Common side effects of DMARDs include injection site inflammation and pain, ecchymo-

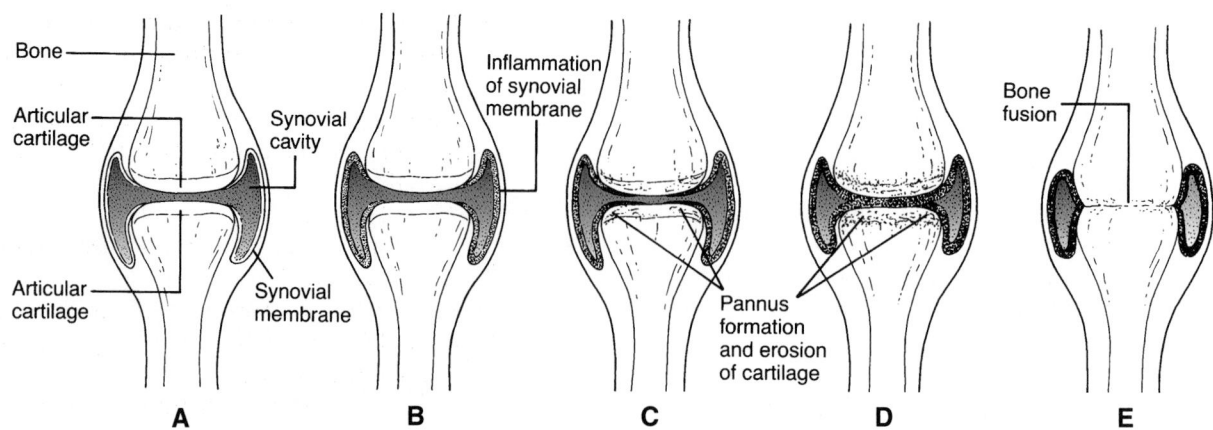

FIG. 68-1 Progressive joint degeneration in rheumatoid arthritis. **A,** Healthy joint. **B,** Inflammation of synovial membrane. **C,** Onset of pannus formation and cartilage erosion. **D,** Pannus formation progresses and cartilage deteriorates further. **E,** Complete destruction of joint cavity together with fusion of articulating bones. (From Lehne, R. [2007]. *Pharmacology for nursing care* [6th ed.]. Philadelphia: W.B. Saunders.)

sis, and edema, pancytopenia and infection, fatigue, headache, nausea, vomiting, and flu-like symptoms, and allergic response.

3. Interventions
   a. Instruct the client to monitor for signs of infection and report signs to the physician.
   b. Monitor the injection site for signs of irritation, pain, inflammation, and swelling.
   c. Instruct the client to consult with the physician before receiving live vaccines and to avoid exposure to infections.
   d. Inform the client about the importance of laboratory tests for neutrophil counts, white blood cell counts, and platelet counts before initiation of treatment and during treatment.
4. Anakinra (Kineret): Injection site reactions are common (pruritus, erythema, rash, pain).
5. Adalimumab (Humira)
   a. Injection site reactions are common.
   b. Has been associated with neurological injury (numbness, tingling, dizziness, disturbed vision, weakness in the legs)
6. Auranofin (Ridaura): Oral gold preparation.
7. Gold sodium thiomalate (Aurolate, Myochrysine), aurothioglucose (Solganal): Intramuscular gold preparations
8. Azathioprine (Imuran): Immunosuppressive and anti-inflammatory actions; toxic effects include hepatitis and blood dyscrasias.
9. Cyclosporine (Neoral): Immunosuppressive actions; can cause nephrotoxicity
10. Etanercept (Enbrel)
    a. Injection site reactions are common.
    b. Poses a risk for heart failure; has been associated with central nervous system demyelinating disorders and hematological disorders

11. Hydroxychloroquine sulfate (Plaquenil): Associated with retinal damage; inform the client to contact the physician if visual disturbances occur.
12. Leflunomide (Arava): Side effects include diarrhea, respiratory infection, reversible alopecia, rash, and nausea; is hepatotoxic.
13. Methotrexate (Rheumatrex, Trexall): Can cause hepatic fibrosis, bone marrow suppression, gastrointestinal ulceration, and pneumonitis
14. Penicillamine (Cuprimine): Can cause bone marrow suppression and autoimmune disorders
15. Infliximab (Remicade): Can cause infusion reactions (fever, chills, pruritus, urticaria, chest pain); is hepatotoxic
16. Sulfasalazine (Azulfidine): Can cause gastrointestinal and dermatological reactions, bone marrow suppression, hepatitis

IV. MEDICATIONS TO PREVENT AND TREAT OSTEOPOROSIS

A. Description
   1. Osteoporosis is characterized by low bone mass and increased bone fragility
   2. Calcium and vitamin D supplementation can reduce the risk of osteoporosis; calcium maximizes bone growth early in life and maintains bone integrity later in life, and vitamin D ensures calcium absorption (see Chap. 54 for information on calcium and vitamin D supplements).
   3. Treatment is aimed at reducing the occurrence of fractures by maintaining or increasing bone strength.
   4. Medications that decrease bone resorption (antiresorptive) and medications that promote bone formation are used.

5. A nurse is providing discharge instructions to a client receiving baclofen (Lioresal). Which of the following would be included in the teaching plan?
   1. Restrict fluid intake.
   2. Avoid the use of alcohol.
   3. Notify the physician if fatigue occurs.
   4. Stop the medication if diarrhea occurs.

6. A nurse is analyzing the laboratory studies on a client receiving dantrolene sodium (Dantrium). Which of the following laboratory tests would identify an adverse effect associated with the administration of this medication?
   1. Creatinine level determination
   2. Platelet count determination
   3. Blood urea nitrogen level determination
   4. Liver function tests

7. A nurse is reviewing the record of a client who has been prescribed baclofen (Lioresal). Which of the following disorders, if noted in the client's history, would alert the nurse to contact the physician?
   1. Seizure disorder
   2. Hyperthyroidism
   3. Diabetes mellitus
   4. Coronary artery disease

8. Cyclobenzaprine hydrochloride (Flexeril) is prescribed for a client for muscle spasms. The nurse is reviewing the client's record. Which of the following disorders, if noted in the record, would indicate a need to contact the physician about the administration of this medication?
   1. Glaucoma
   2. Emphysema
   3. Hypothyroidism
   4. Diabetes mellitus

9. A client is to receive a prescription for methocarbamol (Robaxin). The nurse provides instructions to the client about the medication. Which of the following client statements would indicate a need for further education?
   1. "My urine may turn brown or green."
   2. "I might get some nasal congestion from this medication."
   3. "This medication is prescribed to help relieve my muscle spasms."
   4. "If my vision becomes blurred, I don't need to be concerned about it."

10. A nurse is administering an intravenous dose of methocarbamol (Robaxin) to a client with multiple sclerosis. For which of the following adverse effects would the nurse monitor?
    1. Tachycardia
    2. Rapid pulse
    3. Bradycardia
    4. Hypertension

ALTERNATE ITEM FORMAT: MULTIPLE RESPONSE

In monitoring a client's response to disease-modifying antirheumatic drugs (DMARDs), which assessment findings would the nurse consider acceptable responses? Select all that apply.

❏ 1. Symptom control during periods of emotional stress
❏ 2. Normal white blood cell, platelet, and neutrophil counts
❏ 3. Radiological findings that show nonprogression of joint degeneration
❏ 4. An increased range of motion in the affected joints 3 months into therapy
❏ 5. Inflammation and irritation at the injection site 3 days after the injection is given
❏ 6. A low-grade temperature on rising in the morning that remains throughout the day

ANSWERS

1. **2**

Rationale: Infection and pancytopenia are side effects of etanercept (Enbrel). Laboratory studies are performed prior to and during drug treatment. The appearance of abnormal white blood cell counts and abnormal platelet counts can alert the nurse to a potentially life-threatening infection. Injection site itching and edema are common occurrences following administration. A metallic taste with loss of appetite are not common signs of side effects of this medication.

Test-Taking Strategy: Use the process of elimination. Option 4 can be eliminated, because this is not a common side effect. In early treatment, residual fatigue and joint pain may still be apparent. Option 2 is suggestive of infection, which could indicate a reason for discontinuing this medication and should be reported. Review this medication if you had difficulty with this question.

Level of Cognitive Ability: Analysis
Client Needs: Physiological Integrity
Integrated Process: Nursing Process—assessment
Content Area: Pharmacology
Reference: Ignatavicius, D., & Workman, M. (2006). *Medical-surgical nursing: Critical thinking for collaborative care* (5th ed., p. 405). Philadelphia: W.B. Saunders.

2. **1**

Rationale: Clients taking allopurinol are encouraged to drink 3000 mL of fluid a day. A full therapeutic effect may take 1 week or longer. Allopurinol is to be given with, or immediately after, meals or milk. A client who develops a rash, irritation of the eyes, or swelling of the lips or mouth should contact the physician because this may indicate hypersensitivity.

Test-Taking Strategy: Use the process of elimination. Option 4 can be eliminated easily because it indicates hyper-

sensitivity, which is not a normal expected response. From the remaining options, recalling that this medication is used to treat gout will direct you to option 1. If you had difficulty with this question, review the client instructions related to allopurinol.
Level of Cognitive Ability: Application
Client Needs: Physiological Integrity
Integrated Process: Teaching and Learning
Content Area: Pharmacology
Reference: Hodgson, B., & Kizior, R. (2007). *Saunders nursing drug handbook 2007* (p. 35). Philadelphia: W.B. Saunders.

3. **2**
Rationale: Colchicine is contraindicated in clients with severe gastrointestinal, renal, hepatic, or cardiac disorders and in clients with blood dyscrasias. Clients with impaired renal function may exhibit myopathy and neuropathy manifested as generalized weakness. This medication should be used with caution in clients with impaired hepatic function, the older client, and the debilitated client.
Test-Taking Strategy: Use the process of elimination. Note that options 1, 3, and 4 are endocrine-related disorders. Option 2, the correct option, is different from the others. Review the contraindications associated with this medication if you had difficulty with this question.
Level of Cognitive Ability: Analysis
Client Needs: Physiological Integrity
Integrated Process: Nursing Process—analysis
Content Area: Pharmacology
Reference: Lehne, R. (2007). *Pharmacology for nursing care* (6th ed., p. 844). Philadelphia: W.B. Saunders.

4. **4**
Rationale: Precautions need to be taken with the administration of alendronate to prevent gastrointestinal side effects (especially esophageal irritation) and to increase absorption of the medication. The medication needs to be taken with a full glass of water after rising in the morning. The client should not eat or drink anything for 30 minutes following administration and should not lie down after taking the medication.
Test-Taking Strategy: Knowledge regarding the administration of alendronate is needed to answer this question. Recalling that this medication can cause esophageal irritation will direct you to option 4. Review this medication if you had difficulty with this question.
Level of Cognitive Ability: Application
Client Needs: Physiological Integrity
Integrated Process: Teaching and Learning
Content Area: Pharmacology
References: Ignatavicius, D., & Workman, M. (2006). *Medical-surgical nursing: Critical thinking for collaborative care* (5th ed., p. 1167). Philadelphia: W.B. Saunders.
Lewis, S., Heitkemper, M., & Dirksen, S. (2004). *Medical-surgical nursing: Assessment and management of clinical problems* (6th ed., p. 1711). St. Louis: Mosby.

5. **2**
Rationale: Baclofen is a skeletal muscle relaxant. The client should be cautioned against the use of alcohol and other central nervous system (CNS) depressants because baclofen potentiates the depressant activity of these agents. Constipation rather than diarrhea is an adverse effect. Restriction of fluids is not necessary, but the client should be warned that urinary retention can occur. Fatigue is related to a CNS effect that is most intense during the early phase of therapy and diminishes with continued medication use. The client does not need to notify the physician about fatigue.
Test-Taking Strategy: Use the process of elimination. Recalling that baclofen is a skeletal muscle relaxant will direct you easily to option 2. If you were unsure of the correct option, use general principles related to medication administration. Alcohol should be avoided with the use of medications. Review client teaching points related to this medication if you had difficulty with this question.
Level of Cognitive Ability: Application
Client Needs: Physiological Integrity
Integrated Process: Teaching and Learning
Content Area: Pharmacology
Reference: Lehne, R. (2007). *Pharmacology for nursing care* (6th ed., p. 240). Philadelphia: W.B. Saunders.

6. **4**
Rationale: Dose-related liver damage is the most serious adverse effect of dantrolene. To reduce the risk of liver damage, tests of liver function should be performed before treatment and throughout the treatment interval. Dantrolene is administered in the lowest effective dosage for the shortest time necessary.
Test-Taking Strategy: Use the process of elimination. Eliminate options 1 and 3 because these tests assess kidney function and are comparative or alike. From the remaining options, you must recall that this medication affects liver function. Review this medication if you had difficulty with this question.
Level of Cognitive Ability: Analysis
Client Needs: Physiological Integrity
Integrated Process: Nursing Process—analysis
Content Area: Pharmacology
Reference: Hodgson, B., & Kizior, R. (2007). *Saunders nursing drug handbook 2007* (p. 313). Philadelphia: W.B. Saunders.

7. **1**
Rationale: Clients with seizure disorders may have a lowered seizure threshold when baclofen is administered. Concurrent therapy may require an increase in the anticonvulsive medication. The disorders in options 2, 3, and 4 are not contraindications or cautions for the use of this medication.
Test-Taking Strategy: Use the process of elimination and knowledge about the contraindications and the cautions associated with the administration of baclofen. Remember that baclofen is used with caution for clients with a seizure disorder. If you are unfamiliar with these contraindications and cautions, review this content.
Level of Cognitive Ability: Analysis
Client Needs: Physiological Integrity
Integrated Process: Nursing Process—analysis
Content Area: Pharmacology
Reference: Lehne, R. (2007). *Pharmacology for nursing care* (6th ed., p. 240). Philadelphia: W.B. Saunders.

8. 1

Rationale: Because cyclobenzaprine (Flexeril) has anticholinergic effects, it should be used with caution in clients with a history of urinary retention, glaucoma, and increased intraocular pressure. Cyclobenzaprine should be used only for a short term (2 to 3 weeks).

Test-Taking Strategy: Use the process of elimination. Recalling that this medication has anticholinergic effects will direct you to option 1. If you are unfamiliar with this medication and the contraindications associated with its administration, review this content.

Level of Cognitive Ability: Analysis
Client Needs: Physiological Integrity
Integrated Process: Nursing Process—analysis
Content Area: Pharmacology
Reference: Hodgson, B., & Kizior, R. (2007). *Saunders nursing drug handbook 2007* (p. 297). Philadelphia: W.B. Saunders.

9. 4

Rationale: The client needs to be told that the urine may turn brown, black, or green. Other adverse effects include blurred vision, nasal congestion, urticaria, and rash. The client needs to be instructed that if these adverse effects occur to notify the physician.

Test-Taking Strategy: Use the process of elimination. Note the strategic words *need for further education*. These words indicate a negative event query and ask you to select an option that is incorrect. This will assist in directing you to option 4. If you had difficulty with this question, review this medication.

Level of Cognitive Ability: Analysis
Client Needs: Physiological Integrity
Integrated Process: Teaching and Learning
Content Area: Pharmacology
Reference: Lehne, R. (2007). *Pharmacology for nursing care* (6th ed., p. 237). Philadelphia: W.B. Saunders.

10. 3

Rationale: Intravenous administration of methocarbamol can cause hypotension and bradycardia. The nurse needs to monitor for these side effects. Options 1, 2, and 4 are not a concern with administration of this medication.

Test-Taking Strategy: Use the process of elimination. Eliminate options 1 and 2 first because they are comparative or alike. Knowledge about the specific side effects related to the intravenous use of this medication will direct you to option 3. Remember that hypotension and bradycardia can occur with intravenous administration of methocarbamol. Review this medication if you had difficulty with this question.

Level of Cognitive Ability: Analysis
Client Needs: Physiological Integrity
Integrated Process: Nursing Process—analysis
Content Area: Pharmacology
Reference: Hodgson, B., & Kizior, R. (2007). *Saunders nursing drug handbook 2007* (p. 749). Philadelphia: W.B. Saunders.

ALTERNATE ITEM FORMAT: MULTIPLE RESPONSE

Answer: 1, 2, 3, 4

Rationale: Because emotional stress frequently exacerbates the symptoms of rheumatoid arthritis, the absence of symptoms is a positive finding. DMARDs are given to slow progression of joint degeneration. In addition, the improvement in the range of motion after 3 months of therapy with normal blood work is a positive finding. Temperature elevation and inflammation and irritation at the medication injection site could indicate signs of infection.

Test-Taking Strategy: Use the process of elimination and focus on the subject, acceptable responses to therapy. Recalling that signs of an infection can indicate an unexpected finding will assist in eliminating options 5 and 6. Review the expected effects of this medication if you had difficulty with this question.

Level of Cognitive Ability: Analysis
Client Needs: Physiological Integrity
Integrated Process: Nursing Process—assessment
Content Area: Pharmacology
Reference: Lilly, L., Harrington, S., & Snider, J. (2005). *Pharmacology and the nursing process* (4th ed., pp. 822-826). St Louis: Mosby.

REFERENCES

Hodgson, B., & Kizior, R. (2007). *Saunders nursing drug handbook 2007*. Philadelphia: W.B. Saunders.

Ignatavicius, D., & Workman, M. (2006). *Medical-surgical nursing: Critical thinking for collaborative care* (5th ed.). Philadelphia: W.B. Saunders.

Lehne, R. (2007). *Pharmacology for nursing care* (6th ed.). Philadelphia: W.B. Saunders.

Lewis, S., Heitkemper, M., & Dirksen, S. (2004). *Medical-surgical nursing: Assessment and management of clinical problems* (6th ed.). St. Louis: Mosby.

Lilly, L., Harrington, S., & Snider, J. (2005). *Pharmacology and the nursing process* (4th ed.). St Louis: Mosby.

The Adult Client With an Immune Disorder

PYRAMID TERMS

acquired immunity   Immunity received passively from the mother's antibodies, animal serum, or antibodies produced in response to a disease. Immunization produces active acquired immunity.

allergy   An abnormal, individual response to certain substances that normally do not trigger such an exaggerated reaction.

cellular response   A delayed response against slowly developing bacterial infections; also called delayed hypersensitivity.

humoral response   An immediate response that provides protection against acute, rapidly developing bacterial and viral infections.

immunodeficiency   The absence or inadequate production of immune bodies.

innate immunity   Immunity present at birth.

Kaposi's sarcoma   Skin lesions that occur in individuals with a compromised immune system.

Lyme disease   An infection acquired from a tick bite. Ticks live in wooded areas and survive by attaching to a host.

▲ PYRAMID TO SUCCESS

Pyramid Points focus on the effects of and complications associated with an immune deficiency. Specific focus relates to the nursing care related to the disorder, the impact of the treatment or disorder, and client adaptation. Acquired immunodeficiency syndrome is a pyramid focus, along with protecting the client from infection and preventing the transmission of infection to other individuals. Psychosocial issues relate to social isolation and the body image disturbances that can occur as a result of the immune disorder. The Integrated Processes addressed in this unit include Caring, Communication and Documentation, Nursing Process, and Teaching and Learning.

CLIENT NEEDS

Safe and Effective Care Environment

Acting as an advocate related to the client's decisions
Addressing advance directives
Consulting with members of the health care team
Establishing priorities
Handling hazardous and infectious materials safely
Implementing standard and other precautions
Maintaining asepsis
Maintaining confidentiality regarding diagnosis
Obtaining informed consent for treatments and procedures
Preventing infection
Upholding client rights

Health Promotion and Maintenance

Ensuring that the client receives recommended immunizations
Implementing health screening measures
Monitoring for expected body image changes
Preventing disease related to infection
Providing health promotion programs
Respecting client lifestyle choices

Psychosocial Integrity

Assisting in mobilizing appropriate support and resource systems
Assisting the client and family to cope
Assisting the client to cope, adapt, and problem-solve during illness or stressful events
Considering religious, spiritual, and cultural preferences
Discussing grief and loss related to death and the dying process

Promoting a positive environment to maintain optimal quality of life

Physiological Integrity

Managing pain

Managing medical emergencies

Monitoring for the expected and unexpected responses to treatments

Promoting nutrition

Protecting the client from infection

Providing basic care and comfort

Reviewing diagnostic test and laboratory test results

REFERENCES

Black, J., & Hawks, J. (2005). *Medical-surgical nursing: Clinical management for positive outcomes* (7th ed.). Philadelphia: W.B. Saunders.

Chernecky, C., & Berger, B. (2004). *Laboratory tests and diagnostic procedures* (4th ed.). Philadelphia: W.B. Saunders.

Harkreader, H., & Hogan, M. (2004). *Fundamentals of nursing: Caring and clinical judgment* (2nd ed.). Philadelphia: W.B. Saunders.

Ignatavicius, D., & Workman, M. (2006). *Medical-surgical nursing: Critical thinking for collaborative care* (5th ed.). Philadelphia: W.B. Saunders.

Jarvis, C. (2004). *Physical examination and health assessment* (4th ed.). St. Louis: W.B. Saunders.

Lewis, S., Heitkemper, M., & Dirksen, S. (2004). *Medical-surgical nursing: Assessment and management of clinical problems* (6th ed.). St. Louis: Mosby.

Lilley, L., Harrington, S., & Snyder, J. (2005). *Pharmacology and the nursing process* (4th ed.). St. Louis: Elsevier.

Mosby. (2006). *Mosby's dictionary of medicine, nursing and health professions* (7th ed.). St. Louis: Mosby.

National Council of State Boards of Nursing (Eds.). (2007). *2007 NCLEX-RN® detailed test plan.* Chicago: Author.

Potter, P., & Perry, A. (2005), *Fundamentals of nursing* (6th ed.). St. Louis: Mosby.

Varcarolis, E., Carson, V., & Shoemaker, N. (2006). *Foundations of psychiatric mental health nursing: A clinical approach* (5th ed.). Philadelphia: W.B. Saunders.

Immune Disorders

I. FUNCTIONS OF THE IMMUNE SYSTEM
 A. The immune system provides protection against invasion by microorganisms from outside the body.
 B. The immune system protects the body from internal threats and maintains the internal environment by removing dead or damaged cells.

II. IMMUNE RESPONSE
 A. T lymphocytes and B lymphocytes
  1. Lymphocytes migrate to lymphoid tissue where they remain dormant until they need to form sensitized lymphocytes for cellular immunity or antibodies for humoral immunity.
  2. Some B lymphocytes lie dormant until a specific antigen enters the body, at which time they greatly increase in number and are available for defense.
  3. T lymphocytes are responsible for rejection of transplanted tissue.
  4. T and B lymphocytes are necessary for a normal immune response.
 B. **Humoral response**
  1. **Humoral response** is immediate.
  2. This type of response provides protection against acute, rapidly developing bacterial and viral infections.
 C. **Cellular response**
  1. **Cellular response** is delayed; this is also called delayed hypersensitivity.
  2. This type of response is active against slowly developing bacterial infections and is involved in autoimmune responses, some allergic reactions, and rejection of foreign cells.

III. IMMUNITY
 A. Natural immunity
  1. Natural immunity is also called native or **innate immunity.**
  2. It is present at birth and includes biochemical, physical, and mechanical barriers of defense, as well as the inflammatory response.
 B. **Acquired immunity**
  1. Acquired or adaptive immunity is received passively from the mother's antibodies, animal serum, or antibodies produced in response to a disease.
  2. Immunization produces active **acquired immunity.**

IV. IMMUNIZATIONS (See Chap. 47 for information about immunizations.)

V. LABORATORY STUDIES
 A. Antinuclear antibody (ANA) titer determination
  1. The ANA titer determination is a blood test used for the differential diagnosis of rheumatic diseases and for the detection of antinucleoprotein factors and patterns associated with certain autoimmune diseases.
  2. The test is positive at a titer of 1:20 or 1:40, depending on the laboratory.
  3. A positive result does not necessarily confirm a disease.
  4. The ANA titer is positive in most individuals diagnosed with systemic lupus erythematosus (SLE).
  5. An ANA titer result can be false-positive in a small proportion of the normal population.

B. Anti-dsDNA antibody test
1. The anti-dsDNA (double-stranded DNA) antibody test is a blood test done specifically to identify or differentiate DNA antibodies found in SLE.
2. The test supports a diagnosis, monitors disease activity and response to therapy, and establishes a prognosis for SLE.
3. Values
   a. Negative: Lower than 70 units by enzyme-linked immunosorbent assay (ELISA)
   b. Borderline: 70 to 200 units
   c. Positive: Higher than 200 units
C. See Chap. 11 for testing related to acquired **immunodeficiency** syndrome (AIDS)
D. Skin testing
1. Description
   a. The administration of an allergen to the surface of the skin or into the dermis
   b. Administered by patch, scratch, or intradermal techniques
2. Preprocedure interventions
   a. Discontinue systemic corticosteroids or antihistamine therapy 5 days before the test as prescribed.
   b. Obtain informed consent.
   c. Have resuscitation equipment available if a scratch test is performed, because it may induce an anaphylactic reaction.
3. Postprocedure interventions
   a. Record the site, date, and time of the test.
   b. Record the date and time for follow-up site reading.
   c. Inspect the site for erythema, papules, vesicles, edema, and wheal (Fig. 69-1).
   d. Measure wheal and document size and other findings.
   e. Provide the client with a list of potential allergens, if identified.

VI. IMMUNODEFICIENCY
A. Description
1. **Immunodeficiency** is the absence or inadequate production of immune bodies.
2. The disorder can be congenital (primary) or acquired (secondary).
3. Treatment depends on the inadequacy of immune bodies and its primary cause.
B. Assessment
1. Factors that decrease immune function
2. Frequent infections
3. Nutritional status
4. Medication history, such as use of corticosteroids for long periods
5. History of alcohol or drug abuse
C. Interventions
1. Protect the client from infection.
2. Promote a balanced diet with adequate nutrition.

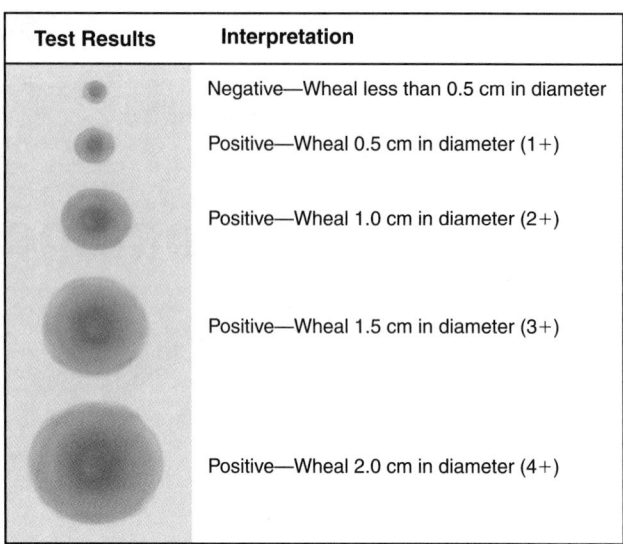

Test Results	Interpretation
	Negative—Wheal less than 0.5 cm in diameter
	Positive—Wheal 0.5 cm in diameter (1+)
	Positive—Wheal 1.0 cm in diameter (2+)
	Positive—Wheal 1.5 cm in diameter (3+)
	Positive—Wheal 2.0 cm in diameter (4+)

FIG. 69-1 Interpretation of intradermal test results based on the size of the wheal after 15 to 30 minutes. (From Phipps, W., Monahan, F., Sands, J., et al. [2003]. *Medical-surgical nursing: Health and illness perspectives* [7th ed.]. St. Louis: Mosby.)

3. Use strict aseptic technique for all procedures.
4. Provide psychosocial care regarding lifestyle changes and role changes.
5. Instruct the client in measures to prevent infection.

VII. HYPERSENSITIVITY AND ALLERGY
A. Description
1. An **allergy** is an abnormal, individual response to certain substances that normally do not trigger such an exaggerated reaction.
2. In some types of allergies, a reaction occurs on a second and subsequent contact with the allergen.
3. Skin testing may be done to determine the allergen.
4. Types of hypersensitivity reactions (Table 69-1)
B. Assessment
1. History of exposure to allergens
2. Itching, tearing, and burning of eyes and skin
3. Rashes
4. Nose twitching, nasal stuffiness
C. Interventions
1. Identification of the specific allergen.
2. Management of the symptoms with antihistamines, anti-inflammatory agents, or corticosteroids
3. Ointments, creams, wet compresses, and soothing baths for local reactions
4. Desensitization programs may be recommended.

TABLE 69-1

Types of Hypersensitivity Reactions

Type	Causative Component	Pathological Process	Reaction
I: Immediate, anaphylactic	IgE	Mast cell degranulation ↓ Histamine and leukotriene release	Anaphylaxis Atopic diseases Skin reactions
II: Cytolytic, cytotoxic	IgG IgM Complement	Complement fixation ↓ Cell lysis	ABO incompatibility Drug-induced hemolytic anemia
III: Immune complex	Antigen-antibody complexes	Deposition in vessels and tissue walls ↓ Inflammation	Arthus reaction Serum sickness Systemic lupus erythematosus Acute glomerulonephritis
IV: Cell-mediated, delayed	Sensitized T cells	Lymphokine release	Tuberculosis Contact dermatitis Transplant rejection

Ig, Immunoglobulin.
From Black, J., & Hawks, J., (2005). *Medical-surgical nursing: Clinical management for positive outcomes* (7th ed.). Philadelphia: W.B. Saunders.

VIII. ANAPHYLAXIS

A. Description
1. Anaphylaxis is a serious and immediate hypersensitivity reaction that releases histamine from the damaged cells.
2. Anaphylaxis can be systemic or cutaneous (localized).

B. Assessment (Fig. 69-2)

C. Interventions
1. Establish a patent airway.
2. Prepare for the administration of epinephrine (Adrenalin), diphenhydramine hydrochloride (Benadryl), or corticosteroids.
3. Provide measures to control shock.
4. Provide emotional support.
5. Instruct the client to wear a Medic-Alert bracelet prior to discharge from emergent care.
6. Instruct the client in the use of prescribed medication such as epinephrine (EpiPen) for immediate treatment of a future reaction.

IX. LATEX ALLERGY

A. Description
1. Latex **allergy** is a hypersensitivity to latex.
2. The source of the allergic reaction is thought to be the proteins in the natural rubber latex or the various chemicals used in the manufacturing process of latex gloves.
3. Symptoms of the **allergy** can range from mild contact dermatitis to moderately severe symptoms of rhinitis, conjunctivitis, urticaria, and bronchospasm to severe life-threatening anaphylaxis.

B. Common routes of exposure (Box 69-1)
1. Cutaneous: Natural latex gloves and latex balloons

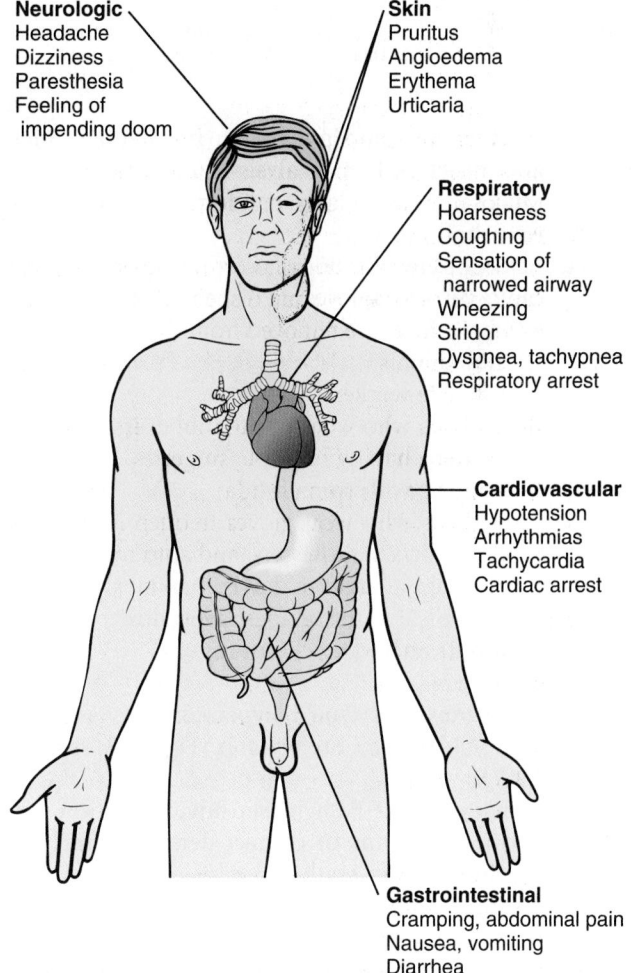

Neurologic
Headache
Dizziness
Paresthesia
Feeling of impending doom

Skin
Pruritus
Angioedema
Erythema
Urticaria

Respiratory
Hoarseness
Coughing
Sensation of narrowed airway
Wheezing
Stridor
Dyspnea, tachypnea
Respiratory arrest

Cardiovascular
Hypotension
Arrhythmias
Tachycardia
Cardiac arrest

Gastrointestinal
Cramping, abdominal pain
Nausea, vomiting
Diarrhea

FIG. 69-2 Clinical manifestations of a systemic anaphylactic reaction. (From Lewis, S., Heitkemper, M., & Dirksen, S. [2004]. *Medical-surgical nursing: Assessment and management of clinical problems* [6th ed.]. St. Louis: Mosby.)

BOX 69-1

Products That May Contain Natural Rubber Latex

Ace bandages (brown)
Adhesive or elastic bandages
Ambu bag
Balloons
Blood pressure cuff (tubing and bladder)
Catheter leg bag straps
Catheters
Condoms
Diaphragms
Elastic pressure stockings
Electrocardiographic pads
Feminine hygiene pads
Gloves
Intravenous catheters, tubing, and rubber injection ports
Levin tubes
Pads for crutches
Prepackaged enema kits
Rubber stoppers on medication vials
Stethoscopes
Syringes

Note: Health care agencies use as many nonlatex products as possible and have nonlatex supplies available for clients with a latex allergy.

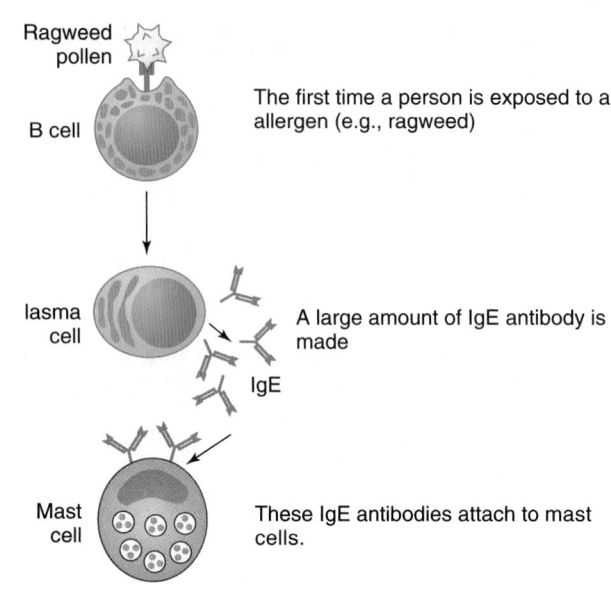

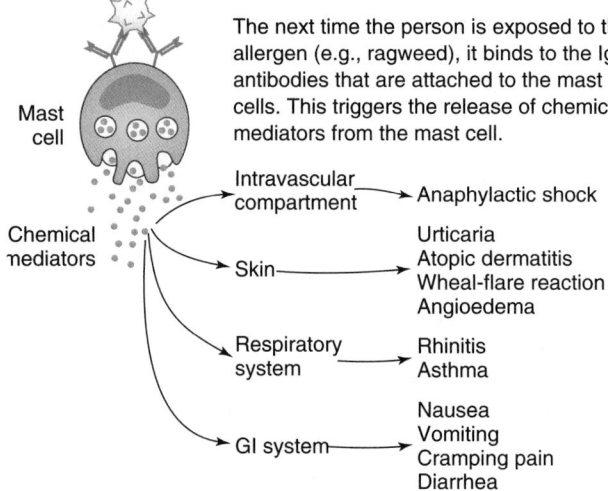

FIG. 69-3 Steps in a type 1 allergic reaction. (From Lewis, S., Heitkemper, M., & Dirksen, S. [2004]. *Medical-surgical nursing: Assessment and management of clinical problems* [6th ed.]. St. Louis: Mosby.)

2. Percutaneous and parenteral: Intravenous lines and catheters; hemodialysis equipment
3. Mucosal: Use of latex condoms, catheters, airways, and nipples
4. Aerosol: Aerosolization of powder from latex gloves can occur when gloves are dispensed from the box or when gloves are removed from the hands.

C. At-risk individuals
1. Health care workers
2. Individuals who work in the rubber industry.
3. Individuals having multiple surgeries
4. Individuals with spina bifida
5. Individuals who wear gloves frequently, such as food handlers, hairdressers, and auto mechanics
6. Individuals allergic to kiwis, bananas, pineapples, tropical fruits, grapes, avocados, potatoes, hazelnuts and water chestnuts

▲ D. Assessment
1. Anaphylaxis or type I hypersensitivity is a response to natural rubber latex (Fig. 69-3; see Fig. 69-2).
2. A delayed type IV hypersensitivity reaction can occur; symptoms of contact dermatitis include pruritus, edema, erythema, vesicles, papules, and crusting and thickening of the skin and can occur within 6 to 48 hours.

▲ E. Interventions (Box 69-2)

X. AUTOIMMUNE DISEASE
A. Description
1. Body is unable to recognize its own cells as a part of itself.

BOX 69-2

Interventions for the Client With a Latex Allergy

Ask the client about a known allergy to latex when performing the initial assessment.
Identify risk factors for a latex allergy in the client.
Use nonlatex gloves and all latex-safe supplies.
Keep a latex-safe supply cart near the client's room.
Apply a cloth barrier to the client's arm under a blood pressure cuff.
Use latex-free syringes, medication containers (glass ampules), and latex-safe intravenous equipment.
Instruct the client to wear a Medic-Alert bracelet.
Instruct the client about the importance of informing health care providers and local and paramedic ambulance companies about the allergy.

2. Autoimmune disease can affect collagenous tissue.

B. Systemic lupus erythematosus (SLE)

1. Description
   a. Chronic, progressive, systemic inflammatory disease that can cause major organs and systems to fail
   b. Connective tissue and fibrin deposits collect in blood vessels on collagen fibers and on organs.
   c. The deposits lead to necrosis and inflammation in blood vessels, lymph nodes, gastrointestinal tract, and pleura.
   d. No cure for the disease is known.

2. Causes
   a. The cause of SLE is unknown, but it is believed to be a defect in immunological mechanisms, with a genetic origin.
   b. Precipitating factors include medications, stress, genetic factors, sunlight or ultraviolet light, and pregnancy.

3. Assessment
   a. Assess for precipitating factors.
   b. Erythema butterfly or rash of the face
   c. Dry, scaly, raised rash on the face or upper body
   d. Fever
   e. Weakness, malaise, and fatigue
   f. Anorexia
   g. Weight loss
   h. Photosensitivity
   i. Joint pain
   j. Erythema of the palms
   k. Anemia
   l. Positive ANA test and lupus erythematosus (LE) preparation
   m. Elevated erythrocyte sedimentation rate (ESR) and C-reactive protein level

4. Interventions
   a. Monitor skin integrity and provide frequent oral care.
   b. Instruct the client to clean the skin with a mild soap, avoiding harsh and perfume substances.
   c. Assist with the use of ointments and creams for the rash as prescribed.
   d. Identify factors contributing to fatigue.
   e. Administer iron, folic acid, or vitamin supplements as prescribed if anemia occurs.
   f. Provide a high-vitamin and high-iron diet.
   g. Provide a high-protein diet if there is no evidence of kidney disease.
   h. Instruct in measures to conserve energy, such as pacing activities and balancing rest with exercise.
   i. Administer topical or systemic corticosteroids, salicylates, and nonsteroidal anti-inflammatory drugs as prescribed for pain and inflammation.
   j. Administer medications to decrease the inflammatory response as prescribed.
   k. Instruct the client to avoid exposure to sunlight and ultraviolet light.
   l. Monitor for proteinuria and red cell casts in the urine.
   m. Monitor for bruising, bleeding, and injury.
   n. Assist with plasmapheresis as prescribed to remove autoantibodies and immune complexes from the blood before organ damage occurs.
   o. Monitor for signs of organ involvement such as pleuritis, nephritis, pericarditis, coronary artery disease, hypertension, neuritis, anemia, and peritonitis.
   p. Note that lupus nephritis occurs early in the disease process.
   q. Provide supportive therapy as major organs become affected.
   r. Provide emotional support and encourage the client to verbalize feelings.
   s. Provide information regarding support groups and encourage the use of community resources.

C. Scleroderma (systemic sclerosis)

1. Description
   a. Scleroderma is a chronic connective tissue disease similar to SLE that is characterized by inflammation, fibrosis, and sclerosis.
   b. This disorder affects the connective tissue throughout the body.
   c. It causes fibrotic changes involving the skin, synovial membranes, esophagus, heart, lungs, kidneys, and gastrointestinal tract.
   d. Treatment is directed toward forcing the disease into remission and slowing its progress.

2. Assessment
   a. Pain
   b. Stiffness and muscle weakness
   c. Pitting edema of the hands and fingers that progresses to the rest of the body
   d. Taut and shiny skin that is free from wrinkles
   e. Skin tissue is tight, hard, and thick, loses its elasticity, and adheres to underlying structures.
   f. Dysphagia
   g. Decreased range of motion
   h. Joint contractures
   i. Inability to perform activities of daily living

3. Interventions
   a. Encourage activity as tolerated.
   b. Maintain a constant room temperature.
   c. Provide small frequent meals, eliminating foods that stimulate gastric secretions, such as spicy foods, caffeine, and alcohol.

d. Advise the client to sit up for 1 to 2 hours after meals if there is esophageal involvement.

e. Provide supportive therapy as the major organs become affected.

f. Administer corticosteroids as prescribed for inflammation.

g. Provide emotional support and encourage the use of resources as necessary.

D. Polyarteritis nodosa
1. Description
   a. Polyarteritis nodosa is a collagen disease; it is a form of systemic vasculitis that causes inflammation of the arteries in visceral organs, brain, and skin..
   b. Treatment is similar to the treatment for SLE.
   c. Polyarteritis nodosa affects middle-aged men.
   d. The cause is unknown, and the prognosis is poor.
   e. Renal disorders and cardiac involvement are the most frequent causes of death.
2. Assessment
   a. Malaise and weakness
   b. Low-grade fever
   c. Severe abdominal pain
   d. Bloody diarrhea
   e. Weight loss
   f. Elevated ESR
3. Interventions
   a. Provide supportive care as required.
   b. Provide a well-balanced diet.
   c. Administer corticosteroids and analgesics to control pain and inflammation.
   d. Provide emotional support and encourage the client to verbalize feelings.
   e. Initiate support services for the client.

E. Pemphigus
1. Description
   a. A group of related disorders, including pemphigus vulgaris, vegetans, foliaceus, and erythematosus.
   b. Pemphigus is a rare autoimmune disease that occurs predominantly between middle and old age.
   c. The cause is unknown, and the disorder is potentially fatal.
   d. Treatment is aimed at suppressing the immune response that causes blister formation.
2. Assessment
   a. Lesions appear as fragile, flaccid bullae.
   b. Partial-thickness wounds bleed, weep, and form crusts when bullae are disrupted.
   c. Debilitation, malaise, and pain
   d. Chewing and swallowing difficulties
   e. Nikolsky's sign: Separation of the epidermis caused by rubbing the skin
   f. Leukocytosis, eosinophilia, foul-smelling discharge from skin

3. Interventions
   a. Provide supportive care.
   b. Provide oral hygiene and increase fluid intake.
   c. Soothe oral lesions.
   d. Assist with oatmeal or potassium permanganate baths, or other soothing baths, as prescribed for relief of symptoms.
   e. Administer topical or systemic antibiotics as prescribed for secondary infections.
   f. Administer corticosteroids and cytotoxic agents as prescribed to bring about remission.

XI. GOODPASTURE'S SYNDROME

A. Description
1. Goodpasture's syndrome is an autoimmune disorder; autoantibodies are made against the glomerular basement membrane and alveolar basement membrane.
2. Goodpasture's syndrome is most common in males and young adults who smoke; the exact cause is unknown.
3. The lungs and the kidneys are affected primarily, and the disorder usually is not diagnosed until significant pulmonary or renal involvement occurs.

B. Assessment
1. Clinical manifestations indicating pulmonary and renal involvement
2. Shortness of breath
3. Hemoptysis
4. Decreased urine output
5. Edema and weight gain
6. Hypertension and tachycardia

C. Interventions
1. Focus on suppressing the autoimmune response with medications such as corticosteroids and plasmapheresis (filtration of the plasma to remove some proteins) to remove the autoantibodies.
2. Provide supportive therapy for pulmonary and renal involvement.

XII. LYME DISEASE

A. Description
1. **Lyme disease** is an infection caused by the spirochete *Borrelia burgdorferi*, acquired from a tick bite (ticks live in wooded areas and survive by attaching to a host).
2. Infection with the spirochete stimulates inflammatory cytokines and autoimmune mechanisms.

B. Assessment (Box 69-3; Fig. 69-4)

C. Interventions
1. Gently remove the tick with tweezers, wash the skin with antiseptic, and dispose of the tick by flushing it down the toilet; the tick may also be placed in a sealed jar so that the health care provider can inspect it and determine its type.

BOX 69-3
Assessment and Stages of Lyme Disease

FIRST STAGE

Symptoms can occur several days to months following the bite.

A small red pimple develops that spreads into a ring-shaped rash.

Rash may be large or small, or may not occur at all.

Flu-like symptoms occur, such as headaches, stiff neck, muscle aches, and fatigue.

SECOND STAGE

This stage occurs several weeks following the bite.

Joint pain occurs.

Neurological complications occur.

Cardiac complications occur.

THIRD STAGE

Large joints become involved.

Arthritis progresses.

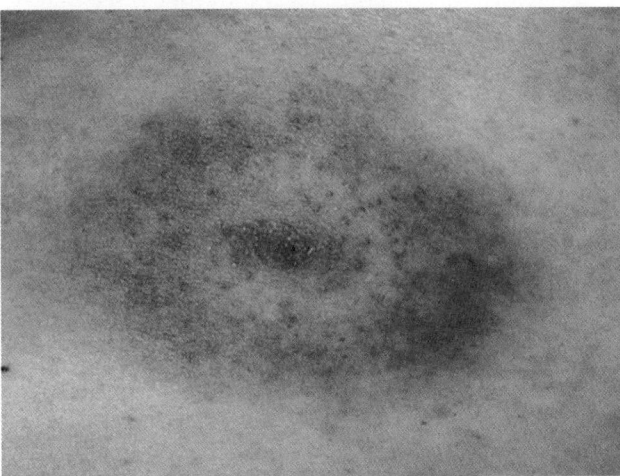

FIG. 69-4 Erythema migrans of Lyme disease. (From Swartz, M. [2006]. *Textbook of physical diagnosis: History and examination* [5th ed.]. Philadelphia: W.B. Saunders.)

2. Obtain a blood test 4 to 6 weeks after a bite to detect the presence of the disease (testing before this time is not reliable).
3. Instruct the client in the administration of antibiotics as prescribed if the disease is confirmed.
4. Instruct the client to avoid areas that contain ticks, such as wooded grassy areas, especially in the summer months.
5. Instruct the client to wear long-sleeved tops, long pants, closed shoes, and hats while outside.
6. Instruct the client to spray the body with tick repellent before going outside.
7. Instruct the client to examine the body when returning inside for the presence of ticks.

XIII. IMMUNODEFICIENCY SYNDROMES

A. Acquired **immunodeficiency** syndrome (AIDS) ▲
   1. AIDS is a viral disease caused by human **immunodeficiency** virus (HIV), which destroys T cells, thereby increasing susceptibility to infection and malignancy (Fig. 69-5).
   2. The syndrome is manifested clinically by opportunistic infection and unusual neoplasms.
   3. AIDS is considered a chronic illness.
   4. The disease has a long incubation period, sometimes 10 years or longer.
   5. Manifestations may not appear until late in the infection.
B. Diagnosis and monitoring the client with AIDS ▲
   1. See Chap. 11 for diagnostic tests.
   2. Refer to Box 69-4 for tests used to evaluate the progression of HIV infection.
C. High-risk groups ▲
   1. Heterosexual or homosexual contact with high-risk individuals
   2. Intravenous drug abusers
   3. Persons receiving blood products
   4. Health care workers
   5. Babies born to infected mothers
D. Assessment ▲
   1. Malaise, fever, anorexia, weight loss, influenza-like symptoms
   2. Lymphadenopathy for at least 3 months
   3. Leukopenia
   4. Diarrhea
   5. Fatigue
   6. Night sweats
   7. Presence of opportunistic infections
   8. Protozoal infections (*Pneumocystis jiroveci* pneumonia, major source of mortality)
   9. Neoplasms (**Kaposi's sarcoma,** purplish-red lesions of internal organs and skin, B-cell non-Hodgkin's lymphoma, cervical cancer)
   10. Fungal infections (candidiasis, histoplasmosis)
   11. Viral infections (cytomegalovirus, herpes simplex)
   12. Bacterial infections
E. Interventions ▲
   1. Provide respiratory support.
   2. Administer oxygen and respiratory treatments as prescribed.
   3. Provide psychosocial support as needed.
   4. Maintain fluid and electrolyte balance.
   5. Monitor for signs of infection.
   6. Prevent the spread of infection.
   7. Initiate standard precautions.
   8. Provide comfort as necessary.
   9. Provide meticulous skin care.
   10. Provide adequate nutritional support as prescribed.
   11. See Chap. 25 and 46 for additional information on AIDS.

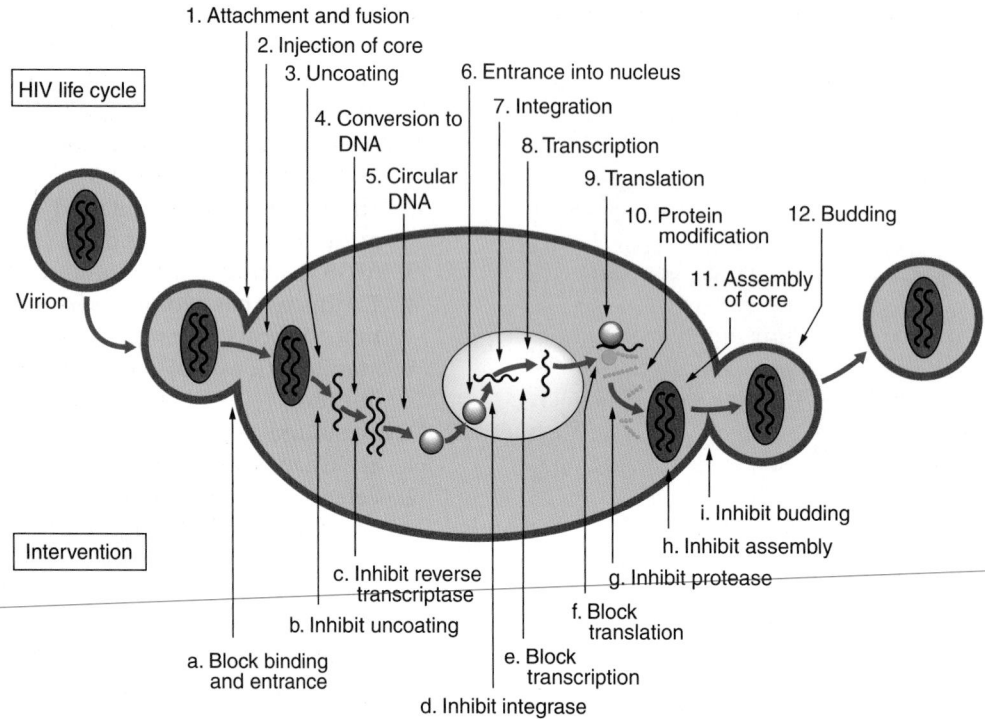

FIG. 69-5 The life cycle of HIV. (From Ignatavicius, D., & Workman, M. [2006]. *Medical-surgical nursing: Critical thinking for collaborative care* [5th ed.]. Philadelphia: W.B. Saunders.)

BOX 69-4

Tests Used to Evaluate Progression of Human Immunodeficiency Virus (HIV) Infection

COMPLETE BLOOD CELL COUNT
White blood cell (WBC) count normal to decreased
Lymphopenia (<30% of the normal number of WBCs)
Thrombocytopenia (decreased platelet count)

LYMPHOCYTE SCREEN
Reduced CD4+/CD8+ T-cell ratio
CD4+ (helper) lymphocytes decreased
CD8+ lymphocytes increased

QUANTITATIVE IMMUNOGLOBULIN
Immunoglobulin G (IgG) increased
IgA frequently increased

CHEMISTRY PANEL
Lactate dehydrogenase level increased (all fractions)
Serum albumin level decreased
Total protein increased

Cholesterol level decreased
*AST and ALT levels elevated

ANERGY PANEL
Nonreactive (anergic) or poorly reactive to infectious
agents or environmental materials (e.g., pokeweed,
phytohemagglutinin mitogens and antigens, mumps,
Candida)

HEPATITIS B SURFACE ANTIGEN TESTING
To detect the presence of hepatitis C

BLOOD CULTURES
To detect septicemia

CHEST RADIOGRAPHY
To detect *Pneumocystis jiroveci* infection or tuberculosis

*AST, Aspartate aminotransferase; *ALT, alanine aminotransferase.
From Copstead, L., & Banasik, J. (2005). *Pathophysiology* (3rd ed.). St. Louis: Mosby.

▲ F. **Kaposi's sarcoma**
   1. Description: Skin lesions that occur primarily in individuals with a compromised immune system
   2. Assessment
      a. **Kaposi's sarcoma** is a slow-growing tumor that appears as raised, oblong, purplish, reddish-brown lesions; may be tender or nontender.

   b. Organ involvement includes the lymph nodes, airways or lungs, or any part of the gastrointestinal tract from the mouth to anus.
   3. Interventions
      a. Maintain standard precautions.
      b. Provide protective isolation if the immune system is depressed.

c. Prepare the client for radiation therapy or chemotherapy as prescribed.

d. Administer immunotherapy, as prescribed, to stabilize the immune system.

XIV. POST-TRANSPLANTATION IMMUNODEFICIENCY

A. Description

1. Secondary **immunodeficiency** is immunosuppression caused by therapeutic agents.

2. The client must take immunosuppression agents for the rest of his or her life post-transplantation to decrease rejection of the transplanted organ or tissue.

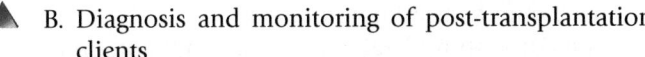 B. Diagnosis and monitoring of post-transplantation clients

1. Check renal and hepatic function.

2. Monitor the complete cell count with differential to determine signs of infection.

3. Assess all body secretions periodically for blood.

▲ C. High-risk clients

1. Clients with a history of malignancy or premalignancy have an increased susceptibility to malignancy if immunosuppressed.

2. Clients with recent infection or exposure to tuberculosis, herpes zoster, or chickenpox have a high risk for severe generalized disease when on immunosuppressive agents.

▲ D. Assessment

1. Assess for signs of opportunistic infections.

2. Assess nutritional status.

3. Assess for signs of rejection (signs will depend on the organ or tissue transplant).

▲ E. Interventions

1. Strict aseptic technique is necessary.

2. Provide teaching regarding asepsis and the signs of infection and rejection.

3. Provide psychosocial support as needed.

4. Provide client teaching about immunosuppressants.

PRACTICE QUESTIONS

1. A female client arrives at the health care clinic and tells the nurse that she was just bitten by a tick and would like to be tested for Lyme disease. The client tells the nurse that she removed the tick and flushed it down the toilet. Which of the following nursing actions is most appropriate?

1. Refer the client for a blood test immediately.

2. Inform the client that there is no test available for Lyme disease.

3. Tell the client that testing is not necessary unless arthralgia develops.

4. Instruct the client to return in 4 to 6 weeks to be tested because testing before this time is not reliable.

2. Following diagnosis of stage I Lyme disease, the nurse would anticipate that which of the following will be part of the treatment plan for the client?

1. No treatment unless symptoms develop

2. A 3-week course of oral antibiotic therapy

3. Daily oatmeal baths for 2 weeks

4. Treatment with intravenously administered antibiotics

3. A Cub Scout leader, who is a nurse preparing a group of Cub Scouts for an overnight camping trip, instructs the scouts about the methods to prevent Lyme disease. Which statement by one of the Cub Scouts indicates a need for further instructions?

1. "I need to bring a hat to wear during the trip."

2. "I should wear long-sleeved tops and long pants."

3. "I should not use insect repellents because it will attract the ticks."

4. "I need to wear closed shoes and socks that can be pulled up over my pants."

4. The client with acquired immunodeficiency syndrome is diagnosed with cutaneous Kaposi's sarcoma. Based on this diagnosis, the nurse understands that this has been confirmed by which of the following?

1. Swelling in the genital area

2. Swelling in the lower extremities

3. Punch biopsy of the cutaneous lesions

4. Appearance of reddish-blue lesions noted on the skin

5. Which of the following individuals is least likely at risk for the development of Kaposi's sarcoma?

1. A kidney transplant client

2. A male with a history of same-gender partners

3. A client receiving antineoplastic medications

4. An individual working in an environment in which he or she is exposed to asbestos

6. The nurse prepares to give a bath and change the bed linens on a client with cutaneous Kaposi's sarcoma lesions. The lesions are open and draining a scant amount of serous fluid. Which of the following would the nurse incorporate into the plan during the bathing of this client?

1. Wearing gloves

2. Wearing a gown and gloves

3. Wearing a gown, gloves, and a mask

4. Wear a gown and gloves to change the bed linens and gloves only for the bath

7. A client is suspected of having systemic lupus erythematous. The nurse monitors the client, knowing that which of the following is one of the initial characteristic signs of systemic lupus erythematous?

1. Weight gain

2. Subnormal temperature

3. Elevated red blood cell count

4. Rash on the face across the bridge of the nose and on the cheeks

8. The nurse provides home care instructions to a client with systemic lupus erythematous and tells the client about methods to manage fatigue. Which statement by the client indicates a need for further instructions?
   1. "I should take hot baths because they are relaxing."
   2. "I should sit whenever possible to conserve my energy."
   3. "I should avoid long periods of rest because it causes joint stiffness."
   4. "I should do some exercises, such as walking, when I am not fatigued."

9. The client with acquired immunodeficiency syndrome has a respiratory infection from *Pneumocystis jiroveci* and a nursing diagnosis of Gas exchange, impaired written in the plan of care. Which of the following indicates that the expected outcome of care has not yet been achieved?
   1. Client limits fluid intake.
   2. Client has clear breath sounds.
   3. Client expectorates secretions easily.
   4. Client is free of complaints of shortness of breath.

10. A client with pemphigus is being seen in the clinic regularly. The nurse plans care based on which of the following descriptions of this condition?
    1. The presence of tiny red vesicles
    2. An autoimmune disease that causes blistering in the epidermis
    3. The presence of skin vesicles found along the nerve caused by a virus
    4. The presence of red, raised papules and large plaques covered by silvery scales

11. The client is brought to the emergency room and is experiencing an anaphylactic reaction from eating shellfish. The nurse implements which immediate action?
    1. Maintaining a patent airway
    2. Administering a corticosteroid
    3. Administering epinephrine (Adrenalin)
    4. Instructing the client on the importance of obtaining a Medic-Alert bracelet

12. The nurse is assisting in planning care for a client with a diagnosis of immunodeficiency. The nurse would incorporate which of the following as a priority in the plan of care?
    1. Protecting the client from infection
    2. Providing emotional support to decrease fear
    3. Encouraging discussion about lifestyle changes
    4. Identifying factors that decreased the immune function

13. A client calls the nurse in the emergency room and tells the nurse that he was just stung by a bumble bee while gardening. The client is afraid of a severe reaction because the client's neighbor experienced such a reaction just 1 week ago. The appropriate nursing action is to:
    1. Advise the client to soak the site in hydrogen peroxide.
    2. Ask the client if he ever sustained a bee sting in the past.
    3. Tell the client to call an ambulance for transport to the emergency room.
    4. Tell the client not to worry about the sting unless difficulty with breathing occurs.

14. The nurse is assisting in administering immunizations at a health care clinic. The nurse understands that an immunization will provide:
    1. Protection from all diseases
    2. Innate immunity from disease
    3. Natural immunity from disease
    4. Acquired immunity from disease

15. The community health nurse is conducting a research study and is identifying clients in the community at risk for latex allergy. Which client population is at most risk for developing this type of allergy?
    1. Hairdressers
    2. The homeless
    3. Children in day care centers
    4. Individuals living in a group home

16. The home care nurse is performing an assessment on a client who has been diagnosed with an allergy to latex. In determining the client's risk factors associated with the allergy, the nurse questions the client about an allergy to which food item?
    1. Eggs
    2. Milk
    3. Yogurt
    4. Bananas

17. The home care nurse is assigned to visit a client who has returned home from the emergency room following treatment for a sprained ankle. The nurse notes that the client was sent home with crutches that have rubber axillary pads and needs instructions regarding crutch walking. On admission assessment, the nurse discovers that the client has an allergy to latex. Before providing instructions regarding crutch walking, the nurse should:
    1. Contact the physician.
    2. Cover the crutch pads with cloth.
    3. Call the local medical supply store and ask for a cane to be delivered.
    4. Tell the client that the crutches must be removed from the house immediately.

18. The home care nurse is ordering dressing supplies for a client who has an allergy to latex. The nurse asks the medical supply personnel to deliver which of the following?
    1. Elastic bandages
    2. Adhesive bandages

3. Brown Ace bandages
4. Cotton pads and silk tape

19. The camp nurse prepares to instruct a group of children about Lyme disease. Which of the following information would the nurse include in the instructions?
    1. Lyme disease is caused by a tick carried by deer.
    2. Lyme disease is caused by contamination from cat feces.
    3. Lyme disease can be contagious through skin contact with an infected individual.
    4. Lyme disease can be caused by the inhalation of spores from bird droppings.

20. The client is diagnosed with stage I Lyme disease. The nurse assesses the client for which characteristic of this stage?
    1. Arthralgias
    2. Flu-like symptoms
    3. Enlarged and inflamed joints
    4. Signs of neurological disorders

ALTERNATE ITEM FORMAT: MULTIPLE RESPONSE

Select the interventions that would apply in the care of a client at high risk for an allergic response to a latex allergy. Select all that apply.

❏ 1. Use nonlatex gloves.
❏ 2. Use medications from glass ampules.
❏ 3. Place the client in a private room only.
❏ 4. Do not puncture rubber stoppers with needles.
❏ 5. Keep a latex-safe supply cart available in the client's area.
❏ 6. Use a blood pressure cuff from an electronic device only to measure the blood pressure.

ANSWERS

1. **4**

Rationale: A blood test is available to detect Lyme disease; however, the test is not reliable if performed before 4 to 6 weeks following the tick bite. Antibody formation takes place in the following manner. Immunoglobulin M is detected 3 to 4 weeks after Lyme disease onset, peaks at 6 to 8 weeks, and then gradually disappears; immunoglobulin G is detected 2 to 3 months after infection and may remain elevated for years. Options 1, 2, and 3 are incorrect.

Test-Taking Strategy: Use the process of elimination. Eliminate option 1 first. The word *immediately* should indicate that this is potentially an incorrect option. A blood test is available; therefore, eliminate option 2. Eliminate option 3 because treatment should begin before the arthralgia develops. If you had difficulty with this question, review the method of diagnosing Lyme disease.

Level of Cognitive Ability: Application
Client Needs: Physiological Integrity
Integrated Process: Nursing Process—implementation
Content Area: Adult health—integumentary
Reference: Ignatavicius, D., & Workman, M. (2006). *Medical-surgical nursing: Critical thinking for collaborative care* (5th ed., p. 418). Philadelphia: W.B. Saunders.

2. **2**

Rationale: Prevention, public education, and early diagnosis are vital to the control and treatment of Lyme disease. A 3-week course of oral antibiotic therapy is recommended during stage I. Later stages of Lyme disease may require therapy with intravenously administered antibiotics, such as penicillin G. Options 1 and 3 are incorrect.

Test-Taking Strategy: Use the process of elimination. Note that the question addresses stage I. Eliminate option 4 because intravenous antibiotics will not be administered in this stage. Eliminate option 3, because although oatmeal baths may be helpful for pruritus, they would not be helpful for a systemic disorder. Waiting for symptoms to develop is an incorrect option. Review the treatment associated with Lyme disease if you had difficulty with this question.

Level of Cognitive Ability: Analysis
Client Needs: Physiological Integrity
Integrated Process: Nursing Process—planning
Content Area: Adult health—integumentary
Reference: Ignatavicius, D., & Workman, M. (2006). *Medical-surgical nursing: Critical thinking for collaborative care* (5th ed., p. 418). Philadelphia: W.B. Saunders.

3. **3**

Rationale: In the prevention of Lyme disease, individuals need to be instructed to use an insect repellent on the skin and clothes when in an area where ticks are likely to be found. Long-sleeved tops and long pants, closed shoes, and a hat or cap should be worn. If possible, heavily wooded areas or areas with thick underbrush should be avoided. Socks can be pulled up and over the pant legs to the prevent ticks from entering under clothing.

Test-Taking Strategy: Use the process of elimination and note the strategic words *need for further instructions*. These words indicate a negative event query and ask you to select an option that is incorrect. Note that option 3 uses the words *should not*. Reading carefully will assist in directing you to this option. If you had difficulty with this question, review the measures to prevent contact with ticks.

Level of Cognitive Ability: Analysis
Client Needs: Safe and Effective Care Environment
Integrated Process: Teaching and Learning
Content Area: Adult health—integumentary
Reference: Ignatavicius, D., & Workman, M. (2006). *Medical-surgical nursing: Critical thinking for collaborative care* (5th ed., p. 418). Philadelphia: W.B. Saunders.

4. **3**

Rationale: Kaposi's sarcoma lesions begin as red, dark blue, or purple macules on the lower legs that change into plaques.

These large plaques ulcerate or open and drain. The lesions spread by metastasis through the upper body and then to the face and oral mucosa. They can move to the lymphatic system, lungs, and gastrointestinal tract. Late disease results in swelling and pain in the lower extremities, penis, scrotum, or face. Diagnosis is made by punch biopsy of cutaneous lesions and biopsy of pulmonary and gastrointestinal lesions.

Test-Taking Strategy: Use the process of elimination. Eliminate options 1 and 2 first because these symptoms occur late in the development of Kaposi's sarcoma. From the remaining options, note the strategic word *confirmed*. This strategic word will assist in directing you to the option that will confirm the diagnosis, the biopsy of the lesions. Review diagnostic measures for Kaposi's sarcoma if you had difficulty with this question.

Level of Cognitive Ability: Analysis
Client Needs: Physiological Integrity
Integrated Process: Nursing Process—assessment
Content Area: Adult health—integumentary
References: Black, J., & Hawks, J. (2005). *Medical-surgical nursing: Clinical management for positive outcomes* (7th ed., p. 2393). Philadelphia: W.B. Saunders.
Huether, S., & McCance, K. (2004). *Understanding pathophysiology* (3rd ed., p. 1157). St. Louis: Mosby.

5. 4
Rationale: Kaposi's sarcoma is a vascular malignancy that presents as a skin disorder and is a common acquired immunodeficiency syndrome indicator. Malignancy is seen most frequently in men with a history of same-gender partners. Although the cause of Kaposi's sarcoma is not known, it is considered to be caused by an alteration or failure in the immune system. The renal transplantation client and the client receiving antineoplastic medications are at risk for immunosuppression. Exposure to asbestos is not related to the development of Kaposi's sarcoma.

Test-Taking Strategy: Use the process of elimination. Note the strategic words *least likely at risk*. Option 2 can be eliminated easily. Note that options 1 and 3 are comparative or alike. These clients are at risk for immunosuppression. With this in mind, these options can be eliminated. If you had difficulty with this question, review the risk factors associated with Kaposi's sarcoma.

Level of Cognitive Ability: Analysis
Client Needs: Physiological Integrity
Integrated Process: Nursing Process—assessment
Content Area: Adult health—integumentary
Reference: Black, J., & Hawks, J. (2005). *Medical-surgical nursing: Clinical management for positive outcomes* (7th ed., p. 2393). Philadelphia: W.B. Saunders.

6. 2
Rationale: Gowns and gloves are required if the nurse anticipates contact with soiled items such as those with wound drainage or is caring for a client who is incontinent with diarrhea or a client who has an ileostomy or colostomy. Masks are not required unless droplet or airborne precautions are necessary. Regardless of the amount of wound drainage, a gown and gloves must be worn.

Test-Taking Strategy: Use the process of elimination and think about the method of transmission of infection when answering a question of this type. Read the question, noting the task that is presented; in this case, it is bathing and changing linens. Eliminate option 3 because the method of transmission is not respiratory. Eliminate options 1 and 4 because neither provide adequate protection based on the method of transmission. If you had difficulty with this question, review standard and transmission-based precautions.

Level of Cognitive Ability: Application
Client Needs: Safe and Effective Care Environment
Integrated Process: Nursing Process—planning
Content Area: Adult health—integumentary
Reference: Potter, P., & Perry, A. (2005). *Fundamentals of nursing* (6th ed., p. 797). St. Louis: Mosby.

7. 4
Rationale: Skin lesions or rash on the face across the bridge of the nose and on the cheeks is an initial characteristic sign of systemic lupus erythematosus (SLE). Fever and weight loss may also occur. Anemia is most likely to occur later in SLE.

Test-Taking Strategy: Use the process of elimination and note the strategic words *characteristic signs*. Recalling the characteristic butterfly rash associated with SLE will direct you to option 4. If you are unfamiliar with this disorder, review this content.

Level of Cognitive Ability: Analysis
Client Needs: Physiological Integrity
Integrated Process: Nursing Process—assessment
Content Area: Adult health—immune
References: Black, J., & Hawks, J. (2005). *Medical-surgical nursing: Clinical management for positive outcomes* (7th ed., p. 2354). Philadelphia: W.B. Saunders.
Ignatavicius, D., & Workman, M. (2006). *Medical-surgical nursing: Critical thinking for collaborative care* (5th ed., p. 410). Philadelphia: W.B. Saunders.

8. 1
Rationale: To help reduce fatigue in the client with systemic lupus erythematosus, the nurse should instruct the client to sit whenever possible, avoid hot baths (because they exacerbate fatigue), schedule moderate low-impact exercises when not fatigued, and maintain a balanced diet. The client is instructed to avoid long periods of rest because it promotes joint stiffness.

Test-Taking Strategy: Note the strategic words *need for further instructions* and focus on the subject, fatigue. By the process of elimination, you should be directed easily to option 1 as the action that would exacerbate fatigue. If you had difficulty with this question, review measures to prevent fatigue in a client with systemic lupus erythematosus.

Level of Cognitive Ability: Analysis
Client Needs: Physiological Integrity
Integrated Process: Teaching and Learning
Content Area: Adult health—immune
References: Black, J., & Hawks, J. (2005). *Medical-surgical nursing: Clinical management for positive outcomes* (7th ed., p. 2357). Philadelphia: W.B. Saunders.
Lewis, S., Heitkemper, M., & Dirksen, S. (2004). *Medical-surgical nursing: Assessment and management of clinical problems* (6th ed., p. 1743). St. Louis: Mosby.

9. 1
Rationale: The status of the client with a diagnosis of Gas exchange, impaired would be evaluated against the standard outcome criteria for this nursing diagnosis. These would include the client stating that breathing is easier and is coughing up secretions effectively, and has clear breath sounds. The client should not limit fluid intake because fluids are needed to decrease the viscosity of secretions for expectoration.
Test-Taking Strategy: Use the process of elimination and note the strategic words *expected outcome* and *has not yet been achieved.* These words indicate a negative event query and ask you to select an option that is incorrect. This will direct you easily to option 1. Review care of the client with acquired immunodeficiency syndrome if you had difficulty with this question.
Level of Cognitive Ability: Analysis
Client Needs: Physiological Integrity
Integrated Process: Nursing Process—evaluation
Content Area: Adult health—immune
Reference: Ignatavicius, D., & Workman, M. (2006). *Medical-surgical nursing: Critical thinking for collaborative care* (5th ed., pp. 443, 447-448). Philadelphia: W.B. Saunders.

10. 2
Rationale: Pemphigus is an autoimmune disease that causes blistering in the epidermis. The client has large flaccid blisters (bullae). Because the blisters are in the epidermis, they have a thin covering of skin and break easily, leaving large denuded areas of skin. On initial examination, clients may have crusting areas instead of intact blisters. Option 1 describes eczema, option 3 describes herpes zoster, and option 4 describes psoriasis.
Test-Taking Strategy: Use the process of elimination. Recalling that pemphigus vulgaris is an autoimmune disorder will direct you easily to option 2. If you had difficulty with this question, review the characteristics of this disorder.
Level of Cognitive Ability: Comprehension
Client Needs: Physiological Integrity
Integrated Process: Nursing Process—planning
Content Area: Adult health—immune
References: Black, J., & Hawks, J. (2005). *Medical-surgical nursing: Clinical management for positive outcomes* (7th ed., p. 1418). Philadelphia: W.B. Saunders.
Ignatavicius, D., & Workman, M. (2006). *Medical-surgical nursing: Critical thinking for collaborative care* (5th ed., p. 1613). Philadelphia: W.B. Saunders.

11. 1
Rationale: If the client experiences an anaphylactic reaction, the immediate action would be to maintain a patent airway. The client then would receive epinephrine. Corticosteroids also may be prescribed. The client will need to be instructed about obtaining and wearing a Medic-Alert bracelet, but this is not the immediate action.
Test-Taking Strategy: Focus on the strategic word *immediate,* which tells you that you need to prioritize your nursing actions. Use the ABCs—airway, breathing, and circulation—to answer the question. The airway is always the priority. Review care of the client experiencing an anaphylactic reaction if you had difficulty with this question.
Level of Cognitive Ability: Application

Client Needs: Physiological Integrity
Integrated Process: Nursing Process—implementation
Content Area: Delegating/Prioritizing
References: Black, J., & Hawks, J. (2005). *Medical-surgical nursing: Clinical management for positive outcomes* (7th ed., p. 2325). Philadelphia: W.B. Saunders.
Lewis, S., Heitkemper, M., & Dirksen, S. (2004). *Medical-surgical nursing: Assessment and management of clinical problems* (6th ed., p. 251). St. Louis: Mosby.

12. 1
Rationale: The client with immunodeficiency has inadequate or absence of immune bodies and is at risk for infection. The priority nursing intervention would be to protect the client from infection. Options 2, 3, and 4 may be components of care but are not the priority.
Test-Taking Strategy: Use Maslow's Hierarchy of Needs theory to answer the question. Remember that physiological needs are the priority. This will direct you to option 1. Review the care of a client with immunodeficiency if you had difficulty with this question.
Level of Cognitive Ability: Application
Client Needs: Physiological Integrity
Integrated Process: Nursing Process—planning
Content Area: Delegating/Prioritizing
Reference: Huether, S., & McCance, K. (2004). *Understanding pathophysiology* (3rd ed., pp. 192-193). St. Louis: Mosby.

13. 2
Rationale: In some types of allergies, a reaction occurs only on second and subsequent contacts with the allergen. The appropriate action, therefore, would be to ask the client if he ever received a bee sting in the past. Option 1 is not appropriate advice. Option 3 is unnecessary. The client should not be told "not to worry."
Test-Taking Strategy: Use the steps of the nursing process to answer the question. Option 2 is the only option that addresses assessment. Review information related to allergic reactions if you had difficulty with this question.
Level of Cognitive Ability: Application
Client Needs: Physiological Integrity
Integrated Process: Nursing Process—implementation
Content Area: Adult health—immune
References: Ignatavicius, D., & Workman, M. (2006). *Medical-surgical nursing: Critical thinking for collaborative care* (5th ed., pp. 453-455). Philadelphia: W.B. Saunders.
Lewis, S., Heitkemper, M., & Dirksen, S. (2004). *Medical-surgical nursing: Assessment and management of clinical problems* (6th ed., pp. 246-248). St. Louis: Mosby.

14. 4
Rationale: Acquired immunity can occur by receiving an immunization that causes antibodies to a specific pathogen to form. Natural (innate) immunity is present at birth. No immunization protects the client from all diseases.
Test-Taking Strategy: Use the process of elimination and knowledge regarding immunity to disease to answer the question. Eliminate option 1 first because of the close-ended word *all.* Next, eliminate options 2 and 3 because they are comparative or alike. Review natural and acquired immunity if you had difficulty with this question.

Level of Cognitive Ability: Comprehension
Client Needs: Health Promotion and Maintenance
Integrated Process: Nursing Process—implementation
Content Area: Adult health—immune
Reference: Huether, S., & McCance, K. (2004). *Understanding pathophysiology* (3rd ed., pp. 210, 130). St. Louis: Mosby.

15. **1**
Rationale: Individuals at risk for developing a latex allergy include health care workers, individuals who work in the rubber industry or those who have had multiple surgeries, have spina bifida, wear gloves frequently, such as food handlers, hairdressers, and auto mechanics, or are allergic to kiwis, bananas, pineapples, tropical fruits, grapes, avocados, potatoes, hazelnuts, and water chestnuts.
Test-Taking Strategy: Focus on the subject, a latex allergy. Recalling the cause and the source of the allergic reaction will direct you easily to option 1. Review the cause of this type of allergy and the individuals at risk if you had difficulty with this question.
Level of Cognitive Ability: Analysis
Client Needs: Health Promotion and Maintenance
Integrated Process: Nursing Process—assessment
Content Area: Adult health—immune
Reference: Ignatavicius, D., & Workman, M. (2006). *Medical-surgical nursing: Critical thinking for collaborative care* (5th ed., p. 461). Philadelphia: W.B. Saunders.

16. **4**
Rationale: Individuals who are allergic to kiwis, bananas, pineapples, tropical fruits, grapes, avocados, potatoes, hazelnuts, and water chestnuts are at risk for developing a latex allergy. This is thought to be to the result of a possible cross-reaction between the food and the latex allergen. Options 1, 2, and 3 are unrelated to latex allergy.
Test-Taking Strategy: Use the process of elimination and knowledge regarding the food items related to a latex allergy. Eliminate options 1, 2, and 3 because they are comparative or alike and relate to dairy products. Review the food items associated with a risk for latex allergy if you had difficulty with this question.
Level of Cognitive Ability: Analysis
Client Needs: Physiological Integrity
Integrated Process: Nursing Process—assessment
Content Area: Adult health—immune
References: Black, J., & Hawks, J. (2005). *Medical-surgical nursing: Clinical management for positive outcomes* (7th ed., p. 2325). Philadelphia: W.B. Saunders.
Ignatavicius, D., & Workman, M. (2006). *Medical-surgical nursing: Critical thinking for collaborative care* (5th ed., p. 512). Philadelphia: W.B. Saunders.

17. **2**
Rationale: The rubber pads used on crutches may contain latex. If the client requires the use of crutches, the nurse can cover the pads with a cloth to prevent cutaneous contact. Option 4 is inappropriate and may alarm the client. The nurse cannot order a cane for a client. Additionally, this type of assistive device may not be appropriate, considering this client's injury. No reason exists to contact the physician at this time.

Test-Taking Strategy: Use the process of elimination and knowledge about alternative resources for a client with a latex allergy. No data in the question support the need to contact the physician. The nurse should not prescribe assistive devices for the client. Option 4 is not a therapeutic action. Review care of the client with a latex allergy if you had difficulty with this question.
Level of Cognitive Ability: Application
Client Needs: Physiological Integrity
Integrated Process: Nursing Process—implementation
Content Area: Adult health—immune
References: Perry, A., & Potter, P. (2006). *Clinical nursing skills and techniques* (6th ed., pp. 218, 291). St. Louis: Mosby.
Potter, P., & Perry, A. (2005). *Fundamentals of nursing* (6th ed., p. 1622). St. Louis: Mosby.

18. **4**
Rationale: Cotton pads and plastic or silk tape are latex-free products. The items identified in options 1, 2, and 3 are products that contain latex.
Test-Taking Strategy: Use the process of elimination and knowledge regarding products that contain latex to answer this question. Eliminate options 1 and 3 first because they are comparative or alike. Noting the strategic words *cotton* and *silk* in option 4 will assist in answering correctly from the remaining options. Review the list of products that contain latex if you had difficulty with this question.
Level of Cognitive Ability: Application
Client Needs: Physiological Integrity
Integrated Process: Nursing Process—implementation
Content Area: Adult health—immune
References: Ignatavicius, D., & Workman, M. (2006). *Medical-surgical nursing: Critical thinking for collaborative care* (5th ed., p. 461). Philadelphia: W.B. Saunders.
Lewis, S., Heitkemper, M., & Dirksen, S. (2004). *Medical-surgical nursing: Assessment and management of clinical problems* (6th ed., p. 253). St. Louis: Mosby.

19. **1**
Rationale: Lyme disease is a multisystem infection that results from a bite by a tick carried by several species of deer. Persons bitten by the *Ixodes scapularis* or *I. pacificus* tick can become infected with the spirochete *Borrelia burgdorferi.* Lyme disease cannot be transmitted from one person to another. Histoplasmosis is caused by the inhalation of spores from bat or bird droppings. Toxoplasmosis is caused by the ingestion of cysts from contaminated cat feces.
Test-Taking Strategy: Use the process of elimination. Recalling that this disease is caused by a tick bite will assist in eliminating the incorrect options. If you had difficulty with this question, review the cause of Lyme disease.
Level of Cognitive Ability: Application
Client Needs: Health Promotion and Maintenance
Integrated Process: Teaching and Learning
Content Area: Adult health—integumentary
References: Ignatavicius, D., & Workman, M. (2006). *Medical-surgical nursing: Critical thinking for collaborative care* (5th ed., p. 418). Philadelphia: W.B. Saunders.
Lewis, S., Heitkemper, M., & Dirksen, S. (2004). *Medical-surgical nursing: Assessment and management of clinical problems* (6th ed., p. 1736). St. Louis: Mosby.

20. **2**

Rationale: The hallmark of stage I Lyme disease is the development of a rash within 2 to 30 days of infection, generally at the site of the tick bite. The rash develops into a concentric ring, giving it a bull's-eye appearance. The lesion enlarges up to 50 to 60 cm, and smaller lesions develop farther away from the original tick bite. In stage I, most infected persons develop flu-like symptoms that last 7 to 10 days; these symptoms may reoccur later. Neurological deficits occur in stage II. Arthralgias and joint enlargements are most likely to occur in stage III.

Test-Taking Strategy: Use the process of elimination and eliminate options 1 and 3 first because they are comparative or alike. Next, note that the question asks for the characteristic of stage I. From the remaining two options, select the least serious one because the subject of the question relates to stage I. Expect neurological disorders to occur with progression of the disease. If you had difficulty with this question, review the stages of Lyme disease.

Level of Cognitive Ability: Analysis
Client Needs: Physiological Integrity
Integrated Process: Nursing Process—assessment
Content Area: Adult health—integumentary
Reference: Ignatavicius, D., & Workman, M. (2006). *Medical-surgical nursing: Critical thinking for collaborative care* (5th ed., p. 418). Philadelphia: W.B. Saunders.

ALTERNATE ITEM FORMAT:
MULTIPLE RESPONSE

Answer: 1, 2, 4, 5

Rationale: If a client is allergic to latex and is at high risk for an allergic response, the nurse would use nonlatex gloves and latex-safe supplies, and would keep a latex-safe supply cart available in the client's area. Any supplies or materials that contain latex would be avoided. These include blood pressure cuffs, medications with a rubber stopper that requires puncture with a needle, latex-safe syringes, and latex-safe intravenous tubing. It is not necessary to place the client in a private room.

Test-Taking Strategy: Focus on the subject, that the client is at high risk for an allergic response to latex. Recalling that items that contain rubber are likely to contain latex will direct you to the correct interventions. Also, noting the close-ended word *only* in options 3 and 6 will assist in eliminating these options. Review care of the client with a latex allergy if you had difficulty with this question.

Level of Cognitive Ability: Application
Client Needs: Safe and Effective Care Environment
Integrated Process: Nursing Process—implementation
Content Area: Adult health—immune
Reference: Harkreader, H., & Hogan, M.A. (2004) *Fundamentals of nursing: Caring and clinical judgment* (2nd ed., p. 1221). Philadelphia: W.B. Saunders.

REFERENCES

Black, J., & Hawks, J. (2005). *Medical-surgical nursing: Clinical management for positive outcomes* (7th ed.). Philadelphia: W.B. Saunders.

Harkreader, H., & Hogan, M. (2004) *Fundamentals of nursing: Caring and clinical judgment* (2nd ed.). Philadelphia: W.B. Saunders.

Huether, S., & McCance, K. (2004). *Understanding pathophysiology* (3rd ed.). St. Louis: Mosby.

Ignatavicius, D., & Workman, M. (2006). *Medical-surgical nursing: Critical thinking for collaborative care* (5th ed.). Philadelphia: W.B. Saunders.

Lewis, S., Heitkemper, M., & Dirksen, S. (2004). *Medical-surgical nursing: Assessment and management of clinical problems* (6th ed.). St. Louis: Mosby.

Perry, A., & Potter, P. (2006). *Clinical nursing skills and techniques* (6th ed.). St. Louis: Mosby.

Potter, P., & Perry, A. (2005), *Fundamentals of nursing* (6th ed.). St. Louis: Mosby.

Immunological Medications

▲ I. **HUMAN IMMUNODEFICIENCY VIRUS (HIV) AND ACQUIRED IMMUNODEFICIENCY SYNDROME (AIDS)**

A. Medications include nucleoside-nucleotide reverse transcriptase inhibitors, non-nucleoside reverse transcriptase inhibitors, protease inhibitors, and fusion inhibitors (Box 70-1; Fig. 70-1).

B. Nucleoside-nucleotide reverse transcriptase inhibitors and non-nucleoside reverse transcriptase inhibitors work by inhibiting the activity of reverse transcriptase.

C. Protease inhibitors work by interfering with the activity of the enzyme protease.

D. Fusion inhibitors work by inhibiting the binding of human immunodeficiency virus to cells.

▲ E. Standard treatment consists of using three or four medications in regimens known as highly active antiretroviral therapy (HAART); this therapy is not curative but can delay or reverse loss of immune function, preserve health, and prolong life.

F. Recommended regimens for initial therapy of established HIV infection are shown in Box 70-2.

G. Other medications include those that are used to treat complications or opportunistic infections that develop (see Box 70-1).

▲ H. Nucleoside-nucleotide reverse transcriptase inhibitors (NNRTIs)

1. Abacavir (Ziagen): Can cause nausea; monitor for hypersensitivity reaction, including fever, nausea, vomiting, diarrhea, lethargy, malaise, sore throat, shortness of breath, cough, and rash.

2. Abacavir; Lamivudine (Epzicom): In addition to the effects that can occur from abacavir and lamivudine, hypersensitivity reactions, lactic acidosis, and severe hepatomegaly can occur.

3. Didanosine (Videx): Can cause nausea, diarrhea, peripheral neuropathy, hepatotoxicity, and pancreatitis

4. Emtricitabine (Emtriva): Can cause headache, diarrhea, nausea, rash, hyperpigmentation of the palms and soles, lactic acidosis, and severe hepatomegaly

5. Emtricitabine; tenofovir (Truvada): In addition to the effects that can occur from emtricitabine and tenofovir, lactic acidosis and severe hepatomegaly can occur.

6. Lamivudine (Epivir): Causes nausea and nasal congestion

7. Lamivudine; zidovudine (Combivir): Can cause anemia and neutropenia and lactic acidosis with hepatomegaly.

8. Lamivudine; zidovudine; abacavir (Trizivir): In addition to the effects that can occur from lamivudine, zidovudine, and abacavir, hypersensitivity reactions, anemia, neutropenia, lactic acidosis, and severe hepatomegaly can occur.

9. Stavudine (d4t, Zerit): Can cause peripheral neuropathy and pancreatitis

10. Tenofovir (Viread): Can cause nausea and vomiting

11. Zalcitabine (ddC, Hivid) Can cause oral ulcers, peripheral neuropathy, hepatotoxicity, and pancreatitis

12. Zidovudine (Retrovir, azidothymidine, AZT, ZDV): Can cause nausea, vomiting, anemia, leukopenia, myopathy, fatigue, and headache

I. Non-nucleoside reverse transcriptase inhibitors ▲ (NRTIs)

1. Delavirdine (Rescriptor): Can cause rash, liver function changes, and pruritis

1122

BOX 70-1

Medications for HIV and AIDS

NUCLEOSIDE-NUCLEOTIDE REVERSE TRANSCRIPTASE INHIBITORS (NNRTIs)
Abacavir (Ziagen)
Abacavir; lamivudine (Epzicom)
Didanosine (Videx)
Emtricitabine (Emtriva)
Emtricitabine; tenofovir (Truvada)
Lamivudine (Epivir)
Lamivudine; zidovudine (Combivir)
Lamivudine; zidovudine; abacavir (Trizivir)
Stavudine (d4t, Zerit XR)
Tenofovir (Viread)
Zalcitabine (ddC, Hivid)
Zidovudine (Retrovir, azidothymidine, AZT, ZDV)

NON-NUCLEOSIDE REVERSE TRANSCRIPTASE INHIBITORS (NRTIs)
Delavirdine (Rescriptor)
Efavirenz (Sustiva)
Nevirapine (Viramune)

PROTEASE INHIBITORS (PIs)
Amprenavir; vitamin E (Agenerase)
Atazanavir (Reyataz)
Fosamprenavir (Lexiva)
Indinavir (Crixivan)
Lopinavir; ritonavir (Kaletra)
Nelfinavir (Viracept)
Ritonavir (Norvir)
Saquinavir (Invirase)
Tipranavir (Aptivus)

FUSION INHIBITOR
Enfuvirtide (Fuzeon)

ANTI-INFLAMMATORY MEDICATION
Sulfasalazine (Azulfidine)

ANTI-INFECTIVE MEDICATIONS
Atovaquone (Mepron)
Metronidazole (Flagyl)
Pentamidine isethionate (Pentam 300)
Sulfamethoxazole; trimethoprim (Bactrim)

ANTIFUNGAL MEDICATIONS
Amphotericin B (Fungizone)
Fluconazole (Diflucan)
Ketoconazole (Nizoral)

ANTIVIRAL MEDICATIONS
Acyclovir (Zovirax)
Foscarnet (Foscavir)
Ganciclovir (Cytovene)

BOX 70-2

Regimens for Initial Therapy of Established HIV Infection

All regimens contain three antiretroviral drugs: NNRTI-based regimens contain an NNRTI combined with two NRTIs, PI-based regimens contain a PI combined with two NRTIs; and one regimen contains three NRTIs.

PREFERRED REGIMENS
NNRTI-Based
Efavirenz + (lamivudine or emtricitabine) + (zidovudine or tenofovir)
PI-Based
Lopinavir; ritonavir [Kaletra] + (lamivudine or emtricitabine) + zidovudine

ALTERNATIVE REGIMENS
NNRTI-Based
Efavirenz + (lamivudine or emtricitabine) + (abacavir, didanosine, or stavudine)
Nevirapine + (lamivudine or emtricitabine) + (abacavir, didanosine, stavudine, tenofovir, or zidovudine)
PI-Based
Atazanavir + (lamivudine or emtricitabine) + (abacavir, didanosine, stavudine, or zidovudine) or (tenofovir + ritonavir, 100 mg/day)
Fosamprenavir + (lamivudine or emtricitabine) + (abacavir, didanosine, stavudine, tenofovir, or zidovudine)
Fosamprenavir; ritonavir + (lamivudine or emtricitabine) + (abacavir, didanosine, stavudine, tenofovir, or zidovudine)
Indinavir; ritonavir + (lamivudine or emtricitabine) + (abacavir, didanosine, stavudine, tenofovir, or zidovudine)
Lopinavir; ritonavir [Kaletra] + (lamivudine or emtricitabine) + (abacavir, stavudine, tenofovir, or zidovudine)
Nelfinavir + (lamivudine or emtricitabine) + (abacavir, didanosine, stavudine, tenofovir, or zidovudine)
Saquinavir/ritonavir + (lamivudine or emtricitabine) + (abacavir, didanosine, stavudine, tenofovir, or zidovudine)

THREE NRTI-BASED
Abacavir + *lamivudine* + *zidovudine*

NNRTI, Nucleoside-nucleotide reverse transcriptase inhibitor; *NRTI,* non-nucleoside reverse transcriptase inhibitor; *PI,* protease inhibitor.
From Lehne, R. (2007). *Pharmacology for nursing care* (7th ed.). Philadelphia: W.B. Saunders.

J. Protease inhibitors (PIs)
1. Amprenavir; vitamin E (Agenerase)
a. Can cause nausea, vomiting, headache, altered taste sensations, perioral paresthesia, rashes, and increased results of liver function studies
b. Oral solution contains an alcohol that can interact with metronidazole (Flagyl); can cause feelings of inebriation.
2. Atazanavir (Reyataz): Can cause nausea, headache, infection, vomiting, diarrhea, drowsiness,

2. Efavirenz (Sustiva): Can cause rash, dizziness, confusion, difficulty concentrating, dreams, and encephalopathy
3. Nevirapine (Viramune): Can cause rash, Stevens-Johnson syndrome, hepatitis, and increased transaminase levels

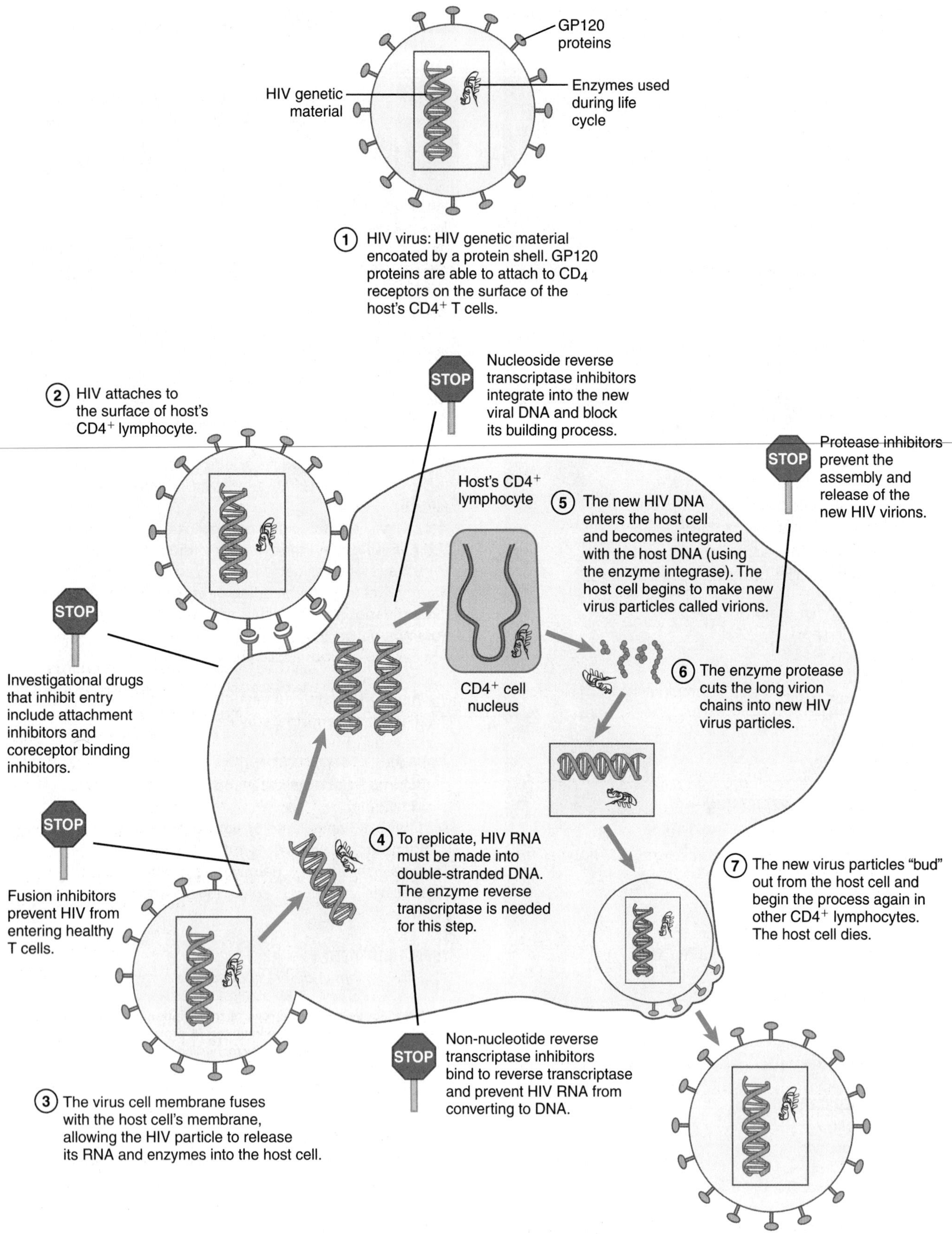

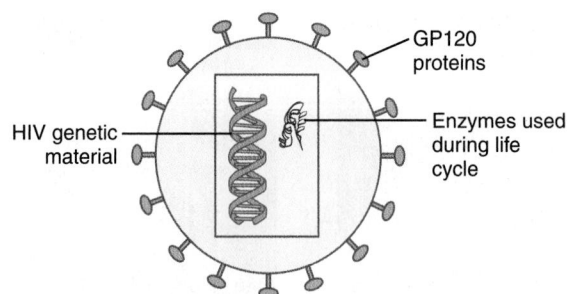

GP120 proteins
HIV genetic material
Enzymes used during life cycle
1 HIV virus: HIV genetic material encoated by a protein shell. GP120 proteins are able to attach to CD4 receptors on the surface of the host's CD4+ T cells.
2 HIV attaches to the surface of host's CD4+ lymphocyte.
STOP
Nucleoside reverse transcriptase inhibitors integrate into the new viral DNA and block its building process.
STOP
Protease inhibitors prevent the assembly and release of the new HIV virions.
Host's CD4+ lymphocyte
5 The new HIV DNA enters the host cell and becomes integrated with the host DNA (using the enzyme integrase). The host cell begins to make new virus particles called virions.
STOP
Investigational drugs that inhibit entry include attachment inhibitors and coreceptor binding inhibitors.
CD4+ cell nucleus
6 The enzyme protease cuts the long virion chains into new HIV virus particles.
STOP
Fusion inhibitors prevent HIV from entering healthy T cells.
4 To replicate, HIV RNA must be made into double-stranded DNA. The enzyme reverse transcriptase is needed for this step.
7 The new virus particles "bud" out from the host cell and begin the process again in other CD4+ lymphocytes. The host cell dies.
STOP
Non-nucleotide reverse transcriptase inhibitors bind to reverse transcriptase and prevent HIV RNA from converting to DNA.
3 The virus cell membrane fuses with the host cell's membrane, allowing the HIV particle to release its RNA and enzymes into the host cell.

FIG. 70-1 Steps in the life cycle of the human immunodeficiency virus (HIV), with correlation to medications. (From Black, J., & Hawks, J., [2005]. *Medical-surgical nursing: Clinical management for positive outcomes* [7th ed.]. Philadelphia: W.B. Saunders.)

insomnia, fever, hyperglycemia, hyperlipidemia, and increased bleeding in clients with hemophilia

3. Fosamprenavir (Lexiva): Similar to amprenavir; can cause nausea, vomiting, headache, altered taste sensations, perioral paresthesia, rashes, and increased results of liver function studies

4. Indinavir (Crixivan): Can cause nausea, diarrhea, hyperbilirubinemia, nephritis, and kidney stones

5. Lopinavir-ritonavir combination (Kaletra): Can cause nausea, diarrhea, altered taste sensations, circumoral paresthesia, and hepatitis.

6. Nelfinavir (Viracept): Can cause nausea, flatulence, and diarrhea.

7. Ritonavir (Norvir): Can cause nausea, vomiting, diarrhea, altered taste sensations, circumoral paresthesia, hepatitis, and increased triglyceride levels.

8. Saquinavir (Invirase): Can cause nausea, diarrhea, photosensitivity, and headache.

9. Tipranavir (Aptivus): Hepatotoxicity (liver damage); can also cause nausea, vomiting, diarrhea, headache, and fatigue

▲ K. Fusion inhibitor: Enfuvirtide (Fuzeon) can cause skin irritation at injection site, fatigue, nausea, insomnia, and peripheral neuropathy.

▲ L. Anti-infective medications: Used to treat opportunistic infections such as *Pneumocystis jiroveci* pneumonia; *Toxoplasma* encephalitis is treated with sulfamethoxazole-trimethoprim (Bactrim; see Box 70-1)

▲ M. Antifungal medications: Used to treat candidiasis, cryptococcal meningitis (see Box 70-1)

▲ N. Antiviral medications: Used to treat cytomegalovirus retinitis, herpes simplex, varicella-zoster virus (see Box 70-1)

▲ II. IMMUNOSUPPRESSANTS (Box 70-3; Fig. 70-2)

▲ A. Description: Immunosuppressants are used for transplant clients to prevent organ or tissue rejection and to treat autoimmune disorders such as systemic lupus erythematosus.

▲ B. Cyclosporine (Sandimmune, Gengraf, Neoral)
1. Used for prevention of rejection following allogenic organ transplantation
2. Usually administered with a glucocorticoid and another immunosuppressant
3. Most common adverse effects are nephrotoxicity, infection, hypertension, and hirsutism.

▲ C. Tacrolimus (Prograf)
1. Used for prevention of rejection following liver or kidney transplantation
2. Adverse effects include nephrotoxicity, neurotoxicity, gastrointestinal effects, hypertension, hyperkalemia, hyperglycemia, hirsutism, and gum hyperplasia.

BOX 70-3

Immunosuppressants

CALCINEURIN INHIBITORS
Cyclosporine (Sandimmune, Gengraf, Neoral)
Tacrolimus (Prograf)

CYTOTOXIC MEDICATIONS
Azathioprine (Imuran)
Cyclophosphamide (Cytoxan, Neosar)
Methotrexate (Rheumatrex, Trexall)
Mycophenolate mofetil (CellCept)
Mycophenolic acid (Myfortic)

ANTIBODIES
Basiliximab (Simulect)
Daclizumab (Zenapax)
Lymphocyte immune globulin, antithymocyte globulin (equine)
Muromonab-CD3 (Orthoclone OKT3)
Rh₀(D) immune globulin (RhoGAM)

OTHER
Sirolimus (Rapamune)

GLUCOCORTICOIDS
See Chap. 54.

D. Azathioprine (Imuran)
1. Generally used with renal transplant clients
2. Can cause neutropenia and thrombocytopenia

E. Cyclophosphamide (Cytoxan, Neosar)
1. Used for its immunosuppressant action to treat autoimmune disorders
2. Can cause neutropenia and hemorrhagic cystitis

F. Methotrexate (Rheumatrex, Trexall)
1. Used for its immunosuppressant action to treat autoimmune disorders
2. Can cause hepatic fibrosis and cirrhosis, bone marrow suppression, ulcerative stomatitis, and renal damage

G. Mycophenolate mofetil (CellCept, Myfortic)
1. Used to prevent rejection following kidney, heart, and liver transplantation
2. Can cause diarrhea, vomiting, neutropenia, sepsis; increased risk of infection and malignancies, especially lymphomas

H. Basiliximab (Simulect); daclizumab (Zenapax)
1. Used to prevent rejection following kidney transplantation
2. Can cause severe acute hypersensitivity reactions including anaphylaxis

I. Lymphocyte immune globulin, antithymocyte globulin (equine)
1. Used to prevent rejection following kidney, heart, liver, and bone marrow transplantation
2. Side effects include fever, chills, leukopenia, and skin reactions.
3. Can cause anaphylactoid reactions

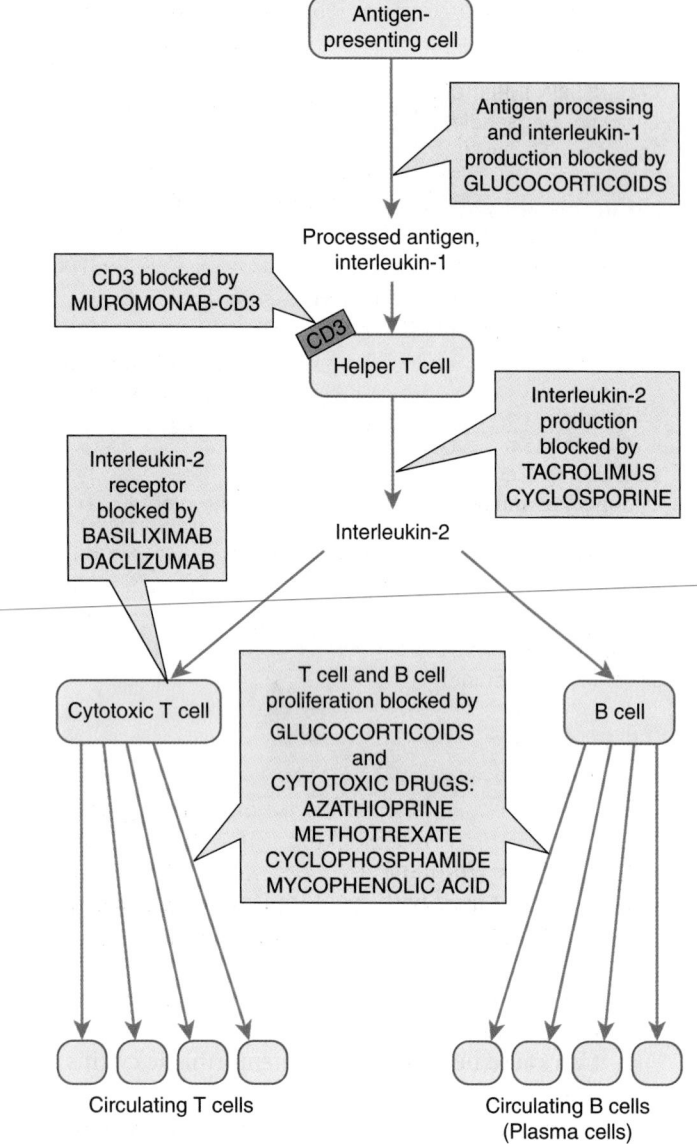

FIG. 70-2 Sites of action of immunosuppressant drugs. (From Lehne, R. [2007]. *Pharmacology for nursing care* [6th ed.]. Philadelphia: W.B. Saunders.)

J. Muromonab-CD3 (Orthoclone OKT3)
  1. Used to prevent rejection following kidney, heart, and liver transplantation
  2. Side effects include fever, chills, dyspnea, chest pain, nausea, and vomiting.
  3. Can cause anaphylactoid reactions
▲ K. Rho(D) immune globulin (RhoGAM; see Chap. 31)
L. Sirolimus (Rapamune)
  1. Used to prevent renal transplant rejection
  2. Increases the risk of infection; raises cholesterol and triglyceride levels; can cause renal injury
  3. Other side effects include rash, acne, anemia, thrombocytopenia, joint pain, diarrhea, and hypokalemia.

BOX 70-4

Antibiotics

AMINOGLYCOSIDES
Amikacin (Amikin)
Gentamicin (Garamycin)
Kanamycin (Kantrex)
Neomycin (Neo-Fradin)
Streptomycin
Tobramycin (Nebcin)

CEPHALOSPORINS
Cefaclor (Ceclor)
Cefadroxil (Duricef)
Cefazolin (Ancef, Kefzol)
Cefdinir (Omnicef)
Cefditoren (Spectracef)
Cefepime (Maxipime)
Cefotaxime (Claforan)
Cefotetan (Cefotan)
Cefoxitin (Mefoxin)
Cefopodoxime (Vantin)
Cefprozil (Cefzil)
Ceftazidime (Ceptaz, Fortaz, Tazicef)
Ceftibuten (Cedax)
Ceftizoxime (Cefizox)
Ceftriaxone (Rocephin)
Cefuroxime (Ceftin)
Cephalexin (Keflex)
Loracarbef (Lorabid)

FLUOROQUINOLONES
Ciprofloxacin (Cipro)
Gatifloxacin (Tequin)
Gemifloxacin (Factive)
Levofloxacin (Levaquin)
Lomefloxacin (Maxaquin)
Moxifloxacin (Avelox)
Norfloxacin (Noroxin)
Ofloxacin (Floxin)
Trovafloxacin (Trovan)

MACROLIDES
Azithromycin (Zithromax)
Clarithromycin (Cleocin)
Dirithromycin (Dynabac)
Erythromycin

LINCOSAMIDES
Clindamycin (Cleocin)
Lincomycin (Lincocin)

MONOBACTAM
Aztreonam (Azactam)

PENICILLINS
Amoxicillin (Amoxil)
Ampicillin (Principen)
Carbenicillin (Geocillin)
Penicillin G (Bicillin L-A, Permapen, Pfizerpen, Wycillin)
Penicillin V (Veetids)
Piperacillin
Ticarcillin (Ticar)

PENICILLINASE-RESISTANT PENICILLINS
Dicloxacillin
Nafcillin
Oxacillin

SULFONAMIDES
Sulfamethoxazole
Sulfadiazine
Sulfasalizine
Sulfisoxazole
Trimethoprim; sulfamethoxazole (TMP-SMZ; Bactrim, Cotrim, Septra)

TETRACYCLINES
Demeclocycline (Declomycin)
Doxycycline (Vibramycin)
Minocycline (Minocin)
Oxytetracycline (Terramycin)
Tetracycline (Sumycin)

ANTIMYCOBACTERIALS
Antituberculosis agents (see Chap. 58)
Leprostatics: Clofazimine (Lamprene) and dapsone

III. **IMMUNIZATIONS** (see Chap. 47)

IV. **ANTIBIOTICS** (Box 70-4)
A. Inhibit the growth of bacteria
B. Include medication classifications of aminoglycosides, cephalosporins, fluoroquinolones, macrolides, lincosamides, monobactams, penicillins and

penicillinase-resistant penicillins, sulfonamides, tetracyclines, and antimycobacterials (see Box 70-4)

▲ C. Adverse effects (Table 70-1)
▲ D. Nursing considerations
    1. Assess for allergies.

TABLE 70-1

Antibiotics and Their Adverse Effects

Classification	Adverse Effects
Aminoglycosides	Ototoxicity
	Confusion, disorientation
	Renal toxicity
	Gastrointestinal irritation
	Palpitations, blood pressure changes
	Hypersensitivity reactions
Cephalosporins	Gastrointestinal disturbances
	Pseudomembranous colitis
	Headache, dizziness, lethargy, paresthesias
	Nephrotoxicity
	Superinfections
Fluoroquinolones	Headache, dizziness, insomnia, depression
	Gastrointestinal effects
	Bone marrow depression
	Fever, rash, photosensitivity
Macrolides	Gastrointestinal effects
	Pseudomembranous colitis
	Confusion, abnormal thinking
	Superinfections
	Hypersensitivity reactions
Lincosamides	Gastrointestinal effects
	Pseudomembranous colitis
	Bone marrow depression
Monobactams	Gastrointestinal effects
	Hepatotoxicity
	Allergic reactions
Penicillins and penicillinase-resistant penicillins	Gastrointestinal effects, including sore mouth and furry tongue
	Superinfections
	Hypersensitivity reactions, including anaphylaxis
Sulfonamides	Gastrointestinal effects
	Hepatotoxicity
	Nephrotoxicity
	Bone marrow depression
	Dermatological effects, including hypersensitivity and photosensitivity
	Headache, dizziness, vertigo, ataxia, depression, seizures
Tetracyclines	Gastrointestinal effects
	Hepatotoxicity
	Teeth (staining) and bone damage
	Superinfections
	Dermatological reactions, including rash and photosensitivity
	Hypersensitivity reactions
Antimycobacterials, leprostatics	Gastrointestinal effects
	Neuritis, dizziness, headache, malaise, drowsiness, hallucinations

2. Monitor appropriate laboratory values before therapy as appropriate and during therapy to assess for adverse effects.
3. Monitor for adverse effects and report to physician if any occur.
4. Determine appropriate method of administration and provide instructions to the client.
5. Monitor intake and output.
6. Encourage fluid intake (unless contraindicated).
7. Initiate safety precautions because of possible central nervous system effects.
8. Teach client about the medication and how to take the medication; emphasize the importance of completing the full prescribed course.

PRACTICE QUESTIONS

1. Amikacin (Amikin) is prescribed for a client with a bacterial infection. The nurse instructs the client to contact the physician immediately if which of the following occurs?
  1. Nausea
  2. Lethargy
  3. Hearing loss
  4. Muscle aches

2. The client who is human immunodeficiency virus seropositive has been taking zalcitabine (ddC, Hivid) as a component of treatment. The nurse plans to monitor which of the following most closely while the client is taking this medication?
  1. Platelet count
  2. Glucose level
  3. Red blood cell count
  4. Liver function studies

3. The nurse is assigned to care for a client with cytomegalovirus retinitis and acquired immunodeficiency syndrome who is receiving foscarnet (Foscavir), an antiviral. The nurse checks the latest results of which of the following laboratory studies while the client is taking this medication?
  1. CD4 cell count
  2. Serum albumin level
  3. Serum creatinine level
  4. Lymphocyte count

4. The client with acquired immunodeficiency syndrome and *Pneumocystis jiroveci* infection has been receiving pentamidine (Pentam 300). The client develops a temperature of 101° F. The nurse does further monitoring of the client, knowing that this sign would most likely indicate:
  1. That the dose of the medication is too low
  2. That the client is experiencing toxic effects of the medication
  3. That the client has developed inadequacy of thermoregulation
  4. That the result of another infection caused by leukopenic effects of the medication

5. Saquinavir (Invirase) is prescribed for the client who is seropositive for human immunodeficiency virus. The nurse reinforces medication instructions and tells the client to:
   1. Avoid sun exposure.
   2. Eat low-calorie foods.
   3. Eat foods that are low in fat.
   4. Take the medication on an empty stomach.

6. The client who is human immunodeficiency virus seropositive has been taking Stavudine (d4t, Zerit). The nurse monitors which of the following most closely while the client is taking this medication?
   1. Gait
   2. Appetite
   3. Level of consciousness
   4. Gastrointestinal function

7. The client with acquired immunodeficiency syndrome has begun therapy with zidovudine (Retrovir, azidothymidine, AZT, ZDV). The nurse carefully monitors which of the following laboratory results during treatment with this medication?
   1. Blood culture
   2. Blood glucose level
   3. Blood urea nitrogen level
   4. Complete blood count

8. The nurse is reviewing the results of serum laboratory studies drawn on a client with acquired immunodeficiency syndrome who is receiving didanosine (Videx). The nurse interprets that the client may have the medication discontinued by the physician if which of the following significantly elevated results is noted?
   1. Serum protein level
   2. Blood glucose level
   3. Serum amylase level
   4. Serum creatinine level

9. The nurse is caring for a post–renal transplantation client taking cyclosporin (Sandimmune, Gengraf, Neoral). The nurse notes an increase in one of the client's vital signs and the client is complaining of a headache. What is the vital sign that is most likely increased?
   1. Pulse
   2. Respirations
   3. Blood pressure
   4. Pulse oximetry

ALTERNATE ITEM FORMAT: MULTIPLE RESPONSE

Ketoconazole (Nizoral) is prescribed for a client with a diagnosis of candidiasis. Select the interventions that the nurse includes when administering this medication. Select all that apply.
   ❑ 1. Restrict fluid intake.
   ❑ 2. Instruct the client to avoid alcohol.
   ❑ 3. Monitor liver function studies.
   ❑ 4. Administer the medication with an antacid.
   ❑ 5. Instruct the client to avoid exposure to the sun.
   ❑ 6. Administer the medication on an empty stomach.

ANSWERS

1. **3**

Rationale: Amikacin (Amikin) is an aminoglycoside. Adverse effects of aminoglycosides include ototoxicity (hearing problems) confusion, disorientation, gastrointestinal irritation, palpitations, blood pressure changes, nephrotoxicity, and hypersensitivity. The nurse instructs the client to report hearing loss to the physician immediately. Lethargy and muscle aches are not associated with the use of this medication. It is not necessary to contact the physician immediately if nausea occurs. If nausea persists or results in vomiting, the physician should be notified.

Test-Taking Strategy: Note the strategic words *contact the physician immediately*. Recalling that this medication is an aminoglycoside (most aminoglycoside medication names end in the letters *-cin*) and that aminogylcosides are ototoxic will direct you to the correct option. Review the adverse effects of aminoglycosides if you had difficulty with this question.

Level of Cognitive Ability: Application
Client Needs: Physiological Integrity
Integrated Process: Teaching and Learning
Content Area: Adult health—immune
Reference: Lehne, R. (2007). *Pharmacology for nursing care* (6th ed., p. 999). Philadelphia: W.B. Saunders.

2. **4**

Rationale: Zalcitabine (ddC, Hivid) is an antiretroviral (nucleoside reverse transcriptase inhibitor) used to manage human immunodeficiency virus infection in combination with other antiretrovirals. Zalcitabine also has been used as a single agent in clients who are intolerant of other regimens. Zalcitabine can cause serious liver damage, and liver function studies should be monitored closely. Options 1, 2, and 3 are not associated specifically with the use of this medication.

Test-Taking Strategy: Focus on the name of the medication. Recalling that this medication is hepatotoxic will direct you to option 4. If you are unfamiliar with this medication, review this content.

Level of Cognitive Ability: Analysis
Client Needs: Physiological Integrity
Integrated Process: Nursing Process—assessment
Content Area: Adult health—immune
Reference: Mosby. (2007). *Mosby's 2007 nursing drug reference* (20th ed., p. 1050). St. Louis: Mosby.

3. **3**

Rationale: Foscarnet (Foscavir) is toxic to the kidneys. The serum creatinine level is monitored before therapy, two or three times per week during induction therapy, and at least weekly

during maintenance therapy. Foscarnet also may cause decreased levels of calcium, magnesium, phosphorus, and potassium. Thus, these levels also are measured with the same frequency.
Test-Taking Strategy: Use the process of elimination. Recalling that this medication is nephrotoxic will direct you easily to option 3. Review this medication if you are unfamiliar with it.
Level of Cognitive Ability: Analysis
Client Needs: Physiological Integrity
Integrated Process: Nursing Process—assessment
Content Area: Adult health—immune
Reference: Hodgson, B., & Kizior, R. (2007). *Saunders nursing drug handbook 2007* (p. 516). Philadelphia: W.B. Saunders.

4. **4**
Rationale: Frequent side effects of this medication include leukopenia, thrombocytopenia, and anemia. The client should be monitored routinely for signs and symptoms of infection. Options 1, 2, and 3 are inaccurate interpretations.
Test-Taking Strategy: Use the process of elimination, focusing on the strategic words *develops a temperature*. Note the relationship between these strategic words and option 4. Review the side effects of this medication if you had difficulty with this question.
Level of Cognitive Ability: Analysis
Client Needs: Physiological Integrity
Integrated Process: Nursing Process—analysis
Content Area: Adult health—immune
Reference: Hodgson, B., & Kizior, R. (2007). *Saunders nursing drug handbook 2007* (p. 913). Philadelphia: W.B. Saunders.

5. **1**
Rationale: Saquinavir is an antiretroviral (protease inhibitor) used with other antiretroviral medications to manage human immunodeficiency virus infection. Saquinavir is administered with meals and is best absorbed if the client consumes high-calorie, high-fat meals. Saquinavir can cause photosensitivity, and the nurse should instruct the client to avoid sun exposure.
Test-Taking Strategy: Use the process of elimination. Options 2 and 3 can be eliminated first, knowing that these dietary measures likely would not be prescribed for this client. From the remaining options, you must know that this medication can cause photosensitivity. Review this medication if you had difficulty with this question.
Level of Cognitive Ability: Application
Client Needs: Physiological Integrity
Integrated Process: Teaching and Learning
Content Area: Adult health—immune
Reference: Hodgson, B., & Kizior, R. (2007). *Saunders nursing drug handbook 2007* (p. 1043). Philadelphia: W.B. Saunders.

6. **1**
Rationale: Stavudine (d4t, Zerit) is an antiretroviral used to manage human immunodeficiency virus infection in clients who do not respond to or who cannot tolerate conventional therapy. The medication can cause peripheral neuropathy, and the nurse should monitor the client's gait closely and ask the client about paresthesia.

Test-Taking Strategy: Focus on the name of the medication. Recalling that this medication causes peripheral neuropathy will direct you to option 1. If you are not familiar with this medication and the important assessment measures, review this content.
Level of Cognitive Ability: Analysis
Client Needs: Physiological Integrity
Integrated Process: Nursing Process—assessment
Content Area: Adult health—immune
Reference: Hodgson, B., & Kizior, R. (2007). *Saunders nursing drug handbook 2007* (p. 1077). Philadelphia: W.B. Saunders.

7. **4**
Rationale: Common side effects of this medication therapy are leukopenia and anemia. The nurse monitors the complete blood count results for these changes. Options 1, 2, and 3 are unrelated to the use of this medication.
Test-Taking Strategy: Focus on the name of the medication. Recalling that zidovudine (AZT) causes leukopenia will direct you to option 4. Review this medication if you had difficulty with this question.
Level of Cognitive Ability: Analysis
Client Needs: Physiological Integrity
Integrated Process: Nursing Process—assessment
Content Area: Adult health—immune
Reference: Hodgson, B., & Kizior, R. (2007). *Saunders nursing drug handbook 2007* (p. 1231). Philadelphia: W.B. Saunders.

8. **3**
Rationale: Didanosine (Videx) can cause pancreatitis. A serum amylase level that is increased to 1.5 to 2 times normal may signify pancreatitis in the client with acquired immunodeficiency syndrome and is potentially fatal. The medication may have to be discontinued. The medication is also hepatotoxic and can result in liver failure.
Test-Taking Strategy: Focus on the name of the medication. Recalling that this medication can cause damage to the pancreas and is hepatotoxic will direct you to the correct option. Review this medication if you had difficulty with this question.
Level of Cognitive Ability: Analysis
Client Needs: Physiological Integrity
Integrated Process: Nursing Process—assessment
Content Area: Adult health—immune
Reference: Hodgson, B., & Kizior, R. (2007). *Saunders nursing drug handbook 2007* (p. 354). Philadelphia: W.B. Saunders.

9. **3**
Rationale: Hypertension can occur in a client taking cyclosporine (Sandimmune, Gengraf, Neoral) and, because this client is also complaining of a headache, the blood pressure is the vital sign to be monitoring most closely. Other adverse effects include infection, nephrotoxicity, and hirsutism. Options 1, 2, and 4 are unrelated to the use of this medication.
Test-Taking Strategy: Focus on the name of the medication and recall that this medication can cause hypertension. Review the adverse effects of this medication if you had difficulty with this question.
Level of Cognitive Ability: Analysis
Client Needs: Physiological Integrity

Integrated Process: Nursing Process—analysis
Content Area: Adult health—immune
Reference: Lehne, R. (2007). *Pharmacology for nursing care* (6th ed., pp. 795-797). Philadelphia: W.B. Saunders.

ALTERNATE ITEM FORMAT: MULTIPLE RESPONSE

Answer: 2, 3, 5
Rationale: Ketoconazole (Nizoral) is an antifungal medication. It is administered with food (not on an empty stomach) and antacids are avoided for 2 hours after taking the medication to ensure absorption. The medication is hepatotoxic and the nurse monitors liver function studies. The client is instructed to avoid exposure to the sun because the medication increases photosensitivity. The client is also instructed to avoid alcohol. There is no reason for the client to restrict fluid intake. In fact, this could be harmful to the client.
Test-Taking Strategy: Use general medication guidelines to assist in selecting the correct interventions. Also, remember that this medication is administered with food and that it is hepatotoxic. Review this medication if you had difficulty with this question.
Level of Cognitive Ability: Application
Client Needs: Physiological Integrity
Integrated Process: Nursing Process—implementation
Content Area: Adult health—immune
Reference: Hodgson, B., & Kizior, R. (2007). *Saunders nursing drug handbook 2007* (p. 654). Philadelphia: W.B. Saunders.

REFERENCES

Black, J., & Hawks, J. (2005). *Medical-surgical nursing: Clinical management for positive outcomes* (7th ed.). Philadelphia: W.B. Saunders.

Hodgson, B., & Kizior, R. (2007). *Saunders nursing drug handbook 2007.* Philadelphia: W.B. Saunders.

Lehne, R. (2007). *Pharmacology for nursing care* (6th ed.). Philadelphia: W.B. Saunders.

Mosby. (2007). *Mosby's 2007 nursing drug reference* (20th ed.). St. Louis: Mosby.

The Adult Client With a Mental Health Disorder

PYRAMID TERMS

abuse   An act of misuse, deceit, or exploitation; the wrong or improper use or action toward another individual that results in injury, damage, maltreatment, or corruption.

addiction   A state of dependence or compulsive use. In relation to drug dependence, addiction incorporates the concepts of loss of control with respect to the use of a drug, taking the drug despite related problems and complications, and a tendency to relapse.

coping mechanisms   Methods of adjusting to environmental stress without altering one's own goals or purposes. These can include conscious and unconscious mechanisms.

crisis   A temporary state of disequilibrium in which an individual's usual coping mechanisms or problem-solving methods fail. Crisis can result in personality growth or personality disorganization.

defense mechanisms   A coping mechanism (protective defense) of the ego that attempts to protect the individual from feelings of inadequacy and worthlessness and prevent awareness of anxiety. When anxiety is too painful, the individual copes by using defense mechanisms to protect the ego and decrease anxiety.

milieu   The physical and social environment in which an individual lives. Milieu therapy focuses on positive physical and social environmental manipulation to produce positive change.

restraints   Physical restraints include any manual method or mechanical device, material, or equipment that inhibits free movement. Chemical restraints include the administration of medications for the specific purpose of inhibiting a specific behavior or movement.

seclusion   Placing a client alone in a specially designed room for protection and close supervision. Seclusion is the last measure in a process to maximize safety to the client and others.

suicide   The ultimate act of self-destruction in which an individual purposefully ends his or her own life.

suicide attempt   Any willful, self-inflicted, or life-threatening attempt by an individual that has not lead to death.

PYRAMID TO SUCCESS

The Pyramid to Success focuses on the therapeutic nurse-client relationship, client rights, hospital admission procedures, the ethical and legal issues related to the care of the client with a mental health disorder, grief and loss, and end-of-life issues. Pyramid Points focus on the use of restraints, seclusion, and electroconvulsive therapy. Focus on care to the client with an addiction, such as an eating disorder or drug or alcohol disorder. Additional focus areas include anxiety, depression, suicide, abuse and violence, rape crisis interventions, post-traumatic stress disorders, obsessive-compulsive disorders, schizophrenia, and bipolar disorders. Pyramid Points address the use of medications prescribed for the client with a mental health disorder, particularly lithium and the benzodiazepines. The Integrated Processes addressed in this unit include Caring, Communication and Documentation, Nursing Process, and Teaching/ Learning.

CLIENT NEEDS

Safe and Effective Care Environment

Ensuring client advocacy
Implementing legal responsibilities related to reporting incidences of violence and abuse

Maintaining confidentiality

Obtaining informed consent related to treatments, such as restraints, seclusion, and electroconvulsive therapy (ECT)

Providing psychiatric consultations and referrals

Providing safety to client and others

Upholding client rights

Using restraints and seclusion appropriately and safely

Health Promotion and Maintenance

Identifying individual lifestyle choices

Performing psychosocial assessment techniques

Providing health promotion programs related to addictions

Psychosocial Integrity

Assessing for abuse and neglect situations

Assessing for chemical dependency

Assessing for domestic violence

Addressing grief and loss and end-of-life issues

Caring for the client who has been sexually abused or raped

Considering religious, cultural, and spiritual influences on health

Developing a therapeutic nurse-client relationship

Identifying appropriate counseling techniques

Identifying coping mechanisms

Identifying support systems

Implementing behavioral interventions

Providing crisis intervention

Providing a therapeutic milieu

Teaching stress management techniques

Physiological Integrity

Administering medications as prescribed

Assessing for abusive and self-destructive behavior

Monitoring elimination patterns

Monitoring for alterations in body systems related to addictions

Monitoring for expected and untoward effects of medications

Monitoring for potential complications related to medications and ECT

Monitoring laboratory values related to medication therapy

Monitoring rest and sleep patterns

Providing adequate nutrition

Providing personal hygiene measures

REFERENCES

Chernecky, C., & Berger, B. (2004). *Laboratory tests and diagnostic procedures* (4th ed.). Philadelphia: W.B. Saunders.

Fortinash, K., & Holoday-Worret, P. (2004). *Psychiatric mental health nursing* (3rd ed.). St. Louis: Mosby.

Ignatavicius, D., & Workman, M. (2006). *Medical-surgical nursing: Critical thinking for collaborative care* (5th ed.). Philadelphia: W.B. Saunders.

Jarvis, C. (2004). *Physical examination and health assessment* (4th ed.). St. Louis: W.B. Saunders.

Keltner, N., Schwecke, L., & Bostrom, C. (2003). *Psychiatric nursing* (4th ed.). St. Louis: Mosby.

Lilley, L., Harrington, S., & Snyder, J. (2005). *Pharmacology and the nursing process* (4th ed.). St. Louis: Mosby.

Mosby (2006). *Mosby's dictionary of medicine, nursing and health professions* (7th ed.). St. Louis: Mosby.

National Council of State Boards of Nursing (Eds.). (2007). *2007 NCLEX-RN® detailed test plan*. Chicago: Author.

Potter, P., & Perry, A. (2005). *Fundamentals of nursing* (6th ed.). St. Louis: Mosby.

Stuart, G., & Laraia, M. (2005). *Principles and practice of psychiatric nursing* (8th ed.). St. Louis: Mosby.

Varcarolis, E., Carson, V., & Shoemaker, N. (2006). *Foundations of psychiatric mental health nursing: A clinical approach* (5th ed.). Philadelphia: W.B. Saunders.

Foundations of Psychiatric Mental Health Nursing

I. THE NURSE-CLIENT RELATIONSHIP

A. Principles
1. Genuineness, respect, and empathic understanding are characteristics important to the development of a therapeutic nurse-client relationship.
2. The client should be cared for in a holistic manner.
3. The nurse considers the religious and spiritual practices of the client and whether these practices may give the client hope, comfort, and support while healing.
4. The nurse considers the client's cultural beliefs and values in assessing the client's response to the nurse-client relationship and his or her adaptation to stressors.
5. Appropriate limits and boundaries define and facilitate a therapeutic nurse-client relationship.
6. Honest and open communication are important cornerstones for the development of trust, an underpinning of the therapeutic nurse-client relationship
7. The nurse uses therapeutic communication techniques to encourage the client to express thoughts and feelings as they address identified problem areas.
8. The nurse respects the client's confidentiality and limits discussion of the client to members of the treatment team.
9. The goal of the nurse-client relationship is to assist the client to develop problem-solving and **coping mechanisms.**

B. Phases of a therapeutic nurse-client relationship
1. Preinteraction phase
   a. The preinteraction phase begins before the nurse's first contact with the client.
   b. The nurse's task in the preinteraction phase is to explore any preconceived ideas, stereotypes, biases, and values that may impinge on the nurse-client relationship.
2. Orientation or introductory phase
   a. Acceptance, trust, and boundaries are established.
   b. Expectations and the time frame of the relationship are identified (establishing a contract).
   c. Client-centered goals are defined.
   d. Termination and separation of the relationship are discussed in anticipation of the time-limited nature of the relationship.
3. Working phase
   a. An attitude of acceptance and active listening assists the client to express thoughts and feelings and to learn about his or her **coping mechanisms.**
   b. Identifying themes and patterns of behavior promotes insight into problem-solving and **coping mechanisms.**
   c. Encouraging independence in the client facilitates recovery and leads to readiness for termination.
4. Termination or separation phase
   a. Prepare the client for termination and separation on initial contact.
   b. Evaluate progress and achievement of goals.
   c. Identify responses related to termination and separation, such as anger, distancing from the relationship, a return of symptoms, and dependency.
   d. Encourage the client to express feelings about termination.

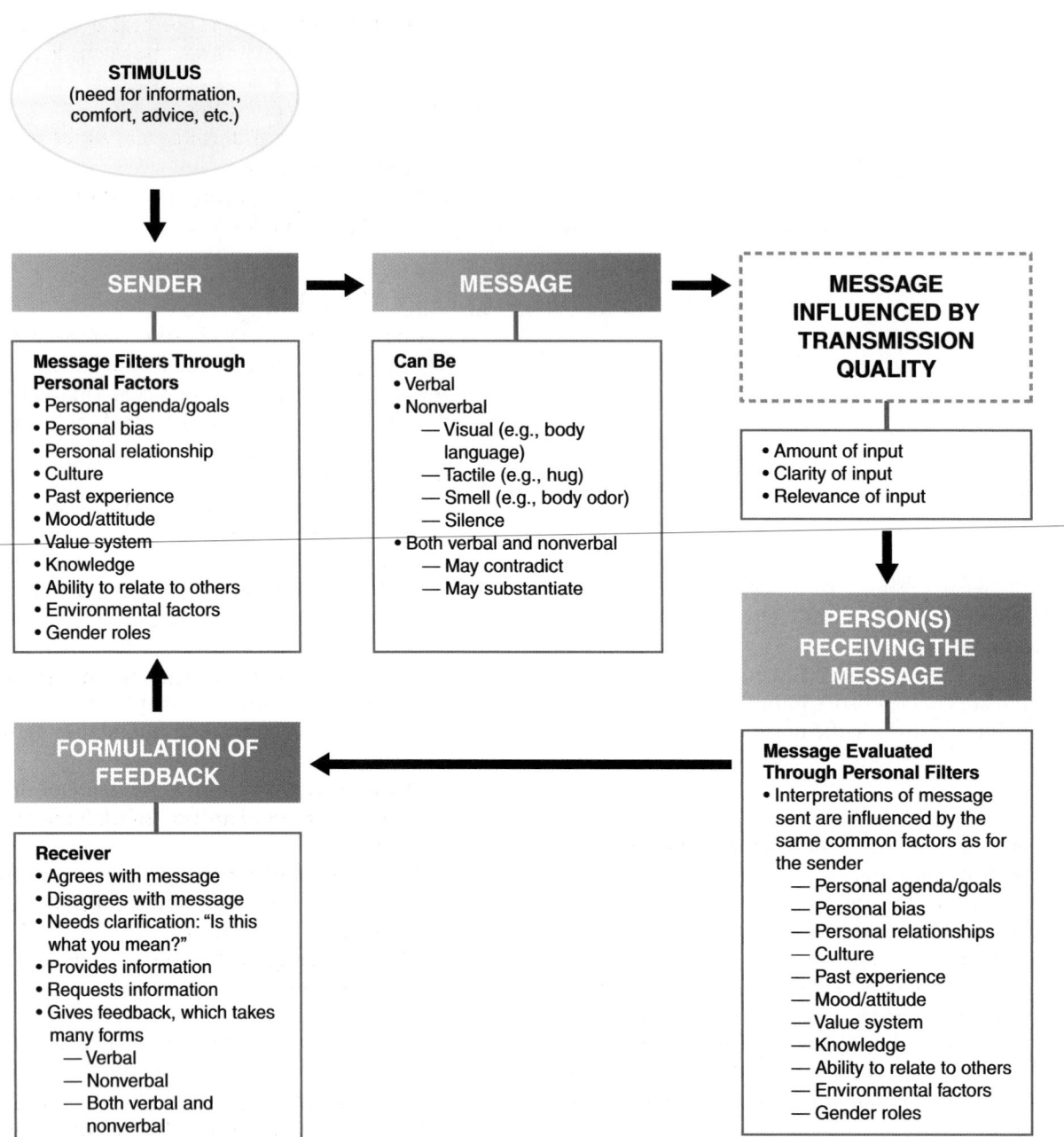

FIG. 71-1 Operational definition of communication. (Varcarolis, E., Carson, V., & Shoemaker, N. [2006]. *Foundations of psychiatric mental health nursing* [5th ed.]. Philadelphia: W.B. Saunders.)

e. Identify the client's strengths and anticipated needs for follow-up care.
f. Refer the client to other support systems.

II. THERAPEUTIC COMMUNICATION PROCESS
A. Principles
1. Communication includes verbal and nonverbal expression (Fig. 71-1).
2. Successful communication includes appropriateness, efficiency, flexibility, and feedback.
3. Anxiety in the nurse or client impedes communication.

4. Communication needs to be goal-directed within a professional framework.
B. Therapeutic and nontherapeutic communication techniques (Box 71-1)

III. MENTAL HEALTH
A. Mental health is a lifelong process of successful adaptation to changing internal and external environments.
B. The mentally healthy individual is *in contact with reality*, can relate to people and situations in their environment, and resolve conflicts within a problem-solving framework.

THERAPEUTIC TECHNIQUES
Clarifying and validating
Encouraging formulation of a plan of action
Focusing and refocusing
Listening
Maintaining neutral responses
Maintaining silence
Providing acknowledgment and feedback
Providing information and presenting reality
Providing nonverbal encouragement
Reflecting
Restating
Sharing perceptions
Summarizing
Using broad openings and open-ended questions

NONTHERAPEUTIC TECHNIQUES
Asking the client "Why?"
Being defensive or challenging the client
Changing the subject
Giving advice or approval or disapproval
Making stereotypical comments
Making value judgments
Placing the client's feelings on hold
Providing false reassurance

C. The mentally healthy individual has psychobiological resilience.

IV. PSYCHIATRIC–MENTAL HEALTH ILLNESS
  A. Description
     1. Psychiatric illness is the loss of the ability to respond to the environment in ways that are in harmony with oneself or the expectations of society.
     2. Psychiatric illness is characterized by thought or behavior patterns that impair functioning and cause distress.
  B. Personality characteristics
     1. Self-concept is distorted.
     2. Perception of strengths and weaknesses is not realistic.
     3. Thoughts and perceptions may not be reality-based.
     4. The ability to find meaning and purpose in life may be impaired.
     5. Life direction and productivity may be disturbed.
     6. Meeting one's own needs may be problematic.
     7. Excessive reliance or preoccupation on the thoughts, opinions, and actions of self or others may be present.
  C. Adaptations to stress
     1. The individual's sense of self-control and environmental mastery may be affected

     2. Perception of the environment may be distorted.
     3. **Coping mechanisms** may be ineffective or non-existent.
  D. Interpersonal relationships
     1. Interpersonal relationships may suffer or even be minimally existent.
     2. The ability to enjoy sustained intimacy in relationships is impaired.

V. COPING AND DEFENSE MECHANISMS
  A. **Coping mechanisms**
     1. Coping involves any effort to decrease anxiety.
     2. **Coping mechanisms** can be constructive or destructive, task-oriented in relation to direct problem solving, or defense-oriented and regulating the response to protect oneself.
  B. **Defense mechanisms**
     1. As anxiety increases, the individual copes by using **defense mechanisms.**
     2. A defense mechanism is a coping mechanism used in an effort to protect the individual from feelings of anxiety (Box 71-2).
  C. Interventions
     1. Assist the client to identify the source of anxiety.
     2. Assist the client to explore methods to reduce anxiety.
     3. Assess the client's use of **defense mechanisms.**
     4. Facilitate appropriate use of **defense mechanisms.**
     5. Determine whether the **defense mechanisms** used by the client are effective for him or her or create additional distress.
     6. Avoid criticizing the behavior and the use of **defense mechanisms.**

VI. DIAGNOSTIC AND STATISTICAL MANUAL OF MENTAL HEALTH DISORDERS
  A. The *Diagnostic and Statistical Manual of Mental Health Disorders* (DSM IV-TR) classifies psychiatric diagnoses according to the American Psychiatric Association.
  B. The manual is a system used in clinical, research, and educational settings, in which diagnostic criteria are included for each diagnosis.
  C. The manual includes a list of culture-bound syndromes that may be associated with a particular diagnostic category.
  D. Knowledge of the characteristics of a particular psychiatric diagnosis will assist the nurse in assessing the client's nursing care needs.

VII. TYPES OF MENTAL HEALTH ADMISSIONS AND DISCHARGES
  A. Voluntary admission
     1. The client (or the client's guardian) seeks admission for care.

BOX 71-2
Types of Defense Mechanisms

COMPENSATION
Putting forth extra effort to achieve in areas where one has a real or imagined deficiency

CONVERSION
The expression of emotional conflicts through physical symptoms

DENIAL
Disowning consciously intolerable thoughts and impulses

DISPLACEMENT
Feelings toward one person are directed to another who is less threatening, thereby satisfying an impulse with a substitute object.

DISSOCIATION
The blocking of an anxiety-provoking event or period of time from the conscious mind

FANTASY
Gratification by imaginary achievements and wishful thinking

FIXATION
Never advancing to the next level of emotional development and organization; the persistence in later life of interests and behavior patterns appropriate to an earlier age

IDENTIFICATION
The unconscious attempt to change oneself to resemble an admired person

INSULATION
Withdrawing into passivity and becoming inaccessible so as to avoid further threatening situations

INTELLECTUALIZATION
Excessive reasoning to avoid feelings; the thinking is disconnected from feelings, and situations are dealt with at a cognitive level

INTROJECTION
A type of identification in which the individual incorporates the traits or values of another into himself or herself

ISOLATION
Response in which a person blocks feelings associated with an unpleasant experience

PROJECTION
Transferring one's internal feelings, thoughts, and unacceptable ideas and traits to someone else

RATIONALIZATION
An attempt to make unacceptable feelings and behaviors acceptable by justifying the behavior

REACTION FORMATION
Developing conscious attitudes and behaviors and acting out behaviors opposite to what one really feels

REGRESSION
Returning to an earlier developmental stage to express an impulse to deal with reality

REPRESSION
An unconscious process in which the client blocks undesirable and unacceptable thoughts from conscious expression

SUBLIMATION
Replacement of an unacceptable need, attitude, or emotion with one more socially acceptable

SUBSTITUTION
The replacement of a valued unacceptable object with an object more acceptable to the ego

SUPPRESSION
The conscious, deliberate forgetting of unacceptable or painful thoughts, ideas, and feelings

SYMBOLIZATION
The conscious use of an idea or object to represent another actual event or object; often, the meaning is not clear because the symbol may be representative of something unconscious.

UNDOING
Engaging in behavior considered to be the opposite of a previous unacceptable behavior, thought, or feeling

2. The voluntary client is free to sign out of the hospital with physician notification and order.
3. Detaining a voluntary client against her or his will is termed *false imprisonment*.
4. Civil rights are retained fully by the client (Box 71-3).

▲ B. Right to confidentiality
1. A client has a right to confidentiality of their medical information; the Health Insurance Por-

tability and Accountability Act (HIPAA) of 1996 ensures client confidentiality with regard to the release and electronic transmission of data.
2. Client information can only be released by the client's informed consent, which specifies the information that can be released and the time frame for which the release is valid.
3. Information sometimes must be released in life-threatening situations without the client's consent.

4. In the event of a specific threat against an identified individual, the health care professional has a legal obligation to warn intended victim(s) of a client's threats of harm.

C. Involuntary admission
1. Involuntary admission may be necessary when a person is mentally ill, is a danger to self or others, or is in need of psychiatric treatment or physical care.
2. Involuntary admission occurs when a client is admitted or detained involuntarily for mental health treatment because of actual or imminent danger to self or others.
3. The client who is admitted involuntarily retains his or her right for informed consent.
4. The client retains the right to refuse treatments, including medications, unless a separate and specific treatment order is obtained from the court.
5. The client loses the right to refuse treatment when he or she poses an immediate danger to self or others, requiring immediate action by the health care team.
6. An order from a judge is required for involuntary admissions except in the case of emergency, which allows time to obtain the necessary order from a judge; in the case of all involuntary ad-

missions, legal counsel must be provided for the client.
7. A court hearing is held by a judge within a specified time period for clients admitted involuntarily; the specific time period varies by state.
8. In most states, the client can institute a court hearing to seek an expedient judicial discharge (a writ of habeas corpus).
9. At the court hearing, a determination is made as to whether the client may be released from the hospital or detained for further treatment and evaluation or committed to a mental health facility for an undetermined time period.
10. The client has the right to treatment in the least restrictive treatment environment; if treatment objectives can be achieved, for example, by court-ordered treatment to an outpatient facility as opposed to an inpatient facility, the client has the right to be treated in the former setting.
11. The client is considered legally competent unless he or she has been declared incompetent through a legal hearing separate from the involuntary commitment hearing.
12. In the course of providing nursing care and carrying out medical orders, if the nurse believes that a client lacks competency to make informed decisions, action should be initiated to determine whether a legal guardian needs to be appointed by the court.

D. Release from the hospital
1. Description
a. A client may be released voluntarily, against medical advice, or with conditions (conditional release).
b. The client who has sought voluntary admission has the right to demand and receive release.
2. Voluntary release
a. In the absence of an act of self-harm or danger to others, a voluntary client should never be detained.
b. If a voluntary client wishes to be discharged from treatment but is considered potentially dangerous to self or others, the physician can order the client to be detained while legal proceedings for involuntary status are sought.
c. Some states provide for conditional release of involuntarily hospitalized clients; this enables the treating physician to order continued treatment on an outpatient basis as opposed to discharging the client to follow-up on his or her own initiative.
d. Conditional release usually involves outpatient treatment for a specified period of time to determine the client's compliance with medication protocol, ability to meet basic needs, and ability to reintegrate into the community.

e. An involuntary client who is released conditionally may be reinstitutionalized while the commitment is still in effect without recommencement of formal admission procedures.

3. Discharge planning and follow-up care
  a. Discharge (unconditional release) is the termination of the client-institution relationship.
  b. This release may be ordered by the psychiatrist, court, or administration for involuntarily admitted clients and may be requested by voluntary clients at any time.
  c. In most states, the client can institute a court hearing to seek an expedient judicial discharge (writ of habeas corpus).
  d. Discharge planning and follow-up care are important for the continued well-being of the client with a mental health disorder.
  e. After-care case managers are used to facilitate the client's adaptation back into the community and to provide early referral if the treatment plan is not successful.

PRACTICE QUESTIONS

1. The nurse is working with a client who has sought counseling after trying to rescue a neighbor involved in a house fire. In spite of the client's efforts, the neighbor died. Which action does the nurse engage in with the client during the working phase of the nurse-client relationship?
   1. Exploring the client's ability to function
   2. Exploring the client's potential for self-harm
   3. Inquiring about the client's perception or appraisal of the neighbor's death
   4. Inquiring about and examining the client's feelings that may block adaptive coping

2. A client who has just been sexually assaulted is quiet and calm. The nurse analyzes this behavior as indicating which defense mechanism?
   1. Denial
   2. Projection
   3. Rationalization
   4. Intellectualization

3. Laboratory work is prescribed for a client who has been experiencing delusions. When the nurse approaches the client to obtain a specimen of the client's blood, the client begins to shout "You're all vampires. Let me out of here!" The appropriate nursing response is which of the following?
   1. "What makes you think that I am a vampire?"
   2. "I'll leave and come back later for your blood."
   3. "I am not going to hurt you; I am going to help you."
   4. "It must be frightening to think that others want to hurt you."

4. Unresolved feelings related to loss most likely may be recognized during which phase of the therapeutic nurse-client relationship?
   1. Working
   2. Trusting
   3. Orientation
   4. Termination

5. A client with a diagnosis of major depression who has attempted suicide says to the nurse, "I should have died. I've always been a failure. Nothing ever goes right for me." The therapeutic response to the client is:
   1. "I don't see you as a failure."
   2. "You have everything to live for."
   3. "Feeling like this is all part of being ill."
   4. "You've been feeling like a failure for a while?"

6. The community health nurse visits a client at home. The client states, "I haven't slept at all the last couple of nights." Which response by the nurse illustrates a therapeutic communication technique for this client?
   1. "Go on."
   2. "Sleeping?"
   3. "You're having difficulty sleeping?"
   4. "Sometimes, I have trouble sleeping too."

7. A client admitted to the mental health unit is experiencing disturbed thought processes and believes that the food is being poisoned. Which communication technique does the nurse plan to use to encourage the client to eat?
   1. Using open-ended questions and silence
   2. Focusing on self-disclosure regarding food preferences
   3. Identifying the reasons that the client may not want to eat
   4. Offering opinions about the necessity of adequate nutrition

8. A client is admitted to a mental health unit for treatment of psychotic behavior. The client is at the locked exit door and is shouting, "Let me out. There's nothing wrong with me. I don't belong here." The nurse analyzes this behavior as:
   1. Denial
   2. Projection
   3. Regression
   4. Rationalization

9. The supervisor reprimands the nurse in charge of the nursing unit because the charge nurse has not adhered to the unit budget. Later that afternoon, the charge nurse accuses the nursing staff of wasting supplies. This behavior is an example of:
   1. Denial
   2. Repression
   3. Suppression
   4. Displacement

10. The client says to the nurse, "I'm going to die, and I wish my family would stop hoping for a cure! I get

so angry when they carry on like this. After all, I'm the one who's dying." The therapeutic response by the nurse is:

1. "Have you shared your feelings with your family?"
2. "I think we should talk more about your anger with your family."
3. "You're feeling angry that your family continues to hope for you to be cured?"
4. "Well, it sounds like you're being pretty pessimistic. After all, years ago, people died of pneumonia."

11. The nurse employed in a mental health unit is assigned to care for a client admitted to the unit 2 days ago. On review of the client's record, the nurse notes that the admission was a voluntary admission. Based on this type of admission, the nurse anticipates which of the following?

1. The client will resist treatment measures.
2. The client will be angry and will refuse care.
3. The client's family will resist treatment measures.
4. The client will participate in the planning of the care and treatment plan.

12. A nurse enters a client's room, and the client is demanding release from the hospital. The nurse reviews the client's record and notes that the client was admitted 2 days ago for treatment of an anxiety disorder and that the admission was a voluntary admission. Which of the following actions will the nurse take?

1. Contact the physician.
2. Call the client's family.
3. Persuade the client to stay a few more days.
4. Tell the client that discharge is not possible at this time.

13. A client has been admitted to the mental health unit. On admission assessment, the nurse notes that the client was admitted by involuntary status. Based on this type of admission, the nurse would most likely expect that the client:

1. Presents a harm to self
2. Requested the admission
3. Consented to the admission
4. Provided written application to the facility for admission

14. The nurse is preparing the client for the termination phase of the nurse-client relationship. The nurse prepares to implement which nursing task appropriate for this phase?

1. Planning short-term goals
2. Making appropriate referrals
3. Developing realistic solutions
4. Identifying expected outcomes

15. During the termination phase of the nurse-client relationship, the clinic nurse observes that the client has made several sarcastic remarks and has an angry affect. The most appropriate interpretation of the behavior is that the client:

1. Needs to be admitted to the hospital.
2. Needs to be referred to the psychiatrist as soon as possible.
3. Requires further treatment and is not ready to be discharged.
4. Is displaying typical behaviors that can occur during termination.

16. The nurse is providing care to a client admitted to the hospital with a diagnosis of acute anxiety disorder. While conversing with the client, the client says to the nurse, "I have a secret that I want to tell you. You won't tell anyone about it, will you?" The appropriate nursing response is which of the following?

1. "No, I won't tell anyone."
2. "I cannot promise to keep a secret."
3. "If you tell me the secret, I will tell it to your doctor."
4. "If you tell me the secret, I will need to document it in your record."

17. The nurse employed in a mental health clinic is greeted by a neighbor in a local grocery store. The neighbor says to the nurse, "How is Carol doing? She is my best friend and is seen at your clinic every week." The appropriate nursing response is which of the following?

1. "I cannot discuss any client situation with you."
2. "If you want to know about Carol, you need to ask her yourself."
3. "I'm not suppose to discuss this, but because you are my neighbor, I can tell you that she is doing great!"
4. "I'm not suppose to discuss this, but because you are my neighbor, I can tell you that she really has some problems!"

18. A home health nurse is talking to the spouse of a client taking an antidepressant. The spouse says, "Now that my husband is responding to the antidepressant, the suicidal risk is over and you can stop making these home visits." After analyzing this statement, which of the following is the appropriate nursing response?

1. "I need to continue with my visits. Your comment reflects a lack of knowledge that this disease runs in families."
2. "I agree with you. Clients who want to kill themselves are only suicidal for a limited time. No one can feel self-destructive forever."
3. "I agree with you. The suicidal threats were really attention seeking. Continuing to visit would reinforce your husband's use of manipulation."
4. "I need to continue with my visits. Most suicides occur within 3 months after improvement begins because the client now has the energy to carry out the suicidal intentions."

19. The nurse is caring for a client who is scheduled for electroconvulsive therapy. The nurse notes that an

informed consent has not been obtained for the procedure. On review of the record, the nurse notes that the admission was an involuntary hospitalization. Based on this information, the nurse determines:

1. That the physician will provide the informed consent
2. That an informed consent does not need to be obtained
3. That an informed consent should be obtained from the family
4. That an informed consent needs to be obtained from the client

20. The client was admitted involuntarily to the mental health unit because of episodes of extremely violent behavior. The client is demanding to be discharged from the hospital and the nurse does not allow the client to leave. Which of the following represents the legal ramifications associated with the nurse's behavior?

1. The nurse will be charged with assault.
2. The nurse will be charged with slander.
3. The nurse will be charged with imprisonment.
4. No charge will be made against the nurse because the nurse's actions are reasonable.

ALTERNATE ITEM FORMAT: MULTIPLE RESPONSE

The nurse in the mental health unit reviews the therapeutic and nontherapeutic communication techniques with a nursing student. Which of the following are therapeutic communication techniques? Select all that apply.

❑ 1. Restating
❑ 2. Listening
❑ 3. Asking the client, "Why?"
❑ 4. Maintaining neutral responses
❑ 5. Giving advice or approval or disapproval
❑ 6. Providing acknowledgment and feedback

ANSWERS

1. 4
Rationale: The client must first deal with feelings and negative responses before the client can work through the meaning of the crisis. Option 4 pertains directly to the client's feelings. Options 1 and 2 do not directly address the client's feelings. Option 3 is more of an assessment question.
Test-Taking Strategy: Focus on the subject of the question, the working phase of the nurse-client relationship. Think about the interventions that occur in this phase. Using the process of elimination, focus on this subject and on the option that focuses on the feelings of the client. This will direct you to option 4. Review the phases of the nurse-client relationship if you had difficulty with this question.
Level of Cognitive Ability: Application
Client Needs: Psychosocial Integrity
Integrated Process: Caring
Content Area: Mental health
References: Fortinash, K., & Holoday-Worret, P. (2004). *Psychiatric mental health nursing* (3rd ed., p. 511). St. Louis: Mosby. Stuart, G., & Laraia, M. (2005). *Principles and practice of psychiatric nursing* (8th ed., pp. 19, 22-23). St. Louis: Mosby.

2. 1
Rationale: Denial is refusal to admit to a painful reality and may be a response by a victim of sexual abuse. Projection is transferring one's internal feelings, thoughts, and unacceptable ideas and traits to someone else. Rationalization is justifying the unacceptable attributes about oneself. Intellectualization is the excessive use of abstract thinking or generalizations to decrease painful thinking.
Test-Taking Strategy: Use the process of elimination and note the strategic words *calm* and *quiet*. These behaviors indicate denial in a sexually abused victim. If you had difficulty with this question, review content related to the sexually abused victim and defense mechanisms.
Level of Cognitive Ability: Analysis

Client Needs: Psychosocial Integrity
Integrated Process: Nursing Process—analysis
Content Area: Mental health
References: Fortinash, K., & Holoday-Worret, P. (2004). *Psychiatric mental health nursing* (3rd ed., p. 9). St. Louis: Mosby. Varcarolis, E., Carson, V., & Shoemaker, N. (2006.) *Foundations of psychiatric mental health nursing* (5th ed., pp. 220, 553). Philadelphia: W.B. Saunders.

3. 4
Rationale: Option 4 helps the client focus on the emotion underlying the delusion but does not argue with it. Option 1 places the client in a position that requires a response. Option 2 avoids the client. Option 3 is an attempt to convince the client to believe another thought. This response may cause the client to hold the delusion more strongly.
Test-Taking Strategy: Use the process of elimination and therapeutic communication techniques to answer the question. Option 4 is the only option that recognizes the client's needs and focuses on the client's feelings. Review therapeutic communication techniques if you had difficulty with this question.
Level of Cognitive Ability: Application
Client Needs: Psychosocial Integrity
Integrated Process: Caring
Content Area: Mental health
References: Fortinash, K., & Holoday-Worret, P. (2004). *Psychiatric mental health nursing* (3rd ed., p. 237). St. Louis: Mosby. Stuart, G., & Laraia, M. (2005,) *Principles and practice of psychiatric nursing* (8th ed., pp. 30-34). St. Louis: Mosby. Varcarolis, E., Carson, V., & Shoemaker, N. (2006). *Foundations of psychiatric mental health nursing* (5th ed., p. 1018). Philadelphia: W.B. Saunders.

4. 4
Rationale: In the termination phase, the relationship comes to a close. Ending treatment sometimes may be traumatic for clients who have come to value the relationship and the

help. Because loss is an issue, any unresolved feelings related to loss may resurface during this phase. Options 1, 2, and 3 are incorrect.
Test-Taking Strategy: Note the strategic words *unresolved, loss,* and *recognized* in the question. Considering the phases of the therapeutic nurse-client relationship will direct you to option 4. Review these phases and the nursing implications if you had difficulty with this question.
Level of Cognitive Ability: Analysis
Client Needs: Psychosocial Integrity
Integrated Process: Caring
Content Area: Mental health
References: Fortinash, K., & Holoday-Worret, P. (2004). *Psychiatric mental health nursing* (3rd ed., p. 437). St. Louis: Mosby.
Stuart, G., & Laraia, M. (2005). *Principles and practice of psychiatric nursing* (8th ed., pp. 23-24). St. Louis: Mosby.

5. **4**
Rationale: Responding to the feelings expressed by a client is an effective therapeutic communication technique. The correct option is an example of the use of restating. Options 1, 2, and 3 block communication because they minimize the client's experience and do not facilitate exploration of the client's expressed feelings.
Test-Taking Strategy: Use the process of elimination and therapeutic communication techniques to direct you to the option that directly addresses the client's feelings and concerns. Also, option 4 is the only option stated in the form of a question and is open-ended; thus, it will encourage the verbalization of feelings. Review therapeutic communication techniques if you had difficulty with this question.
Level of Cognitive Ability: Application
Client Needs: Psychosocial Integrity
Integrated Process: Communication and Documentation
Content Area: Mental health
References: Fortinash, K., & Holoday-Worret, P. (2004). *Psychiatric mental health nursing* (3rd ed., pp. 125-126, 566). St. Louis: Mosby.
Stuart, G., & Laraia, M. (2005). *Principles and practice of psychiatric nursing* (8th ed., pp. 30-34). St. Louis: Mosby.

6. **3**
Rationale: Option 3 uses the therapeutic communication technique of restatement. Although restatement is a technique that has a prompting component to it, it repeats the client's major theme, which assists the nurse to obtain a more specific perception of the problem from the client. Options 1, 2, and 4 are not therapeutic responses.
Test-Taking Strategy: Use the process of elimination. Option 1 is a general lead and allows the client to direct the discussion. Option 2 uses reflection, which simply repeats the client's last words to prompt further discussion. Option 4 focuses on the nurse's problem. Option 3 will provide the perception of the problem from the client's perspective. Review therapeutic communication techniques if you had difficulty with this question.
Level of Cognitive Ability: Application
Client Needs: Psychosocial Integrity
Integrated Process: Communication and Documentation
Content Area: Mental health

References: Fortinash, K., & Holoday-Worret, P. (2004). *Psychiatric mental health nursing* (3rd ed., p. 125). St. Louis: Mosby.
Stuart, G., & Laraia, M. (2005). *Principles and practice of psychiatric nursing* (8th ed., pp. 30-34, 288). St. Louis: Mosby.

7. **1**
Rationale: Open-ended questions and silence are strategies used to encourage clients to discuss their problems. Options 3 and 4 are not helpful to the client because they do not encourage the client to express feelings. The nurse should not offer opinions and should encourage the client to identify the reasons for the behavior. Option 2 is not a client-centered intervention.
Test-Taking Strategy: Use the process of elimination. Eliminate options 3 and 4 first because they do not support client expression of feelings. Eliminate option 2 next because it is not a client-centered response. Focusing on the client's feelings will direct you to option 1. Review therapeutic communication techniques if you had difficulty with this question.
Level of Cognitive Ability: Application
Client Needs: Psychosocial Integrity
Integrated Process: Communication and Documentation
Content Area: Mental health
References: Fortinash, K., & Holoday-Worret, P. (2004). *Psychiatric mental health nursing* (3rd ed., p. 125). St. Louis: Mosby.
Stuart, G., & Laraia, M. (2005). *Principles and practice of psychiatric nursing* (8th ed., pp. 30-34, 112-113). St. Louis: Mosby.
Varcarolis, E., Carson, V., & Shoemaker, N. (2006). *Foundations of psychiatric mental health nursing* (5th ed., p. 190). Philadelphia: W.B. Saunders.

8. **1**
Rationale: Denial is refusal to admit to a painful reality, which is treated as if it does not exist. In projection, a person unconsciously rejects emotionally unacceptable features and attributes them to other persons, objects, or situations. In regression, the client returns to an earlier, more comforting, although less mature, way of behaving. Rationalization is justifying illogical or unreasonable ideas, actions, or feelings by developing acceptable explanations that satisfy the teller and the listener.
Test-Taking Strategy: Use the process of elimination. The strategic words in the question that should direct you to the correct option are *"There's nothing wrong with me."* Select the option that recognizes the client's attempt to avoid looking at the reality of the situation. If you had difficulty with this question, review defense mechanisms.
Level of Cognitive Ability: Analysis
Client Needs: Psychosocial Integrity
Integrated Process: Nursing Process—analysis
Content Area: Mental health
References: Fortinash, K., & Holoday-Worret, P. (2004). *Psychiatric mental health nursing* (3rd ed., p. 9). St. Louis: Mosby.
Varcarolis, E., Carson, V., & Shoemaker, N. (2006). *Foundations of psychiatric mental health nursing* (5th ed., pp. 220-221). Philadelphia: W.B. Saunders.

9. **4**
Rationale: Ego defense mechanisms are operations outside of a person's awareness that the ego calls into play to protect against anxiety. Displacement is the discharging of pent-up

feelings on persons less threatening than those who initially aroused the emotion. Denial is the blocking out of painful or anxiety-inducing events or feelings. Repression is unconsciously keeping unacceptable feelings out of awareness. Suppression is consciously keeping unacceptable feelings and thoughts out of awareness.

Test-Taking Strategy: Use the process of elimination. Read the behavior identified in the question to assist you in determining the type of ego defense mechanism or behavior used. Remember that displacement is the discharging of pent-up feelings on persons less threatening than those who initially aroused the emotion. If you had difficulty with this question, review defense mechanisms.

Level of Cognitive Ability: Analysis
Client Needs: Psychosocial Integrity
Integrated Process: Nursing Process—analysis
Content Area: Mental health
References: Fortinash, K., & Holoday-Worret, P. (2004). *Psychiatric mental health nursing* (3rd ed., p. 9). St. Louis: Mosby. Stuart, G., & Laraia, M. (2005). *Principles and practice of psychiatric nursing* (8th ed., p. 269). St. Louis: Mosby.

10. **3**
Rationale: Restating is the therapeutic communication technique in which the nurse repeats what the client says to show understanding and to review what was said. Option 3 uses the therapeutic technique of restating. In option 1, the nurse is attempting to assess the client's ability to discuss feelings openly with family members. In option 2, the nurse attempts to use focusing, but the attempt to discuss central issues is premature. In option 4, the nurse makes a judgment and is nontherapeutic in the one-to-one relationship.

Test-Taking Strategy: Use therapeutic communication techniques to answer the question. Option 3 is the only option that identifies the use of a therapeutic technique and focuses on the client's feelings. Review these techniques if you had difficulty with this question.

Level of Cognitive Ability: Application
Client Needs: Psychosocial Integrity
Integrated Process: Communication and Documentation
Content Area: Mental health
References: Fortinash, K., & Holoday-Worret, P. (2004). *Psychiatric mental health nursing* (3rd ed., p. 125). St. Louis: Mosby. Stuart, G., & Laraia, M. (2005). *Principles and practice of psychiatric nursing* (8th ed., pp. 30-34). St. Louis: Mosby. Varcarolis, E., Carson, V., & Shoemaker, N. (2006). *Foundations of psychiatric mental health nursing* (5th ed., p. 189). Philadelphia: W.B. Saunders.

11. **4**
Rationale: Generally, the client seeks voluntary admission. A voluntary admission permits a client to make a written application for admission. If the client seeks voluntary admission, the most likely expectation is that the client will participate in the treatment program. Options 1, 2, and 3 are not characteristics of this type of admission.

Test-Taking Strategy: Use the process of admission. Note the strategic words *voluntary admission.* This should direct you to option 4. Additionally, note that options 1, 2, and 3 are com-

parative or alike. Review the various types of hospital admission processes if you had difficulty with this question.
Level of Cognitive Ability: Analysis
Client Needs: Psychosocial Integrity
Integrated Process: Nursing Process—analysis
Content Area: Mental health
References: Fortinash, K., & Holoday-Worret, P. (2004). *Psychiatric mental health nursing* (3rd ed., p. 50). St. Louis: Mosby. Stuart, G., & Laraia, M. (2005). *Principles and practice of psychiatric nursing* (8th ed., p. 150). St. Louis: Mosby.

12. **1**
Rationale: Generally, the client seeks voluntary admission. Voluntary clients have the right to demand and obtain release. If the client is a minor, the release may be contingent on the consent of the parent(s) or guardian. The nurse needs to be familiar with the state and facility policies and procedures. Many states require that the client submit a written release notice to the facility staff members, who reevaluate the client's condition for possible conversion to involuntary status, according to criteria established by laws. The best nursing action is to contact the physician.

Test-Taking Strategy: Use the process of elimination. Noting the type of hospital admission will assist in eliminating option 4. To "persuade" a client to stay in the hospital is inappropriate. Option 2 should be eliminated simply based on the subjects of client rights and confidentiality. Review the various types of hospital admission and discharge processes if you had difficulty with this question.
Level of Cognitive Ability: Application
Client Needs: Psychosocial Integrity
Integrated Process: Nursing Process—implementation
Content Area: Mental health
References: Fortinash, K., & Holoday-Worret, P. (2004). *Psychiatric mental health nursing* (3rd ed., p. 50). St. Louis: Mosby. Stuart, G., & Laraia, M. (2005). *Principles and practice of psychiatric nursing* (8th ed., p. 150). St. Louis: Mosby. Varcarolis, E., Carson, V., & Shoemaker, N. (2006). *Foundations of psychiatric mental health nursing* (5th ed., pp. 120-121). Philadelphia: W.B. Saunders.

13. **1**
Rationale: Involuntary admission is made without the client's consent. Involuntary admission is necessary when a person is a danger to self or others or is in need of psychiatric treatment. Options 2, 3, and 4 describe the process of voluntary admission.

Test-Taking Strategy: Use the process of elimination and note the strategic words *involuntary status.* This should direct you easily to option 1. Also, note that options 2, 3, and 4 are comparative or alike. Review the process of involuntary admission if you had difficulty with this question.
Level of Cognitive Ability: Analysis
Client Needs: Psychosocial Integrity
Integrated Process: Nursing Process—analysis
Content Area: Mental health
References: Fortinash, K., & Holoday-Worret, P. (2004). *Psychiatric mental health nursing* (3rd ed., p. 50). St. Louis: Mosby. Stuart, G., & Laraia, M. (2005). *Principles and practice of psychiatric nursing* (8th ed., p. 150). St. Louis: Mosby.

14. **2**

Rationale: Tasks of the termination phase include evaluating client performance, evaluating achievement of expected outcomes, evaluating future needs, making appropriate referrals, and dealing with the common behaviors associated with termination. Options 1, 3, and 4 identify the tasks of the working phase of the relationship.

Test-Taking Strategy: Use the process of elimination. Noting the strategic words *termination phase* should direct you easily to option 2. If you are unfamiliar with the appropriate tasks of the phases of the nurse-client relationship, review this content.

Level of Cognitive Ability: Application
Client Needs: Psychosocial Integrity
Integrated Process: Nursing Process—planning
Content Area: Mental health
References: Fortinash, K., & Holoday-Worret, P. (2004). *Psychiatric mental health nursing* (3rd ed., pp. 431-437). St. Louis: Mosby.
Stuart, G., & Laraia, M. (2005). *Principles and practice of psychiatric nursing* (8th ed., p. 23). St. Louis: Mosby.

15. **4**

Rationale: In the termination phase of a relationship, it is normal for a client to demonstrate a number of regressive behaviors that can be disturbing to the nurse. Typical behaviors include return of symptoms, anger, withdrawal, and minimizing the relationship. The anger that the client is experiencing is a normal behavior during the termination phase and does not necessarily indicate the need for hospitalization or treatment.

Test-Taking Strategy: Note the strategic words *termination phase.* This alone may assist in directing you to option 4. Additionally, note that options 1, 2, and 3 are comparable. These options address the need for further supervised treatment. If you are unfamiliar with the client behaviors associated with the termination phase, review this content.

Level of Cognitive Ability: Analysis
Client Needs: Psychosocial Integrity
Integrated Process: Nursing Process—analysis
Content Area: Mental health
References: Fortinash, K., & Holoday-Worret, P. (2004). *Psychiatric mental health nursing* (3rd ed., pp. 431-437). St. Louis: Mosby.
Stuart, G., & Laraia, M. (2005). *Principles and practice of psychiatric nursing* (8th ed., pp. 23, 47). St. Louis: Mosby.

16. **2**

Rationale: The nurse should never promise to keep a secret. Secrets are appropriate in a social relationship but not in a therapeutic one. The nurse needs to be honest with the client and tell the client that a promise cannot be made to keep the secret. Options 1, 3, and 4 are inappropriate responses.

Test-Taking Strategy: Use the process of elimination. Option 1 can be eliminated easily because it is inappropriate. Options 3 and 4 are not only inappropriate but are also somewhat threatening and may even block further communication. Review therapeutic communication techniques and the nurse-client relationship if you had difficulty with this question.

Level of Cognitive Ability: Application

Client Needs: Psychosocial Integrity
Integrated Process: Communication and Documentation
Content Area: Mental health
References: Fortinash, K., & Holoday-Worret, P. (2004). *Psychiatric mental health nursing* (3rd ed., pp. 125, 130). St. Louis: Mosby.
Stuart, G., & Laraia, M. (2005). *Principles and practice of psychiatric nursing* (8th ed., pp. 30-34, 275). St. Louis: Mosby.

17. **1**

Rationale: A nurse is required to maintain confidentiality regarding the client and the client's care. Confidentiality is basic to the therapeutic relationship and is a client's right. The most appropriate response to the neighbor is option 1. Option 2 is a rather blunt statement and does not acknowledge the issue that the nurse cannot reveal if the named person is or was a client. Options 3 and 4 identify statements that do not maintain client confidentiality. Option 1 is the most direct and correct.

Test-Taking Strategy: Focus on the subject of the question, maintaining confidentiality. This should assist you easily in eliminating options 3 and 4. From the remaining options, select option 1 over option 2 because it is the most direct and correct. Option 2 is a rather blunt and rude statement. Review confidentiality issues if you had difficulty with this question.

Level of Cognitive Ability: Application
Client Needs: Safe and Effective Care Environment
Integrated Process: Nursing Process—implementation
Content Area: Mental health
Reference: Fortinash, K., & Holoday-Worret, P. (2004). *Psychiatric mental health nursing* (3rd ed., pp. 50-52). St. Louis: Mosby.

18. **4**

Rationale: Most suicides occur within 3 months after the beginning of the improvement, when the client has the energy to carry out the suicidal intentions. Options 1, 2, and 3 are incorrect because they fail to address safety and involve giving false information.

Test-Taking Strategy: Use the process of elimination and knowledge regarding the facts about suicide to answer the question. Recalling that a critical time for a suicidal client is when the client has energy will direct you to option 4. Review the concepts related to suicide and therapeutic communication techniques if you had difficulty with this question.

Level of Cognitive Ability: Application
Client Needs: Physiological Integrity
Integrated Process: Communication and Documentation
Content Area: Mental health
References: Fortinash, K., & Holoday-Worret, P. (2004). *Psychiatric mental health nursing* (3rd ed., pp. 560-561, 566). St. Louis: Mosby.
Stuart, G., & Laraia, M. (2005). *Principles and practice of psychiatric nursing* (8th ed., pp. 30-34). St. Louis: Mosby.

19. **4**

Rationale: Clients who are admitted involuntarily do not lose their right to informed consent. Clients must be considered legally competent until they have been declared incompetent through a legal proceeding. The informed consent needs to be obtained from the client.

Test-Taking Strategy: Knowledge regarding the hospital admission processes and client's rights is necessary to answer this question. If you had difficulty with this question, focus on the subject of client rights to direct you to option 4. Review client rights if you had difficulty with this question.
Level of Cognitive Ability: Analysis
Client Needs: Safe and Effective Care Environment
Integrated Process: Nursing Process—analysis
Content Area: Mental health
References: Fortinash, K., & Holoday-Worret, P. (2004). *Psychiatric mental health nursing* (3rd ed., p. 54). St. Louis: Mosby. Stuart, G., & Laraia, M. (2005). *Principles and practice of psychiatric nursing* (8th ed., pp. 150, 605). St. Louis: Mosby.

20. **4**
Rationale: False imprisonment is an act with the intent to confine a person to a specific area. A nurse can be charged with false imprisonment if the nurse prohibits a client from leaving the hospital if the client has been admitted voluntarily and if no agency or legal policies exist for detaining the client. However, if the client has been admitted involuntarily or had agreed to an evaluation before discharge, the nurse's actions are reasonable.
Test-Taking Strategy: Noting the strategic words *admitted involuntarily* will assist you in eliminating option 3 and direct you to option 4. Options 1 and 2 are unrelated to the subject of the question and can be eliminated easily. Review the subjects related to false imprisonment and hospital admission if you had difficulty with this question.
Level of Cognitive Ability: Analysis
Client Needs: Safe and Effective Care Environment

Integrated Process: Nursing Process—analysis
Content Area: Mental health
References: Fortinash, K., & Holoday-Worret, P. (2004). *Psychiatric mental health nursing* (3rd ed., p. 56). St. Louis: Mosby. Varcarolis, E., Carson, V., & Shoemaker, N. (2006). *Foundations of psychiatric mental health nursing* (5th ed., pp. 128-129). Philadelphia: W.B. Saunders.

ALTERNATE ITEM FORMAT: MULTIPLE RESPONSE

Answer: **1, 2, 4, 6**
Rationale: Some of the therapeutic communication techniques include listening, maintaining silence, maintaining neutral responses, using broad openings and open-ended questions, focusing and refocusing, restating, clarifying and validating, sharing perceptions, reflecting, providing acknowledgment and feedback, giving information, presenting reality, encouraging formulation of a plan of action, providing nonverbal encouragement, and summarizing.
Test-Taking Strategy: Focus on the subject, therapeutic communication techniques. This will assist you in selecting the correct answers. Review therapeutic and nontherapeutic techniques if you had difficulty with this question.
Level of Cognitive Ability: Comprehension
Client Needs: Psychosocial Integrity
Integrated Process: Teaching and Learning
Content Area: Mental health
References: Fortinash, K., & Holoday-Worret, P. (2004). *Psychiatric mental health nursing* (3rd ed., pp. 124-125). St. Louis: Mosby.

REFERENCES

Fortinash, K., & Holoday-Worret, P. (2004). *Psychiatric mental health nursing* (3rd ed.). St. Louis: Mosby.

Potter, P., & Perry, A. (2005). *Fundamentals of nursing* (6th ed.). St. Louis: Mosby.

Stuart, G., & Laraia, M. (2005). *Principles and practice of psychiatric nursing* (8th ed.). St. Louis: Mosby.

Varcarolis, E., Carson, V., & Shoemaker, N. (2006). *Foundations of psychiatric mental health nursing* (5th ed.). Philadelphia: W.B. Saunders.

Models of Care

I. MILIEU THERAPY

A. Description

1. The **milieu** refers to the physical and social environment in which an individual is receiving treatment.
2. **Milieu** therapy uses a safe environment to meet the individual client's treatment needs.
3. Safety is the most important priority in managing the **milieu.**
4. **Milieu** therapy is staffed by persons educated to provide support, understanding and individual attention; all encounters with the client have the goal of being "therapeutic."
5. All members of the treatment team contribute to the planning and functioning of the **milieu;** the team generally includes the registered nurse, social worker, exercise therapist, recreational therapist, psychologist, psychiatrist, occupational therapist, and clinical nurse specialist or nurse practitioner.
6. All treatment team members are viewed as significant and valuable to the client's successful treatment outcomes.

B. Focus of milieu therapy

1. To use the physical and social environment to affect a positive change directed toward accomplishing the client's treatment goals
2. To empower the client through involvement in setting his or her own goals and develop purposeful relations with the staff to assist in meeting these goals.
3. To use community meetings, activity groups, social skills groups, and physical exercise programs to accomplish treatment goals.
4. One-to-one relationships with staff are used to examine client behaviors, feelings, and interactions within the context of the therapeutic group activities.

II. INTERPERSONAL PSYCHOTHERAPY

A. Description

1. A treatment modality that uses a therapeutic relationship to modify the client's feelings, attitudes, and behaviors
2. Therapeutic communication forms the foundation of the therapist-client relationship.

B. Focus of interpersonal psychotherapy

1. To establish a contract, clarify roles, and work within an agreed-on time frame to help meet the client's goals
2. Focusing on the therapist-client relationship is used as a way for clients to examine other relationships in his or her life.

C. Levels of psychotherapy (Box 72-1)

1. Supportive therapy
   a. Allows the client to express feelings, explore alternatives, and make decisions in a safe, caring environment
   b. May be needed briefly or over a period of years
   c. No plan exists to introduce new methods of coping; instead, the therapist reinforces the client's existing **coping mechanisms**.
2. Reeducative therapy
   a. Involves learning new ways of perceiving and behaving

BOX 72-1

Levels of Psychotherapy

Supportive therapy
Reeducative therapy
Reconstructive therapy

b. The client explores alternatives in a planned, systematic way; this requires a longer period of therapy than supportive therapy.

c. The client enters into a contract that specifies desired changes of behavior.

d. May include short-term psychotherapy, reality therapy, cognitive restructuring, behavior modification, and the development of coping skills

3. Reconstructive therapy

a. Involves the use of psychotherapy or psychoanalysis to make major changes in the client's life

b. May require several years of therapy and focuses on all aspects of the client's life

c. Emotional and cognitive restructuring of self takes place.

d. Positive outcomes include a greater understanding of self and others, more emotional freedom, and the development of potential abilities.

III. BEHAVIOR THERAPY

A. A treatment approach that uses the principles of skinnerian (operant conditioning) or pavlovian (classical conditioning) behavior theory to bring about behavioral change

B. The belief is that most behaviors are learned.

C. Operant conditioning refers to the manipulation of selected reinforcers to elicit and strengthen desired behavioral responses; the reinforcer refers to the consequence of the behavior and is defined as anything that increases the occurrence of a behavior (Fig. 72-1).

D. In classical conditioning (respondent conditioning), the individual responds to a stimulus but is basically a passive agent (see Fig. 72-1).

E. Desensitization is a form of behavior therapy whereby exposure to increasing increments of a feared stimulus is paired with increasing levels of relaxation, which helps reduce the intensity of fear to a more tolerable level.

F. Aversion therapy is a form of behavior therapy whereby negative reinforcement is used to change

behavior; for example, a stimulus *attractive* to the client is paired with an *unpleasant* event in hopes of endowing the stimulus with negative properties, thereby dissuading the behavior.

G. Modeling is behavioral therapy whereby the therapist acts as a role model for specific identified behaviors so that the client learns through imitation.

IV. COGNITIVE THERAPY

A. An active, directive, time-limited, structured approach used to treat a variety of disorders, including anxiety, depression, and phobias

B. It is based on the principle that how individuals feel and behave is determined by how they think about the world and their place in it; their cognitions are based on the attitudes or assumptions developed from previous experiences.

C. Therapeutic techniques are designed to identify, reality-test, and correct distorted conceptualizations and the dysfunctional beliefs underlying these cognitions.

D. The therapist helps the individual change the way he or she thinks, thereby relieving symptoms.

V. GROUP DEVELOPMENT AND GROUP THERAPY

A. Description: Group therapy involves a therapist and, ideally, five to eight members working on his or her individual goals within the context of a group, which presumably increases the opportunity for feedback and support.

B. Stages of group development (Box 72-2)

1. Initial stage

a. During this stage, group development involves superficial rather than open and trusting communication.

b. Members become acquainted with each other and search for similarities between themselves and other group members.

c. Members may be unclear about the purpose or goals of the group.

d. Group norms, roles, and responsibilities are established.

2. Working stage

a. During this stage, the real work of the group is accomplished.

b. Members are familiar with each other, the group leader, and the group roles, and feel free to address and attempt to solve their problems.

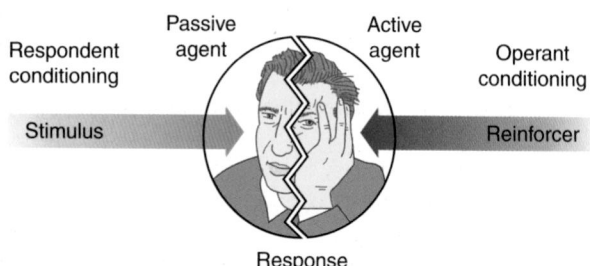

FIG. 72-1 Respondent versus operant conditioning. (From Varcarolis, E., Carson, V., & Shoemaker, N. [2006]. *Foundations of psychiatric mental health nursing* [5th ed.]. Philadelphia: W.B. Saunders.)

Passive agent — Active agent
Respondent conditioning — Operant conditioning
Stimulus — Reinforcer
Response

BOX 72-2
Stages of Group Development

Initial stage
Working stage
Termination stage

c. Both conflict and cooperation surface during the group's work as the members learn to work with each other.

3. Termination stage
   a. Members' feelings are explored regarding their accomplishments and the impending termination of the group.
   b. The termination stage provides an opportunity for members to learn to deal more realistically and comfortably with this normal part of human experience.

C. Group therapy models (*Note:* these models apply to individual or group psychotherapy.)
   1. Psychoanalytical group psychotherapy
      a. The therapist holds a main position.
      b. Each client in the group has a relationship with the therapist.
      c. Communication is focused on three levels—unconscious, semiconscious, and conscious information.
   2. Transactional analysis
      a. The three ego states of the individual—the parent, the child, and the adult—are examined.
      b. The goal is for individuals in the group to communicate from the proper ego states for the situation and responses of others, thereby lessening conflict and promoting mature relationships.
   3. Rational emotive therapy is a type of cognitive therapy in which the therapist focuses on how irrational beliefs and thoughts contribute to psychological distress.
   4. Rogerian therapy
      a. The therapist's goal is to help the members express their feelings toward one another during group sessions.
      b. The therapist's role is one of encouraging the expression of feelings, clarifying these feelings with clients, and accepting clients and their feelings nonjudgmentally.
   5. Gestalt therapy
      a. Emphasis is on the "here and now."
      b. Emphasizes self-expression, self-exploration, and self-awareness in the present
      c. The client and therapist focus on everyday problems and try to solve them.
      d. The individual becomes aware of the total self and the surrounding environment.
      e. Awareness of the problem renders the client capable of change.
      f. The therapist's role is to help the members express their feelings and grow from their experiences.
   6. Interpersonal group therapy: Promotes the individual's comfort with others in the group, which then transfers to other relationships

---

BOX 72-3
Self-help and Support Groups

Adult Children of Alcoholics
Al-Alon
Alcoholics Anonymous
Co-Dependents Anonymous
Gamblers Anonymous
Narcotics Anonymous
Overeaters Anonymous
Cancer Support
Mental illness support groups
Bereavement groups
Parents without Partners
Recovery groups, such as for those who have experienced trauma
Smoking cessation groups
Groups to help deal with unexpected body image changes, such as mastectomy or colostomy

---

   7. Self-help or support groups (Box 72-3)
      a. Support groups are based on the premise that persons who have experienced a similar problem are able to help others who have the same problem.
      b. A prototype support group would be Alcoholics Anonymous, in which alcoholics work together to support each others' recovery through member-run group meetings.

VI. FAMILY THERAPY
   1. Family therapy is a specific intervention mode based on the premise that the member with the presenting symptoms signals the presence of problems in the entire family; also assumed from this premise is that a change in one member will bring about changes in other members.
   2. The therapist works to assist family members to identify and express their thoughts and feelings, define family roles and rules, try new, more productive styles of relating, and restore strength to the family.

PRACTICE QUESTIONS

1. The client asks the nurse about milieu therapy. The nurse responds, knowing that the primary focus of milieu therapy can best be described as which of the following?
   1. A form of behavior modification therapy
   2. A cognitive approach to changing behavior
   3. A living, learning, or working environment
   4. A behavioral approach to changing behavior

2. The nurse is caring for a client with a phobia who is being treated for the condition. The client is introduced to short periods of exposure to the phobic object while in a relaxed state. The nurse understands that this form of behavior modification can best be described as:

1. Milieu therapy
2. Aversion therapy
3. Self-control therapy
4. Systematic desensitization

3. A client with an eating disorder is planning to attend group meetings with Overeaters Anonymous, and the nurse describes this group to the client. The nurse determines that the client needs additional information if the client states which of the following about this self-help group?
   1. "The leader is a nurse or psychiatrist."
   2. "The members provide support to each other."
   3. "People who have a similar problem are able to help others."
   4. "It is designed to serve people who have a common problem."

4. The nurse is conducting a group therapy session, and a client with a manic disorder is monopolizing the group. The appropriate nursing action is which of the following?
   1. Ask the client to leave.
   2. Refer the client to another group.
   3. Tell the client to stop monopolizing
   4. Thank the client for the contribution and tell him or her to allow others a chance to contribute.

5. A nurse employed in a mental health unit of a hospital is the leader of a group psychotherapy session. The nurse's role in the termination stage of group development is to:
   1. Encourage problem-solving.
   2. Encourage accomplishment of the group's work.
   3. Acknowledge the contributions of each group member.
   4. Encourage members to become acquainted with one another.

6. All treatment team members are seen as equally important in helping clients meet their treatment goals. This type of therapy approach is:
   1. Milieu therapy
   2. Interpersonal therapy
   3. Behavior modification
   4. Rational emotive therapy

7. An 18-year-old woman is admitted to an inpatient mental health unit with the diagnosis of anorexia nervosa. A cognitive behavioral approach is used as part of her treatment plan. The nurse understands that the purpose of this approach is to:
   1. Provide a supportive environment.
   2. Examine intrapsychic conflicts and past issues.
   3. Emphasize social interaction with clients who withdraw.
   4. Help the client identify and examine dysfunctional thoughts and beliefs.

8. A client with major depression is considering cognitive therapy. The client asks the nurse, "How does this treatment work?" The nurse responds and tells the client that:
   1. "This type of treatment will help you relax and develop new coping skills."
   2. "This type of treatment helps you confront your fears by gradually exposing you to them."
   3. "This type of treatment helps you examine how your past life has contributed to your problems."
   4. "This type of treatment helps you examine how your thoughts and feelings contribute to your difficulties."

9. The client is preparing to attend a Gambler's Anonymous meeting for the first time. The prototype used by this group is the 12-step program developed by Alcoholics Anonymous. The nurse tells the client that the first step in the 12-step program is which of the following?
   1. Admitting to having a problem
   2. Substituting other activities for gambling
   3. Stating that the gambling will be stopped
   4. Discontinuing relationships with friends who are gamblers

ALTERNATE ITEM FORMAT: MULTIPLE RESPONSE

Select the characteristics of the termination stage of group development. Select all that apply.
- ❑ 1. The group evaluates the experience.
- ❑ 2. The real work of the group is accomplished.
- ❑ 3. Group interaction involves superficial conversation.
- ❑ 4. Group members become acquainted with each other.
- ❑ 5. Some structuring of group norms, roles, and responsibilities take place.
- ❑ 6. The group explores members' feelings about the group and the impending separation.

ANSWERS

1. **3**

Rationale: Milieu therapy, or "therapeutic community," has as its focus a living, learning, or working environment. Such therapy may be based on any number of therapeutic modalities from structured behavioral therapy to spontaneous, humanistically oriented approaches. Although milieu may include behavioral approaches, option 3 describes its primary focus.

Test-Taking Strategy: Use the process of elimination. Note that options 1, 2, and 4 are comparative or alike and that option 3 identifies a comprehensive description. Review milieu therapy if you had difficulty with this question.

Level of Cognitive Ability: Comprehension
Client Needs: Psychosocial Integrity
Integrated Process: Nursing Process—implementation
Content Area: Mental health
References: Fortinash, K., & Holoday-Worret, P. (2004). *Psychiatric mental health nursing* (3rd ed., p. 438). St. Louis: Mosby.
Varcarolis, E., Carson, V., & Shoemaker, N. (2006). *Foundations of psychiatric mental health nursing* (5th ed., pp. 30-31). Philadelphia: W.B. Saunders.

2. **4**

Rationale: Systematic desensitization is a form of therapy used when the client is introduced to short periods of exposure to the phobic object while in a relaxed state. Gradually exposure is increased until the anxiety about or fear of the object or situation has ceased. Options 1, 2, and 3 are incorrect.

Test-Taking Strategy: Use the process of elimination. Focus on the strategic words *introduced to short periods of exposure*. This will direct you to the correct option. If you had difficulty with this question, review systematic desensitization.

Level of Cognitive Ability: Comprehension
Client Needs: Psychosocial Integrity
Integrated Process: Nursing Process—implementation
Content Area: Mental health
References: Fortinash, K., & Holoday-Worret, P. (2004). *Psychiatric mental health nursing* (3rd ed., pp. 326-327). St. Louis: Mosby.
Varcarolis, E., Carson, V., & Shoemaker, N. (2006). *Foundations of psychiatric mental health nursing* (5th ed., pp. 29-30). Philadelphia: W.B. Saunders.

3. **1**

Rationale: The sponsor of a self-help group is an experienced member of the group. A nurse or psychiatrist may be asked by the group to serve as a resource but would not be the leader of the group. Options 2, 3, and 4 are characteristics of a self-help group.

Test-Taking Strategy: Use the process of elimination and focus on the subject, self-help group. Note the strategic words *needs additional information* in the question. Note that options 2, 3, and 4 are comparative or alike. This should direct you easily to option 1, the correct option. Review the characteristics of a self-help group if you had difficulty with this question.

Level of Cognitive Ability: Analysis
Client Needs: Psychosocial Integrity
Integrated Process: Teaching and Learning
Content Area: Mental health

References: Fortinash, K., & Holoday-Worret, P. (2004). *Psychiatric mental health nursing* (3rd ed., pp. 321-322). St. Louis: Mosby.
Varcarolis, E., Carson, V., & Shoemaker, N. (2006). *Foundations of psychiatric mental health nursing* (5th ed., pp. 725-726). Philadelphia: W.B. Saunders.

4. **4**

Rationale: If a client is monopolizing the group, the nurse must be direct and decisive. The best action is to thank the client and suggest that the client stop talking and try listening to others. Although option 3 may be a direct response, option 4 is a more specific and direct statement. Options 1 and 2 are inappropriate.

Test-Taking Strategy: Use the process of elimination. Eliminate options 1 and 2 first because they are comparative or alike. Use therapeutic communication techniques to assist in directing you to option 4. If you had difficulty with this question, review therapeutic communication techniques for the client with a manic disorder.

Level of Cognitive Ability: Application
Client Needs: Psychosocial Integrity
Integrated Process: Nursing Process—implementation
Content Area: Mental health
References: Fortinash, K., & Holoday-Worret, P. (2004). *Psychiatric mental health nursing* (3rd ed., p. 445). St. Louis: Mosby.
Stuart, G., & Laraia, M. (2005). *Principles and practice of psychiatric nursing* (8th ed., pp. 30-34). St. Louis: Mosby.
Varcarolis, E., Carson, V., & Shoemaker, N. (2006). *Foundations of psychiatric mental health nursing* (5th ed., pp. 365-366). Philadelphia: W.B. Saunders.

5. **3**

Rationale: In the termination stage, the group leader's task is to acknowledge the contributions of each member and the experience of the group as a whole. In this stage, the group members prepare for separation and assist each other to prepare for the future. Options 1 and 2 identify the tasks of the working stage. Option 4 identifies the orientation stage.

Test-Taking Strategy: Use the process of elimination. Eliminate options 1 and 2 first because they are comparative or alike. From the remaining options, note the relationship between the words *termination stage* in the question and option 3. Review the stages of group development if you had difficulty with this question.

Level of Cognitive Ability: Application
Client Needs: Psychosocial Integrity
Integrated Process: Nursing Process—implementation
Content Area: Mental health
References: Fortinash, K., & Holoday-Worret, P. (2004). *Psychiatric mental health nursing* (3rd ed., p. 444). St. Louis: Mosby.
Varcarolis, E., Carson, V., & Shoemaker, N. (2006). *Foundations of psychiatric mental health nursing* (5th ed., p. 719). Philadelphia: W.B. Saunders.

6. **1**

Rationale: All treatment team members are viewed as significant and valuable to the client's successful treatment outcomes in milieu therapy. Behavior modification is based on rewards and punishment. Rational emotive therapy deals with the correction of distorted thinking. Interpersonal therapy on the other hand is based on a one-to-one or group therapy approach in which the therapist-client relationship is often used as a way for the client to examine other relationships in his or her life.

Test-Taking Strategy: Focus on the subject. Note the relationship between the words *helping clients to meet their treatment goals* and option 1. Review the types of therapy noted in the options if you had difficulty with this question.

Level of Cognitive Ability: Application
Client Needs: Psychosocial Integrity
Integrated Process: Nursing Process—implementation
Content Area: Mental health
Reference: Varcarolis, E., Carson, V., & Shoemaker, N. (2006). *Foundations of psychiatric mental health nursing* (5th ed., pp. 30-31). Philadelphia: W.B. Saunders.

7. **4**

Rationale: Cognitive behavioral therapy is used to help the client identify and examine dysfunctional thoughts and to identify and examine values and beliefs that maintain these thoughts. Options 1, 2, and 3 are incorrect.

Test-Taking Strategy: Use the process of elimination and note the strategic words *cognitive behavioral.* Focusing on these words should direct you to option 4. If you are unfamiliar with this type of therapy and its purpose, review this content.

Level of Cognitive Ability: Comprehension
Client Needs: Psychosocial Integrity
Integrated Process: Nursing Process—planning
Content Area: Mental health
Reference: Fortinash, K., & Holoday-Worret, P. (2004). *Psychiatric mental health nursing* (3rd ed., pp. 389, 422). St. Louis: Mosby.

8. **4**

Rationale: Cognitive therapy frequently is used for clients with depression. This type of therapy is based on exploring the client's subjective experience. Cognitive therapy includes examining the client's thoughts and feelings about situations and how these thoughts and feelings contribute to and perpetuate the client's difficulties and mood.

Test-Taking Strategy: Focusing on the word *cognitive* will assist you in selecting the correct option. Look for a similar word used in the question and repeated in one of the options. Note the relationship of the word *cognitive* in the question and *thoughts* in option 4. Review this form of therapy if you had difficulty with this question.

Level of Cognitive Ability: Application
Client Needs: Psychosocial Integrity
Integrated Process: Nursing Process—implementation
Content Area: Mental health

References: Fortinash, K., & Holoday-Worret, P. (2004). *Psychiatric mental health nursing* (3rd ed., pp. 201-202, 221, 231). St. Louis: Mosby.
Varcarolis, E., Carson, V., & Shoemaker, N. (2006). *Foundations of psychiatric mental health nursing* (5th ed., p. 333). Philadelphia: W.B. Saunders.

9. **1**

Rationale: The first step in the 12-step program is to admit that a problem exists. Options 3 and 4 are unrealistic as a first step in the process to recovery. Although option 2 may be a strategy, it is not the first step.

Test-Taking Strategy: Use the process of elimination and note the strategic words *first step* in the question. This will assist in directing you to option 1. If you are unfamiliar with the 12-step program, review this content.

Level of Cognitive Ability: Application
Client Needs: Psychosocial Integrity
Integrated Process: Nursing Process—implementation
Content Area: Mental health
References: Fortinash, K., & Holoday-Worret, P. (2004). *Psychiatric mental health nursing* (3rd ed., pp. 321-322). St. Louis: Mosby.
Varcarolis, E., Carson, V., & Shoemaker, N. (2006). *Foundations of psychiatric mental health nursing* (5th ed., p. 566). Philadelphia: W.B. Saunders.

ALTERNATE ITEM FORMAT: MULTIPLE RESPONSE

Answer: 1, 6

Rationale: The stages of group development include the initial stage, the working stage, and the termination stage. During the initial stage, the group members become acquainted with each other and some structuring of group norms, roles, and responsibilities take place. During the initial stage, group interaction involves superficial conversation During the working stage, the real work of the group is accomplished. During the termination stage. the group evaluates the experience and explores members' feelings about the group and the impending separation.

Test-Taking Strategy: Focus on the subject, the termination stage. Reading each item presented and recalling the stages of group development will assist in answering this question. Review these stages if you had difficulty with this question.

Level of Cognitive Ability: Comprehension
Client Needs: Psychosocial Integrity
Integrated Process: Nursing Process—Planning
Content Area: Mental Health
Reference: Fortinash, K., & Holoday-Worret, P. (2004). *Psychiatric mental health nursing* (3rd ed., p. 444). St. Louis: Mosby.

REFERENCES

Fortinash, K., & Holoday-Worret, P. (2004). *Psychiatric mental health nursing* (3rd ed.). St. Louis: Mosby.
Potter, P., & Perry, A. (2005). *Fundamentals of nursing* (6th ed.). St. Louis: Mosby.

Stuart, G., & Laraia, M. (2005). *Principles and practice of psychiatric nursing* (8th ed.). St. Louis: Mosby.
Varcarolis, E., Carson, V., & Shoemaker, N. (2006). *Foundations of psychiatric mental health nursing* (5th ed.). Philadelphia: W.B. Saunders.

73

Mental Health Disorders

I. ANXIETY

A. Description
1. Anxiety is a normal response to stress.
2. A subjective experience that includes feelings of apprehension, uneasiness, uncertainty, or dread
3. Occurs as a result of a threat that may be misperceived or misinterpreted or of a threat to identity or self-esteem
4. May result when values are threatened or preceding new experiences

B. Types of anxiety
1. Normal: A healthy type of anxiety
2. Acute: Precipitated by imminent loss or change that threatens one's sense of security
3. Chronic: Anxiety that persists as a characteristic response to daily activities

C. Levels of anxiety
1. Mild
   a. Associated with the tension of everyday life
   b. The individual is alert.
   c. The perceptual field is increased.
   d. Mild anxiety can be motivating, produce growth, enhance creativity, and increase learning.
2. Moderate
   a. The focus is on immediate concerns.
   b. Moderate anxiety narrows the perceptual field.
   c. Selective inattentiveness occurs.
   d. Learning and problem solving still occur.
3. Severe
   a. Severe anxiety is a feeling that something bad is about to happen.
   b. A significant narrowing in the perceptual field occurs.
   c. Focus is on minute or scattered details.
   d. All behavior is aimed at relieving the anxiety.

e. Learning and problem solving are not possible.
f. The individual needs direction to focus.
4. Panic
   a. Panic is associated with dread and terror and a sense of impending doom.
   b. The personality is disorganized.
   c. The individual is unable to communicate or function effectively.
   d. Increased motor activity occurs.
   e. Loss of rational thoughts with distorted perception occurs.
   f. Inability to concentrate occurs.
   g. If prolonged, panic can lead to exhaustion and death.

D. Interventions: General nursing measures
1. Recognize the anxiety.
2. Establish trust.
3. Protect the client.
4. Do not criticize **coping mechanisms.**
5. Do not force the client into situations that provoke anxiety.
6. Decrease stimulation in the environment.
7. Modify the environment by setting limits or limiting interaction with others.
8. Provide creative outlets.
9. Provide activities that limit the amount of time for destructive behavior.
10. Promote relaxation techniques such as breathing exercises or guided imagery.
11. Monitor vital signs and administer antianxiety medications as prescribed.

E. Interventions: Mild to moderate levels
1. Help the client identify the anxiety.
2. Encourage the client to talk about feelings and concerns.
3. Help the client identify thoughts and feelings that occurred before the onset of anxiety.

1151

4. Encourage problem solving.
5. Encourage gross motor exercise.

F. Interventions: Severe to panic levels
1. Reduce the anxiety quickly.
2. Use a calm manner.
3. Always remain with the client.
4. Minimize environmental stimuli.
5. Provide clear, simple statements.
6. Use a low-pitched voice.
7. Attend to the physical needs of the client.
8. Provide gross motor activity.
9. Administer antianxiety medications as prescribed.

II. GENERALIZED ANXIETY DISORDER

A. Description
1. Generalized anxiety disorder is an unrealistic anxiety about everyday worries that persists over time and is not associated with another psychiatric or medical disorder.
2. Physical symptoms occur.

B. Assessment
1. Restlessness and inability to relax
2. Episodes of trembling and shakiness
3. Chronic muscular tension
4. Dizziness
5. Inability to concentrate
6. Chronic fatigue and sleep problems
7. Inability to recognize the connection between the anxiety and physical symptoms
8. Client is focused on the physical discomfort.

C. Panic disorder
1. Description
   a. Panic disorder produces a sudden onset of feelings of intense apprehension and dread.
   b. The cause usually cannot be identified.
   c. Severe, recurrent, intermittent anxiety attacks lasting 5 to 30 minutes occur.
2. Assessment
   a. Choking sensation
   b. Labored breathing
   c. Pounding heart
   d. Chest pain
   e. Dizziness
   f. Nausea
   g. Blurred vision
   h. Numbness or tingling of the extremities
   i. Sense of unreality and helplessness
   j. Fear of being trapped
   k. Fear of dying
3. Interventions
   a. Remain with the client.
   b. Attend to physical symptoms.
   c. Assist the client to identify the thoughts that aroused the anxiety and identify the basis for these thoughts.
   d. Assist the client to change the unrealistic thoughts to more realistic thoughts.

e. Use cognitive restructuring to replace distorted thinking.
f. Administer antianxiety medications if prescribed.

III. POST-TRAUMATIC STRESS DISORDER

A. Description: After experiencing a psychologically traumatic event, the individual is prone to reexperience the event and have recurrent and intrusive dreams or flashbacks.

B. Stressors
1. Natural disaster
2. Terrorist attack
3. Combat experiences
4. Accidents
5. Victim of rape
6. Victim of crime or violence
7. Victim of sexual, physical, and emotional abuse
8. Reexperiencing the event as flashbacks

C. Assessment
1. Emotional numbness
2. Detachment
3. Depression
4. Anxiety
5. Sleep disturbances and nightmares
6. Flashbacks of the event
7. Hypervigilance
8. Guilt about surviving the event
9. Poor concentration and avoidance of activities that trigger the memory of the event

D. Interventions (Box 73-1)

IV. PHOBIAS

A. Description
1. An irrational fear of an object or situation that persists, although the person may recognize it as unreasonable

---

BOX 73-1

Interventions for Post-Traumatic Stress Disorder

Be nonjudgmental and supportive.
Assure the client that his or her feelings and behaviors are normal reactions.
Assist the client to recognize the association between his or her feelings and behaviors and the trauma experience.
Encourage the client to express his or her feelings; provide individual therapy that addresses loss of control or anger issues.
Assist the client to develop adaptive coping mechanisms and to use relaxation techniques.
Encourage the use of support groups
Facilitate a progressive review of the trauma experience.
Encourage the client to establish and reestablish relationships.
Inform the client that hypnotherapy or systematic desensitization may be used as a form of treatment.

2. Associated with panic level anxiety if the object, situation, or activity cannot be avoided
3. **Defense mechanisms** commonly used include repression and displacement.

B. Types (Box 73-2)

C. Interventions
1. Stay with the client when the anxiety is high to promote safety and security.
2. Identify the basis of the anxiety.
3. Allow the client to verbalize feelings about the anxiety-producing object or situation; frequently talking about the feared object is the first step in the desensitization process.
4. Teach relaxation techniques such as breathing exercises, muscle relaxation exercises, and visualization of pleasant situations.
5. Promote desensitization by gradually introducing the individual to the feared object or situation in small doses.
6. Do not force the client to have contact with the phobic object or situation.

V. OBSESSIVE-COMPULSIVE DISORDER

A. Obsessions: Preoccupation with persistently intrusive thoughts and ideas

B. Compulsions
1. A compulsion is the performance of rituals or repetitive behaviors designed to prevent some event, divert unacceptable thoughts, and decrease anxiety.
2. Obsessions and compulsions often occur together and can disrupt normal daily activities.
3. Anxiety occurs when one resists obsessions or compulsions, and from being powerless to resist the thoughts or rituals.
4. Obsessive thoughts can involve issues of violence, aggression, sexual behavior, orderliness, or religion, and uncontrollably can interrupt conscious thoughts and the ability to function.

C. Compulsive behavior patterns (behaviors or rituals)
1. Compulsive behavior patterns decrease the anxiety.
2. The patterns are associated with the obsessive thoughts.
3. The patterns neutralize the thought.
4. During stressful times, the ritualistic behavior increases.
5. **Defense mechanisms** include repression, displacement, and undoing.

D. Interventions (Box 73-3)

VI. SOMATOFORM DISORDERS

A. Description (Box 73-4)
1. Somatoform disorders are characterized by persistent worry or complaints regarding physical illness without supportive physical findings.
2. The client focuses on the physical signs and symptoms and is unable to control the signs and symptoms.
3. The physical signs and symptoms increase with psychosocial stressors.
4. The anxiety is redirected into a somatic concern.

BOX 73-2
Types of Phobias

Acrophobia	Fear of heights
Agoraphobia	Fear of open spaces
Astraphobia	Fear of electrical storms
Claustrophobia	Fear of closed spaces
Hematophobia	Fear of blood
Hydrophobia	Fear of water
Monophobia	Fear of being alone
Mysophobia	Fear of dirt or germs
Nyctophobia	Fear of darkness
Pyrophobia	Fear of fires
Social phobia	Fear of situations in which one might be embarrassed or criticized; fear of making a fool of oneself
Xenophobia	Fear of strangers
Zoophobia	Fear of animals

BOX 73-3
Interventions for Obsessive-Compulsive Disorder

Ensure that basic needs (food, rest, grooming) are met.
Identify the situations that precipitate the compulsive behavior; encourage the client to verbalize concerns and feelings.
Be empathetic toward the client and aware of his or her need to perform the compulsive behavior.
Do not interrupt the compulsive behaviors unless they jeopardize the safety of the client or others (provide for client safety related to the behavior).
Allow time for the client to perform the compulsive behavior but set limits on behaviors that may interfere with the client's physical well-being to protect the client from physical harm.
Implement a schedule for the client that distracts from the behaviors (structure simple activities, games, or tasks for the client).
Establish a written contract that will assist the client to decrease the frequency of compulsive behaviors gradually.
Recognize and reinforce positive nonritualistic behaviors.

BOX 73-4
Types of Somatoform Disorders

Conversion disorder
Hypochondriasis
Somatization disorder

5. The client may unconsciously use somatization for secondary gains, such as increased attention and decreased responsibilities.

B. Conversion disorder
  1. Description
    a. A physical symptom or a deficit suggesting loss or altered body function related to psychological conflict or a neurological disorder.
    b. Conversion disorder is an expression of a psychological conflict or need.
    c. The most common conversion symptoms are blindness, deafness, paralysis, and the inability to talk.
    d. Conversion disorder has no organic cause.
    e. Symptoms are beyond the conscious control of the client and are directly related to conflict.
    f. The development of physical symptoms reduces anxiety.
  2. Assessment
    a. "La belle indifference": Unconcerned with symptoms
    b. Physical limitation or disability
    c. Feelings of guilt, anxiety, or frustration
    d. Low self-esteem and feelings of inadequacy
    e. Unexpressed anger or conflict
    f. Secondary gain

C. Hypochondriasis
  1. Description
    a. Preoccupation with fears of having a serious disease
    b. No evidence of physical illness exists.
    c. Hypochondriasis significantly impairs social and occupational functioning.
  2. Assessment
    a. Preoccupation with physical functioning
    b. Frequent somatic complaints
    c. Complaints of fatigue and insomnia
    d. Anxiety
    e. Difficulty expressing feelings
    f. Extensive use of home remedies or nonprescription medications
    g. Repeatedly visiting the doctor in spite of repeated reassurance and normal test results
    h. Secondary gain

D. Somatization disorder
  1. Description
    a. The client has multiple physical complaints involving a number of body systems.
    b. The cause of these complaints is presumed to be psychological.
  2. Assessment
    a. Physical complaints of pain, denial of emotional problems, signs of anxiety, fear, and low self-esteem may be present.

    b. Secondary gain—the client may unconsciously use somatization for secondary gains, such as increased attention and decreased responsibilities.

E. Interventions
  1. Obtain a nursing history and assess for physical problems.
  2. Discourage verbalization about physical symptoms by not responding with positive reinforcement.
  3. Allow a specific time period to discuss physical complaints because the client will feel less threatened if this behavior is limited rather than stopped completely.
  4. Explore the needs being met by the physical symptoms with the client.
  5. Assist the client to identify alternative ways of meeting needs.
  6. Assist the client to relate feelings and conflicts to the physical symptoms.
  7. Convey understanding that the physical symptoms are real to the client.
  8. Assure the client that physical illness has been ruled out.
  9. Explore the source of anxiety and stimulate verbalization of anxiety.
  10. Encourage the use of relaxation techniques as the anxiety increases.
  11. Use a pain assessment scale if the client complains of pain and implement pain reduction measures as required.
  12. Report and assess any new physical complaint.
  13. Encourage diversional activities.
  14. Provide positive feedback.
  15. Assist the client in recognizing his or her own feelings and emotions.
  16. Administer antianxiety medications if prescribed.

VII. DISSOCIATIVE DISORDER

A. Description
  1. Dissociative disorder is a disruption in integrative functions of memory, consciousness, or identity.
  2. Dissociative disorder is associated with exposure to an extremely traumatic event.

B. Dissociative identity disorder (multiple personality)
  1. Description
    a. Two or more fully developed distinct and unique personalities exist within the person.
    b. The host is the primary personality and the other personalities are referred to as *alters*.
    c. Alter personalities may take full control of the client, one at a time, and may or may not be aware of each other.
    d. The alters may be aware of the host but the host is not usually aware of the alter(s).

2. Assessment
   a. The client may have an inability to recall important information (unrelated to ordinary forgetfulness).
   b. Transition from one personality to the other is related to stress or a traumatic event and is sudden.
   c. Dissociation is used as a method of distancing and defending one's self from anxiety and traumatizing experiences.

C. Dissociative amnesia
   1. Description
      a. Inability to recall important personal information because it provokes anxiety
      b. Memory impairment may range from partial to almost complete.
   2. Assessment
      a. Localized: The client blocks out all memories about a specified period.
      b. Selective: The client recalls some but not all memories about a specified period.
      c. Generalized: The client has a loss of all memory about past life.

D. Dissociative fugue
   1. Description
      a. The client assumes a new identity in a new environment.
      b. The disorder may occur suddenly.
   2. Assessment
      a. The client may drift from place to place.
      b. The client develops few social relationships.
      c. When the fugue lifts, the client returns home and is unable to recall the fugue state.

E. Depersonalization disorder
   1. Description: An altered self-perception in which one's own reality is temporarily lost or changed
   2. Assessment
      a. Feelings of detachment
      b. Intact reality testing

F. Interventions
   1. Develop a trusting relationship with the client.
   2. Encourage verbal expression of painful experiences, anxieties, and concerns.
   3. Explore methods of coping.
   4. Identify sources of conflict.
   5. Focus on the client's strengths and skills.
   6. Orient the client.
   7. Provide nondemanding simple routines.
   8. Allow the client to progress at his or her own pace.
   9. Implement stress reduction techniques.
   10. Plan for individual, group, and/or family psychotherapy to integrate dissociated aspects of personality or memory and to expand self-awareness.

VIII. MOOD DISORDERS

A. Bipolar disorder
   1. Description (Box 73-5)
      a. Bipolar disorder is characterized by episodes of mania and depression with periods of normal mood and activity in between.
      b. The medication of choice has traditionally been lithium carbonate, which can be toxic and therefore requires the regular monitoring of serum lithium levels.
      c. Other medications such as divalproex (Valproate) or olanzapine (Zyprexa) may be prescribed; carbamazepine (Tegretol) may also be prescribed to reduce the symptoms of acute bipolar manic episodes.

BOX 73-5

Assessment of Bipolar Disorder

MANIA
Becomes angry quickly
Delusional self-confidence
Distracted by environmental stimuli
Extroverted personality
Flight of ideas
Grandiose and persecutory delusions
High and unstable affect
Inability to eat or sleep because of involvement in more important things
Inability to sleep yet still active
Inappropriate affect
Inappropriate dress
Initiation of activity
Pressured speech
Restlessness
Sexually promiscuous
Significant decrease in appetite
Unlimited energy
Urgent motor activity

DEPRESSION
Increased or decreased appetite
Decrease in activities of daily living
Decreased emotion and physical activity
Easily fatigued
Inability to make decisions
Poor concentration
Internalizing hostility
Introverted personality
Social isolation and withdrawn from groups
Lack of energy
Lack of initiative
Lack of self-confidence and low self-esteem
Lack of sexual interest
Psychomotor retardation
Suicidal thinking

2. Interventions for mania (Box 73-6)
   a. Remove hazardous objects from the environment.
   b. Assess the client closely for fatigue.
   c. Use comfort measures to promote sleep.
   d. Provide frequent rest periods.
   e. Monitor the client's sleep patterns.
   f. Provide a private room if possible.
   g. Administer a hypnotic or sedative medication as prescribed.
   h. Encourage the client to ventilate feelings.
   i. Use calm, slow interactions.
   j. Help the client focus on one topic during the conversation.
   k. Ignore or distract the client from grandiose thinking.
   l. Present reality to the client.
   m. Do not argue with the client.
   n. Limit group activities and assess the client's tolerance level.
   o. Provide high-calorie finger foods and fluids.
   p. Supervise the client's choice of clothing.
   q. Reduce environmental stimuli.
   r. Set limits on inappropriate behaviors.
   s. Provide physical activities and outlets for tension.
   t. Avoid competitive games.
   u. Provide gross motor activities such as walking and writing.
   v. Provide structured activities or one-to-one activities with the nurse.
   w. Provide simple and direct explanations for routine procedures.
   x. Supervise the administration of medication.
3. Major depressive disorder
   a. Assessment (see Box 73-5)
   b. Interventions for depressed clients (Box 73-7)

IX. SCHIZOPHRENIA
  A. Description
     1. Schizophrenia is a group of mental disorders characterized by psychotic features (hallucinations and delusions), disordered thought processes, and disrupted interpersonal relationships.
     2. Disturbances in affect, mood, behavior, and thought processes occur.
  B. Assessment (Fig. 73-1)
     1. Physical characteristics
        a. Unkempt appearance
        b. Body image distortions
        c. May be preoccupied with somatic complaints

BOX 73-6

Dealing With Inappropriate Behaviors Associated With Bipolar Disorder

AGGRESSIVE BEHAVIOR
Assist the client in identifying feelings of frustration and aggression.
Encourage the client to talk out instead of acting out feelings of frustration.
Assist the client in identifying precipitating events or situations that lead to aggressive behavior.
Describe the consequences of the behavior on self and others.
Assist in identifying previous coping mechanisms.
Assist the client in problem-solving techniques to cope with frustration or aggression.

DE-ESCALATION TECHNIQUES
Maintain safety for the client, other clients, and self.
Maintain a large personal space and use a nonaggressive posture.
Use a calm approach and communicate with a calm, clear tone of voice (be assertive, not aggressive).
Determine what the client considers to be his or her need.
Avoid verbal struggles.
Provide the client with clear options that deal with the client's behavior.
Assist the client with problem solving and decision making regarding the options.

MANIPULATIVE BEHAVIOR
Set clear, consistent, realistic, and enforceable limits and communicate expected behaviors.
Be clear about the consequences associated with exceeding set limits and follow through with the consequences in a nonpunitive manner, if necessary.
Discuss the client's behavior in a nonjudgmental and nonthreatening manner.
Avoid power struggles with the client (avoid arguing with the client).
Assist the client in developing means of setting limits on own behavior.

BOX 73-7

Interventions for Depressed Clients

Assess for suicidal ideation.
Provide safety from suicidal actions.
Assist with activities of daily living.
Use gentle encouragement to participate in activities of daily living and unit therapies.
Do not push decision making or making complex choices or decisions that the client is not ready to make.
Monitor sleep patterns.
Monitor nutritional intake and weight.
Provide achievable activities in which the client can achieve success (focus on strengths).
Remind the client of times when she or her felt better and was successful.
Spend time with the client to communicate the client's value.
Respond to anger therapeutically.

d. May neglect hygiene, eating, sleeping, and elimination
2. Motor activity (Box 73-8)
    a. Catatonic posturing: Holding bizarre postures for long periods of time
    b. Catatonic excitement: Moving excitedly, with no environmental stimuli present
    c. Possible total immobilization
    d. Inability to respond to commands or responding only to commands
    e. Waxy flexibility
    f. Repetitive or stereotyped movements
    g. Motor activity that may be increased, as evidenced by agitation, pacing, inability to sleep, loss of appetite and weight, and impulsiveness
    h. Possible inability to initiate activity (anergia)
3. Emotional characteristics
    a. Mistrust may be present.
    b. View of the world as threatening and unsafe
    c. Affect may be blunted, flat, or inappropriate
    d. May display feelings of ambivalence, helplessness, anxiety, anger, guilt, or depression in response to hallucinations, delusions, or as a result of the grief related to losses imposed by this illness

4. Compulsive rituals: Performed as an attempt to solve conflicting feelings by constant, repetitive activity
5. Overcompliance: Attempt to deny responsibility for any action by doing only what another person instructs exactly
6. Affective disturbances
    a. Flat or incongruent affect, or inappropriate affect
    b. Altered thought processes

BOX 73-8
Abnormal Motor Behaviors

DESCRIPTION
Abnormal motor behavior or activity displayed by the mentally ill client that occurs as a result of a psychiatric disorder

TYPES OF ABNORMAL MOTOR BEHAVIORS
Echolalia
Repeating the speech of another person
Echopraxia
Repeating the movements of another person
Waxy Flexibility
Having one's arms or legs placed in a certain position and holding that same position for hours

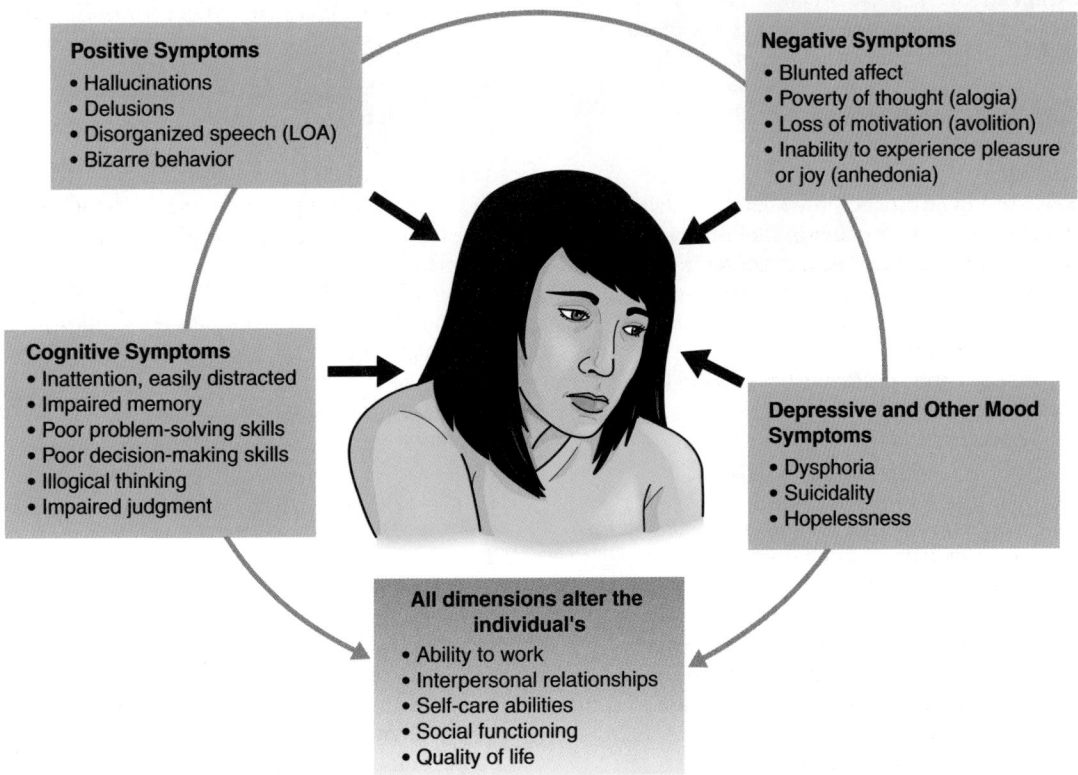

Positive Symptoms
• Hallucinations
• Delusions
• Disorganized speech (LOA)
• Bizarre behavior

Negative Symptoms
• Blunted affect
• Poverty of thought (alogia)
• Loss of motivation (avolition)
• Inability to experience pleasure or joy (anhedonia)

Cognitive Symptoms
• Inattention, easily distracted
• Impaired memory
• Poor problem-solving skills
• Poor decision-making skills
• Illogical thinking
• Impaired judgment

Depressive and Other Mood Symptoms
• Dysphoria
• Suicidality
• Hopelessness

All dimensions alter the individual's
• Ability to work
• Interpersonal relationships
• Self-care abilities
• Social functioning
• Quality of life

FIG. 73-1 Treatment-relevant dimensions of schizophrenia. *LOA,* Looseness of association. (From Varcarolis, E., Carson, V., Shoemaker, N. [2006]. *Foundations of psychiatric mental health nursing* [5th ed.]. Philadelphia: W.B. Saunders.)

7. Abnormal thought processes (Box 73-9)
   a. Impaired reality testing
   b. Fragmentation of thoughts
   c. Thought blocking
   d. Loose associations
   e. Echolalia
   f. Distorted perception of the environment
   g. Neologisms
   h. Magical thinking
   i. Inability to conceptualize meaning in words or thoughts
   j. Inability to organize facts logically
   k. Delusions associated with thought processes or content

8. Types of delusions (Box 73-10)

   a. Loss of reference in which the client believes that certain events, situations, or interactions are related directly to self
   b. Delusions of persecution in which the client believes that he or she is being harassed, threatened, or persecuted by some powerful force
   c. Delusions of grandeur in which the client attaches special significance to self in relation to others or the universe and has an exaggerated sense of self that has no basis in reality
   d. Somatic delusions in which the client believes that his or her body is changing or responding in an unusual way, which has no basis in reality
9. Perceptual distortions
   a. Illusions, which may be brief experiences with a misinterpretation or misperception of reality
   b. Hallucinations (five senses) with no basis in reality (Box 73-11), such as perceiving objects, sensations, or images
10. Language and communication disturbances (Box 73-12)
    a. Related to disorders in thought process
    b. Inability to organize language

BOX 73-9
Abnormal Thought Processes

DESCRIPTION
Abnormal thought processes displayed by the mentally ill client that occur as a result of a psychiatric disorder

CIRCUMSTANTIALITY
Before getting to the point or answering a question, the individual gets caught up in countless details and explanations.

CONFABULATION
Filling a memory gap with detailed fantasy believed by the teller; the purpose of confabulation is to maintain self-esteem; seen in organic conditions such as Korsakoff's psychosis.

FLIGHT OF IDEAS
This is a constant flow of speech in which the individual jumps from one topic to another in rapid succession; a connection between topics exists, although it is sometimes difficult to identify; seen in manic states.

LOOSENESS OF ASSOCIATION
Haphazard, illogical, and confused thinking and interrupted connections in thought; this is seen mostly in schizophrenic disorders.

NEOLOGISMS
An individual makes up words that only have meaning for the individual; often part of a delusional system.

THOUGHT BLOCKING
A sudden cessation of a thought in the middle of a sentence; the client is unable to continue the train of thought; often, sudden new thoughts come up unrelated to the topic.

WORD SALAD
This is a mixture of words and phrases that has no meaning.

BOX 73-10
Delusions

DESCRIPTION
A false belief held to be true, even when there is evidence to the contrary

TYPES
Grandeur
The false belief that one is a powerful and important person
Jealousy
The false belief that one's partner or mate is going out with other persons
Persecution
The thought that one is being singled out for harm by others

INTERVENTIONS
Ask the client to describe the delusion.
Be open and honest in interactions to reduce suspiciousness.
Focus the conversation on reality-based topics rather than on the delusion.
Encourage the client to express feelings and focus on the feelings that the delusions generate.
If the client obsesses on the delusion, set firm limits on the amount of time for talking about the delusion.
Do not argue with the client or try to convince the client that the delusions are false.
Validate if part of the delusion is real.

c. Difficulty communicating clearly

d. Inappropriate responses to a situation

e. A single word or phrase may represent the whole meaning of the conversation such that the client may feel that he or she has communicated adequately.

f. Development of a private language

C. Types of schizophrenia (Box 73-13)

1. Paranoid schizophrenia
   a. Suspiciousness
   b. Hostility
   c. Delusions
   d. Auditory hallucinations
   e. Anxiety and anger
   f. Aloofness
   g. Persecutory themes
   h. Violence

2. Disorganized schizophrenia
   a. Extreme social withdrawal
   b. Disorganized speech or behavior
   c. Flat or inappropriate affect
   d. Silliness unrelated to speech
   e. Stereotyped behaviors
   f. Grimacing mannerisms

g. Inability to perform activities of daily living

3. Catatonic schizophrenia
   a. Psychomotor disturbances
   b. Immobility
   c. Stupor
   d. Waxy flexibility
   e. Excessive purposeless motor activity
   f. Echolalia
   g. Automatic obedience
   h. Stereotyped or repetitive behavior

4. Undifferentiated schizophrenia
   a. Undifferentiated schizophrenia does not meet the criteria for paranoid, disorganized, or catatonic schizophrenia.
   b. Delusions and hallucinations
   c. Disorganized speech
   d. Disorganized or catatonic behavior
   e. Flat affect
   f. Social withdrawal

5. Residual schizophrenia
   a. Diagnosed as schizophrenic in the past
   b. Time limited between attacks but may last for many years
   c. The client exhibits considerable social isolation and withdrawal and impaired role functioning.

BOX 73-11

Hallucinations

DESCRIPTION

A sense perception (occurs with one of the five senses) for which no external stimuli exist; can have an organic or functional cause

TYPES

Auditory
Hearing voices when none are present

Gustatory
Experiencing taste in the absence of stimuli

Olfactory
Smelling smells that do not exist

Tactile
Feeling touch sensations in the absence of stimuli

Visual
Seeing things that are not there

INTERVENTIONS

Ask the client directly about the hallucination.

Avoid reacting to the hallucination as if it were real.

Decrease stimuli or move the client to another area.

Do not negate the client's experience.

Focus on reality-based topics.

Attempt to engage the client's attention through a concrete activity.

Respond verbally to anything real that the client talks about.

Avoid touching the client.

Monitor for signs of increasing anxiety or agitation, which may indicate that the hallucinations are increasing.

BOX 73-12

Language and Communication Disturbances

Clang association	Repetition of words or phrases that are similar in sound but in no other way
Echolalia	Repetition of words or phrases heard from another person
Mutism	Absence of verbal speech
Neologism	A new word devised that has special meaning only to the client
Pressured speech	Speaking as if the words are being forced out quickly
Verbigeration	Purposeless repetition of words or phrases
Word salad	Form of speech in which words or phrases are connected meaninglessly

---

BOX 73-13

Types of Schizophrenia

Catatonic
Disorganized
Paranoid
Residual
Undifferentiated

D. Interventions: See Box 73-14.

E. Interventions: Active hallucinations
  1. Monitor for hallucination cues and assess content of hallucinations. Safety is the first priority—ensure that the client does not have an auditory command telling him or her to harm self or others.
  2. Intervene with one-on-one contact.

BOX 73-14

Interventions for Schizophrenia

Assess the client's physical needs.

Set limits on the client's behaviors when it interferes with others and becomes disruptive.

Maintain a safe environment.

Initiate one-on-one interaction and progress to small groups as tolerated.

Spend time with the client, even if the client is unable to respond.

Monitor for altered thought processes.

Maintain ego boundaries and avoid touching the client.

Limit the time of interaction with the client.

Avoid an overly warm approach; a neutral approach is less threatening.

Do not make promises to the client that cannot be kept.

Establish daily routines.

Assist the client to improve grooming and accept responsibility for personal care.

Sit with the client in silence if necessary.

Provide short, brief, and frequent contact with the client.

Tell the client when you are leaving.

Tell the client when you do not understand.

Do not "go along" with the client's delusions or hallucinations.

Provide simple concrete activities, such as puzzles or word games.

Reorient the client as necessary.

Help the client establish what is real and unreal.

Stay with the client if the client is frightened.

Speak to the client in a simple direct and concise manner.

Reassure the client that the environment is safe.

Remove the client from group situations if the client's behavior is too bizarre, disturbing, or dangerous to others.

Set realistic goals.

Initially, do not offer choices to the client, and gradually assist the client in making his or her own decisions.

Use canned or packaged food, especially with the paranoid schizophrenic client.

Provide a radio or tape player at night for insomnia.

Explain to the client everything that is being done.

Set limits on the client's behavior if the client is unable to do so.

Decrease excessive stimuli in the environment.

Monitor for suicide risk.

Assist the client to use alternative means to express feelings through music or art therapy or writing.

---

  3. Decrease stimuli or move the client to another area.
  4. Avoid conveying to the client that others also are experiencing the hallucination.
  5. Respond verbally to anything real that the client talks about.
  6. Avoid touching the client.
  7. Encourage the client to express feelings.
  8. During a hallucination, attempt to engage the client's attention through a concrete activity.
  9. Accept and do not joke about or judge the client's behavior.
  10. Provide easy activities and a structured environment with routine activities of daily living.
  11. Monitor for signs of increasing fear, anxiety, or agitation.
  12. Decrease stimuli as needed.
  13. Administer medications as prescribed.

F. Interventions: Delusions
  1. Interact based on reality.
  2. Encourage the client to express feelings.
  3. Do not dispute the client or try to convince the client that delusions are false.
  4. Initially initiate activities on a one-on-one basis.
  5. Alter hospital routines as necessary, such as using canned or packaged food or food from home.
  6. Recognize accomplishments and provide positive feedback for successes.

X. **PARANOID DISORDERS**
  A. Description
    1. Paranoid disorder is a concrete, pervasive delusional system characterized by persecutory and grandiose beliefs.
    2. The client demonstrates suspiciousness and mistrust of others.
    3. The client often is viewed by others as hostile, stubborn, and defensive.
  B. Behaviors
    1. Suspicious and mistrustful
    2. Emotionally distant
    3. Distortion of reality
    4. Poor insight and poor judgments
    5. Hypervigilance
    6. Low self-esteem
    7. Highly sensitive, difficulty in admitting own error, and taking pride in being correct
    8. Hypercritical and intolerant of others
    9. Hostile, aggressive, and quarrelsome
    10. Evasive
    11. Concrete thinking
  C. Delusions
    1. Delusions serve a purpose in establishing identity and self-esteem.
    2. Client may have grandiose and persecutory delusions.

3. Process of delusion includes denial, projection, and rationalization.
4. As trust in others increases, the need for delusions decreases.

D. Types of paranoid disorders (Box 73-15)
   1. Paranoid personality disorder (see later)
      a. Suspicious
      b. Nonpsychotic
      c. No hallucinations or delusions
      d. No symptoms of schizophrenia
   2. Paranoia-induced state
      a. Abrupt onset in response to stress; subsides when stress decreases
      b. No hallucinations but experiences paranoid delusions
      c. May be sensitive and suspicious before the development of delusions
      d. No symptoms of schizophrenia
   3. Paranoia
      a. Exhibits an organized delusional system
      b. Not bizarre
      c. No hallucinations
      d. Reserved and sensitive before onset
      e. Psychotic state
      f. No symptoms of schizophrenia
   4. Paranoid schizophrenia
      a. Before the onset, the client becomes cold, withdrawn, distrustful, resentful, argumentative, sarcastic, and defiant.
      b. Bizarre, numerous, and changeable delusions occur.
      c. Delusions become less logical as the client becomes more disorganized.
      d. Persecutory hallucinations occur.
      e. Psychotic state ensues.
      f. All symptoms of schizophrenia are present.

E. Interventions (Box 73-16)

XI. PERSONALITY DISORDERS

A. Description
   1. Personality disorders include various inflexible maladaptive behavior patterns or traits that may impair functioning and relationships.
   2. The individual usually remains in touch with reality and typically has a lack of insight into his or her behavior.
   3. Stress exacerbates manifestations of the personality disorder.

4. In severe cases, the personality disorder may deteriorate to a psychotic state.

B. Characteristics
   1. Poor impulse control
      a. Acting out to manage internal pain
      b. Forms of acting out include physical and verbal attacks, such as yelling and swearing, and self-injurious behaviors. such as cutting own skin, banging the head, punching self, manipulation, substance **abuse,** promiscuous sexual behaviors, and **suicide attempts.**
      c. Client may be preoccupied with self, religion, or sex.
   2. Mood characteristics
      a. May experience abandonment and depression
      b. Moods may include rage, guilt, fear, and emptiness.
   3. Impaired judgment
      a. Difficulty with problem solving
      b. Inability to perceive the consequences of behavior
   4. Impaired reality testing: Distortion of reality and often projection of own feelings onto others

---

BOX 73-16

Interventions for Paranoid Disorders

Assess for suicide risk.
Diminish suspicious behavior.
Avoid direct eye contact.
Establish a trusting relationship.
Promote increased self-esteem.
Remain calm, nonthreatening, and nonjudgmental.
Provide continuity of care.
Respond honestly to the client.
Follow through on commitments made to the client.
Acknowledge the client's feelings but tell the client that you do not share the her or his interpretation of an event.
Provide a daily schedule of activities.
Assist the client to identify diversionary activities.
Gradually introduce the client to groups.
Refocus conversation to reality-based topics.
Use role playing to help the client identify thoughts and feelings.
Provide positive reinforcement for successes.
Do not argue with delusions.
Use concrete, specific words.
Do not be secretive with the client.
Do not whisper in the client's presence.
Assure the client that he or she will be safe.
Involve the client in noncompetitive tasks.
Provide the client with the opportunity to complete small tasks.
Monitor eating, drinking, sleeping, and elimination patterns.
Limit physical contact.
Monitor for agitation and decrease stimuli as needed.

BOX 73-15

Types of Paranoid Disorders

Paranoid personality
Paranoid state
Paranoia
Paranoid schizophrenia

5. Impaired object relations: Rigid and inflexible, with difficulty in intimate relationships
6. Impaired self-perception: Distorted self-perception and experience of self-hate or self-idealization
7. Impaired thought processes
   a. Concrete or diffuse thinking
   b. Difficulty concentrating
   c. Impaired memory
8. Impaired stimulus barrier
   a. Inability to regulate incoming sensory stimuli
   b. Increased excitability
   c. Excessive response to noise and light
   d. Poor attention span
   e. Agitated
   f. Insomnia

C. Cluster A personality disorder types include the odd, eccentric types—schizoid, schizotypal, and paranoid.
1. Schizoid personality disorder is characterized by an inability to form warm, close social relationships.
   a. Social detachment and lack of close relationships
   b. Interest in solitary activities
   c. Aloof and indifferent
   d. Restricted expression of emotions
   e. Lack of interest in others
2. Schizotypal personality disorder is characterized by the display of abnormal or highly unusual thoughts, perceptions, speech, and behavior patterns.
   a. Suspicious
   b. Paranoia
   c. Magical thinking
   d. Odd thinking and speech
   e. Relationship deficits
3. Paranoid personality disorder is characterized by suspiciousness and mistrust of others.
   a. May be suspicious and distrusting
   b. May be argumentative
   c. May be hostile, aloof
   d. May be rigid, critical, and controlling of others
   e. May have thoughts of grandiosity

D. Cluster B personality disorders include the over-emotional, erratic types—histrionic, narcissistic, borderline, and antisocial.
1. Histrionic personality disorder is characterized by overly dramatic and intensely expressive behavior.
   a. Lively and dramatic and enjoys being the center of attention
   b. Has poor and shallow interpersonal relations
   c. May be sexually seductive or provocative
   d. Dramatizes their life and may appear theatrical

e. Overly concerned with appearance
f. Easily bored
2. Narcissistic personality disorder is characterized by an increased sense of self-importance and preoccupation with fantasies and unlimited success.
   a. Need for admiration and inflation of accomplishments
   b. Overestimation of abilities and underestimation of contributions of others
   c. Lack of empathy and sensitivity to needs of others
3. Antisocial personality disorder is comprised of a pattern of irresponsible and antisocial behavior, selfishness, an inability to maintain lasting relationships, poor sexual adjustment, a failure to accept social norms, and a tendency toward irritability and aggressiveness.
   a. Perceives the world as hostile
   b. Superficial charm and hostility
   c. No shame or guilt
   d. Self-centered
   e. Unreliable
   f. Easily bored
   g. Poor work history
   h. Inability to tolerate frustration
   i. View others as objects to be manipulated
   j. Poor judgment
   k. Impulsive
4. Borderline personality disorder is characterized by instability in interpersonal relationships, unstable mood and self-image, and impulsive and unpredictable behavior.
   a. Unclear identity
   b. Unstable and intense
   c. Extreme shifts in mood
   d. Easily angered
   e. Easily bored
   f. Argumentative
   g. Depression
   h. Self-destructive behavior
   i. Manipulation
   j. Inability to tolerate anxiety
   k. Chronic feelings of emptiness and fear of being alone
   l. Splitting—sees others as all good or all bad; creates conflict between individuals by playing one person against another

E. Cluster C personality disorders includes the anxious, fearful types of personality disorders—obsessive compulsive personality, avoidant, and dependent.
1. Obsessive-compulsive personality disorder is characterized by difficulty expressing warm and tender emotions, perfectionism, stubbornness, the need to control others, and a devotion to work.
   a. Overly conscientious

b. Inflexible and preoccupied with details and rules
c. Extremely devoted to work to the exclusion of leisure activities and friendships
d. Miserly and stubborn
e. Hoarding behavior
f. Engages in rituals
2. Avoidant personality disorder is characterized by social withdrawal and extreme sensitivity to potential rejection.
   a. Feelings of inadequacy
   b. Hypersensitive to reactions of others and poor reaction to criticism
   c. Social isolation
   d. Lack of support system
3. Dependent personality disorder is characterized by an intense lack of self-confidence, low self-esteem, and inability to function independently, such that the individual passively allows others to make decisions and assume responsibility for major areas in the person's life; the dependent client has great difficulty making decisions.

▲ F. General interventions for the client with a personality disorder
1. Maintain safety against self-destructive behaviors.
2. Allow the client to make choices and be as independent as possible.
3. Encourage the client to discuss feelings rather than act them out.
4. Provide consistency in response to the client's acting-out behaviors.
5. Discuss expectations and responsibilities with the client.
6. Discuss the consequences that will follow certain behaviors.
7. Inform the client that harm to self, others, and property is unacceptable.
8. Identify splitting behavior.
9. Assist the client to deal directly with anger.
10. Develop a written safety and/or behavioral contract with the client.
11. Encourage the client to keep a journal recording daily feelings.
12. Encourage the client to participate in group activities, and praise nonmanipulative behavior.
13. Set and maintain limits to decrease manipulative behavior.
14. Remove the client from group situations in which attention-seeking behaviors occur.
15. Provide realistic praise for positive behaviors in social situations.

XII. COGNITIVE IMPAIRMENT DISORDERS

A. Autism: See Chap. 35.
B. Attention-deficit/hyperactivity disorder: See Chap. 35.

C. Tourette's disorder: See Chap. 35.
D. Dementia and Alzheimer's disease
1. Dementia
   a. Dementia is a syndrome with progressive deterioration in intellectual functioning secondary to structural or functional changes.
   b. Long- and short-term memory loss occur, with impairment in judgment, abstract thinking, problem-solving ability, and behavior.
   c. Dementia results in a self-care deficit.
   d. The most common type of dementia is Alzheimer's disease.
2. Alzheimer's disease (Box 73-17)
   a. Alzheimer's disease is an irreversible form of senile dementia caused by nerve cell deterioration.
   b. Individuals with Alzheimer's disease experience cognitive deterioration and progressive loss of ability to carry out activities of daily living.
   c. The client experiences a steady decline in physical and mental functioning and usually requires long-term care in a specialized facility in the final stages of the illness.
3. Interventions
   a. Identify and reinforce retained skills.
   b. Provide continuity of care.
   c. Orient the client to the environment.
   d. Furnish the environment with familiar possessions.
   e. Acknowledge the client's feelings.
   f. Assist the client and family members to manage memory deficits and behavior changes.
   g. Encourage family members to express feelings about caregiving.
   h. Provide the caregiver with support and identify the resources and support groups available.
   i. Monitor the client's activities of daily living.
   j. Remind the client how to perform self-care activities.
   k. Help the client maintain independence.
   l. Provide the client with consistent routines.
   m. Provide the client with exercises, such as walking with an escort.

BOX 73-17
Alzheimer's Disease

Agnosia	Failure to recognize or identify objects despite intact sensory function
Amnesia	Loss of memory caused by brain degeneration
Aphasia	Language disturbance in understanding and expressing spoken words
Apraxia	Inability to perform motor activities, despite intact motor function

n. Avoid activities that tax the memory.

o. Allow the client plenty of time to complete a task.

p. Use constant encouragement of the client with a simple step-by-step approach.

q. Provide the client with activities that distract and occupy time, such as listening to music, coloring, and watching television.

r. Provide the client with mental stimulation with simple games or activities.

4. Wandering

a. Provide the client with a safe environment.

b. Prevent unsafe wandering.

c. Provide the client with close supervision.

d. Close and secure doors.

e. Use identification bracelets and electronic surveillance.

5. Communication

a. Adapt to the communication level of the client.

b. Use a firm volume and a low-pitched voice to communicate.

c. Stand directly in front of the client and maintain eye contact.

d. Call the client by name and identify self; wait for a response.

e. Use a calm and reassuring voice.

f. Use pantomime gestures if the client is unable to understand spoken words.

g. Speak slowly and clearly, using short words and simple sentences,

h. Ask only one question at a time and give one direction at a time.

i. Repeat questions if necessary, but do not re-phrase.

6. Impaired judgment

a. Remove throw rugs, toxic substances, and dangerous electrical appliances from the environment.

b. Reduce hot water heater temperature.

7. Altered thought processes

a. Call the client by name.

b. Orient the client frequently.

c. Use familiar objects in the room.

d. Place a calendar and clock in a visible place.

e. Maintain familiar routines.

f. Allow the client to reminisce.

g. Make tasks simple.

h. Allow time for the client to complete a task.

i. Provide positive reinforcement for positive behaviors.

8. Altered sleep patterns

a. Allow the client to wander in a safe place until she or he becomes tired.

b. Prevent shadows in the room by using indirect light.

c. Avoid the use of hypnotics because they cause confusion and aggravate the sundown effect.

9. Agitation

a. Assess the precipitant of the agitation.

b. Reassure the client.

c. Remove items that can be hazardous during the time of agitation.

d. Approach the client slowly and calmly from the front and then speak, gesture, and move slowly.

e. Remove the client to a less stressful environment.

f. Use touch gently.

g. Do not argue with or force the client.

XIII. PSYCHOSEXUAL ALTERATIONS

A. Sexuality

1. One's sense of being a sexual individual

2. Includes how one looks, behaves, and relates to others

B. Sexual expression (Box 73-18)

C. Alterations in sexual behavior

1. Transsexualism: Feeling that one's gender is inappropriate and desiring to acquire sexual characteristics of the opposite gender

2. Exhibitionism: Sexual urges and fantasies that result in exposure of genitals to strangers to bring sexual gratification and/or arousal

3. Fetishism: Using nonliving objects for sexual gratification

4. Pedophilia: Desiring sexual activity with a child younger than 13 years of age

5. Sexual masochism: Sexual gratification that involves receiving pain

6. Sexual sadism: Sexual gratification that involves inflicting pain

7. Voyeurism: Sexual gratification through observing others disrobing or engaging in sexual activity

8. Zoophilia: Intense sexual arousal or desire for sexual contact with animals

9. Frotteurism: Intense sexual arousal or desire when rubbing against a nonconsenting person

---

BOX 73-18

Sexual Expression

Bisexuality	Sexual attraction to and activity with both genders
Heterosexuality	Male-female sexual relationships
Homosexuality	Sexual attraction to a member of the same gender
Transvestism	Obsession with wearing clothing of the opposite gender

▲ D. Interventions
1. Assess sexual history, history of trauma or **abuse**, and precipitating event for the sexual disorder.
2. Encourage the client to explore personal beliefs.
3. Provide a nonjudgmental attitude.
4. Provide supportive psychotherapy.

PRACTICE QUESTIONS

1. The nurse assesses a client with the admitting diagnosis of bipolar affective disorder, mania. The symptom presented by the client that requires the nurse's immediate intervention is the client's:
   1. Outlandish behaviors and inappropriate dress
   2. Nonstop physical activity and poor nutritional intake
   3. Grandiose delusions of being a royal descendent of King Arthur
   4. Constant, incessant talking that includes sexual innuendoes and teasing the staff

2. A client who is delusional says to the nurse, "The federal guards were sent to kill me." The nurse's best response is:
   1. "I don't believe this is true."
   2. "The guards are not out to kill you."
   3. "What makes you think the guards were sent to hurt you?"
   4. "I don't know anything about the guards. Do you feel afraid that people are trying to hurt you?"

3. A woman comes into the emergency room in a severe state of anxiety following a car accident. The appropriate nursing intervention is to:
   1. Remain with the client.
   2. Put the client in a quiet room.
   3. Teach the client deep breathing.
   4. Encourage the client to talk about their feelings and concerns.

4. A male client with delirium becomes disoriented and confused in his room at night. The best initial nursing intervention is to:
   1. Move the client next to the nurse's station.
   2. Use an indirect light source and turn off the television.
   3. Keep the television and a soft light on during the night.
   4. Play soft music during the night, and maintain a well-lit room.

5. The nurse is performing an assessment on a client with dementia. Which data gathered during the assessment indicate a manifestation associated with dementia?
   1. Confabulation
   2. Improvement in sleeping
   3. Absence of sundown syndrome
   4. Presence of personal hygienic care

6. The nurse is discharging a client with a history of command hallucinations to harm self or others. The nurse provides instructions to the client about interventions for hallucinations and anxiety and determines that the client understands the instructions if the client states:
   1. "My medications won't make me anxious."
   2. "I'll go to support group and talk so that I don't hurt anyone."
   3. "I won't get anxious or hear things if I get enough sleep and eat well."
   4. "I can call my therapist when I'm hallucinating so that I can talk about my feelings and plans and not hurt anyone."

7. The nurse develops a nursing diagnosis of self-care deficit for an older client with dementia. Which of the following is an appropriate goal for this client?
   1. The client will function at the highest level of independence possible.
   2. The client will complete all activities of daily living independently within a 1-hour time frame.
   3. The client will be admitted to a long-term care facility to have activities of daily living needs met.
   4. The nursing staff will attend to all the client's activities of daily living needs during the hospital stay.

8. The nurse is caring for a male client diagnosed with catatonic stupor. The client is lying on the bed with his body pulled into a fetal position. The appropriate nursing intervention is which of the following?
   1. Ask direct questions to encourage talking.
   2. Leave the client alone and intermittently check on him.
   3. Sit beside the client in silence with occasional open-ended questions.
   4. Take the client into the dayroom with other clients so that they can help watch him.

9. The client is admitted to the mental health unit with a diagnosis of schizophrenia. A nursing diagnosis formulated for the client is thought processes, disturbed related to paranoia. In formulating nursing interventions with the members of the health care team, the nurse provides instructions to:
   1. Increase socialization of the client with peers.
   2. Avoid laughing or whispering in front of the client.
   3. Begin to educate the client about social supports in the community.
   4. Have the client sign a release of information to appropriate parties so that adequate data can be obtained for assessment purposes.

10. A client is admitted to the mental health unit with a diagnosis of depression. The nurse develops a

plan of care for the client and includes which appropriate activity in the plan?

1. Reading and writing most of the day
2. Several activities from which the client can choose
3. Nothing, until the client asks to participate in milieu
4. A structured program of activities in which the client can participate

11. When planning the discharge of a client with chronic anxiety, the nurse directs the goals at promoting a safe environment at home. The appropriate maintenance goal should focus on which of the following?

1. Ignoring feelings of anxiety
2. Identifying anxiety-producing situations
3. Continued contact with a crisis counselor
4. Eliminating all anxiety from daily situations

12. The client is unwilling to go out of the house for fear of "doing something crazy in public." Because of this fear, the client remains homebound, except when accompanied outside by the spouse. Based on this data, the nurse determines that the client is experiencing:

1. Agoraphobia
2. Social phobia
3. Claustrophobia
4. Hypochondriasis

13. A nurse is conducting a group therapy session. During the session, a client with mania consistently talks and dominates the group session, and her behavior is disrupting group interactions. The nurse would initially:

1. Ask the client to leave the group session.
2. Ask another nurse to escort the client out of the group session.
3. Tell the client that she will not be able to attend any future group sessions.
4. Tell the client that she needs to allow other clients in the group time to talk.

14. A client is admitted to a medical nursing unit with a diagnosis of acute blindness. Many tests are performed, and there seems to be no organic reason why this client cannot see. The nurse later learns that the client became blind after witnessing a hit-and-run car accident, when a family of three was killed. The nurse suspects that the client may be experiencing a:

1. Psychosis
2. Repression
3. Conversion disorder
4. Dissociative disorder

15. The manic client announces to everyone in the dayroom that a stripper is coming to perform this evening. When the nurse firmly states that this will not happen, the manic client becomes verbally abusive and threatens physical violence to the nurse. Based on the analysis of this situation, the nurse determines that the appropriate action would be to:

1. Orient the client to time, person, and place.
2. Tell the client that the behavior is not appropriate.
3. Escort the manic client to her room, with assistance.
4. Tell the client that smoking privileges are revoked for 24 hours.

16. The nurse is planning activities for a client who has bipolar disorder with aggressive social behavior. Which of the following activities would be most appropriate for this client?

1. Chess
2. Writing
3. Ping pong
4. Basketball

17. A client is admitted to the hospital with a diagnosis of major depression, severe, single episode. The nurse assesses the client and identifies a nursing diagnosis of nutrition: less than body requirements, imbalanced related to poor nutritional intake. The appropriate nursing intervention related to this diagnosis is:

1. Weigh the client three times per week before breakfast.
2. Explain to the client the importance of a good nutritional intake.
3. Schedule brief nursing interactions with the client during several meals in which small portions are offered.
4. Report the nutritional concern to the psychiatrist and obtain a nutritional consultation as soon as possible.

18. The depressed client verbalizes feelings of low self-esteem and self-worth typified by statements such as "I'm such a failure. I can't do anything right." The best nursing response would be to:

1. Tell the client that this is not true, that we all have a purpose in life.
2. Identify recent behaviors or accomplishments that demonstrate the client's skills.
3. Reassure the client that you know how the client is feeling and that things will get better.
4. Remain with the client and sit in silence; this will encourage the client to verbalize feelings.

19. A client with a diagnosis of major depression, recurrent, with psychotic features, is admitted to the mental health unit. To create a safe environment for the client, the nurse most importantly devises a plan of care that deals specifically with the client's:

1. Self-care deficit.
2. Imbalanced nutrition.
3. Deficient knowledge.
4. Disturbed thought processes.

20. The nurse observes that a client is pacing, agitated, and presenting aggressive gestures. The client's speech pattern is rapid, and affect is belligerent. Based on these observations, the nurse's immediate priority of care is to:

1. Provide safety for the client and other clients on the unit.
2. Provide the clients on the unit with a sense of comfort and safety.
3. Assist the staff in caring for the client in a controlled environment.
4. Offer the client a less stimulated area to calm down and gain control.

❑ 3. Assist the client in testing out alternative behaviors for obtaining needs.
❑ 4. Follow through about the consequences of behavior in a nonpunitive manner.
❑ 5. Enforce rules and inform the client that he or she will not be allowed to attend therapy groups.
❑ 6. Be clear with the client regarding the consequences of exceeding limits that have been set regarding behavior.

ALTERNATE ITEM FORMAT: MULTIPLE RESPONSE

Select all nursing interventions for a hospitalized client with mania who is exhibiting manipulative behavior. Select all that apply.
❑ 1. Communicate expected behaviors to the client.
❑ 2. Ensure that the client knows that he or she is not in charge of the nursing unit.

ANSWERS

1. **2**
Rationale: Mania is a mood characterized by excitement, euphoria, hyperactivity, excessive energy, decreased need for sleep, and impaired ability to concentrate or complete a single train of thought. Mania is a period when the mood is predominantly elevated, expansive, or irritable. All options reflect a client's possible symptomatology. Option 2, however, clearly presents a problem that compromises physiological integrity and needs to be addressed immediately.
Test-Taking Strategy: Note the strategic word *immediate* and use Maslow's Hierarchy of Needs theory to assist you in answering the question. Option 2 is the only option that reflects a physiological need. Review care of the client with mania if you had difficulty with this question.
Level of Cognitive Ability: Analysis
Client Needs: Physiological Integrity
Integrated Process: Nursing Process—assessment
Content Area: Delegating/Prioritizing
References: Fortinash, K., & Holoday-Worret, P. (2004). *Psychiatric mental health nursing* (3rd ed., pp. 210-211). St. Louis: Mosby.
Varcarolis, E., Carson, V., & Shoemaker, N. (2006). *Foundations of psychiatric mental health nursing* (5th ed., pp. 364-365, 368). Philadelphia: W.B. Saunders.

2. **4**
Rationale: For the nurse to empathize with the client's experience is most therapeutic. Disagreeing with delusions may make the client more defensive, and the client may cling to the delusions even more. Encouraging discussion regarding the delusion is inappropriate.
Test-Taking Strategy: Use therapeutic communication techniques. Eliminate options 1 and 2 because they are comparative or alike and are statements that disagree with the client. Option 3 encourages discussion regarding the delusion. Review communication techniques with the client experiencing delusions if you had difficulty with this question.
Level of Cognitive Ability: Application
Client Needs: Psychosocial Integrity

Integrated Process: Communication and Documentation
Content Area: Mental health
References: Fortinash, K., & Holoday-Worret, P. (2004). *Psychiatric mental health nursing* (3rd ed., p. 125). St. Louis: Mosby.
Stuart, G., & Laraia, M. (2005). *Principles and practice of psychiatric nursing* (8th ed., pp. 30-34). St. Louis: Mosby.
Varcarolis, E., Carson, V., & Shoemaker, N. (2006). *Foundations of psychiatric mental health nursing* (5th ed., p. 407). Philadelphia: W.B. Saunders.

3. **1**
Rationale: If a client with severe anxiety is left alone, the client may feel abandoned and become overwhelmed. Placing the client in a quiet room is also important, but the nurse must stay with the client. Teaching the client deep breathing or relaxation is not possible until the anxiety decreases. Encouraging the client to discuss concerns and feelings would not take place until the anxiety has decreased.
Test-Taking Strategy: Use the process of elimination. Note the strategic words *severe state*. Eliminate options 3 and 4 first, knowing that these actions are not possible when the client is in a severe state of anxiety. From the remaining options, the appropriate action is to remain with the client. Review care of the client with severe anxiety if you had difficulty with this question.
Level of Cognitive Ability: Application
Client Needs: Psychosocial Integrity
Integrated Process: Nursing Process—implementation
Content Area: Mental health
References: Fortinash, K., & Holoday-Worret, P. (2004). *Psychiatric mental health nursing* (3rd ed., pp. 512-514). St. Louis: Mosby.
Varcarolis, E., Carson, V., & Shoemaker, N. (2006). *Foundations of psychiatric mental health nursing* (5th ed., p. 216). Philadelphia: W.B. Saunders.

4. **2**
Rationale: Provision of a consistent daily routine and a low stimulating environment is important when the client is disorientated. Noise, including radio and television, may add to

the confusion and disorientation. Moving the client next to the nurses' station is not the initial action.
Test-Taking Strategy: Use the process of elimination and note the strategic word *initial* in the question. Eliminate options 3 and 4 first because they are comparative or alike. Focusing on the strategic word will direct you easily to option 2. Review measures related to the client who is disoriented and confused if you had difficulty with this question.
Level of Cognitive Ability: Application
Client Needs: Psychosocial Integrity
Integrated Process: Nursing Process—implementation
Content Area: Mental health
References: Fortinash, K., & Holoday-Worret, P. (2004). *Psychiatric mental health nursing* (3rd ed., p. 330). St. Louis: Mosby. Varcarolis, E., Carson, V., & Shoemaker, N. (2006). *Foundations of psychiatric mental health nursing* (5th ed., p. 430). Philadelphia: W.B. Saunders.

5. **1**

Rationale: The clinical picture of dementia varies from the development of mild cognitive defects to severe, life-threatening alterations in neurological functioning. For the client to use confabulation or the fabrication of events or experiences to fill in memory gaps is not unusual. Often, lack of inhibitions on the part of the client may constitute the first indication of anything being "wrong" to the client's significant others (the client may undress in front of others or demonstrate slovenly table manners but was formerly well mannered). As the dementia progresses, the client will have episodes of wandering or sundowning.
Test-Taking Strategy: Use the process of elimination and focus on the client's diagnosis. Noting the subject, a manifestation, will direct you to option 1. If you had difficulty with this question, review the manifestations associated with dementia.
Level of Cognitive Ability: Analysis
Client Needs: Psychosocial Integrity
Integrated Process: Nursing Process—assessment
Content Area: Mental health
References: Fortinash, K., & Holoday-Worret, P. (2004). *Psychiatric mental health nursing* (3rd ed., p. 331). St. Louis: Mosby. Stuart, G., & Laraia, M. (2005). *Principles and practice of psychiatric nursing* (8th ed., pp. 451-452, 459). St. Louis: Mosby.

6. **4**

Rationale: The risk for impulsive and aggressive behavior may increase if a client is receiving command hallucinations to harm self or others. The nurse should ask the client whether he or she has intentions to hurt himself or herself or others. Talking about auditory hallucinations can interfere with subvocal muscular activity associated with a hallucination. Options 1, 2, and 3 will aid in wellness but are not specific interventions for hallucinations, if they occur.
Test-Taking Strategy: Use the process of elimination. Options 1, 2, and 3 are interventions that a client can carry out to aid wellness. Option 4 is a specific agreement to seek help and evidences self-responsible commitment and control over one's own behavior. Review teaching points for a client with a history of hallucinations if you had difficulty with this question.
Level of Cognitive Ability: Analysis
Client Needs: Psychosocial Integrity

Integrated Process: Nursing Process—evaluation
Content Area: Mental health
References: Fortinash, K., & Holoday-Worret, P. (2004). *Psychiatric mental health nursing* (3rd ed., p. 211). St. Louis: Mosby. Varcarolis, E., Carson, V., & Shoemaker, N. (2006). *Foundations of psychiatric mental health nursing* (5th ed., pp. 402-403). Philadelphia: W.B. Saunders.

7. **1**

Rationale: All clients, regardless of age, need to be encouraged to perform at the highest level of independence possible. Independence contributes to the client's sense of control and sense of well-being. Option 3 is incorrect because what the *self-care deficit* entails is not known. To assume that the client requires long-term care based on so little information would be erroneous. Options 2 and 4 are close-ended statements.
Test-Taking Strategy: Use the process of elimination. Eliminate options 2 and 4 first because of the close-ended word *all*. From the remaining options, select option 1 because it is the umbrella option. Review care of the client with dementia if you had difficulty with this question.
Level of Cognitive Ability: Application
Client Needs: Safe and Effective Care Environment
Integrated Process: Nursing Process—planning
Content Area: Mental health
Reference: Fortinash, K., & Holoday-Worret, P. (2004). *Psychiatric mental health nursing* (3rd ed., pp. 333, 339). St. Louis: Mosby.

8. **3**

Rationale: Clients who are withdrawn may be immobile and mute and may require consistent, repeated approaches. Communication with withdrawn clients requires much patience from the nurse. Interventions include the establishment of interpersonal contact. The nurse facilitates communication with the client by sitting in silence, asking open-ended questions, and pausing to provide opportunities for the client to respond.
Test-Taking Strategy: Eliminate option 2 because the client would not be left alone. Option 4 relies on other clients to care for this client, which is an inappropriate expectation. Asking direct questions of this client is not therapeutic. Option 3 provides for client supervision and communication as appropriate. Review care of the client with catatonic stupor if this question was difficult.
Level of Cognitive Ability: Application
Client Needs: Psychosocial Integrity
Integrated Process: Nursing Process—implementation
Content Area: Mental health
References: Fortinash, K., & Holoday-Worret, P. (2004). *Psychiatric mental health nursing* (3rd ed., p. 221). St. Louis: Mosby. Stuart, G., & Laraia, M. (2005). *Principles and practice of psychiatric nursing* (8th ed., p. 404). St. Louis: Mosby. Varcarolis, E., Carson, V., & Shoemaker, N. (2006). *Foundations of psychiatric mental health nursing* (5th ed., p. 414). Philadelphia: W.B. Saunders.

9. **2**

Rationale: Disturbed thought process related to paranoia is the client's problem, and the plan of care must address this problem. The client is experiencing paranoia and is distrustful and suspicious of others. The members of the health care team need to establish a rapport and trust with the client. Therefore, laughing or whispering in front of the client would be counterproductive. Options 1, 3, and 4 ask the client to trust on a multitude of levels. These options are actions that are too intrusive for a client who is paranoid.

Test-Taking Strategy: Use the process of elimination and knowledge regarding this disorder to answer the question. Noting that the client has paranoia will direct you to option 2. Review this disorder if you had difficulty with this question.

Level of Cognitive Ability: Application
Client Needs: Psychosocial Integrity
Integrated Process: Nursing Process—implementation
Content Area: Mental health
References: Fortinash, K., & Holoday-Worret, P. (2004). *Psychiatric mental health nursing* (3rd ed., pp. 249-250, 262). St. Louis: Mosby.
Varcarolis, E., Carson, V., & Shoemaker, N. (2006). *Foundations of psychiatric mental health nursing* (5th ed., p. 418). Philadelphia: W.B. Saunders.

10. **4**

Rationale: A client with depression often suffers a depressed mood and is withdrawn. The person also experiences difficulty concentrating, loss of interest or pleasure, low energy, fatigue, and feelings of worthlessness and poor self-esteem. The plan of care needs to provide successful experiences in a stimulating yet structured environment. Options 1, 2, and 3 are too "restrictive" and offer little or no structure and stimulation.

Test-Taking Strategy: Use the process of elimination. Recall that the depressed client requires a structured and stimulating program in a safe environment. Option 4 is the only option that will provide a safe and effective environment. Review care of the client with depression if you had difficulty with this question.

Level of Cognitive Ability: Application
Client Needs: Psychosocial Integrity
Integrated Process: Nursing Process—planning
Content Area: Mental health
References: Fortinash, K., & Holoday-Worret, P. (2004). *Psychiatric mental health nursing* (3rd ed., p. 221). St. Louis: Mosby.
Stuart, G., & Laraia, M. (2005). *Principles and practice of psychiatric nursing* (8th ed., p. 353). St. Louis: Mosby.

11. **2**

Rationale: Recognizing situations that produce anxiety allows the client to prepare to cope with anxiety or avoid a specific stimulus. Counselors will not be available for all anxiety-producing situations, and this option does not encourage the development of internal strengths. Ignoring feelings will not resolve anxiety. Elimination of all anxiety from life is impossible.

Test-Taking Strategy: Use the process of elimination. Eliminate option 4 first because of the word *all.* Eliminate option 1 next, because feelings should not be ignored. From the remaining options, select option 2 because this option is more client-centered and helps prepare the client to deal with anxiety should it occur. Review home care planning for the client with chronic anxiety if you had difficulty with this question.

Level of Cognitive Ability: Application
Client Needs: Safe and Effective Care Environment

Integrated Process: Nursing Process—planning
Content Area: Mental health
Reference: Fortinash, K., & Holoday-Worret, P. (2004). *Psychiatric mental health nursing* (3rd ed., pp.184, 190-191). St. Louis: Mosby.

12. **1**

Rationale: Agoraphobia is a fear of open spaces and the fear of being trapped in a situation from which there may not be an escape. Agoraphobia includes the possibility of experiencing a sense of helplessness or embarrassment if an attack occurs. Avoidance of such situations usually results in reduction of social and professional interactions. Social phobia focuses more on specific situations, such as the fear of speaking, performing, or eating in public. Claustrophobia is a fear of closed places. Clients with hypochondriacal symptoms focus their anxiety on physical complaints and are preoccupied with their health.

Test-Taking Strategy: Use the process of elimination. Focusing on the strategic words *remains homebound* will direct you to option 1. If you had difficulty with this question, review phobia types and associated client behaviors.

Level of Cognitive Ability: Analysis
Client Needs: Psychosocial Integrity
Integrated Process: Nursing Process—assessment
Content Area: Mental health
References: Fortinash, K., & Holoday-Worret, P. (2004). *Psychiatric mental health nursing* (3rd ed., pp. 178-179). St. Louis: Mosby.
Stuart, G., & Laraia, M. (2005). *Principles and practice of psychiatric nursing* (8th ed., p. 271). St. Louis: Mosby.
Varcarolis, E., Carson, V., & Shoemaker, N. (2006). *Foundations of psychiatric mental health nursing* (5th ed., p. 234). Philadelphia: W.B. Saunders.

13. **4**

Rationale: Manic clients may be talkative and can dominate group meetings or therapy sessions by their excessive talking. If this occurs, the nurse initially would set limits on the client's behavior. Initially, asking the client to leave the session or asking another person to escort the client out of the session is inappropriate. This may agitate the client and further escalate the client's behavior. Option 2 is also an inappropriate initial action because it violates the client's right to receive treatment and is a threatening action.

Test-Taking Strategy: Use the process of elimination and note the strategic word *initially.* Eliminate options 1 and 2 first because they are comparative or alike. Next, eliminate option 3 because it violates the client's right to receive treatment and is a threatening action. Remember that setting firm limits with the client initially is best. Review care of a client with mania if you had difficulty with this question.

Level of Cognitive Ability: Application
Client Needs: Psychosocial Integrity
Integrated Process: Nursing Process—implementation
Content Area: Mental health
References: Fortinash, K., & Holoday-Worret, P. (2004). *Psychiatric mental health nursing* (3rd ed., p. 445). St. Louis: Mosby.
Varcarolis, E., Carson, V., & Shoemaker, N. (2006). *Foundations of psychiatric mental health nursing* (5th ed., p. 364). Philadelphia: W.B. Saunders.

14. 3

Rationale: A conversion disorder is the alteration or loss of a physical function that cannot be explained by any known pathophysiological mechanism. A conversion disorder is thought to be an expression of a psychological need or conflict. In this situation, the client witnessed an accident that was so psychologically painful that the client became blind. A dissociative disorder is a disturbance or alteration in the normally integrative functions of identity, memory, or consciousness. Psychosis is a state in which a person's mental capacity to recognize reality, communicate, and relate to others is impaired, thus interfering with the person's ability to deal with life's demands. Repression is a coping mechanism in which unacceptable feelings are kept out of awareness.

Test-Taking Strategy: Use the process of elimination. The key to the correct option lies in the fact that the client presents no organic reason to account for the blindness—hence, a conversion disorder. If you had difficulty with this question, review defense mechanisms and the concepts associated with a conversion disorder.

Level of Cognitive Ability: Analysis
Client Needs: Psychosocial Integrity
Integrated Process: Nursing Process—analysis
Content Area: Mental health
Reference: Fortinash, K., & Holoday-Worret, P. (2004). *Psychiatric mental health nursing* (3rd ed., p. 183). St. Louis: Mosby. Varcarolis, E., Carson, V., & Shoemaker, N. (2006). *Foundations of psychiatric mental health nursing* (5th ed., pp. 254, 259) Philadelphia: W.B. Saunders.

15. 3

Rationale: The client is at risk for injury to self and others and therefore should be escorted out of the dayroom. Antipsychotic medications are useful to manage the manic client. Hyperactive and agitated behavior usually responds to haloperidol (Haldol). Option 4 may increase the agitation that already exists in this client. Orientation will not halt the behavior. Telling the client that the behavior is not appropriate already has been attempted by the nurse.

Test-Taking Strategy: Use the process of elimination and Maslow's Hierarchy of Needs theory to answer the question. Look for the option that promotes safety of the client, other clients, and staff. If you had difficulty with this question, review the appropriate interventions when dealing with a manic client.

Level of Cognitive Ability: Analysis
Client Needs: Psychosocial Integrity
Integrated Process: Nursing Process—implementation
Content Area: Mental health
References: Fortinash, K., & Holoday-Worret, P. (2004). *Psychiatric mental health nursing* (3rd ed., pp. 210, 221). St. Louis: Mosby.
Varcarolis, E., Carson, V., & Shoemaker, N. (2006). *Foundations of psychiatric mental health nursing* (5th ed., p. 369). Philadelphia: W.B. Saunders.

16. 2

Rationale: Solitary activities that require a short attention span with mild physical exertion are the most appropriate activities for a client who is exhibiting aggressive behavior.

Writing (journaling), walks with staff, and finger painting are activities that minimize stimuli and provide a constructive release for tension. Competitive games should be avoided because they can stimulate aggression and increase psychomotor activity.

Test-Taking Strategy: Use the process of elimination. Options 1, 3, and 4 are comparative or alike in that they are activities that the client cannot do alone. Option 2 identifies a solitary activity. Review care of the client with aggressive behavior if you had difficulty with this question.

Level of Cognitive Ability: Application
Client Needs: Physiological Integrity
Integrated Process: Nursing Process—planning
Content Area: Mental health
References: Fortinash, K., & Holoday-Worret, P. (2004). *Psychiatric mental health nursing* (3rd ed., pp. 220-221, 225, 450). St. Louis: Mosby.
Stuart, G., & Laraia, M. (2005). *Principles and practice of psychiatric nursing* (8th ed., p. 355). St. Louis: Mosby.

17. 3

Rationale: Change in appetite is one of the major symptoms of depression. Other symptoms include a depressed mood, increased fatigue, feelings of worthlessness, diminished ability to think, or indecisiveness and psychomotor agitation or retardation. Option 2 is incorrect because the client is experiencing poor concentration; thus, even if the client does understand the rationale, the client still may not be able to complete tasks. Weighing the client does not address how to increase nutritional intake. Reporting to the psychiatrist and the nutritionist is to some degree correct but does not present a method to increase food intake.

Test-Taking Strategy: Use the process of elimination, focusing on the subject, poor nutritional status. Option 3 is the only option that addresses the imbalanced nutrition concretely and designs a method in which the client feasibly will increase the nutritional intake. Review care of the client with depression if you had difficulty with this question.

Level of Cognitive Ability: Application
Client Needs: Physiological Integrity
Integrated Process: Nursing Process—implementation
Content Area: Mental health
References: Fortinash, K., & Holoday-Worret, P. (2004). *Psychiatric mental health nursing* (3rd ed., p. 215). St. Louis: Mosby.
Stuart, G., & Laraia, M. (2005). *Principles and practice of psychiatric nursing* (8th ed., pp. 529-530). St. Louis: Mosby.
Varcarolis, E., Carson, V., & Shoemaker, N. (2006). *Foundations of psychiatric mental health nursing* (5th ed., pp. 245, 336). Philadelphia: W.B. Saunders.

18. 2

Rationale: Feelings of low self-esteem and worthlessness are common symptoms of the depressed client. An effective plan of care to enhance the client's personal self-esteem is to provide experiences for the client that are challenging but that will not be met with failure. Reminders of the client's past accomplishments or personal successes are ways to interrupt the client's negative self-talk and distorted cognitive view of self. Silence may be interpreted as agreement. Options 1 and 3 give advice and devalue the client's feelings.

Test-Taking Strategy: Use the process of elimination and therapeutic communication techniques. Focus on the client's diagnosis. You can eliminate options 1 and 3 easily. From the remaining options, focusing on the client's diagnosis will direct you to option 2. Review care of the client with depression if you had difficulty with this question.
Level of Cognitive Ability: Application
Client Needs: Psychosocial Integrity
Integrated Process: Nursing Process—implementation
Content Area: Mental health
References: Fortinash, K., & Holoday-Worret, P. (2004). *Psychiatric mental health nursing* (3rd ed., p. 231). St. Louis: Mosby.
Stuart, G., & Laraia, M. (2005). *Principles and practice of psychiatric nursing* (8th ed., pp. 305-306, 350-351). St. Louis: Mosby.
Varcarolis, E., Carson, V., & Shoemaker, N. (2006). *Foundations of psychiatric mental health nursing* (5th ed., pp. 341-342). Philadelphia: W.B. Saunders.

19. 4
Rationale: Major depression, recurrent, with psychotic features, alerts the nurse that in addition to the criteria that designates the diagnosis of major depression, one also must deal with the client's psychosis. Psychosis is defined as a state in which a person's mental capacity to recognize reality and to communicate and relate to others is impaired, thus interfering with the person's ability to deal with the demands of life. Disturbed thought processes generally indicate a state of increased anxiety in which hallucinations and delusions prevail. Although all the nursing diagnoses may be appropriate because the client is experiencing psychosis, option 4 is the correct option.
Test-Taking Strategy: Use the process of elimination. All the nursing diagnoses listed may be appropriate for a client diagnosed with major depression. The strategic words leading to the correct option are *psychotic features,* in which the client often suffers with disturbed thought processes, such as hallucinations and delusions. Review appropriate nursing diagnoses for major depression and psychotic features if you had difficulty with this question.
Level of Cognitive Ability: Analysis
Client Needs: Safe and Effective Care Environment
Integrated Process: Nursing Process—planning
Content Area: Mental health
References: Fortinash, K., & Holoday-Worret, P. (2004). *Psychiatric mental health nursing* (3rd ed., pp. 220, 458). St. Louis: Mosby.
Stuart, G., & Laraia, M. (2005). *Principles and practice of psychiatric nursing* (8th ed., p. 335). St. Louis: Mosby.
Varcarolis, E., Carson, V., & Shoemaker, N. (2006). *Foundations of psychiatric mental health nursing* (5th ed., pp. 385). Philadelphia: W.B. Saunders.

20. 1
Rationale: Safety of the client and other clients is the priority. Option 1 is the only option that addresses the client and other clients' safety needs. Option 2 addresses other clients' needs. Option 3 is not client-centered. Option 4 addresses the client's needs.
Test-Taking Strategy: Note the strategic words *immediate priority* and use Maslow's hierarchy of needs theory to prioritize. Note the words *agitated, aggressive,* and *belligerent.* Safety is the strategic subject. Option 1 is the umbrella option and addresses the safety of all. Review nursing interventions to provide safety to clients if you had difficulty with this question.
Level of Cognitive Ability: Application
Client Needs: Safe and Effective Care Environment
Integrated Process: Nursing Process—implementation
Content Area: Delegating/Prioritizing
References: Fortinash, K., & Holoday-Worret, P. (2004). *Psychiatric mental health nursing* (3rd ed., p. 438). St. Louis: Mosby.
Varcarolis, E., Carson, V., & Shoemaker, N. (2006). *Foundations of psychiatric mental health nursing* (5th ed., pp. 80, 400). Philadelphia: W.B. Saunders.

ALTERNATE ITEM FORMAT: MULTIPLE RESPONSE

Answer: **1, 3, 4, 6**
Rationale: Interventions for dealing with the client exhibiting manipulative behavior include setting clear, consistent, and enforceable limits on manipulative behaviors; being clear with the client regarding the consequences of exceeding limits set; following through with the consequences in a nonpunitive manner; and assisting the client in identifying personal strengths and testing out alternative behaviors for obtaining needs. Enforcing rules and informing the client that he or she will not be allowed to attend therapy groups is a violation of a client's rights. Ensuring that the client knows that he or she is not in charge of the nursing unit is inappropriate; power struggles need to be avoided.
Test-Taking Strategy: Focus on the subject, manipulative behavior. Recalling clients' rights and that power struggles need to be avoided will assist in selecting the correct interventions. Review care of the client with manipulative behavior if you had difficulty with this question.
Level of Cognitive Ability: Application
Client Needs: Psychosocial Integrity
Integrated Process: Nursing Process—implementation
Content Area: Mental health
References: Fortinash, K., & Holoday-Worret, P. (2004). *Psychiatric mental health nursing* (3rd ed., p. 287). St. Louis: Mosby.
Varcarolis, E., Carson, V., & Shoemaker, N. (2006). *Foundations of psychiatric mental health nursing* (5th ed., pp. 292-293). Philadelphia: W.B. Saunders.

REFERENCES

Fortinash, K., & Holoday-Worret, P. (2004). *Psychiatric mental health nursing* (3rd ed.). St. Louis: Mosby.
Potter, P., & Perry, A. (2005). *Fundamentals of nursing* (6th ed.). St. Louis: Mosby.

Stuart, G., & Laraia, M. (2005). *Principles and practice of psychiatric nursing* (8th ed.). St. Louis: Mosby.
Varcarolis, E., Carson, V., & Shoemaker, N. (2006). *Foundations of psychiatric mental health nursing* (5th ed.). Philadelphia: W.B. Saunders.

Addictions

I. EATING DISORDERS

A. Description: Eating disorders are characterized by uncertain self-identification and grossly disturbed eating habits (Fig. 74-1).

B. Compulsive overeating
   1. Compulsive overeating is binge-like overeating without purging.
   2. Food consumption is out of the individual's control and occurs in a stereotyped fashion.
   3. Client may be repulsed by eating, and the eating relieves tension but does not produce pleasure.
   4. Client is aware that eating patterns are abnormal and feels depressed after eating.
   5. Client eats secretly during a binge and consumes high-calorie and easily digestible food.
   6. Client repeatedly tries to diet but without success.
   7. Client feels helpless and hopeless about weight.
   8. When experiencing guilt, anger, depression, boredom, loneliness, inadequacy, or ambivalence, client responds by eating.

C. Anorexia nervosa
   1. Description
      a. The onset often is associated with a stressful life event.
      b. The client intensely fears obesity.
      c. Body image is distorted, and the client has a disturbed self-concept.
      d. Client is preoccupied with foods that prevent weight gain and has a phobia against foods that produce weight gain.
      e. The eating disorder can be life-threatening.
      f. Death can occur from starvation, **suicide**, cardiomyopathies, or electrolyte imbalance.

   2. Assessment
      a. Refusal to eat and appetite loss
      b. Appetite denial
      c. Feelings of lack of control
      d. Self-induced vomiting and self-administered enemas
      e. Compulsive exercising
      f. Overachiever and perfectionist
      g. Decreased temperature, pulse, and blood pressure
      h. Weight loss
      i. Gastrointestinal disturbances
      j. Constipation
      k. Electrolyte imbalances
      l. Scaly, dry skin
      m. Presence of lanugo on extremities
      n. Sleep disturbances
      o. Hormone deficiencies
      p. Amenorrhea for at least three consecutive menstrual periods
      q. Teeth and gum deterioration
      r. Cyanosis and numbness of extremities
      s. Esophageal varices from vomiting
      t. Bone degeneration

D. Bulimia nervosa
   1. Description
      a. The client indulges in eating binges followed by purging behaviors.
      b. Most clients remain within a normal weight range but think that their lives are dominated by the eating-related conflict.
   2. Assessment
      a. Preoccupied with body shape and weight
      b. Consumption of high-calorie food in secret; guilt about secretive eating

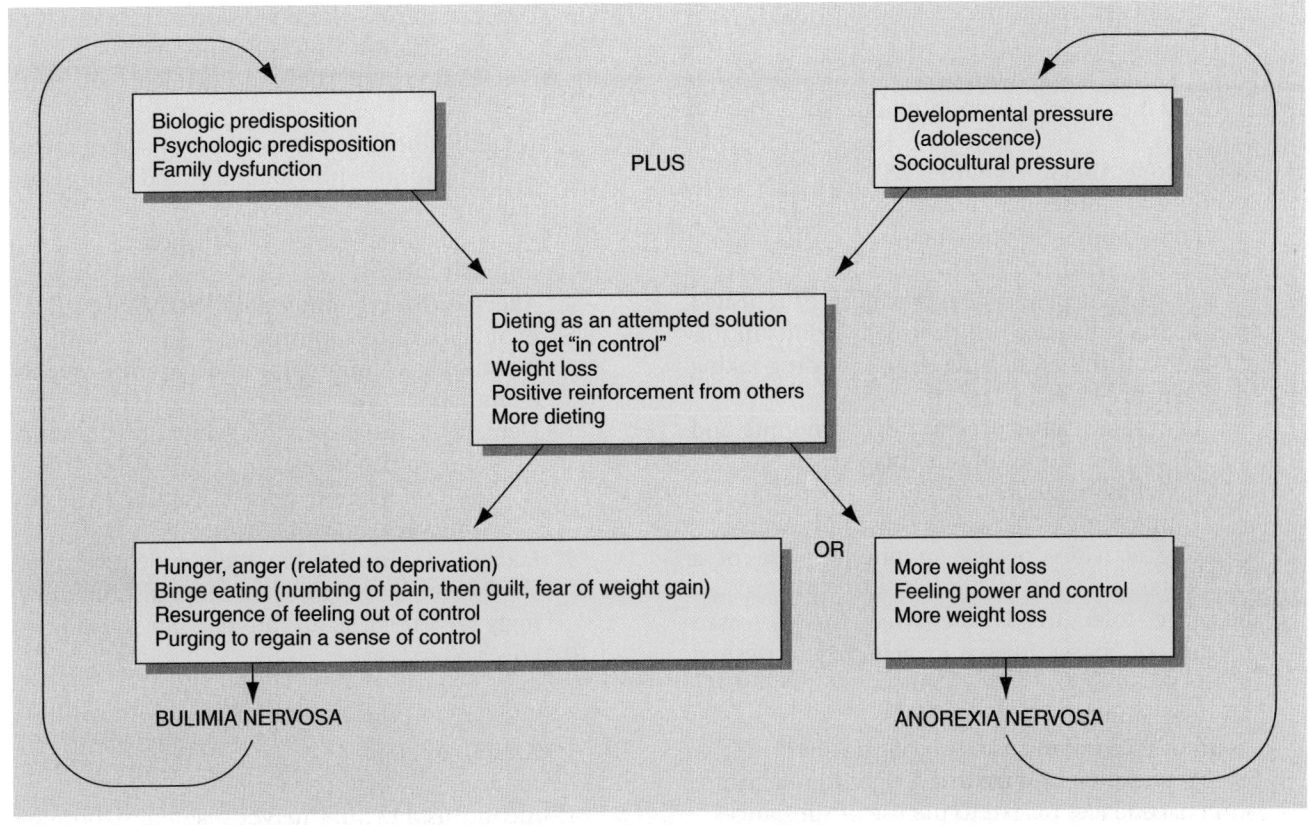

FIG. 74-1 The cycle of eating disorders. (From Fortinash, K., & Holoday-Worret, P. [2004]. *Psychiatric mental health nursing* [3rd ed.]. St. Louis: Mosby.)

c. Binge-purge syndrome
d. Attempts to lose weight through diets, vomiting, enemas, cathartics, and amphetamines or diuretics
e. Has a need to control yet experiences feelings of powerlessness or loss of control
f. Low self-esteem
g. Poor interpersonal relationships
h. Decreased or absence of interest in sex
i. Mood swings
j. Electrolyte imbalances
k. Loss of tooth enamel and dental decay
l. Stomach ulcers and rectal bleeding
m. Esophageal varices from vomiting
n. Cardiac disease and hypertension

E. Interventions: Clients with an eating disorder
1. Assess the client's nutritional status and the severity of any medical problems.
2. Establish a one-to-one therapeutic relationship with client; the nurse needs to establish trust and recognize any client reluctance to establish a relationship.
3. Establish a contract with the client concerning the nutritional plan for the day.
4. Assist the client to identify precipitants to the eating disorder.

5. Encourage the client to express feelings about the eating behavior.
6. Be accepting and nonjudgmental.
7. Work with client on exploring self concept and establishing identity
8. Implement behavior modification techniques.
9. Supervise client during mealtimes and for a specified period after meals.
10. Set a time limit for each meal.
11. Provide a pleasant, relaxed environment for eating.
12. Monitor for signs of physical complications related to the eating disorder.
13. Record intake and output.
14. Weigh the client daily at the same time, using the same scale, after the client voids.
15. When weighing the client, ensure that the client is wearing the same clothing as when the previous weight was taken.
16. Monitor and restore fluid and electrolyte balance.
17. Monitor elimination patterns.
18. Assess and limit the client's activity level.
19. Encourage the client to participate in diversional activities.
20. Assess the client's suicidal potential.

21. Administer antidepressant medication if prescribed.
22. Encourage psychotherapy.
23. Refer the client to support groups.

II. SUBSTANCE ABUSE DISORDERS

A. Description: Substance **abuse** disorders cause behavioral and physiological changes.
B. Substance dependence (Box 74-1)
   1. Substance dependence is a pattern of repeated use of a substance, which usually results in tolerance, withdrawal, and compulsive drug-taking behavior.
   2. Client takes substances in larger amounts and over longer periods of time than was intended.
   3. Client has the desire to cut down but has unsuccessful efforts to decrease or discontinue use.
   4. Daily activities revolve around the use of a substance.
C. Substance tolerance is the need for increased amounts of the substance to achieve the desired effect.
D. Substance **abuse**
   1. Client recurrently uses substances.
   2. Client experiences recurrent, significant harmful consequences related to the use of substances.
   3. Client may have legal issues to resolve, and involvement with the legal system is not uncommon.
E. Substance withdrawal
   1. Physiological and substance-specific cognitive symptoms occur.
   2. Substance withdrawal occurs when an individual experiences a decrease in blood levels of a substance to which they are physiologically dependent.
F. Other factors to consider in the client with a substance-related disorder
   1. Rebellion and peer group pressure in adolescence may contribute to the onset of substance use.
   2. Substance use may become a coping mechanism for decreasing physical and emotional pain.

BOX 74-1

Cage Screening Test

C: Have you ever felt the need to cut down on your drinking/drug use?
A: Have you ever been annoyed at criticism of your drinking/drug use?
G: Have you ever felt guilty about something that you have done when you have been drinking or taking drugs?
E: Have you ever had an eye opener, drinking or taking drugs first thing in the morning to get going or to avoid withdrawal symptoms?

---

3. Depression may precede or occur as a result of or in association with substance use.
4. Grief and loss may be associated with substance use.
G. Dysfunctional behaviors related to substance **abuse**
   1. Preoccupation with obtaining and using substance
   2. Manipulation to avoid consequences of behavior
   3. Impulsiveness
   4. Anger, including physical and verbal **abuse**
   5. Avoidance of relationships
   6. Sense of self-importance and requiring special treatment
   7. Denial; blaming everything but the substance use for their problems
   8. Uses rationalization and projection to justify unacceptable behavior
   9. Likely to be involved in codependent relationships whereby a significant other also unknowingly serves as a significant enabler
   10. Low self-esteem
   11. Depression

III. ALCOHOL ABUSE

A. Description
   1. Alcohol is a central nervous system depressant affecting all body tissues.
   2. Physical dependence is a biological need for alcohol to avoid physical withdrawal symptoms, whereas psychological dependence refers to craving for the subjective effect of alcohol.
B. Risk factors
   1. Biological predisposition; genetic and familial predisposition may also be a risk factor.
   2. Depressed and highly anxious characteristics
   3. Low self-esteem
   4. Poor self-control
   5. History of rebelliousness, poor school performance, delinquency
   6. Poor parental relationships
C. Assessment
   1. Slurred speech
   2. Uncoordinated movements
   3. Unsteady gait
   4. Restlessness
   5. Belligerence
   6. Confusion
   7. Sneaking drinks, drinking in the morning, experiencing blackouts
   8. Binge drinking
   9. Arguments about drinking
   10. Missing work
   11. Increased tolerance to alcohol
   12. Intoxication, with blood alcohol levels of 0.1% (100 mg alcohol/dL blood) or higher
D. Psychological symptoms
   1. Depression

2. Hostility
3. Suspiciousness
4. Rationalization
5. Irritability
6. Isolation
7. Decrease in inhibitions
8. Decrease in self-esteem
9. Denial that a problem exists

▲ E. Complications associated with chronic alcohol use
   1. Vitamin deficiencies
      a. Vitamin B deficiency causing peripheral neuropathies
      b. Thiamine deficiency, causing Korsakoff's syndrome
   2. Alcoholic-induced persistent amnesic disorder, causing severe memory problems
   3. Wernicke's encephalopathy, causing confusion, ataxia, and abnormal eye movements
   4. Hepatitis; cirrhosis of the liver
   5. Esophagitis and gastritis
   6. Pancreatitis
   7. Anemias
   8. Immune system dysfunctions
   9. Brain damage
   10. Peripheral neuropathy
   11. Cardiac disorders

▲ IV. ALCOHOL WITHDRAWAL
   A. Description
      1. Early signs develop within a few hours after cessation of alcohol intake.
      2. These signs peak after 24 to 48 hours and then rapidly disappear, unless the withdrawal progresses to alcohol withdrawal delirium.
      3. At the onset of withdrawal (Box 74-2), follow agency protocol using specified withdrawal assessment scales as indicated by unit or agency policy.

4. Chlordiazepoxide (Librium) is the most commonly prescribed medication for acute alcohol withdrawal and is usually given orally unless a more immediate onset is required (any benzodiazepine will decrease the withdrawal symptoms because of cross tolerance; see Chap. 76 for a list of benzodiazepines).
5. An intramuscular injection of vitamin B_1 (thiamine) followed by several days of oral administration is administered to prevent Wernicke-Korsakoff syndrome.

   B. Withdrawal (see Box 74-2)
   C. Withdrawal delirium (Box 74-3)
      1. Withdrawal delirium is a medical emergency.
      2. Death can occur from myocardial infarction, fat emboli, peripheral vascular collapse, electrolyte imbalance, aspiration pneumonia, or **suicide**.
      3. The state of delirium usually peaks 48 to 72 hours after cessation or reduction of intake (although can occur later) and lasts 2 to 3 days.

   D. Interventions
      1. Provide care in a nonjudgmental manner.
      2. Check the client frequently.
      3. Monitor vital signs and neurological signs (as often as every 15 minutes) and provide one-to-one supervision.
      4. Provide a quiet, nonstimulating environment; encourage a family member (one at a time) to stay with the client to minimize anxiety.
      5. Orient the client frequently.
      6. Explain all treatments and procedures in a quiet and simple manner.
      7. Initiate seizure precautions.
      8. Administer sedating or anticonvulsant medication as prescribed.
      9. Provide small, frequent, high-carbohydrate foods (administer antiemetic before meals as needed).
      10. Monitor intake and output.
      11. Administer vitamins (multivitamin, vitamin B complex including thiamine, and vitamin C)
      12. Assist client with activities of daily living and assist with ambulation if stable.
      13. Allow client to express fears.

BOX 74-2

Early Signs of Alcohol Withdrawal

Anorexia (nausea and vomiting may occur)
Anxiety
Easily startled
Hyperalertness
Hypertension
Insomnia
Irritability
Jerky movements
Possibly experiences hallucinations, illusions, or vivid nightmares
Possibly reports a feeling of "shaking inside"
Seizures (usually appear 7 to 48 hours after cessation of alcohol)
Tachycardia
Tremors

BOX 74-3

Manifestations of Alcohol Withdrawal Delirium

Agitation
Anorexia
Anxiety
Delirium
Diaphoresis
Disorientation with fluctuating levels of consciousness
Fever (temperature of 100° F to 103° F)
Hallucinations and delusions
Insomnia
Tachycardia and hypertension

E. Disulfiram (Antabuse) therapy
1. Description
   a. Disulfiram is an alcohol deterrent used for alcoholic dependence.
   b. The medication sensitizes the client to alcohol, so a disulfiram-alcohol reaction occurs if alcohol is ingested.
   c. The client must abstain from alcohol for at least 12 hours before the initial dose is administered.
   d. Adverse effects usually begin within several to 30 minutes after consuming alcohol and may last ½ to 2 hours.
   e. The client must avoid drinking alcohol for 14 days after disulfiram therapy has been discontinued; otherwise, the client is at risk for a disulfiram-alcohol reaction.
2. Adverse reactions
   a. Facial flushing
   b. Sweating
   c. Throbbing headache
   d. Neck pain
   e. Nausea and vomiting
   f. Hypotension
   g. Tachycardia
   h. Respiratory distress
3. Client education
   a. Educate about the effects of the medication.
   b. Ensure that the client agrees to abstain from alcohol and any alcohol-containing substances.
   c. Instruct the client that the effects of the medication may occur for several days after discontinuance.
   d. Instruct the client to avoid the use of substances that contain alcohol, such as cough medicines, rubbing compounds, vinegar, mouthwashes, and aftershave lotions.
   e. Other medications used to assist with cravings include acamprosate calcium (Campral) and naltrexone (ReVia)

F. Dealing with the client who **abuses** alcohol (Boxes 74-4 and 74-5)

V. DRUG DEPENDENCY

A. Central nervous system (CNS) depressants
1. CNS depressants can include alcohol, benzodiazepines, and barbiturates and act as a depressant, sedative, and/or hypnotic.
2. Intoxication (Box 74-6)
3. Overdose can produce cardiovascular or respiratory depression, coma, shock, convulsions, and death.
4. Overdose: If the client is awake, vomiting is induced and activated charcoal is administered; if the client is comatose, airway establishment and maintenance and gastric lavage with activated

---

BOX 74-4

Dealing With the Client Who Abuses Alcohol

Direct the client's focus to the substance abuse problem.
Identify those situations that precipitate angry feelings with the client.
Set limits on manipulative behavior and verbal and physical abuse.
Hold the client firmly to reasonable limits, consistently reinforcing rules, with reasonable consequences for breaking rules.
Hold the client accountable for all behaviors.
Assist the client to explore strengths and weaknesses.
Encourage time-out if the client is losing control.
Encourage the client to participate in group therapy and support groups.

BOX 74-5

Therapies for Substance Abuse Clients and Their Families

Behavior therapy, aversion conditioning with disulfiram (Antabuse) or another medication
Hospitalization
Psychotherapy (individual, group, family)
Support groups such as Alcoholics Anonymous, Narcotics Anonymous, Pills Anonymous, Al-Anon, Al-a-Teen, or Narc-Anon (for family members and friends of alcoholics or addicts), and Adult Children of Alcoholics
Transitional living programs (halfway houses)

---

charcoal are the priorities; seizure precautions are indicated.
5. Flumazenil (Romazicon) intravenously may be used for benzodiazepine overdose to reverse the effects.
6. Withdrawal effects include nausea, vomiting, tachycardia, diaphoresis, irritability, tremors, insomnia, and seizures; withdrawal must be treated with a carefully titrated similar drug (abrupt withdrawal can lead to death).
7. Withdrawal from CNS depressants such as barbiturates is generally treated with a barbiturate such as phenobarbital or a long-acting benzodiazepine.

B. CNS stimulants
1. CNS stimulants can include amphetamines, cocaine, and crack.
2. Intoxication (Box 74-7)
3. Overdose can produce respiratory distress, ataxia, hyperpyrexia, seizures, coma, cerebrovascular accident, myocardial infarction, and death.
4. Overdose is treated with antipsychotics and management of associated effects.
5. Withdrawal effects include fatigue, depression, agitation, apathy, anxiety, insomnia, disorientation, lethargy, and craving.

BOX 74-6

Intoxication: Central Nervous System Depressants

Drowsiness
Hypotension
Impairment of memory, attention, judgment, and social
  or occupational functioning
Incoordination and unsteady gait
Irritability
Slurred speech

BOX 74-7

Intoxication: Central Nervous System Stimulants

Dilated pupils
Euphoria
Hypertension
Impairment of judgment and social or occupational
  functioning
Insomnia
Nausea and vomiting
Paranoia, delusions, hallucinations
Potential for violence
Tachycardia

BOX 74-8

Intoxication: Opioids

Constricted pupils
Decreased respirations
Drowsiness
Euphoria
Hypotension
Impairment of memory, attention, and judgment
Psychomotor retardation
Slurred speech

BOX 74-9

Intoxication: Hallucinogens

Agitation and belligerence
Anxiety and depression
Bizarre behavior, regressive behavior, or violent behavior
Blank stare
Diaphoresis
Dilated pupils
Elevated vital signs including blood pressure
Hallucinations
Impairment of judgment and social and occupational
  functioning
Incoordination
Muscular rigidity and chronic jerking
Paranoia
Seizures
Tachycardia
Tremors

6. Withdrawal is treated with antidepressants, a dopamine agonist, or bromocriptine (Parlodel); withdrawal is primarily supportive, particularly when dealing with the severe depression and suicidal ideation that accompanies stimulant withdrawal.

C. Opioids
  1. Opioids include opium, heroin, meperidine (Demerol), morphine sulfate, codeine sulfate, methadone (Dolophine), hydromorphone (Dilaudid), OxyContin (oxycodone), and fentanyl (Sublimaze).
  2. Intoxication (Box 74-8)
  3. Overdose can produce respiratory depression, coma, shock, seizures, and death.
  4. Overdose is treated with a narcotic antagonist such as naloxone (Narcan).
  5. Withdrawal effects include yawning, insomnia, irritability, rhinorrhea, diaphoresis, cramps, nausea and vomiting, muscle aches, chills, fever, lacrimation, and diarrhea.
  6. Withdrawal may be treated by methadone detoxification or tapering dosage with other opioids.
  7. Clonidine (Catapres), an α-adrenergic blocker, assists in reducing the severity of sympathetic nervous system–generated withdrawal discomfort.
  8. Specific symptom management measures may also be used, such as bismuth subsalicylate (Kaopectate) for diarrhea and acetaminophen (Tylenol) for muscle aches.

D. Hallucinogens
  1. Hallucinogens include lysergic acid diethylamide (LSD), mescaline (peyote), psilocybin (mushrooms), and phencyclidine (PCP).
  2. Intoxication (Box 74-9)
  3. Overdose effects of LSD, peyote, and psilocybin include psychosis, brain damage, and death; effects of PCP include psychosis, hypertensive crisis, hyperthermia, seizures, and respiratory arrest.
  4. Treatment (LSD, peyote, psilocybin) involves low environmental stimuli (speak slowly, clearly, and in a low voice) and medications to treat anxiety.
  5. Treatment (PCP) involves possible gastric lavage (if alert), acidifying urine to assist in excreting drug, and interventions to treat behavioral disturbances, hyperthermia, hypertension, and respiratory distress.
  6. Withdrawal is primarily supportive and may include medications to target particular problem behaviors, such as agitation.

E. Inhalants
  1. Inhalants can include gases or liquids such as butane, paint thinner, paint and wax removers, airplane glue, nail polish remover, and nitrous oxide.

2. Intoxication (Box 74-10)
3. Overdose can cause damage to the nervous system and death.
4. Withdrawal management is mainly supportive including treating affected body systems.

F. Marijuana (*Cannabis sativa*)
1. Marijuana generally is smoked but can be ingested.
2. Marijuana causes euphoria, detachment, relaxation, talkativeness, slowed perception of time, anxiety, and/or paranoia.
3. Long-term dependence can result in lethargy, difficulty concentrating, memory loss, and possibly chronic respiratory disorders.
4. Withdrawal management is mainly supportive.

G. Other recreational and club drugs
1. Include (methylenedioxymethamphetamine, MDMA) ecstasy, GHB (gamma-hydroxybutyrate), methamphetamine (e.g., crank, meth, crystal meth), ketamine (special K)
2. Effects include euphoria, increased energy, increased self-confidence, and increased sociability.
3. Adverse effects include hyperthermia, rhabdomyolysis, renal failure, hepatotoxicity, depression, panic attacks, psychosis, cardiovascular collapse, and death.
4. The use of over-the-counter medications containing ephedrine or pseudoephedrine to manufacture illegal supplies of methamphetamine has led many states to adopt laws requiring limited sales and signatures for the purchase of these medications.
5. Programs for **addiction** also address nicotine withdrawal and the pharmacological and psychotherapeutic interventions for this problem, such as nicotine patches, nicotine inhalers, and bupropion (Zyban) for the reduction of withdrawal and cravings.
6. Anabolic steroids have also gained increased attention as increasingly adverse events, including death, have become more widely publicized.

H. Interventions: Withdrawal
1. Initiate seizure precautions.
2. Hydrate the client.
3. Monitor vital signs every hour.
4. Monitor intake and output.
5. Orient client frequently.
6. Maintain minimal stimuli.

BOX 74-10

Intoxication: Inhalants

Enhancement of sexual pleasure
Euphoria
Excitation followed by drowsiness, lightheadedness, disinhibition, and agitation
Giggling and laughter

---

7. Approach client in an accepting and nonjudgmental manner.
8. Direct client's focus to the substance **abuse** problem.
9. Assist the client with identifying situations that precipitate angry feelings.
10. Assist client to deal with emotions
11. Limit the client's placing blame or rationalizing to explain the substance **abuse** problem.
12. Assist client to use assertive techniques rather than manipulation to meet needs.
13. Set limits on manipulative behavior and verbal and physical **abuse**.
14. Maintain firm and reasonable limits, consistently reinforcing rules, with reasonable consequences for breaking rules.
15. Hold the client accountable for all behaviors.
16. Assist the client to explore strengths and weaknesses.
17. Encourage time-out if the client is losing control.
18. Encourage the client to participate in unit activities.
19. Encourage the client to participate in group therapy and support groups.
20. Box 74-11 delineates nursing care for clients.

I. Dual diagnoses
1. Sometimes the use of alcohol and drugs masks underlying psychiatric pathology.
2. Psychiatric pathology may also be precipitated by substance use and **abuse**.
3. When psychiatric disorders and substance **abuse** are both present, it is often referred to as dual diagnosis.
4. Separating psychiatric diagnosis from substance dependence can only be done over time following a sustained period of abstinence.

BOX 74-11

Withdrawal: Nursing Care

Obtain information regarding the drug type and amount consumed.
Assess vital signs.
Remove unnecessary objects from the environment.
Provide one-to-one supervision if necessary.
Provide a quiet, calm environment with minimal stimuli.
Maintain client orientation.
Ensure client's safety by implementing seizure precautions.
Use restraints, if necessary and prescribed, to prevent client from harming self and others.
Provide for physical needs.
Provide food and fluids as tolerated.
Administer medications as prescribed to decrease withdrawal symptoms.
Collect blood and urine samples for drug screening.

J. **Addiction** and **abuse** in health care professionals: Suspicious signs
1. Frequently reporting that drugs have been wasted without being witnessed by another nurse
2. Administering maximum dosages of controlled substances when other nurses do not
3. A variance in usual pain relief in the absence of a change in dosage or frequency in their patients
4. Work patterns include the following: Always volunteering to carry narcotic keys, choosing shifts in which less supervision is present, choosing work areas where the use of controlled substances is high, such as critical care units, operating room, anesthesia, trauma.
5. Nurses have a professional and ethical obligation to report impaired coworkers.
6. Most impaired nurses are able to return to work through the State Board of Nursing assistance and monitoring programs; such programs usually require strict adherence to clearly stated rules and regular reports and drug screens.

K. Codependency issues
1. Codependency refers to the presence of coexisting behaviors present in a significant other, which serves to enable the addict or alcoholic to continue the irresponsible patterns of use without experiencing consequences.
2. Examples of codependency: Paying bills for which the addict or alcoholic is responsible, bailing the addict or alcoholic out of jail, helping the addict or alcoholic to call in sick.
3. It is important to address codependency issues with the family to maximize the chance for recovery of both the client with the **addiction** and the person with the codependent behaviors.

PRACTICE QUESTIONS

1. The nurse is monitoring a client who abuses alcohol for signs of alcohol withdrawal. Which of the following would alert the nurse to the potential for withdrawal delirium?
   1. Hypotension, ataxia, hunger
   2. Stupor, agitation, muscular rigidity
   3. Hypotension, coarse hand tremors, agitation
   4. Hypertension, changes in level of consciousness, hallucinations

2. The spouse of a client admitted to the mental health unit for alcohol withdrawal says to the nurse, "I should get out of this bad situation." The most helpful response by the nurse would be:
   1. "Why don't you tell your husband about this?"
   2. "What do you find difficult about this situation?"
   3. "This is not the best time to make that decision."
   4. "I agree with you. You should get out of this situation."

3. The home health nurse visits a client at home and determines that the client is dependent on drugs. Which of the following assessment questions would assist the nurse to provide appropriate nursing care?
   1. "Why did you get started on these drugs?"
   2. "How much do you use and what effect does it have on you?"
   3. "How long did you think you could take these drugs without someone finding out?"
   4. The nurse does not ask any questions for fear that the client is in denial and will throw the nurse out of the home.

4. A female client with anorexia nervosa is a member of a predischarge support group. The client verbalizes that she would like to buy some new clothes, but her finances are limited. Group members have brought some used clothes to the client to replace the client's old clothes. The client believes that the new clothes were much too tight and has reduced her calorie intake to 800 calories daily. The nurse analyzes this behavior as:
   1. Normal behavior
   2. Evidence of the client's disturbed body image
   3. Regression as the client is moving toward the community
   4. Indicative of the client's ambivalence about hospital discharge

5. The nurse determines that the wife of an alcoholic client is benefiting from attending an Al-Anon group when the nurse hears the wife say:
   1. "I no longer feel that I deserve the beatings my husband inflicts on me."
   2. "My attendance at the meetings has helped me to see that I provoke my husband's violence."
   3. "I enjoy attending the meetings because they get me out of the house and away from my husband."
   4. "I can tolerate my husband's destructive behaviors now that I know they are common with alcoholics."

6. A hospitalized client with a history of alcohol abuse tells the nurse, "I am leaving now. I have to go. I don't want any more treatment. I have things that I have to do right away." The client has not been discharged. In fact, the client is scheduled for an important diagnostic test to be performed in 1 hour. After the nurse discusses the client's concerns with the client, the client dresses and begins to walk out of the hospital room. The appropriate nursing action is to:
   1. Call the nursing supervisor.
   2. Call security to block all exit areas.
   3. Restrain the client until the physician can be reached.
   4. Tell the client that the client cannot return to this hospital again if the client leaves now.

7. The nurse is preparing to perform an admission assessment on a client with a diagnosis of bulimia nervosa, and a nursing student will be observing the nurse. The nurse asks the student about the expected assessment findings and determines that the student needs to research the disorder further if the student states that which of the following is a characteristic finding?
   1. Dental decay
   2. Loss of tooth enamel
   3. Electrolyte imbalances
   4. Body weight well below ideal range

8. The nurse is caring for a female client who was admitted to the mental health unit recently for anorexia nervosa. The nurse enters the client's room and notes that the client is engaged in rigorous push-ups. Which nursing action is appropriate?
   1. Interrupt the client and weigh her immediately.
   2. Interrupt the client and offer to take her for a walk.
   3. Allow the client to complete her exercise program.
   4. Tell the client that she is not allowed to exercise rigorously.

9. The nurse is caring for a client with anorexia nervosa. The nurse is monitoring the behavior of the client and understands that the client with anorexia nervosa manages anxiety by:
   1. Engaging in immoral acts
   2. Always reinforcing self-approval
   3. Observing rigid rules and regulations
   4. Having the need always to make the right decision

10. The client with a diagnosis of anorexia nervosa, who is in a state of starvation, is in a two-bed room. A newly admitted client will be assigned to this client's room. Which of the following clients would be an appropriate choice as this client's roommate?
    1. A client with pneumonia
    2. A client receiving diagnostic tests
    3. A client who thrives on managing others
    4. A client who could benefit from the client's assistance at mealtime

ALTERNATE ITEM FORMAT: MULTIPLE RESPONSE

Select the appropriate interventions for caring for the client in alcohol withdrawal. Select all that apply.
❑ 1. Monitor vital signs.
❑ 2. Maintain an NPO status.
❑ 3. Provide a safe environment.
❑ 4. Address hallucinations therapeutically.
❑ 5. Provide stimulation in the environment
❑ 6. Provide reality orientation as appropriate.

ANSWERS

1. **4**

Rationale: Some of the symptoms associated with withdrawal delirium typically are anxiety, insomnia, anorexia, hypertension, disorientation, hallucinations, changes in level of consciousness, agitation, fever, and delusions.
Test-Taking Strategy: Use the process of elimination. Review each option carefully to ensure that all the symptoms in the option are correct. Eliminate options 1 and 3 first, knowing that hypertension rather than hypotension occurs. From the remaining options, recalling that the client who is stuporous is not likely to exhibit withdrawal delirium will direct you to option 4. Review these symptoms if you had difficulty with this question.
Level of Cognitive Ability: Analysis
Client Needs: Physiological Integrity
Integrated Process: Nursing Process—assessment
Content Area: Mental health
Reference: Fortinash, K., & Holoday-Worret, P. (2004). *Psychiatric mental health nursing* (3rd ed., pp. 317, 318). St. Louis: Mosby.

2. **2**

Rationale: The most helpful response is one that encourages the client to solve problems. Giving advice implies that the nurse knows what is best and also can foster dependency. The nurse should not agree with the client, nor should the nurse request that the client provide explanations.

Test-Taking Strategy: Use therapeutic communication techniques. Eliminate option 1 because of the word *why*, which should be avoided in communication. Eliminate option 4 because the nurse is agreeing with the client. Eliminate option 3 because this option places the client's feelings on hold. Option 2 is the only option that addresses the client's feelings. Review therapeutic communication techniques if you had difficulty with this question.
Level of Cognitive Ability: Application
Client Needs: Psychosocial Integrity
Integrated Process: Communication and Documentation
Content Area: Mental health
References: Fortinash, K., & Holoday-Worret, P. (2004). *Psychiatric mental health nursing* (3rd ed., pp. 125, 319-316, 322). St. Louis: Mosby.
Stuart, G., & Laraia, M. (2005). *Principles and practice of psychiatric nursing* (8th ed., pp. 30-34). St. Louis: Mosby.

3. **2**

Rationale: Whenever the nurse carries out an assessment for a client who is dependent on drugs, it is best for the nurse to attempt to elicit information by being nonjudgmental and direct. Option 1 is incorrect because it is judgmental and off focus and reflects the nurse's bias. Option 3 is incorrect because it is judgmental, insensitive, and aggressive, which is nontherapeutic. Option 4 is incorrect because it indicates passivity on the nurse's part and uses rationalization to avoid the therapeutic nursing intervention.

Test-Taking Strategy: Use the process of elimination and therapeutic communication techniques to answer the question. Also, focus on the subject, *provide appropriate nursing care.* Review assessment of a client who is a substance abuser if you had difficulty with this question.

Level of Cognitive Ability: Analysis
Client Needs: Psychosocial Integrity
Integrated Process: Nursing Process—assessment
Content Area: Mental health
Reference: Fortinash, K., & Holoday-Worret, P. (2004). *Psychiatric mental health nursing* (3rd ed., pp. 311-313). St. Louis: Mosby.

4. 2
Rationale: Disturbed body image is a concern with clients with anorexia nervosa. Although the client may struggle with ambivalence and show regressed behavior, the client's coping pattern relates to the basic issue of disturbed body image. The nurse should address this need in the support group.

Test-Taking Strategy: Use the process of elimination, focusing on the information provided in the question, which is related directly to an altered body image. This should direct you to the correct option. Review the needs of the client with anorexia nervosa if you had difficulty with this question.

Level of Cognitive Ability: Analysis
Client Needs: Psychosocial Integrity
Integrated Process: Nursing Process—analysis
Content Area: Mental health
Reference: Fortinash, K., & Holoday-Worret, P. (2004). *Psychiatric mental health nursing* (3rd ed., pp. 322, 382, 384). St. Louis: Mosby.

5. 1
Rationale: Al-Anon support groups are a protected, supportive opportunity for spouses and significant others to learn what to expect and to obtain excellent pointers about successful behavioral changes. Option 1 is the most healthy response because it exemplifies an understanding that the alcoholic partner is responsible for his behavior and cannot be allowed to blame family members for loss of control. In option 2, the nonalcoholic partner should not feel responsible when the spouse loses control. Option 4 indicates that the wife remains codependent. Option 3 indicates that the group is viewed as an escape, not a place to work on issues.

Test-Taking Strategy: Use the process of elimination. Note the strategic words *benefiting from attending an Al-Anon group.* This will direct you to option 1. Review the purpose of this group if you had difficulty with this question.

Level of Cognitive Ability: Analysis
Client Needs: Psychosocial Integrity
Integrated Process: Nursing Process—analysis
Content Area: Mental health
Reference: Fortinash, K., & Holoday-Worret, P. (2004). *Psychiatric mental health nursing* (3rd ed., p. 322). St. Louis: Mosby.

6. 1
Rationale: A nurse can be charged with false imprisonment if a client is made to believe wrongfully that he or she cannot

leave the hospital. Most health care facilities have documents that the client is asked to sign relating to the client's responsibilities when the client leaves against medical advice. The client should be asked to sign this document before leaving. The nurse should request that the client wait to speak to the physician before leaving, but if the client refuses to do so, the nurse cannot hold the client against the client's will. Restraining the client and calling security to block exits constitutes false imprisonment. All clients have a right to health care and cannot be told otherwise.

Test-Taking Strategy: Use the process of elimination. Keeping the concept of false imprisonment in mind, eliminate options 2 and 3 because they are comparative or alike. Eliminate option 4, knowing that all clients have a right to health care. From the options presented, the best action is option 1. Review the points related to false imprisonment if you had difficulty with this question.

Level of Cognitive Ability: Application
Client Needs: Safe and Effective Care Environment
Integrated Process: Nursing Process—implementation
Content Area: Mental health
References: Fortinash, K., & Holoday-Worret, P. (2004). *Psychiatric mental health nursing* (3rd ed., pp. 319-320). St. Louis: Mosby.
Varcarolis, E., Carson, V., & Shoemaker, N. (2006). *Foundations of psychiatric mental health nursing* (5th ed., pp. 128-129). Philadelphia: W.B. Saunders.

7. 4
Rationale: Clients with bulimia nervosa initially may not appear to be physically or emotionally ill. They are often at or slightly below ideal body weight. On further inspection, the client demonstrates dental decay and loss of tooth enamel if the client has been inducing vomiting. Electrolyte imbalances are present.

Test-Taking Strategy: Focus on the subject, bulimia nervosa, and note the strategic words *need to research.* Eliminate options 1 and 2 because they are comparative or alike. From the remaining options, recall that in anorexia nervosa the body weight is normally below 85% of ideal body weight. Option 4 is a characteristic sign of anorexia nervosa, not bulimia nervosa. Review the characteristics of these disorders if you had difficulty with this question.

Level of Cognitive Ability: Analysis
Client Needs: Psychosocial Integrity
Integrated Process: Teaching and Learning
Content Area: Mental health
Reference: Fortinash, K., & Holoday-Worret, P. (2004). *Psychiatric mental health nursing* (3rd ed., pp. 380-381, 383). St. Louis: Mosby.

8. 2
Rationale: Clients with anorexia nervosa frequently are preoccupied with rigorous exercise and push themselves beyond normal limits to work off caloric intake. The nurse must provide for appropriate exercise and place limits on rigorous activities. Options 1, 3, and 4 are inappropriate nursing actions.

Test-Taking Strategy: Use the process of elimination and focus on the client's diagnosis. Also, focus on the need for the nurse to set firm limits with clients who have this disorder. If you had difficulty with this question, review interventions for the client with anorexia nervosa.

Level of Cognitive Ability: Application
Client Needs: Physiological Integrity
Integrated Process: Nursing Process—implementation
Content Area: Mental health
References: Fortinash, K., & Holoday-Worret, P. (2004). *Psychiatric mental health nursing* (3rd ed., pp. 385-386). St. Louis: Mosby.
Stuart, G., & Laraia, M. (2005). *Principles and practice of psychiatric nursing* (8th ed., p. 530). St. Louis: Mosby.

9. 3

Rationale: Clients with anorexia nervosa have the desire to please others. Their need to be correct or perfect interferes with rational decision-making processes. These clients are moralistic. Rules and rituals help the clients manage their anxiety.

Test-Taking Strategy: Use the process of elimination and focus on the subject, managing anxiety. Eliminate options 2 and 4 because of the close-ended word *always*. Option 1 is not characteristic of the client with anorexia. Review the characteristics associated with this disorder if you had difficulty with this question.

Level of Cognitive Ability: Analysis
Client Needs: Psychosocial Integrity
Integrated Process: Nursing Process—assessment
Content Area: Mental health
References: Fortinash, K., & Holoday-Worret, P. (2004). *Psychiatric mental health nursing* (3rd ed., pp. 11, 376-377). St. Louis: Mosby.
Varcarolis, E., Carson, V., & Shoemaker, N. (2006). *Foundations of psychiatric mental health nursing* (5th ed., p. 307). Philadelphia: W.B. Saunders.

10. 2

Rationale: The client undergoing diagnostic tests is an acceptable roommate. The client with anorexia nervosa is most likely experiencing hematological complications, such as leukopenia. Having a roommate with pneumonia would place the client with anorexia nervosa at risk for infection. The client with anorexia nervosa should not be put in a situation in which the client can focus on the nutritional needs of others

or being managed by others because this may contribute to sublimation and suppression of personal hunger.

Test-Taking Strategy: Use the process of elimination and note the strategic words, *in a state of starvation*. Recalling the characteristics associated with anorexia nervosa will direct you to option 2. Review care of the client with anorexia nervosa if you have difficulty with this question.

Level of Cognitive Ability: Analysis
Client Needs: Safe and Effective Care Environment
Integrated Process: Nursing Process—planning
Content Area: Mental health
References: Fortinash, K., & Holoday-Worret, P. (2004). *Psychiatric mental health nursing* (3rd ed., p. 311). St. Louis: Mosby.
Stuart, G., & Laraia, M. (2005). *Principles and practice of psychiatric nursing* (8th ed., p. 521). St. Louis: Mosby.
Varcarolis, E., Carson, V., & Shoemaker, N. (2006). *Foundations of psychiatric mental health nursing* (5th ed., pp. 303-304). Philadelphia: W.B. Saunders.

ALTERNATE ITEM FORMAT: MULTIPLE RESPONSE

Answer: 1, 3, 4, 6

Rationale: When the client is experiencing withdrawal from alcohol, the priority for care is to prevent the client from harming himself or herself or others. The nurse would provide a low stimulating environment to maintain the client in as calm a state as possible. The nurse would monitor the vital signs closely and report abnormal findings. The nurse would reorient the client to reality frequently and would address hallucinations therapeutically. Adequate nutritional and fluid intake need to be maintained.

Test-Taking Strategy: Use therapeutic communication techniques to assist in selecting the correct interventions. Also, recalling the characteristics associated with alcohol withdrawal will assist in answering correctly. Review these interventions if you had difficulty with this question.

Level of Cognitive Ability: Application
Client Needs: Psychosocial Integrity
Integrated Process: Nursing Process—implementation
Content Area: Mental Health
Reference: Fortinash, K., & Holoday-Worret, P. (2004). *Psychiatric mental health nursing* (3rd ed., pp. 319-320). St. Louis: Mosby.

REFERENCES

Fortinash, K., & Holoday-Worret, P. (2004). *Psychiatric mental health nursing* (3rd ed.). St. Louis: Mosby.
Keltner, N., Schwecke, L., & Bostrom, C. (2006). *Psychiatric nursing* (6th ed.). St. Louis: Mosby.

Stuart, G., & Laraia, M. (2005). *Principles and practice of psychiatric nursing* (8th ed.). St. Louis: Mosby.
Varcarolis, E., Carson, V., & Shoemaker, N. (2006). *Foundations of psychiatric mental health nursing* (5th ed.). Philadelphia: W.B. Saunders.

Crisis Theory and Intervention

I. CRISIS INTERVENTION

A. Description
1. **Crisis** is a temporary state of severe emotional disorganization caused by failure of **coping mechanisms** and lack of support.
2. The ability for decision making and problem solving is inadequate.
3. Treatment is aimed at assisting the client and the family through the stressful situation.

B. Phases of a **crisis**
1. Phase 1: External precipitating event
2. Phase 2
   a. Perception of the threat
   b. Increase in anxiety
   c. Client may cope or resolve the **crisis.**
3. Phase 3
   a. Failure of coping
   b. Increasing disorganization
   c. Emergence of physical symptoms
   d. Relationship problems
4. Phase 4
   a. Mobilization of internal and external resources
   b. Goal is to return the individual to at least a precrisis level of functioning.

C. Types of crises (Box 75-1)

D. **Crisis** intervention
1. Treatment is immediate, supportive, and directly responsive to the immediate **crisis.**
2. Interventions are goal-directed.
3. Feelings of the client are acknowledged.
4. Intervention provides opportunities for expression and validation of feelings.
5. Connections are made between the meaning of the event and the **crisis.**
6. Client explores alternative **coping mechanisms** and tries out new behaviors.

BOX 75-1
Types of Crises

Maturational: Relates to developmental stages and associated role changes; examples include marriage, birth of a child, and retirement.
Situational: Arises from an external source, is often unanticipated, and is associated with a life event that upsets an individual's or group's psychological equilibrium; examples include loss of a job or a change in job, change in financial status, death of a loved one, divorce, abortion, and severe physical or mental illness.
Adventitious: Relates to a crisis of disaster or an event that is not a part of everyday life and is unplanned and accidental. This type of crisis may result from a natural disaster or catastrophic event, such as a flood, earthquake, hurricane, fire, tornado, war, riots, or act of terrorism, or a crime of violence, such as rape, assault, murder, or spousal or child abuse.

II. GRIEF

A. Grief is a natural emotional response to loss that individuals must experience as they attempt to accept the loss.
B. Grief usually involves moving through a series of stages or tasks to help resolve the grief (Box 75-2).
C. Feelings associated with grief can include anger, frustration, loneliness, sadness, guilt, regret, and peace.
D. Healing can occur when the pain of the loss has lessened and the survivor has adapted to life without the deceased; the survivor will continue to experience memories of the deceased.
E. Types of grief
1. Normal grief: Physical, emotional, cognitive, or behavioral reactions can occur; the process of resolution can take months to years.

BOX 75-2
The Grief Response

STAGE 1: SHOCK AND DISBELIEF
Survivor may have feelings of numbness, difficulties with decision making, emotional outbursts, denial, and isolation.

STAGE 2: EXPERIENCING THE LOSS
Survivor may feel angry at the loved one who died or may feel guilt about the death.
Bargaining and or depression also may occur in this stage.

STAGE 3: REINTEGRATION
Survivor begins to reorganize his or her life and accepts the reality of the loss.

BOX 75-3
Children's Grief

BIRTH TO 1 YEAR
Infant has no concept of death.
Infant reacts to the loss of mother or caregiver.

1 TO 2 YEARS
Child may see death as reversible.
Grief response occurs only to the death of the significant person in the child's life.
Child may scream, withdraw, or become disinterested in the environment.

2 TO 5 YEARS
Child may see death as reversible.
Child has a sense of loss and is concerned about who will provide care.
Regressive or aggressive behavior may occur.

5 TO 9 YEARS
Child begins to see death as permanent.
Child may feel responsible for the occurrence.
Child has difficulty concentrating.

PREADOLESCENT THROUGH ADOLESCENT
Adolescent sees death as permanent.
Adolescent experiences a strong emotional reaction.
Adolescent may regress.

BOX 75-4
Communication Process

Determine how much the client and family want to know.
Determine whether there is a spokesperson for the family.
Be aware of cultural and religious beliefs and how they may affect the communication process; consider personal space issues, eye contact, and touch.
Obtain an interpreter, if necessary.
Allow opportunity for informed choices.
Assist with the decision-making process if asked; use problem solving to assist in decision making, and avoid interjecting personal views or opinions.
Encourage expression of feelings, concerns, and fears.
Be honest and truthful, and let the client and family know that you will not abandon them.
Ask the client and family about their expectations and needs.
Be a sensitive listener; sit in silence if necessary and appropriate.
Extend touch and hold the client's or family member's hand if appropriate.
Encourage reminiscing.
If you do not know what to do in a particular situation, seek assistance.
If you do not know what to say to a client or family who is talking about death, listen attentively and use therapeutic communication techniques, such as open-ended questions or reflection.
Acknowledge your own feelings; let the client and family know that the topic of conversation is a difficult one and that you do not know what to say.
Realize that it is acceptable to cry with the client and family during the grief process.

III. LOSS
A. Loss is the absence of something desired or previously thought to be available.
B. Actual loss can be identified by others and can arise in response to or in anticipation of a situation.
C. Perceived loss is experienced by one person and cannot be verified by others.
D. Anticipatory loss is experienced before the loss occurs.
E. Mourning
   1. Mourning is the outward and social expression of loss.
   2. Mourning may be dictated by cultural and religious beliefs.
F. Bereavement
   1. Bereavement includes the inner feelings and the outward reactions of the survivor.
   2. Bereavement includes grief and mourning.

IV. NURSE'S ROLE: GRIEF AND LOSS
A. The nurse's role includes communicating with the client, family members, and significant other (Box 75-4).

2. Anticipatory grief occurs before the loss and is associated with an acute, chronic, or terminal illness.
3. Disenfranchised grief occurs when a loss is experienced and cannot be acknowledged openly (societal norms do not define the loss as a loss within its traditional definition).
4. Dysfunctional grief occurs with prolonged emotional instability and a lack of progression to successful coping with the loss.
5. Children's grief is based on their developmental level (Box 75-3).

B. Allow ongoing opportunities for fully informed choices.

C. Facilitate the grief process; assess grief and assist the survivor to feel the loss and complete the tasks of the grief process.

D. Consider the survivor's culture, religion, family structure, individual life experiences, coping skills, and support systems.

E. Grief affects survivors physically, psychologically, socially, and spiritually; therefore, a multidisciplinary team approach, including a bereavement specialist, facilitates the grief process.

▲ V. END-OF-LIFE ISSUES

A. Description: End-of-life refers to issues related to death and dying.

B. Cultural and religious issues (see Chap. 6 and Box 6-4 for information regarding cultural and religious issues)

C. Legal and ethical issues
   1. Outcomes related to care during illness and the dying experience should be based on the client's wishes.
   2. Issues for consideration may include organ and tissue donations, advance directives or other legal documents, withholding or withdrawing treatment, and cardiopulmonary resuscitation.

D. Palliative care
   1. Palliative care focuses on caring interventions and symptom management rather than cure for diseases that no longer respond to treatment.
   2. A pain-controlled and symptom-controlled environment is established (the dying client should be as pain-free and as comfortable as possible).
   3. Hospice care provides support and care for clients in the last phases of incurable diseases so that they might live as fully and as comfortably as possible; client and family needs are the focus of any intervention.

E. Near-death physiological manifestations
   1. As death approaches, metabolism is reduced and the body gradually slows down until all function ends.
   2. Sensory: Client experiences blurred vision, decreased sense of taste and smell, decreased pain and touch perception, and loss of blink reflex, and appears to stare (hearing is believed to be the last sense lost).
   3. Respirations
      a. Respirations may be rapid, slow, shallow, and irregular.
      b. Respirations may be noisy and wet sounding (death rattle).
      c. Cheyne-Stokes respiration is alternating periods of apnea and deep, rapid breathing.
   4. Circulation

   a. Heart rate slows, and blood pressure falls progressively.
   b. Skin is cool to touch, and the extremities become pale, mottled, and cyanotic.
   c. Skin is wax-like very near death.
   5. Urinary output gradually decreases; incontinence may occur.
   6. Gastrointestinal motility and peristalsis diminish, leading to constipation, gas accumulation, and distension; a bowel movement may occur before death or at the time of death.
   7. Musculoskeletal system: Client gradually loses ability to move, has difficulty speaking and swallowing, and loses the gag reflex.

F. Death
   1. Death occurs when all vital organs and body systems cease to function.
   2. Generally, respirations cease first, and then the heartbeat stops a few minutes thereafter.

G. Brain death occurs when the cerebral cortex stops functioning or is irreversibly damaged.

H. Nursing care
   1. Assessment of the client; avoid repeated, unnecessary assessments on the dying client.
      a. Assessment should be limited to obtaining essential data.
      b. Frequency of assessment depends on the client's stability (at least every 8 hours); as changes occur, assessment needs to be done more frequently.
   2. Physical care (Box 75-5)
   3. Psychosocial care
      a. Monitor for anxiety and depression.
      b. Monitor for fear (Box 75-6).
      c. Encourage the client and family to express feelings.
      d. Provide support and advocacy for the client and family.
      e. Provide privacy for the client and family.
      f. Provide a private room for the client.
   4. Postmortem care (Box 75-7)
      a. Maintain respect and dignity for the client.
      b. Determine whether the client is an organ donor; if so, follow appropriate procedures related to the donation.
      c. Consider cultural rituals, state laws, and agency procedures when performing postmortem care.
      d. Prepare the body for immediate viewing by the family.
      e. Provide privacy and time for the family to be with the deceased person.

VI. DEPRESSION
A. Description (see Chap. 73)
   1. Depression affects feelings, thoughts, and behaviors.

BOX 75-5

Physical Care of the Dying Client

PAIN
Administer pain medication.
Do not delay or deny pain medication.

DYSPNEA
Elevate the head of the bed or position the client on his or her side.
Administer supplemental oxygen.
Suction fluids from the airway as needed.

SKIN
Assess color and temperature.
Assess for breakdown.
Implement measures to prevent breakdown.

DEHYDRATION
Maintain regular oral care.
Encourage taking ice chips and sips of fluid.
Do not force the client to eat or drink.
Use moist cloths to provide moisture to the mouth.
Apply lubricant to the lips and oral mucous membranes.

ANOREXIA, NAUSEA, AND VOMITING
Provide antiemetics before meals.
Have family members provide the client's favorite foods.
Provide frequent small portions of favorite foods.

ELIMINATION
Monitor urinary and bowel elimination.
Place absorbent pads under the client and check frequently.

WEAKNESS AND FATIGUE
Provide rest periods.
Assess tolerance for activities.
Provide assistance and support as needed for maintaining bed or chair positions.

RESTLESSNESS
Maintain a calm soothing environment.
Do not restrain.
Limit the number of visitors at the client's bedside.
Allow a family member to stay with the client.

BOX 75-6

Fear Associated With Dying

FEAR OF PAIN
Fear of pain may occur based on anxieties related to dying.
Do not delay or deny pain relief measures to a terminally ill client.

FEAR OF LONELINESS AND ABANDONMENT
Allow family members to stay with the client.
Holding hands, touching (if culturally acceptable), and listening to the client are important.

FEAR OF BEING MEANINGLESS
Client may feel hopeless and powerless.
Encourage life reviews and focus on the positive aspects of the client's life.

Modified from Lewis, S., Heitkemper, M., & Dirksen, S. (2004). *Medical-surgical nursing: Assessment and management of clinical problems* (6th ed.). St. Louis: Mosby.

BOX 75-7

General Postmortem Procedures

Close the client's eyes.
Replace dentures.
Wash the body.
Place pads under the perineum.
Remove tubes and dressings.
Straighten the body and place a pillow under the head in preparation for family viewing.

3. Feeling sad
4. Feeling let down or disappointed
5. Mild alterations in sleep patterns
6. Feeling less alert
7. Irritability
8. Disinterested in spending time with others
9. Increased use of alcohol or drugs

C. Moderate depression
1. Persists over time
2. The person experiences a sense of change and often seeks help.
3. Despondent and gloomy
4. Dejected
5. Low self-esteem
6. Helplessness and powerlessness
7. May experience intense anxiety and anger
8. Diurnal variation: The person may feel better at a certain time of the day, such as in the morning.
9. Slow thought processes and difficulty in concentrating
10. Rumination: Persistent thinking about and discussion of a particular subject
11. Negative thinking and suicidal thoughts
12. Sleep disturbances

2. It can occur after a loss, including loss of self-esteem, the end of a significant relationship, the death of a loved one, or a traumatic event.
3. The loss is followed by grief and mourning; if this process does not resolve, depression results.
4. Depression may be mild, moderate, or severe.
5. Treatment includes counseling, antidepressant medication, and electroconvulsive therapy (ECT).

B. Mild depression
1. Triggered by an external event, this experience follows the normal grief reaction.
2. Lasts less than 2 weeks

13. Social withdrawal
14. Anorexia, weight loss, and fatigue
15. Somatic complaints
16. Menstrual changes
17. Increased use of alcohol or drugs
D. Severe depression
    1. Intense and pervasive
    2. Despair and hopelessness
    3. Guilt and worthlessness
    4. Flat affect
    5. May show agitation and pace about
    6. Poor posture and unkempt appearance
    7. Decreased speech
    8. Self-destructive thoughts; however, the client may lack energy to act on the thought.
    9. Social withdrawal
    10. Poor concentration and overwhelmed by simple tasks
    11. Severe psychomotor retardation
    12. Anorexia and considerable weight loss
    13. Constipation and urinary retention
    14. Lack of sexual interest
    15. Terminal insomnia
    16. Diurnal variation: The person feels worse in the morning and better as the day goes on.
    17. Delusions and hallucinations
E. Interventions
    1. Altered thought processes
       a. Encourage the client to discuss losses or changes in the life situation.
       b. Encourage the client to express sadness or anger and allow adequate time for verbal responses.
       c. Assist the client in developing short-term goals.
       d. Encourage the use of problem solving and positive thinking.
       e. Limit decision making.
       f. Spend short periods of time throughout the day with the client.
       g. Be on time when a schedule is planned with the client.
       h. Sit in silence with the client who is not verbalizing.
       i. Use simple, concrete words when communicating.
       j. Avoid a cheerful attitude.
    2. Risk for self-harm
       a. Assess for **suicide** clues and intervene to provide safety precautions as necessary.
       b. Ask the client directly, "Have you thought of hurting yourself?"
       c. Assess lethality of plans.
       d. Do not leave the client alone for extended periods.
       e. If the client has a suicidal plan, place on one-to-one supervision.
       f. Form a suicidal contract with the client.
    3. Activity intolerance
       a. Encourage daily exercise.
       b. Assist with activities of daily living if the client is unable to perform them.
       c. Begin with one-to-one activities.
       d. Provide activities for easy mastery to increase self-esteem and help in alleviating guilt feelings.
       e. Provide activities that do not require a great deal of concentration (simple card games, drawing).
       f. Engage in gross motor activities (walking).
       g. Eventually bring the client into small group activities and then large groups.
    4. Altered nutrition
       a. Ensure adequate nutrition.
       b. Offer small, high-calorie, high-protein snacks and fluids throughout the day.
       c. Stay with the client during meals.
       d. Weigh the client weekly.
       e. Assess bowel patterns for constipation.
    5. Sleep pattern disturbance
       a. Ensure adequate sleep.
       b. Provide rest periods after activities.
       c. Encourage the client to dress and stay out of bed during the day.
       d. Provide relaxation measures at bedtime.
       e. Decrease environmental stimuli at bedtime.
       f. Spend time with the client before bedtime.

VII. ELECTROCONVULSIVE THERAPY (ECT)
A. Description
    1. An effective treatment for depression that consists of inducing a grand mal (tonic-clonic) seizure by passing an electrical current through electrodes attached to the temples.
    2. The administration of a muscle relaxant minimizes seizure activity, preventing damage to long bones and cervical vertebrae.
    3. The usual course is 6 to 12 treatments given two to three times per week.
    4. Maintenance ECT once a month may help decrease the relapse rate for the client with recurrent depression.
    5. ECT is not a permanent cure.
    6. Not necessarily effective in the client with dysrhythmic depression or the client with depression and personality disorders, those with drug dependence, or those with depression secondary to situational or social difficulties
    7. At-risk clients include those with recent myocardial infarction, stroke, or cerebral vascular malformation, or intracranial mass lesions.
B. Uses
    1. Clients with major depressive and bipolar depressive disorders, especially when psychotic

symptoms are present, such as delusions of guilt, somatic delusions, and delusions of infidelity

2. Clients who have depression with marked psychomotor retardation and stupor
3. Manic clients whose conditions are resistant to lithium and antipsychotic medications and clients who are rapid cyclers (a client with a bipolar disorder who has many episodes of mood swings close together)
4. Clients with schizophrenia (especially catatonia), those with schizoaffective syndromes, and psychotic clients

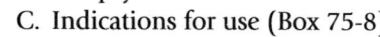 C. Indications for use (Box 75-8)

D. Preprocedure
1. Explain the procedure to the client.
2. Encourage the client to discuss feelings, including myths regarding ECT.
3. Teach the client and family what to expect.
4. Informed consent must be obtained when voluntary clients are being treated.
5. For involuntary clients, when informed consent cannot be obtained, permission may be obtained from the next of kin, although in some states the permission for ECT must be obtained from the court.
6. NPO after midnight or at least 4 hours prior to treatment
7. Baseline vital signs are taken.
8. The client is requested to void.
9. Hairpins, contact lenses, and dentures are removed.
10. Administer preoperative medication if prescribed; glycopyrrolate (Robinul) or atropine sulfate may be prescribed to prevent the potential for aspiration and to minimize bradydysrhythmias in response to electrical stimulation.

E. During the procedure
1. Place a blood pressure cuff on one of the client's arms.
2. As IV line is inserted, electroencephalographic and electrocardiographic electrodes are attached.
3. A pulse oximeter is placed on the client's finger.
4. Blood pressure is monitored throughout the treatment.
5. Medications administered may include a short-acting anesthetic such as methohexital sodium (Brevital Sodium), thiopental sodium (Pentothal), and a muscle relaxant such as succinylcholine (Anectine).
6. 100% oxygen by mask via positive pressure is administered throughout the procedure.
7. An airway or bite block is placed to prevent biting the tongue.
8. An electrical stimulus is administered; the seizure should last 30 to 60 seconds.

F. Postprocedure
1. The client will be transported to a recovery room with the blood pressure cuff and oximeter in place, where oxygen, suction, and other emergency equipment are available.
2. Once the client is awake, talk to the client and take vital signs.
3. The client may be confused; provide frequent orientation (brief, distinct, and simple) and reassurance.
4. Client returns to the nursing unit when a 90% oxygen saturation level is maintained, vital signs are stable, and mental status is satisfactory.
5. Assess the gag reflex prior to giving the client fluids, food, or medication.

G. Potential side effects
1. Major side effects with bilateral treatment are confusion, disorientation, and short-term memory loss.
2. The client may be confused and disoriented on awakening.
3. Memory deficits may occur, but memory usually recovers completely, although some clients have memory loss lasting up to 6 months.

VIII. SUICIDAL BEHAVIOR

A. Description
1. Suicidal clients characteristically have feelings of worthlessness, guilt, and hopelessness that are so overwhelming that they feel unable to go on with life and feel unfit to live.
2. The nurse caring for a depressed client always considers the possibility of **suicide**.

B. High-risk groups
1. Those with a history of previous **suicide attempts**
2. Family history of **suicide attempts**
3. Adolescents
4. Older clients
5. Disabled or terminally ill adults
6. Clients with personality disorders
7. Clients with organic brain syndrome or dementia
8. Depressed or psychotic clients

BOX 75-9
Suicidal Clues

Giving away personal, special, and prized possessions
Canceling social engagements
Making out or changing a will
Taking out or changing insurance policies
Positive or negative changes in behavior
Poor appetite
Sleeping difficulties
Feelings of hopelessness
Difficulty in concentrating
Loss of interest in activities
Client statements indicating an intent to attempt suicide
Sudden calmness or improvement in a depressed client
Client inquires about poisons, guns, or other lethal objects.

BOX 75-10
Suicidal Client: Assessment

THE PLAN
Does the client have a plan?
What is the plan, how lethal is the plan, and how likely
  is death to occur?
Does the client have the means to carry out the plan?

CLIENT HISTORY OF ATTEMPTS
What suicide attempts occurred in the past and what
  were the outcomes?
Was the client accidentally rescued?
Have the past attempts and methods been the same, or
  have methods increased in lethality?

PSYCHOSOCIAL FACTORS
Is the client alone or alienated from others?
Is hostility or depression present?
Do hallucinations exist?
Is substance abuse present?
Has client had any recent losses or physical illness?
Has client had any environmental or lifestyle changes?

9. Substance abusers
C. Clues (Box 75-9)
D. Assessment (Box 75-10)
E. Interventions
   1. Initiate **suicide** precautions.
   2. Remove harmful objects.
   3. Do not leave the client alone.
   4. Provide one-to-one supervision at all times.
   5. Provide a nonjudgmental, caring attitude.
   6. Develop a contract that is written, dated, and signed and that indicates alternative behavior at times of suicidal thoughts.
   7. Encourage the client to talk about feelings and to identify positive aspects about self.
   8. Encourage active participation in own care.
   9. Keep the client active by assigning achievable tasks.

10. Check that visitors do not leave harmful objects in the client's room.
11. Identify support systems.
12. Do not allow the client to leave the unit unless accompanied by a staff member.
13. Continue to assess the client's **suicide** potential.

IX. ABUSIVE BEHAVIORS
A. Anger
   1. Anger is a feeling of annoyance that may be displaced onto an object or person.
   2. Anger is used to avoid anxiety and gives a feeling of power in situations in which the person feels out of control.
B. Aggression can be harmful and destructive when not controlled.
C. Violence is the physical force that is threatening to the safety of self and others.
D. Assessment
   1. History of violence or self-harm
   2. Poor impulse control and low tolerance of frustration
   3. Defiant and argumentative
   4. Raising of voice
   5. Making verbal threats
   6. Pacing and agitation
   7. Muscle rigidity
   8. Flushed face
   9. Glaring at others
E. Interventions
   1. Maintain safety.
   2. Use a calm approach and communicate with a calm, clear tone of voice (be assertive, not aggressive, and avoid verbal struggles).
   3. Maintain a large personal space and use a nonaggressive posture.
   4. Listen actively and acknowledge the client's anger.
   5. Determine what the client considers to be his or her need.
   6. Provide the client with clear options that deal with the client's behavior, set limits on behavior, and make the client aware of the consequences of anger and violence.
   7. Discuss the use of **restraints** or **seclusion** if the client is unable to control angry behavior that may lead to violence.
   8. Assist the client with problem solving and decision making regarding the options.
F. **Restraints** and **seclusion**
   1. Description
      a. Physical **restraints**: Any manual method or mechanical device, material, or equipment that inhibits free movement
      b. **Seclusion**: A process in which a client is placed alone in a specially designed room for protection and close supervision

c. Chemical **restraints**: Medications given for a specific purpose of inhibiting a specific behavior or movement and that have an impact on the client's ability to relate to the environment

2. Use of **restraints** and **seclusion**

a. **Restraints** and **seclusion** should never be used as punishment or for the convenience of the health care staff.

b. **Restraints** and **seclusion** are used when behavior is physically harmful to the client or others and when alternative or less restrictive measures are insufficient in protecting the client or others from harm.

c. The nurse must document the behavior leading to the use of **restraints** or **seclusion**.

d. **Restraints** and **seclusion** are used when the client anticipates that a controlled environment would be helpful and requests **seclusion**.

e. **Restraints** require a written order of a physician, which must be reviewed and renewed every 24 hours; it also must specify the type of restraint to be used, the duration of the restraint or **seclusion**, and the criteria for release (agency policy and procedures need to be followed).

f. In an emergency, the qualified nurse may place a client in **restraints** or **seclusion** and obtain a written or verbal order as soon as possible thereafter.

g. Within 1 hour of the initiation of **restraints** or **seclusion**, the psychiatrist must make a face-to-face assessment and evaluation of the client and must continuously reevaluate the need for continued restraint or **seclusion**.

h. While in **restraints** or **seclusion**, the client must be protected from all sources of harm by having one-to-one supervision with a staff member within an arm's length of the client.

i. The client in **restraints** or **seclusion** needs constant one-to-one supervision; physical, safety, and comfort needs must be assessed every 15 to 30 minutes, and these observations are also documented (e.g., food, fluids, bathroom needs, range-of-motion exercise, and ambulation).

X. **FAMILY VIOLENCE**

A. Description (Fig. 75-1)

1. The violence begins with threats or verbal or physical minor assaults (tension building), and the victim attempts to comply with the requests of the abuser.

2. The abuser loses control and becomes destructive and harmful (acute battering) while the victim attempts to protect himself or herself.

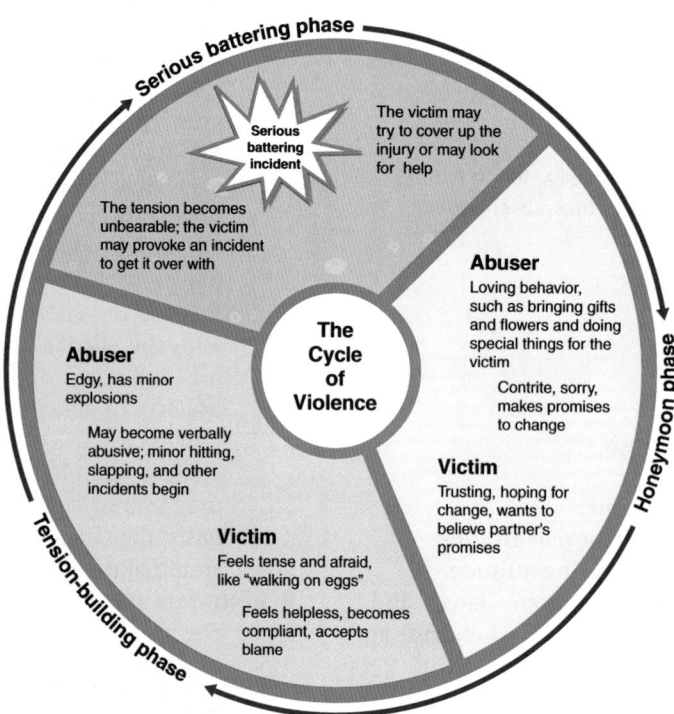

FIG. 75-1 The cycle of violence. (From Varcarolis, E., Carson, V., & Shoemaker, N. [2006]. *Foundations of psychiatric mental health nursing* [5th ed.]. Philadelphia: W.B. Saunders.)

3. Following the battering, the abuser then becomes loving and attempts to make peace (calmness and defusion of tension).
4. The abuser justifies that violence is normal and the victim is responsible for the **abuse.**
5. Outsiders are usually not aware of what is happening in the family.
6. Family members are isolated socially and lack autonomy and trust among each other; caring and intimacy in the family are absent.
7. Family members expect other members of the family to meet their needs, but none are able to do so.
8. The abuser threatens to abandon the family.

B. Types of violence (Box 75-11)

C. The vulnerable person
1. The vulnerable person is the one in the family unit against whom violence is perpetrated.
2. Those most vulnerable are children and older adults.
3. The perpetrator of violence or the person targeted by the violence can be male or female.
4. Battering is a crime.

D. Characteristics of abusers
1. Impaired self-esteem
2. Strong dependency needs
3. Narcissistic and suspicious
4. History of **abuse** during childhood
5. Perceive victims as their property and believe that they are entitled to **abuse** them

E. Characteristics of victims
1. Victims feel trapped, dependent, helpless, and powerless.
2. Victims of **abuse** may become depressed as they are trapped in the abusers' power and control cycle (see Fig. 75-1).
3. As victims' self-esteem becomes diminished with chronic **abuse,** they may blame themselves for the violence and be unable to see a way out of the situation.

F. Interventions
1. Report suspected or actual cases of child **abuse** or **abuse** of the older adult to appropriate authorities (follow state and agency guidelines).
2. Assess for evidence of physical injuries.
3. Ensure privacy and confidentiality during the assessment and provide a nonjudgmental and empathetic approach to foster trust; reassure the victim that he or she has not done anythingwrong. Box 75-12 lists sample assessment questions.
4. Assist the victim to develop self-protective and other problem-solving abilities.
5. Even if the victim is not ready to leave the situation, encourage the client to develop a specific safety plan (a fast escape if the violence returns) and where to obtain help (hotlines, safe houses, and shelters); an abused person is usually reluctant to call the police.
6. Assess suicidal potential of the victim.
7. Assess the potential for homicide.
8. Assess for the use of drugs and alcohol.
9. Determine family coping patterns and support systems.
10. Provide support and assistance in coping with contacting the legal system.
11. Assist in resolving family dysfunction with prescribed therapies.

BOX 75-11

Types of Violence

PHYSICAL VIOLENCE
Infliction of physical pain or bodily harm

SEXUAL VIOLENCE
Any form of sexual contact without consent

EMOTIONAL VIOLENCE
Infliction of mental anguish

PHYSICAL NEGLECT
Failure to provide health care to prevent or treat
physical or emotional illnesses

DEVELOPMENTAL NEGLECT
Failure to provide physical and cognitive stimulation
needed to prevent developmental deficits

EDUCATIONAL NEGLECT
Depriving a child of education

ECONOMIC EXPLOITATION
Illegal or improper exploitation of money, funds,
or other resources for one's personal gain

BOX 75-12

Assessment Questions for Violence and Abuse

"Has anyone ever touched you in a way that made you
    uncomfortable?"
"Is anyone hurting you now?"
"How do you and your partner deal with anger
    (or disagreement)?"
"Has your partner ever hit you?"
"Have you ever been threatened by_____"
"Does your partner prevent you from seeing family or
    friends"
"Does your partner ever use the children to manipulate
    you?"
"Did (or does) anyone in your family deal with anger by
    hitting?"
"Who do you play with most often? Is there anyone you
    do not like playing with? Are there games you don't
    like playing?"

12. Encourage individual therapy for the victim that promotes coping with the trauma and prevents further psychological conflict.
13. Individual therapy that focuses on preventing violent behavior and repairing relationships is encouraged for abusers.
14. Encourage psychotherapy, counseling, group therapy, and support groups to assist family members to develop coping strategies.
15. Assist the family to identify an access to community and personal resources.
16. Maintain accurate and thorough medical health records.

XI. CHILD ABUSE (see Chap. 35)

A. Description: Child **abuse** involves physical, emotional, or sexual **abuse** and also can involve neglect.
B. Assessment
   1. Physical **abuse**
      a. Unexplained bruises, burns, or fractures
      b. Bald spots on the scalp
      c. Apprehensiveness in the child
      d. Extreme aggressiveness or withdrawal
      e. Fear of parents
      f. Lack of crying when approached by a stranger
   2. Physical neglect
      a. Inadequate weight gain
      b. Poor hygiene
      c. Consistent hunger (begs or steals food)
      d. Inconsistent school attendance
      e. Constant fatigue
      f. Reports of lack of child supervision
      g. Delinquency
   3. Emotional **abuse**
      a. Speech disorders
      b. Habit disorders, such as sucking, biting, rocking
      c. Learning disorders
      d. Self-harm behaviors
   4. Sexual **abuse**
      a. Difficulty walking or sitting
      b. Torn, stained, or bloody underclothing
      c. Pain, swelling, or itching of the genitals
      d. Bruises, bleeding, or lacerations in the genital or anal area
      e. Poor peer relations
      f. Delinquency
      g. Changes in sleep patterns
      h. Self-harm behaviors
   5. Shaken baby syndrome
      a. **Abuse** can cause intracranial hemorrhage, leading to cerebral edema and death.
      b. Baby often has respiratory problems.
      c. Nurse would note full bulging fontanelles and a head circumference greater than expected.

6. Child abduction
   a. Many cases involve abduction by a family member (usually a parent) who takes or keeps the child and violates a custody order.
   b. Most vulnerable age for children abduction is younger than 6 years of age.
   c. Parents at risk for abducting their child include those who have made a prior threat of intent, cases in which there is a suspicion of **abuse** of the child, those wanting the child to grow up in their country of origin, or a parent with a mental illness, especially a sociopath.
C. Interventions
   1. Assess injuries; support the child during a thorough physical assessment.
   2. Report cases of suspected **abuse** to appropriate authorities (follow state and agency guidelines); reporting is mandated by federal law.
   3. The child will likely be removed from the abusive environment to a safe place to prevent further injury while the case is being investigated.
   4. Move slowly and avoid any loud noises when near the child.
   5. Communicate with the child at the child's eye level.
   6. Reassure the child that he or she is not "bad" and is not responsible for the abuser's behavior.
   7. Document accurately and completely all information related to the suspected **abuse**.
   8. When working with parents in follow-up care or counseling, assist the parents in identifying stressors and alternative ways to express feelings.
   9. Provide education to the parents, and refer parents to **crisis** hotlines and community support systems such as Parents Anonymous (a group for parents who have been abused or fear that they may **abuse** their child physically) or Parents United International (a group devoted to helping sexually abused families).

XII. ABUSE OF THE OLDER ADULT

A. Description
   1. **Abuse** of an older adult involves physical, emotional, or sexual **abuse** and also can involve neglect or economic exploitation.
   2. Individuals at most risk include those who are dependent because of illness, immobility, or altered mental status.
   3. Factors that contribute to **abuse** and neglect include long-standing family violence, caregiver stress, and the individual's increasing dependence on others.
   4. Victims may attempt to dismiss injuries as accidental, and abusers may prevent victims from receiving proper medical care to avoid discovery.

5. Victims often are isolated socially by their abusers.

 B. Assessment
1. Physical **abuse**
   a. Sprains, dislocations, or fractures
   b. Abrasions, bruises, or lacerations
   c. Pressure sores
   d. Puncture wounds
   e. Burns
   f. Skin tears
2. Sexual **abuse**
   a. Torn or stained underclothing
   b. Discomfort or bleeding in the genital area
   c. Difficulty in walking or sitting
   d. Unexplained genital infections or disease
3. Emotional **abuse**
   a. Confusion
   b. Fearful and agitated
   c. Changes in appetite and weight
   d. Withdrawn and loss of interest in self and social activities
4. Neglect
   a. Disheveled appearance
   b. Dressed inadequately or inappropriately
   c. Dehydration and malnutrition
   d. Lacking physical needs, such as glasses, hearing aids, and dentures
5. Signs of medication overdose
6. Economic exploitation
   a. Inability to pay bills and fearful when discussing finances
   b. Confused, inaccurate, or no knowledge of finances

C. Interventions
1. Assess for physical injuries and treat physical injuries.
2. Report cases of suspected **abuse** to appropriate authorities (follow state and agency guidelines).
3. Separate the older adult from the abusive environment, if possible, and contact adult protective services for assistance in placement while the **abuse** is being investigated.
4. Explore alternative living arrangements that are least restrictive and disruptive to the victim.
5. The older adult who has been abused may need assistance for financial or legal matters.
6. Provide referrals to emergency community resources.
7. When working with caregivers, assess the need for respite care or counseling if needed to deal with caregiver stress.

XIII. **RAPE AND SEXUAL ASSAULT**
A. Description
1. Rape is engaging another person in a sexual act and/or sexual intercourse through the use of force and without the consent of the sexual partner.

2. The victim is not required by law to report the rape or assault.
3. Often, the victim is blamed by others and receives no support from significant others.
4. Acquaintance rapes involve someone known to the victim.
5. Statutory rape is the act of sexual intercourse with a person under the age of legal consent, even if the minor consents.
6. Marital rape
   a. The belief that marriage bestows rights to sex whenever wanted and without consent of the partner contributes to the occurrence of marital rape.
   b. Victims of marital rape describe being forced to perform acts they did not wish to perform, and being physically abused during sex.

B. Assessment
1. Female client
   a. Obtain the date of the last menstrual period.
   b. Determine the form of birth control used and the last act of intercourse before rape.
   c. Determine the duration of intercourse, orifices violated, and whether penile penetration occurred.
   d. Determine whether a condom was used by the perpetrator.
2. Shame, embarrassment, and humiliation
3. Anger and revenge
4. Fear of telling others for fear of not being believed

C. It is important to note that males may be sexually abused both as children and as adults and are the usual targeted victim of pedophiles; males may have more difficulty with disclosing their **abuse.**

D. Rape trauma syndrome
1. Sleep disturbances, nightmares
2. Loss of appetite
3. Fears, anxiety, phobias, suspicion
4. Decrease in activities and motivation
5. Disruptions in relationships with partner, family, friends
6. Self-blame, guilt, shame
7. Lowered self-esteem, feelings of worthlessness
8. Somatic complaints

E. Interventions
1. Perform the assessment in a quiet, private area.
2. Stay with the victim.
3. Assess the victim's stress level before performing treatments and procedures.
4. Victim should not shower, bathe, douche (female), or change clothing until an examination is performed.
5. Obtain written consent for the examination, photographs, laboratory tests, release of information, and laboratory samples.

6. Assist with the female pelvic examination and obtain specimens to detect semen (the pelvic examination may trigger a flashback of the attack); a shower and fresh clothing should be made available to the client after the examination.
7. Preserve any evidence.
8. Treat physical injuries and provide client safety.
9. Document all events in the care of the victim.
10. Reinforce to the victim that surviving the assault is most important; if the victim survived the rape, then he or she did exactly what was necessary to stay alive.
11. Refer the victim to **crisis** intervention and support groups.

PRACTICE QUESTIONS

1. The nurse is planning care for a client being admitted to the nursing unit who attempted suicide. Which of the following priority nursing interventions will the nurse include in the plan of care?
   1. One-to-one suicide precautions
   2. Suicide precautions with 30-minute checks
   3. Checking the whereabouts of the client every 15 minutes
   4. Asking the client to report suicidal thoughts immediately

2. The emergency room nurse is caring for a client who has been identified as a victim of physical abuse. In planning care for the client, which of the following is the priority nursing action?
   1. Adhering to the mandatory abuse reporting laws
   2. Notifying the case worker of the family situation
   3. Removing the client from any immediate danger
   4. Obtaining treatment for the abusing family member

3. The emergency room nurse is caring for an adult client who is a victim of family violence. Which priority instruction would be included in the discharge instructions?
   1. Information regarding shelters
   2. Instructions regarding calling the police
   3. Instructions regarding self-defense classes
   4. Explaining the importance of leaving the violent situation

4. A female victim of a sexual assault is being seen in the crisis center. The client states that she still feels "as though the rape just happened yesterday," even though it has been a few months since the incident. The appropriate nursing response is which of the following?
   1. "You need to try to be realistic. The rape did not just occur."
   2. "It will take some time to get over these feelings about your rape."

3. "Tell me more about the incident that causes you to feel like the rape just occurred."
4. "What do you think that you can do to alleviate some of your fears about being raped again"?

5. The nurse in the emergency department is caring for a young female victim of sexual assault. The client's physical assessment is complete and physical evidence has been collected. The nurse notes that the client is withdrawn, confused, and at times physically immobile. These behaviors are interpreted by the nurse as:
   1. Signs of depression
   2. Normal reactions to a devastating event
   3. Evidence that the client is a high suicide risk
   4. Indicative of the need for hospital admission

6. The nurse has been working with a victim of rape in a clinic setting for the past 4 weeks. Which of the following is unrealistic as a short-term initial goal?
   1. Physical wounds will heal.
   2. The client will participate in the treatment plan.
   3. The client will verbalize feelings about the event.
   4. The client will resolve feelings of fear and anxiety related to the rape trauma.

7. Which of the following is the best approach for the nurse to use in crisis counseling?
   1. Reassuring
   2. Passive listening
   3. Explore early life experiences
   4. Active, with focus on current situation

8. A client comes to the clinic after losing all personal belongings in a hurricane. The nurse develops a nursing diagnosis of Coping, ineffective. Which of the following is the least realistic goal for this client?
   1. The client will develop adaptive coping patterns.
   2. The client will identify a realistic perception of stressors.
   3. The client will express and share feelings regarding the present crisis.
   4. The client will stop blaming himself or herself for the lack of insurance.

9. The nurse is reviewing the assessment data of a client admitted to the mental health unit. The nurse notes that the admission nurse has documented that the client is experiencing anxiety as a result of a situational crisis. The nurse determines that this type of crisis could be caused by:
   1. Witnessing a murder
   2. The death of a loved one
   3. A fire that destroyed the client's home
   4. A recent rape episode experienced by the client

10. The nurse is conducting an initial assessment on a client in crisis. When assessing the client's perception of the precipitating event that led to the crisis, the appropriate question to ask is:
    1. "With whom do you live?"

2. "Who is available to help you?"

3. "What leads you to seek help now?"

4. "What do you usually do to feel better?"

11. The nurse is developing a plan of care for the client in a crisis state. When developing the plan, the nurse considers which of the following?

    1. A crisis state indicates that the individual is suffering from a mental illness.

    2. A crisis state indicates that the individual is suffering from an emotional illness.

    3. Presenting symptoms in a crisis situation are similar for all individuals experiencing a crisis.

    4. A client's response to a crisis is individualized and what constitutes a crisis for one person may not constitute a crisis for another person.

12. The nurse observes that a client with a potential for violence is agitated, pacing up and down the hallway, and is making aggressive and belligerent gestures at other clients. Which statement would be appropriate to make to this client?

    1. "You need to stop that behavior now."

    2. "You will need to be placed in seclusion."

    3. "You seem restless; tell me what is happening."

    4. "You will need to be restrained if you do not change your behavior."

13. During a conversation with a depressed client on an inpatient unit, the client says to the nurse, "My family would be better off without me." The nurse's best response is:

    1. "Have you talked to your family about this?"

    2. "Everyone feels this way when they are depressed."

    3. "You will feel better once your medication begins to work."

    4. "You sound very upset. Are you thinking of hurting yourself?"

14. The nurse has been observing a client closely who has been displaying aggressive behaviors. The nurse observes that the behavior displayed by the client is escalating. Which nursing intervention is least helpful to this client at this time?

    1. Initiate confinement measures.

    2. Acknowledge the client's behavior.

    3. Assist the client to an area that is quiet.

    4. Maintain a safe distance with the client.

15. Which behavior observed by the nurse indicates a suspicion that a depressed female adolescent client may be suicidal?

    1. The client runs out of the therapy group, swearing at the group leader, and runs to her room.

    2. The client gives away a prized CD and a cherished autographed picture of the performer.

    3. The client becomes angry while speaking on the telephone and slams down the receiver.

    4. The client gets angry with her roommate when the roommate borrows the client's clothes without asking.

16. A client is admitted to the mental health unit following a serious attempt of suicide by hanging. The nurse's most important aspect of care is to maintain client safety. This is accomplished best by:

    1. Requesting that a peer remain with the client at all times

    2. Removing the client's clothing and placing the client in a hospital gown

    3. Assigning a staff member to the client who will remain with the client at all times

    4. Admitting the client to a seclusion room where all potentially dangerous articles are removed

17. The police arrive at the emergency room with a client who has seriously lacerated both wrists. The initial nursing action is to:

    1. Administer an antianxiety agent.

    2. Examine and treat the wound sites.

    3. Secure and record a detailed history.

    4. Encourage and assist the client to ventilate feelings.

18. The nursing care plan indicates a nursing diagnosis of Violence, self-directed, risk for suicidal ideations with a plan. An expected outcome of this plan of care would be that the client:

    1. Displays less anxiety and agitation

    2. Establishes a relationship with staff and peers

    3. Develops adequate coping and problem-solving skills

    4. Denies suicidal ideation and identifies options to deal with stressors

19. A client is admitted to the hospital with a nursing diagnosis of Grieving, dysfunctional related to the loss of a spouse. The client progresses well and is approaching discharge. Which of the following is an appropriate outcome for this nursing diagnosis?

    1. The client reports three additional coping strategies.

    2. The client verbalizes stages of grief and plans to attend a community grief group.

    3. The client verbalizes connections between significant losses and low self-esteem.

    4. The client verbalizes decreased desire for self-harm and discusses two alternatives to suicide.

    1. Needs to go to the bathroom.

20. The moderately depressed client who was hospitalized 2 days ago suddenly begins smiling and reporting that the crisis is over. The client says to the nurse, "I'm finally cured." The nurse interprets this behavior as a cue to modify the treatment plan by:

    1. Suggesting a reduction of medication

    2. Allowing increased "in-room" activities

    3. Increasing the level of suicide precautions

    4. Allowing the client off-unit privileges as needed

ALTERNATE ITEM FORMAT: MULTIPLE RESPONSE

A nurse is preparing to care for a dying client, and several family members are at the client's bedside. Select the therapeutic techniques that the nurse will use when communicating with the family. Select all that apply.

❏ 1. Discourage reminiscing.
❏ 2. Make the decisions for the family.
❏ 3. Encourage expression of feelings, concerns, and fears.
❏ 4. Explain everything that is happening to all family members.
❏ 5. Extend touch and hold the client's or family member's hand if appropriate.
❏ 6. Be honest and truthful and let the client and family know that you will not abandon them.

ANSWERS

1. **1**

Rationale: One-to-one suicide precautions are required for the client who has attempted suicide. Options 2 and 3 may be appropriate, but not at the present time, considering the situation. Option 4 also may be an appropriate nursing intervention, but the priority is identified in option 1. The best intervention is constant supervision so that the nurse may intervene as needed if the client attempts to cause harm to self.

Test-Taking Strategy: Use the process of elimination, noting the strategic words *attempted suicide*. Option 1 is the only option that provides a safe environment. Review interventions for the suicidal client if you had difficulty with this question.

Level of Cognitive Ability: Application
Client Needs: Safe and Effective Care Environment
Integrated Process: Nursing Process—implementation
Content Area: Mental health
References: Stuart, G., & Laraia, M. (2005). *Principles and practice of psychiatric nursing* (8th ed., p. 369). St. Louis: Mosby. Varcarolis, E., Carson, V., & Shoemaker, N. (2006). *Foundations of psychiatric mental health nursing* (5th ed., p. 481). Philadelphia: W.B. Saunders.

2. **3**

Rationale: Whenever the abused client remains in the abusive environment, priority must be placed on ascertaining whether the person is in any immediate danger. If so, emergency action must be taken to remove the person from the abusing situation. Options 1, 2, and 4 may be appropriate interventions but are not the priority.

Test-Taking Strategy: Use Maslow's Hierarchy of Needs theory, remembering that if a physiological need is not present, then safety is the priority. This should direct you to option 3, the only option that directly addresses client safety. Review care of the client who is a victim of physical abuse if you had difficulty with this question.

Level of Cognitive Ability: Application
Client Needs: Safe and Effective Care Environment
Integrated Process: Nursing Process—planning
Content Area: Delegating/Prioritizing
Reference: Varcarolis, E., Carson, V., & Shoemaker, N. (2006). *Foundations of psychiatric mental health nursing* (5th ed., p. 521). Philadelphia: W.B. Saunders.

3. **1**

Rationale: Tertiary prevention of family violence includes assisting the victim once the abuse has already occurred. The nurse should provide the client with information regarding where to obtain help. This includes a specific plan for removing self from the abuser, information as to escaping, hotlines, and the location of shelters. An abused person is usually reluctant to call the police. Teaching the victim to fight back is not the appropriate action for the victim when dealing with a violent person.

Test-Taking Strategy: Note the strategic word *priority*. Focus on the subject of the question, which relates to providing the client with a safe environment. Use Maslow's Hierarchy of Needs theory to assist in directing you to option 1. If you had difficulty with this question, review the nursing measures for caring for a victim of family violence.

Level of Cognitive Ability: Application
Client Needs: Safe and Effective Care Environment
Integrated Process: Nursing Process—implementation
Content Area: Mental health
Reference: Varcarolis, E., Carson, V., & Shoemaker, N. (2006). *Foundations of psychiatric mental health nursing* (5th ed., pp. 465, 521). Philadelphia: W.B. Saunders.

4. **3**

Rationale: Option 3 allows the client to express her ideas and feelings more fully, and portrays a nonhurried, nonjudgmental, supportive attitude on the part of the nurse. Clients need to be reassured that their feelings are normal and that they may express their concerns freely in a safe, caring environment. Option 4 places the problem solving totally on the client. Option 2 places the client's feelings on hold. Option 1 immediately blocks communication.

Test-Taking Strategy: Use the process of elimination. Option 3 is the only option that addresses the client's feelings. Always address the client's feelings first. Review therapeutic communication techniques if you had difficulty with this question.

Level of Cognitive Ability: Application
Client Needs: Psychosocial Integrity
Integrated Process: Caring
Content Area: Mental health
References: Fortinash, K., & Holoday-Worret, P. (2004). *Psychiatric mental health nursing* (3rd ed., pp. 546-547). St. Louis: Mosby.
Stuart, G., & Laraia, M. (2005). *Principles and practice of psychiatric nursing* (8th ed., pp. 30-31). St. Louis: Mosby.

5. **2**

Rationale: During the acute phase of the rape crisis, the client can display a wide range of emotional and somatic responses. The symptoms noted indicate a normal reaction to an intensely difficult crisis event.

Test-Taking Strategy: Use the process of elimination and knowledge regarding client responses to devastating events to

answer the question. Focus on the symptoms noted in the question to direct you to option 2. If you had difficulty with this question, review normal and abnormal client responses to dealing with devastating crisis events.
Level of Cognitive Ability: Analysis
Client Needs: Psychosocial Integrity
Integrated Process: Nursing Process—analysis
Content Area: Mental health
Reference: Varcarolis, E., Carson, V., & Shoemaker, N. (2006). *Foundations of psychiatric mental health nursing* (5th ed., pp. 533-534). Philadelphia: W.B. Saunders.

6. **4**
Rationale: Short-term goals include the beginning stages of dealing with the rape trauma. Clients will be expected initially to keep appointments, participate in care, begin to explore feelings, and begin to heal any physical wounds that were in-flicted at the time of the rape.
Test-Taking Strategy: Use the process of elimination and note the strategic words *unrealistic* and *short-term initial goal.* Use the process of elimination, considering each option and the real-ity of the option statement being achieved short term. Note the word *resolve* in option 4. This word should provide you with the clue that this option is a long-term goal. Review ex-pected outcomes in the plan of care for the client who has been raped if you had difficulty with this question.
Level of Cognitive Ability: Analysis
Client Needs: Psychosocial Integrity
Integrated Process: Nursing Process—planning
Content Area: Mental health
Reference: Varcarolis, E., Carson, V., & Shoemaker, N. (2006). *Foundations of psychiatric mental health nursing* (5th ed., pp. 533-534). Philadelphia: W.B. Saunders.

7. **4**
Rationale: During crisis counseling, the best approach for the nurse to use is an active one, with a focus on the current situ-ation. Options 1, 2, and 3 would be inconsistent with the acute needs that emerge in a crisis. Passive listening would be contrary to the individual's acute stress and disorganization. Exploring the past would be insensitive to the current crisis and would be exploitative of a person in acute distress. Al-though reassurance may be needed, what is most associated with the nurse's response in a crisis is the need for a direct focus on immediate needs.
Test-Taking Strategy: Focus on the subject, crisis counseling. Noting the words *current situation* in option 4 will direct you to this option. If you had difficulty with this question, review the principles of crisis intervention and counseling.
Level of Cognitive Ability: Analysis
Client Needs: Psychosocial Integrity
Integrated Process: Nursing Process—planning
Content Area: Mental health
Reference: Fortinash, K., & Holoday-Worret, P. (2004). *Psychi-atric mental health nursing* (3rd ed., pp. 515, 631). St. Louis: Mosby.

8. **4**
Rationale: Options 1, 2, and 3 identify a positive movement toward increased self-esteem and problem solving. Option 4

places undue pressure on the client by implying that the client was negligent and contributed to the loss.
Test-Taking Strategy: Use the process of elimination and note the strategic words *least realistic.* The words *realistic, adaptive,* and *express and share feelings* in options 1, 2, and 3, respec-tively, identify positive goals. This should assist in directing you to option 4. There is no data in the question that indicates that the client lacked insurance, as option 4 reflects. Review expected outcomes for the client who experienced a crisis if you had difficulty with this question.
Level of Cognitive Ability: Analysis
Client Needs: Psychosocial Integrity
Integrated Process: Nursing Process—planning
Content Area: Mental health
References: Stuart, G., & Laraia, M. (2005). *Principles and prac-tice of psychiatric nursing* (8th ed., p. 228). St. Louis: Mosby. Varcarolis, E., Carson, V., & Shoemaker, N. (2006). *Foundations of psychiatric mental health nursing* (5th ed., p. 465). Philadel-phia: W.B. Saunders.

9. **2**
Rationale: A situational crisis arises from external rather than internal sources. External situations that could precipi-tate a crisis include loss of or change of a job, the death of a loved one, abortion, change in financial status, divorce, ad-dition of new family members, pregnancy, and severe ill-ness. Options 1, 3, and 4 identify adventitious crises. An adventitious crisis is not a part of everyday life; it is un-planned or accidental.
Test-Taking Strategy: Use the process of elimination. Eliminate options 1, 3, and 4 because they are comparative types of oc-currences. If you had difficulty with this question, review the types of crisis.
Level of Cognitive Ability: Analysis
Client Needs: Psychosocial Integrity
Integrated Process: Nursing Process—analysis
Content Area: Mental health
References: Fortinash, K., & Holoday-Worret, P. (2004). *Psychi-atric mental health nursing* (3rd ed., pp. 509-510). St. Louis: Mosby.
Varcarolis, E., Carson, V., & Shoemaker, N. (2006). *Foundations of psychiatric mental health nursing* (5th ed., pp. 458-459). Philadelphia: W.B. Saunders.

10. **3**
Rationale: A nurse's initial task when assessing a client in crisis is to assess the individual or family and the problem. The more clearly the problem can be defined, the better the chance a solution can be found. Option 3 will assist in determining data related to the precipitating event that led to the crisis. Options 1 and 2 assess situational supports. Option 4 assesses personal coping skills.
Test-Taking Strategy: Use the process of elimination and note the strategic words *precipitating event.* Focus on these strategic words when selecting the correct option. Eliminate options 1 and 2 because these data will determine support systems. Eliminate option 4 because this question would be asked when determining coping skills. Review assessment tech-niques for the client in crisis if you had difficulty with this question.

Level of Cognitive Ability: Application
Client Needs: Psychosocial Integrity
Integrated Process: Nursing Process—assessment
Content Area: Mental health
References: Fortinash, K., & Holoday-Worret, P. (2004). *Psychiatric mental health nursing* (3rd ed., p. 511). St. Louis: Mosby. Varcarolis, E., Carson, V., & Shoemaker, N. (2006). *Foundations of psychiatric mental health nursing* (5th ed., p. 459). Philadelphia: W.B. Saunders.

11. **4**
Rationale: Although each crisis response can be described in similar terms as far as presenting symptoms are concerned, what constitutes a crisis for one person may not constitute a crisis for another person, because each is a unique individual. Being in the crisis state does not mean that the client is suffering from an emotional or mental illness.
Test-Taking Strategy: Use the process of elimination. Eliminate option 3 because of the word *all.* Next, eliminate options 1 and 2 because a crisis does not indicate "illness." Review the characteristics of a crisis state if you had difficulty with this question.
Level of Cognitive Ability: Analysis
Client Needs: Psychosocial Integrity
Integrated Process: Nursing Process—planning
Content Area: Mental health
References: Fortinash, K., & Holoday-Worret, P. (2004). *Psychiatric mental health nursing* (3rd ed., p. 509). St. Louis: Mosby. Varcarolis, E., Carson, V., & Shoemaker, N. (2006). *Foundations of psychiatric mental health nursing* (5th ed., pp. 459-461). Philadelphia: W.B. Saunders.

12. **3**
Rationale: The best statement is to ask the client what is causing the agitation. This will assist the client to become aware of the behavior and may assist the nurse in planning appropriate interventions for the client. Option 1 is demanding behavior that could cause increased agitation in the client. Options 2 and 4 are threats to the client and are inappropriate.
Test-Taking Strategy: Use the process of elimination. Eliminate option 1 because of the demand that it places on the client. Eliminate options 2 and 4 because they indicate threats to the client. Review appropriate nursing actions for the agitated client if you had difficulty with this question.
Level of Cognitive Ability: Application
Client Needs: Psychosocial Integrity
Integrated Process: Communication and Documentation
Content Area: Mental health
References: Fortinash, K., & Holoday-Worret, P. (2004). *Psychiatric mental health nursing* (3rd ed., p. 509). St. Louis: Mosby. Varcarolis, E., Carson, V., & Shoemaker, N. (2006). *Foundations of psychiatric mental health nursing* (5th ed., p. 502). Philadelphia: W.B. Saunders.

13. **4**
Rationale: Clients who are depressed may be at risk for suicide. For the nurse to assess suicidal ideation and plan is critical. Ask the client directly whether a plan for self-harm exists. Options 1, 2, and 3 do not deal directly with the client's feelings.

Test-Taking Strategy: Using therapeutic communication techniques will assist in directing you to the correct option. Option 4 is the only option that deals directly with the client's feelings. Additionally, clients at risk for suicide need to be assessed directly regarding the potential for self-harm. Review care of the client at risk for suicide if you had difficulty with this question.
Level of Cognitive Ability: Application
Client Needs: Psychosocial Integrity
Integrated Process: Communication and Documentation
Content Area: Mental health
Reference: Stuart, G., & Laraia, M. (2005). *Principles and practice of psychiatric nursing* (8th ed., pp. 30-34, 367). St. Louis: Mosby. Varcarolis, E., Carson, V., & Shoemaker, N. (2006). *Foundations of psychiatric mental health nursing* (5th ed., p. 330). Philadelphia: W.B. Saunders.

14. **1**
Rationale: During the escalation period, the client's behavior is moving toward loss of control. Nursing actions include taking control, maintaining a safe distance, acknowledging behavior, moving the client to a quiet area, and medicating the client, if appropriate. To initiate confinement measures during this period is not appropriate. Initiation of confinement measures is most appropriate during the crisis period.
Test-Taking Strategy: Note the strategic words *behavior, escalating,* and *least helpful.* Recalling that the least restrictive measures should be used will direct you to option 1. Review care of the client with aggressive behavior if you had difficulty with this question.
Level of Cognitive Ability: Application
Client Needs: Psychosocial Integrity
Integrated Process: Nursing Process—implementation
Content Area: Mental health
References: Fortinash, K., & Holoday-Worret, P. (2004). *Psychiatric mental health nursing* (3rd ed., p. 509). St. Louis: Mosby. Varcarolis, E., Carson, V., & Shoemaker, N. (2006). *Foundations of psychiatric mental health nursing* (5th ed., p. 502). Philadelphia: W.B. Saunders.

15. **2**
Rationale: A depressed suicidal client often gives away that which is of value as a way of saying good-bye and wanting to be remembered. Options 1, 3, and 4 deal with anger and acting-out behaviors that are often typical of any adolescent.
Test-Taking Strategy: Use the process of elimination. Eliminate options 1, 3, and 4 because they are comparative or alike. Option 2 is different and is an action that could indicate that the client may be "saying good-bye." Review behaviors that indicate a suicide intent if you had difficulty with this question.
Level of Cognitive Ability: Analysis
Client Needs: Psychosocial Integrity
Integrated Process: Nursing Process—assessment
Content Area: Mental health
References: Stuart, G., & Laraia, M. (2005). *Principles and practice of psychiatric nursing* (8th ed., p. 367). St. Louis: Mosby. Varcarolis, E., Carson, V., & Shoemaker, N. (2006). *Foundations of psychiatric mental health nursing* (5th ed., p. 477). Philadelphia: W.B. Saunders.

16. 3
Rationale: Hanging is a serious suicide attempt. The plan of care must reflect action that will ensure the client safety. Constant observation status (one to one) with a staff member who is never less than an arm's length away is the best selection. Seclusion should not be the initial intervention, and the least restrictive measure should be used. Placing the client in a hospital gown and requesting that a peer remain with the client will not ensure a safe environment.
Test-Taking Strategy: Use the process of elimination. Eliminate option 4 because seclusion should not be the initial intervention. Eliminate option 1 next, because the responsibility to safeguard a client is not the peer's responsibility. Eliminate option 2, because removing one's clothing will not maximize all possible safety strategies. Review nursing interventions for the client at risk for suicide if you had difficulty with this question.
Level of Cognitive Ability: Analysis
Client Needs: Safe and Effective Care Environment
Integrated Process: Nursing Process—implementation
Content Area: Mental health
References: Stuart, G., & Laraia, M. (2005). *Principles and practice of psychiatric nursing* (8th ed., p. 379). St. Louis: Mosby. Varcarolis, E., Carson, V., & Shoemaker, N. (2006). *Foundations of psychiatric mental health nursing* (5th ed., p. 481). Philadelphia: W.B. Saunders.

17. 2
Rationale: The initial nursing action is to assess and treat the self-inflicted injuries. Injuries from lacerated wrists can lead to a life-threatening situation. Other interventions may follow after the client has been treated medically.
Test-Taking Strategy: Use Maslow's Hierarchy of Needs theory to prioritize. Physiological needs come first. Option 2 addresses the physiological need. Review care of the client who attempted suicide if you had difficulty with this question.
Level of Cognitive Ability: Application
Client Needs: Physiological Integrity
Integrated Process: Nursing Process—implementation
Content Area: Delegating/Prioritizing
Reference: Stuart, G., & Laraia, M. (2005). *Principles and practice of psychiatric nursing* (8th ed., pp. 229, 367, 375-376). St. Louis: Mosby.

18. 4
Rationale: A suicidal client may have numerous diagnoses that encompass inadequate coping skills, anxiety, and strained interpersonal relationships. The question, however, directly and clearly designates that the problems that need to be dealt with are the "Risk for self-directed violence" and the client's "suicidal ideations with a plan." The expected outcome is that the client no longer has suicidal ideations and has identified options to deal with stress. Options 1, 2, and 3 are not related directly to the nursing diagnosis as stated in the question.
Test-Taking Strategy: When presented with a question that identifies a nursing diagnosis, use the information in the question to assist in directing you to the correct option. Option 4 is the only option that offers a resolution to the problem of "suicidal ideations with a plan" in that the client denies the "suicidal ideation and identifies options to deal with

stressors." Review the appropriate plan of care for a suicidal client if you had difficulty with this question.
Level of Cognitive Ability: Analysis
Client Needs: Psychosocial Integrity
Integrated Process: Nursing Process—evaluation
Content Area: Mental health
Reference: Stuart, G., & Laraia, M. (2005). *Principles and practice of psychiatric nursing* (8th ed., pp. 377, 381). St. Louis: Mosby.

19. 2
Rationale: The question is focused on the nursing diagnosis of Grieving, dysfunctional. The only option that deals with grief is option 2. Options 1, 3, and 4 are unrelated to this nursing diagnosis.
Test-Taking Strategy: When presented with a question that identifies a nursing diagnosis, use the information in the question to assist in directing you to the correct option. Option 2 is the only option that is focused on the nursing diagnosis of Grieving, dysfunctional. Additionally, note the word *grieving* in the question and the word *grief* in the correct option. Review expected outcomes for the client experiencing dysfunctional grieving if you had difficulty with this question.
Level of Cognitive Ability: Analysis
Client Needs: Psychosocial Integrity
Integrated Process: Nursing Process—evaluation
Content Area: Mental health
Reference: Stuart, G., & Laraia, M. (2005). *Principles and practice of psychiatric nursing* (8th ed., pp. 331, 786-787). St. Louis: Mosby.

20. 3
Rationale: A client who is moderately depressed and has only been in the hospital 2 days is unlikely to have such a dramatic cure. When a depression suddenly lifts, it is likely that the client may have made the decision to harm himself or herself. Suicide precautions are necessary to keep the client safe.
Test-Taking Strategy: Use the process of elimination. Options 1 and 4 support the client's notion that a cure has occurred. Option 2 allows the client to increase isolation and would present a threat to the client's safety. Safety is of the utmost importance; therefore, option 3 is the correct option. Review care of the client with depression if you had difficulty with this question.
Level of Cognitive Ability: Analysis
Client Needs: Safe and Effective Care Environment
Integrated Process: Nursing Process—planning
Content Area: Mental health
References: Fortinash, K., & Holoday-Worret, P. (2004). *Psychiatric mental health nursing.* (3rd ed., pp. 216-217). St. Louis: Mosby. Stuart, G., & Laraia, M. (2005). *Principles and practice of psychiatric nursing* (8th ed., pp. 335, 811). St. Louis: Mosby.

ALTERNATE ITEM FORMAT: MULTIPLE RESPONSE

Answer: 3, 5, 6
Rationale: The nurse must determine whether there is a spokesperson for the family and how much the client and family want to know. The nurse needs to allow the family and

client the opportunity for informed choices and assist with the decision-making process if asked. The nurse should encourage expression of feelings, concerns, and fears, as well as reminiscing. The nurse needs to be honest and truthful and let the client and family know that they will not be abandoned. Extend touch and hold the client's or family member's hand, if appropriate.

Test-Taking Strategy: Recalling therapeutic communication techniques and client and family rights will assist you in answering this question. Review these techniques and care of the dying client if you had difficulty with this question.

Level of Cognitive Ability: Application
Client Needs: Psychosocial Integrity
Integrated Process: Caring
Content Area: Mental health
References: Potter, P., & Perry, A. (2005). *Fundamentals of nursing* (6th ed., pp. 586-587). St. Louis: Mosby.
Varcarolis, E., Carson, V., & Shoemaker, N. (2006). *Foundations of psychiatric mental health nursing* (5th ed., p. 606). Philadelphia: W.B. Saunders.

REFERENCES

Fortinash, K., & Holoday-Worret, P. (2004). *Psychiatric mental health nursing* (3rd ed.). St. Louis: Mosby.

Potter, P., & Perry, A. (2005). *Fundamentals of nursing* (6th ed.). St. Louis: Mosby.

Stuart, G., & Laraia, M. (2005). *Principles and practice of psychiatric nursing* (8th ed.). St. Louis: Mosby.

Varcarolis, E., Carson, V., & Shoemaker, N. (2006). *Foundations of psychiatric mental health nursing* (5th ed.). Philadelphia: W.B. Saunders.

Psychiatric Medications

I. SELECTIVE SEROTONIN REUPTAKE INHIBITORS (SSRIs) (Box 76-1)

A. Description
1. Inhibit serotonin uptake and elicit an antidepressant response
2. The potential for medication interactions is high and complete medication assessments must be obtained and evaluated; inquire about the use of herbal therapies, especially St. John's wort.

B. Side effects
1. Nausea, vomiting, cramping, and diarrhea
2. Dry mouth
3. Central nervous system (CNS) stimulation, including akathisia (restlessness, agitation)
4. Photosensitivity
5. Insomnia, somnolence (sleepy, drowsy)
6. Nervousness
7. Headache, dizziness
8. Seizure activity
9. Weight loss or gain
10. Decreased libido
11. Apathy
12. Tremors
13. Increased sweating

C. Interventions
1. SSRIs interact with a number of medications.
2. Monitor vital signs because SSRIs can potentially lower or elevate blood pressure.
3. Monitor weight.
4. Initiate safety precautions, particularly if dizziness occurs.
5. Instruct the client to avoid alcohol.
6. Administer with a snack or meal to reduce the risk of dizziness and lightheadedness.
7. Monitor the suicidal client, especially during improved mood and increased energy levels.

BOX 76-1
Reuptake Inhibitors

SELECTIVE SEROTONIN REUPTAKE INHIBITORS
Citalopram (Celexa)
Escitalopram (Lexapro)
Fluoxetine (Prozac)
Fluvoxamine
Paroxetine hydrochloride (Paxil, Pexeva)
Sertraline hydrochloride (Zoloft)

SEROTONIN-NOREPINEPHRINE REUPTAKE INHIBITORS
Venlafaxine (Effexor)
Duloxetine (Cymbalta)

ATYPICAL ANTIDEPRESSANTS
Amoxapine
Bupropion hydrochloride (Wellbutrin)
Mirtazapine (Remeron)
Nefazodone
Reboxetine (Vestra)
Trazodone (Desyrel)

---

8. Instruct the client taking fluoxetine (Prozac) and bupropion (Wellbutrin) to take the medication early in the day to prevent interference with sleep.
9. For the client on long-term therapy, monitor liver and renal function test results; altered values may occur requiring dosage adjustments.
10. Monitor white blood cell and neutrophil counts; the medication may be discontinued if levels fall below normal.
11. If priapism (painful, prolonged penile erection) occurs, the medication is withheld and the physician is notified.
12. Inform the client about the possibility of decreased libido.

13. Instruct the client to change positions slowly to avoid a hypotensive effect.
14. Instruct the client to report any visual changes to the physician.
15. Educate the client about the potential for a discontinuation syndrome if medication is stopped abruptly rather than tapered; the syndrome is characterized by gastrointestinal (GI) distress, behavioral or perceptual oddities, movement problems, and sleep disturbances.
16. Be aware of the potential for serotonin syndrome characterized by elevated temperature, muscle rigidity, elevated creatine phosphokinase (CPK) levels; this risk is greatly increased when SSRIs are given with monoamine oxidase inhibitors (MAOIs). Thus, this medication combination needs to be avoided.
17. Instruct the client that over-the-counter (OTC) cold medicines can increase the likelihood of serotonin syndrome.
18. In pregnancy, consultation with an obstetrician is recommended regarding taking these medications.
19. Monitor the medication response in children, adolescents, and the older client because the response may be different than in an adult client.
20. Encourage psychotherapy.

II. TRICYCLIC ANTIDEPRESSANTS (TCAs) (Box 76-2)
A. Description
1. Block the reuptake of norepinephrine (and serotonin) at the presynaptic neuron; used to treat depression
2. May reduce seizure threshold.
3. May reduce effectiveness of antihypertensive agents.
4. Concurrent use with alcohol or antihistamines can cause CNS depression.
5. Concurrent use with MAOIs can cause hypertensive crisis.
6. Cardiac toxicity can occur and all clients should undergo electrocardiographic evaluation prior to treatment and periodically thereafter.
7. Overdose is life-threatening, necessitating immediate treatment (Box 76-3).
8. The tricyclic antidepressant clomipramine (Anafranil) may be used to treat obsessive-compulsive disorder.
B. Side effects
1. Anticholinergic effects: Dry mouth, difficulty voiding, dilated pupils and blurred vision, decreased gastrointestinal motility, constipation
2. Photosensitivity
3. Cardiovascular disturbances such as tachycardia, dysrhythmias

4. Orthostatic hypotension
5. Sedation
6. Weight gain
7. Anxiety, restlessness, irritability
8. Decreased or increased libido with ejaculatory and erection disturbances
C. Interventions
1. Instruct the client that the medication may take several weeks to produce the desired effect (client response may not occur until 2 to 4 weeks after the first dose).
2. Monitor the suicidal client, especially during improved mood and increased energy levels.
3. Instruct the client to change positions slowly to avoid a hypotensive effect.
4. Monitor pattern of daily bowel activity.
5. Assess for urinary retention.
6. For the client on long-term therapy, monitor liver and renal function test results.

BOX 76-2
Tricyclic Antidepressants

Amitriptyline hydrochloride
Clomipramine (Anafranil)
Desipramine hydrochloride (Norpramin)
Doxepin hydrochloride (Sinequan)
Imipramine hydrochloride (Tofranil)
Maprotiline
Nortriptyline hydrochloride (Aventyl, Pamelor)
Protriptyline hydrochloride (Vivactil)
Trimipramine maleate (Surmontil)

BOX 76-3
Symptoms and Interventions for Tricyclic Antidepressant Overdose

SYMPTOMS
Dysrhythmias, including tachycardia, intraventricular blocks, complete atrioventricular block, ventricular fibrillation
Hypothermia
Flushing
Dry mouth
Dilation of the pupils
Confusion, agitation, hallucinations
Seizures followed by coma

INTERVENTIONS
Maintain a patent airway.
Monitor vital signs.
Obtain an ECG.
Gastric lavage with activated charcoal to prevent further medication absorption
Physostigmine (a cholinesterase inhibitor) to counteract anticholinergic actions
Antidysrhythmic medications

7. Administer with food or milk if gastrointestinal distress occurs.

8. Administer the entire daily oral dose at one time, preferably at bedtime.

9. Instruct the client to avoid alcohol and nonprescription medications to prevent adverse medication interactions.

10. Instruct the client to avoid driving and other activities requiring alertness until the response is known; sedation is expected in early therapy and may subside with time.

11. When the medication is discontinued by the physician, it should be tapered gradually.

12. The potential for medication interactions with OTC cold medication exists.

13. Caution the client about photosensitivity and to take measures to prevent exposure to sunlight.

14. Encourage oral hygiene and the use of hard candies and mouth rinses to relieve dry mouth.

15. Encourage psychotherapy.

III. MONOAMINE OXIDASE INHIBITORS (MAOIs) (Box 76-4)

A. Description
   1. Inhibit the enzyme monoamine oxidase, which is present in the brain, blood platelets, liver, spleen, and kidneys
   2. Monoamine oxidase metabolizes amines, norepinephrine, and serotonin, so the concentration of these amines increases with MAOI.
   3. Used for depression in the client who has not responded to other antidepressant therapies, including electroconvulsive therapy
   4. Concurrent use with amphetamines, antidepressants, dopamine, epinephrine, guanethidine, levodopa, methyldopa, nasal decongestants, norepinephrine, reserpine, tyramine-containing foods, or vasoconstrictors may cause hypertensive crisis.
   5. Concurrent use with opioid analgesics may cause hypertension, hypotension, coma, or seizures.

B. Side effects
   1. Orthostatic hypotension
   2. Restlessness
   3. Insomnia
   4. Dizziness
   5. Weakness, lethargy
   6. Gastrointestinal upset
   7. Dry mouth
   8. Weight gain
   9. Peripheral edema
   10. Anticholinergic effects
   11. CNS stimulation, including anxiety, agitation, mania
   12. Delay in ejaculation

C. Hypertensive crisis
   1. Hypertension

BOX 76-4
Monoamine Oxidase Inhibitors

Isocarboxazid (Marplan)
Phenelzine sulfate (Nardil)
Tranylcypromine sulfate (Parnate)
Moclobemide

---

   2. Occipital headache radiating frontally
   3. Neck stiffness and soreness
   4. Nausea and vomiting
   5. Sweating
   6. Fever and chills
   7. Clammy skin
   8. Dilated pupils
   9. Palpitations, tachycardia, or bradycardia
   10. Constricting chest pain
   11. Antidote for hypertensive crisis: 5 to 10 mg phentolamine (Regitine), intravenous injection

D. Interventions
   1. Monitor blood pressure frequently for hypertension.
   2. Monitor for signs of hypertensive crisis.
   3. If palpitations or frequent headaches occur, withhold the medication and notify the physician.
   4. Administer with food if gastrointestinal distress occurs.
   5. Instruct the client that the medication effect may be noted during the first week of therapy, but maximum benefit may take up to 3 weeks.
   6. Instruct the client to report headache, neck stiffness, or neck soreness immediately.
   7. Instruct the client to change positions slowly to prevent orthostatic hypotension.
   8. Instruct the client to avoid caffeine or OTC preparations such as weight-reducing pills or medications for hay fever and colds.
   9. Monitor for client compliance with medication administration.
   10. Instruct the client to carry a Medic-Alert card indicating that an MAOI medication is being taken.
   11. Avoid administering the medication in the evening because insomnia may result.
   12. When the medication is discontinued by the physician, it should be discontinued gradually.
   13. Instruct the client to avoid foods that require bacteria or molds for their preparation or preservation, and those that contain tyramine (Fig. 76-1; Box 76-5).

IV. MOOD STABILIZERS (Box 76-6)

A. Description: Affect cellular transport mechanism and enhance serotonin and/or gamma-aminobutyric acid (GABA) function, which are associated with mood.

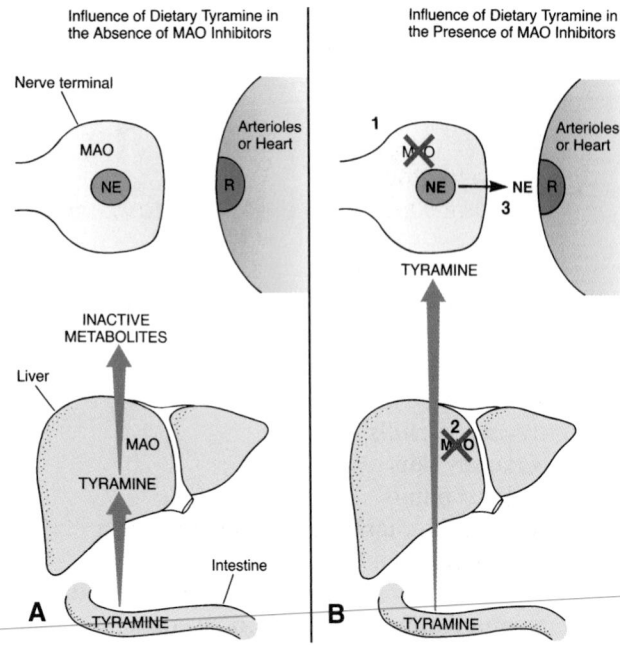

Influence of Dietary Tyramine in the Absence of MAO Inhibitors

Influence of Dietary Tyramine in the Presence of MAO Inhibitors

FIG. 76-1 Interaction between dietary tyramine and monoamine oxidase inhibitors (MAOIs). **A,** In the absence of MAOIs, dietary tyramine is absorbed from the intestine, transported to the liver, and then immediately activated by MAO. No tyramine reaches the general circulation. **B,** Three events occur in the presence of MAOIs: (1) inhibition of neuronal MAO raises levels of norepinephrine (NE) in sympathetic nerve terminals; (2) inhibition of hepatic MAO allows dietary tyramine to pass through the liver and enter systemic circulation intact; (3) on reaching peripheral sympathetic nerve terminals, tyramine promotes the release of accumulated NE stores, thereby causing massive vasoconstriction and excessive stimulation of the heart. *MAO,* Monoamine oxidase; *R,* receptor for NE. (From Lehne, R. [2007]. *Pharmacology for nursing care* [6th ed.]. Philadelphia: W.B. Saunders.)

B. Lithium
  1. Concurrent use with diuretics, fluoxetine (Prozac), methyldopa, or nonsteroidal anti-inflammatory drugs (NSAIDs) increases lithium reabsorption by the kidney or inhibits lithium excretion, either of which increases the risk of lithium toxicity.
  2. Acetazolamide (Diamox), aminophylline, phenothiazines, or sodium bicarbonate may increase renal excretion of lithium, reducing its effectiveness.
  3. The therapeutic dose is only slightly less than the amount producing toxicity.
  4. The therapeutic drug serum level of lithium is 0.6 to 1.2 mEq/L; the actual dose at which the therapeutic effect is achieved and the levels at which toxicity appears is highly variable among individuals.
  5. The causes of an increase in the lithium level include decreased sodium intake, fluid and elec-

---

BOX 76-5
Foods to Avoid That Contain Tyramine

Avocados
Bananas
Beef or chicken liver
Brewer's yeast
Broad beans
Caffeine, such as in coffee, tea, or chocolate
Cheese, especially aged, except cottage cheese
Figs
Meat extracts and tenderizers
Overripe fruit
Papaya
Pickled herring
Raisins
Red wine, beer, sherry
Sausage, bologna, pepperoni, salami
Sour cream
Soy sauce
Yogurt

BOX 76-6
Mood Stabilizers

LITHIUM PREPARATIONS
Lithium carbonate (Eskalith, Lithobid)
Lithium citrate

OTHER MOOD STABILIZERS
Aripiprazole (Abilify)
Carbamazepine (Tegretol)
Gabapentin (Neurontin)
Lamotrigine (Lamictal)
Olanzapine (Zyprexa)
Olanzapine/fluoxetine (Symbyax)
Oxcarbazepine (Trileptal)
Quetiapine (Seroquel)
Risperidone (Risperdal)
Valproate sodium (Depakene, Depakote, Depacon)
Ziprasidone (Geodon)

---

trolyte loss associated with severe sweating, dehydration, diarrhea, or diuretic therapy, and illness or overdose.
  6. Serum lithium levels should be checked every 1 to 2 months or whenever any behavioral change suggests an altered serum level.
  7. Blood samples to check serum lithium levels should be drawn in the morning, 12 hours after the last dose was taken.
C. Side effects
  1. Polyuria
  2. Polydipsia
  3. Anorexia, nausea
  4. Dry mouth
  5. Mild thirst
  6. Weight gain

7. Abdominal bloating
8. Soft stools or diarrhea
9. Fine hand tremors
10. Inability to concentrate
11. Muscle weakness
12. Lethargy
13. Fatigue
14. Headache
15. Hair loss
16. Hypothyroidism

D. Interventions
1. Monitor the suicidal client, especially during improved mood and increased energy levels.
2. Administer the medication with food to minimize gastrointestinal irritation.
3. Instruct the client to maintain a fluid intake of six to eight glasses of water a day.
4. Instruct the client to avoid excessive amounts of coffee, tea, or cola, which have a diuretic effect.
5. Instruct the client to maintain an adequate salt intake.
6. Do not administer diuretics while the client is taking lithium.
7. Instruct the client to avoid alcohol.
8. Instruct the client to avoid OTC medications.
9. Instruct the client that he or she may take a missed dose within 2 hours of the scheduled time; otherwise, the client should skip the missed dose and take the next dose at the scheduled time.
10. Instruct the client not to adjust the dosage without consulting the physician because lithium should be tapered and not discontinued abruptly.
11. Instruct the client of the signs and symptoms of lithium toxicity.
12. Instruct the client to notify the physician if polyuria, prolonged vomiting, diarrhea, or fever occurs.
13. Instruct the client that the therapeutic response to the medication will be noted in 1 to 3 weeks.
14. Monitor the electrocardiogram (ECG), renal function tests, and thyroid tests (ensure that these tests are performed before the start of therapy).
15. Instruct the client to take the medication with food or milk to decrease GI upset.
16. Monitor weight.

E. Lithium toxicity
1. Description
    a. Occurs when ingested lithium cannot be detoxified and excreted by the kidneys
    b. Symptoms of toxicity begin to appear when the serum lithium level is 1.5 to 2 mEq/L.
2. Mild toxicity
    a. Serum lithium level is 1.5 mEq/L.
    b. Apathy

c. Lethargy
d. Diminished concentration
e. Mild ataxia
f. Coarse hand tremors
g. Slight muscle weakness
3. Moderate toxicity
    a. Serum lithium level between 1.5 to 2.5 mEq/L
    b. Nausea, vomiting
    c. Severe diarrhea
    d. Mild to moderate ataxia and incoordination
    e. Slurred speech
    f. Tinnitus
    g. Blurred vision
    h. Muscle twitching
    i. Irregular tremor
4. Severe toxicity
    a. Serum lithium level is higher than 2.5 mEq/L
    b. Nystagmus
    c. Muscle fasciculations
    d. Deep tendon hyperreflexia
    e. Visual or tactile hallucinations
    f. Oliguria or anuria
    g. Impaired level of consciousness
    h. Tonic-clonic seizures or coma, leading to death
5. Interventions for lithium toxicity
    a. Withhold lithium and notify the physician.
    b. Monitor vital signs and level of consciousness.
    c. Monitor cardiac status.
    d. Prepare to obtain samples monitoring lithium, electrolyte, blood urea nitrogen, and creatinine levels and complete blood cell count.
    e. Monitor for suicidal tendencies and institute **suicide** precautions.

V. ANTIANXIETY OR ANXIOLYTIC MEDICATIONS
A. Description
1. Antianxiety medications depress the CNS, thereby increasing the effects of GABA, which produces relaxation and may depress the limbic system.
2. Benzodiazepines have anxiety-reducing (anxiolytic), sedative-hypnotic, muscle-relaxing, and anticonvulsant actions (Box 76-7).
3. Benzodiazepines are contraindicated in clients with acute narrow-angle glaucoma and should be used cautiously in children and older clients.
4. Benzodiazepines interact with other CNS medications, producing an additive effect.
5. Abrupt withdrawal of benzodiazepines can be potentially life-threatening and withdrawal should only be done under medical supervision.

B. Side effects
1. Daytime sedation
2. Ataxia
3. Dizziness
4. Headaches

5. Blurred or double vision
6. Hypotension
7. Tremor
8. Amnesia
9. Slurred speech
10. Urinary incontinence
11. Constipation
12. Paradoxical CNS excitement
13. Lethargy
14. Behavioral change

C. Acute toxicity
1. Somnolence
2. Confusion
3. Diminished reflexes and coma
4. Flumazenil (Romazicon), a benzodiazepine antagonist administered intravenously, will reverse benzodiazepine intoxication in 5 minutes.
5. The client being treated for an overdose of a benzodiazepine may experience agitation, restlessness, discomfort, and anxiety.

D. Interventions
1. Monitor for motor responses such as agitation, trembling, and tension.
2. Monitor for autonomic responses such as cold clammy hands and sweating.
3. Monitor for paradoxical CNS excitement during early therapy, particularly in older and debilitated individuals.
4. Monitor for visual disturbances because the medications can worsen glaucoma.
5. Monitor liver and renal function test results and complete blood cell counts.
6. Reduce the medication dose as prescribed for the older adult client and for the client with impaired liver function.
7. Initiate safety precautions, because the older adult client is at risk for falling when taking the medication for sleep or anxiety.

8. Assist with ambulation if drowsiness or lightheadedness occurs.
9. Instruct the client that drowsiness usually disappears during continued therapy.
10. Instruct the client to avoid tasks that require alertness until the response to the medication is established.
11. Instruct the client to avoid alcohol.
12. Instruct the client not to take other medications without consulting the physician.
13. Instruct the client not to stop the medication abruptly (can result in seizure activity).

E. Withdrawal
1. To lessen withdrawal symptoms, the dosage of a benzodiazepine should be tapered gradually over 2 to 6 weeks.
2. Abrupt or too rapid withdrawal results in the following:
   a. Restlessness
   b. Irritability
   c. Insomnia
   d. Hand tremors
   e. Abdominal or muscle cramps
   f. Sweating
   g. Vomiting
   h. Seizures

VI. BARBITURATES AND SEDATIVE-HYPNOTICS
(Box 76-8)
A. Description
1. These medications depress the reticular activating system by promoting the inhibitory synaptic action of the neurotransmitter GABA.
2. These medications are used for short-term treatment of insomnia or for sedation to relieve anxiety, tension, and apprehension.
B. Side effects
1. Dizziness and drowsiness

BOX 76-7
Benzodiazepines

Alprazolam (Xanax, Niravam)
Chlordiazepoxide (Librium)
Clonazepam (Klonopin)
Clorazepate (Tranxene)
Diazepam (Valium)
Estazolam (ProSom)
Flurazepam (Dalmane)
Lorazepam (Ativan)
Midazolam (Versed)
Oxazepam (Serax)
Quazepam (Doral)
Temazepam (Restoril)
Triazolam (Halcion)

NONBENZODIAZEPINE ANXIOLYTICS
Buspirone (BuSpar)

BOX 76-8
Barbiturates and Sedative-Hypnotics

BARBITURATES
Amobarbital (Amytal)
Butabarbital (Butisol)
Pentobarbital (Nembutal)
Phenobarbital (Luminal)
Secobarbital (Seconal)

SEDATIVE-HYPNOTICS
Chloral hydrate (Aquachloral Supprettes, Somnote)
Eszopiclone (Lunesta)
Meprobamate (Miltown)
Paraldehyde (Paral)
Ramelteon (Rozerem)
Zaleplon (Sonata)
Zolpidem (Ambien)

2. Confusion
3. Irritability
4. Allergic reactions
5. Agranulocytosis
6. Thrombocytopenic purpura
7. Megaloblastic anemia

C. Overdose
1. Tachycardia
2. Hypotension
3. Cold and clammy skin
4. Dilated pupils
5. Weak and rapid pulse
6. Signs of shock
7. Depressed respirations
8. Absent reflexes
9. Coma and death may result from respiratory and cardiovascular collapse.

D. Withdrawal
1. Severe withdrawal symptoms begin within 24 hours after the medication is discontinued in an individual with severe medication dependence.
2. Gradual withdrawal is used to detoxify a dependent client.
3. Anxiety
4. Insomnia
5. Nightmares
6. Daytime agitation
7. Tremors
8. Delirium
9. Seizures
10. Behavioral changes

E. Interventions
1. Administer lower doses as prescribed for the older client.
2. Medications should be used with caution in the client who has suicidal tendencies or has a history of drug addiction.
3. Maintain safety by supervising ambulation and using side rails at night.
4. Instruct the client to take the medication as directed.
5. Instruct the client to avoid driving or operating hazardous equipment if drowsiness, dizziness, or unsteadiness occurs.
6. Instruct the client to avoid alcohol.
7. For insomnia, instruct the client to take the medication 30 minutes before bedtime; avoid taking with a heavy meal to help absorption.
8. Instruct the client that a hangover effect may occur in the morning.
9. Instruct the client not to discontinue the medication abruptly.
10. Instruct the client taking chloral hydrate to take the medication with food and a full glass of water, fruit juice, or ginger ale to prevent gastric irritation.

VII. ANTIPSYCHOTIC MEDICATIONS (Box 76-9)

A. Description
1. Improve the thought processes and the behavior of the client with psychotic symptoms, especially the client with schizophrenia.
2. Affect dopamine receptors in the brain, thereby reducing the psychotic symptoms
3. Typical antipsychotics are more effective for positive symptoms of schizophrenia such as hallucinations, aggression, and delusions; typical antipsychotic medications also block the chemoreceptor trigger zone and vomiting center in the brain, producing an antiemetic effect.
4. Atypical antipsychotics are more effective for the negative symptoms of schizophrenia, such as withdrawal, apathy, and alogia.
5. The effects of antipsychotic medications will be potentiated when given with other medications acting on the CNS.

B. Side effects (Box 76-10)

C. Extrapyramidal syndrome
1. Parkinsonism
   a. Tremors
   b. Mask-like facies
   c. Rigidity
   d. Shuffling gait
2. Dystonia
   a. Facial grimacing
   b. Abnormal or involuntary eye movements
3. Akathisia
   a. Restlessness
   b. Constant moving about
4. Tardive dyskinesia
   a. Protrusion of the tongue
   b. Chewing motions
   c. Involuntary movements of the body and extremities

BOX 76-9
Antipsychotic Medications

TYPICAL ANTIPSYCHOTICS
Chlorpromazine hydrochloride (Thorazine)
Fluphenazine decanoate (Prolixin Decanoate)
Haloperidol (Haldol)
Loxapine (Loxitane)
Molindone hydrochloride (Moban)
Pimozide (Orap)
Thiothixene hydrochloride (Navane)
Trifluoperazine

ATYPICAL ANTIPSYCHOTICS
Aripiprazole (Abilify)
Clozapine (Clozaril)
Olanzapine (Zyprexa)
Quetiapine (Seroquel)
Risperidone (Risperdal)
Ziprasidone (Geodon)

BOX 76-10

Side Effects of Antipsychotic Medications

ANTICHOLINERGIC EFFECTS
Dry mouth
Increased heart rate
Urinary retention
Constipation
Hypotension

EXTRAPYRAMIDAL SIDE EFFECTS
Parkinsonism
Tremors
Mask-like facies
Rigidity
Shuffling gait
Dysphagia
Drooling
Dystonias
Abnormal or involuntary eye movements, including
    oculogyric crisis
Facial grimacing
Twisting of the torso or other muscle groups
Akathisia
Restlessness
Constant moving about
Tardive Dyskinesia
Protrusion of the tongue
Chewing motion
Involuntary movements of the body and extremities

OTHER SIDE EFFECTS
Drowsiness
Blood dyscrasias
Pruritis
Photosensitivity
Elevated blood glucose level
Increased weight
Impaired body temperature regulation
Gynecomastia
Lactation

10. Avoid skin contact with the liquid concentrate to prevent contact dermatitis.
11. Protect the liquid concentrate from light.
12. Dilute the liquid concentrate with fruit juice.
13. Inform the client that a full therapeutic effect of the medication may not be evident for 3 to 6 weeks following initiation of therapy; however, an observable therapeutic response may be apparent after 7 to 10 days.
14. Inform the client that some medications may cause a harmless change in urine color to pinkish to red-brown.
15. Instruct the client to use sunscreen, hats, and protective clothing when outdoors.
16. Instruct the client to avoid alcohol or other CNS depressants.
17. Instruct the client to change positions slowly to avoid orthostatic hypotension.
18. Instruct the client to report signs of agranulocytosis, including sore throat, fever, and malaise.
19. Instruct the client to report signs of liver dysfunction, including jaundice, malaise, fever, right upper abdominal pain.
20. When discontinuing antipsychotics, the medication dosage should be reduced gradually to avoid sudden recurrence of psychotic symptoms.

VIII. NEUROLEPTIC MALIGNANT SYNDROME ▲
  A. Description
    1. A potentially fatal syndrome that may occur at any time during therapy with neuroleptic (antipsychotic) medications
    2. Although rare, neuroleptic malignant syndrome more commonly occurs at the initiation of therapy, after the client has changed from one medication to another, after a dosage increase, or when a combination of medications is used.
  B. Assessment
    1. Dyspnea or tachypnea
    2. Tachycardia or irregular pulse rate
    3. Fever
    4. High or low blood pressure
    5. Increased sweating
    6. Loss of bladder control
    7. Skeletal muscle rigidity
    8. Pale skin
    9. Excessive weakness or fatigue
    10. Altered level of consciousness
    11. Seizures
    12. Severe extrapyramidal side effects
    13. Difficulty swallowing
    14. Excessive salivation
    15. Oculogyric crisis
    16. Dyskinesia
    17. Elevated white blood cell count, liver function results, and creatinine phosphokinase level

▲ D. Interventions
    1. Monitor vital signs.
    2. Monitor for extrapyramidal syndrome.
    3. Monitor for symptoms of neuroleptic malignant syndrome.
    4. Monitor urine output.
    5. Monitor serum glucose level.
    6. Note that the client taking an antipsychotic medication may require long-term medication for parkinsonian symptoms.
    7. Administer the medication with food or milk to decrease gastric irritation.
    8. For oral use, the liquid form might be preferred, because some clients hide tablets to avoid taking them.
    9. Note that the absorption rate is faster with the liquid form of oral medication.

C. Interventions
1. Notify the physician.
2. Monitor vital signs.
3. Initiate safety and seizure precautions.
4. Prepare to discontinue the medication.
5. Monitor level of consciousness.
6. Administer antipyretics as prescribed.
7. Use a cooling blanket to lower the body temperature.
8. Monitor electrolyte levels and administer fluids intravenously as prescribed.

IX. **MEDICATIONS TO TREAT ATTENTION-DEFICIT/ HYPERACTIVITY DISORDER** (Box 76-11)
A. Children with attention-deficit/hyperactivity disorder may require medication to reduce hyperactive behavior and lengthen attention span.
B. Medications that are most effective in controlling this disorder are CNS stimulants.
C. CNS stimulants, which increase agitation and activity in adults, have a calming effect on children with attention-deficit/hyperactivity disorder and increase alertness and sensitivity to stimuli.
D. Side effects
1. Tachycardia
2. Anorexia and weight loss
3. Elevated blood pressure
4. Dizziness
5. Agitation
E. Interventions
1. Monitor for CNS side effects.
2. Obtain a baseline ECG.
3. Monitor the blood pressure
4. Instruct the child and parents that OTC medications need to be avoided.
5. Instruct the child and parents that the last dose of the day should be taken at least 6 hours before bedtime (14 hours for extended-released forms) to prevent insomnia.
6. Monitor height and weight (particularly in children).
7. Reinforce that several weeks of therapy may be necessary before the therapeutic effect is noted.

BOX 76-11

Medications to Treat Attention-Deficit/ Hyperactivity Disorder

---

Amphetamine
Atomoxetine (Strattera)
Dexmethylphenidate (Focalin)
Dextroamphetamine (Dexedrine)
Dextroamphetamine and amphetamine (Adderall XR)
Methamphetamine (Desoxyn)
Methylphenidate (Ritalin, Concerta, Metadate CD, Methylin)
Pemoline (Cylert)

---

8. Instruct the client and parents that a drug-free period may be prescribed to allow growth of the child if the medication has caused growth retardation.

X. **MEDICATIONS TO TREAT ALZHEIMER'S DISEASE** (Box 76-12)
A. Acetylcholinesterase inhibitors may be used to treat Alzheimer's disease to improve cognitive functions in the early stages.
B. Donepezil (Aricept)
1. An inhibitor of acetylcholinesterase used to treat mild to moderate dementia of Alzheimer's disease
2. Side effects include nausea and diarrhea.
3. Donepezil can slow the heart rate through its vagotonic effect. ▲
C. Galantamine (Razadyne)
1. An inhibitor of cholinesterase used to treat mild to moderate dementia of Alzheimer's disease.
2. Side effects include nausea, vomiting, diarrhea, anorexia, and weight loss.
3. Can cause bronchoconstriction; used with caution in clients with asthma and chronic obstructive pulmonary disease ▲
D. Memantine (Namenda)
1. An NMDA (*N*-methyl-D-aspartate) receptor antagonist indicated for moderate to severe Alzheimer's disease
2. Side effects include dizziness, headache, confusion, and constipation.
3. Should not be used in combination with other NMDA antagonists such as amantadine (Symmetrel) or ketamine (Ketalar); such combinations produce undesirable additive effects.
4. Sodium bicarbonate and other medications that alkalinize the urine can decrease renal excretion of memantine; accumulation to toxic levels can result. ▲
E. Rivastigmine (Exelon)
1. Cholinesterase inhibitor used to treat mild to moderate dementia of Alzheimer's disease
2. Side effects include nausea, vomiting, diarrhea, abdominal pain, and anorexia.
3. Use with caution in clients with peptic ulcer disease, bradycardia, sick sinus syndrome, urinary obstruction, and lung disease because it ▲

BOX 76-12

Medications to Treat Alzheimer's Disease

Donepezil (Aricept)
Galantamine (Razadyne)
Memantine (Namenda)
Rivastigmine (Exelon)
Tacrine (Cognex)

enhances cholinergic transmission, thus intensifying symptoms of these disorders.

F. Tacrine (Cognex)
1. A centrally acting cholinesterase inhibitor used to treat mild to moderate dementia of Alzheimer's disease
2. Side effects include ataxia, loss of appetite, nausea, vomiting, and diarrhea.
3. An adverse effect is hepatotoxicity; liver function studies need to be monitored.

PRACTICE QUESTIONS

1. The nurse is performing a follow-up teaching session with a client discharged 1 month ago. The client is taking fluoxetine (Prozac). What information would be important for the nurse to obtain during this client visit regarding the side effects of the medication?
   1. Cardiovascular symptoms
   2. Gastrointestinal dysfunctions
   3. Problems with mouth dryness
   4. Problems with excessive sweating

2. The client who has been taking buspirone (BuSpar) for 1 month returns to the clinic for a follow-up assessment. The nurse determines that the medication is effective if the absence of which manifestation(s) has occurred?
   1. Paranoid thought process
   2. Rapid heartbeat or anxiety
   3. Alcohol withdrawal symptoms
   4. Thought broadcasting or delusions

3. A client taking lithium carbonate (Eskalith) reports vomiting, abdominal pain, diarrhea, blurred vision, tinnitus, and tremors. The lithium level is 2.5 mEq/L. The nurse interprets this level as:
   1. Toxic
   2. Normal
   3. Slightly above normal
   4. Excessively below normal

4. The home health nurse visits the client. The client gives the nurse a bottle of clomipramine (Anafranil). The nurse notes that the medication has not been taken by the client in 2 months. What behaviors observed in the client would validate noncompliance with this medication?
   1. Complaints of insomnia
   2. Complaints of hunger and fatigue
   3. A pulse rate less than 60 beats/min
   4. Frequent hand washing with hot soapy water

6. The hospitalized client has begun taking bupropion (Wellbutrin) as an antidepressant agent. The nurse monitors this client for which adverse effect indicating that the client is taking an excessive amount of medication?
   1. Constipation
   2. Seizure activity
   3. Increased weight
   4. Dizziness when getting upright

6. The client's medication sheet contains an order for sertraline hydrochloride (Zoloft). To ensure safe administration of the medication, the nurse would administer the dose:
   1. On an empty stomach
   2. At the same time each evening
   3. Evenly spaced around the clock
   4. As needed when the client complains of depression

7. The client with schizophrenia has been started on medication therapy with clozapine (Clozaril). The nurse assesses the results of which laboratory study to monitor for adverse effects from this medication?
   1. Platelet count
   2. Blood glucose level
   3. White blood cell count
   4. Liver function studies

8. A client is scheduled for discharge and will be taking phenobarbital (Luminal) for an extended period of time. The nurse would place highest priority on teaching the client which of the following points that directly relates to client safety?
   1. Take the medication only with meals.
   2. Take medication at the same time each day.
   3. Use a dose container to help prevent missed doses.
   4. Avoid drinking alcohol while taking this medication.

9. The 26-year-old female client with schizophrenia has been prescribed chlorpromazine hydrochloride (Thorazine). The client calls the mental health clinic and tells the nurse that her urine has become dark. The client has no other urinary symptoms. The nurse tells the client:
   1. That this indicates medication toxicity
   2. To seek treatment for urinary tract infection
   3. To increase intake of acid-ash foods and liquids
   4. That this is an expected side effect of the medication

10. A client is receiving fluphenazine (Prolixin) daily. The nurse would teach the client to do which of the following to minimize common side effects of this medication?
    1. Monitor the temperature daily.
    2. Use hard sour candy or sugarless gum.
    3. Eat snacks at midmorning and at bedtime.
    4. Have the blood pressure checked once a week.

11. The nurse is describing the medication side effects to a client who is taking oxazepam (Serax). The nurse incorporates in discussions with the client the need to:
    1. Consume a low-fiber diet.
    2. Increase fluids and bulk in the diet.
    3. Rest if the heart begins to beat rapidly.
    4. Take antidiarrheal agents if diarrhea occurs.

12. The nurse is administering risperidone (Risperdal) to a client who is scheduled to be discharged. Prior to discharge, which of the following should the nurse teach the client?
    1. Get adequate sunlight.
    2. Avoid foods rich in potassium.
    3. Continue driving as usual.
    4. Get up slowly when changing positions.
13. A client receiving lithium carbonate (Eskalith) complains of loose watery stools and difficulty walking. The nurse would expect the serum lithium level to be which of the following?
    1. 0.7 mEq/L
    2. 1 mEq/L
    3. 1.3 mEq/L
    4. 1.8 mEq/L
14. The nurse is teaching a client who is being started on imipramine hydrochloride (Tofranil) about the medication. The nurse informs the client that the maximum desired effects may:
    1. Start during the first week of administration
    2. Not occur for 2 to 3 weeks of administration
    3. Start during the second week of administration
    4. Not occur until after 2 months of administration
15. The client receiving tricyclic antidepressants arrives at the mental health clinic. Which observation would indicate that the client is following the medication plan correctly?
    1. Client reports not going to work for this past week.
    2. Client arrives at the clinic neat and appropriate in appearance.
    3. Client complains of not being able to "do anything" anymore.
    4. Client reports sleeping 12 hours per night and 3 to 4 hours during the day.

16. A client begins to experience extrapyramidal side effects from an antipsychotic medication. The nurse anticipates that the physician will prescribe which of the following to treat this condition?
    1. Haloperidol (Haldol)
    2. Benztropine (Cogentin)
    3. Prochlorperazine (Compazine)
    4. Chlorpromazine (Thorazine)
17. The nurse notes that a client diagnosed with schizophrenia is moving her mouth, protruding her tongue, and grimacing as she watches television. The nurse determines that the client is experiencing:
    1. Torticollis
    2. Tardive dyskinesia
    3. Hypertensive crisis
    4. Neuroleptic malignant syndrome

ALTERNATE ITEM FORMAT: MULTIPLE RESPONSE

A hospitalized client is started on phenelzine sulfate (Nardil) for the treatment of depression. The nurse instructs the client to avoid consuming which foods while taking this medication? Select all that apply.
- [ ] 1. Figs
- [ ] 2. Yogurt
- [ ] 3. Crackers
- [ ] 4. Aged cheese
- [ ] 5. Tossed salad
- [ ] 6. Oatmeal cookies

ANSWERS

1. **2**
Rationale: The most common side effects related to this medication include central nervous system and gastrointestinal system dysfunction. Fluoxetine (Prozac) affects the gastrointestinal system by causing nausea and vomiting, cramping, and diarrhea. Excessive sweating, dry mouth, and cardiovascular symptoms are not side effects associated with this medication.
Test-Taking Strategy: Use the process of elimination. Recalling that this medication causes gastrointestinal problems will direct you to option 2. Review the side effects related to this medication if you had difficulty with this question.
Level of Cognitive Ability: Analysis
Client Needs: Physiological Integrity
Integrated Process: Nursing Process—assessment
Content Area: Pharmacology
References: Fortinash, K., & Holoday-Worret, P. (2004). *Psychiatric mental health nursing* (3rd ed., p. 470). St. Louis: Mosby. Keltner, N., & Folks, D. (2005). *Psychotropic drugs* (4th ed., pp. 163-164, 656). St. Louis: Mosby.

2. **2**
Rationale: Buspirone (BuSpar) is not recommended for the treatment of drug or alcohol withdrawal, thought disorders, or schizophrenia. Buspirone hydrochloride most often is indicated for the treatment of anxiety.
Test-Taking Strategy: Note the strategic words *absence of which manifestation(s)*. Recalling that buspirone is an antianxiety medication will direct you to the correct option. Review the action and use of this medication if you had difficulty with this question.
Level of Cognitive Ability: Analysis
Client Needs: Physiological Integrity
Integrated Process: Nursing Process—evaluation
Content Area: Pharmacology
Reference: Keltner, N., & Folks, D. (2005). *Psychotropic drugs* (4th ed., pp. 237, 243). St. Louis: Mosby.

3. **1**
Rationale: Maintenance serum levels of lithium are 0.6 to 1.2 mEq/L. Symptoms of toxicity begin to appear at levels of

1.5 to 2 mEq/L. Lithium toxicity requires immediate medical attention with lavage and possible peritoneal dialysis or hemodialysis.

Test-Taking Strategy: Use the process of elimination. Recalling that the high end of the maintenance level is 1.2 mEq/L will direct you to option 1. Review the maintenance level and signs of toxicity if you had difficulty with this question.

Level of Cognitive Ability: Analysis
Client Needs: Physiological Integrity
Integrated Process: Nursing Process—analysis
Content Area: Pharmacology
References: Fortinash, K., & Holoday-Worret, P. (2004). *Psychiatric mental health nursing* (3rd ed., p. 478). St. Louis: Mosby. Keltner, N., & Folks, D. (2005). *Psychotropic drugs* (4th ed., pp. 214-216). St. Louis: Mosby.

4. 4
Rationale: Clomipramine (Anafranil) is a tricyclic antidepressant used to treat obsessive-compulsive disorder. Weight gain and tachycardia are side effects of this medication. Sedation sometimes occurs and insomnia is a seldom side effect.

Test-Taking Strategy: Recalling that this medication is a tricyclic antidepressant used to treat obsessive-compulsive disorder will direct you to option 4. Review the purpose and use of this medication if you had difficulty with this question.

Level of Cognitive Ability: Analysis
Client Needs: Physiological Integrity
Integrated Process: Nursing Process—evaluation
Content Area: Pharmacology
Reference: Keltner, N., & Folks, D. (2005). *Psychotropic drugs* (4th ed., p. 160). St. Louis: Mosby.

5. 2
Rationale: The nurse monitors for signs of toxicity. Seizure activity is common in bupropion dosages higher than 450 mg daily. This medication does not cause significant orthostatic blood pressure changes. Weight gain is an occasional side effect, whereas constipation is a common side effect of this medication.

Test-Taking Strategy: Use the process of elimination and note the strategic words *adverse effect* and *excessive amount*. These strategic words will direct you to option 2. Review this medication if you had difficulty with this question.

Level of Cognitive Ability: Analysis
Client Needs: Physiological Integrity
Integrated Process: Nursing Process—assessment
Content Area: Pharmacology
Reference: Keltner, N., & Folks, D. (2005). *Psychotropic drugs* (4th ed., p. 169). St. Louis: Mosby.

6. 2
Rationale: Sertraline hydrochloride (Zoloft) is classified as an antidepressant. Sertraline generally is administered once every 24 hours. It may be administered in the morning or evening, but evening administration may be preferable, because drowsiness is a side effect. The medication may be administered without food or with food if gastrointestinal distress occurs. Sertraline is not ordered for use as needed.

Test-Taking Strategy: Use the process of elimination. Recalling that this medication is an antidepressant administered daily

will direct you to option 2. Review this medication if you had difficulty with this question.

Level of Cognitive Ability: Application
Client Needs: Physiological Integrity
Integrated Process: Nursing Process—implementation
Content Area: Pharmacology
Reference: Keltner, N., & Folks, D. (2005). *Psychotropic drugs* (4th ed., pp. 164, 166). St. Louis: Mosby.

7. 3
Rationale: The client taking clozapine (Clozaril) may experience agranulocytosis, which is monitored by reviewing the results of the white blood cell count. Treatment is interrupted if the white blood cell count drops below 3000/mm^3. Agranulocytosis could be fatal if undetected and untreated. The other options are not related specifically to the use of this medication.

Test-Taking Strategy: Use the process of elimination. Recalling that this medication causes agranulocytosis will direct you to option 3. Review the adverse effects of this medication if you had difficulty with this question.

Level of Cognitive Ability: Analysis
Client Needs: Physiological Integrity
Integrated Process: Nursing Process—assessment
Content Area: Pharmacology
References: Fortinash, K., & Holoday-Worret, P. (2004). *Psychiatric mental health nursing* (3rd ed., p. 464). St. Louis: Mosby. Hodgson, B., & Kizior, R. (2007). *Saunders nursing drug handbook 2007* (p. 278). Philadelphia: W.B. Saunders. Keltner, N., & Folks, D. (2005). *Psychotropic drugs* (4th ed., pp. 131-132). St. Louis: Mosby.

8. 4
Rationale: Phenobarbital (Luminal) is an anticonvulsant and hypnotic agent. The client should avoid taking any other central nervous system depressants such as alcohol while taking this medication. The medication may be given without regard to meals. Taking the medication at the same time each day enhances compliance and maintains more stable blood levels of the medication. Using a dose container or "pillbox" may be helpful for some clients.

Test-Taking Strategy: Use the process of elimination. Focus on the subject, client safety and note the strategic words *highest priority*. This tells you that more than one or all the options may be partially or totally correct and that you must prioritize your answer. Remember, alcohol should not be consumed when a hypnotic is taken. Review client teaching points related to this medication if you had difficulty with this question.

Level of Cognitive Ability: Application
Client Needs: Safe and Effective Care Environment
Integrated Process: Teaching and Learning
Content Area: Pharmacology
Reference: Keltner, N., & Folks, D. (2005). *Psychotropic drugs* (4th ed., pp. 309-310). St. Louis: Mosby.

9. 4
Rationale: Chlorpromazine hydrochloride (Thorazine) is an antipsychotic medication. A side effect of this medication is that the color of urine may darken. The client should be aware that this effect is harmless. The other options are incorrect.

Test-Taking Strategy: Use the process of elimination. Eliminate options 2 and 3 first because the question states that the client exhibits no other symptoms of urinary tract infection. From the remaining options, remember that dark urine is a side effect of this medication. Review the side effects of this medication if you had difficulty with this question.
Level of Cognitive Ability: Application
Client Needs: Physiological Integrity
Integrated Process: Nursing Process—implementation
Content Area: Pharmacology
Reference: Hodgson, B., & Kizior, R. (2007). *Saunders nursing drug handbook 2007* (p. 242). Philadelphia: W.B. Saunders.

10. 2
Rationale: Dry mouth is a common side effect. Frequent mouth rinsing with water, sucking on hard candy, and chewing sugarless gum will alleviate this common side effect. Hypotension and hypertension are rare side effects of fluphenazine (Prolixin). Mild leukopenia may occur, but the temperature does not need to be taken daily. Weight gain is a common side effect, and frequent snacks will worsen the problem.
Test-Taking Strategy: Use the process of elimination, noting the strategic words *common side effects*. Eliminate options 1 and 4 because they are assessments rather than interventions. As such, they cannot "minimize" a side effect. From the remaining options, you must recall that a dry mouth is a side effect. Review the common side effects related to this medication if you had difficulty with this question.
Level of Cognitive Ability: Application
Client Needs: Physiological Integrity
Integrated Process: Teaching and Learning
Content Area: Pharmacology
References: Fortinash, K., & Holoday-Worret, P. (2004). *Psychiatric mental health nursing* (3rd ed., p. 461). St. Louis: Mosby. Keltner, N., & Folks, D. (2005). *Psychotropic drugs* (4th ed., p. 118). St. Louis: Mosby.

11. 2
Rationale: Oxazepam (Serax) causes constipation, and the client is instructed to increase fluid intake and bulk (high fiber) in the diet. If the heart begins to beat fast, the physician is notified, because this could indicate overdose. Additionally, diarrhea could indicate an incomplete intestinal obstruction and, if this occurs, the physician is notified.
Test-Taking Strategy: Use the process of elimination. Recalling that constipation is a side effect of this medication will direct you to option 2. Review the side effects and adverse effects of oxazepam if you had difficulty with this question.
Level of Cognitive Ability: Application
Client Needs: Physiological Integrity
Integrated Process: Teaching and Learning
Content Area: Pharmacology
Reference: Keltner, N., & Folks, D. (2005). *Psychotropic drugs* (4th ed., p. 677). St. Louis: Mosby.

12. 4
Rationale: Risperidone (Risperdal) can cause orthostatic hypotension. Sunlight should be avoided by the client taking this medication. Food interaction is not a concern. With any psychotropic medication, caution needs to be taken until the in-

dividual can determine whether his or her level of alertness is affected.
Test-Taking Strategy: Knowledge regarding the nursing considerations related to the administration of risperidone is required to answer this question. Remember that risperidone can cause orthostatic hypotension. Review this medication if you had difficulty with this question.
Level of Cognitive Ability: Application
Client Needs: Physiological Integrity
Integrated Process: Teaching and Learning
Content Area: Pharmacology
References: Fortinash, K., & Holoday-Worret, P. (2004). *Psychiatric mental health nursing* (3rd ed., p. 465). St. Louis: Mosby. Keltner, N., & Folks, D. (2005). *Psychotropic drugs* (4th ed., p. 132). St. Louis: Mosby.

13. 4
Rationale: The therapeutic serum level of lithium is 0.6 to 1.2 mEq/L. A serum lithium level of 1.8 mEq/L indicates moderate toxicity. Serum lithium concentrations of 1.5 to 2.5 mEq/L may produce vomiting, diarrhea, ataxia, incoordination, muscle twitching, and slurred speech.
Test-Taking Strategy: Focusing on the client's symptoms will assist in answering this question. Also, note that option 4 identifies the highest lithium level. Review the normal lithium level and signs of toxicity if you had difficulty with this question.
Level of Cognitive Ability: Analysis
Client Needs: Physiological Integrity
Integrated Process: Nursing Process—analysis
Content Area: Pharmacology
References: Fortinash, K., & Holoday-Worret, P. (2004). *Psychiatric mental health nursing* (3rd ed., p. 479). St. Louis: Mosby. Keltner, N., & Folks, D. (2005). *Psychotropic drugs* (4th ed., pp. 215, 218). St. Louis: Mosby.

14. 2
Rationale: The maximum therapeutic effects of imipramine hydrochloride (Tofranil) may not occur for 2 to 3 weeks after the antidepressant therapy has been initiated. Therefore, options 1, 3, and 4 are incorrect.
Test-Taking Strategy: Focus on the strategic word *maximum*. Recalling that it takes 2 to 3 weeks for a maximum therapeutic effect to occur with most antidepressants will direct you to option 2. Review this medication if you had difficulty with this question.
Level of Cognitive Ability: Application
Client Needs: Physiological Integrity
Integrated Process: Teaching and Learning
Content Area: Pharmacology
Reference: Fortinash, K., & Holoday-Worret, P. (2004). *Psychiatric mental health nursing* (3rd ed., p. 472). St. Louis: Mosby. Keltner, N., & Folks, D. (2005). *Psychotropic drugs* (4th ed., p. 151). St. Louis: Mosby.

15. 2
Rationale: Depressed individuals will sleep for long periods, are not able to go to work, and feel as if they cannot "do anything." Once they have had some therapeutic effect from their medication, they will report resolution of many of

these complaints and demonstrate an improvement in their appearance.

Test-Taking Strategy: Use the process of elimination. The client's behaviors or reports identified in options 1, 3, and 4 are symptoms of depression. The improvement in appearance indicates a therapeutic response to the medication, thus indicating compliance with the medication regimen. Review the expected effect of a tricyclic antidepressant if you had difficulty with this question.

Level of Cognitive Ability: Analysis
Client Needs: Physiological Integrity
Integrated Process: Nursing Process—evaluation
Content Area: Pharmacology
References: Fortinash, K., & Holoday-Worret, P. (2004). *Psychiatric mental health nursing* (3rd ed., p. 472). St. Louis: Mosby. Keltner, N., & Folks, D. (2005). *Psychotropic drugs* (4th ed., p. 148). St. Louis: Mosby.

16. **2**
Rationale: Benztropine (Cogentin) is an anticholinergic medication used to treat drug-induced extrapyramidal reactions, except tardive dyskinesia. Options 1, 3, and 4 are antipsychotic medications. Antipsychotic medications can cause extrapyramidal reactions.

Test-Taking Strategy: Focus on the medications in the options. Recalling the classifications of each will direct you to option 2. Remember that benztropine (Cogentin) is an anticholinergic medication. Review the side effects and extrapyramidal reactions of antipsychotic medications if you had difficulty with this question.

Level of Cognitive Ability: Analysis
Client Needs: Physiological Integrity
Integrated Process: Nursing Process—analysis
Content Area: Pharmacology
Reference: Hodgson, B., & Kizior, R. (2007). *Saunders nursing drug handbook 2007* (p. 128). Philadelphia: W.B. Saunders.

17. **2**
Rationale: Tardive dyskinesia is an adverse reaction that can occur from antipsychotic medication. It is characterized by uncontrollable involuntary movements of the body and extremities, particularly the tongue. Torticollis refers to an extrapyramidal side effect involving the upper body. Hypertensive crisis can occur from the use of monoamine oxidase inhibitors and is characterized by hypertension, occipital headache radiating frontally, neck stiffness and soreness, nausea, and vomiting. Neuroleptic malignant syndrome is a potentially fatal syndrome that may occur at any time during therapy with neuroleptic (antipsychotic) medications. It is characterized by dyspnea or tachypnea, tachycardia or irregular pulse rate, fever, blood pressure changes, increased sweating, loss of bladder control, and skeletal muscle rigidity.

Test-Taking Strategy: Focus on the data in the question. Remember that tardive dyskinesia is characterized by uncontrollable involuntary movements of the body and extremities, particularly the tongue. Review the side effects and extrapyramidal side effects of antipsychotic medications if you had difficulty with this question.

Level of Cognitive Ability: Analysis
Client Needs: Physiological Integrity
Integrated Process: Nursing Process—analysis
Content Area: Pharmacology
Reference: Keltner, N., & Folks, D. (2005). *Psychotropic drugs* (4th ed., p. 222). St. Louis: Mosby.

ALTERNATE ITEM FORMAT: MULTIPLE RESPONSE

Answer: 1, 2, 4
Rationale: Phenelzine sulfate (Nardil) is a monoamine oxidase inhibitor. The client should avoid taking in foods that are high in tyramine. Use of these foods could trigger a potentially fatal hypertensive crisis. Foods to avoid include yogurt, aged cheeses, smoked or processed meats, red wines, and fruits such as avocados, raisins, or figs.

Test-Taking Strategy: Recall that phenelzine sulfate is a monoamine oxidase inhibitor and that foods high in tyramine needed to be avoided. Next, from the food items listed in the question, identify the food that contains tyramine. Review the food items to avoid with monoamine oxidase inhibitors if you had difficulty with this question.

Level of Cognitive Ability: Application
Client Needs: Physiological Integrity
Integrated Process: Nursing Process—implementation
Content Area: Pharmacology
References: Fortinash, K., & Holoday-Worret, P. (2004). *Psychiatric mental health nursing* (3rd ed., p. 472). St. Louis: Mosby. Keltner, N., & Folks, D. (2005). *Psychotropic drugs* (4th ed., p. 176). St. Louis: Mosby.

REFERENCES

Fortinash, K., & Holoday-Worret, P. (2004). *Psychiatric mental health nursing* (3rd ed.). St. Louis: Mosby.

Hodgson, B., & Kizior, R. (2007). *Saunders nursing drug handbook 2007*. Philadelphia: W.B. Saunders.

Keltner, N., & Folks, D. (2005). *Psychotropic drugs* (4th ed.). St. Louis: Mosby.

Stuart, G., & Laraia, M. (2005). *Principles and practice of psychiatric nursing* (8th ed.). St. Louis: Mosby.

Varcarolis, E., Carson, V., & Shoemaker, N. (2006) *Foundations of psychiatric mental health nursing* (5th ed.). Philadelphia: W.B. Saunders.

Comprehensive Test

1. The nurse provides instructions regarding home care to the parents of a 3-year-old child hospitalized with hemophilia. Which statement, if made by the parent, indicates a need for further instructions?
   1. "We will supervise the child closely."
   2. "We will pad corners of the furniture."
   3. "We will remove household items that can easily fall over."
   4. "We will avoid having the child receive immunizations and cancel the scheduled dental appointments."

2. The registered nurse is planning the client assignments for the day. Which of the following is the most appropriate assignment for the nursing assistant?
   1. A client with bladder cancer who will be receiving chemotherapy
   2. A client on bed rest who requires range-of-motion (ROM) exercises every 4 hours
   3. A new diabetes mellitus client scheduled for discharge
   4. A client scheduled to receive a blood transfusion

3. The client is brought into the emergency room in ventricular fibrillation (VF). The advanced cardiac life support (ACLS) nurse prepares to defibrillate by placing conductive gel pads on which part of the chest?
   1. The upper and lower halves of the sternum
   2. The right of the sternum, just below the clavicle and to the left of the precordium
   3. The right shoulder and the back of the left shoulder
   4. Parallel between the umbilicus and the right nipple

4. The nurse reviews the plan of care for a client at 37 weeks of gestation who has sickle cell anemia. The nurse determines that which nursing diagnosis listed on the nursing care plan will receive the highest priority?
   1. Coping, ineffective
   2. Body image, disturbed
   3. Risk for pain, acute
   4. Fluid volume, deficient

5. The nurse provides instructions to a malnourished client regarding iron supplementation during pregnancy. Which statement, if made by the client, would indicate an understanding of the instructions?
   1. "The iron is best absorbed if taken on an empty stomach."
   2. "Meat does not provide iron and should be avoided."
   3. "Iron supplements will give me diarrhea."
   4. "My body has all the iron it needs and I don't need to take supplements."

6. Levothyroxine (Synthroid) is prescribed for a client diagnosed with hypothyroidism. The nurse reviews the client's record and notes that the client is presently taking warfarin (Coumadin). The nurse contacts the physician, anticipating that the physician will prescribe which of the following?
   1. An increased dosage of Coumadin
   2. A decreased dosage of Coumadin
   3. An increased dosage of Synthroid
   4. A decreased dosage of Synthroid

7. The nurse is teaching the client with emphysema about positions that help breathing during dyspneic episodes. The nurse instructs the client to avoid which of the following positions that will aggravate breathing?
   1. Sitting up with the elbows resting on knees
   2. Standing and leaning against a wall
   3. Lying on the back in a low-Fowler's position
   4. Sitting up and leaning on a table

8. The client is about to undergo a lumbar puncture (LP). The nurse describes to the client that which of the following positions will be used during the procedure?
   1. Side-lying with the legs pulled up and the head bent down onto the chest
   2. Side-lying with a pillow under the hip
   3. Prone with a pillow under the abdomen
   4. Prone in slight Trendelenburg

9. The nurse recognizes that which of the following interventions is unlikely to facilitate effective communication between the dying client and family?
   1. The nurse encourages the client and family to identify and discuss feelings openly.
   2. The nurse makes decisions for the client and family to relieve them of unnecessary demands.
   3. The nurse assists the client and family in carrying out spiritually meaningful practices.
   4. The nurse maintains a calm attitude and one of acceptance when the family or client expresses anger.

10. The nurse has given activity guidelines to the client with chronic low back pain. The nurse determines that the client understands the instructions if the client states that he or she will avoid which of the following positions?
    1. Lying on the side, with knees and hips bent
    2. Lying prone
    3. Standing with one foot on a step or stool
    4. Sitting using a lumbar roll or pillow

11. The nurse has just admitted to the nursing unit a client with a basilar skull fracture who is at risk for increased intracranial pressure (ICP). Pending specific physician orders, the nurse would avoid placing the client in which of the following positions?
    1. Neck in neutral position
    2. Head of bed elevated 30 to 45 degrees
    3. Flat, with head turned to the side
    4. Head midline

12. The nurse reviews the arterial blood gas (ABG) results of an assigned client and notes that the laboratory report indicates a pH of 7.30, P_{CO_2} of 58 mm Hg, P_{O_2} of 80 mm Hg, and HCO_3 of 27 mEq/L. The nurse interprets that the client has which acid-base disturbance?
    1. Metabolic acidosis
    2. Metabolic alkalosis
    3. Respiratory acidosis
    4. Respiratory alkalosis

13. The nurse has admitted a client to the clinical nursing unit following a modified right radical mastectomy for the treatment of breast cancer. The nurse plans to place the right arm in which of the following positions?
    1. Elevated above shoulder level
    2. Elevated on a pillow
    3. Level with the right atrium
    4. Dependent to the right atrium

14. On the second postpartum day, a woman complains of burning on urination, urgency, and frequency of urination. A urinalysis is done and the results indicate the presence of a urinary tract infection. The nurse instructs the new mother regarding measures to take for the treatment of the infection. Which of the following statements, if made by the mother, would indicate a need for further instructions?
    1. "The prescribed medication must be taken until it is finished."
    2. "My fluid intake should be increased to at least 3000 mL daily."
    3. "I need to urinate frequently throughout the day."
    4. "Foods and fluids that will increase urine alkalinity should be consumed."

15. The client received 20 units of NPH insulin subcutaneously at 8:00 AM. The nurse should assess the client for a hypoglycemic reaction at:
    1. 10:00 AM
    2. 11:00 AM
    3. 5:00 PM
    4. 11:00 PM

16. The community health nurse is working with disaster relief in a local community following a hurricane that ruined many homes in the community. The nurse is working to find housing for the survivors and is organizing counseling services. The nurse's actions represent which type of level of prevention?
    1. Primary
    2. Secondary
    3. Tertiary
    4. Fourth

17. A pregnant woman in her second trimester calls the prenatal clinic nurse to report a recent exposure to a child with rubella. Which of the following responses by the nurse would be appropriate and supportive to the woman?

18. The breast-feeding mother of an infant with lactose intolerance asks the nurse about dietary measures. The nurse tells the mother to avoid:
    1. Hard cheeses
    2. Green leafy vegetables
    3. Dried beans
    4. Egg yolk

19. A client with diabetes mellitus is told that amputation of the leg is necessary to sustain life. The client is very upset and tells the nurse, "This is all the doctor's fault. I have done everything that the doctor has asked me to do!" The nurse interprets the client's statement as:
    1. An expected coping mechanism
    2. A need to notify the hospital lawyer
    3. An expression of guilt on the part of the client
    4. An ineffective coping mechanism

20. A client brought to the emergency room is dead on arrival (DOA). The family of the client tells the physician that the client had a terminal cancer. The emergency room physician examines the client and asks the nurse to contact the medical examiner regarding an autopsy. The family of the client tells the nurse that they do not want an autopsy performed. Which of the following responses to the family is appropriate?
    1. "It is required by federal law. Why don't we talk about it and why don't you tell me why you don't want the autopsy done?"
    2. "The decision is made by the medical examiner."
    3. "I will contact the medical examiner regarding your request."
    4. "An autopsy is mandatory for any client who is DOA."

21. A pregnant human immunodeficiency virus (HIV)–positive woman delivers a newborn infant and the nurse provides instructions to help the mother regarding the newborn infant care. Which statement by the client indicates the need for further instructions?
    1. "I will be sure to wash my hands before and after bathroom use."
    2. "Support groups are available to assist me with understanding my diagnosis of HIV."
    3. "I need to breast-feed, especially for the first 6 weeks postpartum."
    4. "My newborn infant should be on antiviral medications for the first 6 weeks after delivery."

1. "There is no need to be concerned if you don't have a fever or rash within the next 2 days."
2. "Be sure to tell the doctor on your next prenatal visit, but there is little risk in the second trimester."
3. "You should avoid all school-age children during pregnancy."
4. "You were wise to call. I will check your rubella titer screening results and we can immediately identify if future interventions are needed."

22. An adolescent is diagnosed with conjunctivitis and the nurse provides information to the adolescent about the use of contact lenses. Which statement by the client indicates the need for further information?
    1. "My contact lenses can be worn if they are cleaned as directed."
    2. "I should not wear my contact lenses."
    3. "New contact lenses should be obtained."
    4. "My old contact lenses should be discarded."

23. A client with diabetes mellitus is self-administering NPH insulin from a vial that is kept at room temperature. The client asks the nurse about the length of time an unrefrigerated vial of insulin will maintain its potency. The appropriate response to the client is which of the following?
    1. 2 weeks
    2. 1 month
    3. 2 months
    4. 6 months

24. The nurse is caring for a client scheduled for a transsphenoidal hypophysectomy. The preoperative teaching instructions should include which most important statement?
    1. "Your hair will need to be shaved."
    2. "Deep breathing and coughing will be needed after surgery."
    3. "Brushing your teeth will not be permitted for at least 2 weeks following surgery."
    4. "You will receive spinal anesthesia."

25. During a routine prenatal visit, the client complains of gums that bleed easily with brushing. The nurse performs an assessment and then teaches the client about proper nutrition to minimize this problem. Which statement, if made by the client, indicates an understanding of the proper nutrition to minimize this problem?
    1. "I will eat three servings of cracked wheat bread each day."
    2. "I will eat fresh fruits and vegetables for snacks and for dessert each day."
    3. "I will drink 8 oz of water with each meal."
    4. "I will eat two saltine crackers before I get up each morning."

26. A 6-year-old child has just been diagnosed with localized Hodgkin's disease and chemotherapy is planned to begin immediately. The mother of the child asks the nurse why radiation therapy was not prescribed as a part of the treatment. The appropriate and supportive response to the mother is:
    1. "I'm not sure. I'll discuss it with the physician."
    2. "The child is too young to have radiation therapy."
    3. "It's very costly, and chemotherapy works just as well."
    4. "The physician would prefer that you discuss treatment options with the oncologist."

27. The nurse is preparing to care for a newborn infant who will be returning from surgery with a colostomy that was created for imperforate anus. When the newborn infant returns from surgery, the nurse assesses the stoma and notes that it is red and edematous. Which of the following is the appropriate nursing intervention?
    1. Call the physician.
    2. Document the findings.
    3. Apply ice immediately.
    4. Elevate the buttocks.

28. The nurse in the labor room is performing an initial assessment on a newborn infant. On assessment of the newborn infant's head, the nurse notes that the ears are low-set. Which of the following nursing actions would be appropriate?
    1. Cover the ears with gauze pads.
    2. Document the findings.
    3. Arrange for hearing testing.
    4. Notify the physician.

29. The clinic nurse is assessing the status of jaundice in a child with hepatitis. Which anatomical area will provide the best data regarding the presence of jaundice?
    1. The nail beds
    2. The skin in the abdominal area
    3. The skin in the sacral area
    4. The membranes in the ear canal

30. The nurse is assigned to care for a client who is in traction. The nurse prepares a plan of care for the client and includes which nursing action in the plan?
    1. Monitor the weights to be sure that they are resting on a firm surface.
    2. Check the weights to be sure that they are off of the floor.
    3. Making sure that the knots are at the pulleys.
    4. Making sure the head of the bed is kept at a 45- to 90-degree angle

31. A nurse is setting up the physical environment for an interview with a client and plans to obtain subjective data regarding the client's health. Select all interventions that are appropriate.
    ❑ 1. Set the room temperature at a comfortable level.
    ❑ 2. Provide seating for the client so that the client faces a strong light.
    ❑ 3. Ensure that the distance between the client and nurse is at least 6 feet.
    ❑ 4. Place a chair for the client across from the nurse's desk .
    ❑ 5. Remove distracting objects from the interviewing area.
    ❑ 6. Ensure comfortable seating at eye level for the client and nurse

32. The nurse is caring for an older client who has been placed in Buck's extension traction following a hip

fracture. On assessment of the client, the nurse notes that the client is disoriented. The appropriate nursing intervention is to:

1. Ask the family to stay with the client.
2. Apply restraints to the client.
3. Ask the laboratory to perform electrolyte studies.
4. Reorient the client frequently and place a clock and calendar in the client's room.

33. The nurse is preparing a plan of care for the client in skin traction. The nurse includes in the plan that a priority intervention is to assess the client frequently for:

1. The presence of bowel sounds
2. Signs of infection around the pin sites
3. Signs of skin breakdown
4. Urinary incontinence

34. The home care nurse is visiting a client who is in a body cast. The nurse is performing an assessment and is assessing the psychosocial adjustment of the client to the cast. The nurse would most appropriately assess:

1. The type of transportation available for follow-up care
2. The ability to perform activities of daily living
3. The need for sensory stimulation
4. The amount of home care support available

35. When counseling a female Amish client, the nurse should:

1. Speak only to the husband.
2. Use complex medical terminology.
3. Avoid using scientific or medical jargon.
4. Stand close to the client and speak loudly.

36. A client has refused to eat more than a few spoonfuls of breakfast. The physician has ordered that tube feedings be initiated if the client fails to eat at least half of a meal, because the client had been losing weight for the prior 2 months. The nurse enters the room, looks at the tray, and states, "If you don't eat any more than that, I'm going to have to put a tube down your throat and get a feeding in that way." The client begins crying and tries to eat more. Based on the nurse's actions, the nurse may also be accused of a tort known as which of the following?

1. Assault
2. Battery
3. Slander
4. Invasion of privacy

37. The registered nurse (RN) is planning assignments for the clients on a nursing unit. The RN needs to assign four clients and has a registered nurse, a licensed practical (vocational) nurse, and two nursing assistants on a nursing team. Which of the following clients would the nurse most appropriately assign to the licensed practical (vocational) nurse?

1. The client who requires a 24-hour urine collection
2. An elderly client requiring assistance with a bed bath and frequent ambulation
3. A client on a mechanical ventilator requiring frequent assessment and suctioning
4. A client with an abdominal wound requiring wound irrigations and dressing changes every 3 hours

38. To perform cardiopulmonary resuscitation (CPR), the nurse would use the method shown in Fig. 1 to open the airway in which of the following situations?

1. In all situations requiring CPR
2. If neck trauma is suspected
3. If the client is unconscious
4. If the client has a history of headaches

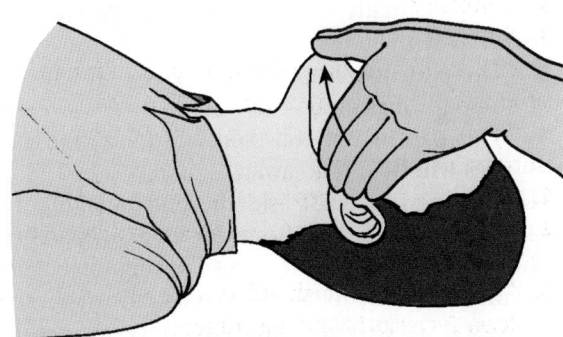

FIG. 1 Opening the airway using the jaw thrust maneuver. (From Harkreader, H., & Hogan, M. [2004]. *Fundamentals of nursing: Caring and clinical judgment* [2nd ed.]. Philadelphia: W.B. Saunders.)

39. The nurse teaches skin care to the client receiving external radiation therapy. Which of the following statements, if made by the client, would indicate the need for further instruction?

1. "I will handle the area gently."
2. "I will avoid the use of deodorants."
3. "I will limit sun exposure to 1 hour daily."
4. "I will wear loose-fitting clothing."

40. A physician's order reads levothyroxine (Synthroid), 150 mcg PO daily. The medication label reads Synthroid, 0.1 mg per tablet. A nurse administers how many tablet(s) to the client?

Answer: _____ tablet(s)

41. Metformin (Glucophage) is prescribed for the client with type 2 diabetes mellitus. The nurse tells the client that the most common side effect of the medication is:

1. Hypoglycemia
2. Gastrointestinal (GI) disturbances
3. Weight gain
4. Flushing and palpitations

42. Select all interventions that apply to the care of a child who is having a seizure.
    - ❑ **1.** Insert an oral airway.
    - ❑ **2.** Place the child in a supine position.
    - ❑ **3.** Loosen clothing around the child's neck.
    - ❑ **4.** Restrain the child.
    - ❑ **5.** Time the seizure.
    - ❑ **6.** Stay with the child.

43. A 13-year-old child is diagnosed with Ewing's sarcoma of the femur. Following a course of radiation and chemotherapy, it has been decided that leg amputation is necessary. Following the amputation, the child becomes very frightened because of aching and cramping felt in the missing limb. Which nursing statement would be appropriate to assist in alleviating the child's fear?
    1. "This aching and cramping is normal and temporary and will subside."
    2. "This normally occurs after the surgery and we will teach you ways to deal with it."
    3. "The pain medication that I give you will take these feelings away."
    4. "This pain is not real pain and relaxation exercises will help it go away."

44. The nursing instructor asks the nursing student to identify the priorities of care for an assigned client. The student correctly identifies the client needs that are the priority by telling the nursing instructor that:
    1. Actual or life-threatening concerns are the priority
    2. Time constraints related to the client's needs are the priority
    3. Obtaining needed supplies to care for the client is the priority
    4. Completing care in a reasonable time frame is the priority

45. A client arrives at the clinic complaining of fatigue, lack of energy, constipation, and depression. Following diagnostic studies, hypothyroidism is diagnosed and levothyroxine (Synthroid) is prescribed. The nurse instructs the client that the expected outcome of the medication is to:
    1. Increase energy levels.
    2. Achieve normal thyroid hormone levels.
    3. Increase blood glucose levels.
    4. Alleviate depression.

46. A community health nurse is preparing a poster for an educational session for a group of women and will be discussing the risk factors associated with breast cancer. Select the risk factors for breast cancer that the nurse will list on the poster. Select all that apply.
    - ❑ **1.** Family history of breast cancer
    - ❑ **2.** Early menarche
    - ❑ **3.** Early menopause
    - ❑ **4.** Previous cancer of the breast, uterus, or ovaries
    - ❑ **5.** Multiparity
    - ❑ **6.** High-dose radiation exposure to chest

47. The nurse is caring for a client with acute pancreatitis and is monitoring the client for paralytic ileus. Which assessment data would alert the nurse to this occurrence?
    1. Firm, nontender mass palpable at the lower right costal margin
    2. Severe, constant pain with rapid onset
    3. Inability to pass flatus
    4. Loss of anal sphincter control

48. The nurse inspects the color of the drainage from a nasogastric tube on a postoperative client approximately 24 hours following a laparotomy. Which of the following findings would indicate the need to notify the physician?
    1. Light yellowish-brown drainage
    2. Dark red drainage
    3. Dark brown drainage
    4. Greenish-tinged drainage

49. The nurse is preparing to discontinue a client's nasogastric (NG) tube. The client is positioned properly and the tube has been flushed with 15 mL of air to clear secretions. Prior to removing the tube, the nurse makes which statement to the client?
    1. "Take a deep breath when I tell you and breathe normally while I remove the tube."
    2. "Take a deep breath when I tell you and bear down while I remove the tube."
    3. "Take a deep breath when I tell you and slowly exhale while I remove the tube."
    4. "Take a deep breath when I tell you and hold it while I remove the tube."

50. The client with a history of lung disease is at risk for developing respiratory acidosis. The nurse assesses this client for which signs and symptoms characteristic of this disorder?
    1. Bradycardia and hyperactivity
    2. Decreased respiratory rate and depth
    3. Headache, restlessness, and confusion
    4. Bradypnea, dizziness, and paresthesias

51. The nurse is caring for a client with a resolved intestinal obstruction who has a nasogastric (NG) tube in place. The client has tolerated the tube being clamped every 2 hours for 1 hour. The physician has now ordered the NG tube to be removed. Prior to removing the tube, the nurse assesses for:
    1. Proper NG tube placement
    2. Normal serum electrolyte levels
    3. The presence of bowel sounds in all four quadrants
    4. Normal pH of the gastric aspirate

52. The nurse has administered approximately half of an enema solution when the client complains of pain and cramping. Which nursing action is the most appropriate?
    1. Raise the enema bag so that the solution can be instilled quickly.
    2. Clamp the tubing for 30 seconds and restart the flow at a slower rate.

3. Reassure the client and continue the flow.
4. Discontinue the enema and notify the physician.

53. The client experiencing a great deal of stress and anxiety is being taught to use self-control therapy. Which statement by the client indicates a need for further teaching about the therapy?
    1. "An advantage of this technique is that change is likely to last."
    2. "This form of therapy can be applied to new situations."
    3. "Talking to oneself is a basic component of this form of therapy."
    4. "It provides a negative reinforcement when the stimulus is produced."

54. A nurse is preparing a list of home care instructions regarding stoma and laryngectomy care to a client who had a laryngectomy. Select all instructions that would be included in the list.
    ❏ 1. Avoid swimming and use care when showering.
    ❏ 2. Keep the humidity in the home low.
    ❏ 3. Avoid exposure to people with infections.
    ❏ 4. Restrict fluid intake.
    ❏ 5. Obtain a Medic-Alert bracelet.
    ❏ 6. Prevent debris from entering the stoma.

55. A physician orders 2000 mL of 5% dextrose and half-normal saline to infuse over 24 hours. The drop factor is 15 drops/1 mL. A nurse sets the flow rate at how many drops per minute? (Round to the nearest whole number.)
    Answer:_____ drops per minute

56. The client is returned to the nursing unit following thoracic surgery with chest tubes in place. During the first few hours postoperatively, the nurse assesses for drainage and expects to note that it is:
    1. Serous
    2. Serosanguineous
    3. Bloody
    4. Bloody, with frequent small clots

57. The client has had radical neck dissection, and begins to hemorrhage at the incision site. Which action by the nurse would be contraindicated?
    1. Lowering the head of the bed to a flat position
    2. Applying manual pressure over the site
    3. Monitoring the client's airway
    4. Calling the physician immediately

58. A sexually active 20-year-old client has developed viral hepatitis. Which of the following statements, if made by the client, would indicate a need for further teaching?
    1. "A condom should be used for sexual intercourse."
    2. "I can never drink alcohol again."
    3. "I won't go back to work right away."
    4. "My close friends should get the vaccine."

59. A nurse would include which interventions in the plan of care for a client with hypothyroidism (myxedema)? Select all that apply.

❏ 1. Instruct the client about thyroid replacement therapy.
❏ 2. Encourage the client to consume fluids and high-fiber foods in the diet.
❏ 3. Provide a cool environment for the client.
❏ 4. Instruct the client to consume a high-fat diet.
❏ 5. Instruct the client to contact the physician if episodes of chest pain occur.
❏ 6. Inform the client that iodine preparations will be prescribed to treat the disorder.

60. The nurse is preparing to care for a client who will be weaned from a tracheostomy tube. The nurse is planning to use a tracheostomy plug and plans to insert it into the opening in the outer cannula. Which of the following nursing interventions are required prior to plugging the tube?
    1. Place the inner cannula into the tube.
    2. Deflate the cuff on the tube.
    3. Ensure that the client is able to swallow.
    4. Ensure that the client is able to speak.

61. The client is diagnosed with glaucoma. Which of the following assessment data gathered by the nurse identifies a risk factor associated with this eye disorder?
    1. A history of migraine headaches
    2. Frequent urinary tract infections
    3. Cardiovascular disease
    4. Frequent upper respiratory infections

62. The client with retinal detachment is admitted to the nursing unit in preparation for a scleral buckling procedure. Which of the following would the nurse anticipate to be prescribed?
    1. Bathroom privileges only
    2. Elevating the head of the bed to 45 degrees
    3. Placing an eye patch over the client's affected eye
    4. Wearing dark glasses to read or watch television

63. The nurse is caring for a client who is on strict bed rest. The nurse develops a plan of care and develops goals related to the prevention of deep vein thrombosis (DVT) and pulmonary emboli. Which of the following nursing actions would be most helpful to prevent these disorders from developing?
    1. Applying a heating pad to the lower extremities
    2. Encouraging active range-of-motion (ROM) exercises
    3. Placing a pillow under the knees
    4. Restricting fluids

64. The nurse is caring for a suicidal client. The appropriate nursing intervention in dealing with this client is to:
    1. Demonstrate confidence in the client's ability to deal with stressors.
    2. Provide hope and reassurance that the problems will resolve themselves.
    3. Display an attitude of detachment, confrontation, and efficiency.
    4. Provide authority, action, and participation.

65. The client with tuberculosis (TB), whose status is being monitored in an ambulatory care clinic, asks the nurse when it is permissible to return to work. The nurse replies that the client may resume employment when:
    1. Three sputum cultures are negative.
    2. Five sputum cultures are negative.
    3. A sputum culture and a chest x-ray are negative.
    4. A sputum culture and a Mantoux test are negative.

66. A client comes to the emergency room following an assault and is extremely agitated, trembling, and hyperventilating. The appropriate initial nursing action would be to:
    1. Encourage the client to discuss the assault.
    2. Place the client in a quiet room alone to decrease stimulation.
    3. Remain with the client until the anxiety decreases.
    4. Begin to teach relaxation techniques.

67. The nurse is caring for a client admitted to the hospital with a suspected diagnosis of acute appendicitis. Which of the following laboratory results would the nurse expect to note if the client does indeed have appendicitis?
    1. Leukopenia with a shift to the right
    2. Leukocytosis with a shift to the right
    3. Leukocytosis with a shift to the left
    4. Leukopenia with a shift to the left

68. The nurse is developing a plan of care for the client experiencing anxiety following the loss of a job. The client is verbalizing concerns regarding the ability to meet their role expectations and financial obligations. The appropriate nursing diagnosis for this client is:
    1. Dysfunctional family process
    2. Disturbed thought process
    3. Risk for anxiety
    4. Ineffective coping

69. The nurse is monitoring the chest tube drainage system in a client with a chest tube. The nurse notes intermittent bubbling in the water seal compartment. Which of the following is the appropriate action?
    1. Change the chest tube drainage system.
    2. Document the findings.
    3. Check for an air leak.
    4. Notify the physician.

70. A client arrives in the emergency room in a crisis state. The client demonstrates signs of profound anxiety and is unable to focus on anything but the object of the crisis and the impact on self. The initial nursing assessment would focus on:
    1. The object of the crisis
    2. The presence of support systems
    3. The physical condition of the client
    4. The client's coping mechanisms

71. After performing an initial abdominal assessment on a client with a diagnosis of cholelithiasis, the nurse documents that the bowel sounds are normal. Which of the following descriptions best describes "normal bowel sounds?"
    1. Waves of loud gurgles auscultated in all four quadrants
    2. Very high-pitched loud rushes auscultated especially in one or two quadrants
    3. Relatively high-pitched clicks or gurgles auscultated in all four quadrants
    4. Low-pitched swishing auscultated in one or two quadrants

72. A nurse is calculating a client's fluid intake for an 8-hour period. The client drank 8 oz of tea and 4 oz of orange juice for breakfast, 4 oz of water at 10:00 AM and at 1:00 PM when taking his medications, and 6 oz of iced tea at lunch. At 8:00 AM and again at 2:00 PM, the client received his intravenous antibiotics in 50 mL of normal saline. What is the client's total intake in mL?
    Answer: _____ mL

73. The client newly diagnosed with diabetes mellitus is instructed by the physician to obtain glucagon for emergency home use. The client asks the home care nurse about the purpose of the medication. The nurse instructs the client that the purpose of the medication is to treat:
    1. Hypoglycemia from insulin overdose
    2. Hyperglycemia from insufficient insulin
    3. Lipoatrophy from insulin injections
    4. Lipohypertrophy from inadequate insulin absorption

74. The nurse is providing care to a Cuban-American client who is terminally ill. Numerous family members are present most of the time and many of the family members are very emotional. The appropriate action is to:
    1. Restrict the number of family members visiting at one time.
    2. Inform the family that emotional outbursts are to be avoided.
    3. Request permission to move the client to a private room and allow the family members to visit.
    4. Contact the physician to speak to the family regarding their behaviors.

75. A client presents to the emergency department with upper gastrointestinal (GI) bleeding and is in moderate distress. In planning care, which nursing action would be the first priority for this client?
    1. Thorough investigation of precipitating events
    2. Insertion of a nasogastric tube and Hematest of emesis
    3. Complete abdominal examination
    4. Assessment of vital signs

ANSWERS

1. 4

Rationale: The nurse needs to stress the importance of immunizations, dental hygiene, and routine well-child care. Options 1, 2, and 3 are appropriate. The parents are also instructed in the measures to implement in the event of blunt trauma, especially trauma involving the joints, and to apply prolonged pressure to superficial wounds until the bleeding has stopped.

Test-Taking Strategy: Use the process of elimination. Note the strategic words *indicates a need for further instructions*. These words indicate a negative event query and ask you to select an option that is incorrect. Knowledge that bleeding is a concern in this disorder will assist in eliminating options 1, 2, and 3, which include measures of protection and safety for the child. If you had difficulty with this question, review home care instructions for the child with hemophilia.

Level of Cognitive Ability: Analysis

Client Needs: Health Promotion and Maintenance

Integrated Process: Teaching and Learning

Content Area: Child health

Reference: McKinney, E., James, S., Murray, S., & Ashwill, J. (2005). *Maternal-child nursing* (2nd ed., p. 1319). St. Louis: W.B. Saunders.

2. 2

Rationale: The nurse must determine the most appropriate assignment based on the skills of the staff member and the needs of the client. In this case, the most appropriate assignment for a nursing assistant would be to care for a client on bed rest who requires range-of-motion (ROM) exercises. The nursing assistant is trained in this procedure. The client receiving chemotherapy and the client receiving a blood transfusion require the assessment skills that a licensed nurse can perform. The client with diabetes mellitus who is being discharged will require predischarge review of diabetic management instructions and potentially coordination of necessary home care services.

Test-Taking Strategy: Note the strategic words *most appropriate* in the question. Use the process of elimination and recall the principles of delegation and supervision of the work of others in answering the question. Work that is delegated to others must be done consistent with the individual's level of expertise and licensure or lack of licensure. Review the principles of delegation if you had difficulty with this question.

Level of Cognitive Ability: Application

Client Needs: Safe and Effective Care Environment

Integrated Process: Nursing Process—planning

Content Area: Delegating/Prioritizing

Reference: Huber, D. (2006). *Leadership and nursing care management* (3rd ed., pp. 551-552). Philadelphia: W.B. Saunders.

3. 2

Rationale: The ACLS nurse would place one gel pad to the right of the sternum just below the clavicle and the other gel pad to the left of the precordium. The nurse would then place the electrode paddles over the pads. Options 1, 3, and 4 identify incorrect positions.

Test-Taking Strategy: Use the process of elimination, considering the anatomical location of the heart. This will easily assist in eliminating options 1, 3, and 4. If you had difficulty with this question, review the correct placement of pads for defibrillation.

Level of Cognitive Ability: Application

Client Needs: Physiological Integrity

Integrated Process: Nursing Process—implementation

Content Area: Adult health—cardiovascular

References: Ignatavicius, D., & Workman, M. (2006). *Medical-surgical nursing: Critical thinking for collaborative care* (5th ed., p. 742). Philadelphia: W.B. Saunders.

Lewis, S., Heitkemper, M., & Dirksen, S. (2004). *Medical-surgical nursing: Assessment and management of clinical problems* (6th ed., p. 875). St. Louis: Mosby.

4. 4

Rationale: For the client with sickle cell anemia, dehydration will precipitate sickling of the red blood cells. Sickling can lead to life-threatening consequences for the pregnant woman and for the fetus, such as an interruption of blood flow to the placenta. Options 1, 2, and 3 may also be appropriate nursing diagnoses for the client with sickle cell anemia but are not the priority.

Test-Taking Strategy: Use Maslow's Hierarchy of Needs theory, remembering that physiological needs come first. Using this principle, eliminate options 1 and 2. From the remaining options, select option 4 because it identifies an actual rather than a potential nursing diagnosis. Review sickle cell anemia if you had difficulty with this question.

Level of Cognitive Ability: Analysis

Client Needs: Physiological Integrity

Integrated Process: Nursing Process—analysis

Content Area: Maternity/Antepartum

Reference: Murray, S., & McKinney, E. (2006). *Foundations of maternal-newborn nursing* (4th ed., p. 678). Philadelphia: W.B. Saunders.

5. 1

Rationale: Iron is needed both to allow for transfer of adequate iron to the fetus and to permit expansion of the maternal RBC mass. During pregnancy, the relative excess of plasma causes a decrease in the hemoglobin concentration and hematocrit, known as physiological anemia of pregnancy. This is a normal adaptation during pregnancy. Meats are an excellent source of iron. Iron supplements usually cause constipation. Iron is best absorbed if taken on an empty stomach.

Test-Taking Strategy: Use the process of elimination, focusing on the strategic words *understanding of the instructions*. Knowledge of basic principles related to nutrition during pregnancy will assist in eliminating options 2 and 4. From the remaining options, remember that iron causes constipation. Review client teaching points related to iron supplementation if you had difficulty with this question.

Level of Cognitive Ability: Analysis

Client Needs: Physiological Integrity

Integrated Process: Nursing Process—evaluation

Content Area: Maternity/Antepartum

Reference: Lowdermilk, D., & Perry, A. (2004). *Maternity and women's health care* (8th ed., p. 379). St. Louis: Mosby.

6. 2

Rationale: Levothyroxine (Synthroid) accelerates the degradation of vitamin K-dependent clotting factors. As a result, the effects of warfarin (Coumadin) are enhanced. Therefore, if thyroid hormone replacement therapy is instituted in a client who has been taking warfarin, the dosage of warfarin should be reduced.

Test-Taking Strategy: Use the process of elimination. Recalling that levothyroxine enhances the effects of warfarin will direct you to the correct option. Review these medication interactions if you had difficulty with this question.

Level of Cognitive Ability: Analysis
Client Needs: Physiological Integrity
Integrated Process: Nursing Process—analysis
Content Area: Pharmacology
Reference: Kee, J., Hayes, E., & McCuistion, L. (2006). *Pharmacology: A nursing process approach* (5th ed., pp. 597, 603). Philadelphia: W.B. Saunders.

7. **3**
Rationale: The client should use the positions outlined in options 1, 2, and 4. These allow for maximal chest expansion. The client should not lie on the back because it reduces movement of a large area of the client's chest wall. Sitting is better than standing, whenever possible. If no chair is available, then leaning against a wall while standing allows accessory muscles to be used for breathing and not posture control.

Test-Taking Strategy: Use the process of elimination, noting the strategic words *dyspneic episodes* and *avoid*. Also, note that options 1, 2, and 4 are comparative or alike in that they all address upright positions. If you had difficulty with this question, review client teaching points related to emphysema.

Level of Cognitive Ability: Application
Client Needs: Physiological Integrity
Integrated Process: Teaching and Learning
Content Area: Adult health—respiratory
Reference: Ignatavicius, D., & Workman, M. (2006). *Medical-surgical nursing: Critical thinking for collaborative care* (5th ed., pp. 597, 603). Philadelphia: W.B. Saunders.

8. **1**
Rationale: The client undergoing lumbar puncture (LP) is positioned lying on the side, with the legs pulled up to the abdomen and the head bent down onto the chest. This position helps open the spaces between the vertebrae and allows for easier needle insertion by the physician. Each of the other options identifies incorrect positions for this procedure.

Test-Taking Strategy: Use the process of elimination. Recalling that an LP is the introduction of a needle into the subarachnoid space will direct you to option 1. It is reasonable that the position of the client must facilitate this and the correct option is the only position that flexes the vertebrae and widens the spaces between them. Review care of the client undergoing an LP if you had difficulty with this question.

Level of Cognitive Ability: Application
Client Needs: Physiological Integrity
Integrated Process: Nursing Process—implementation
Content Area: Adult health—neurological
Reference: Chernecky, C., & Berger, B. (2004). *Laboratory tests and diagnostic procedures* (4th ed., p. 739). Philadelphia: W.B. Saunders.

9. **2**
Rationale: Maintaining effective and open communication among family members affected by death and grief is of the greatest importance. Option 1 describes encouraging discussion of feelings and is likely to enhance communications. Option 3 is also an effective intervention, because spiritual practices give meaning to life and have an impact on how people react to crisis. Option 4 is also an effective technique, because the client and family need to know that someone will be there who is supportive and nonjudgmental. Option 2 describes the nurse removing autonomy and decision making from the client and family, who are already experiencing feelings of loss of control in that they cannot change the process of dying. This is an ineffective intervention, which could further impair communication.

Test-Taking Strategy: Use the process of elimination, noting the strategic words *unlikely to facilitate*. Understanding that people in crisis usually feel helpless and unable to control their circumstances can assist in identifying option 2 as a response that further removes control. Review these therapeutic interventions if you had difficulty with this question.

Level of Cognitive Ability: Comprehension
Client Needs: Psychosocial Integrity
Integrated Process: Caring
Content Area: Fundamental skills
References: Potter, P., & Perry, A. (2005). *Fundamentals of nursing* (6th ed., p. 579). St. Louis: Mosby.
Varcarolis, E., Carson, V., & Shoemaker, N. (2006). *Foundations of psychiatric mental health nursing* (5th ed., p. 603). Philadelphia: W.B. Saunders.

10. **2**
Rationale: The client should avoid positions or activities that place strain on the lower back. The client should not sleep on the abdomen (prone) or on the side if the hips and knees are straight. The client should not lean forward without bending the knees, stand in one position for lengthy amounts of time, or lift anything above elbow level. It may be helpful for the client to stand with a foot elevated on a stool, or to sit using a form of lumbar support.

Test-Taking Strategy: Use the process of elimination, noting the strategic word *avoid*. Use knowledge of body mechanics and low back injury to answer the question. If you had difficulty with this question, review client teaching points related to low back pain.

Level of Cognitive Ability: Analysis
Client Needs: Health Promotion and Maintenance
Integrated Process: Nursing Process—evaluation
Content Area: Adult health—musculoskeletal
References: Ignatavicius, D., & Workman, M. (2006). *Medical-surgical nursing: Critical thinking for collaborative care* (5th ed., pp. 978-979). Philadelphia: W.B. Saunders.
Lewis, S., Heitkemper, M., & Dirksen, S. (2004). *Medical-surgical nursing: Assessment and management of clinical problems* (6th ed. pp. 1700-1701). St. Louis: Mosby,.

11. **3**
Rationale: The head of the client at risk for or with increased intracranial pressure (ICP) should be positioned so that the head is in a neutral, midline position. The nurse should avoid

flexing or extending the neck, or turning the head side to side. The head of the bed should be raised to 30 to 45 degrees. Use of proper positions promotes venous drainage from the cranium to keep intracranial pressure down.

Test-Taking Strategy: Use the process of elimination, noting the strategic words *at risk for increased intracranial pressure* and *avoid.* Visualize each of the positions identified in the options and identify the position that is detrimental to the client with increased ICP. This would be the position that interferes with arterial circulation to the brain or venous drainage from the brain. The only position that meets one of those criteria is option 3. Review care of the client at risk for or with increased ICP if you had difficulty with this question.

Level of Cognitive Ability: Application
Client Needs: Physiological Integrity
Integrated Process: Nursing Process—implementation
Content Area: Adult health—neurological
References: Black, J., & Hawks, J. (2005). *Medical-surgical nursing: Clinical management for positive outcomes* (7th ed., p. 2201). Philadelphia: W.B. Saunders.
Ignatavicius, D., & Workman, M. (2006). *Medical-surgical nursing: Critical thinking for collaborative care* (5th ed., pp. 1044-1045). Philadelphia: W.B. Saunders.

12. **3**
Rationale: The normal pH is 7.35 to 7.45. The normal Pco_2 is 35 to 45 mm Hg. In respiratory acidosis, the pH is low and the Pco_2 is elevated. Options 1, 2, and 4 are incorrect interpretations of the values identified in the question.

Test-Taking Strategy: Remember that in a respiratory imbalance you will find an opposite response between the pH and Pco_2. Also, remember that the pH is low in an acidotic condition. Recalling this information will allow you to eliminate each of the incorrect options. Review interpretation of blood gas results if you had difficulty with this question.

Level of Cognitive Ability: Analysis
Client Needs: Physiological Integrity
Integrated Process: Nursing Process—analysis
Content Area: Fundamental skills
Reference: Ignatavicius, D., & Workman, M. (2006). *Medical-surgical nursing: Critical thinking for collaborative care* (5th ed., p. 283). Philadelphia: W.B. Saunders.

13. **2**
Rationale: The client's operative arm should be positioned so that it is elevated on a pillow, and not exceeding shoulder elevation. This promotes optimal drainage from the limb, without impairing the circulation to the arm. If the arm is positioned flat (option 3) or dependent (option 4), this could increase the edema in the arm, which is contraindicated because of lymphatic disruption caused by surgery.

Test-Taking Strategy: Use the process of elimination. Read each option carefully and attempt to visualize the position identified in the option. Using the principles of circulation and gravity will easily direct you to option 2. Option 2 is the option that avoids the two extremes of height in positioning the limb affected by surgery. Review care of the client following mastectomy if you had difficulty with this question.

Level of Cognitive Ability: Application
Client Needs: Physiological Integrity

Integrated Process: Nursing Process—planning
Content Area: Adult health—oncology
Reference: Ignatavicius, D., & Workman, M. (2006). *Medical-surgical nursing: Critical thinking for collaborative care* (5th ed., p. 1805). Philadelphia: W.B. Saunders.

14. **4**
Rationale: The woman with a urinary tract infection must be encouraged to take the medication for the entire time it is prescribed. The women should also be instructed to drink at least 3000 mL of fluid each day to flush the infection from the bladder and to urinate frequently throughout the day. Foods and fluids that acidify the urine need to be encouraged.

Test-Taking Strategy: Use the process of elimination. Note the strategic words *indicate a need for further instructions.* These words indicate a negative event query and ask you to select an option that is incorrect. Recall that foods and fluids that acidify the urine should be consumed rather than foods and fluids that cause urine alkalinity. If you had difficulty with this question, review nursing considerations for the client with a urinary tract infection.

Level of Cognitive Ability: Analysis
Client Needs: Physiological Integrity
Integrated Process: Teaching and Learning
Content Area: Maternity/Postpartum
References: Black, J., & Hawks, J. (2005). *Medical-surgical nursing: Clinical management for positive outcomes* (7th ed., p. 860). Philadelphia: W.B. Saunders.
Ignatavicius, D., & Workman, M. (2006). *Medical-surgical nursing: Critical thinking for collaborative care* (5th ed., p. 1684). Philadelphia: W.B. Saunders.

15. **3**
Rationale: NPH is an intermediate-acting insulin. The onset of action is 3 to 4 hours, it peaks in 4 to 12 hours, and its duration of action is 16 to 20 hours. Hypoglycemic reactions most likely occur during peak time.

Test-Taking Strategy: Use the process of elimination and knowledge regarding the onset, peak, and duration of action for NPH insulin. Recalling that peak action is between 4 to 12 hours will direct you to option 3. Review the characteristics of NPH insulin if you had difficulty with this question.

Level of Cognitive Ability: Analysis
Client Needs: Physiological Integrity
Integrated Process: Nursing Process—assessment
Content Area: Adult health—endocrine
Reference: Ignatavicius, D., & Workman, M. (2006). *Medical-surgical nursing: Critical thinking for collaborative care* (5th ed., pp. 1519, 1539). Philadelphia: W.B. Saunders.

16. **3**
Rationale: Tertiary prevention involves the reduction of the amount and degree of disability, injury, and damage following a crisis. Primary prevention means keeping the crisis from occurring and secondary prevention focuses on reducing the intensity and duration of the crisis during the crisis itself. There is no known fourth care prevention level.

Test-Taking Strategy: Identify the scenario in the question and the role of the nurse in the question. Focus on these nursing roles and use knowledge regarding the various levels of pre-

vention to answer the question. If you had difficulty with this question, review the levels of prevention.
Level of Cognitive Ability: Comprehension
Client Needs: Safe and Effective Care Environment
Integrated Process: Nursing Process—implementation
Content Area: Fundamental skills
Reference: Varcarolis, E., Carson, V., & Shoemaker, N. (2006). *Foundations of psychiatric mental health nursing* (5th ed., p. 465). Philadelphia: W.B. Saunders.

17. 4
Rationale: Rubella virus is spread by aerosol droplet transmission through the upper respiratory tract and has an incubation period of 14 to 21 days. The risks of maternal and subsequent fetal infection during the second trimester include hearing loss and congenital anomalies. Rubella titer determination is a standard antenatal test for childbearing women during their initial screening and entry into the health care delivery system. Option 4 helps clarify maternal concerns with accurate information based on the acquisition of rubella infection and potential fetal side effects.
Test-Taking Strategy: Use the process of elimination and knowledge regarding the transmission of rubella virus to the fetus. Also, use of therapeutic communication techniques will direct you to option 4. Option 4 addresses the client's concerns. Review concepts related to exposure to rubella during pregnancy if you had difficulty with this question.
Level of Cognitive Ability: Application
Client Needs: Psychosocial Integrity
Integrated Process: Nursing Process—implementation
Content Area: Maternity Antepartum
Reference: Lowdermilk, D., & Perry, A. (2004). *Maternity and women's health care* (8th ed., pp. 210, 212). St. Louis: Mosby.

18. 1
Rationale: Breast-feeding mothers with lactose-intolerance infants need to be encouraged to limit dairy products. Cheese is a dairy product. Alternative calcium sources that can be consumed by the mother include egg yolk, green leafy vegetables, dried beans, cauliflower, and molasses.
Test-Taking Strategy: Use the process of elimination. Note the strategic word *avoid* in the question. Knowledge that lactose is the sugar found in dairy products will easily direct you to option 1. Review the dietary management for the infant with lactose intolerance if you had difficulty with this question.
Level of Cognitive Ability: Application
Client Needs: Physiological Integrity
Integrated Process: Nursing Process—planning
Content Area: Child health
Reference: Murray, S., & McKinney, E. (2006). *Foundations of maternal-newborn nursing* (4th ed., p. 194). Philadelphia: W.B. Saunders.

19. 1
Rationale: The nurse needs to be aware of the effective and ineffective coping mechanisms that can occur in a client when loss is anticipated. The expression of anger is known to be a normal response to impending loss, and the anger may be directed toward the self, God or other spiritual being, or caregivers. Notifying the hospital lawyer is inappropriate. Guilt

may or may not be a component of the client's feelings and the data in the question do not indicate that guilt is present.
Test-Taking Strategy: Focus on the data provided in the question. Note that options 1 and 4 address coping mechanisms. This provides you with the clue that one of these options may be the correct response. Additionally, knowledge of the stages of grief associated with loss will direct you to option 1. Review these stages and expected client responses if you had difficulty with this question.
Level of Cognitive Ability: Analysis
Client Needs: Psychosocial Integrity
Integrated Process: Nursing Process—analysis
Content Area: Fundamental skills
Reference: Varcarolis, E., Carson, V., & Shoemaker, N. (2006). *Foundations of psychiatric mental health nursing* (5th ed., pp. 243, 437). Philadelphia: W.B. Saunders.

20. 3
Rationale: An autopsy is required by state law in certain circumstances, including the sudden death of a client and a death that occurs under suspicious circumstances. A client may have provided oral or written instructions regarding an autopsy following death. If an autopsy is not required by law, these oral or written requests will be granted. If no oral or written instructions were provided, state law determines who has the authority to consent for an autopsy. Most often, the decision rests with the surviving relative or next of kin.
Test-Taking Strategy: Use knowledge regarding the laws and issues surrounding autopsy and therapeutic communication techniques to answer the question. Eliminate options 1 and 4 because these statements are not completely accurate. From the remaining options, option 3 is the therapeutic and appropriate response to the family. Review the issues and laws surrounding autopsy if you had difficulty with this question.
Level of Cognitive Ability: Application
Client Needs: Psychosocial Integrity
Integrated Process: Caring
Content Area: Fundamental skills
Reference: Lynch, V. (2006). *Forensic nursing* (pp. 354-355, 364). St. Louis: Mosby.

21. 3
Rationale: The mode of perinatal transmission of HIV to the fetus or neonate of an HIV-positive woman can occur during the antenatal, intrapartal, or postpartum period. HIV transmission can occur during breast-feeding. Therefore, HIV-positive clients should be encouraged to bottle-feed their neonates. Frequent hand washing is encouraged. Support groups and community agencies can be identified to assist the parents with the newborn infant's home care, the impact of the diagnosis of HIV infection, and available financial resources. It is recommended that newborn infants of HIV-positive clients receive antiviral medications for their first 6 weeks of life.
Test-Taking Strategy: Use the process of elimination. Note the strategic words *need for further instructions* in the question. These words indicate a negative event query and ask you to select an option that is incorrect. Recalling that breast-feeding is discouraged in the HIV-positive woman will direct you to the correct option. Review home care measures for the HIV-positive client if you had difficulty with this question.

Level of Cognitive Ability: Analysis
Client Needs: Safe and Effective Care Environment
Integrated Process: Teaching and Learning
Content Area: Maternity/Postpartum
Reference: Lowdermilk, D., & Perry, A. (2004). *Maternity and women's health care* (8th ed., p. 422). St. Louis: Mosby.

22. **1**
Rationale: If the child wears contact lenses, he or she should be instructed to discontinue wearing them until the infection has cleared completely. Securing new contact lenses will eliminate the chance of reinfection from contaminated contact lenses and will also lessen the risk of a corneal ulceration.
Test-Taking Strategy: Use the process of elimination. Note the strategic words *need for further information* in the question. These words indicate a negative event query and ask you to select an option that is incorrect. Options 2, 3, and 4 are comparative or alike in that they relate to avoiding the use of contact lenses during infection. If you had difficulty with this question, review treatment measures for conjunctivitis.
Level of Cognitive Ability: Analysis
Client Needs: Safe and Effective Care Environment
Integrated Process: Teaching and Learning
Content Area: Child health
Reference: McKinney, E., James, S., Murray, S., & Ashwill, J. (2005). *Maternal-child nursing* (2nd ed., p. 1588). St. Louis: W.B. Saunders.

23. **2**
Rationale: An insulin vial in current use can be kept at room temperature for up to 1 month without significant loss of activity. Direct sunlight and heat must be avoided.
Test-Taking Strategy: Use the process of elimination. Note the strategic word *unrefrigerated* in the question. This word will assist in directing you to the correct option. If you are unfamiliar with the concepts related to insulin stability, review this information.
Level of Cognitive Ability: Application
Client Needs: Physiological Integrity
Integrated Process: Teaching and Learning
Content Area: Pharmacology
Reference: Kee, J., Hayes, E., & McCuistion, L. (2006). *Pharmacology: A nursing process approach* (5th ed., p. 778). Philadelphia: W.B. Saunders.

24. **3**
Rationale: Based on the location of the surgical procedure, spinal anesthesia would not be used. Additionally, the hair would not be shaved. Although coughing and deep breathing are important, specific to this procedure is avoiding brushing the teeth to prevent disruption of the surgical site.
Test-Taking Strategy: Consider the anatomical location and the surgical procedure itself to eliminate options 1 and 4. Although you may be tempted to select option 2, note the strategic words *most important*. Because of the anatomical location of the surgery, option 3 is most important. Review this surgical procedure if you had difficulty with this question.
Level of Cognitive Ability: Application
Client Needs: Physiological Integrity

Integrated Process: Teaching and Learning
Content Area: Adult health—endocrine
Reference: Lewis, S., Heitkemper, M., & Dirksen, S. (2004). *Medical-surgical nursing: Assessment and management of clinical problems* (6th ed., p. 1331). St. Louis: Mosby.

25. **2**
Rationale: Fresh fruits and vegetables will provide vitamins and minerals needed for healthy gums. Cracked wheat bread may abrade the tender gums, drinking water with meals has no direct effect on gums, and eating saltine crackers before arising helps decrease nausea.
Test-Taking Strategy: Use the process of elimination and focus on the subject of the question. Eliminate options 1 and 4 first because these measures could irritate fragile gums. From the remaining options, eliminate option 3, remembering that drinking water with meals has no direct effect on gums. Review measures that promote dental health during pregnancy if you had difficulty with this question.
Level of Cognitive Ability: Analysis
Client Needs: Physiological Integrity
Integrated Process: Nursing Process/Evaluation
Content Area: Maternity/Antepartum
Reference: Lowdermilk, D., & Perry, A. (2004). *Maternity and women's health care* (8th ed., p. 431). St. Louis: Mosby.

26. **2**
Rationale: Radiation therapy is usually delayed until a child is 8 years of age, whenever possible, to prevent retardation of bone growth and soft tissue development. Options 1, 3, and 4 are inappropriate responses to the mother.
Test-Taking Strategy: Note the age of the child in the question. Additionally, use therapeutic communication techniques and knowledge regarding the effects of radiation to answer this question. Options 1 and 4 are nontherapeutic and place the mother's inquiry on hold. From the remaining options, use the child's age as a guide in directing you to option 2. Review the effects of radiation therapy if you had difficulty with this question.
Level of Cognitive Ability: Application
Client Needs: Physiological Integrity
Integrated Process: Nursing Process—implementation
Content Area: Child health
References: McKinney, E., James, S., Murray, S., & Ashwill, J. (2005). *Maternal-child nursing* (2nd ed., p. 1335). St. Louis: W.B. Saunders.
Wong, D., Perry, S., Hockenberry, M., et al. (2006). *Maternal child nursing care* (3rd ed., p. 1631). St. Louis: Mosby.

27. **2**
Rationale: A fresh colostomy stoma will be red and edematous, but this will decrease with time. The colostomy site will then be pink without evidence of abnormal drainage, swelling, or skin breakdown. The nurse would document these findings because this is a normal expectation. Options 1, 3, and 4 are inappropriate interventions.
Test-Taking Strategy: Use the process of elimination. Note the strategic words *returns from surgery*. You would expect redness and edema at this time. Review postoperative colostomy assessment if you had difficulty with this question.

Level of Cognitive Ability: Application
Client Needs: Physiological Integrity
Integrated Process: Nursing Process—implementation
Content Area: Child health
Reference: Hockenberry, M., Wilson, D., & Winkelstein, M. (2005). *Wong's essentials of pediatric nursing* (7th ed., p. 783). St. Louis: Mosby.

28. 4
Rationale: Low or oddly placed ears are associated with a variety of congenital defects and should be reported immediately. Although the findings would be documented, the most appropriate action would be to notify the physician. Options 1, 2, and 3 are inaccurate and inappropriate nursing actions.
Test-Taking Strategy: Use the process of elimination. Knowledge regarding the normal assessment findings in a newborn infant is required to answer this question. Recall that low-set ears is an abnormal finding will easily direct you to option 4. Review normal assessment findings in a newborn if you had difficulty with this question.
Level of Cognitive Ability: Application
Client Needs: Physiological Integrity
Integrated Process: Nursing Process—implementation
Content Area: Maternity/Postpartum
Reference: Wong, D., Perry, S., Hockenberry, M., et al. (2006). *Maternal child nursing care.* (3rd ed., p. 714). St. Louis: Mosby.

29. 1
Rationale: Jaundice, if present, is best assessed in the sclera, nail beds, and mucous membranes. Generalized jaundice will appear in the skin throughout the body. Option 4 is not an appropriate area to assess for the presence of jaundice.
Test-Taking Strategy: Use the process of elimination. Note the strategic word *best* in the question. Option 2 and 3 can be eliminated first because jaundice present in the skin is generalized. From the remaining options, recalling that skin discoloration can best be assessed in the nail beds will direct you to option 1. Review assessment findings related to jaundice if you had difficulty with this question.
Level of Cognitive Ability: Analysis
Client Needs: Health Promotion and Maintenance
Integrated Process: Nursing Process—assessment
Content Area: Child health
Reference: McKinney, E., James, S., Murray, S., & Ashwill, J. (2005). *Maternal-child nursing* (2nd ed., pp. 821,1150). St. Louis: W.B. Saunders.

30. 2
Rationale: To achieve proper traction, weights need to be free-hanging, with knots kept away from the pulleys. Weights are not to be kept resting on a firm surface. The head of the bed is usually kept low to provide countertraction.
Test-Taking Strategy: Use the process of elimination. Attempt to visualize the traction, recalling that there must be weight to exert the pull from the traction setup. This concept will assist in eliminating options 1 and 3. Recalling that countertraction is needed will assist in eliminating option 4. Review care of the client in traction if you had difficulty with this question.
Level of Cognitive Ability: Application
Client Needs: Physiological Integrity

Integrated Process: Nursing Process—planning
Content Area: Adult health—musculoskeletal
References: Black, J., & Hawks, J. (2005). *Medical-surgical nursing: Clinical management for positive outcomes* (7th ed., p. 637). Philadelphia: W.B. Saunders.
Ignatavicius, D., & Workman, M. (2006). *Medical-surgical nursing: Critical thinking for collaborative care* (5th ed., p. 1201). Philadelphia: W.B. Saunders.

31. 1, 5, 6
Rationale: When preparing the physical environment for an interview, the nurse would set the room temperature at a comfortable level. The nurse would provide sufficient lighting for the client and nurse to see each other. The nurse would avoid having the client face a strong light because the client would have to squint into the full light. Distracting objects and equipment should be removed from the interview area. The nurse should arrange seating so that both the nurse and client are seated comfortably at eye level, and the nurse avoids facing the client across a desk or table because this creates a barrier. The distance between the nurse and the client should be set by the nurse at 4 to 5 feet. If the nurse places the client any closer, the nurse will be invading the client's private space and may create anxiety in the client. If the nurse places the client farther away, the nurse may be seen as distant and aloof by the client.
Test-Taking Strategy: Read each intervention carefully. Use the guidelines for preparing the physical environment for conducting an interview to select the appropriate interventions. Review these guidelines if you had difficulty with this question.
Level of Cognitive Ability: Application
Client Needs: Health Promotion and Maintenance
Integrated Process: Nursing Process—planning
Content Area: Fundamental skills
Reference: Jarvis, C. (2004). *Physical examination and health assessment* (4th ed., pp. 53, 165). Philadelphia: W.B. Saunders.

32. 4
Rationale: An inactive older adult may become disoriented because of lack of sensory stimulation. The most appropriate nursing intervention would be to reorient the client frequently and to place objects such as a clock and a calendar in the client's room to maintain orientation. The family can assist with orientation of the client but it is not appropriate to ask the family to stay with the client. It is not the within the scope of nursing practice to prescribe laboratory studies. Restraints may cause further disorientation and should not be applied unless specifically prescribed; agency policies and procedures should be followed prior to the application of restraints.
Test-Taking Strategy: Use the process of elimination. Eliminate option 3 first because it is not within the realm of nursing practice to prescribe laboratory studies. Next, eliminate option 2 because restraints may add to the disorientation that the client is experiencing. It is not appropriate to place the responsibility of the client on the family, so eliminate option 1. Note the relationship between the words *disoriented* in the question and *reorient* in the correct option. Review the measures related to caring for a client who is disoriented if you had difficulty with this question.
Level of Cognitive Ability: Application
Client Needs: Psychosocial Integrity

Integrated Process: Nursing Process—implementation
Content Area: Adult health—musculoskeletal
Reference: Black, J., & Hawks, J. (2005). *Medical-surgical nursing: Clinical management for positive outcomes* (7th ed., p. 641). Philadelphia: W.B. Saunders.

33. **3**

Rationale: Skin traction is achieved by Ace wraps, boots, and slings that apply a direct force on the client's skin. Skin traction is usually removed and reapplied once a day. Traction is maintained with 5 to 8 lb of weight and this type of traction can cause skin breakdown. There are no pin sites with skin traction. Urinary incontinence is not related to the use of skin traction. Although constipation can occur as a result of immobility and monitoring bowel sounds may be a component of the assessment, this intervention is not the priority assessment.
Test-Taking Strategy: Use the process of elimination. Note the strategic word *priority* in the question. Eliminate option 2 first because there are no pin sites with skin traction. Visualizing the traction setup and knowledge of the complications associated with this type of traction will direct you to option 3. Review the complications associated with skin traction and the priority nursing interventions if you had difficulty with this question.
Level of Cognitive Ability: Application
Client Needs: Physiological Integrity
Integrated Process: Nursing Process—planning
Content Area: Adult health—musculoskeletal
References: Black, J., & Hawks, J. (2005). *Medical-surgical nursing: Clinical management for positive outcomes* (7th ed., p. 643). Philadelphia: W.B. Saunders.
Ignatavicius, D., & Workman, M. (2006). *Medical-surgical nursing: Critical thinking for collaborative care* (5th ed., p. 1201). Philadelphia: W.B. Saunders.

34. **3**

Rationale: A psychosocial assessment of the client who is immobilized would most appropriately include the need for sensory stimulation. This assessment should also include such factors as body image, past and present coping skills, and coping methods used during the period of immobilization. Although transportation, home care support, and the ability to perform activities of daily living are components of an assessment, they are not as specifically related to psychosocial adjustment as is the need for sensory stimulation.
Test-Taking Strategy: Use the process of elimination and focus on the strategic words *psychosocial* and *most appropriately*. Option 2 can be eliminated first because it relates to physiological integrity rather than psychosocial integrity. Next, eliminate options 1 and 4 because they are most closely related to physical supports rather than psychosocial needs of the client. Review the components of a psychosocial assessment if you had difficulty with this question.
Level of Cognitive Ability: Analysis
Client Needs: Psychosocial Integrity
Integrated Process: Nursing Process—assessment
Content Area: Adult health—musculoskeletal
Reference: Potter, P., & Perry, A. (2005). *Fundamentals of nursing* (6th ed., p. 1442). St. Louis: Mosby.

35. **3**

Rationale: Complex scientific or medical terminology should be avoided when counseling an Amish client (or any client). Some Amish society's prohibit education after eighth grade. When counseling a female Amish client, most often the husband and wife will want to discuss health care options together. Standing close and speaking loudly is inappropriate in most counseling situations.
Test-Taking Strategy: Use knowledge of the Amish society and therapeutic communication techniques to answer this question. Options 2 and 4 can be eliminated first because option 4 is inappropriate and option 2 is not a therapeutic intervention. Option 1 can then be eliminated because of Amish cultural habits. Review Amish society and cultural beliefs if you had difficulty with this question.
Level of Cognitive Ability: Application
Client Needs: Psychosocial Integrity
Integrated Process: Communication and Documentation
Content Area: Fundamental skills
Reference: Lewis, S., Heitkemper, M., & Dirksen, S. (2004). *Medical-surgical nursing: Assessment and management of clinical problems* (6th ed., p. 28). St. Louis: Mosby.

36. **1**

Rationale: Assault occurs when a person puts another person in fear of harmful or offensive contact and the victim fears and believes that harm will result as a result of the threat. In this situation, the nurse could be accused of the tort of assault. Battery is the intentional touching of another's body without the person's consent. Slander is verbal communication that is false and harms the reputation of another. Invasion of privacy is committed when the nurse intrudes into the client's personal affairs or violates confidentiality.
Test-Taking Strategy: Use the process of elimination. Focusing on the words used by the nurse and noting that the nurse threatens the client will direct you to option 1. Review the descriptions of each item in the options if you had difficulty with this question.
Level of Cognitive Ability: Comprehension
Client Needs: Physiological Integrity
Integrated Process: Nursing Process—implementation
Content Area: Fundamental skills
Reference: Potter, P., & Perry, A. (2005). *Fundamentals of nursing* (6th ed., p. 413). St. Louis: Mosby.

37. **4**

Rationale: When delegating nursing assignments, the nurse needs to consider the skills and educational level of the nursing staff. Collecting a 24-hour urine and frequent ambulation can most appropriately be provided by the nursing assistant, considering the clients identified in each option. The client on the mechanical ventilator requiring frequent assessment and suctioning should most appropriately be cared for by the registered nurse. The licensed practical (vocational) nurse is skilled in wound irrigation and dressing changes, so this client would be assigned to this staff member.
Test-Taking Strategy: Use the principles related to delegations and assignments and consider the education and job position as described by the nurse practice act and employee guidelines. Note the strategic word *assessment* in option 3. This

should alert you that this client should be assigned to the registered nurse. Options 1 and 2 can easily be eliminated because a nursing assistant can easily perform these tasks. This should assist in directing you to option 4. If you had difficulty with this question, review the principles related to a delegation and assignment making.

Level of Cognitive Ability: Application
Client Needs: Safe and Effective Care Environment
Integrated Process: Nursing Process—planning
Content Area: Delegating/Prioritizing
Reference: Huber, D. (2006). *Leadership and nursing care management* (3rd ed., pp. 551-552). Philadelphia: W.B. Saunders.

38. **2**

Rationale: The jaw thrust without the head tilt maneuver is used when head and/or neck trauma is suspected. This maneuver opens the airway while maintaining proper head and neck alignment, thus reducing the risk of further damage to the neck. Option 1 is incorrect. In situations requiring CPR, the client will be unconscious. Option 4 is also incorrect. Additionally, it is unlikely that the nurse will be able to obtain these data.

Test-Taking Strategy: Focus on the data in the question. Eliminate option 1 because of the close-ended word *all*. Noting that the client requires CPR will assist in eliminating options 3 and 4. Review CPR guidelines and the various test-taking strategies if you had difficulty with this question.

Level of Cognitive Ability: Application
Client Needs: Physiological Integrity
Integrated Process: Nursing Process—implementation
Content Area: Adult health—cardiovascular
Reference: Harkreader, H., & Hogan, M.A. (2004). *Fundamentals of nursing: Caring and clinical judgment* (2nd ed., p. 909). Philadelphia: W.B. Saunders.

39. **3**

Rationale: The client needs to be instructed to avoid exposure to the sun. Options 1, 2, and 4 are accurate measures in the care of a client receiving external radiation therapy.

Test-Taking Strategy: Use the process of elimination. Note the strategic words *need for further instruction*. These words indicate a negative event query and ask you to select an option that is incorrect. Eliminate option 1 because of the word *gently* and option 4 because of the word *loose*. From the remaining options, recalling that sun exposure is to be avoided will assist in answering the question. Review skin care measures for the client receiving external radiation if you had difficulty with this question.

Level of Cognitive Ability: Analysis
Client Needs: Physiological Integrity
Integrated Process: Teaching and Learning
Content Area: Adult health—oncology
Reference: Ignatavicius, D., & Workman, M. (2006). *Medical-surgical nursing: Critical thinking for collaborative care* (5th ed., pp. 490-491). Philadelphia: W.B. Saunders.

40. **1.5**

Rationale: It is necessary to convert 150 mcg to mg. In the metric system, to convert smaller to larger, divide by 1000 or move the decimal three places to the left. Therefore, 150 mcg = 0.15 mg. Next, use the formula to calculate the correct dose.

Formula:

$$\frac{\text{Desired}}{\text{Available}} \times \text{tablet} = \text{tablets per dose}$$

$$\frac{0.15 \text{ mg}}{0.1 \text{ mg}} \times 1 \text{ tablet} = 1.5 \text{ tablets}$$

Test-Taking Strategy: In this medication calculation problem, it is necessary first to convert micrograms to milligrams. Next, follow the formula for the calculation of the correct dose. Label each figure, including the answer. Recheck your work, and make sure that the answer makes sense. If you had difficulty with this question, review medication calculation problems.

Level of Cognitive Ability: Application
Client Needs: Physiological Integrity
Integrated Process: Nursing Process—implementation
Content Area: Fundamental skills
Reference: Kee, J., & Marshall, S. (2004). *Clinical calculations: With applications to general and specialty areas* (5th ed., p. 80). Philadelphia: W.B. Saunders.

41. **2**

Rationale: The most common side effect of metformin (Glucophage) is GI disturbances, including decreased appetite, nausea, and diarrhea. These generally subside over time. This medication does not cause weight gain; in fact, clients lose an average of 7 to 8 lb because the medication causes nausea and decreased appetite. Although hypoglycemia can occur, it is not the most common side effect.

Test-Taking Strategy: Use the process of elimination, noting the strategic words *most common side effect*. Remember that the most common side effect of metformin is GI disturbances. Review these side effects if you had difficulty with this question.

Level of Cognitive Ability: Analysis
Client Needs: Physiological Integrity
Integrated Process: Nursing Process—implementation
Content Area: Pharmacology
Reference: Hodgson, B., & Kizior, R. (2007). *Saunders nursing drug handbook 2007.* (pp. 745-746). Philadelphia: W.B. Saunders.

42. **3, 5, 6**

Rationale: During a seizure, the child is placed on his or her side in a lateral position. Positioning on the side will prevent aspiration because saliva will drain out the corner of the child's mouth. The child is not restrained because this could cause injury to the child. The nurse would loosen clothing around the child's neck and ensure a patent airway. Nothing is placed into the child's mouth during a seizure because this could injure the child's mouth, gums, or teeth. The nurse would stay with the child to reduce the risk of injury and allow for observation and timing of the seizure.

Test-Taking Strategy: Visualize this clinical situation. Recalling that airway patency and safety is the priority will assist in determining the appropriate interventions. Review care of the child experiencing a seizure if you had difficulty with this question.

Level of Cognitive Ability: Application
Client Needs: Physiological Integrity
Integrated Process: Nursing Process—implementation

Content Area: Child health
Reference: Hockenberry, M., Wilson, D., & Winkelstein, M. (2005). *Wong's essentials of pediatric nursing* (7th ed., pp. 1051-1052). St. Louis: Mosby.

43. 1
Rationale: Following amputation, phantom limb pain is a temporary condition that some children may experience. This sensation of burning, aching, or cramping in the missing limb is most distressing to the child. The child needs to be reassured that the condition is normal and only temporary. Options 2, 3 and 4 are not appropriate responses to the child.
Test-Taking Strategy: Use therapeutic communication techniques. Note that the subject of the question relates to alleviating the child's fear. Option 1 is the only option that will alleviate fear. Options 2, 3, and 4 imply that this pain may be permanent. Review care to the child following amputation if you had difficulty with this question.
Level of Cognitive Ability: Application
Client Needs: Psychosocial Integrity
Integrated Process: Caring
Content Area: Child health
Reference: Hockenberry, M., Wilson, D., & Winkelstein, M. (2005). *Wong's essentials of pediatric nursing* (7th ed., p. 1164). St. Louis: Mosby.

44. 1
Rationale: Setting priorities means deciding which client needs or problems require immediate action and which can be delayed until a later time because they are not urgent. Client problems that involve actual or life-threatening concerns are always considered first. Although time constraints, obtaining needed supplies, and completing care in a reasonable time frame are components of time management, these items are not the priority in planning care for the client, based on the options provided.
Test-Taking Strategy: Use the process of elimination and principles related to prioritizing to answer the question. Noting the strategic word *life-threatening* in option 1 will assist in directing you to this option. Review the principles related to prioritizing if you had difficulty with this question.
Level of Cognitive Ability: Application
Client Needs: Safe and Effective Care Environment
Integrated Process: Nursing Process—planning
Content Area: Delegating/Prioritizing
Reference: Huber, D. (2006). *Leadership and nursing care management* (3rd ed., p. 167). Philadelphia: W.B. Saunders.

45. 2
Rationale: Laboratory determinations of serum thyroid stimulating hormone (TSH) level are an important means of evaluation. Successful therapy will cause elevated TSH levels to fall. These levels will begin their decline within hours of the onset of therapy and will continue to drop as plasma levels of thyroid hormone build up. If an adequate dosage is administered, TSH levels will remain suppressed for the duration of therapy.
Test-Taking Strategy: Use the process of elimination. Note the strategic words *expected outcome*. Relate the diagnosis hypo*thy*roidism with *thyroid* hormone levels in the correct option. If you had difficulty with this question, review the therapeutic effects of levothyroxine (Synthroid).

Level of Cognitive Ability: Application
Client Needs: Physiological Integrity
Integrated Process: Teaching and Learning
Content Area: Pharmacology
References: Hodgson, B., & Kizior, R. (2007). *Saunders nursing drug handbook 2007* (p. 687). Philadelphia: W.B. Saunders. Skidmore-Roth, L. (2005). *Mosby's drug guide for nurses* (6th ed., pp. 493-495). St. Louis: Mosby.

46. 1, 2, 4, 6
Rationale: Risk factors for breast cancer include family history of breast cancer, age older than 40 years, early menarche, late menopause, or both, previous cancer of the breast, uterus, or ovaries, nulliparity or first child born after age 30 years, and high-dose radiation exposure to chest.
Test-Taking Strategy: Focus on the subject, the risk factors associated with breast cancer. Thinking about the physiology associated with the reproductive system and the most common causes of cancer will assist in answering the question. Review these risk factors if you had difficulty with this question.
Level of Cognitive Ability: Analysis
Client Needs: Physiological Integrity
Integrated Process: Nursing Process—assessment
Content Area: Adult health—oncology
Reference: Ignatavicius, D., & Workman, M. (2006). *Medical-surgical nursing: Critical thinking for collaborative care* (5th ed., pp. 1795-1796). Philadelphia: W.B. Saunders.

47. 3
Rationale: An inflammatory reaction such as acute pancreatitis can cause paralytic ileus, the most common form of nonmechanical obstruction. Inability to pass flatus is a clinical manifestation of paralytic ileus. Option 1 is the description of the physical finding of liver enlargement. The liver is usually enlarged in cases of cirrhosis or hepatitis. Although this client may have an enlarged liver, an enlarged liver is not a sign of paralytic ileus or intestinal obstruction. Pain is associated with paralytic ileus, but the pain usually presents as a more constant generalized discomfort. Pain that is severe, constant, and rapid in onset is more likely caused by strangulation of the bowel. Loss of sphincter control is not a sign of paralytic ileus.
Test-Taking Strategy: Use the process of elimination. Noting the word *paralytic* will assist in directing you to option 3. Review the clinical manifestations of paralytic ileus if you had difficulty with this question.
Level of Cognitive Ability: Analysis
Client Needs: Physiological Integrity
Integrated Process: Nursing Process—assessment
Content Area: Adult health—gastrointestinal
Reference: Ignatavicius, D., & Workman, M. (2006). *Medical-surgical nursing: Critical thinking for collaborative care* (5th ed., p. 1327). Philadelphia: W.B. Saunders.

48. 2
Rationale: For the first 12 hours following a laparotomy, the nasogastric (NG) tube drainage may be dark brown to dark red. Later, the drainage should change to a light yellowish-brown color. The presence of bile may cause a greenish tinge. The physician should be notified if dark red drainage is noted 24 hours postoperatively.

Test-Taking Strategy: Focus on the subject, need to notify the physician. Use the process of elimination and recall that bleeding is a concern in the postoperative client. This concept will easily direct you to option 2. Review the signs of postoperative complications following a laparotomy if you had difficulty with this question.
Level of Cognitive Ability: Analysis
Client Needs: Physiological Integrity
Integrated Process: Nursing Process—analysis
Content Area: Adult health—gastrointestinal
References: Ignatavicius, D., & Workman, M. (2006). *Medical-surgical nursing: Critical thinking for collaborative care* (5th ed., p. 345). Philadelphia: W.B. Saunders.
Potter, P., & Perry, A. (2005). *Fundamentals of nursing* (6th ed., p. 1405). St. Louis: Mosby.

49. **3**
Rationale: The client should take a deep breath because the client's airway will be temporarily obstructed during tube removal. The client is then told to exhale slowly and the tube is withdrawn during exhalation. Bearing down could inhibit the removal of the tube. Breathing normally could result in aspiration of gastric secretions during inhalation. Holding the breath does not facilitate tube removal.
Test-Taking Strategy: Use the process of elimination. Attempt to visualize the process of tube removal to direct you to option 3. Remember, exhaling slowly will facilitate the process of removal. Review the procedure for removal of a nasogastric tube if you had difficulty with this question.
Level of Cognitive Ability: Application
Client Needs: Physiological Integrity
Integrated Process: Nursing Process—implementation
Content Area: Adult health—gastrointestinal
Reference: Potter, P., & Perry, A. (2005). *Fundamentals of nursing* (6th ed., p. 1407). St. Louis: Mosby.

50. **3**
Rationale: When the client is experiencing respiratory acidosis, the respiratory rate and depth increase in an attempt to compensate. The client also experiences headache, restlessness, mental status changes, such as drowsiness and confusion, visual disturbances, diaphoresis, cyanosis as the hypoxia becomes more acute, hyperkalemia, a rapid, irregular pulse, and dysrhythmias.
Test-Taking Strategy: Use the process of elimination and knowledge of the signs and symptoms of respiratory acidosis to answer the question. Remember that restlessness and confusion occur in respiratory acidosis. If this question was difficult, review the clinical manifestations associated with respiratory acidosis.
Level of Cognitive Ability: Analysis
Client Needs: Physiological Integrity
Integrated Process: Nursing Process—assessment
Content Area: Fundamental skills
Reference: Potter, P., & Perry, A. (2005). *Fundamentals of nursing* (6th ed., p. 1145). St. Louis: Mosby.

51. **3**
Rationale: Distention, vomiting, and abdominal pain are a few of the symptoms associated with intestinal obstruction.

Nasogastric tubes may be used to remove gas and fluid from the stomach, thus relieving distention and vomiting. Bowel sounds return to normal as the obstruction is resolved and normal bowel function is restored. Discontinuing the nasogastric tube prior to normal bowel function may result in a return of the symptoms, necessitating reinsertion of the nasogastric tube. Serum electrolyte levels, tube placement, and pH of the gastric aspirate are important assessments for the client with a nasogastric tube in place, but would not assist in determining the readiness for removing the nasogastric tube.
Test-Taking Strategy: Use the process of elimination. Eliminate options 1 and 4 first because they are comparative or alike. Assessing the pH of the gastric aspirate is one method of assessing tube placement. From the remaining options, focus on the subject and the client's diagnosis to direct you to option 3. Review abdominal assessment in the client with an intestinal obstruction if you had difficulty with this question.
Level of Cognitive Ability: Analysis
Client Needs: Physiological Integrity
Integrated Process: Nursing Process—assessment
Content Area: Adult health—gastrointestinal
References: Ignatavicius, D., & Workman, M. (2006). *Medical-surgical nursing: Critical thinking for collaborative care* (5th ed., pp. 1329-1330). Philadelphia: W.B. Saunders.
Potter, P., & Perry, A. (2005). *Fundamentals of nursing* (6th ed., p. 1408). St. Louis: Mosby.

52. **2**
Rationale: The enema fluid should be administered slowly. If the client complains of fullness or pain, the flow is stopped for 30 seconds and restarted at a slower rate. Slow enema administration and stopping the flow temporarily, if necessary, will decrease the likelihood of intestinal spasm and premature ejection of the solution. The higher the solution container is held above the rectum, the faster the flow and the greater the force in the rectum. There is no need to discontinue the enema and notify the physician at this time. Although client reassurance is important, continuing the flow is inappropriate.
Test-Taking Strategy: Use the process of elimination. Eliminate options 1 and 3 first because they are comparative or alike. From the remaining options, focusing on the subject will direct you to option 2. Review the procedure for administering an enema if you had difficulty with this question.
Level of Cognitive Ability: Application
Client Needs: Physiological Integrity
Integrated Process: Nursing Process—implementation
Content Area: Fundamental skills
Reference: Potter, P., & Perry, A. (2005). *Fundamentals of nursing* (6th ed., pp. 1401-1402). St. Louis: Mosby.

53. **4**
Rationale: Option 4 describes aversion therapy. Options 1, 2, and 3 are characteristics of self-control therapy.
Test-Taking Strategy: Use the process of elimination. Note the strategic words *need for further teaching* in the question. These words indicate a negative event query and ask you to select an option that is incorrect. Think about the subject, self-control. This subject should easily direct you to option 4. If you are unfamiliar with self-control therapy, review this content.
Level of Cognitive Ability: Analysis

Client Needs: Psychosocial Integrity
Integrated Process: Teaching and Learning
Content Area: Mental health
Reference: Varcarolis, E., Carson, V., & Shoemaker, N. (2006). *Foundations of psychiatric mental health nursing* (5th ed., pp. 29-30). Philadelphia: W.B. Saunders.

54. **1, 3, 5, 6**

Rationale: The nurse would teach the client how to care for the stoma, depending on the type of laryngectomy performed. Most interventions focus on protection of the stoma and the prevention of infection. Interventions include to avoid swimming, use care when showering, avoid exposure to people with infections, prevent debris from entering the stoma, and obtain a Medic-Alert bracelet. Additional interventions include wearing a stoma guard or high-collared clothing to cover the stoma, increasing the humidity in the home, and increasing fluid intake to 3000 mL/day to keep the secretions thin.
Test-Taking Strategy: Recalling that most interventions focus on protection of the stoma and the prevention of infection will assist in identifying the client instructions for home care. Review these instructions if you had difficulty with this question.
Level of Cognitive Ability: Application
Client Needs: Physiological Integrity
Integrated Process: Teaching and Learning
Content Area: Adult health—oncology
Reference: Ignatavicius, D., & Workman, M. (2006). *Medical-surgical nursing: Critical thinking for collaborative care* (5th ed., pp. 575, 580-581). Philadelphia: W.B. Saunders.

55. **21**

Rationale: Use the IV flow rate formula.
Formula:

$$\frac{\text{Total volume} \times \text{gtt factor}}{\text{Time in minutes}} = \text{gtt per min}$$

$$\frac{2000 \text{ mL} \times 15 \text{ gtt}}{1440 \text{ minutes}} = \frac{30,000}{1440} = 20.8, \text{ or } 21 \text{ drops per minute}$$

Test-Taking Strategy: Use the formula for calculating IV flow rates when answering the question. Verify the answer using a calculator. Review IV infusion rates if you had difficulty with this question.
Level of Cognitive Ability: Application
Client Needs: Physiological Integrity
Integrated Process: Nursing Process—implementation
Content Area: Fundamental skills
Reference: Kee, J., & Marshall, S. (2004). *Clinical calculations: With applications to general and specialty areas* (5th ed., pp. 80, 120). Philadelphia: W.B. Saunders.

56. **3**

Rationale: In the first few hours after surgery, the drainage from the chest tube is bloody. After several hours, it becomes serosanguineous. The client should not experience frequent clotting. Proper chest tube function should allow for drainage of blood before it has the chance to clot in the chest or the tubing.
Test-Taking Strategy: Recall that following thoracic surgery, there may be considerable capillary oozing for some hours in the postoperative period. This would lead you to choose the bloody drainage over serous or serosanguineous. Knowing

that patent chest tubes do not allow blood to collect in the pleural space eliminates the option of blood with clots. Review the assessment measures required for the care of a client with a chest tube if you had difficulty with this question.
Level of Cognitive Ability: Analysis
Client Needs: Physiological Integrity
Integrated Process: Nursing Process—assessment
Content Area: Adult health—respiratory
Reference: Ignatavicius, D., & Workman, M. (2006). *Medical-surgical nursing: Critical thinking for collaborative care* (5th ed., p. 617). Philadelphia: W.B. Saunders.

57. **1**

Rationale: If the client begins to hemorrhage from the surgical site following radical neck dissection, the nurse elevates the head of the bed to maintain airway patency and prevent aspiration. The nurse applies pressure over the bleeding site, and calls the physician immediately.
Test-Taking Strategy: Use the process of elimination, noting the strategic word *contraindicated*. Options 2 and 3 are indicated if the client is hemorrhaging. Calling the physician is also indicated immediately, but lowering the head of bed does not help with airway maintenance. Review nursing actions if a client begins to hemorrhage if you had difficulty with this question.
Level of Cognitive Ability: Application
Client Needs: Physiological Integrity
Integrated Process: Nursing Process—implementation
Content Area: Adult health—respiratory
References: Ignatavicius, D., & Workman, M. (2006). *Medical-surgical nursing: Critical thinking for collaborative care* (5th ed., p. 579). Philadelphia: W.B. Saunders.
Lewis, S., Heitkemper, M., & Dirksen, S. (2004). *Medical-surgical nursing: Assessment and management of clinical problems* (6th ed., p. 585). St. Louis: Mosby.

58. **2**

Rationale: To prevent transmission of hepatitis, a condom is advised during sexual intercourse, as well as vaccination of the partner. Alcohol should be avoided for 1 year because it is detoxified in the liver and may interfere with recovery. Rest is especially important until laboratory studies show that liver function has returned to normal. The client's activity is increased gradually.
Test-Taking Strategy: Use the process of elimination, focusing on the strategic words *need for further teaching*. These words indicate a negative event query and ask you to select an option that is incorrect. Noting the strategic word *never* in option 2 will direct you to this option. Review client instructions regarding hepatitis if you had difficulty with this question.
Level of Cognitive Ability: Analysis
Client Needs: Physiological Integrity
Integrated Process: Teaching and Learning
Content Area: Adult health—gastrointestinal
Reference: Lewis, S., Heitkemper, M., & Dirksen, S. (2004). *Medical-surgical nursing: Assessment and management of clinical problems* (6th ed., p. 1114). St. Louis: Mosby.

59. **1, 2, 5**

Rationale: The clinical manifestations of hypothyroidism are the result of decreased metabolism from low levels of thyroid hormone. Interventions are aimed at replacement of the hormones and providing measures to support the signs and symptoms related to a decreased metabolism. The nurse encourages the client to consume a well-balanced diet that is low in fat for weight reduction and high in fluids and high-fiber foods to prevent constipation. The client often has cold intolerance and requires a warm environment. The client would notify the physician if chest pain occurs because it could be an indication of overreplacement of thyroid hormone. Iodine preparations are used to treat hyperthyroidism. These medications decrease blood flow through the thyroid gland and reduce the production and release of thyroid hormone.

Test-Taking Strategy: Focus on the client's diagnosis, hypothyroidism. Recalling that in this disorder the client has a decreased metabolic rate will assist in determining the appropriate interventions. Review interventions for the client with hypothyroidism and hyperthyroidism if you had difficulty with this question.

Level of Cognitive Ability: Application
Client Needs: Physiological Integrity
Integrated Process: Nursing Process—implementation
Content Area: Adult health—endocrine
Reference: Ignatavicius, D., & Workman, M. (2006). *Medical-surgical nursing: Critical thinking for collaborative care* (5th ed., pp. 1491-1492). Philadelphia: W.B. Saunders.

60. **2**
Rationale: Plugging a tracheostomy tube is usually done by inserting the tracheostomy plug (decannulation stopper) into the opening of the outer cannula. This closes off the tracheostomy, and airflow and respiration occur normally through the nose and mouth. When plugging a cuffed tracheostomy tube, the cuff must be deflated. If it remains inflated, ventilation cannot occur and respiratory arrest could result. The ability to swallow or speak is unrelated to weaning and plugging the tube.

Test-Taking Strategy: Note the strategic word *required* in the question. This should assist in directing you to the option that addresses a priority physiological need. Use the process of elimination to direct you to option 2, because an inflated cuff would cause airway obstruction. Review this procedure if you had difficulty with this question.

Level of Cognitive Ability: Application
Client Needs: Physiological Integrity
Integrated Process: Nursing Process—implementation
Content Area: Adult health—respiratory
References: Ignatavicius, D., & Workman, M. (2006). *Medical-surgical nursing: Critical thinking for collaborative care* (5th ed., p. 558). Philadelphia: W.B. Saunders.
Lewis, S., Heitkemper, M., & Dirksen, S. (2004). *Medical-surgical nursing: Assessment and management of clinical problems* (6th ed., p. 576). St. Louis: Mosby.
Potter, P., & Perry, A. (2005). *Fundamentals of nursing* (6th ed., p. 1114). St. Louis: Mosby.

61. **3**
Rationale: Hypertension, cardiovascular disease, diabetes mellitus, and obesity are associated with the development of glaucoma. Options 1, 2, and 4 do not identify risk factors associated with this eye disorder.

Test-Taking Strategy: Use the process of elimination. Focusing on the subject, a risk factor associated with glaucoma, will

direct you to option 3. If you had difficulty with this question, review the risk factors associated with this disorder.

Level of Cognitive Ability: Analysis
Client Needs: Physiological Integrity
Integrated Process: Nursing Process—assessment
Content Area: Adult health—eye
References: Black, J., & Hawks, J. (2005). *Medical-surgical nursing: Clinical management for positive outcomes* (7th ed., p. 1945). Philadelphia: W.B. Saunders.
Ignatavicius, D., & Workman, M. (2006). *Medical-surgical nursing: Critical thinking for collaborative care* (5th ed., pp. 1097-1098). Philadelphia: W.B. Saunders.

62. **3**
Rationale: The nurse places an eye patch over the client's affected eye to reduce eye movement. Some clients may need bilateral patching. Depending on the location and size of the retinal break, activity restrictions may be needed immediately. These restrictions are necessary to prevent further tearing or detachment and to promote drainage of any subretinal fluid. The nurse positions the client as prescribed by the physician.

Test-Taking Strategy: Use the process of elimination. Remember that the eye needs to be protected and rested. This should direct you to option 3. If you had difficulty with this question, review care of the client with retinal detachment.

Level of Cognitive Ability: Analysis
Client Needs: Physiological Integrity
Integrated Process: Nursing Process—analysis
Content Area: Adult health—eye
Reference: Ignatavicius, D., & Workman, M. (2006). *Medical-surgical nursing: Critical thinking for collaborative care* (5th ed., p. 1103). Philadelphia: W.B. Saunders.

63. **2**
Rationale: Persons at greatest risk for pulmonary emboli are immobilized clients. Basic preventive measures include early ambulation, leg elevation, active leg exercises, elastic stockings, and intermittent pneumatic calf compression. Keeping the client well hydrated is essential because dehydration predisposes to clotting. A pillow under the knees may cause venous stasis. Heat should not be applied without a physician's prescription.

Test-Taking Strategy: Use the process of elimination and basic principles related to the care of the immobile client to answer this question. If you are unfamiliar with these basic measures, review this content.

Level of Cognitive Ability: Application
Client Needs: Physiological Integrity
Integrated Process: Nursing Process—planning
Content Area: Adult health—respiratory
References: Ignatavicius, D., & Workman, M. (2006). *Medical-surgical nursing: Critical thinking for collaborative care* (5th ed., p. 650). Philadelphia: W.B. Saunders.
Potter, P., & Perry, A. (2005). *Fundamentals of nursing* (6th ed., p. 1427). St. Louis: Mosby.

64. **4**
Rationale: A crisis is an acute, time-limited state of disequilibrium resulting from situational, developmental, or societal sources of stress. A person in this state is temporarily unable to cope with or adapt to the stressor by using previous coping

mechanisms. The person who intervenes in this situation (the nurse) "takes over" for the client who is not in control and devises a plan (action) to secure and maintain the client's safety. Once this has occurred, the nurse works collaboratively with the client (participates) in developing new coping and problem-solving strategies.

Test-Taking Strategy: Use the process of elimination. The client who experiences a suicidal crisis is in a state of acute disequilibrium. Remember, in a crisis, an authority figure must emerge to take action. Review care of the client in crisis if you had difficulty with this question.

Level of Cognitive Ability: Application
Client Needs: Psychosocial Integrity
Integrated Process: Nursing Process—implementation
Content Area: Mental health
Reference: Fortinash, K., & Holoday-Worret, P. (2004). *Psychiatric mental health nursing* (3rd ed., pp. 515-517). St. Louis: Mosby.

65. **1**

Rationale: The client must have sputum cultures performed every 2 to 4 weeks after initiation of antituberculosis drug therapy. The client may return to work when the results of three sputum cultures are negative, because the client is considered noninfectious at that point.

Test-Taking Strategy: Use the process of elimination. Knowing that a positive Mantoux test never reverts to negative helps you eliminate option 4. From the remaining options, it is necessary to know that three negative sputum cultures are required. If this question was difficult, review these concepts related to TB.

Level of Cognitive Ability: Application
Client Needs: Safe and Effective Care Environment
Integrated Process: Teaching and Learning
Content Area: Adult health—respiratory
Reference: Ignatavicius, D., & Workman, M. (2006). *Medical-surgical nursing: Critical thinking for collaborative care* (5th ed., p. 644). Philadelphia: W.B. Saunders.

66. **3**

Rationale: This client is in a severe state of anxiety. When a client is in a severe or panic state of anxiety, it is critical for the nurse to remain with the client. Processing the anxiety at this point will further increase the client's level of anxiety. The client in a severe state of anxiety would not be able to learn relaxation techniques.

Test-Taking Strategy: Use the process of elimination and note the strategic words *appropriate initial*. The best action in this situation is to remain with the client. If you are unfamiliar with the symptoms of the different levels of anxiety and the interventions that are indicated, review this information.

Level of Cognitive Ability: Application
Client Needs: Psychosocial Integrity
Integrated Process: Nursing Process—implementation
Content Area: Mental health
Reference: Stuart, G., & Laraia, M. (2005). *Principles and practice of psychiatric nursing* (8th ed., p. 379). St. Louis: Mosby.

67. **3**

Rationale: Laboratory findings do not establish the diagnosis of appendicitis, but there is often a moderate elevation of the

white blood cell (WBC) count (leukocytosis) to 10,000 to 18,000/mm^3 with a shift to the left (an increased number of immature WBCs.).

Test-Taking Strategy: Use the process of elimination. Knowledge that an inflammatory process causes a rise in the WBC count will assist in eliminating options 1 and 4. From the remaining options, it is necessary to understand the significance of a shift to the left. If you are unfamiliar with the meaning of shift to the left, review this content.

Level of Cognitive Ability: Analysis
Client Needs: Physiological Integrity
Integrated Process: Nursing Process—assessment
Content Area: Adult health—gastrointestinal
Reference: Ignatavicius, D., & Workman, M. (2006). *Medical-surgical nursing: Critical thinking for collaborative care* (5th ed., p. 1339). Philadelphia: W.B. Saunders.

68. **4**

Rationale: Ineffective coping may be evidenced by inability to meet basic needs, inability to meet role expectations, alteration in social participation, use of inappropriate defense mechanisms, or impairment of usual patterns of communication. Disturbed thought processes are evidenced by altered attention span, distractibility, and disorientation to time, place, person, and events. A dysfunctional family process may exist when the family has difficulty adapting or responding to the changes or traumatic experience of the member in crisis.

Test-Taking Strategy: Use the data presented in the question to direct you to the correct option. Option 3 can be easily eliminated because the client is presently experiencing anxiety. Eliminate option 1 because there are no data in the question that address the family. Similarly, there are no data to suggest disturbed thought processes, so this option can be eliminated, leaving option 4 as the correct option. Review nursing diagnoses for the client experiencing anxiety if you had difficulty with this question.

Level of Cognitive Ability: Analysis
Client Needs: Psychosocial Integrity
Integrated Process: Nursing Process—analysis
Content Area: Mental health
Reference: Fortinash, K., & Holoday-Worret, P. (2004). *Psychiatric mental health nursing* (3rd ed., pp. 192-193). St. Louis: Mosby.

69. **2**

Rationale: Bubbling in the water seal compartment is caused by air passing out of the pleural space into the fluid in the chamber. Intermittent bubbling is normal. It indicates that the system is accomplishing one of its purposes, removing air from the pleural space. Continuous bubbling during inspiration and expiration indicates that an air leak exists. If this occurs, it must be corrected.

Test-Taking Strategy: Focus on the strategic words *intermittent bubbling* and *water seal compartment*. Recalling that intermittent bubbling is normal will direct you to option 2. If you are unfamiliar with chest tube drainage systems, review this content.

Level of Cognitive Ability: Application
Client Needs: Physiological Integrity
Integrated Process: Nursing Process—implementation

Content Area: Adult health—respiratory
References: Black, J., & Hawks, J. (2005). *Medical-surgical nursing: Clinical management for positive outcomes* (7th ed., pp. 1862-1863). Philadelphia: W.B. Saunders.
Lewis, S., Heitkemper, M., & Dirksen, S. (2004). *Medical-surgical nursing: Assessment and management of clinical problems* (6th ed., p. 623). St. Louis: Mosby.

70. 3
Rationale: The initial nursing assessment of a client in a crisis state is to evaluate the physical condition of the client, the potential for self-harm, and the potential for harm to others. Once this has been determined and appropriate interventions have been initiated, the nurse would then proceed with the mental health interview.
Test-Taking Strategy: Use Maslow's Hierarchy of Needs theory to answer the question. Physiological needs take priority over other needs. Option 3 is the only option that addresses a physiological need. Review care of the client in crisis if you had difficulty with this question.
Level of Cognitive Ability: Analysis
Client Needs: Physiological Integrity
Integrated Process: Nursing Process—assessment
Content Area: Mental health
References: Fortinash, K., & Holoday-Worret, P. (2004). *Psychiatric mental health nursing* (3rd ed., p. 562). St. Louis: Mosby.
Stuart, G., & Laraia, M. (2005). *Principles and practice of psychiatric nursing* (8th ed., pp. 229, 375-376, 367). St. Louis: Mosby.

71. 3
Rationale: Although frequency and intensity of bowel sounds will vary depending on the phase of digestion, normal bowel sounds are relatively high-pitched clicks or gurgles. Loud gurgles (borborygmi) indicate hyperperistalsis. Bowel sounds will be more high-pitched and louder (hyperresonance) when the intestines are under tension, such as in intestinal obstruction. A swishing or buzzing sound represents turbulent blood flow associated with a bruit. Bruits are not normal sounds.
Test-Taking Strategy: Use the process of elimination. Normally, bowel sounds are audible in all four quadrants; therefore, options 2 and 4 can be eliminated. From the remaining options, use knowledge regarding normal findings to direct you to option 3. Review abdominal assessment if you had difficulty with this question.
Level of Cognitive Ability: Comprehension
Client Needs: Physiological Integrity
Integrated Process: Nursing Process—assessment
Content Area: Adult health—gastrointestinal
Reference: Lewis, S., Heitkemper, M., & Dirksen, S. (2004). *Medical-surgical nursing: Assessment and management of clinical problems* (6th ed., p. 957). St. Louis: Mosby.

72. 880
Rationale: The client consumed a total of 26 oz of fluid (12 oz at breakfast, 8 oz with medications, and 6 oz at lunch). This equals 780 mL (1 oz = 30 mL). The client also received a total of 100 mL of intravenous fluid (50 mL at 8:00 AM and 50 mL at 2:00 PM). Therefore, the total intake is 880 mL.
Test-Taking Strategy: Focus on the subject, the client's intake in milliliters. Read the question carefully, noting the client's oral

intake in ounces and then converting the total ounces to milliliters. Remember, 1 oz = 30 mL. Once you have done this, remember to add the 100 mL of intravenous fluid to the oral total. Review procedures for calculating intake and output if you had difficulty with this question.
Level of Cognitive Ability: Comprehension
Client Needs: Physiological Integrity
Integrated Process: Nursing Process—assessment
Content Area: Child health
Reference: Harkreader, H., & Hogan, M.A. (2004). *Fundamentals of nursing: Caring and clinical judgment* (2nd ed., pp. 580-582). Philadelphia: W.B. Saunders.

73. 1
Rationale: Glucagon is used to treat hypoglycemia resulting from insulin overdose. The family of the client is instructed in how to administer the medication. In an unconscious client, arousal usually occurs within 20 minutes of glucagon injection. Once consciousness has been regained, oral carbohydrates should be given. Lipoatrophy and lipohypertrophy result from insulin injections.
Test-Taking Strategy: Use the process of elimination. Noting the word *glucagon* will assist in determining that the medication contains some form of glucose. This relationship should direct you to option 1. Review the purpose of this medication if you are unfamiliar with it.
Level of Cognitive Ability: Application
Client Needs: Physiological Integrity
Integrated Process: Teaching and Learning
Content Area: Pharmacology
Reference: Kee, J., Hayes, E., & McCuistion, L. (2006). *Pharmacology: A nursing process approach* (5th ed., p. 789). Philadelphia: W.B. Saunders.

74. 3
Rationale: In the Cuban-American culture, loud crying and other physical manifestations of grief are considered socially acceptable. Of the options provided, option 3 is the only one that identifies a culturally sensitive approach on the part of the nurse. Options 1, 2, and 4 are inappropriate nursing interventions.
Test-Taking Strategy: Focus on the client(s) of the question, the family members. Use the process of elimination and therapeutic nursing interventions, recalling the characteristics of the culture and the importance of cultural sensitivity. This will direct you to option 3. If you had difficulty with this question, review the characteristics of this culture.
Level of Cognitive Ability: Application
Client Needs: Psychosocial Integrity
Integrated Process: Nursing Process—implementation
Content Area: Fundamental skills
References: Giger, J., & Davidhizar, R. (2004). *Transcultural nursing* (5th ed., pp. 231-233). St. Louis: Mosby.
Ignatavicius, D., & Workman, M. (2006). *Medical-surgical nursing: Critical thinking for collaborative care* (5th ed., p. 56). Philadelphia: W.B. Saunders.

75. 4
Rationale: The priority nursing action is to assess the vital signs. This would indicate the amount of blood loss that has

occurred and also provides a baseline by which to monitor the progress of treatment. The client may not be able to provide subjective data until the immediate physical needs are met. Although an abdominal examination and an assessment of the precipitating events may be necessary, these actions are not the priority.

Test-Taking Strategy: Note the strategic words *first priority.* Use the process of elimination and the ABCs: airway, breathing, and circulation. This will direct you to option 4. Review care

of the client with a GI bleed if you had difficulty with this question.

Level of Cognitive Ability: Application
Client Needs: Physiological Integrity
Integrated Process: Nursing Process—implementation
Content Area: Adult health—gastrointestinal
Reference: Lewis, S., Heitkemper, M., & Dirksen, S. (2004). *Medical-surgical nursing: Assessment and management of clinical problems* (6th ed., p. 1024). St. Louis: Mosby.

REFERENCES

Black, J., & Hawks, J. (2005). *Medical-surgical nursing: Clinical management for positive outcomes* (7th ed.). Philadelphia: W.B. Saunders.

Chernecky, C., & Berger, B. (2004). *Laboratory tests and diagnostic procedures* (4th ed.). Philadelphia: W.B. Saunders.

Cohen, E., & Cesta, T., (2005). *Nursing case management: From essentials to advanced practice applications* (4th ed.). St. Louis: Mosby.

Fortinash, K., & Holoday-Worret, P. (2004). *Psychiatric mental health nursing* (3rd ed.). St. Louis: Mosby.

Gahart, B., & Nazareno, A. (2006). *2006 intravenous medications* (22nd ed.). St. Louis: Mosby.

Giger, J., & Davidhizar, R. (2004). *Transcultural nursing* (5th ed.). St. Louis: Mosby.

Grodner, M., Long, S., & DeYoung, S. (2004). *Foundations and clinical applications of nutrition: A nursing approach* (3rd ed.). St. Louis: Mosby.

Harkreader, H., & Hogan, M.A. (2004). *Fundamentals of nursing: Caring and clinical judgment* (2nd ed.). Philadelphia: W.B. Saunders.

Hockenberry, M., Wilson, D., & Winkelstein, M. (2005). *Wong's essentials of pediatric nursing* (7th ed.). St. Louis: Mosby.

Hodgson, B., & Kizior, R. (2007). *Saunders nursing drug handbook 2007.* Philadelphia: W.B. Saunders.

Huber, D. (2006). *Leadership and nursing care management* (3rd ed.). Philadelphia: W.B. Saunders.

Huether, S., & McCance, K. (2004). *Understanding pathophysiology* (3rd ed.). St. Louis: Mosby.

Ignatavicius, D., & Workman, M. (2006). *Medical-surgical nursing: Critical thinking for collaborative care* (5th ed.). Philadelphia: W.B. Saunders.

Jarvis, C. (2004). *Physical examination and health assessment* (4th ed.). Philadelphia: W.B. Saunders.

Kee, J., Hayes, E., & McCuistion, L. (2006). *Pharmacology: A nursing process approach* (5th ed.). Philadelphia: W.B. Saunders.

Kee, J., & Marshall, S. (2004). *Clinical calculations: With applications to general and specialty areas* (5th ed.). Philadelphia: W.B. Saunders.

Lewis, S., Heitkemper, M., & Dirksen, S. (2004). *Medical-surgical nursing: Assessment and management of clinical problems* (6th ed.). St. Louis: Mosby.

Lowdermilk, D., & Perry, A. (2004). *Maternity and women's health care* (8th ed.). St. Louis: Mosby.

Lynch, V. (2006). *Forensic nursing.* St. Louis: Mosby.

McKinney, E., James, S., Murray, S., & Ashwill, J. (2005). *Maternal-child nursing* (2nd ed.). St. Louis: W.B. Saunders.

Meiner, S., & Leuckenotte, A. (2006). *Gerontologic nursing* (3rd ed) St. Louis: Mosby.

Mosby (2006). *Mosby's medical, nursing, and allied health dictionary* (7th ed.). St. Louis: Mosby.

Murray, S., & McKinney, E. (2006). *Foundations of maternal-newborn nursing* (4th ed.). Philadelphia: W.B. Saunders.

Nix, S. (2005). *Williams basic nutrition and diet therapy* (12th ed.). St. Louis: Mosby.

Pagana, K., & Pagana, T. (2005). *Mosby's diagnostic and laboratory test reference* (7th ed.). St. Louis: Mosby.

Phipps, W., Monahan, F., Sands, J., et al. (2003). *Medical-surgical nursing: Health and illness perspectives* (7th ed.). St. Louis: Mosby.

Potter, P., & Perry, A. (2005). *Fundamentals of nursing* (6th ed.). St. Louis: Mosby.

Skidmore-Roth, L. (2005). *Mosby's drug guide for nurses* (6th ed.). St. Louis: Mosby.

Skidmore-Roth, L. (2007). *Mosby's 2007 nursing drug reference* (20th ed.). St. Louis: Mosby.

Stuart, G., & Laraia, M. (2005). *Principles and practice of psychiatric nursing* (8th ed.). St. Louis: Mosby.

Varcarolis, E., Carson, V., & Shoemaker, N. (2006). *Foundations of psychiatric mental health nursing* (5th ed.). Philadelphia: W.B. Saunders.

Wong, D., Perry, S., Hockenberry, M., et al. (2006). *Maternal child nursing care* (3rd ed.). St. Louis: Mosby.

Index

Page numbers followed by b indicate box(es);
f, figure(s); t, table(s).

1239